INSIGN

BELGIUM · BENIN · BOLIVIA · BOSNIA · BOSNIAN SERBIA · BOTSWANA · BRAZIL · BRUNEI · BULGARIA

CHINA · COLOMBIA · CONGO (PEOPLE'S REPUBLIC) · COSTA RICA · CROATIA · CUBA · CYPRUS · CZECH · DENMARK

FINLAND · GABON · GERMANY · GHANA · GREECE · GUATEMALA · GUINEA · GUINEA-BISSAU · GUYANA

IVORY COAST · JAMAICA · JAPAN · JORDAN · KENYA · KOREA (NORTH) · KOREA (SOUTH) · KUWAIT · LAOS

     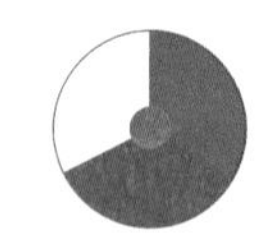  

MAURITANIA · MEXICO · MONGOLIA · MOROCCO · MOZAMBIQUE · NEPAL · NETHERLANDS · NEW ZEALAND · NICARAGUA

      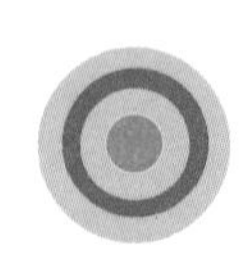      

PHILIPPINES · POLAND · PORTUGAL · QATAR · ROMANIA · RUSSIA · RWANDA · SAUDI ARABIA · SENEGAMBIA

SWEDEN · SWITZERLAND · SYRIA · TAIWAN · TANZANIA · THAILAND · TOGO · TRINIDAD & TOBAGO · TUNISIA

YEMEN · YUGOSLAV REPUBLIC · ZAIRE (NOW CONGO, DEMOCRATIC REPUBLIC) · ZAMBIA · ZIMBABWE

BRASSEY'S

WORLD AIRCRAFT & SYSTEMS DIRECTORY

1999/2000

CHIEF EDITOR: MICHAEL J. H. TAYLOR

Assistant Editor (East European): Piotr Butowski

The inaugural edition of *Brassey's World Aircraft & Systems Directory* was the result of over two years work by a highly-dedicated, international team of specialist contributors headed by Michael Taylor. The new 1999–2000 edition of *WA&SD* has been fully revised in both text and illustrations, taking a year to produce and with final updates being introduced into parts of the text as late as November 1998. Revision has been very widely supported by the world's aerospace companies and organizations.

Chief Editor: Michael J. H. Taylor

Michael Taylor had his first aviation book published when he was 19 years old. At the same time he was also contributing important sections to *Jane's All the World's Aircraft*, *Jane's Fighting Ships* and other books. In 1976 he became Editor of the magazine *Aircraft Illustrated*, while still compiling sections for various Jane's yearbooks and writing on average four books a year. In 1981 he was appointed Editor of *Jane's Aviation Review* and conceived and masterminded the best selling *Jane's Encyclopedia of Aviation*. In the late 1980's Michael Taylor became the Assistant Editor to *Jane's All the World's Aircraft*, by which time his output of aviation books had passed 100. In 1993 he left this position to conceive, develop and become the Chief Editor of *Brassey's World Aircraft and Systems Directory*.

SPECIALIST CONTRIBUTORS

Piotr Butowski: Russian, Ukrainian, Polish & other East European Civil and Military Aircraft

Piotr Butowski is a resident of Gdansk, Poland. He is the author of several important books on Russian aviation history and several hundred articles for a variety of notable periodicals in Polish, English, French, Japanese and Russian. He is in close contact with many chief designers and military officers in Russia and the Ukraine.

Neville Beckett: British Aerospace (Military)

Neville Beckett was an engineer with British Aerospace for 37 years, mostly working at Brough in Humberside but latterly at Warton in Lancashire where his activities related to future projects. Since retirement, he continues to write for a number of aviation publications.

Geoffrey P. Jones: Recreational Aircraft

Currently the Managing Director of a civil engineering company in Guernsey, Geoffrey P. Jones is a private pilot and well-known aviation photographer. He is also European Editor for *Kit Planes* magazine.

Joachim Ewald: Sailplanes and Motorgliders

A renowned sailplane and motorglider test pilot, Joachim Ewald is an experienced writer and is a regular contributor to the German magazine *Fliegermagazin*.

Tim Furniss: Spaceflight

Tim Furniss has been the spaceflight correspondent of *Flight International*, the UK's weekly international aerospace magazine, since 1984, and writes space technology stories for *The Sunday Times*. He has written 25 books about spaceflight, operates the Genesis Space Photo Library, presents spaceflight lectures and offers space consultancy services.

Don Parry: Radars

Don Parry was a Flight Engineer with the RAF between 1949–57, later joining BOAC/BA and flying on Britannia 102s, B707s and B747s and holding training and management posts. He is a Chartered Engineer and a Member of the Royal Aeronautical Society. For more than 30 years he has also worked as a freelance Aerospace writer, contributing to magazines and books published worldwide.

ACKNOWLEDGEMENTS

The invaluable assistance in large or small measure of the following individuals must be acknowledged, though many others (too numerous to list) made important contributions to the fullness and accuracy of the book or helped with support, advice or illustrations: Malcolm English, John W. R. Taylor, Peter Selinger, Arnold W. L. Nayler, Alan Brothers, Susan Midgley, Ulla Weinberg, Kenneth Munson, Susan Young, Susan Bushell, Austin Brown, Simon Watson, Sebastian Zacharias, Paul Jackson, Doris Taylor, Isobel Taylor, Elfan ap Rees. Finally, thanks are due to the employees of the many companies covered in this second edition for the time and effort they expended in fulfilling the requests for information that ultimately make such a publication possible.

Contents

First English Edition 1999

UK editorial offices: Brassey's, 583 Fulham Road, London SW6 5BY
UK orders: Bailey Distribution Ltd, Unit 1, Learoyd Road, New Romney, Kent, TN28 8XU

North American orders: Brassey's Inc. PO Box 960, Herndon, VA 20172, USA

Michael Taylor has asserted his moral right to be identified as the Chief Editor and compiler of this work.

Library of Congress Cataloging in Publication Data available

British Library Cataloguing in Publication Data
A catalogue record for this book is available from the British Library

ISBN 1 85753 245 7 Hardcover

Air Force Insignia illustrations provided by Key Publishing
Designed and produced by Gecko Ltd, Bicester
Printed in Italy

↑ **Announced at the September 1998 Farnborough International Air Show, the Airbus A318 will compete in the 100-seat market** *(courtesy Airbus Industrie)*

↑ **Computer image of the Lockheed Martin proposed joined-wing New Strategic Aircraft (see page 264), intended to replace the KC-135, C-141 and other tanker/transports from 2015** *(courtesy Lockheed Martin)*

Foreword

Picture a time, many millions of years ago, when the Earth was dominated by giant creatures. Some, among the largest, were content to graze uncaringly in the tranquillity of primeval forests and swamps, living in harmony with lesser species off the generous bounties provided. Then there were the predators, in many ways the more successful, hunting vigorously for new opportunities and culling the meek, dominating whole swaths of land. The largest of the predators stalked alone, but just imagine the impact if they had hunted in groups. Then, whole species might have been wiped out and total supremacy achieved!

Millions of years later the giants are back, not huge animals but worldwide corporations and holding groups that each own an ever-increasing number of business units or divisions, some of which had previously been fully independent companies in their own right. A bad thing? Not necessarily, and not entirely new to commercial practice. But, what impact the latest mergers and take-overs among already large companies will have on 'choice', both for the customer and governments wanting to attract competitive tendering, nobody can predict with any certainty.

In-out, in-out, shake it all about

If the last eighteen months are remembered for anything in particular within the aerospace industry, it will be for these multi-billion dollar deals, although others became bogged down by anti-trust law and governmental objections. The opening line of a popular party song perhaps sums this up, *"in-out, in-out, shake it all about"*. An obtuse thought, perhaps, but it fairly well expresses what has recently happened, when the hardest work for onlookers has been to keep pace with change.

Over the months, as the compilers of *WA&SD* picked their way through the vast mountain of material supplied by aircraft manufacturers and the many other sources of data from every corner of the world, it quickly became evident that something special was happening. We had all expected significant updating, but the quantity of change turned out to be hugely greater than anyone could have predicted. More worryingly for the compilers, revision became as much a battle to keep pace with the changes within the companies themselves as updating their product ranges.

Hardly a breath could be drawn before yet another major merger was announced. Household names had become willing victims of corporate expansion, though in the case of McDonnell Douglas operation as a single company with Boeing (under the Boeing name) did not begin until 4 August 1997, after which the fun and games really started as everyone on the outside tried to make sense of what had taken place and how individual operating units functioned under the new scheme. Indeed, so large have some companies become that information officers within those organizations often found it difficult, if not impossible, to keep pace with events and were occasionally unable to answer the most simple questions regarding new corporate structures, divisions or facilities without an initial silence, followed by a polite "I'll get back to you". Thank goodness, they did!

But why did such large and successful companies unite? As the best known name in commercial airliner building, Boeing hardly needed McDonnell Douglas' commercial products, though the MD-95 did fit nicely into Boeing's range and was consequently retitled the 717. Future prospects for the MD-80 and MD-90 looked doomed from the start, but it was perhaps surprising that the MD-11 gained only a brief postponement of execution in Boeing's hands and is set for early retirement from production in the year 2000 despite initial hope of keeping it going, particularly for freighting. The fuss once made by Airbus over Boeing's McDonnell Douglas transport aircraft acquisitions may have been, in retrospect, a little premature. Of course, Globemaster III was a glittering prize and could have caused Airbus concern, having gained the interest of foreign air forces including the RAF, which Airbus might have hoped would eventually commit itself to the originally perceived number of FLAs.

McDonnell Douglas's combat aircraft were, naturally, entirely safe in Boeing's hands and a much welcomed boost to Boeing's military presence on the world stage. But, surprising to many, Boeing made the strategic decision to pull out of commercial helicopters and quickly reached an agreement with Textron for the sale of its newly inherited MD 500, MD 520, MD 530 and MD 600 series, plus its interest in the amazing Bell Boeing 609 tilt-rotor. This move was intended to leave Boeing free to concentrate on its preferred military helicopter programmes within the rotorcraft business, plus the Explorer that Bell Helicopter Textron did not select but which was also put up for sale. Despite the approval of the Textron board of directors in February 1998, the immediate path towards purchase was blocked by a pending US Federal review, although the tiltrotor did pass entirely to Bell. Interestingly, it came to light in September 1998 that Bell had struck an agreement with Agusta of Italy to jointly manufacture and market the 609 tiltrotor as the BA609, while Bell would take on a similar role with Agusta's newly announced 12/15-seat AB139 medium twin helicopter (to be certified in 2002). Both companies had wanted risk-sharing partners for their latest products, and the agreement formed an excellent 'marriage of convenience' that also had the effect of opening new marketing opportunities.

With its acquisition of McDonnell Douglas, and also the aerospace and defence units of Rockwell, Boeing became a company of about 235,000 employees. Little wonder, then, that there was some uncertainly as to 'what was where', as the corporate giant restructured and digested its expanded facilities and products.

If one looks at the merger in a totally dispassionate way, it all made perfect sense. Boeing may not have required McDonnell Douglas' airliners but it did need a much greater presence in the current combat aircraft market, even with its almost simultaneous acquisition of Rockwell. Conversely, McDonnell Douglas had lost out on the massive Joint Strike Fighter programme for the 21st century following the award of Phase II Concept Demonstrator Program contracts to Boeing and Lockheed Martin in November 1996 and had joined the Boeing team. The merged company, under the Boeing name, at a stroke became massively involved in all aspects of the commercial and military scene.

Before the JSF award and the Boeing/McDonnell Douglas merger, it had appeared likely that Lockheed Martin and McDonnell Douglas would be dominant among US combat aircraft manufacturers in the 21st century, with Boeing unrivalled nationally in the commercial sector. The award of the JSF contracts challenged this assumption. Moreover, in July 1997 Lockheed Martin announced its own pending merger with Northrop Grumman, expected to be finalized before the end of that year, in a deal worth a reported US$11.6 billion and expected to lead to an organization with 230,000 employees. This time alarm bells started ringing in government circles, as the prospect of these two military-orientated companies combining appeared to be a somewhat different matter, partly as it reduced further the US industries' ability to tender competitively for particular military contracts. Suddenly this merger was in crisis, with a court hearing then scheduled for September 1998 to sort out the validity of the objections. It seemed that approval by the boards of directors and shareholders was again not sufficient to drive the merger through.

Flying high

Civil aviation is in boom. Commercial airliner orders are soaring and recent achievements in general aviation include certification and first deliveries in 1998 of the Bombardier BD-700 Global Express, a true rival to the superb Gulfstream V. Airline profits have mostly been strong, particularly for those operating domestic routes, investment in new airliners is high, and the first flights of many new aircraft in all categories have taken place, indicating a faith in future markets. Also, on 30 July 1998, the world's most powerful commercial aero-engine, the Pratt & Whitney PW4098 of 98,000 lbf (435.93 kN) and intended for future Boeing 777s, received its Type and Production certificates from the FAA. So, is there a down side to all this optimism? Whilst it was welcome news that the number of airline accidents involving fatalities was slightly lower in the first half of 1998 as compared with the previous year, the actual number of fatalities reportedly more than doubled, with Asia seen as a particular region requiring improvements in safety. And, with Asia suffering economic downturn, airlines and manufacturers connected with that region have begun to find the going tougher.

The incredible upsurge in commercial aviation has left Boeing and Airbus, as the biggest players, with order books bulging to the point of overflowing. Airbus Industrie took an amazing US$20.3 billion worth of orders between January and 30 June 1998 alone, an improvement over the same period of 1997 of nearly 260%. The company recorded a first half-year turnover of US$6 billion, at which time it had a backlog of 1,173 aircraft orders. Similarly, Boeing received orders valued at US$15.459 billion between January and 31 May 1998, when it had a backlog of 1,793 aircraft orders. Such immense sales are likely to continue, with Airbus forecasting the need for some 13,600 newly built jet airliners of over 70 seat capacity up to the year 2017, on the basis of a 5% per year increase in traffic growth, with 8,500 to replace ageing aircraft alone.

The next point of intense interest will be which company manages to launch the first very high capacity airliner, to dwarf even the huge, tremendously successful and long-serving 747. Although several flying-wing proposals have been reported, it was always far more likely that a conventionally configured but full double-deck airliner would be selected for development, and Airbus has taken an early lead with its A3XX. Indeed, Airbus Industrie formed a Large Aircraft Division in 1996 to speed up the A3XX programme, and it is understood that it wants airline launch commitments in 1999. In May 1998 the Engine Alliance offered its GP7200 engine as an alternative to the Rolls-Royce Trent for A3XX, and A3XX service entry could be 2004. According to Airbus, the A3XX will offer passengers (including economy class) wider seats and a more spacious cabin than today's airliners, plus 15-20% lower direct operating costs per seat for the airline, helping to keep the cost of air travel falling in real terms.

As a partial response to A3XX, Boeing, having decided to discontinue development of its 548-seat 747-600X in early 1997, has since formulated the 747-400Y Stretch to carry 500 passengers over 7,700 naut miles as one of the new models

↑ **Computer-aided cutaway image of the double-deck Airbus A3XX, for which launch commitments are sought for 1999** *(courtesy Airbus Industrie)*

↑ **Embraer's newest regional jet for 37 passengers is the ERJ135, first flown on 4 July 1998** *(courtesy Embraer)*

offered or proposed for the next century, and it can be assumed with near certainty that the company will fully respond to any market trends. Russian companies too have proposals for very high capacity airliners, including the workmanlike Sukhoi KR-860 and somewhat more futuristic Tupolev Tu-404, both with capacities around the 850/860-seat mark.

Potential traffic growth has also not gone unnoticed by those interested in manufacturing much smaller capacity turbofan-powered jetliners, in areas of the market generally outside the remit of the largest manufacturers. The newly created Fairchild Dornier Germany set-up is already flying its 328JET turbofan airliner based on the turboprop 328 and has a range of four other JETS of 40 to 90 seat capacities in hand in both high- and low-wing configurations. Similarly, Embraer of Brazil added the ERJ135 to its ERJ145 jetliner in 1998, and has also proposed the 70-seat ERJ170, while IPTN of Indonesia expects to fly its 104/132-seat N2130 in the year 2002. China and ST Aero of Singapore are among others with similar ambitions, while ATR appears still to be proposing to develop its Airjet range of small-capacity turbofan airliners. Interestingly, following this trend, TUSAŞ of Turkey has redesigned its HD-19 turboprop airliner into the low-wing and turbofan HD-XX.

The rivalry to be No 1 in commercial aviation, or be seen as No 1, between the US and European supergiants of Boeing and Airbus is only too apparent, yet there is work for all (possibly too much to keep pace, requiring the continuous support of a worldwide network of subcontractors to supply subassemblies and other components) and it would be almost impossible to view either as dominant in any real sense. Each has its strengths and each continues to establish milestone events; on 31 March 1998 the Airbus A330-200 with CF6-80E1 engines became the first airliner to receive simultaneous triple type certification, from the European Joint Aviation Authorities, Federal Aviation Administration and Transport Canada.

Both companies have also seen the future benefits of expanding their ranges to include the 100-seat market, with Boeing's 717 flying on 2 September 1998, simultaneously with Airbus' announcement of the A318.

There have been other significant mergers and take-overs, including British Aerospace acquiring 35.1% share capital in Saab AB of Sweden for £269 million to "strengthen ties between the two companies and enable a common strategy to be pursued...", part of Daimler-Benz Aerospace (Dornier) being taken over by Fairchild Aerospace and Daimler then merging with Chrysler in November 1998, and Raytheon Company's purchase of Hughes defence to become a company with 118,000 employees and worldwide sales of more than US$20 billion, to name just four. Other significant movements of shares include Boeing taking an interest in Aero Vodochody of the Czech Republic, Ayres taking a huge shareholding in Let of the Czech Republic, and Bell Helicopter agreeing to take a majority shareholding in IAR-SA Brasov of Romania as part of a deal involving the licence manufacture of AH-1W SuperCobras for the Romanian forces (as AH-1RO Draculas). Interestingly, in Great Britain, Pilatus Britten-Norman reverted to its original name in July 1998 after its Swiss master sold the company, while GKN Westland and Agusta have been discussing possible merger through their parent organizations, having agreed an MoU in April 1998 to continue to identify the nature of any alliance and/or joint venture company that could unify assets and interests. In talks with GKN Westland in October 1998, *WA&SD* was told that an announcement was possible at the end of the year or soon after. Interestingly, the recent agreement over the BA609 and AB139 between Agusta and Bell was viewed as strengthening the reasons for merger, with the potential of improving the product range.

The European factor

Having decided that even closer co-operation was desirable, British Aerospace Regional Aircraft and Avions de Transport Regional (ATR) began promoting their aircraft under the Aero International (Regional) banner. Having gone through the due processes, just a short time later the decision was taken to disengage the structure, though keeping representation under the AI(R) generic name. Then, in July 1998, full de-coupling took place. Meanwhile, Airbus has expanded into the military field and sees its future as a fully integrated single European corporate company rather than an organization owned and run as a highly efficient but ultimately multi-fractional entity. If Airbus needs to see the benefits of full integration, it only has to look at Eurocopter, which merged its various international components into what is claimed to have been the first integrated European aeronautical company, with only Eurocopter Deutschland remaining as a 100% subsidiary.

On 19 May Dassault Aviation, which itself became even more closely linked with Aerospatiale in 1998, presented its initial design concept for the supersonic Falcon business jet, to offer a non-stop range of 4,000 naut miles at a cruise speed of Mach 1.8, while carrying 8 passengers. It was unlucky timing that only days later a Concorde sustained damage to an elevon during supersonic flight, which might have put a damper on the perception of civil supersonic flying had it not quickly become evident that the damage caused no major problems and Concordes were quickly cleared for continuing commercial use well into the next century to carry on their unrivalled success story. Little wonder, then, that projects in Europe, the USA, Russia and Japan continue towards a second-generation large supersonic transport, with a revamped and little-used Tupolev Tu-144LL having helped both East and West in their technical programmes as the only type of large civil supersonic aircraft not in regular service and thereby available for research. But, Dassault is not alone in seeing potential for a supersonic business jet. The September 1998 Farnborough International Air Show was the venue for Lockheed Martin's announcement of a joint venture supersonic business jet study with Gulfstream Aerospace, making up a trio of SBJ projects if including Sukhoi's 10-passenger S-21.

Unqualified commercial success in the field of airliners and helicopters is one thing, but Europe as a whole has not found a common military theme so easy to achieve. Of course, Tornado and Jaguar have been outstandingly successful programmes, but these reached only a fraction of the nations within Europe, and difficulties in maintaining a sensible rate of progress with Eurofighter emphasises national differences and preferences. Sweden has never relied on other nations to dictate its needs, and continues to produce outstanding multi-role warplanes on its own, now at long last attracting such international attention that Britain has taken retrospective interest in exports of Gripen. But, to achieve a truly unified European military business, as successful as Airbus in its own way, France at least would need to be wooed away from supporting its wholly national efforts.

More likely than an all-out European military aircraft industry along Airbus lines, with long-term programmes beyond the development and production of single aircraft types, would be much increased co-operation between the industries of two or more nations. The obvious candidates for this are France and the UK, and this idea has been urged at French ministerial level, which sees Dassault and BAe as prime companies for co-operation that could eventually lead to merger. As companies in the USA competing for worldwide defence orders have shrunk in number due to mergers, so it is argued that European companies should not be competing against each other in addition to competing against strengthened US companies and realigned Russian organizations. However, this may take some swallowing if full merger is eventually proposed, as France pulled out of what has become the most important current European combat aircraft programme, Eurofighter, to develop its own rival, and it is hard to see where such a merger could lead. Yet, BAe and Dassault have already taken early steps towards jointly studying a Tornado replacement, and it will be interesting to see where this leads. DASA has also entered talks with BAe.

History is littered with good intentions to produce 'common' designs that failed to satisfy more than a handful of nations within Europe. Examples that come to mind include attempts to conceive and develop common warplanes to suite NATO countries in the 1950s and 60s, even *with* French input. These, at best, were generally only partially successful in attaining substantial European operation, often suffering from that endemic inability within Europe to agree to anything much when faced with hard choices and compromise.

Outside the current NATO and EU, it is well known that the Czech Republic, Hungary and Poland would like to merge their fighter procurement, but at least in the short term this means an agreed 'foreign purchase', rather than jointly developing warplanes. However, it has equally been recognised that whilst it would make economic sense, the needs of the respective armed

↑ **Dassault Supersonic Falcon business jet, unveiled on 19 May 1998** *(courtesy Dassault/Aviaplans J. P. Soton)*

forces and the timescale for procurement of new aircraft could well make the plan unworkable in the near term.

Such common sense does not always appear to be so apparent within the corridors of the European Union. In the opinion of many, the EU has in recent times been too little interested in sorting out its publicly-mandated economic, agricultural and social policies in a determined effort to woo and coerce by peaceful means the peoples of individual nations into a near European single state, with everything of importance centralized.

This, some argue, could be a truly dangerous path, as the former Yugoslavia is evidence of what can eventually happen when the individual aspirations of sovereign nations and separate peoples are merged against the will of the majority or for political expediency. In recent times, several nations have devolved from unions into separate autonomous countries – the Soviet Union and Czechoslovakia being two obvious examples of this – and even the United Kingdom has taken tentative steps towards a form of autonomy for the small individual nations that form the Union. So why is the European Union swimming against the tide? Indeed, if the greatest reason for the existence of the EU is to avoid any possibility of another major European war, rather than merely trading between like-minded nations, then the creation of a type of EU single state may ironically have the opposite effect and be the very catalyst for armed conflict in the next century.

For commercial/civil aviation, the future in Europe is extremely bright. Such success requires the co-operation of European governments and the skills of European aerospace companies. It is unlikely, therefore, that any closer integration of nations would affect this commercial success in any tangible way as co-operation and mergers between the industries of those nations go ahead with or without the relaxation of borders.

Upstaging from the East

Having survived several years of near chaos, Russia's aerospace companies and bureaux have merged, restructured and become highly motivated. The near disappearance of their traditional markets, including the long-gone Warsaw Pact organization, has forced greater commercialization and rationalization. Despite the effects of reduced home markets and slimmer exports, Russia has managed to keep itself at the cutting-edge of design, with many believing that current Russian warplanes, the latest large Sukhois for example, are at least as good as anything in the West and very possibly better. Interestingly, an impression of what many believed to be the anticipated MAPO "MiG" LFI/LFS lightweight fighter (Mikoyan I-2000) turned out to be the Eurasia Integral, a new design to Western observers detailed in this current edition. Other programmes will be new to readers, and to this end *WA&SD*'s expert on Russian aircraft has spent a great deal of time there talking to designers and manufacturers and obtaining the very latest information on current and future programmes.

China, in particular, has made a quantum leap in its capabilities in the aerospace field, moving away from traditionally reverse-engineered aircraft to new types of partly, mostly or entirely indigenous origin. As a nation, it has accepted assistance from many foreign companies in its efforts to update, while developing the Chengdu J-10 and J-12 among other types for future needs. The J-10 flew for the first time in 1998, but clearly China still has not abandoned development of its older stalwarts, having displayed in 1998 a new 'FS' technology demonstrator version of the Chengdu F-7, featuring a nose radome and chin air intake. China has also actively sought participation in new commercial programmes and, despite rumours, remains politically and industrially in favour of producing (with Airbus Industrie) a small airliner of AE31X type or of a similar concept that may eventually replace AE31X once firm requirements are defined. Although AE31X may itself have been side-stepped, China has been compensated by the recent announcement that it is to become the second source for A320 wings.

Both Israel and the UK have been working hard to supply China with airborne early warning aircraft, with Russia hedging its bets by requesting stakes in programmes aimed at China and based on its Beriev A-50 *Mainstay*/Ilyushin Il-76 airframe. Indeed, in general there has been much activity in the field of electronic mission aircraft, particularly as the number of countries requiring an AEW&C capability has increased. Many AEW&C aircraft with fixed antennae in conformal or in non-rotating over-fuselage radomes have recently entered the market in actual or proposed forms, to compete with the more traditional types with rotating radomes, with carrier aircraft ranging in size from the Embraer RJ145 to the Boeing 737 and Airbus A310. Consequently, new AEW&C designs abound in the Special Electronic & Reconnaissance section of this edition. In other fields of activity, excitement has been generated by the first flight of the Scaled Composites Proteus in July 1998, as a multi-purpose, high altitude and long-duration sensor platform of truly unique appearance.

If deterrent is a dirty word, long live the economists!

Before the 1990s, it was easier for governments to focus defence spending. In Europe, as the most likely theatre of any possible widescale conflict involving the main power blocs, defence allocations were more or less dictated by a perceived requirement to hinder, rather than totally prevent, any determined enemy attacking on massive scale before the threat of nuclear strike came into play and negotiations opened. A dangerous policy, perhaps, but it kept the peace through many crises. Moreover, the need for sufficient conventional forces made pulling together assets to meet other totally unexpected challenges a fairly simple task

One of the greatest achievements of the 1990s has been the 'outbreak' of genuine co-operation between the former power blocs on both political and economic levels. Who would have believed just a decade ago that Russia would feel sufficiently at ease with its neighbours to sell China some of its most modern warplanes and sanction their licensed production, or that French, Israeli and other 'western' avionics and weapon systems would be permitted on aircraft of the Russian air force. And, it doesn't end there. RAF Nimrods have been transported on board Antonov An-124s from RAF Kinloss, at the start of Nimrod 2000 refurbishment. There are numerous other examples of co-operation in both commercial and military fields.

The outlook is fine, future prospects are good, and all is well. Perhaps so, but it would be a foolish person who believed the need for some form of credible deterrence has evaporated, not least as the number of nuclear-armed nations demonstrably increased in 1998. The generally cordial relations between countries perhaps makes us forget that vast numbers of massively destructive weapons remain in place, and new weapons are in the pipeline. The new Russian SS-27 ICBM (RS-12M1 and M2 Topol-M for silo and mobile launched versions respectively), for example, is expected to replace all older systems by 2010. A total of 270 is being produced, and initial operational capability was declared as recently as December 1997 with the first two missiles housed in former SS-19 silos. (Interestingly, this is set against reports that the Russian ministry of defence procured only 12 new combat aircraft between 1994 and 1998.) And, any change of government can spell changes to foreign policy. For, whilst possession of the means of massive destruction by a small number of countries hasn't stopped other individual nations around the world from militarily challenging regional neighbours or even confronting major nuclear powers in shows of determination, it is a fundamental truth that by having sufficient assets to face-down such problems, it guarantees that making war rarely pays. Like it or not, under particular circumstances it requires almost as much strength and resolve to prevent a war as to win one.

Maintaining peace on a global scale with mainly conventional arms can be very expensive, but it is a necessity in our evolving world, when the threat of 'mutual destruction' by nuclear deterrent has become a bit of a 'damp squib'. This is well understood by military planners in the USA and Russia, who have seen to it that many strategic and theatre bombers now have a dual-role capability to enable the deployment of conventional weapons when called upon. However, the downside is that once again it becomes a numbers game, requiring more available assets. Scare stories of how few front-line warplanes are serviceable at any given moment make good reading, but do they point to a worrying trend of unpreparedness that upsets the equations of conventional deterrent? In many cases, probably not. For example, in mid 1998 it was thought that the USAF had just over 180 strategic bombers left in its total active inventory (TAI), but of these about half were not in the primary aircraft inventory (PAI) for possible assignment for immediate use. Oh dear! However, many non-PAI aircraft were being used for training purposes, for tests, undergoing upgrade or modification, or were stored against attrition losses, so all is not as it first appears. In terms of fighters and attack aircraft, the USAF's PAI forces amounted to some 84% of the TAI, a very creditable achievement.

When trying to save on defence budgets, it may be folly to reduce spending to a point when the number of first-line and support aircraft available for immediate action falls below acceptable figures due to cash starvation. Some people believe there is evidence of such failings in 1998, and the perceived preparedness of a number of major air forces has been questioned (possibly including those of the UK and Russia, among others). Thankfully, other more sophisticated ways of reducing short-term spending can been found, including lengthening the procurement period of new aircraft to spread costs, by marginally reducing the number ordered in each of several near-term fiscal years. A good example of this approach can be found under the F-22 Raptor entry, whereby the production lots were altered in 1998 (the figures quoted in the book were received from Lockheed Martin on 16 June 1998). Rescheduling, if managed properly, has the benefit of maintaining the total number of new aircraft eventually acquired, without greatly affecting the serviceability of existing forces through lack of funding. Of course, any such delays must be viewed against immediate needs, as certain procurements are time sensitive.

The need for economic constraint has also led some air forces to restrict their pilots to too few flying hours, a particular problem facing any countries wishing to align themselves with NATO. In a report of mid 1998, it was suggested that of the Czech Air Force's 34 most recent accidents, only 24% had been confirmed as caused by technical failure, perhaps 70% due to human error, and the remainder from unknown causes. Significantly, the average number of hours flown by a Czech military pilot in the year had been a mere 30, under half that thought necessary as a minimum and well below the requirements of NATO.

Having a make-over

Alongside new production, business is booming in the upgrade of older aircraft for greatly extended periods of service, or modernizing fairly new aircraft to boost their capabilities. Everyone is used to hearing of Skyhawks, Phantoms, F-5s and MiG-21s receiving major structural and systems upgrading, but with thousands of F-16s and MiG-29s in service, modernization programmes are likely to be of growing importance in the next century as viable alternatives to buying new. Indeed, one might question how many Eurofighters, F-22s and latest Sukhois are likely to be exported when cheaper upgrades using state-of-the-

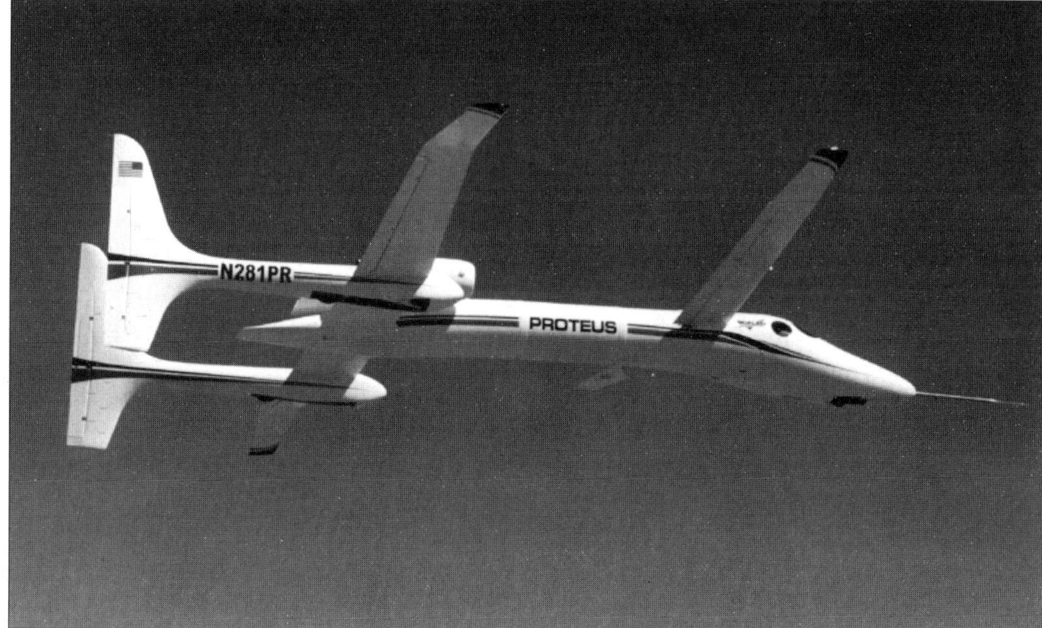

↑ **The highly unique Scaled Composites Proteus, first flown on 26 July 1998** *(courtesy Scaled Composites, Inc)*

↑ **First flight of a production Beech T-6A Texan II on 15 July 1998, the first of 711 intended for the USAF and US Navy under the JPATS programme. Production of so many Texan IIs is indicative of huge opportunities for manufacturers in the replacement of old second-line aircraft within the armed forces** *(courtesy Raytheon Aircraft Company)*

art avionics and new engines offer realistic alternatives for cash-strapped forces.

The Russian air force is anxious to modernize substantial numbers of recent production MiG-29s with long service lives, and this is far from unique. But, when dealing with older aircraft, how realistic is it to maintain a first-line fleet of modernized combat aircraft when others might be flying new aircraft with multi-dimensional thrust vectoring, for example? No problem, or so it would appear. Modernization of the MiG-29 could include adoption of RD-133 engines with 3-D vectoring but, conversely, it is rumoured that even some Mikoyan designers are somewhat sceptical about their necessity given that the greatest advantages are often obtained at speeds of less than Mach 0.5, which under operational conditions is a small fraction of the speed range.

If any aircraft typifies longevity through upgrade and modification, it has to be the B-52. Still the most numerous bomber in the USAF's fleet (in 1998), B-52s average 36 years of age and yet proposals to replace their eight engines with four modern Rolls-Royce turbofans have been made to keep 71 active well into the 21st century. Not far behind in average age come hundreds of C-135 tanker/transports, and these are the tip of an international list of elderly aircraft. Incredibly, because of an on-going programme of update that includes structure and avionics, the T-38 will reappear in its latest T-38C form from 1999, allowing continued service up to the year 2020, by which time the average age of this supersonic trainer in the USAF fleet will be over 52 years. It appears the predictions in the Foreword of the 1996-97 edition of *WA&SD* remain valid; there are still great opportunities for the future.

Brassey's World Aircraft & Systems Directory

Due to the hard work of the contributors, the co-operation of manufacturers, and the help of a huge number of other persons and organizations, *WA&SD* has quickly established itself as a prime source of information on the world's aerospace industry. This new edition carries even more in-depth data than the first, which received very pleasing acclaim throughout the world. As can be seen from a glance at the entries, it also features a large number of aircraft that cannot be found in *any* similar reference book.

WA&SD has justified being called "The World's Most Comprehensive Aviation Reference Work", as no other single book attempts to offer such a wealth of information on so many types of current aircraft plus those under development or being modified, from the largest commercial airliners and bombers to the smallest microlights, gliders and airships, supported by additional sections on engines, radars, missiles and more besides. Responding to requests, illustrations are generally larger and a new Spaceflight section detailing manned spacecraft and commercial launch vehicles has been added.

WA&SD offers an unrivalled package of information at a truly affordable price, with no compromise on quality. Indeed, at the time of publication it is believed to be by far the most up-to-date book of its size and type available anywhere in the world, with many final corrections and updates introduced as late as November 1998.

To all those that have helped in the preparation of the new Second Edition, I offer my sincere thanks.

Michael Taylor
November 1998

Glossary of abbreviations

2-D Two dimensional
3-D Three dimensional

A Amp (normally amp is used, rather than A)
AAM Air-to-air missile
ABM Anti-ballistic missile
AC Alternating current
ACB Air circuit breaker
ACC Air Combat Command (USAF)
ACES Advanced concept ejection seat (plus other meanings)
ACLS Automatic carrier landing system
ACM Air combat manoeuvring, or air combat mission (or mode)
ACN Aircraft classification number
ACO Airborne commanding officer
ACP Audio Control Panel
ACS Air combat simulator, or attitude (or automated) control system
ACT Active control technology
Ada High order computer language for US services
ADC Air data computer
ADF Automatic direction finder, or air defense fighter
ADHS Analog data handling system
ADI Attitude director indicator
ADV Air defence variant
AETC Air Education and Training Command (USAF)
AEW Airborne early warning
AEW&C Airborne early warning & control
AF Air force
AFB Air force base, aramid fibre composite, or automatic frequency control
AFC Augmentor fuel control
AFCS Automatic flight control system
AFDS Autopilot and flight director system
AFL Avionics flying laboratory
AFM Advanced fuel management
AFMC Air Force Materiel Command (USAF)
AFRC Air Force Reserve Command (USAF)
AFSPC Air Force Space Command (USAF)
AFSOC Air Force Special Operations Command (USAF)
Afterburning Augmented thrust
AFTI Advanced fighter technology integration
AGM Air-to-ground missile
AGL Above ground level
AHRS Attitude heading reference system
AIC Air inlet computer
AIDS Airborne integrated data system
AIM Airborne intercept missile, or actuator interface module (or others)
Airstairs Passenger boarding stairs built as an integral part of the aircraft
AIS Automated information system
ALCM Air launched cruise missile
ALCS Active lift control system, or augmented longitudinal control system
ALFS Airborne low frequency sonar
Al-Li Aluminium-lithium
Alt Altitude
AM Amplitude modulation
AMC Air Mobility Command (USAF)
Amp Ampère
ANG Air National Guard (US)
Anhedral Inclined downward from root to tip
AoA Angle of attack
AOAI Angle of attack indicator
AOC Air officer commanding
APGS Auxiliary power generating system
APR Auxiliary power reserve
APS Auxiliary power system (plus others)
APU Auxiliary power unit
ARCS Acquisition radar and control system
ARIA Advanced range instrumentation aircraft
ARINC Aeronautical Radio Inc
ARM Anti-radiation missile
ARPA Advanced research projects agency
ARR Air refuelling receptable
ARS Attack radar set
Articulated rotor With blades able to flap, drag and feather
ARV Air recreational vehicle
ASARS Advanced synthetic aperture radar system
ASI Airspeed indicator
ASIP Aircraft structural integrity programme
ASL Above sea level
ASM Air-to-surface missile
ASO Acoustic systems officer
ASRAAM Advanced short range air-to-air missile
ASST Anti-ship surveillance & targeting. Also, advanced supersonic transport
ASTOVL Advanced short take-off and vertical landing
ASUW Anti surface warfare. See ASV
ASV Anti surface warfare (anti ship)
ASW Anti submarine warfare
ATA Advanced tactical aircraft
ATC Air traffic control. Also, approved type certificate
ATDS Airborne tactical data system
ATF Advanced tactical fighter
ATGW Anti-tank guided weapon
ATHS Airborne target handover system
ATO Assisted take-off. RATO (rocket) and JATO (jet, often meaning rocket)
Autogyro US gyroplane
AUW All up weight
Avionics Aviation electronics
AVLF Airborne very low frequency
AWAC Automatic weapons control system
AWACS Airborne warning & control system
AWR Airborne weather radar

BCAR British Civil Airworthiness Requirements
BERP British experimental rotor programme
BHP Brake horsepower
BIT Built in test
BITE Built in test equipment
BLC Boundary layer control
Bleed air Hot compressed air taken from turbine engines
Blimp Non-rigid buoyant aircraft (airship)
Blind flying Flying using instruments, without outside visual references
BVR Beyond visual range

C Celsius or centigrade
C^2 Command and control
C^3 Command, control and communications
C^3I Command, control, communications and intelligence
CAA Civil Aviation Authority (UK)
CAD Computer aided design
CAF Counter air fighter

CAM Computer aided manufacture
CAMS Computer aided maintenance system
Canard Foreplane
CAP Combat air patrol
CAR Civil airworthiness regulations
CAS Calibrated airspeed, calculated airspeed, or close air support
Casevac Casualty evacuation
Cat Category
CB Chemical biological
CBR Chemical biological radiological, or California bearing ratio
CBU Cluster bomb unit
CBW Chemical, biological warfare
CCD Charge coupled device
CCV Control configured vehicle
CDU Cockpit display unit
CEO Chief executive officer
CEP Concurrent evaluation phase
CFT Conformal fuel tank
CG Centre of gravity
Chord Width between the leading and trailing edges of an aerofoil
CIP Common Integrated Processor
CIS Commonwealth of independent states
CKD Component knock down (parts for assembly)
CLCD Colour liquid crystal displays
Clean Flying with flaps, slats and undercarriage retracted (if u/c retractable). No external stores
cm Centimetre
CNI Communications navigation identification
CO Commanding officer
COD Carrier on-board delivery
C of A Certificate of airworthiness
COIN Counter insurgency
com or **comm** Communications
Combat SAR Combat search and rescue
Combi Combined passengers and freight
Comint Communications intelligence
COTS Commercial off the shelf
CP Core processing
CPCI Computer programme configuration item
CPP Cost per passenger
CPS Central processing system
CPU Central processing unit
CSE Common support equipment
CSP Common signal processor
CRT Cathode ray tube
CVR Cockpit voice recorder
CW Continuous wave. Also chemical warfare
CWR Colour weather radar

DADC Digital air data computer
DADS Digital air data system
dB Decibel
DC Direct current
Dem/val Demonstration/validation
Derated Output power of an engine deliberately restricted to under its full possible rating
DF Direction finder
DFCC Digital flight control computer
DFCS Digital flight control system
DID Data insertion device
Difar Directional acoustic frequency analysis and recording
Dihedral Inclined upwards from root to tip
DIN(S) Digital inertial navigation (system)
DLC Direct lift control
DME Distance measuring equipment
DMU Distance measuring unit. Also data management unit
DoD Department of Defense (US)
DRU Direct reporting unit
DRU Design review update
DTC Data transfer cartridge
DTE Data transfer equipment
DT&E Development test & evaluation
DTU Data transfer unit

EAA Experimental Aircraft Association
EADI Electronic attitude display (or director) indicator
EAS Equivalent airspeed
ECCM Electronic counter countermeasures
ECM Electronic countermeasures
ECR Electronic combat and reconnaissance
EDU Engine diagnostic unit
EEZ Exclusive economic zone
EFIS Electronic flight instrumentation system
EGT Exhaust gas temperature
ehp Equivalent horsepower
EHSI Electronic horizontal situation indicator
EICAS Engine indication/instrumentation and crew alerting system
EICMS Engine in-flight monitoring system
ekW Equivalent Kilowatt
ELF Extremely low frequency
Elint Electronic intelligence
ELT Emergency locator transponder
EM Electromagnetic
EMD Engineering and manufacturing development
EMI Electromagnetic interference
EMS Emergency medical service
EO Electro-optical
EOC Early operational capability
EPNdB Equivalent perceived noise decibel
ER Extended range
ERU Ejector release unit
eshp Equivalent shaft horsepower
ESM Electronic (support or surveillance) measures
Esmo ESM operator
ETOPS Extended range twin operations
EW Electronic warfare

F Fahrenheit
FAA Federal Aviation Administration (US) or Fleet Air Arm (UK)
FAC Forward air control
FADEC Full authority digital engine control
FAR Federal aviation regulations
FBL Fly by light
FBW Fly by wire
FCS Flight control system
FDAS Flight director acquisition system
FDC Flight director coupler
FDI Flight director indicator
FDS Flight director system
ff First flight
FFAR Folding fin (or forward firing or free flight) aircraft rocket
FGA Fighter and ground attack
FGR Fighter, ground (attack) and reconnaissance
FLCC Flight control computer
FLCS Flight control system
FLIR Forward looking infra-red
FM Frequency modulation
FMC(S) Flight management computer (system)
FMD Flight management display
FMS Foreign military sales (US) or flight management system
FOD Foreign object damage (debris)
FSD Full scale development
ft Foot (12 ins)
FY Fiscal year

g Gramme
G limit Acceleration due to gravity
GAC Gust alleviation control
GEO Geostationary Earth orbit, direct reporting unit, or data retrieval unit
glove Non-moving root section of a variable-geometry wing
GMTI Ground moving target indicator
GNS Global navigation system
GP General purpose
GPS Global positioning system
GPU Ground power unit
GPWS Ground proximity warning system
GRP Glass reinforced plastics
GTO Geostationary transfer orbit
GW Guided weapon

HARS Heading and attitude reference system
HDD Head down display
HE High explosive
HF High frequency
HMD or **HMS** Helmet mounted display (or sight)
HOCAC Hands on cyclic and collective
HOTAS Hands on throttle and stick
HOTCC Hands on throttle/collective/cyclic
hp Horsepower
HSD Horizontal situation display
HSI Horizontal situation indicator
HUD Head up display
HUDWAC HUD weapon aiming computer
HUMS Health and usage monitoring system
HVAR High velocity aircraft rocket
Hz Hertz

IAS Indicated airspeed
ICAO International Civil Aviation Organization
IDS Interdiction strike
IF Intermediate frequency
IFF Identification friend or foe
IFR Instrument flight rules
IGE In ground effect
IIR Imaging infra-red
IIRS Instrument inertial reference set
ILS Instrument landing system
IMS Information (or integrated) management system
INAS Integrated nav/attack system
INS Inertial navigation system
ins Inches
IOC Initial operational capability
IR Infra-red
IRCCD Infra-red charged coupled device
IRCM Infra-red countermeasures
IRLS Infra-red linescan
IRS Inertial reference system
IRST Infra-red search track
IRU Inertial reference unit
ISA International standard atmosphere
ISAR Inverse synthetic aperture radar
ISWL Isolated single-wheel

JAA Joint airworthiness authorities
JAR Joint airworthiness requirements
JAR-VLA Joint airworthiness requirements-very light aircraft
JAST Joint advanced strike technology
JATO Jet assisted take off (see ATO)
JPATS Joint primary aircraft training system
JSC Joint stock company
JSF Joint strike fighter
J-STARS Joint-surveillance target acquisition radar system
JTIDS Joint tactical information distribution system

K Kelvin
kg Kilogramme
km Kilometre
km/h Kilometre per hour
kN Kilonewtons
KTAS Knots true airspeed
kts Knots
kVA Kilovolt ampère
kW Kilowatt

LAMPS Light airborne multi-purpose system
LANTIRN Low altitude navigation and targeting infra-red (at) night
LAPES Low-altitude parachute extraction system
lbf Pounds force (engine thrust rating)
LCD Liquid crystal display
LCG Load classification group
LCN Load classification number
LED Light emitting diode
LEO Low Earth orbit
LERX Leading-edge route extension
LF Low frequency
LFC Low fuel consumption, liquid fuel consumption, or laminar flow control
LGB Laser guided bomb
Litres Litres × 0.264177 = US gallons.
Litres × 0.219975 = Imperial gallons
Litter Stretcher
LLL(TV) Low light level (TV)
LO Low observable
Loran Long range navigation
Low observables Stealth
Lox Liquid oxygen
LRU Line replaceable unit
Ltd Limited (company)

m Metre
MAC Mean aerodynamic chord
Mach Mach number
MAD Magnetic anomaly detector
Madge Microwave aircraft digital guidance system
MAWS Missile approach warning system
MCM Mine countermeasures
MCP Maximum continuous power
MCU Management control unit
Medevac Medical evacuation
MEP Mission equipment package
MF Medium frequency
MFD Multi-function display
MGB Main gearbox
MGT Motor gas temperature
MGTOW Maximum gross take-off weight
MIL-STD Military standard
MLS Microwave landing system
MLU Mid-life update (or upgrade)
MLW Maximum landing weight
mm Millimetre
M_{MO} Maximum operating Mach number

MMS Mast mounted sight, or mission management system
mod Modified
MoU Memorandum of understanding
MPA Maritime patrol aircraft
MPD Multi-purpose display
mph Miles per hour
MPR Military power reserve
MR Medium range or maritime reconnaissance
MSIP Multi stage improvement programme
MTBF Mean time between failures
MTBM Mean time between maintenance
MTI Moving target indicator
MTOW Maximum take-off weight
MW Medium wave
MZFW Maximum zero fuel weight

N/A Not applicable
NACA National Advisory Committee for Aeronautics
NAS Naval air station
NASA National Aeronautics and Space Administration
NASP National aero space plane
NATO North Atlantic Treaty Organization
nav Navigation
navaid Navigation aid
nav/com(m) Navigation and communications
NBAA National Business Aircraft Association
NBC Nuclear, biological, chemical
NEDS Narcotics eradication delivery system
Ni-cd Nickel cadmium
NOE Nap of the earth
NOS Night observation surveillance
Notar No tail rotor
NVG Night vision goggles
NVS Night vision system
NWC Naval weapon center

OBIGGS Onboard inert gas generating system
OBOGS On-board oxygen generating system
OBS On board simulation, or omni-bearing selector (also others)
OCU Operational conversion unit
OEI One engine inoperative
OEU Operational evaluation unit
OGE Out of ground effect
Omega Long-range radio navigation aid
OMI Omnibearing magnetic indicator
OTH(T) Over the horizon (targeting)
OTPI On top position indicator
OTU Operational training unit

PACAF Pacific Air Forces (USAF)
Pax Passengers
PCN Pavement classification number
PDR Preliminary design review
PDU Power distribution unit
PFCS Primary flight control (or computer) system
PFD Primary flight display
PGM Precision guided munition
PLC Public limited company
PMFD Primary multi-function display
PRDS Processed radar display system
psi Pounds per square inch. psi × 0.06895 = bars
PWR Passive warning receiver

R&D Research & development
RAF Royal Air Force (UK)
RAM Radar absorbing material. Also random access memory
RAS Radar absorbing structure
RAT Ram air turbine
RAWS Radar altitude warning system. Also radar attack and warning system
RCS Radar cross section
RF Radio frequency
RFP Request for proposals
RHWR Radar homing and warning receiver
RHWS Radar homing and warning system
RMI Remote or radio magnetic indicator
Root Innermost part of an aerofoil where it attaches to the supporting airframe
RPA Remotely piloted airship (or aircraft)
rpm Revolutions per minute
RPV Remotely piloted vehicle (drone/UAV)
RWR Radar warning receiver. Also rear warning radar.
RWS Radar warning system

SALT Strategic arms limitations talks
SAM Surface-to-air missile
SAR Search and rescue. Also synthetic aperture radar and semi-active radar
SARH Semi-active radar homing
SAS Stability augmentation system
Satcom Satellite communications
SCAS Stability and control augmentation system
SEAD Suppression of enemy air defenses
Senso Sensor operator
SFAR Special federal aviation regulations
SFC Specific fuel consumption
shp Shaft horsepower
SIF Selective identification (interrogation) facility
Sigint Signals intelligence
SLAR Side looking airborne radar
SLEP Service life extension programme
SMS Stores management system
SOF Special operations forces
SP Signal processor
SPILS Stall protection and incidence limiting system
SR Short range or strategic reconnaissance
SRAM Short range attack missile
SSB Single sideband
SST Supersonic transport
STA Supplementary Type Approval
STC Supplemental Type Certificate
STD Standard
STE Special test equipment
STO Short take off
STOL Short take off and landing
STOVL Short take off and vertical landing
Swing wing Variable geometry wing

Tacamo Take charge and move out (US Navy)
Tacan Tactical air navigation
Tacco Tactical commander or co-ordinator
TANS Tactical air navigation system
TAS True airspeed, or tactical alerting system
TBO Time between overhauls
TCAS Traffic alert and collision avoidance system
TDS Tactical data system
TET Turbine entry temperature
TFR Terrain following radar
TGT Turbine gas temperature
TGW Terminally guided weapon
TIALD Thermal imaging airborne laser designator
TIAS Target identification and acquisition system
TIT Turbine entry temperature
TLS Tactical landing system
TOGW Take off gross weight
tonne 1,000 kilogrammes
TOW Take-off weight
TRU Transformer-rectifier unit
TSD Tactical situation display
TV Television
TWR Threat warning radar
TWS Track while scan, or tail warning system

UAV Unmanned aerial vehicle
UFD Up-front display
UHF Ultra high frequency
USAF United States Air Force
USAFE US Air Forces in Europe (USAF)
USCG United States Coast Guard
USMC United States Marine Corps
USN United States Navy
UV Ultraviolet

V Volts
VA Volt ampères
V_A Design manoeuvring speed
Variable geometry "Swing" wing
V_D Design diving speed
VDU Visual or video display unit
Vertrep Vertical replenishment
VFR Visual flight rules
VHF Very high frequency
VHSIC Very high speed integrated circuits
VIP Very important person. Also value improvement programme
VISTA Variable in-flight stability test aircraft
VLF Very low frequency
VLO Very low observable
VMC Visual meteorological conditions
V_{MO} Maximum permitted operating speed
VMS Vehicle management system
V_{NE} Never-exceed speed
VOD Vertical on-board delivery
VOR VHF omnidirectional (radio) range
VPU Video processing unit
VSD Vertical situation display
VSI Vertical speed indicator
V/STOL Vertical or short take-off and landing
VTO(L) Vertical take-off (and landing)

WA&SD World Aircraft & Systems Directory
WDNS Weapon delivery and navigation system
WSI Windshear indicator
WSO Weapon system operator

ZFW Zero fuel weight

DIRECTORY USER'S GUIDE

The *Brassey's World Aircraft & Systems Directory 1999–2000* details aircraft in production or under development worldwide – military, commercial, general aviation, helicopters, autogyros, updates and modifications, sporting, homebuilts, microlights, gliders and airships. All categories are important to the industry and enthusiast alike. In addition, some older combat aircraft are detailed when undergoing upgrade, while reference is made to the 1996-97 edition of *WA&SD* for other older types. However, the specification of an aircraft is insufficient knowledge if the performance details of the radar it carries and missiles it launches (if military) are not available at source, for half the knowledge is half the capability revealed. Essential also are details of the engines.

To address all these vital issues, the book contains sections on commercial, military and light aircraft engines, missiles and commercial and military radars, plus runway information. In addition, and new to the book, is an extra section on spaceflight (manned, plus commercial satellite launchers).

The book has been divided into 13 sections, to enable the reader to see and compare at a glance aircraft of similar purpose built throughout the world. Within each section countries are listed alphabetically, and within each country aircraft manufacturers are listed alphabetically.

Important company information (such as address, telephone/facsimile/web site/E-mail contacts and information officer) is provided for each manufacturer, but where a manufacturer's products fall into more than one section (for example, Boeing in Combat, Airliners and Helicopters) the company details are given in the first section containing any of that company's aircraft, with cross references thereafter. A comprehensive index is also provided.

The book has been designed for easy reference and usability. Each new company entry starts with a heading arranged across the entire page with blue tint. This prevents the products of different companies merging. The significant development dates of an aircraft are listed, rather than written in paragraph form, with a distinctive colour icon by each date in the appropriate sections to make it easily distinguished. Therefore, by looking for the ■ blue icon symbol throughout the book, the development dates of aircraft can be found at a glance. Similar distinctive blue icons have been adopted for the various business ■ **Activities** of a company, its ■ **Facilities**, and the design ■ **Aims** of individual aircraft types.

Within the individual aircraft entries, information is presented in a way intended to help resolve readers' queries with ease. For example, there are separate sub-headings for "**fixed**" and "**expendable weapons**" of a combat aircraft, as well as for its "**radar**", "**flight instruments/avionics**" and "**self-protection systems**". Similarly, there are separate sub-headings for the "**engine**", its "**power rating**", "**fuel system**" and "**flight refuelling**". There are many other examples of this approach throughout the pages, aimed at making information easily accessible and fast to find. Specification data (such as dimensions, weights and performance) is provided in shaded boxes for speedy reference and clear display. Where an aircraft is no longer available, reference is made to the entry in the previous edition of *WA&SD*, quoting the exact page number.

Combat Aircraft
(and Modern Turbine Trainers)

Lockheed Martin Aircraft Argentina SA (LMAASA) — Argentina

Corporate address:
Avenida Fuerza Aérea Argentina km 5500, 5010-Córdoba.

Telephone: +54 51 651 706
Facsimile: +54 51 651 706 and 51 661 894

Founded:
15 July 1995 (see Activities), to manage the Fábrica Militar de Aviones SA (FMA) that had first formed in 1927 under Argentine Air Force control via its Area de Material Córdoba (AMC).

CEO:
James Taylor (Managing Director).

Employees: 1,004.

Information:
Victor Hugo Almirón (Marketing Manager).

ACTIVITIES

- On 15 December 1994 the Government of Argentina and former Lockheed Aircraft Service Company (later Lockheed Martin Aircraft Services) of the USA signed contracts to privatize the Government's Fábrica Militar de Aviones SA (FMA) aircraft factory and maintenance depot at Córdoba, to modify A-4M Skyhawk attack aircraft under a $200 million (approximately) contract, and provide aircraft maintenance services for the Argentine Air Force for 5 years under a similarly priced contract. Consequently, Lockheed established LMAASA (Lockheed Martin Aircraft Argentina SA) for operating purposes, beginning management on 1 July 1995 but having 15 July as the official founding date.
- Lockheed Martin's A-4M Skyhawk contract covered the refurbishment and modernization of 36 ex-US Navy aircraft for Argentina (previously in storage in Arizona) over a 3 year period, as A-4AR Fightinghawks. The work included depot level inspections and rewiring, engine refurbishment, avionics upgrade, pilot and mechanic training, spares provisioning and technical documentation. The initial 18 A-4Ms were assigned to be upgraded at Chino, California, USA, and the remainder at LMAASA using Lockheed Martin kits.
- Under depot privatization, LMAASA has a 25-year concession. Córdoba is becoming an international C-130 maintenance centre, attracting also other fabrication, maintenance and modification work, including commercial.
- Supports the IA.58A Pucará, and manufacturers the IA.63 Pampa and parachutes.
- Major repair and overhaul centre for civil and military aircraft, encompassing the Lockheed Martin C-130, Fokker F-27 and F-28, and FMA IA.50 Guaraní II.
- Major repair and overhaul centre for T-56, T-63, TFE731, GTC 85, Spey 555, PT-6, Atar 09C, Marboré, Bastan VI and Astazou XVI-G engines.

FMA IA.58A Pucará

Comments: Production of Pucará ended in 1986. The Chief Editor was informed by Lockheed Martin that the company considered the Pucará to be an ideal low-intensity conflict attack aircraft. A full description of Pucará and a photograph can be found in the 1996-97 edition of *WA&SD*, pages 11 and 12. The Argentine Air Force has approximately 40 operational Pucarás serving with 3 Grupo, III° Brigada Aérea at Reconquista, with at least 25 more stored against attrition or for possible transfer; Colombia has 3 (314 squadron, Grupo 31 at Apiay); Sri Lanka received 4 and held options for a further 6 used aircraft; and Uruguay received 6 (serving with 1 Group). The Sri Lanka Pucarás were based with No 7 Squadron of No 1 Wing at Anuradhapura. An anticipated operational move to Vavuniya was abandoned when 1 aircraft was lost and difficulties with spares hindered deployment of the remainder, since when another has been lost and 1 cannibalized for components to maintain the Pucará flying with the Training Wing (it can still undertake combat missions).

↑ **FMA IA.63 Pampa at Mendoza** *(Denis Hughes)*

FMA IA.63 Pampa

First flight: 6 October 1984.
Role: Basic, advanced and weapon training, and light attack.
Fatigue life: 8,000 flight hours, safe life certified. 14,000 flight hours, damage tolerance.

Aims

- To provide the Argentine Air Force with a modern jet trainer and light attack aircraft to replace the Morane-Saulnier MS.760 Paris and possibly other aircraft.
- Capable of operating from grass and other unprepared strips.
- Apply Alpha Jet technology to realise a 50% development saving.

Development

- 1979. Programme begun. 7 designs submitted in single- and twin-jet configurations, with selection in the following year.
- 1981. Full-scale development initiated after wind-tunnel testing of scale models and further design work. Participation by Dornier of Germany (with Alpha Jet and transonic supercritical wing experience) provided technical back-up in addition to manufacturing the wings and other surfaces for the prototypes. The chosen aerofoil was of advanced Dornier type.
- March 1981. Metal cut for the first of what became 5 prototypes (3 flying and 2 ground test).
- 6 October 1984. First flight of a prototype, although the sixth flight on 10 October marked the recognized first flight date.
- 7 August 1985. First flight of the second prototype. A Government order for production aircraft was placed 2 months later.
- April 1988. 3 of an initial 18 production Pampas ordered were received by the IV Brigada Aérea (the M-S Paris operating Brigada at Mendoza). 1 squadron fully equipped by May 1992, then unarmed and without HUDs or weapon delivery systems (see Avionics).
- May 1990. LTV (later renamed Vought and now part of Northrop Grumman) and FMA became partners to offer the Pampa 2000-International for the USAF's JPATS programme. In the event, not selected.
- 31 August 1992. Second prototype in provisional Pampa 2000-International form was lost in an accident in Britain, while preparing for the Farnborough Air Show.
- 26 May 1993. First flight of a Pampa 2000-International prototype proper, prepared from an Argentine production Pampa.
- 1995. Programme to upgrade Pampa, based around the Elbit lightweight weapon delivery and navigation system (see Avionics), to provide an advanced interface system that familiarizes trainee pilots with a WDNS.

Details

Sales/Users: Initially, 18 ordered for the Argentine Air Force, with up to 46 more expected to be funded later, first joining III Escuadron (III Squadron), 4 Grupo at El Plumerillo (Mendoza). Early consideration by Brazil to buy Pampas did not materialize, but other nations have expressed interest, believed to include Mexico and Israel. The Argentine Navy sought funding for 12-14 naval training variants, modified for landing on the deck of *25 de Mayo* but also for shore use. Not selected for US JPATS. Standard version price, US$3.5 million.
Crew: 2, trainee normally in the front cockpit and instructor in the tandem rear cockpit that is raised to provide improved forward visibility.
Cockpit: Dual controls. Control stick in the front cockpit includes trim switch, bombs release button, VHF pulse button, forward wheel steering system button, and camera/trigger (cannon and rockets). Control stick in the rear cockpit has the same functions plus additionally includes trim priority button. Single-piece windshield. Single-piece upward-hinged canopy with internal screen. Fully pressurised and air conditioned, with AiResearch bootstrap type environmental control system (maximum differential 4.35 psi) using high and low pressure engine bleed air, maintaining a 6,500 ft (1,981 m) cockpit altitude to 18,800 ft (5,730 m).
Crew escape: UPC S-111-S3IA63 zero-zero ejection seats.
Fixed guns: None internally. Fitted with an underfuselage and removable 30-mm DEFA cannon pod containing 145 rounds of ammunition.
Number of weapon pylons: 5, comprising 1 under the fuselage (970 lb, 440 kg maximum weapon load), and 4 under the wings (2 × 970 lb, 440 kg and 2 × 640 lb, 290 kg), all stressed at +4.5/-2 g. Weapon load is restricted to 2,558 lb (1,160 kg) when Pampa carries 968 litres of fuel (normal internal fuel load).
Expendable weapons and equipment: Container for practice bombs or rockets, 250 lb and/or 500 lb bombs (including SITEA

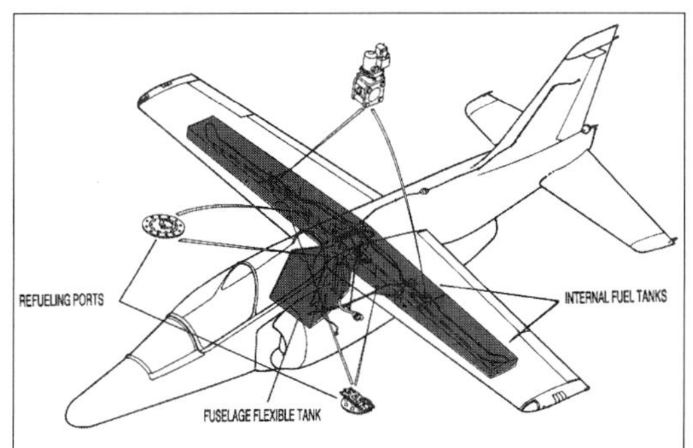

↑ **FMA IA.63 Pampa fuel system diagram** *(courtesy LMAASA)*

BK-BR series of general purpose and BRP/BRPS/FAS parachute retarded bombs), rockets, gun pod with two 7.62-mm machine-guns, or other weapons. See Fixed guns.
Additional stores: Include reconnaissance pod.
Flight/weapon system avionics/instrumentation: Standard Air Force version equipped with 2 Collins VHF transceivers, Becker intercom system for communication, Collins VOR/ILS with marker beacon receiver, Collins DME and Collins ADF for flight. Navigation system capable of complete IFR navigation/landing training. Attitude and heading information by Astronautics 3-gyro platform, with magnetic flux valve compass for additional heading reference. Standard Air Force version equipped with gyro-stabilized Saab RGS 2 sighting system in front cockpit (optional in rear), with recorder in front sight and weapon management system. As part of an upgrade programme, an Elbit head-up display has been fitted to in-service Pampas. For future production aircraft, it is programmed to upgrade the complete system, including a lightweight weapon delivery and navigation system with central mission computer, ring laser gyro/inertial navigation system, video camera and VTR, and multi-function display.
Wing characteristics: High-mounted transonic, straight tapered, with slight anhedral.
Wing control surfaces: Ailerons and single-slotted Fowler flaps.
Tail control surfaces: Slab tailplane. Rudder.
Airbrakes: 2, on sides of upper-rear fuselage near the tail. Can be used at all flight speeds.
Flight control system: Each primary flight control, flaps and airbrakes are powered using 2 separate hydraulic systems. Primary control surfaces are operated by Liebher tandem servo actuators that can function on either system should one system fail. Electrically-operated pitch and yaw trim. Rudder control includes a yaw damper.
Fuselage: Conventional, with 2 lateral air intakes and a slim, almost boom-like aft end carrying the tail, allowing for the efflux from the underfuselage engine nozzle.
Construction materials: All metal.
Engine: AlliedSignal TFE731-2-2N turbofan.
Engine rating: 3,500 lbf (15.57 kN).
Fuel system: 1,383 litres maximum internal fuel, comprising normal 968 litres plus 415 litres in auxiliary wing tanks. 10 seconds of inverted flight permitted.
Electrical system: 28 volt DC supply with engine-driven starter-generator (Lear Siegler 400 A, 11.5 kW). 2 parallel 27 amp-hour SAFT ni-cd batteries. 2 Flite-Tronics 450 VA static inverters for AC supply. 30 minutes emergency electrical power.
Hydraulic system: 3,000 psi for each of 2 independent systems, powered by an engine-driven pump. Bootstrap reservoirs pressurized at 58 psi. No 1 system (16 litres per minute flow rate) for primary flight controls, airbrakes, and undercarriage extension/retraction and braking. No 2 system (8 litres per minute flow rate) for primary flight controls, flaps, nosewheel steering, and emergency/parking brakes. Ram air turbine (AiResearch) for emergency hydraulic power to No 2 system should engine shut down in flight and pressure drop below the minimum allowable.
Braking system: Messier-Bugatti discs on main units, with anti-skid.
Oxygen system: 10 litre lox converter. An emergency system is located on the rear left side of each ejection seat.

Aircraft variants:
IA.63 Pampa is the standard Argentine Air Force version, as detailed. The naval variant is offered in similar configuration.
Pampa 2000-International was the combined Vought/FMA version for the USAF's JPATS competition. Withdrawn on 22 November 1994. See 1996-97 edition of *WA&SD*, page 12.

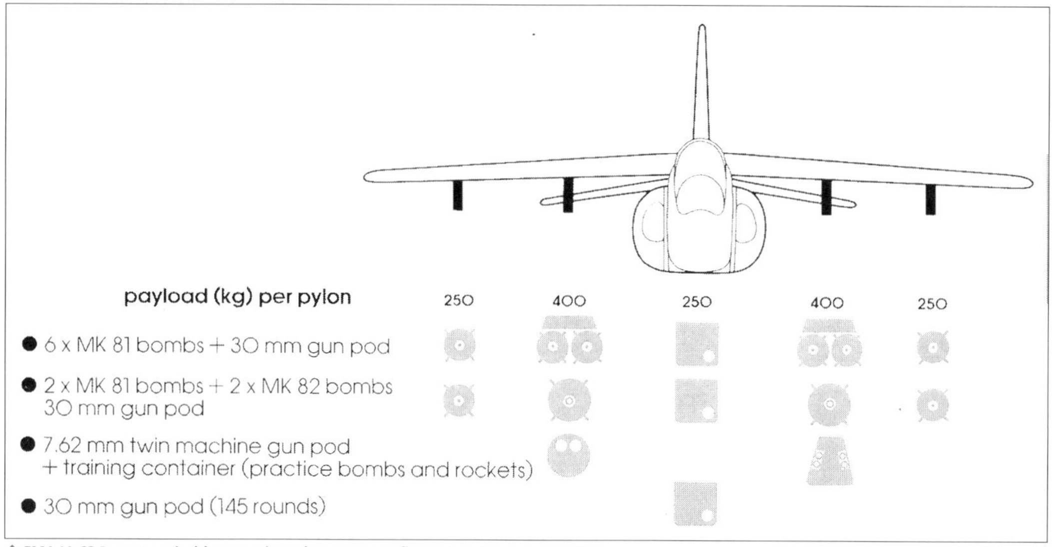

↑ **FMA IA.63 Pampa typical (not maximum) weapon configurations** *(courtesy LMAASA)*

Details for IA.63 Pampa

PRINCIPAL DIMENSIONS:
Wing span: 31 ft 9 ins (9.69 m)
Maximum length: 35 ft 9 ins (10.9 m)
Maximum height: 14 ft 1.25 ins (4.3 m)

WINGS:
Aerofoil section: Dornier/FMA Do/A7/-8
Area: 168.272 sq ft (15.63 m^2)
Aspect ratio: 6.01
Anhedral: 3°

TAIL UNIT:
Tailplane span: 15 ft (4.58 m)
Tailplane area: 46.867 sq ft (4.35 m^2)

UNDERCARRIAGE:
Type: SHL retractable, with steerable nosewheel (±47°), designed for operation from unprepared surfaces. Nosewheel retracts rearward, main wheels into air intakes
Main wheel tyre size: Low pressure Goodrich 6.5 × 10, pressure 95 psi
Nosewheel tyre size: Low pressure, double water deflectors Goodrich 380 × 150 mm, pressure 58 psi
Wheel base: 14 ft 6 ins (4.42 m)
Wheel track: 8 ft 9 ins (2.66 m)

WEIGHTS:
Empty, operating: 6,217 lb (2,820 kg)
Normal take-off: 8,311 lb (3,770 kg)
Maximum take-off: 11,025 lb (5,000 kg)

PERFORMANCE:
Maximum operating Mach number (M_{Mo}): 0.8, *clean*
Maximum speed: 440 kts (507 mph) 815 km/h, *clean*, at 26,200 ft (7,785 m)
Maximum speed at sea level: 405 kts (466 mph) 741 km/h, *clean*
Cruise speed: 350 kts (403 mph) 650 km/h at 30,000 ft (9,145 m), *clean*
Stall speed: 82 kts (95 mph) 152 km/h CAS, *flaps down*
Approach speed at 7,215 lb (3,273 kg) weight: 103 kts (118 mph) 191 km/h CAS, *flaps down*
Take-off distance, at 8,311 lb (3,770 kg) weight: 1,411 ft (430 m), normal internal fuel, at sea level, ISA
Landing distance at 7,716 lb (3,500 kg) weight: 1,510 ft (460 m) at sea level, ISA
Maximum climb rate: 5,200 ft (1,560 m) per minute, at 8,311 lb (3,770 kg) weight
Roll rate: 200° per second, *clean*
G limits: +6, -3 without external stores
Ceiling: 42,300 ft (12,900 m)
Range with full internal fuel: 1,140 naut miles (1,312 miles) 2,112 km at 300 kts and 35,025 ft (10,675 m), ISA with reserves
Radius of action with full fuel and 2,205 lb (1,000 kg) of bombs: 236 naut miles (272 miles) 437 km, Hi-Lo-Lo-Hi air-to-ground profile, with 30 naut mile dash in/out, 5 minutes allowance for weapon delivery and reserves

SABCA — Belgium

Full name:
Société Anonyme Belge de Constructions Aéronautiques.

Corporate address:
Chaussée de Haecht 1470, B-1130 Bruxelles.
Charleroi plant: Rue des Fusillés 11, B-6041 Gosselies.

Telephone: +32 2 729 55 11 or 59 01 (Bruxelles)
+32 71 25 42 11 or 43 39 (Gosselies)
Facsimile: +32 2 705 15 70 (Bruxelles).
+32 71 34 42 14 or 35 48 27 (Gosselies)
Telex: 21237 sabca b (Bruxelles). 51251 sabgo b (Gosselies)

Founded: December 1920. Charleroi plant inaugurated in 1954. Major shareholder is Dassault Aviation (53% holding); it was reported that Fokker's share holding was being sold.

Employees: 1,550.

Information:
M. Humblet (Sales and Marketing).

FACILITIES

▪ Brussels plant (Bruxelles) is the corporate HQ, engineering, design, development and test facility, and manufactures aerospace structures, servo systems and electronics.
▪ Charleroi plant is for assembly and integration, retrofit, mid-life updates, and maintenance and overhaul of aeroplanes and helicopters.
▪ SABCA Limburg NV plant (Dellestraat 32, B-3560 Lummen) was founded in 1989 as a fully-owned subsidiary. It designs, develops and manufactures composite aerofoil skins by automated tape-laying, monolithic and honeycomb structures.

ACTIVITIES

▪ Production of servo actuators (Ariane, B737 and F-16), and is the world's second largest source of integrated servo actuators for the F-16 programme.
▪ Limburg activities include producing the Rafale vertical fin, Boeing AWACS antenna fairings, A330/A340 tailcone access doors, Falcon 900 and 2000 components, Fokker 50 wing trailing edges, and Ariane 5 space booster nosecone and fairings.
▪ Electronics and electro-optics, including SIB 92 controls for the Mirage V MIRSIP (see below).
▪ Research and Development.
▪ Aircraft modernization and repair. This includes or has recently included:
A-109. Designed and developed the military cockpit front panel for the Belgian Army. Weapon system integration, final assembly and test flying.
F-5. Update, including new avionics (HUD, HOTAS, INS and more) and industrial co-operation with the customer. Bulkhead manufacturing and integration. Customers include Indonesia, which is receiving mainly upgrade kits.
F-16. SABCA delivered 222 F-16s to Lockheed Martin and co-operates with Lockheed Martin in the Mid-Life Update programme; it is upgrading F-16As and Bs of European air forces.
Mirage F1. Sub-contracted by Thomson-CSF in the upgrading of Spanish fighters.
Mirage 5. MIRSIP (MIRage System Improvement Programme) upgrade, having previously modernized 10 former Belgium Air Force Mirage 5s under a safety improvement programme. Belgium Mirage 5s were withdrawn from service and many offered for sale. Chile purchased 25, including 4 Mirage 5BRs and a Mirage 5BD. The remaining 15 Mirage 5MA single-seaters and 5 MD 2-seat operational trainers underwent upgrade, becoming Mirage 5M Elkans to serve with Grupo 8 of Ala 1. The first Elkan was rolled-out on 11 October 1994, and Elkans were airlifted to Chile from 1995. The SABCA MIRSIP for Chilean Mirage 5s included canards; nose strakes; HOTAS; new avionics encompassing weapon delivery, navigation, UHF/VHF communications, cockpit displays and IFF; active/passive ECM; a laser designator; zero-zero ejection seats; and system improvements. SABCA claimed that the standardization of equipment and firing performances with the F-16 makes the Mirage 5 MIRSIP a suitable F-16 lead-in aircraft.
Plus ***Alpha Jet*** **and** ***Sea King.***

Embraer

Brazil

Full name:
Empresa Brasileira de Aeronáutica S.A.

Corporate address:
Av. Brig. Faria Lima, 2170, PO Box 8050, 12227-901 São José dos Campos-SP.

Telephone: +55 12 345 1000 or 25 1000/1529
Facsimile: +55 12 345 2411
Telex: 1233589 EBAE BR
Web site: http//www.embraer.com

Founded:
19 August 1969. Privatization of Embraer was completed on 7 December 1994, though the Federal Government of Brazil part retains about 15% of the capital.

Employees: 3,595.

CEO:
Maurício Novis Botelho (President and CEO).

Information:
Marcia Benevides (Press Office – *telephone* +55 12 345 1311, *Facsimile* +55 12 345 1610).

ACTIVITIES

- All-time record turnover for fiscal year ending December 1997, at US $766.5 million, up 84% on the previous full year.
- Design, development, production and marketing of a range of turboprop and jet aircraft for regional airlines and military use (see Airliner section); piston and turboprop engined aircraft for general aviation, corporate and agricultural uses (see General Aviation section); and aviation related mechanical and hydraulic systems.
- Following the original June 1987 contract with McDonnell Douglas (now Boeing), Embraer has been manufacturing carbon/epoxy outboard flaps for the MD-11 airliner and is the sole subcontractor for these.
- Under a 1989 contract with Boeing, Embraer has been supplying machined flap supports for the 747 and 767 airliners.
- Under a 16 December 1991 contract with Boeing, Embraer is producing wing tips and dorsal fins for the 777 airliner, deliveries expected to last until 1999.
- Embraer is a risk-sharing partner in the Sikorsky S-92 programme, signing an agreement in June 1995 for the development and production of the sponson fuel and undercarriage gear systems (see Helicopter section).
- Multi-national programme is the AMX (see Multi-national in this section).
- The ERJ145SA surveillance version of the ERJ145 regional airliner can be found in the Reconnaissance section.
- Awarded in 1997 the International Service Organization (ISO) 9001 Quality Management Systems certificate of compliance for design, production, sales and servicing of commercial aircraft and parts.

↑ Embraer Tucanos with the Brazilian air display squadron

DIVISIONS

EMBRAER DIVISÃO EQUIPAMENTOS

HQ address:
São José dos Campos SP.

Activities:
- Equipment division. Engineering and production processes employing the latest information systems and manufacturing technologies at this 2.73 million sq ft (253,625 m^2) plant.

INDÚSTRIA AERONÁUTICA NEIVA S.A.

HQ address:
See General Aviation section.

Activities:
- Subsidiary of Embraer, producing the EMB-202 Ipanema agricultural aircraft and a line of light aircraft, mostly built under licence from Piper.

EAC-EMBRAER AIRCRAFT CORPORATION

HQ address:
276 South West 34th Street, Fort Lauderdale, FL 33315, USA.

Telephone: +1 954 359 3710
Facsimile: +1 954 359 4755

Activities:
- Subsidiary for sales and after-sale support of Embraer products in North America.

EAI-EMBRAER AVIATION INTERNACIONAL

HQ address:
Aeroport du Bourget, Zone d'Aviation d'Affaires, 93 350 Le Bourget, France.

Telephone: +33 1 49 92 73 04
Facsimile: +33 1 48 35 88 00

Activities:
- Subsidiary for sales and after-sale support of Embraer products in Europe and Asia.

↑ French Air Force Embraer EMB-312F

Embraer aircraft deliveries 1971 to October 1998	
EMB-110 Bandeirante	469
EMB-111 Bandeirante sea patrol	31
EMB-120 Brasilia	336**
EMB-121 Xingu	105
EMB-200 Ipanema	781**
EMB-312 Tucano	633**
EMB-314 Super Tucano/ALX	see entry**
EMB-326 GB Xavante	182
AMX	45 (Embraer production)
EMB-400 Urupema glider	21
EMB-710 Carioca	288
EMB-711 Corisco	477
EMB-712 Tupi	145
EMB-720/D Minuano	294**
EMB-721/D Sertanejo	206**
EMB-810/D Seneca	868**
EMB-820 Navajo	132*
NR-821 Caraja	39
ERJ135	see entry**
ERJ145	79**

**including 6 airframes for turboprop conversion*
***In production, available or new type*

Embraer EMB-312 Tucano

First flight: 16 August 1980.
Role: Basic and advanced training, and capable of armament and target towing, day and night instrument flying, aerobatic visual flights, and ferry flights.
Fatigue life: EMB-312F has 10,000 hour and Shorts Tucano 12,000 hour structural life (see Aims and Aircraft variants).

Aims

- First military trainer designed from the outset to use turboprop engines.
- Operation within the temperature ranges of +50°C and -45°C. Altitude operational range 30,000 ft (9,145 m) to -1,000 ft (-305 m) to sea level.
- Structure designed originally for a safe life of 6,000 hours, based on 82% basic/advanced training, 15% weapon and tactics training, and 3% logistics.

Development

- 1978. Design was initiated, at first intended as a replacement for Brazilian Cessna T-37s.
- 6 December 1978. Brazilian Ministry of Aeronautics awarded a contract for 4 prototypes, 2 flying and 2 test.
- 16 August 1980. First flight of a prototype. Second prototype flew on 10 December that year.
- 16 August 1982. Pre-series Tucano flew.
- September 1983. Deliveries began to the Brazilian Air Force under the designation T-27, with 6 officially handed to the EDA-Esquadrão de Demonstração Aerea (air display squadron). The first export customer was Honduras, which ordered 10.
- October 1983. First major export breakthrough, with Egypt ordering 120 for itself and Iraq, the first 10 delivered from Brazil, leading to the Arab Organization for Industrialization assembling the remainder (later increased to 124 assembled by AOI).
- 21 March 1985. The Tucano was chosen against stiff competition to equip the RAF as the British-built Shorts Tucano (not S312), replacing the Jet Provost (see Aircraft variants). 130 were delivered up to 25 January 1993.
- 14 February 1986. First flight of a Tucano with the RAF's required Garrett engine.
- 30 December 1986. First flight of a Shorts Tucano.
- 7 April 1993. First flight (2 hours duration) of a French Air Force EMB-312F.

Details

Sales/Users: 650 ordered by 14 air forces and 633 delivered by April 1998: Argentina (30), Brazil (133), Colombia (14), Egypt (54, most assembled by AOI), France (50), Honduras (12), Iran (25), Iraq (80, assembled by AOI), Kenya (12, built by Shorts), Kuwait (16, built by Shorts), Paraguay (6), Peru (30), the UK (130, built by Shorts) and Venezuela (31). (See Aircraft variants.).
Crew: 2 in tandem, with rear seat raised to allow a visibility of 4° 30' below horizontal when the aircraft is level.
Crew escape: Martin-Baker MKBR8LC ejection seats, allowing safe ejection at any speed in flight at altitude but at speeds above 70 kts (81 mph) 130 km/h at ground level. Each seat has a pilot parachute and jungle survival kit.

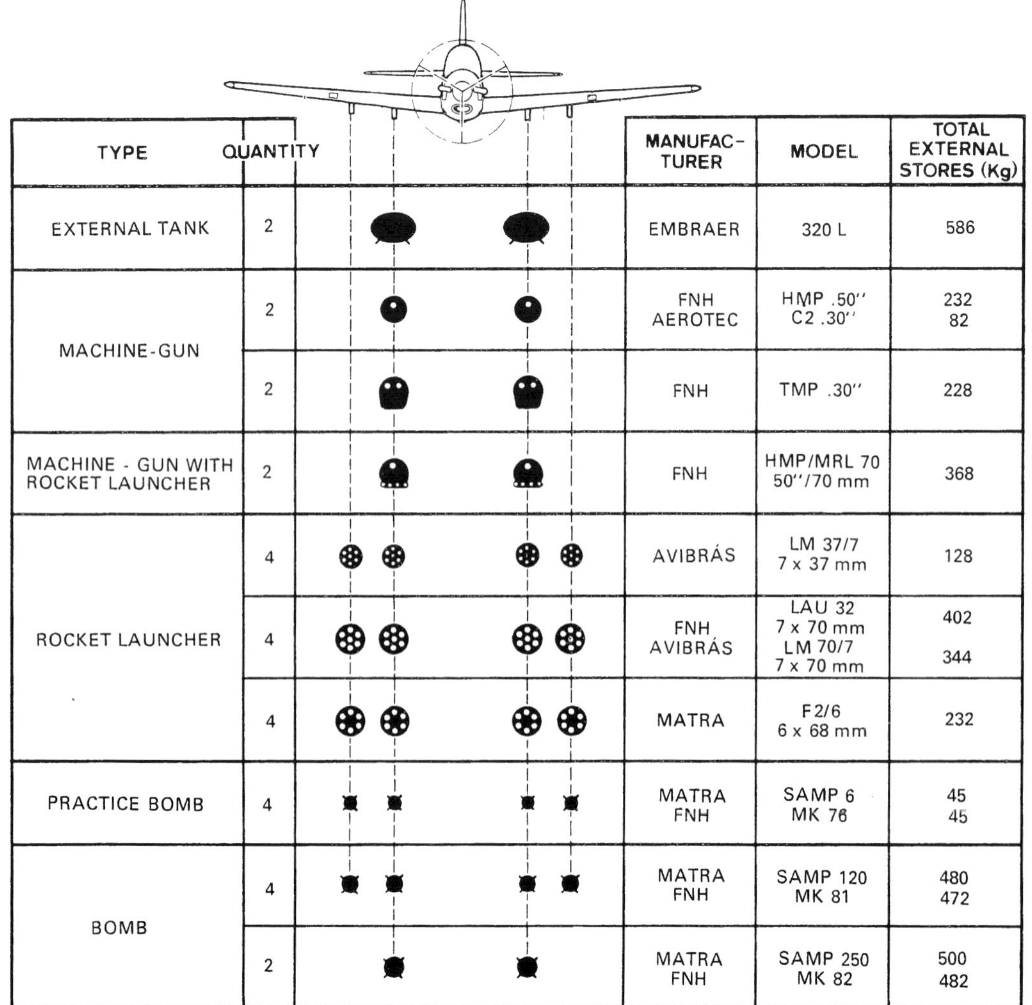

TYPE	QUANTITY	MANUFACTURER	MODEL	TOTAL EXTERNAL STORES (Kg)
EXTERNAL TANK	2	EMBRAER	320 L	586
MACHINE-GUN	2	FNH AEROTEC	HMP .50" C2 .30"	232 82
	2	FNH	TMP .30"	228
MACHINE - GUN WITH ROCKET LAUNCHER	2	FNH	HMP/MRL 70 50"/70 mm	368
ROCKET LAUNCHER	4	AVIBRÁS	LM 37/7 7 x 37 mm	128
	4	FNH AVIBRÁS	LAU 32 7 x 70 mm LM 70/7 7 x 70 mm	402 344
	4	MATRA	F2/6 6 x 68 mm	232
PRACTICE BOMB	4	MATRA FNH	SAMP 6 MK 76	45 45
BOMB	4	MATRA FNH	SAMP 120 MK 81	480 472
	2	MATRA FNH	SAMP 250 MK 82	500 482

↑ **Tucano external weapon/drop-tanks configurations using pylons with standard release unit 2610 (49 lb, 23 kg)** *(courtesy Embraer)*

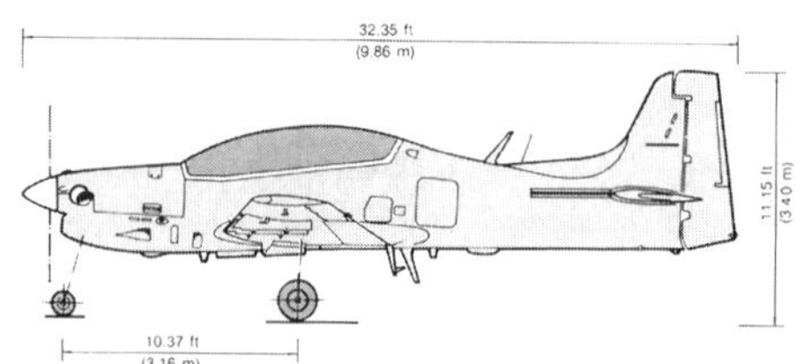

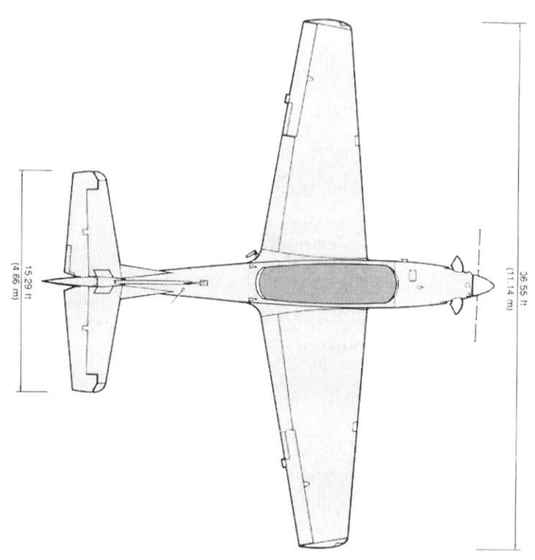

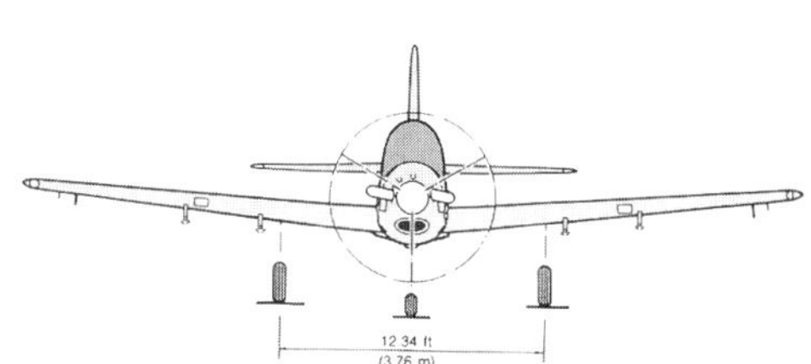

↑ **Embraer EMB-312 Tucano** *(courtesy Embraer)*

Fixed guns: None.
Number of weapon pylons: 4, each limited to 551 lb (250 kg) in weapon configuration, or 408 lb (185 kg) in aerobatic configuration. 2 stores only for ferry flights, each inboard point carrying 694 lb (315 kg).
Expendable weapons and equipment: See diagram.
Radar: None.
Flight/weapon system avionics/instrumentation: Communications (including Collins/Engetronica VHF20B VHF transceiver), navigation and identification. Navigation system consists of a Collins PN-101 gyromagnetic compass, Collins/Engetronica TDR-90 transponder, Collins/Engetronica automatic digital ADF-60A, Collins/Engetronica VIR-30A VOR/ILS/marker beacon receiver and DME-40 subsystems, and Ametek C-5D magnetic compass, among others.
Wing control surfaces: Ailerons (deflection 15° down, 17° up), with tabs. Single-slotted flaps with 35° maximum deflection (25% relative chord).
Tail control surfaces: Elevators (deflection 20° down, 18° up) with port tab, and rudder (25° deflection), with tab.
Airbrakes: Ventral type on French and UK Tucanos.
Flight control system: Mainly mechanical, with electromechanical flaps and tabs.
Construction materials: Basically 2024 aluminium alloy, with steel alloys and glassfibre where advantageous to strength, structure, shape, weight and heat protection.
Engine: Pratt & Whitney Canada PT6A-25C turboprop, with a Hartzell HC-B3TN-3C/T10178-8R 3-blade propeller. Allows 30 seconds of inverted flight, 15 seconds vertical nose up, 20 seconds vertical flight nose down, 10 seconds zero G.
Engine rating: 750 shp (559.3 kW), with 700 shp (522 kW) maximum climb and cruise rating.
Fuel system: 694 litres in 2 wing tanks. Provision for 2 × 330 litre drop tanks, carried on inboard pylons.
Electrical system: 28 volt DC, with a 25.2 volt/26 amp-hours BTCA-9-20 alkaline (ni-cd) battery, an emergency battery, and a 200 amp starter-generator. AC system furnished by a main 250 volt-amp inverter, generating 115 and 26 volt/400Hz. A 125 volt-amp standby inverter supplies some AC essential loads in an electrical emergency.

Details for EMB-312

PRINCIPAL DIMENSIONS:
Wing span: 36 ft 6.5 ins (11.14 m)
Maximum length: 32 ft 4 ins (9.86 m)
Maximum height: 11 ft 2 ins (3.4 m)

COCKPIT:
Length: 9 ft 6 ins (2.9 m)
Width: 2 ft 9.5 ins (0.85 m)
Height: 5 ft 1 ins (1.55 m) stepped
Canopy: 8 ft 4.5 ins (2.55 m) free length, 2 ft 7 ins (0.85 m) maximum free width. Side hinged
Baggage: 6 cu ft (1.17 m^3), with 66 lb (30 kg) capacity, with fixture net

WINGS:
Aerofoil section: NACA 63_2A-415 root at centre line, 63A-212 tip
Area: 208.8 sq ft (19.4 m^2)
Aspect ratio: 6.397
Sweepback: 0° 43′ 26″ at 25% chord
Chord at root: 7 ft 6.5 ins (2.3 m)
Chord at tip: 3 ft 6 ins (1.07 m) structural
Chord at centre line: 7 ft 11.5 ins (2.43 m)
Incidence: 1° 25′ at centre line
Geometric twist: 2° 13′
Dihedral: 5° 30′ at 30% chord

TAIL UNIT:
Tailplane span: 15 ft 3.5 ins (4.66 m)
Tailplane area: 49.19 sq ft (4.57 m^2) without fillets
Fin area: 15.72 sq ft (1.46 m^2)

UNDERCARRIAGE:
Type: Retractable, with nosewheel
Main wheel tyre size: 6.50-10, 8 ply, Type III Nylon, rib, tube
Nose wheel tyre size: 5.00-5, 8 ply, Type III Nylon, rib, tube
Wheel base: 10 ft 4.5 ins (3.16 m)
Wheel track: 12 ft 4 ins (3.76 m)

WEIGHTS:
Empty, equipped: 4,123 lb (1,870 kg) ± 2%
Maximum zero-fuel: 4,519 lb (2,050 kg)
Maximum take-off: 7,000 lb (3,175 kg) or 5,622 lb (2,550 kg) in aerobatic configuration
Maximum landing: 6,173 lb (2,800 kg), or 5,622 lb (2,550 kg) in aerobatic configuration

PERFORMANCE:
Never-exceed speed (V_{NE}): 280 kts (322 mph) 518 km/h, or 291 kts (335 mph), 539 km/h design
Maximum speed: 242 kts (278 mph) 448 km/h at 8,000 ft and 5,622 lb AUW, 227 kts (261 mph) 420 km/h at 7,000 ft and 7,000 lb AUW, ISA
Maximum cruising speed: 222 kts (255 mph) 411 km/h at 10,000 ft, or 240 kts (276 mph) 444 km/h design
Stall speed: 72 kts (83 mph) 134 km/h *clean*, 75 kts (87 mph) 139 km/h *design clean* at 5,622 lb AUW, 67 kts (77 mph) 124 km/h *with flaps*, and 69 kts (80 mph) 128 km/h *design with flaps* at 5,622 lb AUW
Manoeuvring speed: 98 kts (113 mph) 181 km/h *design with flaps* at 5,622 lb AUW
Take-off distance: 1,227 ft (374 m) at 5,622 lb AUW, and 1,811 ft (552 m) at 7,000 lb AUW, ISA; or 1,962 ft (598 m) at 7,000 lb AUW at ISA+15° C
Landing distance: 1,276 ft (389 m) at 5,622 lb AUW, brakes only (no thrust reverse) at sea level, ISA, or 1,493 ft (455 m) at 6,173 lb AUW, brakes only, at sea level, ISA+15° C.
Take-off distance over a 50 ft (15 m) obstacle: 2,103 ft (641 m) at 5,622 lb AUW, sea leval, ISA, or 3,717 ft (1,133 m) at 7,000 lb AUW, sea level, ISA+15° C
Landing distance over a 50 ft (15 m) obstacle: 1,716 ft (523 m) at 5,622 lb AUW, with brakes and reverse thrust, sea level, ISA, or 2,323 ft (708 m) at 6,173 lb AUW, brakes only, sea level, ISA+15° C
Maximum climb rate: 2,230 ft (680 m) per minute at sea level at 5,622 lb AUW, or 1,460 ft (445 m) per minute at sea level at 7,000 lb AUW, ISA
G limits: +4.4, -2.2 weapon configuration, or +6, -3 aerobatic configuration
Ceiling: 30,000 ft (9,145 m)
Range with full internal fuel: 1,111 naut miles (1,278 miles) 2,057 km at long-range cruise speed, 30 minutes reserve, at 25,000 ft altitude, 5,622 lb AUW, ISA; or 1,764 naut miles (2,030 miles) 3,267 km at long-range cruise speed, 30 minutes reserve, at 17,000 ft altitude, 7,000 lb AUW, ISA+15° C

Hydraulic system: 2,100 psi.
Braking system: Single disc on each main unit.
Oxygen system: Low pressure (450 psi) diluter-demand system for both crew members. 6 or 7 × 200 litre cylinders.

Aircraft variants:
EMB-312 is Embraer's designation for the standard PT6A-25C powered version, as detailed.
EMB-312F is the French Air Force model, with extended fatigue life airframe (see Aims), a ventral airbrake, 37 Sextant instruments (including LCD EADI and EHSI), and other changes. First delivery batch comprised 2 pre-series aircraft for evaluation at French Ministry of Defence organizations. Replaced Fouga Magisters.
Shorts Tucano (not S312, as often quoted) is the RAF version, with differences including a 1,100 shp (820.3 kW) Garrett (now AlliedSignal) TPE331-12B turboprop to improve performance, airframe strengthening for 12,000 hours, ventral airbrake, 37 ft (11.28 m) wing span, redesigned cockpits with much UK equipment, and more. Also sold to Kenya and Kuwait. Maximum speed 274 kts (315 mph) 507 km/h.

Embraer EMB-314 Super Tucano and ALX

First flight: 15 May 1993 for genuine Super Tucano prototype (see Development).
Role: Training (similar to Tucano) and day/night operational missions (see Development).
Fatigue life: Structure of Tucano was completely redesigned to incorporate new wings capable of providing a useful life of 18,000 flying hours in a typical primary training role or over 12,000 hours for operational applications.

Aims

- Advanced version of the Tucano, with a strengthened airframe.
- 1,600 shp (1,193 kW) Pratt & Whitney Canada PT6A-68 turboprop engine in the proof-of-concept prototype, with a 5-blade Hartzell propeller (see Engine).
- Fuselage lengthened by 4 ft 6 ins (1.37 m), made up of 1 ft 2 ins (0.37 m) ahead of and 3 ft 4 ins (1 m) aft of the cockpit.
- Reinforced, electrically-actuated, upward hinged canopy, with anti-icing (also propeller de-icing).
- New glass cockpit layout.
- Global Positioning System (GPS), Traffic Collision Avoidance System (TCAS).
- 5 psi Pressurized cockpit.
- Automatic rudder trim.
- On-board oxygen generating system.
- Air-cycle air-conditioning system.
- Crew anti-G system.
- Zero-zero ejection seats.
- Redesigned engine cowling to improve maintainability.
- Single point pressure fuelling.
- Reinforced undercarriage.
- Standard ventral airbrake.
- Kevlar armour protection for cockpits.
- Aircraft logistics concept improved, with enhancements in systems reliability, components accessibility, and revised inspections and intervals.
- Single and 2-seat versions of the ALX, for armed operational missions in addition to training (see Aircraft variants).

Development

- January 1991. Development began, with public disclosure of the programme in June at the Paris Air Show.
- 9 September 1991. First flight of the Super Tucano proof-of-concept aircraft, modified from the RAF Shorts Tucano prototype. Pilot was Gilberto Pedrosa Schittini.
- May 1992. Embraer and Northrop of the USA signed a preliminary agreement to jointly tender a version of Super Tucano for the USAF's JPATS programme.
- 1993. 2 prototype Super Tucanos proper appeared, the first making its maiden flight on 15 May and the second on 14 October. Public deput 20 May at the Embraer works. The second prototype was fitted out to take part in the USAF's JPATS programme, in co-operation with team-member Northrop, the Embraer/ Northrop association having been formalized in July 1993.
- 1993. Studies begun of the ALX derivative model for advanced training (including weapon familiarization and conversion to advanced navigation/attack systems), plus operational light attack missions by day or night.
- 26 August 1994. Provisional certification by the Brazilian CTA. The 2 prototypes had by then flown over 500 flight hours in 396 missions, 20 of which were certification oriented and flown by CTA representatives.
- 1995. New training concept was launched in Canada, as the NFTC – NATO Flying Training in Canada Program, for training NATO and Canadian Armed Forces fighter pilots, for which the Canadian Department of National Defense selected the Super Tucano for basic training. The first pilot will graduate under this programme in the year 2000.
- 18 August 1995. Brazilian Air Force contracted Embraer under a $50 million programme to develop the ALX light attack aircraft derivative, including a single-seat and a 2-seat prototypes produced by modifying Super Tucano prototypes.
- May 1996. First ALX flew.
- 18 April 1997. Elbit contracted to supply mission avionics for ALX.
- 1998. ALX prototypes flown configured with final mission system package.
- 1999. First deliveries of ALXs to the Brazilian Air Force.

Details

Sales/Users: 2 prototype ALXs, in single-seat and 2-seat forms, for flight test and qualification. About 100 ALXs for the Brazilian Air Force, to perform some duties undertaken by Xavantes. Single-seaters to be designated A-29s and 2-seaters AT-29s in Brazilian service. 23 Super Tucanos needed for the NFTC - NATO Flying Training in Canada Program (see Development), bought via Bombardier.
Crew: 2 normally. ALX available in both single- and 2-seat versions.

↑ Prototype Embraer EMB-314 Super Tucano used in the ALX development programme, carrying AAMs

↑ **Prototype Embraer ALX at Paris Air Show 1997 in black paint for night operations, with 2 mock MAA-1 AAMs among its stores** *(Aviation Picture Library)*

Fixed guns: Embraer has performed studies and installation trials of 2 × 0.50-ins machine-guns in Super Tucano wings.
Number of weapon pylons: 5 (see Aims and Aircraft variants).
Expendable weapons and equipment: Armament choices could be expanded to include the MAA-1 air-to-air missile.
Flight/weapon system avionics/instrumentation: See also Aims and Aircraft variants.
Engine: 1,250 shp (932 kW) Pratt & Whitney Canada PT6A-68-1 turboprop for primary/basic training applications; 1,600 shp (1,193 kW) PT6A-68-3 for basic/advanced training and operational roles. Engine has automatic engine monitoring and control system.
Fuel system: 694 litres. ALX prototype ferried across the Atlantic for the 1997 Paris Air Show carried 2 × 379 and 1 × 322 litre external fuel tanks.

Aircraft variants:
ALX is the designation of a special-application version of the Super Tucano for the Brazilian Air Force and export, intended for advanced training, weapons familiarization training, internal security, surveillance and light attack. Structural and system modifications, including 5 hardpoints for weapons/drop tanks, and the cockpit will have crew ballistic protection. Fighter-type suite with HOTAS, including Elbit-supplied central mission modular computer, HUD, 5x5 liquid crystal active matrix multi-function display (1 per station), armament control system, laser inertial reference system with embedded GPS, and an air-data computer. Autopilot. Integrated radio communication and navigation systems. Tactical V/UHF, and VTR. The nav-attack system incorporates an embedded ACMI type capability for debriefing and mission rehearsal. All instrumentation and lighting will be NVG Gen III compatible. Provision for FLIR Systems AAQ-22 in underfuselage turret for night surveillance and attack missions on 2-seat version, a radar warning receiver and chaff dispenser. Able to operate with weapons from unpaved runways. 1,600 shp (1,193 kW) PT6A-68 engine.
EMB-312HJ was the JPATS version with a 1,300 shp (969.4 kW) PT6A-68A engine. Not selected. See Development.
EMB-314 is the designation of the standard dedicated trainer version, capable of carrying weapons. See Aims and Sales/Users.

Details for EMB-314, indicating standard Tucano differences

PRINCIPAL DIMENSIONS:
Maximum length: 37 ft 5.5 ins (11.42 m)
Maximum height: 12 ft 9.5 ins (3.9 m)

UNDERCARRIAGE:
Wheel base: 11 ft (3.36 m)

WEIGHTS:
Empty, operating: 5,335 lb (2,420 kg)
Maximum take-off: 7,032 lb (3,190 kg)

PERFORMANCE:
Maximum speed at height: over 320 kts (368 mph) 593 km/h
Maximum speed at sea level: over 270 kts (311 mph) 500 km/h
Maximum cruising speed: 286 kts (329 mph) 530 km/h at 20,000 ft
Long-range cruising speed: 228 kts (262 mph) 422 km/h at 20,000 ft
Stall speed: 85 kts (98 mph) 157 km/h *clean*, 78 kts (90 mph) 145 km/h *with flaps and undercarriage down*, EAS
Take-off distance: 1,148 ft (350 m)
Landing distance: 1,805 ft (550 m)
Take-off distance over a 50 ft (15 m) obstacle: 1,805 ft (550 m)
Landing distance over a 50 ft (15 m) obstacle: 2,822 ft (860 m)
Maximum climb rate: 2,935 ft (895 m) per minute
G limits: +7, -3.5 aerobatic, +4, -2.2 with 6,106 lb stores load
Ceiling: over 35,000 ft (10,650 m)
Range with full fuel: 847 naut miles (975 miles) 1,568 km at 30,000 ft, with 30 minutes reserve
Ferry range: 1,495 naut miles (1,721 miles) 2,768 km at 25,000 ft, with underwing tanks and 30 minutes reserve
Duration: 6 hours on internal fuel, at long-range cruise speed, 30 minutes reserve

Bombardier Inc — Canada

Corporate address:
800 René-Lévesque Blvd West, Montreal, Quebec H3B 1Y8.
Telephone: +1 514 861 9481
Facsimile: +1 514 861 7053
Employees: Over 41,000 in all groups, with 24,300 in the Aerospace Group.

ACTIVITIES

▪ Motorized consumer products, transportation equipment and aerospace.
▪ Combines the products and services of 4 aircraft manufacturers, namely Canadair and de Havilland in Canada, Learjet in the USA and Shorts in the UK.

DIVISIONS

BOMBARDIER AEROSPACE GROUP
HQ address:
400 Côte-Vertu West, Dorval, Quebec H4S 1Y9.
Telephone: +1 514 855 5000
Facsimile: +1 514 855 7401
Web site: www.aero.bombardier.com
Information:
Josée Vaillancourt (public relations – *telephone* +1 514 855 7989).
Activities:
▪ Specializes in the design, manufacture, sale and support of regional airliners, business jets, amphibians, special mission variants of its commercial aircraft, airframe components and air defence systems.

COMPRISING:

BOMBARDIER INC. CANADAIR
HQ address: 400 Côte-Vertu West, Dorval, Quebec H4S 1Y9.
Telephone: +1 514 855 5000
Facsimile: +1 514 855 7401
Activities:
▪ See Bombardier Regional Aircraft Division and Bombardier Inc, Canadair in the Special Electronic and Airliner sections.

DE HAVILLAND INC
HQ address:
123 Garratt Boulevard, Downsview, Ontario M3K 1Y5.
Telephone: +1 416 633 7310
Facsimile: +1 416 375 4546
Activities:
▪ See also Bombardier Regional Aircraft Division in the Special Electronic and Airliner sections.

→ **Bombardier de Havilland Dash 8 coastal patrol aircraft operated by Surveillance Australia. Note the undernose FLIR, underfuselage search radar, and above fuselage HF antenna**

LEARJET INC

HQ address:
7761 W. Kellogg, Wichita, KS 67209, USA.

Telephone: +1 316 946 2000
Facsimile: +1 316 946 2220, 2163

Activities:
▪ See General Aviation section – USA.

SHORT BROTHERS PLC

HQ address:
Airport Road, Belfast, Northern Ireland BT3 9DZ.

Telephone: +44 1232 458 444
Facsimile: +44 1232 732 974

Activities:
▪ See Airliner section, under UK.

Bombardier de Havilland Dash 8 Maritime Patrol Aircraft

Comments: The Maritime Patrol Aircraft is one of several Multi-Role variants of the Dash 8 currently offered, others encompassing coastal patrol/surveillance, aeromedical, electronic, flight calibration, navigation training, search and rescue, paratroop/military transport and cargo/combi roles. An operator of coastal patrol aircraft is Surveillance Australia, a subsidiary of National Jet Systems of Australia, under the 10 year coastwatch programme contract from the Australian Customs service.

Maritime Patrol Aircraft can have belly-mounted search radar and FLIR to offer 360° scanning, customised navigation suites, air-drop chutes, sensor operator's workstation, blister windows with observer stations, 4 wing hardpoints of 375 lb (170 kg) capacity each for various stores that can include search lights and droppable survival kits, and more. An accompanying illustration shows a Dash 8 Series 200 layout. A Series 300 MPA is the Triton 300, with additional MAD tailboom, ESM in wingtip pods, sonobuoy air-drop chute and weapon racks mounted low on the fuselage. Typical patrol speed for Triton is quoted as 135 kts (155 mph) 250 km/h, and duration is 9 hours.

Further details and illustration of Multi-Role Dash 8s can be found in the Electronics section.

Bristol Aerospace Ltd — Canada

Corporate address:
PO Box 874, 660 Berry Street, Winnipeg, Manitoba R3C 2S4.

Telephone: +1 204 788 2831
Facsimile: +1 204 775 7494

Founded:
Origins in McDonald Brothers Aircraft of 1930 founding. Purchased by Rolls-Royce in 1966 but acquired by Magellan Aerospace Corporation in July 1997.

Information:
Robert C. Walker (public relations).

DIVISIONS

Aircraft

Activities

▪ Modernization of the F-5, though this work is being phased out. A full description of the F-5 Modernization programme, together with 2 photographs, can therefore be found in the 1996-97 edition of *WA&SD*, page 18.
▪ With the decision to retire its fleet of F-5s, Canada appointed Bristol Aerospace to be the exclusive marketing agent for the modernized aircraft.
▪ Development of the Wire Strike Protection System (WSPS®) for helicopters, offering protection against inadvertent flight into horizontal power and communications wires and cables.

Aerocomponents

Activities

▪ Major aero-engine and aero-structure design and manufacturing programmes, working with a wide range of materials. Offers advanced techniques for forming, welding, brazing, heat treat, coating and chemical processing. Comprehensive machining facilities. Manufacture of components using both composite and metal to metal bonding.

Rockets & Space

Activities

▪ Owns and operates Canada's only solid fuel propellant plant, providing motors for many of this division's products. These include Black Brant sounding rockets, space payloads, small satellites, CRV7 rocket weapon system, and remotely controlled targets. Included among 4 air, 1 sea and 2 land targets is the Pop-Up Helicopter land target, aimed at helping air-defence gunners learn and maintain skills needed to meet the challenge of nap-of-the-earth mission combat helicopters that pop-up for target search and missile firing.

Empresa Nacional de Aeronáutica Chile (ENAER) — Chile

Corporate address:
Avda J.M.Carrera, 11087 Paradero 36½, Santiago.

Telephone: +56 2 528 2823, 528 2735 and 528 2599
Facsimile: +56 2 528 2699, 2815
Telex: 645157 ENAER PCT

Founded: 1984.

Employees: 1,700.

Information:
Alejandro Vargas (commercial), and Felipe Fernandez mesa (aircraft maintenance division).

ACTIVITIES

▪ ENAER's first and principal programme was the piston-engined T-35 Pillán basic trainer, developed jointly by ENAER and Piper of the USA but completely manufactured and assembled by ENAER (except for knock-down kits supplied to CASA in Spain). A full description of the T-35 Pillán and an illustration can be found in the 1996-97 edition of *WA&SD*, page 385.
▪ Part manufacture and assembly of A-36 Halcón attack aircraft was completed in 1995, having previously assembled related T-36 jet trainers. This was ENAER's second industrial programme.
▪ Principal programmes in recent years have been the development of the T-35 DT Pillán Turbo trainer and development/production of the Ñamcu lightplane (see General Aviation section), the latter as the first aircraft to be entirely designed and built by ENAER.
▪ Modernization, upgrading and structural life extension programmes are offered for civil and military aircraft, and have encompassed the Hawker Hunter (including self-defence EW equipment), the conversion of the Beech 99 to a maritime surveillance aircraft and also for electronic intelligence (with an ENAER ITATA radar detection sytem), modernization of the Mirage 50 to Pantera 50 form (a description of the Pantera 50 and an illustration can be found in the 1996-97 edition of *WA&SD*, page 20), and upgrade of the Northrop F-5. The latter includes upgrade to F-5 Plus standard of all of the Chilean Air Force's F-5E/Fs (about 16), in co-operation with IAI, having Elta EL/M-2032B Doppler radar, enhanced weapon delivery and navigation systems, inertial navigation system, air data computer, El-Op head-up and 2 head-down displays, HOTAS, radar warning receiver, chaff/flare dispenser, jammer, and deletion of a cannon. 2 modernized by IAI and redelivered in 1993, with all further conversions in Chile.
▪ Other Activities encompass aircraft maintenance and repair (A-37B, C-130, CASA 212, UH-1H and others), engine maintenance (repair, overhaul and inspection of over 20 different types), accessories maintenance, component production (including tail parts for the CN 235 and ERJ145 commercial transports), and commercialization services covering technical training, field support, provision of spare parts and more.
▪ In September 1994 ENAER signed a contract with the Chilean Air Force for the manufacture of mechanical components for FASat-Alfa, the first Chilean satellite (a collaborative programme with Surrey Satellite Technology of the UK), launched in July 1995 carrying experiments for ozone layer monitoring, data transfer, GPS navigation and student educational experiments.

ENAER T-35 DT Pillán Turbo and Pillán 2000

Comments: This programme dates from 1986, when a T-35 Pillán with an Allison engine flew as the first prototype Pillán Turbo, subsequently known as the T-35TX Aucán. In March 1991 the second prototype flew as the Pillán Turbo proper.

Intended for military and civil primary and basic training (including screening, familiarization, aerobatics, formation flying, navigation, instrument and night flying), plus utility and rescue operations, reconnaissance and patrol, it remains available for purchase but only in new form as the Pillán 2000, featuring new wings of increased span designed in Russia by Technoavia . Both piston and turboprop versions are offered. Prototype flew in Russia in 1998. A full description of Pillán Turbo and a photograph can be found in the 1996-97 edition of *WA&SD*, page 19.

ENAER T-36/A-36 Halcón and Halcón II

Role: Advanced jet trainer (T-36) and light tactical attack (A-36).

Aims

▪ Licence built Spanish CASA C-101BB and C-101CC respectively, that became ENAER's second industrial programme.
▪ Chosen for co-production because of the aircraft's characteristics and because it allowed ENAER to take part in a technological exchange programme.
▪ ENAER manufactured the front fuselage, tail unit, flight control surfaces, electric and hydraulic systems, and assembled the entire structure under the final phase of the Halcón programme, having begun by assembling CASA-produced kits for the first few aircraft and thereafter progressively introducing locally-produced components.

Development

▪ 1980. Chilean Air Force signed a Development and co-production contract with CASA for the C-101.
▪ 1983. First of 4 T-36s produced by CASA entered Air Force service with the Escuela de Aviación Capitan Avalos. In November, the first A-36 flew.
▪ 1989. Final phase of production/assembly, with ENAER contributing its highest number of components (see Aims).
▪ 1995. Production/assembly of the A-36 completed, having previously delivered all T-36s.
▪ 1996. A number of Halcóns were reportedly transferred to Honduras, joining that nation's CASA C-101BBs.
▪ 1997. Redelivery to Chile of upgraded A-36s as Halcón IIs, modified by SAGEM of France to have the MAESTRO (Modular Avionics Enhancement Targeted for Retrofit Operations) system

↑ **Chilean ENAER A-36s have been upgraded to Halcón IIs** *(Denis Hughes)*

based upon multifunction navigation and attack units, wide-angle HUD, flat-panel MFDs, an advanced video recording system and HOTAS.

Sales/Users: 14 T-36s and 23 A-36s produced, 10 and 19 respectively under the co-production arrangements. Number remaining is uncertain. Used by the Escuela de Aviación Capitan Avalos as trainers, and by at least Brigada Aérea I and possibly Brigada Aérea IV in A-36 tactical form.
Further details: See CASA entry under Spain.

Aviation Industries of China (AVIC) — China

Corporate address: PO Box 33, 67 Jiao Nan Street, Beijing 100712.
Telephone: +86 10 6401 3322, 3207 **Facsimile:** +86 10 6401 3648
Founded: 26 June 1993.
CEO: Zhu Yuli.

ACTIVITIES

▪ Established to oversee the growth of China's aviation industry, and encourage foreign investment and collaboration. High-level deligations were received from Europe (including BAe, CASA, DASA, GEC-Marconi, Rolls-Royce and many others), North America (including Boeing, GE and P&W), Israel, Japan, South Korea and elsewhere. Risk-sharing joint ventures and sub-contracting agreements have been established with Chengdu, Changhe, Harbin, Shanghai, Shenyang and Xi'an and others. Among recent agreements has been the formation of joint ventures in the aero engine field, including the founding in February 1996 of Chengdu Aerotech Manufacturing Co Ltd with Pratt & Whitney, another at Xi'an with Rolls-Royce that was founded on 20 May 1996, and extended co-operation with Rolls-Royce and BMW Rolls-Royce, agreed on 7 November 1996. In June 1997 AVIC and CFM International formed a joint leadership council to co-ordinate co-operative activities, including long-term business matters, industrial co-operation and support, and review of the AE31X airliner, CFM56-9 engine and CFM56 product strategy. Other possibilities include the assembly of ATR airliners in China and production of ATR 72 rear fuselages by Xi'an.
▪ Co-developing the AE31X series of airliners with Singapore Technologies and Airbus Industrie Asia (see Airliner section).
▪ Is overseeing licensed production of the Sukhoi Su-27 in China, as the J-11, and development of the latest multi-role fighter reportedly known to the US Office of Naval Intelligence as the XXJ, which is expected to enter service during the second decade of the 21st century.
▪ AVIC's principal operating organization is CATIC (which see).

China National Aero-Technology Import & Export Corporation (CATIC) — China

Corporate address: CATIC Plaza, 18 Beichen Dong Lu, Chaoyang District, Beijing 100101.
Telephone: +86 10 6494 1090 **Facsimile:** +86 10 6494 1088, or 0658 **Telex:** 210403 CATIC CN/22318 AEROT CN **Cable:** CAID BEIJING
Founded: 1979, becoming the CATIC Group under AVIC on 26 August 1993.
Employees: 10,000.
CEO: Liu Guomin (President).
Information: Bi Jianfa (Deputy Director, Public Relations Office).

ACTIVITIES

▪ Established to integrate Chinese industry and technology with trade. Deals with the export of aero and non-aero products (including Chinese manufactured aircraft), and imports modern aero and civilian technologies. Also develops co-production and joint-venture programmes.
▪ Has 11 subsidiaries in China (3 in Beijing and others in Shenzhen, Guangzhou, Shanghai, Zhuhai, Fuzhou, Xiamen, Hangzhou and Harbin), and has overseas representatives in 21 countries and regions.
▪ Has over 120 joint ventures and sole ventures operating worldwide. The agreement covering development and production of the K-8 jet trainer (see Multi-national section) was signed by CATIC and the Defence Production Division of the Pakistan Government.
▪ Current international sub-contracting of aircraft, engine and airborne system components is undertaken on behalf of companies from Canada, Europe and the USA, including for ATR airliners, the Airbus A300, A310 and A320, Bombardier Aerospace Dash 8 and CL-415, and Boeing 737, 747, 757 and MD-80/90 series.
▪ The Technical Support Division provides technical services, after-sales service, spares supply, overhaul/repair, flight crew/ground crew training and more.

Chengdu Aircraft Industrial Corporation — China

Corporate address: PO Box 800, Chengdu, Sichuan 610092.
Telephone: +86 28 7401033 **Facsimile:** +86 28 7404984 **Telex:** 60132 **Cable:** 6752
Founded: 1958.
Information: Wang Yinggong.

ACTIVITIES

▪ In addition to building and developing versions of the Jianjiji-7 fighter and modest production of the Jianjiji Jiaolianji-5 (JJ-5) trainer, Chengdu has been entrusted with development of the new FC-1 fighter. It also produces Boeing MD-80 and 90 series airliner nose structures for Chinese and US production.
▪ A description and photograph of the Chengdu JJ-5 advanced lead-in/fighter conversion trainer variant of the MiG-17PF can be found in the 1996-97 edition of *WA&SD*, page 23.

Chengdu J-7 series

First flight: 17 January 1966.
Role: Tactical fighter and air defence interceptor.

Aims

▪ Jianjiji-7 (J-7) was developed from the Mikoyan MiG-21F-13, after the Soviet Government agreed to Chinese manufacture.

Development

▪ 1960-61. Discussions between the USSR and both Czechoslovakia and China on local co-production of the new MiG-21 fighter in its early form started almost immediately after Soviet production began. Interest centred on the second production version, the MiG-21F-13, the first model to have missile armament.
▪ Chinese programme began with the receipt from the USSR of both completed test aircraft and components for Chinese assembly and familiarization. However, technical transfer had not been completed before co-operation ended, forcing a delay in the programme while the extra engineering and development work was undertaken.
▪ 17 January 1966. First J-7 flown, having been assembled from Chinese parts at Shenyang, where most fighter production was then centred and where the first few production J-7s were built. Production at Chengdu started in the following year.
▪ 30 December 1978. Maiden flight of the much improved J-7 II, leading to substantial production for the PLA air force and modest export.
▪ 26 April 1984. Maiden flight of the J-7 III, the final development of the basic MiG-21 concept with the traditional nose intake.
▪ 1989. Co-operation with Grumman of the USA on development of the radically-altered Super-7 was terminated at government level, with Chengdu thereafter joining Pakistan Aeronautical Complex in its development. Engines from Russia.
▪ 1996. Maiden flight of the multi-role Super-7 prototype anticipated but programme cancelled.
▪ November 1996. New F-7MG displayed at the Zhuhai Air Show.

Details *(principally for the F-7M, but not exclusively, as indicated)*

Sales/Users: Chinese production is thought to total about 1,000 aircraft, of which more than half that number remain in Air Force service as interceptors. J-7Es are among PLA naval aviation fighters. All nations to have received exported F-7s appear to continue to operate them. These include Albania (operating about 10 F-7As at Zadrima), Bangladesh (16-20 F-7Ms, operated by No 5 Squadron at Dhaka and No 35 at Chittagong), Egypt (60+ at Fayid), Iran (18-20 F-7Ms), Iraq (over 60), Myanmar (36 F-7Ms – discussions were underway in 1997 with Elbit of Israel to upgrade these), Pakistan (95 F-7P/MPs, received from July 1988 and first serving with No 20 Squadron at Rafiqui – now also with No 18 Squadron at the same base, No 2 at Masroor and No 25 OCU at Mianwali), Sri Lanka (4 F-7BSs operated by No 5 Squadron at Katunayake as part of a mixed squadron with FT-5s), Sudan (15 F-7Bs?), Tanzania (some 11 F-7As), and Zimbabwe (20 or fewer F-7Ms at Gweru).

↑ **Chinese Chengdu J-7 III** *(courtesy Chinese Embassy)*

Crew: Pilot.
Crew escape: Chengdu zero-altitude ejection seat, for use at speeds not less than 70 kts (81 mph)130 km/h. Martin Baker seat in other versions (see Aircraft variants).
Fixed guns: 2 × 30-mm Type 30-1 cannon. 1 × 23-mm cannon in J-7 III.
Ammunition: 120 rounds total.
Number of weapon pylons: 4, plus underfuselage station for an auxiliary fuel tank.
Expendable weapons and equipment: 1 Chinese PL-2 to PL-7, Rafael Python 3 known in China as the PL-8, or French (Matra Magic) air-to-air missile, or a pod for 57-mm or 90-mm rockets (air-to-air or air-to-ground), or a 50-500 kg bomb (full range of Norinco bombs, including fuel-air, concrete penetration cluster, anti-armour cluster, general purpose) under each inboard wing pylon. 1 × 50-150 kg bomb, or rockets or an auxiliary fuel tank under each outboard pylon. F-7P and F-7MG can carry 2 or 4 US Sidewinder AAMs (see Aircraft variants).
Radar: Skyranger. F-7P/MP now with replacement FIAR Grifo, including the Grifo 7 model. F-7MG has Super Skyranger.
Flight/weapon system avionics/instrumentation: GEC-Marconi suite, encompassing Type 956 head-up display and weapon-aiming computer, and air data computer. Other avionics include locally produced Model 602 IFF. See Aircraft variants for more details.
Wing characteristics: Mid-mounted delta. J-7E and F-7MG have radically-redesigned double deltas (see Aircraft variants).
Wing control surfaces: Ailerons and trailing-edge flaps.
Tail control surfaces: Highly swept slab tailplane and rudder.
Airbrakes: 3 mounted on the fuselage.

↑ **Chengdu F-7MG** *(Sebastian Zacharias)*

Flight control system: Hydraulically actuated.
Construction materials: All metal.
Engine: Liyang WP-13F turbojet in F-7M, F-7MG and F-7 III, with power to weight ratio of 6. Single 9,689 lbf dry/13,443 lbf with afterburning (43.1 kN/59.8 kN) WP7B in F-7A, and similarly rated WP7B M batch in F-7B and WP7B (BM) in F-7L and some F-7Ms. Single 9,037 lbf/14,815 lbf (40.2 kN/65.9 kN) in some F-7 IIIs, with 5.9 power to weight ratio. See Aircraft variants for Liming WP7C and F-engined J-7 II and J-7E.
Engine rating: 9,690 lbf (43.1 kN) dry, 14,815 lbf (65.9 kN) with afterburning (WP-13F).
Air intakes: At nose, with a central radar-carrying shock-cone.
Fuel system: 2,385 litres in the wings and fuselage. 1 × 800 litre or 500 litre auxiliary fuel tank under the fuselage, and/or 1 × 500 litre tank under each outboard wing pylon. See also F-7MG entry under Aircraft variants.
Braking system: LS-16 disc brakes on main undercarriage units and LS-15 on nosewheel. Drag-chute carried in a pod under the rudder.

Aircraft variants:
J-7 I (Jianjiji-7 I) was the first major Chinese version, though numbers remained limited. Short range, 2 wing pylons, and an ejection seat and forward-hinged canopy that caused difficulties. Exported in small numbers as the F-7A.
J-7 II (Jianjiji-7 II) was produced with the improved M batch engine of similar rating, the option of a 720 litre auxiliary fuel tank carried under the fuselage, jettisonable rear-hinged canopy, new ejection seat capable of use at lower speed (135 kts, 155 mph, 250 km/h), and other refinements. Exported as the F-7B with optional French AAMs. Another export version was the F-7BS, specially produced for Sri Lanka with 4 underwing pylons. Information received by *WA&SD* from China indicated also the use of the WP7C, rated at 9,590 lbf (42.66 kN) dry and 13,625 lbf (60.6 kN) with afterburning. This is probably fitted to the last production aircraft or by retrofit.
F-7L is an export version about which nothing much is known. It uses a WP7B (BM) engine. It is almost certainly an Airguard variant.
F-7M Airguard became the first truly modernized version, intended to attract export interest. Increased range, advanced weapons control system, greater weapons fit options and improved engine and improved pilot ejection seat. Skyranger ranging radar and other western avionics, including a HUD, requiring a better electrical system. 4 underwing weapon/tank pylons, and the availability of PL-7 missiles. Stronger undercarriage. Remains in production.
F-7P Airguard is an upgrade of the F-7M for Pakistan, sometimes referred to as Skybolt. Martin Baker 10L ejection seat. 4 US Sidewinder AAMs. Grifo 7 radar being retrofitted. Flight testing had almost finished by late 1997. A sub-variant is the F-7MP, featuring an important avionics upgrade and a revised cockpit layout. In addition to Grifo, it has Collins ARN-147 VOR/ILS, ARN-149 automatic direction finder and Pro Line II digital distance measuring equipment.
F-7FS new demonstrator with chin intake (see Foreword).
J-7 III (Jianjiji-7 III) became the first all-weather variant of the J-7 for Chinese service, featuring JL-7 radar, improved fire control system, KJ-11 autopilot, radar warning receiver, GT4 ECM, new Model 605A IFF, WP13F engine with a power-to-weight ratio of 6 and more internal fuel, blown flaps (possibly 25° deflection for take-off and 45° for landing), HTY-4 ejection seat, ability to carry 4 missiles or other loads, 23-mm Type 23-3 twin-barrel cannon carried under the fuselage, and other updates. A further upgraded model has also joined the PLA air force and navy, the designation of which is uncertain. Normal take-off weight 17,968 lb (8,150 kg) with 2 missiles. An export equivalent was offered as the F-7-3.
J-7E (Jianjiji-7E) of 1990 appearance is a variant of the J-7 II but with an entirely new wing shape, in the form of a double delta of 27 ft 4 ins (8.32 m) span and 267.81 sq ft (24.88 m²) area (see Wing characteristics). 57° inboard wing sweepback and 42° outboard sweepback. HUD, air data computer, radar warning receiver, PL-7 missile option (4 underwing pylons), and 9,920 lbf (44.13 kN) dry and 14,330 lbf (63.75 kN) with afterburning Liming WP7F turbojet. Photographed carrying 2 PL-5B AAMs and a drop tank in PLA naval aviation markings and light grey colour

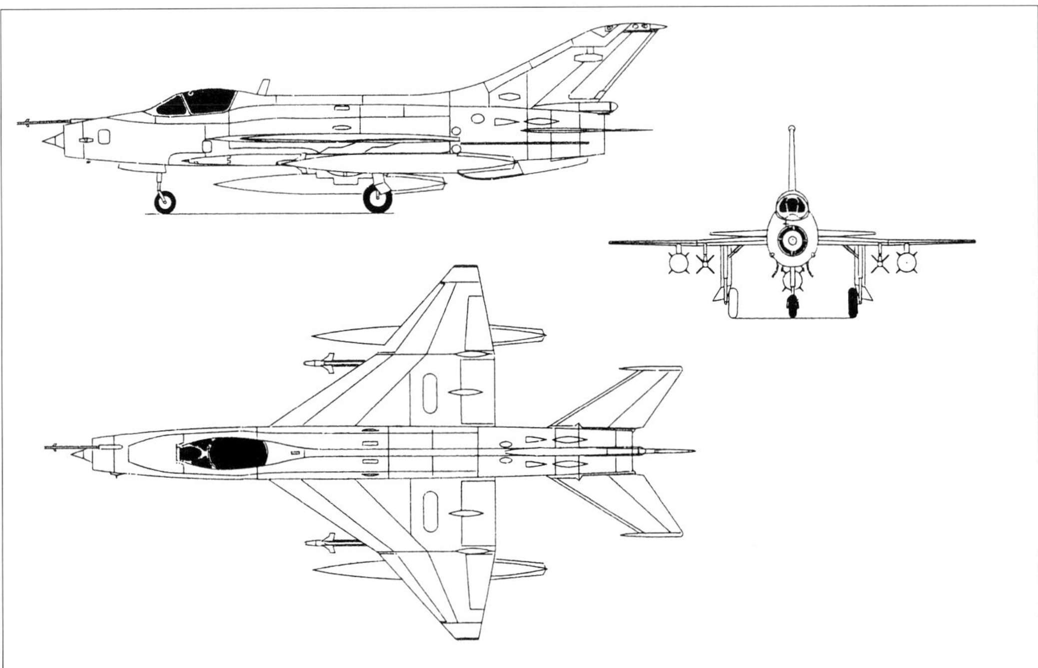

↑ **Chengdu F-7MG with double delta wings** *(courtesy CATIC)*

Details for F-7M, *with F-7MG in italics*

PRINCIPAL DIMENSIONS:
Wing span: 23 ft 5.5 ins (7.154 m), *27 ft 3.5 ins (8.32 m)*
Maximum length: 45 ft 9 ins (13.945 m) tail to shock cone, 48 ft 10 ins (14.885 m) including nose probe, *the same*
Maximum height: 13 ft 5.5 ins (4.103 m), *the same*

WINGS:
Area: 247.57 sq ft (23 m²), *267.8 sq ft (24.88 m²)*
Aspect ratio: 2.225
Sweepback: 49° 6′ at 25% chord
Incidence: 0°
Anhedral: 2°

TAIL UNIT:
Tailplane span: 12 ft 3 ins (3.74 m)
Tailplane area: 42.41 sq ft (3.94 m²)
Fin area: 37.46 sq ft (3.48 m²)

UNDERCARRIAGE:
Type: Retractable, with steerable nosewheel
Main wheel tyre size: 600 × 200 mm
Nose wheel tyre size: 500 × 180 mm
Wheel base: 15 ft 9 ins (4.807 m)
Wheel track: 8 ft 10 ins (2.692 m)
Turning radius: 23 ft 1 ins (7.04 m)

WEIGHTS:
Empty: 11,629 lb (5,275 kg), *11,667 lb (5,292 kg)*
Normal take-off: 16,603 lb (7,531 kg) with 2 PL-7s, *16,623 lb (7,540 kg) with 2 AIM-9Ps*
Maximum take-off: *20,062 lb (9,100 kg)*

PERFORMANCE (F-7M with 2 × PL-7s)**:**
Maximum speed: Mach 2.05, *Mach 2+*
Maximum speed: 1,174 kts (1,351 mph) 2,175 km/h
Take-off distance: 2,300-3,120 ft (700-950 m), *1,970-2,300 ft (600-700 m)*
Landing distance: 1,970-2,955 ft (600-900 m) with drag-chute, *1,970-2,300 ft (600-700 m)*
Maximum climb rate: 35,435 ft (10,800 m) per minute, *38,400 ft (11,700 m) per minute*
Level flight acceleration time from Mach 0.9 to 1.2: 35 seconds at 16,400 ft (5,000 m)
Maximum sustained rate of turn: 14.7° per second at Mach 0.7, 9.5° per second at Mach 0.8 and 5,000 m, *16° per second at 1,000 m altitude*
G limits: +8, *the same*
Ceiling: 59,710 ft (18,200 m) service, 61,350 ft (18,700 m) absolute (static), *57,415 ft (17,500 m) practical*
Range with 2 × PL-7s and 3 × 500 litre drop tanks: 939 naut miles (1,081 miles) 1,740 km
Range with 2 × PL-7s and 2 × 500 litre plus 1 × 800 litre drop tanks: 1,204 naut miles (1,385 miles) 2,230 km
Range for F-7MG with 2 × 480 litre and 1 × 720 litre drop tanks: *944 naut miles (1,087 miles) 1,750 km*
Operational radius of action for F-7MG: *458 naut miles (528 miles) 850 km in air superiority role (Hi-Hi-Hi), 297 naut miles (342 miles) 550 km for ground attack (Lo-Lo-Hi)*

scheme. Can deploy PL-8s. Used by the August 1st aerobatic display team.

F-7MG is the latest variant, first flown in 1993 and first shown at the November 1996 Zhuhai Air Show. Probably based on the F-7M but incorporating J-7E type wings for improved agility, of double delta planform and having leading-edge and rear manoeuvring flaps (integrated manoeuvrability said to be improved by 45% over the original F-7). GEC-Marconi Super Skyranger radar and air data computer, HUD, weapon-aiming computer, VHF/UHF communications system, Tacan, VOR/DME/ILS, ECM system, HOTAS, colour CRT displays and video recording system. Red light cockpit illumination. WP-13F engine. 2 × 30-mm guns. 5 stores attachment points, capable of 3,968 lb (1,800 kg) load in 100 configurations (including AIM-9P Sidewinder AAMs), with improved air-to-ground capability. Maximum climb rate reportedly 38,400 ft (11,700 m) per minute, and combat radius at altitude 459 naut miles (528 miles) 850 km. Standard range can be increased by attachment of 2 × 480 litre and 1 × 720 litre external fuel tanks. Provision for adding air-refuelling system. Possibly only 2 prototypes by early 1998. Said by AVIC to be a light fighter with high performance/price ratio, to meet mission requirements to and beyond the year 2000.

Super-7 was the most radical modernization of the F-7. Was to fly in 1996 but the programme has been terminated in favour of the FC-1. Further details, full specifications and an illustration can be found in the 1996-97 edition of *WA&SD*, pages 21-22.

Chengdu FC-1

First flight: Before the year 2000.
Role: Advanced multi-role fighter, capable of air superiority, interdiction and air support.

Aims

- To become operational early next century as a replacement for the J-7, and possibly also to replace J-6s and Q-5s.
- To have beyond-visual-range radar and missile capability.

Development

- 1991. Development began, with some co-operation from MAPO "MiG" of Russia, and with part funding believed to have come from Pakistan (possibly to be an early export customer).
- 1998. Possible resumption of development, after the programme was subject to funding delays. Several prototypes will be built for flight and static testing.
- 1999. Possible first flight.

Details

Sales/Users: Reportedly, Pakistan will only consider purchasing the fighter once China has made a similar commitment. China requires some 100 and Pakistan up to 150.

↑ **Chengdu FC-1 next-generation fighter** *(courtesy CATIC)*

↑ **Mock-up of the Chengdu FC-1 cockpit depicting GEC-Marconi avionics** *(Sebastian Zacharias)*

Crew: Pilot on zero-zero ejection seat, but with a 2-seater also anticipated.
Fixed guns: Option for 23-mm GSh-23-2 twin-barrel cannon on centreline.
Number of weapon pylons: 7, comprising 2 at the wingtips for AAMs, 4 under the wings and a fuselage centreline hardpoint.
Expendable weapons and equipment: To include wingtip PL-11s. Weapon load 7,716 lb (3,500 kg).
Radar: Phazotron NO-10 S-29 Zhuk type originally expected (Kopyo now offered). Possibly Chinese JL-10A radar for PLA version. Alenia is offering the alternative Grifo 7, GEC-Marconi the Blue Hawk and Thomson-CSF the RD-400, possibly as risk-sharing partners, for the export version.
Flight/weapon system avionics/instrumentation: Modern cockpit layout. Air data computer, stores management system, raster-compatible HUD, 2 MFDs, INS/GPS, communications avionics and databuses are being tendered by Alenia, GEC-Marconi, Thomson-CSF and Sagem for the export version, while the PLA version is likely to have Chinese avionics.
Wing characteristics: Cropped delta type, with swept leading edges and straight trailing edges. Wing root extensions to maintain stability at high angles of attack. Leading-edge manoeuvring and trailing-edge flaps.
Tail control surfaces: All moving tailplane and rudder.
Flight control system: Mechanical, with hydraulic servo-actuated control. Analogue fly-by-wire secondary. Principal mechanical system helps reduce costs but fly-by-wire system could become the principal form of control on developed versions.
Construction materials: Principally aluminium and steel alloys.
Engine: Klimov RD-93 tubofan, to be built by Liyang.
Engine rating: 17,985 lbf (80 kN).
Air intakes: On the fuselage sides with splitter plates, merging into fuselage strakes housing hydraulic lines and fuel.

Details for FC-1

PRINCIPAL DIMENSIONS:
Wing span: 29 ft 6 ins (9 m), or 31 ft 2 ins (9.5 m) over wingtip missiles
Length: 45 ft 9 ins (13.952 m)
Height: 16 ft 5 ins (5.014 m)

UNDERCARRIAGE:
Type: Retractable, with nosewheel
Wheel base: 16 ft 10 ins (5.137 m)
Wheel track: 7 ft 6 ins (2.3 m)

WEIGHTS:
Empty: 20,503 lb (9,300 kg)
Maximum take-off: 26,675 lb (12,100 kg)

PERFORMANCE:
Maximum speed: Mach 1.6-1.8
Take-off distance: 1,640 ft (500 m)
Landing distance: 2,300 ft (700 m)
Ceiling: 52,500 ft (16,000 m)
G limits: +8
Radius of action: 648 naut miles (745 miles) 1,200 km in air-to-air role, 378 naut miles (435 miles) 700 km for attack

Chengdu J-10

First flight: 24 March 1998 (pilot Li Chen).
Role: Advanced multi-role fighter, capable of air superiority, interdiction and air support. Possible carrier fighter role.

Aims

- Expected to follow the Su-27 into Chinese service.
- Quantum leap in Chinese fighter development, producing an aircraft in the magnitude of the Swedish Gripen, French Rafale and European Eurofighter.

Development

- 1980s. Start of the J-10 study programme.
- 1994. A US satellite photographed a new Chinese fighter prototype. Varying reports have suggested that this fighter could have adopted technology from the Israeli Lavi that was abandoned in an advanced stage of development in the1980s.
- 1996. The Chinese People's Liberation Army released a photograph of the J-10 as a model for wind tunnel testing, with the undercarriage lowered and with 4 missiles and 2 drop tanks suspended on pylons under the wings. The Russian engine said to power the actual prototype J-10 is larger, heavier and more powerful than the Pratt & Whitney flown in Lavi, which suggests the J-10 could have a fuselage of greater proportions, while each wing leading-edge may have a 'dogtooth' at the position of the slat and the trailing-edge has a root extension that passes above the ventral fins. Furthermore, while Lavi had 4 underwing pylons and 2 AAM launch rails at the wingtips, it appears J-10 has 6 underwing pylons and no tip rails. At least the inner pair of wing pylons are 'wet'.
- February 1998. Taxi trials began.
- 24 March 1998. First flight, demonstrating short take-off/landing. 40 minutes duration.
- 2001. Possible start of full rate production.
- 2005. Likely initial operational capability with the Chinese forces.

Details *(speculative)*

Sales/Users: 4 prototypes by May 1998. China is said to need 300, probably including a number of 2-seat operational training variants.
Crew: Pilot on zero-zero ejection seat, but with a 2-seater also anticipated.

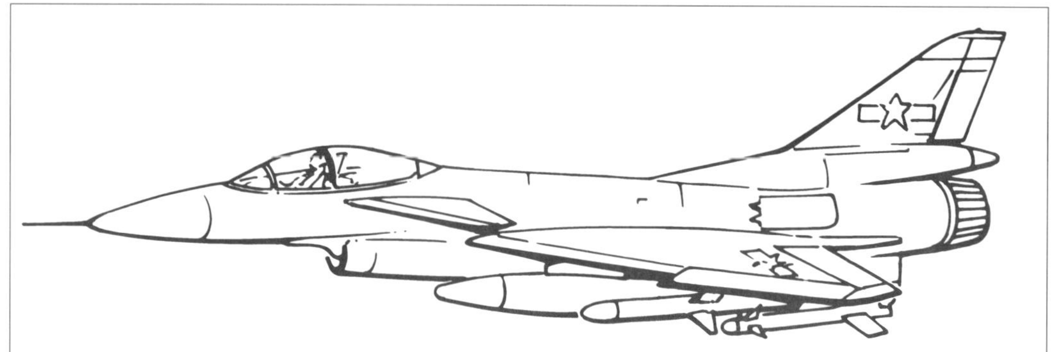

↑ **Artist's impression of the Chengdu J-10** *(Michael Taylor/Bill Hobson)*

Fixed guns: Unknown, but possibly pod-mounted cannon.
Number of weapon pylons: 6 (see Development).
Expendable weapons and equipment: Missiles compatible with the Russian Phazotron radar include AA-10 *Alamo*, AA-11 *Archer*, AA-12 *Adder* and AS-17 *Krypton*. Israeli-supplied missiles could include the Rafael Python 4. Possibly South African Darter type.
Radar: Possibly Russian Phazotron Zhuk PH Improved Pulse Doppler multirole radar, known as Zhemchoug, with a 132 naut mile velocity mode and 99 naut mile range mode, and 10 target tracking capability. Alternatively, the Israeli Elta El/M-2035, originally developed for the Lavi fighter, or Chinese JL-10A.
Flight/weapon system avionics/instrumentation: Advanced technology glass cockpit. Undoubtedly HOTAS, wide-angle HUD, head-down displays, and full range of computer controlled management systems, warning systems and countermeasures.
Wing characteristics: Swept, cropped delta type, above and ahead of which are close-coupled all-moving swept foreplanes. See Development for other features.
Tail control surfaces: Swept fin with inset rudder. 2 outward-canted quadrilateral ventral fins under the rear fuselage.
Airbrakes: Door type, each side of the rear fuselage, approximately in line with the wing trailing edges.
Flight control system: Digital fly-by-wire.
Construction materials: Metal and composites.
Engine: Originally thought to be an NPO Saturn Lyulka AL-31F turbofan (10 delivered from Russia), but also suggested is a Klimov RD-33.
Engine rating: 16,755 lbf (74.53 kN) dry, and 27,558 lbf (122.59 kN) with afterburning if AL-31F, and 11,100 lbf (49.42 kN) dry and 18,300 lbf (81.4 kN) with afterburning if RD-33.
Air intake: Under the forward fuselage.

Chengdu J-12

Comments: Very little is known about this multi-role fighter, dubbed by the US Office of Naval Intelligence as the XXJ. It is suggested that the J-12 has 2 engines and that single-seat and 2-seat versions are in the concept definition phase, which would probably indicate that the first flight could take place in about the year 2005, with service entry between 2015 and 2020. It is also feasible that other Chinese manufacturers are working on rival designs to fulfil the role, though it is known that Chengdu is an active participant in the programme. At the time of writing, there was insufficient hard knowledge of the layout to allow an artist's impression to be drawn with any confidence.

Guizhou Aviation Industry Corporation — China

Corporate address:
PO Box 38, Anshun, Guizhou 561000.
Telephone: +86 853 551027
Telex: 66018 AIMGA CN

ACTIVITIES

▪ Produces 2-seat operational training variants of the Chengdu J-7 fighter, in addition to work on the main J-7 programme.
▪ Other activities include weaponry and turbine engines.

Guizhou JJ-7

First flight: 5 July 1985 (JJ-7).
Role: Supersonic lead-in/fighter conversion trainer, with combat capability.

Aims

▪ JJ-7 and its export counterpart, the FT-7, are capable of duplicating all the flying and combat techniques of the J-7/F-7, and a major part of F-8 training.

Development

▪ 1982. Development work on the JJ-7 started, based on the J-7 II and similar in concept to the Russian MiG-21US.
▪ 1986. Production initiated, with the first series-built FT-7 making its maiden flight at the end of 1987.
▪ 9 November 1990. Maiden flight of a production FT-7P for Pakistan.

↑ **Guizhou JJ-7 in Chinese service** *(courtesy Chinese Embassy)*

▪ 1994. Development began of a lengthened 2-seat operational combat version of FT-7P, with a 23.6 ins (60 cm) fuselage plug.
▪ 1996. The new stretched FT-7P entered service with Pakistan.

Details *(for the FT-7, unless stated)*

Sales/Users: Although it previously appeared that China had not adopted the JJ-7, the accompanying photograph of a Chinese trainer in full markings indicates that it did enter service . Export of the FT-7 to Bangladesh (4), Myanmar, Pakistan (15+ FT-7Ps), Sri Lanka (1) and Zimbabwe (2).
Crew: 2.
Cockpit: Twin tandem cockpits, equipped with duplicated instrumentation and controls, the rear having a retractable periscope for improving the forward view. Red lighting. Starboard-hinged canopies. Cockpit pressure differential 4.35 psi.
Crew escape: Ejection seats.
Fixed guns: Optional weaponry, including a 23-mm twin-barrel 23-3 cannon pack carried under the fuselage. New stretched FT-7P has a fixed internal gun.
Number of weapon pylons: Normally 2 under the wings plus an underfuselage station for a drop tank, but 4 underwing pylons on the FT-7P.
Expendable weapons and equipment: Typical choice of 2 × PL-2B air-to-air missiles, 2 × 18 round 57-2 rocket packs or 2 × 100 kg to 250 kg bombs.
Radar: See J-7 entry.
Flight/weapon system avionics/instrumentation: Includes a "trouble simulator" system. Pakistan's FT-7Ps incorporate avionics in keeping with its F-7 models.
Fuselage: Similar to the J-7 but with larger ventral fins of angular shape. Very slightly shorter overall length including nose probe.
Engine: Liyang WP7B (BM) turbojet.
Engine rating: 9,689 lbf (43.1 kN) dry, 13,443 lbf (59.8 kN) with afterburning.
Air intakes: At fuselage nose.
Flight refuelling probe: None.
Fuel system: 560 litres in wing tanks and 1,880 litres in the fuselage. Removable metal "saddle-back" tank to the rear of the cockpits. Optional 500 litre drop tanks under the wings and/or a 720 litre underfuselage tank. FT-7P has greater tankage.

↑ **New stretched version of the Guizhou FT-7P** *(Sebastian Zacharias)*

Electrical system: 28.5 volt DC supply. 12 kW engine-driven starter-generator, with static inverters.
Hydraulic system: 3,000 psi.
Braking system: See J-7 entry.

Aircraft variants:
JJ-7 is the Chinese designation for the domestic forces.
FT-7 is the standard export version, with only 2 underwing pylons.
FT-7P is a structurally upgraded version for Pakistan, with avionics compatible with its Airguard fighters and 4 underwing pylons. Empty weight reduced by some 418 lb (190 kg), and with a maximum take-off weight of 18,960 lb (8,600 kg), allowing for increased armament and/or fuel.
Stretched FT-7P for Pakistan is 50 ft 9 ins (15.47 m) in length, with a maximum take-off weight of 21,050 lb (9,550 kg). Internal fuel capacity increased to 2,800 litres, while 3 drop tanks can provide for an additional 1,800 litres. Internal fixed gun.

Details for FT-7

PRINCIPAL DIMENSIONS:
Wing span: 23 ft 5.5 ins (7.154 m)
Maximum length: 45 ft 9 ins (13.945 m) tail to shock cone, 48 ft 9.5 ins (14.874 m) including nose probe
Maximum height: 13 ft 5.5 ins (4.103 m)

WINGS:
Area: 247.57 sq ft (23 m^2)
Aspect ratio: 2.225
Sweepback: 49° 6' at 25% chord
Incidence: 0°
Anhedral: 2°

TAIL UNIT:
Tailplane span: 12 ft 3 ins (3.74 m)
Tailplane area: 42.41 sq ft (3.94 m^2)
Fin area: 37.46 sq ft (3.48 m^2)

UNDERCARRIAGE:
Type: Retractable, with steerable nosewheel
Main wheel tyre size: 600 × 200 mm
Nose wheel tyre size: 500 × 180 mm
Wheel base: 15 ft 9 ins (4.807 m)
Wheel track: 8 ft 10 ins (2.6924 m)
Turning radius: 23 ft 1 ins (7.04 m)

WEIGHTS:
Empty, operating: 12,167 lb (5,519 kg)
Maximum take-off: 18,860 lb (8,555 kg)

PERFORMANCE:
Maximum speed: Mach 2.05 (CATIC brochure quotes speed at above 1.25 km altitude or 4,100 ft, 1,250 m, but it is probable that it should be above 12.5 km or 41,000 ft, 12,500 m)
Take-off speed: 170-181 kts (196-208 mph) 315-335 km/h
Landing speed: 165-175 kts (190-202 mph) 306-324 km/h
Stall speed: 135 kts (155 mph) 250 km/h
Take-off distance: 2,955-3,610 ft (900-1,100 m)
Landing distance: 2,790-3,610 ft (850-1,100 m) with drag-chute and braking
Maximum climb rate: 30,512 ft (9,300 m) per minute
G limits: +7
Ceiling: 56,760 ft (17,300 m) service, 58,070 ft (17,700 m) theoretical absolute
Range with full internal fuel: 545 naut miles (627 miles) 1,010 km, at 36,000 ft (11,000 m)
Range with full internal fuel plus a 720 litre drop tank: 788 naut miles (906 miles) 1,459 km, at 36,000 ft (11,000 m)
Range with maximum weapon load: 709 naut miles (816 miles) 1,313 km

Harbin Aircraft Manufacturing Corporation — China

Corporate address:
PO Box 201-29, 15 Youxie Street, Pingfang District, Harbin 150066.

Telephone: +86 451 6501122-83491/82881
Facsimile: +86 451 6502061
Telex: 87082 HAF CN
E-mail: phamcas@hr.hl.cn

Founded: 1952.

Employees: 17,000.

Information:
Xu Zhanbin (Managing Director, Aircraft Sales & Support Division).

ACTIVITIES

▪ Main transport aircraft production centres on the Y-12 (including the latest Y-12 (IV) that obtained its type certificate from the CAAC on 3 July 1994 and from the FAA on 26 March 1995).
▪ The SH-5 amphibian remains important to the PLA Navy but went out of production after a small number of aircraft had been produced.
▪ Helicopter production now includes Z-9Bs, while the new EC-120 has also flown (see Helicopter section).

Harbin H-5 (NATO name *Beagle*)

Comments: Production of this strategic and tactical bomber, reconnaissance and naval anti-shipping aircraft, based on the Ilyushin Il-28, began in 1966 and ended many years ago. In a reply from Harbin for this edition, no changes were made to the existing entry, Full details and a photograph can be found in the 1996-97 edition of *WA&SD*, pages 24-25.

Harbin SH-5

Comments: First flown on 3 April 1976, the SH-5 is principally a large amphibian for anti-submarine work, mine warfare, anti-shipping and maritime patrol, but is also capable of search and rescue and cargo-carrying. On 3 September 1986, the first and only production batch of 4 aircraft in full military form were

↑ **Harbin SH-5 amphibian** *(Xinhua News Agency)*

received by the PLA Navy. In a reply from Harbin for this edition, it was stated that 'no change' should be made to the Sales/Users paragraph, which follows. The reported sale of a small number of British Searchwater radars to China (1996) has given rise to speculation that these were intended to replace the nose-mounted Doppler search radar in the SH-5s. Full details of the SH-5 can be found in the 1996-97 edition of *WA&SD*, page 25.
Sales/Users: 1 static test prototype, 1 flying prototype and 5 production SH-5s (confirmed). 4 of the latter are operated at the Tuandao base. 1 of the non-military aircraft has been tested as a fire-fighter for water bombing, able to carry 17,635 lb (8,000 kg) of water, scooped during a taxi run and taking 15 seconds to fill using this method.

Hongdu Aviation Industry Group — China

Corporate address:
PO Box 5001-506, Nanchang, Jiangxi 330024.

Telephone: +86 791 846 8401, 8402
Facsimile: +86 791 845 1491
Telex: 95068 NAMC CN

Founded: 1951. Formerly Nanchang Aircraft Manufacturing Company, until 28 March 1998.

Employees:
About 20,000.

Information:
Wang Zhiqiang.

ACTIVITIES

▪ Includes the development/production of the N-5A agricultural aircraft and CJ-6A primary trainer (see General Aviation section).
▪ In partnership with Pakistan Aeronautical Complex on the K-8 Karakorum jet trainer programme (see Multi-national in this section). The Chinese version is known as K-8J.

Hongdu Q-5/A-5 (NATO name *Fantan*)

First flight: 5 June 1965.
Role: Supersonic attack and strike aircraft, anti-shipping, and with the capability of limited air defence.

Aims

▪ To develop a dedicated attack aircraft using enhanced Shenyang J-6 technology and based on that airframe.
▪ Transonic speed at low level.
▪ Minimum transonic drag by adopting an area ruled fuselage configuration.
▪ Cockpit armour to protect the pilot from ground fire during low-level close support missions.
▪ To offer the potential of carrying a nuclear weapon at high speed.

Development

▪ 1958. Very limited design work on the Q-5 began at Shenyang, but the project was transferred to Nanchang for further development by the Ministry of Aviation.
▪ 1961. Project cancelled but revived 2 years later.
▪ 1965. First flight of a prototype, but intended early production was deferred after trials indicated that modifications to several of the aircraft's systems should be undertaken.
▪ 1969. Prototypes reappeared, with modifications to the armament, hydraulic and other systems. Production authorized.
▪ 1970. Early production Q-5s appeared as conventionally-armed attack/strike aircraft, each with a fuselage weapon bay. Availability of a small free-fall nuclear bomb soon led to several being modified for trials and service.
▪ 1980. The improved Q-5 I appeared, with greatly increased internal fuel tankage to cure the Q-5's lack of range, but requiring deletion of the bomb bay and addition of 2 more underwing pylons to make good the loss of internal weapon attachment points.
▪ January 1983. First exports, with upgraded A-5Cs being delivered over the next 12 months to the Pakistan Air Force.
▪ 1984. Appearance of the Q-5 IA, also adopting 6 underwing pylons and some other A-5C-type upgrades. Certified early the following year.
▪ 30 August 1988. First flight of an A-5M prototype, produced by modification of a Q-5 II by Aeritalia (now Alenia) of Italy under a CATIC agreement of 1986. Based on the need for a modern navigation/attack system.
▪ 17 September 1988. First Q-5K Kong Yun prototype made its maiden flight, having undergone an extensive navigation/attack avionics upgrade by Thomson-CSF of France (under a CATIC agreement) that included a laser rangefinder, head-up display, INS and much more, together with the required improved electrical supply system. This programme was, however, abandoned in 1990.
▪ 17 October 1988. First A-5M prototype was lost in an accident.
▪ 8 March 1989. First flight of the second A-5M prototype. Development was completed in 1991 but further upgrades were thereafter begun.
▪ 1993. Myanmar became the first A-5M recipient.
▪ 1996. A-5M programme reported to be placed on hold due to inadequate funding.

Details

Sales/Users: Bangladesh (20+ A-5Cs with 2 squadrons at Dhaka and Chittagong), China (well over 500 in air force service, and over 100 with the navy for anti-shipping, the latter confirmed by Hongdu to have no special designation), Myanmar (A-5Cs), North Korea (40 Q-5 IAs), and Pakistan (perhaps 45 A-5Cs, known as A-5 IIIs, remaining with 3 squadrons at Masroor and Peshawar).
Crew: Pilot.
Cockpit: Armoured and pressurized.
Crew escape: The standard Chinese ejection seat is a zero-altitude Type I, with safe operation between 135 and 459 kts (155 and 528 mph) 250 and 850 km/h. A-5C and M use a Martin Baker zero-zero ejection seat.
Fixed guns: 2 × 23-mm Norinco 23-2K cannon in the wing roots.
Ammunition: 100 rounds per cannon.
Number of weapon pylons: 8 on Q-5 (2 in weapon bay, 2 underfuselage and 4 under the wings). 8 on Q-5 I/IA/II, with no weapon bay but 4 externally under the fuselage plus 4 under the wings. 10 on A-5C/A-5 III, all external, including 6 under the wings. 12 on A-5M, including 8 under the wings.
Expendable weapons and equipment: 4,409 lb (2,000 kg) total weight. Early Q-5s could carry up to 2 × 500 kg general-purpose bombs in the bay, plus lighter bombs under the fuselage and wings. However, as the normal operational load was 1,000 kg, it can be supposed that the planned configuration was to remain "clean", with no external stores beyond perhaps drop tanks unless on a close support mission. Fuselage pylons can each carry up to a 250 kg general-purpose bomb, incendiary bomb, or other types including foreign special-purpose weapons such as Durandal penetration bombs for disabling airfields. Inner wing stations for light weapons, including pods for 57-mm, 68-mm, 90-mm or 130-mm rockets, practice or light fragmentation bombs. Centre wing pylons each have the greatest carrying

↑ **Hongdu (Nanchang) Q-5 in Chinese service, carrying 2 underfuselage bombs, 2 rocket launchers and 2 drop tanks. Port wingroot gun is clearly visible** *(courtesy Chinese Embassy)*

↑ **Hongdu (Nanchang) A-5C on display at Zhuhai** *(Sebastian Zacharias)*

capacity, suited to a C-801 or similar anti-ship missile, various types of bombs including 350 kg Norinco anti-tank/anti-runway cluster types or foreign, fuel/air bomb of up to 500 kg, 760 litre (or 1,140 litre on the A-5M) auxiliary fuel tank or other load. Outboard pylons are each normally used to carry an air-to-air missile for self-defence or for limited air-defence duty, including the PL-2/2B or PL-7 range (plus PL-5B for A-5M) of Chinese AAMs, or alternatively Sidewinder or Magic on exported aircraft. A number of Chinese aircraft may carry up to a 20 kiloton nuclear weapon. At least the A-5M could be equipped to carry anti-radiation missiles and laser-guided weapons, but the Q-5 II (Q-5B) could already carry LGBs. See also Q-5 II (Q-5B) under Aircraft variants for other possible weapons.
Radar: No radar is normal for most Q-5 models, except possibly some or all Q-5 IIs (Q-5Bs) that could carry ranging radar compatible with an anti-ship role (see Aircraft variants). Pointer 2500 I-band ranging radar in the modified nose of the A-5M. Russia's Phazotron is offering a radar for Q-5 retrofit.
Flight/weapon system avionics/instrumentation: Conventional instrumentation in all Q-5/A-5C models, including a WL-7 radio compass, AR-3201/CT-3 VHF and HF/SSB transceiver, marker beacon receiver and IFF. Chinese aircraft have a gun camera at the nose. ABS1A or SH-1J optical bombing sight. See also Q-5 II (Q-5B) under Aircraft variants for other possible equipment. Very much improved A-5M has a modern navigation/attack system interfaced with retained Chinese avionics, based on the principal subsystems of: Chinese VHF communications and IFF; Litton LN-39A inertial navigation system; 2 Singer digital computers and dual-redundant 1553B databus, with computer based weapon aiming and delivery, incorporating the Pointer 2500 ranging radar and a new stores management system; Alenia head-up display and other cockpit changes; data processing, with an air data computer; ECM (existing or Italian type) and radar warning receiver. Changes required an improved electrical system. Further A-5M improvements could include (now, or as a later development) night vision systems and a laser rangefinder.
Self-protection systems: Type 930 radar warning receiver. ECM pod can be carried on the centre wing pylon (of Italian manufacture on the A-5M). Chaff/flare dispenser available to at least the A-5M.
Wing characteristics: Sharply swept, mid mounted, with a mid-span fence, configured from J-6 wings.
Wing control surfaces: Ailerons (port tab) and Gouge area-increasing trailing-edge flaps.
Tail control surfaces: Anhedral slab tailplane with anti-flutter devices, and rudder (with tab).
Airbrakes: Under fuselage, hydraulically actuated.
Flight control system: Hydraulic for ailerons, flaps and boosted tailplane, mechanical for rudder, and electric tabs.
Fuselage: Lengthened and considerably altered area-ruled J-6 type for minimum transonic drag, leaving almost no ancestral likeness. "Solid" metal pointed nose on all versions except the A-5M.
Construction materials: Metal, but with the possible use of composites for A-5M developments to reduce the radar signature.
Engines: 2 Liming WP6 turbojets. Alternative WP6As for export A-5s and possibly available for retrofit to Q-5s. Hydraulically operated afterburner nozzle.
Engine rating: Each 5,400 lbf (24.03 kN) dry and 7,165 lbf (31.87 kN) with afterburning. WP6As have an afterburning rating of 8,930 lbf (39.72 kN).
Air intakes: Each side of the forward fuselage, level with the cockpit, with splitter plates.
Flight refuelling probe: A system to allow the Q-5/A-5 to receive fuel from H-6 tankers was designed by Flight Refuelling Ltd in the 1980s but never adopted.
Fuel system: 3,648 litres internally. 2 × 760 litre or 2 × 400 litre auxiliary fuel tanks (middle or outer pylons respectively), or up to 2 × 1,140 litre tanks for the A-5M.
Electrical system: 28 volt DC supply with 2 engine-driven starter-generators. 2 static inverters for the AC supply.
Hydraulic system: Primary and secondary systems, at 3,000 psi. Emergency back-up pressure of 1,565 psi for undercarriage extension.
Braking system: Disc on main units. Drag-chute housed in a tail fairing, typically positioned (except in the oldest aircraft) under the rudder.

Aircraft variants:
Q-5 was the original version with a fuselage bomb bay.
Q-5 I was the first model to have the bay removed and fuel tankage increased, becoming the standard configuration.
Q-5 IA introduced several important refinements, including 2 extra underwing pylons, improved optical sights, and better self protection among other changes.
Q-5 II (Q-5B) appears to be almost identical to the Q-5 IA except for having a RWR. However, it may also have ranging radar, ALR-1 laser rangefinder/designator to operate with newly deployed laser-guided bombs, a HUD, mission computer and ECM. Armament frequently includes 2 torpedoes or C-801 anti-shipping missiles.
A-5C (or A-5 III) is the major export model, with many refinements dictated by the requirements of the Pakistan Air Force. Marginally greater length and span. Refinements include improved avionics, the ability to carry Western-manufactured weapons, and a Martin Baker PKD10 zero-zero ejection seat.
A-5M is the latest model, developed in association with Aeritalia (now Alenia) of Italy. Many avionics improvements, as noted previously, and 12 pylons. WP6A III engines with extended time between overhaul for the engines and greater drop tank capacity.

Details for A-5 models

PRINCIPAL DIMENSIONS:
Wing span 31 ft 10 ins (9.7 m)
Maximum length: 55 ft 0 ins (16.77 m) for A-5C/A-5 III with probe, 51 ft 6 ins (15.695 m) without, or 50 ft 5 ins (15.366 m) for A-5M
Maximum height: 14 ft 10 ins (4.516 m) for A-5C/A-5 III, 14 ft 10.5 ins (4.53 m) for A-5M

WINGS:
Area: 300.9 sq ft (27.95 m^2)
Aspect ratio: 3.366
Sweepback: 52° 30' at 25% chord
Chord at root: 13 ft 7.5 ins (4.15 m)
Chord at tip: 5 ft 1 ins (1.55 m)
Incidence: 0°
Anhedral: 4°

UNDERCARRIAGE:
Type: Retractable, with nosewheel (not steerable) that rotates through nearly 90° during retraction
Main wheel tyre size: 830 × 205 mm
Nose wheel tyre size: 595 × 230 mm
Wheel base: 13 ft 2 ins (4.01 m)
Wheel track: 14 ft 5 ins (4.4 m)

WEIGHTS:
Empty: 14,635 lb (6,638 kg) for A-5C/A-5 III, or 14,625 lb (6,634 kg) for A-5M
Maximum take-off: 26,455 lb (12,000 kg)

PERFORMANCE:
Maximum level flight Mach number: Mach 1.12 for A-5C/A-5 III, or Mach 1.2 for A-5M, at 36,000 ft (11,000 m)
Maximum speed: 653 kts (752 mph) 1,210 km/h for A-5C/A-5 III, or 661 kts (761 mph) 1,225 km/h for A-5M, at sea level
Take-off distance: 4,101 ft (1,250 m) for A-5C/A-5 III, or 3,937 ft (1,200 m) for A-5M, at maximum weight
Landing distance: 2,638-3,478 ft (804-1,060 m) ground roll
Maximum climb rate: 29,125 ft (8,880 m) per minute, at sea level
Maximum climb rate at 16,400ft (5,000 m): 20,275 ft (6,180 m) per minute for A-5C/A-5 III, or 22,640 ft (6,900 m) per minute for A-5M, *clean*
G limits: +7.5 *clean*, +5 *with maximum external armament*
Ceiling: 52,000 ft (15,850 m) for A-5C/A-5 III, or 52,490 ft (16,000 m) for A-5M
Range with full fuel: 980 naut miles (1,131 miles) 1,816 km, with 1,520 litres of auxiliary fuel, at 11,000 m and best range cruise speed
Radius of action: 216-324 naut miles (248-373 miles) 400-600 km for A-5C/A-5 III, or 173-279 naut miles (200-321 miles) 320-518 km for A-5M, depending on mission profile, with a 2,000 kg payload

Shenyang Aircraft Corporation — China

Corporate address:
PO Box 328, Shenyang, Liaoning 110034.
Telephone: +86 24 6896680
Facsimile: +86 24 6896689
Employees:
Approximately 30,000.

ACTIVITIES

- Major division of the Shenyang Aircraft Industrial (Group) Company Ltd.
- Has been responsible for producing the great majority of Chinese fighters and fighter-bombers since the mid-1950s, including huge numbers of J-5s (MiG-17F/PFs) and J-6s (MiG-19s), of which several thousand remain available to the PLA Air Force and to the Navy for various duties including interception, attack, reconnaissance and training. In addition, Shenyang-built JJ-2 2-seat trainers remain active (MiG-15UTIs), as are JJ-6s for a similar role. Current fighter work is based on the J-8 II and F-8 IIM export model. See the 1996-97 edition of *WA&SD* for an export F-6 photograph, page 27.
- Sub-contract work includes components for several European and North American aircraft programmes, including the Airbus A300/319/320, Boeing 757, DHC Dash 8 and Lockheed Martin Hercules transports.
- Chinese source for Sukhoi Su-27CK licensed production, as the J-11. First built from kits to fly late 1998.
- Shenyang Hellenic Aircraft Repair Company was established in 1997 with Hellenic Aerospace Industry (see Greece).

Shenyang J-8 II (NATO name *Finback*)

First flight: 5 July 1969.
Role: Multi-role fighter, all-weather combat aircraft for interception, air superiority, air convoy, battlefield interdiction, and close air support.
Fatigue life: 3,000 flying hours for F-8 IIM.

Aims

- Enlarged, twin-engined development of the J-7, initially with a similar nose air intake and shock-cone.
- J-8 II reconfigured to make space for a more capable fire-control radar, and provide greater airflow via 2 side air intakes to feed engines with higher augmented ratings.

Development

- 1964. Work on the J-8 programme began.
- 1969. Flight trials with the prototypes began and continued over several years, while further development work and construction was halted for political reasons.
- 1979. Construction of 3 pre-series aircraft began, 1 being destroyed before flight.
- 24 April 1981. First flight of a pre-series J-8 I
- 12 June 1984. First flight of the first of four J-8 II prototypes, with 2 others being built for ground testing.
- 1985. Production began of early model J-8s, followed by J-8 Is.
- 5 August 1987. Contract signed between CATIC and Grumman of the USA , covering the development of an upgrade package for the J-8 II funded under a USAF foreign military sales programme named Peace Pearl, involving 50 sets. Included in the upgrade were to be a modified Westinghouse APG-66 radar, fire control computer, a Litton LN-39 inertial navigation system and head-up display. Two J-8 IIs were delivered to the USA for development purposes.
- 1989. Peace Pearl programme was put on hold by the US Government following events in China, leading to Chinese termination of the project in the following year. The prototypes were sent back to China 4 years later. Production of the J-8 II continued despite the lack of upgrade, but in very small numbers.
- 1994. First appearance of the F-8 II export version of the J-8 II, with many upgrades.
- 31 March 1996. First flight of the new F-8 IIM export fighter, incorporating F-8 II development gains. Taking only 2 years to reach first flight after delivery of drawings became a Chinese industrial record.

↑ **Shenyang F-8 IIM on display at Zhuhai, with PL-9 and AA-19 missiles**
(Sebastian Zacharias)

Details *(apply to J-8 II, but with data for F-8 IIM and other versions where indicated)*

Sales/Users: Early J-8 day fighters have largely been withdrawn or were upgraded to J-8 I standard for all-weather operations, joined by small numbers of J-8 IIs. Reported numbers in service in early 1998 with the PLA air force and possibly navy vary greatly from under 100 to well over 200. Development and low volume production is said to continue. Iran is rumoured to be a potential export customer.
Crew: Pilot, under an upward-hinged canopy.
Cockpit: Modern head-up and head-down displays in the export F-8 II (see Avionics and Aircraft variants).
Crew escape: Ejection seat.
Fixed guns: 23-mm twin-barrel 23-3 cannon in the belly of the forward fuselage.
Ammunition: 200 rounds.
Number of weapon pylons: 7, with the single underfuselage pylon typically carrying a drop tank to extend range.
Expendable weapons and equipment: 9,920 lb (4,500 kg) maximum possible load, though normally no more than 5,512 lb (2,500 kg) for J-8 II, including PL-2B and PL-7 air-to-air missiles, HF-16A or B launchers each for 12 × 57-mm air-to-air rockets fired in salvos of 4, 8 or 12, or HF-7 launchers for 90-mm air-to-surface rockets to attack armoured or installation targets, or bombs and/or drop tanks. F-8 IIM weapons include PL-9, AA-10 *Alamo* and AA-12 *Adder* AAMs, and possibly AS-17 *Krypton* ASM. Growth capability to launch anti-ship missiles.
Radar: China Leihua SR-4 I/J-band air-to-air fire control radar with single-target tracking and engagement in the J-8 I, and an unidentified monopulse radar (possibly China Leihua Type 317a) in the J-8 II to offer single target tracking/engagement, ground mapping, terrain avoidance and ranging. Russian Phazotron Zhuk 8 II multi-function pulse Doppler fire control radar in F-8 IIM with lookdown/shootdown, with 37.8 naut mile (43.5 mile) 70 km detection range in the forward hemisphere and 21.6 naut mile (24.8 mile) 40 km in the aft hemisphere for 32.3 sq ft (3 m^2) target RCS, for multiple target track-while-scan (10) and guidance of medium-range AAMs for single and dual target attacks.
Flight/weapon system avionics/instrumentation: Includes tactical air navigation system, instrument landing system, marker beacon receiver, radar altimeter, and IFF. Gun camera. Autopilot for maintaining altitude, heading and level flight. Optical gyro sight. F-8 IIM has a new digital avionics package, with integrated fire control system incorporating combined GPS/INS and IFF; navigation/attack system using a dual redundant ARINC 429 databus; datalink/Tacan; autopilot; head-up display and 2 head-down displays; HOTAS; advanced electronic warfare system; and threat radar data recording. Radio communications.
Self-protection systems: Radar warning receiver and ECM; F-8 IIM has omni-directional RWR, rearward noise jamming against threat (including pulse Doppler radar). Chaff/flare dispensers.
Wing characteristics: Delta, mid mounted, with upper-surface fences towards the wingtips.
Wing control surfaces: Ailerons and 2-section single-slotted trailing-edge flaps. F-8 II has leading-edge flaps.
Tail control surfaces: Slab tailplane and rudder. A large stabilizing fin under the rear fuselage is deployed from its folded position only once the aircraft is airborne.

↑ **PLA air force Shenyang J-8 IIs** *(courtesy Chinese Embassy)*

Airbrakes: 4, under the fuselage.
Flight control system: Hydraulic.
Fuselage: Area-ruled for minimum transonic/supersonic drag, with an upper-surface spine running from the cockpit to the fin-root airscoop. 2 further airscoops on the aft fuselage, 1 each side of the fin.
Construction materials: All metal, principally aluminium alloy, but with some high-tensile steel and titanium, with the ailerons and portions of the tail unit and ailerons of weight-saving honeycomb construction.
Engines: 2 Liyang WP13A II turbojets in the J-8 II, with a power-to-weight ratio of 5.6. 2 WP13Bs (or WP13A IIIs) in F-8 II/IIM, rated at 10,580 lbf (47.07 kN) dry and with augmented thrust raised to 15,437 lbf (68.67 kN).
Engine rating: Each 9,600 lbf (42.7 kN) dry, 14,815 lbf (65.9 kN) with afterburning for WP13A IIs.
Air intakes: Fuselage sides on the J-8 II/F-8 II/IIM, with adjusting ramp angle and splitter plates (in the nose with a shock-cone on the J-8 I).
Flight refuelling probe: Fitted to F-8 II/IIM only.
Fuel system: Estimated to be 4,350-5,400 litres in fuselage and 4 wing tanks, plus optional auxiliary fuel carried under the fuselage and on the outer underwing pylons. F-8 IIM has 9,259 lb (4,200 kg) fuel load.
Electrical system: 28.5 volt DC supply with 2 × 12 kW engine-driven starter generators. 2 alternators for 3-phase AC supply. F-8 IIM incorporates 2 × 15 kVA AC generators.
Hydraulic system: 2 systems, each 3,000 psi.
Braking system: Disc brakes. Drag-chute housed in an under-rudder fairing.

Aircraft variants:
J-8 and J-8 I (*Finback-A*) were early production versions with nose air intakes, the former for day/fair weather operations and equipped with a ranging radar, 2 × 30-mm cannon and 4 × PL-2B missiles or 2 missiles and 2 drop tanks. Probably no J-8s in service, as most were converted to J-8 I standard with a new air-to-air radar in the air intake shock cone (see Radar), 1 ×23-mm cannon and other changes for all-weather use. 2 engines of J-7 type.
J-8 II (*Finback-B*) is the much modified development with multi-role capability, partly due to its change of radar (see Radar) in a new "solid" nose. Side air intakes, new engines and greater weapon carrying capability on 7 pylons.
F-8 II (*Finback-B*) was the original CATIC-advertized export version. New digital avionics package, with a navigation/attack system using a dual redundant MIL-STD-1553B databus and Doppler radar. Head-up display and 2 head-down displays. Possibly higher augmented-thrust engines (see Engines) and in-flight refuelling probe. Leading-edge flaps. Thought to have been incorporated into the latest F-8 IIM programme.
F-8 IIM (*Finback-B*) is the latest export version, based on F-8 II development and produced by Shenyang as a private venture. First flown in 1996 and displayed at the Zhuhai International Air Show later that year. WP13B (or WP13A III) engines. Russian Zhuk 8 II fire control radar and upgraded cockpit avionics with HOTAS. Improved electrical system. Better armament, with improved ability to utilize the maximum load. For maintainability, has 21% openable access area overall, with 32% access area on forward fuselage; quick opening access to equipment bays; built-in testing capability; international standard AC power socket; and anti-error connectors. Heavier than earlier aircraft, said to result in marginally lower manoeuvrability.

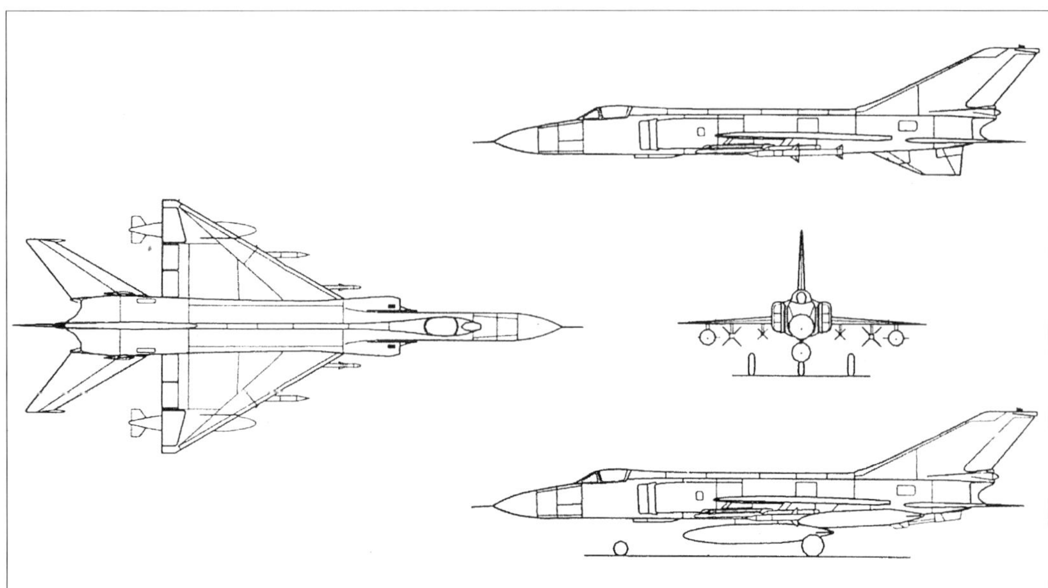

↑ **Shenyang F-8 IIM** *(courtesy CATIC)*

Details for J-8 II, *with F-8 IIM in italics*

PRINCIPAL DIMENSIONS:
Wing span: 30 ft 8 ins (9.344 m), *the same*
Maximum length: 70 ft 10 ins (21.59 m), *70 ft 2 ins (21.389 m)*
Maximum height: 17 ft 9 ins (5.41 m), *the same*

WINGS:
Area: 454.24 sq ft (42.2 m^2), *the same*
Aspect ratio: 2.07
Sweepback: 60°
Anhedral: From roots

UNDERCARRIAGE:
Type: Retractable, with steerable nosewheel
Wheel base: 24 ft 1 ins (7.337 m)
Wheel track: 12 ft 3 ins (3.741 m)

WEIGHTS:
Empty: 21,650 lb (9,820 kg), *22,112-22,864 lb (10,030-10,371 kg)*
Normal take-off: 31,525 lb (14,300 kg), *33,704 lb (15,288 kg)*
Maximum take-off: 39,240 lb (17,800 kg), *40,393-41,621 lb (18,322-18,879 kg)*

PERFORMANCE:
Maximum operating Mach number (M_{MO}): Mach 2.2, *Mach 2*
Maximum indicated speed: 702 kts (808 mph) 1,300 km/h
Take-off speed: 175 kts (202 mph) 325 km/h, *178 kts (205 mph) 330 km/h*
Landing speed: 157 kts (180 mph) 290 km/h, *162 kts (186 mph) 300 km/h*
Take-off distance: 2,203 ft (670 m), *2,067 ft (630 m)*
Landing distance: 3,280 ft (1,000 m), *2,953 ft (900 m)*, both with drag-chute
Maximum climb rate: 39,375 ft (12,000 m) per minute
Maximum climb rate (F-8 IIM): *37,400 ft (11,400 m) per minute, 44,100 ft (13,440 m) per minute at Mach 0.9 and 1,000 m altitude, or 31,500 ft (9,600 m) per minute at Mach 0.9 and 5,000 m*
Acceleration in level flight: *21 seconds from Mach 0.7 to Mach 1 at 1,000 m, 55 seconds from Mach 0.6 to Mach 1.25 at 5,000 m*
G limits at Mach 0.9: +4.83 at 5,000 m altitude, *+6.9 at 1,000 m, + 4.7 at 5,000 m*
Ceiling: over 65,615 ft (20,000 m), *59,055 ft (18,000 m)*
Range with maximum fuel: 1,188 naut miles (1,367 miles) 2,200 km, *1,025 naut miles (1,181 miles) 1,900 km*
Radius of action: 432 naut miles (497 miles) 800 km, *the same*

Xi'an Aircraft Company — China

Full name:
Xi'an Aircraft Industrial Group of China.

Corporate address:
PO Box 140-84, Xi'an 710089.

Telephone: +86 29 6845665
Facsimile: +86 29 6203707
Telex: 70101 XAC CN

Founded: 1958.

Employees: over 21,000.

Information:
Wang Zhigang.

ACTIVITIES

- Xi'an has 4 main activities, the production of military aircraft, commercial aircraft, overseas sub-contracting of aircraft parts and components, and non-aviation products.
- Recent brochures include among Xi'an's military aircraft activities the B-6 bomber and its modified variants (see the separate H-6/B-6 entry below). It has also recently become apparent that the long-awaited JH-7 has reached operational status with PLA naval aviation.
- Current transport manufacturing activities centre on the Y7/Y7H series of military and civil aircraft.
- Has manufactured the Eaglet 100 2-seat light aircraft.
- Sub-contracting work includes manufacture of parts and components on behalf of Boeing, Bombardier/Canadair, Raytheon, Aerospatiale, ATR and Airbus. In April 1994 XAC was certified in accordance with the international ISO9000 for quality.

Xi'an H-6 (NATO name *Badger*)

Comments: First flown on 24 December 1968, the H-6 intermediate-range strategic and tactical bomber, reconnaissance and anti-shipping aircraft was a development of the Russian Tupolev Tu-16, China having received a licence to manufacture the bomber in 1957 and begun by reassembling 2 Russian-supplied aircraft (first flown on 27 September 1959). Originally a Harbin programme, it was taken over by Xi'an in 1961. Approximately 125-150 H-6s remain in service with the PLA air force and naval aviation. This number includes several H-6s modified into flight refuelling tankers to support the air force, while other H-6Ds may be cruise missile carriers. A full description of the aircraft can be found in the 1996-97 edition of *WA&SD*, pages 29-30.

Xi'an JH-7 and FBC-1 Flying Leopard

First flight: 1989.
Role: Supersonic strike, interdiction, ground attack, and maritime strike. Currently in use only in a maritime role.

↑ **Xi'an JH-7 serving with the PLA naval aviation as a dedicated maritime attack aircraft** *(China via Andrei Pinkov)*

Development

- August 1988. First prototype was completed at Xi'an.
- September 1988. News of development of this important aircraft was released at the Farnborough Air Show, UK, in the form of a model and very basic details.
- 1992. Intended service entry, but delayed.
- 1994. Entered service with the PLA naval aviation for early operational use, replacing H-5 torpedo bombers. Used principally for evaluation and over-water missile launch trials.
- October 1995. Service aircraft first displayed on Chinese television, when involved in a naval exercise.
- 1996. JH-7 *(083)* with C-801 and PL-5 missiles was first put on public display in China.
- 1997-98. Development continues to improve both engines and nav-attack system, aimed at very-low-level missions.
- November 1998. FBC-1 export version reveiled.

Details

Sales/Users: 2 prototypes may have been followed by a small pre-series batch for trials, but this is unconfirmed. Reports have suggested that the PLA air force does not plan to field the JH-7, having now received the Su-27, leaving the PLA naval aviation to integrate the aircraft into service; up to 24 may already be in initial operational use in an anti-shipping role. Iran is reportedly an interested export customer.
Crew: 2, in tandem, with substantially raised rear cockpit. Separate upward-hinged canopies, leaving fixed front windshield section and glazed centre section when raised.
Crew escape: HTY-4 zero-zero ejection seats, operable up to 540 kts and 20,000 m.
Fixed guns: 1 × 23-mm twin-barrel cannon.
Number of weapon pylons: 4 underwing and 2 AAM launch rails at the wingtips. The possibility of weapon/stores stations under the fuselage cannot be overlooked.
Expendable weapons and equipment: Up to 11,025 lb (5,000 kg) of bombs of various types, air-to-surface missiles (including C-801 anti-ship) on inner pylons and/or auxiliary fuel tanks (outer pylons) underwing, plus 2 air-to-air missiles (probably PL-5s) at the wingtips for self-defence and limited air defence.
Radar: Navigation/attack and terrain following/clearance.
Flight/weapon system avionics/instrumentation: Probably fitted with Chinese avionics. *Blue Sky* navigation pod, FLIR and laser designator. Blade aerial to the rear of the canopies.

Details for JH-7

PRINCIPAL DIMENSIONS:
Wing span: 42 ft (12.8 m)
Maximum length: 69 ft (21 m)
Maximum height: 20 ft 5 ins (6.22 m)

WINGS:
Area: 563 sq ft (52.3 m^2)
Aspect ratio: 3.13
Anhedral: From roots

UNDERCARRIAGE:
Type: Retractable, with steerable nosewheel/s
Wheel base: 25 ft 7 ins (7.8 m)
Wheel track: 10 ft 1 ins (3.06 m)

WEIGHTS:
Maximum take-off: 60,440 lb (27,415 kg)

PERFORMANCE:
Maximum speed: Mach 1.7
Maximum cruise speed: 485 kts (560 mph) 900 km/h
Take-off distance: 3,018 ft (920 m)
Landing distance: 3,450 ft (1,050 m)
Ceiling: 52,500 ft (16,000 m)
Low-level attack altitude: Approximately 200 ft (60 m)
Radius of combat: 485 naut miles (560 miles) 900 km
Maximum range: 1,672 naut miles (1,925 miles) 3,100 km with full internal and external fuel and no weapons

Wing characteristics: Shoulder mounted anhedral wings, of almost swept-delta planform. Each wing has a compound leading edge, incorporating a dogtooth extension at about two-thirds span, above which is an overwing fence.
Wing control surfaces: Ailerons and flaps of unknown characteristics.
Tail control surfaces: Slab tailplane and swept fin with inset rudder; top of fin on 083 is more rounded than expected from early models, without the fin-top pod. Ventral fin.
Canard: None.
Fuselage: Area-rule design. Large downward-hinged panel under the nose, aft of the nosecone, for access to the forward avionics.
Construction materials: Principally metal.
Engines: 2 Xi'an WS9 turbofans in the prototypes, but it is known that these are giving concern. Reports suggest more powerful Liming engines were intended for production aircraft or higher rated foreign engines, the latter now most likely to be of Russian supply.
Engine rating: Each 12,550 lbf (55.83 kN) dry, 20,515 lbf (91.26 kN) with afterburning.
Air intakes: Fuselage sides, with splitter plates.
Flight refuelling probe: None known.
Fuel system: Internal plus optional auxiliary tanks under the outboard wing pylons.

Aero Holding Joint Stock Company — Czech Republic

Corporate address:
Beranovych 130, 199 04 Praha 9 – Letnany.

Telephone: +420 2 663 10 727, 2 88 40 65, 2 88 27 47 and 2 88 26 56
Facsimile: +420 2 88 65 81, 88 13 40, 88 27 47

Founded:
1 December 1990.

Employees:
27. Over 7,400 employees in the 7 subsidiaries.

Information:
Ing Jan Barton (Executive Director, technical, production and marketing strategy – *telephone* +420 2 88 26 56, *facsimile* +420 2 88 65 81).

ACTIVITIES

- Parent company of the holding group that forms the main part of the Czech aero industry. It has major stakes in Aero Vodochody, Let Kunovice, Letov Praha, Walter Praha, Technometra Praha – Radotín, AXL Semily, and Aeronautical Research and Test Institute (VZLÚ).
- Aero Holding is partly privatized, with 35.2% owned by individual shareholders.
- Principal business is the organization, co-ordination and financing of activities connected with production, sales and operation of aircraft and other aeronautical products.

SUBSIDIARIES

AERO VODOCHODY

HQ address: See next entry.

LET KUNOVICE

HQ address: 686 04 Kunovice.

Telephone: +420 632 512 110, 512 240, 512 351
Facsimile: +420 632 613 52
E-mail: let.otr@brn.pvnet.cz
Web site: www.let.cz

General director:
Ing. Zdenek Pernica.

Employees: 1,723.

Activities:
- L 410 UVP-E, L 420, L 610 regional aircraft and glider production and maintenance.
- Co-operates with foreign aeronautical companies.

LETOV PRAHA

HQ address: Beranovych 65, 199 02 Praha 9 – Letnany.

Telephone: +420 2 858 76 11, 858 76 12
Facsimile: +420 2 858 71 75

General director:
Ing. Vaclav Matousek.

Employees: 1,032.

Activities:
- TL-X flight simulator, NKTL 29/39 ejection seat, LK-2 Sluka and LK-3 Nova ultralights, and maintenance.

WALTER PRAHA

HQ address: Jinonická 329, 158 01 Praha 5 – Jinonice.

Telephone: +420 2 52 11 19, 52 96 20 03
Facsimile: +420 2 52 60 60

General director:
Ing. Vaclav Vanek, CSc.

Employees: 1,187.

Activities:
- Engine production. See Engine section.

TECHNOMETRA PRAHA – RADOTÍN
HQ address: Vrázská 239, 153 04 Praha 5 – Radotín.
Telephone: +420 2 594 4 24, 556 3 28 **Facsimile:** +420 2 549 527
Director: Stanislav Vranek.
Employees: 285
Activities: ■ Undercarriage production and maintenance, and hydraulic equipment production.

AXL SEMILY
HQ address: ulice 3. kvetna, 513 28 Semily.
Telephone: +420 431 621 280 **Facsimile:** +420 431 33 36 **Web site:** AXL@Mikroservis.CZ
Director: Ing. Otokar Pikora.
Employees: 294.
Activities: ■ Undercarriage production and maintenance, and hydraulic equipment production.

VZLÚ – AERONAUTICAL RESEARCH AND TEST INSTITUTE
HQ address: Beranovych 130, 199 05 Praha 9 – Letnany.
Telephone: +420 2 663 11 397, 663 11 428, 663 11 469
Facsimile: +420 2 663 10 518, 859 06 53
Director: Ing. Milan Holl, CSc.
Activities: ■ Development and testing of aircraft aerodynamics and strength, propulsion units, electrical equipment and hydraulic systems; flight tests; charter air transport; joint development projects with Hamilton Standard of the USA, and other work.

Aero Vodochody Ltd — Czech Republic

Corporate address: 250 70 Odolena Voda.
Telephone: +420 2 688 09 71, 688 11 40, 688 17 35, 688 01 22 (sales) **Facsimile:** +420 2 823 172
Founded: Aero was founded in Prague in 1919. The new Vodochody plant was established on 28 April 1953. Vodochody and Aero Vysocany organizations merged on 1 July 1954, becoming Aero Vodochody. On 21 May 1997, the Aero Vodochody Board selected a consortium comprising Boeing (then also McDonnell Douglas) and Czech Airlines (CSA) to become a strategic investor in the company, taking 34-40% of the shares, with the remaining majority held by the Government through the Consolidation Bank and National Property Fund. This arrangement has been approved by the Czech Government, but Aero Vodochody sources suggested 1998 for formal signing.
General director: Ing Adam Stranak.
Employees: 2,240.
Information: Martin Paloda (marketing – *telephone* +420 2 688 00 41, *facsimile* +420 2 687 25 05).

ACTIVITIES

- Produces the L-59, L-139 and L-159 jet trainers and light attack aircraft, and the Ae 270 as part of Ibis Aerospace, plus maintenance.
- Co-operates with foreign aeronautical companies.

Aero L-39 Albatros

First flight: 4 November 1968.
Role: Training and light attack.
Chief designer: Jan Vlcek.
Fatigue life: 6,000 flying hours initially.

Aims

- Rugged and simple design.
- Suited to operations in hard climates and conditions, from hot and dusty to frosty winters or tropical.
- Thoroughly designed airframe and systems for easy maintenance, good reliability, simple pre-flight checks and full autonomy. Mean time between failure in flight is higher than 300 flight hours.
- Low foreign object damage to the engine by the high position of the air intakes, protected by the low-mounted wings.

Development

- 1974. L-39 C entered military service.
- 25 August 1975. Maiden flight of the L-39 ZO.
- 29 September 1976. Maiden flight of the L-39 ZA.

Details

Sales/Users: By June 1998 2,253 L-39 Cs, 347 ZOs, 246 ZAs and 8 Vs had been delivered, with 2 L-39 Cs as the latest deliveries (to Ethiopia), which covers direct deliveries from Aero Vodochody only. Other recent deliveries have included additional L-39 ZA/ARTs shipped to Thailand in 1997, with more orders expected that could raise Thailand's total to 50. 3 L-39 Cs were also delivered to private customers in the USA in 1997, and Ethiopia received a batch of 4 L-39 Cs that same year. Aero direct deliveries have been to Afghanistan (26 L-39 Cs), Algeria (7 L-39 Cs and 32 ZAs), Bangladesh (8 L-39 ZAs), Bulgaria (36 L-39 ZAs), Cuba (30 L-39 Cs), Czech and Slovakia (33 L-39 Cs, 30 ZAs, 8 Vs and 5 MSs), Ethiopia (20 original L-39 Cs plus 6 new aircraft), Germany (former East – 52 L-39 ZOs), Iraq (22 L-39 Cs and 59 ZOs), Libya (181 L-39 ZOs), Nigeria (24 L-39 ZAs), Romania (32 L-39 ZAs), Syria (55 L-39 ZOs and 44 ZAs), Thailand (36 original L-39 ZAs plus 4 in 1996–97), USA (5 private L-39 Cs), the former USSR (2,080 L-39 Cs), and Vietnam (24 L-39 Cs). L-39s are operated by more than 25 air forces worldwide. Non-delivery nations that are operators include some CIS states outside of Russia. Various aircraft have been upgraded, including by Elbit of Israel.
Crew: 2, in tandem, the rear instructor's seat raised.
Cockpit: Pressurized, with automatic pressure and temperature regulation. Windshield and 2 cockpit canopies (manually opening to starboard). Pneumatic canopy seals are supplied by a 2 litre compressed air bottle in the nose compartment. Anti-g suits with automatic regulation protects the crew from the effect of high load factors during manoeuvres.
Crew escape: VS1-BRI ejection seats (with survival kits), suitable at all heights from zero and from 81 kts (93 mph) 150 km/h to the maximum permissible speed.
Fixed guns: L-39 ZA/MP has a 23-mm GSh-23 gun in a detachable fuselage pod.
Ammunition: 150 rounds.
Number of weapon pylons: 2 underwing on L-39 C, 4 on ZO, ZA and ZA/MP.
Expendable weapons and equipment: 626 lb (284 kg) on L-39 C, and up to 2,844 lb (1,290 kg) on ZO, ZA and ZA/MP. Compatibility with NATO standard weapons. See weapon chart for combinations.
Flight/weapon system avionics/instrumentation: Communications equipment includes UHF and VHF AM/FM radios. RV-5M (4400 MHz) radio altimeter and KXP 756 transponder. General avionics configurations at customer's request; customized options can include Aero/Flight Visions Combat Training System, Weapon Delivery and Navigation System, and Advanced Weapons Delivery System options, the latter with a mission computer, HUD, 2 multi-function displays in each cockpit and video display in the rear cockpit, and able to be combined with radar, FLIR, laser rangefinder, warning systems, GPS and more. L-39 ZA/MP is equipped with an integrated digital nav/attack system, incorporating a head-up display. The front pilot's view and HUD symbology are registered by video camera and are displayed in the instructor's rear cockpit. Gyro gunsight or HUD with mission computer for weapon delivery.
Self-protection systems: Offered for upgrades.
Wing characteristics: Straight, low mounted, with tip-tanks.
Wing control surfaces: Ailerons (with tabs) and double-slotted flaps.
Tail control surfaces: Elevators and rudder (with tabs).
Airbrakes: 2 under centre fuselage.
Flight control system: Mechanical for ailerons, elevator and rudder; electrohydraulically for flaps and airbrakes. In case of failure, the functions can be performed by the emergency hydraulic system.
Construction materials: Aluminium alloy.
Engine: Ivchenko PROGRESS AI-25TL turbofan, with hydromechanical control and emergency backup circuit. Saphir 5 APU, mounted in the engine bay; when airborne, the engine can be restarted by both the APU or by autorotation.
Engine rating: 3,792 lbf (16.87 kN).
Fuel system: 1,955 litres usable in 5 fuselage, 2 fixed wingtip and 2 optional drop tanks. Fuselage fuel 1,817 lb (824 kg), 2 × 100 litre wingtip tanks for 344 lb (156 kg), 2 × 150 litre underwing tanks for 516 lb (234 kg) or 2 × 350 litre underwing tanks for 1,221 lb (554 kg).
Electrical system: Main supply is 28 volt DC, with an engine-driven generator (emergency back-up V 910 ram air turbine producing 3kVA). 12 volt 28 amp-hour SAM 28 lead-acid battery for APU starting and standby. AC supply is 3-phase of 3 × 115/200 volt-400Hz.
Hydraulic system: 2,132 psi. Comprises main and emergency circuits, manufactured by Jihlavan Ltd. Main source is LUN 6101.01-8 variable hydraulic pump. Emergency circuit is supplied by an hydraulic accumulator. Operates undercarriage gear and doors, flaps, airbrakes, ram air turbine, and wheel brakes.
Braking system: Hydraulic double disc brakes on main units, with an anti-skid system. Nosewheel has a shimmy damper.
De-icing system: Windshield and air intakes by hot air.
Oxygen system: Oxygen masks in both cockpits.

Aircraft variants:
L-39 C is the basic training version.
L-39 MS was the former designation of the L-59.
L-39 V is a single-seater for target towing.
L-39 ZO is an improved basic trainer with reinforced wings with 4 pylons.
L-39 ZA is the ground attack and reconnaissance version with an underfuselage gun pod and 4 pylons on the reinforced wings.
L-39 ZA/MP is a multi-purpose version with Western avionics and head-up display. ZAs for Thailand (8 delivered in 1993, 28 in 1994, 2 in 1996 and 2 in 1997) are known as L-39 ZA/ARTs and have Elbit avionics (see Elbit). Suited to basic pilot training, combat manoeuvre/attack/weapon training, and light attack.

↑ **Aero L-39 C of 1 Fighter Eskadrile, Lithuanian military air forces at Suauliai in mid-1997** *(Denis Hughes)*

Details for L-39

PRINCIPAL DIMENSIONS:
Wing span: 31 ft (9.46 m)
Maximum length: 39 ft 10 ins (12.13 m)
Maximum height: 15 ft 8 ins (4.77 m)

WINGS:
Aerofoil section: NACA 64A012 mod 5
Area: 202.36 sq ft (18.8 m^2)
Aspect ratio: 4.76
Sweepback: 1° 45′ on leading-edge
Incidence: 2°
Dihedral: 2° 20′

TAIL UNIT:
Tailplane span: 14 ft 5 ins (4.4 m)
Tailplane area: 42.3 sq ft (3.93 m^2)

UNDERCARRIAGE:
Type: Retractable, with castoring/centring nosewheel. Designed to withstand hard conditions and operations from paved/unpaved and grass airfields
Main wheel tyre size: 610 × 185 mm for C, 610 × 215 mm for ZA
Nose wheel tyre size: 430 × 150 for C, 450 × 165 mm for ZA
Wheel base: 14 ft 5 ins (4.39 m)
Wheel track: 8 ft (2.44 m)

WEIGHTS:
Empty, equipped: 7,584-7,892 lb (3,440-3,580 kg)
Maximum ramp: 12,500 lb (5,670 kg) for ZA
Maximum take-off: 10,362 lb (4,700 kg) for C, 12,346 lb (5,600 kg) for ZA

PERFORMANCE (at 9,480 lb, 4,300 kg take-off weight, unless stated)**:**
Maximum dive speed: 491 kts (565 mph) 910 km/h
Maximum speed: 407 kts (469 mph) 755 km/h
Stall speed: 91 kts (104 mph) 169 km/h for C, 103 kts (118 mph) 190 km/h for ZA, both *with flaps.*
Stall speed for L-39 ZA at 9,854 lb (4,470 kg) AUW: 85.5 kts (98 mph) 158 km/h without external stores, 2 crew, *with flaps*, 50% fuel
Take-off distance over a 50 ft (15 m) obstacle: 2,625 ft (800 m)
Landing distance over a 50 ft (15 m) obstacle: 3,051 ft (930 m)
Maximum climb rate: 4,330 ft (1,320 m) per minute, or 4,135 ft (1,260 m) per minute for L-39 ZA at 9,854 lb (4,470 kg) AUW, without external stores, 2 crew
Climb to 16,400 ft (5,000 m): 6 minutes
G limits: +8, -4
Ceiling: 36,000 ft (11,000 m)
Range with full fuel: 971 naut miles (1,118 miles) 1,800 km, or 728 naut miles (839 miles) 1,350 km for L-39 ZA at 9,854 lb (4,470 kg) AUW, without external stores, 2 crew, internal fuel, 10% fuel reserve
Duration: 4 hours, or 2 hours 45 minutes for L-39 ZA at 9,854 lb (4,470 kg) AUW, without external stores, 2 crew

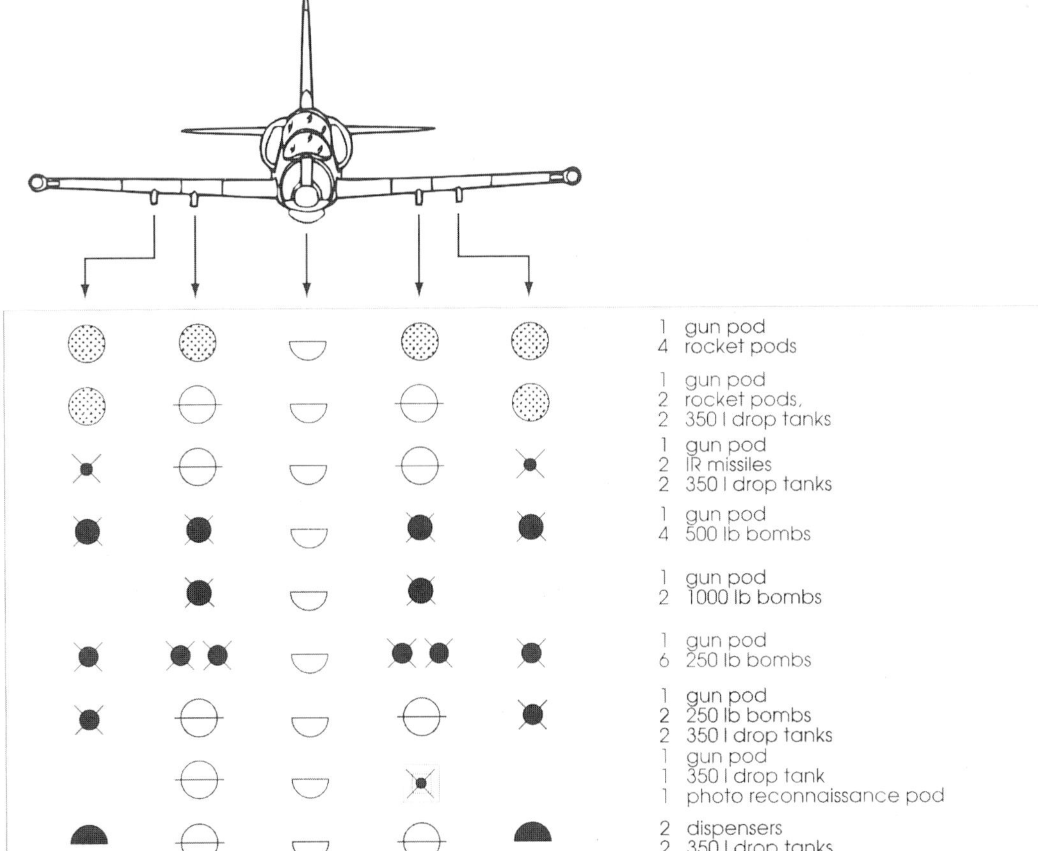

↑ **Aero L-39 ZA armament options** *(courtesy Aero)*

Aero L-59

First flight: 30 September 1986 (in X-22/L-39 MS prototype form).
Role: Training, light attack/COIN, shore defence and limited air defence.
Chief designers: Jan Vlcek and Vlastimil Havelka.
Fatigue life: 10,000 flying hours.

Aims

- Development of the L-39, with additional thrust, modernized cockpit instrumentation, and broader combat capabilities.
- Incorporates diagnostic system for evaluation of technical condition. Maintenance requirements 4.2 hours per flight hour.
- 15 minute turn-around between sorties.
- Comes as a complete training system, with TL-59 flight simulator, ejection seat simulator and ground training aids.

Development

- 3 prototypes, the second and third as X-24/25 flying on 26 June and 6 October 1987.
- 1 October 1989. Maiden flight of a production L-59, with deliveries to the Czech Air Force during 1991-92.
- 29 January 1993. First of 48 L-59 Es for Egypt were delivered.

Details *(generally as for the L-39, except as follows)*

Sales/Users: Czech Republic (3 in L-39 MS form), Egypt (48 L-59 Es), Slovakia (2 in L-39 MS form) and Tunisia (12 L-59 Ts).
Cockpit: Canopy comprises a fixed front shield that can be tilted for assembly and mounting purposes, and a main canopy which is common to both cockpits and can be raised upwards hydraulically.
Crew escape: VS-2 zero-zero ejection seats.
Number of weapon pylons: 4.

↑ Aero L-59 T in Tunisian service

Details for L-59

PRINCIPAL DIMENSIONS:
Wing span: 31 ft 4 ins (9.542 m)
Maximum length: 40 ft (12.203 m)
Maximum height: 15 ft 8 ins (4.77 m)

TAIL UNIT:
Tailplane area: 57 sq ft (5.3 m^2)

WEIGHTS:
Empty: 8,885 lb (4,030 kg)
Maximum take-off: 11,684-12,258 lb (5,300-5,560 kg) clean, 13,196 lb (5,986 kg) with gun and 2 rocket pods, 14,579 lb (6,613 kg) with gun, rockets and 2 drop tanks, and 15,432 lb (7,000 kg) maximum
Maximum take-off from grass: 13,228 lb (6,000 kg)
Maximum landing: 13,228 lb (6,000 kg) concrete, 12,566 lb (5,700 kg) unpaved

PERFORMANCE:
Maximum limiting Mach number: 0.82
Never-exceed speed (V_{NE}): 496 kts (571 mph) 920 km/h
Maximum speed: 469 kts (541 mph) 870 km/h
Stall speed: 117-129 kts (135-148 mph) 216-238 km/h *clean*, 99-110 kts (113-126 mph) 182-203 km/h *with flaps*, 93 kts (107 mph) 172 km/h without stores, *with flaps*, 50% fuel
Take-off distance: 1,936-3,543 ft (590-1,080 m) concrete, 2,822 ft (860 m) unpaved at clean weight
Landing distance: 2,363-2,510 ft (720-765 m) at 5,500 kg weight, 2,100 ft (640 m) at sea level, 50% fuel, clean
Maximum climb rate: 4,920 ft (1,500 m) per minute at sea level, at 5,560 kg weight
Climb to 5,000 m: 3 minutes 30 seconds at 5,560 kg weight
G limits: +8, -4 up to 5,560 kg; +6, -3 to 7,000 kg; in turn at sea level, ISA, 2.25-3.42
Ceiling: 40,000 ft (12,200 m)
Range with full fuel: 653-847 naut miles (752-975 miles) 1,210-1,570 km, depending on weight, at 5,000 m, ISA, 10% reserve, internal fuel
Duration: 2 hours 55 minutes at take-off weight, without stores

↑ **Aero L-59 front cockpit** *(Aero/Jan Kouba)*

Expendable weapons and equipment: 3,307 lb (1,500 kg) of stores, in similar combinations as shown on the L-39 chart, but with no reconnaissance pod indicated and with the option of 4 × 350 litre drop tanks. In weapon training form, typical armament could include 2 × SUU 20s with 12 practice bombs.
Flight/weapon system avionics/instrumentation: VHF and UHF radio communications equipment, and radio-navigation systems. Optional integrated nav/attack system. Up-front control panel, ring laser gyro/INS, video camera and VTR. HUD is basic flight instrumentation, with all data for symbology computed via a central digital computer. System can work in air-to-ground, air-to-air and navigation modes. Attitude and horizontal situations are displayed on 4 × 4 ins (10 × 10 cm) EFIS displays. Options include Stand-Alone Autonomous Air Combat Manoeuvring Instrumentation (A^2CMI), HUD-projected on visor, and full display and sight helmet (DASH).
Self-protection systems: Optional radar warning receiver.
Wing control surfaces: Aileron deflection ±16°.
Tail control surfaces: Elevator deflection +30°, -20°. Rudder deflection ±30°.
Flight control system: Similar to L-39, but irreversible power-operated by actuators.
Fuselage: Strengthened.
Construction materials: Aluminium alloy, with the ailerons and elevators adopting a honeycomb form of construction.
Engine: Povazské Strojárne DV-2 turbofan. Saphir 5M APU.
Engine rating: 4,850 lbf (21.58 kN).
Fuel system: Up to 2,707 litres (5,044 lb, 2,288 kg total weight), as 1,307 litres internal (2,646 lb, 1,200 kg weight, fuselage and wingtip tanks) and 4 underwing drop tanks of 150 or 350 litres each.
Electrical system: Main supply is 27 volt DC, with a 9 kW engine-driven generator. Stand-by source is APU driven. Emergency source is a 25 amp-hour ni-cd battery. AC supply via inverters is 115 volt single-phase and 3 × 36 volt 3-phase.
Braking system: 3 disc brakes with anti-skid system, allowing differential braking for steering.

Aircraft variants:
L-39 MS was the former designation for the L-59.
L-59 is the current designation.

Aero L-139 Albatros 2000

First flight: 10 May 1993.
Role: Basic/advanced training and light attack.
Project Manager: Dobroslav Rak.
Fatigue life: 10,000 flying hours (fatigue monitoring system).

Development

■ Straightforward development of the L-39, customized to use a US engine and avionics.

Details *(generally similar to the L-39, except as follows)*

Crew escape: VS-2 A ejection seats.
Number of weapon pylons: 4, outer pylons 551 lb (250 kg) capacity, inner 1,102 lb (500 kg) capacity.
Expendable weapons and equipment: Weight as for L-59, with similar options.

↑ **Aero L-139 Albatros 2000** *(Aero/Jan Kouba)*

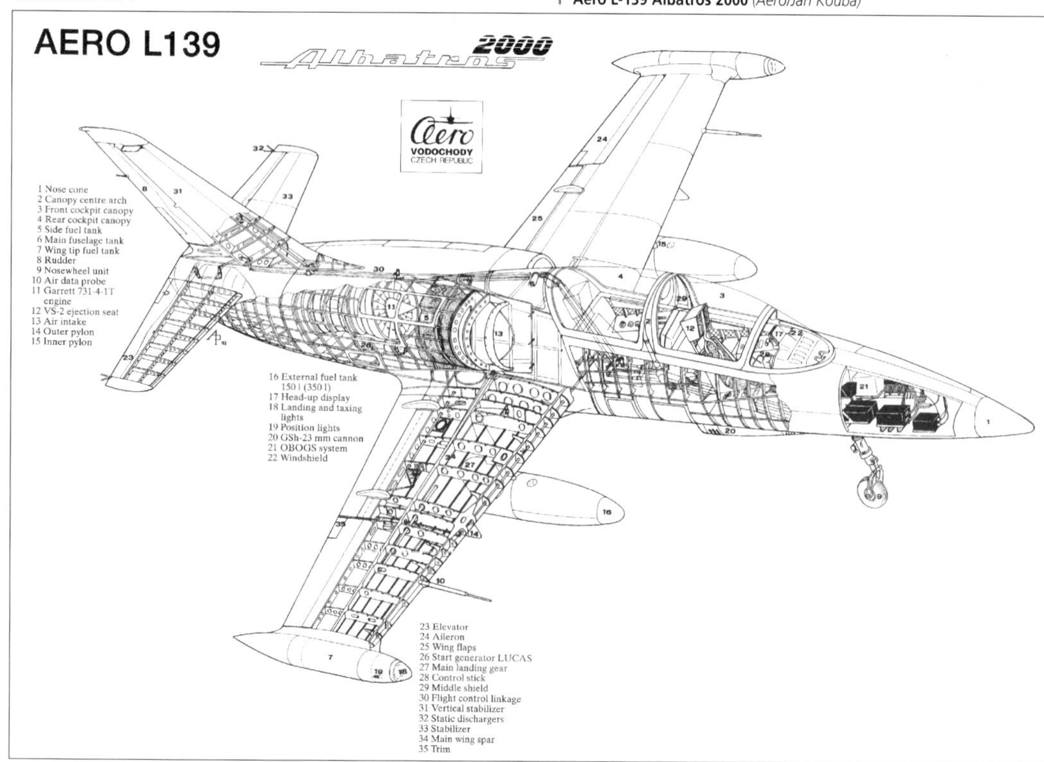

↑ **Aero L-139 Albatros 2000 cutaway** *(courtesy Aero Vodochody)*

Flight/weapon system avionics/instrumentation: VCS 40 A VFF, KTR 909 UHF, MST 67A transponder, RMS 555 central panel radio and identification equipment. Radio-navigation equipment encompasses DFS 43A radio-compass, VNS 41 VOR/ILS, DMS 44 DME, KNS 660 FMS+GPS, EFS 40 EFIS, KAH 560 AHRS, and KAT 480 ADC. Available weapon delivery and navigation system and HUD as detailed for L-59, from Western supplier.
Engine: AlliedSignal TFE731-4-1T turbofan.
Engine rating: 4,080 lbf (18.15 kN).
Fuel system: 1,100 litres in the fuselage, 200 litres in the wingtip tanks, plus optionally 2 × 350 litre drop tanks. Total fuel weight 4,559 lb (2,068 kg). Allowable 20 seconds of inverted flight.
Electrical system: 28 volt/12kW DC system using a Lucas 23080-023 starter-generator with 51539-020A control unit, or 28 volt/6kW Lusas 23081-040A auxiliary generator as a back-up. Emergency 24 volt/43 amp-hour ni-cd battery. 115 volt/400Hz AC supply, using Maraton PC-250 and Mesit LUN 2463.01 converters.
Hydraulic system: 2,175 psi normal pressure, 2,390 psi maximum.
Braking system: Hydraulic discs on mainwheels. No nosewheel brake.
Oxygen system: OBOGS.

Details for L-139

PRINCIPAL DIMENSIONS
As for L-39

WEIGHTS:
Empty: 7,628 lb (3,460 kg)
Ramp: 10,141-13,228 lb (4,600-6,000 kg)
Maximum take-off: 10,031 lb (4,550 kg) clean
Maximum landing: 10,582 lb (4,800 kg)

PERFORMANCE:
Maximum limiting Mach number: Mach 0.8
Never-exceed speed (V_{NE}): 491 kts (565 mph) 910 km/h
Maximum speed: 410 kts (472 mph) 760 km/h at 20,000 ft (6,100 m)
Stall speed: 86 kts (100 mph) 160 km/h
Landing speed: 99 kts (114 mph) 183 km/h
Take-off distance: 1,772 ft (540 m)
Landing distance: 1,837 ft (560 m)
Maximum climb rate: 4,410 ft (1,344 m) per minute
G limits: +8, -4
Ceiling: 39,370 ft (12,000 m)
Range with full internal fuel: 890 naut miles (1,025 miles) 1,650 km, 10% reserves
Duration: 3 hours 19 minutes, internal fuel, 10% reserves

Aero L 159 ALCA

First flight: 2 August 1997. 18 August 1998 for L 159 single-seater.
Role: Single-seat light multi-role combat, and 2-seat training variant, suited to close air support, air defence, tactical reconnaissance, counter insurgency, border patrol, anti-ship, and lead-in fighter and weapons training.

Aims

■ Based on the L-59 configuration but with accommodation for a pilot only in the combat version.
■ Tactical mobility, including ability to use semi-prepared airstrips.
■ LSA in accordance with MIL-STD-1388-1A/2B.
■ Enhanced survivability.
■ Latest generation turbofan engine.
■ On condition maintenance.
■ Computer-based training aids.
■ NATO compatible.
■ Equipped with advanced avionics and sensors, including radar.

Development

■ 1992. Design begun.
■ 1994. Engine selected. Also, Rockwell Collins chosen to head a team (under a US$ 18.6 million contract) to design and fit a new avionics suite into the prototype.
■ 7 April 1995. Government of Czech Republic sanctioned full development.
■ 12 June 1997. Official roll-out of the first prototype in 2-seat configuration at Aero facility.
■ July 1997. Order placed for Czech Air Force.
■ 2 August 1997. First flight of the 2-seat prototype.
■ 1998. First flight of the second prototype, the single-seater.
■ 1999. End of flight testing and start of initial deliveries.
■ 2002. Final delivery of Czech 72-aircraft order.

↑ **Aero L 159 first prototype photographed during its maiden flight on 2 August 1997** *(Aero/Jan Kouba)*

↑ **Aero L 159 front cockpit** *(courtesy Aero Vodochody)*

Details

Sales/Users: 2 flying prototypes and 2 static/ground test aircraft. Czech Air Force is to receive 72, in both single- and 2-seat forms. 4 Venezuelan pilots flew L 159 in February 1998.
Crew: Pilot only in L 159 and A, with armoured cockpit for ballistic protection. 2 seats in L 159 B and T.
Cockpit: NVG compatible. Manually sideways-opening canopy on L 159 and A. For L 159 B and T, canopy comprises a fixed front shield that can be tilted for assembly and mounting purposes, and a main canopy which is common to both cockpits and can be raised upwards hydraulically. AlliedSignal pressurization control system (maximum differential 4.06 psi) using engine bleed air.
Crew escape: VS-2B ejection seat/s.
Number of weapon pylons: 7, 6 under the wings (of 1,212 lb/550 kg, 750 lb/340 kg and 330 lb/150 kg capacity – inboard to outboard) and 1 under the fuselage centreline for a 661 lb (300 kg) load.
Expendable weapons and equipment: 5,159 lb (2,340 kg), comprising selection of air-to-air (including Sidewinder) and air-to-surface (including Brimstone and Maverick) missiles, free-fall and laser-guided bombs, rocket launchers (including LAU-5002) and 1 or 2 Planem 20-mm twin-barrel gun pod/s, or other weapons. Provision for future weapons and special pods.
Other stores: Could include GEC-Marconi thermal imaging airborne laser designator, reconnaissance pod, and the Apollo electronic countermeasures pod.
Radar: FIAR Grifo L pulse Doppler type.
Flight/weapon system avionics/instrumentation: Integration by Boeing via an MIL-STD-1553 databus, allowing future growth. Controls and displays comprise HUD remote control panel, Flight Visions HUD with raster capability and HUD computer, avionics power panel, Mason Electric HOTAS, AlliedSignal 4 × 4 ins liquid crystal colour multi-function head-down displays, HSI and ADI. Targeting sensing system are radar (linked to MFDs and HUD computer) and interference blanking unit. Stores management system has power relay unit and armament control panel. Data loading and recording system, linked to HUD computer, comprises HUD camera, AVTR control panel, video recorder, data transfer system, and flight data acquisition unit. Communication, navigation and identification system comprises AOA transmitter, AlliedSignal air data computer, ring laser gyro INS/GPS, radio altimeter, DME, VOR/ILS, AlliedSignal IFF, 2 Rockwell Collins UHF/VHF radios and autopilot.
Self-protection systems: GEC-Marconi Sky Guard radar warning receiver. Countermeasures dispensers. See Cockpit and Fuel system for OBIGGS elements.

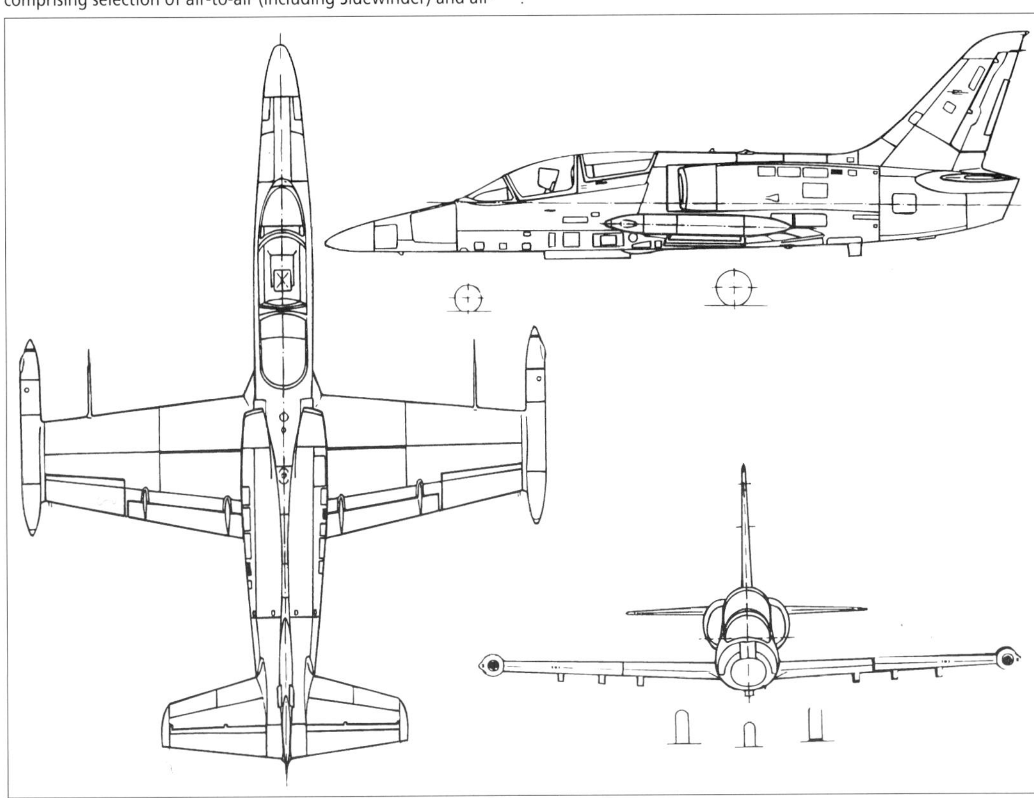

↑ **Aero L 159 ALCA** *(courtesy Aero Vodochody)*

Details for L 159 ALCA & L 159 T

PRINCIPAL DIMENSIONS:
Wing span: 31 ft 4 ins (9.54 m)
Maximum length: 41 ft 9 ins (12.73 m)
Maximum height: 15 ft 8 ins (4.77 m)

WINGS:
Aerofoil section: NACA 64A012 mod 5
Area: 202.36 sq ft (18.8 m^2)
Aspect ratio: 4.84
Sweepback: 6° 30′ on leading-edge
Incidence: 2°
Dihedral: 2° 30′

UNDERCARRIAGE:
Type: Retractable, with steerable nosewheel (±59°). Designed to withstand hard conditions and operations from paved/unpaved and grass airfields
Main wheel tyre size: 610 × 215 mm
Nose wheel tyre size: 460 × 180 mm
Wheel base: 15 ft (4.56 m)
Wheel track: 7 ft 11 ins (2.42 m)
Turning radius: 18 ft 9 ins (5.7 m)

WEIGHTS:
Empty: 9,171 lb (4,160 kg)
Maximum ramp: 17,637 lb (8,000 kg)
Maximum landing: 13,227 lb (6,000 kg)

PERFORMANCE:
Never-exceed speed (V_{NE}): 518 kts (597 mph) 960 km/h
Maximum speed: 502 kts (578 mph) 930 km/h at sea level, KTAS
Stall speed: 100 kts (115 mph) 185 km/h, *with flaps and undercarriage lowered*, at 5,500 kg AUW
Take-off distance: 1,444 ft (440 m)
Landing run: 2,379 ft (725 m)
Maximum climb rate: 9,250 ft (2,820 m) per minute
G limits: +8, -4 structural
Ceiling: 43,300 ft (13,200 m)
Range with full internal fuel: 848 naut miles (975 miles) 1,570 km, 10% reserves for L 159, or 658 naut miles (758 miles) 1,220 km for L 159 T
Range with maximum fuel (internal and external): 1,365 naut miles (1,572 miles) 2,530 km, with 10% reserves for L 159, or 1,241 naut miles (1,429 miles) 2,300 km for L 159 T

Wing characteristics: Straight, low mounted, with tip-tanks.
Wing control surfaces: Ailerons (with tabs) and double-slotted flaps.
Tail control surfaces: Elevators and rudder (with tab).
Airbrakes: 2 under centre fuselage.
Flight control system: Mechanical for rudder; hydraulic for ailerons, double-slotted flaps, elevators and airbrakes. In case of failure, the functions can be performed by the emergency hydraulic system. Electric trim.
Construction materials: Aluminium alloy.
Fuselage: Forward section redesigned for 1 cockpit and a nose radome in single seater.
Engine: AlliedSignal/ITEC F124-GA-100 turbofan. Safir APU.
Engine rating: 6,300 lbf (28.02 kN).
Fuel system: 3,419 lb (1,551 kg) of internal fuel (fuselage and wingtips). 6,338 lb (2,875 kg) of auxiliary fuel in 4 tanks. Tank inerting system for protection (OBIGGS). 2-seat version carries 655 lb (297 kg) less fuel. Optional flight refuelling probe.
Electrical system: 28 volt DC via 6 kW LUN-2134 generator and 25 amp-hour lead-acid battery. AC supply (Sundstrand 25 kVA generator) is 3-phase 115/200 volt-400Hz. Connection of single-phase aggregates to the generator corresponds to MIL-STD-704E.
Hydraulic system: 2 independent systems, each nominally 3,000 psi. Each power supply system has a fluid reservoir, variable-flow constant pressure hydraulic pump driven by the Airframe-mounted Accessory Drive (AAD), a relief valve and pressure accumulator. Both systems power the elevators and ailerons by means of tandem actuators through a corresponding chamber. Both systems have a main and emergency circuit. Also for airbrakes and undercarriage functions.
Braking system: K-52 hydraulic brakes, with anti-skid devices.
Oxygen: On-board oxygen generating system.

Aircraft variants:
L 159 is the single-seat ALCA.
L 159 A is the export single-seat light combat version.
L 159 B is the export 2-seat light combat/lead-in trainer version.
L 159 T is the Czech 2-seat operational training version.

Arab Organization for Industrialization (AOI) — Egypt

Corporate address:
2 D Abbassiya Square, PO Box 770, Cairo – A.R.E.

Telephone: +20 2 932395, 4823377
Facsimile: +20 2 4826010, 4012583
Telex: 92090, 92014 AOI UN

Founded:
November 1975.

Employees:
Some 20,000.

Information:
Mahmoud El-Refai (Director of Operations & Marketing).

DIVISIONS

AIRCRAFT FACTORY

HQ address:
Hammamat Helwan, Cairo.

Telephone: +20 2 5553946, 5553948
Facsimile: +20 2 782408

Founded: 1950.

Information:
Eng Ahmed El Sayed (Chairman).

Activities:
- Assembled both the Alpha Jet and Tucano trainers.
- Currently produces the Helwan 2 and Helwan 3 multi-purpose light aircraft (see General Aviation section), and manufactures Mirage 2000 components plus airframe parts and components for other foreign companies, in addition to auxiliary fuel tanks for F-16s, various Mirages and old Mikoyan types.
- Retrofits military aeroplanes for special missions.
- Among other work, manufactures conventional and retarded bombs.

HELWAN FACTORY

HQ address:
PO Box 162, Heliopolis, Cairo.

Telephone: +20 2 783286, 788509, 873316, 873036
Facsimile: +20 2 788603

Information:
Dr Eng Salah Zaki (Chairman).

Activities:
- Has assembled, ground/flight tested, overhauls and repairs SA-342L Gazelle helicopters (airframe and some dynamic parts).
- Specializes in manufacturing aircraft components from GRP and other composite materials.

KADER FACTORY

HQ address:
PO Box 287, Heliopolis, Cairo.

Telephone: +20 2 4024319, 4024325

Facsimile: +20 2 2608718, 4020986

Founded: 1949.

Information:
Eng Abd El Hameid Wasfy (Chairman).

Activities:
- Contributed to the AOI Tucano programme, and produced the Gomhouria primary trainer.
- Designs and produces training and penetration bombs.
- Armoured vehicle work.

ENGINE FACTORY

HQ address:
PO Box 12, Helwan, Cairo.

Telephone: +20 2 5546092, 5546093
Facsimile: +20 2 781236

Founded: 1960.

Information:
Eng yosry Abo Amer (Chairman).

Activities:
- Assembles the Larzac 04 and PT6A-25E. Overhauls and repairs the Larzac, PT6A-25E, Atar 09C and CT-64. Other work.

ARAB BRITISH ENGINE CO (ABECO)

HQ address:
See Engine section.

Activities:
- Overhauls and repairs helicopter engines, as a joint venture organization.

ELECTRONIC FACTORY

HQ address: PO Box 84, Heliopolis, Cairo.

Activities:
- Avionics, electronic switchboard, electronic sub-assemblies for French airborne radars and French missiles, and other electrical components for aircraft.

AAV FACTORY

HQ address:
PO Box 2419, El-Horreya Heliopolis, Cairo.

Activities:
- Produces and distributes Jeeps for military and commercial uses.

ABD FACTORY

HQ address:
PO Box 2444, El-Horreya Heliopolis, Cairo.

Activities:
- Include guided missile systems, land navigation systems, automatic test equipment, and calibration and measuring equipment.

SAKR FACTORY

HQ address:
PO Box 33, Heliopolis, Cairo.

Activities:
- Artillery systems, mine systems, infantry systems, Sakr Eye man-portable air defence system, and Romh target.

Finavitec OY — Finland

Corporate address:
FIN-35600 Halli.

Telephone: +358 3 58091
Facsimile: +358 3 5809 543

Founded:
1921 for Valtion Lentokonetehdas, becoming Valmet OY in 1958, then Valmet Aviation Industries, and currently Finavitec. To be nationalized.

Information:
Ms Raili Saarinen (Communication Co-ordinator).

ACTIVITIES

- Specializes in maintenance, component and assemblies (Saab 2000 tail surfaces and Hornet fuselage skin panels), and is undertaking assembly of 57 F-18C Hornet fighters for the Finnish Air Force from component knock-down kits, the last to be delivered in the year 2000. Production and worldwide sales of the former Valmet RediGO have been transferred to Aermacchi of Italy. Facilities at Kuorevesi and Linnavuori.

↑ Finnish F-18C Hornet assembled from a knock-down kit *(Simon Watson)*

Dassault Aviation — France

Corporate address:
9 rond-point des Champs-Elysées/ Marcel Dassault, 75008 Paris.

Telephone: +33 1 53 76 93 00
Facsimile: +33 1 53 76 93 20
Web site: www.dassault-aviation.fr

Founded:
14 December 1971 as Avions Marcel Dassault-Breguet Aviation, changing to the present name in 1990. The merger brought together the post-war Dassault company and the Société des Avions Louis Breguet, one of France's oldest established aircraft companies, dating from 1911. 35% of the company's shares have been held by the state-owned Société de Gestion de Participations Aeronautiques (SOGEPA) organization, which performs as a holding company to co-ordinate R&D between France's 2 largest aerospace concerns, Dassault and Aerospatiale. In May 1998 it became known that the French Government's 45.73% shareholding in Dassault was being transferred to Aerospatiale, to bring closer co-operation within the French industry.

Employees:
Approximately 9,250.

Information:
Jean-Pierre Robillard (Vice-President, Communication).
Press communications address: 27 rue du Professeur Victor Pauchet – 92420 Vaucresson.
Telephone: +33 1 47 95 86 90 *Facsimile:* +33 1 47 95 87 40

FACILITIES

▪ Argenteuil, Argonay, Biarritz-Parme, Bordeaux-Mérignac, Cazaux, Istres, Martignas, Poitiers Saint-Cloud, Seclin and Vélizy.

ACTIVITIES

▪ Designs, develops and manufactures military and civil aircraft.
▪ Researches artificial intelligence techniques for the aeronautical and space industries, designs and manufactures flight control systems, undertakes weapon system design and integration, and develops new materials and related technologies.

SUBSIDIARIES

DASSAULT FALCON JET CORP

HQ address:
Teterboro Airport, Box 2000, South Hackensack, NJ 07606, USA.

Telephone: +1 201 440 6700
Facsimile: +1 201 967 4475

CEO:
Jean-Franáois Georges.

Activities:
▪ 100% owned by Dassault Aviation.

DASSAULT SYSTÈMES

HQ address:
24-28 Avenue du Général de Guelle, 92150 Suresnes.

Telephone: +33 1 40 99 40 99
Facsimile: +33 1 42 04 45 81

CEO:
Charles Edelstenne.

Activities:
▪ 45.9% owned by Dassault Aviation.
▪ Computer aided design and manufacturing (CAD/CAM).
▪ Related companies are Dassault Systemes Services (East 15 Midland Avenue, Paramus, NJ 07652, USA) and Dassault Systemes of America (2500 West Empire Avenue, Burbank, CA 91504, USA).

SOGITEC

HQ address:
4 rue Marcel-Monge – Immeuble Nobel, 92158 Suresnes Cedex.

Telephone: +33 1 41 18 57 00
Facsimile: +33 1 41 18 57 18, 18 59 19

Chairman:
Yves Fouché.

Facilities:
▪ Suresnes, Rennes and Bordeaux.

Activities:
▪ 69% owned by Dassault Aviation.
▪ Specializes in simulation and integrated logistics. 2 main divisions, Electronic and Communication.

CORSE COMPOSITES

Activities:
▪ 33% owned by Dassault Aviation.

DASSAULT INTERNATIONAL

Activities:
▪ 56% owned by Dassault Aviation.

Dassault Atlantic, Atlantique 2 and 3

First flight: 8 May 1981 for Atlantique 2, 21 October 1961 for Atlantic.
Role: Long-range maritime patrol, anti-submarine warfare, minelaying and bombing, maritime and signal intelligence, strike aircraft guidance, and search and rescue.
Fatigue life: Under a life-extension programme, German Navy Atlantics are to be capable of over 12,000 flying hours.

Aims

▪ Original Atlantic was designed by Breguet in France, but followed a policy aim of NATO to realize the design of a standardized maritime patrol aircraft to replace the Lockheed Neptune. In the event, the Atlantic was only bought by France, Germany, Italy and the Netherlands, totalling 87 aircraft.
▪ Atlantique 2 is derived from Atlantic. Its main characteristics are, like Atlantic, a sturdy airframe, high aspect ratio wing, single large weapon bay with high load carrying capability, and Tyne Mk 21 turboprops. Mission systems avionics are new and of the latest technology.
▪ Atlantique 2 airframe is produced by a European consortium, comprising Aerospatiale, Dassault, Dornier, MBB, Alenia, and Sabca-Sonaca. A new Atlantique 3 version is being studied.

Development

▪ 19 July 1965. First production Atlantic flew.
▪ 19 July 1974. Final Atlantic delivered, going to the Italian Navy.
▪ September 1978. Development of Atlantique 2 began, born out of the former Atlantic II programme.
▪ 8 May 1981. First flight of the Atlantique 2.
▪ 19 October 1988. First production Atlantique 2 flew.
▪ October 1989. First Atlantique 2 delivery.
▪ 1 February 1991. First Atlantique 2 operational unit, as 23 Flottille of the French Navy.
▪ 1997. Start of the definition phase of a life-extension programme to upgrade German Navy Atlantics, with the intention of continuing service until the year 2010.
▪ 1997. Delivery of the last Atlantique 2 to the French Navy.
▪ 2005. Possible entry into service of the ATL3G, if ordered.

Details *(principally Atlantique 2)*

Sales/Users: France (28 Atlantique 2s), Germany (18 Atlantics remaining operational of 20 received, including 4 modified for signal intelligence – to be upgraded), Italy (18 Atlantics), and Pakistan (4 ex-French Atlantics, plus 2 for spares). Germany and Italy plan to replace Atlantics with a follow-on system from 2007, under the **MPA 2000** programme. See Defense and Civil Systems Group under Daimler-Benz Aerospace.
Crew: 10-12, according to mission. 2 pilots, flight engineer, mission tactical co-ordinator, nav/coms operator, ESM-MAD

Details for Atlantique 2, *with Atlantique 3 in italics*

PRINCIPAL DIMENSIONS:
Wing span: 122 ft 11 ins (37.46 m)
Maximum length: 104 ft 1 ins (31.72 m)
Maximum height: 37 ft 1 ins (11.3 m)

WINGS:
Aerofoil section: NASA 64 type
Area: 1,295.33 sq ft (120.34 m^2)
Aspect ratio: 11
Sweepback: 9° at leading edge
Incidence: 3°
Dihedral: 6°

TAIL UNIT:
Tailplane span: 40 ft 5 ins (12.31 m)
Tailplane area: 260.5 sq ft (24.2 m^2)

UNDERCARRIAGE:
Type: Retractable, with twin nosewheels
Wheel base: 30 ft 10 ins (9.4 m)
Wheel track: 29 ft 6 ins (9 m)

WEIGHTS:
Empty, equipped: 56,659 lb (25,700 kg), with 3,500 kg of mission avionics, *55,777 lb (25,300 kg)*
Maximum zero fuel: *71,650 lb (32,500 kg)*
Basic mission take-off: 97,444 lb (44,200 kg), *the same*
Maximum take-off: 101,853 lb (46,200 kg), *the same*

PERFORMANCE:
Maximum speed: 350 kts (403 mph) 648 km/h at best altitude, *the same at sea level*
Transit speed: *310 kts (357 mph) 574 km/h*
Cruise speed: 300 kts (345 mph) 556 km/h
Economical patrol speed: 170 kts (196 mph) 315 km/h, *the same*
Stall speed: 90 kts (104 mph) 167 km/h with flaps
Balanced runway length: 7,875 ft (2,400 m), at maximum take-off weight, ISA
Take-off distance over a 35 ft (11 m) obstacle: 6,040 ft (1,840 m)
Landing distance over a 35 ft (11 m) obstacle: 4,920 ft (1,500 m)
Maximum climb rate: 2,000 ft (610 m) per minute, at 88,185 lb (40,000 kg) weight
Ceiling: 30,000 ft (9,150 m), *the same*
Range with full fuel: 4,200 naut miles (4,836 miles) 7,778 km
On station duration at normal take-off weight: 8 hours at low altitude, 600 naut miles from base, with 4 torpedoes, 2 Exocets and 100 sonobuoys; or 5 hours at 1,000 naut miles
On station duration with full fuel: 11 hours at 600 naut miles from base; or 8 hours with 2 torpedoes and 1 Exocet, at 1,000 naut miles from base; or 4 hours at 1,500 naut miles from base, same weapons
Maximum duration: 18 hours, *the same*

↑ **Dassault Atlantique 2 with radome lowered**

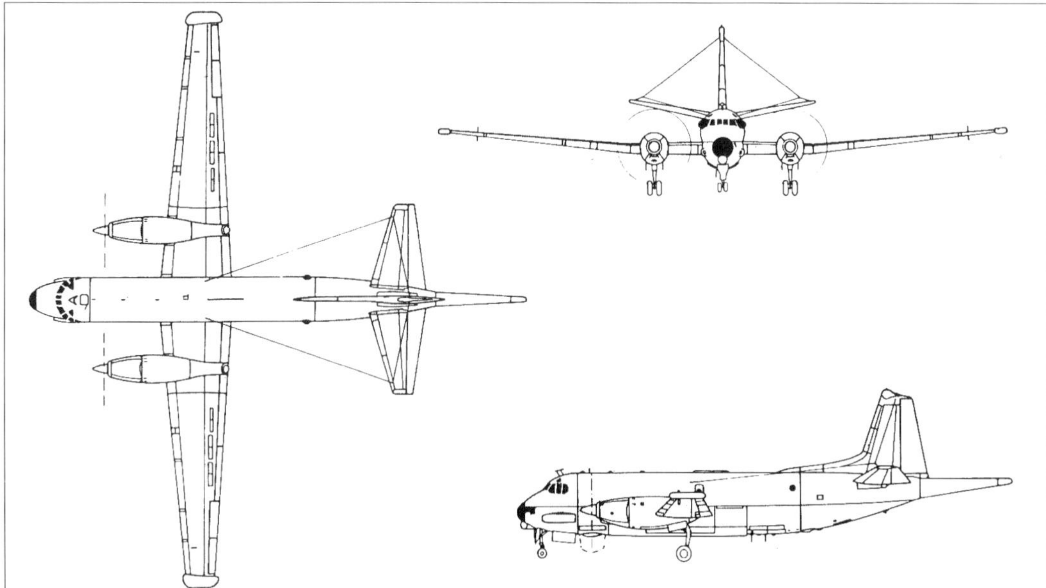

↑ Dassault Atlantique 2 *(courtesy ©Dassault)*

operator, radar operator, 2 acoustic operators, and 1-3 observers. Up to 24 persons (25 for ATL3G) can be carried on deployment flights.
Fixed guns: None.
Number of weapon pylons: 4 under the wings, for a total external stores weight of 7,716 lb (3,500 kg).
Expendable weapons and equipment: Weapon bay of 29 ft 6 ins (9 m) length and 953 cu ft (27 m^3) volume for a 7,936 lb (3,600 kg) load (12,125 lb, 5,500 kg maximum internal load for ATL3G), including up to 8 torpedoes (Mk 46 or V9) , 8 depth charges, 8 bombs (typically 125 kg), 6 × 250 kg mines (or 500 kg mines for ATL3G), 2 Exocet anti-ship missiles, 8 air-sea rescue containers (12 for ATL3G), or a combination that could be, typically, 3 torpedoes or mines or depth charges and an Exocet. Underwing loads can include 2 or 4 Magic, ARMAT or other weapons. The weapons for ATL3G could include 4 AGM-84D Harpoon anti-ship missiles.
Additional stores: Rear fuselage encompasses 4 day/night marker compartments (capacity 69), 4 automatic sonobuoy launchers (capacity 72 A or F size chutes), 4 reloadable sonobuoy launchers of A/F/G size and 1 free-fall chute, sonobuoy storage (60), retro launcher and storage (32), and flare launcher and storage (60). 200 sonobuoys, 70 markers and Signals Underwater Sound (SUS) for ATL3G.
Radar: Thomson-CSF Iguane, in a retractable radome.
Flight/weapon system avionics/instrumentation: Weapon system based on a distributed computer system, and comprising a tactical system with a central processing unit and tactical display, and decentralized sub-systems (detection, navigation, weapons, communications, etc), each with its own control and processing computer. Data exchanges between the sub-systems and to/from the tactical system are made through a digital databus. 2 INS (SEGEM Uliss 53). Mission system avionics sub-systems include 2 acoustic processing units for detecting, locating, identifying and tracking submarines through a network of sonobuoys; a compressed pulse radar able to detect small targets in heavy sea states; a radar emission detection system (ESM – ARAR 13A); a magnetic anomaly detector (MAD), used to classify and locate submarines; and an infra-red sensor under the nose (FLIR – Tango) for long-range, day/night detection of surface vessels. The navigation system includes 2 hybridized redundant inertial platforms, coupled to GPS Navstar satellite receiver, air data computer and automatic navigation plotter. The communications system comprises redundant equipment, such as HF, VHF and UHF (with HAVE QUICK II) with secure devices (voice and TTY). Automatic tactical data transmission system for network interoperability when co-operating with other forces (NATO Link 11). The multi-mission Mission System is designed for tracking and destruction of both submarine and surface ship threats. Omera 35 cameras in the nose and vertically in an aft compartment. Under the proposed life-extension programme, German Atlantics would receive upgraded radar, navigation system and ESM; have FLIR and GMDSS radio fitted; and other work.
Self-protection systems: See above. Capable of carrying air-to-air missiles under the wings.
Wing characteristics: Straight, low mounted. Wingtip pods.
Wing control surfaces: Ailerons, 3-section slotted flaps and 3 spoilers per wing.
Tail control surfaces: Elevators and rudder.
Airbrakes: Use of spoilers.
Flight control system: Hydraulic.
Construction materials: Bi-lope fuselage. Extensive use of bonded light alloy honeycomb panels.
Engines: 2 Rolls-Royce Tyne RTy.20 Mk 21 turboprops.
Engine rating: Each 6,100 eshp (4,549 ekW).
Flight refuelling probe: None. See Aircraft variants.
Fuel system: 23,120 litres (40,785 lb, 18,500 kg maximum). Same for ATL3G.
Electrical system: 28 volt DC supply, with 4 × 6kW transformer/rectifiers and a 40 amp-hour battery. Dual AC supplies, 115/200 volt variable frequency 3-phase, with 2 alternators; 115/200 volt, 400Hz 3-phase , with 4 engine-driven generators. APU-driven emergency AC generator.
Hydraulic system: 2,700 psi (dual), for aerodynamic controls, undercarriage, retractable radome and bay doors.

↑ Dassault Atlantique 3 (ATL3G). Note the underwing missiles

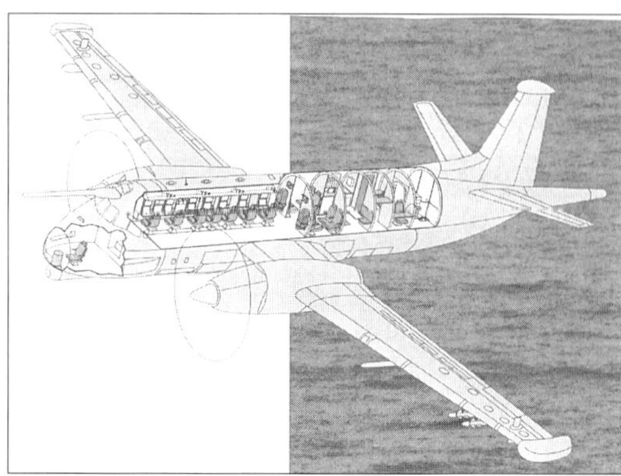

↑ Dassault Atlantique 3 interior layout *(courtesy ©Dassault)*

Braking system: Discs, with anti skid.
Oxygen system: Emergency bottles.
De-icing system: Electric for air intakes and propellers, pneumatic for wing/tail leading edges.

Aircraft variants:
Atlantic is the original version, entering service in 1966 and the fleet having logged over 1,000,000 flight hours. Italian aircraft have undergone, or are undergoing, avionics upgrade, while 4 German aircraft have been modified for sigint.
Atlantique 2 is the newly built upgraded version, for French Navy service, as detailed. 3-crew cockpit. Not all active.
Atlantique 3 is a proposed (Third Generation - ATL3G) new version of Atlantique 2, to take advantage of new off-the-shelf technologies. These could include Allison AE2100 turboprop engines with 6-blade Dowty 945 propellers that could increase duration by up to 1.5 hours and allow an ASW radius of up to 1,000 naut miles (1,151 miles) 1,852 km with 11,023 lb (5,000 kg) of external weapons and remain on-station for 8 hours, in-flight refuelling capability, new or improved sensors (radar with imagery, acoustics with enhanced sonobuoy processing, SATCOM/communications systems, NATO Data Link 11, 14, 16 and 22, and more), and improved self-protection (ESM with DASS, new AAMs, etc). EFIS. Anti-submarine and anti-ship remain principal roles, but increased importance placed on secondary peacekeeping, counter-terrorist, minelaying and mine detection, environmental and economic surveillance, and counter-narcotics uses. 2-crew cockpit. Harpoon among other weapon choices. Proposed as a Nimrod replacement for the RAF but not selected; German interest in doubt because of the proposed Altantic upgrade, and possible Italian interest for service from 2005. Could form the basis of a French Navy Atlantique 2 mid-life upgrade.

Dassault Mirage III, 5 and 50

Comments: Out of production but many have undergone significant upgrade. A description of the basic aircraft and details of upgrades, plus a photograph, appeared in the 1996-97 edition of *WA&SD*, page 36. Upgrades producing newly-named aircraft are the Denel Cheetah, ENAER Pantera and SABCA Elkan.
First flights: 17 November 1956 (Mirage III), 19 May 1967 (Mirage 5), and 15 May 1979 (Mirage 50).

Dassault Mirage IV-P

Comments: The Mirage IV was first flown on 17 June 1959. In 1996 the much upgraded Mirage IV-P finally gave up its strategic/tactical bomber role, when 1 of the 2 remaining squadrons was disbanded. The final IV-P squadron, 1/91 Gascogne at Mont de Marsan, continues to operate strategic reconnaissance missions and has in recent times conducted UN flights over Bosnia and the Hanish Islands. Each aircraft is equipped with the CT52 pod carried on the centreline station, housing the Omera 36 photographic suite with 3 × 600-mm medium/high-altitude cameras, an Omera 35 75-mm panoramic camera, single 152-mm Wild RC8F ground-mapping camera and 2 × 150 mm cameras. A SAT Super Cyclope IR linescanner can be substituted for the 600-mm cameras. Full details of the Mirage IV-P, and a photograph, can be found in the 1996-97 edition of *WA&SD*, pages 36-37.

Dassault Mirage 2000

First flight: 10 March 1978.
Role: Air superiority/defence, long-range strike, multi-role (with priorities according to version – see Aircraft variants), reconnaissance and electronic warfare.

Aims

- Advanced aerodynamics, and extensive use of composites.
- Low wing loading, and high thrust-to-weight ratio.
- Full fly-by-wire control system.
- Extensive use of integrated maintenance to minimize the required ground operations, and thereby the number of technicians and amount of ground equipment (during the 1992 Gulf conflict, a 98% readiness rate was achieved).

Development

- 18 December 1975. Mirage 2000 development approved as the French Air Force's next-generation combat aircraft.
- 10 March 1978. First flight of the first of 4 single-seat and 1 two-seat prototypes.

▪ **11 October 1980.** First flight of a Mirage 2000 B prototype.
▪ **November 1982.** First Mirage 2000 C delivery to the French Air Force, following the first flight on the 20th.
▪ **3 February 1983.** First flight of the Mirage 2000 N.
▪ **1984.** Initial operational capability with the French Air Force's 1/2 Cigognes squadron at Dijon.
▪ **1984.** Delivery and IOC of the Mirage 2000 E.
▪ **1985.** IOC with the first exported Mirage 2000s.
▪ **January 1987.** Initial delivery of the Mirage 2000 N to the French Air Force.
▪ **24 October 1990.** First flight of the Mirage 2000-5.
▪ **19 February 1991.** First flight of a Mirage 2000 D.
▪ **July 1993.** First delivery of a Mirage 2000 D.
▪ **October 1995.** First flight of the first export Mirage 2000-5.
▪ **26 February 1996.** First flight of a Mirage 2000-5 upgrade.
▪ **9 May 1996.** First delivery of an export Mirage 2000-5.
▪ **8 September 1996.** First 3 Mirage 2000-5s handed to Qatar during a ceremony. Remaining 9 for delivery by late 1998.
▪ **December 1997.** First Mirage 2000-5F redeliveries to the French Air Force, with operational service from 1998.
▪ **1998.** OCU with Mirage 2000Bs formed at Orange.

Details

Sales/Users: 557 ordered (including 13 development/company demonstrator aircraft), of which 501 delivered by May 1998. The total includes 109 Mirage 2000-5s (72 new and 37 by conversion of existing aircraft). Customers are Abu Dhabi (36 E and ED, known as EAD, RAD and DAD for interception, reconnaissance and training), Egypt (20 B and E, known as BMs and EMs), French Air Force (315, as 30 Bs, 124 Cs, 86 Ds and 75 Ns – 37 Mirage 2000-5Fs by conversion), Greece (40 Es and Bs, known as BGs and EGs), India (49 Es and Ds known as H and TH Vajras), Peru (12 Es and EDs, known as Ps and DPs), Qatar (12 2000-5s, as DDAs and EDAs), and Taiwan (60 2000-5s, as DIs and EIs; first squadron achieved IOC in November 1997, allowing final stand-down of Starfighters; 60 more 2000-5s requested). Interest shown by Czech Republic, Hungary, Pakistan and Poland. French Mirage 2000 C squadrons at the time of writing are EC-1/2 and EC-2/2 at Dijon (together also operating 17 Bs – this base is to receive upgraded Mirage 2000-5Fs), EC-1/5 and EC-2/5 at Orange (also with 3 Bs – EC-3/5's Mirage 2000 Cs at Orange are among those undergoing conversion to 2000-5Fs), and EC-1/12 and EC-2/12 at Cambrai (also with 3 Bs); Mirage 2000 D squadrons are EC-1/3, 2/3 and 3/3 at Nancy; Mirage 2000 N squadrons are EC-1/4 and 2/4 at Luxeuil, EC-3/4 at Istres and joining Ds at Nancy with EC-2/3.

Crew: Pilot or 2 crew (see Aircraft variants).

Cockpit: Mirage 2000-5 differs from previous versions by having a "glass cockpit" 5-display arrangement and interface intended to lighten the pilot's tasks in a hostile environment (see Aircraft variants). HOTAS. Mirage 2000 N cockpit installations were designed for 2-person missions, the rear cockpit mainly for navigation, ECM management and weapon preparation; 2 head-down displays. 2000 C has head-up and head-down displays. 2000 D has 2 head-down displays.

Crew escape: Martin Baker F10Q zero-zero type.

Fixed guns: 2 × DEFA 554 30-mm cannon in single-seaters.

Ammunition: Each 125 rounds.

Number of weapon pylons: 9, 4 under the wings and 5 under the fuselage (see diagram for capacities).

Expendable weapons and equipment: Maximum load 13,890 lb (6,300 kg). See diagram for weapon options. Mirage 2000-5 can carry 4 Mica and 2 Magic 2 AAMs plus up to 3 drop tanks; other Mirage 2000s can carry Magic 2 and Super 530D missiles. Standard available air-to-surface weapons include up to 18 × 250 kg bombs, 6 × 400 kg modular stand-off/area bombs, 18 × BAP 100 or Durandel anti-runway bombs, up to 6 Beluga or 18 × BAT 120 cluster bombs; laser-guided weapons (1 or 2 × 1,000 kg Matra LGB, or 1 or 2 Aerospatiale AS 30L); 1 or 2 Armat anti-radiation or Exocet anti-ship missiles; 1 × 30-mm CC 630 twin-gun pod; and/or 2 or 4 rocket pods. ASMP available on French Air Force Ns, and Apache submunition missile for late Ds.

Additional stores: Available pods, according to the aircraft version, include 1 or 2 self-defence or 1 offensive ECM, laser designator or FLIR. Alternative optical/IR, SLAR and electronic intelligence reconnaissance pods. Mirage 2000-5 has an integrated FLIR pod and laser designator pod (IR and EO), and EW system.

Radar: Thomson-CSF RDM radar in 16 Mirage 2000 Bs plus the original Mirage 2000-Cs before upgrade, thereafter Thomson-CSF/Dassault Electronique RDIs in Bs and Cs. RDM in 2000 Es. Dassault Electronique Antilope 5 in 2000 N and 2000 D. Thomson-CSF RDY in 2000-5.

Flight/weapon system avionics/instrumentation: Dassault Electronique 2084 digital central computer (2084XR in 2000 D and XR13 in 2000-5), and digital databus. SFENA 605 autopilot (2000 C), 606 (2000 N), 607 (2000 D) and 608 (2000-5). Other systems include Deltac Tacan and Socrat 8900 VOR/ILS. See also Cockpit and Aircraft variants for further details.

Basic details for all Mirage 2000s, or as specified

PRINCIPAL DIMENSIONS:
Wing span: 29 ft 11 ins (9.13 m)
Maximum length: 48 ft 1 ins (14.65 m) for Mirage 2000-5 and D, 47 ft 1.5 ins (14.36 m) for C and E, and 47 ft 9 ins (14.55 m) for 2-seaters
Maximum height: 17 ft 1 ins (5.2 m) for single-seaters, 16 ft 11 ins (5.15 m) for 2-seaters

WINGS:
Area: 441.32 sq ft (41 m^2)
Aspect ratio: 2.033
Sweepback: 58° on the leading edge
Anhedral: From roots

UNDERCARRIAGE:
Type: Retractable, with twin steerable nosewheels
Main wheel tyre size: 750 × 230 mm
Nose wheel tyre size: 360 × 135 mm
Wheel base: 16 ft 5 ins (5 m)
Wheel track: 11 ft 2 ins (3.4 m)

WEIGHTS:
Empty: 16,535 lb (7,500 kg) for single-seaters, 16,755 lb (7,600 kg) for 2-seaters
Typical combat: 21,000 lb (9,525 kg)
Maximum take-off: 23,942 lb (10,860 kg) for single-seaters, 24,163 lb (10,960 kg) for 2-seaters

PERFORMANCE:
Maximum, and maximum sustained speed: over Mach 2.2
Maximum speed at sea level: Mach 1.2
Minimum stable speed: 100 kts (115 mph) 186 km/h
Approach speed: 140 kts (161 mph) 260 km/h
Maximum climb rate: 58,000-60,000 ft (17,680-18,300 m) per minute
Climb to 49,000 ft (14,935 m)/Mach 2: 4 minutes
Roll rate: 270° per second
G limits: +9, -4.5
Operational ceiling: 59,000-60,000 ft (18,000-18,300 m)
Operational loiter time: 150 minutes for Mirage 2000-5 at Mach 0.8/25,000 ft (7,620 m) with 3 drop tanks and 6 AAMs
Operational range for 5 minutes combat (Mirage 2000-5): 780 naut miles (898 miles) 1,445 km at Mach 0.8/30,000 ft (9,145 m), 6 AAMs, drop tanks released
Range (Mirage 2000 E): over 850 naut miles (979 miles) 1,574 km with drop tanks on an air-to-ground mission, ISA
Maximum range: over 1,900 naut miles (2,188 miles) 3,520 km, with drop tanks

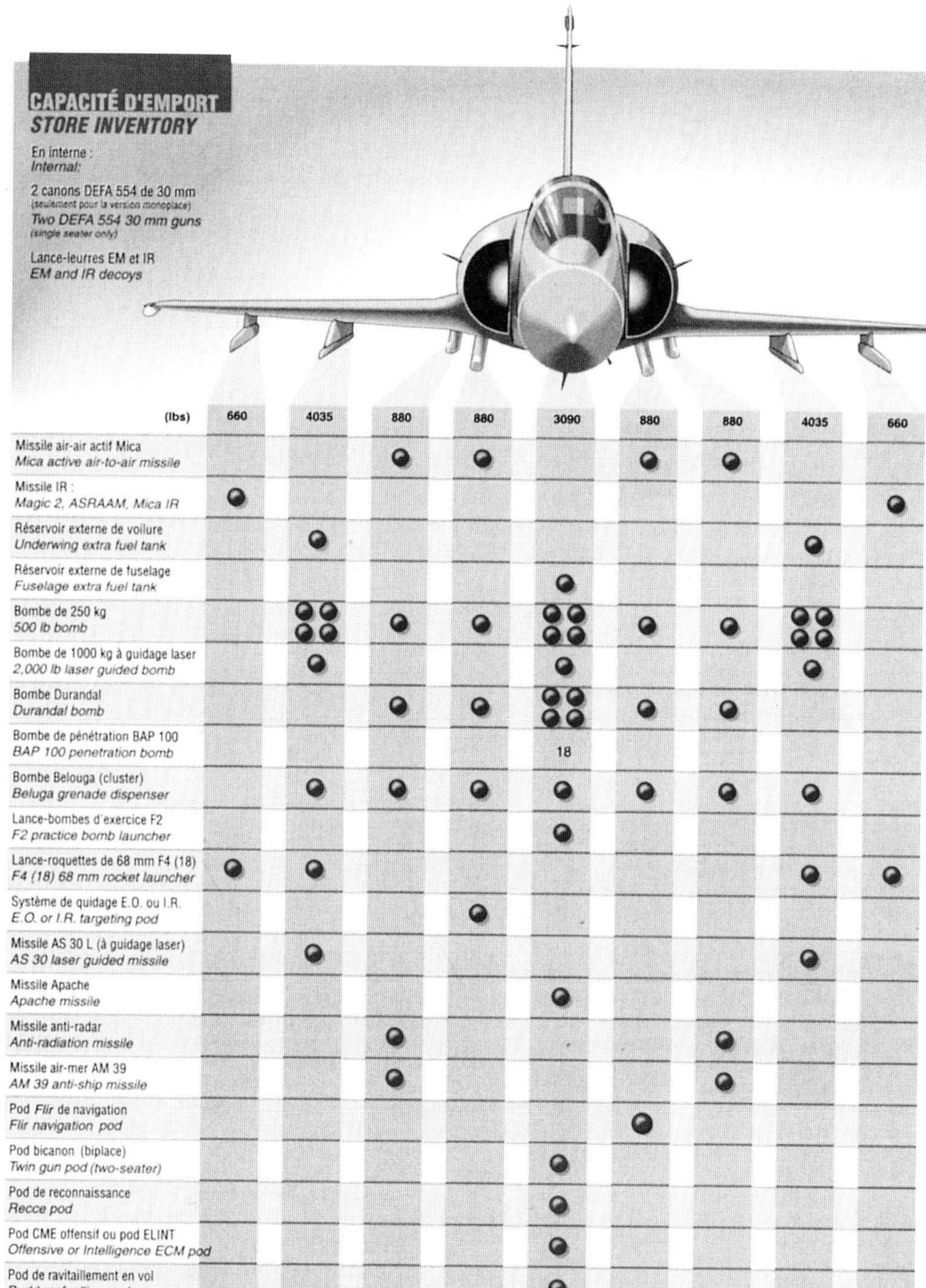

(lbs)	660	4035	880	880	3090	880	880	4035	660
Missile air-air actif Mica / Mica active air-to-air missile			●	●		●	●		
Missile IR : / Magic 2, ASRAAM, Mica IR	●								●
Réservoir externe de voilure / Underwing extra fuel tank		●						●	
Réservoir externe de fuselage / Fuselage extra fuel tank					●				
Bombe de 250 kg / 500 lb bomb		●●●●	●	●	●●●●	●	●	●●●●	
Bombe de 1000 kg à guidage laser / 2,000 lb laser guided bomb		●			●			●	
Bombe Durandal / Durandal bomb			●	●	●●●●	●	●		
Bombe de pénétration BAP 100 / BAP 100 penetration bomb					18				
Bombe Belouga (cluster) / Beluga grenade dispenser		●	●	●	●	●	●	●	
Lance-bombes d'exercice F2 / F2 practice bomb launcher					●				
Lance-roquettes de 68 mm F4 (18) / F4 (18) 68 mm rocket launcher	●	●						●	●
Système de quidage E.O. ou I.R. / E.O. or I.R. targeting pod				●					
Missile AS 30 L (à guidage laser) / AS 30 laser guided missile		●						●	
Missile Apache / Apache missile					●				
Missile anti-radar / Anti-radiation missile			●				●		
Missile air-mer AM 39 / AM 39 anti-ship missile			●				●		
Pod Flir de navigation / Flir navigation pod						●			
Pod bicanon (biplace) / Twin gun pod (two-seater)					●				
Pod de reconnaissance / Recce pod					●				
Pod CME offensif ou pod ELINT / Offensive or Intelligence ECM pod					●				
Pod de ravitaillement en vol / Buddy refuelling pod					●				

↑ **Stores inventory for the Mirage 2000** *(courtesy ©Dassault)*

↑ Dassault Mirage 2000 D with outer Magic 2 AAM, AS 30L ASM and Thomson-CSF PDLCT TV/thermal imaging laser designation pod in view *(SIPA AIR)*

Self-protection systems: Mirage 2000-5 has a comprehensive internal and fully integrated self-protection system (radar warning receiver, advanced jammer, chaff/flare dispensers, etc), with no need for external pods, to be operated in conjunction with a new proficient and programmable mission planning and debriefing system. Mirage 2000 C/N use Serval RWR, Caméléon jamming system, and Spirale chaff/flare. Internal integrated ECM system in E, and some with Spirale. Matra DDM missile launch warning receiver on some French Air Force 2000 D/Ns from Spring 1995.
Wing characteristics: Low-mounted, variable-camber delta type, with high-lift devices.
Wing control surfaces: 2-section elevons (16° up, 25° down). Automatic slats along the entire leading edge, inboard section drooping up to 17° 30', outboard 30°.
Tail control surfaces: Rudder only.
Airbrakes: On upper and lower wing surfaces.
Flight control system: Fly-by-wire.
Fuselage: Area-ruled type.
Construction materials: Metal, including lightweight honeycomb cores for the elevons, rudder and avionics bay cover. Extensive use of carbon and boron fibre, particularly for the rudder, fin and elevon skins, providing a 20% weight reduction for those parts.
Engine: SNECMA M53-5 or M53-P2 turbofan (see Aircraft variants). New version M53-P20 with an augmented rating of 22,050 lbf (98.07 kN) available.
Engine rating: 12,235 lbf (54.43 kN) dry, 19,840 lbf (88.26 kN) with afterburning for M53-5. 14,400 lbf (64.05 kN) dry, 21,400 lbf (95.19 kN) with afterburning for M53-P2.
Air intakes: Side mounted, with moving centrebodies. Externally fixed strakes to create vortices at high AoA.
Flight refuelling probe: Many on-line French Air Force single- and 2-seat Mirage 2000s are capable of in-flight refuelling. Most multi-role Mirage 2000s are capable of flight refuelling, or use as "buddy" system tankers.
Fuel system: 3,978 litres internally in 2000 C/E wing and fuselage tanks, 3,904 litres in other versions. 1,300 litre drop tank under the fuselage and 2 × 1,700 or 2,000 litre tanks under the wings.
Electrical system: Twin 20kVA or 25kVA/400Hz (for current production versions) alternators, twin DC transformers, static inverter and 40 amp-hour ni-cd battery.
Hydraulic system: 4,000 psi (dual).

↑ Dassault Mirage 2000-5 'glass cockpit' *(courtesy Dassault/TEKPHOT – Patrick Darphin)*

Braking system: Disc brakes on main units, with anti-skid system. Provision for a drag-chute or arrester hook.
Oxygen system: Eros type.

Aircraft variants:
Mirage 2000 B is a 2-seat operational trainer, based on the C. The B and C versions are together known as DAs. French Air Force ordered 30 aircraft, all delivered by the end of 1994. Mix of radar fits (see Radar) and 21 aircraft given M53-5 engines and 9 with M53-P2s. Designation **Mirage 2000 BOB** applies to a single electro-optics test aircraft.
Mirage 2000 C is a single-seat air-defence version, the initial 37 produced with the Thomson-CSF RDM radar and SNECMA M53-5 engine, and thereafter with Thomson-CSF/Dassault Electronique RDI radar and M53-P2 engine. Early RDM aircraft having RDI radar retrofitted, taken from a similar number of RDI-equipped aircraft undergoing upgrade to Mirage 2000-5 standard. 2 × 30-mm DEFA cannon, Magic 2 and Super 530D AAMs. Internal countermeasures system. The B and C versions are together known as DAs. French Air Force ordered 124 aircraft, of which 37 were assigned for modification to 2000–50.
Mirage 2000 D ("diversified") is a current production version based on the N but is dedicated to all-weather day and night air-to-surface attack. High speed and very low altitude automatic terrain-following capability, with Antilope 5 radar. Fully redesigned cockpit offers an advanced interface between the crew and the weapons system. Twin INS with GPS. Capable of launching conventional weapons or the most sophisticated modern weapons, including laser-guided and submunitions, but no ASMP capability. 86 ordered by the French Air Force, with deliveries from 1993 and full operational capability from 1994. Final aircraft will be delivered from 1999 with Apache capability. An export variant was offered as the Mirage 2000 S.
Mirage 2000 E is a single-seat multi-role export version of the C, with M53-P2 engine, multimode RDM radar, and Magic 2 and Super 530D AAMs. 2 principal computers with increased memory, new digital databus, ULISS-52 INS, VE-130 head-up display, VMC-180 head-down display, and better ECM. In production for attrition only. Those sold to Abu Dhabi and Greece have better computers among other improvements. Can be used for air-to-air, air-to-ground, air-to-surface and reconnaissance missions. Numerous standard and sophisticated weapon options, including laser guided.
Mirage 2000 ED (or B/ED) is a 2-seat operational training version of the E, similar in concept to the 2000 B.
Mirage 2000 N is a 2-seat all-weather, very low altitude penetration version with nuclear capability, latter 50 also having conventional armament options (later added to some earlier aircraft). Equipped with Dassault Electronique Antilope V terrain-following radar, Sagem twin-inertial navigation system, 2 TRT radar-altimeters, autopilot, Thomson-CSF colour displays, Dassault Electronique ECM, Omera vertical camera and an M53-P2 engine, and carries an ASMP medium-range nuclear missile and 2 × Magic 2 AAMs for self defence. French Air Force ordered 75 aircraft.
Mirage 2000 R is a single-seat reconnaissance variant of the 2000 E, for export customers.
Mirage 2000-5 is the latest and current advanced multi-role combat version, featuring enhanced capabilities. Derived from the 2000 DA (B and C versions), primarily for air superiority/defence but with extensive multi-role capabilities consistent with those developed for the E. Thomson-CSF RDY Doppler radar with automatic selection of waveform, allowing all-altitude and all-weather lookdown/shootdown multi-target detection and tracking (up to 24 targets and track-while-scan 8), capable of interfacing with an IFF. "Glass cockpit" (see Cockpit) and an improved fully integrated ICMS Mk 2 countermeasures system that does not require any external pod; adopts Thomson-CSF VEH 3020 head-up display and combined head-level display collimated to infinity for optimum presentation, 2 colour lateral displays for sensor and system management information, and head-down display. New CPU. Laser designation pod (TV/CT LDP). Matra Mica active interception-combat missiles in an air-to-air role (4 Micas, 2 Magic 2s and up to 3 drop tanks for an additional 5,300 litres of fuel), or choices of Super 530D and Sky Flash. Air-to-surface missiles, laser-guided bombs and Apache in attack configuration. 2-seat version also available. M53-P2 standard engine but M53-P20 engine optional. French aircraft (Mirage 2000-5Fs) are upgrades from 37 Mirage 2000 Cs, redeliveries of which started at the end of 1997 and all are due for return by the year 2000, first serving with EC-2/2.

↑ Dassault Mirage 2000-5 in service with Taiwan, carrying 4 Mica and 2 Magic 2 AAMs *(Dassault/Aviaplans)*

Dassault Mirage F1

Comments: First flown on 23 December 1966, 732 Mirage F1s were produced for the French Air Force and for export. The final variant was the F1 CT high-performance multirole combat aircraft, equipped with a new integrated navigation and weapon system based on inertial sensors and the multifunction Cyrano IV radar. About 55 French Air Force F1 C-200 interceptors were modified into F1 CTs for ground attack. Most work was carried out by Atelier Industriel de l'Air, following a Dassault-produced pattern conversion of 1991. A full description of the Mirage F1 and a photograph appears in the 1996-97 edition of *WA&SD*, pages 39-40.

Dassault Rafale

First flight: 4 July 1986.
Role: Air superiority, air defence, air-to-ground, air-to-surface (anti-ship), reconnaissance, and strike/nuclear strike.

Aims

- Fully digital fighter.
- To equip the French Air Force and Navy with a similar combat aircraft capable of performing a wide range of missions with all present and near future armaments, in all weathers and by day or night. To supersede Jaguars, Mirage F1s and Mirage IV-Ps with the Air Force, and Crusaders and Super Etendards with the Navy.
- 25-30 year life cycle.
- Rapid reconfiguration for changes of role.
- Turnaround time between missions of 15 minutes.
- Survivability through EW systems, terrain masking by very low altitude flying, stealth through the airframe shaping, choice of materials, and design of aerials and external load carriage.
- Inter-operability with NATO air forces.
- Achieve total integration of all conventional aircraft systems: fuel, hydraulics, electrics, air conditioning and communication.

Development

■ 13 April 1983. Decision made to construct a technology demonstrator (ACX/Rafale A), with manufacture beginning in March 1984 and the first flight on 4 July 1986.
■ December 1986. Start of the M88-2 engine development programme.
■ 21 April 1988. Order for Rafale C01, an Air Force prototype. First flown on 19 May 1991.
■ 6 December 1988. Order for the first Rafale M (01), a Navy prototype. The Rafale M02 was ordered on 4 July 1990. M 01 first flown on 12 December 1991, M 02 on 8 November 1993.
■ 19 July 1989. Order for Rafale B 01, an Air Force 2-seat prototype. First flown 30 April 1993.
■ 27 February 1990. First flight of Rafale with an M88-2 engine in place of 1 previous F404.
■ 15 June 1992. First operational evaluation by the CEV, DGA, Air Force and Navy, at Istres, lasting until 26 June.
■ 8 July 1992. Start of Rafale M's USC1 verification programme, lasting until 23 August . Rafale M 01 at Lakehurst (New Jersey, USA) and then Patuxent River (Maryland, USA), undertaking 39 catapults, 69 rolling strand engagements, 14 simulated deck landings on a runway, and 6 deck landings.
■ 30 October 1992. 1,000th Rafale flight (Rafale A 708, C 01 195, and M 01 97).
■ 18 December 1992. Industrialization of the Rafale programme was signed, leading to future production.
■ 31 December 1992. Order for the first production M88 engines.
■ 15 January 1993. Start of the USC2 programme to extend Rafale M's "clean" flight envelope, lasting until 18 February. Included 42 catapults, 19 simulated deck landings on a runway, 23 rolling strand engagements, and 45 deck landings.
■ 5 March 1993. First Rafale gun firing by C 01 at Cazaux, followed by Magic 2 firing on 26 March.
■ 26 March 1993. 2 production aircraft ordered, as B 1 and M 1.
■ 19 April 1993. Start of the PA1 programme covering aircraft carrier compatibility using Rafale M 01 on *Foch*, lasting until 7 May. Included 31 deck landings and 31 catapults.
■ 8 November 1993. Start of the USC3 programme with Rafale M 01 at Lakehurst, lasting until 15 December, to open the flight envelope with external loads (5 configurations). Included 59 catapults, 48 rolling strand engagements and 40 deck landings.
■ 27 January 1994. Start of the PA2 programme with Rafale M 01 and 02, to open the flight envelope, test carrier compatibility with attachments, and VAMOM (inspections of fitness for operation and maintenance). Lasted until 7 February, and then repeated 11 April–3 May. Included 56 deck landings/catapults.
■ 17 February 1994. Orders placed for production Rafale M 2, M 3 and B 2.
■ 5 September 1994. Rafale's 2,000th flight, at Farnborough.
■ June 1995. First self-guided Mica fired from Rafale.
■ July 1995. Front Sector Optronic System and helmet-mounted sight unit installed.
■ November 1995. First Rafale B 01 prototype long-range flight, of 3,020 naut miles.
■ April 1996. Certification of engines, but progress on Rafale production suspended temporarily.
■ 20 September 1996. Spectra protection and fire control avoidance system first flown in a Rafale M.
■ October 1996. Daily Rafale M 01 air demonstrations at Seoul.
■ November 1996. Spectra countermeasures system flight tested.
■ 30 December 1996. First delivery of production engines.
■ 22 January 1997. Production programme restarted, after an agreed reduction in costs.
■ February 1997. Very heavy configuration flight completed by B 01 with Apache.

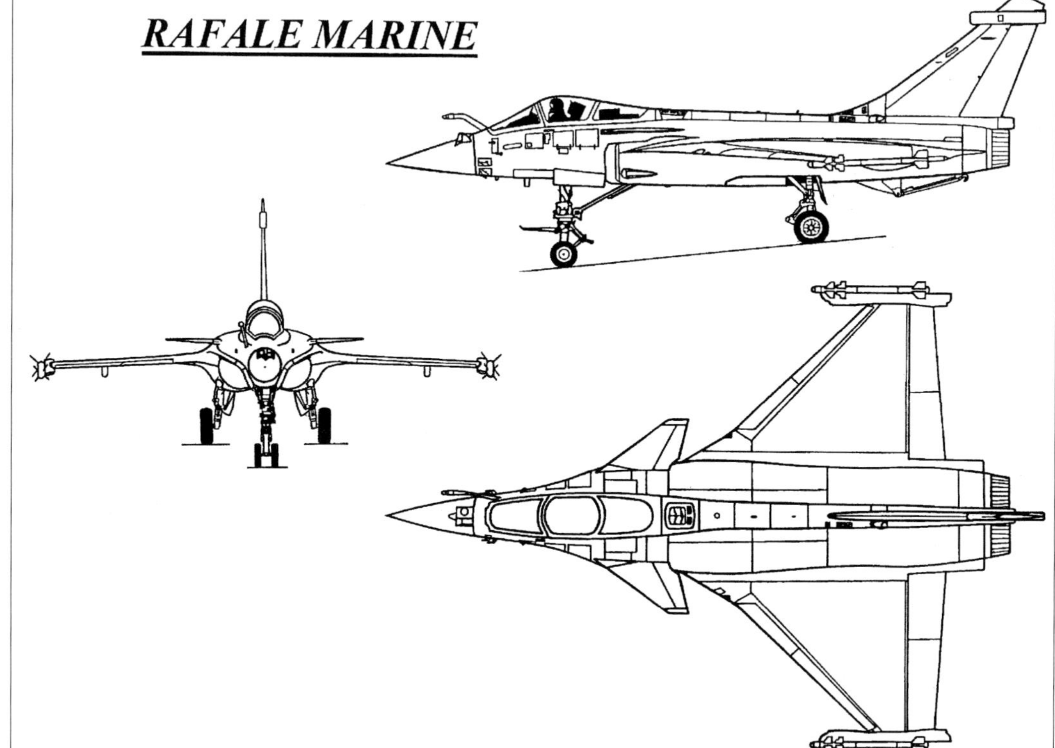

↑ Naval Rafale layout *(© Dassault)*

■ Winter 1998/99. First production Rafale B expected to be ready for trials with CEV.
■ 2000. First deliveries of naval Rafale M production aircraft.
■ June 2001. IOC of the naval Rafale M, with first deployments on *Charles de Gaulle* by 6 aircraft.
■ June 2002. 1 complete naval flotille of 12 aircraft in service.
■ 2005. Likely IOC for Air Force Rafales, following earlier use of promotional and trials aircraft, as 1 squadron of 20 aircraft.

Details

Sales/Users: Single technology demonstrator and 4 prototypes built by May 1998 (see Development). Required for French Air Force (95 single-seat and 139 2-seat) and Navy (86, initially as interceptors and thereafter to replace Super Etendards), with the initial 13 ordered to be joined by 48 more for production up to 2002. Offered for export.
Crew: Pilot, or 2 crew (pilot and weapon system operator, or pilot and trainee) – see Aircraft variants.
Cockpit: Seat tilted 29° to assist the pilot in resisting g loads (by limiting the vertical distance between the heart and the brain). Sextant VEH 3022 30° × 22° field-of-view wide-field holographic collimated head-up display. Images from the sensors and the weapons system status are shown on 2 lateral 5 ins (12.7 cm) square Sextant SLCD 55 colour multifunction polychrome touch-screens. Principal screen is a mid-head TMC 2020 colour display, collimated to avoid too-frequent adjustment, showing elements of the tactical situation. Helmet-mounted display (see Avionics). Controls situated on the single port-side engine-control lever or on the starboard-side mini stick controller, in accordance with HOTAS. Sully Products Spéciaux single-piece canopy is gold coated to reduce signature. Technofan air conditioning system.

↑ Dassault Rafale naval M 02 landing on *Foch* *(F. Robineau – Dassault/Aviaplans)*

Crew escape: SEMMB/Martin Baker Mk 16 zero-zero ejection seat.
Fixed guns: 1 × 30-mm Giat DEFA 791B cannon, with a rate of fire of 2,500 rounds per minute.
Number of weapon pylons: 14 on Rafale B and C, 13 on M, 5 of which are heavy (over 1,000 kg) and wet for drop tanks (underfuselage centre line, and inner/centre underwing pylons).
Expendable weapons and equipment: Up to 17,637 lb (8,000 kg), but recent Dassault-supplied data has stated 9.5 tonnes. Typically 8 Mica air-to-air missiles, or 2 × AS 30L laser-guided missiles and 2 × 1,000 kg laser-guided bombs plus 4 Micas, or 2 Apache submunition missiles and 2 Micas, or 16 × 225 kg bombs and 2 Micas, or 2 anti-ship missiles and 4 Micas, or ASMP, SCALP and AASM missiles, among other options, all in combination with drop tanks and/or mission pods. Initial use of only the radar-homing version of Mica, joined from the year 2002 by the infra-red Mica due to improved operational software on new production Rafales. Air Force Rafales delivered from 2002 will have Apache, SCALP and AASM compatibility. ASMP will not be available for each force until the final level of software becomes operational in about the year 2007.
Additional stores: Photographic or electromagnetic reconnaissance pod, FLIR pod, targeting/navigation pods, etc.
Radar: GIE Radar RBE2, the first European radar to have an antenna with electronic scanning in 2 planes and a very high computing power.
Flight/weapon system avionics/instrumentation: 2 redundant mission computers managing the high-output digital lines to integrate nav/attack, stores management, flight control, engine control and aircraft systems. Sextant Avionique voice-activated controls (not on the first production aircraft – see Weapons) and alarm warning. 2 Sagem Uliss 52X (Sigma RL90 ring-laser gyro) INS, FCS control units and store system interface unit (BISE).

↑ Dassault Rafale B 01 carrying wingtip Micas, Apaches and drop tanks *(F. Robineau - Dassault/Aviaplans)*

Sextant GPS computer coupled to the lasergyro platforms, Mermoz automatic test equipment system, and permanent and back-up instrumentation. Integrated Logistic Support (ILS) to define the aircraft system and the support system. VOR/DME. Thomson-CSF radar altimeter. SFIM/Dassault flight recorder. GIE IFF. Sextant 'Glass cockpit' (see Cockpit) and symbol generator sensors. Images of the external scene from an infra-red camera can be superimposed on the HUD. Thomson-CSF Optronique/Sagem Defence and Security Division/SAT front sector optronic sensor (OSF – not to be fitted initially to the first production aircraft) allows passive visible and infra-red detection at long range, multi-target angular tracking, and ranging on air, sea and ground targets (complements the capabilities of the radar in clear weather or in conditions of very severe electromagnetic jamming, and on penetration missions in clear weather it increases the stealth of the navigation and weapons system by allowing the use of the RBE2 to limited checks). Compatible with the Sextant Topsight helmet-mounted sight. EAS VHF and UHF, and TRT Saturn UHF communication radios, and Thomson-CSF secure radio. TEAM intercommunication system. SFIM crash recorder.

Self-protection systems: Dassault Electronique Spectra (protection and fire control avoidance) is an internal system that is integrated with the navigation and weapons system, to enhance survivability against air-to-air and surface-to-air threats. It monitors the whole range of electromagnetic threats and reports missile launches (by the use of missile departure detectors – DDMs) or laser illuminations (by laser warning detectors – DAL). Following detection and identification, electromagnetic jamming, chaffing or evasive manoeuvres can be effected. This system is unlikely to be fitted to the first production aircraft (see Weapons).
Wing characteristics: Mid-mounted clipped delta, with extended leading-edges near the roots.
Wing control surfaces: Each wing has 2 elevons and 2-section leading-edge slats.
Tail control surfaces: Rudder.
Canard: Active, of swept delta planform, located to optimize aerodynamic efficiency and stability control without impeding the pilot's view. Automatic 20° incidence setting when the undercarriage is lowered.
Airbrakes: 2 on the fuselage, each side of the fin.
Flight control system: Fly-by-wire. 3 digital channels and 1 analog channel, connected to the complete navigation and weapons system. Linked to the control of the engines, the system allows actuation of all control surfaces throughout the flight envelope, from zero speed to Mach 1.8 and -3 to +9g. System allows attitude control in all 3 axes, automatic limitation control, flight control at high angles of attack, co-ordinated turns, speed vector control, and approach with thrust/drag ratio monitoring. It can also be applied to other functions, including low altitude, high speed gust-load alleviation. Control surface deflection results from comparison between the pilot input and the actual motion of the aircraft as detected by the various sensors (accelerometers, rate gyros, probes, etc). Flight controls check between missions is automatic.
Construction materials: Much use of carbonfibre, even for large components such as the rear fuselage, wing panels, elevons, fin, rudder (with aluminium honeycomb core), etc. Kevlar for wing

CAPACITÉ D'EMPORT
EXTERNAL STORE CARRYING CAPABILITY

		TIP R	EXT R	MED R	INT R	AFT LAT R	FWD LAT R	FUS CEN	FWD LAT L	AFT LAT L	INT L	MED L	EXT L	TIP L
	MISSILES													
AIR/AIR	MAGIC	x	x	x								x	x	x
AIR/AIR	MICA	x	x	x		x		x		x		x	x	x
AIR/AIR	SIDEWINDER	x	x	x								x	x	x
AIR/AIR	ASRAAM	x	x	x								x	x	x
AIR/AIR	AMRAAM			x		x		x		x		x		
AIR/SEA	EXOCET/AM 39			x	x						x	x		
AIR/SEA	PENGUIN 3			x	x						x	x		
AIR/SEA	HARPOON			x	x						x	x		
AIR/GROUND	AS 30 L			x	x						x	x		
AIR/GROUND	APACHE				x			x			x			
AIR/GROUND	ALARM			x	x			x			x	x		
AIR/GROUND	HARM			x	x			x			x	x		
AIR/GROUND	MAVERICK			x	x						x	x		
	BOMBS													
LG	1000 kg LG				x			x			x			
LG	400 kg LG			x	x			x			x	x		
LG	GBU 12			x	x			x			x	x		
LG	GBU 10				x			x			x			
CONVENT.	250 kg/Mk 82			x	x	x	x	x	x	x	x	x		
CONVENT.	400 kg/Mk 83			x	x			x			x	x		
CONVENT.	BELOUGA			x	x			x			x	x		
CONVENT.	Bap 100/Bat 120				x			x			x			
CONVENT.	Durandal			x	x			x			x	x		
CONVENT.	Rockets			x	x						x	x		
	TANKS													
FUEL	RL 2000 l Underwing				x						x			
FUEL	RL 2000 l Underfus							x						
FUEL	RL 1250 l Underwing			x								x		
FUEL	RL 1250 l Underfus							x						
	PODS													
NAV	PDLCT - TV						x							
NAV	FLIR								x					
ECM	offensive jammer			x				x				x		
RECCE	IR/opt.RECCE						x	x						
RECCE	SLAR							x						
RECCE	HAROLD							x						
MISC	buddy-buddy refueling							x						
MISC	twin gun pod (600 rounds)							x						

↑ **Dassault Rafale stores inventory** *(© Dassault)*

Details for Rafale

PRINCIPAL DIMENSIONS:
Wing span: 35 ft 5 ins (10.8 m)
Maximum length: 50 ft 2.5 ins (15.3 m)
Maximum height: 17 ft 6 ins (5.34 m) for Rafale D, 17 ft 5 ins (5.3 m) for Rafale M

WINGS:
Area: 491.91 sq ft (45.7 m^2)
Aspect ratio: 2.5
Anhedral: From roots

UNDERCARRIAGE:
Type: Retractable, with twin steerable nosewheels. Naval Rafales are designed to withstand hard landings on deck of 6.5 m per second vertical drop. Rafale M nosewheel leg has energy restitution to optimize take-off at the end of the deck, to create a 'jump'
Main wheel tyre size: Michelin 810 × 275 mm
Nose wheel tyre size: Michelin 550 × 200 mm

WEIGHTS:
Empty, operating: 19,974 lb (9,060 kg) for Rafale D, 21,320 lb (9,670 kg) for M
Maximum ramp: 42,990 lb (19,500 kg) initially. Growth potential to 47,400 lb (21,500 kg), with 54,013 lb (24,500 kg) quoted in 1997 as a potential maximum take-off weight

PERFORMANCE:
Maximum speed: Mach 1.8 to Mach 2
Maximum low-altitude speed: 750 kts (864 mph) 1,390 km/h
Approach speed: 120 kts (138 mph) 222 km/h
Minimum speed: 80 kts (92 mph) 148 km/h
Take-off distance: 1,476 ft (450 m) with AAMs
Landing distance: under 1,312 ft (400 m)
Maximum climb rate: >60,000 ft (18,290 m) per minute
G limits: +9, -3.6 (also quoted as -3.2)
Roll rate: 270° per second
Maximum instant turn rate: >30° per second
Maximum angle of attack: 32°
Ceiling: 55,000 ft (16,765 m) operational
Radius of action: >1,000 naut miles (1,150 miles) 1,850 km with maximum internal/external fuel for penetration mission
Combat air patrol loiter time: >3 hours

root/fuselage fairings and wingtips. Composite materials represent about 24% of the airframe mass and 70% of the wetted surface. Metals include titanium for the slats. Superplastic forming (SPF)-diffusion bonding titanium structures include canards, and SPF aluminium structures. Latécoère fuselage subassemblies.
Engines: 2 SNECMA M88-2 turbofans. (Note: Dassault has deleted the alternative higher-rated M88-3s from the text). Microturbo APU. Engine replacement in 60 minutes.
Engine rating: Each 11,250 lbf (50.04 kN) dry, 16,850 lbf (74.95 kN) with afterburning. During Rafale's first flight, Mach 1 was attained in "super-cruise" (without engine afterburning).
Air intakes: Semi ventral, with no moving parts or bleeds, for optimum performance trade-off at all speeds. Specially designed for stealth qualities.
Flight refuelling probe: Probe on starboard side of nose.
Fuel system: Intertechnique, Lucas Air Equipment and Zenith Aviation fuel system equipment. Over 5,325 litres internally. Refuelling between missions takes 4 to 7 minutes, depending on the configuration. Optional auxiliary fuel comprises Emmen and Secan drop tanks: a 1,700 or 2,000 litre underfuselage drop tank, 2 × 2,000 litre and/or 2 × 1,300 litre underwing tanks, all combinations to a maximum of 6,600 litres (see Number of pylons). Removable (non-retractable) flight refuelling probe.
Electrical system: Auxilec system components and ECE power generation system, with 2 × 30/40kVA alternators.
Hydraulic system: Aviac dual system, with Messier-Bugatti pumps. Lucas Air Equipment hydraulic servo-mechanics. Samm hydraulic filter units. 5,075 psi, for undercarriage actuation and steering.
Braking system: High power carbon brakes on all wheels. Drag-chute available.
Oxygen system: Autonomous oxygen generation (OBOGS). Air Liquide generating equipment and Eros system equipment.

Aircraft variants:
Rafale B was originally intended to be the French Air Force's 2-seat dual-control operational trainer and operational combat aircraft. Now planned as an operational model flown with either 1 or 2 crew. **Rafale D** is the overall name describing both Air Force versions of Rafale.
Rafale C is the French Air Force single-seater.
Rafale M is the French Navy's single-seater for aircraft carrier operations. Only some 1,345 lb (610 kg) heavier than the Rafale C, with the fuselage structure reinforced for carrier operations and the undercarriage modified, plus an arrester hook. Other changes include an electrically-folding ladder, a unit to align gyro platforms with those of the ship, and deck landing aids. Maximum take-off weight is restricted to 36,375 lb (16,500 kg) for operations from *Foch* (which is to have a 1° 30' 'ski jump' ramp), but no restriction on the new *Charles de Gaulle* (when the Rafale M's 'jump' nosewheel leg will be used to assist take-off, giving an ability to carry an additional 900 kg of stores over that possible with a conventional 'flat-deck, no jump' take-off).

Dassault Super Etendard

Comments: The Super Etendard carrier-borne strike-fighter was first flown on 28 October 1974. Production ended in 1983 after 85 aircraft. Argentina retains its 12, and 54 French Navy aircraft were earmarked for upgrade to extend service to 2007-2010, the first upgraded aircraft flying on 5 October 1990 featuring new Dassault Electronique Anémone multi-function radar, computer, INS and more. Full details of the Super Etendard and upgrade, and a photograph, can be found in the 1996-97 edition of *WA&SD*, pages 41-42.

↑ **Dassault Rafale cockpit** *(Dassault/TEKPHOT - Patrick Darphin)*

Dassault Falcon Multirole

Comments: Details of the Falcon Multirole, suited to maritime surveillance and electronic warfare among many other possible applications, can be found with all Falcon aircraft in the General Aviation section.

DaimlerChrysler Aerospace AG (DASA) — Germany

Corporate address:
Postfach 801109, D-81663 Munich.

Telephone: +49 89 6 07-0
Facsimile: +49 89 6 07 26481
Telex: 5287-0 DASAM D

Founded:
Renamed Daimler-Benz Aerospace on 1 January 1995, from the former Deutsche Aerospace AG corporate unit of the Daimler-Benz Group that had been founded in 1989. Oldest operating unit of the Aircraft Group of Daimler-Benz Aerospace was Dornier Luftfahrt GmbH of the Regional Aircraft Division, which dated from 1922; since June 1996, when Fairchild Aircraft of the USA purchased 80% of Dornier Luftfahrt, this has been known as Fairchild Dornier Germany Dornier. Merged with Chrysler 17 November 1998.

Employees:
Over 40,000.

Information:
Christian Poppe (Director of Communications – *telephone* +49 89 607-3 42 50, *facsimile* +49 89 607 3 42 84, *E-mail* yzv0034@dbmail.dasa de), Andreas Breitsprecher (Press Department – *telephone* +49 89 607 3 42 35, *facsimile* +49 89 607 3 42 39), Gregor Kursell (International Media Relations – *telephone* +49 89 607 3 42 55, *facsimile* +49 89 607 3 42 38), Frank E. Rietz (Public Relations – *telephone* +49 89 607 3 42 83, *facsimile* +49 89 607 3 42 85), and Manfred Knappe (Publications – *telephone* +49 89 607 3 46 50, *facsimile* +49 89 607 3 46 55).

ACTIVITIES

▪ In addition to the divisions detailed below, on 9 November 1994 DASA signed an agreement with Hellenic Aerospace Industry of Greece covering future co-operation over civil and military programmes, defence technology and satellite communication (see F-4 programme). Another agreement with the DLR German aerospace research establishment covers co-operation in R&D.

AIRCRAFT GROUP

CIVIL AIRCRAFT

Information:
Dr Theodor Benien (*telephone* +49 89 607 342 59, *facsimile* +49 89 607 256 65, *E-mail* yza9811@dbmail.dasa.de).

DAIMLER-BENZ AEROSPACE AIRBUS GMBH

HQ address:
Postfach 950109, Kreetslag 10, D-21111 Hamburg.

Information:
Rolf Brand (Press Office – *telephone* +49 40 74 37 30 16, *facsimile* +49 40 74 37 25 22, *E-mail* rolf.brand@airbus.dasa.de).

Activities:
▪ Undertakes the German interest in the multi-national Airbus airliner programmes (37.9%). Other interests include the FLA, Super Transporter, work with Tupolev of Russia and Airbus on Cryoplanes powered by liquid hydrogen, C-160 Transall life extension programme, and more.

MILITARY AIRCRAFT

HQ address:
PO Box 801160, D-81663 Munich 80.

Information:
Wolfram Wolff (Press Office – *telephone* +49 89 607 2 57 11, *facsimile* +49 89 607 2 24 55, *E-mail* LMLWW0@dbmail.dasa.de).

Activities:
▪ Undertakes work on the Eurofighter and Panavia Tornado; is overseeing the new AT-2000 programme; has modernized German Air Force F-4F Phantoms under the ICE programme, is upgrading the Hellenic Air Force's F-4Es, and is conducting a Luftwaffe MiG-29 programme; is engaged in conceptual proposals with France and the UK at industrial/ government level aimed at developing a technology demonstrator for a future European stealth fighter; formerly contributed to both the Rockwell Ranger 2000 and the X-31A (latter possibly to be modified and flown from 1998 in the new Vector programme involving also Saab and Boeing); currently manufactures Airbus airliner components; and produces reconnaissance, training/simulation and other systems.

EUROCOPTER DEUTSCHLAND GMBH

HQ address:
D-81663 Munich.

Information:
Christina Gotzhein (Press Office – *telephone* +49 89 60 00 64 88, *facsimile* +49 89 60 00 44 37).

Activities:
▪ Tasked to undertake development and production of helicopters of German origin.

SPACE SYSTEMS GROUP

SATELLITE

Information:
Mathias Pikelj (Press Office – *telephone* +49 75 45 8 91 23, *facsimile* +49 75 45 8 55 89, *E-mail* a01172t@dbmail.dasa.de).

SPACE INFRASTRUCTURE

Information:
Kirsten Leung (Press Office – *telephone* +49 4 21 539 53 26, *facsimile* +49 4 21 539 45 34, *E-mail* kirsten.leung@ri.dasa.de).

DEFENSE AND CIVIL SYSTEMS GROUP

Information:
(Press Office – *telephone* +49 75 45 8 46 13, *facsimile* +49 75 45 8 58 88, *E-mail* rita.monahan@vs.dasa.de).

Activities:
▪ Incorporates Information and Communications Systems (information: Michael Hartwig – *telephone* +49 75 45 8 91 24, *facsimile* +49 75 45 8 58 88), Defense Electronics (information: Peter Schmid – *telephone* +49 731 392 36 81, *facsimile* +49 731 392 37 55, *E-mail* peter.schmid@vs.dasa.de), and Missile Systems (information: Wolfram Lautner – *telephone* +49 89 607 292 33, *facsimile* +49 89 607 255 15). Also Nortel DASA (information: Jackie Simkin – *telephone* +49 69 66 97 16 90, *facsimile* +49 69 66 97 19 97).
▪ Signed an agreement in 1998 with Alenia of Italy to co-operate on the procurement of advanced mission equipment for the planned German-Italian maritime patrol aircraft (**MPA 2000** programme).

PROPULSION SYSTEMS DIVISIONS

AIRCRAFT PROPULSION

Information:
Peter Kellner (Director of Communications – *telephone* +49 89 14 89 25 40, *facsimile* +49 89 14 89 21 72, *E-mail* SMTP:Maria Metz@muc.mtu.dasa.de).

Daimler-Benz Aerospace F-4 and MiG-29 programmes

Comments: DASA was awarded a contract by the German Ministry of Defence to upgrade the avionics systems on more than 150 F-4Fs. In performing this upgrade, known as the

Improved Combat Efficiency (ICE) programme, the company successfully completed the conceptual, definition, development and test phases, and redeliveries of upgraded aircraft began in April 1992. The ICE programme introduced and integrated AIM-120 AMRAAM missiles and launchers, multi-function AN/APG-65GY pulse-Doppler radar, new Litef digital fire control computer, H-423 ring laser IN set, new standard GEC-Marconi CPU-143/A air data computer, modified display system and MIL-STD-1553B multiplex databus. Further details and a photograph can be found in the 1996-97 edition of *WA&SD*, pages 43-44.

In the latter part of 1997 DASA began work on upgrading 39 Hellenic Air Force F-4Es, with Israel's Elbit as sub-contractor to supply the new 'glass cockpit' with colour MFDs and the mission computer. Much of the upgrade has been based on DASA's ICE programme. Most aircraft will be completed by 2000.

DASA is also working on a programme involving the Luftwaffe's MiG-29s.

Daimler-Benz Aerospace AT-2000 Mako

First flight: Not yet flown.
Role: Role-flexible, supersonic-capable family of related aircraft, for advanced, tactical and weapon lead-in training, light fighter and reconnaissance.

Aims

- Family of role-flexible aircraft, incorporating the customer's desired capabilities and levels of performance, by adopting different stages of propulsion, avionics and weapons, while retaining the existing primary structure/airframe.
- New design, allowing a stealth-configured airframe with low RCS. Some shielding by the shelves (see fuselage description) to reduce IR signature.
- A low density airframe design to allow spare volume for growth potential (additional equipment), low structural complexity for low production costs, and good accessibility to reduce maintenance time and in-service costs.
- Sufficient electrical and cooling power for systems' growth.
- Adoption of the Eurojet EJ200 engine family.
- Modular, high-performance mission suite from Denel.
- High external stores capability.
- Overall system design optimized for low Life-Cycle-Cost.
- Maximum usage of off-the-shelf equipment.
- Light Fighter Aircraft models to have single-seat cockpits (except the fighter-bomber), extended mission suite and extended fuel capacity.
- Ground power and replenishing points are designed in accordance with NATO standardization agreement (STANAG) and comply with NATO cross servicing requirements.
- All maintenance work beyond the 'on line' capabilities, mainly the full depth equipment maintenance and major structural repairs, will be performed at industry depot level. The recommended maintenance concept foresees flight line inspections and servicing, scheduled maintenance activities, on aircraft repair activities (in particular, replacement of line replaceable units -LRUs), minimum off aircraft (shop) maintenance tasks as far as required for operational or economic reasons, and battle damage repair capability, to be performed at maintenance levels 'O' and 'I'.

Development

- **2005.** First production deliveries.

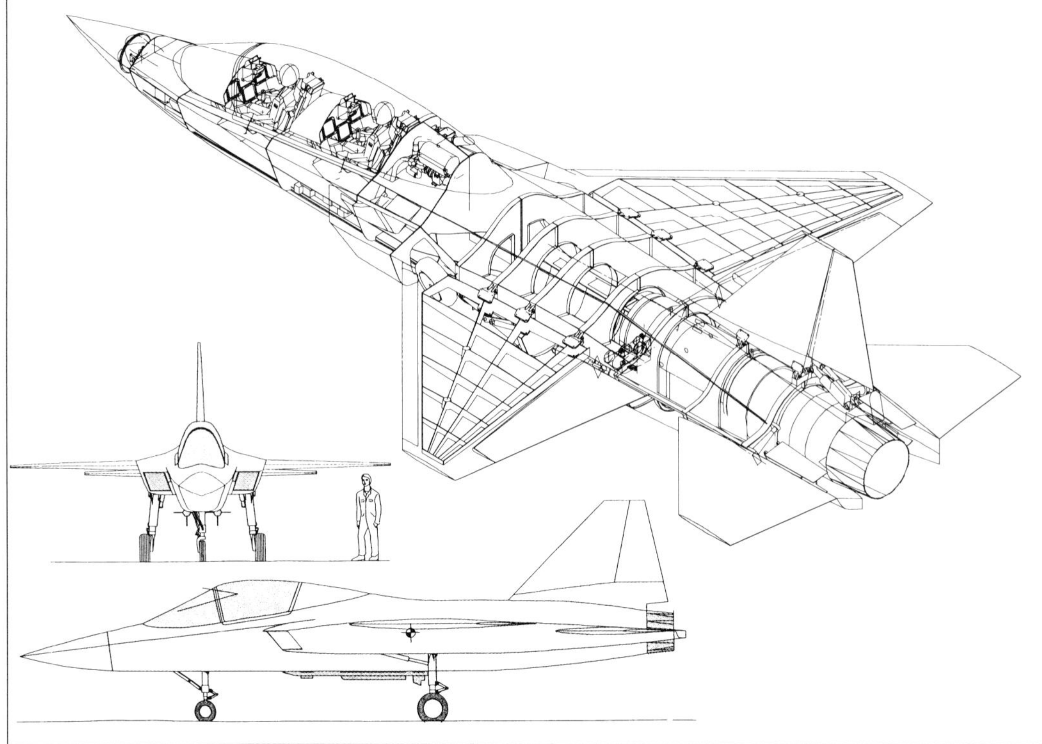

↑ Daimler-Benz Aerospace AT-2000 Advanced Tactical Trainer, with added side and front views of the Light Fighter Aircraft *(courtesy DASA)*

Details

Sales/Users: Anticipated DASA market for up to 700 new advanced trainers and light combat aircraft identified, with overall potential for more than 2,000. DASA has proposed selling 35-40 to South Africa, to replace the Impala. Other nations have expressed interest.
Crew: Pilot only or 2 crew, or pilot instructor and pupil, depending on version. Seat/s tilted at 18°.
Cockpit: Tandem stepped cockpits for 2-seaters, with 15 ° view over the nose and 40 ° to the sides (further improved visibility in single-seaters), and almost identical instrumentation and layout of cockpits. 'Glass cockpits'. Probable centre-stick, though side-stick controller is being investigated. Sideways-opening (to starboard), single-piece canopy. Birdproof windscreen is hinged and opens forward for maintenance. Advanced boot strap type high-pressure environmental control system is located in a compartment behind the rear pressure bulkhead. Cockpit ladder.
Crew escape: Sequence-controlled zero-zero ejection seats, with an ejection angle of 22 °.
Fixed guns: Internal gun for training and close-in combat.
Number of weapon pylons: 7, as 2 at wingtips, 4 under the wings and 1 centreline, of which 2 inboard and centreline are wet. Pylon design and stores installation conform to low RCS.
Radar: Multimode fire-control radar for AT-2000B, with range-while-scan, track-while-scan to detect up to 64 targets and track up to 6 simultaneously, and many other air-to-air and air-to-ground modes. Ranging radar for AT-2000A.
Flight/weapon system avionics/instrumentation: Each cockpit is equipped with 3 colour head-down displays. Front cockpit has a HUD, while the rear cockpit has a HUD repetition facility. All components of the mission system, including the EW system, can be housed internally. Laser rangefinder and ranging radar (instead of FCR) for AT-2000A.
Wing/fuselage characteristics: Shoulder-mounted wings of trapezoidal planform, with main structural boxes containing fuel. Vortex flow from the fuselage forebody and inlet, both with integrated chines, provide good airflow over the fuselage and wings to increase lift and improve drag-due-to-lift while assuring good lateral/directional stability and control during manoeuvres at high angles of attack. Aircraft operates with a low static longitudinal instability at subsonic speeds and low positive stability supersonically to reduce trim drag. Pitch, roll

↑ Daimler-Benz Aerospace AT-2000 Advanced Tactical Trainer impression

Details for AT-2000

PRINCIPAL DIMENSIONS:
Wing span: 26 ft 3 ins (8 m)
Maximum length: 45 ft 1 ins (13.75 m) for both single and 2-seat versions
Maximum height: 14 ft 9 ins (4.5 m)

WINGS:
Area: 270.17 sq ft (25.1 m^2)
Aspect ratio: 2.55
Sweepback: 45° on the leading edge
Anhedral/dihedral: 0°

UNDERCARRIAGE:
Type: Retractable nosewheel type, the main gear retracting forward into bays beside the air intake ducts, while the nose gear retracts forward into a bay below the front cockpit Nosewheel steering
Main wheel tyre size: 25.5 × 8-14
Nose wheel tyre size: 18 × 5.5
Wheel base: 15 ft 9 ins (4.8 m)
Wheel track: 7 ft 10.5 ins (2.4 m)

WEIGHTS:
Empty: 12,306 lb (5,582 kg)
Typical combat: 16,820 lb (7,630 kg)
Maximum take-off: 27,558 lb (12,500 kg)

PERFORMANCE:
Maximum speed: Mach 1.6+
Maximum speed at sea level: Mach 1.1
Minimum stable speed: 100 kts (115 mph) 185 km/h at combat weight
Approach speed: 110-120 kts (127-138 mph) 204-222 km/h
Climb rate: 49,200 ft (15,000 m) per minute
Roll rate: 260 ° per second
G limits: +9, -3
Operational ceiling: 50,000 ft (15,240 m)

and yaw control is provided by the integrated blend of aerodynamic control surface deflections. The elongations of the air intakes along the fuselage (named shelves) accommodate the main undercarriage gear, the gun, APU, major hydraulic components, and flaperon/taileron and airbrake actuators.
Wing control surfaces: Leading-edge flaps. Flaperons with automatic camber adjustment for drag reduction.
Tail control surfaces: All-moving, trapezoidal-configured tailplane. Conventional fin with rudder.
Airbrakes: 4, in the rear upper/lower sides of the shelves.
Flight control system: Quadruplex digital fly-by-wire. For student pilot familiarization, a selectable mode will be installed, with which the flight envelope can be restricted and accelerations and angular rates can be limited.
Construction materials: Light alloy, with carbonfibre reinforced plastics used on the wing and tailplane skins. Tailplane structure comprises a central aluminium box, with aluminium leading edges and sandwich honeycomb trailing edges. Semi-monocoque fuselage structure constructed from load-carrying stiffened skins, supported by longerons, frames and bulkheads which are made from internally stiffened machined aluminium plates. The centre fuselage contains the integral tanks and the 3 main pick-up points for the wings.
Engine: Eurojet EJ200 with variable convergent-divergent nozzle, with options of the SNECMA M88 and General Electric F-404/414. APU.
Engine rating: Nominal 20,230 lbf (90 kN) for EJ200, but can be derated to 16,860 lbf (75 kN) or dry rated at 13,500 lbf (60 kN) for training, thus increasing MTBO; an enhanced performance EJ200 would be 23,155 lbf (103 kN).
Air intakes: Pitot type, on fuselage sides, each with a splitter plate. Boundary layer diverters contain a secondary air inlet for the primary and secondary heat exchangers for the environmental control system.
Flight refuelling probe: Removable probe.
Fuel system: 5 fuselage tanks, wing tanks and 3 external tanks. Centre fuselage tank is located between the air intake ducts, acting as the feed tank, providing pressurized fuel by electric pumps mounted in a negative-g-fuel-cell. 6,283 lb (2,850 kg) of fuel in the 2-seater, with approximately 617 lb (280 kg) of additional fuel likely for the single-seater. For the light fighter aircraft, fuel tanks will be pressurized by nitrogen, provided by an on-board inert gas generating system.
Electrical system: Power generating systems are mounted on an Airframe Mounted Accessory Drive (AMAD), located in a separate compartment below the air intake ducts forward of the engine; a PTO shaft connects the AMAD with the engine drive pad. Thermal battery provides emergency power for an electro-hydraulic pump.
Hydraulic system: For flight controls, undercarriage retraction, nosewheel steering and braking. See above for AMAD.
Braking system: Hydraulically-powered main wheel braking. Arrester hook.
Oxygen system: OBOGS, integrated in the environmental control system.

Aircraft variants:
AT-2000 A is the advanced trainer without radar.
AT-2000 B is the advanced tactical trainer with fire-control radar, giving limited stores/weapon capability.
AT-2000 C is the 2-seat fighter bomber with full mission suite.
AT-2000 D is the single-seat lightweight fighter.
AT-2000 E is a single- or 2-seat reconnaissance aircraft.

RFB Rhein-Flugzeugbau GmbH — Germany

Comments: This company ceased trading on 1st October 1997. Details of its Fantrainer series and the proposed Tiro-Trainer can be found in the 1996-97 edition of *WA&SD*, pages 44-45.

Hellenic Aerospace Industry Ltd — Greece

Corporate address:
Athens Tower, Messogion 2-4, GR-115 270 Athens.
Telephone: +30 1 7799679, 7799654, 7799622 and 7799506
Facsimile: +30 1 7797670
Telex: 219528 HAI GR
Founded: 1975.
Information:
Athanasios Nezis (Chairman and Managing Director).

FACILITIES

▪ Tanagra, PO Box 23, GR-320 09 Schimatari (*telephone* +30 1 8836711, 0262-52000, *facsimile* +30 1 8838714, 0262-52170). Divided into 4 major facilities: *Aircraft* with 33 production shops and capable of supporting virtually all Western fighter, commercial, cargo and helicopter types; *Engine* with 18 shops providing inspection, repair, overhaul, modification, testing and trouble shooting services to over 23 types of engines and their components/accessories; *Electronics* (plus Electronics Manufacturing, producing parts including Hawk radar modules, Stinger missile launch tubes and grip stocks, and AIM-9P Sidewinder missile cable assemblies and upgrade kits) and *Airframe Manufacturing*.

ACTIVITIES

▪ Maintenance, overhaul and modification of fighter and commercial aircraft and helicopters, engines, aircraft and engine accessories and components, avionics, airborne and ground navigation/communication systems and equipment.
▪ Fabrication and assembly of aircraft structural parts and major assemblies, and engine parts.
▪ Manufacturing of complete electronics and telecommunications products and systems, and parts for weapon systems.
▪ Training in a wide range of aviation disciplines at HAI Training Services.
▪ Non-aviation products include an artillery laser range finder, night vision equipment, communications equipment, Hermes digital message device, and more.
▪ On 9 November 1994, DASA of Germany (Daimler-Benz Aerospace) signed an agreement with HAI covering future co-operation over civil and military programmes, defence technology and satellite communication.
▪ In 1997 HAI received a contract to perform structural work on 70 Hellenic Air Force F-4 Phantom IIs as part of a life-extension programme, to keep them in service until after the year 2015.

Aeronautical Development Agency — India

Address:
PO Box 1718, Vimanapura Post, Bangalore 560 017.
Telephone: +91 80 5233060, 5237294
Facsimile: +91 80 5238493, 5234493
Telex: 0845 8114 ADA IN
E-mail: adalib@giasbgO1.vsnl.net.in
Information:
T. Prakash, and Wg Cdr S.J. Joshi (ret'd).

ADA Light Combat Aircraft

First flight: 1998.
Role: Lightweight multi-mission tactical fighter, for close air support and capable of air defence.

Aims

▪ To replace the MiG-21s and MiG-23s in Indian service. Ajeet replacement, as originally intended for LCA, has already taken place (completed 1991 by the MiG-23). LCA is the world's smallest multi-role combat aircraft.
▪ Advanced design, using weight-saving composites materials and with an Indian-developed engine.
▪ Unstable design for high manoeuvrability, requiring computer control.
▪ Small radar signature.
▪ 3,000 hour service life. Less than 10 ground maintenance hours per flight hour.
▪ Capable of operating from paved, unpaved and grass airstrips, and in hot and high conditions.
▪ 95% mission reliability during 1 hour sorties.

↑ ADA Light Combat Aircraft TD-1 Technology Demonstrator

Development

▪ **1983.** Project started following receipt of Indian Government go-ahead. Feasibility studies were assisted by Dornier, MBB and MTU.
▪ 5 January 1985. The Scientific Adviser to the Indian Defence Ministry announced research development of the LCA at the 71st Indian Science Congress.
▪ 1990. Initial design completed, leading to the start of prototype construction by Hindustan Aeronautics Ltd in the following year.
▪ 1993. Mock-up displayed to the public at the Avia India show.
▪ 1 April 1993. The expected roll-out date for LCA was given as June 1996 at the Parliamentary Consultative Committee for Defence, 6 months ahead of schedule (see below).
▪ 1994. First test run of the Kaveri engine.
▪ 1995. LCA flight control software tested in the USA, initially by using an NT-33 and later an F-16.
▪ 17 November 1995. Roll-out of the first Technology Demonstrator TD-1. Construction of TDs by the combined efforts of 12 academic and scientific institutes and 120 companies.
▪ 1998. Flight trials began of the Kaveri engine carried by a Russian Tu-16 test aircraft.
▪ 1998. First flight of the second Technology Demonstrator .

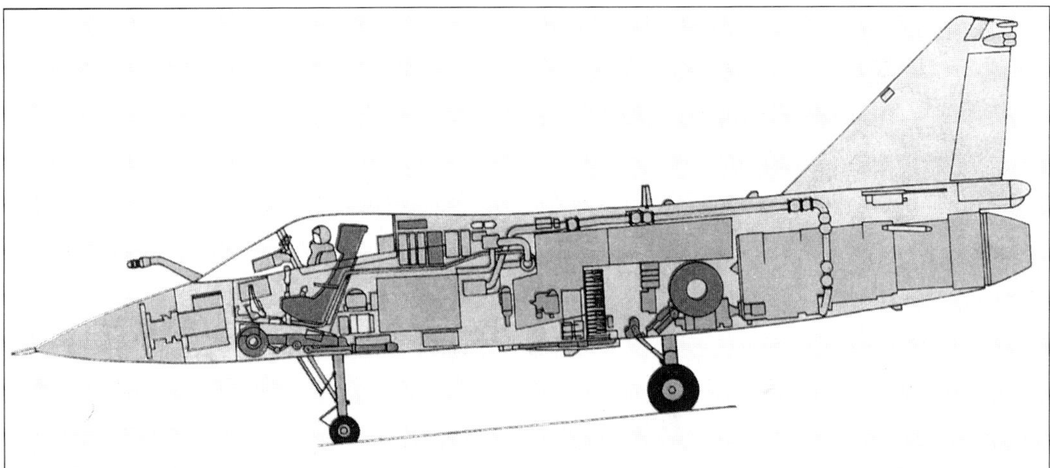

↑ **ADA LCA fuselage systems detail** *(courtesy ADA)*

▪ Late 1999. Roll out and first flight of PV-1.
▪ 2005. Probable operational capability, having gained IOC up to 3 years earlier.

Details

Sales/Users: 2 Technology Demonstrators built (TD-1 and -2), being followed by 5 prototypes (PV-1 to -3 single-seaters, and PV-4 and -5 as examples of the naval variant and 2-seat operational trainer). About 200 production aircraft required.
Crew: Pilot.
Cockpit: See Avionics.
Crew escape: Zero-zero ejection seat.
Fixed guns: 23-mm GSh-23 twin-barrel cannon.
Ammunition: 220 rounds.
Number of weapon pylons: 7 (1 under the fuselage and 6 under the wings).
Expendable weapons and equipment: Over 8,820 lb (4,000 kg), including 2 conventional cruise missiles, cluster bomb dispensers, conventional retarded bombs, laser-guided weapons, anti-ship missile, BVR and short-range AAMs, and rocket pods. Rearmament and refuelling takes under 15 minutes.
Additional stores: Various electronic pods, such as LDP, FLIR, IRST, Recce and more.
Radar: HAL multi-mode pulse-Doppler type, with look-up/look-down, track-while-scan and ground mapping.
Flight/weapon system avionics/instrumentation: Integrated avionics system includes an EFIS cockpit with collimated holographic head-up display and 2 active-matrix colour multi-function displays (MFDs), 2 × 32-bit mission computers (Ada language for mission computer software, complying with MIL-STD-1521 and -2167A) with 3 MIL-STD-1553B-standard databuses, GPS/INS with ring laser gyro, Tacan, IFF and HOTAS. Back-up LED instrumentation. V/UHF and UHF radios. Datalink. Night vision equipment will be available. FLIR and laser designator. Israel was approached to offer both hardware and technical assistance.
Self-protection systems: Radar warning receiver, jammer and chaff/flare dispenser.
Wing characteristics: Mid-to-shoulder mounted compound delta type, with varying degrees of anhedral from the roots, root slots, and considerable twist. Designed for vortex lift, to shed vortex evenly over wings to increase lift and decrease the stalling speed.
Wing control surfaces: Entire trailing-edge is taken up with 2-section elevons. 3-section leading-edge slats.
Tail control surfaces: Rudder.
Flight control system: Lockheed Martin integrated digital, quadruplex redundant fly-by-wire.
Construction materials: Carbonfibre (graphite) wings (single-piece upper and lower skins attached to wing box), elevons, tail unit, airbrakes, undercarriage doors and access panels, constituting at least 30% of the airframe (possibly being increased to 40%). Kevlar radome. Aluminium-lithium and titanium alloys.
Engine: 2 Technology Demonstrators each use a General Electric F404-F2J3 turbofan. Prototypes and production aircraft will have the Gas Turbine Research Establishment Kaveri turbofan (previously designated GTX-35VS), rated at about 11,530 lbf (51.3 kN) dry and 18,750 lbf (83.4 kN) with afterburning, incorporating a digital engine control unit known as KADECU.
Engine rating: 18,100 lbf (80.51 kN) for GE type.
Air intakes: On the fuselage sides, almost level with the wing leading edge. Fixed geometry, with splitter plates.
Flight refuelling probe: Non-retractable type (probably removable), on the starboard side of the nose.
Fuel system: Internal fuel plus up to 5 × 800 litre or larger 1,200 litre drop tanks.

Details for LCA

PRINCIPAL DIMENSIONS:
Wing span: 26 ft 11 ins (8.2 m)
Maximum length: 43 ft 4 ins (13.2 m)
Maximum height: 14 ft 5 ins (4.4 m)

WINGS:
Area: about 413.33 sq ft (38.4 m^2)
Aspect ratio: about 1.79

UNDERCARRIAGE:
Type: Retractable, with twin nosewheels
Wheel base: 14 ft 3 ins (4.34 m)
Wheel track: 7 ft 2.5 ins (2.2 m)

WEIGHTS:
Empty: 12,125 lb (5,500 kg)
Take-off: 18,739 lb (8,500 kg) without stores

PERFORMANCE:
Maximum speed: Mach 1.6
Take-off distance: 2,000 ft (610 m) from a hot and high airfield with full fuel and 5,300 lb (2,400 kg) payload
Sustained turn rate: 13-17° per second; instantaneous 30°
G limits: +9, -3.5
Ceiling: 50,000 ft (15,250 m)

Braking system: Hydraulically-actuated carbon disc type. Kevlar drag-chute in pod beneath rudder.

Aircraft variants:
LCA for the Indian Air Force and to be offered for export.
Naval variant, with a strengthened undercarriage, arrester hook, anti-corrosion materials, and a developed Kaveri engine.
MCA is a projected medium combat aircraft derivative of the LCA, with the potential of replacing Shamshers and Mirage 2000 Hs from about the year 2008. To possess stealth features, a thrust-vectoring variant of the Kaveri engine, and other changes.
2-seat training variant, with full combat capability, planned.

↑ **ADA LCA undergoing structural coupling tests** *(courtesy ADA)*

Hindustan Aeronautics Limited (HAL) — India

Corporate address:
15/1 Cubbon Road, Bangalore 560 001.
Telephone: +91 80 2866701 and 2866902 to 908
Facsimile: +91 80 2867140, 2868758, 5577533
Telex: 0845-2266
E-mail: root@bnghal.kar.nic.in
Founded:
1 October 1964, from the merger of Aeronautics India Ltd and other established manufacturing concerns.
Officiating Chairman:
Dr C.G. Krishnadas Nair (with effect from 31st July 1997).
Employees: over 34,000.
Information:
Cmdr M. Nirmal (Deputy General Manager, Public Relations – *telephone* +91 80 2868629, *facsimile* +91 80 2867140).

FACILITIES

▪ Aircraft activities are divided into 4 Complex groupings, all based in Bangalore but with individual divisions in Bangalore and elsewhere (see below).
▪ Design Complex is charged with the design of aeroplanes, helicopters, avionics and engines.

ACTIVITIES

▪ In addition to the programmes listed, HAL is co-operating internationally in the development of new regional airliners, and has established overhaul facilities for commercial jetliners.
▪ A new programme is to design a new advanced jet trainer, to replace Kiran. Maintenance work includes a 1997 contract to maintain MiG-21s of Laos.
▪ On 25 January 1993 a Memorandum of Understanding was signed between HAL and British Aerospace to establish BAeHAL Software Ltd, to manufacture and export computer software.
▪ See also Special Electronic and Helicopter sections.

COMPLEXES

ACCESSORIES
HQ address: Lucknow.

BANGALORE
HQ address: PO Box 1785, Bangalore 560 017.

DESIGN
HQ address: PO Box 1789, Bangalore 560 017.

MIG
HQ address: PO Box 5150, Bangalore 560 001.

DIVISIONS OF COMPLEXES

AIRCRAFT (part of the Bangalore Complex)
HQ address:
PO Box 1788, Bangalore 560 017.
Telephone: +91 80 5273920
Facsimile: +91 80 5593956
Telex: 845-2234 HALM IN
Activities:
▪ Jaguar/Shamsher programme.
▪ Work on the LCA tactical fighter programme (see Aeronautical Development Agency).
▪ Development of an AWACS aircraft, in co-operation with the Hyderabad Division.
▪ Component manufacturing under contract from various European and US aerospace companies.

HELICOPTER (part of the Bangalore Complex)
HQ address:
PO Box 1790 (Vimanapura), Bangalore 560 017.
Telephone: +91 80 5262924
Facsimile: +91 80 5584717
Telex: 0845-2764
Activities:
▪ Production of ALH. Also Cheetah and Chetak helicopter programmes.

Other Bangalore Complex divisions are:
Aerospace, Engine, Overhaul, and Foundry & Forge.

HYDERABAD, KANPUR, KORWA AND LUCKNOW (parts of the Accessories Complex)
HQ address: PO Box 225, Kanpur 208 008 (for Kanpur Division).
Telephone: +91 512 350361 (for Kanpur Division) **Facsimile:** +91 512 350505 (for Kanpur Division) **Telex:** 325-243 HALK IN
Activities: ▪ Radars, nav/attack systems, INS, and other avionics from Hyderabad and Korwa; Dornier 228, HPT-32 Deepak and other programmes from Kanpur; principally undercarriages from Lucknow.

KORAPUT (part of the MiG Complex)
HQ address: Sunabeda - 763 002, Koraput, Orissa.
Telephone: +91 6853 200, 891 55464 or 54376 **Facsimile:** +91 6853 304 **Telex:** 06601-206 HAL IN, 0495-248 HALE IN
Activities: ▪ Engines and spare engine parts for MiG aircraft (plus overhaul and repair), including the R-11F2 and F2S, R-25 and R-29.

NASIK (part of the MiG Complex)
HQ address: Ojhar 422 207, Maharashtra.
Telephone: +91 2533 75433, 78117 **Facsimile:** +91 2533 75825 **Telex:** 0752-241
Activities: ▪ Production of MiG-27 has ended. MiG-21 and MiG-27 overhaul programmes undertaken. Production of spares, flexible rubber fuel tanks for MiG-21s, metal drop tanks, manufacture and overhaul of ejection seats and canopies, design and manufacture of ground and role support equipment for civil and military aircraft, and more.

Aircraft Design Bureau, Helicopter Design Bureau, Engine Design Bureau and Avionics Design Bureau (parts of the Design Complex).

HAL Jaguar International Shamsher

Details *(those specifications unique to the Shamsher – see also Multi-national)*

Role: Long-range strike, tactical close air support, counter air, interdiction, reconnaissance and maritime strike. Licensed-production version of the SEPECAT Jaguar International (see also Multi-national).
Sales/Users: Following delivery to the Indian Air Force of 40 fly-away SEPECAT Jaguar Internationals built in Europe, HAL began assembly of a further 45 Shamshers (progressively with some indigenous components, including Hyderabad Division avionics), the first making its maiden flight at Bangalore on 31 March 1982 in the hands of the company's Chief Test Pilot. Subsequent manufacturing by HAL has covered a further 46, the last delivered in 1998.
Crew: Pilot.
Fixed guns: 2 × 30-mm Aden cannon in the fuselage, firing at 50 rounds per second.
Ammunition: 300 rounds total.
Number of weapon pylons: 7, as an underfuselage 'wet' centreline pylon for a large store or tandem arrangement for shorter stores, 2 pylons under each wing (the inner 'wet') and 2 over-wing launch rails for air-to-air missiles.
Expendable weapons and equipment: Maximum 8,818 lb (4,000 kg) load. See stores diagram.
Radar: Indian maritime strike Shamshers have Thomson-CSF Agave radar.
Flight/weapon system avionics/instrumentation: Navigation/attack system comprises the ultralight DARIN (Display Attack Ranging Inertial Navigation), with second generation inertial components and digital computers (specification of navigation errors is less than 1.0 nm/hour); large field of vision, high-resolution HUD with rastor facility; head-down combined map and electronic display (COMED); system computers use MIL-STD-1553B dual-redundant databus; interfaced laser ranger and marked target seeker; radio altimeter. Communications system is single main V/UHF, single standby UHF and single HF radios; ADF; and lightweight IFF.
Self-protection systems: Radar warning receiver and active/passive ECM.

↑ **Indian Air Force HAL Shamsher with rocket launchers and overwing Magic AAMs** *(Simon Watson)*

Details for Shamsher

PRINCIPAL DIMENSIONS:
Wing span: 28 ft 6 ins (8.691 m)
Maximum length: 55 ft 7.5 ins (16.955 m)
Maximum height: 15 ft 9.5 ins (4.813 m)

WINGS:
Area: 258.33 sq ft (24.003 m^2)
Aspect ratio: 3.147
Sweepback: 40° 2′ leading edge

WEIGHTS:
Empty: 15,400 lb (6,985 kg)
Normal take-off: 24,250 lb (11,000 kg)
Maximum take-off: 34,613 lb (15,700 kg)

PERFORMANCE:
Maximum speed: 906 kts (1,044 mph) 1,680 km/h above 6,000 m altitude, 648 kts (746 mph) 1,200 km/h at sea level
Take-off distance: 3,085 ft (940 m)
Landing distance: 1,542 ft (470 m)
G limits: +8, -3
Ceiling: 45,000 ft (13,715 m)
Radius of action (Lo-Lo-Lo): 270 naut miles (311 miles) 500 km
Radius of action (Hi-Lo-Hi): 375 naut miles (432 miles) 695 km

↑ **HAL Shamsher representative stores diagram** *(courtesy HAL)*

Engines: 2 Rolls-Royce Turbomeca Adour Mk 811 turbofans.
Engine rating: 5,620 lbf (25 kN) dry, 8,400 lbf (37.37 kN) with afterburning.
Fuel system: 4,171 litres in 6 centre fuselage and wing tanks, or 7,726 litres with 3 drop tanks.

HAL MiG-21 and MiG-27M

MiG-21 assembly in India began with the MiG-21FL, in November 1966, following the import of Soviet-built aircraft that went to No 28 Squadron, IAF. MiGs built entirely from Indian components were delivered from October 1970, with nearly 200 being completed by March 1974. Production subsequently centred on the MiG-21M (delivered from February 1973), followed by the MiG-21bis.

MiG-27M assembly at HAL's MiG Complex began in 1984, leading to manufacture with indigenously-built components from 1988. All production has ended.

The Nasik Division offers repair and overall facilities to the MiGs.

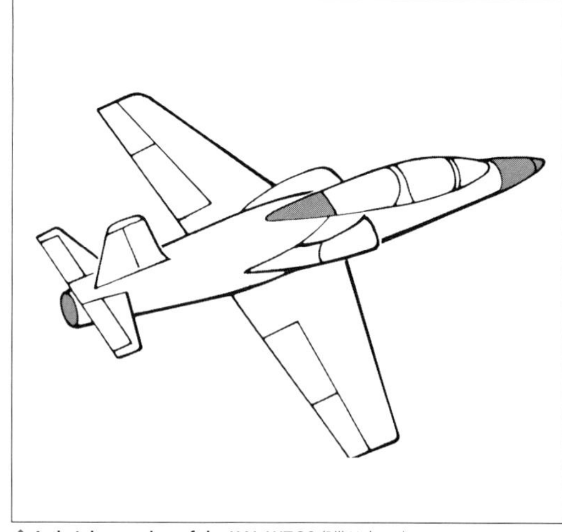

↑ **Artist's impression of the HAL HJT-36** *(Bill Hobson)*

HAL HJT-36 and HTT-38

Comments: These 2 new trainers were announced at the Singapore air show in February 1998. The side-by-side 2-seat HTT-38 is HAL's latest attempt to produce a turboprop-powered and more modern development of the piston-engined HPT-32 Deepak, and has flown in representation form as the repainted HTT-34 (itself an earlier single prototype of a turboprop Deepak). 420 shp (313 kW) Allison 250-B17D turboprop. Wing span 31 ft 2 ins (9.5 m), length 26 ft 6 ins (8.07 m), and MTOW 2,866 lb (1,300 kg). The HJT-36 is a proposed all-new single turbofan-engined, 2-seat (tandem) jet trainer and light attack aircraft (4 underwing pylons, each for 500 lb, 227 kg load), possibly to replace Indian Air Force Kirans. TOW without stores will be about 7,715 lb (3,500 kg), while wing span is expected to be about 32 ft 10 ins (10 m).

Defence Industries Organization — Iran

Reports suggest that Iran has developed an indigenous jet-powered strike fighter over an 11 year period, named **Azarakhsh** (Lightning), of which prototype trials had been completed by mid-1997 and initial production was then imminent for the Air Force. During the Zulfiqar military exercises of September 1997, a prototype is said to have released 2 bombs.

Separately, 2 military training aircraft are also thought to be in production, while a plant has been established in Isfahan for the assembly of Antonov An-140 turboprop transports from Ukrainian-supplied knock-down kits, with plans to eventually introduce indigenously manufactured components. Ilyushin Il-114s are also to be assembled in Iran, with a contract announced at the 1997 Paris Air Show, while contact has also been established with Tupolev regarding aircraft programmes and with Klimov for TV-117 turboprop engine assembly and component manufacture.

Elbit Systems Ltd — Israel

Corporate address:
Advanced Technology Center, PO Box 539, Haifa 31053.

Telephone: +972 4 8315315
Facsimile: +972 4 8550002, 8551623
Also: PO Box 650, Karmiel 20101.
Web site: http://www.elbit.co.il

Founded: 1971.

Information:
Cmdr (Ret'd) Benni Ben-Ari (Vice-President, International Marketing – *telephone* +972 4 8315504, *facsimile* +972 4 8315507).

ACTIVITIES

▪ Modernization programmes for the A-4, F-4, F-5, F-15, F-16, Kfir, L-39, Mirage and MiG-21.
▪ Integrating weapon delivery and navigation, stores management and display systems, mission computers and more.
▪ Current work includes avionics for the New IAR 99 Soim (which see).
▪ Provides ground support, test and training equipment and depot maintenance procedures.
▪ Offers the HALO advanced helicopter avionics suite for safe night-time nap-of-the-earth flying.
▪ Produces a wide range of products, including mission computers, stores management systems, modular multi-role computer, multi-function displays, integrated communication/radio navigation and identification system, digital image processing and communication system, and OPHER autonomous terminal guidance for general purpose bombs.

F-4 Phantom upgrades include Elbit avionics interface computer and missile control system, as selected for the USAF and ANG. Upgrade of the F-4-2000 weapon delivery system includes radar display processor, HUD electronic unit integration, multi-function displays, digital data link (alphanumeric video), avionics interface computer, and operational flight programmes software.

F-5 upgrades are intended to provide a multi-role fire control radar, structural modifications for new aerodynamic capabilities and life extension, electronic warfare suite, HOTAS, head-out flight, reduced pilot workload, improved weapon delivery and navigation system, up-front controls and displays, multi-function colour displays, and incorporation of com and R-nav.

F-16 avionics work has included providing advanced stores management systems (SMS) under sub-contract to Lockheed Martin, multi-function displays as a co-producer and Elbit developed fire control computers. Elbit has also participated in several Israeli Air Force programmes, integrating display and sight helmet systems (DASH), digital communications systems, and supporting the IAF's improved Operational Capability Upgrade (OCU) of F-16A/Bs.

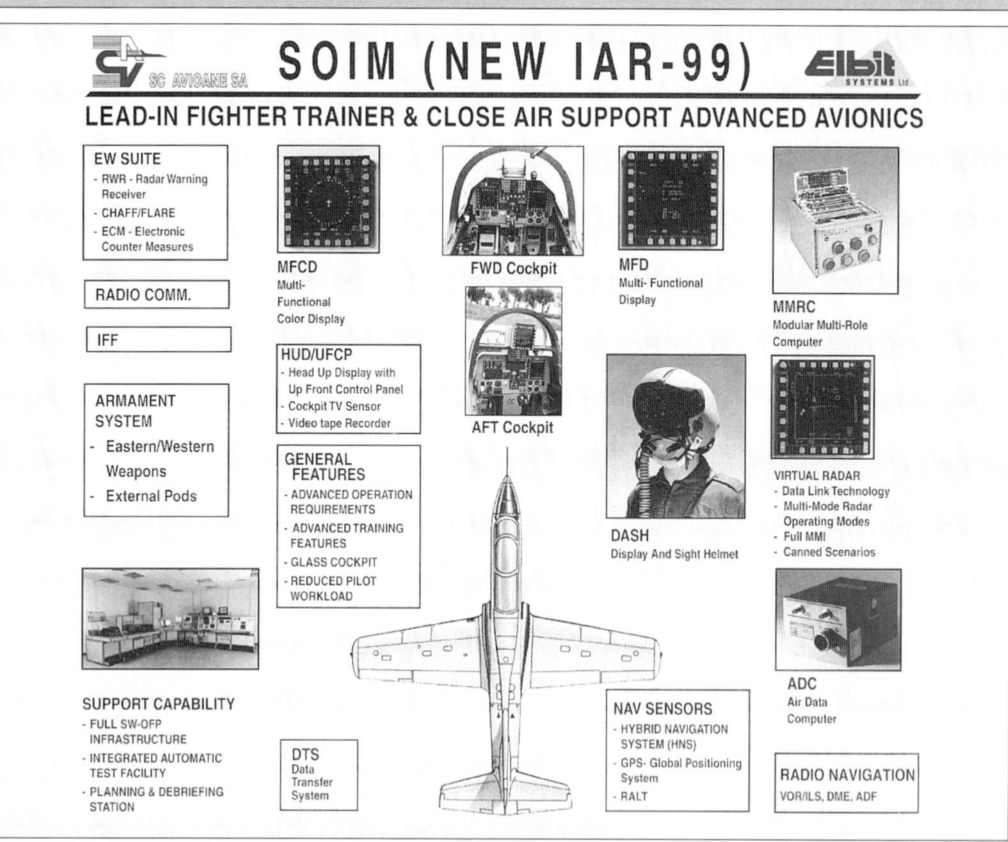

↑ **Advanced avionics suite by Elbit for the New IAR 99 Soim - see Romania** *(courtesy Avioane/Elbit)*

L-39 avionics and cockpit instrumentation upgrade is intended to provide an advanced interface system that familiarizes student pilots with a full weapon delivery and navigation system and HUD. It comprises a HUD, up-front control panel, central mission computer, ring laser gyro/inertial navigation system, video camera and VTR, and multi-function display in the rear cockpit. Additional features that can be integrated include stand-alone autonomous air combat manoeuvring instrumentation (A^2CMI), HUD projected on the pilot's visor, full display and sight helmet, and radar warning receiver.

MiG-21 step-by-step upgrades offer integration of an advanced multi-role radar for air-to-air/range radar for close air support and HUD, navigation sensors (such as INS, ring laser gyro, GPS), computerized air data centre, stores management system for computerized armament management, communications system and radio/ navigation suite, modular multi-role computer, modernized cockpit with HOTAS, advanced display and control systems (including multi-function colour displays, up-front control panel, HUD and helmet mounted display), structural improvements for extended life, enhanced reliability including advanced test equipment and simplified maintenance of aircraft systems, modern integrated briefing/debriefing capability, and experience in operational flight programme software. Elbit and Aerostar of Romania are teamed in the upgrading of Romanian Air Force MiG-21s into Lancers (see Romania). Negotiations between Elbit and Myanmar for the upgrade of 36 Chengdu F-7Ms have taken place.

Israel Aircraft Industries Ltd (IAI) Israel

Corporate address:
Ben-Gurion International Airport, 70100.

Telephone: +972 3 935 8147, 8509, 8514 and 936 8541
Facsimile: +972 3 935 8172, 8512 and 3882
Telex: 381033 ISRAV IL

Founded:
1 April 1967, from the former Bedek Aviation of 1953 founding.

Employees:
Nearly 13,000.

Information:
Doron Suslik (Director of Corporate Communication), Hadassah Paz (Corporate Communication) and Menashe Broder (Vice President of Marketing).

ACTIVITIES

■ Israel's largest aerospace concern, with operations covering a wide range of defence and communication businesses, generating an annual turnover of nearly $1.5 billion, 80% of which is derived from exports.

OPERATING GROUPS

BEDEK AVIATION GROUP

HQ address:
As above.

Telephone: +972 3 935 3743

Facsimile: +972 3 935 7066

Information:
I. Frucht (General Business Manager, Development and Marketing – *telephone* +972 3 935 3640, *facsimile* +972 3 935 3571).

Activities:
■ One-stop maintenance and modification centre for wide- and narrow-body aircraft.

COMPRISING

AIRCRAFT DIVISION

HQ address:
As above.

Telephone: +972 3 935 4930
Facsimile: +972 3 935 3571

Activities:
■ Inspection, repair, upgrading, overhaul, retrofit and conversion of commercial and military aircraft, including: Antonov An-12, An-22 and An-72P; Boeing 707, 727, 737, 747, 757 and 767; Boeing/McDonnell Douglas DC-8, DC-9, DC-10, MD-11 and MD-80; Lockheed Martin L-100 and C-130 Hercules; Airbus A300 and A310; Yakovlev Yak-42; and Tupolev Tu-134 and Tu-154; Westwind, Astra, Arava and Tzukit.
■ Conversion of B 707 and C-130 into aerial tanker/receivers; upgrade of S-2 Tracker; modification for maritime patrol (EW, sigint/comint/elint and reconnaissance); conversion of B747 into special freighter; B747 fire suppression system; B747 strut and wing structural modification and reinforcement, and structural life improvement (Sec 41);
24-hour on site airline support throughout customer network (offers tailored Power-by-the-Hour maintenance services).

ENGINE DIVISION

HQ address:
As above.

Telephone: +972 3 935 7064
Facsimile: +972 3 935 8740

Activities:
■ Overhaul, repair, retrofit, outfitting and testing of more than 30 types of civil and military engines.

COMPONENT DIVISION

HQ address:
As above.

Telephone: +972 3 935 3554
Facsimile: +972 3 935 3311

Activities:
■ Overhaul, repair, test and modification of 6,000 types of components and subsystems for civil and military aircraft.

RAMTA DIVISION

HQ address:
PO Box 323, Industrial Zone Beer-Sheva 84102.

Telephone: +972 7 627 6770
Facsimile: +972 7 627 4851

Activities:
■ Manned and unmanned combat engineering equipment, fighting and support vehicles, minefield breaching equipment, fast patrol boats, ground support equipment and aircraft structures, advanced materials, applications, design and manufacture.

COMMERCIAL AIRCRAFT GROUP

HQ address:
Ben-Gurion International Airport, 70100.

Telephone: +972 3 935 3337
Facsimile: +972 3 935 4226

Information:
Moti Boness (Corporate Vice President and General Manager).

Activities:
■ Concept definition through to prototype construction, testing and certification. Group designs and produces Westwind, Astra and Galaxy business jets. Manufacture and assembly of structures for Boeing.

COMPRISING

ENGINEERING DIVISION

HQ address: As above.

Telephone: +972 3 935 8150
Facsimile: +972 3 935 5050

Activities:
■ Flight sciences, aerodynamics and flight control; airframe design and loads analysis, structural dynamics, weight analysis and control; material and technologies metallurgy, non-metallic materials, radomes, chemistry, and non-destructive testing; mechanical systems design fluid, mechanical and environmental control systems, and turbomachinery; electrical and avionics design and simulators; CAD/CAM and computerized systems, artificial intelligence and expert systems; reliability, maintainability, etc; and test centre, wind tunnels, ground tests and flight tests.

PRODUCTION DIVISION

HQ address: As above.

Telephone: +972 3 935 3132
Facsimile: +972 3 935 3130

Activities:
■ Aircraft assembly and flight line; aerospace structures; jet engine components and nacelle manufacturing; composite structures, radomes and antenna bodies; sheet metal fabrication; metal bonding; complex machined parts; welding of exotic metals; hot forming and titanium machining; chemical processes and heat treatment; and chemical milling.

SHL DIVISION

HQ address:
PO Box 190, Industrial Zone, Lod 71101.

Telephone: +972 8 9222780
Facsimile: +972 8 9222792

Activities:
■ Design; development and manufacture of civil and military hydraulics and electromechanical systems and components; flight control actuation systems, and more.

↑ Crash repair and upgrade to F-4-2000 configuration by IAI

MILITARY AIRCRAFT GROUP

HQ address:
Ben-Gurion International Airport, 70100.

Telephone: +972 3 935 4136
Facsimile: +972 3 935 7843

Information:
M. Shmul (Corporate Vice President and General Manager).

Activities:
■ Upgrades Western and Eastern fighters, offering its **'2000'** modernization programmes to extend capabilities into the next century. These include Kfir 2000 with advanced tactical awareness and capabilities, state-of-the-art radar, BVR capability, modernized 'glass' cockpit with HOTAS, accurate weapon delivery and precision navigation.
■ Major subcontractor to Boeing and Lockheed Martin.
■ Maintains and upgrades helicopters.

COMPRISING

MALAT DIVISION

HQ address:
As above.

Telephone: +972 3 935 7349
Facsimile: +972 3 935 4175

Activities:
■ Specializes in the design, development, integration and manufacturing of UAVs and systems.

LAHAV DIVISION

HQ address:
As above.

Telephone: +972 3 935 3163, 8092
Facsimile: +972 3 935 3687, 7010

Activities:
■ Overhaul, return-to-service, modification, adaptation and all-aspects modernization of combat aircraft and trainers. Includes installation of state-of-the-art avionics and their integration with modern fire-control radars and ECM systems. Existing modernization programmes are offered for the A-4, F-4, F-5, T-38, F-15, F-16, MiG and Sukhoi types, Mirage and Kfir. Responsible for the sale of ex-Israeli Air Force aircraft. Built-to-Print work for aircraft manufacturers. Recent upgrade programmes include Turkish F-4s to '2000' standard (EL/M-2032 radar, ACE-3 type central computer, MIL-STD-1553 databus, 'glass' cockpit, GPS/INS, EW suite and more), the first of 54 re-flown in March 1997; after 32 IAI-upgraded F-4s, the remainder being modified in Turkey using kits.

MATA DIVISION

HQ address:
PO Box 27160, Industrial Zone, Jerusalem 91271.

Telephone: +972 2 584 1350
Facsimile: +972 2 584 1319

Activities:
■ Helicopter structures, systems and components maintenance, crash repair, overhaul, modification and upgrading; CAD/CAM design and production of lightweight, fire resistant electrical harnesses; and design and manufacture of helicopter/aircraft crashworthy crew and passenger seats.

ELECTRONICS GROUP

HQ address:
PO Box 105, Industrial Zone, Yahud 56100.

Telephone: +972 3 531 4021
Facsimile: +972 3 536 3975

Information:
Z. Nahmoni (Corporate Vice President and General Manager).

Activities:
■ Core capabilities in air, ground and sea radar systems, satellite design and integration, launchers, EW, advanced seekers for precision ordnance, attack UAVs, secure communications, navigation systems, stabilized electro-optical payloads, and more.

COMPRISING

TAMAM DIVISION

HQ address:
PO Box 75, Industrial Zone, Yahud 56100.

Telephone: +972 3 531 5003
Facsimile: +972 3 531 5140

Information:
Itzhak Shapira (Director, International Marketing).

Activities:
▪ Upgrades of helicopter electronics and avionics for full night combat capability; wide range of electro-optical payloads for UAVs, helicopters and aeroplanes; inertial navigation systems, and more.

MBT DIVISION

HQ address:
PO Box 105, Industrial Zone, Yahud 5600.

Telephone: +972 3 531 4005
Facsimile: +972 3 531 4130

Activities:
▪ Airborne, naval and ground systems; missiles and guided weapons; and space systems.

MLM DIVISION

HQ address:
PO Box 45, Beer-Yaakov 70350.

Telephone: +972 8 927 2425
Facsimile: +972 3 927 2890

Activities:
▪ Missile programmes (including Anti Tactical Ballistic Missile); small satellite launch vehicles (Shavit) for low Earth orbits; advanced airborne and ground-based telemetry systems; advanced communication systems; military and civil ATC display and processing systems, and Command and Control systems; photovoltaic systems, and more.

ELTA ELECTRONIC INDUSTRIES LTD DIVISION

HQ address:
PO Box 330, Ashdod 77102.

Telephone: +972 8 857 2312, 2410
Facsimile: +972 8 856 4568

Activities:
▪ Design and manufacture of military electronic systems, including radars, EW (sigint, elint, ESM, airborne self-defence, supplementary jamming, and more), communication, information and advanced technologies.

IAI Kfir C2, C7, C10 and Kfir 2000

Comments: First flown in 1973 in C1 prototype form, the Kfir was developed from the basic Mirage 5 airframe and is a multi-role tactical fighter for interception and attack. Late versions were by upgrade. Full details and a photograph can be found in the 1996-97 edition of *WA&SD*, page 49.

↑ **Colombian IAI Kfir TC7** *(P.R. Foster)*

Aeronautica Macchi Group — Italy

Corporate address:
Via Ing Paolo Foresio 1, 21040 Venegono Superiore (Varese).

Telephone: +39 0331 865910
Facsimile: +39 0331 827595

Founded:
1912 origin in the Società Anonima Nieuport-Macchi.

ACTIVITIES

▪ Holding company to Aermacchi (see below), CIRA, Logic SpA (an avionics company; Via Brescia 29, 20063 Cernusco sul Naviglo, MI), Nuova Orione SpA, and SICAMB SpA (a joint-venture with Martin Baker producing ejection seats, crashworthy helicopter seats, and aerostructures including participation in MB-339, AMX, Atlantique, ATR 42, Airbus, MD-11 and Falcon programmes; Via Eschido 1, 04100 Latina).

Aermacchi SpA — Italy

Corporate address:
As for Aeronautica Macchi.

Telephone: +39 0331 813111
Facsimile: +39 0331 813152, 827595

Employees: 1,700

Information:
Viviana Brughera (Marketing Department).

ACTIVITIES

▪ Leading company of the Group, with 2,949,310 sq ft (274,000 m^2) of total airfield/plant area, including 1,205,557 sq ft (112,000 m^2) of covered area and a 1,540 m × 60 m runway.
▪ Apart from the aircraft detailed below, Aermacchi is involved in the Alenia G222 (wing and tailplane), AMX, Dassault Atlantic/Atlantique 2 (flap rails, flight control supports and wing leading-edges), Eurofighter (wing pylons, twin missile carrier, twin store carrier, ECM pods, carbonfibre structures and titanium engine cowlings), Tornado (wing roots, trailing-edges, flaps, wing tips, and wing-mounted swinging pylons) and Yak/Aem-130 programmes.
▪ In February 1996 it signed an agreement with Valmet of Finland, allowing the transfer of production and worldwide sales rights in the RediGO to Aermacchi, now known as the M-290TP RediGO.
▪ In January 1997, Aermacchi took over SIAI Marchetti and thereby acquired all the manufacturing programmes of that company, with the exception of the Canguro transport, including support of out-of-production aircraft and training programmes. Activities involving former SIAI Marchetti aircraft are undertaken at Venegono.
▪ Under an original contract with Daimler-Benz Aerospace, Aermacchi was made responsible for the design and production of the front fuselage of the Dornier (now Fairchild Dornier) 328 airliner and for assembly of the pressurized fuselage.
▪ Among the latest business areas is the production of engine nacelles, including for the Dassault Falcon 900 and 2000, and Airbus A320, A321 and A330.
▪ Has produced test benches to service Tornado and Eurofighter hydraulic systems, designed/qualified firewall bulkheads for rocket booster engines of Ariane 4, and conducts other non-aerospace activities.

↑ **Aermacchi MB-339FD, remaining the offered advanced export version**

Aermacchi MB-339 series

First flight: 12 August 1976 in MB-339X prototype form.
Role: Primary, basic and advanced trainer, lead-in fighter trainer, light attack, aerobatic display and radio calibration.
Fatigue life: Demonstrated 10,000 hours for MB-339C.

Aims

▪ Modern replacement for the MB-326 series.
▪ 12,000 flying hours, 24,000 landings, structural life for the MB-339A.

Development

▪ 20 May 1977. First flight of the second MB-339X prototype.
▪ 20 July 1978. First flight of a production MB-339A, entering service with the Italian Air Force in August that year.
▪ 17 December 1985. First flight of a more powerful MB-339C.
▪ October 1989. A teaming agreement was signed between Aermacchi and Lockheed (LASC) to prepare a missionized version of the MB-339A for entry in the USAF's JPATS competition. Rolls-Royce officially joined the team in 1990, followed by Textron Aerostructures in mid-1993.
▪ May 1992. An MB-339A demonstrator was delivered to Lockheed's Marietta facility for the JPATS competition. Not selected.
▪ September 1994. Aermacchi, Hawker de Havilland and Honeywell Australia signed a Memorandum of Understanding to co-operate in proposing the MB-339FD as a replacement for the MB-326H in the RAAF's Project Air 5367 lead-in fighter trainer programme. Not selected.
▪ 12 April 1996. Roll-out of the MB-339CD prototype, with the first flight 12 days later.
▪ December 1996-1998. Delivery of CDs to the Italian Air Force.

Details

Sales/Users: Some 208 delivered, to Argentina (Navy, 10 As), Dubai (7 As), Eritrea (6 CEs), Ghana (4 As), Italy (122, including 19 delivered to the Frecce Tricolori display team, and 15 MB-339CDs), Malaysia (13 As), New Zealand (18 CBs), Nigeria (12 As) and Peru (16 As). FD ordered by Venezuela in mid-1998.
Crew: 2, with rear instructor's seat raised by 12.8 ins (32.5 cm).
Cockpit: See Avionics.
Crew escape: Martin Baker IT10F, or MK IT10LK on CB, CD and FD, zero-zero ejection seats.
Fixed guns: None.
Number of weapon pylons: 6 under the wings, outboard pylons for up to a 750 lb (340 kg) load each and 4 inner pylons for up to 1,000 lb (454 kg) load each. Centre pylon on each wing is wet for a drop tank.
Expendable weapons and equipment: Many combinations up to 4,500 lb (2,040 kg) for the MB-339A and 4,000 lb (1,815 kg) for MB-339C, CD and FD. Cannon and machine-gun options include 2 Aermacchi pods each with a 12.7-mm Browning M-3 gun and 350 rounds of ammunition or 30-mm DEFA 553 cannon and 125 rounds (each weighing 251 lb, 114 kg and 551 lb, 250 kg respectively), or 6 General Electric SUU-11 Minigun pods each with a 7.62-mm gun and 1,500 rounds (each weighing about 325 lb, 147 kg). Many rocket pod options include 6 Aerea AL-12-80 (each 12 × 81-mm rockets), 6 Aerea AL-18-50 (each 18 × 50-mm rockets), 6 Aerea AL-25-50 (each 25 × 50-mm rockets), 6 Bristol Aerospace LAU launchers (each 7 × 2.75-ins, or 4 × 5-ins, or 6 × 70-mm rockets), 6 Matra launchers (each 18 × 68-mm) or 6 Matra F2 launchers (6 × 68-mm), or 4 TB launchers (each 4 × 100-mm). Missile choices include 2 Magic or Sidewinder air-to-air missiles, Marte Mk-2A anti-ship or AGM-65 Maverick air-to-surface (MB-339C/CD/FD). Other weapon options include 4 × 1,000 lb or 6 × 750 lb general purpose bombs, 6 TBA multi-bomb carriers (each with 6 × BAP 100 airfield attack penetration or BAT-120 anti-tank fragmentation bombs), or 6 dispensers for combinations of bombs and rockets or bombs and flares.

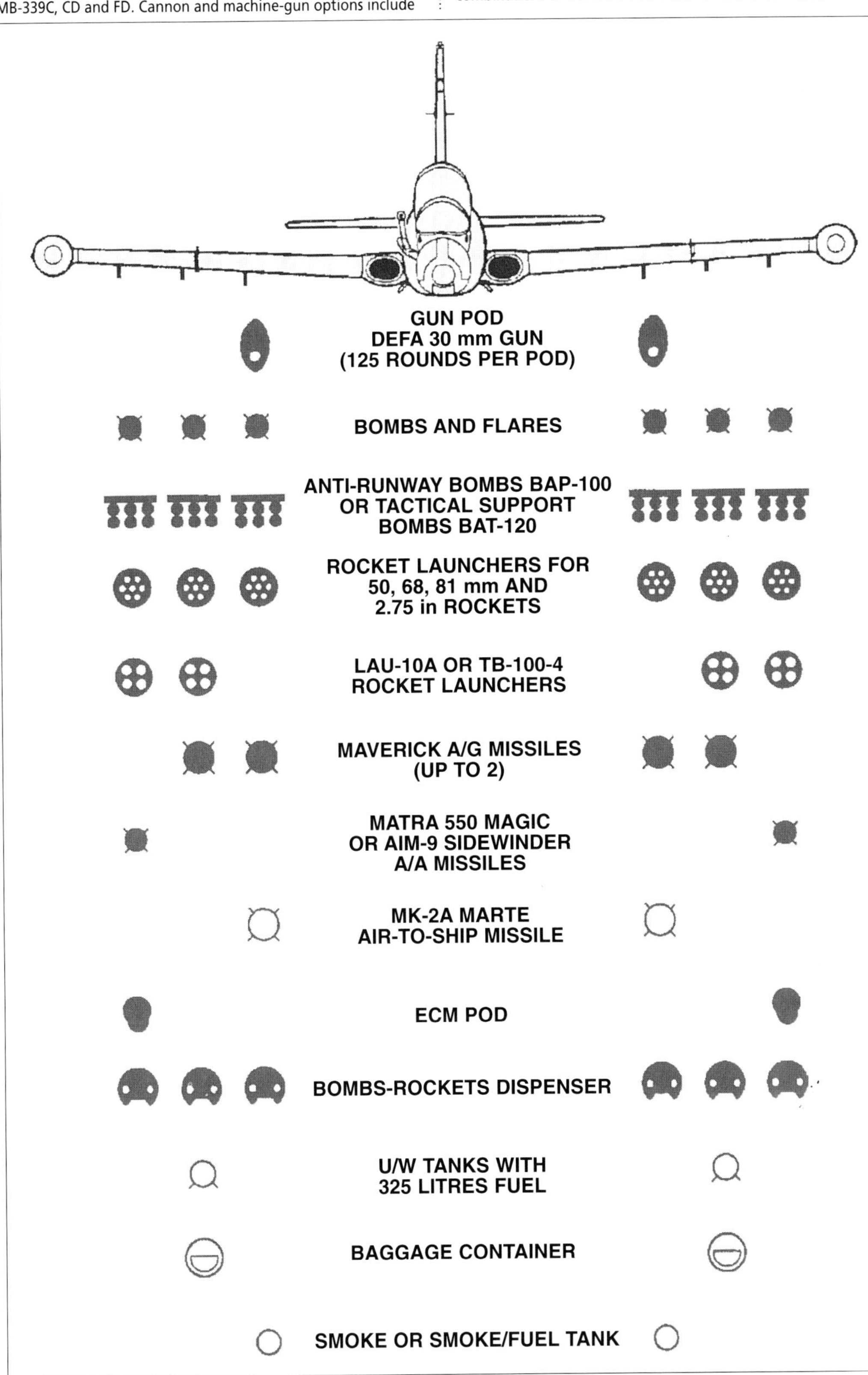

↑ **Typical Aermacchi MB-339 CD/FD stores arrangement** *(courtesy Aermacchi)*

Additional stores: Optional pod with 4 × 70-mm Vinten cameras. See also Avionics and Self-protection.
Radar: MB-339AM carries Doppler radar.
Flight/weapon system avionics/instrumentation: IFR, including Tacan or DME, VOR/ILS, ADF and marker beacon receiver. GEC-Marconi 620C navigation computer in the MB-339A, or 620K in the C which also has inertial reference unit, digital nav/attack system with navigation computer and weapon-aiming computer, HUD, HOTAS, monochrome MFD, stores management system, RWR, ECM, and laser rangefinder. MB-339FD and CD have HOTAS, 3 liquid-crystal multi-function displays in each cockpit, ring laser gyro platform with embedded GPS, powerful mission processor which acts as the main bus controller, HUD in each cockpit, radio navigation systems, air data computer, stores management system, radar altimeter, laser rangefinder, and data recording system; digital data transfer in accordance with MIL-STD-1553B using dual redundant data bus. FLIR and NVG in FD/CD.
Self-protection systems: ELT-156 RWR, ELT-555 ECM pod and ALE-40 chaff/flare dispenser in MB-339C/CD/FD.
Wing characteristics: Straight, low mounted, with fixed tiptanks (2 sizes). 1 upper-surface fence on each wing.
Wing control surfaces: Ailerons (with balance tabs) and single-slotted flaps.
Tail control surfaces: Elevators and rudder, all with balance/trim tabs. Outward-canted shallow ventral fins under the rear fuselage.
Airbrake: Under the mid-fuselage.
Flight control system: Mechanical, with hydraulically-actuated aileron servos and flaps. Electro-hydraulic airbrake. Electrically actuated tabs.

Details for MB-339 series

PRINCIPAL DIMENSIONS:
Wing span: 35 ft 5 ins (10.8 m) for MB-339A, 32 ft 10 ins (10 m) for A (PAN), 36 ft 10 ins (11.22 m) for C/CD/FD over tip-tanks
Maximum length: 36 ft (10.972 m) for MB-339A/A (PAN), 36 ft 10.5 ins (11.24 m) for C/CD/FD
Maximum height: 13 ft 1 ins (3.994 m) for all versions

WINGS:
Aerofoil section: Modified NACA 64A-114 and 64A-212 (tip)
Area: 207.743 sq ft (19.3 m^2)
Aspect ratio: 6.04 for A, 6.52 for C/CD/FD
Sweepback: 11° 18' leading-edge
Dihedral: From roots

UNDERCARRIAGE:
Type: Retractable, with steerable nosewheel
Main wheel tyre size: 545 × 175 mm
Nose wheel tyre size: 380 × 150 mm
Wheel base: 14 ft 4 ins (4.369 m)
Wheel track: 8 ft 2 ins (2.483 m)

WEIGHTS:
Empty, operating: 6,890 lb (3,125 kg) for MB-339A, 7,560 lb (3,430 kg) for MB-339C, 7,527 lb (3,414 kg) for FD
Clean take-off: 11,089 lb (5,030 kg) for FD
Maximum take-off: 13,007 lb (5,900 kg) for MB-339A/A (PAN), 14,000 lb (6,350 kg) for C/CD/FD

PERFORMANCE:
Maximum operating Mach number (M_{MO}): Mach 0.85
Maximum speed: 484 kts (557 mph) 897 km/h for MB-339A/A (PAN), 486 kts (559 mph) 900 km/h for C, and 497 kts (572 mph) 920 km/h for CD and FD
Stall speed: 81 kts (93 mph) 149 km/h for MB-339A, 85 kts (98 mph) 157 km/h for C
Approach speed at 50 ft (15 m) obstacle: 102 kts (118 mph) 190 km/h for FD
Take-off distance: 3,002 ft (915 m) at gross weight for MB-339A, 1,610 ft (490 m) for C at 10,983 lb (4,982 kg) weight with no external weapons/pods/equipment, 1,805 ft (550 m) clean for FD, at sea level
Landing distance: 1,365 ft (415 m) for MB-339A at gross weight, 1,510 ft (460 m) for C, 1,575 ft (480 m) for FD, at above conditions, sea level
Maximum climb rate: 6,600 ft (2,010 m) per minute for MB-339A, 7,100 ft (2,160 m) for C, 6,890 ft (2,100 m) for FD, at sea level
G limits: +8, -4, or +7.33, -4 for FD
Maximum sustained turn rate: 12° per second at 15,000 ft (4,570 m) for FD
Instantaneous turn rate: 20° per second with 2 Sidewinder AAMs, at 15,000 ft (4,570 m) for FD
Ceiling: 48,000 ft (14,630 m) for MB-339A, 46,720 ft (14,240 m) for C, 46,000 ft (14,020 m) for FD
Range with full internal fuel: 950 naut miles (1,094 miles) 1,759 km for MB-339A

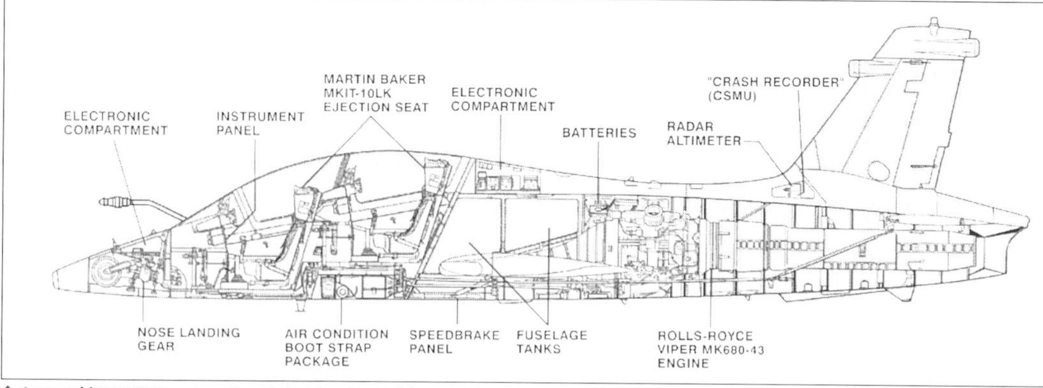

↑ Aermacchi MB-339FD systems layout *(courtesy Aermacchi)*

Construction materials: Metal, with stressed wing and tail skins strengthened by lateral stringers.
Engine: Rolls-Royce Viper 632-43, built by Rinaldo Piaggio SpA. Similar engine for MB-339A (PAN). MB-339C, CD and FD have 4,400 lbf (19.57 kN) Viper 680-43.
Engine rating: 3,970 lbf (17.66 kN) for Mk 632-43.
Air intakes: In the leading edges of the wing roots.
Flight refuelling probe: MB-339FD and CD have a detachable probe; in-flight refuelling probe has become optional on other models.
Fuel system: 1,413-1,781 litres, including tiptanks. 2 drop tanks, each 325 litres capacity. Fuel weight 3,453 lb (1,430 kg) internal and 1,151 lb (522 kg) external for FD.
Electrical system: 28 volt DC supply with 2 engine-driven starter-generators (15 kW total for CD/FD). 2 ni-cd batteries for engine start-up. 2 single-phase static inverters for AC supply.
Hydraulic system: 2,500 psi. Dual circuits, main for ailerons, flaps, airbrake, undercarriage, nosewheel steering and wheel brakes, with accumulator and variable-flow engine-driven pump; and emergency circuit for the nitrogen accumulator, undercarriage and wheel brakes.
Braking system: Hydraulic disc, with anti-skid system.
Oxygen system: Gaseous.

Aircraft variants:
MB-339A is the standard advanced trainer version, capable of light ground attack. Also included are 3 ex-Radiomisure radio calibration aircraft originally used by the Italian Air Force.
MB-339AM is the anti-shipping version, qualified to carry Marte Mk-2A missiles and with upgraded avionics including radar. Test aircraft was an Italian Air Force MB-339A modified to C standard, with trials in collaboration with the force's Experimental Test Centre.
MB-339A (PAN) is the Italian Air Force's aerobatic display team version.
MB-339B was a demonstrator with a 4,400 lbf (19.57 kN) Viper 680 engine and higher-capacity tip tanks.
MB-339C is the advanced and fighter lead-in trainer version, also for light attack, with enhanced avionics (see Avionics). Uprated Viper 680-43 engine.
MB-339CB is the Royal New Zealand Air Force version of C.
MB-339CD is a version of the FD for the Italian Air Force.
MB-339CE is a version of C for Eritrea.
MB-339FD (Full Digital) is the advanced version for export. Originally intended to meet the Royal Australian Air Force's Project Air 5367 Lead-In Fighter requirement but was not chosen. Uses some new materials, new manufacturing technologies (cold working) and different weight distribution coupled with the installation of a strain counter system for expanded life monitoring. Offered to other nations.
T-Bird II was the version for the USAF/USN JPATS competition with Viper 680-582 engine. Not selected.

Aermacchi M-290TP RediGO

First flight: 1 July 1986 as Valmet L-90TP RediGO.
Role: Military and commercial screening, primary and basic training, plus liaison, light transport, medevac, target towing, coastal patrol, SAR, reconnaissance, FAC and light attack.
Fatigue life: 10,000 flight hours and 30,000 landings.

Aims

- Fully aerobatic multirole aircraft, certified to FAR-23.
- Can operate from semi-prepared airstrips.

Details

Sales/Users: Original Valmet RediGOs delivered to Eritrea (8), Finland (10) and Mexico (Navy, 10), with production ending in 1995. Available from Aermacchi since 1996.
Crew: Up to 4 persons (see Aircraft variants). Dual controls.
Cockpit: Rearward-sliding, single-piece, jettisonable canopy. 5-point harnesses for front seats, able to withstand 25g longitudinal and 4g lateral deceleration. 4-point harnesses for rear seats. Baggage shelf of 3.18 cu ft (0.09 m^3) and 88 lb (40 kg) capacity. Heating, ventilation and air conditioning.
Crew escape: Optional zero-zero seats.
Number of weapon pylons: 6 under wings, inner stressed to 551 lb (250 kg), middle/outer to 331 lb (150 kg).
Expendable weapons and equipment: Up to 1,764 lb (800 kg), comprising gun pods, rocket launchers or other weapons.
Additional stores: Special surveillance kit for coastal patrol, with an underwing radar pod (see Avionics).
Radar: See above and below.
Flight/weapon system avionics/instrumentation: Typically 2 VHF communications, with an optional UHF. Radio assisted navigation using VOR/DME/MKR and ADF systems. Tacan and ILS. Relevant information presented to crew through the horizontal situation indicators (HSIs) and radio magnetic indicator (RMI). DME data is provided on a dedicated liquid crystal display. Transponder. Gyro compass system for attitude and direction, shown on the attitude and direction indicators (ADIs), HSIs and turn and slip indicators. All navigation instruments are installed on both sides of the panel. Optional Bendix/King RDR 1400C Colorvision weather radar and a special starboard instrument panel with CRT.
Wing control surfaces: Single-slotted flaps and Frise-type ailerons. Gear/trim tabs.
Tail control surfaces: Horn-balanced elevator and rudder, with gear/trim tabs.
Flight control system: Cable actuated.
Construction materials: Fail-safe. Semi-monocoque fuselage, with frames, stringers and riveted skins. Wings have main and auxiliary spars, ribs, stringers and riveted stressed skin. Aluminium alloy main structure, with CFRP composites for the engine cowling, dorsal fin, wing fillets, wingtips and other non-structural components. Metal control surfaces. Steel tube windshield frame in case of overturn.
Engine: Allison 250-B17F turboprop, with 7 ft 2.4 ins (2.194 m) diameter 3-blade constant-speed Hartzell HC-B3TF-7A/T 10173-15 propeller. Intake and propeller have anti-icing heating system.
Engine rating: 450 shp (335.6 kW).
Fuel system: 4 tanks (2 in each wing), plus collector tank that acts as inverted flight tank (maximum 30 seconds) with about 9 litres capacity. 348 litres usable internal fuel, plus optionally 2 × 80 litre auxiliary tanks.
Electrical system: 28 V DC, using engine-driven 200 A starter-generator. 23 amp-hour ni-cd battery for back-up and engine starting. For safety, an emergency battery powers a dedicated bus bar for essential circuits.
Braking system: Main differential brakes using toe pedals, and parking.
Oxygen system: Optional.

Aircraft variants:
Trainer can typically fly 2 consecutive sorties without refuelling, each (with 2 crew) a 30 naut mile flight to an altitude of 6,000 ft (1,830 m) and incorporating manoeuvres (including 2 touch and go), at 2,976 lb (1,350 kg) take-off weight (clean), with 441 lb (200 kg) of fuel and 15 minutes reserves.
Light attack (anti-guerrilla) missions can be flown at a cruise speed of 170 kts and 10,000 ft (3,050 m) altitude, at a combat radius of 200 naut miles with 10 minutes over target, with the pilot only, at a take-off weight of 4,118 lb (1,868 kg), including 608 lb (276 kg) of fuel (20 minutes reserves), 2 rocket launchers and 2 × 12.7-mm gun pods.
Coastal patrol version can accommodate the pilot and a radar specialist, able to patrol 108 naut miles from the coast for about 3 hours at a cruise speed of 130 kts. With a 12.7-mm machine-gun pod and 2 underwing fuel tanks, the mission can be extended to 5 hours, at 3,928 lb (1,782 kg) take-off weight, with 904 lb (210 kg) of fuel and 20 minutes reserves.
Light transport arrangement has the rear seats removed, enabling 441 lb (200 kg) of freight to be carried in a 35.3 cu ft (1 m^3) space.
Medevac version has rear starboard seat removed and front starboard seat reclined, to accommodate a litter and nurse. Life support equipment can be stowed above the baggage compartment.
Search and rescue version carries a searchlight and up to 5 survival pods on the underwing pylons.

↑ Aermacchi M-290TP RediGO

Basic details for RediGO

PRINCIPAL DIMENSIONS:
Wing span: 34 ft 9 ins (10.6 m)
Maximum length: 28 ft (8.53 m)
Maximum height: 10 ft 6 ins (3.2 m)

WINGS:
Aerofoil section: NACA 63-218 mod at root, 63-412 mod at tip
Area: 159.09 sq ft (14.78 m^2)
Aspect ratio: 7.602
Dihedral: 6°
Incidence: 3°

UNDERCARRIAGE:
Type: Retractable, with self-aligning nosewheel; electro-hydraulic actuation
Main wheel tyre size: 6.00-6
Nose wheel tyre size: 5.00-5
Wheel base: 6 ft 11 ins (2.11 m)
Wheel track: 11 ft (3.365 m)

WEIGHTS:
Empty: 2,138 lb (970 kg)
Maximum take-off: 2,976 lb (1,350 kg) for aerobatics, 3,527 lb (1,600 kg) normal, 4,189 lb (1,900 kg) with external stores

PERFORMANCE:
Maximum operating speed (V_{MO}): 224 kts (258 mph) 415 km/h CAS
Maximum speed: 190 kts (218 mph) 352 km/h at 10,000 ft (3,050 m) aerobatic weight
Cruise speed: 176 kts (202 mph) 326 km/h, at 75% power, normal weight and 10,000 ft (3,050 m)
Stall speed: 50 kts (58 mph) 93 km/h aerobatic, 56 kts (65 mph) 104 km/h normal weight, both with *full flaps*
Take-off distance: 492 ft (150 m) aerobatic, 702 ft (214 m) normal weight
Landing distance: 597 ft (182 m) aerobatic, 712 ft (217 m) normal weight
Climb rate: 2,280 ft (696 m) per minute aerobatic, 1,821 ft (555 m) normal weight
G limits: +7, -3.5 aerobatic
Ceiling: 25,000 ft (7,620 m) aerobatic, 20,800 ft (6,340 m) normal weight
Range: 755 naut miles (870 miles) 1,400 km, aerobatic weight
Ferry range: 1,020 naut miles (1,174 miles) 1,890 km at 140 kts cruise and 20,000 ft (6,100 m), at 3,563 lb (1,616 kg) TOW, with 890 lb (404 kg) of fuel (including 2 external tanks) and 45 minutes reserves
Duration: 5 hours 55 minutes normal weight

Aermacchi S211A

First flight: 10 April 1981 in SIAI Marchetti S211 prototype form; 1992 for S211A.
Role: Trainer (fully aerobatic) and light ground attack.
Fatigue life: 14,400 flying hours structural life.

Development

- 1984. Delivery of S211s to Singapore in component form began in November. Assembly by a subsidiary of Singapore Aircraft Industries (now Singapore Technologies Aerospace) allowed

delivery to the Republic of Singapore Air Force from 1985.
▪ 1992. First flight of the S211A, and delivery of the first of 2 aircraft to Grumman of the USA for the JPATS competition. Not selected.
▪ 1997. Became part of the Aermacchi range, with take over of SIAI Marchetti.

Details

Sales/Users: Deliveries to Philippines (24 S211/S211A) and Singapore (30 S211). All those for Singapore and the majority for the Philippines were assembled/built locally. Haiti received 4 but these were given up and sold to civil owners in the USA.
Crew: 2, with instructor's rear seat raised by 11 ins (28 cm). 15° downward view over the nose from the front cockpit. 5° downward view over the front cockpit seat from the rear cockpit, and 20° forwards beneath the canopy frame.
Cockpit: Integration of freon cycle for cooling with engine bleed air for heating and cockpit pressurization (max differential 3.5 psi). The second JPATS S211A was given an EFIS cockpit layout (see Aircraft variants).
Crew escape: Martin Baker Mk 10 zero-zero ejection seats.
Fixed guns: Uses a detachable 12.7-mm gun pod under the fuselage.
Number of weapon pylons: 4 under the wings, plus an underfuselage centreline position for the gun pod or ferry pod. Inner wing pylons for 551 lb (250 kg) or 772 lb (350 kg) loads, outer for 551 lb (250 kg) loads.
Expendable weapons and equipment: Up to 1,455 lb (660 kg). See diagram for weapon options.
Radar: Capable of having Doppler radar.
Flight/weapon system avionics/instrumentation: Different equipment, according to requirements. Typically VHF/UHF com; AHRS (HSI, ADI), ADF, VOR-ILS/Tacan navigation; ATC/IFF. Capable of having a wide-angle head-up display and ISIS D-211 optical weapon aiming system.
Self-protection systems: Optional radar warning system and ECM.
Wing characteristics: Shoulder-mounted, swept back, with anhedral. Upper surface fences on the leading edge, above the outer pylon positions.
Wing control surfaces: Ailerons and Fowler type flaps.
Tail control surfaces: Variable incidence tailplane, horn-balanced elevators (with tabs) and horn-balanced rudder.
Airbrakes: Under the fuselage.
Flight control system: Push-pull rod primary controls, boosted ailerons, electrically operated flaps and 3-axis trims, and hydraulically operated airbrake.

Details for S211A

PRINCIPAL DIMENSIONS:
Wing span: 27 ft 11 ins (8.51 m)
Maximum length: 31 ft 3 ins (9.53 m)
Maximum height: 12 ft 3 ins (3.73 m)

WINGS:
Aerofoil section: Modified GAW-1
Area: 135.63 sq ft (12.6 m^2)
Aspect ratio: 5.67
Sweepback: 15° 30′ at 25% chord
Chord at root: 7 ft 1 ins (2.151 m)
Chord at tip: 3 ft 3 ins (1 m)
Anhedral: 2°

TAIL UNIT:
Tailplane span: 13 ft (3.96 m)

UNDERCARRIAGE:
Type: Retractable, with steerable nosewheel. Optional powered nosewheel steering
Wheel base: 13 ft 2 ins (4.02 m)
Wheel track: 7 ft 6 ins (2.29 m)

WEIGHTS:
Empty: 4,475 lb (2,030 kg)
Maximum take-off: 6,393 lb (2,900 kg) trainer, 8,267 lb (3,750 kg) armed

PERFORMANCE (trainer at take-off weight, clean, ISA):
Maximum dive speed: Mach 0.8
Maximum speed: 414 kts (477 mph) 767 km/h at 25,000 ft (7,620 m)
Stall speed: 88 kts (102 mph) 163 km/h, *full flaps*
Take-off distance: 1,450 ft (440 m)
Landing distance: 1,362 ft (415 m)
Maximum climb rate: 4,920 ft (1,500 m) per minute
G limits: +7, -3.5; sustained at sea level 4.2; sustained at 15,000 ft (4,570 m) 3.0
Ceiling: 42,000 ft (12,800 m)
Duration: 4 hours 15 minutes, with 10% reserve

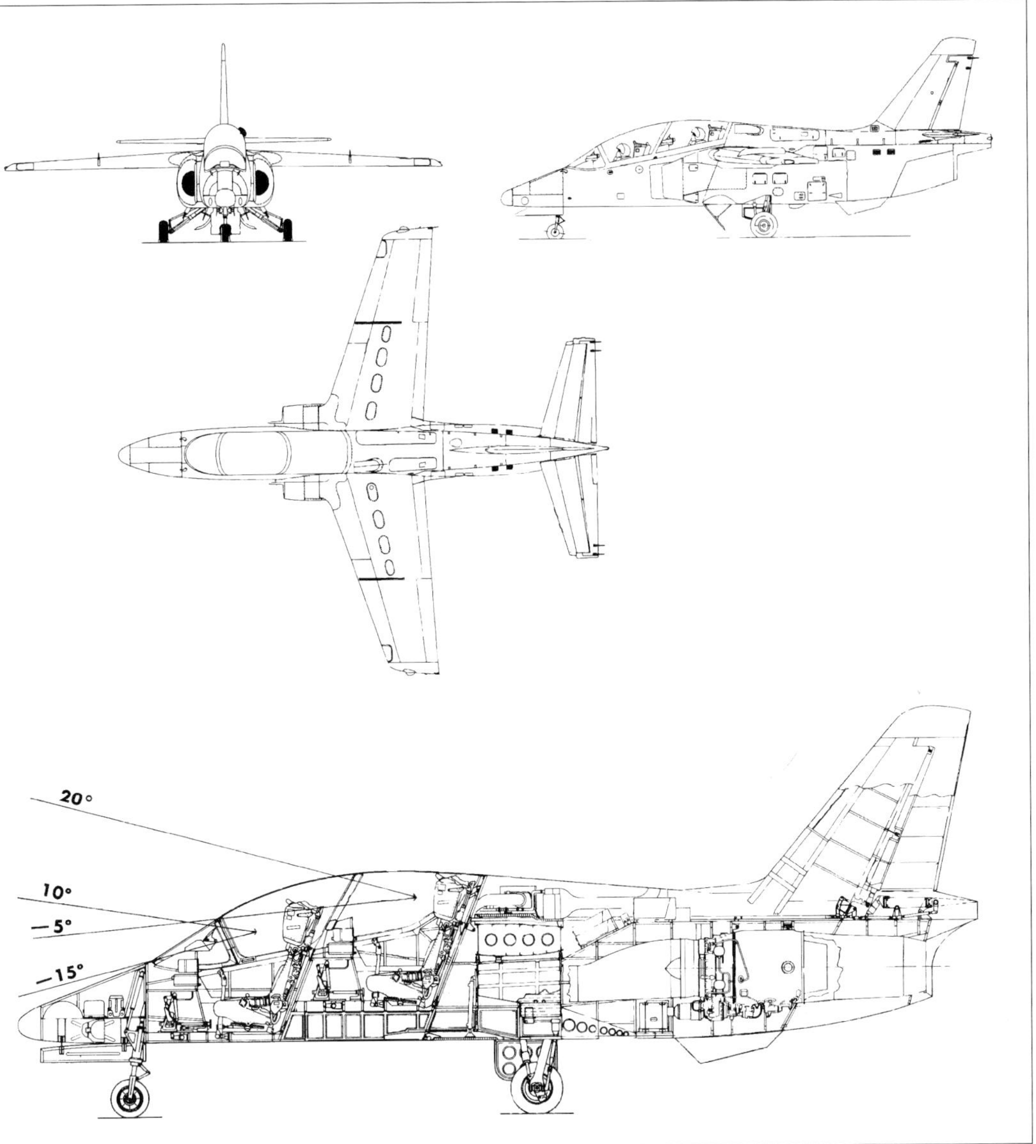

↑ **Aermacchi S211A arrangements** *(courtesy Aermacchi)*

Construction materials: Wide use of structural bonding and composite materials (Kevlar, Nomex and carbonfibre). Metal wings, with one-piece skins.
Engine: Pratt & Whitney Canada JT15D-5C turbofan.
Engine rating: 3,190 lbf (14.19 kN) at take-off.
Air intakes: Ahead of, and below, the wings. Splitter plates.
Flight refuelling probe: Not fitted.
Fuel system: Integral wing tank and fuselage sump, with total capacity of 893 litres. 2 ejection pumps used for fuel transfer from wing to fuselage tank and for engine feed. Electric fuel pump for engine starting and emergency conditions. Refuelling by gravity via a single point in the wing. Provision for 2 × 270 litre drop tanks. Optional pressure refuelling system.
Electrical system: 28 volt DC negative ground system powered by an engine-driven starter-generator. Ni-cd battery for engine starting and operation in emergency conditions. 2 static inverters for the AC supply for the instruments and avionics.

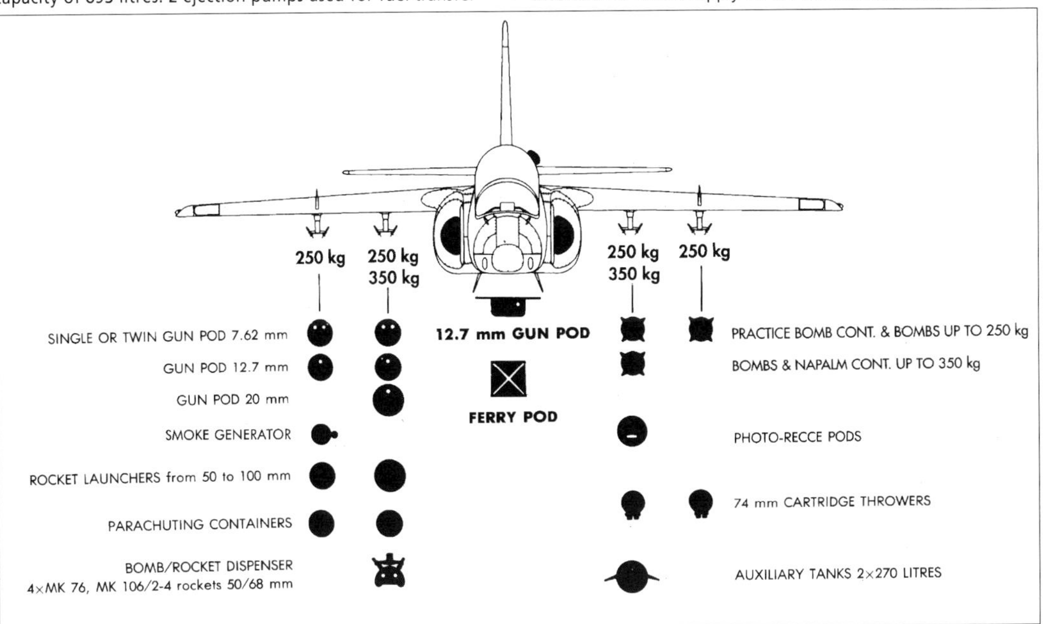

↑ **Aermacchi S211A stores options** *(courtesy Aermacchi)*

↑ **Philippine Air Force Aermacchi S211/211A of 7 Fighter Squadron, 5 Fighter Wing photographed at Basa in September 1997** *(Denis Hughes)*

Hydraulic system: 3,000 psi. For undercarriage, airbrake, freon compressor and aileron booster.
Braking system: Hydraulically actuated.

Aircraft variants:
S211 was the initial version, generally similar to the described S211A but with a 2,500 lbf (11.12 kN) JT15D-4C engine providing lower performance, 800 litres of fuel, and different supercritical wing section.
S211A is the current version, as described.

Aermacchi SF260E/F and SF260TP

First flight: 15 July 1964 in SF250 prototype form.
Role: Fully aerobatic primary military/civil trainer (SF260E/F), armed trainer capable of light attack (SF260E/F Warrior), and turboprop trainer/attack aircraft (SF260TP). Typical training syllabus covers proficiency, solo, aerobatic, instrument, night, formation and navigation.
Fatigue life: ST260TP based on a safe-life philosophy of 8,000 flying hours/20 years, and corresponding to relevant FAA regulations integrated with MIL-A-8866 specifications.

Aims

- Latest available versions of the SF260 series (see Aircraft variants)
- SF260E/F certified to FAA Part 23.

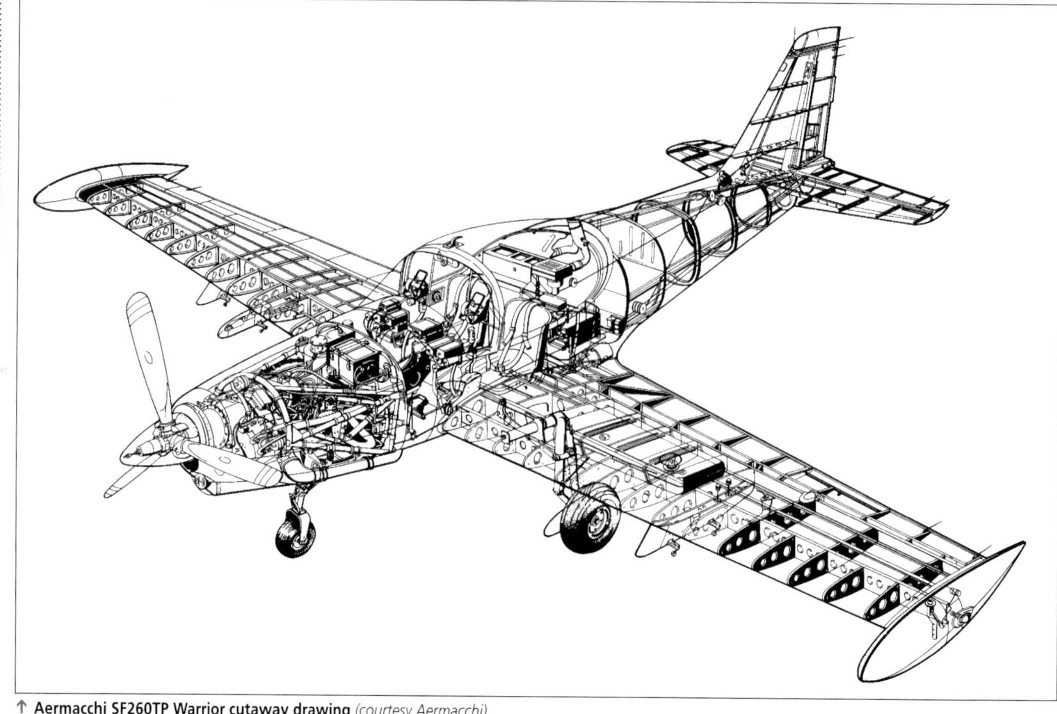

↑ **Aermacchi SF260TP Warrior cutaway drawing** *(courtesy Aermacchi)*

- Internal and external finish in accordance with MIL-F-7179D.

Details *(SF260E/F and SF260TP)*

Sales/Users: Over 870 sold. Current military operators include Belgium (SF260D and M), Bolivia (C), Brunei (Warrior), Burundi (Warrior and TP), Burkina Faso (Warrior), Chad (Warrior), Democratic Republic of Congo (M), Ecuador (ME), Ethiopia (TP), Haiti (TP), Ireland (Warrior), Italy (AM), Libya (Warrior), Myanmar (includes Warrior), Nicaragua (Warrior), Philippines (M Warrior and TP, with currently 18 unserviceable Ms currently being upgraded to TP standard under Project Layang, with a new turboprop engine, new cockpit avionics, 4 underwing pylons and more), Singapore (M and Warrior), Somalia (Warrior), Sri Lanka (M and TP), Thailand (M), Togo (C and Warrior), Tunisia (C and Warrior), Turkey (D), UAE (including TP), Uganda (Warrior),

↑ **Aermacchi SF260E/F Warrior (left) and SF260TP Warrior stores options** *(courtesy Aermacchi)*

Details for SF260E/F, *with SF260TP in italics*

PRINCIPAL DIMENSIONS:
Wing span: 27 ft 5 ins (8.35 m), *the same*
Maximum length: 23 ft 3.5 ins (7.1 m), *24 ft 3.5 ins (7.4 m)*
Maximum height: 7 ft 11 ins (2.41 m), *the same*

WINGS:
Aerofoil section: Modified NACA 64_1212, 64_1210 at root/tip
Area: 108.72 sq ft (10.1 m^2), *the same*
Aspect ratio: 6.9 with tip-tanks

UNDERCARRIAGE:
Type: Retractable, with steerable nosewheel. Electrical retraction
Wheel base: 5 ft 5 ins (1.66 m)
Wheel track: 7 ft 5.5 ins (2.274 m)

WEIGHTS:
Empty: 1,717 lb (779 kg)
Maximum take-off: 2,645 lb (1,200 kg) for SF260E/F, *2,756 lb (1,250 kg) SF260TP as trainer, 2,976 lb (1,350 kg) armed*

PERFORMANCE (SF260E/F at 2,425 lb, 1,100 kg weight, SF260TP at 2,645 lb, 1,200 kg weight):
Maximum speed: 187 kts (216 mph) 347 km/h, *230 kts (265 mph) 426 km/h at 10,000 ft (3,050 m)*
Cruise speed: *216 kts (249 mph) 400 km/h at 10,000 ft (3,050 m)*
Stall speed: 59 kts (68 mph) 109 km/h with full flaps, *61 kts (71 mph) 113 km/h with full flaps*
Take-off distance: 1,575 ft (480 m), *978 ft (298 m)*
Landing distance: 1,460 ft (445 m), *1,008 ft (307 m)*
Maximum climb rate: 1,800 ft (546 m) per minute, *2,165 ft (660 m) per minute*
G limits: +6. -3
Ceiling: 19,000 ft (5,800 m), *24,600 ft (7,500 m)*
Range with full fuel: 805 naut miles (926 miles) 1,490 km, *512 naut miles (590 miles) 950 km*
SF260E/F typical training mission: 50 naut miles (57.6 miles) 93 km distance at 170 kts (196 mph) 315 km/h and 3,000 ft (914 m) altitude (2,513 lb, 1,140 kg take-off weight), with 2 hours 42 minutes over the operating area before return, with total elapsed time of 3 hours 19 minutes, allowing a 44 lb (20 kg) fuel reserve
SF260E/F typical aerobatic training mission: 25 naut miles (29 miles) 46 km distance at 150 kts (173 mph) 278 km/h at 3,000 ft (914 m) altitude (2,293 lb, 1,040 kg take-off weight), with 40 minutes over the operating area before return, with total elapsed time of 1 hour, allowing a 33 lb (15 kg) fuel reserve
SF260TP typical armed mission: Cruise at 180 kts (207 mph) 333 km/h and 200 ft (61 m) altitude to target at 80 naut miles (92 miles) 148 km distance, 20 minutes over target before return at 145 kts (167 mph) 268 km/h and 10,000 ft, with a total elapsed time of 1 hour 25 minutes, allowing a 44 lb (20 kg) fuel reserve

Zambia (M) and Zimbabwe (C and TP Warrior). Civil operators include Sabena. SF260E ordered by Venezuela 1998.
Crew: 3, with side-by-side seating for the pilot and co-pilot/student, and passenger at rear. Heated and ventilated. Optional freon air conditioning.
Cockpit: Ergonomic damper-mounted instrument panel provides space for a complete set of instruments and avionics for dual pilot operation.
Fixed guns: None.
Number of weapon pylons: 2 standard NATO MA4A under the wings on SF260E/F Warrior. 4 similar NATO MA4A pylons on SF260TP.
Expendable weapons and equipment: 661 lb (300 kg) for SF260E/F Warrior and SF260TP Warrior, with release and firing via a trigger on the control stick; selection control on the armament panel. See armament diagram for weapon options.
Flight/weapon system avionics/instrumentation: To customers' requirements. See Cockpit.
Wing characteristics: Straight, low mounted, with dihedral and fixed tip-tanks.
Wing control surfaces: Frise type ailerons (with tabs) and slotted flaps.
Tail control surfaces: Horn-balanced elevators (starboard tab on SF260E/F, port on SF260TP), and horn-balanced rudder (with tab on TP).
Flight control system: Dual cable primary controls, with 3-axis trim. Electric flaps.
Construction materials: Metal, stressed skin.
Engine: 260 hp (194 kW) Textron Lycoming AIO-540-D4A5 in SF260E, O-540-E4A5 for SF260F (with the fuel injected version available as an option), using a Hartzell HC-C2YK-1BF/8477-8R 2-blade constant-speed propeller. SF260TP uses a 350 shp (261 kW) Allison 250-B17D fully aerobatic turboprop, with a 76 ins (1.93 m) Hartzell HC-B3TF-7A/T10173-25R 3-blade propeller.
Engine rating: See above.
Fuel system: 243 litres in 4 aluminium alloy tanks: 2 wing tanks of 99 litres the pair and 2 fixed tip-tanks of 144 litres the pair.

↑ **Aermacchi SF260TP photographed at Fernando AB in September 1997, operating with the 102nd Training Squadron, 100TW, Philippine Air Force** *(Denis Hughes)*

Electric pump transfers fuel from wingtips and starboard wing tank to the main port wing tank, which supplies the engine by an electric booster pump. With selector valve in emergency position, the starboard wing tank can supply the engine.
Electrical system: 24 volt DC, with an alternator-rectifier and 24 amp-hour ni-cd battery.
Braking system: Mainwheel discs.
De-icing system: Electrical for the engine air intake of the SF260TP available.

Aircraft variants:
SF260A*, *B*, *C and ***D*** are unarmed versions principally for civil customers, but are also found in military service. A, B and C are out of production, with the final Ds going to the air forces of Turkey and Belgium from 1992-94.
SF260E and ***F*** are current production versions of the piston trainer, as described, for civil and military use. Different engine models.
SF260M, first flown in 1970, was produced as a military version of the A. Out of production. See also Sales/Users, Philippines.
Warrior is the name of military versions intended to be armed, with stores on NATO standard pylons.
SF260TP is the turboprop version, also available in Warrior form. As described.

Finmeccanica SpA — Italy

Corporate address:
Piazza Montegrappa, 4-00195 Rome.
Telephone: +39 06 324 731
Facsimile: +39 06 320 8621
Telex: 610 371 FINM
Employees: Over 60,000.
Communications office:
Address:
Via Montefeltro, 8-20156 Milan.
Telephone: +39 02 35790 257, 266
Facsimile: +39 02 35790 097

ACTIVITIES

- Parent organization of Agusta SpA, Alenia Aerospazio, FIAR SpA and other companies, with very diverse activities in aircraft design and production, helicopters, avionics and other equipment, space and surface systems.

Alenia Aerospazio — Italy

Corporate address:
Viale Maresciallo Pilsudski, 92 00197 Rome.
Telephone: +39 06 807781
Facsimile: +39 06 8072215, 8075184
Telex: 611395 Alenia I
Founded:
20 December 1990, following the merger of Aeritalia and Selenia. Undergoing further changes, with limited privatization.
Employees:
Approximately 25,000.
Information:
Fabio Dani.

ACTIVITIES

- Commercial and military aircraft programmes, aerostructures, modification, maintenance and overhaul, space programmes and more. Main non-US subcontractor on the MD-11 programme, amounting to 12.11% of the airframe value. Includes 300 series of winglets, fins and rudders, and fuselage panels. Also, the cargo hatch (the largest ever fitted on a commercial aircraft), manufactured at the Capodichino factories, for the combi version. Also contracted to produce fuselage sections for the Boeing 717.
- G222 production and support, currently based around the C-27J Spartan programme with Lockheed Martin (see Freighter section).
- Boeing 707 tanker conversions (see Freighter section).
- Boeing 727 re-engining programme through Dee Howard Co, a subsidiary company (see Freighters section).
- Participation in the Dassault Falcon 2000 programme.
- Multi-national programmes include Airbus A321, AMX, ATR series, Eurofighter, FLA, Tornado, and holds a 38% share in Airbus International Asia working on the AE316 and AE317 programmes (see Airliner section).
- Is co-operating with Daimler-Benz Aerospace over the **MPA 2000** maritime patrol aircraft programme (see Daimler-Benz Aerospace).

Alenia F-104ASA M

Comments: The modernization programme for Aeritalia-built F-104S interceptors and attack aircraft to ASA (Aggiornamento Sistema d'Arma) standard, by upgrading the weapon system (including new FIAR R21G/M1 Setter radar), was detailed and illustrated in the 1996-97 edition of *WA&SD*, page 54. Upgraded aircraft were redelivered to the Italian Air Force between December 1986 and February 1993.

To extend the F-104ASA's operational life until Eurofighter is available, the ASA M (maintainability) modernization programme was drafted to keep 100 or more aircraft operational into the next century. The programme called for the installation of equipment similar to that in Tornado and AMX. The aim was to ensure better maintenance due to the availability of spares, lower costs, and maximum commonality in substitute components. The modernization was to include rewiring of the power system and the substitution of navigation avionics, using Alenia-produced retrofit kits.

Fuji Heavy Industries Ltd — Japan

Corporate address: Subaru Building, 7-2 1-chome, Nishi-Shinjuku, Shinjuku-ku, Tokyo 160.
Telephone: +81 3 3347 2525 (2513 for Aerospace Division) **Facsimile:** +81 3 3347 2588 **Telex:** 232 2268 FUJI J
Founded: 15 July 1953.
Employees: Approximately 15,300, of which over 3,000 in the Aerospace Division.
Information: Publicity office +81 3 3347 2023.

DIVISIONS

AEROSPACE DIVISION

UTSUNOMIYA MANUFACTURING DIVISION
HQ address: 1-11, Yonan 1-chome, Utsunomiya, Tochigi 320.
Telephone: +81 286 58 1111, 1114
Activities: ▪ Subordinate to the Aerospace/Transportation Equipment (Rolling Stock) Division. Major participant in Mitsubishi F-2 development, and manufactures components for Boeing 747 (aileron), 757 (outboard flap), 767 (wing/body fairing and main undercarriage door), 777 (centre wing, wing/body fairing and main undercarriage door), and MD-11 (outboard aileron) airliners. These include over 40,000 hybrid honeycomb panels of carbonfibre/Kevlar for Boeing 767/777 wing/body fairings. ▪ Prime contractor for Japanese-built AH-1S and UH-1J helicopters, and developed the T-5 trainer for the Maritime Self Defence Force. ▪ Undertakes subcontract work within the Japanese industry on the Kawasaki-led P-3C and Mitsubishi-led F-15J programmes, plus the T-4 trainer (fin, tailplane, tailcone, fairings, wingtips, wing/flap trailing edge), and the Patriot air defence system. ▪ Space programmes, including study of exposed structure design for the Japanese Experimental Module (JEM), as part of the NASA space station project. ▪ J/AQM-1 and Flying Forward Observation System UAV systems. Also RPH2 Large Unmanned Helicopter. ▪ Maintenance and overhaul. ▪ Develops high-performance composite materials and structures for space vehicles and plays an important development role in projects of Japan's National Aerospace Development Agency and National Aerospace Laboratories.

Fuji T-7

Fuji T-7 is to be a 400 shp (298 kW) Allison 250 turboprop powered variant of T-3 trainer, with 50 ordered for the JASDF for the year 2000 onwards.

Fuji T-5

First flight: 27 April 1988, following trials with a re-engined KM-2 from 1984.
Role: Primary/basic trainer and utility aircraft, capable of aerobatics.

Aims

▪ Lighter and higher-performing development of the KM-2, with a turboprop engine, sliding blister-type canopy, and upgraded cockpit with more room.

Development

▪ 30 August 1988. First production T-5 was delivered to the JMSDF.

Details

Sales/Users: 36 for the JMSDF. Further 5 aircraft have been requested from FY1998 funding.
Crew: 2 for training and aerobatics, and 4 persons in a utility role.
Cockpit: Dual controls. Heat and ventilation. Upgraded from the KM-2. Rear-sliding canopy, with available IFR hood for training.
Fixed guns: None.
Number of weapon pylons: None.
Flight/weapon system avionics/instrumentation: IFR, including Tacan, ADF, UHF and VHF com, and selective identification facility.
Wing characteristics: Straight, low mounted, with dihedral.
Wing control surfaces: Ailerons (with anti-servo tabs, port also for trim) and single-slotted flaps.
Tail control surfaces: Horn-balanced elevators and rudder, all with tabs.
Flight control system: Mechanical.
Construction materials: Metal.
Engine: Allison 250-B17D turboprop, with Hartzell HC-B3TP-7A/T10173-18 3-blade constant-speed propeller.
Engine rating: 420 shp (313.3 kW), flat rated to 350 shp (261 kW).
Fuel system: 363 litres in 4 bladder wing tanks.

Details for T-5

PRINCIPAL DIMENSIONS:
Wing span: 32 ft 11 ins (10.04 m)
Maximum length: 27 ft 8 ins (8.44 m)
Maximum height: 9 ft 9 ins (2.96 m)

WINGS:
Aerofoil section: NACA 23016.5/23012 (root/tip)
Area: 177.6 sq ft (16.5 m^2)
Aspect ratio: 6.109
Sweepback: 0°
Incidence: 4°/1° (root/tip)
Dihedral: 6°

UNDERCARRIAGE:
Type: Retractable, with steerable nosewheel (±16°)
Main wheel tyre size: 6.50 × 8
Nose wheel tyre size: 5.00 × 5
Wheel base: 7 ft 5 ins (2.27 m)
Wheel track: 9 ft 7 ins (2.92 m)

WEIGHTS:
Empty: 2,385 lb (1,082 kg)
Maximum take-off: 3,980 lb (1,805 kg), or 3,494 lb (1,585 kg) for aerobatics

PERFORMANCE:
Maximum speed: 192 kts (221 mph) 356 km/h
Stall speed: 56 kts (65 mph) 104 km/h *with flaps*
Take-off distance: 991 ft (302 m) at 3,494 lb (1,585 kg) aerobatic weight
Landing distance: 571 ft (174 m) at aerobatic weight
Maximum climb rate: 1,700 ft (518 m) per minute, at aerobatic weight
Ceiling: 25,000 ft (7,620 m)
Range with full payload: 509 naut miles (586 miles) 944 km

Electrical system: 30 volt DC supply via a 150 A starter-generator. 24 amp-hour ni-cd battery for engine starting and operation in emergency conditions. 2 × 160 VA static inverters for AC supply.
Braking system: Hydraulic single-disc type.

→ **Fuji T-5 JMSDF trainer at Shimofusa AB** *(K. Hinata)*

Japan Defence Agency FI-X Programme — Japan

Comments: In fiscal year 1995 the Japanese Government provided funding for a new digitally-controlled 11,240 lbf (50 kN) class turbofan engine with thrust vectoring from Ishikawajima-Harima Heavy Industries (IHI), to be installed and tested in a twin-engined Technology Demonstrator designed by the JDA's Technology Research and Development Institute, as the FI-X. This programme is expected to result in the eventual development of a new-generation small fighter of Japanese design, to replace the Mitsubishi F-15J (which is still in production) well into the 21st Century. It is thought that 4 FI-Xs will be built from funds allocated in fiscal year 1999. Preliminary reports suggest a Technology Demonstrator of even smaller overall dimensions than the current Mitsubishi F-2 (and thereby much smaller than F-15J) but incorporating stealth technologies, with trapezoid wings blended into the fuselage, all-moving canards and twin vertical tails. Other stealth technologies will include construction from radar-absorbent materials and conformal systems (including radar). Flight control will be by fly-by-light.

Japan Defence Agency MPA Programme — Japan

Comments: The JDA and the US Department of Defense are co-operating on proposals for a P-3C Orion maritime patrol aircraft (MPA) replacement, with the signing of a technical review agreement in 1997. Full development could begin in the year 2000, with service from 2008. The JDA is believed to favour an aircraft of about 172,000 lb (78,000 kg) take-off weight, powered by 4 turbofan engines in the 13,050 lbf (58 kN) class. Kawasaki would be the likely main contractor in Japan.

Kawasaki Heavy Industries Ltd — Japan

Corporate address:
Tokyo Head Office: World Trade Centre Building, 4-1, Hamamatsu-cho 2-chome, Minato-ku, Tokyo 105. Kobe Head Office: Kobe Crystal Tower, 1-3, Higashi Kawasaki-cho 1-chome, Chuo-ku, Kobe 650-91.

Telephone: +81 3 3435 2111 (Tokyo), +81 78 371 9530 (Kobe)
Facsimile: +81 3 3436 3037 (Tokyo), +81 78 371 9568 (Kobe)
Telex: 242 4371 KAWAJU J (Tokyo), 5622 355 (Kobe)

Founded:
1918 an aircraft department of Kawasaki Dockyard was founded at the Hyogo Works; 1937 the aircraft department separated from then-Kawasaki Rolling Stock Manufacturing Co at Hyogo to form Kawasaki Aircraft Co Ltd; 1969 Kawasaki Aircraft, Rolling Stock Manufacturing and Dockyard merged to form Kawasaki Heavy Industries.

Employees:
17,400, of which nearly 5,000 are in aerospace activities.

Information:
Toshiyuki Nagai (Helicopter Sales, Aircraft Sales Division).

AEROSPACE DIVISION

FACTORIES

- Gifu (1, Kawasaki-cho, Kakamigahara, Gifu 504) for manufacturing, repair and overhaul of equipment for commercial aircraft, anti-submarine aircraft, fighters, trainers and helicopters, plus missiles and space equipment.
- Nogoya 1 (11, Kusunoki 3-chome, Yatomi-cho, Ama-gun, Aichi 498) and Nagoya 2 (7-4, Kanaoka, Tobishima-mura, Ama-gun, Aichi 490-14), for manufacturing and assembly of airframes.
- Akashi and Seishin for manufacturing and overhaul of jet engines, helicopter transmissions, and more.

ACTIVITIES

- Aerospace accounts for about one-quarter of Kawasaki's total group sales.
- Manufactures the T-4 trainer, and is prime contractor for Japanese P-3C anti-submarine aircraft and Boeing CH-47J Chinook helicopters (following earlier production of 160 KV107IIAs). Undertakes parts production and partial assembly for F-15J fighters, and supplies fuselage components for the Boeing 767 and 777 plus wing ribs for the B737 and outboard flap for the B747, part of the fuselage for the Airbus A321, and flap hinge fairing for the Boeing MD-80.
- Manufactures the BK 117 helicopter (with Eurocopter) plus versions of the Boeing MD 500 helicopter under licence. Also prime contractor for the tandem-seat OH-1 Kongata Kansoku (rolled out on 15 March 1996), the armed small observation helicopter programme, and produces the transmission for the Boeing Explorer.
- Initial study phases for the C-X transport, intended to eventually replace existing C-1s and Hercules, and the MPA (see JDA).
- Engine development and manufacture includes participation in the multi-national V2500 turbofan programme. It is also engaged in research for Supersonic Transport/Hypersonic Transport engines.
- Space activities include overseeing construction of the H-II launch vehicle complex, and development and manufacture of payload fairings. Other space programmes include the HOPE orbiting spaceplanes, Japanese Experiment Module (JEM) as part of the Space Station programme, Hyflex hypersonic flight experiment vehicle for testing design, construction and operating technologies (launched in 1996), Alflex automatic landing flight experiment vehicle (launched to assist in the HOPE programme), and rendezvous and docking systems. A conceptual vehicle is the reusable Single-Stage-to-Orbit Kankoh-Maru (designed by the Transportation Research Committee of the Japanese Rocket Society), able to carry 50 passengers on 24 hour space tours in low Earth orbit.

Kawasaki T-4

First flight: 29 July 1985.
Role: Intermediate trainer and liaison aircraft.

Aims

- To replace the T-33 operating with the JASDF, and subsequently the T-1 primary jet trainer.
- Good flying characteristics over a broad speed range, to ease student pilots from primary trainers and on to advanced trainers.

Development

- 4 September 1981. Japan Defence Agency officially designated Kawasaki prime contractor for development of the T-4, covering FY1981-1988.
- October 1981. Development was initiated, basic design taking 12 months.
- Early 1988. Testing of 4 flying prototypes completed.
- 28 June 1988. Maiden flight of a series-built T-4, with deliveries starting that September.
- 1996. First used by the Blue Impulse aerobatic display team.

Details *(principally for the T-4)*

Sales/Users: Some 200 required by the JASDF, of which 194 have been ordered (including 10 requested in FY1998) and most delivered.
Crew: 2, with rear instructor's seat raised by 10.5 ins (27 cm).
Cockpit: Dual controls. Single-piece side-hinged canopy, opening to starboard, with emergency release. Boot strap air conditioning and pressurization system (maximum differential 4 psi). Baggage hold provided.
Crew escape: UPCO SHIS-3J ejection seats.
Fixed guns: None.
Number of pylons: 5, with underfuselage pylon for EW dispenser, target towing gear or other pod, and 2 under each wing for auxiliary fuel tanks or equipment pods.
Expendable weapons and equipment: Not armed.
Radar: None.
Flight/weapon system avionics/instrumentation: Includes Tokyo Keiki-built ASK-1 air data computer, Shimadzu Corporation-built AVQ-1 head-up display, Nippon Avionics ARN-66 Tacan, Toshiba Electronic ARN-69 VOR/ILS, Tokyo Aircraft Instrument ASH-3 Vgh recorder, Japan Aviation Electronics-built AHRS, and Kanto Aircraft Instruments-built ASH-4 flight data recorder. Mitsubishi Electric ARC-54 VHF/UHF radio.

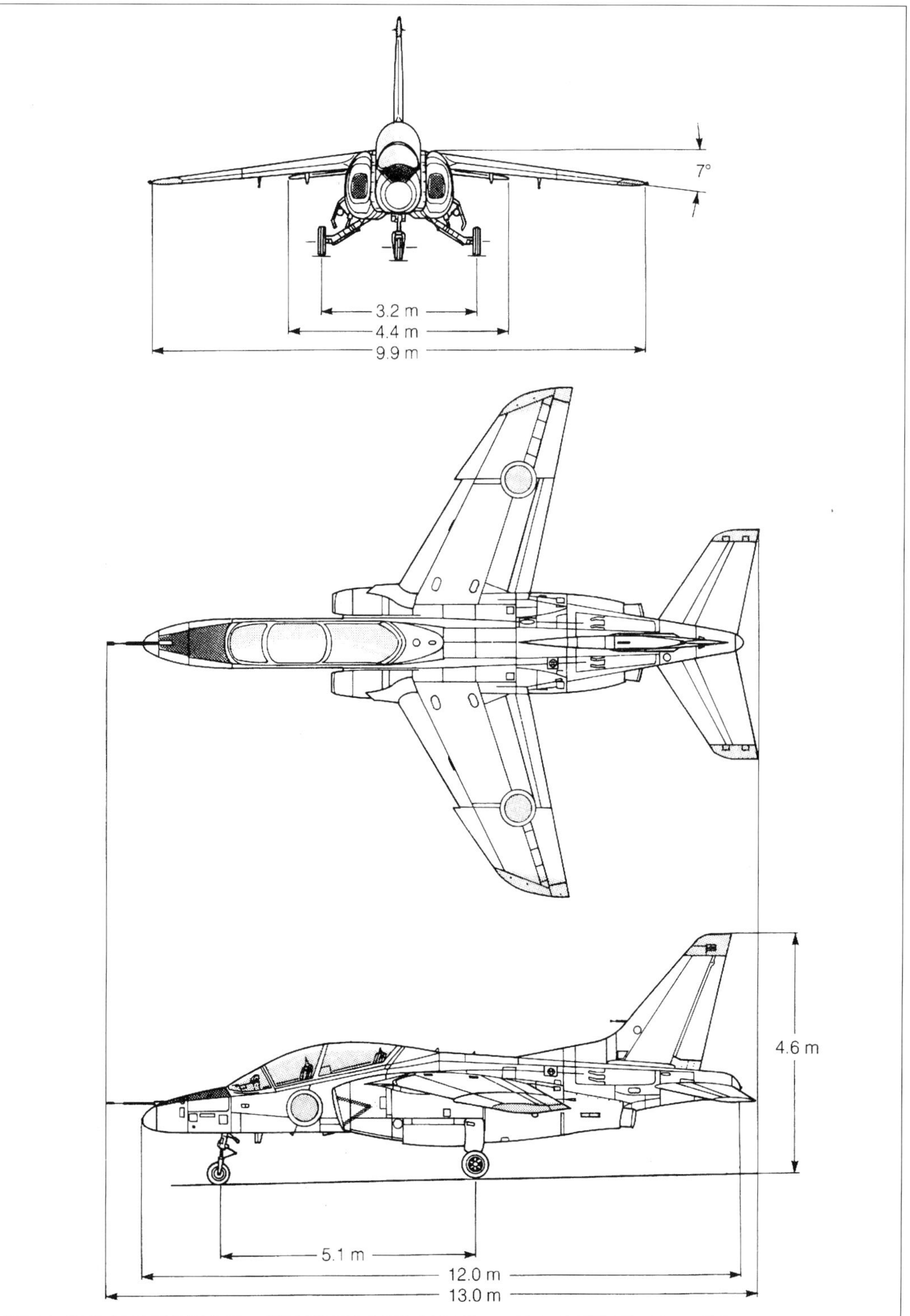

↑ **Kawasaki T-4 arrangement** *(courtesy Kawasaki)*

Details for T-4

PRINCIPAL DIMENSIONS:
Wing span: 32 ft 7 ins (9.94 m)
Maximum length: 42 ft 8 ins (13 m) including probe
Maximum height: 15 ft 1 ins (4.6 m)

WINGS:
Aerofoil section: Supercritical
Area: 226.04 sq ft (21 m^2)
Aspect ratio: 4.67
Sweepback: 27.5° at 25% chord
Incidence: 0°
Anhedral: 7°

TAIL UNIT:
Tailplane span: 14 ft 5 ins (4.4 m)

UNDERCARRIAGE:
Type: Retractable, with steerable nosewheel
Wheel base: 16 ft 9 ins (5.1 m)
Wheel track: 10 ft 6 ins (3.2 m)
Turning radius: 31 ft (9.45 m)

WEIGHTS:
Empty: 8,355 lb (3,790 kg)
Maximum take-off: 12,544 lb (5,690 kg) clean, 16,535 lb (7,500 kg) design

PERFORMANCE:
Maximum speed: Mach 0.9, at 10,692 lb (4,850 kg) all-up weight with 50% fuel load
Maximum speed at sea level: 560 kts (645 mph) 1,038 km/h, weight and fuel as above
Cruise speed: Mach 0.75, at 12,544 lb (5,690 kg) all-up weight
Stall speed: 90 kts (104 mph) 167 km/h at 10,692 lb (4,850 kg) weight
Take-off distance: 2,001 ft (610 m) at 12,544 lb (5,690 kg) weight, 35° C
Landing distance: 2,100 ft (640 m) at 10,692 lb (4,850 kg) weight
Maximum climb rate: 10,000 ft (3,050 m) per minute, at 12,544 lb (5,690 kg) weight
G limits: +7.33, -3
Ceiling: 50,000 ft (15,240 m) at 12,544 lb (5,690 kg) weight
Range with full internal fuel: 700 naut miles (806 miles) 1,297 km, at 12,544 lb (5,690 kg) weight and cruise speed
Range with 2 × 454 litre drop tanks: 900 naut miles (1,036 miles) 1,667 km

↑ **Kawasaki T-4 with 454 litre drop tanks at Hyakuri AB** *(K. Hinata)*

Wing characteristics: Shoulder mounted, sweptback, with anhedral. Dog-tooth leading edges. Root extensions merge leading edges with air intakes.
Wing control surfaces: Ailerons and double-slotted flaps.
Tail control surfaces: Slab tailplane and rudder.
Airbrakes: 2, on the rear fuselage.
Flight control system: Hydraulic.
Construction materials: Metal, except for composites ailerons, airbrakes, fin, sections of the flaps/tailplane, and rudder.
Engines: 2 × Ishikawajima-Harima F3-IHI-30 turbofans.
Engine rating: Each 3,682 lbf (16.38 kN) at take-off.
Air intakes: Fuselage sides, ahead of the wings.
Fuel system: Over 2,240 litres in 2 wing and 2 fuselage tanks. Optional 2 × 454 litre drop tanks.
Electrical system: 2 × 9 kW Shinko engine-driven starter generators.
Hydraulic system: 3,000 psi (dual), for flight control surfaces, undercarriage operation and braking.
Braking system: Mainwheel carbon brakes and anti-skid system.

Aircraft variants:
T-4 is the standard intermediate jet trainer, as described.
AT-X has been a projected advanced training and upgraded derivative of the T-4, to replace the supersonic T-2 trainer early in the next century. Said to be in a study phase by the JDA.

↑ **Kawasaki-built P-3C operated by the JMSDF. In 1997 Kawasaki delivered its 101st and last P-3C anti-submarine and patrol aircraft, based on the US Lockheed Martin Orion, leaving a single EP-3 electronic intelligence aircraft to be delivered in September 1998 and 3 UP-3D electronic training aircraft up to the year 2000. Five P-3Cs are due for conversion into UP-3E surveillance aircraft, each with side-looking airborne radar**

Mitsubishi Heavy Industries Ltd — Japan

Corporate address:
5-1, Marunouchi 2-chome, Chiyoda-ku, Tokyo 100.

Telephone: +81 3 3212 3111
Facsimile: +81 3 3212 9865
Telex: J22282, J22443

Founded:
Aerospace division had its foundations in 1921 and by 1945 had produced over 18,000 aircraft; reorganized in December 1952.

Employees:
Over 44,800 total employees.

Information:
Wataru Tsunefuka (Aerospace & Special Vehicle Administration Department).

AEROSPACE & SPECIAL VEHICLE DIVISION

Activities

▪ Undertaking development of the F-2, leading the nation's team that includes Fuji, Japan Aviation Electronics Industry Ltd (1-21-6 Dogenzaka, Shibuya-ku, Tokyo 150) and Kawasaki among others.
▪ Development of the MH2000 helicopter. Is also prime contractor for Japanese licence-built H-60J helicopters and F-15J fighters (again involving Fuji, Kawasaki and ShinMaywa), and is modernizing the JASDF's F-4EJ fleet.
▪ Active as a risk-sharing partner in development and production of the Canadian Global Express, and developed/produces the fuselage, T-tail and wing/body fairings for the Dash 8 Series 400.
▪ Subcontract activities include parts for the Boeing 737-700/800 (wing flaps), 747 (inboard wing flap), 767 (rear fuselage sections) and 777 (passenger doors and panels), MD-11 (tailcone) and MD-80 (wing trailing edge). Also, has produced fuselage sections for the Kawasaki P-3 series. Undertakes work on the Sikorsky S-92.
▪ Aero engines (including the V2500, and as a 10% partner in the PW4000) and space vehicle construction, serving as systems integrator to Japan's National Space Development Agency.

Mitsubishi F-1 and F-4EJKai

Comments: Photographs and details on these combat aircraft can be found in the 1996-97 edition of *WA&SD*, page 57.

Mitsubishi F-15J and F-15DJ

Comments: 213 being built for the JASDF (a total including 2-seat F-15DJ operational trainers), most of which had been delivered by 1998. No requests for additional F-15s were made by the JASDF in FY1998. F-15J/DJs are equivalent to US Boeing F-15C/Ds, but without conformal auxiliary fuel tanks, and use Japanese ECM and RWR systems and are powered by Ishikawajima-Harima built F100-IHI-100 engines. Future programmes could include incorporation of some F-2 technology into 100 or more F-15Js, including 'stealth materials' and avionics (possibly carrying new active phased-array radar). An ECM escort role is envisaged, allowing mixed squadrons of F-15Js and F-2s to counter heavy electronic jamming during anti-ship missions.

↑ **Mitsubishi F-15Js** *(courtesy JASDF)*

Mitsubishi F-2

First flight: 7 October 1995.
Role: Fighter Support – close support and anti-shipping.

Aims

▪ To replace the F-1 with an aircraft based on the F-16 but incorporating advanced technologies from both Japan and the USA.
▪ Mach 2 performance, approximately a 9 tonne payload, CCV flight mode functions, and ability to launch air-to-surface, medium range and short range missiles, including anti-ship.
▪ Use of advanced materials and structural technology in the airframe, and incorporating cocured composite technology. Increased wing area compared to the F-16C.
▪ Modification of the F-16's nose configuration, lengthened fuselage, adoption of a strengthened windshield, and use of a drag-chute.
▪ Installation of advanced avionics systems, including active phased array radar.
▪ Use of improved performance engine.
▪ First major military aircraft development programme conducted jointly by the USA and Japan.

Development

▪ October 1987. Development initiated after an agreement between Japan and the USA was reached, based on the F-16 but incorporating technology originating in Japan.

▪ November 1988. Memorandum of Understanding signed between the Japanese and US Governments on production work share. Separately, Mitsubishi was made prime contractor by the JDA.
▪ January 1989. Licence agreement signed between Mitsubishi and General Dynamics, allowing some design to start in the following year.
▪ February 1990. Agreement signed between Japan and the USA over technology transfer and work sharing, with the USA receiving a 40% share. General Dynamics (later Lockheed Martin) received the first of 5 development subcontracts, with work including airframe parts, various avionic systems including the stores management system, and ground test equipment.
▪ March 1990. Mitsubishi and Lockheed joint development activity began.
▪ June 1994. The rear fuselage of the first flyable FS-X prototype was handed over to Mitsubishi by Lockheed. In July Lockheed installed an F110-GE-129 engine during "fit checks". Lockheed also provided 16 wing leading-edge flaps (9 left hand and 7 right hand) and left-hand wingbox components, with the first flap delivered on 28 July 1994 and all shipped by mid-1995. These included some for ground testing, prototype flying and spares.
▪ 12 January 1995. Roll out of the first prototype at Mitsubishi's Komaki Minami plant.
▪ February 1995. Ground structural testing of FS-X began at JDA's Tachikawa centre.
▪ 12 September 1995. High speed taxi trials began with first prototype.
▪ 13 December 1995. Second XF-2A prototype flew, followed by third (XF-2B) on 17 April 1996 and last (XF-2B) on 24 May 1996.
▪ 15 December 1995. Japanese Government issued the designation F-2, replacing FS-X.
▪ 22 March 1996. Delivery of the first XF-2A prototype to the Technical Research and Development Agency (TRDI) for a 1,000 hour flight testing and evaluation programme lasting until 1998. 3 other prototypes followed during April-September.

Details for F-2

PRINCIPAL DIMENSIONS:
Wing span: 36 ft 6 ins (11.13 m)
Maximum length: 50 ft 11 ins (15.52 m)
Maximum height: 16 ft 3 ins (4.96 m)

WINGS:
Area: 375 sq ft (34.84 m^2)
Aspect ratio: 3.73
Sweepback: 33° 12′
Incidence: 2° 30′

UNDERCARRIAGE:
Type: Retractable, with steerable nosewheel
Main wheel tyre size: 27.75 × 8.75
Nose wheel tyre size: 18 × 5.7
Wheel base: 13 ft 3 ins (4.05 m)
Wheel track: 7 ft 9 ins (2.36 m)

WEIGHTS:
Empty: 21,003 lb (9,527 kg) for F-2A, 21,237 lb (9,633 kg) for F-2B
Maximum take-off: 48,700 lb (22,100 kg)
Maximum landing: 40,345 lb (18,300 kg)
Payload: 17,824-19,840 lb (8,085-9,000 kg)

PERFORMANCE:
Maximum speed: Quoted by Mitsubishi as approximately Mach 2
Maximum speed at low level: Mach 1
G limits: +9, -3
Combat radius: more than 448 naut miles (516 miles) 830 km for anti-ship mission

↑ **Mitsubishi XF-2A with undercarriage lowered** *(courtesy JASDF)*

▪ April 1996. TRDI flight tests began at Gifu Air Base with XF-2A prototype 001, initially for performance envelope, handling and vibration trials. 002 is being used for EW system trials and loads testing. 003 is undergoing weapon delivery and high AoA trials. 004 is testing the fire-control and navigation systems plus stores releasing.
▪ 30 July 1996. Workshare agreed between Japan and the USA, with 40% value going to the USA (some 120 separate components – see Engine). First production contract issued by Mitsubishi to Lockheed Martin in October, covering the initial 11 production aircraft.
▪ Late 1998. Lockheed Martin delivered its first rear fuselage section for a production F-2.
▪ 2000. Expected roll-out and delivery of the first production aircraft.

Details

Sales/Users: 2 static/fatigue airframes for a 6,000 hour test programme, and 4 flying prototypes (2 single- and 2 two-seaters). 130 production aircraft required, as 83 F-2As and 47 F-2Bs, with 32 ordered/requested up to and including fiscal year 1998. Japan Defence Agency's mid-term defence build-up plan (up to the year 2000) envisages 47 F-2s.
Crew: Pilot, or 2 in the F-2B.
Cockpit: HUD and displays, see Avionics. Strengthened windshield.
Crew escape: Ejection seat/s.
Fixed guns: 1 × 20-mm M61A1 Vulcan multi-barrel cannon mounted in the port wing root.
Number of weapon pylons: 13 possible carrying points using common rails, as 5 under each wing, 2 wingtip launch rails for air-to-air missiles, and 1 under the fuselage.
Expendable weapons and equipment: 17,824-19,840 lb (8,085-9,000 kg) stores load. Drop tanks carried on centreline and inner wing pylons. Next 3 positions under each wing for air-to-surface or anti-ship missiles (including ASM-1 or 2), bombs of up to 350 kg (including Mk 82 and GCS-1), cluster bombs or rocket launchers. Outer underwing pylons for AIM-7F or M Sparrow, AIM-9L Sidewinder or Mitsubishi AAM-3 air-to-air missiles, plus wingtip rails for short-range AAMs, for self defence.
Radar: Mitsubishi Electric active phased array.
Flight/weapon system avionics/instrumentation: Japan Aviation Electronics/AlliedSignal digital flight control computers and Mitsubishi Electric mission computer. Radar with integrated EW system, Japan Aviation Electronics/AlliedSignal laser gyro INS, Shimadzu holographic HUD, and 3 Yokogawa liquid-crystal multi-function displays. Magnavox ARC-164 UHF and NEC VHF/UHF radios. Lockheed Martin has design responsibility for the stores management system and some other avionics and avionics support equipment items, including certain software test stations and factory test equipment.
Self-protection systems: See Avionics, and also the F-15J entry.
Wing characteristics: Built by Lockheed Martin (6 port-side cocured wing boxes and lower skin), Fuji (upper skin and wing fairings).
Wing control surfaces: Flaperons (Fuji built) and 2-section leading-edge flaps (Lockheed Martin built).
Tail control surfaces: Fuji built tail unit. Slab tailplane and rudder.
Flight control system: Japan Aviation Electronics/AlliedSignal digital fly-by-wire system for CCV flight mode function, mounted in the forward fuselage, for relaxed stability mode, control augmentation, manoeuvre enhancement and load control, and decoupled yaw.
Fuselage: Produced by Mitsubishi (forward section), Kawasaki (centre) and Lockheed Martin (rear). Radome manufactured by Fuji.
Construction materials: Includes advanced cocured composites, whereby the wing box and lower skin are cured and bonded in single process. Radar absorbent material for the air intake, surface leading-edges and nose. Flaps have aluminium skins and spars bonded to an aluminium honeycomb core. Titanium in part of rear fuselage and tail.
Engine: General Electric F110-GE-129 twin-shaft turbofan, assembled and tested in Japan by IAI under a 40% workshare arrangement with General Electric.
Engine rating: 17,000 lbf (75.62 kN) dry, 29,600 lbf (131.67 kN) with afterburning.
Air intake: Under the fuselage, F-16 style, with some use of radar absorbent materials (built by Fuji).
Fuel system: 4,675 litres for F-2A (8,470 lb, 3,842 kg), with some 697 litres less for F-2B (6,832 lb, 3,099 kg). Optionally up to 3 drop tanks, 1 × 1,136 litres and 2 × 2,271 litres.
Flight refuelling probe: Not specified at present.
Braking system: Drag-chute in a tail pod.

Aircraft variants:
F-2A is the single-seat combat version, as described.
F-2B is the 2-seat operational training version.
Advanced trainer derivative is possible, based on the F-2B, as a contender in the T-2 replacement programme.

↑ **Mitsubishi XF-2A** *(courtesy Mitsubishi)*

Daewoo Heavy Industries Ltd — South Korea

Corporate address:
6 Manseok-Dong, Dong-gu, Incheon 401702.
Telephone: +82 32 760 1114
Facsimile: +82 32 762 1546
Telex: DHILTD K28473
Cable: DHILTD INCHEON

Founded:
Aerospace Division within the group founded in 1984.

Information:
Kyory Do Park (Manager, Sales Department, Aerospace Division).

AEROSPACE DIVISION
HQ address:
Daewoo Center Building, 22nd Floor, 541-5-ga, Namdaemun-no, Jung-gu, CPO Box 7955, Seoul 100714.
Telephone: +82 2 726 3022, 3298, 3114
Facsimile: +82 2 726 3280, 2679
Telex: DHILTD K23301
E-mail: aero@solar.dhiltd.co.kr (for Changwon factory)
Managing Director: Duck Joo Ra (*telephone* +82 551 80 6530, *facsimile* +82 551 85 8541)
Information:
Steven Kang (Manager, International Marketing – *telephone* +82 2 726 3127, *E-mail* azkang@solar.dhiltd.co.kr)

FACILITIES

▪ Anyang factory at Kyonggi-do (*telephone* +82 343 60 1114), Changwon factory No 1 (*telephone* +82 551 80 4114), and Changwon factory No 2 (*telephone* +82 551 80 6114).

ACTIVITIES

▪ In addition to the various helicopter programmes (including the Korean Light Helicopter and marketing the Polish W-3A Sokól – see the Helicopter section) and UAVs, DHI is developing as prime contractor the KTX-1 Woong-Bee trainer for the indigenous air force, constructs the centre fuselage section, other panels and ventral fins for Samsung F-16 assembly under the Korea Fighter Programme (due to end in 1999), is playing an important role in the Samsung KTX-2 programme, and produces components for the Boeing 747 and Fairchild Dornier 328.

↑ 3 of 4 Daewoo KTX-1 Woong-Bee flying prototypes with revised tail configuration, and cockpit *(courtesy Daewoo)*

▪ Under South Korea's foreign military purchases, DHI has produced components for the BAe Hawk Mk 67, Bell Canada helicopters, Lockheed Martin P-3C Update III and Westland Super Lynx Mk 99.
▪ Other aerospace work includes UAVs and satellite platforms.

Daewoo KT-1 Woong-Bee

First flight: 12 December 1991. Pre-production aircraft believed flown in March 1998.
Role: Primary trainer, capable of aerobatic, instrument, low navigation, night and formation flying. Can be armed.
Fatigue life: 10,000 hours as a trainer.
Programme Director: Duck Joo Ra.

Aims

▪ Design targets were 320 kts maximum diving speed, 11,580 m absolute ceiling, 900 naut mile range, and weapon training capability with guns and rockets.
▪ Developed to comply with US-MIL-SPEC Trainer and Aerobatics/Utility category to FAR 23.
▪ Excellent spin characteristics for high-skill aerobatics.
▪ Good low-speed controllability and stability.
▪ Low operating and maintenance costs.
▪ Simulator and Training System used before actual flight training, offering normal/abnormal training, instrument flight training, flight performance and manoeuvrability analysis. Simulator classified as FAA AC 120-40B Level C, with realistic control feel, 3-D vision system (FOV 150° × 40°), real-time distributed processing system, self-diagnostic system, modular simulation software, monitor/control/evaluation by instructor operation system, and synergestic 6-DOF motion system.

Development

▪ February 1988. Development began under the Korea Trainer Experimental programme, originally named Yeo-Myung. Design by Daewoo and the ADD. Daewoo's first complete aircraft project as prime contractor and South Korea's first indigenous aircraft. Also participating in the programme are Korean Air, Samsung and GSP.
▪ 12 December 1991. First flight of the first of 4 flying prototypes, following November roll-out.
▪ 5 February 1993. First flight of the second prototype. PT6A-25A engine.
▪ 10 August 1995. First flight of the third prototype, featuring the much more powerful PT6A-62A engine (prototypes later modified to have tails similar to the fourth prototype – see below).
▪ November 1995. Named Woong Bee (the great flight for the future).
▪ 10 May 1996. First flight of the fourth and last flying prototype, with substantial aerodynamic refinements that include complete redesign of the tail unit, with the tailplane moved rear and lower and thereby requiring redesign also of the fin and rudder, and shorter nose.
▪ 1998. Ground evaluation and then flight testing of the pre-production trainer, with PT6A-62 engine.
▪ Late 1998. Anticipated Governmental approval for full production in 1999.

↑ Daewoo KTX-1 Woong-Bee fourth prototype *(courtesy Daewoo)*

Details for KTX-1 *(principally with PT6A-62 engine)*

PRINCIPAL DIMENSIONS:
Wing span: 34 ft 9 ins (10.6 m)
Maximum length: 33 ft 8 ins (10.26 m)
Maximum height: 12 ft (3.67 m)

WINGS:
Aerofoil section: Modified NACA 63-218 root, NACA 63-212 tip
Area: 172.33 sq ft (16.01 m^2)
Aspect ratio: 7.02

UNDERCARRIAGE:
Type: Retractable, with engage/disengage steerable nosewheel (±22°). Production aircraft will have new undercarriage designed by Fairey Hydraulics
Main wheel tyre size: 18 × 5.5
Nose wheel tyre size: 14.2 ins maximum – 13.65 ins minimum
Wheel base: 8 ft 5 ins (2.56 m)
Wheel track: 11 ft 9.5 ins (3.59 m)

TAIL UNIT:
Tailplane span: 13 ft 8 ins (4.16 m); tailplane and fin have aerofoil NACA 0012 at root and 0009 at tip

WEIGHTS:
Empty: 3,955 lb (1,794 kg)
Maximum take-off: 7,065 lb (3,205 kg) utility, or 5,399 lb (2,449 kg) aerobatic

PERFORMANCE:
Never-exceed speed (V_{NE}): 350 kts (403 mph) 648 km/h
Maximum speed: 260 kts (299 mph) 482 km/h at 10,000 ft (3,050 m)
Maximum speed at sea level: 250 kts (288 mph) 463 km/h
Stall speed: 70 kts (81 mph) 130 km/h, *flaps down*
Take-off distance over a 50 ft (15 m) obstacle: 800 ft (244 m)
Landing distance over a 50 ft (15 m) obstacle: 1,300 ft (396 m)
Maximum climb rate: 3,500 ft (1,065 m) per minute
G limits: +7, -3
Temperature limit: -25° to +45°
Ceiling: 38,000 ft (11,580 m)
Average flight altitude for training: 14,775 ft (4,500 m)
Range with full fuel: 900 naut miles (1,036 miles) 1,666 km
Duration: At least 2 hours 30 minutes, with 1 hour 30 minutes normal mission

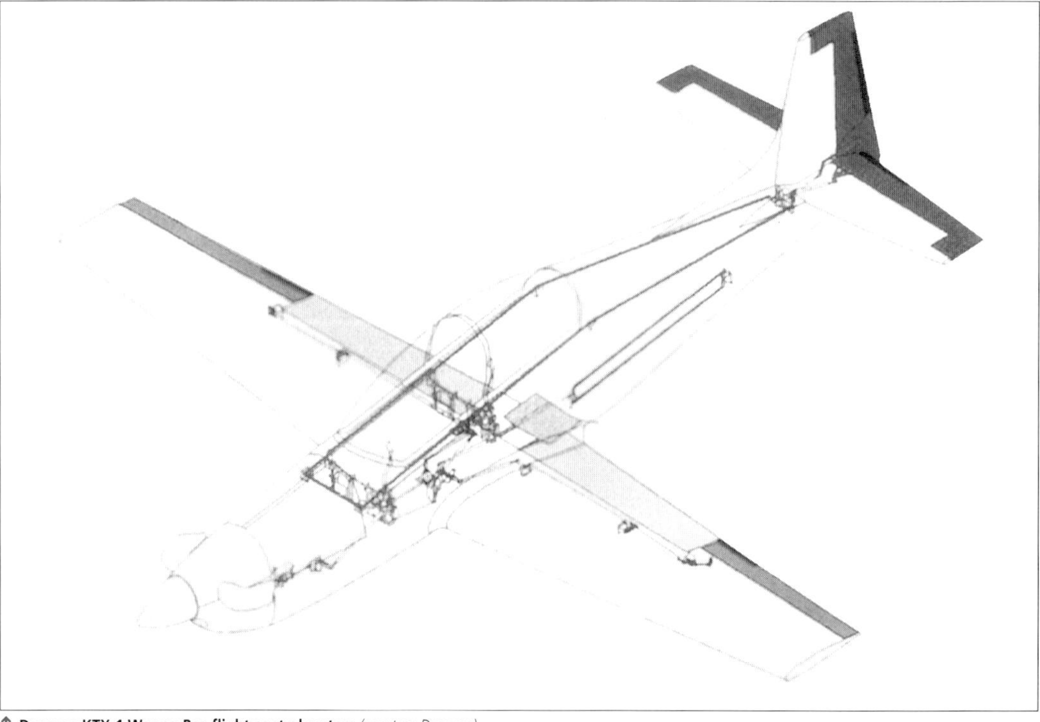

↑ Daewoo KTX-1 Woong-Bee flight control system *(courtesy Daewoo)*

▪ August 1999. Expected start of KT-1 production. These aircraft will feature a Fairey Hydraulics undercarriage among other changes to the prototypes.
▪ 2000. Start of deliveries to the Air Force.

Details

Sales/Users: 7 prototypes, as 4 flying (01 to 04) and 3 static/fatigue for testing (001 to 003), followed by a single pre-production aircraft (flown 1998). 4 flying prototypes had accumulated 1,100 hours by November 1997. 85 KT-1 trainers are expected to be produced, plus 20 armed for FAC, for the Air Force. Export partner being sought.
Crew: 2, in tandem, with the instructor having a raised cockpit to improve forward vision.
Cockpit: Pressurized, with maximum differential of 3 psi. AiResearch 2-wheel boot strap air cycle environmental control system. Independent ram air ventilation in an emergency. Cooling capacity 12,000 btu per hour.
Crew escape: Martin Baker Mk 16L zero-zero ejection seats.
Number of weapon pylons: 4 under the wings; 2 "wet".
Expendable weapons and equipment: Machine-guns and rockets. All necessary control and wiring is installed as standard.
Flight/weapon system avionics/instrumentation: IFR, including Lear Astronics AHRS, Teledyne AN/APX-101 IFF/SIF, Collins AN/ARN-153 Tacan, Collins AN/ARC-186 VHF and Magnovox AN/ARC-164 UHF coms, ADC supplied EADI and EHSI, RA-697 communication control, and optional VOR/ILS. Master warning system.
Wing characteristics: Straight, low mounted, with dihedral.
Wing control surfaces: Ailerons with trim tabs and split flaps.
Tail control surfaces: Elevators (with port trim tab) and rudder (with trim tab). New, larger-area and curved dorsal fin replacing original angular fin.
Airbrake: Under the fuselage. Actuator by Fairey Hydraulics.
Flight control system: Manual, with hydraulically actuated flaps and airbrake, and mechanically actuated ailerons, elevators and rudder. Electrically actuated trim tabs.
Engine: Prototype 01 and 02 each have a 550 shp (410 kW) Pratt & Whitney Canada PT6A-25A turboprop and 3-blade propeller. 03 and 04 have 950 shp (708.4 kW) PT6A-62A, with 95-ins (2.41 m) Hartzell HCE4N-3EX 4-blade constant-speed, variable-pitch and feathering propeller (2,000 rpm fixed velocity regulator). It was originally thought that the AlliedSignal TPE331 turboshaft was also be be flight tested.
Fuel system: 640 litres (990 lb, 449 kg), mainly carried in 4 wing tanks but with a small collector tank in the fuselage that probably acts as an inverted flight tank (maximum 30 seconds). Provision for 2 × 189 litre (total 80 lb, 36.3 kg) drop tanks.
Electrical system: 28V DC, using a combined starter-generator and ni-cd battery (33% power margin).
Hydraulic system: Self-pressurized main and emergency systems, operating at 3,000 psi. Pneumatic back-up system (confirmed as Fairey Hydraulics accumulator, power package, sampling and shut-off valves, selector manifold, and actuators) for the airbrake, flaps and undercarriage. Emergency back-up circuit uses battery.
Braking system: Parker Hannifin hydraulic type on main units. Parking brake. No anti-skid system.
Oxygen system: Gaseous type (2,250 litres).
De-icing system: Only for propeller. Inertial separator for engine intake anti-icing.

Samsung Heavy Industries (SHI) — South Korea

Corporate address: 26th Floor, Samsung Main Building, 250, 2-ga, Taepyung-ro, Chung-gu, Seoul.
Telephone: +82 2 751 2073 **Facsimile:** +82 2 751 2083 **Web site:** http://www.samsung.com
Founded: 1938.

SAMSUNG AEROSPACE INDUSTRIES CO LTD (SSA)
Telephone: +82 2 3467 7114 **Facsimile:** +82 2 3467 7080
Founded: 1977, initially to overhaul and assemble aircraft engines.
Employees: 8,455.

ACTIVITIES

▪ Principal business activities are aircraft production, aircraft parts, gas turbines, and other work as detailed below.
▪ Consortium leader/integrator in the development of the KTX-2, and is developing the Kari 8-seat business aircraft.
▪ Prime contractor in the Korea Fighter Programme, producing 120 Lockheed Martin F-16Cs and Ds under licence for the Republic of Korea Air Force (deliveries to be completed by 1999).
▪ Prime contractor for a consortium of Korean companies collaborating in the development of new commercial airliners.
▪ Collaborates on Bell 427 production and sales, agreed in 1996 to assemble and sell the Russian Mil-26 helicopter, and manufactures components for the Bell Canada 212 and 412, Boeing 757 and 767, and de Havilland DHC-8 Dash 8.
▪ Produces military hardware (including artillery), is working on satellites, and produces a range of machine tools, electronic and semiconductor assembly equipment, lead frames, cameras, opto-electronic devices and factory automation systems. Helicopter shuttle service.

Samsung (Lockheed Martin) KTX-2

First flight: Year 2001.
Role: Lead-in fighter trainer and light combat.

Aims

▪ To replace the T-33A and T-37C, of which some 50 remain.
▪ Mach 1.4 maximum speed and 1,000 naut mile range.
▪ To have the manoeuvrability, duration and systems to prepare future pilots to fly next-generation fighters such as the F-22 and JSF.
▪ Combat capability, allowing the aircraft to be sold as a dual-role force multiplier in many air forces.
▪ Cost-effective, total training system featuring fully integrated ground and flight-based training elements.

Details for KTX-2

PRINCIPAL DIMENSIONS:
Wing span: 29 ft 10.5 ins (9.1 m)
Maximum length: 42 ft 7 ins (12.98 m)
Maximum height: 15 ft 8.3 ins (4.8 m)

WEIGHTS:
Empty: 13,808 lb (6,263 kg)
Maximum take-off: 19,604 lb (8,892 kg)

PERFORMANCE:
Maximum speed: Mach 1.4
Climb rate: 27,000 ft (8,225 m) per minute
Ceiling: 45,000 ft (13,715 m)
G limits: +9. -3
Range with full fuel: 1,000 naut miles (1,150 miles) 1,850 km

Development

▪ 1992. Initial design work started by South Korea's Defence Development Agency and Samsung, with major participation by Lockheed under an F-16C/D offset arrangement.
▪ July 1994. Selection of the present mid-mounted wing and single fin design, over the high-wing and twin fin alternative layout.
▪ 1995. Preliminary design completed.
▪ July 1996. Lockheed Martin became the sought-after foreign partner in the programme through an interim collaboration agreement, with the US company taking responsibility for the avionics, flight control system and wings, plus providing technical expertise.
▪ 3 July 1997. South Korean Government approved the production programme, providing 70% of the US$2 billion development programme costs, with remaining 17% coming from Samsung and 13% from Lockheed Martin.
▪ 17 July 1997. Lockheed Martin signed a full agreement with Samsung for the joint development and production of the KTX-2.
▪ 24 October 1997. Samsung received a contract (worth approximately US$1.27 billion) to develop the KTX-2 and construct prototypes.
▪ 10 November 1997. The US Congress finally gave its approval for a technology export licence, allowing the programme to advance to full-scale development.
▪ 2001. Likely first flight date and start of the test programme.
▪ 2005. Initial operational capability.
▪ 2009. End of production deliveries for the Republic of Korea Air Force.

Details

Sales/Users: 94 trainer versions initially ordered for the Republic of Korea Air Force, from 120 aircraft required. Potential market seen as 600-800 worldwide.
Crew: 2, in tandem stepped cockpits, under a large bubble canopy.
Crew escape: Ejection seats.
Fixed guns: 20-mm cannon.
Number of weapon pylons: 7, as 4 under the wings, 2 wingtip missile rails and 1 centreline under the fuselage.
Expendable weapons and equipment: Range of air-to-air and air-to-surface missiles, bombs, rocket launchers, etc.
Radar: Lockheed Martin APG-67 selected in 1998.
Flight/weapon system avionics/instrumentation: Lockheed Martin is responsible for the avionics and flight control system. Colour multi-function displays, and GEC-Marconi HUD.
Wing characteristics: Mid mounted with leading-edge sweepback and wingtip launch rails. Leading-edge root extensions, and rear 'shelf' extensions.
Wing control surfaces: Leading-edge flaps, and elevons.
Tail control surfaces: Slab tailplane, and single fin and rudder.
Flight control system: Digital fly-by-wire.
Engine: 16,000 lbf (71.2 kN) class turbofan. Competing offers are a version of the General Electric F404 with dual-channel FADEC or single-channel FADEC with hydro-mechanical back-up, and the SNECMA M88-2 (possibly as the locally assembled M88-2K). Possible future upgrade to the General Electric F414.
Air intakes: Fuselage sides, just ahead and below of the wing roots. Size allows upgrade of engines to F414s if required.

↑ **Impression of Samsung (Lockheed Martin) KTX-2s carrying AAMs** *(courtesy Lockheed Martin)*

Pakistan Aeronautical Complex — Pakistan

HQ address:
Kamara, District Attock.

Telephone: +92 51 584212, 580261 to 580265 (5 lines) for AMF
Facsimile: +92 51 583837 for AMF
Telex: 5601 PAC KAMRA PK
E-mail: amf@isb.com.sats-net.pk

Founded: 1978.

Information:
Sqn Ldr S. Zahid Rahman (DCE Technical Co-ordination and Training).

FACILITIES AND ACTIVITIES

▪ *Aircraft Manufacturing Factory* (AMF) produces the Saab MFI 17 Safari Supporter under licence as the Mushshak. A new variant with a 260 hp (194 kW) Textron Lycoming IO-540 engine has been developed as the Super Mushshak (see General Aviation section). In a letter of December 1997, the Chief Editor was informed by AMF that the weapon-carrying capability of Mushshak is optional under the design, but that under the licence agreement for manufacture between Saab and AMF this optional capability is not being offered.

AMF, in collaboration with Nanchang and AVIC of China, has participated in the development of the Karakorum-8 basic jet trainer (see Multi-national section). Present AMF workshare is restricted to 25% but is expected to rise to 45%. AMF already builds the horizontal stabilizer/elevator, vertical tail/rudder and engine cowling. Front fuselage manufacturing capability is being established and co-production plans are being negotiated.

▪ *Kamra Avionics and Radar Factory* (KARF) rebuilds and overhauls ground-based MPDR radars and their associated power generators. It also manufactures avionics components and complete systems, plus other varied work, and has contributed to Mirage III modernization.

▪ *Mirage Rebuild Factory* undertakes structural work, engine, avionics and systems modernization and overhaul for Mirage III and 5 fighters. Upgrade programmes include ex-Australian Mirage IIIs now belonging to Pakistan, receiving Sagem avionics, INS, GPS, upgraded ECM, FLIR, HOTAS and more. This project was still in progress in 1998. Also supports the Air Force's F-16 engine overhaul.

▪ *F-6 Rebuild Factory* is the oldest of the 4 PAC operations and manufactures components for, and overhauls, the Air Force's Chinese-built combat aircraft.

Philippine Aerospace Development Corporation — Philippines

Corporate address:
Box 7395, Domestic Airport Post Office, Lock Box 1300, Domestic Road, Pasay City, Metro Manila.

Telephone: +63 2 832 37 57, 27 41, 27 49
Facsimile: +63 2 832 25 68
Telex: 66019 PADC PN

Founded: 1973.

Information:
Captain Panfilo Villaruel Jr (President).

ACTIVITIES

▪ Recent programmes included assembly of 24 SIAI-Marchetti S211 jet trainers, 18 SF260TP turboprop trainers, and 8 Lancair lightplanes from Pacific Aeronautical kits, for the air force and police.

▪ Following PADC's assembly of Pilatus Britten-Norman Islanders for the armed forces and others, operates a service centre and also maintains the engines.

▪ Following PADC's assembly of BO 105 helicopters for the armed forces and others, Philippine Helicopter Services Inc subsidiary undertakes repair, maintenance and servicing, and acts as a spares depot. Also maintains MD 500 rotor blades.

▪ Undertakes repair and maintenance of Allison turboshaft and turboprop engines, and also reciprocating engines, plus propellers (see above).

▪ Had been involved in sales of the Italian Canguro transport.

▪ Partner in Eurocopter Philippines, to undertake assembly of Eurocopter helicopters from European-supplied kits, plus sales and maintenance.

Instytut Lotnictwa — Poland

Corporate address:
Aleja Krakowska 110/114, 02-256 Warszawa.

Telephone: +48 22 846 0011, 0993
Facsimile: +48 22 846 4432
Telex: 813 537
E-mail: ilot@ilot,edu.pl

Founded: 1926.

Employees: 500.

ACTIVITIES

▪ In addition to wide-ranging research and development, and testing, in the fields of aircraft, engines, instrumentation and materials, several engines (see Engines section) and aircraft have been built (see also IL-23 in the General Aviation and IS-2 in the Helicopter sections).

▪ Details and a drawing of the **Kobra 2000**, first proposed in 1993 as a possible future replacement for Iryda in air-to-ground operations from the year 2005 (if first flown in 1999) and originally designed as a competitor to the PZL-230 Skorpion and M-99 Orkan, can be found in the 1996-97 edition of *WA&SD*, page 61. It is interesting to note that since the 1996-97 edition went to press, 2 Rolls-Royce Turbomeca Adour Mk 871 turbofans mounted in the rear fuselage, each 5,990 lbf (26.65 kN), were among engines proposed. All 3 types have since been cancelled.

WSK "PZL-Mielec" S.A. — Poland

Full name:
Wytwórnia Sprzętu Komunikacyjnego "PZL-Mielec" S.A.

Corporate address:
ul. Wojska Polskiego 3, 39-300 Mielec.

Telephone: +48 17 788 7244, 7243
Facsimile: +48 17 788 6587, 214 785
Web site: http://www.pzl-mielec.com.pl/
E-mail: wskpzlsa@ptcnet.mielec.pl

Founded: 1938.

Employees:
8,700, including 4,360 in aircraft production.

Information:
Danuta Bogdan.

ACTIVITIES

▪ In addition to Iryda variants, PZL-Mielec has manufactured many thousands of An-2 general-purpose transports, and continues to produce the M-28 Skytruck, M-18A/B Dromader agricultural aircraft and M-26 Iskierka piston trainer, plus the M-20 Mewa developed from the Piper Seneca II, and now the Tampico Club TB 9 lightplane under Socata contract.

Instytut Lotnictwa/PZL-Mielec I-22, M-93 and M-96 Iryda

Note: On 25 November 1997, "PZL-Mielec" announced that its contract with the Polish Air Force had been terminated. It remains unclear if the M-96 upgrade programme will be completed.

First flight: 3 March 1985 for the I-22 prototype (pilot Ludwik Natkaniec), 22 December 1992 for the M-93K and 16 August 1997 for the M-96 with all upgrades.
Role: Advanced trainer and light attack.
Fatigue life: I-22 designed for 2,500 flight hours or 10,000 take-off/landings.

Aims

▪ Modern replacement for the TS-11 Iskra.

▪ Capable of day/night and adverse weather flying, and able to use unprepared airfields.

▪ Built according to UK AP-970 regulations. Flight handling characteristics conform to the requirements of US military standards MIL-F-8785 b/ASG.

▪ Roomy cockpits. Oxygen, fire-fighting, de-icing, air-conditioning and other airborne systems are installed.

↑ **Instytut Lotnictwa/PZL-Mielec M-96 Iryda featuring strakes, slats and Fowler flaps, plus higher tailfin** *(Waclaw Holys)*

Development

▪ 1979. Programme started. Air Force requirements were stated as: maximum speed 900 km/h, maximum Mach number 0.85, climb rate 40 metres per second, take-off distance 750 m, landing distance 900 m, and operational radius of 220 km.
▪ 1982. Technical design accepted by the Polish Air Force.
▪ 3 March 1985. First flight by I-22 prototype 02. 2 × SO-3W22 (later renamed PZL-5) turbojets.
▪ 30 January 1987. 02 prototype crashed, killing the pilot.
▪ 1990. Work started on the I-22 M-93 modernized version with Larzac 04C20 engines and Israeli avionics. Later other engines and avionics analyzed.
▪ March 1992. Joint factory and state acceptance tests of I-22 completed.
▪ 14 April 1992. I-22 Iryda officially commissioned by Polish Air Force.
▪ 5 May 1992. First flight of the first production aircraft, side number 103, c/n *AN001-03*.
▪ 24 October 1992. First 2 production aircraft, 103 and 105, ceremonially assigned to Polish Air Force.
▪ 22 December 1992. First flight of the Iryda M-93K, powered by K-15 turbojets (installed in *SP-PWD* prototype).
▪ 25 April 1994. First flight of the Iryda M-93V prototype, powered by Rolls-Royce Viper 545 engines (installed in *SP-PWE* prototype, piloted by Ludwik Natkaniec). Also featured new Martin Baker Mk 10L ejection seats (standard for the M-93).
▪ 26 May 1994. First flight of the M-93S prototype with Sagem avionics (installed in *SP-PWD*)
▪ 6 July 1994. First flight of the first production M-93K with K-15 engines (c/n *AN002-04*, registration *SP-PWF*).
▪ September 1994. Iryda was presented abroad for the first time (*SP-PWE* M-93V prototype) at the Farnborough Air Show in the UK.
▪ 24 January 1996. Accident with an M-93K led to the termination of production of this model.
▪ 21 December 1996. First flight of M-96 prototype with aerodynamic changes.
▪ 23 April 1997. First flight of M-96 prototype with Sextant avionics.
▪ 16 August 1997. First flight of the M-96 with all upgrades.

Details *(principally for the M-96 Iryda)*

Sales/Users: 7 prototypes (including static test); see 1996-97 edition of *WA&SD*, page 62 for details. 6 production aircraft built by the end of 1994 (Nos 103, 105, 201-204); production aircraft up to No 203 are in I-22 Iryda form with PZL-5 turbojets; No 204 (c/n *AN002-04*) was the first production M-93K Iryda with PZL K-15 engines. Next 6 M-93Ks were delivered during 1995, all assigned to the 58th Training Air Regiment of the Dęblin Pilot School. Production terminated after a crash on 24 January 1996, and all military Irydas returned to the manufacturer. Of 19 Irydas built to date, 10 were taken into service by the Polish Air Force and 2 were lost; 7 were development prototypes (including 2 already unflyable and 2 static for ground testing). All military aircraft were to be upgraded according to the new M-96 specification and 6 more M-96 Irydas were to be built during 1997-98. PZL-Mielec anticipated an order for 6 or 7 aircraft from the Polish Navy in 1998.
Crew: 2, in tandem, the instructor's rear seat stepped up by 16 ins (40 cm). See Aircraft variants for single-seat models.
Cockpit: See Aims. Cockpit pressurized (maximum differential 2.75 psi).
Crew escape: Martin Baker Mk 10L zero-zero ejection seats.
Fixed guns: 1 × 23-mm GSz-23L 2-barrel gun in an under-fuselage pack.
Ammunition: 50-200 rounds.
Number of weapon pylons: 4 under the wings, each capable of carrying a 1,100 lb (500 kg) load; 2 are 'wet'.
Expendable weapons and equipment: Up to 3,968 lb (1,800 kg), typically including single bombs of 50 kg to 500 kg weight each or up to 4 × 50 kg to 100 kg bombs on each pylon using multi-store carriers, launchers for 16 or 32 × 57-mm rockets, or 2 R-60 air-to-air missiles, or a combination of weapons. Other options include gun pods or a munition dispenser.
Additional stores: Camera pods.
Radar: None.
Flight/weapon system avionics/instrumentation: Sextant suite, using MIL-STD-1553B databus, includes Totem ring-laser gyro INS/GPS, HUD, SMD54 liquid-crystal multi-function displays, and HOTAS. Instytut Lotnictwa stores management system and altimeter. Radio navigation equipment and flight data recorder.
Self-protection systems: SPO-10 RWR.
Wing characteristics: High mounted, with swept leading-edge and straight trailing edge. Anhedral. Important changes introduced into M-96 wings are small leading-edge root extension strakes, Fowler flaps replacing the former single-slotted flaps, slots along the whole leading-edge of the wings and turbulizers near the ailerons.
Wing control surfaces: Hydraulically boosted ailerons (capable of differential operation, and with ground-adjustable tabs), Fowler flaps and 2-section full-span leading-edge slats. See above.
Tail control surfaces: Variable incidence tailplane, elevators and rudder (with trim tab). In order to reduce by 50% the control stick load, which was a matter of complaint by pilots, an aerodynamic trim tab was fitted to the rudder of M-96. Also, the tailfin was made taller compared with the earlier Irydas in order to obtain necessary stability at low speed.
Airbrakes: 2 aft of the wings plus a new airbrake under the fuselage on M-96. Compared with earlier Irydas, M-96 introduced changes to the shape of the airbrakes.
Flight control system: Mechanical, except for hydraulic flaps, tailplane incidence and airbrakes.
Construction materials: Metal stressed skin, but including minor use of metal honeycomb in the elevators and non-structural composites.
Engines: 2 PZL K-15 Kaszub turbojets. Uprated K-16 of 3,527 lbf (15.69 kN) is under development.
Engine rating: Each 3,307 lbf (14.71 kN).
Air intakes: Fuselage sides, well below and ahead of the wings.
Flight refuelling probe: None.
Fuel system: 4,114 lb (1,866 kg) in wing and fuselage tanks. 30 seconds inverted flight allowable. 2 × 380 litre drop tanks can be carried.
Electrical system: 115 volt/400 Hz single-phase and 36 volt/400Hz 3-phase AC supply using 2 starter generators and principal and stand-by static converters. Emergency DC supply using 2 × 24 volt/25 amp-hour batteries.
Hydraulic system: 3,046 psi, for flaps, tailplane incidence, airbrakes, undercarriage and brakes.
Braking system: Hydraulic disc type on main units. Parking brakes. SH21U-1 drag-chute in the tailcone.
De-icing system: Electrically heated front transparencies, and bleed air for the canopy and air intakes.

Aircraft variants:
I-22 Iryda (code named W-300) was the early training version, with 2 × PZL-5 (SO-3W-22) turbojets.
M-93 Iryda (originally named I-22M-93) is a modified combat trainer with new engines, intended to train pilots in operational flights and also to perform tactical operational missions. Several sub-variants were considered, including 2 produced as the M-93K with K-15 Kaszub engines and M-93V with Rolls-Royce Viper 535 engines.
M-93K Iryda, see M-93 above.
M-93M and ***R Iryda*** were projected maritime attack and reconnaissance versions respectively, similar to the M-93 but with specialized equipment or armament. See M-93 above.
M-93S Iryda was designed with a French Sagem MAESTRO nav/attack system that included Uliss 92 inertial navigation system, multi-channel GPS, wide-view HUD and EFIS colour displays. WDNS allowed actual weapon delivery as well as simulated firing through state-of-the-art technology. HOTAS control. See M-93 above.
M-93V Iryda was the anticipated export sub-variant of the M-93, with Rolls-Royce Viper 535 engines. See the 1996-97 edition of *WA&SD*, page 63, for details. See M-93 above.
M-96 Iryda is the current production/upgrade version with improved flight handling, particularly at take-off and landing, as well as a new Sextant avionics suite. The most important changes are those introduced into the wing design (see Wing characteristics), aerodynamic trim for the rudder and fin size (see Tail control surfaces), and to the airbrakes (which see). Prototype *SP-PWD* (c/n *1ANP01-05*) with first-stage upgrades introduced (strakes, turbulizers and taller fin) first flew on 21 December 1996. Prototype with Sextant avionics first flew 23 April 1997, and prototype with all upgrades flew on 16 August 1997.

Several proposed combat/reconnaissance versions have been cancelled, including:
M-95 Iryda (originally named I-22M-95) 2-seat tactical reconnaissance/ground attack version with new swept wings with supercritical aerofoil sections, modified tail unit, updated avionics, special reconnaissance equipment, fixed 30-mm cannon, and provision for AAMs, ASMs and bombs.
M-97 single-seat derivative of M-95, proposed in 2 sub-variants as the M-97S (szturmowy, attack) and M-97MS (myśliwsko-szturmowy, fighter-attack), differing in armament system only.
M-99 Orkan strengthened single-seat ground attack aircraft, carrying 9,039 lb (4,100 kg) of weapons.

Details for the M-96 Iryda

PRINCIPAL DIMENSIONS:
Wing span: 31 ft 7 ins (9.6 m)
Maximum length: 43 ft 4.5 ins (13.22 m)
Maximum height: 14 ft 1 ins (4.3 m)

WINGS:
Aerofoil section: NACA 64A010, NACA 64A210 (root/tip)
Area, gross: 214.4 sq ft (19.92 m^2)
Aspect ratio: 4.627
Sweepback: 18° on leading edge
Incidence: 0°
Anhedral: 3°
Twist: 1° 44'

TAIL UNIT:
Tailplane span: 16 ft 1 ins (4.9 m)
Tailplane and elevators area: 52 sq ft (4.83 m^2)
Fin and rudder area: 39.6 sq ft (3.68 m^2)
Fin angle: 29° 48' at 25% chord

UNDERCARRIAGE:
Type: Retractable, with steerable nosewheel
Main wheel tyre size: 670 × 210 mm
Nose wheel tyre size: 430 × 170 mm
Wheel base: 16 ft 2 ins (4.92 m)
Wheel track: 8 ft 11 ins (2.71 m)

WEIGHTS:
Empty, operating: 10,251 lb (4,650 kg)
Normal take-off: 15,313 lb (6,946 kg), clean
Maximum take-off: 19,771 lb (8,968 kg)
Maximum landing: 14,550 lb (6,600 kg)

PERFORMANCE (clean)**:**
Maximum operating Mach number (M_{MO}): Mach 0.8
Maximum speed at sea level: 432 kts (497 mph) 800 km/h
Stalling speed: 100 kts (115 mph) 185 km/h
Time to 32,800 ft (10,000 m): 6 minutes 55 seconds
Landing distance: 1,640 ft (500 m)
Maximum climb rate: 8,405 ft (2,562 m) per minute, at sea level
G limits: +8, -4
Service ceiling: 42,000 ft (12,800 m)
Range: 874 naut miles (1,006 miles) 1,620 km

PZL "Warszawa-Okęcie" S.A. — Poland

Full name:
Państwowe Zakłady Lotnicze Warszawa-Okęcie SA.

Corporate address:
Aleja Krakowska 110/114, 00-971 Warszawa.

Telephone: +48 22 846 0031
Facsimile: +48 22 846 6192, 5479, 2701

Founded: 1 January 1928.

Employees: 1,100.

Information: Władyslaw Skorski (MoB, Marketing & Sales – *telephone:* +48 22 846 6152).

ACTIVITIES

▪ Produces a range of light and agricultural aircraft in addition to the trainers detailed here (see also the General Aviation section).
▪ On 2 January 1995 PZL "Warszawa-Okęcie" became a stock company owned by the Ministry of Industry and Trade.

PZL Warszawa-Okęcie PZL-130 Orlik

First flight: 8 October 1984 (original piston-engined Orlik, with pilot Witold Łukomski). 16 July 1986 for the Orlik Turbo (pilot Jerzy Wojnar), now known simply as Orlik. 21 August 1992 for PZL-130TC-1 Orlik.
Role: Fully aerobatic basic, advanced and combat trainer, plus counter-insurgency (TC-3).

↑ **PZL Warszawa-Okęcie PZL-130TC-1 Orlik with armament and auxiliary fuel tanks** *(Cezary Piotrowski, via Piotr Butowski)*

Aims

▪ Original piston-engined Orlik was designed for both civil and military training and limited operational roles, with the cockpit instrumentation configured to permit easy transition to jet aircraft. Difficulty obtaining the required AOOT M-14PM radial engine led to its demise after prototype flying.
▪ Orlik Turbo, already well under development when Orlik was cancelled, offered jet-like handling combined with turboprop efficiency.
▪ Designed to comply with US FAR 23, Amdt 28.

Development

▪ 1979. Design work on the PZL-130 Orlik (Eaglet) piston-engined trainer began. The chief designer was Andrzej Frydrychewicz, assisted by Tomasz Wolf.
▪ July 1982. Full-scale mock-up commissioned.
▪ 12 October 1984. First flight of prototype c/n 002, side-marked *SP-PCA*, powered by an M-14PM radial piston engine.
▪ 1985. *SP-PCC* (c/n 004) was presented at the Paris Air Show.
▪ November 1985. Design of the PZL-130T Orlik Turbo offered.
▪ November 1985. *SP-PCC* shipped to Canada to be fitted with a turboprop engine.

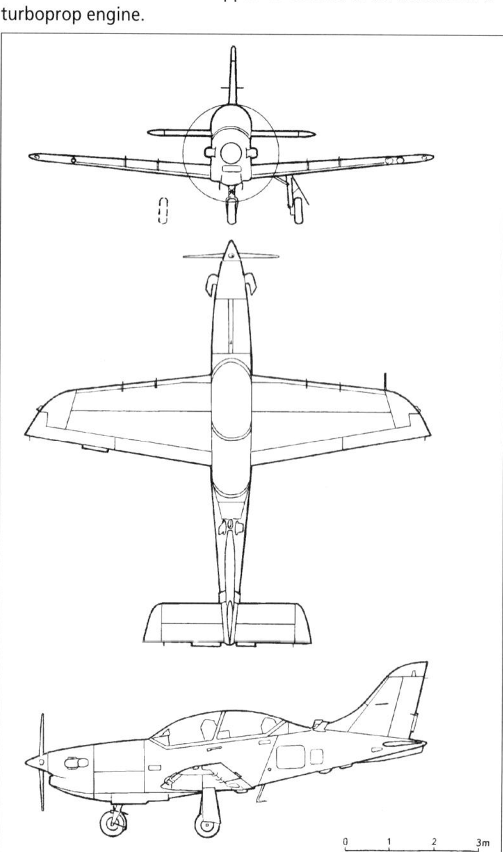

↑ **PZL Warszawa-Okęcie PZL-130TC-1 Orlik** *(courtesy PZL Warszawa-Okęcie)*

▪ 16 July 1986. First flight of *SP-PCC* (later redesignated *SP-RCC*), with a Pratt & Whitney PT6A-25A turboprop.
▪ 20 January 1987. *SP-RCC* was lost in Colombia, killing the pilots.
▪ 19 February and 19 March 1988. Two follow-up piston-engined aircraft built, Nos 005 and 006. Both later converted into PZL-130TMs, re-engined with M-601E turboprops.
▪ 12 January 1989. First flight of the PZL-130TM prototype (007) powered by a Motorlet Walter M-601E turboprop. Pilot Jan Gaw'cki.
▪ January 1990. Polish Air Force acceptance tests of the PZL-130TM began.
▪ 4-9 November 1990. Flight testing of PZL-130T *(SP-WCA*, 008) in Israel. Here, Israeli military pilots made about 100 flights totalling 23 flight hours.
▪ 18 September 1991. First flight of PZL-130TB prototype (009, *SP-PRF*).
▪ October 1992. 2 PZL-130TMs (005 and 006) were delivered to the Polish Air Force for qualification tests.
▪ 2 June 1993. First flight of the PZL-130TC prototype (011, *SP-PCE*), pilots Tadeusz Dunowski and Jerzy Wojnar.
▪ June 1993. PZL-130TB (second production aircraft, 013, *SP-PCF*) displayed at the Paris Air Show.
▪ November 1993. Polish Air Force qualification tests of PZL-130TB completed.
▪ 4 March 1994. First PZL-130TBs delivered to the Polish Air Force.
▪ 7 July 1994. First PZL-130TC-1s delivered to the Polish Air Force.
▪ March 1997. Start of tests with the upgraded PZL-130TC-1, with ventral tailfin, and turbulizers at the wingtips and tailplane.

Details *(principally for the current production PZL-130TC-1 Orlik)*

Sales/Users: Of 45 Orliks built by 1998, including 3 for delivery to the Polish Air Force during that year, 35 are in service with the Polish Air Force (Military Pilot Academy at Dęblin and 60th Training Air Regiment at Radom). First PZL-130T (008) was lent to Dęblin by PZL Warszawa-Okęcie in November 1991, and the next 3 PZL-130TMs (005, 006, 007) were delivered to Dęblin in October 1992 for evaluation tests. Normal deliveries began 4 March 1994, when a batch of 9 PZL-130TBs (012 to 021, excluding 014) was delivered to the Polish Air Force (021 lost on 30 April 1994). All the military aircraft are now converted into TC-1s.
Crew: 2, in tandem, the rear seat raised by 2.5 ins (6.5 cm).
Crew escape: Martin Baker Mk PL11B ejection seats on production TC-1s and converted TBs that formerly had LFK-F1 ejection seats.
Fixed guns: None.
Number of weapon pylons: 6 under the wings (see Aircraft variants), 2 of which are 'wet' for drop tanks.
Expendable weapons and equipment: 1,323 lb (600 kg).
Flight/weapon system avionics/instrumentation: AlliedSignal Bendix/King avionics, including KTR908 VHF communications. See Aircraft variants for navigation avionics. EFIS cockpit layout tested on the TC-2 in 1995 (see Aircraft variants). S-17 gunsight. Gun camera.
Wing characteristics: Straight, low mounted, with dihedral. Removable leading-edges for easy repair or replacement.
Wing control surfaces: Frise type ailerons and 3-position double-slotted flaps, with new servo tabs.
Tail control surfaces: Elevators and rudder, with new servo tabs. A special trim system has been flight tested to counter propeller torque, comprising a Lear Astronics computer controlling a ventral tail fin.
Flight control system: Mechanical, except for electrically-actuated flaps and tabs.
Construction materials: Metal, but with glassfibre wingtips.
Engine: Walter M-601T turboprop, with a 5-blade propeller.
Engine rating: 751 shp (560 kW).
Fuel system: 560 litres. 2 × 340 litre drop tanks can be carried.
Electrical system: 27.5 volt DC supply powered by a starter generator and 2 × 24 volt/15 amp-hour ni-cd batteries. Inverter for 115 volt/26 volt AC supply.
Braking system: Multi-disc type. Parking brakes.

Aircraft variants:
PZL-130 Orlik was the designation of the M-14PM piston-engined prototypes, with a single aircraft (006) tested with Polish K-8AA derivative engine.
PZL-130T Orlik Turbo was given a 550 shp (410 kW) Pratt & Whitney Canada PT6A-25A turboprop. Other changes included increased dorsal fin leading-edge forward sweep, changes to the systems (the pneumatic system replaced by hydraulic, the electric system redesigned, and an oxygen system added). New equipment was fitted, and the wing structure was strengthened in order to allow underwing stores. 2 prototypes only (004, *SP-RCC* converted from PZL-130, and 008, *SP-WCA*).
PZL-130TM was similar to the PZL-130T, but fitted with a Walter M-601E engine of similar power and a 5-blade propeller. Prototype was 007, and later 005 and 006 were converted.
PZL-130TB (originally named Orlik Turbo Bis, currently simply Orlik) became the standard version for the Polish Air Force, with an M-601T engine and 5-blade propeller. Much heavier than the PZL-130T/TM, with the take-off weight increased from 3,527 to 5,952 lb (1,600 to 2,700 kg). The wing span was extended by 3 ft 3 ins (1 m), and new double-slotted flaps of greater span installed. The position of the ailerons changed, and the aerodynamic twist increased, but the torque box remained unchanged. Weapon load and number of pylons increased from the previous 1,411 lb (640 kg) and 4 pylons. Also, to improve visibility, the rear seat was raised and a single-piece canopy adopted (without the fixed windscreen). Lightweight LFK-F1 ejection seats. Main undercarriage was given increased tyre pressure and new multi-disc brakes. The nosewheel was changed to be of similar size to the main wheels, with steering instead of self-centring. Now all converted to TC-1s.
PZL-130TBH was the proposed version for Hungary.
PZL-130TC is the most advanced version, intended for export. 950 shp (708.4 kW) P&WC PT6A-62 with a 4-blade Hartzell

Details for PZL-130TC-1 Orlik (updated June 1998)

PRINCIPAL DIMENSIONS:
Wing span: 29 ft 7 ins (9 m)
Maximum length: 29 ft 7 ins (9 m)
Maximum height: 11 ft 7 ins (3.53 m)

WINGS:
Aerofoil section: Modified NACA 64_2215
Area: 139.9 sq ft (13 m^2)
Aspect ratio: 6.231
Twist: +3° root, -3° tip
Dihedral: 5°

UNDERCARRIAGE:
Type: Retractable, with steerable nosewheel
Main wheel tyre size: 500 × 200 mm
Nose wheel tyre size: 500 × 200 mm
Wheel base: 9 ft 6 ins (2.9 m)
Wheel track: 10 ft 2 ins (3.1 m)

WEIGHTS:
Empty, operating: 4,023 lb (1,825 kg)
Maximum take-off: 5,952 lb (2,700 kg), or 4,740 lb (2,150 kg) for aerobatics

PERFORMANCE:
Maximum speed: 302 kts (348 mph) 560 km/h at 19,700 ft (6,000 m) altitude, 274 kts (315 mph) 508 km/h at sea level
Cruise speed: 243 kts (280 mph) 450 km/h
Stall speed: 71 kts (82 mph) 131 km/h
Take-off distance: 1,165 ft (355 m) aerobatic weight
Landing distance: 1,280 ft (390 m) aerobatic weight
Maximum climb rate: 2,618 ft (798 m) per minute
G limits: +6, -3 aerobatic or +4.4, -1.76 utility
Ceiling: 33,000 ft (10,000 m)
Range: 573 naut miles (660 miles) 1,062 km, internal fuel
Range with full internal and external fuel: 1,079 naut miles (1,243 miles) 2,000 km

propeller. 2 aircraft built so far (010 and 011), one for static tests. AlliedSignal Bendix/King avionics, including KNR634 navigation glideslope, KTU709 Tacan, KDFB06 ADF, KDM706 DME, KXP756 transponder, and Omega navigation system. Flight Vision HUD in the front cockpit. Martin Baker Mk PL11B ejection seats. Maximum take-off weight 5,952 lb (2,700 kg) with 560 litres of fuel and up to 1,764 lb (800 kg) of external stores. Maximum speed 335 kts (385 mph) 620 km/h, take-off distance 722 ft (220 m), landing distance 1,280 ft (390 m), climb rate 3,878 ft (1,182 m) per minute, ceiling 32,800 ft (10,000 m), and range 594 naut miles (684 miles) 1,100 km. Prototype only.

PZL-130TC-1 is similar to the PZL-130TB but with Martin Baker Mk PL11B ejection seats and other minor alterations including AlliedSignal GPS and transponder, and servo tabs on the control surfaces. This is the current production version, and all the PZL-130TBs were converted to this standard. Currently, further alterations are being tested for TC-1, including a ventral tailfin.

PZL-130TC-2 has an EFIS cockpit layout, and it is probable that this upgrade will eventually be adopted by the Polish Air Force. Flight testing took place in 1995 with prototype *SP-PRF* (009), but had an accident on 25 January 1996.

PZL-130TC-3 is a proposed counter-insurgency version of TC-1. Flight Vision HUD, and 1,543 lb (700 kg) of weapons including Zeus 7.62-mm gun pods, rockets, Strela type AAMs, bombs of up to 200 kg weight each, or submunition dispensers.

PZL-130TD is similar to the PZL-130TC but with a less powerful 750 shp (559.3 kW) PT6A-25C turboprop and 3-blade Hartzell propeller. Project only.

PZL-130TE is a proposed economic version, with a 560 shp (417.6 kW) PT6A-25 engine. Due to the available power, this version has no ejection seats and its equipment has been considerably reduced. Project only.

Aerostar S.A. — Romania

Full name:
Grup Industrial Aeronautic Aerostar S.A.

Corporate address:
9 Condorilor Street, Bacau 5500.

Telephone: +40 34 172 006, 175 070
Facsimile: +40 34 172 023, 172 259, 174 500
Telex: 21339

Founded:
1953, taking its current name in 1991.

Employees:
About 4,700 at 6 plants.

Information:
Serban Yosipescu (Programme Manager – *telephone* +40 34 172 102).

ACTIVITIES

▪ In addition to Yak-52 production, the company produces lightplanes (see General Aviation section), M-14P and M-14V26 aero-engines, the RU-19A-300 engine/APU (see Engine section), low-power diesel engines for agricultural machinery and domestic applications, hydraulic equipment, electronics, avionics and other specialized equipment.

▪ Undertakes jet aircraft upgrade and overhaul, and is currently teamed with Elbit of Israel in the upgrade of Romanian MiG-21s; 10 reportedly being diverted to Ethiopia in 1998.

Aerostar MiG-21 Lancer

Comments: The upgrade programme for 110 Romanian Air Force MiG-21s to Lancer standard (75 for ground attack, 25 air defence and 10 two-seat trainers) by Aerostar and Elbit of Israel (see below for MiG-21 upgrade avionics system diagram) began in November 1993. The first single-seater (an MF) flew on 23 August 1995, followed by a 2-seater in May 1996. The modular upgrade enhances the aircraft and extends life by introducing an array of advanced systems and capabilities through structural modifications and wiring installation; improved electrical power, ECS and pylons; avionics systems design through systems engineering, fused avionics, modular hardware, operational flight programmes software and tools, tests and varification; and new avionics that include mission computers, displays, stores management systems, data links, helmet sight tracker, integrated communication and navigation systems, missile control systems and more. Modernization will enable Lancers to remain in service until the year 2010. Some 50 re-delivered by July 1998.

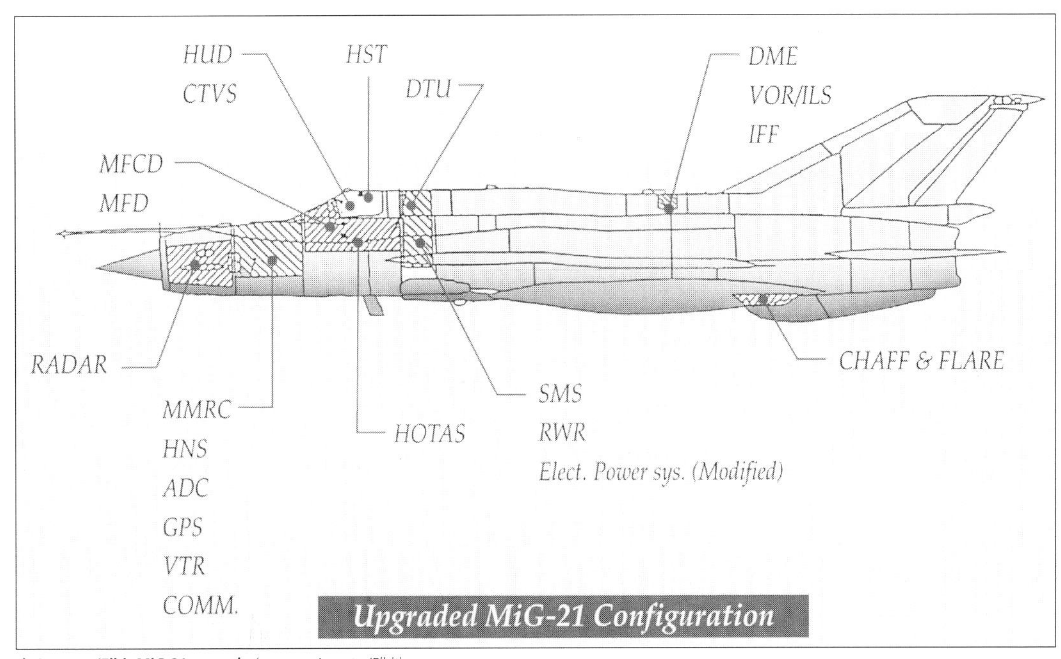

↑ **Aerostar/Elbit MiG-21 upgrade** *(courtesy Aerostar/Elbit)*

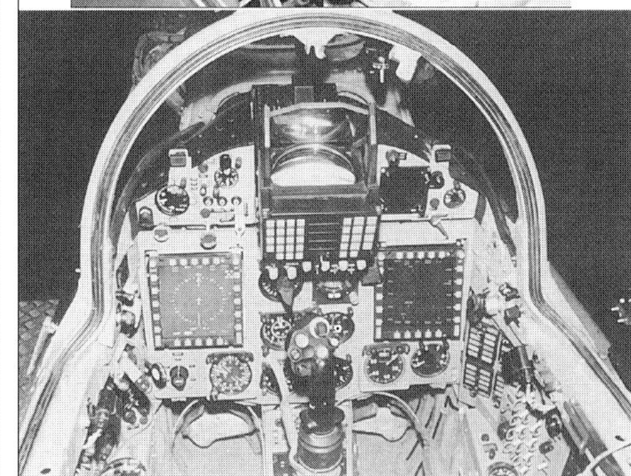

↑ **Romanian Air Force MiG-21 cockpit before and after upgrade to Lancer** *(courtesy Aerostar/Elbit)*

S.C. Avioane S.A.Craiova — Romania

Corporate address:
Aeroportului Street no 1, Craiova, mail code 1100.

Telephone: +40 51 12 4170, 4610
Facsimile: +40 51 12 4382
E-mail: Savioane @ cisnet ro

Founded:
1 February 1972 (named IAv Craiova until 1991).

Information:
Tudor Bistreanu (General Manager).

ACTIVITIES

▪ In addition to the aircraft detailed here, Avioane informed the Chief Editor in late 1997 that work on the IAR-93/J-22 Orao programme with Yugoslavia/Serbia has been terminated. For details and a photograph, see the 1996-97 edition of *WA&SD*, page 170.

▪ For more details of the original IAR 99 Soim than are given here and its upgraded variant, the IAR 109 Swift, see the 1996-97 edition of *WA&SD*, page 65.

▪ The Soim is still being manufactured but in a modern variant named New IAR 99 Soim, as detailed below.

▪ Some manufacturing output has been geared to non-aviation items, including prefabricated buildings.

Avioane New IAR 99 Soim

First flight: 22 May 1997 for New Soim (21 December 1985 for original Soim).
Role: Lead-in fighter trainer and light attack aircraft.

Aims

▪ Totally modernized version of Soim that is compatible to contemporary aircraft, equipped with performance-proven, state-of-the-art avionics resembling that found in most advanced fighters.

▪ Full radar training capability, with virtual radar (see Avionics) that allows training as if operating a multi-mode radar.

▪ Long-range ground attack flight profile.

Details *(New IAR 99 Soim)*

Sales/Users: 2 flying and 1 static test original-version Soim prototypes. Up to 50 original-version Soims ordered for service with the Romanian Air Force. New Soim probably applies to final production aircraft from the 50 already ordered, any further new production, plus upgraded existing original Soims.
Crew: 2, in tandem, with the rear instructor's seat raised by 14 ins (35 cm). Only a pilot is carried during attack missions.
Cockpit: Pressurized. Split canopy appears to be standard.
Crew escape: Zero-zero ejection seats.
Fixed guns: 23-mm GSh-23 cannon in a detachable underfuselage pod.
Ammunition: 200 rounds.
Number of weapon pylons: 4, including 2 'wet' for drop tanks.
Expendable weapons and equipment: Wide array of practice and live ordnance, including smart weapons and pods capability. Up to 2,205 lb (1,000 kg) total load, including 2 pods each with 2 × 7.62-mm guns, bombs of 50 kg to 250 kg weight on single or multi-store carriers, 42-mm or 57-mm rocket launchers, or other options. The gun pods or the drop tanks are suited only to the

↑ **Avioane New IAR 99 Soim with drop tanks**

inner pylons, not a combination of these on all 4 pylons.
Radar: Virtual radar (see Avionics).
Flight/weapon system avionics/instrumentation: Advanced avionics suite integrated by Elbit, including communication (radio and IFF), navigation (VOR/ILS, DME and ADF, GPS and RALT), and identification systems. Advanced cockpit configuration is similar to upgraded MiG-21 and F-16 concepts. Full multi-mode radar training capability, with data link feature that enables generation of virtual radar, providing the capability of full man/machine interface (HOTAS, MFDs, etc) with detection, acquisition and tracking of co-operative airborne targets. Front cockpit has HUD with up-front control panel (UFCP), port MFCD, starboard MFD, ADI and HSI. Instructor monitors trainee performance on aft station HUD monitor (ASHM), enabling on-line mistake correction and demonstration capabilities. Other rear cockpit features include UFCP, audio panel, starboard MFD, ADI and HSI. Display and sight helmet (DASH) system gives instructor constant indication on trainee line-of-sight (LOS) and fast indication to trainee of instructor LOS. Record switch enables instructor to record comments on airborne videotape without the trainee being aware (with event mark), thereby providing advanced debriefing with video and AACMI. Advanced interface system with full computerized (MMR) weapon delivery and navigation systems. Failure injection panel (FIP) simulates failures in the forward cockpit, allowing emergency procedures to be performed. Audio system with voice activation for clear intercommunication. (see Elbit entry under Israel.)

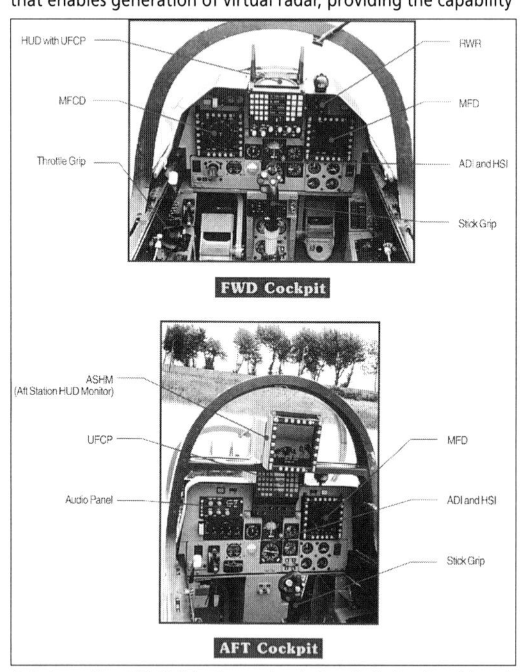

↑ **Avioane New IAR 99 Soim forward and aft cockpits** *(courtesy Avioane)*

Self-protection systems: EW suite with chaff/flare, RWR and ECM pod.
Wing characteristics: Straight, low mounted, with slight dihedral from the roots.
Wing control surfaces: Ailerons (port tab) and single-slotted flaps.
Tail control surfaces: Elevators and rudder, with tabs.
Airbrakes: 2, under the aft fuselage.
Flight control system: Hydraulic ailerons, flaps and airbrakes, mechanical elevators and rudder, electric tabs.
Construction materials: Metal, with honeycomb sandwich construction used for various components including all the control surfaces except for the flaps.
Engine: Rolls-Royce Viper 632-41M turbojet, built indigenously by Intreprinderea Turbomecanica Bucuresti.
Engine rating: 3,970 lbf (17.66 kN).
Air intakes: Fuselage sides, above the wings, with small splitter plates.
Flight refuelling probe: None.
Fuel system: Internal 2,425 lb (1,100 kg). External auxiliary tanks 800 lb (363 kg).
Electrical system: 28 volt DC supply using a starter-generator. Ni-cd battery for engine starting and operation under emergency conditions. AC supply of 115 volt/400Hz and 26 volt/400Hz using 2 static inverters.
Hydraulic system: 2,987 psi.
Braking system: Hydraulic disc type. Anti-skid system.
Deicing system: Bleed air for windshield.

Details for New IAR 99 Soim

PRINCIPAL DIMENSIONS:
Wing span: 32 ft 4 ins (9.85 m)
Maximum length: 36 ft 1.5 ins (11.009 m)
Maximum height: 12 ft 9.5 ins (3.898 m)

WINGS:
Aerofoil section: Modified NACA 64_1A214, 64_1A212 (root/tip)
Area: 201.32 sq ft (18.71 m^2)
Aspect ratio: 5.186
Sweepback: 6° 35′ at 25% chord
Incidence: 1°
Dihedral: 3°

TAIL UNIT:
Tailplane span: 13 ft 6 ins (4.12 m)
Tailplane area: 47.05 sq ft (4.37 m^2)
Sweepback: 9° 8′ at 25% chord
Fin height: 6 ft 5 ins (1.96 m)
Fin sweepback: 34° at 25% chord
Fin area: 27.42 sq ft (42.55 m^2)

UNDERCARRIAGE:
Type: Retractable, with castoring nosewheel
Main wheel tyre size: 552 × 164 mm
Nose wheel tyre size: 445 × 150 mm
Wheel base: 14 ft 4 ins (4.378 m)
Wheel track: 8 ft 10 ins (2.686 m)

WEIGHTS:
Empty, operating: 7,054 lb (3,200 kg)
Maximum take-off: 12,258 lb (5,560 kg) for attack, 9,680 lb (4,391 kg) training

PERFORMANCE (trainer, unless stated)**:**
Maximum operating Mach number (M_{MO}): 0.76
Maximum speed (V max): 467 kts (538 mph) 865 km/h clean, at sea level
Take-off distance: 1,475 ft (450 m)
Landing distance: 1,800 ft (550 m)
Maximum climb rate: 6,900 ft (2,100 m) per minute
G limits: +7, -3.6
Sustained turn rate: Up to >20° per second at 9,700 lb (4,400 lb) weight, 3,280 ft (1,000 m) altitude
Ceiling: 42,300 ft (12,900 m)
Typical attack mission: To target 189 naut miles (217 miles) 350 km from base, outward at 31,170 ft (9,500 m) altitude and Mach 0.55 with 4 × 250 kg bombs, gun pod, full internal fuel and pilot only, at 12,081 lb (5,480 kg) MTOW, with 3-5 minutes over target, and return at 32,800 ft (10,000 m) and Mach 0.6.
Duration: 2 hours 40 minutes

Aeroprogress Inc/Khrunichev State Space Research Center — Russia

Comments: Aeroprogress and Khrunichev (Aviation Department) are closely affiliated. Descriptions of their many current programmes and production aircraft can be found in the General Aviation section. Details and photographs (of models) relating to military concepts that have not progressed into flying prototypes can be found in the 1996-97 edition of *WA&SD*, pages 66 and 67, including the T-501 basic trainer, T-504 Borets combat trainer, T-710 Anaconda STOL strike aircraft, T-720 pusher combat aircraft, T-730 attack aircraft, and T-752 Shtyk wing-in-ground-effect strike and anti-helicopter aircraft. See also Airliners section.

Beriev Taganrog Aviation Complex — Russia

Full name:
Joint Stock Company 'Taganrog Aviation Scientific-Technical Complex named after G.M. Beriev'.

Corporate address:
1 Aviatorov Square, 347928 Taganrog.

Telephone: +7 86344 49839 or 49901
Facsimile: +7 86344 41454

Founded: 1932.

Information:
Gennadiy S. Panatov (Chairman, CEO and General Designer).

Note: Beriev has joined Sukhoi under the AVPK Sukhoi organization.

FACILITIES

- Include the design bureau departments, laboratory complex, flight test complex, experimental production plant, and test base at Gelendzhik on the Black Sea.
- Beriev established Betair Limited Joint Venture (originally Association), along with the Taganrog aircraft production plant, Irkutsk aircraft production plant (IAPO) and Geneva ILTA Trade Finance SA, a Russian-Swiss venture. Through Betair, other western companies have become involved in Be-200 development (see Special Electronic, Airliners and General Aviation sections).

ACTIVITIES

- New aircraft include the propfan Be-42 SAR prototype and A-60 laser-gun testbed.

Beriev Be-12, Be-12P and Be-12P-200 (NATO name *Mail*)

Comments: The Be-12 as an anti-submarine warfare and search and rescue amphibian was manufactured between 1963-73 in Taganrog. Those remaining with the Russian Navy are being withdrawn, leaving only small numbers in service with other forces. A full description of the Be-12 and photographs can be found in the 1996-97 editon of *WA&SD*, pages 67 and 68. The following is a brief account of current operators of the military Be-12 and details of newer models produced by conversion.
Programme Manager: Viktor Ponomaryov is responsible for Be-12 conversions.

↑ **Beriev Be-12P-200 fire-fighting conversion with systems prepared for the Be-200** *(Piotr Butowski)*

First flight: 18 October 1960 first take-off from water (pilot G. Turyanov); 2 November 1960 first take-off from shore (pilot Piotr Bobro).
Role: Shore-based, short-range anti-submarine warfare (ASW) and search and rescue amphibian. Also converted for fire-fighting, civil transport and patrol, and ecological monitoring.

Development

■ 1992. Civil conversion programme started, particularly aimed at the fire-fighting version.
■ 13 July 1993. The effectiveness of the Be-12P fire-fighter was demonstrated, when it dropped 252 tonnes of water in 2 runs during a fire at the village of Listvianka.
■ 1 June 1994. The Russian Government voted the declaration "On Fighting the Forest Fire". According to this declaration, in 1994 naval aviation was to hand over a further 8 Be-12s to be converted to fire-fighting versions. However, this programme was not financially supported.

Details

Sales/Users: Total of 142 built (including prototypes) for military ASW and SAR roles. The Russian Navy had about 40 at time of writing, plus 22 in store as reserve aircraft. 14 are used by the Ukrainian Navy, about 12 by Vietnam (operated since 1980) and Syria. 4 Be-12Ps, a single Be-12P-200 and 2 Be-12NKh conversions had been completed at time of writing, but both NKhs were lost in 1994.
Crew: 4 (2 pilots side-by-side, navigator in the glazed fuselage nose, under the radar antenna, and a radio officer in the cabin) of military versions. Crew of 6 in the Be-12PS (rescue system operator and litter-bearer added).
Engines: 2 Ivchenko PROGRESS/Zaporozhye AI-20D (series 4) turboprops located over the highest point of the wings, with 4-blade variable-pitch propellers. AI-8 auxiliary power unit (APU).
Engine rating: Each 5,180 eshp (3,863 ekW).
Fuel system: 19,842 lb (9,000 kg) of internal fuel. Provision for 2 additional tanks inside the cabin, 1,800 litres each.

Aircraft variants:
Be-12 (izdeliye E) was the initial production ASW version, powered by AI-20s.
Be-12N became the upgraded and current ASW version, with the Nartsiss (narcissus) search/track system.
Be-12NKh (narodno-khoziaystvennyi, economical) was a civil transport/multipurpose conversion. 2 completed, used at Kurile Islands and Sakhalin for airborne search of fish banks, in addition to their operations as cargo/passenger transports, the latter including a regular service to Kunashir Island during 1992-93. In total, the Be-12NKh in Sakhalin District made 260 flights (628 hours), carrying 401.5 tonnes of cargo and 2,055 passengers. The amphibians were pressed into use during the earthquake in the Kuril Islands on 3 October 1994, when neither land-based aircraft nor helicopters were able to come to the rescue due to poor visibility. Carrying aid, *No 96* alighted off the coast, taxiing to the shore at 32 kts in 30 minutes. Thereafter, between 6 and 11 October 1994, the Be-12NKhs delivered 30 tonnes of cargo. However, both aircraft were lost in 1994 at Curile Islands (without casualties), because of operational shortcomings during rescue missions.
Be-12P (pozharnyi, fire-fighting) is the fire-fighting conversion. Prototype (c/n *9601404*, side number *40*) first flew in the Spring of 1992. Work has been financed by the administration of Irkutsk District and by the Federal Forestry Service of Russia. A Be-12P with factory number *2602505* was presented to the public in August and September 1993 in Zhukovsky near Moscow. A further 3 Be-12s were similarly converted. The aircraft takes in 6,000 litres of water during the take-off run which, when released in a single mass from an altitude of 115-130 ft (35-40 metres), blankets an area 490 × 130 ft (150 × 40 m). When extinguishing the Irkutsk District fire, carrying 9,921 lb (4,500 kg) of fuel and flying a distance from the water to the fire equal to 8 naut miles (9.3 miles) 15 km, a Be-12P dropped 120 tonnes of water onto the burning forest (see also Development – 13 July 1993). Be-12Ps were also used for fire-fighting in Tchukotka, in Rostov District, as well as near Yalta and Gelendzhik on the Black Sea.
Be-12P-200 (c/n *8601301*) is a fire-fighting conversion under trials, equipped with a new water-lifting system designed for the Be-200 (see Transport section). First flown in August 1996.

Beriev A-40/Be-40 Albatross, Be-42 and Be-44 (NATO name *Mermaid*)

First flight: 8 December 1986 from land (pilot Yevgeni Lakhmastov), 4 November 1987 from water.
Role: Intermediate-range anti-submarine warfare/mine laying, search and rescue and patrol/reconnaissance amphibian.
Chief designer: Alexei Konstantinov.

Aims

■ Designed as the replacement for both the Be-12 *Mail* amphibian and Il-38 *May*.
■ Ability to alight on water, yet possess a range of 5,000 km needed to satisfy the Il-38-replacement requirement.
■ Ability to take-off from rough sea with wave heights exceeding 2 m.

Development

■ 1983. Work started.
■ 1985. Metal cut for the first prototype.
■ 1988. Design of a search and rescue variant began.
■ June 1991. First international presentation, at the Paris Air Show.
■ Early 1992. The Russian Navy ordered about 20 aircraft, widely publicized to be for search and rescue.
■ 22 June 1993. An A-40 prototype was displayed at the Woodford Air Base in the UK.
■ 30 May 1995. Russian ministry of Defence representative Pavel Grachev visited Taganrog and flew the A-40, indicating renewed interest of the armed forces, possibly for landing marine units.

Details *(based on Be-40, but other versions as indicated)*

Sales/Users: 2 of 3 existing A-40 prototypes are used as flying test-beds, while the third is for static testing. At the time of writing, none of these carried any special equipment or weapons. In 1992, the Russian Navy ordered a certain number of production examples (reportedly 20) but this construction lacks funding. Beriev has obtained the permission of the Russian Government to sell the Be-40 abroad, and the aircraft has visited several international expositions. A third flying prototype was built and probably flew in 1997, representing the Be-42 SAR version powered by 2 D-27A propfans (some reports suggest the provisional designation A-45). If production of the Albatross continues, it will be in Be-42 form for SAR and this will become the standard engine type, whereas a specialized anti-submarine warfare variant of the Tu-204 airliner will now enter service instead of Be-40.
Crew: 5 flight crew (2 pilots, navigator, flight engineer and radio operator), plus mission crew of 3.
Cockpit: Divided into 2 separate 4-seat compartments, with doors at both sides of the rear compartment. Aft of the cockpit is a rest room and toilet.
Fixed guns: None.
Expendable weapons and equipment: Up to 13,228 lb (6,000 kg) but with a 'normal' load of 8,818 lb (4,000 kg), carried in the fuselage bay, including ASW torpedoes and missiles, depth bombs, mines, etc. The list of Be-40 weapons includes 3 Orlan ASW torpedoes or 4 to 6 ASW missiles of Korshun, Yastreb and Oriol types, but no further details are available.
Radar: Undernose radome houses search/attack, surveillance, navigation and wave measuring radar.
Flight/weapon system avionics/instrumentation: Conventional instrumentation. Inertial flight/navigation system. IFF. Magnetic anomaly detector (MAD) will be fitted to the fin-tip of any operational aircraft, protruding to the rear.
Self-protection systems: Probably active electronic jammers standard.
Wing characteristics: Slightly swept, shoulder mounted. No dihedral/anhedral. Wingtip floats and jammer pods. Optimized for 2 speeds: maximum cruising speed (760 km/h) and patrol speed (Mach 0.3-0.35).
Wing control surfaces: Each wing has an aileron, 2-section double-slotted flaps, spoilers and full leading-edge slats.
Tail control surfaces: T-tail with variable incidence swept tailplane, elevators, and swept fin with rudder.
Fuselage: Semi-monocoque, of high length-over-beam ratio. The fuselage height was made as low as possible (maximum height

↑ **Beriev A-40 cockpit** *(Piotr Butowski)*

↑ **Beriev A-40 take-off at Gelendzhik, Black Sea** *(Piotr Butowski)*

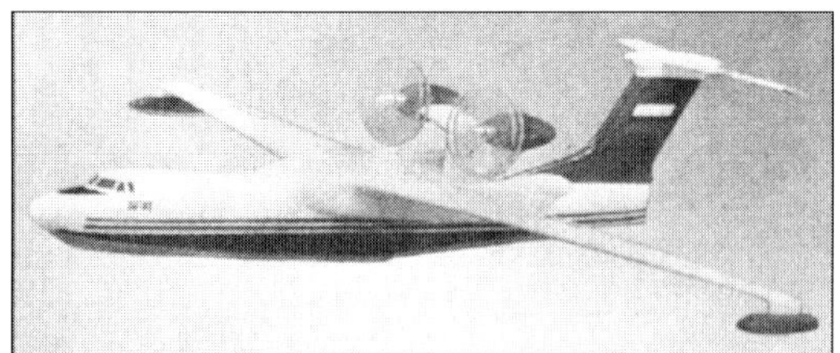

↑ **Beriev third flying prototype has D-27A propfans, as will all future production Be-40/Be-42s** *(courtesy Beriev)*

13 ft 5 ins, 4.1 m), making the planing bottom relatively flat; the so called 'boat pitch' is 1% at the stern and 6.5% at the bow. A flat bottom, however, means much greater dynamic load on the hull when taking-off and alighting. Therefore special profiles were designed to reduce these loads by half, the so-called 'variable-rise bottom'. The hull is of single step type, double-chine forward of the step (like a flattened 'W') and a simple 'V' aft of the step. 2 wedges are attached at the rear of the step, near the bomb bay, to assist take off. Anti-spray strakes are carried near the nose and forward of the step, the forward strakes acting at low speed and the rear at high speed to protect the engines from water inhalation. Main cabin area is divided into 2 pressurized and 1 unpressurized (weapons bay) compartments. Whole fuselage is pressurized in the SAR Be-42 version, except the lower section of the weapons bay.
Construction materials: Mostly metal, but with honeycomb core/composites used where structurally acceptable.
Engines: 2 D-30KPV turbofans carried above the fuselage, aft of the wings. 2 Rybinsk/Novikov RD-38K turbojet boosters (each 6,581 lbf, 29.27 kN) are installed below the main engines. The Be-42 third flying prototype, plus any following production aircraft, will use Ivchenko PROGRESS/Zaporozhye D-27A propfans (each 14,000 shp, 10,440 kW) and a single Klimov/St Petersburg RD-33AS turbofan take-off booster (11,465 lbf, 51 kN). Other engines are also being considered, including PS-90A turbofans and D-27M propfans (see Aircraft variants). TA-12 APU.
Engine rating: Each 26,455 lbf (117.68 kN) at take off and 6,062 lbf (26.97 kN) cruise for D-30KPV.
Engine nozzles: Toed out.

↑ **Beriev-developed A-60 laser-gun testbed** *(courtesy Beriev)*

Flight refuelling probe: Mounted on the nose, forward of the cockpit.
Fuel system: 35,100 litres.
Electrical system: 27 volt DC system, and 115 volt/400Hz single-phase and 115-220 volt/400Hz 3-phase AC systems, using 2 engine-driven 60kVA AC generators, 3 static inverters and 3 batteries.
Hydraulic system: 3,000 psi. 4 circuits.
Braking system: Discs on the main units, with anti-skid.
De-icing system: For cockpit windows, tail, wing slats and air intakes.
Oxygen system: Gaseous.

Aircraft variants:
A-40 (izdelye V) prototypes, used for testing and international presentations/representations. Have established 128 world records.
A-40M is a projected improved version, probably with D-27M propfans, each 16,000 shp (11,931 kW).
Be-40 is the intended production ASW version, as detailed, with both D-30KPV and D-27A engine options. See also Be-44.
Be-40P is a projected passenger version for 105 persons. Flight refuelling probe and bay doors deleted.
Be-40PT is a projected convertible passenger/cargo version of the P, for 37 or 70 passengers plus cargo.
Be-42 (A-42) is the search and rescue variant, with electro-optical sensors and searchlights suspended under the wings. D-27A propfans. Can carry a rescue group of 4-6 persons, boats, pontoons, LPS-6 rafts, ladders, etc. Sophisticated medical equipment can be installed, when the flight crew is joined by 3 medical staff. Accommodation for 53 survivors. Another possible task for the Be-42 is the replacement of ships' crews at sea, 37-70 seats being available in this variant. Larger pressurized cabin than the Be-40, at 2,437 cu ft (69 m^3), instead of 2,048 cu ft (58 m^3), but at the cost of a reduced weapons bay. Expendable stores include KAS-150 rescue packs and SAV illumination bombs carried in the weapons bay.
Be-44 (A-44) was a projected patrol/reconnaissance version. Now cancelled and its tasks transferred to the standard Be-40 which will have extended equipment compared with that originally planned.
A-45 designation has been reported in the western press for the propfan prototype (see Be-42), though *WA&SD* has not received any evidence to support the use of this designation.

Beriev A-60

First flight: 1980s.
Role: Experimental laser-gun carrier testbed. Not data available regarding results of trials.
Based on: Ilyushin Il-76MD *Candid*. Single aircraft converted, *SSSR-86879*.
Features: Large bulge radome at the nose. 2 power supply generators in the forward-extending undercarriage nacelles. Laser-gun turret protruding above the centre section of the fuselage.

Details for A-40/Be-40 with D-30KPV engines; *weights and performance of D-27A-powered version in italics*

PRINCIPAL DIMENSIONS:
Wing span: 143 ft 10 ins (43.839 m)
Maximum length: 138 ft 11 ins (42.33 m), without probe
Fuselage length: 127 ft 8 ins (38.915 m)
Maximum height: 36 ft 4 ins (11.066 m)

WINGS:
Aerofoil section: Supercritical
Area: 2,152.78 sq ft (200 m^2)
Aspect ratio: 8.6
Sweepback: 23° 13'
Incidence: 3° 23' at root
Twist: 4° 30'
Dihedral/anhedral: 0°

TAIL UNIT:
Tailplane span: 38 ft 11 ins (11.87 m)
Tailplane area: 302.31 sq ft (28.086 m^2)
Fin area: 225.93 sq ft (20.99 m^2)

UNDERCARRIAGE:
Type: Retractable, with twin steerable nosewheels. Main units have tandem pairs of wheels. Fixed wingtip floats
Main wheel tyre size: 1,030 × 350 mm
Nose wheel tyre size: 840 × 290 mm
Wheel base: 48 ft 8 ins (14.835 m)
Wheel track: 16 ft 3 ins (4.96 m)
Turning radius: 63 ft 2 ins (19.25 m)

WEIGHTS:
Maximum take-off: 189,597 lb (86,000 kg), *209,439 lb (95,000 kg)*
Maximum landing: 187,393 lb (85,000 kg) on water, 160,937 lb (73,000 kg) on shore, *the same*

PERFORMANCE:
Maximum operating Mach number (M_{MO}): Mach 0.79
Maximum speed: 442 kts (510 mph) 820 km/h
Cruise speed: 410 kts (472 mph) 760 km/h at 19,685 ft (6,000 m), *378 kts (435 mph) 700 km/h*
Patrol speed: Mach 0.3 to 0.35
Stall speed: 146 kts (168 mph) 270 km/h *clean*, 98 kts (113 mph) 182 km/h *with flaps*
Climb rate at sea level: 5,905 ft (1,800 m) per minute
Take-off distance: 3,281-3,937 ft (1,000-1,200 m), *4,100-6,496 ft (1,250-1,980 m)*
Landing distance: 2,300-2,953 ft (700-900 m), *1,312-2,297 ft (400-700 m)*
Ceiling: 31,825 ft (9,700 m)
Range with full fuel: 2,970 naut miles (3,418 miles) 5,500 km, *5,666 naut miles (6,524 miles) 10,500 km*
Range with full payload: 2,536 naut miles (2,920 miles) 4,700 km, *4,479 naut miles (5,157 miles) 8,300 km*
Maximum duration (D-27A propfan engines): *17 hours*
Allowable wave height: 7.2 ft (2.2 m) (the aircraft has been tested at 5.5 ft, 1.68 m)

Eurasia Design Bureau — Russia

Corporate address:
Severnoye Chertanovo 6, korp. 607, Moscow Region.
Telephone: +7 095 319 1191
Facsimile: +7 095 318 4271
President: Dr Fatidin Mukhamedov.
Activities:
▪ Eurasia is developing several aircraft with unusual disc-like wing centre section and short outer wing panels.

Eurasia Integral and Integral-2010

First flight: Project only.
Role: Modern advanced trainer (Integral) or lightweight multirole combat fighter (Integral-2010).

Aims *(Integral-2010)*

▪ Reduced radar and IR visibility, and internal bay for 4 R-77 AAMs.
▪ Very high manoeuvrability, with 70° angles of attack.
▪ Low cost.

Details

Crew: Pilot in Integral-2010, or 2 in the Integral.
Number of weapon pylons (Integral-2010): 6 under the wings, and 1 under the fuselage. Also an internal weapons bay in the wing centre section.
Expendable weapons and equipment (Integral-2010): Basic air combat armament comprises 4 medium-range R-77 (AA-12 *Adder*) AAMs. Also standard short-range AAMs and tactical ASMs can be used.
Engine: Single Klimov/Sarkisov RD-331 non afterburning turbofan, with single round nozzle in Integral and 2 separate flat nozzles in Integral-2010.
Engine rating: 11,573 lbf (51.48 kN).
Fuel system: Maximum 4,409 lb (2,000 kg) in internal tanks, but 2,646 lb (1,200 kg) is the normal fuel capacity. Single underfuselage auxiliary tank.

Aircraft variants:
Integral is a 2-seat trainer, with combat training version possible.
Integral-2010 is its single-seat derivative, with armament.

Details for Eurasia Integral

PRINCIPAL DIMENSIONS:
Wing span: 34 ft 3.5 ins (10.45 m)
Maximum length: 35 ft 7 ins (10.84 m)
Maximum height: 14 ft (4.26 m)

WINGS:
Area: 288.8 sq ft (26.83 m^2)
Sweepback: 27° on outer panels

UNDERCARRIAGE:
Type: Retractable, with single wheels

WEIGHTS:
Normal take-off: 12,125 lb (5,500 kg)
Maximum take-off: 13,889 lb (6,300 kg)
Maximum take-off for combat training variant: 19,180 lb (8,700 kg)

PERFORMANCE:
Maximum operating speed: 620 kts (715 mph) 1,150 km/h
Landing speed, normal landing weight: 86 kts (99 mph) 160 km/h
Maximum climb rate: 21,650 ft (6,600 m) per minute, at sea level
Ceiling: 51,180 ft (15,600 m)
Range with maximum fuel: 1,079 naut miles (1,242 miles) 2,000 km

← **Eurasia Integral-2010 lightweight training and combat aircraft** *(Piotr Butowski)*

Ilyushin Aviation Complex — Russia

Full name:
Aviatsionnyi Kompleks imeni S.V. Ilyushina.

Corporate address:
45G Leningradsky Prospekt, 125190 Moscow.

Telephone: +7 095 943 8325
Facsimile: +7 095 212 2132
Telex: 411956 SOKOL

Founded: 1933.

Employees: 3,800.

Information:
Igor Katyrev (Chief Designer).

ACTIVITIES

▪ In the Summer of 1994 the Ilyushin Aviation Complex joined with the VASO Voronezh aircraft production plant to form the Ilyushin Aircraft Production Association. The Russian Government then retained a 51% majority interest. The Voronezh Aircraft Production Facility manufactures the Il-96, while the Tashkent Aircraft Production Organization (Chkalov Tashkent Aircraft Production Enterprise in Uzbekistan) builds the Il-76. Construction of the Il-103 lightplane has been assigned to MAPO's Lukhovitsky Machine-Building Plant.
▪ Since its founding, Ilyushin has designed over 100 different types of aircraft, accounting for nearly 60,000 aircraft. See Airliners, Reconnaissance and General Aviation sections.

Ilyushin Il-38 (NATO name *May*)

First flight: 28 November 1961 (first prototype with incomplete systems), piloted by Vladimir Kokkinakki.
Role: Shore-based, medium range anti-submarine warfare aircraft.
Based on: Ilyushin Il-18 transport.

Development

▪ 18 June 1960. Governmental order for a medium-range ASW aircraft.

↑ **Ilyushin Il-38 *May* showing the Berkut navigation/attack radar under the forward fuselage**

▪ 1965. Fully equipped Il-38 began flight tests.
▪ 14 May–4 December 1965. State acceptance trials.
▪ 23 December 1967. First production aircraft left factory.
▪ 17 January 1969. Il-38 officially commissioned.
▪ 1970. First recognized in the West.
▪ 22 February 1972. Last aircraft produced.
▪ 20-21 July 1996. First visit to the West, to Fairford Air Tattoo, UK.

Details

Sales/Users: 57 Il-38s were built by Znamya Truda (now MAPO) in Moscow. It is likely that around 35 currently serve with the Russian and Ukrainian navies, though some reports suggest a higher figure. 5 went to India in 1975. Russian Il-38s are divided between the Northern Fleet (ASW aircraft regiment based at Severomorsk), Pacific Fleet (regiment based at Petropavlovsk) and the Baltic Fleet (including squadron based at Ostrov). Indian Navy's 315 squadron at Dabolim has 5, received in 1976.
Crew: 10 according to design bureau, but 7 according to military publications and 7-8 reported when flown to Fairford, comprising 2 pilots, navigator, sensor operator, tactical commander, communications operator and flight engineer, with provision for an instructor (supernumerary crew member). Maximum cabin pressure differential 7.1 psi.
Fixed guns: None.
Number of weapon pylons: None externally.
Radar: Navigation/weather radar in the nose radome. Berkut search/attack radar (NATO name *Wet Eye*) in an egg-shaped radome under the forward fuselage.
Other mission sensors/equipment: Automated Leninets Berkut search/attack system joining radar of the same name, radio sonobuoy system, navigational subsystem, and TsVM-264 Plamya digital computer. APM-73 Bor magnetic anomaly detector (MAD) in the tail sting is a separate system, not included in the Berkut system.
Expendable weapons and equipment: Up to 18,519 lb (8,400 kg) of weapons and stores (nominal load 11,023 lb, 5,000 kg) carried in 2 fuselage weapon bays. The 3 typical load variants are: search with 216 RGB-1 sonobuoys (each 31 lb, 14 kg); search/attack with 144 RGB-1 sonobuoys plus 10 RGB-2 sonobuoys (each 99 lb, 45 kg) and 3 RGB-3 sonobuoys (each 408 lb, 185 kg) and 2 AT-2 torpedoes or 10 PLAB-250-120 depth bombs or a single RYu-2 nuclear depth bomb; mine-laying with 8 AMD-2-500M mines or 4 UDM mines. PSN-6A rescue dinghy and life jackets.
Self-protection systems: Some aircraft carry 4 large packs of chaff/flare dispensers, 1 each side of the nose and 1 on each side of the MAD antenna. Each pack contains 192 projectiles. RWR.
Wing control surfaces: Balanced ailerons with trim tabs and double-slotted trailing-edge flaps.
Tail control surfaces: Elevators and rudder with trim tabs plus spring tab on rudder.
Flight control system: Mechanical, with cables and hydraulic actuators/boost (see Hydraulic system). Electrically-operated trim tabs.
Engines: 4 Ivchenko PROGRESS AI-20M turboprops, with AV-68I 4-blade propellers. TG-16M APU.
Engine rating: Each 4,250 eshp (3,169 ekW) at take-off.
Fuel system: 35,153 litres.
Electrical system: 28 volt DC, 115 volt/400Hz AC, with 8 engine-driven generators.
Hydraulic system: 3,000 psi, for flap/elevator/rudder actuation, antennae, bay doors, undercarriage and brakes.
Braking system: Hydraulically operated.

Aircraft variants:
Il-38 *May-A* is the standard version, as detailed.
Il-38 *May B* has an additional drop-type radome in place of the front bomb bay, as seen in 1986.
Il-38M was a prototype of 1972 with new Korshun search/attack system and provision for in-flight refuelling (another Il-38 was to be used as the tanker). Not accepted in order not to compete with long-range Tu-142.

Details for Il-38 *May-A*

PRINCIPAL DIMENSIONS:
Wing span: 122 ft 9 ins (37.42)
Maximum length: 131 ft 6 ins (40.075 m)
Maximum height: 33 ft 4.5 ins (10.17 m)

WINGS:
Area: 1,507 sq ft (140 m^2)
Aspect ratio: 10
Chord at root: 18 ft 5 ins (5.61 m)
Dihedral: 3°

TAIL UNIT:
Tailplane span: 38 ft 8 ins (11.8 m)
Tailplane area: 172.2 sq ft (16 m^2)

UNDERCARRIAGE:
Type: Retractable, with steerable nosewheels (±45°)
Main wheel tyre size: 930 x 305 mm
Nose wheel tyre size: 800 × 225 mm
Wheel base: 41 ft 11 ins (12.78 m)
Wheel track: 29 ft 6 ins (9 m)

WEIGHTS:
Empty, operating: 75,023 lb (34,030 kg)
Maximum take-off: 145,504 lb (66,000 kg), but 139,993 lb (63,500 kg) quoted by design bureau

PERFORMANCE:
Maximum speed: 354 kts (408 mph) 656 km/h
Cruise speed: 313 kts (360 mph) 580 km/h
Mission speed: 173-216 kts (199-249 mph) 320-400 km/h
Take-off distance: 4,265 ft (1,300 m)
Mission altitude: 98-36,090 ft (30-11,000 m), but usually between 328-3,280 ft (100-1,000 m)
Range with 11,023 lb (5,000 kg) of weapons: 3,615 naut miles (4,163 miles) 6,700 km
Patrol duration: 4 hours at 1,080 naut miles (1,243 miles) 2,000 km from base
Duration: 11 hours maximum

MIG "MAPO-M"
VPK MAPO-M (Military Industrial Group "Moscow Aircraft Production Organization-M") — Russia

Full name:
Voenno-Promyshlennyi Komplex Moscow Aviation Production Organization – Myasishchev.

Corporate address:
7, First Botkinsky Drive, Moscow 125190.

Telephone: +7 095 252 8141
Facsimile: +7 095 250 8819, 202 9447

Information:
Public Relations & Media Centre (*telephone* +7 095 207 0366, *facsimile* +7 095 924 2489).

Founded:
Original aviation factory in Moscow (forerunner of MAPO) was founded in 1893. During WW1 it built Farman and Nieuport aeroplanes, becoming The State Aircraft works No 1 in 1918 and MAPO in 1991. In 1995 the A I Mikoyan Aviation Scientific-Production Complex and MAPO merged as MAPO "MiG" for MiG sales and support. Following a period of difficulty, in January 1996 the MIG "MAPO" organization (Military Industrial Group "MAPO") was established as a state-owned unitary concern by Presidential decree by the merger of a number of leading Russian military and civil aviation-building companies, forming a huge industrial-financial concern. MIG "MAPO" (VPK MAPO in Russian) organization then comprised The Moscow Aircraft Production Organization "MiG", Kamov Public Joint-Stock Company , NPO Klimov Research and Production Company, Tushino Soyuz Machine-Building Plant, Chernyshev Moscow Machine-Building Plant, Krasny Octyabr Machine-Building Plant, Ryazan State Instrument Plant, Perm Instrument-Building Joint-Stock Company, OKB Elektroavtomatika, Pribor (instrument) Joint-Stock Company, NTP Aviatest Scientific-Technical Enterprise, Aviation Repair Plant No 121 at Kubinka, and Aviabank Joint-Stock Commercial Bank. In the Summer of 1997, MIG "MAPO–M" was established as the current organization, having incorporated the Myasishchev Design Bureau.

ACTIVITIES

▪ MAPO "MiG" branch of MIG "MAPO-M" comprises the MAPO production plant and ANPK 'MiG' named after A.I. Mikoyan (the Design Bureau) and produces the MiG-29 fighter and MiG-AT trainer. It is developing the 5th generation multi-role I-42, upgrades early MiG fighters (importantly the MiG-21, including Indian aircraft), offers maintenance and servicing, plus undertakes series production of civil aircraft, including the T-101 Grach, Aviatika-890, Il-103 and I-1L, and continues work on the MiG-110, MiG-115 and MiG-125 general-purpose/transport aircraft. It is developing the MiG 301 and 321, believed to be hypersonic reconnaissance aircraft.
▪ Kamov undertakes development, experimental production, maintenance and upgrading of military and civil helicopters (see Helicopter section).
▪ Klimov, Tushino Soyuz, Chernyshov and Krasny Octyabr undertake development, production, maintenance and upgrading of aircraft engines, gearboxes and other units.
▪ Ryazan, Perm. Electroautomatica, Pribor and Aviatest develop, produce, maintain and upgrade instruments and ground equipment, including radars and weapon control systems.
▪ Aviation Repair Plant No 121 maintains, repairs and upgrades military aircraft, engines, units and airborne equipment, with the capability of repairing over 100 aircraft per year. MAPO-Service was established for guarantee and post-guarantee maintenance for supplied MiG-29s.
▪ Aviabank invests in science-consumable and 'leading-edge' design projects and in the production of new-generation aircraft, aviation techniques and weapon systems.
▪ MIG "MAPO" is the 5th largest Russian enterprise for export sales volume, and the leading machine-building complex.

MAPO "MiG" Russia

Address:
N.6, Leningradskoe Shosse, 125299, Moscow.

Telephone: +7 095 155 2639, 158 0221, 158 8031
Facsimile: +7 095 943 0027

Founded:
8 December 1939.

Information:
Svyatoslav Yu. Ribas (Public Relations).

ACTIVITIES

■ Branch of MIG "MAPO-M" (see above).

Mikoyan MiG-21 and MiG-21-93 (NATO name *Fishbed*)

Note: See Israel, Romania and Multi-national sections for other MiG-21 upgrades.
First flight: 9 January 1956 (E-5 development aircraft); 25 May 1995 for MiG-21-93 (pilot Vladimir Gorbunov).
Role: Lightweight multi-role combat fighter.

Aims

■ See the 1996-97 edition of *WA&SD*, page 71, for MiG-21 Aims.
■ MiG-21-93 to carry new R-27 and R-77 AAMs and guided air-to-surface weapons.
■ MiG-21-93 to have all-weather multi-mode radar, helmet-mounted sight, and 'glass' cockpit.

Development

■ See the 1996-97 edition of *WA&SD*, page 71, for MiG-21 development.
■ May 1994. MiG-21-93 prototype was presented at ILA '94 in Berlin.
■ 1 March 1996. Contract signed between HAL and MAPO "MiG" for upgrade of 125 Indian Air Force MiG-21bis.
■ Late-1998. First MiG-21-93 to enter service with India.

Details

Sales/Users: 10,158 MiG-21s were built at 3 Soviet factories: 5,278 at No 21 in Nizhny Novgorod, 3,203 at No 30 Znamya Truda in Moscow, and 1,677 at No 31 in Tbilisi. In addition, 574 were manufactured by HAL in India (197 MiG-21FLs, 162 MiG-21Ms, 35 MiG-21MFs and 180 MiG-21bis); 194 in Czechoslovakia (MiG-21F-13); and some 2,500 in China where it remains available in J-7/F-7 variants (which see). In early 1998 some 4,500 MiG-21s of many versions were thought to remain in use in 32 countries throughout the world, including over 300 of Indian origin and over 700 from China. The MiG-21 is completely withdrawn from Russian service. Major users are Afghanistan, Algeria, Angola, Bulgaria, China, Cuba, Czech Republic, Egypt, Ethiopia, Hungary, India, Iraq, North Korea, Laos, Libya, Poland (about 217 in 1998), Romania, Slovakia, Syria and Vietnam (over 100). For the Indian upgrade requirement, the Mikoyan tender was forwarded to India in September 1991. The contract between HAL and MiG for updating 125 MiG-21bis (with an option for 50 more) into MiG-21-93s was finally signed on 1 March 1996. The programme is expected to take 4 years and will cost about $340 million. The first 2 Indian MiG-21bis aircraft have been upgraded at the Sokol plant in Nizhny Novgorod, with later aircraft being modified by HAL in India. The first upgraded MiG-21-93 is slated to enter service at the end of 1998. Bulgaria, Syria and Vietnam have expressed interest in the upgrade, and Phazotron has expressed the view that demand for at least 400-500 upgraded aircraft is anticipated. In May 1997, HAL of India signed a contract to upgrade 29 Laotian MiG-21s.
Crew: Pilot; 2 in tandem cockpits on training versions.
Cockpit: Single-piece windscreen on MiG-21-93 for better visibility, replacing former 3-piece canopy.
Crew escape: Standard Mikoyan KM-1 or KM-1M ejection seat.
Fixed guns: Underfuselage mounted GSh-23L 2-barrel 23-mm cannon was standard on all versions from MiG-21M *Fishbed J*.
Ammunition: 200 rounds.
Number of weapon pylons: 4 under the wings.
Expendable weapons and equipment: MiG-21bis can carry up to 2,646 lb (1,200 kg) of stores (2,205 lb, 1,000 kg for older versions). Standard air-to-air armament includes infra-red R-60M (AA-8 *Aphid*), infra-red R-13M (AA-2 *Atoll*), and semi-active radar-homing R-3R. Air-to-surface weapons are unguided only on versions other than MiG-21-93 and other upgrades, such as bombs, rockets and gun pods. Theoretically, MiG-21bis can carry the Kh-28 (AS-9 *Kyle*) heavy anti-radar missile, but only a few MiG-21 users have this missile (including Vietnam and Iraq). MiG-21-93 can carry the alternative armament of 2 R-27R1 or R-27T1 (AA-10 *Alamo*) medium-range AAMs, 4 R-77 (AA-12 *Adder*) medium-range AAMs, 4 R-73 (AA-11 *Archer*) close air combat AAMs, or 6 R-60M close air combat AAMs. Air-to-surface options for MiG-21-93 are a single Kh-31A/P (AS-17 *Krypton*) ASM, 2 Kh-35 anti-ship missiles, 2 Kh-25MP (AS-12 *Kegler*) anti-radar missiles, 2 × 500 kg TV-guided KAB-500Kr bombs, or unguided rockets, bombs, etc. See Israel for MiG-21-2000, with weapon options that include 4 infra-red air-to-air missiles (R-60M, R-73, and Israeli Rafael Python 3), 7 Mk 82E Snakeye laser-guided bombs, 7 free fall 250 kg or 3 free fall 500 kg, or a single 1,000 kg bombs.
Additional stores: V18-329E reconnaissance pod and EL-8202 electronic warfare pod on MiG-21-2000.
Radar: MiG-21bis has RP-22SM or SMA (Sapfir-21, NATO *Jay Bird*), a simplified version of Smerch A used in the MiG-25P *Foxbat A*, in the nose shock cone. Search range is 10.8-13.5 naut miles (12.4-15.5 miles) 20-25 km, tracking range 7.6-9.2 naut miles (8.7-10.6 miles) 14-17 km, and search area 28° in azimuth and 17° 40' in elevation. MiG-21-93 has the small Phazotron Kopyo (Spear), with design and technology gleaned from the MiG-29M's N-010 Zhuk radar. Weight 364 lb (165 kg). Mean time between failures (MTBF) 120 hours. Kopyo can also engage targets at altitudes from 100 ft (30 m), whereas RP-22 detects targets at above 3,280 ft (1,000 m). Kopyo can track-while-scan up to 8 targets simultaneously and engage 2, whereas RP-22 can track only 1.

↑ **MiG-21-93 is a Russian upgrade ordered by India** *(Piotr Butowski)*

Details for MiG-21-93

PRINCIPAL DIMENSIONS:
Wing span: 23 ft 6 ins (7.154 m)
Maximum length: 51 ft 8 ins (15.75 m)
Maximum length without probe: 47 ft 5 ins (14.457 m)
Maximum height: 14 ft 9 ins (4.5 m)

WINGS:
Aerofoil section: TsAGI C-96
Area: 247.6 sq ft (23.0 m^2)
Wing aspect ratio: 2.225
Sweepback: 57° leading edge
Mean aerodynamic chord: 13 ft 2 ins (4.002 m)
Incidence: 0°
Anhedral: 2°

TAIL UNIT:
Tailplane aerofoil section: A6A
Tailplane area (moving sections): 40.3 sq ft (3.74 m^2)
Tailplane sweepback: 55°
Fin aerofoil section: S-11
Fin area: 57.05 sq ft (5.3 m^2)
Fin sweepback: 61° 27'
Rudder area: 10.4 sq ft (0.965 m^2)

UNDERCARRIAGE:
Type: Retractable, with steerable nosewheel (47°)
Main wheels tyre size: 800 × 200 mm
Nose wheel tyre size: 500 × 180 mm
Wheel base: 15 ft 5 ins (4.71 m)
Wheel track: 9 ft 2 ins (2.787 m)

WEIGHTS:
Normal take-off: 19,456 lb (8,825 kg)

PERFORMANCE:
Maximum speed: Mach 2.05 or 1,174 kts (1,351 mph) 2,175 km/h
Maximum speed at sea level: Mach 1.05 or 702 kts (808 mph) 1,300 km/h
Landing speed: 146 kts (168 mph) 270 km/h
Take-off distance: 2,953 ft (900 m)
Landing distance: 2,133 ft (650 m) with drag-chute
Maximum climb rate: 44,300 ft (13,500 m) per minute at sea level
G limits: +8.5
Ceiling: 56,760-59,050 ft (17,300-18,000 m)
Range (internal fuel) with 2 AAMs: 539 naut miles (621 miles) 1,000 km at high altitude, 302 naut miles (348 miles) 560 km at low altitude
Ferry range: 1,133 naut miles (1,305 miles) 2,100 km

It can also be used to detect ground targets and for ground mapping (with freeze frame, zooming, etc).
Flight/weapon system avionics/instrumentation: MiG-21bis has the ASP-PFD-21 gun sight, AP-155SN autopilot (KAP-2K for old versions up to MiG-21PFM *Fishbed-F*), R-832M com radio, RV-UM radio altimeter, ARK-10 radio compass, SOD-57M transponder, MRP-56P beacon receiver, and Lazur-M data link. SRZO-2 IFF standard, although Hungarian MiGs are receiving USAF Electronic Systems Center IFF under the Peace Pannon system. MiG-21-93 has a Shchel-3UM helmet mounted sight, and optional infra-red search/track system combined with a laser rangefinder for close air combat and engagement of ground/sea targets. MiG-21-93s upgraded in India receiving Sextant Avionique Topflight® suite including SHUD, 2 colour LCD MFDs, mission management computer and symbol generator, digital mapping generator, Topsight modular helmet-mounted display, Totem 3000 laser inertial navigation system, and more.
Self-protection systems: MiG-21bis and older versions have SPO-10 Sirena radar warning receiver. SM-1 suspended pod containing SPS-141M response electronic jammer and 2 × 32-cartridge ASO-2I chaff/flare dispensers. MiG-21-93 has BVP-1F chaff/flare dispensers installed on the upper surface of the wingroots, with 120 × 26-mm cartridges.
Wings: Mid-mounted delta, with anhedral.
Wing control surfaces: Ailerons, and blown flaps (deflection 25° for take-off and 45° for landing).
Tail control surfaces: Sweptback slab tailplane (deflection +7° 30', -16° 30') and rudder (±25°).
Airbrakes: 2 airbrakes on lower front fuselage, each 4.76 sq ft (0.442 m^2) and deflected 35°; third airbrake under the rear fuselage, 5.06 sq ft (0.47 m^2), deflected 40°.
Flight control system: Mechanical, hydraulically actuated (BU-210 boosters for tailplane, BU-45 boosters for ailerons).
Fuselage: Semi-monocoque elliptic sections.

Construction materials: Aluminium alloys (mainly D16), steel (mainly 30KhGSNA) and magnesium alloys.
Engine: MiG-21bis and MiG-21-93 each have a Soyuz/Moscow R-25-300 turbojet. See Aircraft variants for other versions.
Engine rating: 9,039 lbf (40.21 kN) dry, 15,100 lbf (67.18 kN) with afterburning. As the result of short duration increase of rpm up to 106% and with second afterburner, the ground level thrust at near sonic speed has been increased to 21,825 lbf (97.09 kN) for several seconds.
Air intake: In the nose, with adjustable cone.
Fuel system: 11 internal tanks (7 fuselage, 4 wings). MiG-21bis capacity is 2,885 litres, plus 3 drop tanks (1 × 800 litres under the fuselage and 2 × 490 litres under the wings). MiG-21SM/M/MF capacity is 2,600 litres plus 1 × 800 litre drop tank. MiG-21PFM capacity is 2,680 litres, plus 1 × 490 litre drop tank.
Flight refuelling probe: None.
Electrical system: DC supply using 1 × 28.5 volt generator and 2 × 24 volt batteries. 115 volt/400 Hz AC supply with a generator.
Hydraulic system: Dual, AMG-10 oil, pressure 3,045 psi.
Braking system: Brake on each wheel. PT-21UK drag-chute of 204.5 sq ft (19 m^2).

Aircraft variants (main versions that are currently used, in order of appearance, not alphabetical, but with U series trainers last – see 1996-97 *WA&SD* for other versions):
MiG-21PFM (izdelye 94) *Fishbed-F* has RP-21M (TsD-30) radar, and 13,614 lbf (60.56 kN) R-11F2S-300 engine (later replaced by 14,308 lbf, 63.65 kN R-13-300 on some aircraft). Manufactured 1964-65 for Soviet Air Force and 1966-68 for export.
MiG-21R (E-7R, izdelye 94R) *Fishbed-H* is a reconnaissance variant. Larger dorsal spine. Provision for 2 underwing drop tanks. Reconnaissance pod suspended under the fuselage. Manufactured 1965-71.
MiG-21M and ***MiG-21MF*** (E-7M, izdelye 96) *Fishbed-J* each have more fuel, RP-21MA radar, built-in GSh-23L cannon, and 4 underwing pylons instead of 2. Manufactured 1968-71 in the former USSR (for export only) and from 1973 in India.
MiG-21bis (E-7bis, izdelye 75) *Fishbed-L* has RP-22SM Sapfir-21 radar, R-25-300 engine and lengthened dorsal spine fuel tank. R-13M, R-55 and R-60 short-range AAMs. Manufactured 1972-74 for Soviet Air Force, later for export. 180 manufactured in India during 1980-87. Izdelye 75A version for WarPact countries, 75B for others.
MiG-21bis (izdelye 75P) *Fishbed-N* is similar to izdelye 75 but with additional RSBN-6S short-range radio navigation and instrument landing system.
MiG-21U (izdelye 66) *Mongol-A* is a 2-seat trainer based on the MiG-21F-13. Manufactured 1962-66 for the USSR, and 1964-68 for export.
MiG-21US (izdelye 68) *Mongol-B* is the training version with blown flaps, R-11F2S-300 engine and KM-1 ejection seats. Manufactured 1966-71.
MiG-21UM (izdelye 69) *Mongol-B* is the modified training version with AP-155 autopilot and ASP-PFD gunsight (trainers have no radar).
MiG-21-93 (initially named MiG-21I for India) is the Mikoyan mid-life upgrade of MiG-21, principally MiG-21bis. It has the airframe and engine of MiG-21bis, and is equipped with new coherent pulse-Doppler Kopyo radar. Armed with R-77 and R-27 AAMs, as well as Kh-31P and Kh-25MP anti-radiation ASMs, and Kh-31A and Kh-35 anti-ship missiles.
Another Russian upgrade offer is targeted at older MiG-21 versions and can be carried out in 3 stages: simplest consists the introduction of R-73 AAMs with insignificant changes to the aircraft's radar and sight; stage 2 provides for a helmet-mounted sight and/or new navigation system including GPS; and the most advanced upgrade additionally introduces Phazotron Moskit (Mosquito) or Lev (Leo) radar, active jammer and new weapons.

↑ **Kopyo radar in the nose of a MiG-21-93** *(Piotr Butowski)*

↑ **Polish MiG-23MF armed with R-23R and R-60 missiles** *(Piotr Butowski)*

Mikoyan MiG-23 (NATO name *Flogger*)

Note: First flown on 10 June 1967 as a variable geometry prototype, the MiG-23 fighter and ground attack (MiG-23B/BN) aircraft was manufactured between 1969 and 1985. A full description of the MiG-23 can be found in the 1996-97 edition of *WA&SD*, pages 73-75, but to keep readers up-to-date a few brief details regarding upgrades have been retained for this edition.

Development

▪ 27 September 1994. India and Russia (Mikoyan) signed a co-operation agreement, covering among several programmes an avionics upgrade of Indian MiG-23s (and MiG-27s).
Sales/Users: Manufactured between 1969 and 1985, as 4,278 single-seaters and 769 trainers. Single-seat versions were manufactured at the Znamya Truda factory in Moscow (now MAPO), and MiG-23UB trainers at Irkutsk. Although withdrawn from first-line service, Russia has about 200 MiG-23s operated by Air Defence Troops (mainly for training purposes), with some 400 preserved for strategic reserve until the year 2000. Belarus has 45 MiG-23s and Ukraine has 175. The first foreign users of MiG-23s (MiG-23BN, MiG-23MS and MiG-23UB) were Egypt and Libya, from 1974. Warsaw Pact countries purchased MiG-23s in the late 1970s; MiG-23MF, MiG-23ML, MiG-23BN and MiG-23UB were used by the air forces of Czechoslovakia and East Germany, while Bulgaria also took the MiG-23MLD. Poland received 42 MiG-23MF/UBs, of which 37 remain in service. Other current MiG-23 operators are Afghanistan, Algeria, Angola, Cuba, Ethiopia, Hungary, India (MiG-23BN Vijay, later as MiG-23MF Rakshak and MiG-23UB), Iraq, Libya, North Korea, Romania, Sudan, Syria, Vietnam and Yemen. Non-typical owners (for non-operational use) of small numbers are the USA, China and Israel; 1 MiG-23 was flown to Israel on 11 October 1989, while China bought at least 2 aircraft from Egypt (paying with spare parts for old type MiGs) and the USA bought more aircraft from Egypt in 1978 and later obtained several others from Germany. A mid-life upgrade programme has begun in India.

Upgrade programmes: (Russian)

MiG-23-98 is the proposed upgrade of export MiG-23MF/MS/MLs. Many options possible, with upgraded Sapfir-23 radar or new Moskit, Kopyo or Zhemchug radars. New cockpit, mission computer, Mil-STD-1553 data bus, weapons, etc, as for MiG-29 upgrade.
MiG-23B-98 is the proposed upgrade for export MiG-23BN attack aircraft, with helmet-mounted sight and R-73 missiles for self-defence, podded Moskit radar, TV-guided air-to-ground weapons, etc.
MiG-23UB-99 is the proposed upgrade for export MiG-23UB trainers.

Mikoyan MiG-25 (NATO name *Foxbat*)

Note: First flown on 6 March 1964 in E-155R-1 reconnaissance prototype form, the multi-mission MiG-25 had been conceived as a 3,000 km/h aircraft for reconnaissance, as an interceptor to counter the US B-70 Valkyrie bomber then under development (later cancelled), and also to perform strike and air-defence suppression missions. On 13 June 1972 the MiG-25P interceptor was officially commissioned into service with Soviet Air Defence Troops, followed in December 1972 by the MiG-25RB, MiG-25RBK and MiG-25RBS reconnaissance-bomber versions. Series production lasted until 1985. In 1994 MiG-25PD/PDS

Details for the MiG-25RB *(applies also to derived versions such as MiG-25RBV, RBK, RBS, etc)*

PRINCIPAL DIMENSIONS:
Wing span: 43 ft 11 ins (13.38 m)
Maximum length: 70 ft 8.5 ins (21.55 m)
Maximum height: 19 ft 8 ins (6 m)

WINGS:
Aerofoil section: P-44M, P-101M root/tip
Area: 660.9 sq ft (61.40 m^2)
Aspect ratio: 2.92
Sweepback at leading edge: 41° 02′
Incidence: 2°
Anhedral: 5°

TAIL UNIT:
Tailplane span: 28 ft 8 ins (8.74 m)
Tailplane area: 105.6 sq ft (9.81 m^2)
Tailplane sweepback: 50° 22′
Fin sweepback at leading edge: 54°
Fins cant angle: outward 8°

UNDERCARRIAGE:
Type: Retractable, with twin nosewheels
Main wheel tyre size: 1,300 × 360 mm
Nose wheel tyre size: 700 × 200 mm
Wheel base: 16 ft 10.5 ins (5.144 m)
Wheel track: 12 ft 7.5 ins (3.85 m)
Stationary angle of pitch: 2° 28′

WEIGHTS:
Take-off: 77,294 lb (35,060 kg) clean
Take-off with drop tank: 87,810 lb (39,830 kg)
Take-off, maximum: 90,830 lb (41,200 kg)

PERFORMANCE:
Max limiting Mach number at 42,650 ft (13,000 m): Mach 2.83
Max speed at 42,650 ft (13,000 m): 1,620 kts (1,864 mph) 3,000 km/h
Supersonic cruise Mach number, at high altitude: Mach 2.35
Supersonic cruise speed, at high altitude: 1,350 kts (1,553 mph) 2,500 km/h
Maximum Mach number with 4 FAB-500T bombs, at 42,650 ft (13,000 m): Mach 2.35
Maximum Mach number with 4 × FAB-500T bombs and drop tank, at 42,650 ft (13,000 m): Mach 1.5
Maximum speed at sea level: 648 kts (746 mph) 1,200 km/h
Time to Mach 2.35 at 65,600 ft (20,000 m) altitude: 6 minutes 36 seconds, clean
Time to Mach 2.35 at 65,600 ft (20,000 m) altitude, with 4 × FAB-500 bombs: 8 minutes 12 seconds
G limit: 3.8, with 4 × FAB-500 bombs
Ceiling: 75,460 ft (23,000 m)
Ceiling with 4 × FAB-500T bombs: 67,900 ft (20,700 m)
Range with 4 × FAB-500Ts, Mach 2.35: 891 naut miles (1,025 miles) 1,650 km
Range with 4 × FAB-500Ts and drop tank, Mach 2.35: 1,150 naut miles (1,324 miles) 2,130 km
Range with 4 × FAB-500Ts, subsonic speed: 1,007 naut miles (1,159 miles) 1,865 km
Range with 4 × FAB-500Ts and drop tank, subsonic speed: 1,296 naut miles (1,491 miles) 2,400 km

↑ 3 MiG-25 photographs showing typical reconnaissance nose configurations: *top* MiG-25RBV with Virazh elint and photo-cameras; *centre* MiG-25RBS/RBSh with Sabla or Shompol side-looking radar; *bottom* MiG-25RBF with Shar elint *(Cezary Piotrowski)*

interceptors were finally withdrawn from service with Russian Air Defence Troops. A full description of the MiG-25 can be found in the 1996-97 edition of *WA&SD*, pages 75-76, but to keep readers up-to-date details of the aircraft's current status among user countries have been retained for this edition, plus some detail specifically relating to reconnaissance versions.
Sales/Users: 1,186 MiG-25s were built. Full-scale production in Gorki (now Nizhny Novgorod) lasted until 1982, and later a small quantity of MiG-25BM anti-radar aircraft were manufactured up to 1985. In 1994 MiG-25PD/PDS interceptors were finally withdrawn by the Russian Air Defence Troops, replaced by MiG-31s and Su-27s. However, Russia still operates reconnaissance versions, since there is no replacement (possibly up to 250, some 143 in Europe but 65 stored, and the remainder in Asian areas of Russia). Of the other ex-Soviet states, Ukraine has 49 MiG-25s and Belarus 1. In the late 1970s several other countries purchased MiG-25s. MiG-25P interceptors were delivered in 1979 to Algeria and Syria and, a little later, to Iraq and Libya (the latter obtained also MiG-25PDs). Reconnaissance MiG-25RBs are used by Algeria, India, Iraq, Libya and Syria. India also obtained 2 training aircraft of MiG-25RU type. Although MiG-25 was offered to the Warsaw Pact countries, only Bulgaria bought 3 MiG-25RBs and 1 MiG-25RU, and these were later returned.
Number of weapon pylons: MiG-25RB has 4 under the wings plus underfuselage stations.
Expendable weapons and equipment: MiG-25RB and its sub-variants are armed with up to 10 FAB-500T demolition bombs (4 under the wings and 6 under the fuselage), or a single nuclear bomb.
Flight/weapon system avionics/instrumentation: Standard equipment includes the SO-69 transponder, SRO-2N and SRZO-15 IFF, RV-3 or RV-4 altimeter, ARK-10 or ARK-19 radio compass, MRP-56P beacon receiver, and RSBN-6S short range radio navigation and approach system. R-832M (or R-802) and R-864 (or R-847) com radio. Radar and Vozdukh-1M ground controlled intercept GCI systems of the interceptors are deleted from reconnaissance/strike versions, but the Peleng-D/DR/DM nav/attack system with TsVM-10-155 Orbita digital computer is added, plus DISS-7 (DISS-3S on early aircraft) Doppler navigation radar.
Self-protection systems: Active ECM jammers (MiG-25RB/BM family only) built into the nose: SPS-141 Siren on early production aircraft, later SPS-151 Lyutik. SPO-10 Sirena or SPO-15 Beryoza radar warning receiver.
Engines: 2 Soyuz/Tumansky R-15BD-300 turbojets, side-by-side in the rear fuselage, or R-15B-300 in early aircraft.
Engine rating: Each 24,692 lbf (109.84 kN) with afterburning.
Fuel system: Fuel located in 6 fuselage compartments (including tanks around the air intakes), 4 wing tanks and in the tailfins. Total of 33,609 lb (15,245 kg) for the reconnaissance MiG-25RB. Provision for extra-large underfuselage auxiliary tank, of 9,855 lb (4,470 kg) capacity. Thermal resistant fuel of T-6 or T-7P type.
Electrical system: 2 engine-driven 27 volt DC generators. 1 or 2 AC generators. 2 emergency batteries and transformers.
Hydraulic system: Main and secondary for flight control units, with main supplying also other systems and secondary for emergency brake back-up.
Braking system: On all units, with main and emergency. Twin drag-chutes, 646 and 538 sq ft (60 and 50 m^2), housed in the tailcone between and above the engine nozzles.

Aircraft variants (reconnaissance) :
MiG-25R (E-155R, izdelye 02) *Foxbat-B* was the initial reconnaissance version. 3 cameras and SRS-4 Romb electronic intelligence (elint) device. Manufactured until 1970.
MiG-25RB (izdelye 02B) *Foxbat-B* is the 1970 reconnaissance-bomber version. As MiG-25R but armed with up to 11,023 lb (5,000 kg) of bombs.
MiG-25RBN (izdelye 02B) *Foxbat-B* is the night reconnaissance version. As MiG-25RB but specialized cameras.
MiG-25RBV (izdelye 02B) *Foxbat-B* is similar to the MiG-25RB but with SRS-9 Virazh instead of Romb.
MiG-25RBK (izdelye 02K or izdelye 51) *Foxbat-D* is similar to MiG-25RB but without cameras. Kub elint. Manufactured 1972-80.
MiG-25RBS (izdelye 02S or izdelye 52) *Foxbat-D* has no cameras but has Sabla side-looking airborne radar (SLAR). Manufactured 1972-77.
MiG-25RBT (izdelye 02T) *Foxbat-D* has Tangazh elint.
MiG-25RBSh *Foxbat-D* is a 1981 version, converted from MiG-25RBS with Shompol SLAR instead of Sabla.
MiG-25RBF (izdelye 02F) *Foxbat-D* is a 1981 version, converted from MiG-25RBK with Shar elint instead of Kub.
MiG-25RU (izdelye 39) *Foxbat-C* is the 2-seat trainer.

Mikoyan MiG-27 (*Flogger-D/J*)

Note: First flown on 20 August 1970 in MiG-23B prototype form, the MiG-27 supersonic ground attack aircraft was based on the MiG-23, featuring a strengthened undercarriage, external steel plate cockpit armour, deletion of the MiG-23's multi-mode radar, reshaping of the shortened nose to improve downward vision, changes to wing sweep and flap control, addition of long wingroot extensions, adoption of non-variable air intakes and 2-position afterburner nozzles, new avionics, and larger low-pressure tyres. By 1983 production in the Soviet Union had ended and manufacturing was transferred to India where on 11 January 1986 the first Indian MiG-27L assembled from Soviet MiG-27M parts (produced at Irkutsk) left the Nasik factory. In 1988 the first all-Indian MiG-27L (export M, also known as ML) was completed. In 1994, the MiG-27 was withdrawn from service by CIS forces (except the Ukraine), and production in India ended later that same year. A full description of the MiG-27 can be found in the 1996-97 edition of *WA&SD*, page 77, but to keep readers up-to-date details of the aircraft's current status among user countries have been retained for this edition, plus some detail relating to upgrades. A photograph of an Indian MiG-27L appears with the HAL entry under India.
Sales/Users: Manufactured at the Irkutsk and Ulan-Ude factories, with a total of about 910 built between 1973 and 1983, including about 550 MiG-27s, 214 of the most sophisticated MiG-27Ks and about 150 MiG-27Ms. During 1982-85, standard MiG-27 *Flogger-Ds* were converted into MiG-27D *Flogger-Js* at the Irkutsk and Ulan-Ude factories. Production of MiG-27, after completion in the USSR, was transferred to India (first 10 MiG-27Ls built at Irkutsk, plus about 80 in kit form for HAL assembly). These were manufactured at Nasik in India until 1994 as Bahadurs, while R-29B-300 engines were put into production at Koraput. The production programme provided for 165 aircraft of this type, the 100th leaving the production line in May 1992. Production had been expected to continue until 1997 but ended early. India has plans to modernize these aircraft, equipping them with Indian or Western avionics such as IFF-405A, VUC-201A com radio, ARC-610A beacon receiver, RAM-700A radio altimeter, flight recorder, etc. Another Indian/Russian upgrade offer includes lightweight Phazotron Komar (Gnat) radar, a 'glass' cockpit with 1 large multifunction colour CRT display at the main panel and 2 small liquid-crystal displays at side panels, new air-to-surface weapons, and R-73/AA-11 *Archer* AAMs coupled with a helmet-mounted sight. An upgraded MiG-27L was shown in Bangalore in December 1996. Restart of MiG-23 production in India, in upgraded form, has been considered. Indian MiG-27s are the only examples still in service, other than 47 or fewer in the Ukraine.

MAPO "MiG" MiG-29 (NATO name *Fulcrum*)

First flight: 6 October 1977, piloted by Alexander Fedotov.
Role: Lightweight close-air combat fighter, and attack.
Chief designer: Rostislav Belyakov until 1982, Mikhail Valdenberg from 1982-93, Valeri Novikov since May 1993.
Fatigue life: 2,500 flight hours (20 years).

Aims

- Extremely high manoeuvrability, with high angles of attack.
- Thrust to weight ratio of 1.1.
- Wide fuselage/wing centre section providing 40% of the lifting force.
- Complex weapon control system comprising radar, infra-red search-track and helmet mounted target designator.
- Operation from rough unprepared runways, due to separate take-off air intakes that allow main intake blanking.

↑ **MiG-29SM** *(Artur Sarkisyan/MIG "MAPO-M")*

Development

▪ 1969. Soviet Air Force competition opened for a PFI (perspektivnyi frontovoi istrebitel – advanced tactical fighter) of similar class to the US F-15. First MiG-29 design was a heavy air-superiority fighter.
▪ 1971. PFI programme was subdivided into 2 independent sections: TPFI (T for tyazholyi– heavy) and LPFI (L for logkiy – lightweight), similar to the US F-15 and F-16. MiG-29 was accordingly designed as a lightweight fighter.
▪ 1974. Preliminary design accepted.
▪ 6 October 1977. First flight of 9-01, the first of 14 prototypes.
▪ March 1979. First information published in the West, provisionally named Ram-L.
▪ 29 April 1981. First flight of the MiG-29UB combat trainer, piloted by Aviard Fastovets.
▪ May 1982. First production aircraft left Moscow's Znamya Truda aircraft plant (now MAPO).
▪ July 1983. First aircraft delivered to the Soviet Air Force (234th Fighter Air Regiment at Kubinka).
▪ 1984. State Acceptance Trials completed.
▪ 13 February 1985. First flight of the izdelye 9-14 experimental version of the MiG-29 with air-to-surface attack systems in a suspended pod. Pilot Toktar Aubakirov. Prototype only.
▪ 25 April 1986. First flight of MiG-29M (MiG-33).
▪ 1 July 1986. MiG-29 first seen abroad, in Finland.
▪ 23 December 1990. First flight of the MiG-29S (type 9-13S).
▪ 1992. Production switched to MiG-29S.
▪ 26 April 1995. First record set by MiG-29: height 90,096 ft (27,460 m) for aircraft of 12,000-16,000 kg take-off weight, flown by Roman Taskayev.
▪ 16 November 1995 – January 1996. Flight refuelling trials, in accordance with a Malaysian requirement.
▪ 1996. Guided air-to-ground weapons introduced (MiG-29SM).
▪ 29 November 1997. First flight of the prototype MiG-29SMT at Zhukovsky, flown by Marat Alykov.
▪ 1998. First flight for the fully upgraded MiG-29 with new avionics, thrust-vectoring engines and extended range.

Details

Sales/Users: Single-seat fighter versions manufactured in Moscow and MiG-29UB combat trainers in Nizhny Novgorod (former Gorki). Total of over 1,300 MiG-29 single-seaters and over 200 MiG-29UBs built at the time of writing, with recent production of only a small number per year (1,216 of the total of single-seaters had been completed by early 1995 and 197 of the 2-seaters by the end of 1991). Since about 1990 production has continued for export only, accounting for nearly 400 aircraft sold. Most recently, 28 MiG-29s have been sold to Hungary, 18 to Malaysia, 13 to Slovakia, 10 MiG-29SEs to India, 5 to Romania and 1 to Iran, in some cases joining others previously purchased. Malaysian aircraft were delivered in simple 9-12B form but are being upgraded to MiG-29SD standard (plus flight refuelling), with the first 2 upgrades with N019ME radar and AAM-AE missiles flying April 1998; another 18 aircraft to be purchased. Bulgaria ordered 8-12 in April 1997, with delivery of 14 MiG–29SMs discussed but later stopped when Bulgaria decided to align with NATO. Indonesia, Myanmar, Philippines, Thailand and others were anticipated customers. At the time of writing the Russian forces had some 600 MiG-29s (including over 430 active with tactical air forces and 35 with naval aviation), while other users were Belarus (80), Bulgaria, Cuba, Germany (23,

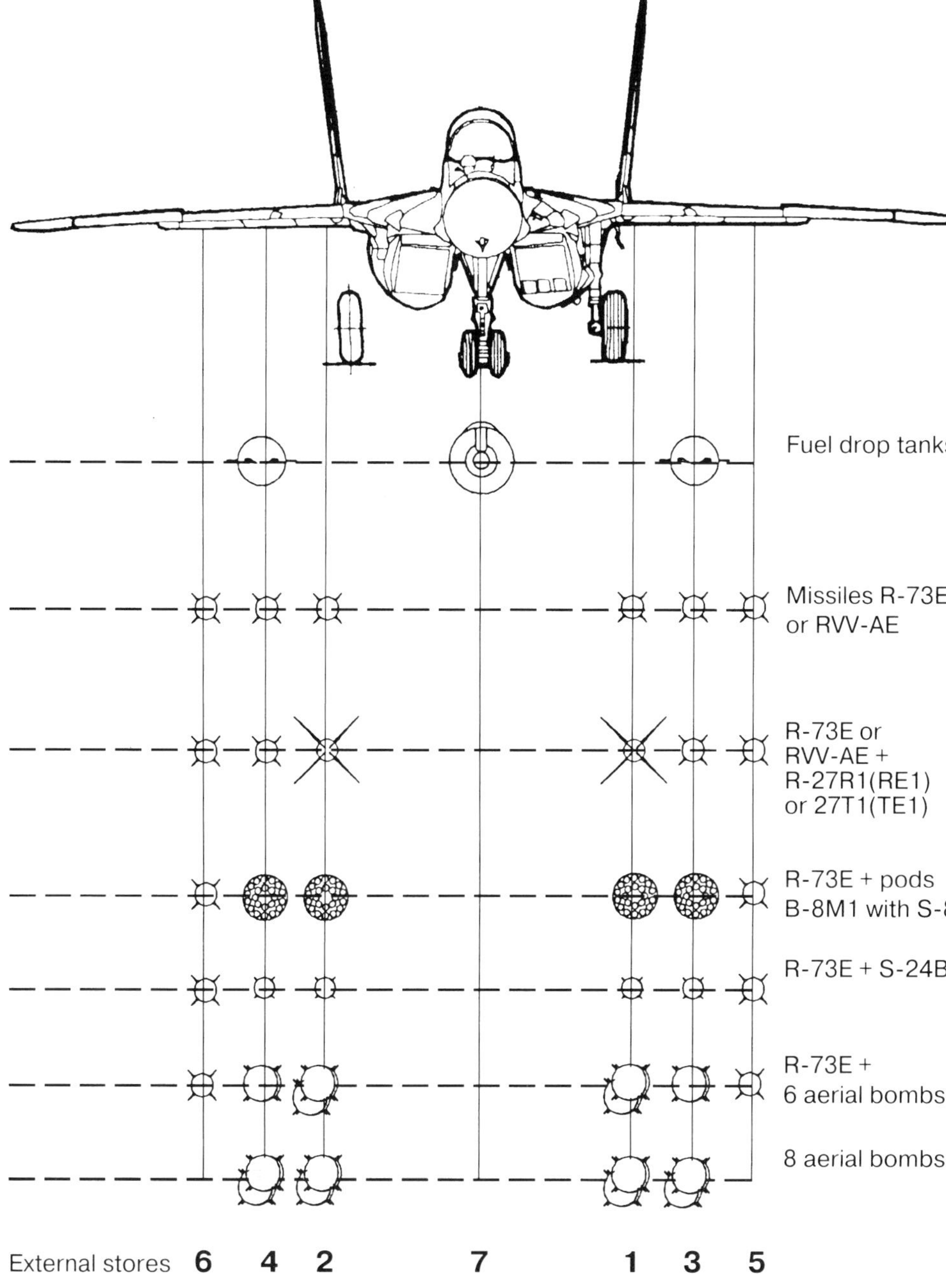

↑ **MiG-29SE weapon options** *(courtesy MAPO "MiG")*

Details for MiG-29SD/SE/SM/SMT *Fulcrum-A/C*

PRINCIPAL DIMENSIONS:
Wing span: 37 ft 3 ins (11.36 m)
Maximum length: 56 ft 10 ins (17.32 m)
Length without probe: 53 ft 5 ins (16.28 m)
Length with probe: 56 ft 10 ins (17.32 m)
Fuselage length: 48 ft 10 ins (14.875 m)
Maximum height: 15 ft 6 ins (4.73 m)

WINGS:
Area: 410.1 sq ft (38.1 m^2)
Aspect ratio: 3.39
Sweepback at leading edge: 42°
Sweepback of LERX, at leading edge: 73° 30′
Incidence: 0°
Anhedral: 3°

TAIL UNIT:
Tailplane span: 25 ft 6 ins (7.78 m)
Fins cant angle: 6° outward
Distance between fins, at roots: 11 ft 1 ins (3.38 m)

UNDERCARRIAGE:
Type: Retractable, with twin steerable nosewheels (±30° maximum, and typically ±8° for taxying, take-off/landing)
Main wheel tyre size: 840 × 290 mm
Nose wheel tyre size: 570 × 140 mm
Wheel base: 12 ft (3.645 m)
Wheel track: 10 ft 2 ins (3.1 m)

WEIGHTS:
Empty, operating: 24,030 lb (10,900 kg) for MiG-29SD
Take-off, clean: 31,526 lb (14,300 kg) for MiG-29SD, 33,731 lb (15,300 kg) for MiG-29SE
Take-off with 2 R-27 and 4 R-60M AAMs: 34,392 lb (15,600 kg)
Maximum take-off for MiG-29: 40,741 lb (18,480 kg)
Maximum take-off for MiG-29S/SE: 43,431 lb (19,700 kg)
Maximum take-off for MiG-29SM: 44,092 lb (20,000 kg)
Maximum take-off for MiG-29SMT: 46,297 lb (21,000 kg)
Maximum landing: 31,306 lb (14,200 kg)
Normal landing: 27,117 lb (12,300 kg)

PERFORMANCE:
Maximum operating Mach number (M_{MO}): Mach 2.3
Maximum operating speed: 1,296 kts (1,491 mph) 2,400 km/h
Maximum Mach number at sea level: Mach 1.2
Maximum speed at sea level: 810 kts (932 mph) 1,500 km/h
Maximum climb rate: 64,960 ft (19,800 m) per minute, at sea level
Stalling speed: 130 kts (149 mph) 240 km/h
Landing speed, normal landing weight: 135 kts (155 mph) 250 km/h
Landing speed, maximum landing weight: 146 kts (168 mph) 270 km/h
Take-off distance, maximum afterburning: 820 ft (250 m)
Take-off distance, without afterburning: 1,805 ft (550 m)
Landing distance, normal landing weight, with drag-chute: 2,165 ft (660 m)
Landing distance, normal landing weight: 2,953-3,117 ft (900-950 m)
Sustained turn rate at 9,840 ft (3,000 m) with 50% internal fuel: 23.5° per second
Acceleration time from 600 to 1,000 km/h at 3,280 ft (1,000 m) height: 13.5 seconds
Acceleration time from 1,100 to 1,300 km/h, at 3,280 ft (1,000 m) height: 8.7 seconds
Maximum angle of attack, Mach < 0.85: 26°
G limits at Mach < 0.85, at 50% internal fuel: +9, -3
G limits at Mach > 0.85, at 50% internal fuel: +7,-1.5
Ceiling, clean: 59,050 ft (18,000 m)
Ceiling, with 2 AAMs: 57,400 ft (17,500 m)
Range at high altitude, Mach 0.8, internal fuel: 809 naut miles (932 miles) 1,500 km for MiG-29SE
Range at 656 ft (200 m), Mach 0.5: 383 naut miles (441 miles) 710 km for MiG-29
Maximum range with underfuselage drop tank: 1,134 naut miles (1,305 miles) 2,100 km for MiG-29SE
Maximum range with 3 drop tanks for MiG-29SE: 1,566 naut miles (1,802 miles) 2,900 km
Maximum range with 3 drop tanks for MiG-29SMT: 1,888 naut miles (2,175 miles) 3,500 km
Maximum range with 3 drop tanks and 1 in-flight refuelling for MiG-29SMT: 3,615 naut miles (4,163 miles) 6,700 km

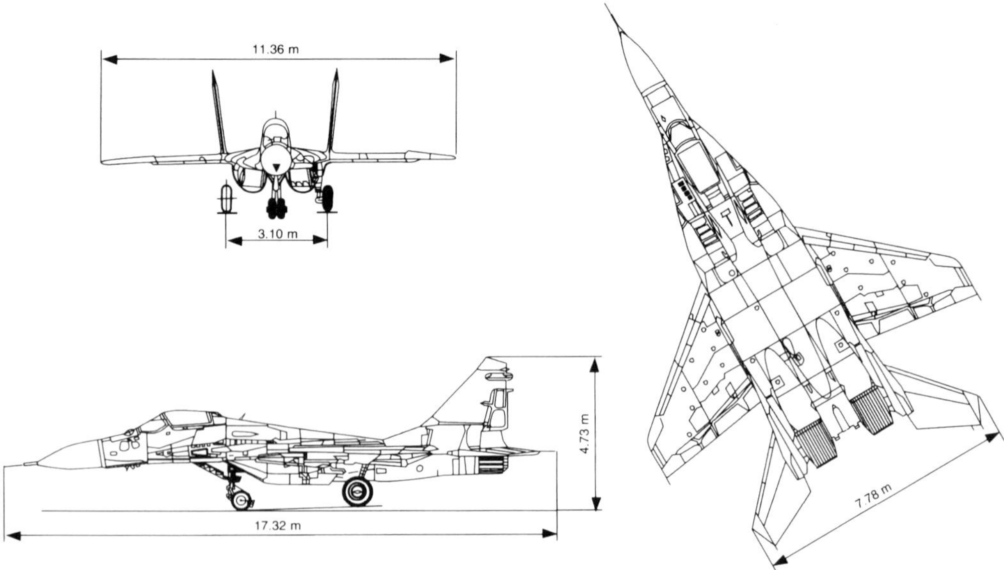

↑ **MiG-29 general arrangement** *(courtesy MAPO "MiG")*

subject to upgrade in Germany by DASA), Hungary (28, including 6 2-seaters), India (94 named Baaz), Iran (including ex-Iraqi aircraft; in 1993 Iran ordered 48 MiG-29s but only 1 was delivered), Iraq (those remaining probably no longer operational), Kazakhstan (22), North Korea, Malaysia (18, including two 2-seaters), Moldova (6 remaining for sale, under repair in Belarus in early 1998; 4 sold to Yemen in 1994, and 21 to the USA in 1997), Peru (Belarus sold 18 to Peru in 1997 under a US$380 million contract), Poland (22, including 10 bought from the Czech Republic in January 1996), Romania (14, including two 2-seaters), Slovakia (24, including 3 2-seaters), Syria, Turkmenistan, Ukraine (230), USA (21 bought from Moldova, as 14 *Fulcrum-Cs*, 6 *'As'* and 1 *'B'*, in 1997), Uzbekistan (reportedly 21 delivered in exchange for Tu-95MS bombers transferred to Russia), Yemen (4 were sold by Moldova in 1994) and Yugoslavia (16 delivered many years ago; recently reported talks have discussed the purchase of up to 20 more). 12 Russian MiG-29s were destined for Ecuador according to November 1997 reports, but denied.

Crew: Pilot, or 2 in the MiG-29UB.

Cockpit: Conventional instrumentation, with HUD. See also MiG-29SMT Modernization programme under Aircraft variants.

Crew escape: Zvezda K-36DM/2-06 zero-zero ejection seat.

Fixed guns: Gryazev/Shipunov GSh-301 (9A-4071K) single-barrel 30-mm cannon, built into the port wing LERX. Rate of fire 1,800 rounds per minute, and effective range of 3,900-5,900 ft (1,200-1,800 m) against air targets and 656-2,625 ft (200-800 m) against ground targets.

Ammunition: 150 rounds.

Number of weapon pylons: 6 under the wings; BD3-UMK2B pylons.

Expendable weapons and equipment: Up to 4,409 lb (2,000 kg) on initial MiG-29s, later gradually increased to 6,614 lb (3,000 kg), 8,818 lb (4,000 kg) and, finally, 9,921 lb (4,500 kg). Standard air-combat armament comprises 2 medium-range radar or infra-red R-27R/R-27T/TE (AA-10 *Alamo*) AAMs (the numeral '1' may be added to indicate the export version; for example R-27R1) on the inner pylons, plus 4 R-73E (AA-11 *Archer*) or R-60M (AA-8 *Aphid*) short-range infra-red missiles on the outer pylons; up to 6 R-73Es may be carried. Air-to-ground weapons include 8 × FAB-250 250 kg or FAB-500 500 kg free-fall bombs, ZB-500 incendiary tank, KMGU-2 submunitions dispenser, and 57-mm to 240-mm unguided rockets (can include 2 to 4 × 240-mm S-24B or 40 to 80 × 80-mm S-8 rockets); no smart weapons on initial MiG-29 and MiG-29S. Because of its improved radar, MiG-29S can be armed with up to 6 new-generation active radar medium-range R-77 (RVV-AE, AA-12 *Adder*) and 2 extended-range R-27ER (AA-10C *Alamo-C*) AAMs. TV-guided bombs (4 KAB-500KR) and ASMs (2 Kh-29T, AS-14 *Kedge*), and 2 active/passive radar Kh-31A/P (AS-17 *Krypton*) ASMs for MiG-29SM/SMT. Rearming with new R-74 short-range missiles is expected, with target indication range by HMS increased to ±90° (±60° for R-73) and with new IR-sensitive element of the homing head enabling twice the search distance.

Radar: RLPK-29 (radiolokatsyonnyi pritselnyi kompleks) radar attack system includes coherent pulse Doppler S-29 (N-019, NATO *Slot Back*) look-down/shoot-down radar and Ts100.02-06 digital computer. Search range (fighter-type target) is 38 naut miles (43.5 miles) 70 km in front hemisphere and 19 naut miles (21.75 miles) 35 km in rear hemisphere, with an increase of about 50% for larger bomber-size targets. Radar can track up to 10 targets simultaneously and engage the one chosen by the computer as the most important. Search angles 67° each side in azimuth, +60°, -38° in elevation. MiG-29S (SD, SE and SM) is equipped with the RLPK-29M (ME) radar attack system which includes the more jam-resistant N-019M (ME) Topaz radar, able to track 10 and engage 2, and the Ts101M weapons computer. See also MiG-29SMT Modernization programmes under Aircraft variants.

Flight/weapon system avionics/instrumentation: RLPK-29 (RLPK-29M) radar system is supported by the OEPrNK-29-1 (optiko-elektronnyi pritselno-navigatsyonnyi kompleks) opto-electronic nav/attack system, which comprises the OEPS-29 sighting system, SN-29 navigation system, Ts100.02-02 (Ts100.02.07 for MiG-29SD/SE/SM) digital computer, SUO-29M2 (M4 for MiG-29SD/SE/SM) weapons control system and SYel-31E2 (SYel-31-1E for MiG-29SD/SE/SM) data presentation system with ILS-31 head-up-display. OEPS-29 (optiko-elektronnaya pritselnaya sistema) comprises the KOLS-29 infra-red/laser search and track device (tracking range 10 naut miles, 11.2 miles, 18 km, rear hemisphere only, distance accuracy 10 ft, 3 m) and Shchel-3UM helmet-mounted target designator. SN-29 (sistema navigatsi) includes the ARK-19 radio compass, A-037/06 altimeter, A-611 marker beacon receiver, and A-323 short-range navigation and instrument landing system. E502-20/04 Turkus data link for target indication from land-based radars. R-862 com radio, SO-69M (SO-69K-11E for MiG-29SD/SE/SM) transponder. Parol IFF (SRO-2 transponder, SRZ-15 interrogator). See also Modernization programmes under Aircraft variants.

Self-protection systems: SPO-15 (L006LM/101 for MiG-29SD, L006LM for MiG-29SE) Beryoza radar warning receiver. 20SP passive countermeasures system with 2 BVP-30-26M (blok vybrosa pomekh) chaff/flare dispensers built into the wing upper surface fence; each dispenser contains 30 × 26-mm PPI-26 flares or PPR-26 chaff cartridges. MiG-29 (9-13) and MiG-29S (9-13S) also have the L203B Gardenia-1 (L203BE Gardenia-1E for MiG-29SE) active electronic jammer built into the airframe.

Wing characteristics: Swept-back, mid mounted. Wide fuselage/wing centre section provides 40% of the lifting force. Leading-edge root extensions (LERX). Outer wing panels of conventional 3-spar construction.

Wing control surfaces: 3-section, full-span (except wingtips) manoeuvring flaps (20°). Slotted trailing-edge flaps (25°), and ailerons (+25°, -15°, neutral +5°) with tabs. Vortex generators on forward fuselage prevent aileron reversal at near maximum angles of attack.

Tail control surfaces: Tail surfaces are mounted on booms alongside the engine nacelles. Slab (taileron) tailplane, deflected +5° 45', -17° 45' evenly or differentially. Twin fins and rudders, outward canted by 6°. Rudders have 25° deflection.

Airbrakes: Above and below the rear fuselage, between the engine nozzles: upper flap deflects 56° and has an area of 7.9 sq ft (0.73 m^2), lower deflects 60° and has an area of 8.6 sq ft (0.795 m^2).

Flight control system: Mechanical, hydraulically actuated. SAU-451-04 (sistema avtomaticheskogo upravlenya – SAU-451-05 for MiG-29SD and SAU-451-06 for MiG-29SE) automatic control system includes SOS-3M (sistema ogranichitelnykh signalov – SOS-3M-3 for MiG-29S/SD/SE/SM) angle of attack/g-load dumper.

Construction materials: Mainly aluminium-lithium alloys, steel, with some composites (used in parts of the ailerons, trailing-edge flaps and tail) and titanium.

Engines: 2 widely spaced Klimov/Sarkisov RD-33 turbofans. Currently manufactured RD-33 series 2 has 700 hours TBO and 1,400 hours service life; RD-33 series 3 will have 1,000 hours TBO and 2,000 hours service life. Thrust vectoring RD-133 with the same rating is expected as a mid-life upgrade.

Engine rating: Each 11,100 lbf (49.42 kN) dry, and 18,300 lbf (81.4 kN) with afterburning.

Air intakes: Wedge main air intakes, which are blanked off by doors with many small apertures when the nosewheel is lowered, at which point air for the engines is supplied via the apertures plus louvres on the upper surface of each LERX. ARV-29D air-intake control. See also Modernization programme under Aircraft variants.

Flight refuelling probe: Can be fitted to any aircraft (currently only Malaysia); transfer rate 900 litres per minute.

Fuel system: 4,300 litres of internal fuel in 3 tanks inside the fuselage/wing centre section (650, 870 and 2,120 litres) and 2 outer wing tanks (each 330 litres). "Humpback' versions of MiG-29 (9.13) have an additional 200 litres inside the fuselage. Standard provision for a single underfuselage drop tank between the engines, of 1,520 litres capacity. 2 more 1,150 litre underwing tanks can be carried by MiG-29S/SD/SE/SM only (and upgraded earlier MiG-29s, such as German aircraft); recently also 1,800 litre tanks offered. Additional internal fuel for MiG-29SMT. See Modernization programme under Aircraft variants.

↑ **Upgraded MiG-29 cockpit with 2 colour liquid-crystal MFDs on the front panel, with a reduced set of conventional instruments between** *(Piotr Butowski)*

↑ **MiG-29SM with Kh-31 and Kh-29 ASMs plus R-77 AAMs. Note the flight refuelling probe which can be retrofitted to any MiG-29** *(Piotr Butowski)*

Hydraulic system: 3,000 psi. 2 independent systems to operate rudders, ailerons and tailplane actuators, air intake ramps, undercarriage (including nosewheel control), trailing-edge flaps, leading-edge flaps, and airbrakes.
Braking system: Main and nose wheel brakes. 183 sq ft (17 m^2) drag-chute housed in a tailcone, aft of the airbrakes.

Aircraft variants:
MiG-29 (also named izdelye 9-12 by design bureau or izdelye 5 by production plant) *Fulcrum-A* was the first production model, early series aircraft having detachable ventral tail fins and no chaff/flare overwing dispensers. Extended-chord rudders later retrofitted on all aircraft. Export variants were designated 9-12A (with N-019EA radar) for WarPact countries, or 9-12B for other countries. Operational MiG-29s of the Russian Air Force have been upgraded to MiG-29S standard at Repair Plant No 121 in Kubinka since 1993.
MiG-29 (izdelye 9-13 or izdelye 7) *Fulcrum-C* is similar to 9-12 but with Gardenia active ECM system installed in the more heavily curved top of fuselage decking.
MiG-29UB (izdelye 9-51 or izdelye 30) *Fulcrum-B* is the 2-seat trainer. Radar removed, and no chaff/flare dispensers. Mikoyan and Phazotron are working on a MiG-29UB upgrade, with the first flight originally scheduled for November-December 1997; radar for full multi-role capability for combat and operational training. See izdelye 9-52 under Aircraft variants.
MiG-29KVP (korotkiy vzlot i posadka, STOL), aircraft 9-18 is a technology demonstrator for the ship-borne MiG-29K, converted from an early production MiG-29 (9-12). Arrester hook added under the tail. Tested on land at Saki, Ukraine, with the first ski-jump take-off on 21 August 1982, piloted by Aviard Fastovets. Prototype only.
MiG-29S (izdelye 9-13S) *Fulcrum-C* is externally similar to MiG-29. Modified N-019M Topaz radar. Improved weapons include R-27RE extended-range and R-77 medium-range missiles; maximum weapons load 8,818 lb (4,000 kg). Improved flight control system, allowing a 28° angle of attack (instead of 22° in early aircraft, later gradually raised to 24° and 26°). Provision for 2 × 1,150 litre drop tanks under the wings, supplementing the previous underfuselage tank, offering a ferry range of 1,566 naut miles (1,802 miles) 2,900 km.
MiG-29SD *Fulcrum-A* is an export version of the MiG-29S in 9-12 configuration.
MiG-29SE (izdelye 9-13SE) *Fulcrum-C* is the export version of MiG-29S with Gardenia jammer. All export versions have Tacan AN/APN-118 navigation system, TNL-1000 GPS receiver, ILS-71, and R-800L1 radio with emergency frequency of 243 MHz.
MiG-29N and ***MiG-29UBN*** are the Malaysian single-seat and 2-seat aircraft. 'N' is equivalent to the Russian MiG-29SD with some changes such as provision for flight refuelling (fitted during overhauls), adaptation of the airframe and equipment for a wet climate, installation of satellite communications and navigation systems, plus extended engine life.
MiG-29SM is similar to MiG-29S/SE but has extended air-to-surface capabilities; TV-guided KAB-500Kr bombs and Kh-29T

↑ **MiG-29SM cockpit** *(Piotr Butowski)*

↑ **Malaysian MiG-29UBN of No 17 Squadron OCU, at Kuantan in late 1997** *(Denis Hughes)*

missiles, plus active radar Kh-31A and anti-radiation Kh-31P missiles. Displayed June 1995, with acceptance trials completed in 1996 with TV-guided weapons and in 1997 with Kh-31. 44,090 lb (20,000 kg) take-off weight.
Modernization programme for MiG-29, named **MiG-29SMT**, or izdelye 9-17, includes new avionics, new weapons, extended range and improved manoeuvrability. The mock-up of MiG-29SMT (incomplete) was shown during MAKS'97 exhibition in Zhukovsky. First flight of prototype (with new cabin only) on 29 November 1997 in Zhukovsky, piloted by Marat Alykov. The same aircraft flew with a 2,020 litre conformal upper fuel tank on 22 April 1998 (with Vladimir Gorbunov at the controls), and was then shown at Berlin ILA'98. Full set of changes planned for the 9-17 programme is presently being introduced into the next test aircraft, which will be the final prototype for mid-life upgrade or new production aircraft. The prototype (c/n 47-10) will be marked 917 and was to fly for the first time at the end of June 1998. Open architecture avionics and 'glass' cockpit are introduced with common data bus compatible with MIL-STD-1553B and STANAG 3910. New cockpit has 2 large colour liquid-crystal displays of MFI-68 type (mnogofunktsionalnyi indikator, multi-function display; 6 × 8 ins, 15 × 20 cm), as well as a set of reduced-size conventional instruments in the centre. HOTAS. Navigation has been improved, due to inertial system with laser gyros and by GPS combined with both US Navstar and Russian GLONASS systems. Avionics system and cockpit of MiG-29SMT were highly praised by the Russian Air Force and are now considered as a universal solution for all future Russian fighter and strike aircraft, as well as for combat helicopters. The modernized N019MP Topaz radar has synthetic aperture mode of operation for ground mapping with resolution up to 50 ft (15 m) and engagement of sea targets with the Kh-31A anti-ship missile. Range of MiG-29SMT is improved by additional external fuel tanks (3 instead of 1), increased internal fuel, and/or by provision for flight refuelling. Total weight of internal fuel for MiG-29SMT with conformal upper tank is 10,527 lb (4,775 kg), some 2,855 lb (1,295 kg) more than in the normal MiG-29 (9-13). With a conformal tank installed to 9-12 aircraft (with smaller back), the fuel weight increase is 3,494 lb (1,585 kg) or 2,020 litres. Flight refuelling system was designed to a Malaysian order; tests began on 16 November 1995. A radical way of improving MiG-29's manoeuvrability is the adoption of the RD-133 engine, a version of the present RD-33 with 3-dimensional thrust vectoring nozzle. Reportedly, Mikoyan designers are rather sceptical about the necessity of such a solution for MiG-29, because greatest advantages are often obtained at low speed (less than Mach 0.5) which under operational conditions is about 5% of the speeds range. The movable nozzles will be installed to the modernized MiG-29, but not necessarily straight away; work is continuing without any technical difficulties. Radar absorbing coatings are being introduced to MiG-29. Airframe service life will be extended from current 2,500 hours to 4,000 hours. Modernization of MiG-29 is considered a priority by the Russian Air Force. According to the Russian armed forces procurement chief, some 150-180 MiG-29 fighters of recent production series (with longest reserve of service life) will be modernized, with the first 10-15 before the end of 1998. The work is being carried out by Repair Works No 121 in Kubinka near Moscow.
'Second stage' of 9-17 upgrade programme provides replacement of Topaz radar with the new Zhemchug, and new weapons including long-range K-37M, medium-range K-77M and short-range K-30 AAMs, Kh-36 and Kh-38 tactical ASMs, as well as any requested type of Western weapons. New Klimov RD-43 turbofan engines are planned, of 22,050 lbf (98.1 kN) thrust each. Kedr-29 (cedar) self-defence system combining warning unit, active jamming unit and trap dispenser will be introduced (at present MiG-29 has no self-defence system, only separate devices). The existing mechanical control system will be replaced by triple digital fly-by-wire. Mikoyan representatives announced that after the 'second stage' of modernization, the combat efficiency of MiG-29SMT over present MiG-29 in air-to-air missions will be 2.1:1, or 1.75:1 in respect of Su-27 and 1.3:1 in respect of F-16C Block 50. The combat potential in air-to-ground missions will be increased by 3.8:1.
MiG-29SMTK or izdelye 9-17K (K for korabelnyi – shipborne) will have folding wings, reinforced undercarriage arrester hook and expanded navigational equipment. This variant is being prepared for the possible purchase by India of the *Admiral* Gorshkov aircraft carrier, modified to have a ski-jump. The 9-17K changes will also be offered to 'shore' users for operation from damaged (shorter) airstrips.
Izdelye 9-52 is a proposed upgrade of the MiG-29UB combat trainer, with changes similar to those given for 9-17 programme, including increased fuel, new cockpits and avionics, and air-to-ground weapons (TV-guided and anti-radiation). The second stage modernization provides for installing a radar, possibly a lightweight Moskit (mosquito) operating within 3 cm band; a millimetre band radar, more suitable for air-to-ground tasks, is being considered. Upgraded MiG-29UBs will be capable of being used as multi-purpose fighters, with a weapons system operator in the rear cockpit.
MiG-33 (MiG-29M) and ***MiG-29K*** – see separate entry.

↑ **MiG-29K for new flight trials in September 1996, with wingtips folded** *(Piotr Butowski)*

MAPO "MiG" MiG-29M, MiG-33 and MiG-29K (NATO name *Fulcrum-E*)

First flight: 25 April 1986, piloted by Valeri Menitsky.
Role: Lightweight tactical fighter and ground attack aircraft; MiG-29K is a ship-borne version.
Chief designer: Mikhail Valdenberg (1982-93) and Valeri Novikov since May 1993.

Aims

- According to data from the design bureau, the close air combat effectiveness of MiG-29M is 1.8 times better than that of MiG-29 and 3.5 times more effective in ground attack.
- Necessary ground service for the MiG-29M is 11.5 man hours per 1 flight hour.
- Mean time for flight preparation of the MiG-29M is 30 minutes.
- 15-25 minutes turnaround between missions.

Development

- 1982. Start of work on a highly modified and advanced MiG-29 derivative with air-to-surface capabilities added. Also start of development of a ship-borne version as the MiG-29K.
- 25 April 1986. First flight of the MiG-29M prototype (side number 151, first aircraft of 9-15 type).
- 23 July 1988. First flight of the MiG-29K, piloted by Toktar Aubakirov (side number 311, first aircraft of 9-31 type).
- September 1992. First seen abroad, at the Farnborough Air Show (MiG-29M side number 156).
- 1993. Programme lacked government financial support and halted.
- 1995. MiG-29M trials restarted, mainly to support the next-generation MiG-35 programme.
- September 1996. MiG-29K flew for the first time after several years break, with trials restarted because of the anticipated purchase of the *Admiral Gorshkov* aircraft carrier by India; the carrier is planned to be modified for conventional aircraft, as at present it can only deploy VTOL types.

Details

Sales/Users: 6 MiG-29Ms and 2 MiG-29Ks built for trials.
Crew: Pilot.
Cockpit: 15° visibility over the nose (1.5° more than MiG-29), due to the higher seat position. 2 cathode-ray tube (CRT) multi-function displays and improved HUD, with conventional instrumentation as stand-by. Cockpit differs from aircraft to aircraft; for example, CRT displays in 156 (sixth aircraft) are located about 8 ins (20 cm) lower than in 155. First MiG with HOTAS.
Crew escape: Zvezda K-36DM zero-zero ejection seat.
Fixed guns: GSh-301 single-barrel 30-mm cannon.
Ammunition: 100 rounds.
Number of weapon pylons: 9, 4 under each wing and 1 under the fuselage.
Expendable weapons and equipment: Up to 12,125 lb (5,500 kg). Air-to-air weapons are those detailed in the previous MiG-29 entry or 2 improved-range R-27ER/R-27ETs (AA-10 *Alamo-C/D*), or up to 8 active-radar medium-range R-77s (AA-12 *Adder*); maximum quantity of R-27R/R-27T1s (AA-10 *Alamo-A/B*) missiles is 4 rather than 2 for MiG-29. Air-to-surface weapon options include up to 6 Kh-25ML/MP (AS-10 *Karen*/AS-12 *Kegler*) laser guided/anti-radar missiles, up to 6 Kh-29L/T (AS-14 *Kedge*) laser/TV guided missiles, up to 4 Kh-31A/P (AS-17 *Krypton*) anti-ship/anti-radar missiles, or up to 6 KAB-500Kr TV-guided bombs, as well as free-fall bombs, submunitions dispensers, rockets, incendiary tanks, etc.
Radar: Phazotron S-29M (N-010) Zhuk lookdown/ shootdown pulse Doppler radar. Search range for fighter-size targets 48.6 naut miles (56 miles) 90 km in the forward hemisphere, 21.6 naut miles (25 miles) 40 km in rear hemisphere. Can track-while-scan 10 targets and engage 4 simultaneously. Mapping with the resolution of 49-66 ft (15-20 m), image freezing and terrain following in the air-to-ground mode.
Flight/weapon system avionics/instrumentation: Improved opto-electronic search and track device has a range of 16.2 naut miles (18.6 miles) 30 km in the rear and 5.4 naut miles (6.2 miles) 10 km in the forward hemispheres. Moreover, it may be used for laser designation of surface targets to be attacked by Kh-25ML and Kh-29L laser-guided missiles. The new TV channel is used for increasing the range of visual observation (for identification of targets without switching-on the radar IFF unit) as well as for designation of targets for TV guided Kh-29T air-to-surface missiles and KAB-500Kr bombs.
Self-protection systems: The improved radar warning receiver is also used for programming the seekers of Kh-25MP and Kh-31P anti-radiation missiles immediately before launch. Gardenia-1 active jammer built into the airframe. Chaff/flare system built into the dorsal spine, with 120 × 26-mm flares/cartridges rather than 60 in MiG-29.
Wing characteristics: Chine type LERX from the wing leading-edge creates strong vortex.
Wing control surfaces: Similar to MiG-29 but with elongated ailerons.
Tail control surfaces: Slab tailplane of greater chord, with dogtooth leading edges.
Airbrakes: Single door-type airbrake on fuselage dorsal spine.
Flight control system: Analog fly-by-wire. Quadruple redundant pitch control; dual roll and yaw control with stand-by mechanical system (up to half of normal deflection of control surfaces).
Fuselage: Enlarged dorsal spine, the fuselage structure ending beyond the engine nozzles.
Construction materials: Lightweight aluminium/lithium alloy centre-section.
Engines: 2 Klimov/Sarkisov RD-33K turbofans (engine life 1,400 hours, including general overhaul after first 700 hours).
Engine rating: Each 19,400 lbf (86.3 kN) with afterburning; 22,050 lbf (98.07 kN) version is under test.
Air intakes: Larger than for MiG-29, in accordance with the increased engine rating. Original MiG-29 blanking doors deleted, as are the overwing louvres and associated ducting (see Fuel system below), replaced by blanking grids and electronically-controlled lower intake lip (to further increase orifice area when required) that together provide sufficient air flow during take off. Curiously, to camouflage MiG-29M against identification, false louvres were painted on the upper surface of the LERX to make the aircraft appear similar to MiG-29.
Fuel system: 5,700 litres (1,400 litres more than MiG-29) of internal fuel, due to the freeing of space in the LERX. Provision for 3 drop tanks, 1 × 1,520 litre under the fuselage and 2 × 1,150 litre under the wings.
Flight refuelling probe: MiG-29K only.
Braking system: Twin drag-chutes, 280 sq ft (26 m²) area.

Aircraft variants:
MiG-29M (izdelye 9-15 or izdelye 9) *Fulcrum-E*, as described.
MiG-29EM (izdelye 9-15E) is the projected export version of MiG-29M, equipped with the radar/weapons of the MiG-29S.
MiG-29MR is the projected reconnaissance version.
MiG-29UM (izdelye 9-16) is the projected 2-seat combat trainer.
MiG-33 is the export version of MiG-29M, with fully rated radar/weapon system.
MiG-29K (izdelye 9-31) *Fulcrum-D* was produced as a carrier-borne version, similar to the MiG-29M. Work began in 1984, and the maiden flight was achieved on 23 July 1988. The first landing on the carrier *Tbilisi* (now *Admiral Kuznetsov*) was made on 1 November 1989. 2 prototypes only, with the programme terminated in the Summer of 1993 in favour of Su-27K (Su-33) but restarted in 1996. Construction commonality between MiG-29K and MiG-29M is 80-85%. RD-33K engines have an additional special mode of operation, offering 20,723 lbf (92.19 kN) of thrust. In-flight refuelling and an emergency fuel tank emptying system are installed. Wing span increased to 39 ft 4.5 ins (12 m); extended chord trailing-edge flaps; leading-edge flaps extended to the wing tips, but the ailerons are unchanged. The wings fold for stowage on board ship (the folded span is 25 ft 7 ins, 7.80 m). The nose radome also folds, reducing length from 56 ft 8 ins (17.27 m) to 49 ft 6.5 ins (15.1 m). Rear fuselage is reinforced, and an arrester hook installed. The S-29K radar is similar to S-29M Zhuk, and the navigation system is improved. Nominal take-off weight is 39,022 lb (17,700 kg); maximum 49,163 lb (22,300 kg). Maximum speed is 1,242 kts (1,429 mph) 2,300 km/h; maximum speed at sea level is 756 kts (890 mph) 1,400 km/h. Ceiling 57,000 ft (17,400 m); climb rate at 1,000 m altitude is 51,180 ft (15,600 m) per minute. G limit at Mach < 0.85 is +8.5; G limit at Mach > 0.85 is +6. Ferry range is 1,620 naut miles (1,864 miles) 3,000 km.
MiG-29KU (korabelnyi uchebnyi) is the projected ship-borne training version of MiG-29K, with a redesigned nose section containing a separate stepped cockpit with individual canopy for the instructor, forward and below of the standard cockpit, as for the MiG-25PU/RU. Programme cancelled.

↑ MiG-29M cockpit with 2 multi-function displays and improved HUD, and conventional instrumentation as stand-by *(Piotr Butowski)*

Details for MiG-29M *Fulcrum-E*

PRINCIPAL DIMENSIONS:
Wing span: 37 ft 3 ins (11.36 m)
Maximum length: 57 ft (17.37 m)
Maximum height: 15 ft 6 ins (4.73 m)

WINGS:
Sweepback: 42° leading edge
Anhedral: 3°

UNDERCARRIAGE:
Type: Strengthened MiG-29 type
Wheel base: 11 ft 11 ins (3.64 m)
Wheel track: 10 ft 2 ins (3.1 m)

WEIGHTS:
Normal take-off: 37,038 lb (16,800 kg)
Maximum take-off: 48,502 lb (22,000 kg)

PERFORMANCE:
Maximum operating Mach number (M_{MO}): Over Mach 2.2
Maximum speed: 1,323 kts (1,522 mph) 2,450 km/h
Maximum speed at sea level: 810 kts (932 mph) 1,500 km/h
Maximum climb rate: 64,960 ft (19,800 m) per minute, at sea level
Turn rate at 9,850 ft (3,000 m): 23° per second
Maximum angle of attack, < Mach 0.85: 30°
G limit at < Mach 0.85: +9
Ceiling: 55,775 ft (17,000 m)
Radius of action, air combat mission with 2 medium-range and 2 short-range AAMs, 3 drop tanks, and 5 × 360° turns during combat: 675 naut miles (777 miles) 1,250 km
Radius of action, air intercept mission with 4 medium-range AAMs, 3 drop tanks, Mach 0.85: 778 naut miles (895 miles) 1,440 km
Radius of action, ground attack mission with 2 ASMs, 2 short-range AAMs, and 3 drop tanks: 642 naut miles (739 miles) 1,190 km
Radius of action, ground attack mission with 4,409 lb (2,000 kg) of bombs, 2 short-range AAMs, and 3 drop tanks: 632 naut miles (727 miles) 1,170 km
Maximum range: 1,188 naut miles (1,367 miles) 2,200 km, on internal fuel
Range at low altitude: 486 naut miles (559 miles) 900 km on internal fuel
Ferry range with 3 drop tanks: 1,728 naut miles (1,988 miles) 3,200 km

MAPO "MiG" MiG-31 (NATO name *Foxhound*)

First flight: 16 September 1975, piloted by Alexander Fedotov.
Role: Long-range interceptor for autonomous operation with or without GCI (ground-controlled interception) system support, mainly for Russia's northern regions for protection against cruise missile attack.

Aims

- Mach 2.35 cruise speed with 4 R-33 long-range AAMs.
- 720 km supersonic combat radius.
- 3 hours 36 minutes subsonic flight endurance.
- All-altitude weapons system.
- Electronically-scanned phased array fire control radar, enabling true multi-target engagement.
- Group operations of up to 4 aircraft, with common

↑ MiG-31M *Foxhound-B* with refuelling probe raised. Note the cylindrical wingtip jammer pods with fins *(Dmitri Grinyuk)*

information area (data exchange system).

- Heaviest, most heavily armed, and fastest fighter aircraft in the world.
- Loss coefficient: 11.7 aircraft for 100,000 flight hours.

Development

- 1972. Work began on a MiG-25 replacement with added all-altitude multi-target capability and extended flight endurance. Chief designer, Gleb Lozino-Lozinski, was replaced in the mid-1970s by Konstantin Vasilchenko; now Anatoli Belosvet.
- 16 September 1975. First flight of MiG-25MP (E-155MP) prototype.
- 1976. First knowledge in the West of a MiG-25 development came from a defecting Soviet MiG-25 pilot.
- December 1976. First pre-production MiG-31 built by Gorki (now Nizhny Novgorod) aircraft plant.
- December 1981. State acceptance trials were completed and the MiG-31-33 intercept system (which includes MiG-31 aircraft, R-33 missiles and control systems) was accepted into service with Soviet Air Defence Troops.
- 1983. Initial operational capability achieved by the first MiG-31 unit, the 786th Air Defence Fighter Regiment in Pravdinsk.
- Autumn 1985. MiG-31 was photographed for the first time by a Norwegian F-16 over the Barents Sea.
- 21 December 1985. First flight of the MiG-31M, piloted by Boris Orlov.
- 1986. First flight of the MiG-31D satellite interceptor.
- 1990. MiG-31B replaced MiG-31 on the production line.
- June 1991. MiG-31 was exhibited for the first time in the West (Paris Air Show).
- Spring 1994. First successful launches of R-37 missiles from the MiG-31M, at a distance of over 162 naut miles (186 miles) 300 km.

Details

Sales/Users: About 400 built, and series production continues in small quantities at Nizhny Novgorod. In service with Russian Air Defence Troops only (229 in Europe as latest figure at time of writing) and never exported.
Crew: 2, in tandem cockpits, pilot (front) and weapons systems officer (rear).
Cockpit: Separate rearward-hinged canopies. Controls in both cockpits. Conventional instrumentation.
Crew escape: Zvezda K-36 zero-zero ejection seats (Mikoyan KM-1M in early aircraft).
Fixed guns: 6-barrel 23-mm GSh-6-23 (9YeYu) cannon at the starboard side of MiG-31's fuselage. No cannon in the MiG-31M.
Ammunition: 260 rounds.
Number of weapon pylons: 8, or 10 for MiG-31M (6 instead of 4 under the fuselage, and 4 under the wings).
Expendable weapons and equipment: 4 semi-active radar R-33 (AA-9 *Amos*) AAMs of 65 naut mile (74.6 mile) 120 km range, carried in tandem pairs under the fuselage (the front pair semi-recessed), plus 2 medium-range R-40TD (AA-6 *Acrid*) or 4 self-defence R-60M (AA-8 *Aphid*) AAMs on the wing pylons. MiG-31B/BS have R-33S instead of R-33 missiles. MiG-31M is armed with 6 active-radar R-37 AAMs of 189 naut mile (217 mile) 350 km range and 4 medium-range R-77s (AA-12 *Adders*).
Radar: Zaslon (or N-007, or S-800, NATO name *Flash Dance*) fire control radar, the first ever operational electronically-scanned phased array type (chief designer Alfred Fedotchenko). Can track 10 targets and engage 4 well-spread targets simultaneously flying at altitudes of 100 m to 27,000 m and with speeds of 3,700 km/h (head-on). Search ranges quoted by NIIP are 151 naut miles (174 miles) 280 km for E-3 AEW&C aircraft, 108 naut miles (124 miles) 200 km for SR-71 type reconnaissance aircraft flying at over 25,000 m altitude, 97 naut miles (112 miles) 180 km for the B-1 bomber, 65 naut miles (74.6 miles) 120 km for the F-16 and 35 naut miles (40.4 miles) 65 km for low-flying AGM-86B cruise missiles. Search angles are 70° each side in azimuth, and +70°, -60° in elevation. Zaslon weighs more than 2,205 lb (1,000 kg), of which 661 lb (300 kg) is the antenna of 43 in (110 cm) diameter. MiG-31M is equipped with Zaslon-M radar, capable of tracking 10 targets and engaging 6 simultaneously flying at altitudes up to 40,000 m and speeds of up to Mach 6. Its maximum search range is estimated at 216 naut miles (248 miles) 400 km. See also MiG-31BM under Aircraft variants.
Flight/weapon system avionics/instrumentation: Argon-K digital weapon computer. Tropik (Loran-type) and Marshrut (Omega-type) long-range navigation systems. 8TP retractable infra-red search and track device under fuselage nose, with search angles of 60° each side in azimuth, and +6°, -13° in elevation.
Self-protection systems: SPO-15 Beryoza radar warning receiver, and active electronic countermeasures.

↑ MiG-31B front and rear cockpits *(Piotr Butowski)*

Details for MiG-31B/MiG-31BS *Foxhound-A*

PRINCIPAL DIMENSIONS:
Wing span: 44 ft 2 ins (13.464 m)
Maximum length: 74 ft 5 ins (22.688 m)
Length without probe: 67 ft 8 ins (20.62 m)
Maximum height: 20 ft 2 ins (6.150 m)

WINGS:
Area: 663 sq ft (61.6 m^2)
Aspect ratio: 2.943
Sweepback at leading edge: 41°
Sweepback at trailing edge: 9° 30′
Twist: 0° root
Anhedral: 4°
Aileron span: 5 ft 7 ins (1.7 m)
Trailing-edge flap span: 8 ft 10 ins (2.682 m)

TAIL UNIT:
Tailplane span: 28 ft 8 ins (8.74 m)
Tailplane sweepback: 50° 22′
Tailplane dihedral: 1° 25′
Fins area: 168 sq ft (15.6 m^2)
Fin sweepback: 54°
Fins cant angle: 8° outward
Rudders area: 22.8 sq ft (2.12 m^2)
Ventral fins area: 32.3 sq ft (3.0 m^2)
Ventral fins cant angle: 12° outward

UNDERCARRIAGE:
Type: Retractable, with twin nosewheels. Each main unit has 2 offset tandem wheels
Main wheel tyre size: 950 × 300 mm
Nose wheel tyre size: 660 × 200 mm
Wheel base: 23 ft 4 ins (7.113 m)
Wheel track: 11 ft 11 ins (3.638 m)

WEIGHTS:
Empty, operating: 48,105 lb (21,820 kg)
Maximum take-off: 101,853 lb (46,200 kg)

PERFORMANCE:
Maximum Mach number: Mach 2.83
Maximum speed at high altitude: 1,620 kts (1,864 mph) 3,000 km/h
Maximum speed at sea level: 810 kts (932 mph) 1,500 km/h
Supersonic cruise Mach number at high altitude: Mach 2.35
Supersonic cruise speed at high altitude: 1,350 kts (1,553 mph) 2,500 km/h
Subsonic cruise Mach number: Mach 0.85
Landing speed: 151 kts (174 mph) 280 km/h
Take-off distance: 3,937 ft (1,200 m)
Landing distance: 2,625 ft (800 m)
Climb time to 32,810 ft (10,000 m): 7.9 minutes
Ceiling: 67,585 ft (20,600 m)
G limit: +5
Combat radius at Mach 2.35, with 4 R-33s and no drop tanks: 389 naut miles (447 miles) 720 km
Combat radius at Mach 0.85, with 4 R-33s, 2 drop tanks, and one in-flight refuelling: 1,188 naut miles (1,367 miles) 2,200 km
Combat radius at Mach 0.85, with 4 R-33s and 2 drop tanks: 756 naut miles (870 miles) 1,400 km
Combat radius at Mach 0.85, with R-33s and no drop tanks: 648 naut miles (746 miles) 1,200 km
Ferry range, unrefuelled: 1,782 naut miles (2,050 miles) 3,300 km
Duration with drop tanks: 3 hours 36 minutes

Wing characteristics: Modestly swept-back, high mounted, with short leading-edge root extensions. Single fence on the upper surface of each wing.
Wing control surfaces: Ailerons (+20°, -20°) and slotted trailing-edge flaps (30°). 4-section leading-edge slats (13°).
Tail control surfaces: Slab (taileron) tailplane, operating both symmetrically (+9°, -30°) and differentially (+1° 50', -1° 50') to simulate elevator and aileron functions when flying at supersonic speed. Twin outward-canted fins with rudders (25° deflection), and 2 ventral stabilizing fins.
Airbrakes: 2, forward-hinged, under the air-intake ducts (44°). Airbrakes area 29.9 sq ft (2.78 m^2)
Flight control system: Conventional, hydraulically actuated.
Construction materials: 50% steel, 33% aluminium and 16% titanium by weight.
Engines: 2 Aviadvigatel/Perm D-30F-6 (izdelye 48) turbofans. MiG-31M uses 2 advanced D-30F-6Ms (izdelye 64) of 38,580 lbf (171.62 kN) with afterburning.
Engine rating: Each 20,944 lbf (93.17 kN) dry, and 34,172 lbf (152 kN) with afterburning.
Air intakes: Wedge-type, with electronically-controlled upper variable 3-shock ram.
Flight refuelling probe: MiG-31B/BS are equipped with a semi-retractable probe on the port side of the nose. MiG-31M has a starboard-side retractable probe.
Fuel system: 36,045 lb (16,350 kg) of fuel inside the fuselage and fins. 2 × 2,500 litre drop tanks can be carried under the wings. MiG-31M has a 39,683 lb (18,000 kg) internal fuel capacity.
Hydraulic system: 2 independent systems to operate undercarriage, wheel brakes, airbrakes, flight control surfaces, flaps and air intake ramps.
Braking system: Main and nose wheel brakes. Twin drag-chute in a fairing between the engine nozzles.

Aircraft variants:
E-155MP (MiG-25MP, izdelye 83) prototype had no wingroot extensions.
MiG-31 (izdelye 01) *Foxhound-A*, as described (see MiG-31B).
MiG-31B (izdelye 01B or izdelye 12) *Foxhound-A* has Zaslon-A radar and R-33S missiles. New navigation system. Flight-refuelling probe added.
MiG-31BS (izdelye 01BS) *Foxhound-A* is similar to the MiG-31B, but upgraded from the MiG-31. A-723 navigation system. Software-enhanced Zaslon radar.
MiG-31E was to be the export version.
MiG-31BM is a proposed mid-life upgrade for interceptors, giving them multi-role capability. Wide range of air-to-ground weapons added, including 6 Kh-31s, 3 Kh-59s, 2 Kh-59Ms, 3 Kh-29T/Ls or other ASMs. New AAMs incorporated from MiG-31M include AA-12 *Adder*, AA-11 *Archer*, and long/ultra-long-range missiles. Zaslon radar will be upgraded using Zaslon-M technology with more target engagement, adaptive control of search zone, detection of Mach 6 targets, better resolution, plus introduction of real-beam and synthetic-aperture ground-mapping mode. MTOW increased to 110,230 lb (50,000 kg).
MiG-31FE was to be the export version of MiG-31BM.
MiG-31M (izdelye 05) *Foxhound-B* has a modified weapons system with Zaslon-M radar, and up to 6 R-37 plus 4 R-77 AAMs. No fixed cannon. Wingroot extensions with lengthened curved leading edges, wider dorsal spine, cylindrical ECM/ECCM wingtip pods on some aircraft, reduced glazing for the rear cockpit and single-piece forward windscreen, and increased-area rudders. More powerful engines, more fuel, and refuelling probe transferred to starboard side. Take-off weight increased to about 114,640 lb (52,000 kg). First 7 built by early 1995, when production continued but total built is uncertain.
MiG-31D (izdelye 07) was developed as an anti-satellite version, armed with 2 Vympel missiles on wing pylons. Cancelled.
Commercial system for space object launching using the MiG-31 interceptor has been under development since early 1997. It will certainly utilize experience gained from experiments with the anti-satellite MiG-31D. The work, sponsored by Russia and Kazakhstan, is in partnership with the Kazakhstan Air Force and Academy of Sciences. First launches of space objects from MiG-31 are expected late 1999 or early 2000.

MAPO "MiG" MiG-35

First flight: Expected late 1998 or early 1999. News of development released May 1996.
Role: Multi-role fighter, now aimed mainly at the export market. Larger development of the MiG-29/MiG-33, originally conceived to replace both the MiG-29 and Sukhoi Su-27 with the Russian Air Force and for export after the year 2005. Thought to have been prepared for a time when Russia may not be able to support both a light (LFI) and heavy (MFI) fighter fleet (see also LFS and MFI entries).

↑ Provisional drawing of the MiG-35. Note the canard foreplanes planned in the early stages of the programme have since been deleted *(Piotr Butowski)*

Aims
- Integrated fire-control/flight/navigation/ECM avionics.
- High manoeuvrability due to thrust vectoring, thrust-to-weight ratio 1.3:1, and low wing loading.
- Range 3,000 km on internal and 4,000 km with auxiliary tanks.

Details
Sales/Users: Expected to become the main Russian export proposal after the year 2005. Believed not to have been chosen for Russian deployment.
Crew: Pilot only.
Fixed guns: Possible Gryazev/Shipunov GSh-301 single-barrel 30-mm cannon.
Number of weapon pylons: 10.
Expendable weapons and equipment: Up to 11,023 lb (5,000 kg), including all current and near future short/medium/intermediate range AAMs and tactical ASMs such as Kh-31, Kh-38 and Kh-59, guided bombs, etc.
Radar: Phazotron RP-35 (formerly Zhuk-Ph) phased-array radar, currently undergoing laboratory testing. Search range (fighter type target) is 75.5 naut miles (87 miles) 140 km in the forward hemisphere and 35 naut miles (40.4 miles) 65 km in the rear hemisphere. Radar can track up to 24 targets simultaneously and engage 4. Search angles 60° each side in azimuth; additionally, antenna can be turned mechanically through an angle of 60°. Radar weight 485 lb (220 kg), volume 500 litres. In air-to-ground mode, the radar generates a ground map, enables terrain avoidance/following, and engages ground targets; 4 ground targets can be tracked simultaneously.
Flight/weapon system avionics/instrumentation: Fully integrated digital avionics suite.
Wing characteristics: New wing, enlarged when compared with MiG-29 due to increased root chord, though with smaller tip chord.
Canard: Canard foreplanes were reportedly planned in the early stages of the programme, but now rejected.
Flight control system: Fly-by-wire.
Engines: 2 widely-spaced Klimov/St Petersburg RD-333 3-D thrust-vectoring turbofans, installed 3 ft (0.92 m) further aft than MiG-29/MiG-33 engines. Air delivery 187 lb (85 kg) per second; temperature at turbine entry 1,527° C. Service life expected to be 2,000 hours to the first general repair. For initial flight trials, less powerful RD-133s may be used, though this may not become necessary due to a delay in the first flight date from late 1997 to late 1998.
Engine rating: Each 22,045 lbf (98.06 kN) thrust with afterburning.
Fuel system: 3,307 lb (1,500 kg) more fuel than MiG-29 provided in the fuselage, due to further aft-positioning of engines.

ANPK "MiG" LFS

Note: A number of the drawings of the so-called Mikoyan I-2000 LFI that appeared in the press in early 1998 were actually of the little known Eurasia Integral (which see).
Role: Lightweight multi-role fighter, weighing less than MiG-29.

Aims
- Reduced radar and IR visibility.
- Very high manoeuvrability.
- New weapon systems.
- Short take-off and landing.
- Low cost.

Development
- 1983. Work began on the new LFI (logkiy frontovoi istrebitel, lightweight tactical fighter), a close-air combat partner for heavy MFI.
- 1995. Work resumed after some 10 years on new technology basis. Now named LFS (S for samolot, aircraft).
- 2005. Possible initial operational capability.

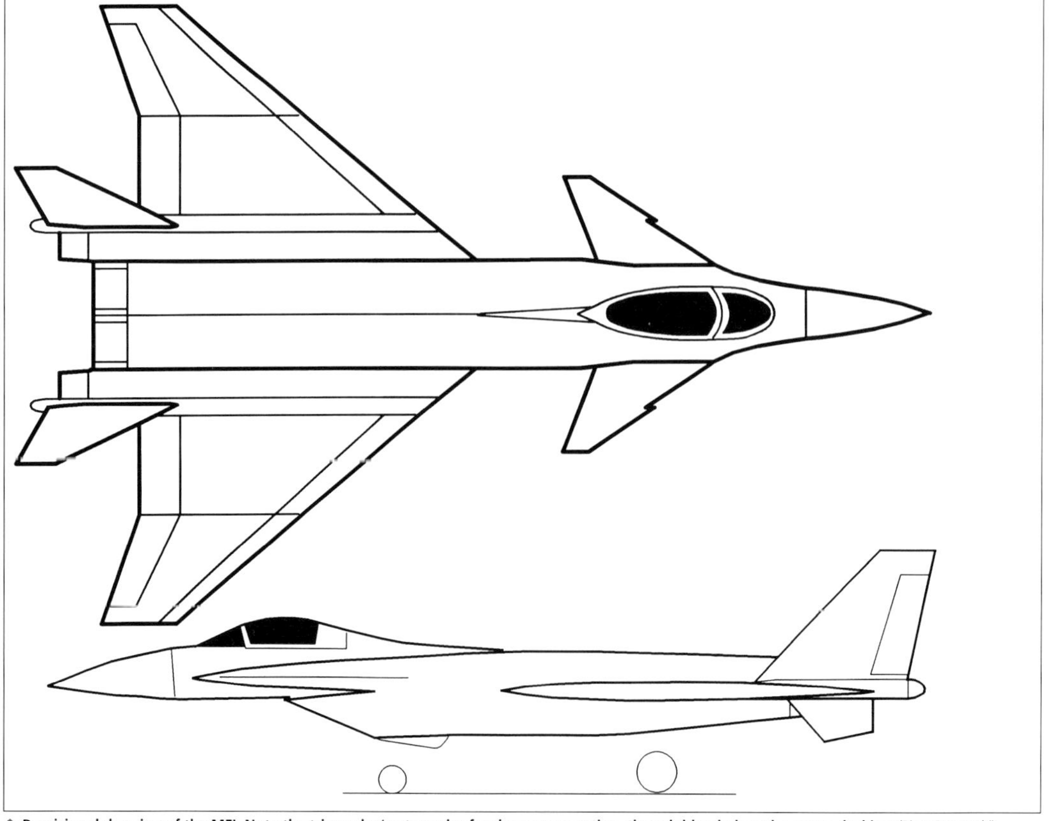

↑ Provisional drawing of the MFI. Note the triangular/rectangular fuselage cross section, though blended on the upper decking *(Piotr Butowski)*

Details

Sales/Users: Russian Air Force as a new 5th-generation fighter.
Engine/s: Single- and twin-engined configurations are being considered, though company Chairman is reported to have a preference for the twin-engined layout. In twin-engined configuration, each would possibly have a thrust in the 22,045 lbf (98.06 kN) class. Thrust vectoring.

MAPO "MiG" MFI (1-42) and 1-44

First flight: Originally expected to fly in 1995. In early 1998, the maiden flight was announced to be August 1998.
Role: "Reconfiguring" combat aircraft of unique aerodynamics (see Aims), intended to be an advanced tactical fighter with attack capability. May become an aerodynamics, avionics and weapon system testbed/demonstrator for the LFS programme.

Aims

- Supersonic cruise speed.
- High manoeuvrability at supersonic speed.
- Control retained at angles of attack up to 60-70° (so called super-manoeuvrability).
- Safe flying at hypercritical angles of attack (about 100-120°), with stability but not controllability (so-called hyper-manoeuvrability).
- Built with so-called "second generation stealth technology" (special radar absorbing materials and coatings, with minimal airframe changes that impair aircraft performance).
- Air-to-air missiles carried in the fuselage weapons bay, in order to reduce the aircraft's radar signature.
- New radars, including a tail unit for rearward coverage.
- New weapon systems with next-generation missiles of each range-class.
- According to Anatoli Belosvet, Deputy General Manager of MAPO-M "MiG", the MFI "is like a bird. It reconfigures itself according to flight range. Unique aerodynamics solutions have been introduced to the aircraft, which no one other aircraft has".

Development

- 1983. Work began on the new MFI (mnogofunktsyonalnyi istrebitel – multifunction fighter) according to programme I-90 (istrebitel, fighter for the nineties).
- 1986. Mikoyan design bureau began the detailed design.
- 1991. First flight originally planned, but completion of the prototypes delayed through financial restrictions, especially for engine development.
- December 1994. High-speed taxi trials performed by the 1-44 prototype.
- August 1997. Russian Ministry of Defence promised limited financial aid "to led MFI to flight condition".

Details

Sales/Users: 2 prototypes (Object 1-44) built by Mikoyan experimental works in Moscow. Any production is now unlikely.
Crew: Pilot.
Fixed guns: Probably a single 30-mm cannon.
Expendable weapons and equipment: Standard air-to-air armament includes 162 naut mile (186 mile) 300 km range R-37 missiles, medium-range R-77M missiles, and R-73 close air combat missiles. Main weapon load is housed in the fuselage. The Vympel design bureau is working on a successor to the R-73 short-range missile for use on 1-42 and other aircraft. The first tests of this new high-manoeuvrability missile are expected in the near future.
Radar: NIIR (Phazotron) N-014 electronically-scanned phased array type in the nose. Rearward-looking self-defence radar in the tail.
Wing characteristics: Shoulder mounted, with moderate sweepback. Little or no anhedral or dihedral. Clipped wingtips.
Wing control surfaces: Multi-segment leading-edge flaps. Trailing-edge ailerons and flaps, with possibly spoilers.
Tail control surfaces: Twin outward-canted dorsal fins and inset rudders, possibly carried on short fuselage booms of MiG-29 type. Twin outward-canted ventral fins.

DETAILS FOR MFI (PROVISIONAL)

WEIGHTS:
Normal take-off: 61,729 lb (28,000 kg)
Maximum take off: 77,162 lb (35,000 kg)

PERFORMANCE:
Maximum speed: 1,349 kts (1,553 mph) 2,500 km/h
G limits: +10
Supersonic range: 1,079 naut miles (1,243 miles) 2,000 km
Maximum range: 2,158 naut miles (2,485 miles) 4,000 km

Canard: Swept, fairly close coupled.
Fuselage: Triangular/rectangular cross section, though blended on the upper decking. Additional flaps, functioning as elevators, are installed on the rear fuselage, thus increasing the allowable centre of gravity range.
Airbrakes: Large airbrake on the upper fuselage.
Engines: 2 Saturn AL-41F thrust-vectoring turbofans.
Engine rating: Each about 39,680 lbf (176.5 kN).
Air intakes: Box-type under the forward fuselage, with large side-by-side inlets.
Nozzles: Vectoring flat nozzles.

Aircraft variants:
MFI (mnogofunktsyonalnyi istrebitel) or 1-42 is an anticipated 5th-generation fighter, as detailed.
1-44 is an aerodynamics demonstrator, without some advanced systems.

MAPO "MiG" 701 and 701P

Note: Details of these programmes can be found in the 1996-97 edition of *WA&SD*, page 83.

MAPO "MiG" MiG-AT, MiG-UTS and MiG-AC

First flight: 16 March 1996, piloted by Roman Taskayev.
Role: Advanced and combat trainer, and light attack. Can be modified for naval aircraft-carrier training, using arrester hook (see Aircraft variants).

Aims

- To replace the L-29 Delfin and L-39 Albatros in Russian Air Force service.
- To be capable of various aspects of training, including flying, air combat and weapons.
- Requirements of the Russian Air Force are (in summarized form):

a) 2 non-afterburning engines, with 0.6-0.7 power-to-weight ratio. Maximum take-off weight 15,432 lb (7,000 kg).
b) 459 kts (528 mph) 850 km/h maximum speed. Landing speed not exceeding 92 kts (106 mph) 170 km/h, and take-off and landing runs not exceeding 1,640 ft (500 m). Provision for operation from unpaved runways.
c) Normal range of 648 naut miles (746 miles) 1,200 km at Mach 0.5 and 19,700 ft (6,000 m) altitude. Ferry range of 1,350 naut miles (1,553 miles) 2,500 km.
d) G limits of +8, -3.
e) High manoeuvrability, similar to that of new generation fighters.
f) Pre-programmable control system imitating aircraft with different longitudinal stability coefficient.
g) 15,000 flying hours structural life over 30 years.

Development

- January 1991. Competition for a new generation jet trainer (UTS, uchebno-trenirovochnyi samolyot) was initiated by the Russian Air Force. UTK (uchebno-trenirovochnyi komplex) training system has been ordered which includes flight simulators.

↑ **MiG-AT2 (MiG-UTS or Type 823) cockpit** *(Piotr Butowski)*

- January 1992. First stage of the competition summarized. Mikoyan 821, Myasishchev M-200, Sukhoi S-54 and Yakovlev Yak-130 took part in the design competition. The designs were judged in 8 technical and economic categories. The Sukhoi S-54 was reportedly judged winner in 4 of the 8 categories (technical perfection, flight safety, combat capability and technical training). But, at the same time, the S-54 was disqualified for having only a single engine. Both Mikoyan and Yakovlev were approved to continue the development of prototypes.
- 14 September 1992. Agreement signed between Mikoyan and SNECMA concerning use of Larzac 04-R20 engines in the MiG-AT. The Larzac powers the 821.1 first prototype and export aircraft. Also, Mikoyan, SNECMA and Sextant Avionique signed an agreement to jointly develop and market the trainer.
- 1995. Despite expected final selection in 1994, the final choice between the MiG-AT and Yak-130 will not be made until after service trials.
- January 1995. Ground testing took place of the MiG-AT prototype in France with production Larzac 04-R20 engines. Aircraft shipped to Russia for the first flight and subsequently returned for exhibition at the 1995 Paris Air Show.

↑ **MiG-AT2 (MiG-UTS or Type 823) second prototype featuring Russian avionics. Although displayed with R-77 AAM and Kh-29T ASM, only unguided weapons can be carried by this aircraft** *(Piotr Butowski)*

▪ January 1997. A first batch of 10 aircraft ordered by the Russian Air Force for service trials.
▪ 28 October 1997. Second prototype first flew and joined the test programme, as a MiG-UTS/MiG-AT2.

Details *(principally MiG-AT, unless stated)*

Sales/Users: Initially, requirement of the Russian Air Force under UTS programme was estimated at 800-1,000 aircraft before the year 2000, later decreased to 500 and now standing at 200. The potential export market is for 1,200-1,300 aircraft over 20 years. Export interest includes that from India and South Africa. Series production at MAPO plant in Moscow. 15 aircraft were planned to be completed by the end of 1997, 6 of which were in final assembly in mid-1997, all of Type 823 standard (Russian systems and avionics, but French engines).
Crew: 2, in tandem, the rear instructor's seat raised by 15.75 ins (40 cm), offering a 17° downward view from the front cockpit and 7° from the rear cockpit.
Crew escape: Zvezda K-93 (K-36LT) ejection seats.
Fixed guns: None.
Number of weapon pylons: 7.
Expendable weapons and equipment: Up to 4,409 lb (2,000 kg), including the usual light weapons.
Flight/weapon system avionics/instrumentation: 821.1 prototype and export MiG-ATFs have Sextant Topflight® avionics, including 5 colour MFD-55 multi-function liquid crystal displays (2 in front cockpit, 3 aft), HUD with built-in computer (SHUD), H341 BSM gyro horizon attitude indicator, H221 CMT standby gyro horizon, 64-032-220 airspeed indicator, 64-963-503 engine rpm indicator, 61-533-133 temperature indicator, ChaM 756 clock, K1-13BS-1 magnetic compass, IXT 565 navigation indicator, 64-142-223 barometric altimeter, and 64-081-320 vertical speed indicator. Totem laser inertial navigation system and mission computer, Topstar GPS/Glonass standalone receiver, UMPT 33 air data computer system, ERT 120 radio altimeter, NR810F101 (stated in brochure as NR810A101) VOR/ILS, NC-12B Tacan, videocamera, CG90 gyro-magnetic compass, flying mission computer and symbols generator, and helmet-mounted target designation system. HOTAS, multifunctional ILS panel, and rear cockpit multifunctional panel (rear UFCP). Flight data insertion unit (KTDU), EVS 915 videotape recorder, and Tester U3A flight data recorder. SG 100D IFF, ERA 200 V/UHF com transceiver, SPU-821 intercom, and Almaz-UBS information voice reporting system. CSU-821 integrated flight control system and SMS weapons control system. Integration using MIL-STD-1553B databus.
Self-protection system: Radar warning receivers.
Wing characteristics: Straight, low-mounted, with slight wingroot extensions.
Wing control surfaces: Ailerons, slotted trailing-edge flaps and 3-section leading-edge slats.
Tail control surfaces: Elevators and rudder. Ventral fin.
Airbrakes: 2, forming the tailcone.
Flight control system: Avionca multi-channel fly-by-wire, with Rodina control actuators and hydraulic units.
Construction materials: Aluminium alloy for the wings (honeycomb core), leading-edge slats, fixed tail and 60% of the fuselage. Remaining fuselage content, plus wing control surfaces, of carbonfibre and glassfibre composites. Titanium for airbrakes and part of the rear fuselage, with minor use of steel for front of air intake areas. See Aircraft variants.
Engines: 2 SNECMA Larzac 04-R20 turbofans for prototype and export aircraft. New Soyuz/Moscow RD-1700 turbofans (fully interchangeable with Larzacs) are projected for the domestic market and are expected in 1999-2000.
Engine rating: Each 3,175 lbf (14.21 kN).
Air intakes: Each side of the fuselage, above the wing roots.
Fuel system: 2,290 litres, 3,704 lb (1,680 kg) maximum capacity, with 1,874 lb (850 kg) nominal and 2,822 lb (1,280 kg) intermediate. Fuel accumulator guarantees 30 seconds of engine operation during changes in aircraft attitude. In case of electric fuel pump failure, fuel supply continues by engine compressed air bleed.
Hydraulic system: Independent booster system fed by port-side engine-driven Messier Bugatti PR70660-20 pump. Independent general system fed by similar starboard-side engine-driven pump. Emergency undercarriage and airbrake/flaps extension via hydraulic accumulators. Hydraulic accumulators additional charging via hand-operated pump. Auxiliary booster system feed line connected to NS-65 emergency hydraulic pump. Booster system for first chamber of electro-hydraulic actuators; general system feeds second chamber of actuators and hydraulic actuators of aircraft systems.
Electrical system: 27V DC and 200/115V 400Hz 3-phase AC. 2 channel DC system with 2 × 8044-21 Auxilec starter-generators (with WDII-014 Auxilec control and protection unit) offering 9 kW nominal power (primary system). 2-channel AC system with 2 static inverters (secondary system). In case of failure of both generators, power supplied by 15CTSS-45B lead-zink batteries of 45 amp-hours each. If a static inverter fails, both AC channels receive power from the remaining unit.

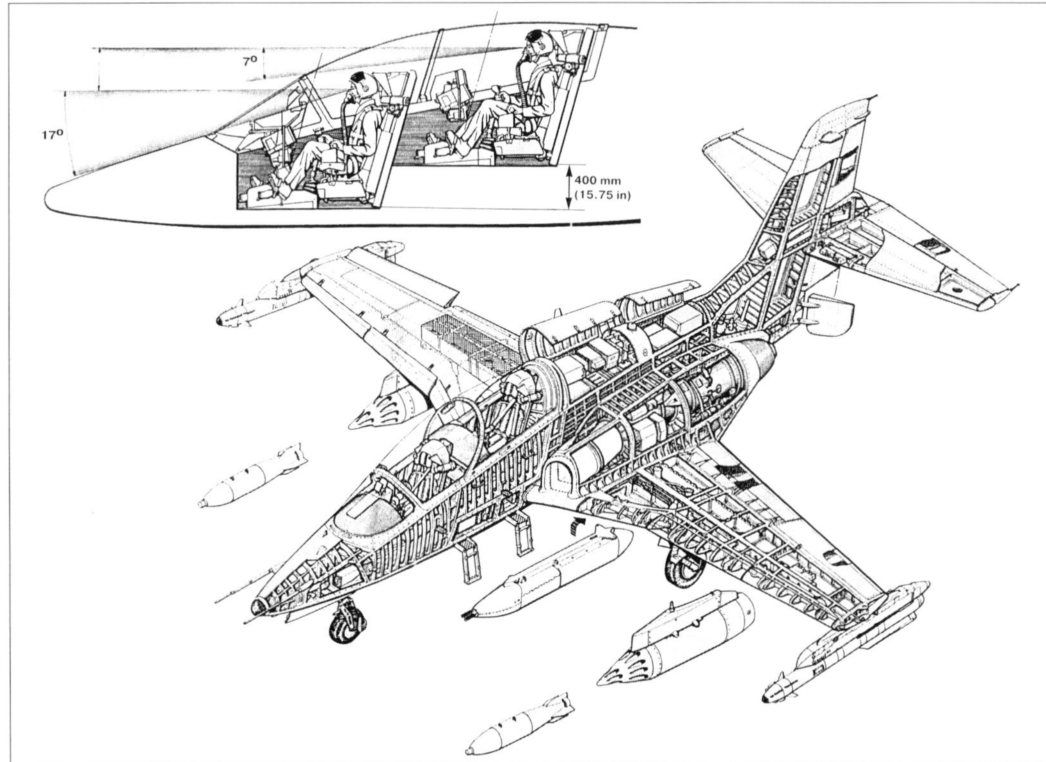

↑ **Structure of MiG-AT and cockpit layout** *(courtesy MAPO-M "MiG"/Terpsichore)*

Details for MiG-AT

PRINCIPAL DIMENSIONS:
Wing span: 33 ft 4 ins (10.16 m), or 21 ft 4 ins (6.5 m) folded on naval version
Maximum length: 39 ft 5 ins (12.01 m)
Maximum height: 15 ft 2 ins (4.623 m)

WINGS:
Aspect ratio: 5.84
Area: 190.2 sq ft (17.67 m^2)

UNDERCARRIAGE:
Type: Retractable, with nosewheel
Main wheel tyre size: 660 × 200 mm
Nose wheel tyre size: 500 × 150 mm
Wheel base: 14 ft 8 ins (4.477 m)
Wheel track: 12 ft 6 ins (3.8 m)

WEIGHTS:
Nominal take-off: 10,163 lb (4,610 kg)
Normal take-off: 11,464-12,544 lb (5,200-5,690 kg)
Maximum take-off: 15,432 lb (7,000 kg) for combat

PERFORMANCE:
Maximum operating Mach number (M_{MO}): Mach 0.85
Maximum speed at sea level: 459 kts (528 mph) 850 km/h
Take-off speed: 97-119 kts (112-137 mph) 180-220 km/h
Flaps/slats retraction speed: 189 kts (217 mph) 350 km/h
Stalling speed: 97 kts (112 mph) 180 km/h
Landing speed: 94-125 kts (109-144 mph) 175-232 km/h for basic/advanced training
Time to 350 km/h: 31.5 seconds for advanced training, 61 seconds for basic training
Take-off distance: typically 1,181 ft (360 m), with 1,771 ft (540 m) quoted for basic training and 1,017 ft (350 m) for advanced training
Take-off distance using ski-jump: 345 ft (105 m)
Climb rate at sea level: 5,510-13,580 ft (1,680-4,140 m) per minute for basic/advanced training
Climb rate at 16,400 ft (5,000 m): 4,330-7,875 ft (1,320-2,400 m) per minute for basic/advanced training
Landing distance: 2,100 ft (600 m) ground roll
G limits: +8, -3
Sustained turn g limit at sea level: +4.5/+8 for basic/advanced training
Sustained turn g limit at 16,400 ft (5,000 m): +3.4/+5 for basic/advanced training
Ceiling: 45,930 ft (14,000 m), but stated in brochure to be 50,850 ft (15,500 m)
Practical range at Mach 0.5, 19,700 ft (6,000 m) altitude: 648 naut miles (746 miles) 1,200 km
Ferry range: 1,403 naut miles (1,615 miles) 2,600 km
Typical ground attack training mission: Visually sighted target, range 43 naut miles (50 miles) 80 km, altitude 655-8,200 ft (200-2,500 m), with 4 diving attacks, 3 advanced manoeuvre attacks and landing from a circle, with 50% fuel and 331 lb (150 kg) fuel reserves

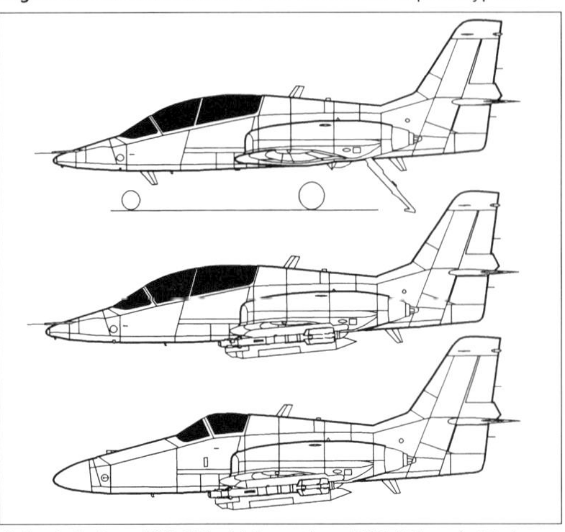
↑ *Top to bottom:* **MiG-AT in shipborne form, MiG-ATC combat trainer and MiG-AC single-seater with Moskit radar** *(Piotr Butowski)*

Aircraft variants:
MiG-AT (advanced trainer, or Type 821) is the basic export variant, as detailed. Prototype 821-1, side number 81, first flew on 16 March 1996.
Type 822 was a developed version proposed for South Korea. The internal wing structure was to be slightly altered and construction was to be of composites. Programme abandoned.
MiG-UTS (uchebno-trenirovochnyi samolot, or Type 823) is a version with Russian avionics and systems. First prototype (second aircraft built) number 83 was displayed at MAKS '97 in Zhukovsky before its first flight on 28 October 1997 (pilot Roman Taskayev).
MiG-ATC proposed 2-seat combat training version.
MiG-AC is the proposed single-seat combat version with Phazotron Moskit-1 (Mosquito) radar weighing 154 lb (70 kg), with a range of 32.4 naut miles (37 miles) 60 km.
Naval Training version applies to any aircraft of the family, modified to perform carrier deck landing/take-offs, combat missions, or renew pilot skills. Can be based in sea conditions up to 6, with weather minimum of 30-400 metres, perform ski-jump take-offs, and land using an arrester hook. Can also have folding outer wing panels (span reduced to 21 ft 4 ins, 6.5 m) and use catapult for launch.

MAPO "Myasishchev" — Russia

Corporate address:
140160 Zhukovsky-5, Moscow Region.

Telephone: +7 095 272 60 41 or 556 77 76
Facsimile: +7 095 556 55 83 or 52 98
E-mail: mdb@mastak.msk.ru

Founded:
1951. On 10 June 1997 Myasishchev was incorporated into the Military Industrial Group MAPO, becoming MAPO-M.

Information:
Stanislav G. Smirnov.

ACTIVITIES

▪ Myasishchev has stopped work on the M-200 Master jet trainer, details and a photograph of which can be found in the 1996-97 edition of *WA&SD*, page 84. It is, however, involved in the upgrade of the Russian Air Force's huge fleet of Czech-built L-39 jet trainers and L-410 light transports, plus UAV programmes. See also Special Electronic and Reconnaissance, Transport, and General Aviation sections for current aircraft programmes.

Novosibirsk Aircraft Production Association (NAPA) — Russia

Corporate address:
15 Polzunova Str, 630051 Novosibirsk.

Telephone: +7 3832 798095 or 773706
Facsimile: +7 3832 772392 or 771035
Telex: 133211 NAPO SU

Founded: 1936.

Information:
Valery Skvortsov (Marketing).

ACTIVITIES

▪ One of the most important aircraft construction enterprises in Russia, having also developed a large number of different aircraft types. Currently, its manufacturing includes the Sukhoi Su-34 combat aircraft and the Ukrainian Antonov An-38 short-haul transport.

SibNIA named after Chaplygin — Russia

Full name:
Sibirsky Nauchno-Issledovatelsky Institute Aviatsii im. Chaplygina.

Corporate address:
630051 Novosibirsk, ul. Polzunova, 21

Telephone: +7 3832 779241, 770361

Founded:
1940s, as a 'reserve' institute for TsAGI in the event of war.

Information:
Vladimir Berns (*telephone* +7 3832 797042).

ACTIVITIES

▪ This Siberian-based Aeronautical Research Institute is generally not a design bureau but is a large scientific centre that has been involved in aerodynamics testing (in wind tunnels) of many Sukhoi projects (including the Su-27). Recently, it displayed a model of a radical single-seat close air support aircraft, of which full-scale development is unlikely. It is believed to represent a Sukhoi project of the 1980s, based on (or using technology similar to that of) the Sukhoi *Frogfoot*, having what appears to be fairly similar straight wings but in this case rear-mounted on an entirely different fuselage, with LERX and just 3 pylons per wing (more pylons under the fuselage). The single turboprop engine is mounted in the rear fuselage or mid-fuselage with a long shaft, fed with air from an over-fuselage intake and driving contra-rotating pusher propellers, each with 6 advanced-design blades around a huge spinner-type tail fairing. A V-tail with ruddervators is joined by smaller fixed ventral fins, while all-moving large canards are mounted just forward of the mid-fuselage and a smaller anhedral pair is carried under the nose on a fairing that could be used to house either cannon or equipment. No further details are necessary.

▪ Except for the Dzhinn lightplane (see General Aviation section) developed in co-operation with the Rastr Scientific-Technical Centre, the organization manufactures full-scale replicas of I-16 and I-153 piston-engined fighters of the interwar/WWII periods. At the time of writing, 6 I-16s had been completed, the first having flown in August 1995 (using ASh-62IR engine from an An-2) and a single I-153 (first flown August 1997). Deliveries include 1 to New Zealand.

Sokol Nizhny Novgorod Aircraft Building Plant, JSC — Russia

Corporate address:
1 Chaadaeva Str, 603035 Nizhny Novgorod.

Telephone: +7 8312 467501

Facsimile: +7 8312 247966

Founded:
1 February 1932.

Information:
Vladimir Pomolov (General Director).

ACTIVITIES

▪ Has manufactured the MiG-29UB and MiG-31 as the most recent models of MiG combat aircraft built since 1949 on behalf of Mikoyan, and undertakes modernization of the MiG-21bis under the MiG-21-93 programme. Civil/commercial aircraft manufactured include the Dingo amphibian with air-cushion landing system, MiG-110, M-101T Gzhel and Accord, F-15F Excalibur and gliders. It also constructs boats/amphibious boats.

AVPK Sukhoi — Russia

Full name:
Aviatsionnyi Voyenno Promyshlennyi Komplex Sukhoi, or Aviation Military Industrial Complex Sukhoi).

Founded:
30 December 1996.

Information:
Mikhail Pogosyan (General Director).

ACTIVITIES

▪ This organization has brought together under a single grouping the Sukhoi and Beriev design bureaux, the production centres at Irkutsk (constructing the Be-200, Su-27UB and Su-30, including India's Su-30MKIs), Komsomolsk-on-Amur (constructing the Be-103, Su-27, Su-33, Su-35, S-80 and T-60S) and Novosibirsk (constructing the An-38 and Su-34), plus the Inkombank and Oneximbank banks. Other programmes include the Su-37, development of a 5th generation fighter, and the proposal for the 860-seat **KR-860** ultra-large airliner (Krylya Rossii or *Wings of Russia*), all from the Sukhoi Design Bureau (which see), plus the **S-237** supersonic attack aircraft and **TKS-25** transport from Sukhoi Shturmovics (which see).

SUKHOI SHTURMOVICS CONSORTIUM

Information:
Vladimir Babak.

Activities:
▪ In March 1992, 47 companies, including the Sukhoi Design Bureau, Tbilisi and Ulan-Ude aircraft factories, Ufa engine factory and many others formed the Sukhoi Shturmovics consortium. The main objective became the manufacturing and sale of Su-25 and Su-25T aircraft, plus later designs. Among current programmes is work on the new 20-25 tonne TOW **S-237** supersonic attack aircraft, a twin-engined derivative of the S-37 project of the 1980s (not to be mistaken for the current S-37 and Su-37 fighters), plus development of the **TKS-25** (transportnyi konteinernyi samolet or transport containerized aircraft) of 25 tonnes take-off weight and powered by 2 D-436 turbofans, able to deliver an 11,023 lb (5,000 kg) payload over a 2,700 naut mile (3,107 mile) 5,000 km range.

SUKHOI ADVANCED TECHNOLOGIES JSC

Founded: 1989.

Information: Boris Rakitin.

Activities:
▪ Development and manufacturing of high-performance competition and training aircraft.

SUKHOI DESIGN BUREAU

Activities:
▪ See next page.

Sukhoi Design Bureau

Russia

Corporate address:
23A Polikarpov Str, Moscow 125284.
Telephone: +7 095 945 65 25 **Facsimile:** +7 095 200 42 43 **Telex:** 414716 SUHOI SU
Founded: 1939.
Information: Mikhail Petrovich Simonov (General Designer).

ACTIVITIES

■ Current Design Bureau programmes include the Su-37, development of a 5th generation S-37 fighter, and the proposed 860-seat **KR-860** ultra-large airliner (Krylya Rossii or *Wings of Russia*). Sukhoi piston-engined trainers and aerobatic aircraft, plus various transports, can be found in the Freighter and General Aviation sections. (See AVPK Sukhoi.)

Sukhoi Su-17, Su-20 and Su-22 (NATO name *Fitter*)

Note: First flown on 2 August 1966, the Su-17 variable-geometry wing derivative of the Su-7 *Fitter-A* was followed by Su-20 and Su-22 export versions. Although principally for ground attack and reconnaissance, some have been used for limited interception (by Peru), while the Su-22M5 upgrade can be a multi-role aircraft offering full air-to-air combat (see Aircraft variants). Production of all versions ended in 1990 and withdrawal from CIS forces was underway by 1995 except in reconnaissance form. Full technical details plus illustrations can be found in the 1996-97 edition of *WA&SD*, pages 84-86. However, to keep readers up-to-date with the current situation regarding these older aircraft, the Sales/Users and Aircraft variant sub-sections have been expanded, updated and reprinted here.

Sales/Users: Some 1,200 Su-17s/20s/22s of all versions were produced at the Komsomolsk-on-Amur plant, including 500 for export. Production ended in 1990 and by 1995 the Su-17 was being withdrawn from service with CIS air forces except in reconnaissance form. Currently, Ukraine has 51 aircraft in service and Russia no more than 100 (some 60 in Europe). Others are in Kazakhstan, Turkmenistan and Uzbekistan. In 1974-76 Poland purchased 27 Su-20s, of which the last was withdrawn in 1996. Other users of Su-20s are Algeria, Egypt and Iraq. In 1985 2 Egyptian aircraft were bought by West Germany for testing in the experimental unit Erprobungsstelle 61 (1 for flying and 1 for spares). The total number of Su-22s currently (at the time of writing) in service throughout the world, except CIS, is over 300, including 99 with Poland. Other Su-22 operators are Afghanistan, Angola, Czech Republic, Hungary, Libya, North Korea, Peru, Slovakia, Syria, Vietnam (64 bought in the 1980s) and Yemen. Vietnam has expressed interest in the Su-22 upgrade with podded Komar-17 (Gnat) radar.

Aircraft variants (in order of appearance):

Su-7IG (S-22I) *Fitter-B* first prototype, used as a variable-wing technology demonstrator.

Su-17 (S-32) *Fitter-B* had a 21,164 lbf (94.15 kN) with full afterburning AL-7F1-250 turbojet. Manufactured 1970-72. 6,614 lb (3,000 kg) weapon load. 6,173 lb (2,800 kg) of internal fuel.

Su-17M (S-32M) *Fitter-C* appeared in December 1971 as the first large-scale production version. 24,692 lbf (109.84 kN) with afterburning AL-21F-3 engine. 8,818 lb (4,000 kg) of weapons. 8,003 lb (3,630 kg) of internal fuel.

Su-20 (S-32MK) *Fitter-C* became the export version of Su-17M, with slightly downgraded equipment and weapons.

Su-17M2 (S-32M2) *Fitter-D* appeared in 1974 and was manufactured 1975-79. 8 ins (200 mm) lengthened nose. Fon-1400 laser rangefinder and DISS-7 Doppler navigation radar added, and new ASP-17 gun sight.

Su-22 (Su-17M2D, S-32M2K) *Fitter-F* became the export version of the Su-17M2, powered by an R-29B-300 engine instead of the standard AL-21F-3. Manufactured 1976-80.

Su-17UM (S-52U, S-52UM) *Fitter-E/G* appeared from 1975 as 2-seat combat trainer, with weapon systems retained but only 1 cannon. Much larger dorsal spine, and new K-36 ejection seats instead of the former KS-4. Early version with short tailfin was named S-52U *Fitter-E*, followed by S-52UM *Fitter-G* with a lengthened fin. Later, all aircraft upgraded to Su-17UM3 standard.

Su-17M3 (S-52) *Fitter-H* is externally similar to the Su-17UM but is a single seater. New weapon system including Klon laser rangefinder/target designator, and new KN-23 navigation system. Manufactured 1976-81.

Su-22M (S-52K) *Fitter-J* became the export derivative of the Su-17M3 but with downgraded avionics of the Su-22. R-29B-300 engine. Manufactured 1979-81.

Su-22M3 (S-52M3K) was offered as an export version similar to the Su-22M but with complete weapons and avionics suite of Soviet Su-17M3. Small quantity manufactured in 1982.

Su-22U (S-52UK) and **Su-22UM** (S-52UMK) *Fitter-E* became the export names of the Su-17U/UM.

Su-17UM3 (S-52UM3) *Fitter-G* appeared in October 1978 as a 2-seat trainer similar to the Su-17UM, but with the weapon system of the Su-17M3.

Su-22UM3 (S-52UM3K) *Fitter-G* appeared as the export version of the Su-17UM3, powered by the R-29BS-300 turbojet.

Su-17M4 (S-54) *Fitter-K* was first flown on 19 June 1980 and manufactured during 1980-90. Most advanced production version.

Su-22UM3K (S-52UM3K) *Fitter-G* is similar to Su-22UM3 but with the AL-21F3 engine. Appeared in 1982.

Su-22M4 (S-54K) *Fitter-K* became the export version of the Su-17M4.

Su-17M3R, Su-17M4R, Su-20R, Su-22R, Su-22M3R and ***Su-22M4R*** are reconnaissance versions with the KKR-1 reconnaissance pod suspended beneath the fuselage and containing photo-cameras (A-39, UA-47 and PA-1), KDF-38 flare dispenser and SRS-9 Virazh elint (as can be carried by any Su-17M3 and M4).

Su-22M5 (S-56, originally named Su-17M4N or S-54N) was a project of the early 1980s, with fixed 45° swept wings, AL-31F turbofan of the Su-27, and new weapons.

Upgrade programmes are currently offered by Sukhoi, as well as by Israel.

First offer of 1994 was prepared jointly by Sukhoi, Thomson-CSF and Sextant Avionique and featured an advanced PrNK-55 nav/attack system including new smart HUD for day and night operations, Thomson-CSF TMV 630 laser rangefinder/target designator, new Sextant Avionique mission computer, Sherloc radar warning receiver (RWR), NSS100-P Navstar/Glonass GPS receiver, AHV6 radio altimeter, Totem inertial navigation system, and ADU 300 air data unit. Optionally, conventional cockpit instrumentation could be replaced by 2 MFD55 multi-function colour 5 ins × 5 ins (13 × 13 cm) liquid crystal active matrix displays derived from the French Rafale. Radio, VOR, navigation and IFF systems could also be improved. ***In the Second Stage***, the aircraft could receive beyond visual range (BVR) air-to-air plus all-weather round-the-clock air-to-surface capability due to the lightweight Phathom radar located in the air intake shock cone (Phathom is a product of the Russian Phazotron and French Thomson-CSF organizations). When used against air targets, upgraded *Fitter* could be equipped with a helmet-mounted display (HMD). During air-to-ground operations the aircraft could carry a Rubis FLIR pod connected to the system through the common databus, a laser target designation pod, and Barem jamming pod. Weapons were to include R-77 (AA-12 *Adder*) and R-27 (AA-10 *Alamo*) AAMs, Kh-31P (AS-17 *Krypton*) anti-radar and Kh-31A and Kh-35 anti-ship missiles. With the laser target designation pod, laser-guided missiles and bombs could be carried (including possibly Western types). The upgrade proposal was rigid and cost US$4.5 million, and generated no interest. Therefore a more flexible offer has been prepared and is currently being presented to Poland, Vietnam and others.

Upgrade offer of 1997 provides 4 packages which can be introduced independently. First modernization package includes GPS (for example, Russian A-737), new IFF and flight data sensors. Next, the self-defence system can be improved by new RWR and electronic jammer. In the third package, the aircraft receives MFDs and helmet-mounted sight. Lastly, the most advanced and expensive package provides for use of a podded RLPK-22 system with Kopyo or Komar radar to enable the aircraft to deploy Kh-31A anti-ship missiles. Except for the Russian radar, all remaining upgrade items can be of different manufacture. Sukhoi also offers the MK-54 computerized mission planning system for the Su-22, allowing the flight path and weapons use to be defined and inserted into the aircraft's computer in 11 minutes 30 seconds rather than the current 3-4 hours. Additionally, the service life can be extended to 3,000 flight hours or 30 years.

↑ **Poland, with 99 aircraft, is the main operator of the Su-22** *(Piotr Butowski)*

Sukhoi Su-24 (NATO name *Fencer*)

First flight: 2 July 1967 for the T6-1 delta-winged prototype, piloted by Vladimir Ilyushin. 17 January 1970 for the T6-2I variable-geometry prototype.

Role: Nuclear strike, tactical bomber, reconnaissance and electronic warfare.

Chief designer: Yevgeni Felsner until 1989, then Leonid Logvinov.

Aims

■ To penetrate enemy defences for 5 minutes at 1,400 km/h and 200 m altitude.

■ Supersonic replacement for the Ilyushin Il-28 and Yakovlev Yak-28, originally intended to be developed from the Su-7.

Development

■ 1961. Initial requirements for an Su-7 development equipped with nav/attack radar.

■ Autumn 1963. Full-scale mock-up of the S-6 project.

■ August 1965. Governmental order for the T-6 (T-58M) tactical nuclear strike aircraft.

■ Autumn 1966. Full-scale mock-up of the T-6 accepted.

■ 2 July 1967. 5 am first flight of the T6-1 prototype with fixed delta wings and 4 lift engines built into the fuselage.

■ August 1968. Official governmental order for a variable-geometry derivative.

■ 17 January 1970. Maiden flight of the T6-2I variable-geometry wing prototype, piloted by Vladimir Ilyushin.

■ 30 December 1971. First production aircraft left the factory in Novosibirsk.

■ July 1974. State Acceptance Trials completed.

■ 1974. Su-24 attained initial operational capability with the first unit.

■ February 1975. Su-24 officially commissioned into Soviet Air Force service.

■ February 1975. Requirements for Su-24M modification issued, including new smart weapons, more precise nav/attack system, powerful self-protection system, and increased range.

- 24 June 1977. Maiden flight of the first Su-24M prototype.
- Summer 1979. First production Su-24M left the factory.
- November 1979. Trials with Su-24M completed.
- December 1979. First flight of the Su-24MP electronic warfare version.
- March 1980 to May 1981. Supplementary tests of the weapon system.
- May 1980. First flight of the first prototype Su-24MR reconnaissance aircraft, piloted by Anatoli Ivanov.
- June 1983. Su-24M officially commissioned.
- 1987. First Su-24MK export aircraft manufactured.
- August 1988. First public showing of the Su-24, at Zhukovsky outside Moscow.

Details

Sales/Users: Some 1,200 Su-24s were all manufactured at Novosibirsk during 1972-92 before production changed to the Su-27IB. In 1990 the Soviet Air Force in Europe had 760 Su-24s, with 99 more in Naval Aviation. A further 120-150 Su-24s were based in the Asian sector of the USSR, bringing the total number then in service to about 1,000, including more than 130 Su-24MR *Fencer-E* reconnaissance and some 12 Su-24MP *Fencer-F* electronic warfare versions. Since then there has been some change in the total number of Su-24s in service, and their basing and operating forces have altered considerably. Many Su-24s were taken over by Belarus (currently operating about 42) and Ukraine (251 in 1996 but currently thought to total just over 200 operational aircraft, including 7 Su-24MPs with the 118th Electronic Warfare Air Regiment), while Kazakhstan is believed to have acquired 37. Russia itself withdrew aircraft from all its foreign bases (except 11 Su-24MRs taken over by Azerbaijan at the Dallyar Air Base in June 1992 – which reportedly are not airworthy). All other flyable former Soviet Su-24s are based in Russia (445 with the Air Force according to official US sources, 413 quoted by official Russian souces and well over 500 according to other calculations, including 80 *Fencer-Es* plus the *Fencer-Fs*; and some 95 with Naval Aviation, mainly for attack but including 20-25 *Fencer-E/Fs*). The Su-24MK export version was acquired by Algeria (10), Iran (number uncertain but including 12 received plus many ex-Iraqi aircraft), Iraq (received 24 aircraft; all active aircraft are now thought to be in Iran), Libya (at least 6, from 15 ordered), and Syria (reportedly 42 but possibly half that number).

Crew: Pilot and navigator/weapons system officer, side-by-side (pilot to port). SPU-9 intercom.

Cockpit: 2 separate rearward-hinged canopies. Dual controls.

Crew escape: Zvezda K-36DM zero-zero ejection seats (K-36D on the first series of *Fencer-As*).

Fixed guns: 6-barrel 23-mm GSh-6-23 or GSh-6-23M (AO-19) cannon in a fairing under the starboard side of the under-fuselage. Similar fairing on the port side contains an AKS-5 camera-gun.

Ammunition: 500 rounds.

Number of weapon pylons: 8 of 4 distinct types with 7 interfaces, as 4 under the fuselage, 2 under the wing gloves, and 2 pivoting pylons under the outer wing panels (see photograph and also Su-24MR under Aircraft variants). Some reports suggest 9 pylons, with 5 under the fuselage (3 in tandem on centreline).

Expendable weapons and equipment: Up to 17,637 lb (8,000 kg) for *Fencer-D*; 15,432 lb (7,000 kg) for *Fencer-A/B/C*. Principal weapons in a nuclear role are tactical nuclear bombs (including the TN-1000 and TN-1200). Conventional options for *Fencer-D* include a wide range of smart weapons such as anti-radiation Kh-58U (AS-11 *Kilter*), Kh-25MP (AS-12 *Kegler*) and Kh-31P (AS-17 *Krypton*) ASMs; laser-guided Kh-25ML (AS-10 *Karen*) and Kh-29L (AS-14 *Kedge*) missiles plus KAB-500L and KAB-1500L bombs; and TV-guided Kh-29T (AS-14 *Kedge*), Kh-59 (AS-13 *Kingbolt*) and Kh-59M (AS-18 *Kazoo*) missiles plus KAB-500Kr and KAB-1500TK bombs. *Fencer-A/B/C* are armed with older weapons such as Kh-28 (AS-9 *Kyle*) anti-radiation missiles, but no laser or TV weapons. Unguided weapons for *Fencer* include bombs of up to 1,500 kg, RBK-250 and RBK-500 cluster bombs, KMGU-2 submunitions dispensers, incendiary tanks, 80-mm to 420-mm rockets, and UPK-23 or SPPU-6 (with flexible GSh-6-23) gun packs. 2 R-60 (AA-8 *Aphid*) AAMs can be carried for self protection, or older R-55s on *Fencer-A/B/C*. Su-24MR *Fencer-E* and Su-24MP *Fencer-F* carry no air-to-surface weapons.

Additional stores: See Aircraft variants, particularly Su-24MR and MP.

Radar: See Flight/weapon system avionics.

Flight/weapon system avionics/instrumentation (principally Su-24M *Fencer-D*): PNS-24M Tigr-NS nav/attack system includes Orion-A air-to-surface radar (81 naut mile, 93 mile, 150 km range), Relyef terrain-avoidance radar, DISS-7 Doppler navigation radar, and Kayra-24 laser-TV sight/target designator. TsVM-10-058K Orbita (tsentralnaya vychislitelnaya mashina) digital weapons system computer. Less sophisticated PNS-24 Puma nav/attack system on *Fencer-A/B/C*. R-862 and R-864G radios, SO-69 transponder, ARK-15M radio compass, RV-21 (A-035) Impuls altimeter, Klistron short-range radio navigation system, and RSDN-10 long-range navigation system. Vstrecha all-weather radio navigation system (range 162 naut miles, 186 miles, 300 km) for automatic search and lead to tanker. Further systems suspended in the pods include Fantasmagoria (L-080 or L-081) passive radar associated with anti-radiation missiles and APK-9 data-link pod associated with Kh-59M (AS-18 *Kazoo*) ASM.

Self-protection systems: *Fencer-A/B/C* have no integrated self-protection systems, but use separate devices such as SPO-10 Sirena RWR (*Fencer-C* has SPO-15 Beryoza) and suspended ECM pods. *Fencer-D* has BKO-2 (L-167) Karpaty computer-controllable self-protection system comprising SPO-15S (L-006) Beryoza radar warning receiver (RWR), Mak (L-082) infra-red launch and approach warning device (small blister on the upper fuselage aft of the cockpit), SPS-161/SPS-162 Geran (L-101/L-102) active response jammer, and APP-50A chaff/flare dispensers (4 cassettes with 3 × 50-mm cartridges each, built into the fuselage near the tailfin root).

Wing characteristics: Shoulder mounted, with small fixed gloves and variable-geometry main panels. Movable outer panels are controlled (4 wing angles – see data table) by SPK-2-3 (sistema povorota kryla) hydraulic actuators. Large aerodynamic fence in line with the weapon pylon on early series Su–24M/MR/MP.

Wing control surfaces: 3-section (4-section on early aircraft) leading-edge slats (27°) over the full span of the outer panels. Double-slotted 2-section (3-section on early aircraft) trailing-edge flaps (34°) on each outer wing panel. 2-section differential spoilers (43°) forward of the flaps for roll control at low speed and lift dumping on landing. No ailerons.

↑ Sukhoi Su-24 *Fencer B* on approach. Note the airbrakes and 4 underfuselage, 2 glove and 2 wing pylon points *(Cezary Piotrowski)*

↑ Under the fuselage of a Sukhoi Su-24M *Fencer-D*, with wide Kayra window, gun fairing (left) and multi-store bomb pylons *(Piotr Butowski)*

Details for Su-24M *Fencer-D*

PRINCIPAL DIMENSIONS:
Wing span: 34 ft (10.366 m) *fully swept*, 57 ft 10.5 ins (17.64 m) *fully spread*
Maximum length: 80 ft 6 ins (24.532 m)
Maximum height: 20 ft 4 ins (6.193 m)

WINGS:
Aerofoil section: SR14S-5.376 for gloves; SR14S–9.226/SR16M–10 movable sections
Area: 549.2 sq ft (51.024 m^2) *swept*, 593.8 sq ft (55.168 m^2) *spread*
Aspect ratio: 2.106 *swept*, 5.64 *spread*
Sweepback of fixed centre-section: 69°, at leading edge
Sweepback of movable panel: 16°, 35°, 45° and 69°, at leading edge
Incidence: 0°
Anhedral: 4.5°
Leading-edge slats area: 32.68 sq ft (3.036 m^2)
Spoilers area: 32.97 sq ft (3.063 m^2)
Trailing-edge flaps area: 109.9 sq ft (10.21 m^2)

TAIL UNIT:
Tailplane span: 27.56 ft (8.40 m)
Tailplane area: 147.6 sq ft (13.707 m^2)
Tailplane sweepback: 55°, at quarter chord
Fin sweepback: 55°, at quarter chord
Ventral fins area, total: 23.7 sq ft (2.2 m^2)

UNDERCARRIAGE:
Type: Retractable, with steerable nosewheel. Twin wheels on each unit. Mudguard on front wheels. Low-pressure tyres on main undercarriage
Main wheel tyres size: KT-172 of 950 × 300 mm
Nose wheel tyres size: KN-21 of 660 × 200 mm
Wheel base: 27.92 ft (8.510 m)
Wheel track: 10.88 ft (3.317 m)

WEIGHTS:
Empty, operating: 49,207 lb (22,320 kg)
Nominal take-off, with 6,612 lb (3,000 kg) of weapons: 79,168 lb (35,910 kg)
Maximum take-off: 87,523 lb (39,700 kg)

PERFORMANCE:
Maximum operating Mach number (M_{MO}): Mach 1.35
Maximum speed: 783 kts (901 mph) 1,450 km/h
Maximum speed at sea level, clean: 737 kts (848 mph) 1,365 km/h
Maximum speed at sea level with armament: 715 kts (823 mph) 1,325 km/h
Take-off distance: 2,789-2,953 ft (850-900 m)
Landing distance with drag-chute: 2,625-2,789 ft (800-850 m)
Landing distance without drag-chute: 4,265 ft (1,300 m)
G limit: +6.5
Ceiling: 54,135 ft (16,500 m)
Maximum range at high altitude with 2 × 3,000 litre drop tanks: 1,350 naut miles (1,553 miles) 2,500 km
Maximum range with single in-flight refuelling: 2,306 naut miles (2,653 miles) 4,270 km
Radius of action, at 650 ft (200 m) altitude, no drop tanks: 221 naut miles (255 miles) 410 km
Radius of action, at 650 ft (200 m), with drop tanks: 302 naut miles (348 miles) 560 km

↑ Sukhoi Su-24M about to take fuel from an Il-78M tanker *(Piotr Butowski)*

Tail control surfaces: All-moving horizontal stabilizer deflected +11°/-25° evenly or differentially; conventional fin with rudder (24° deflection). 2 ventral fins.
Airbrakes: Front covers of main undercarriage bays, hinged 62°; 18.1 sq ft (1.68 m^2) total area.
Flight control system: Mechanical, hydraulically actuated. SAU-6M1 automatic control system (SAU-6 in early aircraft) with terrain avoidance capability using Relyef radar.
Fuselage: Semi-monocoque, of rectangular section. Fuselages of Su-24M/MR/MP *Fencer-D/E/F* are lengthened over earlier versions, by the addition of a 29.5 ins (750 mm) fuselage plug added in front of the cockpit, containing new avionics and the flight refuelling set.
Construction materials: All metal, mainly aluminium alloys.
Engines: 2 Saturn AL-21F-3 or AL-21F-3A (izdelye 89) turbojets.
Engine rating: Each 17,196 lbf (76.49 kN) dry, 24,692 lbf (109.8 kN) with afterburning.
Air intakes: Fixed geometry (standard from the 22nd production series, and later older aircraft similarly modified, with controls removed), with splitter plates.
Flight refuelling probe: Provision for in-flight refuelling on Su–24M/MR/MP *Fencer-D/E/F* only, with the probe mounted centrally in front of the cockpit. Su-24M *Fencer-D* can also act as a buddy tanker to other aircraft through the UPAZ-1A (unifitsyrovannyi podvesnoi agregat zapravki) Sakhalin refuelling pack suspended beneath the fuselage.
Fuel system: 11,860 litres (21,715 lb, 9,850 kg) of fuel in 3 fuselage tanks (10,860 litres in early Su-24 *Fencer-A*). Up to 3 auxiliary tanks, as 2 PTB-3000 (3,000 litres each) on wing pylons and a single PTB-2000 (2,000 litres) under the fuselage, when maximum fuel is 19,860 litres. See also Aircraft variants.
Electrical system: 2 DC and AC generators, plus 2 stand-by batteries.
Hydraulic system: 3 separate systems. AMG-10 liquid, pressure 2,986 psi.
Braking system: PTK-6M twin drag-chutes in the tailfin root, 495 sq ft (46 m^2) total area. KT-69.430 mainwheel brakes, with IA-58 anti-skid devices.

Aircraft variants:
T6-1 was the first prototype with fixed delta wings, powered by 2 R-27 (later AL-21) main engines and 4 R36-35 lift engines inside the fuselage. Now in the Monino museum.
Su-24 was named *Fencer-A, B* and *C* in the West:
Fencer-A covers the first 15 production series. Rectangular rear fuselage box enclosing the engine nozzles. First 4 series powered by 2 AL-21F (izdelye 85) engines of 19,620 lbf (87.28 kN) each; later standard AL-21F3s and widened air intakes. An additional 1,000 litres of internal fuel was provided from the 8th production series. RSDN-10 long-range navigation system retrofitted.
Fencer-B covers aircraft from the 16th to 21st production series. Drag-chute container increased in size and raised, and the rear fuselage rounded. RSDN-10 long-range navigation system retrofitted.
Fencer-C covers aircraft of the 22nd to 27th series. Improved equipment with SPO-15 Beryoza RWR instead of SPO-10 Sirena, RSDN-10 long-range navigation system (later retrofitted to older aircraft), and new IFF. Manufactured up to 1983, parallel with the first Su-24Ms. Fixed air intakes (intake controls removed also from existing aircraft).
Su-24M *Fencer-D* has a modified nav/attack system, new weapons, provision for flight refuelling, and lengthened forward fuselage (by 29.5 ins, 750 mm). Su-24M's combat potential exceeds that of Su-24 by 40%. See general description.
Su-24MK *Fencer-D* is the export version of Su-24M, K standing for kommercheskiy or commercial. As for Su-24M but with minor differences in radio and IFF equipment. Manufactured from 1988.
Su-24MR *Fencer-E* is the reconnaissance version, designed for all-weather, day and night, multi-system reconnaissance operations. Radar, infra-red, TV, laser, radio, radiation and photo-reconnaissance equipment integrated into the united BKR-1 system. Relyef terrain-avoidance radar remains, whereas the Orion nav/attack radar was replaced with Shtyk side-looking radar. A-100 camera under the port air intake. Kayra-24 removed to make room for the AP-402P panoramic camera. Aist-M TV-camera and Zima infra-red scanner installed under the fuselage. Further equipment carried in suspended pods includes Shpil-2M laser or Tangazh electronic intelligence (elint) under the centre fuselage, and the Efir-1M radiation reconnaissance system under the starboard outer wing panel. 2 R-60 self-defence AAMs under the port wing. Inner wing pylons can carry 2 PTB-3000 fuel tanks. Reconnaissance information is transmitted to the ground stations by the ShRK-1 Posrednik-1 transmitter. The photographs are developed on board the aircraft and dropped to the ground in a Kadr container. No air-to-surface attack capabilities since Orion radar and Kayra laser/TV system were removed. NK-24 navigation system.
Su-24MP *Fencer-F* covers only a small number of aircraft (probably 20, including 7 in service with the 118th Electronic Warfare Air Regiment at Chertkov in the Ukraine; others in Russia built up to the end of 1990. Landysh electronic warfare system, comprising the Los, Fasol and Mimoza subsystems built into the fuselage and suspended in pods. Su-24MP can be distinguished externally by a narrow longitudinal fairing under the nose, sword type aerials of the Fasol unit at the sides of the air intakes, and radio transparent fairing at the back of the fuselage just behind the cockpit. No attack capability, but can carry 2 R-60 AAMs for self protection.
Upgrade programme is proposed by Sukhoi, in several variants. These range from simply adding GPS, to the replacement of the entire flight and weapons control avionics with those from the Su-27IB.

Sukhoi Su-25 (and Su-28) (NATO name *Frogfoot)*

First flight: 22 February 1975, piloted by Vladimir Ilyushin.
Role: Subsonic close-air support, and target towing.
Chief designer: Yuri Ivashechkin, replaced in 1983 by Vladimir Babak.

Aims

- 8,818 lb (4,000 kg) of offensive weapons, including laser-guided missiles.
- High manoeuvrability.
- Full armour protection for the pilot.
- Extensive protection of systems, including fuel tanks filled with anti-explosive reticulated polyurethane foam and constructed to prevent large leaks, control system partially doubled with large-diameter steel pushrods, engines spaced widely apart in stainless steel compartments to prevent simultaneous damage from ground fire (capable of using any available fuel), and armour-protection for basic items of equipment.
- Maintenance system/equipment housed in 4 containers fitted to the pylons for 5-day autonomous operation away from base.

Development

- March 1968. Start of work on the T-8 (or SPB) design for a subsonic attack aircraft (without an order for the Air Force). 2 × 3,858 lbf (17.16 kN) AI-25T turbojets, and 18,078 lb (8,200 kg) take-off weight.
- March 1969. Official competition for a close air support aircraft announced by the Soviet Air Force.
- Autumn 1969. Sukhoi T-8 project selected for further development.
- 22 February 1975. First flight of the T8-1 prototype. 2 × 5,512 lbf (24.52 kN) RD-9 turbojets, 26,896 lb (12,200 kg) take-off weight, and 540 kts (621 mph) 1,000 km/h target speed.
- December 1975. T8-2 second prototype began flight tests.
- March 1976. 9,039 lbf (40.21 kN) R-95Sh engines installed in the T8-2, renamed T8-2D.
- 26 April 1978. Aircraft submitted for state acceptance trials.
- 18 June 1979. T8-3 built, the first Su-25 from the Tbilisi aircraft factory.
- 16 April-5 June 1980. T8-1D and T8-3 tested in Afghanistan, based at the Shindand Air Base.
- 30 December 1980. State acceptance trials completed.
- 4 February 1981. First operational unit became the 200th Independent Attack Air Flight, with 12 aircraft formed at the Sital-chai airfield in Azerbaijan.
- 18 June 1981. Su-25s of the 200th Independent Attack Air Flight flew to Shindand in Afghanistan for combat operations.
- 1984. First series of modified aircraft with hydraulic actuators. Maximum speed increased from 459 kts (528 mph) 850 km/h to 540 kts (621 mph) 1,000 km/h.
- 17 August 1984. First flight of the Su-25T tank-buster version (see separate entry).
- 6 August 1985. First flight of the Su-25UB combat trainer.
- 1987. Su-25UB production started.
- 1987. Su-25BM replaced the Su-25 in production at Tbilisi.
- August 1987. First flight of the Su-28/Su-25UT.
- June 1989. Su-25 and Su-25UT (Su-28) displayed abroad for the first time (Paris Air Show).
- 1 November 1989. Su-25UTG landed for the first time on board the aircraft carrier *Tbilisi* (now *Admiral Kuznetsov*).
- 1992. Main production ended.
- 1997/98. Limited production underway for Georgia and a new reconnaissance variant of Su-25UTG (see Sales/Users and Aircraft variants). Also development restarted of the Su-25U3, plus upgrade programme.

Details

Sales/Users: Single-seat combat versions were manufactured at the Tbilisi aircraft plant between 1979 and 1992, while 2-seaters came from the Ulan-Ude factory between 1987 and 1992. More than 700 Su-25s were built. Several dozen early production aircraft manufactured up to 1984 with fully manual flight control systems have recently been withdrawn from service. Russia has between 229 and 250 Su-25s (including 50 with Naval Aviation – the former number quoted from US sources), of which 20 are expected to be upgraded into Su-25TMs (see Su-25T/

↑ Slovakian Sukhoi Su-25UBK *(Piotr Butowski)*

Su-39), Belarus 73 of the 99 it took over, Ukraine about 30, 5 or more operate with Georgia, and Azerbaijan and Kazakhstan have several. About 210 aircraft were exported and serve with Angola (12 Su-25K and 2 Su-25UBK, delivered in 1988-89), Bulgaria (bought a regiment in 1985, comprising 36 Su-25Ks and 4 Su-25UBKs), Czech Republic (24), Iraq, North Korea (18) and Slovakia (14). Of those with the Czech Republic and Slovakia, the former Czechoslovakia received its first Su-25K on 2 April 1984, later also receiving Su-25UBK trainers. Iraq had about 45 Su-25s, which were used during the Iraq-Iran war. On 25 January 1991, 7 Iraqi Su-25Ks flew to Iran; 2 others were lost on 6 February 1991. Afghanistan received aircraft between 1986-90 and it is believed 12 remain operational. Some sources suggest Peru operates about 14 and that Croatia may have a small number. Limited production continues at Tbilisi, for the Georgian Air Force, including Su-25U trainers but also for the new reconnaissance version of Su-25UTG (see Aircraft variants). About 30 Su-25s are stored at Tbilisi in various stages of completion. Reported order for 50 Su-25s for the Georgian Air Force is doubtful and probably applies to an order for 5 Su-25Us. Sukhoi is working on an upgrade programme for the Russian Air Force (see Aircraft variants). Tbilisi plant offers a mid-life upgrade for Su-25s using Israeli avionics and weapon systems. In 1998 negotiations were underway for 12 Su-25UTGs for the Russian Navy.

Crew: Pilot; or instructor (rear) and pupil (front) in the trainer versions. Projected 3-seat tandem trainer was Su-25U3.

Cockpit: Self-contained compartment of welded titanium plates (10 to 24-mm thick). Starboard-opening canopy, and port ladder.

Crew escape: Zvezda K-36L (light) zero-zero ejection seat.

Fixed guns: Double-barrel 30-mm GSh-2-30 (AO-17A) cannon built into the port front fuselage, under the pilot's cockpit.

Ammunition: 250 rounds.

Number of weapon pylons: 8 under the wings, each able to carry a 1,102 lb (500 kg) load, plus 2 small outboard pylons for R-60 (AA-8 *Aphid*) AAMs only.

Expendable weapons and equipment: Normal weapon load is 2,954 lb (1,340 kg), comprising 4 × 250 kg bombs plus 2 × R-60 AAMs. Maximum load is 9,568 lb (4,340 kg). The most advanced weapons are laser-guided Kh-25ML (AS-10 *Karen*) and Kh-29L (AS-14 *Kedge*) ASMs. Unguided weapons include 57-mm to 370-mm rockets, standard Russian free-fall bombs up to 500 kg weight each, KMGU submunitions dispensers, incendiary tanks, and UPK-23-250 and SPPU-22-01 gun containers. R-60 (AA-8 *Aphid*) AAMs for self-protection only. The second model of the new reconnaissance version of Su-25UTG (see Aircraft variants) will be armed with a cruise missile.

Additional stores: Include 4 rocket-propelled PM-6 diving targets, or 4 M-6 parachute targets, or the TL-70 towing system carried under the wings, the latter carried under the port wing and towing a Kometa target.

Radar: Doppler navigation radar (see below).

Flight/weapon system avionics/instrumentation: ASP–17BC–8 gunsight, Klon-PS laser rangefinder/target designator (small window in the nose), and AKS-5 photographic camera. Navigation system derived from the KN-23 system of the MiG-27/Su-17M3; RSBN-6S short-range navigation and instrument landing system, A-031 (early aircraft had RV-5M) altimeter, DISS-7 Doppler navigation radar, and ARK-15M radio compass. SRO-2 Khrom IFF transponder. R-862 radio.

Self-protection systems: SPO 15L Beryoza (early aircraft SPO 10 Sirena) radar warning receiver. 8 (early aircraft 4) ASO-2V chaff/flare dispensers (32 × 26-mm rounds each) mounted on the rear upper fuselage at the tailfin sides and above the rear engine ducts. Provision for a container with SPS-141MVG Gvozdika response electronic jammer.

Wing characteristics: Straight, shoulder mounted, with dogtooth leading edge. Tip pods (see Airbrakes).

Wing control surfaces: Each wing has 5-section leading-edge slats across the full span (12° for landing, 6° for manoeuvring), 2-section double-slotted trailing-edge flaps (40° inner and 35° outer sections for landing, 10° all sections for manoeuvring), and ailerons (+20°, -20°).

Tail control surfaces: Variable incidence tailplane (1° 40', -3° 17' or -7° 56'), with elevators (+23°, -14°) and tabs (15°). 2-section rudder (25° deflection) with tab, upper section operated as an automatic yaw dumper.

Airbrakes: Crocodile-type, forming split wingtip pods (110°), with area of 13 sq ft (1.2 m²).

Flight control system: Manually operated elevators and rudder, and ailerons with BU-45 hydraulic actuators (early series aircraft, up to 1984, fully manually operated).

Construction materials: Aluminium alloys and steel.

Fuselage: Semi-monocoque, with flat sides.

Engines: 2 Soyuz/Moscow R-95Sh turbojets (the non-afterburning version of the MiG-21's R-13-300 engine) in long nacelles at the fuselage sides, each 9,039 lbf (40.21 kN). Upgraded R-195s in the Su-25BM and last series Su-25, offering 9,921 lbf (44.13 kN) and significantly reduced exhaust gas temperature; cool air from a tailpipe is mixed with the hot engine efflux to further reduce the possibility of infra-red detection.

Engine rating: See Engines.

Air intakes: Fuselage sides, under the wings.

Flight refuelling probe: None.

Fuel system: 6,614 lb (3,000 kg), or 6,008 lb (2,725 kg) for the Su-25UB, in 2 centre-fuselage and 1 wing centre-section tanks. Provision for 4 × 820 litre PTB-800 drop tanks beneath the wings.

Electrical system: 2 engine-driven AC generators, 2 × 28 volt DC generators and 2 batteries.

Details for Su-25 *(plus Su-25UB where indicated)*

PRINCIPAL DIMENSIONS:

Wing span: 47 ft 1 ins (14.36 m)
Maximum length: 50 ft 11.5 ins (15.53 m), 50 ft 5 ins (15.36 m) for Su-25UB
Fuselage length: 47 ft 10.5 ins (14.59 m)
Maximum height: 15 ft 9 ins (4.80 m), 17 ft 1 ins (5.2 m) for Su-25UB

WINGS:

Area: 324 sq ft (30.10 m²)
Aspect ratio: 6.85
Taper ratio: 3.38
Sweepback at leading edge: 19° 54'
Sweepback at trailing edge: 0°
Chord at root: 11 ft 4 ins (3.457 m)
Chord at tip: 3 ft 4.5 ins (1.023 m)
Anhedral: 2° 30'
Twist: 0° root
Leading-edge slats area, total: 34 sq ft (3.16 m²)
Ailerons area, total: 16.28 sq ft (1.512 m²)
Trailing-edge flaps area, total: 47.82 sq ft (4.443 m²)

TAIL UNIT:

Tailplane span: 15 ft 3 ins (4.652 m)
Tailplane area: 69.7 sq ft (6.473 m²)
Tailplane dihedral: 5°
Tailplane sweepback: 23° 17'
Elevators area: 20.26 sq ft (1.882 m²)
Fin height: 8 ft 6 ins (2.58 m)
Fin area: 50.05 sq ft (4.65 m²)
Rudder area: 8.11 sq ft + 2.22 sq ft upper section (0.7534 m² + 0.206 m²)
Fin sweepback: 35° 47'

UNDERCARRIAGE:

Type: Retractable, with steerable nosewheel (with mudguard)
Main wheel tyre size: 840 × 360 mm
Nose wheel tyre size: 660 × 200 mm
Wheel base: 11 ft 9 ins (3.574 m)
Wheel track: 8 ft 2 ins (2.506 m)

WEIGHTS:

Normal take-off: 32,023 lb (14,530 kg), or 31,416 lb (14,250 kg) for early aircraft
Maximum take-off: 38,647 lb (17,530 kg), or 38,250 lb (17,350 kg) for early aircraft
Normal landing: 23,810 lb (10,800 kg)

PERFORMANCE:

Maximum allowable Mach number: Mach 0.82, or 0.71 for early aircraft
Maximum operating speed, with 4 × 250 kg bombs plus 2 × R-60 AAMs: 513 kts (590 mph) 950 km/h, or 459 kts (528 mph) 850 km/h for early aircraft
Take-off speed: 130-135 kts (149-155 mph) 240-250 km/h
Landing speed: 121-124 kts (140-143 mph) 225-230 km/h
Take-off distance, normal weight: 1,969 ft (600 m)
Take-off distance, maximum weight: 2,953 ft (900 m)
Landing distance: 1,969 ft (600 m)
G limit with normal weapons load and 80% internal fuel: +6.5
Ceiling: 22,950 ft (7,000 m)
Range with maximum internal fuel, at low altitude: 275 naut miles (317 miles) 510 km, or 270 naut miles (311 miles) 500 km for early aircraft
Maximum range, with drop tanks: 999 naut miles (1,450 miles) 1,850 km, or 1,053 naut miles (1,212 miles) 1,950 km for early aircraft

↑ Sukhoi Su-25UTG shipboard trainer assigned to *Admiral Kuznetsov* *(Piotr Butowski)*

↑ Sukhoi Su-25 with rocket launchers and drop tanks *(Piotr Butowski)*

Hydraulic system: 2 independent engine-driven systems to operate the undercarriage, slats and flaps, ailerons, tailplane incidence, airbrakes, main wheel brakes and nosewheel steering.
Braking system: Main wheel brakes plus a twin drag-chute.

Aircraft variants:
T8-1 and ***T8-2*** prototypes used RD-9 turbojets.
Su-25 *Frogfoot-A* became the standard single-seater, powered by R-95Sh turbojets. Longer wings than the prototypes (wing aspect ratio raised from 5 to 6.85), and weapon system modernized.
Su-25K (kommercheski) became the export version of Su-25.
Su-25BM (buksir mishenei) *Frogfoot-A* is the modernized single-seat attack version, but also specialized for target towing. R-95Sh engines replaced by R-195s with lower IR-signature and higher thrust. 50 built.
Su-25BMK is the export version of Su-25BM.
Su-25U is a trainer developed from the Su-25T by the Tbilisi factory. 5 ordered by Georgia. R-195 engines.
Su-25UB (uchebno-boevoi) *Frogfoot-B* is the tandem 2-seat combat trainer, with weapon systems retained. Larger tailfin.
Su-25UBK is the export version of Su-25UB.
Su-25UT (uchebno-trenirovochnyi, Su-28) is a 2-seat jet aerobatic aircraft based on the Su-25UB, with weapon system and some equipment removed. Only 1 built.
Su-25UTG (G for gak) is a shipborne trainer. Weapon system removed, and instrument landing system and arrester hook added. Series of 10 built at the Ulan-Ude plant during 1989-90. 5 at the Saki (Ukraine) training centre, 4 on board *Admiral Kuznetsov*, and 1 lost in an accident. Su-25UTG is now mentioned by Admiral Deineka as the subject of essential upgrade.
Reconnaissance version of Su-25UTG will have millimetre-wave radar, improved navigation system and TKS secure data link. Prototype (aircraft numbered 11) is now under construction. Following aircraft (number 12) will be used for reconnaissance and target acquisition, and later also armed with a cruise missile.
Su-25U3 was a projected tandem 3-seat trainer of 1991. Work resumed in 1997 after a break of several years. Take-off weight 22,045 lb (10,000 kg). Derated R-195 turbojets of 7,715 lbf (34.32 kN) each.
Sukhoi upgrade programme for the Su-25 is expected to introduce an on-board computer for navigation, new air data system, and new TV-guided weapons (Kh-29T missile and KAB-500Kr bomb).
Su-39 (Su-25T and Su-25TM) is a specialized tank-buster version. See separate entry.

Sukhoi Su-27 (NATO name *Flanker*)

First flight: 20 May 1977, piloted by Vladimir Ilyushin.
Role: Long-range air-superiority fighter.
Programme manager: Naum Chernyakov (up to 1975), Mikhail Simonov (January 1976-December 1979), Artyom Kolchin (December 1979-October 1981), and Alexei Knyshev (since October 1981).

Aims

- To counter the US F-15 and other advanced aircraft.
- To destroy enemy strike aircraft at altitudes from 30 m to 17-18 km
- Attain 1,350-1450 km/h at sea level and 2,300-2,500 km range at height.
- Thrust to weight ratio of 1.2:1.
- To operate from third class airfields with runway lengths of 1,200 m.

Development

- 1969. PFI (perspektivnyi frontovoi istrebitel) advanced tactical fighter programme started to produce a fighter in the class of the US F-15 Eagle.
- 1971. Sukhoi T-10 project selected.
- 20 May 1977. First flight of the T10-1 prototype.
- 7 July 1978. T10-2 second prototype crashed, with the loss of the pilot.
- March 1979. First information published in the West, with the fighter provisionally named Ram-K.
- 23 August 1979. First flight of the AL-31F turbofan-powered prototype, T10-3.
- 1980-82. Series of 5 Su-27s (T-10) built at Komsomolsk-on-Amur.
- 20 April 1981. First flight of the totally redesigned T10S-1 (T10-7) production prototype, piloted by Vladimir Ilyushin.
- 3 September 1981. T10S-1 was lost, but the pilot survived.
- 23 December 1981. T10S-2 second prototype crashed, with the loss of the pilot.
- 1982. Production of the Su-27 (T-10S) began at Komsomolsk-on-Amur.
- December 1984. Initial operational capability of the first Su-27 unit.
- 7 March 1985. First flight of the Su-27UB combat trainer, piloted by Nikolai Sadovnikov.
- 7 January 1987. A Norwegian F-16 made the first contact with an Su-27, over the Barents Sea.
- 13 September 1987. Collision between a Soviet Su-27 and Norwegian P-3B Orion.
- May 1989. Su-27 was displayed abroad for the first time, showing the "Pugachev's cobra" manoeuvre, at the Paris Air Show.
- Spring 1990. First Su-27 military unit sent abroad, 159th Fighter Air Regiment of the Soviet Air Force based at Kluczewo, Poland.
- 19 March 1993. First known combat loss, when a Russian Su-27 was struck by a surface-to-air missile near Sukhumi.

Details

Sales/Users: Production of Su-27 *Flanker-B* started in 1982 at the Komsomolsk-on-Amur plant. Su-27UB *Flanker-C* combat trainer entered production in 1986 at the Irkutsk production plant (about 85 built, including 13 delivered to China and Vietnam). Currently, the Russian Air Force has 330 Su-27s in Europe plus over 100 in Asia, principally as interceptors for home defence units but with over 100 operating as fighters with tactical units. Russian Naval Aviation has 30. Ukraine has 67, Belarus 23, and at least 10 of 32 Su-27s destined for Kazakhstan as debt repayments had been received by 1998. Armenia, Azerbaijan and Georgia are also believed to be future Su-27 operators, and Syria is known to have expressed interest in 14. Greece has been among others to consider the Su-27 as a possible future fighter purchase. However, other than the USA, which received 2 Su-27s from 1995, at the time of writing the only Su-27s outside of the former Soviet Union have been bought by China and Vietnam. China purchased an initial batch of 26 (as 20 Su-27SK single-seaters and 6 Su-27UBK 2-seaters, not 22 and 4 respectively as originally believed) in 1991 for about US$1 billion. These aircraft were reported to have been delivered in June 1992 and operate from Wuhu AFB. In July 1996 the first 11 of a second batch of 24 aircraft (18 single-seaters and 6 2-seaters) were delivered to Suixiu AFB in Southern China. Both Suixiu and Wuhu bases belong to the 3rd Division of the People's Air Force. In August 1995 Chinese Su-27s approached the Senkaku Islands north of Taiwan, which are claimed by China, Japan and Taiwan. In March 1996, Su-27s flew in major Chinese military exercises. On 6 December 1996, Moscow and Beijing reached an agreement for China to begin licensed production at Shenyang of 150-200 Su-27s as J-11s and JJ-11s (trainer); China cannot export any under this agreement. The first licence-built **Su-27CK** to fly in late 1998, assembled from parts supplied from Komsomolsk-on-Amur. The contract does not provide for manufacture of the AL-31F engines, radar or other avionics in China. Also, the purchase of a new batch of 55 Su-27s is now under consideration by China. In March-May 1995, Vietnam received a batch of 6 Su-27s (including 3 trainers), followed in 1997-early 1998 by another 6 (including 4 trainers) under a US$180 million contract signed in January 1997. The next purchase of some Su-27s by Vietnam is expected before the year 2000.
Crew: Pilot, or 2 in the Su-27UB trainer. Crew has the NAZ-8 portable life pack containing Komar-2M radio, PSN-1 dinghy, medicine, food, signal flares, etc.
Cockpit: Conventional, with analog indicators and switches.
Crew escape: K-36DM series 2 zero-zero ejection seat.
Fixed guns: Single-barrel 30-mm GSh-301 cannon in the starboard LERX.
Ammunition: 150 rounds.
Number of weapon pylons: 10 (or 12 for Su-27SMK upgrade), comprising 2 under the fuselage in tandem between the engine nacelles, 2 under the air ducts, 4 (or 6) under the wings, and 2 at the wingtips.
Expendable weapons and equipment: Maximum allowable load is 17,636 lb (8,000 kg), but the maximum load in normal operations is 8,818 lb (4,000 kg). Typical armament for air-combat missions comprises 10 AAMs, including up to 4 extended-range R-27ER/ETs (AA-10 *Alamo-C/D*) and up to 6 medium-range R-27R/Ts (AA-10 *Alamo-A/B*). Outer underwing pylons and wingtip pylons normally carry R-73 close-air combat AAMs. Only unguided air-to-ground weapons can be used, including bombs and rockets. See upgrade under Aircraft variants.
Radar: RLPK-27 (radiolokatsyonnyi pritselnyi kompleks) radar attack system includes NIIP S-27 Myech (N-001) coherent pulse Doppler look-down/shoot-down radar (designed by Tamerlan Bekirbayev) and a Ts-100 digital computer. Search range about 54 naut miles (62 miles) 100 km for a fighter-sized target in a head-on position. Radar can track up to 10 targets simultaneously and engage 1. New Zhuk-27 radar will be fitted to next production aircraft, including the third batch of Su-27s for China. According to Anatoliy Kanashchenkov, Phazotron's General Designer, a Zhuk-27 radar was installed in an Su-27 at the Komsomolsk plant in 1997 and the first flight was then expected in September 1997. Zhuk-27 is the first Russian multifunction radar which can not only track air targets but can also be used for surface mapping including image freezing and zooming as well as terrain following and avoidance. It has a range similar to N-001 but is able to track-while-scan 10 targets and engage 4. See upgrade under Aircraft variants.
Flight/weapon system avionics/instrumentation: RLPK-27 radar system is supported by OEPS-27 (optiko-elektronnaya pritselnaya sistema) which comprises an OLS-27 (optikolokatsyonnaya stantsya, or 36Sh) infra-red search/track device coupled with a laser rangefinder (tracking range 27 naut miles, 31 miles, 50 km in the rearward hemisphere and 8.1 naut miles, 9.3 miles, 15 km in the forward hemisphere), Shchel-3U helmet-mounted target designator and Ts-100 computer. Head-up-display showing integrated information from the various sensors. R-800 and R-864 com radios, Parol IFF, TKS-2 secure data link for group operations, and Spektr data link for target indication from land-based radars. Navigation equipment includes 2 altimeters, ARK-22 radio compass, marker beacon receiver, A-317 short range radio navigation, and SO-69 transponder.
Self-protection systems: SPO-15 Beryoza (L-006) radar warning receiver with sensors on the sides of the air intakes and on the tailboom. Pallad electronic countermeasures (ECM) system (only rearward hemisphere is jammed when radar is active). Provision

↑ Sukhoi Su-27 *Flanker-B* (left) and 2-seat Su-27UB *Flanker-C* have similar weapon systems with N-001 radar *(Piotr Butowski)*

↑ Sukhoi Su-27 *Flanker-B*

for suspended ECM jamming pods, including 2 Sorbtsya-S (L-005) on the wingtips. APP-50 (L-O29) chaff/flare system built into the tailboom. 8 dispensers, each with 3 × 50-mm cartridges in early aircraft; from the 18th production series, 32 dispensers in expanded tailboom sides.

Wing characteristics: Swept, mid-mounted, with 3-spar structure. Low wing loading. Sharp-edged wingroot extensions.

Wing control surfaces: Flaperon (+35°, -20°) occupies about 60% of each wing trailing edge from root. Full-span leading-edge slats (30°).

Tail control surfaces: Mounted on booms alongside the engine nacelles. Twin uncanted fins and rudders (25° deflection). Slab (taileron) tailplane, deflecting symmetrically (+15°, -20°) or differentially (+10°, -10°). Twin ventral fins.

Airbrakes: Single door-type airbrake on the fuselage dorsal spine, hydraulically actuated 54°. Area 28 sq ft (2.6 m^2).

Flight control system: Designed to be inherently unstable. SDU-10-27 (sistema distantsyonnovo upravlenya) quadruple redundant analog fly-by-wire, with no mechanical backup. RPD-1 electro-hydraulic power units. Flaperons and slats are controlled manually for take-off and landing, with computer-assisted control (fly-by-wire) in flight. Tailplane computer controlled, except when operated differentially. Rudder has manual control. Automatic control system includes OPR (ogranichitel predelnykh rezhimov) angle of attack/g-load limiter, which can be overruled manually.

Fuselage: Airframe designed from similar national research that aided the MiG-29. Wide fuselage/wing centre section provides considerable lifting force. Fuselage is of semi-monocoque construction, technologically divided into 3 sections. Nose section contains the radar, cockpit, front undercarriage unit and equipment boxes; sloping centre section houses 2 fuel tanks, airbrake, equipment boxes and main undercarriage compartment; the rear section houses widely spaced engine nacelles and a central rearward-protruding boom containing a

Details for Su-27 *Flanker-B*, with Su-27SK where stated and Su-27UB *Flanker-C* following

PRINCIPAL DIMENSIONS:
Wing span: 48 ft 3 ins (14.7 m)
Wing span with wingtip R-73s: 49 ft 0.5 ins (14.948 m)
Length without probe: 72 ft (21.935 m)
Maximum height: 19 ft 6 ins (5.932 m)

WINGS:
Area: 667.8 sq ft (62.037 m^2)
Aspect ratio: 3.48
Sweepback at leading edge: 42°
Sweepback at trailing edge: 15°
Incidence: 0°
Dihedral/anhedral: 0°
Leading edge slats area, gross: 49.51 sq ft (4.6 m^2)
Trailing-edge flaperons area, gross: 52.74 sq ft (4.9 m^2)

TAIL UNIT:
Tailplane span: 32 ft 5 ins (9.88 m)
Tailplane area: 131.75 sq ft (12.24 m^2)
Distance between fins: 14 ft 1 ins (4.3 m)
Fins area, gross: 165.76 sq ft (15.4 m^2)
Fins cant angle: 0°
Rudders area, gross: 37.57 sq ft (3.49 m^2)
Ventral fins area, gross: 26.91 sq ft (2.5 m^2)

UNDERCARRIAGE:
Type: Retractable, with steerable nosewheel with mudguard
Main wheel tyre size: 1,030 × 350 mm (also quoted as 1,300 × 350 mm)
Nose wheel tyre size: 680 × 260 mm
Wheel base: 19 ft 4 ins (5.88 m)
Wheel track: 14 ft 2.5 ins (4.33 m)

WEIGHTS:
Empty, operating: 36,112 lb (16,380 kg)
Normal take-off: 51,015 lb (23,140 kg)
Maximum take-off: 62,391 lb (28,300 kg)
Maximum allowable take-off for last production series: 72,752 lb (33,000 kg)

PERFORMANCE:
Maximum operating speed: 1,241 kts (1,429 mph) 2,300 km/h (Mach 2.17), or 1,350 kts (1,553 mph) 2,500 km/h (Mach 2.35) for Su-27SK
Maximum speed at sea level: 756 kts (870 mph) 1,400 km/h, same for Su-27SK
Landing speed: 121 kts (140 mph) 225 km/h
Take-off distance: 2,133-2,297 ft (650-700 m)
Landing distance: 2,034-2,297 ft (620-700 m)
Climb rate: 64,960 ft (19,800 m) per minute at sea level for Su-27SK
Minimum radius of turn: 1,477 ft (450 m) for Su-27SK
Roll rate: about 270° per second
G limit: +9
Ceiling: 60,700 ft (18,500 m)
Maximum range, clean: 2,008 naut miles (2,312 miles) 3,720 km, or 1,985 naut miles (2,286 miles) 3,680 km for Su-27SK
Maximum range with 10 AAMs: 1,512 naut miles (1,740 miles) 2,800 km
Radius of action at high altitude: 589 naut miles (677 miles) 1,090 km, or 842 naut miles (969 miles) 1,560 km for Su-27SK
Radius of action at low altitude: 227 naut miles (261 miles) 420 km

PRINCIPAL DIMENSION for Su-27UB *Flanker-C*:
Maximum height: 20 ft 10 ins (6.357 m)

WEIGHTS for Su-27UB *Flanker-C*:
Empty, operating: 39,462 lb (17,900 kg)
Normal take-off: 53,220 lb (24,140 kg)
Maximum take-off: 67,130 lb (30,450 kg)
Maximum allowable take-off for last production series: 73,854 lb (33,500 kg)

PERFORMANCE for Su-27UB *Flanker-C*:
Maximum operating speed: 1,147 kts (1,320 mph) 2,125 km/h
Maximum speed at sea level: 702 kts (808 mph) 1,300 km/h
Landing speed: 124 kts (143 mph) 230 km/h
Take-off distance: 2,461-2,625 ft (750-800 m)
Landing distance: 2,133-2,297 ft (650-700 m)
G limit: +8.5
Ceiling: 57,400 ft (17,500 m)
Maximum range, clean: 1,620 naut miles (1,864 miles) 3,000 km

↑ **Sukhoi Su-27SK general arrangement** *(courtesy Sukhoi)*

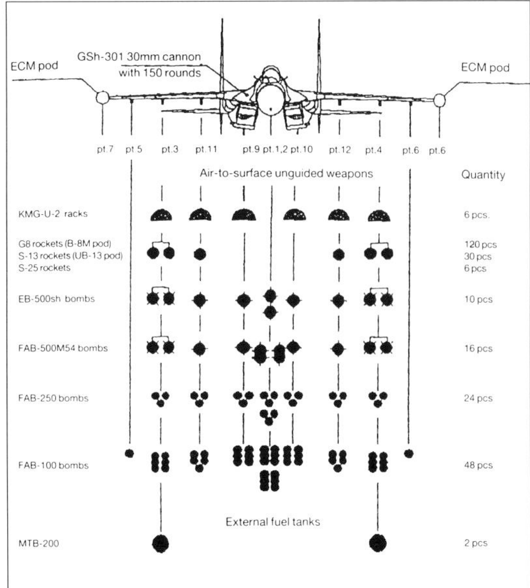

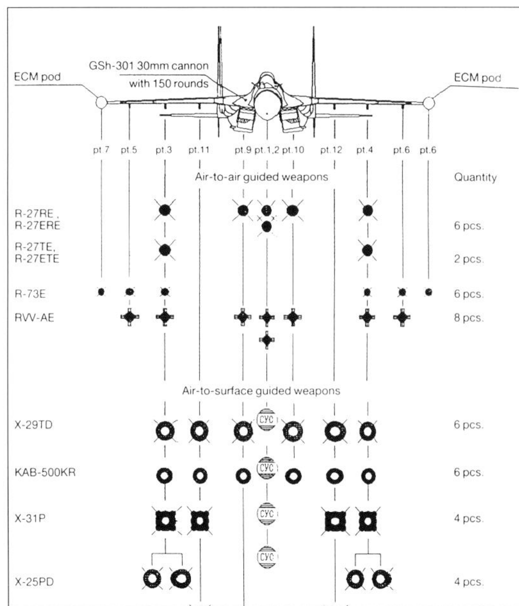

↑ **Sukhoi Su-27SMK air-to-surface unguided weapons (*left*) and air-to-air and air-to-surface guided weapons (*right*). Note that the X designations are known in the West as Kh designations** *(courtesy Sukhoi)*

fuel tank, equipment, chaff/flare dispensers and drag-chute.
Construction materials: All metal, mainly aluminium alloy. The most loaded bottom panel of the centre wing section (4,900 mm × 600 mm) is constructed of titanium.
Engines: 2 Saturn/Moscow AL-31F (izdelye 99V) turbofans.
Engine rating: Each 16,755 lbf (74.53 kN) dry, 27,558 lbf (122.59 kN) with afterburning.
Air intakes: 3 ramp adjustable type. Intakes semi-blanked during take-off and landing by a grid, when additional air is provided by sets of louvres around the intake.
Flight refuelling probe: None.
Fuel system: Up to 12,000 litres (20,723 lb, 9,400 kg) of fuel in 5 tanks: 2 in the wing centre section, 2 in the outer wings and 1 in the tailboom. Nominal fuel is 13,227 lb (6,000 kg), while the remaining 7,496 lb (3,400 kg) is called the "internal auxiliary tank". No external drop tanks are carried, except by Su-27SMK. Tanks are filled with anti-explosive reticulated polyurethane foam.
Electrical system: 27 volt DC supply. 2 AC generators, 115 volt/400 Hz. 2 × 20NKBN-25 stand-by batteries.
Hydraulic system: Dual systems, pressure 3,983 psi, used for the tailplane, rudders, flaperons, slats, airbrake, undercarriage, undercarriage doors, mainwheel brakes, air intakes and air-intake grids (see Flight control system).
Braking system: Carbon disc mainwheel brakes, with anti-skid device and electric cooling fans. Nosewheel brake. Twin drag-chutes, 538.2 sq ft (50 m^2) gross area, housed in the tailboom.

Aircraft variants:
T-10 *Flanker-A* appeared in 1977. 4 prototypes, plus first 5 pre-production aircraft built at Komsomolsk-on-Amur. Ogival wing and AL-21F3 turbojets (except T10-3 and T10-4 with AL-31Fs). First prototype now in the Monino museum. Possibly up to 15 prototype/development aircraft.
Su-27S (T-10S) *Flanker-B* became the basic tactical production model, as described.
Su-27P *Flanker-B* is the basic air defence version of the Su-27S.
Su-27UB *Flanker-C* (Type 10-4) is a 2-seat combat trainer. Prototype appeared in 1985 and the first production aircraft flew in Irkutsk on 10 September 1986. Second cockpit added by reducing fuel capacity. Full combat capability, with radar/weapons system retained.
Su-27 vectoring-thrust test-beds, see Su-35.
Su-27SK (K for kommerchesky) is the export version of Su-27, with 13,668 lb (6,200 kg) weapon load.
Su-27UBK is the export version of Su-27UB.
P-42 is the 3rd prototype (T10S-3) prepared for record flights, with radar, weapons system, antennas, paint, etc removed. During 1986-87 it set a series of 27 records for climb and altitude.
T10-20R became another special conversion (though record-breaking flights were not performed), destined for long-range supersonic flight. Reduced weight, and fuel added in the nose (in place of the radar) and tail (in the "sting" between the engines), offering 26,455 lb (12,000 kg) of fuel at 58,643 lb (26,600 kg) take-off weight. Now in the museum at Khodinka airfield in Moscow.
Su-27PD became the personal aircraft of Anatoli Kvochur, well-known test pilot. Standard Su-27, but with the weapon systems removed and flight-refuelling probe added (D for dozapravka).
Su-27SMK represents an export upgrade package, probably the ***Su-27SM*** if proposed to the Russian Air Force. 'Demonstrator' flew in 1995, simply as a standard Su-27 with 27SMK written on the nose. The main objectives of the upgrade are new avionics and weapons (including guided ASMs), and extended range. The Su-27SMK programme will be in 2 stages. During 1998 (all dates based on receiving proper financial backing) an aircraft will fly with 12 weapon pylons, flight refuelling system, more fuel in the wings (giving a total fuel load of 21,969 lb, 9,965 kg) and provision for 2 × 2,000 litre auxiliary tanks under the wings. Ferry range will increase to 2,369 naut miles (2,728 miles) 4,390 km or 2,806 naut miles (3,231 miles) 5,200 km with a single in-flight refuelling. Due to new software, the N-001 Myech radar will support new R-77 (AA-12 *Adder*) AAMs. In the second stage during 1998-99, the aircraft will receive new avionics and air-to-surface weapons. New navigation system is planned (French system for export), and new self-defence systems. The latter version of Su-27SMK will be capable of carrying Kh-31P or Kh-25MP anti-radar missiles (up to 4), Kh-59M (2) or Kh-29T (6) TV-guided missiles, and KAB-500Kr (6) TV-guided bombs. Control systems for air-to-surface weapons will be carried in pods. Maximum weapon load is 17,637 lb (8,000 kg). According to the manufacturer, Su-27SMK will offer improvements over the Su-27 to the ratio of 1.2-1.4:1 in air-to-air operations (due to R-77 AAMs) and 20-24:1 in air-to-surface operations (due to the use of guided weapons). Although the standard N-001 Myech radar will be retained, there are also plans to install Zhuk-27.
Su-30 (Su-27PU) is a 2-seat interceptor/multi-role fighter derivative. See separate entry.
Su-32FN and ***Su-34*** (or ***Su-27IB***) are 2-seat maritime strike derivatives. See separate entry.
Su-33 (Su-27K) is a shipborne fighter derivative. See separate entry.
Su-35 and ***Su-37*** (or ***Su-27M***) are advanced air-superiority fighters with ground attack capability derivatives. See separate entry.

Sukhoi Su-30 (NATO name *Flanker*)

First flight: 30 December 1989 for prototype (numbered 05) and 14 April 1992 for first production Su-30 (numbered 603), piloted by G. Bulanov and V. Maximenkov. 1 July 1997 for Su-30MKI aerodynamic testbed (numbered 56, piloted by Sergei Averyanov).
Role: 2-seat long-range multi-role interceptor (Su-30), 2-seat fighter with ground attack capability (Su-30MK), and combat trainer.
Chief designers: Alexei Knyshev (supervisor), Igor Yemelyanov (Su-30) and Viktor Galushko (air-to-surface weapon system for Su-30MK).

Aims

- Additional avionics to command a group of fighters (possibly 4 Su-27s).
- In-flight refuelling.
- Ability to carry high-accuracy air-to-ground/surface missiles (Su-30MK).

Development

- 1987. First tests with a flight refuelling system on the Su-27 (Su-27UB side number 02). The aircraft was also used as a buddy tanker with a UPAZ-1A Sakhalin refuelling pack.
- 23 June 1987. Aircraft flew from Moscow to Komsomolsk-on-Amur and back, remaining airborne for 15 hours 31 minutes, after being flight refuelled 4 times. Total distance 7,238 naut miles (8,329 miles) 13,404 km.
- May-June 1993. Su-27UB (ex side number 389, now 321) was presented as an Su-30MK at the Paris Air Show, with suspended weapons and equipment pods, but no flight refuelling probe or ground-attack weapons control system.
- March 1994. Su-30 (side number 603, c/n *1010101*) was displayed for the first time (FIDAE'94, Chile), named Su-30MK.
- 1 July 1997. Su-30MKI aerodynamic prototype with canards and AL-31FP engines with thrust vectoring first flew in 2-seater form at Zhukovsky.

Details

Sales/Users: About 30 were manufactured at Irkutsk during 1992-97, with 1 of those for Russian service going to the Russian Aerobatic team. Reports suggest a number may have joined Su-27 trainers delivered to China. On 30 November 1996, India signed a contract for 40 Su-30MKI multi-role fighters (US$1.72 billion, including weapons and spares). First 8 delivered during Spring 1997, with an introduction ceremony on 11 June at Pune Air Station, are basic Su-30 interceptors with no air-to-ground capability. Next 8 delivered 1998 are Su-30MKs capable of carrying air-to-surface weapons and with infra-red/laser sensor pods and other equipment including foreign-supplied items (Sextant VEH3000 HUD, Totem INS/GPS and liquid-crystal displays). Following 12 have canards and will be delivered to

↑ **Production Sukhoi Su-30** *(Piotr Butowski)*

India in 1999, leaving 12 for delivery in the year 2000 in final Su-30MKI form with thrust vectoring; the earlier aircraft are scheduled to be upgraded to MKIs later. First unit to operate Su-30s was No 24 Hawks Squadron, replacing MiG-21bis at Pune. A licence to allow production of about 120 MKIs at Ozhar near Nasik has been expected. Indonesia announced an order for 12 Su-30MKs on 5 August 1997, and 8 Indonesian flying instructors are to train in Russia.
Crew: 2, in tandem cockpits.
Cockpit: Full avionics/instrumentation in both cockpits. Colour liquid-crystal MFDs in Su-30MK/MKI.
Crew escape: As for Su-27/Su-27UB.
Fixed guns: As for Su-27/Su-27UB.
Number of weapon pylons: 12.
Expendable weapons and equipment: Su-30 maximum load is 17,636 lb (8,000 kg). Typical armament comprises 10 AAMs, including a mix of up to 6 extended-range R-27ER/ET (AA-10 *Alamo-C/D*) and up to 6 R-73 close-air combat AAMs, with option of R-77s (RVV-AE, AA-12 *Adder*). Su-30MK has same maximum load. Besides the standard air-to-air armament, it carries guided air-to-surface missiles and weapon guidance pods. Kh-31P (AS-17 *Krypton*) anti-radar missiles are controlled by the Pastel radar warning receiver (RWR), which detects the targets and programmes the missile before launch. TV-guided Kh-29T (AS-14 *Kedge*) missiles and KAB-500Kr bombs use guidance cameras, the picture from the missile being projected on the TV screen situated on the upper right side of the instrument panel in the cockpit. The longer-range (62 naut mile, 71.5 mile, 115 km) Kh-59M (AS-18 *Kazoo*) TV-guided missile requires an APK-9 data link pod, suspended on the rear centreline pylon. Kh-29L (AS-14 *Kedge*) laser-guided missile uses the laser channel of the OLS-27 for target designation. Unguided weapons include the usual FAB-100/250/500 bombs, B-8M and B-13L packs (20 × 80-mm and 5 × 130-mm rockets respectively), S-25 rockets (each 250-mm), etc.
Radar: Su-30 uses the same radar as Su-27/Su-27UB.
Su-30MK/MKI have a new generation radar, most probably the Phazotron Zhuk-27 with flat slotted antenna, with a range of 54 naut miles (62 miles) 100 km, track-while-scan of 15 targets and engagement 4.
Flight/weapon system avionics/instrumentation: Extended navigation equipment and tactical data link, enabling a group commander on board an Su-30 to assign targets to other fighters. Final version of the Su-30MK/MKI will have a new INS system, ILS/VOR and GPS.
Wing characteristics: As for Su-27/Su-27UB.
Tail control surfaces: As for Su-27UB.
Canard: None for Su-30 and Su-30MK in its current form. Standard Su-33/34/35 canards for final version of Su-30MK and MKI.
Flight control system: Digital fly-by-wire, similar to Su-37.
Fuselage: As for Su-27UB.
Construction materials: As for Su-27/Su-27UB.

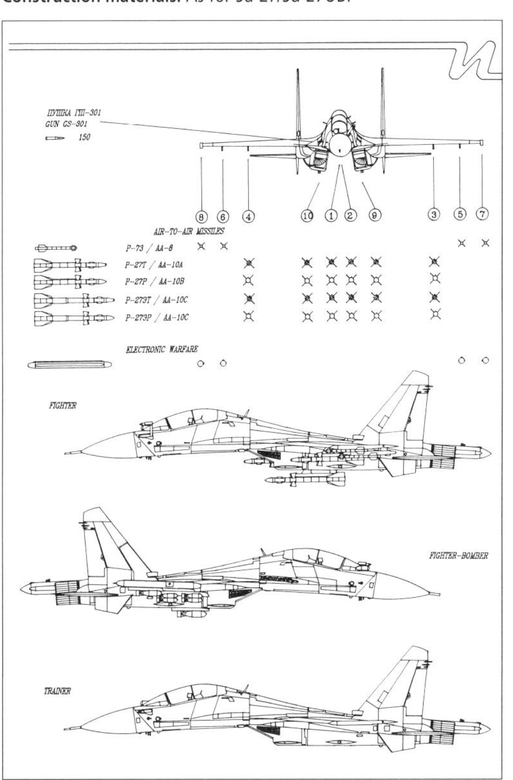

↑ **Air-to-air weapon and electronic warfare arrangement for the Su-30 (top), plus side views of the Su-30, Su-30MK and Trainer (bottom)** *(courtesy Sukhoi)*

↑ **Pilot's front cockpit (*left*) and weapon system operator's cockpit (*right*) of the Su-30. Note the CRT tactical situation display instead of HUD in the WSO cockpit** *(Piotr Butowski)*

Engines: As for Su-27/Su-27UB, except the Su-27MKI and upgraded earlier MKs which will have thrust-vectoring AL-31FP turbofans (same thrust).
Nozzles: Axi-symmetrical 3-D vectoring-thrust nozzles will be fitted to Su-30MKI, actuated hydraulically by the engine's fuel system (not the aircraft's hydraulic system).
Flight refuelling probe: See below.
Fuel system: 20,944 lb (9,500 kg). Provision for in-flight refuelling with a standard probe on the port side of the nose. On the Su-30 (and other versions of the Su-27 equipped with a refuelling probe), the IRST is moved to the right side of the windscreen (instead of centre).

Aircraft variants:
Su-30 (***Su-27PU***, T-10PU or 10-4PU) is a 2-seat long-range interceptor. Normal TOW 52,911 lb (24,000 kg); MTOW 73,855 lb (33,500 kg).
Su-30K is an export version of Su-30.
Su-30MK (T-10PMK) is a multi-role version, announced 1993. Originally, it was a simple derivative with air-to-ground systems added and no changes in the basic weapons system of the Su-30 (probably none was built in this form). Currently, the designation Su-30MK is used for an advanced version with new radar, canards and thrust vectoring (see Sales/Users and description).
Su-30MKI is a derivative of the Su-30MK (final version) built for India. Some Western equipment expected in place of Russian. Aerodynamic prototype (with canards and thrust-vectoring engines) flew on 1 July 1997.
2-seat trainer version is available (see drawing).

Details for Su-30MK, unless stated

As Su-27UB except:

WEIGHTS:
Maximum take-off: 83,775 lb (38,000 kg)

PERFORMANCE:
Maximum operating Mach number (M_{MO}): Mach 2; quoted as Mach 2.35 in brochure for Su-30
Maximum speed: 1,147 kts (1,320 mph) 2,125 km/h; quoted as 1,350 kts (1,553 mph) 2,500 km/h in brochure for Su-30
Maximum speed at low altitude: 729 kts (839 mph) 1,350 km/h
Take-off distance: 1,805 ft (550 m)
Landing distance: 2,198 ft (670 m); quoted as 2,297 ft (700 m) in brochure for Su-30 with drag chute
G limit: +8; +9 quoted in brochure for Su-30
Ceiling: 57,400 ft (17,500 m)
Maximum range without flight refuelling: 1,620 naut miles (1,864 miles) 3,000 km
Range with single flight refuelling: 2,808 naut miles (3,231 miles) 5,200 km
Range with 2 flight refuellings: 3,774 naut miles (4,343 miles) 6,990 km
Combat radius: 809 naut miles (932 miles) 1,500 km for Su-30

↑ **Sukhoi Su-30MK demonstrator with canards and thrust vectoring** *(Piotr Butowski)*

Sukhoi Su-32FN and Su-34/Su-27IB (NATO name *Flanker*)

First flight: 13 April 1990 (pilot Anatoli Ivanov).
Role: Supersonic tactical interdiction (Su-34) and maritime strike (Su-32FN) aircraft to replace MiG-27, Su-17 and Su-24.

Aims

- Developed from the general Su-27 type but with significant airframe redesign offering side-by-side seating.
- Titanium armour plating around cockpit.
- Additional rearward-facing air-to-air radar in a long tailboom.

Development

- 13 April 1990. First flight of the T10V-1 prototype (side number 42).
- 1991. First photograph published by TASS.
- 14 February 1992. T10V-1 displayed at Machulishche, Belarus, to CIS leaders. Officially named Su-27IB.
- 18 December 1993. First flight of pre-production aircraft (T10V-3, side number 43) built at Novosibirsk, piloted by Igor Votintsev and Yevgeni Revunov.
- 28 December 1994. Third aircraft flown at Novosibirsk (number 45).
- June 1995. First international presentation in Paris (as Su-32FN).
- 26 December 1996. Fourth aircraft (number 44) flew at Novosibirsk, as the first to be fully equipped with radar and weapon systems.
- 1998. First production batch of Su-34s for the Russian Air Force completed.

Details

Sales/Users: Series manufacturing of the Su-34 began at Novosibirsk, after a single prototype was built by the Sukhoi works in Moscow. 3 production aircraft built before the end of

↑ Sukhoi Su-34/Su-27IB, the first to be fully equipped with radar and weapon systems *(Piotr Butowski)*

1996, with more then underway. An order for up to 12 Su-34s (Su-27IBs) from the Russian Air Force was reported, to be completed by 1998. Further orders expected, allowing the replacement of all Su-24s by the year 2005. Initial production of the Su-32FN for Russian Naval Aviation (also to replace Su-24s) was believed to have begun as long ago as 1995, but these may have since been cancelled. India has expressed interest.
Crew: Pilot (port side) and weapons operator (starboard), side-by-side.
Cockpit: Very high cockpit, allowing the crew to stand and perform relaxing exercises during long-duration missions. Aft of the cockpit is a toilet and galley compartment. Cockpit conditions at an altitude of 7,875 ft (2,400 m) is maintained up to 32,800 ft (10,000 m), allowing the crew to work without oxygen masks. Crew enter cockpit via the front wheel bay; the canopy is not opened. The entire cockpit is located inside a 17-mm thick titanium alloy armoured 'box', protecting the crew from anti-aircraft fire.
Crew escape: Zvezda K-36DM zero-zero ejection seats.
Fixed guns: GSh-301 30-mm cannon built into the starboard wingroot.
Ammunition: 180 rounds.
Number of weapon pylons: 12, as 2 under the fuselage (centreline), 2 under the intake ducts, 6 under the wings and 2 at the wingtips (see also Expendable weapons for torpedo arrangements on Su-32FN).
Expendable weapons and equipment: Up to 17,637 lb (8,000 kg). The aircraft presented at Machulishche carried Kh-31P (AS-17 *Krypton*) anti-radar, Kh-29L (AS-14 *Kedge*) laser-guided and Kh-29T TV-guided ASMs, KAB-500L laser-guided bombs, plus R-73 (AA-11 *Archer*) and R-77 (AA-12 *Adder*) AAMs. Su-32FN weapons include 2 heavy Moskit (ASM-MSS) anti-ship missiles, 3 new-generation Alpha (ASM-MS) ASMs, 3 Kh-59M (AS-18 *Kazoo*) TV-guided missiles, 6 Kh-35 (AS-20 *Kayak*) anti-ship missiles, and 6 Kh-31s. The aircraft can also carry an ultra-long-range R-37 and KS-172 AAMs as well as Kh-15 of 135 naut mile (155 mile) 250 km range and Kh-65 ASMs. A pack of 72 sonobuoys can be suspended under the fuselage of Su-32FN for anti-submarine warfare, plus 4 ASW torpedoes (on tandem racks under the intake ducts) and depth charges (including new RBK-100 PLAB-10K cluster bombs).
Radar: High-resolution, multi-function nav/attack radar, with terrain following/avoidance.
Flight/weapon system avionics/instrumentation: Digital avionics are integrated via a MIL-STD-1553 databus and controlled by Argon computer. Fire-control system includes radar, opto-electronic system coupling TV, infra-red and laser channels, and other optional devices (see Aircraft variants). Inertial navigation system is integrated with GLONASS satellite navigation. According to Mikhail Simonov, the aircraft navigation system "with principally new computer" is capable of navigation "with accuracy of up to 1 metre". See Aircraft variants, particularly for Su-32FN. See photograph for MFDs, HUD and instruments layout.

↑ Sukhoi Su-34/Su-27IB cockpit for 2-crew seated side-by-side *(Piotr Butowski)*

Self-protection system: Pastel radar warning receiver, Mak infra-red missile launch and approach device, and laser warning device. Sorbtsya-S ECM containers can be mounted at the wingtips. Chaff/flare dispensers.
Wing characteristics: As Su-27.
Tail control surfaces: As Su-27UB for T10V-1 (number 42) prototype, and as Su-27 for production aircraft.
Canard: Similar to Su-33 and Su-35.
Construction materials: 3,263 lb (1,480 kg) of overall weight comprises the protection system (cockpit armour, etc).
Flight control system: Quadruple redundant digital fly-by-wire.
Engines: Currently 2 Saturn/Moscow AL-31F turbofans, each 27,560 lbf (122.59 kN). To be replaced by 30,865 lbf (137.3 kN) derivatives, probably with thrust vectoring (as for all aircraft in the Su-27 family).
Air intakes: Non-adjustable type.
Flight refuelling probe: Fitted as standard, on port side of nose.
Fuel system: Up to 26,676 lb (12,100 kg) of internal fuel plus 15,873 lb (7,200 kg) in auxiliary tanks.
Braking system: Twin drag-chute housed on top of the fuselage, between the engine nacelles.

Aircraft variants:
Su-27IB (istriebitiel-bombardirovshchik, fighter-bomber) is the name used by the Russian Air Force, while T-10V is the Design Bureau name. First flying prototype (T10V-1 – T10-42, side number 42) was produced by Sukhoi in Moscow as a conversion of an Su-27UB, with only the front fuselage replaced (up to frame 18). T10V-3 (number 43) is a newly-built pre-production aircraft constructed at Novosibirsk.
Su-32FN was to have been a Russian Naval Aviation version but is now an export maritime strike derivative with avionics suite comprising Sea Snake radar and other standard systems, anti-submarine warfare devices, radio sonobuoy system and magnetic anomaly detector. According to Sukhoi, at high altitude the radar is able to detect a trace made on the surface by a submerged submarine from a distance of 81 naut miles (93 miles) 150 km.
Su-34 is the designation proposed by the Design Bureau for the Air Force version.
Su-27KUB (korabelnyi uchebno-boyevoi) is a ship-borne combat-trainer derived from the Su-27IB. First flight had been scheduled for 1997.
Reconnaissance version is being developed as a replacement for the Su-24MR *Fencer-E*. Special reconnaissance equipment BKR (bortovoi kompleks rozvedki, on-board reconnaissance complex) is being prepared. This provides for the simultaneous use of side-looking radar, radio intelligence, television, infra-red, laser and photo reconnaissance equipment that is integrated into the BKR system.
Electronic warfare version is being developed as a replacement for the Su-24MP *Fencer-F*.

Details for Su-34/Su-27IB

PRINCIPAL DIMENSIONS:
Wing span: 48 ft 3 ins (14.7 m)
Length without probe: 76 ft 7 ins (23.335 m)
Length overall: 81 ft 4 ins (24.8 m)
Maximum height: 19 ft 11.5 ins (6.084 m)
Canards span: 21 ft (6.4 m)

UNDERCARRIAGE:
Type: Retractable, with twin nosewheels. Single mainwheels on the T10-42 prototype but tandem mainwheels on production aircraft
Main wheel tyre size: KT-206 on production aircraft, 950 × 400 mm
Nose wheel tyre size: KT-27, 680 × 260 mm
Wheel base: 21 ft 8 ins (6.6 m)
Wheel track: 14 ft 5 ins (4.4 m)

WEIGHTS:
Normal take-off: 85,980 lb (39,000 kg)
Maximum take-off: 99,428 lb (44,100 kg)

PERFORMANCE:
Maximum speed: 1,025 kts (1,181 mph) 1,900 km/h
Maximum speed at sea level: 702 kts (808 mph) 1,300 km/h
Take-off distance: 4,134 ft (1,260 m)
Landing distance: 3,610 ft (1,100 m)
Landing distance with drag-chute: 2,953 ft (900 m)
Ceiling: 45,930 ft (14,000 m)
G limit: +7 allowable
Combat radius at low altitude, internal fuel, 8,818 lb (4,000 kg) weapons: 324 naut miles (373 miles) 600 km
Combat radius at low altitude, maximum fuel, 8,818 lb (4,000 kg) weapons: 610 naut miles (702 miles) 1,130 km
Ferry range: 2,428 naut miles (2,796 miles) 4,500 km

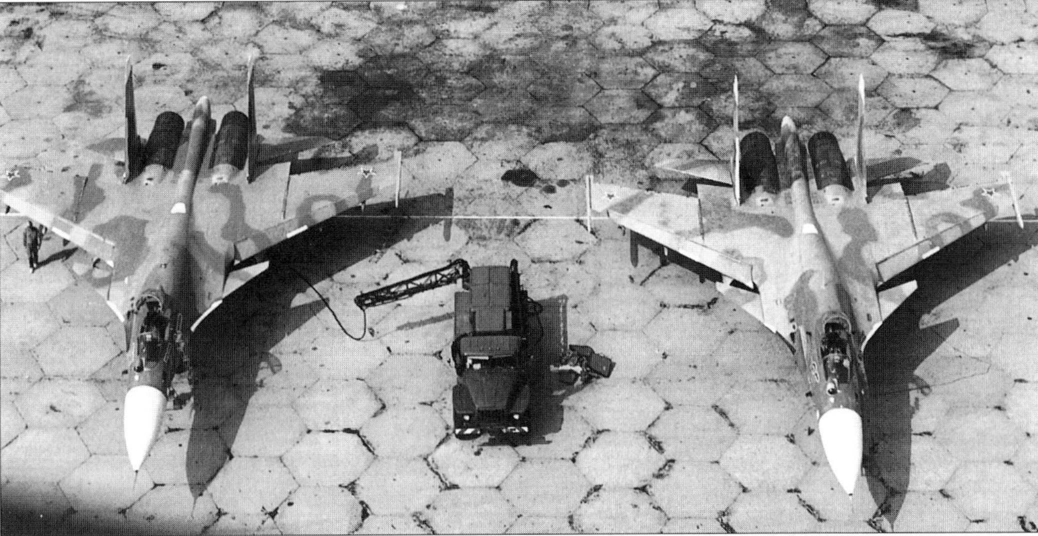

↑ Production Sukhoi Su-29Ks (Su-33s) from the Severomorsk Regiment shore-based on the Kola Peninsula *(Yefim Gordon)*

Sukhoi Su-33 (Su-27K) (NATO name *Flanker-D*)

First flight: 17 August 1987, piloted by Viktor Pugachov.
Role: Carrier-borne air-superiority/air defence and anti-ship aircraft.
Chief designer: Konstantin Marbashev.

Aims

▪ Modified ship-borne derivative of the Su-27. Bureau designation Su-33, Russian Navy designation Su-27K.

Development

▪ 28 August 1982. First take-off of Su-27 (T10-3, third prototype) from a dummy flight deck marked out on the runway at Saki, Ukraine, the Naval aviation test centre. Piloted by Nikolai Sadovnikov.
▪ 18 April 1984. Official government order for the Su-27K and MiG-29K ship-borne fighters.
▪ 1 September 1984. First landing of Su-27 (T10-25 test aircraft) with use of an arrester hook, piloted by Viktor Pugachov.
▪ 25 September 1984. First take-off from the new ski-jump built at Saki, an exact copy of the flight deck of the aircraft carrier *Tbilisi*, by T10-25.
▪ May 1985. First flight of T10-24 test aircraft, the first Su-27 with canard surfaces, piloted by Viktor Pugachov.
▪ 1987. First fully-automatic landings of the Su-27 on the Saki runway using the Rezistor radio system, and the first night landing using the Luna-3 optical-laser system.
▪ 17 August 1987. First flight of T10K-1, the first proper prototype (designated also T10-37, side number 37); this was lost in 1988, the pilot surviving.
▪ Spring 1988. First information published on the Su-27K, named *Flanker-B variant 2*, later *Flanker-D*.
▪ 1 November 1989. First landing on the deck of *Tbilisi*, piloted by Viktor Pugachov. The aircraft was T10K-2 (T10-39, side number 39).
▪ 21 November 1989. First night landing on the deck of Tbilisi.
▪ 17 February 1990. First flight (pilot Igor Votintsev) of the first production aircraft manufactured at Komsomolsk-on-Amur, being the third aircraft of the type (T10K-3).
▪ 18 August 1991. First public presentation, a fly-pass at the Zhukovsky test centre.

↑ Sukhoi Su-29Ks (Su-33s) on *Admiral Kuznetsov*. Note the arrester hook, and the folded wings of other aircraft

▪ 26 September 1991. First flights by military pilots (not test pilots) on the deck of an aircraft carrier; the first was Col Timur Apakidze.
▪ Summer 1994. Saki airfield leased to Russia by Ukraine for aircraft carrier pilot training.
▪ October 1994. State acceptance trials were completed successfully (started Autumn 1992). The aircraft was officially commissioned and accepted into service with the Russian Navy as the Su-27K (names T-10K and Su-33 are from the Design Bureau).
▪ 31 August 1994. Su-27Ks transferred to *Admiral Kuznetsov* at Severomorsk Northern Fleet base.
▪ 23 December 1995 – 25 March 1996. 8 Su-27Ks deployed into the Atlantic on board *Admiral Kuznetsov* during the first operational deployment.
▪ 1997. Probable first flight of the Su-27KUB or Su-33UB (korabelnyi uchebno-boyevoi) shipborne combat-trainer with side-by-side seating.

Details

Sales/Users: After 2 prototypes (T10K-1 and -2) built at the Sukhoi works in Moscow, a pre-peries batch of 7 aircraft (T10-3 to K-9) built at Komsomolsk-on-Amur in 1990. First 4 production aircraft delivered in March-April 1993. In October 1994, when Su-27K officially entered service, Russian Navy had 24 operational aircraft. Subsequent production terminated due to financial cutbacks, but in 1996 restarted and several aircraft have been delivered to the Navy. A total of 72 aircraft is planned: 24 should be assigned to *Admiral of the Fleet Kuznetsov* (an aircraft carrier more often known simply as *Admiral Kuznetsov*) plus 2 reserve units, each with 24 aircraft, to be based on shore.
Crew: Pilot. Current production aircraft have a folding ladder built into the fuselage.
Cockpit: As for Su-27, plus some new navigation instrumentation.
Crew escape: Zvezda K-36DM ejection seat.
Fixed guns: As for Su-27 (single GSh-301 cannon).
Number of weapon pylons: 12.
Expendable weapons and equipment: Maximum weapon load of 14,330 lb (6,500 kg). In addition to standard Su-27 weapons, the Su-27K can carry R-27EM air-to-air missiles specialized for use over the sea against air targets flying at low altitude, as well as 4 × Kh-31A anti-ship missiles of 38 naut mile (43.5 mile) 70 km range and 1 heavy Moskit (ASM-MSS) missile weighing 9,921 lb (4,500 kg) and with a range of 135 naut miles (155 miles) 250 km.
Radar: As for Su-27 (NIIP N-001) for aircraft built until 1997, but Phazotron Zhuk-27 fitted to next production aircraft.
Flight/weapon system avionics/instrumentation: Su-27K carries a special device, allowing fully automatic, command controlled or manual controlled landing. On board ship are 2 landing systems that combine with the aircraft's system: Rezistor automatic radio approach and landing system, and Luna-3 optical-laser system warning the pilot by means of lights of various colours against deviations from the best landing approach path.
Self-protection systems: As for Su-27.
Wing characteristics: In spite of external similarity to Su-27, the internal wing structure of Su-27K is quite different. Outer wing panels fold hydraulically (135°) for stowage on board ship.
Wing control surfaces: A conventional trailing-edge flap and aileron occupy the full trailing edge, instead of the Su-27's approximately 60%-span flaperon.
Tail control surfaces: As for Su-27, but folding outer tailplane panels are standard. The folded tailplane seems to have caused problems, indicated by the alterations to T10K-6 (side number 79); when presented to CIS leaders at Machulishche in February 1992, T10K-6 had a folded horizontal tail, but 2 months later the same aircraft was displayed at the Kubinka Air Base with a one-piece unit.
Canard: All-moving, swept, deflected symmetrically only (about +7°, -70° at leading edge).
Airbrakes: As for Su-27.
Flight control system: Adapted from the Su-27.
Fuselage: Upward folding nose radome. Folding tailboom, which is much shorter than that of Su-27.
Construction materials: Greater use of anti-corrosion materials.
Engines: 2 modified AL-31K turbofans with emergency afterburning added.

Details for Su-33 (Su-27K)

PRINCIPAL DIMENSIONS:
Wing span: 48 ft 3 ins (14.70 m)
Span with wings and tailplane folded: 24 ft 3 ins (7.40 m)
Length without probe: 69 ft 6 ins (21.185 m)
Maximum height: 19 ft 2 ins (5.85 m)

WINGS:
Area: 729.79 sq ft (67.8 m^2)
Aspect ratio: 3.187
Sweepback at leading edge: 42°
Dihedral/anhedral: 0°

TAIL UNIT:
Tailplane span: 32 ft 2 ins (9.80 m)

UNDERCARRIAGE:
Type: Strengthened retractable type, with twin steerable nosewheels (±60°)
Main wheel tyre size: 1,030 × 350 mm
Nose wheel tyre size: 620 × 180 mm
Wheel base: 19 ft 3 ins (5.872 m)
Wheel track: 14 ft 5 ins (4.40 m)

WEIGHTS:
Maximum take-off: 66,000 lb (29,940 kg)
Maximum in flight, after refuelling: 72,752 lb (33,000 kg)

PERFORMANCE:
Maximum speed: Mach 2.165 or 1,242 kts (1,429 mph) 2,300 km/h
Maximum speed at sea level: Mach 1.14 or 756 kts (870 mph) 1,400 km/h
Approach speed: 130 kts (149 mph) 240 km/h
Take-off distance on deck (14° ramp): 394 ft (120 m)
G limit: +9
Ceiling: 55,775 ft (17,000 m)
Maximum range without flight refuelling: 1,620 naut miles (1,864 miles) 3,000 km

↑ Sukhoi Su-29K (Su-33) cockpit *(Piotr Butowski)*

Engine rating: Each 29,320 lbf (130.42 kN).
Flight refuelling probe: Mounted on the port side of the nose. The lights on both sides in the front fuselage are for illuminating the tanker's drogue during night refuelling. UPAZ-A Sakhalin 'buddy' refuelling pod can be carried under the fuselage of Su-27K. Flight refuelling is a very important feature of the Su-27K, since it cannot take-off with full fuel from the carrier if heavily armed.
Braking system: Arrester hook under the tailboom. No drag-chute.

Aircraft variants:
Su-27K (***Su-33***, K stands for korabelnyi, ship-borne), as described.
Su-27MK was a projected shipborne derivative of Su-27M (Su-35), but project abandoned.
Su-27KUB or ***Su-33UB*** (korabelnyi uchebno-boyevoi) is a shipborne combat-trainer with side-by-side seating (but derived from Su-27K, not Su-27IB). In production at Komsomolsk-on-Amur.

Sukhoi Su-35 and Su-37, or Su-27M (NATO name *Flanker*)

First flight: 28 June 1988 for Su-35 (T10M-1) and 2 April 1996 for Su-37 (T10M-11).
Role: Advanced air-superiority fighter, with ground-attack capability.

Aims

- Multi-role capability, including use of 250 km-range ASMs.
- Improved avionics including track-while-scan radar for up to 15-24 targets (see Radar) and rear radar.
- Improved manoeuvrability due to new 'tandem triplane' configuration, instability some 3 to 5 times greater than that for Su-27, and vectored thrust for developed models.

Development

- 28 June 1988. Maiden flight of the T10M-1 first prototype.
- 31 March 1989. Vectored thrust trials began with an Su-27 testbed, piloted by Oleg Tsoi (see Nozzles).
- 14 February 1992. Su-27M (side number 706) was presented to CIS leaders at Machulishche.
- September 1992. First public presentation, with T10M-3 (side number 703, c/n *79371010102*), Sukhoi designated Su-35, at the Farnborough Air Show.
- September 1996. Su-37 (T10M-11) first presented abroad, at the Farnborough Air Show, displaying unbelievable manoeuvres including Kulbit (somersault) which combines rapid deceleration with a full 360° tight-diameter loop.
- 1998/99. Anticipated Russian IOC for Su-35/37.

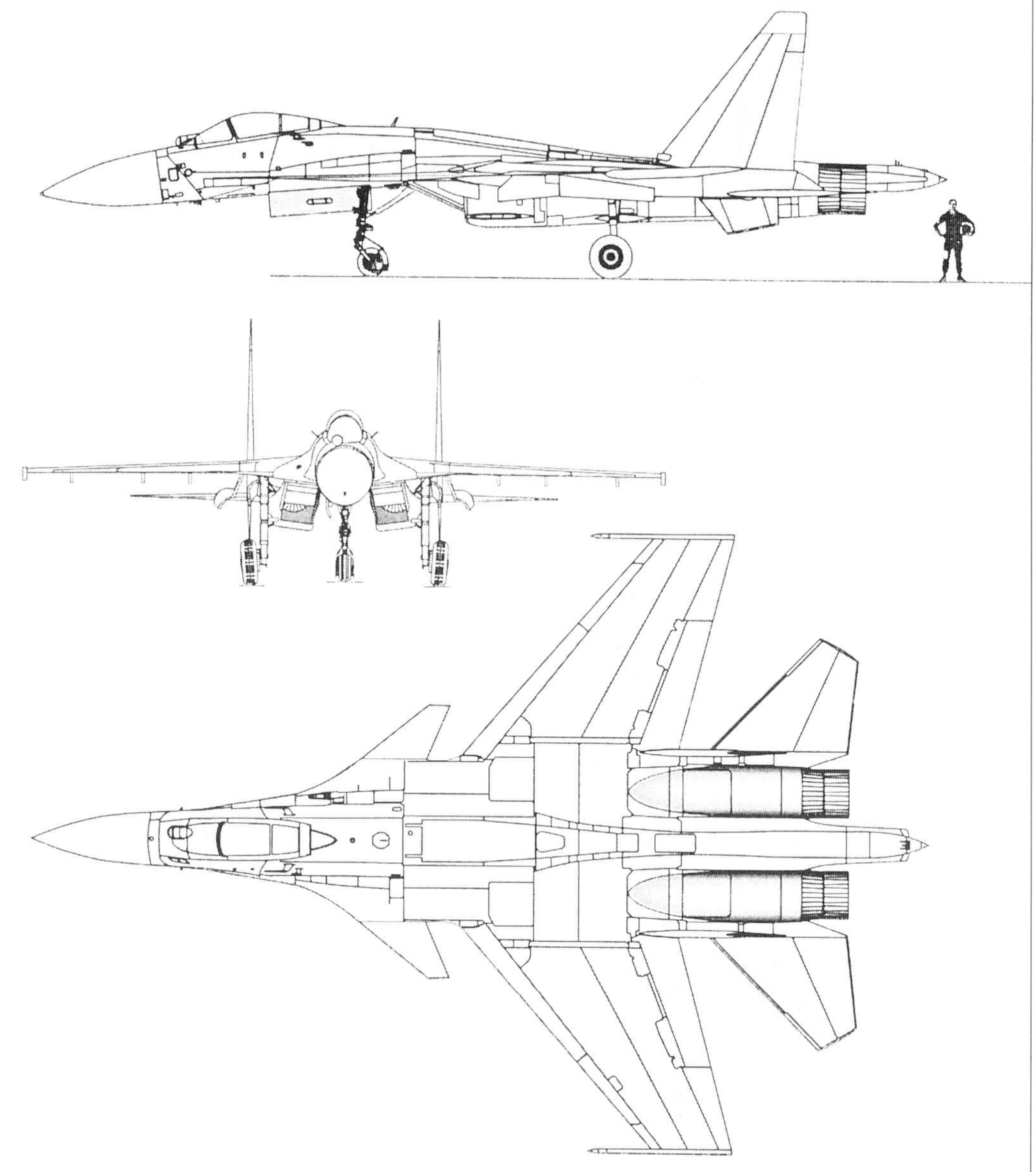
↑ **Sukhoi Su-35 general arrangement** *(courtesy KnAAPO)*

Details

Sales/Users: 11 prototypes and pre-production aircraft built at the Sukhoi test production facility in Moscow and at the Komsomolsk-on-Amur plant. India and the United Arab Emirates expressed interest. Su-35 anticipated for Russian service from late 1990s but may give way to Su-37 instead. Su-37 had been suggested as a variant of the Su-35 for the UAE. Currently, Su-37 is considered an experimental aircraft, aiding the export Su-30MKI and other programmes (probably S-32 also).
Crew: Pilot.
Cockpit: Glass cockpit with 4 multi-function displays (front panel and side panels, the exact positioning varying from aircraft to aircraft). Monochrome displays in current aircraft, colour displays for production aircraft. Starboard side-stick controller introduced on Su-37 (after being tested on Su-27 LMK-2405), while earlier prototypes have conventional central sticks.

↑ **Deflected nozzles of AL-31FP engines in Su-37** *(Piotr Butowski)*

Crew escape: K-36DM zero-zero ejection seat, inclined 30° for better g-force tolerance and adapted for long-duration flights. PPK-15 anti-G suit for pilot.
Fixed guns: As for Su-27 (GSh-301 30-mm cannon).
Number of weapon pylons: 14.
Expendable weapons and equipment: Up to 17,634 lb (8,000 kg) of weapons. All types of modern Russian air-to-air missiles, including 216 naut mile (249 mile) 400 km-range KS-172s, medium-range R-77s (AA-12 *Adder*) and short-range R-73 (AA-11 *Archer*). All types of Russian tactical air-to-surface missiles, including anti-radar/active radar Kh-31 (AS-17 *Krypton*), Kh-59M (AS-18 *Kazoo*) TV-guided, advanced Alpha multi-mode and Kh-65 cruise missiles, plus bombs, rockets, etc.
Radar: NIIP N-011 multi-mode look-down/shoot-down radar with flat slotted antenna, designed by Tamerlan Bekirbayev. Coverage ±85° in azimuth and ±55° in elevation. Maximum search range for a fighter type air target (RCS 21.5 sq ft, 2 m^2) is 43-54 naut miles (50-62 miles) 80-100 km head-on and 16-21.5 naut miles (18.6-25 miles) 30-40 km tail-on. Track-while-scan mode allows tracking of 15 air targets and engaging 4-6 simultaneously (including motionless targets such as helicopters). In an air-to-ground mode, it can acquire surface targets at ranges up to 108 naut miles (124 miles) 200 km, and undertake ground mapping, terrain following and terrain avoidance. N-011M phased-array derivative planned for production aircraft. Phazotron offers the competitive Zhuk-Ph radar with phased-array electronically-scanned antenna (coverage ±60° currently, but to be substantially increased mechanically), with an anticipated detection range of 75.5 naut miles (87 miles) 140 km, and a reported capability to detect 24 targets and engage 6 to 8. Su-35/37 also carry rear-looking N-012 radar in the thicker tailboom.

Details for Su-35

PRINCIPAL DIMENSIONS:
Wing span: 48 ft 3 ins (14.698 m)
Wing span over wingtip ECM pods: 49 ft 9 ins (15.16 m)
Maximum length: 72 ft 9 ins (22.183 m)
Maximum height: 21 ft 1 ins (6.433 m)

WINGS:
Area: 667.36 sq ft (62 m^2)
Aspect ratio: 3.484
Sweepback at leading edge: 42°

UNDERCARRIAGE:
Type: Retractable, with single nosewheel on *706* and *707* prototypes, and twin wheels on the following aircraft
Wheel base: 19 ft 1 ins (5.815 m)
Wheel track: 14 ft 1.5 ins (4.301 m)

WEIGHTS:
Empty, operating: 40,565 lb (18,400 kg)
Normal take-off, air-combat mission: 56,593 lb (25,670 kg) with 3,086 lb (1,400 kg) of weapons and reduced fuel
Maximum take-off: 74,957 lb (34,000 kg)

PERFORMANCE:
Maximum speed: Mach 2.35 or 1,350 kts (1,553 mph) 2,500 km/h
Maximum speed at sea level: Mach 1.14 or 756 kts (870 mph) 1,400 km/h
Required runway length: 3,937 ft (1,200 m)
G limit: +9
Climb rate: 45,275 ft (13,800 m) per minute
Ceiling: 58,400 ft (17,800 m)
Range at low altitude: 750 naut miles (864 miles) 1,390 km
Range with maximum fuel: 1,781 naut miles (2,051 miles) 3,300 km

↑ Final pre-production Sukhoi Su-35 *(Piotr Butowski)*

Flight/weapon system avionics/instrumentation: Improved opto-electronic search/track device includes TV channel, IR channel and laser rangefinder/target designator. Su-35 has 3 MFDs plus HUD; Su-37 has Sextant Avionique 4 liquid-crystal MFDs with HUD, GLONASS GPS and laser-gyro INS.
Self-protection systems: Improved, including wingtip jammer pods, Mak infra-red sensor on the fuselage and Pastel RWR.
Wing characteristics: As for Su-27.
Tail control surfaces: As for Su-27 on first prototypes, but higher and thicker fins with internal fuel tankage on other aircraft.
Canard: All-moving, swept, deflected symmetrically only (+7°, -70° at leading edge).
Airbrakes: As for Su-27.
Fuselage: Longer and thicker nose, with no Pitot tube.
Construction materials: Increased use of composites and aluminium-lithium alloy.
Flight control system: Avionika quadruple redundant digital fly-by-wire for the longitudinal control channel (tailplane when deflected symmetrically), triple redundant digital fly-by-wire in other channels. For Su-37, the engine nozzles are included in the flight control of the aircraft. New software integrates aerodynamic and engine control inputs; therefore, there is no separate control for thrust vectoring in the cockpit.
Engines: 2 Saturn AL-31FP (also designated AL-35F for Su-35 and AL-37FU for Su-37) turbofans on the production version, but the Su-27's standard AL-31F engines are installed in the pre-production aircraft (except T10M-11, which has AL-31FP modification with vectored thrust). When compared with AL-31F, AL-31FP has new larger-diameter fan (increased by 0.79 ins, 20 mm) and increased turbine entry temperature (TET); maximum reheat thrust is 30,865 lbf (137.3 kN), rather than 27,560 lbf (122.6 kN), and its specific fuel consumption is increased from 0.67 lb/lbf/hr (18.98 g/kNs) to 0.685 lb/lbf/hr (19.4 g/kNs).
Engine rating: See Engines.
Nozzles: Axi-symmetrical 2-dimensional vectored-thrust nozzles (±15° deflection) are fitted to Su-37. Each nozzle is actuated hydraulically (from the aircraft's hydraulic system on the prototype, and by the engine's fuel system on production aircraft); there is also an emergency pneumatic system used for immediate setting of nozzles to neutral position in the event of any defect. Service life of AL-31FP's (AL-37FU) controllable nozzle is said by Saturn to be 250 hours at present and 500 hours for production engines. Nozzle is 243 lb (110 kg) heavier and 15.7 ins (40 cm) longer than the standard AL-31F nozzle. In 1989 Sukhoi began trials with 2 vectored-thrust test-beds with manual nozzle control system and nozzle deflected at fixed angles.
Flight refuelling probe: Standard, on the port side of the front fuselage.
Fuel system: Fuel capacity is about 3,307 lb (1,500 kg) greater than for Su-27.

↑ Sukhoi Su-37 N-011M phased-array radar *(Piotr Butowski)*

Aircraft variants:
Su-27M (T-10M) is the only designation used by the Russian Air Force, while Su-35 and Su-37 are used by Sukhoi.
Su-35 has fixed engine nozzles.
Su-37 is the definitive production version with thrust-vectoring nozzles, side-stick controller, and 4 colour MFDs in the cockpit. Also, the designation ***Su-37MR*** has been mentioned by Russian sources.

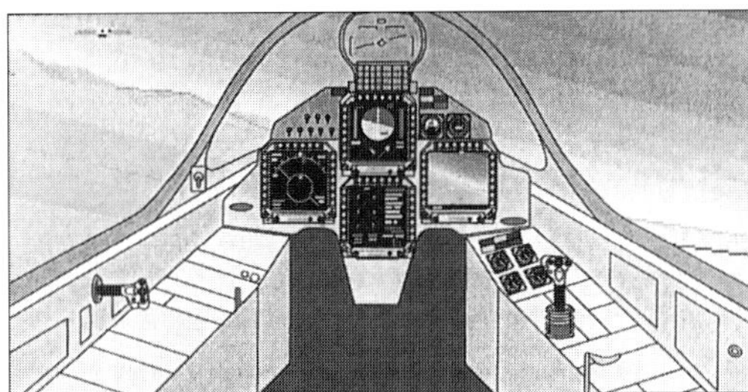
↑ Cockpit layout of Su-37, with 4 large colour MFDs and starboard side-stick controller

Sukhoi Su-39 (Su-25TM) (NATO name *Frogfoot*)

First flight: 17 August 1984, piloted by Alexander Isakov.
Role: Subsonic, armoured close-air support and anti-tank aircraft, used also as lead aircraft for groups of Su-25s.
Chief designer: Vladimir Babak.

Aims

- Expanded navigation/attack system compared with Su-25.
- New smart weapons, including laser-beam riding Vikhr anti-tank missiles.
- Longer range.

Development

- 1980. Work started on a dedicated anti-tank aircraft.
- 17 August 1984. First flight of prototype T8M-1.
- 26 July 1990. First flight of a production Su-25T, at Tbilisi, Georgia.
- November 1991. First public presentation (Dubai, UAE) with the export name Su-25TK. Provisionally designated Su-34 by Sukhoi, later Su-39.
- September 1993. State Acceptance Trials of Su-25T completed.
- First Su-25TM built (also first combat Su-25 built at Ulan-Ude in Russia, where production had been transferred from Tbilisi).
- 1997. Start of State Acceptance Trials of Su-25TM.

Details for for Su-39/Su-25TM

PRINCIPAL DIMENSIONS:
Wing span: 47 ft 7.5 ins (14.52 m)
Maximum length: 50 ft 3.5 ins (15.33 m)
Fuselage length: 46 ft 10 ins (14.28 m)
Maximum height: 17 ft 1 ins (5.20 m)

WINGS:
Area: 324 sq ft (30.10 m^2)
Aspect ratio: 7.004

TAIL UNIT:
Tailplane span: 15 ft 0.5 ins (4.582 m)
Elevators area: 20.26 sq ft (1.882 m^2)
Fin area: 56.84 sq ft (5.28 m^2)

UNDERCARRIAGE:
Type: Retractable, with nosewheel
Nose wheel tyre size: 680 × 260 mm
Wheel track: 8 ft 2.5 ins (2.5 m)
Wheel base: 11 ft 9 ins (3.58 m)

WEIGHTS:
Nominal take-off: 37,192 lb (16,870 kg)
Maximum take-off: 47,400 lb (21,500 kg)
Maximum landing: 29,100 lb (13,200 kg)

PERFORMANCE:
Maximum allowable Mach number: Mach 0.82
Maximum speed: 513 kts (590 mph) 950 km/h, with 2 × 500 kg bombs and 2 × R-60 AAMs
Maximum cruise speed at 656 ft (200 m): 378 kts (435 mph) 700 km/h
Landing speed: 124-127 kts (143-146 mph) 230-235 km/h
Maximum climb rate: 11,400 ft (3,480 m) per minute, at sea level
Turn radius at 4,920 ft (1,500 m) altitude, 50% internal fuel and 3,307 lb (1,500 kg) of weapons: 1,870 ft (570 m) at 248 kts IAS, 2,198 ft (670 m) at 275 kts IAS, and 2,231 ft (680 m) at 302 kts IAS
Take-off distance: 1,969-2,297 ft (600-700 m)
Landing distance: 1,969-2,297 ft (600-700 m)
G limits: +6.5
Ceiling: 32,810 ft (10,000 m)
Radius of action with 2,998 lb (1,360 kg) of weapons at 26,250 ft (8,000 m): 275 naut miles (317 miles) 510 km
Radius of action with 5,203 lb (2,360 kg) of weapons and 2 PTB-1150 auxiliary tanks, at 26,250 ft (8,000 m): 340 naut miles (391 miles) 630 km
Radius of action with 2 Kh-35U ASMs, 2 R-77 AAMs and 4 PTB-800 tanks, at 26,250 ft (8,000 m): 486 naut miles (559 miles) 900 km
Range with 2,998 lb (1,360 kg) of weapons, at 656 ft (200 m): 351 naut miles (404 miles) 650 km
Range: 1,350 naut miles (1,553 miles) 2,500 km with maximum fuel

Details *(Su-39/Su-25TM, unless stated)*

Sales/Users: In 1990-91 the factory in Tbilisi, Georgia, manufactured the first series of 20 Su-25Ts. After the break-up of the USSR, 8 were in Russia, with the rest remaining in Tbilisi (these too were reportedly being transferred to Russia under a recent agreement). Subsequent production was transferred to Ulan-Ude in Russia; at least 3 Su-25TMs had been built in Ulan-Ude by early 1998 (first in 1995, the second by mid-1997 and the third flying in about October 1997). Order for 24 Su-25TMs had been expected for the Russian Air Force for the newly created fast response forces (a number of existing Su-25Ts will be upgraded to TM type, plus 2 newly-built aircraft before the end of 1998 and at least 4 more delivered in 1999). Since 1993 the Sukhoi Shturmovics consortium has been negotiating with Bulgaria and Slovakia over the purchase or leasing of small numbers. With these forces, Su-39s would probably be used as homing and lead aircraft for groups of Su-25Ks. In 1997, the Su-39 was also offered to Poland. Negotiations for an unspecified number are taking place with China. Reports suggest Georgia could require up to 50 but with no known order at the time of writing.
Crew: Pilot. Maximum cockpit pressure differential 3.63 psi.
Crew escape: K-36L ejection seat.
Cockpit: Fully armoured.
Fixed guns: 1 × 30-mm twin-barrel GSh-2-30 cannon installed under the starboard side of the fuselage, requiring the nosewheel leg to be moved 8.7 ins (222 mm) to port.
Number of weapon pylons: 11, including 1 under the fuselage for the radar pod and 2 wingtip stations for air-to-air missiles only.
Expendable weapons and equipment: Up to 13,228 lb (6,000 kg) of weapons and equipment. The basic anti-tank armament is 16 Vikhr missiles carried in 2 × APU-8 clusters under the wings. The

↑ Second production Sukhoi Su-39 (Su-25TM) built at Ulan-Ude in 1997. Note the MSP-410 Omul EW container on the ground under the wing-mounted Kh-58U (*right*), TV-guided Kh-29T and Vikhr anti-tank missiles. See also the Kopyo-25 under fuselage *(Piotr Butowski)*

aircraft can also carry laser or TV-guided Kh-25ML, Kh-29L/T and S-25L ASMs; KAB-500Kr TV-guided bombs; Kh-58U anti-radar missiles; Kh-31A or Kh-35U anti-ship active-radar missiles; R-77, R-27, R-73 and R-60M AAMs; rockets, bombs, gun packs, etc; Su-25T was not able to carry active-radar Kh-31A and Kh-35 ASMs, and medium-range R-27 and R-77 AAMs .

Radar: Phazotron Kopyo-25 (N027) multi-mode radar with slotted flat antenna of 19.7 ins (500 mm) diameter, suspended in an underfuselage pod. Radar's coverage is ±40° in azimuth and +20°, -60° in elevation. Search range for large sea targets is 108 naut miles (124 miles) 200 km, for small sea targets is 40.5 naut miles (46.6 miles) 75 km, and for groups of tanks is 13.5 naut miles (15.5 miles) 25 km. Aerial targets (fighters) are detected from a distance of 31 naut miles (35.4 miles) 57 km. Radar is interconnected with Shkval-M optical-TV aiming system. Originally, a Leninets Kinzhal-S radar was to have been used with the Su-25TM, but this was replaced by Kopyo-25 as some Kinzhal parts were produced in co-operation with Ukrainian factories. No Kopyo-25 in Su-25T.

Flight/weapon system avionics/instrumentation: Inertial stabilized platform with SUV-25TM Voskhod nav/attack system, with 2 Orbita-20 computers (Orbita-20-56M for navigation and Orbita-20-13M for guided weapon system). The system has the I-251M Shkval-M day optical-TV subsystem used for target detection, automatic tracking and homing the laser-guided missiles. The Shkval unit includes 3 interconnected channels: TV channel for observation and tracking, Prichal laser rangefinder/target designator, and laser-beam homing system for the Vikhr missile. A large, common window for the TV camera and laser unit is installed in the aircraft's nose. The viewing angles for the Shkval optical-TV system can be adjusted for wide range (observation) 27° × 36°, or for narrow range (tracking) 0.7° × 1.0°. The optical axis of Shkval can be moved vertically from +15° through to -80°, and horizontally by 35° each side. Shkval can track a movable target (such as a tank) with an accuracy of 2 ft (0.6 m) at a distance of 4.3 naut miles (5 miles) 8 km. Shkval can detect a bridge from 11-13 naut miles (12.5-15 miles) 20-24 km, a single building from 8.1 naut miles (9.3 miles) 15 km, fighter aircraft from 5.4 naut miles (6.2 miles) 10 km, and a helicopter from 3.2 naut miles (3.7 miles) 6 km. A container with Khod FLIR equipment can be suspended under the fuselage for night missions (Merkuriy LLLTV was tested previously, but with little success). Original Su-25T has a day Shkval system only (no radar or Khod FLIR). Navigation subsystem contains A-723 long-range radio navigation, A-312 ILS, ShO-13A Doppler speed and drift meter, and RV-21 radio altimeter. In addition, other equipment not connected to the system include ARK-22 radio compass, R-862 and R-828 com radios, SO-69 transponder, and SRO-1-P IFF. The information is displayed by an SOI-57 Lotos data presentation system on the HUD and IT-23 CRT screen. 5 × 5 ins (13 × 13 cm) colour MFD (see illustration).

Self-protection systems: Irtysh electronic countermeasures system, which includes Pastel radar warning receiver (1.2-18 GHz), L-166S Sukhogruz IR jammer, UV-26 chaff/flare dispenser system (contains 192 × 26-mm PPI-26 infra-red or PPR-26 chaff cartridges), and MSP-410 Omul active electronic jammer. L-166S active infra-red jamming unit generates signals inside the rear cone with apex angle of 50°. The 5 kW unit weighs 62 lb (28 kg). UV-26 is installed in a large fairing at the tailfin root. MSP-410 is installed in 2 pods suspended under the outer underwing pylons and is able to jam ground and airborne radars and missile seekers within the 4-10 GHz range.

Airframe: As for Su-25UB, but with additional equipment and fuel in place of the rear cockpit. BU-45 hydraulic actuators also for elevators (formerly only for ailerons).

Engines: 2 Soyuz R-195 turbojets. Cold air bleed to reduce the infra-red signature. Engine service life 3,000 hours.

Engine rating: Each 9,921 lbf (44.13 kN).

Flight refuelling probe: None.

Fuel system: 4,890 litres (8,466 lb, 3,840 kg) of internal fuel, equivalent to 1,000 litres more than Su-25. Provision for 4 × 820 litre PTB-800 or 2 × 1,150 litre PTB-1150 drop tanks under wings.

Aircraft variants:

Su-25T (T-8M) was the initial version with I-251 Shkval day aiming system. Armament restrictions (see Expendable weapons).

Su-25TK was the export designation, K meaning kommercheskiy or commercial.

Su-25TM (***Su-39***, T-8TM) is the developed production version with Kopyo-25 radar and Khod FLIR pods added for all-weather day/night operations. Missiles can include R-27R, R-27ER and R-77 AAMs, and radar-guided ASMs.

Su-25TP was the projected ship-borne attack version, featuring an arrester hook and strengthened undercarriage. Programme terminated.

↑ Sukhoi Su-39 (Su-25TM) cockpit with wide-view HUD, IT-23 monochrome CRT of Shkval unit (*right*) and colour MFD (*left*)

Sukhoi S-37

Note: This fighter was detailed under S-32 in the 1996-97 edition of *WA&SD*. It has since been redesignated S-37.

First flight: 25 September 1997 (pilot Igor Votintsev).

Role: Fifth-generation heavy tactical fighter. First prototype S-37-1 is an experimental aircraft with provisional engines and no weapons control avionics suite. In February 1996, the Council of the Russian Air Force reportedly did not judge development necessary and has not included this programme among its priorities.

Aims

▪ Competitor to the Russian MAPO "MiG" MFI (1-42) and of similar class to the US F-22 Raptor.
▪ Stealth features include RAM (radar absorbing materials) and weapons carried in a conformal underfuselage pack. 14 weapon stations has been reported.
▪ Outstanding manoeuvrability achieved by 'tandem triplane' configuration with forward swept wing and thrust vectoring.

Development

▪ 1980s. Work started under S-32 designation, initially as a purely experimental aircraft.
▪ 25 September 1997. First flight of the S-37-1 prototype at Zhukovsky test centre in Moscow. After 9 flights, on 27 November 1997, tests stopped and the prototype became the subject of modifications, including increase in the area of the tailfins.
▪ April 1998. Flights re-started.

Details

Wing characteristics: Forward swept wings of 90% composite materials.

Tail control surfaces: First project reported as a pure canard, but currently seen to be of 'tandem triplane' (canard, wing and tailplane) layout. Twin slightly outward-canted fins.

Details for S-37, provisional

PRINCIPAL DIMENSIONS:
Wing span: 54 ft 9.5 ins (16.7 m)
Length: 74 ft 2 ins (16.7 m)
Height: 21 ft (6.4 m)

WEIGHTS:
Normal take-off: 55,115 lb (25,000 kg)
Maximum take-off: 77,162 lb (35,000 kg)

PERFORMANCE:
Maximum speed: 1,079 kts (1,243 mph) 2,000 km/h (1,350 kts, 1,553 mph, 2,500 km/h has also been reported)
Maximum speed at sea level: 755 kts (870 mph) 1,400 km/h
Ceiling: 59,050 ft (18,000 m)
Range: 1,780 naut miles (2,050 miles) 3,300 km

↑ Sukhoi S-37 during early flight trials from September-late November 1997

↑ Sukhoi S-37 *(Piotr Butowski)*

Engines: 2 Aviadvigatel/Perm D-30F-6 turbofans in prototype, with no thrust vectoring. Soyuz/Moscow R-79Ms of 39,680 lbf (176.5 kN) or AL-41Fs of similar rating with thrust vectoring nozzles expected for any following aircraft and possibly later for the first prototype (although AL-37FUs have also been reported).
Engine rating: Each 20,944 lbf (93.17 kN) dry, and 34,172 lbf (152 kN) with afterburning, for D-30F-6.

Sukhoi S-54 and S-55

First flight: Expected 1998.
Role: Lightweight multirole fighter (S-54) and combat trainer (S-55). (Initially S-54 project of 1991 had been for an advanced trainer with light combat capability.)

Development

- August 1992. A model of S-54 in original advanced trainer configuration was shown. R-195FS turbojet engine, weather radar, and no sophisticated weapons. Of Su-27 general layout (without canards).
- August 1995. A model of the S-55 combat trainer was shown. Canards introduced. AL-31F turbofan engine.
- June 1997. A model of what might be the final configuration was shown in S-54 single-seat fighter form. Single underfuselage air intake (instead of 2 under LERX), canards, and reshaped fuselage and tail unit.

Details

Crew: Pilot only in forward-protruding cockpit for S-54. 2 in tandem cockpits for S-55, the rear seat raised.
Crew escape: New Zvezda/Tomilono K-2000 zero-zero ejection system.
Fixed guns: Seen on S-55 model.
Number of weapon pylons: 6 on original S-54 model, comprising 2 under each wing and 2 wingtip AAM launch rails. Only 2 wingtip rails seen on new S-54 and S-55 models.

↑ Sukhoi S-54 lightweight fighter in latest configuration, as displayed in model form in June 1997. Note the S-54 designation on nose, single-seat cockpit and twin EW tailbooms *(Piotr Butowski)*

Expendable weapons and equipment: Air-to-air and air-to-surface missiles, unguided rockets and other light armament.
Radar: Phazotron Sokol (Falcon) with phased-array 1,000-mm antenna for both S-54 and S-55. Search range 97 naut miles (112 miles) 180 km in head-on mode and 43 naut miles (50 miles) 80 km in tail-on mode. 24 targets can be tracked simultaneously and 6 engaged. 4 targets can be tracked simultaneously in an air-to-surface mode. Radar weight 606 lb (275 kg). (Only simple weather radar seen on original S-54 model.)
Flight/weapon system avionics/instrumentation: Instrumentation similar to that of the Su-35/-37, with "glass" cockpit. Video recording of flight for ground analysis in S-55. S-54 has EW systems in twin tailbooms.
Wing characteristics: Swept, mid mounted, with small wingroot extensions. Canards.
Wing control surfaces: Leading-edge flaps, and trailing-edge flaperons.
Tail control surfaces: 2 outward-canted fins and inset rudders are mounted at the wing trailing edges, while the aft-mounted tailplane is slab type.
Airbrake: Fitted.
Flight control system: Fly-by-wire, programmable in S-55 to increase/decrease skill needed to fly and with spin-recovery and straight/level flight recovery buttons.

Details for S-55 (latest model)

PRINCIPAL DIMENSIONS:
Wing span: 31 ft 6 ins (9.595 m)
Maximum length: 43 ft 5 ins (13.24 m)
Maximum height: 14 ft 6 ins (4.41 m)

WINGS:
Chord at root: 15 ft 3 ins (4.64 m)
Chord at tip: 3 ft 11 ins (1.18 m)

TAIL UNIT:
Tailplane span: 18 ft (5.49 m)
Tailplane area: 48 sq ft (4.46 m^2)
Fins area, gross: 69.53 sq ft (6.46 m^2)
Rudders area, gross: 16.6 sq ft (1.54 m^2)

UNDERCARRIAGE:
Type: Retractable, with nosewheel
Wheel base: 11 ft 4 ins (3.45 m)
Wheel track: 8 ft 3 ins (2.52 m)

WEIGHTS:
Empty, operating: 10,560 lb (4,790 kg)
Maximum take-off: 20,745 lb (9,410 kg)
Maximum landing: 15,719 lb (7,130 kg)

PERFORMANCE:
Maximum operating Mach number (M_{MO}): Mach 1.55
Maximum speed: 891 kts (1,025 mph) 1,650 km/h
Maximum speed at sea level: 648 kts (746 mph) 1,200 km/h
Stalling speed: 97 kts (112 mph) 180 km/h
Landing speed: 92 kts (106 mph) 170 km/h
Take-off distance: 1,181 ft (360 m)
Landing distance: 1,640 ft (500 m)
G limits: +9, -3
Ceiling: 59,000 ft (18,000 m)
Range with maximum internal fuel, at high altitude: 1,080 naut miles (1,242 miles) 2,000 km
Range with maximum internal fuel, at sea level: 443 naut miles (509 miles) 820 km

↑ **Sukhoi S-55 combat trainer** *(Piotr Butowski)*

Engine: Saturn/Lyulka AL-31FP turbofan, with 3-dimensional vectoring thrust nozzles for prototype; Soyuz/Moscow R-79M (39,565 lbf; 176 kN) turbofan for production aircraft.
Engine rating: 27,560 lbf (122.6 kN) dry rating.
Flight refuelling probe: None.
S-54 is the single-seat lightweight multirole fighter, with a single air intake under the fuselage.
S-55 is the 2-seat combat-trainer with twin air intakes under the LERX.

Sukhoi T-60S

First flight: After the year 2000.
Role: Medium-range strike bomber.

Aims

▪ Originally, replacement for the Tupolev Tu-16 *Badger* and Tu-22 *Blinder*, plus eventually the Tu-22M *Backfire*.

Development

▪ 1983. Initial design started.

Details

Sales/Users: Komsomolsk-on-Amur factory was constructing the first prototype.
Crew: 2, side-by-side in nose cockpit.
Fuselage: Flattened, with stealth features.
Wing characteristics: Originally thought to have rear-mounted delta type, with LERX and chines, but now believed to have variable-geometry wings.
Canard: None.
Tail unit: All-moving slab tailplane and 2 inward-canted fins with rudders.
Engines: 2 augmented engines, shielded to lower IR signature and possibly with broad 2-D nozzles.
Air intakes: 2, widely spaced, positioned above the broad fuselage, with ducts blending into the top decking.

Sukhoi new generation close-air support aircraft

Comments: Piotr Deinekin, Commander-in-Chief of the Russian Air Force, announced recently that a new "prospective stealth ground-attack aircraft" will enter service after the year 2000. A modern close-air support aircraft named Sh-90 (shturmovic for 1990s) was being developed by Sukhoi some 10 years ago but no more information about this aircraft is available. It is unknown whether Sh-90 (Sukhoi T-12) and the aircraft mentioned by Piotr Deinekin are the same designs.

Sukhoi S-80PT

Comments: This is a light patrol/surveillance transport variant of the twin-boom S-80 multipurpose STOL transport, expected to first fly in 1999. It features a Leninets/St Petersburg Strizh nav/attack radar in an undernose radome and the ability to be armed, the latter including Kh-29T ASMs, R-73 AAMs and Vikhr anti-tank missiles carried on 4 underwing and 1 fuselage pylons. See Special reconnaissance and Airliner sections for full details and photograph.

↑ **Sukhoi Sh-90 (T-12)**

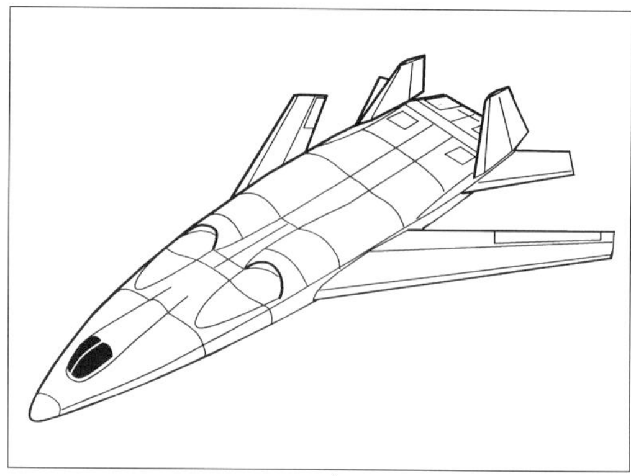

↑ **Artist's impression of Sukhoi T-60S strike bomber** *(Piotr Butowski)*

Tupolev Joint-Stock Company — Russia

Corporate address:
17 Academician Tupolev Embankment (Naberezhnaya Akademika Tupoleva), Moscow 111250.

Telephone: +7 095 267 2508 or 2533 and 261 2436
Facsimile: +7 095 261 7141 or 0868
Telex: 412439 YAUZA SU

Founded:
Lineage can be traced to Andrei Nikolayevich Tupolev's leadership of the AGOS department of the Moscow TsAGI from 1922.

Employees: 10,500.

Information:
Valentin Shoubin (Chief of Information); Elena Kutcherenko (*telephone* +7 095 263 7726).

ACTIVITIES

▪ Tupolev JSC undertakes the design, testing and production of aircraft, plus product support, combining with: Aviacor (International Aviation Corporation) JSCo at 32 Pskovskaya Str, 443052 Samara, producing Tu-154 airliners, Molniya business aircraft and more; the Taganrog Aviation Production Association; and the Aviastar organization producing the Tu-204 among other aircraft at the Ulyanovsk Industrial Complex. Tupolev's flight research centre is at Zhukovsky, where the Tomilino plant is also located.
▪ Military UAV programmes, including Tu-141 Strizh, Tu-143/243 Reys and Tu-300 Korshun.
▪ Co-operating with Daimler-Benz Aerospace on a cryogenic programme.

Tupolev Tu-16 (NATO name *Badger*)

Note: First flown on 27 April 1952, this intermediate-range bomber, reconnaissance, electronic warfare and tanker aircraft is virtually out of service, except in Chinese Xi'an H-6 form (which see). Full details and a photograph can be found in the 1996-97 edition of *WA&SD*, pages 97-98.

Tupolev Tu-22M (NATO name *Backfire*)

First flight: 30 August 1969 (pilot Vasili Borisov).
Role: Intermediate-range bomber/missile carrier, plus small number as reconnaissance aircraft, and an electronic warfare version tested.
Chief designer: Dmitri Markov until January 1992; thereafter Boris Levanovich.

Aims

▪ To replace Tu-16 *Badger* and Tu-22 *Blinder* medium bombers in performing nuclear/conventional strike against targets in Western Europe and China, as well as anti-ship missions (when the main targets are aircraft carriers).
▪ 2,000 km/h dash speed.
▪ Mach 0.9 low-level penetration of enemy air defences with wings fully swept.
▪ 900 km/h high-altitude flight with wings at 30°.
▪ Compatibility with previously used Kh-22 missile system of the Tu-22 *Blinder*.
▪ Maximum armament of 3 Kh-22 (AS-4 *Kitchen*) missiles.

Development

▪ 1965. Tupolev began work on the variable-geometry medium bomber project 145, or izdelye (product) 45, or aircraft A. Target data for project 145 in 1965 were as follows: length 134 ft 6 ins (41.0 m), wing span 77 ft 7 ins to 120 ft 5 ins (23.66 m to 36.7 m), take-off weight 231,485 lb (105,000 kg), and armament of a single Kh-22 missile. The design speed was 2,000 km/h, ceiling 17,000 m, supersonic range 4,000 km, and subsonic range 6,000 km.
▪ 1967. Final design was approved by the State Commission. Required speed 2,000 km/h and maximum range 7,000 km.
▪ 30 August 1969. First flight of Tu-22M0 prototype.
▪ 28 July 1971. First flight of a Tu-22M pre-production aircraft. Series manufacturing carried out at Kazan.
▪ 7 May 1973. First flight of the Tu-22M2 large-scale production version.
▪ 1975. First delivery to 185th Heavy Bomber Regiment of Guards stationed in Poltava, Ukraine.
▪ 1975. Work began on a modernization version designated Tu-22M3 (or aircraft AM, or izdelye 45.03).
▪ 20 June 1977. Maiden flight of the AM prototype.
▪ 18 June 1979. According to SALT-2 treaty, Soviets were obliged to delete the in-flight refuelling capability and not to increase the production rate of the Tu-22M.
▪ 1983. Tu-22M3 officially accepted for service with the Soviet Air Force.
▪ 6 December 1985. First flight of Tu-22MR reconnaissance version.
▪ December 1987-January 1988. Two squadrons of Tu-22M2s of 185th Regiment stationed in Poltava, operating from Mary air base in Turkmenistan, took action against forces blocking Khost, Afghanistan. Other combat missions were performed from October 1988 to January 1989 by 16 Tu-22M3s, including attacks on approaches to the roads being used by departing Soviet troops. Heavy and very heavy bombs (500-3,000 kg) were dropped from high altitude.

Details

Sales/Users: Manufactured between 1971-90 at the Kazan plant named after Sergei Gorbunov. Total of 514 produced (including

↑Russian Air Force Tupolev Tu-22M3 *Backfire-C* with wings spread *(Piotr Butowski)*

222 Tu-22M3 *Backfire-Cs*), only for the Soviet Air Force and Navy and never exported as such. In 1995 2 units belonging to the Black Sea Fleet (5th and 943rd Missile Carrier Regiments) stationed in the Crimea were divided between Russia and the Ukraine (20 for each country). At present, Russia has some 240 Tu-22M2/M3s, plus about 12 of 13 Tu-22MR reconnaissance variants produced. 134 belong to the Air Force, the rest flying with the Navy. Ukraine now has 70 Tu-22Ms, principally operating with the 185th Heavy Bomber Regiment in Poltava and the 260th Heavy Bomber Regiment in Stryi. Much detail of the deployment of Russian Air Force and Navy aircraft in 1995 can be found in the 1996-97 edition of *WA&SD*, pages 98-99. Those stationed in Estonia and Belarus at the time of the break-up of the USSR were assigned to the Russian Air Force.
Crew: 4, with 2 pilots side by side, the navigator and weapon system operator to their rear.
Cockpit: Conventional instrumentation and control wheels. Air conditioning, using engine compressor-stage bleed air; also for maintaining correct temperature for specialized avionics in other parts of the aircraft.
Crew escape: Tupolev KT-1 ejection seats (kreslo Tupoleva, Tupolev's seats), connected into the ASS automatic rescue system. A minimum speed of 70 kts (81 mph) 130 km/h is necessary for safe ejection at below 200 ft (60 m) altitude; at greater altitude there is no speed limit. LAS-5M life saving dinghies.
Fixed guns: Defensive armament of Tu-22M3 includes 23-mm GSh-23 double-barrel cannon (1 barrel above the other), with a firing rate equal to 4,000 rpm, installed in a UK-9A-802 tail turret that is remotely controlled by means of a PRS-4 radar sight (NATO *Fan Tail*) and TP-1 TV sight. Tu-22M2 has 2 × GSh-23 cannon in the tail turret and older *Box Tail* radar (the pre-production Tu-22M was given a large container with jamming equipment instead of cannon).

↑ Tupolev Tu-22M3 modified to carry the MKU6-1 rotary launcher for 6 × Kh-15 missiles *(Dmitri Grinyuk via Piotr Butowski)*

Expendable weapons and equipment: 52,910 lb (24,000 kg) maximum load, including conventional or nuclear free-fall bombs or mines, or 3 × Kh-22 (AS-4 *Kitchen*) missiles, 1 semi-recessed under the fuselage and 2 under the fixed wing gloves. The normal weapon load is 13,228 lb (6,000 kg) of bombs or a single Kh-22. 4 versions of Raduga Kh-22 are used: Kh-22M and Kh-22N with active-radar seeker (350 km range), and nuclear Kh-22MA and Kh-22NA with inertial guidance (510 km range). Since 1988, the Tu-22M3's fuselage Kh-22 can be replaced by an MKU6-1 rotary launcher (MKU stands for mnogozaryadnaya katapultnaya ustanovka, multiple launching device) carrying 6 × Kh-15 (AS-16 *Kickback*) inertial-guidance short-range attack missiles inside the weapon bay. It is also possible to replace all 3 Kh-22s with 10 Kh-15 missiles (6 inside the fuselage and 4 under the wings). Bombs can be carried suspended on KD-3-22R or KD-4-105A pylons inside the bomb bay as well as on 4 external MBD3-U9-68 multiple racks (2 under the engine air intake trunks and 2 under the wings, each rack carrying 6 × 500 kg bombs). Maximum bomb loads are, for instance, 69 × 250 kg, or 42 × 500 kg, or 8 × 1,500 kg (including guided bombs – according to some sources the aircraft carries UPAB-1500s), or 2 × 3,000 kg. The practical armament load does not exceed 12,000 kg, however, and normal is half this, as a greater load compromises the fuel carried.
Radar: Leninets/St Petersburg PN-AD navigation/attack radar (NATO *Down Beat*) installed under dielectric nose cone.
No automatic terrain avoidance capability (Tu-22M5 has terrain avoidance using new radar – see Aircraft variants). See also Fixed weapons for tail radar.
Flight/weapon system avionics/instrumentation: OBP-15 optical bomb sight in the fairing under the crew cockpit. AFA-15 photographic camera installed under the fuselage nose. The Tu-22M3 aircraft together with Kh-22 missiles and respective homing systems form the K-22M missile complex (K for kompleks, complex). Communication equipment (some secure type) includes 2 × UHF R-832M radios, 1 × HF R-846 radio and SPU-10 intercom. Autonomous and highly accurate NK-45 navigation system with automatic high/low altitude pre-programming, and automatic approach, includes a long-range navigation system, short-range navigation system, ARK-15 radio compass, SP-50 instrument landing system, and 2 × RV-18 radio altimeters. RI-65 voice information device.
Self-protection systems: Ural system consists of active and passive jamming, including SPS-171 and SPS-172 response jammers, AG-56 noise jamming generator with automatic tuning, and chaff/flare dispensers installed under the tailplane roots. L-082 Mak infra-red missile launch and approach sensor on top of the fuselage just behind the rear crew, and Sirena-3 radar warning receiver.
Wing characteristics: Variable geometry (see table). Large fixed glove centre-section. Hydraulic wing-sweep motors; wing panels motion synchronized.
Wing control surfaces: Fowler-type trailing-edge flaps (62° deflection) on the fixed glove sections. Each movable panel has 3 sections of double-slotted flaps (deflected by 23° for take-off and 40° for landing), and 3-section full-span leading-edge slats. No ailerons; control is performed by 3 sections of spoilers/lift dumpers on the outer panels and by differential deflection of the elevators.
Tail control surfaces: Slab type (tailerons), deflected +9°/-20° symmetrically or differentially. Large tailfin with rudder.
Flight control system: Hydraulic/electric.
Fuselage: Conventional semi-monocoque type. Circular cross section forward and more rectangular at the centre and rear.
Engines: Tu-22M3 is powered by 2 Samara NK-25 afterburning turbofans (designed by the SGNPP Trud team of Nikolai Kuznetsov in Samara, former Kuibyshev). Time from low to full thrust is 9 seconds; 18 seconds to full thrust with afterburning. TA-6 auxiliary power unit, installed in front of the tailfin root, supplies power for engine starting and for onboard systems. Original Tu-22M and Tu-22M2 used NK-22 turbofans of 44,090 lbf (196.14 kN – see Aircraft variants).
Engine rating: 31,526 lbf (140.2 kN) without afterburning and

Details for Tu-22M3 *Backfire-C*

PRINCIPAL DIMENSIONS:
Wing span: 76 ft 5 ins (23.3 m) *swept* (65°), 112 ft 6 ins (34.28 m) *fully spread* (20°)
Maximum length: 139 ft 4 ins (42.46 m)
Fuselage length: 126 ft 4 ins (38.5 m)
Maximum height: 36 ft 3 ins (11.05 m)

WINGS:
Area: 1,892-1,976 sq ft (175.78-183.58 m^2)
Aspect ratio: 3.088 *swept*, 6.401 *spread*
Sweepback of fixed gloves: 56° at leading edge
Sweepback of movable panels: 20°, 30°, 50°, 60° and 65° at leading edge
Anhedral/dihedral: 0°
Twist: -4° at tip

TAIL UNIT:
Tailplane span: 36 ft 11 ins (11.26 m)
Tailplane area: 664.13 sq ft (61.7 m^2)
Fin area: 355 sq ft (32.98 m^2)
Fin angle: 57° 15′ leading-edge sweepback

UNDERCARRIAGE:
Type: Retractable, with nosewheels. Main legs are attached to the fixed wing gloves, retracted into the wings while the wheels are partly retracted into the fuselage; each main bogie comprises 3 pairs of wheels in tandem. Nose leg has double wheels, rearward-retracted into the fuselage. *Backfire-A* pre-production aircraft had big wing trailing-edge fairings to enclose the retracting gear; the main gear comprised 6-wheel units with the central pair of wheels moved aside by 29.5 ins (75 cm) during extension
Main wheel tyre size: 1,030 × 350 mm
Nose wheel tyre size: 1,000 × 280 mm
Wheel base: 44 ft 4 ins (13.51 m)
Wheel track: 23 ft 11 ins (7.3 m)

WEIGHTS:
Maximum take-off: 273,373 lb (124,000 kg)
Maximum take-off with JATO rockets: 278,665 lb (126,400 kg)
Normal landing: 171,960 lb (78,000 kg)
Maximum landing: 194,007 lb (88,000 kg); can land at full weight in an emergency

PERFORMANCE:
Maximum operating Mach number (M_{MO}): Mach 1.8
Maximum speed at high altitude: 1,080 kts (1,243 mph) 2,000 km/h
Cruising speed: 486 kts (559 mph) 900 km/h
Take-off speed: 200 kts (230 mph) 370 km/h
Take-off distance: 6,562-6,890 ft (2,000-2,100 m)
Landing distance: 4,100-4,757 ft (1,250-1,450 m)
Time to climb to 26,245 ft (8,000 m) without afterburning: 20 minutes
Time to climb to 42,650 ft (13,000 m) without afterburning: 25-30 minutes
Turning radius at supersonic speed: 8.1-10.8 naut miles (9.3-12.4 miles) 15-20 km
Turning radius at subsonic speed: 2.7-3.24 naut miles (3.1-3.73 miles) 5-6 km
G limits: +1.6 *fully spread*, +2.5 *fully swept*
Ceiling at supersonic speed: 45,930 ft (14,000 m)
Ceiling at subsonic speed: 33,465 ft (10,200 m)
Radius of action at high altitude, some supersonic flight, with 1 × Kh-22, unrefuelled: 1,188 naut miles (1,367 miles) 2,200 km
Radius of action with 26,455 lb (12,000 kg) of weapons, subsonic at low altitude, unrefuelled: up to 898 naut miles (1,034 miles) 1,665 km

55,115 lbf (245.18 kN) with afterburning.
Air intakes: Wedge-type on Tu-22M3. Tu-22M/M2 were given slightly inclined intakes, with large vertical splitter plates.
Flight refuelling probe: Above-nose fairing replaced the in-flight refuelling probe after the 1980 treaty, but can be re-equipped.
Fuel system: 118,057 lb (53,550 kg) of fuel in tanks located in the fuselage and wings (including outer panels), plus in the fence in front of the tailfin. Standard fuel: T-1, TS-1 or RT.
Electrical system: 27 volt DC supply with 4 × GSR-20BK engine-driven generators (2 per engine) and 2 ni-cd batteries. AC supply with 2 × GT 60 NZHCH 12P generators for 3-phase 200/115 volt 400Hz, and 2 × TS 350SO4A transformers for 36 volt/400Hz 3-phase.
Hydraulic system: 3 separate systems, each 3,046 psi, for flight controls, wing sweep, undercarriage and brakes. Bottle-supplied pneumatic system, 2,132 psi.
Braking system: Hydraulic wheel brakes. Drag-chute carried in an under rear fuselage bay.
De-icing system: Electro-thermal de-icing of cockpit and sight windows, plus air intakes. Hot air deicing of inlet guide vanes.
Oxygen system: Gaseous type, via bottles.

Aircraft variants:
Tu-22M0 *Backfire-A* (or Tu-22KM, or izdelye 45.00, or 145, or A) prototype of 1969. NK-144-22 turbofans. Range 2,235 naut miles (2,570 miles) 4,140 km. Maximum speed 826 kts (951 mph) 1,530 km/h. Span 103 ft 8 ins (31.6 m).
Tu-22M1 *Backfire-A* (or 45.01) pre-series aircraft of 1971 appearance. Modified NK-22 engines and lengthened movable wing panels (maximum span 112 ft 6 ins, 34.28 m). Maximum range 2,700 naut miles (3,107 miles) 5,000 km, and maximum speed 896 kts (1,031 mph) 1,660 km/h.
Tu-22M2 *Backfire-B* (or 45.02) of 1973 appearance was the first large-scale production version. Equipped with new flight/navigational systems. 2 × GSh-23 cannon in the tail replacing the electronic jamming unit. Maximum range 2,753 naut miles (3,170 miles) 5,100 km, and maximum speed 972 kts (1,118 mph) 1,800 km/h.
Tu-22M2Ye of 1974 was an experimental aircraft powered by NK-25 turbofans.
Tu-22M3 *Backfire-C* (or 45.03, or AM) of 1977 appearance, is the improved version with more powerful NK-25 engines, and redesigned forward fuselage with larger wedge-type air intakes and upturned nosecone. According to Tupolev, the Tu-22M3's combat capabilities are 2.2 times higher than that of Tu-22M2.
Tu-22MP electronic warfare version equipped with Miass jamming system, developed from the Tu-22M3. Identified by US intelligence in February 1986 at Kazan. The second and third prototypes of Tu-22MP, built in 1992, were tested in 1994-95.
Tu-22MR is a reconnaissance version that entered service in 1989, equipped with Shompol SLAR, Tangazh elint, Osen IR sensor and photographic cameras. 13 built from Tu-22M3 airframes.
Tu-22M4 was the next version under development before 1991, when the programme was abandoned.
Tu-22M5 (or *245*) is a mid-life upgrade for Tu-22M3, started in 1992. The upgraded aircraft will be/are fitted with new radar with terrain avoidance capability and new missiles. The navigation systems, and the defence systems, are also thought to be modernized under the programme.

Tupolev Tu-95 (NATO name *Bear*)

First flight: 12 November 1952, piloted by Alexei Perelet. Current Tu-95MS first flew in August 1979.
Role: Long-range bomber, strategic, maritime and photographic reconnaissance, and electronic intelligence.
Programme manager: Nikolai Bazenkov (1951-1976), later Dmitri Antonov.

Aims

- Required speed of 900-950 km/h, and range of 14,000-15,000 km with a single nuclear bomb.

Development

- 11 July 1951. Andrei Tupolev assigned to build the Tu-95 intercontinental bomber.
- 12 November 1952. Maiden flight of the Tu-95/1 first prototype, powered by TV-2F turboprops.
- May 1953. Tu-95/1 was lost in an accident.
- 16 February 1955. First flight of the Tu-95/2 production prototype, with 4 × NK-12 turboprops.
- Summer 1955. First public presentation, during the Tushino Aviation Day fly-pass.
- Autumn 1955. First production aircraft left factory No 18 in Kuibyshev (Samara).
- August 1957. Tu-95M officially entered Soviet Air Force service.

↑ **Tupolev Tu-95MS *Bear-H*** *(Piotr Butowski)*

- 1969. Series production completed (restarted later).
- Summer 1968. First flight of the Tu-142 anti-submarine warfare derivative. See separate entry.
- October 1975. First flight of the Tu-95K-22.
- 1978. First test launches of the Kh-55 (AS-15 *Kent*) cruise missile from a Tu-95M-55 test bed.
- August 1979. First flight of the Tu-95MS.
- 1984. Initial operational capability of the first unit equipped with Tu-95MS heavy bombers, as the 182nd Heavy Bomber Regiment in Uzin-Shepelovka, Ukraine.
- February 1992. Final end to Tu-95MS production announced by President Yeltsin.
- 2005. Tu-95MS to be gradually withdrawn from service, to be replaced by the new stealth strategic bomber (see final Tupolev entry in this section).

Sales/Users: Production at Kuibyshev (becoming Samara) aviation plant. During the first production period (1955-69), 173 were built; 24 of these were in service up to 1997 (Tu-95K-22s of Long-Range Aviation) but it is thought that they have now been withdrawn for eventual scrapping. After a gap of about 13 years, series production of the Tu-95 was re-established at Kuibyshev (Samara). During 1982-92 more than 90 Tu-95MS *Bear-H* bombers were produced and are currently in service with the air forces of Ukraine (5 Tu-95MS6s and 20 MS16s at Uzin-Shepelovka, plus 1 Tu-95U) and Russia (2 Tu-95MS6s and 19 MS16s at Mozdok, and 26 MS6s and 18 MS16s in Ukrainka; see above for Tu-95K-22s). Under an agreement of early 1995, Ukraine was to return all the *Bear-Hs* to Russia, but in 1998 Russia reportedly decided against this move. 40 Tu-95MSs operated earlier by the 79th Heavy Bomber Division in Semipalatynsk (Kazakhstan) were handed back to Russia, with the last 4 returning on 19 February 1994.

Details *(general description applies to the Tu-95MS Bear-H)*

Crew: 2 pilots, navigator with access to astrodome, navigation/offensive weapons operator, defence systems operator, flight engineer, and tail gunner.
Cockpit: 2 separate pressurized compartments (cockpit and the isolated tail gunner's); 3 compartments in early aircraft produced between 1955-69. All crew (except tail gunner) enter the cockpit via the front undercarriage bay. Conventional instrumentation.
Crew escape: No ejection seats.
Fixed guns: 1 or 2 self-defence twin-barrelled 23-mm GSh-23 cannon in the tail turret, controlled by a radar sight (*Box Tail*). Tu-95K-22 had also a ventral turret with 2 guns.
Expendable weapons and equipment: 6 × Kh-55 (AS-15 *Kent*) cruise missiles on the MKU-6 rotary launcher inside the fuselage. Tu-95MS16 has an additional 10 × Kh-55s under the wings in 4 clusters (2 on each inner pylon and 3 on each pylon between the engines). Rearming of Tu-95MS is planned with 2 new subsonic cruise missiles, long-range Kh-101 (8) and medium-range Kh-SD (up to 14) missiles. Normal weapon load is 19,842 lb (9,000 kg), though the maximum is 44,092 lb (20,000 kg).
Radar: Obzor-MS navigation/attack radar (*Clam Pipe*) at the nose, with weather radar above. See Fixed guns.
Flight/weapon system avionics/instrumentation: NPK-VP-021 flight-navigation system. Satellite communication system. The aircraft is capable of taking-off with just 1,312 ft (400 m) visibility, and a 100 ft (30 m) cloud base, and land in under 3,280 ft (1,000 m) and with 328 ft (100 m) respective conditions. IFF antenna is mounted near the root of the in-flight refuelling probe.
Self-protection systems: Meteor-NM self-defence system joining Beryoza radar warning receivers at the nose and tail, Mak infra-red missile launch and approach sensor under the nose, Geran jammers at the nose and rear fuselage, and in pods under the tail turret, and 50-mm chaff/flare dispensers in the undercarriage fairings.
Wing characteristics: Swept, mid mounted, with marginal anhedral. 3 boundary layer fences on each wing. 4-spar 35° (at 25% chord) inner wing panels; 3-spar 33.5° outer wing panels.
Wing control surfaces: 2-section double-slotted trailing-edge flaps (Fowler-type flaps in aircraft produced between 1955-69)

↑ **Tupolev Tu-95MS *Bear-H* weapon bay, with Kh-55 cruise missiles on the rotary launcher** *(Dmitri Grinyuk via Piotr Butowski)*

Details for Tu-95MS *Bear-H*

PRINCIPAL DIMENSIONS:
Wing span: 164 ft 2 ins (50.04 m)
Maximum length: 161 ft 2 ins (49.13 m)
Maximum height: 43 ft 8 ins (13.301 m)
Fuselage diameter: 9 ft 6 ins (2.9 m) maximum

WINGS:
Area: 3,1210.5 sq ft (289.9 m^2)
Aspect ratio: 8.64
Sweepback: 35° (inner panel), 33° 30′ (outer panel), at 25% chord

UNDERCARRIAGE:
Type: Retractable, with steerable twin nosewheels. 4-wheel bogies on each main unit, retracted into the large fairings on the wing trailing edges, in line with the inner engines
Main wheel tyre size: 1,450 × 450 mm
Nose wheel tyre size: 1,140 × 350 mm
Wheel base: 48 ft 8 ins (14.827 m)
Wheel track: 41 ft 2 ins (12.55 m)

WEIGHTS:
Empty: 208,116 lb (94,400 kg)
Maximum take-off: 407,885 lb (185,000 kg)
Maximum in flight: 412,264 lb (187,000 kg), after in-flight refuelling
Maximum landing: 297,624 lb (135,000 kg)

PERFORMANCE:
Maximum speed: 448 kts (516 mph) 830 km/h
Maximum speed at sea level: 297 kts (342 mph) 550 km/h
Cruise speed: 397 kts (457 mph) 735 km/h
Take-off speed at 185,000 kg: 162 kts (186 mph) 300 km/h
Landing speed at 135,000 kg: 148 kts (171 mph) 275 km/h
Take-off distance at 185,000 kg: 8,334 ft (2,540 m)
G limit: +2
Ceiling: 34,450 ft (10,500 m)
Range without in-flight refuelling, normal combat load: 5,670 naut miles (6,524 miles) 10,500 km
Range without in-flight refuelling, maximum combat load: 3,507 naut miles (4,039 miles) 6,500 km
Range with single in-flight refuelling: 7,613 naut miles (8,761 miles) 14,100 km
Flight duration without in-flight refuelling: 14 hours

and 3-section ailerons (with tabs) on each wing. Spoilers on upper wing surface.
Tail control surfaces: Variable incidence tailplane, adjustable in flight according to the fuel used (1° down, 3° up). Elevators and rudder, all with tabs.
Flight control system: Mechanical, hydraulically actuated.
Fuselage: Semi-monocoque, circular section. About a 36 ft (11 m) long bomb bay in the centre.
Construction materials: Metal.
Engines: 4 Samara/Kuznetsov NK-12MP turboprops. Each 8-blade AV-60 K propeller unit comprises 2 × 4-blade co-axial contra-rotating reversible-pitch propellers.
Engine rating: Each 15,000 eshp (11,185 ekW) maximum power, 9,870 eshp (7,360 ekW) cruise.
Flight refuelling probe: Ahead of the cockpit, on the nose.
Fuel system: Maximum 185,188 lb (84,000 kg) of internal fuel in 8 wing and 3 fuselage tanks. No auxiliary tanks.
Hydraulic system: For actuators and undercarriage.
Braking system: Mainwheel brakes.

↑ **Tupolev Tu-95MS *Bear-H* flight deck** *(Peter J. Cooper)*

De-icing system: Thermal for wing and tailplane leading edges.

Aircraft variants (full list of in service and out-of-service versions in the 1996-97 edition of *WA&SD*, page 101):
Tu-95K-22 (izdelye VK-22) *Bear-G* appeared in 1975. Conversion of the Tu-95K/KD/KM armed with 2 Kh-22 (AS-4 *Kitchen*) ASMs. Also for electronic intelligence. SPS-100 Rezeda ECM in the extended tailcone and Siren ECM in the nose thimble. Leninets PN *Down Beat* nose radar. 24 were in service up to 1997 but now withdrawn.
Tu-95MS (izdelye VP-021, prototype designated Tu-142MS) *Bear-H* appeared in 1979. The main operational version, in MS6 and MS16 forms. As described.
Tu-96MS16 *Bear-H* is a variant of MS armed with 16 cruise missiles rather than 6 (MS6) by using underwing stations. In service.
Tu-95U is a training conversion of M series aircraft. Single aircraft in the Ukraine.
Tu-142 *Bear-F*, see separate entry.

Tupolev Tu-142 (NATO name *Bear-F/J*)

First flight: 18 June 1968 (pilot I. Vedernikov).
Role: Long-range anti-submarine warfare and communications relay, derived from the Tu-95. Also used to deploy submarine decoys to assist Russian Navy submarines attempting to leave sensitive areas.

Aims

▪ All-ocean operation at a distance of 5,000 km from base.

Development

▪ 28 February 1963. Governmental order for a long-range ASW aircraft based on the Tu-95 strategic bomber.

↑ **Tupolev Tu-142MR *Bear-J* communications relay aircraft, with underfuselage VLF antenna system** *(Piotr Butowski)*

▪ 27 July 1971. First operational flight over the Norwegian Sea undertaken.
▪ 14 December 1972. Tu-142 *Bear-F* was officially accepted for service with Soviet Naval Aviation.
▪ 1973. First identified in the West.
▪ 4 November 1975. First flight of the modified Tu-142M *Bear-F* mod 2, piloted by I. Vedernikov.
▪ 19 November 1980. Tu-142M with Korshun-K ASW system officially entered service.
▪ 1986. Tu-142MR *Bear-J* communications relay aircraft was first identified in the West.
▪ November 1990. A series of 10 world records set by Tu-142LL.
▪ 1993. Tu-142MZ officially accepted into service with the Russian Navy.
▪ 1994. End of production at Taganrog.

Details *(Tu-142MZ Bear-F mod 4, unless stated)*

Sales/Users: Produced during 1968-72 at Kuibyshev (18 built), with relaunch of second-series production in 1974 at Taganrog which continued until 1994. Some 55 Tu-142 ASW aircraft are thought to remain with Russian Naval Aviation, plus some 10 Tu-142MR *Bear-Js*, though an official US source suggests 72 ASW types, divided between the Pacific and Northern Fleets. 8 Tu-142MK-Es (*Bear-F* mod 3) are operated by India.
Crew: 11, as 2 pilots, 2 navigators, navigator/weapon system operator, 2 radio sonobuoy system operators, communications operator, self-defence operator, technician and rear gunner.
Fixed guns: 2 twin-barrel 23-mm GSh-23 cannon in the tail turret, controlled by a PRS-4 Krypton radar sight.
Expendable weapons and equipment: Maximum 19,842 lb (9,000 kg), normal 9,700 lb (4,400 kg) located in 2 fuselage weapons bays (1 in place of the bomber's ventral gun turret), with options including 3 AT-2M torpedoes or 3 APR-2 ASW missiles, depth charges (nuclear or conventional PLAB-250-120), mines, and up to 96 sonobuoys of RGB-1A (14 kg), RGB-2 (45 kg), RGB-16 (9 kg) and RGB-25 (45 kg) types. New armament of 8 Kh-35U (AS-20 *Kayak*) anti-ship missiles for all operational ASW Tu-142s, carried in pairs under the wings. Submarine decoys (see Role).
Radar: Leninets Korshun-N J-band 360° search/attack radar in an underfuselage radome. Small weather radar in the nose.
Flight/weapon system avionics/instrumentation: Korshun-N search/attack system consists a radar of the same name, Zarechye radio sonobuoy system, MMS-106 Ladoga MAD, on-board computer, and tactical data presentation system. Automatic data link for target acquisition. Satellite communication system.
Self-protection systems: Pastel RWR, Mak infra-red missile launch and approach warning sensor, Geran active electronic

↑ **Tupolev Tu-142MZ *Bear-F mod 4*** *(Piotr Butowski)*

↑ **Tupolev Tu-142MZ tail-gunner's position. Note the 2 twin-barrel cannon, fire control radar antenna above the glazing and the short-range navigation antenna directly below, and 2 ECM pods under the tail** *(Piotr Butowski)*

jammers, and 50-mm chaff/flare dispensers inside the main undercarriage fairings.

Airframe and Engines: As for Tu-95MS *Bear-H* (which see).

Fuel system: 189,597 lb (86,000 kg).

Aircraft variants:

Tu-142 *Bear-F* is a long-range ASW aircraft, with the Leninets Berkut-95 search/attack system of the Ilyushin Il-38 *May*, controlled by TsVM-263 Plamya computer. No magnetic anomaly detector (MAD). First 12 aircraft were able to operate from unprepared runways due to larger nosewheel tyres and 6-wheel rather than 4-wheel main undercarriage bogies (the undercarriage fairings on the wing trailing edges were much larger). Later, the standard undercarriage was fitted (*Bear-F mod 1*). Tu-142 *Bear-F mod 2* was the first version manufactured at Taganrog from 1974, with an airframe of the Tu-142M married to the old Berkut-95 system.

Tu-142M (design bureau name Tu-142MK, for Korshun) *Bear-F mod 3* was given the new Korshun anti-submarine search/attack system capable of detecting low-noise new-generation submarines. MMS-106 Ladoga MAD with an antenna located at the tailfin tip, PNK-142M INS and new Strela-142M communication system. Completely redesigned and more comfortable flight deck, with the fuselage nose lengthened by 3 ft 11 ins (1.2 m). Flight refuelling probe inclined 4° downward.

Tu-142MK-E became the export derivative of Tu-142MK, for India.

Tu-142MP was a prototype with an Atlantida search/attack system.

Tu-142MR *Bear-J* is a relay aircraft with an Oriol communications system. The main task is to ensure a communications link between the Russian authorities and the commanders of

↑ **Tu-142M *Bear-F* Flight Engineer's position, Training Regiment of Russian Navy** *(Peter J. Cooper)*

strategic nuclear missile submarines. The most important features include a ventral pod for the very low frequency trailing wire antenna installed in the forward bomb bay, satellite communications dome on the upper forward fuselage, and a forward-pointing pod on the tailfin. Tu-142MR was prepared by the Beriev design bureau at Taganrog.

Tu-142MRTs of late 1980s – early 1990s was a reconnaissance/target acquisition version expected to replace Tu-95RTs. 1 prototype only.

Tu-142MZ *Bear-F mod 4* was the last production version, appearing in the mid-1980s. New Zarechye (therefore Z in the name) radio sonobuoys system, and new self-defence systems. Chin mounted weather radar reintroduced (having been deleted on *mod 1, 2* and *3* versions). ECM thimble radome on the nose. As described.

Tu-142MZ-K (K from kommerchesky) was a proposed civil transport derivative of Tu-142MZ.

Details for Tu-142MZ *Bear-F mod 4*, unless stated

PRINCIPAL DIMENSIONS:

Wing span: 164 ft 2 ins (50.04 m)
Maximum length: 174 ft 1 ins (53.07 m)
Maximum height: 43 ft 11 ins (13.392 m)

WINGS:

Area: 3,121 sq ft (289.9 m²)

UNDERCARRIAGE:

Type: Similar to Tu-95
Main wheel tyre size: 1,450 × 450 mm
Nose wheel tyre size: 1,140 × 350 mm
Wheel base: 53 ft 6 ins (16.3 m)
Wheel track: 41 ft (12.5 m)

WEIGHTS:

Empty: 202,384 lb (91,800 kg)
Maximum take-off: 407,885 lb (185,000 kg)
Maximum in flight: 413,807 lb (187,700 kg) after an in-flight refuelling
Maximum landing: 297,624 lb (135,000 kg)
Payload of Tu-142MZ-K: 37,479 lb (17,000 kg)

PERFORMANCE:

Maximum speed: 462 kts (531 mph) 855 km/h
Cruise speed: 397 kts (457 mph) 735 km/h
Take-off distance: 8,300 ft (2,530 m) at MTOW
Landing distance: 3,937 ft (1,200 m)
Ceiling: 36,090 ft (11,000 m), practical
Range without flight refuelling: 6,475 naut miles (7,456 miles) 12,000 km
Duration with single flight refuelling: 17 hours

Tupolev Tu-160 (NATO name *Blackjack*)

First flight: 19 December 1981 (pilot Boris Veremey).

Role: Supersonic heavy missile carrier (not yet adapted for free-fall bombing). Projected escort interceptor and Burlak spacecraft launch platform.

Project manager: Valentin Bliznyuk.

Aims

■ Original aim was for a supersonic strategic bomber able to cruise at 3,200-3,500 km/h, and with a 16,000-18,000 km maximum range. Sukhoi T-4MS became the winning design before the requirements were scaled down (see below and Development).

■ 2 flight profiles to overcome enemy air defences: Mach 1.8 at high altitude armed with long-range stand-off missiles, or high subsonic speed at low altitude to defeat defences with short-range missiles or soften defences in preparation for the main attacking force.

■ Cruise at Mach 0.77 at high altitude.

■ Long-range platform for cruise missiles.

Note. Maintains a good safety record in service, with pilots finding the aircraft easy to fly.

Development

■ 1967. Competition opened for a supersonic strategic bomber (see first entry under Aims). Sukhoi T-4MS (winner) and Myasishchev M-20 projects participated.

■ 1970. Revised (scaled down) requirements called for a dash speed of 2,000 km/h, and maximum range of 14,000-16,000 km. At this stage of the competition, the Myasishchev M-18 was judged winner against Tupolev's Tu-144 airliner variant. Reportedly, because of inadequate production capabilities of the Myasishchev team, the design was handed over to Tupolev.

■ Spring 1975. Preliminary design accepted by state commission and technical design work began.

■ 1977. Full-scale mock-up accepted.

■ 25 November 1981. Tu-160 was reportedly photographed at the Zhukovsky test centre by an airline passenger. This was the first Tu-160 photograph published in the West. Provisionally named Ram-P.

■ 19 December 1981. First flight of the 70-01 prototype.

■ 6 October 1984. First flight of the second flying prototype 70-03 (70-02 was used for static tests).

■ February 1985. First supersonic flight.

■ 25 April 1987. First 2 Tu-160s arrived at the 184th Heavy Bomber Regiment of Guards at Priluki, Ukraine. First 10-aircraft Flight established before the end of 1987.

■ June 1987. First launches of Kh-55 (AS-15 *Kent*) cruise missiles from the Tu-160 performed by military pilots.

■ 2 August 1988. Frank C. Carlucci, US Defense Secretary, became the first person from the West to be given a close view of a Tu-160 (aircraft side number 12, Kubinka air base near Moscow).

■ 20 August 1989. Tu-160 was shown to the public for the first time during a fly-pass over Tushino airfield in Moscow.

■ 1989-90. Series of 44 speed, payload and altitude records were claimed, including a speed of 935 kts (1,075.8 mph) 1,731.4 km/h over a 1,000 km closed circuit with a 66,139 lb (30,000 kg) payload (class C-1-r, take-off weight up to 240,000 kg).

■ May 1991. An F-16A of 331 Sqn, Royal Norwegian Air Force, intercepted a Tu-160 off the coast near Tromsø.

■ May 1992. 184th Regiment in Priluki was taken over by Ukraine. Russia formed its own Tu-160 unit at Engels with 6 aircraft (121st Heavy Bomber Regiment). See Sales/Users.

■ August 1992. First public static presentation, at the MosAeroshow'92 exhibition in Zhukovsky.

↑ **Tupolev Tu-160 *Blackjack* with wings set at 20°** *(Piotr Butowski)*

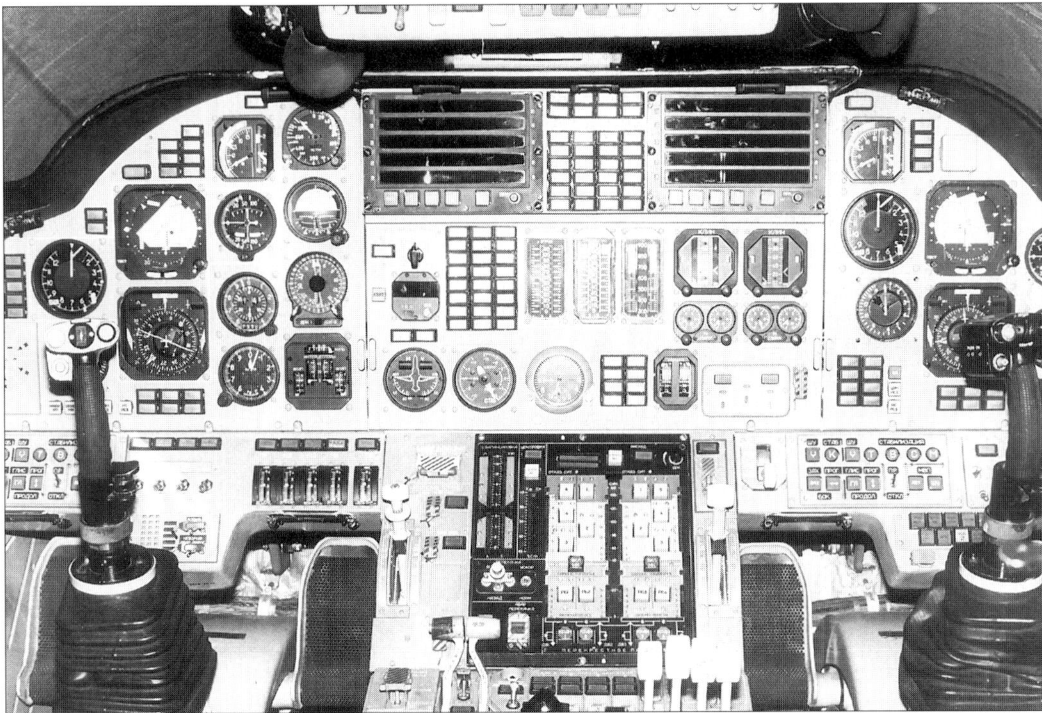

↑ **Cockpit of Tupolev Tu-160** ***Blackjack*** *(Piotr Butowski)*

■ 22 October 1992. First launch of Kh-55 missiles by Russian pilots (Lieutenant Colonel A. Zhikharev, commanding officer of the 121st Regiment).
■ June 1994. Manufacturing of Tu-160 in Kazan was halted due to financial restrictions.
■ Early 1995. Agreement between Russia and the Ukraine covered the return of all 19 available Ukrainian Tu-160s to the Russian Air Force, but this had not taken place at the time of writing.
■ June 1995. First international presentation, at the Paris Air Show.
■ June 1997. First visit to the USA, on the occasion of the 60th anniversary of the ANT-25 flight over the North Pole to the USA in 1937.

Details

Sales/Users: Series manufacturing at the Kazan aircraft plant named after S. Gorbunov. More than 30 built before June 1994. 19 in service with the 184th Heavy Bomber Regiment of the Ukrainian Air Force in Priluki (rarely flying; were to be returned to Russia), 6 with the 121st Heavy Bomber Regiment of the Russian Air Force in Engels (according to Russian TV, a seventh Tu-160 was being completed at Kazan), and 6 are at the Zhukovsky test centre. Mid-life upgrade is planned, comprising the rearming with new high-precision Kh-101 and Kh-SD cruise missiles.
Crew: 4, all in the nose cockpit. The front port-side seat is occupied by the commander-pilot, with the co-pilot at his side. The rear seats are occupied by the navigator/offensive weapons operator and the navigator/EW and communications operator.
Cockpit: Access via the nosewheel undercarriage bay. Small galley and toilet. Fighter-type sticks rather than the usual wheels or yokes. Conventional analog instrumentation, with no CRT displays.
Crew escape: Zvezda K-36LM zero-zero ejection seats, ejecting upwards.
Fixed guns: None.
Expendable weapons and equipment: Weapons are carried exclusively inside the fuselage in 2 tandem weapon bays, each 37 ft (11.28 m) long and 6 ft 4 ins (1.92 m) wide, with a volume of 1,518.5 cu ft (43 m^3). Basic armament comprises 12 Raduga Kh-55 (AS-15B *Kent*) cruise missiles installed on 2 × MKU-6-5U revolving launchers, 1 × 6-round launcher in each of the bays. Each missile is dropped mechanically from the lowest point of the revolving drum and then fired. Afterwards the drum is revolved 60° ready for the next launch. The weight of 12 × Kh-55s is 44,974 lb (20,400 kg). Alternative armament is the Raduga Kh-15 (AS-16 *Kickback*) short-range attack missile. 24 × Kh-15 missiles can be carried on 4 short MKU-6-1 revolving drums (in tandem pairs), the total load weighing 63,493 lb (28,800 kg). Theoretically, the Tu-160 is capable of carrying 88,185 lb (40,000 kg) of free-fall nuclear or conventional bombs but, as yet, has not been adapted for these types of weapons. Rearming is planned with 2 new subsonic cruise missiles, the 4,850-5,291 lb (2,200-2,400 kg) long-range Kh-101 (12 missiles per aircraft) and 3,527 lb (1,600 kg) medium-range Kh-SD (12 missiles).
Radar: Obzor-K navigation/attack radar and Sopka terrain-following radar in the nose.
Flight/weapon system avionics/instrumentation: OPB-15 optical bomb sight in the fairing under the nose. K-042K astro-inertial long-range navigation system, plotting the current position on the map. About 100 computers are used for the control of various onboard systems (including 12 computers for the fire control system). Interestingly, a single central computer concept was considered and abandoned during the course of aircraft design, believing a multi-computer system more reliable.
Self-protection systems: Baykal self-defence system, integrating warning devices, electronic countermeasures system and chaff/flare dispensers in the fuselage tailcone.
Wing characteristics: Variable geometry, with slight anhedral. Outer, movable panels are set for 3 manually-selected positions: 20° for take-off and landing, 35° for Mach 0.77 cruise speed, and 65° for supersonic flight. With the wings fully swept, the inner section of each 3-section trailing-edge flap is raised to become a large aerodynamic fence between the wing and the fixed glove to improve directional stability.
Wing control surfaces: Each movable wing panel has 4-section leading-edge slats, a 3-section double-slotted trailing-edge flap, and aileron. 5-section spoilers ahead of the flaps.
Tail control surfaces: Mid-mounted slab (taileron) tailplane, deflecting symmetrically or differentially. All-moving upper section of the tailfin, above the tailplane, forms the rudder.
Flight control system: Quadruple fly-by-wire, plus stand-by mechanical. Since the aircraft is statically unstable, the use of the mechanical control system is considerably limited.
Fuselage: The long and narrow fuselage/wing centre section (LERX type), blended for maximum radar deflection, is subdivided into 4 compartments: nose (radar unit, crew cockpit and nosewheel undercarriage unit), front (fuel tanks and front weapon bay), centre (main undercarriage units, engine nacelles and rear weapon bay) and rear (fuel tanks and equipment).
Construction materials: Mainly, if not entirely, metal (including 20% titanium).
Engines: 4 Samara NK-321 turbofans in widely separated pairs (to make room in the fuselage for the weapon bay) under the wing centre section, with the nacelles protruding far beyond wing trailing edge.
Engine rating: Each 30,865 lbf (137.3 kN) dry, 55,115 lbf (245.18 kN) with afterburning.
Nozzles/air intakes: Automatically adjustable nozzles. Adjustable air intake with vertical wedge for each pair of engines.
Flight refuelling probe: Retractable probe mounted in the upper part of the nose.
Fuel system: 326,284 lb (148,000 kg) of fuel in 13 tanks installed in the fuselage/wing centre section and the movable wing panels. The fuel transfer system is used to balance the aircraft when accelerating into supersonic speed.
Braking system: 3 drag-chutes of 1,130 sq ft (105 m^2) gross area.

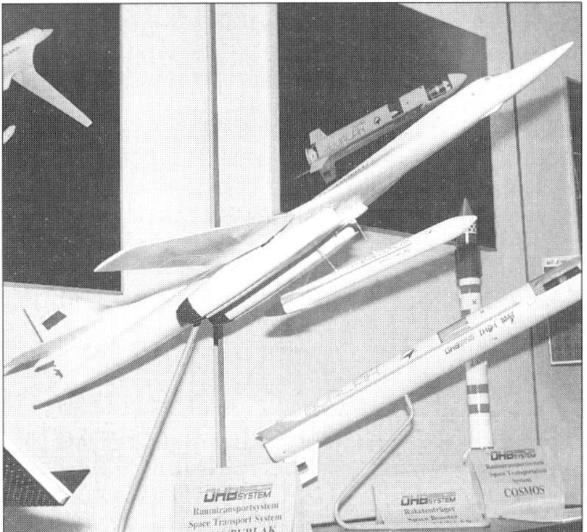

↑ **Model of the Tu-160SK with the Burlak space vehicle suspended under the fuselage** *(Piotr Butowski)*

Aircraft variants:
Tu-160 (izdelye 70, or izdelye K) strategic bomber, as described.
Tu-160P was a projected escort interceptor, armed with medium and long range AAMs. Programme has been cancelled.
Tu-160PP (postanovshchik pomekh) was a projected ECM escort aircraft variant.
Tu-160SK is a projected commercial version for use as a launching platform for the Burlak space vehicle (similar to the US Pegasus), as presented as a full-scale mock-up in Paris in 1995. Burlak was designed by the Raduga missile design bureau as an inexpensive low-Earth-orbital vehicle to carry a 1,819-2,425 lb (825-1,100 kg) load, depending on the orbital altitude. Projected Burlak-M with the additional hypersonic ram-jet engine could carry 50% more

Details for Tu-160 *Blackjack* bomber

PRINCIPAL DIMENSIONS:
Wing span: 116 ft 9.5 ins (35.6 m) *at 65° sweep*, 166 ft 4 ins (50.7 m) *at 35° sweep*, and 182 ft 9 ins (55.7 m) *at 20° sweep*
Maximum length: 177 ft 6 ins (54.1 m)
Maximum height: 44 ft (13.1 m)
Length of engine nacelle: 43 ft 7 ins (13.28 m)

WINGS:
Area: 2,497.2 sq ft (232 m^2)
Aspect ratio: 13.373 *at 20° sweep*
Sweepback: fixed at 20°, 35° or 65°

TAIL UNIT:
Tailplane span: 43 ft 6 ins (13.25 m)

UNDERCARRIAGE:
Type: Retractable, with twin nosewheels. 6-wheel main bogies (3 tandem pairs) retracting into the wing centre section between the weapon bay and engine nacelles
Main wheel tyre size: 1,260 × 425 mm
Nose wheel tyre size: 1,080 × 400 mm
Wheel base: 58 ft 8 ins (17.88 m)
Wheel track: 17 ft 9 ins (5.4 m)
Allowed angle of attack when landing: 12° 30'

WEIGHTS:
Empty: 257,941 lb (117,000 kg)
Normal take-off: 589,956 lb (267,600 kg)
Maximum take-off: 606,270 lb (275,000 kg)
Maximum landing: 341,716 lb (155,000 kg)

PERFORMANCE:
Maximum operating Mach number (M_{MO}): Mach 2.05
Normal maximum speed: 1,080 kts (1,243 mph) 2,000 km/h
Maximum speed at sea level: 556 kts (640 mph) 1,030 km/h
Cruise Mach number: Mach 0.77
Minimum speed at 308,650 lb (140,000 kg): 140 kts (162 mph) 260 km/h
Take-off distance: 2,953-7,218 ft (900-2,200 m) at 150-275 tonnes weight respectively
Landing distance: 3,937-5,250 ft (1,200-1,600 m) at 140-155 tonnes weight respectively
Climb rate: 13,800 ft (4,200 m) per minute, maximum
Practical ceiling: 52,495 ft (16,000 m)
G limit: +2
Practical range without in-flight refuelling, Mach 0.77, and 6 × Kh-55 missiles dropped mid range: 6,641 naut miles (7,643 miles) 12,300 km, with 5% fuel reserve
Maximum theoretical range: 7,532 naut miles (8,668 miles) 13,950 km
Maximum duration without in-flight refuelling: 15 hours
Combat radius at Mach 1.5: 1,080 naut miles (1,243 miles) 2,000 km

payload. Weighing 70,550 lb (32,000 kg), Burlak is suspended under the fuselage of the Tu-160, between the engine nacelles. Range of the Tu-160SK with Burlak will be 2,997 naut miles (3,450 miles) 5,550 km, and the spacecraft will be launched at 44,300 ft (13,500 m) altitude and 972 kts (1,118 mph) 1,800 km/h speed. An Ilyushin Il-76SK radar aircraft will provide control.

Tupolev Tu-204P

First flight: Expected before the year 2000.
Role: Medium-range maritime patrol, anti-submarine warfare, reconnaissance and target acquisition aircraft based on the Tu-204 airliner.

Aims

▪ To supersede a wide range of maritime aircraft, such as the now-retired Tu-16 *Badger*, Tu-22 *Blinder* and Tu-95RT *Bear-D*, plus the Il-38 *May* and Be-12 *Mail*.
Sales/Users: Order from the Russian Navy.
Crew: Probably 3 flight crew and 4 operational crew (including 3 systems operators).
Fixed guns: None.
Expendable weapons and equipment: Missiles, torpedoes, depth charges and sonobuoys inside a fuselage bay.
Radar: Leninets 360° search/attack synthetic aperture radar with air-to-surface and air-to-air modes.
Mission equipment: Leninets/St Petersburg computerized system named Sea Dragon that combines radar, electro-optics (FLIR and LLLTV), MAD, sonobuoy system, and ESM. Signal intelligence and photo reconnaissance equipment. Over-the-horizon mid-course guidance system for ship-to-ship missiles. Mission data shown to 3 operators, each station with 2 large (13.4 ins, 34 cm) colour liquid-crystal MFDs.
Self-protection system: RWR, infra-red missile launch and approach warning sensor, active electronic jammers, and chaff/flare dispensers.
Airframe, engines, dimensions, weights and performance: See Tu-204 airliner, probably Tu-204-200.

Tupolev Tu-2000

First flight: About the year 2010.
Programme Manager: Alexandr Pukhov.
Role: This general designation covers 4 designs projected under the Tupolev hypersonic programme. The Tu-2000A is a relatively small development aircraft, Tu-2000 is a Mach 25 aerospace vehicle, and the third and fourth designs are a Mach 6 bomber and passenger aircraft respectively.

Development

▪ 1986. Programme started.
▪ 1992. Work delayed considerably because of a lack of governmental financial support. Before that, some components of the Tu-2000A had been fabricated, including the 33 ft × 13 ft × 2.6 ft (10 m × 4 m × 0.8 m) wing torque box of nickel alloy, cryogenic fuel tank and fuel pipes of unique composite materials, plus some fuselage elements.
▪ June 1993. Tu-2000 model presented for the first time, at the Paris Air Show.

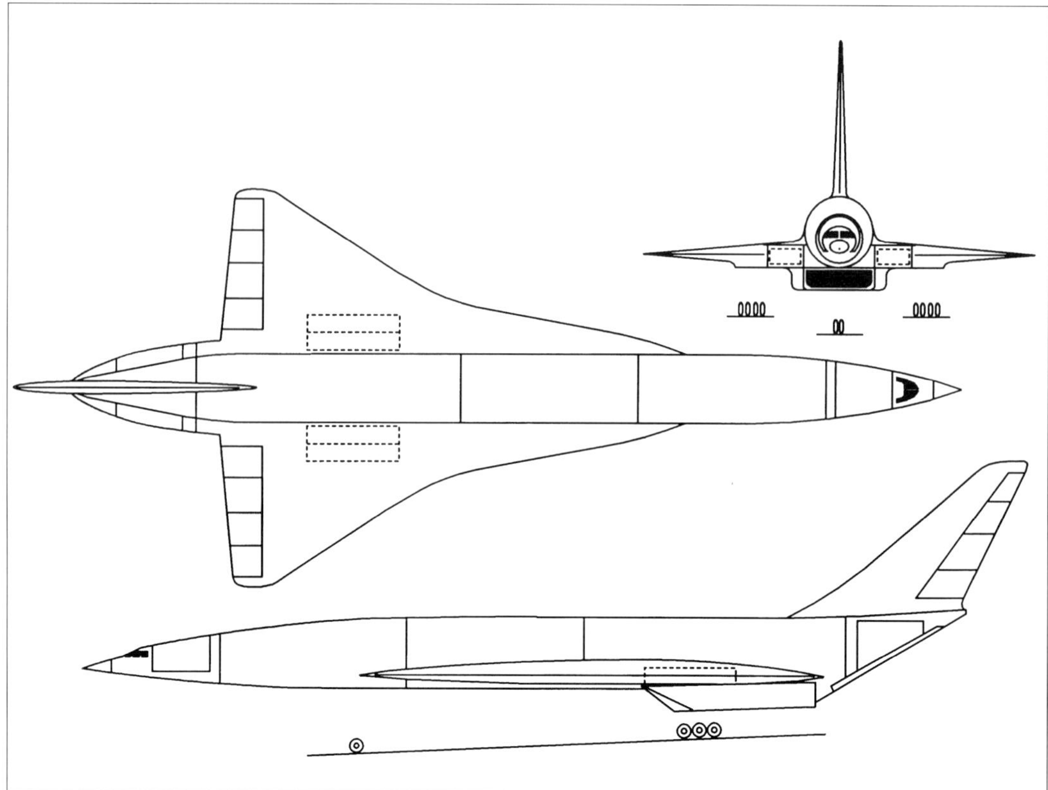

↑ Tupolev hypersonic bomber *(Piotr Butowski)*

Aircraft variants:
Tu-2000A is to be the initial experimental aircraft, reaching Mach 6 at 98,425 ft (30,000 m) altitude to research aerodynamics, propulsion and construction problems for operational hypersonic aircraft. Its weight will be in the region of 154,323-198,416 lb (70,000-90,000 kg), length 180-197 ft (55-60 m), and wing span 46 ft (14 m). 2 crew. Powered by variable-cycle turbojet/ramjet engines with liquid-hydrogen fuel.
Tu-2000 will be a much larger and faster single-stage aerospace vehicle, able to deliver a 17,637-22,045 lb (8,000-10,000 kg) load at a 108 naut mile (124 mile) 200 km orbit. It is said by Tupolev to be a 'multi-role system', featuring short reaction time, autonomy and flexibility of operation. Its maximum weight will be 573,200 lb (260,000 kg) and maximum speed Mach 15-25. It will include liquid-propellant rocket engines. The vehicle will be capable of operating from conventional runways at international airports.
Hypersonic bomber will have an empty weight of 440,900 lb (200,000 kg), take-off weight of 771,600 lb (350,000 kg), length 328 ft (100 m), wing span 133 ft 6 ins (40.7 m), and wing area of 13,455 sq ft (1,250 m^2). Powered by 6 liquid-hydrogen engines, it will reach Mach 6 at 98,425 ft (30,000 m) altitude and have a range of 4,850-5,395 naut miles (5,590-6,210 miles) 9,000-10,000 km. Weapon load will be carried in 2 bays inside the wing roots.
Mach 6 passenger aircraft has also been announced by Tupolev.

Tupolev New Strategic Bomber

Under development to replace the Tu-95MS bombers, which will be gradually withdrawn from service from the year 2005. The new bomber will be a subsonic stealth aircraft, simpler and less expensive than the Tu-160.

Yakovlev Joint Stock Company – A. S. Yakovlev Design Bureau — Russia

Corporate address:
68 Leningradsky Prospekt, 125315 Moscow.
Telephone: +7 095 157 5737
Facsimile: +7 095 157 4726
Founded:
1992 for Yak Aircraft Corporation (see Activities).
Information:
Yuri V. Zasypkin (Head of Information Department & Press Service – *telephone* and *facsimile* +7 095 158 3616).

ACTIVITIES

▪ Yakovlev Design Bureau is associated with the Saratov and Smolensk airframe manufacturing factories, under Yak Aircraft Corporation. Yakovlev itself has produced some 70,000 aircraft in over 100 types and modifications since 1927. See also Airliners and General Aviation sections.
▪ Work on the Yak-41 and Yak-43 VTOL combat aircraft has ended, as well as work on the shipborne Yak-44 AEW&C aircraft. For details and illustrations, see the 1996-97 edition of *WA&SD*, pages 104-105 and 180-181.
▪ It is a partner in Hyundai-Yak Aerospace Co Ltd, a South Korean based company aimed at developing, marketing and selling a wide range of small and medium sized aircraft.
▪ It is a partner with Aermacchi of Italy on the Yak/Aem-130 and Yak-131 programmes (see Multi-national section of Combat).
▪ Yakovlev is also involved in a programme for a new supersonic business jet for 10-12 passengers (preliminary design was complete in September 1997), as well as UAVs for military use.

UTVA — Serbia/Montenegro – Yugoslavia

Corporate address:
Jabucki put bb, 26000 Pančevo.
Telephone: +381 13 512 584
Facsimile: +381 13 519 859

Comments: The Super Galeb jet trainer and light combat aircraft, first flown on 17 July 1978, is thought not to have re-entered production as originally expected. Full details and a photograph can be found in the 1996-97 edition of *WA&SD*, page 106. According to S.C Avioane S.A. Craiova in Romania (partner in the IAR-93/J-22 Orao), the IAR-93/Orao programme has effectively been terminated. More recently, an agricultural aircraft has been put under development as the UTVA-95, said to be based on the UTVA-75 lightplane. This is to have a 2,000 litre hopper. Contact with the company in 1998 did not verify continued development.

Singapore Technologies Aerospace Ltd (ST Aero) Singapore

Note: Divisions, Subsidiaries and Associated companies were updated on 23 June 1998, according to new information received that day.

Corporate address:
540 Airport Road, Paya Lebar 539938.

Telephone: +65 2871111, 3806176
Facsimile: +65 2808213, 2809713
Telex: RS 43255 SAMKG
Web site: http://www.st.com.sg/STAero

Founded:
1975. Added "Technologies" to its name on 31 March 1995.

Employees: About 4,000.

Information:
Shirley Tan (Head, Corporate Communications – *telephone* +65 380 6176, *facsimile* +65 280 8213, *E-mail* shirleyt@st.com.sg).

ACTIVITIES

▪ Aerospace arm of Singapore Technologies Pte Ltd (STPL), recently restructured to concentrate on the core business of aircraft maintenance, systems integration and engineering services, including structural modification and refurbishment, engine and component overhaul, and repair and spares support. STPL has a 15% share in the AE31X airliner programme.

▪ Commercial Business Group (CBG) of STAe built upon its recovery of 1996 by increasing profits in 1997 (sales for 1997 S$674 million), principally due to its maintenance business, while the Military Business Group (MBG) remained its main business-generating division.

▪ Has conducted a re-engining programme on 52 of Singapore's A-4S/S-1 Skyhawk attack aircraft, installing the 11,000 lbf (48.93 kN) General Electric F404-GE-100D non-augmented turbofan. Other modifications included some minor structural changes. Under a later avionics upgrade programme, Super Skyhawks were assigned to receive Litton LN-93 laser inertial navigation, air data computer, GEC-Marconi 4150 head-up display, head-down display, and the ability to launch the Maverick missile. Modified aircraft are designated A-4SUs, with IOC declared in 1992. Details can be found in the 1996-97 edition of *WA&SD*, pages 107-108.

▪ Under the offered F-5 Tiger upgrade programme, a digital mission computer, air data computer, Litton LN-93 inertial navigation system, new wide-angle head-up display, HUD video camera and recorder, and HOTAS are installed. To these can be added the FIAR Grifo F multi-mode pulse-Doppler radar, VOR/ILS, Tacan, data transfer system, multi-function display and more, plus optional Elisra SPS-2000 radar-warning receiver, ECM, FLIR and other systems and expanded weapon options. Republic of Singapore Air Force's F-5 Tiger II interceptors and Venezuela's ex-Canadian CF-5s have been upgraded. Singapore's first squadron of upgraded F-5S/Ts reached IOC on 7 January 1998. ST Aero is to upgrade Turkey's F-5A/Bs, as part of a consortium.

▪ One-stop service centre for the C-130 Hercules, and an authorized service centre for Bell and Eurocopter helicopters. Has a 15% share of the Eurocopter EC 120 programme, for which it produces the tailboom, tailfins, cockpit pedestal and doors. Under a Boeing contract, it produces B777 nosewheel doors (100 sets, with option for an additional 100).

▪ On 16 August 1994, the company signed an agreement with the Russian Academy of Sciences to set up a joint venture company in Singapore to explore and commercialize the many innovative technologies and products developed in Russia.

▪ On 10 August 1994, Singapore Aerospace joined a consortium to establish a commercial aircraft maintenance facility at Shenzhen Airport in China. The joint venture is named Shenzhen Aircraft Maintenance and Engineering Company.

SUBSIDIARIES & ASSOCIATED COMPANIES

ST AEROSPACE ENGINEERING PTE LTD

HQ address:
540 Airport Road, Paya Lebar, Singapore 539938.

Telephone: +65 2871111
Facsimile: +65 2823236

Information:
Ho Yuen Sang (President).

Activities:
▪ Undertakes depot level maintenance, major modifications, structural repairs, retrofits, and assembly work for a wide range of civil and military aircraft.

ST AEROSPACE ENGINES PTE LTD

HQ address:
501 Airport Road, Paya Lebar, Singapore 539931.

Telephone: +65 2851111
Facsimile: +65 2823010

Information:
Chong Kok Pan (Senior Vice President/ General Manager).

Activities:
▪ With about 370 employees, it overhauls/repairs a variety of civil and military turbojet, turboprop and turboshaft engines, including the GE J85 and F404, Allison T56/501, AlliedSignal T53, PW F100 and JT8D, and Turbomeca Makila and Arriel.

ST AEROSPACE SYSTEMS PTE LTD

HQ address:
505A Airport Road, Paya Lebar, Singapore 539934.

Telephone: +65 2872222
Facsimile: +65 2844414

Information:
Ang Chye Kiat (Vice President/General Manager).

Activities:
▪ With about 420 employees, it repairs and overhauls a wide range of civil and military aircraft components and systems including propellers, servo actuators, undercarriages, pneumatic systems, radios, navigation equipment and gyros.

ST AEROSPACE SUPPLIES PTE LTD

HQ address:
540 Airport Road, Paya Lebar, Singapore 539938.

Telephone: +65 380 6282
Facsimile: +65 380 4757, 284 3637

Information:
Ambrose William (Vice President/General Manager).

Activities:
▪ With about 199 employees, it stocks and supplies a wide range of parts for civil and military aircraft, and is the material support specialist for the Singapore Technologies Aerospace Group. Consultancy services on major aerospace and defence programmes to OEMs.

ST AVIATION SERVICES COMPANY

HQ address:
11 Changi North Crescent, Singapore 499611.

Telephone: +65 545 0988
Facsimile: +65 545 6757

Information:
Stephen Low (Vice President/General Manager).

Activities:
▪ With about 430 employees, it provides heavy maintenance, structural repair and modification for wide/narrow-body commercial aircraft. Aircraft serviced include Boeing 707/727/737/747/757, Airbus A300 and (McDonnell Douglas) DC-10.

ST AVIATION RESOURCES PTE LTD

HQ address:
540 Airport Road, Paya Lebar, Singapore 939938.

Telephone: +65 3806192
Facsimile: +65 2809713

Information:
Sew Chee Jhuen (General Manager).

Activities:
▪ Provides aircraft leasing services.

ST AIRPORT GROUND SERVICES PTE LTD

HQ address:
540 Airport Road, Paya Lebar, Singapore 539938.

Telephone: +65 3806192
Facsimile: +65 2809713

Information:
Sew Chee Jhuen (General Manager).

Activities:
▪ Provides airport ground handling services.

ITS TECHNOLOGIES PTE LTD

HQ address:
77 Science Park Drive, #03-23 Cintech III, Singapore Science Park, Singapore 118256.

Telephone: +65 7788168
Facsimile: +65 7745971

Information:
Yong Thiam Chong (President).

Activities:
▪ Develops, markets and maintains advanced simulation and training systems for aircraft and other industries.

VISIONTECH ENGINEERING PTE LTD

HQ address:
540 Airport Road, Paya Lebar, Singapore 539938.

Telephone: +65 3806819
Facsimile: +65 2876164

Information:
Thomas Jeyaseelen (General Manager).

Activities:
▪ Provides engineering services for repair, maintenance and modification of aircraft, aircraft equipment and components.

ASSOCIATED COMPANIES

Asian Aerospace PTE Ltd
Composite Technology International PTE Ltd
Singapore British Engineering PTE Ltd
Singapore Precision Repair and Overhaul PTE Ltd
Turbine Overhaul Services PTE Ltd
Samaero Company PTE Ltd

OVERSEAS ASSOCIATED COMPANY

Aerospace Engineering Services PTY Ltd

OVERSEAS SUBSIDIARIES & INTERNATIONAL NETWORK

AIRLINE ROTABLES LTD

HQ address:
Building 6002, Taylors End, Stansted, Essex, CM24 IRL, UK.

Telephone: +44 1279 681770
Facsimile: +44 1279 681402

Information:
David Erridge (Vice President/General Manager).

Activities:
▪ Specializes in rotable component support for Airbus and Boeing fleets.

ST MOBILE AEROSPACE ENGINEERING INC

HQ address:
2100, 9th Street, Brookley Complex, Mobile, AL 36615, USA.

Telephone: +1 334 438 8888
Facsimile: +1 334 438 8892

Information:
Bob Tan (Executive Director/CEO).

Activities:
▪ Major inspection, heavy maintenance and modification of wide/narrow-bodied commercial aircraft, and conversion from passenger to freight configurations.

SINGAPORE TECHNOLOGIES AEROSPACE (DUBAI)

HQ address:
Suite 214-A, Galleria Hyatt, PO Box 6655, Dubai, UAE.

Telephone: +971 4 710872, 7064214
Facsimile: +971 4 720566

Information:
James Tan (Reg Director).

Activities:
▪ Marketing office for all aerospace related business.

SINGAPORE AEROSPACE KABUSHIKI KAISHA
HQ address: 1-19-3, Wakabacho, Tachikawa, Tokyo 190, Japan.
Telephone: +81 425 37 6005 **Facsimile:** +81 425 37 6882
Information: Taijo Sato (Representative).
Activities: ■ Marketing office for all aerospace related business.

SINGAPORE AEROSPACE (UK) PTE LTD
HQ address: Building 6002, Taylors End, Stansted Airport, Stansted, Essex, CM24 1RL, UK.
Telephone: +44 1279 681770 **Facsimile:** +44 1279 680598
Information: Bernard Cheong (Reg Director).
Activities: ■ Marketing and investment company.

DALFORT AEROSPACE LP INC
HQ address: 7701 Lemmon Avenue, Dallas, TX 75209, USA.
Telephone: +1 214 358 6019 **Facsimile:** +1 214 902 0938
Information: Stephen Lim (President).
Activities: ■ Specializes in complete aircraft and component maintenance, repair, major modification, and avionics services on a wide range of transport aircraft.

ST PAE HOLDINGS PTY LTD
HQ address: PO Box 213, Bullsbrook, Western Australia 6084, Australia.
Telephone: +61 8 9571 6170 **Facsimile:** +61 8 9571 6191
Information: Albert Chan (Director, Operations).
Activities: ■ Investment holding company.

AMD — South Africa

Full name: The South African Aerospace, maritime, and Defence Industries Association.
Address: PO Box 1750, Rivonia 2128.
Telephone: +27 11 315 5203 **Facsimile:** +27 11 315 2103
Founded: 25 September 1996.
Information: Leona Redelinghuys (Communications Manager).

ACTIVITIES

■ Superseded AIRASA (Aerospace Industry Representative Association of South Africa, founded 1992) and SADIA (formed in 1994 by Armscor management and leaders in the defence industry), as merged AMD to represent a wider grouping of companies involved in high technology and complex integrated mobility systems. Now represents approximately 95% of involved South African companies, on the first 2 levels of contracting, in the systems hierarchy, involved in research, development, manufacturing and maintenance of aerospace, maritime and defence equipment.

■ Aims include to encourage, promote, unify and protect the interests of the South African aerospace, maritime and defence industry, independently of the personal interest of any such entity; co-ordinate strategic thinking and planning; stimulate development both nationally and internationally; to offer collective national representation to Government and other interest groups on matters of policy; create a more favourable business environment for the industry; and establish and maintain a code of conduct for the Industry.

Denel Aviation — South Africa

Corporate address: Astro Park, Atlas Road, Bonaero Park, PO Box 11, Kempton Park, 1620.
Telephone: +27 11 927 9111, 9222 **Facsimile:** +27 11 395 1103, 2400 **Telex:** 742403 **Web site:** www.denel.co.za
Founded: 1964 registered as a private company.
Employees: 2,100.
Information: Patricia Wilson (Public Relations Manager – *telephone* +27 11 927 2726, *facsimile* +27 11 395 1524); Rodney Meier (Manager, Helicopter Workshops – *telephone* +27 11 395 1236, *facsimile* +27 11 927 3309); Martin J. Hutchings (Rooivalk Marketing – *telephone* +27 11 927 3304, *facsimile* +27 11 927 2181); Falk Willscher (Oryx programme – *telephone* +27 11 927 3359, *facsimile* +27 395 2346); Albert van Oldenmark (Cheetah programme – *telephone* +27 11 927 4446, *facsimile* +27 11 395 1664).

ACTIVITIES

■ Division of Denel (Pty Ltd), the holding company; Chairperson D.C. Brink and Managing Director Dr S.V.Chonco. In April 1996, Atlas Aviation and Simera of the Aerospace Group were merged into Denel Aviation, operating under the sub-divisions Tactical Aircraft Support, Transport Aircraft Support, Aircraft Manufacturing and Airmotive. A new computerized pilot training system has been developed by Apollo Informatics Training (AIT), a business unit of Denel Informatics, known as PATCOM (Pilot Academic Training Computerisation).

■ Development, production and logistical support of fixed and rotary-wing aircraft, plus production of gas turbine engines and related subsystems.

■ State-of-the-art maintenance services.

■ Products and capabilities include Rooivalk, Puma gunship and related Oryx, and Cirstel Alouette helicopter programmes; modification and upgrading of aircraft and their subsystems; capability to manufacture fixed-wing aircraft, engines, composite material structures and components, and aerospace quality sand castings; precision and vacuum investment castings; service and overhaul of airframes, engines, components and accessories including avionics, hydraulics, pneumatics, navigation and fuel systems; full-scale repair; flight testing under hot and high conditions; logistical support; and provision of manpower and training.

■ Details and illustrations of the ACE all-composite trainer, which has been cancelled, can be found in the 1996-97 edition of *WA&SD*, page 109.

■ Co-operating with DASA of Germany on the AT-2000 programme, with the proposal to sell 35-40 to the South African Air Force to replace the Impala. Also, undertaking closer co-operation with Aerospatiale of France under a March 1997 agreement, including aeroplanes, helicopters and missiles.

Denel Cheetah C and D conversion programme

Comments: See 1996-97 edition of *WA&SD* for standard Cheetah D, E and R details, pages 109-110, plus an illustration of Cheetah D.
First flight: 1986 for original Cheetah D.
Role: Multi-role fighter, fighter-bomber, and reconnaissance. Cheetah D is a 2-seat operational trainer.

Aims

■ Highly modified Mirage III, to maintain combat efficiency at a time when replacement aircraft were unavailable, through very extensive airframe, engine and avionics upgrades.

■ Continued development based on newly designed high-efficiency wings and a further avionics upgrade (including radar).

Development

■ 1984. Launch of the Cheetah programme, as an upgrade of the Mirage IIIEZ, DZ, D2Z, RZ and R2Z. Became almost a totally new design. Subsequent conversions also included 9 or more Cheetah D/Es from ex-Israeli Kfirs.

■ July 1986. First Cheetah was rolled out, as a conversion of a Mirage III-D2Z 2-seat operational trainer.

■ 1987. Initial operational capability.

■ 1994. Funding costs and figures for the continuing Cheetah programme were announced in the South African parliament, confirming the intention to re-wing aircraft and install new Elta radar.

■ 31 January 1995. Roll-out of a Cheetah D with the more

Details for Cheetah C, *with Cheetah D conversion 844 in italics*

WEIGHTS:
Payload: 12,346 lb (5,600 kg)
Maximum take-off: 35,715 lb (16,200 kg)

PERFORMANCE:
Maximum speed: Mach 2
Time to Mach 1.8 at 40,000 ft (12,190 m): *4.8 minutes, instead of 8.2 minutes for standard Cheetah D*
Time for 180° turn at Mach 1.8 and 36,000 ft (10,970 m): *1.1 minutes, instead of 2.1 minutes for standard Cheetah D*
Instantaneous turn rate: 17° per second
Sustained load factor: *6.7g at sea level, 3.8g at Mach 2 and 36,000 ft (10,970 m), instead of 6g and 2.8g respectively for standard Cheetah D*
Typical unrefuelled radius of action (attack mission): 300 naut miles (345 miles) 556 km, with bombs, tanks and AAMs

↑ **Denel Cheetah C releasing fire bombs** *(courtesy Herman Potgieter/Denel)*

powerful SNECMA Atar 09K50 turbojet of the Mirage F1, tail numbered 844. The rear fuselage of this aircraft had been fire damaged after a heavy landing at Louis Trichardt AFB, but examination had shown that the forward half and key systems were not seriously damaged. Starting on 7 July 1994, the rear fuselage and engine were removed, to be replaced by the rear fuselage of a retired Mirage IIIR2Z. A Cheetah C fin was attached, an Atar 09K50 engine installed and Cheetah C type single-piece windshield and undercarriage fitted. 844 flew again on 25 November 1994, with official roll-out the following January. Significant performance increases were displayed, including 16% more thrust at Mach 1.8 and 36,000 ft (10,970 m), and 10-20% shorter take-off distance. See performance box.

▪ 1995. Cheetah C production was completed after a 4-year programme.

▪ 1996-97. As part of the trials for South Africa's MUP-SOW multi-purpose stand-off weapon, the Cheetah was used to carry out a series of drop tests in order to gain data on the flight characteristics and motor performance of the missile.

Details *(principally Cheetah C, unless stated)*

Sales/Users: 38 Cheetahs were ordered for the SAAF under a 6,500 million Rand programme, including 21 of the latest multi-role Cheetah Cs delivered to No 2 Squadron at Louis Trichardt AFB by November 1994 (3 more may have followed in 1995); some 23 operational in early 1998, following the loss of an aircraft on 1 September 1997 close to the base. Cheetah D 2-seat operational trainers, early and unconverted E single-seat interceptors and fighter-bombers, and R and R2 reconnaissance fighters were put up for sale in 1994.
Crew: Pilot, or 2 in operational training versions.
Cockpit: Single-piece windscreen to improve forward vision.
Radar: EL/M-2035 on Cheetah Cs.
Wing characteristics: Advanced Combat Wing, first seen on a modified R2 and standard on Cheetah C, has slightly less sweep over the outer 20% of the leading edge, drooped leading-edges, and a squared-off tip to mount an AAM launch rail. Carries 260 litres of fuel in 4 leading-edge tanks, extending the tactical radius of action by 55 naut miles or loiter time at 150 naut mile radius by 10 minutes. It offers the capability of stable flight at speeds as low as 80 kts (92 mph) 148 km/h at 33° angle of attack, and a higher sustained turn rate.
Canard: Swept, clipped delta type, fixed to the air intake sides.
Engine: SNECMA Atar 09K50 turbojet, taken from decommissioned Mirage F1s, but with improved reliability. The Russian Klimov RD-33 of approximately similar dry thrust but with much higher augmented rating, had been flight tested in a Cheetah as a possible new power source.
Engine rating: 11,060 lbf (49.2 kN) dry, 15,846 lbf (70.49 kN) with afterburning.
Flight refuelling probe: Fixed to the starboard side of the cockpit.

Aircraft variants:
Cheetah C was the final multi-role combat conversion, representing modified Es with Elta EL/M-2035 radar and the new low-drag wings. Avionics installed by IAI's Bedek Aviation.
Cheetah D 844 2-seater, see Development.

Construcciones Aeronáuticas, S.A. (CASA) — Spain

Corporate address:
Avda. de Aragón, 404– 28022 Madrid.

Telephone: +34 91 585 70 00, 73 75
Facsimile: +34 91 585 74 57, 73 66, 76 66
Telex: 41696/41726 CASA E

Founded:
1923.

Employees:
over 8,000.

Chairman/CEO:
Alberto Fernández Fernández (nominated July 1997).

Information:
Jose Mª Sanmillán (Public Relations and Press – *telephone* +34 91 585 72 68, *facsimile* +34 91 585 72 74).

ACTIVITIES

▪ By July 1998, the world distribution of current CASA aircraft amounted to 460 C-212s (209 to 57 civil operators in 24 countries and 251 to 31 military operators in 23 countries), 134 CN 235s (12 to 5 civil operators in 3 countries and 122 to 18 military operators in 16 countries), and 151 C-101s (151 military to 4 operators in 4 countries); CN 235 figures for Spanish production only.

DIVISIONS

AIRCRAFT DIVISION

Activities:
▪ Complete design of aircraft and integrated structures (its own and those related to multi-national manufacturing programmes), with a high degree of industrial automation in the production processes. At the forefront of the design and manufacture of large composite material structural elements.
▪ Product Support Service puts the aircraft into service and integrates it into the operator's organization. Offers an integral package of courses for all levels of flight and ground crews.
▪ Multi-national programmes include Airbus (4.2% share), FLA and Eurofighter.
▪ Research, design and manufacture of structural parts and components for other aircraft, including contracts with Boeing (B757 flaps, plus MD-11 tailplane, F/A-18, and final assembly and flight testing Harrier II Plus), Eurocopter, Northrop Grumman, and Saab (Saab 2000 wings – see Saab entry in Airliners section).
▪ The C-101 Aviojet was confirmed in early 1998 as an on-going programme, together with the C-212 Aviocar in Series 300 and 400 forms, and the CN 235 via Airtech (see also Multi-national sub-section of Combat for Airtech Persuader and the Airliners section).
▪ A proposed attack aircraft is the ATX, which could replace upgraded F-5s early next century.

MAINTENANCE DIVISION

Activities:
▪ Modernization of aircraft and weapon systems. Over 7,900 aircraft have passed through this division's facilities to be serviced, checked or modernized, including AV-8 Harrier, BO 105, SH-3D, Super Puma, F-4, F-5, F-15, F/A-18, and Mirage III/F1s.
▪ Current work includes a life extension programme for Spanish F-5s, and modernization of Mirage F1s and C-130s.

SPACE DIVISION

Activities:
▪ Develops high stability mechanical subsystems, service modules, direct broadcasting reflector antennae, power distribution networks, robotics and animation software.
▪ In co-operation with the European Space Agency, participates on scientific programmes, telecommunications ventures, transport systems, platform and earth tracking instrument programmes, and a large number of technologically related projects.
▪ Produces the first-stage skirts (forward and intertank) for Ariane 4, plus the equipment bay structure, payload adaptors, safety and switching boxes, and a set of POGO valves. For Ariane 5, develops the upper stage EPS-support and equipment-bay structures, and more.
▪ Also participates in the Helios, Spot 4, Eutelsat II, Hispasat, Huygens, Soho, Envisat, Metop, Minisat 01 and Polar Platform programmes.

CASA ATX

First flight: Not yet flown.
Role: Family of aircraft suited to advanced, tactical and weapon lead-in training, plus multi-role missions including interdiction, air defence and reconnaissance.

Aims

▪ Future European trainer/attack aircraft. Based on a requirement of the Spanish Air Force for an F-5B replacement.
▪ Representative of the latest generation of first-line fighters in terms of handling qualities, agility, performance, systems technology and cockpit displays.
▪ Partner being actively sought.

Development

▪ 1989. Original studies began under Spanish Government auspices, adopting the designation AX (see the 1996-97 edition of *WA&SD*, page 110).
▪ 1998. Possible start of the development phase.
▪ 2004. Expected service entry date as an F-5B replacement.

Details

Sales/Users: Being developed initially for the Spanish Air Force.
Crew: 2 in tandem cockpits for trainers; possible single-seat combat versions. Rear cockpit raised to improve forward view.
Cockpit: Modern 'glass' cockpit expected. Single-piece canopy plus moulded forward windshield. No further details at time of writing.
Fixed guns: Possibly an internal starboard-side gun for training and close-in combat, carried in the chine.
Number of weapon pylons: Includes wingtip launch rails for AAMs and an underfuselage centreline 'wet' station.
Expendable weapons and equipment: Wingtip AAMs plus practice/attack weapons, depending on role.
Self-protection systems: Optional passive/active ECM capabilities.
Radar: Optional multi-mode.
Flight/weapon system avionics/instrumentation: 'Glass' cockpit with MFDs in the fully integrated digital avionics system. Front cockpit has a HUD.
Wing/fuselage characteristics: Shoulder-mounted wings of conventional planform, with swept leading edges. Chines at the wingroots, forming LERX forward and continuing the full length of the rear fuselage, almost certainly housing the gun, APU, major hydraulic components, and airbrake actuators.
Wing control surfaces: Leading-edge flaps, and trailing-edge flaps and ailerons.
Tail control surfaces: All-moving tailerons. Conventional fin with inset rudder.
Flight control system: Digital fly-by-wire.
Airbrakes: Mounted to the rear of the fuselage chines.
Engine: Single afterburning engine with an estimated BME of between 11,023-12,125 lb (5,000-5,500 kg) and rating of 16,000 lbf (71.17 kN), but thrust range option of 70-90 kN. Choices include the Eurojet EJ200 and General Electric F-404/414.
Air intakes: On lower fuselage sides, below chines/LERX.

Details for ATX

PRINCIPAL DIMENSIONS:
Length: 43 ft (13.1 m)

WINGS:
Area: 236.81 sq ft (22 m^2)

WEIGHTS:
Take-off: 18,960 lb (8,600 kg) clean
Maximum: 27,117 lb (12,300 kg)

PERFORMANCE:
Maximum Mach number: Mach 1.5
Sustained turn rate: 12° per second at 15,000 ft (4,570 m)
Range, interdiction mission: 300 naut miles (345 miles) 556 km, Lo-Lo-Lo, with 6 × Mk 82 bombs

↑ Concept design for the CASA ATX advanced trainer/attack aircraft

CASA C-101 Aviojet

First flight: 27 June 1977.
Role: Basic, advanced and lead-in trainer, ground attack and tactical support, and special missions including target towing; can undertake reconnaissance, armed patrol, point defence, and forward air control.

Aims

- Optimum cost/efficiency ratio.
- Modular airframe design.
- 10,000 flight hour structural life.
- Minimum maintenance using a Progressive Maintenance Programme, allowing a rate of under 4 man-hours per flight hour, including third level.

Development

- 16 September 1976. Spanish Ministry of Air and CASA signed an agreement for development and 6 prototypes (4 flying, 2 static). Northrop of the USA and MBB of Germany assisted design.
- 27 June 1977. First flight of the first flying prototype.
- 30 September 1977. First flight of the second flying prototype.
- 1978. Third and fourth flying prototypes made their maiden flights on 26 January and 17 April.
- 17 March 1980. First production C-101 EBs entered service with the Spanish General Air Academy to equip Squadron 793.
- 16 November 1983. Maiden flight of the C-101 CC attack version.

Details

Sales/Users: 151 delivered by early 1998. 92 C-101 EBs were delivered to the Spanish Air Force as E.25 Mirlos, serving with the General Air Academy (see Development), plus the Practice Group where refresher courses are undertaken together with a series of special missions including target towing, and also equips the Aguila aerobatic display team. ENAER in Chile assembled examples as Halcóns for the Chilean Air Force (which see), and CASA exported 4 C-101BBs to Honduras (operating from Comayagua) and 16 to Jordan in C-101 CC form.
Crew: 2, the instructor's rear seat raised by 13 ins (32 cm).
Cockpit: HOTAS, etc (see Avionics). Accommodates crew members between the 3rd and 99th percentiles. Front cockpit vision below the horizon is 15°; 9° from the rear seat. Duplicated instruments and controls in the cockpits, with rear cockpit command priority for flight safety. 2 independent canopy sections, hinged sideways. Internal transparent screen protects the instructor in the event of front pilot ejection. Automatic pressurization at 8,000 ft (2,440 m), maintained to 19,685 ft (6,000 m), above which 4.07 psi pressure differential is maintained; bleed air system. Cockpit temperature selectable between 18° and 29° C.
Crew escape: Martin Baker Mk 10 zero-zero ejection seats.
Fixed guns: See below.
Ammunition: 130 cannon rounds, or 220 rounds per machine-gun.
Number of weapon pylons: 6 under the wings (500 kg, 375 kg and 250 kg capacity each wing set) plus a central fuselage station for a 30-mm DEFA 553 cannon or 2 × 12.7-mm Browning machine-gun pod.
Expendable weapons and equipment: 4,000 lb (1,814 kg) at maximum take-off weight. Options include rocket launchers, bombs, 2 Maverick air-to-surface missiles or 2 air-to-air missiles (Magic or Sidewinder).
Flight/weapon system avionics/instrumentation: C-101 CC version includes communication and identification system, as well as a navigation system built around a flight director and Lear Siegler gyroscope platform. DD version is equipped with an integrated nav/attack system built around a HUD, and interconnected through a 1553B digital databus. Standard C-101 communications equipment comprises Andrea intercom, Collins VHF, Magnavox/Collins UHF, Teledyne IFF/SIF and Dorne Margolin ELT. Nav/attack comprises Collins Tacan, VOR/ILS/MK, DME and ADF, plus CASA armament control. C-101 CC has an Avimo gunsight, Lear Siegler gyro platform and Sperry flight director. C-101 DD has a GEC-Marconi FD4513 HUD (incorporating CCIP mode for attack, and CT and CCIL modes for air-to-air combat), Litton inertial platform, Alenia mission computer, Microtecnica air data computer, Alenia radar altimeter, MIL-STD-1553B digital databus, and HOTAS.
Self-protection systems: Optional Gen. Instrument radar warning receiver, and Vinten chaff/flare system.
Wing characteristics: Single-piece, 3-spar, straight, and low mounted, attached to the fuselage by 6 bolts. Use of advanced aerofoil technology offers lower aerodynamic drag with greater thickness and structural strength.
Wing control surfaces: Ailerons (with tabs) and flaps.
Tail control surfaces: Variable incidence tailplane. Elevator and rudder, latter with trim tab. 2 ventral fins at the rear fuselage increase directional stability (particularly for weapon launching).
Airbrakes: Under the central fuselage, hydraulically operated.
Flight control system: Mechanical, except for hydraulically actuated ailerons and flaps. Electric trim tabs and electrically actuated tailplane incidence.
Construction materials: Conventional, but using modern manufacturing techniques and materials such as numerically controlled integral machining, honeycomb and composites.
Engine: AlliedSignal TFE731-5J in the C-101CC and DD (see Aircraft variants for other engines).
Engine rating: 4,300-4,700 lbf (20.91 kN) at take off.
Air intakes: Above the wings, ahead of the leading edges, at sufficient height to eliminate all FOD problems.
Flight refuelling probe: None.
Fuel system: Flexible bag fuselage tank and 3 integral wing tanks. Normal capacity (no outer wing tankage) of 1,730 litres; 2,972 lb (1,348 kg). Total internal capacity 2,414 litres; 4,148 lb (1,881 kg). Single pressure refuelling point, providing 1,670 litres in 3 minutes; also independent gravity point for each tank. Allowable 30 seconds inverted flight. No drop tanks.
Electrical system: 28 volt, 9kW DC starter-generator, driven by the engine high-pressure spool acting through the accessory gearbox. 2 × 24 volt, 23 amp-hour ni-cd batteries for emergency use, and can be used to start the engine. 2 × 700 VA static inverters with 115 volt and 26 volt single-phase current outputs for the AC supply for the lighting and navigation equipment.
Hydraulic system: 3,000 psi for flaps, airbrake, aileron boosters, undercarriage wheel brakes and anti-skid devices. In the event of a failure, back-up systems operate the undercarriage, aileron boosters and wheel brakes. Nitrogen reservoir supplies the pressure needed to lower the undercarriage, the aileron booster subsystem has an accumulator to provide power for roll control in an emergency, and an accumulator provides emergency power for the brakes.
Braking system: Hydraulic brakes, and anti-skid devices.
Oxygen system: Gaseous, in 2 high-pressure bottles, for up to 8 hours for both crew members. An emergency bottle by each seat.

Aircraft variants:
C-101EB trainer, used by Spain as the E.25 Mirlo. 3,500 lbf (15.57 kN) AlliedSignal TFE731-2J turbofan engine.

↑ Jordan received 16 CASA Aviojets in C-101 CC form

Details for C-101 CC and DD

PRINCIPAL DIMENSIONS:
Wing span: 34 ft 9.5 ins (10.6 m)
Maximum length: 41 ft (12.5 m)
Maximum height: 13 ft 11.5 ins (4.25 m)

WINGS:
Aerofoil section: NORCASA-15
Area: 215.28 sq ft (20 m^2)
Aspect ratio: 5.618
Incidence: 1°
Dihedral: 5°

TAIL UNIT:
Tailplane span: 14 ft 2 ins (4.32 m)
Tailplane area: 37.028 sq ft (3.44 m^2)

UNDERCARRIAGE:
Type: Retractable, with nosewheel
Wheel track: 10 ft 5 ins (3.18 m)

WEIGHTS:
Empty: 7,650 lb (3,470 kg) equipped
Typical training weight: 9,590 lb (4,350 kg) with 50% normal fuel
Maximum take-off and landing: 13,889 lb (6,300 kg)

PERFORMANCE:
Maximum dive speed: Mach 0.8
Maximum speed: 450 kts (518 mph) 833 km/h
Take-off speed: 110 kts (127 mph) 204 km/h
Undercarriage retraction speed: 200 kts (230 mph) 370 km/h
Stall speed: 85 kts (98 mph) 158 km/h, *with flaps*
Landing speed: about 90 knots (104 mph) 167 km/h
Take-off distance: 1,838 ft (560 m)
Landing distance: 1,575 ft (480 m)
Maximum climb rate: 6,400 ft (1,950 m) per minute
Time to 25,000 ft (7,620 m): 6 minutes 30 seconds
Roll rate: 180° per second
G limits: +7.5, -3.9
Maximum sustained load factor: 4.6
Ceiling: 44,000 ft (13,400 m)
Training mission time: 2 hours 15 minutes, with full normal fuel
Range with full fuel: 2,000 naut miles (2,300 miles) 3,700 km
Duration: 7 hours

C-101 BB armed trainer, powered by a 3,700 lbf (16.46 kN) TFE731-3J engine. Used by Chile as the Halcón, and Honduras.
C-101 CC is a higher performing attack and training version, operated by Chile as the Halcón and Jordan. TFE731-5J engine.
C-101 DD is the latest version, equipped with an integrated nav/attack system built around a HUD (see Avionics). TFE731-5J engine. The Continuously Computed Impact Point (CCIP) mode for air-to-ground attack and the Continuous Tracking (CT) and Continuous Computed Impact Line (CCIL) modes for air-to-air combat, enable training in most modern combat techniques.

CASA C-212 MP, ASW and DE Patrullero

Role: Maritime patrol, EEZ patrol, anti-submarine, counter-insurgency, search and rescue, environmental/resources, and electronic warfare variants of the Aviocar STOL transport.

Aims

- See C-212 Aviocar entry in the Freighters section for more general Aims and Development.
- High-wing configuration, together with FOD resistant engines and tough, wide-track undercarriage with low-pressure tyres, offer easy operation from unpaved airstrips (up to 150 passes over CBR = 3.5).
- Good low-altitude flight capability, good cabin visibility, and over 9 hours endurance (with drop tanks) for special missions.
- Possible use of FLIR, search radar and related systems, plus weapons capability.
- Effective for electronic warfare, including electronic support measures, electronic countermeasures, electronic intelligence, and airborne early warning. Other missions can include photogrammetric, navigation training, and geophysical survey.

Sales/Users: Derived from the 100, 200, 300 and the latest 400 series Aviocar. Deliveries of at least 54 of these specialized variants (among a total of 250 military/government sales of the C-212) to Angola (MP), Argentina (navy C-212-300MP), Indonesia (navy C-212-200MP and DE), Jordan (C-212-100 for survey), Mexico (navy C-212-200MP), Portugal (C-212-100/300 in MP and DE forms), Spain (customs C-212-200MP, air force C-212-100/200 types), Sweden (coast guard C-212-200 type, navy C-212-200 used for ASW), Uruguay (C-212-200MP), and Venezuela (navy

↑ **Portugal operates C-212-300s in MP and DE forms**

C-212-200/400MP). See full list of military versions of C-212 in the Freighter section.
Crew: 2 pilots, plus a radar operator and 2 observers (with use of bulged windows) in the main MP maritime patrol version; pilots plus a radar/ESM operator, tactical controller with MAD, and acoustic controller, plus 1 more for ASW anti-submarine warfare version; or pilot plus up to 4 persons in the main cabin of the photogrammetric version.
Fixed guns: None.
Number of weapon pylons: 2, on fuselage outriggers.
Expendable weapons and equipment: 1,102 lb (500 kg) load on the outrigger pylons for 2 Sea Skua anti-ship missiles, 2 Mk 46 Sting Ray smart torpedoes, 2 bombs of up to 250 kg each, LAU-3A or LAU-32 rocket launchers, 20-mm cannon pods, or 2 × 12.7 or 2 × twin 7.62-mm machine-gun pods. Alternative AS.15TT anti-ship missile. Equipment for the maritime patrol and anti-submarine versions also includes sonobuoys and smoke markers.
Radar: Aircraft variants.
Flight/weapon system avionics/instrumentation: Communications equipment includes interphone, 2 VHF, HF and ATC/transponder. Navigation includes 2 VOR/ILS, 2 ADF, DME and weather radar. Flight control includes AFCS and radio altimeter. Optional avionics include VHF/UHF- AF/FM com, IFF/SIF, VLF/Omega, Tacan and an emergency locator transmitter. See also Aircraft variants.
Optional equipment: FLIR/TV sensors, data link and searchlight; for environmental/traffic/resources work can have SLAR, IR/UV scanner, microwave radiometer, therman radiometer and other compatible sensors.
Fuel system: 2,000 litres (usable) in the wings, plus 1,000 litres in 2 underwing drop tanks.

Aircraft variants:
MP maritime patrol version has a 360° APS-128 search radar in the nose radome (can be housed under the fuselage, but not typically), with options including FLIR. Also used for search and rescue. Sonobuoys, smoke markers and a searchlight. Bulged observers' windows. Radar operator is positioned immediately behind the flight deck.

See C-212 Aviocar for general specifications *(the following differences come from specific CASA C-212 M literature)*

WEIGHTS:
Maximum take-off: 17,867 lb (8,100 kg)
Normal take-off: 16,975 lb (7,700 kg)
Maximum landing: 16,424 lb (7,450 kg)
Maximum payload: 5,952 lb (2,700 kg)
Maximum weapon load: 1,102 lb (500 kg)

PERFORMANCE:
Maximum cruise speed: 190 kts (219 mph) 352 km/h
Take-off distance over a 50 ft (15 m) obstacle: 1,884 ft (574 m)
Landing distance over a 50 ft (15 m) obstacle: 1,703 ft (519 m)
Maximum climb rate: 1,600 ft (488 m) per minute
Ceiling: 26,000 ft (7,925 m), or 11,400 ft (3,475 m) on single engine
Range with full internal/external fuel: 1,370 naut miles (1,577 miles) 2,537 km
Range with full payload: 430 naut miles (495 miles) 796 km
Search duration: over 9 hours, with drop tanks

DE electronic warfare versions for ESM, electronic countermeasures (including jamming), electronic intelligence, and airborne early warning. Different shape nose thimble.
Photogrammetric version.
ASW anti-submarine version is designed to have a 360° search radar under the fuselage, magnetic anomaly detector (MAD), sonobuoys, ESM, on-top position indicator, and IFF/SIF. This version was not among the cabin layout drawings received from CASA.

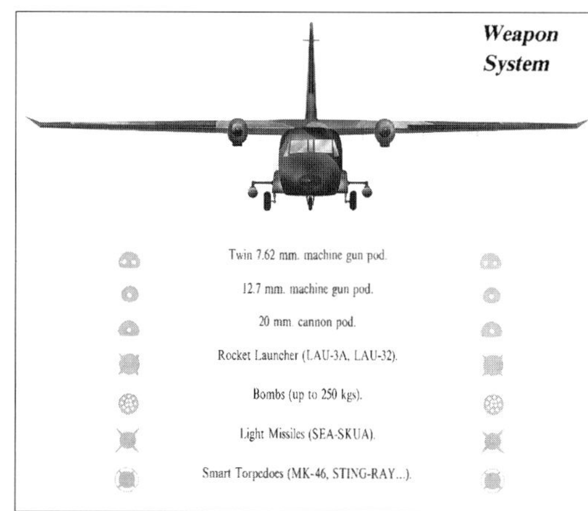

↑ **CASA C-212 weapon arrangement** *(courtesy CASA)*

FFA — Sweden

Full name:
Flygtekniska Försöksanstalten (The Aeronautical Research Institute of Sweden).

Corporate address:
PO Box 11021, S-161 11 Bromma.

Telephone: +46 8 634 10 00
Facsimile: +46 8 25 34 81
E-mail: ffa@ffa.se
Web site: www.ffa.se

Founded: 1940.

Employees: 201.

Information:
Anna Wautil (Information office – *telephone* +46 8 634 11 38, *facsimile* +46 8 25 34 81).

ACTIVITIES

▪ Central government agency for aeronautical research in Sweden. Its principal role is to provide scientific support and technical assistance to Swedish Government authorities, to domestic and foreign industries and to other organizations.
▪ Aeronautical research and testing, as a part of the development of Swedish military and civil aircraft, is the core business. The number of international aerospace customers is also increasing.
▪ Main areas of research are experimental aerodynamics (department head Magnus Linde), conceptual aerodynamics (Ingemar Lindblad), flight systems (Peter Caap), structures (Ragnar Gillberg), acoustics (Peter Göransson), wind energy (Sven-Erik Thor), model manufacturing (Curt Ohlsson), National Laboratory for pressure (Carin Bergström), Technical/Scientific Advisory Group (Pavel Sindelar) and International Relations (Anders Gustafsson).

Industrigruppen JAS AB — Sweden

Founded: 1981, by a number of Swedish companies to create an industry group to develop and produce the Gripen, namely Saab-Scania (now Saab AB), Volvo Aero Corporation, Ericsson Radar Electronics (now Ericsson Microwave Systems AB) and FFV Aerotech AB, with Ericsson-Saab Avionics now also a member (see below). Industrigruppen JAS continues to oversee the programme in Sweden and perform as the contractor for the FMV (Försvarets Materielverk). See below for Saab details, Engine section for Volvo, and Radar section for Ericsson.
Domestic sales: Saab AB Gripen develops and manufactures the JAS 39 Gripen for the domestic market as one of the companies in the Industry group JAS. (Saab has 66% of the programme delivery value, Volvo Aero Corporation 14%, Ericsson Microwave Systems 11%, Ericsson-Saab Avionics 6% and FFV Aerotech 4%.)
International marketing/sales: Gripen is marketed, produced, adapted and supported for the export market by Saab-BAe Gripen AB, a joint venture company between Saab and British Aerospace that was formed in 1995 (operating from November), with 55% and 45% of the workshare respectively.

Saab Group — Sweden

Corporate address:
S-581 88 Linköping.

Telephone: +46 13 18 00 00
Facsimile: +46 13 18 18 02, 18 71 70
E-mail: _._@saab.se
Web site: www.saab.se

Founded:
1937 as the main Swedish aircraft manufacturer. Saab AB is the parent company, consisting of 5 business units.

Employees:
8,500.

Information:
Lars Jagerfelt (Director Corporate Communications and Public Affairs – *telephone* +46 13 18 71 65), Monica Vider Wegmann (Administration – *telephone* +46 13 18 71 61, *facsimile* +46 13 18 72 00).

FACILITIES

▪ Linköping, Malmö, Ödeshög, Göteborg, Jönköping, Huskvarna and Kista.

ACTIVITIES

▪ Gripen production and Viggen upgrade military programmes, plus commercial airliner and electronic derivative programmes (see Special Reconnaissance and Airliner sections). In addition, defence products include guided weapons, electronics and optronics, and training equipment.
▪ Active in developing commercial high technology niches for space, industry, traffic systems and data communications and telecommunications.

DIVISIONS

Note. Saab AB comprises 5 product companies. Since 1991, Saab-Scania (and now Saab AB) has been wholly owned by the private Wallenberg company investor, Sweden's largest industrial holding company.

SAAB AB

Address:
As for Corporate.

Telephone: +46 13 18 00 00
Facsimile: +46 13 18 18 02

Information:
Jan Ahlgren (Public Relations Director for Gripen and IG JAS – *telephone* +46 13 18 39 07, *facsimile* +46 13 18 54 27).

Activities:
▪ From 1 January 1997, operations of previous Saab Military Aircraft, Saab Aircraft and Saab Service Partner have been merged under the parent company, Saab AB.
▪ Develops and produces military and commercial aircraft within the business units of Gripen, General Military Aircraft, Future Products and Technology, Operations Commercial Aircraft, and Collaborative Programmes. Include Gripen development and production, continuous updating of Viggen, and re-engining Sk 60 W trainers. Sub-contracting work includes wing flap support struts for the Boeing 777, and Airbus A340-500/600 floor assemblies on behalf of Aerospatiale (first delivery Autumn 1999).

SAAB DYNAMICS AB

Address:
As for Corporate.

Telephone: +46 13 28 60 00
Facsimile: +46 13 28 60 06

Activities:
▪ Autonomous guided weapons, defence electronics and optronics.

SAAB TRAINING SYSTEMS AB

Address:
S-561 85 Huskvarna.

Telephone: +46 36 38 80 00
Facsimile: +46 36 38 80 80

Activities:
▪ Develops, produces and markets advanced training systems and is a world leader in laser-based simulation systems. Includes the BT 46 laser simulator.

SAAB AIRCRAFT AB

Address:
As for Corporate.

Telephone: +46 13 18 20 00
Facsimile: +46 13 18 27 22

Activities:
▪ Markets commercial aircraft and supports Saab 340 and 2000, plus derivatives and special versions.

SAAB COMBITECH AB

Address:
Box 1017, S-551 11 Jönköping.

Telephone: +46 36 19 40 00
Facsimile: +46 36 19 45 10

Activities:
▪ Develops commercial, high technology niche operations, including products and systems from Saab Ericsson Space, Saab Marine Electronics, Combitech Traffic Systems, Combitech Software and Combitech Network.

ALSO:

SAAB AIRCRAFT INTERNATIONAL LTD

Address:
Leworth House, 14-16 Sheet Street, Windsor, Berkshire SL4 1BG, England.

Telephone: +44 1753 859991
Facsimile: +44 1753 858884

SAAB AIRCRAFT OF AMERICA, INC

Address:
Loudoun Tech Center, 21300 Ridgetop Circle, Sterling, VA 20166, USA.

Telephone: +1 703 406 7224
Facsimile: +1 703 406 7272

ERICSSON-SAAB AVIONICS AB

Activities:
▪ Formed January 1997, concentrating skills in electronic warfare, display and surveillance systems, advanced electronic and mechanical equipment, and electromagnetic technologies, including electrical environment.

Saab J 35J Draken and Sk 60 W

Comments: Details on these aircraft and upgrade programmes, plus photographs, can be found in the 1996-97 edition of *WA&SD*, pages 114-115. A single squadron of J 35J Draken interceptors will remain active with the Swedish Air Force until 1999. The first 9 Sk 60 W upgraded trainers with FJ44 engines were delivered in 1996, beginning 6 September to the FMV, with the remainder by 1998.

Saab 37 Viggen

Comments: First flown 8 February 1967, 329 Viggen all-weather air defence, attack, reconnaissance and training aircraft were delivered to the Swedish Air Force between June 1971 and 29 June 1990. A long and continuous series of upgrades over the years have given Viggen double its original combat efficiency. The first test aircraft with the latest modification, Mod-D, was delivered to FMV in the Summer of 1998. This includes a Gripen compatible communication and weapon system with (among other things) 1553 databuses and integration of AMRAAM. Although JA37s will be the last Viggens to be replaced by Gripens, 75 of the older AJ, SH and SF37 Viggens were also converted to AJS37 form and redelivered between 1993-95, leaving Sweden with a substantial JA37 and AJS37 force for continued service. Full details on the Viggen, plus photographs and drawings, can be found in the 1996-97 edition of *WA&SD*, pages 115-116.

↑ **Saab JA37 Viggens of F4 Wing; Viggen is currently undergoing Mod-D modification, for 1998 delivery** *(Peter Modigh/Swedish Defence Images)*

Saab AB Gripen JAS 39 Gripen

First flight: 9 December 1988.
Role: Lightweight multi-role fighter, maritime or ground attack, and reconnaissance aircraft.

Aims

▪ World's first production combat aircraft of a completely new generation.
▪ First multi-role fighter combining interceptor, attack and reconnaissance roles in a single aircraft.
▪ One aircraft to perform fighter, attack and reconnaissance missions, with the same pilot. By push-button control, the pilot chooses the system function in the computer programmes, giving the Gripen the characteristics needed for that particular mission.
▪ Canard and delta wing configuration with a large number of control surfaces and a digital control system to provide unique handling characteristics. High manoeuvrability.
▪ Small radar cross-section, making detection difficult.
▪ Totally integrated avionics structure, with a common software language for all important functions.
▪ Dispersed operation from short and narrow runways, including Sweden's V90 roads under emergency conditions with 2,625 ft (800 m) long and 30 ft (9 m) wide strip segments.
▪ Under 10 minutes combat turnaround by a single technician and 5 conscripts, including refuelling, rearming, essential servicing and inspection. Built-in AUP, for independent alert and engine start-up.
▪ Built-in test and monitoring system, with any failure localized and displayed on a HDD. Line replaceable units for fast repair. Monitoring system, together with in-depth maintenance analysis (MSG-3), optimizes the balance between preventive and on-condition maintenance.

Development

▪ Mid-1980. Definition phase was initiated.
▪ 3 June 1981. Proposals to the customer, FMV (Försvarets

↑ **Saab JAS 39A Gripen cockpit, with HUD, Flight Data Display, Horizontal Situation Display and Multi-Sensor Display** *(courtesy Ericsson Microwave Systems AB)*

Details for JAS 39A, *with JAS 39B in italics*

PRINCIPAL DIMENSIONS:
Wing span: 27 ft 7 ins (8.4 m)
Maximum length: 46 ft 3 ins (14.1 m) excluding pitot tube, *48 ft 5 ins (14.755 m)*
Maximum height: 14 ft 9 ins (4.5 m)

UNDERCARRIAGE:
Type: Retractable, with steerable twin nosewheels
Wheel base: 17 ft 1 ins (5.2 m), *19 ft 4 ins (5.9 m)*
Wheel track: 7 ft 10.5 ins (2.4 m)

WEIGHTS:
Empty, operating: 14,600 lb (6,620 kg), *17,637 lb (8,000 kg)*
Take-off: about 17,639-18,739 lb (8,000-8,500 kg) clean
Maximum take-off: about 30,865 lb (14,000 kg) according to latest brochure at time of writing; up from 27,558 lb (12,500 kg) quoted in 1995

PERFORMANCE:
Maximum speed: Supersonic at high, medium and low altitudes
Take-off distance: 2,625 ft (800 m) long and minimum 30 ft (9 m) wide strips (see Aims)
G limits: +9
Radius of action: 431 naut miles (497 miles) 800 km

Materielverk – Swedish Defence Materiel Administration).
▪ 30 June 1982. FMV and Industry Group JAS signed a contract to develop Gripen, covering 5 test aircraft and an initial batch of 30 fixed-price production aircraft. Long term intention was to replace AJ, SH, SF, JA and then AJS Viggens plus older J 35J Draken interceptors.
▪ 26 April 1987. Prototype 39-1 roll out, with the first flight at the end of the following year (see First flight).
▪ 2 February 1989. First prototype Gripen was lost in a landing accident.
▪ 4 May 1990–23 October 1991. 4 other prototypes made their maiden flights.
▪ 26 June 1992. Contracts signed for batch 2 production covering 110 aircraft, including development and production of 14 JAS 39B 2-seaters and support systems.
▪ 10 September 1992. Maiden flight of the first production Gripen (JAS 39.101). Replaced JAS 39-1 for trials.
▪ 8 June 1993. First delivery of a Gripen to the FMV (JAS 39.102, first flown 4 March).
▪ 8 August 1993. JAS 39.102 (second production aircraft) crashed during a flying display in Stockholm. The test pilot ejected safely. Following a Swedish Board of Accident Investigation report (dated 18 August) and implementation of the recommendations, a Government Commission report of 11 January 1994 stated that the programme should be continued. Modified flight control software improves low speed and low altitude handling; new non-linear filter has been added and phase-lag deleted.
▪ 29 December 1993. Flight tests resumed with JAS 39-2.
▪ 1994. About 85% of the agreed verification work included in Gripen development was completed in 1994. 443 test flights took place, representing 70% of the planned total. Firing tests of Rb75 Maverick air-to-surface missiles from Gripen were completed at the end of the year. A major part of the cold weather tests had been completed by August, and taxiing in water and slush had also been performed. Weapon tests were undertaken in Northern Sweden.
▪ 1 September 1994. AMRAAM missiles ordered by the FMV for Gripen, following a governmental decision that July.
▪ September 1995. Roll out of the Gripen 2-seater.
▪ December 1995. Test-flight number 2,000 took place; more than 90% of the test flight programme was then concluded.
▪ 7 February 1996. BAe Deputy Chief Test Pilot Paul Hopkins became the first British pilot to fly Gripen.
▪ 29 April 1996. The first test flight of the 2-seat Gripen. The first production 2-seater flew on 22 November 1996 and was used for evaluation flights until handed over to the Swedish Air Force in 1998.
▪ June 1996. Gripen was officially introduced into the Swedish Air Force by the King of Sweden, at a ceremony at F7 Air Force Wing.
▪ December 1996. The last aircraft in batch 1 and the first in batch 2 were delivered to the Swedish Defence Materiel Administration, FMV. The terms for the development work that were signed by FMV and Industry group JAS in 1982 were now fulfilled.
▪ 1997. Evaluation flights began by pilots from other countries, including Austria, Czech Republic, Hungary and Poland.
▪ June 1997. 'Export Baseline Standard' defined. NATO interoperable.
▪ 7 August 1997. A team of specialist military operations and engineering personnel from BAe completed an evaluation of the Czech Caslav Tactical Fighter Base in preparation for a future decision on the purchase of Export Gripens.
▪ 9 September 1997. Commander in Chief of the Hungarian Air Force, General Kositzky, flew in a 2-seat Gripen during a visit to Sweden.
▪ 14 October 1997. A month after the Chilean evaluation team visited Sweden, Commander in Chief of the Chilean Air Force, General Fernando Rojas Vender, flew Gripen.
▪ March 1998. First demonstrations of Gripen in South America (Chile and Brazil).
▪ April 1998. First test firing of AIM-120 AMRAAM from Gripen.
▪ June 1998. Deliveries reached 55 aircraft, including 2 2-seaters.
▪ 2007. All 12 Swedish Gripen squadrons to be equipped.

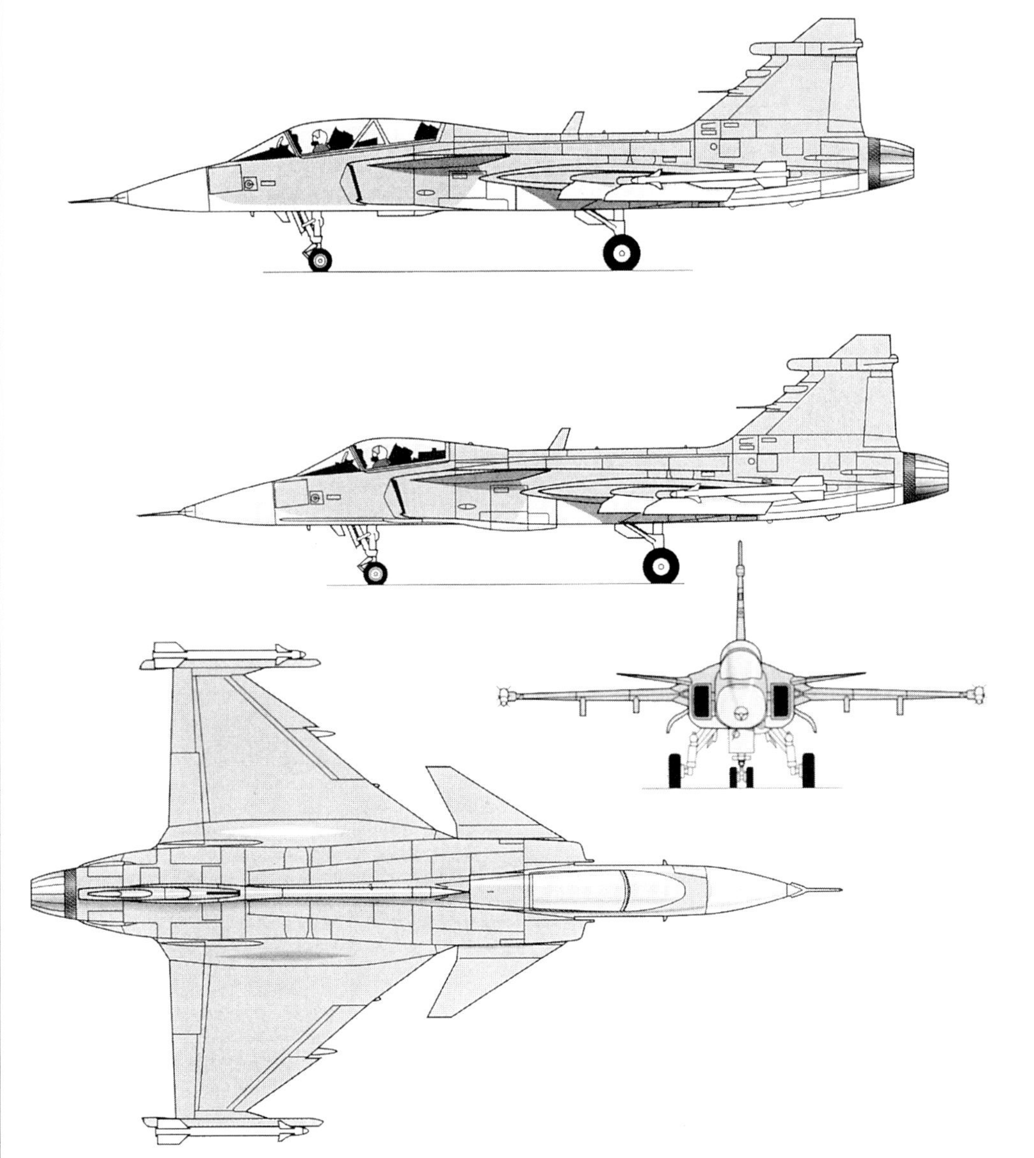

↑ **Saab JAS 39A Gripen, with extra side view (*top*) of JAS 39B** *(courtesy Saab AB Gripen)*

↑ **Saab JAS 39A Gripen** *(Foto Caspersson)*

↑ Saab JAS 39A Gripen with JAS 39B (*foreground*) *(Anders Nylén)*

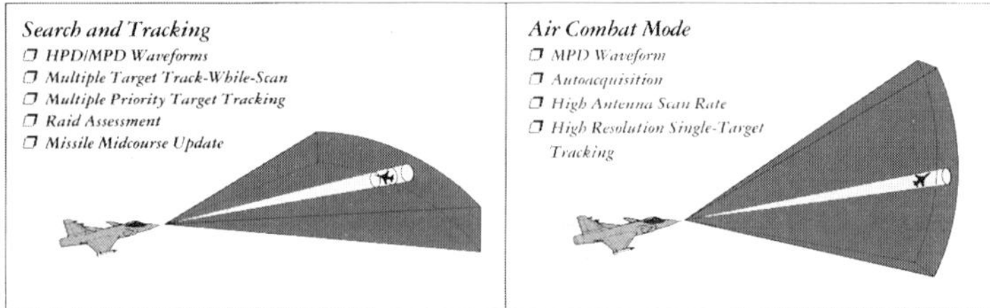

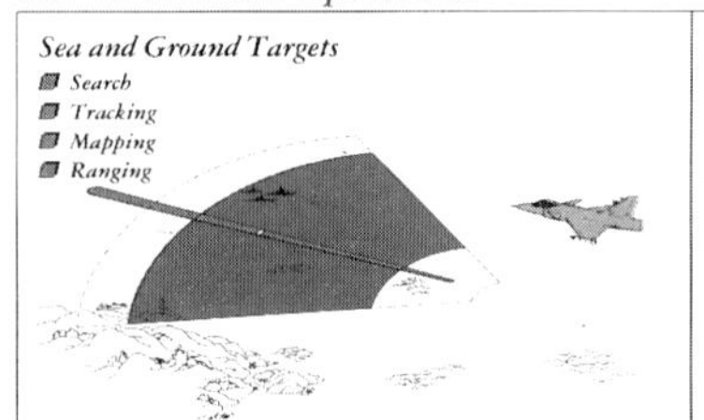

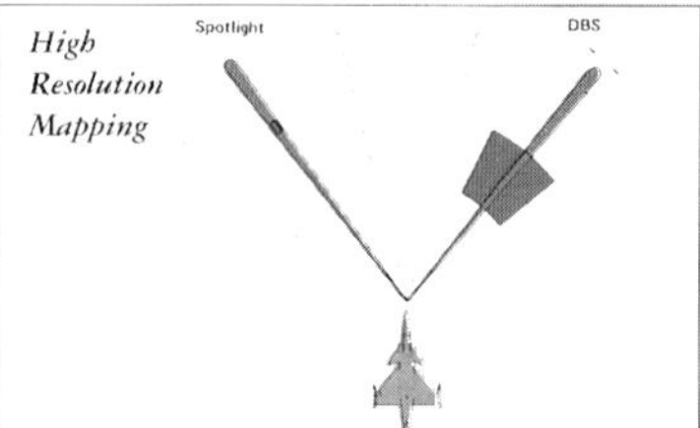

↑ Ericsson PS-05/A radar modes for the Saab JAS 39 Gripen *(courtesy Ericsson Microwave Systems AB)*

Details

Sales/Users: After the signing of a contract between FMV and Industry group JAS in June 1997 concerning a third batch of 64 Gripens, the total number of aircraft ordered for the Swedish Air Force is 204; 28 of these are JAS 39B 2-seat Gripens. Delivery of the first batch of 30 aircraft was completed in 1996. The first Gripen squadron became operational at the Skaraborg Air Force Wing, F7, in 1997. According to the decision of the Swedish Parliament, the Air Force will be equipped with 12 Gripen squadrons by the year 2007. Up to June 1998, 55 aircraft (including 2 2-seaters) had been delivered to the FMV and the Swedish Air Force. The first 2 squadrons have formed at F7, with the following 2 at F10 at Ängelholm and then 2 at F16 in Uppsala. The Export Gripen is marketed by Saab-BAe Gripen in about 10 countries, with potential sales estimated at 200-400 (including Austria, Brazil, Chile, Czech Republic, Hungary, Philippines, Poland and South Africa) . This is supported by the Governments of Sweden and Great Britain and their export credit organizations.
Crew: Pilot, or 2 crew for JAS 39B.
Cockpit: 0.7 ins (17 mm) longer and redesigned HOTAS centrally-mounted hand-stick controller has replaced the original stick to improve pilot comfort. Identical cockpits in the JAS 39B, except the HUD is omitted from the rear cockpit but, instead, the front pilot's HUD and exterior view can be presented on the rear cockpit's Flight Data Display. JAS 39B has larger cockpit canopy. Hymatic environmental control system, with Hughes-Treitler heat exchanger; environmental control system (cockpit and equipment conditioning) of Export Gripen modified to enable operation in hot climates.
Crew escape: Martin Baker S10LS zero-zero ejection seats.
Fixed guns: 27-mm Mauser Bk27 cannon, which can operate in an automatic radar-guided aiming mode.
Number of pylons: 9, comprising 4 under the wings, 2 at the wingtips, 2 under the air intakes (principally for avionics pods), and 1 under the fuselage. Export Gripen has NATO pylons and release units for weapons and other loads presently not in use by the Swedish Air Force.
Expendable weapons and equipment: Wingtip Rb 74 (AIM-9L) Sidewinder air-to-air missiles (plus cannon) is the basic armament of all models. Additional armament can include AMRAAM air-to-air (Mica is an option), RBS-15F anti-ship, Rb75 Maverick air-to-surface or other missiles, DWS39 cluster weapons dispensers, conventional or retarded bombs, rockets and more.
Additional stores: Camera and sensor pods (reconnaissance and electronic warfare).
Radar: Ericsson PS-05/A pulse-Doppler.
Flight/weapon system avionics/instrumentation: Ericsson DS80E system comprising radar (see above), EP-17 electronic display system, SDS 80 computing system with D80 or later D80E computer, and forward-looking TV camera and HI-8mm format video cassette recorder for intelligence gathering and training. Nordmicro air data computer. 3 MIL-STD-1553B databuses. EP-17 comprises 3 Ericsson 120 × 150 mm monochrome (152 × 203 mm colour for Batch 3 and for Export Gripens) head-down displays (in-flight reconfigurable) of 525/675/875 lines, identical/ interchangeable hardware and with soft keys in the front frames for selectable and interchangeable presentations (displays for Export Gripen adapted to common Western formats), plus wide-angle (22° × 28°) diffraction optics Kaiser HUD for both flight and weapon-aiming symbology and, if wanted, raster video images from electro-optical sensors such as the FLIR: Flight Data Display for basic flight, system and weapon data and HUD information backup; Horizontal Situation Display for a tactical overview based on an electronic map, with air-to-air, air-to-surface and emergency checklist modes; Multi-Sensor Display for information from the radar and other sensors, including IR video. A helmet sighting system is under development, and a fully integrated helmet-mounted display including weapon aiming symbology is under consideration for the future. See also Cockpit. Provision for night vision goggles. For all roles (not just attack and reconnaissance, as originally thought), data link permits transfer of tactical information in real or near-real time; radar-derived surface target data can be transferred from one Gripen to another group of "radar silent" attacking aircraft. Honeywell laser inertial navigation system and radar altimeter. BAe standby strapdown gyromagnetic unit. CelsiusTech twin V/UHF com radios; IFF. (Gripen mock-up was fitted with a Saab OTIS infra-red search/track system mock-up on the nose.) Batch 1 Gripens were given PP1 and PP2 display processors; batch 2 have a smaller, lighter and less power consuming processor to provide space for a new radio system. In 1996 Ericsson received 115 million kronor contract from the FMV to supply a new display processor for the first batch of Gripens. Designated PP12, the processor generates the graphic information to the 3 HDD and the HUD, with installation to commence in 1998. Display processing features full software control in computers and symbol generators, all raster graphics provided with anti-aliasing, digital map in 5 scales, and sensor information processing including radar scan conversion. Rafael Litening laser designator pod has been proposed by Zeiss. See also Export Gripen under Aircraft variants. New cockpit under development in 1998 has 3 larger 157 × 211-mm flat-panel head down displays (resolution of 600 × 800 colour pixels).
Self-protection systems: Ericsson EW suite, with radar homing and warning receiver; chaff/flare, jamming and towed decoy.
Wing characteristics: Rear-mounted delta, with clipped tips for missile rails. Dogtooth leading edge.
Wing control surfaces: Automatic, 2-section leading-edge flaps. 2 elevons on each wing trailing edge. Any 2 control surfaces (wing, canard or tail) can be lost without affecting the ability to return to base.
Tail control surfaces: Rudder.
Canard: Close coupled, all moving, swept type. Can be heavily tilted for braking during the landing roll.
Airbrakes: Rear fuselage sides. See Canards.
Flight control system: Initially Lear Astronics triplex redundant fly-by-wire; Lockheed Martin upgraded control computer for later aircraft. Moog servo valves and Saab Combitech motion sensors and throttle actuator.
Construction materials: Carbonfibre used for some 20% of the airframe, including the wings, canards, fin and more. Other materials include aluminium alloy (some 60%) and titanium (6%) of weight. Static load testing of the complete airframe at 230% of load limit has been undertaken.
Engine: Volvo RM12 (F404 type). Early studies have been conducted into higher-thrust engines, such as EJ200, F414 and M88 (see also JAS 39C and Thrust-vectoring Gripen under Aircraft variants). Microturbo APU.
Engine rating: 12,141 lbf (54 kN) dry, 18,105 lbf (80.54 kN) with afterburning.
Nozzles: Variable, below canards, with splitter plates.
Flight refuelling probe: Under development. Retractable, located on the upper fuselage (port side, from earlier starboard position), including for Export Gripen.
Fuel system: 5,000 lb (2,268 kg) capacity in the wings and

JAS 39 GRIPEN

↑ Saab JAS 39A general arrangement cutaway

fuselage, plus optional drop tanks.
Electrical system: Sundstrand 40 kVA, 400Hz system with generator and transformer. Lucas Aerospace back-up AC supply with 10 kVA generator and gearbox-driven turbine. Under emergency conditions, APU or engine bleed air, or thermal batteries, can power turbine.
Hydraulic system: 2 Dowty independent systems.
Braking system: Carbon disc type on all wheels, and ABS anti-skid devices.
Oxygen system: On Board Oxygen Generating System (OBOGS), matching the extended duration offered by air-to-air flight refuelling on Export Gripen.

Aircraft variants:
JAS 39A is the initial production single-seater, as described.
JAS 39B is the 2-seater for tactical training and operational missions requiring a 2-person crew. Identical cockpits, except the HUD is omitted from the rear cockpit (see Cockpit) but HUD data is repeated on the rear cockpit Flight Data Display. No internal cannon. Eventual extra tasks for 2-seaters could include a flying air-defence tactical control centre role. Fuselage lengthened by 2 ft 2 ins (0.655 m), larger cockpit canopy, and ventral air intake for the environmental control system.
JAS 39C is the potential upgraded single-seater, with a more powerful engine and higher weights. Engine options under examination include the Volvo RM12 Plus, Eurojet EJ200, General Electric F414 and SNECMA M88-3 . Also upgraded avionics and other systems.
Export Gripen is to third-phase (JAS 39C type) standard. First presented at the Paris Air Show in 1997. Can be fitted with (among other things) a retractable air-to-air refuelling probe, an On Board Oxygen Generating System (OBOGS), larger and colour displays, environmental control system (cockpit and equipment conditioning) to enable operation in hot climates,and NATO pylons and release units for weapons and other loads presently not in use by the Swedish Air Force. Engineering development activities largely at BAe, Brough site.
Thrust-vectoring Gripen is a possible future development, after discussions regarding the resumption of X-31 (see 1996-97 edition of *WA&SD*, page 153) tests with Germany and the USA indicated Swedish interest.

Pilatus Aircraft Ltd — Switzerland

Full name: Pilatus Flugzeugwerke AG (member of the Oerlikon-Bührle Group).
Corporate address: CH-6370 Stans.
Telephone: +41 41 619 61 11 **Facsimile:** +41 41 610 61 07 **Telex:** 866 202-PIL CH **Cable:** PILATUSAIR STANS
Founded: 1939.
Information: Bill. J. Cato (Manager, Marketing Support Services – *telephone* +41 41 619 64 87, *facsimile* +41 41 610 33 51).

ACTIVITIES

▪ In addition to the trainers detailed here, the PC-6 Turbo Porter and PC-12 can be found in the General Aviation section.

DIVISIONS

PILATUS BRITTEN-NORMAN LTD
HQ address: See UK section.

Pilatus PC-7 Turbo Trainer

First flight: 18 August 1978 (production model).
Role: Basic through to advanced flying training, including aerobatic, tactical and instrument.

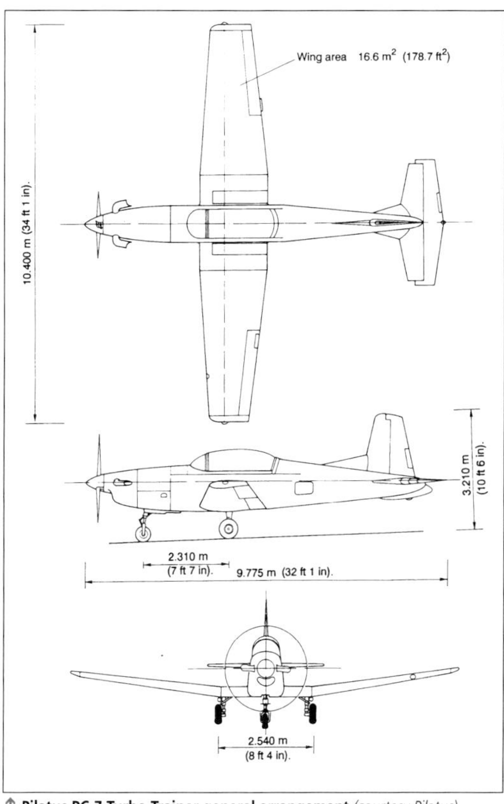

↑ **Pilatus PC-7 Turbo Trainer general arrangement** *(courtesy Pilatus)*

Aims

▪ Noise levels at 2,200 rpm: 73 dB(A) aerobatic weight, 79.5 dB(A) utility weight.
▪ Approved manoeuvres in aerobatic category are steep turn, looping positive, roll off the top (Immelmann), lazy eight, cuban eight, climbing half-roll, aileron roll, barrel roll, hesitation roll, slow roll, wing over, inverted flight (30 seconds maximum), and spins. Manoeuvres in utility category are steep turn, looping positive, roll off the top (Immelmann), lazy eight and roll.

Development

▪ 5 December 1978. FOCA type certification, Aerobatic category.
▪ 6 April 1979. FOCA type certification, utility category.

Details

Sales/Users: Over 440 built at time of writing (not including Mk II, which see). Delivered to Abu Dhabi (UAE), Angola, Austria, Bolivia, Botswana, Brunei, Chile (navy), France, Guatemala, Iran, Iraq, Malaysia, Mexico, Myanmar, Netherlands, Suriname, Switzerland and Uruguay, plus several to civil users including 4 to the French ECCO display team.
Crew: Student pilot and instructor in tandem. Solo flights from the front cockpit.
Cockpit: Freon-type cooling system consisting of an engine-driven compressor, a condenser and an evaporator, with blower in each cockpit. Heated and windshield demisted by hot air bled from engine compressor outlet. Controls in front cockpit allow ram air and/or hot bleed air to be selected to the floor outlets of both cockpits and/or windshield. 55 lb (25 kg) of baggage.
Crew escape: Optional Martin Baker CH 15A ejection seats.
Fixed guns: None.
Number of pylons: 6; 551 lb (250 kg) inboard, 353 lb (160 kg) centre and 243 lb (110 kg) outboard capacities per wing.
Expendable weapons and equipment: 2,293 lb (1,040 kg) total permissible pylon load.
Flight/weapon system avionics/instrumentation: Optional ranges of communications and navigation avionics. Standard instrumentation in each cockpit includes an airspeed indicator, attitude indicator, turn and bank indicator, altimeter, vertical speed indicator, angle of attack indexer, clock, g meter, magnetic compass, trim position indicators and much more.
Self-protection systems: Swiss Air Force aircraft use the Ericsson Erijammer pod for ECM training.
Wing characteristics: Straight, low mounted, with dihedral outboard of the centre section.
Wing control surfaces: Mass-balanced ailerons with tabs, and split flaps.
Tail control surfaces: Mass-balanced elevator and rudder, with tabs.
Flight control system: Manual, but with electrically actuated (mechanically operated) flaps and electric tabs.
Construction materials: Aluminium alloy. Single-piece wing formed by a main spar, auxiliary spar, ribs and stringer-reinforced skin.
Engine: Pratt & Whitney Canada PT6A-25A turboprop, with a 7 ft 9 ins (2.362 m) Hartzell HC-B3TN-2 constant-speed propeller.

Details for PC-7

PRINCIPAL DIMENSIONS:
Wing span: 34 ft 1.5 ins (10.4 m)
Maximum length: 32 ft 1 ins (9.775 m)
Maximum height: 10 ft 6.5 ins (3.21 m)

WINGS:
Aerofoil section: NACA 64_2A-415, 64_1A-612 (root/tip)
Area: 178.68 sq ft (16.6 m^2)
Aspect ratio: 6.516
Dihedral: 7°

UNDERCARRIAGE:
Type: Retractable, with castering nosewheel. Electric operation, with manual back-up
Wheel base: 7 ft 7 ins (2.31 m)
Wheel track: 8 ft 4 ins (2.54 m)

WEIGHTS:
Empty*: typically 2,976 lb (1,350 kg), but depends on avionics fit
Maximum zero fuel: 3,668 lb (1,664 kg)
Maximum take-off: 4,189 lb (1,900 kg) *aerobatic*, 5,952 lb (2,700 kg) *utility*, with underwing stores
Maximum landing (FAR 23): 4,189 lb (1,900 kg) *aerobatic*, 5,655 lb (2,565 kg) *utility* with underwing stores, 10 ft (3 m) per second sink rate
Maximum landing (MIL SPEC): 3,977 lb (1,804 kg) *aerobatic*, 13 ft (4 m) per second sink rate

CENTRE OF GRAVITY RANGE:
Aerobatic: 18 to 28% MGC
Utility: 22 to 28% MGC

PERFORMANCE (EAS at maximum operating weights)**:**
Design diving speed (V_D): 300 kts (345 mph) 556 km/h
Maximum operating Mach number (M_{MO}): Mach 0.55
Maximum operating speed (V_{MO}), and maximum design cruise speed (V_C): 270 kts (311 mph) 500 km/h
Design manoeuvring speed (V_A): 175 kts (202 mph) 324 km/h *aerobatic*, 181 kts (208 mph) 335 km/h *utility*
Maximum speed with flaps and/or undercarriage extended: 135 kts (155 mph) 250 km/h
Maximum cruise speed: 209-225 kts (241-259 mph) 387-417 km/h, *aerobatic*
Maximum range cruise speed: 150-171 kts (173-197 mph) 278-317 km/h
Stall speed, clean: 71 kts (82 mph) 132 km/h *aerobatic*, 83 kts (96 mph) 154 km/h *utility*
Stall speed, flaps and undercarriage down: 63.5 kts (73 mph) 118 km/h *aerobatic*, 74 kts (86 mph) 137 km/h *utility*
Take-off distance: 787 ft (240 m) *aerobatic* with flaps, 2,559 ft (780 m) *utility* with 6 pylon stores and no flaps, both at sea level
Landing distance: 968 ft (295 m) *aerobatic*, 1,657 ft (505 m) *utility* with 6 pylon stores, with brakes, at sea level
Take-off distance over a 50 ft (15 m) obstacle: 1,312-1,936 ft (400-590 m) *aerobatic*, 3,871-5,906 ft (1,180-1,800 m) *utility* with 6 pylon stores, both at sea level to 8,000 ft (2,440 m)
Landing distance over a 50 ft (15 m) obstacle: 1,673-2,051 ft (510-625 m) *aerobatic*, 2,625-3,248 ft (800-990 m) *utility* with 6 pylon stores, both at sea level to 8,000 ft (2,440 m)
Maximum climb rate: 2,150 ft (655 m) per minute *aerobatic*, 1,290 ft (393 m) per minute *utility* with 6 pylon stores, both at sea level
G limits: +6, -3 *aerobatic*; +4.5, -2.25 *utility*; *+2 with flaps*
Ceiling: 25,000 ft (7,620 m) *operating*, 33,000 ft (10,000 m) *service*
Temperature limits: -45° C minimum, +50° C maximum
Still air range with full fuel: 407-730 naut miles (468-840 miles) 754-1,353 km, sea level to 20,000 ft (6,100 m) altitude, with reserve
Still air duration: 1 hour 54 minutes at sea level and maximum cruise speed (*utility*), to 4 hours 22 minutes at 20,000 ft (6,100 m) and maximum range cruise speed (*aerobatic*)
Noise emission: 73.0 dB(A) *aerobatic*, 79.5 dB(A) *utility*, at 2,200 propeller rpm in accordance with ICAO Annex 16
*Empty weight is defined as the complete aircraft, without usable fuel, and no crew, baggage or underwing stores, but including engine oil and unusable fuel

↑ Pilatus PC-7 Turbo Trainer

Engine rating: 560 shp (417.6 kW).
Air intakes: Engine intake air inertial separation system for ice protection.
Fuel system: 474 litres of usable fuel in 2 tanks. 30 seconds maximum inverted flight due to a 12 litre aerobatic tank. Can carry 2 × 152 or 240 litre drop tanks.
Electrical system: 28 volt DC supply via dual-role starter-generator, and a secondary 24 volt supply using a 24 volt 40 amp-hour ni-cd battery. 2 (main and stand-by) AC output static inverters, each providing 2 outputs of 115 volt/400Hz and 26 volt/400Hz.
Hydraulic system: For brakes only (see below).
Braking system: Hydraulic on mainwheels.
De-icing system: See air intakes. Electrically heated pitot tube, static ports, fuel sense lines and angle-of-attack transmitter. Optional propeller de-icing. Flight into known or forecast icing conditions is not approved.
Oxygen system: Gaseous. OBOGS optional.

Pilatus PC-7 Mk II (M) Turbo Trainer

First flight: 28 September 1992.
Role: Civil and military trainer (see PC-7).

Aims

■ Developed to include an advanced airframe with stepped cockpits, better aerodynamics (and including an improved tail unit), improved handling qualities and higher manoeuvrability, a robust undercarriage for grass operation and featuring nosewheel steering, advanced cockpit layout (with EFIS, GPS and HUD), more powerful engine with a 4-blade propeller, addition of an airbrake and standard ejection seats, and improved access for easier maintenance.

Development

■ 1992. Conceived initially to meet a South African Air Force requirement for a Harvard replacement.
■ 1993. Ordered by South Africa against competition from the indigenous Atlas ACE.
■ 1994. Production began.

Details

Sales/Users: Total of 61 operating with 2 customers at time of writing, the major user being South Africa which ordered 60.
Crew: 2, in tandem, the rear seat raised.
Cockpit: ECS has vapour-cycle cooling and bleed air/ram air mix for heating.
Crew escape: Martin Baker CH11A ejection seats fitted as standard.
Fixed guns: None.
Number of pylons: 6; 551 lb (250 kg) inboard and centre, and 243 lb (110 kg) outboard capacities per wing. 2 'wet' pylons on SAAF aircraft, for drop tanks only.

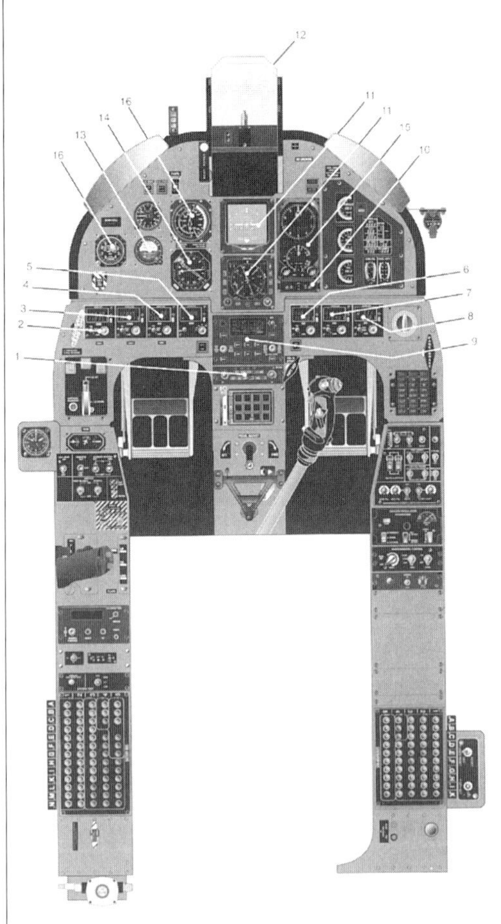

↑ **IFR advanced avionics cockpit configuration for both the Pilatus PC-7 Mk II (M) and PC-9(M), with: 1** Pilatus/Becker AS 3100 Audio/Int, **2** Bendix/King KTR 908/KFS 598A VHF com 1, **3** similar VHF com 2, **4** Bendix/King KTR 909/KFS 599A UHF com, **5** Bendix/King MST 67A/ KFS 578A ATC XPNDR, **5a** Narco ELT 910 ELT, **6** Bendix/King KNR 634A/ KFS 564A VHF nav 1, **7** similar nav 2, **8** Bendix/King KDF 806/KFS 586A ADF, **9** Bendix/King KLN 900 GPS system, **10** Bendix/King KRA 405B digital radar altimeter/CP 470 control panel, **11** Bendix/King SG 465 symbol generators/ED 462 dual EADI/ED 461 EHSI EFIS, **11a** Bendix/King DMS 441B DME, **12** Flight Vision FV 2000 HUD, **13** Sextant H 221 AMN and Litef LCR 92 pitch/roll/yaw/hdg and Bendix/King KMT 112 flux valve for attitude system, **14** Bendix/King KNI 582 RMI, **15** Bendix/King KDC 481 digital air data computer/KAV 485 ALT/VS indicator/KST 488 TAS/TAT/SAT/indicator for ADC system, **16** Thommen A/S 3" sw and A/S 3" and 2nd ALT 2" flight instruments *(courtesy Pilatus)*

Expendable weapons and equipment: 2,293 lb (1,040 kg) total permissible pylon load.
Flight/weapon system avionics/instrumentation: Improved avionics and layout, including optional HUD.
Airbrake: Under the fuselage, directly aft of the wing.
Engine: Pratt & Whitney Canada PT6A-25C turboprop, with a Hartzell 8 ft (2.438 m) 4-blade, variable-pitch propeller.
Engine rating: 700 shp (522 kW) cruise.
Fuel system: 518 litres usable in 2 wing and collector tanks, plus a 12 litre aerobatic tank allowing 30 seconds of inverted flight. Optional 155 or 246 litre drop tanks.
Hydraulic system: 3,002 psi for undercarriage operation and steering, and airbrake.
Oxygen system: Gaseous. Emergency oxygen is fitted to each ejection seat.

↑ Pilatus PC-7 Mk II (M) with auxiliary tanks

Details for PC-7 Mk II (M)

PRINCIPAL DIMENSIONS:
Wing span: 33 ft 2.5 ins (10.124 m)
Maximum length: 33 ft 3 ins (10.137 m)
Maximum height: 10 ft 8.5 ins (3.26 m), typical

WINGS:
Area: 175.34 sq ft (16.29 m^2)
Aspect ratio: 6.287

TAIL UNIT:
Tailplane span: 12 ft 2 ins (3.664 m)

UNDERCARRIAGE:
Type: Retractable, with steerable nosewheel. Life of 30,000 landings
Wheel base: 7 ft 7 ins (2.312 m)
Wheel track: 8 ft 4 ins (2.54 m)

WEIGHTS:
Empty: typically 3,682 lb (1,670 kg), but depending on avionics fit
Maximum zero fuel: 4,189 lb (1,900 kg)
Maximum take-off: 4,960 lb (2,250 kg) *aerobatic*, 6,283 lb (2,850 kg) *utility*
Maximum landing: 4,960 lb (2,250 kg) *aerobatic*, 6,062 lb (2,750 kg) *utility*

CENTRE OF GRAVITY RANGE:
Aerobatic: 22 to 30% MAC up to 4,960 lb (2,250 kg)
With underwing stores: 23 to 28% MAC at 6,283 lb (2,850 kg)

PERFORMANCE (EAS at maximum operating weights)**:**
Design diving speed (V_D): 360 kts (415 mph) 667 km/h
Maximum operating Mach number (M_{MO}): Mach 0.60
Maximum operating speed (V_{MO}), and design cruise speed (V_C): 300 kts (345 mph) 555 km/h
Manoeuvring speed (V_O): 210 kts (242 mph) 389 km/h *aerobatic*, 200 kts (230 mph) 370 km/h *utility*
Maximum speed with flaps and/or undercarriage extended: 150 kts (173 mph) 320 km/h
Maximum cruise speed: 251 kts (289 mph) 465 km/h at 10,000 ft (3,050 m)
Stall speed: 75 kts (87 mph) 139 km/h *clean*, 68 kts (79 mph) 126 km/h *with flaps and undercarriage down, aerobatic*; 84 kts (97 mph) 156 km/h *clean*, 75 kts (87 mph) 139 km/h *with flaps and undercarriage down, utility*
Take-off distance: 850 ft (259 m), at sea level
Landing distance: 1,100 ft (335 m), at sea level
Take-off distance over a 50 ft (15 m) obstacle: 1,360 ft (415 m)
Landing distance over a 50 ft (15 m) obstacle: 2,210 ft (674 m)
Maximum climb rate: 2,840 ft (865 m) per minute
Time to 5,000 ft (1,525 m): 1 minute 50 seconds
Time to 20,000 ft (6,100 m): 10 minutes 55 seconds
G limits: +7, -3.5 *aerobatic*; +4.5, -2.25 *utility*
Sustained load factor: 3.2g at sea level, 2.5g at 10,000 ft (3,050 m) and 1.7g at 20,000 ft (6,100 m)
Ceiling: 25,000 ft (7,620 m) *operating*, 30,000 ft (9,145 m) *service* at 4,960 lb (2,250 kg)
Temperature limits: -55° C minimum, +50° C maximum
Range with full fuel: over 760 naut miles (875 miles) 1,408 km at 25,000 ft (7,620 m) and cruise power

Pilatus PC-9(M) Advanced Turbo Trainer

First flight: 7 May 1984.
Role: Basic to advanced flying training, and target towing.

Aims

▪ Approved manoeuvres in aerobatic category are stall turn, steep turn, loop positive, roll off the top (Immelmann), lazy eight, cuban eight, vertical roll, rolling turn, climbing half-roll, aileron roll, barrel roll, hesitation roll, slow roll, wing over, inverted flight (60 seconds maximum), erect spin and Derry turn. Manoeuvres with underwing stores are steep turn, loop positive, roll off the top (Immelmann), chandelle, aileron roll, barrel roll, cuban eight and lazy eight.

Development

▪ 19 September 1985. FOCA type certificate gained in the aerobatic category.
▪ 2 April 1987. FOCA type certificate gained for operation with underwing stores installed.

Details

Sales/Users: Total of over 220 sold to 12 customers at the time of writing, including those delivered to Angola, Australia (assembled locally), Croatia, Cyprus, Germany, Iraq, Myanmar, Saudi Arabia (original 30, plus 20 more ordered in late 1994), Switzerland, Thailand, and USA (army, non-operational chase aircraft but in 1995 sent to Slovenia). German plus Swiss Air Force aircraft undertake target-towing roles. The PC-9 Mk II was also entered by Raytheon-Pilatus in the US military JPATS competition as the Beech Mk II, being announced winner on 22 June 1995. Up to 711 will be built for the USAF and US Navy at Raytheon's Wichita works, for delivery from November 1998 as T-6A Texan IIs. 10 Slovenian PC-9s being upgraded by IAI.
Details: Principally for the PC-9.
Crew: 2, in tandem stepped cockpits. Pilot in the front cockpit when flying solo.
Cockpit: ECS has vapour-cycle cooling and bleed air/ram air mix for heating.
Crew escape: Martin Baker CH 11A ejection seats, operational from zero height to 40,000 ft (12,200 m), and 60 to 400 kts EAS.
Fixed guns: None.
Number of pylons: 6; 551 lb (250 kg) inboard and centre 'wet', and 243 lb (110 kg) outboard capacities per wing.
Expendable weapons and equipment: 2,293 lb (1,040 kg) total permissible load.
Flight/weapon system avionics/instrumentation: Except for the audio system, the communication system is optional. Standard navigation system comprises a pitot-static system with Mach/airspeed indicators, altimeters, vertical speed indicators, angle of attack system, attitude indicators and stand-by magnetic compass. Other navigation equipment is optional. Each cockpit is equipped with an engine and secondary display panel (ESDP) with liquid crystal displays. PC-9 Mk II has a steerable FLIR system, which displays images in either cockpit.
Wing characteristics: Straight, low mounted, with dihedral outboard of the centre section.
Wing control surfaces: Mass-balanced ailerons with mass-balanced trim tabs, and split flaps.
Tail control surfaces: Mass-balanced elevator and rudder, with mass-balanced trim tabs.
Flight control system: Manual, but with hydraulically operated airbrake, and electric flaps and tabs.
Airbrake: Single, plate type under the fuselage.
Construction materials: Aluminium alloy. Single-piece wing formed by a main spar, auxiliary spar, ribs and stringer-reinforced skin.
Engine: Pratt & Whitney Canada PT6A-62 turboprop, with a Hartzell 8 ft (2.438 m) constant-speed, variable-pitch, 4-blade propeller.
Engine rating: 950 shp (708.4 kW).
Air intakes: Engine intake air inertial separation system for ice protection.
Fuel system: 518 litres of usable fuel in 2 tanks, plus a 12 litre aerobatic tank allowing a maximum 60 seconds of inverted flight. 2 optional 154 litre or 248 litre drop tanks.
Electrical system: 28 volt DC supply via dual-role starter-generator with a 300A output, and a secondary 24 volt supply using a 24 volt 40 amp-hour ni-cd battery. Optional 2 (main and stand-by) AC output static inverters, each providing 2 outputs of 115 volt/400Hz and 26 volt/400Hz.
Hydraulic system: 3,002 psi for undercarriage gear/doors, nosewheel steering and airbrake.
Braking system: Hydraulic mainwheel brakes.
De-icing system: See air intakes. Electrically heated pitot tube, static ports, and angle-of-attack transmitter. Optional propeller de-icing. Flight into known or forecast icing conditions is not approved.
Oxygen system: Gaseous. Emergency oxygen is fitted to each ejection seat. Optional OBOGS.

Aircraft variants:
PC-9 (M) is the standard version, as detailed.
PC-9B is the designation of commercially-operated target-towing aircraft supporting the German forces.
PC-9 Mk II is the version that won the USAF/US Navy JPATS competition in 1995, now known as the Beech T-6A Texan II and first flown in December 1992. Improved performance due to the 1,250 shp (932.1 kW) PT6A-68 turboprop. Pressurized cockpits, improved birdstrike capability, Martin Baker Mk 16 ejection seats, AlliedSignal state-of-the-art optimized avionics and increased crew comfort, plus maintenance features to reduce still further the operating costs. Can carry several types of ordnance utilizing various kinds of optical sight. Complete day/night training with the addition of FLIR. See Raytheon.

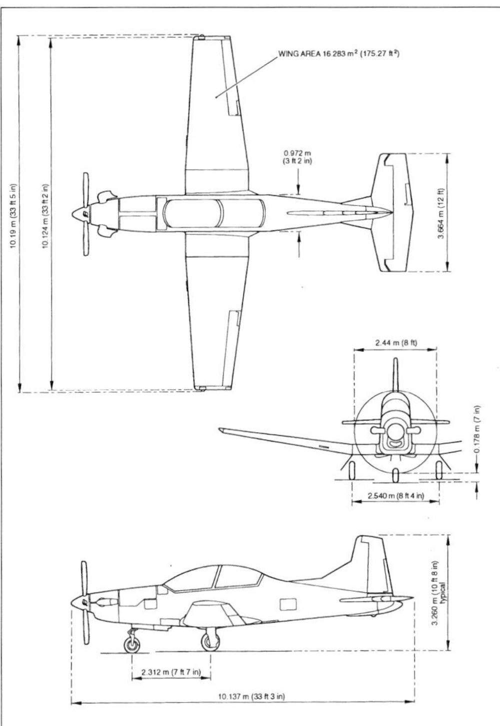

↑ **Pilatus PC-9 (M) Advanced Turbo Trainer general arrangement** *(courtesy Pilatus)*

← **Pilatus PC-9 (M) Advanced Turbo Trainer**

Details for PC-9 (M)

PRINCIPAL DIMENSIONS:
Wing span: 33 ft 2.5 ins (10.124 m)
Maximum length: 33 ft 3 ins (10.137 m)
Maximum height: 10 ft 8 ins (3.26 m)

WINGS:
Aerofoil section: PIL15M825, PIL12M850 (root/tip)
Area: 175.27 sq ft (16.283 m^2)
Aspect ratio: 6.292
Incidence: 1°
Dihedral: 7°

TAIL UNIT:
Tailplane span: 12 ft (3.664 m)
Tailplane area: 19.375 sq ft (1.8 m^2)

UNDERCARRIAGE:
Type: Retractable, with steerable nosewheel. Life of 30,000 landings
Wheel base: 7 ft 7 ins (2.312 m)
Wheel track: 8 ft 4 ins (2.54 m)

WEIGHTS:
Empty*: typically 3,803 lb (1,725 kg), depending on avionics fit
Zero fuel: 4,409 lb (2,000 kg)
Maximum ramp: 5,203 lb (2,360 kg) *aerobatic*, 7,077 lb (3,310 kg) with underwing stores
Maximum take-off: 5,181 lb (2,350 kg) *aerobatic*, 7,055 lb (3,200 kg) with underwing stores
Maximum landing weight: 5,181 lb (2,350 kg) *aerobatic*, 6,834 lb (3,100 kg) with underwing stores

CENTRE OF GRAVITY RANGE:
Aerobatic: 22 to 30% MAC at 4,960 lb (2,250 kg) or less, 25 to 30% MAC at 5,181 lb (2,350 kg)
With underwing stores: 23 to 28% MAC at 7,055 lb (3,200 kg)

PERFORMANCE (EAS at maximum operating weights)**:**
Design diving speed (V_D): 360 kts (414 mph) 666 km/h
Design diving Mach number (M_D): Mach 0.73
Maximum operating Mach number (M_{MO}): Mach 0.65
Maximum operating speed (V_{MO}): 320 kts (368 mph) 593 km/h
Design cruising speed (V_c): 320 kts (368 mph) 593 km/h
Maximum cruise speed: 300 kts (345 mph) 556 km/h at 25,000 ft (7,620 m)
Long-range cruise speed: 208 kts (240 mph) 385 km/h at 25,000 ft (7,620 m)
Manoeuvring speed (V_O): 205 kts (236 mph) 380 km/h *aerobatic*, 200 kts (230 mph) 370 km/h with underwing stores
Maximum speed with flaps and/or undercarriage extended: 150 kts (173 mph) 278 km/h
Stall speed, clean: 77 kts (89 mph) 143 km/h, or 90 kts (104 mph) 167 km/h with underwing stores
Stall speed, flaps and undercarriage down: 69 kts (80 mph) 128 mph, or 80 kts (92 mph) 149 km/h with underwing stores
Take-off distance: 795 ft (242 m) at sea level, *aerobatic*
Landing distance: 1,150 ft (350 m) at sea level, *aerobatic*
Take-off distance over a 50 ft (15 m) obstacle: 1,280 ft (390 m) at sea level, *aerobatic*
Landing distance over a 50 ft (15 m) obstacle: 2,297 ft (700 m) at sea level, *aerobatic*
Maximum climb rate: 4,100 ft (1,250 m) per minute at sea level, 3,500 ft (1,067 m) per minute at 10,000 ft (3,050 m)
Time to 5,000 ft (1,525 m): 1 minute 15 seconds
Time to 20,000 ft (6,100 m): 5 minutes 55 seconds
G limits: +7, -3.5 *aerobatic*; +4.5, -2.25 with underwing stores; +2, -0 with flaps and undercarriage extended
Sustained load factor: 3.8g sea level, 3.2g at 10,000 ft (3,050 m), 2.4g at 20,000 ft (6,100 m)
Ceiling: 25,000 ft (7,620 m) operating, 38,000 ft (11,600 m) service
Temperature limits: -55° C minimum, +50° C maximum
Still-air range with full internal fuel, at sea level: 358-401 naut miles (412-461 miles) 663-743 km, with reserve
Still-air range with full internal fuel, at 25,000 ft (7,620 m): 660 naut miles (760 miles) 1,223 km, with 20 minutes plus 5% reserve
Maximum range at 210 kts, at 25,000 ft (7,620 m): 830 naut miles (955 miles) 1,538 km
Duration: 1 hour 19 minutes to 4 hours 30 minutes, on internal fuel and with reserve, depending on speed and altitude
*see PC-7 for basic weight criteria.

SF

Switzerland

Full name:
Schweizerische Unternehmung für Flugzeuge und Systeme Entreprise Suisse d'Aeronautique et de Systemes Impresa Svizzera d'Aeronautica e Sistemi - Swiss Aircraft And Systems Company.

Corporate address:
CH-6032 Emmen.

Telephone: +41 41 268 41 11
Facsimile: +41 41 260 25 88
Web site: http://www.sfaerospace.ch

Founded:
1996 from the merger of F+W (see 1996-97 edition of *WA&SD*, page 116), the industrial division of SAFLC (Swiss Air Force Logistics Command) and some departments of the Federal Ordnance Office (FOO).

Employees:
1,700.

Information:
Marius Greber (*telephone* +41 41 268 44 01, *facsimile* +41 41 268 39 91).

FACILITIES

- CH-6032 Emmen for Business Management, Systems Management, Aircraft and UAVs; CH-6370 Stans for maintenance, inspection and repair of Jet Engines, plus Missiles and Anti-aircraft Systems; CH-3800 Interlaken for Avionics and related equipment; Lodrino, CH-6703 Osogna-Cresciano for Propeller-driven aircraft servicing; and CH-8600 Dübendorf for Electronic Command and Communication Systems.

ACTIVITIES

- Research and development organization, also undertaking manufacture, component production, maintenance and upgrading.
- Is assembling all but 2 of the 26 F/A-18Cs and 8 F/A-18Ds chosen to replace Swiss F-5Es, plus is developing and constructing low-drag pylons. BAe Hawk Mk 66 assembly has finished.
- Produces components under contract, including A320 airliner wingtips, auxiliary fuel tanks for the Dassault Rafale, wing slats for Boeing (McDonnell Douglas) MD-80 series of airliners and elevators for the Boeing 717.
- Upgrade of various military aircraft.
- Maintenance of military and civil aircraft and helicopters.
- Manufacture of the catapult-launched ADS 95 reconnaissance drone.
- Manufacture of Ariane nose fairings.
- Manufactures various missiles, including the anti-armour Dragon.

AIDC – Aerospace Industrial Development Corporation (Chinese name: Han Hsiang Aerospace Industry Co Ltd)

Taiwan

Corporate address:
No 111-6, Lane 68, Fu-Hsing North Road, Taichung, Taiwan 407 (postal address PO Box 90008-10-14, Taichung).

Telephone: +886 4 2562226, 2562379, 2590001
Facsimile: +886 4 2562282
Telex: 51142AIDC
Web site: http://www.aidc.com.tw/

Founded:
1 March 1969 under the auspices of the Ministry of National Defence. Reorganized under the authority of the Ministry of Economic Affairs on 1 July 1996.

Employees:
About 4,500.

Information:
Christine, Hwei-Ling Cheng (Senior Officer, Public Relations – *telephone* +886 4 2562301, *Facsimile* +886 4 2562370).

FACILITIES

- Chin Chuan Kang for aircraft assembly, development test facilities and flight test centre.
- Taichung for HQ, aeronautical research laboratory, component factories and avionics factory.
- Kaoshiung for the aero engine factory.

ACTIVITIES

- On 17 May 1995 it was announced that AIDC had been granted government approval to widen its activities into civil and component manufacture. Renamed HHAI in Taiwan, it continues to be state owned, but will become privatized by late 1999.
- Present products include manufacture of the Ching-Kuo Indigenous Defence Fighter, while upgraded versions of the AT-3 Tzu-Chiang trainer/light attack aircraft are being promoted. Sub-contracting includes manufacture of the Boeing 717 tail unit, Sikorsky S-92 cockpits, Dassault Falcon 900 and 2000 rudder, F-16 components, and engines (including CT7 & and TFE1042).
- Partnered with Aero Vodochody in Ibis Aerospace, developing the Ae 270 Ibis.

DIVISIONS

AIRCRAFT FACTORY

Activities:
- Over 2,200 employees at 2 complexes with 18 manufacturing plants. Parts fabrication, testing, assembly, maintenance, production planning, support and services facilities.

ENGINEERING DEPARTMENT (AERONAUTICAL SYSTEM DEVELOPMENT)

Activities:
- Research, development and production of numerous aviation programmes, including AT-3 and IDF.

AERO ENGINE FACTORY

Activities:
- Established September 1973 and now with over 600 employees for modern engine manufacturing.

AERONAUTICAL RESEARCH LABORATORY

Activities:
- Founded in 1939 and became part of the former AIDC in 1969. Water and wind tunnels (subsonic and supersonic), fatigue/load/static testing laboratory, electrical power testing laboratory, flight control centre, dual-dome flight simulator, engine test facility, flight test range, material laboratory, computer centre and more.

AVIONICS FACTORY

Activities:
- Founded April 1980 and is responsible for producing high-technology equipment for military purposes. Meets MIL-STD-2000 specifications and ISO-9002 production requirements for the IDF avionics systems. 7 current co-production programmes for the IDF including radar, the digital flight control computer, mission computer, integrated air data computer, bus interface unit, Tacan radio and the fuel measuring and indicating control system.

ADMINISTRATION AND OPERATIONS SUPPORT

AIDC/HHAI AT-3 Tzu-Chiang

First flight: 16 September 1980 for AT-CH-3 prototype.
Role: Advanced trainer, light attack, target towing, electronic countermeasures, maritime patrol and night surveillance.

Development

- 1975. Development began of the AT-CH-3.
- 1977. Construction of 2 prototypes began.
- 1980-81. 2 prototypes appeared, the second making its maiden flight on 30 October 1981.
- 6 February 1984. Maiden flight of a production AT-3, with deliveries beginning the following month.
- 1989. Production ended after 62 examples.
- 1997. First details released at the Paris Air Show of the AT-3S variant (see Flight/weapon system avionics/instrumentation and Aircraft variants).

Details *(AT-3, except where stated)*

Sales/Users: 62 built between 1977 and 1989, 60 for Air Force service. No exports at that time. AT-3 light attack aircraft is in active service with the 35th Squadron and performs electronic countermeasures, maritime patrol, night surveillance and close air support missions. 2 countries were thought to be in early negotiations for upgraded variants of the AT-3 in 1997, but no further details were available at the time of writing.
Crew: 2, in tandem, the rear seat stepped up by 11.8 ins (30 cm).

Details for the AT-3

PRINCIPAL DIMENSIONS:
Wing span: 34 ft 4 ins (10.46 m)
Maximum length: 42 ft 4 ins (12.9 m)
Maximum height: 14 ft 4 ins (4.36 m)

WINGS:
Aerofoil section: Supercritical
Area: 236 sq ft (21.93 m^2)
Aspect ratio: 4.989
Incidence: 1.5°

TAIL UNIT:
Tailplane span: 15 ft 10 ins (4.83 m)

UNDERCARRIAGE:
Type: Retractable, with steerable nosewheel that is also extendable to raise the nose by 3.5° during the ground run to reduce the take-off distance
Main wheel tyre size: 24 × 8 ins
Nose wheel tyre size: 18 × 6.5 ins
Wheel base: 18 ft (5.49 m)
Wheel track: 13 ft (3.96 m)

WEIGHTS:
Empty, operating: 8,500 lb (3,855 kg)
Flying training take-off: 11,500 lb (5,215 kg) clean
Maximum take-off: 17,500 lb (7,940 kg) for attack

PERFORMANCE:
Maximum limiting Mach number: Mach 1.05
Maximum speed: Mach 0.85 at 36,100 ft (11,000 m), 485 kts (558 mph) 899 km/h at sea level
Maximum cruise speed: 476 kts (548 mph) 882 km/h
Stall speed: 100 kts (116 mph) 185 km/h without flaps and with undercarriage retracted, or 90 kts (104 mph) 167 km/h with flaps and undercarriage lowered
Take-off distance: 1,500 ft (460 m)
Landing distance: 2,200 ft (670 m)
Take-off distance over a 50 ft (15 m) obstacle: 2,200 ft (670 m)
Take-off distance, 1 engine: 2,000 ft (610 m)
Maximum climb rate: 10,105 ft (3,080 m) per minute at sea level
Climb rate, 1 engine: 2,350 ft (716 m) per minute
Minimum turning radius: 1,080 ft (330 m) at 5,000 ft (1,525 m)
Ceiling: 48,000 ft (14,630 m)
Radius of action, with 5,000 lb (2,268 kg) external load: 250 naut miles (288 miles) 463 km, with full internal fuel, 5 minutes over target; total 1 hour 40 minutes mission time
Range with full fuel: 1,230 naut miles (1,416 miles) 2,275 km
Ferry range: 1,722 naut miles (1,982 miles) 3,191 km with auxiliary tanks retained, optimum speed at 30,000 ft (9,145 m)
Duration: 3.2 hours, or 5.2 hours with 2 × 568 litres auxiliary tanks

↑ **AIDC/HHAI AT-3 Tzu-Chiang 2-seater, camouflaged for combat** *(courtesy AIDC/HHAI)*

Cockpit: Pressurization differential 5 psi. One-piece canopy (see photograph).
Crew escape: Zero-zero ejection seats.
Fixed guns: See below.
Number of weapon pylons: Underfuselage bay for a machine-gun pack or other equipment. 7 pylons for the usual range of light weapons; 4 under the wings (inner 'wet' each 1,400 lb, 635 kg capacity; outer 600 lb, 272 kg capacity), wingtip launchers for AAMs, and 1 under the fuselage (2,000 lb, 907 kg capacity). Total load must not exceed 6,000 lb (2,722 kg).
Additional stores: Include pylon-mounted target systems or drop tanks.
Radar: See below.
Flight/weapon system avionics/instrumentation: IFR equipped. VOR/ILS and marker beacon indicator. Company produced avionics include IFF (with Teledyne), Tacan (with Collins), undercarriage warning, variable gain control, stability augmentation, radio communication, caution panel, hydraulic pressure/cabin pressure/fuel indicators, and inter-communications. Gunsight and camera. AT-3 brochure received in late 1997 detailed a variant employing a nav/attack system with dual 1553B databuses for such equipment as radar, HOTAS, MFD, HUD, LINS, DADC, anti-ship MCU, SCS, Tacan, radar altimeter, UHF coms, IFF and more. This might refer to the new avionics system for the AT-3B or the anticipated AT-3S. A diagram of the system is shown below.
Wing characteristics: Straight, low-mounted, with slight dihedral from the roots. Thought to be undergoing modification.
Wing control surfaces: Ailerons and single-slotted flaps.
Tail control surfaces: Slab tailplane and rudder (with yaw damper).
Airbrakes: 2 under the centre fuselage.
Flight control system: Hydraulic, but with electric flap actuation.
Construction materials: Mostly metal, including honeycomb sandwich for the ailerons, but with composites airbrakes and some fuselage parts.

↑ **Avionics diagram for an upgraded AT-3** *(courtesy AIDC/HHAI)*

Engines: 2 AlliedSignal TFE731-2-2L non-augmented turbofans.
Engine rating: Each 3,500 lbf (15.57 kN) take-off, 755 lbf (3.36 kN) cruise at 40,000 ft (12,200 m) and Mach 0.8.
Air intakes: Fuselage sides, ahead and above the wing, with splitter plates.
Flight refuelling probe: None.
Fuel system: 1,630 litres in 2 fuselage bag tanks. 2 optional 568 litre drop tanks under the wings.
Electrical system: 28 volt DC supply via engine-driven starter-generators. 40 amp-hour ni-cd battery for engine start-up. AC supply via 2 static inverters.
Hydraulic system: Dual, each 3,002 psi, with the ailerons, tailplane and rudder served by both.
Braking system: Disc type.
Oxygen system: Liquid.

Aircraft variants:
AT-3 is the basic version, as described, some 20 being camouflaged for attack.
AT-3A is a dedicated single-seater for attack and anti-ship roles (latter presumably with Hsiung Feng II), the prototype and so far only confirmed example being prepared from the second AT-3 prototype. Avionics changes included a new nav/attack system. Named Lui-Meng.
AT-3B is an upgrade of a number of AT-3s, retrofitted with AT-3A nav/attack.
AT-3S was a designation revealed by AIDC at the 1997 Paris Air Show for an upgraded variant.

AIDC/HHAI AT-5

Comments: The designations AT-5A and AT-5B mentioned at the 1997 Paris Air Show may refer either to a fully digital variant of the AT-3, with all the modern systems shown in the AT-3 diagram plus digital fly-by-wire flight control, or a new lead-in trainer based on the Ching-Kuo IDF. It is known that the RoCAF requires a fly-by-wire lead-in trainer now that it has IDFs, F-16s and Mirage 2000-5s in service, having found the 2-seat IDF too costly to use in all required stages of training and with too few available for the size of the training programme. AT-5 (presumably A and B refer to single and 2-seat forms, though not necessarily in this order) will use higher-thrust AlliedSignal engines, have the most modern avionics (but without radar and all the mission computers of the IDF), and incorporate modern structural materials and construction processes, knowing that AIDC has accumulated significant skills in manufacturing technologies concerned with CNC machining, sheet metal forming, titanium hot sizing, graphite composite material bonding, shot peening forming, and aluminium alloy and titanium alloy chemical milling.

AIDC/HHAI Ching-Kuo indigenous defence fighter (IDF)

First flight: 28 May 1989.
Role: Air defence fighter, counter-air, anti-ship and ground attack.

Aims

- Replacement for Taiwan's F-5E/F Tiger IIs and Starfighters, following US government blocks on Northrop F-20 Tigershark licence production and (formerly) the sale of other advanced fighters.
- To carry indigenous Sky Sword and Hsiung Feng II missiles.
- 8,000 flying hour structural life.
- Line replacement unit (LRU) modular design.
- Twin engines with digital engine controllers.
- Low wing loading, high thrust-to-weight ratio, and relaxed stability.
- Designed and tested in accordance with US military specifications and practices.
- Integrated logistics support applied to design.
- System growth capability.

Development

- May 1982. IDF programme begun. Allowed assistance came from Garrett (now AlliedSignal) with the engines, General Dynamics with the airframe, Westinghouse with the radar, and others. Newly founded Avionics Factory undertook substantial IDF work.
- 28 May 1989. Maiden flight of the first of 4 flying prototypes, as the 10001/77-8001 single-seater.
- 27 September 1989. Maiden flight of second prototype 10002/78-8002.
- 10 January 1990. Maiden flight of third prototype 10003/78-8003.
- 10 July 1990. Maiden flight of the first 2-seat and final prototype (10004/79-8004).
- 12 July 1991. Second prototype was lost.
- 19 November 1993. Last of 10 pre-series Ching-Kuos was received by the Air Force.
- 10 January 1994. Maiden flight of a production single-seat IDF, with deliveries starting that month.
- 27 February 1994. First production 2-seater delivered.
- January 1995. IOC with No 8 Squadron at Chin Chuan Kang, replacing Starfighters.

↑ **AIDC/HHAI Ching-Kuo indigenous defence fighters in single-seat and 2-seat forms**

■ October 1995. Deliveries temporarily halted to allow changes to the fuel management system.
■ May 1996. Deliveries restarted, with 52nd IDF.
■ 1997. First IDF simulator delivered by AIDC/HHAI, with 180° × 60° display and ESIG-3000 image generator.

Details

Sales/Users: 4 prototypes, including a single 2-seater. Original figure of 250 production IDFs was cut to 130 in 1993 following the availability of F-16s and Mirage 2000-5s and reportedly also because of concerns over engine rating. 2 IDF Wings planned. In 1998, 102 single-seaters and 28 2-seaters remained the number planned, when some 85 were in service, including at least 17 2-seaters. No 8 Squadron was the first to declare operational capability, in January 1995, with 22 aircraft. Fourth squadron operational by 1997. Offered for export, with Philippines approached.
Crew: Pilot, or 2 crew in tandem, with seats tilted 30° to help crew resist g loads.

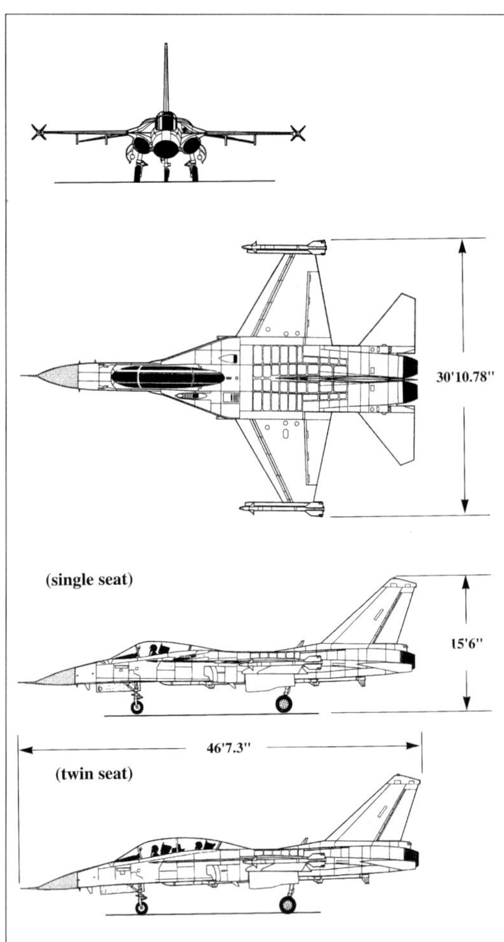

↑ AIDC/HHAI Ching-Kuo general arrangement *(courtesy AIDC/HHAI)*

↑ AIDC/HHAI Ching-Kuo with 2 Sky Sword II/TC-II missiles under the fuselage

Cockpit: Advanced 9g cockpit with 2 head-down displays plus a head-up display. Side-stick controller. Single-piece canopy plus windshield. AiResearch environmental control system, using bleed air from engines.
Crew escape: Martin Baker Mk 12 zero-zero ejection seats.
Fixed guns: 20-mm M61A1 cannon in the fuselage (port).
Ammunition: 511 rounds.
Number of weapon pylons: 6, 2 under the wings, 2 wingtip and 2 in tandem under the fuselage.
Expendable weapons and equipment: 8,600 lb (3,900 kg) maximum load. For air defence, 4 Sky Sword I (TC-I) air-to-air missiles under the wings and on the wingtip launchers, plus 2 Sky Sword IIs (TC-II) under the fuselage. Alternative weapons for attack/anti-ship missions can include 2 Maverick air-to-ground, 3 Hsiung Feng II anti-ship or other missiles, rocket launchers on 4 underwing pylons, cluster bombs or conventional bombs on all pylons except wingtip (including multiple launchers on inner underwing pylons), and fire bombs on underwing and underfuselage pylons.
Radar: Golden Dragon 53 multi-mode pulse-Doppler, based on the US APG-67(V).
Flight/weapon system avionics/instrumentation: Avionics Factory has 7 current co-production programmes for the IDF, including the digital flight control computer, mission computer, radar, integrated air data computer, bus interface unit, Tacan and the fuel measuring and indicating control system. Bendix/King displays (2 MFDs and a HUD). Honeywell H423 INS. All-aspect infra-red tracker. Photo-Sonics gun camera.
Self-protection systems: Radar homing and warning system. ECM.
Wing characteristics: Straight, mid-mounted, with no dihedral/anhedral, blended into the fuselage. LERX. Wingtip launch rails.
Wing control surfaces: Flaperons and leading-edge flaps.
Tail control surfaces: Slab tailplane (tailerons) and inset rudder.
Flight control system: Digital triplex fly-by-wire (Lear Astronics).
Construction materials: Mostly aluminium alloy, but with some composites including the tailplane and airbrakes, plus titanium for engine nozzles and cannon blast deflector.
Engines: 2 AlliedSignal (ITEC) TFE1042-70 turbofans, with FADEC. AlliedSignal C36-120 APU, for engine starting and as part of the ITEC integrated emergency power system.
Engine rating: Each 6,300 lbf (28 kN) dry, 9,250 lbf (41.1 kN) with afterburning.
Air intakes: Oval, fixed geometry, high efficiency type, with splitter plates, on the fuselage sides.
Flight refuelling probe: None.
Fuel system: 2,517 litres in 2 wing and 3 fuselage tanks with halon fire suppression. Provision for up to 3 × 568 litre or 1,041 litre drop tanks under the wings (inner 'wet' pylons) and fuselage, though 2 × 568 litre tanks under the wings or a single centreline 1,041 litre tank is more typical.
Electrical system: Principal AC supply via Westinghouse constant-frequency generators. DC supply using battery.
Hydraulic system: Dual, each 3,104 psi, for leading-edge flaps, control surface actuators, undercarriage (including steering), and airbrakes. 300 psi pneumatic system for emergency undercarriage operation.
Braking system: ABS carbon disc brakes, with anti-skid devices.
Oxygen system: Liquid type.

Details for IDF

PRINCIPAL DIMENSIONS:
Wing span: 28 ft (8.53 m) without wingtip AAMs, 30 ft 10.78 ins (9.42 m) with wingtip AAMs
Maximum length: 46 ft 7.3 ins (14.21 m) with probe, 43 ft 6 ins (13.26 m) without
Maximum height: 15 ft 6 ins (4.72 m)

WINGS:
Aerofoil section: Bi-convex type
Area: 261.13 sq ft (24.26 m^2)
Aspect ratio: 2.999

TAIL UNIT:
Tailplane span: 19 ft 7.4 ins (5.98 m)

UNDERCARRIAGE:
Type: Menasco retractable type, with steerable (±41.5°) nosewheel
Main wheel tyre size: 24 × 8-15 (Goodyear)
Nose wheel tyre size: 18 × 5.7-9.75 (Goodyear)
Wheel base: estimated 17 ft 4 ins (5.3 m)
Wheel track: estimated 6 ft 7 ins (2 m)
Turning radius: 26 ft (7.9 m) around nosewheel

WEIGHTS:
Empty: 14,300 lb (6,486 kg), equipped
Typical take-off: 21,000 lb (9,525 kg)
Maximum take-off: 27,000 lb (12,250 kg)

PERFORMANCE:
Maximum speed: estimated Mach 1.65-1.8
Maximum speed: 700 kts (806 mph) 1,297 km/h at 36,000 ft (11,000 m)
Best cruise speed: Mach 0.8, at 30,000 ft (9,145 m)
Stall speed: 100 kts (115 mph) 185 km/h
Climb rate: 50,000 ft (15,240 m) per minute
G limits: +6.5 at maximum design gross weight, +9/-3 cockpit and structure at basic
Ceiling: over 50,000 ft (15,250 m)

TUSAŞ Aerospace Industries Inc (TAI) — Turkey

Full name:
TUSAŞ Havacilik ve Uzay Sanayii AS.

Corporate address:
PO Box 18, 06692 Kavaklidere, Ankara.

Telephone: +90 312 811 1800
Facsimile:+90 312 811 1425
E-mail: tai-f@servis.net.tr
Web site: http://www.tai.com.tr

Founded:
May 1984. Joint-venture company, with Lockheed Martin of Turkey, Inc (42% shareholding), General Electric (7%), Turkish Armed Forces Foundation and Turkish Air League (2%).

Employees:
Over 2,200.

ACTIVITIES

■ F-16 production. Currently 80 Block 50D production C/Ds for the indigenous Air Force under the US Peace Onyx II programme (ordered 1992). Also constructs wings and fuselage sections for US production lines. Under the original US Peace Onyx I programme, the Turkish Air Force received 136 F-16Cs and 24 F-16Ds from 1987 to 1995, all but 8 assembled by TAI at Mürted, where 2 Ana Jet Ü F-16 squadrons and the OCU are based. Produced 46 C/Ds for Egypt, the first delivered on 29 March 1994. Turkish F-16s are receiving structural work by TUSAŞ under the Falcon-Up programme, and are having Loral ALQ-178 ECM fitted.
■ CN 235M transport production under licence from CASA, with Spain having delivered only 2 of the 52 destined for the Air Force. These include replacements for C-47s, plus 16 assigned to an electronic warfare role.
■ UH-60L Black Hawk production, with TAI assembling 50 of the 95 ordered, mostly for Army service.
■ Co-production of 28 Eurocopter Cougar Mk Is for the Air Force, for delivery from 1999, under Eurotai management.
■ Development of the HD-19 commuter transport (see Airline section).
■ Other work includes aircraft modernization, work on the Airbus FLA, construction of components for the EC 135 and S-76, and UAVs.

TAI TG-X1 Bat

First flight: 17 February 1997, completing ground and flight tests 13-15 May 1997 at Sivrihisar air base.
Role: Single-seat attack-surveillance aircraft, developed from the

↑ TAI TG-X1 Bat prototype

Sadler A-22 Piranha (in association with Sadler Aircraft Corp of Arizona, USA).
Comments: Powered by a 450 hp (335.5 kW) V-8 Chevrolet engine, can carry 1,000 lb (454 kg) of ordnance, and its folding wings and small size make it transportable on a small truck. Wing span 22 ft (6.71 m), length 16 ft 10 ins (5.13 m), MTOW 2,570 lb (1,168 kg), maximum speed 249 kts (287 mph) 462 km/h, range at 130 kts economical cruise speed 781 naut miles (900 miles) 1,448 km, and maximum loiter duration 6 hours. (In addition to the Piranha, Sadler itself offers the T-22 2-seat version.)

British Aerospace plc — UK

Corporate address:
Warwick House, PO Box 87, Farnborough Aerospace Centre, Farnborough, Hampshire GY14 6YU.
Telephone: +44 1252 373232
Facsimile: +44 1252 383000

Founded:
29 April 1977 by the amalgamation of BAC, Hawker Siddeley Aviation, Hawker Siddeley Dynamics and Scottish Aviation.

Employees:
Approximately 44,000.

Information:
Locksley C. Ryan (Director of Communications).

BRITISH AEROSPACE INTERNATIONAL MARKETING & SALES ORGANIZATIONS

HQ address:
Lancaster House, Farnborough Aerospace Centre, Farnborough, Hants GU14 6YU.

Telephone: +44 1252 373232
Facsimile: +44 1252 384812

BUSINESS UNITS

DEFENCE

BRITISH AEROSPACE AUSTRALIA HOLDINGS LIMITED

HQ address:
Regional Headquarters, Suite 2, Level 3, Westfield Towers, Sydney, NSW 2011, Australia.

Telephone: +61 2 9358 2900
Facsimile: +61 2 9358 4816

Activities:
▪ With British Aerospace Australia Limited, and a workforce of 1,800 at 30 locations in Australia and overseas, is a leading Australian defence and aerospace organization specializing in aircraft systems, military vehicles, missiles and decoys, electronic systems and dedicated customer support.

BRITISH AEROSPACE DEFENCE SYSTEMS LTD

Activities:
▪ Acquired Siemens Plessey Defence Systems Ltd as core of this new division.

MATRA BAE DYNAMICS

HQ address:
Six Hills Way, Stevenage, Herts SG1 2DA.

Telephone: +44 1438 312422
Facsimile: +44 1438 753377

Also:
Address:
PO Box 5, Lostock Lane, Lostock, Bolton, Lancashire BL6 4BR.
Telephone: +44 1204 696551
Facsimile: +44 1204 693908

Address:
PO Box 5, Filton, Bristol BS12 7QW.
Telephone: +44 117 9693866
Facsimile: +44 117 9316529

Activities:
▪ A European joint venture company, principally involved in the design, manufacture, sale and support of guided weapon systems. Product range includes ALARM, Sea Eagle, Storm Shadow, Meteor, Trigat, Seawolf, Sea Skua, Rapier and Jernas.

MILITARY AIRCRAFT AND AEROSTRUCTURES

HQ address:
Warton Aerodrome, Preston, Lancashire PR4 1AX.

Telephone: +44 1772 633333
Facsimile: +44 1772 643724

Information:
Dawn James (Head of Public Affairs and Communications – *telephone* +44 1772 852317, *facsimile* +44 1772 852539).

Also:
Address:
Brough, North Humberside HU15 1EQ.
Telephone: +44 1482 667121
Facsimile: +44 1482 666625

Address:
Dunsfold Aerodrome, Godalming, Surrey GU8 4BS.
Telephone: +44 1483 272121
Facsimile: +44 1483 200341

Address:
Hertford House, Farnborough Aerospace Centre, Farnborough, Hampshire GU14 6YU.
Telephone: +44 1252 373232
Facsimile: +44 1252 383000

Address:
Samlesbury Aerodrome, Balderstone, Lancashire BB2 7LF.
Telephone: +44 1254 812371
Facsimile: +44 1254 768000

Address:
Chadderton, Greengate, Middleton, Manchester M24 1SA.

Address:
Filton, PO Box 6, Filton House, Filton, Bristol BS99 7AR.

Address:
Prestwick International Airport, Ayrshire, Scotland KA9 2RW.

Activities:
▪ Specializing in the design, development and production of military aircraft. Also systems engineering and prime contractorship. Produces components and sub-assemblies for civil aircraft and other customers around the world. Supported by advanced test and research facilities.

BRITISH AEROSPACE NORTH SEA RANGE

HQ address:
Gregory House, Harlaxton Road, Grantham, Lincolnshire NG31 7JX.

Telephone: +44 1476 593909
Facsimile: +44 1476 592562

Activities:
▪ Located some 87 naut miles off the east coast of the UK, the North Sea ACMI Range is a dedicated air combat training facility.

ROYAL ORDNANCE

HQ address:
Euxton Lane, Chorley, Lancashire PR7 6AD.

Telephone: +44 1257 265511
Facsimile: +44 1257 242609

Activities:
▪ Principal activities include the design, manufacture and supply of munitions, munition delivery systems, field guns and small arms. Also, a full range of training and support services.

BAeSEMA LTD

HQ address:
Apex Tower, 7 High Street, New Malden, Surrey KT3 4LH.

Telephone: +44 181 942 9661
Facsimile: +44 181 942 9771
(jointly owned by BAe and Sema Group plc.)

Activities:
▪ Naval prime contractorship, naval construction, underwater weapons, and technical consultancy services.

BRITISH AEROSPACE (SYSTEMS & EQUIPMENT) LTD

HQ address:
Clittaford Road, Southway, Plymouth, Devon PL6 6DE.

Telephone: +44 1752 695695
Facsimile: +44 1752 695500

Activities:
▪ Navigation, radomes, recorders, motion sensing, weapon sub-systems, tracking and databus equipment, communications and magnetic components. Recent contracts include those from Lockheed Martin for integration of TERPROM digital terrain system into the F-16.

SYSTEMS & SERVICES

HQ address:
Mill Lane, Warton Aerodrome, Preston, Lancashire PR4 1AX.

Telephone: +44 1772 633333
Facsimile: +44 1772 855286

Activities:
▪ Provision of a range of prime contracting services in support of major defence procurement programmes, including the Al Yamamah contract with Saudi Arabia. Also the provision of battlefield systems, defence systems and systems integration, customer training and flight training.

COMMERCIAL AEROSPACE

BRITISH AEROSPACE AIRBUS LTD

HQ address:
PO Box 77, New Filton House, Filton, Bristol BS99 7AR.
Telephone: +44 117 969 3831
Facsimile: +44 117 936 2828

Also:
Address:
Chester Road, Broughton, nr Chester, Clwyd CH4 0DR.
Telephone: +44 1244 520444
Facsimile: +44 1244 523000

Activities:
▪ 4,300 employees. Designs wings and fuel systems for all Airbus airliners. Manufactures and assembles the primary structure of all Airbus wings. Equips A319, A320 and A321 wings. Airbus maintenance and conversion. See Airbus in the Airliners section. Also the FLA military transport programme through Airbus (see Freighters). Builds fuselage and wings for Hawker range of bizjets for Raytheon of USA.

BRITISH AEROSPACE ASSET MANAGEMENT

Address:
Warwick House (see Corporate address).

Also:
Address:
Asset Management Jets, 1 Bishop Square, St Alban's Road West, Hatfield, Herts.

Address:
Asset Management Turboprops, Washington Technology Park (see above).

Activities:
▪ Employs 130. Responsible for managing BAe's civil aircraft portfolio, consisting of over 500 aircraft for which BAe has financial responsibility.

BRITISH AEROSPACE REGIONAL AIRCRAFT LTD (BARAL)

AVRO INTERNATIONAL AEROSPACE

Address:
Woodford Aerodrome, Chester Road, Woodford, Cheshire SK7 1QR.

Telephone: +44 161 439 5050
Facsimile: +44 161 955 3008

ALSO:

SPARES AND LOGISTICS CENTRE

Address:
Vickers Drive, Brooklands Business Park, Weybridge, Surrey KT13 OUJ.

Telephone: +44 1932 352611
Facsimile: +44 1932 358232

Activities:
▪ Assembles RJ family of regional jets.

JETSTREAM AIRCRAFT LTD

Activities:
▪ Engineering management function for Jetstream customers.

OTHER BUSINESS UNITS

ARLINGTON SECURITIES PLC

HQ address:
Arlington House, Arlington Business Park, Theale, Reading, Berks RG7 4SA.

Telephone: +44 1734 304141
Facsimile: +44 1734 304383

Activities:
▪ Development and management of business parks.

BRITISH AEROSPACE (CONSULTANCY SERVICES) LTD

HQ address:
620-622 Birchwood Boulevard, Birchwood, Warrington, Cheshire WA3 7QW.

Telephone: +44 1925 822337
Facsimile: +44 1925 822483

Activities:
▪ Primarily engineering design, project management, quantity survey and management consultancy services to aerospace related projects.

BRITISH AEROSPACE FLIGHT TRAINING (UK) LIMITED

HQ address:
Prestwick Airport, Ayrshire KA9 2RW.

Telephone: +44 1292 671022
Facsimile: +44 1292 671010

ALSO:

BRITISH AEROSPACE FLIGHT TRAINING (AUSTRALIA) PTY LIMITED

FARNBOROUGH BUSINESS AVIATION

HQ address:
Farnborough Airport, Farnborough, Hampshire GU14 6XA.

Telephone: +44 1252 524440
Facsimile: +44 1252 518771

Activities:
▪ Business aviation centre at Farnborough. Workforce 25 employees.

SOWERBY RESEARCH CENTRE

HQ address:
FPC 267, PO Box 5, Filton, Bristol BS12 7QW.

Telephone: +44 117 969 3831
Facsimile: +44 117 936 3733

Activities:
▪ Research of new technology. 215 employees.

BRITISH AEROSPACE HOLDINGS INC

HQ address:
Washington Technology Park, 15000 Conference Center Drive, Suite 200, Chantilly, Virginia 20151-3819, USA.

Telephone: +1 703 802 0080
Facsimile: +1 703 227 1610

JOINT VENTURES

Airbus Industrie (20%), Asia Pacific Training and Simulation Ltd (63%), BAeHAL (40%), BAeSEMA Ltd (50%), Competence Center Informatik GmbH (30%), Eurofighter Jagdflugzeug GmbH (33%), Euromissile Dynamics Group (33%), Lee Valley Developments Ltd (50%), Liverpool Airport PLC (76%), Orange PLC (21.91%), Orion Network Systems (8.3%), Panavia Aircraft GmbH (42.5%), Reflectone Inc (52.7%), SEPECAT SA (50%), Singapore British Engineering Pte Ltd (51%), Spectrum Technologies (20%), UKAMS (33%).

British Aerospace Future Offensive Aircraft (FOA) of the Future Offensive Air System (FOAS) programme

First flight: Possibly 2005 for Technology Demonstrator.
Role: Primarily long-range interdiction and offensive counter air. Secondary roles include tactical air reconnaissance, suppression of enemy air defences, anti-surface warfare and offensive air support (battlefield interdiction). Involves all-weather, day/night, precision attack at low and medium/high altitudes.

Aims

▪ Replacement for Tornado IDS with RAF beyond the year 2015.
▪ High survivability against sophisticated defences, by exploiting stealth technology, defensive measures and crew protection.
▪ 'First time' mission effectiveness.
▪ Affordability.
▪ Highly integrated weapons/weapon systems.
▪ Self-defence (air combat) capability greater than Tornado GR 4.
▪ Role versatility.
▪ Out of area operation.

Development

▪ 1988-89. First studies for a Tornado replacement incorporating stealth concepts.
▪ 1990-91. Stealth aircraft studies, including Tornado 2000.
▪ 1991-92. Pre FOA (Future Offensive Aircraft) configuration studies.
▪ 1993-July 1996. UK Ministry of Defence pre-feasibility study, involving OR (Air), MoD PE, DERA and UK industry; BAe (MAD), R-R, GEC, Smiths Industries and others participated. Tornado 2000, derivatives of Eurofighter, and JSF included.
▪ 1996. MoD Equipment Approval Committee endorsement of Staff Target (Air) 425 'Future Offensive Air System' (FOAS, formerly FOA), encompassing not only the manned aircraft described, but also unmanned air vehicles and stand-off weapons launched from large airborne platforms. Formation of FOAS Project Board within BAe.
▪ 1997. Research, technology and facilities development and technology demonstration (risk reduction) programmes orientated towards the Future Offensive Aircraft underway in key technology areas: configurational design, stealth, low cost manufacture, sensors, avionics systems and weapons integration, advanced avionics architecture, electronic warfare, crew protection and propulsion. Includes industry-wide participation with MoD.

↑ **British Aerospace Future Offensive Aircraft P145-25 Pre-Feasibility Study multi-role interdictor, released at Farnborough 1996 and the latest known configuration** *(courtesy BAe)*

▪ 1997. Definition of FOAS specific Technology Demonstration Programme content.
▪ 1997-99. Feasibility (option) studies embracing new design multi-role interdictor, Eurofighter derivative, JSF CV-CTOL development, other future 'off the shelf' aircraft, unmanned concepts and large non-penetrating aircraft with ALCMs.
▪ 1998. FOAS funded Technology Demonstration Programme initiation.
▪ 1999. MoD decision expected on preferred solution from the options for Staff Requirement (Air) 425. Start of Project Definition phase.
▪ 2001. Originally envisaged first flight date of possible Technology Demonstrator. In 1998, a more likely estimate would be 2005 to accommodate studies on alternatives and probable international collaboration.
▪ 2005-2012*. Development phase.
▪ 2010*. Investment and production.
▪ 2015*. Envisaged entry into RAF service.
*earliest envisaged dates.

Configuration evolution

▪ 1990. Earliest impressions of subsonic 'flying triangle', thick blended delta planform, with canted wingtips. Presumed internal weapons carriage. Integrated canopy.
▪ September 1994. Impression of Next Combat Aircraft (NCA). Subsonic delta wing configuration with blended wing/body and chined front fuselage, accommodating a pilot only under a 'high field of view' canopy. Sensors in the nose and wingtip pods. No radar? Twin raked and scarfed side intakes for the single engine. Internal weapons carriage, including self-defence AAMs. Trailing-edge flaperons and no tailplane. Twin canted fins.
▪ September 1996. Impressions released and models displayed at Farnborough Air Show of 2 alternative configurations:
1. Subsonic, very low radar cross section (RCS), dedicated interdictor. Single pilot and no radar? Twin raked, scarfed side intakes (shielded) for twin engines. Front fuselage chines integrated into highly swept inner wing to mid span. 'Edge alignment' of untapered outer wing panel resulted in notched trailing-edge planform. Low (radar) observables nozzles. Internal weapons carriage.
2. Supersonic configuration with trapezoidal wing and aft tail offering more manoeuvrability (air-to-air capability), but presumably with RCS penalty. Single pilot and nose radar? Edge alignment on flying surfaces and intake shields. Twin canted fins. Internal weapons carriage.
▪ 1998. Current configuration classified.

Details

Sales/Users: Intended for RAF, to replace Tornado GR 4 phasing out about the year 2015. Multi-national partners being sought (European, or USA as a CTOL JSF derivative).
Crew: Single and 2-crew studies. Single pilot if workload/mission requirements can be shown to be compatible, but 2 crew more likely as lower risk.
Cockpit: Emphasis on crew protection; laser threat? Metallized canopy for low RCS?
Weapons carriage: Bay for internal weapons carriage in stealthiest configuration. Also external carriage capability for larger/additional air-to-surface and air-to-air weapons, and/or fuel (see below).
Expendable weapons and equipment: Medium/long-range stand-off air-to-surface weapons. Precision attack munitions (for example, Paveway III UK). Defence suppression missiles. Air-to-air self-defence missiles. Internal carriage of 2 × 2,000 lb class weapons plus 2 self-defence AAMs. External carriage of up to 8,000 lb (3,629 kg) of weapons/fuel.
Radar: See earlier comments.
Self-protection systems: Active and passive electronic and infra-red countermeasures probable. Towed decoy?
Engines: 2, widely spaced and in the 20,000 lbf (89 kN) class. Possibly variable cycle.

Basic details for Future Offensive Aircraft

PRINCIPAL DIMENSIONS:
Unknown, but probably in Tornado class

WEIGHTS:
Unknown, but probably in Tornado class

PERFORMANCE:
Maximum speed: Transonic and supersonic options
Manoeuvrability: Sufficient agility for credible self-defence with AAMs
Basing concept: Conventional/reduced length runway, but non-STOVL
Radius of action: 750-1,000 naut miles (864-1,151 miles) 1,390-1,853 km estimated for 'platform plus weapon reach'

British Aerospace Hawk T Mk 1/1A, 50, 60 and 100 series

First flight: 21 August 1974; May 1976 for Mk 50 demonstrator, 1 April 1982 for Mk 60, and 1 October 1987 for Mk 100.
Role: Basic and advanced trainer, with operational air defence and attack roles (see Aircraft variants).

Aims

- Modern, high-subsonic, advanced flying trainer, and also weapons and navigation trainer with potential for further development.
- Uncompromized configuration, with tandem seating in an "ideal" cockpit.
- Fuel-efficient turbofan engine.
- 6,000 flying hours safe fatigue life.

Development

- Original design and development was by Hawker Siddeley Aviation (see Founded).
- October 1971. HS 1182 selected to fulfil requirement ASR 397, as a replacement for Folland Gnat and Hawker Hunter advanced trainers.
- October 1973. HS 1182 given the name Hawk.
- 4 November 1976. First deliveries to No 4 Flying Training School at RAF Valley.
- 1980. First export deliveries, as Mk 51s for Finland.
- 18 November 1981. Winner of a US Navy's VTXTS competition for a new carrier-capable trainer. Became the T-45A Goshawk. Full scale development began in 1984. (See Boeing/BAe T-45 Goshawk in the multi-national section).
- 13 July 1982. First Mk 60 delivery, as Mk 61 for Zimbabwe.
- 19 May 1986. First flight of the Hawk Mk 200 single-seater (which see).
- 4 December 1991. First aircraft carrier landing by a Hawk variant, a US Goshawk (which see).
- April 1993. First Mk 100 delivery, as Mk 102 for Abu Dhabi.
- 13 February 1997. First 2 deliveries (from Warton) from batch of 20 Mk 65As for RSAF.
- June 1997. Australia ordered 33 Hawk 100s, first aircraft to have Adour 871s and later aircraft Adour 900s.
- 2000. First batch of 12 Mk 127s for Australia to be delivered, with further 21 by 2006.

Details

Sales/Users: *T Mk 1*: UK (176, with 88 redelivered as T Mk 1As). *Series 50*: Finland (50 Mk 51s and 7 Mk 51As), Indonesia (20 Mk 53s) and Kenya (12 Mk 52s). *Series 60*: Abu Dhabi (12 Mk 63As, 4 Mk 63Bs plus 4 new Mk 63Cs – see end of paragraph for new Mk 63s), Dubai (9 Mk 61s), Kuwait (12 Mk 64s), Saudi Arabia (30 Mk 65s plus 20 65As), Switzerland (20 Mk 66s), South Korea (20 Mk 67s) and Zimbabwe (8 Mk 60s and 5 Mk 60As). *Series 100*: Abu Dhabi (18 Mk 102s), Australia (33 Mk 127s for lead-in fighter training - see Development), Indonesia (8 Mk 109s), Malaysia (10 Mk 108s), Oman (4 Mk 103s) and Qatar (18 Mk 100s). Further orders (to be confirmed at time of writing in 1998) from Canada (17 and possibly 25 for NATO Flying Training in Canada, with deliveries commencing in the year 2000), the UAE (further 12 Mk 63s), and Brunei (4 Mk 100s; 6 others expected, type unclear). 1 Mk 100 used by BAe for development flying. Production rate of all Hawks at time of writing: 22 per year (excluding 12 T-45A Goshawks).
Crew: 2 in tandem, with the rear instructor's seat stepped up. Usually flown as a single-seater in combat.
Cockpit: Single-piece windshield with frame, hinging forward for maintenance only. Single-piece canopy with mid arch, sideways (starboard) opening. Rear cockpit has a protective front screen integral with the canopy arch.
Crew escape: Martin Baker Mk 10B zero-zero ejection seats in early aircraft, Mk 10LH later. Canopy fracturing system (miniature detonating cord - MDC).
Fixed guns: None, although a self-contained single 30-mm Aden cannon pod can be carried on the centreline attachment. *Mk 51* uses a 12.7-mm gun.
Ammunition: Up to 150 rounds.
Number of weapon pylons: T Mk 1/1A have 3 (2 under the wings and 1 under the fuselage), but with the ability to have 2 more under the wings. *Series 50/60* have all 5 in use, each underwing pylon with a 1,135 lb (515 kg) capacity. *Series 50/60* introduced 'wet' pylons and an increased overall load. *Series 100* adds wingtip AAM launch rails, making 7 weapon points. Utilization of twin-store carriers enables Hawk 100 and Mk 63A/C to carry a maximum of 11 stores.
Expendable weapons and equipment: *Mk 1/1A*: typically 1,500 lb (680 kg) of practice bombs or rocket pods on the wing pylons and a gun pod under the fuselage, with optional AIM-9L Sidewinders for Mk 1A. *Series 50/60/100* are able to carry an extensive range of NATO and US stores, including gun pod, rocket launchers (68-mm, 81-mm or 100-mm rockets), bombs (250 lb, 500 lb or 1,000 lb), cluster bombs, runway cratering bombs, practice bomb/rocket carriers, air-to-surface missiles (including Maverick) and Sidewinder AAM. *Series 100* has standard wingtip launch rails for additional Sidewinders, although 12 Abu Dhabi Mk 63s have also been given new wings of Series 100 type plus the higher-rated engine (becoming Mk 63As), as have newly-built Mk 63Cs. Maximum warload for Series 60/100s is 6,600 lb (3,000 kg). Twin-store carriers can be adopted (see above).
Additional stores: Reconnaissance pod, ECM pod or target-towing system.
Radar: None. See Hawk 200.
Flight/weapon system avionics/instrumentation: Conventional dial-type flight instrumentation on all but Series 100 aircraft. *T Mk 1/1A* and *Series 50* have UHF, VHF, VOR/ILS/DME and IFF. No HUD. Gunsight. Tacan. *Series 60* incorporates attitude and heading reference system (AHRS), ISIS gunsight and a comprehensive stores management system. *Series 100* offers an advanced state-of-the-art fit, including wide-angle HUD, new generation weapon aiming computer, and head-down multi-purpose display. HOTAS. Optional FLIR/laser ranging in the nose. Laser inertial navigation. High accuracy air data. MIL-STD-1553B dual redundant digital databus.
Self-protection systems: Radar warning receiver. IR flares and chaff on Series 100. Possible ECM.
Wing characteristics: Slightly swept, low mounted, with dihedral. 2 spar, single-piece continuous wing structure. Skin with integral stiffeners. Undercarriage accommodated ahead of the front spar, avoiding a cut-out in the main wing box. Fences, stall strips and vortex generators. *Series 100* wing has leading-edge droop to enhance lift and manoeuvrability, and full flap vanes.
Wing control surfaces: Ailerons outboard of trailing-edge flaps (single-slotted plus fixed vane, effectively double slotted); *Series 60* and *100* have 4-position flaps, including combat settings, instead of the earlier 3-position.
Tail control surfaces: Slab tailplane and rudder (with tab). 2 canted ventral underfuselage strakes. Aerodynamic "SMURF" surfaces immediately ahead of and lower than the tailplane on Series 100 aircraft, intended to inhibit tailplane stall and thereby increase trimming ability in flapped configurations.

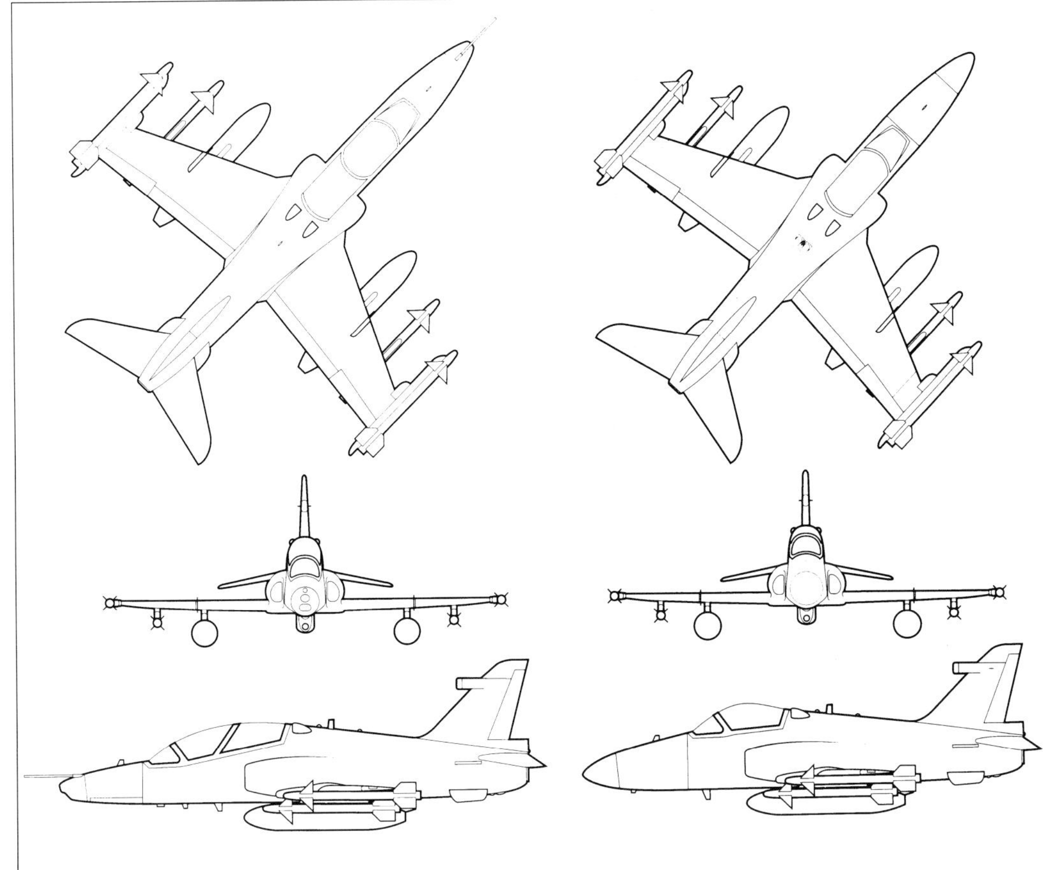

↑ **British Aerospace Hawk Mk 100 general arrangement (*left*), with additional Hawk 200 (*right*) for easy comparison** *(courtesy British Aerospace)*

Details for Hawk (not Hawk 200)

PRINCIPAL DIMENSIONS:
Wing span: 30 ft 10 ins (9.39 m), 32 ft 7.5 ins (9.94 m) over AAMs
Maximum length: 38 ft 10.5 ins (11.85 m), or 40 ft 9 ins (12.42 m) *Series 60/100*
Maximum height: 13 ft 1 ins (3.99 m)

WINGS:
Area: 179.64 sq ft (16.69 m^2)
Aspect ratio: 5.28
Sweepback: 21.5° at 25% chord
Chord at root: 8 ft 8 ins (2.64 m)
Chord at tip: 3 ft (0.91 m)
Dihedral: 2°

TAIL UNIT:
Tailplane span: 14 ft 5 ins (4.39 m)
Tailplane area: 46.6 sq ft (4.33 m^2)
Fin area: 27 sq ft (2.51 m^2), or 28.1 sq ft (2.61 m^2) *Series 100*

UNDERCARRIAGE:
Type: Retractable, with castoring or steerable nosewheel
Main wheel tyre size: 22 × 6.50-10
Nose wheel tyre size: 18 × 5.5-16
Wheel base: 14 ft 9 ins (4.5 m)
Wheel track: 11 ft 5 ins (3.48 m)

WEIGHTS:
Empty: 7,700 lb (3,493 kg) approximately for *Series 50*, 8,845 lb (4,012 kg) *Series 60*, 9,700 lb (4,400 kg) *Series 100*
Design trainer take-off: 11,100 lb (5,035 kg) *Series 50*
Maximum take-off: 17,085 lb (7,750 kg) *Series 50*, 20,062 lb (9,100 kg) *Series 60/100*

PERFORMANCE:
Maximum level Mach number: Mach 0.82 for *Series 100*
Maximum speed (*Series 50*): 540 kts (622 mph) 1,000 km/h *clean*, or 485 kts (558 mph) 898 km/h with 1 crew, 2 Sidewinders and 60% fuel
Stall speed: 96 kts (110 mph) 177 km/h
Take-off distance: 1,500 ft (457 m) *Series 50* at design trainer weight, ISA+ 15°, or 4,200 ft (1,280 m) at 17,000 lb (7,711 kg) weight
Landing distance: 1,800 ft (549 m) *Series 50* at 10,000 lb (4,536 kg) weight, or 1,500 ft (457 m) with drag-chute
Time to 30,000 ft (9,145 m): 8 minutes 30 seconds for *Series 50* with 1 crew, gun, 2 Sidewinders and internal fuel, or 6 minutes 54 seconds for *Series 60*, or 7 minutes 30 seconds for *Series 100*
G limits: +8, -4 for *Series 50*, +6 -3 for *Series 100* with 6 × 1,000 lb bombs and 60% fuel
G limit, sustained: 4.6 for *Series 50* at sea level, mean combat weight
Ceiling: 46,000 ft (14,000 m) for *Series 60*

BAe Hawk typical mission radius, or duration/ferry range

Version	Weapons	Fuel	Mission	naut miles (miles) km
Series 50	2 × 1,000 lb bombs	Internal	Lo-Lo-Lo-Lo	187 (215) 346
	4 × 1,000 lb bombs	Internal	Lo-Lo-Lo-Lo	162 (186) 300
	6 × 1,000 lb bombs	Internal	Lo-Lo-Lo-Lo	140 (161) 259
	2 × 1,000 lb bombs	+2 drop tanks	Lo-Lo-Lo-Lo	278 (320) 515
	4 × 1,000 lb bombs	+2 drop tanks	Lo-Lo-Lo-Lo	250 (288) 463
	2 × 1,000 lb bombs	Internal	Hi-Lo-Lo-Hi	406 (467) 752
	4 × 1,000 lb bombs	Internal	Hi-Lo-Lo-Hi	337 (388) 624
	6 × 1,000 lb bombs	Internal	Hi-Lo-Lo-Hi	280 (322) 519
	2 × 1,000 lb bombs	+2 drop tanks	Hi-Lo-Lo-Hi	608 (699) 1,126
	4 × 1,000 lb bombs	+2 drop tanks	Hi-Lo-Lo-Hi	500 (575) 926
	Gun + 2 Sidewinders	Internal	1 crew, combat air patrol	70 minutes, at 100 naut miles
	Gun + 2 Sidewinders	Internal	1 crew, combat air patrol	40 minutes, at 200 naut miles
	Gun + 2 Sidewinders	+2 drop tanks	1 crew, combat air patrol	130 minutes, at 100 naut miles
	Gun + 2 Sidewinders	+2 drop tanks	1 crew, combat air patrol	98 minutes, at 200 naut miles
			Ferry range	about 1,400 (1,610) 2,593
Series 60	Gun + 4 Sidewinders	+2 drop tanks	Air defence, Hi-Hi	2.7 hours at 100 naut miles
			Interdiction, Hi-Lo-Lo-Hi	415 (478) 768
	2 × rocket pods	+2 drop tanks	Maritime attack	455 (524) 842
			Ferry range	1,575 (1,813) 2,917
Series 100	Gun + 4 Sidewinders	+2 drop tanks	Air defence, Hi-Hi	2 hours at 100 naut miles
			Close air support	125 (144) 231.5
			Interdiction, Hi-Lo-Lo-Hi	345 (397) 639
		+2 drop tanks	Ferry range	1,360 (1,566) 2,519

Airbrake: Single petal type under the rear fuselage. Cannot be used for landing.
Flight control system: Hydraulic for ailerons, tailplane plus flap actuation. Manual only for rudder, but a powered rudder was introduced on Series 60/100, with yaw damper. Electric trimming about all axes.
Fuselage: Manufacture breakdown: cockpit to aft of the rear pressure bulkhead and nose section, centre fuselage, separate intake nacelles, and rear fuselage aft of the wing trailing edge. Equipment (depending on variant) in the nose, under and aft of the rear cockpit, and in the fuselage dorsal spine. Centre fuselage accommodates a large bag fuel tank and intake ducts, the wing being a continuous carry-through structure.
Construction materials: Principally aluminium alloys.
Engine: Rolls-Royce Turbomeca Adour turbofan (see below).
Engine rating: *Mk 1/1A* have Adour 151 of 5,240 lbf (23.31 kN). *Series 50* has Adour 851 of similar rating. *Series 60* has Adour 861 of 5,710 lbf (25.4 kN). *Series 100* has Adour 871 of 5,730 lbf (25.5 kN), as have *Mk 63*s. Later Australian *Mk 127*s to have Adour 900s.
Nozzles: Fixed, plain.
Air intakes: Bifurcated pitots, with vertical bodyside diverters.
Flight refuelling probe: Flight tested on Hawk 100.
Fuel system: 1,659 litres in integral wing and centre section tanks, plus fuselage bag tank. *Series 50/60/100* have 'wet' inner wing pylons; *Series 50* can carry 450 litre combat drop tanks, and *Series 60/100* can carry 591 litre drop tanks. Booster pump in the collector tank delivers fuel to engine under all flight conditions; collector tank can sustain 30 seconds of inverted flight.
Electrical system: Single 9kW DC generator. AC power via 2 × 500 VA inverters. Emergency power from 2 × 18 amp-hour batteries. Increased power on *Series 60* and *100* via a single 12kW 30V DC generator; AC power from 2 × 3KVA 115/26V 400Hz 3-phase inverters. 2 batteries supply 20 minutes power for essential services in the event of primary supply failure.
Hydraulic system: 2 independent systems (each with own engine-driven pump), at 3,000 psi. Both systems power the flying controls by means of tandem actuators at ailerons and tailplane. No 1 system also supplies general services (airbrake, undercarriage, flaps and wheel brakes). No 2 system supplies PCUs in the event of No 1 failure. Ram air turbine supplies power in the event of both systems or engine failure.
Braking system: Main wheel brakes, with anti-skid. Drag-chute on most versions but not on RAF Mk 1/1As.
Oxygen system: Gaseous, capacity 1,400 litres, for up to 4 hours duration. Emergency oxygen cylinder on ejection seat, with demand regulator.

Aircraft variants:
Hawk T Mk 1 is the RAF's advanced flying and weapon training version.
Hawk T Mk 1A covers 88 T Mk 1s modified and redelivered to carry AIM-9L Sidewinders on the inner wing pylons and the option of using outer pylons, for an operational point air defence role under emergency conditions or co-operating with radar-equipped Tornados in a Mixed Fighter Force. All returned to service by 1986.
Hawk Mk 50 is the export trainer, with similarly rated engines to the T Mk 1. Higher weights and with limited attack capability.
Hawk Mk 60 is an export variant with greater engine power and higher performance, significant airframe changes (see Wing characteristics and other headings) and increased weapon options.
Hawk Mk 100 has another increase in engine power, greater operational fighter and attack capabilities through improved weapon system management and avionics, and with further airframe changes including a new wing with leading-edge droop to improve manoeuvrability plus manual combat flaps. HOTAS. Provision for nose-mounted FLIR/laser ranging.

↑ British Aerospace Hawk Mk 100 stores options (similar for Hawk 200) *(courtesy British Aerospace)*

British Aerospace Hawk 200

First flight: 19 May 1986 (demonstrator).
Role: Multi-role for air defence, close air support, battlefield interdiction, maritime support, maritime strike, reconnaissance and more.

Aims

▪ Exploitation of the proven 2-seat Hawk design, producing a single-seat, lightweight, subsonic combat variant with significantly increased air-to-air and air-to-ground capability by the provision of radar. Increased fuel load for longer range.

Development

▪ June 1984. BAe private venture decision to enhance the export potential of the Hawk.
▪ 2 July 1986. First demonstrator was lost barely 8 weeks after the first flight, due to G-induced loss of consciousness.
▪ July 1990. First order placed by Oman.
▪ 13 February 1992. Third Hawk 200 flew (the second in April 1987), featuring a complete avionics fit, including radar.
▪ 11 September 1993. First flight of a full production Hawk 200, as a Mk 203 for Oman.

↑ Malaysian British Aerospace Mk 208 single-seater (*rear*) and Hawk Mk 108 2-seater (*nearest*)

▪ April 1997. Delivery of the last Mk 209 of initial batch of 16 to Indonesia.
▪ 1998. Initial deliveries from second batch of 16 Mk 209s to Indonesia. Include IFR capability.

Details

Sales/Users: Ordered by Indonesia (16 Mk 209s, plus further 16 ordered), Malaysia (18 as Hawk Mk 208s), and Oman (12 as Hawk Mk 203s). Further orders (to be confirmed at time of writing) to Qatar and Brunei (Brunei reaffirmed intention to acquire 10 Hawks, type unclear). 1 Mk 200 used by BAe for development flying.
Crew: Pilot.
Cockpit: Smaller canopy with MDC, retaining good field of view. Sideways opening.
Crew escape: Martin Baker Mk 10LH.
Fixed guns: None, but 30-mm gun pod under the fuselage.
Ammunition: Up to 150 rounds.
Number of weapon pylons: 7, as for Hawk 100. Utilization of twin-store carriers enables a maximum of 11 stores to be carried. Maximum 2,000 lb (907 kg) load on each underwing pylon.
Expendable weapons and equipment: Extensive range of NATO and US stores as detailed under the earlier Hawk entry. Maximum 6,600 lb (3,000 kg).
Additional stores: Reconnaissance pod, target towing system, etc. Optional ECM pod.
Radar: Northrop Grumman APG-66H multi-mode radar, offering 8 air-to-surface and 10 air-to-air modes with fixing, target detection and target ranging sub modes. Derivative of the APG-66 in the F-16.
Flight/weapon system avionics/instrumentation: Based on the Hawk 100 fit, except for the addition of display of radar data.
Self-protection systems: Radar warning receiver, and chaff/flare dispenser.
Wing characteristics: Based on the Hawk 100.
Engine: Rolls-Royce Turbomeca Adour 871 turbofan.
Engine rating: 5,730 lbf (25.5 kN).
Flight refuelling probe: Optional and proven, with fixed probe.
Fuel system: 1,655 litres internal, 1,182 litres external.
Electrical system: Primary power via a 25KVA 200/115V 400Hz 3-phase generator driven from the auxiliary gearbox. DC power via a single transformer rectifier unit. 2 batteries for engine starting and essential services for 20 minutes should primary supply fail.
Hydraulic system: Same as previous 2-seat Hawk entry.
Oxygen system: Gaseous; 1,400 litres capacity, for up to 7 hours duration. Emergency cylinder on ejection seat, with demand regulator.

Details for Hawk 200

PRINCIPAL DIMENSIONS:
Wing span: 30 ft 10 ins (9.39 m), 32 ft 7.5 ins (9.94 m) over AAMs
Maximum length: 37 ft 3 ins (11.35 m)
Maximum height: 13 ft 1 ins (3.98 m)

WINGS:
Area: 179.64 sq ft (16.69 m^2)
Aspect ratio: 5.28
Sweepback: 21.5° at 25% chord, 26° leading edge
Chord at root: 8 ft 8 ins (2.64 m)
Chord at tip: 3 ft (0.91 m)
Thickness/chord ratio: 10.9% root, 9% tip
Dihedral: 2°

TAIL UNIT:
Tailplane span: 14 ft 5 ins (4.39 m)
Tailplane area: 46.6 sq ft (4.33 m^2)

WEIGHTS:
Empty: 9,810 lb (4,450 kg)
Maximum take-off: 20,061 lb (9,100 kg)

PERFORMANCE:
Maximum dive speed: Mach 1.2
Maximum speed: 540 kts (621 mph) 1,000 km/h at sea level
Stall speed: 96 kts (110 mph) 177 km/h IAS, *with flaps*
Take-off distance: 2,070 ft (631 m)
Landing distance: 1,960 ft (597 m)
Time to 30,000 ft (9,145 m): 7 minutes 24 seconds
G limits: +8, -4; +6, -3 with 6,000 lb (2,722 kg) stores load and 60% internal fuel
G limit with 1,102 lb (500 kg) load on individual underwing pylons: +8
Sustained G limit: 5.6
Ceiling: 45,000 ft (13,716 m)

BAe Hawk 200 typical mission radius, or duration/ferry range

Weapons	Fuel	Mission	naut miles (miles) km
4 × 1,000 lb bombs, gun and 2 Sidewinders	Internal	Close air support	100 (115) 185
2,000 lb (907 kg) of bombs and 2 Sidewinders.	+2 drop tanks	Battlefield interdiction	290 (334) 537
2 rocket launchers and 2 Sidewinders	+2 drop tanks	Maritime support	315 (363) 583
Reconnaissance pod and 2 Sidewinders	+2 drop tanks	Fighter reconnaissance	490 (564) 907
4 Sidewinders and gun	+2 drop tanks	Air defence	2 hours loiter at radius of 100 (115) 185
	+2 drop tanks	Ferry range	1,300 (1,497) 2,407

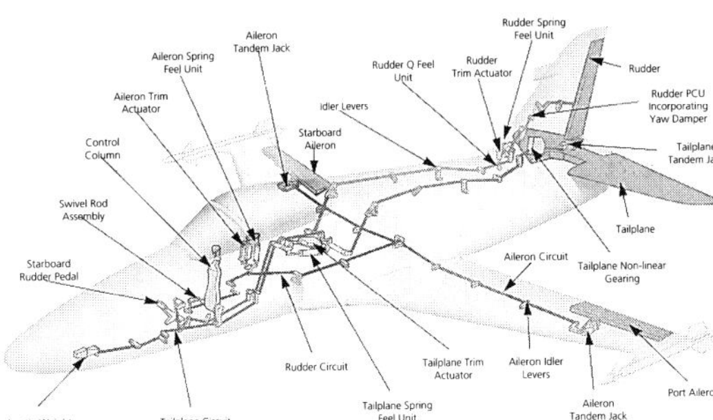

↑ **British Aerospace Hawk 200 flying controls** *(courtesy British Aerospace)*

New Generation British Aerospace Hawk

Comments: Development continues on new variants of Hawk for potential orders circa 2010.

British Aerospace Harrier

Comments: Brief notes on (then) current operators and versions of the original variants of Harrier appeared in the 1996-97 edition of *WA&SD*, page 124. Since then it has become clear that the Royal Thai Navy received 7 AV-8Ss and 2 TAV-8S Matadors, now operating on board the light carrier HMTS *Chakri Naruebet*. These have suffered from spares difficulties and not all are operational in early 1998. It is possible further Matadors may be purchased from Spain.

British Aerospace Sea Harrier F/A Mk 2

Comments: See 1996-97 edition of *WA&SD*, pages 124-125, for details on the Sea Harrier FRS Mk 1 (plus the general Aims and Development of the original Sea Harrier programme), withdrawn from Royal Navy service in 1995. Indian Navy received 23 FRS Mk 51s between 1982-92 plus 6 Harrier T Mk 60 trainers. India's plan to purchase F/A Mk 2s to replace FRS Mk 51s was abandoned, deciding instead on a navalized LCA, although in September 1997 it ordered 2 refurbished ex-Royal Navy T Mk 4 trainers to supplement T Mk 60s. Planned upgrade of FRS Mk 51s to keep them operational until the year 2010 was suspended in 1996, when also the carrier INS *Vikrant* was decommissioned.
First flight: 19 September 1988 (FRS Mk 2 aerodynamic development aircraft).
Role: STOVL ship-based fleet air defence, surface ship attack and reconnaissance.

Aims

▪ Derived from Sea Harrier FRS Mk 1 (newly built or by conversion), with 13.75 ins (35 cm) fuselage plug aft of wing, new Blue Vixen radar in a reshaped radome, ability to carry AMRAAM AAMs on Frazer-Nash launch rails and US-supplied LAU-106A ejector release units, MIL-STD-1553B databus for new integrated weapon system, revised cockpit with multipurpose displays, HOTAS, and more.

Development

▪ 19 September 1988. Under a Ministry of Defence mid-life upgrade contract with BAe, the first flight took place of the FRS Mk 2 aerodynamic development aircraft.
▪ 7 December 1988. MoD contract with BAe to upgrade 29 Royal Navy FRS Mk 1s to Mk 2 standard. Upgraded aircraft were redesignated F/A Mk 2s.
▪ 1990. MoD order for newly built Mk 2s.
▪ 7 November 1990. First carrier landing by a Mk 2, on HMS *Ark Royal*.
▪ 29 March 1993. First AMRAAM air-to-air missile fired from a Mk 2.
▪ 2 April 1993. First F/A Mk 2 conversion for service (second aircraft) was handed over to the Royal Navy at Dunsfold.
▪ 1 June 1993. F/A Mk 2 Operational Evaluation Unit established at Boscombe Down (No 899 Squadron).
▪ 1994. MoD ordered a further 5 F/A Mk 2s.
▪ 24 August 1994. First deployment by 4 aircraft of No 899 Squadron to HMS *Invincible*, becoming operational 5 days later and flown on behalf of United Nations over Bosnia.
▪ 26 January 1995. No 801 squadron deployed with F/A Mk 2s on board HMS *Illustrious*.
▪ 1995. Newly built F/A Mk 2s and T Mk 8N trainers entered service.
▪ April 1995. Royal Navy accepted into service the VEGA F/A Mk 2 training system for maintenance technicians.
▪ 3 July 1996. Award of a contract to install IN/GPS to Royal Navy Sea Harriers. Conversion of 47 F/A Mk 2s during 1999-2000.
▪ September 1997. Under a £16.5 million contract, Indian Navy ordered 2 refurbished ex-Royal Navy Sea Harrier T4 trainers.
▪ 1999. Delivery of refurbished Sea Harrier T Mk 4 trainers to India.

Details

Sales/Users: 57 FRS Mk 1s were delivered to the Royal Navy between 1979-88, of which 29 were upgraded to F/A Mk 2s and a further 18 Mk 2s have been newly built. India's plan to purchase F/A Mk 2s to replace FRS Mk 51s was abandoned.
Crew: Pilot only.
Cockpit: Seat raised by 11 ins (28 cm) compared to the land-based Harrier, to improve view. Manual, rear-sliding canopy, with MDC. Windshield has washing and wiper facilities. Normalair-Garrett pressurization system, with 3.5 psi maximum differential.
Crew escape: Martin Baker Mk 10H zero-zero ejection seat.
Fixed guns: None, but provision for 2 × 30-mm Aden gun pods in a ventral position, replacing strakes.
Number of weapon pylons: 7, 4 under the wings (inner pylons 'wet' and each capable of a 2,000 lb, 907 kg load; outer 1,000 lb, 454 kg) and 3 under the fuselage (standard centreline for 2,000 lb, 907 kg load, plus 2 positions after removing strakes for AMRAAMs instead of gun pods).
Expendable weapons and equipment: Maximum weapon/stores load 8,500 lb (3,856 kg) for STO, or 5,000 lb (2,268 kg) for VTO. Range of free fall, retarded and cluster bombs (or ML CBLS 100 carriers for small 3 or 14 kg practice bombs). Also rockets, flares, etc. Air-to-air armament comprises 4 AMRAAMs (2 under the wings and 2 instead of the underfuselage strakes) or 2 underfuselage AMRAAMs plus 4 AIM-9L or M Sidewinders. Other options include 2 Sea Eagle anti-ship or ALARM anti-radar missiles.
Additional stores: Reconnaissance pod.
Radar: Blue Vixen multi-mode pulse-Doppler.

↑ **British Aerospace Sea Harrier F/A Mk 2**

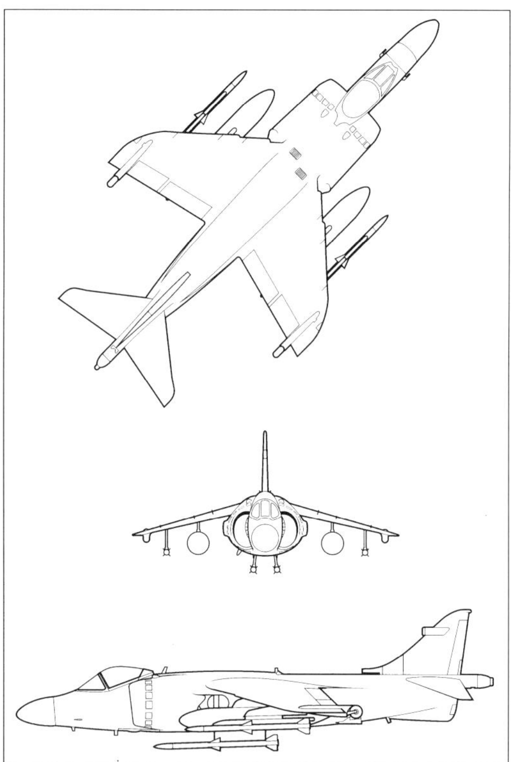

↑ British Aerospace Sea Harrier F/A Mk 2 general arrangement *(courtesy British Aerospace)*

Flight/weapon system avionics/instrumentation: MIL-STD-1553B databus and revised cockpit layout for F/A Mk 2, with TV raster display and HOTAS. Smiths HUD/digital weapon aiming computer, stores management system, Doppler, radar altimeter, Racal-Thorn MADGE (microwave airborne digital guidance equipment), GEC-Marconi AD 2770 Tacan, autopilot, Magnavox ARC-164 UHF and GEC-Marconi AD 120 VHF coms (suppressed VHF aerial on fin) plus Dowty D 403M standby UHF, GEC-Marconi PTR 446 or (later aircraft) AlliedSignal APX-100 Mk 12 IFF and ARI 5983 transponder. Vinten video recorder for displays. New Litton LN-100G INS with embedded GPS, being complemented by Rockwell-Collins (UK) supplied IPG-100F reversionary GPS navigation system to provide full stand-alone navigation capability, with moving waypoints, being installed on 47 F/A Mk 2s during 1998-2000. IPG-100F will usually provide head-down display redundancy for INS symbology on the MPD, allowing the unit to selectively display either INS or autonomous GPS data. Cockpit voice recorder. Joint tactical information distribution system expected. F.95 oblique camera.
Self-protection systems: GEC-Marconi Sky Guardian 200 radar warning receiver. ALE-40 chaff/flare/active radar decoy dispensers.
Wing characteristics: Marginally swept, shoulder-mounted, with heavy anhedral. 3 wing fences and a series of 11 small vortex generators per wing. Variable wing leading edge, plus the dogtooth moved closer to the root. Wing extension panels can be fitted for long-range ferry flights.
Wing control surfaces: The flight control system is a combination of aerodynamic surfaces and reaction controls. Plain ailerons and flaps. Autostabilizer jet reaction control system ("puffer jets"), with valves at the nose, tailpipe and near the wingtips. Bleed air from the engine HP compressor. Stability Augmentation and Attitude Hold System (SAAHS) comprises the Automatic Flight Control System (AFCS) and Stability Augmentation System (SAS), offering stability about all axes over the complete flight envelope.
Tail control surfaces: Variable-incidence slab tailplane and rudder (with trim tab).
Airbrakes: Single petal type under the fuselage.
Flight control system: Hydraulic powered control units.
Fuselage: Folding nose radome for access and below-deck storage ("spotting").
Construction materials: All metal, with enhanced corrosion protection over the land-based Harrier, including elimination of all magnesium components. Single-piece, 3-spar wing. Mainly aluminium alloy (including bonded honeycomb sandwich for parts of the control surfaces) but using titanium in areas of extreme heat.
Engine: Rolls-Royce Pegasus 11 Mk 104 or 106 vectored turbofan. Re-engining with higher-thrust Pegasus 11-61 is being studied in 1997/98. 227 litres of demineralized water to maintain thrust during short take-off and vertical operations in hot conditions.
Engine rating: 21,500 lbf (95.64 kN).
Nozzles: 4 rotatable thrust-vectoring, made of steel, with 98.5° movement from aft to forward of vertical, enabling flight in any direction, including backwards.
Air intakes: Bifurcated, pitots, with internal throat bleed slot; series of 8 auxiliary air intakes (various sizes) around each main intake offers increased airflow during vertical or slow flying.
Flight refuelling probe: None.
Fuel system: 2,864 litres in 5 fuselage and 2 wing tanks. Provision for 2 × 454.6, 863.7 or 1,500 litre drop tanks.
Electrical system: Main AC supply using 2 × 15KVA generators. DC supply via transformer/rectifiers. 2 × 28 volt 25 amp-hour batteries, 1 used to start the Lucas Mk 2 APU via a motor to drive a 6KVA auxiliary alternator (for ground use).
Hydraulic system: 2 independent systems, each 3,000 psi. Fairey actuators. Reservoirs are nitrogen pressurized.
Braking system: Multi-disc brakes, with anti-skid.
Oxygen system: British Oxygen liquid type, of 4.55 litres capacity.

Aircraft variants:
F/A Mk 2 was formerly known as FRS Mk 2. Latest Royal Navy version, upgraded from FRS Mk 1s and newly built.
2-seat trainer is the T Mk 8N, corresponding to Mk 2.

Details for F/A Mk 2

PRINCIPAL DIMENSIONS:
Wing span: 25 ft 3 ins (7.7 m), or 29 ft 8 ins (9.04 m) with ferry flight extensions
Maximum length: 46 ft 5 ins (14.15 m)
Length, nose folded: 42 ft 10 ins (13.06 m)
Maximum height: 11 ft 10 ins (3.61 m)

WINGS:
Aerofoil section: Hawker design (10% t/c root, 5% tip)
Area: 201 sq ft (18.67 m^2)
Aspect ratio: 3.17
Sweepback: 34° at 25% chord
Chord at root: 11 ft 8 ins (3.56 m)
Chord at tip: 4 ft 2 ins (1.27 m)
Incidence: 1° 45′
Anhedral: 12°

TAIL UNIT:
Tailplane span: 13 ft 11 ins (4.24 m)
Tailplane area: 47.5 sq ft (4.41 m^2)
Fin area: 25.8 sq ft (2.4 m^2)

UNDERCARRIAGE:
Type: Retractable bicycle type, with twin main wheels retracting aft and single nosewheel retracting forward. Single outrigger wheel near each wingtip, retracting aft into a fairing
Main wheel tyre size: 27 × 7.74-13
Nose wheel tyre size: 26 × 8.75-11
Outrigger tyre size: 13.5 × 6-4
Wheel base: 11 ft 4 ins (3.45 m)
Wheel track: 22 ft 2 ins (6.76 m)

WEIGHTS:
Empty, operating: 14,050 lb (6,373 kg)
Normal take-off: 21,700 lb (9,843 kg)

SKI-JUMP:
Incremental weight for 12° ski-jump take-off: 2,500 lb (1,134 kg)
Take-off with the VTO payload of 5,000 lb (2,268 kg): 50-60% reduction in run

PERFORMANCE:
Maximum operating Mach number (M_{MO}) at altitude: Mach 1.25
Maximum speed at sea level: 635 kts (731 mph) 1,176 km/h
Maximum cruise speed: >Mach 0.8 at high altitude, 450 kts (518 mph) 834 km/h at low level
STO take-off distance: 1,000 ft (305 m) at maximum weight from land, 300-450 ft (92-137 m) from deck with ski-jump, depending upon type of mission and load
Time to 30 naut mile combat radius: <6 minutes
G limits: +7.8, -4.2
Radius of action (attack): Typically 200-250 naut miles (230-288 miles) 370-463 km, Hi-Lo-Hi mission, depending upon stores carried
Radius of action (intercept): 400 naut miles (460 miles) 741 km, Hi-Hi mission, with 3 minutes combat
Radius of action (reconnaissance): 525 naut miles (604 miles) 973 km, with 2 × 863.7 litre auxiliary tanks
Duration (combat air patrol): 1.5 hours at 100 naut miles (115 miles) 185 km with 4 AMRAAMs, gun pods and 2 × 863.7 litre auxiliary tanks
Duration (reconnaissance): 1.75 hours at 525 naut miles (604 miles) 973 km radius, with 2 × 863.7 litre auxiliary tanks

British Aerospace Nimrod MR Mk 2P and R Mk 1P

Comments: First flown on 23 May 1967 in prototype form utilizing an existing de Havilland Comet 4C airframe, the Nimrod remains the RAF's maritime patrol, anti-submarine warfare, anti-ship attack, maritime reconnaissance, and search and rescue control post aircraft as the MR Mk 2P, and signal/electronic intelligence aircraft as the R Mk 1P. Full details and a photograph can be found in the 1996-97 edition of *WA&SD*, pages 125-126. Upgrade to Nimrod 2000 standard has begun.

British Aerospace Nimrod 2000/MRA Mk 4

First flight: Anticipated in 1999 for the first re-worked airframe from FR Aviation. Year 2000 for the first fully equipped aircraft from BAe Warton.
Role: Anti-submarine warfare, anti-surface unit warfare, maritime reconnaissance, search and rescue, and law enforcement.
Project director: Graham Chisnall.

Aims

- Major re-work of the proven Nimrod basic configuration for the next century, thereby replacing MR Mk 2Ps.
- Re-lifed airframe with only the fuselage shell, tailplane and basic fin box retained (estimated 80% airframe rebuilding/replacement). Service life extended by at least 25 years. New wings, engines, undercarriage and internal systems.
- New mission system, and 2-man 'glass' cockpit.
- Programme involves over 200 British companies and a number of foreign suppliers, including several teaming arrangements with key suppliers including Boeing, Rolls-Royce/BMW, FRA, Short Brothers, Smiths Industries, Lucas Aerospace, Messier-Dowty, Loral, Normalair Garrett, Racal Telephonics, Ultra and Aerosystems International. BAe has a marketing agreement with Boeing to introduce the technological, economic and operational advantages of the Nimrod 2000 state-of-the-art mission system to world markets, matched with BAe's integration expertise.

Development

- 1993. Request for Information issued for an RAF Replacement Maritime Patrol Aircraft (RMPA), to meet Staff Requirement (Air) 420.
- 1995. Invitation to Tender issued.
- 1995-96. Competition involving BAe Nimrod 2000, Lockheed Martin Orion 2000, Loral/Marshall Valkyrie (P-3A/B update) and Dassault Atlantique 3.
- 25 July 1996. Announcement of RMPA contract for Nimrod 2000 system to be awarded to BAe, worth about £2 billion, with launch by the UK MoD that December.
- 14 February 1997. First of 3 Nimrod MR Mk 2Ps was delivered to FR Aviation (FRA) at Bournemouth for airframe re-work, carried inside an Antonov An-124 freighter from RAF Kinloss where it had been in storage. Further 2 flights followed on the 15th and 16th.
- 1999. First BR710-48 engine deliveries.
- December 1999. First re-worked airframe due for delivery to BAe, Warton, for mission equipment fit.
- January/February 2000. Second and third aircraft due at Warton.
- December 2001. First redelivery to the RAF in Nimrod 2000 form.
- 2003. Initial operational capability.

Details

Sales/Users: Initial order for 21 aircraft for RAF only. Fixed price contract over 10 years, including support and training. Potential export sales for the world's only available jet-powered large land-based maritime aircraft.
Crew: Flight crew of 2 (provision for third flight crew member), plus 8 other crew (see Cabin and Avionics).
Cockpit: Flight deck for the pilot and co-pilot only (see Flight instrumentation). Normalair Garrett environmental control system, with 4 modern packs.
Cabin: Main cabin, aft of the flight deck, is divided into 3 areas: forward Tactical Compartment including beam lookout, mid rest quarters, and rear sonobuoy storage and dispensing area. Tactical compartment accommodates the 7 'warfare' operators with similar Boeing work stations, each with reconfigurable, high resolution, colour displays integrated by GEC-Marconi (see Avionics for functions). Air electronics officer, plus single observer/expendables handler in rear. Room for 13 other persons, including spare crew for long duration missions.

↑ Impression of a British Aerospace Nimrod 2000 launching Harpoon

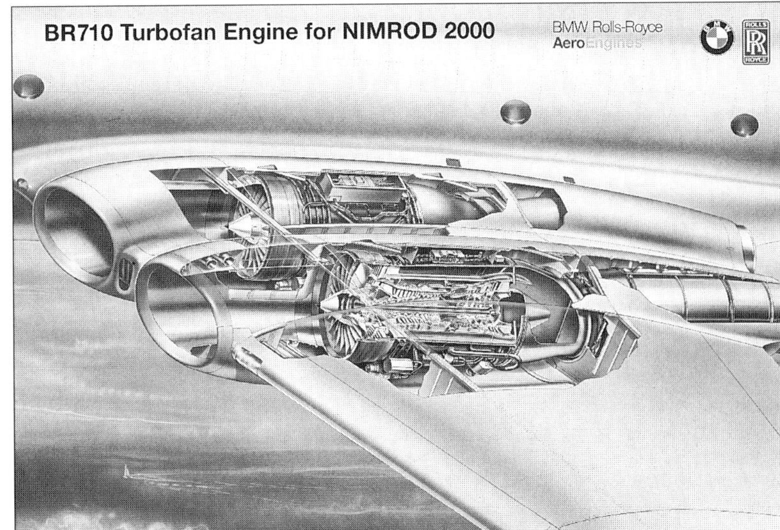

↑ BMW Rolls-Royce BR710-48 turbofans in the new Nimrod 2000 wing

Fixed guns: None.
Number of weapon pylons: 6 rows of store carriers in the roof of the 48 ft 6 ins (14.78 m) weapons bay. 2 pylons under each wing, with multiple release units.
Expendable weapons and equipment: Very large range of weapons (up to about 12,000 lb, 5,443 kg total weight), both underwing and in the bay, including Harpoon anti-ship missiles, Stingray torpedoes and bombs. 2 Sidewinder AAMs for self-protection can be carried with each underwing anti-ship weapon on multiple release units, making 8 in total. Rear sonobuoy/marine marker storage and dispensing area, with 2 Normalair Garrett rotary launchers for low-level dispensing and 2 barrel launchers for higher altitude dispensing when cabin is pressurized.
Radar: Racal Thorn Searchwater 2000 MR multimode radar in the nose. New high power transmitter employing advanced pulse Doppler signal processing techniques and with large antenna.
Flight/weapon system avionics/instrumentation: Sextant Avionique designed and produced Flight Deck Display System and the autopilot; new 'glass' 2-crew cockpit comprising 7 digital full-colour LCD flight information screens. Tactical Command and Sensor System (TCSS) supplied by Boeing. Armament Control System supplied by Smiths Industries. 7 Boeing-supplied crew work stations, each with reconfigurable, high resolution, colour displays: 2 'dry' radar and ESM/MAD; 2 'wet' for ASW acoustics; and 3 for coms and systems management. Each work station is 'user friendly', with 2 programme entry panel key pad, query keyboard and a single numeric quick entry key pad. Tactical 'picture' is relayable to cockpit. Upgraded Elta EL/L-8300 ESM. MAD in tail sting (CAE equipment, modified from MR 2). Electro-optical sensor, derived from Westinghouse 'Night Giant", is turret-mounted under the front fuselage and comprises FLIR and LLTV with 12x magnification. Communication Management System covers LF to UHF, with secure datalink and satellite communication. Smiths Industries navigation and flight management system (see below). Navigation equipment includes new nav-aids and microwave landing system (MLS). Twin Litton LN-100G INS with embedded GPS. Ground proximity/collision avoidance warning systems. Triplex air data system. Non-mission avionics include TCAS II, GPWS, and new auto flight control with integral autothrottle. Some 2 million lines of computer software code are incorporated. IFF Mode S transponder.
Self-protection systems: Defensive Aids Sub-system (DASS), with dedicated ALR-56M radar warning receiver, missile approach receiver and integral chaff/flare dispensers. GEC-Marconi Ariel or Raytheon E-Systems ALE-50 towed active-radar decoy. Racal Radar Defence Systems received a £10 million contract in l997 to supply 21 techniques generators for the DASS system.
Wing characteristics: Slightly swept, low mounted, with marginal dihedral. 2-spar structure, continuous through fuselage. New wingtip ESM pods. All new wing, including carry-through wing box, with 12 ft (3.66 m) span increment. Inner wing section accommodates new, larger diameter and longer engines.
Wing control surfaces: Ailerons outboard of 2-section plain trailing-edge flaps. Spoiler airbrakes, mid span, on upper and lower surfaces immediately ahead of the outer flap sections.
Tail control surfaces: Full-span elevator (with tabs) and rudder. Large dorsal fin extension, needed to offset the directionally destabilizing effect of the pannier. Finlets on the upper and lower surfaces of the tailplane (larger than on MR 2) and a shallow ventral fin, to improve handling when refuelling operations are underway.
Airbrakes: See Wings.
Flight control system: New system, with improved actuators offering better safety, reliability and maintainability.
Fuselage: Pressurized main cabin and unpressurized pannier/weapons bay, similar to MR Mk 2P but with new floor.
Construction materials: Principally aluminium alloy, but with other materials including glassfibre for the radome and various pods. Redux adhesive bonding extensively used in place of riveting. Nimrod 2000 introduces some enhanced materials for added corrosion protection.
Engines: 4 BMW Rolls-Royce BR710-48 turbofans, with FADEC and EICAS. Engine health and usage monitoring system. APU for full autonomous operation (ground use only).
Engine rating: Each 15,500 lbf (68.97 kN) flat-rated at ISA+10° C.
Air intakes: Wing root leading-edge intakes, enlarged from those of the MR Mk 2P for higher mass flow of 48 ins (1.22 m) fan of BR710-48 engines.
Flight refuelling probe: Above the flight deck.
Fuel system: MR Mk 2P has 48,778 litres in the wings, lower fuselage and permanent wing leading-edge (external) tanks. Nimrod 2000 has additional fuel in the new wings. New automated fuel system. MR Mk 2P has provision for up to 6 auxiliary tanks in the weapons bay, and this capability will be retained.
Electrical system: New integrated drive generators (160KVA), control units and wiring.
Hydraulic system: Normalair Garrett supplied. Largely new, with Airbus-type components and architecture.
Braking system: Improved main wheel braking with carbon brakes, and anti-skid system.
Oxygen system: New system and NBC protection.
Anti-icing system: Hot air type.

Details for Nimrod 2000

PRINCIPAL DIMENSIONS:
Wing span: 127 ft (38.71 m)
Maximum length: 126 ft 7.5 ins (38.6 m)
Maximum height: 30 ft (9.14 m)

WINGS:
Area: 2,538 sq ft (235.8 m^2)
Aspect ratio: 6.355
Sweepback: 20° at 25% chord

TAIL UNIT:
Tailplane span: 47 ft 7 ins (14.5 m)
Tailplane area: 435 sq ft (40.41 m^2)
Fin area: 179 sq ft (16.63 m^2), including dorsal fin

UNDERCARRIAGE:
Type: Messier-Dowty retractable type, with twin steerable nosewheels. 4-wheel main bogies. Arrangement is similar to MR Mk 2P but with a totally new gear, designed to cater for a 20% growth in MTOW
Main wheel tyre size: Dunlop, 36 × 10
Nose wheel tyre size: Dunlop, 30 × 9-15
Wheel base: 46 ft (14.02 m)
Wheel track: 35 ft (10.67 m)

WEIGHTS:
Empty, operating: 102,515 lb (46,500 kg)
Maximum take-off: 231,165 lb (104,855 kg)

PERFORMANCE:
Maximum speed: Mach 0.77
Ceiling: 42,000 ft (12,800 m)
Unrefuelled range: over 5,935 naut miles (6,835 miles) 11,000 km
Duration: 15+ hours

Cobham plc — UK

Corporate address:
Brook House, Wimborne, Dorset BH21 2BJ.
Telephone: +44 1202 882020
Facsimile: +44 1202 840523

FACILITIES

■ Incorporates FR Aviation Ltd (FRA, Bournemouth) and Flight Refuelling Ltd (Wimborne), also Chelton, Westwind, Hymatic, Alan Cobham, Carleton and Stanley Aviation.

ACTIVITIES

■ Design and manufacture of equipment, specialized systems and components; and operation, maintenance, modification of aircraft for special mission flight operations, role conversions, and more.
■ FRA specializes in air defence training for the RAF, RN and various NATO countries, using a fleet of Falcon 20s; EW, target towing and aircraft engineering support services. Economic zone (maritime) surveillance with Dornier 228s and PBN Islanders. Navigation aid flight calibration and towing with Cessna Conquests. FRA Serco Ltd for helicopter, flying training and tanker/transport support to the RAF. See Nimrod 2000 entry.
■ Flight Refuelling Ltd for air-to-air IFR systems (probe and drogue technology), plus ship-to-helicopter; surveillance UAVs; airborne and marine towed targets; external tanks; and fuel systems.
■ Chelton for antennae, microwave components and radomes.
■ Other products are air bearing spindle systems, pneumatics and more.

Marshall Aerospace (Marshall of Cambridge Aerospace Ltd) UK

Corporate address:
The Airport, Cambridge CB5 8RX.

Telephone: +44 1223 373263
Facsimile: +44 1223 373373

ACTIVITIES

▪ Design, manufacturing, modification, maintenance, in-service support, and airport operations. Specializes in Lockheed TriStar, Boeing (McDonnell Douglas) MD-11/DC-10, Lockheed Martin C-130, Boeing 707/727/737, BAe 146, Gulfstream and Citation.
▪ Design of large structural components, avionics/specialist systems integration, fluid systems, structural and flight testing.
▪ Extensive manufacturing capabilities, and conventional and sophisticated CNC/DNC machining. Specialist manufacturing skills, treatment and inspection.
▪ Modification and maintenance; special role conversions, avionics equipment and systems, line maintenance, technical support, refurbishment and repair.
▪ C-130 programmes include future C-130J support. TriStar tanker and freighter conversions. Boeing E-3D design authority and maintenance. BAe 146 VIP interiors and refit. Is co-operating with Denel of South Africa to perform mid-life updates on 12 SAAF C-130B/Fs, to extend their service lives by 20 years.
▪ See also Lockheed Martin ASTOR programme in the Electronics section.

The Boeing Company USA

Corporate address:
PO Box 3707, Seattle, WA 98124-2207 (mailing address), or 7755 East Marginal Way South, Seattle, Washington 98108 (street address).

Telephone: +1 206 655 2121
Facsimile: +1 206 655 1177
Telex: 329430
Cable: BOEINGAIR
NYSE: BA
Web site (Boeing): http://www.boeing.com
Web site (Media): http://www.boeingmedia.com

Founded:
15 July 1916, with 26 April 1917 for adoption of the name Boeing Airplane Company, formed out of Pacific Aero Products Company. Merger with McDonnell Douglas announced on 15 December 1996, with operation as a single company under the Boeing name beginning on 4 August 1997. Boeing acquired Rockwell's aerospace and defence units on 6 December 1996, becoming Boeing North American, Inc and later part of the Space Systems business unit reporting to the ISDS Group (see below).

Employees:
234,850 in 1998.

Chairman/CEO: Philip M. Condit.
President/COO: Harry C. Stonecipher.

Information:
Peter Conte (Director, Public Relations (*telephone* +1 206 655 6123, *facsimile* +1 206 655 3987) or Larry Bishop (Vice President Communications and Investor Relations – *telephone* +1 206 655 6300, *facsimile* +1 206 544 1581, *E-mail* larry.bishop@boeing.com).

ACTIVITIES

▪ Boeing operates primarily in 4 market segments: the development, production and marketing of commercial and military aircraft; development and production of commercial and defence missiles and space exploration equipment; development and production of defense electronics systems; and computer services and large-scale information networks. Products are commercial jet transports, military aircraft, rotorcraft, guided missiles, space vehicles, defence and space systems and defence electronics.
▪ In addition to the products detailed below, in November 1997 Boeing was awarded a US$333.4 million contract for the F-15C Contractor Training Simulation Service Program, to provide 2 four-ship sets of F-15C full mission trainers, for basing at Eglin and Langley AFBs, to be networked together to provide realistic combat training between distant locations, as part of the USAF's Distributed Mission Training System programme.
▪ In addition to earlier business agreements, including that signed between McDonnell Douglas and the Hungarian Government in December 1996 for industrial co-operation, in September 1997 an MoU was signed between Boeing's F/A-18 Hornet Industry Team and Instytut Lotnictwa of Poland for potential collaboration on more than 20 advanced technologies.
▪ The pending sale of most of Boeing's civil helicopters to Bell Helicopter Textron was suspended in June 1998, after US Federal Trade Commission reservations. See Helicopter section.

GROUPS

INFORMATION, SPACE AND DEFENSE SYSTEMS GROUP (ISDS)

HQ address:
PO Box 3999, Seattle, WA 98124-2499 (mailing address), or 20403 68th Avenue South, Kent, WA 98032.

Telephone: +1 253 773 2121

President: David A. Sloan (Senior Manager, Public Relations)

COMPRISING:

BUSINESS UNITS

AIRCRAFT AND MISSILE SYSTEMS

HQ address:
PO Box 516, St Louis, MO 63166-0516.

Telephone: +1 314 232 2800
Facsimile: +1 314 234 8296

President: Mike Sears.

Activities:
▪ The company's military aircraft systems (fixed and rotary wing), including JSF, F-22, Harrier II Plus, F-15, Hornet and Super Hornet, C-17, T-45 Goshawk, Airborne Laser, 767 AWACS, B-1B, B-2, RAH-66 Comanche, CH-47 Chinook, AH-64D Apache Longbow and V-22 Osprey, and oversees development of tactical missiles. Includes Boeing Philadelphia for military rotorcraft, and subordinate Boeing Mesa for Apache and commercial helicopters, chain guns, wiring harnesses and more.

BOEING SPACE SYSTEMS

HQ address:
PO Box 2515, Seal Beach, CA 90740-1515.

Telephone: +1 562 797 5630
Facsimile: +1 562 797 5281

President: John McLuckey.

Activities:
▪ Responsible for Boeing's prime and subcontracting roles on a variety of DoD and NASA space programmes, including International Space Station, rocket engines, sub-scale Space Maneuver Vehicle (SMV, that was rolled-out in August 1997 for test flying before the end of that year), Sea Launch, Inertial Upper Stage, Global Positioning System, Delta rockets, and Space Shuttle programme (see Spaceflight section).

INFORMATION AND COMMUNICATION SYSTEMS

HQ address:
PO Box 3999, M/S 8A-15, Seattle, WA 98124-2499 (mailing address), or 20403 68th Avenue South, Kent, WA 98032 (street address).

Telephone: +1 253 773 7900
Facsimile: +1 253 773 1208

President: Jim Evatt.

Activities:
▪ Includes information and surveillance systems such as E-3 and 767 AWACS programmes; communication and information management systems; commercial communication systems, including Boeing's involvement in Teledesic; advanced integrated defence systems; satellite systems which involves the Global Positioning System; Boeing Australia Limited; Airborne Laser programme; Tier III Minus programme; electronic products including commercial avionics systems, cabin management systems, phased-array antenna development and military electronics; and special projects and advanced system concepts.

PHANTOM WORKS

HQ address:
PO Box 516, St. Louis, MO 63166-0516.

Telephone: +1 314 234 1500
Facsimile: +1 314 233 0428

Executive Vice President: David Swain.

Activities:
▪ Advanced research and development organization, to improve the company's competitive position through innovative technologies, improved processes, and the creation of new products. Has an integrated management team with operations in Southern California, Mesa, Philadelphia, St. Louis and Seattle. Cross-functional organization, on par with ISDS.
▪ Programmes include developing the Hyper-X hypersonic experimental research vehicle for NASA (built by Micro Craft), to demonstrate atmospheric flight without rocket engines (using a scramjet) at about Mach 5-10. The first of 4 Hyper-X subscale vehicles is expected to fly in November 1998, after release from a Pegasus launcher. A Mach 10 bomber and reconnaissance aircraft could eventually develop from the programme, having an 11,000 lb (5,000 kg) payload and 8,500 naut mile combat radius.

PLUS:

BUSINESS RESOURCES

Executive Vice President: Scott E. Carson.

BOEING COMMERCIAL AIRPLANE GROUP (BCAG)

HQ address:
PO Box 3707, Seattle, Washington 98124-2207 (mailing address), or North 8th & Park Avenue North, Renton, WA 98055 (street address).

Telephone: +1 425 237 2121
Facsimile: +1 425 237 3544

President: Ronald B. Woodward.

Information:
Mary Foerster (Director, Public Relations and Advertising – *telephone* +1 425 237 0241, *facsimile* +1 425 237 3544, *E-mail* mary.foerster@boeing.com).

COMPRISING:

CUSTOMER SERVICES

Address:
2925 South 112th, Seattle, WA 98168.

Telephone: +1 253 544 8301
Facsimile: +1 253 544 9550

Activities:
▪ Provides training, field support and spare parts to Boeing customers.

DOUGLAS PRODUCTS DIVISION

HQ address:
3855 Lakewood Boulevard, Long Beach, CA 90846.

Telephone: +1 562 982 2603

Vice President & General Manager: Richard H. Pearson.

Information: Doug Jacobsen (General Manager – *telephone* +1 562 496 7473).

Activities:
▪ Manufactures and develops the Boeing 717, MD-11, MD-80 and MD-90.

ENGINEERING DIVISION

HQ address:
North 8th & Park Avenue North, Renton, WA 98055 (street address).

Telephone: +1 425 234 3535
Facsimile: +1 425 237 3544

Vice President: Robert Spitzer.

FABRICATION DIVISION

HQ address:
1002 15th Street Southwest, Auburn, WA 98002.

Telephone: +1 253 931 3330
Facsimile: +1 253 931 9500

Information:
Tom Koehler (Communications - *telephone* +1 253 931 5834, *facsimile* +1 253 931 2144, *E-mail* thomas.koehler@boeing.com).

Activities:
■ Responsible for a wide variety of components for Boeing aircraft.

MATERIEL DIVISION

HQ address:
20818-44th Avenue West, Lynnwood, WA 98036.

Telephone: +1 206 655 2121

Vice President & General Manager: Gerald D. Kearns.

Information:
Patricia E. Riddle (Senior Manager, Communications - *telephone* +1 425 266 0517, *facsimile* +1 425 266 1007, *E-mail* patricia.e.riddle@boeing.com).

Activities:
■ Responsible for the materials and subcontracted components used in Boeing aircraft production.

PROPULSION SYSTEMS DIVISION

HQ address: 7600 212th Avenue Southwest, Kent, WA 98032.

Telephone: +1 425 393 8000

Vice President: Ray Conner.

Activities:
■ Responsible for the preparation of all jet engines for installation on Boeing airliners.

737/757 PROGRAMS

HQ address:
North 8th & Park Avenue North, Renton, WA 98055 (street address).

Telephone: +1 425 237 2121
Facsimile: +1 425 237 1379

Vice President & General Manager: Gary R. Scott.

Information:
Susan Bradley (Senior Manager - *telephone* +1 425 237 0600, *facsimile* +1 425 234 4456, *E-mail* susan.bradley@boeing.com).

Activities:
■ Design and production of Boeing 737 and 757 aircraft.

747/767 PROGRAMS

HQ address:
3303 West Casino Road, Everett, WA 98203.

Telephone: +1 425 294 4088
Facsimile: +1 425 342 1756

Vice President & General Manager: Edward J. Renouard.

Information:
Doug Webb (Senior Manager, Communications - *telephone* +1 425 294 6102, *facsimile* +1 425 294 6200, *E-mail* douglas.webb@boeing.com).

Activities:
■ Design and production of Boeing 747 and 767 aircraft.

777 PROGRAM

HQ address:
PO Box 3707, Seattle, WA 98124 (mailing address), or 3303 West Casino Road, Everett, WA 98204 (street address).

Telephone: +1 425 294 4088

Vice President & General Manager: Ron Ostrowski.

Activities:
■ Design and production of Boeing 777 aircraft.

WICHITA DIVISION

HQ address:
PO Box 7730, M/S K12-12, Wichita, KS 67277-7730 (mailing address), or 3801 South Oliver, Wichita, KS 67210 (street address).

Telephone: +1 316 526 3156

Vice President & General Manager:
Jeffrey L. Turner.

Information:
Dick Ziegler (Senior Manager, Communications - *telephone* +1 316 526 3153, *Facsimile* +1 316 526 1845).

Activities:
■ Responsible for the production of component parts and assemblies used in all Boeing commercial aircraft.

BOEING SHARED SERVICES GROUP

HQ address:
PO Box 24346, Seattle, WA 98124 (mailing address), or 2810 160th Avenue Southeast, Bellevue, WA 98008 (street address).

President: James F. Palmer.

Information:
Karen Burt (Director, PR & Communications - *telephone* +1 425 865 4653, *facsimile* +1 425 865 2953, *E-mail* karen.h.burt@boeing.com).

Activities:
■ Information management services and computing resources to all Boeing operating divisions and to government customers worldwide.

↑ **Impression of a Boeing B-52H Stratofortress powered by 4 Rolls-Royce RB.211-535E-4 turbofans, launching ALCMs**

Boeing B-52H Stratofortress

Comments: First flown on 15 April 1952 in YB-52 prototype form, the B-52 remains operational with the USAF as a conventional and nuclear strategic bomber, suited also to anti-ship missions with Harpoon. Other weapons recently tested include AGM-142 Have Nap/Popeye. Full details of the active B-52H can be found in the 1996-97 edition of *WA&SD*, pages 127-128. Boeing has also proposed re-engining 71 B-52Hs with Rolls-Royce RB.211-535E-4 turbofans, with 4 engines per aircraft in place of the existing 8 TF33-P-3s. In a separate programme, the NASA B-52 has been used to carry the X-38 lifting-body research vehicle from the Dryden Flight Research Center.

Boeing AL-1A Airborne Laser Programme

First flight: Year 2000.
Role: To autonomously acquire and track tactical theatre ballistic missiles in their boost phase and destroy them with an airborne laser, while typically patrolling at above 40,000 ft (12,190 m). Other possible missions could include imaging surveillance, protection of high value airborne assets, cruise missile defence, and suppression of enemy air defences.
Based on: Modified Boeing 747-400F Freighter.

Aims

■ To target and designate the missile at cloud break, 42 seconds after launch; to destroy the missile within 52-70 seconds of launch; to provide a contingency destruction period of 10 seconds. Cost per 'shot' estimated in 1997 at US$1,000.
■ BMDO Commander integrated ABL into TMD architecture.
■ Offer alternative to hit-to-kill TMD systems.
■ Inflight refuellable, and small deployable footprint.
■ Long distance, 360°, autonomous target acquisition, providing real time launch/impact points to the theatre Commander.
■ Each C-17 transport used for re-supply can carry sufficient laser fuel for approximately 140 more engagements by ABL aircraft.

Development

■ Team ABL comprises Boeing, TRW Space & Electronics, and Lockheed Martin.
■ September 1992. Boeing Defense & Space Group received a contract from the USAF Phillips Laboratory to assess how an existing large aircraft would perform while carrying a high-energy laser and beam control system.
■ 13 August 1993. Boeing, TRW and Lockheed Martin submitted a proposal to the USAF's Airborne Laser System Program Office at Kirtland AFB.
■ 12 November 1996. DoD selected ABL for the Program Definition and Risk Reduction (PDRR) phase of the programme.
■ 27-28 February 1997. Flight-weighted Laser Module (FLM) critical design review, Los Angeles (TRW).
■ 19-21 March 1997. Airborne Laser production readiness review, Seattle.
■ Third quarter 1998. Authority to Proceed (milestone 1).
■ 1996-2000. PDRR phase 1, to build a single ABL weapon system.
■ 2000-2001/2. PDRR phase 2, to flight test the YAL-1A demonstrator and shoot down a boosting tactical ballistic missile (year 2002).
■ 2001/2-2004. Engineering, Manufacturing and Development (EMD).
■ 2004-2008. Production.
■ 2005-2006. Initial operational capability with 3 aircraft.
■ 2007-2008. Full operational capability with 7 aircraft.

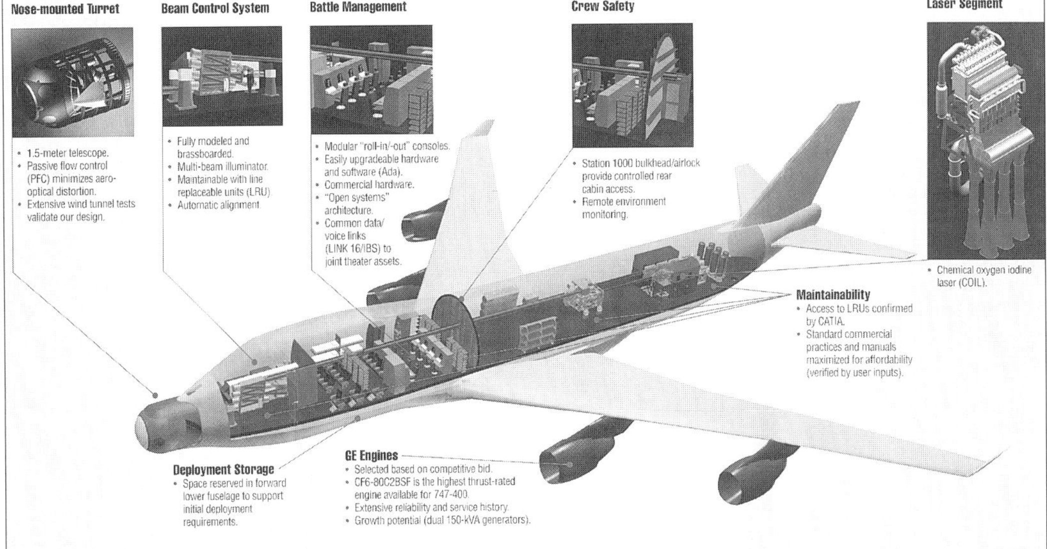

↑ **Boeing AL-1A airborne laser aircraft general arrangement** *(courtesy Team ABL)*

↑ Impression of a Boeing AL-1A destroying a tactical ballistic missile

Details

Laser system: Nose-mounted turret, with 5 ft (1.5 m) telescope. Multi-beam illuminator. Multi-megawatt, chemical oxygen iodine laser (COIL), developed by TRW. FLM total weight using commercial lightweight materials 3,104 lb (1,408 kg). PDRR laser Module 1 with additional weight reduction 2,920 lb (1,324 kg).
Configuration: For PDRR phase, the 747-400F will carry 6 laser modules, 12 crew consoles and a 20-shot magazine. For EMD phase, the aircraft will have 14 laser modules, 4 crew consoles and 20-40 shot magazine.

Boeing Joint Strike Fighter (JSF)

First flight: 1999 for X-32A demonstrator.
Role: Primary US role will be interdiction/strike, but also multi-role including close-air support, suppression of enemy air defences, air defence, combat air patrol, deck launch intercept, anti-ship attack and reconnaissance .

Aims

▪ Largely (approximately 90%) common basic airframe/engine configuration to provide supersonic, alternative CTOL/STOVL variants for multi-service use.
▪ CTOL variant as replacement for F-16 with the USAF; CV/CTOL variant as replacement for F/A-18C/D and already retired A-6E with US Navy.
▪ STOVL variant as replacement for Harrier AV-8B/Harrier II Plus, and F/A-18C/D with USMC and Sea Harrier F/A Mk 2 with Royal Navy.
▪ 'Conventional' airframe and propulsion configuration for 'up and away' and supersonic flight. Cropped delta wings and twin fins configuration with relaxed stability for high manoeuvrability and with pitch only vectoring of rear engine exhaust nozzle. High usable alpha.
▪ Powered vertical lift derived from engine exhaust diverted through 2 vectoring nozzles near aircraft centre of gravity.
▪ Low radar signature achieved by configuration geometry (external and internal shaping), internal carriage of weapons, materials (RAM) and special treatments.

Development

▪ 1990. Common Affordable Lightweight Fighter study launched by US Advanced Research Project Agency (ARPA).
▪ 1991. Phased development programme on Supersonic Strike Fighter (SSF) initiated with contracts from ARPA to Lockheed Martin and McDonnell Douglas for Phase I of 1991-92, including Propulsion Concept Selection. Boeing not formally involved at this stage.
▪ 1993. Boeing entered programme.
▪ 1993-96. PV work by Boeing (subsequently partly funded by ARPA) on Critical Technology Evaluation and Configuration Refinement for SSF/CALF, becoming Joint Advanced Strike Technology (JAST).
▪ 1995-96. Essentially full-scale powered (YF-119 engine) lift model tested in a static rig at Renton, near Seattle and NASA Ames.
▪ March 1996. Request for proposals (RFP) issued to Boeing, Lockheed Martin and McDonnell Douglas.
▪ 16 November 1996. Award of Phase II Concept Demonstrator Programme contract, valued at US$1.1 billion, to Boeing and also Lockheed Martin led teams. McDonnell Douglas, having been eliminated, joined the Boeing team. 51-month programme to produce and flight test 2 demonstrator aircraft, designated X-32A CTOL variant for USAF/USN and X-32B STOVL variant for USMC/Royal Navy.
▪ 1997. Initial design review completed.
▪ April/May 1998. First test run of the P&W SE614 engine.
▪ 1999. First flight of the X-32A CTOL demonstrator.
▪ 1999. Joint Operational Requirement to be issued.
▪ 2000. First flight of the X-32B STOVL demonstrator. Also X-32C CV/CTOL demonstrator, converted from X-32A.
▪ 2001. Engineering and Manufacturing Development (EMD) contract award to winning team.
▪ 2004. First flight of the EMD aircraft.
▪ 2007. First flight of a production aircraft.
▪ 2008. In service date for CTOL variant.
▪ 2010. In service date for STOVL variant. EMD completed.
▪ 2030. Possible end of all JSF production, including any export.

Details

Sales/Users: About 2,900 currently planned for 4 lead services: 1,763 (reduced from 2,036) for USAF to replace A-10 and F-16 (and to complement F-22), 609 (from 642) for USMC to replace AV-8B/Harrier II Plus and F/A-18C/D, 60 for Royal Navy to replace Sea Harrier F/A Mk 2, and 300-480 for US Navy to replace F/A-18C/D. USAF has also expressed interest in some 200 of the STOVL variant. Foreign interest shown by Australia, Canada, Denmark, the Netherlands, Norway and possibly Singapore. Global total sales (especially as a possible F-16 replacement) could be for 5,000+. Unit costs of approximately US$28 millon for CTOL, US$35 million for STOVL, and US$38 million for carrier-based versions.
Crew: Pilot (no 2-seat variant is planned).
Cockpit: Metallized (low RCS), single-piece canopy with no separate windshield, offering 'all-round' field of view. Completely night vision capable. Integrated access steps/ladder.
Crew escape: Advanced Martin Baker zero-zero rocket type ejection seat. Alternatives for at least the USAF version could be the Russian K-36D or a variant of ACES 2.
Fixed guns: Integrated 20-mm M61 improved cannon on USAF variant; optional for USN. USMC/Royal Navy aircraft expected to have external gun pod. Development of a new 25-mm cannon being considered, with the ability for head-on firing within AAM minimum launch range and strike effectively ground targets at 8,200-9,840 ft (2,500-3,000 m) range.
Ammunition: 400 rounds.
Number of weapon pylons: At least 4 external pylons (see below).
Expendable weapons and equipment: In 'stealthy' configuration, internal carriage of 6 AIM-120C AMRAAM (cropped) AAMs or 2 AMRAAMs plus 2 × 2,000 lb class GBU-31 Joint Direct Attack Munitions possible. Serrated leading-edges for weapon doors. External stores (over 12,000-13,000 lb, 5,443-5,896 kg for CTOL/STOVL; over 17,000 lb, 7,711 kg for carrier based) could include JSOW, larger LGBs, bombs, anti-radiation missiles, air-to-surface missiles, auxiliary tanks, etc.
Radar: Advanced multi-mode, electronically scanned array, synthetic aperture radar.
Flight/weapon system avionics/instrumentation: Highly integrated vehicle management system. MIL-STD-1553 databus. Integrated core processor. 3 large MFDs. Active noise cancellation. Helmet integrated display, including laser protection possible. No conventional HUD; Flight Visions Night Hawk HUD for X-32 demonstrator only. HOTAS integrated flight/engine control, driven by STOVL requirements. Internal laser designator. Infra-red sensors.
Self-protection systems: Radar and infra-red warning receivers. ECM and chaff/flare dispensers integrated into airframe. Laser warning?
Wing characteristics: Large area, shoulder-mounted, cropped delta planform, with leading-edge flaps and trailing-edge flaperons. Tip extensions on USAF and USN variants. No wing folding necessary. All internal fuel carried in the 1-piece wing box structure.
Wing control surfaces: 2-piece (inner and outer) trailing-edge flaperons for pitch and roll control. Additional 'vortex flap' near leading-edge to reduce take-off and landing speeds for aircraft carrier operations. (see Wing characteristcs.)
Tail control surfaces: Twin canted fins with conventional rudders; may also provide some pitch control. No tailplane.
Flight control system: Digital fly-by-wire, integrating flight/engine control. Electric actuators replace conventional hydraulic PCUs for all control surfaces.
Fuselage: Chined nose and canopy fairing blended into the

↑ Impression of Boeing JSF in USAF configuration

↑ Impression of Boeing JSF in US Navy configuration, with intake cowl moved forwards and downwards, opening an additional large triple-sided auxiliary intake slot

upper surface of the wing. Fuselage below the wing comprises bottom and inclined flat side facets. Prominent undernose intake. Rear fuselage boom/fairing either side of engine nozzle carry the twin fins and their actuators, and also house yaw reaction control nozzles. Weapon bays in fuselage sides. Lift improvement devices on lower fuselage of STOVL variant.
Construction materials: High proportion of advanced composites and titanium. Aluminium-lithium alloys. SPF/DB and honeycomb used where appropriate.
Engine: Pratt & Whitney F-119 derivative, designated SE614 for demonstrator. Incorporates 30-40% larger fan for increased air mass flow, resulting in higher by-pass ratio of around 0.6. Rolls-Royce and Allison are teamed with General Electric to develop the YF120-FX alternate main engine to be available early in production of JSF.
Engine rating: 35,000 lbf (155.7 kN) class, augmented.
Nozzles: Single, 2-dimensional vectoring (in pitch only) nozzle for non-STOVL flight. Low observable type, with upper and lower trailing-edges having the same sweep as the wing trailing-edge, offering edge alignment for low RCS. For STOVL, the powered lift mode rear nozzle closes and blocks the main propulsion duct. Dry engine exhaust is largely directed downward via twin vectoring (Harrier/Pegasus type) nozzles; with 1 on either side of the engine, and located on the fuselage lower corners, thrust acts through the aircraft's centre of gravity. A 'jet screen' of by-pass air acting as an anti-recirculation (hot gas re-ingestion) device, emerges from a further duct in the fuselage bottom, ahead of the main lift jets. Roll reaction jet nozzles are located in the outboard wings. Yaw nozzles are located in the rear fuselage boom fairings. A pitch control nozzle is located on the lower fuselage centre-line, immediately ahead of the engine nozzle.
Air intakes: For non-STOVL operations a single ventral under-nose intake is used, comprising a lower moderately-swept 2-edge lip and highly-swept side walls. For STOVL operations, the efficiency of the thin, sharp-lip main intake is improved by the whole intake cowl being moved forwards and canted downwards, thereby opening up an additional large triple-sided auxiliary intake slot with thick lips that is ideally shaped for zero/low speed flight.
Fuel system: Over 15,000 lb (6,804 lb) of internal fuel for CTOL/STOVL, and over 16,000 lb (7,257 kg) of internal fuel when carrier based.
Flight refuelling probe: Receptacle is located on the fuselage upper surface of the USAF variant. Retractable probe for USMC, USN and Royal Navy.

Aircraft variants:
X-32A CTOL concept demonstrator for the USAF.
X-32B STOVL concept demonstrator for the USMC and Royal Navy.
X-32C CTOL demonstrator by modification of the X-32A for the US Navy.

↑ Boeing (McDonnell Douglas) F-15Es

Production variants will be based on the features of the individual demonstrators.

Basic details for Boeing JSF

PRINCIPAL DIMENSIONS:
Wing span: 36 ft (10.97 m) for CTOL, 30 ft (9.14 m) for STOVL
Maximum length: 45 ft (13.72 m)

WINGS:
Area: 590 sq ft (54.81 m²)
Aspect ratio: 2.2 for CTOL, 1.53 for STOVL

UNDERCARRIAGE:
Type: Retractable, with single main and nose wheels. Main gear retracts aft into the wing root/fuselage fairings, nose gear aft into the lower fuselage. Messier Dowty units

WEIGHTS:
Empty: 22,046 lb (10,000 kg) for USAF variant and STOVL, 24,030 lb (10,900 kg) for USN version
Normal take-off: 38,000 lb (17,236 kg) for USAF variant
Maximum take-off: 50,000 lb (22,680 kg) for all variants

PERFORMANCE:
Maximum speed: Mach 1.6
Attained and sustained G limits, and turn rate: Similar or better than F-16C and F/A-18C
Radius of action: 600 naut miles (691 miles) 1,110 km for USMC specified mission, 850 naut miles (979 miles) 1,575 km for USAF specified mission, 750 naut miles (863 miles) 1,390 km for USN specified mission

McDonnell Douglas A-4 Skyhawk

Comments: First flown on 22 June 1954, this light (carrier-capable) attack bomber remained in production until 1979. Specifications of the A-4SU Super Skyhawk can be found in the 1996-97 edition of *WA&SD*, pages 107-108, and of the Skyhawk in general (including upgrades) on page 142. See also Argentina for Fightinghawk and Israel in this present edition. In 1996, former McDonnell Douglas (now Boeing) established agreements with Derco Aerospace Inc and Kitco Inc to provide spare parts and components for continued support to operators.

McDonnell Douglas F-4 Phantom

Comments: First flown on 27 May 1958 in F4H-1 Phantom II form, this interceptor, tactical fighter, reconnaissance fighter and radar suppression aircraft went out of production in the USA in June 1979, although production in Japan continued until 1981. Specifications and photographs of the F-4, and upgrade programmes, can be found in the 1996-97 edition of *WA&SD*, pages 43-44, 48, 57 and 142-143. See also Daimler-Benz Aerospace (ICE and related programmes) and Israel (Phantom 2000) in this current edition. In 1996, former McDonnell Douglas (now Boeing) established agreements with Derco Aerospace Inc and Kitco Inc to provide spare parts and components for continued support to operators. Upgrades may keep some F-4s flying until the year 2015. South Korea has recently chosen to deploy both the AGM-130 and AGM-142 on its F-4Es.

Boeing (McDonnell Douglas) F-15 Eagle

Comments: Production of the single-seat F-15C and 2-seat F-15D Eagle ended in the USA in 1992. Licensed production of these models continued thereafter in Japan as Mitsubishi F-15Js and F-15DJs, 213 being built for the JASDF, of which most had been delivered by 1998. No requests for additional F-15s were made by the JASDF in FY1998. F-15J/DJs do not have conformal auxiliary fuel tanks and use Japanese ECM and RWR systems plus Ishikawajima-Harima built F100-IHI-100 engines. Production of Eagle in the USA continues with the dual-role F-15E and its export counterparts. The following details cover principally the F-15E, with some data on the F-15C and D, including upgrades of USAF F-15Cs. Details of the F-15A and B can be found in the 1996-97 edition of *WA&SD*, pages 143-144, plus under Development and Sales in this edition.
First flight: 27 July 1972 for prototype F-15; 11 December 1986 for production dual-role F-15E.
Role: Air superiority fighter with ground attack capability (F-15C/D), and dual-role air superiority/long-range interdiction fighter (F-15E). SEAD (suppression of enemy air defence) role for converted F-15Cs, planned to replace F-4G Wild Weasels at the end of this decade, was reinstated, and flight testing began in August 1996, using the F-15D AFTD (advanced fighter technology demonstrator) carrying PDF and the HARM missile. However, full development of the Litton Amecom/TRW Precision Direction Finding (PDF) system to locate/identify enemy radars has not been authorized by the USAF, although the demonstration/validation phase was allowed to be completed. A reconnaissance pod for the F-15C has also been evaluated on the AFTD.

Aims

- F-15E designed for advanced air-to-air performance combined with improved air-to-ground capability in a single tactical aircraft. 16,000 hour structural life.
- F-15E needs no fighter escort, and can (if required) fly interdiction missions without electronic jamming aircraft or AWACS support.
- F-15E has a strengthened airframe to allow take off at higher weight, and manoeuvre to 9g at combat weight throughout the flight envelope.
- Over 65 design changes incorporated into the F-15E (from the F-15C) to improve reliability and reduce maintenance. 95.9% mission capable rate achieved during the Gulf conflict.

Development

- 11 December 1986. Maiden flight of a production dual-role F-15E at St Louis.
- 12 April 1988. First F-15E handed-over to the USAF, going initially to the 461st Tactical Fighter Training Squadron of the 405th Tactical Training Wing at Luke AFB, Arizona.
- 10 May 1989. First flight with 2D nozzles of the F-15SMTD (Short take-off and landing Manoeuvre Technology Demonstrator), an experimental vectored-thrust conversion of an F-15B.
- 1989. 336th FS of the 4th Wing at Seymour Johnson AFB, became the first operational F-15E unit.
- October 1994. McDD received a USAF contract of $189.8 million to upgrade the AN/APG-63 radar on over 350 F-15C/Ds (full production could start in early 1999, with retrofits to begin soon after at a rate of 72 per year). See 18 July 1997.
- 19 April 1995. First of 2 demonstrations of a manned tactical reconnaissance capability, when the F-15D AFTD (advanced fighter technology demonstrator) took a series of high-resolution tactical images with electro-optical linear array reconnaissance systems in a conformal centreline pod of 23 ft (7.01 m) length. The pod is capable of carrying a complete Loral ATARS (advanced tactical airborne reconnaissance system) sensor suite.
- 12 September 1995. Roll-out of the first F-15S for Saudi Arabia, having previously flown in June.
- 1996. F-15D AFTD used for SEAD programme.
- February 1996. Start of F-15 ACTIVE vectored thrust trials.

▪ April 1997. Flight testing began of General Electric F110-GE-129 engines on 2 F-15Es at the start of a year-long evaluation programme, expected to accumulate at least 1,000 engine flight hours.
▪ 18 July 1997. First USAF F-15 with upgraded APG-63(V)1 radar flew.
▪ 12 September 1997. First flight of the first F-15I for Israel. Official roll-out ceremony took place on 6 November and the first 2 were delivered in January 1998. Delivery of all 25 will be completed by 1999.
▪ 19 January 1998. First 2 F-15Is arrived in Israel.
▪ 1998. Start of F-15 MANX 'tailless' trials (see Aircraft variants).

Details *(principally current production F-15E)*

Sales/Users: Israel (received 81 new and ex-USAF F-15A/B/C/Ds, plus is receiving 25 dual-role F-15Is as Ra'ams or Thunders), Japan (14 F-15J/DJs built in the USA plus Mitsubishi assembly/production – see Comments), Saudi Arabia (received 98 new and ex-USAF F-15C/Ds and ordered 72 dual-role F-15Ss), and the USAF (882 production F-15A/B/C/Ds and 227 F-15Es, with 5 more F-15Es ordered for attrition reserve in FY1998). 617 F-15s of all operational versions were in the USAF's active inventory in mid-1998 (including over 500 up to D version), of which 518 were primary aircraft authorized for combat missions, plus another 116 with the Air National Guard. See Aircraft variants for 'tailless' proposal for South Korea.
Crew: Pilot and weapon systems officer in tandem, under a bubble canopy.
Crew escape: McDonnell Douglas ACES II zero-zero ejection seats.
Fixed guns: 1 × 20-mm M61A1 Vulcan 6-barrel cannon in the starboard wing.
Ammunition: 512 rounds.
Number of weapon pylons: Maximum of 18, comprising 1 under each wing, 1 under each air intake, 2 centreline, and 6 on each of the 2 CFTs. Each CFT (conformal fuel tank) has the ability to carry 6 air-to-ground weapons, 3 on stub pylons and 3 on a long pylon. However, the long pylon more usually carries 2 air-to-air missiles in tandem. CFTs are available to F-15C/D/Es. In addition, the wing and centreline pylons can use multiple ejectors, in the case of the wing pylons each with perhaps 4 bombs plus 2 Sidewinders or a drop tank plus 2 Sidewinders. CFT pylons cause less drag than conventional multi-ejection racks.
Expendable weapons and equipment: 24,500 lb (11,113 kg) stores load, though 23,000 lb (10,432 kg) maximum more typically. Maximum air-to-air missile configurations are 8 AMRAAMs, or 4 Sidewinders under the wings and 4 Sparrows/AMRAAMs on the intakes (F-15Is carry Python 4s and AMRAAMs). Air-to-surface missiles include Maverick (up to 3 per wing) and HARM (F-15Es), with new missiles encompassing AGM-154A JSOW. Another future weapon will be WCMD (wind corrected munitions dispenser), while a large range of current smart guided bombs include the new GBU-31/32 (JDAM). Alternative weapons include up to 5 nuclear bombs, AGM-130 rocket-powered bombs, and conventional free-fall bombs up to the Mk 84 (2,000 lb).
Additional stores: Various mission pods, including LANTIRN (see below) carried on the 2 under front intake pylons, AXQ-14 data link to provide guidance updates for the GBU-15 guided bomb, and Texas Instruments ASQ-213 high-speed anti-radar missile targeting system (HTS). Towed target. F-15D being evaluated with a reconnaissance pod (see Development – 19 April 1995).
Radar: F-15C/D have Raytheon AN/APG-63, except APG-70 was installed in 43 late Cs and Ds; more than 350 USAF F-15C/Ds may be upgraded from 1999 with new APG-63(V)1) radar (some 148 initially), using components from the F/A-18E/F Hornet's AN/APG-73 and the transmitter and some software from the AN/APG-70 radar. F-15E's AN/APG-70 has air-to-air and air-to-ground modes, including high-resolution ground mapping and freezing to permit the crew to create an image of the target location (45° either side of the aircraft) in a short burst of radar activity. Advanced Electronics Company of Saudi Arabia is producing components for the F-15S's radar.
Flight/weapon system avionics/instrumentation: F-15E has 7 software-controlled avionics systems, comprising the IBM CP-1075C VHSIC central computer, multi-purpose display processor, avionics interface unit, radar (see above), Honeywell ring laser gyro INS, programmable armament control system, and Lear Siegler Astronics triple-redundant digital flight control system encompassing automatic terrain following that is linked to the LANTIRN navigation pod. Lockheed Martin LANTIRN (low-altitude navigation and targeting infra-red for night) itself has 2 pods: the navigational pod has FLIR for high-speed and low-altitude flight at night, its images displayed onto the pilot's Kaiser holographic wide-angle HUD, and terrain-following radar; the targeting pod has tracking FLIR and a laser designator for use with smart weapons. LANTIRN targeting pod is integrated with the main radar mapping mode, allowing the tracking FLIR to be slaved to targets selected by the aircrew on the radar display. Honeywell AN/ASK-6 air data computer. Honeywell AN/ASN-108 AHRS, and Rockwell Collins HSI, AN/ARN-118 Tacan, ADF and ILS. Weapon System Officer has 2 Sperry colour and 2 Kaiser monochrome CRTs (to display radar, EW and IR data in addition to aircraft, weapon and threat information), plus a new Honeywell digital map display (previously Bendix/King RP-341/A). Pilot has 1 colour and 2 monochrome CRTs, plus Kaiser IR-2394/A holographic wide-angle HUD. Teledyne AN/APX-101 IFF transponder and Hazeltine AN/APX-76 interrogator. GPS installed, and a weapons-control computer link with spaceborne/airborne sensors. JTIDS/Link 16. Elisra supplies the EW suite for F-15Is.
Self-protection systems: Northrop Grumman AN/ALQ-135(V) fully automatic, software-controlled and reprogrammable, dual-mode internal electronic countermeasures system for radar jamming, covering all major threat bands, with 20 processors. Loral AN/ALR-56C RWR. Magnavox warning system. Chaff/flares.
Wing characteristics: Shoulder mounted, cropped delta type, with slight anhedral.
Wing control surfaces: Plain ailerons and trailing-edge flaps.
Tail control surfaces: Slab tailplane (tailerons), currently with ±12° deflection when the aircraft is at high angle of attack but rising to ± 32° after control system modifications. Pronounced dogtooth leading edges. Twin fins and inset rudders, without inward or outward cant.
Canard: None.
Airbrakes: Single large airbrake above centre fuselage.
Flight control system: Hydraulic actuators. See Avionics. New system evaluated for the F-15E, reportedly to allow the aircraft to go well beyond the 20° angle of attack limit currently imposed to prevent the onset of spin.
Construction materials: Mostly metal (aluminium alloy and titanium, and including honeycomb core for ailerons, flaps, airbrake and wingtips), but composites airbrake skins.
Engines: 2 Pratt & Whitney F100-PW-220 or F100-PW-229 turbofans, latter allowing acceleration from idle to full afterburning in 4 seconds. AlliedSignal APU. General Electric F110-GE-129s were being flight tested on 2 F-15E in 1997-98.
Engine rating: Each 14,590 lbf (64.9 kN) dry, 23,770 lbf (105.74 kN) with afterburning, or 17,800 lbf (79.18 kN) dry, 29,100 lbf (129.445 kN) with afterburning, respectively.
Air intakes: Variable, 2-dimensional, horizontal wedge type on the fuselage sides, with 2 ramps.
Fuel system: 7,836 litres in F-15C, and 7,643 litres in F-15E. Fire retardant foam under the fuselage fuel tanks. Conformal Fuel Tanks (CFTs) on the F-15C house 5,542 litres of fuel, and on the F-15E 5,508 litres. Up to 3 × 2,309 litre drop tanks. CFTs (Conformal Fuel Tanks) are secured to the sides of the air intakes, offering far less drag than drop tanks and with the same g limits as the airframe, and can also house electronic systems (see Weapons).
Electrical system: 2 Lucas generators, either generator able to provide sufficient power for all systems.
Hydraulic system: 3 independent systems of 3,000 psi each, any able to provide safe control.
Braking system: Carbon disc brakes, with anti skid.
Oxygen system: Liquid oxygen systems in F-15A/B/C/D; molecular sieve oxygen generating system in F-15E.

Aircraft variants:
F-15C and ***F-15D*** became the standard production single- and 2-seat models from 1979 (replacing A and B), with F100-PW-100, 200 and 220 engines during production. 100 and 200 series engines upgraded to 220 standard.
F-15E dual-role 2-seater has a modified airframe to allow higher gross weight at take off, and manoeuvre to 9g at gross combat weight throughout the flight envelope. Heaviest version, with weapon-carrying CFTs and larger rear-canopy section.
F-15J and ***DJ*** are Mitsubishi-built F-15C and D versions for the JASDF.
F-15I Ra'am or Thunder is the exported F-15E for Israel, incorporating Elbit display and sight helmet (DASH) system, Elisra EW suite with active jammer and radar/missile warning systems plus chaff/flare. F100-PW-229 engines. AAMs include Python 4s.
F-15S is the exported F-15E for Saudi Arabia, which flew on 19 June 1995 and was officially rolled-out on 12 September that year. Some operational downgrading to conform more to Saudi F-15C/Ds, with 48 specializing in attack and the remainder in air-to-air combat. No high-resolution radar mapping, Sharpshooter LANTIRN, and downgraded ECM.
F-15SE is a potential USAF variant for defence against cruise missiles. Concept only at time of writing. Another new role for an F-15E variant could be theatre missile defence, becoming a boost-to-intercept platform.
F-15U and ***F-15U Plus*** were proposed versions of the F-15E to meet the United Arab Emirates' long-range strike requirement. More radical Plus version was proposed with new larger wings, and increased weapon and fuel loads. Thrust vectoring was considered.
F-15SMTD was a Short take-off and landing Manoeuvre Technology Demonstrator, converted from an F-15B and first flown in the 1980s. F100-PW-229 engines later fitted with new axisymmetric multi-directional thrust-vectoring pitch yaw balanced beam nozzles (PYBBN), under the ACTIVE (Advanced Control Technology for Integrated VEhicles) programme, with subsonic flight testing starting in February 1996. The first supersonic thrust-vectoring test occurred on 24 April that year. Foreplanes.
F-15 MANX is an outgrowth of the ACTIVE programme (see above), being developed with NASA, Pratt & Whitney and the USAF as a 'stealthy' and 'tailless' version of Eagle. Could be offered to South Korea to meet its F-X requirement, and to the USAF for its Replacement Interdictor Aircraft requirement. ACTIVE's tailfins and foreplanes removed, with the tailplane marginally canted up to improve stability in the event of double engine failure.

Details for F-15E, *with F-15C in italics*

PRINCIPAL DIMENSIONS:
Wing span: 42 ft 9.5 ins (13.05 m), *the same*
Maximum length: 63 ft 9.5 ins (19.45 m), *the same*
Maximum height: 18 ft 5.5 ins (5.63 m), *the same*

WINGS:
Aerofoil section: NACA 64A
Area: 608 sq ft (56.49 m^2), *the same*
Aspect ratio: 3.014, *the same*
Sweepback: 38° 42' leading edge, *the same*
Incidence: 0°, *the same*
Anhedral: 1°, *the same*

TAIL UNIT:
Tailplane span: 28 ft 3 ins (8.61 m), *the same*
Tailplane area: 111.36 sq ft (10.346 m^2), *the same*

UNDERCARRIAGE:
Type: Retractable, with nosewheel, *the same*
Main wheel tyre size: 36 × 11-18, *34.5 × 9.75-18*
Nose wheel tyre size: 22 × 7.75-9, *22 × 6.6-10*
Wheel base: 17 ft 9.5 ins (5.42 m), *the same*
Wheel track: 9 ft (2.75 m), *the same*

WEIGHTS:
Empty, operating: 32,000 lb (14,515 kg), *28,600 lb (12,975 kg)*
Maximum take-off: 81,000 lb (36,740 kg), *68,000 lb (30,844 kg)*

PERFORMANCE:
Maximum speed: Mach 2.5, *the same*
Take-off distance: *900 ft (275 m) with AAMs*
Landing distance: *3,500 ft (1,070 m) without drag-chute*
G limits: +9 for F-15E throughout flight envelope, *+9, -3*
Ceiling: 60,000 ft (18,290 m)
Radius of action: 686 naut miles (790 miles) 1,271 km
Range with full fuel: 2,400 naut miles (2,764 miles) 4,445 km
Ferry range: *3,100 naut miles (3,570 miles) 5,740 km*

Boeing (McDonnell Douglas) F/A-18 Hornet and F/A-18E/F Super Hornet

First flight: 18 November 1978 for Hornet prototype, 29 November 1995 for Super Hornet.
Role: Multi-mission, land and carrier-borne fighter, attack and reconnaissance; missions include air superiority, fighter escort, suppression of enemy air defences, forward air control, close air support and day/night strike.

Aims

▪ Original versions of Hornet replaced the A-7 Corsair II and F-4 Phantom with the USN/USMC.
▪ Idle to maximum thrust in 4 seconds, and combat thrust-to-weight ratio greater than 1 to 1.
▪ Built-in test system (BITS) to check the avionics and mechanical systems. 85-89% readiness rate achieved.
▪ Can operate in temperatures ranging from -51° C to +51.7° C, and survive landing descents of over 17 ft (5.2 m) per second.
▪ 12,000 flying hour structural lifetime (demonstrated), equivalent to nearly 30 years USN service.
▪ Super Hornet offers more powerful engines, increased carrier bringback capability, greatly improved fuel and weapons-carrying capability, increased range and duration, increased ability to survive in a wartime environment, and the growth potential to incorporate future systems and technologies to meet new threats.

Development

■ McDonnell Douglas began as prime contractor, with Northrop as principal sub-contractor producing the centre and aft fuselage, twin vertical tails and all associated subsystems.
■ 1974. US Navy VFAX low cost, lightweight fighter programme was superseded by a plan to develop a navalized variant of the General Dynamics F-16 or Northrop F-17, then in prototype form for a USAF competition. McDD's proposal for a navalized derivative of the YF-17 was accepted, with Northrop becoming prime sub-contractor and also prime contractor on the land-based version (later abandoned). Expected separate A-18 attack and F-18 fighter variants were merged to form a single F/A-18 multi-role fighter.
■ May 1980. The US Navy began receiving F/A-18A single-seaters and 2-seat B trainers, initially operated by VFA-125 at NAS Lemoore as a development unit.
■ 8 September 1980. Loss of a TF-18A (original designation of F/A-18B) in the UK, after flying at Farnborough Air Show. Hornet flying resumed on the 20th.
■ 28 July 1982. First of Canada's CF-18s was rolled out. Canada was the first export customer.
■ 1983. F/A-18A/Bs entered US Marine Corps and US Navy operational service, initially with VMFA-314 (7 January) and VFA-113 (October) respectively.
■ 3 September 1987. First production F/A-18C flew.
■ November 1989. Deliveries began of Hornets with night strike capability.
■ February 1992. USMC began receiving Hornets capable of integrating a reconnaissance pallet.
■ June 1992. Award of US$3.7 billion contract for engineering and manufacturing Development (EMD) of the F/A-18E/F advanced versions of Hornet. Also 7.5 year development and support programme. 7 flight test aircraft and 3 ground test.
■ October 1992. Delivery of Hornets with Enhanced Performance Engines.
■ 1993. US Hornets began receiving a laser designator housed within the targeting forward-looking infra-red sensor, for laser-guided bomb carriage.
■ 17 September 1993. 2 million F/A-18 flight hours were recorded, during a USMC flight over Bosnia-Herzegovina.
■ May 1994. Delivery of Hornets to the US Navy with upgraded AN/APG-73 radar.
■ May 1994. Production of the first F/A-18E/F centre/aft fuselage was started by Northrop Grumman.
■ 23 September 1994. F/A-18E/F assembly began at McDD's St Louis facility, marking the establishment of a second Hornet production line.
■ June 1994. Critical Design Review passed for the F/A-18E/F.
■ 1995. See Lockheed Martin P-3C Orion entry for Project Sword information relay trials involving an F/A-18A.
■ 21 April 1995. First flight of a Finnish Hornet, an F/A-18D.
■ 8 May 1995. Final assembly began of the F/A-18E/F.
■ 18 September 1995. Roll-out of the first F/A-18E.
■ 29 November 1995. First flight of the F/A-18E1.
■ 26 December 1995. First flight of the F/A-18E2.
■ 25 January 1996. First of 34 F/A-18C/Ds for Switzerland was rolled out. All for delivery by November 1999.
■ 1 April 1996. First F/A-18F Super Hornet flew, as F/A-18F1, delivered to Patuxent River after a 2.6 hour flight on 21 May.
■ 12 April 1996. First supersonic flight (Mach 1.1) by the F/A-18E1 Super Hornet.
■ 6 August 1996. First 3 catapult launches of Super Hornet at the Naval Air Warfare Center, Patuxent River (F/A-18F1), piloted by Cmdr Tom Gurney.

↑ **Boeing F/A-18E Super Hornet leading an F/A-18C Hornet over Missouri. Note the E's larger wings with dogtooth leading-edges, larger tailerons and larger/reshaped LEX**

■ 7-11 December 1996. 4 day, 7 flight, evaluation of Hornet by Philippine Air Force representatives.
■ 18 January 1997. F/A-18F1 made the type's first landing on an aircraft carrier, USS *John C. Stennis*, at the start of the initial sea trial which ended on the 24th. Production began in 1997.
■ 1 February 1997. First flight of the seventh and last Super Hornet flight test aircraft.
■ 19 February 1997. F/A-18E5 dropped an auxiliary tank from 5,000 ft (1,524 m), in the Super Hornet's first separation test.
■ 26 February 1997. First flight of a Super Hornet (F/A-18E5) with weapons attached (Mk 84 bombs, 2 Sidewinders and anti-radiation missiles, plus 1,817 litre tanks).
■ 26 May 1997. First 4 F/A-18Ds for Malaysia arrived at Butterworth after a 7,145 naut mile flight using a KC-10 refuelling tanker and stop-overs in Hawaii and Guam. The first Malaysian aircraft had made its maiden flight on 1 February, with the official delivery ceremony in St. Louis on 19 March.
■ 12 September 1997. Super Hornet flew its 1,000th flight with Integrated Test Team pilot Cdr Rob Niewoehner at the controls.
■ 22 September 1997. Production of the first operational Super Hornets began at St. Louis. First production Super Hornet appeared in 1998 as an F/A-18E.
■ 9 December 1997. Super Hornet surpassed 2,000 flight hours during its flight test programme (by F/A-18F2).
■ November 1998. Start of operational evaluation of integration of the Advanced Tactical Airborne Reconnaissance System into USMC F/A-18Ds, to allow IOC for March 1999.
■ Late 1998. Expected start of F/A-18E/F deliveries to the US Navy.
■ 2001. IOC of F/A-18E/F.
■ 2002. Possible start of EMD for the F/A-18G.

Details *(principally both F/A-18C/D Hornet and F/A-18E/F Super Hornet, with earlier versions where indicated)*

Sales/Users: More than 1,350 delivered of 1,478 ordered at time of writing (accumulating over 3.3 million flying hours by June 1998), comprising Australia (75 between 1984-90 as AF-18As and

↑ **Boeing F/A-18F Super Hornet during sea/carrier trials, with arrester hook lowered**

↑ **Boeing F/A-18E with 3 × 1,817 litre auxiliary tanks, 2 × Mk 84 bombs, 2 HARM missiles and 2 Sidewinders** *(Vernon Pugh/ US Navy)*

↑ **The sixth Boeing (McDonnell Douglas) F/A-18D of Malaysia's No 18 Squadron, photographed at Butterworth in late 1997** *(Denis Hughes)*

ATF-18As – upgrade plans include improved mission computers, improved coms, APG-73 radar, Link 16 datalink, EW and other systems, plus new AAMs), Canada (138 between 1982-88 as CF-18A/Bs, known as CF-188A/Bs), Finland (64 F/A-18C/Ds, delivered 1995-2000 and first serving with HävLLv 21 at Tampere to replace Drakens; McDD delivered the first 7 structurally complete F/A-18Ds, with Finavitec undertaking final assembly of 57 F/A-18Cs locally), Kuwait (40 between 1992-93), Malaysia (8 F/A-18Ds between 1996-97, with a further 10-16 requested), Spain (72 EF-18A/Bs between 1986-90 and known as C.15s and CE.15s, plus 24 US Navy F/A-18As to fill the gap caused by Eurofighter delays, with 13 delivered by June 1998), Switzerland (2 assembled plus 32 kits for F/A-18C/Ds, all delivered from USA by 1997), Thailand (8, as 4 F/A-18Cs and 4 F/A-18Ds), and USA (1,028, those remaining currently operated by 26 active and 4 reserve Navy and 15 active and 4 reserve Marine Corps squadrons – the US Navy planned an all late-production F/A-18C/D force for carrier operations prior to E/F deliveries). For the F/A-18E/F development programme, 7 flight test aircraft and 3 ground test aircraft were built. US Navy plans call for about 1,000 F/A-18E/Fs by 2015 (12 ordered initially, plus 20 in the 1998 procurement budget), plus the possibility of over 100 F/A-18Gs after the EMD phase (which could begin in the year 2002). Production of the first operational Super Hornets began in September 1997 at St. Louis. Hornet has also been evaluated by Chile, the Philippines, Poland, Hungary, Czech Republic and Austria. Super Hornet is among possibilities to replace Australian Hornets, which could be retired in 2010 for budgetary reasons, though upgrade of systems and deployment of new short- and medium-range AAMs will almost certainly take place.

Crew: Pilot, or 2 in tandem in the F/A-18B/D/F and USMC night attack versions.

Cockpit: AiResearch (Hornet) or Hamilton Standard (Super Hornet) air conditioning system.

Crew escape: Martin Baker SJU-5-6 zero-zero ejection seat/s.

Fixed guns: 20-mm M61A1 Vulcan cannon in the nose. Upgrade will introduce a new lightweight cannon, as to be used in E/F.

Ammunition: 570 rounds.

Number of weapon pylons: 9, as 2 wingtip for Sidewinders, 2 outboard for weapons, 2 inboard 'wet' for drop tanks or weapons, 2 nacelle stations for AMRAAMs/Sparrows or sensor pods, and 1 fuselage centreline for a drop tank or air-to-ground weapon. Super Hornet has 2 extra wing pylons, each for up to a 1,000 lb (454 kg) load.

Expendable weapons and equipment: Current F/A-18C and D have a normal load of 13,700 lb (6,214 kg) and maximum of 14,900-15,500 lb (6,758-7,030 kg). Wingtip Sidewinders, AMRAAM or Sparrow AAMs on the nacelle pylons, and AAMs or attack weapons on the underwing and centreline pylons. Maximum air-to-air armament is 10 AMRAAMs and 2 Sidewinders. Attack weapons include IR Maverick, SLAM, anti-ship Harpoon and HARM missiles, laser-guided/free fall/cluster bombs and including CBU-59 and the GBU-32 (JDAM for the USN), or rocket pods. Future weapons will include JSOW, and could encompass Python 4 and ASRAAM. Super Hornet has a 17,750 lb (8,050 kg) payload, with the following weapons launched during trials in 1997: Sidewinder, Sparrow, AMRAAM, Harpoon, SLAM, GBU-10, HARM and Maverick, plus free-fall weapons including Mk 76, BDU-48, Mk 82LD, Mk 83HD and Mk 84 bombs.

Additional stores: FLIR pod (see Avionics) or Lockheed Martin AN/ASQ-173 laser spot tracker and strike camera.

Radar: Raytheon AN/APG-65 digital multi-mode, superseded by AN/APG-73 with increased speed and memory capacity processors from May 1994 deliveries. AN/APG 73 used on Super Hornet.

Flight/weapon system avionics/instrumentation: Includes MIL-STD-1553B databus, and MIL-STD-1760 to provide a common electrical and digital interface between the weapons and the aircraft. Control Data AN/AYK-14 digital computers. Smiths digital (computer-generated) colour moving map. Hughes AN/AAR-50 thermal imaging navigation set (TINS) and Lockheed Martin ASS-38B Nite Hawk targeting forward looking infra-red sensor, with imagery on the pilot's Kaiser AN/AVQ-28 raster HUD and combined with navigation and weapon delivery symbology (NAVFLIR pod also houses a laser designator and ranger). Loral colour video/TV mission recording system (for US Navy). Boeing is studying an advanced targeting FLIR system (ATFLIR) for Hornet/Super Hornet. Litton AN/ASN-130A INS or more recent ASN-139 ring laser INS, GPS, Rockwell-Collins AN/ARN-118 Tacan, GEC-Marconi FID 2035 horizontal situation display, and AlliedSignal horizontal situation indicator. 2 Kaiser 5 × 5 ins multi-function displays (monochrome, or colour for Night Attack versions), GEC-Marconi central CRT, and HOTAS; 2 existing MFDs plus larger (6.25 × 6.25 ins) colour tactical situation display and 3 × 5 ins touch-screen upfront control panel for Super Hornet. AN/APX-100 IFF. Hazeltine APX-111 combined interrogator transponder for Kuwait and now for currently built aircraft, plus planned retrofit to US aircraft (which are also to receive Litton Embedded GPS/inertial system). AN/ARC-182 U/VHF coms. Harris AN/ASW-25 datalink. Spar flight incident recorder (US aircraft). Horizons Technology integrated mission support system on F/A-18s of Finland, Malaysia, Spain and Switzerland. GEC-Marconi Cat's Eyes night vision goggles for the pilot or weapon systems officer, and compatible cockpit lighting. F/A-18C/D upgrade programmes include mission computer improvements with VHSIC technology (current XN-8), and reconnaissance capability (see F/A-18D[RC]). US Hornets use an automatic carrier landing system. Canadian F/A-18A/Bs and Finnish C/Ds have an instrument landing system.

Self-protection systems: Litton AN/ALR-67 radar warning, Magnavox AN/ALR-50 alerting, and Sanders ALQ-126B jamming. ALQ-162(V) continuous wave jammers fitted to CF-18s and some EF-18s. Westinghouse/ITT (Northrop Grumman) ALQ-165 for Finland and Switzerland; also in limited US use. Goodyear AN/ALE-39 or, later, -47 chaff/flares. ADM-141 TALD (tactical air launched decoys). F/A-18E/F have Integrated Defense Electronic Countermeasures (IDECM) system, with AN/ALR-67(V)3 RWR, jammer and chaff/flares. Raytheon AN/ALE-50 towed radar decoy is being considered for US Navy Hornets/Super Hornets.

Wing characteristics: Straight, shoulder mounted, with long leading-edge extensions; LEX of Hornet 56 sq ft (5.2 m^2) but larger and more rounded LEX of Super Hornet 75.3 sq ft (6.99 m^2). Slots at wing/fuselage blend. Fence added to the LEX of US F/A-18Cs improves longitudinal control during high alpha. Folding wings for carrier stowage, and standard on all aircraft. Super Hornet features larger wings with 100 sq ft (9.3 m^2) more area, outer-section dogtooth, wing root depth increased by 1 ins (2.54 cm), larger control surfaces and 2 extra weapon stations (see Aircraft variants).

Wing control surfaces: Ailerons, automatic trailing-edge flaperons and automatic leading-edge manoeuvre flaps. LEX spoilers on Super Hornet.

Tail control surfaces: Slab tailplane (tailerons, of increased area for Super Hornet) and twin outward-canted fins with inset rudders. Rudders are toed-in during take-off/landing for trimming effect. Super Hornet tailerons adopt neutral position if damaged.

Canard: None.

Airbrakes: 1 above the extreme rear fuselage on Hornet only. LEX spoilers on Super Hornet.

Flight control system: General Electric 4-channel (quadruple-redundant), dual computer, digital fly-by-wire, with automatic reversion to 1g flying should the controls be released. US Hornets use an automatic carrier landing system. Emergency electric provisions. Mechanical link to tailerons for "get home" capability on Hornet only.

Fuselage: Northrop Grumman as principal subcontractor produces the centre and aft fuselage sections (see Development).

Construction materials: Structure has 50% by weight aluminium alloy, 13% titanium, 10% carbonfibre/epoxy composites, and the remainder of steel, glassfibre, aramid and other materials. 40% of the outer skin is carbonfibre/epoxy.

Engines: 2 General Electric F404-GE-400 turbofans, or 402s from 1992, on Hornet. Super Hornet has F414-GE-400s, each of 22,000 lbf (97.86 kN) with afterburning. AlliedSignal GTC36-200 APU. Under ideal conditions, an engine can be changed in under 21 minutes.

Engine rating: 16,000 lbf (71.17 kN) with afterburning or 17,700 lbf (78.73 kN) with afterburning respectively for F404-GE-400 and -420.

Air intakes: Non-variable with splitters, under the wings, each side of the fuselage for Hornet. New angular intakes for Super Hornet, offering greater flow; also reduce radar signature.

Flight refuelling probe: Retractable, in the starboard side of the nose.

Fuel system: 10,860 lb (4,926 kg) internally (some reports suggest 10,381 lb, 4,709 kg), equivalent to about 6,056 litres. Self-seal tanks. No fuel stored between engines. Fire retardant foam under the fuselage fuel tanks. Optional 3 × 1,249 litre drop tanks, while 2,271 litre tanks have been proposed. Some 14,460 lb (6,559 kg), equivalent to about 8,060 litres internal capacity, for Super Hornet, plus 3 × 1,817 litre auxiliary tanks.

Details for F/A-18C/D, *with E/F in italics*

PRINCIPAL DIMENSIONS:

Wing span: 37 ft 6 ins (11.43) without wingtip missiles, 40 ft 5 ins (12.32 m) including missiles. *44 ft 8.5 ins (13.62 m) including missiles*

Span, wings folded: 27 ft 6 ins (8.38 m), *30 ft 7 ins (9.32 m)*

Maximum length: 56 ft (17.07 m), *60 ft 1 ins (18.31 m)*

Maximum height: 15 ft 3.5 ins (4.66 m), *16 ft (4.88 m)*

WINGS:

Area: 400 sq ft (37.16 m^2), *500 sq ft (46.45 m^2)*

Aspect ratio: 3.516, *3.996*

Sweepback: 20° at 25% chord

Anhedral: from root

TAIL UNIT:

Tailplane span: 21 ft 7 ins (6.58 m)

Tailplane area: 88.1 sq ft (8.185 m^2)

UNDERCARRIAGE:

Type: Retractable, with twin steerable nosewheels. Tyre pressures greatly increased for aircraft carrier operations. Can survive landing descents of over 17 ft (5.2 m) per second

Main wheel tyre size: 30 × 11.5-14.5

Nose wheel tyre size: 22 × 6.6-10

Wheel base: 17 ft 9.5 ins (5.42 m)

Wheel track: 10 ft 2.5 ins (3.11 m)

WEIGHTS:

Empty: 23,832 lb (10,810 kg), *29,264-30,560 lb (13,274-13,860 kg)*

Take-off (air superiority): 36,700 lb (16,647 kg)

Maximum take-off: 56,000 lb (25,400 kg), or 51,900 lb (23,540 kg) for typical air-to-surface mission. *Approximately 66,000 lb (29,940 kg) for E/F, with 62,400 lb (28,304 kg) demonstrated on 26 February 1997 test flight*

Bringback: 5,500 lb (2,495 kg), *9,000 lb (4,082 kg)*

Carrier landing: 33,000 lb (14,968 kg), *42,900 lb (19,459 kg)*

PERFORMANCE:

Maximum speed: over Mach 1.8

Maximum speed, intermediate power: over Mach 1

Approach speed: 134 kts (154 mph) 248 km/h, *125 kts (144 mph) 231 km/h*

Take-off distance: less than 1,400 ft (426 m)

Minimum deck wind speed for carrier operations: 35 kts take-off, 19 kts landing, *30 kts take-off, 15 kts landing*

G limits: +7.5, with optional upgrade to +9 manoeuvre

Operating temperatures: -51° C to +51.7° C

Ceiling: 50,000 ft (15,240 m), combat, *the same*

Radius of action (attack): typically over 470 naut miles (541 miles) 871 km, *over 660 naut miles (760 miles) 1,222 km*

Radius of action (interdiction): typically 290 naut miles (334 miles) 537 km, *390 naut miles (449 miles) 723 km with 4 × Mk 83HD bombs, 2 AAMs and 2 auxiliary tanks*, for Hi-Lo-Lo-Hi mission profile

Radius of action (interception): typically over 400 naut miles (461 miles) 741 km, internal fuel

Radius of action (fighter escort): *over 400 naut miles (461 miles) 741 km with 2 AMRAAM and 2 Sidewinder AAMs on internal fuel*

Ferry range: over 1,800 naut miles (2,073 miles) 3,335 km

Electrical system: Hornet's General Electric system replaced by Leland Electrosystems system on Super Hornet, offering a large increase in power.

Hydraulic system: 2 independent systems, each 3,000 psi. Damage isolation of hydraulics.

Braking system: Bendix brakes. Arrester hook.

Aircraft variants:

F/A-18A was the initial production single-seater, delivered up to 1987. XN-5 mission computer.

F/A-18B was the initial 2-seat operational training version of A (originally TF-18A). Similar dimensions but with a second tandem cockpit and 6% less fuel.

F/A-18C and ***F/A-18D*** became the standard production single-seat and 2-seat models from 1987, with night attack capability added from the 139th aircraft. Improved armament options include AMRAAM and IR Maverick, while many important avionics updates include huge leaps in memory for the weapon management system and mission computer (XN-6 and later XN-8). Small airframe changes. Higher rated engines from 1992. APG-73 radar (instead of APG-65) from May 1994 deliveries, with earlier aircraft being upgraded (see earlier paragraphs).

F/A-18D(RC) is the modification for 31 USMC F/A-18Ds, each having an Advanced Tactical Airborne Reconnaissance System comprising a new high-resolution strip mapping mode for the radar, datalink pod, and an infra-red linescanner/electro-optical sensor pod. Operational evaluation November 1998 to January 1999, with operational use from 1999.

F/A-18E/F have greater range and payload, significantly increased carrier suitability and survivability (added defence electronics – see Self protection – and fuel protection). Avionics and software are over 90% common with those of F/A-18C/D. Cockpit upgrades include a larger (6.25 × 6.25 ins) colour tactical situation display and 3 × 5 ins touch-screen upfront control panel. More electrical power. Fuel increased by about 3,600 lb (1,633 kg) to extend mission radius by up to 60%, depending on the mission profile. 34 ins (86 cm) longer fuselage. Larger wings with 100 sq ft (9.3 m^2) more area, outer-section dogtooth, wing root depth increased by 1 ins (2.54 cm), larger control surfaces and 2 extra weapon stations. Larger and more outward-rounded LEX of 75.3 sq ft (6.99 m^2), with spoilers; no air brake, functions being assumed by spoilers and use of rudders/flaps. Tailerons have increased area. More powerful engines (see Engines), and enlarged, more angular, air inlets to provide greater airflow to the engines. Increase in the use of advanced composite materials in the airframe, and greater electrical and hydraulic capacity.

F/A-18G is a proposed 2-seat electronic warfare (C^2W – command and control warfare) variant of F/A-18F, proposed as a future Prowler replacement and with Northrop Grumman's Electronics and Systems Integration Division undertaking systems integration. Features could include a large centreline jammer pod with electronically-scanned antennae to counter radars in the 0.5-18 GHz frequency, and low band antennae in place of RWR in the wing leading-edge. 8 × 10 ins (20 × 25 cm) colour tactical situation display.

AF-18A and ***ATF-18A*** are the Australian designations of its F/A-18A/Bs, most assembled locally by ASTA. All remaining aircraft upgraded with C/D avionics, including Nite Hawk capability.

CF-18A and ***CF-18B*** are the Canadian F/A-18A/Bs, known locally as CF-188A/Bs. Minor differences from US Hornets include some varying expendable weapon options (including deployment of 70-mm submunition rocket pods) , an instrument landing system, and more. 1,817 litre drop tanks. Nite Hawk capability.

EF-18A and ***EF-18B*** are the Spanish F/A-18A/Bs, known locally as C.15 and CE.15. Remaining aircraft upgraded to near C/D standard, sometimes quoted as EF-18A+/B+.

Boeing X-36

First flight: 17 May 1997.
Role: 28% scale, remotely piloted (from a ground station), tailless technology demonstrator, to help in the development of tailless stealth aircraft.
Comments: Developed with NASA, X-36 has no vertical or horizontal tail surfaces and uses split ailerons and thrust vectoring to provide yaw and pitch control, while the ailerons are also used for roll and canards for pitch. This configuration is expected to demonstrate the possibility of reduced airframe weight, drag and radar signature, while increasing range, manoeuvrability and survivability. The demonstrator took 28 months to design, develop and build, costing US$17 million. The first phase of flight testing ended on 30 June 1997, after 8 flights, during which a 20° angle-of-attack and 2g manoeuvres were demonstrated. Having upgraded the flight control software, the first X-36 resumed tests in July, aiming to demonstrate a 35° angle-of-attack and higher levels of g, plus high angles-of-attack at low speeds. Autopilot was used for part of the second, third and fourth flights, due to temporary datalink failures. A second X-36 was built and the 2 X-36s completed the second phase of flying on 12 November 1997, accumulating (over the 2 phases of 31 flights) a total of 15 hours 38 minutes flying time, during which 40° AoA and 4.8 g were achieved.
Engine: 1 Williams F112, of 700 lbf (3.1 kN).
Construction materials: Substructure of machined aluminium, with non-autoclaved carbon-epoxy skins.

Basic details for X-36

PRINCIPAL DIMENSIONS:
Wing span: 10 ft 4 ins (3.18 m)
Maximum length: 18 ft 2 ins (5.54 m), including probe
Maximum height: 3 ft 1 ins (0.94 m)

UNDERCARRIAGE:
Type: Retractable, with nosewheel

WEIGHTS:
Empty: 1,090 lb (494 kg)
Fuel: 180 lb (81.6 kg)
Maximum take-off: 1,270 lb (576 kg)

PERFORMANCE:
Mach number: ≤Mach 0.6
Approach speed: 110 kts (127 mph) 204 km/h
G limits: 5
Duration: up to 45 minutes

Boeing (Rockwell) B-1B Lancer

Comments: First flown on 18 October 1984, the B-1B long-range penetration and stand-off strategic bomber entered USAF service in July 1985, with the final delivery (100th) on 30 April 1988. Some 77 remained on the active inventory of Air Combat Command in June 1998, a B-1B of the 28th Bomb Wing at Ellsworth having been lost on 19 September 1997, of which some 36 are primary aircraft authorized (PAA), for operational use with the 7th Wing at Dyess AFB in Texas and 28th Bomb Wing at Ellsworth AFB in South Dakota (both 8th Air Force), plus the 366th Wing at Mountain Home AFB in Idaho (12th Air Force). A further 17 are with the 116th Bomb Wing, Robins AFB in Georgia and the 184th Bomb Wing at McConnell AFB, Kansas, of the Air National Guard.

Continuing emphasis has been placed on conventional mission enhancement (though remaining nuclear capable), begun in August 1993 when Rockwell, with Boeing as subcontractor, entered a teaming agreement to initiate the USAF's CMUP programme (Conventional Mission Upgrade Program). Phase I of the CMUP, completed in 1995, included Boeing's development of software to provide for manual selection of and insertion of ballistic information into the system to accommodate various free-fall weapons, such as cluster bombs. Current programmes under the Block D upgrade include the integration of the Raytheon AN/ALE-50 towed decoy system (TDS) and the JDAM weapon system with the required MIL-STD-1760 databus, both programmes having been brought forward to allow early deployment on 7 aircraft of the 28th BW by January 1999. TDS is accommodated in fairings under the tailplane, each with 4 decoys. JDAM provides for 8 × 2,000 lb GBU-31(V)1 or (V)3 bombs, each an INS/GPS-guided modification of the Mk 84 fragmentation or BLU-109 penetrator bombs. Flights for the decoy test programme have also been used to assist in the active vibration suppression system programme, which hugely reduces structure vibration by producing oscillatory signals to piezoceramic actuators which cause the vibration to be suppressed. Other Block D upgrades include GPS and improved communications. From the year 2002, Block E upgrades on B-1Bs will include the computing and software changes required to allow simultaneous carriage of 3 different guided and unguided weapons, including WCMD, JASSM and AGM-154A. In a new role, the B-1B is to be capable of deploying Mk 62 Quick Strike underwater mines. Full details of the B-1B can be found in the 1996-97 edition of *WA&SD*, pages 153-155.

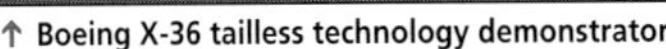
↑ Boeing X-36 tailless technology demonstrator

↑ Boeing (Rockwell) B-1B, currently undergoing Block D upgrades, including a towed decoy system and JDAM integration

Lockheed Martin

On 3 July 1997 Lockheed Martin and Northrop Grumman announced their pending merger under a US$11.6 billion agreement, with Northrop Grumman shareholders to receive Lockheed Martin shares and the new organization forming under the Lockheed Martin name. The merged company would have some 230,000 employees worldwide and be headed by Lockheed Martin's Chairman Vance Coffman, with Northrop Grumman's current Chairman and CEO Kent Kresa becoming the new Vice Chairman. Although the merger had been expected to be finalized before the end of 1997, it was not until February 1998 that shareholders of both companies approved the merger. However, the US Government voiced concerns over the merger, citing anti-trust law, and a high court hearing was scheduled to begin on 8 September 1998. Although it is possible that an outcome could be reached before the end of 1998, it is more likely to be 1999. As a result, the Chief Editor of *WA&SD* was requested by Lockheed Martin representatives to list the companies separately for this edition of *WA&SD*, given that the merger had not gone through at the time of writing, nor the establishment of merged divisions. By July 1998, the merger appeared increasingly unlikely.

In 1997 Lockheed Martin agreed to sell General Electric 3 businesses, namely the part of Aero & Naval Systems dealing with thrust reversers, plus Access Graphics and its stake in Globalstar.

Lockheed Martin Corporation

USA

Corporate address:
6801 Rockledge Drive, Bethesda, MD 20817.

Telephone: +1 301 897 6000
Facsimile: +1 301 897 6028, 6252

Founded:
15 March 1995, as a merger of the Lockheed Corporation (founded 1926) and Martin Marietta (founded 1965 but with roots going back to 1911). In April 1996. Lockheed Martin completed a 'strategic combination' with the defence electronics and systems integration business of Loral.

Employees: 180,000.

Information:
Keith Mordoff (Director, International Public Relations – *telephone* +1 301 897 6387, *facsimile* +1 301 897 6289).

SECTORS AND DIVISIONS

AERONAUTICS SECTOR

HQ address:
Bethesda, MD.

Telephone: +1 301 897 6121
Facsimile: +1 301 897 6252

Employees: About 33,000.

President: James A 'Micky' Blackwell.

COMPRISING:

LOCKHEED MARTIN TACTICAL AIRCRAFT SYSTEMS

HQ address:
(PO Box 748) Lockheed Blvd., Fort Worth, TX 76101.

Telephone: +1 817 777 2000
Facsimile: +1 817 763 4797
Web site: http://www.lmtas.com

Information: Joseph W. Stout (Director of Communications – *telephone* +1 817 763 4086, *E-mail* joe.w.stout@1mco.com)

Activities:
■ Design and production of the F-16, plus F-16 upgrade. One-third of F-22 engineering and development programme. Assisted in the Mitsubishi F-2 development programme. Working on the Joint Strike Fighter.

LOCKHEED MARTIN AERONAUTICAL SYSTEMS

HQ address:
86 South Cobb Drive, Marietta, GA 30063-0264.

Telephone: +1 770 494 4124, 4411
Facsimile: +1 770 494 7656

Information:
Ray Crockett (Director, Public Affairs - *telephone* +1 770 494 3211).
Information (Airlift programmes):
Julius Alexander (*telephone* +1 770 494 9818)
Information (P-3, S-3, MPA/AEW programmes):
Doug Oliver (*telephone* +1 770 494 6208)
Information (F-22, Advanced Tactical programmes, JPATA, L-1011):
Jeff Rhodes (*telephone* +1 770 494 2702)

Activities:
■ Design and production of fighter, military transport and maritime patrol/surveillance aircraft. Engineering and manufacturing development of the F-22, production of Hercules, and P-3 programmes.

LOCKHEED MARTIN SKUNK WORKS

HQ address:
1011 Lockheed Way, Palmdale, CA 93599-3740.

Telephone: +1 805 572 4153
Facsimile: +1 805 572 4163

Information:
Ronald C. Lindeke (Director, Public Affairs).

Activities:
■ Designs 'innovative' aircraft, recently including the F-117A stealth fighter. Upgrades U-2 and F-117A. X-33 reusable launch vehicle programme. Ontario, California branch for design, systems integration and modification of aircraft for electronic warfare; command, control and communications; and special operations missions. Aircraft maintenance, training and support services.

LOCKHEED MARTIN AERO & NAVAL SYSTEMS

HQ address:
103 Chesapeake Park Plaza, Baltimore, MD 21220.

Telephone: +1 410 682 1120
Facsimile: +1 410 682 3276

Information: Don Carson.

Activities:
■ Up to late 1997 encompassed the design, development, production and support of missile launching systems and engine thrust reversers. Believed to be one of 3 businesses sold to General Electric under a recent agreement, though not including the Naval launch systems.

LOCKHEED MARTIN AIRCRAFT CENTER

HQ address:
Greenville, South Carolina.

Activities
Support services for military and commercial customers.

LOCKHEED MARTIN LOGISTICS MANAGEMENT

HQ address:
1600 East Pioneer Pkwy., Arlington, TX 76010-6594.

Information: Kathryn Hayden.

Telephone: +1 817 548 2442
Facsimile: +1 817 860 7930

Activities:
■ Contract field teams for on-site maintenance, modification and support of DoD bases. Fixed base contracts for logistical support at US forces bases.

LOCKHEED MARTIN AERONAUTICS INTERNATIONAL

HQ address:
Ontario, California.

Activities:
■ Specializes in developing and managing international aviation service centres, privatizing aerospace-related depots, establishing joint ventures in foreign countries and marketing modification and maintenance projects worldwide. Subsidiaries and joint ventures in Argentina (which see), China, Hungary and Saudi Arabia.

ELECTRONICS SECTOR

HQ address:
Bethesda, MD.

President & COO: Thomas A. Corcoran.

Information: James Tierney (Vice President, Communications).

Telephone: +1 301 897 6952

COMPRISING:

Lockheed Martin Canada
Lockheed Martin Commercial Electronics
Lockheed Martin Control Systems
Lockheed Martin Electronics & Missiles
Lockheed Martin Fairchild Systems
Lockheed Martin Federal Systems-Manassas
Lockheed Martin Federal Systems-Owego
Lockheed Martin Government Electronic Systems
Lockheed Martin IR Imaging System
Lockheed Martin Ocean, Radar & Sensor Systems
Lockheed Martin Tactical Defense Systems-Akron
Lockheed Martin Tactical Defense Systems-Eagan
Lockheed Martin Vought Systems
Sanders, a Lockheed Martin Company

ENERGY & ENVIRONMENT SECTOR

INFORMATION & SERVICES SECTOR

HQ address:
Bethesda, MD.

President & COO: Peter. B. Teets.

Activities:
■ Information technology services.

COMPRISING:

Lockheed Martin Air Traffic Management
Lockheed Martin Enterprise Information Systems
Lockheed Martin IMS
Lockheed Martin Information Systems
Lockheed Martin Western Development Laboratories

PLUS:

Lockheed Martin Commercial Systems Group
Lockheed Martin Systems Integration Group
Lockheed Martin Technology Services Group
United Space Alliance as 50% joint venture with Boeing (see Spaceflight section).

SPACE & STRATEGIC MISSILES SECTOR

HQ address:
Bethesda, MD.

President and COO: Dr Mel Brashears.

Telephone: +1 301 897 6493

COMPRISING:

LOCKHEED MARTIN MISSILES & SPACE

HQ address:
PO Box 3504, Sunnyvale, CA 94088-3504.

Telephone: +1 408 742 5113
Facsimile: +1 408 743 2239

Information:
Eric DeRitis (*telephone* +1 408 742 8932, *E-mail* eric.deritis@1mco.com).

LOCKHEED MARTIN ASTRONAUTICS

HQ address:
Denver, Colorado.

LOCKHEED MARTIN COMMERCIAL

HQ address:
Sunnyvale, California.

LOCKHEED MARTIN MANNED SPACE SYSTEMS

HQ address:
New Orleans, Louisana.

Lockheed Martin AC-130H Spectre and Rockwell AC-130U Spooky

Comments: These heavy gunship conversions of the C-130 Hercules are operated by the USAF's 16th Special Operations Wing, Special Operations Command, out of Hurlburt Field, Florida (8 AC-130Hs and 13 AC-130Us) for special operations by day or night, including close air support, interdiction, armed reconnaissance, escort and area defence. In 1997, Raytheon Systems received an order for 16 AN/AAQ-26 FLIR sensors to equip 7 Hs and 9 Us. A description and illustrations can be found in the 1996-97 edition of *WA&SD*, page 130. See cover photograph and Lockheed Martin C-130 entry in this 1998-99 edition.

Lockheed Martin (LMTAS) F-16 Fighting Falcon

First flight: 20 January 1974.
Role: Fighter, air superiority, air defence, close air support, precision strike, battlefield interdiction, forward air control, maritime operations, defence suppression and reconnaissance.

Aims

■ Originally intended as a lightweight and low-cost day fighter. Role subsequently expanded to include all-weather operations and ground attack.
■ Relaxed stability for reduced tail drag and improved manoeuvrability, requiring fly-by-wire control.
■ 8,000 hour structural life.
■ Mishap rate per 100,000 flight hours: 4.5 (USAF), 5.4 (worldwide).

↑ **Lockheed Martin F-16 tested in 1997 with about 600 sq ft (55.74 m^2) of surface area treated with a black, pressure sensitive, adhesive applique, instead of paint, to test cost and weight savings among other benefits**

↑ **Lockheed Martin F-16D launching HARM**

Development

▪ 28 February 1972. Proposals for the Lightweight Fighter programme received by the USAF from 5 manufacturers.
▪ 13 April 1972. General Dynamics and Northrop contracted to develop competing prototypes (2 each as YF-16s and YF-17s).
▪ 2 February 1974. Recognized and scheduled first flight at Edwards AFB (but not actual first flight).
▪ 11 March 1974. First Mach 2 test flight.
▪ 13 January 1975. YF-16 chosen for EMD, under the renamed Air Combat Fighter programme. Role expanded to include ground attack, and with provision for radar and navigation avionics suited to all-weather operations.
▪ 8 December 1976. Maiden flight of the first of 8 EMD aircraft (including 2 two-seaters).
▪ 8 August 1977. Maiden flight of the first EMD F-16B 2-seater.
▪ 7 August 1978. Maiden flight of the first full production F-16A.
▪ 6 January 1979. First delivery to the USAF, going to the 388th TFW at Hill AFB.
▪ 26 January 1979. Belgian Air Force became the first foreign recipient. Final assembly of European F-16s was undertaken in Belgium and the Netherlands.
▪ 1983. F-16s joined the US Air National Guard, followed by the US Air Force Reserve the next year.
▪ July 1991. Mid-Life Update for the USAF and EPAF (European Participating Air Forces) was authorized. See MLU under Aircraft variants.
▪ 1993. F-16s were assigned to the new battlefield air support composite Wing at Pope AFB, NC. Also the first AFRES unit deployment on peacekeeping duties.
▪ Late 1993. F-16s around the world passed 5 million flight hours.
▪ December 1993. Lockheed Fort Worth awarded Honeywell Defense Avionics Systems a contract for design of a liquid-crystal flat panel colour display for the F-16.
▪ 11 February 1994. First launch demonstration of high off-boresight missile capability, at Tyndall AFB. Launching an AIM-9 derivative, the pilot used his helmet-mounted display to slew a missile seeker to his line of sight and achieve seeker lock-on at high angles off the nose of the F-16B. .
▪ March 1994. Multi-Axis Thrust Vectoring (MATV) F-16 completed its 95-flight test programme.
▪ March 1994. Integration of Harpoon onto USAF F-16s.
▪ 19 May 1994. AFTI/F-16 launched a HARM missile using off-board sensor data, in the Talon Sword Bravo demonstration. Target data, transmitted to a US Navy Prowler via a satellite, was correlated by the aircrew to identify and locate an appropriate threat emitter, sending the target data through an Improved Data Modem to the AFTI/F-16.
▪ August 1994. F-16 selected by the USAF to perform SEAD (Suppression of Enemy Air Defences) missions, following demonstrations that May.
▪ April 1995. First Mid-Life Update F-16 was flown.
▪ 26 April 1995. First flight of an F-16C of the ANG equipped with a special recon-optical pod.
▪ 27 April 1995. 3,500th F-16 delivered, an F-16C Block 50D.
▪ September 1997. First F-16 with a production MLU fit was taken by the Royal Netherlands Air Force at Leeuwarden. Squadron conversion started December 1997.
▪ 12 May 1998. UAE announced selection of F-16 Block 60s.
▪ July 1998. Expected IOC of F-16 MLUs deployed by 322 squadron, Royal Netherlands Air Force.
▪ 2025. Expected final retirement of F-16s from the USAF.

Details *(principally F-16C Block 50, unless stated)*

Sales/Users: Delivery of 3,779 production F-16s of all versions by 1 June 1998, comprising 2,967 from Lockheed Martin (and earlier General Dynamics; backlog of 247 to fulfil), 222 F-16A/Bs from SABCA, 300 A/Bs from Fokker, 237 from TAI, and 48 from Samsung, of which some 27 aircraft were delivered by Lockheed Martin, 10 by Samsung and 7 by TAI during September-December 1997 alone to Greece (F-16C/D Block 50s), Taiwan (F-16A/Bs Block 20), South Korea (F-16C/Ds Block 52), and Turkey (F-16Cs Block 50). Overall total ordered by Bahrain (12 F-16C/Ds with GE-100 engines, all delivered), Belgium (160 F-16A/Bs with PW-200/220s, all delivered by SABCA), Denmark (70 F-16A/Bs, 58 delivered by SABCA and 12 by Fokker; some assigned to reconnaissance, plus 3 ex-USAF F-16As, with PW-200/220s), Egypt (196 F-16A/B/C/Ds with GE-100/129 and PW-200/220s, including 46 produced by TAI and a single aircraft from SABCA; 128 delivered by the start of 1998), Greece (80 F-16C/Ds with GE-100/129s, some 65 delivered by the start of 1998), Indonesia (12 F-16A/Bs with PW-220s, all delivered), Israel (210 A/B/C/Ds with GE-100 and PW-200s, all delivered, plus 50 ex-USAF F-16s from August 1994), South Korea (160 F-16C/Ds with PW-220/229s – first export customer with Block 52 aircraft; 52 aircraft delivered by Lockheed Martin and some 48 by Samsung by the start of 1998; more F-16s might be required for F-X programme; equipment includes ALQ-165 jammer system), Netherlands (213 F-16A/Bs with PW-200/220s, all delivered by Fokker; 36 AGM-65G Mavericks ordered in 1997 for F-16 deployment; some 21 aircraft used for reconnaissance by 306 Squadron as F-16[R]s), Norway (74 F-16A/Bs with PW-200/220s, all delivered, coming from USA 2 and Fokker 72; Norway has been offered F-16C Block 50Ns as F-5 replacements under the KFA-96 requirement), Pakistan (68 F-16A/Bs with PW-200/220s, all delivered), Portugal (20 F-16A/Bs with PW-220Es, all delivered; has requested 25 ex-USAF F-16A/Bs, which would receive MLU), Singapore (26, as 8 F-16A/Bs with PW-220s and 18 F-16C/Ds with PW-229 engines; 8 A/Bs delivered by the start of 1998; 12 further F-16C/Ds to be acquired, to replace additional leased USAF aircraft), Taiwan (150 F-16A/Bs, of which some 69 delivered by the start of 1998; the Block 20 have been built with MLU improvements; purchasing 28 Pathfinder/Sharpshooter navigation/targeting pods), Thailand (36 F-16A/Bs, all delivered), Turkey (240 with GE-100/129s; 8 from US production and some 191 by TAI delivered by the start of 1998), USA (2,200 A/B/C/Ds for the USAF with all engine options, including 4 F-16A/Bs built by SABCA, 2 A/Bs by Fokker, 778 A/Bs and 1,416 C/Ds by General Dynamics/Lockheed Martin; new Block 50s delivered in 1998 incorporate modular mission computers, digital terrain systems and colour MFDs; some 802 F-16s were in the active USAF inventory in mid-1998 but only 666 primary aircraft authorized (PAA) for combat, plus 71 with the AFRES and 607 with the ANG, including the Thunderbirds display team; 272 A/Bs were modified into F-16ADF air defence fighters for the ANG (most currently stored); other F-16As replaced some A-10As and F-111E/Fs as F-16 CASs or 'F/A-16As' for close air support and battlefield interdiction (CAS/BAI) with the ANG, while current plans call for some 250 modified F-16Cs Blocks 30 and 32 to deploy with 2 Wings for day CAS/BAI operations and F-16Cs Blocks 40 and 42 for over 4 Wings undertaking night operations; 26 F-16N/TFs for US Navy with GE-100s, all delivered), and Venezuela (24 F-16A/Bs with PW-200s, all delivered). USAF F-16C/D fleet averages an 88% mission capable rate. Block 60 F-16s were selected by the UAE, as announced on 12 May 1998, incorporating MLU upgrades and for delivery 2002-4. F-16 C/Ds to be acquired by Saudi Arabia to replace F-5/RF-5s.

Crew: Pilot, reclining at 30° to help withstand high g forces. 2 crew in tandem in 2-seaters.

Cockpit: Single-piece polycarbonate canopy, many NATO aircraft having gold film for radar dissipation. 15° downward visibility for pilot over nose and 40° at sides. Lear Astronics side stick controller (Block 50 and MLUs). Monochrome CRT displays being replaced by colour liquid-crystal displays on some existing aircraft and new production (see Avionics and Aircraft variants). Digitally controlled ECS, using engine bleed air.

Crew escape: McDonnell Douglas ACES II zero-zero ejection seat.

Fixed guns: 20-mm General Electric M61A1 multi-barrel gun in the port wing root. Those USAF F-16s modified for close air support and battlefield interdiction carry a GPU-5/A 30-mm cannon under the fuselage (see Expendable weapons).

Ammunition: 511 rounds.

Number of weapon pylons: 9, as 6 under the wings (capacities for up to 5.5g limit are 4,500 lb, 2,040 kg inner; 3,500 lb, 1,588 kg middle; and 700 lb, 317 kg outer – alternative capacities for maximum g are 2,500 lb, 1,134 kg; 2,000 lb, 907 kg; and 450 lb, 204 kg respectively), 1 under the fuselage (2,200 lb, 998 kg capacity, or 1,200 lb, 544 kg at maximum g), and 2 wingtip AAM launch rails (425 lb, 193 kg at all times).

Expendable weapons and equipment: Typically 12,000 lb (5,443 kg) load; maximum about 15,590 lb (7,071 kg) with GE-129 engine, or 15,930 lb (7,225 kg) with PW-229 engine. Typical air-to-air armament is 6 AIM-9L, M or P Sidewinders (wingtips and 4 outer wing pylons), though other loads include Sparrow and AMRAAM, or Python 3s on Israeli aircraft (6 advanced BVR missiles are positioned as for Sidewinders, with the ability to carry 2 BVR AAMs on the middle wing pylons). The adoption of French Mica air-to-air missiles has been studied against possible foreign requirement. Captive testing of the BAe ASRAAM was completed on an F-16 at Eglin AFB in 1995. Air-to-ground armament includes a 30-mm GPU-5/A cannon on the fuselage centreline (see F-16 CAS under Aircraft variants), free-fall bombs (typically 12 × Mk 82 on 4 multiple release units or 4 × Mk 84, carried on the inner and middle wing pylons), smart bombs, 8 dispensers (carried as 3 on each inner and 2 on each middle wing pylons), and missiles including Shrike and HARM anti-radiation (2 on the middle wing pylons), Harpoon and Penguin anti-ship (up to 4 on the inner and middle wing pylons), and Maverick (up to 6, in 2 clusters of 3 on the middle wing pylons); newly deployed AGM-65G Maverick and PGU-28/20-mm cannon. GBU-22 Paveway III now also cleared for deployment. Other weapons to include JDAM, JSOW and WCMD (wind corrected munition dispenser). South Korea has shown interest in Popeye for its F-16C/Ds.

Additional stores: Pods are usually carried on the fuselage centreline or middle wing pylons. 2 specific pod stations for EO/FLIR/TF are also provided (each 550 lb, 249 kg capacity under any g loading, but not for carrying weapons), 1 each side of the intake. Stores can include LANTIRN, Sharpshooter and GEC-Marconi Atlantic (see Avionics), other FLIR, laser designator,

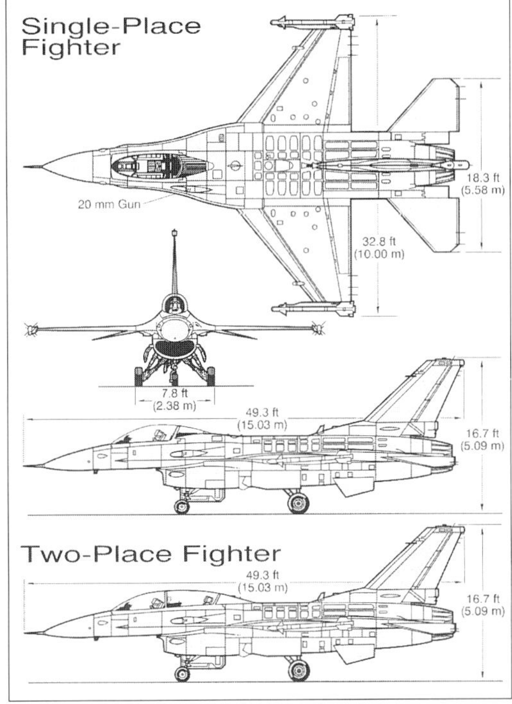

↑ **Lockheed Martin F-16C and F-16D (*bottom*) Block 50** *(courtesy Lockheed Martin)*

↑ South Korean Lockheed Martin F-16C Block 52

reconnaissance and other systems. 16 digital Tactical Airborne Reconnaissance System (TARS) pods going to US Air National Guard squadrons, each with a KS-87 camera, ground station and tape recorder (GPS also being fitted to aircraft).
Radar: F-16C/D have Northrop Grumman AN/APG-68(V) coherent, multi-mode, digital fire control radar, from Block 50 production aircraft incorporating the Westinghouse Advanced Programmable Signal Processor (APSP) as the (V)5 variant (see Aircraft variants). F-16C/D Block 30/40s with APG-68 have demonstrated a mean time between radar failures (MTBF) of over 150 hours in the field; Block 50 aircraft with APSP have over 300 hours MTBF. MLU aircraft have APG-66(V)2A.
Flight/weapon system avionics/instrumentation: Avionics integrated via 2 × 1553B databuses. Improved data modem for faster data transmission and demonstrated near real time linking and receiving data. Litton inertial navigation system (LN-39 or ring-laser gyro LN-93) or latest Honeywell H-523, Rockwell Collins AN/ARN-108 instrument landing system, and Rockwell Collins AN/ARN-118 tactical air navigation system (Tacan). Gould AN/APN-232 radar altimeter. Magnavox AN/ARC-164 UHF and Rockwell Collins AN/ARC-186 VHF radios, or later (Blocks 50/52) Magnavox Have Quick IIA UHF and Have Sync radios, plus AN/ARC-190 HF; VHFVHF/FM antenna with extended operating distance is incorporated into fin leading edge on current F-16C/D Block 50. British Aerospace Terprom digital terrain profile matching system on European and some USAF upgrades and incorporated in new production Block 20 F-16A/Bs plus new USAF Block 50s for delivery in 1998. GPS. Honeywell air data computer. New modular mission computer (MMC) under Mid-Life Update for European F-16A/Bs and retrofit to 223 USAF F-16C/Ds; new USAF Block 50s for delivery in 1998 will also incorporate MMC. 128K data transfer cartridge. Teledyne AN/APX-101 IFF (APX-109 V3 IFF for US FMS sales), or Hazeltine advanced IFF for MLUs. GEC-Marconi wide-angle holographic head-up display, (with raster for LANTIRN). Honeywell Defense Avionics Systems monochrome CRT displays; European aircraft received other new equipment under the MLU (as detailed under Aircraft variants), including 2 Honeywell 4 ins × 4 ins liquid-crystal flat panel colour displays and enhanced upgraded programmable display generator (UPDG) to replaced CRTs; UPDG standard on F-16C/D Block 50, offering 7 × faster processing capability and 4 × greater memory; similar colour fit is being offered to other F-16A/B/C/D operators. Horizontal situation display for increased situation awareness and tactical flexibility on all missions. Lockheed Martin Enhanced Envelope Gunsight now used by some USAF F-16C/Ds, and may be retrofitted to others. USAF IOC in 1994 for the AN/ASQ-213 HARM Targeting System (initially used by 20th FW F-16C/Ds of Block 50); current F-16C/D Block 50 has HARM avionics/launcher interface computer (ALIC) for full autonomous employment of HARM missile. LANTIRN for night and precision-guided weapon capability used by USAF, Greece, South Korea, Thailand and Turkey. Netherlands deploying 10 Lockheed Martin Sharpshooter targeting pods and 60 GEC-Marconi Atlantic forward-looking infra-red navigation to MLUs; Sharpshooter also deployed by Bahrain and Singapore, and Israel has Sharpshooter and Rafael Litening pods. Many variations of equipment on international aircraft.
Self-protection systems: Dalmo Victor AN/ALR-69 RWR or Loral AN/ALR-56M, Westinghouse AN/ALQ-131 jammer pod (or AN/ALQ-184) available, AN/ALQ-126B deceptive ECM, and chaff/flare. Many variations of equipment on international aircraft: Belgium uses Dassault Electronique Carapace ECM; Denmark ALQ-162, and South Korean Block 52s ALQ-165 jammer system; Greece Litton ASPIS; Israel Elta ECM and Elisra SPS 3000 self-protection jammer; and Turkey Rapport III, as examples. TERMA Electronics Warfare Management System for MLU aircraft.
Wing characteristics: Mid mounted, blended with the fuselage, with swept leading edges and no anhedral/dihedral. Vortex control surfaces from the wingroots to a point on the fuselage sides level with the cockpit, to enhance lift and increase stability at high alpha. F-16U proposed with a delta wing (see Aircraft variants).
Wing control surfaces: Flaperons and automatic leading-edge manoeuvring flaps.
Tail control surfaces: Slab tailplane (tailerons) and rudder. VHF/FM antenna, with extended operating distance, incorporated into the leading edge of the fin.
Canard: None.
Airbrakes: Each side between the engine and the tailplane, with 60° movement.
Flight control system: 4-channel digital fly-by-wire.
Construction materials: Principally aluminium alloy, with honeycomb core for the leading-edge flaps, leading-edges of the tailplane, and twin ventral fins. Graphite/epoxy fin and taileron skins. Air intake construction and gold-coated canopy on many F-16C/Ds reduce radar signature.
Engine: General Electric F110-GE-100 or later GE-129, or Pratt & Whitney F100-PW-200, 220 or 229 turbofan. Common Engine Bay (CEB) from Block 30/32, allowing installation of GE or PW engine from 1986. Current Block 50/52 have GE-129 or PW-229. See Operational Capabilities Upgrade under Aircraft variants for F100-PW-220E, as fitted as standard to Portuguese F-16A/Bs and possibly Taiwan's Block 20s. Sundstrand Solar self starter.
Engine rating: 28,000 lbf (124.55 kN), 29,000 lbf (128.93 kN), 23,770 lbf (105.74 kN), the same, and 29,100 lbf (129.445 kN) with afterburning respectively. See Engine section for F100 upgrades.
Air intakes: Large intake under the fuselage, with splitter plate. Internal radar absorbing material. VISTA F-16 flew in May 1997 with an F100-PW-229 engine and the Modular Common Inlet (MCID). The MCID is wider and thereby offers higher airflow, matching that used for General Electric-powered F-16s.
Fuel system: 7,162 lb (3,248 kg) of JP-8 internally for F-16C/D Block 50; 3,986 litres in wing and fuselage tanks, reduced to 3,297 litres on 2-seaters. 3 drop tanks, as 1,135.6 litre tank under fuselage, and a 1,400 litre or 2,271 litre tank under each wing.
Electrical system: 60kVA and 10kVA principal and back-up generators. 17 amp-hour battery, plus 4 stand-by batteries for the fly-by-wire system.
Hydraulic system: 2 systems, each 3,000 psi. Bootstrap reservoirs.
Braking system: ABS brakes with anti-skid. Drag-chute available in a pod beneath the fin (23 ft, 7 m diameter), as used by 6 export customers. Arrester hook.

Aircraft variants:
AFTI/F-16 is an Advanced Fighter Technology Integration aircraft, a one-off operated by the USAF for test programmes (see Development).
F-16A was the initial production version, though still available to foreign users, such as Taiwan in Block 20 form. AN/APG-66 radar. Many upgraded (see below). Originally analog fly-by-wire control system.
F-16B is the 2-seat version of F-16A, still available for export.
F-16ADF was the designation given to 272 USAF F-16A/Bs when modified for air defence with the ANG, armed with Sidewinders, Sparrow and AMRAAM. IOC 1989. Improved AN/APG-66 radar and ECCM, IFF, and other upgrades, and with the ability to receive GPS.
F-16C is the current single-seat production version, developed through a series of multinational staged improvement

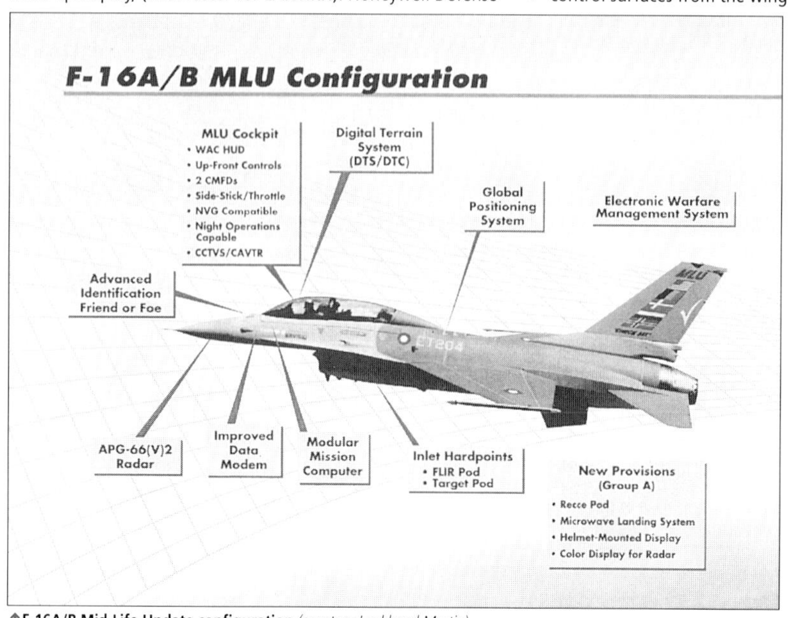

↑F-16A/B Mid-Life Update configuration *(courtesy Lockheed Martin)*

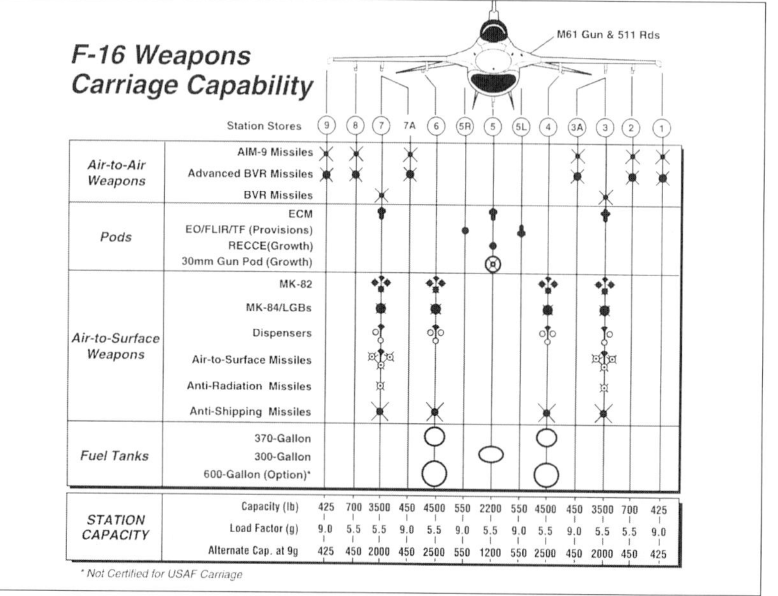

↑Lockheed Martin F-16C weapon configurations *(courtesy Lockheed Martin)*

↑ Cockpit of the Mid-Life Update F-16, now being deployed by European air forces and on new production Block 20s and 50s

programmes (MSIP) to enhance combat efficiency (particularly improving attack by day or night, and beyond-visual range), though Stage 1 affected F-16A/B Block 15s delivered from late 1981 with structural, systems and wiring provisions to permit future multi-role use; Stage 2 was introduced in 1984 for F-16C/Ds of Block 25 with AN/APG-68 radar, structural and core avionics improvements, and revised cockpit; Stage 3 is found in current Block 50/52 forms, though features appear in some earlier Stage 2 types, offering a more powerful engine (GE-129 or PW-229), improved AN/APG-68 radar (see Radar), advanced cockpit displays and other avionics, enhanced situation awareness displays, multi-target AMRAAM capability, and autonomous HARM missile capability (adopted for Blocks 50D/52D), and more. Blocks 40 and 42 introduced specialized night attack capability with smart weapons ("Night Falcon" – see also F-16 CAS), with features including LANTIRN, 4-channel digital flight controls, automatic terrain following system, more memory for core computers, diffractive optics HUD, GPS and more, plus AN/APG-68(V) improved radar, upgraded gunsight, modified drive for the leading-edge flaps, structural and undercarriage strengthening for higher weights and manoeuvring limits plus 8,000 hour airframe life, and revised ergonomics and 'Combat Edge' breathing system to permit the pilot to withstand greater g forces. Block improvements (50 Plus) are to also offer the ability to carry GBU-31/32 JDAM, and have AN/APG-68(I) radar with synthetic aperture and terrain-referenced modes among other features. Stage 4 has been proposed to include a Joint Helmet Mounted Cueing System, Modular Mission Computer, JTIDS, new advanced weapons, and option of 2,271 litre auxiliary tanks.

F-16D is the 2-seat equivalent of F-16C. Same principal dimensions.

F-16ES became the Enhanced Strategic version tested in 1995, offering a radius of action of 890 naut miles (1,025 miles) 1,650 km with 2 × 2,000 lb bombs and 4 AAMs. Features 2 conformal fuel tanks fitted to the above-wing/fuselage blend, adding 3,200 lb (1,451 kg) of fuel, plus 2 drop tanks. Nose-mounted FLIR. Offered to (but not adopted by) Israel. Can be part of the Block 60 configuration, as ordered by UAE. Photograph appeared in the 1996-97 edition of *WA&SD*, page 132.

F-16HTS applies to more than 100 USAF F-16C Block 50D/52D for SEAD missions used in conjunction with Boeing RC-135 Rivet Joint electronic warfare aircraft. AN/ASQ-213 HARM Targeting Systems for autonomous launch.

F-16N and ***TF-16N*** are the US Navy designations for 22 F-16Cs and 4 F-16Ds used as supersonic adversary readiness and training aircraft. AN/APG-66 radar, F110-GE-100 engine and no fitted gun.

F-16U was a unique 2-seat delta-wing and 20 hardpoint variant of F-16, proposed for the United Arab Emirates as a long-range strike aircraft but not taken up. Also being proposed for the USAF as a JAST substitute as the ***Falcon 2000***.

F-16X is a proposed 'next generation' version for service from 2010, featuring wings based on the F-22 design married to a longer fuselage. Conformal stores carriage, requiring a huge increase in internal fuel capacity.

F-16 CAS or 'F/A-16' applied originally to converted F-16As for close air support and battlefield interdiction (CAS/BAI) with the ANG, each with a fuselage centreline 30-mm GPU-5/A cannon; current plans call for some 250 F-16C Blocks 30 and 32 conversions for late 1990s/early 2000, to deploy with 2 Wings for day CAS/BAI operations with 30-mm cannon, steered FLIR, Pave Penny, GPS and more, and F-16C Blocks 40 and 42 for more than 4 Wings undertaking night operations and having LANTIRN, NVG, datalink, new VHF anti-jam radio, improved data modem for faster data transmission and demonstrated near real time linking and receiving data, missile warning receiver, radar warning receiver and chaff/flare for added self protection.

GF-16s are non-operational ground trainers.

VISTA NF-16D is the USAF's F-16D Block 30 Variable Stability In-Flight Simulator Test Aircraft (USAF/Calspan), currently having an axisymmetric thrust vectoring nozzle fitted to the PW-229 engine. Recently used for flight control development in connection with the F-22 and Indian LCA programmes.

Operational Capabilities Upgrade (OCU) was initiated to improve both the USAF's early F-16A/Bs and the aircraft of NATO countries, principally to give them the ability to deploy advanced beyond visual range AAMs and ASMs through update of the radar, fire control computer, stores management computer, and software, while also adding ring laser gyro INS and adopting the PW-220E improved performance engine.

Mid-Life Update kit, originally for 403 European F-16A/B Block 10/15s but currently for Belgium (72, plus possibly 18 more), Denmark (61), Norway (56) and the Netherlands (136) as European Participating Air Forces (EPAF); USAF originally to receive 130 but withdrew (see next entry). Uses Lockheed Martin Tactical Aircraft Systems' developed Mid-Life Upgrade kit in a configuration known as Block 20, with SABCA delivering European-produced kits. With MLU, operational life may be extended by some 15 years. MLU features basically the same cockpit as Block 50/52 aircraft (including GEC-Marconi wide-angle HUD, compatible with FLIR) but with additions of dual colour MFDs and a Modular Mission Computer (MMC) to provide expanded memory and increased speed. Improved data modem. Upfront controller. Side-stick controller and throttle. Has APG-66(V)2A radar improvements (including new Signal Data Processor), 2 Honeywell 4 × 4 ins liquid-crystal flat panel colour displays and enhanced upgraded programmable display generator, British Aerospace Terprom digital terrain profile matching system, ring-laser gyro INS, miniaturized GPS, microwave landing system, night vision goggle compatible cockpit, and more. Terma Electronic Warfare Management System. Hazeltine AN/APX-111 advanced IFF and helmet-mounted display on some aircraft (including those of the Netherlands and Norway). See Avionics. Upgraded aircraft will be capable of carrying advanced AAMs and ASMs. First deliveries began at the end of 1996 and operational testing started in 1997 at the OT&E at Leeuwarden in the Netherlands. MLU is available as an option to other countries operating (or considering purchase of) F-16A/Bs, with Portugal already as a possible purchaser.

USAF upgrade using MLU (as above) for 130 F-16 Block 15s was abandoned, but the USAF continues to perform programme management for the European element, plus technical and test support, while ordering 229 Modular Mission Computers for F–16C/D Block 50/52s. 125 F-16A/Bs flown by the US Air Force Reserve have received the BAe Terprom digital terrain profile matching system. See F/A-16.

F-16 UCAV is one of several Lockheed Martin proposals for an Uninhabited (unmanned) Combat Air Vehicle, in this case converting unwanted F-16s into long-duration, unmanned aircraft with 60 ft (18.3 m) wings to carry extra fuel and more weapons to be released from 50,000 ft (15,240 m) in groups of 2 or 3 aircraft.

F-16 FFD-1 is a projected tailless configuration (1 of several tailless proposals that include a tailless F-22 and a fully delta tailless aircraft), conceived for the USAF's RESTORE (reconfigurable controls) programme.

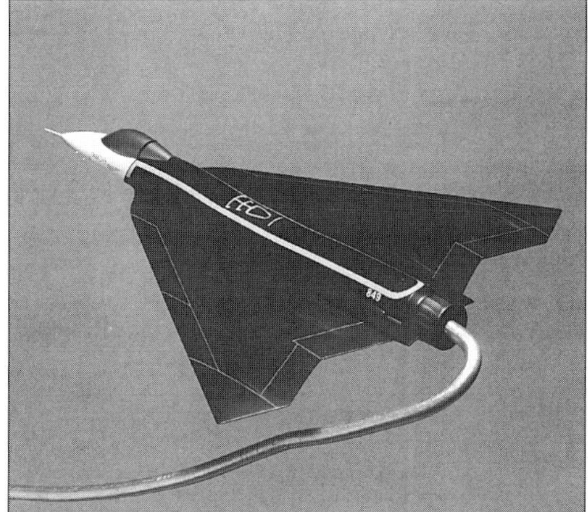

↑ FFD-1 model of a projected tailless F-16 configuration

Details for F-16C Block 50

PRINCIPAL DIMENSIONS:
Wing span: 32 ft 9.5 ins (10 m) over missiles
Maximum length: 49 ft 3.5 ins (15.02 m)
Maximum height: 16 ft 8.5 ins (5.09 m)

WINGS:
Aerofoil section: NACA 64A-204
Area: 300 sq ft (27.87 m^2)
Aspect ratio: 3.2 without missiles
Sweepback: 40° leading edge

TAIL UNIT:
Tailplane span: 18 ft 3.5 ins (5.58 m)
Taileron area: 63.7 sq ft (5.918 m^2)
Fin area: 43.1 sq ft (4.004 m^2) dorsal and ventral

UNDERCARRIAGE:
Type: Menasco retractable, with steerable nosewheel
Main wheel tyre size: Goodyear 27.75 × 8.75-14.5
Nose wheel tyre size: 18 × 5.7-8
Wheel base: 13 ft 2 ins (4 m)
Wheel track: 7 ft 9.5 ins (2.38 m)

WEIGHTS:
Empty: over 18,900 lb (8,573 kg) with GE-129 or 18,590 lb (8,432 kg) with PW-229 engine
Take-off with 2 AAMs, full internal fuel: 27,100 lb (12,292 kg) with GE-129, 26,760 lb (12,138 kg) with PW-229 engine
Maximum take-off: 42,300 lb (19,187 kg)

PERFORMANCE:
Maximum speed: Mach 2+
G limits: +9 design, or +5.5 with full stores load
Ceiling: over 50,000 ft (15,240 m)
Radius of action (CAP): 865 naut miles (997 miles) 1,605 km with 2 AMRAAM and 2 Sidewinder AAMs, maximum internal and 3,936 litres of external fuel
Radius of action (CAS): 677 naut miles (780 miles) 1,255 km with 2 × Mk 84 bombs, 2 AAMs, maximum internal and 3,936 litres of external fuel, Hi-Lo-Lo-Hi mission profile
Ferry range: about 2,275 naut miles (2,620 miles) 4,215 km with 1 × 1,135.6 litre and 2 × 2,271 litre auxiliary fuel tanks

Lockheed Martin F-22 Raptor

First flight: 29 September 1990, and 7 September 1997 for first EMD (*4001*) F-22 (pilot Paul Metz).
Role: Air dominance fighter, with ground attack capability. See Development (April 1995) below.

Aims

- To conform to specific weight and fly-away cost constraints, initially targeted at 50,000 lb take-off gross weight and US$35 million in FY1985 dollars.
- Sufficient fuel for mission radius.
- Supersonic cruise without engine afterburning (supercruise).
- Low supersonic drag.
- Unlimited angle-of-attack capability in conformal configuration.
- Internal weapons carriage in air superiority configuration.
- Unrestricted manoeuvrability, including use of 2-dimensional (2D) convergent/divergent exhaust nozzles (see Engines) for thrust vectoring. Latter used to reduce take-off and landing runs, assist aerodynamic pitch control, and enhance control during high angles of attack and at low flying speed. Sufficient nose-up pitch control power with thrust vectoring and horizontal tails to allow trimmed flight at extreme angles of attack.
- Thrust/weight ratio of 1.4.
- Spin resistance and ability to recover from a spin with control surfaces neutralized.
- Low observables (stealth) through airframe configuration and avionics, including care in design of weapons carriage arrangement, supersonic inlet, augmentor and engine nozzles, canopy, conformal avionics apertures and maintenance areas. Particular emphasis on low radar cross section (RCS).
- High survivability, through low observables, high manoeuvrability and state-of-the-art integrated avionics for first-look/first-shoot/first-kill, with beyond-visual-range (BVR) engagement capability.
- Fully integrated common module avionics. Liquid cooling of avionics for reliability.
- Ada (US DoD) real-time software for all functions, including vehicle management, flight controls, sensors processing and mission avionics integration, as part of VHSIC (very-high-speed integrated circuit) technology.
- Fully integrated cockpit displays and controls.
- High level of reliability and supportability, at least twice as good as current fighters.

↑ Lockheed Martin F-22 Raptor EMD aircraft *4001*

▪ 15 minute turnaround time for high sortie rates.
▪ All maintenance "on the plane" or at depot level, with exceptions of tyres and battery. Ground support equipment not needed as near-elimination of wing-level maintenance shops and personnel. Portable maintenance aid (lap top). Fuselage height from ground 3 ft (0.91 m).
▪ Self sufficiency, with APU, OBOGS, OBIGGS and engine start.
▪ Squadron of 24 F-22s to require less than the capacity of 8 C-141 transports and 258 support personnel for a 30-day airlift deployment.
▪ 8,000 hour structural, systems and avionics life.
▪ Compatible with existing aircraft shelters.

Development

▪ November 1981. USAF identified the requirement for a new air superiority fighter to replace the F-15C.
▪ September 1983. Air Force awarded concept definition contracts to 7 aircraft manufacturers for the ATF (Advanced Tactical Fighter).
▪ September 1985. Formal ATF request for proposals was issued.
▪ May 1986. Edward Aldridge, Secretary of the Air Force, announced that as part of the Packard Commission guidelines, the ATF demonstration/validation programme would include prototype aircraft and engines as well as a prototype avionics demonstration.
▪ September 1986. Lockheed, Boeing and General Dynamics signed an MoU leading to a teaming agreement. Original YF-22 configuration was Lockheed 638.
▪ 31 October 1986. Lockheed/Boeing/GD team and Northrop/McDonnell Douglas team were selected to compete in the dem/val phase. Each was to build 2 prototypes (YF-22A and YF-23A respectively) plus an avionics testbed under $818 million 4 year 6 month study contracts (Lockheed team's own investment totalled $675 million).
▪ 3 November 1986. Lockheed, Boeing and GD exchanged preliminary design data.
▪ 10 July 1987. Original design was determined by the Lockheed team to be technically and competitively unacceptable.
▪ 13 July 1987. Lockheed team initiated a new YF-22 design, approved that October.
▪ April 1988. YF-22 prototype configuration was "unfrozen" to reduce supersonic drag. Redesign of the forebody and aft fuselage took place the following month.
▪ December 1988. First YF119 engine sea level bench test.
▪ 17 July 1989. Initial tests began on YF-22 avionics system in a Lockheed-owned Boeing 757.
▪ 11 October 1989. ATF evaluation phase given a 6-month extension.
▪ November 1989. System review with the USAF.
▪ January 1990. Final assembly of the first YF-22 prototype began at Palmdale, followed by the second in February.
▪ April 1990. Initial Engineering and Manufacturing Development proposals (EMDs) requested. F-22 configuration for EMD proposal frozen that August.

↑ Computer-generated 3 dimensional image of the F-22 main weapon bay, with 6 AIM-120C AMRAAM AAMs

▪ 29 August 1990. YF-22 Prototype Air Vehicle (PAV-1) was unveiled at Lockheed Plant 10 in Palmdale. YF120-GE-100 engines fitted.
▪ 29 September 1990. Lockheed test pilot, Dave Ferguson, made the first flight in YF-22 (PAV-1), during ferry from Palmdale to Edwards AFB flight test center. Test flying by 6511st Test Squadron, USAF.
▪ 25 October 1990. First supersonic flight (PAV-1, test flight 9).
▪ 26 October 1990. First aerial refuelling of the YF-22 (PAV-1, test flight 11) from a KC-135. Aerial refuelling qualification completed on 31 October.
▪ 30 October 1990. Lockheed test pilot, (Tom Morganfield, first flew the second YF-22 prototype PAV-2) from Palmdale to Edwards. YF119-PW-100 engines.
▪ 3 November 1990. PAV-1 first demonstrated supercruise (test flight 14).
▪ 15 November 1990. General Electric-powered PAV-1 first demonstrated thrust vectoring capability (test flight 15).
▪ 19 November 1990. First AFOTEC piloted flight (PAV-1, test flight 19).
▪ 20 November 1990. First in-flight weapon bay opening (PAV-2, test flight 6).
▪ 28 November 1990. General Dynamics' test pilot, Jon Beesley, fired an unarmed AAM at Mach 0.7 at 20,000 ft (6,100 m) over China Lake, California, (PAV-2, test flight 11).
▪ 10 December 1990. PAV-1 began YF-22 high angle of attack (high alpha) trials (test flight 28). Completed 17 December (test flight 38) after attaining unprecedented 60° AoA attitude while remaining in full control. (Production configuration models attained over 85° angle of attack in wind tunnel testing.)
▪ 20 December 1990. PAV-2 fired an unarmed AMRAAM missile over the Pacific Missile Test Range at Point Mugu, California (test flight 24).
▪ 28 December 1990. Mach 2+ was achieved (PAV-1, test flight 43). PAV-1 also demonstrated maximum positive g. During dem/val, PAV-1 was flown 43 times for 52.8 hours and PAV-2 31 times for 38.8 hours. YF-22 flying temporarily ended.
▪ 23 April 1991. Air Force Secretary, Dr Donald Rice, announced at a Pentagon briefing that the F-22/P&W F119 combination was winner of the ATF competition.
▪ 23 June 1991. PAV-1 was flown by C-5 to Marietta, to become a non-flying engineering mockup.
▪ 2 August 1991. USAF awarded the Lockheed team a $9.55 billion contract to begin EMD of the F-22. 11 flyable (including two 2-seat) aircraft, 1 static test and 1 fatigue test airframe to be built (reduced January 1993 to 9 flying, currently in 1998 all single-seaters). Separate $1.4 billion contract to P&W for engine development, including 33 flightworthy engines (reduced January 1993 to 27).
▪ 30 October 1991. PAV-2 began new 100 hour test programme, covering aerodynamic effects of control actuation, aerodynamic loads, vibration and acoustic fatigue, and maximum lift coefficient.
▪ 16 December 1991. External design of the F-22 frozen during air vehicle requirements/design review update. This allowed wind tunnel and radar cross section models to be built, the internal design to be completed and tooling preparations begun.
▪ 25 April 1992. Returning to Edwards AFB after a test flight, PAV-2 experienced series of pitch oscillations at about 40 ft (12 m) above the runway. With the undercarriage retracted, it hit the runway, caught fire and slid about 8,000 ft (2,440 m). No longer flight-worthy, it was taken by C-5 to Rome Air Development Center at Griffiss ARB to be used in antenna tests. External damage was repaired. Over 70 flights, it totalled 100.4 hours.
▪ 4 June 1992. Design review update completed.
▪ January 1993. Resulting from FY1993 funding shortfall, F-22 EMD programme was rephased. Key events were put back between 6 and 18 months and the number of development aircraft and engines reduced. Second rephase in mid-1994.
▪ 30 April 1993. Air vehicle Preliminary Design Review finished. Final development phase covering detailed design began.
▪ May 1993. Addition of ground attack capability.
▪ 8 December 1993. First F-22 parts fabrication began at Boeing's Kent facility.
▪ 24 February 1995. Formal portion of the air vehicle Critical Design Review completed, after 231 critical design reviews of software and subsystems. Production configuration became Lockheed Martin 645.
▪ 20 April 1995. Lockheed received a $9.5 million 2-year contract from the USAF to explore F-22 derivatives, including for SEAD (suppression of enemy air defences), non-lethal suppression of enemy defences, reconnaissance, attack/interdiction, and surveillance.
▪ 27 June 1995. Assembly of the first flyable EMD aircraft started at Lockheed Martin.
▪ February 1996. Testing of the F-22's flight control laws start, using the VISTA F-16.
▪ 6 May 1996. Pratt & Whitney began assembling the first flight test F119-PW-100 engine, delivered to the USAF on 24 September 1996.
▪ 9 April 1997. Roll out of the first F-22 EMD aircraft (*4001*) and F-22 named Rapter.
▪ 10 June 1997. USAF officially granted Pratt & Whitney Initial Flight Release certification for its F119-PW-100 engine.
▪ 7 September 1997. First flight of the initial EMD aircraft, with flight testing from 17 May 1998.
▪ Autumn 1999. Anticipated first flight of an EMD F-22 with full avionics suite.
▪ December 1999. Low-rate initial production expected.
▪ 2002. Expected delivery of first 6 full production aircraft of Lot 2.
▪ 2004. Anticipated end of the flight test programme, after approximately 2,546 flights totalling 4,583 hours using EMDs.
▪ 2004. High-rate production decision (DoD "Milestone III") anticipated (previously July 2001, then March 2002).
▪ 2005. Anticipated IOC with the USAF (32 aircraft).
▪ 2013. Last USAF F-22A delivery.
Note: Approximately 240 US companies are considered to be major subcontractors, with over 1,150 other US firms plus companies in 7 foreign countries participating.

Details

Sales/Users: 9 EMD flying aircraft (see Development, January 1993, and Aircraft variants). Originally planned 750 F-22A/Bs reduced to 648. Number required further reduced in 1993 to 442 (including 4 pre-production aircraft and 58 2-seaters), then 438

↑ Lockheed Martin F-22 Raptor 'all glass' cockpit

↑ Lockheed Martin F-22 Raptor *4001* *(courtesy Lockheed Martin)*

full-production single-seat F-22As only, the first 4 pre-production aircraft and all F-22B 2-seat variants having been cancelled. Currently planned figure in mid 1998 stands at 339 full-production single-seat F-22As. As of 16 June 1998, planned production Lots (Lot sizes and calender year of full contract awards) are Lot 1 (2, 1999), Lot 2 (6, 2000), Lot 3 (10, 2001), Lot 4 (16, 2002), Lot 5 (24, 2003), Lots 6-12 (36 per year, yearly 2004-2010), Lot 13 (29, 2011), with deliveries approximately 2 years after contract award. Operating bases not yet announced, but testing and training will be assigned to Edwards AFB, California (Flight Test Centre); Nellis AFB, Nevada (Fighter Weapons School); and Tyndall AFB, Florida (325th Fighter Wing for pilot training). Total programme cost $US70.9 billion in 'then-year real dollar' costs, equivalent to US$60.8 billion in FY97 dollars. Unit flyaway cost US$90.6 million or US$70.9 million, in 'then-year' and FY97 dollars respectively. Export of F-22 is possible, including potentially under Foreign Military Sales (FMS) funding, with South Korea likely to be approached for its F-X requirement.
Crew: Pilot only. No pilot check list. Cold start to ready to go in 3 steps (typically 17 for other aircraft), namely battery on, APU to start, and both throttles to idle.
Cockpit: All 'glass' cockpit, with no traditional standby or dedicated gauges. NVG compatible; Olin Aerospace interior lighting controller. 15° pilot look-down visibility over the nose through the Sierracin single-piece, tinted monolithic polycarbonate canopy (about 140 ins long × 45 ins wide × 27 ins high, weighing 350 lb; 356 cm × 114 cm × 69 cm, 159 kg respectively), which has an aluminium/titanium frame incorporating 8 latching points. AlliedSignal environmental control system/thermal management system (ECS/TMS): open-loop air-cycle system cools flight-critical avionics and supplies life-support system; primary heat-exchanger cools engine/APU bleed air for supply to air-cycle refrigeration pack; closed-loop vapour-cycle system provides liquid-cooling (polyalphaolephin coolant - PAO) for mission-critical avionics; uses fuel as heat sink; thermal management system cools fuel. Fire protection via infra-red and ultra-violet sensors and helon extinguishers. Cockpit ventilation and canopy de-fogging. ACFC ram-air intake (in boundary-layer diverter) injectors suck air into ram ducts when aircraft is on the ground. Meta Research life support system pressure suit. ILC Dover life support chemical/biological/cold water immersion gear. Lear Astronics HOTAS with throttle (port side) and sidestick (starboard) with 63 functions via 20 separate controls. Pilot-deployable ladder.
Crew escape: McDonnell Douglas modified ACES II zero-zero ejection seat, with fast-acting drogue and restraint webbing over the arms. Non-articulated seat in production F-22A; articulated system conceived for YF-22s.
Fixed guns: General Dynamics 20-mm M61A2 6-barrel rotary cannon, with linear linkless ammunition handling system (LMTAS), concealed behind door in the starboard wing root, with firing rate of 6,000 rounds per minute.
Ammunition: 480 rounds.
Number of weapon pylons: 4 under the wings, plus weapon bays (see below). Each wing pylon has 5,000 lb (2,268 kg) capacity. Side weapons bays with thermoplastic doors also used to store fins from externally-mounted missiles during ferry flights, and have Curtiss Wright hydraulically operated driveshaft mechanism for actuation. Missile launch rails incorporate plume deflector. Main and side weapon bay doors have serrated leading edges, while side bays also have serrated trailing edges.
Expendable weapons and equipment: All air-to-air missiles are carried internally during stealth missions, in 2 side-of-air-intake and 1 underfuselage bays, with missiles fired from LAU-141/A trapeze hydraulic launchers. For non-stealth missions, 8 additional AMRAAMs can be carried in pairs under the wings. 1 AIM-9M Sidewinder AAM in each side bay and 6 AIM-120C AMRAAMs in the underfuselage bay. Underfuselage bay can house 2 × 1,000 lb GBU-32s (JDAM or Joint Direct Attack Munitions); GBU-32s displace 4 AIM-120Cs during attack missions. Provision was also made (mostly software) for AIM-9X. Other possible stores include HARM, WCMD, Paveway III and LOCAAS dispenser. All 4 underwing stations may carry F-15 type 610 US gallon (2,309 litre) drop tanks, using Edo BRU-47A racks. Ground attack provision added just 23 lb (11 kg) to weight. For ferry flights, 4 drop tanks plus 8 external AMRAAMs (inert – fins removed, see above) may be carried in addition to bay weapons.
Radar: Northrop Grumman (former Westinghouse)/Raytheon AN/APG-77 active VLO electrically-scanned active array system integrated with the composite radome design, and integrated with the CIP (common integrated processor); growth provisions for 2 side arrays.
Flight/weapon system avionics/instrumentation: Integrated flight and engine controls via Lear Astronics vehicle management system (VMS) that includes triple-redundant flight control computers, with no back-up; Rosemont air data sensor system with 4 upper and lower Beta sideslip plates and 2 angle-of-attack (Alpha) probes. Lear Astronics integrated vehicle subsystem control (IVSC) to control aircraft subsystems via databus, including electrical, hydraulic, fuel, APU, ECS, undercarriage and brakes, diagnostics and structural-integrity monitoring. VMS, IVSC and Sanders stores management system use 18 × 1750A common processor modules. Highly integrated digital avionics suite, but aircraft has no traditional radios, nor tacan, GPS, ILS or radar in the usually accepted sense; avionics suite is centred on Hughes Common Integrated Processor modules (2 CIPs per aircraft, each with 66 module slots – developed using very high speed integrated circuit technology) that have the ability to emulate any of the electronic functions through automatic reprogramming (for example, if a CIP module performing radio functions fails, another module will automatically reload the radio programme), and thereby CIP modules perform signal and data processing for the radar, TRW communication/navigation/identification (CNI) and Sanders (Lockheed Martin) electronic warfare systems, and combine data from the sensors for display to the pilot. CNI uses multi-function antennae and shared assets (upper steerable, narrow-beam antenna; inter/intra-flight datalink [IFDL] antenna); IFDL allows exchange of information to other F-22s without radio messages, to provide multiple integrated com/nav functions, while also allowing secure monitoring of the fuel and weapon situations, whether radar is active or passive, and what targets have been selected, of accompanying friendly aircraft. All apertures are conformal for LO. CIP has memory of 300 Mbytes and capable of 4 billion signal processing operations each second per CIP (2 CIPs on board, with capacity for 3). CIP uses mission plannable software for sensor emitter management and integration, fed via Fairchild Defense Data Transfer Unit (DTU); CIP is not fully populated, allowing further development (currently 19 slots of CIP 1 and 22 of CIP 2 are not populated). Integrated electronic combat avionics uses multi-function apertures and shared assets to perform multiple functions of radar-track warning, IR warning, missile launch detection, and threat identification. Sorted and fused information is displayed on 6 Sanders/Kaiser (OIS) colour active-matrix, liquid-crystal, multi-function displays; primary multi-function display (PMFD) measuring 8 × 8 ins (20 × 20 cm), 2 up-front displays (UFD) of 3 × 4 ins (7.6 × 10 cm), and 3 secondary multi-function displays (SMFD) of 6.25 × 6.25 ins (16 × 16 cm). Integrated Caution, Advisory and Warning (ICAW) system, with up to 12 filtered messages appearing at any time on the UFD below the glare shield, with additional messages on sub pages of the display; when an ICAW message appears, the pilot can press the checklist push button (bezel button) on the bottom of the UFD and the associated checklist appears on the port-side secondary MFD. 2 Litton LN-100G laser-gyros for the inertial reference system, in normal flight fused with GPS data. GEC-Marconi wide-angle HUD (30° horizontally, 25° vertically), which collapses if canopy hits HUD after a birdstrike to avoid shattering the canopy; HUD has 'shoot' cue, alerting pilot to weapon kill parameters. Sanders Graphics Processor Video Inferface (GPVI), Airborne Video Tape Recorder (AVPR), Operational Debrief System (ODS) and Common Automated Test System (CATS). Fibre network interface unit (FNIU), avionics bus interface (ABI) and fibre optic bus components by Harris Government Aerospace. Glideslope antenna mounted inside nosewheel door. Microwave landing system.
Self-protection systems: Sanders electronic warfare system. IR warning, missile launch detection, AN/ALR-94 RWR/ESM, and AN/ALE-52 flare.
Wing characteristics: Modified diamond planform (see general arrangement drawing). Low wing loading and sufficient wing camber to meet sustained and instantaneous load factor requirements. Scrafed wingtips to house antennae.
Wing control surfaces: Ailerons (±25°), flaperons (+20°, -35°), and leading-edge flaps (+3° and -35° normal, and +5°, -37° maximum).
Tail control surfaces: Virtually all-moving tailplane (+30°, -25°). Twin fins and rudders, outward canted by 28°. Rudders (±30° movement). No airbrake on EMD/production aircraft (though fitted to prototypes); FBW system allows aircraft deceleration at idle engine power through extension and/or movement of control surfaces, primarily asymmetric rudders (fully towed outward – see Aircraft variants). 4-surface tail configuration provides necessary manoeuvrability and control at minimum structural weight. Using thrust vectoring to control pitch at high angle of attack, horizontal tails can be deflected differentially for high roll rates.
Canard: None.
Airbrakes: See Tail control surfaces.
Flight control system: Triple-redundant digital fly-by-wire; no back-up. Integrated electronic flight/propulsion control system, totally controlled by software. Parker Bertea Aerospace flight control actuators. Leading-edge flap drive system by Curtiss-Wright Flight Systems.
Fuselage: Blended fuselage/wing design, with chined forebody and conformal sensors. Freestream fixed geometry supersonic air intakes. All exterior edge angles aligned with either the wing leading or trailing edges. 2 side and 1 main underfuselage weapons bays. Prototypes had retractable spoiler for main bay, used for aircraft deceleration with rudders. Fuselage shields some RCS return from wing trailing edges.
Construction materials: Structural materials by weight are 36% Ti-64 titanium, 24% thermoset composites, 16% aluminium, 15% other materials (see below), 6% steel, 3% Ti-62222

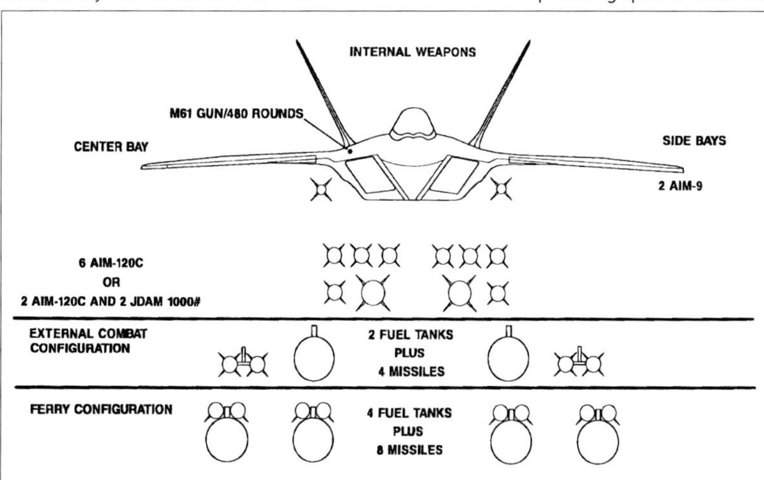

↑ Lockheed Martin F-22 Raptor weapon carriage diagram *(courtesy Lockheed Martin)*

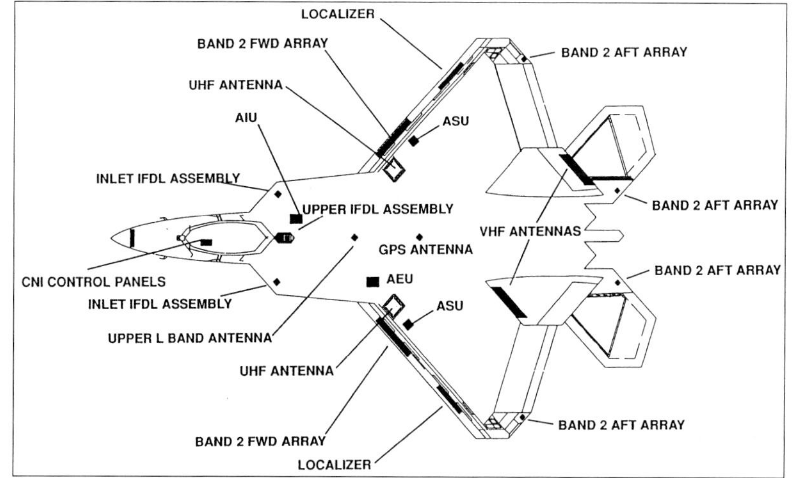

↑ Lockheed Martin F-22 Raptor CNI upper aperture locations *(courtesy Lockheed Martin)*

titanium, and >1% thermoplastic composites. Forward fuselage section of aluminium and composites. Mid-fuselage section of 23.5% composites, nearly 35% titanium, 35% aluminium, plus other materials by weight. Aft fuselage section is 11% composites, 67% titanium and 22% aluminium by weight. Wings 35% composites, 42% titanium, 23% aluminium by weight, excluding steel and other materials for fasteners, clips, etc. Tail fins are of multi-spar configuration internally, and with a hot isostatic pressed (HIP) cast rudder actuator housing. Edges and rudder are of composites, both with embedded VHF and other antennae. Other materials used for coatings, paint, transparency, radome, tyres, brakes, sealant, adhesives, seals, actuators, gases and fluids. Composites components include bismaleimide (BMI) wing skins, mid-fuselage fuel floors and exterior skins, inlet duct skins, thermoplastic weapons bay door skins, dual resin bonded battery access panels, tailplane bonded assembly, RTM bulkheads/frames/spars, co-cured BMI/HC skin panels and doors, and BMI taco shell edge skins and spars. Wing spars and some other components are constructed using the new resin transfer moulding process. Boeing became responsible for development and construction of the wings and aft fuselage, and structures for the installation of the engines, nozzles and APU.
Engines: 2 Pratt & Whitney F119-PW-100 augmented turbofans. All engine accessories placed at the bottom of the engine for easy maintenance. Engine change in under 90 minutes using a single trailer. AlliedSignal G250 APU in port wing root for engine start and electrical power. Stored energy system (SES) bottles for engine-out restart.
Engine rating: Each 35,000 lbf (155.7 kN) range.
Nozzles: 2D convergent/divergent (±20°) with independent throat and exit area actuation and pitch-axis thrust vectoring.
Air intakes: Freestream fixed geometry supersonic intakes with swept cowl lips, boundary layer bleed and overboard bypass systems, and relatively long subsonic diffuser offering 100% line-of-sight RF blockage.
Flight refuelling probe: B.F.Goodrich Aerospace fuel interface set. XAR retractable flight refuelling receptacle; inner guides protect composite external doors from probe damage.
Fuel system: 8 tanks in wings, fuselage and tailbooms. Design allows for later use of additional 'saddle' and fin tanks. Jettisonable external stores pylons with Edo BRU-47A racks for carriage of auxiliary fuel tanks. See Cockpit for TMS.
Electrical system: 3 independent supplies. Sundstrand main electrical power generating system, with Smiths 270 volt DC distribution system. 2 × 65 kW engine-driven generators, a 27 kW APU-driven generator and a 28 volt battery.
Hydraulic system: Dual, high pressure (4,000 psi), non-inflammable system; only 1 Parker Bertea actuator on each control surface.
Braking system: AlliedSignal Carbonex 4000 carbon mainwheel brakes.
Oxygen system: Teledyne onboard inert gas generating system, with Parker Bertea control valve, regulator and pumps; Normalair-Garrett onboard oxygen generating system and breathing regulator anti-g valve.

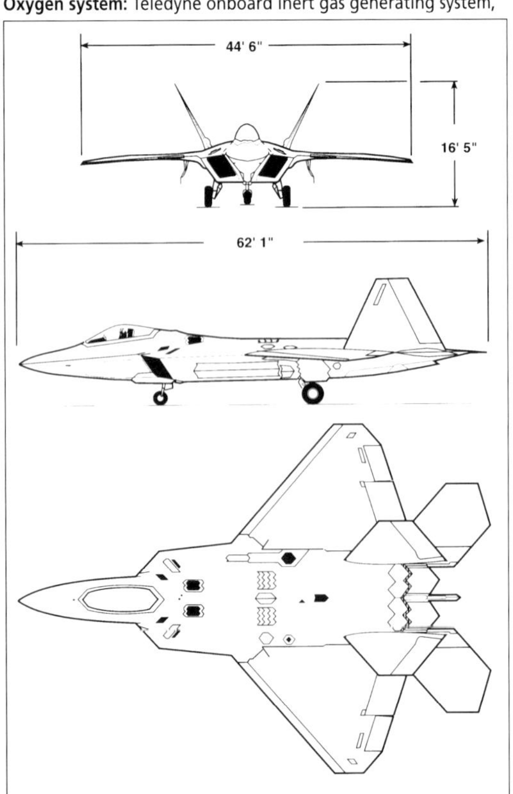

↑ **Lockheed Martin F-22 Raptor general arrangement**
(courtesy Lockheed Martin)

Aircraft variants:
YF-22 designation covers the 2 original prototypes (PAV-1 and -2), both now non-flying. GE YF120 and P&W YF119 engines tested. Straight trailing edges to trapezoid wings and tailplane. More pointed nosecone. Airbrake. Serrated edges to cockpit canopy. Bolt-on spoiler on underfuselage between intakes, permanently hanging in slipstream on some test flights, to assist in collecting weapons bay acoustic and vibration data. Wing span 43 ft (13.11 m), length 64 ft 2 ins (19.56 m), same area as F-22, wing/stabilizer sweepback 48°.
F-22 EMDs (9 aircraft), for testing from 1997. *4001*, *4002* and *4003* (first flying between 1997 and Summer 1999) do not have full tactical avionics and sensors, and are being used for envelope expansion, structural loads, engine, weapons, and other flight tests, including high AoA and arrester gear. Final 6 (*4004-4009*), first flying between Autumn 1999 and Spring 2001, are interchangeable avionics test aircraft, with the avionics suite 'maturing' through 4 Block stages, although all 6 will carry the same avionics configuration at the same time. *4008* and *4009* will later undertake initial operational test and evaluation (IOTE).
F-22A will be the production single-seater, having the reprofiled wings and tail surfaces, and reprofiled ailerons (constant chord) of the EMDs. Compared with prototypes, have reduced wingroot thickness and sweepback, changes to camber and twist, and increased anhedral. Modified undercarriage with shorter wheel track and wheel base, modified legs and doors. Increased fin area. Air inlets farther back, approximately level with the rear of the canopy. Serrated edges to the canopy and nosecone of the prototypes were expected to be retained, but have not (canopy retains some frame shaping but not hard serrations). Airbrake deleted.
F-22B was to have been the 2-seat operational training version, with aft-of-fuselage fuel tank removed. Now cancelled.
Future variants for lethal/non-lethal suppression of enemy defences, reconnaissance, attack/interdiction and surveillance (see Development). Could revive need for a 2-seat configuration, to replace F-15E.
F-22FMS possible export variant (see Sales).

Details for F-22A

PRINCIPAL DIMENSIONS:
Wing span: 44 ft 6 ins (13.564 m)
Maximum length: 62 ft 1 ins (18.923 m)
Maximum height: 16 ft 5 ins (5.004 m)

WINGS:
Aerofoil section: special, biconvex, unspecified
Area: 840 sq ft (78.039 m^2)
Aspect ratio: 2.357
Sweepback: 42° at 25% chord
Chord at root: 32 ft 3.5 ins (9.842 m)
Chord at tip: 3 ft 11 ins (1.194 m)
Twist: 0° 30', 3° 6' (root/tip)
Anhedral: 3° 15'
Ailerons area: 21.4 sq ft (1.988 m^2)
Flaperons area: 55 sq ft (5.11 m^2)
Leading-edge flaps area: 51.2 sq ft (4.757 m^2)

TAIL UNIT:
Tailplane span: 29 ft (8.839 m)
Tailplane area: 136 sq ft (12.635 m^2)
Fin height: 19 ft 7 ins (5.969 m)
Fin area: 178 sq ft (16.537 m^2)
Fin cant angle: 28° outward

UNDERCARRIAGE:
Type: Retractable, with nosewheel. Menasco gear, AlliedSignal wheels and Michelin tyres. Hydraulically actuated, electrically controlled. Steer-by-wire nosewheel steering. Stressed for up to 10 ft (3 m) per second landings
Main wheel tyre size: Michelin 37 × 11.5-R18
Nose wheel tyre size: Michelin 23.5 × 7.5-R10
Wheel base: 19 ft 9.625 ins (6.032 m)

WEIGHTS:
Empty, operating: 32,000 lb (14,515 kg)
Maximum take-off: 55,000 lb (24,950 kg)

PERFORMANCE:
Maximum operating Mach number (M_{MO}): Mach 2+ with afterburning, Mach 1.58 supercruise; USAF quoted in late 1997 Mach number as 1.8+ and supercruise Mach 1.4+
Maximum operating speed: 800 kts (921 mph) 1,483 km/h at sea level
Stall speed: classified.
Take-off/landing distances: less than F-15, otherwise classified
Maximum climb rate: classified
Roll rate: 100° per second at 120 kts, demonstrated
G limits: +9 target, 7.9 achieved by YF-22
Ceiling: over 50,000 ft (15,240 m)
Range with full fuel: over 1,735 naut miles (2,000 miles) 3,220 km

Lockheed Martin (General Dynamics) F-111 Aardvark

Comments: First flown on 21 December 1964 in early F-111A form, this fighter-bomber, nuclear or conventional strike and reconnaissance 'swing-wing' aircraft was retired from the USAF in a ceremony on 27 July 1997, when it was officially named Aardvark. The only other nation to receive F-111s was Australia, which has (at the time of writing) 4 F-111A(C)s, 13 F-111Cs, 15 ex-USAF F-111Gs and 4 RF-111Cs for strike and reconnaissance, all active aircraft having received important avionics upgrades and expected to remain in service until the year 2015. Of the F-111Gs, only some 5 were active/operational in early 1998, the remainder in storage.

Australia has studied plans to upgrade F-111Gs to carry stand-off weapons, matching the F-111Cs, plus the possibility of upgrading the stores management system, mission computer, display generator and adding GPS, while further changes will include improved cockpit lighting and the rewiring of the wings. In 1998, Australia ordered 51 AGM-142 Popeye ASMs for its F-111Cs. In addition, Australia is purchasing some additional ex-USAF Pave Tack laser designator pods. Also, the first F-111Cs retrofitted with Pratt & Whitney TF30-P-109 engines taken from ex-USAF aircraft appeared in 1997, and all A(C)s, Cs and RFs will be similarly re-engined. RAAF F-111Gs will eventually receive a hybrid engine replacement based on the TF30-P-107/109.

Lockheed Martin F-117 Nighthawk

Comments: First flown on 18 June 1981 in FSD form, the subsonic F-117A was developed to fully exploit low observable (LO or stealth) technology, to penetrate dense threat environments at night and attack high-value targets with pinpoint accuracy, using stealth and intelligent mission planning. The 64th and final aircraft (including FSD prototypes) was delivered on 12 July 1990. Of 60 full-production F-117As, only 59 were accepted by the USAF and given serial numbers (as the first was lost on its maiden flight at Groom Lake prior to delivery), of which 54 remain on strength (47 are primary aircraft authorized – PAA – for operational missions), currently operated by the 49th Fighter Wing (12th Air Force), Air Combat Command, USAF, out of Holloman AFB, New Mexico. Upgrade is taking place. Work on the proposed A/F-117X naval variant has ended. Full details of these aircraft, and illustrations, can be found in the 1996-97 edition of *WA&SD*, pages 136-138.

Lockheed Martin (Northrop Grumman and British Aerospace) Joint Strike Fighter (JSF)

First flight: Anticipated for X-35A demonstrator, 1999. Production aircraft circa 2007.
Role: Primarily interdiction/strike, but also multi-role including close air support, suppression of enemy air defences, air defence, combat air patrol, deck-launched intercept, anti-ship attack and reconnaissance.

Aims

- Largely (approximately 80-90%) common basic airframe/engine configuration to provide supersonic, alternative CTOL/STOVL variants of JSF for multi-service use.
- CTOL variant as a replacement for the F-16 with the USAF, also further CV/CTOL variant as a replacement for the F/A-18C/D and already retired A-6E with the US Navy.
- STOVL variant as a replacement for Harrier AV-8B/Harrier II Plus and F/A-18C/D with the USMC, and Sea Harrier F/A Mk 2 with the Royal Navy.
- 'Conventional' airframe and propulsion configuration for 'up and away' and supersonic flight. Trapezoidal wing/aft tail configuration with relaxed stability for high manoeuvrability. Twin fins. High usable alpha.
- Powered vertical lift from aft vectoring propulsion engine nozzle and forward remote shaft-driven lift fan on STOVL variant.

↑ Lockheed Martin JSF in USAF (*top left*), US Navy (*top right*), USMC (*bottom left*) and Royal Navy (*bottom right*) forms

▪ Low radar signature achieved by configuration geometry (external and internal shaping), internal weapons carriage, and materials (RAM and special treatments).
▪ To incorporate Predictive Maintenance Technology, with work started under a US$6.5 million Prognostics and Health Management (PHM) demonstration contract.
▪ Use of Dassault Systems' CATIA computer-aided software, to create a 'Virtual Development Environment' for design and production, integrating management, schedule, cost, design and manufacturing tools.

Development

▪ 1990. Common Affordable Lightweight Fighter (CALF) study launched by Advanced Research Project Agency (ARPA).
▪ 1991. Phased development programme on Supersonic Strike Fighter (SSF) initiated with contracts from ARPA. Phase I of 1991-92 included Propulsion Concept Selection.
▪ March 1993. Phase II Critical Technology Evaluation and Configuration Refinement for SSF/CALF, with a 3 year contract from ARPA running until 1996.
▪ August 1994. ARPA signed an agreement with the UK Ministry of Defence to co-operate in the flight demonstration programme, with the objective of developing a supersonic successor to the Sea Harrier.
▪ 1994. Canard configuration rejected in favour of a lower risk, aft tail configuration to meet carrier approach requirements.
▪ 1995. Joint Advanced Strike Technology (JAST) Concept Study contract placed (incorporating CALF).
▪ 1995-96. 86% scale powered (P&W F100-PW-220+ engine) lift model was statically tested in a hover rig and in the NASA/Ames wind tunnel.
▪ March 1996. Request for Proposals (RFP) issued to Boeing, Lockheed Martin and McDonnell Douglas led teams.
▪ 16 November 1996. Award of Phase III Concept Demonstrator Programme contract, valued at US$1.1 billion, to both Lockheed Martin and Boeing teams; McDD/Northrop Grumman/BAe team had been eliminated. 51-month programme to produce and flight test 2 demonstrator aircraft, designated as X-35A in CTOL form for USAF variant and X-35B in STOVL form for USMC/RN.
▪ 8 May 1997. Northrop Grumman joined Lockheed Martin team.
▪ 18 June 1997. Announcement at the Paris Air Show of BAe joining the team.
▪ 1997. Lockheed Martin completed the initial design review, after some 11,000 hours of scale model testing.
▪ 13 June 1997. X-35 design frozen.
▪ September 1997. Release of engineering drawings for the X-35 demonstrators, indicating the start of long-lead large parts production at the Skunk Works.
▪ January 1998. Completion of a 48 ft long by 31 ft wide (14.6 × 9.4 m) steel assembly fixture required for large-scale manufacturing operations.
▪ April/May 1998. First test run of a P&W SE611 engine.
▪ 1999. First flight of the X-35A CTOL demonstrator. Also, Joint Operational Requirement to be issued.
▪ 2000. First flight of the X-35B STOVL demonstrator. Also X-35C CV/CTOL demonstrator, converted from X-35A.
▪ 2001. Engineering and Manufacturing Development (EMD) contract award to the winning team.
▪ 2004. First flight of an EMD aircraft.
▪ 2007. Production aircraft flight test.
▪ 2008. In service date for the CTOL aircraft.
▪ 2010. In service date for the STOVL aircraft. EMD completed.

Details

Sales/Users: About 2,900 currently planned for 4 lead services: 1,763 (reduced from 2,036) for USAF to replace A-10 and F-16 (and to complement F-22), 609 (from 642) for USMC to replace AV-8B/Harrier II Plus and F/A-18C/D, 60 for Royal Navy to replace Sea Harrier F/A Mk 2, and 300-480 for US Navy to replace F/A-18C/D. USAF has also expressed interest in some 200 of the STOVL variant. Foreign interest shown by Australia, Canada, Denmark, the Netherlands, Norway and possibly Singapore. Global total sales (especially as a possible F-16 replacement) could be for 5,000+.
Crew: Pilot only. No 2-seat variant currently planned.
Cockpit: Metallized (low RCS) canopy, offering 'all-round' field of view, with exceptional look-down angle over the side and excellent forward view over the nose. Completely night vision capable. Integrated access steps/ladder.
Crew escape: Advanced Martin Baker zero-zero rocket type ejection seat.
Fixed guns: Integrated 20-mm M61 improved cannon on USAF variant; optional for USN. USMC/Royal Navy aircraft expected to have external gun pod. Development of a new 25-mm cannon being considered.
Ammunition: 400 rounds.

↑ Lockheed Martin JSF model under test, showing the lift fan of the USMC/Royal Navy variants

↑ Lockheed Martin JSF in (*top to bottom*) USMC Configuration 220B, US Navy Configuration 220C and Royal Navy Configuration 220B forms, plus USAF Configuration 220A plan view

Number of weapon pylons: At least 4 external pylons (see below).
Expendable weapons and equipment: In 'stealthy' configuration, internal carriage of 6 AIM-120C AMRAAM (cropped) AAMs or 2 AMRAAMs plus 2 × 2,000 lb class GBU-31 Joint Direct Attack Munitions possible. External stores could include JSOW, larger LGBs, bombs, anti-radiation missiles, air-to-surface missiles, auxiliary tanks, etc.
Radar: Northrop Grumman advanced multi-mode, electronically scanned array, synthetic aperture radar.
Flight/weapon system avionics/instrumentation: Highly integrated vehicle management system. MIL-STD-1553 databus. Texas Instruments integrated core processor. 3 large MFDs. Active noise cancellation. Helmet integrated display, including laser protection possible. No conventional HUD; Flight Visions Night Hawk HUD for X-35 demonstrator only. HOTAS integrated flight/engine control, driven by STOVL requirements. Internal laser designator. Infra-red sensors.
Self-protection systems: Radar and infra-red warning receivers. ECM and chaff/flare dispensers integrated into airframe. Laser warning?
Wing characteristics: Thin trapezoidal wing planform of medium sweep and taper, mid/shoulder-mounted on fuselage with 'carry through' wing box. 'Planform alignment' with tailplane for low RCS. Wingtip and chord extensions (larger leading-edge flaps) for US Navy version. Wings fold on US Navy/Royal Navy versions.
Wing control surfaces: Full-span leading-edge manoeuvre flaps, and trailing-edge flaperons, for high lift and roll control.

↑ Lockheed Martin JSF in USMC Configuration 220B, during vertical operations

Tail control surfaces: Twin outward-canted fins with conventional rudders. Conventional all-moving trapezoidal aft tailplane, providing both pitch and roll control. Larger tailplane on US Navy version.
Flight control system: Digital fly-by-wire, integrating flight/engine control. Electric actuator system ('power by wire') replaces conventional hydraulic system for all control surfaces, and uses Parker Bertea electro-hydrostatic actuators.
Fuselage: Wing position results in blended wing/fuselage upper surface and 3 flat fuselage facets, the latter comprising fuselage bottom and sloping sides. Nose radome with similarly shaped cross-section blends in aft. Air intakes form bifurcated inlet duct to the main propulsion engine. Integral weapon bays, with twin doors, integrated into both sides of the fuselage. Lower bay doors act as lift improvement devices (LIDs) on STOVL variant. Main undercarriage bays aft of weapons bays. All bay doors, access panels and sensor apertures incorporate 'saw tooth' leading- and trailing-edges to minimize RCS. Rear fuselage aft of wing blends into the wide and deep twin boom configuration, providing mounting and actuation for fins and tailplanes. Carrier-suitable tail hook on US Navy variant.
Construction materials: High proportion of advanced composites and titanium. Aluminium-lithium alloys. SPF/DB and honeycomb used where appropriate.
Engine: Pratt & Whitney F-119 derivative, designated SE611, incorporates increased by-pass ratio and turbine entry temperature and also variable guide vanes for the LP turbine. FADEC. Adapted for STOVL powered lift mode. Forward, remote, Rolls-Royce/Allison designed 2-stage lift fan, shaft-driven from the main engine via a clutch and gearbox. Engine fan by-pass air bleed for roll reaction control jets emerging from wing lower surface outboard of wing/fuselage root junction. Alternative production engine source being developed through the General Electric YF120-FX programme.
Engine rating: 35,000 lbf (155.7 kN) class, augmented. Lift fan can absorb up to 25,000 shp (18,643 kW), corresponding to 18,000 lbf (80 kN).
Nozzles: CTOL propulsion engine has low observable axisymmetric nozzle (LOAN), with 'saw tooth' petal terminators and of variable area, con-di type. Non-vectoring STOVL propulsion system incorporates a nozzle with 3 annular bearings (similar to that of R-79 V-300 of Russian Yak-141), designed by Rolls-Royce and capable of vectoring through 110° downward in STOVL mode. Lift fan nozzle incorporates vectoring to 60° aft and 20° forward. Engine efflux may be vectored laterally for yaw control. Pitch control is effected by modulating lift fan and engine nozzle area.
Air intakes: Twin main engine intakes of essentially 2-dimensional type, with no moving parts, canted to blend with the nose and centre fuselage sections. Scarfed and raked form, with no boundary layer splitter plate or diverter (a fuselage side 'aerodynamic bump' replaces these) for low RCS. 2 auxiliary intakes in fuselage dorsal position immediately forward of the engine face open to feed the main inlet duct in STOVL mode. Lift fan intake in fuselage dorsal position with twin, folding, side-hinged, doors.

Details for Lockheed Martin JSF

PRINCIPAL DIMENSIONS:
Wing span: 40 ft (12.19 m) in CV/CTOL form, or 33 ft (10.06 m) in STOVL/CTOL form
Wing span, folded: 29 ft 10 ins (9.09 m) for USN/RN versions
Maximum length: 50 ft 11 ins (15.52 m)

WINGS:
Area: 540 sq ft (50.17 m^2) for CV/CTOL, or 450 sq ft (41.8 m^2) for STOVL/CTOL
Aspect ratio: 2.96 for CV/STOL, 2.42 for STOVL/CTOL
Sweep: 35° sweepback on the leading edge, 13° sweep forward on the trailing edge

UNDERCARRIAGE:
Type: Retractable, with twin nosewheels that retract forward into the lower fuselage; main wheels retract forward into the fuselage sides aft of the weapons bay; Navy variant has longer stroke and higher capacity plus nosewheel catapulting attachment

WEIGHTS:
Empty: approximately 25,000 lb (11,340 kg)
Maximum take-off: 50,000 lb (22,680 kg)

PERFORMANCE:
Maximum speed: >Mach 1.4
G limits and turn rate: Sustained and attained g, and turn rate, said to be similar to or better than F-16C and F/A-18C
Radius of action (attack): 540 naut miles (622 miles) 1,000 km for USMC-specified mission, 600 naut miles (691 miles) 1,112 km for US Navy specified mission
Notes: STOVL variant has more than twice the radius of action of AV-8B on internal fuel and carries a heavier payload. Navy variant has almost twice the radius of action of F/A-18C on internal fuel.

Flight refuelling probe: Receptacle is located on the fuselage upper surface of the USAF variant. Retractable probe for USMC, USN and Royal Navy.
Electrical system: Possibly 2 independent supplies, with Sundstrand engine-driven starter/generator system, for 270 volt DC.

Aircraft variants:
X-35A in Configuration 220A is the CTOL concept demonstrator for the USAF.
X-35B in Configuration 220B is the STOVL concept demonstrator for the USMC and Royal Navy.
X-35C in Configuration 220C is the CV/CTOL concept demonstrator for the US Navy, converted from the X-35A.
Production variants will be based on the features of the individual demonstrators.

Lockheed Martin P-3 Orion and Orion 2000

Comments: Lockheed Martin production of P-3 Orion has (at present) ended, leaving newly-built aircraft coming only from Kawasaki in Japan. For Aims and a longer Development section for the P-3, see the 1996-97 edition of *WA&SD*, page 138-139.
First flight: 19 August 1958 (Electra N1883 aerodynamic prototype with simulated MAD tail boom), 25 November 1959 (YP3V-1, becoming YP-3A from 1962).
Role: Maritime patrol, anti-submarine, anti-surface vessel, sea control and fisheries protection, mine-laying, search and rescue, over the horizon targeting, and much more including airborne early warning.

Development

▪ 23 July 1962. Production deliveries began to the US Navy, initially to VP-8 at NAS Patuxent River, followed by VP-44.
▪ January 1966. Initial deliveries of the P-3B, to VP-8 at NAS Moffett Field.
▪ 18 September 1968. Maiden flight of the P-3C, with deliveries first going to VP-56 in June 1969.
▪ June 1994. The first of 8 P-3Cs for South Korea was rolled-out, representing the first newly built Orions from Marietta (where production had been transferred).
▪ 1994. Under Project Sword, a US Navy P-3C was used as a command, control, communications and intelligence aircraft to relay real-time information to the cockpit instrumentation of a USAF F-16. A Navy Hornet was used in a similar demonstration in 1995.
▪ September 1995. Final newly-built P-3C from Lockheed Martin production was delivered, to South Korea.
▪ 1996. Final P-3C delivery, with 3 P-3C Update II.75s going to

Pakistan that had been embargoed for several years.

■ 1997. Agreement signed between the Australian Department of Defence and Raytheon Systems to promote worldwide a P-3 upgrade, as adopted by the RAAF's aircraft. Other involved companies include Boeing Australia, British Aerospace Australia and Honeywell Australia. Also suited to other aircraft.

Details *(P-3C, unless stated)*

Sales/Users: Total sales were 649 from US production, the final 8 going to South Korea. Argentina (ex-US Navy P-3s), Australia (AP-3C Update II/II.5; 18 had avionics upgrade, the first by Raytheon Systems in the USA and the remainder in Australia), Canada (CP-140 Aurora plus CP-140A Arcturus for long-range coastal surveillance), Chile (P/UP-3A), Greece (ex-US Navy P-3Bs, plus P-3As for training and 2 for spares), Iran (P-3F), Japan (Kawasaki P-3C Update II.5/III, EP-3, UP-3 – only 3 came from Lockheed, the remainder built or being built by Kawasaki), South Korea (P-3C Update III), Netherlands (P-3C Update II.5), New Zealand (P-3K), Norway (P-3C Update III and P-3N), Pakistan (P-3C Update II.75), Portugal (P-3P), Spain (P-3A and B), Thailand (ex-US Navy as 3 P-3T and 2 UP-3T, plus 2 for spares – all based on the P-3A), and USA (Navy, P-3C Update IIIs on strength with active squadrons and Navy Reserve, plus specialized variants as detailed under Aircraft variants, and including US Customs P-3 AEW).

Crew: Typically 10, as pilot, co-pilot and flight engineer in the flight station, tactical co-ordinator (TACCO) and navigator/communicator aft, MAD operator next in a separate cabin, then a large cabin for the 2 acoustic sensor stations, and finally the ordnance station, plus the flight technician. Observer stations aft, followed by a toilet, galley and rest area with bunks and seats. Up to 13 other persons can be carried, including a relief crew for extended missions.

Fixed guns: None.

Number of weapon pylons: 10 under the wings, plus a 12 ft 10 ins (3.91 m) long weapons bay in the forward fuselage.

Expendable weapons and equipment: Up to 20,000 lb (9,072 kg). Weapon options include 8 Harpoon anti-ship missiles under the wings, 8 × Mk 46 or 6 × Mk 50 torpedoes in the bay or 6 × Mk 60s under the wings, 3 nuclear depth bombs in the bay, up to 20 depth bombs, 11 Mk 83 bombs, up to 20 destructors, up to 11 mines underwing and in the bay, rockets, flares and sonobuoys (52 launch chutes, of which 51 computer controlled – 48 can be loaded before take-off). AGM-65D Maverick capability added to US Navy P-3C-IIIs. 2 AIM-9L Sidewinders can be carried for self protection.

Radar: AN/APS-115 search radar, with 360° scanning, or AN/APS-137 ISAR for upgraded US Navy P-3C-IIIs. Australian AP-3Cs have Elta EL/M-2022A radar.

Flight/weapon system avionics/instrumentation: AN/AYA-8 data processing system comprises the central digital computer, 3 or 4 logic units, 2 magnetic tape transports, and signal data converter. Navigation system includes dual LTN-72 INS, LTN-211 Omega, AN/APN-227 Doppler radar, AN/ARN-81 Loran A/C, true airspeed computer, AN/ARN-118 Tacan, VOR/ILS, AN/ARN-83 LF-ADF, AN/ARA-50 UHF-DF, AN/AJN-15 flight direction indicator and OTPI. Communications system includes 2 AN/ARC-143 UHF transceivers, AN/ARC-101 VHF transceiver, 2 AN/ARC-161 HF transceivers, AN/ACQ-5 data link, AN/AGC-6 teletype, integrated acoustic com system, and secure KY-75 HF and UHF voice. US Navy P-3C-IIIs received a communications upgrade. Australian upgraded AP-3Cs have Lockheed Martin DDC-060 data management system, plus new navigation and communication systems. IFF/SIF. Acoustic sensors are 2 AN/AQA-7 sonar computer recorders or an IBM AN/UYS-1 Proteus acoustic processor in Update III (upgraded Australian AP-3Cs have UYS-503), 2 AN/ARR-72 or -78 (Update III) sonobuoy receivers, command actuated sonobuoy system, time code generator, acoustic tape recorder, ambient sea noise meter, bathythermograph recorder and acoustic source signal generator. Non-acoustic sensors are radar (see Radar), AN/ALQ-78 (or AN/ALR-66(V)3 for upgraded US Navy P-3C-III) electronic support measures in a pod on the port inboard wing pylon (interfaces with the computer which aids in the automatic classification and analysis of radiated electron signals), AN/ASQ-81 magnetic anomaly detector (MAD) or CAE Electronics MAD for Australian upgraded P-3Cs, MAD compensation group adapter, AN/ASA-64 submarine anomaly detector, and retractable infra-red detecting set (scans for surface or partially submerged targets and resolves a target image for visual presentation on the Sensor Station 3 and TACCO displays). US Navy P-3C Update IIIs further upgraded by Unisys to have AN/APS-137 Inverse Synthetic-Aperture Radar, improved infra-red detection, improved communications to allow co-ordinated operations with surface and sub-surface vessels, and standard Loral AN/ALR-66 ESM. KA-74 camera and KB-18A strike assessment camera. A US Navy P-3B was tested with laser airborne depth sounding (LADS) equipment.

↑ Last P-3Cs built in the USA were 8 for South Korea, as shown

Self-protection systems: See above and Weapons.

Wing characteristics: Straight, low mounted, with dihedral.

Wing control surfaces: Ailerons (with tabs) and flaps.

Tail control surfaces: Elevators and rudder, with tabs.

Flight control system: Hydraulic, with boosters.

Construction materials: Metal.

Engines: 4 Allison T56-A-14 turboprops, with Hamilton Standard 56H60-77 propellers. APU.

Engine rating: Each 4,910 shp (3,661 kW).

Flight refuelling probe: Not fitted as standard. See Aircraft variants.

Fuel system: 34,825 litres usable.

Electrical system: 24 volt DC supply. 120/208 volt 400 Hz AC supply.

Hydraulic system: 3,000 psi.

Braking system: Hydraulic brakes.

De-icing system: Bleed air for wings, and electric for tail unit and propeller spinners.

Aircraft variants:

CP-140 Aurora is the Canadian version of Orion. AYK-10 computer, APS-126 radar, ASQ-501 MAD, and other systems from the S-3 Viking. ALR-66(V)3 displays.

CP-140A Arcturus is a Canadian P-3C-based long-range coastal surveillance and EEZ protection variant, with no ASW equipment.

EP-3 is Kawasaki's electronic surveillance version.

EP-3E Aries II is the US Navy designation of 12 P-3Cs modified for electronic surveillance.

EP-3J became a US Navy EW trainer (2).

NP-3 applies to US Navy Orions modified into testbed aircraft.

P-3A was the first production model, upgraded for current operators. Fitted with 4,500 shp (3,356 kW) T56-A-10W turboprops. P-3T/UP-3Ts became modernized P-3As.

P-3B was the first model to use T56-A-14 engines. Most US Navy aircraft in storage, the remainder with Reserve units. P-3K and P–3Ps are upgraded P-3Bs.

P-3C version was initiated with the development of the A-NEW advanced ASW avionics system at the Naval Air Development Center at Warminster. Became the first ASW aircraft in the world with a centralized computer. Directional acoustic frequency analysis and recording processing (Difar). With this computer-integrated system, crew were relieved of the heavy task of interpreting the raw intelligence data provided by the aircraft's sensors. Instead of charts, logs and other data, the computer handled the data, allowing the crew to concentrate on tactical planning.

P-3C Update I was introduced to the US Navy in January 1975, with new avionics and software designed to increase effectiveness. Added equipment included a magnetic memory drum that expanded the computer memory 7-fold, Difar improvements, Omega navigation, and AN/ASA-66 tactical displays for 2 sensor stations.

P-3C Update II was introduced in August 1977, with new infra-red detection and sonobuoy reference systems (IRDS/SRS); Harpoon anti-ship missiles; AQH-4(V)2 28-channel magnetic tape recorder/reproducer; LTN-72 inertial navigation system; VHF/VOR, Tacan, Doppler replacement; Triple Vernier Difar; Mad-CGA; and DMTS.

P-3C Update II.5 was an interim modernization, with improved nav/com, IACS communications link with submarines, wing pylons and other changes. Version for Kawasaki production, beginning with 5 aircraft produced from Lockheed knockdown components (5004-5008); Kawasaki-produced aircraft being modernized to Update III standard. ALR-66(V)3 displays (similar displays are also used by Australia, Canada and Norway).

P-3C Update II.75 refers to Pakistan's aircraft, based on the Update III but with some minor downgrade of equipment.

P-3C Update III was the final version, as flown by the active US Navy, entering service in 1984. Features an IBM Proteus acoustic processor and new sonobuoy receiver (supplanting Difar), and other changes including LTN-211 Omega and KY-75 secure HF voice. Newly built and produced by retrofit as Update IIIR.

P-3F is the version received by Iran; similar to P-3C base but with in-flight refuelling.

P-3K is New Zealand's version. Planned to receive new wings built by Daewoo of South Korea under Project Kestrel. Systems and airframe modernization programme anticipated.

P-3N refers to 2 Norwegian P-3Bs operated by the Coast Guard without ASW capability.

P-3P is the designation of 6 ex-RAAF P-3Bs operated by Portugal, with ALR-66(V)3 displays.

P-3T is Thailand's version.

P-3 AEW is the airborne early warning and control variant, with AN/APS-138 surveillance radar in a 24 ft (7.32 m) rotating dome antenna. 4 delivered to the US Customs Service, the last in 1993.

RP-3A/C are US Navy variants for oceanographic research.

RP-3D is operated by the US Navy for atmospheric research and magnetic survey work.

TP-3A became a US Navy pilot trainer, converted from P-3As.

UP-3 designation covers various mission training, ECM training, utility transport and test aircraft versions.

VP-3A became a US Navy VIP transport.

WP-3D is an atmospheric and weather research variant of P-3C, used by the US Department of Commerce.

Orion 2000 was a modernized version offered to the RAF (see Nimrod 2000 entry under UK). Is being offered to the US Navy for its Large Land Based Aircraft requirement. Advanced sensors and avionics.

Loral/Marshall Valkyrie was proposed as a P-3A/B update to meet the RAF's Nimrod replacement requirement. Not selected.

Details for P-3C Update III

PRINCIPAL DIMENSIONS:

Wing span: 99 ft 8 ins (30.38 m)

Maximum length: 116 ft 10 ins (35.61 m)

Maximum height: 33 ft 8.5 ins (10.27 m)

WINGS:

Aerofoil section: Modified NACA 0014, 0012 (root/tip)

Area: 1,300 sq ft (120.77 m²)

Aspect ratio: 7.64

Incidence: 3° and 0.5° (root/tip)

Dihedral: 6°

TAIL UNIT:

Tailplane span: 42 ft 10 ins (13.06 m)

Tailplane area: 241 sq ft (22.39 m²)

UNDERCARRIAGE:

Type: Retractable, with twin wheels on each unit

Wheel base: 29 ft 9 ins (9.07 m)

Wheel track: 31 ft 2 ins (9.5 m)

WEIGHTS:

Empty: 61,491 lb (27,892 kg)

Normal take-off: 139,760 lb (63,394 kg)

Maximum take-off: 142,000 lb (64,410 kg)

PERFORMANCE:

Maximum speed: 405 kts (466 mph) 750 km/h at 15,000 ft (4,570 m)

Long-range cruise speed: 350 kts (403 mph) 648 km/h at 25,000 ft (7,620 m)

Patrol speed: 209 kts (241 mph) 387 km/h

Stall speed: 133 kts (153 mph) 248 km/h *clean*, 112 kts (129 mph) 208 km/h *with flaps*

Take-off distance: 4,240 ft (1,292 m)

Landing distance over a 50 ft (15 m) obstacle: 2,770 ft (844 m)

Maximum climb rate: 2,600 ft (792 m) per minute at sea level

Ceiling: 34,400 ft (10,485 m)

Maximum radius of action: 2,070 naut miles (2,384 miles) 3,836 km

Ferry range: 4,500 naut miles (5,182 miles) 8,334 km

Duration: 14 hours 30 minutes on all engines, 17 hours 12 minutes on 2 engines

Lockheed Martin S-3B, ES-3A and US-3A Viking

Comments: First flown on 21 January 1972, the Viking has been out of production for many years. In US Navy service, it undertakes carrier-borne sea control (S-3B for anti-submarine, anti-ship, mine warfare, over-the-horizon targeting and strike support), electronic reconnaissance and signal/communications intelligence (ES-3A), and carrier onboard delivery (US-3A) roles, while all S-3B/EA-3As have aerial refuelling receiver/tanker capabilities. Full details and illustrations can be found in the 1996-97 edition of *WA&SD*, pages 139-140 and 189-190.

Northrop Grumman

On 3 July 1997 Lockheed Martin and Northrop Grumman announced their pending merger. Although the merger had been expected to be finalized before the end of 1997, this had not taken place by mid-1998 because of US Government concerns and anti-trust law. See Lockheed Martin preamble for further details.

Northrop Grumman Corporation USA

Corporate address:
1840 Century Park East, Los Angeles, CA 90067-2199.

Telephone: +1 310 553 6262
Facsimile: +1 310 201 3023, 553 2076

Founded:
18 May 1994, following Northrop's (founded 1939) purchase of Grumman (founded 1929).

Employees: 51,800.

Information:
James Hart (Public Information Manager – *telephone* +1 310 201 3458, *facsimile* +1 310 556 4561).

DIVISIONS

COMMERCIAL AIRCRAFT DIVISION

HQ address:
9314 West Jefferson Blvd, Dallas, TX 75211.

Telephone: +1 972 266 2011
Facsimile: +1 972 266 5761

Corporate Vice President and General Manager:
Ralph D. Crosby Jr.

Activities:
■ Aerostructures, including fuselage sections, tail sections, control surfaces, nacelles and thrust reversers for a variety of aircraft, including Boeing 747, 757, 767 and 777; Airbus A340; and Gulfstream IV and V. Also major components for C-17 and General Electric CF6-80 engines. Operates facilities in Hawthorne, CA; Milledgeville, GA; Perry, GA; and Stuart, FL. Also manages Northrop Grumman Allied Industries.

DATA SYSTEMS AND SERVICES DIVISION

HQ address:
2411 Dulles Corner Park, Suite 500, Herndon, VA 22071.

Telephone: +1 703 713 4000
Facsimile: +1 703 713 4067

Corporate Vice President and General Manager:
Herbert W. Anderson.

Activities:
■ Information systems solutions. Facilities in Bohemia, NY; Lawton, OK; Pico Rivera, CA; and Titusville, FL.

ELECTRONIC SENSORS AND SYSTEMS DIVISION

HQ address:
1580-A West Nursery Road, Linthicum, MD 21290.

Telephone: +1 410 765 1000
Facsimile: +1 410 765 0789

Corporate Vice President and General Manager:
James G. Roche.

Activities:
■ Produces radars and electronics. Facilities in Hunt Valley, MD; Sunnyvale, CA; Norwalk, CT; Melville, NY; Annapolis, MD; Sykesville, MD; Cleveland, OH; Cincinnati, OH; Pittsburgh, PA; Huntsville, AL; Knoxville, TN; College Station, TX; Burlington, Canada; and Santa Isabel, PR.

ELECTRONICS AND SYSTEMS INTEGRATION DIVISION

HQ address:
PO Box 9650, 2000 NASA Blvd, Melbourne, FL 32902.

Telephone: +1 407 951 5000
Facsimile: +1 407 951 5923

Corporate Vice President and General Manager:
John E. Harrison.

Activities:
■ Surveillance and battlefield management systems including J-STARS and E-2C Hawkeye, precision weapon systems, EW systems including airborne radar and infra-red countermeasures, and electronics and readiness support systems. Facilities in Benton Park, PA; Clarksburg, West VA; Great River, NY; Hawthorne, CA; Melbourne, FL; New Town, ND; and Rolling Meadows, IL.

MILITARY AIRCRAFT SYSTEMS DIVISION

HQ address:
One Hornet Way, El Segundo, CA 90245-2804.

Telephone: +1 310 332 1000
Facsimile: +1 310 332 3396

Corporate Vice President and General Manager:
William H. Lawler.

Activities:
■ B-2 programme, principal subcontractor on F/A-18, E-2C airframe manufacturer, unmanned aerial targets, remanufacture and modification of Boeing 707s into E-8Cs; EA-6B remanufacturing, F-14 work, and F-5/T-38 upgrades. Facilities in Bethpage, NY; Hawthorne, CA; Lake Charles, LA; Palmdale, CA; Pico Rivera, CA; Point Mugu, CA; and St Augustine, FL.

WHOLLY OWNED SUBSIDIARIES

Logicon Inc
Northrop Grumman Allied Industries Inc
Northrop Grumman International Inc
Northrop Worldwide Aircraft Services Inc
Perceptics Corporation
Remotec Inc
Xetron Inc

Northrop Grumman A-6E/TRAM Intruder

Comments: First flown on 9 April 1960 in original A-6A form and in 1970 as the A-6E, the Intruder carrier-borne all-weather attack-bomber has been withdrawn from US Navy service. Details and a photograph can be found in the 1996-97 edition of *WA&SD*, page 147.

Northrop Grumman (Fairchild Republic) A-10A/OA-10A Thunderbolt II

Comments: First flown on 10 May 1972 as the YA-10A, this close air support and forward air control aircraft went out of production in 1984 after 713 had been built. Expected to remain in service until about the year 2028, the USAF has an active inventory in mid-1998 of 130 A-10A combat aircraft and 90 OA-10 FAC aircraft, of which 117 and 69 are primary aircraft authorized, with 18 aircraft in a squadron. In addition, the Air National Guard operates 100 A-10As and the Air Force Reserve about 51. Full details and a photograph can be found in the 1996-97 edition of *WA&SD*, pages 147-148. The results of an industry competition for long-term support of the fleet was won by Lockheed Martin in 1998.

Northrop Grumman B-2A Spirit

First flight: 17 July 1989.
Role: Subsonic strategic stealth bomber.

Aims

■ To supplement existing bomber forces with Air Combat Command, USAF (originally intended to eventually replace the B-1B).
■ To strike maximum defended and moving targets prior to the deployment of the main non-stealth combat assets, with growing emphasis on conventional weaponry.
■ High survivability through low observable technology and defensive avionics systems.
■ Very wide wheel track, enabling the bomber to use any runway suited to a B727 airliner.
■ Requires less tanker support than other bombers.
■ 77% mission capability rate with an all Block 30 force.

Development

■ Northrop Grumman became prime contractor on the B-2 programme, with Boeing, Vought, Hughes, CAE-Link and General Electric as principal team members, plus approximately 4,000 subcontractors.
■ 1978. Programme was initiated, originally to be a high altitude bomber but revised in 1983 to include low level.
■ October 1981. Development contract issued by the US Air Force Systems Program Office.
■ January 1987. Flight testing of the integrated navigation and radar systems began, using a modified C-135 out of Edwards AFB.
■ 22 November 1988. Roll-out of the first B-2 (AV-1) at Palmdale, under strict security.
■ 17 July 1989. First B-2 (AV-1) made its maiden flight, of 2 hours 20 minutes, landing at Edwards AFB.
■ 8 November 1989. First daytime flight refuelling test, using a KC-10 Extender.
■ 13 June 1990. Block 1 testing completed (16 flights, accumulating 67 flight hours), verifying the B-2's basic flight worthiness (certified by the US General Accounting Office).
■ 19 October 1990. First flight of the second B-2 (AV-2). Heavily instrumented and serving as the loads test aircraft, in addition to performance and weapons carriage and further envelope expansion trials. Undertook flutter (air flow induced resonance) tests, proving the B-2 to be flutter-free for its entire operational envelope.
■ 23 October 1990. Block 2 trials began, including low observable tests (AV-1). In March 1991, Secretary of Defense certified that early Block 2 testing, including flying qualities and performance, were satisfactory, with no significant technical or operational problems. AV-1 went on to complete its development test programme before entering long-term "temporary" storage, awaiting future flight test assignments, having flown 81 times and accumulating more than 352 flight hours. Currently undergoing upgrade to full Block 30 operational standard.
■ 5 June 1991. First cross-country flight.
■ 18 June 1991. Third B-2 (AV-3) first flew. First B-2 to be equipped with a full complement of avionics equipment (initially radar and navigation avionics, with defensive aids added in February 1993).
■ 17 April 1992. Fourth B-2 (AV-4) first flew, used for avionics and armament testing.
■ 4 June 1992. First night flight.
■ 2 July 1992. First night refuelling flight.
■ 3 September 1992. First bomb (inert) release.
■ 5 October 1992. First flight of the 5th B-2 (AV-5), used for armament, climatic and low observable test phases.
■ December 1992. The static test airframe was intentionally taken to the breaking point of 161% of the operational load as a test of ultimate strength. Testing confirmed that the B-2 airframe can safely take 150% of the operational load and in-flight stress that it will endure in operational service. This airframe was 1 of 2 ground test airframes (durability and static) that had been funded alongside the full-scale development aircraft. These were essentially airframes without internal components. Durability test airframe completed its second lifetime of fatigue testing, which simulated 20,000 flight hours or about 30 years of operational use.
■ 2 February 1993. Sixth and last development B-2 flew as AV-6, used for technical order validation, weapons and avionics testing, including terrain following.
■ 1-5 March 1993. The highest number of B-2 flights in a week were recorded, at 8.
■ December 1993. A B-2 completed a 6-month programme at the Climatic Testing Laboratory at Eglin AFB, Florida.
■ 11 December 1993. A production B-2A Block 10 (AV-8 *Missouri*) was first delivered to the 509th Bomb Wing at Whiteman AFB. The first Block 10, AV-7 *Texas*, had previously that year undergone electromagnetic-interference and ECM trials, delaying delivery until 1994.
■ 22 December 1993. First training flight by the 509th.
■ August 1994. 40% of the B-2 flight test hours had been completed, using the 6 full-scale development aircraft at Edwards Air Force Base, logging over 1,800 hours in more than 395 flights (see June 1990 and March 1991).
■ 10-11 June 1995. AV-8 *Missouri* flew from Whiteman AFB to Paris, France, and return, recording the bomber's first overseas flight.
■ 25 April 1996. Longest flight by this time, at 16 hours 54 minutes (see July 1997).

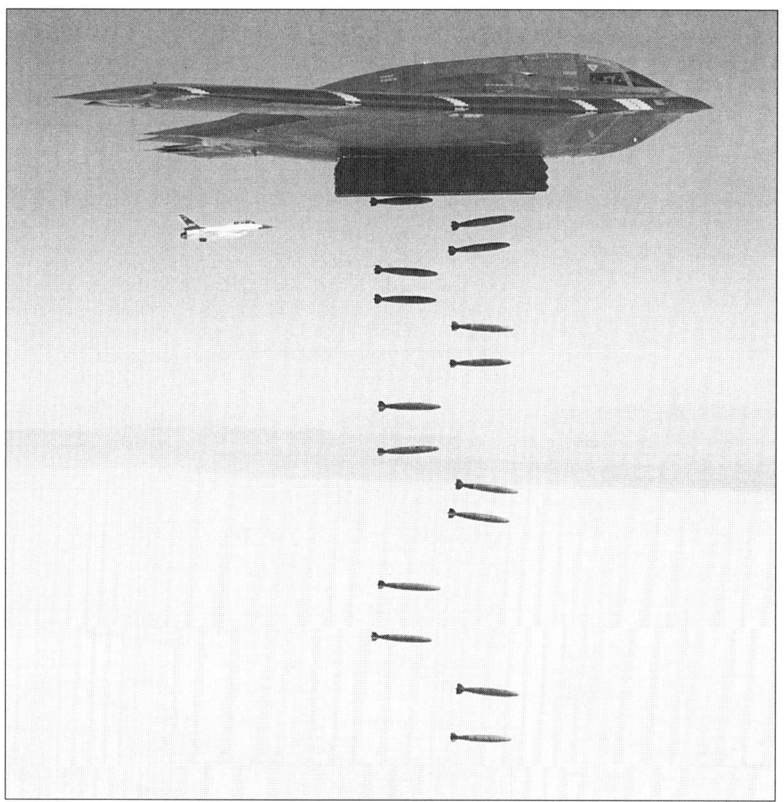

↑ **Northrop Grumman B-2A Spirit dropping 16 bombs during a single pass**

↑ **Northrop Grumman B-2A Spirit general arrangement**

■ 4 February 1996. AV-9 *California* and AV-11 *Washington* undertook the first B-2A overseas deployment, to Guam. 2 training sorties were undertaken on the 6th, including *California* making an appearance at the Singapore Air Show.
■ 3 July 1996. First delivery of a Block 20 B-2A to the 509th (AV-17 *Florida*), having first gone to the Combined Test Force at Edwards AFB on 29 March that year for operational trials.
■ July 1996. USAF took delivery of GAM weapons.
■ 1996. Qualification to carry B-61 and B-83 nuclear weapons.
■ 8 October 1996. 3 B-2As released 16 GBU-36s (GAMs) during trials, from an altitude of 35,000 ft (10,670 m).
■ February 1997. First test drop of a GAM-113 deep-penetration bomb from a B-2A.
■ 1 April 1997. Initial Operational Capability by the 393rd Bomb Squadron of the 509th Bomb Wing.
■ 1997. A B-2A dropped 16 JDAMS in a single pass during trials over the White Sands Missile Range, New Mexico, from an altitude of 39,000 ft (11,900 m).
■ 30 June 1997. Scheduled completion of B-2A flight testing, though AV-3 is continuing flights at Edwards AFB and will be replaced by an operational aircraft when it undergoes Block 30 upgrade in 1998.
■ 30 June 1997. The 6 EMD aircraft (AV-1 to AV-6) had accumulated a total of some 975 missions since July 1989, accumulating 5,000 flight hours.
■ 8-9 July 1997. Longest flight to date, when AV-15 *Alaska* flew for 25 hours 30 minutes.
■ 1 August 1997. First delivery of a Block 30 B-2A (AV-20 *Virginia*).
■ 1998. Final B-2A delivery, as Block 20 AV-21.
■ 1999. Full operational capability with the 715th Bomb Squadron.

Details

Sales/Users: Currently 21 B-2As (including all 6 of the B-2 development aircraft brought up to operational standard), the final 4 B-2As having been funded under FY1994 budget. By the start of 1998, all B-2As operating with the 509th Bomb Wing are Block 20s or final configuration Block 30s. Funding for further production aircraft was first blocked in early 1995; the House of Representatives reportedly wanted 9 more purchased in the FY1998 defence budget but this too was not achieved, but the B-2 industrial base tooling is being preserved. Original plans had envisaged 132 aircraft. 6 flying development B-2s (AV-1 to AV-6) were operated by the 420th Test Squadron of Materiel Command, at the Air Force Flight Test Centre, Edwards AFB (formerly 6520th TS) as part of the Combined Test Force fleet, but are all now being upgraded to Block 30 standard (see Development, 30 June 1997). Initial Block 10 full production aircraft (10 B-2As), were followed by Block 20s (from AV-17), leaving 2 final Block 30s. The entire fleet will be brought up to Block 30 standard by the year 2000 (see Weapons and Avionics, and below). 509th Bomb Wing at Whiteman AFB has 2 squadrons, 393rd and 715th. In mid-1998, 20 B-2As were on the active inventory, of which 8 were primary aircraft authorized, with others involved in further testing or refurbishment to the required Block standard. Upgrade of AV-1-AV-6 to Block 30 standard is underway and is scheduled to be completed by July 2000, taking place at Palmdale, CA; all others are being brought up to Block 30 standard during depot maintenance, for total fleet completion by the first half of 2000, although AV-12 *Kansas*, AV-13 *Nebraska*, AV-14 *Georgia*, AV-15 *Akaska* and AV-16 *Hawaii* were first modified to Block 20 standard. An additional US$331 million in B-2A funding in the FY1998 DoD budget will be used to enhance LO material maintainability, provide battlefield communications and survivability improvements, and possibly to upgrade some cockpit displays.

Crew: 2, pilot on the port side of the flight deck and mission commander to starboard. Provision for a 3rd person as an extra pilot or EW officer. Some 40 B-2A USAF pilots have a monthly routine that includes mission planning, 3 or 4 simulator missions, about 5 T-38 proficiency flights and 2 actual B-2A flying missions.

Cockpit: Rounded windshield glazing, with integral mesh to disperse radar. Centre sticks with artificial feel. Self-contained ladder in the crew entrance hatch.

Crew escape: McDonnell Douglas ACES II zero-zero ejection seats.

Fixed guns: None.

↑ **Northrop Grumman B-2A Spirit**

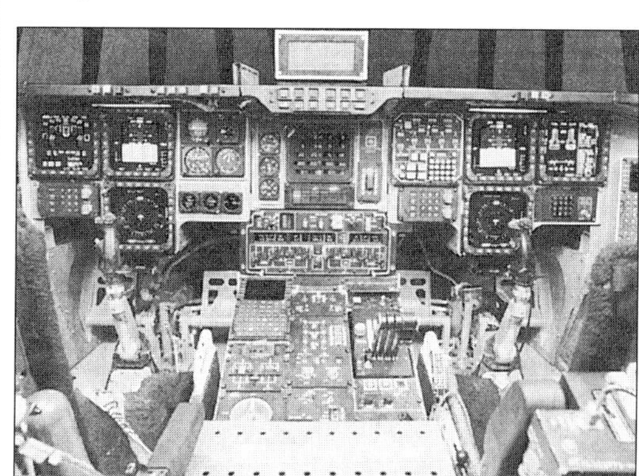

↑ **Northrop Grumman B-2A 2-crew cockpit**

Number of weapon pylons: None.
Expendable weapons and equipment: Up to a 40,000 lb (18,145 kg) load in 2 side-by-side bays in the centre fuselage area, carried on racks or detachable rotary launchers. Vortex-generating spoilers in front of the bays are lowered when the saw-tooth (serrated) edged doors are opened. Under the US Single Integrated Operational Plan (SIOP), the normal nuclear load would be about 25,000 lb (11,340 kg). Original Block 10 B-2As carried 16 × B-83 nuclear or Mk 84 conventional weapons on rotary launchers (or a mixed load), with room for other weapons remaining in the bay. Block 20s added the B-61 nuclear weapon (16 quoted elsewhere but up to 20 thought possible, a figure not altered by Northrop Grumman in its reply) to the options, or 36 CBU-87/89/97/98 cluster bomb munitions, 8 × GAM-113 4,700 lb near-precision deep-penetration bombs for use against underground hard targets such as command-and-control bunkers, or 16 GBU-36s (GAMs or GPS-Aided Munitions) until the full deployment of GBU-31/32 JDAM (certified as 'Operational Capable' in 1997). Block 30 aircraft add the opportunity to carry 80 × 500 lb Mk 82 bombs, or 36 × 750 lb M117 fire bombs, or 80 × Mk 36 or Mk 62 aerial mines, plus full GBU-31/32 capability. Future weapons will include AGM-154A JSOW (from 1999) and JASSM. Typically, 3 B-2As would undertake an attack, with the first 2 releasing their weapons during a single pass, and the third bomber carrying the Mission Commander following behind to make a strike assessment with the synthetic aperture radar and carry out any required further attack, thereby striking up to 32 targets simultaneously.
Radar: Raytheon AN/APQ-181 low-probability-of-intercept radar, with 21 modes.
Flight/weapon system avionics/instrumentation: Lockheed Martin digital computers. Rockwell Collins TCN-250 Tacan, VIR-130A ILS, Milstar satcom and VLF/LF coms. Radar altimeter. EFIS cockpit displays (4 per side, including vertical situation display, port MDU with engine instrumentation data, and starboard MDU for status including control surface position). IFF transponder. No HUD. Selector on the panel provides easy transition from normal flight to an operational "penetration mode", that restricts flight control surface movement and use of avionics to minimize radar and other signals. On-board test system. Angle-of-attack limiter. Hughes GPS-Aided Targeting System or GATS (using the synthetic aperture mode of the radar) allows conventional bombing (with GBU-31/32 or GBU-36) to 20 ft (6 m) accuracy. Special software support for the B-2A comes from Tinker AFB, OK.
Self-protection systems: Loral AN/APR-50 RWR. Northrop Grumman ZSR-63 defensive aids system, possibly to defeat incoming radar energy by emitting radar waves.
Wing characteristics: Flying-wing airframe, with straight leading edges and "saw tooth" trailing edges (see drawing). Entire leading edge and wingtip returns comprise dielectric panels that mask the radar-deflecting triangulated internal wing structure. 2 large dielectric panels on the undersurface, each side of the nose, cover the radar antennae. Northrop Grumman claim that manufacturing was done to the tightest tolerances ever achieved on an aircraft system, with the B-2 accurate to within one-quarter of an inch wingtip-to-wingtip.
Wing control surfaces: All control surfaces are horizontal and form the entire trailing edges of the large outer V sections. The inboard control surfaces are 2-section elevons (functioning as ailerons and elevators), all 4 sections deployed during low-speed flight but with only the outer sections used thereafter. The two 2-section outer control surfaces perform the functions of drag rudders, spoilers and airbrakes, and are split horizontally into upper and lower sections. These are normally in use during flight, with a lower section deflecting up to 90° and an upper section as needed to perform the turn. During landing, the outer surfaces are each deployed at 45° (up and down) as airbrakes, via a panel button. Beaver tail gust load alleviation system (GLAS) with hydraulic actuator forms the centre trailing-edge point of the airframe, aft of the "fuselage"; it is set at about 11° down with the undercarriage deployed, and is also used for pitch trimming in normal flight.
Tail control surfaces: No vertical tail surfaces.
Airbrakes: See Wing control surfaces.
Flight control system: Lockheed Martin quadruple redundant fly-by-wire. Control stick steering.
Fuselage: Blended into the centre section of the wing.
Construction materials: Principally composite materials, including some newly developed, with wide use of graphite and epoxy. Internal honeycomb structure and honeycomb skin, with triangulated leading edges, help deflect and reduce radar returns. RAM top skin and coating, except for the dielectric leading edges; coatings reportedly contribute only some 10% to the B-2A's low RCS and comprise bottom primer, lower coating, top primer, top coating and top tape/adhesion promoter, with foam-filled vertical gaps. Titanium heat protection for the upper wing immediately aft of the nozzles. Nearly 900 new materials and processes were developed in the B-2 programme. Approximately 119 hours of maintenance for each flight hour in 1997, partly to repair the radar absorbing materials that are said to require climate controlled facilities for slow curing; goal is for 60 maintenance hours per flight hour. Despite media reports, there is now no (or virtually no) low-observability degradation to the B-2A due to bad weather, with stronger adhesive tape used to seal seams. 8 portable shelters have been purchased for B-2A maintenance and protection while deployed at forward bases without facilities, while full shelters have been built at some overseas bases, such as Guam.
Engines: 4 General Electric F118-GE-100 non-afterburning turbofans. New tailpipe coating tested from September 1994 to remedy a low observable problem. APU.
Engine rating: Each 19,000 lbf (84.518 kN) class.
Air intakes: 2 paired S-duct intakes of W planform, rounded and blended into the upper wing surface. Saw-tooth boundary layer splitter plates, also to provide cool air for lower infra-red detectability. Auxiliary air inlets about one-third the way back along the intake nacelles open during take-off and low speed flight.
Nozzles: Paired in the wing upper surface, well forward of the wing trailing edges, to mask the efflux from IR detection from below. Nozzles probably produce a wider and thinner plume than usual, possibly directed marginally upward, for fast dispersion in the aircraft's wake.
Flight refuelling probe: Rotating receptacle, aft of cockpit.
Fuel system: Normally 130,000 lb (58,967 kg) of JP-8 in 8 tanks, with automatic fuel management (manual back-up). Pressure refuelling in port wheel well. Possible maximum believed to be up to 200,000 lb (90,718 kg) but not confirmed by Northrop Grumman (previous figure confirmed).
Hydraulic system: 4,000 psi.
Braking system: Brakes, with anti-skid system.

Details for B-2A

PRINCIPAL DIMENSIONS:
Wing span: 172 ft (52.43 m)
Maximum length: 69 ft (21.03 m)
Maximum height: 17 ft (5.18 m)
Height to wingtip: 9 ft (2.74 m)
Height to nose: 10 ft (3.05 m)

WINGS:
Area: 5,140 sq ft (477.52 m^2) estimated
Aspect ratio: 5.76 estimated
Sweepback: 33°

UNDERCARRIAGE:
Type: Retractable Boeing 767 type of extremely wide track, with twin nosewheels. Tandem twin main bogies (4 wheel). Saw-tooth nosewheel door
Wheel track: 40 ft (12.19 m)

WEIGHTS:
Empty: 125,000-153,700 lb (56,700-69,715 kg)
Unarmed take-off: 277,000 lb (125,644 kg)
Normal maximum take-off: 336,500 lb (152,633 kg)
Maximum take-off: 305,000 lb (138,345 kg) initially, increased to 376,000 lb (170,550 kg)

PERFORMANCE:
Maximum speed: Mach 0.8
Cruise speed: Mach 0.78 at 37,000 ft (11,275 m)
Low level training speed: 420 kts (484 mph) 778 km/h
Ecomonic cruise speed: 300-320 kts (345-368 mph) 556-593 km/h
Rotation speed: 139 kts (160 mph) 257 km/h at 277,000 lb weight
Climb-out speed: 280 kts (322 mph) 519 km/h
In flight refuelling speed: 255 kts (294 mph) 472 km/h, with a KC-135 tanker
Approach/landing speed: 130-145 kts (150-167 mph) 240-269 km/h
Take-off distance: 5,500 ft (1,676 m) at 277,000 lb weight
Maximum climb rate: 3,000 ft (915 m) per minute at sea level, at 277,000 lb weight
G limits: 2
Ceiling: 50,000 ft (15,240 m)
Range: 6,000 naut miles (6,900 miles) 11,110 km with a 32,000 lb (14,515 kg) payload, at high altitude
Range with 1 air refuelling: over 10,000 naut miles (11,515 miles) 18,520 km

Northrop Grumman F-5 series and Modernization Programmes

Comments: First flown on 30 July 1959 as the N-156 prototype for the original F-5A version, the F-5 is a lightweight tactical fighter and fighter-bomber that was developed as an inexpensive and simple supersonic aircraft. Development was funded by the US Government, for export under Military Assistance Programmes. Iran became the first MAP nation to operate the F-5, from 1 February 1965. On 11 August 1972, the first flight of the much improved F-5E Tiger II took place, funded by the US Government as an International Fighter Aircraft to replace the F-5A. First deliveries to the USAF to train foreign personnel began in 1973.

↑ Northrop Grumman F-5E Tiger IV cockpit. Note the additional circular gauges to the right of the HUD would be replaced on production upgrades

It is estimated by Northrop Grumman that about 1,500 F-5 variants remain in use, and Paraguay (which is receiving 10 F-5Es and 2 F-5Fs from Taiwan) and Sudan with E/Fs should be incorporated into the list of operators given in the 1996-97 edition of *WA&SD*. Interestingly, the Philippines has recently acquired additional F-5A/Bs from South Korea, Jordan and Taiwan, to be used as lead-in fighters, and is studying proposals for structural and avionics upgrade. In addition to those nations that no longer use F-5s (including Canada), Uruguay (then indicated as a potential operator) should also be deleted. To the list of F-5 upgrade programmes given in the previous edition should be added the F-5E Tiger IV avionics and structural upgrade, performed by a team including AIDC, CASA, Northrop Grumman and Samsung. Turkey is among nations actively exploring upgrades, again for use as lead-in trainers. A description and several illustrations of F-5 programmes can be found in the 1996-97 edition of *WA&SD*, pages 150-151.

Northrop Grumman F-14 Tomcat

Comments: First flown on 21 December 1970, the F-14 variable-geometry carrier-borne long-range air superiority fighter with secondary air-to-ground capability and reconnaissance, has been

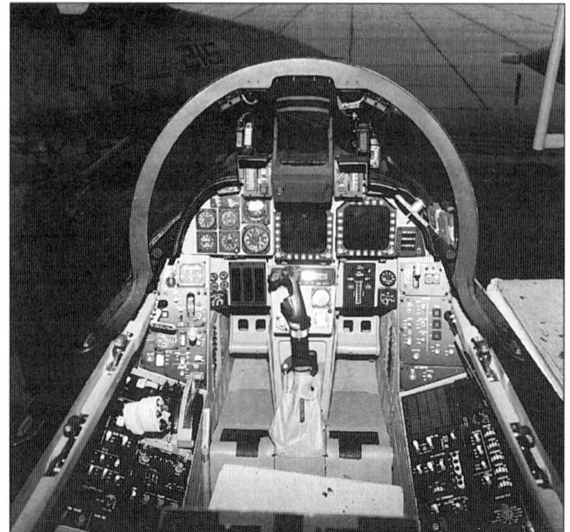
↑ Pilot's cockpit of the Northrop Grumman F-14D Tomcat

deployed with the US Navy since October 1972. Others have served with Iran as land-based aircraft since 1976. On 20 July 1992 the final newly built F-14 was handed over to the US Navy, as the last of 37 F-14Ds (others were produced by conversion). To permit some US Navy F-14s to undertake strike missions using laser-guided bombs and to perform forward air-control duties by day or night, partly to compensate for the withdrawal of the A-6E/TRAM Intruder, 75 F-14s were given Lockheed Martin Low Altitude Navigation and Targeting Infrared for Night (LANTIRN) pods. In 1998 a further 25 pods were purchased. In addition, in late 1996 sea trials took place of an F-14 installed with a new GEC-Marconi digital flight control system (DFCS), using similar fly-by-wire computers as used in Eurofighter. All F-14s are expected tc be equipped, with IOC for the second half of 1998. DFCS has many advantages, not least making recovery easier from inertia-coupled departures.

Northrop Grumman has made only minor changes to the F-14 entry that appeared in the 1996-97 edition of *WA&SD*, namely the addition of LANTIRN, wing span of 38 ft 2 ins (11.63 m) swept (instead of 38 ft 2.5 ins, 11.65 m), maximum length of 61 ft 11 ins (18.87 m), empty weight of 41,500 lb (18,824 kg), maximum take-off weight 70,000 lb (31,751 kg), and take-off distance on land 1,150 ft (350 m) minimum. For a full description of F-14, refer to the 1996-97 edition of *WA&SD*, pages 151-152.

Raytheon Aircraft Company — USA

Corporate address:
PO Box 85, Wichita, KS 67201-0085.

Telephone: +1 316 676 7111
Facsimile: +1 316 676 8286
Web site: http://raytheon.com

Founded:
1994, as a division of Raytheon International Inc, to merge the Beech Aircraft Corporation (acquired in 1980 but previously operated as an independent company) and Raytheon Corporate Jets (former British Aerospace Corporate Jets purchased on 6 August 1993).

Employees: 13,800.

Information:
Jim Gregory (Director of Corporate Affairs – *telephone* +1 316 676 7689, *facsimile* +1 316 676 8867); Pat Zerbe (Media Manager, *telephone* +1 316 676 7603); Corporate Affairs Department (*telephone* +1 316 676 8674, *facsimile* +1 316 676 5687).

FACILITIES

▪ Final assembly, engineering and support activities for the Hawker corporate jets are being relocated from the UK to Wichita. BAe continues to provide fabricated parts and major subassemblies. The Little Rock, Arkansas facility of the former Raytheon Corporate Jets operates an aircraft painting operation, and supplies custom interiors and avionics for the Hawker line.

ACTIVITIES

▪ A subsidiary of the Raytheon Company.
▪ Designs, manufactures, markets and supports business jets, turboprop and piston-engined aircraft, for commercial/civil, military and regional airline markets. Raytheon's propeller-driven aircraft continue to be marketed under the name Beech, while its business jets retain the name Hawker, with the exception of the Raytheon-designed Premier I. See Airliners and General Aviation sections. New Training Systems Division for Texan II production and support, and for export sales.
▪ Produces the AQM-37C, MQM-107D and Super MQM missile targets.

Beech T-6A Texan II/PC-9 Mk II

First flight: 15 July 1998 for T-6A Texan II.
Role: Primary undergraduate flight trainer and undergraduate navigator trainer for the USAF and US Navy, based on the Pilatus PC-9.
Fatigue life: 18,720 flying hours.

Aims

▪ To replace the USAF's T-37s at AETC (Air Education and Training Command) bases as a primary trainer.
▪ To replace US Navy T-34s.
▪ PC-9 Mk II based on the Swiss PC-9 but with significant modifications (estimated 90% redesign), including a pressurized cockpit, Martin Baker zero-zero ejection seats, single-point refuelling, Raytheon-patented computer-controlled trim-aid device, improved bird-strike protection, a cockpit that accommodates 95% of eligible pilots, and more (see below).

Development

▪ 2 Swiss-built Pilatus PC-9s initially delivered to Beech to assist in development work for the JPATS competition, 1 becoming the PT-1 as the engineering development aircraft and accumulating over 260 flying hours during its test programme.
▪ 23 December 1992. Maiden flight of the first of 2 Beech-built PC-9 Mk II prototypes (PT-2).
▪ 29 July 1993. First flight of PT-3 prototype, subsequently used for the official JPATS evaluation programme.
▪ 22 June 1995. Announced winner of the USAF/US Navy JPATS competition (Joint Primary Aircraft Training System).
▪ 5 February 1996. Contract awarded to Raytheon.
▪ June 1996. Completion of the Preliminary Design Review.
▪ November 1996. Critical design review completed.
▪ January 1997. Completion of the Critical Design Review, freezing the aircraft's configuration.
▪ October 1997. Raytheon and the USAF signed a contract modification for the Ground Based Training System (GBTS) element of the JPATS programme. Valued at US$71 million, it covers 4 years of engineering and manufacturing development for GBTS components, US$55 million will go to FlightSafety Services Corp, which Raytheon selected as the GBTS subcontractor in April 1997 to produce aircraft training simulators, the Operational Support System and coursework for the GBTS.
▪ December 1997. 24 T-6A-1s were ordered for the NATO Flying Training Canada (NFTC) programme.
▪ November 1998. First Texan II deliveries.
▪ April 1999. Randolph AFB, headquarters of AETC, will receive the first production Texan IIs.
▪ August 2001. IOC for the GBTS at Laughlin AFB, TX.
▪ 2002. Expected peak rate production, at 43 aircraft per year.
▪ 2003. Start of US Navy training with the Texan II, at Whiting Field.
▪ 2017. Final Texan II deliveries.

Details

Sales/Users: Requirements are for 372 for the USAF and 339 for the US Navy for pilot training, plus 29 for the joint specialized undergraduate navigator training programme. 46 production aircraft ordered by March 1998 for the services, with the latest 22 to be delivered from February 2000. Initial contract estimate is US$4 billion. Scheduled USAF pilot training bases are Randolph AFB,TX (from 1999); Laughlin AFB, TX (from May 2001); Vance AFB, OK (from June 2004); and Columbus AFB, MS (from September 2006). Sheppard AFB, TX, to operate the Euro-NATO Joint Jet Pilot Training programme (from November 2008). US Navy training will begin at Naval Air Station Whiting Field, FL.

↑ Raytheon Beech PC-9 Mk II in PT-3 form

Details for PC-9 Mk II/T-6A Texan II

PRINCIPAL DIMENSIONS:
As for Pilatus PC-9

UNDERCARRIAGE:
Retractable, with hydraulic nosewheel steering. Permits a 13 ft (3.96 m) per second sink rate
Main wheel tyre size: 20 × 4.4
Nose wheel tyre size: 16 × 4.4
Wheel base: 8 ft 7 ins (2.61 m)
Wheel track: 7 ft 7 ins (2.31 m)

WEIGHTS:
Empty: 4,415 lb (2,002 kg)
Maximum take-off: 6,300 lb (2,858 kg)

PERFORMANCE:
Maximum speed: 345 kts (397 mph) 639 km/h
Maximum maintained speed: 320 kts (368 mph) 593 km/h, or 302 kts (348 mph) 560 km/h at 31,000 ft (9,450 m), or 270 kts (311 mph) 500 km/h at sea level
Minimum level flight speed: 120 kts (138 mph) 222 km/h
Rotation speed: 80-90 kts (92-104 mph) 148-167 km/h IAS
Take-off speed: 95 kts (109 mph) 176 km/h IAS
Landing speed: 90 kts (104 mph) 167 km/h IAS
Stall speed: 77 kts (89 mph) 143 km/h IAS
Climb speed: 140 kts (161 mph) 259 km/h IAS
Field length: 4,000 ft (1,220 m) with safe training margin
Maximum climb rate: 3,144 ft (958 m) per minute
Roll rate: 130° per second
Operational ceiling: 31,000 ft (9,450 m)
G limits: +7, -3.5
Range: 900 naut miles (1,036 miles) 1,668 km
Duration: 4 hours

Additional 24 T-6A-1s ordered by Bombardier Services for the NATO Flying Training Canada (NFTC) programme. Chilean Air Force to purchase up to 25 PC-9 Mk IIs. Entire Texan II production at the new 191,000 sq ft (17,744 m^2) Training Systems Division.
Crew: Pupil and instructor, the rear seat raised and front seat modified to offer good forward vision from the rear cockpit. Said to be suitable for 95% of eligible pilots, ranging from about 5 ft to 6 ft 3 ins (1.5-1.9 m) in height and about 105-245 lb (48–110 kg) in weight.
Cockpit: Bird-strike resistant and enlarged canopy, to withstand a 4 lb (1.8 kg) bird hitting at 270 kts. Opens to starboard, via 1 handle, and encompasses a miniature detonating cord (MDC) with automatic and manual detonation (via a handle). Pressurized cockpit (maximum differential 3.5 psi), with digital displays.
Crew escape: Modified Martin Baker Mk US16LA zero-zero ejection seats, each with an emergency oxygen bottle that is automatically activated on ejection. Should the MDC fail to work, seat protrusions penetrate the canopy to prevent injury to the crew on ejection.
Flight/weapon system avionics/instrumentation: Almost identical cockpits. Principally AlliedSignal Bendix/King digital avionics, with

↑ Raytheon Beech PC-9 Mk II instrument panel

active matrix liquid crystal displays comprising a top-central primary flight display (PFD) and a horizontal situation display (HSI) below. AHRS, flight data recorder, GPS, collision warning and more. Includes some analogue back-up instrumentation.
Wing control surfaces: Aileron movement +20°, -11°. Split flap, movement 23° take-off and 50° landing. 10 ins (254 mm) stall strips on leading-edges (inboard).
Tail control surfaces: Computer-controlled Trim Aid Device (TAD) automatically minimizes the torque effect of the turboprop engine, without requiring constant rudder control from the pilot; rudder movement ±24°. Elevator movement +18°, -16°. Reshaped, repositioned and larger ventral fin.
Airbrake: Hydraulically-operated, perforated type, under the mid fuselage (70° maximum).
Flight control system: Manual, with cables, pullies, bellcranks and tubes.
Construction: Strengthened aft fuselage, tailplane and wings for extended service life and to improve birdstrike protection (see Cockpit).
Engine: Pratt & Whitney Canada PT6A-68 turboprop engine, with Power Management System (PMS). Power Management Unit (PMU) of the PMS is a Motorola 68020 microprocessor-based, digital electronic engine control unit, setting the engine power based on the Power Control Lever (PCL) setting, engine operating conditions, and ambient temperature and pressure conditions sensed by the engine; PMU also provides signal conditioning for automatic starting, computation and output drive functions, propeller control, gas generator power control and exceedance protection; software contains system fault reporting, fault accommodation and diagnostic routines. Electro-hydromechanical Propeller Interface Unit (PIU) mounted to the reduction gearbox, provides a propeller speed signal to the PMU and responds to speed control signals.
Engine rating: 1,700 shp (1,268 kW) at 2,000 rpm, flat rated to 1,100 shp (820 kW) to increase time between overhauls.
Air intakes: Fixed geometry and constant bypass.
Fuel system: 700 litres. Fuel Management Unit (FMU) is an electro-hydromechanical control unit to schedule fuel flow to the engine. Up to 45 seconds of inverted flight via a collector tank. Single-point refuelling, although overwing points remain. Pressure fuelling takes 3 minutes; or 6 minutes to remove fuel.
Electrical system: 28 volt DC.
Hydraulic system: 3,000 psi.

Multi-national

Aircraft Technology Industries (Airtech) — Indonesia/Spain

Corporate address:
Founded by IPTN of Indonesia and CASA of Spain as an equal joint venture. See Spain in this section for CASA company details, and IPTN in the Airliners section.

Founded: 1980.

ACTIVITIES

▪ The CN 235 is basically an airliner and freighter, and full details of these are given in the Airliners section. The following information applies only to the maritime versions.

Airtech CN 235 Persuader MP and ASW/ASUW, and CN 235 MPA

Role: Medium-range maritime patrol, maritime surveillance for fishing control and EEZ protection, and search and rescue in MP form. Short-range submarine detection/tracking/attack, anti-surface vessel, and over-the-horizon targeting in ASW/ASUW form.

Aims

▪ Based on the CN 235 M military transport.
▪ Persuader system comprises the aircraft and a ground Mission Support Facility.
▪ User friendly integrated and modular mission system.
▪ Highly interoperable software – Ada high level soft language.
▪ Mission sensor NATO compatible.
▪ Built-in expansion capability.
▪ Ready to launch weapons in the torpedo bay.
▪ C^3I interoperable system, with data link.
▪ Maritime surveillance time on target >10 hours. ASW/ASUW range up to 500 naut miles (576 miles) 926 km, and 4 to 8 hours time on target.

Details *(based on CN 235 Persuader, unless stated)*

Sales/Users: Among 174 military CN 235s ordered by 1998, the Royal Brunei Air Wing requested 3 MPAs and the Indonesian Air Force 3 MPAs from IPTN production lines, while the Irish Air Corps has 2 CN 235 Series 100 Persuader MPs and Spain ordered 6 Persuader MPs from CASA. An undisclosed Asian customer is negotiating for MPA.

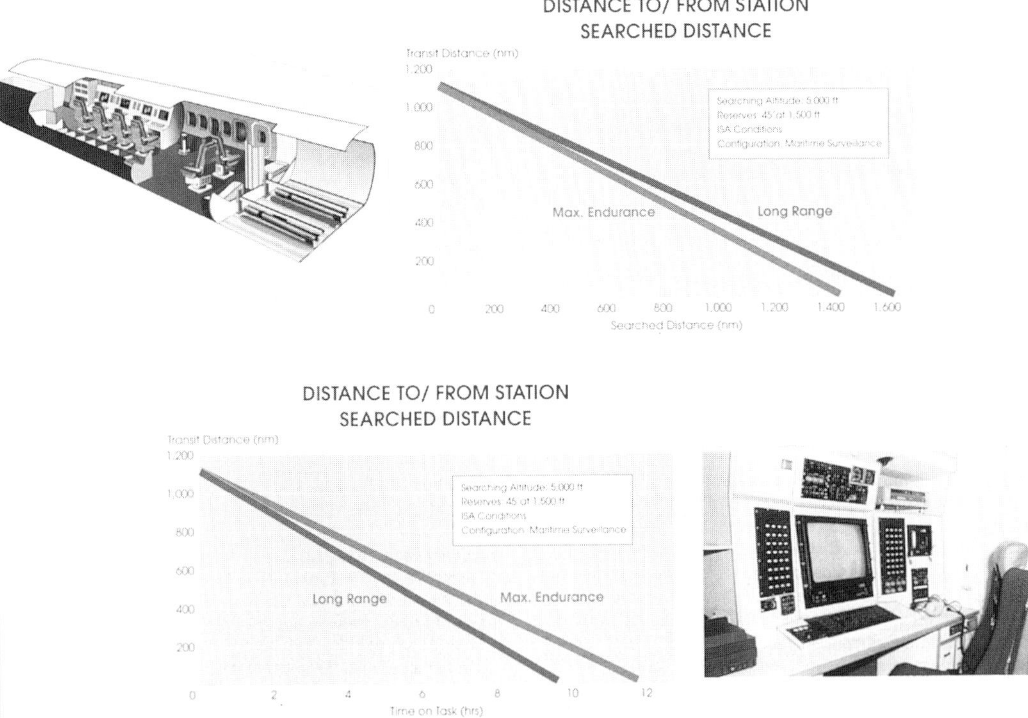

↑ **CN 235 Persuader patrol mission search distance and time on task graphs, plus a typical MP operators' cabin layout (*top, left*) and a sensor operator station with a port-side programmable display keyboard (PDK), colour display, starboard PDK, keyboard and cursor control** *(courtesy CASA)*

Aircraft variants:
CN 236 Persuader is the CASA version and has a mission system structured around the CASA/Litton Tactical Central Processor (based on a Motorola 68040 MP inside a VME) via a MIL-STD-1553B digital databus, with work stations (up to 4, as tactical console, non-acoustic consoles and acoustic console), allowing different missions to be performed by adding to or integrating those specific sensors required. The integrated mission system controls and emulates all the navigation and tactical sensor controls, the recording equipment and the tactical communications with the C^3I centres and other co-operating units. Central computer is a modular processor based on commonly used NATO systems. Typical for Persuader MP is a 360° scan Litton APS-504(V)5 search radar in an underfuselage radome with high detection performance in sea states 1 to 4 plus anti-jamming capability and a track-while-scan mode for up to 20 targets simultaneously, FLIR Systems FLIR-2000HP in a 'chin' ball turret (integrated with radar for better mission co-ordination), Litton/CASA TDMS mission processor, AGI Agiflite hand-held camera, and liferaft/survival

↑ **CASA-built CN 235 Series 100 Persuader MP of the Irish Air Corps**

↑ **IPTN-built CN 235 MPA with nose radar**

kit deployment for maritime surveillance and SAR missions. Normal crew of 6. For ASW/ASUW, the mission equipment can include ISAR/SAR search radar, IFF interrogator, FLIR/TV, Litton ALR-85(V) ESM, acoustic package, MAD, data link and a dedicated navigation package. Weapons bay. Bubble windows for observers that can be opened in flight. Crew rest area for long missions.

CN 235 MPA is the IPTN version, offered with either a similar underfuselage radome as the Persuader (though of different shape) or the newer nose radome. Avionics suite according to customer's requirements. Specified or known radar choices include Raytheon APS-134, GEC-Marconi Seaspray 4000 and Thomson-CSF Ocean Master, while other avionics choices include GEC-Marconi MRT or FLIR Systems Safire FLIR (carried in an undernose turret on the version with nose radar), Litton LN-92 ring laser gyro INS, Trimble TNL 7900 Omega/GPS, and Cossor 3500 IFF. Argosystems AR-700 ESM sensors in an above-cockpit fairing and at the tail, with alternatives being GEC-Marconi Sky Guardian or Litton ALR-93(V)4.

AMX International Ltd — Brazil/Italy

Corporate address:
AMX International is a partnership of Aermacchi and Alenia of Italy and Embraer of Brazil. Addresses and Telephone/Facsimile numbers can be found under the individual companies in the earlier pages of this section.

ACTIVITIES

▪ The original agreement defined the workshare in the AMX programme at 23.6% Aermacchi (front fuselage and tail cone), Aeritalia (which became Alenia) at 46.7% (central fuselage, stabilizers, rudder, ailerons and radome), and 29.7% Embraer (wings, engine air intakes, pylons and drop tanks). The workshare was assigned according to the number of aircraft originally required by the Italian and Brazilian air forces.

AMX International AMX/A-1

First flight: 15 May 1984.
Role: Close air support, interdiction, close interdiction against forces behind the battlefield area, and reconnaissance, with secondary counter-air role. Developments include variants for electronic combat, anti-ship and night attack.

Aims

▪ Series production integrated and based at 3 final assembly lines, 2 in Italy and 1 in Brazil, also covering production of 2-seaters.
▪ Survival in a hostile environment, with minimal vulnerability, aided by low-level flight and good low-level flying characteristics, high speed, low detectability, low infra-red signature, integrated ECM, IR warning, radar warning, chaff and flares.
▪ High state of readiness and safety. Pre-flight built-in test equipment. 15-minute reaction time can be maintained for 30 days with only limited servicing being provided. With systems activated on standby, AMX can be held at 5 minutes readiness for 6 hours at full performance or, with systems not activated, can be scrambled in 5 minutes with decreased performance.
▪ Good take-off and landing performance: self-starting, high-lift wing devices and brakes.
▪ High speed penetration with heavy military loads.
▪ High navigation and attack accuracy.
▪ Post-failure operability. Ability to recover to base even if damaged. Multipath structures and systems protection. Should a double failure of both the hydraulic and electrical systems occur, the aircraft remains controllable through manual back-up of flight controls.
▪ Integrated penetration aids.

Development

▪ 1977. A weapon system specification was issued by the Italian Air Force for a tactical fighter-bomber to replace the F-104G Starfighter and G91, and the resulting programme involved Aermacchi and Alitalia. About the same time the Brazilian Air Force defined a requirement for a similar aircraft to replace the Xavante. The common need resulted in Embraer's involvement in the joint programme.
▪ July 1980. Aermacchi, Aeritalia and Embraer signed an agreement defining their respective participation in the development phase. An industrial agreement was then ratified by a Memorandum of Intent between the Brazilian and Italian Governments. The agreement included provisions for performing an intensive flight test programme based on 6 prototypes, 4 operating in Italy and 2 in Brazil. A seventh was built (see 1 June).
▪ 15 May 1984. First flight of an AMX, performed from Aeritalia's Turin-Caselle facility.
▪ 1 June 1984. The first prototype was lost in an accident on its fifth test flight.
▪ 19 November 1984. First flight of the second prototype, assembled by Aermacchi.
▪ 16 October 1985. First flight of a Brazilian prototype (FAB YA-1 4200) from Embraer's facility, the fifth aircraft to fly but officially the fourth prototype. Officially presented to Brazilian and Italian authorities on the 22nd.
▪ 11 May 1988. First flight of a production AMX in Italy.
▪ April 1989. The Italian Air Force began receiving its first AMXs.
▪ 12 August 1989. First flight of a Brazilian production A-1.
▪ 17 October 1989. Brazil's 1° Esquadrão, 16° Grupo of Comando Aérotático (1°/16° GAv) received the first 2 production A-1s. This unit had been created at Santa Cruz to operate AMX.
▪ 14 March 1990. First flight of an AMX-T 2-seater.
▪ 1995. First SCP-01-equipped A-1 entered Brazilian service (see Radar), the radar having been tested on a modified BAe 125.
▪ 1999. End of Brazilian production according to current orders.

Details

Sales/Users: 192 AMX/A-1s delivered by 1998. Brazil has so far ordered 45 single-seaters (A-1s) and 11 2-seaters from an overall stated requirement of 79 and 15 respectively, first going to 1°/16° GAv at Santa Cruz. Embraer production charts for the AMX indicate 42 were built up to April 1998, with 12 for delivery in 1998 and 1 for 1999, with none scheduled thereafter. Italy had received 149 AMXs by early 1998, from 238 required. Italy is expected to convert 10 2-seaters to an EW role (see Aircraft variants), while reports suggest the Air Force might sell 18 early-batch AMXs rather than update them to latest standard. New AMX ATAs ordered by Venezuela.
Crew: Pilot, with an 18° below horizon downward view over the nose. Tandem seats for the 2-seater (see Aircraft variants).
Cockpit: HOTAS. Microtecnica ECS system.
Crew escape: Martin Baker Mk 10L zero-zero ejection seat, cleared up to 560 kts and 50,000 ft.
Fixed guns: 2 × 30-mm DEFA 554 cannon in A-1s, and 1 × 20-mm M61A1 Vulcan multi-barrel cannon in Italian AMX.
Ammunition: 350 rounds for M61.
Number of weapon pylons: 5, each station able to have twin carriers (2 inboard wing stations able to have triple), plus wingtip rails. See diagram.
Expendable weapons and equipment: Up to 8,378 lb (3,800 kg) weight. Can include Mk 82/83/84 free-fall or retarded bombs, cluster bombs, rockets, stand-off weapons dispenser, precision-guided munitions (requiring electro-optical guidance), air-to-ground missiles, anti-radiation missiles, or anti-ship missiles (requires radar or electro-optical guidance - see Aircraft variants), plus short-range air-to-air missiles on the wingtip stations (Mol for Brazil and AIM-9L Sidewinders for Italy).
Additional stores: Reconnaissance packages (Aeroeletrônica photographic or other sensors) are carried internally, often leaving the centreline and underwing hardpoints free for weapons or fuel tanks. Palletized camera sets can be supported by an infra-red and optical reconnaissance pod installed on the centreline station (some Italian AMXs carry Orpheus). Thomson-CSF CLDP laser designator pods for Italian AMXs. Other options include infra-red/electro-optical pods for smart weapons. See Fuel System.
Radar: SMA/Tecnasa SCP-01 Scipio multi-mode coherent radar in the A-1. FIAR Grifo X plus multi-mode pulse Doppler radar in Italian AMX. Grifo ASV P2801 has been developed for the maritime strike version of AMX, with 65 naut mile range against large warships (see Radar section).
Flight/weapon system avionics/instrumentation: Databus and modular concept of the avionics system provide the capacity for future growth or new roles. 2 electronic flight computers (including Microtechnica air data computer)/digital bus system (MIL-STD-1553B) to provide redundancy to tolerate battle damage; stores management system. Brazilian A-1s have VOR/ILS. Italian AMXs have Litton INS with AHRS and Tacan. Instrumentation includes IR/TV (FLIR system and associated TV camera) and map head-down displays, and OMI/Alenia HUD (GEC-Marconi colour TV head-down display repeater in the rear cockpit of AMX-Ts, providing HUD data). U/VHF coms. IFF. NVG capable.
Self-protection systems: Elettronica active and passive ECM. Radar warning devices, missile launch and approach warning receiver, chaff and IR flares.
Wing characteristics: Shoulder-mounted, moderately sweptback, with high-lift devices.
Wing control surfaces: Ailerons, double-slotted Fowler trailing-edge flaps and leading-edge slats. Twin spoilers ahead of each pair of flaps.

↑Italian Air Force AMXs carrying AIM-9L Sidewinders and auxiliary tanks

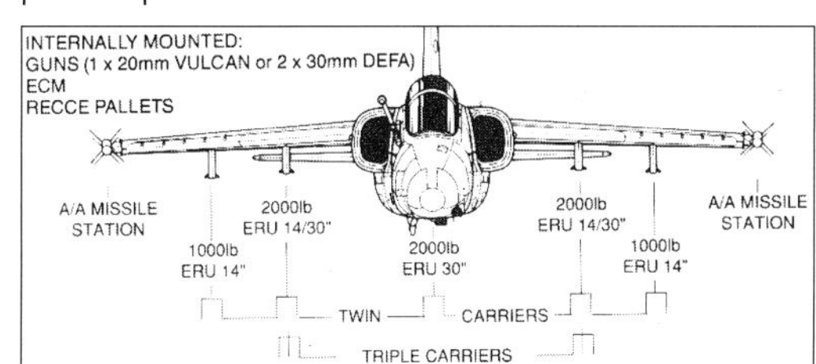

↑Weapon arrangement diagram for AMX/A-1 *(courtesy Embraer)*

Details for AMX/A-1

PRINCIPAL DIMENSIONS
Wing span: 32 ft 8.5 ins (9.97 m) with wingtip missiles, 29 ft 1.5 ins (8.87 m) without
Maximum length: 43 ft 5 ins (13.23 m)
Maximum height: 14 ft 11 ins (4.55 m)

WINGS:
Area: 226 sq ft (21 m^2)
Aspect ratio: 3.75
Sweepback: 27° 30' at 25% chord

TAIL UNIT:
Tailplane span: 17 ft 1 ins (5.2 m)
Tailplane area: 54.9 sq ft (5.1 m^2)
Fin area: 45.9 sq ft (4.27 m^2)

UNDERCARRIAGE:
Type: Retractable, with steerable (±60°) and self centring nosewheel
Main wheel tyre size: 670 × 210-12
Nose wheel tyre size: 457 × 140
Wheel base: 15 ft 5 ins (4.7 m)
Wheel track: 7 ft 1 ins (2.15 m)
Turning radius: 24 ft 9 ins (7.53 m)

WEIGHTS:
Empty, operating: 14,771 lb (6,700 kg)
Maximum take-off: 28,660 lb (13,000 kg)
Landing: 15,430 lb (7,000 kg) typically

PERFORMANCE:
Maximum speed: Mach 0.86 at 30,000 ft (9,145 m), Mach 0.84 at sea level
Take-off distance: 3,222 ft (982 m) at sea level
Landing distance: 1,523 ft (464 m) at sea level
Maximum climb rate: 10,250 ft (3,124 m) per minute at sea level
G limits: +7.33, -3
Ceiling: 42,650 ft (13,000 m)
Radius of action: up to 500 naut miles (575 miles) 926 km
Ferry range: 1,800 naut miles (2,073 miles) 3,335 km

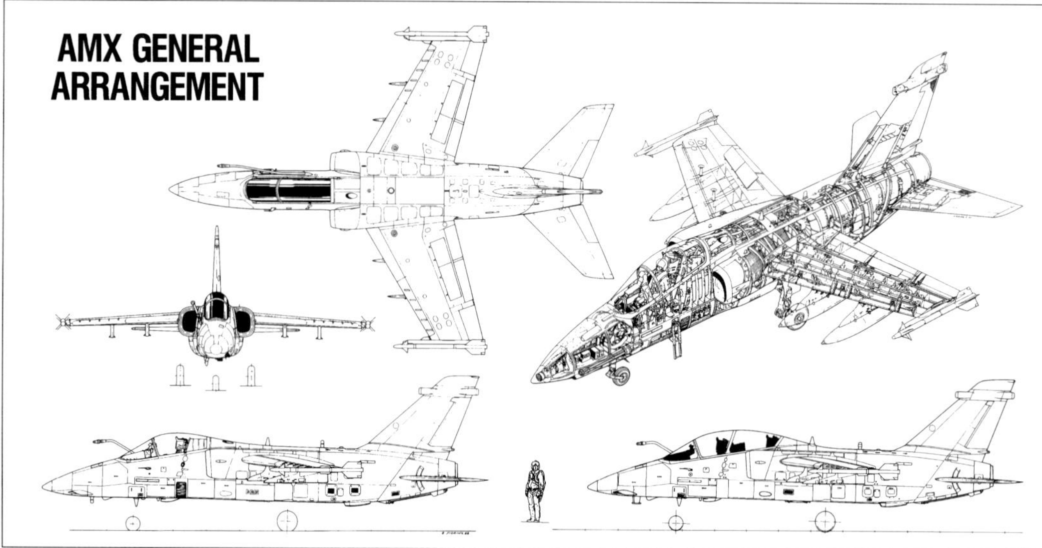

↑ AMX general arrangement (including AMX-T/A-1B side view, *right*), and cutaway *(courtesy Embraer)*

Tail control surfaces: Elevators, rudder and variable-incidence tailplane.
Airbrakes: See spoilers under Wing control surfaces.
Flight control system: Fly-by-wire system for tailplane, rudder and spoilers. Hydraulically actuated ailerons and elevators. Electro-hydraulic flaps and slats. Mechanical back-up of principal surfaces (see Aims).
Construction materials: Principally aluminium alloy, with composites fin and elevators.
Engine: One Rolls-Royce Spey RB168-807 turbofan, built by FiatAvio and Celma-Cia. Fiat Argo APU for engine starting and ground power.
Engine rating: 11,030 lbf (49.06 kN).
Flight refuelling probe: Probe to the starboard side of the cockpit when fitted.
Fuel system: 3,500 litres. Inboard wing pylons can carry 1,100 litre drop tanks, and outboard 580 litre.
Electrical system: Main AC supply using 2 × 30kVA generators, offering 115/200 volts at 400Hz, with 2 transformer/rectifiers to produce 28 volt DC power. In a total electrical loss, electro-avionic loads are fed by a 36 amp-hour ni-cd emergency battery.
Hydraulic system: 2 independent systems (3,000 psi) powered by engine-driven pumps. In the event of damage or failure of the pumps, accumulators provide emergency supply for undercarriage extension, braking and steering, and flight control actuation in critical phases.
Braking system: Hydraulic with anti-skid, plus ground arrester hook capability.

Aircraft variants:
AMX and ***A-1*** are the Italian and Brazilian single-seaters respectively, used for attack and reconnaissance, with secondary counter-air.
AMX-T and ***A-1B*** are the Italian and Brazilian 2-seat advanced trainers respectively, suited to operational conversion and full combat use. Internal cannon, wingtip missiles, internal electronic warfare equipment, and chaff and flares of the single-seater, with extensive avionics. The second cockpit is placed in tandem with the normal single-seat cockpit, having had 1 fuel tank deleted and the environmental control system repositioned. It has full duplication of displays and controls (but no HUD), plus a colour TV head-down display repeater. See next for Italian EW modifications.
Developments of AMX/A-1/AMX-T could include models for: *Electronic combat* with anti-radiation missiles, emission location system, data link and soft-kill jammer pod (it is believed 10 Italian 2-seaters were assigned to be modified for this role, as replacements for Piaggio PD808GEs); *Anti-ship* with Grifo ASV P2801 radar offering sea search and possibly armed with Exocet, Marte, Kormoran, Harpoon or Sea Eagle missiles; and *Night attack* carrying FLIR, wide-angle HUD, laser designator and night vision goggles.
Super AMX proposed by Alenia for export with 'glass' cockpit, new avionics including global positioning navigation, helmet-mounted displays, new multi-mode radar and wide-angle HUD, upgraded HOTAS, integrated defence aids, and possibly a non-afterburning variant of EJ200 engine.

AI(R) – Aero International (Regional) France/Italy/UK

Comments: AI(R) was founded on 1 January 1996, when Avions de Transport Regional (ATR) merged its activities with British Aerospace Regional Aircraft (comprising Avro International Aerospace and Jetstream Aircraft). AI(R) became responsible for all marketing, sales, customer support and product development. However, on 3 July 1998 AI(R) was dissolved and ATR and British Aerospace Regional Aircraft (BARAL) re-assumed responsibility for their own aircraft, though BARAL retains an office in Toulouse.

Avions de Transport Regional (ATR) France/Italy

Corporate address:
1 Allée Pierre-Nadot, 31712 Blagnac Cedex, France.
Telephone: +33 5 62 21 62 21
Facsimile: +33 5 62 21 63 18
Web site: http://www.atregional.com
Founded: 1982.
Information:
Gian Carlo Fré (Press & Information Director - *telephone* +33 5 62 21 66 01, *facsimile* +33 5 62 21 63 18)

ACTIVITIES

- Owned by Alenia of Italy and Aerospatiale of France.
- The current product range comprises the ATR 42 and ATR 72. (see Airliners section).

Avions de Transport Regional ATR 42 and ATR 72 Maritime Patrol

Role: EEZ enforcement, search and rescue, surveillance vessel search and identification, maritime and coastal surveillance, pollution detection and control, anti-surface vessel, and anti-submarine warfare. Additional missions can be medevac and transport.

Aims

- Basic aircraft platform is the ATR 42-400, although ATR 42-500 and ATR 72-210A are also proposed.
- Detect, localize and track 1 or several targets simultaneously, by day or night and in rough sea conditions.
- State-of-the-art search radar for long-distance detection by limiting sea clutter effect, an electro-optical device for day/night close detection, and an accurate navigation system.
- Collaboration with other military/paramilitary units using dedicated communications to transmit voice and data, the information coded.

Details

Sales/Users: Developed initially for the Guardia di Finanza (Italian customs service), ordering 2.
Crew: 2 flight crew, with optional third seat in cockpit. 2 modular-type workstations in basic configuration, with third and fourth if required, fitted directly on the airliner's passenger seat tracks and are easily removed for configuration changes (see Avionics). Debriefing and rest area with a table and passenger-type seats.
Number of weapon pylons: Provision for external load attachment on the fuselage.
Expendable weapons and equipment: Weapons and stores for anti-ship and anti-submarine roles, unspecified in early 1998. Thiokol LUU-2A/B flare launcher.
Additional stores: CFE Agiflite or Kodak hand-held camera for observers. Spectrolab SX 16P searchlight.
Radar: Raytheon (TI) SV 2022, offering high resolution pulse-compression and scan-to-scan processing to reduce sea and rain clutter while optimizing small target detection (less than 54 sq ft, 5 m^2), and 32 target track-while-scan capability.
Flight/weapon system avionics/instrumentation: Avionics systems interconnected via a MIL-STD-1553B databus, and general management of all sensors performed by the mission

↑ ATR 42 Maritime Patrol operated by the Guardia di Finanza

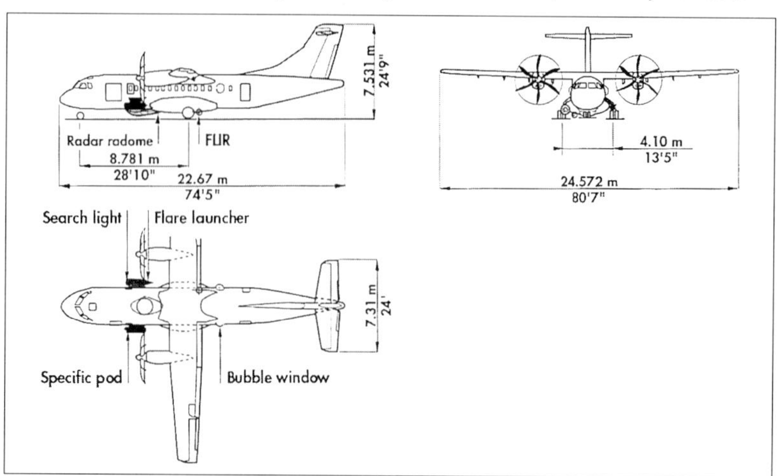

↑ ATR 42 Maritime Patrol *(courtesy ATR)*

software in the GFSA Mission Management System (MMS). Software of the Mission Data Handling System (MIDAHS) provides interface and manages the surveillance and search sensors, mission communications and other equipment; manages the tactical video presentations, including information from the radar, ESM, flight plan and digital map; presents, digitalizes and memorizes the video information from the sensors; stores collected mission information in a data base; plans the mission in accordance with the flight pattern stored in the Honeywell FMZ 2000 Flight Management System (FMS); and allows use of a range of specific sensors by means of a modular concept and through the databus based on an open type architecture. All workstation consoles have a 19 ins (48 cm) multifunction display, 10 ins (25 cm) sensor monitor, keyboard, track ball and joystick.

Details for ATR 42-400 Maritime Patrol

WEIGHTS:
Maximum take-off: 39,462 lb (17,900 kg)
Maximum landing: 38,801 lb (17,600 kg)
Typical payload: 1,323 lb (600 kg), with maximum fuel*

PERFORMANCE:
On station duration: 8 hours, with maximum fuel, 200 naut miles from base
*payload available beyond the basic Maritime Patrol configuration based on 2 crew configuration, for additional workstations and crew and/or internal/external loads.

A common rack equipped with the mission computer, floppy disc driver, printer and inverters is positioned between the 2 basic workstations. 2 additional racks, the first devoted to specific items of equipment such as the radar receiver, processor and transmitter, the ESM receiver and processor unit, and the FLIR control unit; second rack for the mission communication components (Elmer RT-470/L HF, Elmer SRT-651XT V/UHF/AM-FM, CFE data link processor, GEC-Marconi ART 152 VHF/AM, and GFSA TLC management). Proposed Galileo IR/TV (FLIR system and associated TV camera with long-range zoom lense) for detection/classification at night and visual identification of surface vessels. Elettronica ESM for detection of long-range radar targets, identification of long-range targets (even in dense signal environment) and recording data on intercepted radar and loading multiple libraries. Navigation system includes a digital ring laser gyro Inertial Navigator with embedded and tightly coupled GPS receiver. IFF with transponder function only. Rockwell Collins MDF 124F or Chelton 931 direction finder. Rockwell Collins TCN 500 Tacan. TEAC V-250 video recorder.
Structural modifications: Compared with the commercial airliner, the basic passenger entry door with integrated airstairs is replaced by a 3 ft (0.9 m) width by 5 ft 8 ins (1.72 m) height door that is openable in flight, used to launch SAR package (BFE type equipment). 2 bubble windows on the rear fuselage sides for observers, each 13.7 ins (35 cm) diameter. Launcher in rear part of cabin to drop markers. Belly radome, and FLIR turret on starboard side of main undercarriage fairing. See Pylons.
Fuel system: 9,920 lb (4,500 kg) of fuel, maximum.

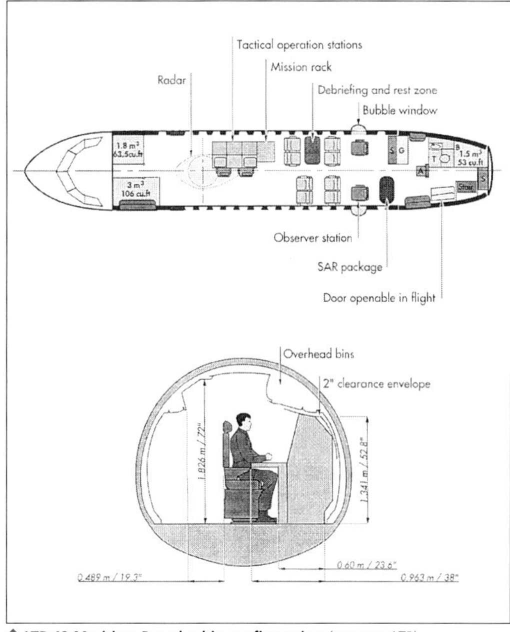

↑ **ATR 42 Maritime Patrol cabin configuration** *(courtesy ATR)*

Boeing/British Aerospace — USA/UK

Corporate address:
See under UK and USA for company details.

ACTIVITIES

▪ Co-operative programmes between these companies follow. Company details can be found in the UK and USA sections under individual headings.

Boeing/British Aerospace Harrier II

First flight: 5 November 1981 (full-scale development AV-8B).
Role: Close air support and interdiction, with unique basing flexibility offered by STOVL capability (including small and/or remote forward fields and small ships).

Aims

▪ Extensively modified and developed derivative of the Harrier I (GR Mk 3/AV-8A), incorporating much technological innovation, including lift improvement devices, larger wings with LERX, and wide use of composites.
▪ Offers twice the payload/range by means of new wings, increased engine thrust, and overall performance improvements.
▪ Increased operational effectiveness due to improved avionics.

Development

▪ Originally a joint BAe/McDonnell Douglas programme. Now Boeing is prime contractor, with BAe as sub-contractor for the AV-8B/EAV-8B. BAe is prime contractor and Boeing sub-contractor for RAF aircraft.
▪ October 1976. Harrier II programme was instituted, following the success of the Harrier I. Full scale development funded.
▪ 9 November 1978. Maiden flight of the first of 2 YAV-8B aerodynamic prototypes, modified from AV-8As.
▪ 1981. UK selected Harrier II for service with the RAF.
▪ 5 November 1981. First of 4 full-scale development AV-8Bs flew.
▪ 29 August 1983. First flight of a production AV-8B, delivered in November 1983 and officially entering USMC service with VMAT-203 on 12 January 1984.
▪ 30 January 1985. USMC commissioned VMA-331 as its first non-training AV-8B squadron, at MCAS Cherry Point in North Carolina, gaining initial operational capability in August of the following year.
▪ 30 April 1985. Maiden flight of an RAF Harrier GR Mk 5 development aircraft.
▪ 21 October 1986. Maiden flight of a TAV-8B.
▪ 1 July 1987. GR Mk 5 entered RAF service, joining No 233 OCU at Wittering.
▪ 24 July 1987. First production TAV-8B was received by VMAT-23 at MCAS Cherry Point.
▪ September 1987. Maiden flight of a Spanish EAV-8B.
▪ 18 May 1990. Maiden flight of an RAF production GR Mk 7.
▪ 17 January 1991. 4 aircraft of VMA-311, USMC, undertook the first AV-8B sorties of the Gulf War. During this conflict, 86 AV-8Bs flying from Saudi Arabia and off an amphibious assault ship in the Persian Gulf, flew 3,383 sorties, accumulating 4,112 combat hours.
▪ 7 April 1994. Maiden flight of an RAF T Mk 10 trainer.
▪ 27 June 1994. First RAF GR Mk 7 to land on HMS *Illustrious*.
▪ 30 November 1994. Maiden flight of McDonnell Douglas's (McDD) technology demonstrator, used initially for trials with inert wingtip Sidewinder AAMs.
▪ February 1995. McDD technology demonstrator began evaluation of "zero scarf" rear nozzles to boost engine thrust, as already used for the forward nozzles.
▪ March 1995. Flight testing began of improved underfuselage lift improvement devices (LIDS) on the McDD demonstrator, intended to maximize VTO lift to allow higher take-off weight, by catching efflux gases under the fuselage that have reflected off the ground. LIDS encompassed small strakes positioned near the nosewheel doors and a crossways fence.
▪ 1 August 1995. RAF GR Mk 7 deployment on patrols over the former Yugoslavia began, undertaking actual ground attack operations between 30 August and 21 September. 3 RAF squadrons (1, 3 and 4) assigned to NATO Reaction Force from the beginning of 1996.
▪ 26 October 1995. Final Harrier II delivery to the RAF, as a T Mk 10 trainer.
▪ October 1996. GR Mk 7 shipborne flight trials.
▪ 1998. Evaluation to take place of a lengthened centre fuselage section (see Fuselage).

Details

Sales/Users: Ordered by the Italian Navy (2 TAV-8Bs plus Harrier II Plus aircraft, initially diverted from USMC orders), Spanish Navy (12 EAV-8Bs and 1 TEAV-8B, operated as VA.2s and to become Plus standard), RAF (96 built in all forms, comprising 2 development batch, 60 GR Mk 5/5As, since converted to

↑ **Boeing/British Aerospace Harrier GR Mk 7 testing 2 Paveway IIIs and TIALD pod**

↑ **RAF GR Mk 7 with rocket launchers**

↑ Italian Navy TAV-8B Harrier II

GR Mk 7s, 34 newly-built GR Mk 7s and 13 T Mk 10s), and USMC (252 production AV-8Bs and 24 TAV-8Bs were ordered, of which 24 were later changed to Plus versions; remanufacture of 72 to Plus version is underway).
Crew: Pilot, or 2 in the 'T' training versions.
Cockpit: Single piece front screen. Single piece bubble canopy, sliding up and aft to open on single-seaters, with MDC fragmentation for ejection. Much improved all-round view compared with Harrier I, with the pilot sitting 12 ins (30 cm) higher. Separate sideways opening canopies on 2-seaters. Vertical stagger affords the instructor a good view in the 2-seaters.
Crew escape: Martin Baker Mk 12H zero-zero ejection seat for GR Mk 7s and UPC/Stencel for USMC.
Fixed guns: None, but with provision for 2 × 25-mm Aden cannon pod on RAF aircraft and a 25-mm multi-barrel cannon on USMC variants, in ventral fuselage location.
Ammunition: 100 rounds per cannon for GRs, 300 rounds for AV-8Bs.

Details for Harrier II

PRINCIPAL DIMENSIONS:
Wing span: 30 ft 4 ins (9.25 m)
Maximum length: 47 ft 8 ins (14.53 m) *for GR Mk 7*, 46 ft 4 ins (14.12 m) *for AV-8B*, 50 ft 3 ins (15.32 m) *for TAV-8B*, and 51 ft 9 ins (15.77 m) *for T Mk 10*
Maximum height: 11 ft 8 ins (3.56 m) *for GR Mk 7* and *AV-8B*, and 13 ft 5 ins (4.1 m) *for T Mk 10*

WINGS:
Aerofoil section: Thick supercritical (root thickness/chord ratio 11.5%, tip 7.5%)
Area: 230 sq ft (21.37 m^2)
Aspect ratio: 3.99

TAIL UNIT:
Tailplane span: 13 ft 11 ins (4.24 m)

UNDERCARRIAGE:
Type: Generally as for Sea Harrier, except outriggers moved inboard to reduce track
Wheel track: 17 ft (5.18 m)

WEIGHTS:
Empty: 15,060 lb (6,831 kg) *GR Mk 7* basic mass; 15,409 lb (6,989 kg) *GR Mk 7* operating, for first 68 built; 15,705 lb (7,123 kg) *GR Mk 7* operating, for later aircraft with larger LERX; 13,971 lb (6,337 kg) AV-8B
Maximum vertical take-off: 19,180 lb (8,700 kg) *GR Mk 7*, 20,595 lb (9,341 kg) *AV-8B* with Pegasus 11-61 engine
Maximum short run take-off: 31,000-32,000 lb (14,061-14,515 kg)
Maximum vertical landing mass: about 19,940 lb (9,044 kg)

PERFORMANCE:
Maximum speed at altitude: Mach 0.91-0.98
Maximum speed at sea level: 585 kts (674 mph) 1,083 km/h *for AV-8B*
Take-off distance: 1,720 ft (524 m) ground run at maximum take-off weight, ISA
G limits: +8, -3
Radius of action (attack – Hi-Lo-Hi): 600 naut miles (691 miles) 1,111 km with 2 × 1,000 lb bombs, 3 × BL 755s and 2 drop tanks
Combat air patrol duration: about 3 hours, 100 naut miles (115 miles) 185 km from base, with 2 Sidewinders and 2 drop tanks
Ferry range: over 1,600 naut miles (1,842 miles) 2,963 km quoted *for GR Mk 7*, over 1,800 naut miles (2,073 miles) 3,334 km) quoted by manufacturer *for AV-8B*, with 1,965 naut miles (2,263 miles) 3,642 km as maximum

Number of weapon pylons: 9 on GR Mk 7 and 7 on AV-8B. Increased wing span over Harrier I allows 3 or 4 per wing, plus fuselage centreline (capacity 1,000 lb, 454 kg). Intermediate and inboard wing pylons are 'wet'.
Expendable weapons and equipment: 13,234 lb (6,003 kg) maximum load for Pegasus 11-61–engined aircraft, 9,200 lb (4,173 kg) normal load for early AV-8Bs and 10,800 lb (4,900 kg) for GR Mk 7 and similarly engined aircraft for STO. VTO payload up to 4,000 lb (1,814 kg). Range of free fall and retarded bombs, including 1,000 lb, laser guided, cluster and practice. Alternatively, or as a mix, rocket launchers, ASMs, AIM-9L Sidewinder/Magic AAMs or other stores. AV-8B has, typically, a choice of 15 × Mk 82 500 lb bombs, 7 BL-755 cluster bombs, 5 × Mk 83 1,000 lb bombs, 4 AGM-65E Maverick ASMs, 6 Sidewinders or 6 rocket pods. Boeing technology demonstrator has flown with wingtip Sidewinders. Future USMC weapons include AGM-154A JSOW, while the RAF has recently received or will receive Brimstone, Paveway III and Storm Shadow among other types.
Additional stores: Sanders AN/ALQ-164 deceptive ECM pod carried on the centreline, for protection against pulse radar threats, power modulated jamming and multiple programmable jamming techniques (ALQ-126B sub-system) and for protection against terminal CW radar threats, with threat ID techniques and priorities programmed by user (ALQ-162 sub-system). Vinten VICON 18 reconnaissance pod for RAF. GEC-Marconi TIALD (Thermal Imaging and Laser Designation) pod (see Avionics).
Radar: None (see Harrier II Plus).
Flight/weapon system avionics/instrumentation: Integrated, computer controlled navigation/attack system. Hughes ASB-19(V)2 or 3 Angle Rate Bombing System (ARBS), with tracking by laser spot or TV. Litton ASN-130A (AV-8B) or GEC-Marconi FIN 1075/1075G (GR.Mk 7) inertial navigation system (INS). ARN-118 (AV-8B) or ARI 23368 (GR Mk 7) Tacan, but USMC AV-8Bs now have integrated Tacan/GPS. GEC-Marconi Moving Map Display (not on AV-8B). AlliedSignal digital air data computer. Unisys AYK-14(V) mission computer. MIL-STD-1553 databus. Smiths AYQ-13 stores management system (SMS) with combining HUD (for flight, threat and weapon delivery information) and display computer, and digital display indicator; SMS control via panel, MPD and HOTAS. APN-194(V) (AV-8B) or ARI 23388 (GR Mk 7) radar altimeter. VHF/UHF radio (Rockwell Collins ARC-182 for AV-8B, GEC-Marconi AD3500 for GR Mk 7). ARA-63 landing receiver for AV-8B. Multi-Purpose Displays (MPD) for ARBS data, radar warning, navigation, stores management, etc. IFF (Bendix/King APX-100 for AV-8B, Cossor for GR Mk 7). GR Mk 7 and AV-8B Night Attack have GEC-Marconi FLIR, with images on a wide-angle HUD or either of 2 head-down Multi-Purpose Colour Displays, including Honeywell (USMC) or GEC-Marconi (RAF) digital colour map. Night vision goggles and compatible instrumentation in cockpit. See also Flight controls. Upgrade to some RAF GR Mk 7s has begun, including addition of Terprom, TIALD, and Advanced Mission Planning Aid (AMPA). Future upgrades could add ring laser gyro INS with embedded GPS, AHRS, upgraded stores management system and mission computer, and MIL-STD-1760 databus for weapons integration.
Self-protection systems: GEC-Marconi Zeus electronic warfare system on RAF aircraft, including radar warning receiver and electronic jamming. Also Plessey PVS 2000 pulse Doppler missile approach warner, and Tracor flare and Bofors BOL 304 chaff dispensers. See also Additional stores. USMC aircraft carry Litton ALR-67(V)2 forward/backward radar warning receiver, optical missile approach warning, FLIR receiver and ALE-39 chaff/flare.
Wing characteristics: Shoulder mounted, with swept leading edges and swept trailing edges outboard of the undercarriage outriggers. Considerable anhedral. Wing gross area increased by some 14% and span 20% relative to Harrier I, and with increased thickness/chord ratio. Outriggers moved inboard from tip (Harrier I) to nearer mid-span. Leading-edge root extensions (LERX) ahead of wing root to increase manoeuvre lift and improve handling. Continuous one-piece wing with multiple spars.
Wing control surfaces: Ailerons (outboard and "droopable"), and inboard slotted flaps for "positive circulation" (lift) and also with auto manoeuvre mode. Reaction controls at the wingtips, as for Harrier I, for lateral control in jet borne flight/transition.
Tail control surfaces: Slab tailplane and rudder.
Airbrakes: Single petal type under the rear fuselage.
Flight control system: Combination of conventional aerodynamic surfaces and reaction controls ("puffer jets"). Ailerons, tailplane and rudder operated by powered flying control units. Reaction control jets at each wingtip, in the nose and tail; bleed air from the engine HP compressor. Honeywell ASW-46(V)2 Stability Augmentation and Attitude Hold System (SAAHS), comprising Automatic Flight Control System (AFCS) and Stability Augmentation System (SAS), provides stability augmentation about all axes over the complete flight envelope; also provides attitude, altitude and heading hold.
Fuselage: Redesigned forward fuselage and stretched rear

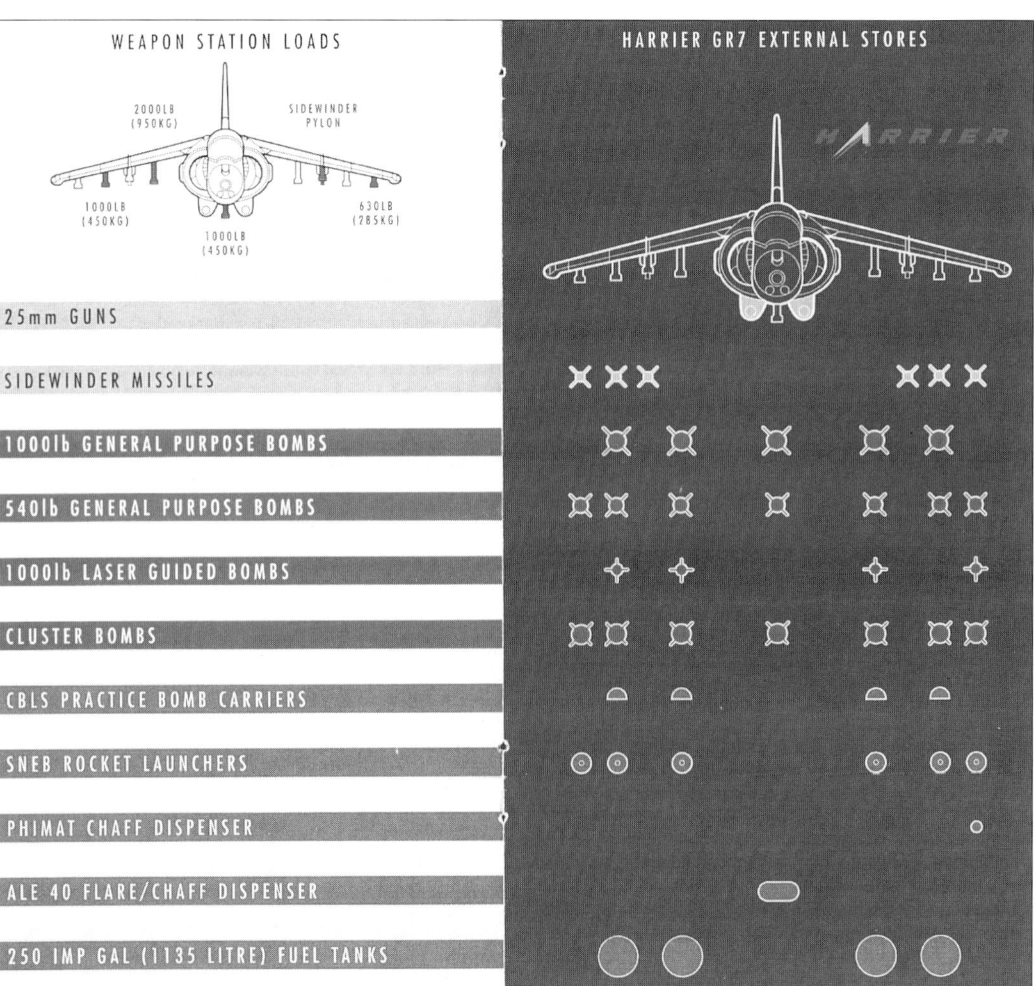

↑ Weapon arrangements for the Harrier GR Mk 7 *(courtesy British Aerospace)*

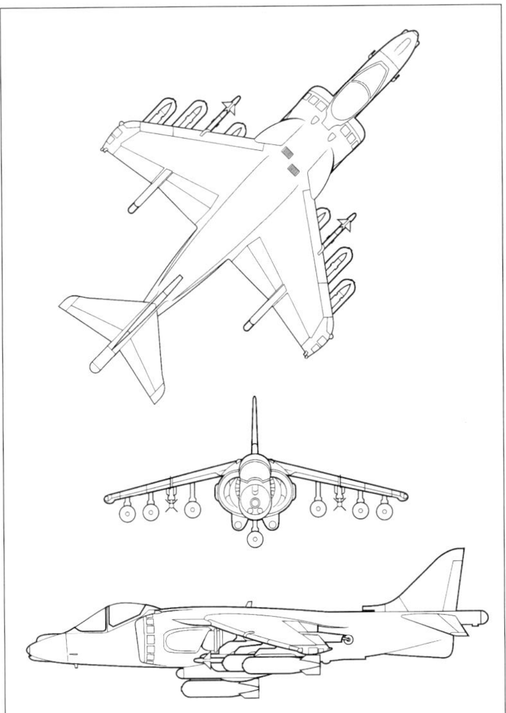

↑ Harrier GR Mk 7 general arrangement *(courtesy British Aerospace)*

fuselage compared with Harrier I. Underfuselage Lift Improvement Devices (LIDS); improvements under test in 1995 (see Development). A redesigned centre fuselage will be evaluated in 1998, with 12 ins (30 cm) plug and lengthened air inlets.
Construction materials: First production combat aircraft to make extensive use of composite materials (graphite epoxy), offering considerable weight saving compared with conventional aluminium alloy airframe of Harrier I. Wing structure/LERX largely graphite epoxy, with claimed saving of 330 lb (150 kg) relative to metal. Leading edges and tips of aluminium alloy for bird strike resistance; also house hot, high pressure reaction control ducting. Tailplane, rudder and flaps, cockpit, nose section and access panels are also constructed of composites. More than 26% of structure weight comprises carbon epoxy composites, resulting in 480 lb (218 kg) weight saving.
Engine: Rolls-Royce Pegasus 11 high-bypass ratio, non-afterburning, vectoring thrust turbofan. See below. Gas turbine starter and APU.
Engine rating: 21,550 lbf (95.86 kN) for Pegasus 11 Mk 105 in RAF aircraft, with future upgrade to Mk 106 possible. Similar rating for Spanish Mk 152-42. Early USMC AV-8Bs use 21,450 lbf (95.42 kN) Pegasus 11-21 (F402-RR-406A), as also for some Italian used aircraft. 23,800 lbf (105.89 kN) Pegasus 11-61 (F402-RR-408A) for USMC aircraft from No 167; also later for Spanish Matador IIs and Italian re-engined trainers.
Air intakes: Bifurcated, pitots, with internal throat bleet slot. New inlet featuring increased capture area, new lip profile, improved internal shaping, and only a single row of auxiliary inlet doors. These revisions produce 300 lbf (1.33 kN) additional static thrust.
Nozzles: 4 rotatable nozzles for thrust vectoring. Front pair are of zero-scarf type (cut off square) producing 200 lbf (0.89 kN) increase in static thrust. Rear zero-scarf nozzles are under test (see Development). Steel construction. See Sea Harrier for details of movement. A ceramic matrix composite blast shield for the rear nozzles was to be tested in late 1995 (titanium blast shield at present).
Flight refuelling probe: Provision for extendable probe mounted externally on the port upper intake nacelle.
Fuel system: 5 fuselage and 2 integral wing tanks. Internal capacity 7,798 lb (3,537 kg) for GR Mk 7 or 4,406 litres in single-seaters, 4,149 litres in 2-seaters. 4 × 1,136 litre drop tanks can be carried underwing on inner and intermediate pylons.
Electrical system: Single engine-driven AC generator.
Hydraulic system: 2 independent systems, each with an engine-driven pump and delivering 3,000 psi. Each is capable of operating power controls should the other system fail.
Braking system: Multi-disc carbon brakes, with anti-skid devices.
Oxygen system: On-board oxygen generating system.

Aircraft variants:
AV-8B is the USMC designation, with differences as noted previously. Night Attack equipped from the 167th production aircraft, which also received the uprated Pegasus 11-61 engine.

↑ Boeing/British Aerospace Harrier II Plus

TAV-8B is the USMC's 2-seat training version, also used by Italy.
EAV-8B is the Spanish Navy version, Spanish military designated VA.2 Matador II. Operated from the aircraft carrier *Principe de Asturias*. These are to be upgraded to Harrier II Plus (which see).
TEAV-8B is the single Spanish 2-seat trainer.
GR Mk 7 is the RAF's current version, suited to night attack. First production GR Mk 5s and then 5As have been modified to Mk 7 standard, making this the sole single-seat version in RAF service.
T Mk 10 is the RAF's 2-seat training version of the GR Mk 7. Effective for day and night operational missions.

Boeing/British Aerospace Harrier II Plus

First flight: 22 September 1992.
Role: All-weather, day and night, attack and air-to-air STOVL combat.

Aims

- Radical extension of Harrier II's combat effectiveness by the addition of proven multi-mode radar.
- Enhanced air-to-air capability includes BVR missile engagement.

Development

- June 1987. Launched as a private venture by the 2 companies.
- 28 September 1990. Tri-national Memorandum of Understanding between USA, Italy and Spain. Funding for development and integration of radar. Funding came from all 3 countries, with $17 million of US investment from Nunn Amendment funding (for military programmes developed with NATO allies).
- 3 December 1990. US Navy contract awarded for the construction of a prototype and completion of a batch of AV-8Bs then on order to Plus standard.
- 1992. Tri-national production MoU.
- 1993. Entry into USMC service.
- December 1994. Initial deliveries to the Italian Navy, for Gruppo Aeri Imbarcati.
- January 1995. 3 Italian Navy Harrier II Plus aircraft left Brindisi on the carrier *Guiseppe Garibaldi* (alongside 4 Army Mangusta attack helicopters) to provide part of the air cover for UN forces leaving Somalia.
- 11 December 1995. First flight of a CASA-produced VA.2 Matador II, with deliveries to Escuadrilla 009 of the Spanish Navy from 15 January 1996.
- 29 May 1998. USMC Harrier II Plus flew with avionics centred on a commercial processor, under the Open Systems Core Avionics Requirement (OSCAR) programme.

Details *(principal differences to Harrier II)*

Sales/Users: Italian Navy (16, with final assembly of 13 by Alenia in Italy), Spanish Navy (8 assembled by CASA), and USMC (original 24, plus 6 against Gulf conflict Harrier II attrition; 3 diverted to Italy, making 27 received; remanufacture of 72 AV-8Bs to Plus underway).
Number of weapon pylons: 9.
Expendable weapons and equipment: 13,234 lb (6,003 kg), including gun and ammunition. Enhanced capabilities include ability to launch AMRAAM, SRAAM, Harpoon and Maverick; Italian Navy has ordered AMRAAMs and Mavericks.
Additional stores: ECM pods.
Radar: Raytheon AN/APG-65 multi-mode, pulse Doppler.
Flight/weapon system avionics/instrumentation: Similar to Harrier II but radar replaces ARBS. Enhancements include GPS and an automatic target handoff system (ATHS).
Self-protection systems: ECM, infra-red suppression and 3 times more upward and downward firing chaff/flares are available than for earlier Harriers. Survivability enhancements will include missile approach warning system.
Engine: Rolls-Royce Pegasus 11-61 (F402-RR-408).

Details for Harrier II Plus

PRINCIPAL DIMENSIONS:
Maximum length: 47 ft 9 ins (14.55 m)

WEIGHTS:
Empty, operating: 14,867 lb (6,743 kg)
Maximum useful load: 16,133 lb (7,318 kg)
Maximum vertical take-off: 20,753 lb (9,413 kg)
Maximum take-off: 31,000 lb (14,062 kg)

PERFORMANCE:
Radius of action (close air support, Lo-Lo-Lo): 200 naut miles (230 miles) 370 km, with 4 bombs, gun pod and ammunition, and 2 drop tanks
Radius of action (interdiction): 400 naut miles (461 miles) 741 km, with 4 bombs, 2 missiles and 2 drop tanks
Radius of action (anti-ship): 540 naut miles (621 miles) 1,000 km, with 2 anti-ship missiles, 2 other missiles and 2 drop tanks
Duration (combat air patrol, Hi): over 2 hours at 100 naut miles (115 miles) 185 km, with 4 AMRAAMs, 2 other missiles and 2 drop tanks; 2.7 hours at 100 naut miles, with 4 AMRAAMs and 2 tanks; 2.1 hours at 200 naut miles (230 miles) 370 km, with 4 AMRAAMs and 2 tanks; or 1.5 hours at 100 naut miles with 6 AMRAAMs and 2 other missiles

Boeing/British Aerospace T-45 Goshawk

First flight: 16 April 1988.
Role: Carrier-capable undergraduate jet pilot trainer.

Aims

- To replace the T-2C Buckeye and TA-4J Skyhawk, under the US Navy's VTXTS programme. Developed initially from the Hawk 60.
- Part of the general T45TS training system, which encompasses the trainer itself, flight simulators, instructional programmes using computer-assisted techniques, a computerized training integration system, and a contractor logistics support package.
- 14,400 hour fatigue life.

Development

- 18 November 1981. Winner of a US Navy's VTXTS competition for a new carrier-capable trainer. Became the T-45A Goshawk.

↑ Boeing/British Aerospace T-45A Goshawk of Training Wing Two

Full scale development began in 1984.
▪ October 1989. Expected Goshawk production deliveries to the US Navy, but delayed due to performance and flying shortcomings identified in operational flight testing and evaluation. Subsequent modifications included an uprated engine of Hawk 100 type, addition of wing leading-edge slats, fin and tailplane modifications, improved control harmonization, and airbrake/tailplane movement interconnected.
▪ October-November 1990. 2 US production Goshawks were delivered to the Naval Air Test Center at Patuxent River.
▪ 4 December 1991. First development Goshawk made a trial landing on the aircraft carrier USS *John F. Kennedy*. Declared "safe and suitable" after testing.
▪ 23 July 1992. First production aircraft were officially handed over to the US Navy at St Louis.
▪ 1994. Training system approved for service early in the year, following operational evaluation.
▪ 11 February 1994. First US Navy student flight in a Goshawk, with the first solo on 23 March.
▪ 19 March 1994. First Cockpit 21 Goshawk demonstrator flew, introducing a "glass" cockpit and digital avionics. This improved cockpit is expected to become the standard fit for all production

↑ Boeing/British Aerospace T-45C Goshawk with Cockpit 21 layout *(courtesy Boeing)*

Goshawks from the 84th aircraft, with earlier Goshawks to be upgraded from 1998.
▪ 5 October 1994. The first class of US Navy pilots to use the T-45 training system (T45TS) received their "Wings of Gold".
▪ 17 January 1995. Authorization for full-rate production following a successful DoD Milestone III review of the T45TS.
▪ February 1996. T-45A fleet at Kingsville had accumulated 62,541 flying hours, rising thereafter at about 3,000 hours per month. 68 T-45s in service by July 1997.
▪ 7 October 1996. First flight (90 minutes duration) of a T-45 with the F124 engine, ostensibly and originally as an alternative engine for a proposed Royal Australian Air Force version.
▪ 31 October 1997. First T-45C with Cockpit 21 improvements was presented at St. Louis.
▪ 15 December 1997. Introduction of the T-45C Goshawk, at a ceremony at the US Naval Air Station Meridian, MS, thereby entering Training Wing One.
▪ July 1998. Start of instruction on T-45C with Training Squadron 23.
▪ 2002. Start of upgrade programme to convert T-45As to T-45C standard, to be completed by 2007.
▪ 2003. 104 T-45Cs to make full complement at NAS Meridian.

Details *(see British Aerospace Hawk entry for general details)*

Sales/Users: US Navy. 83 T-45As built before the first T-45C, these still in active use serving with Training Wing Two at Naval Air Station Kingsville. Delivery of T-45Cs underway to Training Wing One at Naval Air Station Meridian, which will eventually have a full complement of 104. T-45As to be upgraded to C standard from the year 2002.
Crew: 2, in tandem, with the rear instructor's seat stepped up.
Cockpit: Retractable step/foot/hand hold for cockpit access.
Crew escape: Martin Baker Mk 14 Navy Aircrew Common Ejection Seats. Canopy fracturing system (miniature detonating cord - MDC).
Number of weapon pylons: Single pylon under each wing, stressed for 1,000 lb (454 kg) load, plus a centreline pylon.
Expendable weapons and equipment: Practice bombs or rocket pods under wings.
Additional stores: Optional baggage pod.
Radar: None.
Flight/weapon system avionics/instrumentation: Revised cockpit layout, with avionics including attitude and heading reference system (AHRS), Smiths Industries mini HUD in front cockpit only, Rockwell Collins AN/ARN-182 UHF/VHF coms, Rockwell Collins AN/ARN-144 VOR/ILS, Sierra AN/ARN-136A Tacan, Honeywell AN/APN-194 radar altimeter, AlliedSignal Bendix/King AN/APX-100 IFF and GPS, and more. T-45C with digital 'Cockpit 21' upgrades has 2 Elbit 5 ins × 5 ins (12.7 × 12.7 cm) multi-function monochrome displays in each cockpit for navigation, weapon delivery, aircraft performance and communications data, MIL-STD-1553B databus, Litton LN-100G ring laser gyro, HUD velocity vector and Rockwell Collins GPS.
Self-protection systems: Radar warning receiver. IR flares and chaff on Series 100. Possible ECM.
Wing characteristics: Hawk wing but with completely straight leading-edges and addition of leading-edge slats (for lower approach speeds). No wing fences, but with stall strip and vortex generators.
Wing control surfaces: See Aircraft variants.
Tail control surfaces: See Aircraft variants.
Airbrakes: 2 airbrakes (with ventilation slots) on the fuselage sides.
Engine: Rolls-Royce Turbomeca F405-RR-401 engine (Adour Mk 871) with strengthened casing for carrier-borne operations.
Engine rating: 5,845 lbf (26 kN).
Fuel system: 1,768 litres of fuel (2,900 lb, 1,315 kg). Planned modest increase in fuel capacity through use of 'wet' air intakes has been dropped.
Hydraulic system: 2 independent systems, each 3,000 psi.
Braking system: Goodrich, hydraulically operated.
Oxygen system: Onboard oxygen generation system (OBOGS).

Aircraft variants:
T-45A Goshawk is the US Navy's carrier-capable version of the BAe Hawk, built by McDonnell Douglas. Increased tailplane span, and 6 ins (15 cm) fin height increase. Revised wings. Single large vertical underfin (strake) in place of Hawk's 2 smaller strakes. SMURFs. Aileron/rudder interconnect, airbrakes/tailplane (with autotrim) interconnect, improved yaw damper and aileron gearing for lower flight speeds.
T-45B Goshawk is a land-based variant of T-45A, excluded from the US Navy programme but being offered on the export market by Boeing.
T-45C Goshawk is the latest version with Cockpit 21 improvements, which entered service in December 1997.

Details for T-45 Goshawk

PRINCIPAL DIMENSIONS:
Wing span: 30 ft 10 ins (9.39 m)
Maximum length: 39 ft 4 ins (11.99 m)
Maximum height: 14 ft (4.27 m)

WINGS:
Area: 190.1 sq ft (17.66 m^2)
Aspect ratio: 4.993
Sweepback: 21.5° at 25% chord
Dihedral: 2°

TAIL UNIT:
Tailplane span: 15 ft 1 ins (4.6 m)

UNDERCARRIAGE:
Type: Strengthened, high sink rate undercarriage with lengthened main oleos and twin steerable (digital) nosewheels, plus arrester hook
Main wheel tyre size: 24-7.7-10
Nose wheel tyre size: 19 × 5.25-10
Wheel base: 14 ft 0.375 ins (4.28)
Wheel track: 12 ft 9 ins (3.89 m)

WEIGHTS:
Empty: 9,834 lb (4,461 kg)
Normal take-off: 12,750 lb (5,783 kg)
Maximum take-off: 14,080 lb (6,386 kg)

PERFORMANCE:
Maximum speed: 542 kts (625 mph) 1,005 km/h at 8,000 ft (2,440 m)
Stalling speed: 93 kts (107 mph) 172 km/h
Catapult launch speed: 121 kts (139 mph) 224 km/h typically
Carrier approach speed: 115 kts (132 mph) 213 km/h typically
Take-off distance to 15 m (50 ft): 3,610 ft (1,100 m) on land
Landing distance from 15 m (50 ft): 3,310 ft (1,010 m) on land
Climb rate: 8,000 ft (2,440 m) per minute
G limits: +7.33, -3
Ceiling: 40,000 ft (12,190 m)
Duration: over 3 hours
Typical carrier training mission: 100 naut miles (115 miles) 185 km radius of action, Hi-Lo-Hi, with several arrested landings, catapult launches and waveoffs

Dassault Aviation/Daimler-Benz Aerospace — France/Germany

Dassault/Daimler-Benz Alpha Jet

Comments: First flown on 26 October 1973, this basic and advanced jet trainer, suited also to ground support, probably remains available, though no new production has taken place for some considerable time; 504 were delivered to Belgium, Cameroon, Egypt (many assembled by the Arab Organization for Industrialization), France, Germany, Ivory Coast, Morocco, Nigeria, Qatar and Togo. Details recently received from Dassault specify the same 3 versions: the Alpha Jet basic trainer and ground support aircraft, the Alpha Jet 2 strike version and the Alpha Jet ATS advanced trainer. The ATS features an advanced man/system interface, front cockpit HUD and rear cockpit repeater display, 2 lateral MFDs and real-time controls on stick and throttle (HOTAS concept), plus FLIR/video system, laser designation, ECM and more. Full details, plus a photograph and diagrams, can be found in the 1996-97 edition of *WA&SD*, pages 157-158.

EuroFighter Jagdflugzeug GmbH — Germany/Italy/Spain/UK

Corporate address:
im Airport Business Centre, Am Söldnermoos 17, 85399 Hallbergmoos, Germany.

Telephone: +49 811 80 1555
Facsimile: +49 811 80 1557

Founded: 1986.

Information:
Germany (*telephone* +49 89 607 25711), Italy (*telephone* +39 6 807781), Spain (*telephone* +34 1 5857268), and UK (*telephone* +44 1772 854839).

ACTIVITIES

▪ Design, development and production of Eurofighter has been undertaken as a collaborative programme between Daimler-Benz Aerospace of Germany (33% shareholding), Alenia of Italy (21%), CASA of Spain (13%) and British Aerospace of the UK (33%). See earlier pages for company details. The programme management structure means that the 4 companies report to NETMA, which co-ordinates the interests of the respective governments. NETMA also oversees the Eurojet engine programme.
Note: The aircraft is now renamed Eurofighter, having dropped the '2000' part of its name in 1997.

Eurofighter (RAF Typhoon)

First flight: 27 March 1994 (development aircraft 1 or DA1).
Role: Air superiority fighter, with the capability of surface attack and reconnaissance; Germany has specified a multi-role variant.

Aims

▪ Optimized for supersonic, Beyond-Visual-Range (BVR) air defence.
▪ High performance and agility in subsonic close air combat.
▪ Short field capability, also dispersability to unimproved strips.
▪ Canard-delta configuration for optimum supersonic performance.
▪ Naturally longitudinally unstable for high lift/drag with full authority, digital, quadruplex fly-by-wire flight control system.
▪ Low radar cross section.
▪ Double engine change by 4 persons in 45 minutes. Also, 9 maintenance hours per flying hour.

Development

▪ 1983. Feasibility studies were initiated by UK, Germany, Italy, Spain and France for a European Fighter Aircraft (EFA). Initial Staff Requirements were issued on 16 December.
▪ 1984. France technically withdrew to pursue Rafale as a carrier-capable fighter, made official in the following year prior to the founding of the EuroFighter company.
▪ 2 August 1985. Project definition commenced after agreement between Germany, Italy and the UK, completed in September of the following year.
▪ 1987. European Staff Requirement was formulated and issued that September with envisaged in-service date of 1997.
▪ 23 November 1988. Airframe and engine (development only) contracts were placed for work to the year 2000.
▪ 1992. Renamed Eurofighter 2000, but essentially unchanged, following programme review including alternative possible solutions.
▪ 27 March 1994. Maiden flight of DA1 at Manching in Germany, piloted by Peter Weger.
▪ 6 April 1994. Maiden flight of DA2 at Warton in the UK, piloted by Chris Yeo.
▪ 1994. Following 9 flights each on DA1 and DA2, both aircraft were stood down in June for fit of updated FCS and certain avionics.
▪ 15 May 1995. Flying resumed, in time for display at the June Paris Air Show.
▪ 17 March 1995. Fatigue tests on the static Eurofighter airframe at Ottobrunn exceeded 5,000 hours. Tests were to continue until 1997, accumulating some 18,000 hours.
▪ 4 June 1995. DA3 first flew at Turin - Caselle, the first Eurofighter with Eurojet EJ200 engines.
▪ June 1995. Paris Air Show debut, with static display of DA2.
▪ 1996. Schonefeldt debut, with first true public flying display by DA1.
▪ 31 August 1996. First flight of the 2-seater, by DA6 at Madrid.
▪ September 1996. Farnborough debut, with the first true public flying display in the UK, by DA2 (earlier, Eurofighter had made an appearance during a test flight at Air Tattoo '94).
▪ 27 January 1997. First flight of DA7 at Turin - Caselle.
▪ 24 February 1997. First flight of DA5 at Manching. First aircraft with ECR 90 radar.
▪ 14 March 1997. First flight of DA4 at Warton. Second 2-seater and last of 7 development aircraft.
▪ September 1997. During the Flight Development Programme to this date, 475 flights had been made, with achievements including Mach 1.83, alpha 25° and +6g. More than 21 pilots have flown Eurofighter during the trials programme.
▪ November 1997. Production Investment Phase formal approval.
▪ 23 December 1997. Mach 2 achieved for the first time by DA2.
▪ January 1998. First in-flight refuelling trial, by DA2 with an RAF VC10 tanker. Also first supersonic flight trials with GEC-Marconi towed radar decoy.
▪ July 1998. Thrust vectoring nozzle test on EJ200 by ITP (not currently planned for Eurofighter).
▪ November 1999. Planned certification for EJ200 engine.
▪ 2000. Instrumented production standard aircraft; 2 for UK, and 1 for each other partner.
▪ 2002. Planned in-service date for Italy and the UK.
▪ 2003. Possible in-service date for Spain and Germany.
▪ 2014. Last delivery to Germany.
Note: By June 1998, a total of 613 flying hours had been accumulated by Eurofighter in 722 flights. The flight envelope covered included Mach 2, 40,000 ft (12,190 m), 28° alpha, and 'supercruise' (supersonic cruise without afterburning).

↑ **Eurofighter production standard advanced cockpit layout**
(courtesy British Aerospace)

↑ **Eurofighter DA2 carrying a spin recovery chute assembly in 1997**

↑ **Eurofighter DA6, the second 2-seater**

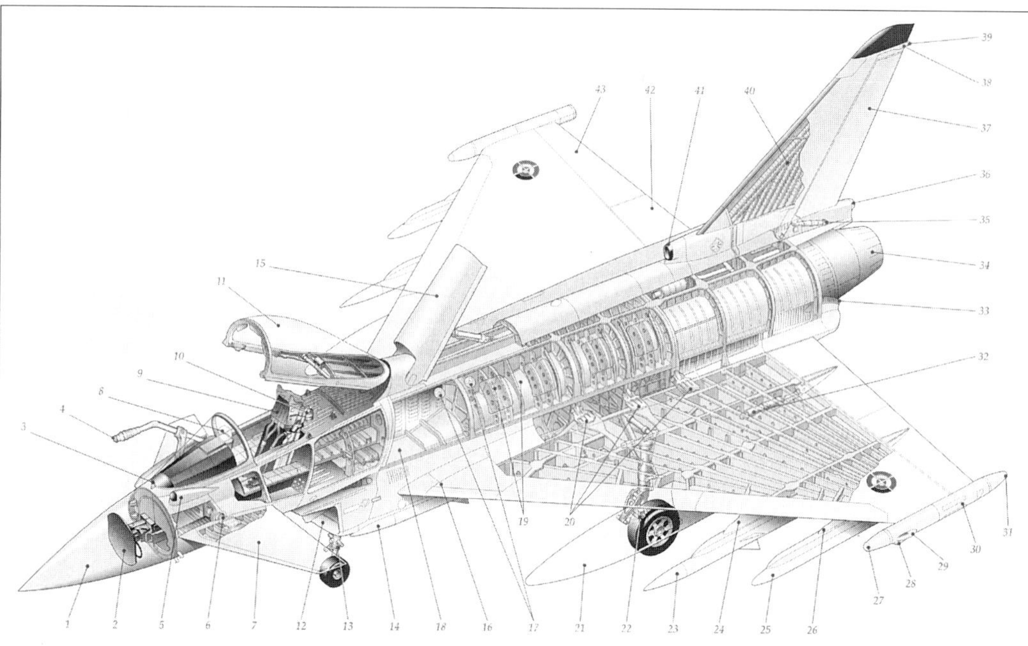

↑ **Eurofighter cutaway** *(courtesy British Aerospace)*

1 *Glass Reinforced Plastic (GRP) Radome*
2 *ECR 90 Multi-Mode Pulse Doppler Radar*
3 *Temperature Probe*
4 *Retractable Flight Refuelling Probe*
5 *Forward Looking Infra Red (FLIR)*
6 *Pivot Bearing*
7 *Port Canard*
8 *Wide Angle Head Up Display*
9 *Martin Baker MK16A Ejection Seat*
10 *Cockpit Pressurization Valves*
11 *Upward Hinging Cockpit Canopy*
12 *Variable Capture Air Intake*
13 *Aft Retracting Nose Undercarriage*
14 *Semi-Recessed Medium Range Active Missile*
15 *Spine Airbrake*
16 *Fixed Inboard Wing Leading Edge*
17 *Gravity Fuel Fillers*
18 *Forward Fuselage Fuel Tank*
19 *Centre Fuselage Integral Fuel Tanks*
20 *Titanium Wing Attachment Fittings*
21 *External Fuel Tank*
22 *Leg Door Mounted Landing/Taxying Lamp*
23 *Medium Range Active Missile*
24 *Outboard Pylon*
25 *Advanced Short Range Air to Air Missile (ASRAAM)*
26 *Integrated Tip Stub Pylon*
27 *Forward DASS Antenna*
28 *Ventral Cooling Air System*
29 *Port Navigation Light*
30 *Port Wing Defensive Aids Sub-System (DASS) Pod*
31 *Rear RWR Antenna*
32 *Inboard Flaperon Hydraulic Actuator*
33 *Airframe/Engine Finger Seals*
34 *Convergent/Divergent Nozzle*
35 *Rudder Hydraulic Actuator*
36 *Brake Parachute*
37 *Rudder*
38 *Fuel Vent*
39 *Tail Navigation Light*
40 *Aluminium/Lithium 'Sine-Wave' Finspars*
41 *Heat Exchanger Ram Air Intake*
42 *Inboard Flaperons*
43 *Outboard Flaperons*

Details for Eurofighter

PRINCIPAL DIMENSIONS:
Wing span over tip-pods: 35 ft 11 ins (10.95 m)
Wing span, reference: 34 ft 5.5 ins (10.5 m)
Overall length: 52 ft 4.5 ins (15.96 m)
Height: 17 ft 4 ins (5.28 m)

WINGS:
Aerofoil section: Modified standard type, approximately 4% mean thickness/chord
Area (gross): 551.1 sq ft (51.2 m^2)
Aspect ratio: 2.153
Sweepback: 53° leading edge
Chord at root: 23 ft 7.5 ins (7.2 m)
Chord at tip: 4 ft 1.5 ins (1.26 m)
Incidence: 0°
Dihedral: 1-2°

CANARD:
Span: 12 ft 6 ins (3.8 m)
Area: 25.83 sq ft (2.4 m^2) exposed

TAIL UNIT:
Fin area: 69.97 sq ft (6.5 m^2)

UNDERCARRIAGE:
Type: Retractable, with steerable nosewheel. Main gear pintle in inner wing, lateral retraction of each single wheel to horizontal in centre fuselage below air duct. Nose gear retraction aft, with wheel vertical below intake duct
Main wheel tyre size: 28 × 9.5-15
Nose wheel tyre size: 18 × 7.75-6
Wheel base: 13 ft 9.5 ins (4.2 m)
Wheel track: 13 ft 2 ins (4 m) approximately

WEIGHTS:
Empty: 22,043 lb (9,999 kg) basic mass
Take-off: 34,282 lb (15,550 kg) estimated, with full internal fuel and 6 AAMs
Maximum take-off: 46,297 lb (21,000 kg)

PERFORMANCE:
Maximum speed: Mach 2, with 6 AAMs
Landing speed: 130-135 kts (150-155 mph) 241-250 km/h, estimated
Normal take-off distance: 984 ft (300 m)
Operating strip length: 2,297 ft (700 m)
Time to Mach 1.5 and over 35,000 ft (10,670 m): <2 minutes 30 seconds from brakes off
Time from 200 kts to Mach 1: 30 seconds, at low level
G limits: +9, -3
Radius of action (Lo-Lo)*: >350 naut miles (403 miles) 649 km
Radius of action (Hi-Lo-Hi)*: >1,000 naut miles (1,151 miles) 1,852 km
Radius of action (air-to-air)*: >1,000 naut miles (1,151 miles) 1,852 km
Combat air patrol time*: >3.25 hours
*unspecified load and mission profile.

Details

Sales/Users: Procurement envisaged as UK (232, plus options for 65), Germany (180 long term, with 140 for air defence and 40 multi-role), Italy (130, plus options for 9) and Spain (87). Sales prospects include Australia, Norway (up to 40 as F-16 replacements), Saudi Arabia, Greece, Singapore and Canada. UK share of the total programme is estimated in 1998 to be about £16 billion.
Crew: Pilot, or 2 in tandem in the operational training variant.
Cockpit: Excellent all-round view, exceeding that of current operational fighters. Fixed front screen with anti-bird strike canopy arch. Rear-hinged clamshell canopy. Access by integral ladder on port side. Pressurized. Normalair-Garrett ECS. Centre stick. Pilot back angle limited to 18°, for good view over the nose. Enhanced pilot G protection by full coverage anti-G trousers and chest counter pressure garment.
Crew escape: Martin Baker Mk 16A zero-zero lightweight ejection seat of advanced design. Crew escape trials have been carried out to 600 kts.
Fixed guns: 27-mm Mauser cannon in starboard wing root.
Ammunition: 150 rounds.
Number of weapon pylons: 13, as 5 under the fuselage and 4 under each wing. 3 stations are 'wet', as centreline and second wing pylons from roots.
Expendable weapons and equipment: 14,300 lb (6,500 kg) load. 4 MRAAMs semi-recessed under the fuselage in low-drag configuration (AMRAAM or Aspide). FMRAAM/Meteor BVR AAMs? Centreline bomb or 1,000 litre drop tank. 2 ASRAAMs on dedicated outboard pylons. MRAAM, SRAAM or bombs on other pylons. A mix of at least 10 air-to-air missiles can be carried. 2 × 1,500 litre tanks on 'wet' wing pylons. Attack stores include 1,000 lb or 500 kg bombs, BL755, laser-guided bombs (GBU-24 and Paveway III), ALARM and Storm Shadow missiles, and most NATO standard weapons.
Additional stores: Laser designator pod or reconnaissance pod.
Radar: ECR 90 radar from the Euroradar consortium led by GEC-Marconi (UK), also comprising Telefunken Systemtechnik (Germany), FIAR (Italy) and INISEL (Spain). Multi-mode, pulse Doppler, with look-up and look-down capability. Long range detection and tracking of airborne targets, with also air-to-surface mode. Multi-target search and track while scan. ECM resistant. Threat analysis and identification and target prioritization. Power and antenna size for active AMRAAM but provision for continuous wave illumination for semi-active missiles also.
Flight/weapon system avionics/instrumentation: 7 displays comprise a GEC-Marconi wide-angle HUD for flight reference, weapon aiming and FLIR imagery; 3 Smiths Industries large Multi-function Head-Down Displays (MHDD), full colour, for tactical, navigation, radar and systems information; a Helmet Mounted Symbology System (HMSS), a Dedicated Warning Panel (DWP) and Multi-Information Distribution System (MIDS) display. The helmet mounted visor display incorporates night vision aids and protection from flash and optical (laser) threats. VTAS (Voice Throttle And Stick), with 44 total functions related to sensor and weapons control, defense aids management and in-flight handling; Direct Voice Input (DVI) for "non flight safety critical" systems allows the pilot to perform certain moding and data entry functions by voice command as an alternative to manual methods, including manual data entry, HUD/MHDD moding, radio/navigation aids selection, and target selection. Automation of systems and mission management; Teldix interface. MIL-STD-1553 databus. Eurofirst PIRATE Passive Infra-Red Airborne Track Equipment (search and track) sensor in a fairing on the port side of the nose, adjacent to the canopy front screen. Dual mode for airborne targets and air-surface role. Target identification facility is incorporated. Saturn V/UHF coms. Computing Devices video/voice recording system. Health and usage monitoring system, for real time fatigue calculations and to determine the life consumed by the airframe, plus monitors significant structural events and flight performance parameters.
Self-protection systems: Integrated into the airframe, making add-on pods unnecessary. Defensive Aids Sub System (DASS) comprises radar warning, missile approach warning, active ECM, and laser threat warning (latter item only for Spain and the UK). Chaff/flare dispensers. Auto or manual defensive control. GEC-Marconi towed decoys carried in starboard wing tip-pod.
Wing characteristics: Low mounted, cropped delta, with integral tip-pods for DASS. 3 main body side joints.
Wing control surfaces: Full-span, inner and outer trailing-edge flaperons, and automatic leading-edge flap (zero slot slat), per wing.
Tail control surfaces: Fin with rudder. Cooling air intake in root.
Canard: All moving (symmetrically).
Airbrakes: Single, forward hinged, dorsal petal immediately behind the canopy.
Flight control system: Full authority, digital, quadruplex fly-by-wire. Carefree handling control of incidence and G. Auto-recovery mode on pilot selection in case of disorientation. Air speed and flow angle data transducers under the nose. Primary control system comprises the canards, flaperons and rudder; pitch and roll control by canards and flaperons, yaw control by the rudder. Secondary control surfaces comprise the slats and airbrake, the former providing optimum wing camber at all angles of attack. The airbrake, intake cowls and nosewheel steering comprise the secondary control system. The entire flying control system is integrated with the aircraft's other systems by means of avionics and utilizes control system databuses, including fibre optic.
Fuselage: Manufacture breakdown is radome and cockpit, centre fuselage with tanks and air intake ducts and with nose and main undercarriage stowage, rear fuselage housing engines.
Construction materials: Extensive use of carbon reinforced composites, comprising 70% of the total aircraft surface area (or about 40% of structure weight). Remainder of surface area is metal (15%, including titanium for the canards, flaperons and areas around the engine nozzles), glassfibre reinforced plastics (12%) and other (3%). Wings have CFC skins and multiple spars with alloy ribs. Leading-edge flaps are aluminium-lithium, and

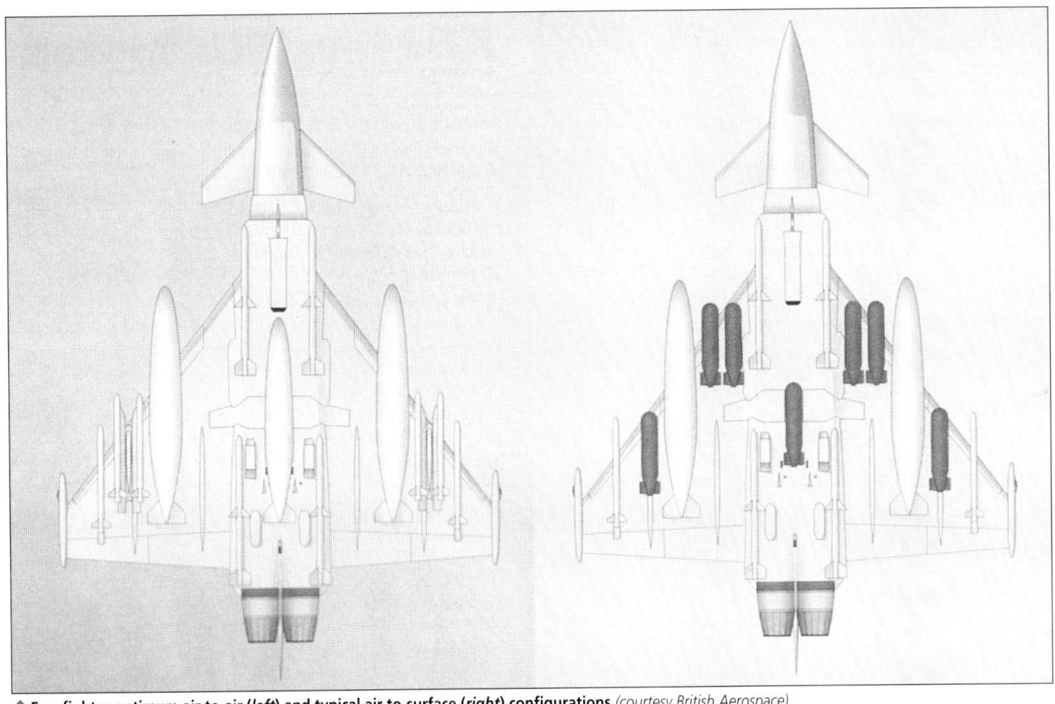

↑ **Eurofighter optimum air-to-air (*left*) and typical air-to-surface (*right*) configurations** *(courtesy British Aerospace)*

outer flaperons are titanium. Canards are superplastic formed, diffusion bonded, titanium. Fin has CFC skins and multiple spars with aluminium-lithium leading edges. British Aerospace is responsible for the forward fuselage section, canards and wing moving surfaces; CASA and BAe are together responsible for one wing; DASA is responsible for the mid-fuselage section and vertical tail; Alenia is responsible for the other wing and its moving surfaces; and CASA and Alenia are together responsible for the rear fuselage section housing the engines. Main airframe fatigue tests to 13,500 hours had been completed by mid-1997.
Engines: 2 Eurojet EJ200 turbofans, with DASA FADEC. Designed specifically for Eurofighter and optimized for air-to-air missions. Thrust/weight >9. DA1 and 2 fitted with Turbo Union RB199s.
Engine rating: Each 13,500 lbf (60 kN) dry, 20,250 lbf (90 kN) with afterburning, rising to 23,000 lbf (102.31 kN).
Air intakes: Single fixed-wedge in ventral position, incorporating bleed holes. Bleed slot at throat. "Varicowl" drooping leading edge for high incidence manoeuvring and take-off/landing. Bifurcated, with vertical external splitter. Horizontal diverter with system air intake in leading edge. No auxiliary intakes for ground running. "Arched" duct path to obscure engine face.
Nozzles: Fully variable, convergent-divergent, to maximize thrust at supersonic speed and high altitude.
Flight refuelling probe: Retractable probe on the starboard side, adjacent to the front canopy screen. Using in-flight refuelling, the longest flight by early 1998 lasted 4 hours.
Fuel system: Integral tanks in the centre fuselage and in the wings for about 5,640 litres. Up to 3,500 litre total in drop tanks (see Weapons). BAe is developing upper fuselage conformal auxiliary fuel tanks, plus greater capacity underwing tanks, to permit a combat radius of over 1,500 naut miles in the strike role.
Electrical system: Lucas Aerospace system, with variable speed, constant frequency engine-driven generators and transformer/rectifier. AlliedSignal APU.
Hydraulic system: Magnaghi fully duplicated system. Engine-driven pumps. All primary and secondary control surfaces, and the undercarriage, actuated by power control units.
Braking system: Carbon disc brakes on the main wheels only. Drag-chute of 13 ft (4 m) diameter in the fin root fairing.
Oxygen system: Molecular Sieve Oxygen Concentrator (MSOC).

Aircraft variants:
Single-seater, as described, with some differences between national variants in capability, avionics and weapon system for the development programme.
2-seater is the training variant, with a modest reduction in internal fuel and repositioning of avionics. Retains full operational capability.

Hongdu Aviation Industry Group/Pakistan Aeronautical Complex — China/Pakistan

Corporate address:
See Hongdu under China and Pakistan Aeronautical Complex under Pakistan.

Hongdu/PAC K-8 and K-8J Karakorum

First flight: 21 November 1990.
Role: Basic jet trainer, also suited to more advanced training and light attack.
Fatigue life: 8,000 flying hours.

Aims

- Developed to MIL-F-8785C IV requirements.
- Low purchase cost and minimum operational costs.

Development

- 1987. Programme initiated, with the first metal cut at the start of 1989.
- 18 October 1991. Maiden flight of the second of 3 flying and static test prototypes.
- 1992. US Government halted TFE731 engine sales to China, reportedly because of transfer of technology considerations, but allowed sales to resume from 1994.
- 9 April 1994. CATIC and the Pakistan Government signed an agreement covering the purchase of the first 6 K-8s for Pakistan.
- 21 September 1994. Acceptance of the first 6 K-8s for the Pakistan Air Force, at Nanchang.
- 1997-98. Flight trials in progress of the Chinese K-8J. China ordered an initial 30 AI-25TL engines in 1997, 10 for delivery in 1997 and 20 in 1998. As many as 300 engines might be ordered, indicating the possible scope of Chinese orders for the K-8J.

Details

Sales/Users: 6 ordered initially for the Pakistan Air Force from a first production batch of 15; deliveries started in September 1994. These being used by the Air Force Academy at Risalpur for a 1,200 hours evaluation, pending further orders. Further purchases likely after the evaluation phase. China has developed the K-8J version for the PLAAF, for which flight trials are in progress (see Development for possible size of requirement). Export opportunities as Bangladesh, Malaysia, Myanmar, Sri Lanka, Syria, Thailand and African nations.
Crew: Student and instructor in tandem, with rear seat raised by 11 ins (28 cm) to improve forward vision.
Cockpit: AlliedSignal ECS 51833 environmental control system. Pressurized cockpit (maximum differential 3.9 psi).
Crew escape: Martin Baker Mk 10LZ zero-zero ejection seats, for use up to 485 kts (560 mph) 900 km/h
Fixed guns: None, but 23-mm gun pod can be installed on the centreline, with 80 rounds of ammunition.
Number of weapon pylons: 4 under the wings, outer pylons 'wet', plus centreline for gun pod or possibly other store (up to 1,543 lb, 700 kg).
Expendable weapons and equipment: 2,080 lb (943 kg) load, including bombs up to a 610 lb BL755 cluster bomb, rocket pods or 2 PL-7 AAMs. See diagram.
Flight/weapon system avionics/instrumentation: AlliedSignal Bendix-King flight avionics, VHF, UHF or VHF/UHF coms, intercom, KTU-709 Tacan or WL-7 radio compass, KNR 634A VOR/ILS with marker beacon receiver, and ADF. Air data computer. AHRS. Rockwell Collins EFIS-86 display set, manufactured (and software altered) in China at the Sushi Aircraft Instrument Factory, incorporating 2 CRTS in each cockpit. Computing optical gunsight. A HOTAS system is under study.

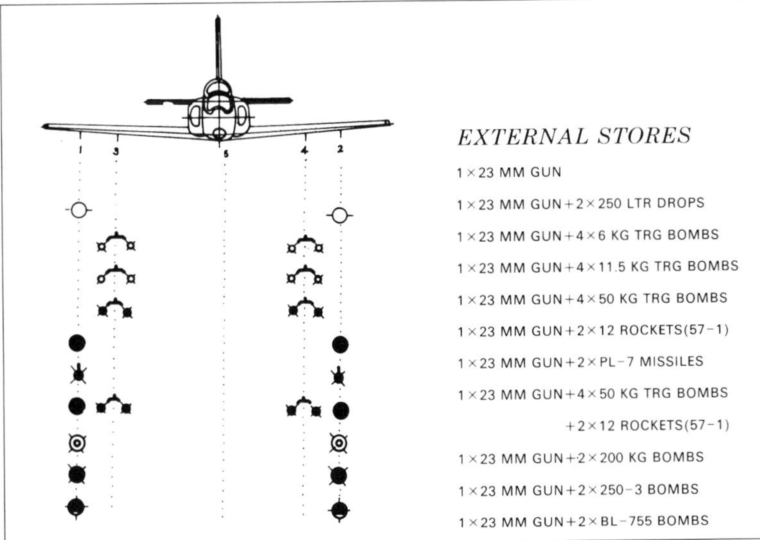

↑ **Hongdu/PAC K-8 Karakorum weapon options** *(courtesy PAC)*

↑ **Hongdu/PAC K-8 Karakorum in service with the Air Force Academy at Risalpur in Pakistan**

Wing characteristics: Straight, low mounted, with slight dihedral.
Wing control surfaces: Boosted ailerons and Fowler type flaps (2 position).
Tail control surfaces: Variable incidence tailplane with horn-balanced elevators (port tab). Rudder with tab.
Airbrakes: 1, beneath the rear fuselage.
Flight control system: Mechanical, with hydraulic aileron, flap and airbrake actuation.
Construction materials: Primarily metal, including honeycomb core for the ailerons, but with composites vertical tail. Present PAC's AMF workshare is restricted to 25% but is expected to rise to 45%. AMF factory already builds the horizontal stabilizer/elevator, vertical tail/rudder and engine cowling. Front fuselage manufacturing capability is being established and co-production plans are being negotiated.
Engine: AlliedSignal TFE731-2A-2A turbofan. Chinese K-8Js to use the Ivchenko PROGRESS AI-25TL turbofan of 3,792 lbf (16.87 kN).
Engine rating: 3,764 lbf (16.74 kN) take-off, 755 lbf (3.36 kN) cruise.
Air intakes: Fuselage sides, level with rear of canopy, with splitter plates.
Fuel system: 1,720 lbs (780 kg) in the wings and 2 bag tanks in the fuselage. 2 × 250 litre drop tanks optional.
Electrical system: 28.5 volt DC supply, with 24 volt back-up. AC supply comprises 400Hz frequency single-phase and 3-phase. Power-generated through engine-driven generator and static invertors.

Details for K-8

PRINCIPAL DIMENSIONS:
Wing span: 31 ft 7 ins (9.63 m)
Maximum length: 38 ft 1 ins (11.6 m)
Maximum height: 13 ft 10 ins (4.21 m)

WINGS:
Aerofoil section: NACA 64A-114, NACA 64A-412 (root/tip)
Area: 183.2 sq ft (17.02 m^2)
Aspect ratio: 5.449
Sweepback: 2.219° at 25% chord
Incidence: 1.5°
Dihedral: 3°

TAIL UNIT:
Tailplane span: 13 f 9 ins (4.2 m)

UNDERCARRIAGE:
Type: Retractable, with steerable nosewheel
Main wheel tyre size: 561 × 169 mm
Wheel base: 14 ft 4.5 ins (4.38 m)
Wheel track: 8 ft (2.43 m)

WEIGHTS:
Empty: 5,924 lb (2,687 kg)
Normal take-off: 8,003 lb (3,630 kg)
Maximum take-off: 9,850 lb (4,468 kg)

PERFORMANCE:
Maximum speed: 432 kts (497 mph) 800 km/h
Unstick speed: 100 kts (115 mph) 185 km/h
Landing speed: 89 kts (103 mph) 165 km/h
Take-off distance: 1,345 ft (410 m)
Landing distance: 1,680 ft (512 m)
Maximum climb rate: 5,900 ft (1,800 m) per minute at sea level
G limits: +7.33, -3
Maximum roll rate: 200° per second
Ceiling: 42,650 ft (13,000 m)
Range with full internal fuel: 756 naut miles (870 miles) 1,400 km
Ferry range: 1,214 naut miles (1,398 miles) 2,250 km
Duration: 3 hours, or 4.4 with drop tanks

Hydraulic system: 3,002 psi, for undercarriage operation, nosewheel steering, wheel brakes, ailerons and flaps. ABEX Aerospace (of California, USA) AP09V-8-01 pump.
Braking system: Hydraulically actuated disc brakes, with anti-skid devices.
Oxygen system: Gaseous supply.

Aircraft variants:
K-8 is the PAC version, as detailed, with AlliedSignal TFE731-2A-2A turbofan.
K-8J is the Chinese version for the PLAAF, with Ivchenko PROGRESS AI-25TL turbofan.

Panavia Aircraft GmbH

Germany/Italy/UK

Corporate address:
im Airport Business Centre, Am Söldnermoos 17, 85399 Hallbergmoos, Germany.

Telephone: +49 811 80 0 (main switchboard)
Facsimile: +49 811 80 1386
Telex: 5 29 825

Founded: 26 March 1969.

Information:
Folkhard Oelwein (Communications – *telephone* +49 811 80 232, *facsimile* +49 811 80 1386).

ACTIVITIES

- Partnership of Alenia of Italy (15%), Daimler-Benz Aerospace of Germany (42.5%) and British Aerospace of the UK (42.5%); see these companies in the earlier pages of this section for individual details.
- Formed for the management of the Tornado design programme, initial build, full production, marketing, public relations, mid-life update and in-service support, on behalf of the tri-national customer organization NETMA.

Panavia Tornado Interdictor Strike (IDS) and Electronic Combat and Reconnaissance (ECR)

First flight: 14 August 1974.
Role: Interdiction, strike, maritime strike and reconnaissance (IDS), and electronic combat and reconnaissance (ECR).

Aims

- European tri-national collaborative programme to satisfy the needs of the UK, Germany and Italy. Netherlands withdrew.
- Multi-role potential basic airframe, reconciling the design requirements of transonic flight at sea level, good field performance, manoeuvrability, high supersonic speed and loiter.
- 2 crew to ease workload, and 2 engines for survivability.
- Radar and comprehensive avionics for all weather operations, with auto-terrain following for enhanced survivability.
- Advanced high by-pass turbofan engines optimized for aircraft, offering low cruise fuel consumption with high augmentation.
- Design fatigue life 16,000 flying hours; scatter factor 4; minimum service life 4,000 flying hours.

Development

- 26 March 1969. Panavia formed to handle the MRCA (Multi-Role Combat Aircraft) contract from the involved governments. Originally comprised BAC, MBB, Fiat (later Aeritalia) and Fokker-VFW, with the Netherlands withdrawing that July (now BAe, Daimler-Benz Aerospace and Alenia).
- May 1969. Project definition phase began.
- 1 June 1969. Turbo Union Ltd formed to design, develop and produce the MRCA engine.
- July 1970. Pre-development phase began.
- September 1971. Intention To Proceed (ITP) declared by the involved governments.
- 27 September 1971. First ground test run of the RB199 engine at Bristol.
- August 1972. Full development contract awarded.
- March 1973. Production investment decision made.
- 14 August 1974. First flight of prototype PO1 at Manching in Germany, crewed by Paul Millet (pilot) and Nils Meister.
- 30 October 1974. First flight of prototype PO2 at Warton in the UK.
- 5 December 1975. First flight of prototype PO5 at Turin in Italy.
- 29 July 1976. Signature of a contract covering the first production batch of 40 aircraft.
- 5 February 1977. First flight of a pre-series IDS (P11).
- 5 June 1979. First Tornado IDS handed over to the RAF at Warton, followed the next day by the first to the Luftwaffe at Manching.
- 29 January 1981. The Tri-national Tornado Training Establishment was officially opened at RAF Cottesmore, Tornados having been received since July 1980.
- 25 September 1981. First production IDS for Italy flew.
- 6 January 1982. Tornado IDSs joined 9 Squadron, RAF, followed by the German Navy and Italy that Summer.
- 8 November 1982. An RAF GR Mk 1 of 9 Squadron made a non-stop return flight between England and Cyprus, refuelled by Victors and a Buccaneer. No 9 Squadron had gained IOC on 1 June.

↑ RAF Tornado GR Mk 4 development aircraft

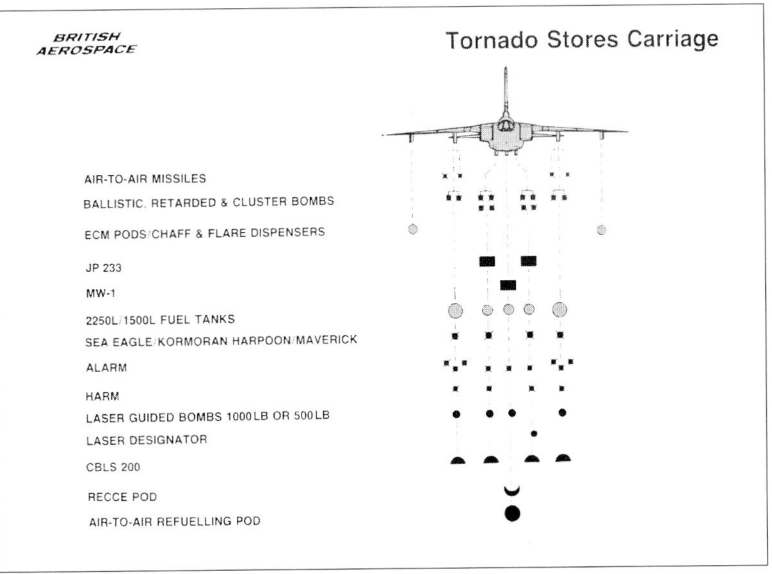

↑ **Panavia Tornado IDS stores carriage diagram** *(courtesy British Aerospace)*

↑ **German Tornado IDS Mid-Life Improvement programme diagram** *(courtesy British Aerospace)*

▪ May 1984. SR (A) 417 Requirement for Tornado upgrade issued.
▪ 11 July 1985. First flight of an RAF Tornado GR Mk 1A, deliveries starting on 3 April 1987.
▪ 26 September 1985. MoU signed between the UK Government and HRH Prince Sultan Bin Abdul Aziz of Saudi Arabia, covering 48 IDS and 24 ADV Tornados, worth an estimated £5 billion (including support).
▪ 26 March 1986. First flight of a Royal Saudi Air Force IDS.
▪ March 1989. Mid-Life Upgrade Development and Investment Contract place with Panavia.
▪ 24 May 1989. The first Tornado Squadron, Germany's MFG 1, completed 50,000 Tornado flying hours.
▪ 21 May 1990. First Tornado ECR was handed over to the Luftwaffe's JaboG 38.
▪ 17 March 1992. Roll-out of the first Italian IDS conversion into an ECR test aircraft took place at Alenia's Caselle test centre.
▪ 1993. SR (A) 417 Requirement for Tornado upgrade re-issued. Scope of modifications and the number of aircraft reduced.
▪ 29 May 1993. First flight of the RAF's GR Mk 4 development aircraft (*ZD 708*).
▪ June 1993. Order placed for follow-on batch of 48 IDS for RSAF.
▪ 14 February 1994. Delivery of the first GR Mk 1B Maritime Strike Tornado to the RAF.
▪ 14 July 1994. £640 million order placed with BAe for conversion of 80 aircraft to GR Mk 4 standard. Options for 62 more for delivery 2000-2002.
▪ 29 July 1994. UK contracts for the Mid-Life Update of GR Mk 1/1As to GR Mk 4/4A standard were signed with Panavia.
▪ 14 October 1996. First of follow-on batch of 48 IDS for the RSAF handed over at Warton.
▪ 4 April 1997. First GR Mk 4 upgraded aircraft flew for the first time (*ZG 750*). Total of 142 upgrades scheduled.
▪ 31 October 1997. Hand-over of the first GR Mk 4 to the RAF.
▪ March 1998. RAF GR Mk 4 entered service. 2 Squadrons to be equipped by the end of 1998.
▪ 1998. In-service date for the first of 40 Luftwaffe Tornados with new reconnaissance pods (see Aircraft variants).
▪ 2002. Completion of GR Mk 4 deliveries to the RAF.

Details

Sales/Users: 781 production IDS/ECR aircraft ordered, of which 750 had been delivered at the time of writing in 1998. Only remaining production aircraft are for delivery to Saudi Arabia. Ordered by Germany (air force 210 IDS and 35 ECR; navy 112), Italy (99), Saudi Arabia (48 originally, with 48 more currently being delivered), and UK (228). 40 German Navy maritime strike aircraft were transferred to the Luftwaffe, and Italy has modified 15 IDSs into ECRs. 142 aircraft being upgraded for the RAF as GR Mk 4/4As.
Crew: Pilot and navigator in tandem.
Cockpit: Front screen in 3 panels, and hinges forward for maintenance access. Single-piece clamshell canopy, hinged at rear. "2 stick" trainer variant retains operational capability. Normalair-Garrett air cycle ECS; pressurization maximum differential 5.2 psi.
Crew escape: Martin Baker Mk 10A fully automatic ejection seats, zero-zero to 625 kts CAS/Mach 2 and 50,000 ft (15,240 m). Canopy jettisons prior to ejection, but MDC assists egress in unlikely case of jettison failure.
Fixed guns: 2 × 27-mm Mauser cannon, in the sides of the lower fuselage. Selectable high and low rate of fire. No guns in the GR Mk 1A reconnaissance version or ECR.
Ammunition: 180 rounds per gun.
Number of weapon pylons: 7. Flat fuselage underside is suited to the carriage of long-range weapons, and has 3 'wet' stations (centreline and 2 outer). Dependent on the stores carried, all 3 may be used simultaneously. Each moving wing panel has inner and outer swivelling pylons; inner are 'wet' and outer dedicated to ECM and chaff/flare pods. Twin or triple stores carriers can be fitted. Inner wing pylons have adapters for Sidewinders in addition to the main store.
Expendable weapons and equipment: Maximum payload of about 19,842 lb (9,000 kg) for both IDS and ECR. Extremely wide range of weapons, including all standard high-explosive bombs, cluster bombs, retarded and low-drag bombs, and laser-guided bombs; programme completed in 1997 to integrate Paveway III low-level LGB. WE177B tactical nuclear weapon available to the RAF until 1998. Practice bomb carriers. Alternative weapons include rocket pods, large weapon dispensers including JP233 and MW-1 for airfield attack and Matra Apache for stand-off attack, and various air-to-surface missiles including Maverick, anti-ship Kormoran and Sea Eagle, and ALARM and HARM for anti-radar. Future weapons will include the US AGM-154A JSOW. Sidewinders provide self defence. Typical configurations are: 8 × 1,000 lb bombs plus 2 Sidewinders, 2 ECM pods and 2 drop tanks; 2 JP-233 dispensers, 2 Sidewinders, 2 ECM pods and 2 tanks; 4 HARM missiles and 2 ECM pods; 2 Kormoran or Sea Eagle missiles and 2 tanks; MW-1, 2 AIM-9L Sidewinders, ECM pod, chaff/flare dispenser and 2 tanks; and 7 ALARM missiles, ECM pod, chaff/flare dispenser and 2 tanks. Future weapons for the RAF's GR Mk 4s include Storm Shadow (CASOM – conventionally armed stand-off missile) and Brimstone anti-armour weapon. German MLIs and Italian Enhancement upgrades to have next-generation ASMs, Paveway IIIs and deployment of the HARM III anti-radiation missile.
Additional stores: Reconnaissance pod on centreline, equipped with wide-angle cameras and infra-red linescan, developed by MBB for German service. 16 Zeiss/Rafael Litening laser designator pods being delivered to the Luftwaffe from 1998 (see Aircraft variants). RAF GR Mk 1A has VICON 2-camera medium-altitude photographic reconnaissance pod; GR Mk 4A to have Hughes Raptor reconnaissance pod with DB-110 electro-optical/infra-red dual-band sensor to offer near real-time imagery, management system and tape recorder (8 plus 2 ground stations ordered). Buddy-buddy refuelling pod available on centreline. Thermal Imaging and Airborne Laser Designator (TIALD) pod. RSAF IDSs have Thomson-CSF designator pod.
Radar: TI developed multi-mode, Ground Mapping Radar (GMR) for blind navigation and targeting, and Terrain Following Radar (TFR) with auto-terrain following capability. Signals from the high resolution mapping radar and TF radar are processed in a shared LRU. Doppler radar for navigational use.
Flight/weapon system avionics/instrumentation: Principal to the avionics system is a 256 kilobyte Litef Spirit 3 digital main computer (being replaced on German and Italian IDSs by an 8 megabyte computer with Ada software), which handles the navigation, flight direction and terrain following, weapon aiming and delivery, computing, communications and defensive aids sub-systems. The sub-systems are interlinked with the GMR and TRF (see Radar), autopilot and flight director system (AFDS), digital inertial navigation system (INS), Tacan, Doppler radar, secondary altitude and heading reference system (SAHRS), air data computer, laser ranger/marked target seeker (LRMTS), ECM/ECCM, communications transmitters and receivers, IFF and ILS. Later production aircraft were also given MIL-STD-1553B (see German MLI under Aircraft variants) databus architecture, enlarged main computer memory, digital missile control unit, advanced displays, new stores management system, a solid state mission data transfer system, improved radar warning system and active ECM. On-board check-out and monitoring system (OCAMS). German ECR is equipped with FLIR, which has been introduced on the RAF's GR Mk 4 variant. Pilot's displays are HUD, head-down moving map, terrain-following E-scope and radar threat warning. Navigator's displays are centrally-located combined mapping radar and moving map display, with identical CRT display either side for navigation and mission planning. May also be used to display electro-optic sensor data (such as FLIR). 3 internal sideways-looking Infra-Red (SLIR) sensor system with signal processing, comprehensive video recording and replay facility on RAF GR Mk 1A (see Aircraft variants). "2 stick" trainer variants have port CRT display removed and flight instruments installed in the rear cockpit. See Mid-Life Update/Improvement and Enhancement programmes under Aircraft variants for new avionics and systems. Italian upgraded aircraft are receiving (among other items) a microwave landing system.
Self-protection systems: Threat radar warning receivers are incorporated, forward and rearward antennae of which are mounted high on the fin leading and trailing edges. A mix of active ECM pods and chaff/flare pods is normal. RAF aircraft usually carry Sky Shadow ECM pod on the port outer wing pylon and BOZ chaff/flare on the starboard wing. German aircraft carry

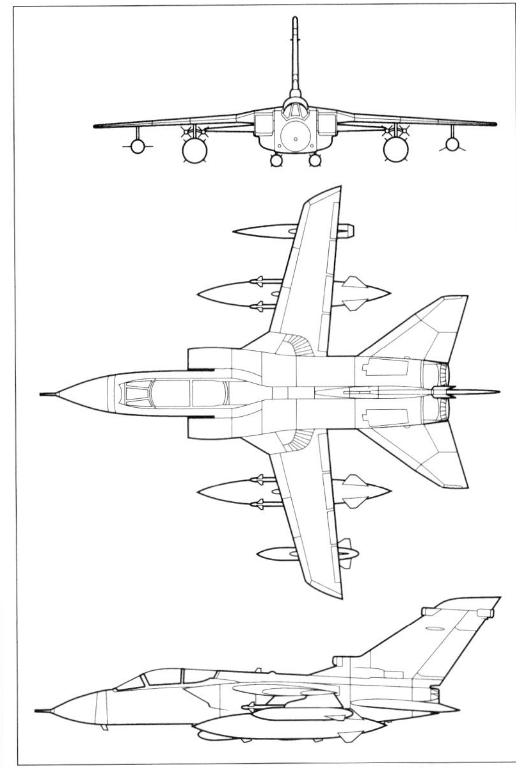

↑ **Panavia Tornado IDS general arrangement** *(courtesy British Aerospace)*

CERBERUS ECM pod and BOZ pod. Italian aircraft are equipped with internally carried self protection jammer and may carry 2 BOZ pods. RAF has deployed an infra-red towed decoy system, as also anticipated for German and Italian aircraft.
Wing characteristics: Variable-geometry outer wing panels. Inboard fixed highly swept 'nibs' (gloves), housing the bodyside wing pivots. 2 spars and machined skin/ribs with integral stiffeners. Swivelling pylon spigots.
Wing control surfaces: Full-span, 4-segment, double-slotted trailing-edge flaperons. Full-span, 3-segment, leading-edge slats. 2-segment lateral control spoilers/lift dumpers at mid span ahead of the flaps. Krueger flaps on the 'nib' leading-edges. Fixed 'nib' has feather fairings to conform to wing contour change with sweep.
Tail control surfaces: Slab tailplane (tailerons), actuated symmetrically for pitch control and differentially for roll. Characteristically large area dictated by short 'tail arm' when wings swept and need to trim effective wing flaps. Tall and large area fin with rudder, dictated by short "fin arm" when wings swept fully aft at supersonic speeds.
Airbrakes: Petal type, in shoulder position each side of the rear fuselage.
Flight control system: All electrical, triplexed fly-by-wire system, with electrical and mechanical back-up modes. Command Stability Augmentation System (CSAS) employs Manoeuvre Demand control and optimizes aircraft flying qualities regardless of speed, height and stores load. Also Gust Alleviation. In the event of multiple failure, mechanical back-up allows a "get home" capability. Spin Prevention and Incidence Limiting System (SPILS) prevents loss of control or spin entry at high incidence. Autopilot and Flight Director System (AFDS).
Fuselage: Manufacture breakdown as: front fuselage, comprising cockpit aft of the rear pressure bulkhead to nose radome (accommodating radar, guns and nose undercarriage); centre fuselage with fuel tankage, intakes and inlet ducting, wing carry-through structure and undercarriage bays, dorsal fairing for services; rear fuselage comprising engine installation with bottom drop-out doors and fin and tailplane spigot mountings.
Construction materials: By weight, aluminium alloy (72%), titanium (17%), steel (6%) and non-metallics (5%). Titanium mainly in the wing carry-through structure incorporating wing pivots, which are Teflon coated, and the engine compartment. Alenia constructs the wings, DASA the centre fuselage section and BAe the remainder of the airframe.
Engines: 2 Turbo Union RB199 turbofans. APU.
Engine rating: 9,100 lbf (40.5 kN) dry, 16,000 lbf (71.2 kN) with afterburning in Mk 103 form for IDS, and 9,550 lbf (42.5 kN) dry and 16,700 lbf (74.3 kN) with afterburning for Mk 105 form for ECR.
Air intakes: Variable 2-dimensional, horizontal wedge type, with fixed first ramp and controlled second ramp and diffuser ramp beyond the throat bleed slot. Swept side walls. 2 auxiliary intake doors on the outer nacelle walls. Bodyside diverter.
Flight refuelling probe: Retractable (and removable) probe on the starboard side of the cockpit.
Fuel system: 5,842 litres in fuselage bag tanks and integral wing tanks, except for RAF and RSAF aircraft which have additional fuel in the fin, making 6,393 litres. Optional drop tanks in 2 underfuselage and 2 wing positions, of 1,500 or 2,250 litre capacities; RAF aircraft can carry 2,250 litre tanks (but wing sweep restricted to 63°). Maximum external fuel weight 12,897 lb (5,850 kg).
Electrical system: 115/220 volt AC 3-phase, 400 Hz constant frequency sub-system and a 28 volt DC sub-system. Power generated by 2 automatically controlled, brushless AC engine-driven generators integrated with a constant speed drive unit. Ni-cd battery for basic flight line servicing functions and APU starting. Emergency power system comprises a single shot battery, emergency hydraulic pump and emergency fuel pump, providing hydraulic power and/or fuel pressure following a double engine flame-out, double generator failure or a double transformer/rectifier unit failure.
Hydraulic system: Fully duplicated, 4,000 psi system, with Vickers pumps.
Braking system: Anti-skid wheel braking, supplemented by thrust reversal and lift dumping. Target type thrust reversers are deployable from a "pre-armed" condition following main wheel contact. Emergency arrester hook. Studies into a new main undercarriage and braking system are underway, to allow increased take-off weight.
Oxygen system: Normalair-Garrett 10 litre liquid oxygen converter. Each seat has an emergency supply.

Aircraft variants:
GR Mk 1 is the basic RAF combat type, with "2 stick" trainer variant. As described. Being upgraded to GR Mk 4 standard.
GR Mk 1A is the RAF reconnaissance version, retaining external stores capability and operational characteristics. Day and night, low-level, high speed, horizon to horizon coverage by 3 internal sideways-looking Infra-Red (SLIR). VICON camera pod. Displaces guns and ammunition. Being upgraded to GR Mk 4A standard. This type is also used by the RSAF.
GR Mk 1B is the RAF maritime attack variant, carrying 2 Sea Eagles on the outer fuselage pylons and with drop tanks on the inner wing pylons. 4 missiles are possible.
GR Mk 4/4A are the RAF's Mid-Life Update versions of the Mk 1/1A to provide covert operational capability. The programme began in 1996 and will be completed in 2002. 142 to be updated from 1/1As in 3 equipment stages. FLIR sensor giving image on a wide-angle HUD, installed in an external fairing on the front fuselage. Hughes Raptor reconnaissance pod (see Additional stores). Night Vision Goggles compatible cockpit. New colour multi-function HDD for pilot. TIALD for autonomous target acquisition, designation and weapon guidance. GPS. New avionics integration system, with MIL-STD-1553B databus controlled by the main computer to link the new systems and permit full integration of an improved defensive aids suite. A 1760 weapons bus is introduced, which controls release of a wide range of weapons and provides improved adaptability for future weapons through the missile control and weapons programming units. Possible future HOTAS.
German IDS, as generally described previously. Luftwaffe force now includes many ex-naval aircraft. Mid-Life Improvement is underway under ("Neue Avionsstruktur") to enhance the low level and high precision weapon delivery capability of the aircraft, together with optimizing the deep penetration tactical capability. Also, to enhance survivability against ground and air threats, the autonomous navigation capability and its interoperability and deployment capability are being improved. New 8-megabyte computer (see avionics) with Ada software and MIL-STD-1760 databus (or operating the laser designator pod, combined laser inertial navigation/GPS and HARM III). FLIR, defensive aids computer, missile warner, and digital cockpit displays, plus next-generation ASMs, Zeiss/Rafael Litening laser designator pod with Paveway III laser-guided bombs, and deployment of the HARM III anti-radiation missile. Industrial studies are continuing for the Enhanced Radar Warning Equipment (ERWE). To include a new reconnaissance role with a podded day/night sensor package with 2 optical cameras and infra-red line-scanner for 40 aircraft. The remaining Navy force is operated for missions against ship (with Kormoran missiles) and land targets, plus reconnaissance (using pods).
Italian IDS force is being enhanced with the German IDSs, with new features including a laser designator pod, laser-guided bombs, deployment of HARM III, advanced radar warning equipment, and microwave landing system.
RSAF IDSs may also receive GR Mk 4-type upgrade at a future time.
ECR is the dedicated electronic combat version, German ECR aircraft having also had a secondary reconnaissance capability until the Honeywell infra-red imaging system was removed to form part of a podded system for German IDSs. Suite of EW equipment is housed in the front fuselage, displacing the guns and ammunition. Threat radar emitter located in the wing root, infra-red imaging linescan, ODIN operational data link (air-to-air and air-to-ground), FLIR and HARM missiles. 35 received by the Luftwaffe, and 16 produced for Italy as IDS conversions.

↑ Luftwaffe Tornado ECR of Einsatzgeschwader No 1, for missions over the former Yugoslavia

Details for Tornado IDS

PRINCIPAL DIMENSIONS:
Wing span: 45 ft 7.5 ins (13.91 m) *spread*, 28 ft 2.5 ins (8.6 m) *fully swept*
Maximum length: 54 ft 9.5 ins (16.7 m) with probe
Maximum height: 19 ft 6 ins (5.95 m)

WINGS:
Area: 286.3 sq ft (26.6 m^2)
Aspect ratio: 7.274 *spread*
Sweepback: 25° *spread*, 67° *fully swept*

TAIL UNIT:
Tailplane span: 22 ft 4 ins (6.81 m)

UNDERCARRIAGE:
Type: Retractable, with twin steerable nosewheels
Main wheel tyre size: 30 × 11.5-14.5
Nose wheel tyre size: 18 × 5.5
Wheel base: 20 ft 4 ins (6.2 m)
Wheel track: 10 ft 2 ins (3.1 m)

WEIGHTS:
Empty: 30,864 lb (14,000 kg)
Take-off, clean: 45,000 lb (20,410 kg), maximum internal fuel
Maximum take-off: 61,729 lb (28,000 kg)

PERFORMANCE:
Maximum operating Mach number (M_{MO}): Mach 2.2 *clean*, Mach 1.8 *with stores*
Maximum speed: 800 kts (921 mph) 1,482 km/h IAS
Take-off distance: 1,510 ft (460 m), or under 1,970 ft (600 m) with heavy weapon load
Landing distance: less than 1,640 ft (500 m)
G limits: +7.5, -1.5
Ceiling: above 50,000 ft (15,240 m)
Radius of action (interdiction, Lo-Lo-Lo-Lo): 600 naut miles (691 miles) 1,111 km*
Radius of action (interdiction, Hi-Lo-Lo-Hi): 800 naut miles (921 miles) 1,482 km*
Radius of action (maritime attack, Hi-Lo-Lo-Hi): over 700 naut miles (806 miles) 1,296 km
Ferry range: 2,050 naut miles (2,360 miles) 3,797 km
*with 4 × 1,000 lb bombs, 2 Sidewinders and 2 drop tanks.

Panavia Tornado Air Defence Variant (ADV)

First flight: 27 October 1979 (pilot David Eagles).
Role: Long-range/duration air defence interceptor.

Aims

■ Significantly different variant of the Tornado airframe, exploiting the multi-role potential. High commonality with IDS, about 80% achieved.

▪ Variable sweep wing for high supersonic speed and high loiter duration, ideally suited to over-ocean intercepts of attacking bombers.
▪ Autonomous all-weather and day/night air defence, with beyond-visual-range engagement.
▪ Patrols for over 3 hours at 300 naut miles from base with 4 Sky Flash and 4 Sidewinder AAMs.

Development

▪ 4 March 1976. FSD initiated, with 3 prototypes included in the first Tornado production contract.
▪ 9 August 1979. Roll-out of the first ADV prototype at Warton (F Mk 2).
▪ 5 November 1984. Delivery of the first F Mk 2 to RAF Coningsby.
▪ 26 September 1985. MoU signed with Saudi Arabia for Tornados (see IDS), including 24 ADVs.
▪ 20 November 1985. Maiden flight of an F Mk 3 for the RAF.
▪ 9 February 1989. First ADV for the RSAF handed over.
▪ 24 March 1993. 170th and last full production ADV delivered to the RAF.
▪ July-December 1995. Initial batch of 12 F Mk 3s on lease to Italy were delivered.
▪ March 1996. Capability Sustainment Programme (CSP) announced by the UK MoD, to enable carriage of ASRAAM and AMRAAM. Contract signed November 1996, valued at about £125 million. Upgrade of up to 100 aircraft.
▪ February-August 1997. Second batch of 12 F Mk 3s delivered to Italy.
▪ Late 1998. 2 RAF squadrons to be operational with CSP-modified F Mk 3s.

Details *(similar to IDS except as follows)*

Sales/Users: 3 development Block 1s. RAF received 18 F Mk 2s (not in service) and 152 F Mk 3s, including 52 in "2 stick" operational training configuration; 24 being leased by the Italian Air Force pending Eurofighter deliveries, with the first handed over on 7 July 1995 for use by 36° Stormo at Gioia del Colle, with 37° at Trapani following with later deliveries. Royal Saudi Air Force received 24.
Fixed guns: 1 × 27-mm Mauser cannon, on starboard side.
Ammunition: 180 rounds.
Number of weapon pylons: Flat underside of the fuselage modified to accommodate 4 medium-range missiles in a semi-recessed, staggered, low-drag arrangement. Special long stroke Frazer Nash ejector/launchers provide safe launch throughout the entire flight envelope. Inner wing pylons only, for external tanks or missiles. Twin Sidewinders may be carried on each wing pylon, using adaptors.
Expendable weapons and equipment: Maximum stores load 18,739 lb (8,500 kg). 4 Sky Flash and 4 AIM-9L Sidewinders; Aspide for Italian aircraft. AMRAAM and ASRAAM compatibility under CSP (see Development).
Additional stores: See Self-protection.
Radar: GEC-Marconi AI-24 Foxhunter multi-mode, track-while-scan, pulse Doppler, with frequency modulated interrupted continuous wave (FMICW). ECCM features. Integrated IFF.

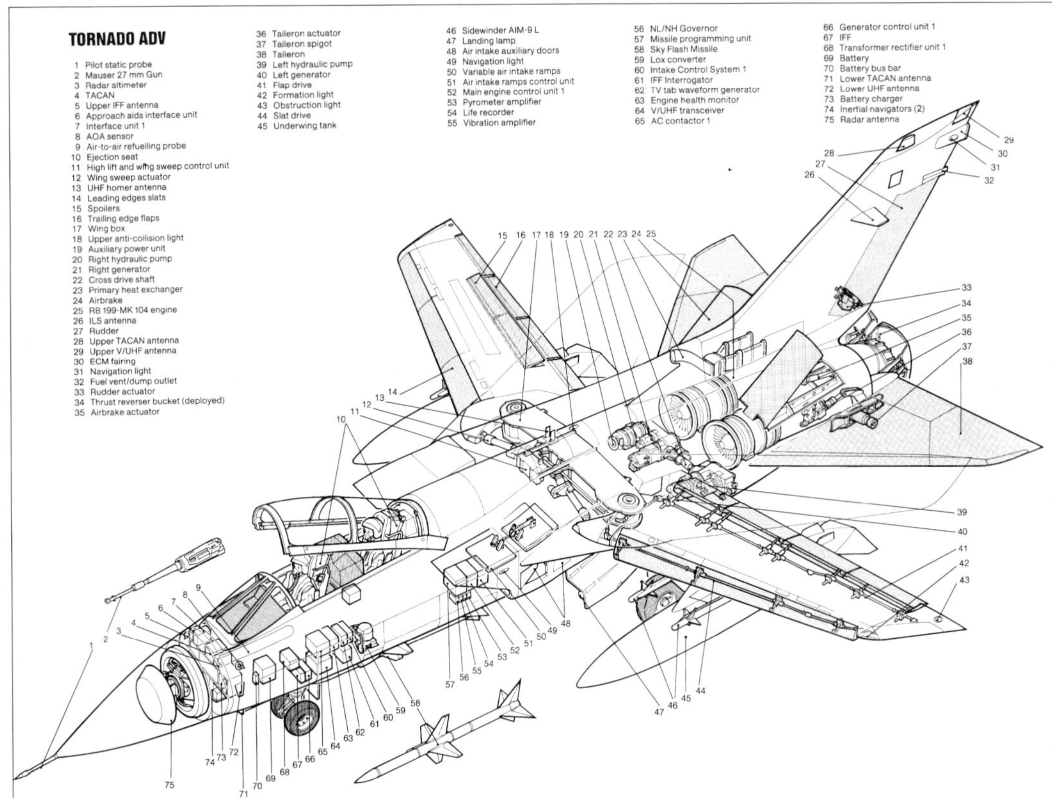

↑ **Panavia Tornado ADV cutaway** *(courtesy British Aerospace)*

Ground mapping mode.
Flight/weapon system avionics/instrumentation: Much of the IDS hardware used, but software optimized for ADV role. Pilot has Smiths Industries HUD, electronic HDD and threat warning displays. Weapon system operator has 2 multi-function display screens with multi-function keys, threat warning display and radar control panel. HOTAS in front cockpit. Secure data link (JTIDS). Litef main computer upgraded to provide dual ported RAM (224kb) for Spirit III processor plus addition of single board computer with Motorola 68040 processor running at 20 MHz with 2 Mb Electrically Erasable Programmable ROM and 1 Mb RAM. In development is an upgrade to the computer display generation system which will replace the discrete Wave Form Generators with modern graphics cards housed in the Litef Main Computer Line Replaceable Unit. This allows computer displays to be enhanced. Cockpit lighting has been modified to provide capability for night vision goggles.
Self-protection systems: Hermes radar homing and warning receivers, with antennae on the fin and in the fixed 'nib' (glove) leading edges. Vinten VICON 78 flare dispensers on engine bay doors. Celsius Tech chaff dispensers on inboard wing pylons. Tracor ALE-40(V) chaff/flare for RSAF.
Wing characteristics: Wing root 'nib' (glove) extended forward, with leading edge sweep increased from 60° to 67°. No outer wing pylons. See Flight control system.
Wing control surfaces: Krueger flaps deleted.
Flight control system: Automatic wing sweep (AWS) and automatic manoeuvre device system (AMDS), to optimize close combat performance. Spin prevention and incidence limiting system (SPILS). Changes to the Command Stability Augmentation System (CSAS) and Autopilot and Flight Director System (AFDS) to enhance rate of roll for air-to-air mission.
Fuselage: Plug of some 1 ft 9 ins (0.54 m) inserted aft of the rear cockpit for ADV, allowing an increase in internal fuel and the carriage of under-fuselage missiles. Longer radome, and small changes at the rear to allow for lengthened jetpipes.
Engines: 2 Turbo Union RB199 Mk 104 turbofans.
Engine rating: Each 9,100 lbf (40.5 kN) dry, 16,410 lbf (73 kN) with afterburning.
Fuel system: Internal capacity increased to 7,270 litres. Maximum auxiliary fuel 7,500 litres.

Details for F Mk 3, *mainly where different to IDS*

PRINCIPAL DIMENSIONS:
Maximum length: 61 ft 1 ins (18.62 m)
Sweepback: 25° *spread*, 67° *fully swept*, with intermediate angles of 45° and 58° via AWS system. Fully spread for speeds below Mach 0.73 and fully swept above Mach 0.95

WEIGHTS:
Empty: 31,967 lb (14,500 kg)
Maximum take-off: 61,729 lb (28,000 kg)

PERFORMANCE:
Maximum operating Mach number (M_{MO}): Mach 2.2 *clean*, Mach 1.8 *with stores*
Maximum speed: 800 kts (921 mph) 1,482 km/h IAS
Time to 30,000 ft (9,145 m): under 2 minutes from brakes off
Take-off distance: less than 3,000 ft (915 m) in full combat configuration
Landing distance: less than 2,130 ft (650 m), or 1,214 ft (370 m) using brakes and thrust reversers
Roll rate: 180° per second at 750 kts (863 mph) 1,389 km/h
G limits: +7.5, -3
Ceiling: 50,000-70,000 ft (15,240-21,300 m)
Radius of action (point intercept): 900 naut miles (1,036 miles) 1,667 km *subsonic**, or 200 naut miles (230 miles) 370 km supersonic*
Duration (combat air patrol): 3 hours at 300 naut miles (345 miles) 556 km from base*
*4 Sky Flash missiles, Sidewinders, gun/ammunition and 2 drop tanks.

↑ **RAF Panavia Tornado F Mk 3 dispensing infra-red jamming flares**

SEPECAT France/UK

Full name:
Société Européene de Production de l'Avion Ecole de Combat et d'Appui Tactique.

Founded:
1966.

ACTIVITIES

■ SEPECAT founded to manage the Anglo-French Jaguar programme. See British Aerospace (UK) and Dassault Aviation (France) for company details.

SEPECAT Jaguar

Comments: First flown on 8 September 1968, this strike fighter and maritime strike aircraft (plus advanced/operational trainer) has been out of production in Europe since 1985, though it continued to be manufactured in India thereafter (see HAL Shamsher under India). A full description of the Jaguar can be found in the 1996-97 edition of *WA&SD*, pages 169-170.

Various modification and upgrade programmes are underway, and to keep readers up to date with developments, the following amendments should be made to the earlier description.

Development

■ 1996-98. RAF aircraft underwent modification to incorporate new weapon and avionics improvements, including GEC-Marconi TIALD (thermal imaging airborne laser designation) pod, HOTAS, GPS, and wide-angle HUD. Upgraded variants are known as GR Mk 3s and T Mk 4s. The first upgrade to Jaguar '96 standard flew in January 1996, prior to '97 upgrade.

■ 1997. £40 million contract signed between the UK Government and Oman to upgrade 19 of Oman's Jaguar Internationals to Jaguar '97 standard. Included are 6 TIALD pods.

Expendable weapons and equipment: Future weapons will include JSOW, Paveway III laser-guided bomb and ASRAAM. The Lockheed Martin Minimum Collateral Damage Weapon (MCDW) has been tested.

Additional stores: Self contained reconnaissance pack available, carried on the centreline pylon, with up to 5 low and high altitude cameras plus infra-red linescan and the addition of the Vinten VICON system incorporated on the GR Mk 3 variant.

Flight/weapon system avionics/instrumentation: RAF GR Mk 1A and Mk 2A variants upgraded to new GR Mk 3 and T Mk 4 respectively, to include additional features such as HOTAS, wide-angle HUD, new 6 ins × 8 ins (15 × 20 cm) active matrix liquid crystal head-down display, colour MFD, video HUD camera, X1553B databus, GPS, twin Have Quick radios, digital moving map, Alpha helmet-mounted sight (12 ordered initially from GEC-Marconi/Honeywell), TIALD pod, Auto Voice Alert Device, Terprom ground proximity warning system, and Mk 12 IFF. To complement these hardware enhancements, software packages are being updated and introduced. These changes are incorporated into programmes known as Jaguar '96 and Jaguar '97.

Self-protection systems: New Sky Guardian RWR and towed radar decoy.

Engines: 2 Rolls-Royce Turbomeca Adour turbofans, to be upgraded to Mk 106s (see below).

Engine rating: Complementary to the avionics upgrade, the RAF intends to further upgrade its Jaguar engines to the more powerful and economical Mk 106 standard, of 8,249 lbf (36.69 kN), between 1998 and 2005.

Aircraft variants:
Jaguar A is the French single-seater.
Jaguar B is the RAF 2-seater, originally designated T.Mk 2 but upgraded with FIN 1064 to Mk 2A standard and now further upgraded to Mk 4 with inclusion of updates from the Jaguar '96 and '97 programmes (see above).
Jaguar E is the French 2-seater.
Jaguar S is the RAF single-seater, originally designated GR Mk 1, upgraded with FIN 1064 to Mk 1A standard and now further upgraded to GR Mk 3 with inclusion of updates from the Jaguar '96 and '97 programmes (see above).
Jaguar International is the exported version, with more engine power and other changes as detailed previously. Overwing AAMs.
Shamsher is the Indian Air Force name for its Jaguar Internationals. See HAL.

↑ **RAF Jaguars are being upgraded to GR Mk 3 standard**

S.C. Avioane S.A.Craiova/Soko/UTVA Romania/Bosnia-Herzegovina/Serbia/Yugoslavia

Corporate address:
For company details, see earlier part of Combat section and General Aviation section.

Avioane IAR-93 and Soko J-22 Orao

Comments: Avioane has informed the Chief Editor that work on the IAR-93/J-22 Orao programme with Yugoslavia/Serbia has been terminated. For details and a photograph, see the 1996-97 edition of *WA&SD*, page 170.

Yakovlev Joint Stock Company/Aermacchi SpA Russia/Italy

Corporate address:
See Yakovlev and Aermacchi in the main Russian and Italian sections.

Yakovlev/Aermacchi Yak/Aem-130 and Yak-131, Yak-133 and Yak-135

First flight: 25 April 1996 at Zhukovsky (Yak-130D, piloted by Andrei Sinitsin).
Role: 2-seat jet trainer, and light combat and reconnaissance aircraft (see Aircraft variants).

Aims

■ To replace the L-29 Delfin and L-39 Albatros in Russian Air Force service.
■ To be capable of various aspects of training, including flying, air combat and weapons.
■ Requirements of the Russian Air Force are (in summarized form):
a) 2 non-afterburning engines, with 0.6-0.7 power-to-weight ratio. Maximum take-off weight 15,432 lb (7,000 kg).
b) 459 kts (528 mph) 850 km/h maximum speed. Landing speed not exceeding 92 kts (106 mph) 170 km/h, and take-off and landing runs not exceeding 1,640 ft (500 m). Provision for operation from unpaved runways.
c) Normal range of 648 naut miles (746 miles) 1,200 km at Mach 0.5 and 19,700 ft (6,000 m) altitude. Ferry range of 1,350 naut miles (1,553 miles) 2,500 km
d) G limits of +8, -3.
e) High manoeuvrability, similar to that of new generation fighters.
f) Pre-programmable control system imitating aircraft with different longitudinal stability coefficient.
g) 15,000 flying hours structural life over 30 years.

Development

■ January 1991. Competition for a new generation jet trainer (UTS, uchebno-trenirovochnyi samolyot) was initiated by the Russian Air Force. UTK (uchebno-trenirovochnyi komplex) training system has been ordered which includes (besides the UTS aircraft) flight simulators.
■ January 1992. First stage of the competition summarized. Mikoyan 821, Myasishchev M-200, Sukhoi S-54 and Yakovlev Yak-130 took part in the design competition. The designs were judged in 8 technical and economic categories. The Sukhoi S-54 was reportedly judged winner in 4 of the 8 categories (technical perfection, flight safety, combat capability and technical-training). But, at the same time, the S-54 was disqualified for having only a single engine. From the remaining designs, the Yak-130 reportedly came out best, but its advantage over the Mikoyan 821 was not decisive and it was decided to postpone the competition result. Both Mikoyan and Yakovlev were approved to continue the development of prototypes.
■ 30 November 1994. The first Yak-130D prototype under construction was displayed, prior to having its engines and avionics installed. Aermacchi of Italy co-operated in development.
■ June 1995. Yak-130D was presented at the Paris Air Show (in the static park).
■ 25 April 1996. Maiden flight of the Yak-130D.
■ Late 1996. Slovakia announced its intention to order the Yak-130.
■ January 1997. Initial order for 10 aircraft from the Russian Ministry of Defence.
■ 11-31 July 1997. Display and familiarization flights to Italy and Slovakia.
■ Summer 1998. Start of flight trials with the Russian Air Force.
■ 2000. First prototype of the Yak/Aem-130 international version.
■ 2002. First deliveries of the Yak/Aem-130.
■ 2009. Final delivery of the initial 100 to the Russian Air Force.

Details

Sales/Users: The Yak-130 is being developed in co-operation with Aermacchi of Italy and Povazské Strojárne of Slovakia (engine). On the basis of a 1993 agreement, Aermacchi contributes financially to the programme and adapts the aircraft for the Western market. Yak-130 is manufactured at the Sokol plant in Nizhny Novgorod in Russia and will be sold by Yakovlev throughout the CIS and by Aermacchi elsewhere in the world. The Yak-130D prototype was built at the Yakovlev works in Moscow and made some 120 flights in its first 15 months. 10 aircraft have been ordered for service trials with the Russian Air Force. The first production aircraft was scheduled to begin flight tests in 1998. Production rate of 4 aircraft per year. The prototype of the international version is expected to appear in the year 2000. Initially, the Russian requirement was estimated at 800-1,000 aircraft, later reduced to 500 and now said to be 200, with the first 100 for delivery by the year 2009 and the second 100 after this date. At the end of 1996, Slovakia announced its intention to purchase 40 Yak-130s in the training version, as well as some in the single-seat combat variant to replace MiG-21s. Yakovlev and Aermacchi estimate the potential export market at 1,300 aircraft, and a market for 770 combat variants.

Crew: Student-pilot (front) and instructor (rear) in tandem cockpits. 16° look-down visibility from front seat and 6° from rear raised seat.

↑ Yakovlev Yak-130D demonstrator for the Yak/Aem-130 *(Piotr Butowski)*

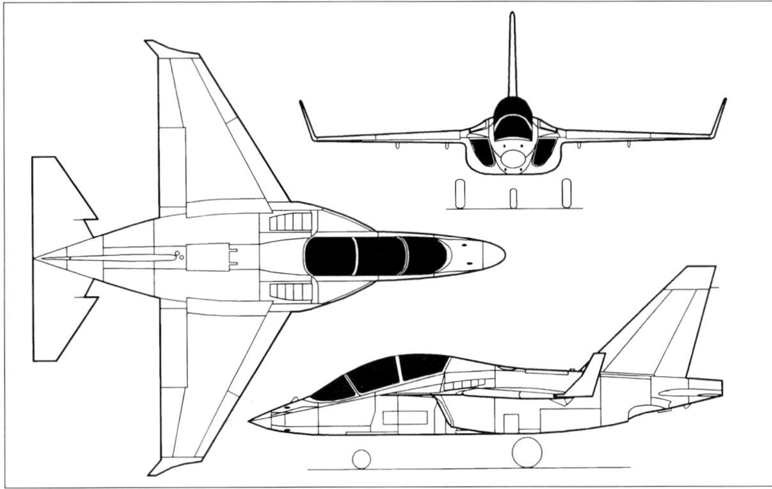
↑ Yakovlev Yak-130 in expected production form, with shorter LERX and dog-tooth horizontal tail surfaces *(Piotr Butowski)*

Crew escape: Zvezda K-93 or Martin Baker Mk 10L/Mk 16 zero-zero ejection seats.
Fixed guns: Laser imitation of cannon for training.
Number of weapon pylons: 7.
Expendable weapons and equipment: 6,614 lb (3,000 kg) load. Can include guided missiles, unguided rockets, bombs and gun pods.
Radar: Phazotron Moskit-2 (Mosquito) planned for the Yak-131. Search range 32 naut miles (37 miles) 60 km and weighing 110 lb (50 kg).
Flight/weapon system avionics/instrumentation: Mission avionics to be developed jointly by GFSA (Finmeccanica)/FIAR of Italy and Leninets of Russia. MIL-STD-1553B architecture. Automatic flight and training procedure control system with 2 digital computers. HUD in the front cockpit. 3 liquid crystal MFDs in each cockpit, with conventional instrumentation as stand-by. Navigation system including GPS, short range radio navigation and instrument landing, radio-compass, radio altimeter, etc. The aircraft has a combat simulator system which includes close air combat with use of infra-red and other guided missiles and cannon, attack against ground targets with various types of guided missiles, as well as passive and active jamming. Helmet mounted sight. Com radio, intercom, IFF, flight data recorder, and video recording of student-pilot behaviour.
Wing characteristics: Mid-mounted, thin wing with variable camber, swept leading edges and wingroot extensions. Winglets (temporarily removed in 1996).
Wing control surfaces: Automatic slats on leading edges. Ailerons and Fowler type trailing-edge flaps.
Tail control surfaces: All-moving slab tailplane, with dogtooth extended chord leading edges. Tall fin and rudder.
Airbrakes: Door-type on the upper fuselage.
Flight control system: Quadruple digital fly-by-wire. Longitudinal stability can be programmed within 0-10% range.
Engines: 2 Povazské Strojárne RD-35/DV-2S turbofans, with digital control (FADEC). Garrett GTCP 36-150 or Russian Saphir 5 APU.
Engine rating: Each 4,850 lbf (21.58 kN).
Air intakes: Main air intakes are located under the leading-edge root extensions (LERX). Take-off intakes for unpaved runway operations are on the upper surface of LERX (solution similar to that of the MiG-29 but much simpler).
Flight refuelling probe: None.
Fuel system: Up to 3,638 lb (1,650 kg) of fuel in 3 internal tanks (1 in the fuselage behind the cockpit and 1 inside each wing). Provision for auxiliary conformal tank containing 1,213 lb (550 kg) of fuel. Normal fuel load is 1,874 lb (850 kg).
Electrical system: 200/115 volt AC, 400Hz.
Hydraulic system: 3,000 psi.

Aircraft variants:
Yak-130D (demonstrator) is the first prototype. Length 39 ft (11.9 m), wing span 35 ft (10.66 m), longer LERXs and no dogtooth at tailplane. Maximum speed limited to 505 kts (581 mph) 935 km/h. G limit 7.
Yak-130 is the basic Russian training version, as detailed.
Yak/Aem-130 is an export derivative, marketed by Aermacchi. Avionics and cockpit arrangement similar to MB-339CD.
Yak-131, ***Yak-133*** and ***Yak-135*** are single-seat or 2-seat lightweight combat aircraft, suited to fighter, close air support and reconnaissance roles. Technical documentation for Yak-131 will be completed in 1998, in both Russian and export forms. Equipment could include Moskit-2, Osa or Grifo radar.
Specialized variants of the Yak-130 trainer are:
Air Defence interception training.
Ship-borne training with arrester hook, strengthened undercarriage and folding wings.
Bomber/transport pilot training, with side-by-side widened cockpit.
Single-seat lightweight combat aircraft (fighter, close-air support, reconnaissance).
4-seat civil executive version, cruising at 351 kts (404 mph) 650 km/h, normal range 621 naut miles (715 miles) 1,150 km, and maximum range 1,080 naut miles (1,243 miles) 2,000 km.
4-seat ship-borne VIP aircraft.
Upon retirement, the aircraft will be converted into pilotless flying targets.

↑ Yakovlev Yak-130D demonstrator. Note the unusual shape of the air intakes, and the height of the rear cockpit

Details for Yak-130 (unless stated)

PRINCIPAL DIMENSIONS:
Wing span: 34 ft 2.5 ins (10.424 m)
Maximum length: 36 ft 11 ins (11.245 m)
Maximum height: 15 ft 8 ins (4.783 m), quoted as 15 ft 7.5 ins (4.76 m) for Yak/Aem-130

WINGS:
Wing area: 252.95 sq ft (23.5 m²)
Wing aspect ratio: 4.62
Sweepback at leading edge: 31°
Sweepback at trailing edge: 0°

UNDERCARRIAGE:
Type: Retractable, with nosewheel
Main wheel tyre size: 650 × 260 mm
Nose wheel tyre size: 500 × 150 mm
Wheel base: 12 ft 9.5 ins (3.95 m)
Wheel track: 8 ft 4 ins (2.53 m)

WEIGHTS:
Normal take-off (1,874 lb, 850 kg of fuel): 11,905 lb (5,400 kg)
Maximum take-off, clean: 13,669 lb (6,200 kg)
Maximum take-off: 19,841 lb (9,000 kg)

PERFORMANCE:
Maximum speed: 567 kts (652 mph) 1,050 km/h
Take-off speed: 108 kts (124 mph) 200 km/h, quoted as 110 kts (127 mph) 205 km/h for Yak/Aem-130
Landing speed: 105 kts (121 mph) 195 km/h, quoted as 95 kts (109 mph) 175 km/h for Yak/Aem-130
Take-off distance: 1,017 ft (310 m) at sea level, ISA
Landing distance: 1,591 ft (485 m) at sea level, ISA, 20% fuel
Time to 35,000 ft (9,145 m): 4 minutes 12 seconds
G limits: +8, -3
Sustained g-limit: 4.9 at 15,000 ft (4,572 m), Mach 0.8
Allowable angle-of-attack: 35°
Ceiling: over 41,010 ft (12,500 m)
Ferry range: 1,149 naut miles (1,323 miles) 2,130 km, quoted as 1,200 naut miles (1,382 miles) 2,224 km for Yak/Aem-130

Special Electronic & Reconnaissance Aircraft

Note: This section details specially developed electronic and reconnaissance aircraft, and generally not the sub-variants of operational combat aircraft used for similar tasks (which can be found under the main aircraft headings in the Combat section). Highly specialized electronic variants of freighters and airliners are detailed here, but not electronic and other special helicopters, which remain with all other helicopters in that section.

Embraer — Brazil

Corporate address:
See Combat section for full company details.

Embraer EMB-120EW and SR

Comments: Development of these sensor platforms, based on the EMB-120 Brasilia, has ended, their tasks having now been transferred to variants of the larger ERJ145 (which see). For details of the EMB-120EW and SR programme, and a photograph, see the 1996-97 edition of *WA&SD*, page 171.

Embraer RJ145 AEW&C, RJ145SA and RS

Note: When the name Embraer is not used before the aircraft designation, the designation becomes ERJ145.
Prime contractor: Raytheon (see Development below). Embraer and Ericsson are jointly marketing the AEW&C internationally.
First flight: 1999.
First delivery: 2000, to the Brazilian Air Force.
Role: *ERJ145 AEW&C*: Airborne early warning and control. *ERJ145SA*: Aerial surveillance for the Brazilian SIVAM programme, optimized for air traffic monitoring and general surveillance duties. *ERJ145RS*: Remote sensing for the Brazilian SIVAM programme, including exploitation of natural resources, environmental control, river pollution control, economic activities and ground occupation monitoring, and illegal activities surveillance; principal mission is to collect data from the ground.
Based on: ERJ145 regional airliner (formerly known as EMB-145 – see Airliners section). Structural changes for the installation of mission systems, including an over-fuselage radar scanner housing for the AEW&C and SA versions, and an under-fuselage fairing for the RS version. Reinforced airframe, navigation and communications systems, enhanced APU, increased fuel capacity and revised interior layout.

Aims

- To produce a derivative of the ERJ145 airliner, with the airframe modified for the integration of an advanced mission system designed for Airborne Early Warning applications. Under the Brazilian SIVAM programme, the AEW&C version is known as ERJ145SA.
- To produce a second electronic ERJ145 variant as the ERJ145RS, for remote sensing under the SIVAM programme.
- Under the SIVAM programme, to co-ordinate and support actions for the protection, rational exploitation of natural resources and sustained development of the Amazonian region.
- Special attention given to the particularly severe environmental conditions for aircraft in the operational area under the SIVAM programme, and their impact in systems design and reliability. Typical missions in the Amazon will exceed 8 hours duration.
- With the ERJ145SA system, data are transmitted real-time over VHF data-link. Target data from primary and secondary radar and communications scanner are combined. Final identification, situation evaluation and decisions are made in the 3 regional co-ordination centres (CRVs), to be established in the Amazonian region, and the central co-ordination centre stationed in Brasilia. Direction of intercept aircraft onto targets can be carried out from the aircraft or from the CRVs.
- Embraer's effective participation in the SIVAM programme is 30%, while development of the SA and RS aircraft is seen as an important step in its ability to develop and market an AEW&C aircraft on the international military market, in co-operation with Ericsson.
- Total cost of SIVAM programme is about US$1.4 billion, funded by foreign resources.

Development

- 1990. SIVAM-Sistema de Vigilância da Amazônia (Amazon Surveillance System) programme conceived.
- September 1994. News released of Embraer's selection by the Brazilian Government to develop versions of the EMB-120 Brasilia as mission aircraft for SIVAM.
- Development in co-ordination with Raytheon of the USA, the prime contractor, providing Brazil with an advanced Air Traffic Control (ATC) environmental surveillance and early warning system for the EMB-120 (later for the ERJ145, see below).
- 1996. EMB-120 effectively replaced by ERJ145 as the airframe configuration of the electronic versions, with Raytheon continuing to act as prime contractor. A communications network, remote earth-sensing satellite information, and other ground and airborne sensor systems form the SIVAM system.
- March 1997. Contract signed between Embraer and the SIVAM Co-ordination Committee (CCSIVAM) for the development and production of 8 aerial surveillance and remote sensing systems, based on the ERJ145.
- 1998. First flight of an ERJ145SA with a mock radar installation for aerodynamic testing.
- 1999. Delivery of the first of 5 Ericsson Erieye radars to Embraer, under a US$145 million contract signed in 1997.

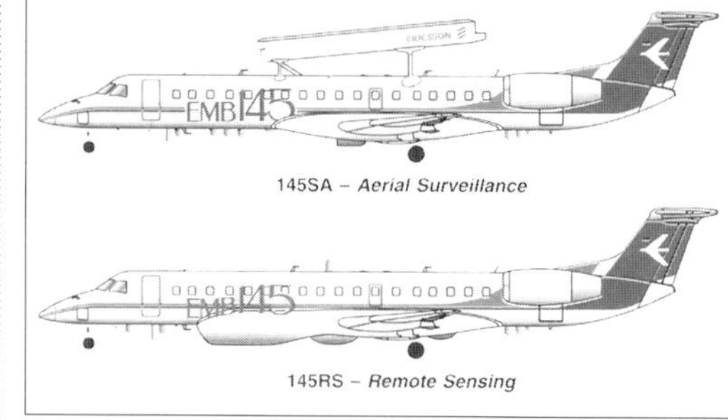

↑ Embraer RJ145SA (*top*) and RJ145RS (*bottom*) *(courtesy Embraer)*

- 1999. First flight of an ERJ145RS, with systems integration that year. Also ERJ145SA systems integration.
- 2000. First ERJ145RS and SA deliveries to the Air Force.
- Raytheon, and the ATECH Foundation (Application of Critical Technology) responsible for the integration services, have been contracted to take part in the SIVAM programme.
- 2002. Final delivery of the last of 8 RS/SAs.

Details

Sales/Users: Brazil (5 ERJ145SAs and 3 ERJ145RSs initially).
Crew: 2 pilots and 1 to 3 system operators, depending on the mission; can carry a relief crew, for a total of 7 crew members. All information in the command and control system is available to all 3 work stations, which are programmable to allow an operator to use any station.
Radar: ERJ145 AEW&C and SA use a new-generation Ericsson Microwave Systems Erieye mission system comprising an active phased-array Doppler surveillance radar and a modular open C^2 system (see Other mission sensors). Major differences from the version of Erieye used by the Swedish Air Force are optimization to lower speed targets and adaptation of the man-machine interface to the roles of the SIVAM operators. Radar control functions are performed in the aircraft instead of at ground centres, in case the data link to the ground centres fails or is out of range. All changes are software related. The fixed S-band radar antenna is said to place much less demand on aircraft size, thereby offering a high-performance AEW&C system for use from relatively small commercial and military aircraft. Antenna is 26 ft 3 ins (8 m) long, providing a narrow main beam and extremely low sidelobe levels. The electronically scanned beam enables beam-steering flexibility, said to offer extended range and enhanced tracking performance compared to a rotodome solution. By directing radar energy in any wanted direction, assigning can be made to priority areas of interest. Erieye detects air and sea targets out to the horizon and beyond, with an instrumented range of 242 naut miles (280 miles) 450 km and a typical detection range against a fighter size target of more than 189 naut miles (217 miles) 350 km. It has coverage to about

↑ Embraer RJ145SA aerial surveillance aircraft

↑ Embraer RJ145SA workstation *(courtesy Ericsson)*

82,000 ft (25,000 m) altitude. Mission avionics system creates a real-time air situation picture for local display as well as for transmission to the ground-based CRVs. ERJ145RS has a Canadian MacDonald Dettwiler IRIS type Synthetic Aperture Radar (SAR). Systems and ground equipment supplied by Raytheon. This provides all-weather day and night maps of the ground over all terrain, allowing observation, classification, localization and eventual movement over ground and water.
Other mission sensors: The ERJ145 AEW&C and SA have an on-board command and control system, said to be the world's first using Commercial Off-The-Shelf (COTS) computers, providing open architecture for flexibility and growth potential. 3 multi-function operator work stations, each equipped with a large colour display and user-friendly man-machine interface; a high degree of automation and computer support minimizes the operator workload. Watkins Johnson communications and non-communications exploitation system (COMMS/ NON-COMMS). The ERJ145RS has a Daedalus ultraviolet/visible/infra-red line scanner, Versatron SA-144 Skyball high-sensitivity TV/FLIR and the COMMS/NON-COMMS system. Line scanner allows a high-resolution image and simultaneously collects and records up to 6 spectral bands.
Fuel system: Adoption of an additional fuel tank.
Flight avionics/instrumentation: Adoption of new navigation and communication systems, including laser gyro, GPS, FMS and VHF data-link. Integrated IFF.
Aircraft variants: See Role.

de Havilland Inc — Canada

Corporate address:
Unit of Bombardier Aerospace Group, Bombardier Inc (see Combat section for company details).

Notes: The US Army is deploying 3 de Havilland RC-7Bs, with 2 more for 1999, installed with Crazy Hawk Airborne Reconnaissance Low-Multi-function (ARL-M) radar systems to patrol the demilitarized zone between North and South Korea. These have been prepared by California Microwave, with the synthetic aperture radars based on the Raytheon HISAR system. See Hughes and California Microwave under USA.

A Dash 8 Series 200B is in operation in Australia for hydrographic survey in coastal waters, using the Vision Systems laser airborne depth sounder (LADS – similar LADS systems are also operated on a Royal Australian Navy Fokker F27 and US Navy P-3 Orion).

de Havilland E-9A and CT-142

Role: *E-9A*: Airborne over-the-horizon telemetry relay, to relay manned/unmanned air vehicle control data, and gather data, during missile trials at the Gulf Test Range. Also used to sea-search for intruders during tests. Can relay data from 5 pairs of vehicles flying at over Mach 5. *CT-142*: Navigation trainer.
Based on: DHC-8 Dash 8M series 100.
Sales/Users: Canada (4 CT-142s) and USA (USAF 2 *E-9As*, operated by the 475th Weapons Evaluation Group at Tyndall AFB, Florida).
Crew: *E-9A*: 2 pilots and a systems operator.
Radar: *E-9A*: Telephonics AN/APS-128D sea surveillance radar in an underfuselage radome. *CT-142*: Mapping radar in the extended nose.

↑ de Havilland E-9A with steerable phased-array telemetry antenna housed behind the fuselage fairing

Other mission sensors: *E-9A*: 5 beam, 75 ft (22.86 m) steerable phased-array telemetry antenna in a box fairing on the starboard side of the fuselage (photograph with telemetry antenna exposed can be found in the 1996-97 edition of *WA&SD*, page 171).

Chinese AEW&C programmes — China

Note: China is actively involved in the development of AEW&C aircraft for the PLAAF, using foreign assistance with the radar and installation. Varied reports formerly suggested the Shaanxi Y8 or Ilyushin Il-76 as the carrier aircraft. Either was possible, but it is known that both competing foreign radar suppliers (IAI and GEC-Marconi) have worked on the basis of the Il-76/A-50. In 1993 representatives from GEC-Marconi visited China to present details of the Argus S-band AEW radar system (see UK), derived from the Nimrod AEW Mk 3 programme that had been cancelled in 1986. The Argus 2000 presumably requires large radomes on the nose and tail to house the antennae and avoid interference from the airframe, each with a 180° scan in azimuth. GEC-Marconi actively sought an Il-76 airframe for prototype installation plus technical documents, with British Aerospace probably to assist in actual structural modification. Reports suggest Russia offered an Il-76, but wants to be involved in the programme. Negotiations with China over the cost of the Argus system installation continued into 1998 (see GEC-Marconi). The second company is Israel Aircraft Industries, using its Phalcon system. The Phalcon usually has conformal antennae, but a dorsal arrangement has been adopted, with 3 triangularly arranged arrays housed in an above-fuselage radome, with the first mounted in a Beriev A-50 *Mainstay* airframe from Russia (see IAI entry) in 1998 under an Israeli/Russian co-operation agreement (see Beriev entry). Likely participation in both programmes by China Leihua Electronic Technology Research Institute at Wuxi:

Reims Aviation S.A. — France

Corporate address:
Aérodrome de Reims-Prunay, BP 2745, 51062 Reims Cedex.

Telephone: +33 3 26 48 46 46
Facsimile: +33 3 26 49 13 60
Telex: 870 754F
E-mail: www;champ;ing;fr/reims_aviation

Founded:
Out of Max Holste, originally (but no longer) with Cessna as a 49% shareholder after a February 1960 agreement to produce small Cessna aircraft for European and African markets.

Information:
Gildas Illien (Vice President, Sales & Marketing) and Max Boirame (Public Relations).

ACTIVITIES

- Manufacturing, assembly and customization of the F 406 and system integration.
- Plans to manufacture and assemble single-engined F172 and F182 lightplanes under Cessna licence were abandoned in 1998.
- Subcontracting for main customers (Dassault Aviation and Aerospatiale) in major European programmes in which Reims plays an active role: Airbus A300/A310; Falcon series; Mirage 2000; Atlantique 2; and ATR 42/72.
- Partnership work on A330/A340 belly fairing.
- Aircraft maintenance and servicing through RAMS (Reims Aviation Maintenance Service), a 100% subsidiary of Reims Aviation.

Reims Vigilant series

Role: Maritime surveillance, border surveillance and customs control, maritime and land pollution control, aerial photography, calibration, and comint (communications intelligence).
Based on: Reims Caravan II (see General Aviation section). Specific characteristics of Vigilant in the basic version include, apart from mission equipment, heavy duty marine corrosion protection, air conditioning and internal ventilation system, de-icing equipment, special operator seats, photo window, and emergency exits with opening controls.
Crew: Typically 3 for surveillance missions.
Sales/Users: Includes the custom services of Australia (Vigilant) and France (Vigilant Polmar and Vigilant Surmar), plus Scottish Fisheries (Vigilant).
Number of stores pylons: In 1996 Reims developed wing hard points to make the aircraft suitable for carrying light weapons (such as machine-gun pod or rocket launcher), camera pods or SAR life raft.

Aircraft variants:
Vigilant in basic form can have GEC-Marconi Seaspray 2000 maritime surveillance radar, although Raytheon APS-134 is used by the Australian customs.
Calibration for in-flight control of navigation and landing aids, to calibrate ILS, VOR, DME, VHF, NDB, GONIO, PAPI, VASI, radar and Tacan.
Comint/Intelligence is the electronic warfare version, first unveiled at the 1997 Paris Air Show and jointly developed with Thomson-CSF. SAS airborne ECM. On-board workstation used for interception, listening, analysis and goniometry of radioelectric emissions. Options include transmission of data to a ground control station, radioelectric emissions jamming capacity, and self-protection via a threat analyser and a decoy launching system. Uses advanced technology to home onto radio signals (voice or data transmission), with PPT processing and a high scanning rate, which allow intercept of fixed and mobile radios and message sending systems.
Vigilant Frontier is for border surveillance and anti-drug control, with surveillance radar, FLIR and datalink for detection, display of movement on land, sea or air, to record activity and transmit the data in real time to other units. For anti-drug control, is equipped with APG-66 surveillance system and turret FLIR.
Geo Survey for cartography and geo-surveillance, with spacious cabin for high-definition cameras, workstations and technical

equipment. Cameras in cabin or in optional exterior cargo pods.
Vigilant Polmar is for land and sea pollution control and surveillance, by day and night, equipped with SLAR, radiometer, IR and UV scanner, and a datalink system. Optional underwing equipment.
Vigilant Surmar is for maritime surveillance of coastal regions, with possible equipment including Raytheon APS-134 maritime surveillance radar, FLIR and datalink system. Optional underwing equipment.
Principal dimensions: See similar Reims F 406 Caravan II in the General Aviation section.

↑ **Reims Vigilant with new wing hard points for carrying various stores, including camera pods and life raft, as shown** *(J.N. Sirot)*

Example surveillance mission profiles

	1	2	3	4	5
Location of the zone of intervention in relation to base	100 naut miles	200 naut miles	Base located in the patrol area	Base located in the patrol area	500 naut miles
Weather conditions	ISA + 20° C, no wind	ISA + 20° C, no wind	ISA + 20° C, no wind	ISA + 20° C, no wind	ISA + 20° C, no wind
Flight altitude over zone	500 ft (152 m)	1,000 ft (305 m)	1,000 ft (305 m)	1,000 ft (305 m)	1,000 ft (305 m)
Flight altitude in transit	500 ft (152 m)	FL 120	1,000 ft (305 m)	1,000 ft (305 m)	FL 180
Patrol speed	140 kts	140 kts	140 kts	140 kts	130 kts
Time over zone	4 hours 50 minutes	3 hours 58 minutes	6 hours 6 minutes	6 hours 58 minutes	1 hour 24 minutes
Transit distance/speed	200 naut miles/ 170 kts	400 naut miles/ 185 kts	140 kts	130 kts	1,000 naut miles/ 203 kts
Transit time	1 hour 15 minutes	2 hours 10 minutes	0	0	5 hours 6 minutes
Fuel consumed in transit	584 lb (265 kg)	926 lb (420 kg)	0	0	2,028 lb (920 kg)
Fuel consumed on patrol	1,929 lb (875 kg)	1,587 lb (720 kg)	2,425 lb (1,100 kg)	2,425 lb (1,100 kg)	485 lb (220 kg)
Reserve fuel	275 lb (125 kg) (45 minutes at 5,000 ft, 1,525 m)	275 lb (125 kg) (45 minutes at 5,000 ft, 1,525 m)	275 lb (125 kg) (45 minutes at 5,000 ft, 1,525 m)	275 lb (125 kg) (45 minutes at 5,000 ft, 1,525 m)	275 lb (125 kg) (45 minutes at 5,000 ft, 1,525 m)
Total flight time	6 hours 5 minutes	6 hours 8 minutes	6 hours 6 minutes	6 hours 58 minutes	6 hours 30 minutes
Equipped weight empty	6,592 lb (2,990 kg)	6,592 lb (2,990 kg)	6,592 lb (2,990 kg)	6,592 lb (2,990 kg)	6,592 lb (2,990 kg)
Crew	3, at 540 lb (245 kg)	3, at 540 lb (245 kg)	3, at 540 lb (245 kg)	3, at 540 lb (245 kg)	3, at 540 lb (245 kg)
Fuel	2,800 lb (1,270 kg)	2,800 lb (1,270 kg)	2,800 lb (1,270 kg)	2,800 lb (1,270 kg)	2,800 lb (1,270 kg)

Socata Groupe Aerospatiale — France

Full name:
Société de Construction d'Avions de Tourisme et d'Affaires.

Corporate address:
Le Terminal, Bâtiment 413, Zône d'Aviation d'Affaires, F-93352 Aéroport du Bourget.

Telephone: +33 1 49 34 69 69, or 69 70
Facsimile: +33 1 49 34 69 71
Telex: 520 828 F
Web site: http://www.socata.com

Founded: 1966.

Employees: Approximately 1,000 technicians at Tarbes.

Information:
Anne-Sophie Zobenbueler (*telephone* +33 1 49 34 69 93, *facsimile* +33 1 49 34 69 96).

FACILITIES

▪ Production unit: Aéroport de Tarbes Ossun-Lourdes, BP 930, 65009 Tarbes Cedex (*telephone* +33 5 62 41 73 00, *Facsimile* +33 5 62 41 73 55). Customer operations and product support also at Tarbes.

ACTIVITIES

▪ Socata is Aerospatiale's general aviation subsidiary, producing a range of light aircraft (see General Aviation section). The Epsilon trainer was also detailed in that section in the 1996-97 edition of *WA&SD*, page 396.
▪ A current programme is the development of the HALE high-altitude long-endurance aircraft for communications and electronic intelligence, optical/radar observation, and anti-ballistic missile warning.
▪ Pre-project activities include CAD designing, computing, static endurance testing, in-flight testing and more, networked to Aerospatiale's computing centre and computerized design and engineering departments.
▪ Sub-contract work includes parts for Eurocopter Dauphin and Ecureuil/AStar helicopters; Airbus A320, A340 and A300-600ST; ATR 42 and 72; Dassault Falcon 50 and 900; Lockheed Martin Hercules, and the CFM56 engine. Also satellite assembly tools.

SUBSIDIARIES

SOCATA AIRCRAFT

HQ address: North Perry Airport, 7501 Pembroke Road, Pembroke Pines, FL 33023, USA.

Telephone: +1 954 964 6877
Facsimile: +1 954 964 1668

SOCATA GMBH

HQ address:
Siegerland Flughafen, Werfstrasse 1 - Halle D, D-57299 Burbach, Germany.

Telephone: +49 2736 49 690
Facsimile: +49 2736 491 147

Socata Omega

Comments: First flown on 30 April 1989, this turboprop-powered military trainer has also been offered for aerobatic, patrol and surveillance work. A full description and photograph can be found in the 1996-97 edition of *WA&SD*, pages 42-43.

Socata High-Altitude Long-Endurance (HALE) Aircraft

First flight: The year 2004.
Role: Communications and electronic intelligence (comint/elint), optical/radar observation, and anti-ballistic missile warning (launch detection and warning, location of threat launcher,

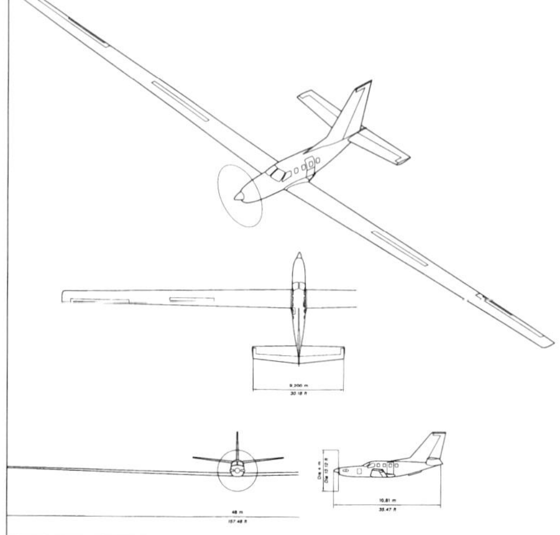

↑ **Socata High-Altitude Long-Endurance (HALE) Aircraft** *(courtesy Socata)*

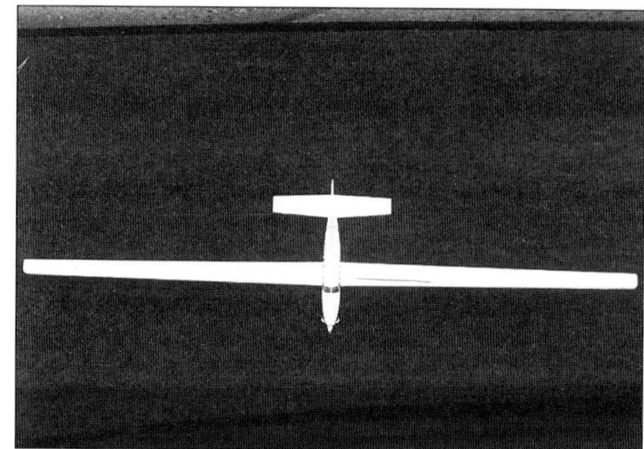

↑ **Socata High-Altitude Long-Endurance (HALE) Aircraft**

Details for HALE

PRINCIPAL DIMENSIONS:
Wing span: 157 ft 5.75 ins (48 m)
Maximum length: 35 ft 5.6 ins (10.81 m)

WINGS:
Area: 753.47 sq ft (70 m²)
Aspect ratio: 32.91

TAIL UNIT:
Tailplane span: 30 ft 2 ins (9.2 m)

UNDERCARRIAGE:
Type: Retractable, with nosewheel

WEIGHTS:
Maximum take-off: 9,921 lb (4,500 kg)
Payload: 882 lb (400 kg)

PERFORMANCE:
Cruise speed: 165 kts (190 mph) 306 km/h
Time to ceiling: 1 hour 30 minutes
Time to 55,000 ft (16,765 m): 45 minutes
Ceiling: 60,000 ft (18,288 m), service
Range with maximum fuel and full payload, at 165 kts and 60,000 ft, manned: 3,184 naut miles (3,666 miles) 5,900 km
Range with maximum fuel and full payload, at 165 kts and 60,000 ft, unmanned: 3,831 naut miles (4,412 miles) 7,100 km
Duration with maximum fuel and full payload, at 165 kts and 60,000 ft, manned: 19 hours 42 minutes
Duration with maximum fuel and full payload, at 165 kts and 60,000 ft, unmanned: 23 hours 36 minutes

estimation of missile flight path, and computation of impact zone).
Based on: Socata TBM 700, but with new very high aspect ratio wings and similarly enlarged tail surfaces.
Crew: 2 crew, or optional unmanned variant.
Fuselage: 123.6 cu ft (3.5 m^3) usable pressurized volume.
Wing control surfaces: Ailerons with trim tab, and lift-dumping spoilers.
Tail control surfaces: Horn-balanced elevators, and very large fin with horn-balanced rudder.
Engine: Pratt & Whitney Canada PW127C turboprop, driving a 13 ft 1.5 ins (4 m) propeller.
Engine rating: 3,100 shp (2,312 kW) thermodynamic, flat rated at 1,050 shp (783 kW).
Fuel system: 1,275 litres, or 1,500 litres for unmanned operations.

Fairchild Dornier Germany Dornier Luftfahrt GmbH — Germany

Corporate address:
PO Box 1103, D-82230 Wessling.

Telephone: +49 81 53 300
Facsimile: +49 81 53 30 20 07, or 29 01
Web site: www.fairchilddornier.com

Founded:
June 1996, following Fairchild Aerospace's purchase of 80% of Dornier Luftfahrt from Daimler-Benz Aerospace. Fairchild Aerospace thereby owns 80% and Daimler-Benz Aerospace owns 20% of Fairchild Dornier Germany, while Fairchild Aerospace owns 100% of Fairchild Dornier USA.

Information:
Peter Klonk (*telephone* +49 81 53 30 20 25, *facsimile* +49 81 53 30 20 07).

ACTIVITIES

▪ Development, production and support of Regional aircraft (see Fairchild Dornier Germany and Fairchild Dornier USA in the Airliners section, under Germany and USA respectively, plus Fairchild Dornier USA in this section).
▪ Manufacture of components and subassemblies for all Airbus types.
▪ Dornier 228 is part of a marketing campaign for new and pre-owned aircraft.

Fairchild Dornier 228 special missions versions

Role: Day/night maritime patrol, border patrol and surveillance, pollution control, aerial survey and mapping, long-range observation, Polar research, environmental and scientific research, and navaid flight inspection.
Based on: Dornier 228 (see Airliners section). Optional mission equipment for surveillance aircraft includes VHF/Omega navigation system with search pattern mode, GPS, hand-held camera system with navigation interface, camera operator's seat, radar console with flight/navigation instrumentation, 'wet' outboard wing with a fuel capacity of 4,960 lb (2,250 kg), observer's seat, observer's desk/worktop/intercom, map table with laptop computer, toilet, bubble windows, anti-skid floor, quilted cabin wall lining, wide roller door, wing hardpoints, openable photo windows, steerable searchlight in underwing pod, 7 and 10 person liferafts, stowage and chute for markers and flares, small galley, and pods for spraying oil-binding agents. EFIS cockpit (Finnish Frontier Guard 228s have 5-tube AlliedSignal Bendix/King EFIS and a display screen for sensor imagery).

↑ Fairchild Dornier 228 operated by the Finnish Frontier Guard for surveillance, with radome clearly visible under the fuselage

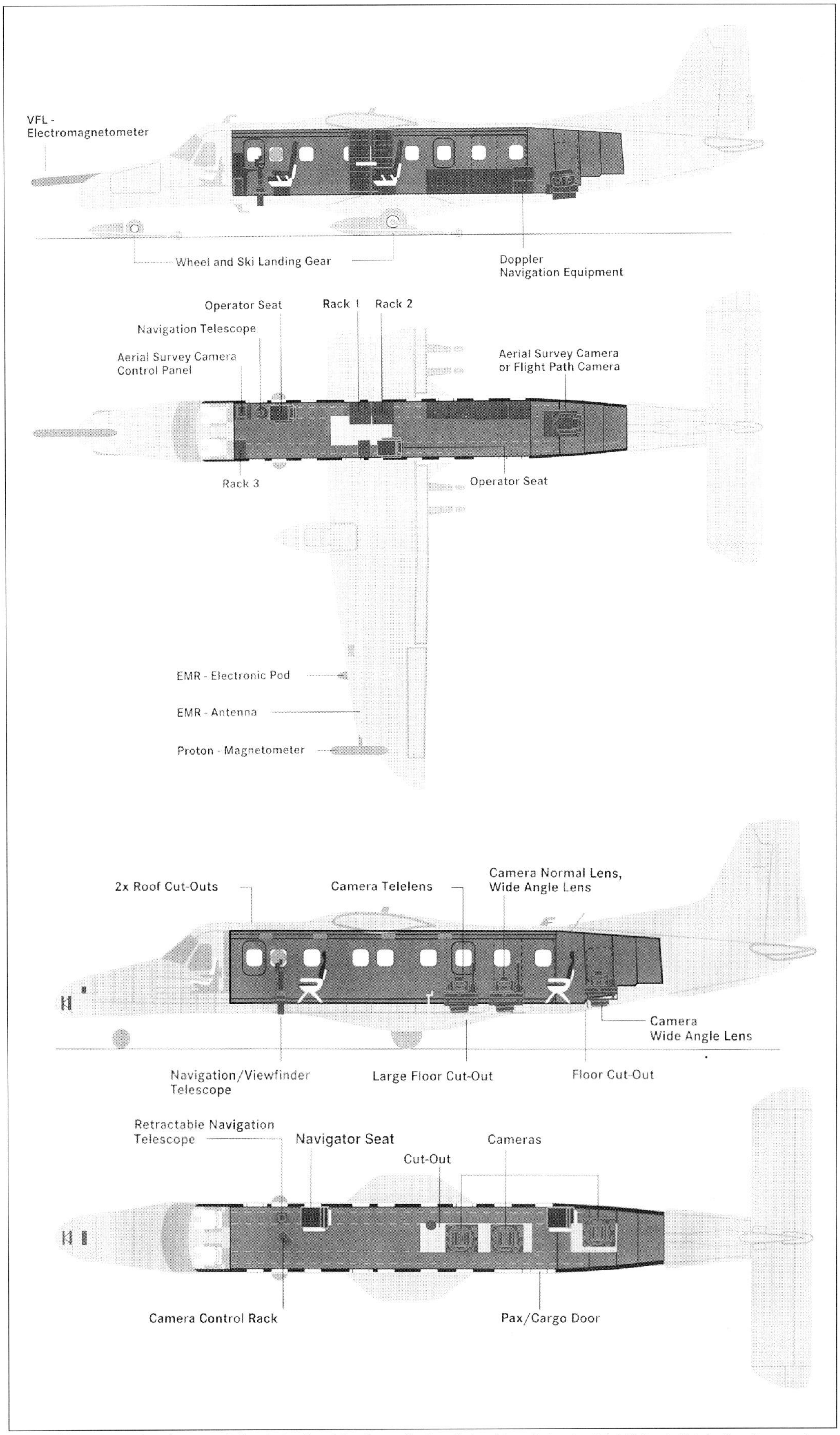

↑ Fairchild Dornier 228 in Polar Research (*top 2 views*) and Geo Survey (*bottom 2 views*) layouts *(courtesy Fairchild Dornier/Daimler-Benz Aerospace)*

Crew: Typically, Finnish Frontier Guard 228s have crew of 4, with the pilot as the mission commander, co-pilot acting also as observer, an operator in cabin for the primary surveillance equipment (search radar and FLIR) and communications, while the other operator is responsible for the SLAR and IR/UV scanner in addition to visual lookout and photography.
Radar: See Aircraft variants for surveillance radars. Terma Elektronik SLAR. Forward-looking airborne radars are Honeywell Primas 500, AlliedSignal Bendix/King 1400 and RDS-82VP, Narco KWX-56 and Rockwell Collins WXR-270.
Other mission sensors: See Aircraft variants.

Aircraft variants:
Border patrol version has an integrated sensor suite comprising a stabilized long-range observation system (SLOS), FLIR (with a gimballed sensor head under the fuselage), remotely stabilized (Forward Motion Compensation) aerial survey camera in a floor cut-out and which can be controlled by a viewfinder/navigation sight (with 4 different lens assemblies, and interfaced to the VLF-Omega navigation system to provide navigational data on the film), night vision goggles, plus work stations for sensor control and real-time imagery exploitation, data recording, communications equipment, and C-band real-time air-to-ground data link. SLOS consists of a stabilized telescope unit (STU) with remote-mounted joystick, 2 monitors for image display which are coupled to the video tape recorder, interface to the VLF-Omega navigation system (to allow annotation of the images with the navigation data), turret for the STU, and SLOS operator console.
Maritime patrol version has been offered with AlliedSignal Bendix/King RDR-1500B, Racal (MEL/Thorn EMI) Super Searcher, Litton APS-504(V)5, GEC-Marconi Seaspray 2000, Thomson-CSF/Daimler-Benz Aerospace Ocean Master 100 or Telephonics (Eaton) APS-128 surveillance radar. Other optional equipment includes FLIR/TV, SLOS, night vision goggles, camera, searchlight, smoke markers and flares, etc. Currently also built in India by HAL for the Indian Coast Guard as the Maritime Surveillance but covering maritime patrol over a wide spectrum of activities, including surveillance of EEZ, pollution monitoring and control, SAR, aerial survey and casevac; 33 228-101s in the process of being delivered to the Indian Coast Guard, joining 3 German built aircraft for India, originally with Thorn EMI Marec 2 radars offering 360° coverage but Racal Super Marec radars were ordered by India for both upgrading Indian maritime aircraft and equipping new anti-shipping 228s (see below). Other Indian Coast Guard equipment includes bubble windows, IR/UV linescanner, Omega navigation, Agiflite camera system (ONS interface), searchlight, marine markers, roller door, double litters and rafts, plus the ability to field anti pollution Micronair spraypods under the wings. Other operators of maritime patrol 228s include Finland (Frontier Guard), Thailand (Navy, in Coast Guard version) and FRA (see Cobham plc under UK in Combat section, for economic zone surveillance/fisheries protection).

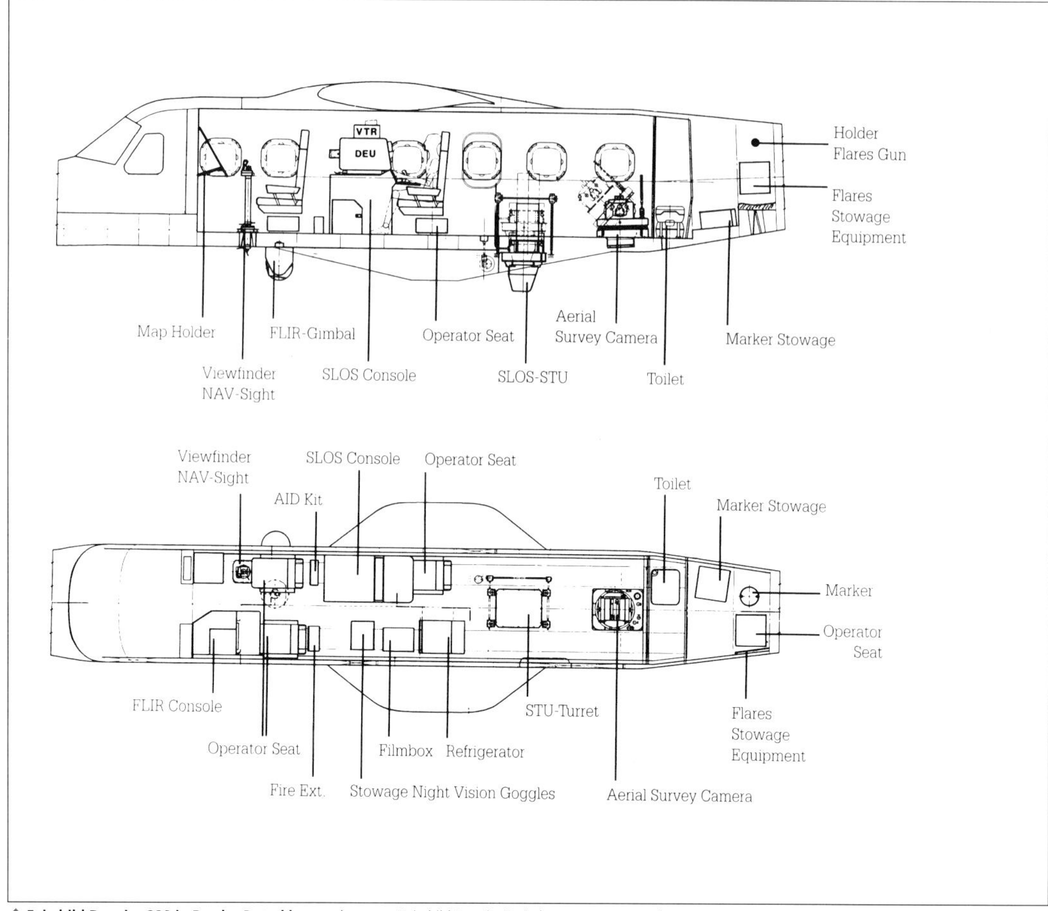

↑ **Fairchild Dornier 228 in Border Patrol layout** *(courtesy Fairchild Dornier/Daimler-Benz Aerospace)*

Pollution surveillance version can have Terma Elekronik SLAR, Daedalus IR/UV scanner, IR camera, microwave radiometer, laser fluorescent sensor, video/photo camera/recording media, navigation system with R Nav II, and GPS. Operated by the German Navy and Netherlands coast guard (AlliedSignal RDR-1400C radar). Integrated system control and information display, with large high-resolution colour monitor.
Anti-ship version is currently being delivered to the Indian Navy from HAL production (27 expected), carrying Racal Super Marec radar and appropriate missiles.
Other versions include Long-Range Observation with a sensor suite comprising SLOS, camera system, FLIR and NVG; Polar Research with options of magnetometers, electromagnetic reflection equipment, gravimeters, meteorological sensors, viewfinder telescope, and photogrammetry and survey cameras; Environmental and Scientific Research; Geo Survey; and Navaid Flight Inspection.

Burkhart Grob Luft- und Raumfahrt GmbH & Co KG — Germany

Corporate address:
Lettenbachstrasse 9, 86874 Tussenhausen.

Telephone: +49 82 68 998-0
Facsimile: +49 82 68 998-124
Web site: http://www.grob-aerospace.com
E-mail: grob_aerospace.info@t-online.de

Founded:
1971 (aviation activities).

Information:
Dipl-Ing Roland Rischer (Sales Manager - *E-mail* rischer.roland@t-online.de)

ACTIVITIES

▪ See also General Aviation and Glider sections.

DIVISIONS

GROB-WERKE GMBH & CO KG

Addresses:
Industriestrasse 4, 87719 Mindelheim and Westendstrasse 193, 80686 München.

GROB SYSTEMS INC

HQ address:
1-75 + Airport Drive, Bluffton, OH 45817, USA.

Telephone: +1 419 358 9015
Facsimile: +1 419 358 3660

B. GROB DO BRASIL S/A

HQ address:
Av. Caminho do Mar, 1811 S. Bernardo do Campo, Sao Paulo, Brazil.

Telephone: +55 11 4552522
Facsimile: +55 11 4552878

Grob G-520 Egrett and Strato 1

First flight: 24 June 1987 (G 500 Egrett).
Role: High-altitude, long-duration research platform capable of carrying various payloads to high altitude for up to 13 hours in 12 purpose-designed, operator-configurable and air-conditioned equipment bays in the fuselage. Also for traffic control management and vehicle tracking, pollution monitoring, weather and fire observation, reconnaissance, surveillance, and aerial communications monitoring and relay. Suited to all-weather, day and night operations, including flight into known icing conditions.

Development

▪ The name Egrett came from the 3 companies co-operating in development of the proof-of-concept aircraft, namely E-Systems (since Raytheon Systems, of the USA), Grob and Garrett (since AlliedSignal).
▪ 1986. Development began.
▪ 1 September 1988. G 500 Egrett 1 proof-of-concept aircraft set an FAI absolute altitude record without payload in its class at 53,574 ft (16,329 m), altitude in horizontal flight without payload of 53,276 ft (16,238 m), and time to climb to 15,000 m at 40 minutes 47 seconds.
▪ 20 April 1989. First longer-span and higher-weight prototype G 520 Egrett 2 (*D-FGEE*) flew, with modified rear fuselage and equipped with pressurized cabin, lightning protection, retractable undercarriage and ice protection systems.
▪ 9 September 1990. First flight of the second G 520 Egrett 2 (*D-FGEO*, becoming *D-FEGR* and later *D-FSTN*), used initially to integrate the electronic systems.

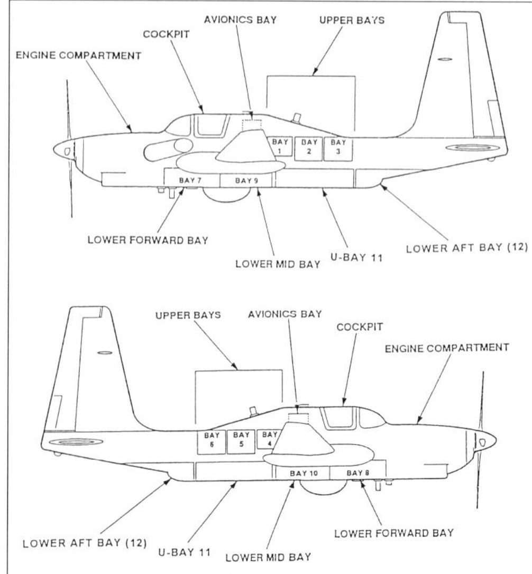

↑ **Grob G 520 Egrett 2 equipment compartment arrangement** *(courtesy Grob)*

Details for G 520, *with 520T in italics*

PRINCIPAL DIMENSIONS:
Wing span: 108 ft 3 ins (33 m)
Maximum length: 39 ft 4.5 ins (12 m), *44 ft 10 ins (13.67 m)*
Maximum height: 18 ft 8 ins (5.68 m), *18 ft 7 ins (5.66 m)*

WINGS:
Aerofoil section: Modified Eppler E580
Area: 427.08 sq ft (39.677 m^2)
Aspect ratio: 27.445

UNDERCARRIAGE:
Type: Operation from unpaved runways is not authorized
Wheel base: 12 ft 2 ins (3.71 m), *14 ft (4.26 m)*
Wheel track: 15 ft 4 ins (4.68 m), *15 ft (4.57 m)*

WEIGHTS:
Empty: 6,393 lb (2,700 kg), *the same*
Maximum zero fuel weight: 8,988 lb (4,077 kg)
Maximum take-off: 10,362 lb (4,700 kg), *the same*
Maximum landing: 9,843 lb (4,465 kg)
Payload: 2,205 lb (1,000 kg)

PERFORMANCE:
Maximum operating speed (M_{MO} or V_{MO}): Mach 0.448 or 153 kts (176 mph) 283 km/h IAS
Cruise speed: 180-250 kts (207-288 mph) 333-463 km/h, *179-240 kts (206-276 mph) 332-444 km/h*
Recommended rotation speed: 65-77 kts (75-89 mph) 120-143 km/h IAS
Recommended climb speed: 95 kts (109 mph) 176 km/h IAS from sea level to 30,000 ft (9,145 m), reducing by 1 kts per 1,000 ft (305 m) thereafter
Stall speed: 66 kts (76 mph) 123 km/h *clean*, 61 kts (70 mph) 113 km/h *with flaps*
Landing approach speed: 75-85 kts (86-98 mph) 139-158 km/h *with flaps*, at 6,614-9,843 lb (3,000-4,465 kg) MLW
Take-off distance: 1,545 ft (471 m) at MTOW, ISA and sea level, *the same*
Take-off distance over a 50 ft (15 m) obstacle: 2,245 ft (684 m) at MTOW, ISA and sea level, *the same*
Landing distance: 1,000 ft (305 m) at 7,716 lb (3,500 kg) AUW, ISA and sea level, *the same*
Landing distance over a 50 ft (15 m) obstacle: 1,801 ft (549 m) at 7,716 lb (3,500 kg) AUW, ISA and sea level, *the same*
Climb rate: 1,400 ft (427 m) per minute, *the same*
Time to climb from 10,000 to 35,000 ft (3,050 to 10,670 m): 21 minutes at maximum weight
G limits: +3.28, -1.31 *clean*
Ceiling: 52,500 ft (16,000 m)
Range with full fuel: 1,930 naut miles (2,222 miles) 3,574 km
Duration: 13 hours, *11 hours*

▪ 4 January 1991. First flight of the G 520 Egrett 2 (*D-FDEM*) for E-Systems (now Raytheon Systems). Later equipped for sigint.
▪ 22 March 1991. LBA certification of G 520 Egrett. Currently certified to LBA/FAA FAR Pt 23 Amendment 34 all-weather IFR/icing requirements.
▪ 5 June 1991. First flight of the G 520 Strato 1 (*D-FGRO*).
▪ 21 April 1993. First flight of the G 520T Egrett 2 trainer (*D-FDST*, later *D-FARA*).
▪ 31 March 1994. G 520 Strato 1 set 2 more absolute altitude with payload world records for turboprop-powered aircraft in the Open Weight and Medium Weight Classes, at 51,024 ft (15,552 m).

Details *(G-520, unless stated)*

Users: Present family comprises 4 single-seaters and a 2-seater, as 3 G 520 Egrett 2s, 1 G 520 Strato 1 (Grob and Raytheon Systems operated) and the G 520T 2-seater. G 500 Egrett proof-of-concept aircraft is not operated. Egrett 2 was anticipated to re-enter production in 1997-98. First Egrett 2 operated at time of writing by Aurora Flight Sciences in the USA, currently for use in the Atmospheric Radiation Enhanced Short-wave Experiment programme on behalf of the US Department of Energy. *D-FSTN* used by STN Atlas Elekronik GmbH for surveillance. Third Egrett 2 is owned by Raytheon Systems in the USA and is presently involved in an Environmental Research Aircraft and Sensor Technology programme for NASA. 2-seat Egrett 2 currently used by Airborne Research Australia and has undertaken atmospheric and geophysical programmes.
Crew: Pilot, or 2 in G-520T (raised rear seat). S-1031 pressure suit for flights above 25,000 ft (7,620 m).
Cockpit: Maximum pressurization differential 6 psi.
Mission equipment: 6 payload compartments in the upper fuselage, 4 in the lower forward fuselage sides, an aft fuselage bay (number 12 on the drawing) and the main removable U-shaped bay (number 11) as part of the lower centre fuselage. Capacities in mm/kg: 1 and 4 (615 × 940 × 450/68), 2 and 5 (625 × 940 × 415 or 540/102), 3 and 6 (645 × 940 × 545/102), 7 and 8 (1,450 × 250 × 500/68), 9 and 10 (1,100 × 250 × 500/68), 12 (1,000 × 750 × 530/22) and 11 (1,950 × 800 × 530/238).
Wing characteristics: Mid-mounted, high aspect ratio. Removable wingtips, allowing winglets. Inner section fairings to house undercarriage.
Wing control surfaces: Ailerons, split flaps and leading-edge slats.
Tail control surfaces: Horn-balanced elevators and rudder, all with tabs.
Flight control system: Mechanical/manual.
Construction materials: Carbonfibre, glassfibre and Kevlar-reinforced plastics.
Engine: AlliedSignal TPE331-14F-801L turboprop, with a 10 ft (3.05 m) Hartzell HC-E4P-5/E11990K 4-blade, constant-speed, variable-pitch propeller.
Engine rating: Derated to 750 shp (559.3 kW) continuous.
Fuel system: 1,117 litres, of which 1,090 litres are usable. Optional 1,382 litres (1,355 litres usable). G-520T has 1,345 litres.
Flight avionics/instrumentation: AlliedSignal Bendix/King KFC325 flight director and autopilot system standard. Tacan, UHF, IFF/SIF, nav/com and identification equipment optional.
Electrical system: DC supply as a 250 amp starter-generator, 24 volt lead-acid battery, 24 volt sealed lead-acid emergency battery, and DC external power connection. AC supply as 115 volt, 400 Hz 3-phase generator (10kVA, or 40 kVA optionally), 250 volt inverter and external power connection.
Oxygen system: 10 litre liquid system (LOX), with pressurized oxygen for emergency supply. G 520T has double the amount of breathing oxygen.

Aircraft variants:
G 520 Egrett 2, as described.
G 520T Egrett 2 is the 2-seat trainer version for high-altitude pilot training and 2-crew missions. Almost identical payload weight and installation capabilities. More fuel and oxygen.
G 520 Strato 1 was the fourth aircraft built, used on some record breaking flights.

↑ Grob G 520 Egrett 2

Grob G 850 Strato 2C

First flight: 31 March 1995 (in proof of concept form, without mission avionics fitted).
Role: High-altitude, long-duration atmospheric/stratospheric/climatic research, earth observation and communications, to operate up to 78,740 ft (24,000 m) altitude and 48 hours duration.

Development

▪ Built under contract from the Deutsche Forschungsanstalt für Luft- und Raumfahrt (DLR). IABG became responsible for the propulsion system and sub-systems.
▪ April 1992. Design initiated, with manufacture of airframe moulds starting in mid-November.
▪ April 1993. Construction began, initially the tailplane.
▪ 1994. Construction completed and engine installation undertaken.
▪ 1995. Mission avionics fit completed.
▪ 4 August 1995. World altitude record for manned piston-engined aircraft set on the 29th flight, at 60,867 ft (18,552 m).
▪ June 1996. Grob and foreign interests took over the Strato 2C from the DLR.

Details

Users: Proof-of-Concept Strato 2C originally developed for DLR (see Development); now owned by Grob. Production standard

Details for Strato 2C

PRINCIPAL DIMENSIONS:
Wing span: 185 ft 4.5 ins (56.5 m)
Maximum length: 78 ft 8 ins (23.975 m)
Pressure cabin length: 28 ft 1 ins (8.565 m) including cockpit, 18 ft 2.5 ins (5.55 m) for cabin only
Pressure cabin diameter: 7 ft 5.75 ins (2.28 m)
Pressure cabin height: 6 ft 1 ins (1.85 m)
Maximum height: 25 ft 5.5 ins (7.76 m)

WINGS:
Aerofoil section: Laminar flow, high lift, resulting in low Reynolds numbers down to 400,000; no supersonic regions despite thickness and high lift; thickness 17.5% for high stiffness and volume
Area: 1,614.59 (150 m^2)
Aspect ratio: 21.28

TAIL UNIT:
Tailplane span: 32 ft 9.7 ins (10 m)

UNDERCARRIAGE:
Type: Retractable, with hydraulic nosewheel steering and twin wheels on each unit. Cabin air vents into gear pods for ozone protection

WEIGHTS:
Empty: 14,660 lb (6,650 kg)
Maximum take-off: 29,432 lb (13,350 kg)
Payload: 2,205 lb (1,000 kg), or 331 lb (150 kg) to 26,000 m altitude

PERFORMANCE:
Maximum operating Mach number (M_{MO}): Mach 0.56
Cruise/climb speed: 140 kts (161 mph) 259 km/h at 59,000 ft (17,980 m) altitude, 270 kts (311 mph) 500 km/h at 78,740 ft (24,000 m)
Ceiling: 52,500-85,300 ft (16,000-26,000 m), *design 78,740 ft (24,000 m)*
Range with full fuel: 9,773 naut miles (11,246 miles) 18,100 km
Typical 18,000 m mission: 2,205 lb (1,000 kg) payload, cruising at 200 kts (230 mph) 370 mph TAS, ceiling of 75,460 ft (23,000 m) but loitering at 59,000 ft (18,000 m) for 20 hours, offering a 27 hour total flight time and maximum range of 4,695 naut miles (5,406 miles) 8,700 km
Typical 22,000 m mission: 1,764 lb (800 kg) payload, cruising at 250 kts (288 mph) 463 mph TAS, ceiling of 75,460 ft (23,000 m) but loitering at 72,180 ft (22,000 m) for 6 hours, offering a range of 4,586 naut miles (5,280 miles) 8,500 km
Duration: 48 hours at 59,000 ft (18,000 m) altitude, 8 hours at 24,000 m

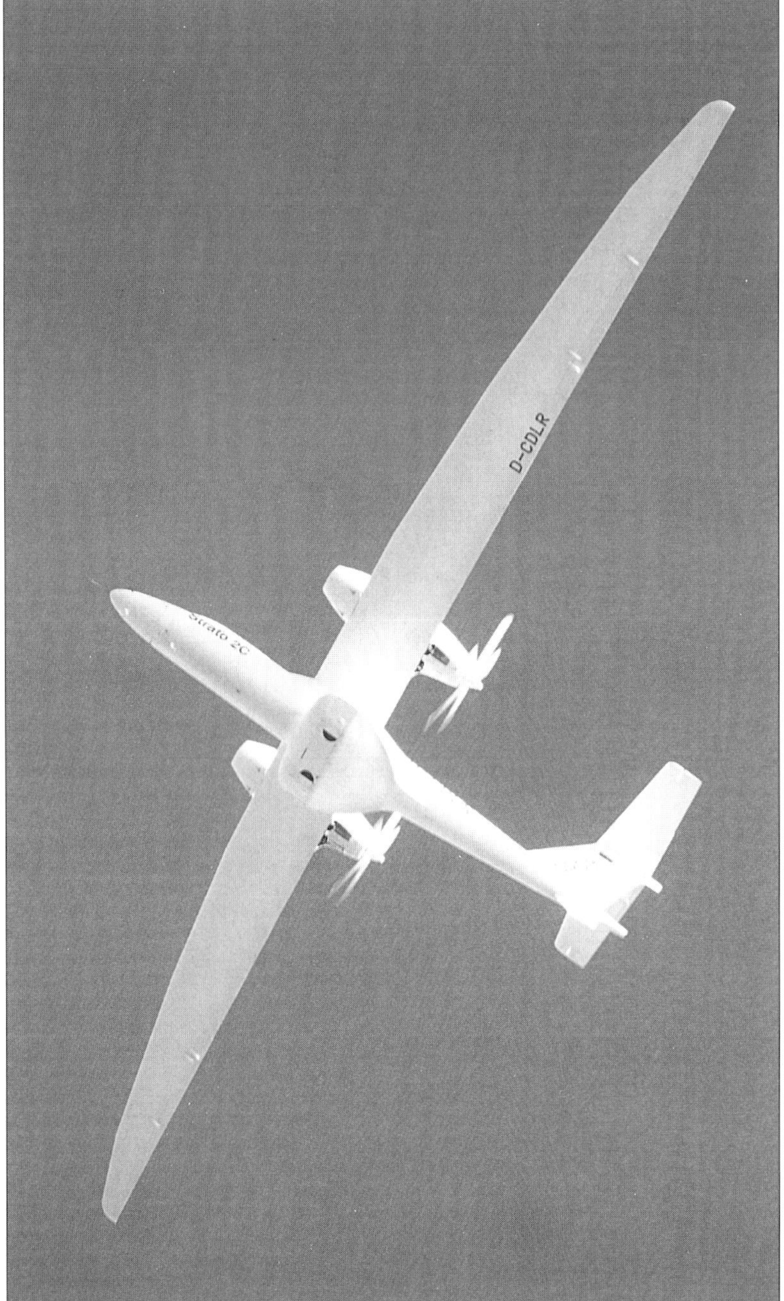

↑ Grob G 850 Strato 2C

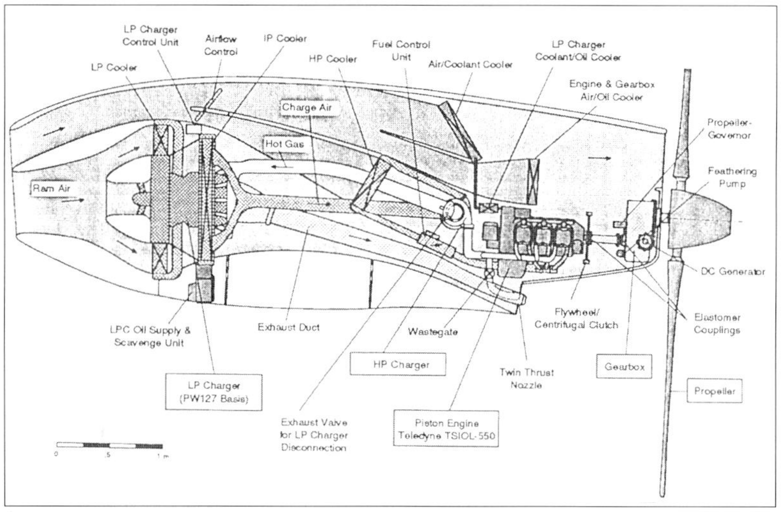

↑ Grob G 850 Strato 2C compound propulsion system *(courtesy Grob)*

↑ Grob G 850 Strato 2C cockpit *(courtesy Grob)*

Mission Aircraft anticipated.
Crew: 2 pilots (can be flown by 1 pilot while the other rests during long missions) and 2 scientists. Oxygen and pressure suit systems.
Cockpit/cabin: Large pressure cabin (including flight deck), with work stations for scientists. Easy access door of 2 ft 11 ins × 5 ft 3 ins (0.9 × 1.6 m). Toilet, galley and rest facilities. Pressurized, at 8,000 ft (2,440 m) pressure altitude and 10.6 psi maximum differential.
Mission equipment: External payload bays (2 payload spaces in the nose section and 1 behind rear bulkhead), 12 hard points under the fuselage, 4 under the wings, plus wingtip and fin hard points. Available equipment includes cryogen collectors for air samples, pyranometers and pyrgeometers, scanning radiometers, mass spectrometers, and sensors for pressure, temperature and wind measurement. New equipment might include infra-red interferometers, microwave radiometers and scanners, long-distance absorption cells, active chemical ionization spectrometers, optical multi-zone analyzers, Lyman alpha equipment, light detection and ranging (LIDAR), and fast ozone probes. Provision for optical windows at 6 positions for remote sensing instruments.
Wing characteristics: High mounted, straight, with dihedral. Winglets. High aspect ratio and low loading.
Wing control surfaces: Ailerons with tabs, outboard spoilers, and 2-section speed brakes.
Tail control surfaces: T-tail with horn-balanced elevators and rudder, with tabs.
Flight control system: Mechanical.
Construction materials: Composites, mainly carbonfibre but also glassfibre and aramid reinforced plastics. See Aircraft variants. World's largest single-piece all-composite wing in early 1998. Hand layup/vacuum bagging/low and high temperature curing. Sandwich or plain shells. Computer controlled fabric impregnation.
Engines: Compound propulsion system, suited to very high altitude, based around 2 Teledyne Continental TSIOL-550 turbocharged piston engines with reduction gearboxes and 2 Pratt & Whitney Canada PW127 gas generators, providing about 12% jet thrust in addition to the propeller thrust. Each of the 2 propulsion units of the overall propulsion system comprises 2 major equipment groups. The first group encompasses the piston engine with a standard AlliedSignal turbocharger, the reduction gearbox and the propeller, allowing conventional power during take-off and landing. For higher altitudes the second group (the LP charger) provides charged air at a pressure that allows the piston engine to maintain 402.3 hp (300 kW) shaft power to the aircraft's ceiling. The LP charger has its own oil system and integrated charge air coolers. Piston engine and HP charger are controlled by a standard exhaust wastegate at the turbine inlet, which is operated by engine oil; while the turbine sections of both chargers are controlled by the exhaust wastegate of the HP charger, matching of the LP and HP charger compressors is achieved by LP and IP bleed. 5-blade Mühlbauer variable-pitch pusher propellers of 19 ft 8 ins (6 m) diameter, with 636 rpm. See Aircraft variants.
Engine rating: Each 402.3 hp (300 kW).
Fuel system: 12,566 lb (5,700 kg) Avgas, Jet A1.
Hydraulic system: Low temperature/low pressure environment.
Electrical system: Payload power 8.4 kW (300 amp at 28 volt DC) with ARINC 429 datalink to payload.
Braking system: 4 multi-disc self-adjusting steel brakes. Anti-skid system.
Flight avionics/instrumentation: See Aircraft variants.

Aircraft variants:
Proof-of-Concept aircraft has a 'quick' solutions wing structure with high safety margin, using available materials; safe load test. Propulsion system has many 'off the shelf' components. Electrical system offers full power at altitude. Full differential pressure and environmental control; sensors and windshield de-icing. No rails, windows, inlets or galley. IFR instrumentation (no ADF); yaw damper; standard com/nav. VVZ (LBA preliminary flight worthiness certification).
Mission Aircraft would have optimized wing structure with higher allowables and expensive materials; ultimate load and fatigue evaluation. Propulsion system of increased power, reduced weight and sfc, and better efficiency with optimized components. Mission bus added to electrical system. Wing and tail surface de-icing. Payload features installed. IFR instrumentation, with 3-tube 'glass' cockpit, long-range nav/com, air data computer, autopilot, IRS/GPS, FMS and weather radar. Improved aerodynamics. For LBA/FAR 23 Am 42/commuter certification.

Hindustan Aeronautics Limited (HAL) — India

Corporate address:
See Combat section for full company details.

HAL (BAe/Avro) 748 ASWAC and CABS Phase II

First flight: 5 November 1990 (748 ASWAC for aerodynamic trials).
Role: ASWAC technology demonstrator.
Based on: British Aerospace (Avro) 748 airliner (ASWAC).
Radar/mission avionics: Under development by the Defence Research and Development Organization, Electronics and Radar Development Establishment, and Bharat Electricals.

Development

▪ 1985. Development was initiated by the Aerospace Surveillance Warning and Control (ASWAC) organization, under the auspices of the Defence Research and Development Organization. Modification of the borrowed BAe (Avro) 748 took place at the Aeronautical Development Agency (ADA) in Bangalore. The 15.75 ft (4.8 m) above-fuselage rotating 'saucer' radome was designed and manufactured jointly with MBB of Germany (now Daimler-Benz Aerospace). However, the aircraft had no surveillance radar, nor other substantial mission equipment or sensors.
▪ 1989-90. ASWAC programme "went on hold", though some flying took place from 1990, but work on an ASWAC system continued at low pace at the Centre for Airborne Systems (CABS) at Bangalore.
▪ August 1993. First flight of the 748 under the rejuvenated programme. Phase II of the programme was to be an ASWAC system on a Boeing 737, Airbus A310/A320 or similar transport.
▪ 2-6 December 1996. The repainted BAe 748 (known in India as the Avro 748 *H2175*, no longer in camouflage – see 1996-97 edition of *WA&SD* for one of the first photographs to appear in the west, page 174) was shown at the Aero India 1996 air show at Yelanhanka Air Station near Bangalore as an airborne surveillance platform, though again it is generally expected that a larger aircraft will eventually form the basis of a new system unless the arrays of the active phased-array radar being developed are to be carried in a fixed overfuselage container (like the Embraer RJ145 and Saab 360 AEW&C) or in a conformal arrangement similar to the Israeli Phalcon. However, more likely is the original plan to purchase a previously-used B737, Airbus or Il-76. It is known that development of the 748 ASWAC has been hampered by mission suite overheating.

↑ **HAL (BAe/Avro) 748 ASWAC at Aero India 1996** *(Simon Watson)*

HAL/Fairchild Dornier 228 special missions versions

Comments: See Fairchild Dornier under Germany for HAL-built versions of the 228, plus the Airliners section.

↑ **HAL-produced 228-101 maritime surveillance aircraft with Racal Super Marec radar, operated by the Indian Coast Guard**

Israel Aircraft Industries Ltd (IAI) — Israel

Corporate address:
See Combat section for company details.

IAI Phalcon and derivatives

First flight: 12 May 1993.
First delivery: 2 May 1995.
Role: Airborne early warning, and intelligence.
Based on: First conversion based on a Boeing 707-320C. Other platforms being considered are the B767, possibly the Il-76/A-50 (see China), and A310 under an international programme (see Raytheon Systems).

Development

▪ Co-operation with Elta Electronics Industries of IAI's Electronics Group produced the Phalcon radar system, suited for installation on aircraft of varying sizes.

Details *(original B707 Phalcon)*

Sales/Users: Chilean Air Force B707-320C converted to Phalcon configuration, handed over in May 1994 but returned for further work, with redelivery a year later. The Israeli Air Force has an undeclared number of Phalcon 707 AEWs with conformal arrays, taking on added importance since its Hawkeyes were withdrawn, and may well require a more sophisticated Phalcon configuration using an over-fuselage radome and triangulated arrays (see below), possibly based on a more modern and larger airframe. It is rumoured that 2 South African B707-320 tanker/transports, possibly of No 60 Squadron at Waterkloof, were installed with some elements of the Phalcon system for early-warning, elint and sigint, including only the fuselage-side antennae. Raytheon Systems Company of the USA is proposing an AEW aircraft based on an Airbus A310 airframe to meet the Royal Australian Air Force's Project Wedgetail requirement, using the IAI/Elta radar with arrays triangularly arranged in a more traditional but fixed over-fuselage radome (see Raytheon Systems Company), while a similar configuration was put under development for China but this time based on the Il-76/A-50; prototyping of the latter used a Russian-supplied Beriev A-50 (see China) but some of the mission avionics were to be fitted in Taganrog, under an Israeli/Russian agreement to eventually market the aircraft internationally; Israel reached agreement with Russia regarding the purchase of several Il-76 airframes for

↑ **IAI Phalcon fitted to a Chilean Boeing 707-320C, with 3 antennae only in forward fuselage sides and nose positions, providing 260° scan coverage**

Phalcon use, with the first for China expected to be converted in 1998. South Korea is being offered a similar A310-based system plus a second system based on a Boeing 767 platform (possibly in 767-300ER form) for its 4-aircraft requirement, with the Phalcon system of the B767 employed as 2 side-of-fuselage conformal L-band arrays plus nose and tail radomes, providing 360° coverage out to about 200 naut miles over the forward and side sectors (260°) and marginally less in the rear sector. The B767 would accommodate 11 operator workstations, use similar Elta ESM and IFF to the B707 Phalcon but incorporate a datalink compatible with US aircraft flying in the area, probably supplied by Raytheon Systems Company. Unrefuelled duration could be well over 10 hours, offering a range of 5,400 naut miles and operational ceiling of 35,000 ft (10,670 m). Lockheed Martin has also expressed interest in Phalcon as an option for its C-130J AEW aircraft, with South Korea and Turkey as potential customers, among others. Selection of the South Korean AEW aircraft, against competing designs, was expected in 1998. India is also believed to have considered the Phalcon solution (see HAL entry).

Crew: Flight crew, plus operators for 6 mission stations, each having 2 graphic colour displays and associated equipment. Stations comprise 4 radar, 1 electronic support measures/ electronic intelligence, and 1 communications support measures/ communications intelligence. Data link management and communications do not have a specific operator. Capacity for up to about 11 consoles.

Radar: Elta EL/M-2075 L-band radar, with up to 6 conformal airframe-mounted solid-state phased arrays (carried in 2 × 12 m and 2 × 4 m separate fuselage-side container fairings, 1 under the tail and 1 in the nose radome). Each electronically-scanned array covers a given sector in azimuth and elevation, thereby requiring all 6 arrays to provide 360° coverage. Partial fits are considered suitable to certain applications, and it is believed the Chilean B707-320C was originally delivered with 3 arrays. Maximum radar range is reportedly 215 naut miles (249 miles) 400 km, though this would depend on the profile of the targets; modes are medium PRF search and track, low PRF for helicopter detection, and long-range search.

Other mission sensors: Monopulse IFF, integrated with the radar arrays. Elta EL/L-8312 0.5-18 GHz ESM/elint with wingtip, nose and tail antennae, Elta EL/K-7031 HF/UHF/VHF communications intelligence, C-band datalink and other systems, with MIL-STD-1553B databus.

Rinaldo Piaggio — Italy

Full name:
Industrie Aeronautiche E Meccaniche Rinaldo Piaggio SpA.
Corporate address: Via Cibrario 4, 16154 Genova Sestri, Genoa.
Telephone: +39 010 64811 **Facsimile:** +39 010 6520160
Founded: 29 February 1964.
Employees: Over 1,000.
Information: Paulo Barberies (Sales and Public Relations – *telephone* +39 010 6481308).

Comments: In 1994 Piaggio was placed under insolvency protection, with 3 Government commissioners overseeing the company. However, in May 1998 it was announced that the company had been sold and the protection would be lifted in November 1998. 51% of shares are now held by a consortium led by Turkish state-holding company Tushav.

ACTIVITIES:

- Subcontractor to AMX International, Alenia, Dassault and Panavia.
- Produces the Rolls-Royce Gem, Spey and Viper, and AlliedSignal T53 and T55 engines under licence, and has a share in the RTM 322.
- See General Aviation section for Avanti.

SUBSIDIARY

PIAGGIO AVIATION INC:
HQ Address: Dover, DE, USA.

Piaggio P.166-DL3-SEM Maritime

First flight: 3 July 1976.
Role: Maritime search and surveillance, coastal patrol, SAR, long-range search, anti-smuggling, aerial photogrammetry, air ambulance, paratroop dropping, cargo and passenger transport.
Based on: P.166-DL3-SEM.
Users: Italian Capitanerie coast guard and Guardia di Finanza, totalling 27. Production of all versions of the P.166-DL3-SEM multi-role aircraft is now only to order. Italian utility P.166s are being upgraded, having P&WC PT6A-121 turboprops, new avionics and systems.
Crew: Typically 2, plus up to 8 passengers.
Mission equipment: 2 colour displays, for the pilot and operator console. FIAR/AlliedSignal Bendix/King RDR-1500B radar, interfaced (or compatible) with Loran-C ANI-7000, VOR, Sierra AN/ARN-136A Tacan, B & B TAS/Plus 2504M computer, and Rockwell Collins compass. Also Daedalus AA 3500 IR/UV digital scanner, or Daedalus AADS 1268 12-channel airborne thematic mapper, FLIR, video recorder, twin Vinten 618 70-mm view cameras (viewing angles –20° to –60° for side installation, –60° to –100° for vertical installation, when taking the horizon as 0°), and Optical Radiation Corp gimbled searchlight. Possible enhancements include NMS with GPS/VLF, remote sensing equipment, and video and data link.
Engines: 2 AlliedSignal LTP101-700A-1A turboprops.
Engine rating: 700 eshp (522 ekW), flat rated to 600 shp (447.4 kW).
Fuel system: 2,504 lb (1,136 kg).
Flight avionics/instrumentation: Communication equipment comprises HF/SSB, Cripto HF, V/UHF (AM and FM), VHF/FM low band, VHF/FM high band, VHF/AM, UHF/AM and intercom. Navigation/identification equipment comprises Loran-C, Tacan, VOR/ILS, ADF, integrated Doppler navigator, TAS computer (for Doppler and Loran-C), direction finder, homing, IFF/transponder, compass, strap-down AHRS, radar altimeter, radio altimeter, 3-axis autopilot and flight director (see Mission equipment).

Details for P.166-DL3-SEM Maritime

PRINCIPAL DIMENSIONS:
Wing span: 48 ft 2 ins (14.69 m)
Maximum length: 40 ft 8 ins (12.39 m)
Maximum height: 16 ft 5 ins (5 m)

WINGS:
Area: 285.9 sq ft (26.56 m^2)
Aspect ratio: 8.12

TAIL UNIT:
Tailplane span: 16 ft 9 ins (5.1 m)

UNDERCARRIAGE:
Type: Retractable, with nosewheel
Wheel base: 15 ft 2 ins (4.62 m)
Wheel track: 8 ft 9 ins (2.66 m)

WEIGHTS:
Empty, basic: 5,996 lb (2,720 kg)
Maximum zero fuel: 8,377 lb (3,800 kg)
Maximum take-off: 9,480 lb (4,300 kg)
Maximum landing: 8,377 lb (3,800 kg)
Payload: 2,407 lb (1,092 kg) maximum, or 979 lb (444 kg) with maximum fuel
Maximum useful load: 3,483 lb (1,580 kg), including crew

PERFORMANCE:
Maximum speed: 224 kts (258 mph) 415 km/h, at 10,000 ft (3,050 m)
Maximum cruise speed: 210 kts (242 mph) 389 km/h, at 12,000 ft (3,660 m)
Economic cruise speed: 162 kts (186 mph) 300 km/h, at 12,000 ft (3,660 m)
Minimum control speed: 90 kts (104 mph) 167 km/h
Stall speed: 69 kts (80 mph) 128 km/h
Take-off distance: 2,000 ft (610 m)
Take-off distance over a 50 ft (15 m) obstacle: 1,362 ft (415 m)
Maximum climb rate: 2,580 ft (786 m) per minute, or 1,732 ft (528 m) per minute using 1 engine
Ceiling: 30,500 ft (9,295 m) service, or 16,000 ft (4,875 m) using 1 engine
Range: 1,109 naut miles (1,277 miles) 2,056 km, 30 minutes reserve, at 12,000 ft (3,660 m)

↑ **Piaggio P.166-DL3-SEM Maritime** *(courtesy Rinaldo Piaggio)*

↑ **Operator console on the Piaggio P.166-DL3-SEM Maritime** *(courtesy Rinaldo Piaggio)*

Fokker — Netherlands

Fokker Maritime Enforcer Mk 2, Black Crow Mk 2, KingBird Mk 2, Maritime Mk 2 and Sentinel Mk 2

Comments: See Airliners section for current position of the Fokker company. Details of the Maritime Enforcer Mk 2 and a photograph can be found in the 1996-97 edition of *WA&SD*, page 60. Details of the other electronic, reconnaissance and surveillance aircraft listed above can also be found in the 1996-97 *WA&SD*, pages 175-176.

Beriev Taganrog Aviation Complex — Russia

Corporate address:
See Combat section for all company details.

Beriev A-50 and 976 (NATO name *Mainstay*)

First flight: 19 December 1978, piloted by Vladimir Demyanovsky.
Role: Strategic airborne early warning and control aircraft.
Based on: Ilyushin Il-76MD *Candid*.

Aims

- Replace Tu-126 *Moss*, based around the new Shmel radar system.
- Effective operation over land and sea.

Development

- 1965. Vega radar design bureau started work on the Shmel AEW&C system (chief designer of the system was Vladimir Ivanov, radar by V. Pogreshayev, and on-board computer by O. Rezepov).
- 1984. Initial operational capability.
- 1987. First photographs published.
- August 1992. Presented for the first time in public (MosAeroshow in Zhukovsky).
- 17 June 1997. At the Paris Air Show, the Russian Rosvooruzheniye and Israel Aircraft Industries' Elta division signed an agreement to jointly develop an AEW&C system based on the A-50, using Israeli Phalcon radar. This will undoubtedly initially help Israel compete for Chinese orders, but eventually the aircraft will be marketed internationally (see China and Israel).

Details

Sales/Users: Manufactured at Taganrog using Il-76MD airframes constructed at Tashkent. About 16 in service with Russian Air Defence Troops, all with the 144th Regiment at Berezovka over the Polar Circle, providing interception data to the latest Russian defence fighters. Also available to tactical forces. Production and development continues. The A-50 was used during the Gulf conflict of 1991; 2 crews under command of Major Alexei Serebrov and Major Vasili Kubasov flew by rotation over the Black Sea to monitor the situation and track cruise missiles.
Flight crew: 4, comprising 2 pilots, navigator and engineer.
Mission crew: 11 systems operators, comprising the commander, engineer, 3 detection operators, 4 control operators and 2 communications operators.
Radar: Rotating dome of 34 ft 5 ins (10.5 m) diameter and 8 ft 2 ins (2.5 m) maximum thickness carried above the fuselage, housing the Shmel radar S-band antenna. Rotation rate is 6 revolutions per minute. The radar can track up to 50-60 targets simultaneously; search range is 124 naut miles (143 miles) 230 km for fighter size targets at low altitude, 162-189 naut miles (186-218 miles) 300-350 km for targets at high altitude, and 216 naut miles (249 miles) 400 km for a large sea target. 10-12 friendly fighters can be guided to the targets simultaneously. Total weight of the Shmel mission system is 44,092 lb (20,000 kg).
Other mission sensors: 4 R-863 radio communication sets (for friendly aircraft control), 2 R-866 radio coms, 3 metre and decametre wavelength datalinks of 189 naut miles (217 miles) 350 km range and 1 of unlimited range via a satellite. New type of IFF.
Self-protection systems: Oborona system with integrated warning devices, active electronic jammers, and packs of chaff/flares on the fuselage sides.
Fixed weapons: None.
Expendable weapons and equipment: None.
Flight refuelling probe: On the nose, ahead of the cockpit. See Aircraft variants – A-50.

Aircraft variants:
A-50 *Mainstay*, as detailed. Based on the Il-76MD transport but without nose glazing. Stub-wings added to the undercarriage nacelles and small surfaces near the fuselage tail (both undoubtedly to help prevent known buffeting during flight refuelling operations), and a fin-root air intake to cool the avionics.
A-50M is an updated version with the Shmel-2 radar system and more powerful computer.
A-50U is a further improved version, with Shmel-M radar. Probably has triple tailfin. Maximum take-off weight increased to 462,970 lb (210,000 kg) and patrol duration is about 6 hours. First reportedly seen in 1995 at the Chkalovskaya air base outside Moscow.
976 is a civil derivative, used as a 'picket' control and data recording station during the test flights of aircraft at the Flight Test Institute in Zhukovsky. Named also **Il-76SK** when proposed as an airborne control post for the Tu-160/Burlak aerospace system. It has, unlike the A-50, the glazed nose of the Il-76, but no in-flight refuelling capability and thereby no added aerodynamic surfaces at the undercarriage nacelles and fuselage tail. The 976's radar can track aerial vehicles at a distance of 324 naut miles (373 miles) 600 km and space vehicles at 540 naut miles (621 miles) 1,000 km. 6 experimental vehicles can be tracked simultaneously. The 976 also carries a satellite-based communications and datalink system, which relays data to ground posts. The weight of the electronic systems is 44,092 lb (20,000 kg). 5 built in the latter 1980s (*SSSR-76452* to *SSSR-76456*) , but possibly only 1 in current use.

Details for A-50

WEIGHTS:
Take-off: 418,878 lb (190,000 kg)
Maximum landing: 334,000 lb (151,500 kg)
Fuel: 142,903 lb (64,820 kg)

PERFORMANCE:
Patrol speed: 324 kts (373 mph) 600 km/h
Typical patrol altitude: 26,250-32,810 ft (8,000-10,000 m)
Ceiling: 33,465 ft (10,200 m), service
G limit: 2
Maximum range: 2,698 naut miles (3,107 miles) 5,000 km
Patrol duration at 540 naut miles (621 miles) 1,000 km from base: 4 hours
Patrol duration at 1,080 naut miles (1,242 miles) 2,000 km from base: 1 hour 24 minutes
*See Ilyushin Il-76 for general details in the Airliners section.

↑ **Beriev A-50 *Mainstay*** *(Piotr Butowski)*. Note: an underview of A-50 was illustrated in the 1996-97 edition of *WA&SD*, page 176

↑ **Beriev 976, a civil derivative of the A-50 for use as a 'picket' control and data recording station** *(Piotr Butowski)*

Ilyushin Aviation Complex — Russia

Corporate address:
See Combat section for all company details.

Ilyushin Il-20 and Il-24 (NATO name *Coot-A*)

Comments: The Il-20 reconnaissance, electronic intelligence (elint) and communications relay aircraft is no longer operational. The Il-24N became the civil derivative, used for oversea fishery observation; Nit radar retained but Igla radar and elint sensors removed. Details of these aircraft and a photograph can be found in the 1996-97 edition of *WA&SD*, page 177.

Ilyushin Il-80 (NATO name *Maxdome*)

First flight: Summer 1985.
Role: Strategic command post, subordinated to the General Staff of the Russian armed forces.
Based on: Ilyushin Il-86 airliner. No main cabin windows, and hardened against the effects of electromagnetic pulse following a nuclear exchange.

Development

- 5 March 1987. First flight of a fully equipped prototype.
- 1992. Noticed by Western observers at the Zhukovsky test centre.

Details

Sales/Users: 4 aircraft converted, all with civil markings and registered *RA-86146* to *RA-86149*. Usually based on Chkalovskaya airfield outside Moscow.
Mission equipment: The most outstanding external feature is a large canoe-shaped fairing on top of the front fuselage, believed to house a satellite communication systems. The first 2 (*-146* and *-147*) have large sword-type aerials installed in various positions on the fuselage, particularly in the upper section, whilst the remaining 2 have small aerials. Longitudinal fairings are mounted in front of the tailfin and under the rear part of the fuselage. Extremely long trailing wire antenna is used for very low frequency radio (for instance, for communication with submerged submarines), released from the pod installed on the port side of the rear fuselage. See Self-protection systems.
Self-protection systems: A large, cigar shaped container is suspended near the root of each wing. The air intakes suggest electronic equipment, probably an electronic warfare system.
Flight refuelling probe: Fitted.

Ilyushin Il-82

Role: Communications relay aircraft associated with the Il-80 command post.
Based on: Ilyushin Il-76MD.

Development

- 1992. Seen by Western observers at the Zhukovsky test centre.

Details

Sales/Users: 2 aircraft built, civil registered Aeroflot Il-76MD *CCCP-76450* and *76451*. Used as relay aircraft for Il-80 command posts, usually based at Chkalovskaya outside Moscow.
Mission equipment: The most outstanding feature of its external appearance (like the Il-80 command post) is a large canoe-shaped fairing containing a set of aerials, above the forward fuselage. 2 x AI-24 turbine engines are used to supply power for the onboard equipment, installed in long undercarriage nacelles. 2 additional long and narrow fairings are carried under the front fuselage and 2 more ahead of the tailfin. A trailing wire antenna with stabilization cone, used for low frequency radio communication, is released from beneath the rear fuselage. A sword-type aerial is fitted each side of the wire antenna. Streamlined containers, with long forward protruding rods, are installed near the wingtips. The usual nose glazing of the Il-76 has been deleted.

↑ Ilyushin Il-80 *Maxdome* (Piotr Butowski)

↑ Ilyushin Il-82 communications relay aircraft associated with Il-80 operations (Piotr Butowski)

Ilyushin Il-114 special electronic versions

First flight: 1998 (prototype Il-114P was under construction at the Ilyushin works in Moscow in late 1997).
Role: Il-114FK is the aerial photographic/photogrammetry version, planned to replace the An-30 (also for 'Open Skies' missions). Il-114P is a Russian Federal Border Guard patrol aircraft. Il-114RT had been planned as a military radio relay aircraft to replace the An-26RT, but since abandoned.
Based on: Ilyushin Il-114 airliner.

Details *(Il-114P, unless stated)*

Mission crew: 2 operators, each having a bubble window for observation. Passenger cabin is sub-divided into 2 compartments. Front compartment is used for carrying litters, survivors or other loads up to 6,614 lb (3,000 kg). The rear compartment contains the Strizh system equipment, accommodates the 2 operators, and has seating for a reserve crew.
Radar: Leninets/St Petersburg Strizh (Swift) carried in the nose. Search area ±135°. See Sukhoi S-80PT for radar data.

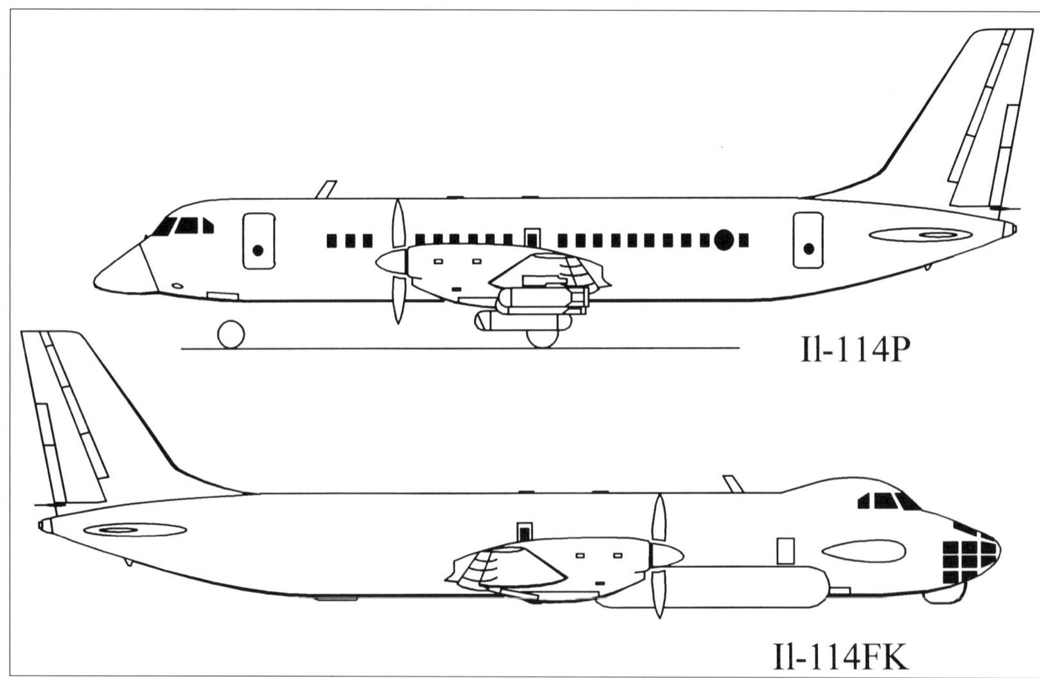

↑ Ilyushin Il-114P (*top*) and Il-114FK special mission versions of the Il-114 airliner (Piotr Butowski)

Other mission sensors: Mission equipment is integrated into the Strizh electronic system, comprising the radar of the same name, LLTV and FLIR, as well as GPS, communication and datalink systems. Flight/navigation equipment provides for automatic navigation, preset position finding, detection of ships and determining their position within an accuracy of 100-165 ft (30-50 m).
Fixed weapons: None.
Expendable weapons and equipment: SPPU-687 gun pack with GSh-301 flexibly-mounted cannon, 2 podded searchlights, high-

Details for Il-114P, as for Il-114 except

PRINCIPAL DIMENSIONS:
Maximum length: 89 ft 11 ins (27.4 m)
Fuselage length: 87 ft 8 ins (26.725 m)

PERFORMANCE:
Patrol speed: 189-270 kts (217-311 mph) 350-500 km/h
Patrol altitude: 330-19,685 ft (100-6,000 m)
Range: 1,888 naut miles (2,175 miles) 3,500 km
Duration: 8-10 hours

power loudspeakers, plus liferafts, marker buoys and marker beacons carried on standard pods under the wings and fuselage.

Aircraft variants:
Il-114FK (fotokartografichesky) is planned to replace the Il-20 (already withdrawn) in a peacetime role and An-30, and will be used for inspection flights under the 'Open Skies' programme. It will have the navigation equipment for automatic and accurate flights along the programmed routes, plus photographic equipment in the cabin. The most obvious external feature is a large glazed nose and raised flight deck resembling that of the An-30. More advanced reconnaissance versions will be equipped with SLAR. First flight was targeted for 1998.
Il-114P is the patrol version for Russian Federal Border Guard use, intended for patrols over the 200-mile economic zone during 8 to 10 hour flights. Prototype was under construction in 1997. See general description.
Il-114RT military relay version has been abandoned.

MAPO "MiG" — Russia

Corporate address:
See Combat section for company details.

Mikoyan 301 and 321

Comments: Brief details of these projected hypersonic aircraft, probably intended for reconnaissance and bombing, can be found in the 1996-97 edition of *WA&SD*, page 178.

→ **Mikoyan 301 hypersonic reconnaissance aircraft and bomber** *(Piotr Butowski)*

MAPO "Myasishchev" — Russia

Corporate address:
See Combat section for full company details.

↑ **Myasishchev Il-22 featuring a long underfuselage antenna housing** *(Piotr Butowski)*

Myasishchev Il-22 (NATO name *Coot-B*)

Role: Airborne command post.
Based on: Ilyushin Il-18D airframe.

Development

▪ Conversion of the Il-18D airliner, undertaken by Myasishchev.

Details

Sales/Users: About 20 aircraft were converted and are used by the Russian armed forces. The mission equipment has been modernized many times. All Il-22/Il-22Ms are flying in civil Aeroflot markings and inscribed Il-18.
Mission equipment: Il-22 can be identified by the bullet-shaped fairing on top of the tailfin, and the shallow pod under the fuselage, about 65 ft 8 ins (20 m) long for the Il-22 and about 29 ft 7 ins (9 m) for the Il-22M. Numerous other blade-type antennae can be seen on the fuselage.

Aircraft variants:
Il-22 and ***Il-22M***, as detailed above.

Myasishchev M-17 and M-55 (NATO name *Mystic*)

First flight: 26 May 1982 (M-17), piloted by Eduard Cheltsov.
Role: M-17RM (M-55) *Mystic-B* is a high-altitude reconnaissance aircraft. M-55.2 Geophysica is for ecological monitoring. Original M-17 *Mystic-A* was a high-altitude reconnaissance balloon interceptor.

Aims

▪ 5 hours operation at an altitude of 55,775 ft (17,000 m), with long loiter.
▪ 3,307 lb (1,500 kg) of inter-changeable reconnaissance and data transfer equipment.
▪ Basing at second-category airfield (concrete).

Development

▪ 1970. Start of work on the M-17 high-altitude balloon interceptor, intended to intercept US unmanned reconnaissance balloons.
▪ 24 December 1978. Loss of the M-17 prototype before its first flight.
▪ 26 May 1982. First flight of an M-17 (civil registration *CCCP-17103*).
▪ 1982. M-17 detected in the West and provisionally named Ram-M.
▪ 16 August 1988. First flight of the M-17RM (M-55) reconnaissance aircraft (registration *CCCP-01552*, now *RF-01552*). Piloted by Eduard Cheltsov.
▪ 1989. M-17 (*CCCP-17103*) displayed at the Monino museum.
▪ 28 March-14 May 1990. M-17 (*CCCP-17401*) set 25 world records in Class C-1i/j.
▪ November 1993. M-55 was shown for the first time abroad (in Italy). ILS-80 system installed for flights abroad. Displayed at the Farnborough Air Show in the UK the following year.
▪ 19 December 1996–16 January 1997. M-55.2 Geophysica participated in an international Polar experiment to study the chemistry and physics of the Polar stratosphere relating to ozone depletion. Based at Rovaniemi, northern Finland, the aircraft undertook 6 research flights, accumulating 30 flying hours, reaching an altitude of 69,880 ft (21,300 m), when the outside temperature was -81.3° C. Pilot was Viktor Vasenkov.
▪ 1998-2000. Similar research flights to the above entry will be made over Antarctica and the Indian Ocean.

Details *(M-17RM/M-55, unless stated)*

Sales/Users: First prototype M-17-1 was built at the Kumertau aircraft production plant in 1978. Later, manufacturing was transferred to Smolensk, where 2 more M-17s (plus 1 for static testing) and at least 5 M-55s were built. Production at the Smolensk factory has been terminated due to a lack of funding, although the Russian Air Force has expressed interest in more aircraft. Some reports stated that 2 aircraft are currently being tested by the military. See Development, 2 final entries.
Crew: Single pilot, except in the M-55U and Geophysica-2 2-seaters. VKK-6D or VK-3M pilot suit.
Cockpit: Pressurized. At maximum altitude the conditions inside the cockpit are the same as external conditions at 16,400 ft (5,000 m) altitude. Rearward hinged canopy.
Crew escape: Zvezda/Tomilino K-36L zero-zero ejection seat/s.
Mission equipment: Up to 3,968 lb (1,800 kg) of interchangeable reconnaissance sensors, including SLAR (side-looking airborne radar), infra-red scanner and photographic cameras housed inside the unpressurized fuselage nose compartment of 318 cu ft (9 m^3) volume. Datalink.
Fixed guns: See Aircraft variants.
Wing characteristics: High aspect ratio, high-wing monoplane. Built in 5 sections (centre-section plus 2 outer panels each side). Torsion box construction, with integral fuel tanks.
Wing control surfaces: No high-lift devices. Ailerons at outer trailing edge (+20°, -16°). 3-section spoilers on the upper surface of each wing (+50°).
Tail control surfaces: T-type, carried on twin tailbooms, with 2-section elevator (+13° 30', -7° 30') and 2 rudders (±20°). Tabs on elevator and rudders.
Flight control system: Manual (without boosters); push-pull rods.
Fuselage: Nacelle type, built in 3 sections and housing the cockpit, sensors and engines. Dense framing without longitudinals. Twin tailbooms.

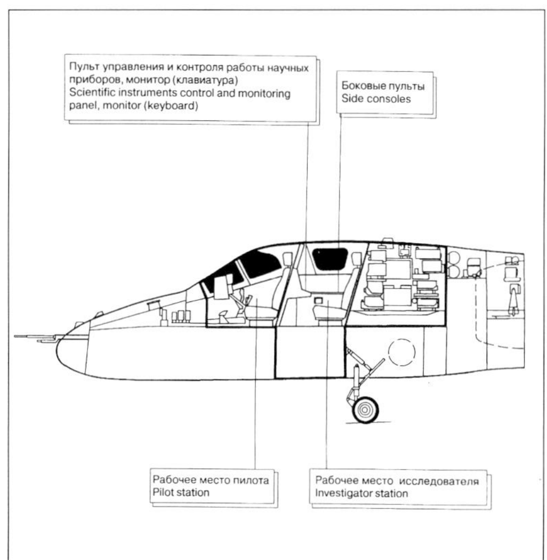

↑ **2-seat cockpit in the lengthened nose of the Myasishchev Geophysica-2** *(courtesy Myasishchev)*

↑ Myasishchev M-55.2 Geophysica that participated in the 1996-97 international Polar experiment, flying with an M-101T Gzhel. Note the box antenna housing aft of the cockpit *(Piotr Butowski)*

Details for M-17RM (M-55) *Mystic-B*

PRINCIPAL DIMENSIONS:
Wing span: 122 ft 11 ins (37.464 m)
Maximum length without probe: 75 ft (22.8675 m)
Maximum height: 15 ft 10 ins (4.83 m)

WINGS:
Aerofoil section: Supercritical P-173-9
Area, gross: 1,417 sq ft (131.6 m^2)
Aspect ratio: 10.665
Incidence: 5°
Anhedral: 2° 30′

TAIL UNIT:
Tailplane span: 39 ft 3 ins (11.96 m)
Tailplane area: 297 sq ft (27.62 m^2)
Fin area: 156.8 sq ft (14.57 m^2)

UNDERCARRIAGE:
Type: Retractable, with twin steerable nose wheels
Main wheel tyre size: 660 x 200 mm
Nose wheel tyre size: 520 x 125 mm
Wheel base: 18 ft 10 ins (5.735 m)
Wheel track: 21 ft 8 ins (6.6 m)

WEIGHTS:
Empty, operating: 30,865 lb (14,000 kg)
Maximum take-off: 52,470 lb (23,800 kg)
Payload: 3,968 lb (1,800 kg)

PERFORMANCE:
Maximum and cruise speed: 405 kts (466 mph) 750 km/h at 65,620 ft (20,000 m)
Take-off distance: 2,953 ft (900 m)
Landing distance: 2,560-5,742 ft (780-1,750 m)
Ceiling: 68,900 ft (21,000 m)
Range: 2,681 naut miles (3,085 miles) 4,965 km maximum
Duration with payload: 4 hours 12 minutes at 65,620 ft (20,000 m), 5 hours at 55,775 ft (17,000 m)
Duration without payload: 6 hours 30 minutes at 55,775 ft (17,000 m)

Construction materials: All-metal, mainly D16 aluminium alloy.
Engines: 2 Aviadvigatel/Perm D-30V (izdelye 75) non-afterburning turbofans (D-30V10 in the prototype and D-30V12 in production aircraft). Engines mounted side-by-side in the rear fuselage. *Mystic-A* had a single RD-36-51V (see Aircraft variants).
Engine rating: Each 9,921 lbf (44.13 kN) maximum thrust at sea level and 739 lbf (3.29 kN) at 68,900 ft (21,000 m).
Fuel system: 10,000 litres of internal fuel in 5 wing tanks; 17,416 lb (7,900 kg) of special high altitude T-8V fuel or 18,298 lb (8,300 kg) of standard RT fuel.
Electrical system: Large reserve of power for the mission systems (60 kVA at 115V AC and 3 kW at 27.5V DC).
Braking system: On main units.
Flight avionics/instrumentation: Korall short-range navigation system, R-863 and R-864 radios, Parol IFF, and digital computer.

Aircraft variants:
M-17 *Mystic-A* was the original version, built as a high-altitude balloon interceptor. PrNK-17 nav/attack system with opto-electronic search and track device, and armed with a flexibly-mounted GSh-23 cannon with 500 rounds of ammunition in a turret. Single 15,432 lbf (68.65 kN) RD-36-51V high-altitude engine. Wing span 132 ft 3 ins (40.32 m), length overall 73 ft 1 ins (22.27 m), maximum take-off weight 40,565 lb (18,400 kg), service ceiling 70,700 ft (21,550 m), maximum speed 401 kts (462 mph) 743 km/h at 65,625 ft (20,000 m), maximum range 710 naut miles (817 miles) 1,315 km with 5% fuel reserve, and duration of 2 hours 14 minutes. Military programme terminated in 1987. Later renamed *Stratosphere* and used as a research aircraft for ozone-layer analysis. 2 flying prototypes built, 1 now in the Monino museum and 1 scrapped.
M-17RM (razvedchik modifitsirovannyi, modified reconnaissance aircraft) or ***M-55*** *Mystic-B* has a significantly redesigned airframe and twin engines. Weapon system removed. Lengthened and raised front fuselage with special equipment compartment. Planned as a component of a Russian reconnaissance and strike system equivalent to the US Assault Breaker or Precision Location Strike System. The system comprises the M-17RM used for reconnaissance and target indication, a ground control post, launchers for surface-to-surface missiles, and strike aircraft. Due to real-time updating of reconnaissance information, the accuracy of hit is better than 'several metres'.
M-55.2 Geophysica is the civil version of the military M-55 used with several equipment suites. These comprise:
M-55A designed for lower-stratosphere ecological monitoring.
M-55B uses the following systems for Earth surface monitoring: 2-frequency synthetic aperture side-looking radar with 16.4-32.8 ft (5-10 m) resolution at 1.6 ins (4 cm) wavelength or 65.6-131.2 ft (20-40 m) resolution at 49 ins (1.25 m) wavelength; A-84 photographic camera with 2.6-5.3 ft (0.8-1.6 m) resolution; Argos optical scanner with 98.4 ft (30 m) resolution; or infra-red scanner with 45.9 ft (14 m) resolution and Radius scanning radiometer.

Geophysica can also be used for weather control, by spraying chemical agents into cloud to generate rain (used to prevent potential hailstorm clouds damaging cultivation). In this role the aircraft flies above the cloud and drops the container with chemical agent, which is opened automatically at isotherm level. Cloud height is 7-14 km and isotherm -6°C is at 4 km altitude. In development of this role, Myasishchev is in partnership with Krasnodar (The Application of Civil Aviation in National Economy) and Nalchik (Alpine Geophysic Research Institute). See the 1996-97 edition of *WA&SD*, page179, for an artist's impression.
Geophysica-2 is a follow-up civil research version, initially expected to become operational in 1997 but now considerably delayed. Has increased possibilities by carrying a second crew member (researcher), 4,409 lb (2,000 kg) of equipment, and with range and flight duration increased by 25%. The forward section of the fuselage is lengthened and redesigned, using a pressurized 4.9 ft (1.50 m) plug inserted between the cockpit and equipment compartment, allowing for the installation of the second cockpit in the upper part and additional equipment in the lower. Accordingly, the front undercarriage leg has been moved forward, thereby increasing the wheel base to about 24 ft (7.3 m). The lengthened fuselage and tailbooms provide 399 cu ft (11.3 m^3) of space for special equipment, including 46 cu ft (1.3 m^3) in a pressurized segment (the M-55 has only 318 cu ft, 9 m^3 of available space, all unpressurized). Moreover, the Geophysica-2 can carry measuring equipment in 2 containers, 53 cu ft (1.5 m^3) each, suspended under the wings. The wings themselves are longer, at 131 ft 4 ins (40.0 m), with upper winglets. Wing fuel capacity is increased to 22,267 lb (10,100 kg). Maximum take-off weight is 59,525 lb (27,000 kg), and maximum flight duration at an altitude of 62,335-65,625 ft (19,000-20,000 m) is 6 hours 30 minutes.
M-55U is a projected 2-seat trainer.

Sukhoi Design Bureau — Russia

Corporate address:
See Combat section for company details.

Sukhoi S-80PT

First flight: Expected 1999, though prototype S-80 seen 1998.
Role: Light military patrol/surveillance and transport. See also Airliners section.
Based on: Sukhoi S-80 general-purpose aircraft.
Sales/Users: In 1996 Sukhoi accelerated work on the S-80PT, which is the subject to great interest of the Russian Air Force, Federal Border Guard and Ministry of Emergency Situations.
Crew: 2, if the co-pilot also operates the Strizh surveillance/weapon control system, otherwise 3.
Passengers: 20 folded seats or 10 litters in the cabin.
Freight hold capacity: 6,614 lb (3,000 kg) of cargo.
Freight hold access: Rear loading ramp/door plus door on the port side of the mid fuselage.
Radar: Leninets/St Petersburg Strizh nav/attack radar in an egg-shaped undernose radome. Search range for a sea object of 3.2 sq ft (0.3 m^2) radar cross section is 10.8 naut miles (12.4 miles) 20 km when flying at 328 ft (100 m) altitude and sea state 3. Large ships with an RCS of 32,292-53,820 sq ft (3,00-5,000 m^2) are detected at 108-119 naut miles (124-137 miles) 200-230 km. Up to 20 targets can be tracked simultaneously. In addition to Strizh, the Phazotron Gukol and Vega-M Shtyk radars are under consideration.
Other mission equipment: Strizh surveillance-attack system with a radar of the same name, and FLIR at the port side of the fuselage. FLIR unit is able to detect a person's head in water from a distance of 985 ft (300 m), a liferaft from 4,920-6,560 ft (1,500-2,000 m), and

↑ Model of the Sukhoi S-80PT with bulged radome, FLIR turret, ASMs and rocket packs *(Piotr Butowski)*

a ship from 16 naut miles (18.6 miles) 30 km. In an air-to-air mode, the FLIR can detect a fighter from about 10.8 naut miles (12.4 miles) 20 km and a transport aircraft from 27 naut miles (31 miles) 50 km. Datalink to coastal or airborne command posts.
Self-protection systems: Optional flare dispensers.
Fixed guns: None.
Number of weapon pylons: 5, as 4 under the wings and 1 at the starboard side of the fuselage.
Expendable weapons and equipment: Kh-29T (AS-14 *Kedge*) TV-guided ASMs, APU-8V 8-tube clusters of Vikhr (AT-16) anti-armour missiles and B8M rocket pods can be suspended from the inner underwing pylons, with 2 self-defence R-73 (AA-11 *Archer*) AAMs on the outer pylons, and an SPPU-22-01 gun on the fuselage pylon.

Details for S-80PT *powered by General Electric CT7-9B engines*

PRINCIPAL DIMENSIONS:
Wing span: 76 ft (23.16 m)
Maximum length: 58 ft 7 ins (17.85 m)
Maximum height: 18 ft 4 ins (5.58 m)

CABIN:
Length: 20 ft 8 ins (6.3 m), or 25 ft 7 ins (7.8 m) with ramp
Width: 7 ft 1 ins (2.15 m) maximum, 6 ft 0.5 ins (1.84 m) at floor
Height: 6 ft (1.83 m)
Volume: 745.1 cu ft (21.1 m^3)

UNDERCARRIAGE:
Type: Retractable, with steerable nosewheels (38°). Twin wheels on each unit
Main wheel tyre size: 660 x 200 mm
Nose wheel tyre size: 500 x 180 mm
Wheel base: 21 ft 4 ins (6.5 m)
Wheel track: 18 ft 4.5 ins (5.6 m)

WEIGHTS:
Empty, operating: 19,048 lb (8,640 kg)
Maximum take-off and landing: 27,558 lb (12,500 kg), or 25,353 lb (11,500 kg) from an unpaved strip
Payload: 6,614 lb (3,000 kg)

PERFORMANCE:
Maximum cruise speed: 275 kts (317 mph) 510 km/h
Economic cruise speed: 205 kts (236 mph) 380 km/h
Landing speed: 97 kts (112 mph) 180 km/h
Take-off distance: 2,297 ft (700 m)
Landing distance: 919 ft (280 m)
Ceiling: 29,525 ft (9,000 m)
Maximum range: 1,392 naut miles (1,603 miles) 2,580 km
Range with full payload, at 275 kts: 362 naut miles (416 miles) 670 km, at 19,685 ft (6,000 m) altitude, with 30 minutes reserves
Range with full payload, at 205 kts: 1,335 naut miles (1,538 miles) 2,475 km, at 19,685 ft (6,000 m) altitude, with 30 minutes reserves
Range with 3,417 lb (1,550 kg) payload: 944 naut miles (1,087 miles) 1,750 km, at 275 kts and 19,685 ft (6,000 m) altitude, with 30 minutes reserves
Patrol duration: 6-9 hours, at 189 naut miles (217 miles) 350 km from base

Tupolev Joint-Stock Company — Russia

Corporate address:
See Combat section for company details.

Tupolev Tu-135

Comments: Brief details and 2 photographs of this military high command executive transport with long-range communications system can be found in the 1996-97 edition of *WA&SD*, page 180.

Yakovlev Joint Stock Company – A. S. Yakovlev Design Bureau — Russia

Corporate address:
See Combat section for company details.

Yakovlev Yak-44

Comments: Programme ended. Details and a photograph of this carrier-borne early warning and control aircraft, intended also for land-based surveillance, can be found in the 1996-97 edition of *WA&SD*, page 180-181

Saab Group — Sweden

Corporate address:
See Combat section for company details.

Saab AEW&C/S 100B Argus and SAR-200

First flight: 1 July 1994 (AEW&C with radar).
First delivery: 1995 (S 100B).
Role: Airborne early warning and control, intended in Swedish service to be a reporting radar post linked to ground C^2 command and control centres via a secure data link. SAR-200 is a search and rescue/transport aircraft for the Japan Maritime Safety Agency.
Based on: Saab 340B airliner (Saab 340Plus for SAR-200).

Development

- 1982. Development began with Fairchild Aircraft of the USA receiving an order from the Swedish Defence Materiel Administration (FMV) to develop a trials AEW&C aircraft based around the Swedish Ericsson Erieye radar then under development. Initial plans covered the adaptation of a Fairchild Metro III with an over-fuselage box radome for the radar antenna, able to scan over a 120° sector.
- January 1991. Following wind-tunnel testing in 1983 and flight trials of the Metro III with an empty radome during 1986-87, trials began with a prototype radar installed.
- 8 January 1993. Plans for an operational system involved changing the carrier aircraft to the Saab 340, the prototype of which was ordered.
- February 1993. 6 Erieye radars were ordered by the FMV, plus work on new adaptive control.
- 23 December 1993. 5 production Saab 340 AEW&Cs were ordered for the Swedish Air Force, to be joined by the prototype.
- 17 January 1994. Maiden flight of a strengthened Saab 340 intended as the pre-series prototype to the AEW&C variant. Also featured enlarged ventral fins, and a new tailcone to house the APU for electrical power generation and cooling air for the avionics, but no radar or antenna.
- 1 July 1994. Maiden flight of the complete working system at Linköping. Used for trials by the FMV while production deliveries were underway.
- February 1996. First 2 SAR-200s ordered by the Japan Maritime Safety Agency.

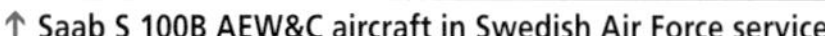
↑ Saab S 100B AEW&C aircraft in Swedish Air Force service

↑ Saab SAR-200 search and rescue aircraft for the Japan Maritime Safety Agency

▪ March 1996. First production delivery of Erieye radar system to the FMV, for continued testing and evaluation. Second delivery also in 1996. Swedish Air Force designation is PS 890.
▪ 1997. Delivery of 2 SAR-200s to the Japan Maritime Safety Agency.
▪ November 1997. First 3 S 100Bs transferred from the FMV to the Swedish Air Force.
▪ 1999. Final 3 S 100Bs delivered to the Swedish Air Force by Ericsson.

Details *(AEW&C, unless stated)*

Sales/Users: Japan (SAR-200; 10 required for JMSA) and Swedish Air Force (6 S 100Bs).
Crew: Up to 3 operator workstations.
Radar: Ericsson FSR-890 Erieye mission system (Swedish military PS 890) has flexible architecture using a MIL-STD-1553B databus and includes command and control, the active phased array radar, IFF interrogator, ESM (2-18 GHz), INS/GPS navigation system and data link (ESM/comint can be integrated into the Erieye system). Radar has a 26 ft 3 ins (8 m) antenna in a 29 ft 6 ins (9 m) box radome on struts above the fuselage, with sector scanning to provide a narrow main beam and very low sidelobe levels. Said to detect and track air and sea targets out to the horizon and beyond, with an instrumented range of 243 naut miles (279 miles) 450 km. Typical detection range against a fighter size target is 189 naut miles (217 miles) 350 km in a 150° sideways sector (Erieye provides 360° coverage, with performance optimized in 150° sideways sectors). Outside this sector, performance is reduced in forward and aft directions. According to Ericcson, the electronically scanned beam is controlled by an automatic and intelligent energy management system. This system was developed to utilize the features of phased-array technology, programmed to intelligently use its inherent ability to transmit in any direction from pulse-to-pulse. A target is automatically illuminated with extra pulses interlaced in the radar's normal pattern. The system is said to optimize the beam position and give faster detection verification, increased range and improved tracking performance compared to a rotodome layout. The radar's ability to instantaneously direct energy in any direction is used to optimize resources for a particular scenario. By assigning priorities to areas of interest, more energy can be directed to that area, thereby enhancing system performance.

Aircraft variants:
AEW&C is the airborne early warning and control aircraft, as detailed, initially operated by the Swedish Air Force as the S 100B. APU in tail for additional electrical supply.
SAR-200 is a search and rescue aircraft for the Japan Maritime Safety Agency, also suited to the transportation of personnel and supplies to remote stations. Telephonics APS-143(V) X-band sea surveillance radar carried in an underfuselage radome, AAQ-22 FLIR, VLF/Omega and GPS. Other equipment includes marine markers, flares and rescue pack, the latter released using a dropping hatch.

Details for Saab AEW&C

PERFORMANCE:
On-station duration: about 6 hours, at 100 naut miles (115 miles) 185 km from base

Antonov ASTC (Aviation Scientific-Technical Complex) — Ukraine

Corporate address:
1 Tupolev Street, Kiev 252062.
Telephone: +380 44 442 70 98
Facsimile: +380 44 449 99 96
Telex: 131309 ozon
Founded: 1946.
Information:
Oleg Bogdanov (Deputy General Designer).

ACTIVITIES

▪ Principally known for transport aircraft (see Airliners section). Created more than 100 aircraft types and modifications.
▪ Performs a wide range of scientific and research work, including wind-tunnel, structural, laboratory and flight tests.
▪ After-sale and engineering support to extend aircraft service life.
▪ Carries out international cargo carrying operations, including oversize loads, on a charter basis using An-124 heavy transports.
▪ Co-operates with Israel Aircraft Industries to offer an upgraded maritime patrol variant of the An-72P.

Antonov/Beriev An-30 (NATO name *Clank*)

Comments: First flown on 21 August 1967, 115 examples of this civil and military photogrammetric aircraft were manufactured at Kiev between 1971 and 1980, including 65 going to Soviet civil aviation, 26 to the Air Force and 18 exported to Afghanistan (1), Bulgaria (2), China (7), Cuba (2), Mongolia (1), Romania (3) and Vietnam (2). A Bulgarian An-30 was sold to the Czech Republic in 1988. One aircraft, now the An-30B (side number *81*), was prepared in March 1993 by Antonov for 'Open Skies' missions, serving with the Ukrainian Blakitna Stezha unit (alongside An-26s). The first inspection flight was carried out in April 1994 over the UK. In Russia from 1995, 6 An-30s have been adapted for a similar role by the Russian Avionics Design Bureau (part of MIG MAPO), fitted with new computerized navigation/data equipment, including GPS, ILS/VOR, and new com radio. Interestingly, the designation An-30D applies to a 1990 An-30 conversion offering extended range and carrying the Kvitok-2 long-range radio navigation system, the An-30FG became a Czech photogrammetric version with new cameras, and An-30M is a weather control aircraft of 1985 appearance, carrying 8 containers of dry carbon dioxide in the fuselage and 2 packs of chemical cartridges on the fuselage sides to prevent crop-damaging hailstorms and also to maintain good weather during important events, the latter including the recent 850th anniversary of Moscow in September 1997. The An-30R has an additional filtration device for radiation reconnaissance.

↑ Russian Air Force Antonov An-30, recently converted to undertake 'Open Skies' missions *(Piotr Butowski)*

Antonov An-71 (NATO name *Madcap*)

First flight: 12 July 1985 in Kiev, piloted by Alexander Tkachenko.
Role: Tactical airborne early warning and control. Can operate autonomously during 30 days away from base. Now offered also for civil use as an airborne air traffic control post.

Development

▪ 1982. Work started as a result of a study of combat over the Bekkaa Valley (Lebanon).
▪ March 1983. Antonov An-72 chosen as a platform for an AEW&C system, partly but not exclusively for possible operation from aircraft carriers (latter in An-71K form - see Aircraft variants).
▪ 9 January 1984. Official government order issued.
▪ 12 July 1985. First flight, though not fully completed.
▪ 28 February 1986. First flight of the second prototype, piloted by Georgi Lysenko.
▪ May 1986. AEW&C system installed.
▪ Late 1990. Tests abandoned.
▪ 1995. Relaunch offered, for roles including civil air traffic control.

Details

Sales/Users: 2 flying prototypes built in Kiev, both with civil Aeroflot registration (*SSSR-780151* as the rebuilt first An-72 flying prototype and *SSSR-780361* as a conversion of a production An-72). Tests abandoned at the end of 1990, when the first prototype had made 387 flights and the second aircraft 362 flights. Now relaunch of the programme by Antonov for roles that include civil air traffic control.
Crew: 3 flight crew (2 pilots and a navigator), plus 3 mission crew. Screens to protect the crew against electromagnetic radiation.
Radar: Rotating dome of 23 ft 11 ins (7.3 m) diameter carried above the tailfin, housing the Moscow Vega-M Kvant radar with S-band antenna (2 other systems were tested before Kvant). Rotation rate is 6 revolutions per minute. Radar can track up to 120 targets simultaneously; search range is 108 naut miles (124 miles) 200 km for fighter size targets (radar cross section of 21.5 sq ft, 2 m^2) at 0-98,425 ft (0-30,000 m), and maximum search range is 189-200 naut miles (217-230 miles) 350-370 km. The target position is detected with an accuracy of 1.35 naut miles (1.6 miles) 2.5 km.
Other mission sensors: Metre and decametre wavelength datalink.

↑ Antonov An-71 *Madcap 780361* second flying prototype, converted from a production An-72

Details for An-71 *Madcap*

PRINCIPAL DIMENSIONS:
Wing span: 104 ft 7.5 ins (31.89 m)
Maximum length: 77 ft 1 ins (23.5 m)
Maximum height: 30 ft 2 ins (9.2 m)

WINGS:
Area: 1,060.6 sq ft (98.53 m^2)
Aspect ratio: 10.32

UNDERCARRIAGE:
Type: Minor changes to An-72 type

WEIGHTS:
Maximum take-off: approximately 88,185 lb (40,000 kg)

PERFORMANCE:
Maximum operating speed: 351 kts (404 mph) 650 km/h
Patrol speed: 270-286 kts (311-329 mph) 500-530 km/h
Ceiling: 31,170-35,435 ft (9,500-10,800 m), service
Required runway length: 4,593 ft (1,400 m) concrete, 5,906 ft (1,800 m) unpaved
Patrol altitude: 26,245 ft (8,000 m)
Duration: 4 to 4 hours 30 minutes, with 1 hour reserve

Wing characteristics: Similar to that of An-72 transport.
Tail control surfaces: High dihedral, low-mounted tailplane (An-72 has T tail). Forward-swept tailfin of extended chord. 4-section rudder.
Fuselage: Forward section to frame 23, as for An-72. Rear section entirely new and shortened by 13 ft 1 ins (4 m). Fuselage is divided into 3 compartments, with flight and mission crew in the front compartment, mission computer and flight avionics in the centre compartment, and radar boxes, take-off booster and flight control system in the rear compartment.
Engines and rating: 2 Ivchenko PROGRESS/Zaporozhye D-436K turbofans, each 16,535 lbf (73.55 kN). Since the aircraft's weight was increased considerably, as the result of additional equipment, a Kolesov/Rybinsk RD-38A turbojet (6,393 lbf, 28.44 kN) was added for take-off boost, installed in a diagonal position in the rear fuselage.
Flight refuelling probe: None.
Electrical system: Basic systems are similar to An-72, except 4 GP-23 generators (instead of 2 GP-21s) provide 4 times the power, as required for the Kvant. Cooling system has been increased accordingly.
Flight avionics/instrumentation: Similar to that of An-72 transport.

Aircraft variants:
An-71 is the basic air force-type AEW&C aircraft, as described,
An-71K was the proposed shipborne version for *Admiral Kuznetsov*, prepared in 1982-83. This work has not continued, as it is clearly too heavy and could not easily be adapted for this role without major modification. Take-off from a carrier was to be assisted by 3 RD-38A turbojet boosters and five JATO rockets.

Antonov An-72P (NATO name *Coaler*)

Role: Armed surveillance and maritime patrol (day-and-night, and all-weather), especially for the 200 naut mile (230 mile) 370 km coastal zone.

Development

- Late 1980s. Entered service with the Soviet armed forces.
- August 1992. Presented to the public for the first time, at Zhukovsky.
- September 1992. Presented at the Farnborough Air Show.
- February 1994. Co-operation between Antonov and Israel Aircraft Industries (IAI) announced during Asian Aerospace in Singapore. Israel is supplying complete equipment, including EL/M-2022A maritime surveillance radar (installed in the nose), stabilized opto-electronic system for observation and tracking, programmed chaff/flare system, Elisra EW suite, etc. Upgraded cockpit with digital avionics. The aircraft will be armed with the Rafael Popeye missile; former armament will remain.

Details

Sales/Users: Manufactured at the Kharkov aircraft plant. Dozen or so aircraft in Russian military service. Being marketed by IAI under a co-operation agreement, with new equipment (see Development).
Crew: 5, comprising 2 pilots, navigator, onboard engineer and radio operator. Navigator has a port side station and the radio operator a starboard station aft of the pilots, with bulged blister windows. Rear cabin compartment, length 22 ft 11.5 ins (7.0 m), remains a cargo hold.
Radar: Standard navigation/weather radar in the nose, replaced by Israeli EL/M-2022A in IAI upgraded version.
Mission equipment: OTV-124 optical-TV sensor (weighing 551 lb, 250 kg), with resolution of 33 ft (10 m) at a distance of 9,843 ft (3,000 m), is installed in the port undercarriage nacelle for

↑ Antonov An-72P with fixed UPK-23-250 cannon pod on the starboard undercarriage nacelle *(Piotr Butowski)*

observation (including night observation). It has an automatic tracking system that keeps the target in the sight. The recording equipment consists of 3 photographic cameras; 2 of type A-86P are used for daylight photography, with 1 installed in the tail (used when the cargo hold is opened) and the other in the port side. The third camera, a UA-47, is used for night photography and is installed near the A-86P camera in the tail. This camera is used after dropping SFP-2A flares carried inside the cargo hold (instead of bombs). Communication equipment is expanded, including instrument target indication to assist supporting coast guard ships.
Payload: Up to 11,023 lb (5,000 kg), and can include 40 troops or 22 paratroops, or 16 litter patients.
Fixed guns: UPK-23-250 cannon pod containing a twin-barrel 23-mm GSh-23 cannon, housed in the starboard side of the lower fuselage, just in front of the undercarriage nacelle.
Ammunition: 250 rounds.
Expendable weapons and equipment: Up to 1,433 lb (650 kg), suspended on 2 underwing pylons (100 kg bombs or UB-32M rocket packs) and 4 racks inside the cargo cabin above the ramp (100 kg bombs) which can be used when the ramp is slid under the cabin.
Airframe and Engines: As for the An-72.
Flight avionics/instrumentation: Inertial navigation system added.

Details as for the An-72, except

CABIN:
Length: 23 ft (7 m)

WEIGHTS:
Payload: 11,023 lb (5,000 kg)

PERFORMANCE:
Patrol speed: 162-189 kts (186-217 mph) 300-350 km/h
Required runway length: 6,400 ft (1,950 m)
Ceiling: 33,135 ft (10,100 m), at 72,732 lb (33,000 kg) TOW
Patrol altitude: 1,640-3,280 ft (500-1,000 m)
Range: 1,510 naut miles (1,740 miles) 2,800 km with maximum payload
Patrol duration: 6 hours 18 minutes to 7 hours 18 minutes, with reserve

Antonov An-88 (An-72R)

Role: Tactical battlefield surveillance aircraft, probably to replace An-71. Seen in 1995 at the Air Force Flight Test Centre in Akhtubinsk (registration *CCCP-783573*).
Based on: An-72 transport. An-88 is bureau designation, An-72R military.
Radar: Conformal phased-array side-looking radar antennae, built into each side of the rear fuselage.

↑ Antonov An-88 tactical AEW&C/tactical battlefield surveillance aircraft with conformal radar *(Eric Bannworth)*

Britten-Norman Ltd UK

Corporate address:
Bembridge, Isle of Wight PO35 5PR.

Telephone: +44 1983 872511
Facsimile: +44 1983 873246
Telex: 86866
Web site: www.britten-norman.com

Founded:
Late 1950s (as Britten-Norman), becoming Pilatus Britten-Norman in 1979. Sold to Litchfield Continental Ltd July 1998, adopting original name.

Information:
Sheila Dewart (Marketing Communications Manager).

ACTIVITIES

▪ See also Airliners section for the BN2B and BN2T Islander.

↑ One of 2 Britten-Norman BN2T Defenders operated by the Pakistan Maritime Security Agency

Britten-Norman Defender

First flight: 1971 introduction of the Defender based on the piston-engined BN2B, and 1981 based on the turbine-engined BN2T.
Role: Includes border surveillance, battlefield observation, maritime patrol, urban/rural policing, customs and coast guard, EEZ and fishery protection, smuggling interdiction, and search and rescue.
Based on: BN2B and BN2T Islander STOL transports, but now principally the latter. For a general description of Islander/Defender, see the Airliners section.

Aims

▪ Maximum surveillance capability at minimum cost, with the options of a wide range of simple to sophisticated equipment and sensors.
▪ High wing permits unobstructed all-round downward view. Cabin blister windows for observation stations.
▪ Operates from 1,150 ft (350 m) unprepared strips (including beaches, jungle clearings and grass).

Development

▪ Developed from the Islander for specific government and law enforcement agency requirements.

Details

Sales/Users: Large number of operating countries. Operators of Defenders as surveillance/observation and photography platforms include Belgium, Cyprus, Netherlands, Oman, Pakistan (Maritime Security Agency) and the UK (including Army Air Corps Defenders, which were used on active service during the Gulf conflict). Coast guard and customs versions include those with Australia (6 delivered May-August 1995), Mauritius and Pakistan, while full naval operators include India.
Radar and mission sensors: Detection equipment can be mounted externally on 4 underwing pylons or on/in the fuselage. Sector-scan low-cost radar can be fitted, or full 360° scanning systems with advanced processing and display units, integrated with video and thermal imaging cameras. Vertically mounted cameras can also be installed for photography through floor apertures. Other available systems include FLIR (see photograph). For *monitoring and tracking*, electronic sensors can be data-linked with the ground. *Surveillance data collection* uses video tapes and film for future intelligence assessment or as evidence in prosecutions. If required for *military surveillance and tactical support*, Defender can act as a targeting system for long-range weapons and land-based aircraft. Specialist trials variants have included a Skymaster radar-equipped Defender, developed with Thorn EMI, to offer standoff battlefield surveillance, and an Elint Defender for locating and identifying radio and radar transmissions, carrying a Racal Kestrel electronic warfare suite.
Mission equipment: For *search and rescue*, survival packs and extra dinghies can be carried and dropped through the sliding door.
Flight avionics/instrumentation: Omega, GPS, DME, VOR and ILS, and can be combined in a flight management system coupled to an autopilot to minimize pilot workload. Radar altimeter. Optional communications equipment covers UHF, VHF, MF and HF. Night vision goggles among other options.
Self-protection systems: Northrop Grumman infra-red based system tested on a British Army BN2T during 1997, with an underfloor turret and sensors at the aircraft extremities, to detect and locate any IR threat.

Defender details as for Islander (which see), except

PRINCIPAL DIMENSIONS:
Maximum length: Length may vary, according the use of nose radar

WEIGHTS:
Payload with maximum fuel: 1,096 lb (497 kg) *for Defender based on the BN2B-26*, 966 lb (438 kg) *for BN2B-20*, and 1,520 lb (689 kg) *for BN2T*
Disposable load: 2,386 lb (1,082 kg) *for Defender based on the BN2B-26*, 2,256 lb (1,023 kg) *for BN2B-20*, and 2,960 lb (1,343 kg) *for BN2T*

PERFORMANCE:
On task duration: typically 4 hours at 10 naut miles (115 miles) 185 km from base

Britten-Norman Defender 4000 (BN2T-4S)

First flight: 17 August 1994 (piloted by Iain Young).
Role: Maritime surveillance, border patrol/urban surveillance, electronic intelligence and support/liaison.
Based on: BN2T Defender.
Fatigue life: Over 40,000 hours.

Aims

▪ To carry sophisticated navigation and sensor systems, including thermal imaging and radar.
▪ Lengthened fuselage, larger wings and tailplane, and enhanced visibility cockpit with deep windshield.
▪ Anti-corrosion airframe.
▪ Powerful turbine engines for greater sortie time and payload.
▪ Good low-speed handling and manoeuvring, allowing continuous turns at low level for close inspection and photography.
▪ Advanced avionics, including EFIS and a full range of communication equipment.
▪ Patrol of 150 naut miles (173 miles) 278 km for each flying hour, by day or night.
▪ Transit speed of 160 kts (184 mph) 296 km/h from base to the patrol area.

Development

▪ 13 November 1995. Certification by the UK CAA.
▪ 12 December 1996. Contract signed with the Irish Ministry of Justice for the first production Defender 4000.
▪ 14 August 1997. Delivery of the first Defender 4000 to the Garda Siochana hEireann (Irish Police), for operations from Baldonnell.
▪ November 1997. Delivery of a BN2T-4S to Sabah Air in Malaysia.

Details

Sales/Users: First aircraft to Irish Garda. First civil-registered BN2T-4S delivered to Sabah Air in Malaysia for aerial photographic survey work in 1997, followed by a second in 1998 (third on option).
Crew: Airline-type seating. Space for at least 2 consoles and operators in tandem along 1 side of the cabin. Tactical seating for up to 16 personnel. Static line or free-fall parachuting fit. Deep windshield, giving pilot and observer 240° visual look-out.
Radar: Wide range of radars, from weather to surveillance types. Accommodates 27 ins (68.6 cm), 360° rotating antenna in a new nose structure. Alternatively weather or simple search radar, and possible additional sensors. Radar search area 8,000 sq naut miles per hour at 140 kts search speed. Prototype installed with Seaspray 2000 radar.

Details for Defender 4000

PRINCIPAL DIMENSIONS:
Wing span: 53 ft (16.15 m)
Maximum length: 40 ft 0.5 ins (21.21 m)
Maximum height: 14 ft 3.5 ins (4.35 m)

WEIGHTS:
Empty, equipped: 4,900 lb (2,222 kg)
Maximum zero fuel: 8,300 lb (3,764 kg)
Maximum take-off and landing: 8,500 lb (3,855 kg)
Payload with maximum fuel: 1,598 lb (724 kg)
Disposable load: 3,600 lb (1,633 kg); or 1,598 lb (725 kg) with maximum fuel

PERFORMANCE:
Maximum cruise speed: 176 kts (203 mph) 326 km/h at 10,000 ft (3,048 m)
Transit speed: 160 kts (184 mph) 296 km/h from base to the patrol area
Economic cruise speed: 150 kts (173 mph) 278 km/h
Search speed: 140 kts (161 mph) 259 km/h
Stall speed: 53 kts (61 mph) 98 km/h *clean, power off*, or 47 kts (54 mph) 87 km/h *with flaps, power off*
Take-off distance: 1,167 ft (356 m)
Landing distance: 1,012 ft (308 m)
Take-off distance over a 50 ft (15 m) obstacle: 1,855 ft (565 m)
Landing distance over a 50 ft (15 m) obstacle: 1,934 ft (589 m)
Maximum climb rate: 1,250 ft (381 m) per minute, or 223 ft (68 m) per minute with 1 engine inoperable
Ceiling: 25,000 ft (7,620 m) absolute, or 12,000 ft (3,660 m) with 1 engine inoperable
Range: 861 naut miles (991 miles) 1,595 km *IFR*, 1,006 naut miles (1,158 miles) 1,864 km *VFR*
Duration: 7-8 hours, or 4 hours on task 100 naut miles (115 miles) 185 km from base

Other mission sensors: Options include thermal imaging system, FLIR, video and film cameras (hand-held or podded).
Number of pylons: 4 (2 under each wing); 750 lb (340 kg) inboard and 350 lb (159 kg) outboard.
Expendable weapons and equipment: Anti-submarine and anti-ship weapon systems on 4 underwing pylons (750 lb and 350 lb, 340 kg and 159 kg capacities each side).
Fuselage: New nose, able to fit a 27 ins (68.6 cm), 360° rotating antenna.
Airframe: In addition to the adoption of a single fence on each wing, the Defender 4000 now has a stabilon (winglet) on the fin.
Engines: 2 Allison 250-B17F/1 turboprops, with 6 ft 8 ins (2.03 m) Hartzell 3-blade constant-speed propellers.
Engine rating: Each flat-rated to 400 shp (298 kW).
Fuel system: 2,002 lb (908 kg) usable, or 1,131 litres.
Electrical system: 200 amp engine-driven generators.
Flight avionics/instrumentation: EFIS cockpit. Full range of UHF/VHF/HF/VHF(FM) communications. Open radio or secure voice. Fully integrated autopilot. GPS integrated with Omega or INS.

Aircraft variants:
Border surveillance/internal security role uses visual search, thermal imaging systems, and video and fixed cameras. Can patrol 130 naut miles (150 miles) 241 km of border per flying hour, by day or night, or conduct a fixed patrol along a 43.4 naut mile (50 mile) 80 km sector for up to 6 hours, revisiting each point every 30 minutes.
Environmental role, surveying at least 1,000 sq miles (2,590 km^2) per hour.
Maritime role for fishery protection, pollution detection, search and rescue, sovereignty patrol, maritime surveillance with search radar and visual identification of each target and covering up to 3,000 sq miles (7,770 km^2) per hour in average sea traffic density, radar-only survey using a modern maritime radar and covering 6,000 sq miles (15,540 km^2) per hour, and anti-submarine/anti-ship.

Britten-Norman MSSA (Multi-Sensor Surveillance Aircraft)

Comments: This STOL battlefield surveillance, border/maritime patrol, AEW, smuggling interdiction, law enforcement, environmental protection, and disaster control/relief management aircraft, with APG-66SR multi-mode radar in a large nose radome, is no longer marketed. Details and 3 illustrations can be found in the 1996-97 edition of *WA&SD*, page 184.

↑ **Britten-Norman Defender 4000 operated by the Irish Police (Garda). Note the addition of the stabilon on the fin**

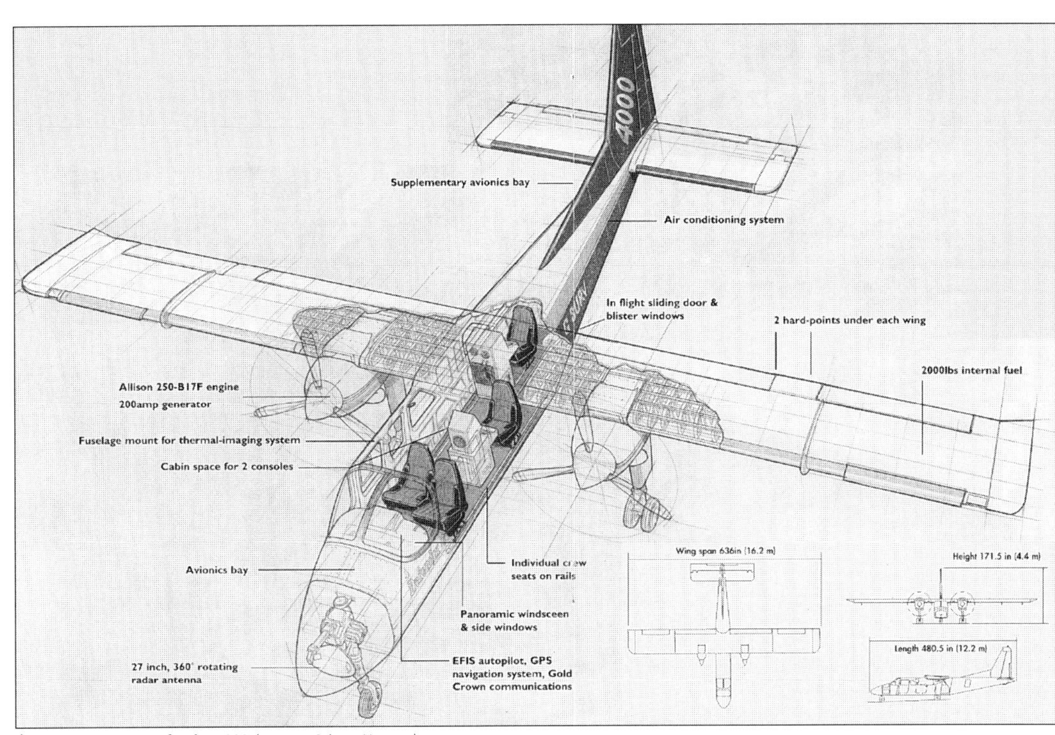

↑ **Britten-Norman Defender 4000** *(courtesy Britten-Norman)*

GEC-Marconi Avionics Ltd — UK

Corporate address:
Crewe Toll, Ferry Road, Edinburgh EH5 2XS, Scotland.

Telephone: +44 131 332 2411
Facsimile: +44 131 343 4011
E-mail: steve.marlow@gecm.com

ACTIVITIES

▪ The GEC-Marconi Argus 2000 modular AEW system may be configured for a basic airborne surveillance platform or as a very sophisticated, multi-sensor, multi-role system. When fitted in a suitable aircraft, it offers 360° scan cover, and can provide AEW, tactical control of friendly forces, and perform a wide range of missions. It is a new generation, high performance, pulse-Doppler radar system incorporating fully-programmable signal processing, optional IFF and ESM, ergonomically efficient data processing and communications, and advanced multi-function colour displays. Argus 2000 is currently being offered to China against its AEW&C requirement, with negotiations continuing in early 1998 for 4 systems to be installed in Ilyushin Il-76s. It is believed Russia has offered to supply Il-76 airframes and technical documentation (for participation in the programme).

Raytheon Systems Ltd — UK

HQ address:
Kings House, Kymberley Road, Harrow, Middx HA1 1YD.

Telephone: +44 181 861 2525
Facsimile: +44 181 863 0599
E-mail: randerson@resl.cossor.com (Programme Manager, ASTOR).

Employees: 1,800.

Information:
Mike Brown (*telephone* +44 181 427 3520, *facsimile* +44 181 427 4866, *E-mail* mike.brown@rcj.ray.com).

Note: On 22 December 1997, Raytheon Company in the USA announced the creation of Raytheon Systems Ltd in the UK, following the merger of Raytheon with Hughes. Raytheon Systems Ltd will initially include 2 operating divisions: Electronic Systems incorporating Raytheon Cossor's Harlow and Hughes Microelectronic's Glenrothes operations; and Systems Integration incorporating Hughes Flight Training at Crawley and Hughes ATC Simulation and Training at Burgess Hill. UK operations merging into Raytheon Systems Ltd are Raytheon Cossor Electronics, Raytheon TI Systems, Raytheon E-Systems, Raytheon Computer Products Europe; and Hughes Microelectronics, Hughes Defence Systems, Hughes Flight Training, Hughes ATC Simulation and Training (all divisions of former Hughes UK Ltd). In addition, Raytheon Marine Europe Limited and Raytheon Aircraft Services Limited (formerly Raytheon Corporate Jets, Inc) will become subsidiaries. Systems Integration Division is the prime contractor or partner for major UK and European programmes including ASTOR, BVRAAM and SIFF, and will manage current contracts such as RAPTOR.

Raytheon Systems ASTOR programme

Comments: Raytheon Systems Ltd is leading a team proposing a Global Express-based ground surveillance and intelligence gathering aircraft for the British forces under the ASTOR (Airborne Stand-off Radar) programme, to fulfil Ground & Air Staff Requirement 3956, competing with the Lockheed Martin led team and a new bid from Northrop Grumman based on the JSTARS system in a Global Express or similar business jet. It is also suited to the NATO Alliance Ground Surveillance (AGS) programme. Adopts the Raytheon ASARS 2 radar, Motorola mobile ground stations for imagery exploitation (some 9 ground stations required under ASTOR) and Bombardier Global Express aircraft with airframe modifications (about 5 aircraft required under ASTOR). Other Raytheon Systems team members are Data Sciences, Short Brothers, GEC-Marconi, GRC International, DRA Malvern, Motorola UK, Marshall Specialist Vehicles, BMW Rolls-Royce, Cubic Defense Systems, Lucas UK, Messier-Dowty UK and Thomson-CSF. Operational requirements include a patrol altitude of 50,000 ft (15,240 m), and synthetic-aperture radar/moving target indicator (SAR/MTI) imagery at 135-162 naut mile (155-186.4 mile) 250-300 km ranges. The Raytheon Global Express ASTOR has a 51,000 ft (15,545 m) patrol altitude, 14 hour duration, and a range of 6,700 naut miles (7,715 miles) 12,416 km with IFR reserves. Selection of the winning team was expected in 1998, with an in-service date set for the year 2003.

↑ **Raytheon Systems ASTOR contender, based on the Bombardier Global Express** *(courtesy Raytheon Systems Ltd)*

The Boeing Company USA

Corporate address:
See Combat section for company details.

Boeing 737 Airborne Early Warning & Control system (AEW&C)

First flight: Not yet flown.
Based on: Boeing 737-700.
Comments: This system blends the high performance and '21st century' avionics of the 737-700 airliner platform with a modular Northrop Grumman Multi-role Electronically Scanned Array (MESA) radar system. The 360° steerable beam arrays (3 L-band, with 288 modules) are designed to provide scanning range to about 190 naut miles (or over twice that for long-range sector scanning), jamming, tracking accuracy and growth. The radar is able to track air and sea targets simultaneously and can help the operator maintain control of high-performance aircraft while continuously scanning the operational area. One array is housed in the top of the 35 ft (10.7 m) long, 5 ft (1.52 m) wide and 7 ft 10 ins (2.4 m) high fixed dorsal "top hat" radome for fore/act scanning, while 2 arrays are carried on the sides of the mounting, providing side scanning (the radome size could vary, that quoted being for Project Wedgetail). More than 400 hours of wind tunnel testing have demonstrated the compatibility of the aircraft and radar. The dorsal "top hat" position of the upper array is said to provide a practical solution for fore and aft coverage, while maintaining the low drag profile. It enables the system to be installed on a medium-sized aircraft (737-700) without significant impact on aircraft performance. Another innovation is the integrated IFF, sharing the primary radar arrays to further reduce weight, improve reliability and simplify target correlation. Also, the aircraft has an expanded passive surveillance system, advanced open system architecture (OSA) with a standards-based design for cost-effective commonality and maximum flexibility, and an effective self-defence capability. Maximum take-off weight will be about 170,000 lb (77,110 kg), maximum speed Mach 0.8, ceiling over 40,000 ft (12,190 m), and 8 hours on station at a range from base of 300 naut miles.

The 737 AEW&C has been offered to the Royal Australian Air Force under that nation's Project Wedgetail (Air 5077), for which a production contract decision for 4 aircraft is expected in 1999 and operational service from 2002. Competing designs for Project Wedgetail are being offered by Lockheed Martin and Raytheon Systems Company. On 2 December 1997, Boeing announced that it had been awarded 1 of 3 Initial Design Activity contracts by the Australian Defence Force under Project Wedgetail, worth $6.5 million. Boeing Australia is providing system engineering and aircraft modification support, and is leading the product support and ground support systems teams. British Aerospace Australia is providing the passive surveillance system, electronic warfare self-protection system, operational mission and mission support segment and the AEW&C support facility.

↑ **Boeing 737 AEW&C, in Australian Project Wedgetail markings**

Boeing 767 Airborne Warning & Control System (AWACS) (E-767)

First flight: 10 October 1994 in unmodified transport form, and 9 August 1996 with structural AWACS features.
First delivery: 1998.
Role: Airborne early warning and control, for surveillance and C^3 (command, control and communications) functions for tactical and air defence forces.
Based on: Boeing 767-200ER (basic aircraft); 767-27C (modified for AWACS configuration).

Aims

- 50% more floor space and nearly twice the volume of the B707/E-3, with a heavier payload, and greater range and operating altitude.
- Uses similar proven mission avionics to the E-3, with which it will be interoperable.

Development

- December 1991. Following the end of Boeing 707 airframe production in May, Boeing announced the 767 would become the next-generation AWACS platform.

↑ Boeing 767 Airborne Warning & Control System for Japan

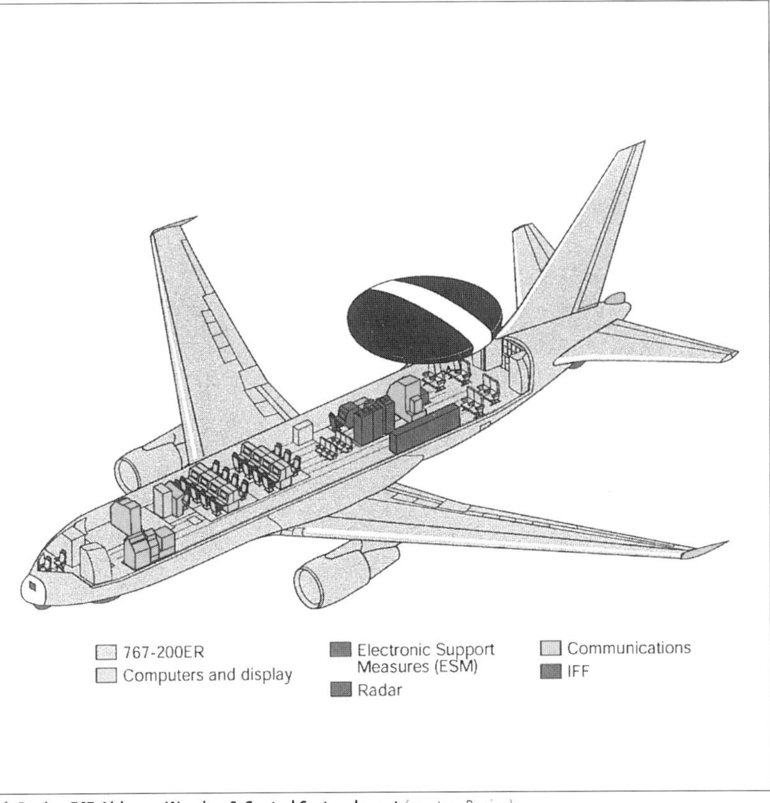

↑ Boeing 767 Airborne Warning & Control System layout *(courtesy Boeing)*

▪ Spring 1992. Wind tunnel testing took place, including rotodome location.
▪ November 1993. First order for two 767 AWACS (as E-767s) from the Japanese Defence Agency, for JASDF service. Separate contracts covered the air vehicle and mission system equipment.
▪ 10 October 1994. First Boeing 767 (for AWACS installation) for Japan made its first flight, thereafter in November flying from Everett to Wichita, where the Product Support Division assisted the Electronic Systems Division in adapting the aircraft for its role by undertaking engineering design for the environmental control, oxygen, hydraulics and fuel systems, and for wiring integration and aircraft interiors. In addition, PSD undertook extensive airframe modification, with structural changes to Section 46 of the fuselage which carries the rotodome.
▪ 28 October 1994. 2 further E-767s ordered by the Japanese Defence Agency through Itochu Corporation, Boeing's representative in Japan.
▪ 18 July 1995. First flight of the second 767 airframe for AWACS adoption.
▪ 18 August 1995. Second 767 arrived at Wichita for structural modifications. On return to Seattle, it became the first 767 AWACS to have mission avionics fitted.
▪ June 1996. First 767 AWACS returned to Seattle and had its rotodome installed in July.
▪ 9 August 1996. First 767 AWACS flew from Boeing Field International in Seattle with rotodome fitted, piloted by Charles Gebhardt and Gerald Whites. Beginning of a 7-month test programme. The rotodome contained mass simulators, to began conducting aerodynamic tests in Seattle prior to installation of the prime mission equipment (displays and computers, radar, sensors and communication equipment) in May 1997.

Details for 767 AWACS

PRINCIPAL DIMENSIONS:
Wing span: 156 ft 1 ins (47.57 m)
Maximum length: 159 ft 2 ins (48.51 m)
Maximum height: 52 ft (15.85 m)
Rotodome diameter: 30 ft (9.14 m)
Rotodome thickness: 6 ft (1.83 m)

WEIGHTS:
Maximum take-off: 385,000 lb (174,633 kg)

PERFORMANCE:
Maximum speed: over 434 kts (500 mph) 804 km/h
Ceiling: 34,000-40,100 ft (10,360-12,220 m)
Range: 4,500-5,000 naut miles (5,182-5,758 miles) 8,330-9,260 km
Duration: 8 hours on station, at 1,000 naut miles (1,150 miles) 1,850 km radius, or 12 hours at 300 naut miles (345 miles) 556 km radius. Extended possibilities with air refuelling
Maximum duration: 22 hours with air refuelling

▪ January 1997. Flight test programme completed 3 weeks ahead of schedule, accumulating 383 flying hours during 130 flights.
▪ 11 March 1998. Delivery of the first two 767 AWACS to Japan.
▪ January 1999. Second 2 aircraft to be delivered to Japan.
Sales/Users: Japan (4, designated E-767). Interest has been expressed from Italy, South Korea, Saudi Arabia and Turkey.
Crew: 21, comprising 2 flight crew plus 19 AWACS mission specialists (including 7 surveillance operators and a surveillance controller). Crew rest area with galley.
Radar: Northrop Grumman AN/APY-2 (see E-3 entry).
Other mission sensors and equipment: Similar to E-3, which see. Optional AN/AYR-1 electronic support measures (see E-3 entry) and infra-red countermeasures. Loral CC-2E multi-processing computer. Hazeltine colour high-resolution situation display consoles and auxiliary display units. 2 Litton LN-100G INS/GPS. Telephonics AN/APX-103 unit with IFF interrogator and Selective Identification Facility (SIF), and data-link fighter control Tactical Digital Information Link/Command (TADIL-C), with IFF/TADIL-C antennae in the rotodome (see E-3 entry). HF/VHF/UHF coms, with optional Have Quick, JTIDS and satellite communications. Hughes Technology audio distribution systems.
Expendable weapons and equipment: No armament.
Airframe: See Boeing 767-200ER in the Airliners section.
Engines: 2 General Electric CF6-80C2B6FA turbofans. APU.
Engine rating: Each 61,500 lbf (273.57 kN).
Flight refuelling probe: None.
Electrical system: 4 engine-driven 150kVA 3-phase 400Hz AC generators. APU-driven 90kVA generator.

Aircraft variants:
767 AWACS, as detailed.
Other future 767 military derivatives could include Joint-STARS, tankers, freighters and executive transports.

Boeing EC-135/RC-135 and OC-135

Comments: The USAF has contracted many companies in addition to Boeing to modify these Boeing aircraft to specialized roles, the latter which include advanced range instrumentation, strategic command and control post, tactical control, monitor of the Open Skies Treaty, and specialized reconnaissance/intelligence gathering. Among the most important are those used for Measurement and Signature Intelligence (MASINT), including the RC-135S Cobra Ball, which has infra-red telescopes with associated wide-angle tracking/high resolution cameras, 4 optical ports, and a series of horizontal fairings and a box fairing on the port front fuselage side for its role of tracking and recording ballistic missile re-entry vehicles and tactical ballistic/cruise missile detection; RC-135V and W Rivet Joints for electronic surveillance; and EC-135U Cobra Sents for analysis of detected systems. Further details and a photograph can be found in the 1996-97 edition of *WA&SD*, page 185.

Boeing E-3 Sentry Airborne Warning & Control System (AWACS)

First delivery: 22 March 1977.
Role: Airborne early warning and control, for surveillance and C^3 (command, control and communications) functions for tactical and air defence forces.
Based on: Boeing 707-320B.

Aims

▪ Quick-reaction surveillance and C^3 needed to manage tactical and defensive fighter forces in a tactical role. Detect, identify, track and control the interception of airborne threats in a strategic role, with mobility for rapid deployment where needed.

Development

▪ 26 January 1973. Full-scale development began.
▪ 1978. USAF declared initial operational capability with Core E-3As.
▪ May 1987. Long-term improvement programme began with a USAF award of the ICON (Integration Contract) to Boeing, to provide USAF and NATO E-3s with an ESM passive surveillance capability, and offer other block enhancements including upgrading of the Joint Tactical Information Distribution System (JTIDS) to TADIL-J (Tactical Digital Information Link-J) or Link 16 (NATO) standard, increased computer capacity, and worldwide use of GPS. To the USAF, it is known as the Extend Sentry Program. Following the first upgrade and testing of a NATO E-3 with colour displays, Have Quick radios and Link 16 (see Mission equipment) in 1994-95, Daimler-Benz Aerospace began retrofitting the remaining NATO fleet in 1996 and completed the work in 1997.
▪ 26 March 1991. First delivery of an E-3D to the RAF.
▪ January 1997. Long-lead production contracts awarded to Boeing for the radar system improvement program (RSIP), to provide a major update to the radar capability. Northrop Grumman's Electronic Sensors and Systems Division began the production phase of the US Air Force Materiel Command's Electronic Systems Center contract. RSIP kits are going to the USAF, NATO and UK.
▪ November 1997. Daimler-Benz Aerospace began installation of the first RSIP kit on a NATO E-3A.
▪ 1998. Further USAF, NATO and UK fleets are scheduled to begin incorporation of RSIP, with the programme running until about 2004.
▪ 1998. Under a USAF contract, Boeing is testing an IRST system for the E-3 (see Other mission sensors).
Note. Since 1992, E-3s have flown more than 5,200 missions in support of United Nations' resolutions for the former Yugoslavia.

↑ Impression of a composite strike package, comprising both manned and unmanned aircraft co-ordinating air-to-air and air-to-surface attack missions. Using Control Automation and Task Allocation (CATA) technology developed by Boeing, a pilot (assisted by his situation awareness decision-aiding system) could co-ordinate and conduct all attacks *(courtesy Boeing)*

Sales/Users: 66 E-3s in use with the USAF (32 E-3B/Cs on the active inventory, of which 26 are primary aircraft authorized for operational missions, serving with the 552nd Air Control Wing based at Tinker AFB, Oklahoma; the 961st and 962nd Airborne Air Control Squadrons are deployed to Japan and Alaska), NATO (17 E-3As, with main operating base at Geilenkirchen, Germany), Saudi Arabia (5 AWACS plus 6 related KE-3 in-flight refuelling tankers under the Peace Sentinel programme, delivered June 1986-September 1987), France (4 E-3Fs, delivered May 1991-February 1992, operating with 36e Escadre), and the UK (7 E-3D Sentry AEW Mk 1s, delivered March 1991 to May 1992, serving with 8 Squadron at RAF Waddington).
Crew: 21, comprising 4 flight crew plus 17 AWACS specialists.
Radar: Northrop Grumman AN/APY-2 S-band, high-PRF, pulse-Doppler, multi-mode lookdown radar (with inherent ECCM), able to separate maritime and airborne targets from ground and sea clutter (E-3Bs have upgraded AN/APY-1s). Radar comprises 3 major subsystems, the slotted planar array antenna, radar receivers and processors located in the centre of the aircraft cabin, and the radar transmitter located in the lower cargo bay. Operating modes are pulse-Doppler nonelevation with high-PRF Doppler to provide lookdown surveillance to the radar horizon but does not measure target elevation, pulse-Doppler elevation scan which is similar to the previous mode but includes electronic vertical scan of the radar beam to provide target elevation (vertical scanning and height finding using ferrite phase-shifters), beyond the horizon operation for long-range surveillance of medium and high altitude aircraft (as the radar beam is above the horizon, there is no ground clutter and a low-PRF radar pulse is used to obtain range and azimuth of the target), passive scanning with the radar transmitter off and the receiver on to obtain ECM information (such as enemy jammer location), and maritime mode using a very short radar pulse to provide the high resolution required to detect moving or anchored surface ships. Liquid-cooled, slotted planar array surveillance antenna (the antenna face comprises 30 slotted waveguide sticks) and IFF/data-link fighter-control TADIL-C (tactical digital information link/command) or TADIL-J antennae are housed in the glassfibre rotodome, which turns at 6 rpm during active use but only 1 revolution every 4 minutes when unused to maintain bearing lubrication. 360° scanning, able to detect targets about 213 naut miles (245 miles) 394 km away when flying at 30,000 ft (9,145 m) operating altitude. Mission equipment can separate, manage and display these targets individually on situation displays. See radar system improvement program (RSIP) under Development, aimed at maintaining operational capability against growing threats from smaller radar cross section targets, cruise missiles and electronic countermeasures, and improving the man-machine interface, reliability and maintainability, and ECCM. Major part of RSIP is to increase radar sensitivity against small targets through replacement of the digital Doppler processor and radar data correlator with a state-of-the-art surveillance radar computer (SRC), and translation of the associated software into Ada language. In addition to handling the upgraded radar processing load, the SRC contains adequate growth reserves to accommodate further radar upgrades. The man-machine interface is improved by modification of the radar control and maintenance panel, to incorporate a spectrum analyser, special test equipment, and new displays for monitoring the surveillance environment as well as the maintenance status of the radar system.

↑ RAF Boeing E-3D Sentry Airborne Warning & Control System (AWACS)

Other mission sensors: AN/AYR-1 electronic support measures (ESM) fitted to US/NATO aircraft, indicated by radomes on the fuselage sides forward of the wings, for passive listening and detection, enabling aircraft to detect, identify and track electronic transmissions from ground, airborne and maritime sources (enabling radar and weapon system type to be determined). Testing of a fuselage roof-mounted Eagle infra-red search and track system began in 1998, as a possible means of detecting and targeting ballistic missiles. French E-3Fs are to receive ESM upgrade. See Radar for RSIP.
Mission equipment: Navigation, communications, data processing, identification and display equipment. Central to the processing network is the Lockheed Martin CC2 command and control multi-processing computer (NATO E-3 computers upgraded since 1993 to CC2E model, with 380% increase in memory using bubble memory technology; further upgrade under RSIP). Boeing produced Have Quick A-NETS, an improved communications system that provides secure, anti-jam radio contact with other AWACS, friendly aircraft and ground stations for US and NATO aircraft. Also JTIDS is being upgraded to TADIL-J (US) and Link 16 (NATO) standards to increase the amount of information that can be collected and distributed among other AWACS, friendly aircraft and ground stations. See Radar for RSIP.
Self-protection systems: Can carry self-defence AAMs.
Fixed guns: None.
Engines: US and NATO E-3s have 4 Pratt & Whitney TF33-PW-100 or 100A turbofans (each 21,000 lbf, 93.41 kN). Others use CFM56-2A-2 or 3 turbofans (each 24,000 lbf, 106.76 kN) offering higher operating altitudes to extend the surveillance horizon (over 35,000 ft, 10,668 m).
Flight avionics/instrumentation: Includes weather radar, dual Delco AN/ASN-119 IN, and Northrop Omega. Boeing is reportedly looking into the possibility of upgrading the cockpits of USAF E-3s to 737-700 standard. See Radar for RSIP.

Details for E-3B/C

PRINCIPAL DIMENSIONS:
Wing span: 145 ft 9 ins (44.42 m)
Maximum length: 152 ft 11 ins (46.61 m)
Maximum height: 41 ft 9 ins (12.73 m)
Rotodome diameter: 30 ft (9.14 m)
Rotodome thickness: 6 ft (1.83 m)
Rotodome height above fuselage: 11 ft (3.35 m)
Radar antenna face width: 24 ft (7.32 m)
Radar antenna face height: 5 ft (1.52 m)

WEIGHTS:
Maximum: 335,000 lb (151,953 kg)
Radar system: 8,250 lb (3,742 kg)

PERFORMANCE:
Maximum speed: 460 kts (530 mph) 853 km/h
Ceiling: about 30,000 ft (9,145 m)
Range with full fuel: over 5,000 naut miles (5,760 miles) 9,260 km, without in-flight refuelling
Duration: 11 hours unrefuelled

Aircraft variants:
E-3A is the NATO standard, representing an improved version of the original (and since upgraded) USAF Core E-3A, featuring the larger memory CC2 computer, etc.
E-3B represents 24 earliest production USAF E-3As upgraded with a CC2 computer, much improved radio communications, austere maritime capability for the radar, 14 (instead of 9) display consoles, and more.
E-3C is the other USAF version, produced by conversion of the 10 E-3As originally built to improved standard (as for NATO aircraft), featuring better command and control capability. Redelivered 1984-88.
E-3D is known to the RAF as Sentry AEW Mk 1. Wing span increased to 147 ft 7 ins (44.98 m) due to wingtip Loral Yellow Gate ESM pods.
E-3F is the French variant.

Boeing E-4B

Comments: First flown on 13 June 1973 in E-4A form and in 1979 as the current E-4B, this National Airborne Operations Center (NAOC) aircraft operates as a survivable airborne link between the national command authorities and strategic forces during an attack. The USAF has 4 on the active inventory, of which 3 are primary aircraft authorized for operational use with the 55th Wing of ACC out of Offutt AFB, Nebraska. Details and a photograph can be found in the 1996-97 edition of *WA&SD*, page 187.

Boeing E-6A/B Mercury

Comments: First flown on 19 February 1987, 16 Mercury survivable airborne communications system aircraft were delivered to the US Navy between August 1989 and 28 May 1992, to support its ballistic missile submarine force by providing a link between the force and national command authorities, with continuous airborne alert coverage for both Atlantic and Pacific Oceans. In 1997, a Boeing 707 fuselage tested the structural modifications needed to enable the Mercury aircraft to be fitted with the roof-mounted high-frequency antenna associated with the Milstar secure satellite communication system then to be retrofitted to E-6s. Details of the Mercury, and a photograph, can be found in the 1996-97 edition of *WA&SD*, page 187.

Boeing EC-18B and D

Comments: Details of the advanced range instrumentation aircraft (EC-18B ARIA) and cruise missile mission control aircraft (EC-18D CMMCA), operated by the USAF, can be found in the 1996-97 edition of *WA&SD*, page 187.

Boeing common support aircraft

Comments: Details and an illustration of this formerly proposed carrier and land based airborne early warning and surveillance aircraft, to replace the E-2C Hawkeye in the 21st century, can be found in the 1996-97 edition of *WA&SD*, pages 187-188.

Fairchild Dornier USA Fairchild Aircraft Incorporated — USA

Corporate address:
PO Box 790490, San Antonio, TX 78279-0490.

Telephone: +1 210 824 9421
Facsimile: +1 210 820 8656

Founded:
1959 formation of predecessor company, sold to Fairchild Hiller in 1972. Parent company is Fairchild Aerospace, which in June 1996 purchased 80% of Dornier Luftfahrt from Daimler-Benz Aerospace. Thereby, Fairchild Aerospace owns 80% and Daimler-Benz Aerospace owns 20% of Fairchild Dornier Germany (which see), while Fairchild Aerospace owns 100% of Fairchild Dornier USA.

Information:
Michael E. Cardellichio (*telephone* +1 703 444 8300, *facsimile* +1 703 430 5416).

ACTIVITIES

▪ See Airliners section for regional aircraft development, production and support.

SUBSIDIARIES

FAIRCHILD AIRCRAFT SERVICES

HQ address:
9623 W. Terminal Drive, San Antonio, TX 78216.

Telephone: +1 800 327 2313, 210 824 2313
Facsimile: +1 210 824 3462

Activities:
▪ Supplies technical, spare parts and training support for Metro, Fairchild Dornier 228 and 328 operators. Also operates an aircraft repair station capable of major repairs and refurbishment of Metros, as well as other aircraft types. Prime source for Metro sales and after-market service, and supports the sale of new Metro 23s and pre-owned Metros.

FAIRCHILD GEN-AERO

Activities:
▪ Fixed-base operation, providing aviation services to private and corporate operators at San Antonio International Airport.

↑ Fairchild Dornier MMSA with a Lockheed Martin underfuselage pod

FAIRCHILD FINANCIAL

MERLIN EXPRESS INC

Activities:
▪ Responsible for operation, maintenance and management of the UPS Express Package Expediter fleet, and provides Contractor Logistics Support for the military C-26 fleet; awarded a 10 year contract for the maintenance and supply support of USAF C-26s serving with the Air National Guard. Also a charter cargo/passenger airline.

Fairchild Dornier MMSA

Based on: Metro 23.

Aircraft variants:
MMSA is a Multi-Mission Surveillance Aircraft that can be reconfigured in under 2 hours for C^3, surveillance, reconnaissance, maritime patrol, contraband interdiction, 18 passenger or VIP, medical evacuation, cargo, utility or other roles. Avionics and sensors, according to the customer's requirements, can include tactical air-to-air, sea surveillance or weather avoidance radar, plus equipment for visual and infra-red surveillance and reconnaissance (carried in an underfuselage sensor pod and including camera, FLIR and linescan), sigint system for electronic reconnaissance, multi-spectral mapping, and near real-time image transmission. 8 hour duration.

Gulfstream Aerospace Corporation — USA

Corporate address:
PO Box 2206, Savannah, GA 31402-2206.

Telephone: +1 912 965 3000
Facsimile: +1 912 965 3775

Information:
Julie Stone (Marketing Communications – *telephone* +1 912 965 3865, *facsimile* +1 912 965 3084).

FACILITIES

▪ Production facilities at Savannah (Georgia), Oklahoma City (Oklahoma) and Mexicali (Mexico), with service and completion centres in Savannah and Long Beach (California).

ACTIVITIES

▪ See also General Aviation section.

SRA-4 is a little used generic term for aircraft modified for special missions (mainly military). Current aircraft are based on IV-SP. These can include electronic warfare training and support, carrying a jammer, chaff and other equipment to simulate enemy aircraft or missile activity in a training or evaluation role; electronic surveillance and reconnaissance, with optional sensors including side-looking synthetic aperture radar, infra-red countermeasures in the enlarged tailcone, chaff, ESM and oblique camera; airways flight inspection; SAR; training; special weather applications; anti-submarine, carrying nose-mounted radar, FLIR, MAD in a tailcone, sonobuoys and acoustic processor, ESM, and weapons in the fuselage bay and under the wings, including torpedoes and anti-ship missiles; ship attack with 2 anti-ship missiles and equipment including some or all of that for the anti-submarine variant; maritime patrol, with search radar, FLIR, ESM, flares, marine markers and more; medevac, carrying 15 litters; transport and more. The US Army operates a C-20F for communications (alongside older C-20Es and Js based on the Gulfstream II/III), the US Navy and USMC C-20Gs (see

↑ Swedish Air Force has received 3 Gulfstream SRA-4s as S 102Bs for sigint with undernose fairings housing sensors and a Tp 102 for communications. Note the antennae under the wings and fuselage and other features including ventral fin

Gulfstream IV-MPA in General Aviation section for similar loads) and the USAF 2 C-20H Special Air Mission types based on the IV-SP and assigned to Andrews AFB (other USAF special missions C-20s are 3 C-20As based on the Gulfstream III, 5 C-20Bs and 3 C-20Cs). Other users include Japan (Civil Aviation Bureau for airways flight inspection), Sweden (Air Force, 2 as S 102Bs for signals intelligence, linking to ground C^2 command and control centres via a secure data link and operating with Saab S 100Bs, plus a Tp 102 communications aircraft), and Turkey (3, as 1 in Air Force markings and 2 civil registered).

Gulfstream IV-MPA is a Multi-Purpose Aircraft, detailed in the General Aviation section. Operators include the JASDF, which requires up to 9 for service in transport, training and medevac roles. 4 ordered at time of writing, delivered via the Okura agency, with service from 1997.

Gulfstream V is being promoted as the aircraft platform for a contender in the UK's ASTOR programme, fitted with Racal radar, under a Lockheed Martin-led team to fulfil Ground & Air Staff Requirement 3956 (see also Raytheon Systems under UK and Lockheed Martin under USA).

↑ SRA-4 with a ventral pannier under the forward fuselage for electronic sensors

Lockheed Martin Corporation USA

Corporate address:
See Combat section for company details.

↑ Lockheed Martin EC-130H Compass Call C^3 jamming aircraft

Lockheed Martin ASTOR programme

Comments: Proposing a Gulfstream V-based ground surveillance and intelligence gathering aircraft for the British Army and RAF under the ASTOR (Airborne Stand-off Radar) programme, competing with the Raytheon Systems Ltd-led Global Express competitor and a new bid from Northrop Grumman based on the JSTARS system in a Global Express or similar business jet, to fulfil Ground & Air Staff Requirement 3956. It also meets key requirements of the proposed NATO Alliance Ground Surveillance (AGS) system. For the ASTOR development and possible future production phase, the Gulfstream V would be modified by Marshall Aerospace, including installation of the radar-based mission system together with a defensive aids suite, in-flight refuelling capability and sophisticated data and communications links. Other elements of the programme include data and communications links, mobile ground stations and advanced imagery exploitation and mission planning tools. The dual-mode radar comes from Racal, designed specifically for ASTOR but using proven technology. Lockheed Martin ground station modules use standard service trucks and shelters. Lockheed Martin UK Government Systems was assigned to provide systems integration and prime contract management for UK programmes. Selection of the winning team was expected in 1998, with an in-service date set for the year 2003.

Lockheed Martin EC-130 series

Role: See Aircraft variants.
Based on: C-130E or H Hercules, except EC-130J which is based on the latest C-130J version of Hercules.
Sales/Users: Morocco (2 civil-registered Hercules carrying side-looking airborne radar for border surveillance duties) and USA (Coast Guard, USAF and ANG, as detailed).

Aircraft variants:

EC-130E ABCCC III is the designation of 7 recently upgraded (by Unisys) USAF Airborne Battlefield Command and Control Center aircraft operated by the 42nd Electronic Combat Squadron at Davis-Monthan AFB. Based on the C-130E, but with underfuselage antennae, podded ABCCC equipment carried in the cargo cabin, and some with replacement T56-A-15 engines. Deployed over Bosnia.

EC-130E Commando Solo is operated by the 193rd Special Operations Squadron of the 193rd Special Operations Wing of the US Air National Guard, from Harrisburg IAP, Pennsylvania, for psychological warfare operations by broadcasting radio or television pictures over targeted areas, but also for broadcasting during time of national emergencies. Lockheed Martin upgraded 6 to WWCTV (World Wide Color Television) configuration. Each currently has 4 tailfin-mounted antennae and underwing pods for UHF/VHF antennae. Previously known in earlier configurations as Rivet Rider and Volant Solo. A photograph appeared in the 1996-97 edition of *WA&SD*, page 189. 3 aircraft were deployed to Italy in September 1997, for operations over Bosnia during the elections, to jam any possible transmissions from outside of Bosnia.

EC-130H Compass Call is a C^3 jamming aircraft, of which 14 are operated by the 41st and 43rd EC squadrons of the 355th Wing, USAF, from Davis-Monthan AFB.

EC-130J Commando Solo is a new psychological warfare version for the 193rd Special Operations Squadron, based on the C-130J Hercules. 1 ordered to date under the FY1997 defence budget, for delivery to the ANG in 1999.

EC-130V first flew on 31 July 1991 as a single HC-130H conversion to AEW role for the US Coast Guard, using an above-fuselage radome and radar of E-2C Hawkeye type; 8 Hawkeyes had been received by the USCG for use in its anti-smuggling operations but lacked the range offered by the EC-130V. Budget cutbacks saw the EC-130V transfer to USAF service, however, going to the 514th Test Squadron at Hill AFB. Currently the US Coard Guard operates only HC-130H versions of Hercules for SAR and surveillance.

EC-130Q was the US Navy's TACAMO version for airborne strategic communications relay between the national command authority and ballistic missile submarines up to 1992. With the arrival of the Boeing E-6 Mercury, some were mothballed (presumably recoverable or stored for conversion), 3 converted to transports for NASA and 2 modified into TC-130Q support transports.

C-130 Samson is Lockheed Martin's own name for the C-130H carrying the Samson "Open Skies" pod. The Lockheed Martin-manufactured Samson surveillance pod, used by Belgium and 9 other countries to verify the new European Open Skies Treaty, carries 3 Recon-Optical KS-87B framing film cameras, a KS-116A panoramic film camera and 2 video cameras.

Lockheed Martin C-130J Airborne Early Warning variants

Comments: Australia, Greece, Italy, South Korea, Spain and Turkey are among countries interested in new AEW&C aircraft, plus possibly Israel, with versions based on the latest C-130J or C-130J-30 Hercules 2 in contention; Romania also requires an AEW system, though possibly to be based on an older airframe. The currently offered AEW version is designed for either standard or open system architecture (OSA) for flexibility, on a palleted system to allow easy reconfiguration. With Northrop Grumman as the principal subcontractor for systems integration, the baseline version has Lockheed Martin AN/APS-145 or possibly -145 Plus radar, combined with IFF to allow automatic target detection and tracking of ships out of the radar horizon and aircraft at ranges greater than 300 naut miles. Other features are believed to include an integrated passive detection system to augment target identification, HF, VHF and UHF radios (including secure), datalink systems for the transmission of radar pictures to the ground and other AEW&C aircraft, Have Quick, satcom, JTIDS, management information and decision support (MIDS), and more. Up to 12 workstations (perhaps typically 9), with displays and communication accessibility. 10 hour on-station duration, 300 naut miles from base, or 11 hours 30 minutes on station at 150 naut miles from base (C-130J-30), in the latter case taking 25 minutes 'time-to-climb' and adopting an initial orbiting altitude of 29,000 ft (8,840 m). The Wedgetail programme includes Australia's Tenix Defence Systems in the team; the Lockheed Martin team was 1 of 3 awarded an Initial Design Activity contract by the Australian Defence Force in December 1997, worth $6.5 million.

A second AEW configuration envisages using the Israeli Elta EL/M-2075 Phalcon radar system with electronically-scanned phased arrays, which could meet with interest from Israel, South Korea and Turkey.

A third proposed configuration sees the use of the Swedish Ericsson Erieye radar, carried in an above-fuselage container of similar configuration (but possibly with a larger antenna with 360° scanning) to that adopted for the ERJ145 and Saab S 100B. This too was, reportedly, initially seen as a possible configuration for the Wedgetail bid.

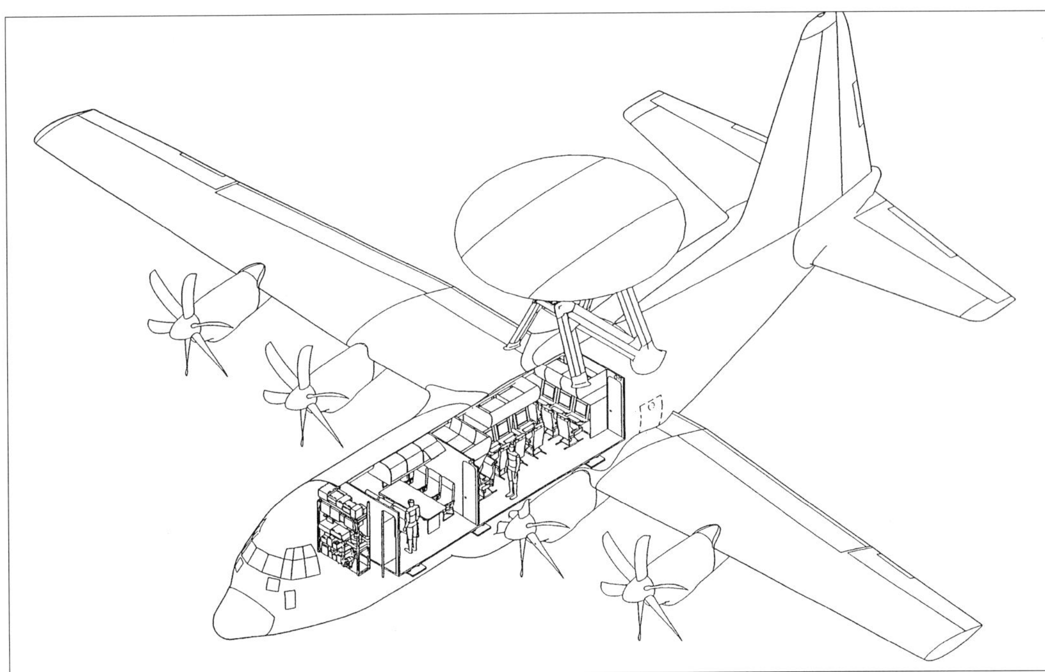

↑ Lockheed Martin C-130J Airborne Early Warning aircraft with AN/APS-145 radar *(courtesy Lockheed Martin)*

Lockheed Martin ES-3A and S-3 AEW Viking

Comments: First flown in August 1991, the ES-3A intelligence gathering/processing/evaluation/reporting, airborne command and control, over-the-horizon targeting and battlefield management aircraft was produced for the US Navy by conversion of S-3A Vikings. The S-3 AEW was conceived as a carrier AEW aircraft to replace Hawkeye, again based on the S-3 airframe, but was not developed. Details and photographs of these aircraft can be found in the 1996-97 edition of *WA&SD*, page 189.

Lockheed Martin P-3 AEW, CEC, ASARS and Slicks, and Kawasaki EP-3

Comments: In 1997 Kawasaki delivered its 101st and last P-3C ASW and patrol aircraft, leaving a single EP-3 electronic intelligence aircraft to be delivered in September 1998 and 3 UP-3D electronic training and support aircraft up to March 2000 as the only remaining Orion new production either in Japan or the USA. However, 5 Kawasaki P-3Cs are due for conversion into UP-3E surveillance aircraft for image data collecting, each with side-looking airborne radar (SLAR), long-range oblique camera pod, IR detection system, GPS and satcom, able to relay images in real time. Further details of the both US and Japanese electronic versions of Orion can be found in the 1996-97 edition of *WA&SD*, page 190.

↑ Kawasaki license-built EP-3C electronic intelligence aircraft at Atsugi, operated by the JMSDF *(K. Hinata)*

Lockheed Martin U-2S and ST Dragon Lady

Comments: Re-delivery of all 35 USAF U-2s under the latest U-2S (31 single-seaters) and U-2ST (4 2-seat trainers) designations was completed in 1998. These have the 19,000 lbf (84.518 kN) General Electric F118-GE-101 turbofan engine offering weight reduction of 1,200 lb (544 kg), fuel saving of over 15%, increase of range by 1,200 naut miles (1,380 miles) 2,200 km, increase of duration by 3 hours, and increase of altitude by 3,500 ft (1,060 m), plus new electro-optical multi-spectral cameras. Details of the U-2S/ST can be found in the 1996-97 edition of *WA&SD*, pages 190-191, together with a photograph.

Northrop Grumman Corporation — USA

Corporate address:
See Combat section for company details.

Northrop Grumman E-2C Hawkeye, Group II E-2C Hawkeye II and Hawkeye 2000

First flight: 21 October 1960 (original W2F-1 prototype). 11 April 1998 for Hawkeye 2000.

Role: Carrier-borne and land-based airborne early warning/command and control (AEW/CC), primarily for wide-area air defence intercept and strike control. Secondary missions include surface surveillance, search-and-rescue, air traffic control, tanker co-ordination, electronic signal monitoring, drug interdiction and communications relay.

Aims

- Highly automated system, requiring a small crew.
- 10,000 flight hour design life for Group II aircraft, calculated at 55,000 lb (24,947 kg) gross weight.

Development

- 19 April 1961. First flight of a W2F-1 prototype with full avionics suite.
- 19 January 1964. Initial delivery of an E-2A, the first operational US Navy squadron becoming VAW-11.
- 20 January 1971. Maiden flight of the E-2C prototype, followed by a production aircraft on 23 September 1972.
- December 1994. US Navy awarded Northrop Grumman a $122.5 million contract for long-lead procurement and production start-up for 7 new Group II E-2C Hawkeyes (all Group II types known by Northrop Grumman as Hawkeye IIs), for delivery during 1997-98. Further US Navy procurement will take place to keep Hawkeye in production into the next century. New USN Hawkeye IIs were the first built at the new E-2C production facility in St Augustine, Florida. These aircraft will be retrofitted to the latest Hawkeye 2000 configuration, and all new production switched over to Hawkeye 2000 (see Aircraft variants).
- 29 April 1996. US Navy squadron VAW-123 'Screwtops' based at Norfolk Naval Air Station, Virginia, became the first squadron on the East Coast of the USA to deploy the next-generation Group II E-2C.
- 24 January 1997. First flight of the Hawkeye 2000 test aircraft with a mission computer upgrade, allowing CEC, sent after contractor flight tests to Patuxent River Naval Air Test Center for extensive testing.
- 24 February 1997. First new Group II E-2C (Hawkeye II) produced at St Augustine facility was rolled out.
- 11 April 1998. Hawkeye 2000 first airframe test flight, lasting 1 hour 45 minutes.

Details

Sales/Users: 166 E-2Cs delivered up to the 1995 end of production at the Calverton, New York, facility. Total of 139 (see USCC below) was received by the US Navy by 1995 (82 in the US Navy inventory at time of writing), with production restarted – instead of older aircraft modernization – to provide an additional 36 new Group II aircraft into the next century, beginning with 7 ordered under an initial 2 year programme from FY1995, with funding for 4 more in FY1997 and long-lead funding for an additional 3 in FY1998, all becoming Hawkeye 2000 configuration. In addition, upgrade is taking place of 12 Group I Hawkeyes to Group II configuration for the US Navy, redelivered from the end of 1995. US Navy has 11 E-2C air wings. US Coast Guard operated 4 Hawkeyes but these were returned to the US Navy. 33 exported to date when including Taiwan's refurbished S-2Bs, going to Egypt (5 + 1 replacement, and was looking to buy another), Israel (4 received but no longer used, with APS-125 radar), Japan (13 Group 0s with APS-138 radar, to be upgraded to near Group II standard), Singapore (4) and Taiwan (4 E-2Ts, delivered 1994-96 as refurbished ex-US Navy E-2Bs and not new production). France ordered 2 for operation from the aircraft carrier *Foch* and later for transfer to *Charles de Gaulle*, delivered in 1997, with 2 more possibly to follow. Other interested nations include Thailand and Turkey.

Crew: 5, comprising pilot, co-pilot, combat information centre officer, air control officer, and radar operator. The 3 system

↑ US Navy squadron VAW-123 'Screwtops' became the first squadron on the East Coast of the USA to deploy the next-generation Group II E-2C

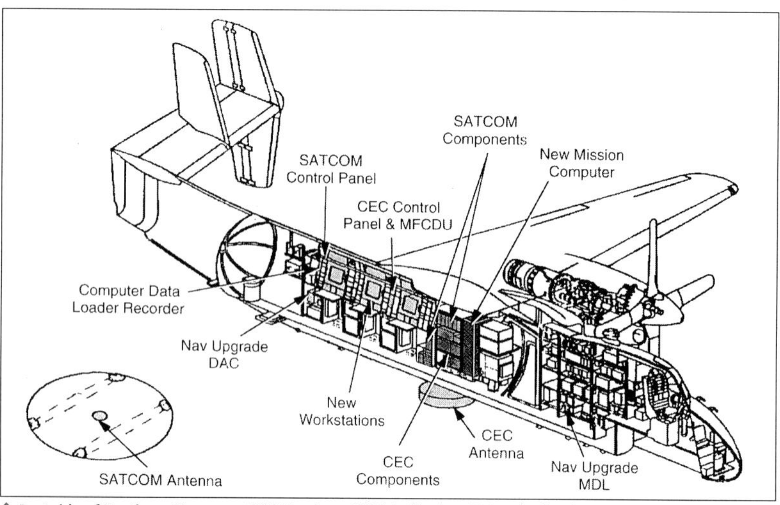

↑ **Port side of Northrop Grumman E-2C Hawkeye 2000, indicating CEC and other improvements** *(courtesy Northrop Grumman)*

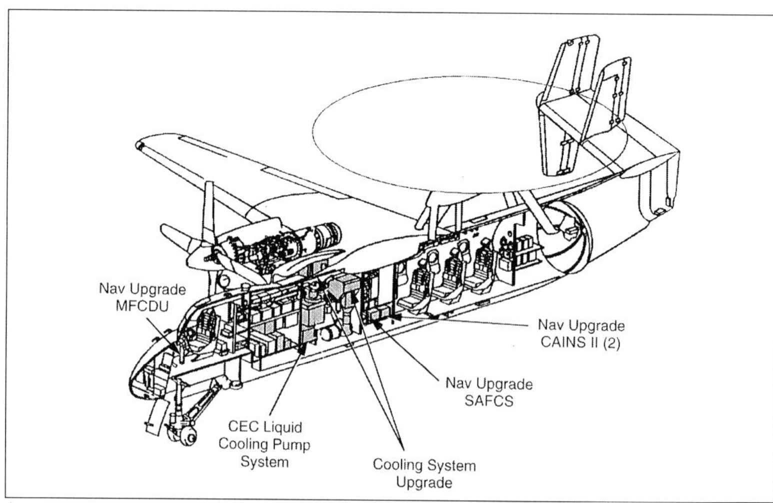

↑ **Starboard side of Northrop Grumman E-2C Hawkeye 2000, with improvement features** *(courtesy Northrop Grumman)*

operators work independently in all operational roles (sensor utilization, monitoring/control of the tactical situation, and data exchange).
Crew escape: Ditching hatches above the pilots, pulled by handles into the cockpit and moved aft. CIC compartment ditching hatch on starboard side of the fuselage. For airborne escape, main port door is blown using explosive charges, after alarm has been sounded and cabin unpressurized.
Radar: Currently Lockheed Martin AN/APS-145 radar with fully automatic system optimization for continuous overland and overwater detection and tracking. Can track over 2,000 targets and simultaneously control friendly forces to over 40 interceptions. Operating at above 30,000 ft (9,145 m), can automatically detect, identify and track air and maritime targets over water, and air targets over land at ranges of more than 260 naut miles (300 miles) 483 km. Radar, working with the IFF and passive detection systems through associated computers, can monitor 6 million cubic miles of airspace and more than 150,000 square miles of ocean surface. APS-145 uses Loral-Randtron AN/APA-171 rotating antennae for the radar (TRAC-A – Total Radiation Aperture Control Antenna) and IFF. Majority of production E-2Cs (118 to the USN) were delivered with earlier and less capable APS-120, -125, -138 and recent -139 (latter for Group I E-2C variant) radars; APS-120 and -125 (latter the first digital version) are out of USN service.
Mission equipment: More than 12,000 lb (5,443 kg) of electronic equipment (including radar). With the latest APS-145 radar comes enhanced high-speed processors, new high-target-capacity colour displays, JTIDS for improved secure anti-jam voice and data communications, and GPS. Also, Northrop Grumman received a development contract for a mission computer upgrade (MCU) for 'new-build' aircraft and retrofit (see Development and Aircraft variants), to replace the Litton L-304, offering improved memory and processing capabilities in a smaller and lighter (300 lb, 136 kg instead of 750 lb, 340 kg) unit that is easier to maintain (subcontracted to Raytheon's Equipment Division, as the Model 940). This is based on the DEC Alpha chip processing element. MCU flight testing began in 1997. Northrop Grumman has also worked on a CEC suite (co-operative engagement capability) based around an underfuselage fixed active array antenna, for high speed and secure passing of radar reports between ship and air elements of the carrier battle group. Another programme which is part of the MCU programme is the substitution of the current operators' displays and panels with 3 new lightweight operator stations in the rear compartment, each with a flat-panel plasma screen and processor. In addition, a small workstation was proposed for the co-pilot who can often be under utilized during typical operations, allowing the co-pilot to undertake data processing.
Fixed guns: None.
Wing characteristics: Shoulder mounted, straight, with dihedral. Wings fold and turn to stow horizontally (hydraulically).
Wing control surfaces: Ailerons and Fowler flaps, the former with automatic drooping when the flaps are operated. Leading-edge de-icing boots.
Tail control surfaces: Dihedral tailplane supporting 4 sets of fins, the largest outer fins having dorsal and ventral surfaces and double-hinged rudders. 2 smaller inboard fins, only 1 having a horn-balanced double-hinged rudder. All fins cant inward.
Fuselage: Above fuselage heat exchanger for avionics cooling, being upgraded by 50% capability from 1996 production. Pylon-mounted radome.
Construction materials: All metal, except for some composites in the tail unit.
Engines: 2 Allison T56-A-427 turboprops, with 4-blade constant-speed propellers.
Engine rating: Each 5,100 eshp (3,803 ekW).
Flight refuelling probe: Retrofitted to Israeli aircraft. US Navy system has been designed but not funded.
Fuel system: 12,400 lb (5,624 kg).
Electrical system: Primary 3-phase 400 Hz AC system using 2 x 90kVA engine-driven generators and 28 volt rectifier for instruments. Emergency 10kVA generator for unfeathering the propellers. Hawkeye 2000 is receiving 225kVA generators.
Braking system: Hydraulic brakes and arrester hook.
Flight avionics/instrumentation: Manual/automatic landing system with AN/ARA-64 enhancer, using a data link with the aircraft carrier to allow the pilot to put the aircraft on the glideslope. See Mission equipment for mission computer. Navigation update for Hawkeye 2000 includes GEC-Marconi CP-140/A air data computer, and dual Litton AN/ASN-139 laser ring gyro INS (in place of single ASN-92) under the ECP (Engineering Change Proposal) with backing HARS. AN/ALR-73 passive detection unit. Satcom kits already supplied for voice mini-dama hardware. Under MCU, permanent digital Satcom links (with MATT) will follow. ADF and radar altimeter. Lockheed Martin autopilot as part of the current navigation upgrade. Communications equipment on latest aircraft comprises 2 HF and 6 UHF radios, 3 of the latter also for VHF and 1 usable for SATCOM. See Mission equipment for JTIDS (which incorporates Tacan) and CEC. Several 1553 buses and new high speed bus allows expansion of systems.

↑ **First new Northrop Grumman Group II E-2C Hawkeye (Hawkeye II) built at St Augustine**

Aircraft variants:
E-2C is the standard service version, in Group II (Hawkeye II) form. No longer in production.
TE-2C is a training variant, of which 2 are in active USN service.
Hawkeye 2000 is the latest 'advanced generation' configuration, applying to the last newly built Group II E-2C Hawkeyes for the US Navy after retrofit to this configuration and all new production examples. Mission computer upgrade, advanced control indicator set (workstation), co-operative engagement capability, AlliedSignal vapour-cycle cooling system and more (see diagrams for further features).

Details for E-2C latest configuration

PRINCIPAL DIMENSIONS:
Wing span: 80 ft 7 ins (24.56 m)
Width, wings folded: 29 ft 4 ins (8.94 m)
Maximum length: 57 ft 8.75 ins (17.6 m)
Maximum height: 18 ft 3.75 ins (5.58 m)
Radar dome diameter: 24 ft (7.32 m)

WINGS:
Area: 700 sq ft (65.032 m^2)
Aspect ratio: 9.276

UNDERCARRIAGE:
Type: Retractable, with steerable twin nosewheels
Wheel base: 23 ft 2 ins (7.06 m)
Wheel track: 19 ft 6 ins (5.94 m)

WEIGHTS:
Empty: 40,484 lb (18,363 kg)
Maximum take-off: 54,426 lb (24,687 kg) for Group II aircraft, with 55,000 lb (24,947 kg) as the design maximum

PERFORMANCE:
Maximum speed: 338 kts (389 mph) 626 km/h
High cruise speed: 325 kts (374 mph) 600 km/h
Average cruise speed: 259 kts (298 mph) 480 km/h
Typical low cruise speed: 200 kts (230 mph) 370 km/h
Approach speed: 103 kts (119 mph) 191 km/h
Stall speed: 75 kts (87 mph) 139 km/h
Climb rate: 3,360 ft (1,024 m) per minute at sea level
Take-off distance: 1,850 ft (564 m)
Landing distance: 1,440 ft (439 m)
Landing distance over a 50 ft (15 m) obstacle: 2,420 ft (738 m) required runway length
G limits: +3 design, +2 normal
Ceiling: 37,000 ft (11,278 m), service
Ferry range: 1,541 naut miles (1,774 miles) 2,855 km
Duration: 5.3 hours at service ceiling, 200 naut miles (230 miles) 370 km from base/ship, with USN reserve

Northrop Grumman EA-6B Prowler

Comments: Although out of production, Prowler took on new significance in 1998 following the withdrawal from service of USAF EF-111A Ravens and the decision to merge the stand-off jamming needs of both the USAF and US Navy/USMC into the EA-6B Prowler. Also, ICAP-3 is a proposed designation for the next war-fighting sufficiency upgrade currently being formulated by the US Navy. Thus, the following entry has been fully revised and expanded by Northrop Grumman for inclusion in this edition of *WA&SD*.
First flight: 25 May 1968; ICAP-2 prototype first flew on 24 June 1980.
First delivery: 1971.
Role: Carrier-based electronic warfare, command and control aircraft to degrade/suppress enemy defences; also deployed from land.
Based on: A-6 Intruder and the EA-6A 2-seat ECM development.

Aims

▪ More specialized, capable and lengthened development of EA-6A, with 2 additional crew to operate the ECM systems.

Development

▪ See Mission equipment.

Details

Sales/Users: US Navy, US Marine Corps and USAF. Total of 127 existing aircraft in early 1998, as 103 with the US Navy and 24 with the USMC; 1 USMC Prowler was damaged in an accident at an Italian ski resort on 3 February 1998 during a low-level flight training flight. Each of 5 EA-6B squadrons (VAQ-128, 133, 134, 137 and 142) designated for joint service operations will include USAF aircrew; other US Navy squadrons are VAQ-129 (training), 130, 131, 132, 135, 136, 138, 139, 140 and 141 at Whidbey NAS, Washington, including 1 squadron 'home ported' in Atsugi, Japan. 1 US Navy reserve unit activated in 1991 and located at Andrews AFB, MD. USMC has 4 squadrons as VMAQ-1, 2, 3 and 4, all located at Cherry Point, NC, including an alternating squadron on continuous deployment.
Crew: 4, comprising the pilot, a navigation/communications and defensive ECM operator to his right, and 2 specialist ECM officers (ECMOs) in a separate heavily-glazed cabin aft of the cockpit.
Crew escape: Martin Baker ejection seats.
Mission equipment: AN/ALQ-99F tactical jamming system, with 5 integrally powered pods, and HARM missiles. Sensitive surveillance receivers in the fin-top pod for long-range detection of radars. Emitter information is fed to the AN/AYK-14 central digital computer that processes the signal for display and recording. Detection, identification, direction of arrival and jammer response are performed either automatically or manually by the ECMOs. There have been 4 generations of EA-6B Prowlers produced: Basic Capability (BASCAP), Expanded Capability (EXCAP), Improved Capability-1 (ICAP-1), and the current ICAP-2 version which provides additional jamming capabilities. ICAP-2 prototype first flew on 24 June 1980. All previously delivered aircraft were modified to ICAP-2 configuration. First production aircraft delivered on 3 January 1984. Universal Exciter in each of 5 external jamming pods, generating signals in 7 different frequency bands, with each pod capable of jamming in 2 frequency bands simultaneously. Enhancements provided for the development and integration of the Navy standard computer (AYK-14), Carrier Airborne Inertial Navigation System (CAINS), Digital Display Group (ASN-123) and the development of a replacement of the Multi-Band Exciter (MBE) with a Universal Exciter capable of generating modulation techniques in all transmitter frequencies. Subvariants of ICAP-2 include Block 82, Block 86 and Block 89/89A. The first ICAP-2 aircraft with HARM capability was delivered on 21 January 1986. The Block 86 aircraft expanded the communications system (ARC-182 VHF/UHF/KY-58 and ARC-199 HF/KY-75), enhanced signal processing (CIU/E), and integrated the ALQ-126 of the self-protection system B variant and a digital fuel quantity system/fuel system improvement. Deliveries began on 29 July 1988. The Block 89 deliveries, beginning in July 1991, included hydraulic system pressure switches/caution lights, yaw rate indication, a new fire detection and extinguishing system and several other safety modifications, while the first Block 89A upgrade flew on 8 June 1997 and incorporates commercial EFIS, computer enhancements, new ILS with embedded GPS/INS, and new coms, all for eventual installation in the fleet. ICAP-3 is a proposed designation for the next war-fighting sufficiency upgrade currently being formulated by the US Navy, to include reactive jamming, datalink and displays for improved situation awareness. 1996 Congressional Authorization Act directed that some elements of connectivity and a reactive jamming system upgrade be started, and it is anticipated to be included in this configuration.
Self-protection systems: Include chaff dispensers (see above).
Fixed guns: None.
Expendable weapons and equipment: 4 underwing pylons standard, for pods, HARM anti-radar missiles or drop tanks. Underfuselage pylon for pod or tank.
Wing characteristics: Mid mounted, slightly swept, with root extensions.
Wing control surfaces: Fowler type flaperons, similar-span spoilers and leading-edge slats.
Airbrakes: Split type.
Engines: 2 Pratt & Whitney J52-P-408 or 409 turbojets.
Engine rating: Each 11,200 lbf (49.82 kN) or 12,000 lbf (53.38 kN) respectively.
Flight refuelling probe: At nose.
Fuel system: 15,422 lb (6,995 kg) plus optional drop tanks.

↑ **Northrop Grumman EA-6B Prowler of VAQ-136** *(K. Hinata)*

Details for Prowler

PRINCIPAL DIMENSIONS:
Wing span: 53 ft (16.15 m)
Maximum length: 59 ft 10 ins (18.24 m)
Maximum height: 16 ft 3 ins (4.95 m)

WEIGHTS:
Empty: 31,572 lb (14,320 kg)
Maximum take-off: 65,000 lb (29,480 kg)
Maximum landing: 45,500 lb (20,638 kg)

PERFORMANCE:
Maximum speed: 565 kts (651 mph) 1,047 km/h
Cruise speed: 417 kts (481 mph) 774 km/h
Stall speed: 124 kts (143 mph) 230 km/h *clean*
Take-off distance: 2,670 ft (814 m)
Landing distance: 2,150 ft (656 m)
Maximum climb rate: 12,900 ft (3,930 m) per minute
G limits: 5.5
Ceiling: 41,200 ft (12,560 m)
Range with full payload: 955 naut miles (1,100 miles) 1,770 km

Northrop Grumman E-8C Joint STARS

First flight: December 1988 (fully configured E-8A prototype); 17 August 1995 for first production E-8C.
First delivery: 1996.
Role: Joint Surveillance Target Attack Radar System (Joint STARS or JSTARS) platform, as a powerful airborne surveillance and target acquisition system to provide real-time, accurate, battle management information, plus natural disaster management.
Based on: Remanufactured ex-commercial Boeing 707-300 airframes. Remanufacturing at Lake Charles, LA, and electronics installed/tested at the Integration and Test Facility at Melbourne, FL.

Aims

▪ From a stand-off position, to detect, locate, classify, track and target hostile ground movement in all weather conditions. Operates around-the-clock, in constant communication through secure data links with Air Force command posts, Army mobile ground stations or centres of military analysis away from the point of conflict, which can call upon aircraft, missiles and artillery for fire support.
▪ Determine direction, speed and patterns of activity of ground vehicles and helicopters. Track the evolution of conditions across borders or around areas of dispute, for pre-conflict crisis management and the rapid deployment of assets to counter conflict or conduct actual operations.

Development

▪ Co-operative USAF and US Army programme, managed by the US Air Force Materiel Command's Electronic Systems Center at Hanscom AFB, MA.
▪ 1985. Work began under an initial full-scale development contract.
▪ November 1990. USAF awarded Northrop Grumman a follow-on full-scale development (NET) contract that included enhancements to the system and a third Joint STARS platform (E-8C).
▪ 17 December 1990. Request for deployment of available E-8As in the Gulf by US Army General H. Norman Schwarzkopf.
▪ 11 January 1991. 2 E-8As with combined USAF/Army/contractor crews left Melbourne, Florida, for Saudi Arabia, landing the following day.
▪ March 1991. The 2 E-8As returned to the USA after Gulf deployment, having accumulated nearly 535 flying hours over 49 sorties during the Gulf conflict, operated by the 4411th Joint STARS Squadron.
▪ 24 April 1992. Northrop Grumman signed a low-rate initial production advanced procurement contract with the USAF, for 2 E-8Cs. Remanufacturing began in May 1993.
▪ December 1993. Joint STARS development programme completed, when the USAF accepted 2 E-8A demonstrator prototypes for testing at Edwards AFB.
▪ 27 December 1995. The second E-8A development aircraft and the E-8C testbed began operations over Bosnia-Herzegovina from Rhein-Main AFB, Germany, logging 1 sortie each day until 14 February 1996, completing 95 sorties in over 100 flights during the deployment. Returned to the USA in March 1996.
▪ 22 March 1996. First production E-8C delivered to the USAF.
▪ 25 September 1996. Approved for full-rate production.
▪ October 1996. 2 E-8Cs (first production E-8C and the testbed until 25 December, when the second production E-8C replaced testbed) of the 93rd Air Control Wing were deployed to Europe in support of NATO peacekeeping forces in Bosnia-Herzegovina, starting operations on 15 November and returning on 4 January 1997 after flying 39 missions.
▪ 11 June 1997. First occasion an E-8C provided moving target indicator (MTI) target data to an F-16 fighter flying over Bosnia-Herzegovina.
▪ 18 December 1997. Initial Operational Capability with the USAF.
▪ 2004. 13 E-8s to be in USAF service.
Sales/Users: USAF (2 E-8A development aircraft for upgrading to Cs, 1 E-8C test aircraft and 19 production E-8Cs required - of the latter, 8 contracted and 2 more under advance procurement at the time of writing). USAF to have 3 squadrons within the 193rd Air Control Wing at Robins AFB. Was evaluated by NATO for its Alliance Ground Surveillance (AGS) requirement but not selected.
Crew: 21 for a standard mission, comprising 3 flight crew and 18 operators. 34 for a long-duration mission, comprising 6 flight crew and 28 operators (including relief crew).
Radar: Northrop Grumman AN/APY-3 side-looking, phased array radar with antenna scanned electronically in azimuth and steered mechanically in elevation from either side of the aircraft, with wide-area surveillance, fixed target indication, synthetic aperture, moving target indicator and target classification modes. Remainder of Joint-STARS system includes 3 load-sharing, programmable signal processors (each containing 5 high-speed, fixed point distributed processors*, capable of over 600 million operations per second), operator consoles, secure voice and data

↑ Northrop Grumman E-8C Joint STARS. Note the side-looking phased array radar antenna in the underfuselage radome

↑ Joint STARS provides real-time battle management information to on-board operators, enabling them to distinguish moving or fixed targets from other types of objects on the ground and relay that information to other airborne or ground assets

links, and other subsystems. Data from the 24 ft (7.32 m) long radar antenna (which is housed under the fuselage) is processed and displayed to the operators as moving or fixed target reports, target tracks, and synthetic aperture radar images. This radar data is distributed simultaneously to ground stations. In addition to ground targets, the radar can detect helicopters and has a limited maritime capability.

*Under a 1997 US$132 million contract from the USAF, Northrop Grumman is to replace 5 central processors with 2 advanced processors in the E-8C testbed, to be completed by October 1999. Similar computer upgrades for production aircraft may follow under other contracts.

Mission equipment: 18 consoles, comprising 17 identical operation station consoles and a navigation/self-defence console (E-8A prototypes have 10 operations consoles and 2 communications consoles). Each operator workstation can undertake flight path planning and monitoring, generation and display of cartographic and hypsographic map data, radar management, surveillance and threat analysis, radar data review, time-of-arrival calculation, jammer location, distance and azimuth calculation, pairing of weapons and targets, and other functions. Digital data links are surveillance and control link (SCDL) for transmission to mobile ground stations, JTIDS for Tacan operation and TADIL-J (tactical data information data link J) generation and processing, and satellite communications (satcom) link. Voice communications encompass 12 encrypted UHF radios, 2 encrypted HF radios, 3 encrypted VHF radios with provision for single channel ground and airborne radio system (SINCGARS), and multiple intercom nets. Industry team comprises Computing Devices International for the Programmable Signal Processors, Cubic Defense Systems for Surveillance and Control Data Link, Greenwich Air Services for engine refurbishment, Interstate Electronics Corporation for graphic displays, Litton Guidance & Control Systems for Inertial Measurement System, Raytheon Company for UHF communications system equipment, Miltope Corporation for message page printer, Motorola Government Electronics Group for ground stations, Orbit International Corporation for workstation keyboards, PAR Government Systems Corp for software engineering, Raytheon Company for RAYVAX Mod 860/866 computers and AXP-3000/500 workstations, RF Products Inc for VHF collocation filter, Rockwell Collins for Flight Management System, and Telephonics Corporation for intercommunication control systems.

Engines: 4 Pratt & Whitney JT3D-3B turbojets.
Engine rating: Each 18,000 lbf (80.07 kN).
Fuel system: 155,000 lb (70,307 kg)

Details for E-8C

PRINCIPAL DIMENSIONS:
Wing span: 145 ft 9 ins (44.42 m)
Maximum length: 152 ft 11 ins (46.61 m)
Maximum height: 42 ft 6 ins (12.95 m)
Underfuselage antenna length: 24 ft (7.32 m)

WINGS:
Area: 3,050 sq ft (283.35 m^2)
Aspect ratio: 6.965

WEIGHTS:
Empty: 171,000 lb (77,560 kg)
Maximum take-off: 336,000 lb (152,400 kg)

PERFORMANCE:
Maximum speed: Mach 0.84
Ceiling: 42,000 ft (12,800 m)
Duration: 11 hours, or 20 hours with in-flight refuelling

Northrop Grumman EF-111A Raven

Comments: First flown on 17 May 1977 as a full prototype conversion of an F-111A fighter-bomber, the EF-111A Raven entered service in 1981 to become the USAF's primary tactical radar jamming (defence suppression) aircraft, to perform standoff jamming or to escort armed fighter-bombers. With the decision to merge the stand-off jamming needs of the USAF and US Navy into the Navy's EA-6B Prowler, the Raven was assigned for retirement, with just 12 remaining with the 429th Electronic Combat Squadron at Cannon AFB for final service in 1998. Details of the Raven and a photograph appeared in the 1996-97 edition of *WA&SD*, page 194.

Northrop Grumman OV-1D and RV-1D Mohawk

Comments: First flown on 14 April 1959 in YOV-1A development aircraft form, the Mohawk became a standard US Army observation, surveillance, forward air control and electronic intelligence aircraft. Some 23 ex-US Army OV-1Ds also joined the Argentine Army from 1993. Details of the Mohawk and a photograph appeared in the 1996-97 edition of *WA&SD*, page 195.

Raytheon Aircraft Company — USA

Corporate address:
See Combat section for company details.

↑ Raytheon Beech RC-12N Guardian Common Sensor, one of the US Army's first fixed-wing platforms to include an integrated Aircraft Survivability Equipment suite and 'glass' cockpit

Comments: Raytheon Aircraft offers a range of Special Mission aircraft based on its General Aviation business aircraft (see General Aviation section). The King Air B200 has formed the

↑ 2 JASDF Raytheon Hawker 800s in U-125A form, of which 10 have been ordered from a requirement of 27 *(courtesy JASDF)*

↑ Raytheon Beech King Air in photo mapping configuration

basic platform for more than 50 US Army RC-12 Special Electronics Mission aircraft delivered since 1971 in Guardrail and Guardian Common Sensor forms, for intelligence gathering and including communications intercept and direction finding roles. The latest version is the RC-12Q, covering 3 existing RC-12Ps recently converted to carry data link for wide band aircraft-to-aircraft, aircraft-to-ground and aircraft-to-satellite communications to work alongside remaining RC-12Ps and increase their area of operations. King Air B200s are also offered for Maritime Patrol and further specialist tasks, such as photo mapping.

The King Air 350 also forms the basis for special mission versions, including the RC-350 Guardrail elint demonstrator that is equipped to locate and monitor communications in the 20-1,400 MHz band widths and radar emissions in the in the 20 MHz-18 GHz range, plus the JGSDF LR-2 for both liaison and reconnaissance roles.

The Raytheon Hawker 800 business jet has also spawned special mission variants, including the U-125 flight inspection and U-125A SAR aircraft taken by the JASDF, plus flight inspection aircraft currently flown by the FAA (ex-USAF C-29As). Others are the Hawker 800RA surveillance and 800SIG sigint, 4 of each having been ordered by South Korea in 1996. On 16 November 1996, a JASDF U-125A equipped with belly-mounted search radar and nose FLIR, attached to the Chitose Air Rescue Station, helped save the lives of 22 civilian Russian sailors, whose ship had foundered in the Sea of Japan.

Raytheon Systems Company — USA

Corporate address:
(For parent Raytheon Company): 141 Spring Street, Lexington, MA 02173.

Telephone: +1 617 862 6600
Facsimile: +1 617 860 2520 (Public Relations)

Information:
Robert S. McWade (*telephone* +1 617 860 2846).

Note:
On 18 December 1997 Raytheon Company announced the completion of its merger with Hughes Defense. At the same time, Raytheon Systems Company was formed, to include the Hughes defense operations and the operations of Raytheon Electronic Systems, Raytheon TI Systems, and Raytheon E-Systems. Headquarters for Raytheon Systems Company will be in the Washington DC area, with public relations probably handled out of Lexington.

Chairman & CEO: William H. Swanson.

BUSINESS UNITS OF RAYTHEON SYSTEMS COMPANY

DEFENSE SYSTEMS

Activities:
■ Focus on anti-tactical ballistic missile systems; air defence; air-to-air, surface-to-air and air-to-ground missiles; naval and maritime systems; ship self-defence systems; torpedoes; strike, interdiction and cruise missiles; and advanced munitions.

SENSORS AND ELECTRONIC SYSTEMS

Activities:
■ Ground, shipborne and airborne fire control and surveillance systems; primary and secondary air traffic control radars; ground, space-based, night vision, and reconnaissance sensors; electronic warfare; and GPS systems.

HISAR PROGRAMME:

Address:
PO Box 902, El Segundo, CA 90245.
Telephone: +1 310 334 4727
Facsimile: +1 310 334 6278
Activities:
■ A Raytheon Beech King Air B200T has been used to demonstrate the Raytheon Systems' HISAR (Hughes) Integrated Surveillance And Reconnaissance System, an advanced X-band radar mapping and surveillance system that can be accommodated into executive class aircraft. Weighing 496 lb (225 kg), it offers a wide area search that covers 2,160 sq miles (5,600 sq kilometres) every 75 seconds with a resolution of 65 ft (20 m), can strip map a swath of 23 miles (37 km) with a resolution of 20 ft (6 m) (with moving target indicator), spot a 3.8 sq mile (10 sq kilometre) area with a resolution of 6 ft (1.8 m), undertake sea surveillance, and detect and monitor low-flying aircraft in an air-to-air role. All equipment for mission and collection planning, data collection, and real-time image formation and display requires only 4,930 watts and 29.3 cu ft (0.83 m^3) volume in the aircraft. Current platforms include the US Army's 3 de Havilland RC-7Bs, with 2 more for 1999, to patrol the demilitarized zone between North and South Korea.

COMMAND, CONTROL AND COMMUNICATIONS (C^3) SYSTEMS

Activities:
■ C^3 systems; air traffic control systems; tactical radios; satellite communication ground terminals; wide area surveillance systems; advanced transportation systems; and simulators and simulation systems.

↑ **Raytheon Systems HISAR on a Beech King Air B200T** *(courtesy Raytheon Systems Company)*

INTELLIGENCE, INFORMATION AND AIRCRAFT INTEGRATION SYSTEMS

Activities:
■ Ground-based information processing systems; large scale information retrieval, processing and distribution systems; global broadcast systems; airborne surveillance and intelligence systems integration; aircraft modification; and head-of-state aircraft systems. Current programmes include the refurbishment of 18 Royal Australian Air Force Lockheed Martin AP-3C Orions under the Sea Sentinel Program, to include upgraded data management system; communications system (new UHF, VHF, HF, satcom and intercommunications); advanced acoustic processing capabilities that include use of colour for rapid target acquisition, classification and tracking; added GPS; and upgraded modular radar system. Also Project Wedgetail (see below).

PROJECT WEDGETAIL PROGRAMME:

Address: Majors Field, Greenville, TX 75402.
Telephone: +1 903 455 3450
Activities:
■ Raytheon Systems Company as team leader has proposed an AEW&C aircraft based on the Airbus A310-300 to meet the requirements of the Royal Australian Air Force under that nation's Project Wedgetail (Air 5077), for which a production contract decision for 4 aircraft is expected in 1999 and operational service from 2002. It adopts the IAI/Elta Phalcon radar, with arrays triangularly arranged in a more traditional but fixed over-fuselage radome that would contribute to overall 'lift'. Competing designs for Project Wedgetail are being offered by Boeing and Lockheed Martin. In late 1997, Raytheon was awarded 1 of 3 Initial Design Activity contracts by the Australian Defence Force under Project Wedgetail, worth $6.5 million. Members of the Raytheon team include Israel Aircraft Industries/Elta, Airbus Industrie, Raytheon Systems Australia, Honeywell Australia (roles to include avionics systems and training), Hawker de Havilland (roles to include installation of mission systems), Adacel (for software/engineering design, development and support), and ADI (for C^3 and computer development, integration and support). A310-300 AEW&C operating weight could be about 249,600 lb (113,217 kg), and it is expected to offer more than 10 hours duration on station at 300 naut miles from base without inflight refuelling. Economical cruise speed will be Mach 0.8 and cruise altitude 41,000 ft (12,500 m).

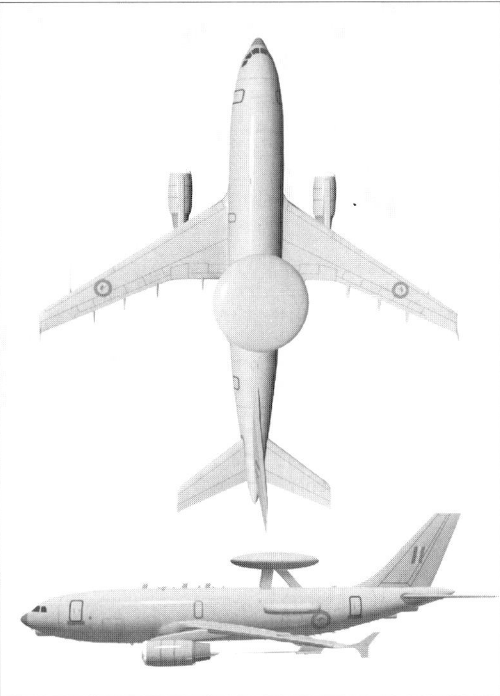

↑ **Raytheon Systems Company A310 AEW&C design for the RAAF's Project Wedgetail programme. Note the communications antennae mounted on the fuselage and wings** *(courtesy Raytheon Systems Company)*

↑ **Radome of the Raytheon Systems Company A310, with the Phalcon electronically-scanned phased arrays mounted in a triangular configuration** *(courtesy Raytheon Systems Company)*

TRAINING AND SERVICES

Activities:
■ Training services and integrated training programmes; technical services; and logistics and lifetime support.

Scaled Composites, Incorporated

USA

Corporate address:
1624 Flight Line, Mojave, CA 93501-1663.

Telephone: +1 805 824 4541
Facsimile: +1 805 824 4174
Web site: http://www.scaled.com/

Information:
Kaye LeFebvre.

Scaled Composites Proteus

First flight: 26 July 1998.
Role: Multi-purpose, high-altitude, long-endurance, sensor platform, for civil and military applications including communications relay, remote sensing, real-time FEMA monitoring, Earth and ocean resources monitoring, atmospheric sciences and so on. Optional unmanned UAV form.

Aims

- Modular configuration, designed to be easily reconfigured for a wide range of missions, using the most recent technologies in aerodynamics, structures, power plants and manufacturing techniques.
- Modular concept allows near-complete development and qualification of new payloads without tying up an entire flying platform.
- In addition to HALO application (see Development), other missions are detailed under Aircraft variants.
- To offer airline reliability and fast mission turnaround.

Development

- Designed and built by Scaled Composites under development funding from Scaled's parent company, Wyman-Gordon.
- 1998. First flight of the proof-of-concept vehicle.
- First commercial application is being developed for Angel Technologies, Corporation of Magna Place, Suite 760, 1401 South Brentwood Blvd, St. Louis, MO 63144 (*telephone* +1 314 918 1700, *facsimile* +1 314 918 1710 – Diane Murphy for Public Relations *telephone* +1 703 893 0740). To be known as HALO (High Altitude, Long Operation), it will carry a 20 ft (6.1 m) suspended antenna pod for communications use, offering a very rapid and cost-effective means of providing nationwide telecommunications and data relay. It is said 1 aircraft can provide cellular telephone and "broad band on demand" data relay services over an area of thousands of square miles, remaining on station by flying a 5-8 naut mile circle, while a pivoting pylon maintains the antenna in a level attitude. Thereby, the communications package can be considerably more powerful than that of an orbiting satellite. The aircraft can generate up to 45 kW of electrical power, in addition to payload cooling. A typical operation would use 3 aircraft, to provide 24-hour coverage and back-up.

Sales/Users: First commercial application for Angel Technologies, Corporation. Expected initial demand for 100 aircraft for communications relay use.
Crew: 2, in a near-sea-level environment (including ozone scrubbing and humidification). Crew to alternate duty and on-station rest cycles.
Airframe: Modular, all-composites, canard type. Varying wing span, according to mission and payload, through 4 extendable wingtips. Consists of 3 sections: nose section includes the crew compartment, forward wing, forward fuselage tank and nose undercarriage unit; payload-dedicated centre section 'barrel', of 45 ins (1.14 m) diameter and varying length (according to mission requirements); and the aft section that includes the aft fuselage with its fuel tank, the main wing, main undercarriage units, tail-booms and engines. Payload 'barrels' are easily interchangeable and incorporate quick connections for controls and electronics.
Engines: 2 Williams-Rolls FJ44-2 turbofans.
Engine rating: Each 2,300 lbf (10.23 kN).

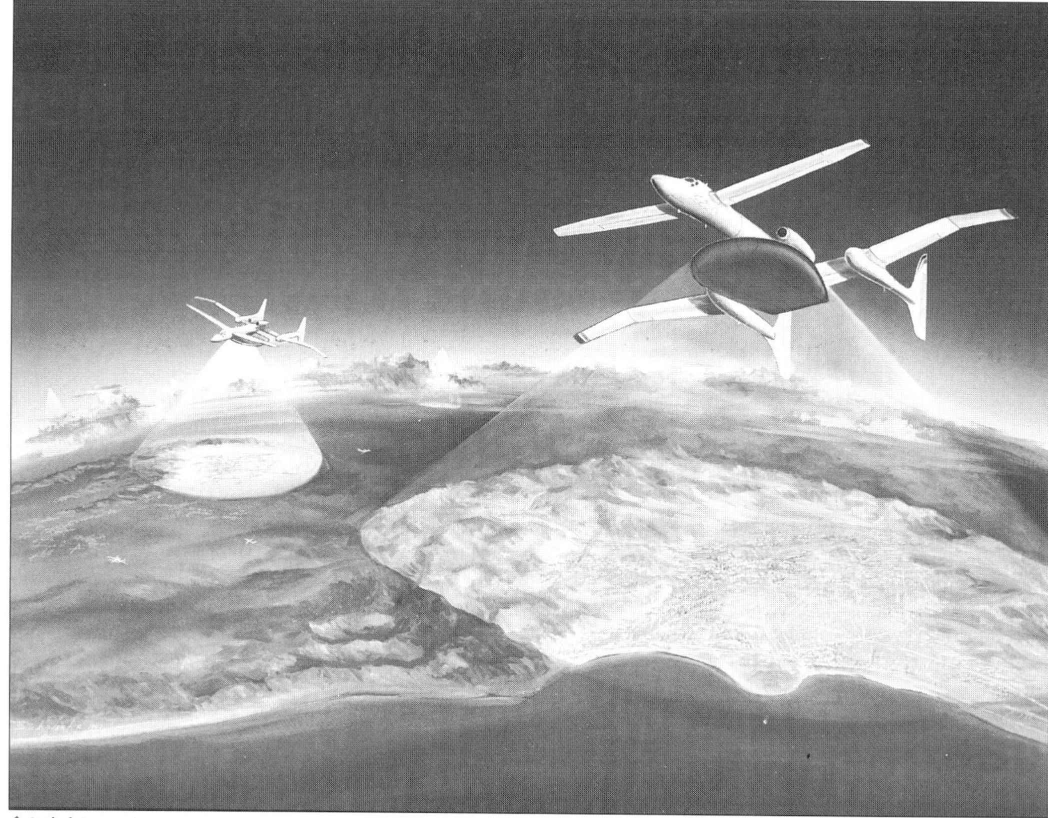

↑ Scaled Composites Proteus in Angel Technologies HALO telecommunications form

Aircraft variants:
HALO, see Development.
Atmospheric research mission could see Proteus take-off from a general aviation airfield, fly 500 naut miles, loiter at 60,000 ft (18,290 m) for 18 hours and return. Alternatively, fly 3,000 naut miles, loiter for 6 hours and return. This allows such missions as ozone depletion measurement over the South Pole from a base in South America, Antarctic overflights from South America, New Zealand or South Africa, or long-duration hurricane research.
Reconnaissance and surveillance missions could include long-duration battlefield surveillance and imaging, elint or JTIDS data relay. It can carry and support Global Hawk (Tier 2+) payloads, and can be operated in unmanned UAV form.
Space launch support, by changing fuselage barrel sections (and perhaps also wing extensions for asymmetric loads) to allow reconfiguration to carry large external payloads such as orbital and sub-orbital boosters, allowing 'point to shoot' capability by manoeuvring the aircraft to any required attitude before booster separation and ignition.

Details for Proteus

PRINCIPAL DIMENSIONS:
Wing span: 79 ft (24.08 m), increased up to 92 ft (28.04 m) for some missions

PERFORMANCE: See also Aircraft variants
Normal operating altitude: 50,000-65,000 ft (15,240-19,800 m)
Available time on station: up to 18 hours

↑ In late June 1998 *WA&SD* received these photographs of the actual Proteus proof-of-concept vehicle while in the late stage of construction, awaiting the canards and flaps. Because Proteus is so large, the photographer was unable to photograph the whole aircraft while indoors

Schweizer Aircraft Corporation

USA

Corporate address:
Box 147, Elmira, NY 14902.

Telephone: +1 607 739 3821
Facsimile: +1 607 796 2488
Telex: 932459

Founded: 1939.

Information:
Barbara J. Tweedt (Manager, Marketing/Communications).

ACTIVITIES

■ See also Helicopter, General Aviation and Glider sections.

Schweizer SA 2-37A

Comments: First flown in 1986, this low-noise special missions aircraft for surveillance, EEZ protection, pollution control, training, towing and cargo carrying was described and illustrated in the 1996-97 edition of *WA&SD*, pages 195-196.

Schweizer SA 2-38A (RU-38A Twin Condor)

First flight: 31 May 1995 (unofficial technical) and June 1995 (official).
Role: Covert day/night patrol and surveillance. Also EEZ protection, pollution patrol and more, and will be able to jettison payloads for SAR at a later date. For USCG operation over the Gulf of Mexico and Caribbean for the above-mentioned roles.
Based on: SA 2-37A/RG-8A.

Aims

■ Initially a modification of a USCG RG-8A (SA 2-37A type) to twin-engined configuration, providing for an increased payload and improved sensor arrangement, increased over-water safety (especially at night), and better engine maintenance through geared engines to prevent valve coking at low power settings for slow-speed mission flight.

Development

■ 24 January 1994. First USCG RG-8A received by Schweizer for conversion into a RU-38A under USAF contract. First of a planned 2 RG-8As for conversion, to be joined by a further newly built aircraft for the USCG.
■ June 1995. Flight testing began at Edwards AFB.
■ December 1996. Agreement reached to supply only 2 RU-38As to the USCG, instead of the originally expected 3 (see below).
■ May 1997. Resumption of flying, after a delay of many months following the loss off the coast of Puerto Rico of the intended second USCG RG-8A donor aircraft in 1996, reportedly due to engine problems.

Sales/Users: US Coast Guard (2 RU-38As, only 1 by conversion of an RG-8A). It is believed that Schweizer has at least 1 other national and an international customer.
Crew: 2, comprising pilot and sensor operator in wider cabin. 3-seat 'new build' version is under development for a customer.
Radar: AlliedSignal AN/APN-215(V) multi-function X-band sea search, mapping and weather radar in a radome below the nose of the port fuselage boom.
Other mission sensors: FLIR in the starboard boom, plus LLTV and dual recorder. Boom pod sensors are interchangeable.
Wing characteristics: SA 2-37A wings, with span increased by the addition of the fuselage booms.
Wing control surfaces: As for SA 2-37A, with ailerons and upper/lower airbrakes. No flaps.
Tail control surfaces: Twin fins and horn-balanced rudders, and single joining tailplane with elevator.
Fuselage: Pod and twin-boom type, using only the forward section of the SA 2-37A.
Engines: 2 Teledyne Continental GIO-550A piston engines in 'push and pull' tandem layout for the first USCG aircraft, but with only 1 engine used during typical cruise flight. 3:2 gear reduction to 2,267 rpm. Engines 'muffled' to reduce sound; since allocated turbochargers.
Engine rating: Each 350 hp (261 kW).
Fuel system: 375 litres.
Flight avionics/instrumentation: Typical USCG avionics include Omega, GPS, AlliedSignal Bendix/King KY58 and KY75 communications encryption devices, Wolfsberg RT9600 Maritime band radio, Rockwell Collins ARC-182 VHF/UHF, AlliedSignal HF-900 radios, and VHF/UHF direction finders. Night vision goggles optional.

Details for RU-38A

PRINCIPAL DIMENSIONS:
Wing span: 64 ft (19.51 m)
Maximum length: 30 ft 2 ins (9.19 m)

WINGS:
Aerofoil section: Wortmann FX-61-163 and modified FX-60-126 (root/tip)
Area: 225.86 sq ft (20.98 m^2)
Aspect ratio: 18.135

UNDERCARRIAGE:
Type: Fixed, with nosewheel

WEIGHTS:
Empty: 3,360 lb (1,524 kg)
Maximum take-off: 5,300 lb (2,404 kg)
Payload: 900 lb (408 kg)

PERFORMANCE:
Cruise speed: 136 kts (157 mph) 253 mph, at 75% power
Mission speed: 85-95 kts (98-110 mph) 157-176 km/h
Stall speed: 76 kts (87 mph) 140 km/h
Take-off distance: 960 ft (293 m)
Landing distance: 1,350 ft (412 m)
Climb rate: 2,200 ft (671 m) per minute, or 1,150 ft (351 m) per minute with rear engine stopped
Mission altitude: Below 10,000 ft (3,050 m)
Ceiling: 24,000 ft (7,315 m)
Duration: 6-10 hours

↑ Schweizer RU-38A surveillance aircraft for the US Coast Guard

Airliners, Freighters and Tankers

As a guide, the term 'airliner' has been determined to mean transport aircraft with seating capacities of 18/19 seats or more, though there are a number of exceptions where deemed necessary. Many component manufacturing and upgrade/modification companies are also included for added reference value.

Boeing Australia Limited — Australia

Corporate address:
Level 6, 3 Thomas Holt Drive, North Ryde, NSW 2113.

Telephone: +61 2 9805 5555
Facsimile: +61 2 9805 5599

Founded:
1960, becoming Rockwell Australia before being renamed Boeing Australia.

Employees: 1,700.

Information:
Tony Hill (Manager, Public Affairs) or Leanne Vroonland (Marketing Support Co-ordinator – *facsimile* +61 2 9888 2795).

ACTIVITIES

- Boeing Australia Limited is a wholly owned subsidiary of Boeing North American, Inc of Seal Beach, California, USA, which in turn is owned by The Boeing Company (see Combat section). It has an annual turnover of about $250 million.
- Design, development, manufacture, installation and support of defence combat and communication systems, aircraft repair and modification, and through life support of electronic systems. It is a member of the Boeing team proposing a 737-700 AEW&C aircraft to meet the RAAF's Project Wedgetail requirement, providing system engineering and aircraft modification support, and is leading the product support and ground support systems teams.
- Products include integrated aircraft systems; submarine combat and communications systems; and military ground/ship/airborne communications, navigation, control systems and equipment. Also military and civil air traffic control switching systems, processors, telemetry, acoustic imaging, ASW, navigation sound ranging, countermeasures, decoys and unattended acoustic sensors, commercial aircraft, space systems, helicopters, military aircraft, missile systems, electronic products and software products.

OTHER OFFICES

AUSTRALIAN CAPITAL TERRITORY

Address:
First Floor, 99 Northbourne Avenue, GPO Box 397, Canberra, ACT 2601.

Telephone: +61 2 6257 4441
Facsimile: +61 2 6257 4774

VICTORIA

Address:
Cnr Sheep Road & Maroondah Highway, PO Box 200, Lilydale, Victoria 3140.

Telephone: +61 3 9727 9711
Facsimile: +61 3 9726 5920

AIRCRAFT SYSTEMS DIVISION

Address:
Private Bag No 4, Beach Road, Lara, Victoria 3212.

Telephone: +61 3 5227 9444
Facsimile: +61 3 5282 3345

Employees: 250.

Activities:
- See below, as division of ASTA.
- Specializes in the design, manufacture and maintenance of military aerospace equipment. Prime customers are the Australian Defence Force and overseas Original Equipment Manufacturers.

ASTA COMPONENTS

Address:
226 Lorimer Street (Private Bag No 4 for postal address), Port Melbourne, Victoria 3207.

Telephone: +61 3 9647 3111
Facsimile: +61 3 9646 2253, or 9645 3424

Employees:
560 at the single site of operation at Fishermen's Bend, Melbourne.

Activities:
- See below, as division of ASTA.
- Established manufacturer of aerospace components for Aerospatiale and Boeing. Long-term contracts covering production of the A330/A340 floor support structure, and main and central undercarriage doors; 737-700 and 747-400 Krueger flaps; 757 and 777 rudder; 767 slat wedges; and the F/A-18C/D Hornet trailing-edge flap. In addition, in February 1997 was awarded trailing-edge flap manufacture from ship set 1 of the F/A-18E/F Super Hornet.

SUBSIDIARY

AEROSPACE TECHNOLOGIES OF AUSTRALIA LIMITED (ASTA)

Address:
226 Lorimer Street, Port Melbourne, Victoria 3207.

Telephone: +61 3 9647 3111
Facsimile: +61 3 9646 2253

Founded:
1939 as GAF (Government Aircraft Factories), succeeded by Aircraft Technologies of Australia in 1987. Acquired by present owner in 1995.

Information:
Jo Staines (Business Department).

Activities:
- Wholly owned subsidiary of Boeing Australia Limited.
- Manufacturing aerostructure components for commercial and military aircraft. Capable of structural bonding (both composite and metallic), metal fabrication and processing, and airframe assembly.
- 2 divisions, as ASTA Components at the same address, and ASTA Defence Avalon, trading as Boeing Australia's Aircraft Systems Division.

Hawker de Havilland Ltd — Australia

Corporate address:
361 Milperra Road, Bankstown, NSW 2200.

Telephone: +61 2 9772 8111
Facsimile: +61 2 9792 3604

Information:
Ken Sayers (New Projects Manager).

ACTIVITIES

- Activities include production of aerostructures for various Airbus and Boeing civil/military aeroplanes and helicopters, aircraft upgrading (including current participation in the RAAF F-111C/G and P-3 Orion programmes), and has undertaken complete licence production of aircraft for the RAAF.
- Member of the Raytheon Systems Company team proposing an AEW&C aircraft based on the Airbus A310-300, to meet the requirements of the Royal Australian Air Force under Project Wedgetail.

SONACA S.A. — Belgium

Full name:
Société Nationale de Construction Aérospatiale.

Corporate address:
Parc Industriel – Route Nationale Cinq – B-6041 Gosselies.

Telephone: +32 71 25 51 11
Facsimile: +32 71 34 40 35
Telex: 51241

Founded: 1978.

Employees: 1,200.

Information:
Marcel Devresse (Marketing and Programmes Director – *telephone* +32 71 25 54 85).

ACTIVITIES

- Full scope design, development and certification expertise. Also, production facilities and skills for both metal and advanced composite structures.
- Various fabrication, overhaul and modification programmes include fabrication of the leading-edge moving surfaces and systems for the A310/A319/A320/A321/A330/A340, fuselage sections/wing leading edge/anti-icing system for the ERJ145, wing flaps/leading edge/trailing edge for the Atlantique, doors for the A 109 and A119 Koala, reinforcing frames for the Saab 340/2000, and aft fuselage/fin plus final mating and repair, overhaul and modification for the F-16.
- Space activities include contributions to ESA's manned space infrastructure, SPOT5 Earth observation satellite and more.

Embraer

Brazil

Corporate address:
See Combat section for company details.

Embraer EMB-110 Bandeirante and C-95 series

Comments: First flown on 26 October 1968 (EMB-100/YC-95 2130 prototype), this short-haul transport for both commercial and military use went out of production in 1994. Full details, plus various illustrations, can be found in the 1996-97 edition of *WA&SD*, pages 197-198.

Embraer EMB-120 Brasilia

First flight: 27 July 1983.
Certification: Designed to comply with FAR 25 requirements. 10 May 1985 for Brazilian CTA. 9 July 1985 for FAA Type Approval, followed in 1986 by European certification. 26 August 1986 for hot-and-high version with PW118A engines, which maintain maximum output up to a temperature of ISA+15°C at sea level. On 12 March 1996, Brasilia received a special certificate of recognition from the FAA for initiating an intensive and comprehensive test of Brasilia wing de-icing, which demonstrated the aircraft's safety.
First delivery: May 1985 to Atlantic Southeast Airlines of the USA; December 1986 for first PW118-powered version, to Skywest; April 1996 for first PW118B-powered version to Skywest.
Role: Regional airliner and cargo transport, with corporate and other special versions.
Airframe life: Designed for 40,000 flight hours or 60,000 flights with minimum structural repairs or replacements due to fatigue.
Noise levels: 82.0 EPNdB take-off, 83.5 EPNdB sideline, 92.3 EPNdB approach, with PW118 engines.
Sales: 332 Brasilias had been delivered by April 1998, flown by at least 29 companies in 13 countries; the 300th went to InterBrasil Star in ER Brasilia Advanced form. World fleet has accumulated more than 4 million flight hours and carried over 60 million passengers. At the time of writing, the Brasilia commanded a 24.2% share of the worldwide sales market in its class. Lead time to build the Brasilia went from 14 months in 1994 to 8 months in 1996.

Details *(principally for the latest EMB-120 Brasilia Advanced, unless stated)*

Crew: 2 pilots, 1 flight observer.
Passengers: Normally 30. Passenger or cargo quick-change cabin layout is available in aircraft with a forward galley and toilet, offering 30 passengers plus 1,543 lb (700 kg) of baggage, or 7,716 lb (3,500 kg) of cargo. Conversion takes about 50 minutes by 3 persons. Removable bulkhead. Cargo restraint net system. Combi layout allows for 19 passengers and 2,425 lb (1,100 kg) of cargo.
Seat pitch: 31 ins (79 cm) except last 2 seats on starboard side.
Baggage compartment: 6-section overhead compartment, each section 5.3 cu ft (0.15 m^3) and with 73 lb (33 kg) capacity. Main compartment complies with class D of FAR-25.857. Volume 222.5 cu ft (6.3 m^3) and 1,543 lb (700 kg) capacity. Service door 4 ft 5.5 ins × 4 ft 3 ins (1.36 × 1.3 m).
Pressurization: AiResearch, 7 psi differential maintains the cabin at sea level up to 17,000 ft (5,200 m), or at 8,000 ft (2,440 m) at ceiling. Control by electropneumatic system (automatic) or by pneumatic system (manual).
Wing control surfaces: Ailerons (with trim tabs), outboard and inboard double-slotted Fowler flaps, plus nacelle flap.
Tail control surfaces: T-tail, with 2-segment rudder (tandem) and elevators (with trim tabs).
Flight control system: Mechanical, except for hydraulically-operated rudder and flaps.
Construction materials: Mostly metal, the fuselage having chemically milled skin reinforced by extruded stiffeners. Composite wing and tailplane leading edges (detachable/interchangeable), fin leading edge and dorsal fin.

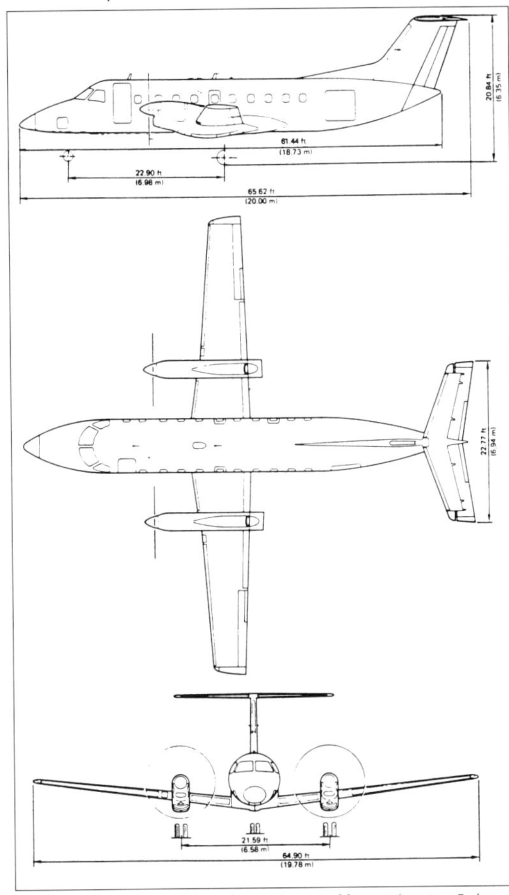

↑ Embraer EMB-120 Brasilia Advanced general layout *(courtesy Embraer)*

↑ Embraer EMB-120ER Brasilia Advanced in Rio-Sul service

Details for EMB-120 Brasilia Advanced with PW118 engines, except where indicated *(for PW118A engines, 9 lb, 4.08 kg should be added to equipped empty and basic operating weights, and the same amount deducted from the payload).*

PRINCIPAL DIMENSIONS:
Wing span: 64 ft 11 ins (19.78 m)
Maximum length: 65 ft 8 ins (20 m)
Maximum height: 20 ft 10 ins (6.35 m)

CABIN:
Length: 30 ft 9 ins (9.38 m)
Width: 6 ft 11 ins (2.1 m)
Height: 5 ft 9 ins (1.76 m)
Volume: 967.62 cu ft (27.4 m^3)
Main door size: 66.9 × 30.57 ins (1.7 × 0.77 m)

WINGS:
Aerofoil section: NACA 23018 modified/23012 (root/tip)
Area: 424.42 sq ft (39.43 m^2)
Aspect ratio: 9.923
Incidence: 2°
Dihedral: 6° 30'

TAIL UNIT:
Tailplane span: 22 ft 9 ins (6.94 m)
Tailplane area: 107.64 sq ft (10 m^2)
Vertical tail area: 74.27 sq ft (6.9 m^2)

UNDERCARRIAGE:
Type: Retractable, with steerable nosewheels (steering handle control permits ±50°, and the rudder pedals control has its authority limited to ±7°). Nosewheel centring made by castoring effect whenever the hydraulic supply is interrupted
Main wheel tyre size: 24 × 7.25-12 12PR
Nose wheel tyre size: 18 × 5.5
Wheel base: 22 ft 1 ins (6.98 m)
Wheel track: 21 ft 7 ins (6.58 m)
Turning radius: 51 ft 8 ins (15.76 m) wingtip, no slip angle

WEIGHTS:
Empty, equipped: typically 15,807 lb (7,170 kg)
Basic operating: 16,711 lb (7,580 kg)
Maximum ramp: 26,609 lb (12,070 kg)
Maximum take-off: 26,433 lb (11,990 kg)
Maximum landing: 25,794 lb (11,700 kg)
Payload: 7,319 lb (3,320 kg)

PERFORMANCE (ISA, unless stated):
Maximum cruise speed: 298 kts (343 mph) 552 km/h at 25,110 lb (11,390 kg) weight, or 315 kts (363 mph) 584 km/h with PW118A engines
Long-range speed: 264 kts (304 mph) 489 km/h, at 25,110 lb (11,390 kg) weight
Stall speed: 90 kts (104 mph) 167 km/h *with full flaps*, 17%CG
Take-off distance: 5,118 ft (1,560 m)
Landing field length: 4,528 ft (1,380 m)
Maximum climb rate: 2,000 ft (610 m) per minute, sea level
Maximum climb rate, 1 engine: 540 ft (165 m) per minute, sea level
Ceiling: 30,000 ft (9,145 m), or 27,000 ft (8,230 m) ISA+15° C, at 25,794 lb (11,700 kg), or 32,000 ft (9,750 m) with PW118As
Ceiling, 1 engine: 15,400 ft (4,700 m) or 11,600 ft (3,535 m) ISA+15° C, at 25,794 lb (11,700 kg)
Range with full fuel: 1,640 naut miles (1,887 miles) 3,037 km, basic operating weight of 16,711 lb (7,580 kg), at 29,000 ft (8,840 m),with IFR reserves; 1,370 naut miles (1,577 miles) 2,539 km at ISA+15°C; 1,460 naut miles (1,681 miles) 2,705 km ISA+20°C with PW118As
Range with 30 Passengers: 850 naut miles (978 miles) 1,575 km, or 800 naut miles (920 miles) 1,481 km with PW118As, at 30,000 ft (9,145 m), with reserves for 100 naut mile diversion and 45 minute hold

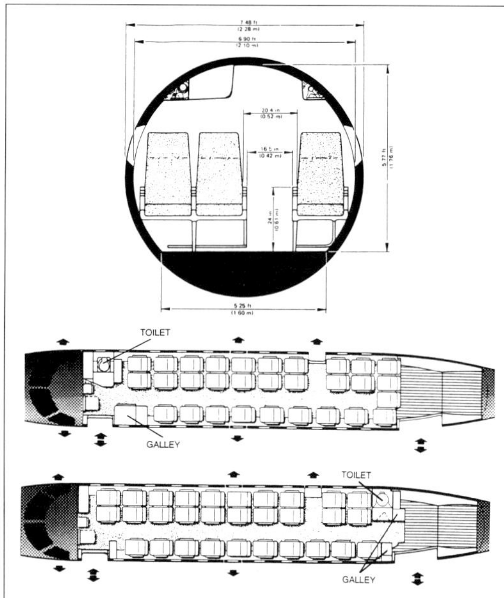

↑ **Embraer EMB-120 Brasilia Advanced cabin cross section (*top*), 30-passenger cabin layout with forward galley/toilet (*centre*), and 30-passenger aft layout (*bottom*)** *(courtesy Embraer)*

Engines: 2 Pratt & Whitney Canada PW118, PW118A or latest PW118B (for improved hot and high performance) turboprops, with 10 ft 6 ins (3.2 m) Hamilton Standard 14 RF-9 propellers. AlliedSignal GTCP36-150(A) APU can be installed in the fuselage tail to provide electrical/pneumatic power.
Engine rating: Each 1,800 shp (1,342 kW).
Fuel system: 3,312 litres usable, of 3,340 litres capacity.
Electrical system: Primary 28 volts DC supply. Power sources are 2 × 400 amp, 28 volt DC starter-generators; 2 × 150 amp, 28 volt DC auxiliary generators. The AC supply (115 and 26V) is by 2 × 250 volt-amp/400Hz single-phase static inverters, 1 as a standby. 24 volt/40 amp-hour ni-cd battery is connected to the central DC bus in parallel with the starter-generators, assisting each starter-generator during engine starting in case of no external power supply.
Hydraulic system: 3,000 psi normal pressure. 2 independent systems, each powered by a variable delivery, pressure compensated hydraulic pump, driven by the propeller gearbox, and a standby DC electric motor driven pump. Latter, and hand pump, for extending undercarriage in an emergency. First system for undercarriage retraction/extension, normal brakes (outboard pair), flaps (outboard pair), rudder powered system, nosewheel steering and airstair door actuation. Second system for emergency and parking brakes, normal brakes (inboard pair), flaps (inboard and nacelle pairs), and rudder powered system.
Braking system: Hydraulically-operated disc (see above). Parking brake by full displacement of emergency brake handle followed by a 90° locking turn.
De-icing system: Electrically-heated windshields and electrically de-iced propeller blades. Wings, fin and tailplane leading edges, air inlet and induction by-pass ducts are protected by inflatable de-icers.
Oxygen system: Option 1: Chemical, with 979 litres of usable oxygen for the crew and 11 oxygen generators for the passenger cabin. Option 2: Gaseous, with 11 dispensing units for the passenger cabin.
Fire system: Halon 1301.
Radar: See below.
Flight avionics/instrumentation: Digital navigation and communications systems. Rockwell Collins configuration is based on the Pro Line II, with 4 × 4 ins (10 × 10 cm) main navigation displays (2 EHSIs and 2 electromechanical ADIs with attitude display monitoring) and WXR-270 colour weather radar (alternative WXR-300). Options to this include a complete set of 6 × 5 ins (15.2 × 12.7 cm) EFIS. Alternative AlliedSignal Bendix/King configuration centres on the CNI-3 and EFIS-10 lines, with weather radar.

Aircraft variants:
EMB-120 was the initial production version, with 1,500 shp (1,118.6 kW) Pratt & Whitney Canada PW115 engines.
EMB-120RT quickly became the standard version, offered with either PW118 or PW118A engines. Maximum take-off weight 25,353 lb (11,500 kg). Take-off distance reduced to 4,659 ft (1,420 m). Maximum cruising speed 300 kts and 315 kts with PW118 and 118A engines respectively.
EMB-120 Cargo is the all-cargo version with a 8,818 lb (4,000 kg) payload, currently based on the EMB-120ER.

↑ **The new Embraer RJ135 regional jet for 37 passengers on roll-out in May 1998**

EMB-120QC is the quick-change version available from 1993, with floor plus sidewall protection, fire protection system, smoke curtain separating the cockpit from the cargo compartment, a 9g removable rear bulkhead and cargo restraint net. Conversion takes about 50 minutes by 3 persons.
EMB-120 Combi layout allows for 19 passengers and 2,425 lb (1,100 kg) of cargo as a mixed load, based on QC features.
EMB-120ER Basilia Advanced (provisionally known as EMB-120X) became available from 1994 as an enhanced range version, with PW118 and PW118A engines (currently also offered with PW118Bs) and, most importantly, increased take-off weight. Redesigned interchangeable leading edges for all flying surfaces, changes in flap fixing, changes in bleed air insulating materials, improved passenger door sealing for better noise reduction, redesigned interior with new double-door overhead bins of increased capacity, new passenger cabin and cockpit air-conditioning circulation, new cockpit dividing panel, frame equipped windows and windshield, improved crew seating, redesigned cockpit floor, increased cargo compartment capacity and more. Earlier Brasilias can be upgraded to Advanced form.
EMB-120EW and ***SR*** were surveillance versions, since superseded by the ERJ145SA and RS, described in the Reconnaissance section of the 1996-97 edition of *WA&SD*.

Embraer RJ135 (ERJ135)

Comments: On 16 September 1997 Embraer announced the development of this 37-passenger regional jet. It embodies the Embraer 'jet family' concept, being based on the ERJ145 design and with 90% commonality in the engines (though using the derated AE 3007A-3 model), main systems, cockpit, wings, tail unit and fuselage (though 11 ft 7 ins, 3.53 m shorter). Development is expected to require an investment of US$100 million, funded by industrial development institutions, risk-sharing suppliers and Embraer's own resources. Demand for 500 aircraft is anticipated over the next 10 years. The prototype was rolled out on 12 May 1998 and first flew on 4 July that year, allowing the first delivery in October 1999. On 9 October 1997,

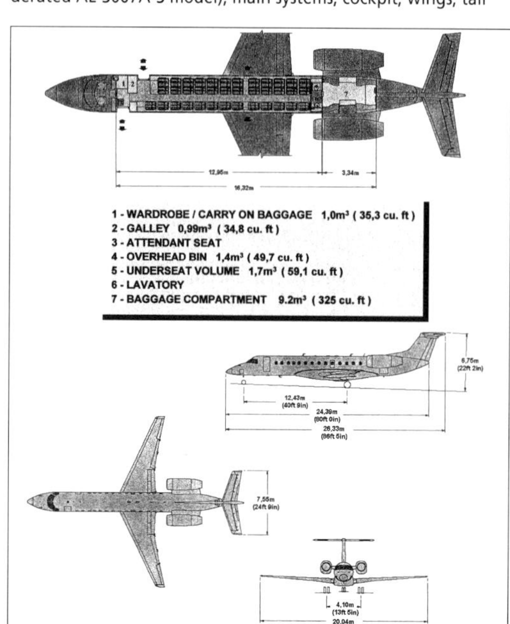

↑ **Embraer RJ135 interior arrangement and general arrangement** *(courtesy Embraer)*

Details for ERJ135

PRINCIPAL DIMENSIONS:
Wing span: 65 ft 9 ins (20.04 m)
Length: 86 ft 5 ins (26.33 m)
Maximum height: 22 ft 2 ins (6.75 m)

CABIN:
Length: 42 ft 6 ins (12.95 m)
Width: 6 ft 11 ins (2.1 m), and 5 ft 1 ins (1.56 m) at floor
Height: 6 ft (1.82 m)
Main door size: 5 ft 7 ins × 2 ft 4 ins (1.7 × 0.71 m)
Height to sill: 5 ft 4 ins (1.63 m)
Baggage compartment volume: 325 cu ft (9.2 m^3)

WINGS:
Aerofoil section: Supercritical
Area: 551 sq ft (51.18 m^2)
Aspect ratio: 7.85
Sweepback: 22° 43' 48" at 25% chord

TAIL UNIT:
Tailplane span: 24 ft 9 ins (7.55 m)
Tailplane area: 120.6 sq ft (11.2 m^2)
Fin and rudder area: 77.5 sq ft (7.2 m^2)

UNDERCARRIAGE:
Type: Retractable, with steerable nosewheels (steering controlled by both steering handle on the pilot's lateral console and rudder pedals; handle permits ±50°, and the rudder pedals permit additional ±7°). Nosewheel centring made by castoring effect whenever the hydraulic supply is interrupted
Wheel base: 40 ft 9 ins (12.43 m)
Wheel track: 13 ft 5.5 ins (4.1 m)

WEIGHTS:
Basic operating: 24,471 lb (11,100 kg)
Maximum zero fuel: 34,392 lb (15,600 kg)
Maximum take-off: 41,887 lb (19,000 kg)
Maximum landing: 40,785 lb (18,500 kg)
Payload: 9,921 lb (4,500 kg)
Maximum fuel: 9,200 lb (4,173 kg)

DESIGN PERFORMANCE:
Maximum cruise speed: Mach 0.78
Take-off field length: 5,415 ft (1,650 m) at MTOW, ISA, sea level
Take-off field length for 800 naut mile range: 4,134 ft (1,260 m), ISA, sea level
Landing field length: 4,462 ft (1,360 m) at MLW, sea level
Time to climb to 35,000 ft (10,668 m): 23 minutes
Range with 37 passengers at 100 kg each: 1,350 naut miles (1,553 miles) 2,500 km
Range with 37 passengers at 100 kg each, ISA + 31° C: 620 naut miles (714 miles) 1,149 km

Embraer announced that the French regional airline Flandre Air will be the European launch customer, having placed 8 firm orders and 12 options, which could be either the ERJ135 or ERJ145. Unit cost for the ERJ135 in early 1998 was US$11.8 million. On 26 January 1998, Embraer closed a preliminary commercial agreement with Wexford Management LLC of Greenwich, Connecticut, USA, for the sale of the airliner, having signed a letter of intent to buy 20, with 20 options. The first US regional airline to order was Business Express (20 plus 40 options). By 27 May 1998, 73 on firm order and 122 options, with Continental Express ordering 25 (50 options).

Embraer RJ145 (ERJ145)

Note: When the name Embraer is not used before the aircraft designation, the designation becomes ERJ145.
First flight: 11 August 1995.
Certification: FAR and JAR Pt 25, FAR Pt 36, ICAO Annex 16 and FAR Pt 121; November 1996 for Brazilian CTA, 16 December 1996 for FAA, 15 May 1997 for European Joint Aviation Authorities. 10 March 1997 for FAA approval to fly safely into known icing conditions and operate in cold weather environment.
First delivery: To Continental Express in the USA, which began regular revenue flights on 6 April 1997. May 1997 to Regional Airlines of France and Rio-Sul of Brazil.
Role: 50-seat regional airliner.
Airframe life: Designed for 75,000 flight hours or 60,000 flights, with minimum structural repairs or replacement due to fatigue, when used in the commuter role.
Airport limits: Standard version maximum take-off weight and main LDG tyres (30 × 9.5-14) at 130 psi:

RIGID PAVEMENT	K(M N/m³)	ACN
	150	11.0
	80	11.7
	40	12.3
	20	12.9
FLEXIBLE PAVEMENT	California Bearing Ratio	ACN
	15%	9.4
	10%	10.1
	6%	11.6
	3%	13.1

Noise levels: Expected levels were 82 EPNdB take-off, 87 EPNdB sideline, 92 EPNdB approach. Expected average cabin noise level during maximum cruise was 75.7 dBA.
Sales: 182 firm orders by 27 May 1998, with options for 246. Some 55 then delivered, to Continental Express of the USA (25, against 50 firm orders and 150 options), Regional Airlines of France (6, against 10 firm orders), British Regional Airlines (5, against 15 firm and 5 options), PGA – Portugália Airlines of Portugal (6, against 6 firm and 2 options), Rio-Sul Linhas Aéreas of Brazil (7, against 15 firm and 15 options), SIVAM of Brazil (8 ordered), American Eagle of the USA (5 delivered of 42 ordered and 25 options), Luxair of Luxembourg (2 ordered plus 2 options), City Airlines of Sweden (1 ordered plus 4 options), Wexford Management LLC of USA (20 ordered plus 20 options), European Regional Airlines of Spain (2 ordered plus 3 options), Trans States Airlines of the USA (1 delivered of 9 ordered and 18 options), plus 2 orders and 2 options from undisclosed customer/s.
Crew: 2 pilots and 1 flight observer.
Passengers: 50, at 31 ins (79 cm) seat pitch.
Baggage compartment: 325 cu ft (9.2 m³), 2,205 lb (1,000 kg). Overhead bin in 11 sections with 67.1 cu ft (1.9 m³) of space, originally intended to have 635 lb (288 kg) capacity but now 789 lb (358 kg). Under-seat volume 79.8 cu ft (2.26 m³), 992 lb (450 kg). Wardrobe and stowage compartment 48.9 cu ft (1.38 m³). Total volume 520.8 cu ft (14.74 m³).
Galley: 42 cu ft (1.2 m³), catering 353 lb (160 kg) normal. Optional configurations allow 50, 56 and 81 cu ft (1.4, 1.6 and 2.3 m³) of volume, with catering 441, 529 and 705 lb (200, 240 and 320 kg) respectively, retaining 50 passengers but reducing to 48-49 with increased half trolley capacity and/or increased wardrobe space.
Pressurization: Liebherr system of 7.8 psi differential to maintain cabin at maximum 8,000 ft (2,440 m) to an operational ceiling of 37,000 ft (11,275 m).
Wing control surfaces: Aileron, 2 double-slotted flaps and 2 ground spoilers (external panel also acts as a flight speed brake) per wing.
Tail control surfaces: 2-segment rudder (tandem) where the trailing rudder is automatically deflected as a function of the forward rudder deflection, and elevators (with tabs).

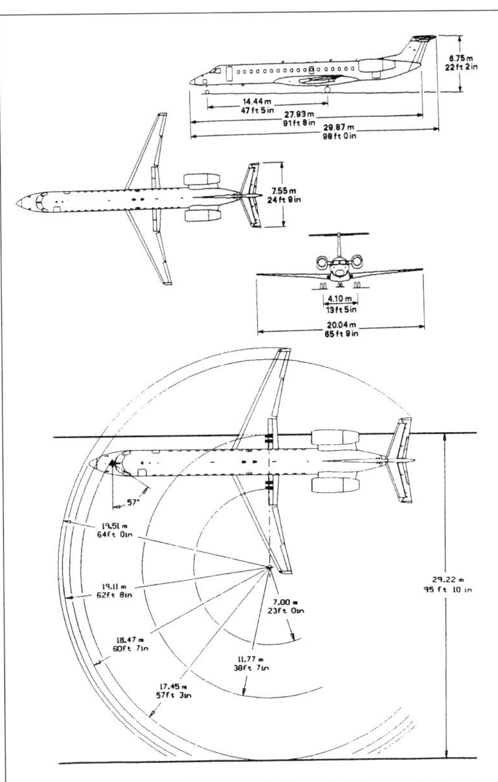

↑ Embraer RJ145 general arrangement (*top*) and turning circles (*bottom*) *(courtesy Embraer)*

Fuselage: Basically a lengthened Brasilia structure, with 3 × 7050 hand forged/machined frames providing the necessary basis for the continuous wing to fuselage attachments, and special 7050 machined frames at the tail cone providing the basis for similar attachments of the pylons and fin.
Flight control system: Mechanically actuated elevators, and the dual rudder and ailerons are power operated. For the rudder and aileron control systems, artificial feel and centring units are provided. All trims are electrically actuated. Flap panels are electrically actuated and electronically controlled. Speed brake/ground spoilers are hydraulically actuated and electronically controlled. Automatic flight control system. Stall protection system with stick shaker and stick pusher.

Details for ERJ145 *(versions as stated)*

PRINCIPAL DIMENSIONS:
Wing span: 65 ft 9 ins (20.04 m)
Maximum length: 98 ft (29.87 m)
Maximum height: 22 ft 2 ins (6.75 m)

CABIN:
Length: 54 ft 1 ins (16.49 m)
Width: 6 ft 11 ins (2.1 m), and 5 ft 1 ins (1.56 m) at floor
Height: 6 ft (1.82 m)
Volume: 1,871.7 cu ft (53 m³)
Main door size: 5 ft 7 ins × 2 ft 4 ins (1.7 × 0.71 m)
Height to sill: 5 ft 4 ins (1.63 m)

WINGS:
Aerofoil section: Supercritical
Area: 551 sq ft (51.18 m²)
Aspect ratio: 7.85
Sweepback: 22° 43′ 48″ at 25% chord

TAIL UNIT:
Tailplane span: 24 ft 9 ins (7.55 m)
Tailplane area: 120.6 sq ft (11.2 m²)
Fin and rudder area: 77.5 sq ft (7.2 m²)

UNDERCARRIAGE:
Type: Retractable, with steerable nosewheels (steering controlled by both steering handle on the pilot's lateral console and rudder pedals; handle permits ±50°, and the rudder pedals permit additional ±7°). Nosewheel centring made by castoring effect whenever the hydraulic supply is interrupted
Main wheel tyre size: 30 × 9.5-14
Nose wheel tyre size: 19.5 × 6.75-8
Wheel base: 47 ft 5 ins (14.45 m)
Wheel track: 13 ft 5.5 ins (4.1 m)
Turning radius: 95 ft 10 ins (29.22 m) for 180° turn

DESIGN WEIGHTS:
Empty, equipped: 24,436 lb (11,084 kg) for standard and ER
Ramp: 42,549 lb (19,300 kg) standard, 45,645 lb (20,700 kg) for ER
Basic operating: 25,540 lb (11,585 kg) for standard and ER
Maximum zero fuel weight: 37,700 lb (17,100 kg) for standard and ER, 39,463 lb (17,900 kg) for LR
Maximum take-off: 42,328 lb (19,200 kg) standard, 45,415 lb (20,600 kg) for ER, 48,501 lb (22,000 kg) for LR
Maximum landing: 41,226 lb (18,700 kg) for standard and ER, 42,549 lb (19,300 kg) for LR
Payload: 12,158 lb (5,515 kg) for standard and ER

DESIGN PERFORMANCE:
Maximum operating speed: Mach 0.78
Maximum cruise speed: 451 kts (519 mph) 836 km/h
High cruise speed: Mach 0.75, or 430 kts (495 mph) 796 km/h standard, 416 kts (479 mph) 770 km/h for ER, 95% power
Long-range cruise speed: 360 kts (415 mph) 667 km/h
Stall speed: 117 kts (135 mph) 217 km/h *clean*, 97 kts (112 mph) 180 km/h *with flaps*
Take-off field length (FAR Pt 25): 4,921 ft (1,500 m) standard, 5,741 ft (1,750 m) for ER at sea level, ISA
Landing field length (FAR Pt 121): 4,232 ft (1,290 m) for standard and ER, 45° *flaps*, sea level, typical 50 passenger weight
Maximum climb rate: 2,560 ft (780 m) per minute standard, 2,150 ft (655 m) per minute for ER
Maximum climb rate, 1 engine: 660 ft (201 m) per minute standard, 520 ft (158 m) per minute for ER
Time to climb to 30,000 ft, MTOW: 16 minutes
Ceiling: 37,000 ft (11,280 m)
Ceiling, 1 engine: 20,000 ft (6,095 m)
Range with full fuel: 1,430 naut miles (1,645 miles) 2,648 km at sea level, with 15 passengers, with reserve
Range with 50 Passengers: 800 naut miles (920 miles) 1,480 km standard, 1,270-1,330 naut miles (1,462-1,531 miles) 2,353-2,465 km for ER, 1,600 naut miles (1,842 miles) 2,965 km for LR

↑ PGA – Portugália Airlines received its third Embraer RJ145 on 6 November 1997 and fourth the next month

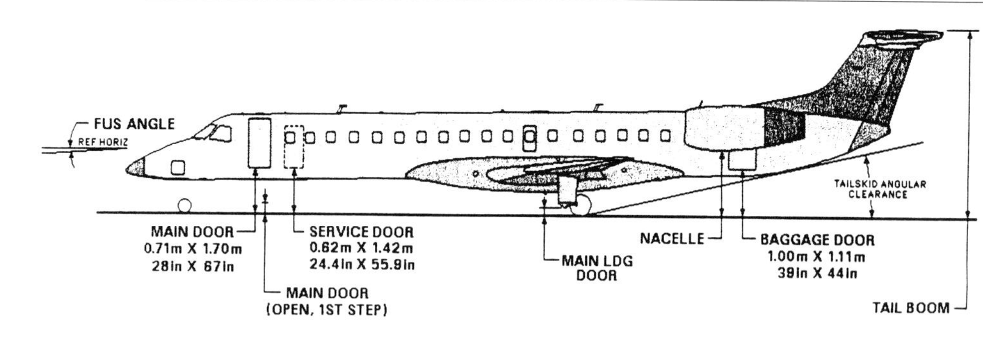

	FUS ANGLE	MAIN DOOR	MAIN DOOR (OPEN, 1ST STEP)	SERVICE DOOR	MAIN LDG DOOR	NACELLE	BAGGAGE DOOR	TAIL BOOM	TAILSKID ANGULAR CLEARANCE
MAXIMUM	1° 21′ 24″	1.628 m 5 ft 4 in	0.480 m 1 ft 7 in	1.592 m 5 ft 2¾ in	0.279 m 11 in	2.405 m 7 ft 10¾ in	1.760 m 5 ft 9¼ in	6.748 m 22 ft 1¾ in	12° 41′ 0″
MINIMUM	0° 52′ 0″	1.508 m 5 ft 11¼ in	0.360 m 1 ft 2¼ in	1.479 m 4 ft 10¼ in	0.206 m 8 in	2.296 m 7 ft 6½ in	1.644 m 5 ft 4¾ in	6.588 m 21 ft 7¼ in	11° 43′ 59″

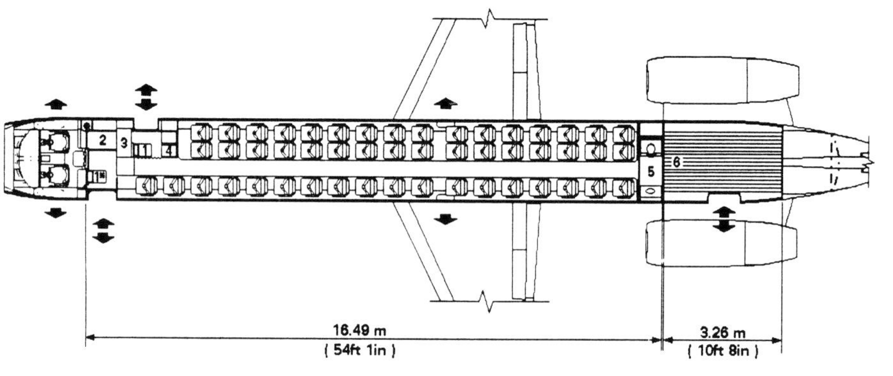

↑ Embraer RJ145 ground clearances (*top*), and basic 50-passenger layout with *1* attendant seat (1 optional), *2* wardrobe/carry-on baggage, *3* stowage compartment, *4* galley, *5* toilet, and *6* baggage compartment *(courtesy Embraer)*

Construction materials: Mostly metal (generally aluminium alloy), with extensive chemical milling. Composites aft wing-stub cell upper skin (carbonfibre/Nomex honeycomb sandwich), wing control surfaces, fin leading edge and dorsal fin (Kevlar/glassfibre/Nomex honeycomb sandwich), fin-to-tailplane fairing (Kevlar/glassfibre) and elevator tabs.
Engines: 2 Allison AE 3007A turbofans for ERJ145 and ERJ145ER, with optional hydraulically-actuated thrust reversers;
AE 3007A1s with more thermodynamic thrust for ERJ145LR for improved climb and hot weather cruise performance, and optional for ER.
Engine rating: Each AE 3007A offers 7,040 lbf (31.32 kN) sea level static, ISA, with FADEC.
Fuel system: In wing tanks, each half wing tank holding 2,621 litres of usable fuel. Tank capacity 9,200 lb (4,173 kg) for ERJ145ER and 10,986 lb (4,983 kg) for LR.
Electrical system: 4 × 28 volt DC, 400 amp brushless generators. Also 400 amp/28 volt DC APU starter-generator. AC power (115 VAC) using 1 × 250 volt-amps/400Hz single-phase static inverter. 2 × 24 VDC/43 amp-hour ni-cd batteries. An independent back-up 24 VDC lead-acid sealed battery is installed to supply stabilized power for equipment that may be affected by electrical transients in the main generation system.
Hydraulic system: 3,000 psi normal pressure. 2 independent systems, each powered by an engine-driven pump and a back-up electric motor driven pump. System 1 for the rudder, nosewheel steering, undercarriage, main door, ailerons, outboard brakes and ground spoiler. System 2 for rudder, inboard brakes, emergency/parking brake, ailerons, thrust reversers (optional) and speed brake/ground spoiler.
Braking system: Multi-disc type, with hydraulic and mechanical actuation, with carbon heatsink. Main brake system and an emergency/parking brake subsystem.
De-icing system: Air intake of the nacelles, and wing and tailplane leading edges use bleed air anti-icing. Electrically heated windshields, pitot-static tubes, angle-of-attack sensors, total air temperature probe, etc.
Oxygen system: Gaseous crew system. Passenger system consists of chemical generators.
Radar: Weather radar.
Flight avionics/instrumentation: Main characteristics are dual central integrated avionics computer, encompassing functions such as displays driving, autopilot/flight director, and EICAS. All glass cockpit based on Honeywell Primus 1000 EFIS suite with five 8 × 7 ins (20 × 18 cm) CRT displays with multi-reversionary capabilities (2 primary flight displays, 2 multi-function displays and 1 EICAS display). Standard and optional equipment satisfies FAR-25, IFR operation and FAR-121.

Aircraft variants:
ERJ145 is the standard version, with an 800 naut mile range with 50 passengers. AE 3007A engines.
ERJ145ER is the extended range version, offering a full-passenger range of 1,270+ naut miles. Increased ramp and MTO weights, but basic operating, maximum zero fuel, landing and payload weights unchanged. Optional AE 3007A1 engines.
ERJ145LR is the new long-range version with AE 3007A1 engines for improved climb and hot weather cruise performance. Higher weights.
ERJ145 AEW&C, ERJ145SA and RS are special mission airborne early warning and control, surveillance and remote sensing versions, as detailed in the Electronic section.

Embraer RJ170 (ERJ170)

Comments: A decision whether or not to begin development of this 70-seat regional airliner had not been made by June 1998. Though still embodying the Embraer 'jet family' concept, it would have a new wider fuselage, allowing a possible 4-abreast seating arrangement, while the wing would be based on that of the ERJ145 but of increased area due to a 2 ft (0.61 m) wing-root extension; leading-edge slats would be added. Power is likely to be 2 uprated AE 3007s, in the 10,000 lbf (44.5 kN) class. Maximum cruise speed could be about Mach 0.8, and range 1,597 naut miles (1,839 miles) 2,960 km.

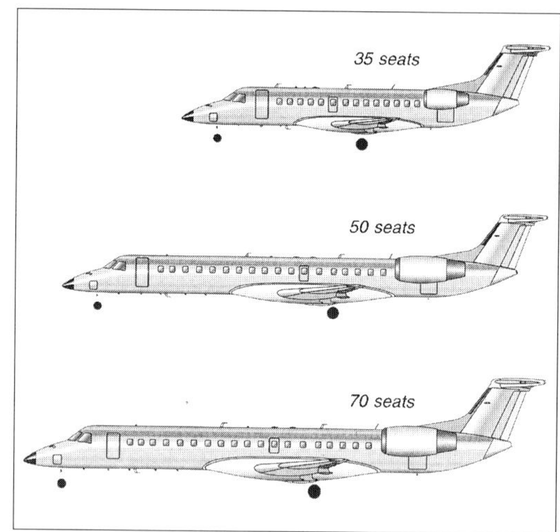

↑ Embraer RJ135 (*top*), RJ145 (*centre*) and RJ170 (*bottom*) *(courtesy Embraer)*

Bombardier Aerospace — Canada

Corporate address:
See Combat section for company details under Bombardier Inc.

BOMBARDIER REGIONAL AIRCRAFT DIVISION

Corporate address:
123 Garratt Boulevard, MS N42-43, Downsview, Ontario M3K 1Y5.

Founded: August 1992.

Information:
Colin S. Fisher (Manager, Public Relations – *telephone* +1 416 375 3026, *facsimile* +1 416 375 4529).

Activities:
▪ Marketing, sales, contracts and customer support for the Canadair Regional Jet and de Havilland Dash 8 series.

Bombardier Canadair Regional Jet, Corporate Jetliner and CRJ Series 700

Details: For Regional Jet Series 200 (except where indicated).
First flight: 10 May 1991.
Certification: 31 July 1992 (Transport Canada Type Approval based on FAA FAR 25, Amendment 62), 14 January 1993 for European JAA change 13, and 21 January 1993 for FAA.
First delivery: 19 October 1992 to Lufthansa CityLine of Germany, starting services on 1 November.
Role: Medium-range regional airliner.
Airframe life: Economic repair life of 80,000 cycles, crack free life of 40,000 cycles, and service life 30 years (based on 2,400 flights per year).
Noise levels: 78.6 EPNdB take off, 92.1 EPNdB approach, 82.4 EPNdB sideline. Average measured cabin noise approximately 77 dBA.
Sales: Total of 360 Regional Jets, Corporate Jetliners and CRJ Series 700s ordered by 19 March 1998, of which 221 had been delivered. Orders from Adria Airways (3), Air Canada (26, all delivered), Air Littoral (19, all but 4 delivered), Air Nostrum (5), American Eagle (25 Series 700, delivery from 2001), Atlantic Coast Airlines (23, of which 7 delivered), Atlantic Southeast Airlines (30, of which 8 delivered), BRIT AIR (14 Series 100s and 2 Series 700s, of which 12 Series 100s delivered), Canadair Regional Jet (Corporate variants 12, all delivered), COMAIR (80, of which 57 delivered), DAC Air (2 delivered), Lauda Air (8 delivered), Lufthansa (35, of which 32 delivered), Maersk (5), Mesa (32, of which 13 delivered), Midway (10), Saeaga (1 delivered), SkyWest (10 delivered), South African Express (6, 4 delivered), Southern Winds (2 delivered) and Tyrolean (10, of which 8 delivered).
Crew: 2 pilots.
Passengers: 50. Drop-down air stair for open ramp parking; collapsible handrails for airbridge capability.
Seat pitch: Universal interior has generally 31 ins (79 cm), but with 32 ins (81.3 cm) overwing pitch in FAA configuration and 37 ins (94 cm) overwing pitch in optional JAA and Alternate configurations.

↑ Bombardier Canadair Regional Jet operated by Atlantic Coast Airlines

Galley: 'Optimized G1' option with facilities including 4 standard containers and 4 half-size carts. Return Catering option for JAA configuration adds a second galley with 4 containers and 2 half-size carts in the aft baggage area. Alternate configuration has an aft-facing forward galley with 4 Atlas standard containers (each set of 2 containers can be replaced with optional oven) and 6 half-size carts, and a forward-facing forward galley with 5 Atlas standard containers and 2 half-size carts.
Pressurization: 8.3 psi maximum cabin differential.
Baggage volume: 9.7 cu ft (0.28 m^3) per passenger, comprising wardrobe, overhead bin, under seat and in the 318 cu ft (9 m^3) aft baggage hold (FAA configuration). Aft baggage hold of 306 cu ft (8.66 m^3) in optional JAA configuration, or 277 cu ft (7.84 m^3) in the Return Catering configuration with fore and aft galleys, or 229 cu ft (6.48 m^3) in Alternate configuration with 2 forward galleys.
Baggage hold capacity: 3,500 lb (1,588 kg) in FAA configuration, or 3,350 lb (1,520 kg) in optional JAA configuration, or 2,700 lb (1,225 kg) in optional Alternate configuration.
Size of baggage door: 2 ft 9 ins height × 3 ft 7 ins width (0.84 × 1.09 m). Height to sill 5 ft 3.5 ins (1.61 m).
Wing control surfaces: Ailerons, and double-slotted flaps with 2 independent motors and 2 channel electric control unit. Flight spoilers, spoileron and 2 ground spoilers per wing.
Tail control surfaces: Elevators and rudder with 2 channel yaw dampers.
Flight control system: Multiple redundancy. 2 or 3 power control units per surface. Mechanical, except for fly-by-wire spoilers/spoilerons. Automatic flight control system, with 2 independent flight directors and a fail-safe autopilot.
Construction materials: Metal, with use of composites for the winglets, wing to fuselage fairings, tailcone, various doors and panels, main cabin floor, and more.
Engines: 2 General Electric CF34-3B1 turbofans. AlliedSignal GTCP 36-150 APU, capable of starting main engines at 13,000 ft (3,960 m), 30 kVA generator power available at FL370.
Engine rating: Each 8,729 lbf (38.83 kN) normal take-off (flat rated ISA+6.1°C), or 9,220 lbf (41 kN) APR (flat rated ISA+6.1°C).

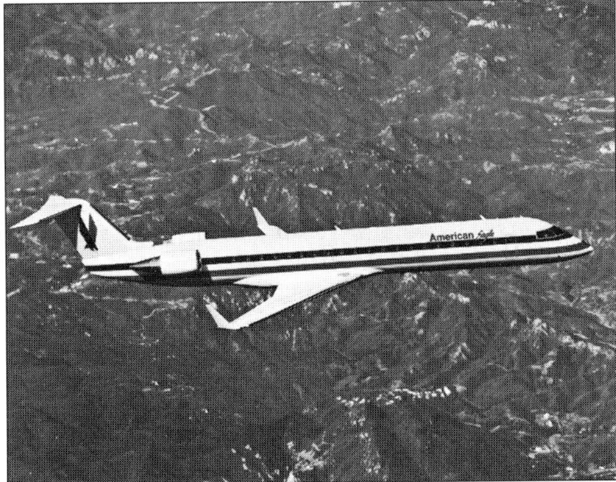

↑ Impression of the Bombardier Canadair CRJ Series 700, to be delivered to American Eagle from the year 2001

Fuel system: 9,380 lb (4,255 kg) or 5,500 litres for Series 200, 14,305 lb (6,489 kg) or 8,082 litres for Series 200ER/LR.
Electrical system: 3-phase 115 volt/400 Hz AC supply with 2 × 30 kVA engine-driven generators, with APU and air-driven generator back-up. 28 volt DC supply using transformer/rectifiers. 17 amp-hour ni-cd battery.

Hydraulic system: 3 systems, each 3,000 psi.
Braking system: Multiple discs and anti skid.
De-icing system: Bleed air anti-icing for wing leading edges and engine air intakes, and electric system for cockpit glazing and sensors.
Fire system: Engine and APU fire protection comprises 2 loop detection and 3 extinguishing bottles.
Radar: Weather radar standard. Optional Rockwell Collins split-scan radar.
Flight avionics/instrumentation: Rockwell Collins Pro Line 4 integrated digital avionics, with standard equipment of 2 primary flight displays, 2 multi-function displays, and 2 engine indication and crew alert system displays (EICAS), each 7 ins × 6 ins (18 × 15 cm). Autopilot, flight management and central avionics maintenance functions are handled by an integrated avionics processing system (IAPS). Dual automatic flight control system (AFCS), with dual independent flight directors, Category II approach capability, single fail passive autopilot, dual yaw damper, dual ADF receivers, dual DME transceivers, 2 radio tuning units (RTU), 2 Mode S transponders, digital weather radar (see Radar), dual digital air data computers, 2 data concentrator units (DCU), dual VHF coms radios, and dual navigation radios (VOR, ILD, MKR). Standard avionics are Rockwell Collins TCAS, Artex emergency location, Avtech digital audio system, Sextant stall protection system, Fairchild cockpit voice recorder, Loral flight data recorder, Avtech passenger address system, Sundstrand ground proximity warning system and windshear detection and recovery guidance. Other avionics upon request, including optional Rockwell Collins single or dual flight management system, third DCU, third VHF, dual Litton inertial reference system, Rockwell Collins split scan radar, Coltech selective calling (Selcal), and Rockwell Collins HF transceiver. Optional Cat IIIa capability with head-up guidance system, flight management system, INS and second radio altimeter.

Aircraft variants:
Series 100 was the initial standard version, with CF34-3A1 engines. Superseded by the Series 200. Weights and

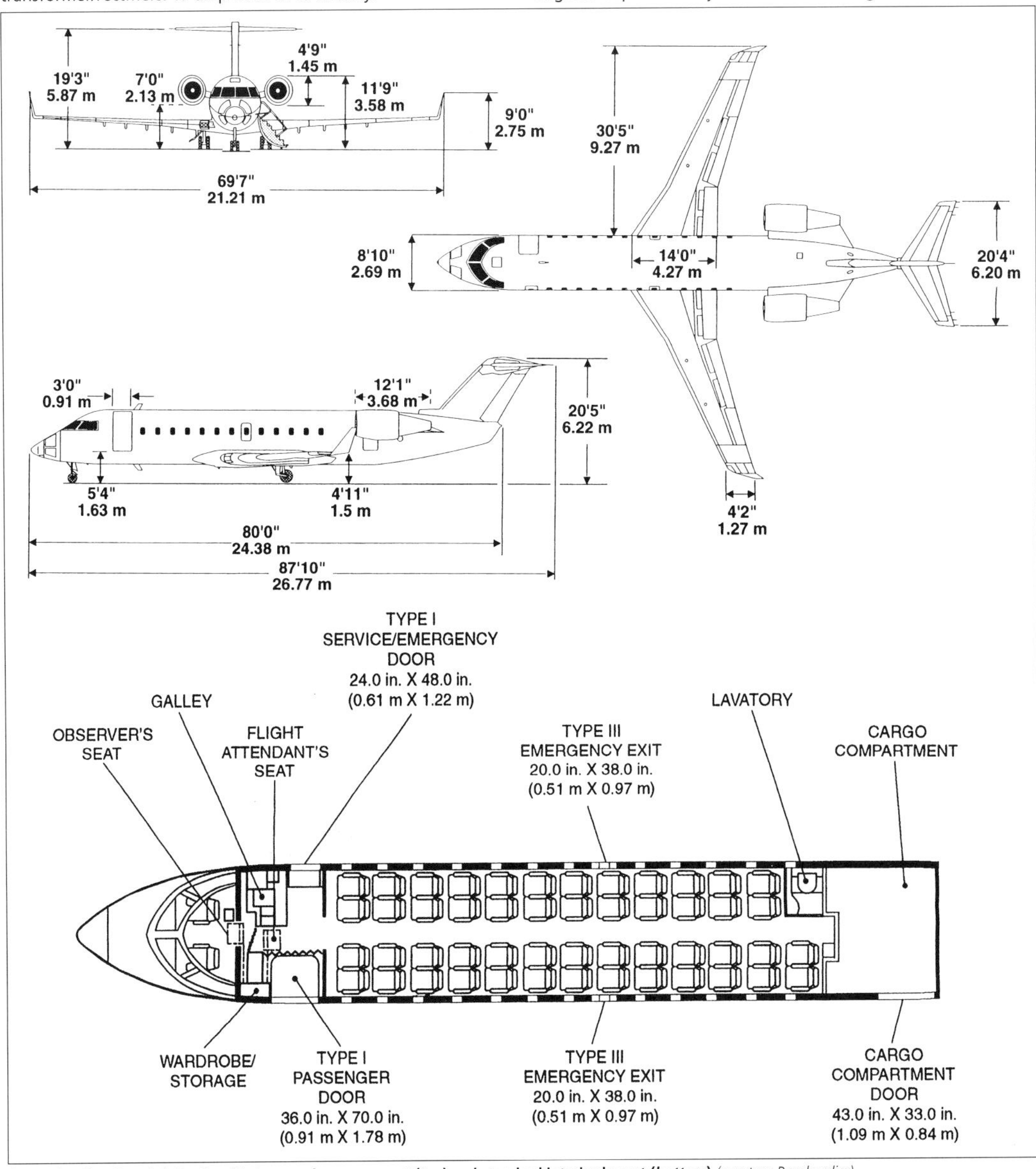

↑ Bombardier Canadair Regional Jet general arrangement (*top*) and standard interior layout (*bottom*) *(courtesy Bombardier)*

performance were detailed in the 1996-97 edition of *WA&SD*, page 202.
Series 100ER was the increased weight version to offer a higher fuel load for extended range, with CF34-3A1 engines. Superseded by the Series 200ER. Weights and performance were detailed in the 1996-97 edition of *WA&SD*, page 202.
Series 100LR was the initial long-range version, certificated in 1994. CF34-3A1 engines. Take-off weight increased to 53,000 lb (24,040 kg). Superseded by the Series 200LR.
Series 200 is the current standard version, with higher operating empty weight and slightly reduced payload compared with Series 100. More powerful CF34-3B1 engines. Same fuel capacity as Series 100, but engines have lower SFC to offer greater range and improvements to initial cruise altitude and cruise speed. Introduced 8° flap setting to better climb. First delivered to Tyrolean in January 1996. New Universal interior, with retrofit capability between FAA and JAA configurations, with benefits including the potential for added galley capacity.
Series 200ER is the current extended range version. CF34-3B1 engines. Higher operating empty weight and slightly reduced payload compared with Series 200ER. Reduced take-off and landing distances.
Series 200LR is the current long-range version. CF34-3B1 engines.
Series 200B, 200B ER and 200B LR are 'hot and high' options to the current Series 200 models.
Corporate Jetliner is a business version of the Regional Jet, with 2+1 crew and seating for 18-35 persons. CF34-3B1 engines. Rockwell Collins Pro Line 4 6-tube EFIS. In 30 passenger form it has a basic operating weight of 31,800 lb (14,424 kg), maximum take-off weight of 51,000 lb (23,133 kg) plus options for up to 53,250 lb (24,154 kg), cruise speeds of Mach 0.74-0.8, and a maximum range of 2,250 naut miles (2,590 miles) 4,167 km. First delivery to the Xerox Corporation in June 1993.
Canadair Special Edition (SE), is a version of Regional Jet for trans-Atlantic corporate travel, available to special order and offering a cabin of similar size to the Global Express. 3,000 naut miles (3,455 miles) 5,556 km range with original CF34-3A1 engines and 3,120 naut miles (3,593 miles) 5,782 km range with currently offered CF34-3B1s. State-of-the-art avionics, with dual Rockwell Collins FMS 4200 flight management system, dual Litton inertial reference system, third VHF, Coltech selective calling (Selcal), and dual Rockwell Collins HF transceiver as part of the extra features of the Rockwell Collins Pro Line 4 6-tube EFIS suite. Rockwell Collins digital weather radar. 2+1 crew and 14 to 19 passengers with armchairs, club seating and divans. First customer was TAG Aeronautics Ltd. Same external principal dimensions as Regional Jet and same cabin sizes, except maximum cabin width (centreline) is given as 8 ft 2 ins (2.49 m), floor area 326 sq ft (30.29 m^2) and cabin volume at 1,900 cu ft (53.8 m^3), both excluding cockpit and baggage, while baggage volume is 275 cu ft (7.79 m^3). Maximum ramp weight 53,250 lb (24,154 kg), maximum take-off weight 53,000 lb (24,040 kg), maximum landing weight 47,000 lb (21,319 kg), maximum zero-fuel weight 39,500 lb (17,917 kg), basic operating weight 33,900 lb (15,377 kg), maximum payload 5,600 lb (2,540 kg), and maximum fuel weight 18,305 lb (8,303 kg), the additional 4,000 lb (1,814 kg) of fuel in 2 new aft auxiliary tanks. Long-range cruise speed and ceiling are the same as for Regional Jet, but high speed cruise is Mach 0.8, balanced field length 6,294 ft (1,918 m) at sea level (ISA, MGTOW), and landing distance is 2,910 ft (887 m) at sea level (MLW). Take-off EPNdB is 78.7.
CRJ Series 700 (CRJ-700) is a 70-passenger 'stretched' derivative of the RJ, to be available in standard and ER versions, with a B Model option for 74 passengers. Programme launched 21 January 1997. Initial orders from BRIT AIR and American Eagle. Expected to first fly in 1999 and receive US and European airworthiness certification in 2000. Deliveries to American Eagle in early 2001. Powered by General Electric CF34-8C1 turbofans, of 12,670 lbf (56.36 kN) take-off and 13,790 lbf (61.34 kN) APR ratings each. Baggage volume 832 cu ft (23.56 m^3). Rockwell Collins Pro Line 4 6-tube EFIS/EICAS, dual AHRS, TCAS and Rockwell Collins digital weather radar. Flight Dynamics HGS 2000 head-up guidance system. Sextant Avionique is prime contractor for the integrated secondary flight control system, which comprises the spoiler and the horizontal stabilizer control systems, including actuators. Sextant also supplies the stall protection system. Also the first application of Sextant's solid-state LCD integrated standby instrument (ISI) on a regional transport. Noise levels 84.8 EPNdB at take-off, 93.0 EPNdB approach, and 87.4 EPNdB sideline.

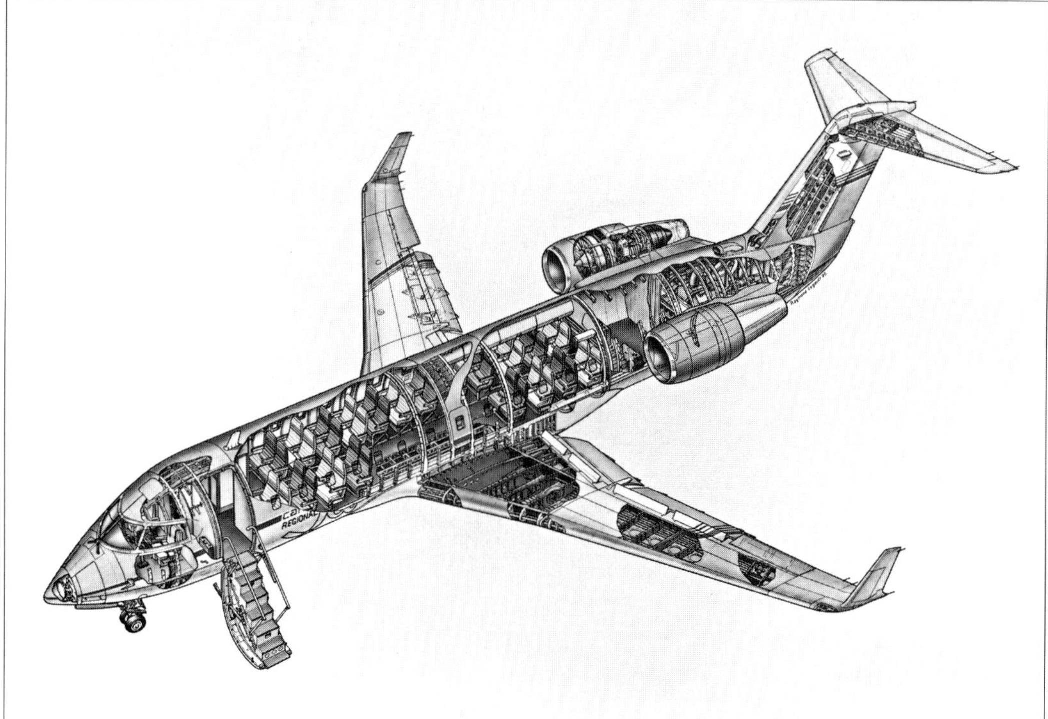

↑ **Bombardier Canadair Regional Jet cutaway** *(courtesy Bombardier)*

Details for Regional Jet series and CRJ Series 700 (CRJ-700)

PRINCIPAL DIMENSIONS:
Wing span: 69 ft 7 ins (21.21 m), except 75 ft 6 ins (23.01 m) *for CRJ-700*
Maximum length: 87 ft 10 ins (26.77 m), except 106 ft 4 ins (32.41 m) *for CRJ-700*
Maximum height: 20 ft 5 ins (6.22 m), except 23 ft 11 ins (7.29 m) *for CRJ-700*

CABIN:
Length: 48 ft 5 ins (14.76 m), 68 ft 2 ins (20.78 m) *for CRJ-700*, both excluding cockpit
Width: 8 ft 5 ins (2.57 m) maximum, 7 ft 2 ins (2.18 m) floor, except 7 ft (2.13 m) floor *for CRJ-700*
Height: 6 ft 1.5 ins (1.87 m) maximum
Floor area: 346 sq ft (32.14 m^2), except 477 sq ft (44.31 m^2) *for CRJ-700*, both excluding cockpit
Volume: 2,015 cu ft (57.06 m^3), except 2,872 cu ft (81.32 m^3) *for CRJ-700*
Main passenger door: 5 ft 10 ins height × 3 ft width (1.78 m × 0.91 m). Height to sill 5 ft 3.5 ins (1.61 m), except 5 ft 7.5 ins (1.71 m) *for CRJ-700*
Cargo door: airliners only
Emergency exits: Type III in each side of fuselage, plus Type I for main entrance and service doors. Overhead crew exit

WINGS:
Area: 520.4 sq ft (48.35 m^2) net, except 738.7 sq ft (68.63 m^2) *for CRJ-700*
Aspect ratio: 8.85
Sweepback: 24.8° at 25% chord
Dihedral: 2.33°

TAIL UNIT:
Tailplane span: 20 ft 4 ins (6.2 m)

UNDERCARRIAGE:
Type: Retractable, with steerable nosewheels. Twin wheels on each unit
Wheel base: 37 ft 4.5 ins (11.39 m)
Wheel track: 10 ft 5 ins (3.18 m)
Turning radius: 75 ft (22.86 m) for 180° turn, with 11 ft (3.35 m) margin, except 74.1 ft (22.6 m) *for CRJ-700*

WEIGHTS:
Empty, operating: 30,270 lb (13,730 kg) *for Series 200*, 30,292 lb (13,740 kg) *for Series 200ER and Series 200LR*, 43,200 lb (19,595 kg) *for CRJ-700 and CRJ-700ER*
Maximum zero fuel: 42,200 lb (19,142 kg) *for Series 200*, 44,000 lb (19,958 kg) *for Series 200ER and Series 200LR*
Maximum ramp: 51,250 lb (23,247 kg) *for Series 200ER*, 53,250 lb (24,154 kg) *for Series 200LR*, 72,750 lb (32,999 kg) *for CRJ-700*, 75,250 lb (34,133 kg) *for CRJ-700ER*
Maximum take-off: 47,450 lb (21,523 kg) *for Series 200*, 51,000 lb (23,133 kg) *for Series 200ER*, 53,000 lb (24,040 kg) *for Series 200LR*, 72,500 lb (32,885 kg) *for CRJ-700*, and 75,000 lb (34,019 kg) *for CRJ-700ER*
Maximum landing: 44,700 lb (20,276 kg) *for Series 200*, 47,000 lb (21,319 kg), *for Series 200ER and Series 200LR*, 67,000 lb (30,390 kg) *for CRJ-700 and CRJ-700ER*
Payload: 11,930 lb (5,411 kg) *for Series 200*, 13,708 lb (6,218 kg) *for Series 200ER and Series 200LR*, 18,800 lb (8,527 kg) *for CRJ-700 and CRJ-700ER*
Payload with full fuel: 6,653 lb (3,018 kg) *for Series 200ER*, 8,653 lb (3,925 kg) *for Series 200LR*, 9,130 lb (4,141 kg) *for CRJ-700*, and 11,630 lb (5,275 kg) *for CRJ-700ER*
Design payload: 10,000 lb (4,536 kg) for all versions
Maximum fuel: See main discription for Regional Jet. 20,420 lb (9,262 kg) *for CRJ-700*

PERFORMANCE:
Maximum operating Mach number (M_{MO}): Mach 0.85
High cruise speed: Mach 0.81, 464 kts (534 mph) 860 km/h *for Series 200, 200ER, 200LR, CRJ-700 and CRJ-700ER*
Normal (long-range) cruise speed: Mach 0.74, 424 kts (488 mph) 786 km/h *for Series 200, 200ER and 200LR*, or Mach 0.77, 442 kts (508 mph) 819 km/h *for CRJ-700 and CRJ-700ER*
FAR take-off field length at MTOW: 5,010 ft (1,530 m) *for Series 200*, 5,800 ft (1,770 m) *for Series 200ER*, 6,290 ft (1,920 m) *for Series 200LR*, 5,135 ft (1,565 m) *for CRJ-700*, and 5,500 ft (1,676 m) *for CRJ-700ER*, all at sea level, ISA
Landing distance at MLW: 4,670 ft (1,425 m) *for Series 200*, 4,850 ft (1,480 m) *for Series 200ER and Series 200LR*
FAR 121 landing field length at MLW: 4,950 ft (1,509 m) *for CRJ-700 and CRJ-700ER*, at sea level
Time to climb to FL350 at MTOW: 19.2 minutes *for Series 100*, 22.3 minutes *for Series 100ER*
Ceiling: 41,000 ft (12,496 m), maximum operating, all versions
Range at design payload: 985 naut miles (1,135 miles) 1,825 km *for Series 200*, 1,645 naut miles (1,895 miles) 3,045 km *for Series 200ER*, and 2,005 naut miles (2,309 miles) 3,715 km *for Series 200LR*
Range at long-range cruise speed: 1,702 naut miles (1,959 miles) 3,154 km *for CRJ-700*, 2,032 naut miles (2,339 miles) 3,765 km *for CRJ-700ER*, both 70 passengers, FAR 121

Bombardier de Havilland Dash 8Q

First flight: 20 June 1983 (Series 100), 15 May 1987 (Series 300), and 31 January 1998 (Series 400).
Certification: September 1984 (Series 100 – Transport Canada), 14 February and 8 June 1989 (Series 300 – Transport Canada and FAA respectively). Certification for Series 400 expected in the first quarter of 1999.
First delivery: December 1984 service entry for Series 100 (norOntair), 27 February 1989 first delivery for Series 300 (Time Air), 1995 for Series 200.
Role: Short-range regional airliner.
Airframe life: Economic life of 160,000 landings. Dash 8Q-400 has crack-free life of 40,000 flying hours or 80,000 flights, and economic life of 80,000 hours or 160,000 flights.

Noise levels: 81 EPNdB take off, 95 EPNdB approach, 86 EPNdB sideline.
Sales: 547 ordered by 19 March 1998 (297 Series 100, 82 Series 200, 136 Series 300 and 32 Series 400), with 486 delivered (296, 58, 132 and 0 respectively). Largest orders from Air Atlantic (15 Series 100s), AirBC (12 Series 100s and 6 Series 300s), Air Ontario (30 Series 100s and 6 Series 300s), Air Wisconsin (5 Series 100s and 7 Series 300s), America West (12 Series 100s), GPA Jetprop (16 Series 100s and 14 Series 300s), Great China Airlines (4 Series 100s, 14 Series 300s and 6 Series 400s; actual total of 12 Series 400 orders and options), Horizon Air (21 Series 100s and 35 Series 200s), Mesa Air (12 Series 200s), Northwest Airlines (25 Series 100s), SA Express (12 Series 300s), Time Air (4 Series 100s and 10 Series 300s), SAS Commuter (15 series 400s, plus 38 options), Tyrolean (11 Series 100s, 15 Series 300s, and 4 Series 400s), USAir Express (including Piedmont Airlines and Allegheny Commuter; 56 Series 100s and 10 Series 200s), and Wideroe (15 series 100s and 1 series 400).
Crew: 2 pilots plus attendant.
Passengers: See table.
Seat pitch: 31 ins (79 cm) for Series 100/200, 32 ins (81 cm) for Series 300, 33-31 ins (84-79 cm) for Series 400A (depending on interior layout and 456-548 cu ft, 12.91-15.46 m^3 baggage volume) and 31-30 ins (79-76.2 cm) for Series 400B (depending on interior layout and 456-502 cu ft, 12.91-14.22 m^3 baggage volume), with an option for Series 400B for 10 seats at 34 ins (86.4 cm) and 62 at 31 ins (79 cm) with 429 cu ft (12.15 m^3) of baggage.
Galley: Buffet type.
Pressurization: 5.5 psi cabin differential.
Baggage compartment volume: 300 cu ft (8.495 m^3) for Series 100/200, 320 cu ft (9.06 m^3) for Series 300, and up to 502-548 cu ft (14.22-15.46 m^3) for Series 400, depending on interior configuration and seat pitch selected.
Size of baggage door: 4 ft 2 ins × 5 ft (1.27 × 1.52 m)

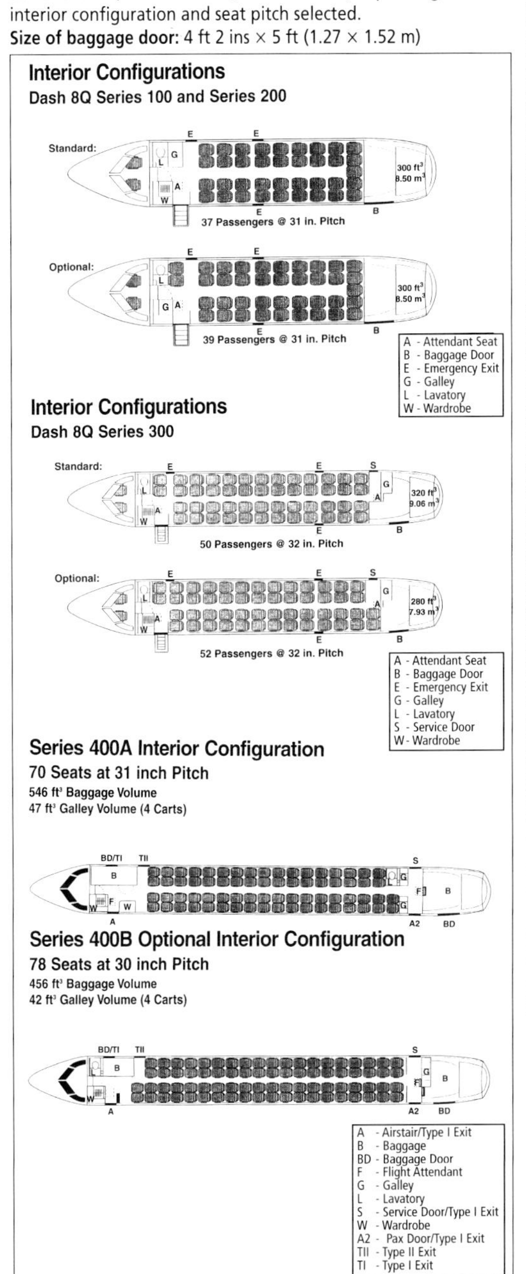

↑ **Bombardier de Havilland Dash 8Q Series 100, 200, 300 and 400A/B typical cabin configurations** *(courtesy Bombardier)*

↑ **Bombardier de Havilland Dash 8Q Series 400**

Baggage compartment: 2,000 lb (907 kg) capacity for Series 100/200, 2,500 lb (1,134 kg) for Series 300, and 3,500 lb (1,588 kg) for Series 400.
Wing control surfaces: Horn-balanced ailerons (with tabs), 2-section slotted flaps, spoilers and lift dumpers. Leading-edge stall strips. Flap settings 0°, 5°, 15° and 35° for Series 100 and 200; 10° additional setting introduced on Series 300.
Tail control surfaces: Horn-balanced elevator (with 4 tabs) and 2-section rudder.
Flight control system: Mechanical/hydraulic.
Construction materials: Include allodyned alloys, carbonfibre, Kevlar, and Nomex honeycomb. Composites for fin/tailplane fairing, tailplane/fin leading edges, elevator tips, tailcone, dorsal fin, cabin bulkhead, luggage bins, floor panels, engine nacelles, flap shrouds and trailing edges, wingtip fairings, wing leading edges, wing/fuselage fairings, nose bay and radome.
Engines: See table. 13 ft (3.96 m) diameter Hamilton Standard 14SF-7 4-blade propellers for Series 100/200, 14SF-23 propellers for Series 300, and 13 ft 6 ins (4.11 m) diameter Dowty R408 6-blade slow-turning composite propellers for Series 400.
Fuel system: 3,160 litres standard for Series 100/200/300, and 5,700 litres optional for Series 100/200/300. 6,707 litres standard for Series 400.
Electrical system: DC supply via dual starter-generators, supplemented by dual transformer rectifier units (TRU) and dual ni-cd batteries. 115 volt AC supply via dual engine-driven generators and 3 static inverters (AC buses provide power for electrical de-icing). Series 400 has 3 batteries to support DC bus system. Equipped with AC and DC ground power receptacles. Optional APU providing 28 volt DC power.

Details for Dash 8Q, *with further information in the main table on page 184*

CABIN:
Length: 30 ft (9.14 m) *for Series 100/200*, 41 ft 6 ins (12.65 m) *for Series 300*, 61 ft 8 ins (18.8 m) *for Series 400*
Width: 8 ft 2 ins (2.49 m) centreline, 6 ft 8 ins (2.03 m) floor
Height: 6 ft 5 ins (1.95 m)
Volume: 1,328 cu ft (37.6 m^3) *for Series 100/200*, 1,838 cu ft (52 m^3) *for Series 300*, and 2,740 cu ft (77.6 m^3) *for Series 400*
Main passenger door: 2 ft 6 ins × 5 ft 5.5 ins (0.762 × 1.66 m) airstair

TAIL UNIT:
Tailplane span: 26 ft (7.92 m) *for Series 100/200/300* and 30 ft 5 ins (9.27 m) *for Series 400*
Horizontal area: 150 sq ft (13.94 m^2) *for Series 100/200/300*, and 180 sq ft (16.72 m^2) *for Series 400*
Vertical area: 152 sq ft (14.12 m^2)

UNDERCARRIAGE:
Type: B.F. Goodrich wheels. Retractable (8 seconds main gear retraction time, or 5 seconds for Series 400), with steerable nosewheels (powered ±60°, or ±70° for Series 400; 120° for towing). Twin wheels on each unit. Main gears interchangeable (left to right)
Wheel base: 26 ft 1 ins (7.95 m) *for Series 100/200*, 32 ft 10 ins (10 m) *for Series 300*, 28 ft 10 ins (8.79 m) *for Series 400*
Wheel track: 25 ft 10 ins (7.87 m), 45 ft 9 ins (13.94 m) *for Series 400*

↑ **Bombardier de Havilland Dash 8Q Series 100 operated by Ryukyu Air Commuter**

Hydraulic system: Dual independent systems plus third system providing redundancy to powered elevator. Electric pump provides redundant power source for system 1. Power Transfer Unit (PTU) provides redundant power source for system 2. Hand pump, with separate fluid reservoir, for emergency undercarriage extension. No hydraulic fluid transfer between systems.
Braking system: B.F. Goodrich carbon disc brakes with high heat sink capacity and fade resistance, with anti-skid system.
Deicing system: Boots for wing, tailplane and fin leading edges, and nacelle air intake. Electric for stall warning transducers, propellers, pitot/static ports, windshield and engine intake adapter.
Radar: Honeywell Primus 800 weather radar. Integral scavenge oil heating for engine intake. Windshield wipers with available optional washer system.
Flight avionics/instrumentation: Certified for Category II approaches. Now all Dash 8Q variants certified for Category IIIa weather operations with the Flight Dynamics Head-Up Guidance System offered as an option; Horizon Air Dash 8Q-100 was the first to be certified by the FAA for Category IIIa operations, using a Flight Dynamics HGS 2000. Bendix/King Gold Crown III communication/navigation suite and Honeywell EFIS, with optional Rockwell Collins suite, except Series 400 which has Sextant suite with five 6 ins × 8 ins (15.2 × 20.3 cm) LCD active matrix high-resolution displays. Standard full complement of

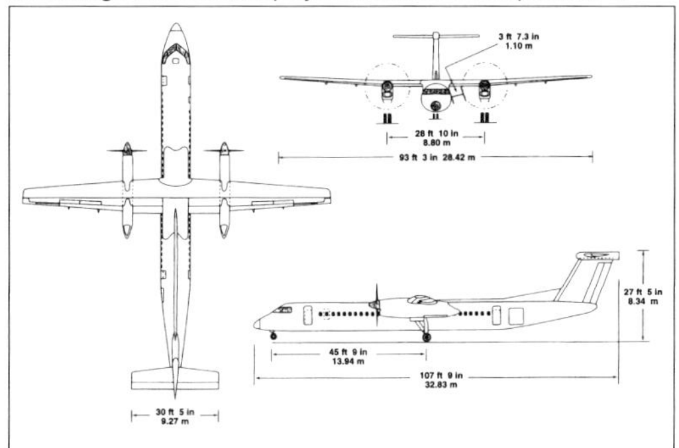

↑ **Bombardier de Havilland Dash 8Q Series 400 general arrangement** *(courtesy Bombardier)*

Dash 8Q basic configurations

	Series 100A	Series 100B	Series 200A	Series 200B	Series 300A	Series 300B	Series 300E	Series 400A	Series 400B
Passengers (data for lower number)	37-39	37-39	37-39	37-39	50-56	50-56	50-56	70	72-78
Engines (2 turboprops)	P&WC PW120A	P&WC PW121	P&WC PW123C	P&WC PW123D	P&WC PW123	P&WC PW123B	P&WC PW123E	P&WC PW150A	P&WC PW150A
Rating (each)	2,000 shp (1,491 kW)	2,150 shp (1,603 kW)	2,150 shp (1,603 kW)	2,150 shp (1,603 kW) to 45° C OAT @ SL	2,380 shp (1,775 kW) to 35° C OAT @ SL	2,500 shp (1,864 kW) to 30° C OAT @ SL	2,380 shp (1,775 kW) to 40° C OAT @ SL	5,071 shp (3,781 kW) to 37.4° C OAT @ SL	5,071 shp (3,781 kW) to 37.4° C OAT @ SL
Wing span	85 ft (25.91 m)	85 ft (25.91 m)	85 ft (25.91 m)	85 ft (25.91 m)	90 ft (27.43 m)	90 ft (27.43 m)	90 ft (27.43 m)	93 ft 3 ins (28.42 m)	93 ft 3 ins (28.42 m)
Length	73 ft (22.25 m)	73 ft (22.25 m)	73 ft (22.25 m)	73 ft (22.25 m)	84 ft 3 ins (25.68 m)	84 ft 3 ins (25.68 m)	84 ft 3 ins (25.68 m)	107 ft 9 ins (32.84 m)	107 ft 9 ins (32.84 m)
Height	24 ft 7 ins (7.49 m)	24 ft 7 ins (7.49 m)	24 ft 7 ins (7.49 m)	24 ft 7 ins (7.49 m)	24 ft 7 ins (7.49 m)	24 ft 7 ins (7.49 m)	24 ft 7 ins (7.49 m)	27 ft 5 ins (8.34 m)	27 ft 5 ins (8.34 m)
Wing area	585 sq ft (54.35 m^2)	585 sq ft (54.35 m^2)	585 sq ft (54.35 m^2)	585 sq ft (54.35 m^2)	605 sq ft (56.21 m^2)	605 sq ft (56.21 m^2)	605 sq ft (56.21 m^2)	679 sq ft (63.08 m^2)	679 sq ft (63.08 m^2)
Wing aspect ratio	12.35	12.35	12.35	12.35	13.39	13.39	13.39	12.8	12.8
Empty weight, operating	22,730 lb (10,310 kg)	22,778 lb (10,332 kg)	23,004 lb (10,434 kg)	23,020 lb (10,442 kg)	25,814 lb (11,709 kg)	25,836 lb (11,719 kg)	25,814 lb (11,709 kg)	36,458 lb (16,537 kg)	36,549 lb (16,578 kg)
Maximum take-off weight	34,500 lb (15,649 kg)	36,300 lb (16,465 kg)	36,300 lb (16,465 kg)	36,300 lb (16,465 kg)	41,100 lb (18,643 kg)	43,000 lb (19,505 kg)	41,100 lb (18,643 kg)	60,250-63,250 lb (27,329-28,690 kg)	60,250-63,250 lb (27,329-28,690 kg)
Maximum landing weight	33,900 lb (15,377 kg)	33,900 lb (15,377 kg)	34,500 lb (15,649 kg)	34,500 lb (15,649 kg)	40,000 lb (18,144 kg)	42,000 lb (19,051 kg)	40,000 lb (18,144 kg)	59,750-60,500 lb (27,102-27,442 kg)	59,750-60,500 lb (27,102-27,442 kg)
Payload	8,570 lb (3,887 kg)	9,222 lb (4,183 kg)	9,396 lb (4,262 kg)	9,380 lb (4,255 kg)	11,386 lb (5,165 kg)	13,664 lb (6,198 lb)	11,386 lb (5,165 kg)	17,292-18,792 lb (7,844-8,524 kg)	17,201-18,701 lb (7,802-8,483 kg)
Payload with maximum fuel	6,127 lb (2,779 kg)	7,879 lb (3,574 kg)	7,673 lb (3,480 kg)	7,657 lb (3,473 kg)	9,663 lb (4,383 kg)	11,541 lb (5,235 kg)	9,663 lb (4,383 kg)	11,821 lb (5,362 kg)	
Cruise speed kts (mph) km/h	265 (305) 491	270 (311) 500	295 (340) 546	295 (340) 546	287 (330) 532	285 (328) 528	287 (330) 532	350 (403) 648	351 (404) 650
Stalling speed, with flaps kts (mph) km/h	72 (83) 133	72 (83) 133	72 (83) 133	72 (83) 133	77 (88) 142	77 (88) 142	77 (88) 142		
Take-off field length, SL, ISA (for 200 naut miles)	2,740 ft (835 m)	2,635 ft (803 m)	2,680 ft (817 m)	3,957 ft (1,206 m) at ISA +30°C, elevation 5,000 ft	3,085 ft (940 m)	2,980 ft (908 m)	4,640 ft (1,415 m) ISA +20°C, elevation 5,000 ft	3,335 ft (1,016 m) ISA, sea level, FAR 25	4,050 ft (1,234 m) ISA, sea level, MTOW
Take-off distance at MTOW	3,100 ft (945 m)	3,255 ft (992 m)	3,255 ft (992 m)	3,255 ft (992 m)	3,600 ft (1,097 m)	3,865 ft (1,178 m)	3,600 ft (1,097 m)	4,050 ft (1,235 m)	
Landing field length, SL, ISA, @ MLW	2,580 ft (786 m)	2,580 ft (786 m)	2,605 ft (794 m)	2,757 ft (840 m), ISA +30°C, elevation 5,000 ft	3,315 ft (1,010 m)	3,415 ft (1,041 m)	3,735 ft (1,138 m), ISA +20°C, elevation 5,000 ft	4,215 ft (1,285 m) ISA, sea level, FAR 25	4,215 ft (1,285 m) ISA, sea level, FAR 25
Operating ceiling	25,000 ft (7,620 m)	25,000 ft (7,620 m)	25,000 ft (7,620 m)	25,000 ft (7,620 m)	25,000 ft (7,620 m)	25,000 ft (7,620 m)	25,000 ft (7,620 m)	25,000 ft (7,620 m)	25,000 ft (7,620 m)
Range naut miles (miles) km	737 (848) 1,365	1,041 (1,198) 1,928	969 (1,115) 1,795	969 (1,115) 1,795	801 (922) 1,483	1,228 (1,414) 2,275 with optional long-range tanks	801 (922) 1,483	1,296 (1,492) 2,401 at high gross weight, reserves, MCR	878 (1,011) 1,627 at basic weight, 1,291 (1,486) 2,392 at high gross weight, 74 passengers

digital avionics, including dual channel autopilot/flight director system. Primary flight information can be displayed on EFIS. Can accommodate an expansion of navigational capability to include MLS, RNAV, and long-range systems. Upgrade of the cockpit of the Series 300 to Series 400 standard is thought to be under consideration as an option, as the Series 300X.

Aircraft variants:
Dash 8Q Series 100 has been offered in basic 100, improved range 100A and additional take-off power/payload 100B versions. Good rough field capability and hot-and-high performance.
Dash 8Q Series 200 was designed for 300 kts cruise and high commonality with Series 300A, and superior payload-range capability. 200A is the basic model, with 200B offering additional take-off power for improved take-off and single-engine ceiling performance out of hot-and-high airfields.
Dash 8Q Series 300 is offered in 3 versions, as A and additional take-off power B and E, the latter with a further increase in hot-and-high capability. Intended for more densely travelled routes requiring higher capacity. Upgrade of the cockpit to Series 400 standard is thought to be under consideration as an option.
Dash 8Q Series 400 is the latest 'stretched' version, seating 70 in A version for the North American market and up to 78 in B version. Sextant avionics suite. Length increased by 23 ft 6 ins (7.16 m), wing span increased, new cargo and baggage doors, and new main undercarriage. PW150 engines with 6-blade propellers (moved 13 ins, 33 cm further from the fuselage). 3 configurations, basic gross weight at 60,250 lb (27,329 kg), intermediate at 61,720 lb (27,996 kg) and high at 63,250 lb (28,690 kg), with respective payloads of 17,292 lb (7,844 kg), 18,042 lb (8,184 kg) and 18,792 lb (8,524 kg). First order for 12 from Great China Airlines (including 6 options) launched the programme in April 1995. First aircraft began taxi trials in October 1997 and flew on 31 January 1998. Second and third aircraft followed in 1998. Certification 1999 and with deliveries to Great China Airlines that year.
Dash 8M is the military version. See E-9A and CT-142 in the Electronic section and Dash 8 Maritime Patrol in the Combat section.
Dash 8 Multi-Role can be a military Dash 8M or civil version, with roles including search and rescue, aero-medical transport, navigation training, paratroop transport, VIP transport, flight calibration, freighter, and cargo/combi convertible.

Bombardier Business Aircraft

Canadair Challenger 604

Note: Details of the Challenger 600 and 601-1A/3A/3R, all of which are out of production, can be found in the 1996-97 edition of *WA&SD*, pages 204-205, and briefly under Aircraft variants below.
First flight: 8 November 1978 for original Challenger 600, and 18 September 1994 for current Challenger 604.
Certification: 20 September 1995 (Canada) and October 1995 (FAA), to FAR Pt 25.
First delivery: January 1996 (Challenger 604).
Role: Wide-body business jet for executive and government transport. Also used for other military and civil applications, including cargo, surveillance and air ambulance.
Noise levels: 80.9 EPNdB take-off, 90.3 EPNdB approach, 86.2 EPNdB sideline.
Sales: 48 Challenger 604s delivered at time of writing (making 391 of all Challenger versions). List price US$21.25 million.

Details *(Challenger 604)*

Crew: 2 (flight).
Passengers: Up to 19.
Galley: Buffet type.
Baggage volume: 115 cu ft (3.26 m^3).
Pressurization: Maximum 8.8 psi differential.
Wing control surfaces: 2-section double-slotted flaps, ailerons, inner spoiler/lift dumper and outer spoiler/airbrake.
Tail control surfaces: Variable incidence tailplane. Elevators and rudder.
Flight control system: Hydraulic, except for electrically actuated tailplane incidence.
Engines: 2 General Electric CF34-3B turbofans.
Engine rating: Each 8,729 lbf (38.83 kN), with APR rating of 9,220 lbf (41 kN), flat rated to 30° C.

↑ Bombardier Canadair Challenger 604

Fuel system: 20,000 lb (9,072 kg).
Electrical system: 3-phase 115/200 volt, 400 Hz AC supply via 2 × 30 kVA engine-driven generators. 28 volt DC supply via 4 transformer/rectifiers. 43 amp-hour ni-cd battery. APU and stand-by air-driven generator.
Hydraulic system: 3 systems, each 3,000 psi.
Braking system: Multiple disc brakes with anti-skid.
De-icing system: Bleed air for wing leading edges and engine air intakes. Electric de-icing for cockpit glazing and pitots.
Oxygen system: Gaseous.
Radar: Rockwell Collins RTA-854 weather radar.
Flight avionics/instrumentation: Rockwell Collins Pro Line 4 fully-integrated suite. Standard equipment includes 6 EFIS displays, digital EICAS, maintenance and diagnostic computer, dual autopilot, dual FMS, dual DCU, dual air data computer system, dual Litton Flagship inertial reference systems, dual radio tuning units, plus dual VHF com, Nav, DME, ADF, Mode S transponders, dual HF receiver/transmitter and improved Avtech audio controls. Optional equipment includes Flight Dynamics Head-up Guidance System, a third FMS, third DCU, third IRS, third VHF transceiver, second radio altimeter, dual channel GPS, GPWS, TCAS II, lightening detection system, AFIS, and flight data recorder.

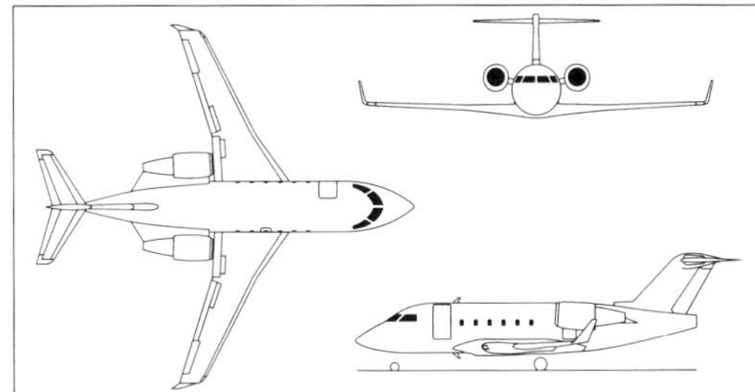
↑ Bombardier Canadair Challenger 604 general arrangement *(courtesy Bombardier)*

Aircraft variants:
Challenger 600 was the initial version, with 7,500 lbf (33.36 kN) Textron Lycoming ALF502L-2 turbofans. 11,142 litres of fuel with optional 1,186 litre tank included. Range 2,800 naut miles. 84 delivered, the last on 22 June 1983.
Challenger 601-1A was built with 8,650 lbf (38.48 kN) General Electric CF34-1As. Standard fuel capacity of 11,142 litres, for 3,440 naut mile range. Winglets added. 66 delivered between 6 May 1983 and 29 May 1987.
Challenger 601-3A was delivered with 8,650 lbf (38.48 kN) General Electric CF34-3As, offering 9,220 lbf (41 kN) with APR. Digital avionics suite including 5-tube EFIS, turbulence detecting 4-colour digital radar (other avionics as detailed for 601-3R). 134 delivered between 6 May 1987 and 29 October 1993. Version also offered with 11,979 litres of fuel for 3,585 naut mile range.
Challenger 601-3R was evolved from the 601-3A with new CF34-3A1 airliner-proven engines, intercontinental 3,585 naut mile range, and increased take-off weight. 59 delivered between July 1993 and January 1996.
Challenger 604 offers 4,077 naut mile intercontinental range and new all-glass, fully integrated flight deck. New CF34-3B engines, flat rated to a higher temperature for better hot and high performance. Better fuel consumption. Increased maximum fuel, maximum take-off weight and maximum landing weight. New stronger undercarriage, brake and anti-skid system derived from the Canadair Regional Jet. 27ins (68.58 cm) diameter wheels and low pressure (177 psi) tyres. New MSG-3 task-oriented maintenance programme with general inspections at every 400 flight hours. CF34-3B engines on task-oriented maintenance programme does not require hard-time hot section inspections or overhauls. Visual borescope inspection every 3,200 hours and data from the computerized engine trend monitoring software provide advance warning for required engine repair. General Electric anticipates the first unscheduled shop visit for the CF34-3B to take place, on average, after 9,000 flight hours. New optional extended cabin layout adding 18 ins (46 cm) and 2 windows to the seating area. Improved passive noise insulation system. Optional Active Noise and Vibration Control (ANVC) system.
Challenger Cargo Variant was announced in June 1995, offered jointly with Pemco World Air Services which performs the installation.

↑ Bombardier Canadair Challenger 604 flight deck, with Pro Line 4 avionics system

Details for Challenger 604

PRINCIPAL DIMENSIONS:
Wing span: 64 ft 4 ins (19.6 m)
Maximum length: 68 ft 5 ins (20.85 m)
Maximum height: 20 ft 8 ins (6.3 m)

CABIN:
Length: 28 ft 4 ins (8.64 m)
Width: 8 ft 2 ins (2.49 m) centreline, 7 ft 2 ins (2.18 m) floor
Height: 6 ft 1 ins (1.85 m)
Volume: 1,150 cu ft (32.56 m^3)
Main passenger door: 5 ft 10 ins × 3 ft (1.78 × 0.91 m)

WINGS:
Area: 492 sq ft (45.71 m^2)
Aspect ratio: 8.41

UNDERCARRIAGE:
Type: Retractable, with steerable/self-centring nosewheels. Twin wheels on each unit
Wheel base: 26 ft 2.5 ins (7.99 m)
Wheel track: 10 ft 5 ins (3.18 m)
Turning radius: 40 ft (12.19 m)

WEIGHTS:
Empty, operating: 26,630 lb (12,079 kg)
Maximum ramp weight: 47,700 lb (21,636 kg)
Maximum take-off: 47,600 lb (21,591 kg)
Maximum landing: 38,000 lb (17,237 kg)
Payload: 5,370 lb (2,436 kg)

PERFORMANCE:
High cruise speed: Mach 0.83, 476 kts (548 mph) 882 km/h
Normal cruise speed: Mach 0.8, 459 kts (528 mph) 850 km/h
Long-range cruise speed: Mach 0.74, 425 kts (489 mph) 787 km/h
Balanced field length: 5,700 ft (1,738 m) at MTOW, sea level, ISA
Landing distance: 2,775 ft (846 m) at MLW, sea level
G limits: 2.6 design
Initial cruise altitude: 37,500 ft (11,430 m) at MGTOW, ISA
Time to initial cruise altitude: 22 minutes
Ceiling: 41,000 ft (12,497 m)
Range with full fuel, 2 crew and 5 passengers, at Mach 0.74: 4,077 naut miles (4,692 miles) 7,551 km with NBAA IFR reserves, ISA
Range with full fuel, 2 crew and 5 passengers, at Mach 0.80: 3,769 naut miles (4,337 miles) 6,980 km with NBAA IFR reserves, ISA

↑ Fourth Bombardier Global Express (*9004*)

Bombardier BD-700 Global Express

First flight: 13 October 1996.
Certification: June 1998.
First delivery: 1998 to US corporate customer.
Role: Long-range and high-speed business and VIP transport, with a very large cabin.
Noise levels: 80 EPNdB take-off, 91 EPNdB approach and 90 EPNdB sideline.

Development

- October 1991. Project Global Express was introduced at the National Business Aircraft Association meeting in Texas.
- 20 December 1993. Programme was launched with 30 orders and 8 options.
- February 1995. End of joint definition phase. Mitsubishi cut metal for first aircraft.
- January 1996. Final assembly began of first aircraft (9001).
- 26 August 1996. Official unveiling.
- 10 November 1996. Flight test programme began in Wichita, KS, USA.
- 7 February 1997. First flight of the second aircraft (9002).
- 22 April 1997. First flight of the third aircraft (9003).
- 8 September 1997. First flight of the fourth aircraft (9004).

Details

Sales: 75 ordered by mid-February 1998.
Crew: 3 + 1, with forward rest area (for 1 or 2) and toilet.
Passengers: 8-19 typically. 8 passengers with maximum fuel load.
Galley: Fully equipped in the forward part or rear of the cabin.
Pressurization: 9.64 psi maximum differential.
Baggage volume: Flexible, according to the customer, but typically 324 cu ft (9.17 m^3).
Wing characteristics: New wing and winglets, having an advanced aerofoil section with thick chord and low taper ratio to increase lift, lower drag and provide good low/high speed performances. Features 14 composite control surfaces.
Wing control surfaces: Ailerons (deflected +26.5°, -23°, maximum), 3-segment single-slotted Fowler flaps and 4-segment leading-edge slats, driven by dual-redundant electric motors. Electronically controlled spoilers; 4 spoilers and 2 ground spoilers per side to enhance lateral and directional control, improve altitude management and reduce landing distances.
Tail control surfaces: Elevators (deflected +34°, -19°, maximum) and rudder (30° maximum). Variable incidence tailplane (+2° to –13°).
Flight control system: Sextant Avionique multiple-redundant, hydraulically powered primary system, with a system of cables and pulleys transferring inputs from the pilots' control columns to the Power Control Units (PCUs). Artificial feel mechanisms using spring-loaded roller system. Aileron PCUs also provide trim through electrical actuators within the cable control system. 2 or 3 Parker Hannifin hydraulic PCUs per control surface. Fly-by-wire back-up for primary surfaces (with manual reversion). Flaps and slats driven by dual-redundant electric motors.
Construction materials: Subcontractors include Mitsubishi of Japan for wing and centre fuselage sections, Canadair, de Havilland and Shorts.
Engines: 2 BMW Rolls-Royce BR710-48-C2 turbofans.
Engine rating: Each 14,750 lbf (65.61 kN), flat rated to ISA + 20°.
Fuel system: Parker Hannifin system. 43,350 lb (19,664 kg) maximum, or 37,750 lb (17,123 kg) with maximum payload.
Electrical system: Lucas Aerospace and Leach Corporation system with variable frequency generating and advanced automated power management system; 5 generators, 2 × 40 kVA per engine for 115/200 volt 3-phase AC supply, plus 1 × 45 kVA driven by APU. Emergency 9 kVA air-driven generator. 4 TRUs to provide 28 volt DC supply, with 25 amp-hour and 42 amp-hour ni-cd batteries for emergency DC supply. AlliedSignal (team leader) RE220(GX) APU with FADEC for electrical power and engine starting bleed air at altitudes of up to 45,000 ft (13,715 m); can be started in flight at altitudes up to 37,000 ft (11,275 m).

Details for Global Express

PRINCIPAL DIMENSIONS:
Wing span: 94 ft (28.65 m)
Maximum length: 99 ft 5 ins (30.3 m)
Maximum height: 24 ft 10 ins (7.57 m)

CABIN:
Length: 48 ft 4 ins (14.73 m)
Width: 8 ft 2 ins (2.49 m) centreline, 6 ft 11 ins (2.11 m) floor
Height: 6 ft 3 ins (1.91 m)
Floor area: 335 sq ft (31.12 m^2)
Volume: 2,140 cu ft (60.6 m^3)

WINGS:
Area: 1,022 sq ft (94.94 m^2) basic
Aspect ratio: 8.65
Sweepback: 35°
Incidence: 4° at root
Dihedral: 2.5°

UNDERCARRIAGE:
Type: Messier-Dowty retractable, with steerable nosewheels (±75°), with twin wheels on each unit
Main wheel tyre size: Goodyear , H38 × 12-19
Nose wheel tyre size: Goodyear
Wheel base: 41 ft 11 ins (12.78 m)
Wheel track: 13 ft 8 ins (4.17 m)
Turning radius: 45 ft 3 ins (13.78 m) minimum

WEIGHTS:
Maximum zero fuel: 56,000 lb (25,401 kg)
Basic operating: 48,800 lb (22,136 kg)
Maximum ramp: 93,750 lb (42,525 kg)
Maximum take-off: 93,500 lb (42,412 kg)
Maximum landing: 78,600 lb (35,653 kg)
Payload: 1,600 lb (726 kg) with maximum fuel, 7,200 lb (3,266 kg) maximum

PERFORMANCE:
High cruise speed: Mach 0.88, 505 kts (581 mph) 935 km/h
Normal cruise speed: Mach 0.85, 488 kts (561 mph) 904 km/h
Long-range cruise speed: Mach 0.80, 459 kts (528 mph) 850 km/h
Stall speed: 102 kts (117 mph) 189 km/h
Approach speed: 125 kts (144 mph) 232 km/h
Balanced field length: 5,550 ft (1,692 m) ISA, sea level, MGTOW
Landing distance: 2,600 ft (792 m), sea level, MLW
G limit: 2.5 design
Initial cruise altitude: 41,000 ft (12,497 m) at MTOW
Time to initial cruise altitude: 25 minutes
Ceiling: 51,000 ft (15,545 m) operating
Range: 5,000-6,700 naut miles (5,754-7,710 miles) 9,260-12,408 km

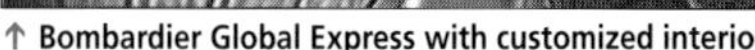
↑ Bombardier Global Express with customized interior

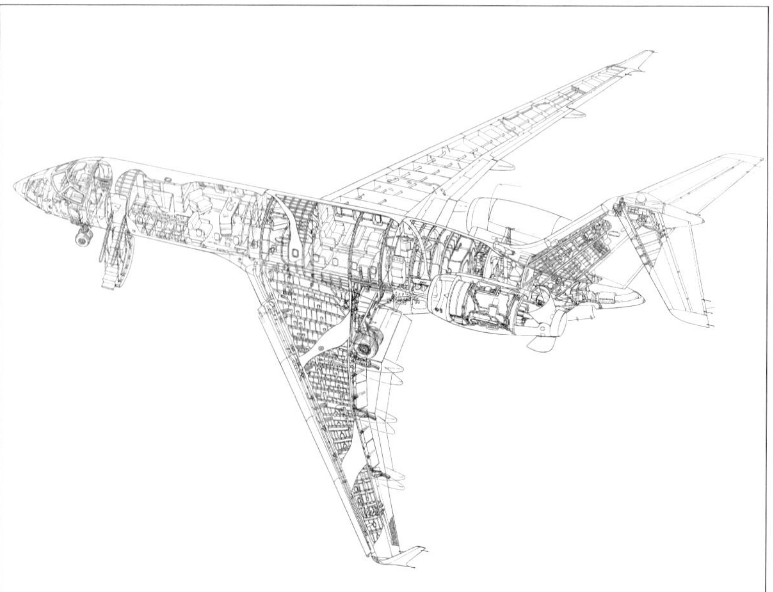
↑ Bombardier Global Express cutaway *(courtesy Bombardier)*

Hydraulic system: Abex NWL Aerospace system. 3 fully independent systems, each 3,000 psi, fully segmented and isolated for maximum safety, each system powered by 2 pumps.
Braking system: Messier-Dowty supplied, with B.F. Goodrich/HydroAire hydraulic brake-by-wire system, having electrically-signalled carbon brakes with anti-skid. System features a pilot-selectable, auto-braking mode with controllable deceleration.
Environmental control system: ABG-Semca air management system, integrating bleed air, anti-icing, avionics cooling, air conditioning, and cabin pressurization.
Radar: Honeywell Primus weather radar.
Flight avionics/instrumentation: Honeywell Primus 2000 XP suite (suited to ETOPS), including dual fail-operational automatic autopilot and dual fail-passive autothrottles, six 8 ins × 7 ins (20.3 × 17.8 cm) CRT EFIS, an engine indication and crew alerting system (EICAS) with synoptics, a dual (optional triple) flight management system with "SmartPerf" software for performance calculations and dual auto-throttles. GPS, 3 Laseref III inertial reference systems, 3 air data computers, 2 Honeywell VHF navigation and communications systems, and traffic collision avoidance and ground proximity warning systems (TCAS II). Optional Sextant Avionique head-up flight display system (HFDS) for Category IIIa operations, comprising 4 LRUs, combiner, flight display computer, optical projector unit and head-up control panel.

Bombardier Canadair CL-215 and CL-215T

First flight: 23 October 1967 (CL-215), and 8 June 1989 (CL-215T).
Certification: 27 March 1969 (CL-215), and 28 March 1991 (Transport Canada, restricted category – CL-215T), 24 December 1991 (utility category – CL-215T), 30 March 1993 (FAA, restricted category – CL-215T).
First delivery: 6 June 1969 (CL-215), and June 1991 (CL-215T, to Spain).
Role: Firefighting, transport, utility, and search and rescue amphibian.
Sales: 124 piston-engined CL-215s were delivered to customers in Canada (49), Spain (30), Greece (16), France (15), Italy (5), former Yugoslavia (5), Thailand (2) and Venezuela (2), the final delivered to Greece on 3 May 1990. 17 CL-215T retrofits were ordered (Spain 15 and Province of Quebec 2), all delivered. In 1995 Croatia became the first customer for a refurbished CL-215.

Aircraft variants:
CL-215 was the original version, powered by 2 × 2,100 hp (1,566 kW) Pratt & Whitney R-2800-83AM piston engines. Firefighting productivity, at 10 naut miles water-to-fire distance, is 26,730 litres per hour.
CL-215T is the designation of CL-215s retrofitted with 2,380 shp (1,775 kW) P&WC PW123AF turboprops using kit modification and added improvements. Firefighting productivity, at 10 naut miles water-to-fire distance, is 32,080 litres per hour. 58,000 drops recorded by start of 1998.

Details for CL-215/CL-215T

PERFORMANCE:
Maximum speed: 165 kts (190 mph) 306 km/h *for CL-215*, 197 kts (227 mph) 365 km/h *for CL-215T*
Maximum climb rate: 1,000 ft (305 m) per minute *for CL-215*, 1,375 ft (419 m) per minute *for CL-215T*
Water drop pattern: 400 ft (122 m)

Bombardier Canadair CL-415

First flight: 6 December 1993.
Certification: 24 June 1994 (Canada), 14 October 1994 (FAA).
First delivery: November 1994 (to France).
Role: Turboprop amphibian for firefighting, plus multi-role including EEZ protection, transport, and search and rescue. Incorporates significant modernization and upgrading compared to CL-215/T.

Aims

▪ Scooping water for firefighting from nearby sources and providing sustained water-bombing to contain fires. An average mission could be 5.2 naut miles (6 miles) 10 km from water to fire, with the CL-415 making 9 drops in an hour, delivering 55,170 litres of fire suppressant.
▪ Land, loiter and take-off in sea conditions of 4 to 6 ft (1.22 to 1.83 m) waves and gusting winds of 35 kts, and operate from water only 6 ft (1.83 m) deep.

↑ Bombardier Canadair CL-215T belonging to Quebec's Fond du service aérien gouvernement *(John de Leon, Los Angeles Fire Dept)*

Details

Sales: Governments of Quebec (8), Croatia (1), France (12, with 11 in use in 1998), and Italy (8). Italy first used its aircraft to fight fires in March 1995. 56,000 drops recorded by start of 1998.
Crew: 2. CL-415 Multi-Role may have 3 flight crew, 2 observers and a specialist.
Passengers: 8-30 passengers (with toilet, galley, etc) with water tanks deleted, or 14 troops with quick-change fittings.
Firefighting capacity: 6,140 litres of water in 4 compartments. Foam chemical is located in left and right-hand reservoirs feeding respective tanks. Total 600 litres of usable concentrate should provide 16 foam drops at 0.6:99.4 mix ratio before replenishment. Scoop reloading of water or on the ground via adapters on the fuselage sides. Drop options are selectable by the flight crew.
Wing characteristics: High mounted, straight, with endplates and fences. Strengthened over CL-215. Leading edge extended and drooped locally just outboard of engine nacelles.
Wing control surfaces: Powered aileron (with tabs), and single-slotted flaps.
Tail control surfaces: Powered elevators and rudder (all with tabs), plus automatic rudder trim compensator. Small slat on starboard side of tailplane, inboard of finlet, to eliminate flow separation. Finlets canted 5° to port to improve directional stability. Bullet fairing at junction of tailplane/fin to eliminate airflow separation.
Construction materials: Metal.

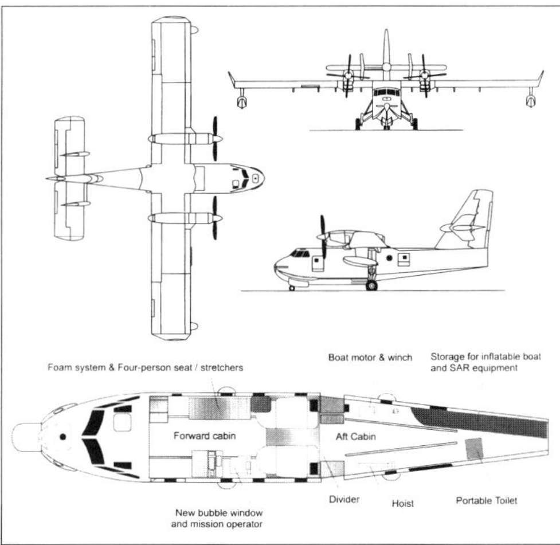

↑ **General arrangement (*top*) and possible hull layout for the Bombardier Canadair CL-415 Multi-Role** *(courtesy Bombardier)*

Details for CL-415

PRINCIPAL DIMENSIONS:
Wing span: 93 ft 11 ins (28.63 m)
Maximum length: 65 ft 0.5 ins (19.82 m)
Maximum height: 29 ft 5.5 ins (8.98 m)

CABIN:
Length: 30 ft 9.5 ins (9.38 m), excluding cockpit
Width: 7 ft 10 ins (2.39 m) maximum
Height: 6 ft 3 ins (1.9 m)
Floor area: 212 sq ft (19.69 m^2), excluding cockpit
Volume: 1,257 cu ft (35.59 m^3), excluding cockpit

WINGS:
Area: 1,080 sq ft (100.335 m^2)
Aspect ratio: 8.17

UNDERCARRIAGE:
Type: Retractable, with steerable and self-centring twin nosewheels. Non-retractable wingtip floats
Wheel base: 23 ft 9 ins (7.24 m)
Wheel track: 17 ft 4 ins (5.28 m)

WEIGHTS:
Empty, operating: 28,373 lb (12,861 kg)
Maximum zero fuel: 43,000 lb (19,505 kg)
Maximum ramp: 44,000 lb (19,958 kg) land, 38,000 lb (17,237 kg) water
Pre-water scooping weight: 37,000 lb (16,783 kg)
Maximum take-off (from land): 43,850 lb (19,890 kg) *with disposable load*, 37,850 lb (17,168 kg) *with non-disposable load*
Maximum lift, after scooping: 47,000 lb (21,320 kg)
Maximum landing: 37,000 lb (16,783 kg)
Payload: 13,500 lb (6,123 kg)

PERFORMANCE:
Maximum cruise speed: 203 kts (234 mph) 376 km/h at 5,000 ft (1,525 m), ISA
Take-off distance: 2,700 ft (823 m) *disposable load*, 2,300 ft (701 m) *non-disposable load (land)*, 2,670 ft (814 m) *non-disposable load (water)*
Landing distance: 2,210 ft (674 m) *land*, 2,180 ft (664 m) *water*
Scooping distance: 3,900 ft (1,190 m), total
Scooping time: 12 seconds to refill tanks
Initial climb rate: 1,375 ft (419 m) per minute at sea level, at 46,000 lb (20,865 kg) weight
Operating ceiling: 20,000 ft (6,100 m)
Water drop productivity: 36,800 litres per hour at 10 naut miles water-to-fire distance
Ferry range: 1,310 naut miles (1,508 miles) 2,426 km
Typical time on fire: 3 hours

↑ Bombardier Canadair CL-415 Multi-Role with nose radar, deploying a motorboat

Engines: 2 Pratt & Whitney Canada PW123AF turboprops, with Hamilton Standard 14SF-19 4-blade, reversible pitch, composite propellers.
Engine rating: Each 2,380 shp (1,775 kW).
Fuel system: 5,796 litres.
Electrical system: Split AC-DC bus-bar system. 2 × 400 amp, 28 volt engine-driven starter-generators. 2 × 800 volt-amp static inverters. 2 × 40 amp-hour 20-cell ni-cd batteries and battery chargers.
Braking system: Hydraulic disc, with increased reservoir capacity over CL-215.
De-icing system: Pneumatic boot for engine air intakes, plus electric anti-ice adapter at engine inlets.
Fire system: Detection system in fire zones of engines, with 2 Halon 1301 bottles.
Flight avionics/instrumentation: Honeywell EDZ-605 4-tube EFIS, and 3-tube Integrated Instrument Display System (IIDS). Dual Honeywell Primus 2 radio nav/com management system, plus Global Wulfsberg V-UHF/FM radio, Collins HF-230 HF radio, and Honeywell AA-300 radio altimeter. Angle-of-attack indicator. Flight data recorder, radar, and GPS among options.
Mission equipment: CL-415 Multi-Role can carry searchlight, litters, liferafts and other disaster relief/search and rescue equipment. Many other options include stores on 4 available underwing pylons.

Aircraft variants:
CL-415 is the standard firefighting version, as detailed.
CL-415 Multi-Role is a new variant, for military and non-military uses.

Kelowna Flightcraft Group — Canada

Corporate address:
#1 5655 Kelowna Airport, Kelowna, British Columbia VIV 1S1.

Telephone: +1 250 491 5500
Facsimile: +1 604 765 1489

President:
Barry Lapointe.

Information:
Bill De Meester (CV5800 Project Manager – *telephone* +1 250 491 5568, *facsimile* +1 604 765 8397).

ACTIVITIES

■ Marketing has been initiated to promote the CV5800 based on company operational data. Promotional work has also begun on a Kelowna Flightcraft CV580A programme, which will provide CV580 operators with the means to continue their present operations with a better engine reliability programme.
■ Exclusive Allison repair station for the CV580, CV580A and CV5800.

DIVISIONS

KELOWNA FLIGHTCRAFT AIR CHARTER LTD

Activities:
■ Operates 19 Boeing 727s (7 passenger, 12 freight), 12 Convair CV580s (5 passenger, 7 freight), 2 CV5800s (freight), Cessna 402Bs (freight), 1 Piper Cheyenne (passenger), 1 Westwind (passenger), and 1 DC-3C (freight).

KELOWNA FLIGHTCRAFT LTD

Activities:
■ Maintains Kelowna Flightcraft Air Charter fleet, performs third party work, holder and installer of various STA/STCs such as the Convair 122 ins (3.1 m) cargo door, CV-580A upgrade, manufacturer of the Convair CV5800 'stretch' aircraft, modification to 'glass' cockpits, electrical systems and depot maintenance inspections to the Lockheed T-33 Silver Star.

KELOWNA FLIGHTCRAFT R&D

Activities:
■ R&D of major aircraft modifications, including STC/STAs. Current programmes include long-range fuel capacity for the CV580/CV5800, avionics engineering, development of the CV5800, electronics modification for the T-33, avionics and electrical integration/modification to the Mi-17KF helicopter.

↑ Kelowna Flightcraft CV5800

Kelowna Flightcraft CV5800

First flight: 11 February 1992.
Certification: Gained December 1993. Designed to meet Stage III noise level and Cat II landing standards.
First delivery: February 1994; aircraft had accumulated over 5,000 flying hours by early 1998.
Role: Lengthened and modernized Convair CV580 for freight or passenger uses. Similar conversions can be accomplished on the CV340 and CV440 airframes.
Airframe life: Modification is claimed to extend the aircraft life by a further 100,000 hours.

Conversion includes:

■ Complete removal of all components, including flight controls, stabilizers, systems and all wiring.
■ Extension of the fuselage by 14 ft 3 ins (4.34 m), with intensive structural work as per Convair Engineering to accept the increased gross weight of 63,000 lb (28,576 kg).
■ Incorporation of a Honeywell SPZ-4500 digital AFCS, EDZ-803 4 tube EFIS, and a Primus II nav/com/ident radio package. These avionics include dual FZ-450 flight guidance computers, manually switching into a single control surface servo drive system, Primus 650 weather radar, dual VG-14A/C-14A attitude/heading package and an A-A300 radio altimeter.
■ Installation of Allison 501-D22G turboprop engines with Hamilton Standard 54H60-164(-77) propellers. Fuel capacity 6,549 litres standard, 7,874 litres optional.

Other features include:

■ Dual point underwing pressure refuelling, GTC with 95 amp auxiliary DC alternator, roller floor system, cabin floor loading of 150 lb/sq ft (732.36 kg/m^2), and 9g tie-down system.

Details for CV5800

PRINCIPAL DIMENSIONS:
See general arrangement drawing

CABIN:
Length: 62 ft 6 ins (19.05 m)
Width: 7 ft 9.7 ins (2.37 m) at floor
Height: 6 ft 6 ins (1.98 m)
Floor area: 518 sq ft (48.12 m^2)
Volume: 3,096 cu ft (87.67 m^3)
Underfloor volume (optional): 150 cu ft (4.25 m^3) forward, 58 cu ft (1.64 m^3) aft

WEIGHTS:
Empty, operating: 33,200 lb (15,059 kg)
Maximum zero fuel: 55,000 lb (24,948 kg)
Maximum take-off: 63,000 lb (28,576 kg) MTOGW
Maximum landing: 58,000 lb (26,308 kg)
Payload: 21,800 lb (9,888 kg)

PERFORMANCE:
Range: 700 naut miles (806 miles) 1,297 km with 21,534 lb (9,768 kg) payload, with 45 minutes reserve and allowance for 100 naut mile alternate
Range with full fuel: 1,475 naut miles (1,698 miles) 2,733 km with optional fuel load, or 1,150 naut miles (1,324 miles) 2,131 km with standard fuel load, with 45 minutes reserve and allowance for 100 naut mile alternate

Sales: 2 CV5800 freight versions completed, which have accumulated over 8,000 flying hours at a 99+% dispatch reliability rate. Production has begun of a third CV5800, with plans for continued production for several more.

Aircraft variants:
CV5800 cargo version is configured to a Class 'E' standard and is available with a cargo conveyance system. It has a cabin volume of 3,096 cu ft (87.67 m^3), operating empty weight of 33,166 lb (15,044 kg), and payload of 21,834 lb (9,904 kg).
CV5800 passenger version is for 76 passengers at 32 ins (81 cm) seat pitch.

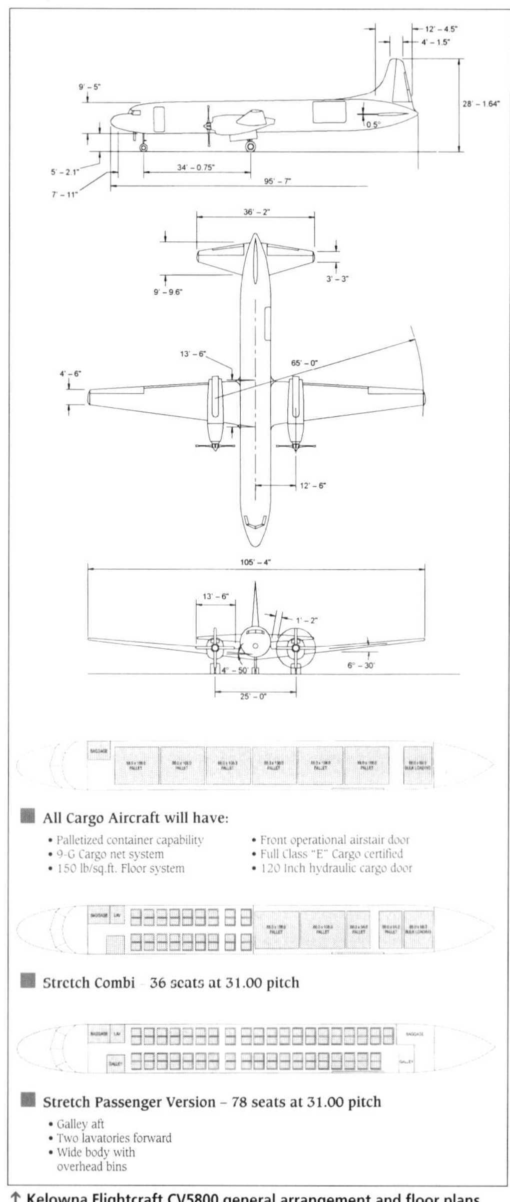

↑ Kelowna Flightcraft CV5800 general arrangement and floor plans *(courtesy Kelowna Flightcraft)*

Aviation Industries of China — China

Corporate address:
See Combat section for organization details.

Comments: AVIC is co-developing the Air Express 100/A316 and A317 airliner range with Singapore Technologies and Airbus Industrie Asia. Details can be found in the multi-national part of this section. The Special Vehicle Institute is a subsidiary of AVIC, specializing in R&D of seaplanes, wing-in-ground-effect aircraft, and airships (see Airship section).

Harbin Aircraft Manufacturing Corporation — China

Corporate address:
See Combat section for company details.

ACTIVITIES

■ See also Y-11B in the General Aviation and EC-120 in the Helicopter sections.

Harbin Y-12 (II), Y-12 (IV) and Harbin/ Canadian Aerospace Group Twin Panda

First flight: June 1984.
Certification: *Y-12 (II)*: 25 December 1985 (Tc from CAAC), December 1986 (Pc from CAAC), and 20 June 1990 (Tc from CAA). *Y-12 (IV)*: 3 July 1994 (Tc from CAAC) and 26 March 1995 from FAA. Designed to the requirements of FAR Pt 23 and FAR Pt 135 Apdx A. Conforms to CCAR-23 and BCAR-K (CAA).
First delivery: September 1985.
Chief designer: Song Hongxing.
Structural life: 20,000 flying hours or 20 years.
Role: Light general purpose transport with STOL characteristics, for passengers or cargo, air dropping, parachute jumping, forest seeding and agricultural, cloud seeding, geological survey, aerial photography, maritime surveillance (illustrated in the 1996-97 edition of *WA&SD*, page 208) and more. AEW and calibration versions are under development.
Airport limits: LCN 7.
Sales: Well over 100 Y-12s sold by Harbin (see Aircraft variants), with Chinese operators including Flying Dragon Aviation (9), China General Aviation Corporation (5), China Southwest Airlines (4), Guizhou Aviation Corporation (1) and No 630 Institute of AVIC (1). Exports by Harbin include Air Kiribati Ltd (1), Aero Bengal Airlines Ltd (2), Cambodia Air Force (2), Eritrea Air Force (3), Fiji Air (3), Kenya Air Force (6), Lao Aviation (7), Malaysia (Berjaya Air Charter, 2), Ministry of Defence of Mauritania (2), Middle East (9), Mongolian Airlines (6), Ministry of Defence of Namibia (2), Nepal Airlines (5), Pakistan Army (2), Pakistan Air Force (2), Peruvian Air Force (6), Ministry of Internal Affairs of Peru (3), Philippines (Island Holding, 3), Sri Lanka Air Force (9), Ministry of Defence of Tanzania (3), Ministry of Defence – Government of Zambia (4), and Zimbabwe Airlines (1). In 1998, agreement reached with the Canadian Aerospace Group for 50 Y-12(IV) airframes over 3 years for completion for the North American market, with 150 options, as Twin Pandas.

Details *(for Y-12 (II), except under Aircraft variants and boxed details)*

Crew: 2 (flight).
Passengers: 17, or 15 parachutists.
Seat pitch: 29.5 ins (79 cm).
Size of baggage doors: Front: 1 ft 7 ins × 2 ft 4.5 ins (0.48 × 0.72 m). Rear: 4 ft 1 ins × 1 ft 10 ins (1.25 × 0.55 m).
Baggage compartments: Front: 27.2 cu ft (0.77 m^3) volume, and 220 lb (100 kg) load. Rear: 66.6 cu ft (1.89 m^3), and 573 lb (260 kg) load.
Wing control surfaces: Ailerons (starboard tab) and 2 section double-slotted flaps.
Tail control surfaces: Horn-balanced elevators and rudder (with tabs).

↑ One of 3 Fiji Air Harbin Y-12s

Flight control system: Mechanical, but with electrically actuated flaps.
Construction materials: Metal. Composite materials may be introduced later.
Engines: 2 Pratt & Whitney Canada PT6A-27 turboprops.
Engine rating: Each 620 shp (462.3 kW), with Hartzell 8 ft 2 ins (2.49 m) 3-blade propellers.
Fuel system: 2,712 lb (1,230 kg).
Hydraulic system: 2 independent sets (normal and emergency) of pressure supply and brake distribution system.
Electrical system: 2 × 28 volt 6,000W DC starter-generators, 2 × 600VA 400Hz single-phase static inverters supplying AC power (115V and 26V), and 1 × 28 volt DC receptacle for external power.
Braking system: Hydraulic.
De-icing system: Can fly into icing conditions when optional de-icing equipment for the wings and tail unit is installed.
Radar: Optional AlliedSignal Bendix/King RDR-1400C weather radar.
Flight avionics/instrumentation: VFR and IFR. Standard com/nav equipment is VHF-251 radio, HF-230 SSB radio, ADF-650A radio compass, AUD-251H intercom, ALT-50A radio altimeter, TDR-950 transponder, DME-451 distance-measuring equipment, MKR-350 beacon marker receiver, VOR-351, PN-101 gyro magnetic compass, 101420-11934 encoding altimeter, GLS-350 glideslope receiver, and G8400A-36-24 anti-collision light. Options include APS-65 autopilot and GNS-500A-4 Omega. Y-12 (IV) has traffic alert and collision avoidance system (TCAS 1), and voice/digital flight data recorders.
Mission equipment: Depends on role. Forest seeding and agricultural equipment includes a 1,200 litre hopper. Radar in a bulbous nose for AEW.

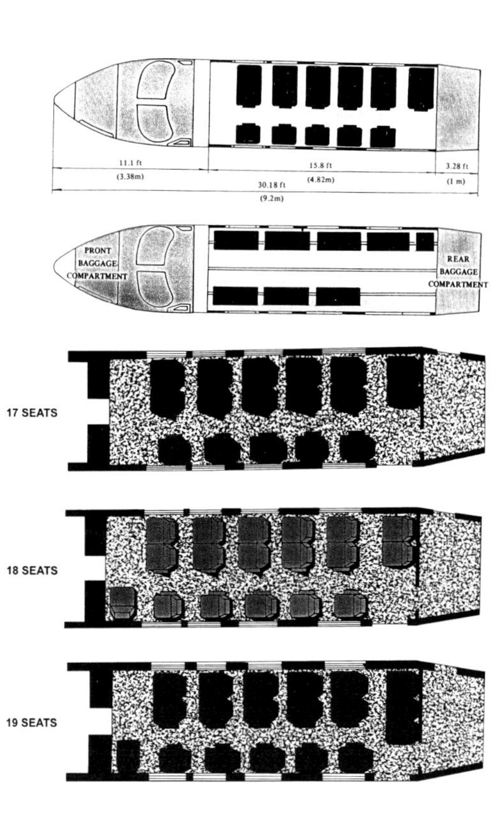

↑ *Top to bottom:* **Y-12 (II) cabins in Commuter and Cargo layouts, Y-12 (IV) 17/18/19-seat cabin layouts** *(courtesy Harbin)*

Aircraft variants:
Y-12 (II) is the standard current version, as detailed.
Y-12 (IV) was developed from the Y-12 (II) and has new 'shearing' wingtips to increase take-off weight to 12,500 lb (5,670 kg). 19 passenger seats, 4,374 lb (1,984 kg) payload, and the addition of an external baggage door in the rear fuselage to ease loading/unloading.
Twin Panda is the name for Y-12 (IV)s fitted out in Canada by the Canadian Aerospace Group and marketed as a possible replacement for the Twin Otter. Western instruments, wheels/brakes and cabin interior. PT6A-34 engines.

Details for Y-12 (II), *with Y-12(IV) in italics where different*

PRINCIPAL DIMENSIONS:
Wing span: 56 ft 6.5 ins (17.235 m), *63 ft (19.2 m)*
Maximum length: 48 ft 9 ins (14.86 m)
Maximum height: 18 ft 7.5 ins (5.675 m)

CABIN:
Length: 15 ft 10 ins (4.82 m)
Width: 4 ft 9.5 ins (1.46 m)
Height: 5 ft 7 ins (1.7 m)
Volume: 454.7 cu ft (12.9 m^3)
Main passenger/cargo door: 4 ft 6 ins × 4 ft 9 ins (1.38 × 1.45 m)

WINGS:
Aerofoil section: LS(1)-0417
Area: 368.9 sq ft (34.27 m^2)
Aspect ratio: 8.668

UNDERCARRIAGE:
Type: Fixed, with nosewheel. Suited to grass, sand, earth, or prepared airstrips
Main wheel tyre size: 640 × 230 mm
Nose wheel tyre size: 480 × 200 mm
Wheel base: 15 ft 5 ins (4.698 m), *15 ft 5.1 ins (4.702 m)*
Wheel track: 11 ft 10 ins (3.61 m)
Turning radius: 55 ft (16.75 m)

WEIGHTS:
Maximum zero fuel: *11,438 lb (5,188 kg)*
Maximum take-off: 11,684 lb (5,300 kg), *12,500 lb (5,670 kg)*
Maximum landing: 11,684 lb (5,300 kg), *11,905 lb (5,400 kg)*
Payload: 3,748 lb (1,700 kg), *4,374 lb (1,984 kg)*

PERFORMANCE:
Maximum cruise speed for Y-12 (II): 177 kts (204 mph) 328 km/h, at 9,840 ft (3,000 m)
Maximum operating speed for Y-12 (IV): *162 kts (186 mph) 300 km/h*
Economic cruise speed: 135 kts (155 mph) 250 km/h, at 9,840 ft (3,000 m)
Cruise speed for Y-12 (IV): *135-140 kts (155-162 mph) 250-260 km/h*
Take-off distance: 1,395 ft (425 m), *1,575 ft (480 m)*, both *with 15° flaps*
Take-off ground run: 1,115 ft (340 m), *1,247 ft (380 m)*, both *with 15° flaps*
Landing distance: 2,034 ft (620 m) with brakes only, 1,575 ft (480 m) with brakes and reversed propellers, 1,214 ft (370 m) STOL *with 20° flaps*
Landing ground run: 1,115 ft (340 m) with brakes only, *1,083 ft (330 m) with brakes only*, 657 ft (200 m) with brakes and reversed propellers plus *20° flaps*
Maximum climb rate: 1,595 ft (486 m) per minute, *1,535 ft (468 m) per minute*
Maximum climb rate, 1 engine: 276 ft (84 m) per minute, *295 ft (90 m) per minute*
Cruise altitude and 1-engine ceiling: 9,840 ft (3,000 m)
Ceiling: 23,000 ft (7,000 m)
Range: 723 naut miles (832 miles) 1,340 km, at economic cruise speed and 3,000 m, 45 minutes reserve, *728 naut miles (839 miles) 1,350 km*
Duration for Y-12 (II): 5.2 hours, with above conditions

Shaanxi Aircraft Company — China

Corporate address:
PO Box 34, Chenggu, Shaanxi 723213, or PO Box 35, Chenggu, Shaan-Xi 723215.

Telephone: +86 916 2202156, 2216301-457
Facsimile: +86 916 216302
Cable: 3400, 3500

Information:
Li Yousheng (Marketing Manager).

ACTIVITIES

▪ Production of standard and special mission aircraft, ground support equipment, and offering improvements and modifications. In addition to the Y8, Shannxi produces the Hanjiang 1,323 lb (600 kg) small commercial vehicle, SFJ6800 36-seat coach, and SFJ6120 tourist bus.

Shaanxi Y8

First flight: 25 December 1974 (prototype Y8); 17 December 1990 for Y8C.
First delivery: 1986 in Y8B form.
Role: Medium-range transport, with special mission variants. Developed from the Antonov An-12B.
Airport limits: ACN rating of 15.
Sales: Some 60 received by military and commercial customers, the PLA Air Force thought to have about half those currently flying.
Crew: 2 pilots, flight engineer, navigator and radio operator.
Passengers: 121 passengers in the Y8K. 96 troops, or 80 paratroops, or 72 litters, 20 seated casualties and 3 attendants in Y8 and Y8C. Other transport versions can accommodate 14 persons in a pressurized forward compartment.
Pressurization: Fully pressurized cabin in Y8C, Y8D, Y8K and Y8X. See Environmental control system.
Freight hold capacity: Y-8 accommodates 2 trucks, Y8C 2 trucks plus a jeep. Y8C accommodates size A and M standard containers or pallets (thirteen 1-m cargo pallets, two 4-m cargo pallets, two 6-m cargo pallets), and is also suited to carrying perishable goods and livestock.
Size of rear ramp door: Y8 has 2 inward-opening cargo doors and ramp of 25 ft 2 ins (7.67 m) length, 7 ft 1 ins to 10 ft 2 ins (2.16 to 3.1 m) width, that hinges upward inside the hold to provide direct loading. Ramp of Y8 is otherwise used for loading/unloading on the ground. New cargo ramp/door for Y8C and other newer variants, opening outward and with closing automatically controlled by hydraulic and electrical systems; door can be lowered to the ground for drive-in loading of vehicles, and can be adjusted to track bed height for straight-in handling of standard containers, pallets and other cargo with the roller system.
Loading facilities: Electric winch with tow and hoist capacity of 5,070 lb (2,300 kg), and optional 4-track roller mats.
Wing control surfaces: Double-slotted trailing-edge Fowler flaps, 2-section aileron (with trim tab) on each outer panel, and spoilers.
Tail control surfaces: Elevators (with trim tabs) and rudder (with trim tab).
Flight control system: Mechanical; trailing-edge flaps are hydraulically actuated.
Construction materials: Metal.
Engines: 4 South Aero Engine Company WJ6 turboprops, with J17-G13 4-blade reversible-pitch propellers (feathering angle 83° 30'; blades pitch angle range 0° to 83° 30'; 1,075 operating rpm; electric de-icing). Engines equipped with anti-icing and fire extinguishing devices. WDZ-1 APU for engine starting and electrical power.
Engine rating: Each 4,250 eshp (3,169 ekW).
Fuel system: 50,505 lb (22,909 kg), except Y8C which has 32,112 lb (14,566 kg).
Hydraulic system: 2 independent systems, of 2,204 psi and 2,132 psi, with electric and manual emergency back-up.
Electrical system: 28.5 volt DC supply via 8 × 12 kW generators, the WDZ-1 APU and 4 × 28 amp-hour batteries. 115 volt 400Hz AC supply via 4 × 12kVA alternators.
Environmental control system: For Y8, oxygen equipment and air conditioning facilities, the latter assuring pressurization (2.9 psi differential above 4,300 m), heating and ventilation of cabins. For Y8C, 2 air-conditioning facilities and oxygen equipment, the former modified type with high pressure water removing system. Cabin temperature is adjustable between 16 and 28° C.
Braking system: Hydraulically operated discs, with inertial anti-skid system.
De-icing: Anti-ice devices on the wing leading edges, tail unit and engine intakes, propeller blades, spinners and windshield.
Radar: Honeywell colour weather radar in an undernose radome.
Flight avionics/instrumentation: Y8C has a communications system that includes KHF 950 HF radio, VHF 22B radio, SSCVR cockpit voice recorder and JT-6A earphones; navigation system with VIR-32 VOR/ILS, AHS-85E attitude heading system, TNL 8100 GPS, DME-42, KJ-6C autopilot and AI-804u ATT indicator; TDR-90 ATC responder and ROR-1400L CWR; instruments including ALT-55 radio altitude, ADF-60 automatic direction finder, ADS-85 air data system, EFIS-85A electronic flight, and 811B-24 digital clock.
Expendable weapons and equipment: Small bomb rack (2 on older aircraft) thought possible under each main undercarriage nacelle for flare bombs to light the landing area at night. At least 2 former Sri Lankan aircraft carried bombs.

↑ Shaanxi Y8C pressurized transport *(Sebastian Zacharias)*

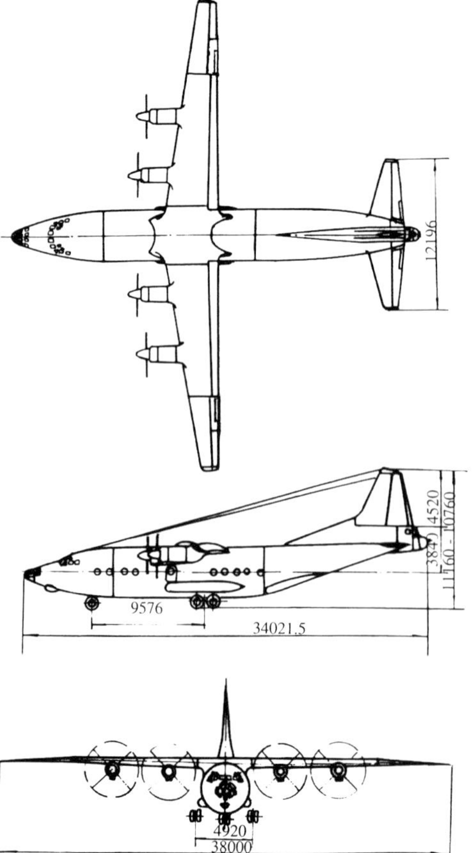

↑ Shaanxi Y8 general arrangement *(courtesy Shaanxi)*

Aircraft variants:
Y8 was the original unpressurized-hold version, sometimes with tail gun turret. Prototype and production aircraft.
Y8A became a helicopter and general unpressurized-hold transport, the cabin height slightly increased by removal of the unnecessary internal cargo handling system.
Y8B was produced for civil use, with empty weight reduced by 3,792 lb (1,720 kg) by removal of military gear. First flown in 1990 and certified in 1993.
Y8C introduced pressurization for the lengthened cargo cabin of 51 ft 6 ins (15.7 m), new cargo ramp/door opening outward and automatically controlled by hydraulic and electrical systems, conveyor system for standard containers, modified undercarriage for increased airframe fatigue life, new fuel burn sequence for longer wing life, improved avionics (which see), and new environmental control system. 32,112 lb (14,566 kg) fuel capacity. First flown in 1990.
Y8D is an export version, with some western avionics, reportedly operated by Myanmar, Sri Lanka and Sudan.
Y8D II is the current export version, with similar avionics to Y8C.
Y8E is a UAV launch/control aircraft, first flown in 1989.
Y8F is a livestock transport, for 500 sheep or other animals. Certification by CAAC on 26 January 1994.

Details for Y8, *with Y8C in italics*

PRINCIPAL DIMENSIONS:
Wing span: 124 ft 8 ins (38 m), *the same*
Maximum length: 111 ft 7.5 ins (34.0215 m), *the same*
Maximum height: 36 ft 7 ins (11.16 m), *the same*

CARGO COMPARTMENT:
Length: 44 ft 3.5 ins (13.5 m), *51 ft 6 ins (15.7 m)*
Width: 9 ft 10 ins to 11 ft 6 ins (3 to 3.5 m), with 3 to 3.5 m between frames 9 to 13, 3.5 m between frames 13 and 25, 3 m between frames 25 and 30, and 3.5 m up to frame 43
Height: 7 ft 4.5 ins to 8 ft 6.5 ins (2.25 to 2.6 m), with 2.25 to 2.5 m between frames 9 and 13, 2.5 m between frames 13 and 25, 2.4 m between frames 25 and 30, and 2.6 m up to frame 43
Volume: 4,354 cu ft (123.3 m^3), *4,859 cu ft (137.6 m^3)*

WINGS:
Aerofoil section: TsAGI-based C-5-18, C-3-16, C-3-14 (root to tip)
Sweepback: 0° centre section; middle and outer panels 9° 41' at leading edge and 6° 50' at quarter chord

TAIL UNIT:
Tailplane span: 40 ft (12.196 m)

UNDERCARRIAGE:
Type: Retractable, with steerable twin nosewheels (±35°). 4-wheel main bogies with low-pressure tyres suited to unpaved airfields
Main wheel tyre size: 1,050 × 300 mm
Nose wheel tyre size: 900 × 300 mm
Wheel base: 31 ft 5 ins (9.576 m), *the same*
Wheel track: 16 ft 2 ins (4.92 m), *the same*
Turning radius: 45 ft 1 ins (13.75 m)

WEIGHTS:
Empty, operating: 76,059-77,382 lb (34,500-35,100 kg), *76,632 lb (34,760 kg)*
Maximum zero fuel: 121,867 lb (55,278 kg), *122,440 lb (55,538 kg)*
Maximum take-off: 134,482 lb (61,000 kg), *the same*
Maximum landing: 127,868 lb (58,000 kg), *the same*
Payload: 44,092 lb (20,000 kg) distributed, 35,274 lb (16,000 kg) concentrated bulk item, *the same*
Airdrop payload: 29,100 lb (13,200 kg), or 16,314 lb (7,400 kg) for a single item

PERFORMANCE:
Maximum speed: 357 kts (411 mph) 662 km/h, *345 kts (398 mph) 640 km/h*
Cruise speed: 297 kts (342 mph) 550 km/h, *the same*
Take-off distance: 4,035-4,167 ft (1,230-1,270 m) at sea level, MTOW, *the same*
FAR take-off field length: 6,234 ft (1,900 m)
Landing distance: 3,445 ft (1,050 m) at sea level, MLW, *the same*
FAR landing field length: 5,414 ft (1,650 m)
Cruise altitude: 26,245 ft (8,000 m)
Ceiling: 34,120 ft (10,400 m), *32,975 ft (10,050 m)*, service
Range with full fuel: 3,032 naut miles (3,489 miles) 5,615 km, *1,857 naut miles (2,138 miles) 3,442 km*

Y8F100 is a cargo only variant of Y8F, with Y8C type rear ramp/door. Users include China Postal Airlines.
Y8F200 is a totally pressurized aircraft, based on the Y8C but used for cargo operations only. Y8C type rear ramp/door.
Y8H carries survey equipment.
Y8K was offered as an airliner version, with rear ramp/door deleted. 121 passengers.
Y8X is a maritime surveillance version, with Litton APS-504(V)3 or 5 surveillance radar, infra-red sensors, cameras, sonobuoys and other equipment. 1 built at time of writing.
Y8 AEW is a speculated version, though now to be an unlikely candidate for China's known AEW requirement (see Reconnaissance section – China, Israel and UK).

Shanghai Aviation Industrial Corporation — China

Corporate address:
PO Box 436-840, Shanghai 200436.
Telephone: +86 21 566 81122
Facsimile: +86 21 556 84336

ACTIVITIES

▪ Shanghai Aircraft Manufacturing Factory division produced 35 MD-82 and MD-83 airliners under licence from McDonnell Douglas of the USA, mostly for Chinese operation but including 5 MD-83s purchased by TWA. The first MD-82, built using US supplied assemblies, made its maiden flight on 2 July 1987 and entered service with China Northern Airlines on 31 July that year. Late aircraft are of mostly Chinese manufacture and assembly. On 25 April 1994, SAIC signed a sales agreement with China Northern Airlines and China Aviation Supplies Corporation, covering the last of the 35 MD-80s (going to CNA on 18 October 1994, with roll-out on 31 August). A further 20 MD-82T Trunkliners were under negotiation in 1994 but plans were subsequently abandoned due to MD-90 production; Trunkliner differed from the other versions in having 4-wheel main undercarriage bogies to allow operation from low bearing strength runways.

▪ On 25 June 1992 the MD-90-30 was chosen to be the second form of Trunkliner for Chinese assembly, with Shanghai as prime contractor (also mostly Chinese manufacture of subassemblies, with subcontracts to Chengdu, Shenyang and Xi'an), having 25,000 lbf (111.21 kN) International Aero Engines V2525 engines. Negotiations were concluded and contracts signed on 4 November 1994 covering co-production of 20 from 1995, for delivery from April 1998, of which China Northern and China Eastern were expected to receive 11 and 9 respectively under a July 1996 agreement, though firm commitments covered only 15 almost a year later. The last MD-90-30 will be delivered in December 2000.

Xi'an Aircraft Company — China

Corporate address:
See Combat section for company details.

Xi'an Y7 and Y7H

First flight: 25 December 1970 for Y7, 26 December 1993 for Y7-200A, and 24 March 1992 for Y7H-500.
Certification: 1980, and 30 December 1993 for Y7H-500.
First delivery: 1984.
Role: Y7/Y7-100/200B are short/medium-range passenger, executive commuter, and civil/military cargo transports, developed from the Antonov An-24. Also for scientific research, pilot and crew training (including aircrew training with the PLA Navy), rescue, aerial mapping and more. Y7-200A is a convertible passenger/cargo or cargo variant. Y7H/Y7H-500 are military/civil freighters based on the An-26 (with rear ramp/door), also suited cargo carrying, air-dropping, parachuting and medevac. In addition, Y7H-500 can be use for aerial mapping, geological survey, air seeding/rain making and forest firefighting. All versions listed by Xi'an as the Y7 family.
Airframe life: 30,000 flight hours or 15,000 landings or 15 years.
Airport limits: LCN/radius of relative stiffness for Y7-100 at MTOW (rigid runway): 64/16.5, 79/17 and 94/17.3.
Noise levels: Average below 85 dB for Y7-100.
Sales: Some 70 Y7s of all versions are believed to be in commercial airline service with 18 operators, the largest number (11) with China Northern Airlines and those exported including Lao Aviation (5 Y7-100 series). Military users include the PLA Air Force (about 30) and PLA Navy (about 10, including 2 used for training).
Crew: 2 flight crew for Y7-200A plus observer; pilot, co-pilot and flight engineer for Y7/-100/-200B; or 5 crew for Y7-100C series. Y7H has 2 pilots, navigator, radio operator and flight engineer; Y7H-500 has pilot, co-pilot and flight engineer.
Passengers: Y7/-100/-200B accommodate 48, 50 or 52 passengers, or 20-22 for the executive commuter variant and 38 for VIP, and Y7-200A has 52, 56 or 60. Environmental control system automatically controls cabin temperature within 20° C ±2°. Y7H can carry 39 paratroops, 38 fully-armed troops, or 24 litters and an attendant.
Seat pitch: 30.7 ins (78 cm) for 52 seats and 28.3 ins (72 cm) for 56 or 60 seats in Y7-200A.
Galley: With food cabinets and electric kettles, aft of passenger cabin.
Pressurization: Cockpit and cabin pressurized.
Freight hold access: Y7H and Y7H-500 have a rear ramp/door, which can also be retracted under the fuselage (belly position) for direct loading from trucks. Door operation can be normal, emergency and manual, and open door setting can be at any position between fully down and belly position.
Loading facilities: For freight handling, a DJC-2 electric winch (with 4,409 lb, 2,000 kg lifting capacity, and maximum 4m/minute powered speed with a 1,168 lb, 530 kg load) and floor-mounted KSY-1 hydraulic conveyor (10,031 lb, 4,550 kg capacity) are in the Y7H/Y7H-500 cabin.
Baggage holds: 2, totalling 370.8 cu ft (10.5 m^3).
Wing control surfaces: Ailerons (21° up, 16° down, ±1°) with servo/trim tabs, single-slotted inboard and double-slotted outboard flaps (all 15° for take-off and 38° landing). Winglets reduce drag by 4%, offering 5% fuel saving.
Tail control surfaces: Elevators (30° up, 15° down, ±1°) with balance tabs, and rudder (25°, ±1°) with trim/spring tabs.
Flight control system: Mechanical for ailerons/elevators/rudder, with electric servo motor for autopilot operation. Hydraulic flap actuation.
Construction materials: Fuselage has 49 frames. Metal, but Y7-200B has carbonfibre tailplane and fin tips.
Engines: Y7-100 has 2 × 2,900 eshp (2,162 ekW) Dongan WJ5A-1 turboprops with J16-G10A 4-blade auto-feathering propellers. Y7-200A has 2,750 shp (2,051 kW) Pratt & Whitney Canada PW127Cs with Hamilton Standard 247F-3 4-blade propellers. Y7-200B has WJ5A-1G engines, with 4-blade propellers. Y7H has 2 × 2,790 shp (2,080 kW) WJ5A-1(M)s. All have a 1,984 lbf (8.826 kN) PY19A-300 turbojet for engine starting and performance boosting. Y7H-500 has 3,050 eshp (2,275 ekW) WJ5Es. APU (AlliedSignal GTCP-150CY for Y7-200A).
Fuel system: 10,560 lb (4,790 kg) for Y7-100, 12,125 lb (5,500 kg) for Y7H-500.
Electrical system: 28.5 volt DC supply via 2 engine-driven QF-18 generators (each 18kW). Emergency 24 volt power via 2 × 12HK-28 batteries. Main single-phase 115 volt, 400 Hz AC supply via JF-30A generator system, but also with 3 static inverters

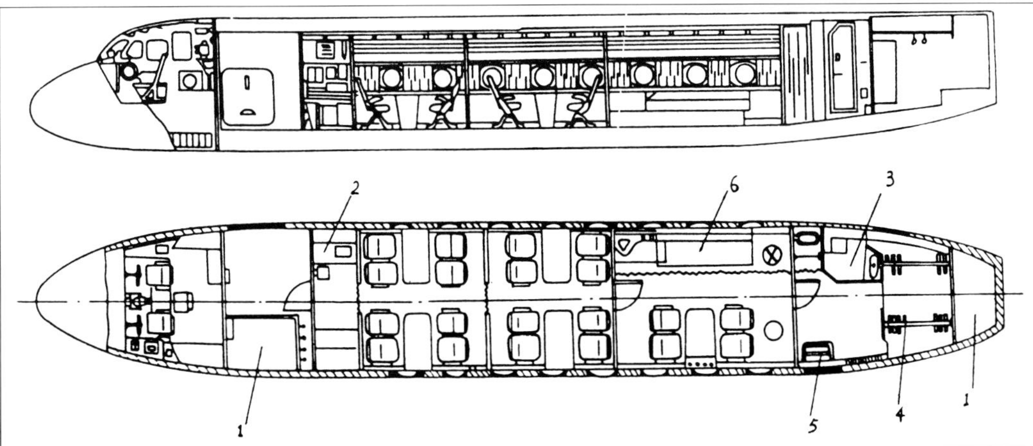

↑ **Xi'an Y7-100 in 20-seat executive commuter layout, with *1* baggage compartment, *2* galley, *3* toilet, *4* wardrobe, *5* airstair and *6* sofa** *(courtesy Xi'an)*

Details for Y7-100, *with Y7H-500 in italics*

PRINCIPAL DIMENSIONS:
Wing span: 97 ft 4 ins (29.666 m), *95 ft 9.5 ins (29.2 m)*
Maximum length: 79 ft 5.5 ins (24.218 m), *79 ft 9 ins (24.31 m)*
Maximum height: 28 ft 1 ins (8.553 m), *29 ft 2 ins (8.89 m)*

CABIN:
Length: 32 ft 6 ins (9.91 m), *37 ft 6 ins (11.43 m)*
Width: 9 ft 1 ins (2.76 m), *9 ft 1.5 ins (2.78 m)*
Height: 6 ft 1 ins (1.86 m), *6 ft 3 ins (1.91 m)*
Volume: 1,822 cu ft (51.6 m^3), *2,118.9 cu ft (60 m^3)*
Main passenger door: *2 ft × 4 ft 7 ins (0.6 × 1.4 m)*
Cargo door: *10 ft × 7 ft 10.5 ins (3.05 × 2.4 m), with sill height of 5 ft 8.5 ins (1.74 m)*

WINGS:
Area: 810.09 sq ft (75.26 m^2), also documented as 812.78 sq ft (75.51 m^2), *807.08 sq ft (74.98 m^2)*
Aspect ratio: 11.694, *11.37*
Sweepback: 6° 50' at 25° outer-section chord
Incidence: 3°
Anhedral: 2° 12'

UNDERCARRIAGE:
Type: Retractable, with steerable (±45°) and castoring nosewheels. Twin wheels on each unit, with low-pressure tyres. Can operate from grass, soil, crushed stone or paved runways
Main wheel tyre size: 900 × 300 to 370 mm, *1,050 × 400 mm*
Nose wheel tyre size: 700 × 250 to 350 mm, *700 × 250 mm*
Wheel base: *27 ft 5 ins (8.366 m)*
Wheel track: *25 ft 11 ins (7.9 m)*
Turning circle: *36 ft 11 ins (11.25 m) radius minimum*

WEIGHTS:
Empty, operating: 33,153 lb (15,038 kg), with 3 crew, *34,773 lb (15,773 kg)*
Maximum ramp: *53,241 lb (24,150 kg)*
Maximum take-off: 48,060 lb (21,800 kg), *52,910 lb (24,000 kg)*
Maximum landing: *51,808 lb (23,500 kg)*
Payload: 10,362 lb (4,700 kg), *12,125 lb (5,500 kg)*

PERFORMANCE:
Maximum speed: 272 kts (312 mph) 503 km/h, *255 kts (294 mph) 471 km/h*
Cruise speed: 257 kts (296 mph) 476 km/h, at 21,000 kg at 6,000 m, *237 kts (272 mph) 438 km/h*
Economic cruise speed: 228 kts (263 mph) 423 km/h, at 21,000 kg and 6,000 m, *229 kts (263 mph) 424 km/h*
Stall speed: 85-110 kts (98-126 mph) 157-203 km/h, with 38° and 0° flaps respectively, at MTOW
Take-off field length: *4,594 ft (1,400 m)*
Take-off distance: 2,100 ft (640 m), at 21,800 kg, *2,812 ft (857 m)*
Landing distance: 2,116 ft (645 m), at 21,800 kg, *2,080 ft (634 m)*
Maximum climb rate: 1,503 ft (458 m) per minute, at 21,000 kg, *1,680 ft (512 m) per minute*
Climb rate, 1 engine: *577 ft (176 m) per minute*
Ceiling: 28,700 ft (8,750 m), at 21,000 kg, *26,905 ft (8,200 m)*
Ceiling, 1 engine: 12,630 ft (3,850 m), at 19,000 kg, *13,125 ft (4,000 m)*
Range with full fuel: 1,297 naut miles (1,493 miles) 2,403 km, *1,160 naut miles (1,336 miles) 2,150 km*
Range with full payload: 491 naut miles (565 miles) 910 km, *539 naut miles (621 miles) 1,000 km*
Duration: *5.38 hours*

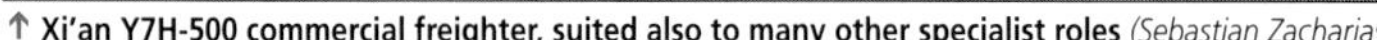

↑ Xi'an Y7H-500 commercial freighter, suited also to many other specialist roles *(Sebastian Zacharias)*

↑ Xi'an Y7H-500 flight deck *(Sebastian Zacharias)*

(1 for emergency) and 3-phase 36 volt, 400 Hz supply via an SBL-500 converter. Y7H-500 differs in having an additional DC-24B generator for auxiliary power supply (9kW) and 3 batteries.
Hydraulic system: Main system pressure 2,205 psi (±71), and emergency 2,275 psi (±213).
Braking system: Electronic anti-skid system on Y7-200B.
De-icing system: Hot air for wings and tail leading edges, turbine generator oil, engine guide vanes and inlet lips. Electric for propeller blades, spinners, windshield, air pressure sensors and more.
Fire system: HG-11 and HG-12 fire warning sensors and 4 extinguisher bottles for engines, and portable extinguishers on bulkheads of frames 7 and 34 for cabin in Y7-100.
Radar: Primus 90 colour weather radar.
Flight avionics/instrumentation: Y7-100 principal navigation and air data equipment comprises Honeywell VG-311 dual attitude reference system and dual MHRS; Rockwell Collins DF-206, ILS with 51Z-4 marker beacon receiver, AL-101 radio altimeter, DME-42, dual 51RV-4B VOR/ILS, ADI-84A, dual EHSI-74, 2 RMI-36, FGS-65 and CWS-80; Litton LTN-211 Omega/VLF; SFENA H321AKM emergency horizon, IDC air data instrument, Sundstrand 980-4100-FWXS flight data recorder, and Chinese KJ-6A autopilot and XLG-2A stall warning system with stick shaker. Y7-200A has Rockwell Collins EFIS-85 or 86. Y7-200B has EFIS-85B14, APS-85 digital flight control system, AHS-85 strapdown heading attitude system, and ADC-82A air data system, with data bus. Communication equipment for Y7-100 comprises Rockwell Collins 628T-3 HF, 618M-3 VHF, Becker 3100 audio system and Sundstrand AV-557C voice recorder. Rockwell Collins 621A-6A air traffic control transponder. Y7H-500 has KHF-950 HF and FJ-30 flight data recorder. All information on a CRT.

Aircraft variants:
Y7 was the basic 3-crew version, based on the An-24. Some retrofitted with winglets. Production ended. Also produced as a full freighter, the first delivered on 24 June 1992.
Y7-100 is an upgraded Y7 that conforms to BCAR requirements, featuring winglets, and updated cockpit and cabin systems of Western origin. 3 crew. Also for combi loads.
Y7-100C1, C2 and C3 are 5-crew versions with different levels of equipment.
Y7-200A is a newer convertible commuter passenger/cargo or all cargo aircraft with lower empty weight, developed with Boeing consultation. 2 flight crew plus optional observer. P&WC PW127C engines, lengthened fuselage (81 ft 1 ins, 24.708 m), redesigned forward fuselage to improve view from the cockpit, modified wing leading edges and flaps, vertical control sticks, and more.
Y7-200B has a fuselage lengthened by 29 ins (74 cm) compared with Y7-100 series, new wing leading-edge profile, ground spoilers, and 1% larger tailplane. Some use of composites (see Construction). Anti-skid system for undercarriage. Forward cargo door and emergency exit enlarged. EFIS cockpit instrumentation. WJ5A-1G engines.
Y7E first flew on 5 July 1994. Believed able to take-off with full load under hot and high conditions.
Y7H is a 5-crew military cargo transport, based on the Antonov An-26. Has external suspension points for airdropping loads of up to 4,409 lb (2,000 kg). Rear ramp/door.
Y7H-500 is a civil version of Y7H. Certified for full production 15 June 1994. Wide range of possible roles, as detailed under Role. More powerful 3,050 eshp (2,275 ekW) WJ5E engines. Can take-off with full load under hot and high operations.

Let A.S. — Czech Republic

Corporate address:
686 04 Kunovice.

Telephone: +420 632 51 1111 (exchange), 61 616 (sales), or 51 3780
Facsimile: +420 632 61 352, 62 530
E-mail: let@let.cz
Web site: www.let.cz

Founded:
1950 under its own name, though an enterprise in Kunovice started in 1936 as Avia Aviation Works.

Information:
Milan Morkus (Marketing Manager – *telephone* +420 642 51 3344, *E-mail* morkus@let.cz)

ACTIVITIES

▪ See also Gliders section. Ayres Corporation of the USA was completing a 93% shareholding stake in July 1998.

Let L 410 UVP-E9 and -E20, L 420 and L 430

First flight: 16 April 1969 (L 410 prototype), 30 December 1984 for L 410 UVP-E, and 10 November 1993 for L 420.
Certification: 1986 in UVP-E form (Russian NLGS-2). L 410 UVP-E20 improved version certified July 1990 in Sweden (according to FAR 23/Amendment 34). UVP-E meets JAR 25 and FAR 23 requirements, also satisfying all FAR 36 and ICAO Annex 16 noise requirements. L 420 certified to FAA FAR 23 Amendment 41 requirements in 1994.
Role: STOL short-haul commuter, executive and cargo transport, with medevac, paratroop, photogrammetric and surveillance special mission versions. Operating temperatures -50° to +42° C.
Airframe life: 20,000 flight hours or 20,000 cycles or 20 years.
Airfield limits: Minimum strength of 6 kg/cm^2 for L-420.
Noise levels: Reduced on L 420.
Sales: Approaching 1,100 L 410s of all types delivered to civil and military customers in Europe, Africa, Asia and the Americas by 1998. Over 80% of all L 410s produced are still in operation.

Details *(L 410 UVP-E, except where stated)*

Crew: 2.
Passengers: 19 standard, with optional 17 passenger layout. Executive Shuttle has 8, 11 or 13 passenger interiors. See also Aircraft variants.
Seat pitch: 29.9 ins (76 cm) in 17 passenger layout.
Pressurization: None.
Baggage compartment: 24.72 cu ft (0.7 m^3) front, 27.2 cu ft (0.77 m^3) rear.
Freight hold capacity: For cargo operations, a stationary goods container of 106.3 × 46.9 × 11.8 ins (270 × 120 × 30 cm) is standard. Loading and unloading via large cargo doors with a width of 4 ft 1 ins (1.25 m) and height to sill of 2 ft 7.2 ins (0.792 m).

↑ Let L 410 UVP-E20 operated by Metavia Airlines *(Pavel Lukes)*

Details for L 410 UVP-E, *with L 420 in italics*

PRINCIPAL DIMENSIONS:
Wing span: 65 ft 6.5 ins (19.98 m) with tip tanks, 63 ft 11 ins (19.48 m) without. *L 420 the same*
Maximum length: 47 ft 3.75 ins (14.424 m), *the same*
Maximum height: 19 ft 1.5 ins (5.829 m), *the same*

CABIN:
Length: 20 ft 10 ins (6.345 m), *the same*
Width: 6 ft 3.5 ins (1.92 m), *the same*
Height: 5 ft 5.5 ins (1.66 m), *the same*
Volume: 632.13 cu ft (17.9 m^3), *the same*
Main passenger/cargo door: 4 ft 9.5 ins (1.46 m) high, and 2 ft 7.5 to 4 ft 1 ins (0.8 to 1.25 m) extendable width, *the same*

WINGS:
Aerofoil section: NACA 63A418, 63A412 (root/tip), *the same*
Area: 375.23 sq ft (34.86 m^2), *the same*
Aspect ratio: 10.89 without tip tanks, *the same*
Dihedral: 1° 45', *the same*
Incidence: 2°, -0° 30' root/tip

UNDERCARRIAGE:
Type: Retractable, with steerable nosewheel. Low pressure tyres for use from rain soaked, grassy and unpaved runway surfaces, *the same*
Main wheel tyre size: 718 × 306 mm, *720 × 310 mm*
Nose wheel tyre size: 548 × 221 mm, *550 × 225 mm*
Wheel base: 12 ft 0.25 ins (3.666 m), *the same*
Wheel track: 11 ft 11.5 ins (3.65 m), *the same*

WEIGHTS:
Empty: 8,730 lb (3,960 kg) for UVP-E9, 8,796 lb (3,990 kg) for UVP-E20, *8,962 lb (4,065 kg)*
Empty, operating: 9,083 lb (4,120 kg) for UVP-E9, 9,149 lb (4,150 kg) for UVP-E20, *9,314 lb (4,225 kg)*
Maximum zero fuel weight: 12,941 lb (5,870 kg), *13,007 lb (5,900 kg)*
Empty: 8,862 lb (4,020 kg) with tip tanks, *9,094 lb (4,125 kg)*
Maximum take-off: 14,550 lb (6,600 kg), *the same*
Climb limited take-off weight: 14,550 lb (6,600 kg) with 18° flaps, ISA + 15° C, 3,400 ft (1,036 m); 14,550 lb (6,600 kg) with 0° flaps, ISA + 15° C, 5,400 ft (1,645 m); *14,550 lb (6,600 kg) with 18° flaps, ISA + 15° C, 1,900 ft (579 m)*
Maximum landing: 14,110 lb (6,400 kg), *the same*
Payload: 3,770 lb (1,710 kg), *the same*
Fuel: 2,866 lb (1,300 kg) maximum, *the same*

BLOCK DATA (300 naut miles, ISA, FL140):
Block fuel: 1,093 lb (496 kg), *1,102 lb (500 kg)*
Block time: 98 minutes, *the same*

PERFORMANCE:
Maximum cruise speed: 208 kts (240 mph) 386 km/h at 14,000 ft (4,267 m), *209 kts (241 mph) 388 km/h* at 14,000 ft (4,267 m) altitude
Take-off field length to 35 ft (11 m), MTOW: 3,068 ft (935 m) ISA, at sea level for UVP-E9; 3,281 ft (1,000 m) ISA + 15° C, sea level for UVP-E9; 3,182 ft (970 m) ISA, at sea level for UVP-E20; 3,412 ft (1,040 m) ISA + 15° C, sea level for UVP-E20; *2,707 ft (825 m) ISA, at sea level; 3,035 ft (925 m) ISA + 15° C, sea level*
Take-off distance over a 35 ft (11 m) obstacle: 1,854 ft (565 m), sea level, ISA, MTOW, *1,820 ft (555 m)*
Landing field length over a 50 ft (15 m) obstacle, MLW: 2,756 ft (840 m) ISA at sea level; 2,855 ft (870 m) ISA + 15° C at sea level, *the same*
Maximum climb rate: 1,300 ft (396 m) per minute, *1,378 ft (420 m) per minute*, both ISA, sea level
Maximum climb rate, 1 engine: 335 ft (102 m) per minute, *354 ft (108 m) per minute*, both ISA, sea level
Ceiling: 23,785 ft (7,250 m) for 100 ft (30 m) per minute climb
Ceiling, 1 engine: 14,765 ft (4,500 m), *13,780 ft (4,200 m)*, both ISA, 95% MTOW, climb at 50 ft (15 m) per minute climb
Operating altitude: 13,780 ft (4,200 m) maximum
Range with full fuel (UVP-E): 711 naut miles (818 miles) 1,317 km, ISA, at 14,000 ft (4,267 m), ISA, 45 minutes hold
Range with full fuel (L 420): *733 naut miles (844 miles) 1,358 km, ISA, at 14,000 ft (4,267 m),with 45 minutes hold*
Range (L 420): *367 naut miles (422 miles) 680 km without tip tanks, 17 passengers and 45 minutes reserve*

Wing control surfaces: Double-slotted flaps, ailerons, ground spoilers and ABC tabs.
Tail control surfaces: Elevators and rudder with tabs. Small ventral fin.
Flight control system: Mechanical, except for hydraulic flaps and spoilers.
Construction materials: Aluminium alloy, except for fabric-covered flaps, rudder and elevators.
Engines: 2 Walter M 601E (for UVP-E9) and M 601E-21 (for UVP-E20) turboprops, with 90.55 ins (2.3 m) diameter Avia Hamilton V 510 5-blade, reversible-pitch, constant-speed propellers. L 420 has 778 shp (580 kW) M 601Fs.
Engine rating: Each 751 shp (560 kW).
Fuel system: 2,866 lb (1,300 kg) maximum (with wingtip tanks); wingtip tanks 200 litres each are optional. Fuel capacity without wingtip tanks 2,127 lb (965 kg).
Braking system: Disc brakes with ABS anti-skid on mainwheels only.
De-icing system: Wing leading-edge rubber boots. Tailplane and fin leading edges have pneumatic de-icing. Electric propeller de-icing.
Radar: Optional AlliedSignal Bendix/King RDS-81 weather radar.
Flight avionics/instrumentation: IFR. AlliedSignal Bendix/King Silver Crown or optional Gold Crown EFIS nav avionics, with optional KFC 325 autopilot, or Silver Crown with optional KFC 275 autopilot. Standard are ADF, VOR/ILS/MKR, NAV/RNAV/IL, transponder, DME, 2 VHF transceivers, 2 intercom, 2 public address, 2 gyro-compass, and standby head set. Other options include GPS, HF transceiver, radio altimeter, and ground proximity warning system (GPWS).

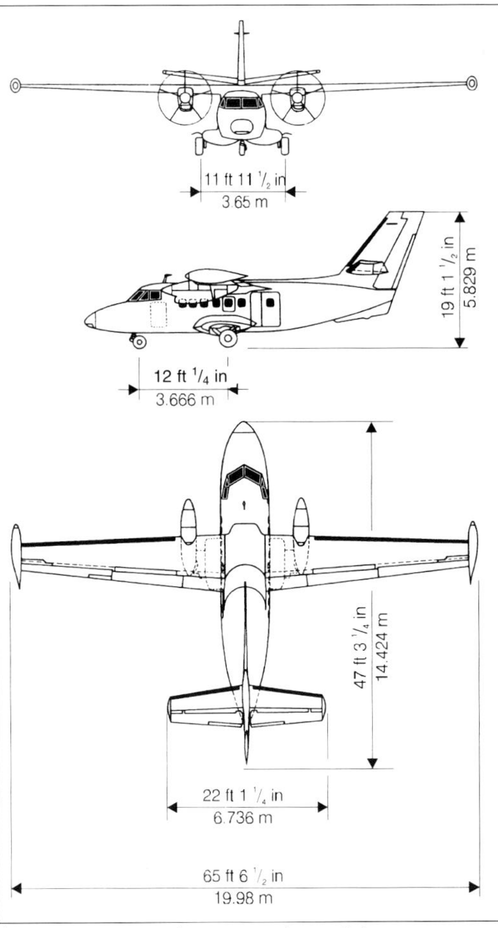

↑ Let L 410 UVP-E general arrangement *(courtesy Let)*

Aircraft variants:
UVP-E Commuter has 19 passengers plus 24.72 cu ft (0.7 m^3) front, 27.2 cu ft (0.77 m^3) rear baggage holds with inside access. Alternatively 17 passengers plus 24.72 and 47.7 cu ft (0.7 and 1.13 m^3) holds with outside access, tables and seats for attendant and stewardess. Toilet.
UVP-E Executive Shuttle has 8, 11 or 13 passenger interiors, choice of holds as for commuter, tables, buffet and toilet.
UVP-E Cargo for a 106.3 × 46.9 × 11.8 ins (270 × 120 × 30 cm) container, accompanying passenger seats and toilet.
UVP-E Fast Medical Aid with adjustable table and bed, 4 patient seats, foldable seats, doctor and attendant seats, toilet, and equipment. Alternatively 3 litters instead of patient seats.
UVP-E Medevac with 6 litters, 5 seated patients and an attendant, a table and toilet.
UVP-E Paratroop with in-flight openable door, toilet and observation blisters. 15 persons.
UVP-E Photogrammetric with apertures for 2 vertical cameras, camera control unit, aiming device and side camera. 2 operator control panels, navigator workstation, blister, 551 lb (250 kg) auxiliary fuel tank, and toilet.
L 420 is a derivative of L 410 with higher-rated 778 shp (580 kW) Walter M 601F engines and other improvements.
L-430 is a proposed lengthened version with Pratt & Whitney Canada PT6 turboprop engines, with higher weights and performance.

↑ Let L 610G at the Paris Air Show in 1997

Let L 610G

First flight: 30 December 1988 (prototype L 610M with M602 engines); 18 December 1992 for L 610G (technical) and 6 January 1993 (official).
Certification: 1998 to FAR Pt 25. ICAO Annex 16, section 5 and FAR Pt 36 noise requirements.
First delivery: 1998.
Role: Short/medium haul regional airliner, with quick change for cargo carrying.
Airframe life: 50,000 flight hours.
Sales: 7 flying L 610Ms delivered to the Czech Air Force (trials at Kbely). Further production halted. Production version is the L 610G.
Crew: 2.
Passengers: 40.
Seat pitch: 30 ins (76.2 cm).
Pressurization: 5.22 psi cabin differential.

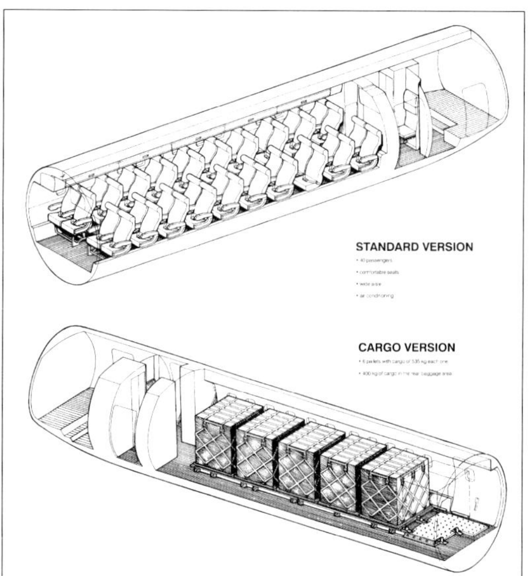

↑ **Let L 610G standard seating arrangement for 40 passengers, and cargo arrangement for 6 pallets with 1,179 lb (535 kg) load each and 882 lb (400 kg) of additional cargo in the rear baggage area** *(courtesy Let)*

Baggage compartment: 6 ft 4.6 ins (1.95 m) length, 6 ft 0.6 ins (1.845 m) height. 226.015 cu ft (6.4 m^3) aft of the toilet. Volume of overhead bins 70.63 cu ft (2 m^3).
Wing control surfaces: Ailerons (port tab), single-slotted flaps (12° take-off, 26° landing) and ground/lateral control spoilers ahead of flaps.
Tail control surfaces: Elevators (each with trim and geared tabs) and rudder (trim and spring balance tabs).
Flight control system: Mechanical, except for hydraulic flaps and spoilers.
Construction materials: Aluminium alloy, with some composites.
Engines: 2 General Electric CT7-9D turboprops, with 11 ft (3.35 m) diameter Hamilton Standard HS-14RF-23 reversible-pitch 4-blade propellers. APU.
Engine rating: Each 1,750 shp (1,305 kW).
Fuel system: 3,420 litres in 2 wing tanks. Total usable 5,952 lb (2,700 kg). Signalized fuel reserve allows at least 45 minutes further operation at cruise power and flight altitudes.
Electrical system: Primary DC power supplied by 2 engine-driven starter-generators, 28 volt DC at 400A each, and 2 × 37 amp-hour ni-cd batteries for ground and emergency operation. Starter-generator is connected to the 2 main busbars. Distribution buses are supplied via circuit breakers. 2 brushless, air-cooled 26kVA alternators (wild frequency), 1 on each engine, supply heating and de-icing circuits and serve as emergency power supplies.
Hydraulic system: Main and emergency systems, each 3,046 psi. Main system for flaps, undercarriage, brakes, spoilers, windshield wiper, and nosewheel steering. 2 piston pumps driven by the engines; at 6,145 rpm they have an output of 18 litres per minute. Emergency system is fed by an electrically driven pump, which delivers 6 litres per minute, providing power for the flaps, undercarriage extension, brakes, door and ground spoiler controls.

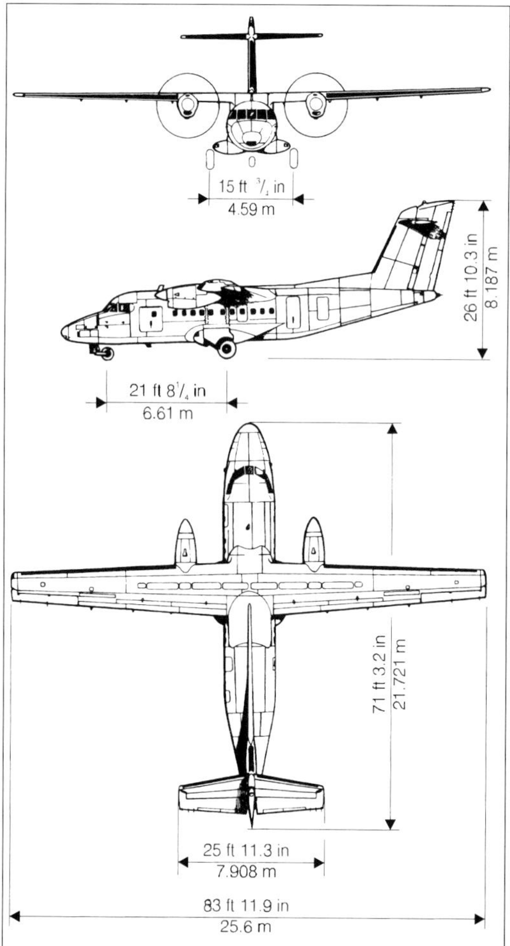

↑ **Let L 610G general arrangement** *(courtesy Let)*

Braking system: Hydraulic disc, with anti-skid system.
De-icing system: Pneumatic for wing, fin, tailplane, and elevator aerodynamic balances. Automatic, operating in 1 and 3 minute cycles and with built-in function check. Electric heating for windshield, propellers, pitot heads and air intakes. Ice detector is ultrasonic type and its sensing element is periodically de-iced, which enables the icing rate to be continually evaluated.
Environmental control system: Dual ECS of circulation type. 2 air conditioning packs with 3-wheel air cycle machines and a high pressure water separator which enhances the effectiveness of cooling on the ground and shortens the preparation of the aircraft for flying in hot weather conditions.
Radar: Rockwell Collins WXR-250 weather radar.
Flight avionics/instrumentation: Rockwell Collins Pro Line 2, with 5-tube EFIS, flight director, autopilot, 2 gyro AHRS, and air data system. Category II landing minimum capability. Options include flight management system, GPS, ground proximity warning system, and traffic alert and collision avoidance system.

Details for L 610G

PRINCIPAL DIMENSIONS:
Wing span: 84 ft (25.6 m)
Maximum length: 71 ft 3.2 ins (21.721 m)
Maximum height: 27 ft 10.3 ins (8.187 m)

CABIN:
Length: 36 ft 5 ins (11.1 m)
Width: 8 ft 4 ins (2.54 m)
Height: 6 ft 0.25 ins (1.835 m)
Volume: 1,578.6 cu ft (44.7 m^3)
Passenger door: 5 ft 4 ins (1.625 m) high, and 2 ft 6 ins (0.76 m) wide
Cargo door: 4 ft 1.2 ins (1.25 m) high, 4 ft 3 ins (1.3 m) wide

WINGS:
Aerofoil section: MS(1)-0318D, 0312 (root/tip)
Area: 602.78 sq ft (56 m^2)
Aspect ratio: 11.703
Sweepback: 1° at 25% chord
Dihedral: 2°
Incidence: 3° 8′ 38″ root, 0° tip

UNDERCARRIAGE:
Type: Retractable, with steerable nosewheel. Low pressure tyres for use from rain soaked, grassy and unpaved runway surfaces with minimum strength of 85 lb/sq ins (6 kg/cm^2)
Nose wheel tyre size: 720 × 310 mm
Wheel base: 21 ft 8.25 ins (6.61 m)
Wheel track: 15 ft 1 ins (4.59 m)
Turning circle: 60 ft 2 ins (18.33 m)

WEIGHTS:
Empty: 19,731 lb (8,950 kg)
Empty, operating: 20,326 lb (9,220 kg)
Maximum zero fuel weight: 29,101 lb (13,200 kg)
Maximum take-off: 31,967 lb (14,500 kg)
Climb limited take-off weight: 31,967 lb (14,500 kg) with 12° flaps, ISA + 15° C, 2,600 ft (792 m); 31,967 lb (14,500 kg) with 0° flaps, ISA + 15° C, 5,700 ft (1,737 m)
Maximum landing: 31,305 lb (14,200 kg)
Payload: 10,000 lb (4,536 kg)

BLOCK DATA (300 naut miles, ISA, FL240)**:**
Block fuel: 1,323 lb (600 kg)
Block time: 92 minutes

PERFORMANCE:
Maximum cruise speed: 243 kts (280 mph) 450 km/h at 20,000 ft (6,100 m)
Cruise speed at 24,000 ft (7,315 m): 236 kts (272 mph) 438 km/h
Stall speed: 76 kts (87.5 mph) 140.5 km/h CAS, *with 26° flaps*
Take-off field length (MTOW): 3,300 ft (1,006 m) ISA, sea level; 3,642 ft (1,110 m) ISA + 15° C, sea level
Landing field length (MLW): 3,504 ft (1,068 m) without thrust reversers, 3,209 ft (978 m) with thrust reversers, ISA, sea level
Maximum climb rate: 1,673 ft (510 m) per minute
Operating altitude: 24,000 ft (7,315 m)
Ceiling, 1 engine: 15,750 ft (4,800 m), ISA, 95% MTOW, climb at 50 ft (15 m) per minute
Range: 1,305 naut miles (1,503 miles) 2,420 km, ISA, 45 minutes plus 100 naut mile reserve

DaimlerChrysler Aerospace AG (DASA) — Germany

Corporate address:
See Combat section for company details.

Note: In 1996 Fairchild Aerospace purchased 80% of Dornier Luftfahrt from Daimler-Benz Aerospace. Thereby, Fairchild Aerospace owns 80% and Daimler-Benz Aerospace owns 20% of Fairchild Dornier Germany (which see).

Daimler-Benz Aerospace Airbus Cryoplanes

Comments: Daimler-Benz Aerospace Airbus, with Russian (Tupolev and Samara) and German partners, has been researching hydrogen fuel for aircraft. The combustion of hydrogen produces water vapour and only small amounts of nitrogen oxides when the fuel is burned in a specially optimized combustion chamber, and thereby also avoiding CO_2 emissions. Experiments in hydrogen fuel burning using such chambers were carried out as part of the 'Euro-Quebec Hydro-Hydrogen Pilot Project', which was supported by the province of Quebec and the European Union, with the view to eventually using Quebec's surplus hydroelectricity to produce hydrogen that could be shipped to Europe for fuel. In addition to work on aero engine hydrogen combustion by Pratt & Whitney Canada, MTU, AlliedSignal, the German Aerospace Research Institute and DASA, experiments with large-cross-section combustion chambers are in progress at DASA's Hydrogen Centre at Ottobrunn. Also, the Aaachen Technical College has developed a new procedure for pre-mixing hydrogen with air before it is introduced into the chamber, expected to offer very low nitrogen oxides emissions. The new chamber design was installed in an APU of the type found on the Airbus A320 and is under test.

Liquid hydrogen (at -253°C) has 3 times the energy of kerosene, weight for weight, but requires 4 times the tankage volume. Fuel for a first-generation Airbus Cryoplane is therefore to be stored in special over-cabin tanks, leaving the main cabin free for revenue payload. In the event of an accident or leak, the hydrogen evaporates upwards. Prior to the production of an Airbus demonstrator, DASA has constructed a smaller test-bed aircraft based on the Fairchild Dornier 328. The hydrogen is stored in additional tanks under the wings, and for initial trials only one of the P&WC PW119 engines has been converted to use hydrogen. Flight trials were scheduled to begin in 1998.

↑ **Impression of the DASA produced Dornier Fairchild 328 Cryoplane test-bed, with the projected Airbus Cryoplane in the background**

Fairchild Dornier Germany Dornier Luftfahrt GmbH — Germany

Corporate address:
See Reconnaissance section for company details.

Fairchild Dornier 228

Comments: First flown on 28 March 1981, the 228 STOL light commuter and cargo transport, with special mission variants, is currently part of a marketing campaign by Fairchild Dornier for new and pre-owned aircraft. Details of special mission versions can be found in the Reconnaissance section, both under Germany and India.

Details *(228-212)*

Crew: 1 or 2 pilots.
Passengers: 19 in commuter version. Other layouts provide for up to 22 troops or 21 parachutists and a jumpmaster, or 6 litters and 9 seated persons in a medevac role.
Baggage compartments: 463 lb (210 kg) in rear cabin, plus 265 lb (120 kg) in nose.
Wing control surfaces: Drooping ailerons, and single-slotted flaps.
Tail control surfaces: Variable incidence tailplane, elevators (port tab) and rudder (with tab).
Flight control system: Mechanical.
Construction materials: Mainly aluminium alloy, but with composites contributing to the wing structure, and for the undercarriage nacelles, fuselage nose, and the tips of the wings and all fixed/moving tail surfaces.
Engines: 2 AlliedSignal TPE331-5-252D turboprops.
Engine rating: Each 840 shp (626 kW) for take off, with 776 shp (578 kW) gearbox limit.
Fuel system: 4,156 lb (1,885 kg), or 4,960 lb (2,250 kg) with optional tank.
Electrical system: 28 volt DC supply by 2 engine-driven starter-generators. 2 × 25 amp-hour ni-cd batteries. 2 static inverters for AC supply.
Hydraulic system: 3.002 psi.

Details for 228-212

PRINCIPAL DIMENSIONS:
Wing span: 55 ft 8 ins (16.97 m)
Maximum length: 54 ft 4 ins (16.56 m)
Maximum height: 15 ft 11 ins (4.86 m)

CABIN:
Length: 23 ft 3 ins (7.08 m)
Width: 4 ft 5 ins (1.346 m)
Height: 5 ft 1 ins (1.55 m)
Volume: 519 cu ft (14.7 m^3)
Main passenger door: 4 ft 5 ins × 2 ft 1 ins (1.34 × 0.64 m)
Cargo door: airliners only

WINGS:
Aerofoil section: A-5
Area: 344.44 sq ft (32 m^2)

UNDERCARRIAGE:
Type: Retractable, with steerable nosewheel
Wheel base: 20 ft 8 ins (6.29 m)
Wheel track: 10 ft 10 ins (3.3 m)

WEIGHTS:
Empty: 8,243 lb (3,739 kg)
Maximum take-off: 14,109-14,550 lb (6,400-6,600 kg)
Maximum landing: 13,448 lb (6,100 kg)
Payload: 4,852 lb (2,201 kg)

PERFORMANCE:
Maximum cruise speed: 234 kts (269 mph) 433 km/h at 10,000 ft (3,050 m)
Long-range cruise speed: 170 kts (196 mph) 315 km/h at 2,000 ft (610 m)
Maximum duration speed: 105 kts (121 mph) 195 km/h
Minimum control speed: 73 kts (84 mph) 135 km/h, *clean*
Stall speed: 80 kts (92.5 mph) 148 km/h, *with flaps*
Take-off distance: 2,600 ft (793 m)
Take-off distance Mil STOL: 1,477 ft (450 m)
Landing distance: 1,477 ft (450 m)
Maximum climb rate: 1,870 ft (570 m) per minute
Ceiling: 28,000 ft (8,535 m)
Range with full payload: typically 600 naut miles (691 miles) 1,111 km with reserve
Range with 1,709 lb (775 kg) payload: up to 1,320 naut miles (1,520 miles) 2,444 km

↑ Fairchild Dornier 228-212 for ozone layer measuring

Braking system: Carbon disc brakes on main units.
De-icing system: Engine intakes. Others items optional.
Radar: Optional weather radar.
Flight avionics/instrumentation: IFR equipped. Standard equipment includes VOR/ILS, marker beacon receiver, transponder, DME, RMI, HSI and ADI.
Mission equipment: See Reconnaissance section.

Aircraft variants:
Dornier 228-212 current version, which succeeded the 228-202 from aircraft No 176. Forms the basis for all currently offered special versions (see Passengers, and below).
Cargo layout provides for up to 5,158 lb (2,340 kg) of freight in the cabin.
Border Patrol and ***Maritime Patrol*** are among several special mission military/civil variants on offer and in service. See Reconnaissance section.

Fairchild Dornier 328

First flight: 6 December 1991.
Certification: 15 October 1993 (JAR 25), 10 November 1993 (FAR 25). 3/4 November 1994 LBA/FAA certification for the Improved Performance 328-110. May 1995 for 328-120.
First delivery: 21 October 1993 to Air Engiadina. First 328-120 to Formosa Airlines.
Role: Regional transport, with air ambulance and other potential uses.
Noise levels: 82 EPNdB take-off, 84 EPNdB sideline, and 94 EPNdB approach. Interior below 78 dB(A) over 75% of the cabin.
Sales: 100 ordered, with 43 further options at time of writing, of which 80 had been delivered. Largest orders to date are from PSA Airlines/US Airways Express with 25 delivered and 15 more on option, Mountain Air Express with 12 ordered and 12 on option (4 delivered), and Horizon Air with 12 delivered, all from the USA.
Crew: 2.
Passengers: 30-34 in 328-110/120/130, or 37-39 in 328-210/220/230. Cabin arrangements on a modular design, allowing adaptability to changing market needs. Air ambulance version can have 31 seats, leg rests for patients with leg injuries, 4 litters and 12 seats, or up to 3 intensive care units and seats.
Seat pitch: 30-31 ins (76-79 cm) for 33-34 passengers, and 31 ins (79 cm) for 30-32 passengers. 31 ins (79 cm) for 37-39 passengers in 328-210/220/230 series.
Galley: Holds 2 airline-standard trolleys. See diagrams.
Toilet: Walk-in compartment.
Pressurization: Maximum 6.75 psi cabin differential, providing

30 Seats
31 in seat pitch
31 Seats
31 in seat pitch
37 Seats
31 in Seat pitch
39 Seats
31 in Seat pitch
Utility
Flying Sensor Platform
NAVY

↑ Fairchild Dornier 328 typical cabin layouts, with (*top to bottom*) 328-110 in 30 and 31 seat configurations, 328-200 series in 37 and 39 seat configurations, plus the projected Flying Sensor Platform utility configuration *(courtesy Fairchild Dornier)*

low cabin altitude (5,400 ft, 1,645 m) at normal cruising altitude. Pre-pressurization at take-off.
Baggage compartment: Rear compartment 8 ft 6 ins × 6 ft (2.6 × 1.83 m), of 229.5 cu ft (6.5 m^3) volume, with 1,653 lb (750 kg) available capacity. Sill height 3 ft 8.5 ins (1.13 m). Door size 3 ft × 4 ft 7 ins (0.92 × 1.4 m). Overhead bins, underseat stowage and wardrobe (if fitted) offer each passenger in a 32-seat layout 2.83 cu ft (0.08 m^3) of carry-on volume.
Wing control surfaces: Ailerons (with geared tabs), flaps and available spoilers (ground/lateral control). Improved Performance 328-110 and -120 offer option of ground spoilers among other changes (see Aircraft variants). 328-130 and -230 have ground spoilers as standard and 20° flaps for take-off.
Tail control surfaces: Elevators and rudder, with geared tabs. 328-130 and -230 have a Rudder Enhanced Deflection System (REDS).
Flight control system: Mechanical, except for hydraulic (mechanically interconnected) flaps, spoilers and electric tabs.
Construction materials: Composites make up 25% of the structural weight. Aluminium alloy used for the wings and fuselage, except for: Kevlar for the upper fuselage/wing fairing, fin/fuselage fairing, unpressurized fuselage side fairings housing the main undercarriage units, and part of the wing skin; carbonfibre reinforced plastics (CFRP) for part of the rear fuselage, part of the wings, wingtips, ventral fins and parts of the tail; and titanium-alloy for the tailcone. Doors of aluminium-

↑ Fairchild Dornier 328 of Horizon Air

alloy sandwich. Titanium framework and CFRP covering engine nacelles. CFRP and Kevlar for the leading and trailing edges of the fin (including rudder and tabs), part of the elevators and ailerons. Glassfibre reinforced plastics (GFRP) for the nosecone and tailplane leading edges. Daewoo of South Korea produces fuselage shells, Aermacchi of Italy builds cockpit shells and undertakes fuselage assembly, and Westland of the UK produces engine nacelles and doors. Main wing box milled from a single billet; integrally machined with stringers, ribs and spar flanges. Wing contour formed by applying controlled, hydraulic pressure at stringer/rib joints, giving a smooth, rivetless wing surface.
Engines: 2 Pratt & Whitney Canada PW119B or C turboprops (see Aircraft variants), with 11 ft 10 ins (3.6 m) Hartzell 6-blade composite propellers (1,050 rpm in cruise). See Electrical system for APU.
Engine rating: Each 2,180 shp (1,626 kW).
Fuel system: Usable 4,290 litres (7,530 lb, 3,416 kg) in 2 tank groups in the wings. 2 engine-driven ejectors, boost pumps and electrical emergency pump. Cross-feed system. Single-point pressure refuelling/defuelling; under 8 minute pressure refuelling. Gravity fuelling/defuelling possible.
Electrical system: Primary DC system with 2 engine-driven starter-generators of 28 volt/400 A each. Secondary DC with 2 × 40 amp-hour ni-cd batteries. AC system has 2 × 20kVA brushless alternators. Optional AlliedSignal 36-150(DD) APU in tailcone for air conditioning bleed air, generator back-up and battery assistance during engine starting; can provide higher climb rates.

Details for 328-110, unless stated

PRINCIPAL DIMENSIONS:
Wing span: 68 ft 10 ins (20.98 m)
Maximum length: 69 ft 10 ins (21.28 m)
Maximum height: 23 ft 9 ins (7.24 m)

CABIN:
Length: 33 ft 8 ins (10.27 m)
Width: 7 ft 2 ins (2.18 m) maximum, 5 ft 11 ins (1.82 m) at floor
Height: 6 ft 2.5 ins (1.89 m)
Volume: 1,183 cu ft (33.5 m^3)
Main passenger door: 5 ft 7 ins × 2 ft 3.5 ins (1.7 × 0.7 m)
Service door: 4 ft 1 ins × 1 ft 8 ins (1.25 × 0.51 m), with 3 ft 8 ins (1.13 m) sill height

UNDERCARRIAGE:
Type: Retractable, with electro-hydraulically steerable nosewheels (±60°). Twin wheels on each unit
Wheel base: 24 ft 4 ins (7.42 m)
Wheel track: 10 ft 7 ins (3.22 m)
Turning circle: under 49 ft 4 ins (15 m) for 180°

WEIGHTS:
Maximum take-off: 30,843 lb (13,990 kg), and same for 328-120 and -130
Climb limited take-off (hot and high): 29,894 lb (13,560 kg), ISA + 20° C, at 6,000 ft (1,830 m), or 30,843 lb (13,990 kg) for 328-120 and -130 (latter with *12° flaps*)

BLOCK DATA (300 naut mile sector, ISA, at FL250)**:**
Block fuel: 1,455 lb (660 kg) for 328-110, -120 and -130
Block time: 70 minutes (ground time 6 minutes) for 328-110, -120 and -130

PERFORMANCE:
Maximum cruise speed: 335 kts (386 mph) 620 km/h, ISA, 95% MTOW, at 20,000 ft (6,100 m), and same for 328-120 and -130
Take-off field length, ISA (JAR 25/FAR 25): 3,570 ft (1,088 m), sea level, at MTOW, same for 328-120 without ground spoilers, 3,490 ft (1,065 m) for 328-120 with ground spoilers, and 3,270 ft (995 m) for 328-130
Take-off field length, ISA + 20° C (JAR 25/FAR 25): 5,675 ft (1,730 m) at 6,000 ft (1,830 m), MTOW for 328-120 without ground spoilers, or 5,545 ft (1,690 m) for 328-120 with ground spoilers and 328-130 with 12° flaps
Landing field length (JAR 25/FAR 25): 3,820 ft (1,164 m) ISA, sea level, at MLW, Factor 0.6, or 3,825 ft (1,166 m) for 328-120 without ground spoilers, and 3,525 ft (1,074 m) for 328-120 with ground spoilers and 328-130
Glideslope: -5.5° for steep approach capability
Gross climb gradient, second segment: 5.4%, ISA, sea level, at MTOW
Maximum operating altitude: 25,000-31,000 ft (7,600-9,450 m), standard and optional respectively for 328-110, -120 and -130
Single engine ceiling: 15,620 ft (4,760 m), ISA, 95% MTOW, or 16,800 ft (5,120 m) for 328-120 and -130
Range: 900 naut miles (1,036 miles) 1,668 km, with 30 passengers (93 kg each), ISA, at 25,000 ft (7,620 m), 100 naut mile alternate, 45 minutes reserve and 10 minute allowances; or optional 1,000 naut miles (1,151 miles) 1,853 km at 31,000 ft (9,450 m), and same for 328-120 and -130

Hydraulic system: Main system for undercarriage, brakes, flaps and spoilers when fitted. Auxiliary system with cockpit hand-pump for emergency undercarriage extension. Separate, unpressurized reservoirs.
Braking system: Segmented, steel brake pad on mainwheels, with 2,000 landings design life.
De-icing system: Pneumatic boots for wing and tail leading edges, and air intakes. Electric mats for propeller leading edges, and electric windscreen de-icing.
Environmental control system: 2 air conditioning packs. Automatic and manual temperature control (cockpit and cabin separated), with possible override by flight attendants. Individual air outlets. Temperature and airflow for floor and ceiling outlets controlled individually. See Pressurization. APU for cabin climatization as option. Ground connection for cabin preheating/precooling as option.
Radar: Honeywell Primus 650 weather radar, or optional Primus 870.
Flight avionics/instrumentation: Honeywell Primus 2000 system, including EFIS/EICAS with five 7 × 8 ins (18 × 20 cm) CRTs, flight management system (database including VOR, VORTAC, VOR/DME, airport reference points, etc), Primus II integrated radio system, dual integrated avionics computer, flight director and autopilot, dual digital air data reference unit, dual AHRS, Mode S transponder and fault recording. Full range of options, including traffic alert and collision avoidance system, GPS (with GPS approach), microwave landing system, laser INS, head-up guidance system allowing Cat IIIa landings, and VLF/Omega nav.

Aircraft variants:
328-100 was the initial version. Superseded by the 328-110.
328-110 is the current basic Improved Performance version, with changes including option of spoilers, larger dorsal and ventral fins, increased rudder travel, larger-diameter propellers and more. PW119B engines. Flaps can be extended to 32° on approach. MTOW increased, take-off distance reduced, and other performance gains.
328-120 offers further improvements in take-off/landing performance, with 5% extra thermodynamic engine power from the PW119C engines. Certified May 1995.
328-130 features a Rudder Enhanced Deflection System (REDS) for improved field performance for short field markets, including inner city and remote airports. Ground spoilers and 20° flaps for take-off.
328-210 is a high-density variant of 328-110, with 4-abreast seating for 37-39 passengers.
328-220 is a high-density variant of 328-120, with 4-abreast seating for 37-39 passengers. Also better hot and high performance, and higher single-engine service ceiling.

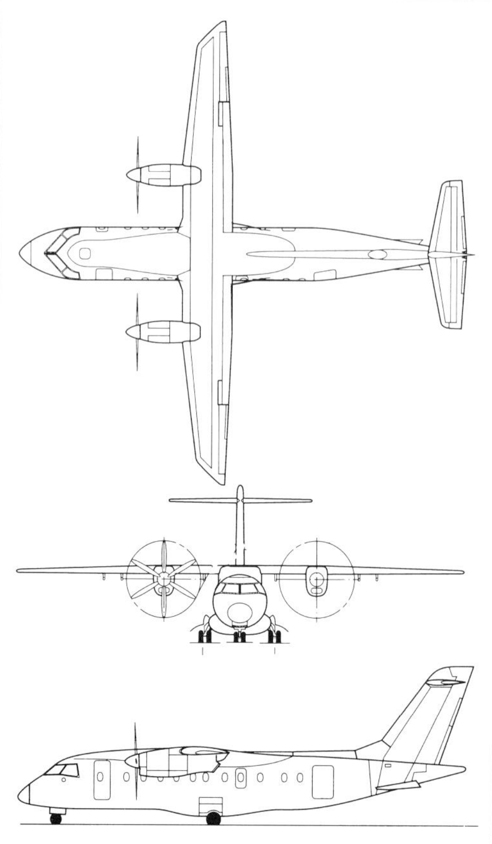

↑ **Fairchild Dornier 328 general arrangement** *(courtesy Fairchild Dornier)*

328-230 is a high-density variant of 328-130, with 4-abreast seating for 37-39 passengers, plus better airfield performance.
328 Utility is a projected version suited to several very different roles, from quick-change cargo carrying to flying sensor platform.
328 hydrogen-powered testbed will fly in 1998, with a possible production version in 2005. P&WC engines.

Fairchild Dornier 328JET, 428JET, 528JET, 728JET and 928JET

First flight: 20 January 1998 for 328JET (first prototype converted from the second 328 turboprop prototype, while the second 328JET prototype has been newly built).
Certification: 1999 for 328JET.
First delivery: First quarter of 1999 for 328JET.
Role: Regional transport, corporate shuttle and air ambulance.

Details *(328JET, unless stated)*

Sales: 17 firm orders and 15 options for 328JET at the time of writing, with Proteus Airlines as launch customer (6). Expected 728JET launch orders from Crossair and Lufthansa CityLine (each 60 firm plus 60 options), Eurowings (30) and Proteus Airlines (15).
Crew: 2.
Passengers: 30-34 with 3-abreast seating, or 37-39 at 4-abreast. Cabin arrangements on a modular design, allowing adaptability to changing market needs. Air ambulance version can have 31 seats, leg rests for patients with leg injuries, 4 litters and 12 seats, or up to 3 intensive care units and seats. 10+ passengers for Business Jet.
Seat pitch: 30-31 ins (76-79 cm) for 33-34 passengers, 31 ins (79 cm) for 30-32 passengers and 31 ins (79 cm) for 37-39 passengers.
Baggage hold capacity: As for 328.
Engines: 2 Pratt & Whitney Canada PW306/9 (306B) turbofans, with FADEC. AlliedSignal 36-150 (DD) APU standard.
Engine rating: Each 6,050 lbf (26.9 kN) uninstalled, up to ISA + 20°C.
Fuel system: 7,800 lb (3,538 kg).
Braking system: Strengthened.
Flight avionics/instrumentation: Honeywell Primus 2000 system (see 328).

Aircraft variants:
328JET is basically a turbofan-powered variant of the Fairchild Dornier 328, for regional use or other roles including air ambulance, corporate shuttle/VIP transport, air ambulance and more. To enter service in 1999.
428JET is a 40-43 seat stretched version, launched in 1998 and expected to enter service in January 2001. 11 ft (3.35 m) longer fuselage than 328JET, and 3 ft (0.9 m) increased wing span. 7,716 lb (3,500 kg) increased MTOW. P&WC PW308 turbofans.
528JET is a projected 55-seat (5-abreast), 76 ft (23.17 m) length version of the low-wing 528/728/928JET series. 10,500 lbf (46.71 kN) General Electric CF34-8D (derated) engines. 67,570 lb (30,650 kg) MTOW and 13,340 lb (6,050 kg) maximum payload. MMO Mach 0.83, maximum cruise speed Mach 0.81 target, field length 4,000 ft (1,220 m), and design range 1,600 naut miles.
728JET is the 70-seat initial version of the low-wing JET range, with certification/first deliveries in 2001. Programme launched 1998. 13,300 lbf (59.16 kN) General Electric CF34-8D1, with other possibilities of Allison AE 3012 and P&WC/Snecma SPW14. Possible fly-by-wire FCS. 75,550 lb (34,270 kg) MTOW and 16,975 lb (7,700 kg) maximum payload. Same speeds as 528JET. T-O field length 5,000 ft (1,524 m) and landing field length 4,500 ft (1,372 m) targets. 1,600 naut miles design range at FL370 or 2,000 naut miles for extended-range version. Length 85 ft 5 ins (26.03 m), wing span 87 ft 4 ins (26.62 m), height 27 ft 8 ins (8.44 m), wing area 807.3 sq ft (75 m^2), aspect ratio 9.48 and sweepback 23.5°.
928JET is a projected 90-seat version, with 14,040 lbf (62.45 kN)

↑ **Fairchild Dornier 328JET, first flown in 1998**

↑ **Fairchild Dornier 728JET, the first of the low-wing JET series**

General Electric CF34-8XX engines. 86,035 lb (39,025 kg) MTOW, and 21,825 lb (9,900 kg) maximum payload. Same speeds and range as 528JET. T-O field length 6,000 ft (1,829 m), and landing field length 5,500 ft (1,677 m). Length 96 ft 1 ins (29.28 m), with same wing span and height as 728JET.

Details for 328JET

PRINCIPAL DIMENSIONS: Same as 328
CABIN: Same as 328
WINGS: Same as 328
TAIL UNIT: Same as 328
UNDERCARRIAGE: Similar to 328, but strengthened

WEIGHTS:
Empty, operating: 20,282 lb (9,200 kg)
Maximum zero fuel: 27,800 lb (12,610 kg)
Maximum take-off: 33,047 lb (14,990 kg) European standard, 33,510 lb (15,200 kg) for US standard and Business Jet
Climb limited take-off: 33,047 lb (14,990 kg) at ISA + 20° C, 6,000 ft (1,830 m)
Maximum landing: 31,063 lb (14,090 kg)
Payload: 7,518 lb (3,410 kg)

BLOCK DATA:
Block fuel: 1,501 lb (681 kg) for 200 naut mile sector, 2,079 lb (943 kg) for 300 naut mile sector, and 2,980 lb (1,352 kg) for 500 naut mile sector
Block time: 44.2 minutes for 200 naut mile sector, 59.5 minutes for 300 naut mile sector, and 91.3 minutes for 500 naut mile sector, all with 10 minutes ground/manoeuvring allowances

PERFORMANCE:
Maximum cruise speed: 400 kts (461 mph) 741 km/h
Cruise speed at 25,000 ft (7,620 m): 387 kts (446 mph) 717 km/h
Take-off field length: 4,070 ft (1,240 m), ISA, at sea level, MTOW
Landing field length: 3,890 ft (1,185 m), ISA, at sea level, MLW, Factor 1/0.6
Ceiling, 1 engine: 20,500 ft (6,250 m), ISA, 98% MTOW
Time to 31,000 ft (9,450 m): 14 minutes 12 seconds
Design range: 900 naut miles (1,036 miles) 1,668 km, with 32 passengers, at 31,000 ft (9,450 m)
Range for extended-range version: 1,200 naut miles (1,382 miles) 2,223 km with 32 passengers, at increased MTOW

Aeronautical Development Agency (ADA) — India

Corporate address:
See Combat section for company details.

Comments: At Aero India '96, a model was displayed of the MTA 120, a projected 120-seat airliner for development in India under the auspices of the ADA. As can be seen from the photograph, it will have 2 rear-mounted turbine engines and a T-tail. Intended for commercial and military roles, spin-off versions will include a freighter with a 29,760 lb (13,500 kg) payload and a multi-role variant.

↑ **Model of the projected Aeronautical Development Agency MTA 120**
(Simon Watson)

PT Industri Pesawat Terbang Nusantara (IPTN) — Indonesia

Corporate address:
PO Box 1562 BD, Jalan Pajajaran 154, Bandung 40174.

Telephone: +62 22 633900, 633911
Facsimile: +62 22 632145
Telex: 28295 IPTNBD IA

Founded: 24 August 1976.

Employees: over 15,000.

Information:
Soleh Affandi (International Public Relations Manager – *telephone* +62 22 634526, *facsimile* +62 22 631696).

ACTIVITIES

▪ Partner in the Airtech CN-235 programme and has developed a Maritime Patrol Aircraft variant. Undertakes licence production of the CASA C-212 (as the NC-212), Eurocopter BO-105 (as NBO-105) and Super Puma (as NSA-332), and Bell 407, 412 and 430 (NBell-407, 412 and 430). Also produces FFAR (fin folded air rocket) and SUT (surface underwater torpedo).

▪ Has developed the N-250 turboprop transport, the first commuter aircraft ever designed by Indonesia, and is developing the N-2130 turbofan airliner. In 1997, it was reported that a new military transport was being developed; according to IPTN in 1998, experimental models are in design stage. However, IPTN wished no further publicity at this stage, and so no further details are provided here. IPTN is also in the design stage for new helicopters.

▪ IPTN's UMC (Universal Maintenance Centre) has undertaken engine maintenance, overhaul and repair. In 1998 it is expected to become an independent subsidiary, known as the Aviation Propulsion and Turbine Company, entering the field of engine design and production.

▪ Subcontract work includes components for the Boeing 737 and 767, and Lockheed Martin F-16.

SUBSIDIARIES

IPTN NORTH AMERICA INC

Address:
IPTN Building, 1035 Andover Park West, Suite B, Tukwila, Seattle, WA 98188-7681, USA.

Telephone: +1 206 575 6507
Facsimile: +1 206 575 0318

Information: Satya Wibowo.

IPTN EUROPE AIRCRAFT & LOGISTICS GMBH

Address:
Heuberg 1, 20354 Hamburg, Germany.

Telephone: +49 40 357 6840
Facsimile: +49 40 357 68444

AMERICAN REGIONAL AIRCRAFT INDUSTRY (AMRAI)

Address:
19 Triangle Park Drive, Suite 1901, Cincinnati, OH 45246, USA.

Telephone: +1 513 771 2672
Facsimile: +1 513 326 7088

Activities:
▪ Facilities at Mobile, Alabama, USA, as an IPTN after-sales support service for the Americas and possible future second assembly line; for the latter, all primary subassemblies would be built in Indonesia, for shipping to the USA in knock-down form. IPTN retains a 40% holding and General Electric has 10%.

AVIATION PROPULSION AND TURBINE COMPANY

Comments: See Activities.

↑ **IPTN N-250 prototype PA1** *(courtesy Austin J. Brown)*

IPTN N-250 and N-270

Details *(for N-250-100, except where stated)*

First flight: 10 August 1995; roll-out of the prototype took place on 10 November 1994. First flight of the first N-250-100 development aircraft (PA2) 19 December 1996.
Certification: To FAA Pt 25, Pt 36 and ICAO Annex 16 standards.
First delivery: 1999.
Role: Regional/Commuter airliner.
Airframe life: 60,000 hours or 56,000 cycles.
Noise levels: Community noise, FAR 36 Stage 3. Interior 78 dB.
Sales: 50-seat 'short fuselage' N-250 prototype (PA1 *Gatotkoco*), 3 N-250-100 flying development aircraft (PA2-PA4), 2 static development aircraft for the 120,000 hour fatigue test programme at the National Research Centre in Serbong, plus an N-250-50 development aircraft (PA5). PA2-PA4 have production-standard lengthened fuselages; first development aircraft for handling and performance envelope testing, second for avionics trials and systems certification, and third for final certification (1,600-2,000 hour flight test programme using the prototype and all 3 development aircraft). Total of 287 orders/MoU options or under negotiation by early 1998, comprising 5 firm orders from Bouraq Airlines, 15 firm orders and 60 options in a 20 year planning period from Merpati Nusantara, 6 firm and 10 options from Sempati Air, MoU for 20 from Mandala, MoU for 2 from Gatari Air Service, MoU for 4 from Air Venezuela, MoU for 15 from Pakistan International Airlines and 150 in negotiation from undisclosed US Airlines (thought to include Gulfstream International Airlines). Projected sales of over 700.
Crew: 2 (flight).
Passengers: 60-68.
Seat pitch: 32 ins (81 cm) for 60-64 seat layouts, or 30 ins (76 cm) for 68-seat layout.
Pressurization: AlliedSignal cabin control pressure system, with 6 psi maximum differential. ECSs provide cabin pressurization for 25,000 ft (7,620 m), equivalent to 8,000 ft (2,440 m) atmospheric pressure.
Baggage volume: 7.06 cu ft (0.2 m^3) per passenger, plus a further 1.73 cu ft (0.049 m^3) per passenger in overhead bins.
Wing control surfaces: Horn-balanced ailerons with tabs, double-slotted Fowler flaps and 2-section spoilers.
Tail control surfaces: Elevators with tabs and 2-section rudder.
Flight control system: Lucas Aerospace/Liebherr-Aero-Technik active fly-by-wire for ailerons, spoilers, flaps, elevators and rudder. Mechanically signalled back-up for the ailerons and elevators. Stand-by fly-by-wire for rudder.
Construction materials: Mostly metal, but with 10% composites used for control surfaces, wing leading edges and tips, wingroot fairings, various parts of the tail unit, tailcone and more.
Engines: 2 Allison AE 2100C turboprops, with dual channel FADEC, and driving 12 ft 6 ins (3.81 m) diameter Dowty Rotol R384 6-blade composite propellers. APIC originally, now Sundstrand APS 1000 auxiliary power unit.
Engine rating: Each 3,271 shp (2,365 kW) at 1,100 propeller rpm.
Fuel system: 9,259 lb (4,200 kg). Cobham system.
Electrical system: 115 volt 400Hz 3-phase AC supply via a 40kVA state-of-the-art integrated drive generator. 28 volt DC supply via 2 transformer-rectifiers, plus 2 × 43 amp-hour ni-cd batteries for emergency DC supply. Flight-rated APU (see engines).
Hydraulic system: 3 systems, each 3,000 psi, for flight control and undercarriage systems.

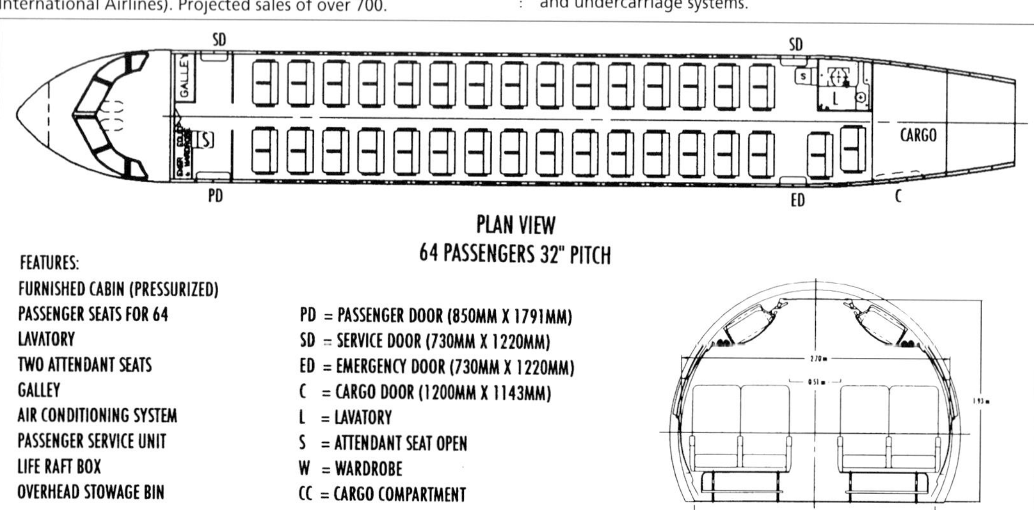

↑ **IPTN N-250-100 64-passenger cabin layout and cabin cross section** *(courtesy IPTN)*

Details for N-250-100

PRINCIPAL DIMENSIONS:
Wing span: 91 ft 10 ins (28 m)
Maximum length: 92 ft 4 ins (28.155 m)
Maximum height: 28 ft 10 ins (8.785 m)

CABIN:
Length: 43 ft 5 ins (13.23 m)
Width: 8 ft 9.5 ins (2.7 m) maximum, 7 ft 11 ins (2.41 m) at floor
Height: 6 ft 4 ins (1.93 m)

WINGS:
Aerofoil section: MS-0317 at root
Area: 699.65 sq ft (65 m^2)
Aspect ratio: 12.062
Incidence: 2°
Dihedral: 3°

TAIL UNIT:
Tailplane span: 30 ft 10 ins (9.4 m)

UNDERCARRIAGE:
Type: Retractable, with FBW steerable nosewheel (±65°). Twin wheels on each unit
Main wheel tyre size: 37 × 11.75
Nose wheel tyre size: H21 × 7.25
Wheel base: 33 ft 8 ins (10.253 m)
Wheel track: 13 ft 5.5 ins (4.1 m)

WEIGHTS:
Empty, operating: 34,612 lb (15,700 kg)
Maximum zero fuel: 48,281 lb (21,900 kg)
Ramp: 54,895 lb (24,900 kg)
Maximum take-off: 54,875 lb (24,800 kg)
Maximum landing: 54,233 lb (24,600 kg)
Payload: 13,669 lb (6,200 kg)

PERFORMANCE:
Maximum operating speed: 350 kts (403 mph) 648 km/h
Cruise speed: 330 kts (380 mph) 611 km/h, at 20,000 ft (6,100 m), ISA
Long-range cruise speed: 300 kts (345 mph) 555 km at 20,000 ft (6,100 m)
Stall speed: 105 kts (121 mph) 195 km/h EAS *clean*, or 90 kts (104 mph) 167 km/h EAS *with 20° flaps*
Take-off and landing: 4,000 ft (1,219 m), sea level, ISA +20°C
Landing field length: 4,350 ft (1,325 m), ISA +20°C
Maximum climb rate: 1,850 ft (564 m) per minute
Maximum climb rate, 1 engine: 520 ft (158 m) per minute
Ceiling: 25,000 ft (7,620 m)
Ceiling, 1 engine: 20,000 ft (6,100 m)
Range with 64 passengers: 800 naut miles (921 miles) 1,481 km
Range with 68 passengers: 685 naut miles (789 miles) 1,270 km

Environmental control system: Dual Hamilton Standard, using engine bleed air and APIC originally, now Sundstrand APS 1000 auxiliary power unit.
Radar: Rockwell Collins WXR-840, with TWR-850 doppler turbulence weather radar optional.
Flight avionics/instrumentation: Rockwell Collins Pro Line 4, with five 8 ins × 8 ins (20 × 20 cm) CRTs including EICAS; additional CRT optional with GPS. Advanced aircraft management system incorporates the flight management system, navigation and guidance system, communication systems, engine system (dual channel FADEC) and engine related systems into a network that allows each subsystem to interface with the others. Integrated digital suite, based on ARINC 429 interfaces. Communications suite comprises 2 basic and optional third VHF, 1 HF, 2 radio management units (RMU) with back-up, optional selective calling (Selcal), and optional aircraft communications and addressing system (ACARS). Navigation suite comprises 1 basic and 1 optional radio altimeters, 2 VOR/ILS/MB, 2 ADFs, 1 basic and 1 optional DME, 1 optional flight management computer system, space for 1 Omega navigation system, and optional GPS. 1 basic and 1 optional air traffic control radar beacon systems/Mode S, 1 ground proximity warning system (GPWS), 1 emergency locating transmitter (ELT), and optional TCAS-94 traffic alert and collision avoidance system. Guidance system comprises 2 attitude heading reference systems (AHRS), 2 air data systems, and 1 automatic flight control system (AFCS). Audio system comprises 1 3-channel integrated communication system, 1 passenger address and cabin interphone system, 1 cockpit voice recorder, and 1 optional boarding music system. Recording equipment comprises 1 digital flight data acquisition unit (DFDAU), direct FADEC interface to display units, and 2 electronic flight instrument systems with 5 displays (PFD, MFD and EICAS).

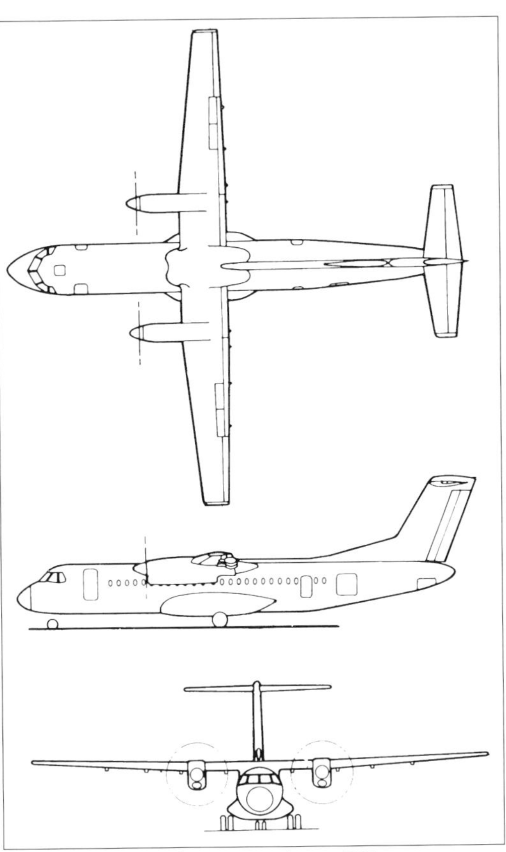

↑ **IPTN N-250-100 general arrangement** *(courtesy IPTN)*

Aircraft variants:
N-250-50 is the 50-54 passenger version, with a fuselage of 87 ft 4.5 ins (26.63 m) length and of wider cross section. Wing box lowered. PA5 is the development aircraft.
N-250-100 is the initial 60-68 passenger production-standard version, longer than the first PA1 prototype (with 1 ft 8 ins and 3 ft 4 ins, 0.51 m and 1.01 m plugs).
N-250-200 is a projected longer range/payload variant for delivery in the next century.
N-250-300 was announced in 1997.
N-250 Cargo is a proposed all-cargo variant of the -100, with reinforced cabin floor and a large side-loading door.
N-250 special mission variants could include an AEW version with Erieye radar or other system.

N-270 is the projected stretched version for 70 passengers, which is expected to enter airline service in the USA from the year 2000 or later. Could be assembled in the USA at Mobile (see Activities) but programme delayed through the N-250 scheduling.

IPTN N2130

First flight: Year 2002.
Certification: Year 2004.
First delivery: Year 2004.
Role: Medium-range airliner.
Sales: Programme was initiated in October 1994 by the start of the 'N2130 Technology Programme' (NTP) conceptual design phase, which was completed in March 1997. Entered the Preliminary Design Stage in 1997. Anticipated domestic sales in Indonesia are for 170 aircraft. IPTN forecasts that 3,237 aircraft in the 100-130-seat range from around the world will require replacement with newer types during 2005-2025. MoUs reportedly from Garuda Indonesia Airways for 20 and Sempati Air for 15.
Crew: 2 (flight).
Passengers: 104 to 132 passengers, 5 or 6 abreast. N2130-100 accommodates 114 tourist-class passengers or 104 mixed class. N2130-200 accommodates 132 tourist-class or 122 mixed class passengers.
Seat pitch: 32 ins (81 cm).
Wing control surfaces: Ailerons, 2-section trailing-edge flaps, and 5-section spoilers ahead of the flaps.
Tail control surfaces: Conventional elevators and rudder.
Flight control system: Fly-by-wire.
Engines: 2, in the 19,300–23,000 lbf (85.9–102.3 kN) class range, with FADEC. Request for engine proposals to BMW Rolls-Royce, CFM International and Pratt & Whitney, with selection expected in 1998. Anticipated engines to be offered are the BR715-56, CFM56-9 and PW6000 respectively.

↑ **IPTN N2130** *(courtesy Austin J. Brown)*

Aircraft variants:
N2130-100 is the baseline version for 100 passengers, with the capacity to carry 114 tourist-class passengers or 104 mixed class. 19,300–20,100 lbf (85.9–89.4 kN) class engine range.
N2130-200 is a stretched version for 130 passengers, with the capacity for 132 tourist-class or 122 mixed-class passengers. 22,050–22,895 lbf (98.1–101.85 kN) class engine range.
Increased Gross Weight variants (2) are planned for both versions.

Details for N2130

PRINCIPAL DIMENSIONS:
Wing span: 98 ft 5 ins (30 m)
Maximum length: 102 ft 6 ins (31.25 m) for N2130-100, or 111 ft 1 ins (33.86 m) for N2130-200
Height: 38 ft 3 ins (11.65 m)

CABIN:
Width: 12 ft 2 ins (3.71 m)

WINGS:
Area: 1,183 sq ft (109.9 m^2)
Aspect ratio: 8.19
Sweepback: 25° at 25% chord
Dihedral: 5°

UNDERCARRIAGE:
Wheel base: 36 ft 1 ins (11 m) for N2130-100, or 39 ft 8 ins (12.09 m) for N2130-200

WEIGHTS:
Maximum take-off: 109,239 lb (49,550 kg) for N2130-100, 124,715 lb (56,750 kg) for N2130-200, 113,538 lb (51,500 kg) for N2130-100 Increased Gross Weight, and 129,455 lb (58,720 kg) for N2130-200 Increased Gross Weight
Payload: 25,132 lb (11,400 kg) or 25,221 lb (11,440 kg) IGW for N2130-100, and 29,100 lb (13,200 kg) for N2130-200

PERFORMANCE:
Long-range cruise speed: Mach 0.8
Approach speed: 125 kts (144 mph) 232 km/h
Field length: 4,922 ft (1,500 m) or 5,086 ft (1,550 m) at IGW for N2130-100, and 5,578 ft (1,700 m) or 5,742 ft (1,750 m) at IGW for N2130-200, all ISA +18°C, dry runway, at sea level
Ceiling: 39,000 ft (11,890 m)
Design range: 1,200 naut miles (1,382 miles) 2,224 km for N2130-100 and -200
Range, at Increased Gross Weight: 1,600 naut miles (1,842 miles) 2,965 km for N2130-100 and -200

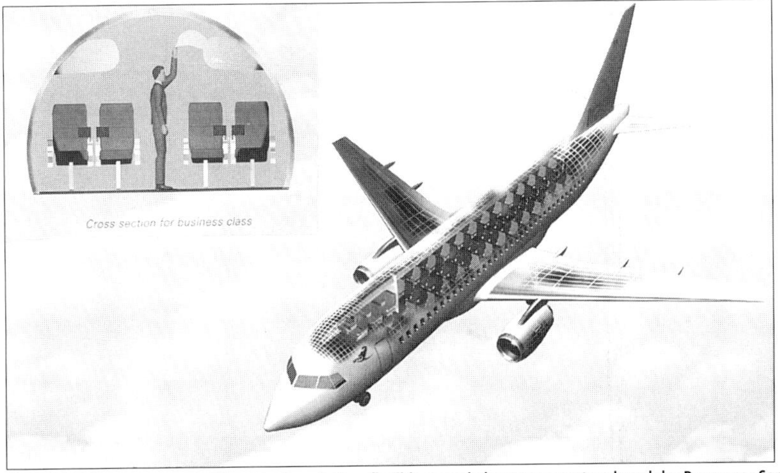

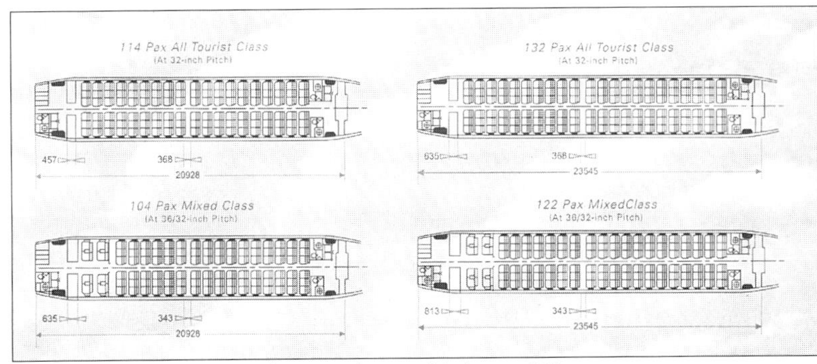

↑ **IPTN N2130 arrangements. Movable class divider, flexible seat pitch arrangement and modular Passenger Service Units allow changes in business and economy class overnight** *(courtesy IPTN)*

Alenia Aerospazio — Italy

Corporate address:
See Combat section for company details.

ACTIVITIES

- See Combat section for activities.
- Brief details and a photograph of Alenia's Capodichino Nord factories conversion of ex-TAP Boeing 707s into flight refuelling tankers/transports for the Italian Air Force, between 1989-93, can be found in the 1996-97 edition of *WA&SD*, page 215. Other modification work has included converting McDonnell Douglas (now Boeing) DC-10/MD-11s into freighters by Alenia's Aeronavali Venezia subsidiary, and upgrading the UPS B727/DC-8 parcel-carrier fleet by its Dee Howard Co subsidiary in the USA (see the 1996-97 edition for details).
- Alenia is a 38% shareholder in Airbus International Asia (which see under Multi-national).
- Alenia and Lockheed Martin of the USA are equal partners in the development and marketing of the C-27J Spartan tactical transport, based on the G222.

↑ Impression of the Lockheed Martin Alenia Tactical Transport System (LMATTS) C-27J *(courtesy LMATTS)*

↑ Alenia/Chrysler Technologies C-27A Spartan, for which Raytheon Systems provides maintenance and logistics support under a contract to last until December 1999 *(courtesy Raytheon Systems Company)*

Alenia G222, C-27A Spartan, and Lockheed Martin Alenia Tactical Transport System (LMATTS) C-27J

Details *(based on G222, except where stated)*

First flight: 18 July 1970.
First delivery: 1976 (G222 to Dubai). First C-27J expected in year 2000.
Role: Medium-range tactical military transport, with STOL characteristics. Also used for firefighting, calibration, EW and more.
Sales: Last G222 order for 6 for the Royal Thai Air Force, all delivered within 18 months of the 1994 contract date. 87 previously built, including 46 for the Italian Air Force in transport (30 aircraft), G222SAA firefighting (10, convertible between firefighting and transport roles), G222RM navaid calibration and G222VS electronic countermeasures versions, plus 5 to the Italian Ministry of Civil Defence. 20 G222Ts with Rolls-Royce Tyne engines went to Libya, while other recipients were Argentina (3), Congo (3), Dubai (1), Nigeria (5), Somalia (2) and Venezuela (7). In August 1990, 10 G222-710s were ordered by the USAF as C-27A Spartans, of which 7 remain in the inventory. Chrysler Technologies Airborne Systems became prime contractor for C-27As, responsible for installation of communication and navigation equipment. C-27As are based with the 24th Wing at Howard AFB in Panama, flying rapid response missions within Central and South America to transport cargo and personnel to remote areas with 1,800 ft × 45 ft (549 × 13.7 m) semi-prepared airfields and requiring a STOL type. Capable of air-dropping containers without special equipment; with special equipment, can air-drop heavy items and undertake low altitude parachute extraction system (LAPES) missions. Stated potential sales of more than 200-300 C-27Js worldwide, with possible customers including Australia and Brazil.

Details *(standard G222 transport)*

Crew: 2 or 3, plus loadmaster.
Passengers: Typically 34 fully-equipped troops on side seats but with provision for 46 or a maximum of 53. Alternatively, typically 24 paratroops but with provision for up to 40 or 42, or 24 litters plus 4 medical attendants (possible 36 litters).
Pressurization: 5.95 psi cabin differential.
Freight hold volume: 2,048.25 cu ft (58 m^3).
Freight hold capacity: 19,840 lb (9,000 kg). Can include 2 trucks or 1 truck towing a trailer or 105-mm howitzer gun, armoured vehicle, or many other varied loads including 5 × A-22 containers or pallets of up to 7 ft 4 ins (2.24 m) wide. Items up to 11,020 lb (5,000 kg) weight can be air dropped.
Freight hold access: Door and ramp (hydraulically operated) under the rear fuselage.
Size of freight doors: Full height and width of cabin, at 8 ft 0.5 ins × 7 ft 4.5 ins (2.45 × 2.25 m).
Wing control surfaces: Ailerons (with tabs), double-slotted flaps and 2-section spoilers.
Tail control surfaces: Variable-incidence tailplane. Elevators (with tabs) and rudder.
Flight control system: Hydraulic flaps, spoilers and rudder. Mechanical ailerons and elevators.
Construction materials: Aluminium alloy, with some honeycomb cores.
Engines: 2 General Electric/FiatAvio T64-P4D turboprops.
Engine rating: Each 3,400 shp (2,535 kW).
Fuel system: 12,000 litres.
Electrical system: 28 volt DC supply via AC system using 2 transformer/rectifiers. 24 volt ni-cd battery and static inverter for back-up. 115/200 volt, 400 Hz 3-phase AC supply via 2 engine and 1 APU driven alternators.
Hydraulic system: 2 systems, each 3,002 psi.
Braking system: Hydraulic multi-disc type.
De-icing system: Pneumatic boots for wing, tailplane and fin leading edges. Electric for propellers, and electric plus bleed air for engine intakes.
Oxygen system: Liquid standard, with gaseous as option.
Radar: Meteo weather and mapping radar.
Flight avionics/instrumentation: Navigation suite includes autopilot, Omega, dual VOR, dual ILS, dual Tacan or DME, ADF, marker beacon receiver, HSI, flight director and more. Communications suite includes HF/SSB, UHF, VHF-AM and FM.
Mission equipment: 3 life-rafts as standard equipment.

Aircraft variants:
G222 versions, see Sales and above.
C-27A Spartan is the USAF version, delivered from April 1991. Chrysler Technologies Airborne Systems integration of new Tacan, GPWS, IFF, INS, flight instrumentation, external/internal communications suites, aeromedical oxygen and power provisions, cargo box lighting and loadmaster station.
C-27J is the new Alenia/Lockheed Martin variant, following an agreement to become partners in its development in February 1996 (LMATTS – see heading). Lockheed Martin to integrate the avionics and engines, and undertake marketing and product support; Alenia to construct the airframes, undertake final assembly and carry out certification and flight testing. To offer enhanced performance, combined with lower operating, maintenance and life-cycle costs. Intention to apply C-130J Hercules technology, and adopt 4,200 shp (3,132 kW) Rolls-Royce Allison AE 2100D3 turboprop engines fitted with Dowty R391 6-blade composite propellers. EFIS 5-tube 'glass' cockpit, with Honeywell suite.

Details for C222, *with C-27 in italics where different*

PRINCIPAL DIMENSIONS:
Wing span: 94 ft 2 ins (28.7 m)
Maximum length: 74 ft 6 ins (22.7 m)
Maximum height: 34 ft 8 ins (10.57 m)

CABIN:
Length: 28 ft 2 ins (8.58 m)
Width: 8 ft 0.5 ins (2.45 m)
Height: 7 ft 4.5 ins (2.25 m)
Floor area: 276.42 sq ft (25.68 m^2), including ramp/door

WINGS:
Area: 882.64 sq ft (82 m^2)
Aspect ratio: 10.045

UNDERCARRIAGE:
Type: Can operate from semi-prepared and grass airstrips
Wheel base: 20 ft 5 ins (6.23 m)
Wheel track: 12 ft 0.5 ins (3.67 m)

WEIGHTS:
Empty, operating: 34,612 lb (15,700 kg), *or 35,500 lb (16,103 kg) for C 27A* or *36,375 lb (16,500 kg) for C-27J*
Maximum take-off: 61,729 lb (28,000 kg), *56,879 lb (25,800 kg) for C-27A* or *66,139 lb (30,000 kg) for C-27J*
Maximum landing: 58,422 lb (26,500 kg)
Payload: 19,840 lb (9,000 kg)

PERFORMANCE:
Maximum speed: 263 kts (303 mph) 487 km/h
Cruise speed: 238 kts (273 mph) 440 km/h, or *250 kts (288 mph) 463 km/h for C-27A*
Stall speed: 92 kts (106 mph) 170 km/h
Take-off distance: 2,251 ft (686 m), or *1,500 ft (458 m) for C-27A with 4,000 lb (1,814 kg) cargo, 2,000 ft (610 m) PA, ISA + 15°, unpaved*
Landing distance: 2,861 ft (872 m) at MLW, or *under 2,000 ft (610 m) for C-27A*
Maximum climb rate: 1,250 ft (380 m) per minute
Ceiling: 24,935 ft (7,600 m), or *22,000 ft (6,705 m) for C-27A*
Range with full fuel: 2,160 naut miles (2,485 miles) 4,000 km
Range with full payload: 680 naut miles (783 miles) 1,259 km
Operating/ferry range (C-27A): *300/1,500 naut miles (345/1,727 miles) 556/2,780 km*
Range (C-27J): *540 naut miles (621 miles) 1,000 km with a 17,639 lb (8,000 kg) payload, or 1,350 naut miles (1,553 miles) 2,500 km with an 11,023 lb (5,000 kg) payload, at 270 kts cruise speed*

Partenavia Costruzioni Aeronautiche SpA — Italy

Comments: See General Aviation section regarding fate of this company and products. Details and an illustration of the projected PD 90 Tapete Air Truck light transport can be found in the 1996-97 edition of *WA&SD*, pages 216-217.

ShinMaywa Industries Ltd — Japan

Corporate address:
Nihon Building, 2-6-2 Ohtemachi, Chiyoda-Ku, Tokyo 100.

Telephone: +81 3 3245 6611
Facsimile: +81 3 3245 6616

Founded: October 1949.

ACTIVITIES

- Manufactures aircraft and subassemblies, industrial machinery and truck bodies.
- Components include contributions to aeroplanes and helicopters being assembled in Japan. Boeing MD-11 engine pylon, is a risk-sharing partner on the Boeing 717 (pylons and horizontal stabilizers), builds trailing edges and other components for Boeing 757s and 767s, 777 wing/body fairings and components for Gulfstream business aircraft.

ShinMaywa US-1A and US-X

First flight: 16 October 1974.
First delivery: 5 March 1975.
Role: STOL search and rescue amphibian, and firefighting.
Sales: 17 US-1s and US-1As were received by the JMSDF, mainly for search and rescue with No 71 Squadron (not all remaining in service); a former PS-1 anti-submarine amphibian and more recently a US-1A were modified for firefighting, the latter carrying over 30,000 lb (13,600 kg) of water. A new version, the US-X, has been proposed for service in the next century, to replace US-1As.

Details *(US-1A, except under Aircraft variants)*

Crew: 4 for SAR.
Passengers: Can accommodate 12 litters or 20 seated persons in the cabin.
Wing control surfaces: Ailerons, inner and outer flaps, leading-edge slats, and spoilers. Flaps blown using a BLC system powered by a 1,500 shp (1,118 kW) T58-IHI-10M2 engine.
Tail control surfaces: T-tail with tailplane inverted slats. Elevators (with tabs) and rudder, using BLC system (see above).
Flight control system: Hydraulic.
Engines: 4 Ishikawajima T64-IHI-10J turboprops.
Engine rating: Each 3,400 eshp (2,535 ekW).
Fuel system: About 22,490 litres usable.
Radar: APS-115-2 search radar. APN-187C-N doppler radar.
Flight avionics/instrumentation: Includes bearing/distance and heading indicator, dead-reckoning plotting board, ADF, Tacan, VOR/ILS receiver, GPS, IFF transponder, and wave height meter.

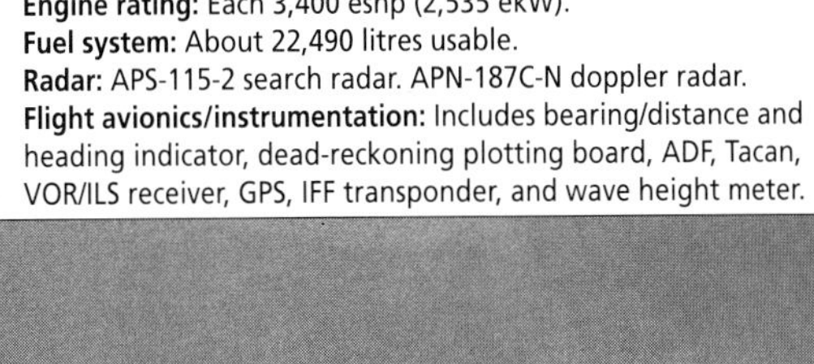

↑ **ShinMaywa US-1A SAR amphibian** *(courtesy ShinMaywa)*

Aircraft variants:
US-1A is the current version, as detailed.
US-1Kai is the designation for US-1As under a planned upgrade, with Rolls-Royce Allison AE 2100 turboprop engines with FADEC and upgraded avionics including 'glass' displays and a flight management system.
US-X is a projected replacement for US-1As, with the first flight in about the year 2000 or 2001, allowing production to start some 3 years later. New engines, pressurized hull, EFIS cockpit and improved weights and performance.

Details for US-1A

PRINCIPAL DIMENSIONS:
Wing span: 108 ft 9 ins (33.15 m)
Maximum length: 109 ft 9.3 ins (33.46 m)
Maximum height: 32 ft 8 ins (9.95 m)

WINGS:
Area: 1,462 sq ft (135.82 m^2)
Aspect ratio: 8.091

UNDERCARRIAGE:
Type: Retractable, with steerable nosewheels. Twin wheels on each unit
Wheel base: 27 ft 4 ins (8.33 m)
Wheel track: 11 ft 8 ins (3.56 m)

WEIGHTS:
Empty: 56,217 lb (25,500 kg)
Maximum take-off and landing (land): 99,208 lb (45,000 kg)
Maximum take-off and landing (water): 94,798 lb (43,000 kg) sheltered water, 79,366 lb (36,000 kg) open ocean
Payload: 30,000 lb (13,600 kg) of water in firefighting role

PERFORMANCE:
Cruise speed: 230 kts (265 mph) 426 km/h
Take-off over a 50 ft (15 m) obstacle: 2,198 ft (670 m) at MTOW from land, 2,412 ft (735 m) MTOW from water
Landing distance over a 50 ft (15 m) obstacle: 2,658 ft (810 m) to land, 1,838 ft (560 m) to water, both at 79,366 lb (36,000 kg)
Ceiling: 23,600 ft (7,200 m) at MTOW
Maximum range: 2,300 naut miles (2,648 miles) 4,260 km
Open ocean sea state capability: Sea state 5
Typical mission: Outboard cruise at 227 kts and 3,000 m altitude to search area, with 135 kts search speed at 300 m search altitude, water landing to rescue personnel, and return at 173 kts and 2,400 m altitude

Fokker Aircraft B.V. (see Rekkof Restart below) — Netherlands

Corporate address:
PO Box 7600, NL-1117ZJ Schiphol Oost.

Telephone: +31 20 605 2730
Facsimile: +31 20 605 2929

Founded:
Original Fokker company was founded on 21 July 1919.

Information:
Frank Ellemers (Marketing/Sales – *telephone* +31 20 605 2577).

Comments: On 15 March 1996 Fokker Aviation filed for bankruptcy. In July 1996 the Stork Group purchased Fokker Aviation, which continues in July 1998 as Fokker Aircraft with the activities of the following companies: Fokker Services (product support) and Fokker Elmo B.V. (electronic systems and components), both now based at Woensdrecht, Fokker Aerostructures B.V. at Papendrecht, and Fokker Special Products B.V. at Hoogeveen. The former Fokker Aircraft Services B.V. at Hoogerheide no longer operates. Under the trustees, a total of 33 new aircraft was built after the bankruptcy and up to May 1997 (with 3 Fokker 50s and 7 Fokker 70s in 1997 alone), when the final aircraft (a Fokker 50 for Ethiopian Airlines) was delivered. Thus, worldwide, Fokker had sold 768 Fokker F27s (including those by Fairchild in the USA), 241 F28s (programme to re-engine F28s as F28REs has been developed based on the Rolls-Royce Tay 620, with other options including new cockpit avionics, adoption of Fokker 100 wing leading-edges and tips, AlliedSignal RE220 APU, and some new airframe panels and fairings), 212 Fokker 50s and 60s, 47 Fokker 70s and 278 Fokker 100s.

From March 1996, various attempts were made to restart full manufacturing of the Fokker 50, 70 and 100, but much foreign interest did not lead to the company being purchased. However, in July 1998 negotiations were still underway to restart manufacturing under the name **Rekkof Restart** (Fokker backwards), Rekkof Restart being a company owned by Mr Rosen Jucobson. Rekkof has bought the tooling, rented the factory for production, and bought assets from Short Brothers PLC for wing production. This would see restart of Fokker 70 and 100 production, but not Fokker 50 or 60, nor development of the formerly proposed Fokker 130.

Fokker 50

Comments: First flown on 28 December 1985, this short-range airliner and multi-purpose government/military/corporate utility transport was built up to May 1997, when the last of 208 aircraft was delivered to Ethiopian Airlines. There are no plans to restart production. Full details and illustrations can be found in the 1996-97 edition of *WA&SD*, pages 217 and 218. A cargo conversion programme has been proposed, featuring an electrically operated side door of 7 ft 10 ins × 5 ft 10 ins (2.34 m × 1.78 m).

Fokker 60 Utility

Comments: First flown on 2 November 1995, this was basically a utility version of the Fokker 50. Just 4 aircraft were delivered, going to No 334 Squadron of the Royal Netherlands Air Force at Eindoven from June 1996. There are no plans to restart production. Full details and illustrations can be found in the 1996-97 edition of *WA&SD*, pages 218 and 219.

Fokker 70

First flight: 2 April 1993.
Certification: 14 October 1994 (RLD and FAA).
First delivery: 25 October 1994 (to Ford Motor Company).
Role: Short-medium range regional airliner, as reduced-length variant of the Fokker 100.
Airframe life: 45,000 cycles, and economic repair life of 90,000 cycles or hours.
Noise levels: 76.8 EPNdB fly-over, 89.9 EPNdB sideline, 87.7 EPNdB approach, standard weights; 80.1 EPNdB fly-over, 89.5 EPNdB sideline, 88.3 EPNdB approach, maximum optional weights.
Sales: 47 delivered before end of production in May 1997, including 7 built in 1997. Among Fokker aircraft expected to

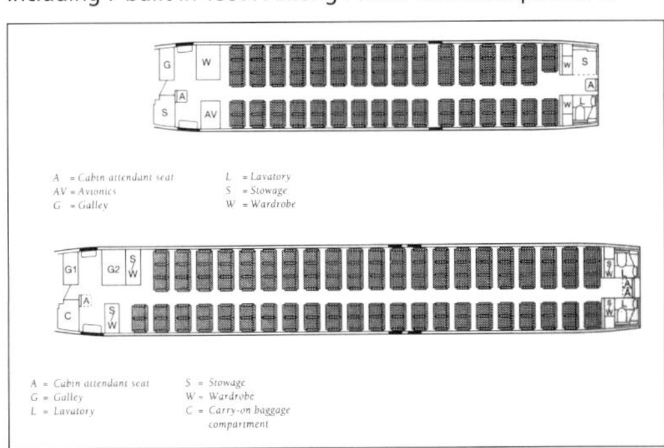

↑ **Fokker 70 cabin layout for 79 passengers (*top*), with Fokker 100 layout for 107 passengers (*below*)** *(courtesy Fokker)*

Details for Fokker 70

PRINCIPAL DIMENSIONS:
Wing span: 92 ft 1.5 ins (28.08 m)
Maximum length: 101 ft 5 ins (30.91 m)
Maximum height: 27 ft 11 ins (8.51 m)

CABIN:
Length: 54 ft 4.5 ins (16.57 m)
Width: 10 ft 2 ins (3.1 m)
Height: 6 ft 7 ins (2.01 m)
Volume: 2,966 cu ft (84 m^3)

WINGS:
Area: 1,006.42 sq ft (93.5 m^2)
Aspect ratio: 8.433
Sweepback: 17° 27' at 25% chord
Dihedral: 2.5°

TAIL UNIT:
Tailplane span: 32 ft 11.5 ins (10.04 m)
Tailplane area: 191.17 sq ft (17.76 m^2)

UNDERCARRIAGE:
Type: Retractable, with steerable nosewheels (±76°); nosewheel steering can be disconnected for greater angles. Twin wheels on each unit
Main wheel tyre size: H40 × 14-19
Nose wheel tyre size: 24 × 7.7-10
Wheel base: 37 ft 10.5 ins (11.54 m)
Wheel track: 16 ft 6.5 ins (5.04 m)

WEIGHTS:
Empty, operating: 49,984 lb (22,673 kg)
Maximum taxi: 81,494 lb (36,965 kg) *standard*, 84,492 lb (38,325 kg) *intermediate optional*, or 88,493 lb (40,140 kg) *high optional*
Maximum take-off: 81,000 lb (36,740 kg) *standard*, 83,996 lb (38,100 kg) *intermediate optional*, or 87,997-92,000 lb (39,915-41,730 kg) *high optional*
Maximum landing: 75,000-78,992 lb (34,020-35,830 kg) *standard*, 78,992-81,000 lb (35,830-36,740 kg) *intermediate optional*, or 81,000 lb (36,740 kg) *high optional*
Payload: 20,507 lb (9,302 kg) *standard*, 22,007 lb (9,982 kg) *intermediate optional*, or 24,008 lb (10,890 kg) *high optional*

PERFORMANCE:
Maximum permitted operating speed (V_{MO}): 320 kts (368 mph) 593 km/h CAS
Maximum operating Mach number (M_{MO}): Mach 0.77
Maximum speed: 462 kts (532 mph) 856 km/h TAS
Take-off field length: 3,675-5,160 ft (1,120-1,573 m), *at sea level*, 4,660-5,415 ft (1,420-1,650 m) *at 2,000 ft (610 m) elevation*
Landing field length: 3,822 ft (1,165 m) sea level, 3,970 ft (1,210 m) at 2,000 ft (610 m) elevation
Maximum operating altitude: 35,000 ft (10,670 m)
Range at 36,740 kg MTOW: 1,080 naut miles (1,243 miles) 2,000 km, with 79 passengers, minimum fuel speed schedule, reserves for overshoot to 1,500 ft, 200 naut mile diversion and 45 minutes hold
Range at 38,100 kg MTOW: 1,415 naut miles (1,629 miles) 2,620 km, passengers and reserves as above
Range at 39,915 kg MTOW: 1,840 naut miles (2,118 miles) 3,407 km
Range at 41,730 kg MTOW: 2,015 naut miles (2,320 miles) 3,734 km
Out and return range: 825 naut miles (950 miles) 1,528 km at 39,915 kg MTOW

↑ Fokker 70 operated by Malev Hungarian Airlines

re-enter production. Launch customers were Sempati Air and Pelita Air Service, ordered in mid-1993. Ford Motor Company became Executive Jet 70 launch customer (48-seat version). Kenyan Government became 70ER launch customer.
Crew: 2 (flight).
Passengers: 70-79. Alternatively, 30-52 in the Executive Jet version.
Seat pitch: 31/32 ins (79/81 cm) in 79-seat form.
Pressurization: 7.5 psi cabin differential.
Freight hold volume: 287.8 cu ft (8.15 m^3) forward, 163.5 cu ft (4.63 m^3) aft.
Baggage capacity: 310.8 cu ft (8.8 m^3) in overhead bins, stowages and wardrobes.
Engines: 2 Rolls-Royce Tay Mk 620 turbofans. AlliedSignal GTCP36-150RR APU.
Engine rating: Each 13,850 lbf (61.61 kN).
Fuel system: 9,640 litres (17,064 lb, 7,740 kg) standard or 13,365 litres (23,658 lb, 10,731 kg) optional.
Radar: Weather radar.
Flight avionics/instrumentation: ARINC 700 avionics. Automatic flight control and augmentation system, EFIS, multi-function display system and flight warning system. Cat II approach capability. Avionics can be extended to full Fokker 100 level, including Cat III autoland and flight management system.

Aircraft variants:
Fokker 70 is the basic airliner, as detailed. Variant (particularly for the North American market) is 70A, with 70 seats but greater freight capacity.
Fokker 70ER is the Extended Range version, with 4 modular fuel tanks in the forward cargo hold, providing over 3,240 naut miles (3,728 miles) 6,000 km range. 1 delivered on 15 December 1995 to Kenya.
Fokker Executive Jet 70 is the corporate shuttle (30-52 passengers), business and VIP (up to 30) version. Intercontinental range in the Extended Range version. Cat III capability.

Fokker 100

First flight: 30 November 1986.
Certification: 20 November 1987 (RLD), 30 May 1989 (FAA).
First delivery: 29 February 1988, to Swissair.
Role: Short-medium range airliner.
Airframe life: 45,000 cycles, and economic repair life of 90,000 cycles or hours.
Noise levels: 81.8 EPNdB fly-over, 91.7 EPNdB sideline and 93 EPNdB approach, certificated, at 98,000 lb (44,450 kg) MTOW and 88,000 lb (39,915 kg) MLW.
Sales: 278 delivered before the end of production. Among Fokker aircraft expected to re-enter production.
Crew: 2 (flight).

↑ Fokker 100 operated by American Airlines, the largest operator with 75

↑ Fokker 100 EFIS cockpit

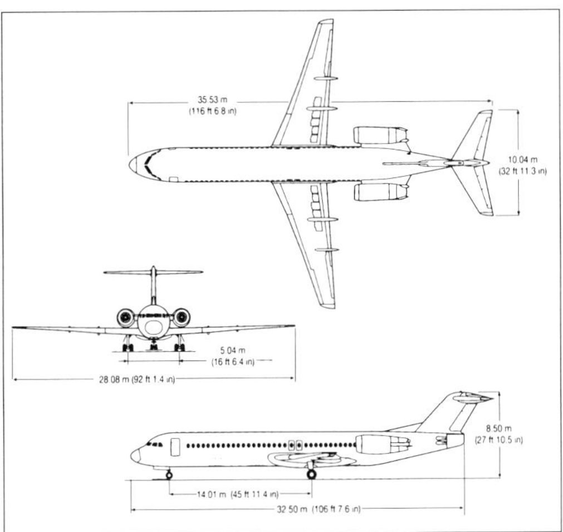

↑ **Fokker 100 general arrangement** *(courtesy Fokker)*

Passengers: 107 standard, with options from 97-109.
Seat pitch: 32 ins (81 cm) standard layout.
Galleys: 2.
Pressurization: 7.5 psi cabin differential.
Freight capacity: 334.7 cu ft (9.48 m^3) forward hold, or 437.9 cu ft (12.4 m^3) if avionics are repositioned to the main deck. 255.7 cu ft (7.24 m^3) aft hold.
Baggage capacity: 287.8 cu ft (8.15 m^3) in overhead bins, stowages, wardrobes and carry-on baggage compartment.
Wing control surfaces: Ailerons (with servo tabs), double-slotted Fowler flaps, and 5-section lift dumpers. (Prototype with laminar flow wing section was used in the ELFIN European research project during 1991-92.)
Tail control surfaces: Variable incidence tailplane, elevators and inset rudder.
Flight control system: Hydraulic/manual for the principal control surfaces, with hydraulic/electric for flaps.
Construction materials: Metal, except for composites ailerons, flaps, rudder, fin extension, wing-to-fuselage fairings, floor panels and other non-structural components.
Engines: 2 Rolls-Royce Tay 620 or Tay 650 turbofans. See Electrical system for APU.
Engine rating: Each 13,850 lbf (61.61 kN) or 15,100 lbf (67.17 kN) respectively.
Fuel system: 13,365 litres (23,658 lb, 10,731 kg).

Details for Fokker 100

PRINCIPAL DIMENSIONS:
Wing span: 92 ft 1.5 ins (28.08 m)
Maximum length: 116 ft 7 ins (35.53 m)
Maximum height: 27 ft 10.5 ins (8.5 m)

CABIN:
Length: 69 ft 6.2 ins (21.19 m)
Width: 10 ft 2 ins (3.1 m)
Height: 6 ft 7 ins (2.01 m)
Volume: 3,799.2 cu ft (107.58 m^3)
Main passenger door: 6 ft × 2 ft 7 ins (1.82 × 0.78 m)

WINGS:
Area: 1,006.42 sq ft (93.5 m^2)
Aspect ratio: 8.433
Sweepback: 17° 27' at 25% chord
Dihedral: 2.5°

TAIL UNIT:
Tailplane span: 32 ft 11.5 ins (10.04 m)
Tailplane area: 191.17 sq ft (17.76 m^2)

UNDERCARRIAGE:
Type: Retractable, with steerable nosewheels (±76°); nosewheel steering can be disconnected for greater angles. Twin wheels on each unit
Main wheel tyre size: H40 × 14-19
Nose wheel tyre size: 24 × 7.7-10
Wheel base: 45 ft 11.5 ins (14.01 m)
Wheel track: 16 ft 6.5 ins (5.04 m)
Turning circle: 73 ft (22.2 m) for 180° turn

WEIGHTS:
Empty, operating: 54,218 lb (24,593 kg) *with Tay 620s*, 54,514 or 54,558 lb (24,727 or 24,747 kg) *with Tay 650s*
Maximum ramp: 95,500 lb (43,320 kg) *standard*, 98,500 lb (44,680 kg) *intermediate optional*, and 101,500 lb (46,040 kg) *high optional with Tay 650s only*
Maximum take-off: 95,000 lb (43,090 kg) *standard*, 98,000 lb (44,450 kg) *intermediate optional*, or 101,000 lb (45,810 kg) *high optional with Tay 650s*
Maximum landing: 85,500 lb (38,780 kg) *standard*, 88,000 lb (39,915 kg) *intermediate and high optional*
Payload: 24,784 lb (11,242 kg) *standard with Tay 620s*, 26,780 lb (12,147 kg) *optional with Tay 620s*, 24,489 lb (11,108 kg) *standard with Tay 650s*, 26,484 lb (12,013 kg) *maximum optional with Tay 650*

PERFORMANCE:
Maximum permitted operating speed (V_{MO}): 320 kts (368 mph) 593 km/h CAS
Maximum operating Mach number (M_{MO}): Mach 0.77
Maximum speed: 462 kts (532 mph) 856 km/h TAS
Landing field length: 4,183 ft (1,275 m) at sea level, 6,365 ft (1,330 m) at 2,000 ft (610 m) elevation
Maximum operating altitude: 35,000 ft (10,670 m)
Range with Tay 620s, at 43,090 kg MTOW: 1,290 naut miles (1,485 miles) 2,389 km, with 107 passengers, minimum fuel speed schedule, reserves for overshoot to 1,500 ft, 200 naut mile diversion and 45 minutes hold
Range with Tay 620s, at 44,450 kg MTOW: 1,575 naut miles (1,813 miles) 2,917 km, conditions as above
Range with Tay 650s, at 43,090 kg MTOW: 1,260 naut miles (1,451 miles) 2,333 km
Range with Tay 650s, at 45,810 kg MTOW: 1,680 naut miles (1,934 miles) 3,111 km

Electrical system: Includes engine-driven generators. AlliedSignal GTCP36-150RR APU.
Braking system: Carbon multi-disc type, with anti-skid. Clamshell speed brakes in the tailcone.
Radar: Weather radar.
Flight avionics/instrumentation: ARINC 700 avionics plus built-in test equipment. Not more than 18 instruments, including 6 colour displays, present information. EFIS and fully digital cockpit, with "dark cockpit philosophy" with no indication lights on during normal operations. Dual flight management system. Cat IIIb autoland.

Aircraft variants:
Fokker 100 is the basic version, as detailed.
Fokker 100 Quick Change version for 88 passengers on palletized seats or containers (11 × LD3, or 5 × LD7 or LD9), and with a large cargo door of 11 ft 2 ins × 6 ft 4 ins (3.4 × 1.93 m). Structural modifications contracted out.
Fokker Executive Jet 100 is the corporate shuttle, business and VIP version. Intercontinental range in the Extended Range version with 4 modular fuel tanks in the forward cargo hold. Cat III capability.
Fokker 130 was a proposed 'stretched' 116–137-passenger derivative. Not being developed.

WSK "PZL-Mielec" S.A. — Poland

Corporate address:
See Combat section for company details.

PZL-Mielec/Antonov An-28 and M28 Skytruck (NATO name *Cash*)

First flight: 23 April 1975 (Antonov prototype), 22 July 1984 (Polish built An-28), 24 July 1993 for An-28PT Piryt (renamed M28 Skytruck in 1995 when the certificate was obtained).
Certification: 7 February 1986 for An-28. M28 Skytruck gained Temporary Polish Type Certificate in March 1994 and full IKCSP certification to FAR Pt 23 in mid-1995.
Role: Light passenger or cargo transport capable of short take-off and landing, with special military versions. An-28 now redesignated M28. Suited to hot and high operations (up to 8,530 ft, 2,600 m and at -50° to +60° C).
Sales: 197 built at time of writing (including a dozen Skytrucks plus specialized versions). About 160 An-28s had been delivered to the USSR before 1989, when production for Russia terminated, leaving several aircraft at the factory. 6 An-28s were purchased by the Polish armed forces, including 4 by the Navy. In 1995, 6 M28 Skytrucks were ordered for the Venezuelan National Guard (first delivered December 1996, c/n 1AJE001-03, registered GN-96105), with another 6 ordered in April 1997 for the Venezuelan Army and Air Force, with options for 12 to 16 more. An order for 6 to 8 M28RM Bryza-1Rs is expected from the Polish Navy, to join the single example received in 1994. M28TD Bryza-1 is operated by the Polish Air Force (see Aircraft variants).

Details *(mainly M28 Skytruck)*

Crew: 2 (flight).
Passengers: 18 in M28 Skytruck, 17 in An-28 with 2 TWD-10B engines, or cargo (seats folded along cabin wall). Provision for a 661 lb (300 kg) baggage container fitted under the fuselage.
Freight hold access: Clamshell rear doors or sliding doors (M28TD).
Wing control surfaces: Ailerons (port trim tab), 2-section double-slotted flaps (15° for take-off, 40° for landing), manual/automatic spoilers, and leading-edge slats.
Tail control surfaces: Elevators (with trim tabs) and twin horn-balanced rudders (with trim tabs).
Flight control system: Cable-pushrod type, with electrically operated tabs.
Engines: 2 Pratt & Whitney Canada PT6A-65B turboprops, with 5-blade autofeathering and reversible-pitch Hartzell propellers.
Engine rating: Each 1,100 shp (820.3 kW).
Fuel system: 1,940 litres (3,351 lb, 1,520 kg) in wings standard, or 3,891 lb (1,765 kg) for the extended-range version. Provision for a 3,549 lb (1,610 kg) fuel tank in the cabin for long ferry flights.
Electrical system: 3-phase 200/115 volt AC via engine-mounted alternators, and 3-phase 36 volt AC using T5105O4B transformer. Under emergency conditions, PO-250A converter can supply single-phase 115 volt, 400 Hz AC power. 27 volt DC via rectifiers. 20NKBN-25 batteries for emergency power and engine start when needed.
Hydraulic system: 2,233 psi, to operate flaps, spoilers, mainwheel brakes, and nosewheel steering.
Braking system: Hydraulic multi-disc, with anti-skid system.
De-icing system: Thermal/pneumatic for slats, tail unit, inlet ducts, oil coolers and air intakes. Electric for propellers/spinners, windshield and pitot heads.
Radar: RDS-81 digital weather radar.
Flight avionics/instrumentation: AlliedSignal Bendix/King KFC 275 or 325 automatic flight control, radar altimeter and transponder. Navigation suite comprises dual VOR/ILS, DME, ADF, marker beacon, RMI, and dual KCS-55A plus KNS 81 digital area navigation system and GC 381A radar graphics computer. Communications suite comprises VHF/AM (KY 196/KX 165), HF com, audio selector panel and interphone, and dual emergency VHF.

Aircraft variants:
M28 (formerly An-28) is the standard transport version, with 945 shp (705 kW) PZL TWD-10B engines with 3-blade AW24AN propellers.
M28A is a Polar region transport, with increased fuel capacity.
M28P (Pozarniczy) is a paratroop version for firefighting.
M28TD Bryza-1 (transportowo-desantowy, cargo-assault) is a military transport/paratroop version, tested in 1992. Prototype was the converted 23rd aircraft of the seventh production series. First production M28TD (side number *1003*) was delivered in October 1994 to the 13th Transport Air Regiment of the Polish Air Force. Rear clamshell doors replaced by ramp sliding forward under the fuselage. 4 variants, accommodating 13 paratroops and 2 × 100 kg parachute containers, or 17 parachutists, or 6 litters and 7 seated persons, or 3,858 lb (1,750 kg) of cargo, or a special version for transporting air-to-air missiles (up to 1,102 lb, 500 kg each).

↑ **Polish Navy An-28 fitted with Golden Crow avionics** *(Piotr Butowski)*

M28RM Bryza-1R (ratowniczy morski, sea rescue) is the maritime patrol/rescue co-ordination version for the Polish Navy. 2 pilots, technician and 3 systems operators. Prototype tested in Autumn 1992, equipped with Polish made ARS-100 navigation radar (derived from the naval SRN-441XA) in an underfuselage radome. Radar has modified X-band antenna, rotating 7.5 or 15 times per minute. Maximum search range is 60 naut miles (69 miles) 111 km. First (and only, at the time of writing) production aircraft (*1002*) was delivered on 27 October 1994 to the Polish Navy. Chelton DF-707-1 radio system is also used for locating shipwrecked persons. Can carry ACR/RLB-14 radio marker buoys, and 2 × 100 kg SAB-100NM bombs to illuminate the rescue area (racks are on undercarriage supports, and a light PKV bombsight is located at the convex window at rear starboard of fuselage). AFA-39 photo-camera. Can also drop 3 × 6-person Mewa-6 dinghies (in addition to crew dinghies). Flight/navigation equipment includes AlliedSignal Bendix/King Silver Crown suite with RDS-81 weather radar, KNS-815 navigation system, KLN-90A GPS receiver, KT-71 transponder, and ARK-15 radio-compass. 2 PZL-10B turboprop engines, each rated at 900 shp (671 kW). First prototype is now being tested with the ARS-400 radar, and new data transfer and command system. An order for 6 to 8 aircraft is expected from the Polish Navy (all with ARS-400 radar). Illustrated in the 1996-97 edition of *WA&SD*, page 221.

M28RF Bryza-2 was a projected military electronic warfare version. Prototype tested with new Gold Crown navigation suite, including KFC-325 automatic flight control, Litton LTN-101 GPS, KNS-660 navigation computer, EFIS displays, etc. Mission equipment never installed. Programme abandoned and the prototype (*1007*) used as a passenger aircraft.

M28PT Piryt prototype (*SP-PDF*) first flew on 24 July 1993. Westernized version with PT6 engines and more comfortable cabin. Put into series production as the M28 Skytruck.

M28 Skytruck is the current production version (see Piryt), with PT6A-65B turboprop engines, as detailed.

M28.03 and M28.04 Skytruck Plus will carry 30 passengers in an enlarged fuselage. See next entry.

Details for M28 Skytruck PT

PRINCIPAL DIMENSIONS:
Wing span: 72 ft 4.5 ins (22.063 m)
Maximum length: 43 ft (13.1 m)
Maximum height: 16 ft 1 ins (4.9 m)

CABIN:
Length: 17 ft 3 ins (5.26 m)
Width: 5 ft 8.5 ins (1.74 m)
Height: 5 ft 3 ins (1.6 m)
Cargo door: Clamshell 7 ft 10.5 ins (2.4 m) length, with 4 ft 7 ins (1.4 m) width at sill, narrowing at top to 3 ft 3.25 ins (1 m)

WINGS:
Area: 427.54 sq ft (39.72 m^2)
Aspect ratio: 12.26
Flaps area, total: 85.96 sq ft (7.986 m^2)
Ailerons area, total: 46.61 sq ft (4.33 m^2)

TAIL UNIT:
Tailplane span: 16 ft 10.5 ins (5.14 m)
Tailplane and elevator area, total: 95.26 sq ft (8.85 m^2)
Tailfins and rudders area, total: 107.64 sq ft (10 m^2)

UNDERCARRIAGE:
Type: Fixed, with castoring nosewheel
Main wheel tyre size: 720 × 320 mm
Nose wheel tyre size: 595 × 185 mm
Wheel base: 14 ft 3.5 ins (4.354 m)
Wheel track: 11 ft 2 ins (3.405 m)
Turning circle: 45 ft 11 ins (14 m) for 180° turn

WEIGHTS:
Empty: 8,635 lb (3,917 kg)
Maximum take-off: 15,432 lb (7,000 kg)
Maximum landing: 14,661 lb (6,650 kg)
Payload: 4,409 lb (2,000 kg)
Maximum payload plus fuel: 6,327 lb (2,870 kg)
Maximum unit cargo floor handling: 882 lb (400 kg)

PERFORMANCE:
Maximum speed: 197 kts (227 mph) 365 km/h
Maximum cruise speed: 181 kts (208 mph) 335 km/h
Economic speed: 146 kts (168 mph) 270 km/h
Stall speed: 71 kts (81.5 mph) 131 km/h
Maximum airfield elevation: 8,530 ft (2,600 m)
Take-off distance: 870 ft (265 m) at sea level, MTOW, concrete runway
Take-off distance over a 35 ft (11 m) obstacle: 1,198 ft (365 m)
Landing distance: 607 ft (185 m)
Landing distance over a 50 ft (15 m) obstacle: 1,920 ft (585 m)
Maximum climb rate: 2,657 ft (810 m) per minute, at 9,845 ft (3,000 ft) altitude, MTOW
G limits: +3, -1
Cruise altitude: 9,840 ft (3,000 m)
Ceiling: 24,935 ft (7,600 m)
Ceiling, 1 engine: 16,400 ft (5,000 m)
Range with full fuel: 765 naut miles (881 miles) 1,417 km, with 1,984 lb (900 kg) cargo
Range with 18 passengers: 539 naut miles (621 miles) 1,000 km

PZL-Mielec M28.03 and M28.04 Skytruck Plus

First flight: Expected in Summer 1998. Full-size mock-up of M28.03 was presented for the first time on 30 August 1997 in Mielec.
Certification: Expected 1999, to FAR Pt 23.
Role: 30-passenger or cargo transport, developed as an enlarged-fuselage derivative of the M28 Skytruck. Originally designated PZL M34.
Crew: 2 (flight) in passenger version, 1 or 2 in cargo version.
Passengers/cargo: 19 in the commercial version with airliner seats, 27-30 in the military version, or up to 5,952 lb (2,700 kg) of cargo (including 3 standard LD-3 containers).
Freight hold access: Clamshell rear doors (M28.03) or large side hatch (M28.04). Provision for a 1,102 lb (500 kg) weight and 70.63 cu ft (2 m^3) volume baggage container fitted under the fuselage.
Fuselage: Compared with M28 Skytruck, lengthened by 6 ft 0.5 ins (1.84 m), using 2 fuselage sections, and height increased by 10 ins (0.25 m).
Engines: 2 uprated Pratt & Whitney Canada PT6A-65B turboprops, with 9 ft 3 ins (2.82 m) diameter Hartzell 5-blade propellers.
Engine rating: 1,175 shp (876 kW) each.
Fuel system: 2,277 litres (3,891 lb, 1,765 kg) in the wings. Provision for 2,100 litre (3,549 lb, 1,610 kg) fuel tank inside the cabin for long ferry flights.
Radar: Weather radar optional.
Flight avionics/instrumentation: Automatic flight control system, radar altimeter and transponder. Navigation suite includes dual VOR/ILS, DME, and ADF marker beacon. Communications suite comprises 2 VHF coms, audio selector panel and interphone. GPS optional.
Weapons and equipment: Small weapons rack at each main undercarriage strut for small bombs and rocket packs.

Aircraft variants:
M28.03 will have clamshell rear doors, as for current M28.
M28.04 will have a large side hatch sufficient for loading an LD-3 container.

Details for Skytruck Plus

PRINCIPAL DIMENSIONS:
Wing span: 72 ft 4.5 ins (22.063 m)
Maximum length: 49 ft (14.94 m)
Maximum height: 16 ft 11 ins (5.15 m)

CABIN:
Width: 5 ft 11 ins (1.8 m)
Height: 5 ft 3 ins (1.6 m)
Volume: 847.55 cu ft (24 m^3)
Cargo door: Clamshell 7 ft 10.5 ins (2.4 m) length, with 5 ft 9 ins (1.75 m) width at sill for M28.03

UNDERCARRIAGE:
Type: Fixed, with castoring nosewheel

WEIGHTS:
Empty: 9,458 lb (4,290 kg)
Maximum zero fuel: 15,598 lb (7,075 kg)
Maximum take-off: 18,960 lb (8,600 kg)
Maximum landing: 18,012 lb (8,170 kg)
Payload: 5,952 lb (2,700 kg)

PERFORMANCE:
Maximum cruise speed: 189 kts (217 mph) 350 km/h
Take-off distance: 1,214 ft (370 m), at sea level, MTOW, concrete runway
Landing distance: 542 ft (165 m)
Cruise altitude: 9,845 ft (3,000 m) for passenger version
Ceiling: 24,935 ft (7,600 m)
Range with full payload: 593 naut miles (683 miles) 1,100 km
Range with 19 passengers: 782 naut miles (901 miles) 1,450 km, with 1 hour reserves
Ferry range with fuselage fuel tank: 1,619 naut miles (1,864 miles) 3,000 km

↑ **PZL-Mielec M28.03 Skytruck Plus mock-up. Note the 500 kg baggage container under the fuselage and rocket pods at the undercarriage struts** *(Wacław Hołyś)*

Romaero S.A. — Romania

Corporate address:
Bulevardul Ficusului Nr 44, Sector 1, Code 71544, Bucharest.

Telephone: +40 1 633 50 82, 666 60 90
Facsimile: +40 1 212 20 82
Telex: 11691 IAVB-R

Founded: 1920.

Information:
Constatin Dinischiotu (Sales and Marketing Executive Director).

ACTIVITIES

■ Manufacture of the Britten-Norman BN2 Islander (including BN2T and Defender 4000) under a subcontracting agreement (over 500 completed and delivered to B-N).
■ Aircraft, engine and component maintenance and repair.
■ Manufacture of subassemblies and components for Boeing under an agreement signed in March 1994.
■ Supplied design services for IAI's Galaxy, and has reportedly been subcontracted by Sogerma to manufacture Galaxy Aerospace Galaxy rear fuselage sections (Galaxy Aerospace Corporation being the marketing company).
■ See next entry for 1-11 and Airstar 2500 status.

Romaero 1-11 and Airstar 2500

Comments: Romaero assembled nine 1-11s from British Aerospace-supplied kits, all of Series 561RC type and going to Tarom and Romavia Romanian Aviation (the first flew on 18 September 1982). Development of the much-modernized Airstar 2500 variant has been terminated. Details of these aircraft can be found in the 1996-97 edition of *WA&SD*, pages 221-222.

Aeroprogress Inc/Khrunichev State Space Research Center — Russia

Comments: Aeroprogress and Khrunichev (Aviation Department) are closely affiliated. See Combat section for status of some military concepts. Details and illustrations relating to civil programmes can be found in the General Aviation section of this edition, while various other transport programmes that have not progressed to prototype stage can be found in the 1996-97 edition of *WA&SD*, pages 222 to 225. Among the largest projected transports from Aeroprogress is the T-274 Titan, a 28,660 lb (13,000 kg) payload T-tailed STOL freighter with 4 TV7-117 turboprop engines and a rear ramp/door for straight-in loading. Prototype construction was said to have originally been scheduled to start in 1995, allowing a first flight in 1996, but the present status of the programme is uncertain (details in the 1996-97 edition).

Aviaspetstrans Consortium — Russia

Corporate address:
Zhukovsky 5, Box 230 AST, Moscow Region 140160.

Telephone: +7 095 556 59 93
Facsimile: +7 095 292 65 11

Founded: 1990.

Aviaspetstrans (Myasishchev) Yamal

First flight: Anticipated for 1998.
Role: Multi-purpose amphibian for passenger/cargo transportation into remote areas, medevac, ice and EEZ patrol, ecological survey, firefighting, air/sea rescue and more.

Development

■ Under the auspices of Gosaviaregistr, involving 4 Russian scientific/research organizations, and with Myasishchev undertaking actual aircraft development.

Details

Crew: 2.
Passengers: 15 passengers as a flying-boat, 18 when operated from land. Alternatively, medevac and other layouts.
Wing control surfaces: Ailerons (with tabs) and 2-section flaps.
Tail control surfaces: T-tail, with elevators (with tabs) and split rudder, the lower half with tab (rudder split each side of the propeller housing).
Fuselage: Single-step hull, with side sponsons for stability and to house the main undercarriage units.
Engines: 2 Rybinsk RD-600 turboshafts, driving a single tail-mounted 6-blade pusher propeller through a combining reduction gearbox.
Engine rating: Each 1,300 shp (969.4 kW).
Fuel system: 5,291 lb (2,400 kg).

↑ Aviaspetstrans (Myasishchev) Yamal *(Piotr Butowski)*

Details for Yamal

PRINCIPAL DIMENSIONS:
Wing span: 70 ft 2.5 ins (21.4 m)
Maximum length: 55 ft 2.5 ins (16.825 m)
Maximum height: 17 ft 7 ins (5.367 m)

CABIN:
Length: 57 ft 4 ins (17.47 m)
Width: 6 ft 8 ins (2.025 m)
Volume: 826.36 cu ft (23.4 m^3)
Main passenger door: On the port side of the upper hull, above the sponson

WINGS:
Area: 558.65 sq ft (51.9 m^2)
Aspect ratio: 8.824

UNDERCARRIAGE:
Type: Retractable main wheels and fixed tailwheel. Nosewheel undercarriage being developed. Maximum ground pressure 64 psi

WEIGHTS:
Maximum take-off: 21,165 lb (9,600 kg)
Fuel: 5,291 lb (2,400 kg)
Payload: 4,409 lb (2,000 kg)

PERFORMANCE:
Maximum cruise speed: 235 kts (270 mph) 435 km/h, at 24,600 ft (7,500 m)
Long-range cruise speed: 202 kts (233 mph) 375 km/h
Take-off distance: 738 ft (225 m) *land*, 755 ft (230 m) *water*
Operating altitude: 24,600 ft (7,500 m)
Range with full payload: 632 naut miles (727 miles) 1,170 km, at maximum cruise speed, or 756 naut miles (870 miles) 1,400 km at long-range cruise speed

Beriev Taganrog Aviation Complex — Russia

Corporate address:
See Combat section for company details. See also Reconnaissance and General Aviation.

Beriev Be-32 (NATO name *Cuff*)

First flight: 8 July 1968 for Be-30 commuter transport with TVD-10 turboprops (pilot M. Nikhailov), March 1976 for Be-32 with TVD-10Bs, 12 May 1993 for renewed Be-32 with TVD-20s, and 15 August 1995 for Be-32K with Pratt & Whitney – Klimov PK6A-65B turboprops.
Certification: Planned for 1997-98 for Be-32, to AP-23 regulations.
Role: Light passenger/cargo commuter transport, 7-passenger business aircraft, and with adaptation to ambulance and forest/economic monitoring.
Sales: 3 prototypes and 5 production Be-30s built in late 1960s and early 1970s. In 1976, the second Be-30 prototype was converted into the Be-32 with shaft-connected engines and weather radar installed. Programme restarted after 17 years, targeted at the CIS market to fill a gap after the reduction of Polish An-28 and Czech L 410 deliveries. Current Be-32 prototype is the restored Be-32 No 1 of 1976. Production planned at Tananrog, although also Komsomolsk-on-Amur and Kraiova (Romania) plants have been under construction. Expected price $2.6 to 2.8 million. Possible sales are estimated at 250-300 aircraft by Beriev, but no firm order had been announced at the time of writing. Russian Federal Border Guard intends to order 50-75 Be-32Ps.
Crew: 2.
Passengers/cargo: 16 in the passenger version, 7 passengers in the business model, 6 litters plus 10 seats and a medical attendant in an ambulance role, 15 paratroops/parachutists, or 4,189 lb (1,900 kg) of cargo.
Seat pitch: 29 ins (73.75 cm) for 16-passenger layout.
Freight hold access: 2 large port-side freight doors.
Wing control surfaces: Ailerons and double-slotted flaps.

↑ Beriev Be-32K *(Piotr Butowski)*

Tail control surfaces: Elevators (port tab) and rudder (with tab).
Construction materials: Mostly metal, including honeycomb panels for part of the wings and tail unit. Glassfibre for non-structural wing and tail tips plus wing-root fillets.
Engines: 2 Pratt & Whitney – Klimov PK6A-65B turboprops.
Engine rating: 1,100 shp (820.3 kW).
Fuel system: 2,250 litres.
Electrical system: DC power by 25.5 volt/12 kW rectifiers. AC power by 115/200 volt, 400Hz 3-phase system with 2 × 16 kW alternators.
Braking system: On main units.
De-icing system: Electro-thermal for cockpit windows and propellers. Hot air for wing/tail leading edges, air intakes and oil cooler.

Details for Be-32K

PRINCIPAL DIMENSIONS:
Wing span: 55 ft 9 ins (17 m)
Maximum length: 51 ft 6 ins (15.7 m)
Maximum height: 18 ft 1.5 ins (5.52 m)

CABIN:
Length: 18 ft 7 ins (5.66 m), or 23 ft 4 ins (7.1 m) for the cargo version, when the rear area is used
Width: 5 ft (1.52 m)
Height: 5 ft 11 ins (1.81 m)
Floor area: 39.18 sq ft (3.64 m^2)
Volume: 459.1 cu ft (13 m^3), or 600.3 cu ft (17 m^3) for the cargo version
Door size: 4 ft 3 ins × 2 ft 5.5 ins (1.3 × 0.75 m)

WINGS:
Aerofoil section: P-20
Area: 344.44 sq ft (32 m^2)
Aspect ratio: 9.03
Twist: 3°
Anhedral: On outer panels

UNDERCARRIAGE:
Type: Retractable, with twin nosewheels. Can operate from natural ground airfields, or in Northern and Arctic regions using floats and skis
Main wheel tyre size: 720 × 320 mm
Nose wheel tyre size: 500 × 150 mm
Wheel base: 15 ft 7 ins (4.75 m)
Wheel track: 17 ft 1 ins (5.2 m)

WEIGHTS:
Empty: 10,494 lb (4,760 kg)
Maximum take-off: 15,432-16,094 lb (7,000-7,300 kg)
Maximum landing: 14,991 lb (6,800 kg)
Payload: 4,189 lb (1,900 kg)

PERFORMANCE:
Maximum cruise speed: 275 kts (317 mph) 510 km/h
Economic cruise speed: 200 kts (230 mph) 370 km/h
Take-off distance: 1,608 ft (490 m)
Landing distance: 1,641 ft (500 m)
Maximum climb rate: 1,476 ft (450 m) per minute at sea level
Range with 16 passengers: 477 naut miles (550 miles) 885 km
Range with 7 passengers: 1,106 naut miles (1,274 miles) 2,050 km
Duration: 5 hours 24 minutes maximum

Radar: Kontur-10 weather type.
Flight avionics/instrumentation: Automatic flight control system.

Aircraft variants:
Be-30 was the initial version of the 1960s. See Sales.
Be-32 is an Omsk TVD-10B or TVD-20 engined version.
Be-32A is a projected version, powered by Rybinsk TVD-1500 turboprops of 1,500 shp (1,118 kW) each.
Be-32K has PK6A-65B engines. As detailed.
Be-32P (patrulnyi) is a patrol version for Russian Federal Border Guard service, ordered in September 1997. A prototype Be-32K (RA-67205) will be upgraded into the Be-32P, featuring blisters, external hardpoints and a machine-gun in the cabin. Maximum take-off weight 16,094 lb (7,300 kg), and increased fuel volume to allow an 8-10 hour duration. Border Guard intends to order 50-75 aircraft.
Be-32PV (vooruzhonnyi, armed) is a proposed armed derivative of Be-32P.

Beriev Be-102

First flight: Project only; design began in 1993.
Role: Multi-purpose amphibian, mainly for firefighting but to be offered also for passenger and/or cargo carrying, search and rescue, environmental and maritime patrol, and ice reconnaissance.
Crew: 2.
Passengers: 44 in the passenger version.
Firefighting tanks volume: 282.5 cu ft (8 m^3) of water in underfloor tanks. 130 tonnes of water can be dropped without refuelling during repeated missions, assuming an airfield to reservoir distance of 27 naut miles (31 miles) 50 km and a reservoir to fire distance of 22 naut miles (25 miles) 40 km.
Freight hold capacity: Up to 9,259 lb (4,200 kg) of cargo in freighter configuration.
Wing characteristics: Shoulder mounted, with slight sweepback and anhedral on the outer sections. Winglets.
Wing control surfaces: Ailerons with tabs, single-slotted flaps, and spoilers.
Tail control surfaces: T-tail. Elevators and rudder.
Engines: 2 turboprops, each rated at 2,500 shp (1,864 kW).
Radar: Weather radar.

PLAN VIEW (16 PASSENGERS)

PLAN VIEW (14 PASSENGERS)

EXECUTIVE

CARGO

AMBULANCE

PARADROP

↑ Beriev Be-32 general arrangement and cabin layouts *(courtesy Beriev)*

Details for Be-102

PRINCIPAL DIMENSIONS:
Wing span: 110 ft 6 ins (33.67 m)
Maximum length: 85 ft 4 ins (26 m)
Maximum height: 30 ft (9.15 m)

CABIN:
Main cargo door: 5 ft 7 ins × 4 ft 11 ins (1.7 × 1.5 m)

UNDERCARRIAGE:
Type: Retractable, with twin wheels on each unit. Small underwing floats

WEIGHTS:
Maximum take-off: 46,297 lb (21,000 kg)
Payload: 9,259 lb (4,200 kg) of cargo, or 17,637 lb (8,000 kg) of water in the firefighting version

PERFORMANCE:
Maximum speed: 248 kts (286 mph) 460 km/h
Maximum cruise speed: 203 kts (234 mph) 376 km/h
Take-off distance: 2,107 ft (642 m) from shore, 3,281 ft (1,000 m) from water
Landing distance: 2,461 ft (750 m) to shore, 2,297 ft (700 m) to water
Maximum wave height: 2.3 ft (0.7 m)
Range with maximum payload: 1,230 naut miles (1,417 miles) 2,280 km

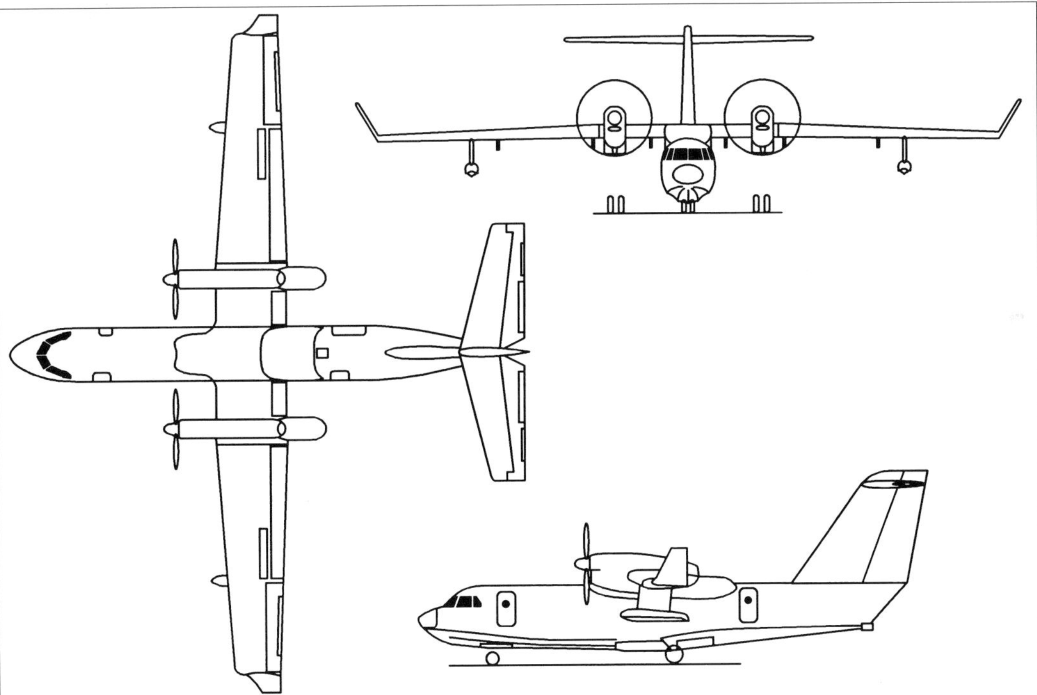

↑ Beriev Be-102 multi-purpose amphibian *(Piotr Butowski)*

Beriev Be-112 Pelican

Comments: Be-112 is a 22,046-26,455 lb (10,000-12,000 kg) MTOW class multi-purpose amphibian project, designed for passenger/cargo carrying, ambulance and veterinary support to far-off regions, geological support, ice and fishery surveillance, EEZ patrol, and ecological monitoring. 24-27 passengers or 6,173 lb (2,800 kg) of cargo could be carried to a distance of 540 naut miles (621 miles) 1,000 km, with a cruise speed of 216-243 kts (249-280 mph) 400-450 km/h. 2 × 1,300-1,500 shp (969-1,119 kW) turboprops will be provided, possibly of Pratt & Whitney PT6A-67, Omsk TVD-20, or Rybinsk TVD-1500 types. The design of the aircraft is still evolving, making the publication of firm data meaningless. Nevertheless, all designs for the Be-112 maintain a similar short and thick boat-shaped fuselage, long unswept wings and 2 engines installed above the rear fuselage on special supports or carried by the twin tailfins. See the 1996-97 edition of *WA&SD*, page 227, for specifications of one design.

↑ Beriev Be-112 Pelican

Beriev Be-200

First flight: 24 September 1998 (pilot Konstantin Babich).
Certification: Planned for the end of 1998.
Role: Multi-purpose amphibian, initially for firefighting but to be offered for passenger and/or cargo carrying, search and rescue, environmental and maritime patrol, and ice reconnaissance.
Sales: No prototype built by Beriev experimental works, but 4 (including 2 for static/fatigue tests) pre-series Be-200s have been/are being built at Irkutsk. First of these was rolled-out on 11 September 1996. First Be-200 has been completed as a firefighter, as this configuration has the highest priority and also does not require full certification. Second aircraft has been build in Be-200ChS form, according to an order from Russia's Ministry of Emergency Situations (total of 7 aircraft has been ordered by MES). More than 100 preliminary orders are reported from Russia plus many foreign options including 15 from Italy. Possible sales are estimated at 300 aircraft by Beriev. Price has been quoted as US$ 22-24 million.
Crew: 2 flight crew for each version.
Passengers: 2 cabin attendants and 32 passengers in mixed first/business class layout, or 64, 66 or 68 passengers in all-tourist layout. 18-23 seats in business-jet configuration. 19 passengers and 6,614 lb (3,000 kg) of cargo in combi configuration. Ambulance version has 30 litters and seats for 7 casualties/attendants. See Firefighting tanks volume for firefighters.
Seat pitch: 29.5-31.5 ins (75-80 cm) in tourist layout, 35.4-37.4 ins (90-95 cm) in business layout, and 40.2 ins (102 cm) in first class layout.
Firefighting tanks volume: 423.8 cu ft (12 m^3) of water in 2 tanks, and 42.38 cu ft (1.2 m^3) of liquid chemical in 4 tanks. 26 seats for firefighters in the cabin. 260 tonnes of water can be dropped without refuelling during repeated missions, assuming an airfield to reservoir distance of 108 naut miles (124 miles) 200 km and a reservoir to fire distance of 5.4 naut miles (6.2 miles) 10 km.
Freight hold capacity: Up to 17,637 lb (8,000 kg) of cargo in freighter configuration; LD-1, LD-2 and AKS containers, and PA-1.5 and P-8 pallets.
Freight hold access: 6 ft 9 ins × 5 ft 9 ins (2.05 × 1.76 m) door in starboard side of forward fuselage.
Wing control surfaces: Ailerons, single-slotted flaps, spoilers and leading-edge slats. Winglets.
Tail control surfaces: Elevators and rudder.
Engines: 2 Ivchenko PROGRESS/Zaporozhye D-436TP turbofans, carried as for the A-40/Be-40 (which see in Combat section). BMW Rolls-Royce BR715s are proposed as alternative engines. APU based on the TA12-60.
Engine rating: Each 16,535 lbf (73.55 kN).
Fuel system: 27,589 lb (12,514 kg).

Details for Be-200

PRINCIPAL DIMENSIONS:
Wing span: 107 ft 7 ins (32.78 m) over winglets
Maximum length: 105 ft 2 ins (32.049 m)
Maximum height: 30 ft 4 ins (9.25 m), originally quoted as 29 ft 2 ins (8.9 m)

CABIN:
Length: 61 ft 4 ins (18.7 m)
Width: 8 ft 2.5 ins (2.5 m)
Height: 6 ft 3 ins (1.895 m)
Volume: 2,853.4 cu ft (80.8 m^3)
Main passenger door: 5 ft 7 ins × 2 ft 11.5 ins (1.7 × 0.9 m)

WINGS:
Aerofoil section: Supercritical
Area: 1,264.1 sq ft (117.44 m^2)
Aspect ratio: 9.1
Sweepback: 19° at 25% chord

TAIL UNIT:
Tailplane span: 33 ft 2 ins (10.114 m)
Tailplane area: 268.24 sq ft (24.92 m^2)
Tailfin area: 185.14 sq ft (17.2 m^2)

UNDERCARRIAGE:
Type: Retractable, with twin steerable nosewheels
Main wheel tyre size: 950 × 300 mm
Nose wheel tyre size: 620 × 180 mm
Wheel base: 36 ft 6.5 ins (11.143 m)
Wheel track: 14 ft 1 ins (4.3 m) outline
Turning radius: 45 ft 1.5 ins (13.75 m)

WEIGHTS:
Empty, operating: 55,380 lb (25,120 kg) for passenger, 55,865 lb (25,340 kg) for firefighting, and 56,350 lb (25,560 kg) for cargo versions
Maximum: 94,799 lb (43,000 kg) lift weight after water scooping for firefighting
Normal maximum take-off: 82,012 lb (37,200 kg)
Maximum landing: 77,162 lb (35,000 kg)
Payload: 17,637 lb (8,000 kg) of cargo, or 26,455 lb (12,000 kg) of water in firefighting version

PERFORMANCE:
Maximum speed: 405 kts (466 mph) 750 km/h
Maximum cruise speed: 383 kts (441 mph) 710 km/h
Economic cruise speed: 297 kts (342 mph) 550 km/h
Stall speed: 116 kts (134 mph) 215 km/h *clean*, 84 kts (97 mph) 155 km/h *with flaps*
Take-off distance: 2,297 ft (700 m) from shore, 3,281 ft (1,000 m) from water, at 79,366 lb (36,000 kg) weight
Landing distance: 3,445 ft (1,050 m) to shore, 3,609 ft (1,100 m) to water, at MLW
Maximum wave height: 3 ft 1 ins (1.2 m)
Required water depth: 6.6 ft (2 m)
Maximum climb rate: 2,756 ft (840 m) per minute
Ceiling: 36,000 ft (11,000 m)
Range with 64 passengers: 1,674 naut miles (1,926 miles) 3,100 km
Range with 6 tonnes of cargo: 1,620 naut miles (1,864 miles) 3,000 km
Range with 7 tonnes of cargo: 917 naut miles (1,056 miles) 1,700 km

↑ Beriev Be-200 in firefighting configuration *(courtesy IAPO)*

Electrical system: As for Be-40.
Hydraulic system: 3,000 psi.
De-icing system: As for Be-40.
Radar: RDR-4A weather radar.
Flight avionics/instrumentation: ARIA (joint venture between AlliedSignal and National Institute of Aircraft Equipment) ARIA-200 integrated avionics, including 6 EFIS flat-panel displays, each 6 × 8 ins (15 × 20 cm), and a flight management system. Satellite communication for ecological role.
Mission equipment: For search and rescue, the aircraft carries appropriate sensors, searchlights for night illumination and medical equipment.

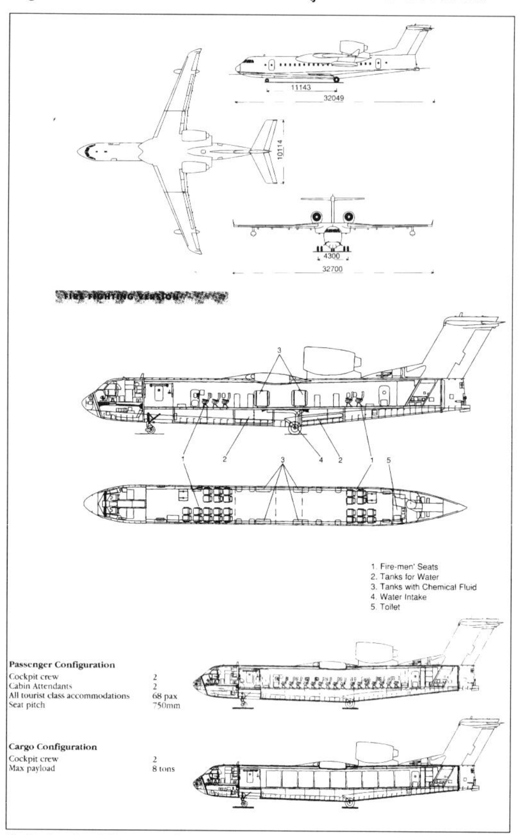

↑ **Beriev Be-200 general arrangement, plus (*lower*) firefighting, passenger and cargo configurations** *(courtesy Beriev)*

Aircraft variants:
Be-200 is the basic version which can be completed in firefighting, passenger, cargo and other versions.
Be-200ChS (Cherezvychainykh Situatsiy, emergency situations) is a specially equipped version ordered by Ministry of Emergency Situations.
Be-200M is an unspecified modernized version.
Be-200P is a maritime patrol version, with extended search and communications equipment. Also some weapons capability expected.

Beriev Be-1200 and Be-2500

Role: Futuristic projects for very-heavy-lift cargo and passenger amphibians, with features of a wing-in-ground effect vehicle in some configurations.
Wing characteristics: Wide fuselage/wing centre section with water-displacing characteristics. Moderately swept outer wing panels.
Tail control surfaces: 2 T-tails fitted to the beams at the side edges of wing centre section.
Engines: 6 Trud/Samara NK-116 high bypass ratio turbofans, each 231,485 lbf (1,030 kN), for the Be-2500; or 6 Rolls-Royce Trents, each 110,230 lbf (490 kN), for Be-1200. Various engine arrangements have been analyzed, including 2 engines pylon-mounted on the wing centre section and 4 mounted above the canards giving an air-cushion effect under the wing (see accompanying photograph of Be-1200).

Aircraft variants:
Be-1200 is a 1,200-tonne MTOW project with a maximum payload of 450 tonnes and range of 5,396 naut miles (6,214 miles) 10,000 km.
Be-2500 is a 2,500-tonne project, as described.

↑ **Beriev Be-1200 heavy-lift amphibian** *(Piotr Butowski)*

Details for Be-2500

PRINCIPAL DIMENSIONS:
Wing span: 482 ft 3 ins (147 m)
Maximum length: 397 ft (121 m)
Maximum height: 90 ft 1 ins (27.46 m)

UNDERCARRIAGE:
Type: Retractable, with 2 × 4-wheel bogies at the nose and 4 × 6-wheel main units retracted into the fuselage and wing centre-section
Wheel track: 114 ft 10 ins (35 m)

WEIGHTS:
Maximum take-off: 5,511,550 lb (2,500,000 kg)
Payload: 2,204,620 lb (1,000,000 kg)

PERFORMANCE:
Cruise speed: 432 kts (497 mph) 800 km/h
Ceiling: 32,800 ft (10,000 m)
Range with full fuel: 9,173 naut miles (10,563 miles) 17,000 km
Range with 1,058,218 lb (480,000 kg) payload: 5,396 naut miles (6214 miles) 10,000 km
Range with 1,543,234 lb (700,000 kg) payload: 3,777 naut miles (4,350 miles) 7,000 km

EKIP Aviation Concern — Russia

Corporate address:
141070, Kaliningrad, Moskovskaya oblast, ul. Pionerskaya, 8a, korp. 1.

Telephone: +7 095 5136307, 5166673
Facsimile: +7 095 5136307, 5166673

Information:
Lev Shchukin (General Designer of EKIP), Aleksandr Yermishin (General Manager of Saratov Aircraft Plant).

Note:
EKIP is an abbreviation for EKologia I Progress (ecology and progress).

EKIP series

First flight: Project announced in 1992. An L1 model has been flying since November 1991; L2-1 and L2-2 remotely piloted testbeds are under construction by Saratov aircraft plant, but not completed at time of writing.
Role: Cargo/passenger aircraft suitable also for patrol, firefighting and other roles; able to operate from any type of surface due to its air cushion landing system. Can also fly near the ground as a wing-in-ground effect craft. Series of various-size vehicles proposed.

Aims

- Lift-to-drag ratio of 17-18 during high altitude flight or up to 25 in wing-in-ground effect flight.
- Internal volume 1.5-2 times larger than that of a conventional aircraft of the same payload.
- Empty weight 25-30% of maximum take-off weight.
- Use of active boundary layer control to reduce friction drag.

Details

Fuselage/wing characteristics: Lifting saucer-shaped fuselage/wing body of large thickness, plus short outer wings.
Tail unit: Widely fitted V-type.
Propulsion system: 2 groups of engines: high-bypass ratio turbofans (PROGRESS/Zaporozhye D-436s of 15,430 lbf/68.64 kN, or D-18Ts of 51,655 lbf/229.78 kN, or Kuznetsov/Samara NK-15As of 33,720 lbf/150 kN) used as cruise engines, and Saturn/Moscow AL-34s generating the air-cushion when working in full-power mode, and supplying a boundary layer control system in level flight when working in economy mode. AL-34 is a variable power engine, with 2 gas generators powering a single shaft.

Aircraft variants:
L1 is the small-size experimental model, with an 8 ft 10 ins (2.7 m) span and 110 lb (50 kg) weight.
L2-1 and ***L2-2*** are remotely controlled experimental vehicles. L2-1 is equipped for taking-off from ground, while L2-2 takes off from water.
L2-3 should be the first piloted aircraft suitable for service.
L3 and ***L4*** are larger vehicles, as shown in the chart below.

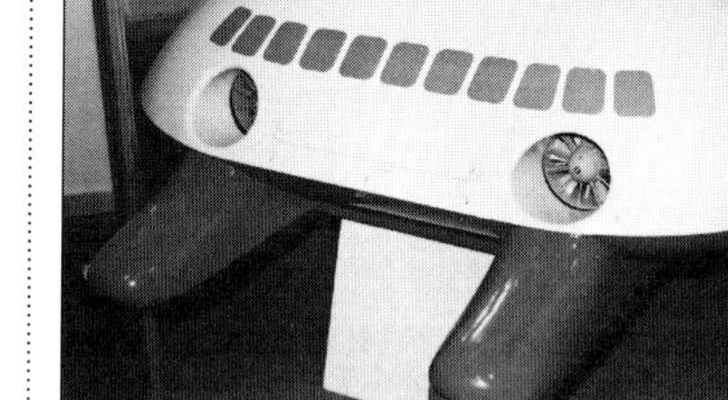
↑ **Model of an EKIP aircraft** *(Piotr Butowski)*

Details for the EKIP series

	L2-3	L3-1	L3-2	L4-1	L4-2
Cruise engines	PW300	2 × D-436	2 × D-18T	6 × D-18T	10 × D-18T
Thrust/weight ratio	0.46	0.41	0.35	0.36	0.3
Passengers	18-20	100	300-400	1,000	2,000
Wing span ft-ins (m)	47-3 (14.4)	102-8 (31.3)	182 (55.5)	300-6 (91.6)	420 (128)
Length ft-ins (m)	36-1 (11)	65-8 (20)	116-10 (35.6)	193-7 (59)	269 (82)
Height ft-ins (m)	8-2 (2.5)	16-5 (5.0)	38.9 (11.8)	64-4 (19.6)	90-3 (27.5)
Air-cushion area sq ft (m^2)	538 (50)	2,152 (200)	7,105 (660)	18,298 (1,700)	37,674 (3,500)
Take-off weight lb (kg)	19,842 (9,000)	88,184 (40,000)	264,554 (120,000)	661,385 (300,000)	1,322,770 (600,000)
Payload lb (kg)	5,510 (2,500)	24,250 (11,000)	88,185 (40,000)	220,460 (100,000)	440,920 (200,000)
Fuel lb (kg)	4,409 (2,000)	30,865 (14,000)	88,185 (40,000)	220,460 (100,000)	440,920 (200,000)
Cruise speed kts (mph) km/h	256-324 (295-373) 475-600	350 (404) 650	350-378 (404-435) 650-700	350 (404) 650	350 (404) 650
Take-off run ft (m)	1,313 (400)	1,477 (450)	1,640 (500)	1,640 (500)	1,640 (500)
Ceiling ft (m)	26,250 (8,000)	32,800 (10,000)	32,800 (10,000)	32,800 (10,000)	32,800 (10,000)
Range naut miles (miles) km	1,349 (1,553) 2,500	2,482 (2,858) 4,600	4,047 (4,660) 7,500	4,640 (5,343) 8,600	4,640 (5,343) 8,600

Ilyushin Aviation Complex

Russia

Corporate address:
See Combat section for all company details. See also Reconnaissance and General Aviation sections.

Ilyushin Il-76 (NATO name *Candid*) and Il-84

Note: For Il-84, see Aircraft variants – Il-76PS.
First flight: 25 March 1971 (piloted by Eduard Kuznetsov). 8 May 1973 for the first production aircraft, manufactured at the Tashkent plant.
First delivery: June 1974 to Soviet military transport aviation. Commercial services with Aeroflot began December 1976.
Chief designer: Radiy Papkovsky.
Role: Medium/long-range civil and military transport, also used for firefighting, medical evacuation, astronaut training, electronic countermeasures and more. Able to operate in severe weather conditions.
Sales: In production since 1973 at the Tashkent aircraft factory named after V. Chkalov. More than 900 manufactured, of which CIS air forces have 460, including 248 in Russia, 30 in Belarus and perhaps 180 with Ukraine. About 200 are with commercial companies in the CIS. 137 exported to Algeria, China (25, including 15 sold in 1994-95 by Uzbekistan)), Cuba (2), India (24 named *Gajaraj*, operated since July 1985), Iraq (more than 30), Libya (21) and Syria (4); some returned to Russia, leaving about 100 abroad. In May 1997, Israel reached an agreement about the purchase of several Il-76 airframes, to be fitted with Phalcon AEW systems by IAI and delivered to China.

Details *(principally for Il-76MD, unless stated)*

Crew: 6/7. Twin-deck: upper for pilots, lower for navigator.
Passengers: See Freight hold capacity.
Pressurization: 7.25 psi differential for freight hold.
Freight hold capacity: For payload, see Aircraft variants. Typical loads include standard Russian containers, each 8 ft (2.44 m) width and height by the following lengths: 40 ft (12.19 m) (UAK-20), 19 ft 11 ins (6.06 m) (UAK-10 and UUK-20), and 9 ft 10 ins (2.99 m) (UAK-5 and UUK-10). Also smaller UAK-5A and UAK-2.5 containers and PA-6.8, PA-5.6, PA-4.5, PA-3.6, PA-2.5 pallets. Alternatively up to 126 paratroops, or 167 troops, or 245 troops when the second deck is installed. It takes 30 minutes to convert the standard Il-76 into a passenger aircraft using 3 modules installed in the cabin (105 passengers), or into an evacuation aircraft for litter patients.
Freight hold access: Rear loading ramp, and a small door each side of the front cabin.
Size of freight doors: Rear opening 11 ft 2 ins × 11 ft 4 ins (3.4 × 3.45 m).
Loading facilities: 2 floor electrical winches, each 6,614 lb (3,000 kg), and 4 electrical telphers, each 5,512 lb (2,500 kg). Roller tracks on the floor. Rear loading ramp can lift up to 66,139 lb (30,000 kg). 4 toe plates to load self-propelled and towed vehicles.
Wing control surfaces: Full-span leading-edge slats (15% of wing chord, deflected 25°). Each wing has 2 sections of triple-slotted trailing-edge flaps, occupying 73.5% of the span, with maximum deflection of 43° for the inner section and 40° for the outer. Ailerons (+16°, -28°) with tabs. Forward of the flaps are 4 sections of spoilers (20°, deflected differentially to support ailerons or evenly as airbrakes when landing) and 4 sections of airbrakes (40°).
Tail control surfaces: T-tail, with a variable incidence tailplane (+2°, -8°), elevators (+15°, -21°) with tabs, and rudder (± 27°) with tab.
Flight control system: Mechanical, power operated; manual control as stand-by. A version with digital fly-by-wire is projected.
Construction materials: All-metal; aluminium alloy, steel and titanium. Metal honeycomb used for the detachable panels of the wings, tail unit, pylons and undercarriage fairings.
Engines: 4 Rybinsk D-30KP II turbofans, with thrust reversers. TA-6A auxiliary power unit in the starboard main undercarriage fairing. The Il-76M/Il-76T are powered by D-30KP turbofans of the same thrust but inferior high temperature characteristics (take-off thrust to ISA +15° C, while D-30KP IIs are to ISA +23°C). Proposed mid-life upgrade by installing CFM International CFM56-5C2s (31,217 lbf, 138.87 kN) or Pratt & Whitney PW 2037s. Another upgrade offer uses Russian PS-90A12 turbofans, each 26,455 lbf (117.68 kN), as Il-76TD-90, as well as D-30KP IIIs with higher thrust.
Engine thrust: Each 26,455 lbf (117.68 kN) at take-off.
Fuel system: Up to 109,480 litres (187,040 lb, 84,840 kg) of fuel in 12 tanks along the whole span of the wings.
Flight refuelling: None.
Electrical system: 115/120 volt, 400Hz AC supply has 4 × 60kVA generators (1 on each engine). 1 × 40kVA generator (AC 115/220 volt, 400 Hz), and 1 × DC 12 kW generator on APU, as stand-by. 4 batteries and converters as an emergency power source.
Hydraulic system: 2 independent systems, with 2 hydraulic pumps each. Operating pressure 2,990 psi.
Braking system: Hydraulically operated, with anti-skid system.
Radar: Leninets/St Petersburg Kupol-3-76 navigation radar in an undernose radome that is also used as a sight when paradropping. Kupol-2-76 for civil aircraft.
Flight avionics/instrumentation: SAU-76 automatic control system. R-838 and R-847 communication radios. IL-76MF introduced 2 CRT displays.
Fixed weapons: Many military aircraft and a few civil have a rear gun turret with 2 twin-barrel GSh-23 cannon.
Expendable weapons and equipment: Up to 4 × 500 kg flares for illumination of the landing area.
Self-protection systems: See cannon under Fixed weapons. Some military aircraft have radar warning receivers in large fairings on the sides of the nose, as well as SPS-5 Fasol electronic jammers. During the conflict in Afghanistan, chaff/flare dispensers were carried (pack of 96 × 50-mm projectiles on each side of the fuselage and/or on the undercarriage fairings).

Aircraft variants:
Il-76 *Candid-A* prototypes had a maximum take-off weight of 374,785 lb (170,000 kg) and a payload of 72,752 lb (33,000 kg).
Il-76K, ***Il-76MDK*** and ***Il-76MDK-2*** (K for kosmos) versions were prepared for cosmonaut training. In the cabin of the diving aircraft a state of weightlessness can be created, lasting 22-24 seconds a dozen or so times during each flight.
Il-76LL (letayushchaya laboratoria or flying test bed) covers 6 aircraft used at the Russian Flight Test Centre in Zhukovsky as engine (4) and equipment (2) test beds. D-18T, D-236, D-27, etc

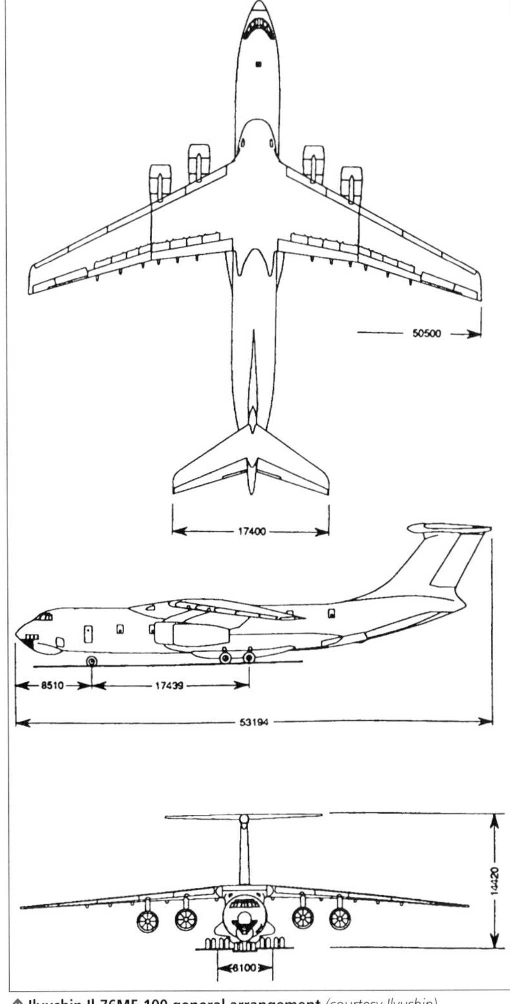

↑ **Ilyushin Il-76MF-100 general arrangement** *(courtesy Ilyushin)*

have been installed in place of the standard starboard inner engine. Measurement equipment in the cabin.
Il-76M *Candid-B* military transport features slight strengthening of the wings, wider rear fuselage, new equipment, and a maximum take-off weight of 374,785 lb (170,000 kg) but a maximum payload of 103,617 lb (47,000 kg). Range 3,510 naut miles (4,039 miles) 6,500 km with a 44,092 lb (20,000 kg) payload. Tail gun turret on some aircraft. Production switched to this version and its Il-76T civil derivative in 1977.
Il-76MD *Candid-B* (D for dalniy or long range) was given considerably strengthened wings. Maximum allowable take-off weight increased to 418,878 lb (190,000 kg), which made possible provision for more fuel (this tankage volume was left unused in previous versions). Range 3,942 naut miles

↑ **Ilyushin Il-76MF** *(Piotr Butowski)*

↑ **Ilyushin Il-76MD used by the Flight Research Institute in Zhukovsky for avionics testing. Note the fairing in front of the undercarriage nacelle** *(Piotr Butowski)*

(4,536 miles) 7,300 km with a 20,000 kg payload. Improved D-30KP II engines.
Il-76MF (f for fuselage) has a fuselage lengthened by 21 ft 8 ins (6.6 m) by the insertion of 2 plugs, becoming 164 ft 8 ins (50.2 m) fuselage length and 174 ft 6 ins (53.194 m) overall length. The cargo hold is 102 ft 2 ins (31.14 m) long, including the ramp. The basic Russian variant is powered by 4 Aviadvigatel/Perm PS-90A76 turbofans, each 35,300 lbf (157 kN). Fuel efficiency improved by 12%, Take-off weight 462,970 lb (210,000 kg), operating empty weight 222,667 lb (101,000 kg), and maximum payload 114,640 lb (52,000 kg). Practical range with a 88,185 lb (40,000 kg) load is 3,130 naut miles (3,604 miles) 5,800 km with 1 hour reserve. Cruise speed 405-421 kts (466-485 mph) 750-780 km/h. Updated avionics include 2 CRT displays, Kupol-3-76MF radar, SAU-76Ts automatic control system and BASK-124 flight data recorder borrowed from the Antonov An-124. 3 aircraft built at the time of writing, the first of which flew on 1 August 1995 at Tashkent, Uzbekistan, piloted by Anatoli Knyshov.
Il-76MF-100 will be the Il-76MF derivative with CFM56-5C turbofans (-5C2 with take-off thrust of 31,200 lbf, 138.79 kN, or -5C4 with 34,000 lbf, 151.24 kN). Data as for Il-76MF except the range 3,777 naut miles (4,350 miles) 7,000 km with 88,185 lb (40,000 kg) payload (with CFM56-5C2 engines).
Il-76P or ***Il-76TP*** (P stands for pozharnyi or firefighting) was developed in 1989. 97,003 lb (44,000 kg) of fire-extinguishing mixture, in 2 tanks, can be released from 66-330 ft (20-100 m) at 150-160 kts. Time of discharge is 6-7 seconds, covering an area of 1,640 × 328 ft (500 × 100 m). Refill takes between 10 and 15 minutes. Any Il-76 can be converted to a firefighting version in the field. Equipment weight is about 11,023 lb (5,000 kg). Can carry 40 paratroopers/firefighters and 384 weather cartridges with silver iodide. Leading designer Nikolai Talikov. Demonstrated to the US Forest Service and British officials at Boscombe Down, UK, on 9 September 1994. Cost about US$9,000 to US$10,000 per hour.
Il-76PP (postanovshchik pomekh or jammer) is the electronic countermeasures aircraft, conceived as an escort aircraft for the A-50 AEW&C. Prototype only, appearing in about 1985.
Il-76PS or ***Il-84*** (PS for poiskovo-spasatelnyi or search and rescue) is able to patrol for 3 hours at a distance of 1,620 naut miles (1,864 miles) 3,000 km from base. Group of 40 rescue paratroopers can be dropped as well as a Gagara motor boat (22,046 lb, 10,000 kg weight, with a crew of 3 – allowable wave height 10 ft, 3.0 m) plus dinghies for 1,000 people. Prototype only, first flown on 18 December 1984 but abandoned in 1989.
Il-76PSD is a new project for a SAR aircraft.
Il-76 Scalpel-MT was developed as a medical version, using 3 container-type modules with a surgical room, recovery room, etc, mounted inside the cabin. Medical crew of 12 persons. 2 produced (*CCCP-86905* and *86906*) and used during the conflict in Afghanistan.
Il-76T Candid-A became the civil derivative of the Il-76M, with assault/paratroop equipment removed and no tail turret. Maximum payload 110,231 lb (50,000 kg).
Il-76TD *Candid-A* is the civil derivative of the Il-76MD.
Il-76TD-90 is a proposed mid-life upgrade of the Il-76TD, with PS-90A12 turbofans. Order for 20 upgrades reported.
Il-76TD-S appeared in 1991 and is a civil variant of the military Scalpel-MT.
Il-76TF is a projected commercial MF.
Il-78 Midas – see separate entry.
Il-82 relay aircraft – see Electronic/Reconnaissance section.

↑ Ilyushin Il-76MF cockpit, featuring 2 CRT displays not found on earlier versions *(Piotr Butowski)*

Details for Il-76MD *Candid-B, unless stated*

PRINCIPAL DIMENSIONS:
Wing span: 165 ft 8 ins (50.5 m)
Maximum length: 152 ft 10 ins (46.594 m)
Maximum height: 48 ft 5 ins (14.76 m)

CABIN:
Length, maximum: 80 ft 6 ins (24.54 m)
Length without ramp: 65 ft 7 ins (20 m)
Width: 11 ft 4 ins (3.45 m) at floor
Height, maximum: 11 ft 2 ins (3.4 m)
Main door: 11 ft 2 ins × 11 ft 4 ins (3.4 × 3.45 m)
Side doors: 6 ft 3 ins × 2 ft 10 ins (1.9 × 0.86 m)

WINGS:
Aerofoil section: TsAGI P-151
Area, gross: 3,242 sq ft (301.2 m^2)
Aspect ratio: 8.467
Sweepback: 25° at 25% chord
Twist: +3° root, 0° tip
Anhedral: 3°
Ailerons area: 142.84 sq ft (13.27 m^2)
Spoilers area: 116.9 sq ft (10.86 m^2)
Airbrakes area: 170.07 sq ft (15.8 m^2)
Trailing-edge flap area: approx 710.4 sq ft (66 m^2)

TAIL UNIT:
Tailplane span: 57 ft 1 ins (17.4 m)
Tailplane area: 678.1 sq ft (63 m^2)
Elevators area: 184.8 sq ft (17.17 m^2)
Fin height: 23 ft 9 ins (7.245 m)
Fin sweepback: 38° 10' at 25% chord
Fin area: 538.2 sq ft (50 m^2)

UNDERCARRIAGE:
Type: Retractable, with steerable nosewheel unit consisting of a 4-wheel bogie. Each main unit consists of 2 such bogies in tandem
Main wheel tyre size: 1,300 × 480 mm
Nose wheel tyre size: 1,100 × 330 mm
Wheel base: 46 ft 6 ins (14.17 m)
Wheel track: 26 ft 9 ins (8.16 m)

WEIGHTS:
Empty, operating: 196,211 lb (89,000 kg)
Maximum take-off: 418,878 lb (190,000 kg)
Maximum allowable take-off: 462,970 lb (210,000 kg) for no more than 15% of take-offs
Maximum take-off from unprepared runway: 347,228 lb (157,500 kg)
Maximum landing: 341,716 lb (155,000 kg)
Payload: 103,617 lb (47,000 kg) maximum

PERFORMANCE:
Maximum allowable Mach number: 0.77
Maximum cruise speed: 405-421 kts (466-485 mph) 750-780 km/h at 39,370 ft (12,000 m)
Take-off distance: 5,578 ft (1,700 m)
Landing distance: 2,953-3,281 ft (900-1,000 m)
Cruise altitude (Il-76MF): 29,525-39,370 ft (9,000-12,000 m)
Range with maximum fuel: 4,212 naut miles (4,847 miles) 7,800 km
Range with 44,092 lb (20,000 kg) payload: 3,942 naut miles (4,536 miles) 7,300 km
Range with 88,184 lb (40,000 kg) payload: 2,570 naut miles (2,958 miles) 4,760 km
Range with maximum payload: 2,052 naut miles (2,361 miles) 3,800 km

Beriev A-50 *Mainstay*/Be-976 – see Electronic/Reconnaissance section.
Beriev A-60 – see Combat section.
Bagdad-1 and Adnan-1 are AEW&C derivatives developed in Iraq. See Electronic/Reconnaissance section of the 1996-97 edition of *WA&SD*, page 174.

Ilyushin Il-78 series (NATO name *Midas*)

First flight: June 1983.
Role: In-flight refuelling tanker.
Based on: Il-76MD.
Sales: About 40 in service, divided equally between Ukraine (409th Air Tanker Regiment at Uzin; first unit, gaining IOC in 1987) and Russia (230th Regiment at Engels). Production completed. Some Ukrainian Il-78s (not Il-78Ms) have been converted back to transport configuration, with refuelling equipment removed. Delivery of 4 Il-78s to India is planned for 1998 (6 according to some sources).
Crew: 6, including refuelling operator in the place usually occupied by the tail gunner.
Freight holds: The Il-78 is similar to the Il-76 when the additional fuel tanks are removed. The Il-78M version carries no freight, as the fuel tanks are fixed.
Size of freight doors: Il-78 is similar to the Il-76. The Il-78M has no doors.
Fuel system: 2 cylindrical fuel tanks mounted inside the cabin (removable in Il-78, fixed in Il-78M), each carrying 30,865 lb (14,000 kg) of fuel for the Il-78 and 39,683 lb (18,000 kg) for the Il-76M. Both versions can also transfer fuel from the standard wing torsion box tanks.
Fuel transfer: Fuel is transferred via 3 refuelling pods, designed by the Zvezda bureau. 2 UPAZ-1A Sakhalin (unifitsirovannyi podvesnoi agregat zapravki – unified suspended refuelling gear) are installed under the wings, each at a distance of 53 ft 10 ins (16.40 m) from the aircraft centreline and have a transfer rate of 2,340 litres per minute each. The third pod, a PAZ-1 with a transfer rate of 4,000 litres per minute, is suspended from the port side of the rear fuselage at a distance of 9 ft 10 ins (3 m) from the centreline. The central pod was designed for refuelling 1 heavy aircraft, whereas the underwing pods transfer fuel to 2 lighter aircraft (in combat conditions, 3 tactical aircraft can be refuelled simultaneously). At least 85 ft (26 m) of the UPAZ-1A's hose has to be unwound prior to the start of refuelling, which starts automatically after the drogue has captured the probe and is stopped after transferring the preset volume of fuel. The refuelling operation can also be stopped manually by the operator, or automatically after the whole hose length is unwound or when the difference in speed of the aircraft exceeds 591 ft (180 m) per minute. Refuelling can only be carried out with direct visibility (for night operations, lights are used). Il-78 can also be used as a ground refuelling station for 4 aircraft, usually on front line airfields. The refuelling pods are then replaced by 4 hoses connected directly to the valves of the internal fuel storage tanks.
Flight avionics/instrumentation: As for Il-76, except RSBN-7S short-range radio navigation system has added Vstrecha (rendezvous) mode for all weather, day and night mutual

↑ Ilyushin Il-78M *Midas* tanker about to refuel a Tu-95MS bomber, accompanied by a MiG-29 fighter *(Piotr Butowski)*

detection and approach from 162 naut miles (186 miles) 300 km distance. The system automatically controls the distance between the aircraft and generates a warning signal if the aircraft are too close (closest allowable distance is 42.8 ft, 13 m).

Aircraft variants:
Il-78 *Midas* was the initial version, with a maximum allowable take-off weight of 418,878 lb (190,000 kg). Convertible between transport/tanker.
Il-78M *Midas* is the standard, strengthened production version. First flown 7 March 1987, piloted by Vyacheslav Belousov. Maximum allowable take-off weight is 462,970 lb (210,000 kg). Non-convertible. No cabin doors or ramp, resulting in a reduced structural weight.
Il-78MK (kommerchesky) is the export version.
Il-78V has modified refuelling pods of MK-32B type.

Details for Il-78 and Il-78M

PRINCIPAL DIMENSIONS:
As for Il-76MD

WEIGHTS:
Maximum allowable take-off (Il-78): 418,878 lb (190,000 kg)
Maximum allowable take-off (Il-78M): 462,970 lb (210,000 kg)
Maximum from unprepared runway: 347,228 lb (157,500 kg)
Maximum landing: 334,000 lb (151,500 kg)
Maximum fuel in standard wing tanks: 187,040 lb (84,840 kg)
Maximum fuel in additional cabin tanks (Il-78): 61,729 lb (28,000 kg)
Maximum fuel in additional cabin tanks (Il-78M): 79,366 lb (36,000 kg)

PERFORMANCE:
Cruise speed: 405 kts (466 mph) 750 km/h
Refuelling speed: 232-319 kts (267-367 mph) 430-590 km/h IAS
Take-off distance (Il-78): 5,578 ft (1,700 m) at MTOW
Take-off distance (I-78M): 6,824 ft (2,080 m) at MTOW
Landing distance: 2,953 ft (900 m)
G limit: 2.0 at 379,195 lb (172,000 kg)
Refuelling altitude: 6,562-29,525 ft (2,000-9,000 m)
Refuelling radius, 44,092 lb (20,000 kg) of fuel delivered (Il-78): 1,998 naut miles (2,299 miles) 3,700 km
Refuelling radius, 44,092 lb (20,000 kg) of fuel delivered (Il-78M): 2,727 naut miles (3,138 miles) 5,050 km
Refuelling radius, 66,139 lb (30,000 kg) of fuel delivered (Il-78): 1,080 naut miles (1,243 miles) 2,000 km
Refuelling radius, 66,139 lb (30,000 kg) of fuel delivered (Il-78M): 2,268 naut miles (2,610 miles) 4,200 km
Refuelling radius, 88,185 lb (40,000 kg) of fuel delivered (Il-78): 1,134 naut miles (1,305 miles) 2,100 km
Refuelling radius, 88,185 lb (40,000 kg) of fuel delivered (Il-78M): 1,863 naut miles (2,144 miles) 3,450 km
Refuelling radius, 110,231 lb (50,000 kg) of fuel delivered (Il-78): 756 naut miles (870 miles) 1,400 km
Refuelling radius, 110,231 lb (50,000 kg) of fuel delivered (Il-78M): 1,404 naut miles (1,616 miles) 2,600 km

Ilyushin Il-86 (NATO name *Camber*)

Comments: First flown on 22 December 1976, the Il-86 was in production until December 1995. A total of 103 was built at Voronezh; 80 are in current airline service in Russia, 10 in Uzbekistan, 7 in Kazakhstan, and 3 in Armenia. Largest operators are Aeroflot Russian International Airlines (23) and Vnukovo Air Lines (22). Details and an illustration can be found in the 1996-97 edition of *WA&SD*, pages 229-230. See also Il-80 strategic airborne command post in the Electronic section.

Ilyushin Il-96 series (including Il-96-500, -550, -750)

First flight: 28 September 1988 for Il-96-300 piloted by Stanislav Bliznyuk. See Aircraft variants. 16 May 1997 for Il-96T.
Certification: 29 December 1992 for Il-96-300.
First delivery: 1993 to Aeroflot, with services starting on 14 July 1993 between Moscow and New York.
Role: Long-range widebody airliner.
Airframe life: 60,000 flying hours.
Noise levels: Meets ICAO Chapter 3 Annex 16.
Sales: Manufactured at Voronezh. 12 Il-96-300s had been delivered at the time of writing, including 6 to Aeroflot Russian International Airlines and 2 to Domodedovo Airlines. Il-96M is likely to become the main production version. On 3 December 1996, 17 Il-96Ms and 3 Il-96Ts were ordered by Aeroflot Russian International Airlines, for delivery between 1997 (Il-96T) and 2002. 10 Il-96Ms were ordered by Transaero during the June 1997 Paris Air Show, with deliveries starting in 2001. On 20 August 1997, Volga-Dnepr ordered 4 Il-96Ts. Expected price for the Il-96T is $63 million. Russian charter cargo airline Aviaross is to purchase 3 Il-96-300s.

Details *(Il-96-300)*

Crew: 2 pilots and an engineer, with 2 optional seats.
Passengers: Passengers on upper deck, with Il-86's 'Luggage by themselves' system abandoned. Typical layouts are 22 first (6 abreast), 40 business (8 abreast) and 173 economy (9 abreast) classes, or 300 economy (9 abreast).
Seat pitch: 40.2 ins (102 cm), 35.5 ins (90 cm), 34.3 ins (87 cm) and 34.3 ins (87 cm) respectively.
Galley: On lower deck.
Freight hold capacity: Up to 32 LD3 containers or pallets on lower deck.
Wing control surfaces: Inner and outer ailerons, the latter to provide damping moment. Double-slotted and 2-section single-slotted trailing-edge flaps. Multi-section leading-edge slats. 3-section airbrakes and multi-section spoilers.
Tail control surfaces: Variable-incidence tailplane. Elevators and inset 2-section rudder.
Flight control system: Triplex fly-by-wire, with manual back-up.
Construction materials: Metal, but with composites for areas of the tail unit, wing flaps, cabin floors and cargo holds.
Engines: 4 Aviadvigatel PS-90A turbofans. APU. New Perm/Pratt & Whitney PS-95 turbofans are under consideration for Il-96-300. See Aircraft variants.
Engine rating: Each 35,274 lbf (157 kN), with thrust reversers.
Fuel system: 148,260 litres or 253,315 lb (114,900 kg) in 9 wing tanks.
Hydraulic system: 3,000 psi, for all control surfaces, undercarriage, mainwheel brakes, nosewheel steering, engine thrust reversers, and freight hold doors.
Braking system: Rubix wheels and brakes on Il-96M and T, featuring AlliedSignal Carbenix advanced carbon composite friction material.
Radar: Weather/navigation.

Details for Il-96-300

PRINCIPAL DIMENSIONS:
Wing span: 197 ft 2.3 ins (60.105 m)
Maximum length: 181 ft 7 ins (55.35 m)
Maximum height: 57 ft 8 ins (17.57 m)

CABIN:
Volume: 12,360 cu ft (350 m^3)
Main passenger doors: 3, each 6 ft × 3 ft 6 ins (1.83 × 1.07 m)

WINGS:
Aerofoil section: Supercritical
Area: 4,215.14 sq ft (391.6 m^2) accepted, with 350 m^2 quoted by a Moscow source
Aspect ratio: 9.225
Sweepback: 30° at 25% chord

TAIL UNIT:
Tailplane span: 67 ft 6 ins (20.57 m)

UNDERCARRIAGE:
Type: Retractable, with twin steerable nosewheels and 3 sets of 4-wheel main bogies to reduce runway loading
Main wheel tyre size: 1,300 × 480 mm
Nose wheel tyre size: 1,260 × 460 mm
Wheel base: 65 ft 10 ins (20.065 m)
Wheel track: 34 ft 1 ins (10.4 m)

WEIGHTS:
Empty: 262,350 lb (119,000 kg)
Maximum take-off: 529,109 lb (240,000 kg)
Maximum landing: 385,808 lb (175,000 kg)
Payload: 88,185 lb (40,000 kg)

PERFORMANCE:
High cruise speed: 486 kts (560 mph) 900 km/h
Typical cruise speed: 448-459 kts (515-528 mph) 830-850 km/h
Take-off distance: 9,843 ft (3,000 m)
Landing distance: 6,890 ft (2,100 m)
Cruise altitude: 32,800-39,370 ft (10,000-12,000 m)
Maximum range: 7,554 naut miles (8,700 miles) 14,000 km
Range with 300 passengers: 5,396 naut miles (6,213 miles) 10,000 km

Flight avionics/instrumentation: Electronic flight deck with 3 pairs of colour CRT screens. Satellite navigation receivers, Omega, INS and flight management system. Head-up flight display system (HFDS) for Category IIIa operations.

Aircraft variants:
Il-96 (originally named Il-86M) was the first projected version of 1978, to carry 350 passengers over a 4,856 naut miles (5,592 miles) 9,000 km range. To retain the Il-86 fuselage, married to new wings. However, as a result of a government decision to standardize engines for new passenger aircraft, less powerful PS-90s had to be selected and the reduced-size Il-96-300 (for 300 passengers) thereby came into being.
Il-96-300 is the initial production version, as detailed.
Il-96-300 Russian Presidential Transport (*RA-96012*, probably named ***Il-96PU***) has an extended communications suite in rear fuselage (weighing 14 tons), surgical module and VIP interior fitted-out in Switzerland, and was painted by KLM in the Netherlands. Replaced the former presidential Il-62M in 1996.
Il-96-300D will be an Il-96-300 re-engined with Pratt & Whitney PW2337 turbofans. Russian avionics. MTOW increased to

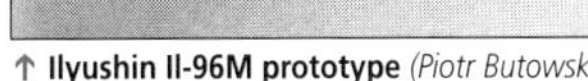
↑ **Ilyushin Il-96M prototype** *(Piotr Butowski)*

↑ **Ilyushin Il-96T flight deck, with 6-tube 'glass' cockpit** *(Piotr Butowski)*

595,247 lb (270,000 kg), and range 7,015 naut miles (8,078 miles) 13,000 km with a 55,115 lb (25,000 kg) of payload.
Il-96-500 is a projected double-deck derivative for 500 passengers.
Il-96-550 is a projected 550-seat double-deck version with 4 NK-92s or PW 2337s. MTOW 595,247 lb (270,000 kg), maximum payload 154,323 lb (70,000 kg), and practical range 4,856 naut miles (5,592 miles) 9,000 km.
Il-96-750 is a projected 750-seat triple-deck version (lower deck for baggage and containers, middle deck with 9-abreast seating, and upper deck with 6-abreast seating).
Il-96M (initially named Il-96-350) is a westernized version for Category IIIb operations, using 38,250 lbf (170.1 kN) Pratt & Whitney PW2337 turbofans and Rockwell Collins avionics (ARINC 700). 2-crew flight deck. First flown 6 April 1993, piloted by Stanislav Bliznyuk, as the ***Il-96MO*** (O for opytnyi, test) prototype, being the rebuilt first prototype of the Il-96-300. First flight of a production Il-96M had been expected late 1997. Lengthened to 209 ft 9.3 ins (63.939 m) to accommodate up to 384 passengers. Empty weight 291,892 lb (132,400 kg), MTOW 595,250 lb (270,000 kg) and maximum payload 127,868 lb (58,000 kg). Cruise speed 448-459 kts (516-528 mph) 830-850 km/h, take-off distance 11,000 ft (3,350 m) and range 5,396 naut miles (6,214 miles) 10,000 km with 384 passengers.
Il-96MD was a projected twin-engined derivative, currently reworked into the Il-98, which see.
Il-96MK is a proposed variant using the Il-96M airframe and Trud/Samara NK-93 ducted engines.
Il-96MR will have an Il-96M airframe and Russian Aviadvigatel/Perm PS-90A or Trud/Samara NK-92 turbofans. MTOW and payload as for Il-96M; practical range of 5,936-6,745 naut miles (6,835-7,767 miles) 11,000-12,500 km.
Il-96T is a freighter conversion of Il-96M, with a 202,825 lb (92,000 kg) payload and 15 ft 11 ins × 9 ft 5 ins (4.85 × 2.875 m) loading door on the port side of the fuselage, ahead of the wing. PW2337 engines and Rockwell Collins avionics. Total volume of 27,405 cu ft (776 m^3), including 20,483 cu ft (580 m^3) upper and 6,922 cu ft (196 m^3) lower deck. Standard loads are 25 P-6 plus 1 P-2 pallets on the upper deck and 32 LD3 containers on the lower deck. MTOW 595,250 lb (270,000 kg), range with maximum payload 2,805 naut miles (3,231 miles) 5,200 km. First aircraft (*RA-96101*) ceremonially rolled-out on 26 April 1997 in Voronezh and first flown on 16 May. First international presentation at the Paris Air Show in June 1997.

Ilyushin Il-98

First flight: Project only.
Role: Long-range widebody airliner, proposed as a twin-engined derivative of the Il-96M.
Passengers: 384 in economy class layout.
Engines: 2 large turbofans in the 88,125-110,150 lbf (392-490 kN) class range (Samara NK-44, Pratt & Whitney PW 4000, or Rolls-Royce Trent).

Aircraft variant:
Il-98 is currently the only version planned, although initially 2 versions were proposed as the ***Il-98*** (earlier named ***Il-96MD***) with the airframe of the Il-96-300 and the Il-98M with the lengthened fuselage of the Il-96M.

Details for Il-98 with PW4384 engines

PRINCIPAL DIMENSIONS:
Wing span: 197 ft 2.3 ins (60.105 m)
Maximum length: 209 ft 9.3 ins (63.939 m)
Fuselage length: 198 ft 6 ins (60.5 m)
Maximum height: 57 ft 7 ins (17.55 m)

WEIGHTS:
Empty: 282,191 lb (128,000 kg)
Maximum take-off: 584,224 lb (265,000 kg)
Landing: 485,016 lb (220,000 kg)
Payload: 127,868 lb (58,000 kg)

PERFORMANCE:
Cruise speed: 459-469 kts (528-540 mph) 850-870 km/h
Take-off distance: 9,515 ft (2,900 m)
Landing distance: 7,875 ft (2,400 m)
Cruise altitude: 29,530-42,650 ft (9,000-13,000 m)
Range with 384 passengers: 6,475 naut miles (7,456 miles) 12,000 km
Maximum range: 8,903 naut miles (10,252 miles) 16,500 km

↑ Model of the projected Ilyushin Il-106 heavy military transport *(Piotr Butowski)*

Ilyushin Il-106

First flight: Not before the year 2000.
Role: Heavy military transport.
Wing control surfaces: Each wing has 6 sections of leading-edge slats, 2 sections of trailing-edge flaps and an aileron. 6 sections of spoilers/airbrakes forward of the flaps.
Engines: 4 Samara/Kuznetsov NK-92 turbofans, each 39,685 lbf (176.53 kN), or Rybinsk/Reshetnikov D-100s, each 41,888 lbf (186.33 kN).

Ilyushin Il-106

PRINCIPAL DIMENSIONS:
Wing span: 191 ft 11 ins (58.5 m)
Wing span, without winglets: 182 ft 8 ins (55.68 m)
Maximum length: 189 ft (57.6 m)
Fuselage length: 182 ft 1 ins (55.5 m)
Maximum height: 65 ft 4 ins (19.925 m)

CABIN:
Length: 111 ft 7 ins (34 m)
Width: 19 ft 8 ins (6 m)
Height: 15 ft 1 ins (4.6 m)

WEIGHTS:
Maximum take-off: 568,792 lb (258,000 kg)

PERFORMANCE:
Cruise speed: 443-459 kts (510-528 mph) 820-850 km/h
Take-off distance: 5,085 ft (1,550 m)
Landing distance: 4,593 ft (1,400 m)
Range with maximum payload: 2,700 naut miles (3,107 miles) 5,000 km

Ilyushin Il-112

First flight: Project.
Role: Short-haul regional airliner, VIP transport and freighter.

Development

▪ 1994. Preliminary design began. Programme received Governmental backing according to Resolution No 1119 of 4 November 1994, but reportedly lacking financial support.

Details

Crew: 2.
Passengers: 40 maximum.
Pressurization: Flight deck and cabin.
Freight hold access: Freighter version will have a rear ramp/door and large side-loading door.

↑ Ilyushin Il-112 in model form *(Piotr Butowski)*

Wing characteristics: Straight, high mounted, with no dihedral/anhedral.
Wing control surfaces: Ailerons, long-chord flaps, and 2-section spoilers.
Tail control surfaces: T tail, with elevators and rudder.
Engines: 2 Klimov TV7-117 turboprops.
Engine rating: Each 2,500 shp (1,864 kW).

Aircraft variants:
Il-112 will be the standard passenger version.
Il-112T is the projected freighter derivative with rear loading ramp. Payload 9,920 lb (4,500 kg), which can include 4 × LD3 type containers or 5 × PA-1.5 pallets among choices.
Il-112 corporate/VIP transport will offer accommodation for 8 in the forward section of the cabin, with inward-facing seats and tables; 7 can be accommodated in the centre section, with a 3-seat sofa and 4 armchairs, tables and cabinets; and the rear utility area includes buffets.

Details for Il-112

PRINCIPAL DIMENSIONS:
Wing span: 74 ft (22.55 m)
Maximum length: 71 ft 6 ins (21.78 m)
Fuselage length: 65 ft 7 ins (20 m)
Maximum height: 23 ft 5 ins (7.14 m)

UNDERCARRIAGE:
Type: Retractable, with nosewheel. Main units to retract into fairings on the fuselage sides
Wheel track: 12 ft 5 ins (3.8 m)

WEIGHTS:
Empty: 16,755 lb (7,600 kg)
Empty, operating: 20,060 lb (9,100 kg)
Maximum take-off: 32,030 lb (14,530 kg)
Payload: 8,818 lb (4,000 kg), or 9,920 lb (4,500 kg) for Il-112T

PERFORMANCE:
Maximum cruise speed: 324 kts (373 mph) 600 km/h
Take-off distance: 1,706 ft (520 m)
Landing distance: 1,313 ft (400 m)
Cruise altitude: 26,245 ft (8,000 m)
Cruise altitude, 1 engine: 16,405 ft (5,000 m)
Range with 32 passengers: 810 naut miles (932 miles) 1,500 km
Range with 11 passengers: 1,944 naut miles (2,237 miles) 3,600 km, at 270 kts (311 mph) 500 km/h

Ilyushin Il-114

First flight: 29 March 1990 (piloted by Vyacheslav Belousov).
Certification: ARMAC airworthiness certification 26 April 1997.
First delivery: 1993, to Uzbekistan Airlines.
Chief designer: G. V. Novozhilov.
Role: Short-haul pressurized transport to replace the An-24, able to operate from airfields with low support levels.

Development

▪ 1986. Work started on a twin-turboprop transport capable of carrying 64 passengers over a distance of 1,000 km with a fuel consumption of 20 grammes per passenger/km.

Details

Sales: 4 prototypes were constructed by Ilyushin at Moscow-Khodynka, including prototype 02 for static tests and 04 for fatigue tests. 01 prototype remains airworthy; 03 crashed on 5 July 1993. The accident to 03 was caused by accidental feathering of the propeller blades during take-off. The first production aircraft, c/n *01-05* built at the Tashkent plant, first flew on 7 August 1992. The next 5 aircraft of the first series, *01-06* through to *01-10*, were completed before January 1995. Production of second series started after this date; *02-01* is flying, while the next 9 aircraft were under construction at the time of writing. First aircraft of the third series (*03-01*) is a prototype for the Il-114T, while the next 2 are also under construction. The factory is capable to completing 60-80 Il-114s a year. 4 Il-114s (01 prototype, 2 production Il-114s and the first Il-114T) were allocated to certification tests at Zhukovsky near Moscow. At the time of writing, 3 aircraft were being tested at the factory airfield in Tashkent, and 2 have been purchased by Uzbekistan Airlines. Firm orders for 15 aircraft were received from Uzbekistan, Kazakhstan and Turkmenistan, while the eventual sale of some 350 is anticipated for domestic services in CIS. Originally, manufacturing was also expected to take place at Moscow's MAPO factory (it was ready to construct a series of 5 aircraft), but this was later abandoned. Il-114 is now produced and marketed (since 1998) by an Uzbekistan-Russian consortium which includes Ilyushin, TAPO and VASO, with financial backing from the Incombank.

↑ Ilyushin Il-114 *(Piotr Butowski)*

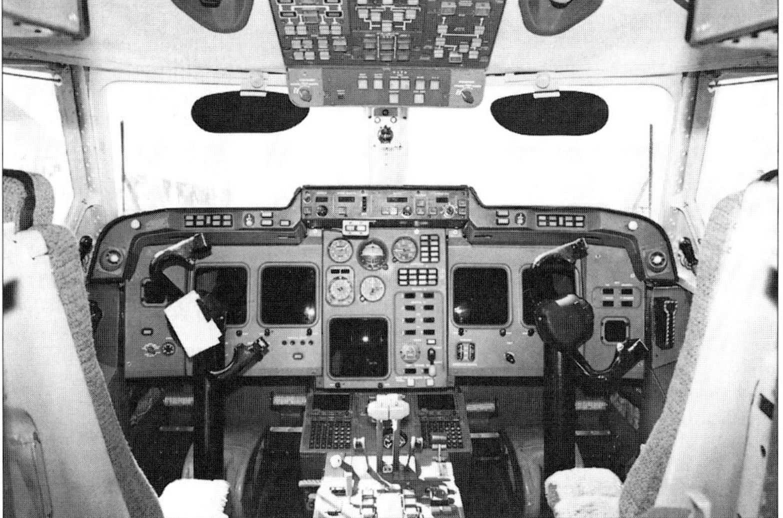
↑ EFIS cockpit of the Ilyushin Il-114T *(Piotr Butowski)*

Crew: 2 (flight) and 1 cabin attendant.
Passengers: 52-64 standard (4 abreast); 2 travel cots. Il-114MA will accommodate 74 passengers. See Aircraft variants.
Seat pitch: 30 ins (76.2 cm) for 64 passengers, or 32 ins (81 cm) for 52 passengers.
Pressurization: 6.4psi cabin differential.
Galley: Buffet type in the rear of the cabin.
Toilet: In the rear of the cabin.
Baggage compartments: 2; the smaller compartment to the starboard side of the forward fuselage area can be accessed from the passenger cabin or from the outside via a 37.8 × 51.2 ins (96 × 130 cm) hatch; the larger compartment is located in the rear part of the fuselage with access via a 28.3 × 54.33 ins (72 × 138 cm) hatch at the starboard side which doubles as another emergency exit. In the 'carry on' baggage version, passengers place their own baggage into the compartment, while racks are provided in the cabin for hand luggage. In the other version, baggage is loaded by the usual cargo handling facilities and devices through the forward and rear cargo doors.
Wing control surfaces: Ailerons (with servo and trim tabs), double-slotted flaps, spoiler and 2 airbrakes.
Tail control surfaces: Elevators (with trim tabs) and rudder (with trim and servo tabs).
Flight control system: Mechanical, but with hydraulic flaps.
Construction materials: Principally metal, but with 10% by weight composites.
Engines: 2 Klimov TV7-117-3 turboprops, with 11 ft 10 ins (3.6 m) diameter SV-34 6-blade high-technology composites propellers. APU housed in the tailcone for engine starting. Western engines to be available as an option for export aircraft (see Aircraft variants).
Engine rating: Each 2,500 shp (1,864 kW) at take off, 1,800 shp (1,342 kW) cruise.
Fuel system: 8,360 litres in 2 wing tanks.
Electrical system: 115/220 volt, 400Hz AC supply via 2 × 40kVA generators. 24 volt DC supply.
Hydraulic system: Dual systems, each 3,002 psi.
Braking system: Hydraulic disc.
De-icing system: Bleed air for engine inlets and electro/thermal for propellers and cockpit glazing.
Radar: Weather radar.
Flight avionics/instrumentation: IFR. Modern TsPNK-114 digital suite. Meets ICAO Cat I and II standards. Glass cockpit, with 5 CRT displays presenting navigation (2 displays, 1 for each pilot), flight (2) and engine/systems (1, central) information. Western avionics to be made available as an option for exported aircraft.

Details for Il-114

PRINCIPAL DIMENSIONS:
Wing span: 98 ft 5 ins (30 m)
Fuselage length: 85 ft 11.5 ins (26.2 m)
Fuselage diameter: 9 ft 4.6 ins (2.86 m)
Maximum length: 88 ft 2 ins (26.877 m)
Maximum height: 30 ft 7 ins (9.324 m)

CABIN:
Length: 73 ft (22.24 m)
Height: 6 ft 3.5 ins (1.92 m)
Main passenger door: 2, each 5 ft 7 ins × 2 ft 11.5 ins (1.7 × 0.9 m)
Emergency door: 2, each 20 ins × 36 ins (51 × 91 cm) on the fuselage sides

WINGS:
Area: 881.56 sq ft (81.9 m^2)
Aspect ratio: 10.99

TAIL UNIT:
Tailplane span: 36 ft 5 ins (11.1 m)
Tailfin height: 30 ft 7 ins (9.324 m)

UNDERCARRIAGE:
Type: Retractable, with steerable (±55°) nosewheels. Twin wheels on each unit. Can operate from unpaved airfields
Main wheel tyre size: 880 × 305 mm
Nose wheel tyre size: 620 × 180 mm
Wheel base: 29 ft 11 ins (9.125 m)
Wheel track: 27 ft 7 ins (8.4 m)

WEIGHTS:
Empty, operating: 33,069 lb (15,000 kg)
Maximum take-off: 50,045-51,809 lb (22,700-23,500 kg)
Payload: 14,330 lb (6,500 kg)

PERFORMANCE:
Cruise speed: 270 kts (311 mph) 500 km/h
Approach speed: 107 kts (123 mph) 198 km/h
Take-off distance: 4,430 ft (1,350 m)
Take-off distance over a 50 ft (15 m) obstacle: 5,100 ft (1,550 m), MTOW, concrete runway
Landing distance: 4,265-4,430 ft (1,250-1,350 m)
Cruise altitude: 24,935 ft (7,600 m)
Range with 3,307 lb (1,500 kg) cargo: 2,592 naut miles (2,982 miles) 4,800 km
Range with 64 passengers: 540 naut miles (621 miles) 1,000 km

Aircraft variants:
Il-114 is the standard TV7-117-3 version, as detailed.
Il-114M was to have higher rated TV7M-117 engines and 74 passengers in a lengthened fuselage. Lengthened fuselage via 2 plugs, 1 of 48.8 ins (1,240 mm) in front of the wing torque box and the other of 33.86 ins (860 mm) just behind the box. Length would thereby be increased to 92 ft 10 ins (28.30 m), while other dimensions remained unchanged. Project abandoned, as the TV7M engines are still paper projects and the version is thereby being replaced by Western-engined versions.
Il-114MA is a derivative of the lengthened Il-114M project, powered by Allison GMA 2100 turboprops (4,850 shp, 3,617 kW each) and driving 12 ft 8 ins (3.86 m) diameter Russian-made SV-36-05 propellers. Take-off weight 59,767 lb (27,110 kg) and payload increased to 16,182 lb (7,340 kg). The practical range with 74 passengers is expected to be 1,080 naut miles (1,243 miles) 2,000 km, and cruise speed 324-351 kts (373-404 mph) 600-650 km/h. Programme suspended at time of writing.
Il-114MAK will be a convertible cargo/passenger version of Il-114MA. Programme suspended at time of writing.
Il-114MAT is a planned cargo version of the Il-114MA. Programme suspended at time of writing.
Il-114PC is a version with 2,750 shp (2,051 kW) Pratt & Whitney Canada PW127F turboprops. Range 971 naut miles (1,118 miles) 1,800 km with 64 passengers. Contract signing between Ilyushin Aviation Complex and Pratt & Whitney Canada was announced at Paris on 14 June 1997. The first flight is targeted for Autumn 1998. Earlier, the same Il-114PC designation had been applied to a projected PW127C-engined version featuring also Rockwell Collins Pro Line 4 avionics and improved systems.
Il-114T is a cargo variant that made its first flight on 14 September 1996 at Tashkent, piloted by Igor Zakirov (aircraft c/n *03-01*). The cargo hold is 62 ft 1 ins (18.93 m) long, 6 ft 4 ins (1.92 m) high and 7 ft 6 ins (2.294 m) wide at floor level. The cargo door, 10 ft 10 ins (3.31 m) wide and 5 ft 10 ins (1.78 m) high, is positioned at the port side of the rear fuselage at the sill height of 6 ft 11 ins (2.1 m) from ground level. No cabin windows. With take-off weight increased to 51,809 lb (23,500 kg), it carries up to a 15,432 lb (7,000 kg) payload. Range with a 13,228 lb (6,000 kg) load is 540 naut miles (621 miles) 1,000 km and cruise speed is 254 kts (292 mph) 470 km/h.
Il-114K (konvertiruyemyi, convertible) is a hybrid of the passenger and cargo versions, and may be converted in the field for the carriage of cargo or passengers. As far as the overall design is concerned, it is nearer the passenger version, the main difference being that the starboard front cargo door has been increased in size to 5 ft 11 ins × 7 ft 4 ins (1.8 × 2.23 m).
Il-114A (Arkticheskiy, Arctic) will be a modification of the Il-114K, adapted for operation in polar regions. It will be equipped with a ski undercarriage as well as special navigation equipment and systems.
Il-114FK (fotokartograficheskiy, photo-cartographic), ***Il-114P*** (patrol) and ***Il-114RT*** (retranslator, radio-relay) are electronic versions, described in the Electronic section of this edition.

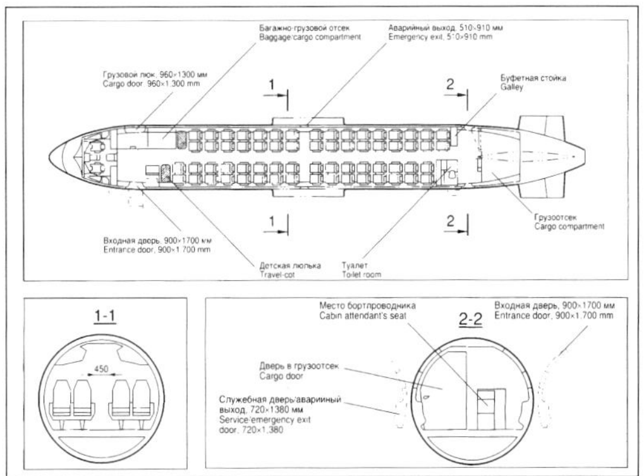

↑ Ilyushin Il-114 cabin layout for 64 passengers at 762-mm pitch, plus fuselage cross sections *(courtesy Ilyushin)*

↑ Ilyushin Il-114T with rear cargo door raised *(Piotr Butowski)*

Inalet Company — Russia

Corporate address:
ul. Svobody, d. 95, k. 2, R4, 123481 Moscow.

Telephone: +7 095 4964660, 4955040
Facsimile: +7 095 4964652

Founded:
1990 (formerly named VIST).

Information:
Viktor Mikhailovich Kapin (President), Viktor Vladimirovich Subbotin (Chief Designer).

Inalet-4, -8 and -18

First flight: Projects only in June 1998, having been announced in 1992.
Role: Air-cushion or/and vertical take-off and landing aircraft, suitable for cargo/passenger transportation, patrol, ambulance, agricultural, and other roles. Series of various-size vehicles proposed, including 4-passenger Inalet-4, 8-passenger Inalet-8, and 18-passenger Inalet-18.

Aims

- Vertical take-off, horizontal take-off on air-cushion (from any type of surface), and conventional take-off from a concrete runway to obtain maximum payload.
- Cruise speed higher by 30-40% and specific fuel consumption reduced by 40-50% compared with helicopters.
- Aerodynamic offset of countertorque by control surfaces in propeller airstream.

Details

Crew: 1 or 2.
Passengers: See Role.
Fuselage/wing characteristics: Blended lifting fuselage/wing centre section, and short delta/trapezoid outer wings. Fuselage houses the lift fan within a ring-shaped channel and the hovering 'skirt' which retracts in flight.
Tail unit: Various arrangements, depending on version, including T-tail for Inalet-4, and twin fins and rudders with adjoining horizontal tailplane and elevator carried on twin booms for Inalet-18.
Engines: Inalet-4 will have 2 Allison 250-C20R turboshafts carried in the fuselage, Inalet-8 will have 2 × 600 shp (447.4 kW) Pratt & Whitney Canada PW206 turboshafts, and Inalet-18 will have 4 Klimov TV3-117 turboshafts (in side-by-side pairs), the power being switched between the take-off fan and the 2 cruise propellers. Cruise propellers are mounted in various positions, depending on the version, including in pusher configuration on pylons above the wings for Inalet-4 and carried on the tailfins in tractor configuration for Inalet-18. Propeller cyclic pitch mechanism to provide control and stabilization in hover/transition modes.

↑ **Inalet-8 (*nearest*) for 1 or 2 crew and 6 or 7 passengers. Cabin will be 6 ft 7 ins (2 m) long, 14 ft 5 ins (4.4 m) wide and 4 ft 2 ins (1.28 m) high. Alternative accommodation for up to 1,543 lb (700 kg) of cargo or layouts for ambulance, patrol, rescue, environmental, aerial photography and ice monitoring roles. Vertical take-off/landing from sites 82 × 82 ft (25 × 25 m), or conventional take-off when overloaded from Class E airports. Advanced avionics with automated monitoring and control of all flight modes. Operational empty weight 4,409 lb (2,000 kg), MTOW for VTO 6,834 lb (3,100 kg) and MTOW for conventional take-off 8,157 lb (3,700 kg). Maximum cruise speed 270 kts (311 mph) 500 km/h. Wing area 281.37 sq ft (26.14 m²). To the rear is the Inalet-32** *(Piotr Butowski)*

Details for Inalet-4, *with Inalet-18 in italics*

PRINCIPAL DIMENSIONS:
Wing span: 37 ft 3 ins (11.34 m), *76 ft 4 ins (23.26 m)*
Maximum length: 39 ft 1 ins (11.92 m), *78 ft 5 ins (23.89 m)*

WINGS:
Area: 430.6 sq ft (40 m²), *1,453 sq ft (135 m²)*

WEIGHTS:
Empty: 3,362 lb (1,525 kg), *23,149 lb (10,500 kg)*
Normal take-off: 4,630 lb (2,100 kg), *34,171 lb (15,500 kg)*
Payload: 882 lb (400 kg), *5,512 lb (2,500 kg)*
Fuel: 606 lb (275 kg), *8,818 lb (4,000 kg)*

PERFORMANCE:
Maximum cruise speed: 200 kts (230 mph) 370 km/h, *232 kts (267 mph) 430 km/h*
Economic cruise speed: 146 kts (168 mph) 270 km/h, *178 kts (205 mph) 330 km/h*
Cruise altitude: 9,840-13,125 ft (3,000-4,000 m), *the same*
Maximum range: 809 naut miles (932 miles) 1,500 km, *917 naut miles (1,056 miles) 1,700 km*
Range with full payload: 512 naut miles (590 miles) 950 km, *540 naut miles (621 miles) 1,000 km*

Inalet-32

Role: 32-passenger regional airliner, with main cabin seating 6-abreast.
Airframe: Aerodynamically shaped fuselage with 'stub' wings and highly-swept T-tail. Combination said to provide high aerodynamic characteristics with uninterrupted stability up to 20–22° angle of attack and makes it possible to reduce mass compared with traditional designs. Will comply to FAR requirements.
Engines: 2 × 650 shp (485 kW) Pratt & Whitney Canada PW206 turboshafts in the fuselage, driving 4-blade tractor propellers mounted above the fuselage. Maintains symmetrical thrust with 1 engine operating, due to close loop gasdynamic transmission drive which continues to operate both engines.

Inalet-60

Certification: Expected 2001 for baseline version, to 2003 for Corporate.
Role: 62/68-passenger regional airliner (Inalet-60A), freighter for 7 tonnes of containerized/palleted cargo (Inalet-60T), and 20-30 passenger business/corporate aircraft or executive transport (Inalet-60B).
Engines: 2 × 8,650 lbf (38.48 kN) General Electric CF34-1A turbofans.

↑ **Inalet-60** *(Piotr Butowski)*

Details for Inalet-60 baseline version

PRINCIPAL DIMENSIONS:
Wing span: 78 ft 9 ins (24 m)
Length: 77 ft 9 ins (23.7 m)
Height: 27 ft 3 ins (8.3 m)

CABIN:
Length: 30 ft 10 ins (9.4 m)
Width: 11 ft 8 ins (3.55 m)
Height: 7 ft 1 ins (2.15 m)

WINGS:
Area: 645.83 sq ft (60 m²)

WEIGHTS:
Empty, operating: 31,746 lb (14,400 kg)
Maximum take-off: 52,910 lb (24,000 kg)
Payload: 14,392 lb (6,528 kg)

PERFORMANCE:
Maximum speed: 464 kts (534 mph) 860 km/h
Required runway length: 4,659 ft (1,420 m)
Service ceiling: 33,135 ft (10,100 m)
Range with full fuel: 2,833 naut miles (3,262 miles) 5,250 km
Range with full payload: 636 naut miles (733 miles) 1,180 km

Details for Inalet-32

PRINCIPAL DIMENSIONS:
Length: 44 ft (13.4 m)
Height: 16 ft 7 ins (5.05 m)

CABIN:
Height: 6 ft 5 ins (1.95 m)

WINGS:
Area: 364.7 sq ft (33.88 m²)

WEIGHTS:
Empty, operating: 8,686 lb (3,940 kg)
Maximum take-off: 16,623 lb (7,540 kg)
Payload: 6,349 lb (2,880 kg)
Maximum fuel: 3,351 lb (1,520 kg)
Fuel with maximum payload: 1,587 lb (720 kg)

PERFORMANCE:
Maximum speed: 248 kts (286 mph) 460 km/h, near land
Cruise speed: 205 kts (236 mph) 380 km/h
Minimum speed: 81 kts (94 mph) 150 km/h
Take-off distance over a 35 ft (10.7 m) obstacle: 1,772 ft (540 m)
Landing distance over a 50 ft (15 m) obstacle: 1,247 ft (380 m), with reverse thrust
Service ceiling: 19,685 ft (6,000 m)
Cruise ceiling: 13,125 ft (4,000 m)
Range with full fuel: 1,521 naut miles (1,752 miles) 2,820 km
Range with full payload: 658 naut miles (758 miles) 1,220 km

MAPO "MiG" — Russia

Corporate address:
See Combat section for company details. See also General Aviation section for the new MiG-125 business jet.

MAPO "MiG" MiG-110

First flight: Originally planned for 1996, but now about 1999.
Role: Light multi-purpose civil/military transport.
Airframe life: 25,000 flying hours.

Development

- 1980. Counter-insurgency (COIN) aircraft similar to the US OV-10 Bronco was thrown open to competition to meet the needs of the Afghanistan conflict. The Mikoyan design, called izdelye 101, won the competition against Sukhoi and Ilyushin designs. Later, when interest in the COIN aircraft diminished, the 101 was transformed into 101M and 101N designs for general

purpose aircraft with a 4,409 lb (2,000 kg) payload.
▪ February 1992. Design work on izdelye 110 (MiG-110) began on the basis of 101, with the maximum payload increased to 11,023 lb (5,000 kg).
▪ 30 December 1993. The Russian Government decided to offer financial aid and preferential loans to the Nizhny Novgorod factory to prepare for series manufacture of the MiG-110.
▪ 1997. Progress accelerated when the main work on the MiG-AT was finished and the design group moved to the MiG-110. Current project is a little larger than the previous design, with payload increased to 12,125 lb (5,500 kg).

Details

Sales: Demand estimated at more than 1,000 aircraft for CIS civil aviation and more than 300 for the armed forces.
Crew: 2.
Passengers: 48 (from previously planned 39) or mixed passenger/cargo layout. See Freight hold capacity.
Pressurization: Flight deck and cabin.
Freight hold capacity: Up to 12,125 lb (5,500 kg – increased from previous 5,000 kg), including a UAZ-452 truck/pickup, LD3 and 1AK-1.5 containers, or bulk freight. See Passengers.
Freight hold access: Beaver-tail rear fuselage, with built-in ramp in the hinged lower section. Side door of 2 ft 4 ins × 1 ft 8 ins (0.7 × 0.5 m) for crew and passengers is located in port side of the forward fuselage.
Wing characteristics: High mounted, with approximately 7° anhedral for the inner sections from the fuselage to the booms, thereafter 0° or slight anhedral only for the outer panels. Winglets.
Wing control surfaces: Aileron, 2-section double-slotted trailing-edge flaps, and leading-edge slats.
Tail control surfaces: 2-section elevator (with tab) on the adjoining tailplane. Twin fins and rudders, canted slightly inward.
Engines: 2 Klimov/Sarkisov TV7-117-3V turboprops.
Engine rating: Each 2,500 shp (1,864 kW).

↑ MAPO "MiG" MiG-110 *(Piotr Butowski)*

Details for MiG-110

PRINCIPAL DIMENSIONS:
Wing span: 81 ft 11 ins (24.96 m)
Maximum length: 61 ft (18.6 m)
Maximum height: 17 ft 8.5 ins (5.4 m)

CABIN:
Length: 29 ft 6 ins (9 m) *with ramp*, 24 ft 3 ins (7.4 m) *without ramp*
Width: 9 ft 1 ins (2.76 m) *maximum*, 7 ft 3 ins (2.2 m) *at floor*
Height: 7 ft 3 ins (2.2 m)

UNDERCARRIAGE:
Type: Retractable, with twin wheels on each unit

WEIGHTS:
Maximum take-off: 39,683 lb (18,000 kg)
Payload: 12,125 lb (5,500 kg)

PERFORMANCE:
Cruise speed: 270 kts (311 mph) 500 km/h
Required runway length, concrete: 1,970 ft (600 m) with full payload
Required runway length, unprepared: 1,542 ft (470 m) with a 7,716 lb (3,500 kg) payload
Required runway length, hot and high conditions: 2,395 ft (730 m) with 7,716 lb (3,500 kg) payload
Ceiling: 26,245-36,090 ft (8,000-11,000 m)
Range with full fuel and 5,864 lb (2,660 kg) payload: 2,037 naut miles (2,345 miles) 3,775 km, with 30 minutes reserve
Range with 9,920 lb (4,500 kg) payload: 906 naut miles (1,044 miles) 1,680 km, with 30 minutes reserve

NPO Molniya — Russia

Full name:
Molniya Research and Industrial Corporation.

Corporate address:
6 Novoposelkovaja, Moscow 123459.

Telephone: +7 095 493 5053, 3335, and 497 4760
Facsimile: +7 095 492 9371, 497 4511
E-mail: Alex@molniya.msk.ru

Founded:
1976, to develop the first Russian reusable spacecraft. Founded on the basis of 2 design bureaus, Burevestnik (Chief Designer A.V. Potopalov) and Molniya (Chief Designer M. R. Bisnovat).

Information:
Michail Gofin (Marketing Director – *telephone* +7 095 497 4723).

ACTIVITIES

▪ To supplement reduced work on the Buran Space Shuttle programme, Molniya now develops civil aircraft. Most are of 'tandem 3-plane' configuration, a layout which makes aircraft spinproof and unloads the main wing.
▪ Molniya-1 is being series built, and Molniya-100 and -300 have undergone design study; Aist lightplane, Ladoga amphibian, Vityaz, Molniya-400 and Molniya-1000 Heracles are still at the feasibility or design stages (see also General Aviation section).
▪ Molniya is also involved in many space programmes, including aircraft-launched MAKS project (see An-225 under Ukraine).
▪ Molniya markets some projects of Aviacor JSC (which see), including Aist and Kasatik (see General Aviation section).

Molniya-400

Role: Freighter, with possible passenger/cargo combi derivative. Possible competitor to the Antonov An-70 and Tupolev Tu-330.
Airframe life: 60,000 hours at 3,500 hours per year, or 20,000 landings.

Development

▪ 1994. Feasibility study completed, leading to preliminary design.

Details

Crew: 5, comprising 2 pilots, flight engineer and 2 cargo operators.
Passengers: 250 on the upper deck when containers are carried on the lower deck in a combi layout.
Freight hold access: Ramp/door under the rear fuselage on freighter version. Airliner does not have this facility.
Wing characteristics: Swept, high mounted, with drag-reducing winglets. Slightly swept, low-mounted canards with winglets.
Wing control surfaces: Appears to have ailerons, flaps and multi-section spoilers.
Tail control surfaces: Mid-mounted tailplane with 2-section elevators. Rudder.
Engines: 2 Aviadvigatel PS-90A turbofans.

↑ Molniya-400 in airliner configuration *(Piotr Butowski)*

Details for Molniya-400

PRINCIPAL DIMENSIONS:
Wing span: 140 ft 1 ins (42.7 m)
Maximum length: 136 ft 2 ins (41.5 m)
Maximum height: 51 ft 0.5 ins (15.56 m)

CABIN:
Length: 65 ft 8 ins (20 m)
Width: 13 ft 2 ins (4 m)
Height: 13 ft 6 ins to 14 ft 5 ins (4.1 to 4.4 m)

UNDERCARRIAGE:
Type: Retractable, with twin nosewheels and 6-wheel main bogies

WEIGHTS:
Maximum take-off: 242,067 lb (109,800 kg)
Overload take-off weight: 266,979 lb (121,100 kg)
Payload: 66,139 lb (30,000 kg)
Overload payload: 110,230 lb (50,000 kg)

PERFORMANCE:
Maximum speed: 502 kts (578 mph) 930 km/h
Cruise speed: 410-432 kts (472-497 mph) 760-800 km/h at ceiling
Take-off distance: 4,035 ft (1,230 m)
Required runway length at overload weight: 8,530 ft (2,600 m)
Ceiling: 36,745 ft (11,200 m), service
Range with full payload: 2,700 naut miles (3,106 miles) 5,000 km
Range at overload weight: 1,620 naut miles (1,864 miles) 3,000 km

Engine rating: Each 35,274 lbf (156.9 kN).
Fuel system: 106,924 lb (48,500 kg).
Flight avionics/instrumentation: IFR and ICAO Category II landing. Modern suite.

Molniya-1000 Heracles

Role: Super-heavy freighter, passenger aircraft and space payload carrier.

Aims

▪ To develop a 450 tonne payload transport that can be built using current Russian industrial potential and technologies (except the engines, which should be of new type). Due to the 'triple-plane' configuration, the aircraft's size is expected to be similar to that of the An-225, though payload could be greater. Considered also as a launcher for MAKS aerospace system, instead of the An-225 (a Presidential decree is expected on this).

Development

▪ Early 1990s. An initial impetus came from a Saudi Arabian preliminary requirement. Model has been displayed in desert markings with a huge water tank as payload.
▪ 2005. Possible production start-up, if funded.

Details

Crew: 4 plus 4 relief crew. Unique crew accommodation, with a cockpit in each of the 2 fuselage boom noses.
Payload/passengers: Quickly attachable/detachable modules, cargo containers and pallets, or super heavy/outsized loads (for example, hydro turbines, chemical reactors, petrol/chemical industry equipment, tanks, etc) carried externally between the fuselage booms; maximum length 197 ft (60 m), width 36 ft (11 m), and height 30.8 ft (9.4 m). Possible passenger capsule for 1,200 seats.

↑ Molniya-1000 Heracles in desert paintwork, with water tank between fuselage booms *(Piotr Butowski)*

Loading facilities: Lifting and lowering system, without the need for bulky cranes. After landing, the aircraft would be taxied to a working area, where 2 self-propelled trolleys would come to the aircraft, the first empty to accept the existing payload and take it to the terminal, and the second carrying the new payload.

Details for Molniya-1000

PRINCIPAL DIMENSIONS:
Wing span: 296 ft 7 ins (90.4 m)
Maximum length: 240 ft 10 ins (73.4 m)
Maximum height: 57 ft 5 ins (17.5 m)

UNDERCARRIAGE:
Type: Retractable, with 5 rows of 4 wheels under each fuselage boom plus nosewheels
Wheel track: 52 ft 6 ins (16 m)

WEIGHTS:
Maximum take-off: 1,984,150 lb (900,000 kg)
Payload: 992,080 lb (450,000 kg)

PERFORMANCE:
Cruise speed: 394-442 kts (454-510 mph) 730-820 km/h
Take-off distance: 7,710 ft (2,350 m)
Landing distance: 3,281 ft (1,000 m)
Range with full fuel: 4,478-6,367 naut miles (5,157-7,332 miles) 8,300-11,800 km, with 529,109 lb (240,000 kg) payload
Range with full payload: 1,242-1,674 naut miles (1,430-1,926 miles) 2,300-3,100 km
Ferry range: 9,712 naut miles (11,185 miles) 18,000 km

Wing characteristics: Large single-piece canard on fin-type pylons at the nose, above the cockpits. Huge high-mounted wing, forming an inverted V at the centre section and with anhedral outer panels, with winglets.
Wing control surfaces: Multi-section leading- and trailing-edge control surfaces on both the wings and canard.
Tail control surfaces: Huge twin fins supported on the booms, with rudders, carring a single-piece high-mounted tailplane with full-width elevator.
Engines: 6 Samara NK-44 turbofans in pods under the wing. Alternatively, General Electric CF6-90VH, Pratt & Whitney PW4084, or Rolls-Royce Trent turbofans. 10 current PS-90A turbofans are planned for first-stage prototype aircraft.
Engine rating: 88,185 lbf (392.3 kN) for production aircraft in this application.
Fuel system: 771,617 lb (350,000 kg), although 789,250 lb (358,000 kg) is quoted in some documentation.

Aircraft variants:
Prototype is proposed to have 10 PS-90A turbofans, each 35,274 lbf (156.9 kN). Maximum take-off weight reduced to 1,521,188 lb (690,000 kg), payload 771,617 lb (350,000 kg), and range 2,000-2,500 naut miles with a 551,155 lb (250,000 kg) cargo payload.
Production version will have 6 × 392.3 kN turbofan engines.

Molniya Vityaz

Comments: Vityaz will be a much smaller transport aircraft based of the Heracles configuration, with a crew of 2. Maximum length will be 82 ft (25 m), wing span 131 ft 3 ins (40 m), height 20 ft 8 ins (6.3 m), maximum weight 110,230 lb (50,000 kg), and payload 66,138 lb (30,000 kg). It will have passenger cabins inside the 2 fuselage booms and cargo suspended between. Medevac, firefighting and flying tanker versions are also under consideration. Powered by 4 Saturn 2AL-34 turboprops (each 1,400 shp, 1,044 kW) with ducted propellers mounted at the rear of the fuselage booms, cruising speed is expected to be 405-459 kts (466-528 mph) 750-850 km/h and maximum range 3,507 naut miles (4,039 miles) 6,500 km or 2,158 naut miles (2,485 miles) 4,000 km when an external load is attached, with a normal fuel load of 13,228 lb (6,000 kg). Ferry range 10,792 naut miles (12,427 miles) 20,000 km. Cruise altitude 29,525-36,090 ft (9,000-11,000 m), landing speed 86 kts (99 mph) 160 km/h, and required runway length 3,940 ft (1,200 m).

↑ Molniya Vityaz passenger and cargo transport *(Piotr Butowski)*

MAPO "Myasishchev" — Russia

Corporate address:
See Combat section for company details. See also Electronic and General Aviation sections.

Myasishchev 3MS-2 and VM-T Atlant (NATO name *Bison*)

Comments: The 3MS-2 tanker conversion of the *Bison-B* bomber is no longer operational. Details and illustrations of this, and the 2 VM-T Atlant freighter conversions of the bomber for transporting the Buran space shuttle and Energia rocket components in support of the Baikonur cosmodrome, can be found in the 1996-97 edition of *WA&SD*, pages 233-234.

Myasishchev M-90 Air Ferry (MGS)

Comments: Details and an illustration of the projected M-90 multi-purpose very-heavy-lift transportation system for outsized equipment, cargo containers, liquid/granular loads and passengers, now abandoned through lack of funding, can be found in the 1996-97 edition of *WA&SD*, page 234.

Myasishchev M-112 (MM-1)

Comments: Details and an illustration of the M-112 multi-purpose wide-body transport, now abandoned through lack of funding, can be found in the 1996-97 edition of *WA&SD*, pages 234-235.

Myasishchev M-150

Comments: Details and an illustration of the M-150 convertible commuter/cargo transport, now abandoned through lack of funding, can be found in the 1996-97 edition of *WA&SD*, page 235.

Myasishchev GP-60

Comments: GP-60 (gruzo-passazhirsky, cargo-passenger) is the generic title for a series of projected high-altitude transport aircraft based on the former M-60 high-altitude reconnaissance aircraft project. It features a wide fuselage (width-to-height ratio 2.5), high aspect ratio unswept low-mounted wings, twin tailfins, and engines carried above the rear fuselage. GP-60 aircraft are offered with a passenger capacity from 5 to 500 seats and range from 5,000 to 15,000 km. 2 models were shown at Zhukovsky in August 1997, the twin-engine GP-60d (see photograph) and triple-engine GP-60s. For reference value and as a guide, the basic M-60 reconnaissance/battlefield control aircraft had to have a take-off weight of 35,000-40,000 kg, mission load of 5,000-7,000 kg and crew of 6. Required cruise altitude was 20,000 m, cruise speed Mach 0.7 and a duration of 8 hours. Work on M-60 was stopped due to a lack of funding in the early 1990s.

↑ Model of the Myasishchev GP-60d shown at Zhukovsky in August 1997 *(Piotr Butowski)*

NIAT (National Institute of Aviation Technologies) JSC — Russia

Corporate address:
24 Petrovka Street, Moscow 103051.
Telephone: +7 095 200 7601
Facsimile: +7 095 292 6511
Telex: 411700 PTB SV FOR NIAT
Information:
V. P. Pushkov.

↑ NIAT-2.5ST Freighty *(Piotr Butowski)*

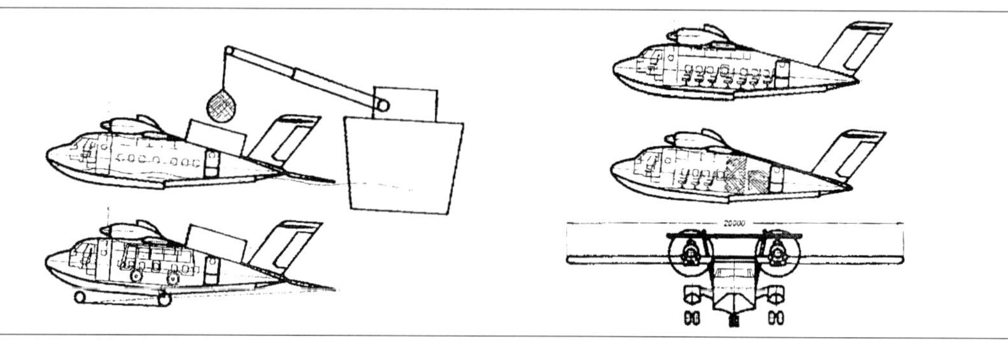
↑ NIAT-2.5ST Freighty showing the cargo version interacting with shipping (*top left*), cargo version having loaded a minibus (*bottom left*), passenger version with 7 rows of passengers 4-abreast (*top right*), combi/convertible version (*centre right*), and the front view with wheels lowered (*bottom right*) *(courtesy NIAT)*

ACTIVITIES:

▪ Following the projected NIAT-1 Gruzovichok (Freighty) of 1994, the organization designed the NIAT-2.5ST Freighty, as detailed below.
▪ On 1 June 1995, NIAT completed the initial design phase of the **NIAT-2.5ST Freighty** amphibious transport, intended to operate in remote areas (such as Siberia and South-East Asia). The domestic Russian market alone is estimated to be for 350 aircraft, while foreign sales could total about 300, with 7 Freightys produced in the first year, rising to 15 in the second

and 25 in the third. Certification had been scheduled for 1997, but this depended on required investment. Powered by 2 × 1,380 shp (1,029 kW) Omsk/Glushenkov TVD-20 turboprop engines, it is constructed of composite materials, aluminium-lithium and titanium alloys, and has a single-step flying-boat hull and T-tail mounted on twin fins. Loading is via a rear ramp/door, with extra headroom provided at the entrance of the tapering rear fuselage by upward-hinging roof sections, allowing straight-in loading of a vehicle. Wing span is quoted as 65 ft 7 ins (20 m), length 53 ft (16.152 m), height 17 ft 8 ins (5.4 m), speed 189-216 kts (217-249 mph) 350-400 km/h, take-off distance from land/water 1,739/2,149 ft (530/655 m) respectively, landing distance on land/water 2,035/2,297 ft (620/700 m) respectively, and range with 5,511 lb (2,500 kg) cargo or 28 passengers is 323 naut miles (373 miles) 600 km or with 2,204 lb (1,000 kg) cargo is 809 naut miles (932 miles) 1,500 km.

Sukhoi Design Bureau — Russia

Corporate address:
See Combat aircraft section for company details. See also General Aviation section.

Sukhoi S-80

First flight: Had been expected in 1994. Now end of 1998.
Role: Light military/civil multi-purpose cargo and passenger transport, with STOL features. Also suitable to patrol, surveillance, survey, medevac and more.

Development

- 1988. Work began against a requirement of the Ministry of Health for a light medevac aircraft for use during natural disasters.
- 1992. Government financial support stopped. Development continued as a general-purpose aircraft, shared by Sukhoi and Komsomolsk-on-Amur.

Details

Sales: 2 aircraft (1 for flight testing and 1 for static testing) under construction at the Komsomolsk-on-Amur plant since early 1995 (no prototype is being built by the Sukhoi design bureau). With demand in the CIS for 1,800-2,000 aircraft of this class, Sukhoi hopes to capture one-third of this market plus up to 10-15% of the world market. Some 30 orders reported from Russia (probably in patrol version for the Russian Federal Border Guard Service) as well as preliminary orders from South Korea, Indonesia and Brazil (also in military S-80PT version). See also the Electronic section.
Crew: 1 or 2.
Passengers: Up to 25 airline-type seats in the civil passenger and convertible versions. Also offered in 9, 12 or 16-seat business configurations. Military transport version will have 20 folded seats in the cabin, while the medevac version accommodates 10 litters and 3 attendants.
Freight hold capacity: 6,834 lb (3,100 kg) of cargo.
Freight hold access: Rear loading ramp/door, plus door on the port side of the mid fuselage.
Wing control surfaces: Ailerons (with trim tabs), single-slotted trailing-edge flaps (20° for take-off and 40° for landing), and leading-edge slats between engine nacelles and wingtips. Winglets.
Tail control surfaces: Tail unit supported by twin booms. Slightly inward canted fins. Additional aerodynamic surface/support between the rear fuselage and booms. Horn-balanced rudders with tabs and narrow-chord elevator.
Flight control system: Pushrods and cables, except for electric trim tabs.
Construction materials: Mainly aluminium alloys (67-71% of airframe weight), composites (7-9%), steel (7-9%) and titanium (4-6%).
Engines: 2 General Electric CT7-9B turboprops, with 11 ft (3.35 m) diameter Hamilton Standard 4-blade propellers. Engines will be licence built by Rybinsk in Russia. Initially, 1,300 shp (969.4 kW) RKBM/Rybinsk TVD-1500S turboprops with 6-blade AV-36 propellers had been planned.
Engine rating: Each 1,750 shp (1,305 kW).
Fuel system: 3,000 litres (5,192 lb, 2,355 kg) in 4 wing tanks. Provision for auxiliary fuel tank.
Electrical system: 27 volt DC supply via 2 Auxilec starter/generators. AC supply via 2 Lucas alternators, 115/200 volt 300-900Hz, and 2 PTS-800BN converters, 115/200 volt 400Hz. 2 stand-by Varta batteries. To supply avionics, external and internal lighting, de-icing system and more.
Hydraulic system: Main and emergency systems, pressure 3,000 psi, used for undercarriage extension/retraction, nosewheel steering, rear ramp control and wheel brakes.
Pneumatic system: Emergency undercarriage lowering.
Flight avionics/instrumentation: Rockwell Collins suite on the first aircraft. Pro Line 2 EFIS. ICAO Cat II operations. Automatic systems testing.

Aircraft variants:
S-80 was the original design of 1988 with 2 wings in tandem. Czech Walter M-601E turboprops. Abandoned in 1990 when aerodynamic testing indicated insufficient lift-to-drag ratio. More conventional S-80M design begun thereafter, having single high aspect ratio wing (now renamed **S-80**, when S-80M became the ambulance version – see below).
S-80A (arkticheskiy) is for Arctic operations.
S-80GP (gruzo-passazhirskiy) is the convertible cargo-passenger version.
S-80GR (geologicheskoi razvedki) is for geological exploration.
S-80M (meditsinsky) is an air ambulance for 10 litters and 3 attendants.
S-80P is a 25-seat passenger version.
S-80PT (patrulno-transportnyi) is a military patrol/transport, with an electronic surveillance system including radar, FLIR, and weapons. See separate entry and photograph in the Electronic aircraft section.
S-80R (rybopoiskovyi) is for EEZ/fishery surveillance.
S-80TD (transportno-desantnyi) is the military assault transport.

↑ **Sukhoi S-80 multi-purpose transport** *(Piotr Butowski)*

Details for S-80 with CT7-9B engines

PRINCIPAL DIMENSIONS:
Wing span: 76 ft (23.16 m)
Maximum length: 55 ft 4 ins (16.86 m)
Maximum height: 18 ft 4 ins (5.58 m)

CABIN:
Length: 20 ft 8 ins (6.3 m), or 25 ft 7 ins (7.8 m) with ramp
Width: 7 ft 1 ins (2.15 m) maximum
Height: 6 ft (1.83 m) maximum
Volume: 745 cu ft (21.1 m^3)

WINGS:
Area: approximately 473.61 sq ft (44 m^2)
Aspect ratio: approximately 12.19

TAIL UNIT:
Tailplane span: 16 ft (4.88 m)
Fin area: 71.47 sq ft (6.64 m^2)

UNDERCARRIAGE:
Type: Retractable, with steerable nosewheels (38°). Twin wheels on each unit
Main wheel tyre size: 660 × 200 mm
Nose wheel tyre size: 500 × 180 mm
Wheel base: 21 ft 4 ins (6.5 m)
Wheel track: 18 ft 4.5 ins (5.6 m)

WEIGHTS:
Empty, operating: 18,078 lb (8,200 kg) cargo, 18,408 lb (8,350 kg) passenger
Maximum take-off: 27,558 lb (12,500 kg), or 25,353 lb (11,500 kg) from an unpaved runway
Maximum landing: 27,558 lb (12,500 kg), or 25,353 lb (11,500 kg) to an unpaved runway
Payload: 7,716 lb (3,500 kg)

PERFORMANCE:
Maximum cruise speed: 289 kts (332 mph) 535 km/h
Economic cruise speed: 216 kts (249 mph) 400 km/h
Landing speed: 97 kts (112 mph) 180 km/h
Take-off distance: 1,821 ft (555 m) at MTOW, ISA, sea level
Landing distance: 919 ft (280 m) with brakes and reverse
Required runway length, ISA: 2,789 ft (850 m), MTOW, at sea level
Required runway length, ISA + 34°: 2,986 ft (910 m), MTOW, at sea level
Required runway length, ISA + 30°: 3,314 ft (1,010 m), MTOW, at 4,920 ft (1,500 m)
Maximum climb rate: 2,953 ft (900 m) per minute
Ceiling: 29,525 ft (9,000 m)
Maximum range: 1,392 naut miles (1,603 miles) 2,580 km
Range at maximum cruise speed, at 19,685 ft (6,000 m) altitude: 350 naut miles (404 miles) 650 km with 7,716 lb (3,500 kg) payload, or 1,214 naut miles (1,398 miles) 2,250 km with 4,299 lb (1,950 kg) payload, both with 45 minutes reserve
Range at economic cruise speed, at 19,685 ft (6,000 m) altitude: 378 naut miles (435 miles) 700 km with 7,716 lb (3,500 kg) payload, or 1,392 naut miles (1,603 miles) 2,580 km with 4,299 lb (1,950 kg) payload, both with 45 minutes reserve
Ferry range: 1,559 naut miles (1,796 miles) 2,890 km

Sukhoi KR-860

Role: Proposed 860-seat ultra-large airliner.

↑ **Sukhoi KR-860**

Tupolev Joint-Stock Company — Russia

Corporate address:
See Combat section for company details. See also General Aviation section.

Tupolev C-Prop

Role: Project for a light passenger or cargo transport using liquid gas cryogenic fuel.
Passengers/cargo: 32 passengers or 3 pallets of 88 ins × 125 ins (2.24 × 3.175 m) or 88 ins × 108 ins (2.24 × 2.74 m) each.
Freight hold access: Rear ramp/door under the tail.
Wing characteristics: Low-mounted, straight main wings, with dihedral. High-mounted canards, joined to the 2 booms that are supported at the rear on wing-mounted pylons.
Wing control surfaces: Horn-balanced ailerons (with port tab) and flaps on the main wings. Canards carry trailing-edge surfaces.
Tail control surfaces: T-tail with elevators (port tab) and rudder (with tab).
Engines: 2 Pratt & Whitney Canada PT6A-67 turboprops, with pusher propellers.
Engine rating: Each 1,500 shp (1,118 kW).
Fuel system: 5,291 lb (2,400 kg) of liquid gas fuel.

↑ **Tupolev C-Prop cryogenic fuelled transport** *(Piotr Butowski)*

Details for C-Prop

PRINCIPAL DIMENSIONS:
Wing span: 73 ft 10 ins (22.5 m)
Maximum length: 68 ft 11 ins (21 m)
Maximum height: 21 ft 8 ins (6.6 m)

CABIN:
Length: 31 ft 9 ins (9.68 m)
Width: 8 ft 6.5 ins (2.6 m)
Height: 7 ft 3 ins (2.2 m)

WEIGHTS:
Maximum take-off: 29,762 lb (13,500 kg)
Payload: 7,496 lb (3,400 kg)

PERFORMANCE:
Cruise speed: 243 kts (280 mph) 450 km/h
Required runway length: 2,035 ft (620 m)
Cruise altitude: 26,250 ft (8,000 m)
Range with full payload: 809 naut miles (932 miles) 1,500 km

Tupolev Tu-130

First flight: Project announced in 1993.
Role: Light civil/military convertible cargo/passenger transport, for autonomous operation.
Crew: 2.
Passengers: As an alternative to freight, can be configured for 53 passengers.
Seat pitch: 30.7 ins (78 cm).
Freight hold volume: 1,850.5 cu ft (52.4 m^3).
Freight hold capacity: Cargo, including 4 containers, pallets or light vehicles.
Freight hold access: Beaver-tail rear fuselage, with rear loading ramp for straight-in loading. Ramp size 11 ft 6 ins × 9 ft 2 ins (3.5 × 2.8 m). Side loading door in forward fuselage, port side.
Wing control surfaces: Aileron, 2-section flaps and 2-section spoiler per wing. No slats.
Tail control surfaces: Conventional elevators and rudder.
Fuselage: Circular front fuselage cross-section, squaring off towards the rear.

↑ **Tupolev Tu-130 display model (*bottom*), alongside the Tu-230 and Tu-330 (*top*)** *(Piotr Butowski)*

Engines: 2 Klimov/St Petersburg TV7-117-3 turboprops.
Engine rating: Each 2,500 shp (1,864 kW).
Fuel system: 7,937 lb (3,600 kg) for Tu-130, 15,432 lb (7,000 kg) for Tu-130LNG, and 4,409 lb (2,000 kg) for Tu-130LNG North.

Aircraft variants:
Tu-130 is the standard propulsion version, as detailed.
Tu-130LNG is being developed to use liquid natural gas (LNG) fuel, in a programme of co-operation with Daimler-Benz Aerospace (which see) that sees some commonality of components. Greater fuel capacity but reduced payload. Maximum range 1,079 naut miles (1,243 miles) 2,000 km with 15,432 lb (7,000 kg) of LNG fuel and 11,023 lb (5,000 kg) payload. Has been attributed also with the designation Tu-132.
Tu-130LNG North is another liquid natural gas project, this time adapted for Polar regions and Siberia. 2 LNG tanks mounted above the rear fuselage. Payload increased but LNG fuel reduced.

Details for Tu-130

PRINCIPAL DIMENSIONS:
Wing span: 87 ft 1 ins (26.54 m)
Maximum length: 74 ft 8 ins (22.75 m)
Maximum height: 26 ft 9 ins (8.15 m)

CABIN:
Length: 27 ft 11 ins (8.5 m)
Width: 9 ft 2 ins (2.8 m)
Height: 7 ft 3 ins (2.2 m)
Floor area: 256.18 sq ft (23.8 m^2)

WINGS:
Area: 753.47 sq ft (70 m^2)
Aspect ratio: 10.06

UNDERCARRIAGE:
Type: Retractable, with twin steerable nosewheels. Twin wheels on each main unit, in tandem, retracted into fairings on the fuselage sides

WEIGHTS:
Empty: 28,439 lb (12,900 kg)
Maximum take-off: 46,297 lb (21,000 kg)
Payload: 11,020-14,330 lb (5,000-6,500 kg)

PERFORMANCE:
Cruise speed: 270 kts (311 mph) 500 km/h
Required runway length: 5,910 ft (1,800 m)
Ceiling: 22,965 ft (7,000 m)
Range with full payload: 1,079-1,349 naut miles (1,243-1,553 miles) 2,000-2,500 km

Tupolev Tu-134 and Tu-135

Comments: First flown on 29 July 1963 and making its first scheduled flight between Moscow and Adler on 9 September 1967, Tu-134 medium-range airliner was manufactured at Kharkov, Ukraine, between 1966-1984 (852 built). It is also remembered as the first Soviet passenger aircraft to be widely exported (134 delivered to 14 countries). Although some 208 remained in civil use at the time of writing, this number was widely expected to fall to 139. Nevertheless, an upgrade programme under the designation Tu-134M has been proposed to extend the service life beyond 2010. About 180 Tu-134s are also in CIS military aviation, mainly as trainers. Tu-135 is a military high command transport. Details of Tu-134M are given below among a general listing of Tu-134/-135 versions, provided for reference interest and comparison.

Aircraft variants:
Tu-124A was a 52-seat prototype with 2 D-20P-125 engines, each 12,785 lbf (56.87 kN).
Tu-134 was an initial production version for 72 passengers, powered by 2 D-30 series I engines, each 14,990 lbf (66.68 kN). 78 manufactured.
Tu-134A became the most numerous version, having entered production in June 1970. Fuselage lengthened by 6 ft 11 ins (2.1 m), take-off weight increased to 103,617 lb (47,000 kg), 76 passengers as standard (some with 86 seats, when the crew rest area and galley was kept to a minimum), new D-30 series II turbofans (same thrust), and TA-8 APU. From the mid-1970s a new ABSU-134 flight/navigation system was introduced to meet ICAO Cat II requirements.

↑ **Tupolev Tu-134A used as an executive transport by the Bulgarian Air Force** *(Piotr Butowski)*

Tu-134A-3 became an upgrade of the Tu-134A, with D-30 series III engines.
Tu-134AK is a space-crew training version. 2 built.
Tu-134B entered production in 1980. D-30 series II engines. Standard accommodation for 80 passengers. Groza M-134 weather radar, improved cockpit layout, flight crew reduced from 4 to 3. Modified spoilers.
Tu-134B-1 became a modification of the Tu-134B for 84 or 90 passengers (due to a reduced galley). Later, a version for 96 passengers (with 5 seats in row) was developed.
Tu-134B-3 became an upgrade of Tu-134B/B-1, with D-30 series III engines.
Tu-134BU became a civil and military training conversion, equipped for ICAO Cat IIIA automatic landings.
Tu-134BV was a test aircraft supporting the Buran space shuttle programme.
Tu-134 Imark is a geology/cartography/ecology research aircraft with Vega-M side-looking radar.
Tu-134LL is the common designation for a dozen flying test beds used for radar, FLIR, communications testing and more.
Tu-134M is a proposed mid-life upgrade with Ivchenko PROGRESS/Zaporozhye D-436T turbofans.
Tu-134OL (optomological) is a medical laboratory of Sviatoslav Fyodorov, a Russian eye surgeon.
Tu-134Sh (shturmansky) is a navigational training version. 122 Tu-134s were converted to this version; includes Tu-134Sh-1 based on the Tu-134, and Tu-134Sh-2 based on the Tu-134A. Externally similar to a standard passenger Tu-134, but has an enlarged radar antenna under the nose and bomb pylons under the wings. 12 navigator stations inside the cabin.
Tu-134SKh (selsko-khozaistvennyi) is an agricultural and economic survey version, based on the Tu-134A-3. 12 built between 1982 and 1984. 2 large removable underwing nacelles containing side-looking radar (originally Toros, from May 1987 replaced by Nit'-S1-SKh). Other equipment located inside 3 pressurized and 1 unpressurized compartments in the bottom of the fuselage, includes scanning radiometer and photocameras. 10 operator stations in the cabin. Extended navigation system.
Tu-134UB-K was a training version for naval aviation pilots. Prototype only, 1982.
Tu-134UB-L (uchebno-boevoi dla lotchikov) is a trainer for Tu-22M and Tu-160 pilots, converted at the Kharkov factory from the Tu-134B. Some dozens are in service with CIS military aviation. Nose lengthened and pointed, with the total length increased to 137 ft 6 ins (41.92 m). Because stability reportedly decreased at high angle-of-attack, the allowable take-off weight was reduced to 97,554 lb (44,250 kg). Maximum speed 464 kts (534 mph) 860 km/h at 32,800 ft (10,000 m). Illustrated in the 1996-97 edition of *WA&SD*, page 236.
Tu-135 is a military high command executive transport. Long-range communications system added, including Balkany radio, distinguished by the long antenna 'sting' protruding from the rear fuselage. Passenger cabin divided into 3 compartments, with tables, charts, rest area and communication system room. Several used by the CIS armed forces (carrying civil registrations and marked as Tu-134As).

Tupolev Tu-144LL (NATO name *Charger*)

First flight: 29 November 1996 from Zhukovsky airfield, piloted by Sergei Borisov. Original Tu-144 prototype first flew 31 December 1968, piloted by Eduard Elyan.
Role: Research aircraft based on a converted Tu-144D airliner. Used by the US aircraft industry to assist in the development of a High-Speed Civil Transport (HSCT) aircraft capable of carrying 300 passengers at Mach 2.4. Russia has also used the aircraft to help in the final design of its second-generation supersonic aircraft, the Tu-244 (which see). The US industry team has been led by Boeing (as selected by NASA), with other participants including Pratt & Whitney and General Electric. British companies have also participated in the programme. Tu-144 was chosen because it was available for modification and test, can cruise at 1,349-1,457 kts (1,553-1,678 mph) 2,500-2,700 km/h, and has ample space inside the fuselage for installing the necessary measuring equipment. This particular model of the Tu-144 has the additional benefit of an ejection seat rescue system for the crew. Russian tests of Tu-144LL have been carried out by Tupolev's team, headed by Aleksandr Pukhov.

Development

- 21 May 1997. Tu-144LL flew supersonically on its 6th flight, reaching Mach 1.42 at 39,370 ft (12,000 m) during the 1 hour 3 minute flight from Zhukovsky. During the 7th flight, on 28 May, the aircraft attained Mach 1.8.
- 11 February 1998. Made its 19th and last flight during the test programme.

Details *(Tu-144LL)*

Users: In addition to the prototype of 1968, the Voronezh factory constructed 11 Tu-144s, each powered with 4 Nikolai Kuznetsov NK-144A augmented turbojets (44,080 lbf, 196.1 kN each) and 5 Tu-144Ds with Piotr Kolesov RD36-51A engines (same thrust, but achieved without afterburning). 4 further aircraft were built for static tests. Only 2 Tu-144s remain airworthy, belonging to the eighth production series (each series encompassed 2 aircraft), having the serial numbers *08-01* and *08-02* and registrations *RA-77113* and *RA-77114* respectively. The current Tu-144LL is the converted Tu-144D *RA-77114*, originally completed on 13 April 1981 as the 15th Tu-144 type. *RA-77114* did not make any passenger flights, but was used instead for various test purposes. In July 1983, S. Agapov used this aircraft to set a series of records under the designation Type 101 (its engines were recorded as Type 57s). Before the actual conversion to Tu-144LL, the aircraft had accumulated only 82 hours and 40 minutes flying time.
Tu-144LL test programme schedule: During the first stage of Tu-144LL testing, carried out entirely in Russia and planned for 6 months, the aircraft had been scheduled to perform 32 flights in connection with 6 programmes. However, according to Aleksandr Pukhov, the research programme only required 18 flights to test the following:
- temperature of airframe skin and structure.
- temperature of the engines.
- the effect of ground surface on small aspect ratio wings during the landing approach.
- passenger cabin noise generated by outer air flow.
- characteristics of aircraft stability and manoeuvrability.
- boundary layer friction and pressure coefficients.

In addition, 2 ground tests were completed during September and October 1996, devoted to the aircraft's engines and air intakes, which in the second-generation Tu-244 are entirely redesigned. Conversion of the other airworthy aircraft, *RA-77113*, is also considered.
Crew: 5, including 2 pilots, navigator, flight engineer and test engineer, each occupying an ejection seat. No passengers.
Fuselage: Seats removed from the passenger cabin in order to make space for the laboratory equipment; numerous sensors were installed on the airframe surface.
Construction materials: Light VAD-23 aluminium alloy, steel, and titanium used for the wing leading edges, elevons, rudder and the lower area of the rear fuselage.
Engines: 4 Kuznetsov/Samara NK-32 turbofans, developed originally for Tu-160.
Engine rating: Each 30,865 lbf (137.3 kN) dry, 55,115 lbf (245.18 kN) with afterburning.

Details for Tu-144LL

PRINCIPAL DIMENSIONS:
Wing span: 88 ft 7 ins (27 m)
Maximum length: 196 ft 10 ins (60 m)
WEIGHTS:
Take-off: 440,924 lb (200,000 kg)
Fuel: 224,871 lb (102,000 kg)
PERFORMANCE:
Maximum operating speed: 1,511 kts (1,740 mph) 2,800 km/h
Range with maximum fuel, at supersonic speed: 3,507 naut miles (4,039 miles) 6,500 km

Tupolev Tu-154 (NATO name *Careless*)

First flight: 3 October 1968 for Tu-154 prototype (*CCCP-85000*, piloted by Yuri Sukhov); 1982 for the Tu-152M.
First delivery: May 1971 to Aeroflot (Tu-154 for early cargo, airmail and passenger flights, with scheduled services by Aeroflot from 9 February 1972). Tu-154M first delivered on 27 December 1984.
Role: Medium-range airliner.
Airframe life: 20,000 flying hours or 15,000 cycles.
Sales: Some 1,027 Tu-154s of all versions built at Kuibyshev (now Samara) at time of writing; 158 have been exported to 17 foreign airlines, including those in Afghanistan, Bulgaria, China, Cuba, Czech Republic and Slovakia, Egypt, former East Germany, Hungary, Iraq, North Korea, Latvia, Mongolia, Poland (resold), Romania and Syria. More than 20 leased to Iranian carriers, and another 12 Tu-154Ms have been delivered against an order placed on 3 August 1996. In 1997, Slovakia bought 4 Tu-154Ms in VIP configuration, scheduled for delivery from February 1998.

Details *(Tu-154M)*

Crew: 2 pilots and a flight engineer.
Passengers: Various layouts including 24 first and 154 tourist class, 164 all-tourist class, and 180 all-economy class (6 abreast).
Galley: To the customer's requirements.
Pressurization: 8.41 psi.
Freight hold volume: 176.6 cu ft (5 m^3) under the cabin floor, at

↑ **Tupolev Tu-144LL, used by Russia and the USA as a test-bed** *(Piotr Butowski)*

rear. Unpressurized.
Size of freight doors: 3 ft × 3 ft 7 ins (0.9 × 1.1 m).
Baggage holds: 759.3 cu ft (21.5 m^3) forward, 582.7 cu ft (16.5 m^3) aft. Pressurized. 2 access doors, each 3 ft 11 ins × 4 ft 5 ins (1.2 × 1.35 m).
Wing control surfaces: Ailerons (with tabs), triple-slotted trailing-edge flaps (28° or 15° at take-off, 45° or 36° at landing), leading-edge slats and 4-section spoilers. 4 overwing fences.
Tail control surfaces: T tail, with variable incidence tailplane, elevators with tabs, and rudder.
Flight control system: Hydraulic, but with electric slat, tailplane incidence and tab actuation.
Construction materials: Metal, with tail moving surfaces using honeycomb cores.
Engines: 3 Rybinsk D-30KU-154 II turbofans, 2 with thrust reversers. See Aircraft variants for other engines.
Engine rating: Each 23,149 lbf (103 kN) at take-off. TA-92 APU.
Fuel system: 87,634 lb (39,750 kg). To ensure reliability, fuel from all 6 wing tanks is routed via a collector tank.
Electrical system: 3-phase AC supply via a 40kVA alternator to each engine, producing 200/115 volt at 400Hz. 36 volt, 400Hz stand-by AC supply. 27 volt DC supply. 4 batteries.
Hydraulic system: Triple, each 3,002 psi.
Braking system: Disc, with anti-skid on main units.
De-icing system: Bleed air for engine inlets, wing and tail unit leading edges. Electric for slats.
Radar: Weather radar.
Flight avionics/instrumentation: Meets ICAO Cat II. Includes autopilot, triple inertial navigation system, ground proximity warning system, and HF/VHF communications.

Aircraft variants:
Tu-154 was the initial version, powered with 3 Kuznetsov/Kuibyshev NK-8-2 engines, each 20,943 lbf (93.16 kN). Maximum take-off weight 198,416 lb (90,000 kg). Up to 152 passengers. Range 1,360 naut miles (1,566 miles) 2,520 km with maximum payload. Later upgraded into the more modern versions.
Tu-154A was manufactured from 1973 and introduced NK-8-2U turbofans, each 23,146 lbf (102.96 kN). Maximum take-off weight 207,234 lb (94,000 kg). Up to 158 passengers. Range 1,727 naut miles (1,988 miles) 3,200 km with 35,274 lb (16,000 kg) payload. Later upgraded into the more modern versions.
Tu-154B of 1975 appearance introduced improved high-lift devices and Thomson CSF/SFIM avionics enabling ICAO Cat II

↑ Tupolev Tu-154M when used by the Luftwaffe for Open Skies missions

landings. Maximum take-off weight increased to 216,053 lb (98,000 kg). Up to 158 passengers. Range 2,698 naut miles (3,107 miles) 5,000 km with maximum fuel and 12,677 lb (5,750 kg) payload.
Tu-154B-1 became a Soviet domestic sub-variant for 160 passengers.
Tu-154B-2 manufactured from 1980 became the most numerous version. Similar to B/B-1 but cabin configured for 180 passengers (reduced galley). Many former versions have been upgraded to the B-2 standard.
Tu-154M is a completely upgraded version with new D-30KU-154 II turbofans, and had originally been designated Tu-164. Entered production in 1984 and is the current standard airliner. As detailed.
Tu-154M model 1995 is another current production version, introducing Zhasmin (Jasmine) flight/navigation system which enables ICAO Cat II landing as well as anti-collision radar and GPS. Optional western navigation systems.
Tu-154M for Open Skies missions had been adapted by the German Luftwaffe and entered service on 19 April 1995. It was an ex-GDR Tu-154M (*11+02*) fitted with 3 LMK 2015 photocameras and 3 VOS 60 videocameras. Further installation of infra-red linescanner and synthetic-aperture radar were planned, but the aircraft was lost over the Atlantic on 13 September 1997.
Tu-154M-ON (Otkrytoye Nebo, Open Skies) was to be a Russian adaptation for Open Skies missions, featuring a Vega-M surveillance system including photocameras, TV cameras, RONSAR synthetic-aperture side-looking radar, and Raduga linescan IR sensor. 3 aircraft had been planned to be converted but work stopped when the Russian Duma did not ratify the Open Skies treaty.
Tu-154M2 had been planned as a modification of Tu-154M with PS-90A turbofans for improved fuel economy and to meet noise limits. Maximum take-off weight increased to 229,280 lb (104,000 kg) and maximum landing weight 181,881 lb (82,500 kg). Programme ended.
Tu-154-100 is a higher comfort derivative of Tu-15M, with the first aircraft expected 1998. Modern avionics suite, new passenger cabin arrangement with wider windows, and improved seats and interior.
Tu-154-200 is a projected version powered by 2 Kuznetsov/Samara NK-93 ducted propfans.
Tu-152M-LK1 is an experimental aircraft for cosmonaut training.
Tu-154S appeared in 1981 and is a freighter conversion of the Tu-154B. 10 aircraft converted. 4,061.2 cu ft (115 m^3) useful volume in the Tu-154B conversion, comprising 2,542.7 cu ft (72 m^3) in the cabin (loading via a 9 ft 2 ins × 6 ft 2 ins, 2.8 × 1.87 m port-side cargo door), and 1,518.5 cu ft (43 m^3) under the floor. Roller tracks and ball matting to ease loading of pallets or other cargoes into the main cabin.
Tu-155 and Tu-156 are the Tu-154 derivatives with cryogenic-fuel engines. See separate entry.

Details for Tu-154M

PRINCIPAL DIMENSIONS:
Wing span: 123 ft 2.4 ins (37.55 m)
Maximum length: 157 ft 3 ins (47.925 m)
Maximum height: 37 ft 5 ins (11.4 m)

CABIN:
Width: 11 ft 9 ins (3.58 m)
Height: 6 ft 7.5 ins (2.02 m)
Volume: 5,763.4 cu ft (163.2 m^3)
Main passenger doors: 5 ft 8 ins × 2 ft 7.5 ins (1.73 × 0.8 m)

WINGS:
Area: 2,168.4 sq ft (201.45 m^2)
Aspect ratio: 6.999
Sweepback: 35° at 25% chord

TAIL UNIT:
Tailplane span: 44 ft (13.4 m)

UNDERCARRIAGE:
Type: Retractable, with steerable (±63°) twin nosewheels. 6-wheel main bogies
Main wheel tyre size: 950 × 300 mm (earlier versions 930 × 305 mm)
Nose wheel tyre size: 800 × 225 mm
Wheel base: 62 ft 1 ins (18.92 m)
Wheel track: 37 ft 9 ins (11.5 m)

WEIGHTS:
Empty, operating: 121,915 lb (55,300 kg)
Maximum take-off: 220,462 lb (100,000 kg)
Maximum landing: 176,370 lb (80,000 kg)
Payload: 39,683 lb (18,000 kg)

PERFORMANCE:
Maximum cruise speed: 505 kts (581 mph) 935 km/h
Required field length: 8,205 ft (2,500 m)
Operating ceiling: 39,040 ft (11,900 m)
Range with full fuel: 3,564 naut miles (4,100 miles) 6,600 km
Range with 28,660 lb (13,000 kg) payload: 2,752 naut miles (3,168 miles) 5,100 km
Range with full payload: 2,050 naut miles (2,361 miles) 3,800 km

Tupolev Tu-155 and Tu-156

First flight: 15 April 1988 for Tu-155 (pilot Vladimir Sevankayev). First flight of Tu-156 with NK-89 engines was scheduled for 1997 but was delayed (possibly until 1999).
Role: Derivatives of the Tu-154 featuring cryogenic-fuel engines. Tu-155 is an experimental aircraft, while Tu-156 is planned for cargo (to gain experience) and later passenger carrying (Tu-156M/M2). Cryogenic-fuel programme (originally liquid hydrogen) began in 1979 and was targeted at military hypersonic aircraft, but later switched to cargo/passenger aircraft using liquid natural gas (LNG) fuel, with liquid hydrogen as the next-stage fuel.
Sales: According to Governmental resolution No 368 of 23 April 1994, Samara plant had to convert 3 Tu-154Ms into Tu-156s with NK-89 engines in 1997. Lack of financial allocations caused significant delays in the programme. Currently, the first flight is not expected before 1999, and only 1 aircraft will be converted.

↑ Tupolev Tu-156M2 *(Piotr Butowski)*

Details *(Tu-156S/M)*

Passengers: 135 (Tu-156M) or 31,067 lb (14,500 kg) of cargo (Tu-156S).
Engines: 3 Samara NK-89 turbofans, based on NK-8-2U of Tu-154B.
Engine rating: Each 23,150 lbf (102.97 kN).
Fuel system: LNG fuel is carried in 1 rear fuselage tank, 23 ft (7 m) long and 10 ft (3 m) in diameter (28,660 lb, 13,000 kg), and 2 × 23 ft (7 m) long and 3 ft 3 ins (1 m) diameter underfloor tanks in the front of fuselage (each 4,189 lb, 1,900 kg), all of welded aluminium, covered by 50-mm thermal insulation. Additional 23,369 lb (10,600 kg) of kerosene is carried inside usual wing tanks. Specific fuel flow at 36,100 ft (11,000 m), Mach 0.8 with LNG 0.74; fuel flow 400 g/t-km for LNG, 438.8 g/t-km for kerosene. The kerosene is used for flights to airfields not equipped with LNG infrastructure, as well as being a stand-by fuel. In emergency, the engines can be switched to kerosene in 5 seconds.

Aircraft variants:
Tu-155 is a Tu-154B (*CCCP-85035*) with starboard-side engine replaced by Samara NK-88 working with deep-cooled (lower than 120K) liquid hydrogen fuel. Shown publicly in 1990 at ILA in Hannover.
Tu-156 (Tu-156S) is a projected cargo conversion of the Tu-154S, but powered by 3 NK-89s. As detailed.
Tu-156M is based on the Tu-154M, as a passenger version of the Tu-156 with 3 NK-89s. As detailed.
Tu-156M2 would be a derivative of the Tu-154M2 with LNG fuel (44,092, 20,000 kg in 2 large saddle tanks above the fuselage) and 2 (not 3) PS-90A or NK-94 turbofans. Maximum range 2,158 naut miles (2,485 miles) 4,000 km with 160 passengers.

Details for Tu-156S/M

PRINCIPAL DIMENSIONS:
As for Tu-154M

CABIN:
Length: 60 ft (18.3 m)
Cargo door (Tu-156S): 8 ft 2.5 ins × 5 ft 4 ins (2.5 × 1.62 m)

WEIGHTS:
Empty, operating: 129,191 lb (58,600 kg)
Maximum take-off: 220,462 lb (100,000 kg)
Payload: 30,865 lb (14,000 kg)

PERFORMANCE:
Speed: 459 kts (528 mph) 850 km/h
Required runway length: 8,203 ft (2,500 m) at sea level, ISA
Range with full payload: 1,403 naut miles (1,615 miles) 2,600 km with 37,038 lb (16,800 kg) of LNG fuel; 1,770 naut miles (2,038 miles) 3,280 km with 37,038 lb (16,800 kg) of LNG fuel plus 23,369 lb (10,600 kg) of kerosene; 1,619 naut miles (1,864 miles) 3,000 km with 60,407 lb (27,400 kg) of kerosene

Tupolev Tu-204 and Tu-206

First flight: 2 January 1989 (piloted by Andrey Talalakin).
Certification: 29 December 1994 for Tu-204-100; April 1997 for Tu-204C; 15 July 1997 for Tu 204 120.
First delivery: 1994, when it entered trial operations with Vnukovo Airlines. First scheduled flight on 23 February 1996, flying from Moscow to Mineralnye Vody.
Role: Medium-range airliner, and freighter conversion.
Airframe life: 60,000 flying hours or 45,000 cycles.
Sales: In production by Aviastar Aviation Industrial Complex at Ulyanovsk (Tu-204, Tu-204-100 and Tu-204-300 series). Some 30 aircraft of all Tu-204 versions had been manufactured at the time of writing (including Tu-204-200 series from second production line at Kazan). Users throughout CIS include

↑ Tupolev Tu-204-120 of Sirocco *(Piotr Butowski)*

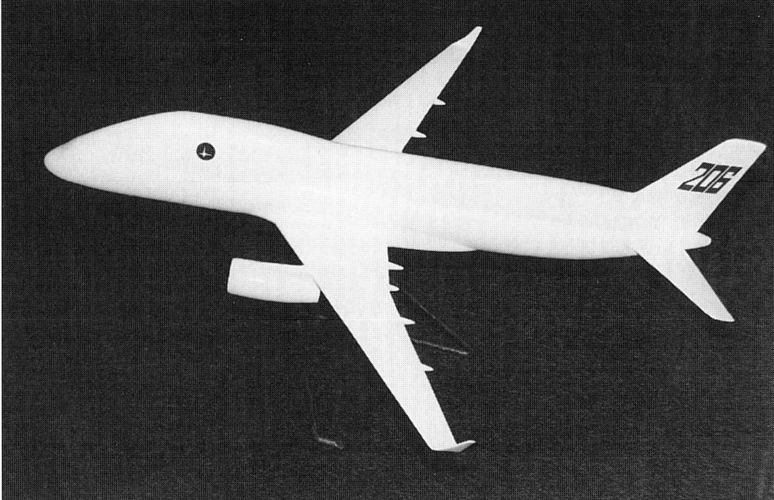

↑ Model of the proposed Tupolev Tu-206 cryogenic-fuel derivative of the Tu-204 *(Piotr Butowski)*

Vnukovo Airlines, Rossiya, Uzbekistan Airways (20 Tu-204-100s leased in March 1997), Oriol-Avia, Aeroflot Russian International Airlines (the first received on 7 April 1995), Kazakhstan Airlines, and Aviastar/Volga Dnepr (2 Tu-204-120Cs ordered in 1997). Also, other CIS operators have expressed interest in the Tu-204, including Khabarovsk Airlines (for 3), KrasAir (10), Tatar Air Lines and Aviastar Asia. Production expected to rise to 35 per year (including Kazan-built versions). Up to 500 Tu-204s are expected to be built for CIS operators. Delivery of 6 Tu-204-100s is expected to Bulgarian Balkan Airlines. Talks with Iranian officials over licensed manufacturing of the Tu-204 in Iran (together with Tu-334 and Antonov An-140) were reported in 1997. Major maintenance facility for Russian and East European aircraft at Minsk aviation repair factory. An order is expected from China for 50 PS-90-powered Tu-204-102s, fitted with the Rockwell-Collins avionics suite.

On 23 March 1996, Tupolev, Aviaexport, Aviastar and Kato Group of Egypt signed a contract, under which Kato Group has exclusive rights for sales of Rolls-Royce powered Tu-204-120 aircraft for 5 years. Kato declared a firm order for 13 aircraft, with another 17 on option. In total, Kato Group expects to sell 150-200 aircraft "initially in Russia and CIS, then in China and the Middle East, then in Europe and the USA". Sirocco consortium was formed for the execution of the programme. Cairo Air, a private airline has been formed by 20 Egyptian entrepreneurs to operate Tu-204-120s ordered by the Kato Group. 6 Tu-204-120s are expected to be ordered by the Egyptian Air Force in 1998 (including 2 in VIP configuration). Tu-204-120 price is $36-38 million.

Details for Tu-204-100

PRINCIPAL DIMENSIONS:
Wing span: 137 ft 10 ins (42 m)
Maximum length: 150 ft 11 ins (46 m)
Maximum height: 45 ft 7 ins (13.9 m)

CABIN:
Length: 99 ft (30.18 m)
Width: 11 ft 8.5 ins (3.57 m)
Height: 7 ft 6 ins (2.28 m)
Main passenger doors: 6 ft 1 ins × 2 ft 9 ins (1.85 × 0.84 m)
Cargo door: See Aircraft variants for freighter conversions

WINGS:
Area: 1,959 sq ft (182 m^2), or 1,980.6 sq ft (184 m^2) for Tu-204-120
Aspect ratio: 9.69, or 9.59 for Tu-204-120
Sweepback: 28°

TAIL UNIT:
Tailplane span: 49 ft 3 ins (15 m)

UNDERCARRIAGE:
Type: Retractable, with twin steerable nosewheels (±70°). 4-wheel main bogies
Main wheel tyre size: 1,070 × 390 mm
Nose wheel tyre size: 840 × 290 mm
Wheel base: 55 ft 9 ins (17 m)
Wheel track: 25 ft 8 ins (7.82 m)

WEIGHTS:
Empty, operating: 129,632 lb (58,800 kg), or 130,734 lb (59,300 kg) for Tu-204-120
Maximum take-off: 227,075 lb (103,000 kg)
Maximum landing: 194,447 lb (88,200 kg)
Payload: 46,297 lb (21,000 kg)

PERFORMANCE:
Cruise speed: 437-459 kts (503-528 mph) 810–850 km/h
Required runway length: 7,382 ft (2,250 m), at 30° C, 730 mm Hg
Cruise altitude: 39,700 ft (12,100 m)
Range with full payload: 2,644 naut miles (3,045 miles) 4,900 km

Details *(Tu-204 and Tu-204-100. See Aircraft variants)*

Crew: 2 pilot operation. Engineer and observer can be carried.
Passengers: 170-214. Typically 214 in all-tourist class layout (6 abreast), or 190 in mixed layout with 12 first class (4 abreast), 35 business and 143 tourist classes (6 abreast). The Ulyanovsk Aviation Industrial Complex Aviastar has formed a joint company with Diamonite Aircraft Furnishings of the UK as Aviastar Interior Corp, to design, develop, certify and manufacture new interiors for the Tu-204, to FAR Pt 25 standards.
Seat pitch: 31.9 ins (81 cm) tourist, 37.8 ins (96 cm) business and 39 ins (99 cm) first class.
Galleys: 2 buffet galleys standard, forward and rear of the passenger cabins, but with customer options.
Freight/baggage hold volume: 388.46 cu ft (11 m^3) nose for 3 × LD3-46 containers, and 543.85 cu ft (15.4 m^3) tail for 5 × LD3-46s, both under the cabin floor.
Wing control surfaces: Aileron, 2-section double-slotted trailing-edge flap, 5-section spoiler, 4-section leading-edge slat, and 2-section airbrake per wing. Drag reducing winglets.
Tail control surfaces: Elevators and rudder.
Flight control system: Triplex digital fly-by-wire, with analog stand-by.
Construction materials: Metal, including aluminium-lithium and titanium, but with composites used for the wingroot fairings, parts of the tail unit, plus various skins and panels, representing some 18% of the structural weight.
Engines: 2 Aviadvigatel PS-90A turbofans. TA-12-60 APU housed in the tailcone.
Engine rating: Each 35,583 lbf (158.3 kN) at take-off.
Fuel system: 72,090 lb (32,700 kg) for Tu-200-100; 71,430 lb (32,400 kg) for Tu-204-120.
Electrical system: 200/115 volt AC supply at 400Hz via 2 generators. 27 volt DC supply.
Hydraulic system: Triple system, each 3,002 psi.
Braking system: Carbon discs, with anti-skid system. Rubix wheels and brakes successfully completed flight testing on the Tu-204-100 in June 1997.
Fire system: 2 litre Halon portable extinguisher in the cockpit, 3 × 6 litre extinguishers on the 9g bulkhead restraint barrier in the courier compartment, 2 × 2 litre Halon and water extinguishers in the emergency equipment closet, and 6 litre Halon extinguisher in the main cargo compartment of the freighter versions.
Radar: Weather radar.
Flight avionics/instrumentation: ICAO Cat IIIa standards. 6 CRT displays for flight, navigation, engine and systems information, triplex autopilot, Honeywell inertial reference system, VOR, DME, satellite navigation, and more. HF/VHF communications.

Aircraft variants:
Tu-204 was the initial version built, with PS-90A engines, 208,557 lb (94,600 kg) take-off weight, 46,297 lb (21,000 kg) payload and 52,910 lb (24,000 kg) of fuel.
Tu-204C is a convertible cargo version, with an 11 ft 2 ins (3.405 m) wide and 7 ft 2 ins (2.19 m) high door added on the port side of the front fuselage. First prototype converted from Tu-204 No 10.
Tu-204-100 is a principal PS-90A-engined version with a maximum take-off weight of 227,075 lb (103,000 kg), allowing an increase in fuel load for longer range.
Tu-204-100F will be a windowless (cabin) freighter variant. Large port-side cargo door. Floor-mounted ball mat at the cargo door entrance and roller tracks thereafter.
Tu-204-102 will be similar to the Tu-204-100 but with Rockwell Collins avionics suite.
Tu-204-120 is a derivative with Rolls-Royce RB211-535E4 engines. Maiden flight was made on 14 August 1992 (prototype *RA-64006*), piloted by Sergei Popov. Became the standard export version. The first series-built Tu-204-120 (No 27, registered *RA-64027*), being the first airframe for Egypt's Kato Aromatic, made its first flight from Aviastar factory on 6 March 1997. The production aircraft differs from the prototype in the design of the pylons, aerodynamics and the avionics.
Tu-204-120C is a cargo variant of the -120.
Tu-204-122 is similar to the Tu-204-120 but features Rockwell Collins avionics.
Tu-204-200 series (Tu-214 and Tu-224) have increased take-off weight, increased payload and more fuel (additional fuel tank in the wing centre section). Manufactured at Kazan. See separate entry.
Tu-204-300 (Tu-234) is a shortened fuselage version, manufactured at Ulyanovsk. See separate entry.
Tu-204-400 will be a 250-passenger version, with a fuselage lengthened to 170 ft 7 ins (52 m).
Tu-204P is a maritime patrol version of Tu-204, now under construction. See Combat section.
Tu-206 is a projected cryogenic-fuel derivative, with PS-92 or NK-94 engines. Gas fuel stored in a large streamline tank superimposed on the fuselage. MTOW 244,161 lb (110,750 kg), maximum payload 55,556 lb (25,200 kg), and fuel 49,604 lb (22,500 kg) of gas plus 12,125 lb (5,500 kg) of kerosene. Range 2,860 naut miles (3,293 miles) 5,300 km with 210 passengers.

Tupolev Tu-214 and Tu-224 (Tu-204-200 series)

Note: Tupolev designates the aircraft as Tu-204-200 series, while Tu-214 and Tu-224 are the commercial names from the Kazan plant.
First flight: 21 March 1996 for Tu-214, piloted by Aleksander Kosyrev.
Certification: April 1997 for a first-stage certificate issued by the Russian Air Register (for flights with a MTOW of 103,000 kg). Certification tests at 110,750 kg were to be completed in October 1997.
Role: Medium-range airliner and freighter conversion. Variant of Tu-204 with take-off weight increased to 244,162 lb (110,750 kg), allowing the payload to be increased to 55,556 lb (25,200 kg) and fuel load to rise to 40,730 litres.
Airframe life: 60,000 flight hours or 45,000 landings.
Sales: Manufactured by Gorbunov KAPO plant at Kazan, Tatarstan. During the Summer of 1997, a Tu-214 was tested, while the second and third airframes were being completed, and KAPO then started assembly of a fourth aircraft. Khabarovsk Airlines

↑ Tupolev Tu-214 *(Piotr Butowski)*

↑ Tupolev Tu-214 6-screen EFIS cockpit *(Piotr Butowski)*

bought 2 aircraft for delivery in 1997. In September 1997, Aeroflot Russian International Airlines placed a firm order for 4 Tu-214C³s. 4 aircraft are to be delivered to Bulgarian Balkan up to the year 2000. Iran has expressed an intention to order 4 Tu-214s. Basic price stated to be up to $30 million (Tu-214).

Details *(Tu-214 [Tu-204-200], unless stated)*

Crew: 2 pilot operation. Engineer and observer can be carried.
Passengers: Standard 210 in single-class layout and 164 in 2-class layout. Also 3-class 170-seat and 2-class 182-seat layouts are available.
Seat pitch: 31.9 ins (81 cm) tourist, 37.8 ins (96 cm) business and 39 ins (99 cm) first class.
Galleys and toilets: 5 buffet galleys and 4 toilets in the 164-seat layout, but with customer options.
Freight hold volume: 1,191.9 cu ft (33.75 m^3). Volume of bulk cargo 201.29 cu ft (5.7 m^3).
Flight control system: Triplex digital fly-by-wire, with analog stand-by.
Engines: 2 Aviadvigatel PS-90A turbofans. TA-12-60 APU housed in the tailcone.
Engine rating: Each 35,583 lbf (158.3 kN) at take-off.
Fuel system: 40,730 litres (72,091 lb, 32,700 kg).
Flight avionics/instrumentation: ICAO Cat IIIa standards. 6 CRT displays for flight, navigation, engine and systems information, triplex autopilot, Honeywell inertial reference system, VOR, DME, satellite navigation, and more. HF/VHF communications.

Aircraft variants:
Tu-214 or ***Tu-204-200*** is the standard passenger version with PS-90A engines, as described.
Tu-214C or ***Tu-204-200C*** is a cargo/combi version, cabin windows retained. Large port-side cargo door.
Tu-214C³ or ***Tu-204-200C³*** (Cargo/Converted/Containerized) is a convertible cargo/combi/passenger version, which can be converted in 1 day. In cargo configuration it carries 8 LD3-46 containers on the lower baggage deck plus 18 in the passenger cabin. First aircraft was under construction at the time of writing. It is expected to be a basic production version.
Tu-214F or ***Tu-204-200F*** is a proposed freighter version without passenger cabin windows. Large port-side cargo door. Floor-mounted ball mat at the cargo door entrance and thereafter roller tracks.
Tu-204-210 is a proposed Tu-214 derivative with Pratt & Whitney PW2240 engines.
Tu-214A was an early name for the Rolls-Royce-engined version.
Tu-224 or ***Tu-204-220*** is a variant with Rolls-Royce RB211-535E4 engines, marketed by Bravia (British Russian Aviation Corp), an organization comprising Tupolev, Aviastar, Avia-export and the Russian branch of Flemings (UK). Integrated avionics system developed for Tupolev by AVIA, the joint venture of Russia's Avionics Research Institute (NIIAO) and AlliedSignal of the USA. EFIS with 6 liquid-crystal displays, dual ARINC 739 flight management system with GPS and associated multi-purpose control and display units, advanced radio management system, traffic alert and collision avoidance system (TCAS II), wide range of CNI options, and Litton or Honeywell inertial reference system. AlliedSignal/Liebherr/Teploobmennik pressurization and air-conditioning systems, 10-15% more effective than Tu-204's, and 20-30% lighter. Wheel brakes fitted with AlliedSignal Landing Systems-developed Carbenix 4000 (carboncarbon material).
Tu-204-222 and ***Tu-204-223*** are variants of the Tu-224 with Rockwell Collins and Sextant Avionique avionics suites respectively.
Tu-224C cargo/combi variant of the Tu-224.
Tu-224C³ cargo/converted/containerized variant of the Tu-224.
Tu-224F windowless freighter versions are under consideration.
Tu-204-230 is a projected variant with 2 × NK-93 propfans, in standard and cryogenic fuel versions.

Details for Tu-214

PRINCIPAL DIMENSIONS:
Wing span: 137 ft 10 ins (42 m)
Maximum length: 150 ft 11 ins (46 m)
Maximum height: 45 ft 7 ins (13.9 m)

WINGS:
Area: 1,980.6 sq ft (184 m^2)
Aspect ratio: 9.59

UNDERCARRIAGE:
Type: Reinforced when compared with Tu-204, with modified wheels with higher brake kinetic energy and Goodyear tyres

WEIGHTS:
Empty, operating: 130,073 lb (59,000 kg)
Maximum take-off: 244,162 lb (110,750 kg)
Payload: 55,556 lb (25,200 kg)

PERFORMANCE:
Cruise speed: 437-459 kts (503-528 mph) 810-850 km/h
Required runway length: 8,629 ft (2,630 m), ISA, sea level
Cruise altitude: 33,135-39,700 ft (10,100-12,100 m)
Range with full payload: 3,416 naut miles (3,933 miles) 6,330 km

Tupolev Tu-230

First flight: Project announced Summer 1995. No anticipated flight date known at the time of writing.
Programme manager: Valentin Bliznyuk.
Role: Light-medium freighter to replace the An-72 and, partly, An-12.
Sales: Will be manufactured at Samara. The possible sales are estimated by Tupolev at 700-1,000 aircraft worldwide.

Details for Tu-230

PRINCIPAL DIMENSIONS:
Wing span: 107 ft 7 ins (32.8 m)
Maximum length: 101 ft 6.5 ins (30.95 m)
Maximum height: 34 ft 9 ins (10.6 m)

CABIN:
Length: 52 ft 6 ins (16 m)
Width: 10 ft 4 ins (3.15 m)
Height: 9 ft 10 ins (3 m)

WINGS:
Area: 1,087.15 sq ft (101 m^2)
Aspect ratio: 10.65

UNDERCARRIAGE:
Type: Retractable, with twin steerable nosewheels. 4-wheel main bogies

WEIGHTS:
Maximum take-off: 116,404 lb (52,800 kg)
Payload, maximum: 39,683 lb (18,000 kg)

PERFORMANCE:
Cruise speed: 432-459 kts (497-528 mph) 800-850 km/h
Required runway length: 7,218 ft (2,200 m)
Cruise altitude: 36,090 ft (11,000 m)
Range with full fuel: 4,640 naut miles (5,344 miles) 8,600 km
Range with 26,455 lb (12,000 kg) payload: 1,619 naut miles (1,864 miles) 3,000 km
Range with 22,046 lb (10,000 kg) payload: 1,942 naut miles (2,237 miles) 3,600 km

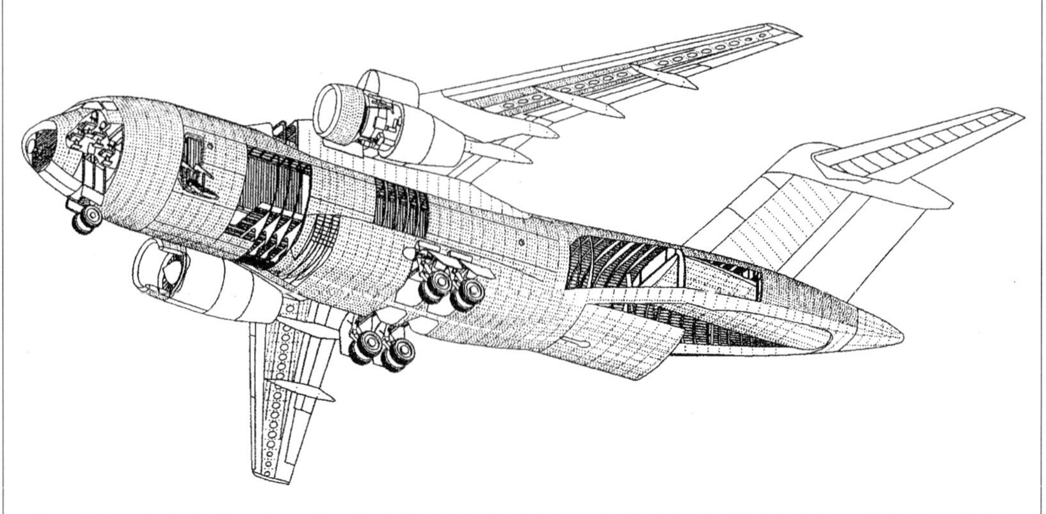
↑ Tupolev Tu-230 *(courtesy Tupolev)*

Crew: 2 pilots and a flight engineer. Cockpit is similar to that in the larger Tu-330 transport.
Freight hold access: Rear loading ramp/door, 10 ft 4 ins (3.15 m) wide and 9 ft 10 ins (3 m) high.
Wing characteristics: High-mounted supercritical, based on the Tu-334 wing. Large over-fuselage fairing to blend the carry-through structure. Substantial leading-edge sweepback, and trailing-edge sweepback on the outer panels only.
Wing control surfaces: Ailerons, 2-section flaps and multi-section leading-edge slats.
Tail control surfaces: T-tail, with sweptback tailplane, elevators and 2-section rudder.
Construction materials: About 75% of assemblies come from the Tu-334 airliner, to reduce design and construction cost and time.
Engines: 2 Ivchenko PROGRESS/Zaporozhye D-436T2 turbofans. Alternatively CFM56-3Cs.
Engine rating: Each 18,078 lbf (80.42 kN).

Aircraft variants:
Tu-230 is the standard civil and military transport, as detailed.
Tu-230LNG is a projected version with liquid gas fuelled T-436T2 engines.

Tupolev Tu-234 (Tu-204-300 series)

Note: Tupolev designates the aircraft as Tu-204-300 series, while Tu-234 is the commercial name from the Kazan plant.
First flight: Rolled-out at the MosAeroshow on 25 August 1995 but it had not flown at the time of writing, when Tupolev declined to specify any expected date (is likely to be in 1998).
Role: Shorter length variant of the Tu-204. To be manufactured at Aviastar plant at Ulyanovsk.
Passengers: 166.
Seat pitch: 31.9 ins (81 cm).
Engines: 2 Aviadvigatel PS-90P turbofans (Tu-204-300) or Rolls-Royce RB211-535E4s (Tu-204-320).
Engine rating: Each 35,585 lbf (158.3 kN) at take-off.

Aircraft variants:
Short-range version with 186,950 lb (84,800 kg) MTOW, 39,863 lb (18,000 kg) payload, maximum payload range of 1,295 naut miles (1,491 miles) 2,400 km, and design range of 1,835 naut miles (2,112 miles) 3,400 km.
Medium-range version with 227,075 lb (103,000 kg) MTOW, 39,863 lb (18,000 kg) payload, and maximum payload and design ranges of 3,590 naut miles (4,132 miles) 6,650 km and 4,075 naut miles (4,691 miles) 7,550 km respectively.
Long-range version with 227,075 lb (103,000 kg) MTOW, 35,274 lb (16,000 kg) payload, and maximum payload and design ranges of 3,885 naut miles (4,473 miles) 7,200 km and 4,991 naut miles (5,747 miles) 9,250 km respectively.

Details for Tu-234

PRINCIPAL DIMENSIONS:
Wing span: 137 ft 9.5 ins (42 m)
Maximum length: 131 ft 3 ins (40 m)
Maximum height: 45 ft 7 ins (13.9 m)

WEIGHTS:
See Aircraft variants

PERFORMANCE:
Cruise speed: 448-459 kts (516-528 mph) 830-850 km/h
Approach speed: 121 kts (140 mph) 225 km/h
Take-off distance: 6,726 ft (2,050 m), 30° C
Landing distance: 8,203 ft (2,500 m)
Operating altitude: 39,700 ft (12,100 m)
Range: See Aircraft variants

↓ Tupolev Tu-234 rolled-out at the MosAeroshow in Zhukovsky *(Piotr Butowski)*

Tupolev Tu-244

Role: Supersonic airliner.
Noise levels: To meet FAR Pt 36 Chapter 3.

Aims

- To comply with the latest sonic boom, noise and ecology requirements.
- High fuel-to-weight ratio, quoted by Tupolev as 51-52% fuel to take-off weight, which is 1.5-2% greater than for first-generation SSTs.
- High lift/drag ratio, quoted by Tupolev as K=10 at Mach 2 and K=15 at Mach 0.9.

Development

- Project stage. Design is still under development, so the specific characteristics vary; for example, early data quoted MTOW of 674,614-683,432 lb (306,000-310,000 kg) and 249 passengers, and later MTOW of 771,617 lb (350,000 kg) and 300 passengers. Current data (at time of writing) are quoted below.

↑ Model of the Tupolev Tu-244 *(Piotr Butowski)*

Passengers: 269.
Cockpit: No pivoting nose as for Tu-144 and Concorde; visibility necessary for taxiing, take-off and landing will be provided by opto-electronic day-and-night all-weather system.
Wing characteristics: Cranked delta, with 7 trailing-edge control surfaces per wing and 4-section leading-edge slats.
Tail control surfaces: 2-section rudder.
Fuselage: Long, narrow and pointed, as for Tu-144 and Concorde first-generation SSTs.
Construction materials: Mainly aluminium alloys and composite materials, but with VT-6Ch titanium alloy for wing torque box.
Engines: 4 in separate nacelles. Engines have not been selected, and 2 categories are being considered: new-generation variable-cycle engines or more conventional 1:1 bypass-ratio turbofans with effective noise suppressors.
Engine rating: Each 59,520 lbf (264.76 kN).

Details for Tu-244

PRINCIPAL DIMENSIONS:
Wing span: 147 ft 8 ins (45 m)
Maximum length: 288 ft 9 ins (88 m)
Maximum height: 49 ft 3 ins (15 m)
Fuselage diameter: 12 ft 10 ins (3.9 m)

WINGS:
Area: 10,064 sq ft (935 m^2)
Aspect ratio: 2.166

UNDERCARRIAGE:
Type: 4-point type with 2-wheel nose unit, 2 × 8-wheel bogies under the wing centre-section, and single 8-wheel bogie under the fuselage

WEIGHTS:
Maximum take-off: 716,500 lb (325,000 kg)
Payload: 55,115 lb (25,000 kg)
Fuel: 352,740 lb (160,000 kg)

PERFORMANCE:
Maximum speed: Mach 2
Required runway length: 9,845 ft (3,000 m)
Operating altitude: 59,055-65,615 ft (18,000-20,000 m)
Range with full fuel: 4,964 naut miles (5,716 miles) 9,200 km

Tupolev Tu-304 and Tu-306

First flight: Planned for 2001.
Role: Long-range airliner. Freighter version possible.
Airport limits: ACNR (A=80 mN/m3) <68.
Passengers: 282 to 392.
Construction materials: Metal, except 15% composites.
Engines: 2 Samara NK-44 turbofans. Possible use of Rolls-Royce Trent 884 or 890 turbofans.
Engine rating: Each 86,500 lbf (384.78 kN).
Fuel system: 198,415 lb (90,000 kg).
Flight avionics/instrumentation: Suited to ICAO Cat IIIa landing.

Aircraft variants:
Tu-304 is a conventionally powered airliner, as detailed. Several configurations have been shown, the most recent at Farnborough 1996 being a convertible passenger/cargo aircraft with twin fins and rear ramp (details for this design are quoted).
Tu-306 is a cryogenic fuel derivative with TV7-46 engines, 132,277 lb (60,000 kg) of liquid gas fuel, 450 passengers and 4,856 naut miles (5,592 miles) 9,000 km range.

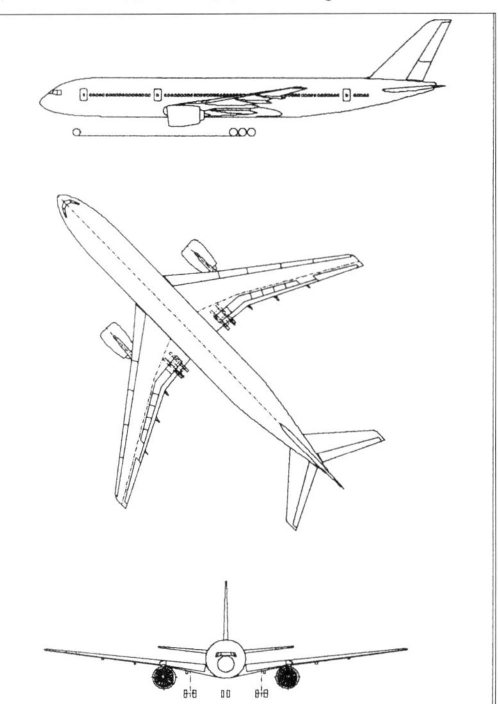

↑ Tupolev Tu-304 general arrangement with Rolls-Royce engines *(courtesy Tupolev)*

Details for Tu-304

PRINCIPAL DIMENSIONS:
Wing span: 187 ft (57 m)
Maximum length: 180 ft (54.86 m)
Maximum height: 49 ft 3 ins (15 m)

WINGS:
Area: 3,713.5 sq ft (345 m²)
Aspect ratio: 9.42
Sweepback: 33° 18'

UNDERCARRIAGE:
Type: Retractable, with twin steerable nosewheels. 6-wheel main bogies

WEIGHTS:
Maximum take-off: 551,155 lb (250,000 kg)
Payload: 176,370 lb (80,000 kg)

PERFORMANCE:
Maximum speed: Mach 0.85
Required runway length: 10,500 ft (3,200 m) at 30° C and 1,115 ft (340 m) above sea level
Cruise altitude: 36,090 ft (11,000 m)
Range with full payload: 3,777 naut miles (4,350 miles) 7,000 km
Range with 392 passengers: 5,935 naut miles (6,835 miles) 11,000 km

Tupolev Tu-324

First flight: Expected 2000.
Role: Regional and business transport. A priority programme of Tupolev, with series manufacturing under preparation at Kazan. Government decree of 28 February 1996 expected state support.
Airframe life: 60,000 flying hours or 30,000 cycles.
Passengers: 50 tourist-class (31.9 ins, 81 cm seat pitch) or 44 mixed (10 seats at 36.6 ins, 93 cm pitch and the rest at 31.9 ins, 81 cm) for the Tu-324 regional transport, or 8-9 business or 1-4 VIPs for the Tu-324A business jet version.
Wing control surfaces: Aileron, 2-section flap, 4-section leading-edge slat, 2-section spoiler (with aileron functions) and 2-section airbrakes ahead of inboard flap section.
Tail control surfaces: Elevators and rudder with tab.
Engines: 2 General Electric CF34-3VB1 or 8,532 lbf (37.95 kN) Ivchenko PROGRESS/Zaporozhye AI-22 turbofans. Soyuz R-126-300s were considered initially.
Fuel system: 13,227 lb (6,000 kg).
Flight avionics/instrumentation: ICAO Cat IIIa standards.

Aircraft variants:
Tu-324 (sometime named ***Tu-324R***) is the standard regional airliner.

↑ **Tupolev Tu-324** *(Piotr Butowski)*

Details for Tu-324

PRINCIPAL DIMENSIONS:
Wing span: 76 ft 1 ins (23.2 m)
Maximum length: 82 ft 8 ins (25.2 m)
Maximum height: 23 ft 4 ins (7.1 m)

WEIGHTS:
Maximum take-off: 52,249 lb (23,700 kg)
Payload: 12,125 lb (5,500 kg)

PERFORMANCE:
Cruise speed: 448 kts (516 mph) 830 km/h
Required runway length: 5,910 ft (1,800 m)
Range with 50 passengers: 1,350 naut miles (1,553 miles) 2,500 km
Range with 44 passengers: 1,619 naut miles (1,864 miles) 3,000 km

Tu-324A (administrativnyi) is a business/VIP version with shortened fuselage. Range 3,777 naut miles (4,350 miles) 7,000 km with 8-9 passengers. Tupolev estimates demand for the Tu-324A at 250 aircraft throughout CIS.

Tupolev Tu-330 and Tu-338

First flight: Initially scheduled for 1996, now probably 1998.
Certification: Scheduled for 1998 but will be delayed.
Programme manager: Valentin Bliznyuk.
Role: Medium freighter, as a replacement for the An-12 and possible competitor to the An-70. See Aircraft variants.

Development

- Spring 1993. Project announced.
- 23 April 1994. Russian Prime Minister, Victor Chernomyrdin, signed a Governmental resolution to finance the Tu-330 programme. According to this, the Tupolev Design Bureau and KAPO production plant in Kazan are obliged to complete the tests and obtain the certificate for the Tu-330 in 1998.

Details

Sales: Possible sales inside CIS are estimated at 140-170 aircraft for civil use and an unspecified number for military, plus 40-50 outside CIS for both military and civil use. According to the Governmental resolution (see above), a series of 10 aircraft should have been completed at the Gorbunov plant in Kazan before 1998, but during 1997 Governmental financial support for this programme fell short of that required (amounting to only 5% of the needed 50 billion roubles).
Crew: 2 pilots and a flight engineer. Fighter-type sticks rather than the usual wheels or yokes.
Freight hold access: Rear loading ramp/door of 13 ft 2 ins × 13 ft 2 ins (4 × 4 m). Side loading door.
Wing characteristics: High-mounted supercritical, with anhedral, based on the Tu-204 wing. Large over-fuselage fairing to blend the carry-through structure. Substantial leading-edge sweepback (probably 28°), and trailing-edge sweepback on the outer panels only. Winglets.
Wing control surfaces: Ailerons, 2 or 3-section trailing-edge double-slotted flaps, multi-section airbrakes and 5-section spoilers, plus 4-section leading-edge slats.
Tail control surfaces: 2-section elevators on the dihedral tailplane, and 2-section rudder.
Construction materials: About 75% of construction elements are taken from the Tu-204-200 airliner, to reduce design and construction cost and time.
Engines: 2 Aviadvigatel PS-90AT turbofans. Alternative engines could be Rolls-Royce RB211-535s or Pratt & Whitney PW2000s.
Engine rating: Each 35,585 lbf (158.3 kN).
Radar: Gukol navigation/weather radar.

Aircraft variants:
Tu-330 is the standard medium transport, as detailed.
Tu-330VT (voyenno-transportnyi) is a military version equipped with specialized communications and self-protection systems. Tanker, radio relay, medevac, firefighting and other versions are being considered.
Tu-338 is a projected version with liquid gas-fuelled NK-94 engines.

Details for Tu-330

PRINCIPAL DIMENSIONS:
Wing span: 142 ft 9 ins (43.5 m)
Maximum length: 137 ft 9.5 ins (42 m)
Maximum height: 45 ft 11 ins (14 m)

CABIN:
Length: 64 ft (19.5 m)
Width: 13 ft 2 ins (4 m)
Height: 11 ft 8 ins to 13 ft 2 ins (3.55 to 4 m)

WINGS:
Area: 1,913.8 sq ft (177.8 m²)
Aspect ratio: 10.64

UNDERCARRIAGE:
Type: Retractable, with twin steerable nosewheels. 6-wheel main bogies

WEIGHTS:
Maximum take-off: 228,178 lb (103,500 kg)
Payload: 77,162 lb (35,000 kg)

PERFORMANCE:
Cruise speed: 432-459 kts (497-528 mph) 800-850 km/h
Cruise altitude: 36,090 ft (11,000 m)
Range with full fuel: 4,644 naut miles (5,344 miles) 8,600 km
Range with 66,139 lb (30,000 kg) payload: 1,620 naut miles (1,864 miles) 3,000 km using 7,218 ft (2,200 m) concrete runway
Range with 44,092 lb (20,000 kg) payload: 3,024 naut miles (3,480 miles) 5,600 km using 7,218 ft (2,200 m) concrete runway

Tupolev Tu-334, Tu-336 and Tu-354

First flight: Airframe (without engines and some systems) rolled-out at MosAeroshow on 26 August 1995. Most recent announcement (at time of writing) claimed that the first flight would be made in late 1998. Pilot Vladimir Matveyev.
Programme manager: Igor Kalygin.
Certification: Planned 1997, but expected in September 1999.
Role: Medium-range airliner.

Aims

- To replace the Tu-134 and Yak-42.
- Planned as a family of aircraft with varying range/payload specifications, plus freighter variants

Development

- 1994. Intended first flight, but delayed. First prototype fitted out at the Zhukovsky Flight Test Centre. Static testing at TSAGI.

Details

Sales: 3 flying prototypes plus 2 static test airframes under construction; 2 prototypes constructed at the Tupolev works in Moscow (including 1 for static tests), 2 others in Kiev (including 1 for fatigue tests) and 1 at Taganrog. Series production tooling is ready. Currently, the only funds for the programme have come from Ukraine (Tu-334 manufacturing at Kiev is included into the

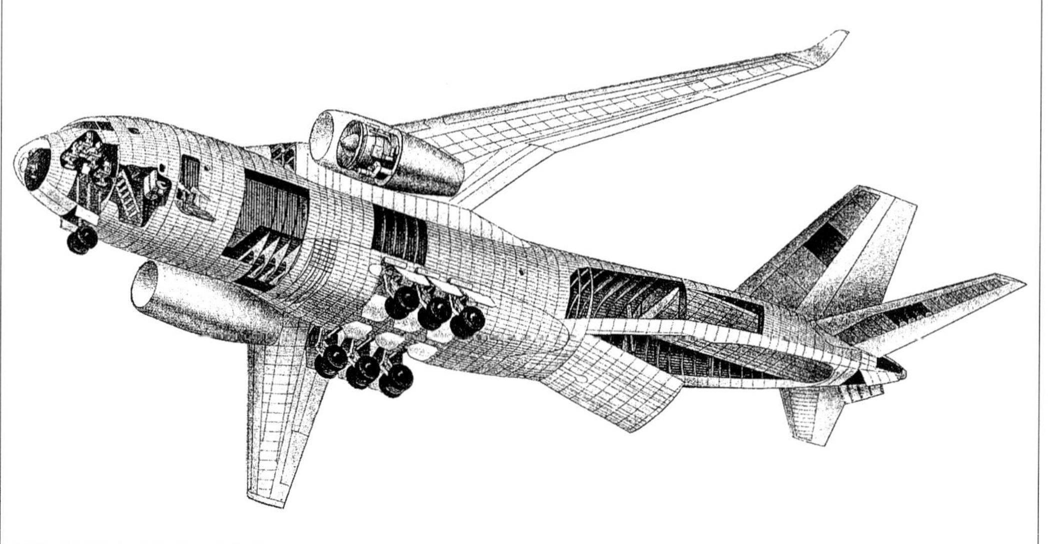

↑ **Tupolev Tu-330** *(courtesy Tupolev)*

Ukrainian Governmental programme). At least 14 options from Russian airlines, including the Siberian Tyumenaviatrans, Komi-Avia and Moscow's Vnukovo Airlines. Tupolev estimates that the Russian market will need 160 Tu-334s in the coming few years; approximate price is $14-15 million. Talks with Iranian officials over licensed manufacturing of the Tu-334 in Iran were reported in 1997. Long-range Tu-354 (Tu-334-100D) derivative is planned to be manufactured at the Aviakor aircraft plant in Samara.

Details *(Tu-334-100 [see Aircraft variants])*

Crew: 2 or 3, with additional provision for an observer or instructor.
Passengers: 102 in all-tourist class layout. Passenger doors in the forward and aft port fuselage side. Alternatives include 92 mixed class, comprising 8 first class (4 abreast) and 84 tourist (6 abreast), or 72 comprising 12 first class and 60 tourist.
Seat pitch: 30.7 ins (78 cm) tourist, 40 ins (102 cm) first class, and 37.8 ins (96 cm) business class when provided. See Aircraft variants.
Galleys: Buffet galley aft of cockpit, with a second in the tail section.
Freight hold access: Starboard side doors for underfloor baggage/cargo compartments.
Baggage compartment/hold: 572.1 cu ft (16.2 m^3) volume, length 13 ft 5.5 ins (4.1 m) + 9 ft 11 ins (3 m), and height 3 ft 11 ins (1.2 m).
Wing characteristics: Derived from the Tu-204 wing. Dihedral. Winglets.
Wing control surfaces: Ailerons, 2-section flaps, 4-section leading-edge slats, 2-section spoilers (with aileron functions) and 2-section airbrakes ahead of inboard flap sections.
Tail control surfaces: Elevators and 2-section rudder.
Flight control system: Fly-by-wire. Emergency mechanical/hydraulic back-up for elevators and rudder.
Construction materials: Principally metal, but with 20% composites and other materials by structure weight.
Engines: 2 Ivchenko PROGRESS/Zaporozhye D-436T1 turbofans. Alternative BMW Rolls-Royce BR715-55s. See Aircraft variants.
Engine rating: Each 16,535 lbf (73.55 kN).
Fuel system: 21,032 lb (9,540 kg).
Flight avionics/instrumentation: Meets ICAO Cat IIIa for landing. EFIS cockpit with 6 displays.

Aircraft variants:
Tu-334-100 is the standard version with D-436T1 engines, as detailed.
Tu-334-100C is a convertible cargo/passenger version. As Tu-334-100 but with a large cargo door on the port side of the front fuselage.

Details for Tu-334-100, *with Tu-334-200 in italics*

PRINCIPAL DIMENSIONS:
Wing span: 97 ft 8 ins (29.77 m), *107 ft (32.607 m)*
Maximum length: 102 ft 7 ins (31.26 m), *115 ft 4.5 ins (35.164 m)*
Maximum height: 30 ft 9 ins (9.38 m) or 28 ft 4 ins (8.625 m), *29 ft 9 ins (9.05 m)*

CABIN:
Length: 58 ft 6 ins (17.84 m)
Width: 11 ft 8 ins (3.57 m) at floor, *the same*
Height: 7 ft 1 ins (2.155 m), *the same*
Volume: 4,167.13 cu ft (118 m^3)

WINGS:
Aerofoil section: Supercritical
Area: 895.84 sq ft (83.226 m^2), *1,076.4 sq ft (100 m^2)*
Aspect ratio: 10.649, *10.632*
Sweepback: 24°

UNDERCARRIAGE:
Type: Retractable, with twin wheels on each unit. Lever type main legs. *Tu-334-200 has 4-wheel main bogies*
Wheel base: 38 ft 7 ins (11.75 m)

WEIGHTS:
Empty: 66,249 lb (30,050 kg), *75,783 lb (34,375 kg)*
Maximum take-off: 101,633 lb (46,100 kg), *120,813 lb (54,800 kg)*
Maximum landing: 95,900 lb (43,500 kg)
Payload: 24,251 lb (11,000 kg), *29,762 lb (13,500 kg)*

PERFORMANCE:
Cruise speed: 432-443 kts (497-510 mph) 800-820 km/h, *432 kts (497 mph) 800 km/h*
Balanced runway length: 7,546 ft (2,300 m) at 30° C
Cruise altitude: 34,775-36,420 ft (10,600-11,100 m), *the same*
Range with 21,363 lb (9,690 kg) payload: 971 naut miles (1,118 miles) 1,800 km, *1,187 naut miles (1,367 miles) 2,200 km*

↑ **Tupolev Tu-334 at Zhukovsky** *(Piotr Butowski)*

Tu-134-100M has an extended range (1,683 naut miles, 1,938 miles, 3,120 km with 102 passengers) due to increased take-off weight (105,160 lb, 47,700 kg).
Tu-334-100D or ***Tu-354*** has the same seating capacity as the -100, but has D-436T2 engines (see below). Wing span increased to 107 ft (32.6 m), wing area 1,076.4 sq ft (100 m^2), length 104 ft 2 ins (31.76 m), and height 30 ft 10 ins (9.4 m). Take-off weight 119,975 lb (54,420 kg). Fuel capacity increased to 34,613 lb (15,700 kg) for a 2,214 naut mile (2,547 mile) 4,100 km range with 102 passengers. 4-wheel main undercarriage bogies.
Tu-334-120 is similar to the Tu-334-100 but has BMW Rolls-Royce BR710-48 engines. Range 1,484 naut miles (1,709 miles) 2,750 km with 102 passengers.
Tu-334-120D is similar to the Tu-334-100D but has BR715-55 engines. Range 2,266 naut miles (2,610 miles) 4,200 km.
Tu-334-200 is derived from -100D but with an extended fuselage for 126 passengers in an all-tourist layout at 31.9 ins (81 cm) seat pitch, or 110 in a mixed layout with 8 first class at 39 ins (99 cm) pitch and 102 tourist (aircraft length is 115 ft 2 ins, 35.1 m). It has 18,078 lbf (80.42 kN) D-436T2 engines, 30,402 lb (13,790 kg) fuel, 120,813 lb (54,800 kg) take-off weight, and range of 1,187 naut miles (1,367 miles) 2,200 km with 126 passengers.
Tu-334-200C is a cargo derivative of Tu-334-200.
Tu-334-220 is a version of Tu-334-200 with BR715-55 engines.
Tu-336 is a projected cryogenic-fuel derivative.

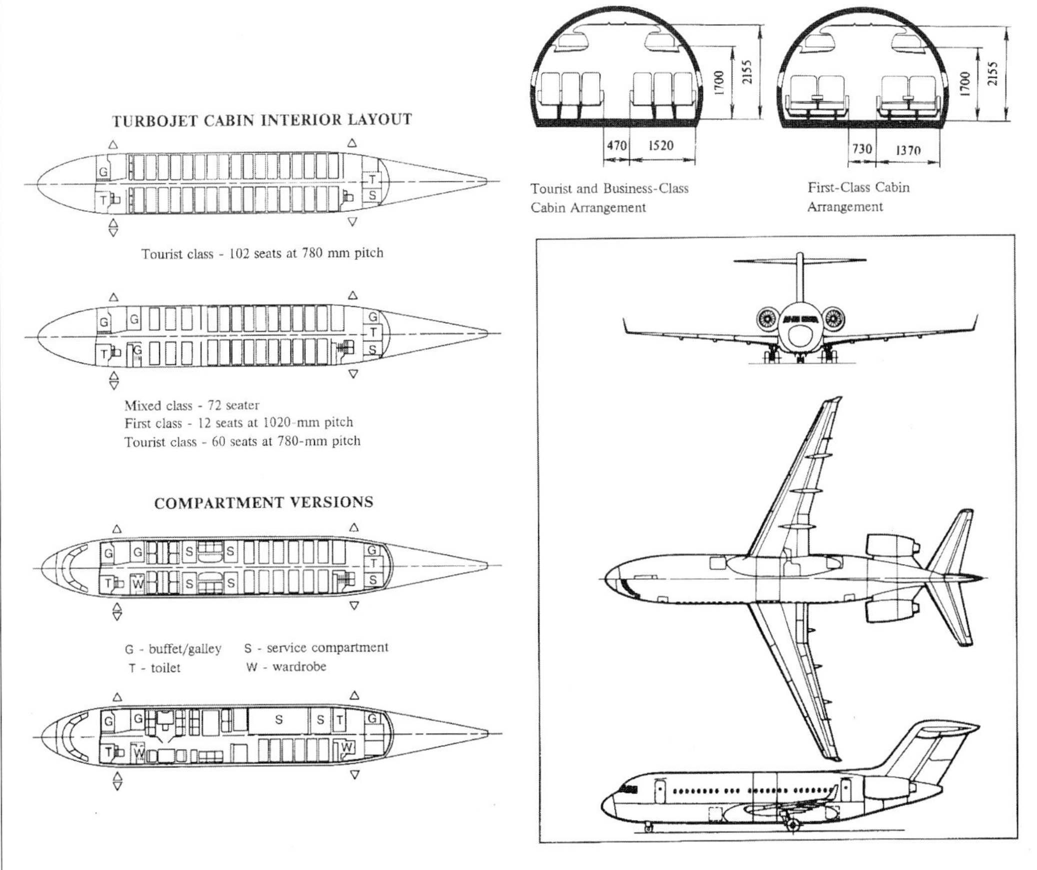

↑ **Tupolev Tu-334-100 cabin layouts and general arrangement** *(courtesy Tupolev)*

Tu-334

1 Nose radom
2 Short-range radio navigation system antenna
3 Meteorological radar
4 ILS antenna
5 Front pressure bulkhead
6 Flight compartment
7 Windshield (triplex acrylic plastic)
8 Side DV-window
9 Forward instrument panel
10 Centre console with throttle levers
11 Fully adjustable crew seats
12 Overhead aircraft systems panel
13 Pre-flight test panel
14 Cabin air-conditioning duct
15 Noze undercarriage bay
16 NLG with one-chamber shock strut and steering control assembly
17 Antenna units
18 Galley
19 Toilet
20 Passenger service doors, incorporating escape chutes
21 Forward bulkhead with curtains (honeycomb composite)
22 Aircraft identification system antenna
23 MLS antenna
24 CAS antenna
25 Overhead panel (prepreg)
26 Passenger windows oriented acrylic plastic
27 Accessory compartment
28 Equipment rack
29 Tourist-class cabin (102 seats at 810 mm pitch)
30 VHF radio antenna
31 SNS antenna
32 Overhead passenger luggage stowage bins
33 Forward freight hold (11.7 cu.m)
34 Freight door 1165×1373 mm (vertical size-1030 mm)
35 Transverse floor beams, supporting floor panels
36 Seat rails
37 Flooring with silicon rubber based carpet (honeycomb)
38 Passenger cabin air conditioning duct
39 AIR COND unit (air cooling unit)
40 Ground AIR COND connection
41 Warm-air duct for passenger cabin heating
42 SatCom antenna
43 Upper ANTI-COOL LT
44 TRSP antenna
45 Fuselage frames (riverted)
46 Strong frames (built-up)
47 Cabin sidewall panels (prepreg)
48 Wing center section (built-up)
49 Main landing gear bay
50 Rear bulkhead with curtains (honeycomb composite)
51 Toilet
52 Cabin attendant coat room
53 Rear pressure dome
54 Rear accessory compartment
55 Hydraulic system components
56 APU section fireproof baffle
57 APU
58 APU section
59 APU cooling shutters
60 Exhaust and tailcone cooling shutters
61 Fin front spar attachment lugs
62 Fin front spar (built-up)
63 Detachable vertical stabilizer leading edge (composite)
64 Rear vertical stabilizer spar (built-up)
65 Two-section rudder (honeycomb with composite skins)
66 Machined panels
67 Vertical stabilizer ribs (riveted)
68 All-moving two-spar tailplane
69 Tailplane hydraulic actuators
70 Detachable tailplane leading edge
71 Elevator (honeycomb with composite skins)
72 Tailplane ribs (rivetcd)
73 Static dischargers
74 Engine nacelle
75 Air intake with soundproof panels
76 Cowl panels
77 Two-shaft turbofan with thrust reverser in bypass duct
78 Engine starter air supply duct
79 Multi-section wing/fuselage fairing
80 Fairing structural elements
81 Machined main undercarriage support beam
82 Undercarriage support beam hingle fitting bell crank
83 Undercarriage support beam rod
84 Main landing gear
85 Two-spar wing box (built-up)
86 Front wing spar (built-up)
87 Accessory door panel
88 Rear spar (built-up)
89 Machined stringers (pressed sections)
90 Box stringer for fuel tank drain
91 Supporting ribs (built-up)
92 Sealed ribs (built-up)
93 Ribs (built-up)
94 Four-piece slat (built-up metal) with tail section (composite)
95 Structural walls with slat attachment fitting load carrying pulleys
96 Leading edge slat tracks
97 Leading edge slat drive shafts
98 Leading edge actuator (balled-screw)
99 Machined lower central wing panel with access doors
100 Low wing panel (built-up)
101 Fuel system components
102 Two-segment air brake (composite)
103 Aft of the spar wing panels (composite)
104 Two-segment spoiler (composite)
105 Two-segment flap (composite)
106 Flap actuator fairing
107 Aileron (honeycomb with composite skins)
108 End flap-track fairing
109 Drain fuel tank
110 Fuel system drain intake
111 "Dry" cell
112 Rear wing-tip navigation light
113 Navigation lights
114 Vertical winglet
115 Static dischargers

↑ **Tupolev Tu-334 cutaway** *(courtesy Tupolev)*

Tupolev Tu-404

First flight: Active project, but no expected first flight date has been received.
Role: 700-850 seat giant airliner, called also 'mega-carrier'. Also a freighter version is proposed in newest configuration.

Aircraft variants:
3 fundamentally different configurations have been shown since June 1993, when first announced in Paris, as follows:
Flying wing with some 100 ft (30.5 m) wide fuselage/wing centre section, moderately-swept outer wings and twin fins. Overall span is about 312 ft (95 m), length 164 ft (50 m), and capacity 700-750 passengers. 6 pusher propfan engines or high-bypass ratio turbofans (each 48,560-55,075 lbf, 216-245 kN) fitted at the fuselage/centre wing trailing edge.
Conventional low-wing monoplane with 4 extra-large turbofans in the 88,125-110,150 lbf, 392-490 kN thrust class (Samara NK-44, Pratt & Whitney PW4000, or Rolls-Royce Trent) on underwing pylons. 3-deck arrangement, with 2 upper decks for passengers (750 passengers in 3-class layout). Wing span 252 ft 7 ins (77 m), length 284 ft 1 ins (86.6 m), maximum take-off weight 1,333,800 lb (605,000 kg), cruise speed 486 kts (559 mph) 900 km/h, and range with maximum payload 4,964 naut miles (5,717 miles) 9,200 km.
2 wings in tandem was the last configuration shown in September 1996 at Farnborough. Front wing is high-mounted, rear is low-mounted. 2 engines of the same type as for the previous design, suspended under each wing. The design is proposed in a convertible passenger/cargo version with a wide rear loading ramp. 2 fins. Following details apply to this configuration.

↑ **Tupolev Tu-404 in flying-wing configuration** *(Piotr Butowski)*

Details for Tu-404

PRINCIPAL DIMENSIONS:
Maximum length: 203 ft 5 ins (62 m)
Maximum height: 51 ft 10 ins (15.8 m)
Front wing span: 107 ft 7 ins (32.8 m)
Rear wing span: 183 ft 9 ins (56 m)

WEIGHTS:
Maximum take-off: 1,031,762 lb (468,000 kg)
Payload: 220,462 lb (100,000 kg)
Maximum fuel: 318,127 lb (144,300 kg)

PERFORMANCE:
Mach number: 0.85
Cruise altitude: 39,370 ft (12,000 m)
Range: 4,802 naut miles (5,530 miles) 8,900 km with 850 passengers

Tupolev Tu-414

Role: Project for a regional and business transport.
Crew: 2.
Passengers: 70 for the regional transport version, 19 in business layout or 1-4 VIPs.
Wing control surfaces: Ailerons, multi-section flaps, leading-edge slats and spoilers.
Tail control surfaces: Elevators and rudder.
Engines: 2 Ivchenko PROGRESS/Zaporozhye D-436T1 turbofans. Alternative BMW Rolls-Royce BR710s.
Engine rating: 16,535 lbf (73.55 kN).

Aircraft variants:
Tu-414 is the basic regional transport for 70 passengers, as detailed. Originally, the name Tu-414 was assigned to the business version, when the regional transport was known as Tu-424.
Tu-414A (administrativnyi) is a long-range VIP/business version, as detailed.
Tu-414D (dalnyi) is a longer range (5,342 naut miles, 6,152 miles, 9,900 km with a 2,205 lb, 1,000 kg payload) VIP/business version,

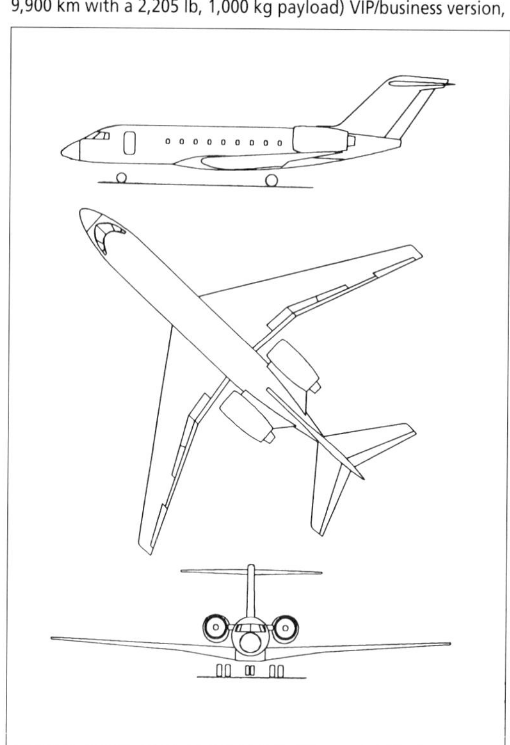

↑ **Tupolev Tu-414** *(courtesy Tupolev)*

Details for Tu-414, *with 414A in italics*

PRINCIPAL DIMENSIONS:
Wing span: 92 ft (28.04 m), *the same*
Maximum length: 99 ft 1 ins (30.2 m), *85 ft 11.5 ins (26.2 m)*
Maximum height: 27 ft 9 ins (8.15 m), *the same*

WEIGHTS:
Maximum take-off: 77,382 lb (35,100 kg), *75,398 lb (34,200 kg)*
Payload: 15,430 lb (7,000 kg), *4,409 lb (2,000 kg)*

PERFORMANCE:
Cruise speed: 432 kts (497 mph) 800 km/h, *the same*
Required runway length: 5,900 ft (1,800 m), *the same*
Range with full payload: 1,889 naut miles (2,174 miles) 3,500 km, *3,453 naut miles (3,977 miles) 6,400 km*
Range with reduced payload: 2,428 naut miles (2,796 miles) 4,500 km with 50 passengers, 4,155 naut miles (4,785 miles) 7,700 km with a 2,205 lb (1,000 kg) payload

with a maximum take-off weight of 97,003 lb (44,000 kg). New wing enables a maximum cruise speed of 464-486 kts (534-559 mph) 860-900 km/h.

Tupolev Tu-136

Role: Project for a light passenger or cargo transport, using liquid gas cryogenic fuel; presented for the first time in 1997. Development of the lighter C-Prop project (which see).
Passengers: 53 (seat pitch 31.9 ins, 81 cm).

↑ Tupolev Tu-136 *(Piotr Butowski)*

Freight hold access: Rear ramp/door under the tail.
Wing characteristics: High-mounted, straight main wings, with no anhedral/dihedral. High-mounted canards of basically constant chord, joined to the 2 engine nacelles that extend back to meet the main wings.
Wing control surfaces: Ailerons (with starboard tab) and flaps on the main wings.
Tail control surfaces: T-tail with horn-balanced elevators (starboard tab) and rudder.
Engines: 2 Pratt & Whitney Canada PW150 turboprops, with 12 ft 9 ins (3.9 m) diameter 6-blade Hartzell propellers.
Engine rating: Each 3,600 shp (2,685 kW) cruise power.
Fuel system: 8,113 lb (3,680 kg) of liquid natural gas fuel plus 9,524 lb (4,320 kg) of kerosene.

Details for Tu-136

PRINCIPAL DIMENSIONS:
Wing span: 71 ft 5 ins (21.765 m)
Maximum length: 74 ft 3 ins (22.625 m)
Maximum height: 26 ft 8 ins (8.127 m)
Distance between propeller hubs: 26 ft (7.912 m)

CABIN:
Width: 9 ft 10 ins (3.006 m) maximum, 8 ft 8 ins (2.644 m) at floor
Height: 6 ft 7 ins (2 m)
Ramp sill height: 4 ft 6 ins (1.374 m)

TAIL UNIT:
Tailplane span: 22 ft (6.7 m)

UNDERCARRIAGE:
Type: Retractable, with twin (side-by-side) nosewheels and twin (tandem) mainwheel units
Wheel track: 12 ft 1 ins (3.684 m)

WEIGHTS:
Maximum take-off: 44,092 lb (20,000 kg)
Payload: 11,023 lb (5,000 kg)

PERFORMANCE:
Cruise speed: 270 kts (311 mph) 500 km/h
Required runway length: 5,906 ft (1,800 m)
Cruise altitude: 23,620 ft (7,200 m)
Range with full payload: 1,079 naut miles (1,243 miles) 2,000 km
Range with 4,409 lb (2,000 kg) payload: 2,698 naut miles (3,106 miles) 5,000 km
Ferry range: 3,237 naut miles (3,728 miles) 6,000 km

Yakovlev Joint Stock Company – A.S. Yakovlev Design Bureau — Russia

Corporate address:
See Combat section for all company details. See also General Aviation section.

Yakovlev Yak-40 and Yak-40TL (NATO name *Codling*)

Comments: First flown on 21 October 1966, well over 1,000 Yak-40s were built before production ended. Details of this short-haul regional and VIP transport, together with the Yak-40TL twin-engined conversion, can be found in the 1996-97 edition of *WA&SD*, pages 241-242.

Yakovlev Yak-42 and Yak-142 (NATO name *Clobber*)

First flight: 6 March 1975 (Yak-42 prototype registered *CCCP-1974*, piloted by Arseni Kolosov).
Certification: New Yak-42D-100 was certified on 15 July 1997.
First delivery: 22 December 1980 start of Yak-42 scheduled services with Aeroflot, between Moscow and Krasnodar.
Role: Short-medium range airliner, with freighter version. Able to operate in remote regions, in temperatures of ±50° C.

Details *(current production Yak-42D, unless stated)*

Airframe life: 20,000 flying hours before general overhaul.
Sales: Production started in 1976 at Smolensk plant (first flight of first production aircraft was made on 8 November 1976, piloted by Valentin Mukhin), later also at Saratov. Production stopped in 1982 but restarted in 1984, at Saratov only. Total of about 191 built by early 1998 (including about 115 Yak-42Ds), 15 of them in Smolenck, the remainder in Saratov. Yak-42D output in recent years has been 10 in 1991, 18 in 1992, 15 in 1993, 8 in 1994, 1 in 1995, 4 in 1996 and some 10 in 1997. Up to 180 Yak-42 types were operating at the time of writing, mostly by civil companies, including at least 87 flying in Russia, 27 in Ukraine, 11 in Lithuania, 9 in China (first delivered January 1990), 5 in Kazakhstan, 4 in Turkmenistan, and 4 in Cuba (first delivered June 1990 to Cubana). First production Yak-142 expected 1998.
Crew: 2 pilots plus optional flight engineer.
Passengers: 80 in mixed first class/business/tourist layout, 102 in mixed first class/tourist layout, and maximum 120 in all-tourist layout.
Seat pitch: 30 ins (76 cm) in tourist class layout.
Galley: 1, aft of the cockpit.
Freight holds: 2 under the cabin floor of all versions, for a total of 8 × 77.69 cu ft (2.2 m^3) containers, or baggage or other loads.
Freight capacity: 26,455 lb (12,000 kg) for the Yak-42T.
Size of freight door: Standard passenger Yak-42 hold door (starboard side) of 4 ft 5 ins × 3 ft 9 ins (1.35 × 1.145 m). Convertible version has a 6 ft 8 ins × 10 ft 7 ins (2.025 × 3.23 m) port-side cargo-loading door. Yak-42T has an 8 ft 2 ins × 6 ft 7 ins (2.5 × 2 m) access door to the main cabin in addition to the undercabin hold door.
Loading facilities: Floor-mounted chain drive in the under-cabin holds.
Wing control surfaces: 2-section ailerons (with tabs), 2-section single-slotted trailing-edge flaps and full-width leading-edge flaps, plus 3-section spoilers.
Tail control surfaces: T-tail with a variable incidence tailplane, elevators (with tabs) and rudder (with tab).
Flight control system: Hydraulic.
Construction materials: Metal.
Engines: 3 Ivchenko PROGRESS/Zaporozhye D-36 series I turbofans.
Engine rating: Each 14,330 lbf (63.745 kN) at take off and 3,527 lbf (15.69 kN) ideal cruise.
Fuel system: 23,200 litres (40,785 lb, 18,500 kg).
Electrical system: Includes TA-12 APU.
Braking system: Hydraulic disc on main units.
Radar: Groza-42 (Thunderstorm) weather radar. See Yak-142 under Aircraft variants.
Flight avionics/instrumentation: Olkha-1 (Alder) navigation system. SAU-42-1 Cat II flight control system.

Aircraft variants:
First prototype carried 102 passengers and had a wing with 11° sweepback.
Yak-42 was the standard production version up to 1987, available in all-passenger or passenger/cargo configurations. MTOW 119,050 lb (54,000 kg). Range with 120 passengers is 826 naut miles (951 miles) 1,530 km.
Yak-42A appeared December 1992, in 1993 renamed Yak-142. See below.
Yak-42D (dalniy) has been a standard production version since 1988 and carries extra fuel. MTOW increased to 124,561 lb (56,500 kg), and range with a 23,148 lb (10,500 kg) payload increased to 1,160 naut miles (1,336 miles) 2,150 km. On 19 May

↑ Yakovlev Yak-142VIP, also known as Yak-142S *(Piotr Butowski)*

1995 it was certified with a MTOW of 126,765 lb (57,500 kg), allowing the normal range to be increased to 1,505 naut miles (1,733 miles) 2,790 km.

Yak-42D-100 is a version of Yak-42D with an AlliedSignal avionics suite but Russian autopilot that appeared in early 1993. Certified on 15 July 1997.

Yak-42F is a multispectral resources/environmental survey aircraft, with 2 underwing equipment pods. 17 equipment operators. Several are operated in Aeroflot markings. MTOW 124,560 lb (56,500 kg).

Yak-42LL (or ***Yak-42E***) is an engine testbed, with an Ivchenko PROGRESS/Zaporozhye D-236 propfan replacing the starboard turbofan.

Yak-42 radar testbed was used to test the radar of the Yak-41 VTOL fighter.

Yak-42ML (mezhdunarodnye linii, international routes) is a higher-comfort version of the standard Yak-42, which appeared in 1981.

Yak-142 (originally named ***Yak-42A***) is the latest version based on the Yak-42D, featuring a full range of AlliedSignal digital avionics, plus some new Russian avionics for Cat II landings. New wing spoiler system, and intermediate positions in the trailing-edge flaps. ICAO Appendix 16, Chapter 3 noise levels. Improved cabin features, including drop-down oxygen masks, improved seats, uprated galley equipment and more. Greater fuel capacity in the wings. First production aircraft expected 1998. MTOW 126,765 lb (57,500 kg). 1,505 naut miles (1,733 miles) 2,790 km range with 120 passengers.

Yak-142K will be a convertible passenger/cargo version of Yak-142. Range 755 naut miles (870 miles) 1,400 km with 31,967 lb (14,500 kg) of cargo. Cargo door 10 ft 6 ins × 6 ft 7 ins (3.2 × 2 m).

Yak-142D will have extended range (1,619 naut miles, 1,864 miles, 3,000 km with 120 passengers) due to MTOW increased to 132,277 lb (60,000 kg).

Yak-142S (salon) or ***Yak-142VIP*** is a business jet for 70 passengers (range 2,050 naut miles, 2,361 miles, 3,800 km) based on the Yak-142D. 2 aircraft delivered (1 to the Lukoil company and the other to the Ministry of Emergency Situations, the latter with

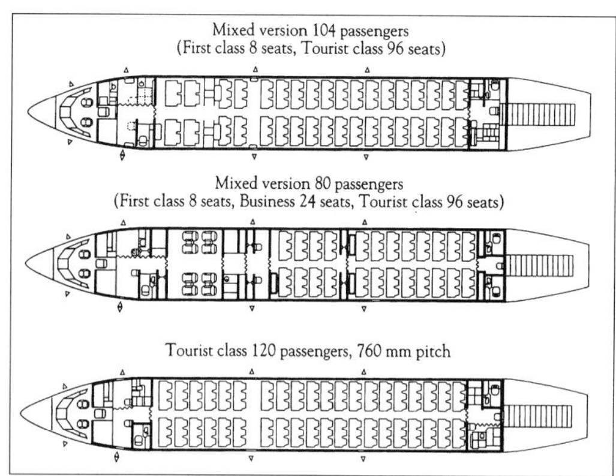

↑ **Yakovlev Yak-142 cabin layouts** *(courtesy Yakovlev)*

Satcom-906 coms, TCAS-II and Rockwell Collins ACARS); next 4 ordered (3 going to the Czech Republic, 1 to Gazpromavia).

Yak-142-100 will have a fuselage extended by 11 ft 1 ins (3.38 m) for 144 passengers. Unchanged MTOW of 132,277 lb (60,000 kg), but range of 944 naut miles (1,087 miles) 1,750 km.

Yak-142M (or ***Yak-42-200***) will be a version for 150 passengers. Range 1,403 naut miles (1,615 miles) 2,600 km. Fuselage lengthened by 19 ft 9 ins (6.03 m) compared with Yak-142D. MTOW of 143,300 lb (65,000 kg). New D-436 turbofans, and more comfortable cabin.

Details for Yak-42D

PRINCIPAL DIMENSIONS:
Wing span: 114 ft 5 ins (34.88 m)
Maximum length: 119 ft 4 ins (36.38 m)
Maximum height: 32 ft 3 ins (9.83 m)
Fuselage diameter: 12 ft 6 ins (3.8 m)

CABIN:
Length: 65 ft 3 ins (19.89 m)
Width: 11 ft 10 ins (3.6 m)
Height: 6 ft 10 ins (2.08 m)
Main passenger door size: 4 ft 11 ins × 2 ft 9 ins (1.5 × 0.83 m). *5 ft 7 ins × 2 ft 10 ins (1.7 × 0.85 m) for Yak-142*

WINGS:
Area: 1,614.6 sq ft (150 m^2)
Aspect ratio: 8.11
Sweepback: 23° at 25% chord

TAIL UNIT:
Tailplane span: 35 ft 5 ins (10.8 m)

UNDERCARRIAGE:
Type: Retractable, with twin steerable nosewheels and 4-wheel main units. Able to land on prepared or unimproved runways under ICAO Category II
Tyre size: 930 × 305 , for all
Wheel base: 48 ft 6 ins (14.786 m)
Wheel track: 18 ft 6 ins (5.63 m)

WEIGHTS:
Empty, operating: 72,752 lb (33,000 kg)
Maximum take-off: 126,765 lb (57,500 kg)
Maximum landing: 111,333 lb (50,500 kg)
Payload, normal: 23,810 lb (10,800 kg) for 120 passengers
Payload, maximum: 29,762 lb (13,500 kg)

PERFORMANCE:
Maximum cruise speed: 437 kts (503 mph) 810 km/h
Economic cruise speed: 399 kts (460 mph) 740 km/h
Take-off speed: 119 kts (137 mph) 220 km/h
Approach speed: 111 kts (127 mph) 205 km/h
Required runway length: 7,218 ft (2,200 m), ISA
Cruise ceiling: 31,500 ft (9,600 m)
Range with full fuel: 2,158 naut miles (2,485 miles) 4,000 km
Range with normal payload: 1,505 naut miles (1,733 miles) 2,790 km, with 5,512 lb (2,500 kg) fuel reserve
Range with maximum payload: 1,057 naut miles (1,218 miles) 1,960 km, with 5,512 lb (2,500 kg) fuel reserve

Yakovlev Yak-46-1

Role: Short-medium range passenger airliner, with convertible, evacuation and other versions planned.

Development

▪ 1992. Received Russian Government approval for full development.

Details

Flight crew: 2, with optional flight engineer.
Passengers: 126 (12 first class and 114 economy), and 178 maximum.
Wing characteristics: Ailerons, double-slotted trailing-edge flaps and leading-edge surfaces. Winglets.
Tail control surfaces: 2-section elevators and rudder.
Flight control system: Digital fly-by-wire.
Engines: 2 Samara turbofans.
Engine rating: Each 24,251 lbf (107.88 kN).
Flight avionics/instrumentation: ICAO Category IIIa landing.

Details for Yak-46-1

PRINCIPAL DIMENSIONS:
Wing span: 118 ft 11 ins (36.25 m)
Maximum length: 127 ft 3.5 ins (38.8 m)

WINGS:
Aerofoil section: Supercritical
Area: 1,291.7 sq ft (120 m^2)
Aspect ratio: 10.95
Sweepback: 25°

WEIGHTS:
Empty, operating: 76,809 lb (34,840 kg)
Maximum take-off: 132,718 lb (60,200 kg)
Payload: 38,581 lb (17,500 kg)

PERFORMANCE:
Cruise speed: 429 kts (528 mph) 850 km/h
Required runway length: 6,890 ft (2,100 m)
Cruise ceiling: 36,425 ft (11,100 m)
Range with 178 passengers: 2,158 naut miles (2,485 miles) 4,000 km
Fuel efficiency: 15-16 g/passenger/km

Yakovlev Yak-46-2

Role: Short-medium range airliner.

Development

▪ 1990. Model shown at MosAeroshow.

Details

Wing characteristics: Very similar configuration and control surfaces to the Yak-46-1.
Tail control surfaces: T-tail, with 2-section elevators and multi-section rudder.
Flight control system: Digital fly-by-wire.
Fuselage: Similar to Yak-46-1.
Engines: 2 rear-mounted Ivchenko PROGRESS D-227 propfans, possibly with 12 ft 6 ins (3.8 m) 8-blade and 6-blade coaxial contra-rotating composites pusher propellers.

Details for Yak-46-2

PRINCIPAL DIMENSIONS:
Wing span: 116 ft 6 ins (35.5 m)
Maximum length: 134 ft 6 ins (41 m)

WINGS:
Area: 1,291.7 sq ft (120 m^2)
Aspect ratio: 10.5

WEIGHTS:
Empty, operating: 82,232 lb (37,300 kg)
Maximum take-off: 135,143 lb (61,300 kg)
Payload: 38,581 lb (17,500 kg)

PERFORMANCE:
Cruise speed: 448 kts (516 mph) 830 km/h
Required runway length: 6,890 ft (2,100 m)
Cruise altitude: 36,425 ft (11,100 m)
Range with full payload: 2,158 naut miles (2,485 miles) 4,000 km
Fuel efficiency: 13-14 g/passenger/km

↑ **Yakovlev Yak-46-2** *(Piotr Butowski)*

Yakovlev Yak-77

Comments: Development of the Yak-77 small regional airliner and executive/business transport has ended. Details and a photograph can be found in the 1996-97 edition of *WA&SD*, page 243.

Yakovlev Yak-242

Details for Yak-242

PRINCIPAL DIMENSIONS:
Wing span: 118 ft 11 ins (36.25 m)
Maximum length: 124 ft 8 ins (38 m)

WINGS:
Aerofoil section: Supercritical
Area: 1,291.7 sq ft (120 m^2)
Sweepback: 25° at 25% chord
Aspect ratio: 10.95
Dihedral: From roots

UNDERCARRIAGE:
Type: Retractable, with twin steerable nosewheels and 4-wheel main units

WEIGHTS:
Empty, operating: 84,657 lb (38,400 kg)
Maximum take-off: 142,418 lb (64,600 kg)
Payload, maximum: 39,683 lb (18,000 kg)
Payload, normal: 32,628 lb (14,800 kg)

PERFORMANCE:
Cruise speed: 459 kts (528 mph) 850 km/h
Required runway length: 7,218 ft (2,200 m)
Cruise altitude: 36,415-38,060 ft (11,100-11,600 m)
Range with full fuel: 2,158 naut miles (2,485 miles) 4,000 km
Range with full payload: 1,079 naut miles (1,242 miles) 2,000 km

Comments: A mock-up of this airliner was accepted in April 1993 and the first flight had been expected in about 1995. However, during 1997 it was reported that only about 30% of the design work had been completed and that the programme had been postponed, although it could be revived if financed. Before these developments, the most likely first flight date appeared to be 1999.
Role: Short-haul airliner.
Crew: 2, with optional flight engineer.
Passengers: Typically 132 (including 12 first and 26 business classes), 138 (including 12 first class), 156, 162 or 180 maximum.
Seat pitch: 29.5 ins (75 cm) in 180 passenger layout, 32 ins (81 cm) in 156 passenger layout. First class pitch 37.75 ins (96 cm) and business 34.25 ins (87 cm).
Wing control surfaces: Ailerons, double-slotted trailing-edge flaps and leading-edge surfaces. Winglets.
Tail control surfaces: 2-section elevators and rudder.
Flight control system: Digital fly-by-wire.
Fuselage: Based on the Yak-42 but lengthened.
Engines: 2 Aviadvigatel/Perm PS-90A12 turbofans. Western V2500 and CFM56-5A were under consideration.
Engine rating: Each 26,455 lbf (117.68 kN) at take off, 5,070 lbf (22.56 kN) cruise.
Fuel system: 48,502 lb (22,000 kg).
Radar: Weather radar.
Flight avionics/instrumentation: IFR. Meets ICAO Category IIIa. AlliedSignal EFIS.

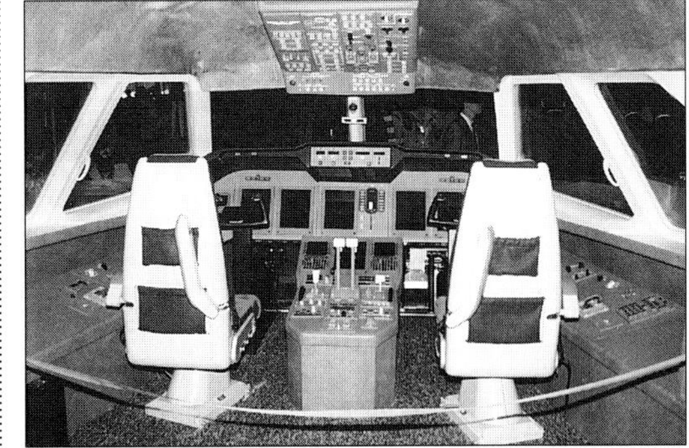
↑ **Proposed flight deck of the Yakovlev Yak-242** *(Piotr Butowski)*

Professional Aviation Services (Pty) Ltd — South Africa

Corporate address:
Terminal Building, Lanseria Airport, PO Box 515, Lanseria 1748, Johannesburg.

Telephone: +27 11 701 3320, 659 2860 (24 hrs: +27 82 455 1305)
Facsimile: +27 11 659 1336
E-mail: profav@iafrica.com

Information:
R. C. H. Garbett.

ACTIVITIES

- Charter services (with 1 AMI-converted turbine and lengthened DC-3, Cessna Citation II, King Airs, CL-44 and Learjets), sales, aircraft broking and management.
- According to correspondence in March 1998, the company is not currently involved in DC-3 modifications (as previously undertaken), but could possibly be so in the future.

Construcciones Aeronáuticas, S.A. (CASA) — Spain

Corporate address:
See Combat section for company details.

CASA C-212 Series 300 and 400 Aviocar

First flight: 26 March 1971 in original C-212 prototype form. Series 400 first flight on 4 April 1997 at San Pablo, Seville.
Certification: 1987 for Series 300, to FAR Pt 25/121/135.
First delivery: 1974 in original C-212A production form.
Role: STOL light passenger and cargo transport, and military freighter. Special purpose military versions are detailed in the Combat section. Other roles currently employed include medevac and civil protection, emergency hospital, aerial photography, rainmaking, geophysical survey, remote areas support, and aerial delivery.
Noise levels: FAR Pt 36.
Sales: 460 of all versions ordered (457 delivered) by July 1998, including 191 aircraft to 51 civil operators in 21 countries and 269 aircraft to 36 military/government users in 24 countries, the latter including Angola (8 Series 200 and 4 Series 300), Argentina (1 Series 200 and 5 Series 300), Bolivia (1 Series 100 and 1 Series 300), Botswana (2 Series 200), Chile (10 Series 100, 2 Series 200 and 5 Series 300), Colombia (2 Series 300 plus 6 to Satena), France (5 Series 300), Indonesia (26 Series 200s), Jordan (4 Series 100s), Lesotho (3 Series 300s), Mexico (10 Series 200s), Nicaragua (4 Series 200s), Panama (4 Series 200s and 3 Series 300s), Portugal (24 Series 100s and 2 Series 300s, plus 4 to TAM), South Africa (3 Series 200s and 2 Series 300s), Spain (2 prototype Series 100s, 69 Series 100s, and 9 Series 200s for SAR, plus 1 to ministry of agriculture and 6 to Servicio Vigilancia Advanera), Suriname (2), Sweden (4 Series 200s), Thailand (2 Series 300s), Uruguay (3 Series 200s), USA (1 Series 200 and 1 Series 300 to the DEA, 1 Series 200 and 1 Series 300 to the US State Department, and 1 Series 200 to the US Army), Venezuela (8 Series 200s and 3 Series 400s) and Zimbabwe (14 Series 200s).
Crew: 2 (flight).
Passengers: 26, with optional air conditioning and noise isolation kit; cabin noise 10 dB. Airstairs. Refurbished cabin to reduce noise level in Series 400. C-212M can carry 25 fully armed troops or paratroops on foldable seats, or 26 passengers in airline-style seats. Can deploy and give air support to advanced patrols of 10 troops and light vehicles, air-drop loads up to 4,409 lb (2,000 kg) at high or low altitudes (HAD, LAPES), or carry 12 litters and 4 attendants for medevac.
Seat pitch: 28.3 ins (72 cm).
Galley: Optional galley and toilet.
Freight hold volume: 22 cu ft (777 m^3).
Freight hold capacity: Optional full-freighter kit, allowing 3 LD3 containers, LD-1 or LD-727/DC-8 containers, standard 88 × 54 ins (2.24 × 1.37 m) pallets, light vehicles, military engines in their cradles, or other loads.
Freight hold access: Rear 2-section ramp/door (see below).
Size of freight doors: 95.67 × 66.14 ins (2.43 × 1.68 m) upper ventral door section, plus 54.33 × 66.14 ins (1.38 × 1.68 m) rear ramp lower door section.
Loading facilities: Roller system for cargo handling. Series 400 has introduced an optional 2,205 lb (1,000 kg) winch.
Baggage compartment: 123.6 cu ft (3.5 m^3).
Wing control surfaces: Ailerons (port trim tab) and double-slotted flaps. Winglets. Series 400 has introduced improved inspection illumination of the wings.
Tail control surfaces: Elevators and rudder with trim/servo tabs.
Flight control system: Mechanical (including servo tabs), but with hydraulic flaps and electric trim tabs.
Construction materials: Aluminium alloy, stressed skin.
Engines: 2 AlliedSignal TPE331-10R-513C turboprops for Series 300 and 2 AlliedSignal TPE331-12JR-701Cs for Series 400, with 9 ft 2 ins (2.79 m) Dowty R.334/4-82-F/13 4-blade propellers.
Engine rating: Each 900 shp (671 kW) for Series 300, and 925 shp (690 kW) for Series 400.
Fuel system: 2,040 litres, of which 2,000 litres are usable (equivalent to 3,527 lb, 1,600 kg usable). C-212M can carry 2 auxiliary tanks, providing 1,000 litres.
Electrical system: DC supply by 2 engine-driven generators. AC supply via inverters. 2 × 24 volt, 40 amp-hour batteries for self-start and aircraft operability under any conditions.
Hydraulic system: 2,000 psi for brakes, nosewheel steering, flaps, rear cargo ramp/door, and emergency and parking brakes. Fed by an electric pump, with emergency manual pump and several accumulators for supply to all subsystems.

↑ **CASA C-212 Series 400**

↑ **CASA C-212 Series 400 EFIS cockpit**

Braking system: Hydraulic discs on mainwheels. Anti-skid system available. Parking brakes.
De-icing system: Pneumatic boot and bleed air for wing and tail unit leading edges. Electric for windshield and propellers.
Oxygen system: Standard.
Fire system: Fire extinguishing system standard.
Radar: AlliedSignal Bendix/King weather radar standard.
Flight avionics/instrumentation: *Series 300:* Interphone, 2 VHF com, 2 VOR-ILS, 2 ADF, DME, transponder, AFCS, radio altimeter and ELT. Optional Omega, CVR, FDR and HF. C-212M has interphone, 2 VHF, HF, ATC/transponder, 2 VOR-ILS, 2 ADF, DME, AFCS and radio altimeter plus options of VHF/UHF-AM/FM com. IFF/SIF, VLF/Omega, Tacan and ELT.
Series 400: Fully modernized compared with Series 300, with former electro-mechanical instruments replaced by an EFIS suite with 4 CRTs. Former engine instrumentation has been replaced with a modern integrated engine data system (IEDS), which displays the information concerning engines and fuel on 2 liquid-crystal displays, additionally providing information to monitor the main aircraft systems (hydraulic, electrical, etc) together with the warning system. The IEDS also follows up the engine basic parameters, by storing the information in a memory to facilitate maintenance work. Flight management system (FMS), including a GPS receiver, allowing navigation planning by integrating the information provided by several sensors (VOR, ADF, DME, GPS and so on). Avionics black boxes have been relocated in the nose compartment to facilitate maintenance inspections.
Expendable weapons and equipment: C-212M can carry up to 1,102 lb (500 kg) of external stores on 2 outrigger pylons, including twin 7.62-mm machine-gun pod, 12.7-mm gun pod, 20-mm cannon pod, LAU-3A or 32 rocket launcher, up to 250 kg bomb, Sea Skua or similar light missile, or smart torpedo on each outrigger.

Aircraft variants:
C-212 Series 300 was the standard version until introduction of the Series 400, as detailed.
C-212 Series 400 is the latest 'glass' cockpit and higher-powered version, as detailed.
C-212M is the military version for transport and many other roles. In addition to troops, pallets and other loads, is capable of deploying and giving air support to advanced patrols (commando groups of 10 persons and light vehicles) with minimum time on the ground. Capable of HAD or LAPES aerial deliveries.
C-212 MP, ASW and DE Patrullero are more specialized variants of the C-212M for maritime patrol, EEZ patrol, anti-submarine, counter-insurgency, search and rescue, environmental/resources, and electronic warfare. Currently based on the Series 300 but will in the future be based on the Series 400. See Combat section.

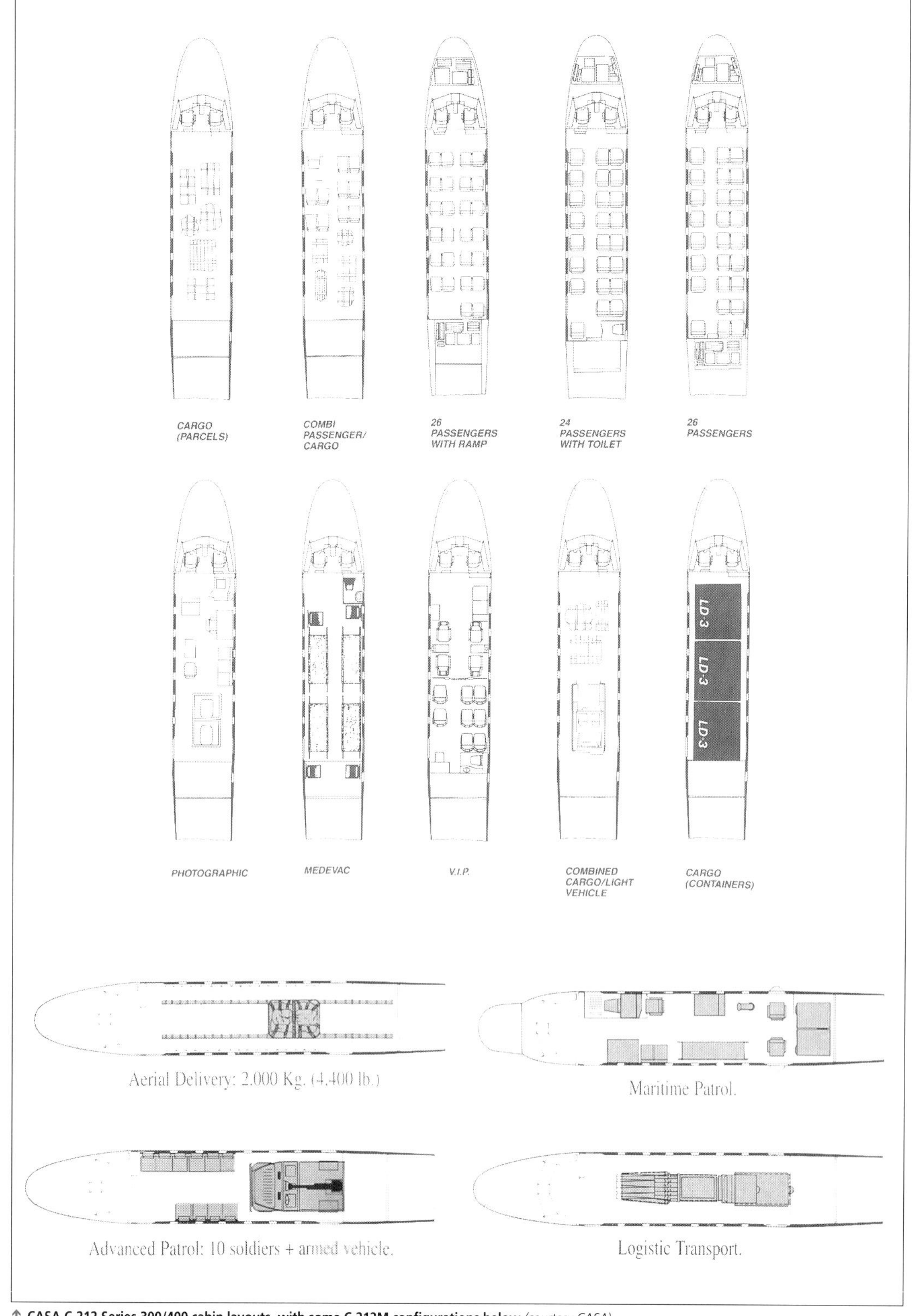

↑ **CASA C-212 Series 300/400 cabin layouts, with some C-212M configurations below** *(courtesy CASA)*

Details for C-212 Series 300 and Series 400, *with C-212M based on Series 300 in italics*

PRINCIPAL DIMENSIONS:
Wing span: 66 ft 6 ins (20.275 m)
Maximum length: 53 ft (16.154 m)
Maximum height: 21 ft 8 ins (6.59 m)

CABIN:
Length: 23 ft 10.5 ins (7.275 m) passenger layout, 21 ft 6 ins (6.55 m) cargo layout, *21 ft 6 ins (6.55 m)*
Width: 6 ft 11 ins (2.1 m), or 6 ft 2 ins (1.87 m) at floor, *the same*
Height: 5 ft 11 ins (1.8 m)
Volume: 840.5 cu ft (23.8 m^3)
Main passenger door: 5 ft 2 ins × 2 ft 3.5 ins (1.58 × 0.7 m)

WINGS:
Area: 441.32 sq ft (41 m^2)
Aspect ratio: 10.026

TAIL UNIT:
Tailplane span: 27 ft 7 ins (8.4 m)
Tailplane area: 96.98 sq ft (9.01 m^2)

UNDERCARRIAGE:
Type: Fixed, with steerable nosewheel
Wheel base: 17 ft 11 ins (5.46 m)
Wheel track: 10 ft 2 ins (3.1 m)

WEIGHTS:
Empty: 8,333 lb (3,780 kg) for Series 300
Max zero-fuel weight: 15,653 lb (7,100 kg) for Series 300, 16,534 lb (7,500 kg) for Series 400, *15,653 lb (7,100 kg)*
Maximum take-off: 17,857 lb (8,100 kg), *the same*
Maximum landing: 16,424 lb (7,450 kg) for Series 300, 17,857 lb (8,100 kg) for Series 400, *16,424 lb (7,450 kg)*
Payload: 5,115 lb (2,320 kg) passengers and 6,172 lb (2,800 kg) cargo for Series 300, 6,504 lb (2,950 kg) for Series 400, *5,952 lb (2,700 kg)*

PERFORMANCE:
Maximum cruise speed: 191 kts (220 mph) 354 km/h, ISA, 10,000 ft (3,050 m) altitude, 97% MTOW for Series 300, 195 kts (225 mph) 361 km/h for Series 400, *190 kts (218 mph) 352 km/h, 97% MTOW*
Stall speed: 78 kts (90 mph) 145 km/h
Balanced field length: 2,936 ft (895 m), hard runway surface
Take-off distance: 2,680 ft (817 m), hard surface, TORA=ASDA criterion, FAR 25-121, *1,307 ft (398 m) ground roll*
Take-off distance over a 50 ft (15 m) obstacle: *1,950 ft (594 m)*
Climb gradient second segment: 3.3%
Approach climb gradient: 3.9%, conditions as above
Landing distance: 2,840 ft (865 m), ISA, sea level, hard surface, FAR 25-121, *810 ft (247 m) ground roll*
Landing distance over a 50 ft (15 m) obstacle: *1,610 ft (490 m)*
Maximum climb rate: 1,630 ft (497 m) per minute
Maximum climb rate, 1 engine: 311 ft (95 m) per minute
Ceiling: 26,000 ft (7,925 m), *the same*
Ceiling, 1 engine: 11,100 ft (3,383 m), *11,400 ft (3,475 m)*
Range with 3,776 lb (1,713 kg) payload (Series 300): 769 naut miles (885 miles) 1,424 km, at 10,000 ft (3,050 m), reserves
Range with 25 passengers (Series 300): 190 naut miles (219 miles) 352 km, at 10,000 ft (3,050 m), reserves
Range with a 5,952 lb (2,700 kg) payload (Series 400): 400 naut miles (460 miles) 741 km, ISA + 20°, at 2,000 ft (610 m)
Range with full fuel (Series 400): 860 naut miles (990 miles) 1,594 km, ISA + 20°, at 2,000 ft (610 m)
Duration: *over 9 hours with underwing tanks*

Saab Group — Sweden

Corporate address:
See Combat section for company details. See also Electronic section.

ACTIVITIES

■ On 15 December 1997 Saab AB decided that manufacturing of the Saab 340 and 2000 regional aircraft will end in mid-1999, due to declining demand. Thereafter Saab AB's aircraft operations will focus on customer support and finance for the existing Saab fleet and on contracting for international manufacturers.

Saab 340B and Saab 340BPlus

↑ **400th production Saab 340, a Saab 340BPlus, delivered to AMR Eagle for the American Eagle fleet**

First flight: 25 January 1983 in Saab-Fairchild 340 prototype form.
Certification: 15 May 1984.
First delivery: June 1984 in Saab 340A form.
Role: Regional airliner, business and cargo transport.
Airframe life: 90,000 landings.
Airport limits: Rigid pavement ACN 7.9 medium subgrade and 7.3 high subgrade. Flexible pavement ACN 6.8 medium subgrade and 6.1 high subgrade.
Noise levels: ICAO: 78.4 EPNdB flyover, 85.9 EPNdB sideline and 91.8 EPNdB approach. FAR Pt 36 Appendix C: 78.5 EPNdB flyover, 85.9 EPNdB sideline and 91.6 EPNdB approach.

Details *(principally based on Saab 340B)*

Sales: By February 1998, 454 Saab 340 models had been ordered plus 15 options held, of which 428 had been delivered.
Crew: 3, as 2 pilots plus a cabin attendant.
Passengers: 30-37, with typically 33-35, all 3 abreast with aisle.
Seat pitch: 30 ins (76 cm) standard, 33 ins (84 cm) business class.
Pressurization: 7 psi cabin differential, allowing 4,500 ft (1,372 m) cabin altitude up to 25,000 ft (7,620 m).
Baggage compartment: At rear of passenger cabin, with volume varying between 220 and 295 cu ft (6.2 and 8.3 m^3) depending upon a forward or rear positioned toilet. Additional baggage stowing in the overhead bins and optional wardrobes.
Wing control surfaces: Ailerons with geared tabs, and single-piece flaps.
Tail control surfaces: Elevators with geared tabs, and rudder with spring tab.
Flight control system: Primary flight controls are all manual. Hydraulic flaps, and electric tabs for trimming.
Construction materials: Metal to metal bonding is used extensively, and aluminium alloy honeycomb for doors, wing flaps, and areas of the tail unit. Kevlar, GFRP and CFRP composites for the control surfaces, fairings, nose and cabin fittings.
Engines: 2 General Electric CT7-9B turboprops, with Dowty 4-blade composite propellers. Optional propeller brake.
Engine rating: Each 1,870 shp (1,394 kW) APR.
Fuel system: 3,220 litres total, in 2 integral tanks in each wing.
Electrical system: Primary split-busbar system giving regulated DC supply via 2 × 28 volt, 400 amp starter-generators mounted on the engine accessory gearboxes, with 2 ni-cd batteries providing back-up power and engine starting. 24 volt, 5 amp-hour lead-acid battery for supply to an emergency bus. 2 static inverters supply 26 volt and 115 volt, 400Hz AC power for certain instrumentation and avionics. 2 variable frequency 115/200 volt AC generators power a separate system for ice protection.
Hydraulic system: 3,000 psi. Designed around a single electric pump and 4 accumulators, with all feedlines located outside the pressure fuselage.
Braking system: Hydraulically operated carbon disc brakes, with anti-skid. See Engines.
De-icing system: Pneumatic boots actuated by engine bleed air for wing and tail unit leading edges. Electric for cockpit glazing, pitot tubes, engine intakes and propellers.
Radar: Rockwell Collins weather radar, with optional turbulence detection.
Flight avionics/instrumentation: Digital avionics suite with autopilot and EFIS (pilot and co-pilot with an HSI and ADI CRT display, with an optional fifth display for secondary information). Rockwell Collins Pro Line 2 navigation and communications equipment. Provision for additional equipment, including second DME, ADF and transponder, HF and FMS/GPS. Air data computer is linked to the flight director, and information on attitude and heading is generated by the AHRS. Digital autopilot.

Aircraft variants:
340A was the standard version between 1984 and 1989.
340B was the standard version between 1989-94.
340BPlus is the current version, introducing a Generation III interior of modern design and with new lighting. Other Plus improvements include 20% increase in overhead luggage bins volume, improved short field and hot-and-high performance using 2 ft (0.6 m) wingtip extensions to reduce field length by up to 400 ft (122 m) and increase take-off weight at restricted airfields by up to 1,500 lb (680 kg), extended maintenance intervals, and optional active noise control to lower cabin noise levels.
340BPlus-wt is the 340BPlus with extended wingtips which increase span to 74 ft 8 ins (22.75 m) and add 44 lb (20 kg) to the empty weight.
340QC is the quick-change version, allowing operators the option to fly passengers by day and cargo by night. Conversion takes under an hour by 2 persons. Up to 24 cargo containers can be loaded with no structural reinforcement.
340 Combi is another layout for the convertible interior, offering 19 passengers plus 3,307 lb (1,500 kg) of cargo.
340 AEW&C, see Electronic section.

Details for Saab 340BPlus, *with 340BPlus-wt with optional extended wingtips in italics*

PRINCIPAL DIMENSIONS:
Wing span (standard): 70 ft 4 ins (21.44 m)
Wing span (optional wingtips): *74 ft 8 ins (22.75 m)*
Maximum length: 64 ft 9 ins (19.73 m)
Maximum height: 22 ft 11 ins (6.97 m)

CABIN:
Length: 34 ft 1 ins (10.39 m)
Width: 7 ft 1 ins (2.16 m)
Height: 6 ft (1.83 m) maximum
Volume: 1,180 cu ft (33.4 m^3)
Main passenger door: 5 ft 3 ins × 2 ft 3 ins (1.6 × 0.69 m)
Cargo door: 4 ft 3 ins × 4 ft 5 ins (1.3 × 1.35 m)

WINGS:
Aerofoil section: NASA MS(1)-0313
Area: 450 sq ft (41.81 m^2)
Aspect ratio: 11
Sweepback: 3° 36′ at 25% chord
Dihedral: 7°

TAIL UNIT:
Tailplane span: 30 ft 4 ins (9.24 m)
Tailplane area: 121.42 sq ft (11.28 m^2)
Fin area: 83.64 sq ft (7.77 m^2)

UNDERCARRIAGE:
Type: Retractable, with steerable (±60°) nosewheels. Twin wheels on each unit
Main wheel tyre size: 24 × 7.7 ins
Nose wheel tyre size: 17.5 × 6.25 ins
Wheel base: 23 ft 5 ins (7.14 m)
Wheel track: 22 ft (6.71 m)
Turning circle: 29 ft 3 ins (8.9 m) minimum

WEIGHTS:
Empty, operating: 18,135 lb (8,225 kg), *or 44 lb (20 kg) more with wingtip extensions*
Maximum zero-fuel: 26,500 lb (12,020 kg)
Maximum take-off: 29,000 lb (13,155 kg)
Maximum landing: 28,505 lb (12,930 kg)
Payload: 8,366 lb (3,795 kg)

PERFORMANCE:
Typical cruise speed: 285 kts (278 mph) 528 km/h
Long-range cruise speed: 242 kts (290 mph) 448 km/h
Stall speed: 106 kts (122 mph) 197 km/h *clean*, 89 kts (102 mph) 164 km/h *in landing configuration*
Balanced field length for take-off (sea level): 4,222 ft (1,287 m) JAR and 4,325 ft (1,318 m) FAR, *3,705 ft (1,129 m) JAR/FAR*, all ISA
Balanced field length for take-off (5,000 ft, 1,525 m): 5,333 ft (1,625 m) JAR and 5,493 ft (1,674 m) FAR, *4,581 ft (1,396 m) JAR/FAR*, all ISA
Landing field length (sea level): 3,390 ft (1,033 m) JAR and 3,499 ft (1,067 m) FAR, *3,258 ft (993 m) JAR/FAR*, all ISA
Landing field length (5,000 ft, 1,525 m): 3,805 ft (1,160 m) JAR and 3,931 ft (1,198 m) FAR, *3,660 ft (1,115 m) JAR/FAR*, all ISA
Maximum climb rate: 2,000 ft (610 m) per minute
Ceiling: 25,000 ft (7,620 m), with 31,000 ft (9,450 m) as option.
Ceiling, 1 engine: 15,920 ft (4,852 m) ISA or 14,155 ft (4,414 m) at ISA + 10°, *16,520 ft (5,035 m) ISA or 14,750 ft (4,495 m) at ISA + 10°*, all at 85% MTOW, 1.1% climb gradient
Range with 35 passengers (200 lb, 91 kg each): 837 naut miles (964 miles) 1,551 km, *745 naut miles (858 miles) 1,380 km*

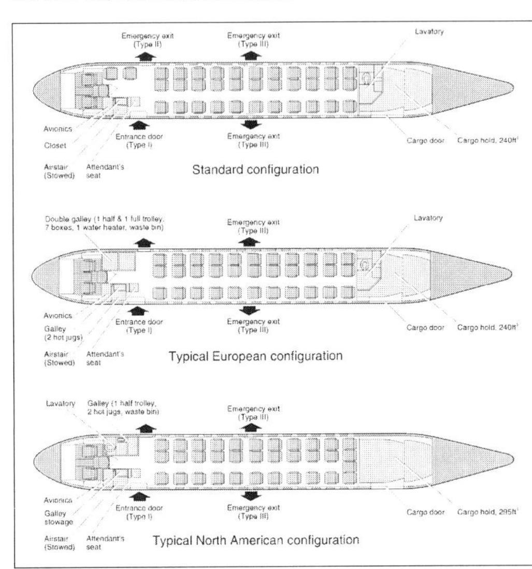

↑ **Saab 340BPlus cabin layouts** *(courtesy Saab)*

Saab 2000

First flight: 26 March 1992.
Certification: 31 March 1994 (JAA) and 29 April 1994 (FAA).
First delivery: 30 August 1994 to Crossair.
Role: Regional airliner and business transport.
Airframe life: 60,000 flight hours or 75,000 landings.
Airport limits: Rigid pavement ACN < 16, unpaved (5,000 passes) CBR < 18.
Noise levels: ICAO: 78.6 EPNdB flyover, 86.9 EPNdB sideline, and 87.9 EPNdB approach. FAR: 78.4 EPNdB flyover, 87.5 EPNdB sideline, and 87.9 EPNdB approach. Below 76 dB(A) cabin noise levels through standard active noise control system.
Sales: By February 1998, 57 firm orders and 4 options, of which 47 had been delivered.
Crew: 2 (flight) plus 1 or 2 cabin attendants.
Passengers: 50-58, 3 abreast with aisle.
Seat pitch: 32 ins (81 cm) and 30 ins (76 cm) for 50 and 58 passengers respectively.
Galley: See diagrams.
Pressurization: 7 psi cabin differential, allowing 7,500 ft (2,286 m) cabin altitude up to 31,000 ft (9,450 m).
Freight/baggage hold volume: 360 cu ft (10.2 m^3), or 300 cu ft (8.5 m^3) with extended galley.
Wing control surfaces: Ailerons (with geared tabs) and single-piece flaps.
Tail control surfaces: Elevators and rudder.
Flight control system: Mechanical ailerons. Dual hydraulic fly-by-wire controlled rudder and elevator system. All controls have electric trim. Hydraulic flaps.
Construction materials: Similar to Saab 340B Plus.
Engines: 2 Allison AE 2100A turboprops, with Dowty 6-blade composite propellers. Standard APU.
Engine rating: Each 4,152 shp (3,096 kW) APR.
Fuel system: 5,300 litres total, in 2 integral tanks in each wing.
Electrical system: 3-phase AC supply via 2 × 45kVA engine-driven generators. DC supply via 4 × 28 volt batteries.
Braking system: Hydraulic carbon disc brakes and anti-skid system.
De-icing system: Similar to Saab 340B, except bleed air for engine intakes.
Radar: Rockwell Collins weather radar, with optional turbulence detection.

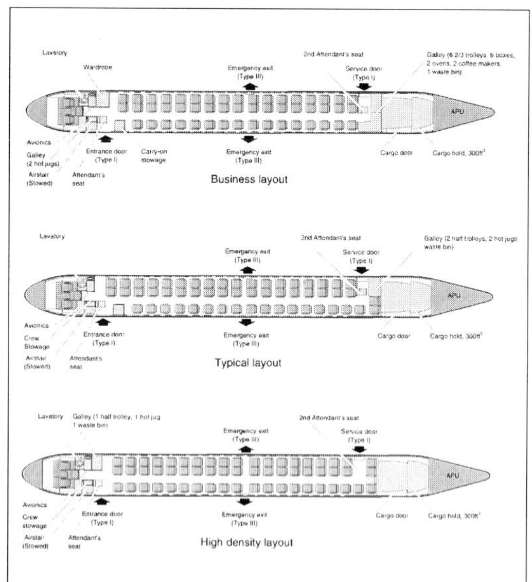

↑ **Saab 2000 cabin layouts** *(courtesy Saab)*

Flight avionics/instrumentation: Integrated digital Rockwell Collins Pro Line 4 avionics suite. 2 primary flight displays, 2 multi-function displays (primarily for navigation), and 2 EICAS displays for engine and aircraft systems and crew alerts. Options include TCAS, ACARS, IRS, FMS/GPS and Cat IIIa landing capability through a head-up guidance system.

↑ **Saab 2000 in Scandinavian Commuter 'Swelink' service** *(Saab/Norman Pealing Ltd)*

Details for Saab 2000

PRINCIPAL DIMENSIONS:
Wing span: 81 ft 3 ins (24.76 m)
Maximum length: 89 ft 6 ins (27.28 m)
Maximum height: 25 ft 4 ins (7.73 m)

CABIN:
Length: 54 ft 9 ins (16.7 m)
Width: 7 ft 1 ins (2.16 m)
Height: 6 ft (1.83 m)
Volume: 1,860 cu ft (52.7 m^3)

WINGS:
Aerofoil section: NASA MS(1) 0313
Area: 600 sq ft (55.7 m^2)
Aspect ratio: 11
Sweepback: 3° 36' at 25% chord
Dihedral: 7°

TAIL UNIT:
Tailplane span: 34 ft (10.36 m)
Tailplane area: 209.99 sq ft (19.51 m^2)
Fin area: 140 sq ft (13.01 m^2)

UNDERCARRIAGE:
Type: Similar to Saab 340BPlus
Wheel base: 36 ft 10 ins (11.22 m)
Wheel track: 27 ft (8.23m)
Turning circle: 42 ft 6 ins (12.96 m)

WEIGHTS:
Empty, operating: 30,424 lb (13,800 kg)
Maximum zero fuel: 43,431 lb (19,700 kg)
Maximum take-off: 50,265 lb (22,800 kg)
Maximum landing: 48,502 lb (22,000 kg)
Payload: 13,007 lb (5,900 kg)

PERFORMANCE:
Typical cruise speed: 370 kts (426 mph) 685 km/h
Balanced field length for take-off (sea level): 4,235 ft (1,291 m)
Balanced field length for take-off (5,000 ft, 1,525 m): 5,367 ft (1,636 m)
Landing field length (sea level): 4,078 ft (1,243 m) JAR, 4,193 ft (1,278 m) FAR
Landing field length (5,000 ft, 1,525 m): 4,620 ft (1,408 m) JAR, 4,748 ft (1,447 m) FAR
Maximum climb rate: 2,250 ft (686 m) per minute
Ceiling: 31,000 ft (9,450 m)
Ceiling, 1 engine: 22,800 ft (6,950 m) ISA , or 20,700 ft (6,309 m) at ISA + 10°, both at 85% MTOW, 1.1% net gradient
Range with 50 passengers: 1,180 and 1,549 naut miles (1,358 and 1,782 miles) 2,185 and 2,869 km, at maximum cruise speed and long-range cruise speed respectively

TUSAŞ Aerospace Industries Inc (TAI) — Turkey

Corporate address:
See Combat section for company details and general information.

ACTIVITIES

▪ Development of the pressurized, STOL capable **HD-XX** (formerly HD-19) medium-range regional passenger/cargo aircraft family, pending full financing. Fuselage section mock-ups completed. Intended to be a low-wing transport of conventional layout, the core version will accommodate 19-passengers (at 31.5 ins, 80 cm pitch) in a wide-body cabin of 6 ft 9 ins (2.05 m). In addition to the forward entrance door, it will have a large cargo door towards the rear of the fuselage. 2 flight crew. 2 turbofan engines (formerly to be 2 × 1,800 shp turboprops). Wing span 65 ft 8 ins (20 m), length of fuselage 55 ft 9 ins (17 m), MTOW 18,835 lb (8,544 kg), payload 4,000 lb (1,814 kg), and range is estimated at 743 naut miles (855 miles) 1,376 km. A 30-seat stretched version may follow. First flight of the 19-seat version will take place 30 months after programme start and certification 12 months later, with the 30-seater flying 12 months after the earlier aircraft's certification (its own certification 8 months thereafter).
▪ Construction of the CN 235M for the Air Force and Croatia.
▪ Other work includes aircraft modernization and work on the Airbus FLA.

↑ **TUSAŞ Aerospace Industries HD-XX in latest form**

Antonov ASTC (Aviation Scientific-Technical Complex) Ukraine

Corporate address:
See Reconnaissance section for full company details and specifications of Antonov transports converted for specialized missions.

Antonov An-12 (NATO name *Cub*)

Comments: First flown on 16 December 1957 (piloted by Yakov Vernikov), the An-12 entered service with Soviet Military Transport Aviation in 1959. Series production took place at 3 production plants in the former USSR: Irkutsk Factory No 39 (155 built between 1957 and 1962), Voronezh Factory No 64 (258 built between 1960 and 1965) and Tashkent Factory No 84 (840 built between 1962 and 1972). A total of 1,253 was built, 130 of which remain in service with CIS air forces (most replaced by the Il-76). 183 exported to 14 countries, many of which remain in use. Continues to be built in China, as the Shaanxi Y8 (which see). On 6 September 1994 the final Russian An-12 based in Germany (Sperenberg) was withdrawn. Antonov offers a service-life extension programme. For full details and 2 illustrations, see the 1996-97 edition of *WA&SD*, pages 247 and 248.

Antonov An-22 (NATO name *Cock*)

Comments: First flown on 27 February 1965 as a prototype (piloted by Yuri Kurlin), the first production example of this heavy strategic military transport flew from the Tashkent factory on 27 January 1966. State Acceptance Trials followed in October 1967, when a 221,344 lb (100,400 kg) payload was lifted to 25,750 ft (7,848 m). Deliveries to the Soviet Air Force began in 1969 (preparations for series production had begun in Tashkent in Uzbekistan in 1962, with the construction of a new large assembly facility as Factory No 84). 68 were produced between 1966 and 1976 (including 2 prototypes in Kiev and 66 in Tashkent, 28 of which were in An-22A version). First participation in the extensive Dvina exercises took place in March 1970. 7 aircraft have been lost during service, in 1970 (2), 1976, 1977, 1980, 1992 and 1994. Not exported. An An-22 was the final Russian military aircraft to leave former bases in Germany, on 7 September 1994. 45 (some 30 flyable) are still operated by the Russian Air Force by 2 units, the 8th Military Transport Air Regiment in Tver and the 81st MTAR in Ivanovo. 2 aircraft (An-22PZs – *UR-64460* and *UR-09307*) are also used by Antonov for the transportation of outsized cargoes carried above the fuselage. For full details of the An-22 and an illustration, see the 1996-97 edition of *WA&SD*, pages 248 and 249.

Antonov An-24 (NATO name *Coke*)

Comments: First flown on 20 October 1959 (piloted by Georgiy Lysenko), commercial services by this short-haul passenger or cargo transport by Aeroflot began in September 1963, between Moscow and Voronezh and Saratov. Some 1,100 were built up to 1979 at factories No 99 at Ulan-Ude, No 39 at Irkutsk (164 An-24Ts) and No 473 at Kiev. Nearly 750 remained in commercial and military use at the time of writing. 218 were sold to 23 countries and Xi'an in China continues to offer its own derivatives as the Y7 (which see). Antonov offers a life extension programme, increasing life from 22,000 flying hours or 20,000 cycles to 45,000 hours or 40,000 cycles. For full details of the An-24 and an illustration, see the 1996-97 edition of *WA&SD*, pages 249 and 250.

Antonov An-26 (NATO name *Curl*)

First flight: 21 May 1969 (piloted by Yu. Ketov).
First delivery: Entered service with the Soviet Air Force in early 1970s.
Role: Light, short-haul transport based on the An-24; also specialist mission versions, as detailed under Aircraft variants.
Airframe life: Antonov offers a service-life extension programme.
Sales: 1,410 An-26s were manufactured at Kiev. Adopted by the Soviet military and Aeroflot, and exported to 27 countries for military and civil use, including the military operators of Afghanistan, Angola, Benin, Cape Verde, China, Cuba, Czech Republic, Germany, Hungary, Iraq, Laos, Libya, Madagascar, Mali, Mongolia, Mozambique, Peru, Poland, Romania, Slovakia, Syria, Yemen, and Yugoslavia. These remaining with CIS armed forces are used as auxiliary aircraft assigned individually to Air Force regiments or to staffs at various levels of command, and for special electronic and other roles (see Aircraft variants). Some 440 commercial An-26s were in service worldwide at the time of writing, the majority used commercially in the CIS, with Aeroflot aircraft forming a reserve for the armed forces. In the Ukraine itself, Air Ukraine counts An-26s among 80 Antonov transports in regular use. Also produced in China as the Y7H/Y7H-500.
Crew: 3-5 (2 pilots and an onboard technician as standard; additionally a navigator and communications operator).
Passengers: See Freight hold capacity.
Pressurization: 4.27 psi cabin differential.
Freight hold volume: 2,118.9 cu ft (60 m^3).
Freight hold capacity: Up to 12,125 lb (5,500 kg) of cargo, including small military cars (up to 2,866 lb, 1,300 kg weight) or 40 troops (folding seats along the cabin sides), or 30 paratroops. In rescue configuration, 24 litter patients and 1 to 3 litter-bearers.
Freight hold access: Hydraulically opened rear loading ramp. When opened, the ramp can take 2 positions: lowered for roll-on from the ground or slid back horizontally under the fuselage for air-dropping or for loading directly from trucks. Door 2 ft × 4 ft 7 ins (0.6 × 1.4 m) at the starboard side of the front freight hold, used also by the crew. Emergency exits in the floor and in starboard and port sides of the hold.
Size of freight door: Rear ramp entrance width 7 ft 10.5 ins (2.4 m) at floor, 6 ft 11 ins (2.1 m) at top; height 10 ft 4 ins (3.15 m), or 5 ft 2 ins (1.564 m) in a vertical line.
Loading facilities: Single cabin-top electrical telpher, 3,306 lb (1,500 kg) capacity. 2 roller tracks on the floor (can be stowed against the cabin walls), tie-down positions and mats. Early An-26s were given a 9,921 lb (4,500 kg) electric/manual floor conveyor system.
Wing control surfaces: Single-slotted trailing-edge flaps on the centre section, tracked double-slotted flaps on the middle panels (15° for take-off, 38° for landing). 2-section ailerons (+24°, –16°) on each wing outer panel.
Tail control surfaces: Elevators (+30°, -15°). Rudder (±25°).
Flight control system: Mechanical.
Engines: 2 Ivchenko PROGRESS/Zaporozhye AI-24VT turboprops, with 12 ft 9.5 ins (3.9 m) 4-blade AV-72T propellers. In the rear of the right engine nacelle is housed a Soyuz/Tumansky RU-19A-300 turbojet (1,984 lbf, 88.3 kN) to provide additional thrust during take-off and climb, or in case of failure of 1 of the main engines. It is also used as an APU for starting the main engines and to drive the electric generators.
Engine rating: Each 2,820 eshp (2,103 ekW).
Fuel system: 7,100 litres in 14 wing tanks (12,125 lb, 5,500 kg).
Flight refuelling probe: None.
Electrical system: 28 volt DC. 115 volt 400Hz and 36 volt 400Hz AC supply.
Hydraulic system: 2 independent systems (basic and stand-by), pressure 2,204 psi.
Braking system: On main undercarriage units.
Radar: RPSN-3N Emblema navigation/weather radar in the nose.
Flight avionics/instrumentation: Typical flight/navigation instruments include ARK-11 radio compass, MRP-56P marker

Details for *Curl-A*

PRINCIPAL DIMENSIONS:
Wing span: 95 ft 9.5 ins (29.2 m)
Maximum length: 78 ft 1 ins (23.8 m)
Maximum height: 28 ft 1.5 ins (8.575 m)

CABIN:
Length: 36 ft 5 ins (11.1 m)
Length, including ramp: 51 ft 5 ins (15.68 m)
Width: 9 ft 1.5 ins (2.78 m) maximum
Height: 6 ft 3 ins (1.91 m) maximum
Volume: 2,118.9 cu ft (60 m^3)

WINGS:
Area, gross: 807.1 sq ft (74.98 m^2)
Aspect ratio: 11.37
Sweepback: 0° at centre section, outer panel leading edge 9° 41′, outer panel at quarter chord 6° 50′
Incidence: 3°
Anhedral: 2° outer panels

TAIL UNIT:
Tailplane span: 32 ft 8.5 ins (9.973 m)
Tailplane area: 213.45 sq ft (19.83 m^2)
Fin area, including dorsal fin: 170.61 sq ft (15.85 m^2)

UNDERCARRIAGE:
Type: Retractable, with steerable (±45°) nosewheels. Twin wheels on each unit
Main wheel tyre size: 1,050 × 400 mm
Nose wheel tyre size: 700 × 250 mm
Wheel base: 25 ft 1 ins (7.651 m)
Wheel track: 25 ft 11 ins (7.9 m)
Turning circle: 36 ft 11 ins (11.25 m)

WEIGHTS:
Empty: 34,943 lb (15,850 kg)
Maximum take-off: 52,910 lb (24,000 kg)
Payload: 12,125 lb (5,500 kg)

PERFORMANCE:
Maximum speed: 292 kts (336 mph) 540 km/h
Cruise speed: 232-235 kts (267-270 mph) 430-435 km/h at 19,685 ft (6,000 m)
Take-off speed, MTOW: 111 kts (127 mph) 205 km/h
Landing speed, MTOW: 105 kts (121 mph) 195 km/h
Take-off distance, concrete runway, at MTOW: 2,854 ft (870 m)
Take-off distance, concrete runway at 20,000 kg take-off weight: 1,739 ft (530 m)
Take-off distance over a 50 ft (15 m) obstacle, concrete runway: 4,495 ft (1,370 m)
Landing distance: 3,806 ft (1,160 m)
Maximum climb rate: 1,417 ft (432 m) per minute at sea level, nominal engine rating, MTOW
Ceiling: 25,260 ft (7,700 m) at MTOW
Ceiling at 20,000 kg: 29,530 ft (9,000 m)
Range with full fuel: 1,458 naut miles (1,678 miles) 2,700 km

↑ **Antonov An-26D with additional fuel tanks fitted to the fuselage sides** *(Piotr Butowski)*

beacon receiver, and SP-50M instrument landing system. IFF. UHF R-802GM and HF R-836/US-SK com radios. OPB-1R bomb sight for paratroop operations.
Fixed weapons: None.
Expendable weapons and equipment: 2 racks can be mounted on each side of the fuselage, usually for SAB-100 100 kg flare bombs for illuminating the landing area.

Aircraft variants:
An-26 *Curl-A* was presented at the 1969 Paris Air Show as the An-24RT with enlarged loading doors. Entirely redesigned rear fuselage with flat ramp and reinforced structure. See general description.
An-26B is a civil version that appeared in 1978 with parachute dropping equipment and improved freight handling gear, enabling 2 persons to load 3 standard freight pallets in 30 minutes.
An-26D (dalnyi, long-range) had additional fuel tanks fitted to the fuselage sides.
An-26L (laboratornyi) is a calibration aircraft.
An-26LR (ledovoi razvedki) is the designation of 5 An-26Bs modified to carry out surveillance of surface ice or assist in the navigation of ship convoys. Increased fuel capacity for 11 hours duration.
An-26P is the fire-fighting version, with 8,818-9,700 lb (4,000-4,400 kg) of fire-extinguishing mixture.
An-26PS (pasazhirsky, svyaz) is the military executive version, with cabin seating and improved communication equipment.
An-26M Spasatel (rescuer) appeared in 1980 and was prepared specially for the conflict in Afghanistan. Surgical cabin.
An-26RR (radiorazvedchik) is a signal intelligence version. Together with the An-26RT, was often used during the conflict in Afghanistan.
An-26RT (relay) *Curl-B* is operated for increasing the range of communications at the tactical level of command. Externally, it differs from the standard An-26 by having a great number of sword-type aerials installed on the airframe. Large number in use.
An-26Sh (shturmansky) appeared in 1975 as a training version for navigators destined for transport aircraft and bombers.
An-26Z-1 (zastavba) is for electronic intelligence, prepared in the Czech Republic. Large bulbous radomes on both sides of the centre fuselage.
Xi'an Y7H/Y7H-500 are Chinese derivatives, still in production and development (which see).

Antonov An-32 (NATO name *Cline*)

First flight: 9 July 1976 (piloted by Vladimir Tkachenko).
First delivery: 1984, to India.
Role: Light short/medium-range freighter or airliner. Based on the An-26, with hot-and-high features added for operation from airfields at 4,500 m above sea level. Built specially against an order from India.
Sales: 337 built since 1984 at Kiev, Ukraine at the time of writing and still in production (including 41 sold between 1993–97). Only a relatively small number in Russian Air Force use and perhaps more than 60 with CIS airline operators plus many others with the Russian Department of Agriculture. 123 accepted by India with the local name Sutlej. Others in Afghanistan, Angola, Bangladesh, Cuba, Kazakhstan, Peru (which ordered 3 more and 3 on option in 1994), and Sri Lanka.
Crew: 2 pilots and a navigator, plus optional on-board technician. Antonov offers new avionics to allow 2-crew operation.
Pressurization: 4.27 psi cabin differential.
Freight hold volume: 2,331 cu ft (66 m^3).
Freight hold capacity: Up to 14,771 lb (6,700 kg), with possible loads including 50 troops, 42 paratroops, 24 litter patients plus 1-3 litter bearers, 4 × PAV-2.5 pallets, 12 MG paradropping platforms (1,102 lb, 500 kg each), or 2 × BG modular paradropping platforms (6,614 lb, 3,000 kg each).
Freight hold access: Rear loading ramp, 18 ft 6 ins (5.633 m) length, 7 ft 10.5 ins (2.4 m) bottom to 6 ft 7 ins (2 m) top width. Side doors 2 ft × 4 ft 7 ins (0.60 × 1.40 m).
Loading facilities: Single cabin-top electric telpher of 6,612 lb (3,000 kg) capacity. 2 stowable roller tracks on the floor, tie-down positions and mats.
Wing and tail control surfaces: As for An-26 except for triple-slotted trailing-edge flaps, and automatic slats along the entire leading-edge span.
Engines: 2 Ivchenko PROGRESS/Zaporozhye AI-20D Series 5 turboprops of 5,180 eshp (3,863 ekW) for hot climates. Engine version for longer service life is the AI-20M of 4,250 eshp (3,169 ekW) for temperate climates. 15 ft 5 ins (4.7 m) 4-blade propellers. TG-16M APU.
Fuel system: 12,004 lb (5,445 kg). Fuel load with maximum payload 4,998 lb (2,267 kg).
Flight avionics/instrumentation: NK-32 navigation system, NKPB-7 sight (for paradropping), Mikron HF com, ARK-15M radio compass, DISS-013-26Sh Doppler speed and drift meter.
Fixed weapons: None.
Expendable weapons and equipment: Provision for 4 × 100 kg flare bombs.

Aircraft variants:
An-32 standard version, as detailed.
An-32B is a civil version with reduced empty weight due to the removal of paradropping and other military equipment, and thereby offers 1,102 lb (500 kg) more payload.
An-32P Firekiller (pozharnyi) is a firefighting version, in prototype form only. Carries up to 17,637 lb (8,000 kg) of water and extinguishing agents in 2 side-of-fuselage nacelles. Maximum take-off weight 65,477 lb (29,700 kg). Typical speed when releasing water is 117-124 kts (135-143 mph) 217-230 km/h at 98 ft (30 m) altitude. Can also carry 27-30 firefighters to be parachuted near the fire. An-32P can also be used for weather adjustment purposes, with rain produced by means of MP-26 chemical cartridges (UVP-26 containers fixed to the fuselage sides) shot into clouds.

↑ **Antonov An-32P Firekiller *UR-48086*** *(Piotr Butowski)*

Details for An-32 *Cline*

PRINCIPAL DIMENSIONS:
Wing span: 95 ft 9.5 ins (29.2 m)
Maximum length: 77 ft 8 ins (23.68 m)
Maximum height: 28 ft 8.5 ins (8.75 m)

CABIN:
Length, including ramp: 51 ft 6 ins (15.685 m)
Length, excluding ramp: 40 ft 11 ins (12.48 m)
Width: 9 ft 1.5 ins (2.78 m) maximum, 7 ft 7 ins (2.3 m) at floor
Height: 6 ft 0.5 ins (1.84 m) maximum
Volume: 2,331 cu ft (66 m^3)

WINGS:
Area, gross: 807.1 sq ft (74.98 m^2)
Aspect ratio: 11.37
Sweepback: 0° centre section, 9° 41′ outer panel leading edges
Mean aerodynamic chord: 9 ft 3 ins (2.813 m)
Anhedral: 2° outer panels
Incidence: +3°

TAIL UNIT:
Tailplane span: 33 ft 7 ins (10.235 m)
Tailplane area: 218.5 sq ft (20.3 m^2)
Fin height: 21 ft 6 ins (6.56 m)
Fin area: 185.35 sq ft (17.22 m^2)

UNDERCARRIAGE:
Type: as for An-26
Main wheel tyre size: 1,050 × 390 mm
Nose wheel tyre size: 700 × 250 mm
Wheel base: 25 ft 1 ins (7.652 m)
Wheel track: 25 ft 11 ins (7.9 m)
Turning circle: 83 ft 1 ins (25.335 m) at wingtip

WEIGHTS:
Empty, operating: 38,140 lb (17,300 kg)
Maximum take-off: 59,525 lb (27,000 kg)
Maximum landing: 55,116 lb (25,000 kg)
Payload: 14,771 lb (6,700 kg)

PERFORMANCE (with AI-20D engines; *data in italics for An-32 with AI-20M engines if different;* all ISA):
Cruise speed: 254-286 kts (292-329 mph) 470-530 km/h
Take-off speed: 116 kts (134 mph) 215 km/h
Landing speed: 100 kts (115 mph) 185 km/h
Take-off distance: 3,937 ft (1,200 m). *4,101 ft (1,250 m)*
Landing distance: 3,117 ft (950 m). *3,215 ft (980 m)*
Time to 19,685 ft (6,000 m): 11 minutes. *15 minutes*
Ceiling: 30,840 ft (9,400 m). *27,890 ft (8,500 m)*
Range with full fuel: 1,349 naut miles (1,553 miles) 2,500 km
Range with full payload: 701.5 naut miles (808 miles) 1,300 km

Antonov An-38

First flight: 23 June 1994 for the An-38-100 (piloted by Anatoli Khrustitsky from Novosibirsk).
Certification: 24 April 1997. Certification by the Russian Interstate Registry according to AP-25 standards.
First delivery: 3 aircraft delivered to Vostok Airlines in 1997 from 8 to be received by the year 2000.
Role: Commuter airliner, utility and special mission aircraft. Capable of operating in vastly differing temperatures, from −50° C to +45° C. Expected to replace many An-24s and Let L 410s.
Airframe life: 30,000 flying hours.
Sales: Launch customer is Vostok Airlines (see Role). Letters of intent from several aviation enterprises. Series production at the Novosibirsk Aircraft Production Association (NAPA) plant in Siberia, with initial capability to produce 32 aircraft per year, rising to 50. First 2 aircraft (the second having first flown in November 1995) are both in An-38-100 form, which accumulated their first 1,000 flights in 1997. Market for 585 is anticipated within the CIS to the year 2007 (including some 95 by the year 2000). Interest from India (An-38 undertook a 3-week tour of India), Thailand and Latin America is also reported. Development in association with NAPA and AlliedSignal, the latter integrating the entire power plant package, encompassing the engines, propellers, starter generators, cockpit indicators, Hartman power switching equipment, Weldon unfeathering pumps, and Hydra-Electric pressure switches (integrated by AlliedSignal's AirSupply Operations).
Crew: 2 flight crew.
Passengers: 27 in commuter layout. Executive An-38VIP layout provides for 8-10. An-38S ambulance layout for 6 litters, 8 seated casualties and an attendant. An-38D assault transport version for 26 troops or 22 paratroops.
Seat pitch: 29.5 ins (75 cm) in 27-passenger commuter layout.

↑ **Antonov An-38-100** *(Piotr Butowski)*

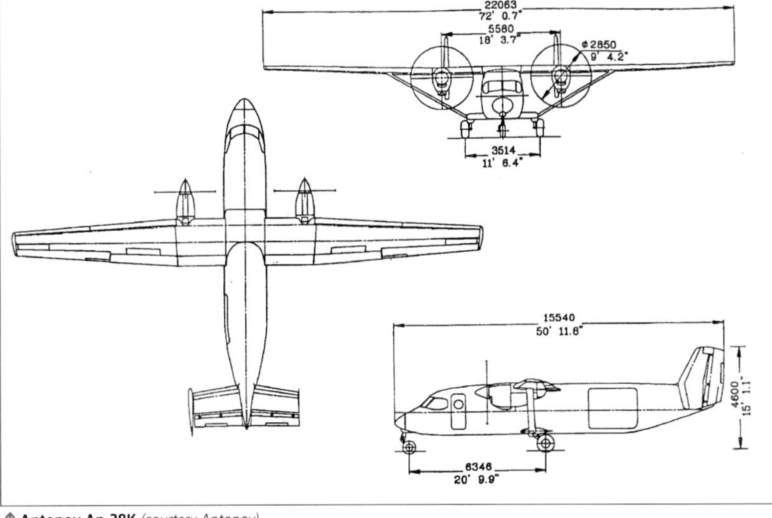

↑ **Antonov An-38K** *(courtesy Antonov)*

Galley: Warm drinks from a position immediately aft of the flight deck.
Baggage area: At the rear of the cabin, aft of the toilet.
Freight capacity: 5,512 lb (2,500 kg) of freight, either with passenger seats and baggage hold stowed against the cabin sides or in an unrestricted freighter layout for containerized cargo (see Aircraft variants).
Size of freight door: Door under the rear of the fuselage is 7 ft 3 ins × 4 ft 7 ins (2.2 × 1.4 m), which can be slid under the cabin for straight-through loading at sill height.
Wing control surfaces: Ailerons, 2-section slotted flaps, and leading-edge slats over the entire wing outboard of the engines, plus spoilers.
Tail control surfaces: Elevators and twin rudders, with tabs.
Engines: 2 AlliedSignal TPE331-14GR-801E turboprops for An-38-100 and An-38K, with 9 ft 4.2 ins (2.85 m) diameter Hartzell HC-B5MA 5-blade propellers. Omsk TVD-20Bs for An-38-200 (see Aircraft variants, particularly for TVD-1500B version).
Engine rating: 1,760 shp (1,312.4 kW), with 1,650 shp (1,230 kW) gearbox limit, for TPE331s.
Fuel system: 4,872 lb (2,210 kg). 2,860 litres for An-38K.
Electrical system: Lucas starter-generators.
Radar: Weather radar.
Flight avionics/instrumentation: AlliedSignal Bendix/King flight and navigation equipment to category II minimums. Ametek cockpit indicators. Alternative avionics include those of Russian origin.

Details for An-38-100, *with An-38K where indicated*

PRINCIPAL DIMENSIONS:
Wing span: 72 ft 5 ins (22.063 m)
Maximum length: 51 ft (15.54 m)
Maximum height: 14 ft 1 ins (4.3 m), 15 ft 1.1 ins (4.6 m) for An-38K

CABIN:
Width: 6 ft 3 ins (1.9 m)
Height: 7 ft (2.14 m)

TAIL UNIT:
Tail span: 16 ft 10 ins (5.14 m), or 18 ft 3.7 ins (5.58 m) for An-38K

UNDERCARRIAGE:
Type: Retractable, with nosewheel. Alternative ski gear
Wheel base: 20 ft 9.9 ins (6.346 m) for An-38K
Wheel track: 11 ft 6.4 ins (3.514 m) for An-38K

WEIGHTS:
Empty: 12,566 lb (5,700 kg)
Maximum take-off: 20,944 lb (9,500 kg)
Payload: 5,512 lb (2,500 kg), or 7,055 lb (3,200 kg) for An-32K

PERFORMANCE:
Maximum cruise speed: 219 kts (252 mph) 405 km/h at 9,850 ft (3,000 m), same for An-38K
Economic cruise speed: 183 kts (211 mph) 340 km/h
Required runway length: 2,953 ft (900 m)
Maximum range: 1,188 naut miles (1,367 miles) 2,200 km
Range with 27 passengers: 486 naut miles (559 miles) 900 km
Range with 5,512 lb (2,500 kg) payload: 445 naut miles (512 miles) 825 km

Aircraft variants:
An-38 was to be a version with Rybinsk TVD-1500B turboprops (1,300 shp, 969.4 kW). Development stopped due to delay in engine development.
An-38-100 is the designation of the initial production version with AlliedSignal engines, becoming the first completely new CIS aircraft to be launched with Western engines. See general description.
An-38-200 is powered with Omsk TVD-20B turboprops (1,380 shp, 1,029 kW). First flight 1998.
An-38K (konteinernyi) will be a cargo version with a new fuselage. Freight door (7 ft 7 ins × 5 ft 10 ins, 2.3 × 1.78 m) at port side of fuselage, and roller tracks/ball mats. TPE331-14GR-801E engines. Maximum payload increased to 7,055 lb (3,200 kg). The aircraft accommodates up to 4 standard LD3 containers. The range will be 183 naut miles (211 miles) 340 km with maximum cargo.
Special variants will include:
An-38T cargo version.
An-38VIP 8-10 seat business aircraft.
An-38D (desantnyi) forest patrol and assault version for 26 troops or 22 paratroops/smoke jumpers.
An-38S (sanitarnyi) ambulance version.
An-38LR (ledovoi razvedki) ice/fishery patrol aircraft.
An-38F photographic version.
An-38GF (geofizichesky) geophysical surveillance version.

Antonov An-70 (and An-77, An-170 and An-177)

First flight: 16 December 1994 (pilot Sergei Maksimov).
First delivery: 1998.
Role: Medium transport to replace remaining An-12 *Cubs*, and take over some tasks from heavier Il-76 *Candids*. Offered also as a replacement for the C-130 Hercules and C-160 Transall.
Chief designer: Vasiliy Teplov.
Airframe life: 45,000 flying hours and 20,000 cycles life over 25 years.

Aims

▪ Ability to carry a 44,092 lb (20,000 kg) payload over 1,620 naut miles (1,864 miles) 3,000 km when operated from unprepared runways with allowed surface pressure of 0.8 MPa and with a take-off run of 1,969 ft (600 m).
▪ Range of 2,700 naut miles (3,107 miles) 5,000 km with a 66,120 lb (30,000 kg) payload when operated from a concrete runway 5,905-7,220 ft (1,800-2,200 m) long.
▪ Unusually large cargo cabin, the internal volume equal to that of the An-22, exceeding by one-third the volume of the Il-76, and 2 or 3 times greater than that of the An-12.
▪ Specific fuel consumption of 165 g per tonne kilometre, 25% less than that of the An-12 and about 50% less than for the Il-76.

Development

▪ 1975. Work began. Original design was to be powered by 4 D-236 turboprop engines, fuselage diameter was to be 16 ft 5 ins (5 m), and the structure was to be all metal.
▪ 1985. New requirements issued, including STOL capability and new payload specifications. Work began on a new design at much higher technological level, including fly-by-wire control system, fuselage diameter increased to 18 ft 4.5 ins (5.6 m), wide use of composite materials, and adoption of D-27 propfan engines.
▪ 24 June 1993. Prime Ministers of Russia and Ukraine signed the agreement covering a joint development programme and financial support for the An-70 (80% from Russia, 20% from Ukraine).
▪ 20 January 1994. Roll-out of the prototype at the Antonov works in Kiev.

↑ **Antonov An-70. Note the propfan arrangement** *(Piotr Butowski)*

■ 14 July 1994. Establishment of a consortium of design bureaux, production plants and banks from Ukraine, Russia and Uzbekistan, for development and manufacturing of the An-70.
■ 16 December 1994. First flight lasting 25 minutes.
■ 10 February 1995. First prototype crashed at Kiev during its fourth test flight, with the loss of its crew of 7. Cause was a collision with a video recording aircraft which landed safely.
■ 24 April 1997. First flight of the second prototype, with Alexander Galunenko at the controls. This has a modified control system (with vital parts moved from the tailfin) and some systems improvements. First 40 flights were accumulated by August 1997.

Details

Sales: Kiev aircraft production plant was designated to be the manufacturer in 1988. Later, following the regional changes, it was decided to have simultaneous production in Kiev (Ukraine) and Samara (Russia). The wings are constructed in Tashkent (Uzbekistan). The first 2 An-70 prototypes were built by the experimental plant of Antonov in Kiev. The demand is estimated by Antonov to be for 400 in Russia and 100 in the Ukraine.
Crew: 3 (2 pilots and an on-board engineer).
Passengers: See Freight hold capacity.
Pressurization: Cockpit and freight hold are pressurized.
Freight hold capacity: 77,162 lb (35,000 kg) nominal, 103,617 lb (47,000 kg) maximum payload (see data column). Loads can include UAK-2.5, -5 and -10 containers, PA-3, 4, 5.6 and 6.8 pallets, vehicles or many other combinations, 110 paratroops, or double-deck configuration for 300 troops.
Freight hold access: Under-tail doors and ramp for straight-in loading.
Loading facilities: Full cargo handling system.
Wing characteristics: Slightly sweptback, with thick supercritical profile. High lift devices assisted by strong airflow from the propfans which double the lifting force during take-off and landing (the lifting force coefficient then becomes 5.6).

Details for the An-70

PRINCIPAL DIMENSIONS:
Wing span: 144 ft 6.5 ins (44.06 m)
Maximum length: 133 ft 7.5 ins (40.73 m)
Fuselage length: 130 ft 11 ins (39.91 m)
Maximum height: 53 ft 9 ins (16.38 m)

CABIN:
Length: 62 ft 8 ins (19.1 m)
Length, including ramp: 73 ft 6 ins (22.4 m)
Width, maximum: 15 ft 9 ins (4.8 m)
Width, at floor: 13 ft 1.5 ins (4 m)
Height: 13 ft 5.5 ins (4.1 m)
Volume: 15,009 cu ft (425 m^3)

WINGS:
Aerofoil section: Supercritical
Area: about 2,196 sq ft (204 m^2)
Aspect ratio: 9.5

UNDERCARRIAGE:
Type: Retractable, with steerable nosewheels. Multi-wheel of typical Antonov type. Nose leg has 1 twin-wheel bogie; main units comprise 3 such bogies
Wheel base: 59 ft 6.6 ins (18.15 m)
Wheel track: 17 ft 1 ins (5.2 m)

WEIGHTS:
Maximum take-off: 286,600 lb (130,000 kg)
Payload, maximum: 103,617 lb (47,000 kg)
Payload, nominal: 77,162 lb (35,000 kg)

PERFORMANCE:
Maximum operating speed: 405-432 kts (466-497 mph) 750-800 km/h
Landing speed: 86-89 kts (99-103 mph) 160-165 km/h
Take-off and landing distance: 5,906 ft (1,800 m)
Ceiling: 29,530-39,370 ft (9,000-12,000 m)
Range from 5,905-7,218 ft (1,800-2,200 m) concrete runway: 728.5 naut miles (839 miles) 1,350 km with a 103,617 lb (47,000 kg) payload, 2,050.5 naut miles (2,361 miles) 3,800 km with a 77,162 lb (35,000 kg) payload, 2,698 naut miles (3,107 miles) 5,000 km with a 66,139 lb (30,000 kg) payload, and 3,993 naut miles (4,598 miles) 7,400 km with a 44,092 lb (20,000 kg) payload
Range from a 2,953 ft (900 m) unprepared runway: 782 naut miles (901 miles) 1,450 km with a 77,162 lb (35,000 kg) payload, 1,403 naut miles (1,616 miles) 2,600 km with a 66,139 lb (30,000 kg) payload, 2,644 naut miles (3,045 miles) 4,900 km with a 44,092 lb (20,000 kg) payload
Range, maximum: 4,694 naut miles (5,406 miles) 8,700 km

Wing control surfaces: Ailerons, multi-slotted trailing-edge flaps, 3-section spoilers and leading-edge slats.
Tail control surfaces: Multi-section rudder and elevators, appearing to be of more conventional single-surface type on the twin-engined variants.
Construction materials: Composites account for about 24% of the aircraft weight, used not only for fairings and other non-structural elements but also for important structures including the entire tail unit, wing flaps and ailerons of Organit composite material. Structural elements using composites are made as 'integral structures' whereby, for instance, the tailplane structure forms an integral assembly without mechanical connections by means of bolts or rivets.
Engines: 4 Ivchenko PROGRESS/Zaporozhye D-27 propfans, with 14 ft 9 ins (4.5 m) Aerosila/Stupino SV-27 propellers each comprising 2 coaxial contra-rotating fans with 8 and 6 composite blades (front and rear fans respectively). Blades are attached diagonally to the hub (the blade axis does not intersect the hub axis). Propeller efficiency 0.9. See Aircraft variants.
Engine rating: each 14,000 shp (10,440 kW) take-off power.
Flight control system: Fly-by-wire type with multiple redundancy (3 digital and 6 analog channels). A special hydraulic stand-by system is connected to the main control system in such a way as to allow changeover in an emergency without any noticeable alteration for the pilots, the commands of the crew or autopilot being relayed to the actuators via hydraulic control channels that are impervious to disturbances such as electromagnetic radiation. By virtue of this control system, a fixed, non-adjustable tailplane could be adopted.

↑ **Antonov An-70 payload arrangements** *(courtesy Antonov)*

Radar: Leninets Kupol was originally planned, but now Phazotron Gukol navigation radar derived from the MiG-29M's Zhuk radar is also proposed.
Flight avionics/instrumentation: Integrated digital system by Aviapribor (FMS and navigation system, incorporating laser inertial navigation and satellite systems among others), NPO Elektroavtomatika (EFIS) and Leninets/St Petersburg (probably OBDMS), with common databus (for the first time in the CIS); due to this system, the length of connections could be reduced by 70% and their weight by 40%, and it makes for easy adoption of foreign equipment. 10 multi-function active liquid crystal colour cockpit displays, the 6 large primary displays for flight, navigation and systems data. SKI-77 head-up display for

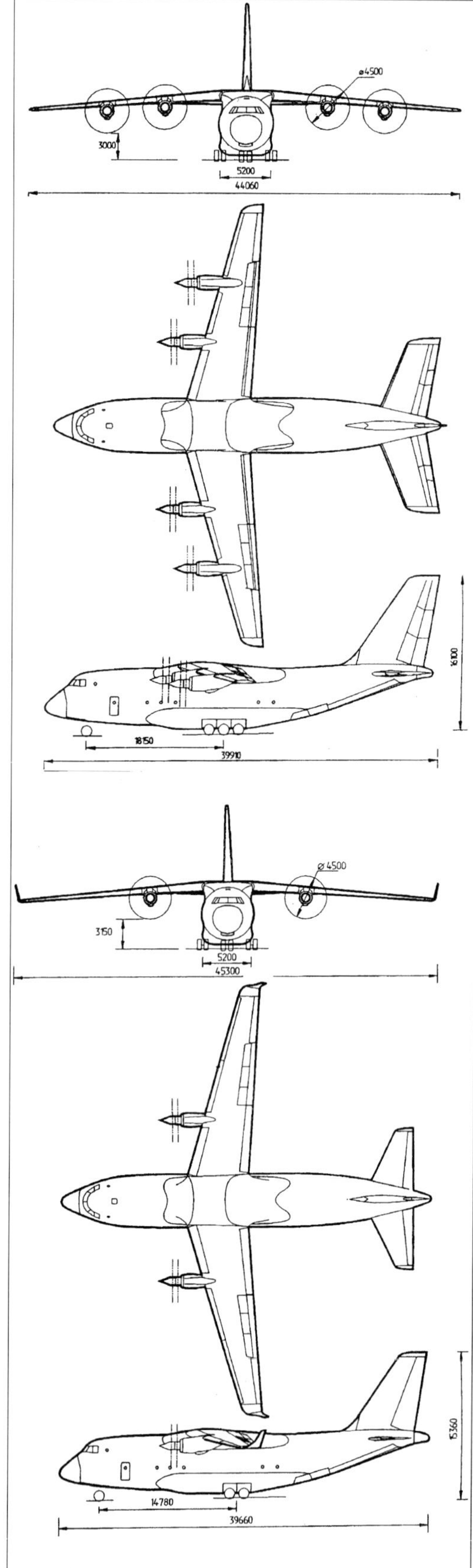

↑ **Antonov An-70T (*top*) and An-70T-100 (*bottom*)** *(courtesy Antonov)*

greater accuracy when taking-off and landing. The navigation system allows the aircraft to fly inside and outside the air traffic lines at any time and in any geographical region, with programmable flight path and optimization of fuel consumption. The instrument landing system meets the requirements of ICAO categories II and IIIa. The BASK-70 integrated in-flight automatic inspection system records and processes 8,000 parameters from all on-board systems (this is a version of the BASK-124 used on the An-124).

Aircraft variants:
An-70 (izdelye 77) is the basic military version.
An-70-100 is a projected military version with new avionics and crew reduced to 2-4.
An-70PS is a projected sea search-and-rescue version intended for paradropping of 17 rescuers and Yorsh motor boat with a crew of 3, as well as life-rafts, and medicine/clothing containers. Patrol duration 5 hours at 809 naut miles (932 miles) 1,500 km from base.
An-70T is the commercial transport version, without military landing/troop equipment or military communication systems. 2 prototypes under construction. Length 130 ft 11 ins (39.91 m), and height 52 ft 10 ins (16.1 m).
An-70T-100 is a projected twin-engined low-cost civil derivative of the An-70T, with no STOL capabilities and lower cruising speed. 2 × D-27 propfans. Fuselage as for the An-70T, but each main undercarriage unit has 4 (instead of 6) mainwheels. Winglets and tail unit changes. Crew of 2. Cruising speed 100 km/h less than for the An-70T, and payload at 5,000 km range is reduced to 44,092 lb (20,000 kg). Specific fuel consumption reduced from 165 to 125 g per tonne kilometre. Aircraft length 130 ft 1.5 ins (39.66 m), wing span 148 ft 7.5 ins (45.30 m), height 50 ft 5 ins (15.36 m) and wheelbase 48 ft 6 ins (14.78 m).
An-70T-200 will be powered by 2 Russian Trud/Samara NK-93 turbofans. Range 1,780 naut miles (2,050 miles) 3,300 km with a 77,162 lb (35,000 kg) payload.
An-70T-300 will be powered by 2 CFM56-5C4 turbofans. Range 890 naut miles (1,025 miles) 1,650 km with a 77,162 lb (35,000 kg) payload.
An-70T-400 will be powered by 4 CFM56-5C4s. Range 1,754 naut miles (2,019 miles) 3,250 km with a 77,162 lb (35,000 kg) payload.
An-70TK is the projected convertible cargo/passenger version, using fully-equipped and removable passenger containers in the cargo cabin.
Other projected versions are a flying tanker, firefighter, anti-submarine warfare, and airborne early warning aircraft.
An-77 (export model) was the former designation of the export An-70; when work began the designation An-70 was classified and so izdelye 77 was adopted for the export version. Now just An-70. Possible use of CFM56 turbofan engines and Western avionics.
An-170 is a projected heavy transport derivative (former export name An-177), with lengthened fuselage and wings (from the An-225). Nominal payload of 99,208-110,231 lb (45,000-50,000 kg).

Antonov An-72 and An-74 (NATO name *Coaler*)

First flight: 31 August 1977 (piloted by Vladimir Tersky). 22 December 1985 for the first flight of a production An-72, manufactured at the Kharkov aircraft plant. December 1989 for the first flight of a production An-74.
Certification: Type certificate issued on 4 August 1995 for the An-74TK-100 by the Russian Interstate Registry.
Role: Light freight and passenger transport, and military executive aircraft. Various special mission variants (see Aircraft variants).

↑ Antonov An-74 (*left*) and An-74TK-200 *(Piotr Butowski)*

Sales: 7 prototypes built at the Kiev aircraft plant (including 2 for static tests). Because the Kiev factory was occupied with the export-capable An-32, production of the An-72 was transferred to Kharkov, which previously built the Tupolev Tu-104/124/134 series. Different technology caused significant delay. Kharkov plant is a manufacturer of military versions (An-72), as well as the civil An-74, An-74-200D, An-74T-100/-200, and An-74TK-100/-200. About 150 aircraft of all versions have been built in Kharkov, mostly for military service. 12 An-74T-200As and TK-200s were ordered in 1995 for Iran's armed forces for $135 million (6 delivered by the start of 1998). In 1993, production of the An-74 was undertaken by the Polyot plant at Omsk, Russia, but only 5 had been built at the time of writing (4 An-74s and 1 An-74-200); current production offers include the An-74, An-74 Salon, An-74-200 and An-74TK-200.

Details *(principally for the An-72 Coaler-C)*

Crew: 3, comprising pilot, co-pilot/navigator and on-board engineer. Other versions may have different numbers of crew (for instance, An-72V has 2, while An-74 has 5).
Passengers: Standard military An-72 can carry 57 paratroops or 68 troops on folding or removable seats, or 36 wounded (including 24 litter cases). Up to 52 passengers for the An-74TK-100/-200. For other configurations, see Aircraft variants.
Pressurization: Maximum differential 7.1 psi for cockpit and cabin.
Freight hold access: Hydraulically opened rear loading ramp. When opened, the ramp can take 2 positions: lowered for roll-on from the ground or slid back horizontally under the fuselage for air-dropping or for loading directly from trucks. See diagram for entrance height and ramp angle.
Size of freight door: Rear ramp door is 23 ft 4 ins (7.1 m) long and 7 ft 10.5 ins (2.4 m) wide.
Freight hold capacity: Pressurized cargo hold is also air conditioned, the latter also used to cool perishable loads when necessary. The various internal configurations, according to requirement and variant, allow for 22,046 lb (10,000 kg) of freight, including 4 × PAV-2.5 pallets or a similar number of UAK-2.5 containers. Comfortable executive versions exist. See Aircraft variants for An-72AT and An-74 combi layout.
Loading facilities: A travelling crane, 5,512 lb (2,500 kg) lifting capacity, is attached to the ceiling and can work in conjunction with a removable winch of similar capacity. Floor-mounted roller tracks are optional.
Wing characteristics: High-mounted with anhedral. Position of the engines forward of the wing leading edges allows the efflux to flow over the wing and flaps to increase lift.
Wing control surfaces: Double-slotted trailing-edge flaps on the wing centre section, triple-slotted flap and 4 sections of spoilers on each middle panel (2 raised prior to landing and 2 open automatically on landing via an undercarriage sensor), and 2-section aileron (with 2 tabs on port side, 1 on starboard) on each outer panel. 3 sections of slats occupy the entire leading-edge span outboard of engine nacelles.
Tail control surfaces: T-tail has the tailplane located beyond the zone of exhaust gas and aerodynamic disturbances behind the wing; tailplane has a unique inverted leading-edge slat co-ordinated with the wing flaps. 2-section rudder; the rear section is subdivided into 2 parts, the lower (with tab) activated manually by the pilot and used for directional control in normal flight, the other adjusted by means of actuators. The upper part of the rear section is used for low speed flying, whereas the front section is used only for compensation for thrust asymmetry in case of failure of 1 engine. Elevators (with 2 tabs each side).
Construction materials: Mainly metal, but with 2,161 lb (980 kg) of composite materials.
Engines: 2 Ivchenko PROGRESS/Zaporozhye D-36 turbofans (Series 1A initially, some current production aircraft having Series 2A, but the main version is Series 3A with added emergency mode when 1 engine is shut down; all engines are of the same thrust). Thrust reversers.
Engine rating: Each 14,330 lbf (63.745 kN).
Fuel system: 7 tanks inside the wing torsion box, for a total of 16,250 litres (28,550 lb, 12,950 kg).
Flight refuelling probe: None.
De-icing system: Thermal for cockpit glazing, wing and tail leading edges, and air intakes.
Radar: Navigation/weather radar in the nose.
Flight avionics/instrumentation: Malva-4 Doppler navigation. PK-72 (PK-72-03 on An-74) system provides flight along a programmed path and landing approach to an altitude of 98 ft (30 m).
Fixed weapons: None.

Aircraft variants:
An-72 (izdelye 72) *Coaler-A* was the prototype; the first prototype had a shorter wing span (84 ft 9 ins, 25.83 m), shorter rear fuselage, 2 ventral fins and a braking chute.
An-72 *Coaler-C* is the standard military transport, as detailed. Initially with D-36 Series 1A engines but currently with Series 3As.
An-72-100 is a commercial upgrade of 'demobilized' military An-72s. Some systems improvements, civil navigation/communications added. Certified in early 1997.

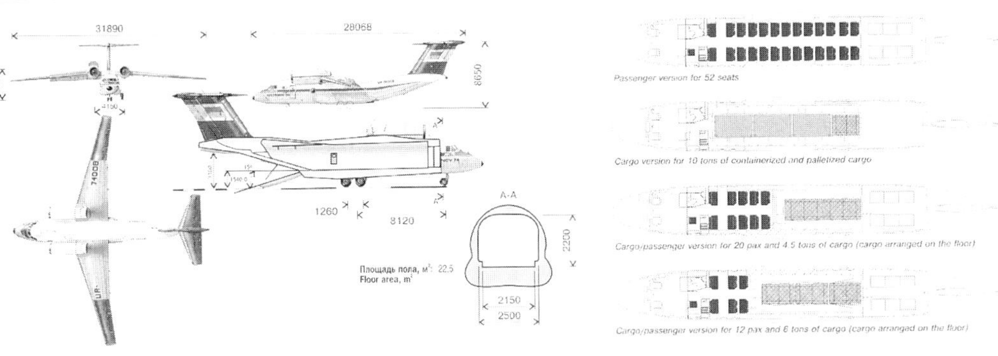

↑ Antonov An-74 general arrangement (*left*) and An-74TK-200 layouts *(courtesy Antonov)*

An-72AT is a freighter adapted for standard airborne containers.
An-72V is an export version with crew of 2.
An-72M is a projected improved version.
An-72PS is a proposed search and rescue version.
An-72P was an electronic countermeasures prototype, tested in mid-1980s.
An-72P patrol version (using the same designation as the EW prototype). See Electronic section.
An-72S is the military executive version with 38 passenger seats and a small cargo compartment large enough for a small vehicle or other load.
An-71 *Madcap* airborne early warning and control aircraft was based on the An-72. See Electronic section.
An-74 (prototype named An-72A, for Arktichesky or Arctic) is a civil version for use in polar regions, announced in February 1984. First production aircraft manufactured December 1989 in Kharkov. The de-icing systems as well as cabin heating and ventilation have been improved in respect of the An-72. The cabin layout has been changed, with 8 armchair-type seats forward, a small bedroom and 3 stations for hydrologists carrying out surveillance of surface ice or navigating the ship convoys. The undercarriage can have ski/wheel units. Fuel capacity has been increased considerably. Navigation system improved. Also, special equipment for precise dropping of loads (for instance, to ice floes). During tests, the crew of S. Gorbik landed the aircraft with a 4,409 lb (2,000 kg) load of scientific equipment on a 1,969 ft (600 m) long icefield and then took off taking a group of polar scientists. Maximum take-off weight of 76,721 lb (34,800 kg), maximum payload of 16,535 lb (7,500 kg), and D-36 Series 2A engines.
An-74P-100 is an executive transport for 16 passengers.
An-74P or ***An-74 Salon*** is a 16-seat VIP derivative of the An-74. Certified in 1996.
An-74P-100 is similar to An-74P but with a crew of 4.
An-74T (transportyi) is a standard civil freight version of the An-74, with no Arctic equipment or systems. Crew of 3.
An-74TK (konvertiruyemyi) is a convertible cargo/passenger version of the An-74T, with 52 folding seats.

Details for An-72 *Coaler-C*

PRINCIPAL DIMENSIONS:
Wing span: 104 ft 7.5 ins (31.89 m)
Maximum length: 92 ft 1 ins (28.068 m)
Maximum height: 28 ft 4.5 ins (8.65 m) still quoted, but often accepted as 28 ft 8.5 ins (8.75 m)

CABIN:
Length, including ramp: 34 ft 5.5 ins (10.5 m)
Width: 7 ft 1 ins (2.15 m) at floor, 8 ft 2 ins (2.5 m) maximum
Height: 7 ft 3 ins (2.2 m)

WINGS:
Area, gross: 1,060.6 sq ft (98.53 m^2)
Aspect ratio: 10.32
Sweepback: 17°
Anhedral: 10°

UNDERCARRIAGE:
Type: Retractable, with steerable twin nosewheels. Low-pressure tandem mainwheels
Main wheel tyre size: 1,050 × 390 mm
Nose wheel tyre size: 720 × 310 mm
Wheel base: 26 ft 8 ins (8.12 m)
Wheel track: 13 ft 7.5 ins (4.15 m)

WEIGHTS:
Empty, operating: 44,533 lb (20,200 kg)
Maximum take-off: 80,469 lb (36,500 kg)
Take-off from a 3,281 ft (1,000 m) runway: 60,627 lb (27,500 kg)
Payload, nominal: 11,023 lb (5,000 kg)
Payload, maximum: 22,046 lb (10,000 kg)

PERFORMANCE:
Maximum speed: 381 kts (438 mph) 705 km/h at 32,810 ft (10,000 m)
Cruise speed: 297-324 kts (342-373 mph) 550-600 km/h at 32,810 ft (10,000 m)
Landing speed: 97 kts (112 mph) 180 km/h
Take-off distance at 72,732 lb (33,000 kg) weight: 3,051 ft (930 m)
Take-off distance at 60,627 lb (27,500 kg) weight: 2,034 ft (620 m)
Landing distance: 1,378-1,526 ft (420-465 m)
Ceiling, at 72,732 lb (33,000 kg) weight: 35,105 ft (10,700 m)
Ceiling, at 60,627 lb (27,500 kg) weight: 38,715 ft (11,800 m)
Range with full fuel: 2,592 naut miles (2,983 miles) 4,800 km, with 45 minutes reserve
Range at full payload: 728.5 naut miles (839 miles) 1,350 km, with 60 minutes reserve

An-74T-100 and ***An-74TK-100*** are the An-74T and TK (respectively) with a navigator completing a crew of 4. An-74TK-100 first flew in April 1995 and received a Russian type certificate in August 1995.
An-74-200, ***An-74T-200A*** and ***An-74TK-200*** are the An-74, T and TK with changes in equipment, MTOW of 80,469 lb (36,500 kg), and Series 3A engines. Crew of 2 in T-200A and TK-200; 5 in -200.
An-74-200D (delovoi, business) is a business aircraft for 10 to 16 passengers. Range 2,698 naut miles (3,107 miles) 5,000 km.
An-74-300 is currently under development, with engines moved to below wings. Because of better aerodynamics, range will increase by 600 km. First flight expected late 1999.
An-74Ts (tsiklon) is a meteorological research version.
An-74GF is a geophysical research version.

Antonov An-124 (NATO name *Condor*)

First flight: 26 December 1982 (prototype *CCCP-680125* commanded by Vladimir Tersky).
Certification: 30 December 1992. Civil certification was awarded to the An-124-100 by the Aviaregistr of the Interstate Aviation Committee, CIS.
First delivery: First aircraft (*01-06*) was delivered on 10 February 1987 to Soviet Voyenno-Transportnaya Aviatsya's (Military Transport Aviation) 566th Regiment based at Seshcha.
Role: Very heavy, long-range military/civil freighter.

Development

- 24 January 1977. Government resolution to begin work on the An-124 (izdelye 400). First project had wings with sweepback of 25°, but a projected later passenger version required higher speed and the wings were redesigned to 30°. The passenger version never materialized.
- Early 1980s. First information published in the West, quoted as An-40, later An-400.
- 26 July 1985. 21 records set, including a 377,473 lb (171,219 kg) payload lifted to 35,270 ft (10,750 m). Pilot V. Tersky.
- 6-7 May 1987. Closed distance of 10,881 naut miles (12,521 miles) 20,151 km achieved.
- September 1990. 451 refugees were emergency airlifted from Amman to Dacca in a single An-124, with only basic amenities.
- 1993. The heaviest single load ever transported by air up to that time was a 124 tonne power plant generator core secured on a specially built load-spreading skid, totalling 135.2 tonnes. This was carried from Dusseldorf in Germany to New Delhi in India on an An-124-100 on behalf of Siemens AG.

Details

Sales: Production started at the Kiev aircraft plant (now Aviant), later joined by the newly-constructed Ulyanovsk factory (now Aviastar – originally, the factory was built for Tu-160 production). First Ulyanovsk-built An-124 flew in October 1985. Wings are produced in Tashkent, Uzbekistan. During 1984 to 1997, 54 aircraft were built, comprising 18 at Kiev and 36 at Ulyanovsk. Russian Air Force currently has 26 An-124s in operation, with 21 others (all now converted into An-124-100s) in use with civil operators (see below). 5 aircraft have been lost, the most recent at Irkutsk on 6 December 1997. Budget restraints have meant that the Russian Air Force is not purchasing further An-124s. Production is continuing for civil operation only at the Ulyanovsk plant (3 under construction during 1997 for Samara Airlines); production at Kiev ended with An-124-100 (*03-03*) built in 1997. Civil operators include Volga-Dnepr of Russia which operates 7 (2 based in the UK), Rossiya (the Russian Government Air Services unit in Aeroflot) for Presidential/VIP use (they can be used commercially when not officially required), Antonov design bureau (5), AJAX (an Aeroflot subsidiary), Air Foyle of the UK which leases 3, and HeavyLift of the UK.
Crew: 6 or 7, comprising pilot, co-pilot, navigator, communications officer, on-board engineer and electrical engineer, with additional loadmaster for the military version. For long distance flights the aircraft carries a rest crew. Up to a dozen cargo handlers may accompany commercial loads. Crews vary for different models (for example, An-124-102 will have a 3-crew cockpit).
Passengers: See Fuselage.
Pressurization: Normal pressure differential 7.8 psi in the crew and passenger compartments but lowered to 3.6 psi in the cargo hold. The lower hold pressure allowed structural weight savings.
Freight hold volume: 35,315 cu ft (1,000 m^3).
Freight hold capacity: 4 platforms of P-7 or P-16 type, when equipment or cargo can be paradropped. Alternatively 12 ISO containers or other heavy/bulky cargoes including battle tanks, construction vehicles, heavy guns, missile systems, Shtil-3A ballistic satellite launcher, generators, etc. Paratroop operations are limited by the low hold pressurization, but when conducted the paratroopers exit in 2 files via the rear hatch with D-5 parachutes of forced opening type. (See Fuselage for passenger capacity.)
Freight hold access: Cargo is rolled or drawn into the hold via a visor-type upward-hinging fuselage nose (7 minute opening time). Unloading (or simultaneous loading) is via the standard rear door ramp.
Loading facilities: 2 travelling cranes, 22,046 lb (10,000 kg) capacity each, are installed on the cargo hold ceiling. 2 electric winches each have a 6,614 lb (3,000 kg) pulling capacity. The floor height may be adjusted in order to make cargo handling easier: the main undercarriage unit oleos may be compressed to lower the cargo hold threshold; alternatively, the nose unit can retract after extendable 'rests' have been deployed, offering a sloping hold of 3° 30'. Due to 2 APUs, cargo handling can be carried out without ground power sources.
Wing control surfaces: Each wing trailing edge has 3 sections of extended-area single-slotted flaps, with diversified deflection angle, and 2 sections of ailerons (with dampers). 12 spoilers on the upper surface of each wing. 6 sections of leading-edge flaps.
Tail control surfaces: 2-section elevators and 2-section rudder. Fixed incidence tailplane.
Flight control system: Near-zero static stability. Quadruple-redundant fly-by-wire with mechanical backup. Control-wheels for pilots.
Fuselage: Double-deck fuselage, the upper diameter 12 ft 5.5 ins (3.8 m) and the lower 23 ft 7 ins (7.2 m). The upper contains the crew cockpit and a compartment for a relief crew with a galley and toilet. A cabin for 88 persons is located on the upper deck behind the wings. The lower deck contains the cargo hold.
Construction materials: Mainly light metal alloys, but with a

↑ **Antonov An-124 of Russian military transport aviation** *(Piotr Butowski)*

titanium cargo hold floor and about 12,125 lb (5,500 kg) of composites.
Engines: 4 Ivchenko PROGRESS/Zaporozhye D-18T turbofans. Current production aircraft have Ivchenko PROGRESS D-18T Series 3Ss with longer service life, lower fuel consumption and better reliability. Thrust reversers of outer (cold) flow type are standard for all engines. 2 TA-12 APUs in the main undercarriage nacelles. Volga-Dnepr has proposed replacing D-18Ts with Rolls-Royce RB211-524Gs, while Antonov has proposed General Electric CF6-80C2s. Another possibility is the Kuznetsov NK-93 ducted propfan.
Engine rating: Each 51,654 lbf (229.78 kN).
Fuel system: 10 integral tanks in the wings, with a total capacity of 471,215 lb (213,740 kg). Maximum practical fuel weight for the An-124-100 is 468,151 lb (212,350 kg).
Flight refuelling probe: None.
De-icing system: Bleed air for wing leading edges and electro-impulse for tailplane leading edges and the fin.
Radar: 2 radars under a common nose radome, comprising a navigation unit and weather unit. (See An-124-100M below.)
Flight avionics/instrumentation: SAU-3-400 automatic control system, inertial navigation, Loran and Omega navigation. Programmed flight path with more than 30 waypoints. Cockpit instrumentation is conventional. BASK-124 integrated automatic inspection system records and processes parameters picked up from more than 1,200 sensors. An-124-100M has Russian 3A822-10M navigation radar; Rockwell Collins SAT-906 satellite communications, ACARS and TCAS-2; and Litton LTN-101 INS, LTN-2001 GPS, and LTN-450.

Aircraft variants:
An-124 (izdelye 400, Ruslan) *Condor* is the basic military transport version for autonomous operation.
An-124-100 is the civil version adapted to extended loading infrastructure of commercial airports.
An-124-100M has the crew reduced to 4 (no communication operator or on-board engineer) due to new avionics which includes Russian 3A822-10M navigation radar; Rockwell Collins SAT-906 satellite communications, ACARS and TCAS-2; Litton LTN-101 INS, LTN-2001 GPS, and LTN-450. First An-124-100M (08-03) was being constructed at Ulyanovsk in 1997.
An-124-100V has noise-reducing covers on the engine nacelles to comply with Chapter 3 Appendix 16 of ICAO standards. Noise cover certified in 1996, with the first aircraft converted in April 1997 (*01-08*); all An-124-100s will be converted before the end of 1998.
An-124-100MV will be a merging of -100M with -100V types.
An-124-102 will have a 3-crew cockpit. Preliminary project only.
An-124-200 is a projected upgrade of the An-124-100M with General Electric CF6-80C2 turbofans. No orders for such an upgrade, as it has been reported that the upgrade cost would take 15 or more years to return, whereas upgrade costs with new D-18T Series 3S turbofans would be returned after 5 years.
An-124A became a projected military version for second-class airfields. 6 tandem wheel sets rather than 5.
An-124AK is a version designed as a platform for the Shtil-3A ballistic missile that is used for launching satellites into Earth orbit. The missile can be carried in the aircraft hold to a distance of 2,214 naut miles (2,548 miles) 4,100 km. Then, at an altitude of 36,090 ft (11,000 m) and speed of 410 kts (472 mph) 760 km/h, it is withdrawn from the cargo hold by means of a parachute. It is then stabilized in a vertical position and its engines started. The weight of Shtil-3A is 100,531 lb (45,600 kg), and length 61 ft 4 ins (18.7 m); it was originally designed for strategic submarines by the V. Makeyev bureau. A similar project based on older type ballistic missiles is Oril (Eagle).
An-124FFR was put under development in 1994 as a firefighting version, capable of delivering 200 tonnes of water plus retardants, using the cargo hold plus 70 tonnes stored in the wing centre section. A kit would be provided to re-convert the aircraft to cargo carrying for off-season operations. An estimated 16 could be required in the next 5 years, at about $100-120 million each.

Details for the An-124, *with An-124-100 in italics for weights*

PRINCIPAL DIMENSIONS:
Wing span: 240 ft 6 ins (73.3 m)
Maximum length: 226 ft 8.5 ins (69.1 m)
Maximum height: 69 ft 2 ins (21.08 m)

CABIN:
Length, at floor: 119 ft 9 ins (36.5 m)
Length, including front and rear ramps: 142 ft 7 ins (43.45 m)
Width, maximum: 21 ft 11 ins (6.68 m)
Width at floor: 21 ft (6.4 m)
Height, maximum: 14 ft 5 ins (4.4 m)

WINGS:
Aerofoil section: Supercritical
Area, gross: 6,760 sq ft (628 m^2)
Aspect ratio: 8.556
Sweepback at quarter chord: 25°
Sweepback at leading edge: 33° root, 30° outer
Incidence: +3° 30′

UNDERCARRIAGE:
Type: Retractable, with steerable nosewheels. Each main unit comprises 5 tandem sets of twin wheels housed inside nacelles on the fuselage sides (each set of twin wheels is independent of the others). Despite its size, the An-124A could have the ability to operate from unprepared strips and other surfaces. For height and slope adjustments, see Loading facilities
Main wheel tyre size: 1,270 × 510 mm
Nose wheel tyre size: 1,120 × 450 mm
Wheel track: 29 ft (8.84 m)
Turning circle: Requires a 147 ft 8 ins (45 m) wide area

WEIGHTS:
Empty, operating: 385,800 lb (175,000 kg)
Maximum take-off: 892,871 lb (405,000 kg)
Maximum ramp: *877,439 lb (398,000 kg)*
Normal maximum take-off: 864,210 lb (392,000 kg), *same for An-124-100 as maximum certificated take-off*
Maximum landing: 727,525 lb (330,000 kg), *same for An-124-100*
Payload, maximum: 330,693 lb (150,000 kg)
Payload, normal maximum: 264,554 1b (120,000 kg), *same for An-124-100*

PERFORMANCE:
Maximum Mach number: 0.77
Maximum speed: 459 kts (528 mph) 850 km/h
Cruise speed: 432 kts (497 mph) 800 km/h
Landing speed: 119-151 kts (137-174 mph) 220-280 km/h
Required runway length: 9,843 ft (3,000 m)
Ceiling: 31,170 ft (9,500 m)
Range with 330,693 lb (150,000 kg) payload: 2,430 naut miles (2,796 miles) 4,500 km
Range with 264,554 lb (120,000 kg) payload: 2,700 naut miles (3,107 miles) 5,000 km
Range with 88,185 lb (40,000 kg) payload: 6,480 naut miles (7,456 miles) 12,000 km
Maximum range: 8,688 naut miles (9,998 miles) 16,090 km
Duration, maximum: 20 hours

Antonov An-140 and An-142

First flight: 17 September 1997 in Kiev (pilot Anatoli Khrustitsky, co-pilot Yevgeni Galunenko, test flight engineer Alexander Makiyan).
Certification: According to AP-25 (FAR-25) anticipated about 18 months after the first flight.
Role: Short-haul regional airliner to replace An-24. Should offer twice the fuel efficiency, 2.2 times the maximum range and 1.4 times the cruise speed of the An-24, plus improve comfort.
Airframe life: Design life of 40,000 cycles or 50,000 flight hours, or 25 years.
Sales: First prototype was rolled-out on 6 June 1997 and flew on 17 September that year. Second (for flight tests) and third (static tests) aircraft have been constructed. Series production is being undertaken at Kharkov (launch manufacturer), Kiev in the Ukraine, and Samara in Russia. First production aircraft will fly in 1998 in Kharkov. In 1997 Ukrainian Airlines ordered 40 An-140s, with the first 4 to be delivered in 1998. On 25 September 1997, Aviacor of Samara and Atlas Project Management signed a contract for the production, marketing and leasing of the An-140 commuter in production at Aviacor. The first An-140 to be assembled in Samara should be flown in 1998. Total demand within Russia is estimated at 430 aircraft, Ukraine 70, and the total for other countries between 900 and 1,000. Antonov won a tender from Iran to complete the HESA aircraft plant at Isfahan for An-140 production (contract signed on 2 December 1995), expected to offer a production rate of 12 aircraft per year in both civil and military transport versions; the factory had been started by America but remained uncompleted. The present contract provides for Ukraine to fit out the factory, train Iranian aircraft specialists in the Ukraine, implement An-140 production, and establish an aircraft design bureau in Iran.
Crew: 2.
Passengers and seat pitch: Basic configuration for 52 (pitch 30 ins, 76.2 cm) or 46 (pitch 32 ins. 81 cm) passengers. Mixed layout for 20 passengers and 8,047 lb (3,650 kg) of cargo. Maximum payload 13,228 lb (6,000 kg).
Galley: Aft of cabin.
Pressurization: Standard.
Freight hold volume: 106 cu ft (3 m^3) under the forward cabin floor.
Baggage holds: 212 cu ft (6 m^3) aft.
Wing control surfaces: Horn-balanced ailerons (with 2 tabs on port aileron and single tab on starboard) and 2-section flaps. 2-section spoilers.
Tail control surfaces: Elevators and rudder, both with tabs.
Engines: 2 Ivchenko PROGRESS/Zaporozhye TV3-117VMA-SB2 turboprops (later TV3-117VMA-SBM rated at 3,000 shp, 2,237 kW are expected) developed from Klimov/St Petersburg TV3-117 helicopter engine, with 6-blade AV-140 advanced propellers. Ground tests of TV3-117VMA-SB2 started in March 1997 in Zaporozhye. Pratt & Whitney Canada PW127A engines are also under consideration. AI-9-3B APU.
Engine rating: Each 2,500 shp (1,864 kW).

↑ **Antonov An-140 regional transport**

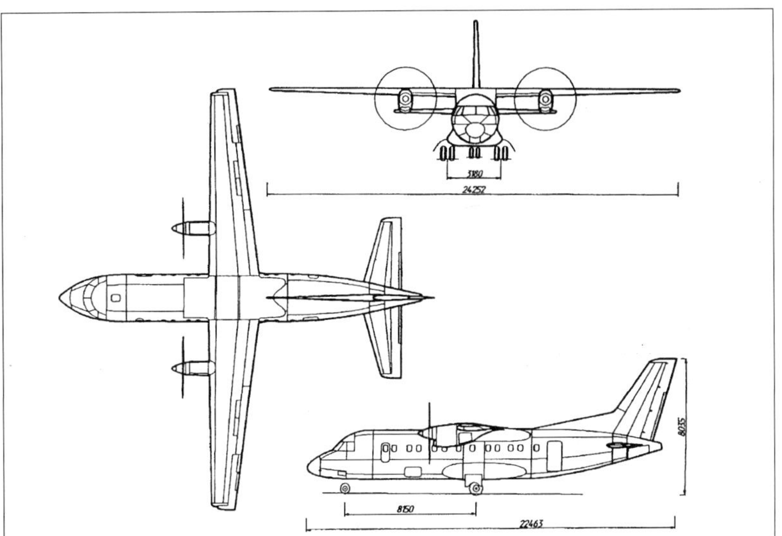

↑ **Antonov An-140 general arrangement** *(courtesy Antonov)*

Aircraft variants:
An-140 is the standard version with Ivchenko PROGRESS engines.
An-140T will have a cargo door added to the port side of the rear fuselage.
An-140TK will be a convertible passenger/cargo version. According to Piotr Balabuyev, Antonov general designer, this is a 'most desirable' version.
An-140VIP will be a business version.
An-140-100 is a projected 68-seat derivative with the fuselage stretched by 12 ft 5 ins (3.8 m), more powerful engines and insignificantly larger wing.
An-142 is a projected military and commercial transport version of the An-140 with rear ramp, to replace the An-26.

Details for An-140

PRINCIPAL DIMENSIONS:
Wing span: 79 ft 7 ins (24.252 m)
Maximum length: 73 ft 8 ins (22.463 m)
Maximum height: 26 ft 4 ins (8.035 m)

CABIN:
Length: 34 ft 5 ins (10.5 m)
Main passenger doors: 5 ft 3 ins × 3 ft 3 ins (1.605 × 0.98 m)

UNDERCARRIAGE:
Type: Retractable, with twin steerable nosewheels
Wheel track: 10 ft 5 ins (3.18 m)
Wheel base: 26 ft 9 ins (8.15 m)

PERFORMANCE (estimated)**:**
Cruise speed: 310 kts (357 mph) 575 km/h
Cruise altitude: 23,625 ft (7,200 m)
Required runway length: 4,429 ft (1,350 m)
Range with full fuel and 34 passengers: 1,985 naut miles (2,286 miles) 3,680 km
Range with 52 passengers: 1,133 naut miles (1,305 miles) 2,100 km

Antonov An-180

First flight: Not yet flown. Design was completed in 1994 but the programme was put on hold due to a lack of funding.
Role: Medium-range propfan airliner. To meet ICAO Category IIIa requirements.
Airframe life: 60,000 flying hours.
Flight crew: 2 or 3.
Passengers: 150-175. Also to be made available in combi form with passengers and freight in the main cabin.
Seat pitch: 32 ins (81 cm) in 163 passenger single class layout.
Freight hold capacity: 7 × LD3 containers under the cabin floor. An all-cargo version has been projected.
Wing control surfaces: Ailerons, flaps and 3-section spoilers.
Tail control surfaces: Multi-section elevators and single-piece rudder.
Engines: 2 Ivchenko PROGRESS/Zaporozhye D-27 propfans, with co-axial contra-rotating tractor propellers, mounted at the tips of the swept tailplane.
Engine rating: Each 13,819 eshp (10,305 ekW) at take-off.
Flight avionics/instrumentation: Automated navigation throughout the flight regime.

Details for the An-180

PRINCIPAL DIMENSIONS:
Wing span: 117 ft 6.5 ins (35.83 m)
Maximum length: 134 ft 2 ins (40.9 m)
Maximum height: 36 ft 7 ins (11.148 m)

UNDERCARRIAGE:
Type: Retractable, with twin steerable nosewheels and tandem pairs of mainwheels

WEIGHT:
Payload: 39,683 lb (18,000 kg)

PERFORMANCE:
Cruise speed: 432 kts (497 mph) 800 km/h
Required runway length: 6,398-7,546 ft (1,950-2,300 m)
Cruise ceiling: 29,855-33,135 ft (9,100-10,100 m)
Range with full fuel: 4,586 naut miles (5,281 miles) 8,500 km
Range with 163 passengers: 3,049 naut miles (3,511 miles) 5,650 km
Range with full payload: 2,212 naut miles (2,547 miles) 4,100 km

Antonov An-218

First flight: Originally expected 1996, but the programme is considerably delayed. The mock-up is ready and production instrumentation is nearing completion.
Role: Medium/long-range airliner, of the class of the Boeing 767. Intended to meet ICAO Category IIIa.
Sales: 1998 was possibly the earliest date for production to have begun.
Flight crew: 2.
Passengers: 195, or 292 in a mixed class layout (comprising 210 economy class, 64 business and 18 first), or 350/400 (all economy), depending on the version (see Aircraft variants).
Seat pitch: 29.5 or 31.9 ins (75 or 81 cm) economy, 40.2 ins (102 cm) first class and 34.3 ins (87 cm) business.
Freight hold volume: Possible 6,367.2 cu ft (180.3 m^3) in 2 main under-cabin holds plus the baggage hold.
Freight hold capacity: 24 containers beneath the cabin floor.
Wing control surfaces: Ailerons, flaps, 7-section spoilers, and leading-edge slats.
Tail control surfaces: Elevators and 2-section rudder.
Engines: 2 Ivchenko PROGRESS/Zaporozhye D-18TM turbofans. See Aircraft variants for D-18TRs and other engines.
Engine rating: Each 57,320 lbf (254.98 kN) max contingency, 48,149 lbf (214.18 kN) take-off.
Fuel system: Low fuel-burn, anticipated at about 18g per passenger-km.
Flight avionics/instrumentation: Electronic cockpit displays.

Aircraft variants:
An-218-100 is the base version with D-18TM turbofans, as detailed.
An-218-200 is a long-range 220 passenger version with more powerful 60,627 lbf (269.7 kN) D-18TR engines, with alternative General Electric CF6-80C2B6, Pratt & Whitney PW4060 or Rolls-Royce RB211-524H4s. Increased fuel capacity.
An-218-300 is the projected extended range model, carrying sufficient fuel in the standard and new freight-hold tanks for 6,048 naut miles (6,959 miles) 11,200 km. Length reduced to 158 ft 5 ins (48.29 m), with consequent reduction in passenger capacity to 195.
An-218-400 is a projected 400-seater, with lengthened fuselage.

Details for the An-218-100

PRINCIPAL DIMENSIONS:
Wing span: 164 ft (50 m)
Maximum length: 196 ft 2 ins (59.79 m)
Maximum height: 58 ft 1 ins (17.7 m)

UNDERCARRIAGE:
Type: Retractable, with twin steerable nosewheels. Each main unit comprises 3 pairs of wheels in tandem

WEIGHT:
Payload: 92,594 lb (42,000 kg)

PERFORMANCE:
Typical cruise speed: 470 kts (541 mph) 870 km/h
Required runway length: 9,515 ft (2,900 m)
Range with 350 passengers: 4,532 naut miles (5,219 miles) 8,400 km
Range with 220 passengers (An-218-200): 5,724 naut miles (6,587 miles) 10,600 km

Antonov An-225 Mriya (NATO name *Cossack*), An-224 and An-325

Comments: The only An-225 very heavy-lift transport built to date first flew on 21 December 1988, piloted by Aleksandr Galunienko. Conceived specially for carrying the Buran space shuttle and Energia rocket elements from the production plant in Moscow to the Baykonur cosmodrome, the design philosophy had been to use as many components from the An-124 as possible. This original task is no longer of the same importance, though the An-225 could later continue to make flights with elements of Buran/Energia but on a reduced scale. An-225 was also used for other tasks; for example, in May 1990 for its first commercial flight, it airlifted a 100-tonne T-800 tractor from

↑ **Antonov An-325 8-engined test model, during tests at TsAGI to assess the aircraft as a launching platform for Hotol** *(courtesy TsAGI)*

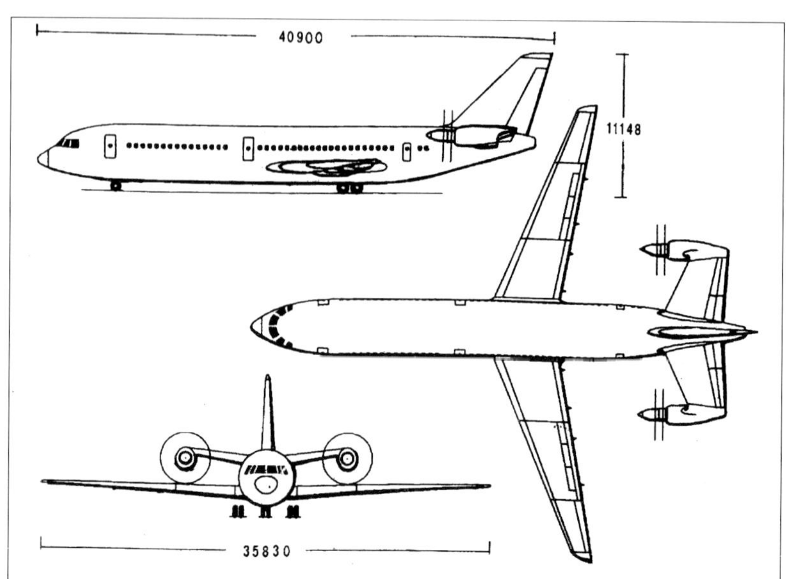

↑ **Antonov An-180 general arrangement** *(courtesy Antonov)*

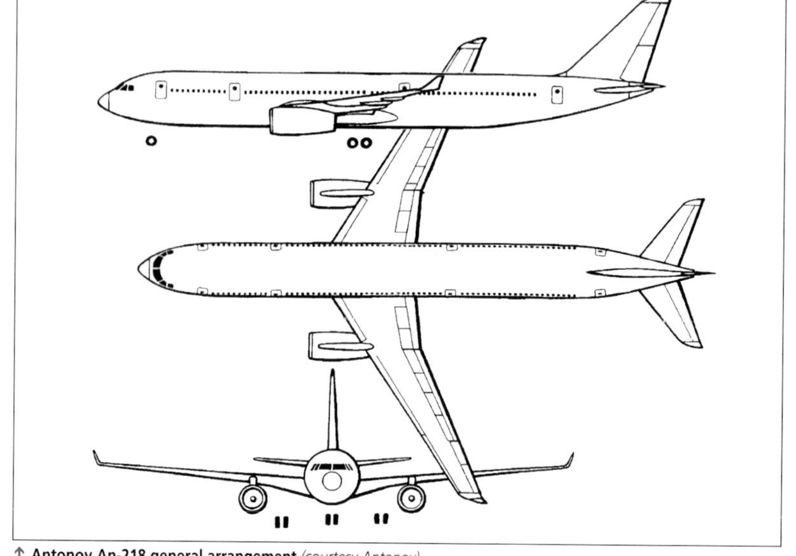

↑ **Antonov An-218 general arrangement** *(courtesy Antonov)*

↑ Antonov An-225 Mriya *(Piotr Butowski)*

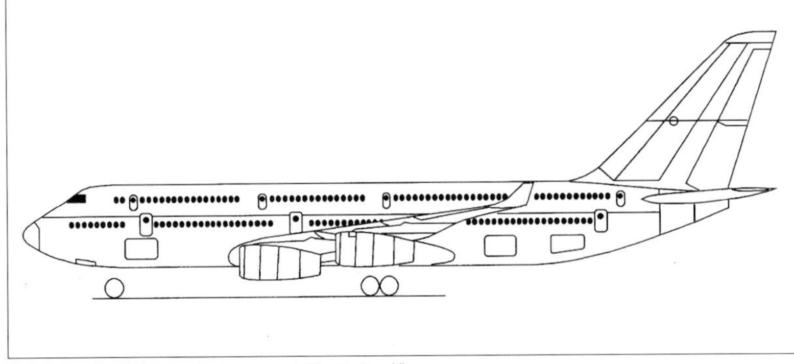
↑ Antonov An-418 general arrangement *(Piotr Butowski)*

Chelabinsk to Yakutia, and in 1991-92 made 9 flights with humanitarian aid from Canada and the USA to the Ukraine. It could also offer a launching platform for space vehicles. The flown An-225 has, however, been in storage for over 2 years and cannibalized. A second An-225 could be ready to be assembled from 1999 (its wing centre section was delivered from Tashkent to Kiev on the back of an An-22 in March 1993). Antonov, in association with the cargo charter airline Air Foyle, has proposed returning the An-225 back into service for commercial use, with proposals for possibly an eventual fleet of 3. A full description of the An-225 can be found in the 1996-97 edition of *WA&SD*, pages 256-257. A list of aircraft variants, including the An-325, follows.

Aircraft variants:
An-224 was an initial project with both An-124-type nose and rear cargo entrances.
An-225 *Cossack*, as detailed.
An-225-100 will be a commercial conversion of the An-225 (as for An-124-100 converted from An-124). Conversion of the first An-225 is planned for 1999 and then construction of the second aircraft could be completed (there is an investor for the programme). Payload 440,924 lb (200,000 kg) internally or 551,155 lb (250,000 kg) externally.
An-325 is an increased-payload version equipped for the MAKS aerospace system (see below). 8 engines, with 2 side-by-side engines on common inner pylons.
Various projects are envisaged using the An-225 and An-325 as launching platforms. These include:
1) British Aerospace Interim Hotol space shuttle which, launched from an An-225 at 29,530 ft (9,000 m) altitude, would reach any Earth orbit. Project companies from UK, Russia and Ukraine.
2) MAKS, where an An-225 or An-325 would carry a Russian Molnia-1 space vehicle built by the Gleb Lozino-Lozinski team. A Russian-Ukrainian project.
3) Svityaz ballistic missile, based on the military Zenit type, proposed as a space launcher.
4) Mriya-Orlyonok as a sea rescue system, with an A-90 Orlyonok wing-in-ground effect craft carried on the back of an An-225. The weight of Orlyonok, built by the Rostislav Alekseyev team, is equal to 110 tonnes.
5) Radem testbed for space technologies.

Antonov An-418

Comments: The An-418 is a projected 4-engined variant of the An-218, to carry 690 passengers over a range of 5,396 naut miles (6,214 miles) 10,000 km, or 500-550 passengers over 6,475-7,015 naut miles (7,456-8,078 miles) 12,000-13,000 km.

British Aerospace Regional Aircraft — UK

Note: See British Aerospace plc in the Combat section.

Corporate address:
Woodford Aerodrome, Chester Road, Woodford, Manchester SK7 1QR.

Telephone: +44 161 439 5050
Facsimile: +44 161 955 3008
E-mail: terry.taylor@bae.co.uk

Information:
Terry Taylor (Public Affairs & Communications Manager – *telephone* +44 161 955 4131, *facsimile* +44 161 957 4630).

ACTIVITIES

▪ The RJ family of regional jets was marketed and customer supported by Aero International (Regional) until July 1998, when AI(R) operations ended. See Combat section for further details.
▪ British Aerospace Regional Aircraft manufactures the RJ family at its Avro facility in Woodford and was also delivering the final 3 Jetstream 41s in 1998 from its Jetstream facility at Prestwick, Scotland, having already completed production of its Super 31 and ATP aircraft (final completed ATPs were awaiting customers at the time of writing in 1998). By 24 July 1998, 147 RJs had been ordered and 109 delivered.
▪ Operates a repair and maintenance facility (Avrotec) and a flight and engineering test business (Avrotest), both at Woodford.

Avro Jetstream 31 and Super 31

Comments: The first production Jetstream 31 flew on 18 March 1982, followed by the first Jetstream Super 31 on 13 April 1988. 381 Jetstream 31s and Super 31s had been delivered by August 1997, when 1 additional aircraft was on order and up to 3 new aircraft were available. In 1998 it was confirmed that production had ended. For details and an illustration, see the 1996-97 edition of *WA&SD*, pages 259-260.

Avro Jetstream 41

Comments: First flown on 25 September 1991, the 30-seat Jetstream 41 was first delivered to Manx Airlines in November 1992. A total of 98 had been ordered by August 1997, with all but 2 then delivered. Further sale meant that a total of 3 was scheduled for delivery in 1998, when production finally ended. For details and an illustration, see the 1996-97 edition of *WA&SD*, pages 260-261.

Avro ATP and Jetstream 61

Comments: First flown on 6 August 1986, the ATP is no longer in production. 62 were delivered by 1998, among the last being 2 for British World and 1 for Ireland Airways. Several completed ATPs then remained available for purchase. A development of the ATP, the Jetstream 61, was flown in 1994 but none was sold and the aircraft is no longer available.

Avro RJ Family

First flight: 23 March 1992 (RJ85 development aircraft – see Development).
Certification: 4 February 1983 for original BAe 146 Series 100; CAA certification of all RJs completed by 1 October 1993, and FAA by 10 June 1994.
First delivery: 2 April 1993 (RJ85 for Crossair).
Role: Short-range regional airliner and freighter.
Noise levels: See tables.

Development

▪ Developed from, and succeeding, the British Aerospace 146 (first flown 3 September 1981), with principal changes including LF507 engines; all digital avionics including Cat IIIa, updated EFIS displays, windshear detection, digital flight guidance system and optional TCAS; and new wide-look 'Spaceliner' interior with new overhead bins, centralized Passenger Service Units and more (for 4, 5 or 6 abreast seating).

Details

Sales: Total of 12 RJ70s (all delivered), 79 RJ85s (56 delivered, with 13 remaining to the largest customer Northwest Airlines), and 56 RJ100s (41 delivered) by 24 July 1998.
Crew: 2 (flight).
Passengers: See tables.
Seat pitch: See tables.
Galleys: 2 basic cold galleys standard (1R/4R). Optional galleys with ovens for a hot meal service.
Pressurization: 7.46 psi.
Baggage compartments: 479 cu ft (13.6 m^3) total for RJ70,

↑ Avro RJ85 in Northwest Jet Airlink livery *(Ian Lowe/British Aerospace Regional Aircraft)*

↑ Avro RJ70 cockpit layout for Air Malta

645 cu ft (18.3 m^3) total for RJ85, and 812 cu ft (23 m^3) total for RJ100, comprising front and rear baggage holds.
Wing control surfaces: Aileron (with trim and servo tabs), Fowler flap, roll spoiler and 3 automatic lift-spoilers per wing.
Tail control surfaces: T-tail with elevators (with trim and servo tabs) and rudder.
Flight control system: Manual/mechanical, except for hydraulic flaps and spoilers.
Construction materials: Conventional metal alloy.
Engines: See tables. Sundstrand/APIC APS1000 APU.
Fuel system: 11,729 litres standard for RJ70, RJ85 and RJ100, with 12,901 litres optional.
Electrical system: 3-phase 115/200 volt AC supply at 400 Hz, via 2 × 40 kVA integrated drive generators. 28 volt DC supply, via 2 transformer/rectifiers. Second battery option for on-board engine start.
Hydraulic system: 2 independent systems, each at a nominal 3,000 psi. Each system has an independent hydraulic tank, pressurized by regulated air bleed from its respective engine. Hydraulically operated services are flaps, flap asymmetry brakes, lift spoilers, roll spoilers, rudder, airbrakes, undercarriage, nose gear steering, wheel brakes (including parking), Airstairs (through the AC pump), standby AC/DC generator, and standby fuel pumps (right and left). On freighter variants, the freight door is hydraulically powered.
Braking system: Carbon multi-discs, with anti-skid system. Split tailcone airbrakes.
De-icing system: Bleed air for wing and tailplane leading edges. Electric for cockpit glazing.
Oxygen system: Chemical.

RJ Family details	RJ70	RJ85	RJ100
Noise levels: take-off, sideline, approach (EPNdB)	81.8, 87.3, 97.5	83.3, 88.1, 97.6	84.9, 87.8, 97.6
Passengers (typically). 5-abreast business and 6-abreast economy; 4-abreast first class layout is available.	70 business or 82 economy	85 business or 100 economy	100 business, 112 economy, or up to 128 high capacity
Seat pitch	31 ins (79 cm)	31 ins (79 cm)	31 ins (79 cm), 32 ins (81 cm) or 29 ins (74 cm) respectively
Engines	4 AlliedSignal LF507-1F turbofans	4 AlliedSignal LF507-1F turbofans	4 AlliedSignal LF507-1F turbofans
Engine rating (each)	7,000 lbf (31.14 kN)	7,000 lbf (31.14 kN)	7,000 lbf (31.14 kN)
Wing span	86 ft 5 ins (26.34 m)	86 ft 5 ins (26.34 m)	86 ft 5 ins (26.34 m)
Length	85 ft 10 ins (26.16 m)	93 ft 8 ins (28.55 m)	101 ft 8 ins (30.99 m)
Maximum height	28 ft 3 ins (8.61 m)	28 ft 3 ins (8.61 m)	28 ft 2 ins (8.59 m)
Cabin length	50 ft 7 ins (15.42 m)	58 ft 5 ins (17.81 m)	66 ft 3 ins (20.19 m)
Cabin maximum width	11 ft 2.8 ins (3.42 m)	11 ft 2.8 ins (3.42 m)	11 ft 2.8 ins (3.42 m)
Cabin height	6 ft 9.3 ins (2.07 m)	6 ft 9.3 ins (2.07 m)	6 ft 9.3 ins (2.07 m)
Main passenger doors	6 ft × 2 ft 9.5 ins (1.83 × 0.85 m)	6 ft × 2 ft 9.5 ins (1.83 × 0.85 m)	6 ft × 2 ft 9.5 ins (1.83 × 0.85 m)
Wing area	832 sq ft (77.295 m^2)	832 sq ft (77.295 m^2)	832 sq ft (77.295 m^2)
Wing aspect ratio	8.98	8.98	8.98
Undercarriage: RJ70 and RJ85 can operate from unpaved runways	Retractable, with steerable nosewheels (±70°). Twin wheels on each unit	Retractable, with steerable nosewheels (±70°). Twin wheels on each unit	Retractable, with steerable nosewheels (±70°). Twin wheels on each unit
Wheel base	33 ft 1.5 ins (10.1 m)	36 ft 9 ins (11.2 m)	41 ft 1 ins (12.52 m)
Wheel track	15 ft 6 ins (4.72 m)	15 ft 6 ins (4.72 m)	15 ft 6 ins (4.72 m)
Empty weight, typical operating	53,100 lb (24,085 kg)	54,400 lb (24,675 kg)	56,600 lb (25,673 kg)
Maximum zero-fuel weight	71,500 lb (32,432 kg) standard, 74,500 lb (33,793 kg) optional	79,000 lb (35,834 kg)	82,500 lb (37,421 kg)
Maximum take-off weight	84,000 lb (38,102 kg) standard, up to 95,000 lb (43,091 kg) optional	93,000 lb (42,184 kg) standard, 97,000 lb (43,998 kg) optional	97,500 lb (44,225 kg) standard, up to 101,500 lb (46,040 kg) optional
Maximum landing weight	83,500 lb (37,875 kg)	85,000 lb (38,555 kg)	88,500 lb (40,143 kg)
Maximum operating Mach number (M_{MO}), JAR/FAR	Mach 0.72/0.73	Mach 0.72/0.73	Mach 0.72/0.73
Maximum permitted operating speed (V_{MO}), IAS kts (mph) km/h	300 (345) 555	300 (345) 555	300 (345) 555
Cruise speed kts (mph) km/h	356-432 (410-497) 659-800	364-432 (419-497) 674-800	371-432 (427-497) 687-800
Take-off field length, ISA, sea level, 350 naut mile sector, JAR reserves, 150 naut mile diversion	3,255 ft (993 m) with 70 passengers at 209 lb (95 kg) each	3,445 ft (1,050 m) with 85 passengers at 209 lb (95 kg) each	3,570 ft (1,088 m) with 100 passengers at 209 lb (95 kg) each
Landing field length, ISA, sea level, 350 naut mile sector, JAR reserves, 150 naut mile diversion	3,455 ft (1,053 m) dry, 3,973 ft (1,211 m) wet	3,605 ft (1,099 m) dry, 4,146 ft (1,264 m) wet	3,860 ft (1,177 m) dry, 4,439 ft (1,354 m) wet
Still air range, standard fuel, optional weights, JAR reserves, 150 naut mile diversion naut miles (miles) km	1,440 (1,657) 2,667 with 70 passengers, 1,395 (1,605) 2,583 with 82 passengers	1,350 (1,553) 2,500 with 85 passengers, 1,290 (1,484) 2,389 with 100 passengers	1,225 (1,410) 2,269 with 100 passengers, 1,190 (1,369) 2,204 with 112 passengers
Still air range, optional fuel, optional weights, JAR reserves, 150 naut mile diversion naut miles (miles) km	1,610 (1,853) 2,982 with 70 passengers, 1,560 (1,795) 2,889 with 82 passengers	1,520 (1,749) 2,815 with 85 passengers, 1,360 (1,565) 2,519 with 100 passengers	1,380 (1,588) 2,556 with 100 passengers, 1,240 (1,427) 2,296 with 112 passengers

Environmental control system: Fed by bleed air from the 4 engines or the APU. Bleed air supply is cooled by 2 identical air conditioning packs, before distribution to the flight deck and cabin. Packs are 3-wheel, air cycle machines located in the rear air conditioning bay. Pressurization (which see) is achieved by regulating the air flow leaving the cabin through 2 discharge valves.
Radar: AlliedSignal weather radar.
Flight avionics/instrumentation: Standard avionics are Honeywell digital flight guidance system, Honeywell IRS, Rockwell Collins ARINC 700 dual VHF com/nav, Rockwell Collins radio altimeter, AlliedSignal Mk 5 GPWS, Rockwell Collins ARINC 700 DME and ARINC 700 mode S transponder, Honeywell windshear detection and guidance, Rockwell Collins ADF, AlliedSignal GNS FMS, and Gables radio management panel. Dual Honeywell EFIS displays (4, each 5 × 6 ins, 12.7 × 15.24 cm), and Smiths LED engine data displays. Options include ACARS, third VHF, TCAS and displays, single/dual HF, selcal, GPS, checklist facility, engine health and monitoring, quick access recorder, and ELT.

Aircraft variants:
RJ70 airliner for typically 70 business class or 82 economy class passengers is no longer in production, but can be built to special order. As detailed.
RJ85 and ***RJ100*** passenger airliners are available and in production. As detailed.
RJ115 116-128-passenger airliner is no longer marketed as a separate model but its features are available as options on the RJ100. Details can be found in the 1996-97 edition of *WA&SD*, pages 257-258.
VIP variants of the RJs are available with custom interiors.
QC quick-change passenger/cargo and **QT 'Quiet Trader'** dedicated freighter variants of the earlier BAe 146 have been supplied, and RJ variants are possible. Typical QT could carry a 28,195 lb (12,789 kg) payload, including LD3 containers in 1,422 cu ft (40.27 m^3) volume and pallets in 2,145 cu ft (60.74 m^3) volume. Cargo door for this version would be 6 ft 4 ins × 10 ft 11 ins (1.93 × 3.33 m).

Avro RJ-X

Comments: This designation was confirmed in June 1998 to relate only to a speculative concept study for a twin-engined follow-up to the RJ family of improved concept. Possible engines could be the P&WC PW308 or AlliedSignal AS907. Airframe/aerodynamic improvements, and use of composites.

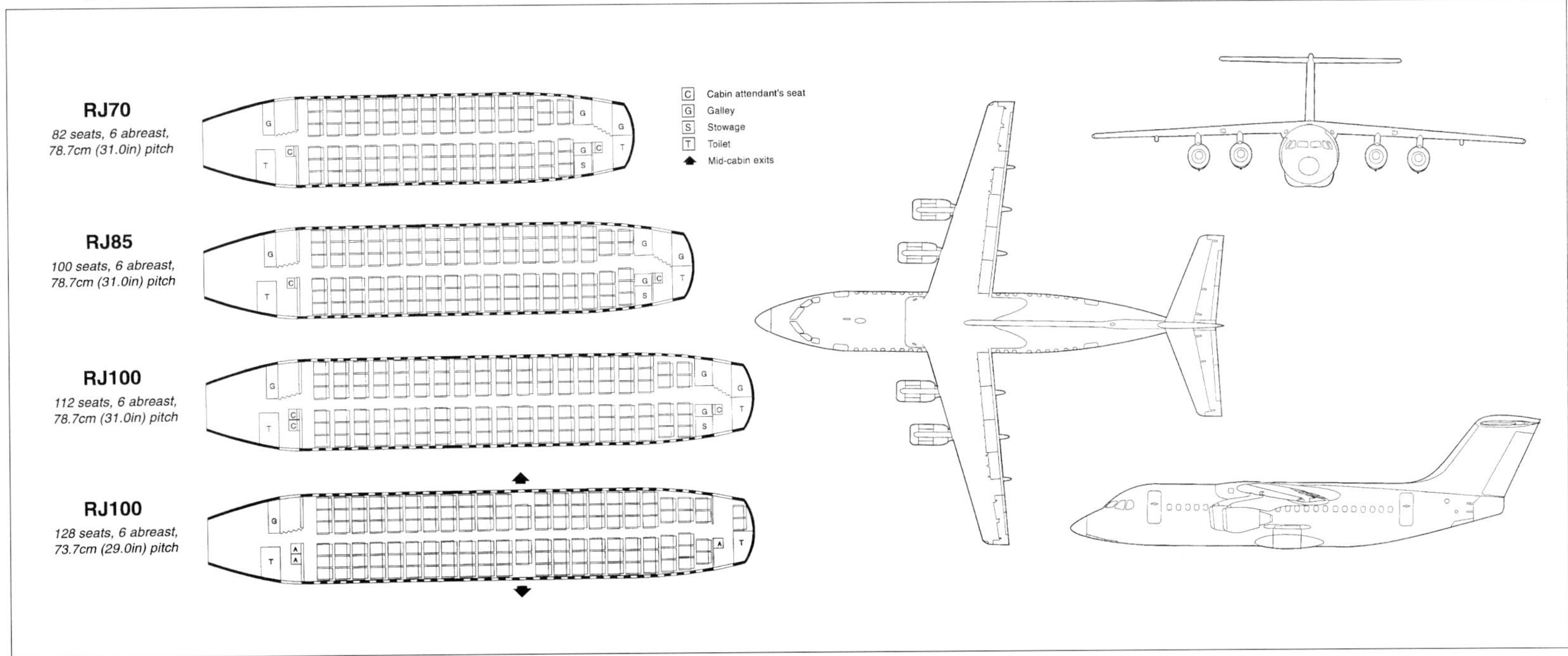

↑ **Avro RJ85 general arrangement, with RJ Family interior layouts below** *(courtesy British Aerospace Regional Aircraft)*

Britten-Norman Ltd — UK

Corporate address:
See Reconnaissance section for company details.

ACTIVITIES

▪ The Defender and Defender 4000 can be found in the Reconnaissance section.

Britten-Norman BN2B and BN2T Islander series

First flight: 13 June 1965.
Certification: 10 August 1967 (UK), 19 December 1967 (USA). Manufactured in accordance with BCAR Section K and FAR Pt 23 with Pt 135 approval.
First delivery: 1967, to Loganair and Aurigny.
Role: STOL, piston- or turboprop-engined unpressurized commuter, feederline, cargo and executive transport, ambulance, crop spraying, parachuting and more.
Sales: Total Islander and Defender deliveries by July 1998 stood at 1,219, including 81 triple-engined Trislanders build between 1971 and 1984. Military operators of Islanders and Defenders in 1998 were the US Army (BN2T), Belize Defence Force (BN2B), Jamaica Defence Force (BN2B), Falkland Island Government Air Service (BN2B), Guyana Defence Force Air Corps (BN2B), Surinam Air Force (BN2B), Venezuelan Army Aviation (BN2B), Belgian Army (BN2B), Cyprus Defence Force (BN2B), Rhine Army Parachute Association (BN2T), Armed Forces of Malta (BN2B), British Army Air Corps (BN2T, upgraded to have a deeper acrylic windscreen and 2 cabin roof transparencies to improve the field of view), British Army Parachute Association (BN2B/T), Royal Air Force (BN2T), Royal Air Force Sport Parachute Association

↑ **Britten-Norman BN2B Islander in British Airways Express livery, operated by Loganair as a BA franchise partner** *(British Airways/John Dibbs)*

Details for Islander

PRINCIPAL DIMENSIONS:
Wing span: 49 ft (14.94 m)
Maximum length: 36 ft (10.97 m)
Maximum height: 13 ft 8.7 ins (4.19 m)

CABIN:
Length: 15 ft 2 ins (4.62 m) including baggage bay, 10 ft (3.05 m) for main passenger area only
Width: 3 ft 7 ins (1.09 m)
Height: 4 ft 2 ins (1.27 m)
Floor area: 47.2 sq ft (4.38 m^2)
Volume: 183.5 cu ft (5.2 m^3) including baggage bay, 130 cu ft (3.68 m^3) for main passenger area
Main passenger doors: 3 ft 7.5 ins × 2 ft 10 ins (1.1 × 0.86 m) starboard, and 3 ft 7.5 ins × 2 ft 1 ins (1.1 × 0.64 m) port

WINGS:
Aerofoil section: NACA 23012
Area: 325 sq ft (30.19 m^2)
Aspect ratio: 7.388
Incidence: 2°

TAIL UNIT:
Tailplane span: 15 ft 5 ins (4.7 m)
Tailplane area: 73 sq ft (6.78 m^2)

UNDERCARRIAGE:
Type: Fixed, with steerable nosewheel. Twin mainwheels. Can operate from beaches, grass and other surfaces. Low pressure tyres (35 psi) for soft-field operation
Tyre size: 16 × 7-7 ins
Wheel base: 13 ft 1.5 ins (4 m) for BN2B, 13 ft 1.22 ins (3.99 m) for BN2T
Wheel track: 11 ft 10 ins (3.61 m)
Turning radius: 30 ft 7 ins (9.32 m) minimum

(BN2T), Royal Jordanian Air Force (BN2B), United Arab Emirates Armed Forces (BN2T), Air Force of Angola (BN2B), Ghana Air Force (BN2T), Mauritanian Air Force (BN2B), Mauritius National Coast Guard (BN2T), Moroccan Ministry of Fisheries (operated by Gendarmerie – BN2T), South African Air Force (BN2B), Air Force of Zimbabwe (BN2B), Government of Cambodia (BN2B), Indian Navy (BN2B/T), Indonesian Army (BN2B), Pakistan Maritime Security Agency (BN2T), Philippine Navy (BN2B), and Army Air Corps/National Police of the Republic of Ireland (BN2T-4S). Typical commercial users are third level airlines operating high frequency, short sector services.
Crew: Pilot.
Passengers: 9 commuter passengers or 6 in executive layout, or 3 litters and attendant, or 10 parachutists plus a jumpmaster.
Freight hold volume: 166 cu ft (4.7 m^3) with all seats removed behind pilot.
Baggage area: 49 cu ft (1.388 m^3).
Wing control surfaces: Ailerons (with starboard ground-adjustable tab) and single-slotted flaps.
Tail control surfaces: Single piece elevator and rudder, both with trim tabs.
Flight control system: Manual, except for electric flaps.
Construction materials: Aluminium alloy.
Engines: See tables. 6 ft 6 ins (1.98 m) diameter Hartzell 2- or 3-blade constant-speed, fully feathering propellers for BN2B-26 and -20, and 6 ft 8 ins (2.03 m) for BN2T.
Fuel system: See tables. In addition, underwing tanks can be installed for extended operation.
Electrical system: DC supply via 2 × 24 volt, 50 amp engine-driven alternators. 24 volt, 17 amp-hour lead-acid battery for emergency power.
Braking system: Cleveland hydraulic.
De-icing system: Optional pneumatic boot in wing and tail unit leading edges. Optional electric propellers and windshield.
Oxygen system: Optional.
Radar: Optional weather radar.
Flight avionics/instrumentation: Standard avionics are dual VHF nav/com with ILS, marker beacon receiver, ADF, VOR, DME, transponder and encoding altimeter. Options include ELT, autopilot, HF/MF radios, RNAV, Omega and GPS.

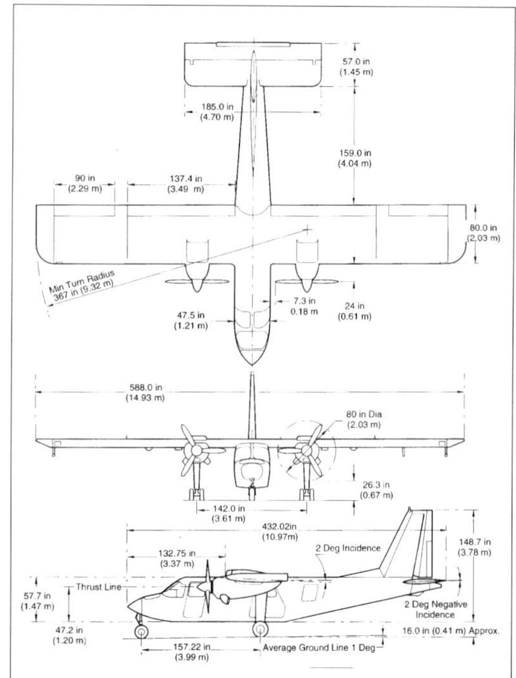

↑ **Britten-Norman BN2T Islander general arrangement** *(courtesy Britten-Norman)*

Aircraft variants:
Islander refers to both the piston- and turboprop-powered versions, though the name Turbine Islander is commonly used for the Allison-engined model. In civil and military/government use. As detailed.
Defender and ***Defender 4000*** are detailed in the Reconnaissance section.

	BN2B-26	BN2B-20	BN2T
Engines	2 Textron Lycoming O-540-E4C5 piston engines	2 Textron Lycoming IO-540-K1B5 piston engines	2 Allison 250-B17C turboprops
Engine rating (each)	260 hp (194 kW)	300 hp (224 kW)	320 shp (238.6 kW)
Weight empty, equipped: a) with full equipment and instrument package, oil and usable fuel b) with optional transfer tip tanks	a) 4,114 lb (1,866 kg) b) 4,214 lb (1,911 kg)	a) 4,244 lb (1,925 kg) b) 4,344 lb (1,971 kg)	4,040 lb (1,832 kg)
Maximum zero fuel weight	6,300 lb (2,857 kg)	6,300 lb (2,857 kg)	6,600 lb (2,994 kg)
Maximum take-off weight	6,600 lb (2,994 kg) with or without tip tanks	6,600 lb (2,994 kg) with or without tip tanks	7,000 lb (3,175 kg), tip tanks standard
Maximum landing weight	6,600 lb (2,994 kg) with or without tip tanks	6,600 lb (2,994 kg) with or without tip tanks	6,800 lb (3,084 kg)
Payload with maximum fuel	1,706 lb (774 kg), or 1,096 lb (497 kg) with tip tanks	1,576 lb (715 kg), or 966 lb (438 kg) with tip tanks	1,520 lb (689 kg)
Disposable load	2,486 lb (1,128 kg), or 2,386 lb (1,082 kg) with tip tanks	2,356 lb (1,069 kg), or 2,256 lb (1,023 kg) with tip tanks	2,960 lb (1,343 kg)
Usable fuel	492 litres, or 814 with tip tanks	492 litres, or 814 with tip tanks	814 litres
Maximum cruise speed at 8,000 ft (2,440 m), unless stated kts (mph) km/h	142 (164) 263	143 (165) 265	170 (196) 315, at 10,000 ft (3,050 m)
Economic cruise speed at 8,000 ft (2,440 m), unless stated kts (mph) km/h	126 (145) 233	128 (147) 237	150 (173) 278, at 10,000 ft (3,050 m)
Stall speed, clean, power off, IAS kts (mph) km/h	50 (58) 93	50 (58) 93	52 (60) 96
Stall speed, with flaps, power off, IAS kts (mph) km/h	40 (46) 74	40 (46) 74	45 (52) 83
Take-off distance (ground roll)	621 ft (189 m)	704 ft (215 m)	837 ft (255 m)
Take-off distance over a 50 ft (15 m) obstacle	1,218 ft (371 m)	1,166 ft (355 m)	1,250 ft (381 m)
Landing distance (ground roll)	459 ft (140 m)	459 ft (140 m)	747 ft (228 m)
Landing distance over a 50 ft (15 m) obstacle	980 ft (299 m)	980 ft (299 m)	1,110 ft (338 m)
Climb rate, at sea level	860 ft (262 m) per minute	1,130 ft (344 m) per minute	1,050 ft (320 m) per minute
Climb rate, 1 engine	145 ft (44 m) per minute	198 ft (60 m) per minute	215 ft (66 m) per minute
Ceiling	13,600 ft (4,145 m) absolute, 11,300 ft (3,444 m) service	19,700 ft (6,005 m) absolute, 17,200 ft (5,242 m) service	25,000 ft (7,620 m) absolute, 23,000 ft (7,010 m) service
Ceiling, 1 engine	4,400 ft (1,340 m) absolute	6,150 ft (1,875 m)	10,000 ft (3,050 m) absolute
IFR range naut miles (miles) km	539 (620) 998, or 952 (1,096) 1,763 with tip tanks	503 (579) 932, or 896 (1,032) 1,659 with tip tanks	590 (679) 1,093
VFR range naut miles (miles) km	675 (777) 1,250, or 1,130 (1,301) 2,093 with tip tanks	639 (736) 1,183, or 1,075 (1,238) 1,991 with tip tanks	728 (838) 1,348

Britten-Norman Trislander

Comments: A total of 81 triple-engined Trislanders was built between 1971 and 1984. Of these, 12 were produced in kit form and sold in 1979 to a customer in the USA. 10 of these kits were subsequently returned to Britten-Norman and sold to an Australian concern, while 2 kits were bought by the Exxtor Group in 1995 for assembly by Anglo Normandy Aero Engineering in Guernsey. The first of these made its maiden flight on 29 March 1996 and is operated by Aurigny Air Services as the air operator of the Exxtor Group. The second kit is under assembly and in March 1998 was approximately half completed. According to Britten-Norman in 1998, the Trislander has been the subject of studies regarding reintroduction into production, and this could happen at a future date if there was sufficient market demand.

↑ **Britten-Norman Islander, 1 of several operated by Aurigny Air Services, in the colours of its new sponsor, Hambros Bank** *(Aurigny Air Services)*

Short Brothers plc — UK

Corporate address:
PO Box 241, Airport Road, Belfast BT3 9DZ, Northern Ireland.

Telephone: +44 1232 458444
Facsimile: +44 1232 454406, 732974

Founded:
1908, becoming a division of Bombardier Inc in 1989. Now forms part of the Bombardier Aerospace and Bombardier Services Groups.

Employees:
About 9,000 worldwide.

Information:
Alec McRitchie (communications and public affairs – *telephone* +44 1232 733514, *facsimile* +44 1232 733399).

ACTIVITIES

■ Under Bombardier Aerospace Group, Shorts has 3 main business areas: **Aerospace**, which incorporates *Aerostructures* in which the company designs and manufactures major aerostructures for Bombardier aircraft programmes, for the Lockheed Martin C-130, for all Boeing commercial aircraft programmes, and to include components for the GKN Westland Apache, and *Nacelle Systems* in which Shorts is a market leader in the design, development, manufacture and support of aircraft engine nacelles; **Missile Systems**, operating as a joint venture with Thomson-CSF of France as Shorts Missile Systems Ltd/Thomson Shorts Systémes; and **Belfast City Airport**, which is owned and operated by the company. Under Bombardier Services Group, Shorts operates its **Support Services** Division (headquartered in Bournemouth, UK), to provide a wide range of military and civil technical support services, including the management of facilities, provision of aircraft maintenance, air traffic control and flying training for customers in the UK, USA and the Middle East.

Ayres Corporation — USA

Corporate address:
PO Box 3090, 1 Ayres Way, Albany, GA 31707.

Telephone: +1 912 833 1440
Facsimile: +1 912 439 9790
Telex: 547629
Web site: www.ayres-corp.com
E-mail: webmaster@ayres-corp.com

Information:
Terry Humphrey.

ACTIVITIES

■ In addition to the Loadmaster detailed below, Ayres produces a range of agricultural aircraft which are described and illustrated in the General Aviation section. See also Let AS.

Ayres Loadmaster LM 200 and LM 250

First flight: 2 LM 200 prototypes expected to be flying by late 1998.
Certification: 1999 for LM 200. Designed to FAR Pt 23 Commuter category, and will be certified for day/night, VFR, IFR, and flight into known icing conditions.
First delivery: 1999 for LM 200.

Details *(for LM 200, except under Aircraft variants)*

Role: Multi-purpose aircraft in 5 basic configurations, namely bulk/containerized freight, 19-passenger commuter and freight, 34-passenger high-density, 28-troop/jump, and reconnaissance with work stations for surveillance operators. Also to be offered in fire-bomber configuration. Quick change between cargo and passenger roles, with cargo including airline-type containers or other high-priority containerized or bulk freight. Intended to be low cost and simple to maintain. Other identified roles could include communications, medevac and command/control.
Sales: 50 firm orders and 200 options from launch customer FedEx of the USA (expected to rise to 350 by the year 2012), 10 firm and 20 options from Corporate Air of the USA, 5 firm and 5 options from Duijvestijn Aviation of the Netherlands, and 2 firm from Orsmond Aviation of South Africa, reported at the time of writing. Projected market for 600 Loadmasters by the year 2010. 12 Loadmasters to be built in 1999, rising to 48 in the year 2000. Interest for the LM 250 has been expressed by Thailand, Venezuela and 2 other nations. Basic cost of the LM 200 is

↑ **Ayres Loadmaster LM 200 loading 4 containers**

↑ **Projected Ayres Amphibious Loadmaster**

expected to be in the US$4 million range, while the LM 250 will be in the US$5 million range. Interest has been expressed in the Amphibious Loadmaster from a Twin Otter floatplane operator based in New York. Production at Dothan, Alabama.
Crew: Pilot and co-pilot, with access to the flight deck via a ladder/stairway (see Fuselage layout). Emergency door to the starboard side of the co-pilot; port emergency door is to be determined.
Passengers: Can be configured for 34 passengers in a high-density layout, or 19 passengers and 4,000 lb (1,814 kg) of freight in combi layout, or for 28 troops/parachutists/smoke jumpers. Operations with more than 19 passengers will be limited to countries that issue a FAR Pt 23 19-passenger waiver.
Baggage hold capacity: Overhead baggage compartments in passenger configuration.
Fuselage layout: Forward section contains the flight deck and forward cargo area below. Aft of the flight deck is a small baggage/cargo area. Main cockpit access door is in the port side of the forward fuselage. Main cargo area is of constant section, and has 3 vertical nets to partition bulk freight. Tie down provisions in the floor and side wall structure. Cargo door in the port side of the fuselage aft of the wing. Optional passenger door can be incorporated into the cargo door to permit loading of passengers in a high-density configuration. Transitional aft section tapers to mate with the aft fuselage section and has a baggage/cargo compartment with vertical net to partition bulk freight between the main cargo compartment and aft compartment (plus tie-down provisions and a door). Aft fuselage section, with access for inspection and repair of the flight control system.
Freight hold capacity: Main cargo area has 4 longitudinal seat tracks for the installation of a cargo loading system or passenger seats. Large fuselage and oversized cargo door to enable loading of 4 AYY ('Demi') or 4 AKE (LD3) containers, or a combination of bulk cargo and containerized freight. See Passengers for combi layout. Tail stand (provision for stowing in the aft cargo area) to prevent the aft fuselage from contacting the ground during loading operations.
Wing control surfaces: Aerodynamically balanced ailerons (span 11 ft 8 ins, 3.56 m), with cable/pulley-operated 3 ft (0.91 m) span trim tab on the starboard aileron; mass balance will be installed to prevent flutter. Interconnected, electro-mechanically operated slotted flaps (span 14 ft 11.45 ins, 4.57 m), with 37° of rotation; will have a back-up actuating system if required by FAR Pt 23.
Tail control surfaces: Rudder, and elevators with cables/bell cranks-operated trim tabs.
Flight control system: Primary system by non-boosted conventional push rods and cables.
Construction materials: Mainly aluminium alloy, but with alloy steels and stainless steels where required. Semi-monocoque aluminium alloy fuselage skins, frames and stringers; no spot welding. Cockpit canopy, wingtips and tailplane tips are of moulded composites construction.
Engine: LHTEC CTP800-4T turboprop engine. Comprises 2 engines operating through a single propeller; 12.9 ft (3.93 m) Hamilton Standard 568F 6-blade propeller.
Engine rating: 2,700 shp (2,013 kW), flat rated to 2,400 shp (1,790 kW).

Details for Loadmaster LM 200, *with LM 250 in italics*

PRINCIPAL DIMENSIONS:
Wing span: 64 ft (19.51 m)
Maximum length: 69 ft (21.03 m)
Maximum height: 22 ft 6 ins (6.86 m)

CABIN:
Length: 22 ft 1 ins (6.73 m) for main area
Width: 8 ft (2.44 m)
Height: 7 ft 1.5 ins (2.17 m)
Floor area: 171 sq ft (15.89 m^2) for main area
Volume: 1,350 cu ft (38.23 m^3) for main cabin/cargo area, 285 cu ft (8.07 m^3) for aft cargo area, 284 cu ft (8.04 m^3) for forward cargo area, and 85 cu ft (2.41 m^3) for upper cargo area
Main cargo door opening: 6 ft 11 ins (2.11 m) high and 6 ft 2 ins (1.88 m) wide

WINGS:
Aerofoil section: ALM 201
Area: 458 sq ft (42.55 m^2)
Aspect ratio: 8.94
Chord: 10 ft 3 ins (3.12 m) at BL 0, 4 ft 1 ins (1.24 m) at tip
Thickness: 20% at root, 12% at tip
Dihedral: 1° 30' effective

TAIL UNIT:
Tailplane/fin aerofoil: NACA 0012
Tailplane span: 25 ft 2 ins (7.67 m)
Tailplane chord: 6 ft 3 ins (1.905 m) at root (theoretical fuselage centreline), 2 ft 10 ins (0.86 m) at tip (theoretical)

UNDERCARRIAGE:
Type: Fixed steerable/centring nosewheel type; main gear is a trailing-link type with oleo shock-absorbers, attached to sponsons mounted on the fuselage; nose gear has a steering damper unit and is designed to allow towing angles up to 90° with pin removed. Vertical travel of main axle 0.5 ins (1.3 cm); vertical travel of nose axle 11 ins (28 cm)
Main wheel tyre size: 39.8 ins (1,011 mm)
Nose wheel tyre size: 22 ins (559 mm)
Wheel base: 21 ft 10.5 ins (6.67 m)
Wheel track: 14 ft (4.27 m)

WEIGHTS (estimated)**:**
Empty: 9,000 lb (4,082 kg), *11,750 lb (5,330 kg)*, including unusable fuel and oil
Maximum ramp: 19,190 lb (8,704 kg)
Maximum take-off: 19,000 lb (8,618 kg), *25,000 lb (11,340 kg)*
Maximum landing: 19,000 lb (8,618 kg), *25,000 lb (11,340 kg)*
Payload: 8,800 lb (3,992 kg), *over 12,000 lb (5,443 kg)*

PERFORMANCE (estimated, ISA)**:**
Maximum cruise speed: 196 kts (226 mph) 363 km/h, *220 kts (253 mph) 408 km/h*, at 10,000 ft (3,050 m)
Normal cruise speed: 165 kts (190 mph) 306 km/h, *183 kts (211 mph) 339 km/h*, at 10,000 ft (3,050 m)
Maximum range cruise speed: 150 kts (173 mph) 278 km/h, *160 kts (184 mph) 297 km/h*, at 10,000 ft (3,050 m)
Take-off distance over a 50 ft (15 m) obstacle: 1,525 ft (465 m), *2,310 ft (704 m)*, at MTOW
Landing distance over a 50 ft (15 m) obstacle: 1,745 ft (532 m), *2,164 ft (660 m)*, at MLW
Climb rate: 1,861 ft (567 m), *the same*, per minute at sea level, at MTOW
Climb rate at 5,000 ft (1,525 m): 1,721 ft (525 m), *the same*, per minute at MTOW
Climb rate at 5,000 ft (1,525 m), ISA + 20° C: 1,661 ft (506 m), *the same*, per minute at MTOW
Manoeuvring load factors: +2.927 and -1.1708
Ceiling: 25,000 ft (7,620 m)
Range with 6,000 lb (2,721 kg) payload: 1,030 naut miles (1,186 miles) 1,908 km
Maximum range: 1,120 naut miles (1,290 miles) 2,075 km, zero payload

Fuel system: 2,271 litres (4,020 lb, 1,823 kg) maximum carried in integral wing tanks, or 3,407 litres (6,030 lb, 2,735 kg) optional long-range fuel. Pressure refuelling, gravity filling.
Electrical system: Dual bus, 28 volt DC, with 2 × 300A engine-driven starter-generators, either capable of supplying power for the major electrical loads in the event of an engine or generator failure. 2 × 24 volt lead-acid or optional ni-cd batteries for engine starting and emergency power back-up. Single small auxiliary 24 volt lead-acid or optional ni-cd battery for lighting of the cargo and main cargo door areas, independent of the primary electrical system but charged by the generators. 28 volt DC external power receptacle.
Hydraulic system: For main wheel brakes and nosewheel steering. Main wheel brakes powered through dual brake valves (master cylinders), 1 for each main wheel. Single reservoir for each main wheel brake.
Braking system: Hydraulically operated brakes, plus parking/emergency brake.
De-icing system: Pneumatic rubber boots (using engine bleed air) on the wing and tail unit leading edges. Electrically-heated windshield. Impulse de-icing is being investigated. Electrically-powered propeller anti-ice heating system.
Environmental control system: Cockpit heating by pneumatic supply system (engine bleed air), directed into a heat exchanger and distribution system for the cockpit and windshield defrosting. Electric heat and ventilation system also provided, powered from the electrical system or from ground power units. Air for ventilation supplied to controllable outlets and will be exhausted to the avionics compartments. Electric force fan/s for cooling . Optional air conditioning.
Radar: Honeywell Primus 440 weather radar.
Flight avionics/instrumentation: Honeywell SPZ-5000 avionics and flight control system, with IC-500 Display Guidance Computer (DGC) for the EFIS, flight director (FD), and automatic flight control system (AFCS) functions; EFIS has 2 ED-600 CRT displays, each 5 ins × 5 ins (12.7 × 12.7 cm). APIRS F206 AHRS, B.F. Goodrich GH-3000 integrated standby instrument system, Honeywell Primus II integrated radio system (with 2 × RCZ-851 integrated communications units with VHF coms and Mode S transponders; 2 × RNZ-851 integrated navigation units providing dual VOR, ILS and marker beacon and 6-channel scanning DME; single RM-850 radio management unit; single CD-850 clearance delivery head; and single AV-850A audio panel), Trimble 2101 I/O GPS navigation system, and Honeywell AA-300 altimeter. Primary air data displays are standard pneumatic airspeed, altitude and vertical speed instruments. To provide altitude alerting and altitude pre-select functionality with the EFIS and FD, the altimeter must contain an encoder and baro set potentiometer; B.F. Goodrich ADC-3000 Air Data Computer connects to the pitot/static system and provides ARINC 429 pressure altitude and airspeed information to the GH-3000. B.F. Goodrich TCAS791 TCAS I is proposed as an option.

Aircraft variants :
Loadmaster LM 200 has an 8,800 lb (3,992 kg) payload. 5 basic configurations, namely bulk/containerized freight, 19-passenger commuter and freight, 34-passenger high-density, 28-troop/jump configuration, and a reconnaissance configuration with work stations for surveillance operators. Also being offered in fire-bomber configuration. As detailed.
Loadmaster LM 250 is a derivative of LM 200 with a rear loading ramp to carry over 12,000 lb (5,443 kg) of cargo or passengers. 3,200 shp (2,386 kW) CTP800-50 turboprop engine. See table.
Amphibious Loadmaster is a projected twin-float version.

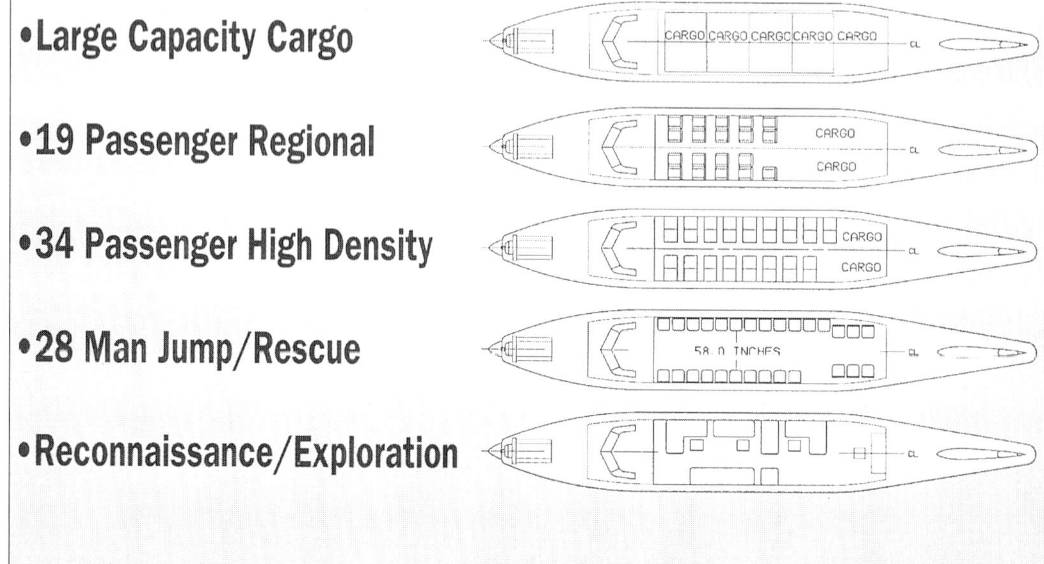

↑ Ayres Loadmaster LM 200 cabin configurations *(courtesy Ayres)*

Basler Turbo Conversions Inc — USA

Comments: Basler Turbo Conversions of Oshkosh, WI, developed the Turbo-67 as a DC-3 conversion with Pratt & Whitney Canada PT6A-67R turboprop engines and a fully engineered, strengthened and stretched airframe to provide 35% more cabin volume, 43% increase in useful load and 24% higher speed, amounting to 76% more productivity than the DC-3, and many other improvements. It also developed the Basler Turbo-34, a lengthened Cessna Model 337 Skymaster with the twin piston engines replaced by a single rear-mounted P&WC PT6A turboprop. A full description of the Turbo-67, and photograph, appeared in the 1996-97 edition of *WA&SD*, pages 263-264.

The Boeing Company — USA

Corporate address:
See Combat section for all company, Group and Business Unit details.

ACTIVITIES

- See also Combat, Reconnaissance and Helicopter sections.
- Following the merger of Boeing and McDonnell Douglas (see Combat section for details), the former McDonnell Douglas MD-95 programme has been redesignated Boeing 717. In 1998 Boeing verified that following delivery of the remaining MD-80s and MD-90s, these production lines will be closed down in 1999, while MD-11 production is expected to end in the year 2000 (although Boeing had earlier anticipated retaining MD-11 production, with emphasis on the Freighter).

New Small Airplane (NSA)

Comments: In 1994, Boeing announced studies for a sub-Boeing 737 size regional airliner in the 70-80 seat range, with potential for larger capacities, to be developed with partners. Then expected to enter service after the year 2002, exploratory discussions are believed to have taken place with China, Japan, South Korea, Taiwan and other potential partners, with CATIC of China and the Japan Aircraft Development Corporation taking a more active role in studies to determine the configuration and sales potential of the aircraft. At the time, Brassey's was informed that NSA was likely to have some commonality with the third-generation 737 to keep costs low, mainly systems, but not in any form that would compromize the design of an otherwise totally new airliner. How the NSA project might be affected by development of the Boeing 717 was uncertain at the time of writing.

Boeing 707 and C-135/C-137 series

Comments: 1,010 Boeing 707s and related B720s in airliner and military guises were built up to 1992, since 1982 only as airframes for various military developments (the last an RAF AWACS aircraft). Details of re-engined KC-135s and other modification programmes can be found in the 1996-97 edition of *WA&SD*, page 264. Under the USAF's Lightning Bolt programmes, Rockwell Collins is currently upgrading the flight decks of some 600 KC-135s using a blend of advanced military and commercial avionics. This Pacer Compass, Radar and Global Positioning System programme (known as KC-135 Pacer CRAG) involves integration and installation of the FMS-800 Flight Management System, FDS-255 flat panel multifunction Flight Display System, WXR-700X forward-looking windshear weather radar, and an embedded INS/GPS navigation system. 3 upgraded KC-135 prototypes were delivered to the USAF in July 1996, and authorization for fleet upgrade followed flight operations testing. 4 KC-135s recently purchased by the Republic of Singapore Air Force from USAF storage are being re-engined with CFM56-2Bs and upgraded for delivery in 1999, after which they are expected to receive a flight deck similar to Pacer CRAG.

Boeing 717 (formerly McDonnell Douglas MD-95)

First flight: First of 3 development aircraft (T1) rolled out on 10 June 1998, for 2 September 1998 first flight.
Certification: FAA and JAA certification scheduled for April 1999.
First delivery: Expected June 1999.
Role: Short-to-medium range airliner.
Airframe life: Anticipated 100,000 hours.
Noise levels: 9.2 dB sideline, 8.1 dB take-off with cutback, and 6.2 dB approach below ICAO Annex 16 Chapter 3 and FAR Pt 36 Stage 3 requirements for Boeing 717-300.

Aims

- Replacement for Stage 2/Chapter 2 aircraft.
- New interior design, with quiet cabin and high-level 100-passenger seating comfort.
- Hydrocarbons 80%, carbon monoxides 70%, oxides of nitrogen 40% and smoke 42% below ICAO emission limits.

Development

- Launched in October 1995 by McDonnell Douglas as an advanced technology aircraft for high frequency, short-to-medium routes. Similar in size to the DC-9 Series 30.
- Major partners include Alenia of Italy (fuselage), AlliedSignal (environmental control system, wheels and brakes), British Aerospace (tail unit), BMW Rolls-Royce (engines), Hyundai (later wing sets), Honeywell (avionics), Korean Air (nose with forward door area), ShinMaywa of Japan (engine pylons and horizontal stabilizers), SHL Servo Systems of Israel (undercarriage), and Sundstrand (electrical system).

Details

Sales: 50 firm and 50 options by launch customer AirTran Airways (formerly ValuJet), plus 5 others (firm, non-US), all 717-200 by June 1998. Boeing envisages a market for approximately 2,300 aircraft of this class over 20 years. 12 expected to be delivered in second half of 1999, with 43 in year 2000, 58 in 2001, and 60 in 2002. Final assembly at Long Beach.
Crew: 2 (flight).
Passengers: 106, typically as 8 first class (4 abreast) and 98 economy (5 abreast). Optionally 117 in all-economy seating, 111 in Euro class layout (53 business and 58 economy), or 129 in a high density layout. Projected Regional version could carry 80 passengers. All new interior (by Fischer Advanced Composite Components) with illuminated hand rails and larger overhead baggage racks. To reduce the cost of custom interiors, a variety of selectable options are available.
Galleys/toilets: Flexible option to provide the freedom to move galleys, toilets and class dividers within a prescribed zone without affecting major systems.
Freight hold volume: 945 cu ft (26.76 m^3) for 717-200, and 689 cu ft (19.51 m^3) for ER.
Wing control surfaces: Ailerons, double-slotted flaps, 2-position and 5-section full-span leading-edge slats, and 3-section spoilers (functioning as speed brakes).
Tail control surfaces: T-tail with elevators (2 tabs each) and rudder (with tab).

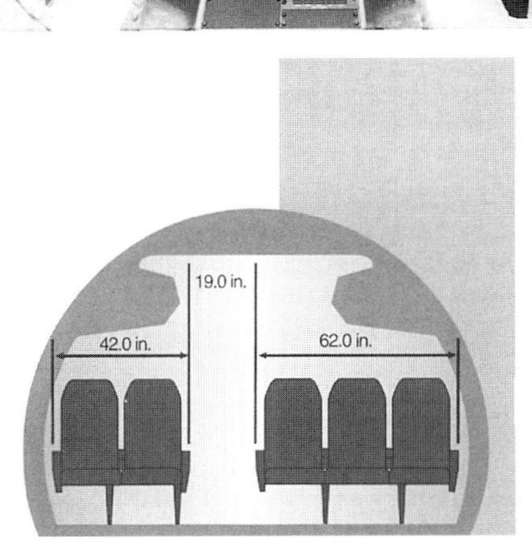

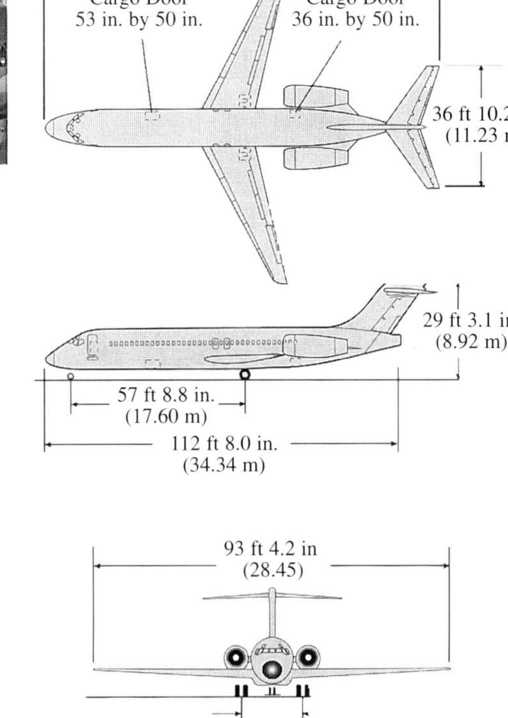

INTERIOR ARRANGEMENTS

Mixed Class – 106 Passengers (Baseline)

Single Class – 117 Passengers

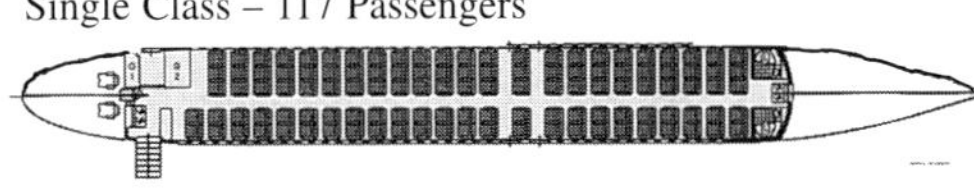

↑ **Boeing 717 general arrangement (*right*), with flight deck layout (*left, top*), economy class seating cross section (*left, centre*), and typical interior arrangements (*left, bottom*)** *(courtesy Boeing)*

↑ Boeing 717-200 roll-out on 10 June 1998

Flight control system: Cable operated ailerons and elevators. Hydraulically actuated rudder, with manual reversion.
Construction materials: Lightweight airframe.
Engines: 2 BMW Rolls-Royce BR715 turbofans. Pivot-type thrust reversers.
Engine rating: Each 18,500 lbf (82.29 kN), with increase to 21,000 lbf (93.41 kN) for the ER version.
Fuel system: 13,892 litres (24,589 lb, 11,153 kg) for 717-200, 18,170 litres (32,160 lb, 14,588 kg) for ER.
Flight avionics/instrumentation: Avionics integrated by the Honeywell VIA 2000 computer and configured around 6 interchangeable liquid crystal displays (each 8 × 8 ins, 20.3 × 20.3 cm) for engine and system monitoring. Electronic instrument system, dual Honeywell Flight Management System (FMS) and a Central Fault Display System (CFDS) to allow mechanics to quickly isolate and correct malfunctions. Full flight regime autopilot, flight director, and autothrottle capable of performing a Cat IIIa automatic landing. GPS, Cat IIIb, onboard maintenance terminal, and Future Air Navigation System (FANS) are optional.

Aircraft variants:
Boeing 717-200 for a range of 1,547 naut miles.
Boeing 717-200 ER extended range with 2 auxiliary fuel tanks for up to 2,001 naut miles.
Boeing 717-500 is under evaluation as a 129-passenger version with increased range.
Regional version is being studied, for 80 passengers.

Details for 717-200, *with ER in italics where different*

PRINCIPAL DIMENSIONS:
Wing span: 93 ft 4.2 ins (28.45 m)
Maximum length: 124 ft 0.4 ins (37.8 m)
Fuselage length: 112 ft 8 ins (34.34 m)
Maximum height: 29 ft 3.1 ins (8.92 m)

CABIN:
Cargo doors: 53 × 50 ins (1.35 × 1.27 m) forward, 36 × 50 ins (0.91 × 1.27 m) aft

WINGS:
Area: 1,000.7 sq ft (92.97 m^2), including ailerons
Aspect ratio: 8.7
Sweepback: 24.5 ° at 25% chord

TAIL UNIT:
Tailplane span: 36 ft 10.2 ins (11.23 m)

UNDERCARRIAGE:
Type: Retractable, with steerable nosewheels. Twin wheels on each unit
Wheel base: 57 ft 8.8 ins (17.6 m)
Wheel track: 16 ft 0.1 ins (4.88 m)

WEIGHTS:
Empty, operating: 67,870 lb (30,785 kg), *69,401 lb (31,480 kg)*
Maximum zero fuel: 96,000 lb (43,544 kg), *98,000 lb (44,452 kg)*
Maximum ramp: 115,000 lb (52,163 kg), *122,000 lb (55,338 kg)*
Maximum take-off: 114,000 lb (51,709 kg), *121,000 lb (54,885 kg)*
Maximum landing: 102,000 lb (46,266 kg), *104,000 lb (47,174 kg)*
Space limited payload: 26,940 lb (12,220 kg), *24,380 lb (11,059 kg)*

PERFORMANCE:
Maximum speed: Mach 0.76, or 438 kts (504 mph) 811 km/h
FAA take-off field length: 6,400 ft (1,950 m), *6,600 ft (2,012 m)*, MTOW, sea level, 30 ° C
FAA landing field length: 4,740 ft (1,445 m), *4,820 ft (1,469 m)*, MLW, sea level
Design range with 106 passengers: 1,547 naut miles (1,781 miles) 2,866 km, 2,001 naut miles (2,304 miles) 3,708 km, domestic reserve

Boeing 737-300 to 737-900 series, and Boeing Business Jet

First flight: 9 April 1967 in original 737-100 form. 24 February 1984 for 737-300, 19 February 1988 for 737-400, 30 June 1989 for 737-500, 9 February 1997 for 737-700, and 30 June 1997 for 737-800.
Certification: 15 December 1967 in original 737-100 form. 14 November 1984 for 737-300, 2 September 1988 for 737-400 and 12 February 1990 for 737-500.
First delivery: 28 November 1984 to USAir for 737-300; 15 September 1988 to Piedmont for 737-400; 28 February 1990 to Southwest for 737-500; October 1997 to Southwest for 737-700; March 1998 to Hapag-Lloyd for 737-800 and August 1998 to SAS for 737-600.
Role: Short/medium range airliner.
Noise levels: Meets FAR Pt 36 Stage 3/ICAO Annex 16 Chapter 3 requirements in take-off, sideline and approach with 30° flaps, but marginally exceeds the approach limit with 40° flaps. 85 dBA at take-off.
Sales: Total of 4,039 B737s had been ordered by June 1998, comprising 30 B737-100s, 1,114 B737-200s, 1,118 B737-300s, 484 B737-400s, 386 B737-500s, 116 B737-600s, 393 B737-700s, 373 B737-800s and 25 B737-900s. Of these, 3,059 had been delivered by that date, leaving 63 B737-300s, 28 B737-400s, 18 737-500s, 116 B737-600s, 363 B737-700s, 367 B737-800s and 25 B737-900s still to be delivered. Boeing Business Jet costs US$32 million at time of writing, when 18 had been ordered, including 1 ordered by golfer and businessman Greg Norman.
Crew: 2 (flight).
Passengers: 128-149 seats for 737-300 (typically 128 in 2-class and 149 inclusive tour layouts), 146-168 seats for 737-400 (typically 146 in 2-class and 168 in inclusive tour layouts), 108-132 seats for 737-500 (typically 108 in 2-class and 132 in inclusive tour layouts), 108-140 for 737-600, 128-149 for 737-700 and 162-189 for 737-800. 4 abreast seating with aisle for first class layout, 5 abreast with aisle for business class, and 6 abreast with aisle for economy. Movable cabin divider (can be repositioned by 1 person between flights) to adjust the ratio of premium and economy seating. Variable-geometry convertible seats are available to change the seat counts and seating proportions, the latter by increasing/decreasing spaces between the individual seats. Airstairs. See Aircraft variants for Boeing Business Jet.
Seat pitch: 36 ins (91 cm) first class, 32 ins (81 cm) economy, and 30 ins (76 cm) inclusive tour.
Galleys: 2, forward and aft of cabin. Options available.
Toilets: 3 typically in forward and aft positions. Options available.
Pressurization: 7.5 psi cabin differential.
Freight hold volume: Lower deck volume of 1,068 cu ft (30.24 m^3) basic, or 917 or 792 cu ft (25.97 or 22.43 m^3) when auxiliary fuel tanks are installed for 737-300. 1,373 cu ft (38.88 m^3) basic, or 1,222 or 1,097 cu ft (34.6 or 31 m^3) when auxiliary fuel tanks are installed for 737-400. 822 cu ft (23.28 m^3) basic, or 671 or 546 cu ft (19 or 15.46 m^3) when auxiliary fuel tanks are installed for 737-500. 756 cu ft (21.41 m^3) for 737-600, 1,002 cu ft (28.37 m^3) for 737-700, and 1,591 cu ft (45.05 m^3) for 737-800. See Aircraft variants for Boeing Business Jet.
Size of freight doors: 35 × 48 ins (89 × 122 cm) forward, and 33 × 48 ins (84 × 122 cm) aft.
Loading facilities: Partial provisions (wiring and relays) are available in all models to permit aftermarket installation of the Air Cargo Equipment (ACE) telescoping-shelf baggage handling equipment. Accommodates ACE in the aft compartment when auxiliary fuel tanks are not installed. Optional sliding carpet loading system for both holds.

↑ Boeing 737 Next Generation flight deck

Wing control surfaces: Ailerons with tabs, triple-slotted trailing-edge flaps, Krueger leading-edge flaps, 3-section leading-edge slats, multi-section spoilers (assisting ailerons and functioning as speed brakes) and 2 lift-dumpers/speed brakes. Next Generation 737-600/700/800/900 have new double-slotted flaps with 37% fewer parts and 33% fewer bearings.
Tail control surfaces: Variable incidence tailplane. Elevators with servo tabs, and rudder.
Flight control system: Hydraulic.
Construction materials: Incorporates advanced aluminium alloys in the wings; glassfibre or glassfibre/graphite in the flap track fairings, other wing parts, wing/body fairing, nosecone, and fin tip and extension; graphite/Kevlar/glassfibre in the tailfin; Kevlar in some interior components; and graphite in the ailerons, elevators and rudder.

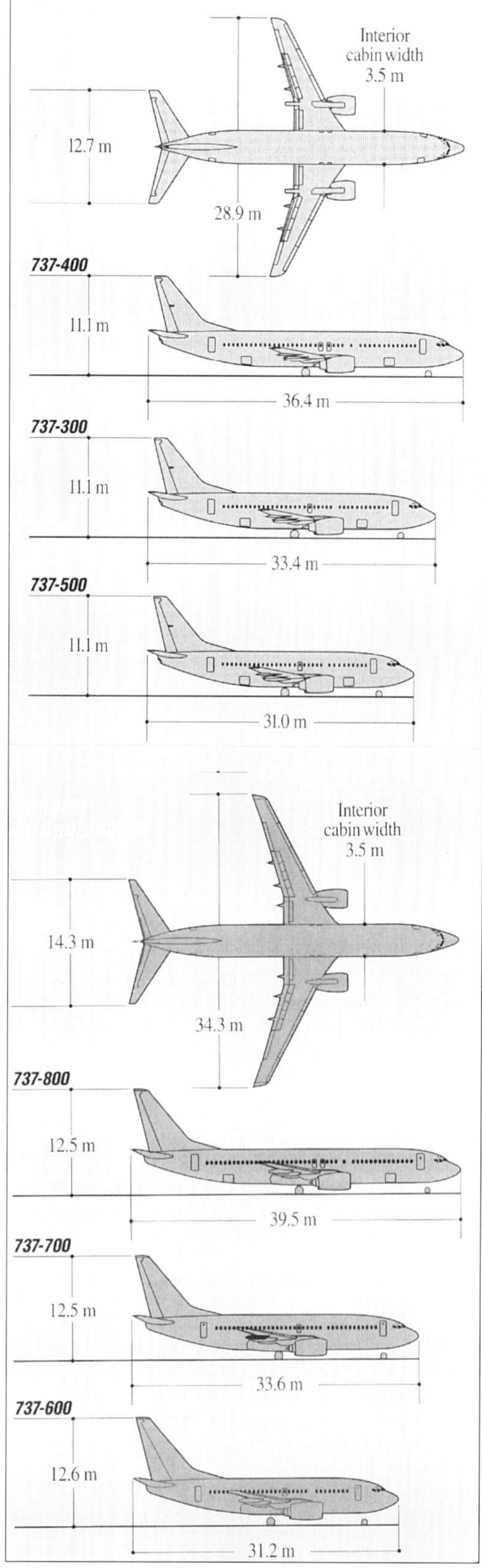

↑ Boeing 737 general arrangements *(courtesy Boeing)*

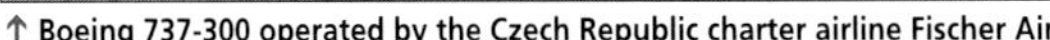

↑ Boeing 737-300 operated by the Czech Republic charter airline Fischer Air

↑ Boeing 737-700 Next Generation airliner

Engines: 2 × CFM International CFM56-3B or 3C1 turbofans operated at 20,000 lbf (88.97 kN) basic or 22,000 lbf (97.86 kN) optional for 737-300, CFM56-3B or 3C at 22,000 lbf (97.86 kN) basic or 23,500 lbf (104.54 kN) optional for 737-400 and 737-400 high gross weight model, and CFM56-3B1 or 3C1 turbofans derated to 18,500 lbf (82.29 kN) basic or 20,000 lbf (88.97 kN) optional for 737-500. Customer unique engine options are CFM56-3B1 of 20,000 lbf (88.97 kN) or CFM56-3B2 of 22,000 lbf (97.86 kN) for 737-300, and CFM56-3B2 of 22,000 lbf (97.86 kN) for 737-400. APU. 120-minutes ETOPS. CFM56-7Bs for Next Generation versions, rated at 18,500 lbf (82.29 kN) basic or 20,000/22,000 lbf (88.97/97.86 kN) for higher gross weight variants of the 737-600; 20,000 lbf (88.97 kN) basic or 22,000/24,000 lbf (97.86/106.8 kN) for higher gross weight variants of the 737-700; and 24,000 lbf (108.6 kN) basic or 26,400 lbf (117.43 kN) for the higher gross weight variant of the 737-800.
Engine rating: See above.
Fuel system: 20,104 litres basic or 21,967 or 23,829 litres optional with auxiliary tanks for 737-300/400/500. 26,036 litres for 737-600/700/800/900.
Electrical system: 2 engine-driven 50 kVA generators.
Hydraulic system: 2 independent systems, each 3,000 psi.
De-icing system: Bleed air.
Radar: Colour weather radar.
Flight avionics/instrumentation: EFIS with EADI and EHSI (with map, flight plan, nav partial compass rose, VOR/ILS full compass rose and weather modes). Wide choice of PIN-selectable display options. Flight management system (single or dual flight computers providing performance and navigation data, with GPS), full-range digital autothrottle, laser gyro inertial reference system, LED engine instrument system, aircraft condition monitoring system/ACARS, windshear alerting and guidance, time-control navigation (T-NAV), and centralized built-in test equipment (BITE) on CDU. Cat II landing standard, with Cat IIIa optional. New Generation 737s have Common Display System flight decks, using Honeywell 6-screen flat panel liquid crystal display technology, offering the ability to emulate electromechanical, EFIS or Primary Flight Display-Navigation Display (PFD-ND) formats for customers wanting commonality and to use the same pilot type rating. Overhead panel with digital electrical metering and pressurization control panels, standby instruments (attitude indicator, altimeter/airspeed indicator and RMI), flight management control display, engine control display, and navigation radio tuning panel with dual scanning DME (see photograph). See also Boeing Business Jet under Aircraft variants.

Aircraft variants:
737-300 is the currently available 128-149 passenger version. Programme launched in March 1981. Compared with earlier 737-200, introduced an 8 ft 8 ins (2.64 m) longer fuselage, larger and more powerful CFM56-3 engines, advanced technology flight deck, and construction and aerodynamic improvements adapted from the 757 and 767 aircraft. High Gross Weight version optional. As detailed.
737-400 is the currently available 146-168 passenger version, with 10 ft (3.05 m) fuselage stretch. Programme launched in June 1986. High Gross Weight version optional. As detailed.
737-500 is the currently available 108-132 passenger version. Programme launched 20 May 1987. Intended as a replacement for the 737-200, but with a fuselage 10 ins (25.4 cm) longer and incorporating -300/-400 advanced technologies. Redesigned interior, with increased cabin space. High Gross Weight version optional. As detailed.
737-600 was known as the 737-500X before programme launch in 1995. Launch customer is SAS, which ordered 35 on 15 March 1995. Smallest Next Generation version, accommodating 108-140 passengers. CFM56-7B engines with ratings of 18,500 lbf, 20,000 lbf and 22,000 lbf (82.29, 88.97 and 97.86 kN). As with all Next Generation models, introduced wings with increased chord and span, thereby increasing fuel capacity, fuel efficiency and range.
737-700 was the first of the new Next Generation 737s to enter service. The programme was launched in November 1993. 128-149 passengers. New wings of increased chord and span, increased fuel capacity (26,136 litres), new CFM56-7B engines with noise improvements, and more. About 3,000 naut mile range. Engine ratings 20,000 lbf, 22,000 lbf and 24,000 lbf (88.97, 97.86 and 106.76 kN).
737-700 Increased Gross Weight Quick Change is a version selected by the US Navy to replace the Reserve force's C-9Bs in a passenger/cargo role under the Navy Unique Fleet Essential Airlift Replacement Aircraft programme. 2 ordered initially, for delivery by the end of 2001. Modified wing featuring continuous double-slotted flaps and new leading-edge slats, and will also have a large cargo door in the forward fuselage. A commercial version could follow, but no decision had been made at the time of writing.
737-800 was officially launched on 5 September 1994, with commitments for over 40 aircraft. First delivery to Hapag-Lloyd in 1998. Longest version, with seating for 162-189 passengers. Engine ratings 24,000 lbf and 26,400 lbf (106.76 and 117.44 kN).
737-900 is a stretched Next Generation model, accommodating 18 more passengers. 10 orders received at the time of writing.
Boeing Business Jet is a corporate aircraft based on the 737-700, with accommodation for 8 to 63 passengers typically, though up to 100 passengers would be possible. It is a joint venture between Boeing and General Electric Company. Avionics include a fully integrated GPS and satcom, plus the 1997 addition of a Flight Dynamics Head-Up Guidance System and second HF radio as standard. Programme launched on 2 July 1996. Auxiliary fuel tanks available, balancing non-stop range with lower-hold storage requirements: 11 auxiliary tanks offering 16,277 litres of fuel, for 6,200 naut mile range and 70 cu ft (1.98 m^3) of cargo

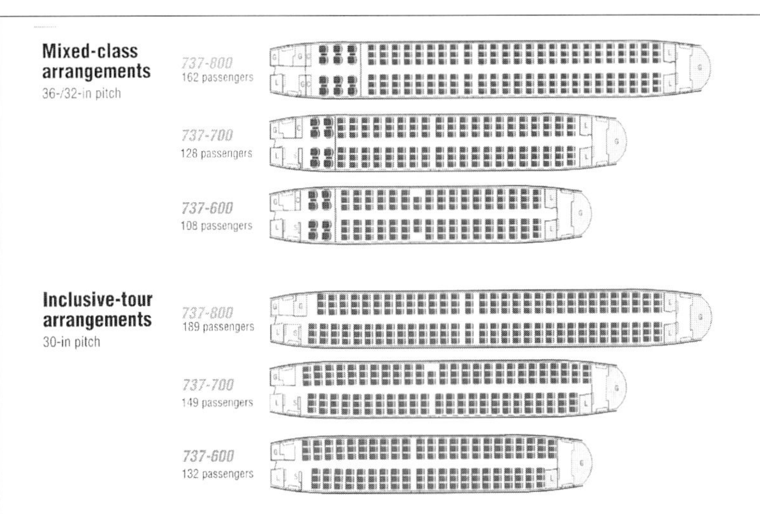

↑ Boeing 737 Next Generation cabin layouts *(courtesy Boeing)*

↑ Boeing Business Jet, in one of many possible configuations

	737-300	737-400	737-500	737-600	737-700	737-800
Wing span	94 ft 9 ins (28.88 m)	94 ft 9 ins (28.88 m)	94 ft 9 ins (28.88 m)	112 ft 7 ins (34.32 m)	112 ft 7 ins (34.32 m)	112 ft 7 ins (34.32 m)
Maximum length	109 ft 7 ins (33.4 m)	119 ft 7 ins (36.45 m)	101 ft 9 ins (31.01 m)	102 ft 6 ins (31.24 m)	110 ft 4 ins (33.63 m)	129 ft 6 ins (39.47 m)
Maximum height	36 ft 6 ins (11.13 m)	36 ft 6 ins (11.13 m)	36 ft 6 ins (11.13 m)	41 ft 3 ins (12.57 m)	41 ft 2 ins (12.55 m)	41 ft 2 ins (12.55 m)
Cabin length	77 ft 2 ins (23.52 m)	89 ft 2 ins (27.18 m)	71 ft 6 ins (21.79 m)	71 ft 6 ins (21.79 m)	79 ft 2 ins (24.13 m)	98 ft 6 ins (30.02 m)
Cabin width	11 ft 7 ins (3.53 m)	11 ft 7 ins (3.53 m)	11 ft 7 ins (3.53 m)	11 ft 7 ins (3.53 m)	11 ft 7 ins (3.53 m)	11 ft 7 ins (3.53 m)
Cabin height	7 ft (2.13 m)	7 ft (2.13 m)	7 ft (2.13 m)	7 ft (2.13 m)	7 ft (2.13 m)	7 ft (2.13 m)
Passenger doors	6 ft × 2 ft 10 ins (1.83 × 0.86 m) and 6 ft × 2 ft 6 ins (1.83 × 0.76 m)	6 ft × 2 ft 10 ins (1.83 × 0.86 m) and 6 ft × 2 ft 6 ins (1.83 × 0.76 m)	6 ft × 2 ft 10 ins (1.83 × 0.86 m) and 6 ft × 2 ft 6 ins (1.83 × 0.76 m)			
Wing area	1,135 sq ft (105.44 m^2)	1,135 sq ft (105.44 m^2)	1,135 sq ft (105.44 m^2)	1,340 sq ft (124.5 m^2)	1,340 sq ft (124.5 m^2)	1,340 sq ft (124.5 m^2)
Wing aspect ratio	7.91	7.91	7.91	9.46	9.46	9.46
Tailplane span	41 ft 8 ins (12.7 m)	41 ft 8 ins (12.7 m)	41 ft 8 ins (12.7 m)	47 ft 2 ins (14.38 m)	47 ft 1 ins (14.35 m)	47 ft 1 ins (14.35 m)
Undercarriage type	Retractable, with steerable nosewheels. Twin wheels on each unit	Retractable, with steerable nosewheels. Twin wheels on each unit	Retractable, with steerable nosewheels. Twin wheels on each unit	Retractable, with steerable nosewheels. Twin wheels on each unit	Retractable, with steerable nosewheels. Twin wheels on each unit	Retractable, with steerable nosewheels. Twin wheels on each unit
Wheel base	40 ft 10 ins (12.45 m)			36 ft 10 ins (11.23 m)	41 ft 3 ins (12.57 m)	51 ft 2 ins (15.6 m)
Wheel track	17 ft 2 ins (5.23 m)	17 ft 2 ins (5.23 m)	17 ft 2 ins (5.23 m)	18 ft 9 ins (5.72 m)	18 ft 8 ins (5.69 m)	18 ft 9 ins (5.72 m)
Weight empty, operating	72,100 lb (32,704 kg) basic, 73,340 lb (33,266 kg) optional for long range	75,800 lb (34,382 kg) basic, 77,520 lb (35,162 kg) optional for long range	70,510 lb (31,983 kg)	81,285 lb (36,870 kg)	83,600 lb (37,920 kg)	91,450 lb (41,480 kg)
Maximum taxi or brake release weight	125,000 lb (56,700 kg) basic, to 139,000-140,000 lb (63,050-63,500 kg) optional taxi	139,000 lb (63,050 kg) basic, to 150,500 lb (68,265 kg) optional taxi	116,000 lb (52,616 kg) basic, to 134,000 lb (60,780 kg) optional taxi	124,000 lb (56,700 kg) standard, 143,500 lb (65,090 kg) high gross weight	133,000 lb (60,328 kg) standard, 153,000 lb (69,400 kg) high gross weight	155,500 lb (70,533 kg) standard, 172,500 lb (78,244 kg) high gross weight
Maximum zero fuel weight	105,000 lb (47,627 kg) basic, 109,600 lb (49,713 kg) optional	113,000 lb (51,255 kg) basic, 117,000 lb (53,070 kg) optional	102,500 lb (46,493 kg) basic, 103,000 lb (46,720 kg) optional	114,500 lb (51,930 kg)	121,500 lb (55,110 kg)	136,000 lb (61,688 kg)
Maximum take-off weight	124,500 lb (56,472 kg) basic, to 138,500 lb (62,822 kg) optional	138,500 lb (62,822 kg) basic, to 150,000 lb (68,040 kg) optional	115,500 lb (52,390 kg) basic, 133,500 lb (60,555 kg) optional	125,000 lb (56,700 kg) basic, 144,490 lb (65,540 kg) optional	133,820 lb (60,700 kg) basic, 154,000 lb (69,850 kg) optional	155,500 lb (70,534 kg) basic, 172,500 lb (78,245 kg) optional
Maximum landing weight	114,000 lb (51,710 kg) basic, 116,600 lb (52,888 kg) optional	121,000 lb (54,885 kg) basic, 124,000 lb (56,245 kg) optional	110,000 lb (49,895 kg)	121,500 lb (55,110 kg)	129,000 lb (58,510 kg)	144,000 lb (65,317 kg)
Typical cruise speed	Mach 0.745 economic	Mach 0.745 economic	Mach 0.745 economic	Mach 0.79 economic cruise speed, Mach 0.82 maximum speed	Mach 0.79 economic cruise speed, Mach 0.82 maximum speed	Mach 0.79 economic cruise speed, Mach 0.82 maximum speed
Approach speed kts (mph) km/h	133 (153) 246 or 135 (155) 250 at long-range weight	137 (158) 254, or 139 (160) 257	128 (147) 237			
Take-off field length (sea level, 29° C or 30° C for -600/-700/-800)	6,660-7,500 ft (2,030-2,286 m) with 128 pax	7,730-8,740 ft (2,356-2,664 m) with 146 pax	6,100-8,640 ft (1,860-2,634 m) with 108 pax	6,160 ft (1,878 m)	6,700 ft (2,043 m)	7,400 ft (2,256 m)
Landing field length	4,580-4,700 ft (1,396-1,433 m) with 128 pax	4,880-5,050 ft (1,488-1,540 m)	4,450 ft (1,357 m)	4,160 ft (1,268 m)	4,500 ft (1,372 m)	5,250 ft (1,600 m)
Initial cruise altitude (or as specified)	35,700 ft (10,880 m), or 33,450 ft (10,195 m) at long-range weight	33,400 ft (10,180 m), or 31,700 ft (9,662 m) at long-range weight	37,000 ft (11,275 m), or 34,250 ft (10,440 m) at long-range weight	39,100 ft (11,920 m)	37,500 ft (11,430 m)	35,200 ft (10,730 m)
Altitude, OEI	17,400 ft (5,210 m)	16,200 ft (4,938 m), or 17,000 ft (5,180 m) at long-range weight	18,400 ft (5,610 m), or 18,100 ft (5,515 m) at long-range weight	17,800 ft (5,425 m)	16,600 ft (5,060 m)	13,800 ft (4,210 m)
Range naut miles (miles) km	2,258 (2,600) 4,184 with 128 pax	2,075 (2,390) 3,846 with 146 pax	2,401 (2,765) 4,450 with 108 pax	1,505-3,195 (1,733-3,679) 2,787-5,917	1,585-3,200 (1,825-3,685) 2,935-5,926	1,925-2,900 (2,216-3,339) 3,565-5,370

Note: Pax = Passengers

volume; 9 auxiliary tanks offering 14,839 litres of fuel, for 6,000 naut mile range and 144 cu ft (4.08 m^3) of cargo volume; 8 auxiliary tanks offering 14,233 litres of fuel, for 5,940 naut mile range and 178 cu ft (5.04 m^3) of cargo volume; 6 auxiliary tanks offering 11,697 litres of fuel, for 5,570 naut mile range and 325 cu ft (9.2 m^3) of cargo volume; 4 auxiliary tanks offering 7,722 litres of fuel, for 5,070 naut mile range and 555 cu ft (15.7 m^3) of cargo volume; and 3 auxiliary tanks offering 6,019 litres of fuel, for 4,830 naut mile range and 655 cu ft (18.5 m^3) of cargo volume. Cabin length 79 ft 2 ins (24.13 m). Maximum take-off weight 171,000 lb (77,564 kg). Normal cruise speed Mach 0.8. Take-off distance for 6,000 naut mile range is 7,050 ft (2,150 m) and landing distance at typical landing weight is 3,600 ft (1,098 m).

Boeing 747-400 series

First flight: 29 April 1988 for 747-400 (original 747 prototype on 9 February 1969). 4 May 1993 for the 747-400 Freighter.
Certification: 10 January 1989 with PW4000 engines, 18 May 1989 with CF6-80C2s, and 8 June 1989 with RB211-524Gs (original 747 prototype certification 30 December 1969).
First delivery: 26 January 1989 for 747-400 to Northwest Orient Airlines, with initial services on 9 February 1989 (original 747 delivery 12 December 1969 to Pan Am). 17 November 1993 for first 747-400 Freighter (to Cargolux).
Role: Long-range (International model) and short-range (Domestic), high capacity, airliner and freighter.
Noise levels: Meets FAA Stage 3 and ICAO Chapter 3 requirements.

Development

▪ Compared with earlier versions, the 747-400 features a new interior (plus longer upper deck), advanced APU, reduced weight, aerodynamic improvements (wing extensions and winglets on International models), advanced flight deck, advanced engines with reduced fuel burn, and increased fuel capacity and range.

Details *(airliner, unless stated. See Sales and Aircraft variants for Combi and Freighter)*

Sales: Total of 1,305 B747s of all models ordered by June 1998, of which 1,155 had been delivered. The total ordered includes 459 B747-400s, of which 77 are from US operators and 382 from non-US; 19 B747-400Ds, all US; 44 B747-400Fs, of which 12 are from US and 32 from non-US; and 59 B747-400Ms, all non-US. Of these, 119 B747-400s, 26 B747-400Fs and 5 B747-400Ms were still to be delivered at the time of writing in June 1998.
Crew: 2 (Captain and 1st Officer), with 2 observer seats. 2-bunk crew rest area accessible from the flight deck, or optional larger rest area with 8 bunks and 2 seats or other layouts in an overhead position (no loss of passenger seats) in the rear fuselage.

Passengers: Typical 3 class arrangement is 420 passengers as 21 first class, 77 business and 322 economy. Alternative layouts include 566-568 passengers in the Domestic short-range model (24 first class at 39 ins seat pitch and 544 economy at 32 ins pitch). 4 abreast with single aisle and 6 abreast with 2 aisles normal first class sleeper seating, 7 abreast business class on main deck with 2 aisles and 4 abreast with single aisle on upper deck, and 10 abreast economy class with 2 aisles. Combi version accommodates typically 266 passengers and 7 pallets on the main deck.
Seat pitch: 61 ins (155 cm) first, 39 ins (99 cm) business and 32 ins (81 cm) economy. See above for first class alternative.
Galleys: 1 upper deck galley. 9 or 10 main deck galleys in centre-line and sidewall positions in 293 possible positions.
Toilets: 2 upper deck toilets in 10 possible positions. 14 main deck toilets in 11 possible positions.
Freight hold volume and capacity: In underfloor container configuration, the forward hold has a 2,768 cu ft (78.38 m^3) capacity for 16 × LD1 containers and the aft hold has a 2,422 cu ft (68.58 m^3) capacity for 14 containers, plus 835 cu ft (23.64 m^3) of bulk cargo, making 6,025 cu ft (170.6 m^3). In mixed pallet (96 × 125 ins, 244 × 318 cm) and container configuration, forward hold has a 2,075 cu ft (58.76 m^3) capacity for 5 pallets and the aft hold a 2,422 cu ft (68.58 m^3) capacity for 14 containers, plus bulk cargo, totalling 5,332 cu ft (150.98 m^3). Optionally, the aft hold can carry 16 LD1 containers for 2,768 cu ft (78.38 m^3) capacity, but then the bulk cargo volume is reduced to 490 cu ft (13.88 m^3), totalling 5,333 cu ft (151 m^3). Maximum lower hold payloads are 58,400 lb (26,490 kg) forward, 50,570 lb (22,938 kg) aft, and 14,880 lb (6,749 kg) bulk, totalling 123,850 lb (56,177 kg). Domestic model can carry 5 pallets and 14 LD1 containers plus bulk in the lower holds, at 5,332 cu ft (150.98 m^3) volume.
Wing characteristics: Compared with earlier 747s, 747-400 International (not Domestic) has a 6 ft (1.8 m) wingtip extension and 6 ft winglet, improving take-off characteristics and offering higher cruise speed and lower drag. Domestic can had wingtip extensions and winglets added for long-range operations.
Wing control surfaces: Each wing has inner and outer ailerons, with outer used only during low-speed flight. 2 flaps per wing, each sub-divided into forward/mid/rear sections; each flap operates as a single unit up to 5° deflected angle, thereafter separating into triple-slotted. 6 spoiler sections, the inner used as a ground spoiler only. Krueger leading-edge flaps inboard, and 2 sections of leading-edge variable camber slats.
Tail control surfaces: Variable incidence tailplane. 2-section elevators. 2-section rudder of improved design, with ±30° movement (instead of 25°), new actuators (triple for upper section and dual for lower), with the former upper-section balance weights deleted.
Flight control system: Mechanical/hydraulic.
Construction materials: Includes advanced aluminium alloys for the wing upper/lower spar chords and stringers, graphite composites for the winglets and main deck passenger compartment floor panels, advanced thermoplastics for the PSUs and window reveals, and hybrid composites (graphite/phenolic or Kevlar/graphite) for the engine nacelles, cabin sidewall panels, ceiling panels and stowage bins.
Engines: 4 ×
- General Electric CF6-80C2B1F (57,900 lbf, 257.56 kN).
- CF6-80C2B1F1 or B7F (59,750 lbf, 265.79 kN).
- Pratt & Whitney PW4056 (56,750 lbf, 252.4 kN).
- PW4060 (60,000 lbf, 266.9 kN).
- PW4062 (62,000 lbf, 275.8 kN).
- Rolls-Royce RB211-524G (58,000 lbf, 258 kN).
- RB211-524H (60,600 lbf, 269.6 kN).

Engine rating: See above.
Fuel system: 204,355 litres basic with P&W and R-R engines or 203,522 litres basic with GE engines, with options of 216,847 litres for P&W and R-R engines or 216,000 litres with GE engines using the optional 12,478 litre fuel tank in the horizontal tail.
Electrical system: AC supply via 4 engine-driven 90 kVA generators. Pratt & Whitney Canada PW901A APU, offering 180 kVA power generation.
Hydraulic system: 4 independent systems.
Braking system: Carbon (replacing steel) brakes with anti-skid system. Domestic model has brake cooling fans.
De-icing system: Bleed air for wing leading-edge and engine inlet.
Radar: Weather radar.
Flight avionics/instrumentation: Flight management system (see illustration) with EFIS and EICAS. 6 CRTs (each 8 × 8 ins, 20.3 × 20.3 cm) display flight control, navigation, engine and crew alerting functions. Dual digital air data computers, triple ring laser inertial reference system, triple ILS, dual VOR with marker receiver, dual ADF, dual DME, GPWS and TCAS. Central maintenance computer monitors over 75 aircraft systems, with

Details for 747-400 airliner

PRINCIPAL DIMENSIONS:
Wing span: 211 ft 5 ins (64.44 m), becoming 213 ft (64.92 m) fully loaded. Domestic model has no winglets and 195 ft 8 ins (59.64 m) span
Maximum length: 231 ft 10 ins (70.66 m), or 225 ft 2 ins (68.63 m) for the fuselage
Maximum height: 63 ft 8 ins (19.41 m)

CABIN:
Width: 20 ft 1 ins (6.12 m)
Main passenger door: 6 ft 4 ins × 3 ft 6 ins (1.93 × 1.07 m)
Cargo door: 10 ft × 11 ft 2 ins (3.05 × 3.4 m)

WINGS:
Area: 5,600 sq ft (520.25 m^2)
Aspect ratio: 7.98
Sweepback: 37.5 ° at 25% chord
Incidence: 2 °
Dihedral: 7 °

TAIL UNIT:
Tailplane span: 72 ft 9 ins (22.17 m)

UNDERCARRIAGE:
Type: Retractable, with twin steerable nosewheels. 4 main units comprise 4-wheel bogies, the 2 inner units steerable (±13°) when nosewheels are steered between 20-70° (20 kts speed restriction)
Main wheel tyre size: 22 ins (55.9 cm) diameter wheels, instead of former 20 ins (50.8 cm). 32-ply tyres for international model, 24-ply for Domestic
Wheel base: 84 ft (25.6 m)
Wheel track: 36 ft 1 ins (11 m)
Turning radius: 159 ft (48.46 m) wingtip

WEIGHTS (International model, unless stated to be Domestic)**:**
Empty, operating (PW4056s): 402,400 lb (182,526 kg), or 403,500 lb (183,025 kg) for heaviest option, both when including overhead crew rest area
Empty, operating (CF6-80C2B1Fs): 401,800 lb (182,253 kg), or 402,900 lb (182,752 kg) for heaviest option, both when including overhead crew rest area
Empty, operating (RB211-524G/Hs): 404,000 lb (183,251 kg), or 405,100 lb (183,750 kg) for heaviest option, both when including overhead crew rest area
Maximum zero fuel: 535,000 lb (242,670 kg)
Maximum take-off: 800,000 lb (362,880 kg) basic, with options for 833,000/850,000 lb (377,840/385,555 kg), or 870,000 lb (394,625 kg) maximum, but 875,000 lb (396,893 kg) possible with loading restrictions
Maximum take-off (Domestic): 600,000 lb (272,155 kg)
Maximum landing: 574,000 lb (260,360 kg) basic, and 630,000 lb (285,760 kg) optional
Maximum landing (Domestic): 574,000 lb (260,360 kg)

PERFORMANCE (International model, unless stated to be Domestic)**:**
Typical cruise speed: Mach 0.85
Approach speed: 146 and 153 kts (168 and 176 mph) 270 and 283 km/h at basic and all optional MTOWs respectively
Approach speed (Domestic model): 148 kts (170 mph) 274 km/h
Take-off field length (PW4056s): 9,250, 10,550 and 11,000 ft (2,819, 3,216 and 3,353 m) at basic MTOW and 850,000 lb/875,000 lb options respectively, at 30° C
Take-off field length (CF6-80C2B1Fs): 9,200, 10,550 and 11,000 ft (2,804, 3,216 and 3,353 m) at basic MTOW and 850,000 lb/875,000 lb options respectively, at 30° C
Take-off field length (RB211-524Gs): 9,300, 10,650 and 11,100 ft (2,835, 3,246 and 3,383 m) at basic MTOW and 850,000 lb/875,000 lb options respectively, at 30° C
Take-off field length (RB211-524Hs): 8,800, 10,050 and 10,500 ft (2,682, 3,063 and 3,200 m) at basic MTOW and 850,000 lb/875,000 lb options respectively, at 30° C
Take-off field length (CF6-80C2B1Fs), Domestic model: 5,850 ft (1,783 m), at 30° C, VMCG limit
Landing field length: 6,250, 6,800 and 6,800 ft (1,905, 2,073 and 2,073 m) at MTOW basic and options respectively
Landing field length (Domestic model): 6,350 ft (1,935 m)
Initial cruise altitude: 34,700, 33,400 and 32,800 ft (10,577, 10,180 and 9,997 m) at MTOW basic and options respectively
Initial cruise altitude (Domestic model): 39,100 ft (11,920 m)
Cruise altitude: 41,000 ft (12,500 m)
Design range (PW4056s): 6,055, 6,900 and 7,270 naut miles (6,972, 7,943 and 8,371 miles) 11,214, 12,779 and 13,464 km at MTOW basic and options respectively
Design range (CF6-80C2B1Fs): 6,050, 6,880 and 7,245 naut miles (6,966, 7,922 and 8,342 miles) 11,205, 12,742 and 13,418 km at MTOW basic and options respectively
Design range (RB211-524G/Hs): 5,930, 6,765 and 7,130 naut miles (6,828, 7,790 and 8,210 miles) 10,982, 12,529 and 13,205 km at MTOW basic and options respectively
Design range (CF6-80C2B1Fs), Domestic model: 1,720 naut miles (1,980 miles) 3,185 km

↑ Cargolux Boeing 747-400F Freighter with the nose door partially open

↑ Boeing 747-400 operated by Malaysia Airlines

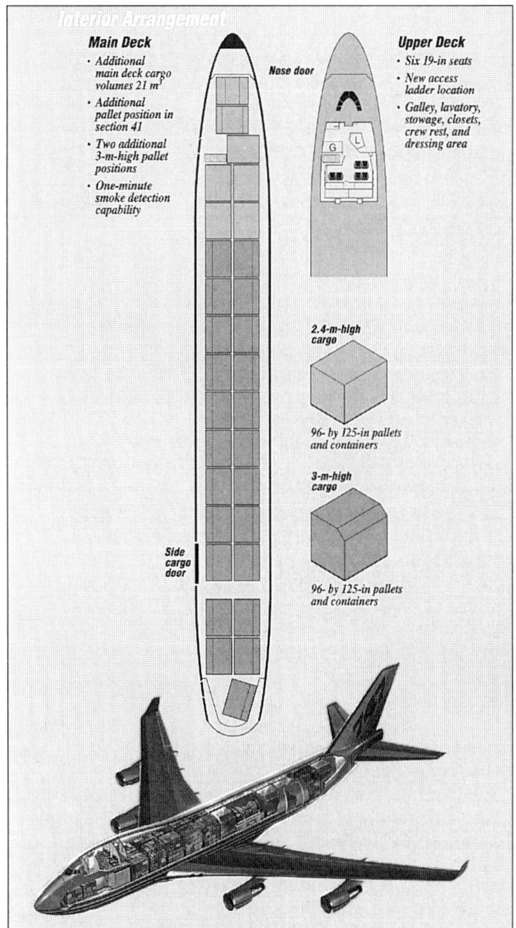

↑ Boeing 747-400F Freighter typical interior arrangements *(courtesy Boeing)*

satcom datalink to ground crews. GPS and FANS (future air navigation system).

Aircraft variants:

747-400 International with winglets, as detailed.

747-400D Domestic models without wingtip extensions and winglets (having 747-200/300 tip fairings), added upper deck windows (3 starboard, 2 port), revised avionics software and cabin pressure schedules, strengthened upper deck floor, 24-ply tyres and brake cooling fans, rear spar bulkhead fitting, re-rated engine thrust, reinforced trailing-edge flap tracks, and reinforced fuselage frames and crown stringers. Up to 566-568 passengers. Can be converted for long-range operations by adding the wingtip extensions and winglets.

747-400F Freighter first went to Cargolux in 1993. Can fly 4,300 naut miles with 244,000 lb (110,675 kg) of revenue payload. Standard maximum take-off weight 800,000 lb (362,873 kg), allowing a 3,200 naut mile range with a 124 ton payload. Optional MTOWs are 833,000 lb (377,842 kg) for a 3,760 naut mile range, 850,000 lb (385,553 kg) for a 4,050 naut mile range, and 875,000 lb (396,893 kg) for a 4,450 naut mile range, all with 124 ton payloads. Main deck volume is 21,347 cu ft (604.48 m^3), supplemented by 5,600 cu ft (158.57 m^3) in the lower hold and 520 cu ft (14.72 m^3) of bulk. Cabin interior 20 ft 3 ins (6.17 m). Main deck nose (upward opening) and side cargo doors are standard.

↑ Boeing 747-400 cockpit

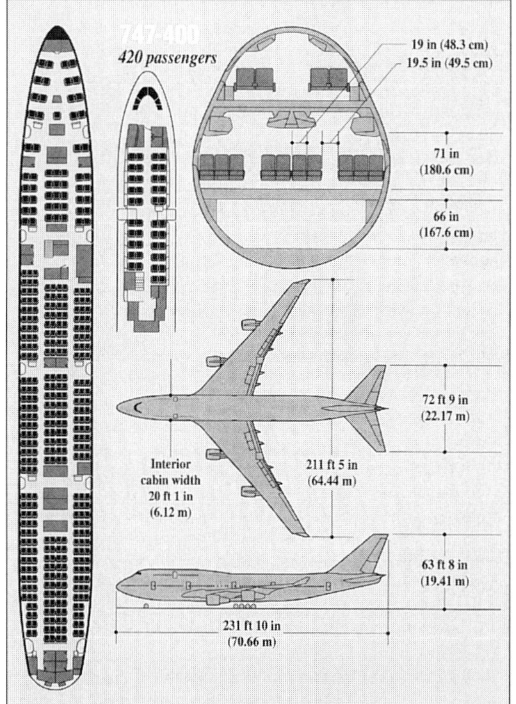

↑ Boeing 747-400 general arrangement, cabin cross section and seating layout for 420 passengers *(courtesy Boeing)*

747-400M Combi is the mixed passenger/cargo version, with typically 268 passengers in a 3-class layout plus up to 40 tons of cargo (typically 6 or 7 pallets on the main deck). Maximum passenger capacity is 413 with no main deck cargo, though lower hold capacity is similar to the standard airliner. Maximum 60,000 lb (27,216 kg) of palleted cargo on the main deck. Large cargo door 11 ft 2 ins × 10 ft (3.4 × 3.05 m). Maximum taxi weight up to 878,000 lb (398,253 kg). MTOW 875,000 lb (396,893 kg).

747-400IGW is offered with a 910,800 lb (413,140 kg) increased gross weight. Announced December 1997.

747-400X and -400LRX are studies for 495 and 375 passenger versions respectively. -400X features strengthened 747-400F type outer wing panels, strengthened fuselage and undercarriage, plus 1 or 2 × 12,040 litre auxiliary fuel tanks in the fuselage for a 7,700 naut mile range; MTOW 910,000 lb (412,770 kg) and will have 65,000 lbf (289 kN) engines. 8,000 naut mile-range for 747-400LRX.

747-400Y is a proposed 500-seat version with the fuselage stretched by about 31 ft (9.4 m), wing span increased, over a 1,000,900 lb (454,000 kg) MTOW and over 7,700 naut mile range. Possible deliveries from 2003.

747-500X and -600X 462 passenger/8,700 naut mile and 548 passenger/7,750 naut mile versions were discontinued in January 1997. Were to incorporate 777 technology.

See also Combat and Electronic sections.

Boeing 757

First flight: 19 February 1982 (Rolls-Royce engines).
Certification: 21 December 1982 (FAA), 14 January 1983 (CAA).
First delivery: 22 December 1982, with Eastern Air Lines starting scheduled services on 1 January 1983. First delivery of a 757-200F Freighter to UPS as a Package Freighter in September 1987. First 757-300 to Condor Flugdienst in January 1999.
Role: Medium-range airliner and freighter.

Details *(757-200 variants, unless stated. See Sales and Aircraft variants)*

Airport limits: LCN 36 at 221,000 lb (100,244 kg) taxi weight and grade C flexible pavement.
Noise levels: 86.2 EPNdB (PW2037s) and 82.2 EPNdB (RB211-535E4s) take-off, 94 EPNdB and 93.3 EPNdB (PW and R-R) sideline, 97.7 EPNdB and 95 EPNdB (PW and R-R) approach.
Sales: 920 sold by June 1998 of all models, of which 802 had by then been delivered. Orders comprise 824 B757-200s (566 from US operators and 258 from non-US), 1 B757-200M Combi (non-US), 80 B757-200PFs (75 US and 5 non-US), and 15 B757-300s (all non-US). Of these, 98 B757-200s, 5 PFs and 15 B757-300s had still to be delivered at this time. 4 757-200s are used by the USAF as C-32A Government VIP transports.
Crew: 2 pilots plus optional observer.
Passengers: 150 or 178 (16 first class and 162 economy) to a maximum of 239 in all inclusive tour layout, with typical intermediate layouts including 194 (12 first and 182 economy), 217 (all economy) and 231 (inclusive tour). 4 abreast first class, 5 abreast business and 6 abreast economy layouts, all with an aisle. Movable cabin divider (can be repositioned by 1 person between flights) to adjust the ratio of premium and economy seating. 757-300 accommodates 240-289 passengers.
Seat pitch: 38 ins (96.5 cm) first, 32 ins (81 cm) economy, and 28/29 ins (71/73.7 cm) inclusive tour.
Galleys: 2 to 4 galleys in 7 possible locations, with 2 standard positions (at the extreme front and extreme rear of the cabin). See drawing.
Toilets: 3 or 4 in 12 possible locations.
Freight hold volume: 1,790 cu ft (50.69 m^3) underfloor for 757-200 and 2,387 cu ft (67.6 m^3) for 737-300.
Freight hold volume (757-200F): See Aircraft variants.
Size of freight doors (757-200F): 134 × 86 ins (340 × 218 cm)

↑ Boeing 757-200 operated by TWA, the 757th example built

main cargo door, and 2 lower deck doors of 105 × 97 ins (267 × 246 cm) and 99 × 93 ins (251 × 236 cm).
Loading facilities: Lower hold can have hand loading for bulk cargo, Air Cargo Equipment (ACE) telescoping-shelf system, sliding carpet as a continuous-belt-with-backstop system, or Aeroveyor belt-driven system. Aeroveyor system for container loading.
Wing control surfaces: Aileron, double-slotted trailing-edge flaps, 6-section spoilers (for aileron, speed brake and ground functions), and 5-section leading-edge slats per wing.
Tail control surfaces: Variable incidence tailplane, elevators and rudder.
Construction materials: Employs advanced aluminium alloys for wing skins, wing spars and spar chords, and composites for wing trailing-edge control surfaces, wing/body fairings, undercarriage doors, engine struts and nacelles, elevators and rudder.
Engines: 2 × 40,100 lbf (178.38 kN) Rolls-Royce RB211-535E4, 43,100 lbf (191.72 kN) RB211-535E4-B, 37,400 lbf (166.37 kN) RB211-535C (not Freighter), 38,250 lbf (170.1 kN) Pratt & Whitney PW2037, or 41,700 lbf (185.5 kN) PW2040s engines. 180 minutes ETOPS with all engines. 757-300 has RB211-535E4-Bs or 43,850 lbf (195.06 kN) Pratt & Whitney PW2043s.
Engine rating: See above.
Fuel system: 42,684 litres for all 200 Series models, and 43,490 litres for 757-300.
Hydraulic system: 3,000 psi.
Braking system: Carbon.
De-icing system: Bleed air for wing leading edges.
Radar: Colour weather radar.
Flight avionics/instrumentation: Cat IIIb instrument landing system. EFIS-700 with 6-colour CRT displays, featuring selectable modes and ranges, moving map. weather radar image over map/VOR/ILS displays, EICAS, and built-in test features. Windshear system with visual and audio warning. Rockwell Collins FCS-700 AFDS.

Details for 757-200 with PW2037s, *and 757-200 with RB211-535E4s in italics.*
(See Aircraft variants for 757-300 data)

PRINCIPAL DIMENSIONS:
Wing span: 124 ft 10 ins (38.05 m), *the same*
Maximum length: 155 ft 3 ins (47.32 m), *the same*
Maximum height: 44 ft 6 ins (13.56 m), *the same*

CABIN:
Length: 118 ft 5 ins (36.09 m), *the same*
Width: 11 ft 7 ins (3.53 m), *the same*
Height: 7 ft (2.13 m), *the same*
Volume: 8,140 cu ft (230.5 m^3), *the same*
Main passenger door: 6 ft × 2 ft 9 ins (1.83 × 0.84 m) forward, and 6 ft × 2 ft 6 ins (1.83 × 0.76 m) rear, *the same*

WINGS:
Area: 1,994 sq ft (185.25 m^2), *the same*
Aspect ratio: 7.815
Sweepback: 25° at 25% chord, *the same*
Incidence: 32°, *the same*
Dihedral: 5°, *the same*

TAIL UNIT:
Tailplane span: 49 ft 11 ins (15.21 m), *the same*
Tailplane area: 542 sq ft (50.35 m^2), *the same*

UNDERCARRIAGE:
Type: Retractable, with twin steerable nosewheels. 4-wheel main bogies
Wheel base: 60 ft (18.29 m), *the same*
Wheel track: 24 ft (7.32 m), *the same*

WEIGHTS:
Empty, operating: 127,800 lb (57,970 kg) standard or 128,900 lb (58,468 kg) optional, *128,100 lb (58,105 kg) standard or 129,200 lb (58,604 kg) optional*
Maximum zero fuel: 184,000 lb (83,460 kg) standard or 186,000 lb (84,368 kg) optional, *184,000 lb (83,460 kg) standard or 188,000 lb (85,275 kg) optional*
Maximum taxi: 221,000 lb (100,244 kg) standard or 256,000 lb (116,120 kg) optional
Maximum take-off: 220,000 lb (99,790 kg) standard or 255,000 lb (115,666 kg) optional, *the same*
Maximum landing: 198,000 lb (89,811 kg) standard or 210,000 lb (95,255 kg) optional, *the same*

PERFORMANCE:
Maximum operating Mach Number (M_{MO}): Mach 0.86
Maximum cruise speed: Mach 0.8 (512 kts, 590 mph, 950 km/h) at 27,000 ft (8,230 m), *the same*
Cruise speed at 34,000 ft (10,365 m): 278 kts (320 mph) 515 km/h
Approach speed: 132 kts (152 mph) 244 km/h, *the same*
Take-off field length: 5,900 ft (1,800 m) or 10,000 ft (3,048 m) at optional weight, *5,430 ft (1,655 m) or 7,580 ft (2,310 m) at optional weight*, all at sea level, 29 ° C
Landing field length: 4,800 ft (1,463 m), *4,650 ft (1,418 m)*, both with 194 passengers
Initial cruise altitude: 38,300 ft (11,675 m) standard weight or 35,400 ft (10,790 m) optional weight, *38,750 ft (11,810 m) standard weight or 35,700 ft (10,880 m) optional weight*
Altitude, OEI: 23,650 ft (7,210 m) standard weight or 23,600 ft (7,195 m) optional weight, *23,850 ft (7,270 m) standard weight or 23,800 ft (7,255 m) optional weight*
Range with full payload: 2,720 naut miles (3,132 miles) 5,037 km standard weight or 3,930 naut miles (4,525 miles) 7,278 km optional weight, *2,550 naut miles (2,936 miles) 4,722 km standard weight or 3,710 naut miles (4,272 miles) 6,870 km optional weight*, both with 194 passengers

Aircraft variants:
757-200 is the passenger airliner, as detailed.
757-200F Freighter can fly 3,360 naut miles (3,869 miles) 6,222 km with a maximum revenue payload of 87,500 lb (39,690 kg); normal revenue payloads of 72,210 lb (32,755 kg) based on 9 lb/cu ft cargo density or 7 lb/cu ft bulk, 79,850 or 79,400 lb (36,220 or 36,015 kg) containers (P&W and R-R engines respectively), or 84,350 or 83,900 lb (38,260 or 38,056 kg) pallets (with P&W and R-R engines respectively). Main deck container volume is 6,600 cu ft (186.89 m^3), with 15 positions for containers/pallets of 88 × 125 ins (2.24 × 3.18 m) each (typical tare weight 3,307 lb, 1,500 kg per pallet and 7,716 lb, 3,500 kg per container), while the lower holds provide 1,830 cu ft (51.82 m^3) bulk cargo volume. Similar engine options, except for 535C. 112,350-112,800 lb (50,960-51,165 kg) empty weight (tare not included), 200,000 lb (90,718 kg) maximum zero-fuel weight, 250,000-255,000 lb (113,400-115,665 kg) maximum take-off weight, and maximum landing weight 210,000 lb (95,250 kg). See earlier text for door sizes. Volume limited payload 72,100 lb (32,700 kg), and structural limit payload 84,215 lb (38,200 kg).
757-200PF Package Freighter was the original cargo model, as developed for UPS.
757-200M Combi offers combined accommodation for passengers and cargo, typically 150 passengers and 3 containers on the main deck. Large cargo door as detailed for 757-200F.
757-300 is a stretched version (23 ft 4 ins, 7.11 m longer), launched on 2 September 1996. Accommodation for 240-289 passengers, depending on configuration; typically 243 passengers in mixed class or 289 for charter use. Same flight deck and operating systems, but new interior, new tyres, wheels and brakes, a tail skid, and strengthened wings and undercarriage. RB211-535E4-B or PW2043 engines. 43,490 litres of fuel. Range of 3,474 naut miles (4,000 miles) 6,437 km when carrying 240 passengers and powered by PW2043 engines. Maximum length 178 ft 7 ins (54.43 m). Lower hold cargo volume increased to 2,387 cu ft (67.6 m^3). MTOW 270,000 lb (122,470 kg). FAR take-off field length 9,000 ft (2,743 m) at sea level (30° C). Rolled out 31 May 1998 and first flown July 1998. First delivery 1999.
757 FTB is a flying avionics testbed to support the F-22 fighter programme.

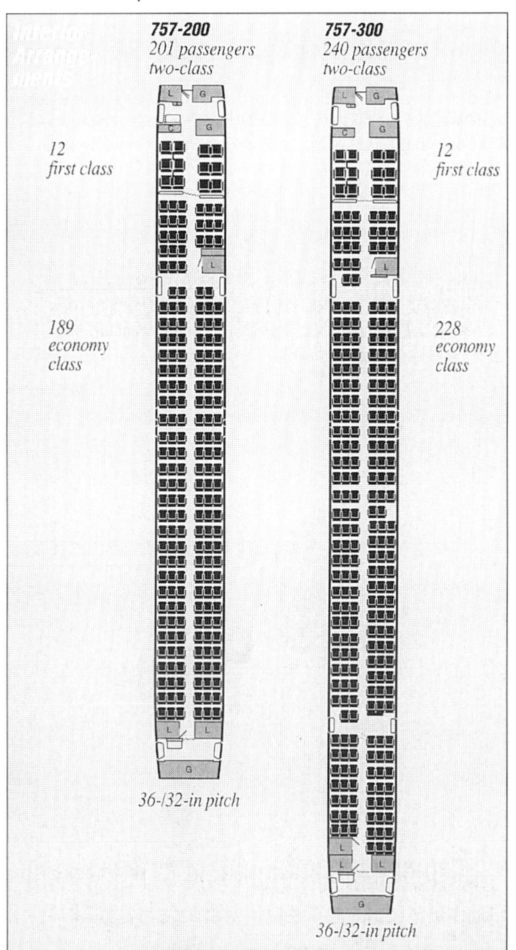

↑ **Boeing 757-200 and -300 typical interior arrangements** *(courtesy Boeing)*

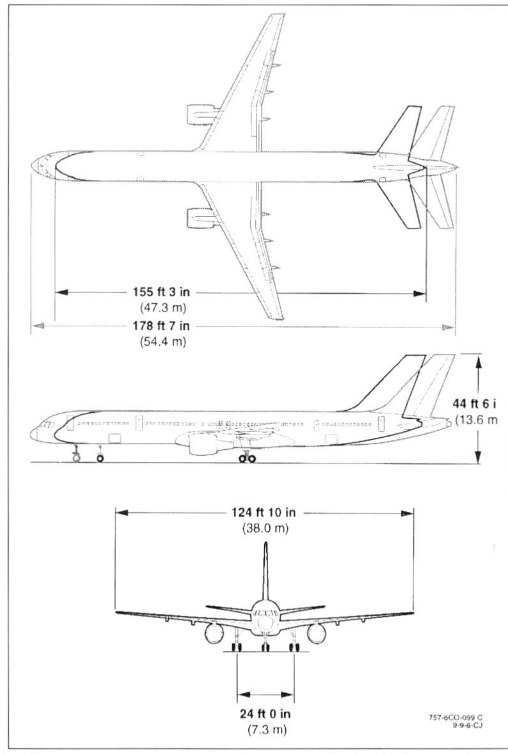

↑ **General arrangements of the 757-200 and 757-300, indicating the larger size of the -300**

Boeing 767

First flight: 26 September 1981. 21 June 1995 for 767-300 Freighter.
Certification: 30 July 1982 with Pratt & Whitney JT9D engines, September 1982 with General Electric engines, February 1990 with Rolls-Royce engines, January 1984 for 767-200ER, September 1986 for 767-300, December 1987 for 767-300ER, and October 1995 for 767-300 Freighter.
First delivery: 19 August 1982 to United Airlines, starting scheduled services on 8 September 1982. First 767-300 delivery on 25 September 1986 to Japan Airlines. First 767-300 Freighter went to United Parcel Service in October 1995.
Airframe life: 40 years of service life; tested through 19 months, consisting of 100,000 simulated flights and 100,000 hours.
Role: Medium-long range airliner and freighter.
Noise levels: 90.4 EPNdB take-off, 96.6 EPNdB sideline, 101.7 EPNdB approach for 767-200ER with CF6-80C2B4 engines.
Sales: 828 ordered of all versions by June 1998, comprising 128 B767-200s (58 by US operators and 70 by non-US operators, of which all delivered), 101 B767-200ERs (34 to US and 67 to non-US, all delivered), 107 B767-300s (28 US and 79 non-US, with 9 then awaiting delivery), 409 B767-300ERs (185 US and 224 non-US, with 58 then awaiting delivery), 32 B767-300Fs (30 US and 2 non-US, with 9 then awaiting delivery), and 51 B767-400ERs (all US, and all then awaiting delivery).
Crew: 2 or 3 (flight).
Passengers: 767-200/200ER typical 3-class 181-seat layout provides for 15 first class (60 ins, 152 cm seat pitch), 40 business (38 ins, 96.5 cm) and 126 economy (32 ins, 81 cm) passengers; or 2-class 224-seat layout for 18 first class (38 ins, 96.5 cm) and 206 economy (32 ins, 81 cm); or 1 class 247-seat layout (32 ins, 81 cm); or inclusive tour 285-seat layout (30 ins, 76 cm). First class double and single sleeper seats (5 abreast), 6 abreast business class, 7 abreast economy class, and 8 abreast inclusive-tour seating, all with 2 aisles. 767-300/300ER typical 3-class 218-seat layout provides for 18 first, 46 business and 154 economy passengers

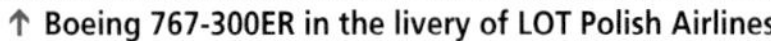
↑ Boeing 767-300ER in the livery of LOT Polish Airlines

↑ Boeing 767-300 flight deck

(same pitches); or 2-class 269-seat layout for 24 first class (38 ins, 96.5 cm) and 245 economy (32 ins, 81 cm); or 1-class 290-seat (32 ins, 81 cm); or inclusive tour 325-seat layout (30 ins, 76 cm). 767-300 can accommodate up to a maximum of 350 passengers.
Seat pitch: See above.
Galleys: 767-200 has forward and aft galleys and a mid-cabin service station offered in 104 possible positions, and 767-300 has 116 possible positions.
Toilets: 5 toilets, with 767-200 having 56 possible positions, and 767-300 having 69.
Pressurization: 8.6 psi cabin differential.
Freight hold capacity: *767-200/200ER:* Typically 3 pallets (96 × 125 ins, 2.44 × 3.18 m) or 6 half-pallets (96 × 61.5 ins, 2.44 × 1.56 m) in forward hold and 10 LD2 containers plus bulk in aft hold, with 2,800-2,875 cu ft (79.2-81.4 m^3) volume, or alternatively 22 LD2 containers plus bulk in holds, volume 3,070 cu ft (86.9 m^3). *767-300/300ER:* Typically 4 pallets or 8 half-pallets in forward hold and 14 LD-2 containers plus bulk in aft hold, volume 3,670-3,770 cu ft (103.9-106.8 m^3), or alternatively 30 LD2 containers plus bulk in holds, volume 4,030 cu ft (114.1 m^3). Alternative LD3 or LD4 containers. *767-400ER* volume 4,904 cu ft (138.87 m^3). Freight hold payloads are 21,600 lb (9,798 kg) forward compartment, 18,000 lb (8,165 kg) aft compartment and 6,450 lb (2,926 kg) bulk compartment for the 767-200/200ER, with alternates of 33,750 lb (15,309 kg), 27,000 lb (12,247 kg) and 6,450 lb (2,926 kg) depending on the number of passengers and galley weights. For the 767-300/300ER, these are 28,800 lb (13,063 kg), 25,200 lb (11,431 kg) and 6,450 lb (2,926 kg) standard, or 45,000 lb (20,412 kg), 38,745 lb (17,575 kg) and 6,450 lb (2,926 kg) alternate respectively. See Freighter under Aircraft variants.
Size of freight doors: 70 ins (178 cm) or 134 ins (340 cm) width, when raised providing a vertical access height of 66 ins (168 cm).
Loading facilities: Ball mat at entrance and roller tracks in holds.
Wing control surfaces: Inner and outer ailerons, double-slotted inner and single-slotted outer trailing-edge flaps, multi-section spoilers (speed brakes and lift dumper functions), and leading-edge slats.
Tail control surfaces: Variable incidence tailplane, elevators and rudder.
Flight control system: Hydraulic.
Construction materials: Metal (including advanced aluminium alloy in the wings and keel beam chords), except for graphite used in parts of the floor panels, shock strut doors, ailerons, spoilers, rudder and elevators; aramid in the engine pylons and flaps; and hybrid composites in the engine nacelles, main undercarriage doors, wing root/tailplane fairings, and part of the wings and fin.
Engines: 2 ×
– General Electric CF6-80C2B2 (52,500 lbf, 233.5 kN) on 200/200ER/300
– CF6-80C2B4 (57,900 lbf, 257.6 kN) on 200ER/300/300ER/400ER
– CF6-80C2B6 (61,500 lbf, 273.6 kN) on 200ER/300ER/400ER
– CF6-80C2B2F (52,500 lbf, 233.5 kN) on 200/200ER/300/400ER
– CF6-80C2B4F (57,900 lbf, 257.6 kN) on 200ER/300/300ER/400ER
– CF6-80C2B6F (61,500 lbf, 273.6 kN) on 200ER/300ER
– CF6-80C2B7F (61,500 lbf, 273.6 kN +2/3% at take-off)
– Pratt & Whitney PW4050 (50,000 lbf, 222.4 kN) on 200/200ER/300
– PW4052 (52,000 lbf, 231.3 kN) on 200/200ER/300
– PW4056 (56,750 lbf, 252.4 kN) on 200ER/300ER/400ER
– PW4060 (60,000 lbf, 266.9 kN) on 200ER/300ER/400ER
– PW4062 (62,000 lbf, 275.8 kN) on 200ER/300ER/400ER
Also available to 767-300ER and -400ER are:
– Rolls-Royce RB211-524G4 (58,000 lbf, 258 kN)
– RB211-524H (60,600 lbf, 269.6 kN)
Available to 767-300 Freighter are:
– CF6-80C2B6F, CF6-80C2B7F, PW4060, PW4062, and RB211-524H.
ETOPS approval of 120 or 180 minutes with certain engine options.
Fuel system: 63,216 litres (767-200), 77,412 or optional 91,378 litres (-200ER), 63,216 litres (-300), and 91,378 litres (-300ER and Freighter).
Electrical system: 115/200 volt, 400 Hz 3-phase AC supply, via 2 × 90 kVA engine-driven generators. APU with 90 kVA generator.
Hydraulic system: 3 systems, each 3,000 psi.
Braking system: Steel or carbon brakes, with electronic anti-skid system.
De-icing system: Wing outer leading-edges, engine inlets, cockpit glazing and data sensors.
Oxygen system: Nitrogen chlorate generators for passengers, gaseous for crew.
Radar: AlliedSignal Bendix/king RDR-4A colour weather radar or similar.
Flight avionics/instrumentation: Cat IIIb instrument landing system. All-digital electronic flight deck with EFIS colour displays, CRT engine instrument display, integrated caution/warning system and display on CRT, "Quiet dark" flight deck concept, and common pilot type rating between multiple models technologies. Full flight management system with laser gyro inertial reference system, EADI, EHSI, EICAS, ARINC 700 (digital databus), navigation radio autotuning, and certified windshear system. TCAS, ACARS, satcom, and GPS.

↑ Impression of the new extended range Boeing 767-400

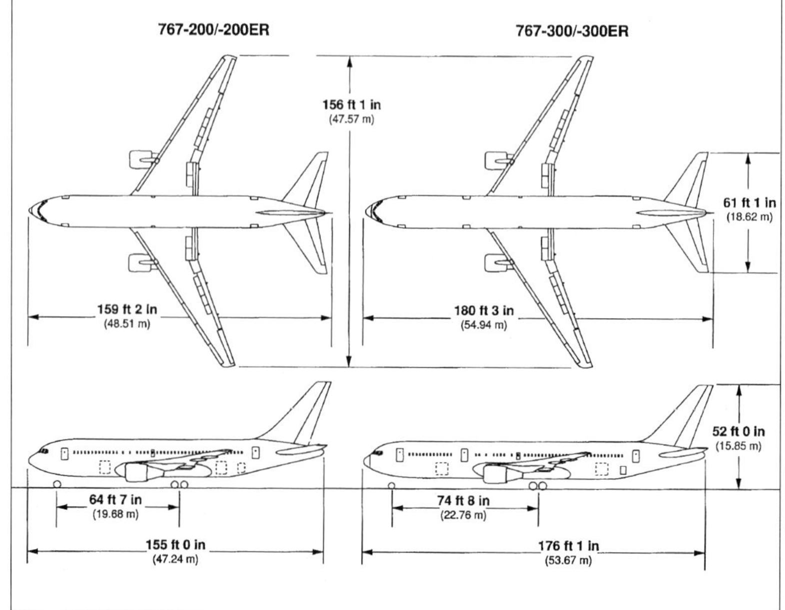

↑ Boeing 767-200/-200ER and 767-300/-300ER general arrangements *(courtesy Boeing)*

	767-200ER	767-300	767-300ER	767-400
Wing span	156 ft 1 ins (47.57 m)	156 ft 1 ins (47.57 m)	156 ft 1 ins (47.57 m)	168 ft (51.21 m)
Maximum length	159 ft 2 ins (48.51 m)	180 ft 3 ins (54.94 m)	180 ft 3 ins (54.94 m)	201 ft 1 ins (61.3 m)
Maximum height	52 ft (15.85 m)	52 ft (15.85 m)	52 ft (15.85 m)	55 ft 1 ins (16.79 m)
Cabin length	111 ft 4 ins (33.93 m)	132 ft 5 ins (40.36 m)	132 ft 5 ins (40.36 m)	
Cabin width	15 ft 6 ins (4.72 m)	15 ft 6 ins (4.72 m)	15 ft 6 ins (4.72 m)	15 ft 6 ins (4.72 m)
Cabin height	9 ft 5 ins (2.87 m)	9 ft 5 ins (2.87 m)	9 ft 5 ins (2.87 m)	9 ft 5 ins (2.87 m)
Cabin volume	15,121 cu ft (428.18 m^3)	17,088 cu ft (483.88 m^3)	17,088 cu ft (483.88 m^3)	
Passenger doors	6 ft 2 ins × 3 ft 6 ins (1.88 × 1.07 m)	6 ft 2 ins × 3 ft 6 ins (1.88 × 1.07 m)	6 ft 2 ins × 3 ft 6 ins (1.88 × 1.07 m)	6 ft 2 ins × 3 ft 6 ins (1.88 × 1.07 m)
Wing area	3,050 sq ft (283.35 m^2)	3,050 sq ft (283.35 m^2)	3,050 sq ft (283.35 m^2)	3,050 sq ft (283.35 m^2)
Wing aspect ratio	7.98	7.98	7.98	7.98
Wing sweepback	31.5 ° at 25% chord	31.5 ° at 25% chord	31.5 ° at 25% chord	31.5° at 25% chord
Incidence	4.25 °	4.25 °	4.25 °	4.25 °
Dihedral	6 °	6 °	6 °	6 °
Tailplane span	61 ft 1 ins (18.62 m)	61 ft 1 ins (18.62 m)	61 ft 1 ins (18.62 m)	
Tailplane area	644.5 sq ft (59.876 m^2)	644.5 sq ft (59.876 m^2)	644.5 sq ft (59.876 m^2)	
Undercarriage type	Retractable, with twin steerable nosewheels. 4-wheel main bogies	Retractable, with twin steerable nosewheels. 4-wheel main bogies	Retractable, with twin steerable nosewheels. 4-wheel main bogies	
Main wheel tyre size	45 × 17-20	45 × 17-20	45 × 17-20	
Nose wheel tyre size	37 × 14-15	37 × 14-15	37 × 14-15	
Wheel base	64 ft 7 ins (19.69 m)	74 ft 8 ins (22.76 m)	74 ft 8 ins (22.76 m)	
Wheel track	30 ft 6 ins (9.3 m)	30 ft 6 ins (9.3 m)	30 ft 6 ins (9.3 m)	
Weight empty, operating	186,200 lb (84,460 kg) standard, 186,600 lb (84,642 kg) optional	191,700 lb (86,954 kg)	199,600 lb (90,537 kg)	
Maximum ramp weight	388,000 lb (175,993 kg)	347,000 lb (157,936 kg)	401,000 lb (181,890 kg)	
Maximum zero fuel weight	253,000 lb (114,760 kg) standard, 260,000 lb (117,936 kg) optional	278,000 lb (126,100 kg)	278,000 lb (126,100 kg) standard, 295,000 lb (133,812 kg) optional	
Maximum take-off weight	345,000 lb (156,492 kg) standard, 387,000-395,000 lb (175,543-179,172 kg) optional	345,000 lb (156,492 kg) standard, 351,000 lb (159,213 kg) optional	380,000 lb (172,368 kg) standard, 408,000-412,000 lb (185,068-186,883 kg) optional	440,000 lb (199,580 kg)
Maximum landing weight	278,000 lb (126,100 kg) standard, 285,000 lb (129,276 kg) optional	300,000 lb (136,080 kg)	300,000 lb (136,080 kg) standard, 320,000 lb (145,152 kg) optional	
Typical cruise speed	Mach 0.8	Mach 0.8	Mach 0.8	
Approach speed kts (mph) km/h	139 (160) 257	141 (162) 261	145 (167) 268	
Take-off field length (sea level, 29° C)	8,600-9,300 ft (2,621-2,835 m)	8,100 ft (2,470 m)	9,800-10,200 ft (2,987-3,109 m)	
Landing field length	4,900 ft (1,494 m), 181 pax, PW4056s		5,200 ft (1,585 m), 218 pax, PW4060s	
Initial cruise altitude (or as specified)	34,800-35,300 ft (10,600-10,760 m), 181 pax, PW4056s	37,200 ft (11,340 m), with CF6-80C2B2s	33,400-33,700 ft (10,180-10,270 m), 218 pax, PW4060s	
Altitude, OEI	24,000 ft (7,315 m)	20,200 ft (6,157 m)	22,500 ft (6,860 m)	
Range naut miles (miles) km	6,652 (7,660) 12,328	3,734 (4,300) 6,920	5,931 (6,830) 10,992	5,645 (6,500) 10,460

Note: Pax = Passengers

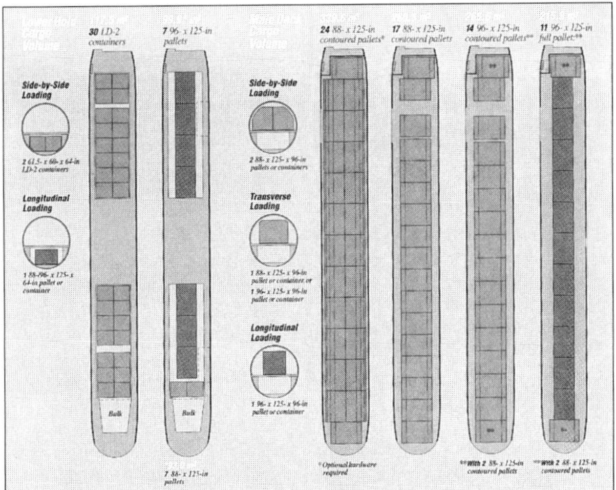

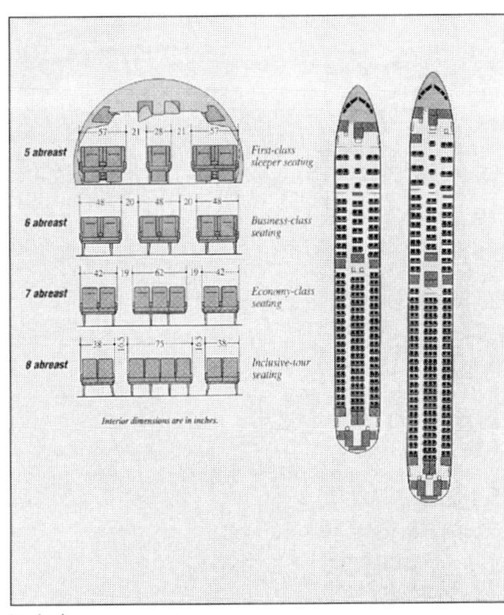

↑ **Boeing 767-300 Freighter layouts (*left*), with 767-200/-300 cabin layouts (*right*)** *(courtesy Boeing)*

Aircraft variants:
767-200 is the basic medium-range version (see Passengers). Maximum take-off weight typically 300,000 lb (136,077 kg). Typical range 4,568 naut miles (5,260 miles) 8,465 km. 767 has considerable commonality with the 757.
767-200ER offers extended range through higher weight and fuel options.
767-300 is a stretched variant of the 767-200, with increased seating capacity as detailed under Passengers. Higher weights, as detailed in table.
767-300ER is an extended range variant of 767-300.
767-300F Freighter has an interior diameter of 15 ft 6 ins (4.72 m), main deck cargo compartment of 130 ft 7 ins (39.8 m), and a 8 ft 9 ins × 11 ft 8 ins (2.67 × 3.456 m) main deck cargo door. First for United Parcel Service flew on 21 June 1995 (deliveries to UPS from 12 October 1995). Cargo volume 15,272 cu ft (432.45 m^3); up to 24 containers or pallets, each 88 × 125 ins (2.24 × 3.18 m) on main deck, 30 lower hold LD2 containers plus 430.8 cu ft (12.2 m^3) of bulk. Total 112,500 lb (51,029 kg) maximum revenue payload; can carry 112,000 lb (50,800 kg) over 3,000 naut miles or 100,800 lb (45,720 kg) over 4,000 naut miles. MTOW of UPS Freighter is 408,000 lb (185,065 kg); Boeing offers a payload enhancement for the Freighter up to 412,000 lb (186,880 kg). No passenger windows or doors and, with the exception of a crew galley and toilet, no interior amenities.
767-400 (formerly known as the -400ERX) was launched on 28 April 1997 as an extended range and higher capacity version, seating 303 passengers in 2-class layout and 245 in 3-class. Range of 5,645 naut miles. An extended range (ER) version is being studied, to offer about 6,000 naut miles range.
767 AWACS is detailed in the Electronic section. 767 tanker/transport also developed, based on the 767-200ER/300ER. 767-300ER tanker has up to 7 cargo hold tanks, each 3,748 litres.

Boeing 777

First flight: 12 June 1994 (lasting 3 hours 48 minutes). October 1997 for 777-300 and 4 February 1998 for 777-300 with PW4098 engine. January 2000 for 777-200X and May 2000 for 777-300X.
Certification: 19 April 1995 (simultaneous FAA and JAA). Received 180 minutes ETOPS approval on 30 May 1995. May 1998 for 777-300.
First delivery: 15 May 1995 to United Airlines (official ceremony, following 15 May actual delivery). Revenue services began 7 June. First 777-300 to Cathay Pacific Airways in Spring 1998. Early 2001 for 777-200X and 777-300X.
Role: Long-range wide-body airliner.
Sales: 392 ordered by June 1998, of which 133 have been delivered. These comprise 345 B777-200s (136 for US operators and 209 for non-US operators, of which 132 have been delivered), and 47 B777-300s for non-US operators (46 to be delivered at time of writing).
Crew: 2 (flight).
Passengers: 777-200 accommodates 305-328 in 3-class layout (typically 24 first, 54 business and 227 economy), 375-400 in

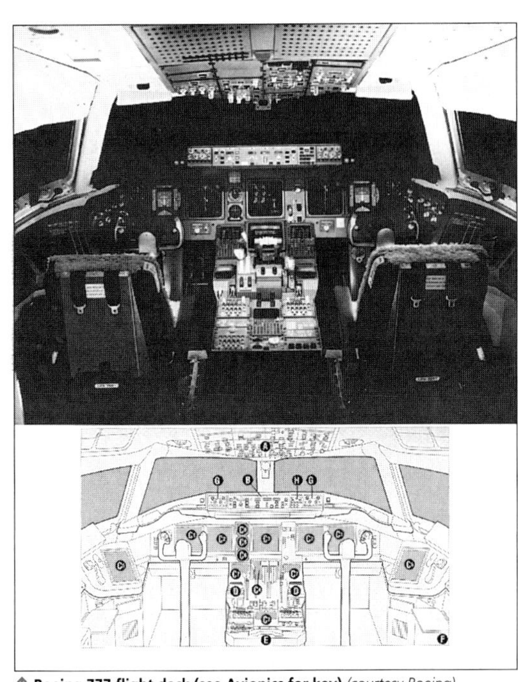

↑ **Boeing 777 flight deck (see Avionics for key)** *(courtesy Boeing)*

↑ **Boeing 777-200 IGW with Rolls-Royce Trent 800 engines, operated by Emirates**

↑ **Boeing 777-200 and -300 general arrangement (*top*), with typical interior arrangements** *(courtesy Boeing)*

2-class layout (typically 30 first and 345 economy), and 418-440 all-economy. 777-300 will carry 368-394 passengers in 3-class layout, or 451-479 in 2-class, or 500-550 in high-density layouts.
Seat pitch: 60 ins (152 cm) first class, 38 ins (96.5 cm) business, and 32 ins (81 cm) economy.
Freight hold volume: 5,656 cu ft (160.16 m^3) with LD3 containers, or 5,302 cu ft (150.14 m^3) with 96 × 125 ins (2.44 × 3.18 m) pallets and containers for 777-200/-200 IGW. 7,552 cu ft (213.85 m^3) with LD3 containers, or 7,080 cu ft (200.48 m^3) with 96 × 125 ins (2.44 × 3.18 m) pallets and containers for 777-300.
Freight hold capacity: 32 LD3 containers plus 600 cu ft (16.99 m^3) of bulk cargo for 777-200. 8 pallets of 96 × 125 ins (2.44 × 3.18 m) each in forward lower hold, 20 LD3 containers in aft lower hold and 600 cu ft (16.99 m^3) of bulk cargo for 777-300.
Size of freight doors: 8 ft 10 ins × 5 ft 7 ins (2.69 × 1.7 m) forward, 5 ft 10 ins × 6 ft 2 ins (1.78 × 1.88 m) aft.
Loading facilities: Mechanized handling system.
Wing characteristics: Long span of increased thickness (compared with 757/767 wings) and offering higher cruise speeds, allowing full passenger loads out of many high elevation and high temperature airfields. Optional feature is a hinge and actuation mechanism to enable almost 22 ft (6.7 m) of each wingtip to fold upwards, reducing wing span to 155 ft 3 ins (47.32 m) when on the ground, to allow it to use existing gate and taxiway space.
Wing control surfaces: Aileron (30° up, 10° down), outboard Fowler-type single-slotted and inboard Fowler-type double-slotted trailing-edge flaps (6 settings), flaperon (10° up, 36° droop), 7-section spoilers (speed brakes and lift dumper functions – 60° up), Krueger leading-edge flap, and 7-section leading-edge slats (3 position) per wing.
Tail control surfaces: Variable incidence tailplane (4° up, 11° down) , elevators (30° up, 25° down), and rudder (27.3° either way) with anti-servo tab.
Flight control system: Digital fly-by-wire.
Construction materials: Use of new lightweight structural materials, including 7055 aluminium alloy for the upper wing skin and stringers. Carbonfibre and toughened carbonfibre reinforced plastics for sections of the tail unit, wing trailing-edge control surfaces, fin, elevators, engine nacelles main undercarriage doors and nosewheel doors. Hybrid composites for the floor beams, wing/body fairings and flap track fairings. Glassfibre for the nose radome, parts of the engine pylons, and areas of the wings and tail unit. Composites account for 9% of structural weight.
Engines: 2 General Electric GE90-75B (78,700 lbf, 350.08 kN), Pratt & Whitney PW4074 (74,000 lbf, 329.17 kN) or Rolls-Royce Trent 875 (75,000 lbf, 333.62 kN) turbofans for 777-200; or GE90-76B (76,400 lbf, 339.9 kN), PW4077 (77,000 lbf, 342.52 kN), or Trent 877 (77,000 lbf, 342.52 kN) at high MTOW. GE90-85B (84,700 lbf, 376.77 kN), PW4084 (84,000 lbf, 373.66 kN) or Trent 884 (86,000 lbf; 373.66 kN) for 777-200 IGW; or GE90-90B (92,100 lbf, 409.67 kN), PW4090 (90,000 lbf, 400.35 kN) or Trent 890 (90,000 lbf, 400.35 kN) at high MTOW. GE90-98B, PW4098 (98,000 lbf; 435.93 kN) and Trent 895 for 777-300. AlliedSignal GTCP331-500 APU.
Engine rating: See above.
Fuel system: 117,348 litres for 777-200, 171,176 litres for 777-200 IGW and 777-300.
Electrical system: AC supply using 2 engine-driven and 1 APU-driven 120 kVA constant-frequency generators. VSCF units generate 20 kVA per engine, while the shafts also produce fly-by-wire power via separate magnet systems. Emergency ram-air turbine system.
Hydraulic system: 3 independent systems, each 3,000 psi.
Braking system: AlliedSignal multi-disc carbon brakes.
De-icing system: Thermal for engine intakes and wing slats. Electric for cockpit glazing and pitot heads.
Radar: Honeywell weather radar.
Flight avionics/instrumentation: See diagram: **A** overhead panel with larger nomenclature, cool LED lighted switches and lightplates, and flight deck lighting master brightness control; **B** full-time, triple-channel autopilot mode control panel with new method of selecting flight path angle and track modes; **C** colour flat-panel liquid-crystal displays (6, each 18 ins, 45.7 cm) comprising **C1** primary flight displays (PFD), **C2** navigation/multifunction displays (ND/MFD), **C3** engine

Details for 777-200, *with 777-300 in italics*

PRINCIPAL DIMENSIONS:
Wing span: 199 ft 11 ins (60.93 m), 155 ft 3 ins (47.32 m) folded, *the same*
Maximum length: 209 ft 1 ins (63.73 m), *242 ft 4 ins (73.86 m)*
Maximum height: 60 ft 9 ins (18.52 m), *60 ft 8 ins (18.49 m)*

CABIN:
Length: 160 ft 8 ins (48.97 m)
Width: 19 ft 3 ins (5.87 m), *the same*
Main passenger door: 6 ft 2 ins × 3 ft 6 ins (1.88 × 1 m)

WINGS:
Area: 4,605 sq ft (427.82 m^2)
Aspect ratio: 8.68
Sweepback: 31.6 ° at 25% chord

TAIL UNIT:
Tailplane span: 70 ft 7.5 ins (21.53 m)

UNDERCARRIAGE:
Type: Retractable, with twin steerable nosewheels (±70°) 6-wheel main bogies, with rear wheel steering (±8°)
Main wheel tyre size: 49 × 19-22
Nose wheel tyre size: 44 × 18-18
Wheel base: 84 ft 11 ins (25.88 m)
Wheel track: 36 ft (10.97 m)

WEIGHTS:
Empty, operating (typical): 304,400 lb (138,073 kg) for 777-200, 311,700 lb (141,385 kg) for 777-200 IGW, and *348,600 lb (158,122 kg)*
Maximum zero fuel: 420,000 lb (190,510 kg) for 777-200, 430,000 lb (195,050 kg) for 777-200 IGW, and *495,000 lb (224,528 kg)*
Maximum take-off: 506,000-545,000 lb (229,518-247,207 kg) for 777-200, 580,000-632,500 lb (263,083-286,900 kg) for 777-200 IGW, and *580,000-660,000 lb (263,082-299,370 kg)*
Maximum landing: 445,000 lb (201,850 kg) for 777-200, 460,000 lb (208,652 kg) for 777-200 IGW, and *524,000 lb (237,682 kg)*

PERFORMANCE:
Maximum cruise speed: Mach 0.87, *Mach 0.89*
Economic cruise speed: Mach 0.84
Approach speed: 136-138 kts (157-159 mph) 253-255 km/h, *148 kts (171 mph) 275 km/h*
Take-off distance: up to 8,300 ft (2,530 m) for 777-200, 10,800 ft (3,295 m) for 777-200 IGW, and *11,000 ft (3,355 m)*
Landing field length: 5,600 ft (1,706 m), *6,100 ft (1,859 m)*
Ceiling: over 43,000 ft (13,100 m)
Range: 3,777-5,145 naut miles (4,350-5,925 miles) 7,000-9,535 km for 777-200, 5,957-7,143 naut miles (6,860-8,225 miles) 11,040-13,237 km for 777-200 IGW, or *5,700 naut miles (6,563 miles) 10,556 km with 368 passengers*

indicating and crew alerting system (EICAS), C4 multifunction display (MFD), C5 optional side LCDs, C6 standby flight instruments, and C7 flight management control display units (CDU); D touch-pad cursor control devices; E full-size printer; F maintenance station; G EFIS control panel; and H display select panel. ARINC 629 2-way digital data bus (11 such pathways to connect computers with systems). Common crew rating.

Aircraft variants:
777-100X was a projected short fuselage version for 259 passengers in 3-class layout, for ranges of up to 8,600 naut miles (9,903 miles) 15,927 km. Not developed.
777-200 is the initial standard version, with a 4,000-4,820 naut mile range in initial form.
777-200 IGW is an increased gross weight variant of 580,000-632,500 lb (263,083-286,900 kg) MTOW, first delivered in February 1997. Carries the same number of passengers over a range up to 7,143 naut miles. IGW+ with MTOW up to 648,160 lb (294,000 kg), offering a range up to 7,487 naut miles, was first put into service by Air France in 1998.
777-200X is an ultra long-range (8,600 naut mile) version for 298 passengers, to be developed following cancellation of the 747-500X/600X. Launch customer is Malaysia Airlines, having signed an MoU on 4 March 1997. Greater fuel capacity (181,500 litres) in the modified wings of slightly increased span and 2 × 9,200 litre auxiliary lower hold tanks. MTOW 720,650-736,250 lb (326,880-333,960 kg). General Electric GE90-100B/102B engines have been reportedly proposed among possible choices, in the 100,000-102,500 lbf (444.83-456 kN) range, with other possibilities including the Trent 8102 of 102,000 lbf (453.73 kN).
777-300 is a stretched version, with the length increased by 33 ft 3 ins (10.13 m), for delivery from May 1998. Programme launched 26 June 1995. Rolled-out on 8 September 1997. In 3-class layout, it will carry 368 passengers up to 5,700 naut miles (6,563 miles) 10,556 km. Accommodation in 2-class layout is 451-479 passengers, allowing ranges of 3,740-4,000 naut miles (4,307-4,606 miles) 6,926-7,408 km. Maximum 550 passengers in all-economy layout.
777-300X is a proposed very long-range (6,790 naut mile) version for 355 passengers in a 3-class layout, to be developed following cancellation of the 747-500X/600X. Greater fuel capacity (181,500 litres) in the modified wings of slightly increased span and 2 × 9,200 litre auxiliary hold tanks. PW4098 or Trent 8104 engines, the latter engine allowing a further 2,200 litres of fuel. MTOW 700,625-715,620 lb (317,800-324,500 kg). See 777-200X for engine proposals.

Boeing C-17A Globemaster III, KC-17 and MD-17

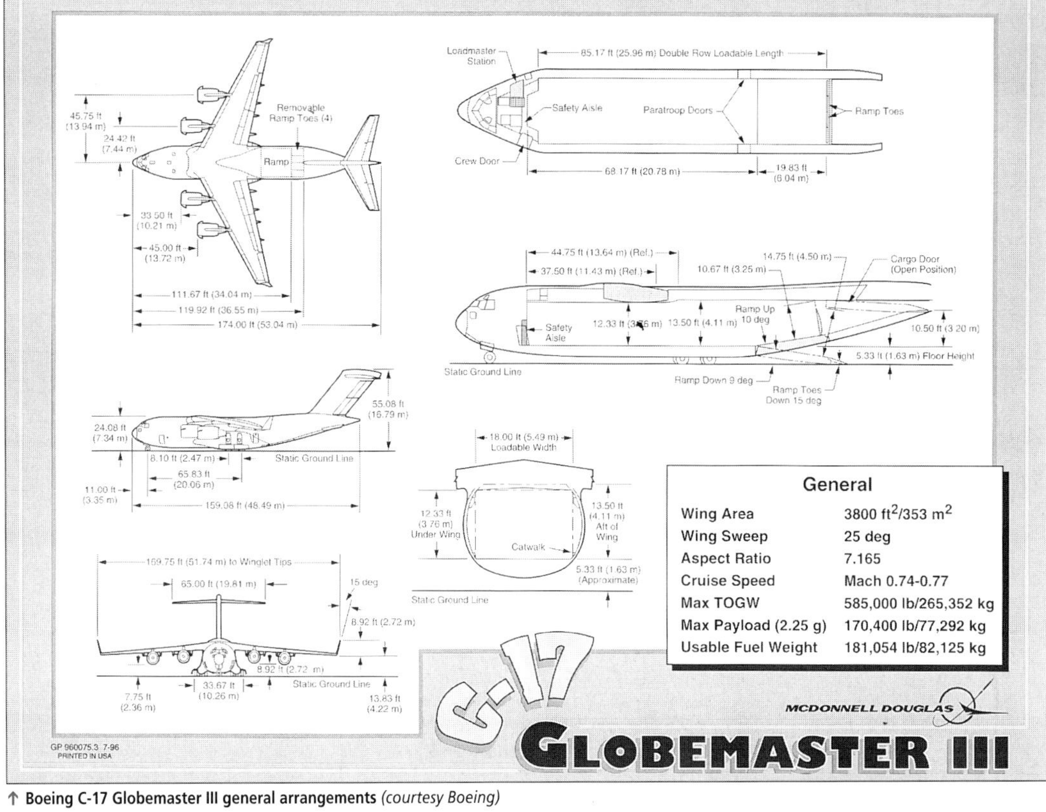

↑ Boeing C-17 Globemaster III general arrangements *(courtesy Boeing)*

First flight: 15 September 1991.
First delivery: First operational delivery on 14 June 1993 to the 437th Air Wing. First actual delivery to the 6517th Test Squadron on 15 September 1991.

Role: Heavy lift, long-range and air refuellable military transport, for intertheatre and intratheatre airlift. Tanker variant proposed as the KC-17. MD-17 is a proposed commercial variant.
Airframe life: C-17 airframe reached 45,000 hours of simulated flight on 28 November 1994 (12,819 flights/ 28,500 landings).

Development

■ Stems from the original C-X transport programme, for which McDonnell Douglas was chosen to be prime contractor on 28 August 1981, although the full-scale engineering and development contract was not signed until December 1985.

Details *(C-17A, unless stated)*

Sales: 1 prototype (T-1). DoD requirement for the USAF is for 120 aircraft (P-1 to P-120), to be delivered through to the year 2004. 25th aircraft (5th aircraft from the Lot VI batch of 6) was delivered on 1 April 1996, with the 38th delivered on 6 March 1998. P-36 to P-40 had contract dates from January to July 1998. First operational unit was the 17th Airlift Squadron, 437th Airlift Wing at Charleston AFB, with initial operational capability achieved on 17 January 1995. Second unit was the Air Force Reserve's 315th AW. Reported RAF interest (perhaps 6).
Crew: 2 flight, plus 2 observer positions. Loadmaster in cargo crew compartment.
Passengers: 54 troops along sidewalls (27 each side; 18 ins/46 cm wide, 24 ins/61 cm spacing centre to centre), 48 troops along centreline in 8 sets of 6 seats back-to-back, or 100 troops on 10 palleted passenger packs plus 54 on sidewalls. Total capacity depending on layout 102-154. In an aeromedical evacuation role, 3 on-board litter kits (each with 4 litters) can be joined by 9 additional kits, making 48 litters in total. Contingency allows for 102 ambulatory seated patients to be carried in addition to the litters. See also Aerial delivery system for paratroops.
Pressurization: See Environmental control system.
Freight hold volume: 20,900 cu ft (591.82 m³).
Freight hold capacity: 18 × 463L pallets, including 4 on ramp. See also Passengers. Can alternatively carry Army wheeled vehicles in 2 side-by-side rows, 3 Bradley infantry fighting

↑ Boeing C-17 Globemaster III

↑ Boeing C-17 Globemaster III unloading a large cargo container at the US controlled Bosnian Air Base in 1997

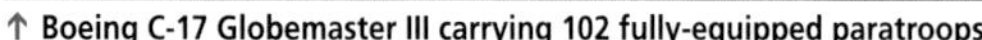
↑ Boeing C-17 Globemaster III carrying 102 fully-equipped paratroops

↑ Boeing MD-17 commercial heavylifter

vehicles, an Abrams M1 series main battle tank at weights up to 135,000 lb (61,235 kg) with other vehicles, or other loads such as Apache helicopters and missile systems. Tracked vehicles weighing 65,000 lb (29,484 kg) or more must be loaded so that the vehicle's centreline is within 8 ins (20.3 cm) of the aircraft's centreline.
Freight hold access: Rear lower ramp/door, 10° internal upsweep when closed, 9° to ground when lowered, and with ramp toes of 15° to bridge the ground with the ramp sill. Ramp capacity 40,000 lb (18,144 kg). Ramp toe capacity (unsupported) is 5,000 lb (2,268 kg) for wheel load (single toe), 10,000 lb (4,536 kg) for single axle load (pair of toes), and 10,355 lb (4,697 kg) for pallet loading or combat offload. Cabin floor height to the ground 5 ft 4 ins (1.62 m). Rear upper door is hinged to the cabin ceiling when open, to provide a total vertical freight loading opening of 10 ft 6 ins (3.2 m). Side doors for paratroop dropping of 43 ins × 80 ins (1.09 × 2.03 m).
Loading facilities: Rails, rollers and tiedown rings (295 on an average 29 ins, 74 cm grid, all 25,000 lb, 11,340 kg capacity). Hydraulic cargo winch, with variable speed of 0-80 ft (0-24.4 m) per minute; 6,500 lbf (28.9 kN) drawbar pull at 30 ft (9.14 m) per minute. Cargo restraint criteria is longitudinal (3g forward, 1.5g aft), lateral (1.5g), and vertical (4.5g down, 2g up).
Aerial delivery system: 9 × 463L pallets plus 2 on ramp. Single load airdrop limit 60,000 lb (27,215 kg) platform. Sequential loads drop 110,000 lb (49,896 kg), 60 ft (18.29 m) of platform. Container delivery system for up to 40 containers of 2,350 lb (1,066 kg) total rigged weight each. Alternatively, 102 paratroops plus 8 equipment bundles.
Wing control surfaces: Externally blown flap system which allows a steep, low-speed final approach and low landing speeds for routine short field landings. With this powered lift system, the engine exhaust flow is directed through the double-slotted fixed-vane simple-hinged flaps to produce additional lifting force. 4 leading-edge slats over full span, aileron and 4 spoilers per wing. Flaps and spoilers deploy simultaneously to act as in-flight airbrakes.
Tail control surfaces: T-tail with trimmable tailplane, with 2-section elevators and 2-section rudder further split into upper and lower portions.
Flight control system: Quadruple-redundant fly-by-wire, with mechanical back-up. Conventional control surfaces, hydraulically actuated. Flight control surfaces with mechanically controlled hydraulic actuation as back-up are tailplane, elevators, lower rudder, and ailerons.
Construction materials: Aluminium alloy, steel and titanium, but with 8.1% composites (particularly for the control surfaces).
Engines: 4 Pratt & Whitney F117-PW-100 (PW2040) turbofans. Direct-flow thrust reversers capable of deployment in flight. On the ground, a fully loaded aircraft using thrust reversers can back up a 2% slope. See Electrical system for APU.
Engine rating: Each 40,440 lbf (179.9 kN).
Fuel system: 181,054 lb (82,125 kg) usable. 4 independent wing tanks, with 2 boost pumps per tank. Any tank can feed any engine. Tanks are inerted with nitrogen from onboard inert gas generating system (OBIGGS). 2 outboard tanks of 21,335 litres each, 2 inboard of 29,742 litres each, and engine feed lines with 143 litres, providing a total of 102,297 litres of usable fuel.
Flight refuelling: Provision.
Electrical system: 90kVA generator on each engine and the APU to provide 115/200 volt, 3-phase, 400Hz power. 4 × 200 amp transformer-rectifiers provide 28 volt DC power. Single-phase 1,000VA inverter powers ground refuelling and emergency AC systems. 2 × 40 amp-hour ni-cd batteries for APU starting and emergency DC power. System accepts 3-phase, 115/200 volt, 400Hz ground power. Onboard 60Hz power for aeromedical equipment. AlliedSignal GTCP 331-250(G) APU in the starboard main undercarriage gear pod.
Hydraulic system: 4 independent systems, each 4,000 psi; each engine drives 1 system. 2 pumps on each engine plus electrical motor-driven pump for redundancy. Fail-safe protection from RAM-air turbine (RAT) pump. Control to safe landing with any single system.
Braking system: Carbon type.
Fire system: Detection and suppression systems. Onboard inert gas generating system, pressurized by bleed air at 60 psi, for explosion protection.
Environmental control system: Bleed air from the 10th and 17th stages of all engines. Maintains 10,000 ft (3,050 m) cabin pressure up to 45,000 ft (13,715 m). 2 air-conditioning units. Environmental control system permits avionics cooling without noticeable contamination of occupied areas of the aircraft during chemical warfare operations; cargo compartment has been designed for ease of decontamination.
Oxygen system: 25 litre converter for flight deck. 75 litre converter for cargo compartment plus provisions for second 75 litre converter. Passenger/troop provisions.
Radar: AlliedSignal AN/APS-133(V) weather and mapping radar, with rendezvous beacon.
Flight avionics/instrumentation: 2 full-time all-function GEC-Marconi HUDs. 4 Honeywell colour multi-function CRT displays plus conventional instruments as a backup. 3 Delco mission computers with 4 displays (MCDs) and 2 keyboards (MCKs). Central aural warning system (CAWS), Jet Electronics and Tech standby navigation and performance indicators, Lockheed Martin electronic flight control system, Hamilton Standard aircraft/propulsion data management computer (A/PDMC), Parker Hannifin primary flight control system, Parker Hannifin-Gulf standby engine display/thrust rating (DE/TRP), Parker Hannifin-Gulf standby position indicators (SRI), and Litton warning annunciator panel (WAP) and warning caution computer (WCC). Communication system comprises Magnavox UHF and Satcom, Rockwell Collins VHF-AM/FM, Rockwell Collins HF, jam resistant (UHF) and secure voice (UHF/VHF/HF), Telephonics wireless intercom system, IFF/SIF, secure UHF and Satcom hookup in cargo compartment, and Telephonics integrated radio management system (IRMS). Navigation system comprises 4 Honeywell IRUs, Rockwell Collins VHF VOR/DME, Rockwell Collins Tacan, Rockwell Collins ILS/marker beacon, Rockwell Collins GPS, Rockwell Collins UHF direction finding, and Sierra station keeping equipment (SKE); also see radar. Lockheed Martin ground proximity warning system, Honeywell radar altimeter, Fairchild Weston cockpit voice recorder, Honeywell air data computer, Smiths standard flight data recorder, aircraft diagnostic and integrated test system (ADITS), Hamilton Standard airborne integrated data system recorder, and drogue parachute video system (DPVS).
Self-protection systems: Provisions for Tracor AN/ALE-47 flare dispensing system and Hercules AN/AAR-47 missile warning system; being installed. See Environmental control system.

Aircraft variants:
C-17A Globemaster III is the standard USAF version, as detailed.
KC-17 is a proposed tanker version, also using the 37,854 litre fuel capacity in the unused centre wing tank and/or a 25,362 litre palletized modular tank carried in the fuselage, offering a maximum usable capacity of 165,513 litres. Refuelling boom

Details for C-17 Globemaster III

PRINCIPAL DIMENSIONS:
Wing span: 165 ft (50.29 m), or 169 ft 9 ins (51.74 m) to winglet tips
Maximum length: 174 ft (53.04 m)
Maximum height: 55 ft 1 ins (16.79 m)

CABIN:
Length: 68 ft 2 ins (20.78 m) aft of flight deck to start of ramp. Ramp adds a further 19 ft 10 ins (6.045 m) length. Double row loadable length 85 ft 2 ins (25.96 m) including ramp
Width: 18 ft (5.49 m) loadable width (not maximum)
Height: 13 ft 6 ins (4.11 m) aft of the wing, 12 ft 4 ins (3.76 m) forward of the wing

WINGS:
Aerofoil section: Supercritical
Area: 3,800 sq ft (353.03 m^2)
Aspect ratio: 7.165
Static ground height to wingtips: 13 ft 10 ins (4.22 m)
Sweepback: 25°

WINGLETS:
Span: 9 ft 2.5 ins (2.8 m)
Area: 35.85 sq ft (3.33 m^2)
Sweepback: 30°
Angle: 15° from vertical

TAIL UNIT:
Tailplane span: 65 ft (19.81 m)
Tailplane area: 845 sq ft (78.5 m^2)
Sweepback: 27°

UNDERCARRIAGE:
Type: Retractable high-sink-rate undercarriage (landing sink rate up to 12.5 ft, 3.81 m per second), with twin nosewheels and 2 tandem twin-strut main bogies, each strut carrying 3 wheels. Can operate from unpaved airfields
Main wheel tyre size: 50 × 21-20 (pressure 138 psi)
Nose wheel tyre size: 40 × 16-14 (pressure 155 psi)
Wheel base: 65 ft 10 ins (20.07 m)
Wheel track: 33 ft 8 ins (10.26 m)
Turning circle: 180° turn in 116 ft (35.4 m). 180° star turn (with backing) in 80 ft (24.4 m)

WEIGHTS:
Empty: 277,000 lb (125,645 kg)
Maximum ramp: 586,000 lb (265,805 kg)
Maximum take-off: 585,000 lb (265,351 kg)
Payload: 170,400 lb (77,292 kg) for 2.25g

PERFORMANCE:
Maximum speed: Mach 0.875
Cruise speed: Mach 0.74-0.77
Take-off field length: 7,740 ft (2,360 m), at MTOW
Landing field length: 3,000 ft (915 m), with 160,000 lb (72,575 kg) payload
Ceiling: 45,000 ft (13,715 m) service, 41,000 ft (12,500 m) operating
Range: 2,400 naut miles (2,763 miles) 4,445 km, with 160,000 lb (72,575 kg) payload
Ferry range: 4,700 naut miles (5,412 miles) 8,710 km

and/or hose unit on an interchangeable rear ramp door plus optional underwing pods. Palletized modular operators' station, with CCTV equipment attached under the rear fuselage to provide an outside view. Potential customers include the USAF, Japan, Saudi Arabia, the UK and others.

MD-17 is a proposed commercial heavylifter variant, capable of carrying a 170,000 lb (77,110 kg) payload over a range of more than 5,000 naut miles. Roll-on/roll-off cargo. Normal ground time 2 hours 15 minutes. Expected programme launch 1998.

McDonnell Douglas KDC-10

Comments: Details of this advanced flight refuelling tanker/transport conversion of the commercial DC-10-30 convertible freighter can be found in the 1996-97 edition of *WA&SD*, page 277.

Boeing (McDonnell Douglas) MD-11

First flight: 10 January 1990.
Certification: 8 November 1990 (FAA), April 1991 for Cat IIIb and September 1991 for JAA.
First delivery: 7 December 1990 to Finnair, starting operations on 20 December.
Role: Medium-long range passenger airliner, freighter and tanker/transport.
Sales: 192 ordered, of which 178 delivered by June 1998. These include 137 MD-11s (136 delivered), 50 MD-11F Freighters (37 delivered) and 5 MD-11M Combis (all delivered). Production expected to end in February 2000.
Crew: 2 (flight).
Passengers: 250 to 410, with typical 298 passenger 3-class arrangement as 16 first class (60 ins, 152 cm seat pitch), 56 business (38 ins, 96.5 cm pitch) and 226 economy (32 ins, 81 cm pitch). Typical 2-class arrangement for 323 passengers comprising 34 first (41/42 ins, 104/107 cm pitch) and 289 economy (33/34 ins, 84/86 cm pitch). All economy layout for 410 (30/31/32 ins, 76/79/81 cm pitch). 6 to 10 abreast seating with 2 aisles. Combi accommodates 150-250 passengers (more typically 214 passengers comprising 34 first or business class and 180 economy class plus 6 cargo pallets, or 181 passengers comprising 16 first class, 41 business class and 124 economy class plus 6 pallets), and Convertible Freighter in passenger mode 350-410.
Seat pitch: See above.
Galleys and toilets: Track-mounted, interchangeable equipment.
Pressurization: 8.6 psi cabin differential.
Lower hold volume: Up to 5,566 cu ft (157.61 m^3), comprising 2,844 cu ft (80.53 m^3) in forward hold, 2,212 cu ft (62.64 m^3) in centre hold and 510 cu ft (14.44 m^3) of aft bulk. Maximum of 32 LD3 containers plus bulk, or 10 pallets of 96 × 125 ins (2.44 × 3.18 m), or 10 pallets of 88 × 125 ins (2.24 × 3.18 m) plus 2 LD3s and bulk. 5,164 cu ft (146.23 m^3) taken in Freighter and Convertible Freighter by 6 pallets and 14 LD3 containers. All bulk cargo volume for each model 6,850 cu ft (194 m^3).
Main deck capacity (Combi/Freighter/Convertible Freighter): Up to 5,950, 15,722 and 14,508 cu ft (169.05, 445.2 and 410.82 m^3) respectively.
Wing control surfaces: Inner and outer ailerons (outer for low speeds only) which droop with the double-slotted flaps at take off, leading-edge slats, and 5 spoilers per wing.
Tail control surfaces: Variable-incidence tailplane, 2-section slotted elevators, and 2-section split rudder.
Flight control system: Hydraulic/electric actuation.
Construction materials: Metal, but with substantial use of composites in the control surfaces, winglets, tailplane trailing edge, wing/body fairings, engine inlets, nacelles and more.
Engines: 3 × 61,500 lbf (273.57 kN) General Electric CF6-80C2D1F, 60,000 lbf (266.9 kN) Pratt & Whitney PW4460 or 62,000 lbf (275.8 kN) PW4462 turbofan engines.

↑ Swissair Boeing (McDonnell Douglas) MD-11 *(courtesy Swissair)*

↑ Boeing (McDonnell Douglas) MD-11 flight deck

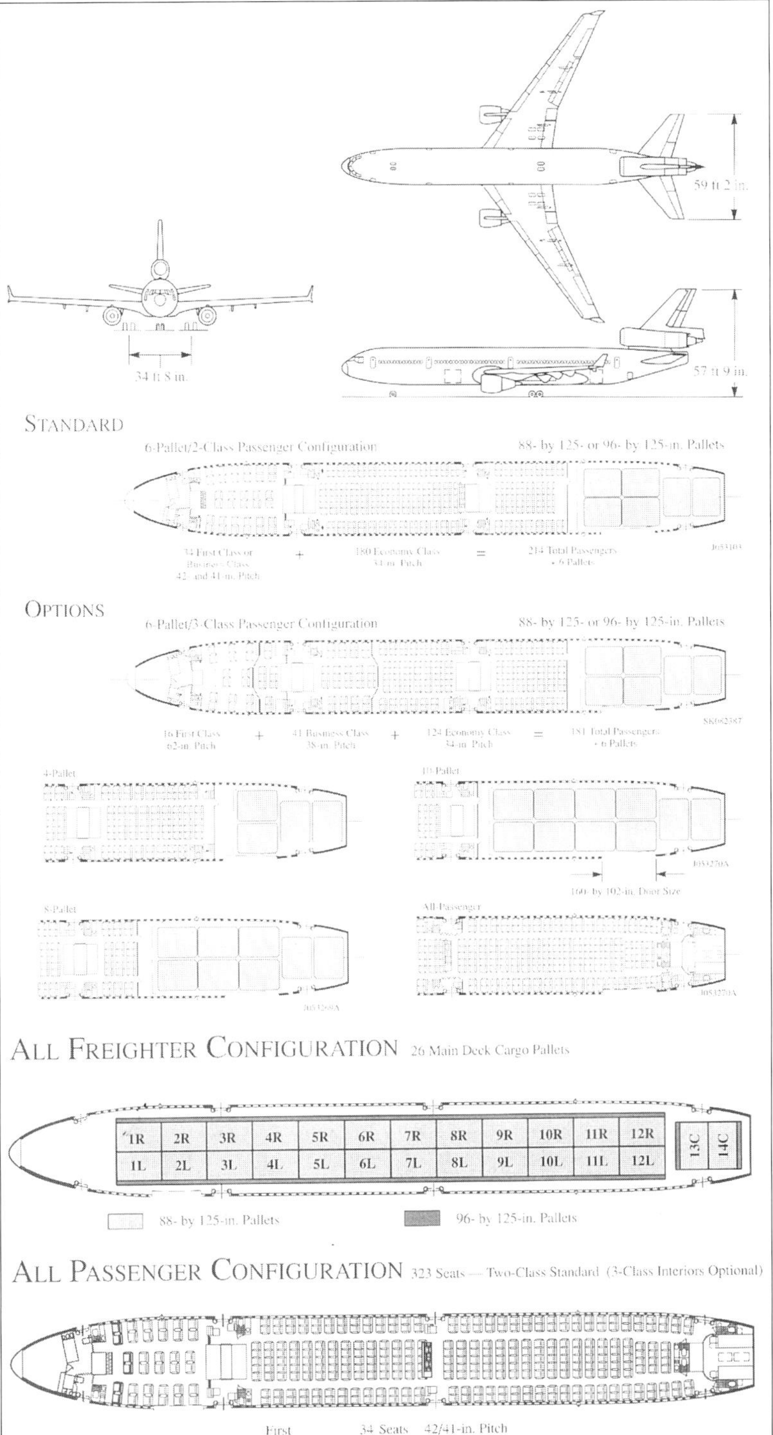

→ Boeing (McDonnell Douglas) MD-11 general arrangement (***top***), with main deck standard layout and options for the MD-11 Combi (***centre***), and all-passenger/all-cargo main deck configurations for the MD-11 Convertible Freighter (***bottom***) *(courtesy Boeing)*

	MD-11 with 298 passengers	MD-11 Combi with 183 passengers and 6 pallets on main deck	MD-11 Freighter	MD-11 Convertible Freighter
Wing span	169 ft 6 ins (51.7 m)	169 ft 6 ins (51.7 m)	169 ft 6 ins (51.7 m)	169 ft 6 ins (51.7 m)
Maximum length	202 ft 2 ins (61.62 m) with GE engines, 200 ft 10 ins (61.21 m) with P&W engines	202 ft 2 ins (61.62 m) with GE engines, 200 ft 10 ins (61.21 m) with P&W engines	202 ft 2 ins (61.62 m) with GE engines, 200 ft 10 ins (61.21 m) with P&W engines	202 ft 2 ins (61.62 m) with GE engines, 200 ft 10 ins (61.21 m) with P&W engines
Maximum height	57 ft 10 ins (17.62 m)	57 ft 10 ins (17.62 m)	57 ft 10 ins (17.62 m)	57 ft 10 ins (17.62 m)
Cabin length	152 ft 7 ins (46.51 m)			
Cabin width	18 ft 9 ins (5.72 m)	18 ft 4 ins (5.59 m) at floor	18 ft 4 ins (5.59 m) at floor	18 ft 4 ins (5.59 m) at floor
Cabin height	7 ft 11 ins (2.41 m)	8 ft 1.5 ins (2.47 m) stack height	8 ft 1.5 ins (2.47 m) stack height	8 ft 1.5 ins (2.47 m) stack height as freighter
Main doors	6 ft 4 ins × 2 ft 8 ins (1.93 × 0.81 m) forward, and 6 ft 4 ins × 3 ft 6 ins (1.93 × 1.07 m) rear	13 ft 4 ins × 8 ft 6 ins (4.04 × 2.59 m) main rear cargo door	11 ft 8 ins × 8 ft 6 ins (3.56 × 2.59 m) main forward cargo door	11 ft 8 ins × 8 ft 6 ins (3.56 × 2.59 m) main forward cargo door
Wing area, not including winglets but including ailerons	3,648 sq ft (338.91 m^2)	3,648 sq ft (338.91 m^2)	3,648 sq ft (338.91 m^2)	3,648 sq ft (338.91 m^2)
Winglet height and area	7 ft (2.13 m) and 40 sq ft (3.72 m^2)	7 ft (2.13 m) and 40 sq ft (3.72 m^2)	7 ft (2.13 m) and 40 sq ft (3.72 m^2)	7 ft (2.13 m) and 40 sq ft (3.72 m^2)
Wing aspect ratio	7.876, calculated at *span and above area criterion	7.876, calculated at *span and above area criterion	7.876, calculated at *span and above area criterion	7.876, calculated at *span and above area criterion
Wing sweepback	35°	35°	35°	35°
Tailplane span	59 ft 2 ins (18.03 m)	59 ft 2 ins (18.03 m)	59 ft 2 ins (18.03 m)	59 ft 2 ins (18.03 m)
Tailplane area	920 sq ft (85.47 m^2)	920 sq ft (85.47 m^2)	920 sq ft (85.47 m^2)	920 sq ft (85.47 m^2)
Undercarriage type	Retractable, with twin steerable (±70°) nosewheels. Main units have 4-wheel bogies, plus twin-wheel bogie under the mid fuselage	Retractable, with twin steerable (±70°) nosewheels. Main units have 4-wheel bogies, plus twin-wheel bogie under the mid fuselage	Retractable, with twin steerable (±70°) nosewheels. Main units have 4-wheel bogies, plus twin-wheel bogie under the mid fuselage	Retractable, with twin steerable (±70°) nosewheels. Main units have 4-wheel bogies, plus twin-wheel bogie under the mid fuselage
Main wheel tyre size	54 × 21-24	54 × 21-24	54 × 21-24	54 × 21-24
Nose wheel tyre size	40 × 15.5-16	40 × 15.5-16	40 × 15.5-16	40 × 15.5-16
Wheel base	80 ft 10 ins (24.64 m)	80 ft 10 ins (24.64 m)	80 ft 10 ins (24.64 m)	80 ft 10 ins (24.64 m)
Wheel track	34 ft 8 ins (10.57 m)	34 ft 8 ins (10.57 m)	34 ft 8 ins (10.57 m)	34 ft 8 ins (10.57 m)
Operating empty weight, without auxiliary tank	286,965 lb (130,165 kg)	288,885 lb (131,036 kg)	251,149 lb (113,919 kg)	289,965 lb (131,526 kg) passenger mode, 254,372 lb (115,381 kg) freight
Operating empty weight, with auxiliary tank	290,498 lb (131,768 kg) with GE engines, 290,182 lb (131,624 kg) with P&W engines			
Maximum zero fuel weight	400,000 lb (181,437 kg)	430,000 lb (195,045 kg)	451,300 lb (204,706 kg)	451,300 lb (204,706 kg)
Maximum take-off weight	602,555 lb (273,314 kg) standard, 630,500 lb (285,990 kg) optional	602,555 lb (273,314 kg) standard, 630,500 lb (285,990 kg) optional	602,555 lb (273,314 kg) standard, 630,500 lb (285,990 kg) optional	602,555 lb (273,314 kg) standard, 630,500 lb (285,990 kg) optional
Maximum landing weight	430,000 lb (195,045 kg)	458,000 lb (207,745 kg)	471,500 lb (213,868 kg) standard, 481,500 lb (218,405 kg) optional	471,500 lb (213,868 kg) standard, 481,500 lb (218,405 kg) optional
Weight limited payload	113,035 lb (51,272 kg)	141,115 lb (64,009 kg)	200,151 lb (90,787 kg) including tare weight	161,335 lb (73,180 kg) passenger mode, 196,928 lb (89,325 kg) cargo mode, including tare weight
Maximum speed	Mach 0.87 or 511 kts (588 mph) 946 km/h at 31,000 ft (9,450 m)	Mach 0.87 or 511 kts (588 mph) 946 km/h at 31,000 ft (9,450 m)	Mach 0.87 or 511 kts (588 mph) 946 km/h at 31,000 ft (9,450 m)	Mach 0.87 or 511 kts (588 mph) 946 km/h at 31,000 ft (9,450 m)
FAA take-off field length	10,220 ft (3,115 m) at MTOW, sea level, 30° C, with PW4462s	10,220 ft (3,115 m) at MTOW, sea level, 30° C, with PW4462s	10,220 ft (3,115 m) at MTOW, sea level, 30° C, with PW4462s	10,220 ft (3,115 m) at MTOW, sea level, 30° C, with PW4462s
FAA landing field length, MLW, sea level	6,950 ft (2,118 m)	7,330 ft (2,234 m)	7,620 ft (2,323 m)	7,620 ft (2,323 m)
Range, international reserve naut miles (miles) km	6,835 (7,871) 12,668	6,715 (7,733) 12,445	3,947 (4,545) 7,315 with weight limited payload	6,795 (7,825) 12,594 with 298 passengers, 3,947 (4,545) 7,315 with weight limited payload
Range, with auxiliary tanks naut miles (miles) km	7,245 (8,343) 13,427	5,736 (6,605) 10,630 with space limited payload		

Note: Pax = Passengers

Fuel system: 258,721 lb (117,354 kg) without auxiliary tank, 272,014 lb (123,383 kg) with auxiliary tank. 30% fuel burn/seat improvement over DC-10. See MD-11ER.
Electrical system: AC supply via 3 × 100/120 kVA, 400 Hz engine-driven generators and 1 × 90 kVA APU-driven generator. DC supply via transformer rectifiers. 50 amp-hour battery. Emergency 25 kVA ram-air generator.
Hydraulic system: 3 independent systems.
Braking system: Carbon.
De-icing system: Bleed air for wing and tailplane leading edges. Electric for windscreen and sensors.
Oxygen system: Chemical for passengers, gaseous for flight crew and portable bottles for cabin crew.
Fire system: See Aircraft variants.
Radar: Weather radar.
Flight avionics/instrumentation: EFIS, with six 8 ins (20 cm) colour CRT flight, engine and systems displays. Dual advanced flight management systems with multifunction control/display units. Dual advanced digital flight control systems. Pilot has full override authority (not computers), and control column always indicates actual flight control position. Windshear detection. See also Aircraft variants.

Aircraft variants:
MD-11 is the standard passenger version.
MD-11ER Extended Range has the availability of an 11,583 litre removable auxiliary fuel tank in the forward cargo hold for longer ranges. Reduced drag, reduced empty weight by 1,500 lb (680 kg), increased take-off weight to 630,500 lb (285,990 kg), satcom, future air navigation system (FANS) and GPS provisions, low noise levels, electronic flight manual, and improved brakes. Announced 1994 and entered service in March 1996. Range of over 7,193 naut miles (8,283 miles) 13,330 km. CF6-80C2, PW4460 or PW4462 engines.
MD-11 Combi can carry 4, 6, 8 or 10 pallets on the main deck in addition to reduced passenger loads of about 150-250 (see Passengers). Class C fire detection and extinguishing in main deck cargo space.
MD-11 Convertible Freighter can accommodate all passengers or all cargo (323 in 2-class or 298 in 3 class layouts, or 196,928 lb, 89,325 kg gross weight-limited cargo). Total cargo volume of 19,672 cu ft (557.05 m^3) for pallets/containers. Conversion from passenger to cargo interior takes 2.24 days; reverse conversion takes 4 days. Complete palletized cargo capability. Main deck engine transportation capability.
MD-11 Freighter has a main deck volume of 14,630-15,722 cu ft (414.27-445.2 m^3) depending upon the type of cargo carried, plus 5,566-6,850 cu ft (157.61-193.97 m^3) on the lower deck, for pallets/containers/bulk (gross weight-limited payload 201,851 lb, 91,558 kg).
Performance Enhancement Programmes:
Phase I drag reduction with 0.7% benefit, restored initial drag deficiency by outboard wing trailing-edge splitter of 1.5 ins (3.8 cm) inboard and 0.5 in (1.3 cm) outboard.
Phase II drag reduction with 1.5% benefit, encompassing outboard slat seals and outboard ailerons drooped 4°.
CPIP Phase IIIa with 0.2% benefit introducing aileron seal plates, and 0.8% benefit with pylon fillets.
Engine and Nacelle improvements, 1.5%-2.7% benefit.
Maximum take-off weight options of 605,500 lb, 610,000 lb, 618,000 lb and 625,500 lb (274,650, 276,691, 280,320 and 283,722 kg).
Take-off field length shortened by 500-900 ft (152-274 m).
Supplemental fuel tanks made available, with 1,984 or 3,969 US gallon (7,510 or 15,024 litre) options. Quick removal capability, or 2 to 4 LD3 containers.
KMD-11 is a flight refuelling/cargo transport variant, offered as a modern development of the KC-10 Extender.

Boeing (McDonnell Douglas) MD-80 series

First flight: 18 October 1979.
Certification: 26 August 1980 (FAA).
First delivery: 12 September 1980 to Swissair, for services from October 1980.
Role: Short-medium range airliner.
Noise levels: MD-81, -82 and -83 (possibly -88) are take-off 90.4 EPNdB, sideline 94.6 EPNdB, and approach 93.3 EPNdB.
Sales: 1,191 ordered by June 1998, of which 1,159 had been delivered. Production reportedly to close after the remaining 32 aircraft have been delivered. Orders comprise 132 MD-81s, 562 MD-82s, 264 MD-83s, 75 MD-87s and 158 MD-88s.
Crew: 2 flight, plus 2 cabin attendants.
Passengers: 172 maximum, 155 typical economy for MD-81, -82,

	MD-81 with 155 pax + baggage	MD-82 and MD-88 with 155 pax + baggage	MD-83 with 155 pax + baggage	MD-87 with 130 pax + baggage
Wing span	107 ft 10 ins (32.87 m)	107 ft 10 ins (32.87 m)	107 ft 10 ins (32.87 m)	107 ft 10 ins (32.87 m)
Maximum length	147 ft 10 ins (45.06 m)	147 ft 10 ins (45.06 m)	147 ft 10 ins (45.06 m)	130 ft 5 ins (39.75 m)
Maximum height	29 ft 7 ins (9.02 m)	29 ft 7 ins (9.02 m)	29 ft 7 ins (9.02 m)	30 ft 6 ins (9.3 m)
Cabin length	101 ft (30.78 m)	101 ft (30.78 m)	101 ft (30.78 m)	
Cabin width	10 ft 4 ins (3.15 m)	10 ft 4 ins (3.15 m)	10 ft 4 ins (3.15 m)	10 ft 4 ins (3.15 m)
Cabin height	6 ft 9 ins (2.06 m)	6 ft 9 ins (2.06 m)	6 ft 9 ins (2.06 m)	6 ft 9 ins (2.06 m)
Cabin volume	6,778 cu ft (191.93 m^3)	6,778 cu ft (191.93 m^3)	6,778 cu ft (191.93 m^3)	
Main passenger door	6 ft × 2 ft 10 ins (1.83 × 0.86 m)	6 ft × 2 ft 10 ins (1.83 × 0.86 m)	6 ft × 2 ft 10 ins (1.83 × 0.86 m)	6 ft × 2 ft 10 ins (1.83 × 0.86 m)
Wing area, including ailerons	1,209 sq ft (112.32 m^2)	1,209 sq ft (112.32 m^2)	1,209 sq ft (112.32 m^2)	1,209 sq ft (112.32 m^2)
Wing aspect ratio	9.61	9.61	9.61	9.61
Wing sweepback	24.5° at 25% chord	24.5° at 25% chord	24.5° at 25% chord	24.5° at 25% chord
Tailplane span	40 ft 2 ins (12.24 m)	40 ft 2 ins (12.24 m)	40 ft 2 ins (12.24 m)	40 ft 2 ins (12.24 m)
Undercarriage type	Retractable, with steerable nosewheels. Twin wheels on each unit	Retractable, with steerable nosewheels. Twin wheels on each unit	Retractable, with steerable nosewheels. Twin wheels on each unit	Retractable, with steerable nosewheels. Twin wheels on each unit
Main wheel tyre size	44.5 × 16.5-20	44.5 × 16.5-20	44.5 × 16.5-20	44.5 × 16.5-20
Nose wheel tyre size	26 × 6.6-14	26 × 6.6-14	26 × 6.6-14	26 × 6.6-14
Wheel base	72 ft 5 ins (22.07 m)	72 ft 5 ins (22.07 m)	72 ft 5 ins (22.07 m)	62 ft 11 ins (19.18 m)
Wheel track	16 ft 8 ins (5.08 m)	16 ft 8 ins (5.08 m)	16 ft 8 ins (5.08 m)	16 ft 8 ins (5.08 m)
Maximum zero fuel weight	118,000 lb (53,524 kg)	122,000 lb (55,339 kg)	122,000 lb (55,339 kg)	118,000 lb (53,524 kg)
Maximum ramp weight	141,000 lb (63,956 kg)	150,500 lb (68,266 kg)	161,000 lb (73,028 kg)	141,000 lb (63,956 kg)
Maximum take-off weight	140,000 lb (63,503 kg)	149,500 lb (67,812 kg)	160,000 lb (72,575 kg)	140,000 lb (63,503 kg) or 149,500 lb (67,812 kg) with auxiliary fuel tanks
Maximum landing weight	128,000 lb (58,060 kg)	130,000 lb (58,967 kg)	139,500 lb (63,276 kg)	128,000 lb (58,060 kg)
Space limited payload	38,105 lb (17,284 kg)	38,105 lb (17,284 kg)	35,705 lb (16,196 kg)	30,820 lb (13,980 kg)
Maximum speed	Mach 0.76 or 438 kts (504 mph) 811 km/h	Mach 0.76 or 438 kts (504 mph) 811 km/h	Mach 0.76 or 438 kts (504 mph) 811 km/h	Mach 0.76 or 438 kts (504 mph) 811 km/h
FAA take-off field length	7,250 ft (2,210 m) MTOW, sea level 30° C	7,450 ft (2,271 m), MTOW, sea level 30° C	8,375 ft (2,553 m), MTOW, sea level 30° C	6,100 ft (1,859 m), MTOW, sea level 30° C
FAA landing field length	4,850 ft (1,478 m) , MLW, sea level	4,920 ft (1,500 m), MLW, sea level	5,200 ft (1,585 m), MLW, sea level	4,690 ft (1,430 m), MLW, sea level
Design range, international reserves	1,563 naut miles (1,800 miles) 2,897 km	2,049 naut miles (2,360 miles) 3,798 km	2,501 naut miles (2,880 miles) 4,635 km	2,371 naut miles (2,730 miles) 4,394 km

Note: Pax = Passengers

↑ Crossair put 8 MD-82/83s into service

-83 and -88. 139 maximum and 130 typical economy for MD-87.
Pressurization: 7.8 psi cabin differential.
Freight hold volume: 1,253 cu ft (35.48 m^3) for MD-81, -82 and -88. 1,013 cu ft (28.68 m^3) for MD-83, and 937 cu ft (26.53 m^3) for MD-87.
Wing control surfaces: Ailerons, double-slotted flaps, full-span 3-position leading-edge slats, and 3 section spoilers (2 functioning as speed brakes and 1 for lift dumping).
Tail control surfaces: Variable incidence tailplane. Elevators and rudder, with tabs.
Flight control system: Manual ailerons and elevators. Hydraulic rudder, flaps and slats. Electric tailplane and tabs.
Construction materials: Mostly metal, but with composites used in areas of the wings, control surfaces, wing/body fairings, cabin floor and more.
Engines: 2 × 18,500 lbf (82.29 kN) Pratt & Whitney JT8D-209 turbofans for MD-81, 20,000 lbf (88.97 kN) JT8D-217A/Cs for MD-82/88, 21,000 lbf (93.41 kN) JT8D-219s for MD-83, and 20,000 lbf (88.97 kN) JT8D-217Cs for MD-87. Target type reversers, for ground operation only.
Engine rating: See above.
Fuel system: 22,107 litres for MD-81, -82 and -88. 26,498 litres for MD-83. 22,107 litres for MD-87, with optional 26,498 litres.
Electrical system: 3-phase 400 Hz supply via 2 engine-driven and 1 APU-driven 40 kVA alternators.
Hydraulic system: 2 independent systems, each 3,000 psi.
Braking system: Disc brakes, with anti-skid system.
De-icing system: Bleed air for wing and tailplane leading edges and engine inlets. Electrical for windscreen.
Radar: Colour weather radar.
Flight avionics/instrumentation: Digital, with integrated flight systems. Cat IIIa. Late versions have EFIS, FMS, windshear detection system and more.

Aircraft variants:
MD-81 high-capacity short-range version, with JT8D-209 engines.
MD-82 and ***MD-88*** are more powerful versions, of higher weights for longer range. MD-82 appeared in 1981 and MD-88 in 1987. See also Shanghai Aviation Industrial Corporation for MD-82/83 and Trunkliner versions built in China.
MD-83 is the most powerful long-fuselage version, with the highest weights for longest range. Appeared 1984.
MD-87 is the short-fuselage version with reduced accommodation, with standard fuel capacity of the MD-82/83/88 but with optional auxiliary tanks. Appeared 1986.
Executive and business versions of the MD-83 and MD-87 became available, with luxurious cabins for small numbers of passengers (many configurations possible).

Boeing (McDonnell Douglas) MD-90 series

First flight: 22 February 1993, with the first production aircraft (third to fly) on 21 September 1994.
Certification: November 1994.
First delivery: February 1995, to Delta Air Lines, entering revenue service in April 1995.
Role: Medium range airliner.
Airframe life: 90,000 hours or 60,000 landings.
Noise levels: 86 EPNdB take-off, 92 EPNdB sideline, 96 EPNdB approach.

Aims

▪ Compared with MD-80, was given electronic engine controls, updated flight deck, stretched fuselage for 10 extra passengers,

↑ Boeing (McDonnell Douglas) MD-90-30

all-new cabin interior, vacuum toilets, upgraded digital environmental control system, carbon brakes with digital anti-skid system, improved hydraulic system, new APU, new VSCF electrical power system, V2500 engines, and powered flight controls.
Sales: 131 ordered by June 1998, of which 73 had by then been delivered. These comprise 111 MD-90-30s and 20 MD-90-30 Trunkliners. Production to close after the remaining 58 aircraft have been delivered.
Crew: 2 (flight).
Passengers: 153 mixed class or 172 maximum, 5 abreast. MD-90-55 can have a high-density layout for up to 187 passengers. Airstair.
Seat pitch: 35 ins (90 cm) first class, 31 ins (80 cm) coach.
Galleys: 2 forward and 2 rear.
Toilets: 3, 1 forward and 2 aft.
Freight hold volume: 1,300 cu ft (36.81 m^3) for MD-90-30, and 822 cu ft (23.28 m^3) for MD-90-50 with optional 6,738 litre auxiliary tank installed.
Wing control surfaces: Ailerons with tabs, double-slotted fixed-vane Fowler-type flaps, full-span 3-position leading-edge slats, and spoilers (functioning as speed brakes and lift dumpers).
Tail control surfaces: T-tail, with elevators (with tabs) and rudder (with tab).
Engines: MD-90-30 has 25,000 lbf (111.21 kN) International Aero Engines V2525-D5 turbofans, and MD-90-55 has 28,000 lbf (124.55 kN) V2528-D5 turbofans. Cascade type thrust reversers for ground operation only. AlliedSignal 131-9(D), with 75 kVA generator (90 kVA for 5 minutes).
Fuel system: 22,107 litres for MD-90-30, and 28,845 litres for MD-90-50. MD-90-30ER has provision for a 2,139 litre auxiliary tank.
Electrical system: Variable speed/constant frequency system.
Hydraulic system: 2 systems, each 3,000 psi.
Braking system: Carbon brakes, with digital anti-skid system. Parking brake.
De-icing system: Overwing ice sensors. Electric heating of nose strakes. Warm fuel from engine oil coolers is recirculated to the wing tanks.
Radar: Weather radar.
Flight avionics/instrumentation: Advanced flight deck with EFIS (6 × 5 ins, 15 × 13 cm screens), including PFDs for radio altitude and navigation data. Full-flight management system (FMS), electronic overhead annunciator panel, INS, and LED dot-matrix displays for engine and systems monitoring. Altimeter, airspeed and vertical speed indicators. Modified windshear computer, new air data computers, and new master warning and caution system (compared with MD-80).

Aircraft variants:
MD-90-30 is the baseline version, as detailed.
MD-90-30ER has a 166,000 lb (75,296 kg) maximum gross weight, providing a range of 2,171 naut miles (2,500 miles) 4,023 km or, with the addition of a 2,139 litre auxiliary tank, a range of 2,388 naut miles (2,750 miles) 4,425 km.
MD-90-30 Trunkliner was chosen on 25 June 1992 to be the

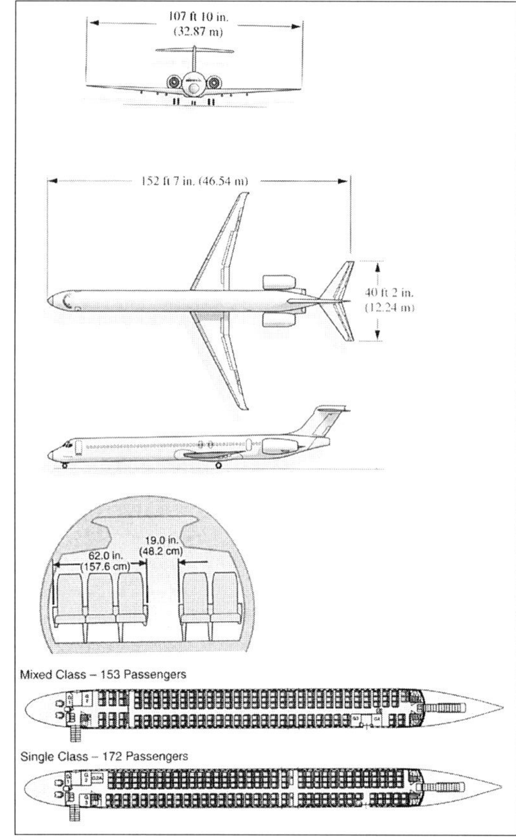

↑ **Boeing (McDonnell Douglas) MD-90-30 general arrangement and cabin layouts for 153 and 172 passengers** *(courtesy Boeing)*

second form of Trunkliner for Chinese assembly, with Shanghai as prime contractor (also mostly Chinese manufacture of subassemblies, with subcontracts to Chengdu, Shenyang and Xi'an), and with Chinese-assembled 25,000 lbf (111.21 kN) International Aero Engines V2525 engines. Negotiations were concluded and contracts signed on 4 November 1994 covering co-production of 20 from 1995, for delivery from 1998.
MD-90-50 has, compared with the MD-90-30, a heavier gross weight for a substantial increase in range; strengthened wings, tail unit and fuselage; strengthened undercarriage, provisions for up to 6,738 litres of auxiliary fuel, and 28,000 lbf (124.55 kN) V2528-D5 turbofan engines.
MD-90-55 is similar to MD-90-50 but has additional emergency exits, permitting higher density charter configurations of up to 187 passengers.

Details for MD-90-30, *with MD-90-50 in italics where different*

PRINCIPAL DIMENSIONS:
Wing span: 107 ft 10 ins (32.87 m)
Maximum length: 152 ft 7 ins (46.51 m)
Maximum height: 30 ft 7 ins (9.32 m)

CABIN:
Length: 105 ft 9 ins (32.23 m)
Width: 10 ft 4 ins (3.14 m)
Height: 6 ft 9 ins (2.06 m)
Main passenger door: 6 ft × 2 ft 10 ins (1.83 × 0.86 m) forward
Cargo doors: 4 ft 5 ins × 4 ft 2 ins (1.35 × 1.27 m)

WINGS:
Area: 1,209 sq ft (112.32 m^2)
Aspect ratio: 9.61
Sweepback: 24.5° at 25% chord

TAIL UNIT:
Tailplane span: 40 ft 2 ins (12.24 m)

UNDERCARRIAGE:
Type: Retractable, with steerable nosewheels. Twin wheels on each unit
Tyre sizes: Based on MD-80
Wheel base: 77 ft 2 ins (23.52 m)
Wheel track: 16 ft 8 ins (5.08 m)

WEIGHTS:
Empty, operating: 88,000 lb (39,916 kg), *91,900 lb (41,685 kg)*
Maximum zero fuel: 130,000 lb (58,967 kg), *135,000 lb (61,235 kg)*
Maximum ramp: 157,000 lb (71,214 kg), *173,500 lb (78,698 kg)*
Maximum take-off: 156,000 lb (70,760 kg), *172,500 lb (78,245 kg)*
Maximum landing: 142,000 lb (64,410 kg), *150,000 lb (68,039 kg)*
Space limited payload: 38,250 lb (17,350 kg), *33,500 lb (15,195 kg)*

PERFORMANCE:
Maximum speed: Mach 0.84
Economic cruise speed: Mach 0.76, or 438 kts (504 mph) 811 km/h at 35,000 ft (10,670 m), ISA standard day
Landing speed: 138 kts (159 mph) 256 km/h
FAA take-off field length: 7,105 ft (2,165 m), *7,990 ft (2,435 m)*, at MTOGW, sea level
FAA landing field length: 5,250 ft (1,600 m), *5,480 ft (1,670 m)*, at MLW, sea level
Climb rate: 2,200 ft (670 m) per minute at 17,500 ft (5,335 m)
Ceiling: 37,000 ft (11,275 m)
Design range: 2,084 naut miles (2,400 miles) 3,862 km, *2,783 naut miles (3,205 miles) 5,158 km*, with international reserves

Burbank Aeronautical Corporation II — USA

Corporate address:
3000 North Clybourn Avenue, Hangar 34, Burbank, CA 91505.
Telephone: +1 818 843 8242
Facsimile: +1 818 843 4510
Founded: 1988.
Employees: 250.
Information:
Thomas J. McGuire (*telephone* +1 818 843 8049).

ACTIVITIES

- Prerequisite hardware for ABS DC-9 Stage 3 Hustkit; partner in the ABS Partnership.
- Inlet cowls for FedEx STC Boeing 727 Hushkit.
- Stage 3 Hushkit for DC-8 Series 62/63 aircraft.
- Stage 3 Hushkit for Boeing 707-300 series aircraft.
- Winglets for Boeing 707 aircraft.

DIVISION

BURBANK NACELLE CORPORATION

↑ **Burbank Aeronautical Corporation II Boeing 707 Stage 3 Hushkit** *(courtesy BAC II)*

Fairchild Dornier USA Fairchild Aircraft Incorporated USA

Corporate address:
See Reconnaissance section for company details.

Fairchild Dornier Metro 23, C-26 and Expediter

Certification: June 1990 to FAR Pt 23 Commuter Category, following earlier SFAR 41 and CAA for Metro III. Also ICAO Annex 8.
Role: Commuter airliner, with special mission variants, including cargo carrying.

Details *(Metro 23 in latest SA-227-DC form, unless stated)*

Airframe life: 35,000 flight hours.
Airport limits: 19-passenger operations into airports under FAR Pt 23 Commuter Category requirements without off-loading.
Sales: Over 1,040 of all Metro and Expediter variants have been built, including 11 C-26As and 30 C-26Bs for the USAF Air National Guard and 10 for the US Army National Guard as quick-change support transport aircraft; some recently diverted under military aid to at least Colombia (air force and police), Mexico, Peru and Venezuela (USAF ANG inventory of 16 in 1998). European marketing and support facility in Belgium (Henneaulaan 366, 1930 Zaventem, Brussels).
Crew: 1 or 2 pilots.
Passengers: Typically 19 (mainly 2 abreast), or 20 with 1 pilot.
Seat pitch: Typical 30 ins (76 cm).
Pressurization: 7 psi cabin differential. Sea level cabin is maintained to 16,800 ft (5,120 m).
Baggage compartments: Nose compartment of 30 cu ft (0.85 m^3) volume, for 600 lb (272 kg) of baggage/cargo/equipment, with door of 18 × 25 ins (46 × 64 cm). Aft pressurized compartment of 143.5 cu ft (4.063 m^3) volume, for 850 lb (385.5 kg) of baggage/cargo, with a large cargo door as detailed in the table. Carry-on closet opposite the passenger door.
Freight hold volume: 623 cu ft (17.64 m^3) in all-cargo configuration.
Wing control surfaces: Ailerons (with trim tabs) and double-slotted flaps.
Tail control surfaces: Variable incidence tailplane. Elevators and rudder (with trim tab).
Flight control system: Mechanical, except for hydraulic flaps and electrically actuated tailplane.
Construction materials: Aluminium alloy except for nosecone.
Engines: 2 AlliedSignal TPE331-12UHR turboprops, with 8 ft 10 ins (2.69 m) diameter McCauley 4-blade full-feathering and reversible-pitch aluminium propellers.
Engine rating: Each 1,100 shp (820.32 kW) with continuous alcohol/water injection and reserve power or 1,000 shp (745.7 kW) dry.
Fuel system: 2,453 litres, equivalent to 4,342 lb (1,969 kg).
Electrical system: 28 volt DC supply via 2 × 300 amp starter-generators. 2 × 24 volt and 23 amp-hour ni-cd batteries. 115 volt and 26 volt AC supply via 2 inverters.
Hydraulic system: 2,000 psi.
Braking system: Hydraulic disc brakes.
De-icing system: Electrically heated windscreen.
Oxygen system: 49 cu ft or optional 178 cu ft (1.39 or 5.04 m^3) capacity.
Fire system: Includes fire zone isolation and a dual engine fire extinguisher system.
Radar: Weather radar.
Flight avionics/instrumentation: Equipped with full array of instrumentation for monitoring engines, flight conditions and systems. SA227-DC/C-26 specifications include basic IFR nav/com package with dual VHF coms/navs, dual audio panels, dual glideslope, marker beacon, ADF, Tacan, RMI, transponder, dual compass systems and gyros, long-range nav system, cockpit voice recorder, flight data recorder and ELT. Off the shelf equipment and custom/specialized items may be specified to meet customer requirements; fully engineered avionics packages include 3 and 5 tube Bendix/King EFIS, Rockwell Collins avionics, HF/SSB radios, IFF systems, ground proximity warning systems, radar altimeters and weather/search radars. Global communications, navigation and positioning systems, and flight management packages can be accommodated.

Aircraft variants:
Metro 23 commuter airliner. Current versions are the SA227-CC with TPE331-11U-612G turboprops (similarly rated) and the SA227-DC as detailed above. Special mission configurations for combi, air ambulance, photographic, airborne early warning, sigint or other electronic roles, and more. See also specialized MMSA.
C-26 was the US military designation given to 13 original C-26As delivered for the Air National Guard Operational Support Transport Aircraft role since 1989, with quick-change interiors, and 36 C-26Bs (plus options) ordered by the National Guard Bureau from 1991 for the ANG and Army National Guard (latter 8), featuring TCAS II, GPS and microwave landing systems. 40 C-26s were stated to be operational with the ANG in 1997 but many have since diverted under military aid to overseas forces (see Sales). 2 crew and 18 passengers, all cargo or mixed.
Expediter 23 is an all-cargo version, with 623 cu ft (17.64 m^3) volume for over 5,500 lb (2,500 kg) of package payload, with package densities as low as 8.26 lb/cu ft.
Merlin 23 is the executive version, for 12-14 passengers with tables.
Merlin 23E applies to EFIS-equipped Metro 23s, delivered from 1996 and also featuring digital autopilot as standard.
MMSA Multi-Mission Surveillance Aircraft. See Reconnaissance section.

↑ Fairchild Dornier Metro 23 commuter airliner

Details for Metro 23 in SA-227-DC form

PRINCIPAL DIMENSIONS:
Wing span: 57 ft (17.37 m)
Maximum length: 59 ft 5 ins (18.1 m)
Maximum height: 16 ft 8 ins (5.08 m)

CABIN:
Length: 25 ft 5 ins (7.75 m)
Width: 5 ft 2 ins (1.57 m)
Height: 4 ft 9 ins (1.45 m)
Floor area: 140 sq ft (13.006 m^2)
Volume: 490 cu ft (13.88 m^3)
Main passenger door: 2 ft 1 ins × 4 ft 5 ins (0.64 × 1.35 m)
Cargo door: 4 ft 5 ins × 4 ft 3.25 ins (1.35 × 1.3 m)

WINGS:
Area: 309 sq ft (28.707 m^2)
Aspect ratio: 10.515

TAIL UNIT:
Tailplane span: 16 ft (4.88 m)
Tailplane area: 54.7 sq ft (5.08 m^2)

UNDERCARRIAGE:
Type: Retractable, with steerable (±63°) nosewheels; optional tiller steering system for optimum ground handling. Twin wheels on each unit
Main wheel tyre size: 19.5 × 6.75-10
Nose wheel tyre size: 18 × 4.4-10
Wheel base: 19 ft 1 ins (5.82 m)
Wheel track: 15 ft (4.57 m)
Turning radius: 38 ft 6 ins (11.73 m) wingtip radius

WEIGHTS:
Empty, operating: 9,500 lb (4,309 kg), including crew
Maximum zero fuel: 14,500 lb (6,577 kg)
Maximum ramp: 16,600 lb (7,530 kg)
Maximum take-off: 16,500 lb (7,484 kg)
Take-off weight for conditions stated below for Performance: 14,560 lb (6,604 kg)
Mid-cruise weight: 14,365 lb (6,516 kg), under conditions stated below for Performance
Maximum landing: 15,675 lb (7,110 kg)
Useful load: 7,100 lb (3,220 kg)
Payload: 5,000 lb (2,268 kg)

PERFORMANCE (for 200 naut mile sector with 19 passengers at 3,800 lb, 1,723 kg payload, ISA, sea level, zero wind and IFR reserves, unless stated)**:**
Cruise speed: 287-290 kts (330-334 mph) 531-537 km/h, at 14,232 lb (6,455 kg) mid-cruise weight
Stall speed: 103 kts (119 mph) 191 km/h IAS *clean*, 89 kts (102 mph) 165 km/h IAS *with flaps and undercarriage lowered*
Take-off distance: 4,400 ft (1,341 m) balanced field
Landing distance over a 50 ft (15 m) obstacle: 2,500 ft (762 m), factored (1.67) 4,175 ft (1,273 m)
Maximum climb rate: 2,700 ft (823 m) per minute at sea level (engine bleed on)
Maximum climb rate, 1 engine: 800 ft (244 m) per minute, sea level (engine bleed off)
Typical cruise altitude: 14,000 ft (4,267 m)
Ceiling: 25,000 ft (7,620 m)
Ceiling (C-26A): 26,700 ft (8,140 m)
Ceiling, 1 engine: 11,600 ft (3,535 m)
Sector totals: flight time 54.8 minutes, average flight speed 219 kts (252 mph) 406 km/h, and 665 lb (301.6 kg) Jet A fuel burn (including 10 minutes taxi, 375.9 litres)*
Range: over 1,000 naut miles (1,151 miles) 1,852 km with IFR reserves
Range with full payload: more than 534 naut miles (615 miles) 990 km
Range (C-26A): 1,063 naut miles (1,224 miles) 1,970 km with 19 passengers
Typical profile: 4 × 150 naut mile sectors without refuelling
*Metro 23 can fly this sector carrying up to 1,200 lb (544 kg) of additional payload. An additional 0.9 of a minute of flight time and 11 lb (5 kg) of fuel are required

Metro 23

↑ **Fairchild Dornier Metro 23 commuter airliner general arrangement** *(courtesy Fairchild Dornier USA Fairchild Aircraft Incorporated)*

Lockheed Martin Corporation USA

Corporate address:
See Combat section for company details.

Comments: The USAF's **C-5 Galaxy** transport aircraft (see also the 1996-97 edition of *WA&SD*, page 273) is to receive an avionics upgrade, with the contract expected to be awarded in September 1998. It may become the first aircraft to operate under the USAF's FANS/Global Air Traffic Management systems.

AlliedSignal and Raytheon Systems Company are engaged in upgrading the avionics on many USAF C-130 Hercules and **C-141 StarLifter** transports (see also the 1996-97 edition of *WA&SD*, page 273). Upgrading for the C-141 includes 6 × 8 ins (15.24 × 20.3 cm) active-matrix liquid crystal displays (AMLCD), as also retrofitted to Spanish C-130s, smaller digital avionics management units, plus display processor units and reference set panels, GPS, fuel quantity indicating systems, defensive systems, and state-of-the-art digital autopilot and ground collision avoidance, the package including AlliedSignal auto throttle actuator and clutch pack for the autopilot, longitudinal accelerometers and column wheel force sensors. C-130 upgrades include AMLCDs on some aircraft and state-of-the-art digital autopilot with ground collision avoidance system, the new automatic flight control system also including an automatic flight control processor, aileron and elevator servo actuators, select mode and flight control panels, and test operations panels.

Under the USAF's Lightning Bolt programmes, Rockwell Collins is currently upgrading the flight decks of some 600 **KC-135s** using a blend of advanced military and commercial avionics (see Boeing entry).

↑ **AlliedSignal automatic flight control system, featuring liquid crystal displays fitted to a C-141, as part of the USAF's C-130/C-141 avionics upgrade programme** *(courtesy AlliedSignal)*

↑ **Lockheed Martin has flown a model joined-wing radio-controlled aircraft, to assist in its New Strategic Aircraft project that could eventually provide a joined-wing replacement for the KC-135 tanker/transport**

Lockheed Martin C-130 and L-100 Hercules, and C-130J and L-100J Hercules

First flight: 23 August 1954 (YC-130 prototype). 7 April 1955 for first production aircraft (C-130A). 5 April 1996 for C-130J (a C-130J-30 for the RAF).
Certification: 16 February 1965 for commercial L-100 Hercules in original FAA class A category, 4 October 1968 in L-100-20 form, and 1970 in L-100-30 form.
Deliveries: 9 December 1956 to November 1959 for C-130A, 1959 to March 1963 for C-130B, 1962 to March 1974 for C-130E, 1964 to 1996 for C-130H, 1980 to 1996 for C-130H-30, and from 1996 for C-130J/C-130J-30 at the start of a year-long flight evaluation programme. First RAF C-130J-30 for active RAF service has joined No 24 Squadron at Lyneham after 26 August 1998 delivery, after trials with the DERA at Boscombe Down.
Role: Tactical military and medium commercial freighter, with many specialized variants. For firefighting, see Mission equipment.
Airport limits: Typically LCN 22 at landing weight of 122,950 lb (55,770 kg) for C-130H-30, with tyre deflections of 39% assuming rigid pavement stiffness of L=30 and flexible pavement thickness of 20 ins over CBR 6 subsurface.
Noise levels: 96.7 EPNdB take-off sideline, 97.8 EPNdB take-off flyover at take-off power, 94.8 take-off flyover at cutback power, and 98.1 approach flyover, all for L-100 at MTOW and MLW.
Sales: Total of 2,237 military and commercial Hercules had been ordered by March 1998, of which 83 remained to be delivered. These comprise 938 delivered to the USAF, 86 to the USMC, 39 to the US Navy, 20 to the US Navy Reserves, 48 to the US Coast Guard and 240 to the US Air National Guard and Air Force Reserve, making a total of 1,371 purchased by the US Government for its own forces. In addition, 670 aircraft have been sold abroad, comprising 260 bought via the US Government for foreign military sales/military assistance programmes and 410 by direct foreign purchase. Commercial sales total 113. Customers have been Abu Dhabi, Algeria, Angola, Argentina, Australia, Belgium, Bolivia, Brazil, Cameroon, Canada, Chad, Chile, China, Colombia, Denmark, Dubai, Ecuador, Egypt, Ethiopia, France, Gabon, Germany, Greece, Indonesia, Iran, Ireland, Israel, Italy, Japan, Jordan, Kuwait, Libya, Malaysia, Mexico, Morocco, Netherlands, New Zealand, Niger, Nigeria, Norway, Oman, Pakistan, Peru, Philippines, Portugal, Saudi Arabia, Singapore, South Africa, Spain, Sudan, Sweden, Switzerland, Taiwan, Thailand, Tunisia, Turkey, Uganda, UK, USA, Venezuela, Yemen, Zaire (now Congo, Democratic Republic), and Zambia. The final C-130H was completed in 1996, leaving the C-130J as the only available model. First flight of a C-130J-30 for the RAF on 5 April 1996 (25 ordered, as 10 C-130Js and 15 C-130J-30s); first flight of a C-130J for the USAF on 4 June 1996 (C-130Js, EC-130J, KC-130Js and WC-130Js ordered); first flight of a C-130J-30 for the Royal Australian Air Force on 16 February 1997 (12 ordered); aircraft from all 3 nations used in the flight evaluation/test programme.

Details *(C-130H and C-130H-30, plus C-130J or other versions where stated)*

Crew: 4, comprising 2 pilots, flight engineer and navigator. Advanced 2-pilot flight deck for C-130J variants.
Passengers: 64 paratroops, 92 ground troops or 74 litters and 2 attendants for the C-130H/J, and 92, 128 and 97/2 respectively for the C-130H-30/C-130J-30. Alternative palletized seating modules for C-130J variants, accommodating 54 and 79 respectively. See Freight hold capacity.
Pressurization: 7.5 psi cabin differential. Maintains sea level cockpit/cabin altitude to 18,000 ft (5,485 m).
Freight hold capacity: In place of troops/paratroops, palleted, containerized or bulk cargo can be carried, or wheeled, self-propelled, pushed or towed vehicles and equipment. See Loading facilities and Aircraft variants. Similar capacities for C-130H and C-130J versions. Can airdrop loads of 42,000 lb (19,051 kg).
Freight hold access: Straight-in loading via the rear ramp/door. Floor sides of hold are strengthened as vehicle treadways, and have aluminium slide strips. Auxiliary ground loading ramps and truck loading ramps are supplied to bridge the sill height from the ground to the ramp.
Size of freight doors: Lower ramp/door 123 ins (3.12 m) wide and 124 ins (3.15 m) long, plus upper door. Lower door can be opened to any position, with a slope of 11.5° when fully lowered on level ground. When fully raised, the internal slope is 21°. Maximum ramp load in flight is 5,000 lb (2,268 kg), and during

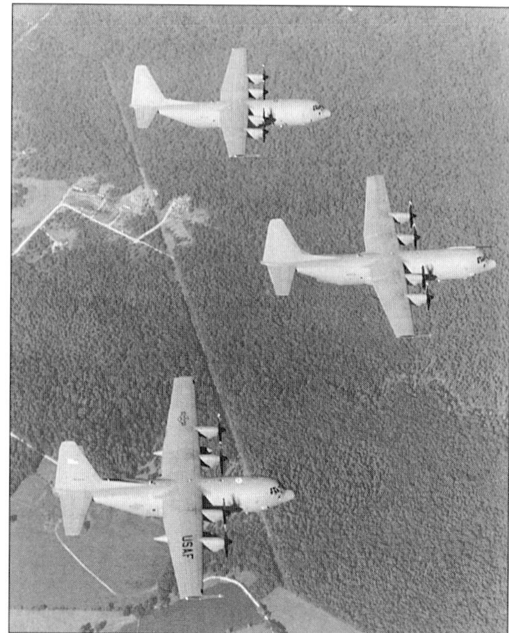

↑ **USAF Lockheed Martin C-130J (*bottom*) flying alongside 2 longer RAF C-130J-30s during the flight test programme. An advanced propulsion system, instrumentation and avionics, all driven by mission computers and sophisticated software, makes the 'J' significantly different from the previous 'H' version**

↑ Royal Air Force Hercules C Mk 4 (C-130J-30) photographed in October 1998 at delivery. C Mk 5 is the designation of standard fuselage-length C-130Js for the RAF

airdrop operations it is lowered level with the floor, with curbs to restrict the width of airdrop items to 9 ft 6 ins (2.9 m).
Loading facilities: A/A32H-4A mechanical dual-rail cargo handling system for pallets of 88 × 54 ins (2.24 × 1.37 m) and 88 × 108 ins (2.24 × 2.74 m) or containers. Portable electric winch of 4,000 lb (1,814 kg) capacity, wheeled pray bar of 2,000 lb (907 kg) capacity, and 2 snatch block pulleys. 10,000 lb (4,536 kg) capacity D-ring tiedown fittings on the floor, 25,000 lb (11,340 kg) capacity rings along the sides of the floor, and 5,000 lb (2,268 kg) capacity rings along the fuselage sides and on the ramp. Fitting provided for troop seats and litter racks. C-130H has 242 tiedown rings and C-130H-30 has 305.
Wing control surfaces: Aileron (with trim tab) and 2 Fowler-type flaps (inboard and outboard) per wing; all-composite flaps for C-130J variants.
Tail control surfaces: Elevators and rudder, all with trim tabs. Same for C-130J.
Flight control system: Mechanical primary controls, with hydraulic boosters. Hydraulic flaps and electric tabs. For C-130J, controls are integrated with the autopilot and flight director.
Construction materials: Metal. Carbonfibre flaps and some graphite/epoxy wing panels for C-130J variants.
Engines: 4 Allison T56-A-15LFE turboprops for C-130H variants, with 13 ft 6 ins (4.11 m) diameter propellers. 4 × 4,591 shp (3,424 kW) Allison AE 2100D3 engines with Lucas FADEC, using Dowty R391 6-blade composite propellers for C-130J variants. APU.
Engine rating: Each 4,508 shp (3,362 kW) for T56-A-15LFE, rated in technical specification documents as 4,300 shp (3,207 kW). For AE 2100D3 rating, see above.
Fuel system: 35,961 litres for C-130H, or 36,416 for C-130H-30, when including 2 optional 5,300 litre underwing auxiliary tanks. Improved/simplified fuel system for C-130J, offering 24,363 or 25,551 litres of fuel internally (with or without fire protection respectively), while 2 × 5,220 litre underwing auxiliary tanks are available.
Flight refuelling/fuel transfer: See Aircraft variants. First in-flight refuelling of a C-130J (RAF C-130J-30 *LM5408*) on 17 February 1997, using a VC-10 tanker over the Atlantic.
Electrical system: AC supply via 5 × 40 kVA alternators (on engines and APU), with conversion to DC via transformer-rectifiers.
Hydraulic system: Booster, utility and auxiliary systems, at 3,000 psi. Similar for C-130J.
Braking system: Hydraulic multi-disc on mainwheels, with anti-skid system.
De-icing system: Bleed air for windscreen defogging, and deicing of engine air and oil cooler inlets, forward radome, and wing and tail unit leading edges. Electric for forward and lower cockpit windscreens, propeller blades and spinners, and pitot static heads.
Oxygen system: 300 psi liquid system providing 96 hours of oxygen at 25,000 ft (7,620 m). Gaseous system optional.
Fire system: Engines, APU and bleed air powered systems are monitored for fire and overheat. Engines and APU are protected by a fire suppression system.
Radar: RDR-1F weather radar for C-130H variants. 2 Rockwell Collins 621A-6A air traffic control radar transponders. C-130J has new low-power Northrop Grumman AN/APN-241 colour radar.
Flight avionics/instrumentation: *C-130H variants:* Communications equipment includes AN/AIC-18 intercommunication, AN/AIC-13 public address, 2 Rockwell Collins 628T-2A HF transceivers and 2 × 618M-3A VHF command transceivers, and provision for AN/ARC-164(V)4 UHF transceiver. Navigation equipment includes Litton LTN-72 INS and LTN-211 Omega, 2 Rockwell Collins 51RV-4B VHF nav/ILS, 2 × 860E-5 DME, 2 DF-206 AFDS, and 51Z-4 marker beacon. Flight displays are dual Rockwell Collins FD-109 flight director system, 2 C-12 gyro compass systems, 860F-4/AL-101 radio altimeter, GPWS Mk II, and Kollsman altitude alerter/preselect system. Automatic flight control system with AP 105V autopilot, guidance display and sensors (2 ADI, 2 HSI). See the Lockheed Martin introductory paragraphs for USAF C-130 avionics upgrade programme. Royal Danish Air Force C-130s are receiving an avionics upgrade by Rockwell Collins, including FDS 255 liquid crystal displays, colour weather radar, APS-85 digital autopilot, FMS-800 flight management system, and new air data systems. In 1997 Marshall Aerospace awarded Sextant Avionique a development and production contract for a C-130 modernization avionics suite, to be installed by Marshall on aircraft deployed by countries wishing to upgrade their aircraft. Known as Topdeck®, it includes 5 liquid crystal displays (each 6 × 8 ins, 15.24 × 20.3 cm), 3 multi-function displays, keyboards to control the navigation functions and communicate with the 2 FMSs, an autopilot, 2 Totem 3000 laser gyro INSs with integrated GPS receiver, and 2 air data modules with their associated probes. *C-130J variants:* Advanced 2-pilot flight deck with fully integrated digital avionics, MIL-STD-1553B databus architecture, 4 (Sanders, a Lockheed Martin Company) colour multi-function liquid crystal displays (each 6 × 8 ins, 15.24 × 20.3 cm) plus 5 smaller digital monochrome units, and 2 Flight Dynamics holographic head-up-displays; modern navigation systems with dual Honeywell laser INS/GPS, AN/ARN-153(V) Tacan, Doppler velocity sensor, mission planning system, digital moving map display, new digital autopilot with ground collision avoidance system, flight director, automatic direction-finder, Sierra station keeping system, VOR, ILS, marker beacon, and radar altimeter; optional microwave landing system; built-in test equipment (BITE) and integrated diagnostics with a maintenance data recorder; AN/ARC-222 VHF,

Details for C-130H, *with C-130H-30 in italics where different*, plus C-130J where stated

PRINCIPAL DIMENSIONS:
Wing span: 132 ft 7 ins (40.41 m); same for C-130J
Maximum length: 97 ft 9 ins (29.79 m), *112 ft 9 ins (34.366 m)*; the same for C-130J and C-130J-30 respectively
Maximum height: 38 ft 1 ins (11.61 m); and 38 ft 10 ins (11.84 m) for C-130J

CABIN:
Length: 41 ft (12.5 m) actual and 40 ft 5 ins (12.32 m) usable to ramp, *56 ft (17.07 m) actual and 55 ft 5 ins (16.89 m) usable*, with additional 10 ft (3.05 m) available on the ramp
Width: 10 ft 3.2 ins (3.13 m) maximum and 9 ft 11.5 ins (3.03 m) adjacent to mainwheels; the same for C-130J
Height: 9 ft (2.74 m) maximum, with slight drop at wing point; the same for C-130J
Floor area: 425 sq ft (39.48 m^2), without ramp
Volume without ramp: 3,621 cu ft (102.53 m^3), *4,966 cu ft (140.62 m^3)*, clear cube volume
Volume with ramp: 4,351 cu ft (123.2 m^3), *5,696 cu ft (161.29 m^3)*, clear cube volume
Cheek volume: 200 cu ft (5.7 m^3), *326 cu ft (9.23 m^3)*

WINGS:
Aerofoil section: NACA 64A318, 64A412 (root/tip); the same for C-130J
Area: 1,745 sq ft (162.116 m^2); the same for C-130J
Aspect ratio: 10.08; the same for C-130J
Incidence: 3°, 0° (root/tip); the same for C-130J
Dihedral: 2° 30'; the same for C-130J

TAIL UNIT:
Tailplane span: 52 ft 8 ins (16.05 m); the same for C-130J

UNDERCARRIAGE:
Type: Retractable, with twin steerable nosewheels (±60°). Tandem mainwheel units. Same for C-130J
Main wheel tyre size: 56 × 20.00-20
Nose wheel tyre size: 39 × 13
Wheel base: 29 ft 6 ins (8.99) from nosewheels to forward main wheels
Wheel track: 14 ft 3 ins (4.34 m), the same for C-130J
Turning radius: 85 ft (25.91 m) wingtip for C-130H and C-130J; 90 ft (27.43 m) wingtip for C-130H-30 and C-130J-30

WEIGHTS:
Empty, operating: 76,505 lb (34,702 kg), *80,152 lb (36,356 kg)*; or 75,562 lb (34,274 kg) for C-130J and 79,291 lb (35,965 kg) for C-130J-30
Maximum zero fuel: 119,142 lb (54,042 kg); 117,350 lb (53,229 kg) for C-130J
Maximum take-off: 155,000 lb (70,307 kg) for 2.5g, 175,000 lb (79,379 kg) for 2.25g; same for C-130J
Maximum landing: 155,000 lb (70,307 kg), for 5 ft per second sink rate
Normal landing: 130,000 lb (58,967 kg), for 9 ft per second sink rate; same for C-130J
Payload: 42,637 lb (19,340 kg), *38,990 lb (17,686 kg)*; or 41,790 lb (18,956 kg) for C-130J and 38,060 lb (17,263 kg) for C-130J-30

PERFORMANCE:
Maximum cruise speed: *335 kts (385 mph) 620 km/h*; 347 kts (400 mph) 643 km/h for C-130J
Long-range cruise speed: 300 kts (345 mph) 556 km/h; 339 kts (390 mph) 627 km/h for C-130J
Stall speed: 100 kts (115 mph) 185 km/h; the same for C-130J
Normal take-off distance: 3,585 ft (1,093 m); or 1,950-3,125 ft (595-953 m) for C-130J
Typical take-off distance for C-130J: 3,050 ft (930 m)
Maximum effort take-off distance for C-130J: 1,800 ft (549 m)
Take-off distance over a 50 ft (15 m) obstacle: *4,700 ft (1,433 m)*; the same for C-130J
Landing distance over a 50 ft (15 m) obstacle: 2,750 ft (839 m) at 130,000 lb (58,967 kg) landing weight, *2,370 ft (723 m) at 122,950 lb (55,769 kg) landing weight*; 2,550 ft (778 m) at 130,000 lb (58,967 kg) landing weight for C-130J
Maximum climb rate: 1,900 ft (579 m) per minute at sea level; 2,100 ft (640 m) per minute at sea level for C-130J
Time to 23,000 ft (7,010 m) for C-130H: 22 minutes
Time to 28,000 ft (8,535 m) initial cruise altitude for C-130J: 14 minutes
Cruise altitude: 24,000 ft (7,315 m), 33,000 ft (10,058 m) ceiling; 28,000 ft (8,534 m) for C-130J
Range: 1,945 naut miles (2,240 miles) 3,602 km with 40,000 lb (18,143 kg) payload, *1,740 naut miles (2,003 miles) 3,222 km with maximum payload, or 4,200 naut miles (4,836 miles) 7,778 km with an 8,430 lb (3,824 kg) payload*
Range for C-130J: 2,835 naut miles (3,265 miles) 5,250 km

↑Lockheed Martin C-130J flight deck

HF/UHF and optional satcom communications system; IFF. Displays are night vision imaging system compatible, enabling the crew to operate the aircraft into and out of areas of total darkness with special night vision devices.
Mission equipment: See Aircraft variants. US Air National Guard and Reserve Hercules can be equipped (in 2 hours) with special aerial firefighting apparatus known as Modular Airborne Fire Fighting Systems or MAFFS, to disperse Phos-Chek D-75 retardant in a solution.
Self-protection systems: Some military versions carry missile warning system and chaff/flare dispensers. Integrated defense system for C-130J variants, with AN/AAR-47 missile warning and AN/ALR-69 radar warning systems, AN/ALQ-157 infra-red jammers and AN/ALE-47 chaff/flare dispensers.
Fixed guns: See AC-130 in the Combat section.

Aircraft variants:
C-130A was the original version, though later aircraft were considerably improved. Initially T56-A-1A turboprops with 3-blade propellers. MTOW 124,200 lb (56,336 kg). Some still in use with foreign air forces.
C-130B entered service from 1959, featuring 4,050 eshp (3,020 ekW) T56-A-7 engines with 4-blade propellers, additional fuel, 135,000 lb (61,235 kg) gross weight and strengthened undercarriage. Some still in use with foreign air forces.
C-130E was delivered from 1962 with T56-A-7 engines, many structural improvements, extra fuel for longer range by introducing a pylon tank under each wing, plus avionics improvements. 155,000 lb (70,307 kg) gross weight. Still in US inventory plus other air forces.
MC-130E Combat Talon I became a USAF special operations version, used for day, night and adverse weather, low-level and deep penetration missions, including air-refuelling of helicopters, aerial delivery and exfiltration, psychological warfare and other roles. Much specialized equipment, including AN/APQ-122(V)8 terrain-following radar and night vision equipment. 14 operated by the 8th and 711th Special Operations Squadrons.
WC-130E became a USAF weather reconnaissance variant.
C-130H appeared in 1964 and remained the main production version until 1996, when the last aircraft was completed. In 1974 a more advanced C-130H was introduced, equipped with a modern auxiliary power unit to replace the gas turbine compressor, and a redesigned air-conditioning system. Known as C-130Ks for the RAF, with Marshall of Cambridge 'stretching' the fuselages to become Hercules Mk 3s.
C-130H-30 Super Hercules was first delivered in 1980 to the Indonesian Air Force, as a variant of the C-130H with a 100 ins (2.54 m) plug inserted aft of the cockpit and an 80 ins (2.03 m) plug just forward of the ramp, to increase its airlift capability. Can carry 7 pallets, 2 more than the C-130H, or 92 paratroops (28 more).
AC-130H and ***U Spectre*** are gunships. See Combat section.
DC-130s are UAV control aircraft with the USAF/USN.
EC-130s are electronic warfare variants. See Reconnaissance section.
HC-130H, N and ***P Combat Shadow*** are special operations versions with the USAF, ANG, AFRES and US Coast Guard, for refuelling helicopters and rescue and recovery of equipment and personnel.
JC-130H was built for the USAF to recover parachute-borne space capsules.
KC-130F/R/T are probe-and-drogue flight refuelling tankers used by the USMC and acquired in KC-130H form by Argentina, Brazil, Israel, Morocco, Saudi Arabia, Singapore and Spain. The US Navy has KC-130T-30s.
LC-130 is a ski/wheel-equipped transport for Arctic operations with the US ANG and Antarctic with the USN.
MC-130H Combat Talon II is an improved USAF special operations version, based on the C-130H. 24 aircraft delivered from 1991, used to supplement Combat Talon Is. Much specialized equipment, including AN/APQ-170 terrain-following/avoidance radar and night vision equipment. Upgrade of the communications and navigation systems underway. Operated by the 1st, 7th and 15th Special Operations Squadrons of the USAF, plus the 58th Special Operations Wing for training.
C-130T is a transport and tanker with the US Navy Air Reserve.
C-130J is the latest and current production version, delivered from 1996. Also offered in **C-130J-30** lengthened form. Advanced 2-pilot flight deck with fully integrated digital avionics and other improved systems. NVG compatible lighting. Allison AE 2100D3 engines with composite propellers. Improved/simplified fuel, environmental control and ice protection systems; integrated defence system. Modern technology enables a reduction of manpower requirements by 37%, improves reliability and maintainability by 50%, and lowers operating costs by 27%, while also improving performance.
EC-130J Commando Solo is a new psychological warfare version for the 193rd Special Operations Squadron, based on the C-130J Hercules. 1 ordered to date under the FY1997 defence budget, for delivery to the ANG in 1999.
KC-130J is a tanker variant of C-130J, with the first 4 ordered for the USMC under the FY97 defence budget. Could have both a fuselage-mounted flying-boom fuel transfer system and 2 wingtip hose-and-drum units. A variable-speed drogue currently under development could allow either fixed-wing aircraft or helicopters to use the same unit. Expected to transfer up to 3,000 litres of fuel per minute via the boom while flying at 240 kts and 20,000 ft (6,100 m), and 1,150 litres per minute via the wingtip units, with a maximum aircraft speed for fuel transfer operations of 270 kts.

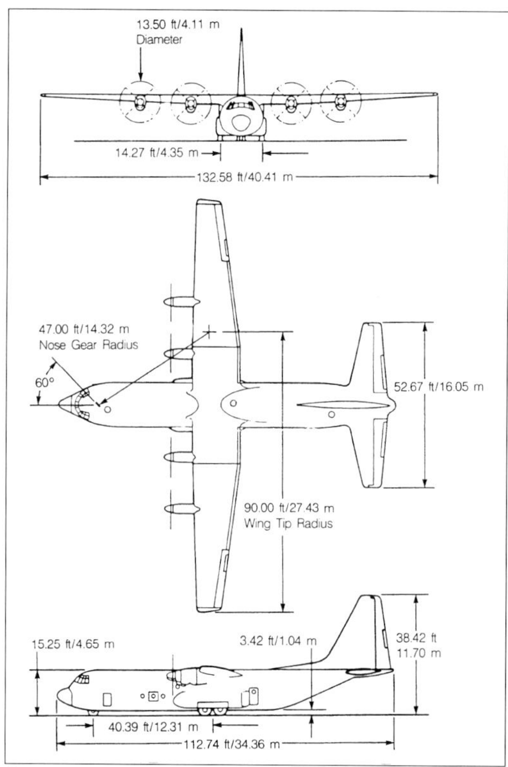

↑ Lockheed Martin L-100-30 Super Hercules general arrangement *(courtesy Lockheed Martin)*

WC-130J is a weather reconnaissance version. 6 on order at the time of writing.
C-130J AEW variant, see Electronic section.
C-130 Floatplane has been proposed, using removable twin-float 'catamaran type' gear that could be attached to existing E, H or J variants of Hercules, with conversion back to a wheeled undercarriage possible in a few hours. Interest has been expressed for US Navy special forces. Required water depth of 5 ft (1.52 m). Estimated payload of 26,800 lb (12,156 kg) and range of 2,200 naut miles.
L-100 and ***L-100-30 Super Hercules*** are commercial versions of Hercules, finally based on the C-130H and C-130H-30 military equivalents. Externally similar to military versions, except for the absence of lower windows on the flight deck. First flown as the L-100 in April 1964 (stretched L-100-20 was certified in 1968, followed by the stretched L-100-30 in 1970). Currently 4,508 shp (3,362 kW) Allison 501-D22A turboprops. L-100-30 ramp weight, MTOW, MLW and payload are 155,800 lb (70,670 kg), 155,000 lb (70,307 kg), 135,000 lb (61,235 kg), and 50,676 lb (22,986 kg) respectively. Special variants include an HS hospital model operated in Saudi Arabia.
L-100J is a commercial variant of the new C-130J-30.

Pemco World Air Services — USA

Corporate marketing and Sales address:
12000 East 47th Avenue, Suite 400, Denver, CO 80239.

Telephone: +1 303 307 0156
Facsimile: +1 303 307 0171
Web site: www.pemcoair.com

Employees:
2,500 corporate wide.

Information:
Suzanne Smith (Manager, Public Relations).

ACTIVITIES

▪ Has provided maintenance and modification services for aircraft since 1951. Military facilities located in Birmingham, Alabama, and commercial facilities in Dothan, Alabama; Victorville, California; and Copenhagen, Denmark. Services include cargo conversions, aircraft maintenance, interior refurbishment, exterior and structural modification, ageing aircraft modifications, component repair, avionics system upgrades and installation, line maintenance, nacelle thrust reverser repair, SB and AD compliance services and EPA-approved stripping and painting. In-house manufacturing capabilities enables Pemco to design, certify and manufacture the vast majority of the components required for conversion and modification, such as cargo handling systems, cargo doors, surrounding structure and all applicable hardware.

▪ Has performed nearly 300 combi, quick-change (QC) and full freighter conversions on wide and narrow body aircraft, including every BAe 146 ever converted, the only aftermarket DC-9 conversions, the only B727-100 freighter to quick-change conversions, the first B727-200 Class C convertible combi, and the only B737-300 quick-change and pure freighter conversions. Pemco holds nearly 100 STCs related to these conversions.

OTHER PEMCO COMPANIES

PEMCO ENGINEERS

Activities:
▪ Located at Corona, California, manufactures aircraft cargo handling systems, main deck barrier nets, precision springs and component parts for the international aviation industry.

PEMCO AIR SUPPORT SERVICES

Activities:
▪ Sales offices and warehouses in Clearwater, Florida and Copenhagen, Denmark to provide its cargo conversion customers with a centralized 24-hour source for spares support and component overhaul.

→ Pemco World Air Services Boeing 737-300 quick-change conversion

PEMCO NACELLE SERVICES

Activities:
▪ Occupies 40,000 sq ft (3,716 m^2) of hangar space adjacent to the St Petersburg/Clearwater International Airport in Clearwater, Florida and operates as an approved Limited Airframe, Powerplant and Accessory Repair Station.

PEMCO AEROPLEX, INC

Activities:
▪ Located at the Birmingham, Alabama International Airport, Pemco Aeroplex provides a full range of maintenance and modification services. Primary mission is to keep military aircraft such as the C-141, C-130, F-15, F-16, H-3 and KC-135 operational. Provides programmed depot maintenance, including structural modifications such as wing swaps and reskins, avionics systems integration, complete overhaul and repair of major components such as undercarriage and flight controls, corrosion inspection, interior refurbishment and stripping painting.

SPACE VECTOR CORPORATION

Activities:
▪ Established in 1972 and located in Fountain Valley and Chatsworth, California, provides missiles, launch vehicles and low-cost launch services for scientific and military missions. Maintains a large research, development and engineering staff to support engineering and manufacturing activities. This work includes the design and manufacture of spacecraft, rockets, inertial guidance and control systems, instrumentation and telemetry subsystems, payload recovery systems and rocket launch support.

HAYES TARGETS

Activities:
▪ Located in Leeds, Alabama, Hayes Targets is one of the world's leading manufacturers of aerial targets and infrared augmenting devices.

Quiet Technologies Venture Ltd — USA

Corporate address:
8000 North-West 56th Street, Miami, FL 33166.

Telephone: +1 305 593 0731
Facsimile: +1 305 592 8265
E-mail: QTV@FLA.NET

Founded: 1984.

Employees: 100.

Information:
Martin Gardner (Director of Engineering).

ACTIVITIES

▪ DC-8 Stage 3 hushkit (FAA approved), USAF C-135B hushkit (USAF approved), Boeing 707 Stage 3 hushkit (FAA approved), and BAC One-Eleven Stage 3 hushkit (development started July 1997, with certification expected at the end of 1998). Plans to develop a Gulfstream II/III Stage 3 hushkit during 1998.

Raytheon Aircraft Company — USA

Corporate address:
See Combat section for company details.

Beech 1900D Airliner

First flight: 1 March 1990.
Certification: March 1991 to FAR Pt 23 Amendment 34.
First delivery: 1991, to Mesa Air Group.
Role: Regional airliner and executive shuttle.
Sales: More than 500 Beech 1900 series aircraft delivered by June 1998, with the 300th current Beech 1900D delivered to Proteus Airlines in March 1998. First Executive shuttle was delivered to Ashanti Goldfields Company Ltd of Ghana in April 1995.
Crew: 1 or 2 pilots.
Passengers: Up to 19 passengers, 2 abreast.
Seat pitch: 30 ins (76 cm).
Galley: Optional self-service commissary and toilet.
Pressurization: 5 psi cabin differential.
Baggage compartments: 17 cu ft (0.48 m^3) forward cabin, for 250 lb (113.4 kg) of baggage. 175 cu ft (4.96 m^3) aft area, for 1,630 lb (739 kg).
Wing control surfaces: Ailerons (with port trim tab) and 2-section single-slotted Fowler-type flaps. Winglets.
Tail control surfaces: T-tail, with tailets, and stabilons to improve pitch stability and widen CG range (4% to 40% of MAC). Elevators and rudder, all with trim tabs.
Flight control system: Mechanical for primary controls, trimmed by mechanical servo tabs. Flaps are electro-mechanically controlled and automatically protected against asymmetric actuation. Standard electric elevator trim.
Construction materials: Aluminium alloy.
Engines: 2 Pratt & Whitney Canada PT6A-67D turboprops, with Hartzell 4-blade composite propellers.
Engine rating: Each derated to 1,279 shp (953.75 kW).
Fuel system: 2,517 litres usable.
Electrical system: 28 volt DC quadruple bus system supplied by 2 engine-driven generators and a 34 amp-hour ni-cd battery. 2 solid state 250VA SPC-10(P) inverters with failure lights supply 115 volt AC and 26 volt AC power for the avionics and instruments.
Hydraulic system: 3,000 psi, with dual reservoir and driven by 28 volt DC electric pump.
Braking system: Goodyear multiple disc brakes on main wheels. Optional electro-hydraulic anti-skid.
De-icing system: Electric for propellers, brakes, windshield, pitot/static masts, alternate static sources and stall warning vanes. Pneumatic for wing and tail unit leading-edges. Engine intake protected from ice and FOD by inertial separators.
Oxygen system: Automatic overhead drop-down passenger system, deployed from the cockpit. Crew masks. 2 × 76.5 cu ft (2.17 m^3) bottles supply crew and passengers for 68 minutes at 25,000 ft (7,620 m).
Fire system: Continuous fire detection loop and 1-shot fire extinguisher in each nacelle. Self monitoring system discriminates between true and false warnings.
Radar: Rockwell Collins WXR-350 colour weather radar, with WXR-840 digital radar and TWR-850 turbulence radar optional.
Flight avionics/instrumentation: Rockwell Collins Pro-Line. Flight director systems comprising dual EFIS-84 4-tube EFIS, with 4 × 4 ins (10 × 10 cm) colour CRT displays for attitude director instrument (EADI) and horizontal situation instrument (EHSI), and dual ADS-65 air data computers. Communications suite has VHF-22A transceiver with CLT-222 control and antenna. Navigation suite has VIR-32 VOR/LOC/glideslope/marker beacon receiver with CLT-32 control and antenna, ADF-462 with CLT-62 control and antenna, dual DME-42, dual RMI-36s with

↑ Air Labrador Beech 1900D Airliner, delivered in 1997

VOR-1/ADF on single needle and VOR-2/ADF on double needle, dual MCS-65 digital compass systems, and dual TDR-94 transponders. Sundstrand Mk VI GPWS. Provision for Goodrich TCAS 791. Other non-Rockwell Collins equipment includes standby gyro horizon, cockpit voice recorder, flight data recorder, cabin briefer, and altimeters. Audio system. Optional available avionics include Rockwell Collins APS-65H autopilot and AlliedSignal Bendix/King KLN-90B GPS.

Aircraft variants:
1900D Airliner is the regional transport. Quick change interior allows conversion from passenger to cargo configuration.
1900D Executive is a business version, the first going to Ashanti Goldfields Company Ltd in April 1995. This has 8 airline seats and 6 club seats, plus galley and toilet.

Details for 1900D Airliner

PRINCIPAL DIMENSIONS:
Wing span: 57 ft 10 ins (17.63 m)
Maximum length: 57 ft 10 ins (17.63 m)
Maximum height: 15 ft 6 ins (4.72 m)

CABIN:
Length: 33 ft 11 ins (10.34 m)
Width: 4 ft 6 ins (1.37 m), or 4 ft 1 ins (1.24 m) at floor
Height: 5 ft 11 ins (1.8 m)
Volume: 584 cu ft (16.54 m^3) main cabin, 103 cu ft (2.92 m^3) crew station
Main passenger door: 5 ft 4.2 ins × 2 ft 3 ins (1.63 × 0.69 m)
Cargo door: 4 ft 4 ins × 4 ft 4 ins (1.32 × 1.32 m) aft door, and 4 ft 9 ins × 4 ft 4 ins (1.45 × 1.32 m) forward door

WINGS:
Aerofoil section: Modified NACA 23018, 23012 (root/tip)
Area: 310 sq ft (28.8 m^2)
Aspect ratio: 10.79
Incidence: 3° 29′ root, -1° 4′ tip
Dihedral: 6°

TAIL UNIT:
Tailplane span: 18 ft 5.75 ins (5.63 m)

UNDERCARRIAGE:
Type: Retractable, with steerable nosewheel. Twin main wheel units
Wheel base: 23 ft 9.5 ins (7.25 m)
Wheel track: 17 ft 2 ins (5.23 m)
Turning radius: 41 ft 1 ins (12.53 m) wingtip

WEIGHTS:
Empty, operating: 10,550 lb (4,785 kg) typically
Maximum zero fuel: 15,000 lb (6,804 kg)
Maximum ramp: 17,060 lb (7,738 kg)
Maximum take-off: 16,950 lb (7,688 kg)
Maximum landing: 16,100 lb (7,303 kg)
Useful load: 6,510 lb (2,953 kg)
Payload: 1,887 lb (856 kg) with full fuel

PERFORMANCE:
Maximum cruise speed: 281 kts (324 mph) 520 km/h *at 10,000 ft (3,050 m)*, 288 kts (332 mph) 533 km/h *at 15,000 ft (4,570 m)*, 285 kts (328 mph) 528 km/h *at 20,000 ft (6,100 m)*, 278 kts (320 mph) 515 km/h *at 25,000 ft (7,620 m)*, all at 15,000 lb (6,804 kg)
Stall speed: 82 kts (95 mph) 152 km/h, with 35° flaps, at 16,100 lb (7,303 kg)
Field length at sea level, ISA: 3,470 ft (1,058 m) with 17° flaps, at 16,000 lb (7,257 kg)
Field length at 5,000 ft (1,525 m), ISA +30° C: 5,717 ft (1,743 m) with 17° flaps, at MTOW
Maximum climb rate: 2,625 ft (800 m) per minute at MTOW
Maximum climb rate, 1 engine: 675 ft (206 m) per minute at MTOW
Ceiling: 25,000 ft (7,620 m) certified, 33,000 ft (10,060 m) service, at MTOW, ISA
Ceiling, 1 engine: 17,500 ft (5,335 m)
Range: 481 naut miles (554 miles) 891 km *at 8,000 ft (2,440 m)*, 518 naut miles (596 miles) 959 km *at 12,000 ft (3,660 m)*, 571 naut miles (657 miles) 1,057 km *at 16,000 ft (4,875 m)*, 705 naut miles (812 miles) 1,305 km *at 25,000 ft (7,620 m)*, all at high cruise power, at typical operating weight with 19 passengers, and 45 minutes reserve

Multi-national

Airbus Industrie

France/Spain/Germany/UK

Corporate address:
1 Rond Point Maurice Bellonte, 31707 Blagnac Cedex, France.

Telephone: +33 5 61 93 33 33
Facsimile: +33 5 61 93 37 92
Telex: AIRBU 530526 F
Web site: http://www.airbus.com

Founded: 1970.

Employees:
About 32,000 work directly on Airbus aircraft within the participating companies, including some 2,700 (of 33 nationalities) at its headquarters and subsidiaries.

Information:
Barbara Kracht (Manager, Press and Information – *telephone* +33 5 61 93 33 87, *facsimile* +33 5 61 93 49 55).

ACTIVITIES

▪ Airbus Industrie is a consortium company owned by Aerospatiale of France (37.9%), Daimler-Benz Aerospace of Germany through its Daimler-Benz Aerospace Airbus GmbH division (37.9%), British Aerospace (20%) and CASA of Spain (4.2%). They not only own the shares but are industrial participants, conducting most of the design and all manufacture, co-ordinated and managed by Airbus Industrie. Belairbus of Belgium is an associate member, as is the Stork Group after its purchase of Fokker Aviation of the Netherlands in July 1996.
▪ Airliner sections produced in the various countries are transported to Aerospatiale in Toulouse (headquarters) for final assembly (A300/310, A320 and A330/A340) or Daimler-Benz Aerospace in Hamburg (A319/A321). Sections were, until mid-1997, transported by Super Guppy aircraft or by road, but new SATIC A300-600ST Super Transporters (Beluga) have taken over (which see).
▪ Four partners signed an MoU on 13 January 1997 to restructure Airbus Industrie into a limited liability company by 1999.

DIVISIONS

CUSTOMER SERVICES DIRECTORATE

Activities:
▪ Undertakes support services, engineering and technical support, transition and recurrent training (formerly by Aeroformation but since May 1994 as part of CSD's activities – conducted at Toulouse in France and Miami in the USA) and flight operations support, materiel support, and business management.

AIRBUS INDUSTRIE ASIA (AIA)

Activities:
▪ Established on 18 June 1997 by Airbus Industrie and Alenia Aerospazio of Italy (62% and 38% of shares respectively), to represent European interests in the development of the AE31X in partnership with AVIC of China and ST Aero of Singapore, producing 2 airliners initially, the A316 and A317. The Joint Venture Company was to be established in 1998, with its headquarters in Hong Kong. See AE3IX entry for latest details of the project and participants.

AIRBUS INDUSTRIE CHINA

Activities:
▪ Was established to represent European interests in the China Aviation Supplies Import & Export Corporation (CASC)/Airbus Industrie Training and Support Centre at Beijing, which has its own A320 and A340 simulators and Mandarin-speaking personnel. The Centre was inaugurated on 17 May 1997.

AIRBUS MILITARY COMPANY

Activities:
▪ Established to take over the FLA military transport programme initiated by Euroflag. In addition to the existing Airbus partners, Alenia of Italy also has an interest in FLA.

LARGE AIRCRAFT

Activities:
▪ This division was founded in 1996 to speed up work on the Airbus A3XX, undertaking all pre-development activities. Belairbus and the Stork Group signed MoUs in January 1997 for the study phase of the A3XX project, and are expected to lead to business agreements to become risk-sharing partners. On 14 October 1997 similar MoUs were signed with Saab of Sweden and Finavitec of Finland. Alenia of Italy is also expected to become involved.

Airbus A300B2 and B4 freighter conversions

Role: Freighter conversion of A300 ex-passenger airliners.
Sales: Deliveries of the A300B2/B4 early series airliners took place between 1974 and 1986. Since 1992, conversion kits have been available to permit any A300B2/B4 model to be retrofitted as freighters. British Aerospace gained its STC from the FAA for A300B4 conversions in 1997, having flown its first converted A300B4 freighter on 23 January 1997; the first delivery to Channel Express took place that July. The largest orders have come from C-S Aviation Services of New York, which has 31 orders and options. DASA undertakes similar conversions in Germany and expected to produce 12 conversions at Dresden in 1998, while others have been subcontracted to Sogerma.
Freight hold capacity: Main deck can accommodate 9 pallets of 88 or 96 ins × 125 ins (2.23 or 2.44 × 3.18 m) plus 3 or 5 pallets of 88 × 125 ins (2.24 × 3.18 m). Lower deck can accommodate 4 pallets plus 8 LD3 containers, or 20 LD3s.
Conversion kit: Comprises an upper deck cargo door of 141 × 101 ins (3.58 × 2.57 m) with 70° or 145° opening angle, floor reinforcements to increase running loads, Class E fire protection on the main deck including a smoke detection system, safety barrier net and smoke curtain, and systems adaptation/simplification for weight reduction. Optional packs include a selection of cargo loading system packages (single row or side-by-side, engine transportation pack).
Fuel system: 43,000 litres for B2-200, and 62,000 litres for B4-100/-200.

Airbus A300-600

First flight: 8 July 1983.
Certification: 9 March 1984 with original JT9D engines.
First delivery: 26 March 1984 to Saudi .
Role: Medium-long range widebody airliner and freighter.
Airport limits: Flexible runway ACN (Cat B) for A300-600 is 56 with standard undercarriage and 52 with optional wider main bogies. For A300-600R is 59 standard and 55 optional.
Noise levels: A300-600R with GE/P&W engines: 91.1/92.2 EPNdB at take-off, 98.6/97.7 EPNdB sideline, 99.8/101.7 EPNdB approach.
Sales: 488 A300s of all versions ordered by June 1998, of which 469 had been delivered and 439 were operating.

Details *(passenger versions; see Aircraft variants for convertible and freighter details)*

Crew: 2 (flight).
Passengers: Typically 266 seats in 2-class layout (26 first at 40 ins/103 cm seat pitch and 240 economy at 32 ins/81 cm pitch), 231 in 3-class (18 sleeper first at 57 ins/145 cm pitch, 35 business at 40 ins/103 cm pitch and 178 economy at 32 ins/81 cm pitch), 298 all-economy (at 32 ins/81 cm pitch), and 361 high-density (current certification limit, at 29 ins/73.7 cm or 30 ins/76 cm pitch). 6-abreast first class, 7-abreast executive or business, 8-abreast economy, and 9-abreast high-density, with 2 aisles.
Seat pitch: See above.

↑ Airbus A300-600R delivered to China Northern Airlines

Details for A300-600, *with -600R in italics where different*

PRINCIPAL DIMENSIONS:
Wing span: 147 ft 1 ins (44.84 m)
Maximum length: 177 ft 5 ins (54.08 m)
Maximum height: 54 ft 2 ins (16.52 m)
Fuselage diameter: 18 ft 6 ins (5.64 m)

CABIN:
Length: 131 ft 11 ins (40.21 m)
Width: 17 ft 4 ins (5.28 m)
Height: 8 ft 4 ins (2.54 m)
Main passenger doors: 6 ft 4 ins × 3 ft 6 ins (1.93 × 1.07 m)

WINGS:
Area: 2,798.61 sq ft (260 m^2)
Aspect ratio: 7.733
Sweepback: 28° at 25% chord

TAIL UNIT:
Tailplane span: 53 ft 4 ins (16.26 m)
Tailplane area: 482.2 sq ft (44.8 m^2)

UNDERCARRIAGE:
Type: Retractable, with twin steerable nosewheels. 4-wheel main bogies of standard 3 ft 1 ins × 4 ft 7 ins (0.927 × 1.397 m) size, but optional wider units with larger low-pressure tyres to reduce runway ACN
Main wheel tyre size: 49 × 17-20 standard, or 49 × 19-20
Nose wheel tyre size: 40 × 14-16
Wheel base: 61 ft (18.6 m)
Wheel track: 31 ft 6 ins (9.6 m)
Turning radius: 114 ft (34.75 m) wingtip

WEIGHTS:
Empty, operating: typically 198,636 lb (90,100 kg), *199,077 lb (90,300 kg)*
Maximum zero fuel: 286,600 lb (130,000 kg), *the same standard and 271,168 lb (123,000 kg) optional*
Maximum take-off: 363,762 lb (165,000 kg), *375,888 lb (170,500 kg) standard or 378,533 lb (171,700 kg) optional*
Maximum landing: 304,238 lb (138,000 kg), *308,647 lb (140,000 kg)*

PERFORMANCE:
Maximum cruise speed: Mach 0.82 at 30,000 ft (9,145 m)
Economic cruise speed: Mach 0.8
Approach speed: 135 kts (155 mph) 250 km/h, *136 kts (157 mph) 252 km/h*
Take-off field length: up to 7,480 ft (2,280 m), *7,515 ft (2,290 m)*, but depends on engines fitted
Landing field length: 5,040 ft (1,536 m), *5,100 ft (1,555 m)*
Initial cruise altitude: 35,000 ft (10,670 m) westbound, 33,000 ft (10,060 m) eastbound
Operating ceiling: 40,000 ft (12,200 m)
Range with 266 passengers and GE engines: 3,700 naut miles (4,260 miles) 6,852 km, *4,050 naut miles (4,663 miles) 7,500 km*, with reserve
Range with 266 passengers and P&W engines: 3,650 naut miles (4,203 miles) 6,760 km, *4,050 naut miles (4,663 miles) 7,500 km or 4,150 naut miles (4,778 miles) 7,690 km maximum with optional fuel*, with reserve

Pressurization: 8.3 psi cabin differential.
Freight hold volume: 5,205 cu ft (147.4 m^3).
Freight hold capacity: LD3 containers are carried 2-abreast in the underfloor holds, and full-sized pallet capability is a standard feature of the forward hold. Full range of existing containers and pallets can be loaded. Forward underfloor hold loads can be 12 LD3 containers or 4 pallets (88 or 96 × 125 ins, 2.23 or 2.44 × 3.18 m), and rear hold can be 10 LD3s and 610 cu ft (17.3 m^3) of bulk or optionally 11 LD3s and 318 cu ft (9 m^3) of bulk.

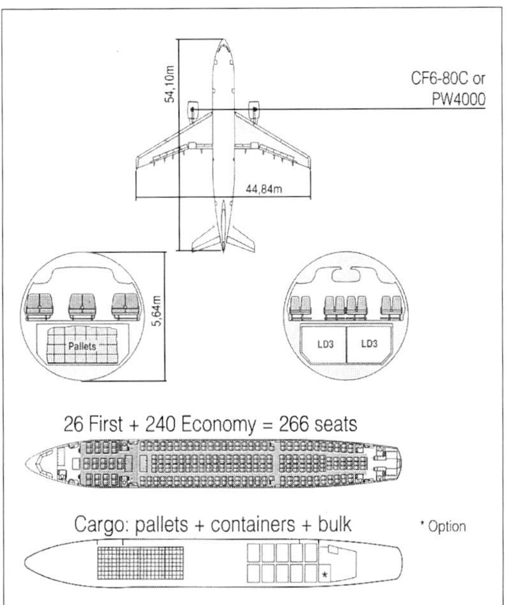

↑ Airbus A300-600 configurations *(courtesy Airbus Industrie)*

Freight hold access: 106 ins × 67.5 ins (2.69 × 1.71 m) forward cargo door.
Wing characteristics: Wing derived from the previous A300B but with aerodynamic improvements by introducing a new inner wing section and also wingtip fences to reduce cruise drag (1°), while deleting the slat fence and outboard aileron.
Flight controls and system: Mechanically controlled and hydraulically operated ailerons, elevators and rudder. Fly-by-wire for tailplane incidence (with mechanical back-up), flaps and Krueger flaps, 2 position slats, spoilers/speedbrakes and lift-dumpers.
Construction materials: Includes 14,550 lb (6,600 kg) of composites for some primary and secondary structures, including fin (carbonfibre), floor struts and panels, spoilers and main undercarriage doors.
Engines: 2 × 56,000 lbf (249.1 kN) Pratt & Whitney PW4156 or 58,000 lbf (258 kN) PW4158 turbofans. Alternatively 59,000 lbf (262.45 kN) General Electric CF6-80C2A1, 60,200 lbf (267.79 kN) CF6-80C2A3, or 61,500 lbf (273.57 kN) CF6-80C2A5 turbofans. AlliedSignal APU.
Engine rating: See above.
Fuel system: 62,000 litres. A300-600R adds a 6,150 litre tank in the tailplane, with a computerized fuel transfer system for active centre-of-gravity control. Optional 73,000 litres for -600R.
Electrical system: AC supply via 2 engine-driven and 1 APU-driven 90 kVA generators, with time-limited overload ratings up to 150 kVA. Fourth hydraulically-driven AC generator (5 kVA) for ETOPS. 28 volt DC supply from AC system via 3 transformer rectifiers. 3 × 25 amp-hour ni-cd batteries for APU start-up and emergency power.
Hydraulic system: 3 independent systems, each 3,000 psi. 1 also provides for ETOPS generator (see Electrical).
Braking system: Carbon discs, with anti-skid. Optional automatic system.
De-icing system: Bleed air for wing leading edges and engine intakes. Electric for cockpit glazing, sensors, static vents and pitots.
Fire system: See Aircraft variants.
Radar: Weather radar.
Flight avionics/instrumentation: Fully digital avionics and flight management systems. EFIS with primary flight displays (PFD) and navigation displays (ND) CRTs. Electronic centralized aircraft monitor (ECAM). Cat IIIb autoland. Windshear warning and guidance system. Common type rating with A310.

Aircraft variants:
A300-600 was launched as the basic passenger model, also available in convertible passenger/freight versions.
A300-600R is the extended range model, available in passenger and convertible passenger/freight versions. Active centre-of-gravity control system. 180 minutes ETOPS equipped, with fourth AC generator and extra cargo hold fire suppression bottle.
A300-600C is the convertible passenger or freight version of either the standard A300-600 or -600R. Maximum structural payload is 106,042 lb (48,100 kg) in freighter mode.
A300-600F is the dedicated all-freight version of the A300-600 or -600R. Main deck compartment can be configured to carry a single row of 88/96 × 125 ins pallets or a double row of 88 × 125 ins pallets. Differences from the passenger aircraft are the addition of a large cargo door on the main deck, reinforced main deck floor, deletion of passenger doors numbers 2, 3 and 4 (left and right), deletion of cabin windows except as required for maintenance, deletion of all passenger-associated systems and equipment, addition of a semi-automatic cargo loading system, Class E main deck fire protection and Class C lower deck, and active centre-of-gravity control system on the maximum-range model. Main deck accommodates 9 pallets of 88/96 × 125 ins (2.23/2.44 × 3.18 m) and 6 of 88 × 125 ins (2.23 × 3.18 m). Lower deck accommodates 4 pallets plus 10 LD3 containers or 22 LD3s. Powered by 58,000 to 61,500 lbf (258 to 273.57 kN) CF6-80C2A5 or PW4158 engines. Maximum take-off weights are 375,888 lb (170,500 kg) for the basic maximum range version, and 363,982 lb (165,100 kg) for the optional maximum payload version. Maximum-range version range is 2,650 naut miles (3,051 miles) 4,908 km, and maximum-payload version range is 1,950 naut miles (2,245 miles) 3,611 km. Standard fuel 68,150 litres, with 44,400 litres optional. First example to Federal Express in April 1994.

Airbus A310

First flight: 3 April 1982.
Certification: 11 March 1983.
First delivery: 29 March 1983 to Swissair and Lufthansa, starting commercial services that April.
Role: Short-medium range widebody airliner.
Airport limits: Flexible runway ACN (Cat B) for A310-200 is 43 with standard undercarriage and 41 with optional wider main bogies.
Noise levels: *A310-200 with GE engines:* 89.6 EPNdB at take-off, 96.4 EPNdB sideline, 98.6 EPNdB approach.
Sales: Total of 261 had been ordered by June 1998, of which 254 had been delivered and 251 were in operation.

Details *(A310 passenger versions)*

Crew: 2 (flight).
Passengers: Typically 220 in 2-class layout (20 first class at 40 ins/103 cm seat pitch, and 200 economy at 32 ins/81 cm pitch), 191 in 3-class layout (12 first at 62 ins/157 cm pitch, 32 business at 40 ins/103 cm pitch, and 147 economy at 32 ins/81 cm pitch), 240 in 2-class regional layout (28 business at 36 ins/91 cm pitch, and 212 economy at 30 ins/76 cm or 31 ins/79 cm pitch), and 280 high-density layout (all economy at 29/30 ins, 73.7/76 cm pitch). Emirates A310 was (in 1992) the first airliner to offer every passenger in all classes their own video display and choice of programmes. Same airline pioneered multichannel telephone calls (via satellite) in 1993. 6-abreast first class seating, 7-abreast business, 8-abreast coach/economy, and 9-abreast high-density, all with 2 aisles.
Pressurization: 8.3 psi cabin differential.
Freight hold capacity: LD3 containers are carried 2-abreast in the underfloor holds, and full-sized pallet capability is a standard feature of the forward hold. Full range of existing containers and pallets can be loaded. Forward underfloor hold loads can be 8 LD3 containers, or 4 LD6 containers, or 3 pallets (88 or 96 × 125 ins, 2.23 or 2.44 × 3.18 m). Rear hold loads can be 6 LD3s or 3 LD6s plus 610 cu ft (17.3 m^3) of bulk, or optionally 7 LD3s and

↑ Airbus A310-300 in Kenya Airways livery

318 cu ft (9 m^3) of bulk.
Freight hold access: 106 ins × 67.5 ins (2.69 × 1.71 m) forward cargo door.
Wing characteristics: Outer wing design is aerodynamically clean, with no vortex generators.
Wing control surfaces: Generally similar to A300-600.
Tail control surfaces: Generally similar to A300-600.
Flight control system: Generally similar to A300-600.
Construction materials: Includes 13,670 lb (6,200 kg) of composites for some primary and secondary structures, including fin (carbonfibre), floor struts and panels, spoilers and main undercarriage doors. A310 was the first commercial airliner to be certified with a composite primary structure (fin). Wing/body, wing/pylon/nacelle, and inner wing areas incorporate an advanced 3-dimensional aerodynamic design.
Engines: 2 × 52,000 lbf (231.3 kN) Pratt & Whitney PW4152 or 56,000 lbf (249.1 kN) PW4156A turbofans. Alternatively 53,500 lbf (238 kN) General Electric CF6-80C2A2 or 59,000 lbf (262.45 kN) CF6-80C2A8 turbofans. AlliedSignal APU.
180 minutes ETOPS.
Fuel system: A310-200 has 54,920 litres usable. A310-300 adds a 6,150 litre tank in the tailplane, with a computerized fuel transfer system for active centre-of-gravity control. In addition, extra fuel volume for -300 can be provided by fitting 1 or 2 × 7,200 litre usable fuel ACTs (additional centre tanks) in the aft main cargo compartment, raising usable fuel to 68,470 or 75,470 litres. ACTs can be fitted/removed overnight, with a removable bulkhead installed behind the tanks, and feed to/from the centre wing tank.

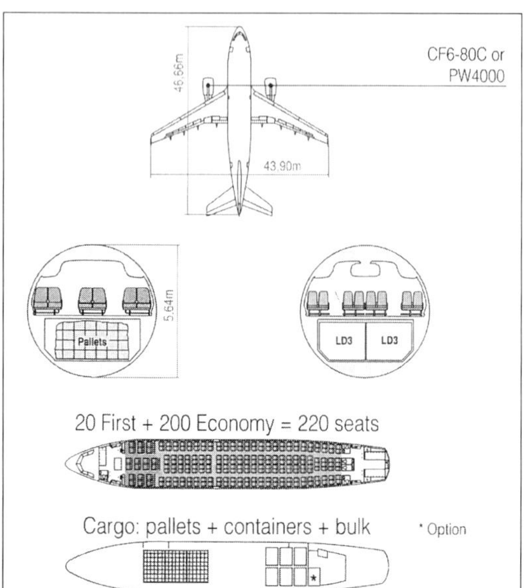

↑ Airbus A310 configurations *(courtesy Airbus Industrie)*

Details for A310-200, *with A310-300 in italics where different*

PRINCIPAL DIMENSIONS:
Wing span: 144 ft (43.9 m)
Maximum length: 153 ft 1 ins (46.66 m)
Maximum height: 51 ft 10 ins (15.8 m)

CABIN:
Length: 109 ft (33.24 m)
Width: 17 ft 4 ins (5.28 m)
Main passenger door: 6 ft 4 ins × 3 ft 6 ins (1.93 × 1.07 m)

WINGS:
Area: 2,357.29 sq ft (219 m^2)
Aspect ratio: 8.8

TAIL UNIT:
Tailplane span: As for A300-600

UNDERCARRIAGE:
Type: As for A300-600, but with smaller main wheel tyres standard and both A300-600 tyre sizes as options to reduce runway ACN
Main wheel tyre size: 46 × 16-20
Nose wheel tyre size: As for A300-600
Wheel base: 49 ft 11 ins (15.21 m)
Wheel track: As for A300-600
Turning radius: 108 ft 3 ins (33 m) wingtip

WEIGHTS:
Empty, operating: typically 177,692 lb (80,600 kg), *178,133 lb (80,800 kg)*
Maximum zero fuel: 249,122 lb (113,000 kg) standard, 251,326 lb (114,000 kg) optional
Maximum take-off: 313,056 lb (142,000 kg), *330,693 lb standard or 337,307 lb, 346,125 lb, or 361,558 lb options (150,000 kg, 153,000 kg, 157,000 kg, or 164,000 kg)*
Maximum landing: 271,168 lb (123,000 kg) standard, 273,373 lb (124,000 kg) optional

PERFORMANCE:
Economic cruise speed: Mach 0.8
Approach speed: 135 kts (155 mph) 250 km/h
Take-off field length: 5,900-6,100 ft (1,800-1,860 m) depending on engines, *7,300-about 9,600 ft (2,225-2,926 m), depending on engines and standard/optional weights*, sea level and ISA +15°
Landing distance: under 4,500 ft (1,375 m) at typical landing weight, and just over 5,000 ft (1,525 m) at optional MLW, sea level
Initial cruise altitude: 37,000 ft (11,275 m) eastbound, 35,000 ft (10,670 m) westbound.
Range with 220 passengers and GE engines: 3,600 naut miles (4,145 miles) 6,667 km, *4,300-5,150 naut miles (4,951-5,930 miles) 7,963-9,538 km*
Range with 220 passengers and P&W engines: 3,650 naut miles (4,203 miles) 6,760 km, *4,350-5,200 naut miles (5,009-5,988 miles) 8,056-9,630 km*

Electrical system: AC supply via 2 engine-driven and 1 APU-driven 90 kVA generators, with time-limited overload ratings up to 180 kVA. Fourth hydraulically-driven AC generator (5 kVA) for ETOPS. 28 volt DC supply from AC system via 3 transformer rectifiers. 3 × 25 amp-hour ni-cd batteries for APU start-up and emergency power.
Hydraulic system: 3 independent systems, each 3,000 psi. 1 also provides for ETOPS generator (see Electrical).
Braking system: Generally similar to A300-600.
De-icing system: Generally similar to A300-600.
Flight avionics/instrumentation: Same cockpit as the A300-600.

Aircraft variants:
A310-200 is the standard version, with many features of the larger A300.
A310-300 is the extended-range version with 2 further fuel options. Active centre-of-gravity control system. 180 minutes ETOPS equipped, with fourth AC generator and extra cargo hold fire suppression bottle.
A310C is the convertible version of either model, with a large main deck door, for all-passenger or all-freight operations. Maximum structural payload is 91,490 lb (41,500 kg). 3,000 naut mile (3,454 mile) 5,556 km range with a 40 tonne load.
A310F is the dedicated freighter variant. Same range as Convertible.
Freighter Retrofit conversion kit, as detailed under A300B2/B4, is also available for the A310. DASA's freighter conversions on order in 1998 included A310s.

Airbus Multi Role Tanker Transport (MRTT)

Comments: This is a conversion of the Airbus A310-300, designed and marketed by the Airbus partners. Produced either from a newly-built aircraft or an existing A310, it combines the roles of flight refuelling tanker and military transport. In the tanker role it carries nearly 77 tonnes of fuel for air-to-air refuelling, delivered via 2 underwing pods, a rear fuselage hose drum kit, or a refuelling boom. It can also receive fuel through a receptacle or probe mounted above the cockpit. As a military freighter it features the addition of a main-deck cargo door and strengthened floor, an efficient cargo loading system, and the possibility of palletized seating for a quick role change. Palletized and containerized freight can include 17 military pallets, each 88 ins × 108 ins (2.24 × 2.74 m), in a convertible role. As a medical transport, up to 60 litters plus 32 seats can be accommodated, or portable First Aid centres.

↑ Airbus Multi Role Tanker Transport (MRTT) impression

Airbus A318 and A319

First flight: 29 August 1995 for A319 (as described below).
Certification: 10 April 1996 for JAA with CFM56-5B engines and 18 December 1996 with IAE V2524 engines.
First delivery: 25 April 1996 for Swissair operations (CFM engines).
Role: Short-medium range, reduced-length and lower-capacity variant of the A320.
Airframe life: Service life before major repair of 48,000 flights of 1.25 hours average, 24,000 flights crack-free fatigue life, and 20,000 flights initial threshold for inspection.
Airport limits: Flexible runway ACN (Cat B) is 34 at standard MTOW and 37 at optional MTOW with standard undercarriage, or 19 and 18 respectively with 4-wheel main bogie undercarriage option.
Noise levels: Estimated for CFM/IAE engines as FAR 36 Stage 3 and ICAO Annex 16 Chapter 3 limits –4.5/–7.9 take-off, –3.2/–5.4 sideline, and –4.4/–4.7 approach.

↑ Airbus A319 in Lufthansa livery

Sales: Total of 461 ordered by June 1998, of which 84 had been delivered.

Details *(see A320 entry for other common details)*

Passengers: Typically 134 seats in single-class layout (32 ins, 81 cm seat pitch), 124 seats in 2-class layout (8 first at 36 ins, 91 cm pitch and 116 economy at 32 ins, 81 cm pitch), 129 seats in alternative 2-class layout (55 business at 34 ins, 86 cm pitch and 74 economy at 31ins, 79 cm or 32ins, 81 cm pitch), or 145 seats in high-density layout (29 ins, 74 cm or 30 ins, 76 cm pitch). 4-abreast first class, 5-abreast international business class, and 6-abreast economy, the latter with either 19 ins (48 cm) or alternative 25 ins (64 cm) aisle. All single aisle. See Aircraft variants for A319CJ.
Freight hold capacity: 11 ft (3.35 m) long forward hold with a capacity of 301 cu ft (8.52 m^3), and 25 ft 2 ins (7.67 m) long aft hold with a capacity of 675 cu ft (19.12 m^3), giving a total of 976 cu ft (27.64 m^3) or 4 LD3-46 or LD3-46W containers plus bulk.
Loading facilities: Optional widebody-compatible mechanized semi-automatic cargo container system.
Fuselage: 3 frames removed forward of the wings (5 ft 3 ins, 1.6 m) and 4 frames aft of the wings (7ft, 2.13 m) compared with the A320. Modified rear cargo hold door, with deleted bulk hold door. Forward overwing emergency exit deleted.
Engines: 2 × 22,000 lbf (97.86 kN) CFM International CFM56-5A4 turbofans, or similarly rated International Aero Engine V2522-A5s. Optional 23,500 lbf (104.54 kN) CFM56-5A5s, 22,000 lbf (97.86 kN) CFM56-5B5s, 23,500 lbf (104.54 kN) CFM56-5B6s or 23,500 lbf (104.54 kN) V2524-A5s. AlliedSignal 36-300 APU.
Fuel system: 23,860 litres.
Flight avionics/instrumentation: Almost identical to the A320/A330/A340. Similar pilot type rating for A319, A320 and A321. Sextant Avionique multi-mode receiver (MMR) approach and landing aid system offered from the latter part of 1997, integrating 3 landing guidance systems (ILS, MLS and GLS) and also offering a continuous GPS satellite navigation function.

Aircraft variants:
A318 (formerly A319M5) is a new 107–117 seat derivative of A319, revealed at the September 1998 Farnborough Air Show. Shorter than A319 by 4.5 frames, and carrying no containerized cargo. PW6000 engines. 1,500–2,000 naut mile range.
A319 airliner, as detailed.
A319CJ is a corporate jet variant, capable of carrying 8 to 50 passengers in widebody comfort over ranges exceeding 6,300 naut miles (7,254 miles) 11,675 km. Modular cabin concept for flexibility on main deck and cargo hold. Containerized cargo hold and outward opening cargo door permit easy rearrangement of auxiliary fuel tanks. Cruise speed Mach 0.82 and 41,000 ft (12,500 m) maximum altitude. Orders include 2 for the Italian Air Force, replacing VIP DC-9s, and 1 for a Kuwaiti customer.

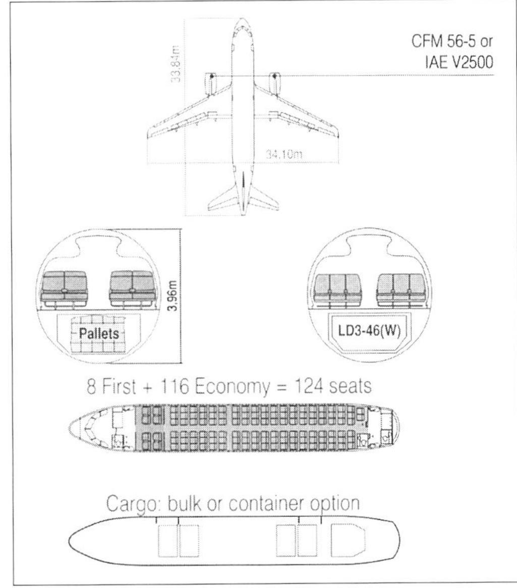

↑ Airbus A319 configurations *(courtesy Airbus Industrie)*

Details for A319, unless stated

PRINCIPAL DIMENSIONS:
Wing span: 111 ft 10 ins (34.1 m)
Maximum length: 111 ft (33.84 m)
Maximum height: 38 ft 7 ins (11.76 m)
Fuselage width: 12 ft 11 ins (3.95 m)

UNDERCARRIAGE:
Turning radius: 39 ft 8 ins (12.1 m) from centre of turn to nose gear. Nosewheels steering angle 75°, with 70° effective turn. 67 ft 7 ins (20.6 m) minimum pavement width for a 180° turn

WEIGHTS:
Empty, operating: typically 88,538 lb (40,160 kg)
Maximum zero fuel: 125,663 lb (57,000 kg)
Maximum take-off: 141,110 lb (64,000 kg) basic, 149,914-162,040 lb (68,000-73,500 kg) optional
Maximum landing: 134,448 lb (61,000 kg) basic, 137,788 lb (62,500 kg) optional

PERFORMANCE:
Cruise speed: Mach 0.82 for A319CJ
Take-off field length: 5,118-8,793 ft (1,560-2,680 m), sea level, ISA + 15 ° C, depending on engines and weights
Landing field length (CFM-56-5 engines): 4,000 ft (1,220 m) at typical landing weight of 120,000 lb (54,430 kg), sea level
Landing field length at MLW (CFM56-5 engines): 4,500 ft (1,372 m), at sea level
Maximum altitude: 41,000 ft (12,500 m) for A319CJ
Initial cruise altitude: 37,000 ft (11,275 m) eastbound, 35,000 ft (10,670 m) westbound
Range with 124 passengers: 1,850 naut miles (2,130 miles) 3,428 km at basic MTOW, or 3,500 naut miles (4,030 miles) 6,486 km at optional MTOW
Range for A319CJ: over 6,300 naut miles (7,254 miles) 11,675 km

Airbus A320

First flight: 22 February 1987.
Certification: 26 February 1988.
First delivery: 28 March 1988 to Air France.
Role: Short-medium range airliner.
Airframe life: Service life before major repair of 48,000 flights of 1.25 hours average, 24,000 flights crack-free fatigue life, and 20,000 flights initial threshold for inspection.
Airport limits: Flexible runway ACN (Cat B) is 41 at standard MTOW and 42 at optional MTOW with standard undercarriage, or 22 and 23 respectively with 4-wheel main bogie undercarriage option.
Noise levels: CFM/IAE engines as FAR 36 Stage 3 and ICAO Annex 16 Chapter 3 limits -3.7/-4.9 take-off, -2.5/-4 sideline, and -4.1/-3.9 approach, at basic MTOW. For derated A321 (IAE) type engines at 75,500 kg MTOW the figures are -5.9 take-off, -4.1 sideline and -4.7 approach.

Details

Sales: Total of 987 ordered by June 1998, of which 642 had been delivered and 636 were in service.
Crew: 2 (flight).
Passengers: Typically 164 seats in single-class layout (32 ins, 81 cm pitch), 150 seats in 2-class layout (12 super first class at 36 ins, 91 cm pitch, and 138 economy at 32 ins, 81 cm pitch), 137 in alternative 2-class layout (30 business at 38 or 39 ins, 97 or 99 cm pitch, and 107 economy at 32 ins, 81 cm pitch), and 180 in high-density layout (29 ins, 74 cm pitch). 4-abreast in super first class seating arrangement, with 57 ins (145 cm) double seats and 27 ins (69 cm) aisle. 5-abreast in business class and 6-abreast in economy, the latter with standard 19 ins (48 cm) aisle or alternative 25 ins (64 cm) aisle. A320 pioneered digital cabin management systems with cabin intercommunication data system (CIDS). The CIDS is responsible for the operation of cabin lighting, pre-recorded messages, emergency evacuation signalling and other tasks. It can also verify the amount of portable water on board and allow cabin staff to preselect the quantity to be uplifted. CIDS is linked to the centralized fault display system.
Galleys and toilets: Modular concept for interior fittings, easing reconfiguration.
Freight hold volume: Forward hold of 16 ft 3 ins (4.95 m) length for 469 cu ft (13.28 m^3) volume, and 32 ft 2 ins (9.8 m) length aft hold for 900 cu ft (25.48 m^3), giving a total bulk volume of 1,369 cu ft (38.76 m^3).
Freight hold capacity: 3 LD3-46 or -46W containers in the forward hold and 4 aft, plus 208 cu ft (5.89 m^3) of bulk.
Loading facilities: Optional semi-automatic container system.
Wing characteristics: Introduced a totally new higher aspect ratio wing. Winglets.
Wing control surfaces: Aileron, 2-section Fowler flaps, 5-section leading-edge slats and 5 spoilers per wing. Spoilers are divided as 4 on the swept wing panels and 1 on the inner panel, functioning for auxiliary roll control, wing load alleviation in gusts (with the ailerons), lift dumpers, and speedbrakes.
Tail control surfaces: Trimmable tailplane, elevators and rudder.

↑ Air Canada Airbus A320

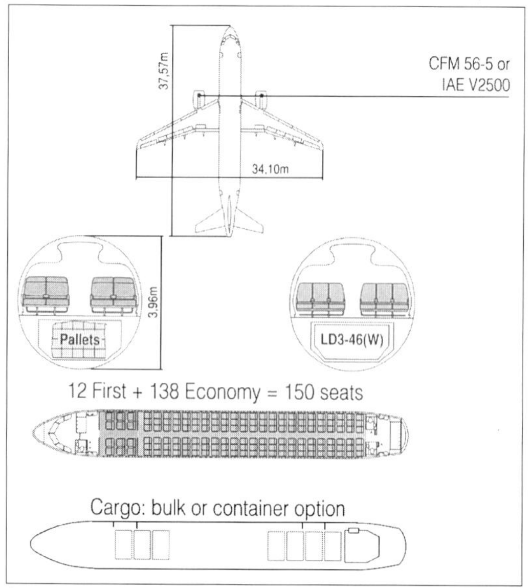

↑ **Airbus A320 configurations** *(courtesy Airbus Industrie)*

Flight control system: Electronic flight control system (EFCS) with fly-by-wire control for all wing and tail surfaces, with hydraulic actuation, except for the rudder which is mechanically operated but connected to the EFCS system via the flight augmentation computer (FAC). Mechanical signalling is also retained as a stand-by mode for the trimmable tailplane. High level of redundancy, with 5 EFCS computers installed, of which 2 are ELAC (elevator and aileron computer) and 3 SEC (spoiler and elevator computer). Spoiler and elevator reversionary mode has been retained as an independent system. The EFCS system is said to offer total flight envelope protection, as the aircraft cannot be stalled or overspeeded, and offers windshear protection. It also prevents structural overstressing, offers better obstacle avoidance capability, and the load alleviation system reduces wing loads in gusts by aileron and spoiler deflection.
Construction materials: Includes improved aluminium alloys and extensive use of composites, the latter for the tail unit, wing control surfaces, wing/body fairings, engine pylons and nacelles, undercarriage doors and fairings, nosecone, and furnishings and floor panels. Weight saving of 1,764 lb (800 kg).
Engines: 2 × 25,000 lbf (111.21 kN) CFM International CFM56-5A1 or International Aero Engines V2500-A1 turbofans standard, with options of 26,500 lbf (117.88 kN) CFM56-5A3s, 26,500 lbf (117.88 kN) CFM56-5B4s, and 26,500 lbf (117.88 kN) V2527-A5s, with FADEC.
Engine rating: See above.
Fuel system: 23,860 litres.
Electrical system: 115/200 volt, 400 Hz AC supply via 2 engine-driven and 1 APU-driven 90 kVA generators. DC supply via transformer rectifiers.
Braking system: Carbon wheel brakes.
Flight avionics/instrumentation: ARINC 700 digital suite, incorporating SFENA autopilot. Advanced flight deck with sidestick controllers for the pilots and only 12 front-panel instruments, with CRTs that are identical and interchangeable, with automatic display reconfiguration in the event of a CRT failure. Thomson-CSF/VDO EFIS has 6 CRT displays, comprising 2 primary flight displays (PFDs), 2 navigation displays (NDs), and 2 multi-purpose displays for engine/warning (ECAM upper screen) and systems data (lower screen). The multi-purpose displays access the Honeywell flight management system (FMS) and are also used to provide maintenance data in the air and on the ground, upon request. The system is coupled to a printer and can also be coupled to an optional Aircraft Communication Addressing and Reporting System (ACARS) link. Common crew type rating with A319 and A321, and cross-crew qualification with the A330 and A340. Centralized fault display system.

Details for A320

PRINCIPAL DIMENSIONS:
Wing span: 111 ft 10 ins (34.1 m)
Maximum length: 123 ft 3 ins (37.57 m)
Maximum height: 38 ft 7 ins (11.76 m)
Fuselage width: 12 ft 11 ins (3.95 m)

CABIN:
Length: 89 ft 10 ins (27.38 m)
Width: 12 ft 1 ins (3.7 m)
Height: 7 ft 3.5 ins (2.22 m)
Main passenger doors: 6 ft 1 ins × 2 ft 8 ins (1.85 × 0.81 m)

TAIL UNIT:
Tailplane span: 40 ft 10 ins (12.45 m)

UNDERCARRIAGE:
Type: Retractable, with twin steerable nosewheels. Standard twin main wheel units but optional 4-wheel bogies to reduce runway ACN
Main wheel tyre size: 45 × 16-R20 standard, but various options available
Nose wheel tyre size: 30 × 8.8-R15, but options available
Wheel base: 41 ft 5.25 ins (12.63 m)
Wheel track: 24 ft 11 ins (7.59 m)

WEIGHTS:
Empty, operating: typically 92,153 lb (41,800 kg)
Maximum zero fuel: 134,480 lb (61,000 kg)
Maximum take-off: 162,040 lb (73,500 kg) basic, 166,450 lb or 169,755 lb (75,500 kg or 77,000 kg) optional
Maximum landing: 142,200 lb (64,500 kg)

PERFORMANCE:
Cruise speed: Mach 0.78 to 0.8
Take-off field length: Minimum 6,700 ft (2,337 m) and maximum over 8,000 ft (2,440 m) with 150 passengers, sea level, ISA + 15° C, depending on engines fitted
Landing field length: Meets FAR Pt 25 Amendment 42 requirements
Cruise altitude: 37,000 ft (11,275 m) eastbound, with full passenger load on sectors up to 2,500 naut miles
High cruise altitude: 35,000-39,000 ft (10,670-11,890 m), former achievable at all weights
Range (CFM engines): 2,700-2,850 naut miles (3,109-3,282 miles) 5,000-5,278 km, standard to maximum optional take-off weights
Range (IAE engines): 2,750-2,950 naut miles (3,166-3,397 miles) 5,093-5,463 km, standard to maximum optional take-off weights

Airbus A321

First flight: 11 March 1993 (as first Airbus assembled in Germany). 12 December 1996 for A321-200.
Certification: 17 December 1993 (European certification, with IAE V2530 engines). European certification with CFM56-5Bs 17 February 1994.
First delivery: 27 January 1994, to Lufthansa.
Role: Lengthened version of the A320, with major changes relating principally to size and capacity.
Airframe life: As for A320.
Airport limits: Flexible runway (Cat B) ACN 48 at basic weight.
Noise levels: CFM56-5B1/V2500-A5 engines as FAR 36 Stage 3 and ICAO Annex 16 Chapter 3 limits –5.3/–6.8 take-off, –1.7/–2.7 sideline, and –5.5/–5.5 approach.

Aims

- Offers 24% more seats and 40% more hold volume than A320, whilst retaining maximum commonality with the A320/A319. Uprated undercarriage, modified wing trailing edges, local structural reinforcement, repositioned and larger emergency exits, and uprated engines.

Details for A321-100

PRINCIPAL DIMENSIONS:
Wing span: 111 ft 10 ins (34.1 m)
Maximum length: 146 ft (44.51 m)
Maximum height: 38 ft 9 ins (11.81 m)
Fuselage width: 12 ft 11 ins (3.95 m)

CABIN:
Length: 112 ft 10 ins (34.39 m)
Width: 12 ft 1 ins (3.7 m)
Height: 7 ft 3.5 ins (2.22 m)
Main passenger doors: 6 ft 1 ins × 2 ft 8 ins (1.85 × 0.81 m)

UNDERCARRIAGE:
Type: Uprated from A320 type, with larger tyres
Turning radius: 59 ft (18 m) radius from centre of turn to nose gear. Minimum pavement width for a 180° turn is 95 ft (29 m)

WEIGHTS:
Empty, operating: typically 105,600 lb (47,900 kg)
Maximum zero fuel: 153,220 lb (69,500 kg) basic, 155,425 lb (70,500 kg) optional
Maximum take-off: 182,983 lb (83,000 kg) basic, 187,393 lb (85,000 kg) optional
Maximum landing: 162,039 lb (73,500 kg) basic, 164,244 lb (74,500 kg) optional

PERFORMANCE:
Cruise speed: Mach 0.78 to 0.8
Take-off field length: typically 4,925-5,580 ft (1,500-1,700 m), sea level, ISA + 15° C, for 500-1,000 naut miles ranges
Landing field length: typically 4,925 ft (1,500 m)
Initial cruise altitude: 37,000 ft (11,275 m) eastbound, 35,000 ft (10,670 m) westbound
Range with 185 passengers (CFM engines): 2,200-2,300 naut miles (2,533-2,648 miles) 4,074-4,259 km, basic-optional MTOW
Range with 185 passengers (IAE engines): 2,250-2,350 naut miles (2,591-2,706 miles) 4,167-4,352 km, basic-optional MTOW
Maximum range: 2,650 naut miles (3,051 miles) 4,908 km

Details *(A321-100)*

Sales: 215 ordered by June 1998, of which 96 had been delivered and all 96 were in operation.
Crew: 2 (flight).
Passengers: Typically 199 seats in single-class layout (32 ins, 81 cm pitch), 185 seats in 2-class layout (16 super first class at 36 ins, 91 cm pitch, and 169 economy at 31 or 32 ins, 79 or 81 cm pitch), and 220 in high-density layout (28 or 29 ins, 71 or 74 cm pitch). 4-abreast in super first class seating arrangement, with 57 ins (145 cm) double seats and 27 ins (69 cm) aisle. 5-abreast in business class and 6-abreast in economy, the latter with standard 19 ins (48 cm) aisle or alternative 25 ins (64 cm) aisle. CIDS as for A320.
Seat pitch: See above.
Freight hold volume: Forward hold of 27 ft 1 ins (8.27 m) length for 806 cu ft (22.82 m^3) volume, and 37 ft 5 ins (11.39 m) length aft hold for 1,022 cu ft (28.94 m^3), giving a total bulk volume of 1,828 cu ft (51.76 m^3).

↑ **Austrian Airlines Airbus A321**

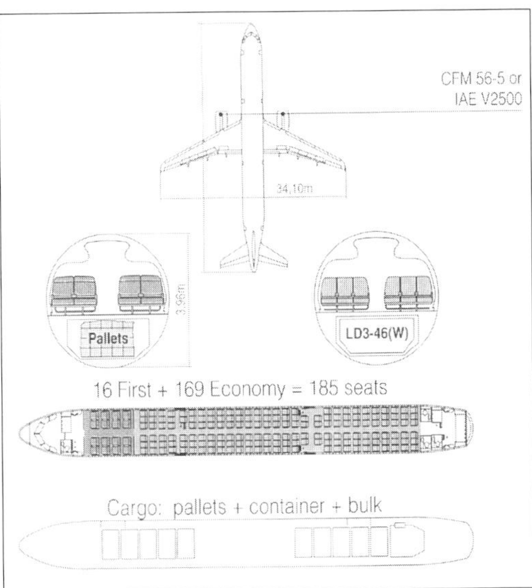

↑ **Airbus A321 configurations** *(courtesy Airbus Industrie)*

Freight hold capacity: 5 LD3-46 or -46W containers in the forward hold and 5 aft, plus 208 cu ft (5.89 m^3) of bulk.
Loading facilities: Optional semi-automatic container system.
Flight control system: As for A320.
Fuselage: A320 fuselage lengthened by the addition of 8 frames forward of the wings (14 ft, 4.26 m) and 5 frames aft (8 ft 9 ins, 2.67 m).
Construction materials: As for A320.
Engines: 2 CFM International CFM56-5B1 or International Aero Engines V2530-A5 turbofans, each 30,000 lbf (133.45 kN). Optional 31,000 lbf (137.9 kN) CFM56-5B2s. A321-200 options of 33,000 lbf (146.29 kN) CFM56-5B3s or V2533-A5s of similar rating. AlliedSignal or APIC APU.
Engine rating: See above.
Fuel system: 23,700 litres.
Systems: Generally as for A320 but adapted as necessary.
Flight avionics/instrumentation: As for A320.

Aircraft variants:
A321-100 is the original version, as detailed.
A321-200 is the extended range version, with 33,000 lbf (146.79 kN) V2533-A5 or CFM56-5B3 turbofans and an additional 2,900 litre fuel tank. First flown 12 December 1996. Launch customer was Aero Lloyd of Germany, which placed firm orders for 4 in 212-seat single-class layout. Maximum take-off weight is 196,200 lb (89,000 kg), maximum landing weight 166,450 lb (75,500 kg), and maximum zero fuel weight 157,630 lb (71,500 kg). Range is extended by about 400-600 naut miles.

Airbus A330

First flight: 2 November 1992 (CF6 engines). 13 August 1997 for A330-200 version.
Certification: 21 October 1993 with GE engines, the first aircraft ever to gain simultaneous European and US certification. 3 June 1994 with PW4000 engines, and 22 December 1994 with Trent 700 engines. Certification for A330-200 with GE, P&W and R-R engines in 1998, with the CF6-80E1-engined version becoming the first airliner to gain triple certification (JAA, FAA and Transport Canada) on 31 March 1998.
First delivery: 30 December 1993 to Air Inter, starting commercial services in January 1994. April 1998 for A330-200 (to Canada 3000).
Role: Medium-extended range widebody airliner, with some airlines operating short-haul high-density routes.
Airport limits: A330-300 flexible pavement (Cat b) ACN is 59 at MTOW, and 64 for the higher gross weight version.

Aims

▪ A330 technologies include advanced aerofoil sections, high-lift devices from root to tip on both leading and trailing edges to ensure optimum low-speed efficiency, centre-of-gravity management system via fuel in the tailplane and a computerized fuel transfer system, extended fly-by-wire/computer system, maximum use of new airframe materials and processes, and increased thrust versions of proven engines.

Details *(A330-300)*

Sales: 238 ordered by June 1998, of which 69 had been delivered.
Crew: 2 (flight).
Passengers: Typically 335 seats in 2-class layout (30 first class at 40 ins, 103 cm seat pitch and 305 economy at 33 or 34 ins, 84 or 86 cm pitch), 295 seats in 3-class layout (18 sleeperette at 60 ins, 152 cm pitch, 81 business at 36 ins, 91 cm pitch, and 196 economy at 34 ins, 86 cm pitch), and 398 or 440 seats in high-density layouts (31 ins, 79 cm pitch). 6-abreast sleeperette/international first class, 7-abreast business, 8-abreast economy, and 9-abreast high-density, all with 2 aisles. CIDS system (see A320). See Aircraft variants.
Galleys: Alternative galley locations.
Toilets: Many possible cabin positions. Special facilities for handicapped passengers.
Freight hold capacity: Forward hold accommodates 18 LD3 containers or 6 pallets (each 88 or 96 ins, 2.24 or 2.44 m), and rear hold accommodates 14 LD3s or 5 pallets of 88 ins. Alternative rear hold layouts for 3 larger 96 ins and 2 small 88 ins pallets, or 4 large pallets and 2 LD3s. Optional additional LD3 in the separate 695 cu ft (19.7 m^3) rear bulk hold, reducing bulk volume to 486 cu ft (13.8 m^3).
Loading facilities: Large cargo doors are standard in both forward and aft holds, allowing any mix of pallets and containers in either hold. Can carry any standard unit load device, using standard ground equipment.
Wing characteristics: All-new wing with high levels of efficiency. High-lift devices over the root-to-tip of both leading and trailing edges, with leading-edge slats (typically 21°), flaps (typically 26°) and aileron droop (typically 15°). Winglets.
Wing control surfaces: 2-section outboard ailerons, 2-section single-slotted flaps, 7-section leading-edge slats, and 6 spoiler sections (latter functioning for roll control with the ailerons, and as speed brakes and lift dumpers).
Tail control surfaces: Trimmable tailplane, elevators and rudder.
Flight control system: Electronic flight control system (EFCS) with fly-by-wire control for all wing and tail surfaces, with hydraulic actuation (3 hydraulic systems), except for the rudder which is connected to the EFCS system but has a mechanical link, while stabilizer trimming is also mechanically backed-up. The pilots' sidestick controllers and the autopilot link to 3 flight control primary computers (FCPC), which serve the spoilers, ailerons, elevators, rudder and stabilizer. The sidestick controllers also link to 2 flight control secondary computers (FCSC), which serve the spoilers, rudder (trim/travel limit), and are stand-by for the ailerons and elevators. The EFCS system is said to offer total flight envelope protection, as the aircraft cannot be stalled or overspeeded, and offers windshear protection. It also prevents structural overstressing, and offers better obstacle avoidance capability.
Construction materials and processes: Include aluminium-lithium, and superplastic forming and diffusion bonding techniques for the inspection hatches, tailcone cap, slat mechanism cans and canopy parts. Composites used on the vertical and horizontal tail, moving surfaces, fairings and cabin floor panels.
Engines: 2 × 67,500 lbf (300.26 kN) General Electric CF6-80E1A2, 64,000 lbf (284.7 kN) Pratt & Whitney PW4164, or 67,500 lbf (300.26 kN) Rolls-Royce Trent 768 turbofans are standard on the A330-300. Optional engines for the A330-300 and standard for the higher gross weight version are 72,000 lbf (320.28 kN) CF6-80E1A3s, 68,000 lbf (302.48 kN) PW4168s, and 71,100 lbf (316.27 kN) Trent 772s. 180 minutes ETOPS approval with CF6-80E1 engines, 120 minutes with PW4164/4168s and 90 minutes with Trent 700s by February 1995.
Engine rating: See above.
Fuel system: 93,500 litres. Tailplane trim tank.
Radar: Weather radar.
Flight avionics/instrumentation: Flight deck derived from the A320. Cross-crew qualification with the A320, A321 and A340. Central Maintenance System (CMS) (first used on the A340 and derived from the A320's CFDS) incorporates the central

Details for A330-300, *with A330-200 version in italics*

PRINCIPAL DIMENSIONS:
Wing span: 197 ft 10 ins (60.3 m), *the same*
Maximum length: 208 ft 11 ins (63.69 m), *193 ft 7 ins (59 m)*
Maximum height: 54 ft 11 ins (16.74 m)
Fuselage diameter: 18 ft 6 ins (5.64 m), *the same*

WINGS:
Area: 3,908.37 sq ft (363.1 m^2)
Aspect ratio: 10.014

UNDERCARRIAGE:
Type: Retractable, with twin steerable nosewheels and 4-wheel main bogies
Wheel track: 34 ft 5 ins (10.5 m)

WEIGHTS:
Empty, operating: typically 261,250 lb (118,500 kg), 266,760 lb (121,000 kg) higher gross weight version, *265,000 lb (120,200 kg)*
Maximum zero fuel: 361,560 lb (164,000 kg)
Maximum take-off: 467,380 lb (212,000 kg), *451,950-507,060 lb (205,000-230,000 kg)*
Maximum landing: 383,600 lb (174,000 kg), *396,830 lb (180,000 kg)*

PERFORMANCE:
Maximum operating Mach number (M_{MO}): *Mach 0.86*
Best cruise speed: Mach 0.82
Take-off field length: about 7,350-9,000 ft (2,240-2,745 m) with CF6-80E engines, sea level, ISA + 15° C
Landing field length: about 5,365 ft (1,635 m) at MLW, sea level, ISA + 15° C
Initial cruise altitude: 37,000 ft (11,275 m) eastbound, 39,000 ft (11,890 m) westbound
Range with 335 passengers (GE or P&W standard engines): 4,750 naut miles (5,470 miles) 8,797 km
Range with 335 passengers and 33,290 lb (15,100 kg) of cargo (GE standard engines): 3,300 naut miles (3,800 miles) 6,110 km
Range with 335 passengers and 32,408 lb (14,700 kg) of cargo (P&W standard engines): 3,300 naut miles (3,800 miles) 6,110 km
Range with 335 passengers (R-R standard engines): 4,650-4,750 naut miles (5,355-5,470 miles) 8,611-8,797 km, depending on pre or post-1996 delivered engines
Range with 335 passengers and 33,950 lb (15,400 kg) of cargo (R-R standard engines): 3,250-3,350 naut miles (3,742-3,857 miles) 6,019-6,204 km, depending on pre or post-1996 delivered engines
Range for A330-200: *6,475 naut miles (7,456 miles) 12,000 km with 253 passengers*

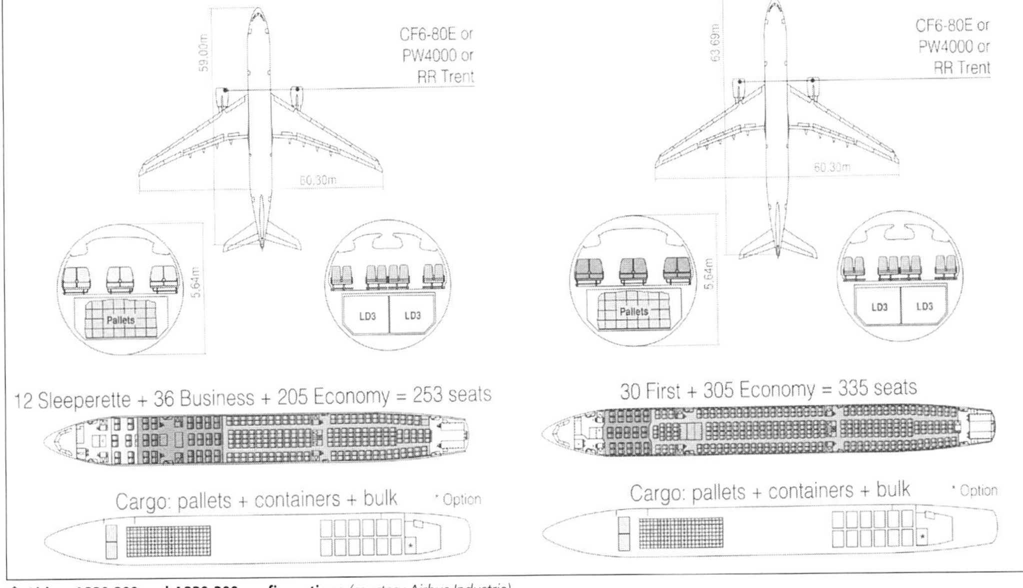

↑ **Airbus A330-200 and A330-300 configurations** *(courtesy Airbus Industrie)*

↑ Airbus A330-300 in Aer Lingus livery

maintenance computer (CMC), which is the interface between the aircraft systems, built-in test equipment (BITE) and the multi-purpose control and display unit (MCDU) located on the centre pedestal. CMC reports on the air conditioning, autopilot, electrical power, fire protection, flight controls, fuel, hydraulics and undercarriage systems among others, with data display, data print-out and real-time reporting to the ground; optional ACARS.

Aircraft variants:
A330-200 is a longer-range version of the A330-300, of 10 fuselage frames (15 ft 5 ins, 4.7 m) shorter fuselage length. 253 passengers in 3-class (12 sleeperette, 36 business and 205 economy), 293 in 2-class and 380/400 in high-density layouts. 139,100 litres of fuel, the additional capacity in a centre-section tank. First flown 13 August 1997. Certification with GE, P&W and R-R engines in 1998. GE-engined version received 180 minutes ETOPS certification before service entry.
A330-300 is the basic version, as detailed.
Higher gross weight version was previously designated A330-300X. 478,400 lb (217,000 kg) MTOW. Can carry 335 passengers over a range of 4,850 naut miles, or 335 passengers plus 20.3 to 21 tonnes of cargo over 3,350-3,400 naut miles.

Airbus A340

First flight: 25 October 1991.
Certification: 22 December 1992 (European). May 1993 for FAA.
First delivery: February 1993 to Lufthansa, entering service in March. 1,000th Airbus of all types was an A340-300 for Air France.
Role: Long-range, medium-density airliner.

Aims

- 4-engined A340 and twin-engined A330 were developed simultaneously after joint launch on 5 June 1987, but with the A340 making the first flight.
- A340-300 and A330 of the same dimensions, but with A340-200 having 8 fewer frames for reduced length. Common flight deck, fuselage, wings except for engine installations, undercarriage, tail unit, and systems except for differences caused by engine interface.

Details

Sales: Total of 229 had been ordered by June 1998, of which 137 had been delivered and 136 were operating.
Crew: 2 (flight).
Passengers: Typically 250 to 350 passengers, depending on version, but with the A340-300 able to accommodate up to 440 in single-class high-density layout (see Aircraft variants). 6-abreast sleeperette/international first class, 7-abreast business, 8-abreast economy, and 9-abreast high-density, all with 2 aisles. CIDS system (see A320).
Wing and tail control surfaces: Similar to A330.
Engines: 4 CFM International CFM56-5C2 turbofans initially, with optional -5C3 (32,500 lbf, 144.57 kN) or -5C4 (34,000 lbf, 151.24 kN) turbofans. See Aircraft variants for A340-500, -600 and -8000 engines.
Engine rating: Each 31,200 lbf (138.79 kN) for CFM56-5C2s.
Fuel system: 138,600 litres.
Flight avionics/instrumentation: As for A330.

Aircraft variants:
A340-200 is the reduced capacity version, with 8 fewer fuselage frames for a length of 194 ft 10 ins (59.39 m). Underfloor cargo holds accommodate a total of 26 LD3 containers or 9 pallets. Optional additional LD3 in the separate 695 cu ft (19.7 m^3) rear bulk hold, reducing bulk volume to 486 cu ft (13.8 m^3). First flown in 1992 and began service in 1993.
A340-300 is the standard length version, corresponding in size to the A330 and with similar underfloor holds. As detailed.
A340-300E ultra-long-range and higher gross weight version of the A340-300, previously designated A340-300X. 597,452-606,270 lb (271,000-275,000 kg) maximum take-off weight. 34,000 lbf (151.24 kN) CFM56-5C4 engines certified in late 1994. Typically to carry 295 passengers over a 7,300 naut mile range. Delivery of the first to Singapore Airlines on 25 April 1996.
A340-400E is a variant of A340-300 with a 21 ft (6.4 m) longer fuselage and CFM56-5C4 engines. 606,270 lb (275,000 kg) MTOW. 6,000 naut mile range with 336 passengers in a 3-class arrangement. Variant proposed with an additional 47 seats on the forward lower deck.
A340-500 is a new longer-range variant, basically a shorter-fuselage version of the A340-600. PW4500 or Rolls-Royce Trent 500 engines, with 56,000 lbf (249.1 kN) Trent 553s being installed

Details for A340-300, *with A340-200 in italics*

PRINCIPAL DIMENSIONS:
Wing span: 197 ft 10 ins (60.3 m), *the same*
Maximum length: 208 ft 11 ins (63.69 m), *194 ft 10 ins (59.39 m)*
Maximum height: 54 ft 11 ins (16.74 m), *the same*
Fuselage diameter: 18 ft 6 ins (5.64 m), *the same*

WINGS:
Area: 3,908.37 sq ft (363.1 m^2)
Aspect ratio: 10.014

UNDERCARRIAGE:
Type: As for A330, but with additional twin-wheel bogie under the fuselage, between the main units

WEIGHTS:
Empty, operating: 279,700 lb (126,870 kg) basic, *271,168 lb (123,000 kg)*
Maximum zero fuel: 383,600 lb (174,000 kg), *372,580 lb (169,000 kg)*
Maximum take-off: 566,587 lb (257,000 kg), *the same*
Maximum landing: 410,000 lb (186,000 kg), *399,000 lb (181,000 kg)*

PERFORMANCE:
Cruise speed: Mach 0.82
Range: 6,600 naut miles (7,600 miles) 12,225 km, 7,350 naut miles (8,463 miles) 13,610 km
Range (in airline service): typical long-range are 5,730 and 5,990 naut miles (6,598 and 6,897 miles) 10,610 and 11,090 km, quoted for Gulf Air's Bahrain-New York and Air France's Paris-Buenos Aires routes respectively

↑ Singapore Airlines Airbus A340

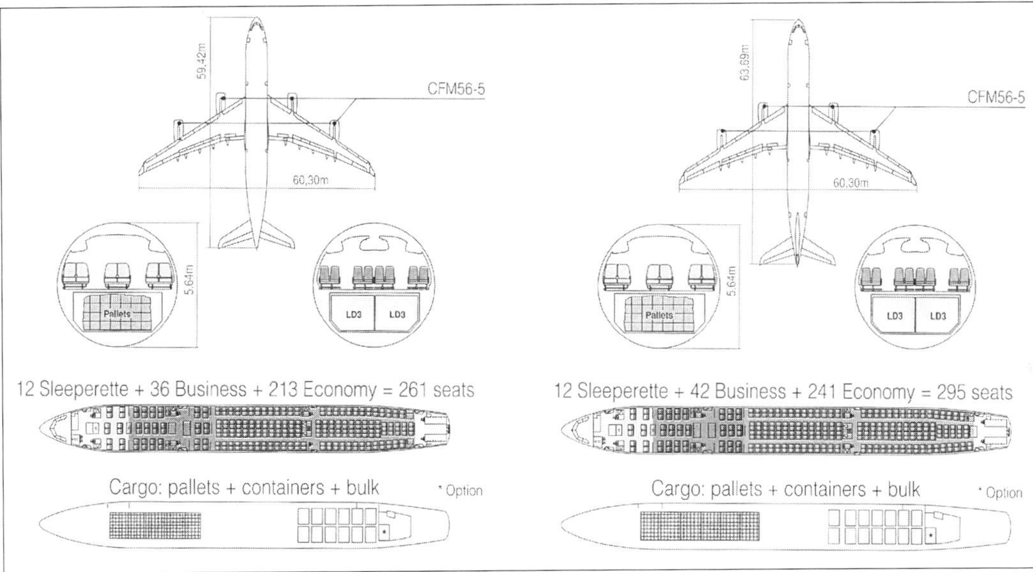

↑ **Airbus A340-8000 and A340-300 configurations** *(courtesy Airbus Industrie)*

↑ **Airbus A340-600 impression**

initially. Commercial programme launched 15 June 1997. Future air navigation system (FANS) equipment and the latest FMS as standard. Will carry 313 passengers in 3-class layout over a range of up to 8,500 naut miles (was originally to be 8,300 naut miles); increase in structural payload capability and freedom from ETOPS constraints. Additional underfloor cargo volume, allowing an additional 2 pallets of 96 ins × 125 ins (2.44 × 3.18 m) each, by retracting the centre undercarriage gear forward (not aft). 804,686 lb (365,000 kg) MTOW and 520,290 lb (236,000 kg) MLW. ***A340-600*** is a new stretched version, with more powerful PW4500 or Rolls-Royce Trent 500 engines, 53,000 lbf (223.75 kN) Trent 553s being installed initially. Commercial programme launched 15 June 1997. Will carry 378 passengers in a 3-class layout up to 7,500 naut miles (was originally to be 7,300 naut miles); increase in structural payload capability and freedom from ETOPS constraints. 35 ft (10.7 m) longer fuselage than the A340-300, and will also feature an enlarged and refined wing, increased design weights, and a revised undercarriage and tail unit. Additional underfloor cargo volume, allowing an additional 2 pallets of 96 ins × 125 ins (2.44 × 3.18 m) each. 529,100 lb (240,000 kg) maximum zero fuel weight, 804,686 lb (365,000 kg) MTOW and 560,000 lb (254,000 kg) MLW. Future air navigation system (FANS) equipment and the latest FMS as standard. Launch customer will be Virgin Atlantic, which ordered 8 plus 8 options in August 1997 (Trent 500 engines) for service from early 2002, and Egyptair (2 orders plus 2 options placed in November 1997). Virgin aircraft to feature double beds in private rooms for its premium fare paying passengers on the forward lower deck, a pub/lounge, a casino, showers, and an exercise and massage area on the aft lower deck.

↑ **Airbus A340 flight deck**

A340-8000 is a growth version, offering an 8,100 naut mile range with 232 passengers in 3 classes or 7,800 naut mile range with 261 passengers. Maximum 400 passengers. CFM56-5 turbofans, and 3 rear hold tanks for increased fuel capacity. Up to 2 ACTs and MTOW of 606,270 lb (275,000 kg). Wing span the same as other A340 versions but length 194 ft 11 ins (59.42 m); wings and fuselage strengthened. A second variant adds an additional tank (making 4) for improved range.

Airbus A3XX

First delivery: 2004, subject to development.
Role: Very high capacity, double-deck, long-range airliner.

Aims

- To share maximum commonality with A320 and A330/A340.
- Possible use of new GLARE (Fibre Metal Laminate) materials for the fuselage structure.

Development

- 1989. Initial studies started for a 500-1,000 seat airliner, with potential fuselage cross-sections including 'double bubbles'.
- 1993. Feasibility studies initiated by Airbus Industrie and a partner for the more conventional A3XX layout.
- 26 May 1994. Feasibility study continued to June 1995.
- 1996. Large Aircraft Division founded within Airbus Industrie to speed up development of the A3XX (see introduction).
- 1999. Programme to be launched.
- 2004. Entry into service.

↑ **Airbus A3XX computer-aided image**

Details for A3XX versions as stated

PRINCIPAL DIMENSIONS:
Wing span: 261 ft 10 ins (79.8 m) for all versions
Maximum length: 221 ft 1 ins (67.4 m) for A3XX-50, 237 ft 10 ins (72.5 m) for A3XX-100 and -100R, 253 ft 11 ins (77.4 m) for A3XX-200
Maximum height: 79 ft 9 ins (24.3 m) for all versions
Fuselage diameter: 22 ft 10 ins (6.95 m) for all versions

CABIN:
Middle deck cabin height: 8 ft (2.44 m)

WEIGHTS:
Empty, typical operating: 597,450 lb (271,000 kg) for A3XX-100, 606,270 lb (275,000 kg) for A3XX-100R, and 630,520 lb (286,000 kg) for A3XX-200
Maximum zero fuel: 707,700 lb (321,000 kg), *771,600 lb (350,000 kg)*
Maximum take-off: 1,102,300 lb (500,000 kg) for A3XX-50, 1,190,500 lb (540,000 kg) for A3XX-100, 1,285,293 lb (583,000 kg) for A3XX-100R and -200
Payload: 187,393 lb (85,000 kg) for A3XX-100 and -100R, and 209,439 lb (95,000 kg) for A3XX-200

PERFORMANCE:
Best cruise speed: over Mach 0.85
Range: See Aircraft variants

Details

Sales: Expected requirement for over 1,300 very high capacity airliners by year 2020. Airline launch commitments sought 1999.
Passengers: Initially to accommodate 555 passengers in a 3-class layout. See also Aircraft variants for passenger numbers. *Upper deck:* 4-abreast first class, 6-abreast business class, and 7/8-abreast economy class. *Main deck:* 6-abreast first class, 7-abreast business class, and 9/10-abreast economy class. All with 2 aisles. Double staircase.
Freight hold capacity: Underfloor capacity for 34 LD3 containers or 10 pallets plus 530 cu ft (15 m^3) of bulk in A3XX-100 and -100R. 42 LD containers or 12 pallets plus 530 cu ft (15 m^3) of bulk in A3XX-200. See Combi and Freighter.
Engines: 4 Rolls-Royce Trent 900s; alternative 67,000–80,000 lbf (293-356 kN) Engine Alliance GP7200 following May 1998 signing of MoU.
Engine rating: In the 69,000-78,000 lbf (307-347 kN) range. 63,850 lbf (284 kN) engines for A3XX-50.
Fuel system: 310,000 litres for A3XX-100 and Study version, and 335,000 litres for A3XX-100R and -200.

Aircraft variants:
A3XX-50 is a proposed shortened version to appear after A3XX-100 and variants, for 480 passengers. Similar range. Lower-powered engines.

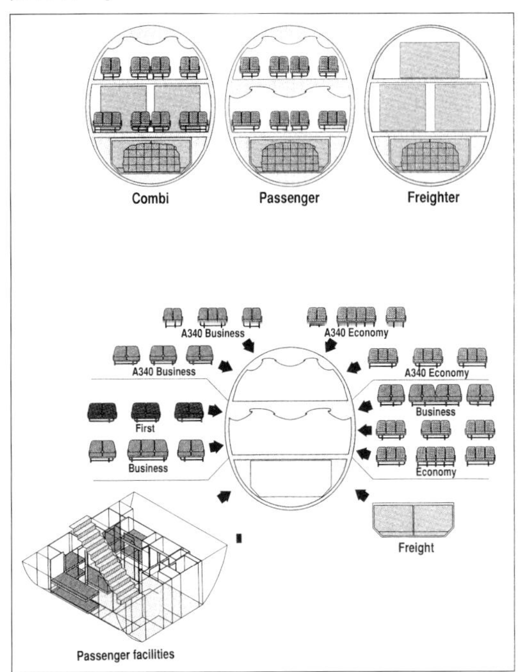

↑ **Airbus A3XX fuselage cross-sections for Combi, passenger and Freighter variants** *(courtesy Airbus Industrie)*

A3XX-100 will be the basic version to cruise at Mach 0.85 and carry 530-570 passengers (typically 555 passengers in a 3-class layout) over a 7,650-8,750 naut mile (8,809-10,075 mile) 14,177-16,215 km range. High-density layout for 854 passengers.
A3XX Combi will have seating for between 350 and 450 passengers and a storage capability of 7-11 pallets on the main deck and up to 11 pallets on the lower deck. The 11-pallet version will be able to carry a full passenger load plus 110,231 lb (50,000 kg) of freight.
A3XX Freighter variants will have 3 cargo decks. The upper deck will hold 18 pallets and the main deck 28, with up to 11 pallets on the lower level. Total of up to 330,690 lb (150,000 kg) payload. Upper deck cargo door in the forward fuselage, in addition to the main deck door.
A3XX-100R extended range development, to carry 555 passengers (typical load) over an 8,750 naut mile (10,075 mile) 16,215 km range.
A3XX-200 could carry 656 passengers. High-density layout for 960 passengers. Length increased to 253 ft 11 ins (77.4 m). 7,650 naut mile (8,809 mile) 14,177 km range.
A3XX Study for a 480 passenger version of 1,190,500 lb (540,000 kg) MTOW, with 310,000 litres of fuel. 8,400 naut mile (9,673 mile) 15,567 km range.
A3XX with canards configuration wind-tunnel tested by BAe.

Airbus Military Company Future Large Aircraft (FLA)

Role: Long-range logistic and tactical transport, tanker/transport and possibly maritime patrol.

Aims:

▪ Requirements reportedly include a short take-off capability, 32 tonne payload carried in a 4 metre wide cargo hold, 700 km/h cruise speed, low speed of 139 kts with 3° AoA, and range of 4,000-5,000 km.
▪ To be contracted in a Single Phase commercial approach, running from the signature of contracts between Industry and the individual national customers, through to first deliveries and beyond. This allows a high level of flexibility in the way the programme is financed in each nation. Contracts with the military will be based on a basic transport aircraft specification and a set of contractual documents covering price, deliveries, optional equipment and associated performance guarantees.

Development

▪ 1993. Year-long pre-feasibility study was completed into a European transport to replace the C-160 Transall and C-130 Hercules. Additional associate partners on the project became Flabel (SABCA and Sonaca) of Belgium, OGMA of Portugal and TUSAŞ of Turkey.

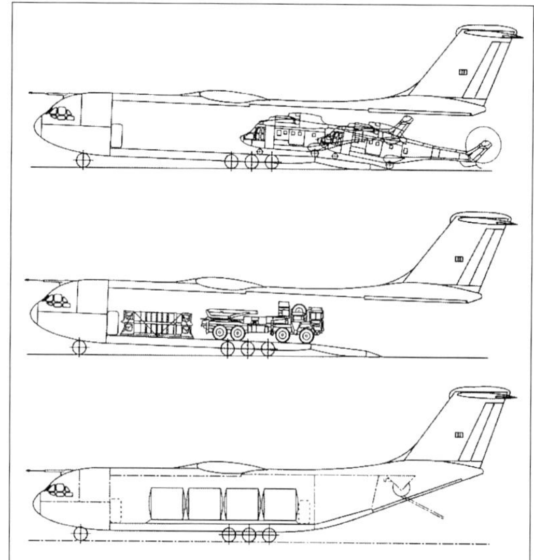

↑ **Airbus Military Company FLA with Super Puma, Patriot missile and tanker payloads** *(courtesy AMC)*

▪ October 1993. Following the signing of inter-government agreements, a feasibility study was initiated, completed under the auspices of Airbus in 1995.
▪ September 1994. A full-scale mock-up was displayed at Farnborough air show.
▪ 1996. Definition phase began, following establishment of an Airbus Military Company to take over from Euroflag srl.
▪ 1998. Full development phase expected to begin.
▪ 2004. Expected service entry.

Details

Sales: Anticipated sales of up to 750-900 aircraft, with perhaps one-third (273) going initially to the participating nations 'home market' of Belgium, France, Germany, Italy, Portugal, Spain, Turkey and the UK. The RAF is now expected to require only half the original 50 anticipated.
Crew: 2 pilots and 1 loadmaster. Optional third crew member on flight deck.
Passengers: Can accommodate 126 paratroops, or a detachment of 62 troops plus 8 pallets of equipment or relief supplies. See Freight hold capacity.
Freight hold capacity: Can accommodate all major army vehicles, armoured vehicles, helicopters (2 of Super Puma size), air defence missile units and other loads. Light vehicles can be loaded side-by-side. Alternatively, up to 9 pallets of 88 × 108 ins (2.24 × 2.74 m) 463L or 96 × 125 ins (2.44 × 3.18 m) 3610 types. See also Passengers.

↑ **Airbus Military Company FLA impression**

Details for FLA

PRINCIPAL DIMENSIONS:
Wing span: 135 ft 10 ins (41.4 m); 133 ft 1.8 ins (40.584 m) quoted previously
Maximum length: 137 ft 9 ins (42 m); 133 ft 7 ins (40.717 m) quoted previously
Maximum height: 47 ft 7 ins (14.5 m); 43 ft 1 ins (13.1086 m) quoted previously
Fuselage diameter: 17 ft 10 ins (5.424 m)

CABIN:
Length: 56 ft 7 ins (17.25 m) from aft of the cockpit to the ramp/door
Width: 13 ft 1.5 ins (4 m)
Height: 12 ft 7.5 ins (3.85 m)
Volume: 12,254 cu ft (347 m^3) with ramp

WINGS:
Anhedral: 2°

TAIL UNIT:
Tailplane span: 48 ft (14.6286 m)

UNDERCARRIAGE:
Type: Retractable, with twin nosewheels and 6-wheel main units. Cargo hold floor height can be lowered to make handling easier by main wheel 'kneeling'. Can operate from unprepared strips
Wheel base: 46 ft 10 ins (14.274 m)
Wheel track: 21 ft 11.5 ins (6.692 m)

WEIGHTS:
Maximum take-off: 244,382 lb (110,850 kg)
Normal payload: 55,115 lb (25,000 kg) for a typical tactical mission of over 2,000 naut miles range
Maximum payload: 70,548 lb (32,000 kg)

PERFORMANCE (estimated)**:**
Maximum speed: Mach 0.72
Cruise speed: Mach 0.68
Design long-range cruise speed: possibly 378 kts (435 mph) 700 km/h
Take-off distance: can operate from unprepared runways over 3,500 ft (1,067 m)
Ceiling: 40,000 ft (12,190 m)
Range with full payload: 2,400 naut miles (2,764 miles) 4,447 km
Ferry range: over 4,000 naut miles (4,606 miles) 7,408 km

Size of freight doors: Rear ramp/door, 15 ft 7 ins (4.74 m) length.
Loading facilities: Autonomous loading and cross loading capability.
Wing control surfaces: Ailerons, 2-section flaps and multi-section spoilers.
Tail control surfaces: T-tail with elevators and a 2-section rudder.
Flight control system: Fly-by-wire.
Construction materials: Will include composites.
Engines: 4 advanced turboprops in the 8,000-9,000 shp (5,966-6,711 kW) range, with options including the SNECMA M138 (M88-2 military core engine), BMW Rolls-Royce BR700-TP (using the core of the BR710 turbofan), and AlliedSignal AS812F (using the core of the TFE1042 turbofan). FADEC. 17 ft (5 m) diameter 8-blade propellers.
Flight refuelling: Over-cockpit central probe.
Flight avionics/instrumentation: Advanced flight deck with integrated avionics. EFIS system, with 5 multi-function displays. HUD for pilot and co-pilot. Possible adoption of Sextant Topdeck® avionics suite, with both civil and military systems. To be capable of night missions at low level into hostile environments.

Aircraft variants:
FLA transport, as detailed. Capable of operations from unprepared runways, low and high altitude air-dropping of cargo or paratroops, casualty evacuation, flying hospital, and more.
FLA convertible tanker/transport could offer 2-point refuelling.
FLA tanker could offer 3-point refuelling, 3 hour loiter at 450 naut miles, and transfer 81,570 lb (37,000 kg) of fuel. Fuel capacity 98,251 litres in 8 ft 6 ins × 8 ft 10 ins (2.6 × 2.7 m) fuselage tanks.
FLA maritime patrol variant could offer 11 hours 30 minutes patrol time at 1,000 naut miles.

AIA/AVIC/ST Aero — Airbus partners/Italy/China/Singapore

Important note. Despite reports that the AE31X project had folded, Airbus confirmed to *WA&SD* on 10 July 1998 that political and industrial collaboration between Airbus Industrie and AVIC of China (plus ST Aero of Singapore, though requiring more time to reappraise its position given the financial climate of the region) continues. AE31X is only in the definition phase and might, at some future date, be replaced by a new project if desirable as requirements are defined, but common interest in such a project remains.

Corporate address:
See Airbus Industrie (Airbus Industrie Asia – AIA) in this section, Alenia Aerospazio under Italy in the Combat section, AVIC under China in Combat and Singapore Technologies Aerospace Ltd in the Combat section.

AIA/AVIC/ST Aero AE31X

First flight: Could (but unlikely to) fly in the year 2002.
First delivery: Could (but unlikely) to enter service in 2003.
Role: Regional airliner.

Aims

- Suited to typical 500 naut mile operations but with range capabilities of up to 1,800 or 2,750 naut miles. Will be offered in standard and higher take-off weights.
- Fully integrated with the Airbus A320 family.

Development

- The original project study for a 100-seat regional airliner was a South Korean/Chinese government undertaking, joined in 1994

↑ AIA/AVIC/ST Aero AE317 regional airliner computer-aided image

Details for AE316, *with AE317 in italics*

PRINCIPAL DIMENSIONS:
Wing span: 101 ft 1 ins (30.8 m), *the same*
Maximum length: 100 ft 8.5 ins (30.7 m), *113 ft 2 ins (34.5 m)*
Maximum height: 34 ft 5.5 ins (10.5 m)

CABIN:
Width: 10 ft 1.1 ins (3.15 m)
Height: 6 ft 10.7 ins (2.1 m)

WEIGHTS:
Empty, operating: 65,697-65,852 lb (29,800-29,870 kg), *69,335-69,490 lb (31,450-31,520 kg)*
Maximum zero fuel: 93,255 lb (42,300 kg), *104,058 lb (47,200 kg)*
Maximum take-off: 110,010-118,168 lb (49,900-53,600 kg), *119,049-127,868 lb (54,000-58,000 kg)*
Maximum landing: 102,515 lb (46,500 kg), *111,333 lb (50,500 kg)*

PERFORMANCE:
Range for AE316: 1,997-2,750 naut miles (2,300-3,166 miles) 3,700-5,096 km
Range for AE317: 1,800-3,130 naut miles (2,072-3,604 miles) 3,335-5,800 km

by Daimler-Benz Aerospace Airbus and in 1995 by the Korean Commercial Aircraft Development Consortium headed by Samsung, at which time it became known as the Air Express 100 to AVIC and dubbed the Asian Airbus in the West. Fokker was then also a reported interested party. In 1996 Singapore Technologies Aerospace joined the grouping but the Korean consortium left. The new designation for the programme is AE31X.

- Pre-development period from 1998 to mid-1999, possibly to be followed by full development, flight testing, certification and service entry. Final assembly could be at Xi'an in China.

Details

Crew: 2 (flight).
Passengers: AE316 accommodates 95 passengers in 2-class layout (4- or 5-abreast) or 105 in single-class layout (5-abreast). AE317 accommodates 115 passengers in 2-class layout (4- or 5-abreast) and 125 passengers in single-class layout (5-abreast).
Seat pitch: 32 ins (81 cm) in single-class layout.
Freight hold volume: Underfloor capacity of 828.5 cu ft (23.46 m^3) for A316, and 1,118.8 cu ft (31.68 m^3) for AE317.

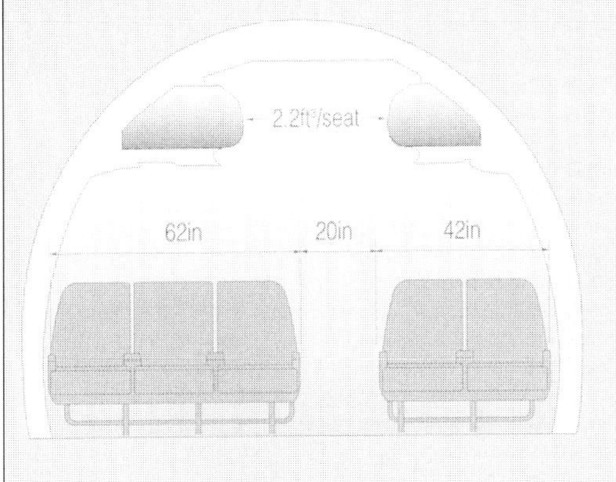

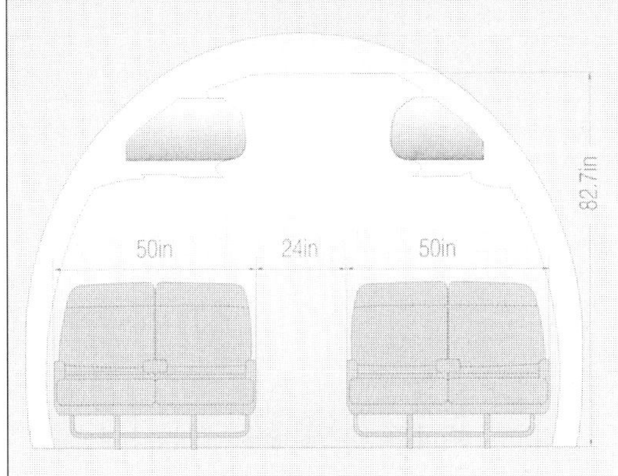

↑ AIA/AVIC/ST Aero AE31X economy class (*top*) and business-class cabin cross sections *(courtesy AIA)*

Engines: Choices are BMW Rolls-Royce BR715, CFM International CFM56-9 and Pratt & Whitney PW6000.
Fuel system: 21,815 litres.
Flight avionics/instrumentation: Features an Airbus A320 family flight deck concept.

Aircraft variants:
AE316 is the 95-105 seat version.
AE317 is the 115-125 seat version, lengthened by 7 frames.

Aircraft Technology Industries (Airtech) — Indonesia/Spain

Corporate address:
See CASA of Spain in the Combat section and IPTN of Indonesia in this section for company details.

Airtech CN 235

First flight: 11 November 1983.
Certification: 20 June 1986. Certified under FAA Pt 25 and Pt 36, and ICAO Annex 16, and designed to meet JAR requirements. Series 100 and 200 certified in 1992.
First delivery: 15 December 1986.
Airframe life: 50,000 hours or 60,000 cycles economic repair life for at least CN 235 M.
Role: Regional transport. Military versions for transport and other more specialized roles (see Aircraft variants).
Noise levels: FAR Pt 36: 84 EPNdB take off, 86 EPNdB sideline, and 87 EPNdB approach.
Sales: Total of 221 CN 235s had been delivered at the time of writing (including 122 military/government and 12 civil by July 1998 from CASA production alone), as 47 civil to 8 operators in 5 countries (Indonesia, Argentina, South Korea, Spain and the USA), and 174 military to 21 operators in 20 countries (Abu Dhabi, Brunei, Indonesia and Malaysia from IPTN production, and Botswana, Colombia, Chile, Ecuador, France, Gabon, Ireland, Morocco, Oman, Papua New Guinea, Saudi Arabia, South Africa, South Korea, Spain, Thailand and Turkey from CASA production).

Details *(current production CN 235, with CN 235 M under Aircraft variants)*

Crew: 2 (flight).
Passengers: 44 maximum. Integral stairs.

↑ Airtech CN 235 with rear ramp/door lowered for LAPES operations

Seat pitch: 30 ins (76 cm) with 44 passengers, or 33 ins (84 cm) with 40 passengers.
Pressurization: 3.64 psi cabin differential.
Freight hold capacity: 4 LD3 containers, plus optional ramp container, or 2 pallets of 88 ins × 125 ins (2.24 × 3.18 m).
Size of freight doors: Hydraulically actuated rear lower ramp/door, 10 ft × 7 ft 8.5 ins (3.04 × 2.35 m). Upper section door 7 ft 9 ins × 7 ft 8.5 ins (2.37 × 2.35 m).
Wing control surfaces: Ailerons (with servo and trim tabs) and single-slotted flaps.
Tail control surfaces: Elevators (trim tab in port, servo and trim tabs in starboard) and rudder (servo and trim tabs).
Flight control system: Mechanical, except for hydraulic flaps and electric trim tabs.
Construction materials: Includes wide use of composites (glassfibre, carbonfibre and Kevlar).
Engines: 2 General Electric CT7-9C turboprops, with Hamilton Standard 14RF-21 4-blade propellers. Optional propeller brake. APU.
Engine rating: Each 1,750 shp (1,305 kW) normal take-off power.
Fuel system: 5,264 litres.
Electrical system: Primary DC supply, using 2 engine-driven generators. AC power via inverters to supply circuits with constant-frequency requirements. In the event of failure in the DC generators, power can be obtained from the variable frequency AC systems through transformer rectifiers. 2 × 24 volt, 37 AH ni-cd batteries for engine starting and emergency use.
Hydraulic system: 3,000 psi, with 2 parallel axial pumps, with either pump able to maintain system pressure in the event of a pump failure. Operates the undercarriage, brakes, rear ramp/door, propeller brake, flaps, nosewheel steering, and emergency and parking brakes.
Braking system: Hydraulic disc with anti-skid system. Optional nosewheel anti-spin brake.
De-icing system: Optional ice detection system.
Environmental control system: Air conditioning system is of recirculation cycle cooling type, to minimize the engine bleed air requirement. Keeps the cabin temperature between 18-29° C.
Radar: Rockwell Collins WXR-350 weather radar.
Flight avionics/instrumentation: Avtech DADS and PACIS; Rockwell Collins EFIS-85 electronic flight instruments (5 CRTs), VHF-22B, dual TDR-90 ATC transponder, dual VIR-32 VOR/ILS/marker beacon, dual ADF-60A, dual DME-42, ALT-55B radio altimeter, APS-65 FD & AP; Motorola N-1335B selcal; Dorne & Margolin DM ELT 8.1 ELT; Fairchild A-100 A CVR and F-800 FDR; and Sundstrand Mk II GPWS. Optional Rockwell Collins HF and Omega with GPS.

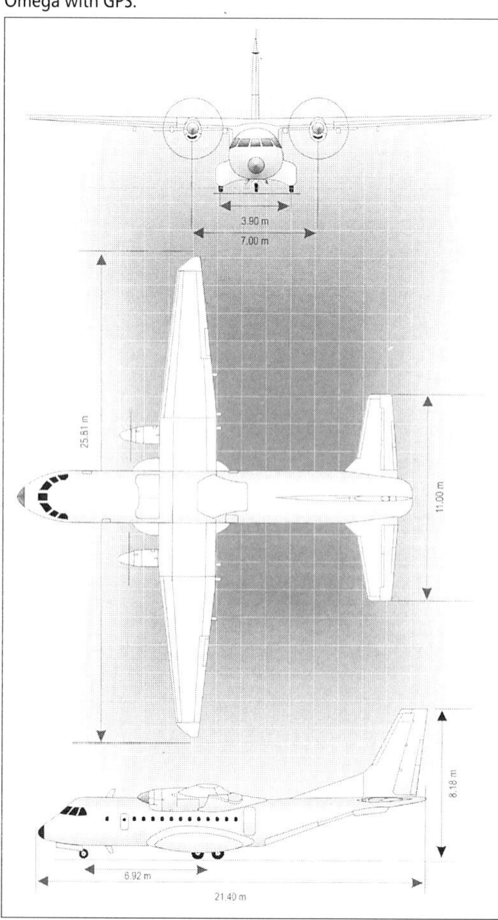

↑ **Airtech CN 235 commercial version from IPTN general arrangement** *(courtesy IPTN)*

Details for current CASA built CN 235, *with CN 235 M in italics where different*

PRINCIPAL DIMENSIONS:
Wing span: 84 ft 8 ins (25.81 m)
Maximum length: 70 ft 2.5 ins (21.4 m)
Maximum height: 26 ft 9.8 ins (8.17 m)

CABIN:
Length: 32 ft 9 ins (9.98 m), *31 ft 7.9 ins (9.65 m)*
Width: 8 ft 10.3 ins (2.7 m), 7 ft 9.1 ins (2.36 m) at floor
Height: 6 ft 2 ins (1.88 m) at aisle
Volume: 1,578 cu ft (44.68 m^3)
Main passenger doors: 2 ft 3.6 ins × 5 ft 7 ins (0.7 × 1.7 m), and 1 ft 11.6 ins × 4 ft 2 ins (0.6 × 1.27 m)

WINGS:
Aerofoil section: NACA65$_3$-218
Area: 636.15 sq ft (59.1 m^2)
Aspect ratio: 11.272
Dihedral: 3°

TAIL UNIT:
Tailplane span: 34 ft 9 ins (10.6 m)
Tailplane area: 273.4 sq ft (25.4 m^2)

UNDERCARRIAGE:
Type: Retractable, with single steerable nosewheel and tandem twin mainwheel units. Optional low-pressure tyres
Main wheel tyre size: 28 × 9.0-12
Nose wheel tyre size: 24 × 7.7
Wheel base: 22 ft 8 ins (6.919 m)
Wheel track: 12 ft 9.5 ins (3.9 m)
Turning radius: 62 ft 3 ins (18.98 m) wingtip

WEIGHTS:
Empty, operating: 21,605 lb (9,800 kg) in passenger configuration
Maximum zero fuel: 31,085 lb (14,100 kg), *32,628 lb (14,800 kg)*
Maximum ramp: 34,943 lb (15,850 kg)
Maximum take-off: 34,833 lb (15,800 kg), *36,376 lb (16,500 kg)*
Maximum landing: 34,392 lb (15,600 kg), *36,376 lb (16,500 kg)*
Payload: 11,067 lb (5,020 kg) cargo version, 9,480 lb (4,300 kg) passenger version, *13,228 lb (6,000 kg)*

PERFORMANCE:
Maximum cruise speed: 244 kts (281 mph) 452 km/h, at 15,000 ft (4,570 m), ISA, *240 kts (276 mph) 445 km/h, 95% MTOW*
Stall speed: 100 kts (115 mph) 185 km/h *clean*, 84 kts (97 mph) 156 km/h *with flaps*, IAS
Take-off balanced field length: 4,180 ft (1,274 m), ISA, sea level, MTOW
Take-off ground roll: *1,680 ft (512 m), MTOW, sea level, ISA*
Take-off distance over a 50 ft (15 m) obstacle: 2,657 ft (810 m), MTOW, sea level, ISA
Landing distance: 2,198 ft (670 m), *1,234 ft (376 m)*, ISA, sea level, MLW
Landing distance over a 50 ft (15 m) obstacle: *2,025 ft (617 m), MLW, sea level, ISA*
Maximum climb rate: 1,525 ft (465 m) per minute
Ceiling: 25,000 ft (7,620 m) service, *27,000 ft (8,230 m) service*, 95% MTOW
Ceiling, OEI: 14,750 ft (4,500 m) ISA, 90% MTOW, *12,800 ft (3,900 m) ISA, at 95% MTOW*
Range with 44 passengers: 957 naut miles (1,102 miles) 1,772 km at maximum cruise speed, 1,079 naut miles (1,242 miles) 1,998 km at long-range cruise speed, with reserves
Range with 22 passengers: 1,974 naut miles (2,273 miles) 3,656 km at maximum cruise speed, 2,291 naut miles (2,638 miles) 4,243 km at long-range cruise speed
Range with maximum cargo: 843 naut miles (971 miles) 1,561 km
Range with 5,635 lb (2,556 kg) cargo: 2,474 naut miles (2,848 miles) 4,582 km
Range with 7,826 lb (3,550 kg) payload: *2,400 naut miles (2,763 miles) 4,445 km*

Aircraft variants:
CN 235 series commercial version, available in passenger, cargo, and quick-change (QC) passenger/cargo variant with a reconfiguration time by 2 groundcrew of under 30 minutes using a low-weight roller system over which the passenger configuration can be installed (baggage container, modular galley and seat platforms). Series 100 is a current CASA built version, with the corresponding Series 110 from IPTN having systems improvements (ECS, electrical and more). CASA built Series 200 introduced aerodynamic refinements and structural reinforcements to allow increases in operative weights, range improvements, and better ground performance. Series 220 is the Indonesian variant, incorporating also Series 110 modifications. QC has a range of 1,075 and 2,340 naut miles (1,238 and 2,694 miles) 1,990 and 4,333 km, with 40 and 17 passengers respectively at long-range cruise speed, or 843 and 2,474 naut miles (970 and 2,848 miles) 1,561 and 4,581 km, with a 10,648 lb (4,830 kg) and 5,216 lb (2,366 kg) payload respectively at long-range cruise speed.
CN 235 M is the military version. Airdrop capability in HAD or LAPES missions. 48 troops/paratroops with 2 jump doors. Medevac version for 21 stretchers and 4 seated attendants. 2 pallets of 88 × 108 ins (2.24 × 2.74 m) or 6 pallets of 88 × 54 ins (2.24 × 1.37 m), or vehicles, etc. Payload 13,228 lb (6,000 kg). Also suited to SAR, electronic warfare, photographic, firefighting, and other more specialized roles.
CN 235 Phoenix is an IPTN Series 330 version of the CN 235, developed for the Australian market. Offered to the RAAF to replace the de Havilland Canada Caribou transport and featuring Honeywell avionics and an EW protection suite. Participation in the programme by Australian companies, principally Hawker de Havilland. Similar payload to other M versions but MTOW increased to 37,038 lb (16,800 kg).
CN 235 MP, ASW/ASUW and ***MPA*** are maritime patrol versions. See Combat section.

Airtech C 295

First flight: Scheduled for 1998.
Certification: Scheduled for FAA FAR Pt 25 in November 1999. Military operations certification during the year 2000.
First delivery: Expected in the year 2000.
Role: Stretched version of the CN 235, produced by CASA.

Aims

▪ 50% more load capacity due to the longer fuselage and new operative weights.
▪ Structurally, has 2 main modifications: the introduction of 6 new frames (3 each side of the wing-to-fuselage attachment); and a reinforced wing structure to withstand the new operating weights (also increased fuel capacity).

Details

Passengers: 69 fully-equipped troops or 27 litters and 4 attendants.
Pressurization: 5.52 psi cabin differential, maintaining the cabin at 7,850 ft (2,393 m) up to 25,000 ft (7,620 m).
Freight hold capacity: Up to 4 pallets of 88 × 108 ins (2.24 × 2.74 m) each, with a maximum of 21,385 lb (9,700 kg) payload. Alternatively 3 light vehicles or troops/litters.
Engines: 2 Pratt & Whitney PW127G turboprops, with 12 ft 11 ins (3.93 m) Hamilton Standard RF 568F 6-blade propellers.
Engine rating: Each 2,645 shp (1,972 kW) take-off power.
Fuel system: 2,380 litres more fuel than CN 235.
Flight avionics/instrumentation: Redesigned and updated, incorporating a Flight Management System (FMS), enabling navigation planning by integrating the signals from several sensors and including GPS. Engine indicators are integrated in a new Engine Data System (IEDS), which presents the information on 2 liquid crystal displays that replace not only the traditional engine indicators but also part of the systems panel (hydraulic, electrical, fuel, etc), including the failure warning panel. Among other modes, the IEDS stores information to assist maintenance.
Number of wing pylons: Provision for 3 hard points under each wing, of 662 lb (300 kg), 1,103 lb (500 kg) and 1,765 lb (800 kg) capacities.

↑ **CASA developed Airtech C 295**

Details for C 295

PRINCIPAL DIMENSIONS:
Maximum length: 41 ft 7.5 ins (12.69 m)

UNDERCARRIAGE:
Type: Reinforced, with twin nosewheels, improving unprepared runway operations

WEIGHTS:
Maximum take-off: 51,147 lb (23,200 kg)
Maximum landing: 51,147 lb (23,200 kg)
Payload: 21,385 lb (9,700 kg)

PERFORMANCE:
Cruise speed: 260 kts (299 mph) 482 km/h
Ceiling: 25,000 ft (7,620 m) service
Range with full payload: 728 naut miles (838 miles) 1,349 km
Range with maximum fuel: 2,250 naut miles (2,591 miles) 4,169 km

Avions de Transport Regional (ATR) France/Italy

Corporate address:
See Combat section for company details.

ATR 42

First flight: 16 August 1984.
Certification: 24 September 1985 (JAR Pt 25), 25 October 1985 (FAR Pt 25).
First delivery: October 1989.
Role: Regional airliner, or cargo transport. Can be adapted for nav aid calibration, VIP transport and other uses (see Aircraft variants).
Noise levels: 82.8 EPNdB take-off, 83.7 EPNdB sideline, 96.7 EPNdB approach for ATR 42-300/-320. ATR 42-500 has about 75 EPNdB take-off, about 80 EPNdB sideline, and about 92 EPNdB approach. Typical cabin noise level for ATR 42-500 is under 80 dBA.
Sales: Total ATR 42 sales amounted to 341 aircraft by March 1998, of which 53 are for the latest ATR 42-500.
Crew: 2 (flight).
Passengers: Basic version for 48 seats (30 ins, 76 cm pitch). Alternative 42 seats (33 ins, 84 cm pitch), 46 seats (30 ins, 76 cm pitch), and 50 seats (30 ins, 76 cm pitch). With the latter configuration, the forward cargo areas are reduced.
Seat pitch: See above.
Galley: At the rear of the cabin (see diagram).
Toilets: At the rear of the cabin (see diagram).
Pressurization: 5.95 psi cabin differential.
Freight hold volume: All seating arrangements allow for 169.5 cu ft (4.8 m^3) of cargo area aft of the cabin. 2 forward cargo areas each provide 106 cu ft (3 m^3) of space, except in 48-seat layout when 1 area is reduced to 63.57 cu ft (1.8 m^3), or in 50-seat arrangement when each forward area is reduced to 63.57 cu ft (1.8 m^3).
Freight hold capacity: Simple operational system can be installed to convert the aircraft into a 9-container transport, with an 8,818 lb (4,000 kg) payload.

↑ ATR 42-500 in Air Littoral livery

↑ Latest ATR flight deck, photographed from the simulator

Wing control surfaces: Aileron (with trim tab), 2 double-slotted flaps and a spoiler per wing, the latter assisting the aileron.
Tail control surfaces: Horn-balanced elevators and rudder, with trim tabs.
Flight control system: Mechanical, except for hydraulic flaps and spoilers, and electric tabs.
Construction materials: Aluminium alloy, but with substantial use of composites (see diagram for the ATR 52C, to which ATR 42 is similar except for the degree of carbonfibre in the wings).
Engines: 2 Pratt & Whitney Canada PW120s for the ATR 42-300, each 1,800 shp (1,342 kW) at take-off and 2,000 shp (1,491 kW) take-off with 1 engine out. 2 PW121s for the ATR 42-320, each 1,900 shp (1,417 kW) at take off and 2,100 shp (1,566 kW) take-off with 1 engine out. 2 PW121As for the ATR 42-400, each 2,000 shp (1,491 kW) at take-off and 2,200 shp (1,640 kW) take-off with 1 engine out. 2 PW127Es for the ATR 42-500, each 2,160 shp (1,611 kW) at take-off and 2,400 shp (1,790 kW) take-off with 1 engine out. 13 ft (3.96 m) diameter Hamilton Standard 14SF5 4-blade propellers for ATR 42-300 and -320; 12 ft 11 ins (3.93 m) diameter Hamilton Standard 568F 6-blade propellers for ATR 42-400 and -500.
Engine rating: See Engines.
Fuel system: 9,920 lb (4,500 kg) for all versions.
Electrical system: Principal 28 volt DC supply, via 2 engine-driven starter-generators. 2 ni-cd batteries, of 15 amp-hour and 43 amp-hour. 115/26 volt single-phase AC supply via 2 static inverters. 115/200 volt 3-phase AC supply via 20 kVA engine-driven alternators.
Hydraulic system: 2 independent systems, each 3,000 psi.
Braking system: Hydraulic discs, with anti-skid system.
De-icing system: Pneumatic boots for outer wing and tailplane leading edges, and engine intakes. Fin and wing inner sections

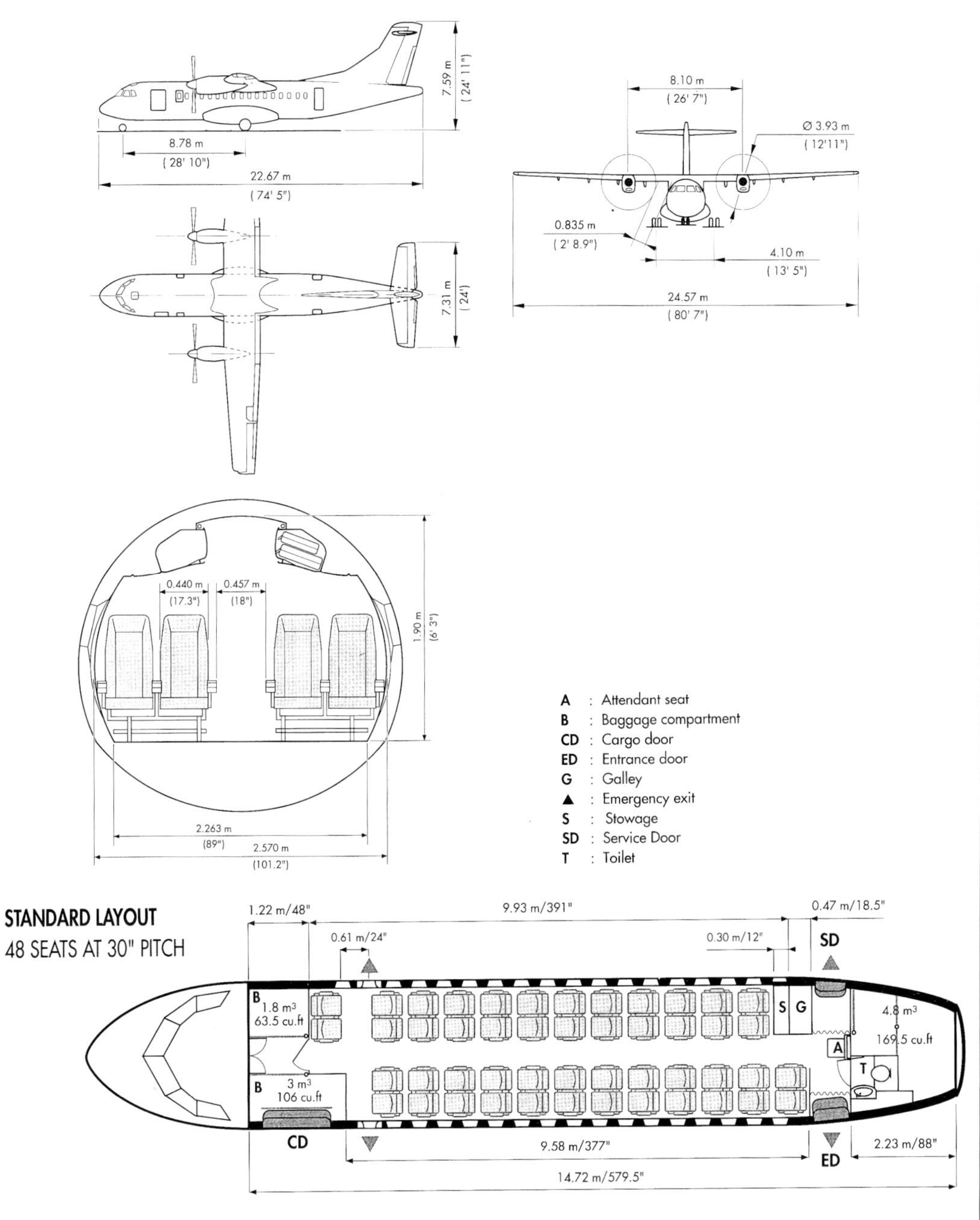

↑ ATR 42-500 general arrangement, cabin cross-section and 48-seat cabin layout *(courtesy ATR)*

can have similar system. Larger boots fitted to US operating aircraft by June 1995, under FAA instruction, certified on 20 March 1995. Electric for cockpit glazing, pitots, propeller blades, and aileron/fin/elevator horn balances.
Environmental control system: ATR 42-500 has a new, quieter air conditioning system similar to that of ATR 72-210A, providing 35% additional cooling capacity compared with ATR 42-300.
Radar: Honeywell weather radar.
Flight avionics/instrumentation: Fully digital avionics suite, organized around the bi-directional ASCB bus. AlliedSignal Bendix/King Gold Crown III, but Rockwell Collins Pro Line II is optional. 2 AZ 800 air data computers, 2 AH 600 AHRS systems, DFZ 600 automatic flight control system for Cat I approaches or as an option for Cat II approaches, and EDZ 820 EFIS with 4 CRTs and 2 symbol generator units (each SGU drives 2 CRTs). AlliedSignal Bendix/King KLN 90A GPS available, coupled to the EFIS and autopilot. ATR 42-500 has 2 multi-function computers replacing 12 separate line replaceable units.

Aircraft variants:
ATR 42-300 uses PW120 engines. See Freight hold capacity for quick-change capabilities.
ATR 42-320 uses PW121 engines.
ATR 42-400 uses PW121A engines. Higher weights and longer range.
ATR 42-500 is currently the main production version, with PW127E engines. Can operate with full payload from hot-or-high runways. Shares many features with the ATR 72-210A. Fuselage structural treatment with installation of dynamic vibration absorbers, new look interior with acoustically absorbent materials, suppression of noise sources such as pressurization outflow valves and hydraulic pumps, optional Active Noise Control system, 40% larger overhead baggage bins to accommodate items up to 6 ft 6 ins (2 m) length, and additional handrail embedded in the overhead bins. New, quieter air conditioning system. 2 multi-function computers replacing 12 separate line replaceable units. First flown 16 September 1994.
ATR 42 C is a cargo version that accommodates 9 containers for a 8,818 lb (4,000 kg) payload. Can be reconfigured for passengers in 1 hour.
ATR 42 F is a military freighter, featuring a strengthened floor, 8,378 lb (3,800 kg) cargo payload or up to 42 troops. Port side door openable in flight for paradropping.
ATR 42 Maritime Patrol, see Combat section.

Details for ATR 42 versions as specified

PRINCIPAL DIMENSIONS:
Wing span: 80 ft 7 ins (24.57 m)
Maximum length: 74 ft 4.5 ins (22.67 m)
Maximum height: 24 ft 11 ins (7.59 m)

CABIN:
Length: 34 ft 1.5 ins (10.4 m) from front to rear seats in 48-seat layout, 41 ft (12.49 m) from rear of cockpit to start of aft toilet/baggage area, and 48 ft 4.5 ins (14.72 m) from rear of cockpit to rear of aft baggage area (see diagram)
Width: 8 ft 5.2 ins (2.57 m), 7 ft 5 ins (2.263 m) at floor
Height: 6 ft 3 ins (1.9 m)
Volume: 2,048.3 cu ft (58 m^3)
Main passenger door: 5 ft 9 ins × 2 ft 5.5 ins (1.75 × 0.75 m)

WINGS:
Area: 586.63 sq ft (54.5 m^2)
Aspect ratio: 11.077
Incidence: 2° at root
Dihedral: 2.5° on outer wing panels

TAIL UNIT:
Tailplane span: 26 ft 7 ins (8.1 m)

UNDERCARRIAGE:
Type: Retractable, with steerable nosewheels. Twin wheels on each unit
Main wheel tyre size: 32 × 8.8-10
Wheel base: 28 ft 10 ins (8.78 m)
Wheel track: 13 ft 5.5 ins (4.1 m)
Turning radius: 56 ft 1 ins (17.08 m) minimum

WEIGHTS:
Empty, operating: 22,675 lb (10,285 kg) for ATR 42-300 and -320, with optional 22,685 lb (10,290 kg); 24,361 lb (11,050 kg) for ATR 42-400; 24,801 lb (11,250 kg) for ATR 42-500
Maximum zero fuel: 33,510 lb (15,200 kg) for ATR 42-300 and -320, with optional 34,259 lb (15,540 kg); 35,935 lb (16,300 kg) for ATR 42-400; 36,817 lb (16,700 kg) for ATR 42-500
Maximum take-off: 36,817 lb (16,700 kg) for ATR 42-300 and -320, with optional 37,258 lb (16,900 kg); 39,462 lb (17,900 kg) for ATR 42-400; 41,005 lb (18,600 kg) for ATR 42-500
Maximum landing: 36,155 lb (16,400 kg) for ATR 42-300 and -320; 38,801 lb (17,600 kg) for ATR 42-400; 40,344 lb (18,300 kg) for ATR 42-500
Payload: 10,835 lb (4,915 kg) for ATR 42-300 and -320, with optional 10,825 lb (4,910 kg); 11,574 lb (5,250 kg) for ATR 42-400; 12,015 lb (5,450 kg) for ATR 42-500

BLOCK DATA (200 naut mile sector)**:**
Block fuel: 1,305 lb (592 kg) for ATR 42-500
Block time: 59 minutes for ATR 42-500
Flight time: 49 minutes for ATR 42-500

PERFORMANCE:
Maximum cruise speed: 265 kts (304 mph) 490 km/h for ATR 42-300, 269 kts (309 mph) 498 km/h for ATR 42-320, 266 kts (306 mph) 492 km/h for ATR 42-400, and 304 kts (350 mph) 563 km/h for ATR 42-500
Stall speed: 104 kts (120 mph) 193 km/h *clean*, 81 kts (93 mph) 150 km/h *with 30° flaps* for ATR 42-300
Balanced take-off field length, sea level, ISA: 3,576 ft (1,090 m) for ATR 42-300, 3,412 ft (1,040 m) for ATR 42-320, 3,954 ft (1,205 m) for ATR 42-400, and 3,822 ft (1,165 m) for ATR 42-500, all at MTOW
Balanced take-off field length, 3,000 ft (915 m), ISA +10°: 4,265 ft (1,300 m) for ATR 42-300, 4,052 ft (1,235 m) for ATR 42-320, 4,823 ft (1,470 m) for ATR 42-400, and 4,613 ft (1,406 m) for ATR 42-500, all at MTOW
Landing field length, sea level, ISA: 3,380 ft (1,030 m) for ATR 42-300 and -320, 3,675 ft (1,120 m) for ATR 42-400, and 3,695 ft (1,126 m) for ATR 42-500, all at MLW
Maximum operational cruise ceiling: 25,000 ft (7,600 m)
Climb from 1,500 ft to 17,000 ft (457 to 5,180 m): under 10 minutes for ATR 42-500
Range with 48 passengers (each 209 lb, 95 kg): 640 naut miles (737 miles) 1,186 km for ATR 42-300, with 760 naut miles (875 miles) 1,408 km at optional weight; 630 naut miles (725 miles) 1,167 km for ATR 42-320, with 750 naut miles (863 miles) 1,390 km at optional weight; 825 naut miles (950 miles) 1,529 km for ATR 42-400; 870 naut miles (1,002 miles) 1,612 km for ATR 42-500

ATR 52C

First flight: Not yet flown.
Role: Multi-purpose transport, suited to civil and military operations. Uses include cargo and vehicle carrying, troop or passenger transport, paratroop and load airdropping, and medevac.

Aims

■ Derivative of the ATR 72-210, using the same wings, tail unit and engines, while the fuselage has been shortened and a rear loading ramp fitted. Identical systems to the ATR 72-210.
Passengers: 47 troops plus 1 loadmaster, 41 paratroops plus 2 jumpmasters and a loadmaster, 45 paratroops and a jumpmaster, or 27 litters (NATO 2040 type) plus 4 attendants. Up to 54 passengers at 30 ins (76.2 cm) pitch, plus 2 attendants. In the latter layout, the paratroops can be dropped in 2 rows through the large rear doors. See Freight capacity.
Pressurization: 6 psi, providing 6,750 ft (2,060 m) cabin altitude pressure up to 25,000 ft (7,620 m).
Freight capacity: In cargo configuration, can carry 6 LD3 containers, 4 pallets of 88 × 108 ins (2.24 × 2.74 m) size, or 3 pallets 88 × 125 ins (2.24 × 3.18 m). Available volume with containers is 953 cu ft (27 m^3), with 4 pallets 1,271 cu ft (36 m^3) and 3 larger pallets 1,165 cu ft (33 m^3). Conversion from cargo configuration to troop/paratroop layout takes about 30 minutes by a team of 4, or under 1 hour for passenger/medevac.
Freight hold access: Rear ramp cargo door, capable of 4 preselected positions: closed (ramp and rear door), axial loading and airdropping (ramp in line with cabin floor and rear door opened), wheeled vehicles loading (ramp tilted down with ramp extension installed at 15° constant angle and rear door closed), and ramp fully down (ramp on the ground, at 23°, with no ramp extension and rear door opened); any other intermediate position can be achieved by the manual driving of the hydraulic actuator. All opening/closing operations can be performed by a control panel located in the rear fuselage close to the ramp.

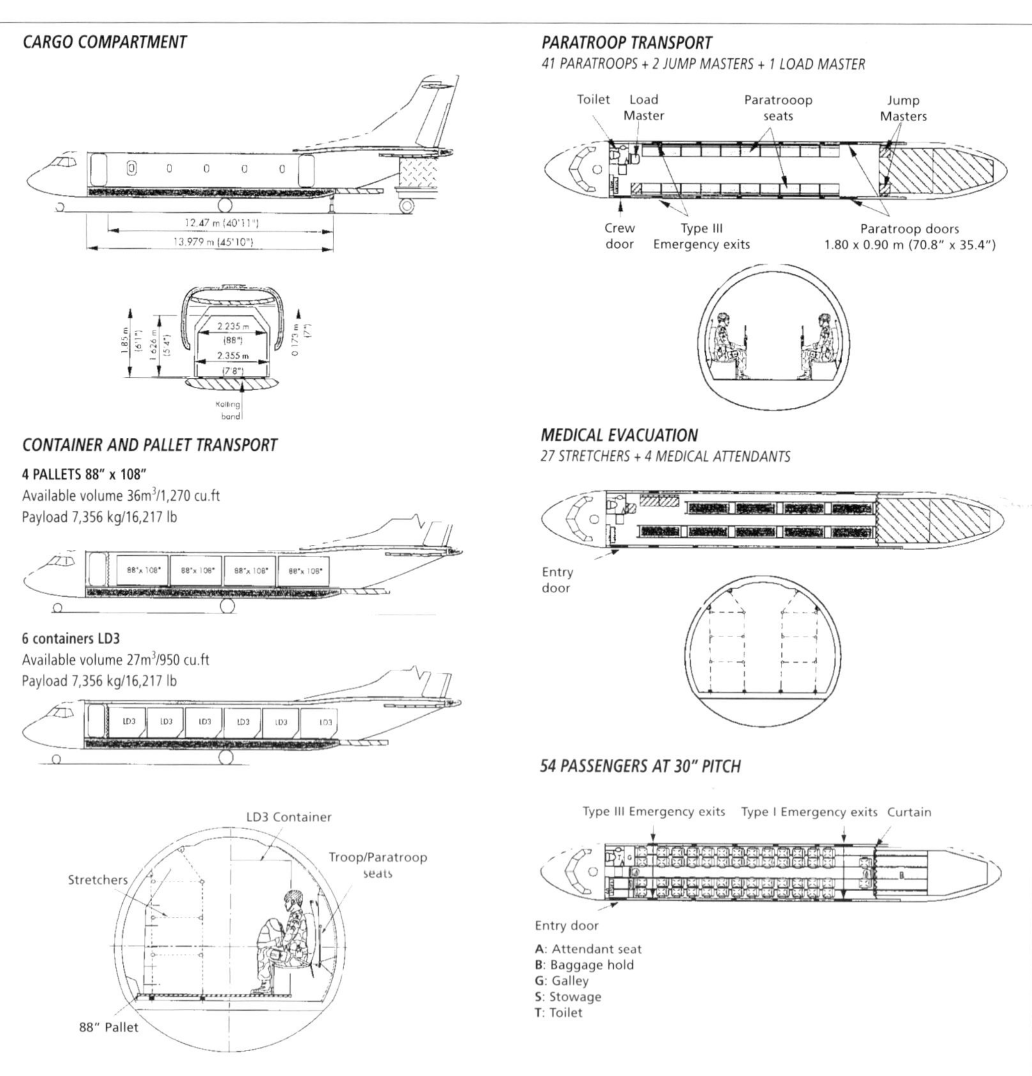

↑ **ATR 52C interior layouts** *(courtesy ATR)*

↑ ATR 52C impression *(courtesy ATR)*

Carbon/Nomex sandwich
Carbon monolithic structure
Kevlar/Nomex sandwich
Kevlar/Nomex sandwich with stiffening carbon plies
Fibreglass/Nomex sandwich
PROPELLER BLADES : Kevlar Shell / carbon fiber spar
BRAKES : Carbon

↑ ATR 52C composite material diagram, for which the ATR 72 is similar *(courtesy ATR)*

Airdropping position can also be selected directly from the cockpit. Ramp extensions (pair) are laterally adjustable (20 ins, 0.51 m width) and stowed into the ramp structure for self or winch loading of vehicles. Floor heavily reinforced to accommodate bulky loads such as vehicles. 2 large lateral doors are openable in flight for paradropping. Bulk freight is secured through rings (5,510 lb, 2,500 kg capacity) that are quickly installable on the floor rails. For heavy items, hard rings of 10,000 lb (4,536 kg) capacity are installed at suitable locations on the frames.

Construction materials: Conventional materials such as aluminium alloys generally used, but composites in the secondary structure and outer wing box offer a weight saving of 794 lb (360 kg) and is identical to the ATR 72-210.

Engines: 2 Pratt & Whitney Canada PW127 turboprops, with Hamilton Standard 247 F propellers.

Engine rating: Each 2,475 shp (1,846 kW) for take-off, or 2,750 shp (2,051 kW) reserve take-off power (1 engine out or tactical operations).

Fuel system: 11,023 lb (5,000 kg) in 2 integral wing tanks, delivering fuel to each engine. 2 feeder tanks for negative G conditions. Both tanks can be pressure refuelled below 50 psi, allowing complete refuelling in 15 minutes.

Mission equipment: Allowance of 882 lb (400 kg).

Electrical system: Based on DC and AC wild frequency currents with high redundancy (4 generators). DC power from 2 starter-generators actuated through the auxiliary gearbox of each engine (28 volt, 400A, 12 kW). Wild frequency AC power from 2 generators (3-phase, 20kVA, 115/200V, 341/488Hz), driven by each propeller gearbox. Constant frequency AC power supplied by DC system via 2 static inverters (each 500VA). 2 batteries (43 amp-hour main and 15 amp-hour emergency) are protected by the battery protection unit. TRU provides an extra DC source from AC power.

Hydraulic system: 2 independent systems, each system comprising an hydraulic pump with 3,000 psi pressure. Main system incorporates 2 hydraulic accumulators and supplies the wing flaps, spoilers, propeller brake, nosewheel steering and parking (emergency) braking. Rear ramp actuation is also through this system, using the AC hydraulic pump (in flight) or DC pump on the ground (electrical power is provided by the Hotel Mode or the main battery). Second hydraulic system has 1 hydraulic accumulator and supplies the undercarriage and normal braking system.

Environmental control system: 2 air conditioning packs, located in the main undercarriage fairing and fed with engine bleed air.

Radar: Honeywell weather radar.

Flight avionics/instrumentation: Honeywell SPZ-6000 package for the main equipment (air data system, autoflight control system, AHRS, EFIS and weather radar). Rockwell Collins Pro Line II radio communication and radio navigation standard civil equipment; for military requirements, can be equipped with specific radios. Optional GPS nav system, coupled to the EFIS and autopilot. Navigation system comprises 2 AHRS, 2 EADI (EFIS), 2 EHSI (EFIS), 2 SGU, 2 ADC, 2 VOR-ILS, 1 marker, 2 RMI, 1 ATC, 1 ADF, 1 DME, 1 radio altimeter, 1 GPWS, and 1 AP/FD Cat I. Communications equipment comprises 2 VHF AM, 1 flight interphone system, 1 public address system and 1 cockpit voice recorder. Others are DFDR and 1 ELT. Options include second ATC, second ADF, second DME, HF, Omega nav system and FMS/GPS. In addition to the standard civil com/nav, can receive specific military equipment such as Tacan, IFF, VHF/UHF AM/FM and NVG capability.

Details for ATR 52C

PRINCIPAL DIMENSIONS:
Wing span: 88 ft 9 ins (27.05 m)
Maximum length: 81 ft 4.2 ins (24.796 m)
Maximum height: 27 ft 5.6 ins (8.372 m)

CABIN:
Length: 45 ft 10 ins (13.98 m)
Height: 6 ft 1 ins (1.85 m)
Main Type 1 doors: 5 ft 10.8 ins × 2 ft 11.4 ins (1.8 × 0.9 m)

UNDERCARRIAGE:
Nose wheel tyre size: 450 × 190-5TL (64 psi)
Main wheel tyre size: 34 × 10-R16 (110 psi or 95 psi for operations on semi-prepared airfields) standard, 37 × 11.75-16 (78 psi or 65 psi for operations on semi-prepared airfields) optional
Wheel base: 31 ft 7.5 ins (9.64 m)
Wheel track: 13 ft 5.5 ins (4.1 m)

WEIGHTS:
Empty, operating: 26,100 lb (11,839 kg)
Maximum zero fuel: 44,092 lb (20,000 kg) standard logistic, 37,700 lb (17,100 kg) tactical, or 47,399 lb (21,500 kg) overload logistic
Maximum take-off: 48,500 lb (22,000 kg) standard logistic, 43,100 lb (19,550 kg) tactical, or 52,469 lb (23,800 kg) overload logistic
Maximum landing: 47,070 lb (21,350 kg) standard logistic, 42,990 lb (19,500 kg) tactical, or 52,469 lb (23,800 kg) overload logistic
Payload: 17,110 lb (7,761 kg) standard logistic, 10,714 lb (4,860 kg) tactical, or 20,415 lb (9,260 kg) overload logistic

BLOCK DATA (200 naut mile logistic mission, FAR/JAR 25, standard operating weights)**:**
Block fuel: 1,410 lb (640 kg)
Block time: 58 minutes, with 7.3 minute terminal allowances

PERFORMANCE (logistic, FAR/JAR 25, standard operating weights)**:**
Maximum cruise speed: 272 kts (313 mph) 504 km/h
Balanced take-off field length: 4,530 ft (1,380 m), sea level, ISA, MTOW
Landing field length: 3,740 ft (1,140 m) at sea level, ISA, MLW
Maximum operating altitude: 25,000 ft (7,620 m)
Ceiling, 1 engine: 9,000 ft (2,743 m)
Range: 500 naut miles (575 miles) 926 km with a 16,976 lb (7,700 kg) payload, or 1,500 naut miles (1,727 miles) 2,780 km with an 11,905 lb (5,400 kg) payload

PERFORMANCE (tactical)**:**
Take-off distance: 1,690 ft (515 m) ISA at sea level, or 2,297 ft (700 m) ISA + 20° at 6,000 ft (1,830 m), both with 15° flaps
Landing distance: 1,150 ft (350 m) ISA at sea level, 1,395 ft (425 m) ISA at 6,000 ft (1,830 m), both with reverse
Ceiling, 1 engine: 14,500 ft (4,420 m) at 41,800 lb (18,960 kg), ISA + 10°
G limits: +3, −1
Range: over 700 naut miles (806 miles) 1,297 km with a 10,582 lb (4,800 kg) payload at maximum tactical take-off weight

ATR 72

First flight: 27 October 1988.
Certification: 25 September 1989.
First delivery: 27 October 1989.
Role: Regional airliner.

Aims

▪ Larger development of the ATR 42, incorporating additional composites (more carbonfibre in the wings).

Details

Sales: Total ATR 72 sales amounted to 221 by March 1998, of which 34 are for the latest ATR 72-210A version.

↑ ATR 72-210A in American Eagle livery

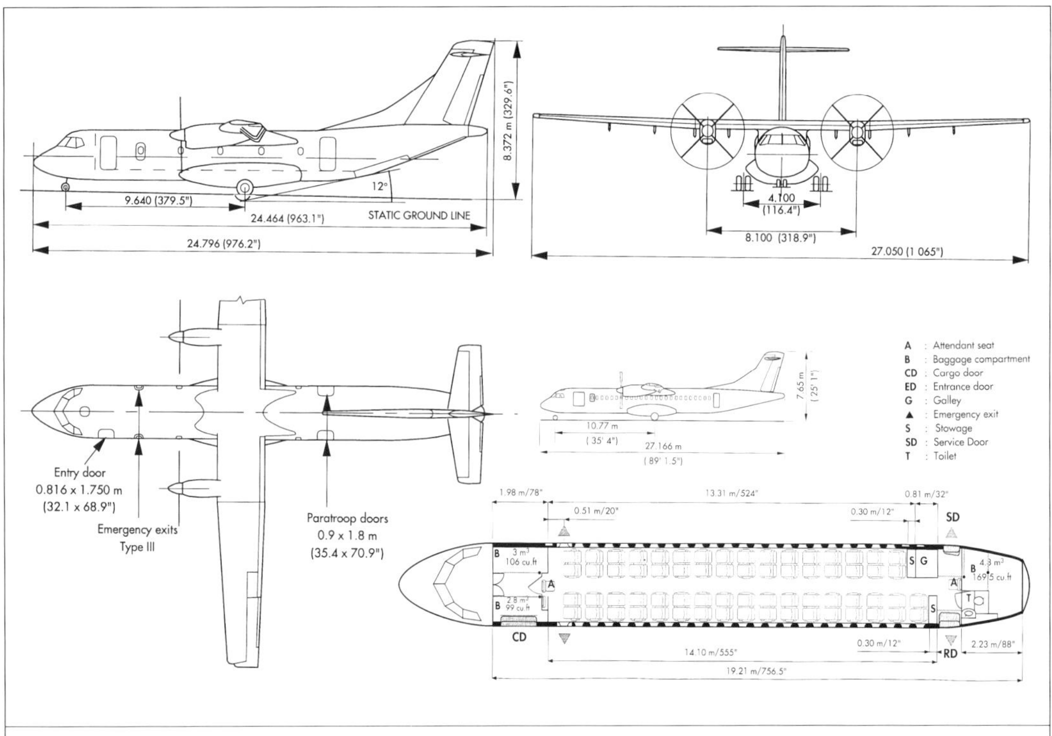

↑ **ATR 52C general arrangement, with smaller (*inset*) ATR 72 side view and (*lower*) ATR 72-210A seating layout for 66 passengers. Note, dimensions are in meters (inches) in the ATR 52C diagram, and door dimensions are clear apertures** *(courtesy ATR)*

Passengers: Typically 66 passengers at 31 ins (79 cm) seat pitch and with either 137.5 cu ft (3.9 m^3) forward cargo area or 2 separate forward areas of 106 cu ft (3 m^3) and 99 cu ft (2.8 m^3); 74 passengers at 30 ins (76 cm) seat pitch and with 56.5 cu ft (1.6 m^3) forward cargo area; or 70 passengers at 31 ins (79 cm) seat pitch and with 2 separate forward cargo areas of 74 cu ft (2.1 m^3) and 67 cu ft (1.9 m^3). All have a rear cargo area of 169.5 cu ft (4.8 m^3).
Wing control surfaces: Similar to ATR 42 but with the addition of vortex generators on the wings and tailplane. See also ATR 52C.
Engines: 2 Pratt & Whitney Canada PW124B turboprops for ATR 72-200, and PW127s for ATR 72-210, with Hamilton Standard 14 SF 11 and 247 F 4-blade propellers respectively. 2 PW127Fs for ATR 72-210A, with 12 ft 11 ins (3.93 m) diameter Hamilton Standard 568F 6-blade propellers.
Engine rating: Each 2,160 shp (1,611 kW) and 2,475 shp (1,846 kW) respectively for PW124B and PW127. 2,750 shp (2,050 kW) maximum take-off power for PW127F.
Fuel system: 11,023 lb (5,000 kg).
Other systems: Similar to ATR 52C, which see.

Aircraft variants:
ATR 72-200 has PW124B engines.
ATR 72-210 has PW127 engines and a more advanced flight deck among other improvements. French certified 15 December 1992, US certified 18 December 1992, and German certified 24 February 1993.
ATR 72-210A has PW127F engines with 6-blade Hamilton Standard 568F propellers. Shares many features with the ATR 42-500. Fuselage structural treatment with installation of dynamic vibration absorbers, new look interior with acoustically absorbent materials, suppression of noise sources such as pressurization outflow valves and hydraulic pumps, 40% larger overhead baggage bins compared with ATR 72-200 to accommodate items up to 6 ft 6 ins (2 m) length, and additional handrail embedded in the overhead bins.
ATR 52C is a shortened variant of the ATR 72 with rear loading door, for cargo carrying and other loads. See earlier entry.

Details for ATR 72-200, *with ATR 72-210 in italics where different*, and ATR 72-210A where stated. Dimensions are similar for all versions

PRINCIPAL DIMENSIONS:
Wing span: 88 ft 9 ins (27.05 m)
Maximum length: 89 ft 1.5 ins (27.166 m)
Maximum height: 25 ft 1 ins (7.65 m)

CABIN:
Length: 63 ft (19.21 m) from aft of cockpit to rear of baggage area (see diagram)
Width: 8 ft 5.2 ins (2.57 m), 7 ft 5 ins (2.263 m) at floor
Height: 6 ft 3 ins (1.9 m)
Volume: 2,683.9 cu ft (76 m^3)

WINGS:
Area: 656.6 sq ft (61 m^2)
Aspect ratio: 12

UNDERCARRIAGE:
Wheel base: 35 ft 4 ins (10.77 m)
Wheel track: 13 ft 5.5 ins (4.1 m)
Turning radius: 64 ft 10 ins (19.76 m)

WEIGHTS:
Empty, operating: 27,337 lb (12,400 kg), *27,447 lb (12,450 kg)*, or 28,329 lb (12,850 kg) for ATR 72-210A
Maximum zero fuel: 43,430 lb (19,700 kg), or 44,092 lb (20,000 kg) basic and 44,753 lb (20,300 kg) optional for ATR 72-210A
Maximum take-off: 47,400 lb (21,500 kg), or 48,501 lb (22,000 kg) basic and 49,604 lb (22,500 kg) optional for ATR 72-210A
Maximum landing: 47,070 lb (21,350 kg), or 48,170 lb (21,850 kg) basic and 49,273 lb (22,350 kg) optional for ATR 72-210A
Payload: 16,093 lb (7,300 kg), *15,983 lb (7,250 kg)*, or 15,763 lb (7,150 kg) basic and 16,424 lb (7,450 kg) optional for ATR 72-210A

PERFORMANCE:
Maximum cruise speed: 279 kts (321 mph) 516 km/h, *280 kts (322 mph) 518 km/h*, or 276 kts (318 mph) 511 km/h for ATR 72-210A at 97% basic MTOW, 17,000 ft (5,180 m)
Balanced take-off field length: 4,626 ft (1,410 m), *3,953 ft (1,205 m)*, or 4,012 ft (1,223 m) at basic and 4,232 ft (1,290 m) at optional weight for ATR 72-210A, all at MTOW, sea level, ISA
Balanced take-off field length (at 3,000 ft, 915 m): 5,735 ft (1,748 m) at 21,100 kg take-off weight, *4,845 ft (1,477 m)*, or 4,140 ft (1,262 m) for ATR 72-210A, all at TOW, ISA + 10° C
Landing field length required at destination: 3,963 ft (1,208 m), *3,451 ft (1,052 m)*, sea level, ISA
Landing field length for ATR 72-201A: 3,438 ft (1,048 m) basic and 3,500 ft (1,067 m) optional weight, at sea level, ISA, MLW
Maximum operational cruise altitude: 25,000 ft (7,600 m)
Range with 66 passengers: 1,200 naut miles (1,382 miles) 2,222 km, or 820 naut miles (944 miles) 1,519 km at basic and 1,030 naut miles (1,186 miles) 1,908 km at optional weight for ATR 72-210A

ATR Airjet series

Comments: A feasibility study for this twin-turbofan regional transport family was started in 1995, but the project was terminated in late 1997, only to be reconsidered in mid-1998. It had been anticipated that the Airjet 70 70-passenger base model could have made its first flight in mid-2000, for service entry in late 2001, followed by the 58-passenger Airjet 58 some 6 months later. An 84-seat 'stretched' version was also anticipated. Programme launch could be soon if a partner is found.

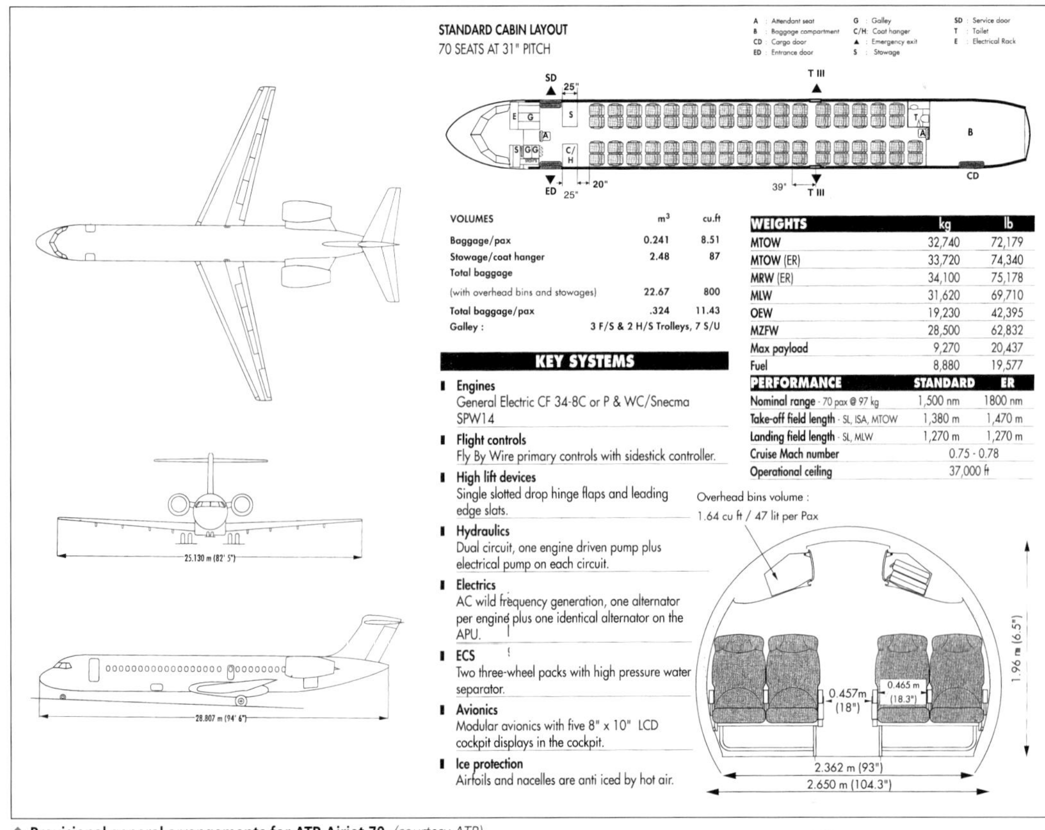

VOLUMES	m^3	cu.ft
Baggage/pax	0.241	8.51
Stowage/coat hanger	2.48	87
Total baggage (with overhead bins and stowages)	22.67	800
Total baggage/pax	.324	11.43
Galley :	3 F/S & 2 H/S Trolleys, 7 S/U	

WEIGHTS	kg	lb
MTOW	32,740	72,179
MTOW (ER)	33,720	74,340
MRW (ER)	34,100	75,178
MLW	31,620	69,710
OEW	19,230	42,395
MZFW	28,500	62,832
Max payload	9,270	20,437
Fuel	8,880	19,577

PERFORMANCE	STANDARD	ER
Nominal range - 70 pax @ 97 kg	1,500 nm	1800 nm
Take-off field length - SL, ISA, MTOW	1,380 m	1,470 m
Landing field length - SL, MLW	1,270 m	1,270 m
Cruise Mach number	0.75 - 0.78	
Operational ceiling	37,000 ft	

KEY SYSTEMS

- **Engines**
  General Electric CF 34-8C or P & WC/Snecma SPW14
- **Flight controls**
  Fly By Wire primary controls with sidestick controller.
- **High lift devices**
  Single slotted drop hinge flaps and leading edge slats.
- **Hydraulics**
  Dual circuit, one engine driven pump plus electrical pump on each circuit.
- **Electrics**
  AC wild frequency generation, one alternator per engine plus one identical alternator on the APU.
- **ECS**
  Two three-wheel packs with high pressure water separator.
- **Avionics**
  Modular avionics with five 8" x 10" LCD cockpit displays in the cockpit.
- **Ice protection**
  Airfoils and nacelles are anti iced by hot air.

↑ **Provisional general arrangements for ATR Airjet 70** *(courtesy ATR)*

Special Aircraft Transport International Company GIE (SATIC) France/Germany

Corporate address:
Joint venture of Aerospatiale of France and Daimler-Benz Aerospace Airbus of Germany (which see).

Founded: October 1991.

↑ Third SATIC A300-600ST (Super Transporter), with a conventional Airbus freighter to its rear

SATIC A300-600ST (Super Transporter) 'Beluga'

First flight: 13 September 1994 (lasting 4 hours and 21 minutes).
Certification: September 1995, after a test programme lasting about 400 hours.
First delivery: January 1996.
Role: Freighter for outsized cargoes, based on the Airbus A300-600R.

Aims

▪ To replace Super Guppy outsized freighters used to transport sections of Airbus airliners between manufacturing companies and the Toulouse and Hamburg assembly plants; Super Guppies were finally retired in October 1997. Airbus Transport International (ATI) was founded in 1996 to operate the Super Transporters on ad hoc charter operations, following the granting of a commercial operating licence. Charters use the spare capacity from the primary Airbus work, and the first such charter was undertaken on 24 November 1996, when a 40-tonne mini pressurized logistics module that is part of the International Space Station Alpha was flown from Toulouse to Turin.
▪ Relocation of the cockpit to a position below and 4 ft 11 ins (1.5 m) forward of the main cargo deck, allowing roll-on loading and roll-off unloading of the aircraft section payloads. This reduces turnaround times to just 45 minutes, compared with 2 to 3 hours for the Super Guppy.
Sales: 5 ordered by Airbus Industrie, the 4th joining the fleet in June 1998 and the last in 2001. Assembled by Sogerma-Socea at Toulouse. Expectations are to sell a further 15-20 to other operators, military and civil.
Freight hold volume: Larger fuselage cross-section than any other aircraft, offering a main-deck volume of 49,440 cu ft (1,400 m^3).
Freight hold capacity: Largest cargo in terms of volume will be A330 and A340 rear fuselage sections, while heaviest will be A330 and A340 wings. In addition to commercial Airbus loads, a military derivative could carry 2 CH-53 or 8 BO 105 helicopters. Lower deck capacity for 10 LD3 or 5 LD1/6 containers.
Freight hold access: Largest door ever installed on an aircraft.
Tail surfaces: Taller (3 ft 8 ins, 1.12 m) vertical tail, modified from the A340, with a leading-edge extension. The tailplane is strengthened and given auxiliary fins to improve stability in flight.
Fuselage: Upper fuselage cross-section of 24 ft 3 ins (7.4 m). In addition to the basic Airbus airframe for modification, new airframe components are produced by Latécoère (also lead contractor for integration), Aerostructures of the UK (nose door), CASA, Daimler-Benz, Elbe Flugzeugwerke, Hurel-Dubois and Sogerma-Socea.
Engines: 2 General Electric CF6-80C2A8 turbofans.
Engine rating: Each 59,000 lbf (262.45 kN).

↑ SATIC A300-600ST (Super Transporter) 'Beluga' loading an outsized tank

Details for A300-600ST

PRINCIPAL DIMENSIONS:
Wing span: 147 ft 1 ins (44.836 m)
Maximum length: 184 ft 3 ins (56.158 m)
Height with nose door raised: 56 ft 7 ins (17.247 m)

CABIN:
Length: 123 ft 8 ins (37.7 m)
Width: 24 ft 3 ins (7.4 m)
Volume: 49,440 cu ft (1,400 m^3)

WEIGHTS:
Maximum take-off: 330,693 lb (150,000 kg)
Payload: 100,310 lb (45,500 kg)

PERFORMANCE:
Cruise speed: 420 kts (484 mph) 778 km/h
Range: 900 naut miles (1,035 miles) 1,666 km

Helicopters, Autogyros and Tiltrotors

VTOL Aircraft Pty Ltd — Australia

Corporate address:
17 Irvine Street, Garden Suburb, 2289 NSW.
Telephone: +61 2 4943 5348
Facsimile: +61 2 4943 5348
E-mail: maloneyb@bigpond.com
Founded: 1971.
Employees: 5.
Information:
Duan A. Phillips (Chairman of Directors).

ACTIVITIES

- Research and development of rotorcraft and vertical lift.

VTOL Aircraft Phillicopter

First flight: 1971. Upgraded development model first flew in 1992.
Role: Light utility helicopter.
Crew/passengers: 2.
Cockpit: Dual controls. Independent collective throttle. Removable doors. Insulated, heated and ventilated.
Optional equipment: Night lights, cabin heater, cargo hook, sprayboom, spray tanks, cargo racks, and auxiliary fuel tanks.
Rotor system: 2-blade main rotor with semi-rigid underslung teetering hub to reduce rotor vibration and control force feed-back. Main blades are mounted 3° above horizontal to minimize blade flexing. Main rotor blades are foam-filled metal, with straight chord and zero twist. Primary gearbox is coupled to the engine by gear flex coupling. Drive shaft from the reduction box to the tail rotor is coupled to the main rotor by an overrun clutch and automatic centrifugal clutch. Rotor brake may be fitted to the clutch drum. Spiral bevel gears in primary and tail rotor gearboxes. Helical gears in the reduction box drive to the main rotor. Spiral bevel gears for tail rotor take-off. Main rotor/engine rpm ratio is 1:5.66.
Tail rotor characteristics: 2-blade teetering. No rotor brake fitted at present. Tail rotor/engine ratio is 1:1.
Tail surfaces: Horizontal and vertical stabilizers, 3 sq ft (0.28 m^2) and 2 sq ft (0.186 m^2) respectively.
Engine: Textron Lycoming O-360 piston engine. Alternative Teledyne Continental O-300 or fuel-injected IVO-360-A1A.
Engine rating: 180 hp (134 kW), 175 hp (130.5 kW) and 180 hp (134 kW) respectively.
Fuel system: 91 litres. Optional 91 litre central tank for fuel or for crop spraying chemicals.
Electrical system: 12 volt engine-driven generator/alternator.
Flight avionics/instrumentation: Range of conventional instruments.

→ Latest upgraded version of the VTOL Aircraft Phillicopter

Details for Phillicopter

PRINCIPAL DIMENSIONS:
Rotor diameter (main): 25 ft 6 ins (7.77 m)
Maximum length, rotors turning: 29 ft (8.84 m)
Fuselage length: 23 ft 2.5 ins (7.07 m)
Maximum height: 8 ft 6 ins (2.59 m)

CABIN:
Width: 3 ft 10 ins (1.17 m)

MAIN ROTOR:
Blade chord: 8 ins (20.3 cm)
Blade area: each 8 sq ft (0.74 m^2)
Rotor disc: 510 sq ft (47.38 m^2)

TAIL ROTOR:
Diameter: 4 ft 8 ins (1.42 m)

UNDERCARRIAGE:
Type: Fixed skid type, with elastomeric anchorage. Ground handling wheels
Skid track: 6 ft (1.83 m)

WEIGHTS:
Empty, operating: 1,000 lb (453.6 kg)
Maximum take-off and landing: 1,550 lb (703 kg)

PERFORMANCE:
Never-exceed speed (V_{NE}): 110 kts (126 mph) 203 km/h
Cruise speed: 75 kts (86 mph) 139 km/h
Maximum climb rate: 1,200 ft (366 m) per minute at 40 kts forward speed, 400 ft (122 m) per minute vertical at sea level
IGE hovering ceiling: 8,000 ft (2,440 m)
Ceiling: 16,000 ft (4,875 m) service OGE
Range with full payload: 375 naut miles (432 miles) 694 km/h, including optional tanks

Masquito Aircraft n.v. — Belgium

Corporate address:
Reigersbaan 31, 1760 Roosdaal.
Telephone: +32 54 343008
Facsimile: +32 54 343009
E-mail: info@masquito.be
Web site: http://www.masquito.be
Information:
John Pescod (Director).

ACTIVITIES

- Test flying at Moorsele airfield.

Masquito M58 and M80

First flight: May 1996 for M58.
Role: Ultralight helicopters.

↑ Masquito M58 production and kit-built helicopter

Aims

- M80 certificated for sale in completed form, and available also as an advanced kit. Meets FAR Pt 27 specifications.

Development

- November 1994. Programme started, with construction of the M58 prototype beginning in December 1995.
- 16 June 1997. Gained second place (behind the Eurocopter EC 120) in the Flight International Aerospace Industry awards, at the Paris Air Show.

Details

Sales: M58 prototype built and flying (now used for M80 development). Second prototype is M80 type with Jabiru engine. As of April 1998, preliminary ground testing of M80 still to do, and flights were not to restart for some time. Anticipated cost of BFr1.5 million.
Crew/passengers: 2 seats, side-by-side in a semi-reclined position. Dual controls. Series built examples have doors, and cabin heating and ventilation.
Rotor system: Laminar profile 2-blade teetering type main rotor. Each blade has a uni-directional composites spar and an aft portion

Details for M80, unless stated

PRINCIPAL DIMENSIONS:
Rotor diameter (main): 15 ft 1 ins (4.6 m)
Maximum length, rotors turning: 20 ft 4 ins (6.2 m)
Length, without rotors: 16 ft 3 ins (4.95 m)
Maximum height: 7 ft 4.5 ins (2.25 m)

CABIN:
Width: 3 ft 10.5 ins (1.18 m)

MAIN ROTOR:
Aerofoil section: Wortmann S (modified); 13% t/c constant profile
Blade chord: 6.5 ins (16.5 cm)
Blade area: each 8.17 sq ft (0.759 m^2)
Rotor disc: 178.896 sq ft (16.62 m^2)
Twist angle: 8° 25′
Rpm: 750

TAIL ROTOR:
Blade area: 0.571 sq ft (0.053 m^2)
Diameter: 3 ft 3 ins (1 m)
Rpm: 3,400

UNDERCARRIAGE:
Type: Twin fixed skids of 6061 aluminium alloy, with energy attenuation by linear deflection of the uni-directional glassfibre and epoxy cross tube supports
Skid track: 5 ft 7 ins (1.7 m)

WEIGHTS:
Empty: 331 lb (150 kg) for M58, 375 lb (170 kg) for M80
Maximum take-off and landing: 838 lb (380 kg) for M58, 860 lb (390 kg) for M80
Payload: 485 lb (220 kg)

PERFORMANCE:
Never-exceed speed (V_{NE}): 97 kts (111 mph) 180 km/h
Maximum speed: 81 kts (93 mph) 150 km/h for M58, and 97 kts (111 mph) 180 km/h for M80 at sea level
Long-range cruise speed: 70 kts (81 mph) 130 km/h
Maximum climb rate: 1,295 ft (395 m) per minute for M58, 1,950 ft (594 m) per minute for M80, both at sea level
IGE hovering ceiling: 2,000 ft (610 m) for M58, 10,000 ft (3,045 m) for M80
Range: 243 naut miles (280 miles) 450 km for M58, 378 naut miles (435 miles) 700 km for M80 without reserve
Duration: 5 hours

of PVC foam, with bidirectional composites skin. Composite virtual hinge rotor head with elastomeric collective thrust bearing not subject to cyclic loads. Primary reduction (1.07) de-clutchable V-belts, lower pulley cont' free wheeling unit; secondary reduction (3.6) crown and pinion hypoid perpendicular gears.
Tail rotor characteristics: Hydraulically-driven 2-blade, with over-torque protection. Conventional hub.
Tail surfaces: Single ventral fin, canted 2° off centre, with small tailguard skid and 35° dihedral stabilizer.
Flight control system: Mechanical, with Hiller servo for cyclic pitch control. Manually correlated rpm control, with constant speed as option.
Fuselage: Pod and boom type, with streamlined, heavily glazed cockpit enclosure.
Airframe materials: 6061 aluminium alloy and chrome molybdenum steel welded, glued and riveted glued triangulations structure, with 3.5 ins (9 cm) diameter tailboom and composites cabin enclosure.
Engines: Rotax 582 piston engine with reduction gearbox and Gates aramid belts for secondary reduction in the M58 prototype. Following development aircraft and production aircraft use the 80 hp (59.7 kW) Jabiru 2200 piston engine with V-belt primary drive and hypoid perpendicular secondary reduction gears.
Engine rating: 64.4 hp (48 kW) for Rotax.
Transmission rating: More than 100 hp (74.6 kW).
Fuel system: 2 tanks, with total capacity of 52 litres.

Soko Air Ltd — Bosnia-Herzegovina

Corporate address:
See General Aviation section for company details.

Soko Air LH1

Comments: This light general purpose/utility helicopter is in an advanced stage of engineering design. The programme was initiated in 1994 and by June 1998 prototype production drawings were virtually complete. Full development funding had not (by then) been released and construction therefore had not then begun. Designed to FAR 27 requirements.

↑ Soko Air LH1 2/3-seat light helicopter

Crew/passengers: 2/3 on bench seat. Dual controls. Co-pilot's cyclic control stick removable for improved comfort in 3-seat layout.
Rotor system: 3-blade fully-articulated main rotor, with foldable blades. Blades have metal spar and composite rear section, with foam core and GFRP skin. Combined V-belt and single-stage bevel gear main rotor drive. Rpm 490.
Tail rotor characteristics: 2-blade; diameter 3 ft 11 ins (1.2 m).
Transmission shaft driven directly from upper pulley incorporating an overrunning clutch. Rpm 4,400.
Tail surfaces: Fixed horizontal stabilizers and ventral fin.
Airframe materials: Welded steel tube truss fuselage, with light alloy and plexiglas cabin and tubular light alloy tailboom. Light alloy tail surfaces.
Engine: 180 hp (134 kW) Textron Lycoming HIO-360B1A piston engine.
Fuel system: 90 litres, carried externally.

Details for LH1

PRINCIPAL DIMENSIONS:
Rotor diameter (main): 26 ft 3 ins (8 m)
Maximum length, rotors turning: 30 ft 4 ins (9.25 m)
Length, blades folded: 22 ft 11.5 ins (7 m)
Width: 4 ft 3 ins (1.3 m)
Maximum height: 8 ft 2.5 ins (2.5 m)

UNDERCARRIAGE:
Type: Fixed skid
Skid track: 6 ft 7 ins (2 m)

WEIGHTS:
Empty: 970 lb (440 kg)
Design gross: 2,046 lb (928 kg)

PERFORMANCE:
Never-exceed speed: (V_{NE}): 86 kts (99 mph) 160 km/h
Cruise speed: 65 kts (75 mph) 120 km/h
Climb rate: 985 ft (300 m) per minute, at sea level
IGE hovering ceiling: 5,905 ft (1,800 m)
OGE hovering ceiling: 2,756 ft (840 m)
Service ceiling: 10,170 ft (3,100 m)
Range: 189 naut miles (217 miles) 350 km
Duration: 3 hours

Helicópteros do Brasil SA (Helibras) — Brazil

Corporate address:
Av. Paulista, 1499 – 10° Andar, 01311-928 São Paulo, SP.
Telephone: +55 11 251 1722
Facsimile: +55 11 283 2978
Founded:
1978. Shareholders are MGI Participações, Grupo Bueninvest and Eurocopter.
Employees: 220.
Information:
Patrick de la Revelière (Sales Director).

FACILITIES

Plant address:
Rua Santos Dumont 200, Distrito Industrial CP 184, 37500-000 Itajubá, MG.
Telephone: +55 35 623 2000
Facsimile: +55 35 623 2100

ACTIVITIES

■ With a production capacity of 33 helicopters per year, Helibras assembles the civil Eurocopter AS 350 Ecureuil (known in Brazil as the Esquilo) and equivalent military AS 550 Fennec, plus the civil AS 365 Dauphin and equivalent military AS 565 Panther.
■ Commercialization and customer support to all Eurocopter helicopters (AS 350, AS 355, BK 117, BO 105, EC 120 Colibri, EC 135, AS 365 and AS 332) in civil and military forms.
■ Services include a training centre with more than 50 different courses, authorized service centres located in the main areas of the country, special bond store carrying many millions of dollars of spare parts, workstation for dynamic assemblies and blade repair, and technical documentation in Portuguese.
■ Main markets in Brazil, Uruguay, Paraguay and Argentina. 280 Helibras helicopters in operation, with some 10% exported.

Bell Helicopter Textron Canada — Canada

Corporate address:
12,800 rue de l'Avenir, Mirabel, Quebec J7J 1R4.
Telephone: +1 514 437 2763
Facsimile: +1 514 437 6010
Telex: 05-52827
Founded: 1984.
Employees: Over 1,800.
Information:
Carl L. Harris (Director of Public Affairs in the USA – *telephone* +1 817 280 2425, *facsimile* +1 817 280 8221, *E-mail* charris@bellhelicopter.textron.com), or Bob Leder (Manager, Public Relations in the USA – *telephone* +1 817 280 6440).

ACTIVITIES

■ Bell Helicopter Textron Inc (see USA) moved its assembly line for commercial helicopters to Canada in 1986, where a production facility had been completed the previous year as a division of Textron Canada Ltd.

On 25 February 1998 the Board of Directors of Textron Inc approved the company's plan to purchase a substantial portion of the commercial helicopter business of The Boeing Company. Under the terms of the proposed sale, Bell Helicopter Textron was to acquire the Boeing (former McDonnell Douglas) MD 500 and MD 600 series product lines. The agreement also included spare parts and support for Boeing's MD Explorer helicopter, though this was not being purchased by Bell. Production of the MD 500 and MD 600 helicopters was to be relocated to Mirabel. However, the purchase had (in July 1998) still to clear US Federal review, and until that approval has been given the helicopters cannot be detailed under the Bell Helicopter Textron Canada product line. See also Bell Helicopter Textron under the USA.

Bell 206B-3 JetRanger III and TH-67 Creek

First flight: 8 December 1962 for the original JetRanger prototype. JetRanger III appeared in 1977.
Role: Light civil helicopter, with military variants.
Sales: Over 8,000 Model 206B JetRangers and derivatives have been built, including OH-58s and TH-67s for the US Army (and TH-57s for the US Navy). 38 206B-3s and 4 TH-67s were delivered in the last full year, plus 13 OH-58Ds (see US section). Taiwan is receiving 30 TH-67s.

↑ Bell 206B-3 JetRanger III used by the Fort Worth Police

Details (*JetRanger III*)

Crew/passengers: Pilot and 4 passengers.
Cabin access: 4 doors, forward hinged with dual point latching.
Freight, internal: Aft cabin cargo volume about 40 cu ft (1.133 m^3). Baggage compartment about 16 cu ft (0.453 m^3), with 250 lb (113.4 kg) capacity.
Optional equipment: High undercarriage skids or emergency flotation gear, dual controls, external cargo hook (or provisions only), flight instrument group (attitude indicator, directional gyro, rate of climb, turn and bank), bleed air heater/defogger, environmental control system, rescue hoist, litter installation, particle separator, engine intake baffles, searchlight (Nightsun), wire strike protection system, and engine fire protection system. Navigation/communication equipment (see Avionics).
Rotor system: Semi-rigid, 2-blade, see-saw (teetering) type main rotor with precone and underslung feathering axis. All-metal, moisture proofed and epoxy encapsulated blades. Flap restraints. Hydraulic boost system (pump and reservoir module). Mechanical flight control linkages throughout. Transmission drive system comprises focused pylon mounting; freewheeling unit between engine and main transmission; gearbox, tail rotor with 2.3:1 spiral bevel gear reduction; hydraulic pump for boost controls; main transmission 2-stage 15.22:1 planetary reduction; oil cooler; oil filter with replaceable cartridge; and constant-pressure oil pump. Tie-down assemblies for main and tail rotors.
Tail rotor characteristics: Semi-rigid, 2-blade, see-saw type.
Tail surfaces: Vertical fin (6 ft 6 ins, 1.98 m) and fixed horizontal stabilizer.
Airframe: Cabin is a semi-monocoque structure using bonded aluminium honeycomb. Monocoque tailboom structure. Provisions for mooring, jacking and single point lifting.
Engine: Allison 250-C20J turboshaft. Engine mount struts with noise dampers. Wet spline starter-generator.
Engine rating: 420 shp (313 kW) take-off, 370 shp (275 kW) maximum continuous.
Transmission rating: 317 shp (236 kW) take-off, 270 shp (201 kW) maximum continuous. See Rotor system.
Fuel system: 344 litres usable, standard tanks. 2 canister-type fuel boost pumps submerged in fuel tanks. Bendix fuel control.
Electrical system: 28 volt DC system with 150 amp starter-generator, and 17 amp-hour ni-cd heavy duty battery. Volt regulator. 28 volt outlet in cabin. Heated pitot tube. External power and grounding receptacles.
Flight avionics/instrumentation: Conventional flight and engine instrumentation and monitoring systems standard. Options include VHF transceiver/VOR with audio switching panel and more, Omni/LOC, ADF, encoding altimeter, and transponder.

Aircraft variants:
JetRanger III is the current civil version, still in production despite appearance of the new Model 407.
TH-57 is the US Navy's initial training helicopter.
TH-67 Creek is the US Army single-rotor pilot trainer, with an advanced cockpit display system embedded in the rear of the right-hand seat to provide a second student with a full view of primary flight and navigation instruments. Commercial avionics suite, providing dual pilot IFR capability. Crashworthy seats. 135 delivered to US Army between 15 October 1993 and February 1996. Deliveries underway to Taiwan.
OH-58, see Bell Helicopter Textron in the USA.

Details for JetRanger III

PRINCIPAL DIMENSIONS:
Rotor diameter (main): 33 ft 4 ins (10.16 m)
Maximum length, rotors turning: 39 ft 1 ins (11.91 m)
Fuselage length: 31 ft 2.5 ins (9.51 m) to tailguard
Maximum height: 9 ft 6 ins (2.896 m) standard skid, 10 ft 5 ins (3.18 m) high skid, 10 ft 6 ins (3.2 m) emergency floats, all to above rotor head
Height to top of fin: 8 ft 4 ins (2.54 m)

CABIN:
Length: 7 ft 9.5 ins (2.37 m), from forward seats and leg room to (and including) aft baggage shelf
Width: 4 ft 2 ins (1.27 m)
Height: 4 ft 2 ins (1.27 m)
Floor area: 23.2 sq ft (2.15 m^2)

MAIN ROTOR:
Blade chord: 1 ft 1 ins (0.33 m)
Blade area: each 18.05 sq ft (1.677 m^2)
Rotor disc: 872.7 sq ft (81.08 m^2)
Rpm: Up to 394

TAIL ROTOR:
Diameter: 5 ft 5 ins (1.65 m)

UNDERCARRIAGE:
Type: Fixed twin tubular skids (standard and high) with replaceable skid shoes; inflatable emergency floats optional. Optional ground handling wheels with lift tube
Skid base: 8 ft 3.5 ins (2.53 m) standard
Skid track: 6 ft 5 ins (1.955 m) standard skids

WEIGHTS:
Empty: 1,678 lb (761 kg), including 12 lb (5.4 kg) of engine oil
FAA normal take-off: 3,200 lb (1,451 kg)
FAA take-off, external load: 3,350 lb (1,519 kg)
External payload: 1,500 lb (680 kg)

PERFORMANCE (normal gross weight, *with data for 2,600 lb, 1,179 kg take-off weight in italics*, both with 2 ft, 0.61 m skid height)**:**
Never-exceed speed (V_{NE}): 122 kts (140 mph) 226 km/h, *130 kts (150 mph) 241 km/h*, IAS
Maximum allowable speed at 5,000 ft (1,525 m): 115 kts (132 mph) 213 km/h, *124 kts (143 mph) 230 km/h*, IAS
Maximum continuous speed at sea level: 115 kts (132 mph) 213 km/h, *121 kts (139 mph) 224 km/h*
Maximum continuous speed at 5,000 ft (1,525 m): 115 kts (132 mph) 213 km/h, *128 kts (147 mph) 237 km/h*
Maximum climb rate: 1,280 ft (390 m) per minute, *2,080 ft (634 m) per minute*, sea level
IGE hovering ceiling, ISA: 12,800 ft (3,900 m), *18,800 ft (5,730 m)*
IGE hovering ceiling, ISA +20° C: 10,200 ft (3,110 m), *16,400 ft (5,000 m)*
OGE hovering ceiling, ISA: 8,800 ft (2,680 m), *14,600 ft (4,450 m)*
OGE hovering ceiling, ISA +20° C: 4,400 ft (1,340 m), *12,000 ft (3,660 m)*
Certified altitude: 13,500 ft (4,115 m), *20,000 ft (6,095 m)*
Service ceiling (MCP): 13,500 ft (4,115 m), *over 20,000 ft (6,095 m)*
Range at sea level: 365 naut miles (420 miles) 676 km, *385 naut miles (443 miles) 713 km*, sea level at long-range cruise speed, no reserves
Range at 5,000 ft (1,525 m): 395 naut miles (455 miles) 731 km, *435 naut miles (501 miles) 805 km*, at long-range cruise speed, no reserves

Bell 206L-4 LongRanger IV

First flight: 11 September 1974 in original form. Current LongRanger IV was certified in October 1992.
Role: Multi-mission light helicopter, for corporate transport, medical support, law enforcement, off-shore support and more, developed as a lengthened JetRanger.
Sales: Nearing 1,600 at time of writing, including 17 delivered during the last full year.
Crew/passengers: Pilot plus 6 passengers. 4-passenger executive and 2 litter/2 sitting casualty medevac layouts optional.
Cabin access: 5 doors, as 1 hinged double door and co-pilot door on port side, and pilot and passenger door on starboard side.
Freight, internal: Aft cabin space 80 cu ft (2.26 m^3). Left forward cabin space 20 cu ft (0.57 m^3). Baggage compartment about 16 cu ft (0.453 m^3), with 250 lb (113.4 kg) capacity.
Optional equipment: Dual controls. Cargo hook with 2,000 lb (907 kg) capacity.
Rotor system: Focused pylon mounted with Noda-Matic cabin suspension system to reduce rotor-induced vibration and cabin noise levels. Freewheeling unit (between engine and main transmission). Kaflex (non-lubricated) input drive shaft. Gearbox, tail rotor with 2.3:1 spiral bevel gear reduction; hydraulic pump for cyclic and collective boost controls; main transmission 2-stage 15.22:1 planetary reduction; oil cooler; oil filter with replaceable cartridge; and constant-pressure oil pump. Tie-down assemblies for main and tail rotors. Flapping ±8° 30'. See Tail rotor.
Tail rotor characteristics: Semi-rigid, 2-blade, see-saw type. Equipped with Bell's new advanced tail rotor system and wide chord main rotor blades, LongRanger (on demonstration to the Pakistan Army in the Himalayas) climbed to an altitude of 19,300 ft (5,883 m).
Tail surfaces: Similar to JetRanger but with fixed stabilizer with sweptback endplates canted to port and synchronized elevator.
Engine: Allison 250-C30P turboshaft.
Engine rating: 650 shp (485 kW) take-off, 557 shp (415 kW) maximum continuous.
Transmission rating: 490 shp (365 kW) take-off, 370 shp (276 kW) maximum continuous.
Fuel system: 419 litres.
Electrical system: 28 volt DC system with 180 amp starter-generator, and 17 amp-hour ni-cd heavy duty battery. Volt regulator. 28 volt outlet in cabin. Heated pitot tube. External power and grounding receptacles.
Flight avionics/instrumentation: Single pilot IFR with Rockwell Collins or SFENA autopilot.

↑ Bell 206L-4 LongRanger IV

Details for LongRanger IV

PRINCIPAL DIMENSIONS:
Rotor diameter (main): 37 ft (11.28 m)
Maximum length, rotors turning: 42 ft 8.5 ins (13.02 m)
Fuselage length: 33 ft (10.06 m)
Fuselage width: 4 ft 4 ins (1.32 m)
Maximum height: 10 ft 3.5 ins (3.14 m) to above rotor head

CABIN:
Length: 9 ft (2.74 m)
Width: 4 ft 2 ins (1.27 m)
Height: 4 ft 2 ins (1.27 m)
Floor area: 29 sq ft (2.7 m^2)

MAIN ROTOR:
Blade chord: 1 ft 1 ins (0.33 m)
Rotor disc: 1,075 sq ft (99.89 m^2)
Rpm: 394

TAIL ROTOR:
Diameter: 5 ft 4.9 ins (1.65 m)

UNDERCARRIAGE:
Skid track: 7 ft 8.1 ins (2.34 m)
Skid base: 9 ft 10.9 ins (3.02 m)

WEIGHTS:
Empty: 2,307 lb (1,046 kg), including 13 lb (5.9 kg) of engine oil
FAA normal take-off: 4,450 lb (2,018 kg)
FAA take-off with external load: 4,550 lb (2,064 kg)
External payload: 2,000 lb (907 kg)

PERFORMANCE (normal gross weight, *with data for 3,600 lb, 1,633 kg take-off weight in italics*)**:**
Never-exceed speed (V_{NE}): 130 kts (150 mph) 241 km/h
Long-range cruise speed at average gross weight (sea level): 112 kts (129 mph) 207 km/h, *116 kts (134 mph) 215 km/h*, ISA
Maximum continuous power (MCP) cruise speed at gross take-off weight (5,000 ft, 1,525 m), at ISA + 20° C: 107 kts (123 mph) 198 km/h, *122 kts (140 mph) 226 km/h*
IGE hovering ceiling, ISA: 10,000 ft (3,050 m), *over 20,000 ft (6,100 m)*
IGE hovering ceiling, ISA + 30 ° C: 6,600 ft (2,010 m), *16,700 ft (5,090 m)*
OGE hovering ceiling, ISA: 6,500 ft (1,980 m), *16,600 ft (5,060 m)*
OGE hovering ceiling, ISA + 30 ° C: 3,100 ft (945 m), *11,500 ft (3,505 m)*
Service ceiling (MCP), ISA: 10,000 ft (3,050 m), *over 20,000 ft (6,100 m)*
Service ceiling, ISA+ 30 ° C: 6,600 ft (2,010 m), *over 20,000 ft (6,100 m)*
Range at average gross weight, at sea level: 321 naut miles (370 miles) 594 km, *334 naut miles (385 miles), 619 km*, ISA
Range at average gross weight at 5,000 ft (1,525 m): 357 naut miles (411 miles) 661 km, *382 naut miles (440 miles) 707 km*
Duration: 3.7 hours loiter at sea level at 52 kts, *4.5 hours loiter at 5,000 ft at 52 kts*

Bell 206LT TwinRanger

Certification: 19 November 1993 (twin-engine Category A capability and Category B operations).
Role: Twin-engined production version of the LongRanger.

Development

■ Production version of the Tridair Helicopters Gemini ST conversion of LongRanger (see Tridair), produced under an agreement with Tridair and the Tridair/Kawada Industries limited partnership.

Details *(similar to LongRanger except as follows)*

Tail surfaces: Similar to LongRanger but with endplates toed inward by 5°.
Engines: 2 Allison 250-C-20R turboshafts.
Engine rating: Each 450 shp (335.6 kW) 5-minute rating, 380 shp (283.4 kW) maximum continuous. OEI rating 450 shp (335.6 kW).
Transmission rating: 490 shp (365.4 kW) 5-minute rating, 370 shp (276 kW) maximum continuous. OEI rating 490 shp (365.4 kW).
Fuel system: 418 litres usable.
Electrical system: 28 volt DC system with 2 × 150 amp starter-generators, and 24 amp-hour ni-cd battery. Volt regulator. Heated pitot tube. 28 volt outlet in cabin.

↑ Bell 206LT TwinRanger

Details for TwinRanger are similar to LongRanger, except as follows

PRINCIPAL DIMENSIONS:
Maximum length, rotors turning: 42 ft 6.2 ins (12.96 m)

WEIGHTS:
Empty: 2,913 lb (1,321 kg), including 23 lb (10.43 kg) of engine oil
FAA normal take-off: 4,550 lb (2,064 kg)*
FAA take-off with external load: 4,550 lb (2,064 kg)
External payload: 2,000 lb (907 kg)

PERFORMANCE (normal gross weight, *with data for 3,600 lb, 1,633 kg take-off weight in italics*):
Maximum continuous cruise speed: 105 kts (121 mph) 195 km/h, *110 kts (127 mph) 204 km/h*, sea level
Economic cruise speed: 107 kts (123 mph) 198 km/h, *112 kts (129 mph) 207 km/h*, average gross weight, sea level
IGE hovering ceiling, ISA: 3,000 ft (915 m), *over 20,000 ft (6,100 m)*
IGE hovering ceiling, ISA + 20° C: 900 ft (274 m), *over 20,000 ft (6,100 m)*
OGE hovering ceiling, ISA: 3,000 ft (915 m), *over 20,000 ft (6,100 m)*
OGE hovering ceiling, ISA + 20° C: 900 ft (274 m), *18,900 ft (5,760 m)*
Service ceiling (MCP), ISA: 3,000 ft (915 m), *over 20,000 ft (6,100 m)*
Service ceiling, OEI continuous, ISA: 3,000 ft (915 m), *over 20,000 ft (6,100 m)*
Service ceiling, OEI continuous, ISA + 20° C: 900 ft (274 m), *18,800 ft (5,730 m)*
Range: 257 naut miles (296 miles) 476 km, *270 naut miles (311 miles) 500 km*, long-range cruise speed, sea level, no reserves
Duration: 2.9 hours with standard tanks
*Operation at 4,550 lb MGW only permitted at density altitude of 3,000 ft and below

Bell 212

Role: Multi-purpose, including offshore support, executive transport, air taxi, border patrol, search and rescue, and more.

Development

■ Commercial version of the US forces UH-1N and Canadian CH-135 military helicopters, also operated by other armed forces (including by the Israeli Defence Force as Anafas).

Details

Sales: Well over 700 in worldwide commercial operation, including many certified for IFR; it is IFR certified in the USA, UK, Norway and Canada. 1 delivered during last full year. Originally from US production lines, it was the first US-manufactured helicopter to be ordered by China (1979), operated by the CAAC in offshore support, geophysical applications and forestry work.
Crew/passengers: Pilot and 14 passengers.
Freight, internal: Cabin space 220 cu ft (6.23 m^3) available, with cargo floor loading 100 lb/sq ft (488 kg/m^2); tie-down fittings (51 on aft cabin floor) strength 1,250 lb (567 kg) vertical, 500 lb (227 kg) horizontal load per fitting. Baggage compartment in tailboom of 28 cu ft (0.79 m^3), with 400 lb (181.4 kg) capacity.
Cabin access: 2 forward cabin swingout jettisonable doors. 2 aft cabin sliding doors, with 2 emergency exit panels on each door. Swingout panels for extended access to aft cabin (2). Fixed step on skids to forward cabin; retractable steps for aft cabin access.
Size of main loading door: 6 ft 2 ins × 4 ft 1 ins (1.88 × 1.24 m) sliding doors to the main cabin.
Rotor system: Semi-rigid, all-metal, 2-blade, thin-tip and high performance type, with gyroscopic stabilizer bar and dampers. See-saw (teetering), with underslung feathering axis. Flapping ±11°.
Tail rotor characteristics: Semi-rigid, 2-blade, all-metal.
Flight control system: All controls hydraulically boosted (dual systems). Force-trim system and artificial feel (electrically set). RPM governor selector control.
Tail surfaces: Automatic variable incidence horizontal stabilizer of 9 ft 4.48 ins (2.86 m) span and 2 ft 6.58 ins (0.78 m) chord. Synchronized with fore and aft cyclic control.
Airframe: Aluminium alloy fuselage. Semi-monocoque tailboom.
Engines: Pratt & Whitney Canada PT6T-3B Twin Pac twinned turboshafts.
Engine rating: Combined rating of 1,800 shp (1,342 kW) at take-off, 1,600 shp (1,193 kW) maximum continuous.
Transmission: Ratings of 1,290 shp (962 kW) take-off, 1,134 shp (845.6 kW) maximum continuous, 1,025 shp (764 kW) single engine. Transmission drive system features vibration isolation mounts; lift link (single point suspension); freewheeling unit (between each engine and main transmission); 42° and 90° gearbox with sight gauges and magnetic plug/chip detector; hydraulic pumps for controls (2 independent systems); transmission oil cooler.
Fuel system: 818 litres standard usable capacity, with 2 optional auxiliary tanks of either 75.7 or 341 litres each.
Electrical system: 30 volt, 200 amp DC starter-generators (2) derated to 150 amp, and 40 amp-hour ni-cd battery. Single-phase AC supply via 3 Class B 250VA solid-state inverters. External power receptacle.
Hydraulic system: 2 supplies, each 1,000 psi.
Braking system: Optional rotor brake.
Environmental control system: Fresh air ventilators with adjustable outlets (8 cockpit and 12 aft cabin). Bleed air heater and defroster with noise suppression.
Radar: Optional weather radar.

↑ IFR-equipped Bell 212s have an above-fuselage fin for better roll-yaw control during manual flying

Flight avionics/instrumentation: Full range of flight and engine instruments. Some IFR equipped with ADF, DME, marker beacon/glideslope, transponder, VHF transceivers, and VOR/LOC/RMI receivers. Standard configuration has a communications and navigation suite comprising Bendix/King KTR 908 720-channel VHF rec/trans, VHF antenna, Astronautics horizontal situation indicator, Astronautics attitude director indicator, Tarsyn 333 3-axis gyro system, provisions for a cockpit voice recorder, and microphones/headset/interphone controls for 2 front seat stations. Automatic flight stabilization. Optional flight director. See end of data table.

Details for 212

PRINCIPAL DIMENSIONS:
Rotor diameter (main): 48 ft (14.63 m)
Maximum length, rotors turning: 57 ft 1.68 ins (17.41 m)
Fuselage length: 42 ft 1.67 ins (12.84 m) from nose to tail rotor hub
Maximum height: 12 ft 6.83 ins (3.83 m) to above rotor head

CABIN:
Length: 7 ft 8 ins (2.34 m)
Width: 8 ft (2.44 m)
Height: 4 ft 1 ins (1.24 m)
Volume: 220 cu ft (6.23 m^3)

MAIN ROTOR:
Blade chord: 1 ft 11.38 ins (0.59 m)
Rotor disc: 1,810 sq ft (168.12 m^2)

TAIL ROTOR:
Diameter: 8 ft 6 ins (2.59 m)

UNDERCARRIAGE:
Type: Fixed skids, with replaceable wear shoes. Optional emergency inflatable floats or full floats. Ground handling wheels available
Skid base: 12 ft 1 ins (3.68 m)
Skid track: 8 ft 8.4 ins (2.65 m)

WEIGHTS:
Empty: 6,176 lb (2,801 kg), VFR standard configuration weight*; 6,346 lb (2,878 kg) IFR standard configuration weight**
Normal take-off and external load gross weight: 11,200 lb (5,080 kg)
Useful load: 5,024 lb (2,279 kg) VFR standard configuration, 4,854 lb (2,202 kg) IFR standard configuration
External payload: 5,000 lb (2,268 kg)

PERFORMANCE (normal gross weight, *with data for 9,000 lb, 4,082 kg in italics*):
Maximum continuous cruise speed at sea level: 111 kts (128 mph) 206 km/h, *121 kts (139 mph) 224 km/h*
Maximum continuous cruise speed at 5,000 ft (1,525 m): 102 kts (117 mph) 189 km/h, *121 kts (139 mph) 224 km/h*
Long-range cruise speed at 5,000 ft (1,525 m): 104 kts (120 mph) 193 km/h, *115 kts (132 mph) 213 km/h*
Maximum climb rate: 1,320 ft (400 m) per minute
IGE hovering ceiling, ISA: 4,750 ft (1,448 m), *11,800 ft (3,597 m)*
IGE hovering ceiling, ISA + 20° C: 2,500 ft (762 m), *9,600 ft (2,926 m)*
OGE hovering ceiling, ISA: *12,000 ft (3,660 m)*
OGE hovering ceiling, ISA + 20° C: *9,600 ft (2,926 m)*
Service ceiling: 14,200 ft (4,328 m)
Ceiling, OEI (30 minutes power): 3,900 ft (1,189 m), *12,500 ft (3,810 m)*
Range at 5,000 ft (1,525 m), no reserves: 243 naut miles (280 miles) 450 km, *277 naut miles (319 miles) 513 km*
Duration: 2.5 hours
*Includes basic VFR configuration weight, co-pilot seat, 13 deluxe passenger seats, and electrical provisions for optional avionic and IFR modifications; includes 25 lb (11.3 kg) of engine oil.
**Includes IFR (FAA) modifications, AFCS, co-pilot seat and instruments, Nos 1 and 2 VOR/LOC, ADF, transponder, No 2 VHF, DME, GS/Marker beacon, No 2 3-axis gyro, dual controls and 13 deluxe passenger seats; includes 25 lb (11.3 kg) of engine oil.

Bell 230

First flight: 12 August 1991 (first prototype as a converted Bell 222).
Role: Commercial helicopter for utility, air ambulance, off-shore support, executive transport and other roles. Special multi-purpose military, paramilitary and police version has been

demonstrated, carrying search radar and suited to search and rescue, maritime surveillance, over-the-horizon targeting, EEZ control, transport, inter-ship liaison and more.

Development

■ Certified under Transport Canada and the FAA in 1992 as a greatly improved derivative of the Bell 222.

Details

Sales: Deliveries started in 1992. 4 delivered during last full year.
Crew/passengers: Typically 10 seats in utility layout (including the crew) with foldable seatbacks, 6 or 8 seats in executive, or 2 litters and 3 seated persons in air ambulance. Floor fittings designed for quick disconnect of seats or equipment.
Cockpit: Collective-mounted throttles.
Cabin access: 4 doors, forward hinged. Aft doors have over 170° opening.
Baggage compartment: 500 lb (227 kg) capacity, 37.2 cu ft (1.05 m^3) compartment aft of cabin.
Optional equipment: Emergency flotation system with watertight tailboom, life jackets and stowage of a life-raft; primary flotation actuation system consists of immersion switch assemblies mounted in the belly of the helicopter. Particle separator. 2,800 lb (1,270 kg) cargo hook.
Rotor system: Advanced 2-blade design, with high-inertia rotor blades with quiet, swept tips and 9 ft 2 ins (2.79 m) rotor-to-ground clearance. Elastomeric pitch change. Flapping bearings (±9°). Mast moment springs. Noda-Matic cabin suspension system to reduce rotor-induced vibration and cabin noise levels. Main rotor mast torque measurement. Rotor system is capable of starts and stops in winds up to 60 kts. Main rotor blades have stainless steel spars, stainless steel leading- and Nomex honeycomb trailing-edges, and glassfibre skins. Glassfibre straps in each blade for structural redundancy.
Tail rotor characteristics: 2-blade, stainless steel.
Flight control system: Mechanical control linkages; adjustable friction controls on cyclic and collective; adjustable anti-torque pedals; dual hydraulic system with separate pumps, reservoirs and filters, dual for main and rotor collective and cyclic and single for tail rotor; ground test provisions; and rotor brake with independent and flapping bearings.
Tail surfaces: Vertical tailfin with tail skid and rotor guard. Horizontal stabilizer, with endplates, has leading-edge slats.
Airframe: Aluminium alloy fuselage, with integral tailboom. Frahm vibration absorber in nose compartment.
Safety features: Energy-absorbing crew seats. Rupture-resistant, drop-tested, fuel cells with self-sealing break-away fittings.
Engines: 2 Allison 250-C30G/2 turboshafts. Electrically operated bleed air engine anti-ice.
Engine rating: Each 700 shp (522 kW) take-off for 5 minutes, and 622 shp (464 kW) maximum continuous. OEI 779 shp (581 kW) for 2.5 minutes and 742 shp (553 kW) for 30 minutes. Engine containment/fire protection systems.

↑ Bell 230 operated by Petroleum Helicopters Inc for support of offshore oil operations

Transmission: Ratings of 925 shp (690 kW) take-off, 875 shp (652 kW) maximum continuous, at mast. Single engine 735 shp (548 kW). Transmission and drive system have 2 bevel and 1 planetary gear reduction transmission; 6 (fuzz burning) main transmission chip detectors; internal wet-sump transmission lubrication with external oil cooler; 2 transmission-mounted hydraulic pumps; freewheeling unit at each power input; segmented tail rotor drive shaft; single-stage, bevel gear, 90° tail rotor gearbox with splash lubrication; and 1 (fuzz burning) tail rotor gearbox chip detector.
Fuel system: Dual interconnect system. 710 litres usable in stub-wings, with 182 litre auxiliary fuel option. 935 litres usable with skid gear, with same auxiliary option, in 5 crash-resistant cells with breakaway fittings at wing to fuselage connections.
Electrical system: Dual 28 volt DC supply with 2 DC buses and 2 emergency buses. 2 engine-mounted 30 volt, 200A starter-generators de-rated to 180 amps. 28 amp-hour ni-cd battery. 2 voltage regulators. Ground fault detection system.
Hydraulic system: Standard dual hydraulic systems.
Environmental control system: Nose-mounted twin ram-air systems for ventilation and defogging in crew compartment, each electric blower assisted. Roof-mounted ram-air ventilation system with 2 adjustable vents in cockpit and 8 in aft cabin.
Radar: See Aircraft variants.
Flight avionics/instrumentation: Single-pilot IFR certified without autopilot. Bell 230 was the world's first commercial helicopter to receive full IFR certification using a head-up display (HUD). Standard avionics include AlliedSignal Bendix/King Gold Crown III communications. Standard instruments include GH-206 4 ins (10 cm) attitude indicator, airspeed indicator, turn and slip indicator, altimeter, vertical speed indicator, Bendix/King KCS 305 compass system, Bendix/King Gold KPI 552B horizontal situation indicator with course pointer, course deviation bar and glideslope, standby magnetic compass and more. Optional EFIS and automatic flight control system.

Aircraft variants:
Bell 230 commercial helicopter, as detailed.
Bell 230 Special Mission demonstrator resulted from a combined effort by Bell and Heli-Dyne Systems Inc. Options for the Special Missions version included Honeywell SPZ-7000 digital automatic flight control system; Honeywell EDZ-705 digital EFIS; Trimble Navigation TNL 7880 airborne VLF/Omega/GPS navigation system; a tactical communications suite with UHF, VHF/AM/FM, HF/SSB transceivers and IFF transponder; AlliedSignal Bendix/King RDR 1500B search and surveillance radar in the nose; Electro Optical System 2602 airborne infra-red imaging system; Flight Visions FV 2000/H HUD; Spectrolab SX-5 Starburst searchlight; 300 lb (136 kg) capacity rescue hoist powered by a 28 volt electric motor; and starboard-side sliding door that folds for clearing sponson. 6-month trial by the demonstrator with the Chilean Navy (leased) included operating off ships at sea, high altitude operations and cold-weather evaluations in the Antarctic Ocean. This was followed by a demonstration tour of South America.

Details for 230

PRINCIPAL DIMENSIONS:
Rotor diameter (main): 42 ft (12.8 m)
Maximum length, rotors turning: 49 ft 11.5 ins (15.23 m)
Fuselage length: 42 ft 7 ins (12.98 m) nose to tailguard
Maximum height: 12 ft 1.5 ins (3.7 m)

CABIN:
Length: 7 ft 1 ins (2.16 m)
Width: 4 ft 10 ins (1.47 m)
Height: 4 ft 9 ins (1.45 m)

MAIN ROTOR:
Blade chord: 2 ft 2 ins (0.66 m)
Rotor disc: 1,385 sq ft (128.7 m^2)

TAIL ROTOR:
Diameter: 6 ft 10.5 ins (2.09 m)

UNDERCARRIAGE:
Type: Fixed skid gear, with retractable wheels with hydraulic mainwheel brakes optional
Skid track: 7 ft 10 ins (2.39 m)

WEIGHTS:
Empty: 5,049 lb (2,290 kg) skid undercarriage, 5,157 lb (2,339 kg) with wheels, both with 35 lb (16 kg) engine oil
Normal take-off: 8,400 lb (3,810 kg), the same with external load
Useful load (standard configuration): 3,351 lb (1,520 kg)
External payload: 2,800 lb (1,270 kg)

PERFORMANCE (normal take-off weight, *with data for 7,000 lb, 3,175 kg take-off weight in italics*, wheel or skid undercarriage as detailed):
Never-exceed speed (V_{NE}): 150 kts (173 mph) 278 km/h
Maximum continuous cruise speed: 141 kts (162 mph) 261 km/h with wheels, 137 kts (158 mph) 254 km/h with skids, *142 kts (164 mph) 263 km/h with skids*, all at sea level
Economic cruise speed: 138 kts (159 mph) 256 km/h with wheels, 134 kts (154 mph) 248 km/h with skids, *135 kts (155 mph) 250 km/h with skids*, all at sea level, average cruise weight and standard fuel
IGE hovering ceiling, ISA: 12,400 ft (3,780 m), *17,700 ft (5,395 m)*
IGE hovering ceiling, ISA + 20° C: 9,500 ft (2,895 m), *15,400 ft (4,694 m)*
OGE hovering ceiling, ISA: 7,300 ft (2,225 m), *13,400 ft (4,085 m)*
OGE hovering ceiling, ISA + 20° C: 4,000 ft (1,220 m), *10,600 ft (3,230 m)*
Service ceiling (MCP): 15,500 ft (4,725 m), *20,000 ft (6,100 m)*
Ceiling, OEI (30-minute power), ISA: 7,700 ft (2,347 m), *14,100 ft (4,300 m)*
Ceiling, OEI (30-minute power), ISA + 20° C: 4,500 ft (1,372 m), *11,500 ft (3,505 m)*
Range at long-range cruise speed: 301 naut miles (346 miles) 557 km with wheels, 385 naut miles (443 miles) 713 km with skids, *398 naut miles (458 miles) 737 km with skids*, all at sea level, no reserves, standard fuel
Range at long-range cruise speed (with auxiliary fuel): 379 naut miles (436 miles) 702 km with wheels, at sea level, no reserves
Duration: 4 hours

Bell 407

First flight: 21 April 1994 (modified LongRanger). 29 June 1995 for prototype. 10 November 1995 for first production 407.
Role: Light helicopter, to complement and later replace the LongRanger.

Aims

■ Based on the 206L-4 LongRanger but with new fuselage side panels to provide an extra 7 ins (18 cm) of cabin width, and using the 4-blade flight dynamics of the US Army's OH-58D.

Development

■ 9 February 1996. Certification (Canadian), with first deliveries in February that year.

Details

Sales: Said to be the fastest selling helicopter in the world, with 140 delivered to customers around the world during the last full year, when a further 110 were on order. First delivery to Niagara Helicopters. Also licensed assembled by IPTN of Indonesia.
Crew/passengers: Pilot plus 6 passengers, with main cabin having 2 backward-facing and 3 forward-facing seats. Corporate interior has 4 seats in main cabin.
Cabin: Larger windows than LongRanger.

Details for 407

PRINCIPAL DIMENSIONS:
Rotor diameter (main): 35 ft (10.67 m)
Maximum length, rotors turning: 41 ft 9.5 ins (12.74 m)
Maximum length, rotors in X: 36 ft 7 ins (11.15 m)
Fuselage length: 34 ft 8.5 ins (10.58 m)
Maximum height: 11 ft 9.5 ins (3.6 m) with low skids, or 12 ft 6 ins (3.81 m) with high skids

MAIN ROTOR:
Blade chord: 10.75 ins (0.273 m)

TAIL ROTOR:
Diameter: 5 ft 5 ins (1.65 m)
Blade chord: 6.4 ins (0.163 m)

UNDERCARRIAGE:
Type: Fixed tubular skids, with replaceable shoes
Skid track: 7 ft 6 ins (2.29 m)

WEIGHTS:
Empty: 2,614 lb (1,186 kg) with 13 lb (6 kg) engine oil, standard configuration
Normal take-off: 5,000 lb (2,268 kg)
External load gross weight: 5,500 lb (2,495 kg)
Useful load, standard configuration: 2,386 lb (1,082 kg)
Maximum external load: 2,646 lb (1,200 kg)

PERFORMANCE (normal take-off weight, *with data for 4,000 lb, 1,814 kg take-off weight in italics*)**:**
Maximum cruise speed, sea level: 128 kts (147 mph) 237 km/h, *132 kts (152 mph) 245 km/h*, ISA
Maximum cruise speed, 4,000 ft (1,220 m): 131 kts (151 mph) 243 km/h, *137 kts (158 mph) 254 km/h*, ISA
Long-range cruise speed: 112 kts (129 mph) 208 km/h at sea level
IGE hovering ceiling, ISA: 12,200 ft (3,719 m), *19,200 ft (5,852 m)*, both with 4 ft 6 ins (1.37 m) skid height
IGE hovering ceiling, ISA + 30°: 4,550 ft (1,387 m), *13,250 ft (4,039 m)*, both with 4 ft 6 ins (1.37 m) skid height
OGE hovering ceiling, ISA: 10,400 ft (3,170 m), *17,500 ft (5,334 m)*
OGE hovering ceiling, ISA + 30°: 1,950 ft (594 m), *11,300 ft (3,444 m)*
Service ceiling (MCP), ISA: 18,690 ft (5,697 m), *over 20,000 ft (6,100 m)*
Range at long-range cruise speed, sea level: 312 naut miles (359 miles) 578 km, *324 naut miles (373 miles) 600 km*, both ISA and standard fuel
Range at long-range cruise speed, 4,000 ft (1,220 m): 342 naut miles (394 miles) 633 km, *359 naut miles (413 miles) 665 km*, both ISA and standard fuel
Duration: 3.7 hours, *3.8 hours*, at sea level; or 4.1 hours, *4.3 hours*, at 4,000 ft (1,220 m)

Cabin access: 5, comprising 1 hinged double door and co-pilot door on port side, and pilot and passenger doors on the starboard side, all of composite materials.
Baggage compartment: 16 cu ft (0.453 m^3) volume and 250 lb (113 kg) capacity, with composite door.
Rotor system: 4-blade main rotor and dynamic system taken from the military Bell OH-58 Kiowa Warrior. Flapping ±6°. Soft inplane flex beam, with glassfibre blades.
Tail rotor characteristics: Semi-rigid, 2-blade type, with glassfibre fabric skins, unidirectional glassfibre/epoxy spar, and Nomex honeycomb core; inboard stainless steel reinforcing plates bonded to the blade root for strength at the attachment points; full length leading-edge stainless steel abrasion strips, and blade tip covered with a stretch formed nickel plated stainless steel shield to protect from erosion. 5,000 hour life.
Tail surfaces: Vertical fin and fixed stabilizer with swept endplates. Tail skid/tail rotor guard on ventral fin.
Flight control system: Hydraulic boost system for main and tail rotors (pump and reservoir module). Mechanical flight control linkages throughout.
Airframe: Bonded aluminium honeycomb cabin, with semi-monocoque structure with composite side panels and aft fuselage skins. Monocoque tailboom.
Engine: Allison 250-C47B turboshaft, with FADEC.
Engine rating: 813 shp (606 kW) at take-off, 701 shp (523 kW) maximum continuous, both uninstalled thermodynamic ratings.
Transmission: Ratings 674 shp (503 kW) take-off for 5 minutes, 630 shp (470 kW) maximum continuous. Drive system has soft-mounted pylon isolation system; freewheeling unit (between engine and main transmission); Kaflex input drive shaft; gearbox, tail rotor, 90° reduction; main transmission; oil cooler; oil filter with replaceable type cartridge; and oil pump (constant pressure).

↑ Bell 407 in Police service and specially equipped for its role

Fuel system: 477 litres standard, with optional 76 litres auxiliary fuel. Engine-driven fuel pump. Fuel boost pumps (4 canister type), with 2 submerged in each main and forward tanks.
Electrical system: 28 volt DC, plus 17 amp-hour ni-cd battery. External power and grounding receptacle. 180 amp starter generator, solid-state voltage regulator, 28 volt outlet in cabin, and heated pitot tube and static ports.
Flight avionics/instrumentation: Standard flight and engine instruments are digital clock (with OAT and amp meter), magnetic compass, dual tachometer, inclinometer, airspeed indicator, altimeter, IVSI indicator, LCD indicator for engine oil pressure/temperature, LCD indicator for free air temperature, LCD indicator for fuel quantity, LCD indicator for fuel pressure/generator load meter, LCD indicator for torquemeter pressure, LCD indicator for turbine outlet temperature, hour meter, and maintenance download ports (FADEC and LCDs).

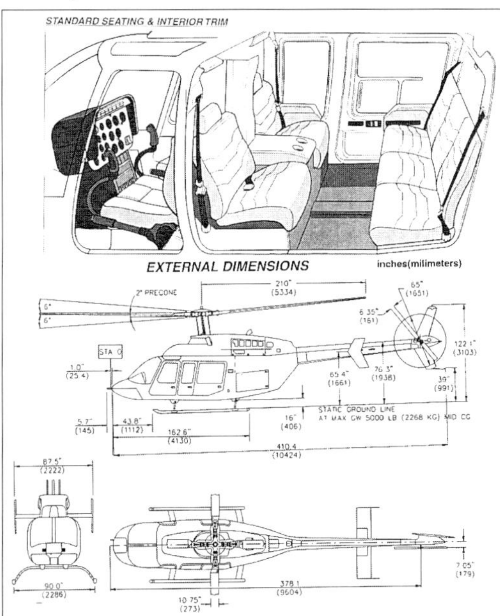

↑ **Bell 407 standard seating and interior trim, with general arrangement below** *(courtesy Bell Helicopter Textron)*

Bell 412EP

First flight: 1979 (development helicopter, as a modified Bell 212).
Role: Civil and military utility, plus specialized search and rescue, law enforcement, emergency medical service (EMS) and more.
Sales: Including those built under licence by Agusta of Italy and IPTN of Indonesia, well over 400 Bell 412s are in operation in 6 continents. 38 delivered during last full year, plus 34 Bell 412CFs (see next). Delivery of 100 412EPs began in August 1994 to the Canadian Department of National Defence as CH-146 Griffons (otherwise known as 412CFs) under the utility tactical transport programme (deliveries ended in 1998) and operated for SAR, emergency medical transport and other missions; first squadrons were No 417 at Cold Lake and No 439 at Bagotville for SAR, entering service in Spring 1995. Recently, 11 (originally 9) to the UK Defence Helicopter Flying School as Griffin HT.Mk 1s. Other SAR versions include 2 to the Japan Maritime Safety Agency, each configured with Honeywell dual-digital, 4-axis automatic flight control system (AFCS), EFIS and Primus 700 radar. Some 30 EMS versions are operated by about 2 dozen major hospitals, public service agencies and ambulance service companies in North America alone. Original deliveries began with the 412 in 1981, followed by the 412SP Special Performance in 1985 and 412HP High Performance in 1990. The 412EP (electric modification) was introduced in 1993.
Crew/passengers: Pilot plus 14 passengers/troops, or 1 or 2 pilots plus 2 patient advanced life support systems and 3 attendants or 6 litters and 2 attendants in EMS role, or cargo.
Cockpit: Collective-mounted throttles.
Freight, internal: 220 cu ft (6.23 m^3) in the cabin, and 28 cu ft (0.79 m^3) in the tailboom baggage compartment. Left crew seat removed provides 20 cu ft (0.56 m^3) of available volume. 51 aft cabin floor cargo tie-down fittings.
Cabin access: 2 swingout jettisonable doors for forward cabin, and 6 ft 2 ins × 4 ft 1 ins (1.88 × 1.24 m) sliding doors (2) to the main cabin (with 2 emergency exit panels on each door). Swingout panels for extended access to aft cabin.
Optional equipment: Cargo hook, with 4,500 lb (2,041 kg) capacity, searchlight, rotor brake, high skid undercarriage, emergency floats, snow skis, heated windshield, heavy duty heater, loudspeakers, hydraulic or electric rescue hoist, FLIR, weather/search radar, wire strike protection system, and more.
Rotor system: Advanced 4-blade main rotor system, with elastomeric bearings that eliminate both mechanical hinges and viscous dampers. New pendulum dampers on the rotor hub to reduce 4/rev vibrations at higher cruise speed. Composite main blades are individually interchangeable and easily foldable for

storage. Main and tail rotor hubs and blades have 5,000 hour retirement lives. Main rotor droop restraint.
Tail rotor characteristics: Semi-rigid, 2-blade, all metal.
Tail surfaces: Automatic variable incidence horizontal stabilizer, 9 ft 5 ins (2.87 m) span and 2 ft 2 ins (0.66 m) chord.
Flight control system: Collective, cyclic and anti-torque system with self-adjustable elevator, hydraulically servo-assisted system with dual servo actuators for pitch and roll, and single anti-torque servo actuator. Electrically set force trim system and artificial feel. Cyclic stick centring. RPM governor selector control. Dual digital 3-axis AFCS (2 pilots); see also Sales and Avionics.
Safety features: Energy absorbing seats, and rupture resistant fuel cells.
Airframe: Aluminium alloy. Semi-monocoque tailboom.
Engines: Pratt & Whitney Canada PT6T-3D Twin Pac turboshafts. Helicopter operating range -40° to +52° C.
Engine rating: Combined 1,800 shp (1,342 kW) take-off, 1,600 shp (1,193 kW) maximum continuous power, 1,140 shp (850 kW) OEI for 2.5 minutes, and 970 shp (723 kW) OEI continuous.
Transmission: Ratings of 1,370 shp (1,022 kW) for 5 minutes at mast, 1,110 shp (828 kW) maximum continuous at mast, and 1,140 shp (850 kW) single engine. 5,000 hours time between overhauls. Main rotor transmission with chip detectors/debris collectors; vibration isolation mounts; single-point suspension lift link; 42° gearbox and 90 ° gearbox (both with sight gauge and magnetic drain plug/chip detector); and transmission oil cooler. See Hydraulic system.

Details for 412EP, unless stated

PRINCIPAL DIMENSIONS:
Rotor diameter (main): 46 ft (14.02 m)
Maximum length, rotors turning: 56 ft 2 ins (17.11 m)
Fuselage length: 41 ft 8 ins (12.7 m) from nose to tailrotor hub
Maximum height: 11 ft 5 ins (3.48 m) to above rotor head

MAIN ROTOR:
Blade chord: 1 ft 4 ins (0.406 m), narrowing to 8.5 ins (0.215 m) at the tip
Rotor disc: 1,662 sq ft (154.4 m^2)
Rpm: 314

TAIL ROTOR:
Diameter: 8 ft 7 ins (2.62 m)

UNDERCARRIAGE:
Type: Fixed skids with replaceable wear shoes, with fixed nosewheel type optional
Skid base: 12 ft 1 ins (3.68 m)
Skid track: 9 ft 4 ins (2.84 m)

WEIGHTS:
Empty, equipped (basic VFR configuration): 6,789 lb (3,079 kg) with AFCS, co-pilot seat, utility trim, 13 deluxe passenger seats and electrical provisions for optional avionics and IFR modifications, plus 25 lb (11 kg) of engine oil; fully equipped CH-146 7,511 lb (3,407 kg); Agusta-Bell AB412EP 6,425 lb (2,914 kg)
Empty, equipped (basic IFR configuration): 6,887 lb (3,124 kg), passengers, trim and oil as above
Normal take-off and external load gross weight: 11,900 lb (5,398 kg)
Useful load: 5,111 lb (2,318 kg) VFR, 5,013 lb (2,274 kg) IFR
Payload: 4,500 lb (2,041 kg) on the cargo hook

PERFORMANCE (normal take-off weight, *with data for 9,500 lb, 4,309 kg take-off weight in italics*):
Never-exceed speed (V_{NE}): 140 kts (161 mph) 259 km/h
Maximum continuous cruise speed, at sea level: 122 kts (140 mph) 226 km/h, *126 kts (145 mph) 234 km/h*
Maximum continuous cruise speed, at 5,000 ft (1,525 m): 124 kts (143 mph) 230 km/h, *133 kts (153 mph) 246 km/h*
Long-range cruise speed: 118 kts (136 mph) 219 km/h at sea level, 130 kts (150 mph) 241 km/h at 5,000 ft (1,525 m), *131 kts (151 mph) 243 km/h at 5,000 ft (1,525 m)*
Maximum climb rate: 1,780 ft (542 m) per minute
IGE hovering ceiling, ISA: 10,200 ft (3,109 m), *17,400 ft (5,300 m)*
IGE hovering ceiling, ISA + 20° C: 6,200 ft (1,890 m), *14,400 ft (4,390 m)*
OGE hovering ceiling, ISA: 5,200 ft (1,585 m), *13,800 ft (4,206 m)*
OGE hovering ceiling, ISA + 20° C: 10,300 ft (3,139 m)
Service ceiling, OEI, continuous power*: 6,300 ft (1,920 m), *13,100 ft (3,993 m)*
Range: 350 naut miles (403 miles) 648 km at sea level, 402 naut miles (463 miles) 745 km at 5,000 ft (1,525 m), *423 naut miles (487 mph) 784 km/h at 5,000 ft (1,525 m)*
Duration: 3.7 hours
*Increased capability available with PT6T-3DE (30 minute OEI Power) kit.

↑ **Bell 412EP with emergency flotation gear and rescue hoist**

Fuel system: 2 fuel systems. 1,249 litres usable, plus 2 optional auxiliary tanks for either 617 or 151 litres each. Rupture resistant cells and breakaway vent fitting. Pumps on engines and submerged in fuel tanks. RPM warning system, 2 starter-generators, and 2 overriding clutches.
Electrical system: 2 × 200 amp, 30 volt DC starter-generators, derated to 150 amps. 2 × 450 volt-amp, 115/26 volt, 400 Hz single-phase solid-state inverters to power AC buses. 40 amp-hour ni-cd battery.
Hydraulic system: 2 redundant flight control hydraulic systems, each capable of operating flight control servo-actuators in case of the failure of the other. Directional control system servo-actuator operated by 1 system.
Environmental control system: Fresh air ventilators with adjustable outlets (8 cockpit and 12 aft cabin).
Radar: Optional. JMSA helicopters, for example, carry Primus 700 (see Sales). See Avionics below.
Flight avionics/instrumentation: Standard communications and navigation equipment encompasses 720-channel VHF rec/trans transceiver, VHF antenna, pilot/co-pilot microphones and headsets, interphone, HSI, ADI, 3-axis gyro systems (2) and cockpit voice recorder provisions. Full range of flight and engine instruments. Can be IFR equipped; AlliedSignal Bendix/King Gold Crown III communications. Optional dual digital AFCS configurations are: Level 1 with 3-axis stability augmentation/altitude hold system, and 2 computer operated digital automatic flight control subsystems (AFCS) which operate simultaneously in roll/pitch control capabilities (1 with short term yaw control capability) and without EFIS; Level 2 with 4-axis flight directors and coupled EFIS; and Level 3 with 4-axis flight directors, EFIS (with colour displays, sensor sources and navigation mapping capabilities) and integrated search and rescue, programmed search patterns, mark on target, auto approach to hover and more. Level 3 SAR equipment includes SAR kit, No 2 radar altimeter, Doppler 91, GNS-X (with VLF), weather/search radar with 5 ins (12.7 cm) display, and Data Nav III. Typical avionics can be dual VHF-AM/FM, HF com, dual VOR/ILS/MB, ADF, DME, IFF or TDR and encoding ALT, area nav or Doppler or inertial system navigation, radar altimeter, weather radar and ELT.
Expendable weapons and equipment: Can be armed with rocket and gun pods, missiles and more (see also Agusta).

Aircraft variants:
412EP is the current production model, as detailed, featuring PT6T-3D instead of PT6T-3B engines, improvements to the main transmission and better utilization of engine power. Also licensed to Agusta in Italy and IPTN in Indonesia (latter as NBell-412). Agusta versions include the FP, FP Maritime Patrol with FLIR and low-light-level TV and more, and EP Griffon.
CH-146 Griffon is a version of the 412EP (sometimes referred to as the 412CF) for the Canadian Forces, with fully integrated cockpit designed and manufactured by Canadian Marconi, with dual ARC-210 VHF/UHF, ARC-217 HF, and ARC-164 UHF/AM communications equipment, and ADF, DME, VOR/ILS/marker, Doppler, IFF transponder, and GPS navigation equipment. Other features are a rescue hoist, cargo hook, wire strike protection system, armoured floor and seat provisions, plus FLIR, Nightsun, skis and a heavy duty cabin heater for cold weather operations.

Bell 427

First flight: 11 December 1997.
Certification: Anticipated Transport Canada certification in December 1998, and FAA certification to FAR 27 for normal category operations in January 1999. Will be approved for VFR operations and Appendix C criteria for Category A; certification for IFR operations and Category A anticipated for 1999.
First delivery: Anticipated January 1999.
Role: Twin-turbine light helicopter for corporate, medical, public service and utility operations.

Aims

- 13 ins (33 cm) longer than the Bell 407, and it will meet anticipated ICAO and JAR twin-engine requirements.
- Designed for single pilot operation (dual pilot configuration available).
- Operating conditions -45° to +51.7° C.

Development

- Under a license agreement, Samsung Aerospace Industries of South Korea will be the sole manufacturer of the cabin and tailboom, plus will undertake final assembly and completion for customers in the Korean and Chinese markets.
- February-May 1998. Flight test programme at Thermal, California.

Details

Sales: 2 development aircraft completed, both taking part in the flight certificate programme. More than 75 ordered at the time of writing.
Crew/passengers: Pilot and 7 passengers, with seating in the main cabin of either 3-abreast facing each other in corporate club style, or 2 rows of 3 abreast all facing forward. 2 cockpit seats are energy-attenuating type, designed for vertical load of 20*g*s on a 170 lb (77 kg) occupant. Main cabin seating easily removable, allowing quick conversion for utility operations. For emergency medical service (EMS), can carry 1 or 2 litters plus attendants (see Fuel system).

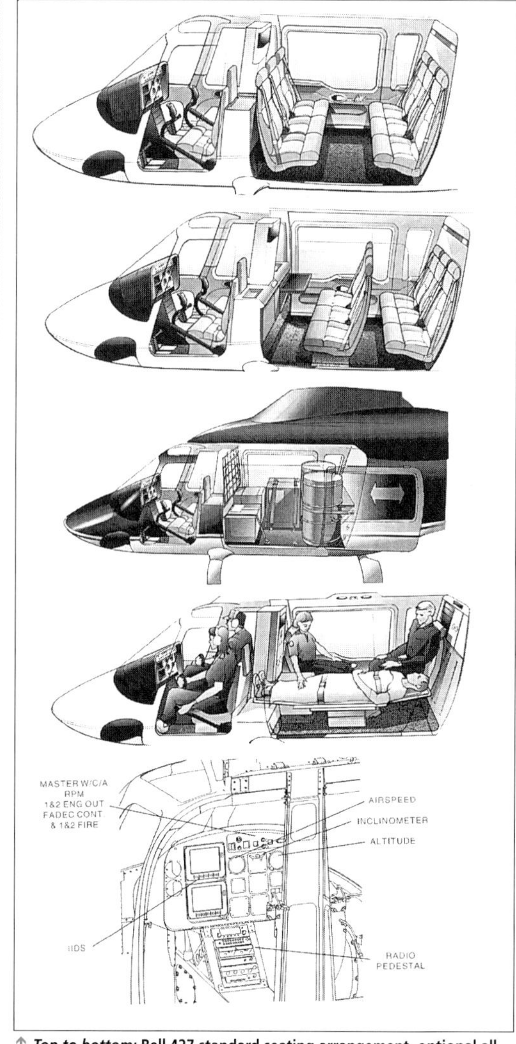

↑ *Top to bottom:* **Bell 427 standard seating arrangement, optional all forward facing seating, cargo configuration, dual pilot medical with 1 litter, and cockpit layout** *(courtesy Bell Helicopter Textron)*

↑ Bell 427 light twin-turbine helicopter, first flown on 11 December 1997

Cockpit: Single set of pilot controls at starboard seat, with dual controls optional. Door windows, chin bubbles, and bulged skylights provide a wide pilot field of vision. The roof above the pilot and co-pilot/passenger is bulged 3 ins (7.6 cm) to give additional headroom.
Freight, internal: 27 cu ft (0.76 m^3) baggage compartment, accessed from outside the helicopter, with hinged door on the starboard side of the aft fuselage, for a maximum of 250 lb (113.4 kg). With cabin seats removed, can be configured for cargo carrying. Optional removable flat cargo floor for all-cargo operations, when passenger seats removed, providing a level floor with the door sills and with integral tie-downs. Without the cargo floor, 8 fittings are located on each of the forward and aft main cabin bulkheads to secure cargo. All tie-downs are stressed for 600 lb (272 kg). Cargo floor area can be loaded to a maximum 75 lb/sq ft (366 kg/m^2). Maximum internal cargo load is 1,313 lb (596 kg).
Cabin access: Optional sliding door kit.
Optional equipment: Includes sliding door, Nightsun searchlight, wire strike protection system, EMS installation and rescue hoist.
Rotor system: Based on the 4-blade main rotor system of the OH-58D. 4 individually-replaceable main rotor blades of composite materials (glassfibre spar, Nomex honeycomb core, glassfibre skins and trailing-edge strips, and a leading-edge stainless steel abrasion strip); blade has a thrust weighted aerodynamic chord of 10.7 ins (27.178 cm) and square tip shape; designed for infinite life (10,000 hour minimum life for DOC estimate). Soft-in-plane hub employs a composite flexbeam yoke, elastomeric dampers and lead-lag/pitch change bearings, metallic pitch horns, grips, and mast and blade attachment components. Soft-mounted pylon isolation system, contributing to lower cabin vibration. Optional main rotor blade folding and rotor brake.
Tail rotor characteristics: Semi-rigid, 2-blade, teetering type from the Bell 407, with glassfibre fabric skins, unidirectional glassfibre/epoxy spar, and Nomex honeycomb core; inboard stainless steel reinforcing plates bonded to the blade root for strength at the attachment points; full length leading-edge stainless steel abrasion strips, and blade tip covered with a stretch formed nickel plated stainless steel shield to protect from erosion. 5,000 hour life.
Tail surfaces: See Airframe.
Flight control system: Push-pull tubes and bellcranks to the roof-mounted single hydraulic servo actuators.
Airframe: Completely new, with extensive use of lightweight advanced composite (graphite and Nomex honeycomb) construction. Main fuselage structure consists of 2 large composite sidebodies, a composite floor panel, nose section and control support structure and 4 internal composite 'roll over' bulkhead/fuel cell enclosures. To eliminate autoclave bonding of the complete fuselage, the main sections are assembled in a master fixture by special corrosion resistant high-strength mechanical fasteners. The major longitudinal structural members (roof beams) are of 7050 aluminium alloy and have been located above the fuselage roof to provide increased cabin headroom. The flat cabin roof panel is constructed from bonded aluminium honeycomb panels along with the nose and control support structures, which also incorporate some aluminium sheet metal. Advanced materials make up 70% of the airframe structure. The engine area top cowlings are designed for light weight and easy inspection and maintenance of aircraft systems. All forward and inlet cowlings are of carbonfibre/graphite with Nomex core; aft engine cowling and fairing are of solid laminate. BMI (Bismalimide) is used in the 'hot section' engine cowling and exhaust fairing. Titanium firewall sections. Aluminium alloy full monocoque tailboom, except for the forward 10 ins (24.4 cm) where the loads are redistributed by means of 4 intercostal load carrying members. Tailboom supports the tail rotor drive shafting, tail rotor gearbox, vertical fin and horizontal stabilizer.
Engines: 2 Pratt & Whitney Canada PW206D turboshafts with FADEC. Optional engine air particle separator kit available which adds Centrisep panels in place of the standard screens.
Engine rating: Each 640 shp (477 kW) take-off (5 minutes) and 567 shp (423 kW) maximum continuous power, both uninstalled thermodynamic ratings, or 550 shp (410 kW) engine rated power.
Transmission: New transmission with direct input from the twin engines. Transmission is a 2-stage reduction gearbox of flat-pack design with dual inputs spaced 21 ins (53 cm) apart. Each of the two 6,000 rpm spiral bevel input pinions mate with a separate spiral bevel gear which is electron beam welded to a single helical pinion that mates with a single helical collection gear (Bull gear) that transmits power to the mast. The right and left gearshafts are of different length to accommodate the 1° left mast tilt within the gearbox. The spiral bevel gearset shaft angle allows for the mast to have a 5° forward tilt. The first stage reduction ratio is 2.45:1 and the second stage reduction is 6.19:1, for a total reduction ratio of 15.18:1. Single row overrunning sprag clutches are located on each transmission input. The tail rotor drive located on the aft side of the transmission consists of a spur gear splined onto the right input spiral bevel pinion, a spur idler gear, and a spur output gear. The main rotor gearbox drives an hydraulic pump and has provisions for driving a rotor brake and a second hydraulic pump for dual boost. Drive system includes the main rotor gearbox (transmission), tail rotor gearbox, input driveshafts, and the tail rotor driveshafting. Power transmitted from each engine to the main rotor gearbox through a Kaflex input driveshaft whch contains flexible plate couplings to accommodate the pylon motions. Main rotor gearbox is rated for 800 shp (597 kW) at the input at 395 rpm for maximum continuous and take-off power, and for 645 shp (481 kW) at the engine for 30 second OEI power.
Fuel system: 719 litres in 3 crash-resistant tanks located within the fuselage, the forward tanks of 113.5 litres capacity each and the aft tank of 492 litres capacity. Fuel capacity reduced by 56.75 litres in EMS configuration, because of removal of the left forward fuel cell and bulkheads to provide litter length, replaced by a tank of half the volume.
Electrical system: Primary system is 28 volt DC, using a single 17 amp-hour heavy-duty ni-cd battery and dual engine-driven starter-generators. 28 amp-hour battery optional for extreme climatic conditions. Electrical distribution through 2 main buses and 2 emergency buses. 28 volt DC external power may be supplied to the DC essential bus through a standard external power receptacle on the nose.
Hydraulic system: Single system, providing boost power to control the main rotor actuators (1 collective and 2 cyclic) and the 1 tail rotor actuator. Pressure 1,250 psi.

Details for 427

PRINCIPAL DIMENSIONS:
Rotor diameter (main): 37 ft (11.28 m)
Maximum length, rotors turning: 42 ft 11 ins (13.08 m)
Maximum length, rotor in X: 37 ft 11 ins (11.55 m)
Fuselage length: 35 ft 11 ins (10.95 m), to tip of tail guard
Width, blades in X: 27 ft 0.5 ins (8.23 m)
Maximum height: 11 ft 5.3 ins (3.49 m) to top of fin, low skid

MAIN ROTOR:
Aerofoil section: Varies along span
Blade chord: 10.64 ins (27.178 cm)
Twist angle: 14°
Rpm: 395, with tip speed of 765 ft (233 m) per second

TAIL ROTOR:
Diameter: 5 ft 8 ins (1.73 m)
Blade chord: 7.35 ins (18.67 cm)
Rpm: 2,375, with tip speed of 705 ft (215 m) per second

UNDERCARRIAGE:
Type: Skid type of 7075 aluminium alloy tubing, designed for energy attenuation of vertical descent speeds up to 6.55 ft (2 m) per second by elastic deflection of the forward and aft cross tubes. Yielding of the cross tubes in combination with elastic deflection, further attenuates energy up to 8.02 ft (2.44 m) per second. Removable for shipping. Standard low skid, but high skid and emergency flotation gear available as options
Skid track: 7 ft 9 ins (2.36 m)

WEIGHTS:
Empty: 3,485 lb (1,581 kg), including 35 lb (16 kg) of engine oil
Normal take-off: 6,000 lb (2,722 kg)
External gross weight: 6,500 lb (2,948 kg)
Useful load: 2,515 lb (1,141 kg) standard configuration
Maximum external load: 3,000 lb (1,361 kg)

PERFORMANCE (normal take-off weight, *with external gross weight in italics*, preliminary):
Maximum continuous speed: 135 kts (155 mph) 250 km/h, *132 kts (152 mph) 245 km/h*, both ISA and sea level
Long-range cruise speed: 130 kts (150 mph) 241 km/h, *129 kts (149 mph) 239 km/h*
IGE hovering ceiling, ISA: 16,200 ft (4,938 m), *13,800 ft (4,206 m)*
IGE hovering ceiling, ISA + 20° C: 12,750 ft (3,886 m), *9,950 ft (3,032 m)*
OGE hovering ceiling, ISA: 13,900 ft (4,237 m), *5,500 ft (1,676 m)*
OGE hovering ceiling, ISA + 20° C: 10,600 ft (3,231 m), *3,250 ft (991 m)*
Service ceiling (MCP), ISA: 18,900 ft (5,761 m), *16,500 ft (5,029 m)*
Service ceiling (MCP), ISA + 20° C: 15,950 ft (4,862 m), *13,450 ft (4,100 m)*
Service ceiling, OEI (30 minutes), ISA: 13,200 ft (4,023 m), *8,750 ft (2,667 m)*
Service ceiling, OEI (30 minutes), ISA + 20° C: 9,950 ft (3,033 m), *6,450 ft (1,966 m)*
Range: 358 naut miles (412 miles) 663 km, *353 naut miles (406 miles) 654 km*, both at long-range cruise speed, no reserves
Duration: 4 hours maximum

Flight avionics/instrumentation: Flight instrument system includes pitot/static system, airspeed indicator, altimeter, inclinometer and airspeed limitation panel. Navigation instrument system includes the standby magnetic compass. Room for additional flight and navigation system equipment and indicators. Factory-installed optional avionics include Bendix/King KX 155 or KX 165 VHF transceiver/VOR, No 2 KY 196A VHF transceiver, GPS and more. The Integrated Instrument Display System (IIDS) comprises 2 liquid crystal display units and a Data Acquisition Unit (DAU). Displays utilize colour active matrix liquid crystal technology, the upper display being the primary and the lower being the secondary.

Bell 430

First flight: 25 October 1995 (54 minute flight).
Certification: February 1996.
First delivery: February 1996.
Role: Evolved from the Bell 230 for commercial use. Current uses include corporate transport, electronic news gathering, pilot training and more.

Aims

▪ Based on the 230 intermediate twin, but with changes including a 4-blade bearingless composite main rotor system, more power, an enlarged cabin (18 ins, 46 cm extension aft) and redesigned cockpit with IIDS and EFIS.

Development

▪ 17 August-2 September 1996. Record-breaking around the world flight by John Williams and Ron Bower, taking 17 days, 6 hours, 14 minutes and 25 seconds.

Details

Sales: 10 delivered during last full year. IPTN of Indonesia is also to assemble the helicopter under licence.
Crew/passengers: 1 or 2 crew (optional dual controls) in the cockpit plus up to 8 passengers in the main cabin or various other main cabin arrangements including an executive layout for 6 passengers on facing seats, fewer seats with 1 or 2 refreshment/entertainment cabinets, or an EMS layout for single or dual pivoting litter installations plus attendants.
Freight, internal: Nose compartment volume 14.2 cu ft (0.402 m^3) and aft 37.2 cu ft (1.053 m^3).
Cabin access: 4 doors, 2 each side for crew compartment and passenger cabin (left hand hinged panel door for litter access available as an option).
Rotor system: Composites hingeless and bearingless main rotor hub with 4 composite main rotor blades having rectangular tips (±6° flapping), based on the 680 rotor design. Rotor brake with independent hydraulic system.
Tail rotor characteristics: 2-blade, stainless steel.
Tail surfaces: Vertical tailfin with tail skid and rotor guard. Horizontal stabilizer, with endplates, has leading-edge slats.
Flight control system: Mechanical control linkages; adjustable friction controls on cyclic and collective; adjustable anti-torque pedals; dual hydraulic system with separate pumps, reservoirs and filters, dual for main and rotor collective and cyclic and single for tail rotor; ground test provisions; and rotor brake with independent and flapping bearings.
Airframe: Aluminium alloy fuselage, with integral tailboom. Compared with 230, has a 1 ft 6 ins (0.46 m) plug aft of the cockpit, providing increased cabin space (particularly useful for the emergency medical transport capability).
Engines: 2 Allison 250-C40B turboshafts, with FADEC.
Engine rating: Each 808 shp (603 kW) take-off (5 minutes), 695 shp (518 kW) maximum continuous power, 940 shp (701 kW) OEI for 30 seconds, and 808 shp (603 kW) OEI continuous, all uninstalled thermodynamic power. 715 shp (533 kW) engine rated power for take-off (5 minutes) and OEI continuous.
Transmission: Ratings of 1,045 shp (779 kW) take-off and 989 shp (738 kW) continuous. OEI for 30 seconds 844 shp (629 kW) and 714 shp (532 kW) continuous. Transmission and drive system have 2 bevel and 1 planetary gear reduction transmission; fluid filled pylon mounts suspension with elastomeric pads and dual inputs from engines; 6 (fuzz burning) main transmission chip detectors; internal wet-sump transmission lubrication with external oil cooler; 2 transmission-mounted hydraulic pumps ; freewheeling unit at each power input; segmented tail rotor drive shaft; single-stage, bevel gear, 90° tail rotor gearbox with splash lubrication; and 1 (fuzz burning) tail rotor gearbox chip detector.
Fuel system: 935 litres usable with skid undercarriage, and 710 litres usable with wheels. Optional 182 litre auxiliary tank. Fuel housed in 5 crash-resistant cells in the wings with breakaway fittings at wing to fuselage connections.
Electrical system: Dual 28 volt DC supply with 2 DC buses and 2 emergency buses. 2 engine-mounted 30 volt, 200A starter-generators, de-rated to 180 amps. 28 amp-hour ni-cd battery. Single 250VA 26/115 V AC inverter. 2 voltage regulators. Ground fault detection system. External power receptacle.
Radar: Optional weather radar.
Flight avionics/instrumentation: Standard instruments include 2 electrically heated pitot/static systems; 4 ins (10 cm) GH-206 attitude indicator; airspeed indicator; turn and slip indicator; altimeter; vertical speed indicator; Bendix/King KCS 305 compass system; Bendix/King Gold Crown KPI 552B HSI with course pointer, course deviation bar and glideslope; standby magnetic compass, and integrated instrument display system (IIDS). Standard communication and navigation instruments encompass KMA 24H-71 ICS/audio panel, Bendix/King Gold Crown III KTR 908 VHF radio, VHF antenna, and headset. Wide range of optional avionics. FAA certified for operation under IFR conditions when equipped with optional dual controls and the SCAS/ATT (stability and control augmentation system/automatic attitude hold) system or the AFCS/KFC 500 autopilot (either 2 or 4 tube EFIS) and the appropriate communication and navigation avionics. Factory and customized optional IFR configurations vary from a layout with AFCS, SCAS/ATT, E/M instruments and no flight director to a layout with AFCS and KFC 500 autopilot with flight director and 4-tube EFIS. A single pilot IFR option was subject to certification at the time of writing, featuring dual AFCS and KFC 500 with flight director and 2-tube EFIS.

Details for 430

PRINCIPAL DIMENSIONS:
Rotor diameter (main): 42 ft (12.8 m)
Maximum length, rotors turning: 50 ft 1.8 ins (15.284 m)
Maximum length, rotor in X: 44 ft 7 ins (13.59 m)
Fuselage length: 44 ft 1 ins (13.44 m), nose to tail guard
Airframe width: 11 ft 3.9 ins (3.453 m)
Maximum height: 13 ft 1.8 ins (4.008 m) to top of fin with standard skids, or 13 ft 11 ins (4.24 m) with high skids, 12 ft 1.6 ins (3.697 m) with wheels

CABIN:
Length: 7 ft 9 ins (2.36 m)
Width: 4 ft 10 ins (1.47 m)
Volume: 158 cu ft (4.47 m^3) cabin, 65.9 cu ft (1.87 m^3) cockpit

MAIN ROTOR:
Blade chord: 1 ft 2.2 ins (0.361 m)

TAIL ROTOR:
Diameter: 6 ft 10.5 ins (2.096 m)
Blade chord: 10 ins (0.254 m)

UNDERCARRIAGE:
Type: Fixed skid gear (standard or high), with retractable wheels with hydraulic mainwheel brakes optional
Skid base: 6 ft 10.1 ins (2.085 m)
Wheel base: 17 ft 9.6 ins (5.424 m)
Skid track: 8 ft 4 ins (2.54 m)
Wheel track: 9 ft 1.6 ins (2.784 m)

WEIGHTS:
Empty: 5,265 lb (2,388 kg) skids, 5,305 lb (2,406 kg) with wheels, both with 35 lb (16 kg) of engine oil
Normal take-off: 9,000 lb (4,082 kg)
External gross weight: 9,300 lb (4,218 kg)
Useful load: 3,735 lb (1,694 kg) standard configuration
Maximum external load: 3,500 lb (1,587 kg)

PERFORMANCE (standard skid undercarriage; normal take-off weight, *with data for 7,000 lb, 3,175 kg in italics*):
Maximum continuous cruise speed: 135 kts (155 mph) 250 km/h, *139 kts (160 mph) 257 km/h*, both ISA, sea level
Long-range cruise speed: 128 kts (147 mph) 237 km/h, *127 kts (146 mph) 235 km/h*, both ISA, sea level
IGE hovering ceiling, ISA: 11,350 ft (3,459 m), *19,200 ft (5,852 m)*
IGE hovering ceiling, ISA + 20° C: 6,850 ft (2,088 m), *15,600 ft (4,755 m)*
OGE hovering ceiling, ISA: 8,750 ft (2,667 m), *16,800 ft (5,121 m)*
OGE hovering ceiling, ISA + 20° C: 4,300 ft (1,311 m), *13,300 ft (4,054 m)*
Service ceiling (MCP), ISA: 18,340 ft (5,590 m), *20,000 ft (6,096 m)*
Service ceiling OEI (30 minutes), ISA: 6,990 ft *(2,130 m), 15,666 ft (4,775 m)*
Range: 348 naut miles (401 miles) 644 km, *365 naut miles (420 miles) 676 km*, both at long-range cruise speed, ISA, sea level, no reserves

↑ Bell 430 with optional retractable wheel undercarriage

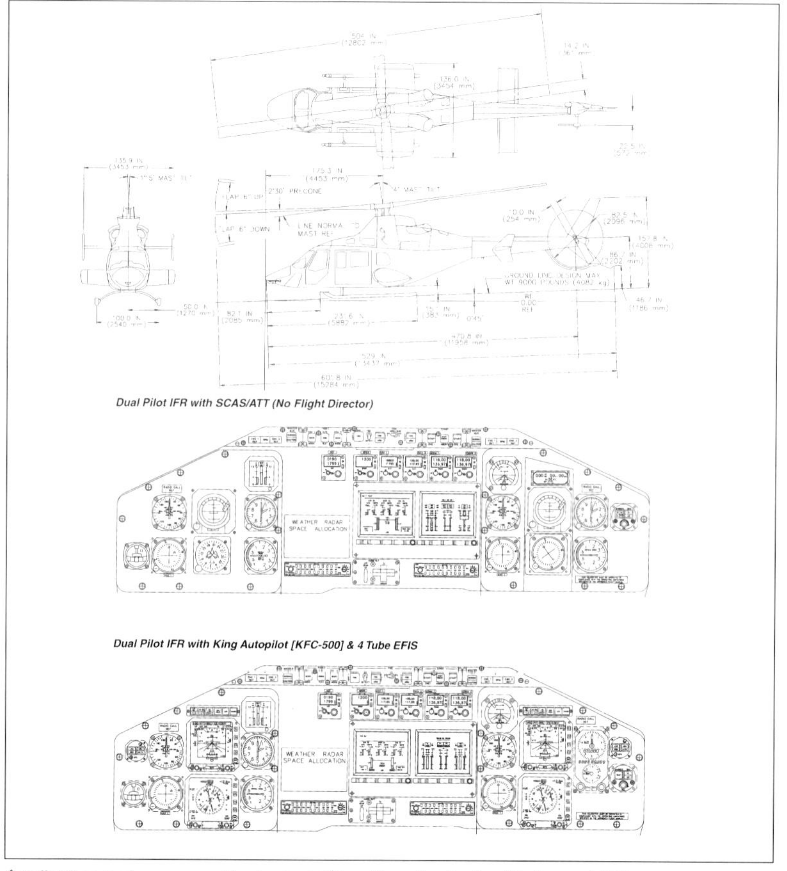

↑ Bell 430 general arrangement in standard skid configuration *(top)* and 2 of several IFR instrument configurations *(bottom)* *(courtesy Bell Helicopter Textron)*

Canadian Home Rotors Inc — Canada

Corporate address:
4 Roy Street, Ear Falls, Ontario P0V 1T0.

Telephone & facsimile: +1 807 222 2474

Information:
Doug Fulford (Vice President).

Canadian Home Rotors Baby Belle

First flown: 1986.
Role: 2-seat light homebuilt helicopter.
Cockpit: Bubble enclosure.
Sales: Made available as plans and kits for home construction/assembly. US$43,009 (as of March 1998) for complete kit, or can be purchased as a series of smaller kits. Building time estimated at 1,200 hours.
Rotor system: 2-blade stainless steel main rotor with bonded and riveted skins. Main transmission is supplied assembled ready to bolt on. Includes swashplate, slider cross, cooling fan, over-running clutch and drum. Nickel-plated balance beam assembly. Tailrotor driveshaft kit contains everything to couple the main transmission to the tail rotor gearbox, including pillow block bearings and constant velocity coupling.
Airframe materials: Principally 4130 chromoly tubing, aluminium sheet, and aluminium alloy skids.

↑ Canadian Home Rotors Baby Belle

Engine: Textron Lycoming O-320 piston engine, with the engine modification kit supplied with everything needed to convert it to vertical operation.
Engine rating: 150-160 hp (112-119.3 kW).
Fuel system: 68 litres.
Electrical system: Engine starter-generator.
Flight avionics/instrumentation: Dual engine and rotor tachometer, manifold pressure, vertical airspeed, compass, hour meter, airspeed indicator, sensitive altimeter, Quad-4 cylinder head temperature, and bank indicator instrumentation.

Details for Baby Belle

PRINCIPAL DIMENSIONS:
Rotor diameter (main): 25 ft (7.62 m)
Maximum length: 29 ft 8 ins (9.04 m)
Maximum height: 8 ft 9 ins ((2.67 m)

MAIN ROTOR:
Blade chord: 8 ins (0.203 m)

TAIL ROTOR:
Diameter: 4 ft (1.22 m)

WEIGHTS:
Empty: 900 lb (408 kg)
Maximum take-off: 1,400 lb (635 kg)
Payload: 500 lb (227 kg)

PERFORMANCE:
Maximum speed: 87 kts (100 mph) 161 km/h
Cruise speed: 74 kts (85 mph) 137 km/h
Normal climb rate: 1,000 ft (305 m) per minute
IGE hovering ceiling: 7,000 ft (2,133 m)
Ceiling: 10,000 ft (3,050 m)
Range: 174 naut miles (200 miles) 322 km

Eurocopter Canada Limited — Canada

Corporate address:
1100 Gilmore Road, PO Box 250, Fort Erie, Ontario L2A 5M9.

Telephone: +1 800 267 4999 or +1 905 871 7772
Facsimile: +1 905 871 3599 or 3320
Web site: www.eurocopter.com

Founded: 1984, originally as MBB Helicopter Canada.

Employees: Approximately 100.

Information:
Contact Customer Support.

ACTIVITIES

▪ As a subsidiary of Eurocopter International, Eurocopter Canada has the mandate for Canada and undertakes marketing, repair and overhaul of Eurocopter helicopters, including the AS 350 BA and B2 Ecureuil, AS 355 Ecureuil, AS 365 Dauphin 2, BO 105 LS A-3 and CBS, and BK 117. New programmes include the preparation and development of options for the EC-135. It also has production facilities, where assembly of helicopters is undertaken, including the BO 105 LS for which it is the principal authority. Details of Eurocopter helicopters can be found in the Multi-national section.

IMP Group International Inc – Aerospace Divisions — Canada

Corporate address:
Suite 400, 2651 Dutch Village Road, Halifax, Nova Scotia B3L 4T1.

Telephone: +1 902 873 2250
Facsimile: +1 902 873 2290
E-mail: impaero@impgroup.com
Web site: http://www.impgroup.com/impaero

Founded: 1970.

Information:
Derek W. Kinsman, P.Eng (Director, International Marketing – *facsimile* +1 902 873 2003).

ACTIVITIES

▪ Depot level maintenance and engineering for the Canadian Forces' H-3 Sea King and P-3C Aurora aircraft.
▪ Manufacturer of sheet metal and composite aerostructures.
▪ Design and manufacture of wire harness assemblies for military and civil aircraft and spacecraft applications.
▪ Licensed by Hamilton Standard on H-3 and S-76 helicopter flight control systems (engineering, manufacture and repair).
▪ Communication equipment repair and overhaul.
▪ Manufacture of precision machined components.

Rotary Air Force Marketing, Inc — Canada

Corporate address:
PO Box 1236, Kindersley, Saskatchewan S0L 1S0.

Telephone: +1 306 463 6030
Facsimile: +1 306 463 6032

Rotary Air Force 1000, 2000 and GTX

Role: Single- and 2-seat kit-built autogyros respectively.

↑ **Rotary Air Force 2000GTX SE** *(courtesy RAF)*

Details *(RAF 2000, except under Aircraft variants)*

Rotor system: RAF 2-blade foam/aluminium/composites rotor, with pre-rotator to reduce take-off distance.
Airframe materials: Aluminium alloy tubing and composites.
Engine: Subaru EA82 modified auto engine, with the 2000GTX SE having the most powerful Subaru EJ 2.2 Legacy engine with 2.1:1 cog belt reduction unit and 5 ft 8 ins (1.73 m) Warp Drive composites propeller.
Engine rating: 98-130 hp (73-97 kW).
Fuel system: 87 litres.

Aircraft variants:
RAF 1000 is the single-seat version, with a 98 hp (73 kW) Subaru engine and 475 lb (215.5 kg) empty weight.
RAF 2000STD SE is the basic 2-seater.
RAF 2000GTX SE is a version of the basic model with the most powerful EJ 2.2 Legacy balanced engine, modified exhaust systems and improved levels of trim.

Details for RAF 2000GTX SE

PRINCIPAL DIMENSIONS:
Rotor diameter (main): 30 ft (9.14 m)
Fuselage length: 13 ft 7 ins (4.14 m)
Maximum height: 8 ft 5.5 ins (2.59 m)

MAIN ROTOR:
Rotor disc: 706 sq ft (65.59 m^2)

WEIGHTS:
Empty: 730 lb (331 kg)
Maximum take-off: 1,540 lb (699 kg)

PERFORMANCE:
Maximum operating speed: 87 kts (100 mph) 161 km/h
Cruise speed: 70 kts (80 mph) 128 km/h pilot only, or 65 kts (75 mph) 121 km/h with 2 crew
Take-off speed: 22 kts (25 mph) 40 km/h pilot only, or 26-31 kts (30-35 mph) 48-56 km/h with 2 crew
Minimum speed: 9-13 kts (10-15 mph) 16-24 km/h with 2 crew
Maximum climb rate: 1,000 ft (305 m) per minute with 2 crew, at sea level
Take-off distance: 75-300 ft (23-92 m)
Landing distance: 1-10 ft (0.3-3 m)
Ceiling: 10,000 ft (3,050 m)
Duration: 3 hours, with 30 minutes reserve

China National Helicopter Corporation — China

ACTIVITIES

▪ A department of AVIC which administers China's helicopter activities, including those of Jingdezhen, Harbin and the Chinese Helicopter Research and Development Institute. It oversees conceptual studies, R&D, testing, production, after sales service, marketing and modifications.

Harbin Aircraft Manufacturing Corporation — China

Corporate address:
See Combat section for company details.

Note: Brief details of the abandoned Polar Star can be found in the 1996-97 edition of *WA&SD*, page 304.

Harbin Z-9 (or Zhi-9) Haitun

Certification: Meets FAR 29 categories A and B for IFR and VFR operations.
Role: Light twin-turboshaft multi-purpose helicopter, as a license-built Eurocopter AS 365N1 Dauphin 2, for passenger or cargo transport, medevac, off-shore support, aerial photography, maritime surveillance, rescue, forestry protection, survey, calibration and more, plus anti-tank, reconnaissance, communications, 'interference', anti-submarine, assault transport and other military roles.
Sales: Assembly of 50 Z-9/-9As covered under the technical licence originally signed with Aerospatiale were completed in 1992. Z-9A-0100 (*B-572L*) is believed to be the HAMC demonstrator. Current production of a second quantity of 30 helicopters is based on the Z-9B, first flown on 16 January 1992 and certified on 30 December that year. PLA Army is thought to operate some 20 or more Z-9 types, including anti-tank variants in full camouflage with roof sights and Hongjian missiles. PLA Navy has a similar number for ship-borne communications and assault roles.

↑ Harbin Z-9B Haitun during off-shore work

Details for Z-9A

PRINCIPAL DIMENSIONS:
Rotor diameter (main): 39 ft 2 ins (11.93 m)
Maximum length, rotors turning: 44 ft 10.5 ins (13.68 m)
Maximum height: 11 ft 6.5 ins (3.52 m) above rotor head

CABIN:
Area: 45.2 sq ft (4.2 m^2), with loading of 125 lb/sq ft (610 kg/m^2)

MAIN ROTOR:
Aerofoil section: OA2
Blade chord: 1 ft 3 ins -1 ft 4 ins (0.385-0.406 m)
Rotor disc: 1,204.5 sq ft (111.9 m^2)
Twist angle: 10°
Rpm: 349 rpm (at 6,000 rpm engine shaft speed), with 350-360 rpm in flight

TAIL ROTOR:
Aerofoil section: NACA 63A
Diameter: 2 ft 11 ins (0.89 m)
Twist angle: -7°

UNDERCARRIAGE:
Type: Hydraulically retractable, with castoring/self-centring twin nosewheels

WEIGHTS:
Empty: 4,519.5 lb (2,050 kg) standard helicopter, excluding any optional equipment
Minimum take-off weight: 5,291 lb (2,400 kg)
Maximum take-off: 9,039 lb (4,100 kg)
Payload: 4,493 lb (2,038 kg)
Maximum slung payload: 3,527 lb (1,600 kg)

PERFORMANCE:
Maximum speed: 165 kts (190 mph) 306 km/h
High cruise speed: 151 kts (174 mph) 280 km/h
Normal cruise speed: 135 kts (155 mph) 250 km/h
Maximum climb rate: 827 ft (252 m) per minute vertical, 1,300 ft (396 m) per minute normal
IGE hovering ceiling: 7,055 ft (2,150 m), ISA
OGE hovering ceiling: 3,775 ft (1,150 m), ISA
Ceiling: 19,685 ft (6,000 m) service
Range: 464 naut miles (534 miles) 860 km with standard fuel, 539.5 naut miles (621 miles) 1,000 km with auxiliary tank, both without reserves

Details *(Z-9A)*

Crew/passengers: 2 crew plus 10-12 passengers, or 4 litters and 2 seats, or 2 litters and 5 seats.
Cockpit: Dual controls.
Cabin access: 6 jettisonable doors.
Loading facilities: 12 tie-down rings flush on the cabin floor, with maximum 3,307 lb (1,500 kg) loading each. Baggage hold between the cabin and the tailboom, with starboard door.
Optional equipment: Includes rescue hoist.
Rotor system: 4-blade composites main rotor. Rotor head comprises a glassfibre starflex, glassfibre clamping plate, elastomeric bearing and frequency matcher with no flapping/clamping hinges and no need for lubrication. Each blade (Nomex honeycomb core, glassfibre spar leading-edge, glassfibre/carbonfibre skin and stainless steel leading-edge strip) is attached to the hub by 2 pins.

↑ PLA Army Harbin Z-9 in anti-tank form, with roof-mounted sight and Hongjian 8 missiles *(courtesy Helicopter International)*

Airframe materials: Semi-monocoque, with some metal honeycomb sandwich construction, and composites for inspection panels and fairings.
Engines: 2 CNSAC WZ-8A (licensed Turbomeca Arriel 1C or 1C1) turboshafts. Fire detection and extinguishing systems installed. Oil 26.5 lb (12 kg).
Engine rating: 669 shp (499 kW) take-off, 594 shp (443 kW) maximum continuous, 696 shp (519 kW) intermediate emergency power, and 734 shp (547 kW) maximum emergency power.
Fuel system: 1,140 litres standard, with 180 litre optional auxiliary tanks and 475 litre optional ferry tanks.
Braking system: Hydraulic disc, for differential or symmetrical braking to main wheels.
Flight avionics/instrumentation: 3-axis autopilot, coupler flight governor, and appropriate instruments and control boxes for single-pilot IFR use of the radio systems.
Weapon system avionics: Roof-mounted sight on military anti-tank version.
Expendable weapons and equipment: Anti-tank variant for PLA Army carries Hongjian 8A and/or 8B missiles on fuselage-side pylons. Anti-submarine version would carry appropriate weapons.

Harbin Z-?

Comments: Harbin and AVIC are studying the possibility of developing a new 5 or 5.5 tonne class helicopter, derived from the Z-9. MTU Turbomeca Rolls-Royce has proposed 2 MTR 390 turboshafts as the power plant. Eurocopter reportedly could become a partner if the programme is launched.

Jingdezhen Helicopter Corporation — China

Corporate address:
PO Box 109, Jingdezhen City, Jianhxi 333002.
Telephone: +86 798 844 2019 or 2023
Facsimile: +86 798 844 1460

Note: This organization was formerly known as the Changhe Aircraft Industries Corporation.

Jingdezhen Z-8

First flight: 11 December 1985.
Certification: 8 April 1989.
Role: Heavy transport helicopter, suited also to search and rescue, firefighting and survey; though described in the brochure as a commercial helicopter, military uses could include anti-submarine, anti-ship and minelaying with the appropriate equipment installed.

Development

- Based on the French Aerospatiale SA 321 Super Frelon, of which the air force retains more than 13 for transport, anti-submarine, and search and rescue roles.

Details

Sales: Underwent military trials from 1989 with the PLA Navy and at least 8 are thought to be in PLA Navy service. Civil version believed also in use, though in very small numbers (possibly 4), conceivably for firefighting in addition to transport.
Crew/passengers: 2 or 3 flight crew plus 39 passengers, or 27 equipped troops, 15 litters and attendant, 11,023 lb (5,000 kg) of cargo, wheeled vehicles or other loads.

Details for Z-8

PRINCIPAL DIMENSIONS:
Rotor diameter (main): 62 ft (18.9 m)
Maximum length, rotors turning: 75 ft 6.8 ins (23.035 m)
Maximum height: 21 ft 10 ins (6.66 m) above rotating rotors

MAIN ROTOR:
Blade area: each 54.89 sq ft (5.1 m^2)
Rotor disc: 3,019.06 sq ft (280.48 m^2)

TAIL ROTOR:
Diameter: 13 ft 1 ins (4 m)

WEIGHTS:
Empty: 15,388 lb (6,980 kg)
Empty, operating: 16,644 lb (7,550 kg)
Normal take-off: 23,350 lb (10,592 kg)
Maximum take-off: 28,660 lb (13,000 kg)
Payload: 11,023 lb (5,000 kg)

PERFORMANCE (MTOW, except where shown):
Never-exceed speed (V_{NE}): 148 kts (171 mph) 275 km/h
Maximum cruise speed: 134 kts (154 mph) 248 km/h
Long-range cruise speed: 125 kts (144 mph) 232 km/h
Climb rate, 1 engine out: 1,300 ft (396 m) per minute, sea level
IGE hovering ceiling: 6,230 ft (1,900 m), or 18,000 ft (5,500 m) at 19,840 lb (9,000 kg) weight
OGE hovering ceiling: 14,435 ft (4,400 m) at 19,840 lb (9,000 kg) weight
Ceiling: 10,000 ft (3,050 m), or 19,700 ft (6,000 m) at 19,840 lb (9,000 kg) weight
Range with full fuel: 432 naut miles (497 miles) 800 km
Duration: 4.1 hours

↑ **Jingdezheng Z-8 in PLA Navy colours** *(courtesy Jingdezhen Helicopter Corporation)*

Cabin access: Hydraulic rear ramp/door for straight-in loading, plus starboard-side sliding door.
Optional equipment: 605 lb (275 kg) rescue hoist, suppressant tank for firefighting, and other equipment appropriate to its role.
Rotor system: 6-blade main rotor, with drag and flapping hinges and damper. Zhongnan gearbox.
Tail rotor characteristics: 5-blade type.
Fuselage: Hull type, with high-mounted tailboom and side-mounted stabilizing floats, to permit safe alighting on water in an emergency. Not believed to be intended for fully amphibious operations, due in part to the fixed undercarriage.
Airframe materials: Metal stressed skin.
Engines: 3 Changzhou Lan Xiang WZ6 turboshafts.
Engine rating: Each 1,550 shp (1,156 kW) OEI rating.
Transmission rating: 4,120 shp (3,072 kW).
Fuel system: 3,900 litres standard, with 1,900 litres of auxiliary fuel available in optional cabin tanks for ferry flights.
Radar: Sea surveillance radar for military maritime and search and rescue roles.
Flight avionics/instrumentation: Includes KJ-8 autopilot.
Expendable weapons and equipment: Could include sonobuoys, missiles, torpedoes, depth bombs, mines and other weapons and equipment appropriate to role.

Jingdezhen Z-11

First flight: 26 December 1996, with reported (but unconfirmed) 1994 first flight date for a possible Ecureuil/AStar rebuild used in the development programme (see Development).
Certification: Anticipated for 1999.
First delivery: Anticipated for 1999.
Role: Multi-purpose light helicopter for civil, paramilitary and military uses, including touring, pilot training, communication, rescue, forest guard, police work, survey, and fire missions.

Development

- Said to be the first helicopter designed and manufactured in China, though clearly bearing a resemblance to the Eurocopter AS 350. Study began in 1991. Reports suggest the acquisition by China of 2 AStar helicopters from the USA in 1994 (presumably used), which may have assisted the development programme, plus 8 Ecureuils from Eurocopter in 1996. Further unconfirmed

↑ **Jingdezhen Z-11** *(courtesy China Aviation News)*

reports suggest some difficulty has been experienced in developing the Z-11's rotor dynamics.
Sales: Possibly the prototype plus 4 development helicopters for the test programme, with 3 others completed (may include ground test airframes). AVIC anticipates production deliveries to begin in 1999. The PLA Army is expected to receive the first examples for observation and training roles.
Crew/passengers: 6 or 7 persons.
Rotor system: 3-blade main rotor.
Tail rotor characteristics: 2-blade.
Tail surfaces: Vertical fins, the ventral supporting a tail guard. Horizontal stabilizer.
Engine: Single CNSAC WZ-8D turboshaft.
Engine rating: 684 shp (510 kW).

Details for Z-11

UNDERCARRIAGE:
Type: Fixed skid type

WEIGHTS:
Empty: 2,770 lb (1,256 kg)
Maximum take-off: 4,851 lb (2,200 kg) class

PERFORMANCE:
Maximum cruise speed: 130 kts (149 mph) 240 km/h
Service ceiling: 17,225 ft (5,250 m)
Range: 323 naut miles (372 miles) 598 km
Duration: 3.7 hours

UNIS, obchodní spol, sro — Czech Republic

Corporate office address:
Jundrovská 33, 624 00 Brno.
Telephone: +420 5 41515 205
Facsimile: +420 5 4121 0361
E-mail: namisnak@unis.cz
Information:
Ing Jan Námisňák, CSc.

ALSO:

UNIS-Aero
Address: Hviezdoslavova 53, 627 00 Brno.
Telephone: +420 5 45321 532
Facsimile: +420 5 4521 6319

UNIS NA 40-Bongo

Certification: Anticipated for late 1998. Normal category, conforming to FAR 27, 33, 34 and 36 regulations.
Role: Twin-turbine light helicopter, without a tail rotor. Possible uses include civil and military flying and navigation training, rescue, city flying (due to small size and twin-engine layout), external cargo carrying, surveillance/observation, and various other military applications (assisted by its very low radar signature, low infra-red signature, and bullet damage resistant airframe).

Aims

- Low maintenance and operating costs.
- Smooth flight due to the reduction in all mechanical and interference vibration, increased directional stability and enhanced directional and lateral manoeuvrability. No tail rotor.

Details

Sales: Priced at approximately US$500,000 (quoted in March 1998).
Crew/passenger: 2 persons, side by side, in semi-reclined position. Baggage space aft of folding seats, of approximately 80 litres capacity.
Freight, external: Up to 529 lb (240 kg) of cargo or baggage space by installing a special aerodynamic container under the fuselage.
Cabin access: Large upward-opening combined window/door for each person.
Rotor system: 2-blade main rotor, the rotor head of elastomeric type constructed with a laminated vacuum-manufactured composite body (see Safety features). Composite blades can move in 3 axes and have significant geometric torsion.
Tail characteristics: COCOMO system, offering complete momentum compensation without the need for a tail rotor, making it possible to reduce the complexity of mechanical transmission as well as fuel consumption, and simplified maintenance.
Tail surfaces: Twin outward-canted curved ventral fins and a dorsal fin.
Flight control system: Dual joysticks. Cyclic and collective control systems are equipped with adjustable alleviation and loading functions. Unique trimming system operating in all 3 axes.
Safety features: Rocket-activated emergency parachute system in the rotor head, suitable for use from as little as 98 ft (30 m) altitude and at speeds up to 108 kts (124 mph) 200 km/h.
Airframe: Basic airframe constructed as a 3D primary bearing sandwich construction, vacuum manufactured under high temperatures.
Engines: 2 PBS Velká Bítes TE 50B turboshafts. Exhausts protrude from the top of the rear fuselage, the efflux providing torque control without the need for a tail rotor. FADEC.

↑ **UNIS NA 40-Bongo tail-rotorless helicopter**

Engine rating: Each 67-94 shp (50-70 kW).
Transmission: Reduction gear and transmission group (RTG) forms an independent construction unit including the output rotor shaft, cyclic ring controller and reducing transmission from the floating self-centring wheel. The RTG is connected to a common gearbox, serving both engines, featuring automatic mechanical clutches combined with overrunning clutches, and an output shaft of the compressor. Gearbox equipped with a real time performance measuring system and has been designed to facilitate safe OEI flight. Engine brake is also part of the transmission group.
Fuel system: Duplicated system. 184 litre capacity rubberized flexible tank located aft of the central bulkhead in the lower half of the fuselage.

Details for Bongo

PRINCIPAL DIMENSIONS:
Rotor diameter (main): 24 ft 3.5 ins (7.4 m)
Fuselage length: 19 ft 3 ins (5.86 m)
Fuselage width: 4 ft (1.22 m)
Maximum height: 8 ft 4 ins (2.54 m) to top of rotor head

UNDERCARRIAGE:
Type: Twin fixed skids, with ground handling wheels. Optional emergency flotation gear and optional floats
Skid track: 5 ft 9.5 ins (1.76 m)

WEIGHTS:
Empty, equipped: 727.5 lb (330 kg)
Maximum take-off: 1,433 lb (650 kg)
Maximum take-off with external load: 1,587 lb (720 kg)

PERFORMANCE:
Never-exceed speed (V_{NE}): 151 kts (174 mph) 280 km/h
Maximum speed: 135 kts (155 mph) 250 km/h
Maximum climb rate: 1,772 ft (540 m) per minute
Ceiling: 13,125 ft (4,000 m)
Maximum range: 378 naut miles (435 miles) 700 km

Electrical system: Dual system, of 27 volt DC. External source connection.
Flight avionics/instrumentation: VFR; equipped with airspeed indicator, altimeter, rate-of-climb indicator, gyroscopic horizon, bank indicator, compass, dual battery and generator indicator, overload indicator, 2 × T_G thermometers, dual oil temperature power unit indicator, tachometric and induction rotor speed indicators.

Aerospatiale Group — France

Corporate address:
37 boulevard de Montmorency, 75781 Paris Cedex 16.
Telephone: +33 1 42 24 24 24
Facsimile: +33 1 42 24 26 19
Founded:
1 January 1970.
Information:
André Bloch or Sophie Roukline (Press relations – *telephone* +33 1 42 24 24 53, *facsimile* +33 1 42 24 21 32, *E-mail* sophie.roukline@siege.aerospatiale.fr).

ACTIVITIES

▪ In February 1998 Aerospatiale announced its reorganization plan, to take effect during the second half of that year, to support its role as a major French organization in the construction of a Europe-wide civil and military aerospace industry. This reorganization was planned with 3 main objectives: to prepare for link-ups with its European partners, due to the spinning off of Aerospatiale Group's activities; strengthen strategic co-ordination of Aerospatiale entities; and revamp the corporate management structure to carry out this mission.
▪ Under the reorganization, Aerospatiale's activities were spun off as subsidiaries and organized in 2 sectors, *Aircraft* and *Space & Defence*.
▪ 2 new subsidiaries were created in the *Aircraft* sector, namely Aerospatiale Airbus and Aerospatiale ATR. Aerospatiale Airbus will team up with partners in the Airbus consortium to constitute the future Airbus corporate entity; this subsidiary comprises 3 operating units, Airbus, Aerostructures, and Systems and Services (excluding the Automatic Test Centre). Aerospatiale ATR, comprising the ATR operating unit, is teaming with its Italian partner to form the ATR company. Also consolidated within the Aircraft sector are Sogerma and its subsidiaries, Socata and its subsidiaries, the other subsidiaries and consortiums which were previously part of the Aircraft Business, and the Eurocopter Group and its subsidiaries.
▪ The *Space & Defence* sector has 4 subsidiaries: Aerospatiale Ballistics and Space Transport, to group the Space, Defence, Systems and Industry operating units; Aerospatiale Missiles, comprising the previous missile division; Aerospatiale ISTI, to consolidate systems engineering (the systems programme group from the Space & Defence Business and the Automatic Test Centre from the Aircraft Business), and all information technology subsidiaries and departments (eg, Fleximage); and Aerospatiale Satellites, which will become part of the joint satellite company formed by Alcatel and Thomson. Also consolidated within Space & Defence are the subsidiaries, consortiums and affiliates that were previously part of Space & Defence Business.
▪ Corporate Management was also reorganized to handle its expanded mission as overall co-ordinator of Group strategy.

Techno Sud Industries (TSI) — France

Corporate address:
178, Boulevard Haussmann, 75008 Paris.
Telephone: +33 1 40 76 90 00
Facsimile: +33 1 42 25 77 58

ACTIVITIES

▪ In addition to offering the helicopter for the roles detailed below (in the configuration detailed), TSI is partnered with ONERA in experiments aimed at developing an autonomous navigation system. ONERA has assumed responsibility for the definition of the on-board computer and development of the navigational software, while TSI is manufacturing hardware integrating software and conducting flight tests using the Vigilant helicopter.

Techno Sud Industries Vigilant F 2000 C

Role: Small, unmanned, light robot helicopter system for civil surveillance, environmental monitoring and assistance support roles.

↑ **Techno Sud Industries Vigilant F 2000 C robot helicopter system** *(courtesy Techno Sud Industries)*

Aims

▪ High quality imagery due to vibration filtering.

Details

Sales: Available, offering turnkey system with training and maintenance, system rental with range of services, and leasing.
Crew/passengers: None.

Details for Vigilant F 2000 C

PRINCIPAL DIMENSIONS:
Maximum length: 7 ft 6.5 ins (2.3 m)
Fuselage width: 1 ft 8 ins (0.5 m)
Maximum height: 2 ft (0.6 m)

WEIGHTS:
Maximum take-off: typically 70.5 lb (32 kg)
Payload: 17.6 lb (8 kg)

PERFORMANCE:
Maximum speed: 54 kts (62 mph) 100 km/h
Ceiling: 9,845 ft (3,000 m)
Range: approximately 10.8 naut miles (12.4 miles) 20 km
Duration: 1 to 2 hours

Flight control system: Autostabilized flight with GPS. Mobile ground control station with 2 computers, a control panel and display screens (flight monitoring and cartography), offering computer-aided flight, protected remote control radio links, and real time data and image receiving and recording. Allows beyond visual range flying. See Activities.
Mission avionics: All types of cameras, environmental probes, radio monitoring or other payloads up to 17.6 lb (8 kg).

Bruno Guimbal — France

Comments: Details of the G2 Cabri 2-seat light helicopter can be found in the 1996-97 edition of *WA&SD*, page 304.

MK Helicopter GmbH — Germany

Corporate address:
Hans-Böcklerstrasse 30, D-65468 Trebur.

Telephone: +49 6147 919128
Facsimile: +49 6147 919129

Information:
Uwe Mathes (Director).

MK Helicopter MKII

First flight: Flight testing to start in January 1999. Earlier ultralight version flew in 1996 and was marketed as an assembled helicopter.
Certification: Anticipated to JAR 27 in 1999.
First delivery: 1999 or 2000 in certified form.
Role: Light helicopter.

Development

▪ Developed from the earlier ultralight version, with many changes: former Mid-West rotary engine replaced by Rotax 914 (new version with more power being tested in 1998); adoption of crashworthy seating; new rotor head and blades, and much more, with virtually only the fuselage remaining largely the same.

Details

Crew/passenger: 2 persons, side by side.
Cabin access: Forward-hinging heavily glazed doors of carbonfibre/Nomex sandwich and Plexiglas.
Rotor system: Semi-articulated, 2-blade main rotor of new design. Each blade is constructed of Rohacell foam, with glassfibre/carbonfibre reinforced plastics covering.
Tail rotor characteristics: Aluminium alloy, 2-blade tail rotor.
Tail surfaces: Fixed, sweptback, dorsal and ventral fins. Horizontal stabilizer.
Airframe: Aluminium alloy load-bearing chassis, with carbonfibre/Nomex sandwich cabin and boom.
Engine: More powerful version of the Rotax 914 piston engine, being tested for General Aviation version.
Engine rating: 140 hp (104.4 kW) take-off, 125 hp (93.2 kW) continuous.
Transmission: With polymer belts and centrifugal clutch. Hydraulically mounted gearbox.
Fuel system: 80 litres, in 2 tanks.

Details for MKII

PRINCIPAL DIMENSIONS:
Rotor diameter (main): 26 ft 5 ins (8.06 m)
Fuselage length: 22 ft 11 ins (6.99 m)
Width: 4 ft 4 ins (1.32 m), fuselage
Maximum height: 8 ft 4 ins (2.54 m)

MAIN ROTOR:
Rotor disc: 549.17 sq ft (51.02 m^2)

TAIL ROTOR:
Diameter: 4 ft 11 ins (1.5 m)

UNDERCARRIAGE:
Type: Fixed skid type, using steel tubing

WEIGHTS:
Empty, equipped: 794 lb (360 kg)
Maximum take-off: 1,366 lb (620 kg)

PERFORMANCE:
Never-exceed speed (V_{NE}): 108 kts (124 mph) 200 km/h
Cruise speed: 92 kts (105 mph) 170 km/h, at sea level
Maximum climb rate: 1,575 ft (480 m) per minute
Ceiling: 14,760 ft (4,500 m)
IGE hovering ceiling: 9,843 ft (3,000 m)
OGE hovering ceiling: 4,921 ft (1,500 m)
Range: 324 naut miles (373 miles) 600 km

↑ **MK Helicopter MKII in ultralight form, with different undercarriage, rotor head and blades than intended for GA version**

Hindustan Aeronautics Limited (HAL) — India

Corporate address:
See Combat section for company details.

ACTIVITIES

▪ The Helicopter division of the Bangalore Complex has been the last production centre for the French Aerospatiale SA 315B Lama and SA 316B Alouette III helicopters, known by the Indian names Cheetah and Chetak respectively. However, production of Cheetah for various civil and military roles (including agricultural) and of Chetak in basic military, naval/match-role, Coast Guard and passenger roles had almost stopped at the time of writing, giving way to the ALH.

HAL Advanced Light Helicopter

First flight: 20 August 1992 (30 August officially) for PT1 first prototype, April 1993 for PT2 second prototype, 28 May 1994 for third PTA Air Force/Army prototype and 23 December 1995 for fourth PTN Navy prototype. First production aircraft flew during the first quarter of the production year 1998-99.
Certification: 1998.
First delivery: Commenced in the latter half of the production year 1998-99, starting with the Indian Army, followed by the other services.
Role: Multi-role civil and military helicopter for commuter and VIP transport, disaster relief, medevac/medecare, offshore support, search and rescue, firefighting, aerial line laying, and underslung load carrying. Armed military versions for anti-tank, close air support, anti-ship, and anti-submarine. Unarmed military versions for observation, casualty evacuation, assault, logistic support, and training.

Aims

▪ Intended for domestic and export markets.
▪ Capable of deck operations, in tricycle undercarriage version.
▪ Integrated dynamic system (IDS) for reduced weight, low vulnerability, increased safety and reliability. Anti-resonance isolation system (ARIS) to isolate rotor-induced vibrations from the fuselage.
▪ Maximum 5,000 kg take-off weight, with growth potential.
▪ Good hot and high performance and good flight handling qualities.
▪ Various hardpoint stations for underslung load, winch operations and mooring.

Development

▪ Designed and developed by HAL in partnership with Eurocopter Deutschland (formerly MBB).
▪ Full-scale wooden mock-up was followed by a metal mock-up, an interface check rig, and finally a ground test vehicle as a non-flying helicopter to prove the endurance of the drive train and test systems.

Details

Sales: Indian Government signed a letter of agreement for 300 utility, attack and naval production helicopters, thereafter placing an initial firm order for 100. Production deliveries scheduled from 1998, starting with utility helicopters for the Indian Army (4 from 110 required). Indian Air Force to receive 4 in 1998 from 150 required, and Navy and Coast Guard 4 from 40 joinly required. Anticipated total civil and military sales could be over 600. Production of 36 in 1999 expected. No name had been given to the ALH by the Indian forces by late March 1998, at which date HAL said that it had received interest from several countries and it had also been responding to tenders.

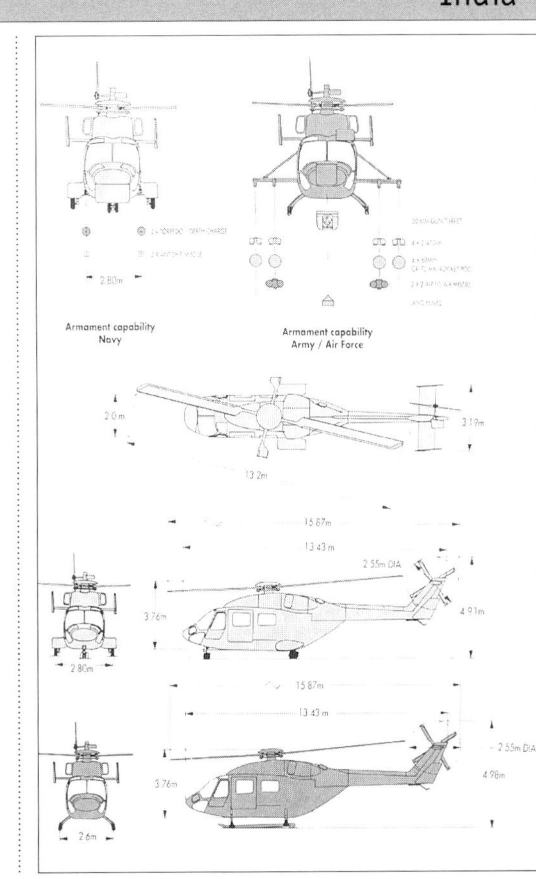

→ **HAL Advanced Light Helicopter, with Naval *(top left* – showing a nose sea-search radar installation) and Army/Air Force *(top right)* weapon choices, Naval general arrangement *(centre)*, standard skid general arrangement *(bottom)*** *(courtesy HAL)*

↑ HAL Advanced Light Helicopter PTA, featuring sighting system, Nag anti-armour missiles and associated system, 20-mm chin gun with turret housing removed, and 2 rocket launchers *(Simon Watson)*

↑ HAL Advanced Light Helicopter PTN, the naval prototype with wheels

Crew/passengers: 2 crew plus 12 seats, or 2 crew plus 14 passengers in high-density layout, or 6 VIPs with foldable table, or 4 litters and 2 ambulatory patients plus all essential medical equipment, spotlights and rescue hoist in medical layout.
Cockpit: Ergonomically designed to offer good all-round visibility, easy access to controls, minimum reflections of illuminated instruments at night, and adjustable crash-protected crew seats.
Freight, internal/external: Maximum 3,307 lb (1,500 kg). Baggage volume 76.3 cu ft (2.16 m^3).
Cabin access: Sliding doors to main cabin, with hinged doors to cockpit. 2 clamshell rear doors for cargo compartment and provisions for rear loading.
Optional equipment: To include rescue hoist, cargo hook, emergency medical equipment, oxygen for high altitude operation, special furnishings for VIP seats, pressure refuelling, and sprag brakes on the nose wheels.
Rotor system: Advanced hingeless system, soft in plane, with 4-blade main rotor (flexible glassfibre blades). FEL type (fibre elastomeric) rotor hub with composite upper and lower starplates, titanium centre piece and elastomeric bearings. Blades have advanced aerofoils and specially designed tip shape for improved performance and low noise, and can be folded manually in 15 minutes by 5 persons. Blades have ballistic tolerance against 12.7 mm bullet strikes. Integrated dynamic system (IDS) comprises rotor hub, main transmission, upper controls and main rotor flight control hydraulics (hydraulic actuators are mounted directly on the gearbox housing), with all upper controls enclosed in the main gearbox housing, to offer some protection against small arms fire; upper control system comprises the mixing unit assembly, swash plate mast, swash plate, rotating control rods, rotating and non-rotating scissors and tracking unit assembly.
Tail rotor characteristics: 4-blade, stiff in plane, bearingless, incorporating flex beam concept with a high thrust capability.
Tail surfaces: Horizontal stabilizer of 10 ft 5.5 ins (3.19 m), with endplates canted to port.
Flight control system: Dual controls. Pilot and co-pilot inputs are coupled through linkage rods in cyclic longitudinal, cyclic lateral and directional channels, and the torque tube for the collective channel. Push/pull rods are used to transmit pilot inputs to control actuators. The integration of Control and Stability Augmentation System (CSAS) series actuators with hydraulic servos leads to a compact flight control actuator module. 4-axis automatic flight control system.
Airframe: 4 main sections, as cockpit, mid-fuselage, rear fuselage and tailboom with tail surfaces. Composites (Kevlar, Carbon, Kevlar/carbon and glassfibre) used in all secondary and some parts of the primary structures, comprising some 29% of structural weight and 60% surface area. Tailboom can be folded for offshore operation.
Safety features: 4 nitrogen gas inflatable floats for the skids optional, for emergency alighting on water. Kinetic energy absorption through undercarriage and controlled deformation of the fuselage, plus crew crashworthy seats in military versions, allowing for 9.5 m/second vertical impact, 6 m/second lateral and 4.6 m/second longitudinal. Frangible couplings give protection against post crash fires. For operation in threat areas, optional armour protection from 7.62-mm bullets. IR suppressors for engines. Self-sealing fuel tanks against 7.62-mm strikes. Optional chaff/flare dispensers.
Engines: First 3 prototypes each have 2 Turbomeca TM333-2B turboshafts, each engine rated at 1,000 shp (746 kW) take-off and 30 minute OEI, 889 shp (663 kW) maximum continuous, and 1,141 shp (851 kW) super contingency for 30 seconds. In January 1995, HAL contracted LHTEC for CTS800-4Ns (each 1,360 shp, 1,014 kW) and CTS800-54s (each 1,656 shp, 1,235 kW) for testing. As verified in late March 1998, both Turbomeca TM333-2Bs and LHTEC CTS800s will be offered as a choice by HAL to customers for production versions.
Transmission: Ratings 1,663 shp (1,240 kW) take-off for 5 minutes, 1,435 shp (1,070 kW) maximum continuous, 1,073 shp (800 kW) OEI super contingency for 30 seconds, 831 shp (620 kW) OEI for 30 minutes, and 717 shp (535 kW) OEI maximum continuous. System comprises the main gearbox, auxiliary gearbox, intermediate gearbox, tail gearbox, tail rotor drive shaft, and rotor brake. Power from both engines is combined in the main gearbox and transmitted to the main rotor. Tail drive shaft is driven by the main gearbox and transmits power via flexibly coupled shafts, the auxiliary gearbox, the intermediate gearbox and the tail gearbox to the tail rotor. Power tap-offs from the main gearbox and auxiliary gearbox are used to power the accessories. See Rotor system for IDS. A 6° of freedom Anti-Resonance Vibration Isolation System (ARIS) is used for isolating the fuselage from rotor vibrations; ARIS connects the main transmission to the fuselage; carbonfibre spring unit; model tests have shown a capability of providing 98% vibration isolation.
Fuel system: 3 main tanks and 2 supply tanks, with total usable 1,400 litres (2,293 lb, 1,040 kg). Each supply tank supplies fuel independently to the engines.
Electrical system: 2 AC subsystems, each with a 5/10 kVA alternator, alternator control power unit and a master box. AC generation system is configured to provide adequate safeguards in case of alternator failure. 2 DC subsystems, each with a 6 kW starter-generator and associated control and protection system, with a battery back-up for 15 minutes under emergency conditions.
Hydraulic system: 3 systems, at 2,988 psi. Systems 1 and 2 for duplicated main and tail rotor flight control actuators. System 3 powers undercarriage, brakes, deck lock harpoon, and optional utility equipment and services.
Braking system: Hydraulic.
Radar: Optional weather radar and Doppler navigation, depending on mission.
Flight avionics/instrumentation: First production batch of ALHs have conventional instrumentation. The standard instrumentation and com/nav package meets BCAR definition of minimum IFR kit and includes V/UHF com, UHF standby, intercom, ADF, gyromagnetic compass with RMI, radio altimeter, IFF, flight and navigation instruments, ASI, VSI, barometric altimeter, LCD panel for systems, centralized warning panel, and AFCS. Range of optional equipment, including Omega, VHF (FM), HF (SSB), V/UHF homing, FLIR, sighting system, night vision goggles and RWR. From the second production batch onwards, a 5 multi-function display (MFD) screen cockpit layout is being considered, but the supplier had not been chosen at the time of writing in late March 1998. BITE facility in major systems.
Expendable weapons and equipment: See Aircraft variants. Expendable weapons carried on cabin-mounted pylons.

Aircraft variants:
Naval variant has a tricycle undercarriage, main rotor blade folding, harpoon system for deck lock, pressure refuelling, and stub wings/sponsons to accommodate undercarriage, floats and batteries. With sonar/sonics, radar, ESM, 2 torpedoes, or 2 depth charges or 4 anti-ship missiles, for ASW, ASV and other roles.
Army/Air Force variant can have Lockheed Martin turreted 3-barrel 20-mm chin gun, 2 pods for 68-mm or 70-mm rockets, 4 air-to-air missiles, or 8 third-generation anti-tank missiles, with significant self-defence and protection systems.
Unarmed military variant for heliborne assault, logistic support, reconnaissance, air observation post, casualty evacuation and training.
Civil version on skids (see Roles).
Dedicated attack version with tandem seats may be developed using ALH dynamics for post 2000.

Details for ALH

PRINCIPAL DIMENSIONS:
Rotor diameter (main): 43 ft 4 ins (13.2 m)
Maximum length, rotors turning: 52 ft 1 ins (15.87 m)
Fuselage length: 42 ft 4 ins (12.89 m)
Width of fuselage: 6 ft 7 ins (2 m), with 10 ft 4 ins (3.15 m) for wheel gear version over sponsons
Maximum height: 16 ft 1.5 ins (4.91 m) rotors turning with wheel gear or 16 ft 4 ins (4.98 m) with skids, or 12 ft 9 ins (3.89 m) to top of tailfin with skid gear and 12 ft 8.75 ins (3.88 m) with wheel gear

CABIN:
Width: 6 ft 5.5 ins (1.97 m)
Height: 4 ft 8 ins (1.42 m)
Volume: 258.86 cu ft (7.33 m^3)

MAIN ROTOR:
Aerofoil section: DMH4 up to 0.8R, DMH3 from 0.9242R to 1.0R
Blade chord: 1 ft 8 ins (0.5 m) up to 0.9242R, 6.57 ins (0.167 m) at tip
Rotor disc: 1,473 sq ft (136.85 m^2)
Rpm: 314

TAIL ROTOR:
Aerofoil section: S 102C up to 0.8R, S 102E from 0.927R to 1.0R
Diameter: 8 ft 4.5 ins (2.55 m)
Rpm: 1,564

UNDERCARRIAGE:
Type: Retractable nosewheel type (twin nosewheels and single main wheels) or fixed skids
Wheel base: 14 ft 4 ins (4.37 m) for wheel gear
Wheel track: 9 ft 2 ins (2.8 m) wheels or 8 ft 6.5 ins (2.6 m) skids

WEIGHTS:
Empty: 5,511 lb (2,500 kg)
Maximum take-off: 11,023 lb (5,000 kg), or 12,125 lb (5,500 kg) in naval form
Maximum sling load: 3,307 lb (1,500 kg) naval, 2,204 lb (1,000 kg) army/air force

PERFORMANCE (MTOW, *or at 8,818 lb, 4000 kg at ISA + 15° C in italics*)**:**
Never-exceed speed (V_{NE}): 165 kts (180 mph) 305 km/h, *178 kts (205 km/h) 330 km/h*
Maximum cruise speed: 151 kts (174 mph) 280 km/h, *156 kts (180 mph) 290 km/h*
Cruise speed: 132 kts (152 mph) 245 km/h, *the same*
Maximum climb rate: 1,770 ft (540 m) per minute, *2,560 ft (780 m) per minute*
Service ceiling: 19,685 ft (6,000 m)
Range with full fuel: 432 naut miles (497 miles) 800 km. with 20 minutes reserve
Duration: 3 hours 48 minutes, *4 hours*, both with 20 minutes reserve

PT Industri Pesawat Terbang Nusantara (IPTN) — Indonesia

Corporate address:
See Airliners section for company details.

ACTIVITIES

■ Undertakes licensed production of the Eurocopter BO 105 (as NBO-105) and Super Puma (as NSA-332), and Bell 407, 412 and 430 (NBell-407, -412 and -430). Two indigenous light helicopters, the NH2 and NH5 have been reported and scale models displayed. However, in a communication to the Editor in late March 1998, IPTN stated that reports regarding these projects were incorrect, to a point, but confirmed that it did have experimental models in the design stage. IPTN asked that these experimental designs should not be given any publicity at this time. In consequence, *WA&SD* will honour this request and nothing more will be published in this edition.

Aviation Industries of Iran (AII) — Iran

Corporate address:
Ministry of Industries, Building No 2, 56 Gharani Avenue, Tehran 15815.

Telephone: +98 21 817 2570, 2572
Facsimile: +98 21 889 7658, 7659

Founded: 1993.

Information:
S. Pourtakdoust.

ACTIVITIES

■ In addition to the aircraft detailed in the General Aviation and Glider sections, AII has been developing a 5-seat helicopter known as the IR-H5 (possibly the Shahed X5), which is almost certainly the helicopter reportedly funded by the Institute of Industrial Research and Development. Designed to meet FAR 27 regulations, it is of conventional layout, with 2-blade main and tail rotors and a heavily glazed and streamlined cabin for the 5 occupants. Construction is principally of aluminium alloy. Maximum speed is estimated at 115 kts (132 mph) 213 km/h and range 215 naut miles (249 miles) 400 km. Some reports in the West have suggested that it could be partly based on the Bell JetRanger, of which Iran had received very large numbers, but equally it could be a totally indigenous effort.

Agusta — Italy

Corporate address:
Via Giovanni Agusta 520, 21017 Cascina Costa di Samarate (VA).

Telephone: +39 0331 229111
Facsimile: +39 0331 229605
Web site: www.agustacorp.com

Founded:
1907. Currently part of the Finmeccanica group.

Employees: About 5,200.

Information:
G.L. Ghezzi (Vice-President, Corporate Affairs – *telephone* +39 0331 229563, *facsimile* +39 0331 229984) or A. Giovannini (Marketing Promotion Manager – *telephone* +39 0331 229935, *facsimile* +39 0331 229920).

FACILITIES

■ In the north of Italy, Cascina Costa di Samarate (VA), Sesto Calende (VA), Somma Lombardo (VA) and Vergiate (VA); in central and southern Italy, Anagni (FR), Benevento, Brindisi, Frosinone and Monteprandone (AP).

ACTIVITIES

■ In addition to the helicopters detailed here, Agusta collaborates with GKN Westland of the UK in the EH 101 programme, has teamed with Bell on the BA 609 tiltrotor, and participates in the 4-nation NH90 programme (see Multi-national at the end of this section).

■ Since first signing an agreement with Bell of the USA in 1952, Agusta has produced various Bell helicopters under licence. This collaboration continues, currently joined also by helicopters from Boeing and Sikorsky. Agusta has also recently announced development of the new **AB 139** with Bell (see Foreword).

■ Agusta Service has a customer support network based in 3 main centres in Italy, Belgium and the USA, plus 23 Service Centres in other countries. 2 new Maintenance and Support facilities at Manila (Philippines) and Bierset (Belgium). The Components Overhaul Centre is in Zaventem, (Belgium), opened in February 1994. Spare parts distribution is based on 3 computer-linked supply centres at Somma Lombardo, Philadelphia and Bierset.

■ Agusta Service Engineering, in co-operation with the ILS organization, updates configurations of Agusta helicopters, developing mid-life improvement packages, avionics upgrades and other modifications.

SUBSIDIARIES

AGUSTA AEROSPACE CORPORATION
HQ address:
Travose, Philadelphia, PA 19114, USA.

AGUSTA AEROSPACE SERVICES SA
HQ address:
Liege Airport, Belgium.

ASSOCIATED COMPANIES

E.H. INDUSTRIES LTD
HQ address:
Farnborough, UK.

E.H. INDUSTRIES INC
HQ address:
Washington, USA.

NH INDUSTRIES
HQ address:
Aix-en-Provence, France.

Agusta A 109 series

First flight: 4 August 1971.
First delivery: A 109A in May 1976.
Role: Civil and military multi-purpose light twin helicopter, currently available in 6 individual versions with 3 different engine options.
Sales: Over 600 of all versions.

Details *(A 109 Power, with other versions detailed under Aircraft variants. A 109 Power and A 109C data in the specification box)*

Crew/passengers: Pilot and passenger or 2 pilots in the cockpit, with main cabin accommodation for 6 persons. Additional space aft of the rear seats allows for extra baggage, ferry tanks, or easy conversion to an EMS role with 1 or 2 longitudinal litters and 2 medical attendants. Cabin width permits a seat between the litters, and the co-pilot seat is reversible for an additional medical attendant. Optional 4/5-seat VIP, 6-seat executive or 6-seat utility layouts.
Baggage compartment: 33.55 cu ft (0.95 m^3) aft of cabin.
Optional equipment: Dual controls, rotor brake, 2,205 lb (1,000 kg) fixed cargo hook, 441 lb (200 kg) rescue hoist, windshield wiper, snow skis, removable emergency floats, slump protection pads, sliding doors, extended-range fuel tanks, particle separator, engine fire extinguishers, bleed air heating, air conditioning, and sound proofing. See also Avionics.
Rotor system: 4-blade main rotor, with interchangeable and high-inertia composite blades with drooped leading edges. Fully articulated rotor head with titanium hub connected to composite grips through a single elastomeric bearing on each blade.
Tail rotor characteristics: Full authority 2-blade semi-rigid tail rotor.
Flight control system: Collective, cyclic, anti-torque system with collective-synchronized elevator. Hydraulically servo assisted by dual hydraulically-actuated swashplate cylinders.
Airframe materials: Aluminium alloy and honeycomb structure.
Engines: 2 Pratt & Whitney Canada PW206C turboshafts with FADEC. Alternative Turbomeca Arrius 2K1s, each 670.5 shp (500 kW) take-off or 751 shp (560 kW) OEI for 2.5 minutes.
Engine rating: For PW206Cs, each 640 shp (477 kW) take-off for 5 minutes, 566 shp (422 kW) maximum continuous, 732 shp (546 kW) OEI for 2.5 minutes and 670 shp (500 kW) OEI for 30 minutes.
Transmission rating: 900 shp (671 kW) maximum continuous, 560 shp (418 kW) OEI maximum continuous, and 640 shp (477 kW) OEI for 2.5 minutes.
Fuel system: 605 litres, with provision for an additional 273 litres of auxiliary fuel for extended range.

Details for A 109 Power, *with A 109C in italics where different*

PRINCIPAL DIMENSIONS:
Rotor diameter (main): 36 ft 1 ins (11 m)
Maximum length, rotors turning: 42 ft 9.5 ins (13.035 m)
Maximum length, rotors stopped: 37 ft 7 ins (11.46 m), *37 ft 6.5 ins (11.44 m)*
Maximum height: 11 ft 6 ins (3.5 m)

CABIN:
Length: 6 ft 11 ins (2.1 m), *5 ft 4 ins (1.63 m)*
Width: 5 ft 2 ins (1.58 m), *4 ft 9 ins (1.44 m)*
Height: 4 ft 2.5 ins (1.28 m)
Volume: 180.1 cu ft (5.1 m^3), *156.1 cu ft (4.42 m^3)*

MAIN ROTOR:
Aerofoil section: NACA 23011
Blade area: each 19.81 sq ft (1.84 m^2)
Rotor disc: 1,022.89 sq ft (95.03 m^2)

TAIL ROTOR:
Diameter: 6 ft 7 ins (2 m)

UNDERCARRIAGE:
Type: Heavy duty retractable, with nosewheel. See Optional equipment
Wheel base: *11 ft 7 ins (3.535 m)*

WEIGHTS:
Empty, basic: 3,461 lb (1,570 kg)
Maximum take-off: 6,283 lb (2,850 kg)
Maximum take-off, external load: 6,614 lb (3,000 kg)
Useful load: *2,822 lb (1,280 kg)*

PERFORMANCE:
Never-exceed speed (V_{NE}): 168 kts (193 mph) 311 km/h
Maximum cruise speed: 156 kts (180 mph) 289 km/h, *152 kts (175 mph) 282 km/h at 5,000 ft (1,525 m)*
Maximum climb rate: 2,080 ft (634 m) per minute, *1,693 ft (516 m) per minute*
Climb rate, OEI: 900 ft (274 m) per minute, *354 ft (108 m) per minute*
IGE hovering ceiling: 16,585 ft (5,055 m), *11,400 ft (3,474 m)*
OGE hovering ceiling: 11,800 ft (3,596 m), *8,000 ft (2,438 m)*
Service ceiling: 20,000 ft (6,100 m), *15,000 ft (4,572 m)*
Service ceiling, OEI: 13,100 ft (3,993 m), *7,000 ft (2,133 m)*
Range: 502 naut miles (578 miles) 930 km, at 5,000 ft (1,525 m), best speed, 878 litres of fuel and no reserve; *420 naut miles (483 miles) 778 km, at 5,000 ft and long-range cruise speed*
Duration: 5 hours 10 minutes, *4 hours 20 minutes*, conditions as for range

↑ Agusta A 109K2 operated by the Toyama Police

↑ Agusta A 109CM with anti-armour missiles and gyrostabilized sight *(courtesy Agusta)*

Electrical system: 2 fully independent AC and DC systems. See Aircraft variants.
Hydraulic system: 2 independent flight control hydraulic systems, each capable of operating swashplate actuators in the event of a failure. 2 utility hydraulic systems with 2 accumulators for undercarriage, rotor brake, wheel brakes and nosewheel centring device.
Radar: Optional colour weather radar.
Flight avionics/instrumentation: Single or dual pilot IFR capability is expandable with a flight director and autotrim, and GPS, integrated with the 3-axis AFCS. Other options include radar altimeter and ELT. Liquid crystal displays available for navigation management or for engines monitoring and for caution and warning presentation. See Aircraft variants.

Aircraft variants:
A 109C is a pilot and 6-7 passenger executive/corporate helicopter, suited also to Medevac. 2 × 450 shp (335.6 kW) take-off rating Allison 250-C20R/1 turboshafts. 550 litres of usable fuel, with 150 litres optional for extended range. Certified for single pilot IFR operation. IFR equipment includes 3-axis autopilot, dual VHF, dual VOR, DME, ADF, TDR and EHSI. Optional flight director and colour weather radar.
Coastal Patrol variant of the A 109C has armoured seats; 550 litres of usable fuel plus optional 150 or 200 litre auxiliary tank and optional self-sealing; pintle-mounted 7.62-mm machine-gun; 4-axis autopilot with automatic approach to hovering to permit easy rescue operations; FLIR; 360° search radar with display information interfaced with LRN 85 VHF Omega, VOR, DME and flight path computer; chaff/flare dispensers; radar warning, and more. Electrical power with 2 × 150 amp (28 volt DC) starter-generators, 3 × 250 volt-amp (115/26 volt AC, 400 Hz) static inverters, and 22 amp-hour battery.
A 109CM is a multi-role military version with 2 Allison 250-C20R/1 turboshaft engines, for such missions as patrol and reconnaissance, light attack, anti-armour, escort/area suppression, liaison and command, transport and medical evacuation. Capable of carrying 4 or 8 TOW 2A missiles and HeliTOW 2. Alternative weapons include 70/81-mm rocket launchers or 12.7/7.62-mm gun pods. APX334 or Herlis or Helios gyrostabilized sight. Available FLIR, radar warning, infra-red jamming, chaff/flare dispenser, self-sealing tanks, armoured crew seats and night vision goggles. Rockwell Collins CMS-80 cockpit management system. Electrical power with 2 × 160 amp (28 volt DC) starter-generators, 2 × 250 volt-amp or high-load 600 volt-amp (115/26 volt AC, 400 Hz) static inverters, and 27 amp-hour (24 volt) ni-cd battery. Users include the Belgian Army.
A 109 G. di. F is a coast guard version with several of the surveillance and detection systems of the Coastal Patrol, and can have a pintle-mounted MG-3 machine-gun. Allison 250-C20R/1 turboshafts.
A 109K2 is a multi-purpose helicopter for hot-and-high operations, using 2 × 632 shp (471 kW) maximum continuous rated Turbomeca Arriel 1K1 engines. AlliedSignal Bendix/King Silver Crown avionics package. Typical roles are medevac and rescue. Can operate up to 20,000 ft (6,100 m) and in 50° C temperature, and meets Category A requirements.
A 109K2 Law Enforcement is based on the A 109K2 but has removable equipment suited to its police work, including cargo hook, rescue hoist, wire strike protection, SX16 searchlight, MA3 retractable light, external loudspeakers, emergency floats, EMS options, rappelling kit, and more.
A 109KM is a military high altitude and high temperature version based on the A 109K2, and was developed with the European army light multi-role helicopter philosophy in mind. Equipment and armament options are similar to those of the A 109CM, but with performance differences due to the Arriel 1K1 engines. Electrical power with 2 × 160 amp (28 volt DC) starter-generators, 2 × 250 volt-amp or high-load 600 volt-amp (115/26 volt AC, 400 Hz) static inverters or alternative 6 kVA alternator plus a standby 250 volt-amp inverter, and 22 amp-hour (24 volt) ni-cd battery.
A 109MAX is a dedicated Emergency Medical Service helicopter, allowing full exploitation of its capabilities and accommodation. 1 or 2 pilots, 1 litter plus 3 assistants or 2 litters and 2 assistants, and medical equipment. Allison 250-C20R/1 turboshafts.
A 109 Power is the latest version of the A 109 family. Take-off in Category A without any load reductions from elevated helipads. A-109K2 cabin length, redesigned retractable undercarriage that increases available internal space, improved aerodynamics, new digital control engines, and new cockpit instrumentation with LCDs.

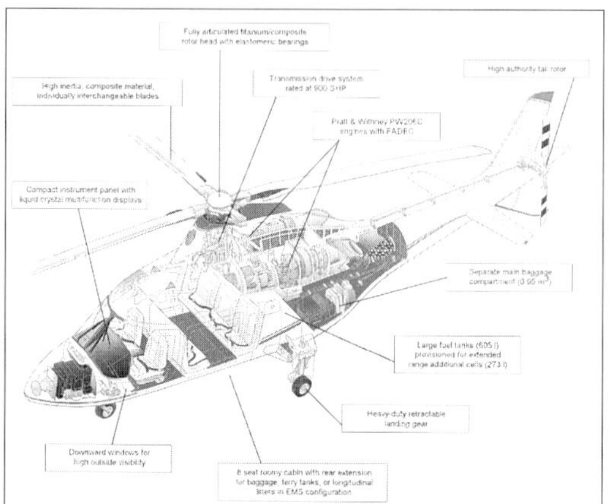

↑ Agusta A 109 Power technical features *(courtesy Agusta)*

Agusta A 119 Koala

First flight: February 1995.
Certification: July 1997.
First delivery: September 1997.
Role: Single-engined, widebody passenger and utility helicopter.
Sales: Approximately $1.78 million in basic form at time of writing.
Crew/passengers: Pilot and 7 passengers. EMS configuration for 1 or 2 litters and 2 medical attendants, without interference with the cockpit. Said by Agusta to be 30% larger than any other lightweight single-turbine helicopter.
Baggage compartments: Small compartment of 'almost half a cubic metre' accessible from inside the cabin. External access to the main 33.55 cu ft (0.95 m^3) baggage area in the tail section, of 7 ft 6.5 ins (2.3 m) length.

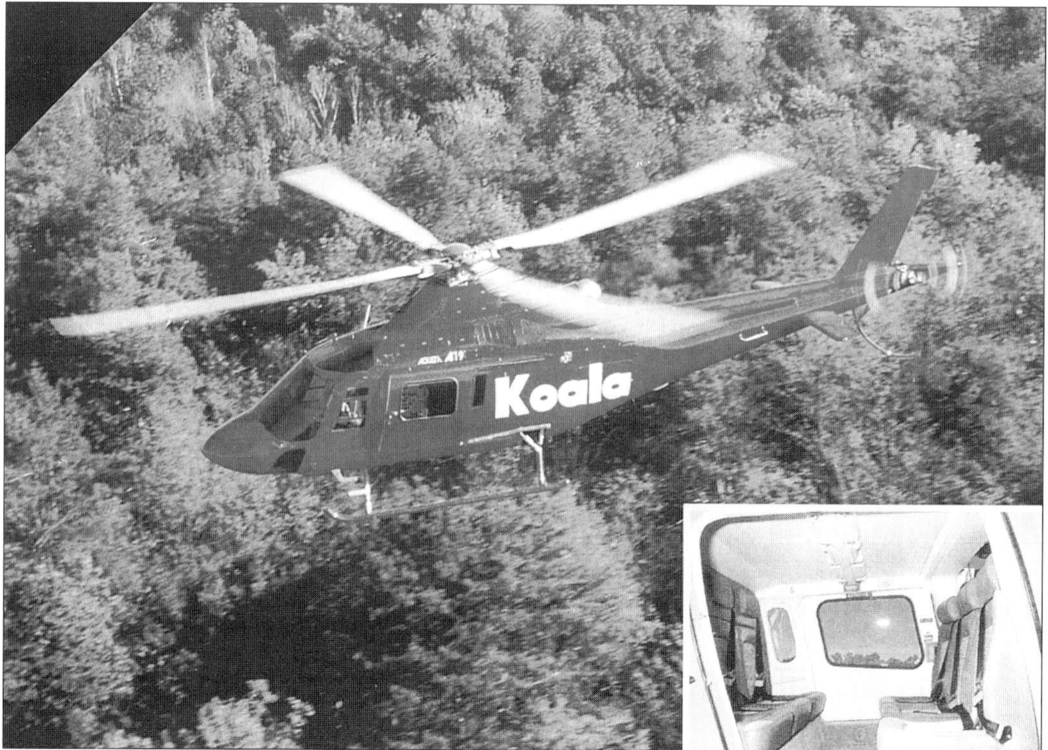

↑ Agusta A119 Koala, with inset cabin view *(courtesy Agusta)*

Cabin access: Large sliding doors.
Rotor system: High inertia main rotor with 'on condition' blades of composite materials. Low vibration, low maintenance, fully-articulated main rotor hub, of titanium, with composite grips and elastomeric bearings.
Airframe materials: Aluminium alloy.
Engine: Pratt & Whitney Canada PT6B-37 turboshaft for the second prototype and all production helicopters (first prototype used a Turbomeca Arriel 1). FADEC.
Engine rating: 1,002 shp (747 kW) at take-off, 872 shp (650 kW) maximum continuous.
Fuel system: 605 litres, with optional 273 litres in auxiliary tank.

Details for Koala

PRINCIPAL DIMENSIONS:
Rotor diameter (main): 36 ft 1 ins (11 m)
Maximum length, rotors turning: 43 ft (13.1 m)
Fuselage length: 36 ft 4 ins (11.07 m)
Maximum height: 10 ft 10 ins (3.3 m)

CABIN:
Length: 6 ft 11 ins (2.1 m) main area, or 11 ft 7 ins (3.53 m) maximum
Width: 5 ft 3.5 ins (1.61 m)
Height: 4 ft 2.5 ins (1.28 m)
Volume: 121.84 cu ft (3.45 m^3) main area, or 175.16 cu ft (4.96 m^3) maximum

TAIL ROTOR:
Diameter: 6 ft 7 ins (2 m)

WEIGHTS:
Maximum take-off: 5,732 lb (2,600 kg)
Maximum take-off, external load: 5,997 lb (2,720 kg)
Useful load: 2,645 lb (1,200 kg), or 2,910 lb (1,320 kg) with external load

PERFORMANCE (MTOW):
Never-exceed speed (V_{NE}): 150 kts (173 mph) 278 km/h
Maximum cruise speed: 140 kts (161 mph) 260 km/h
IGE hovering ceiling: 10,900 ft (3,320 m)
OGE hovering ceiling: 8,038 ft (2,450 m)
Service ceiling: 17,915 ft (5,460 m)
Range: 340 naut miles (391 miles) 630 km
Duration: 3 hours 34 minutes

Agusta A 129 Mangusta and International

First flight: 11 September 1983. 9 January 1995 for the A 129 International.
Role: Day and night attack and reconnaissance, escort, fire support, area suppression, and air-to-air combat.

Aims

- Low detectability (visual, acoustic, IR and radar signatures), good detection of the enemy (visual, electronic warning), high agility and manoeuvrability, nap-of-the-earth performance, and passive/active electronic countermeasures.
- High survivability (see Safety features).
- Major inspections at organizational level can be performed in remote and unprepared areas.
- On-board integrated management system (IMS), providing monitoring, fault isolation, maintenance data recording and self-diagnostics.
- 3.5 working hours for preparation to embark on a C-130 transport, and 6 working hours for flight readiness thereafter.
- Sea portable, and ship operational.

Details

Sales: Deliveries to the Italian Army began in October 1990 against 60 ordered, with all 45 in standard anti-armour configuration delivered by 1996. Remaining 15 Italian Mangustas delivered in upgraded multi-role form, having the International's 5-blade main rotor, uprated transmission providing 1,700 shp (1,268 kW) maximum take-off rating, IR exhaust suppression, undernose gun in a Breda turret and Stinger AAMs. Additional 30 required in both attack and scout configurations, the latter with mast-mounted sights. International version proposed to Turkey under a joint offer with IAI, with an IAI avionics suite incorporating night targeting and EW systems, plus the ability to launch Rafael NT-D anti-armour missiles as an option.
Crew: 2, in tandem stepped cockpits, with pilot at rear. Martin Baker crashworthy seats with adjustable side armour (composites).

↑ Italian Army 'upgraded' Agusta A 129 Mangusta firing its nose gun, with expended shells falling away

Cockpit: Separated cockpits for the crew, each with flat-plate canopy glazing, starboard door (hinged at top) and emergency exit panels on the port side.
Rotor system: 4-blade main rotor (with blade folding from Lot 2 16th example) on first 45 Mangustas and 5-blade on upgraded Mangustas and Internationals, each blade having a Nomex and carbonfibre main spar, Nomex honeycomb leading/trailing edges, composites skin and stainless steel leading-edge strip. Fully articulated rotor head with titanium hub connected to composite grips through a single elastomeric bearing on each blade.
Tail rotor characteristics: 2-blade, delta hinged.
Airframe materials: Wide use of composites for the fuselage, amounting to some 45% of structural weight.
Safety features: 12.7-mm ballistic tolerance by double/triple vital systems redundancy, system separation, components designed to operate after being hit, armour plating, composites materials, transmission operation without oil, protected flight controls, and automatic reconfiguration. Crew protected against ground fire of up to 23-mm calibre. Can operate in contaminated (NBC) environments without the crew wearing special protective suits. MIL-STD-1290 crashworthiness, with crew survival and minimum aircraft damage after a 36 ft (11 m) per second crash impact, achieved through energy absorbing undercarriage, Martin Baker seats, fuel cells and airframe; crew protection via roll bars, A-shaped reinforced frame and cyclic stick installation; and energy egress (pyrotechnic, both sides).
Engines: *Mangusta:* 2 Rolls-Royce Mk 1004 turboshafts, each 881 shp (657 kW) take-off and 825 shp (615 kW) maximum continuous. *International:* 2 LHTEC (Allison/AlliedSignal) T800-LHT-800 turboshafts, each 1,335 shp (996 kW) take-off, 1,240 shp (925 kW) intermediate, and 1,404 shp (1,045 kW) OEI contingency. Sand and NBC filters. Infra-red suppressor system.
Transmission rating: 1,300 shp (970 kW) for the first 45 Mangustas and 1,700 shp (1,268 kW) maximum take-off rating for the remaining 15, and 1,797 shp (1,340 kW) for International.
Fuel system: 1,653 lb (750 kg).
Hydraulic system: 2 independent flight control hydraulic systems of 3,000 psi, each capable of operating swashplate actuators in the event of a failure. 2 utility hydraulic systems with 2 accumulators for rotor brake and wheel brakes.
De-icing system: Blades and engines.
Flight avionics/instrumentation: Computerized, digital integrated management system (IMS), based on the MIL 1553B digital databus architecture, with automatic performance

Agusta A129 International
Dimensions in mm

↑ Agusta A 129 International general arrangement *(courtesy Agusta)*

Details for Mangusta, *with International in italics*

PRINCIPAL DIMENSIONS:
Rotor diameter (main): 39 ft 0.5 ins (11.9 m), *the same*
Maximum length, rotors turning: 47 ft 0.5 ins (14.33 m)
Fuselage length: 40 ft 10 ins (12.452 m), *the same*
Width over stub wings: 11 ft 8 ins (3.55 m)
Maximum height: 11 ft (3.35 m) above rotor head

MAIN ROTOR:
Rotor disc: 1,197 sq ft (111.2 m^2)

TAIL ROTOR:
Diameter: 7 ft 7.5 ins (2.32 m), *8 ft 2.5 ins (2.5 m)*

UNDERCARRIAGE:
Type: Fixed tailwheel type (see Safety features)
Wheel base: 23 ft 1 ins (7.03 m)
Wheel track: 7 ft 4 ins (2.23 m), *the same*

WEIGHTS:
Empty, operating: 5,575 lb (2,529 kg)
Maximum take-off: 9,039 lb (4,100 kg), *11,023 lb (5,000 kg)*
Anti-tank mission weight: 8,708 lb (3,950 kg)

PERFORMANCE (Mangusta for anti-tank mission, sea level, ISA + 20° C, *and International at MTOW in italics*)**:**
Maximum speed: 149 kts (172 mph) 275 km/h, *161 kts (185 mph) 298 km/h*
Cruise speed: 135 kts (155 mph) 250 km/h, *150 kts (173 mph) 278 km/h at sea level, ISA or 137 kts (158 mph) 254 km/h at ISA + 25° C, maximum continuous power*
Maximum climb rate: 2,009 ft (612 m) per minute, *2,225 ft (678 m) per minute at ISA or 2,205 ft (672 m) per minute at ISA + 25° C, sea level*
Vertical climb rate: *1,062 ft (324 m) per minute at ISA, or 846 ft (258 m) per minute at ISA + 25° C, both sea level*
Climb rate, OEI: *905 ft (276 m) per minute at ISA or 453 ft (138 m) per minute at ISA + 25° C, both at sea level*
IGE hovering ceiling: 10,300 ft (3,140 m), *13,800 ft (4,200 m) ISA or 7,800 ft (2,380 m) ISA + 25° C, maximum continuous power*
OGE hovering ceiling: 6,200 ft (1,890 m), *10,800 ft (3,290 m) ISA or 4,400 ft (1,340 m) ISA + 25° C, maximum continuous power*
Ceiling: 15,500 ft (4,725 m)
G limits: +3.5, -0.5
Range: *303 naut miles (349 miles) 561 km at ISA, or 305 naut miles (351 miles) 565 km at ISA + 25° C, both with internal fuel, no reserve, sea level*
Self-deploy range: *over 540 naut miles (621 miles) 1,000 km using external fuel tanks and carrying 4 AAMs*
Typical mission duration: 2 hours 30 minutes, or 3 hours 5 minutes maximum

computation, systems monitoring, weapon control, autonomous navigation, and dual automatic flight control that allows hands-off operation (manual reversion) and encompassing autopilot, automatic heading hold, autohover and autostabilization. Information is presented in both cockpits on graphic/alphanumeric multi-function displays (with keyboards), but conventional instrumentation is provided for back-up. Integrated INS, GPS and Doppler navigation. Night vision system comprises thermal image cameras, integrated helmet and display, sighting system, flight symbology, and NVG cockpit. Sight and pilot night vision system integration allows the crew to detect, identify and engage targets at extended stand-off ranges during day or night or in adverse weather conditions. HeliTOW sight, or mast-mounted sight. Loral FLIR carried in the steerable Ferranti/OMI nose turret is slaved to the crew's integrated helmet and display sighting systems (IHADSS). International version has a new second generation FLIR (83 × mag), state-of-the-art CCD TV (126 × mag), laser rangefinder/designator, automatic target tracker, and video recorder. See also Sales.
Self-protection systems: Chaff/flare dispensers, IR and radar

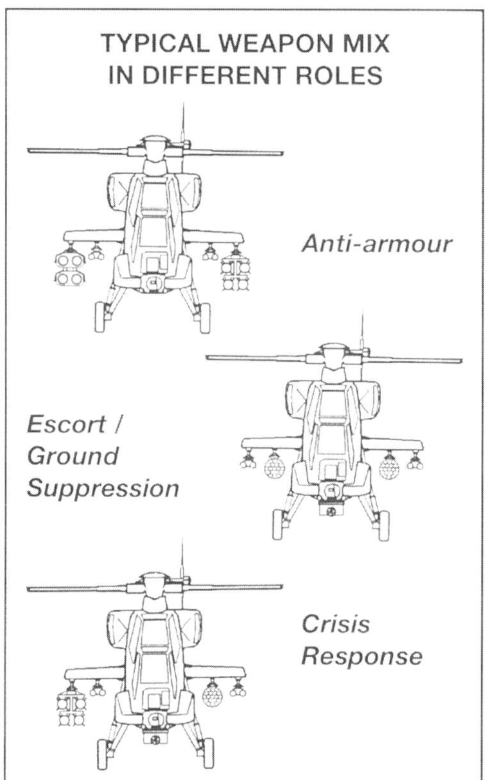

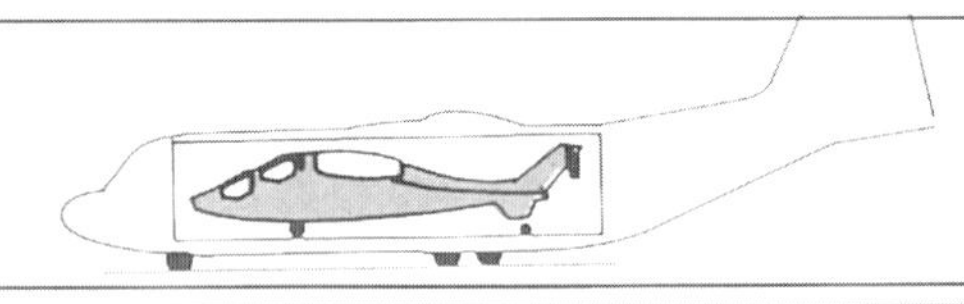

↑ **Agusta A 129 International typical weapon mix for various roles, with C-130 loading diagram and shipborne Mangusta below** *(courtesy Agusta)*

jammers, and radar and laser warning receivers.
Fixed guns: Only final 15 Italian upgraded Mangustas and all Internationals have a 3-barrel 20-mm Gatling-type gun under the nose in a Breda turret as standard, to allow quick off-axis engagement.
Ammunition: 500 rounds.
Number of weapon pylons: 4 under the stub-wings, each outer of 441 lb (200 kg) capacity and each inner of 661 lb (300 kg) capacity, although the outer can carry 661 lb (300 kg) if the total load per wing does not exceed 882 lb (400 kg); 2° up and 10° down outer pylon movement to assist weapon launching.
Expendable weapons and equipment: Up to a 2,646 lb (1,200 kg) load. Choice of up to 8 TOW 2A or Hellfire anti-armour missiles (or mix), or alternative Hot for Mangusta; 4 launchers for 76 × 70-mm or 38 × 81-mm rockets (Mangusta can also deploy 68-mm rockets); air-to-air missiles (Javelin, 8 Mistral, AIM-9L Sidewinder or 4 Stinger for Mangusta, but Mistral or Stinger for International); and 7.62-mm, 12.7-mm or 20-mm gun pods. On-the-field armament reconfiguration, and armament mixing capability.

Aircraft variants:
Mangusta is the standard Italian Army version, with Rolls-Royce engines. First 45 with 4-blade main rotors, the remaining 15 helicopters having 5-blade main rotors and other changes as detailed under Sales.
International uses more powerful LHTEC engines, 5-blade main rotor, higher transmission rating, standard undernose gun, some avionics upgrading and other changes as noted elsewhere.

Agusta-Bell AB-206B JetRanger III

Comments: Licensed-built version of the Bell JetRanger III, with a 450 shp (335.6 kW) Allison 250-C20R/4 turboshaft engine. Sometimes referred to as the AB-206R. Among recent customers has been the Turkish Army, which ordered 20 for training.

Agusta-Bell AB-212 Naval/Skyshark

Comments: Though based on the Bell 212, the *Naval* is an Agusta-missionized version which operates with the Italian Navy and the armed forces of various other NATO countries and in South America. Roles can include shore or corvette/frigate-based anti-submarine search and attack, anti-ship, OTHT, surface surveillance, SAR, transport and liaison. Can undertake independent electronic warfare, anti-submarine and anti-ship missions. An upgraded version was developed as the *Skyshark*, with engine and airframe improvements, including the use of PT6T-3D Twin Pac engines. It has digital MIL 1553B databus architecture, 4-axis AFCS, autonomous navigation (INS, GPS, air data systems), 360° search/track radar, FLIR/TV, variable depth sonar, and torpedoes or Sea Skua missiles. Maximum take-off weight is 11,200 lb (5,080 kg), cruise speed is 110 kts (127 mph) 204 km/h, and it has a range of 308 naut miles (355 miles) 571 km.

Agusta-Bell AB-412EP, Griffon and Maritime Patrol

Comments: Licensed-built versions of the Bell 412EP and Griffon, plus an Agusta-developed dedicated maritime patrol version with a 600 lb (272 kg) rescue hoist, FLIR, high-resolution TV camera, 4-axis AFCS, high-intensity night search light, 360° search radar, and new integrated avionics system. The Maritime Patrol version accommodates 2 pilots, plus a radar/FLIR/LLLTV console operator and a rescue hoist operator. Can still transport 14 equipped troops or 3 to 6 litters plus 2 attendants. A battlefield surveillance version of AB-412 has been developed

↑ **Agusta-Bell AB-412EP of the Finnish Frontier Guard**

for the Italian Army, as part of the CATRIN C³I system. Main feature is a FIAR Creso P2132 radar in an undernose radome for land surveillance, MTI target detection and tracking, plus nose and tail emitter locators and a roof FLIR.

Agusta-Boeing CH-47C

Comments: The Italian licensed-built version of the CH-47C Chinook was originally produced under the Elicotteri Meridionali SpA company name, which acquired the production rights a year after forming with Agusta assistance. Powered by 2 × 3,750 shp (2,796 kW) 10-minute take-off rated AlliedSignal T55-L-712E turboshafts, it has a maximum take-off weight of 50,000 lb (22,680 kg), a useful load of 27,015 lb (12,254 kg), and maximum external cargo load of 28,000 lb (12,700 kg). Typical 3 flight crew plus 33 troops, but optional 44-50 or 59 in high-density arrangements. Alternatively, 24 litters and 2 attendants. Agusta has also developed firefighting and Emergency Surgery Flying Centre variants.

Agusta-McDonnell Douglas (Boeing) AMD-500E

Comments: 50 McDonnell Douglas MD 500Es were produced by Agusta for use as basic trainers by the Italian Air Force, which is responsible for training helicopter pilots for all branches of the Italian armed forces. All delivered.

Agusta-Boeing 520N

Comments: This is a licensed-built MD 520N, characterized by having a NOTAR anti-torque system. It incorporates graphite and Kevlar lightweight composite components. Has 13% more power than the AMD-500, allowing it to carry an extra 280 lb (127 kg) of payload. Due to its higher safety and low noise level, it is particularly suited to police operations, passenger carrying and aerial work. Available.

Agusta-Sikorsky SH-3D, S-61N and HH-4F Combat SAR

Comments: SH-3Ds built by Agusta are operated by the Italian Navy and other NATO, plus Latin America and Middle/Far East nations. The HH-3F, typically for search and rescue, remained in production into the mid-1990s in the modernized Combat SAR version, meeting the requirements of the Italian Air Force and having a night rescue capability. Agusta is also modernizing SH-3Hs to extend their operating life into the next century.

Dragon Fly srl — Italy

Corporate address: Via Raffaello 1/A, 22060 Cucciago (Co).
Telephone: +39 031 351 8101, 8111 **Facsimile:** +39 031 351 8133
Founded: 1993.
Employees: 35.
Information: Arnaldo P. Ratto.

Dragon Fly mod 333 and HELIOT

Certification: 16 June 1996 from Italian Civil Air Board (RAI) under the Very Light Rotorcraft specifications (for Dragon Fly).
Role: Civil and military 2-seat light helicopter. In addition, the company has worked with the French companies EDT and CAC Sistèmes to develop the HELIOT, capable of operating as a normal helicopter or as a robotic craft on autonomous special missions.

Details *(Dragon Fly mod 333, except under Aircraft variants)*

Sales: 5 prototypes and 4 pre-series helicopters. First full production helicopter was delivered to an Italian operator in April 1994 and the 50th production example was delivered in the first half of 1997. By 26 March 1998, 55 had been delivered, 50 of which have gone to Italian customers. Now also used in Abu Dhabi, Australia, Belgium, Brazil, France, Germany, New Zealand, Portugal, and Turkey.

Details for Dragon Fly mod 333

PRINCIPAL DIMENSIONS:
Rotor diameter (main): 22 ft (6.7 m)
Maximum length, rotors turning: 25 ft 9.5 ins (7.86 m)
Fuselage length: 18 ft 3 ins (5.561 m)
Maximum height: 7 ft 9 ins (2.358 m) to above rotor head

MAIN ROTOR:
Aerofoil section: NACA 0012
Blade area: 6.46 sq ft (0.6 m^2)
Rotor disc: 379 sq ft (35.21 m^2)
Rpm: 500

TAIL ROTOR:
Diameter: 3 ft 8 ins (1.12 m)
Chord: 7.87 ins (20 cm)

UNDERCARRIAGE:
Type: Fixed twin skids, with ground handling wheels. Optional floats
Skid base: 7 ft 5 ins (2.26 m)
Skid track: 5 ft 1 ins (1.55 m)

WEIGHTS:
Empty: 573 lb (260 kg)
Take-off: 992 lb (450 kg) typically, or 1,102 lb (500 kg) maximum
Useful load: 441 lb (200 kg)

PERFORMANCE:
Never-exceed speed (V_{NE}): 80 kts (92 mph) 150 km/h
Maximum speed: 73 kts (84 mph) 135 km/h with 32 litres fuel
Cruise speed: 59-70 kts (68-81 mph) 110-130 km/h
Maximum climb rate: 1,870 ft (570 m) per minute at typical TOW, 1,280 ft (390 m) at MTOW
IGE hovering ceiling: 6,725 ft (2,050 m) at MTOW
OGE hovering ceiling: 4,200 ft (1,280 m) with 32 litres of fuel
Service ceiling: 10,000 ft (3,050 m)
Range: 178 naut miles (205 miles) 330 km at cruise speed, 60 litres of fuel
Duration: 2.8 hours

Crew/passengers: 2, with dual controls.
Freight, internal: Baggage compartment.
Optional equipment: Electric trim (lateral). Chip detectors for the main and tail rotor transmission.
Rotor system: 2-blade, semi-rigid of see-saw (teetering) type. Metal blades. Transmission uses a centrifugal clutch and 2 V belts.
Tail rotor characteristics: 2-blade, metal.
Tail surfaces: T-tail, with horizontal stabilizer above the fin.
Flight control system: Conventional mechanical.
Airframe materials: Welded titanium frame. Tailboom and undercarriage skids of aluminium alloy. Composite cabin and engine bay structures.
Engine: Dragon Fly/Hirth F30A26AK 2-stroke piston engine, certified to JAR 22.
Engine rating: 105 hp (78 kW) take-off, 95 hp (71 kW) maximum continuous.
Transmission: Centrifugal clutch and V-belts (2).
Fuel system: 64 litres, all but 7 litres usable.
Electrical system: 12 volt system with starter-generator and 24 amp-hour battery.
Flight avionics/instrumentation: Full VFR instrumentation and including altimeter, airspeed indicator, bank indicator and compass. Engine and fuel instruments, and malfunction warning lights. Optional fuel pressure indicator, engine fire warning light, radio transceiver, and cabin intercom.

Aircraft variants:
Dragon Fly mod 333 is the standard current version, as detailed.
HELIOT is a variant for manned or unmanned military and civil operations (see Role), with a useful load exceeding 661 lb (300 kg). Removable external module for remotely piloted operations, with high-definition camera. Colour monitor on the instrument pedestal.
Training target variant of HELIOT is being developed, in simplified form.

↑ **Dragon Fly mod 333 2-seat light helicopters, with Elite Fly written on the bottom helicopter**

CH-7 Helicopters Heli-Sport srl — Italy

Corporate address:
Strada Traforo del Pino, 102, 10132 Torino.
Telephone: +39 011 899 6730
Facsimile: +39 011 899 5550
Information:
Claudio Barbero.

CH-7 Angel

Role: Single-seat ultralight helicopter. Can also be used for agricultural work.

Development

- Developed from the Augusto Cicarè CH-6.

Details

Sales: Since 1992, more than 130 Angels have been built and flown in 5 continents. Information package 70,000 lire. Kit 57,000,000 lire without 2-stroke engine or 63,900,000 without 4-stroke engine. Building time approx 200 working hours.
Rotor system: 2-blade semi-rigid main rotor, with composite blades.
Tail rotor characteristics: 2-blade, aluminium. NACA 63014, symmetrical aerofoil.
Tail surfaces: Fixed dorsal/ventral fin, with tailskid. Starboard horizontal stabilizer.
Flight control system: Push-pull, without cables.
Fuselage: Pod and boom type.
Airframe materials: Welded 4130 steel tube frame, and bolted aluminium alloy tailboom and skids. Composites cabin.
Engine: Rotax 582 or 912.
Engine rating: 64.4 or 80 hp (48 or 59.6 kW).
Transmission: Cardanic gear and transmission box.
Fuel system: 40 litres.
Flight avionics/instrumentation: Instruments for altitude, vertical speed, engine/rotor rpm, water temperature, gearbox oil temperature, and dual EGT.

↑ **CH-7 Helicopters Heli-Sport Angel**

Details for Angel

PRINCIPAL DIMENSIONS:
Rotor diameter (main): 19 ft (5.8 m)
Length: 23 ft (7.01 m)
Fuselage width: 2 ft 8 ins (0.82 m)
Maximum height: 6 ft 10 ins (2.08 m)

CABIN:
Width: 2 ft 6 ins (0.76 m)

MAIN ROTOR:
Aerofoil section: NACA 8-H-12, asymmetric
Rotor disc: 321.6 sq ft (29.88 m^2)

TAIL ROTOR:
Diameter: 3 ft 4.5 ins (1.03 m)

UNDERCARRIAGE:
Type: Fixed twin skids, with ground handling wheels
Skid track: 5 ft 4 ins (1.64 m)

WEIGHTS:
Empty: 451 lb (205 kg)
Maximum take-off: 793 lb (360 kg)

PERFORMANCE:
Maximum speed: 87 kts (100 mph) 161 km/h
Cruise speed: 69 kts (80 mph) 129 km/h
Maximum climb rate: 1,900 ft (580 m) per minute
IGE hovering ceiling: 6,890 ft (2,100 m)
OGE hovering ceiling: 4,920 ft (1,500 m)
Service ceiling: 11,000 ft (3,350 m)
Range: 148 naut miles (170 miles) 275 km
Duration: 3 hours

CH-7 Kompress

Role: Tandem 2-seat ultralight helicopter, based on the Angel design.
Sales: Delivery of kits began June 1998. Building time approximately 250 working hours. Kit costs 79,900,000 lire without engine.
Engine: Rotax 914 Turbo.
Engine rating: 115 hp (85.75 kW).
Fuel system: 40 litres standard, plus 19 litre auxiliary tank.

↑ CH-7 Helicopters Heli-Sport Kompress

Details for CH-7 Kompress

PRINCIPAL DIMENSIONS:
Rotor diameter (main): 20 ft 4 ins (6.2 m)
Length: 24 ft 7 ins (7.5 m)
Maximum height: 7 ft 8 ins (2.34 m)

UNDERCARRIAGE:
Type: Fixed twin skids, with ground handling wheels

WEIGHTS:
Empty: 540 lb (245 kg)
Maximum take-off: 992 lb (450 kg)
Useful load, equipped: 452 lb (205 kg)

PERFORMANCE:
Maximum speed: 112 kts (129 mph) 209 km/h
Normal cruise speed: 86 kts (100 mph) 160 km/h
Maximum climb rate: 1,475-2,000 ft (450-610 m) per minute
IGE hovering ceiling: 13,125 ft (4,000 m) with pilot only, 11,485 ft (3,500 m) with 2 persons
OGE hovering ceiling: 10,825 ft (3,300 m) with pilot only, 8,200 ft (2,500 m) with 2 persons
Service ceiling: 16,400 ft (5,000 m)
Range: 388 naut miles (447 miles) 720 km with pilot only, 298 naut miles (343 miles) 552 km with 2 persons, both with 19 litre auxiliary fuel tank
Duration: 4.5 hours with pilot only, 3.8 hours with 2 persons, both with 19 litre auxiliary fuel tank

Fuji Heavy Industries Ltd — Japan

Corporate address:
See Combat section for company details.

Fuji-Bell 205B and UH-1J

First flight: 1988 for 205B.
Role: Intermediate civil and military general-purpose helicopters.

Development

▪ Having manufactured 56 civil Model 204B/B-2s under a licensing agreement with Bell (sold co-operatively by Fuji and Mitsui Bussan Aerospace Co), plus military UH-1Hs, Fuji began production of the Model 205B civil helicopter (upgraded Bell 205) primarily for utility and flying-crane work. Production 205Bs became available in the latter part of 1995. Earlier, in 1993, deliveries began of the UH-1J, an upgraded version of the UH-1H for the JGSDF and powered by a 1,500 shp (1,118.6 kW) T53-K-70 turboshaft engine built by Kawasaki.

Details for 205B

PRINCIPAL DIMENSIONS:
Rotor diameter (main): 48 ft (14.63 m)
Maximum length, rotors turning: 57 ft 3.25 ins (17.46 m)
Width: 9 ft 4.8 ins (2.86 m), skids
Maximum height: 12 ft 9.8 ins (3.91 m)

WEIGHTS:
Empty: 5,324 lb (2,415 kg)
Maximum take-off: 10,500 lb (4,763 kg)

PERFORMANCE (estimated):
Maximum speed: 130 kts (150 mph) 241 km/h
Cruise speed: 122 kts (140 mph) 226 km/h
Maximum climb rate: 2,530 ft (770 m) per minute
IGE hovering ceiling: 19,500 ft (5,945 m)
OGE hovering ceiling: 15,200 ft (4,635 m)
Service ceiling: 20,000 ft (6,100 m)
Range: 310 naut miles (357 miles) 574 km

Details *(Model 205B)*

Crew/passengers: 1 pilot plus 14 passengers.
Engine: AlliedSignal T5317B turboshaft.
Engine rating: 1,800 shp (1,342 kW).

Aircraft variants:
205B is the current civil version, with emphasis on good hot-and-high performance.
UH-1J is a military transport, for up to 13 troops. Slightly larger than the UH-1H, uses AH-1S rotors, has upgraded avionics integrated via the 1553B databus, improved armour protection, IR suppression, wire strike protection system, NVG capability, and more.

Fuji-Bell AH-1S

Comments: Licence-built version of the Bell AH-1S (actual AH-1F) HueyCobra, following evaluation of 2 US-built helicopters during 1979-80. Agreement was signed in 1982, and 91 are planned for the JGSDF, most of which have been delivered. 1,800 shp (1,342 kW) Kawasaki T53-K-703 turboshaft offers a never-exceed speed of 170 kts (196 mph) 315 km/h and a mission radius of 123 naut miles (142 miles) 228 km.

↑ Fuji-Bell AH-1S *(courtesy JGSDF)*

Kawasaki Heavy Industries Ltd — Japan

Corporate address:
See Combat section for company details.

ACTIVITIES

▪ In addition to the details below, the BK117 developed jointly with Germany (now Eurocopter as partner) can be found in the Multi-national section. Currently, Kawasaki is offering an active vibration reduction system for new BK117s or retrofit to those already in use, comprising 2 Moog hydraulic actuators, a side spring and cabin 3-axis accelerometers, the former replacing the rear transmission mounts. In addition, and in association with Furono, Kawasaki is marketing a combined GPS and 3-D moving map display for the BK117.

▪ The military/civil twin-rotor Kawasaki-Boeing KV107IIA has been out of production for some years, with the final delivery having taken place on 16 February 1990. Manufacture of CH-47J Chinooks continues, however, to replace KV107s with the Japan Air and Ground Self-Defence Forces. Deliveries started in 1986 and all 16 JASDF CH-47Js have been delivered, plus about 40 (at the time of writing) of the 52 required for the JGSDF as CH-47JAs. Production also continues of the OH-6DA, a licence-built Boeing (former McDonnell Douglas) MD 500D for the JGSDF/JMSDF, plus civil examples. In addition, Kawasaki is prime contractor on the OH-1 scout/observation helicopter programme for the JGSDF, replacing the OH-6D with the JGSDF.

↑ Kawasaki XOH-1 prototype light scout and observation helicopter for the JGSDF

Kawasaki OH-1 Kogata Kansoku

First flight: 6 August 1996.
Role: Armed scout and observation, with attack capabilities.

Development

▪ Contracts were awarded to Kawasaki (prime contractor, with 60% stake), Fuji (20%) and Mitsubishi (20%) by Japan Defence Agency's Technical Research and Development Institute (TRDI) for the development and construction of 4 flying and 2 static test OH-X prototypes plus 20 engines for the flying prototypes, ground testing and certification.

▪ 1991. OH-X airframe and XTSI-1 engine development started. Mitsubishi MG-5 was developed as a prototype to the XTSI-1 engine, developing about 600 shp (447 kW).

▪ October 1992. Design began, completed the following year.

▪ September 1994. A mock-up of the OH-X was put on show by Kawasaki, having been built the previous year.

▪ 6 August 1996. First flight of the redesignated XOH-1 at Gifu factory, starting at 10.46 am and lasting 16 minutes. Maximum speed and height attained during this first lift off were about 30 kts and 35 ft (10 m) respectively. Crewed by Yoshinori Inayama and Takayoshi Yuasa. Second prototype flew that November.

▪ 9 January 1997. First flight of the third prototype, followed by the fourth 2 months later.

▪ June 1997. Delivery of the first prototype to Akeno Air Base prior to the start of Japan Defence Agency testing, by which time the prototypes had accumulated their first 150 flying hours. Operational testing to take 2 years. Delivery of remaining 3 XOH-1s by August. Over 400 flight hours accumulated by Spring 1998.

▪ Mid 1998. Start of series production at Gifu.

▪ January 2000. Initial deliveries to the JGSDF.

Details

Sales: 4 flying prototypes, the first used initially for flight envelope trials, second initially for load/vibration trials, third for avionics testing, and fourth for operational suitability and weapons integration. JGSDF is expected to acquire up to 200, with first 3 production OH-1s ordered in FY97, 2 in FY98 and 5 in FY99.
Crew: 2, in tandem stepped cockpits, with the pilot in the forward cockpit.
Cockpit: Each cockpit has a starboard side upward-hinged entry door. Probably emergency exit via port windows. Flat-plate, glint reducing glazing.
Rotor system: 4-blade hingeless and bearingless rotor system, with composites blades, for high response and agility.
Tail rotor characteristics: 8-blade ducted, providing safety in NOE flight and narrow/confined area operation.
Tail surfaces: Tall tailfin and constant-chord horizontal stabilizers.
Airframe: Carbonfibre reinforced plastics used for about 40% of the airframe in terms of weight.
Safety features: Rotor and transmission systems are ballistic damage tolerant. Dry-run capable XMSN. Crashworthy armoured seating. Other armour protection. Wire cutter just ahead of the roof sight.
Engines: 2 Mitsubishi TSI-10 turboshafts, with FADEC. IR suppressors at the engine nozzles. Alternative engines could include the MTU Turbomeca Rolls-Royce MTR 390.
Engine rating: Each TSI-10 is rated at 884 shp (660 kW) IRP.
Fuel system: In addition to main tanks, 160 litres of auxiliary fuel can be carried under the stub wings.
Flight avionics/instrumentation: Fully integrated via a redundant MIL-STD-1553B databus, with 2 Yokogawa flat-panel liquid crystal colour multi-function displays in each cockpit and a Shimadzu head-up display. AFCS, including stability-control augmentation system and holding functions. HOCAS. Roof-mounted stabilized target acquisition/designation sighting system (110° azimuth and 40° elevation) for accurate reconnaissance and targeting in all weathers and by night, housing a Fujitsu FLIR, NEC laser rangefinder and NEC colour TV camera.
Self-protection systems: Radar warning receiver in the nose. IR jammer on the rear fuselage, aft of the rotor pylon fairings.
Fixed guns: No turreted gun on prototypes.
Number of weapon pylons: 4, under the stub wings, including wet stations for auxiliary fuel tanks.
Expendable weapons and equipment: Known armament will be Toshiba Type 91 IR-homing air-to-air missiles for self-defence. Clearly, will have the ability to carry a range of attack weapons, including anti-armour missiles, rocket launchers and gun pods.

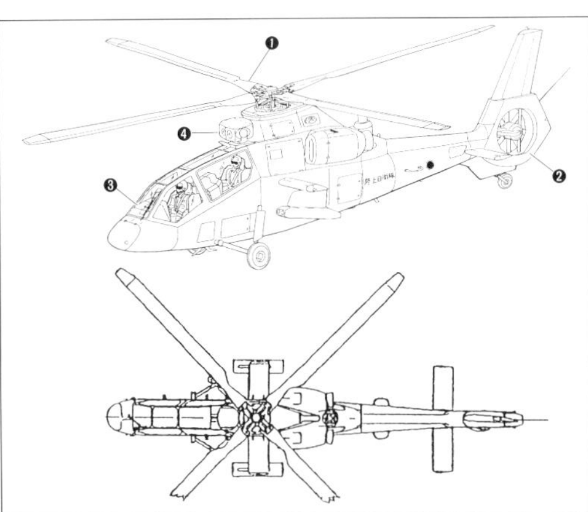

↑ Kawasaki OH-1 with *(1)* fully composite hingeless main rotor *(2)* ducted tail rotor *(3)* integrated displays and *(4)* target acquisition/designation sighting system *(courtesy Kawasaki)*

↑ Fourth prototype in full camouflage, with sighting system represented *(courtesy Kawasaki)*

Details for XOH-1

PRINCIPAL DIMENSIONS:
Rotor diameter (main): 37 ft 9 ins (11.5 m)
Fuselage length: 39 ft 5 ins (12 m)
Fuselage width: 3 ft 3 ins (1 m) at cockpit
Maximum height: 12 ft 5.5 ins (3.8 m) over tailfin

UNDERCARRIAGE:
Type: Fixed tailwheel type

WEIGHTS:
Maximum take-off: about 7,716 lb (3,500 kg)

PERFORMANCE:
Maximum level speed: 140 kts (161 mph) 259 km/h
Maximum design altitude: 10,000 ft (3,050 m)
Radius of action: 108 naut miles (124 miles) 200 km

Mitsubishi Heavy Industries Ltd — Japan

Corporate address:
See Combat section for company details.

ACTIVITIES

▪ In addition to its fixed-wing and engine programmes, and a 20% stake in the new OH-1 helicopter programme (see Kawasaki), Mitsubishi is constructing the Sikorsky SH-60J (S-70B-3) anti-submarine helicopter for the JMSDF to replace the HSS-2B (last HSS-2B was delivered in 1990), the UH-60J search and rescue helicopter for the JMSDF/JASDF, and the UH-60JA for the JGSDF. The first SH-60J flew on 10 May 1991, with deliveries from August 1991; first flight of a component-assembled UH-60J was on 20 December 1989. The JMSDF requires 18 UH-60Js and some 100 SH-60Js, while the JASDF requires 46 UH-60Js, of which nearly half have been delivered. 14 UH-60JAs had been funded for the JGSDF at the time of writing. All H-60J helicopters are powered by T700-IHI-401C turboshafts. Some details of the Mitsubishi RP1 technology demonstrator and a photograph can be found in the 1996-97 edition of *WA&SD*, page 311.

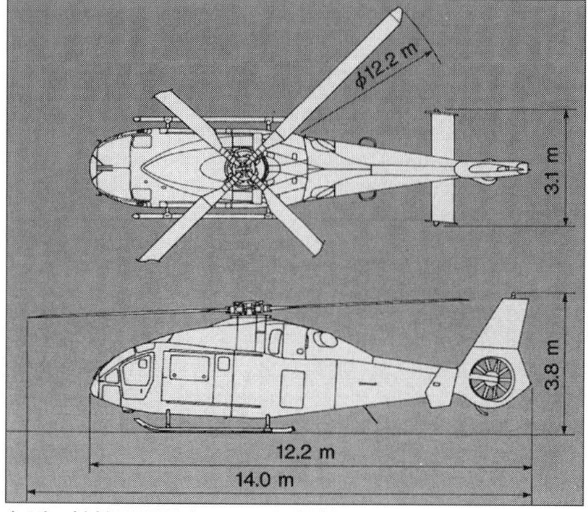

↑ **Mitsubishi MH2000** *(courtesy Mitsubishi)*

Mitsubishi MH2000

First flight: 29 July 1996.
Certification: 26 June 1997 (JCAB).
Role: Twin-turbine, multi-purpose helicopter for transport, EMS, SAR and law enforcement among other roles.

Development

▪ 1995. Programme launched (see 1996-97 *WA&SD* for early artist's impression).

Details

Sales: 4 flying prototypes (JQ6001-6004). Mitsubishi anticipates selling about 100 by the year 2008. Price under ¥400 million at time of writing.
Crew/passengers: 1 or 2 pilots plus 6 or 7 passengers in deluxe executive layout, or 10 for the standard version, or high-density utility seating for 12. Single litter can be accommodated in the SAR version, with further litters anticipated for EMS version.
Cabin access: Sliding door each side of main cabin, each of 3 ft 11 ins (1.2 m) width.
Freight, internal: 79.1 cu ft (2.24 m^3) volume baggage compartment in the aft fuselage, to the rear of the fuel tanks, with an outside access door.

↑ **Third and fourth prototypes of the Mitsubishi MH2000**

Details for MH2000

PRINCIPAL DIMENSIONS:
Rotor diameter (main): 40 ft (12.2 m)
Maximum length, rotors turning: 45 ft 11 ins (14 m)
Fuselage length: 40 ft (12.2 m)
Maximum height: 12 ft 5 ins (3.8 m), previously 4.1 m

MAIN ROTOR:
Rotor disc: 1,258 sq ft (116.9 m^2)

UNDERCARRIAGE:
Type: Fixed twin skids of low height
Skid track: 8 ft 10 ins (2.7 m)

WEIGHTS:
Empty: 5,511 lb (2,500 kg)
Maximum take-off: 9,921 lb (4,500 kg)

PERFORMANCE:
Maximum cruise speed: 151 kts (174 mph) 280 km/h
Economic cruise speed: 135 kts (155 mph) 250 km/h
IGE hovering ceiling: 8,858 ft (2,700 m)
Range: 420 naut miles (485 miles) 780 km, standard fuel, no reserve
Duration: 4 hours

Rotor system: 4-blade bearingless main rotor, with composite blades.
Tail rotor characteristics: 10-blade ducted type, with composite blades.
Tail surfaces: Integral fin, and horizontal stabilizer (10 ft 2 ins, 3.1 m span) with swept endplates canted to starboard. Tail guard below duct.
Engines: 2 Mitsubishi MG5-110 turboshafts, with FADEC. 'One touch' dual speed mode, allowing reduced vibration/noise by selecting 90% power output.
Engine rating: Each 876 shp (653 kW).
Transmission: Mounted above and aft of the passenger cabin to reduce internal vibration and noise.
Fuel system: 1,140 litres usable in crash resistant tanks. Auxiliary fuel available.
Flight avionics/instrumentation: To customer's requirements, including AFCS and integrated GPS/CAS.

Korean Air — South Korea

Corporate address:
Namdaemun Ro 2KA, 118 Marine Centre, Seoul.
Telephone: +82 2 751 7114
Founded: Aerospace Division was founded in 1976.
Employees: About 2,100.

ACTIVITIES

▪ The Aerospace division of the commercial airline operator, Korean Air Lines (KAL), undertakes aircraft maintenance and upgrading, the licensed manufacture of helicopters, constructs light aircraft of its own development (see General Aviation), and produces components for a large number of the world's major aircraft manufacturers, the latter including components for the Airbus A330/340, new generation Boeing 737s and the 777, the new Boeing 717 and Boeing (former McDonnell Douglas) MD-11.
▪ Helicopter activities initially centred on the McDonnell Douglas MD 500, completing over 300 and thereafter continuing to manufacture airframes for the US company. It jointly developed the 520MK Black Tiger, an armed MD 500 with a larger main rotor, many avionics upgrades to enhance day and night capability, and extra fuel for longer range. Currently, it is assembling Sikorsky UH-60Ps for the South Korean forces (138 to be delivered by the end of 1999, with further production anticipated thereafter) and, with Sikorsky assistance, has designed its own helicopter for military and civil roles.

Korean Air Multi-Purpose Helicopter (KMH)

First flight: Possibly year 2000.
Role: Multi-purpose helicopter, suited to civil uses in addition to armed scouting and attack.

↑ **Korean Air Multi-Purpose Helicopter (KMH) mock-up** *(courtesy Avia Press Associates)*

Aims

▪ Originally conceived for the Korean Military Helicopter (KMH) programme but since widened to include civil versions, now known as the Korean Multi-Purpose Helicopter. Korean Air and Sikorsky said to be investing US$400 million in development.

Development

▪ October 1996. Mock-up unveiled at Seoul. Sikorsky provided design assistance; a partner may be sought.
▪ 2003. Possible delivery date for the first production helicopter.

Details

Sales: 2 separate production lines proposed, 1 for the armed military version and the other for the certificated civil variant. Anticipated domestic sales of 100 to 150 in civil form and up to 500 military examples.
Crew/passengers: Crew of 2 on side-by-side crashworthy seats, possibly with armour protection in military version. 6 passengers/troops in the main cabin.
Cabin access: Large partially-glazed door on each side of the fuselage. Triangular forward-hinged doors for access to the cockpit.
Rotor system: 4-blade main rotor.
Tail rotor characteristics: 8-blade ducted tail rotor.
Tail surfaces: T-tail, comprising tall sweptback fin and constant-chord stabilizer.
Flight control system: Dual redundant fly-by-light/hydraulic.
Engines: 2 turboshafts mounted side by side above the cabin, still to be selected at the time of writing, with options including MTU Turbomeca Rolls-Royce MTR 390s.
Engine rating: Each in the 900 to 1,100 shp (671 to 820 kW) range.
Flight avionics/instrumentation: FLIR and sighting system in a nose-mounted turret.
Self-protection systems: Infra-red jammer and radar warning receiver.
Number of pylons: Outriggers for the military version carried on fuselage-mounted lower curved supports and upper bracing struts, each with 2 pylons; possibly detachable.
Expendable weapons and equipment: Weapons will include 4 Hellfire anti-armour or 4 Stinger air-to-air missiles, plus twin machine-gun pods or twin launchers for 14 or 38 × 70-mm rockets.

Details for KMH, provisional

UNDERCARRIAGE:
Type: Fixed tailwheel type, with single wheel on each unit

WEIGHTS:
Maximum take-off: 7,495 lb (3,400 kg)
Payload (external, sling): 2,998 lb (1,360 kg)

PERFORMANCE:
Maximum design speed: 165 kts (190 mph) 305 km/h in military form
Maximum climb rate: 2,100 ft (640 m) per minute in military form
Service ceiling: 20,000 ft (6,100 m)
IGE hovering ceiling: 13,500 ft (4,000 m)
Range: 350 naut miles (403 miles) 650 km in military form

Delta-V srl — Moldova

Corporate address:
6 Lenin Street, 3200 Bender (Moldova, g. Bendery, ul. Lenina 6).

Telephone: +373 232 47112
Facsimile: +373 232 43159

Information:
Vyacheslav F. Barinov (Chief Designer).

Delta-V AK-21

First flight: Originally planned for Autumn 1997.
Role: Light cabin autogyro.
Crew: Pilot only, in heated cabin.
Cabin access: Starboard side door.
Rotor system: 2-blade rotor pylon-mounted above the fuselage.
Tail surfaces: Rudder aft of the propeller ring.
Engine: Rotax 912 piston engine, driving a 4-blade pusher propeller in a shroud ring.
Engine rating: 80 hp (59.7 kW).

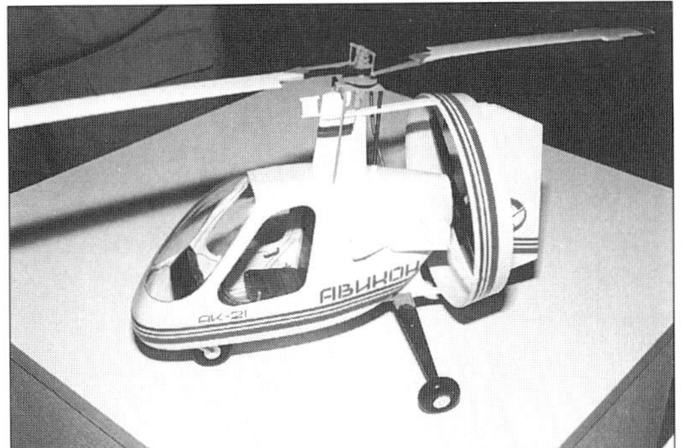

↑ Model of the Delta-V AK-21 autogyro from Moldova *(Piotr Butowski)*

Details for AK-21

PRINCIPAL DIMENSIONS:
Rotor diameter (main): 23 ft 7.5 ins (7.2 m)
Length, without rotor: 10 ft 5 ins (3.18 m)
Maximum height: 7 ft 8.5 ins (2.35 m)

UNDERCARRIAGE:
Type: Fixed nosewheel type, with all wheels of similar size
Wheel base: 5 ft (1.53 m)
Wheel track: 5 ft 11 ins (1.8 m)

WEIGHTS:
Maximum take-off: 750 lb (340 kg)

PERFORMANCE:
Maximum speed: 70 kts (81 mph) 130 km/h
Cruise speed: 54 kts (62 mph) 100 km/h
Minimum speed: 19 kts (22 mph) 35 km/h
Landing speed: 11 kts (12 mph) 20 km/h
Maximum climb rate: 984 ft (300 m) per minute
Take-off distance: up to 33 ft (10 m)
Service ceiling: 13,125 ft (4,000 m)
Range: 146 naut miles (168 miles) 270 km with maximum fuel

Instytut Lotnictwa — Poland

Corporate address:
See Combat section for company details.

Instytut Lotnictwa PZL IS-2

Role: Light helicopter for training, sport, patrol and transport.
First flight: Anticipated for Spring 1999.
Certification: To JAR 27.
Chief designer: Maciej Romicki.

Development

▪ January 1996. Full-scale mock-up accepted.

Details

Crew/passengers: 2 persons, side-by-side, in heated and ventilated cabin. Baggage area to the rear of the seats.
Cabin access: Forward hinged door each side.
Rotor system: 3-blade fully-articulated main rotor, with tall pylon. Glassfibre, epoxy and carbonfibre blades.
Tail rotor characteristics: 4-blade ducted type, with blades of similar composite materials to main rotor.
Tail surfaces: Fixed dorsal fin above tail rotor and horizontal stabilizer (3 ft 10.5 ins, 1.18 m span).
Flight control system: Mechanical, with push-pull tubes.
Airframe: Aluminium alloys and steel fuselage structure, with glassfibre cabin shell. Semi-monocoque tapered tailboom of aluminium alloy, with integral glassfibre tail-rotor duct and fin.
Engine: Single 180 hp (134 kW) Textron Lycoming O-360 piston engine.
Fuel system: 55 litres in each of 2 fuselage tanks.
Electrical system: 28 volt, DC.
Flight avionics/instrumentation: VFR and IFR. AlliedSignal Bendix/King suite, including automatic direction finder, transponder and GPS. Range of conventional instruments.

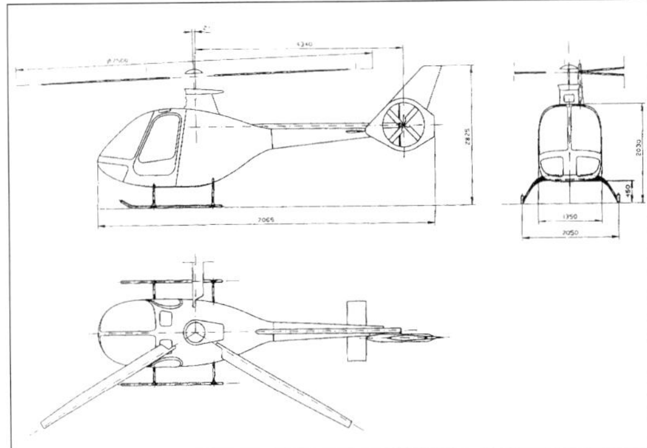

↑ Instytut Lotnictwa PZL IS-2

Details for IS-2

PRINCIPAL DIMENSIONS:
Rotor diameter (main): 24 ft 7 ins (7.5 m)
Maximum length, rotors turning: 29 ft 3.6 ins (8.93 m)
Fuselage length: 23 ft 2.5 ins (7.065 m)
Maximum height: 9 ft 3 ins (2.825 m)

CABIN:
Length: 5 ft 5 ins (1.66 m)
Width: 4 ft 5 ins (1.35 m)
Height: 4 ft 5 ins (1.35 m)
Volume: 77.7 cu ft (2.2 m^3)

MAIN ROTOR:
Aerofoil section: IL HX4A1
Blade chord: 8 ins (20 cm)
Blade area: 6.79 sq ft (0.631 m^2)
Rotor disc: 475.54 sq ft (44.179 m^2)
Twist angle: 10°
Rpm: 483.8

TAIL ROTOR:
Diameter: 2 ft 10 ins (0.864 m)
Rpm: 4,004

UNDERCARRIAGE:
Type: Fixed tubular skid type constructed of metal, with ground handling wheels
Skid track: 6 ft 9 ins (2.05 m)

WEIGHTS:
Empty: 1,213 lb (550 kg)
Empty, operating: 1,393 lb (632 kg)
Normal take-off: 1,730 lb (785 kg)
Maximum take-off: 1,887 lb (856 kg)

PERFORMANCE:
Maximum speed: 104 kts (120 mph) 193 km/h
Cruise speed: 83-94 kts (96-109 mph) 155-175 km/h
IGE hovering ceiling: 4,100 ft (1,250 m) ISA
OGE hovering ceiling: 3,280 ft (1,000 m)
Maximum rate of climb: 1,276 ft (389 m) per minute
Service ceiling: 11,320 ft (3,450 m)
Duration: 3 hours 23 minutes to 4 hours 10 minutes

PZL-Świdnik S.A. — Poland

Full name:
Wytwórnia Sprzetu Komunikacyjnego "PZL-Świdnik" S.A.

Corporate address:
AL. Lotników Polskich 1, 21-045 Świdnik.

Telephone: +48 81 680 901, 751 2071
Facsimile: +48 81 680 919, 751 2173
Telex: 0642301 WSK PL

Founded: 1951.

Employees: 4,300.

Information:
Ryszard Cukierman (Sales Manager).

PZL-Świdnik/Mil Mi-2 (NATO name *Hoplite*)

Comments: First flown on 22 September 1961 as the Soviet-built Mi-2 prototype, with the first Polish-built example following on 4 November 1965, production in Poland continued until 1996, by which time more than 5,450 had been manufactured in many versions (and other versions produced by conversion) and exported to a large number of countries. Full details of the Mi-2 and its versions can be found in the 1996-97 edition of *WA&SD*, pages 312-313. In addition, Mi-2B, Mi-2V, Mi-2G and Mi-2M are Russian proposals for upgraded helicopters, conceived when in the 1990s problems arose with spares from Poland. These Russian versions differ by equipment; for example, the Mi-2M is a version adapted for the Russian Border Guard to carry 6 armed troops and a dog over a distance of 97 naut miles (112 miles) 180 km, featuring sliding doors, Peleng gyrostabilized goggles for observation, and other changes. In the next stage, Allison engines, composite rotor blades, GPS, searchlights and more are proposed.

PZL-Świdnik Kania

First flight: 3 June 1979.
Role: Light, twin-turbine, multi-purpose helicopter, as a 'westernized' development of the Mi-2.
Certification: 1 October 1981 (supplementary); 21 February 1986 to conform to FAR Pt 29 as a transport Category B helicopter with Category A engine isolation.

↑ PZL-Świdnik Kania operated by the Polish Border Guard, equipped with FLIR *(Piotr Butowski)*

Aims

▪ Extensive modification of the Mi-2, retaining a similar robust structure, simplicity of maintenance and spacious interior, combined with new Allison engines, composite blades, new western avionics and other improvements.

Details

Sales: 13 delivered, including 2 to Cyprus in 1989, 1 to Slovakia, 1 to Venezuela, and 4 to the Polish Ministry of the Interior for border patrol and policing (ordered 1995 and delivered 1996). Of the remainder, 2 were involved in accidents, 2 remained unsold at the Świdnik factory (at time of writing), and 1 was used for ground tests.
Crew/passengers: Pilot plus 9 passengers in the standard version, 8 in the business layout and 5 in executive layout. Alternatively, 2 litters and 1 sitting patient plus 2 attendants for EMS.
Freight, internal: 2,645 lb (1,200 kg) of internal freight in cargo layout. Baggage volume in passenger version is 17.66 cu ft (0.5 m^3), with 220 lb (100 kg) capacity. Tie-down rings are standard on all versions of Kania.
Rotor system: 3-blade, fully articulated, glassfibre/epoxy main rotor with hydraulic dampers and electric blade de-icing.
Tail rotor characteristics: 2-blade glassfibre/epoxy, with electric blade de-icing.
Flight control system: Cyclic and collective systems have hydraulic pitch control boosters operating at 943 psi. Variable incidence horizontal stabilizers, using collective pitch lever.
Airframe: Based on the Mi-2 but with some refinements of the structure and cabin layout, of duralumin. Glassfibre/epoxy stabilizer (6 ft, 1.84 m span).
Engines: 2 Allison 250-C20B turboshafts.
Engine rating: Each 420 shp (313 kW).
Transmission: Rated at 874 shp (652 kW) take-off. 3-stage main, intermediate and tail rotor gearboxes. Accessories driven by main gearbox.
Fuel system: 600 litres in an underfloor rubberized tank. Optional 2 × 238 litre auxiliary tanks carried on the fuselage sides.
Electrical system: Principal AC supply via 2 engine-driven 3 kW starter-generators and a 16 kVA 3-phase alternator. 2 × 24 volt, 28 amp-hour lead-acid batteries for DC supply.
Braking system: Pneumatic on main wheels.
Flight avionics/instrumentation: IFR equipped, using AlliedSignal Bendix/King suite as standard, but with option of Becker, Rockwell Collins or other suites at the customer's request.
Additional equipment: Can include BSS FLIR 4000 in a gyrostabilized turret on the starboard side of the fuselage, Nightsun NX-5 searchlight, loudspeakers, electric hoist and more, depending on role.

Aircraft variants:
Passenger version has high standard of comfort, with equipment including individual vents and lighting. Audio system optional. See Passengers for seating arrangements.

Details for Kania

PRINCIPAL DIMENSIONS:
Rotor diameter (main): 47 ft 9.25 ins (14.56 m)
Maximum length, rotors turning: 56 ft 11 ins (17.35 m)
Fuselage length: 39 ft 5.5 ins (12.03 m)
Maximum height: 12 ft 4 ins (3.75 m) to above rotor head

CABIN:
Length: 8 ft 5.6 ins (2.59 m)
Width: 3 ft 5 ins (1.05 m)
Height: 5 ft 4 ins (1.62 m)
Area: 61.14 sq ft (5.68 m^2)
Volume: 274.4 cu ft (7.77 m^3)

MAIN ROTOR:
Aerofoil section: NACA 230-12M
Rotor disc: 1,791 sq ft (166.4 m^2)

TAIL ROTOR:
Diameter: 8 ft 10 ins (2.7 m)
Rotor disc: 61.7 sq ft (5.73 m^2)

UNDERCARRIAGE:
Type: Fixed, with twin nosewheels. Options include attached skis and possibly emergency flotation aids
Main wheel tyre size: 600 × 180 mm
Nose wheel tyre size: 300 × 125 mm
Wheel base: 8 ft 11 ins (2.71 m)
Wheel track: 10 ft (3.05 m)

WEIGHTS:
Empty: 4,409 lb (2,000 kg)
Normal take-off: 7,385 lb (3,350 kg)
Maximum take-off: 7,826 lb (3,550 kg)
Payload: 1,764 lb (800 kg) external, 2,645 lb (1,200 kg) internal
Chemical load for agricultural versions: 2,205 lb (1,000 kg)

PERFORMANCE:
Maximum cruise speed: 113-116 kts (130-133 mph) 210–215 km/h
Economic cruise speed: 103 kts (118 mph) 190 km/h
Maximum climb rate, take-off power: 1,725 ft (525 m) per minute, sea level
Maximum climb rate, normal cruise power: 1,371 ft (418 m) per minute, sea level
Climb rate, OEI, maximum continuous power: 199 ft (601 m) per minute, sea level
IGE hovering ceiling: 8,200 ft (2,500 m)
OGE hovering ceiling: 4,510 ft (1,375 m)
Service ceiling: 13,125 ft (4,000 m), limited
Range, with standard fuel: 259 naut miles (298 miles) 480 km
Range, with standard fuel (30 minutes reserve): 235 naut miles (270 miles) 435 km
Range, with auxiliary fuel: 450 naut miles (519 miles) 835 km
Duration: 4 hours maximum

Executive version accommodates the pilot and 5 passengers on luxury seats. High levels of noise insulation. Standard audio system.
Cargo version is an easy conversion of the standard passenger model, for internal or sling loads. Distribution of loading in the cabin is facilitated by the provision of loading placards, specifying the cg positions of particular load values. Tie-down rings, securing nets and ropes.
Medevac (EMS, air ambulance) version with accommodation as detailed above, plus medical equipment.
Agricultural version is available in 4 basic variants designed for specific types of operations, for low-volume spraying, ultra-low-volume spraying, dusting and spreading.

PZL-Świdnik S-1W Huzar

First flight: Anticipated about 1999.
Role: Anti-tank and attack helicopter.

Development

▪ 1993. Initial requirements issued.
▪ August 1995. Governmental programme for development accepted.
▪ Late 1997-early 1998. Originally scheduled first flight, but now delayed for at least 18 months due to overrunning negotiations concerning the choice of anti-armour missiles and avionics suite.
▪ 1999. Anticipated first flight.

Details

Sales: Purchase of some 100 helicopters planned for the Polish armed forces, with 10-12 per year starting after the year 2000.
Rotor system: As for W-3 Sokół or, more probably, improved SW-5.
Engines: Probably 2 new PZL-Rzeszów free-turbine turboshafts, each in the 1,000 shp (746 kW) class.
Flight avionics/instrumentation: Will include systems to permit night operations and night firing of weapons.
Expendable weapons and equipment: Basic weapons are to be the anti-armour missiles: Hellfire, Rafael NT-D and Hot are under consideration. Other weapons will include a gun and rockets.

PZL-Świdnik SW-4

First flight: 26 October 1996, with 29 October as the 'official' first flight date.
Certification: Expected 1999 to FAR/JAR Pt 27.
Role: Light utility helicopter. Passenger transport, law enforcement, training, patrol, EMS and military surveillance layouts are planned.
Sales: 2 flying prototypes built, plus 1 for static tests and another for dynamic testing, each in its own colour scheme (first flying prototype *600103*, *SP-PSW* is red; ground test prototypes white). Yellow-painted second flying prototype (*600104*) shown at Le Bourget in June 1997 and currently used for certification tests. Red third prototype had accumulated 70 flying hours at the time of writing.
Crew/passengers: Pilot and 3-4 passengers, or alternative layouts according to role, including the pilot, 1 litter and an attendant in EMS form. See table for cargo loads.
Cabin access: Sliding door each side and a hinged door panel just forward of each sliding door, opening outward and forward to increase the total width of the opening.
Rotor system: 3-blade fully articulated main rotor, with glassfibre/epoxy blades. Elastomeric hub.
Tail rotor characteristics: 2-blade, of glassfibre/epoxy.
Tail surfaces: Horizontal stabilizer with small endplates, probably variable incidence. Dorsal and ventral sweptback tailfins, the latter with tailguard.

↑ PZL-Świdnik SW-4 instrument panel *(Piotr Butowski)*

Details for SW-4

PRINCIPAL DIMENSIONS:
Rotor diameter (main): 29 ft 7 ins (9 m)
Maximum length, rotors turning: 34 ft 7 ins (10.55 m)
Fuselage length: 27 ft (8.238 m)
Fuselage width: 4 ft 11.5 ins (1.51 m)
Maximum height: 9 ft 8 ins (2.939 m) to top of rotor head

CABIN:
Length: 7 ft (2.14 m)
Width: 4 ft 8 ins (1.42 m)
Height: 4 ft 2 ins (1.27 m)

MAIN ROTOR:
Rotor disc: 685 sq ft (63.62 m^2)

TAIL ROTOR:
Diameter: 4 ft 11 ins (1.5 m)

UNDERCARRIAGE:
Type: Fixed twin skids (see Safety features). Fourth prototype (yellow) has improved skids
Skid track: 6 ft 7 ins (2 m)

WEIGHTS:
Empty, operating: 1,656 lb (751 kg)
Maximum take-off: 3,527 lb (1,600 kg) with Allison engine, 3,968 lb (1,800 kg) with PW200/9
Payload, internal: 882 lb (400 kg)
Payload, external: 1,653 lb (750 kg)

PERFORMANCE (Allison engines)**:**
Never-exceed speed (V_{NE}): 155 kts (179 mph) 288 km/h
Maximum speed: 132 kts (152 mph) 245 km/h
Cruise speed: 130 kts (149 mph) 240 km/h at 1,640 ft (500 m), 70% power
Climb rate: 1,969 ft (600 m) per minute
IGE hovering ceiling: 11,500 ft (3,500 m)
OGE hovering ceiling: 9,500 ft (2,900 m)
Service ceiling: 19,685 ft (6,000 m)
Range with standard fuel: 485 naut miles (559 miles) 900 km
Duration: 5 hours 30 minutes

Flight control system: Mechanical, with hydraulic boosters introduced to the fourth (yellow) prototype. Third (red) prototype was ftted with a SAMM hydraulic flight control system in 1998.
Safety features: Undercarriage enables survivable landings at a vertical speed equal to 10 ft (3.1 m) per second, by elastic deflection of the crosstubes during hard impact landing. See Fuel system and Transmission.
Airframe: Mainly aluminium alloys, but about 20% of the airframe comprises glassfibre composites.
Engine: Allison 250-C20R/2 free-turbine turboshaft in economy version. Optional 615 shp (459 kW) Pratt & Whitney Canada PW200/9 for the high-performance version. Engine access by removing upper fuselage fairing. See also Aircraft variants for twin-engined version.
Engine rating: 450 shp (335.6 kW), 380 shp (283 kW) for normal cruise, for Allison engine.
Transmission: Located directly forward of the engine and with the same rating as the engine. 2 planetary gear stages provide a speed reduction of 14:1. Main gearbox design provides for 30 minutes operation after loss of oil.
Fuel system: 500 litres in a tank located under the main gearbox and made of high-strength elastic material with good energy attenuating characteristics for safety. Auxiliary tank optional.

↑ PZL-Świdnik SW-4 fourth prototype during its international debut at the 1997 Paris Air Show *(Piotr Butowski)*

Flight avionics/instrumentation: AlliedSignal Bendix/King radio/navigation instruments for VFR/IFR flight, day and night, under all weather conditions.

Aircraft variants:
SW-4 was unveiled in December 1994, when the first ground test example was rolled out. 2 variants are under development, as the economy and high performance with different engines. As detailed.
Twin-engined version is under study because of pending restrictions on the use of single-engined helicopters over built-up areas. Would fulfil OEI requirements (including hover) in accordance with ICAO regulations.

PZL-Świdnik W-3 Sokól and SW-5

First flight: 16 November 1979 (piloted by Wieslaw Mercik); see 6 May 1982 under Development.
Certification: See Development, September 1988, April 1990, 1992 and 1993.
Role: Civil and military intermediate multi-purpose helicopter.

Development

- 1971. Polish-Soviet agreement signed covering an order for a Polish-designed intermediate-sized helicopter. Chief designer Stanislaw Kaminski, now Cezary Kaminski.
- 16 November 1979. First prototype (c/n 30.01.02) used for ground fatigue tests performed the first hovering flight.
- 6 May 1982. First true flight of the W-3 (prototype c/n 30.01.03).
- May 1984. New higher technical requirements prepared.
- 1987. First flight of a production helicopter (c/n 30.02.01).
- 26 September 1988. Temporary Polish certificate.
- 17 March 1990. First flight of a combat version, the W-3U Salamandra.
- 10 April 1990. Full Polish certification.
- December 1992. Russian certification.
- 31 May 1993. US FAA certification for the PZL W-3A.

Details

Sales: 118 built at the time of writing, including 2 for static tests, 6 flying prototypes and 34 for export to Myanmar (12 in November 1990 and 1 in May 1992), 11 W-3As to Czech Republic (exchanged for 10 MiG-29s, delivered between September 1996 and February 1997), 2 W-3As to Germany (c/n 37.05.03, registration *D-HSNA* and 37.07.08, *D-HSNP*), 3 to Citiair of South Korea (in late 1995/early 1996), 4 to Daewoo of South Korea, and 1 to Nigeria. Of 20 delivered to Aeroflot between 1988 and 1990, 2 were involved in accidents and 18 were returned to Poland. First delivery for the Polish armed forces took place in July 1989 (standard W-3 for the 18th Rescue-Communication Flight of Naval Aviation). At the time of writing the Polish armed forces (including the Ministry of Internal Affairs) operated 24 W-3Ws and 2 W-3WAs (25th Air Cavalry Division, with first 5 delivered on 12 May 1994), 11 W-3s, 2 W-3As and 5 W-3RMs. Since 1991, leased W-3s have undertaken a forest firefighting role in Spain.
Crew/passengers: 2 crew in basic transport layout, with single pilot VFR operation for the W-3A. Typically 12 passengers, or 5 VIPs, or 4 litters and an attendant in medevac role. See Aircraft variants for other layouts.
Freight, external: Up to 4,630 lb (2,100 kg) sling load.
Cabin access: Sliding door on the port side of the cabin, 3 ft 10.5 ins × 3 ft 1 ins (1.18 × 0.94 m). Additional and larger starboard door of 3 ft 10.5 ins × 4 ft 1 ins (1.18 × 1.25 m).
Optional equipment: Dual controls, and flat plate windshield.
Rotor system: 4-blade fully-articulated main rotor of glassfibre/epoxy, with Salomon damper to delete oscillatory loads for minimal vibration. Blade de-icing. Optional blade folding (manual). Rotor brake.
Tail rotor characteristics: 3-blade glassfibre/epoxy.
Tail surfaces: Non-moving vertical and horizontal.
Engines: 2 PZL-Rzeszów PZL-10W free-turbine turboshafts. Air inlets have de-icing. Intake particle separators. Series III engine will have MTBO of 3,000 hours.
Engine rating: Each 887.7 shp (662 kW) take-off, or 1,134 shp (846 kW) 2.5 minutes OEI.
Transmission: 1,800 shp (1,342 kW) take-off and 1,560 shp (1,163 kW) maximum continuous. Emergency OEI rating

↑ PZL-Świdnik W-3W Sokól in Polish Army Aviation service *(Piotr Butowski)*

↑ Standard IFR cockpit for the PZL-Świdnik Sokól *(courtesy PZL-Świdnik)*

1,150 shp (857 kW). Main, intermediate and tail rotor gearboxes.
Fuel system: 1,720 litres standard. Optional 1,100 litre auxiliary tank available to some versions. Electronic fuel control.
Hydraulic system: Dual systems, each 1,305 psi, for 3 main rotor control boosters and tail rotor control booster.
Braking system: Main wheel discs.
Radar: See Aircraft variants.
Flight avionics/instrumentation: IFR equipped. See also Aircraft variants. 2-axis flight control system, with 3-4 axis optional. See Aircraft variants.
Expendable weapons and equipment: See Aircraft variants.

Aircraft variants:
W-3 Sokól (Falcon) became the standard version. Single example of a mountain rescue version with skis added to the undercarriage, a 595 lb (270 kg) electric winch and equipped to carry paratroops, was involved in an accident on 11 August 1994. VIP version accommodates 5 persons.
W-3 Erka is a medical helicopter. Single example (*SP-SUE*, c/n 32.02.10) was built in 1988.
W-3A was modified to meet US FAR 29 regulations. First flight 30 July 1992, with FAA certification 31 May 1993. Changes to the hydraulic (dual) and electrical systems. Avionics include AlliedSignal Bendix/King KTR 908 and KHF 950 com radios, KDF 806 radiocompass, KRA 405 radio altimeter, weather radar, KNR 63A VOR/LOC/GS/ MB receiver, KA 35A marker beacon receiver, and KXP 756 transponder. Larger main wheels. New de-icing system. First prototype (c/n 36.04.20, side number *420*; ex *SP-PSK*, ex *SP-SSK*) is currently used by the Polish Ministry of Internal Affairs in VIP form.
W-3RM Anakonda (ratowniczy morski, sea rescue) has 3 inflatable flotation bags on each side of the fuselage, plus a fixed float beneath the tailboom, additional door glazing, a containerized dinghy, French electric winch of 595 lb (270 kg) capacity, starboard racks for 3 marker bombs, and 3 searchlights. First prototype (c/n 39.04.11, side number *0411*) flew in April 1991 and production started in 1992. Polish Navy has 4 and the Ministry of Internal Affairs has 1.
W-3L Traszka (Newt, nickname Long) was to be a stretched version for 14 troops. Cabin length increased by 4 ft 5 ins (1.35 m), 1,000 shp (746 kW) engines, and provision for armament. Abandoned through lack of orders.
W-3U Salamandra (U for uzbrojony, armed) had the armament system of the Mil Mi-24V *Hind-E*. Each outrigger carried 2 Polish Mars-8 rocket pods and 2 Russian tube-launched 9M114 Shturm (AT-6 *Spiral*) anti-tank missiles. GSh-23 twin barrel 23-mm cannon was installed in the starboard side of the nose. Single W-3U Salamandra was built in 1990 (c/n 36.03.17, side number *0317*). Because of lack of interest from the Polish Air Force, in 1992 it was stripped of armament and exported to Myanmar.
W-3U-1 Aligator is an anti-submarine version, expected about 1998, to replace the Mi-14PL *Haze-A*.
W-3WB (WB for wsparcia bojowego, combat support) is the most developed armed version of the W-3. Single prototype was tested in South Africa, where the Kentron company (thereafter sometimes named W-3K) provided the weapon system, including the GA-1 20-mm cannon installed in an undernose turret with 300 rounds of ammunition (angle of fire 90° azimuth, +12°/–60° elevation), and ZT-35 Grot (Arrowhead) anti-tank missiles, plus the fire control system with helmet sight. Standard armament on outriggers comprises 2 Polish-made Mars-2 rocket packs with 16 × 57-mm rockets each, and 2 × 4-tube launchers for ZT-35 laser-guided anti-tank missiles. 1 Grot launcher may be replaced by a Gad (Reptile) launcher with 2 × 9M32M Strzaía (SA-7 *Grail*) AAMs or similar. Can alternatively carry Polish ZR-8 submunition dispensers and Platan mine-laying packs. Fire control system is based on a roof-mounted sight with monochrome TV camera and IR imager, while a laser rangefinder is optional. Other options are IR suppressors, light crew armour and upgraded navigation system. Programme halted through lack of orders.
W-3W Sokól (wsparcia, support; commonly but incorrectly thought to be named Huzar) is a low-cost variant of W-3WB, purchased by Polish Army Aviation. Polish-built systems only and no anti-tank missiles. Standard armament comprises a fixed GSh-23L twin-barrel 23-mm cannon plus outrigger stores. Each of the 4 pylons can carry a 4-tube Grom (Thunder; a Polish-built weapon derived from the Russian Igla-1 and Igla-M portable SAMs) or 2-tube Gad system, or Mars-2 16-round 57-mm rocket pod or S-8 80-mm launcher, or ZR-8MB1 submunition dispensers.
W-3WA is similar to W-3W but based on the certified W-3A helicopter.
W-3RR Procjon is a reconnaissance/electronic warfare version, under development.
W-3RWC is a projected naval reconnaissance and target acquisition version.
SW-5 is a projected improved version, with Sextant Avionique avionics and new 1,000 shp (746 kW) engines. First flight expected in the year 2000.
S-1W Huzar is a projected anti-tank/attack version, detailed separately.

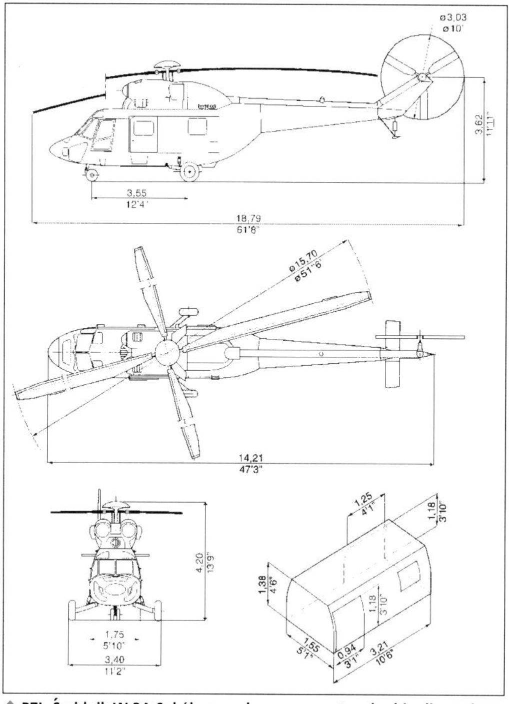

↑ **PZL-Świdnik W-3A Sokól general arrangement and cabin dimensions** *(courtesy PZL-Świdnik)*

Details for W-3A Sokól

PRINCIPAL DIMENSIONS:
Rotor diameter (main): 51 ft 6 ins (15.7 m)
Maximum length, rotors turning: 61 ft 8 ins (18.79 m)
Fuselage length: 46 ft 7.5 ins (14.21 m)
Fuselage width: 5 ft 9 ins (1.75 m)
Maximum height: 19 ft 9 ins (4.2 m) to above rotor head, or 11 ft 10.5 ins (3.62 m) to top of fin

CABIN:
Length: 10 ft 6.5 ins (3.21 m)
Width: 5 ft 1 ins (1.55 m)
Height: 4 ft 6.5 ins (1.38 m)
Volume: 242.16 cu ft (6.89 m^3)

MAIN ROTOR:
Aerofoil section: NACA 23012M
Blade chord: 1 ft 5 ins (0.44 m)
Blade area: each 31.2 sq ft (2.9 m^2)
Rotor disc: 2,084 sq ft (193.6 m^2)
Rpm: 268

TAIL ROTOR:
Diameter: 9 ft 11 ins (3.03 m)
Rpm: 1,342

UNDERCARRIAGE:
Type: Fixed, with twin castoring/self-centring nosewheels. Options include attached skis and emergency flotation aids
Main wheel tyre size: 700 × 250 mm
Nose wheel tyre size: 400 × 150 mm
Wheel base: 11 ft 8 ins (3.55 m)
Wheel track: 11 ft 2 ins (3.4 m)

WEIGHTS:
Empty, operating: 8,488 lb (3,850 kg)
Normal take-off weight: 13,448 lb (6,100 kg)
Maximum take-off: 14,100 lb (6,400 kg)
Payload: 4,630 lb (2,100 kg)

PERFORMANCE (at 12,786 lb, 5,800 kg weight, ISA, at 1,640 ft, 500 m)**:**
Never-exceed speed (V_{NE}): 140 kts (161 mph) 260 km/h
Cruise speed: 131 kts (151 mph) 243 km/h
Cruise speed with suspended armament: 116 kts (134 mph) 215 km/h
Maximum climb rate: 2,008 ft (612 m) per minute
IGE hovering ceiling: 11,485 ft (3,500 m)
OGE hovering ceiling: 8,070 ft (2,460 m)
Service ceiling: 16,075 ft (4,900 m) with armament, 19,685 ft (6,000 m)
Practical ceiling: 17,815 ft (5,430 m)
Range: 431 naut miles (496 miles) 798 km
Range with 20 minutes reserve: 398 naut miles (458 miles) 737 km
Duration: 4.56 hours, or 4.2 hours with 20 minutes reserves
Operating temperatures: -40° C to +43° C

CPCA (Aviation Design & Consulting Center) — Romania

Corporate address:
See General Aviation section for company details.

CPCA ADC-H1

First flight: Expected 1999.
Certification: To meet FAR Pt 27 requirements.
Role: 2-seat light helicopter.
Rotor system: 2-blade main rotor.
Tail rotor characteristics: 2-blade tail rotor.
Tail surfaces: Fixed horizontal stabilizer to starboard and dorsal/ventral fins.
Flight control system: Mechanical.
Airframe materials: Metal and glassfibre.
Engine: 160 hp (119.3 kW) Textron Lycoming O-320-B2C piston engine.
Fuel system: 72 litres.
Electrical system: 14 volt 70 amp alternator, and 14 volt 25 amp-hour battery.
Flight avionics/instrumentation: AlliedSignal Bendix/King KY 197 com transceiver.

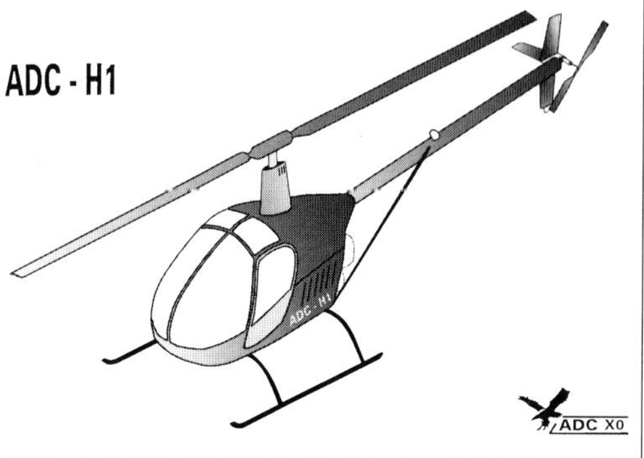

↑ **CPCA ADC-H1 2-seat light helicopter**

Details for ADC-H1

PRINCIPAL DIMENSIONS:
Rotor diameter (main): 25 ft 3 ins (7.7 m)
Maximum length, rotors turning: 28 ft 9 ins (8.76 m)
Fuselage length: 20 ft (6.1 m)
Width: 3 ft 11 ins (1.2 m) over cabin
Maximum height: 8 ft 6 ins (2.6 m)

TAIL ROTOR:
Diameter: 3 ft 7 ins (1.1 m)

UNDERCARRIAGE:
Type: Fixed skid
Skid track: 6 ft 5 ins (1.96 m)

WEIGHTS:
Empty: 846 lb (384 kg)
Maximum take-off and landing: 1,404 lb (637 kg)
Payload: 430 lb (195 kg)

PERFORMANCE (provisional):
Maximum speed: 95 kts (109 mph) 176 km/h
Maximum climb rate: 886 ft (270 m) per minute, at sea level
Ceiling: 11,480 ft (3,500 m)
Range: 197 naut miles (227 miles) 366 km

IAR-SA Brasov — Romania

Corporate address:
1 Aeroportului, 2200 Brasov, PO Box 198.

Telephone: +40 68 15 00 15
Facsimile: +40 68 15 13 04, 15 06 23
Telex: 61266

Founded:
Established in 1968 as ICA Brasov, with foundations in IAR of 1925. 70% of shares in the privatizing company were assigned to be sold to Bell Helicopter Textron under an agreement of 1997.

Employees: 2,400.

Information:
Stefan Paunescu (Marketing Manager).

ACTIVITIES

▪ Aircraft manufacturing and repair, including production of various lightplanes and gliders/motorgliders of its own design (see General Aviation and Glider sections). Agreement with Beriev of Russia to licence build the Be-32K at a plant at Kraiova.

▪ Produces spare parts for the IAR 316B (Alouette), having built 280 (including 70 for export to France and Angola), and spares for the IAR 330L Puma which is still believed to be available as a newly-built helicopter from the company, though no new customers are known. An upgrade programme (SOCAT) for 24 Romanian Air Force Pumas is currently underway.

▪ Component manufacturing for the Rombac 1-11 airliner has ended, as has development of the Noga VI business Jet (see the 1996-97 edition of *WA&SD*, page 417).

▪ Under an agreement of 1996, IAR can licence build up to 80 Eurocopter AS 350BA and AS 355N helicopters.

▪ Under a very significant agreement with Bell Helicopter Textron dating from August 1996 but requiring the share deal (the agreement was tied to Bell's purchase of a majority shareholding in the privatizing company, set at 70%), IAR is to licence manufacture AH-1W SuperCobras for the Romanian forces, using the new designation AH-1RO Dracula. Bell is expected also to use IAR as a production source for other items. Financing was, however, still to be agreed in mid-1998.

IAR AH-1RO Dracula

Comments: The total requirement is for 96 Draculas for the Romanian forces, for delivery between 1999 and 2005. Avionics will be locally produced by A-E Electronics, a joint-venture company founded by Elbit Systems of Israel and Aerostar of Romania (see Aerostar in the General Aviation section). Dracula is expected to incorporate some SOCAT systems (see Puma below).

IAR 330L Puma and Puma 2000

Comments: Full details of the IAR-Brasov built IAR 330L Puma and illustrations can be found in the 1996-97 edition of *WA&SD*, pages 314-315. The upgraded Puma 2000 is an ongoing programme and details follow, together with details of the SOCAT upgrade programme for the Romanian Air Force.

Aircraft variants:
IAR 330L Puma entered production in 1977 and some 180 have been delivered, of which approximately half were exported to France, Pakistan, South Africa and Sudan.
SOCAT is an acronym for Anti-tank Optronic Search and Combat System, being applied to 24 Romanian Air Force IAR 330Ls for a tactical support role. The first SOCAT prototype was rolled out in June 1997 and was displayed at that year's Paris Air Show. Flight testing started in May 1998. The second prototype was completed in 1998 and full 'production' upgrading is now underway, with most avionics coming from the newly formed A-E Electronics company (see Dracula above for company details). New avionics and weapon systems are being integrated via a computer and MIL-STD-1553 digital databus, and encompass monochrome MFDs for the pilot and gunner, digital colour moving map display, and an integrated inertial navigation system/GPS. Other equipment includes nose-mounted laser rangefinder and TV/FLIR camera system, Giat Industries THL20 chin turret 20-mm gun, and expendable weapons including anti-tank missiles, 57-mm unguided rockets, and A-95-MH IR-guided air-to-air missiles.
Puma 2000 is a company-developed upgraded variant of the IAR 330L (that pre-dates the SOCAT programme), with higher powered engines, Hellfire anti-armour missiles among other weapon options, modernized flight deck, and greatly enhanced avionics integrated by Elbit (possibly now A-E Electronics) and using the MIL-STD-1553B databus. Hands on cyclic and stick (HOCAS) controls. EFIS displays and HUD. Optional El-Op MSIS (multi-sensor stabilized integrated system) including FLIR and TV imaging. Laser rangefinder and target designator.

↑ IAR 330L Puma with SOCAT upgrade for the Romanian Air Force *(Aviation Picture Library)*

Autogyro Design Bureau — Russia

Corporate address:
141100 Shczelkovo-3, Moscow Region, ul. Zhukovskogo 4-57.

Telephone: +7 095 526 5019

Information:
Igor Zaytsev.

Autogyro Ariel

First flight: 18 September 1991 (Pelegrim, see Aircraft variants), piloted by Boris Lvov. 19 June 1997 for Ariel-212, piloted by Igor Zaytsev.
Role: Light autogyro, with potential applications including sport and leisure, pipeline and border patrol, surveillance, rescue, air ambulance, and armed.
Sales: Prototype built by Igor Zaytsev. Looking for a partner (at the time of writing) to assist in series production at the Air Force Science and Research Institute in Chkalovskaya near Moscow. Price $24,000 for a production autogyro.
Crew/passenger: 2 persons in tandem in a fully enclosed cabin. Pilot and 1 litter in an air ambulance role.
Rotor system: 2-blade composite main rotor.
Tail surfaces: Triple vertical tail unit carried on a twin tubular structure, with a central rudder aft of the propeller and 2 outer fixed fins, and an adjoining horizontal surface.
Engine: Arrow GP-500 2-stroke piston engine, with 3-blade pusher propeller.

↑ Autogyro Ariel-212 *(Piotr Butowski)*

Engine rating: 65 hp (48.5 kW).

Aircraft variants:
Pelegrim (Pilgrim) was the prototype of 1991, powered by a motorcycle engine. 1 built.
Boomerang (or XA2, Experimental Autogyro, 2-seat) was built in 1993 but suffered an accident in September 1994. After repair, renamed Ratnik and marketed by the Kamerton-N Ltd company.

Details for Ariel-212

PRINCIPAL DIMENSIONS:
Rotor diameter (main): 25 ft 3 ins (7.7 m)
Maximum length, without rotor: 11 ft 9 ins (3.58 m)
Width, without rotor: 6 ft 3 ins (1.9 m)
Maximum height: 8 ft 9.5 ins (2.68 m)

UNDERCARRIAGE:
Type: Fixed nosewheel type

WEIGHTS:
Empty: 518 lb (235 kg)
Maximum take-off: 992 lb (450 kg)

PERFORMANCE:
Maximum speed: 92 kts (106 mph) 170 km/h
Cruise speed: 65 kts (75 mph) 120 km/h
Take-off distance over a 50 ft (15 m) obstacle: 262 ft (80 m)
Landing distance over a 50 ft (15 m) obstacle: 98 ft (30 m)
Service ceiling: 9,845 ft (3,000 m)
Range with full payload: 291 naut miles (335 miles) 540 km
Duration: 5 hours

Ariel-211 (2-seats, 1 engine, 1st version) was next, which was developed into the Ariel-212.
Ariel-212 (2 seats, 1 engine, 2nd version) has a passive flight stabilization system added. First flown on 19 June 1997.

Kamerton-N Ltd — Russia

Comments: Details of the Ratnik light autogyro can be found in the 1996-97 edition of *WA&SD*, page 315. See also Aircraft variants under the previous Autogyro Ariel entry.

Kamov Company — Russia

Full name:
Vertoletnyi Nauchno-Tekhnicheskiy Kompleks Imeni N.I. Kamova.

Corporate address:
8a, The 8th March Street, Liubertsy 140007, Moscow Region.

Telephone: +7 095 700 32 04
Facsimile: +7 095 700 30 71
Telex: 206112 Kamov

Founded:
1948, since 1996 as a branch of Military Industrial Group MAPO-M.

Employees: 3,000.

Information:
V. Kasianikov (Vice President).

ACTIVITIES

■ Development, experimental production, maintenance and upgrading of helicopters, as the helicopter enterprise of MIG MAPO-M. **Ka-37** is a new pilotless helicopter.

Kamov Ka-25 (NATO name *Hormone*)

Comments: Making its first hovering flight on 26 April 1961 (piloted by Dmitri Yefremov), the Ka-25 became the standard Soviet ship-borne anti-submarine warfare (ASW) helicopter, used also in sea target acquisition, minesweeping, SAR and other roles. About 460 were manufactured between 1965-77 at the Ulan-Ude plant. In 1995, the Ka-25 was withdrawn from active service with the Russian Navy, though several dozen remained in reserve. 7 went to India, 9 to Syria, others to the former Yugoslavia (about 5), and Vietnam (about 5). Bulgaria acquired a Ka-25Ts in 1979 but this has not flown since 1991. For full details, plus an illustration, see the 1996-97 edition of *WA&SD*, page 316.

Kamov Ka-27 and Ka-28 (NATO name *Helix-A* and *D*)

First hovering flight: 8 August 1973 (piloted by Yevgeni Laryushin). First full circle flight 24 December 1973.
Role: Ship-based ASW, search and rescue, and armed surveillance.
Chief designer: Yuri Lazarenko.

Aims

■ Ability to destroy a submarine cruising at a depth of 1,640 ft (500 m) and speed of 40.5 kts.
■ Patrol duration of 2 hours at a distance of 200 km from the ship.
■ Overall dimensions could not exceed those of the Ka-25, so that the new helicopter could use the same ship-borne facilities.
■ Ability to operate from a 10 × 10 m platform/deck at head-on wind speeds of 20 m per second or 10 m per second side on, with the vessel heeling at 10° and 3° trim.

↑ Kamov Ka-27 deploying Ros-V dipping sonar *(Piotr Butowski)*

Development

■ 1968. Design started.
■ April 1972. Official Government order for an ASW helicopter.
■ 8 August 1974. First flight of the Ka-27PS rescue version, pilot L. Pantelei.
■ November 1977-December 1978. State acceptance trials of the ASW version.
■ August 1978-February 1979. Acceptance trials for the Ka-27PS.
■ 14 April 1981. Ka-27 officially accepted into Soviet Navy service.

Details

Sales: 267 built at the Kumertau (Kirgizstan) aviation plant. About 200 are in service with the Russian Navy, plus a small number in Ukraine. Ka-28s exported to India (14), the former Yugoslavia (1) and Vietnam (10). Since October 1994, Kamov has participated in a tender to provide an ASW helicopter to South Africa, and has recently tendered for a SAR helicopter for Canada. An order for Ka-28s is expected from China, together with the purchase of 2 destroyers.
Flight crew: Pilot and navigator side-by-side, with a dipping sonar operator in the cabin.
Cabin access: Rearward sliding doors on both sides, with bulged windows, or through the cabin.
Passengers/troops: 12 troops in Ka-27PS.
Loading facilities: Ka-27PS has an LPG-300 winch at the port cabin door, of 661 lb (300 kg) capacity.
Main rotor characteristics: 2 coaxial, contra-rotating, 3-blade fully-articulated rotors. Asymmetric blade aerofoils, with ground adjustable tabs. Bottom rotor has vibration dampers. D2-4 composite blades with automatic folding. Titanium/steel rotor head. Rotor brake. Electrical de-icing of the blades.
Tail surfaces: Tailplane with elevators. Inward toed endplates, each with a rudder and fixed leading-edge slat.
Flight control system: Hydraulic, with no manual back-up. Differential collective pitch yaw control.
Fuselage: Watertight, in case of an emergency ditching.
Construction materials: Aluminium alloy, but also with extensive use of titanium and composite materials.
Engines: 2 Klimov/St Petersburg TV3-117KM turboshafts side-by-side above the cabin compartment. High altitude TV3-117VKs for Ka-28 and late series Ka-27s. Air intake de-icing. APU.
Engine rating: Each 2,225 shp (1,659 kW) maximum, 1,700 shp (1,268 kW) normal, and 2,400 shp (1,790 kW) OEI emergency rating for 2.5 minutes.
Transmission: VR-252 main gearbox.
Fuel system: Ka-27 has 8 fuel tanks under the cabin floor (on both sides of the weapon bay), plus 2 inside the cabin, offering a total of 2,940 litres. Ka-27PS has no cabin tanks, but has 2 additional tanks in place of the Ka-27's weapon bay plus 2 auxiliary tanks fitted externally on the cabin sides, offering a total of 3,450 litres. Ka-28 has larger internal tanks, as well as external cabin tanks, offering a total of 4,760 litres.
Electrical system: Principal AC supply via 2 generators. DC supply via AC using 2 rectifiers. 2 batteries, able to back-up either supply, with inverters for AC.
Hydraulic system: 3, 2 of which are principally main and stand-by systems for the servos. See Braking system.
Braking system: Hydraulic, as a second function of the main hydraulic system and with back-up from the third.
Radar: Osminog radar in the undernose radome. A large ship can be detected from a distance of 97 naut miles (112 miles) 180 km from an altitude of 6,890-7,875 ft (2,100-2,400 m), or a submerged submarine (RCS of 2,691 sq ft, 250 m^2) from a range of 16 naut miles (19 miles) 30 km.
Flight avionics/instrumentation: NKV-252 navigation system using DISS-15 Doppler nav radar mounted under the tailboom. Pre-programmed flight path, and autonomous flight back to the ship. Privod ILS combined with ship systems, automatic radio-compass, Greben-1 heading system, MGV-1V gyroscopic system and A-031 radio-compass. PKV-252 flight system includes VUAP-1 4-channel autopilot and provides automatic hovering at an altitude of more

Details for Ka-27 *Helix-A*, unless stated

PRINCIPAL DIMENSIONS:
Rotor diameter: 52 ft 2 ins (15.9 m) each
Maximum length, rotors folded: 40 ft 2 ins (12.25 m)
Fuselage length: 37 ft 1 ins (11.3 m)
Width, blades folded: 12 ft 6 ins (3.8 m)
Height: 17 ft 8 ins (5.4 m) to above rotor head

CABIN: See Ka-32

MAIN ROTOR:
Blade chord: 1 ft 7 ins (0.48 m)
Rotor disc: 2,136.6 sq ft (198.5 m^2)
Rpm: 252

UNDERCARRIAGE:
Type: 4 fixed legs, each with a single wheel; forward pair castoring. Large flotation gear on each side of the lower fuselage and ahead of the main undercarriage legs. Optional wheel/skis
Main wheel tyre size: 600 × 180 mm, or 620 × 180 mm for later series
Nose wheel tyre size: 400 × 150 mm, or 480 × 200 mm for later series
Wheel base: 9 ft 11 ins (3.02 m)
Main wheel track: 11 ft 6 ins (3.5 m)
Front wheel track: 4 ft 7 ins (1.4 m)

WEIGHTS:
Normal take-off: 23,589 lb (10,700 kg)
Maximum take-off: 24,251 lb (11,000 kg)
Payload (Ka-27PS): 6,614 lb (3,000 kg)

PERFORMANCE:
Maximum operating speed, at normal take-off weight: 156 kts (180 mph) 290 km/h
Maximum operating speed, at MTOW: 146 kts (168 mph) 270 km/h
Cruise speed: 124 kts (143 mph) 230 km/h, at MTOW
OGE hovering ceiling, with TV3-117KM engines: 7,220 ft (2,200 m)
OGE hovering ceiling, Ka-28 with TV3-117VK engines: 9,515 ft (2,900 m)
Service ceiling: 11,480 ft (3,500 m)
Range with maximum fuel: 648 naut miles (745.6 miles) 1,200 km
Normal range: 378 naut miles (435 miles) 700 km
Patrol duration at a distance of 200 km: 2 hours 15 minutes in search variant, 1 hour 25 minutes in search-attack variant
Maximum duration: 3 hours 30 minutes

than 82 ft (25 m). Minimum weather conditions for landing are 197 ft (60 m) cloud base and 1,970 ft (600 m) visual range. R-832M and Zhuravl com radios, SPU-8 intercom, and a coded data exchange system enabling the operation of the host ship and group of helicopters under a common data network.
Fixed weapons: None.
Mission equipment (standard): Osminog search/attack system, built around a radio sonobuoy system (with A-100 Pankhra on-board receiver) and comprising also a radar, tactical indicator, and digital computer. VGS-3 Ros-V dipping sonar (not connected to the system) housed in the bottom of the fuselage, aft of the cabin. Sonar detection range is 23,950 ft (7,300 m). APM-73V Bor MAD (detection range 1,312 ft, 400 m) can be suspended under the tailboom when the sonar is removed.
Expendable weapons and equipment: Normal 1,323 lb (600 kg), maximum 2,205 lb (1,000 kg) in the heated weapons bay. Single AT-1MV torpedo or APR-2 ASW missile, or 6-8 PLAB-250-120 depth charges, KAB-250PL guided depth charges, or nuclear depth charge. Up to 36 RGB-NM, or RGB-N or RGB-16 sonobuoys. Kh-35 (AS-20 *Kayak*) anti-ship missiles have recently been offered for Ka-28 upgrade to India, and probably also for Russian Ka-27s.

Aircraft variants:
Ka-27 (Ka-252PL or izdelye D2, or izdelye 500) *Helix-A*, incorrectly named Ka-27PL by some, is the basic anti-submarine version, as detailed.
Ka-27K ASW version has the new Kamerton-1M search/attack system. Widened flight deck with flat-plate glazing as for Ka-29. Prototype only. Programme terminated.
Ka-27M is an upgraded ASW version with new weapons. Fully tested but not introduced due to lack of funding.
Ka-27PK (protivokorabelnyi, anti-ship) is a version armed with the Kh-35 (AS-20 *Kayak*) anti-ship missile. Status unknown.
Ka-27PS (Ka-252PS or izdelye 501) *Helix-D* is the search and rescue version, with ASW equipment removed. 2 radio signal buoys suspended under the tailboom, and an LPG-300 winch at the cabin door. Carries life-rafts, and containers with clothes, food, medicines, etc.
Ka-27PV (pogranichnyi variant) is intended for armed border surveillance, particularly over coastal areas. Currently presented as the Ka-327 (see Ka-32 entry).
Ka-28 is the export version of Ka-27 *Helix-A*, first flown in 1982 and originally built against an order from India. Maximum allowable take-off weight increased to 26,455 lb (12,000 kg) due to having no requirement for dipping the sonar in a long hovering manoeuvre immediately after take-off from the deck, which was required by the Soviet Navy for the Ka-27. Maximum fuel increased to 4,760 litres (8,113 lb, 3,680 kg), normal combat load 1,765 lb (800 kg), and maximum range 669 naut miles (770 miles) 1,240 km.
Ka-28PS is the export version of Ka-27PS, named also Ka-32PS.
Ka-29 is an assault helicopter. See separate entry.
Ka-31 is an airborne early warning helicopter. See separate entry.
Ka-32 is a civil derivative. See separate entry.

Kamov Ka-29 (NATO name *Helix-B*) and Ka-33

First flight: 28 July 1976, piloted by Yevgeni Laryushin.
Role: Ship-based assault and transport helicopter.

Details for Ka-29

PRINCIPAL DIMENSIONS:
Rotor diameter: 52 ft 2 ins (15.90 m) each
Maximum length, rotors folded: 40 ft 2 ins (12.25 m)
Fuselage length: 37 ft 1 ins (11.3 m)
Width, blades folded: 19 ft 1 ins (5.82 m)
Width, blades folded, outriggers removed: 12 ft 5 ins (3.8 m)
Maximum height: 17 ft 10 ins (5.44 m)

TAIL UNIT:
Span : 11 ft 11.5 ins (3.65 m)

UNDERCARRIAGE:
Main wheel tyre size: 600 × 180 mm
Nose wheel tyre size: 400 × 150 mm
Wheel base: 9 ft 11 ins (3.02 m)
Main wheel track: 11 ft 6 ins (3.5 m)
Front wheel track: 4 ft 7 ins (1.4 m)

WEIGHTS:
Empty: 12,170 lb (5,520 kg)
Normal take-off: 24,471 lb (11,100 kg)
Maximum take-off: 25,353 lb (11,500 kg)
Maximum take-off with external load: 27,778 lb (12,600 kg)
Payload: 3,968 lb (1,800 kg) maximum internal, 8,816 lb (4,000 kg) maximum external

PERFORMANCE:
Maximum operating speed: 151 kts (174 mph) 280 km/h
Cruise speed: 127 kts (146 mph) 235 km/h
OGE hovering ceiling: 9,843 ft (3,000 m)
Service ceiling: 14,108 ft (4,300 m)
Maximum climb rate: 3,050 ft (930 m) per minute, sea level
Radius of action: 54 naut miles (62 miles) 100 km, with 2,425 lb (1,100 kg) of weapons
Normal range: 248 naut miles (286 miles) 460 km, with 16 troops
Ferry range: 400 naut miles (460 miles) 740 km

Development

▪ 1974. Official request for the Soviet Navy.
▪ 1985. Initial deployment with the Northern and Pacific fleets of the Soviet Navy.

Details

Sales: 59 Ka-29s built at Kumertau (Kirgizstan) aviation plant by mid-1998. About 50 in service with the Russian Navy. 6 Ka-33s reportedly ordered by Bulgaria.
Flight crew: Pilot and weapon system operator side-by-side. Access to the cockpit via rearward sliding doors on the sides of the fuselage or through the cabin. Flight deck is about 15.75 ins (40 cm) wider than for the Ka-27, with 3 flat-plate front glazed panels.
Passengers/troops: Up to 16 troops on folding seats inside the cabin, or 4 litters and 8 sitting casualties/attendants in a medevac role.
Freight, internal: 3,968 lb (1,800 kg).
Freight, external: 8,818 lb (4,000 kg).
Cabin access: Doors at port side, divided horizontally into 2 sections.
Main rotor characteristics: As for Ka-27.
Tail surfaces: As for Ka-27.
Safety features: Armoured flight deck and engine compartment.
Engines: As for Ka-27. Optional heat suppressors on the nozzles.
Radar: None.
Flight avionics/instrumentation: As for Ka-27.
Weapon system avionics/instrumentation: Shturm-V anti-tank guided missile system, with electro-optical sight window under the starboard side of the fuselage nose and radio guidance sensor to port. ASP-17VK gun sight. Optional laser rangefinder. ESM.
Self-protection systems: UV-26 chaff dispensers fitted to the fuselage sides (4 × 32 cartridges on each side). L-166V (NATO *Hot Brick*) infra-red jammer on some aircraft, located aft of the APU compartment.
Fixed weapons: NUV-1UM stand with flexible GShG-7.62 4-barrel Gatling type 7.62-mm machine-gun and 1,800 rounds of ammunition at the starboard door. Fire angles –31°/0° in elevation, 28° to port and 30° to starboard. Optional 2A42 30-mm single-barrel cannon with 250 rounds on the port weapon rack.
Number of weapon pylons: 4.
Expendable weapons and equipment: Up to 8 × 9M114 (AT-6 *Spiral*) tube-launched, guided anti-tank missiles of the Shturm-V system, in 2 × 4-tube clusters. Unguided weapons include 2 or 4 B8V-20A rocket launchers, each with 20 × 80-mm rockets, UPK-23-250 gun packs, bombs, incendiary tanks, etc. Maximum weapon load is 3,968 lb (1,800 kg).

Aircraft variants:
Ka-29 (Ka-252TB, transportno-boyevoi, combat-transport, or izdelye D2B or 502) *Helix-B* is a ship-borne transport and assault helicopter. As detailed.
Ka-29RS (razvedyvatelno-svyaznoi) is a ship-borne reconnaissance version with Leninets millimetre-wave radar, TKS secure data link, and new RWR.
Ka-33 is an export transport with weapons removed. 6 reportedly ordered by Bulgaria.
See also Ka-31 Airborne Early Warning and Control (AEW&C) helicopter.

Kamov Ka-31

First flight: October 1987 for 208 prototype with incomplete systems, and 1990 for fully-equipped helicopter.
Role: AEW&C helicopter based on the Kamov Ka-29 *Helix B*. Designed for the detection of aircraft and surface ships, plotting their position and sending the information to the command post on board ship. Originally 2 different systems were designed, 1 for land forces and the other for the Navy, but later E-801 Oko was chosen for all purposes.

Development

▪ 1992. 031 and 032 (see Sales) spotted on the *Admiral Kuznetsov* aircraft carrier. State acceptance trials completed.
▪ 1995. Ka-31 officially accepted into Russian Navy service.
▪ August 1995. Presented publicly for the first time, MAKS in Zhukovsky.

Details

Sales: 3 helicopters are known, bearing side numbers 208, 031 and 032. The 208 was probably used only for testing the

↑ **Kamov Ka-29 with Shturm-V anti-tank missile system and unguided rockets** *(Piotr Butowski)*

↑ **Kamov Ka-31 with E-801 Oko antenna lowered** *(courtesy Rosvoorouzhenie)*

↑ Kamov Ka-31 cockpit, with navigator's post to the right *(Piotr Butowski)*

mechanism for lowering the underfuselage rectangular radar antenna and for testing the undercarriage retracting system (having reduced equipment and aerials compared with 031 and 032 helicopters; an example of the former being the equipment cooling fan). Ka-31 passed State acceptance trials and is now in series production at Kumertau, with systems fitted thereafter at Liubertsy and Nizhny Novgorod. India is reportedly receiving 4.
Flight crew: 2, as pilot and navigator.
Mission equipment: The NNIIRT/Nizhny Novgorod E-801 Oko (Eye) radar detects and tracks small targets, including air targets flying at very low altitude. The 19 ft 8 ins × 3 ft 3 ins (6 × 1 m) rectangular radar antenna weighs 441 lb (200 kg). In cruise position the antenna is folded away horizontally against the bottom of the fuselage. When operating, the antenna is lowered, put into a vertical position and rotated about the axis every 10 seconds. The undercarriage legs are raised in order to avoid the disturbances found with Ka-25Ts *Hormone-B*. In an emergency, the antenna can be raised manually or blown away. The radar unit operates in decametre range. The unit is capable of tracking up to 20 targets simultaneously; it detects a fighter aircraft at a distance of 54-81 naut miles (62-93 miles) 100-150 km, whereas surface ships can be detected at up to 135 naut miles (155 miles) 250 km. After lowering the antenna and selecting the operation mode, which is done by the navigator, the operation of Oko is entirely automatically controlled. The target co-ordinates, speed, heading and nationality, found by the radar, are transmitted via a coded radio data link to shipborne (and/or shore-based) command posts, as well as directly to fighter aircraft. The information on detected targets is processed on-board ship, so that the only task of the helicopter's navigator is to observe the targets on the radar screen.
Flight avionics/instrumentation: Designed by Instrument Design Bureau at Saratov. Due to the autopilot, helicopter vibration with antenna lowered and operating does not exceed 2°, equivalent to flying in turbulence; piloting the helicopter in operating mode without autopilot is practically impossible. The flight navigation system, apart from stabilizing the helicopter with antenna operating, maintains the pre-set heading and altitude, follows the selected path, performs the landing approach and finds the exact position of the helicopter without external sources of information.
Fixed weapons: None.
Expendable weapons and equipment: None.
Engines, rotors, transmission: As for Ka-29. TA-8-Ka APU installed for independent supply for the radar system.

Details for Ka-31

PRINCIPAL DIMENSIONS:
Rotor diameter: 52 ft 2 ins (15.9 m) each
Length, blades folded: 40 ft 2 ins (12.25 m)
Fuselage length: 36 ft 11 ins (11.25 m)
Width, blades folded: 12 ft 5.5 ins (3.8 m)
Maximum height: 17 ft 10.5 ins (5.45 m)

UNDERCARRIAGE:
Type: 4 legs, partially retractable to avoid signals interference
Wheel base: 10 ft (3.05 m)
Main wheel track: 11 ft 6 ins (3.5 m)
Front wheel track: 7 ft 11 ins (2.41 m)

WEIGHTS:
Maximum take-off: 27,558 lb (12,500 kg)

PERFORMANCE:
Maximum speed: 135 kts (155 mph) 250 mph
Cruise speed: 119 kts (137 mph) 220 km/h
Operating speed: 54-65 kts (62-75 mph) 100-120 km/h
Operating altitude: up to 11,485 ft (3,500 m)
Range: 324 naut miles (373 miles) 600 km
Operation radius: up to 54 naut miles (62 miles) 100 km
Operation duration: 2 hours 30 minutes

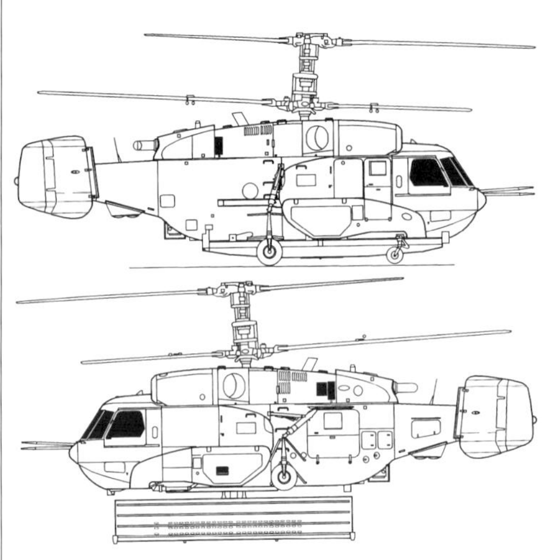

↑ Kamov Ka-31 general arrangement, showing the antenna and wheel position when landed ***(top)*** and when operating *(Piotr Butowski)*

Aircraft variants:
Ka-31 (Ka-252RLD, radio-lokatsyonnogo dozora, radar surveillance), as detailed.

Kamov Ka-32 and Ka-327 (NATO name *Helix-C*)

First flight: 8 October 1980 for Ka-32, piloted by Yevgeni Laryushin.
Role: Civil transport, flying-crane, offshore support, vertrep, rescue, maritime patrol and firefighting.
Sales: 132 Ka-32s built by mid-1998, the Ka-32S and Ka-32T at the Kumertau factory since 1986, with other versions assembled by Kamov at Liubertsy. In addition to Russian-operated helicopters, exports include those to Canada (first 2 delivered in April 1997 of 15 ordered), Ireland (1), South Africa (2), South Korea (12 delivered as payment of Russian debt), Switzerland (1) and Yemen (1). On 7 December 1994, a joint venture company named Lucky-Kamov (with Lucky-Goldstar of South Korea) was established for the sale and servicing of Ka-32Ts in the Asian market.

Details *(generally similar to Ka-27PS, except as described below)*

Crew/passengers: 2 flight crew plus optional third crew member. Up to 14 passengers in the Ka-32A and 16 in Ka-32T. Alternative layouts include litters for a medevac role.
Engines: 2 Klimov/St Petersburg TV3-117V or VMA turboshafts side-by-side above the cabin compartment. Air intake de-icing. APU.
Engine rating: Each 2,200 shp (1,641 kW).
Fuel system: Maximum 3,300-3,450 litres, including 2 × 481 litre auxiliary tanks carried at the fuselage sides. Further auxiliary tanks have been made available as outrigger-mounted external containers (see Ka-32SI and Ka-327 under Aircraft variants).
Radar: Osminog for Ka-32S and Ka-327; none for other versions.
Flight avionics/instrumentation: Similar to Ka-27.

Aircraft variants:
Ka-32A is an upgrade to obtain Cat A and B certification under Russian NLGV-2 and US FAR 29/33 regulations. Certified in Russia on 16 July 1993 (together with TV3-117VMA engines) and available since 1994. New cockpit instrumentation, additional flight control equipment, SO-72M transponder co-operating with air traffic system, new emergency lighting, and improved general systems (mainly electric and fire-protection). Total of 250 alternatives. Electronic flight deck optional, with Canadian Marconi EFIS, AFCS, GPS and Doppler. First flight September 1990, piloted by Dmitri Avtukhov.
Ka-32A1 of 1993 is a firefighting variant, used initially for rescue from high buildings. Carries an external rescue cabin of any of 3 types: TSK-1 for 2 persons, TSK-3 for 10 persons, and TSK-2 for 20 persons, used to evacuate people from the roof of buildings or, in the case of TSK-1, from balconies. TSK cabins can also be used for landing firefighters. Other equipment includes firefighting gear, a flexible 5,000 litre water tank suspended on a long cable under the fuselage, 2 additional searchlights, loudspeakers and special communication equipment, as well as first-aid kits, fire extinguishers and more. Cockpit windows are very bulged for good downward vision. Optional wheel/skis. First flown 12 January 1994. 2 operated with the Moscow fire brigade, organized on 10 March 1994.
Ka-32A2 is a police helicopter, designed for special units of the Home Office. Equipped with 2 radio stations for coded communication, 2 × L-2AG searchlights, and VZS-85 loudspeaker. Cabin can accommodate 12 police/troops. Brackets for machine-gun and for automatic rifles, to provide covering fire, and rope air-landing gear on both sides of the fuselage (5 points). Fuel tanks are protected against explosion resulting from ground fire. 1 built, first flown on 21 March 1995 piloted by O. Krivoshein.
Ka-32A3 is a rescue helicopter ordered by the Russian Ministry of Emergency Situations, to carry salvage and rescue equipment to disaster areas (for example, 10 liferafts) and for evacuation of the sick and injured.
Ka-32A4, A5 and ***A6*** are projected civil derivatives, including the A6 VIP transport.
Ka-32A7 is now known as Ka-327, as it is based on a non-certified military helicopter. See next page.
Ka-32A11 underwent Canadian certification in 1997.
Ka-32A12 received Swiss certification in June 1996.
Ka-32K (kran) is a utility/flying-crane variant, with a retractable gondola to allow the co-pilot to visually take control of delicate

↑ Kamov Ka-32T transport *(Piotr Butowski)*

Details for Ka-32A

PRINCIPAL DIMENSIONS: See Ka-27

CABIN:
Length: 14 ft 10 ins (4.52 m)
Width: 4 ft 3 ins (1.3 m)
Height: 4 ft 1 ins (1.24 m)
Volume: 258 cu ft (7.3 m^3)

WEIGHTS:
Empty: 14,991 lb (6,800 kg)
Normal take-off: 24,251 lb (11,000 kg)
Maximum take-off, external load: 27,999 lb (12,700 kg)
Fuel, standard: 4,145 lb (1,880 kg)
Fuel, maximum: 5,842 lb (2,650 kg), with 2 auxiliary tanks
Maximum internal useful load with standard fuel: 5,093 lb (2,310 kg), including crew
Payload: 11,000 lb (5,000 kg) sling load, 8,157 lb (3,700 kg) internal

PERFORMANCE:
Never-exceed speed (V_{NE}): 140 kts (162 mph) 260 km/h
Never-exceed speed (V_{NE}), with sling load: 103 kts (118 mph) 190 km/h
Cruise speed: 124 kts (143 mph) 230 km/h, at sea level
Climb rate: 2,953 ft (900 m) per minute, maximum
OGE hovering ceiling, ISA: 12,140 ft (3,700 m)
OGE hovering ceiling, ISA + 20° C: 8,530 ft (2,600 m)
Service ceiling: 14,765 ft (4,500 m)
Range with maximum fuel: 485 naut miles (559 miles) 900 km, no reserve
Range with standard fuel: 351 naut miles (404 miles) 650 km
Range with full payload: 59.5 naut miles (68.5 miles) 110 km
Duration: 4.3 hours, standard fuel, no reserve

manoeuvring. Same bulged windows as Ka-32A1. 1 built against an order for the Krasnodar Institute of Civil Aviation. First flown December 1991.
Ka-32PS, see Ka-28.
Ka-32S (sudovoi, shipborne) *Helix-C* is a civil modification of the Ka-27PS, with very little difference, intended for maritime roles including SAR, vertrep, ice surveillance and patrol.
Ka-32SI (issledovatelskiy, exploratory) is a derivative of Ka-32S, equipped with geological and ecological monitoring systems. Additional external fuel tanks. 1 built.
Ka-32T (transportnyi) *Helix-C* is the land-based utility version of 1986 appearance, developed from the Ka-32S and with a considerable reduction of equipment, including removal of the radar.
Ka-327 is a maritime patrol derivative, designed for guarding border and economic zones but with secondary rescue and transport roles (carrying 10 liferafts and 12 life jackets, or 8-10 persons, or 4,409 lb, 2,000 kg of cargo internally, or 6,614 lb, 3000 kg of cargo externally as a sling load). Similar to Ka-27PS but with armament carried on 4 pods at the fuselage sides, including B8V20 rocket launchers and UPK-23-250 gun pods. PKT flexibly-mounted machine-gun at the cabin door. Powerful searchlights, photo-cameras for recording violations, and optional FLIR. Extra fuel by using auxiliary tanks suspended under the weapons racks, allowing a 593 naut mile (683 mile) 1,100 km range. Originally designated Ka-27PV, later Ka-32A7. First flown in 1995 and shown at Zhukovsky that August armed also with 2 Kh-35 anti-ship missiles.
Ka-32M is a planned upgrade, with more powerful TV3-117VMA-SB3 turboshaft engines, each 2,500 shp (1,864 kW).

Kamov Ka-40

First flight: Project only at the time of writing.
Role: Ship-based multi-role helicopter, including anti-submarine warfare, mine-sweeping, anti-ship, SAR, reconnaissance and target acquisition, and electronic warfare, plus airborne early warning. Projected replacement for Ka-27/-29/-31/-32.

↑ **Kamov Ka-40** *(Viktor Drushlyakov)*

Aims

■ More powerful avionics and weapons, better economy and reliability, and easier operation compared with Ka-27 to -32.
Rotor system: 2 coaxial, contra-rotating rotors.
Engines: 2 Klimov/St Petersburg TVa-3000 turboshafts.
Engine rating: Each 2,500 shp (1,864 kW) take-off and 3,750 shp (2,796 kW) 30-seconds emergency power, the latter sufficient for emergency landing with OEI.
Flight avionics/instrumentation: Integrated digital flight/weapon system avionics, enabling all-weather, day and night operation. Mission systems are to be of modular design.
Expendable weapons and equipment: New generation of torpedoes and missiles (including APR-3 ASW missile), guided depth charges and sonobuoys for ASW version.

Kamov Ka-50 and Ka-50N Black Shark (NATO name *Hokum*)

First hovering flight: 17 June 1982 (piloted by Nikolai Bezdetnov). First full circle flight 27 July 1982 (piloted by Yevgeni Laryushin). 5 March 1997 for Ka-50N.
Role: Single-seat anti-tank and attack helicopter.

Development

■ 16 December 1976. Government order for a new generation combat helicopter issued.
■ December 1977. Preliminary design accepted.
■ May 1980. Full-scale mock-up accepted by common committee of the Air Force and Ministry of Air Industry.
■ 16 August 1983. First flight of a fully equipped and armed helicopter (V-80-02, side number *011*).
■ July 1984. Factory tests accomplished.
■ 3 April 1985. First prototype crashed; pilot Laryushin killed.
■ September 1985-August 1986. Comparative tests with Mi-28.
■ December 1987. Government decision to start series production of the Ka-50 and to develop a night version (Ka-50N).
■ 22 May 1991. First flight of a production helicopter at Arsenyev (side number *018*).
■ August 1992. First public presentation at MosAeroshow.
■ August 1993. State acceptance trials completed.
■ 28 August 1995. President Yeltsin signed a decree officially accepting the Ka-50 into service with the Russian Army.
■ September 1996. Ka-50 attained a speed of 210 kts (242 mph) 390 km/h in a shallow dive.
■ 4 March 1997. First flight of the Ka-50N night version.
■ 31 July 1997. A Ka-50 reportedly crashed but the pilot survived, during a presentation demonstration to a Malaysian deligation.
■ June 1998. Fatal loss of a Ka-50, when co-axial rotors touched during NOE flight.

Details *(Ka-50, unless stated)*

Sales: 5 prototypes built (1 lost) by Kamov test facility in Liubertsy outside Moscow; production started 1991 at Arsenyev plant. Due to financial cuts, production was suspended after 12 had been built but restarted in 1996. Production rate for 1997 was set at 1 per month, probably retained for 1998. It is thought probable that India will be the first foreign user, as deliveries were discussed in August 1995. As early as 1993, an Algerian pilot flew Ka-50, but tests in Algeria planned for late 1993 were suspended, however, due to the internal political situation in that country at that time. Another country believed to be interested in the purchase of 6 is Slovakia (although later denied by Slovakian officials); at the end of October 1996 a firing demonstration with Ka-50 took place for Slovakian military commanders at the Kuchyna airfield. Offered to Finland, Singapore and Turkey. Other reported potential customers are believed to be Malaysia (see Development), Myanmar, South Korea and Syria. At IDEX'97 in Abu Dhabi, Alexander Kotyolkin, head of Rosvooruzheniye, announced that an export sale of 2 batches (12 and 15 helicopters) was expected soon.

Details for Ka-50 *Hokum-A*

PRINCIPAL DIMENSIONS:
Rotor diameter: 47 ft 4 ins (14.43 m) each
Maximum length, rotors turning: 52 ft 4.5 ins (15.96 m)
Wing span: 24 ft 1 ins (7.34 m)
Maximum height: 16 ft 2 ins (4.93 m)

UNDERCARRIAGE:
Type: Retractable nosewheel type in order to reduce the aerodynamic drag and radar signature. Twin nosewheels and single main wheels. Nosewheels semi-retract. See Safety features
Main wheel tyre size: 700 × 250 mm
Nose wheel tyre size: 400 × 150 mm
Wheel base: 16 ft 1 ins (4.91 m)
Wheel track: 8 ft 9 ins (2.67 m)

WEIGHTS:
Empty: 16,958 lb (7,692 kg)
Normal take-off: 21,605 lb (9,800 kg)
Maximum take-off: 23,810 lb (10,800 kg)
External load: 6,614 lb (3,000 kg)

PERFORMANCE:
Maximum speed in a shallow dive: 189 kts (217 mph) 350 km/h
Maximum level flight speed: 167 kts (193 mph) 310 km/h
Cruise speed: 146 kts (168 mph) 270 km/h
Backward flight speed: 49 kts (56 mph) 90 km/h
Sideways flight speed: 43 kts (50 mph) 80 km/h
Maximum climb rate at sea level: 2,835 ft (864 m) per minute
Maximum climb rate at 2,500 m: 1,970 ft (600 m) per minute
G limit: 3.5
OGE hovering ceiling: 13,125 ft (4,000 m)
Service ceiling: 18,045 ft (5,500 m)
Practical range: 245 naut miles (283 miles) 455 km
Ferry range: 626 naut miles (721 miles) 1,160 km

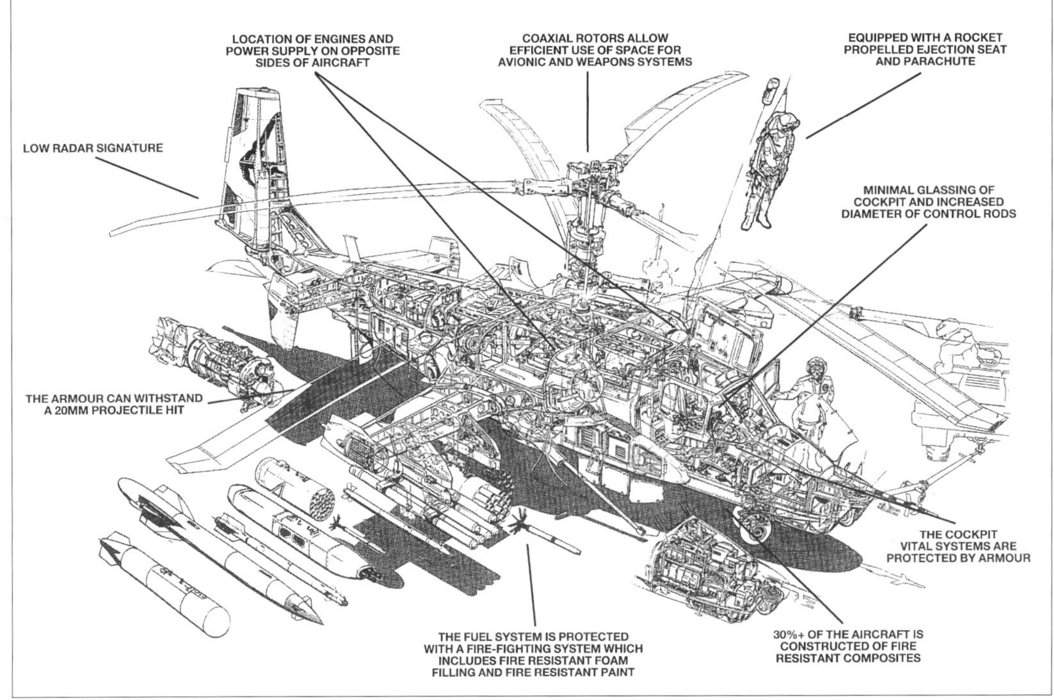

↑ **Kamov Ka-50 cutaway** *(courtesy Kamov)*

↑ Kamov Ka-50 with auxiliary fuel tanks, in camouflage *(Piotr Butowski)*

↑ Kamov Ka-50N with the latest nose arrangement, showing Shkval-V above and Samshit-50 below *(Piotr Butowski)*

Crew: Single pilot. MKS-3 or VMKS-4 suit.
Cockpit: Hermetic, fully protected by 2-layer steel/aluminium armour. 2 flat-plate side windows and a single plate 55-mm windscreen, all armoured. Cockpit protected from 20-mm calibre ammunition fired from a distance.
Ejection seat: Zvezda K-37-800, operated at speeds from zero to 189 kts (217 mph) 350 km/h, and from zero altitude. Rotor blades are detached by means of explosive charges installed in the blade fastenings. Ka-50 was the first operational helicopter to provide a fully integrated rocket-powered pilot escape system, providing safe ejection over the whole flight range envelope.
Main rotor characteristics: 2 coaxial contra-rotating 3-blade rotors, with swept tips. All-composite blades; titanium heads.
Wing/tail surfaces: 2-spar stub-wings, with no high-lift devices. Each wing has 2 armament pylons, and ECM/flare fairings at the wingtips with small vertical plates. All-moving, slightly swept tailfin. The tail unit is not a main structural element, and tests proved that the helicopter can fly after the tailboom has been torn off.
Flight control system: Mechanical, with hydraulic actuators.
Fuselage: Main structural element is a composite glassfibre box beam, 3 ft 3 ins (1 m) in both width and height. Inside this structure are fuel tanks and cannon ammunition. Outside, at both sides, are attached the equipment modules covered by external panels that form the external outline of the airframe.
Construction materials: Mainly aluminium alloys, but with 36% by weight composite materials.
Safety features: Armour protection (about 739 lb, 335 kg total weight) for the cockpit, engine bays, etc. Ejection seat (see earlier description). Undercarriage provides for vertical landings of 33 ft (10 m) per second. Crashworthy seat. Fuel tanks filled with polyurethane foam.
Engines: 2 widely separated Klimov/St Petersburg TV3-117VMA turboshafts. AI-9K APU. Dust filters. Infra-red suppression cool air mixers can be fitted to the engine nozzles. Uprated TV3-117VMA-SB3s, each 2,500 shp (1,864 kW), are planned for the final version.
Engine rating: Each 2,200 shp (1,640.5 kW).
Fuel system: 1,870 litres inside the fuselage. Provision for 4 underwing fuel tanks, each 550 litres.
Transmission: VR-80 main gearbox.
Flight refuelling probe: None.
Flight avionics/instrumentation: Integrated PrPNK-80 Rubikon (K-041) flight-navigation-attack system, which uses 5 Orbita digital computers (4 of TsVM-20-751 type for combat, navigation, data presentation and remote target indication systems, and a single TsVM-80-30201 for the weapon control system). PNK-800 Radian flight-navigation subsystem contains inertial navigation, short-range radio navigation, DISS-32-28 Doppler navigation radar, ARK-22 radio compass, A-036A radio altimeter, and SOS-V1 angle-of-attack dumper. ILS-31 head-up display (HUD). R-800L1 and R-868 com radios and a data link for transmitting information to and receiving from other helicopters and ground posts. PA-4-3 navigation plotting board with paper map on early helicopter replaced by a digital map projected on a liquid crystal colour display on current Ka-50s and Ka-50Ns. GPS compatible with Russian GLONASS and US NAVSTAR is fitted to current production helicopters.
Mission avionics: I-251V Shkval-V fire control unit designed for detecting and automatically tracking small movable targets (such as tanks and helicopters) as well as for aiming and automatic homing of Vikhr guided missiles. The electro-optical Shkval-V unit includes 3 coupled modes: a TV channel for observation and tracking targets, Prichal laser rangefinder/target designator, and laser beam riding system for the Vikhr missile. The widow of the Shkval-V system is located in the helicopter nose. The pilot has an Obzor-800 helmet mounted target designator slaved to the Shkval-V unit. In August 1995, a helicopter equipped with a Saturn FLIR pod (housing French Thomson-CSF Victor FLIR) was presented. The system has 2 observation channels, wide channel (5.7° × 8.6°) and narrow channel (1.9° × 2.9°), capable of detecting a tank at a distance of 19,685-22,965 ft (6,000-7,000 m) and aim at 14,765-16,400 ft (4,500-5,000 m). Final Ka-50N night helicopter has a nose-mounted Ural Optical-Mechanical Plant Samshit-50 (Boxwood; see Ka-52 for further description) gyrostabilized turret. Samshit-50 of Ka-50N is a little different from Samshit for Ka-52; the Ka-52 unit has 3 circular windows, 2 of greater diameter and a third smaller window, whereas the Ka-50N unit has 4 windows as 1 large, 2 small and 1 very small. The FLIR sensor of Samshit-50 unit has been integrated with the basic Shkval-V weapon system. Mast-mounted Phazotron FH-01 Arbalet radar is also planned for Ka-50N, but only a mock-up of the radar was available at the time of writing. Ka-50N's Arbalet is reduced to decimetre wavelength circuit only when compared to the radar of Ka-52, and is used mainly for defence purposes. See also Ka-50N under Aircraft variants for other systems, or modifications.
Radar: See above.
Fixed weapons: Shipunov 2A42 30-mm cannon, originally built for the BMP-2 armoured personnel carrier, mounted on the starboard side of the fuselage. An hydraulic control system moves the barrel in elevation (+3.5°/–37°); aiming in azimuth is effected by means of positioning the whole helicopter. This gun aiming system was chosen because the angular speed of the helicopter is much greater than the horizontal speed of the cannon barrel. However, the barrel can also be moved by +9°/–2.5° in azimuth, but for cannon stabilization only.
Ammunition: 500 rounds.
Number of weapon pylons: 4
Expendable weapons and equipment: Typical weapon load includes 2 UPP-800 6-round clusters of 9A4172 Vikhr (AT-16) supersonic laser-beam riding anti-tank guided missiles (ATGM) on the inner wing pylons and 2 × B-8V20A launchers (containing 20 × 80-mm S-8 unguided rockets) on the outer pylons. ATGM clusters are carried in adjustable pods; they can be lowered by 10°, thus reducing the length of the missile path to the target. Vikhr is a supersonic laser-beam riding missile of 8-10 km range. Modified Vikhr-M, with a 12-15 km range, is under development. Alternative weapons include laser-guided Kh-25ML (AS-10 *Karen*) and anti-radar Kh-25MP (AS-12 *Kegler*) ASMs, UPK-23-250 gun packs, rocket launchers, bombs, etc. Against an airborne target, R-73 (AA-11 *Archer*) AAMs and Igla-V portable SAMs can be carried. Typical weapon load is 1,345 lb (610 kg), maximum 3,993 lb (1,811 kg).
Self-protection systems: Infra-red suppression cool-air mixers on engine nozzles. UV-26 chaff/flare dispensers with 26-mm PPI-26 flares or PPR-26 radar decoys at the wingtips (2 × 32-round dispensers in each wingtip fairing). Infra-red jammer and electronic jammer. The work of the jamming systems is controlled by the L-136 Mak infra-red, L-140 Otklik laser, and L-150 Pastel radar warning receivers.

Aircraft variants:
Ka-50 (V-80Sh1, izdelye 800) *Hokum-A*, as detailed. Black Shark is a commercial name, formerly Werewolf.
Ka-50N (nochnoi, night) is a night attack version, which first flew on 5 March 1997 and was shown at IDEX in Abu Dhabi the same month (first production Ka-50 *018* upgraded to Ka-50N form). Features nose-mounted Samshit-50 FLIR/LLTV/laser station and mast-mounted Arbalet radar (experimental version of Samshit and Arbalet mockup were first shown). A second TV display has been added in the cockpit. Black-painted cockpit is compatible with night vision goggles. Prototype shown during MAKS'97 in Zhukovsky in August 1997 had reshaped nose and no Arbalet radar. Samshit-50 ball-turret has been lowered (below the nose) in order to extend look-down area. At Zhukovsky, Samshit-50 contained a Swedish FLIR from Agema. Also French Sagem and Thomson-CSF FLIRs are being tested, while indigenous FLIR is expected for the Russian service.
Ka-52 *Hokum-B* is a side-by-side 2-seat version. See separate entry.

Kamov Ka-52 Alligator (NATO name *Hokum-B*)

First flight: 25 June 1997, piloted by Alexander Smirnov and Dmitri Titov, with second flight on 1 July.
Role: 2-seat, day and night, all-weather modernized derivative of the Ka-50. Roles include battlefield command and control (reconnaissance and target acquisition), combat, electronic warfare and training.

Development

- September 1994. Announced during the Farnborough Air Show.
- August 1995. Full-scale mock-up presented at Zhukovsky.
- December 1996. Ready-to-fly prototype was displayed at Bangalore, India (side number *061*).

Details

Sales: Prototype constructed from the 11th production Ka-50 by replacing the front fuselage. Several production helicopters were constructed at the Progress plant at Arsenyev in 1997-98. Reported export interest from Iran and others.
Crew: 2 side-by-side, with the commander at port and mission officer at starboard. Dual controls.
Ejection seats: Zvezda K-37 zero-zero type for both crew

↑ Kamov Ka-52 cockpit with 4 colour MFDs and ATGM controls, later replaced by conventional instruments for flight testing *(Alexei Kalinovsky)*

Details for Ka-52

PRINCIPAL DIMENSIONS:
Rotor diameter: 47 ft 4 ins (14.43 m) each
Maximum length, rotors turning: 52 ft 4.5 ins (15.96 m)
Fuselage length: 44 ft 5 ins (13.53 m)
Wing span: 24 ft 1 ins (7.34 m)
Maximum height: 16 ft 3 ins (4.95 m)

UNDERCARRIAGE:
Type: Retractable nosewheel type in order to reduce the aerodynamic drag and radar signature. Twin nosewheels and single main wheels. Nosewheels semi-retract. See Safety features under Ka-50
Wheel base: 16 ft 2 ins (4.92 m)
Wheel track: 8 ft 9 ins (2.67 m)

WEIGHTS:
Normal take-off: 22,928 lb (10,400 kg)

PERFORMANCE:
Maximum speed in a shallow dive: 189 kts (217 mph) 350 km/h
Maximum level flight speed: 167 kts (193 mph) 310 km/h
Backward flight speed: 49 kts (56 mph) 90 km/h
Sideways flight speed: 43 kts (50 mph) 80 km/h
Maximum climb rate at 8,200 ft (2,500 m): 1,575 ft (480 m) per minute
G limit: 3
OGE hovering ceiling: 11,810 ft (3,600 m)
Practical range: 248 naut miles (286 miles) 460 km
Ferry range: 647 naut miles (745 miles) 1,200 km

members, with simultaneous use.
Cockpit: Reduced armour protection.
Rotor system: As for Ka-50.
Airframe: As for Ka-50, except for widened cockpit section. 80-85% parts commonality.
Engines: As for Ka-50.
Radar: Phazotron FH-01 Arbalet radar system coupling 2 radars: millimetre-wave circuit used for air-to-ground (targeting, ground mapping, terrain following/avoidance) and air-to-air tasks, and has an antenna in the fuselage nose; and decimetre-wave circuit for air-to-air tasks (mainly self-defence), with a small eye-shaped antenna at the tip of the rotor's axis.
Flight and mission avionics/instrumentation: Integrated computer-controlled flight-navigation-attack system. 4 colour liquid crystal displays (French CMD 66 screens on prototype). During flight tests, however, the prototype had the LCDs replaced by conventional instruments. Mission avionics differ according to mission. Basic equipment for the battlefield control helicopter is Samshit (Boxwood) reconnaissance-observation unit (export version is Samshit-E), installed within a triple-glazed spherical turret on the top of the fuselage, just aft of the pilot's cockpit. Samshit is used for day and night search, reconnaissance and target indication. The unit includes TV channel, FLIR and laser with rangefinder/illuminator/mark detector, and is gyrostabilized in 3-axes, with operating angles of ±135° azimuth, +10°/-30° elevation and ±5° position angle; rotational speed is 60° per second; dimensions 25.2 × 31.5 ins (640 × 800 mm), and total weight of 331 lb (150 kg) which includes 143 lb (65 kg) of inner equipment. Extended data link for exchange of tactical information with other helicopters and ground posts. Combat version will have Zenit/Krasnogorsk Tor (path, trajectory) wide-window rotary electro-optical search/aiming unit under the nose instead of Samshit. The unit includes TV and FLIR channels for target observation and tracking, laser rangefinder and target designator, and laser beam-riding system for the Vikhr missile. Tor differs from the Shkval unit (see Ka-50) by additional FLIR channel and greater angles of observation (±110° in azimuth). Head-up display (HUD) is installed for the pilot, while the system operator has use of a gyrostabilized optical visor with great magnification (probably 25x); the visor, installed in a small sphere directly under the system operator's post, is combined with axis of the laser rangefinder/target designator, as an additional device for TV and FLIR systems. Both crew have helmet-mounted target indicators and night vision goggles. For export, the Ka-52 will be fitted with a combination of Russian and French equipment, which includes Thomson-CSF FLIR and Sextant Navigation and Attack System for Helicopters (NASH) incorporating the Topowl® binocular HMS/D, Thomson-CSF Victor IR camera, Nadir 10 navigation and mission management system linked to Topstar GPS receiver, Stratus laser gyro attitude/heading reference system, Doppler navigation radar, HUD, and 4 MFDs.
Self-protection systems: As for Ka-50.
Fixed weapons: Same Shipunov 2A42 30-mm cannon as Ka-50.
Number of weapon pylons: 4
Expendable weapons and equipment: As for Ka-50, plus new-generation radar-guided air-to-surface missiles.

↑ **Kamov Ka-52 with Tor removed. Note the above-fuselage Samshit ball turret** *(Piotr Butowski)*

Aircraft variants:
Ka-52 *Hokum-B* has the design bureau designation V-80Sh2 and commercial name Alligator. Basic version for battlefield command and control, and combat version with differing equipment (see details above).
Training variant expected, with reduced equipment.
Electronic warfare variant will be equipped with a powerful active jamming suite.

Kamov Ka-60, Ka-62, and Ka-64 Sky Horse

First flight: Originally planned for 1993; now September 1998; roll-out 29 July 1998.
Role: Civil and military multi-purpose helicopter.

Development

▪ September 1990. Full-scale mock-up of the Ka-62 presented for the first time. Officially adopted under Russia's 'Civil aviation for the year 2000' planning.
▪ August 1993. First Ka-62 prototype shown at Zhukovsky while awaiting its first flight, which had not taken place by mid-1998, mainly due to delays in engine development.
▪ 1994. General Electric followed Rolls-Royce Turbomeca in providing engines for export versions.
▪ 2000-2001. Expected service entry date for Ka-60.
Sales: 3 prototypes built at the Kamov works in Liubertsy, including 1 for static testing. Production planned at the Ulan-Ude plant in Siberia. Ka-60 expected to enter Russian service. Interest reported from Iran.
Crew/passengers: 1 or 2 crew, plus a maximum of 16 passengers. Alternatively, 6 litters and 3 attendants in the ambulance/medevac version. 10 armed troops in the military Ka-60.
Freight, internal: Up to 4,409 lb (2,000 kg). 46 cu ft (1.3 m^3) of baggage in the rear of the fuselage.
Freight, external: Up to 5,511 lb (2,500 kg).
Cabin access: 4 ft 3 ins × 4 ft 1 ins (1.3 × 1.25 m) doors on both sides of the fuselage, plus smaller doors.
Main rotor characteristics: 4-blade main rotor on helicopters with engines up to 1,500 shp (1,119 kW); 5-blade rotor for more powerful engines. Rotor blades and heads taken from the Ka-50.
Tail fan characteristics: Fan-in-fin type, with 11 carbonfibre/Kevlar blades. Larger fan for Ka-62.
Tail surfaces: T-tail, comprising tall fin and small horizontal surface. Larger horizontal stabilizers with sweptback endplates on the fuselage sides (9 ft 10 ins, 3 m span).

↑ **Kamov Ka-62 under construction** *(Alexei Kalinovsky)*

Construction materials: Wide use of composites (52% of airframe weight), including rotor blades, fuselage panels, tailboom, vertical tail and tail fan.
Safety features: Crashworthy seats and undercarriage (up to 6g). Cockpit and cabin framing allows a hard landing descent rate of 33-39 ft (10-12 m) per second. Ka-60 control linkage is able to withstand 7.62-mm and 12.7-mm bullets, whereas the main rotor blades remain serviceable after being hit by a 23-mm shell.
Engines: 2 RKBM/Rybinsk RD-600V turboshafts in Ka-60 and Ka-62 (see Aircraft variants for other).
Engine rating: 1,300 shp (969 kW) each at 6,000 rpm take-off, 1,000 shp (745.7 kW) cruise, and 1,550 shp (1,156 kW) OEI emergency rating.
Transmission: VR-60 main gearbox.
Fuel system: 1,450 litres standard. Provision for 2 × 390 litre auxiliary tanks.
Radar: Military Ka-60 has a Phazotron Arbalet radar in a nose radome, with an antenna width of up to 47.25 ins (120 cm).
Expendable weapons and equipment: Ka-60 has 2 × B-8V7 rocket launchers, each with 7 × 80-mm S-8 rockets.

Aircraft variants:
Ka-60 (V-60) is a military light multi-purpose helicopter, with various uses including training. Accommodates 10 armed troops or litters as given under Crew/passengers. Weapons on side pylons. Reduced infra-red, optics and radar signatures due to special coatings on the fuselage.
V-60R is a projected reconnaissance/target designation/combat helicopter, equipped with Samshit (see Ka-50/52 for description of Samshit).
Ka-62 (V-62) is the civil multi-purpose helicopter for the CIS domestic market, powered by 2 RD-600s.
Ka-62G (named also ***Ka-62M***) was a projected export version with 2 General Electric CT7-2D1 turboshafts, each 1,625 shp (1,212 kW).
Ka-62R was a projected export version with Rolls-Royce Turbomeca RTM322 turboshafts, each 2,100 shp (1,566 kW). Announced September 1990 but now abandoned.
Ka-64 Sky Horse is a joint project of Kamov and Agusta of Italy, being a version of Ka-62 powered by General Electric CT7-9s. Currently under development.

Details for Ka-62 production version

PRINCIPAL DIMENSIONS:
Rotor diameter: 44 ft 3.5 ins (13.5 m)
Maximum length, rotors turning: 51 ft 10 ins (15.8 m)
Fuselage length: 44 ft 2 ins (13.465 m)
Fuselage width: 6 ft 3 ins (1.9 m)
Maximum width, no rotor: 9 ft 10 ins (3 m)
Maximum height: 15 ft 1 ins (4.6 m)
Height to above rotor head: 11 ft 5 ins (3.48 m)

CABIN:
Length: 11 ft 2 ins (3.4 m)
Width: 5 ft 10 ins (1.78 m)
Height: 4 ft 3 ins (1.3 m)
Volume: 265 cu ft (7.5 m^3)

MAIN ROTOR:
Blade chord: 1 ft 9 ins (0.53 m)
Rpm: 294

TAIL ROTOR:
Diameter: 4 ft 7 ins (1.4 m)
Blade chord: 3.5 ins (8.9 cm)
Rpm: 3,056

UNDERCARRIAGE:
Type: Retractable, with single mainwheels and twin small tailwheels
Wheel base: 17 ft 10.5 ins (5.445 m)
Wheel track: 8 ft 2.5 ins (2.5 m)

WEIGHTS:
Empty: 8,223 lb (3,730 kg)
Maximum take-off: 14,330 lb (6,500 kg)
Maximum take-off, with sling load: 14,881 lb (6,750 kg)

PERFORMANCE:
Never-exceed speed (V_{NE}): 162 kts (186 mph) 300 km/h
Cruise speed: 132 kts (152 mph) 245 km/h
Maximum climb rate: 2,047 ft (624 m) per minute, sea level
IGE hovering ceiling, ISA: 9,515 ft (2,900 m)
OGE hovering ceiling: 6,890 ft (2,100 m)
Service ceiling: 18,965 ft (5,150 m)
Range with standard fuel: 378 naut miles (435 miles) 700 km
Range with full payload: 186 naut miles (214 miles) 345 km
Maximum range, with auxiliary tanks: 628 naut miles (724 miles) 1,165 km, no reserve
Duration, with standard fuel: 3.8 hours

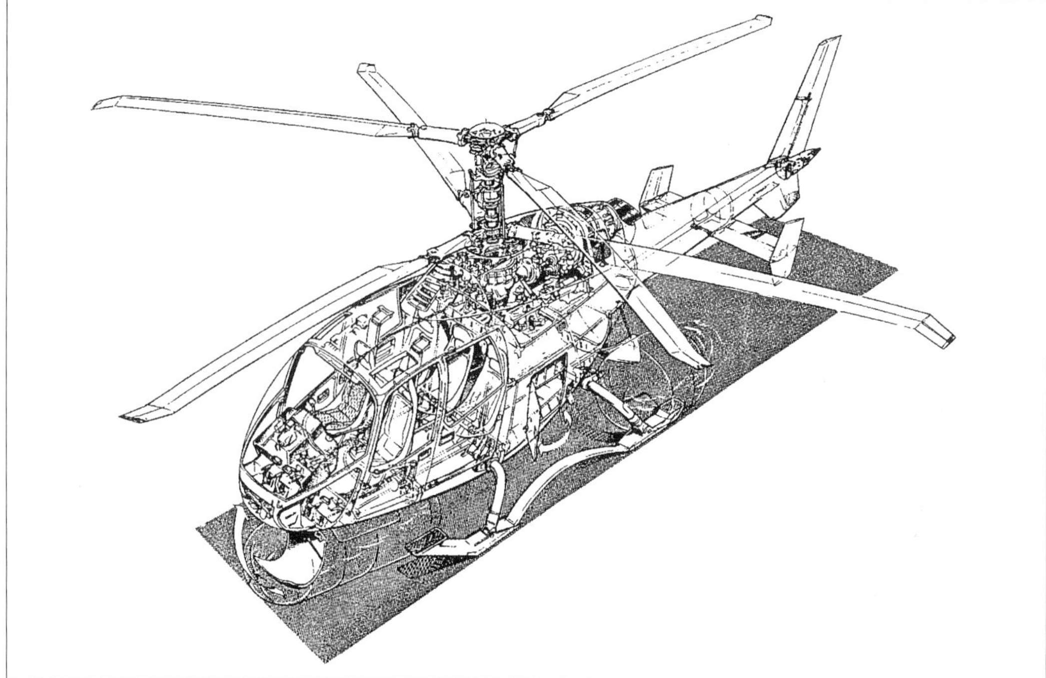

↑ **Kamov Ka-115** *(courtesy Kamov)*

Kamov Ka-115

First flight: Not before 1999.
Role: Light multi-purpose helicopter. Intended uses include training, law enforcement, EMS, SAR and transport.
Sales: Production at St Petersburg's Severnyi Zavod. Full-size mock-up shown at MAKS'97 in Zhukovsky.
Crew/passengers: Pilot plus 3-4 passengers, or a litter and 2 attendants in medevac/EMS role.
Cabin: Heated and ventilated.
Freight, internal: Large cargo compartment (see tables for volume) behind and at the same floor level with the passenger cabin. Long items of up to 13 ft (4 m) can be accommodated.
Cabin access: 2 doors on each side of the cabin (rear sliding), making a 4 ft 11 ins wide × 3 ft 11 ins high (1.5 × 1.2 m) opening. Cargo compartment can be accessed from the cabin and through 2 ft × 2 ft 4 ins (0.6 × 0.7 m) hatches, or 2 ft 2 ins × 2 ft (0.65 × 0.6 m) rear hatch (under the tailboom).
Optional equipment: Electric winch to carry 2 persons for SAR operations.
Rotor system: 2 coaxial, contra-rotating rotors, each with 3 blades and elastomeric bearings. Blades have swept tips. Rotor hub and rotor control system similar to Ka-50. New TsAGI blade aerofoil section. Blade de-icing.
Tail rotor characteristics: No tail rotor.
Tail surfaces: Large, sweptback fin with horn-balanced and smaller ventral fin. Constant-chord horizontal stabilizer with endplates fitted to the tailboom at some 40% from the rear.
Safety features: Shock-absorbing crashworthy seats for crew and passengers. Engine located in the failure-safe area. Crashworthy structure, preventing reduction gear and rotor hub from penetrating the cabin; crashworthy keel beam; injury-safe controls. Crash resistant and self-sealing fuel tank. Shock-absorbing undercarriage. Emergency floats.
Airframe: Wide use of composite materials.
Engine: Pratt & Whitney/Klimov PK206D turboshaft was planned as the basic engine, but is now doubtful following termination of co-operation over the engine. Other engines in the 550-650 shp (410-485 kW) range are under consideration, including those from Allison and Turbomeca. Intake dust separators.
Electrical system: 27 volt DC supply.
Flight avionics/instrumentation: Includes GPS.

Details for Ka-115

PRINCIPAL DIMENSIONS:
Rotor diameter: 31 ft 2 ins (9.5 m) each
Fuselage length: 30 ft 2 ins (9.2 m)
Width, without rotors: 6 ft 7 ins (2 m)
Maximum height: 11 ft 10 ins (3.6 m)

CABIN:
Volume: 106 cu ft (3 m^3) plus cargo compartment of 42.4 cu ft (1.2 m^3)

MAIN ROTOR:
Aerofoil section: New TsAGI section
Rotor disc: 762.9 sq ft (70.88 m^2)

UNDERCARRIAGE:
Type: Fixed spring skid type, with integral foot rests
Skid track: 6 ft 7 ins (2 m)

WEIGHTS:
Maximum take-off: 4,079 lb (1,850 kg)
Payload, internal: 1,543 lb (700 kg)
Payload, external: 1,984 lb (900 kg)

PERFORMANCE:
Maximum speed: 135 kts (155 mph) 250 km/h
Cruise speed: 124 kts (143 mph) 230 km/h
Maximum climb rate: 2,264 ft (690 m) per minute
IGE hovering ceiling: 10,170 ft (3,100 m)
OGE hovering ceiling: 7,710 ft (2,350 m)
Service ceiling: 17,060 ft (5,200 m)
Range, standard fuel: 421 naut miles (485 miles) 780 km
Ferry range, with auxiliary tanks: 647 naut miles (745 miles) 1,200 km

Kamov Ka-126 and Ka-128 (NATO name *Hoodlum-B*)

First flight: 19 October 1987 (piloted by G. Isayev).
Role: Light transport and agricultural helicopter.
Chief designer: S. V. Mikheev.

Aims

▪ Turboshaft developments of the twin piston-engined older Ka-26, offering reduced weight, higher performance, lower fuel consumption, and reduced noise/vibration levels.

Details

Sales: 15 built by mid-1998 (12 in Romania and 3 in Russia).
Crew/passengers: Pilot, but with provision for a co-pilot or passenger in the non-detachable cockpit. Detachable cabin module

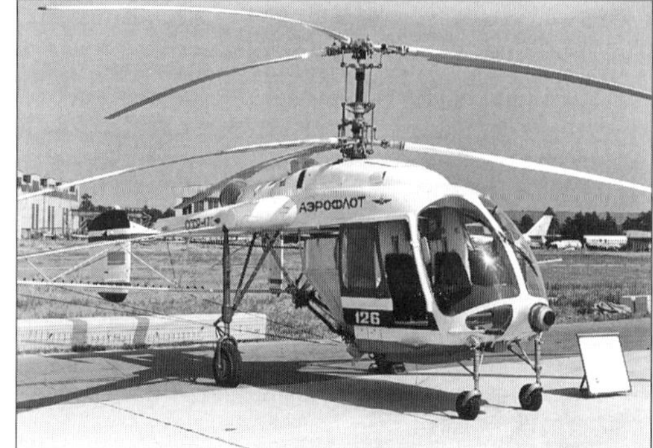

↑ **Kamov Ka-126 with agricultural gear** *(Piotr Butowski)*

for up to 6 persons, or the seats can be folded against the sides for cargo loading via the rear clamshell doors. Medevac module can accommodate 2 litters and 3 sitting casualties/attendants.
Optional equipment: Dual controls, 1,000 litre chemical hopper and spraybars/spreader for agricultural purposes, cargo hook, and more.
Rotor system: 2 non-folding, contra-rotating, 3-blade rotors with hydraulic dampers and standard de-icing. Rotor brake. Standard filters. System borrowed from Ka-26. For production examples, the original plastics blades and hinged rotor head are upgraded to newly designed glass/carbon fibre blades and a composites/titanium hingeless rotor head.
Tail surfaces: Tailplane, and twin inward-toed endplate fins with rudders.
Flight control system: Hydraulic control actuators, with manual reversion.
Fuselage: Pod and twin boom type, with the area aft of the cockpit left free for the optional attachment of 1 of various cabin modules or equipment loads. Leaving the area open permits lighter-weight crane operations. Detachable cabin modules can include those for passenger transport or medevac roles, or the space can be occupied by agricultural equipment including a chemical hopper with spraybars or dry chemical spreader, a cargo platform, or sling cargo.
Airframe materials: Mostly aluminium alloy, with some use of composites and steel.
Engine: OMKB/Omsk TV-O-100 free-turbine turboshaft for the Ka-126 and Arriel 1D1 for Ka-128. Bleed air intake de-icing.
Engine rating: 720 shp (537 kW) for TV-O-100 and 732 shp (546 kW) for Arriel 1D1.
Transmission: VR-126 3-stage gearbox, with a reduction radio of 20.865:1.
Fuel system: 802 litres in 3 standard fuselage tanks. Capacity can rise to 1,120 litres with 2 cabin-side auxiliary tanks.
Electrical system: 27 volt DC supply, with 40 amp-hour stand-by battery. AC supply via a 16 kVA generator, used in part for powering the agricultural gear. Secondary AC supply with 2 static inverters.
Hydraulic system: Single system for rotor control, with manual override.
Braking system: Pneumatic brakes on rear wheels.
Flight avionics/instrumentation: Basic equipment includes ADF, emergency locator beacon and radar altimeter. Optional autopilot.

Aircraft variants:
Ka-126 is the TV-O-100-powered helicopter, as detailed. Originally, both helicopter and engine were to be manufactured in Romania, but this is no longer taking place after the end of Comecom. Subsequent plans to switch to Orenburg plant, but eventually stopped. Additionally, the engine required further funding to complete development, so Ka-126 programme was switched to Ka-128 and the more promising Ka-226 (which see).
Ka-128 is the Turbomeca Arriel 1D1 turboshaft powered derivative, but not flown at the time of writing. See 1996-97 edition of *WA&SD* for weight and performance details.

Details for Ka-126, *with Ka-128 in italics where different*

PRINCIPAL DIMENSIONS:
Rotor diameter: 42 ft 8 ins (13 m) each
Maximum length, rotors turning: 42 ft 8 ins (13 m)
Airframe length: 25 ft 5 ins (7.75 m)
Width, without rotors: 10 ft 7 ins (3.224 m)
Maximum height: 13 ft 7.5 ins (4.15 m) to top of rotor head

CABIN MODULE:
Length: 6 ft 8 ins (2.04 m)
Width: 4 ft 2 ins (1.28 m)
Height: 4 ft 7 ins (1.4 m)

MAIN ROTOR:
Blade chord: 10 ins (0.25 m)
Rotor disc: 1,428.4 sq ft (132.7 m^2) each

UNDERCARRIAGE:
Type: 4-leg fixed type, with single wheels on each unit. Small forward castoring/self-centring wheels. Optional wheel/skis and flotation gear at the fuselage nose and rear legs
Main wheel tyre size: 595 × 185 mm
Nose wheel tyre size: 300 × 125 mm
Wheel base: 11 ft 5 ins (3.48 m)
Wheel track: 8 ft 5 ins (2.56 m) main, 2 ft 11 ins (0.9 m) nose

WEIGHTS:
Empty: 4,221 lb (1,915 kg), *4,012 lb (1,820 kg)*
Normal take-off: 6,614 lb (3,000 kg)
Maximum take-off: 7,165 lb (3,250 kg)
Maximum payload: 2,204 lb (1,000 kg) internal or external
Normal payload: 1,323 lb (600 kg)

PERFORMANCE:
Maximum speed, with normal payload: 103 kts (118 mph) 190 km/h, *108 kts (124 mph) 200 km/h*
Cruise speed, with normal payload: 92 kts (106 mph) 170 km/h, *103 kts (118 mph) 190 km/h*
Maximum climb rate: 1,575 ft (480 m) per minute, *the same*
IGE hovering ceiling: 3,280 ft (1,000 m), *5,250 ft (1,600 m)*, both ISA
Service ceiling: 15,255 ft (4,650 m), *18,600 ft (5,670 m)*
Range with full standard fuel: 356 naut miles (410 miles) 660 km, *383 naut miles (441 miles) 710 km*
Duration: 5.3 hours, *the same*

Kamov Ka-226 (and Ka-228)

First flight: 4 September 1997 for first hovering flight (11 minutes duration) for Ka-226 (piloted by Vladimir Lavrov).
Certification: Expected mid-1999 (Russian), initially for Category B operations. FAR 29 will be sought later.
Role: Twin-engined and refined development of the Ka-126/-128, for similar uses.

Aims

▪ Design life of 18,000 flying hours.

Development

▪ 1991. Programme started.

Details

Sales: Series manufacturing prepared at Strela plant in Orenburg as well as in Kumertau. At the end of 1997, an agreement was signed between Kamov, the Ministry of Emergencies and the Kumertau production plant for manufacture of "several hundred" Ka-226s. Options held by Gazprom company (up to 75) and Moscow's mayor (15 for police and EMS use). First production helicopter expected at the end of 1998. Expected price $1.5 million.
Crew/passengers: Pilot plus 7 passengers.
Optional equipment: Dual controls, 1,000 litre chemical hopper and spraybars/spreader for agricultural purposes, cargo hook, and more.
Rotor system: Similar to Ka-128. New system with glass/carbon fibre blades and a composites/titanium hingeless rotor head is under development.
Tail surfaces: Reconfigured surfaces of less angular form.
Airframe: More streamlined fuselage, with lengthened nose and small ventral windows deleted. Larger passenger cabin module.

Details for Ka-226

PRINCIPAL DIMENSIONS: As for Ka-126/-128 except:
Airframe length: 26 ft 7 ins (8.1 m)

CABIN MODULE:
Length: 7 ft 8.5 ins (2.35 m)
Width: 5 ft 1 ins (1.54 m)
Height: 4 ft 7 ins (1.4 m)
Volume: 160.3 cu ft (4.54 m^3)

MAIN ROTOR:
Blade chord: 10 ins (0.25 m)
Rotor disc: 1,428.4 sq ft (132.7 m^2) each
Rpm: 283

UNDERCARRIAGE: As for Ka-126/-128

WEIGHTS:
Empty, operating: 4,303 lb (1,952 kg)
Maximum take-off: 7,495 lb (3,400 kg)
Fuel, standard: 1,323 lb (600 kg)
Payload: 2,866 lb (1,300 kg)

PERFORMANCE:
Never-exceed speed (V_{NE}): 110 kts (127 mph) 205 km/h
Cruise speed: 104 kts (119 mph) 192 km/h
Maximum climb rate: 1,771 ft (540 m) per minute
IGE hovering ceiling: over 6,625 ft (2,020 m), ISA
OGE hovering ceiling: 4,200 ft (1,280 m), ISA
Service ceiling: 16,570 ft (5,050 m), with 18,700 ft (5,700 m) absolute
Range with standard fuel: 325 naut miles (374 miles) 602 km
Range with maximum fuel: 471 naut miles (542 miles) 873 km, no reserve
Range with full payload: 20 naut miles (23 miles) 37 km
Duration: 4.64 hours with standard fuel, no reserve

Engines: 2 Allison 250-C20R/1 turboshafts, with R/2s optional. See Aircraft variants.
Engine rating: Each 450 shp (335.6 kW) at take-off.
Transmission: Rated at 840 shp (626 kW).
Fuel system: 770 litres standard, with 2 × 160 litre auxiliary tanks.
Flight avionics/instrumentation: AlliedSignal Bendix/King suite for VFR or IFR operation, including KY 196A radio, KN 53 ILS and KLN 90B GPS.

Aircraft variants:
Ka-226 is the basic version with Allison engines, as detailed.
Ka-226A is a rescue version ordered by Russia's Ministry of Emergency Situations.
Ka-228 was to be powered by Ivchenko PROGRESS/Zaporozhye AI-450 turboshafts, but development has ended.

↑ Kamov Ka-226A with passenger pod *(Piotr Butowski)*

Kazan Helicopter Plant — Russia

Corporate address:
420085, Kazan.

Telephone: +7 8432 54 45 52, 54 46 41, 54 46 91
Facsimile: +7 8432 54 52 52
Telex: 22 48 48 AGAT RU

Founded: 1939.

Employees: 10,000.

Information:
Marat Ayupov (Marketing Department Manager) and Mikhail A. Tikhonov (Director of Marketing).

ACTIVITIES

- Principal past (since 1951) and current manufacturer of Mil helicopters, including exports from 1956.
- Uses computer-aided design, some robotic and other advanced manufacturing techniques, and has extensive engineering and test facilities, but until 1994 undertook production only. However, it has now added helicopter design and development to its business activities, and has introduced the Ansat and Aktay.
- Has a 25% shareholding in Euromil (which see).

Kazan Aktay

First flight: Expected in the year 2000.
Certification: To meet AP-29/FAR 29 regulations.
Role: Single-engined light multi-purpose helicopter, with anticipated roles including passenger or cargo transport, rescue, patrol, and training.

Development

- August 1997. Mock-up displayed at MAKS in Zhukovsky.

Details for Aktay

PRINCIPAL DIMENSIONS:
Rotor diameter (main): 32 ft 10 ins (10 m)
Fuselage length: 27 ft 5 ins (8.35 m)
Maximum height: 8 ft 10 ins (2.69 m) to above rotor head

TAIL ROTOR:
Diameter: 4 ft 10.25 ins (1.48 m)

UNDERCARRIAGE:
Type: Fixed twin skids, with integral foot rests
Wheel track: 6 ft 10.5 ins (2.1 m)

WEIGHTS:
Normal take-off: 2,315 lb (1,050 kg)
Payload: 661 lb (300 kg)

PERFORMANCE:
Maximum speed: 103 kts (118 mph) 190 km/h
Cruise speed: 84 kts (96 mph) 155 km/h
OGE hovering ceiling: 4,265 ft (1,300 m)
Ceiling: 15,420 ft (4,700 m)
Range with full payload: 54 naut miles (62 miles) 100 km
Range with 419 lb (190 kg) payload: 324 naut miles (373 miles) 600 km
Duration: 6 hours

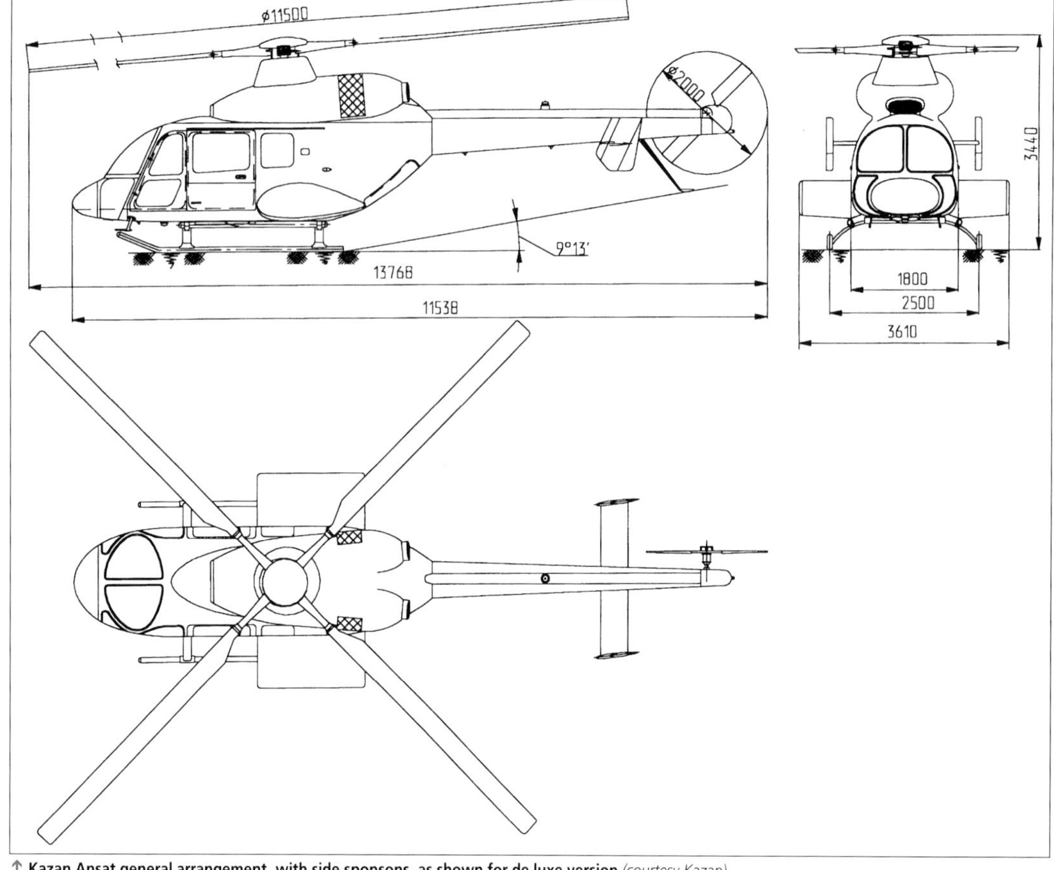

↑ Kazan Ansat general arrangement, with side sponsons, as shown for de luxe version *(courtesy Kazan)*

Details

Crew/passengers: Pilot plus 2 passengers side-by-side or 661 lb (300 kg) of cargo.
Cabin access: Large forward-hinged glazed door each side of the cabin. Clamshell doors at the rear of the fuselage pod, under the tailboom.
Rotor system: 4-blade main rotor with elastomeric bearings.
Tail rotor characteristics: 2-blade tail rotor on the starboard side.
Tail surfaces: T-tail, with sweptback dorsal fin and small constant-chord stabilizer, and sweptback ventral fin with tailguard.
Engine: Wankel type.
Engine rating: 240 hp (179 kW).
Fuel system: AI-92 and AI-93 motorcar fuel. Consumption 62-77 lb (28-35 kg) per hour.

Kazan Ansat

First flight: 1998.
Certification: To meet AP-29/FAR 29 regulations.

Development

- 1994. Design started.
- June 1997. Prototype shown at the 1997 Paris Air Show.

Details

Role: Twin-turboshaft light multi-purpose helicopter, with roles including passenger or cargo transport, rescue, patrol, armed military, firefighting and training.
Chief designer: Alexei Stepanov.
Sales: Demand for 600 expected for the domestic market, including those in police, border guard and EMS forms; 20 helicopters are expected to be built in the first year of production. 2 prototypes built at time of writing, the first for ground testing.
Crew/passengers: 1 or 2 pilots and 4-6 passengers, with the option of 9 passengers for short journeys, or 2 litters and 2 attendants.
Cabin access: Rearward sliding door each side, 3 ft 7 ins wide and 3 ft 11 ins high (1.09 × 1.2 m). Access to the cockpit via a forward-hinged door each side or through the cabin, though a vertical strut prevents the 2 doors each side of the fuselage

↑ Kazan Aktay mock-up *(Piotr Butowski)*

↑ Kazan Ansat prototype without sponsons *(Piotr Butowski)*

forming a single large access area when both are opened.
Freight, internal: 2,866 lb (1,300 kg) in the main cabin with the seats removed.
Freight, external: 2,866 lb (1,300 kg) sling load.
Optional equipment: Includes rescue winch on starboard side.
Rotor system: 4-blade main rotor, with elastomeric bearings.
Tail rotor: 2 blades.
Tail surfaces: Mock up had dorsal and ventral sweptback fins and a fairly small horizontal stabilizer near the top of the dorsal surface. Actual prototype has a new tail arrangement, with a larger horizontal stabilizer with endplates (toed to port) further forward under the boom and a large tailguard. Revised mock-ups and models have a ventral fin as well as the new stabilizer arrangement, but this is not shown on the prototype.
Flight control system: Fly-by-wire.
Airframe: Metal alloys, but with 18-20% composites. A de luxe version of Ansat has been shown in scale model form with different fuselage top cowling for the engines, presumably indicating more engine power (PW207s?), and the optional side sponsons.
Engines: 2 Pratt & Whitney Canada PW206C turboshafts, with FADEC. Alternative 710 shp (529 kW) PW207s from late 1998.
Engine rating: Each 630 shp (470 kW) take-off.
Fuel system: 760 litres in 2 tanks.
Expendable weapons and equipment: Fuselage mock-up in camouflaged military-transport form was shown with 2 rocket launchers and a machine-gun.
Flight avionics/instrumentation: Canadian Marconi CMA-2055 integrated instrument display system (IIDS) in Ansat prototype. Similar Russian NPKV-A flight-navigation system for day and night all-weather operation is expected later. SAU-A autopilot and autohover. 3 MFDs in cockpit.

Details for Ansat

PRINCIPAL DIMENSIONS:
Rotor diameter (main): 37 ft 9 ins (11.5 m)
Maximum length, rotors turning: 45 ft 2 ins (13.768 m)
Fuselage length: 37 ft 7.5 ins (11.47 m), or 37 ft 10.5 ins (11.538 m) nose to end of turning tail rotor
Fuselage width: 5 ft 11 ins (1.8 m), or 11 ft 10 ins (3.61 m) over sponsons
Maximum height: 11 ft 3.5 ins (3.44 m), to above rotor head

CABIN:
Length: 11 ft 6 ins (3.5 m) including cockpit, or 5 ft 11 ins (1.8 m) without cockpit
Width: 5 ft 5 ins (1.65 m)
Height: 4 ft 3 ins (1.3 m)
Volume: 268.4 cu ft (7.6 m^3) including cockpit, or 187.2 cu ft (5.3 m^3) without cockpit

MAIN ROTOR:
Aerofoil section: NACA 230-012
Blade chord: 12.6 ins (0.32 m), constant
Rotor disc: 1,118 sq ft (103.87 m^2)
Rpm: 365.4

TAIL ROTOR:
Diameter: 6 ft 7 ins (2 m)

UNDERCARRIAGE:
Type: Fixed skids type
Skid track: 8 ft 2.5 ins (2.5 m)

WEIGHTS:
Empty: 3,616 lb (1,640 kg) in cargo version, 3,748 lb (1,700 kg) in passenger version
Normal take-off: 6,614 lb (3,000 kg)
Maximum take-off: 7,275 lb (3,300 kg)
Payload: 2,866 lb (1,300 kg) normal, 3,637 lb (1,650 kg) of cargo

PERFORMANCE:
Never-exceed speed (V_{NE}): 151-156 kts (174-180 mph) 280-290 km/h, depending on weight
Maximum speed at normal take-off weight: 150 kts (173 mph) 278 km/h
Maximum cruise speed at normal take-off weight: 128 kts (148 mph) 238 km/h
Economic cruise speed: 76 kts (87 mph) 140 km/h
Climb rate at normal take-off weight: 3,150 ft (960 m) per minute
OGE hovering ceiling: 8,858 ft (2,700 m) at normal take-off weight, or 5,905 ft (1,800 m) at maximum take-off weight
Service ceiling: 19,685 ft (6,000 m) at normal take-off weight, 18,045 ft (5,500 m) at maximum take-off weight
Maximum range, cargo/passenger version: 280/291 naut miles (323/335 miles) 520/540 km, with 30 minutes reserve, depending on weight
Maximum range, rescue/emergency version: 102/113 naut miles (118/130 miles) 190/210 km
Maximum range, patrol version: 205 naut miles (236 miles) 380 km
Range with 3,637 lb (1,650 kg) of cargo: up to 54 naut miles (62 miles) 100 km
Ferry range: 335 naut miles (385 miles) 620 km
Duration: 2.3 hours passenger, 2.4 hours cargo, 1.8 hours emergency/rescue and 2.7-2.9 hours patrol

Mil Moscow Helicopter Plant — Russia

Corporate address:
2 Sokolnichesky val, 107113, Moscow.
Telephone: +7 095 2649083, 2699255
Facsimile: +7 095 2645571, 2649174
Telex: 412144 Mil RU
Founded: 26 March 1947.
Information:
Georgiy Sinelshchikov (General Designer).

ACTIVITIES

▪ Some 25,000 Mil-designed helicopters have been manufactured.
▪ Mil-designed helicopters are produced in association with various closely-linked production facilities, including the Arsenyev Aviation Production Plant (Pl. Lenina 5, Arsenyev 692335 – *telephone* +7 42361 24897, *facsimile* +7 42361 26130) which produces the Mi-34; Kazan Helicopter Plant that produces the Mi-8, Mi-14, Mi-17 and Mi-172 (which see); Rostvertol PLC (5 Novatorov, 344038, Rostov-on-Don – *telephone* +7 8632 317493/317371, *facsimile* +7 8632 310039/317491) which produces the Mi-26, Mi-28 and Mi-24/Mi-35; and the Joint Stock Company Ulan-Ude Aviation Manufacturing Plant (1 Khorinskaya Street, Ulan-Ude 670009 – *telephone* +7 30122 3-74-75, *facsimile* +7 30122 3-01-47) which produces the Mi-8AT, Mi-8AMT and Mi-171.
▪ Mil (with a 25% shareholding) participates in Euromil with Eurocopter, Kazan and Klimov, to develop, produce and market the Mi-38 (which see).

Mil Mi-6 and Mi-22 (NATO name *Hook*)

Details *(for Mi-6A, except where stated)*

First flight: 5 June 1957 (piloted by Rafail Kaprelyan).
Role: Heavy transport, medevac, firefighting, and airborne command post.

Aims

▪ Cabin cargo hold is compatible with the An-12 *Cub*.

Development *(see 1996-97 edition of WA&SD, page 322)*

Sales: Production of 864 helicopters at Rostov-on-Don Factory No 168 (now Rostvertol) during 1959-80. Additionally, 50 also built at Factory No 23 in Moscow-Fili during 1960-62. Over 300 still in service with the CIS armed forces (270 in Russia, the remainder in Belarus, Kazakhstan, Ukraine and Uzbekistan), and more than 60 went to Algeria, Egypt, Ethiopia, India, Indonesia, Iraq, Laos, Pakistan, Peru, Poland, Syria and Vietnam, of which India, Indonesia, Pakistan and Poland are believed no longer to be users. Mi-22 variants are operated by Russia, Belarus, Ukraine and Uzbekistan. Out of production.
Crew/passengers: 5 flight crew (2 pilots, navigator, radio operator and engineer), plus an assault equipment operator in military versions. Standard Mi-6 can carry 61 fully-armed troops. Mi-6TP has 65 folding seats, Mi-6P has 80 seats, and Mi-6S has 41 litters and 2 attendants. See Aircraft variants, and Freight, internal.
Freight, internal: ATL and ATP artillery vehicles, trucks, jeeps, etc.
Cabin access: Hydraulically-operated rear clamshell doors. Single passenger door and 9 windows on starboard side, and 2 doors and 7 windows on port side of the fuselage.
Size of main loading door: 8 ft 10 ins × 8 ft 8 ins (2.7 × 2.65 m) rear opening. Largest side door 5 ft 7 ins × 2 ft 7 ins (1.7 × 0.8 m).
Rotor system: 5-blade steel main rotor with flapping and drag hinges. Fixed tabs. Metal swashplate. Electric blade de-icing.
Tail rotor characteristics: 4-blade metal AV-63-Kh6 tail rotor.
Wing/tail surfaces: Adjustable wings (2 position) attached to the fuselage sides to relieve the rotor by producing some 20% of required lift in cruise flight. For powered cruise the port wing is set to +14° 15′. With the engines off (autorotation), the port wing is set to +4° 15′. Since the rotor generated air flow is not symmetrical, the angle of the wings has to be asymmetrical; the starboard wing setting is always greater by 1° 30′. Ground adjustable horizontal stabilizer (+5° 30′, –7° 30′). Tailboom tip acts as the vertical fin. Wings are detached for flying-crane duties.
Airframe materials: Metal.
Engines: 2 Aviadvigatel/Solovyov D-25V turboshafts. First small series of helicopters powered by Aviadvigatel/Solovyov TV-2V

↑ Mil Mi-6VKP *Hook-B* airborne command post. Note the tailboom aerials, rear clamshell doors, wings and external tanks *(Piotr Butowski)*

engines, based on the Kuznetsov TV-2 turboprop core, the same rating but heavier than later D-25Vs.
Engine rating: Each 5,500 shp (4,100 kW) take-off.
Transmission rating: R-7 (R-6 for helicopters with TV-2V engines) main gearbox, designed by Pavel Solovyov.
Fuel system: 8,150 litres (13,922 lb, 6,315 kg) standard in 11 bag tanks inside the fuselage, plus 4,500 litres (7,694 lb, 3,490 kg) in 2 metal tanks on the fuselage sides. Provision for 4,500 litres of auxiliary fuel in a metal cabin tank. Maximum fuel weight 29,310 lb (13,295 kg).
Flight avionics/instrumentation: Typical Russian flight/navigation/communications equipment for all-weather operations (no radar), plus astrocompass. AP-34B autopilot (AP-31 earlier). SRO-2 IFF.
Self-protection systems: Some military helicopters have a pack of 2 ASO-2 chaff/flare dispensers on each side of the fuselage, with a total of 128 projectiles.
Fixed guns: NUV-1M turret with flexibly-mounted 12.7-mm machine-gun in the glazed nose.
Ammunition: 150 rounds.
Number of weapon pylons: None.

Aircraft variants:
Mi-6 (izdeliye 50) covers the initial production helicopters.
Mi-6A (izdeliye 50A) basic production version from 1971, with longer service life and MTOW increased to 44,000 kg.
Mi-6BUS (bortovoi uzel svyazi, on-board communication interchange) is a modification, externally similar to Mi-22 but having no operational command crew, and extended communication equipment only.
Mi-6M was an ASW prototype of 1964.
Mi-6P (passazhirskiy) has airliner-type seats for 80 passengers, and rectangular instead of circular windows. 1965 appearance.
Mi-6PP became an ECM helicopter, built in several different configurations between 1960s and 1980s.
Mi-6PRTBV and ***Mi-6RVK*** were developed in the early 1960s for the transportation of ballistic missiles.
Mi-6PS (poiskovo-spasatelnyi) or ***Mi-6APS*** (when based on the Mi-6A) of 1977 appearance are military rescue/evacuation versions.
Mi-6PZh (1967) and ***Mi-6PZh2*** (1971) are firefighting versions. 21,000 litres of water in a single 12,000 litre metal cabin tank plus 6 × 1,500 litre bag tanks suspended beneath the fuselage.
Mi-6S (sanitarnyi) is a medevac version for 41 litters and 2 attendants.

Details for Mi-6/6A

PRINCIPAL DIMENSIONS:
Rotor diameter (main): 114 ft 10 ins (35 m)
Maximum length, rotors turning: 136 ft 11 ins (41.739 m)
Fuselage length: 108 ft 10 ins (33.165 m)
Maximum height: 32 ft 4 ins (9.86 m)
Wing span: 50 ft 2 ins (15.3 m), with 376.74 sq ft (35 m^2) area

CABIN:
Length: 38 ft 5 ins (11.726 m)
Width: 9 ft 11 ins (3.014 m)
Height: 6 ft 7 ins to 8 ft 8 ins (2.012 to 2.647 m)
Volume: 2,825 cu ft (80 m^3)

MAIN ROTOR:
Aerofoil section: NACA 230M and high-speed TsAGI P-57-9 (root/centre and tips)
Rotor disc: 10,356 sq ft (962.1 m^2)

TAIL ROTOR:
Diameter: 20 ft 8 ins (6.3 m)

UNDERCARRIAGE:
Type: Fixed, with twin nosewheels
Main wheel tyre size: 1,325 × 480 mm
Nose wheel tyre size: 720 × 310 mm
Wheel base: 29 ft 10 ins (9.095 m)
Wheel track: 24 ft 7 ins (7.502 m)

WEIGHTS:
Empty: 60,054 lb (27,240 kg)
Normal take-off: 89,287 lb (40,500 kg)
Maximum take-off: 93,696 lb (42,500 kg), raised to 97,003 lb (44,000 kg) for final production helicopters (Mi-6A)
Payload: 13,228-26,455 lb (6,000-12,000 kg), normal/maximum

PERFORMANCE:
Maximum speed: 162 kts (186 mph) 300 km/h
Cruise speed: 135 kts (155 mph) 250 km/h
OGE hovering ceiling: 3,280 ft (1,000 m)
Service ceiling: 14,765 ft (4,500 m)
Range with 17,632 lb (8,000 kg) payload: 335 naut miles (385 miles) 620 km, without auxiliary fuel, 5% reserve
Range with auxiliary fuel: 783 naut miles (901 miles) 1,450 km

Mi-6TP (transportno-passazhirskiy) is a convertible cargo/passenger version of 1963 appearance, with 65 folding seats.
Mi-6TZ (toplivo-zapravshchik) and ***Mi-6ATZ*** (when based on the Mi-6A) of 1977 are tanker versions (ground use), used during the Afghan conflict.
Mi-6VKP (vozdushnyi komandnyi punkt, airborne command post) or ***Mi-6VzPU*** (vozdushnyi punkt upravlenya, airborne control post) are command posts named *Hook B* by NATO. 4 small plate-type aerials arranged symmetrically around the tailboom plus a rectangular frame aerial. Usual starboard metal fuel tank is deleted, its place taken by a cooler in front of the undercarriage gear and a small tank behind. Some have additional small aerials.
Mi-22 *Hook-C* or ***Mi-6AYa*** (Mi-6A with Yakhont) is an airborne command post, equipped with Yakhont command system used by tank divisions. Sword type aerial under the front fuselage and no tailboom aerials. Mi-6VKP fuselage cooler deleted, with the starboard metal fuel tank reinstated.
Mi-22M differs from Mi-22 by having an improved power supply, allowing extended working time.
Mi-22 *Hook-D* or **Mi-6AYaSh** has additionally a flat antenna, probably SLAR, on the starboard front fuselage. Based at Novosibirsk-Severniy.

Mil Mi-8 (NATO name *Hip*)

First flight: 24 June 1961 (piloted by B. Zemskov).
Role: Medium civil/military transport, armed assault, minelaying, reconnaissance, airborne command/control post, electronic warfare, firefighting, ambulance, agricultural, and more.

Development

- 20 February 1958. V-8 ordered as a turbine powered replacement for Mi-4 *Hound*.
- 30 May 1960. Twin-engined V-8A ordered.
- 24 June 1961. First flight of the single-engined (Ivchenko AI-24V) V-8 prototype.
- 2 August 1962. First hovering flight of the twin-engined (Isotov TV2-117s) prototype, piloted by N. Leshin.
- 9 October 1963. First flight of the prototype with a 5-blade main rotor.
- 3 November 1964. State acceptance trials completed.
- 26 October 1965. First production Mi-8 helicopter left Factory No 387 in Kazan.

Details

Sales: About 7,300 TV2-117-powered helicopters have been built by the Kazan (4,500 since 1965) and Ulan-Ude (2,800 since 1970) factories, and production continues at Ulan-Ude only (note also that 5 pre-series helicopters were built by Factory No 23 in Moscow, now Khrunichev, 1961-62). Some 1,400 have been exported to 57 countries, with more recent recipients including Algeria (47 combat equipped) and Mexico (12 for Army). Mi-8s took part in the first phase of the Afghanistan conflict but were soon replaced by Mi-8MTs with more powerful engines. In some countries local improvements have been applied; for instance, in Egypt the air intakes of Mi-8Ts are protected by British particle separators, whereas nav/weather radar units have been installed on Finnish Mi-8Ts.
Crew/passengers: 2 pilots, plus flight engineer between the cockpit and main cabin. 28 passengers in the Mi-8P (seat pitch 29 ins, 74 cm, with 12 ins, 30 cm aisle), and 24 equipped troops on tip-up seats or 8,818 lb (4,000 kg) of cargo in the Mi-8T. In an air ambulance role, the helicopter can carry 12 litters, 1 attendant and all necessary equipment. See Aircraft variants.
Freight, external: Both passenger and cargo versions can be fitted with external slings for carrying bulky loads or for use as air cranes. Set of available cables makes it possible to select the suspension height of a sling load. The crane boom installed enables the helicopter to be used for rescue, using the electric winch.
Cabin access: Clamshell freight loading doors at the rear of the cabin, are considerably larger on military variants than civil. Mi-8P has a central airstair door of 2 ft 7 ins × 4 ft 3 ins (0.785 × 1.285 m). Port-side sliding door of 2 ft 8 ins × 4 ft 7 ins (0.82 × 1.4 m).
Optional equipment: 331 lb (150 kg) LPG-150M electric hoist, typically on Mi-8T.
Rotor system: Aluminium alloy, 5-blade main rotor, with balance tabs. Flapping and drag hinges. Forward incline off horizontal of 4° 30'. Current helicopters have pendulum vibration damping. Nitrogen pressurized blade spar crack warning system.
Tail rotor characteristics: 3-blade metal, on starboard side.
Tail surfaces: Ground adjustable horizontal stabilizer. Tailfin formed from the rear of the tailboom.
Flight control system: Mechanical, with hydraulic boosters.
Airframe materials: D16AT and V95 duralumin, other aluminium alloys, magnesium alloy and steel.
Engines: Currently 2 Klimov/Isotov TV2-117AG (formerly TV2-117A) turboshafts, side-by-side above the cabin.
Engine rating: Each 1,500 shp (1,119 kW).
Transmission: 3-stage VR-8A main reduction gearbox, ratio 62.5:1. Weight 1,730 lb (785 kg).
Fuel system: Fuel in a 445 litre collector tank above the cabin and 2 fixed external tanks at the fuselage sides. External tanks are of 2 variants; short tanks are 745 litres (starboard) and 680 litres (port); long tanks are 1,140 litres (starboard) and 1,030 litres (port). For ferrying, 1 or 2 additional tanks (915 litres each) can be carried in the cabin, raising volume to 4,445 litres (weighing 7,599 lb; 3,447 kg) and fairly easily installed/removed under field conditions.
Electrical system: 27 volt DC system via 2 × 18 kW starter-generators plus 6 × 28 amp-hour batteries. AC system at 400 Hz via a generator, plus 3-phase back-up.
Hydraulic system: Basic and stand-by systems operating on AMG-10 oil, pressure 653 to 943 psi.
Braking system: Pneumatic brakes.

↑ **Mil Mi-8PS VIP transport** *(Piotr Butowski)*

Radar: Weather radar in the nose for some versions, including current production.
Flight avionics/instrumentation: AP-34B autopilot for course, altitude, roll and pitch stabilization. ARK-9 and ARK-U2 automatic radio compass, A-037 (earlier RV-3) altimeter, and DIV-1 Doppler navigation. Standard communications equipment includes R-842 (or Yadro-1 in civil versions) and R-860 (earlier R-833, or Baklan-20 for civil versions) radios, and SPU-7 intercom.
Fixed guns: Mi-8TV/TB have 7.62-mm nose-mounted PKT flexible machine-gun. Second version Mi-8TV has 12.7-mm gun.
Ammunition: 700 rounds.
Number of weapon pylons: Military Mi-8Ts can have outriggers with a total of 4 pylons, while Mi-8TV/TBs have 6 plus an additional 4 or 6 anti-armour missiles on over-rigger launch rails.
Expendable weapons and equipment: Military Mi-8T usually carries 4 × UB-16-57UD rocket packs, each with 16 × 57-mm S-5 rockets. Mi-8TV usually carries 6 UB-32 rocket packs (total 192 rockets) and 4 × 9M17 (AT-2 *Swatter*) anti-armour missiles, while Mi-8TB has 6 UB-32s and 6 × 9M14M Malyutka (AT-3 *Sagger*) missiles. Bombs. See Aircraft variants.

Aircraft variants:
V-8 *Hip-A* prototype had a single AI-24V engine and 4-blade main rotor.
V-8A *Hip-B* prototype of 1962 had 2 × TV2-117 engines and a 4-blade rotor.
Mi-8AD is a mine-laying version (anti-personnel) of 1978 appearance.
Mi-8AT *Hip-C* is a current production transport version (Ulan-Ude factory), with TV2-117AG engines (G for graphite sealing).
Mi-8AV of 1975 appearance deploys anti-tank mines.
Mi-8BT is a mine-sweeping version. 5 built in 1974.

Details for *Hip-C*

PRINCIPAL DIMENSIONS:
Rotor diameter (main): 69 ft 10 ins (21.288 m)
Maximum length, rotors turning: 82 ft 9 ins (25.244 m)
Fuselage length: 59 ft 7 ins (18.168 m) or 60 ft 7 ins (18.31 m) with weather radar in nose
Maximum height: 18 ft 7 ins (5.654 m), or 14 ft 4 ins (4.38 m) to above rotor hub

CABIN (Mi-8T, *with Mi-8P in italics*):
Length: 25 ft 8 ins (7.82 m) including rear doors, 17 ft 6 ins (5.34 m) excluding doors, *20 ft 10 ins (6.36 m)*
Width: 7 ft 8 ins (2.34 m) maximum
Width at floor: 6 ft 9 ins (2.06 m)
Height: 5 ft 11 ins (1.8 m)

MAIN ROTOR:
Aerofoil section: NACA 230
Blade chord: 1 ft 8.5 ins (0.52 m)
Rotor disc: 3,832 sq ft (356 m^2)
Rpm: 192

TAIL ROTOR:
Diameter: 12 ft 9.75 ins (3.908 m)

UNDERCARRIAGE:
Type: Fixed, with twin steerable nosewheels. Tyre pressure can be autonomously increased using the pneumatic system and air in the struts. Optional streamline fairings for mainwheels
Main wheel tyre size: 865 × 280 mm (KT 97-3 type)
Nose wheel tyre size: 595 × 185 mm (K2-116 type)
Wheel base: 14 ft (4.258 m)
Wheel track: 15 ft 9 ins (4.8 m)

WEIGHTS:
Empty: 16,248 lb (7,370 kg) for Mi-8P, 15,069-16,006 lb (6,835-7,260 kg) for Mi-8T
Normal take-off: 24,471 lb (11,100 kg)
Maximum take-off: 26,455 lb (12,000 kg)
Payload: 8,818 lb (4,000 kg) internal, 6,614 lb (3,000 kg) external

PERFORMANCE:
Maximum speed: 135 kts (155 mph) 250 km/h at normal take-off weight, 124 kts (143 mph) 230 km/h at maximum
Cruise speed: 121 kts (140 mph) 225 km/h at normal take-off weight
IGE hovering ceiling: 5,905 ft (1,800 m)
OGE hovering ceiling: 2,790 ft (850 m)
Service ceiling: 14,765 ft (4,500 m)
Range with ferry fuel: 532 naut miles (612 miles) 985 km at 1,640 ft (500 m), 30 minutes reserve
Range with 4,469 lb (2,027 kg) fuel: 281 naut miles (323 miles) 520 km, altitude/reserve as above
Range with passengers: 229 naut miles (264 miles) 425 km, 20 minutes reserve

Mi-8K or ***Mi-8TG*** is an artillery spotting helicopter.
Mi-8KP (kommandnyi punkt) is a command post for search and rescue operations, equipped with Saygak communications suite. 1978 appearance.
Mi-8MB is a medevac helicopter of 1973.
Mi-8MT, ***MTV*** and ***AMT*** are helicopters with TV3-117 engines and a port-side tail rotor, and are described separately (see Mi-17 entry).
Mi-8P (V-8AP in prototype form) *Hip-C* is a passenger version. Rectangular cabin windows. See also Mi-8T.
Mi-8PA appeared in 1980. Export version of Mi-8P for a Japanese customer, with TV2-117F engines (emergency rating of 1,700 shp, 1,267 kW introduced). 1 only.
Mi-8PD (punkt dowodzenia) is a Polish airborne command post conversion. Several built.
Mi-8PS, see Mi-8S below.
Mi-8R or ***Mi-8Gr*** is a tactical reconnaissance version with large window in the rear cabin doors.
Mi-8S and ***Mi-8PS*** (S for salon) *Hip-C* are VIP versions based on the Mi-8T and Mi-8P respectively. Sub-versions are PS-7, PS-9 and PS-11 (for 7, 9 or 11 passengers respectively). Current production VIP versions are Mi-8TP (which see), APS, AP-2 and AP-4 with TV2-117AG engines.
Mi-8SP and ***Mi-8SPA*** are rescue helicopters for cosmonauts.
Mi-8T (V-8AT in prototype form) *Hip-C* is a standard civil and military transport version. Circular cabin windows. Both Mi-8T and Mi-8P have many sub-variants depending on equipment, including crane, medical, firefighting (4,409 lb, 2,000 kg of water in suspended rubber tank), and agricultural. Replaced in production at Ulan-Ude by Mi-8AT.
Mi-8TB *Hip-F* became the export version of Mi-8TV (second), with 6 × 9M14M missiles plus other weapons. Received by Germany and Nicaragua.
Mi-8TG has TV2-117TG turboshaft engines adapted for liquid methane fuel, standard aircraft fuel and any mixture of the 2. Flew 1987 as the first methane fuelled helicopter in the world.
Mi-8TM is an Ulan-Ude helicopter with uprated TV2-117F engines and extended avionics, including nose radar. Vibration damper at rotor head. Prototype shown at Zhukovsky in August 1995.
Mi-8TP is a current production military executive helicopter, with upgraded communication equipment, produced by Ulan-Ude. Additional R-832 radio equipment (2 sword-type aerials under the front fuselage and tailboom) plus R-111 unit with rod type aerial lowered under the fuselage.
Mi-8TS (tropichesky sukhoi, tropical dry) is an export version for hot and dusty climates, used by Syria from 1973.
Mi-8TV (vooruzhonnyi, armed) *Hip-C* appeared in 1968. As Mi-8T but with provision for weapon pylons carrying 4 × UB-16-57UD rocket packs or bombs. In service it was named merely Mi-8T (allowing another Mi-8TV version).
Mi-8TV (second use of name) *Hip-E* appeared in 1974 as a military assault transport with extended armament, including 6 rocket packs and 4 ATGMs. A-12.7 machine-gun.
Mi-8TZ is a tanker version (on the ground) of 1977 appearance.
Mi-8VD is for radiation reconnaissance.
Mi-8VKP (vozdushnyi komandnyi punkt, airborne command post) or ***Mi-8VzPU*** (vozdushnyi punkt upravlenya, airborne control post) *Hip-D* carries distinctive equipment boxes on the racks. 2 frame type aerials installed symmetrically above the rear fuselage, plus a new aerial installed under the tailboom. Early 1970s appearance.
Mi-8PP, ***Mi-8PPA***, ***Mi-8SMV*** and other ECM helicopters are detailed in a separate entry, after Mi-17.
Mi-9 *Hip-G* is an airborne command post. See separate entry.

Mil Mi-9 (NATO name *Hip-G*) and Mi-19

First flight: 1977.
Role: Tactical airborne command posts.
Sales: More than 100 Mi-9s are used by CIS land forces. Some are with Hungary and 8 were supplied to the former East Germany for service from May 1984 (now withdrawn). Mi-19 and Mi-19R are used by commanding officers of Russian infantry, tank and rocket units (other users unknown).
Mission equipment: Mi-9 has Ivolga (golden oriole, therefore Mi-8IV) command system, including R-826 HF radio equipment (2 plate-type aerials along the bottom of the fuselage), R-802 UHF (mast-type aerial under the front fuselage), R-405 radio-link (hockey-type aerial on the port side of the rear fuselage and another under the tailboom), R-856 and R-832 (aerials on the tailboom), plus R-111 relay equipment (aerial normally folded along the bottom of the fuselage ready for unfolding in flight).

Aircraft variants:
Mi-9 or ***Mi-8IV*** *Hip-G* command post is based on Mi-8 *Hip-C*.
Mi-19 command post is based on the Mi-8MT (Mi-17) *Hip-H*. Appeared 1987 and used by commanding officers of infantry and tank divisions.
Mi-19R is a specialized version for commanding officers of tactical rocket units.

Mil Mi-14 (NATO name *Haze*)

First flight: 1 August 1967 for prototype with TV2-117 engines (piloted by Yu Shvachko), 1970 for TV3-117-powered prototype.
Role: Shore-based anti-submarine amphibious helicopter, with mine-countermeasures and search and rescue variants. Some converted to passenger and firefighting roles (see Aircraft variants).

Aims

▪ To destroy a submarine operating at a depth of 1,310 ft (400 m) and speed of 32 kts.

Development

▪ 24 January 1974. First flight of the first production helicopter built at the Kazan plant.
▪ 11 May 1976. Mi-14PL officially accepted into Soviet Navy service.

Details

Sales: Production ended in 1986, after 273 had been manufactured at Kazan (including about 120 exported). Officially withdrawn from the Russian Navy, more than 100 remain in reserve. Other recipients were Bulgaria (7 PL/BTs), Cuba (14 PLs), former East Germany (14 PL/BTs; no longer operational; 2 shipped to the USA in November 1991), Libya (43), Nicaragua, North Korea (10 PLs), Poland (17, including some PSs), Romania, Syria (20 PLs), Vietnam, and former Yugoslavia (4 PLs).
Crew/passengers: 2 pilots, technician, and navigator/weapon systems or rescue equipment operator in ASW role. See Aircraft variants for passenger accommodation for converted helicopters, plus SAR version.
Cabin access: Sliding port door.
Standard equipment: MSK-3M sea suits, LAS-5M-3 dinghy, and electric winch; Mi-14PL and Mi-14BT have an LPG-2 (early series) or LPG-150 external winch with a lifting capacity of 331 lb (150 kg), while Mi-14PS has an LPG-300 winch that is retracted inside the cabin, with a 661 lb (300 kg) lifting capacity.
Rotor system: Mi-17 dynamics.
Fuselage: Watertight boat-type hull with side sponsons.
Engines: 2 Klimov/Isotov TV3-117M turboshafts (M for morskoi, sea, with special corrosion-resistant coating for some components). First 3 prototypes used TV2-117 turboshafts (each 1,500 shp, 1,119 kW). AI-9V APU.
Engine rating: Each 1,950 shp (1,454 kW) at take-off, with emergency rating of 2,225 shp (1,659 kW).
Transmission: VR-14 3-stage main gearbox. Weight 1,857 lb (842.5 kg), ratio 78.1:1.
Fuel system: 3,795 litres of fuel in a single collector tank in the engine bay aft of the main gearbox and 6 tanks under the cabin floor. Additional 500 litre tank can be installed inside the cabin for ferry flights.
Radar: Initsiativa-2M (I-2M, or I-2ME for export) nav/search/attack radar in an undernose radome. See below.
Flight avionics/instrumentation: SAU-14 automatic control system, with autohover in Mi-14PL but not in Mi-14PS. ARK-9 and ARK-U2 radio compasses, RV-3 radio altimeter, and DISS-15 Doppler navigation radar. SRZO-2 IFF. Radio communication equipment comprises R-842M and R-860 in Mi-14PL, Karat M-24 and R-832M in Mi-14PS. SPU-7 intercom.
Mission equipment: Mi-14PL *Haze-A* has a Kalmar attack system that interfaces the Initsiativa radar, radio sonobuoys system with A-100 Pankhra receiver (SPARU-55 Baku on early helicopters), Oka-2 sonar, and APM-60 Orsha magnetic anomaly detector (APM-73 Bor-1 on last production series). PK-025 data link for group operations. Sura IR sensor fitted to some Russian helicopters.
Expendable weapons and equipment: Mi-14PL *Haze-A* has a weapons bay, with armament choices of a single AT-1 ASW torpedo or APR-2 torpedo, 8 PLAB-250-120 depth bombs, or a nuclear depth bomb. For search operations, 2 cassettes can be carried, each containing 18 RGBN-MN-1 sonobuoys.

Aircraft variants:
Mi-14PL (protivo-lodochnyi, or V-14 or V-14E for export, or izdeliye 140)) *Haze-A* is the standard ASW version, powered by TV3-117M engines. Tail rotor on the port side. MAD antenna mounted in a lower position on final examples.
Mi-14PLM (V-14M) *Haze-A* was an improved ASW version with Osminog nav/attack system from Ka-27 and new weapons. 1 built in 1975.
Mi-14BT (buksir-tralshchik) *Haze-B* is the mine countermeasures version, equipped with a towed SKT trawl for cutting the cables

↑ Mi-14P passenger conversion of the Mi-14BT by the Konvers Avia *(Piotr Butowski)*

of anchored mines, other types of trawls (acoustic, electromagnetic, etc). Can also tow small boats (for instance, landing and rescue craft).
Mi-14PS (poiskovo-spasatelnyi) *Haze-C* is a search and rescue version. ASW equipment is removed from the cabin, providing room for 20 liferafts, which can be dropped to survivors and towed in a train. Also deploys floating containers with clothes, food, medicines, etc. On-board accommodation for 19 survivors. Compared with the Mi-14PL, it has no magnetometer, the tail rotor is to starboard, 2 large searchlights are installed on the front fuselage and another under the tailboom (some have another in the nose), the port-side cabin door is enlarged, and a 661 lb (300 kg) 3-person rescue hoist is installed. Last production Mi-14PSs were given a third fairing under the tailboom, housing a TV camera (the other 2 are for the DISS-15 and searchlight). Some helicopters were upgraded in Kazan, by fitting additional windows below the cockpit (about 1985-87), and some equipped with electro-optical search sensors (1987).
Mi-14PX is the Polish Mi-14PL converted in June 1990 for search and rescue (Poland had previously lost half its fleet of 4 Mi-14PSs). Searchlights added, some rescue equipment located inside the cabin, but all the ASW equipment retained, allowing its use only for training purposes. 1 only, side number *1003*.
Many testbeds were produced from Mi-14, including V-14R for testing Ros-V sonar, while other helicopters were used to testing new Bor-M MAD, Strizh-M wire-guided ASW torpedoes, anti-ship missiles (Mi-14PL in 1983), and FLIR (Mi-14PS in 1987).
Mi-14 Eliminator III (designated ***Mi-14PZh***, pozharnyi, in Russia) is a German-Russian (Aerotec GmbH and Mil) conversion of the ex-GDR mine-sweeping Mi-14BT *Haze-B* for firefighting, with internal tanks for 4,500 litres of water and 500 litres of foam suppression agents. With 2 pumps capable of a combined 3,900 litres per minute working rate, the helicopter sucks water when afloat and releases it through the weapon bay doors. First flown in March 1994, first shown publicly during ILA-94 in Berlin in May 1994, and employed to fight fires in Portugal and Spain.
Mi-14P and ***Mi-14GP*** are passenger and passenger-cargo conversions respectively of Mi-14BTs. Programme is managed by the Konvers Avia company (101000 Moscow, Ulansky per., d. 22 – *telephone* +7 095 2070721, *facsimile* +7 095 2070372). Cabin accommodates 22-24 airliner seats or 11,023 lb (5,000 kg) of cargo when seats removed. Stairs in the rear of the fuselage. Additional safety equipment includes 3 LAS-5M3 dinghies, 25 ASZh-85 life jackets and an R-855A1 emergency radio. Lightweight Kontur weather radar is fitted in the nose in place of the previous Initsiativa radar. TNL-2000T GPS. 5 conversions 1995-97. Firefighting conversion (Mi-14PZh) is also planned.
Mi-14GER is another conversion by Konvers Avia, equipped with geological and ecological-reconnaissance sensors which can determine offshore drilling positions to an accuracy of about 16 ft (5 m). 1 conversion in 1997 for use in the Caspian Sea.

Details for Mi-14PL *Haze-A*, unless stated

PRINCIPAL DIMENSIONS:
Rotor diameter (main): 69 ft 10 ins (21.294 m)
Maximum length, rotors turning: 83 ft 1 ins (25.315 m)
Fuselage length: 60 ft 3 ins (18.376 m)
Maximum height: 22 ft 9 ins (6.936 m)

MAIN ROTOR:
Aerofoil section: NACA 23012

TAIL ROTOR:
Diameter: 12 ft 10 ins (3.908 m)

UNDERCARRIAGE:
Type: Retractable 4-unit type, with single nosewheels and twin mainwheels, retracted into the fuselage (nosewheels) or side nacelles (mainwheels). Tail rotor is protected from the ground by a tail support with a float of 6.53 cu ft (0.185 m^3) volume. 2 inflatable floats of 141 cu ft (4 m^3) volume on the fuselage sides to keep the helicopter stable when alighting on water. Can float in sea state 2, with side winds up to 33 ft (10 m) per second
Main wheel tyre size: 600 × 180 mm
Nose wheel tyre size: 480 × 200 mm
Wheel base: 13 ft 6 ins (4.128 m)
Wheel track: 9 ft 3 ins (2.82 m) main, 3 ft 10 ins (1.17 m) nose

WEIGHTS:
Empty: 19,620 lb (8,902 kg), or 19,400 lb (8,800 kg) for Mi-14BT *Haze-B*, or 19,447 lb (8,821 kg) for Mi-14PS *Haze-C*
Normal take-off: 28,660 lb (13,000 kg)
Maximum take-off: 30,865 lb (14,000 kg)
Payload: 6,614 lb (3,000 kg) for Mi-14PS *Haze-C*

PERFORMANCE:
Maximum permissible speed: 135 kts (155 mph) 250 km/h
Maximum speed: 124 kts (143 mph) 230 km/h at sea level, or 130 kts (149 km/h) 240 km/h at 3,280 ft (1,000 m)
Service ceiling: 13,125 ft (4,000 m)
Normal range: 432 naut miles (497 miles) 800 km
Maximum range: 613 naut miles (705 miles) 1,135 km, with 7% reserve
Duration: 5 hours 56 minutes maximum

Mil Mi-17 (Mi-8MT), Mi-18, Mi-171, Mi-172 and Mi-173 (NATO name *Hip-H*)

First flight: 17 August 1975.
Role: Medium transport, ambulance, rescue and assault helicopter, derived from the Mi-8 but with TV3-117 engines and a port tail rotor.

Development

- 1977. Entered service with Soviet armed forces.

Details

Sales: Some 2,800 built at Kazan since 1977 and 100 at Ulan-Ude since 1991, with 810 exported. Presently, production for the domestic market is going slowly (for instance, in 1994 no helicopters were ordered by Russian Army Aviation, and only 15 were delivered to the Russian Ministry of Interior), but according to the Russian Ministry of Economy, 80 Mi-8/Mi-17s were exported in 1995 and the first half of 1996. New markets have been explored, including Argentina (shown there in Spring 1996), Brazil (Mi-17 was tested by the Brazilian Air Force during 6-16 December 1994), Colombia (10 Mi-17-1Vs bought in 1997 for $42.8 million, the first 2 delivered April 1997), Ecuador (7 Mi-171s recently delivered), Egypt (20 Mi-17-1Vs), Mexico (4 Mi-17s for Army; 13 Mi-8MTV-1s as ex-Russian civil helicopters now operated by the Mexican Navy for search and rescue duties, usually based at Vera Cruz and which, in 1997, undertook emergency missions), Venezuela, Pakistan (first 3 Mi-17s from 12 ordered delivered in May 1996), Indonesia (8 Mi-17-1Vs ordered in 1997), Sri Lanka (12), Turkey (19 Mi-17-1Vs), Myanmar (6 delivered in 1995, with 6 more ordered thereafter), and Bangladesh (8 delivered in 1996). During 1996-97 Ulan-Ude delivered 30 Mi-171s to China and was scheduled to deliver the next 5 in early 1998. Daily Air of Taiwan ordered 10 Mi-17s, the first 2 for delivery in March 1998 and the rest at a rate of 1 every 2 months.
Crew/passengers: As for Mi-8 *Hip-C*, except optional 6 extra seats installed along the cabin centreline, making 30 seats (latest cabin configuration of Mi-17MD prototype shows 36-40 seats). 12 litters and 1 attendant in a medevac role. 26-28 airliner seats in the passenger version, or 7-11 in the VIP version.
Engines: 2 Klimov/St Petersburg TV3-117MT turboshafts (or 117VMs for the Mi-8MTV and derivatives), usually fitted with dust filters (compressor blades are narrow and need to be protected against particles, while older TV2-117 engine was given wide compressor blades and was not usually fitted with filters). AI-9V APU. Infra-red suppression cool air mixers can be fitted to the engine nozzles.
Engine rating: Each 1,900 shp (1,417 kW) take-off, or 2,200 shp (1,641 kW) for OEI emergency power.
Transmission: VR-14 3-stage main gearbox, weighing 1,857 lb (842.5 kg), with ratio 78.1:1.
Fuel system: As for Mi-8 *Hip-C*. 4 additional 915 litre tanks can be installed inside the cabin of Mi-17MD; 2 for earlier versions. 4 external auxiliary tanks (at weapon racks) for Mi-17MD only.
Radar: Optional 8A-813 weather radar in the nose. Mi-17MD has 8A-813Ts radar. See below.
Flight avionics/instrumentation: DISS-32-90 Doppler navigation radar under tailboom, Kurs MP-70 ILS/VOR, and A-723 long-range radio navigation system (Loran, Omega compatible). R-842 (or Yadro-1 for civil versions) and R-863 (or Baklan-20 for civil

↑ Mil Mi-17MD Night equipped for rescue operations, showing ***(left)*** the reshaped nose, inflatable pontoons, electric winch and underfuselage LLLTV camera, and ***(right)*** the single-section flat rear ramp *(Piotr Butowski)*

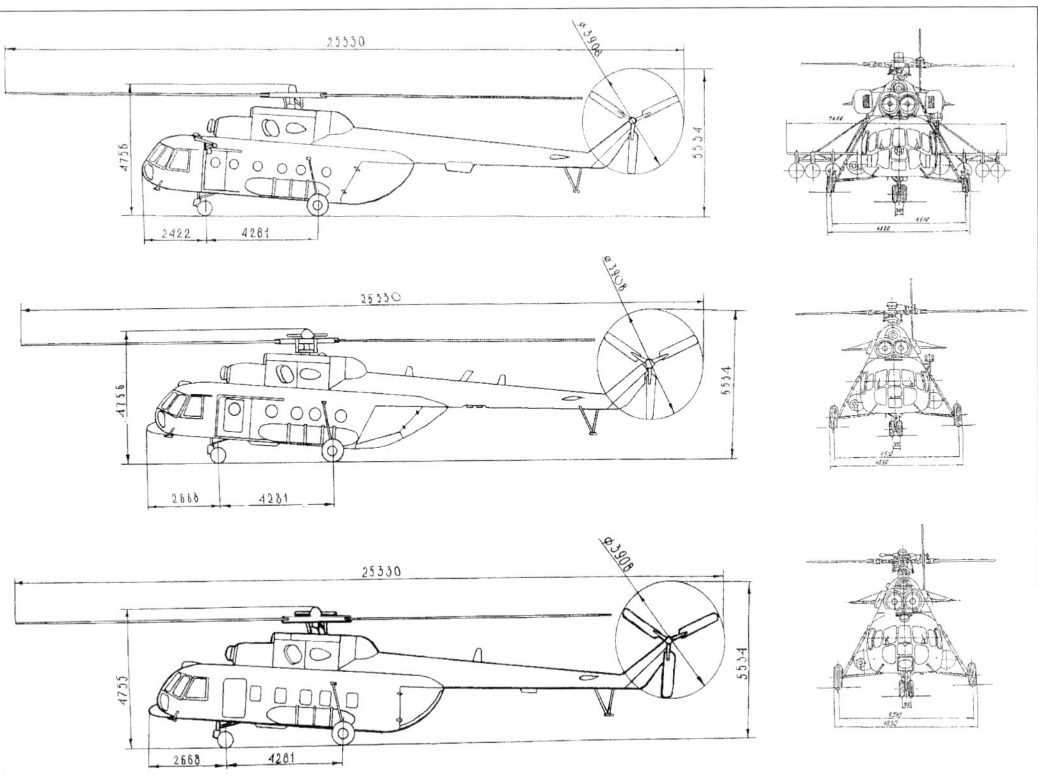

↑ Mil Mi-17-1V with and without armament *(top)*, Mi-17M *(centre)* and Mi-172 *(bottom)* *(courtesy Kazan)*

Details for Mi-8MT (Mi-17) *Hip-H, except where indicated*

PRINCIPAL DIMENSIONS:
Rotor diameter (main): 69 ft 10 ins (21.294 m)
Maximum length, rotors turning: 83 ft 1 ins (25.33 m)
Fuselage length: 59 ft 9 ins (18.219 m) without nose radar, 60 ft 7 ins (18.465 m) with radar
Width, with weapon outriggers: 24 ft 6 ins (7.466 m)
Maximum height: 18 ft 2 ins (5.534 m) over tail rotor, or 15 ft 7 ins (4.756 m) to above rotor head

CABIN:
Length: 17 ft 6 ins (5.34 m) excluding doors
Width: 7 ft 8 ins (2.34 m) maximum
Height: 5 ft 11 ins (1.8 m)

TAIL ROTOR:
Diameter: 12 ft 10 ins (3.908 m)

UNDERCARRIAGE:
Nose wheel tyre size: 595 × 185 mm
Main wheel tyre size: 865 × 280 mm
Wheel base: 14 ft 1 ins (4.281 m)
Wheel track: 14 ft 10 ins (4.51 m)

WEIGHTS:
Empty: 15,554-15,873 lb (7,055-7,200 kg)
Normal take-off weight: 24,471 lb (11,100 kg)
Maximum take-off: 28,660 lb (13,000 kg)
Maximum take-off, Mi-17MD: 29,762 lb (13,500 kg)
Payload: 11,023 lb (5,000 kg) or 9,921 lb (4,500 kg) for early examples internal, 8,818 lb (4,000 kg) external

PERFORMANCE (without outriggers and IR suppressors):
Maximum speed: 135 kts (155 mph) 250 km/h at 1,650 ft (500 m), normal take-off weight
Cruise speed: 119-130 kts (137-149 mph) 220-240 km/h, or 116-124 kts (134-143 mph) 215-230 km/h for Mi-171 at normal/maximum take-off weights respectively
OGE hovering ceiling: 5,775 ft (1,760 m), or 13,060 ft (3,980 m) for Mi-8MTV
Ceiling: 16,405 ft (5,000 m), 19,685 ft (6,000 m) for Mi-8MTV, 18,700 ft (5,700 m) for Mi-8MTV with de-icing operating, and 19,685 ft (6,000 m) for Mi-171 at normal take-off weight
Range with normal fuel: 313 naut miles (360 miles) 580 km
Maximum range: 594 naut miles (684 miles) 1,100 km, 624 naut miles (718 miles) 1,155 km for Mi-171, or 863 naut miles (994 miles) 1,600 km for Mi-17MD with 4 additional fuel tanks

versions) radios. Modern avionics proposed for Mi-17KF and Mi-8MTV-5, which see.
Self-protection systems: Some military helicopters have ASO-2V chaff/flare dispensers (4 cassettes under the tailboom or 6 on the rear fuselage sides, each cassette containing 32 PPI-26-1 flares). Provision for L-166V infra-red jammer (NATO *Hot Brick*) on top of the fuselage aft of the engine bay. See Engines.
Fixed guns: PKT flexibly-mounted 7.62-mm single-barrel machine-gun in the nose on some military versions. AKS-2A photo gun.
Number of weapon pylons: 6 BD3-57KRVM pylons on fuselage truss outriggers.
Expendable weapons and equipment: Armed military versions can typically have 4 × B-8V20A rocket launchers, each with 20 × 80-mm S-8 rockets. Other weapon options include up to 3,307 lb (1,500 kg) of bombs, KMGU-2 submunitions dispensers, incendiary tanks, and UPK-23 gun packs. Provision for a flexibly-mounted PKT machine-gun at the cabin rear emergency door and troops firing through the cabin windows. See Mi-17MD and Mi-8AMT-Sh under Aircraft variants for guided anti-armour and air-to-air weapons.

Aircraft variants:
Mi-18 (first use of this designation; see below) was the first prototype with TV3-117 engines. Mi-8 airframe combined with engines, transmissions and rotors of Mi-14 Haze. Appeared 1975.
Mi-8MT *Hip-H* became the standard version for the Russian armed forces. TV3-117MT turboshafts, as detailed.
Mi-8MD is a military VIP version; other 'Salons' include ***Mi-8MO***, ***MS***, ***MSD***, ***MSO*** and ***Mi-17S*** for export.
Mi-8MTA is a tactical reconnaissance version. Others include ***Mi-8MTF*** for photo-reconnaissance, and ***Mi-8MTS*** and ***MTT*** for radiation reconnaissance.
Mi-8MTB Bissektrisa of 1978 appearance is a rescue/medical version, using during the Afghanistan conflict. Civil/export derivative is Mi-17-1VA, which see. Other medevac versions are ***Mi-8MTN*** (1979) for space crews search and rescue, and ***Mi-8MTM***. Further ***Mi-8MTV-3G***, ***Mi-8MTV-M*** and ***Mi-8MTV-MPS*** are based on Mi-8MTV with high-altitude engines. Offered as ***Mi-17G*** for export.
Mi-8MTD is a SAR version (1979), followed by the ***Mi-8MN*** and ***Mi-8MA Arktika***, the latter equipped for Polar region operations.
Mi-8MTV *Hip-H* is the hot-and-high equivalent of Mi-8MT, but powered by TV3-117VM engines. Produced by Kazan in several subversions, including the civil ***Mi-8MTV-1***; military ***Mi-8MTV-2*** with military communication equipment and optional armoured flight deck, plus provision for fuselage-side weapon racks and a flexibly-mounted machine-gun at the nose; ***Mi-17-1V*** export equivalent of Mi-8MTV-1; ***Mi-17-1VA*** export medical version of the Mi-17-1V (flying ambulance with operating table, 5 medical personnel and 3 wounded); and ***Mi-8MTV-3*** with new electrical system using GT-40PCh8B brushless generators (former SGS-40PU generators caused interference with radios).
Mi-8MTV-5 is a projected final derivative of MTV for the Russian armed forces, similar to Mi-17MD but with new digital avionics and a 'glass' cockpit.
Mi-8MPS (PS for poiskovo-spasatelnyi, search and rescue) is intended mainly for SAR of spacecraft crews at sea and other similar operations. Based on Mi-8MTV-3, has wider side door, added fuselage hatches, extended PNKV-8PS flight/navigation system, YuR-40.1 radar and TAPAS search FLIR.
Mi-8AMT is similar to the Mi-8MTV-3, but manufactured at Ulan-Ude.
Mi-8AMT-Sh is an armed derivative of Mi-8AMT shown at Farnborough in September 1996. Incorporates a weapon system similar to the most recent version of Mi-24 *Hind*, with 9M114 Shturm (AT-6) and 9M120 Ataka (AT-9) ATGMs, as well as 9M39 Igla (SA-18) missiles in an air-to-air form. The helicopter usually carries 2 × 4-tube launchers for Shturm/Ataka missiles, 1 launcher with 2 or 4 Igla missiles, and a single B-8V20A unguided rocket pod. Raduga-Sh gyrostabilized optical sight (in the cruise position protected by a steel cover) and an antenna for the missile radio guidance system installed under the front fuselage (originally, the guidance antenna was installed in the nose). Mi-8AMT-Sh has also been equipped for self-protection, including plate armour in the sides and bottom of the fuselage,

↑ Mil Mi-8MTV-3 with weather radar and armour plates on the nose. Note also armour plates in the cockpit and searchlight near the front undercarriage leg *(Piotr Butowski)*

flare dispensers, and heat suppressors for the engine nozzles. Fuel tanks have polyurethane foam filling.
Mi-17 *Hip-H* is the export Mi-8MT.
Mi-17M is the export version built by Kazan for both civil and military use. TV3-117VM engines. Up to an 11,023 lb (5,000 kg) external load and wider port cabin door (1,250 mm instead of 830 mm). Single prototype shown at ILA in Berlin in 1992 (c/n 95448, *CCCP-95448*). In Paris in 1993 the same prototype (re-registered *RA-70937*) had reconfigured rear main doors (similar to Mi-26) and DISS Doppler antenna concealed in the tailboom. In Dubai in November 1993, this same helicopter featured a sliding cabin door (830 mm width) added to the starboard side.
Mi-17MD (D for desantnyi, air landing) is a derivative of Mi-17M to carry 36-40 troops. Reconfigured nose housing 8A-813Ts weather radar. Prototype (the same *RA-70937*) was shown at the June 1995 Paris Air Show.
Mi-17MD Night is again *RA-70937* with a further upgrade, shown for the first time at ILA in Berlin in May 1996. It has been adapted to night operations by installation of a gyrostabilized LLL TV and night vision goggles. Cockpit painted black. Rear ramp area has been further modified and replaced by a single flat ramp/platform. In September 1996, Mi-17MD Night appeared at Farnborough with armament fitted (only at the port side), comprising Malutka-2 anti-armour missiles and 4 Igla IR AAMs.
Mi-17KF Kittiwake is a version of Mi-17MD tendered to the Canadian Armed Forces for a SAR helicopter to replace CH-113. In Summer 1996, Kelowna Flightcraft of Canada received from Kazan a single Mi-17, for conversion to Kittiwake form by installation of modern Honeywell avionics that include EDZ-765 flight instrumentation, AA-300 radio altimeter, P-700 colour weather radar, Primus II communications and Canadian Marconi Doppler navigation. Prototype first flew in July 1997. Kelowna owns the design data for the avionics and provides modification kits that the customer or the participating companies can install. Kelowna was negotiating (in July 1998) the rights to have the spares facility and also the rights to service helicopters throughout the world.
Mi-17Z-2 (Z for zastavba) is an electronic intelligence version of Mi-17 prepared in the Czech Republic. 2 large drum antennae on outriggers each side of the fuselage.
Mi-18 (second use of the designation) covered 2 prototypes converted by Kazan from Mi-8MTs (c/n 93038 and 93114) in 1980 to Afghan conflict requirements. Fuselage lengthened by 39.3 ins (100 cm), and later given a retractable undercarriage and an additional starboard sliding door. Maximum speed 146 kts (168 mph) 270 km/h, and payload 11,023 lb (5,000 kg). Type has been resurrected as the Mi-173, which see.
Mi-171 is the export Mi-8AMT built at Ulan-Ude.
Mi-171B is a sub-version of Mi-171, in production.
Mi-172 is the export version of Mi-8MTV-3 (see Mi-8MTV) built at Kazan. Certified to the requirements of India and featuring Series 2 engines, upgraded avionics with GPS, DME, ILS, VOR, weather radar and more, has full de-icing, and air conditioning.
Mi-172A is a passenger version which obtained Russian State certification in 1997. A special VIP version has been developed for the President of Russia.
Mi-171TP and ***Mi-172TP*** (transportno-passazhiskiy, cargo-passenger) are derivatives of Mi-171 and Mi-172 respectively, certified to FAR Pt 29. Square windows. 24-28 airliner seats, or 7-11 in VIP form. Access to the cabin via lowered stairs at the port doors and at the rear (instead of a cargo ramp).
Mi-173 is a lengthened-fuselage version offered by JSC Mil Helicopters (former branch of the Mil design bureau) in Kazan. Very similar to Mi-18.
MK-30, see Daewoo of South Korea in the 1996-97 edition of *WA&SD*.
Mi-17P and other electronic warfare versions, see separate entry.

↑ **Mil Mi-8PPA EW helicopter, showing pack of 6 cruciform dipole antennae** *(Miroslav Gyurosi)*

Mil Mi-8 (Mi-13) and Mi-17 electronic warfare variants (NATO name *Hip-J* and *K*)

Role: Electronic countermeasures and electronic intelligence, based on *Hip-C* and *Hip-H*.
Sales: Mi-8SMV serves only with CIS armed forces (more than 50), while Mi-8PPAs are in Czech (2), Slovakian (1) and Syrian service. More than 30 Mi-8MT derivatives are in service with CIS armed forces, in Hungary (2 Mi-17PPs) and Syria (Mi-8MTP and MTU).
Mission equipment (Mi-8MT/Mi-17 derivatives): Jamming equipment with active phase scanning aerials in several configurations, mounted on the fuselage (large vertical panel each side) and tailboom. Digital signal processing.

Aircraft variants:
Mi-8SMV *Hip-J* is a radar jamming helicopter with Smalta-V system of 1971 appearance, based on Mi-8T. 2 box-shaped transmitting antennae on each side of the fuselage in place of the windows. Designed to jam SAM radar sites.
Mi-8PP of 1974 received Pole (field) jamming system, and is based on the Mi-8T.
Mi-8PPA *Hip-K* is a radar jamming version with Akatsiya (acacia) system. Pack of 6 cruciform dipole antennae on each side of the rear fuselage. Row of 6 heat-exchangers under the fuselage nose, with boxes for batteries ahead of the main undercarriage. Appeared early 1980s.
Mi-8MTD, Mi-8MTI (Mi-13), Mi-8MTP, Mi-8MTPB, Mi-8MTPI, Mi-8MTR-1 and ***-2, Mi-8MTSh-1/-2/-3, Mi-8MTPSh, Mi-8MTU, Mi-8MTYa*** and ***Mi-8MT-1S***, all *Hip-K*, are designations of EW versions of Mi-8MT *Hip-H* used by the Russian armed forces. The designations originate from the respective jamming systems (for example, Mi-8MTSh has the Shakhta system, Mi-8MTI the Ikebane and Mi-8MTPB the Bison).
Mi-17P is a designation stated in official Kazan material (Mi-17PI and PG are of same source). Equipped with izdelye 1, izdelye 2 and izdelye 3 jamming units. Izdelye 1, operating in F frequency (wavelength 7.5 through 10 cm), generates jamming signals in the sector covered by 30° azimuth and 12° elevation. Izdelye 2 operates in D frequency (15-30 cm) in the same sectors. Izdelye 3 operates in B frequency (60-100 cm), generating jamming signals over 120° azimuth and 30° elevation. Maximum 4 hours continuous operation. Mi-17P also has electronic intelligence equipment, able to detect F and D band radars in sector 180° × 30°.
Mi-17PI has 1 unit capable of jamming up to 8 sources simultaneously. It operates in D frequency (15-30 cm) and over a 30° azimuth and 11° elevation sector.
Mi-17PG operates in frequency ranges H and I (3-5 cm) and jams up to 8 sources over a sector 25° azimuth and 12° elevation. The principal characteristic of this unit is its capability of jamming not only the pulse type radars (as former types) but also continuous and quasi continuous radars.
Mi-17PP is the designation of Hungarian helicopters, externally similar to Mi-8MTPB.

↑ **Hungarian Mil Mi-17PP EW helicopter** *(Denis Hughes)*

Mil Mi-24, Mi-25 and Mi-35 (NATO name *Hind*)

First flight: 19 September 1969 (piloted by Herman Alfyorov).
Role: Helicopter gunship with assault capability, observation and spotting, reconnaissance, and NBC sampling.

Development

- 1967. Competition opened for a combat-transport helicopter, virtually a flying personnel carrier. Between Kamov Ka-25F and Mil V-24.
- 6 May 1968. Government order issued.
- November 1970. First flight of a production helicopter in Arsenyev
- 1973. Mi-24D with separated pilot and WSO cockpits appeared.
- 1974. Shturm-V anti-armour missile system introduced (Mi-24V).
- 29 March 1976. Mi-24D and Mi-24V officially commissioned by armed forces, although production of Mi-24V did not start until 1978 because of delays in weapon system development.
- 1978. Mi-24V appeared, with new weapon system and high-altitude engines.
- 1980-87. During Afghanistan conflict, Mi-24 introduced TV3-117VM high-altitude engines, heat suppression devices, flare launchers, IR jammers and new weapons.

↑ Hungarian Mil Mi-24D *Hind-Ds*, recently photographed at Vesprem *(Denis Hughes)*

Sales: Manufactured between 1970-89 at Arsenyev (for Soviet use), and since 1976 at Rostov-on-Don (mainly for export, although small quantities for Soviet use). Production tooling in Arsenyev has been replaced by Ka-50 tooling, while in Rostov-on-Don production continues in very small quantities for special orders (about 20 built during 1994-96). More than 2,500 have been produced in total, of which about 1,250 are currently in service with CIS armed forces, and about 600 were exported. Russia currently has nearly 900 helicopters, Ukraine 270, Belarus 60, and Azerbaijan, Kazakhstan and Uzbekistan have between 1 and 2 dozen each. Former WarPact countries (except Romania) received Mi-24Ds from 1978 and later Mi-24Vs, while former East Germany also received Mi-24Ps (East Germany received 51 Mi-24s, which were withdrawn from service after Germany united, 2 going to the USA for testing and others to Hungary and Poland). Czechoslovakia bought 61 Mi-24s, survivors now split as about 36 in the Czech Republic and about 19 in Slovakia. Poland currently has 29 Mi-24s plus the first few of 18 ex-German Mi-24Ds received and put into repair (first put into service with the 49th Combat Helicopter Regiment at Pruszcz Gdanski on 30 November 1996). Mi-24As, Mi-24Ds (designated Mi-25) and Mi-24Vs (designated Mi-35) were sold to Afghanistan, Algeria, Angola, Bulgaria (see below), Cambodia, Chad, Cuba, Ethiopia, India, Iran, Iraq, North Korea, Libya, Mozambique, Nicaragua, Peru, Sri Lanka, Syria, Vietnam, and both Yemens. A few Mi-24s taken in Chad by the French Army were delivered to the USA, while in December 1988 a Nicaraguan Mi-25 flew to Honduras and was later passed to the USA. A single Mi-24 is in the UK (originally flown from Afghanistan to Pakistan in 1988). According to some reports, Croatia is said to have received a number of used Mi-24s. Russian Ministry of Internal Affairs has contracted Rostvertol to convert a number of Mi-24s into unarmed helicopters for an internal security role. In 1995, the sale of 12 used Mi-24s to Bulgaria was agreed (joining 38 previously purchased Mi-24Ds and 6 Mi-24Vs). 8 helicopters were delivered from Russia to Peru in 1996.

Details *(generally for Mi-24V* Hind-E, *unless stated)*

Crew/passengers: 2 crew, as a weapon system operator (WSO) in the front lower cockpit and pilot to his rear. Room for a mechanic on a jump seat in the passage between the flight deck and cabin. 8 troops on 2 × 4-place benches along the sides of the aft cabin, with horizontally divided (upward/downward opening) doors on both sides, the lower sections forming steps for rapid troop deployment and airborne operations.
Cockpits: Tandem stepped cockpits, each having a bulletproof flat plate windscreen and rounded canopy. Armour fragmentation shield between the cockpits. Armoured seats. Dual controls.
Rotor system: 5-blade main rotor. Hydraulic dampers. Steel rotor head. De-icing. Mi-28's rotor system with 5-blade composite main rotor with elastomeric bearings and titanium head used on upgraded Mi-24M/Mi-35M/Mi-35D.
Tail rotor characteristics: 3-blade, on starboard side of tailfin (port side on Mi-24 and first Mi-24A helicopter). Adjustable blade angle-of-attack, between 7° 55' and –25°. De-icing standard. Mi-28's 4-blade 'scissors' tail rotor used on upgraded Mi-24M/Mi-35M/Mi-35D.
Wing/tail surfaces: Trapezoid anhedral wings, with ventral endplates carrying the outer missile pylons. Shortened wings on Mi-24M/Mi-35M/Mi-35D.
Flight control system: Mechanical.
Fuselage: All metal, semi-monocoque, with hermetic troop cabin connected to the cockpits.
Airframe materials: Steel, aluminium alloys, magnesium alloys and titanium.
Safety features: Armour protection (661 lb, 300 kg weight) for the cockpit, engine bays, etc.
Engines: Typically 2 × 2,225 shp (1,659 kW) Klimov/Isotov TV3-117VM high-altitude turboshafts, side-by-side above the cabin, with TV3-117s (same rating) in helicopters built up to about 1982, and TV3-117VMAs (same rating) in the last production series. 2,500 shp (1,864 kW) TV3-117VMA-SB3s proposed for Mi-24M/Mi-35M/Mi-35D upgrades. Dust filters standard since 1976. Infra-red suppression cool air mixers can be fitted to the exhaust outlets. 5-mm armour protection. APU.
Transmission: VR-28 3-stage main transmission gearbox, weight 1,830 lb (830 kg), ratio 62.5:1.
Fuel system: 5 bag tanks, Nos 1 and 2 located side-by-side inside the fuselage above the wings, vertical No 3 below them, and Nos 4 and 5 under the cabin floor. Total capacity is 2,130 litres. Provision for 2 or 4 × 500 litre underwing auxiliary fuel tanks. Early versions, up to Mi-24D, can carry 2 auxiliary tanks (total 1,700 litres) inside cabin (not with external fuel).
Electrical system: 36/115/208 volt, 400 Hz, AC supply via 3 generators. 27 volt DC supply.
Flight avionics/instrumentation: SAU-V24-1 automatic control system, including VUAP-1 autopilot plus autohover. US-450K speedometer, War-30MK climb meter, KI-13K compass, UKT-2 roll/pitch angle indicator, RV-5 altimeter, ARK-15M and ARK-U2 radio compasses, and DISS-15D Doppler nav radar. R-860 (or R-863) and Karat-M24 communication radios, SPU-8 intercom, and RI-65 voice warning device.
Weapon control system: Shturm-V anti-tank system with Raduga-Sh aiming/missile control system consisting of electro-optical sight under the starboard side of the fuselage nose and radio guidance antenna on the port side. Falanga-P anti-tank system with Raduga-F unit featuring smaller RG antenna on Mi-24D. ASP-17 gun sight. SRO-2 Khrom IFF transponder (NATO name *Odd Rods*). See also Mi-24M, Mi-35M and Mi-35D under Aircraft variants.
Self-protection systems: SPO-15 Beryoza radar warning receiver (SPO-10 Sirena on early versions). L-166V-1A Lipa infra-red countermeasures jammer (NATO name *Hot Brick*) aft of engine/APU compartment. ASO-2 chaff/flare dispensers, originally as 4 × 32 round cassettes under the tailboom, later as 3 cassettes on each side of the fuselage aft of the wings. See Engines and Mi-24M, Mi-35M and Mi-35D under Aircraft variants.
Fixed guns: 4-barrel 12.7 mm Yakushev/Borzov YakB-12.7 (9A624) machine-gun in a USPU-24 undernose turret (60° azimuth, 60° downward and 20° upward movement). USPU-24 and Aist sight make up the SPSV-24 gun armament system. (See Mi-35M under Aircraft variants.)
Ammunition: 1,470 rounds.
Number of weapon pylons: 2 under each wing, plus 1 beneath each wingtip endplate with dual launchers for ATGMs only (no wingtip endplates for Mi-24M, Mi-35M and Mi-35D).
Expendable weapons and equipment: 4 tube-launched 9M114 (AT-6 *Spiral*) anti-armour missiles of the Shturm-V system are suspended beneath the wingtip pylons, while a further 4 missiles can be carried on the 2 outer underwing pylons. Strela and Igla missiles or R-60 (AA-8 *Aphid*) AAMs can be carried for use against low-speed airborne targets. Unguided weapons carried on the 4 wing pylons include bombs, KMGU submunition dispensers, UPK-23-250 cannon packs, rocket packs, incendiary tanks, etc. Maximum weapons load is 2,646 lb (1,200 kg). Mi-24D and earlier versions are armed with 4 × 9M17P (AT-2 *Swatter*) anti-armour missiles of the Falanga-V anti-tank system. (See Mi-24M and Mi-35M under Aircraft variants.)

Aircraft variants:
V-24 or izdeliye 240 was the prototype.
Mi-24 *Hind-B* was the pre-series model. Conventional wide flight deck with side-by-side seating for the crew behind flat-plate glazing, TV3-117 engines, wings with no anhedral, and no wingtip ATGM pylons. K-4V weapons system of older Mi-4AV *Hound* helicopter, with 9M17M Falanga-M manually-controlled ATGMs fitted to fuselage sides.
Mi-24A (izdeliye 245) *Hind-A* was the first large-scale production version (240 built during 1970-74). Anhedral wings, and wingtip pylons added. Falanga-P semi-automatic ATGM system introduced.

↑ Impression of the Mil Mi-35D2 upgrade with Shkval in nose. Note Vega AAMs at wingtips

↑ Nose of Mil Mi-24PS with FLIR, searchlight and loudspeakers *(left)* and Mi-35M (Mi-24M) with mock-up of the gyrostabilized GOES-342 *(Piotr Butowski)*

Mi-24U (izdeliye 244) *Hind-C* became the training variant of Mi-24A.
Mi-24B (izdeliye 241) was similar to the Mi-24A, but with a 4-barrel YakB-12.7 machine-gun instead of the A-12.7. Small quantity production during 1971-72.
Mi-24D (izdeliye 246) *Hind-D* introduced a major fuselage redesign that characterized all *Hinds* thereafter. Front fuselage was completely reshaped, with separate tandem cockpits for the pilot and WSO. Production started in 1973 at Rostov-on-Don and some 350 were built.
Mi-24DU (izdeliye 249) *Hind-D* is the training version of Mi-24D, but with the nose machine-gun deleted. 1980 appearance.
Mi-24V (izdeliye 242) *Hind-E* is similar to Mi-24D, but introduced the Shturm-V ATGM system. During the 1980s TV3-117V high-altitude engines introduced. Became the most widespread version, with about 1,000 built between 1976 and 1986. Test derivatives with different weapon and search-aiming systems were ***Mi-24N*** and ***Mi-24F***.
Mi-24VP (izdeliye 258) *Hind-E* is similar to Mi-24V, but with a nose-mounted flexible twin-barrel 23-mm GSh-23 cannon instead of the YakB-12.7 machine-gun. Prototype 1985, with production in 1989. 25 built.
Mi-24P (izdeliye 243) *Hind-F* is similar to Mi-24V, but with a fixed twin-barrel 30-mm GSh-2-30 cannon on the starboard side of the front fuselage instead of the flexible YakB-12.7 machine-gun. 620 built between 1981 and 1989.
Mi-24R (izdeliye 2462) *Hind-G1* is a nuclear, biological and chemical (NBC) reconnaissance/sampling version. No weapon system. Ground material retrieving mechanisms under the modified wingtip endplates, for scientific analysis. 152 built between 1983 and 1989. In 1995, redesignated ***Mi-24RA*** after equipment update.
Mi-24K (izdeliye 201) *Hind-G2* is an artillery spotting and combat reconnaissance helicopter. No weapon system. Computer-controlled Ruta system with undernose Iris electro-optical sight and radio data link. Large AFA-100 photographic camera inside the cabin. 163 built between 1983 and 1989.
A-10 is the official designation of the first Mi-24 prototype when used to set a series of world records.
Mi-24M (first use of this designation; M for morskoi, sea, or izdeliye 247) of 1970 was a project for a multi-role ship-borne version.
Mi-24BMT (izdeliye 248, BMT for buksir minnykh tralov, mine-sweeper) of 1973 remained a prototype only.
Mi-24TS (tamozhennoi sluzhby, custom service) was a single prototype converted from an Mi-24P in 1993 against an order of Russia's customs service, later rebuilt into an Mi-24PS.
Mi-24PS (patrulno-spasatelnyi, patrol rescue) is a helicopter used to support police groups, including transport and air-landings. With GPS, coded communications, 7A813 weather radar in the nose, FPP-7 searchlights, and a powerful loudspeaker, the first prototype had been converted from the Mi-24TS but later returned to its original form as an Mi-24P and given back to the Army. Another and considerably different prototype of the Mi-24PS was shown at Zhukovsky in August 1995. No weapons, with shortened wings to carry only 2 fuel tanks. Nose radar replaced by a French-supplied ball FLIR. Cabin accommodates an assault group of 6, the air-landing equipment including brackets and supports for simultaneous rope landing by 4 persons. 265 lb (120 kg) LPG-4 winch and protective belts. The characteristics of Mi-24PS are similar to those of other Mi-24s. Having completed factory testing, it entered State acceptance trials.
Mi-24M is a proposed upgrade for helicopters of the Russian armed forces, known as ***Mi-24VM*** when applied to Mi-24V/VPs and ***Mi-24PM*** when applied to Mi-24Ps. Rostvertol signed the modernization contract with the Russian Ministry of Defence and the first Mi-24M flew in 1998. The aims of the upgrade are to improve performance and flight handling by reduction of weight and use of more powerful engines; introduce more modern weapons; enable night/adverse weather operations, both flight and weapon systems; and improve maintenance characteristics and extend the service life. Weight reduction will be achieved by reducing the span of the wings to 15 ft 8 ins (4.77 m) span, adopting a fixed undercarriage (saving 187-198 lb, 85-90 kg), and use of the Mi-28's main and tail rotors (new rotors are 661 lb, 300 kg lighter, producing 661 lbf, 2.94 kN more thrust). Improved TV3-117VMA engines with increased power during hot-and-high operations. Further plans provide for the use of new 2,500 shp (1,864 kW) TV3-117VMA-SB3 engines. New weapons will include 9M120 missiles of the Ataka-V system loaded to APU-8/4-U 8-tube missile clusters, and Igla-V AAMs. To enable night operations, the pilot will have ONV-2 night vision goggles and the search/aiming system will be replaced or supplemented by a new system with FLIR. The final arrangement of the helicopter's avionics/weapons control suite had not been specified by early 1998. The most advanced variant under consideration includes use of new PNK-24 flight/navigation system and Zenit/Krasnogorsk Tor-24 electro-optical search/aiming system. One of Rostvertol's offers mentions also a millimetre-wave phased-array antenna radar and terrain avoidance system. Most probably, however, more modest improvements are likely to be selected. Rostvertol, together with Uralsky Optiko-Mekhanichesky Zavod (UOMZ) of Yekaterinburg, offers to replace the existing Raduga optical aiming unit with GOES-342 ball-shaped gyrostabilized unit containing optical channel, FLIR and laser rangefinder, and fitted at the starboard side of the weapon operator's cockpit. The FLIR will be a joint development of UOMZ and Agema of Sweden, while the UOMZ laser rangefinder works at 1.52 mkm wavelength (instead of the current 1.06 mkm). A helicopter with a GOES-342 mock-up (Mi-35M) was shown for the first time during MAKS'97 in Zhukovsky. A competitive offer has come from Zenit/Krasnogorsk and comprises a podded Iris FLIR (under the wing) integrated with the current Raduga-Sh ATGM aiming system (with insignificant alterations of Raduga only). Self-defence is also being upgraded and Mi-24M will receive a Mak-UFM infra-red missile launch and approach sensor, Pastel radar warning receiver (in place of Beryoza), and the UV-26 flare launching system (instead of ASO-2). The upgrade programme is proposed in 3 stages, designated Mi-24M1, M2 and M3. The most advanced (M3) will offer an empty weight of 17,835 lb (8,090 kg), normal take-off weight of 23,810 lb (10,800 kg), MTOW of 25,353 lb (11,500 kg), maximum speed of 167 kts (193 mph) 310 km/h, cruise speed of 140 kts (162 mph) 260 km/h, climb rate of 2,460 ft (750 m) per minute, service ceiling of 18,700 ft (5,700 m), OGE hovering ceiling of 10,170 ft (3,100 m) ISA, and normal range of 270 naut miles (310 miles) 500 km. At the time of writing, the fully upgraded prototype was under construction, while separate items of equipment were under test on Mi-24 testbeds, including new rotors and the shortened wings.
Mi-25 is the export designation of the Mi-24D, mainly for Third World countries, but among WarPact countries the original Soviet designations were retained.
Mi-25U is an export version of the Mi-24DU trainer.
Mi-35 is the export designation of the Mi-24V.
Mi-35P is the export designation of the Mi-24P.
Mi-35M is the designation for the proposed export upgrade of existing Mi-24/Mi-25/Mi-35s, similar to Mi-24M. Prototype (not flying) was exhibited at the June 1995 Paris Air Show, featuring Mi-28 main and tail rotors, shortened wings, fixed undercarriage, and armed with the Ataka-V anti-tank guided missile system and 9M39 Igla-V AAMs. Prototype Mi-35M had a fire control system developed by Sextant Avionique and Thomson-TTD Optronic which integrates Chlio FLIR with TWM 1410 displays for night operations and VH-100 HUD. However, co-operation with France over the programme was reportedly ended recently and Russian systems are now proposed for export upgrades also. *3 basic upgrade stages proposed, as follows:*
Mi-35M1 brings older Mi-25s to the standard of the last production Mi-24VP, introducing a GSh-23L cannon with 450 rounds, Shturm-V anti-tank missile system (and with 9M120 Ataka AAMs) on APU-8/4-U clusters, L-166V infra-red active jammer, Beryoza RWR, and more. Older engines can be replaced

Details for Mi-24V *Hind-E*

PRINCIPAL DIMENSIONS:
Rotor diameter (main): 56 ft 9 ins (17.3 m)
Maximum length, rotors turning: 70 ft 1 ins (21.35 m)
Fuselage length: 57 ft 5 ins (17.51 m)
Maximum height: 17 ft 11 ins (5.47 m), or 14 ft 7 ins (4.44 m) to above rotor head
Wing span: 22 ft 5 ins (6.84 m)

CABIN:
Length: 9 ft 3 ins (2.825 m)
Width: 4 ft 9 ins (1.46 m)
Height: 3 ft 11 ins (1.2 m)

MAIN ROTOR:
Aerofoil section: NACA 230
Blade chord: 1 ft 11 ins (0.58 m) constant
Rotor disc: 2,530 sq ft (235.06 m^2)
Rpm: 240

TAIL ROTOR:
Diameter: 12 ft 10 ins (3.908 m)
Weight: 260 lb (118 kg)

WINGS:
Incidence: 19°
Anhedral: 12°

UNDERCARRIAGE:
Type: Retractable, with twin steerable nosewheels (see Mi-24M and Mi-35M under Aircraft variants)
Main wheel tyre size: 720 × 320 mm
Nose wheel tyre size: 480 × 200 mm
Wheel base: 14 ft 5 ins (4.39 m)
Wheel track: 9 ft 11 ins (3.03 m)

WEIGHTS:
Empty: 18,387 lb (8,340 kg)
Normal take-off: 24,692 lb (11,200 kg)
Maximum take-off: 25,353 lb (11,500 kg)
Maximum overload: 26,015 lb (11,800 kg)
Payload: 5,291 lb (2,400 kg), or 1,764-3,307 lb (800-1,500 kg) internal load

PERFORMANCE:
Maximum speed: 181 kts (208 mph) 335 km/h
Cruise speed: 151 kts (174 mph) 280 km/h
OGE hovering ceiling: 6,560 ft (2,000 m)
Service ceiling: 15,090 ft (4,600 m)
G limits: 1.8
Normal range: 243 naut miles (280 miles) 450 km
Ferry range: 607 naut miles (699 miles) 1,125 km
Duration: 2 hours 35 minutes

by TV3-117VMAs. New KAU-115 hydraulic actuators replace old KAU-110 units to improve manoeuvring. Additional oil coolers will be installed in the main gear lubricating system. New BD3-UV armament pylons have built-in mechanical hoisting devices. Optional GPS and other navigation upgrades. Many of the modifications have already been tested and are ready for implementation.
Mi-35M2 offers 9M39 Igla-V (SA-18 *Grouse*) based AAMs, GSh-23V cannon with water cooling (eliminating cooling pauses), and new radio equipment for communication with ground troops as well as new anti-tank missile radio guidance link.
Mi-35M3 will have the advanced flight/navigation and weapons control systems in one of several offered versions (see Mi-24M). As for Mi-24M, also Mak-UFM infra-red warning device, Pastel RWR, and UV-26 flare system replacing older systems.
Mi-35D is an export upgrade proposal using the Shkval/Vikhr armament system of the Ka-50, announced in the Summer of 1996 and marketed by Rostvertol. *3 modernization variants offered as follows:* Mi-35D is based on the Mi-35 (Mi-24V) and differs from the original version by Raduga-V optical aiming unit replacing Raduga-Sh. The Raduga-V has additional laser channel for Vikhr missile guidance. A container with French supplied Saturn FLIR may be carried under the wing. Up to 4 Vikhr missiles, the remaining armament being similar to the Mi-24. Performances are the same as the original version.
Mi-35D1 is a more advanced upgrade and like Mi-35M (Mi-24M) has shorter wings and new rotors. Developed from the Mi-35P (Mi-24P) with fixed side cannon, thereby there is space in the forward fuselage for installing Saturn FLIR. Due to the use of multi-tube clusters, 8 Vikhr missiles can be carried. Lighter weight airframe (take-off weight reduced from 24,692 lb, 11,200 kg to 23,589 lb, 10,700 kg) improves performances. Hovering ceiling increased from 7,218 ft (2,200 m) to 9,843 ft (3,000 m), practical ceiling from 14,764 ft (4,500 m) to 18,700 ft (5,700 m), climb rate from 1,890 ft (576 m) to 2,440 ft (744 m) per minute, and maximum range from 540 naut miles (621 miles) 1,000 km to 593 naut miles (683 miles) 1,100 km.
Mi-35D2 will have the same airframe as D1 but the armament will be modernized. Raduga-V will be replaced by Shkval TV-laser system, while Saturn FLIR will be placed in an underwing container. Due to Shkval and Saturn, Vikhr missiles will be capable of being launched from a distance of 6.5 naut miles by day and 2.7 naut miles by night (4.2 naut miles by day and 2.4 naut miles by night with Raduga-V). Other new armament offered for Mi-35D1 and D2 includes new G3-X Vega AAMs with combined semi-active laser and IR guidance. Performances similar to Mi-35D1. According to the manufacturer's information, the total combat efficiency factor of Mi-35D2 (number of targets hit in a group) will be 4.8 versus 3.4 for Mi-35D/D1 and 1.6 for Mi-35 (Mi-24V).
Mi-24 Sled (trace) is an ecological monitoring version used for surveying water levels and oil spills, with special equipment. Modified from a military helicopter by Polyot. First flight expected in 1998.

Mil Mi-26 and Mi-27 (NATO name *Halo*)

First flight: 14 December 1977 (piloted by Gurgen Karapetyan). First production Mi-26 on 25 October 1980.
Role: Very heavy transport, tanker, medevac and firefighting helicopter. Airborne command post version is the Mi-27.

Aims

- Range of 800 km with a 15,000 kg payload.
- Empty weight equal to half of the maximum take-off weight.

Development

- 1985. Initial operational capability.
- 28 September 1995. FAA certification for Mi-26TC.

Details *(principally Mi-26, except where stated)*

Sales: Produced by Rostvertol since 1980, and still in production. Some 276 built at the time of writing, mainly for Soviet/Russian military aviation (10 delivered in the past 5 years). Russian armed forces have about 141 Mi-26s and some 49 are in civil use, Belarus has 14 (65th Air Base in Kobryn), Ukraine 20 (344th Helicopter Regiment in Kalinov) plus 2 civil, and Kazakhstan 20. A further 4 are operational with the 126th Squadron of the Indian Air Force (first delivered in June 1986), 2 sold to Peru, 1 to Singapore, 2 to North Korea, and 1 to Cyprus. In November 1996 Samsung Aerospace of South Korea ordered a single Mi-26TC. Both Rostvertol and Mil have surplus Mi-26s in store. Mi-26Ts are currently undertaking United Nations humanitarian operations. Rostvertol's own Mi-26s have worked in Belgium, Switzerland, Malaysia, Somalia, Cambodia, Iran, South Korea and the UAE.

↑ Mil Mi-26TM flying crane, with the latest port-side operator's gondola *(Piotr Butowski)*

Crew/passengers: Pilot, co-pilot, navigator, engineer and assault systems operator, or 4 crew in the civil Mi-26T. Pressurized cockpit. Unpressurized cabin accommodates 68 fully-equipped paratroops (can jump from above 1,640 ft, 500 m altitude at speeds up to 159 kts, 183 mph, 295 km/h), or 82 troops. Medevac layout, see Aircraft variants.
Freight, internal: Alternative to passengers can be up to 44,092 lb (20,000 kg) of containers, pallets, weapons or vehicles.
Cabin access: Rear loading ramp, plus doors on the port side of the fuselage.
Loading facilities: Roller tracks and 2 LG-1500 electric winches inside the cabin. 11,023 lb (5,000 kg) capacity hoist, with second optional.
Rotor system: 8-blade main rotor, with metal/composites blades (glassfibre reinforced plastics/honeycomb, with steel tube spar and titanium abrasion strip; ground tabs). Flapping and drag hinges. Dampers (hydraulic) and droop stops (mechanical). Titanium rotor head. Electric de-icing.
Tail rotor characteristics: 5-blade, glassfibre. Titanium rotor head. Electric de-icing.
Flight control system: Hydraulic. Fly-by-wire system has been under development.
Airframe materials: Includes aluminium-lithium alloys.
Engines: 2 Ivchenko PROGRESS/Zaporozhye D-136 turboshafts side-by-side above the cabin. Dust filters standard, and infra-red suppression cool air mixers optional for military helicopters. TA-8V APU.
Engine rating: Each 11,400 eshp (8,501 ekW) at take-off.
Transmission: VR-26 main gearbox, weight 8,025 lb (3,640 kg), with ratio 62.5:1. Rating 22,000 eshp (16,405 ekW).
Fuel system: 20,194 lb (9,160 kg) of fuel in 10 main tanks located under the cabin floor (6) and above the cabin (4), plus 26,455 lb (12,000 kg) of auxiliary fuel in 4 tanks inside the cabin for ferry flights.
Electrical system: 28 volt DC supply.
Hydraulic system: Dual, each 3,002 psi.
Radar: Optional 7A813 Groza weather radar in the nose radome.
Flight avionics/instrumentation: PKV-26-1 flight control system, with autohover. DISS Doppler navigation. Transponder. Optional GPS and ILS/VOR. Military variants have coded radio communication equipment. Closed circuit TV provided to monitor external payloads.
Self-protection systems: Provision for armour plating to protect the flight deck, fuel tanks, engines and main gearbox. Chaff/flare dispensers on the fuselage sides. Infra-red jammer.
Fixed guns: Provision for flexible mounting of troop machine-guns (7.62-mm) in the blisters of the cargo compartment.

Aircraft variants (in order of appearance):
Mi-26 (izdeliye 90) is the basic military transport/assault helicopter, as detailed.
Mi-26T (izdeliye 209) is the civil transport helicopter of 1983 appearance. Assault equipment, armour, flare dispensers, IR jammer and military communications systems removed. Some

Details for Mi-26

PRINCIPAL DIMENSIONS:
Rotor diameter (main): 105 ft (32 m)
Maximum length, rotors turning: 131 ft 4 ins (40.025 m)
Airframe length: 110 ft 8 ins (33.727 m)
Width, blades folded: 26 ft 9 ins (8.15 m)
Maximum height: 26 ft 9 ins (8.145 m) to above rotor head

CABIN:
Length: 39 ft 8 ins (12.1 m) excluding ramp, or 49 ft 3 ins (15 m) including ramp
Width: 10 ft 8 ins (3.25 m)
Height: 9 ft 7 ins to 10 ft 5 ins (2.91 to 3.17 m)
Volume: 4,273 cu ft (121 m^3)

MAIN ROTOR:
Aerofoil section: TsAGI
Blade length: 45 ft 11 ins (14 m)
Blade chord: 2 ft 7.5 ins (0.8 m)
Blade weight: 826 lb (375 kg)
Rotor disc: 8,656.9 sq ft (804.25 m^2)
Rpm: 132.7

TAIL ROTOR:
Diameter: 25 ft (7.61 m)
Rpm: 552

UNDERCARRIAGE:
Type: Fixed, with steerable nosewheels. Twin wheels on each unit. Main legs of hydraulically-adjustable length to make loading easier. Protective support under tailboom
Main wheel tyre size: 1,120 × 450 mm
Wheel base: 29 ft 4 ins (8.95 m)
Wheel track: 23 ft 6 ins (7.17 m)

WEIGHTS:
Empty: 62,325 lb (28,270 kg)
Normal take-off: 109,349 lb (49,600 kg)
Maximum take-off: 123,459 lb (56,000 kg)
Payload: 33,069 lb (15,000 kg) normal, 44,092 lb (20,000 kg) maximum internal, external or mix

PERFORMANCE:
Maximum speed: 159 kts (183 mph) 295 km/h
Cruise speed: 138 kts (158 mph) 255 km/h, at 1,640 ft (500 m)
IGE hovering ceiling: 3,280 ft (1,000 m), with 11,245 lb (5,100 kg) payload, ISA
OGE hovering ceiling: 5,900 ft (1,800 m), at normal take-off weight, ISA
Service ceiling: 15,090 ft (4,600 m) at normal take-off weight, 11,810 ft (3,600 m) at MTOW
Range with full fuel: 362 naut miles (416 miles) 670 km, with 30 minutes reserve (also quoted by Rostvertol as 800 km with 5% reserve)
Range with full payload: 254 naut miles (292 miles) 470 km
Ferry range: 712 naut miles (820 miles) 1,320 km, with 4 auxiliary tanks, sea level

civil communication and navigation systems added.
Mi-26/Mi-26T medevac helicopter has 4 sub-versions, depending on equipment installed in the cabin: most advanced has a surgical module plus 22 litters; when only a small first-aid room is installed, 47 litters plus 8 attendants can be accommodated; 61 litters plus 3 attendants in the simple evacuation version; or 3 modules (surgical, rehabilitation and laboratory) in field hospital version working on the ground.
Mi-26A was an upgraded military version of 1985 appearance, successfully tested but not ordered by Russian armed forces. NPK-26-1 flight/navigation system, 1A813 radar, and GS-1 gyrostabilized platform with TV and FLIR. Glassfibre rotor blades. UV-26 flare dispensers, Mak IR missile launch sensor, and IR jammer.
Mi-26K (kran, crane) was a projected flying crane version of the 1980s, with a 'thin' fuselage similar to previous Mi-10K.
Mi-26S was a version prepared during the Chernobyl nuclear power station accident in 1986 for spraying de-activation liquid.
Mi-26TZ (toplivozapravshchik, fuel tanker) delivers over 14,040 litres of fuel and 1,040 litres of lubricants to 4 ground-based aircraft or 10 tanks, vehicles, etc, to inaccessible areas. In service since 1988.
Mi-26TM (M for montazhnyi, instalment) is a flying-crane version prepared by Rostvertol, with a glazed gondola for the pilot/sling load operator at the port front cabin door (formerly under the front fuselage, aft of the nosewheels, or a larger gondola under the upswept tail). Shown in 1993 at Paris.
Mi-26TP (P for pozharnyi, firefighting) has 3 sub-versions: with 4 tanks fitted inside the cabin and a single outflow in the bottom, allowing 15,000 litres to be released within 35-45 seconds; with soft externally suspended 17,000 litre tank, able to be emptied in 5 seconds; or 2 EP-8000 rigid externally suspended tanks, with a total of 15,000 litres, emptied in 50 seconds.
Mi-26PP was an ECM version of 1986 appearance to suppress early warning radars.
Mi-27 was produced as an airborne command post, intended to replace the Mi-6VKP/Mi-22. Built in 1988, and details first released in 1990 by the US Department of Defense. 2 prototypes.
Mi-26NEF-M was a prototype ASW version of 1990, with sonar carried on an external sling.
Mi-26P (pogranichnyi) was produced as a border-guard version with 1A813 radar and extended communications. Tested since 1992.
Mi-26TC (C for certified, or izdeliye 219) of 1995 appearance is similar to Mi-26T but adapted for international certification.
Mi-26TK is another flying-crane version, built by Mil in Moscow in 1997.
Mi-26TM1 (modernized, 1st) is offered by Rostvertol and contains some items formerly developed for Mi-26A (which see) and now introduced to the standard Mi-26T. These include integrated night/adverse weather flight/navigation system with millimetre-wave phased-array radar, terrain avoidance system, pilot's night vision system, GPS receiver, Doppler navigation radar and more.
Mi-26M is a projected upgraded basic version with 14,000 eshp (10,440 kW) turboshafts (early project had Ukrainian Ivchenko PROGRESS/Zaporozhye D-127 derivatives of the D-27 propfan, but now Aviadvigatel/Perm engines are planned), all-composite main rotor blades, and self-lubricating rotor heads. New generation flight/navigation system. Maximum payload raised to 48,500 lb (22,000 kg), OGE hovering ceiling 9,185 ft (2,800 m), and service ceiling 19,350 ft (5,900 m).
Mi-26MP is a projected 70 passenger version.
Mi-26MS is a projected flying hospital version, with surgical, pre-operating, ambulance and other compartments in the cabin.
Mi-26 Salon-1 is an offered VIP version with extended communications.

Mil Mi-28 (NATO name *Havoc*)

First flight: 10 November 1982 for first hovering flight (experimental helicopter *012*, crewed by Gurgen Karapetyan and V. Tsygankov). First circle flight 19 December 1982 with the same crew.
Role: Attack. Can operate for 15 days away from base.

Development

- 16 December 1976. Governmental order issued for a new generation combat helicopter.
- May-June 1981. Initial design accepted by State commission.
- 14 December 1987. Government decision to develop a night version (Mi-28N).
- 7 January 1988. First hovering flight of the Mi-28A prototype (*032*). First circle flight on 19 January.
- Autumn 1990. Agreement signed regarding the delivery of Mi-28s to Iraq and subsequent licensed manufacturing in Iraq under the designation Mi-28L. Programme later abandoned.

↑ **Mil Mi-28N with Almaz-28 radar above the rotor, and showing various nose sensors (*top to bottom:* radio-command missile guidance antenna, 2 small cones of RWR, Stolb pilot's FLIR, and Tor in a rotating turret** *(Alexei Mikheyev)*

- Early 1992. Full-scale mock-up of Mi-28N accepted.
- 6 May 1993. Loop performed by *012*, piloted by G. Karapetyan, with a roll a few days later.
- August 1995. Mi-28N prototype (*014*) under construction shown publicly at Zhukovsky.
- October 1995. Mi-28A (*042*) tested in Sweden by Swedish pilots.
- August 1996. Completed Mi-28N left Mil works.
- 14 November 1996. First hovering flight of Mi-28N, still with old VR-28 gearbox, piloted by Vladimir Yudin and S. Nikulin.
- 26 April 1997. First circle flight of Mi-28N, with new VR-29 gearbox. Same crew.

Details *(based generally on Mi-28A, unless stated)*

Sales: 2 experimental Mi-28 helicopters (*012* and *022*), 2 Mi-28As (*032* and *042*) and 1 Mi-28N prototype (*014*) built by Moscow Mil design bureau works. Rostvertol at Rostov-on-Don prepared for series production (see Aircraft variants). Foreign interest (see Development).
Crew/passengers: 2 crew in tandem, with the weapon system operator/navigator forward and the pilot at the rear (see Safety features for seat type and features) . The WSO enters the cockpit via a port side rearward opening jettisonable door, while the pilot uses a similar starboard door. Cockpit is armoured with titanium and ceramic plates, and bullet resistant flat plate glazing; wipers are installed on the front panels. Cockpit can withstand direct hits from 7.62-mm and 12.7-mm machine-gun bullets, or fragments from 20-mm cannon shells. Armour fragmentation shield between the cockpits. A small fuselage hatch can be used, if necessary, for loading cargo or 2 or 3 passengers for ferrying, or for removing downed pilots from a battle area. See Safety features.
Rotor system: 5-blade high-lift main rotor, with elastomeric bearings (2° freedom), dampers (hydraulic) and droop stops (mechanical). Each blade is entirely composites constructed, with a glassfibre spar and honeycomb core, the leading edge protected by titanium. Full-span trailing-edge tab. Titanium rotor head. 5° forward shaft tilt. Blades electrically de-iced. Main rotor blades and wings are detached for transportation by An-22 or Il-76 (requiring 1.5 hours to reassemble), but only the rotor is removed with the An-124 (requiring 30 minutes to reassemble). New rotor with swept blade tips for Mi-28N (currently, at the time of writing, being tested on an Mi-24 testbed helicopter).
Tail rotor characteristics: 4-blade rotor, comprising 2 separate 2-blade rotors (glassfibre) set in 'scissors' configuration, with 45° between the closest intersection. Elastomeric bearings. Electrically de-iced. 3-blade rotor on the first Mi-28s.
Wing/tail surfaces: Anhedral wing (of light alloy except for composites leading/trailing edges) on each side of the mid-fuselage, each with 2 stores pylons and a streamlined container housing electronic sensors and IR flare dispensers. 2-position port-side horizontal stabilizer at the top of the fin. Manually-operated weapon winching system built into the wings.
Flight control system: Mechanical, with hydraulic actuators. Pilot flight controls are arranged for maximum ease, on the pitch-throttle lever, stick and port-side panel.

Details for Mi-28A, *with Mi-28N in italics*

PRINCIPAL DIMENSIONS:
Rotor diameter (main): 56 ft 5 ins (17.2 m)
Maximum length, rotors turning: 69 ft 4 ins (21.133 m)
Fuselage length: 55 ft 10 ins (17.01 m)
Fuselage width: *10 ft 3 ins (3.12 m) at engine nacelles*
Wing span: *19 ft 4 ins (5.89 m)*
Width with APU-8-4U clusters: 19 ft 1 ins (5.824 m)
Maximum height: 15 ft 5 ins (4.7 m), or 12 ft 7 ins (3.823 m) to above rotor head, *11 ft 1.5 ins (3.395 m) without radar*

MAIN ROTOR:
Blade chord: 2 ft 2.5 ins (0.67 m)
Rotor disc: 2,500 sq ft (232.3 m^2)
Rpm: 242

TAIL ROTOR:
Diameter: 12 ft 7 ins (3.84 m)

UNDERCARRIAGE:
Type: Fixed, with castoring tailwheel. Single wheels, with low pressure tyres
Main wheel tyre size: 720 × 320 mm
Tail wheel tyre size: 480 × 200 mm
Wheel base: 36 ft 1 ins (11 m)
Wheel track: 7 ft 6 ins (2.29 m)

WEIGHTS:
Empty: 17,846 lb (8,095 kg)
Normal take-off: 22,928 lb (10,400 kg), *23,589 lb (10,700 kg)*
Maximum take-off: 25,353 lb (11,500 kg), *26,676 lb (12,100 kg)*
Maximum overload: 25,706 lb (11,660 kg)
Useful load: 5,180 lb (2,350 kg)

PERFORMANCE:
Maximum speed: 162 kts (186 mph) 300 km/h, *173 kts (199 mph) 320 km/h**
Cruise speed: 143 kts (165 mph) 265 km/h, *146 kts (168 mph) 270 km/h*
Rearward/sideways speed: 54 kts (62 mph) 100 km/h
Maximum climb rate: 2,677 ft (816 m) per minute, sea level
OGE hovering ceiling: 11,810 ft (3,600 m), *the same**
Service ceiling: 19,030 ft (5,800 m), *the same*
Hover turn rate: 45° per second
G limits: +2.8, -0.5; *+2.6, -0.5*
Normal range: 248 naut miles (286 miles) 460 km, *235-243 naut miles (270-279 miles) 435-450 km*
Combat radius: 108 naut miles (124 miles) 200 km, no auxiliary fuel, 10 minutes at target, 5% reserve
Ferry range: 599 naut miles (690 miles) 1,110 km with auxiliary fuel, at 25,706 lb (11,660 kg) weight, 5% reserve, *534 naut miles (615 miles) 990 km*
Duration: 2 hours
**Higher performance for Mi-28N (including at higher weights) is because of swept rotor blade tips*

Airframe materials: Light alloy, except for composites wing and tail unit leading/trailing edges, and a small number of non-structural components including the fuselage access door. Titanium and ceramic plate armour for the cockpit, and titanium protecting other vital areas.
Safety features: Armour protection (772 lb, 350 kg total weight) for the cockpit, engine bays, etc. Undercarriage has strong energy-absorbing shock absorbers to enable survivable landings at vertical speed equal to 39 ft (12 m) per second. Zvezda/Tomilino Pamir-K crew seats with belts that tighten automatically at high g loading. If a failure occurs at altitude, allowing crew escape by parachute, the cockpit doors are jettisoned, the wings are also jettisoned together with their loads, and a door sill sleeve is air-inflated to protect the crew from protruding structures and help them clear the helicopter.
Engines: 2 Klimov/St Petersburg TV3-117VMA turboshafts (each 2,200 shp, 1,641 kW) for Mi-28A and first 2 Mi-28Ns. Following helicopters have TV3-117VMA-SB3 engines, each 2,500 shp (1,864 kW). The first 2 prototypes have TV3-117VMs, each 1,950 shp (1,454 kW). IR suppression cool air mixers on the exhaust outlets. Air intake dust filters are standard. Engines are set apart and low down in order to reduce the profile and to help survivability of the other engine should one be hit. AI-9V APU between the engines at the tailboom root; can be used to power the electric, hydraulic and pneumatic systems for autonomous operations away from base.
Engine rating: See Engines.
Transmission: VR-28 3-stage main transmission gearbox for Mi-28A, and new VR-29 (based on the Mi-26's gearbox) of higher torque for Mi-28N.
Fuel system: Standard internal capacity of 2,948 lb (1,337 kg) in self-sealing polyurethane foam filled tanks, with self-tightening latex protectors. Optional 4 underwing auxiliary tanks, raising total capacity to 6,876 lb (3,119 kg).
Electrical system: All Mi-28 systems are duplicated. 200 volt/400 Hz AC supply via 2 generators attached to the main gearbox; by this system (rather than engine-driven), electrical power is not interrupted should both engines fail and the helicopter rely on autorotation. 26 volt DC supply. See Engines.
Hydraulic system: Duplicated, at 2,204 psi.
Flight avionics/instrumentation: Mi-28A has PrPNK-28 weapon/flight/navigation control system (PrPNK means pritselno-pilotazhno-navigatsionnyi kompleks). KOPS (meaning kombinirovannaya obzorno-pritselnaya sistema) precision electro-optical unit to identify, acquire and track targets at long range and establish the optimum positioning for rockets or missile launch via the airborne digital computer, is installed on a gyrostabilized platform at the nose and has 2 optical channels (wide and narrow) and a very narrow optical TV channel. The axis of observation is adjustable in azimuth within ±110°, and vertically from 13° elevation through to 40° downward. Laser rangefinder is combined with KOPS. Operator can use a helmet-mounted target designator. Conventional cockpit instrumentation.

Mi-28N is equipped with the IKBO (integrirovannyi kompleks bortovogo oborudovaniya) integrated avionics suite, integrating the mast-mounted 360° scan and 5.4 naut mile (6.2 mile) 10 km range twin antennae (millimetre and decametre wavelength) Almaz-28 radar designed by NPO Almaz (most probably, the Phazotron Arbalet radar will be used on production helicopters), operator's Zenit/Krasnogorsk Tor search-aiming unit with optical/TV/FLIR channels (each wide and narrow), laser rangefinder, Geofizika/Moscow Stolb pilot's FLIR, operator's helmet-mounted target designator, pilot's night vision goggles, radio-command missile guidance link, navigation subsystems (inertial and satellite), communications, and data presentation subsystem with colour MFDs. IKBO system allows night and bad weather observation, navigation and fire control. Mi-28N can fly nap-of-the-earth (NOE) missions at 15-50 ft (5-15 m) altitude in automated mode. On-board fault monitoring system.
Self-protection systems: Pastel RWR, Mak infra-red missile launch and approach sensor, Otklik laser warning receiver, and UV-26 flare/chaff dispensers. Later, all will be joined by an electronic active jammer in the Vitebsk system.
Fixed guns: Single-barrel 30-mm 2A42 cannon is mounted in the NPPU-28 undernose turret and can be moved within the same azimuth/elevation/downward range as the search/aiming unit, in synchronization. Weight of the turret with ammunition is 1,366 lb (620 kg).
Ammunition: 250 rounds in 2 boxes on the cannon sides and moving with the cannon to delete the need for flexible feed chutes. Standard land force ammunition.
Number of weapon pylons: 4 under the wings.
Expendable weapons and equipment: Up to 4,409 lb (2,000 kg). Standard anti-tank armament comprises 16 × 9M114 (AT-6 *Spiral*) missiles of the Shturm-V system or improved 9M120 (AT-9) ATGMs of the Ataka-V system (including 9M120D with a range increased to 3.8 naut miles, 4.3 miles, 7 km). Other weapons include S-8 (80-mm) and S-13 (122-mm) rocket packs, incendiary tanks, KMGU submunition dispensers, minelaying containers, UPK-23, GSh-23 and GUV cannon/gun packs, etc. 9M39 Igla-V (SA-18 *Grouse*) tube-launched AAMs for use against slow-flying aircraft and helicopters. See weapons diagram.

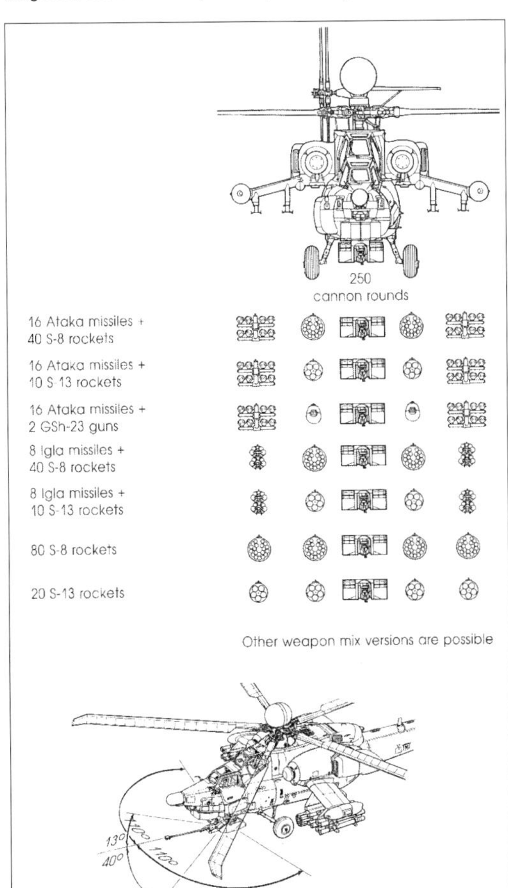

↑ **Mil Mi-28N weapon choices (other mixes are possible), plus chin turret travel diagram *(bottom)*** *(courtesy Mil)*

Aircraft variants:
Mi-28 (izdeliye 280) *Havoc* applies to the original experimental helicopter version. 2 built (*012* and *022*).
Mi-28A (izdeliye 286) is the fully-equipped production day version. 2 built (*032* and *042*). State acceptance trials were terminated in 1993 and Mil's efforts thereafter concentrated on the Mi-28N.
Mi-28N (izdeliye 294) is the all-weather day and night version with IKBO avionics and mast-mounted radar. Full-scale mock-up accepted in 1992. First prototype (*014*) flew on 26 April 1997. To be the principal production version.
Mi-40 assault helicopter is projected on the basis of the Mi-28N. See separate entry.
Mi-58 passenger/cargo helicopter is expected to use the Mi-28's rotors and transmission. See separate entry.

Mil Mi-34 (NATO name *Hermit*)

First flight: 17 November 1986 for first hovering flight (piloted by Boris Savinov). First full circle flight on 26 December 1986.
Certification: May 1995 for Mi-34C by the Russian Interstate Aviation Committee Registry, to FAR 27 requirements.
Role: Light training and sport helicopter, suited also to transport, police, ambulance and other work. Aerobatic version available, capable of manoeuvres including the loop.

Development

▪ December 1980. Development started as a training helicopter for DOSAAF paramilitary organization.
▪ 4 November 1993. First flight of a production helicopter.
▪ September 1994. A police variant, the Mi-34P, began operations with the Moscow City Police under the auspices of the Russian Ministry of Internal Affairs.

Details

Sales: In production since 1993 at Arsenyev. Production was expected to be 150 per year, but only 18 built at the time of Mil's reply (3 at Mil works and 15 at Arsenyev). Basic price at the time of writing about US$350,000. Over 60 orders reported. The first 3 delivered to the Moscow Mayor's office and used for police road traffic control work (Mi-34P). 3 delivered to Bashtransgas company in Bashkortostan, to patrol gas pipelines. Shown at the Sao Paulo Air Show against Brazil's requirement for a military trainer. Mi-34VAZ is a Rostvertol variant.

↑ **Mil Mi-34P used by Moscow's police** *(Piotr Butowski)*

Crew/passengers: Pilot and 3 passengers, with other layouts for training, cargo carrying and EMS hospital (litter plus attendant).
Optional equipment: Dual controls.
Cabin access: Forward hinged door each side of the fuselage, 1 ft 10 ins to 2 ft 4 ins (0.55 to 0.7 m) width, and 3 ft 9 ins (1.15 m) height.
Rotor system: 4-blade composites rotor, with only flapping and cyclic pitch hinges, connected to the rotor head via flexing steel straps. De-icing standard.
Tail rotor characteristics: 2-blade, composites. De-icing standard.
Tail surfaces: Starboard tail rotor and port dorsal/ventral fixed fin with tailskid, plus a constant-chord horizontal stabilizer.
Flight control system: Mechanical for Mi-34 and its derivatives, and hydraulic for Mi-34 VAZ.

Details for Mi-34C, *with Mi-34VAZ in italics*

PRINCIPAL DIMENSIONS:
Rotor diameter (main): 32 ft 10 ins (10.008 m), *37 ft 5 ins (11.4 m)*
Maximum length, rotors turning: 37 ft 5.5 ins (11.414 m)
Fuselage length: 28 ft 7 ins (8.712 m), *31 ft 2 ins (9.5 m)*
Fuselage width, maximum: 4 ft 8 ins (1.42 m), 4 ft 9 ins (1.45 m)
Maximum height: 9 ft (2.75 m), *10 ft (3.05 m) to above rotor head*

CABIN:
Length: 7 ft 10 ins (2.4 m)
Width: 5 ft 3 ins (1.6 m)
Height: 4 ft 3 ins (1.3 m)

MAIN ROTOR:
Blade chord: 9 ins (0.22 m)
Rotor disc: 845 sq ft (78.5 m^2)

TAIL ROTOR:
Diameter: 4 ft 10 ins (1.48 m), *4 ft 11 ins (1.5 m)*

UNDERCARRIAGE:
Type: Fixed skids. Trainer variant has 3-wheel gear
Skid track: 7 ft 3.5 ins (2.22 m), *7 ft 10 ins (2.4 m)*

WEIGHTS:
Empty: 2,094 lb (950 kg)
Normal take-off: 2,822 lb (1,280 kg), or 2,425 lb (1,100 kg) for aerobatics
Maximum take-off: 3,197 lb (1,450 kg), *4,321 lb (1,960 kg)*
Payload: See Performance. Can have sling loads

PERFORMANCE:
Maximum speed: 121 kts (140 mph) 225 km/h, *108-119 kts (124-137 mph) 200-220 km/h*
Cruise speed: 97 kts (112 mph) 180 km/h, *the same*
Time to 3,280 ft (1,000 m): 3 minutes 6 seconds
OGE hovering ceiling: 3,280 ft (1,000 m), *5,250 ft (1,600 m) at MTOW, ISA, or 2,625 ft (800 m) at ISA + 25° C*
Service ceiling: 16,400 ft (5,000 m), *the same*
G limits: +3
Range: 200 naut miles (230 miles) 371 km with a 564 lb (256 kg) payload, maximum fuel and cruise speed at 1,640 ft (500 m) altitude, *324 naut miles (373 miles) 600 km with a 705 lb (320 kg) payload and 30 minutes reserve, or 43 naut miles (50 miles) 80 km with a 1,213 lb (550 kg) payload and 30 minutes reserve*
Duration: 2 hours 19 minutes with maximum fuel and cruise speed at 1,640 ft (500 m), *5 to 5 hours 30 minutes with maximum standard fuel, 705 lb (320 kg) payload, with 30 minutes reserve*
Operating temperature range: -35° C to +45° C

Fuselage: Mi-34 has a more rounded appearance than Mi-34VAZ, the latter featuring reduced lower nose glazing and a more sharply swept windshield.
Airframe materials: Light alloy.
Engines: Mi-34 has a 325 hp (242 kW) OKBM/Voronezh M-14V26 9-cylinder radial piston engine (68 litres per hour fuel consumption in cruise flight at 1,640 ft, 500 m). Certified M-14V26V of same rating for Mi-34C. 2 new uprated derivatives of M-14V26 have been under development for Mi-34, the first of 375 hp (280 kW). See Aircraft variants.
Fuel system: 176 litres (291 lb, 132 kg) for Mi-34C. 245 litres for Mi-34VAZ. Optional similar capacity auxiliary fuel. Permits inverted flight.
Electrical system: Primary DC power supplied by 27 volt generator installed at the engine shaft. Secondary AC power is 36/115 volt, 400 Hz.
Flight avionics/instrumentation: Conventional instruments, including ARK-22 radio compass and A-037 radio altimeter, according to VFR. Mi-34VAZ to have a navigation system suited to day/night and poor weather flying.

Aircraft variants:
Mi-34 (izdeliye 300) with M-14V26 engine is an early version. MTOW 2,976 lb (1,350 kg).
Mi-34A (or ***Mi-134***) was conceived to have an Allison 250-C20R turboshaft engine, rated at 450 shp (336 kW) at take-off. MTOW 3,197 lb (1,450 kg). 340 litres of fuel. Maximum range 281 naut miles (323 miles) 520 km. Not flown at time of writing. Reports suggest work has stopped.
Mi-34C (certified) is the current production version to FAR Pt 27. Originally, Arsenyev-built Mi-34 airframes were converted into Mi-34Cs by Mil in Moscow but now fully completed at Arsenyev. As detailed.
Mi-34L is a projected version with a Textron Lycoming engine.
Mi-34P (patrulnyi, patrol) is a police version of Mi-34C. Equipped with loudspeakers and Elbit FLIR for night observation. See Development and Sales.
Mi-34VAZ (designated ***Mi-34M*** by the military) is being marketed by Rostvertol, featuring twin VAZ modified motorcar engines as VAZ-430 rotary piston engines (Wankel type), each of 230 hp (171.5 kW). Engine is capable of starting without pre-heating at -25° C and of using different fuels (150 lb, 68 kg per hour fuel consumption). First flight scheduled for 1998.
Mi-34M1 and ***Mi-34M2*** are projected versions with twin turbine engines of Russian or foreign type. Take-off weight 5,291-5,511 lb (2,400-2,500 kg); payload 1,984 lb (900 kg) or 6 passengers.

Mil Mi-38

See Euromil under Multi-national.

Mil Mi-40

First flight: Project only. Full scale wooden mock-up built.
Role: Assault helicopter.

Aims

- 'Flying armoured personnel carrier', based on the Mi-28N but with an armoured cabin for 8 troops added.
- High combat survivability due to duplicated systems, critical components masked by non-critical parts, low IR visibility, self-defence system, and 360° gunfire coverage.
- All-weather, day and night operations.

Development

- 1983. Project started, later stopped in favour of Mi-42.
- 1992. Project restarted and announced during the September MosAeroshow in Zhukovsky.

↑ **Model of the Mil Mi-40. Note the mast radar, nose gun, missiles, and Mi-28N type rotors** *(Piotr Butowski)*

Crew/passengers: 2 flight crew plus up to 8 troops (10 originally). Provision for a rear gunner in a heavily glazed rear-of-cabin position.
Cabin access: Horizontally split cabin door each side, allowing rapid troop deployment and use of the lower doors as airsteps.
Rotor system: Similar to Mi-28.
Engines: Similar to Mi-28.
Fuel system: 2,579 lb (1,170 kg). Provision for auxiliary tanks.
Flight avionics/instrumentation: Weapon system avionics similar to Mi-28, including 8-millimetre-wave mast-mounted radar.
Fixed guns: Flexibly-mounted 23-mm GSh-23 cannon in an undernose turret, plus a 12.7-mm machine-gun under the rear of the cabin.
Expendable weapons and equipment: 2 anti-tank missiles on launch rails attached to each side sponson.

Details for Mi-40

PRINCIPAL DIMENSIONS:
Rotor diameter (main): 56 ft 5 ins (17.2 m)
Fuselage length: 52 ft 6 ins (16 m)
Width, blades folded: 13 ft 7 ins (4.15 m)
Maximum height: 15 ft 1 ins (4.6 m) without tail rotor

TAIL ROTOR:
Diameter: 12 ft 7 ins (3.84 m)

UNDERCARRIAGE:
Type: Retractable, with twin nosewheels
Wheel base: 13 ft 7 ins (4.15 m)
Wheel track: 9 ft 10 ins (3 m)

WEIGHTS:
Empty: 18,012 lb (8,170 kg)
Normal take-off: 24,471 lb (11,100 kg)
Maximum take-off: 26,235 lb (11,900 kg)

PERFORMANCE:
Maximum speed: 170 kts (195 mph) 314 km/h
Cruise speed: 140 kts (162 mph) 260 km/h
OGE hovering ceiling: 10,825 ft (3,300 m)
Service ceiling: 18,210 ft (5,550 m)
Range with standard fuel: 216 naut miles (249 miles) 400 km, with 5% reserve
Range with auxiliary tanks: 518 naut miles (597 miles) 960 km, with 5% reserve

Mil Mi-46

First flight: Not yet flown.
Role: Heavy transport helicopter.

Aims

- Exact replacement for old Mi-6s and Mi-10s (12,000 kg payload).
- Service time 1,500-1,800 hours per year.

Development

- 1990. Work started against an order from the Soviet Ministry of Civil Aviation.

Details

Sales: Estimated requirement for 200-270 helicopters for CIS use and 60-70 for export.

Details for Mi-46T

PRINCIPAL DIMENSIONS:
Rotor diameter (main): 90 ft 7 ins (27.6 m)
Fuselage length: 86 ft 3 ins (26.3 m)
Maximum height: 22 ft 6 ins (6.95 m) without tail rotor

TAIL ROTOR:
Diameter: 20 ft 4 ins (6.2 m)

UNDERCARRIAGE:
Type: Fixed, with twin wheels on each unit
Wheel track: 16 ft 5 ins (5 m)

WEIGHTS:
Empty: 35,715 lb (16,200 kg)
Maximum take-off: 66,139 lb (30,000 kg)
Payload: 26,455 lb (12,000 kg)

PERFORMANCE:
Cruise speed: 146 kts (168 mph) 270 km/h
OGE hovering ceiling: 7,545 ft (2,300 m), at MTOW
Range with full fuel: 405 naut miles (466 miles) 750 km
Range with 22,046 lb (10,000 kg) payload: 216 naut miles (249 miles) 400 km, with 30 minutes reserve

Rotor system: 7-blade main rotor.
Tail rotor characteristics: 5-blade.
Engines: 2 Aviadvigatel/Perm D-215 turboshafts, each 7,600 shp (5,667 kW) at take-off.

Aircraft variants:
Mi-46 is the military transport version.
Mi-46T is the civil freight/passenger version.
Mi-46K was a flying crane version, without the normal cargo cabin. Envisaged in 2 and 3 engined forms. Abandoned.

Mil Mi-52

First flight: Possibly 1998.
Role: Very light helicopter.

Development

- 1990. Work started.
- 1993. Displayed in model form.
- 1997. In active development.

Details

Crew/passengers: Pilot forward and 2 passengers on a rear bench seat.
Rotor system: 4-blade composites main rotor.
Tail rotor characteristics: 2-blade, composites.
Tail surfaces: T-tail, with fixed dorsal/ventral fin and horizontal stabilizer. Tail guard under the fin.
Fuselage: Conventional pod and boom type.
Engine: Single 270 hp (201 kW) VAZ-430 rotary piston engine (Wankel type) for Mi-51-1 version. Twin-engined layout under consideration as the Mi-52-2, with 240 hp (179 kW) rotary engines.

↑ **Mil Mi-52 model** *(Piotr Butowski)*

Details for Mi-52

PRINCIPAL DIMENSIONS:
Rotor diameter (main): 32 ft 10 ins (10 m)
Fuselage length: 28 ft 7 ins (8.71 m)

UNDERCARRIAGE:
Type: Fixed nosewheel type, with cantilever legs and wheel fairings

WEIGHTS:
Maximum take-off: 2,535 lb (1,150 kg)
Payload: 550 lb (250 kg)

PERFORMANCE:
Maximum speed: 116 kts (134 mph) 215 km/h
Cruise speed: 92 kts (106 mph) 170 km/h
OGE hovering ceiling: 5,250 ft (1,600 m)
Service ceiling: 16,400 ft (5,000 m)
Range with 551 lb (250 kg) payload: 216 naut miles (248.5 miles) 400 km, with 30 minutes reserve
Range with full fuel: 431 naut miles (497 miles) 800 km, with 30 minutes reserve

Mil Mi-54

Comments: Civil and military light utility helicopter, suited to Category A operations. Project started in 1992, aimed principally to offer a more modern alternative to the Mi-2 and replace helicopters of Mi-4 size. Manufacturing planned at Kazan but development reportedly halted through lack of availability of planned engines. Further details in the 1996-97 edition of *WA&SD*, pages 331-332.

Mil Mi-58

First flight: Not flown at time of writing.
Role: Medium civil helicopter, using the engines, transmission and rotor system of the Mi-28N.

Aims

- Probably to complement the smaller 10/12-seat Mi-54 and 30-seat Mi-38. Possibly encourages the Mi-28 programme by introducing elements into other programmes.
- Certification to AP-29 and FAR 29 requirements.

Development

- 1995. Details first given at the Paris Air Show.

Details

Crew/passengers: 2 pilots plus up to 20 passengers in 3 or 4 abreast cabin layout. VIP and medevac versions are likely.
Rotor system: As Mi-28N.
Tail rotor characteristics: As Mi-28N, with 2 × 2-blade rotors in 'scissors' configuration.
Engines: 2 Klimov/St Petersburg TV3-117VMA-SB3 turboshafts.
Engine rating: Each 2,500 shp (1,864 kW) at take-off.

Mil Mi-60MAI

First flight: Not flown at time of writing.
Role: Very light helicopter, mainly for training.

Development

- Autumn 1993. Work started at the Moscow Aviation Institute (MAI) under the designation V-1MAI, under the direction of Marat Tishchenko, professor at MAI and former general designer at Mil. Later, the Mil design bureau joined in the programme and the helicopter was redesignated Mi-60MAI.
- January 1998. Initial project was ready, and some $30 million was then required for further development, including $15 million for prototype construction and series production tooling, and $1.2 million for certification.

Details

Crew/passengers: Pilot and passenger side by side.
Rotor system: 3-blade composites main rotor.
Tail rotor characteristics: 2-blade, composites.
Tail surfaces: T-tail, with fixed dorsal/ventral fin and horizontal stabilizer.
Fuselage: Conventional pod and boom type.
Engine: Single Textron Lycoming O-360-F1AD piston engine of 190 hp (141.7 kW) or Volzhsky Avtomobilnyi Zavod VAZ-426 rotary piston engine of 240 hp (179 kW). Also 2 Rotax 914Fs are under consideration, each 115 hp (85.7 kW).

Details for Mi-60MAI

PRINCIPAL DIMENSIONS:
Rotor diameter (main): 26 ft 11 ins (8.2 m)
Fuselage length, with tail rotor turning: 24 ft (7.32 m)

TAIL ROTOR:
Diameter: 4 ft 0.5 ins (1.23 m)

UNDERCARRIAGE:
Type: Fixed skid type
Wheel track: 6 ft 6 ins (1.98 m)

WEIGHTS:
Empty: 1,067 lb (484 kg) with Rotax engines, or 1,155 lb (524 kg) with VAZ engine
Normal take-off: 1,763 lb (800 kg)
Maximum take-off: from 2,443 lb (1,108 kg) with Textron Lycoming engine to 2,853 lb (1,294 kg) with VAZ engine

PERFORMANCE:
Maximum speed: from 108 kts (124 mph) 200 km/h with Textron Lycoming engine to 121 kts (140 mph) 225 km/h with VAZ engine
Cruise speed: from 94 kts (109 mph) 175 km/h with Textron Lycoming engine to 105 kts (121 mph) 195 km/h with Rotax engines
Maximum climb rate: from 1,456 ft (444 m) per minute with Textron Lycoming engine to 2,067 ft (630 m) per minute with VAZ engine
OGE hovering ceiling: from 5,900 ft (1,800 m) with Textron Lycoming engine to 10,500 ft (3,200 m) with VAZ engine
Range with full fuel: 216 naut miles (248 miles) 400 km, 5% reserve
Duration: 3.2 to 3.4 hours, with 5% reserve

Denel Aviation — South Africa

Corporate address:
See Combat section for company details. See also Eurocopter entry for co-operation agreements.

Denel AH-2A Rooivalk (Red Kestrel)

First flight: 11 February 1990.
First delivery: 1999, to 16th Squadron of the SAAF at Bloemspruit AFB.
Role: Anti-armour, close air support/ground suppression, anti-helicopter/aircraft, reconnaissance, and counter-insurgency. Capable of self-deployment/ferrying.

Aims

- Designed in accordance with accepted military standards, with design drivers of fire power, survivability, high-mobility warfare, high-intensity operations, day and night operations and affordable availability.
- State of the art weaponry, with multi-mode long-range anti-armour missiles, high-velocity articulated cannon, air-to-air missiles, and high-velocity rockets.
- Highly automated state of the art systems, with fully integrated glass cockpit, helmet display and sighting systems, radar, laser and other electronic warfare equipment, 1553 databus with dual mission computers, and HUMS.
- Low radar, infra-red, noise and visual signatures.

Development

- 1984. Experimental Development Model XDM design began.
- 1988. Advanced Development Model (ADM) contract awarded.
- 11 February 1990. First flight of the XDM.
- 1992. First flight of the ADM.
- 1994. Contract award for Engineering Development Model (EDM).
- 18 November 1996. First flight of the EDM.
- 1996. Production contract for first customer.
- 31 July 1997. First production airframe out of jigs.

Details *(apply to production AH-2A)*

Sales: First order for 12 presently in production for the South African Air Force. MoU with Airod of Malaysia provides for co-operation on Rooivalk. Serious interest being shown by numerous other countries, including Malaysia (8 being negotiated at the time of writing), Saudi Arabia and Singapore. British Aerospace Australia is teamed with Denel to promote Rooivalk to Australia (Army Project Air 87). Strategic alliance signed between Denel and Eurocopter on 25 April 1997 for collaboration on Rooivalk (and Oryx).
Crew: 2 in tandem, with pilot in the rear cockpit and weapon system officer (WSO) in front. Option for interchanged cockpits.

↑ **Denel Cirstel tail-rotorless helicopter, which was expected to complete its full flight envelope tests in 1998. An acronym for Combined Infra-red Suppression and Tail Rotor Elimination System, Cirstel is a technology demonstrator based on an Alouette, combining anti-torque with IR and acoustic stealth capability, a technology possibly to be applied to future military and civil helicopters. The Cirstel anti-torque system incorporates a dual flow path, with high pressure air being fed to circulation control slots on the tailboom and low pressure air fed to a differential thruster at the aft end of the tailboom. Low pressure air fed to the tailboom is also mixed with engine exhaust gases**

Cockpit: Choice of a glass cockpit results in an uncluttered layout, while meeting all crashworthiness and crew safety requirements. Each cockpit conforms to MIL-STD-1333, designed to comply with the 5th to 95th percentile US Army aviator anthropometric data. A high degree of commonality exists between cockpit fittings and controls, permitting considerable flexibility for task sharing. Aircraft can be flown from either cockpit. Flight control grips comprise the collective lever and cyclic control. Rudder pedals control the yaw of the aircraft and are used to disengage the AFCS sight mode; the yaw pedals incorporate toe brakes. The collective lever grip, used to control the lift of the aircraft and also used to fly through certain AFCS modes, is equipped with the following control switches: landing light controls – controls the infra-red and white light in all axes; height and heading trim (autopilot) – allows trimming of stickloads; emergency stores jettison; air self-defence (ASD) mode selection switch – allows selection of all ASD modes; ground self-defence (GSD) mode control – selects and deselects the GSD function; caution/warning acknowledge; autopilot hydraulic release – isolates the flight control system during hydraulic malfunctions. The cyclic control grip is used to control aircraft pitch and roll and is equipped with the following: weapons manual ranging and cueing – allows manual selection of preselected GSD and Continuously Calculated Impact Point (CCIP) rocket ranges and cueing of weapon systems; AFCS disengage – disengagement of stability augmentation during AFCS electronic malfunctions; beeper/hover trim – engages control augmentation and allows trimming of the aircraft in the

↑ Denel AH-2 Rooivalks, in pre-production (nearest, with air data boom for trials only), ADM and XDM configurations. Note the pre-production Rooivalk has its PNVS above the nose

AFCS hover mode; communications transmit frequency scroll – scrolling of frequencies viewed on the CDU; trim release – neutralizes stick forces in any selected flight condition; electronic warfare trigger – manual release of chaff/flares; weapon firing trigger – allows firing of all CDU and ASD/GSD selected weapons through both trigger detents; and communications press-to-transmit. Cockpit windows and canopy provide maximum vision under combat conditions. Flat frontal windshields fitted to both cockpits are of bi-layer type, comprising high-strength chemically-toughened glass, an energy-absorbing polyurethane film, and an anti-abrasion self-healing urethane liner on the inner side. Inner surface of glass is coated to reduce radar reflections and the laminate is framed between 2 Kevlar epoxy retainers. Windshields are designed to resist the force of a 4 lb (1.8 kg) bird strike at 150 kts. Side and overhead near-flat windows are of the stretched acrylic type. Emergency exit system via side glazing (when exit through the gull-type starboard doors is not possible), comprising an explosive charge around the edge of both door windows plus the port-side windows. 23° forward downward view.

Rotor system: Main rotor system is based on components from the SA 332 Super Puma, with adaptations to accommodate Rooivalk requirements. 4-blade fully-articulated main rotor. Composite blades. Rotor brake is hydraulically operated from the pilots' cockpits.

Tail rotor characteristics: 5-blade, composites, starboard mounted.

Tail surfaces: Vertical and horizontal stabilizers provide yaw and pitch stability and comprise dorsal and ventral sweptback fins, and a horizontal stabilizer fitted to the upper port side of the dorsal fin.

Stub wings: Each has 3 hardpoints for external stores. Wings have upward-inclined leading-edges to minimize aerodynamic drag in cruise attitude.

Flight control system: Manual flight control system (MFCS) consists of mechanical bellcranks and linkages that are hydraulically assisted to ensure that the control inputs are light and irreversible. The hydraulically actuated autopilot servo-actuators are mounted in series in the flight control linkages. Flying and ground handling qualities are the same in both cockpits. For AFCS, see Avionics.

Safety features: In addition to the extensive damage tolerance designed into the systems, features include crashworthy undercarriage (designed for up to 20 ft, 6 m per second landing impact), crashworthy airframe design, crashworthy self-sealing fuel system, dual fire extinguishing system, and emergency shut-down system. See Cockpit.

Airframe: Simple and rugged, incorporating crashworthy design, conventional semi-monocoque and I-beam construction. Aluminium alloy riveted structure, with Kevlar epoxy composites used in secondary structure.

Engines: 2 Turbomeca Makila 1K2 turboshafts. IR suppressors. Each engine has its own air intake and particle separator assembly; dust, sand and foreign objects are collected in a scavenge plenum chamber from where they are vented overboard by extractor fans, aft of the intakes. Continuous filtering efficiency is better than 95%.

Engine rating: Each 1,845 shp (1,376 kW) take-off, 1,657 shp (1,236 kW) maximum continuous, 2,109 shp (1,573 kW) OEI for 30 seconds, 1,967 shp (1,467 kW) OEI for 2 minutes, and 1,904 shp (1,420 kW) OEI maximum continuous.

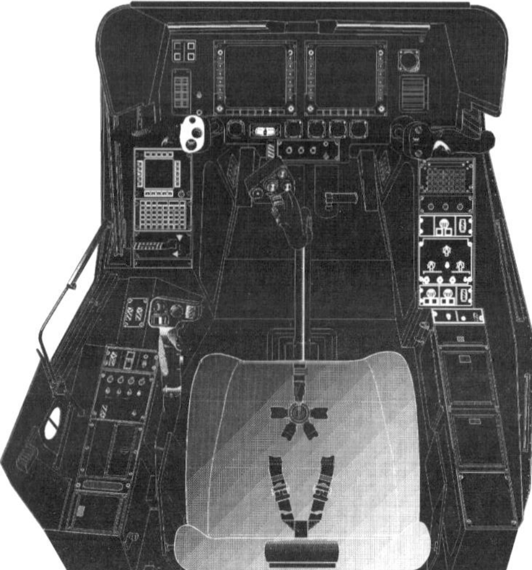

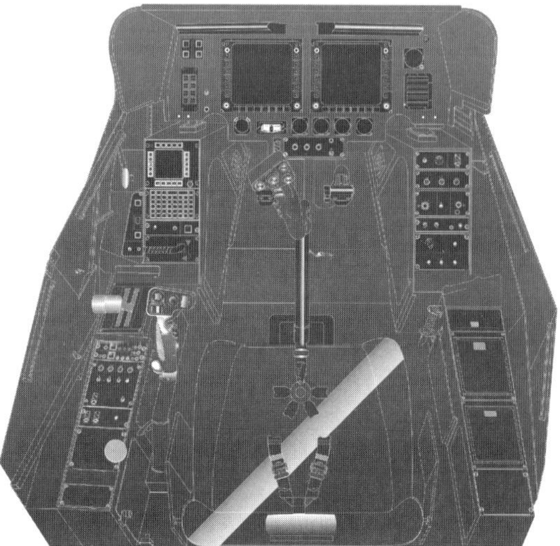

↑ Denel AH-2A Rooivalk WSO's *(left)* and pilot's cockpits *(courtesy Denel Aviation)*

Transmission: Main gearbox dual input is 2,436 shp (1,817 kW) maximum continuous and 3,010 shp (2,245 kW) maximum take-off. Main gearbox OEI is 1,986 shp (1,481 kW) maximum continuous and 2,109 shp (1,573 kW) maximum take-off.

Fuel system: Total internal fuel capacity is 1,854 litres, in 3 fuselage tanks located in 3 separate bays. Fuel management system, located within the HUMS units, is controlled via the MFDs in the cockpits and through the refuelling control panel. The fuel management system incorporates the following features: longitudinal balance of the feed tanks; lateral balance of the external tanks; transfer of fuel from a leaking tank; upstream and downstream feed-line leakage detection; cross feed system; and pressure refuel/defuel system. The aircraft can be refuelled by 3 methods: pressure refuelling using a fuel tanker; from standard 200-litre drums and flexible fuel storage tanks using the onboard refuelling system; and gravity refuelling by the tank mounted gravity filler caps. Jettisonable, rigid-type

Details for AH-2A Rooivalk

PRINCIPAL DIMENSIONS:
Rotor diameter (main): 51 ft 1.5 ins (15.58 m)
Maximum length, rotors turning: 61 ft 5.5 ins (18.73164 m)
Fuselage length: 53 ft 9 ins (16.389 m)
Maximum height: 17 ft (5.1873 m), or 14 ft 7 ins (4.4476 m) over tail rotor
Wing span: 17 ft 1 ins (5.198 m)

MAIN ROTOR:
Rotor disc: 2,052 sq ft (190.6 m^2)

TAIL ROTOR:
Diameter: 10 ft 0.25 ins (3.051 m)

UNDERCARRIAGE:
Type: Fixed, with tailwheel (castoring tailwheel with lock). 2-stage, energy absorbing main legs for survivability in a vertical crash (see Safety features)
Wheel base: 38 ft 7.5 ins (11.7723 m)
Wheel track: 9 ft 1.5 ins (2.7802 m)

WEIGHTS:
Empty, operating: 12,632 lb (5,730 kg)
Maximum take-off: 19,290 lb (8,750 kg)
Payload: 3,446 lb (1,563 kg) when carrying full internal fuel (341 naut mile range)
Maximum weapon load: 5,357 lb (2,430 kg) stub wing carriage capability

PERFORMANCE:
Never-exceed speed (V_{NE}): 167 kts (192 mph) 309 km/h
Maximum speed: 148 kts (170 mph) 274 km/h at 8,000 ft (2,440 m) dense altitude
Typical cruise speed: 138 kts (159 mph) 256 km/h, ISA, sea level, at 16,045 lb (7,278 kg) weight
Sideways speed: 45 kts (52 mph) 83 km/h
Sideslip angle: ±10° for symmetrical store configurations at the design limit speed
Maximum climb rate: 2,000 ft (610 m) per minute, ISA, sea level, at 16,045 lb (7,278 kg) weight, maximum continuous rating
Vertical climb rate: 2,600 ft (792 m) per minute, ISA, sea level, at 16,045 lb (7,278 kg) weight, take-off rating
IGE hovering ceiling: 12,600 ft (3,840 m), ISA, sea level, at 16,045 lb (7,278 kg) weight
OGE hovering ceiling: 11,300 ft (3,445 m), ISA, sea level, at 16,045 lb (7,278 kg) weight
Service ceiling: 19,900 ft (6,065 m)
G limits: +2.9, -0.5
Range with full internal fuel: 413 naut miles (475 miles) 765 km
Range with auxiliary fuel: 680 naut miles (783 miles) 1,260 km, or 610 naut miles (702 miles) 1,130 km with 45 minutes reserve
Duration: 3.6 hours at sea level, ISA, without drop tanks
Missile profiles:
Anti-armour – prime mission configuration, at 17,328 lb (7,860 kg) weight, 124 naut mile combat radius, with 8 anti-armour missiles, 4 AAMs and 400 rounds of 20-mm ammunition
Anti-armour – multiple target configuration, at 18,541 lb (8,410 kg) weight, 112 naut mile combat radius, with 16 anti-armour missiles, 4 AAMs and 400 rounds of 20-mm ammunition
Anti-armour – long range configuration, at 18,739 lb (8,500 kg) weight, 216 naut mile combat radius, with 4 anti-armour missiles, 4 AAMs, 2 × 750 litre drop tanks, and 400 rounds of 20-mm ammunition
Ground suppression – standard configuration, at 17,394 lb (7,890 kg) weight, 124 naut mile combat radius, with 2 × 19 round FZ90 rocket launchers, 4 AAMs and 400 rounds of 20-mm ammunition

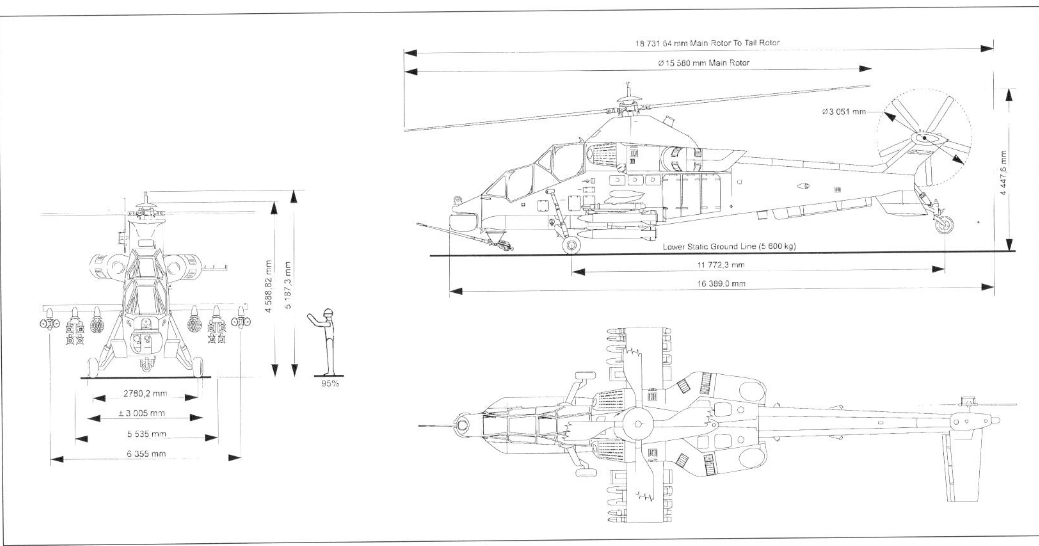

↑ **Denel AH-2A Rooivalk general arrangement** *(courtesy Denel Aviation)*

external fuel tanks can be fitted to the 'wet' inboard wing stations, each standard drop tank having a capacity of 750 litres.
Electrical system: Power generation and distribution system is fully independent and dual redundant. Redundancy of the supply for mission critical and flight critical equipment is at equipment level (eg. down stream of the distribution bus bars). AC supply via 2 × 20 kVA alternators for 200 volt 3-phase and 115 volt single-phase, at 400 Hz. 28 volt DC supply via 2 transformer-rectifiers. 2 × 24 volt 31 amp-hour batteries.
Hydraulic system: Comprises a left-hand main system, right-hand main system and an auxiliary system. Each main system operates at 2,538 psi. Design ensures the survivability of the supply to the main servo-controls. RH main system operation sees fluid drawn from a separate reservoir and pressurized by the RH MGB pump; pressurized fluid is then supplied directly to the lower cylinders of the main servo-controls and the RH cylinder of the tail servo-control. With the auxiliary electrical system operation, the auxiliary electric pump only operates under the following conditions: if the demand on the LH MGB driven pump exceeds its output capacity; if the LH MGB driven pump fails; and if hydraulic power is required when the aircraft is on the ground during rigging or maintenance operations.
Braking system: Independent toe-operated hydraulic wheel brakes fitted to the main wheels; system incorporates a park brake facility. See Rotor system.
Flight avionics/instrumentation: Avionics system has been designed for low crew workload and high reliability, with multiple fall-back modes of operation. The constituent parts communicate through a MIL-STD-1553B data bus, and has a glass cockpit interfacing to real time controls embodying HOCAS (see Cockpit). The avionics comprise an Integrated Management System (IMS), navigation system, digital Automatic Flight Control System (AFCS), Health and Usage Monitoring System (HUMS), communications system, and electronic warfare (EW) suite. The IMS has 2 helicopter mission computers (HMC), 4 Sextant Avionique MFD 66 liquid crystal colour MFDs of 6.25 ins (16 cm) square (2 per cockpit), 2 multi-function keyboards (1 per cockpit), 2 monochrome displays (1 per cockpit), 2 communications status displays (1 per cockpit) and a data transfer unit (DTU) for mass storage. IMS components are NVG compatible. The navigation system comprises a Doppler radar velocity sensor (DRVS), GPS, heading sensor unit (HSU) and air data unit (ADU). The AFCS comprises 2 AFC computers and a Pilot Control Unit (PCU). The AFCS provides rate stabilization in pitch, roll and yaw, attitude hold, altitude hold, turn co-ordination and automatic trimming. The AFCS's higher modes include: control augmentation for more responsive flight control and better quick reaction during NOE flight (NOE mode is implemented by using trim follow-up); hover hold (captures and maintains zero velocity); height hold (captures and maintains radar altimeter height); sight hold (coupled to the TDATS sight); and auto-nav (Flight Director), allowing the aircraft to be flown on a course directed according to the flight plan in the IMS. The communications suite has 2 VHF/UHF transceivers with associated logic converter units and broad-band antennas, for use under normal flying conditions (communication modes such as FM, AM and digitized speech are selectable on these radios); single HF radio with a short-loop antenna for use during NOE manoeuvres; 2 audio control units (ACU), 1 providing intercom and the other audio to the crew; single dedicated control unit (DCU) providing alternative control to 1 VHF/UHF radio and HF radios; and an IFF transponder. The Weapon system features TDATS and HMSD; TDATS (target detection and tracking system) sight is a nose-mounted, stabilized sight unit for target detection, identification and tracking tasks, by day or night, and is equipped with a TV sensor, FLIR, autotracker, laser rangefinder and laser designator; HMSD (helmet-mounted sight system) provides head-up information during NOE flight, especially at night, and allows quickly accessible 'look and shoot' capability. For the helmet, 2 cathode-ray tubes, integrated into a detachable module, generate video or symbology which is superimposed onto the helmet visor by projection; for night operations, the Pilot Night Vision System (PNVS) is used to provide video information to the pilot, while 2 independent image intensification modules supply a NVG type image to both crew members.
Self-protection systems: Fully integrated electronic warfare suite has radar warning, laser warning and countermeasures dispensing. The EW system is HOCAS controlled.
Fixed guns: Universal cannon interface with single-barrel Armscor F2 high speed 20-mm cannon in a chin turret. 90° per second slew rate. Effective range 6,560 ft (2,000 m) against ground and air targets.
Ammunition: 400 or 700 rounds of HS820 ammunition (TP, TPT, HEI, HEIT, SAPHEI, APCI and APCIT rounds available). Selectable dual feed from separate ammunition bins.
Number of weapon pylons: See Stub wings. Total of 6 stores pylons conform to 14" NATO standard and to MIL-STD-1760. Inner pylons of each stub wing are wet.
Expendable weapons and equipment: 5,357 lb (2,430 kg) stub wing carriage capability. Combinations of the following weapons are possible: outer pylon AAMs with 2 × V3P (all sector IR homing with 2-colour seeker slaved to HMSD) or 4 × Mistral types; 16 anti-armour missiles on the middle and inner pylons, comprising ZT-6 Mokopa (semi-active laser homing with articulated seeker head or millimetre-wave homing missile), ZT-3 (automatic command to line of sight type), or Hot 3; 76 × 70-mm FFAR rockets on the middle and inner pylons in 4 × 19-round FZ90 launchers. See Mission profiles in the table.

Denel Oryx

Comments: This medium transport helicopter was developed from the French SA 330 Puma and built for the South African Air Force, which received 50 production examples by 1996 to replace earlier Pumas. It is currently being offered for export, and may eventually be assembled from kits in Malaysia if ordered by that nation. More recently, Oryx was displayed at LIMA 1997. It is offered in several configurations, including *search and rescue* with self contained navigation systems and *armed missions*. In a *maritime role* it is equipped with blade folding, ship tie-down, stick restrainers, emergency flotation gear and sponson fuel tanks. Other options include *ambulance*, and the *customized* version with 10 comfortable seats with reading lights, air-conditioning, toilet and bar facilities. Oryx can be equipped with a sling or fixed hoist and may also be employed in a *tank ferrying* role. As a *troop transport* it accommodates up to 16 troops and their equipment, in addition to a crew of 3.

New technological advances have been incorporated into Oryx, including composite rotor blades, major mechanical components with modular design, IFR capability in virtually all weather conditions, and 'on condition' maintenance for most equipment items and several mechanical assemblies. It is powered by 2 Topaz turboshafts (licence built Turbomeca Makila 1A1s of 1,877 shp, 1,400 kW each).

Denel Puma Gunship

Comments: The Puma Gunship, with nose-mounted sighting system for target acquisition and to guide the cannon and missiles during daylight, with optional night capability, was fully described and illustrated in the 1996-97 edition of *WA&SD*, page 333. The brief details that follow describe only the role and weapon systems.
Role: Anti-armour, long-range troop deployment, heliborne escort, reconnaissance, area suppression and self defence.
Fixed guns: Computer-controlled, hydraulically actuated turreted TC-20 20-mm cannon (400 rounds of MG-151 ammunition), aimed by a helmet sighting system (HSS) or helicopter stabilized optronic sight (HSOS). Firing angles ±110° azimuth, -60° downward and 0° upward. Weight of system 365 lb (165.5 kg).
Expendable weapons and equipment: Choice of weapons carried on 2 pylons on each tubular weapons beam, according to role. For area suppression, HR-68 pods each with 18 × 68-mm rockets (or other rockets) plus the cannon. For anti-armour, 8 × ZT-3 laser-guided missiles in 2 × 4-round packs (option of TOW or similar) on the outer pylons, aimed by the HSOS, plus 2 rocket pods and the cannon.

↑ **Denel Oryx medium transport helicopter**

Light's American SportsCopter Inc — Taiwan

Corporate address:
26, Ta Ho Street, Taichung 407.

Telephone: +886 4 3118003
Facsimile: +886 4 3118001
E-mail: lasi@ms11.hinet.net
Web site: http://www.ultrasport.rotor.com

Founded: 1990.

Employees: 15.

Information:
Charles Lin (Director – *telephone* ext 25).

ACTIVITIES

▪ Design, manufacture and marketing the Ultrasport range of ultralight and Experimental helicopters.

SUBSIDIARY

AMERICAN SPORTSCOPTER INC

Corporate address:
875 Middle Ground Blvd, Newport News, VA 23606, USA.

Telephone: +1 757 873 4914
Facsimile: +1 757 873 3711

Information:
Michael Hagerty (Sales Administrator, Marketing Office for North and South America).

Light's American SportsCopter Ultrasport 254, 331 and 496

First flight: July 1993 for Ultrasport 254 prototype, 1994 for Ultrasport 331, and July 1995 for Ultrasport 496.
Certification: Ultrasport 254 meets FAA FAR Pt 103 as an ultralight, Ultrasport 331 meets FAR Pt 21.191(g) as a homebuilt/Experimental helicopter, and Ultrasport 496 meets the FAA regulation as an ultralight trainer. At the time of writing, FAR Pt 21 Primary Category certification was underway.
First delivery: 1995.
Role: Single-seat (UltraSport 254 and 331) and 2-seat (UltraSport 496) helicopters for sport, recreational, educational, agricultural and tactical applications, including a long-range UAV (unmanned) version.
Sales: Kit (meeting FAA 51% amateur built requirements) deliveries started in December 1995, with at least 10 per month thereafter planned. Kit price US$35,000 for Ultrasport 254, US$36,000 for Ultrasport 331, and US$49,500 for Ultrasport 496. Quoted assembly time of 60-80 working hours.
Rotor system: 2-blade main rotor of underslung, teetering type. Blades constructed using a graphite spar, Nomex honeycomb, an outer glassfibre skin, and polyurethane leading-edge erosion tape. Blades autorotation capability assisted by tungsten weights in the outer half of the blades that help hold inertia in the event of loss of engine rpm. The hub yoke (main body) is a 1-piece CNC machined aluminium component. Pitch change bearings are mounted to the yoke spindles which are inclined 3° to each other (preconed). The blades are retained against centrifugal force with a tension/torsion pack, requiring no lubrication and has infinite life. The entire hub assembly has been structurally tested to conform with FAA FAR Pt 27 levels. The control system uses an overhead cyclic stick which connects directly to the swashplate. A walking beam on the rotor hub reverses the movements of the cyclic stick, causing the rotor to respond in a conventional sense. Combined collective and throttle control to the pilot's left. 2 foot pedals control the tail rotor collective via push/pull cable running along the tailboom.
Tail rotor characteristics: 2-blade, protected by a flat ring tail to guard the tail rotor blades during autorotation or in extreme tail-low manoeuvres. Blade construction similar to the main blades, except by having hard foam in the trailing edge.
Airframe: Seatback is the rigid 'strongback' of the helicopter and forms a strong torque box to which everything else is attached. The seat is assembled from sandwich panels of epoxy resin, graphite fabric and Nomex honeycomb core. The forward fuselage is essentially a non-structural pilot fairing made from layers of graphite. Aluminium tailboom. Composite horizontal stabilizer and vertical ring tail. See Undercarriage.
Engine: Göbler-Hirthmotoren Hirth 2703 and 2706 piston engine for UltraSport 254 and 331 respectively, and F30 for 496. Electric starting for Hirth 2706 and F30.
Engine rating: 55 hp (41 kW) for Hirth 2703/2706 and 95 hp (71 kW) for Hirth F30.
Transmission: Drive system has the engine vertically mounted to the seatback and connected directly to the clutches and main rotor shaft drive. There are no belts. Light weight achieved on the drive system by using an aluminium gearbox, main rotor hub and titanium main rotor shaft. Main rotor gearbox is a 12:1 planetary type (12:1 2-stage type for Ultrasport 496) which also turns the tail rotor at a ratio of 1:1. Gearbox is oil cooled and wet lubricated with an internal sump and pump, and is manufactured to the American Gear Manufacturing Class 11 standards, rated for 2,000 hours TBO. Engine start up is simple due to a centrifugal clutch which does not engage the rotors until the engine reaches 2,000 rpm. The sprag clutch is a 1-way clutch which enables the rotors to continue running in the event of a loss of engine rpm. Rating 65 hp (48.5 kW) main, and 15 hp (11.2 kW) spiral bevel tail.
Fuel system: 19 litres for Ultrasport 254, 38 litres for Ultrasport 331 and 60.5 litres for Ultrasport 496.

Aircraft variants:
Ultrasport 254 is the single-seat ultralight version. Hirth 2703.
Ultrasport 331 is a single-seat growth version of 254, meeting FAA Experimental FAR Pt 21.191(g). Hirth 2706.
Ultrasport 496 is the 2 seater, with Hirth F30 engine.

Details for Ultrasport 254, *with 496 in italics*

PRINCIPAL DIMENSIONS:
Rotor diameter (main): 21 ft (6.4 m), *23 ft (7.01 m)*
Maximum length, rotor folded: 19 ft 2 ins (5.842 m), *19 ft 9 ins (6.02 m)*
Maximum height: 7 ft 10 ins (2.39 m), *the same*

CABIN:
Length: 4 ft 4 ins (1.32 m), *4 ft 5 ins (1.35 m)*
Width: 2 ft 6 ins (0.76 m), *4 ft (1.22 m)*
Height: 4 ft 11 ins (1.5 m), *the same*

MAIN ROTOR:
Blade chord: 6.7 ins (17 cm), *the same*
Twist angle: 8° linear for improved hover performance

TAIL ROTOR:
Diameter: 2 ft 6 ins (0.76 m), *the same*
Blade chord: 2 ins (5 cm), *the same*

UNDERCARRIAGE:
Type: Fixed twin skids, with sandwich structure bows of aluminium honeycomb with glassfibre and epoxy laminate face plies. Ply thickness is tailored to provide maximum energy absorption and impact attenuation for 2.5g ground contact without structural failure. Skids are aluminium tubes with steel skid shoes
Skid track: 8 ft (2.438 m)

WEIGHTS:
Empty: 252 lb (114.3 kg), *495 lb (225 kg)*
Maximum take-off: 525 lb (239 kg), *1,085 lb (492 kg)*
Useful load: 273 lb (124 kg), *590 lb (268 kg)*

PERFORMANCE:
Maximum speed: 55 kts (63 mph) 102 km/h, *85 kts (98 mph) 158 km/h*
Cruise speed: 55 kts (63 mph) 102 km/h, *56 kts (65 mph) 105 km/h*
Maximum climb rate: 1,000 ft (305 m) per minute
IGE hovering ceiling: 10,800 ft (3,290 m), *the same*
OGE hovering ceiling: 7,000 ft (2,135 m), *the same*
Ceiling: 12,000 ft (3,660 m), *the same*
Duration: 1 hour 15 minutes, *2 hours 15 minutes*

↑ Light's American SportsCopter 496 2-seat ultralight helicopter

↑ Light's American SportsCopter Ultrasport 254 with floats

Intora-Firebird plc — UK

Corporate address:
PO Box 8000, Aviation Way, London-Southend Airport, Southend-on-Sea, Essex SS2 6DE.

Telephone: +44 1702 561 818
Facsimile: +44 1702 561 819
E-mail: mail@intora-firebird.com

Comments: Introduced to the public at the September 1998 Farnborough International Air Show, this company offers single- and 2-seat tip-jet powered helicopters. The **Firebird** single-seater is available in both manned and UAV forms, having an open structure, while the side-by-side 2-seat **Atlas Firebird** has a fully enclosed cabin, larger tailboom (also with the option of a manoeuvring tail rotor, which is standard for Firebird of 1 ft 11.5 ins, 0.597 m diameter) and larger fixed tail surfaces. Rotor diameter for Firebird is 18 ft (5.49 m), height to rotor head 6 ft 10.5 ins (2.1 m), and width over skids 4 ft 9 ins (1.45 m). Firebird has a maximum speed of 87 kts (100 mph) 161 km/h, cruise speed of 30 kts (35 mph) 56 km/h, climb rate of 2,000 ft (610 m) per minute, maximum operating ceiling of 30,000 ft (9,145 m), and standard cruise duration of 30 minutes but with various opportunities to greatly extend duration (up to 4 hours with adoption of an optional piston engine with pusher propeller). The helicopters have been designed to be flown after only minimal training, controlled by a single Monotrol handle.

The helicopters use no conventional engine, having instead rotor tip-jets (rockets) fed by 85% hydrogen peroxide which is converted within the jets into super-heated steam and oxygen at about 630° C and expelled rearward (and is therefore free from the usual fuselage-turning torque), providing similar power to a 100 hp (74.6 kW) engine. This power system is said to allow Firebird/Atlas Firebird to offer many times the useful load per empty weight factor of conventional piston/turbine engine-powered helicopters. Many potential military and civil roles include tactical intelligence surveillance, target acquisition and more. Can also be armed.

↑ Intora-Firebird and Atlas Firebird, first displayed to the public at the September 1998 Farnborough International Air Show

Pall Aerospace Ltd — UK

Corporate address:
Europa House, Havant Street, Portsmouth PO1 3PD.

Telephone: +44 1705 303303
Facsimile: +44 1705 302498

Information:
Kenneth P. Smith, F.INSTD, MSLEAT (Export Sales Director – *telephone* +44 1705 302283, *E-mail* ken_smith@pall.com).

ACTIVITIES

■ Division of Pall Europe Ltd. Markets the 'Centrisep' sand filter used by helicopters worldwide, including among many applications the Mil Mi-8, Mi-17 and Mi-24. Compact self-scavenging particle separator, suited also to non-helicopter applications.

GKN Westland Limited — UK

Corporate address:
Yeovil, Somerset BA20 2YB.

Telephone: +44 1935 475222
Facsimile: +44 1935 702131, 702133
Web site: gkn-whl.co.uk
Telex: 46277 WHLYEO G

Founded:
4 July 1935 as Westland Aircraft Ltd, having begun aviation activities as Westland Aviation Works on 3 April 1915.

Information:
Chris Loney (Director of Public Relations – *facsimile* +44 1935 702319).

DIVISIONS

GKN WESTLAND AEROSPACE LTD

HQ address:
East Cowes, Isle of Wight PO32 6RH.

Telephone: +44 1983 294101
Facsimile: +44 1983 291006

Activities:
■ Now incorporates also the former Engineering and Industries divisions, and split into 2 principal parts, as Structures and Transmissions. In addition, Design Services undertakes subcontracted design and engineering for aerospace, rail and engineering industries; and Systems Assessment for operational analysis and systems assessment.
■ Structures oversees the design, manufacture and qualification of advanced composite and metallic flight critical structures and components, including airframe structures for the Lynx (fuselage), EH 101 (cockpit glazing structure, sponsons and engine nacelles), Airbus A330 (wing panels) and A340 (IFS), Boeing 737 (wing panels), 747 (wing panels), C-17 (vanes) and MD-11 (vanes), and Saab 2000 (rear fuselage); doors for the Fairchild Dornier 328, Bombardier Global Express and Dash 8, and Boeing 737 and 747; nacelle manufacture for the C-130J, Dash 8, Fairchild Dornier 328, IPTN N250, and Saab 340B and 2000; and jet nacelle components for A330 and A340, and Boeing 747, 767 and MD-11.
■ Transmissions for Lynx (main drive gearbox), Sea King (main), EH 101 (intermediate), Apache (intermediate), Sikorsky CH-54 (gears and shafts) and Black Hawk (main), Puma/Super Puma (gears and shafts), BR710 (internal) and BR715 (internal).

GKN WESTLAND HELICOPTERS LTD

HQ address:
Yeovil, Somerset BA20 2YB.

Telephone: +44 1935 475222
Facsimile: +44 1935 702131, 702133
Telex: 46277 WHLYEO G

Activities:
■ Manufactures helicopters, including the Sea King based on the US Sikorsky design and Apache from Boeing; 67 WAH-64 Apaches were selected for the British Army Air Corps on 13 July 1995, differing mainly from the US helicopter in having Rolls-Royce Turbomeca RTM322 engines.
■ GKN Westland Heliport for operating London Heliport, and GKN Westland Industrial Products.
■ 50% stake in EH Industries EH 101, with Agusta of Italy.

GKN WESTLAND TECHNOLOGIES LTD

HQ address:
PO Box 27, Yeovil, Somerset BA20 2YJ.

Telephone: +44 1935 475181
Facsimile: +44 1935 427600

Activities:
■ Principal subsidiary is Normalair-Garrett, producing control systems and associated aerospace components.

GKN Westland Lynx, Battlefield Lynx and Super Lynx

First flight: 21 March 1971 (first of 13 prototypes).
Role: Army general-purpose, utility and armed attack/support; naval anti-submarine, anti-surface-vessel, EEZ and convoy protection, vertrep, over-the-horizon targeting, electronic surveillance and warfare, search and rescue, pollution control and VIP transport.

Aims

■ Naval versions can operate in sea state 6 and in 40 kts side or tail winds and up to 50 kts winds from ahead for take-off and landing. In ASW role, can be used for autonomous operations or with other aircraft and ships, for submarine detection, classification, localization and attack in all weathers, by day or night.

Development

■ 2 April 1968. Lynx became 1 of 3 helicopters covered under an Anglo-French agreement between Westland (70% workshare) and Aerospatiale (30%).
■ 1986. Lynx set an absolute world helicopter speed record at 216.45 kts (249.1 mph) 400.87 km/h.

Details *(principally based on newest naval Super Lynx, except where indicated)*

Sales: 394 production Lynx of all versions by 22 July 1998 (including 7 ordered for the German Navy as Mk 88As for delivery from 1999 and 13 new Mk 99As for the South Korean Navy), delivered to the Argentine (2 Mk 23 for ASW), Brazilian (9 Mk 21 and 9 Mk 21A Super Lynx for ASV), Danish (8 Mk 80 and 2 Mk 90 for SAR/patrol, actually ordered by the Air Force, with uses including recent flying from new IS86 Thetis class offshore patrol vessels), French (26 HAS Mk 2(FN) and 14 HAS Mk 4(FN) for ASW/ASV), German (19 Mk 88 for ASW, of which the 17 remaining operational are being upgraded; to receive 7 Mk 88As), South Korean (12 Mk 99 Super Lynx for ASW/ASV; to receive 13 Mk 99As), Netherlands (6 Mk 25 for SAR, 10 Mk 27 and 8 Mk 81 for ASW), Nigerian (3 Mk 89 for ASW/SAR), Portuguese (5 Mk 95 Super Lynx for ASW) and British (60 HAS Mk 2 and 30 HAS Mk 3) navies. Army versions to the British Army Air Corps (113 AH Mk 1, 4 AH Mk 5 and 11 AH Mk 7 for utility/anti-tank, plus 16 AH Mk 9 as Battlefield type), Norwegian Air Force (6 Mk 86 for SAR) and Qatar Police (3 Mk 28 for utility). Of these, only Argentina and Qatar no longer operate the helicopter. The export Battlefield Lynx is generally similar to the British AH Mk 9, while export Super Lynx customers are Brazil (9 Mk 21As, with 5 existing Lynx Mk 21/21As being upgraded to the new standard), South Korea (Mk 99) and Portugal (Mk 95), as already detailed. Pakistan now operates 3 ex-Royal Navy HAS Mk 3s from Type 21 frigates, and Portugal has received 2 ex-Royal Navy HAS Mk 3s. Unconfirmed reports suggest that Malaysia is to purchase 6 Super Lynx with LHTEC engines for its navy, to replace Wasps from 1999-2000 onwards.
Crew/passengers: 2 or 3 crew. Up to 8 passengers in a VIP role, or 8 survivors for SAR, or 3 litters (typically) and an attendant.
Freight, external: 3,000 lb (1,360 kg) cargo hook.
Cabin access: Sliding door, with entrance of 4 ft 6 ins × 3 ft 11 ins (1.37 × 1.19 m).

↑ GKN Westland Lynx Mk 9 of the British Army's 24 Airmobile Brigade on UN duty in Bosnia

Optional equipment: Includes dual controls, harpoon deck securing system, and a 600 lb (272 kg) hydraulic or electric rescue hoist above the large sliding door.
Rotor system: Advanced BERP, aerodynamically efficient, 4-blade, semi-rigid main rotor with swept tips. Provides low vibration, high performance, and the high control power and quick response needed for control in turbulence over a rolling flight deck. Negative pitch facility provides 3,000 lb (1,360 kg) downward thrust to hold the helicopter steady on deck until secured, aided by the low centre of gravity of the low profile gearbox and minimal rotor height. Blades evolved from the British Experimental Rotor Programme (BERP), and made of carbon and glassfibre composite components protected from erosion by titanium and nickel shields. These offer a threefold increase in fatigue life over the original steel blades, a 70% reduction in operator maintenance effort, and the potential to increase the maximum thrust by up to 40%. Standard on Super Lynx, the blades have been retrofitted to British, French, German, Netherlands, Norwegian and Portuguese Lynx helicopters. Main rotor folds for stowage. A new main rotor head has been developed by Westland to reduce maintenance, first fitted to Brazil's Super Lynx. Available also as a retrofit replacement, the new head reduces life cycle costs. Comprising several major sub-assemblies (compared with the existing monobloc), the head is fabricated in a new enhanced grade of titanium alloy.
Tail rotor characteristics: 4-blade, metal or composite, on port side of fin.
Tail surfaces: Starboard, fixed.
Flight control system: Hydraulic rotor head controls. Full authority rotor speed control by each engine.
Fuselage: Folding tail pylon option.
Airframe materials: Light alloy, with limited use of composites for fairings, doors and panels.
Engines: 2 Rolls-Royce Gem 42 series turboshafts, or 2 LHTEC CTS800-4Ns.
Engine rating: Each 1,120 shp (835 kW) for Gem 42s or 1,620 shp (1,208 kW) for CTS800-4Ns.
Transmission rating: 1,840 shp (1,372 kW). Optional engine diffusers for IR suppression.
Fuel system: 990 litres in 5 main tanks, with the option of 2 × 436 litre tanks for long-endurance missions.
Electrical system: 28 volt DC supply via 2 engine-driven starter-generators and alternator. 24 volt ni-cd battery for back-up and emergency engine start (23 or 40 amp-hour). 200 volt, 400 Hz, 3-phase AC supply via 2 alternators.
Hydraulic system: 2 principal systems, each 2,050 psi, plus a third if sonar, hoist or MAD is part of the equipment.
Braking system: Sprag pivoting and locking type, to prevent movement on deck.
Radar: Chin-mounted 360° track-while-scan radar, able to detect small targets among strong sea clutter and electronic counter-measures. Typically GEC-Marconi Seaspray Mk 3 (as fitted to South Korean Mk 99s), Seaspray Mk 3000 (as for South Korean Mk 99As) or AlliedSignal RDR-1500 (as fitted to Portuguese Mk 95s).
Flight avionics/instrumentation: GEC-Marconi automatic flight control system, providing transition to and from hover and Doppler hover control. Tactical air navigation system (TANS N or Super TANS) and Doppler. Typical other instrumentation includes DME, VOR/ILS, Tacan, and I-band transponder. IFF. Mission equipment to suit customer, with the recommended suite now upgraded, with options including MAD, passive radar detection system, and dipping sonar (AlliedSignal Bendix/King AQS-18 or Thomson-Sintra HS-312); Super Lynx has the capability of carrying future advanced low-frequency sonar. Target classification is assisted by electronic support measures and the radar. A major cockpit upgrade was launched by Westland in 1996, designed to progressively introduce glass cockpit elements to ease Super Lynx flying and operations. The upgrade has panel mounted displays to enhance tactical and situation awareness. Radar is enhanced using liquid crystal displays. FLIR can also be integrated into the cockpit display, while tactical navigation is enhanced by GPS. New equipment will be NVG compatible. Multi-sensor reconnaissance pod, camera and night viewing devices for an electronic surveillance/warfare role (typically Vinten or Agiflite), with cabin space and electrical capacity for a range of passive and active EW systems.
Self-protection systems: Vinten Vicon 78 chaff dispenser.
Number of weapon pylons: Detachable rack each side of the cabin, with 2 pylons per rack.
Expendable weapons and equipment: 4 Sea Skua anti-ship missiles for ASV, 2 homing torpedoes (Sting Ray, Mk 44, Mk 46) and depth charges for ASW.

Aircraft variants (currently used only):
AH Mk 7 improved British Army version, with Gem 42 engines, enhanced systems, BERP main blades, composite tail rotor blades

↑ GKN Westland Lynx HMA Mk 8 in service with the Royal Navy

Details for Super Lynx

PRINCIPAL DIMENSIONS:
Rotor diameter (main): 42 ft (12.8 m)
Maximum length, rotors turning: 50 ft (15.24 m)
Maximum length, rotor and tail folded: 35 ft 7 ins (10.85 m)
Width, blades folded: 9 ft 8 ins (2.95 m)
Maximum height: 12 ft 0.5 ins (3.67 m), or 10 ft 8 ins (3.25 m) with rotor and tail folded

CABIN:
Length: 6 ft 9 ins (2.06 m)
Width: 5 ft 10 ins (1.78 m)
Height: 4 ft 8 ins (1.42 m)
Volume: 5.21 cu ft (184 m^3)

MAIN ROTOR:
Rotor disc: 128.71 sq ft (1,385.4 m^2)

TAIL ROTOR:
Diameter: 7 ft 9 ins (2.36 m)

UNDERCARRIAGE:
Type: Fixed, with twin steerable nosewheels. Main units toe outward by 27°, but are manually aligned and locked for deck handling. Optional flotation equipment. Maximum vertical descent rate 7.5 ft (2.3 m) per second
Wheel base: 9 ft 11 ins (3.02 m)
Wheel track: 9 ft 2 ins (2.8 m)

WEIGHTS:
Empty: 7,255 lb (3,291 kg)
Empty, equipped: 7,782 lb (3,530 kg) ASW, 8,495 lb (3,853 kg) ASW search and attack with 3 crew and 1 torpedo, 7,984 lb (3,621 kg) ASV, 7,813 lb (3,544 kg) OTHT, 7,789 lb (3,533 kg) SAR
Operating, minus fuel: 9,226 lb (4,185 kg) for ASW with 2 Mk 46 torpedoes, 9,577 lb (4,344 kg) ASW search and attack, 9,640 lb (4,373 kg) for ASV with 4 Sea Skua, 8,311 lb (3,770 kg) OTHT with 2 auxiliary tanks, 8,329 lb (3,778 kg) SAR
Maximum take-off: 11,750 lb (5,330 kg)
Take-off (SAR): 10,063 lb (4,564 kg)

PERFORMANCE (MTOW)**:**
Cruise speed: 137 kts (158 mph) 254 km/h
Maximum climb rate: 1,776 ft (541 m) per minute at 90 kts
Climb rate, OEI: 396 ft (121 m) per minute at 80 kts
IGE hovering ceiling: 8,859 ft (2,700 m) ISA, or 3,874 ft (1,180 m) at ISA + 15° C
OGE hovering ceiling: 6,726 ft (2,050 m) ISA, 1,116 ft (340 m) at ISA + 15° C
Range: 285 naut miles (328 miles) 528 km *standard tanks*, 437 naut miles (503 miles) 810 km *with 1 auxiliary tank*, 590 naut miles (679 miles) 1,093 km *with 2 auxiliary tanks*, all with 20 minutes reserve
Maximum range (SAR): 340 naut miles (391 miles) 630 km
Radius of action (ASV): Typically up to 160 naut miles (184 miles) 300 km with missiles, at sea level, ISA + 15° C, 20 minutes fuel reserve
Radius of action (ASW): Typically up to 120 naut miles (138 miles) 220 km with 2 torpedoes, at sea level, ISA + 15° C, 20 minutes fuel reserve
Radius of action (SAR): Typically up to 150 naut miles (173 miles) 280 km with standard fuel, or 260 naut miles (299 miles) 480 km with auxiliary tanks, carrying 3 crew, hoist and 4 survivors, at sea level, ISA + 15° C, 20 minutes fuel reserve
Duration (ASV): Typically 3.25 hours at sea level, ISA + 15° C, 20 minutes fuel reserve
Time on station (ASW): Typically 2 hours at 20 naut miles (23 miles) 37 km from ship, with dipping sonar and 1 torpedo, at sea level, ISA + 15° C, 20 minutes fuel reserve
Duration (SAR): Typically 3.7 hours at sea level, ISA + 15° C, 20 minutes fuel reserve

and more. All but 11 produced by conversion of AH Mk 1s; 7 newly built and 2 conversions further modified to Mk 9s.
AH Mk 9 is the latest British Army version, similar to Battlefield Lynx. 16 newly built plus 9 Mk 7 conversions. First Army version with wheel undercarriage. Advanced composite rotor blades. Gem 42 engines with exhaust diffusers for IR suppression.
HAS Mk 3 is a Royal Navy version, being upgraded by Westland to HAS Mk 8 standard. Seaspray Mk 1 radar. Gem 41 engines. Includes sub-variants for Antarctic and Gulf operations.
HMA Mk 8 (HMA = helicopter maritime attack) is a Royal Navy version by conversion of Mk 3s and sub-variants, with Racal RAMS 4000 central tactical system with CRTs, GEC-Marconi Sea Owl passive thermal identification system, upgraded ESM, GPS and much more, integrated by the MIL-STD-1553B databus. Primarily for an anti-surface vessel attack role. First of 44 entered service in January 1995. Initial conversions by Westland, thereafter by the Royal Navy's Fleetlands works using Westland kits. Under an £18.8 million contract from the British Ministry of Defence, Westland provided a new radar processor, entering service with the Royal Navy from October 1994.
Super Lynx, is the latest version, as detailed. A major cockpit upgrade was launched by Westland in 1996, designed to progressively introduce glass cockpit elements. Therefore: Series 100 with conventional instrumentation; Series 200 with option of LHTEC CTS800-4N engines with FADEC and electronic engine system displays; Series 300 with LHTEC CTS800-4Ns and full EFIS with 6 screens.
Battlefield Lynx is the export Army equivalent of Super Lynx. No orders to date, though British AH Mk 9 is similar. Gem 42-1 engines. BERP main rotor. Wheel undercarriage. Cabin pintle 7.62-mm machine-guns. Enhanced flight and defence aid avionics. Empty weight 7,006 lb (3,178 kg). Same maximum take-off weight as Super Lynx.

GKN Westland Sea King and Commando

First flight: 7 May 1969 (HAS Mk 1).
Role: Medium multi-role. Variants include ASW, ASV, SAR, troop/VIP transport, logistic support, airborne early warning, electronic warfare, and Commando assault.

Aims

▪ Licence developed and manufactured variants of the US Sikorsky S-61.

Development

▪ 19 August 1969. First HAS Mk 1 entered service with No. 700S Squadron, RNAS Culdrose, of the Royal Navy.

Details *(advanced version of Sea King, unless stated)*

Sales: 326 delivered (1 built for Germany and 1 for India crashed before delivery, making 328 built) as Australia (navy, 10 Mk 50s and 2 Mk 50As for utility/SAR), Belgium (air force 5 Mk 48s for SAR), Egypt (navy, 6 Mk 47s for ASW; air force 5 Mk 70s and 19 Mk 72s for utility, and 4 Mk 73s for ECM, as Commando Mk 1s, 2/2Bs and 2Es respectively; upgrade programme is being proposed), Germany (navy, 22 Mk 41s for SAR/ASW), India (navy, 12 Mk 42s and 3 Mk 42As for ASW, 20 Mk 42Bs for ASW/ASV, and 6 Mk 42Cs for utility), Norway (air force, 10 Mk 43s, 1 Mk 43A, 3 Mk 43Bs and 2 new Mk 43Bs for SAR), Pakistan (navy, 6 Mk 45s for ASV), Qatar (air force, 8 Mk 74s for ASV and 4 Mk 92s for utility/VIP), and UK (air force, 19 HAR Mk 3s and 6 new Mk 3As for SAR with SN500 AFCS; navy, 56 HAS Mk 1s, 21 Mk 2s, 30 HAS Mk 5s and 5 HAS Mk 6s for ASW, plus 40 HC Mk 4s for utility; ETPS 1 HC Mk 4 for utility; and RAE [now DERA] 2 HC Mk 4X for utility). In addition, Australia and Pakistan have received 1 ex-RN HAS Mk 5 each. 7 Australian Sea Kings (used during the 1994 Sydney bush fires) were upgraded under a £27.6 million contract, with a Life of Type Extension (LOTE) programme that included an avionics update and airframe modifications to extend service life to at least 2008. 5 Belgium SAR Sea Kings were upgraded under a £4.5 million contract with AlliedSignal RDR-1500B search radar, FLIR Systems 2000F FLIR, and Racal RNS-252 navigation computer system integrated with the Canadian Marconi CMA 3012 GPS; under a 1997 contract, the 5 helicopters are receiving Smiths Newmark SN500 AFCS to keep them operational beyond the year 2015.
Crew/passengers: 4 crew and 16 (22 possible) survivors in SAR version; 2 crew and 28 troops (can be extended by some 50% for seated/standing troops), or 9 litters and 2 attendants or cargo (see below) in transport/logistic version; 3 crew and up to 15 VIPs with luxurious interior fittings in VIP transport version; 4 crew in AEW version; 3 crew in ASV and 4 crew in ASW versions.
Cockpit: Dual controls.
Freight, internal: 8,682 lb (3,943 kg) in transport version.
Freight, external: 8,000 lb (3,629 kg) cargo sling instead of troops or internal freight in transport role.

↑ **GKN Westland Sea King Mk 43B for SAR with the Royal Norwegian Air Force**

Cabin access: Sliding cargo door.
Size of main loading door: 5 ft × 5 ft 8 ins (1.52 × 1.73 m) starboard side, with smaller door to port.
Optional equipment: Includes fixed head undercarriage, no sponsons for overland operations, troop seats, 1 or 2 × 600 lb (272 kg) hoists, cargo hook, litters, waterproof floor, and parachute monorail.
Rotor system: Fixed main rotor head with 5 composite blades. Rotor brake. Optional powered folding main rotor head weighing 165 lb (75 kg).
Tail rotor characteristics: 5 or 6-blade.
Fuselage: Semi-monocoque with sponsons (overland version can have sponsons deleted). Folding tail for shipborne use.
Construction materials: Light alloy (stressed skin) airframe.
Engines: 2 Rolls-Royce Gnome H1400-1 turboshafts. Electric and hot air anti-icing. Optional sand filters and foreign object deflector.
Engine rating: 1,660 shp (1,238 kW).
Transmission rating: Main gearbox has an emergency lubrication system.
Fuel system: 6,456 lb (2,928 kg), with gravity and pressure refuelling/ defuelling and fuel jettison system. Optional auxiliary fuel system (864 litres).
Electrical system: 2 × 20 kVA 200/115 Hz alternators, 2 × 200 amp transformer rectifiers, and a 40 amp-hour battery. Optional

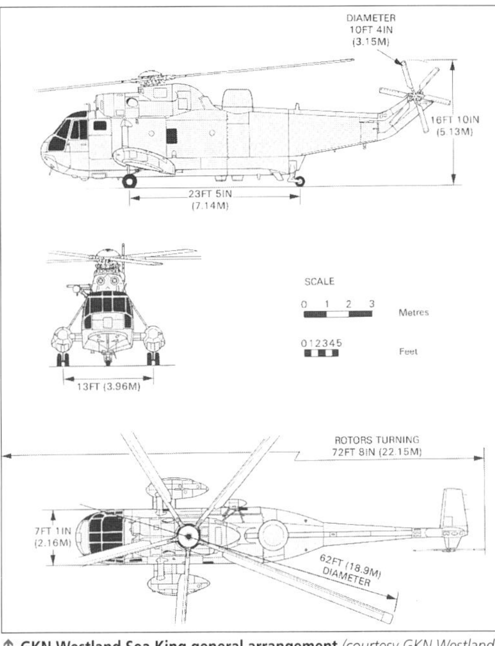

↑ **GKN Westland Sea King general arrangement** *(courtesy GKN Westland)*

third 20 kVA alternator.
Hydraulic system: 2 systems for rotor control at 1,500 psi, plus system for undercarriage retraction, rotor folding and brake, and equipment operation at 3,000 psi.
Braking system: Mainwheel brakes.

Details for currently offered Sea King

PRINCIPAL DIMENSIONS:
Rotor diameter (main): 62 ft (18.9 m)
Maximum length, rotors turning: 72 ft 8 ins (22.15 m)
Fuselage width: 7 ft 1 ins (2.16 m)
Maximum height: 16 ft 10 ins (5.13 m) to top of tail rotor

CABIN:
Length: 24 ft 11 ins (7.59 m)
Width: 6 ft 6 ins (1.98 m)
Height: 6 ft 3.5 ins (1.92 m)
Volume: 990 cu ft (28.03 m^3)

MAIN ROTOR:
Aerofoil section: NACA 0012
Blade chord: 1 ft 6.2 ins (0.46 m)
Blade area: each 43 sq ft (3.99 m^2)
Rotor disc: 2,921 sq ft (271.4 m^2)
Rpm: 209

TAIL ROTOR:
Diameter: 10 ft 4 ins (3.15m)

UNDERCARRIAGE:
Type: Retractable twin mainwheels (into sponsons) and fixed tailwheel. Optional emergency flotation system for overwater operations, and sea anchor
Wheel base: 23 ft 5 ins (7.14 m)
Wheel track: 13 ft (3.96 m)

WEIGHTS:
Empty: 12,009 lb (5,447 kg), except overland version without sponsons is 11,963 lb (5,426 kg)
Maximum take-off: 21,400 lb (9,707 kg)
Payload: 8,692 lb (3,943 kg) maximum

PERFORMANCE (ISA)**:**
Never-exceed speed (V_{NE}): 122 kts (140 mph) 226 km/h
Cruise speed: 110 kts (127 mph) 204 km/h
Maximum climb rate: 1,850 ft (564 m) per minute
IGE hovering ceiling: 5,600 ft (1,707 m)
OGE hovering ceiling: 3,500 ft (1,067 m)
Operating ceiling: 10,000 ft (3,050 m)
Range with full fuel: 800 naut miles (921 miles) 1,482 km
Duration: 7 hours maximum, no reserve
On station: 1 hour 45 minutes for ASV at 100 naut miles (115 miles) 185 km from base, or 2 hours for ASW at 125 naut miles (144 miles) 231 km from base

Radar: AlliedSignal RDR-1300 forward looking or RDR-1500 360° dorsal radar for SAR. Racal Radar Defence Systems Searchwater for AEW (fully stabilized and scanning through 360°), including third alternator. Thomson Thorn Supersearcher for ASW and ASV role.
Flight avionics/instrumentation: Dual pilot IFR. 2 sets of flight instruments, 2 sets of engine instruments, 1 set of general instruments, fire warning, advisory fuel management, caution and identification panels. Automatic flight control system, with fully automatic transition from forward flight to hover and an ability to hover precisely at heights up to 140 ft (43 m) reference to Doppler; auxiliary hover trim facility enables the helicopter to be accurately positioned. Radio equipment comprises dual Rockwell Collins ARC-182 VHF/UHF and HF9000 HF; Racal Doppler 91 and B6922-1 intercom; and IFF. Navigation equipment comprises Racal RNS-252 tactical navigation computer; AlliedSignal Bendix/King KDF 806 ADF, KNR 634R VOR/ILS, and KDM 706A DME; Smiths/Honeywell APN-198 radar altimeter; Chelton 7 UHF and VHF homing; and ARNAV Series 7000 Loran-C. FLIR 2000 for SAR role. Racal MIR 2 ESM for AEW role. I-band transponder for ASW and ASV role; optional MAD (as used by Royal Navy). AlliedSignal Bendix/King AQS-18(V) or Thomson Sintra HS 312 dipping sonar for ASW role.
Fixed guns: Optional cabin-mounted machine-gun.
Expendable weapons and equipment: Exocet, Sea Eagle, Sea Skua, Harpoon, Otomat or Penguin anti-ship missiles, torpedoes (including Sting Ray), 4 Mk 11 depth charges, Clevite simulator, 2 marine markers, 4 smoke floats, and Ultra Electronics mini sonobuoys.

Aircraft variants:
Sea King AEW Mk 2A is the Royal Navy's airborne early warning version for operations from *Invincible* class carriers (converted from 11 former HAS Mk 2As). Searchwater radar scanner in an external air-pressurized Kevlar fabric container, which is hydraulically rotated to the horizontal when the helicopter is in transit or static, and to the vertical, below wheel level, when deployed. See below.
Sea King AEW Mk 7 is the designation for AEW Mk 2A upgrades entering Royal Navy service from the year 2000. Planned in 2 stages with Racal as prime contractor, eventually providing Searchwater 2000AEW radar, central tactical suite with colour displays, JTIDS data link, ring laser gyro INS, GPS, second Have Quick II radio, Hazeltine APX-113(V) interrogator/transponder, and video recorder. 10 upgrades, with options for up to a further 6.
HAR Mk 3A is an RAF SAR version with Racal AR15955/2 radar.
HAR Mk 5 is a SAR only version, 4 converted from HAS Mk 5s.
HAS Mk 5 is a Royal Navy ASW and SAR version with Racal Sea Searcher radar, built new and by conversion of older model Sea Kings. Racal Orange Crop ESM. See Mk 6.
HAS Mk 6 is the latest Royal Navy version for ASW, operated from 1989. Some new, others upgraded from HAS Mk 5s using Westland kits. GEC-Marconi 2069 dipping sonar with enhanced digital processing and with sonar and sonobuoy information presented on a CRT, Orange Reaper ESM, internally mounted MAD, Supersearcher radar and many other improvements.
HC Mk 4 is a Commando type with the Royal Navy, as are the ETPS (Empire Test Pilots' School) Mk 4 and former RAE Mk 4Xs (RAE is now named Defence Evaluation & Research Agency).
Exported Sea Kings are to varying equipment standards, according to roles detailed under Sales. Advanced model is detailed.
Commando is a tactical assault derivative of Sea King, to which it differs in equipment. Fixed head undercarriage and no sponsons for its mainly overland role. Commando operators include Egypt, Qatar and India.
Note: According to information received in July 1998, Sea King is no longer being marketed as a newly built helicopter.

Wombat Gyrocopters — UK

Comments: Details and a photograph of the Gyrocopter single-seat autogyro can be found in the 1996-97 edition of *WA&SD*, page 337.

Air Command International Inc — USA

Corporate address:
PO Box 1345, 702 Cooper Drive, Wylie, TX 75098.
Telephone: +1 972 442 6694
Facsimile: +1 972 442 9174

ACTIVITIES

■ Currently produces 8 different autogyro versions in kit form, with bolt-together components that require no special tools to assemble (50 to 135 hours working time, depending upon the version).

Air Command Commander series

Role: Single and 2-seat kit-built autogyros. Prices quoted were received in May 1998; upgrade kits to convert single-seaters into 2-seaters and many other options are available.

Aircraft variants:
Commander 447 was designed to be a single-seat ultralight autogyro, with a 40 hp (30 kW) Rotax 447 engine and 5 ft (1.52 m) Warp Drive propeller. 23 ft (7.01 m) Skywheels rotor. Gross weight 552 lb (250.4 kg). Maximum speed 55 kts (63 mph) 101 km/h. Kit US$8,500.
Commander 500 is a single-seater with a 65 hp (48.5 kW) Arrow 500 engine and 5 ft (1.52 m) or 5 ft 8 ins (1.73 m) Warp Drive propeller. 23 ft (7.01 m) Skywheels rotor. Gross weight 700 lb (317.5 kg). Maximum speed 82 kts (95 mph) 153 km/h.
Commander 503 is a single-seat Experimental category autogyro with a 47 hp (35 kW) Rotax 503 engine and 5 ft (1.52 m) Warp Drive propeller. 23 ft (7.01 m) Skywheels rotor. Gross weight 590 lb (268 kg). Maximum speed 65 kts (75 mph) 121 km/h. Kit US$9,700.
Commander 582 is a single-seater with a 65 hp (48.5 kW) Rotax 582 engine and 5 ft (1.52 m) or 5 ft 8 ins (1.73 m) Warp Drive propeller. 23 ft (7.01 m) Skywheels rotor. Gross weight 750 lb (340 kg). Maximum speed 82 kts (95 mph) 153 km/h. Kit US$10,870.
Commander 1000 is a single-seater with a 100 hp (74.6 kW) Arrow 1000 engine and 5 ft 4 ins (1.63 m) Warp Drive propeller. 23 ft (7.01 m) Skywheels rotor. Gross weight 900 lb (408 kg). Maximum speed 100 kts (115 mph) 185 km/h.
Commander 147A is a side-by-side 2-seat autogyro with a 160 hp (119.3 kW) Mazda 13B engine and 5 ft 8 ins (1.73 m) Warp Drive propeller. 31 ft (9.45 m) Skywheels rotor. Gross weight 1,500 lb (680 kg). Maximum speed 104 kts (120 mph) 193 km/h. Kit US$30,000, or US$21,500 without engine.
Commander 582 Side-by-Side is a 2-seater with a 65 hp (48.5 kW) Rotax 582 engine and 5 ft (1.52 m) or 5 ft 8 ins (1.73 m) Warp Drive propeller. 25 ft (7.62 m) Skywheels rotor. Gross weight 750 lb (340 kg). Maximum speed 65 kts (75 mph) 121 km/h.
Commander 582 Tandem is a tandem 2-seater with a 65 hp (48.5 kW) Rotax 582 engine and 5 ft 8 ins (1.73 m) Warp Drive propeller. 25 ft (7.62 m) Skywheels rotor. Gross weight 790 lb (358 kg). Maximum speed 78 kts (90 mph) 145 km/h. Kit US$14,095, or US$9,062 without engine.
Commander 1000 Side-by-Side and ***Tandem*** are not currently available. Both designed with 100 hp (74.6 kW) Arrow 1000 engines.

↑ **Air Command International Commander 503** *(Geoffrey P. Jones)*

Air & Space America Inc – See Farrington Aircraft Corporation

Aircraft Designs Inc — USA

Corporate address:
5 Harris Court, Building S, Monterey, CA 93940.
Telephone: +1 408 649 6212
Facsimile: +1 408 649 5738

ACTIVITIES

■ See also Recreational section.

Aircraft Designs Bumble Bee

Role: Single-seat ultralight autogyro.
Sales: Available in plans and kit forms, the latter at about $US5,500. Typical assembly time is 400 working hours.
Rotor system: 2-blade rotor, using NACA 8-H-12 aerofoil. Aluminium alloy and composites construction (foam, glassfibre and epoxy). Pre-rotator.
Tail surfaces: Horizontal and vertical surfaces.
Airframe materials: Aluminium alloy tube open structure. Composite tail.
Engine: 40 hp (30 kW) Rotax 447 piston engine, with 2-blade pusher propeller.
Fuel system: 19 or 38 litres.

→ **Aircraft Designs Bumble Bee ultralight autogyro**

Details for Bumble Bee

PRINCIPAL DIMENSIONS:
Rotor diameter: 23 ft (7.01 m)
Airframe length: 12 ft 6 ins (3.81 m)
Maximum height: 7 ft 6 ins (2.29 m)

WEIGHTS:
Empty, operating: 213-230 lb (97-104 kg)
Maximum take-off: 500 lb (227 kg)

PERFORMANCE:
Maximum speed: 56 kts (65 mph) 105 km/h
Cruise speed: 35 kts (40 mph) 64 km/h
Maximum climb rate: 1,500 ft (457 m) per minute
Ceiling: 12,000 ft (3,660 m)
Range: 56 naut miles (65 miles) 105 km
Duration: 1 hour

Aircraft Designs Sportster

Role: 2-seat (side-by-side) Experimental category autogyro.
Sales: Plans only. Typical construction time is 1,500 working hours.
Rotor system: 2-blade rotor, using NACA 8-H-12 aerofoil. Pre-rotator. Rotor brake.
Tail surfaces: Twin fins and rudders.
Airframe materials: Aluminium alloy tubing and sheet, except for composites used for the wheel fairings and part of the tail.
Engine: Typically Textron Lycoming O-320 piston engine, but with other possibilities.
Engine rating: 150 hp (112 kW) for the O-320.
Fuel system: 64 litres.

Details for Sportster

PRINCIPAL DIMENSIONS:
Rotor diameter: 28 ft (8.53 m)
Airframe length: 12 ft (3.66 m)
Maximum height: 8 ft (2.44 m)

WEIGHTS:
Empty: 650 lb (295 kg)
Maximum take-off: 1,100 lb (499 kg)

PERFORMANCE:
Maximum speed: 78 kts (90 mph) 145 km/h
Cruise speed: 65 kts (75 mph) 121 km/h
Maximum climb rate: 1,000 ft (305 m) per minute
Service ceiling: 12,000 ft (3,660 m)
Range: 130 naut miles (150 miles) 241 km

Alturair — USA

Corporate address:
1405 North Johnson, El Cajon, CA 92020.
Telephone: +1 619 449 1570
Facsimile: +1 619 442 0481
Information:
Frank G. Verbeke (President).

ACTIVITIES

- Offers factory completed or components for the BD-5 Experimental category aircraft, Globe Swift components, and air pressure jet helicopters, the Rotorair 2 being detailed below.
- See also Engine section for the Alturdyne A650 and AT62.

Alturair Rotorair 2

First flight: 1986.
Role: 2-seat air-pressure helicopter, without need of a conventional transmission or tailrotor. Intended to be a simple-to-operate homebuilt.

Aims

- See diagram: Gas turbine engine *A* drives an air compressor *B* to produce compressed air. This air is ducted via a flexible pipe *C* into a rotor distribution hub *D*. Hollow rotor blades *E* and *F* direct this air to the fixed jet nozzles *G*. These nozzles are orientated tangentially to the rotor disc and expel the compressed air to produce blade rotation. Exhaust from the turbine is directed over the tailfin *H* to provide yaw and directional control.

Details

Rotor system: All-metal hollow blades. Rotor hub is simple, as no transmission is required. A series of torsion, tension straps unload all centrifugal stresses from the hub and there is no hinging of the blade roots.
Airframe materials: Lightweight glassfibre fuselage shell.
Engine: The gas turbine engine drives a load compressor directly. A load control valve is installed at the compressor intake for simple power control. Operation of the turbine is automatic from a single switch.
Engine rating: 250 shp (186.4 kW).
Fuel system: 227 litres.

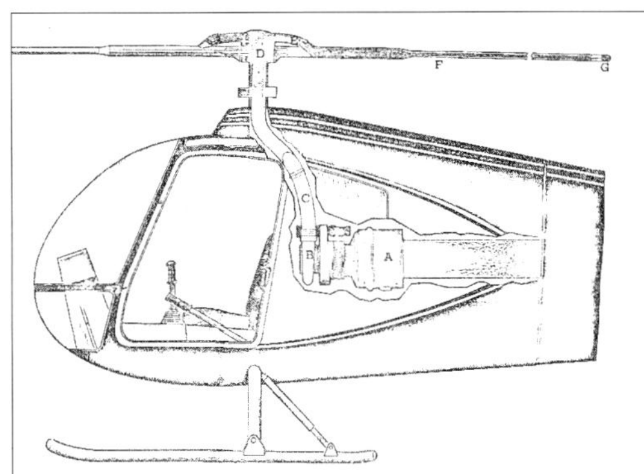

↑ Alturair Rotorair 2 air pressure jet helicopter *(courtesy Alturair)*

Details for Rotorair 2

PRINCIPAL DIMENSIONS:
Rotor diameter: 36 ft (10.97 m)
Airframe length: 10 ft (3.05 m)
Fuselage width: 4 ft (1.22 m)
Maximum height: 7 ft 6 ins (2.29 m)

ROTOR:
Blade chord: 8 ins (20.3 cm)
Rpm: 350

UNDERCARRIAGE:
Type: Fixed skids
Skid track: 6 ft (1.83 m)

WEIGHTS:
Empty: 600 lb (272 kg)
Maximum take-off: 1,400 lb (635 kg)

PERFORMANCE:
Maximum speed: 87 kts (100 mph) 161 km/h
Cruise speed: 74 kts (85 mph) 137 km/h
Maximum climb rate: 900 ft (274 m) per minute
Hovering ceiling: 6,000 ft (1,830 m)
Ceiling: 16,000 ft (4,875 m)
Range: 217 naut miles (250 miles) 402 km

Barnett Rotorcraft Co — USA

Corporate address:
4307 Olivehurst Avenue, Olivehurst, CA 95961.
Telephone: +1 916 742 7416
Facsimile: +1 916 743 6866

ACTIVITIES

- Supplies plans, raw material kits, welded 4130 steel airframes and finished components for the J4B and J4B2.

Barnett J4B

Role: Single-seat homebuilt autogyro. Baggage space aft of seat, capacity 30 lb (13.6 kg).
Sales: Plans and kits are available; material kits cost approximately US$7,000, taking typically 300 working hours to assemble. Factory finished assemblies would total about US$14,000. Available kit allows conversion into a J4B2.
Rotor system: 2-blade, aluminium alloy. Offset rotor head.
Tail surfaces: Fin, large rudder and tailplane.
Airframe materials: Welded 4130 steel tube, glassfibre nacelle, and Dacron fabric covered tail surfaces. Polycarbonate windshield.
Engine: Standard Teledyne Continental A65 to O-200 piston engine, with Barnett 57.5/56P propeller. Subaru with Barnett gearbox, Mazda and Textron Lycoming engines are becoming popular.
Engine rating: 65-100 hp (48.5-74.6 kW) for Teledyne Continental.
Fuel system: 51 litres in a welded aluminium tank (fuel weight 94.5 lb, 43 kg).

↑ Barnett J4B single-seat homebuilt autogyro

Barnett J4B2

Role: 2-seat homebuilt autogyro. Baggage space aft of seats, capacity 20 lb (9 kg).
Sales: Plans and kits are available; see J4B for price guide. A factory finished J4B2 for overseas export costs about US$30,000 ready to fly.
Rotor system: Similar to J4B.

Details for J4B with O-200 engine

PRINCIPAL DIMENSIONS:
Rotor diameter: 23 ft (7.01 m)
Airframe length: 12 ft 4 ins (3.76 m)
Width: 6 ft 6.75 ins (2 m)
Maximum height: 7 ft 8 ins (2.34 m)

MAIN ROTOR:
Rotor disc: 416.59 sq ft (38.7 m^2)
Rpm: 425 (±10)

UNDERCARRIAGE:
Type: Spring or shock-absorber nosewheel type, with small tailwheel. Steering with rudder pedals. Separate pedal (between rudder pedals) for disc brakes, either hydraulic or mechanical
Main wheel tyre size: 5.30/4.50 × 6
Nose wheel tyre size: 4.10/3.50 × 4
Tailwheel size: 4 ins (10 cm) diameter

WEIGHTS:
Empty: 512 lb (232 kg)
Pilot: 180 lb (81.6 kg) ±20 lb (9 kg)
Maximum take-off: 800 lb (363 kg)

PERFORMANCE:
Never-exceed speed (V_{NE}): 122 kts (140 mph) 225 km/h
Maximum speed: 108 kts (125 mph) 201 km/h
Cruise speed: 91 kts (105 mph) 169 km/h at 75% power
Take-off distance: 350 ft (107 m)
Landing distance: up to 20 ft (6 m)
Maximum climb rate: 1,500 ft (457 m) per minute
Service ceiling: 12,000 ft (3,660 m)
Glide ratio: 5:1
Range: 234 naut miles (270 miles) 434 km
Duration: 2 hours 15 minutes, with 20 minutes reserve

Airframe materials: Welded 4130 steel tube, glassfibre nacelle, and fabric covered tail surfaces. Polycarbonate canopy.
Engine: Typically Teledyne Continental O-200 or Textron Lycoming O-360 piston engine, with Barnett 57.5/56P propeller. Subaru EJ 22 or EJ 25 with Barnett gearbox and Mazda engines are becoming popular.
Engine rating: 100-180 hp (74.6-134 kW) for Teledyne Continental or Textron Lycoming.
Fuel system: 64.4 litres in a welded aluminium tank (fuel weight 110.5 lb (50 kg).

Details for J4B2 with O-200 engine

PRINCIPAL DIMENSIONS:
Rotor diameter: 25 ft 4 ins (7.72 m)
Airframe length: 13 ft 8 ins (4.17 m)
Width: 6 ft 6.75 ins (2 m)
Maximum height: 8 ft 1 ins (2.46 m)

MAIN ROTOR:
Rotor disc: 505.39 sq ft (46.95 m^2)
Rpm: 395 (±10)

UNDERCARRIAGE:
Type: Spring or shock-absorber nosewheel type, with small tailwheel. Steering with rudder pedals. Separate pedal (between rudder pedals) for disc brakes, either hydraulic or mechanical
Main wheel tyre size: 5.30/4.50 × 6
Nose wheel tyre size: 4.10/3.50 × 4
Tailwheel size: 4 ins (10 cm) diameter

WEIGHTS:
Empty: 577 lb (262 kg)
Crew: 360 lb (163 kg)
Maximum take-off: 1,085 lb (492 kg)

PERFORMANCE:
Never-exceed speed (V_{NE}): 120 kts (138 mph) 222 km/h
Maximum speed: 104 kts (120 mph) 193 km/h
Cruise speed: 81 kts (93 mph) 150 km/h at 75% power
Take-off distance: 600 ft (183 m)
Landing distance: up to 25 ft (8 m)
Maximum climb rate: 500 ft (152 m) per minute
Service ceiling: 8,000 ft (2,440 m)
Glide ratio: 4:1
Range: 173 naut miles (199 miles) 320 km
Duration: 2 hours 30 minutes

↑ Barnett J4B2 2-seat homebuilt autogyro

Bell Helicopter Textron Inc — USA

Corporate address:
PO Box 482, Fort Worth, TX 76101.
Telephone: +1 817 280 2011
Facsimile: +1 817 280 2321
Web site: http://www.bellhelicopter.textron.com
Founded:
1935 as Bell Aircraft Corporation, with Bell Helicopter Company becoming an operating branch of Textron Inc in 1960 and a fully-absorbed subsidiary on 3 January 1982.
Employees: 8,200 worldwide.
Information:
Carl L. Harris (Director of Public Affairs – *telephone* +1 817 280 2425, *facsimile* +1 817 280 8221, *E-mail* charris@bellhelicopter.textron.com), or Bob Leder (Manager, Public Relations in the USA – *telephone* +1 817 280 6440). Also *telephone* +1 817 280 4686 for international marketing, and +1 817 280 3259 for military business development.

ACTIVITIES

■ More than 33,000 helicopters built over nearly 50 years. Bell Helicopter Textron moved its assembly line for commercial helicopters to Canada in 1986, where a production facility had been completed the previous year as a division of Textron Canada Ltd. Details of the JetRanger III, LongRanger IV, TwinRanger, 212, 230, 407, 412EP, 427 and 430 can, therefore, be found under Canada, including military versions of these helicopters such as the TH-67 Creek trainer. In addition, IPTN of Indonesia, Agusta of Italy and Fuji of Japan produce licence-built variants of Bell helicopters (which see). See Agusta for **AB 139**.
■ Under an agreement with IAR-SA Brasov dating from August 1996 but requiring a share deal (the agreement was tied to Bell's purchase of a majority shareholding in the privatizing company, set at 70%), IAR is to licence manufacture AH-1W SuperCobras for the Romanian forces, using the new designation AH-1RO Dracula. Bell is expected also to use IAR as a production source for other items.
■ The US Army is to have 131 National Guard UH-1s re-engined with LHTEC T800s. See also H-1 Programme.
■ During the last full year (at the time of writing) Bell delivered 320 new helicopters, plus 35 OH-58D retrofits and 28 AH-1W canopy modifications.

On 25 February 1998 the Board of Directors of Textron Inc approved the company's plan to purchase a substantial portion of the commercial helicopter business of The Boeing Company. Under the terms of the proposed sale, Bell Helicopter Textron was to acquire the Boeing (former McDonnell Douglas) MD 500 and MD 600 series product lines. The agreement was also to include spare parts and support for Boeing's MD Explorer helicopter, though this was not being purchased by Bell. Production of the MD 500 and MD 600 helicopters was to be relocated to Mirabel. However, the purchase had (at the time of writing) still to clear US Federal review, and until then the helicopters remain under the Boeing heading. In addition, Bell also agreed to assume Boeing's 49% interest in the Bell Boeing 609 civil tiltrotor as of 1 March 1998. Bell and Boeing remain partnered on the V-22.

Bell H-1 Programme (AH-1Z and UH-1Y)

Comments: Major upgrade to remanufacture 180 AH-1W (4BW) SuperCobras (as AH-1Zs) and 100 UH-1Ns (as UH-1Ys) of the USMC to an advanced configuration featuring common engines and flight dynamics, to operate beyond the year 2020. At the time of writing in 1998, Bell was in the EMD phase. The upgrades include much commonality between the helicopters, including General Electric T700 engines; 4-blade all-composite, hingeless and bearingless main rotor system and tail rotor; and identical drive trains, hydraulics and electrical distribution systems. Litton is to provide the common cockpit configuration. In mid-1998 Lockheed Martin was selected to develop the advanced target sight system (TSS) for the AH-1Z, incorporating Wescam imaging and Lockheed Martin Sniper FLIR. Zero-time airframes are remanufactured with the latest technology. The upgrade increases speed, range, manoeuvrability and lift capability of both aircraft. In addition to major savings in maintenance, ground handling, support and spare parts inventories by the commonality, the advanced technology provides the helicopters with increased battlefield survivability and greater mission success. In addition, crashworthiness is improved, with the 4BN said to be superior to the H-60. First flight of the 4BW is scheduled for October 2000, with 4BN the following month, allowing deliveries to the USMC between 2004 and 2013. See AH-1W SuperCobra entry for more details.

Bell UH-1H-II (Huey II)

First flight: 1992. First flight of a Colombian upgraded Huey II September 1997.
First delivery: June 1997 to the Colombian Air Force as a kit.
Role: Upgrade of the UH-1H.

Aims

■ Joint modernization programme between Bell and AlliedSignal to extend the life of the UH-1H for service into the next century.
■ Engine and airframe upgrade package offered as parts kits to military and civil operators, with the option of the operator undertaking the work.
■ Huey II has the internal payload increased by 642 lb (291 kg), and has good hot day/high altitude performance.

↑ Bell AH-1W (4BW) SuperCobra and UH-1N (4BN) after the H-1 Programme upgrade

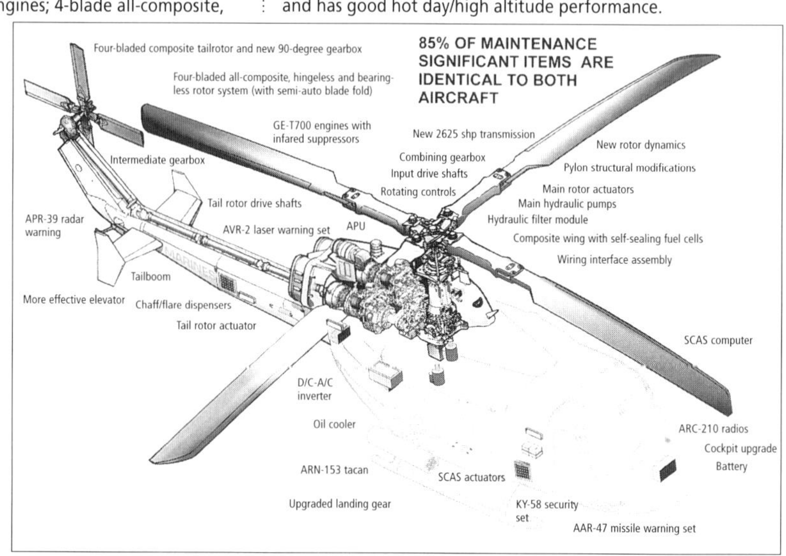

↑ Bell UH-1N (4BN) under the H-1 Programme upgrade. Annotation indicates identical parts with the AH-1W (4BW) SuperCobra under the programme

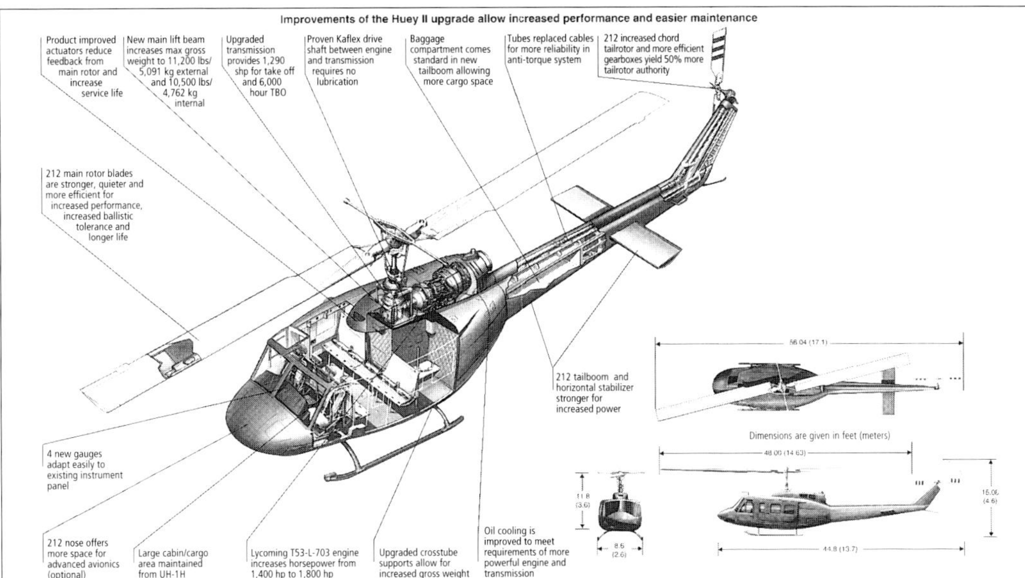

↑ **Bell UH-1H-II (Huey II) modernization diagram** *(courtesy Bell Helicopter Textron)*

■ Upgraded engine (see Engine), and upgraded transmission, gearbox, rotor blades, tailboom and drive system to handle the additional 400 shp (298 kW) of power.

Details

Sales: The Colombian Air Force contracted to upgrade 5 UH-1Hs to Huey II configuration.
Standard equipment: Breeze-Eastern hoist for rescue capability.
Optional equipment: Numerous kits and items are available as optional equipment for Huey II, to include NVG cockpit, FLIR, integrated avionics suite, GPS, rescue hoist, cargo hook, HUMS, engine particle separator and wash kit, and auxiliary fuel tanks.
Rotor system: Upgrades include use of Bell 212 main and tail rotor blades. See diagram.
Engine: AlliedSignal T53-L-703 turboshaft. Heli-Conversions particle separator.
Engine rating: 1,800 shp (1,342 kW) military for 30 minutes, 1,500 shp (1,118 kW) normal.
Transmission rating: 1,290 shp (962 kW) for 5 minutes, 1,134 shp (846 kW) maximum continuous.
Fuel system: 1,435 lb (651 kg). Auxiliary fuel tanks available.
Flight avionics/instrumentation: Rockwell Collins suite. Night vision capability is enhanced with FLIR and a NVG compatible cockpit. Avionics Specialties Inc turbine monitoring system.

Details for Huey II

PRINCIPAL DIMENSIONS:
Rotor diameter (main): 48 ft (14.63 m)
Maximum length, rotors turning: 56 ft 0.5 ins (17.1 m)
Fuselage length: 44 ft 10 ins (13.67 m) including tail rotor
Maximum height: 15 ft 1 ins (4.6 m)

MAIN ROTOR:
Blade chord: 1 ft 11.38 ins (0.59 m)
Rotor disc: 1,810 sq ft (168.12 m^2)
Rpm: 324

WEIGHTS:
Empty: 5,440 lb (2,468 kg)
Maximum take-off: 10,500 lb (4,762 kg) with internal payload, or 11,200 lb (5,080 kg) with external payload
Useful load: 5,060 lb (2,295 kg)

PERFORMANCE:
Never-exceed speed (V_{NE}): 130 kts (150 mph) 240 km/h at 9,500 lb (4,309 kg) gross weight, or 106 kts (122 mph) 196 km/h at 10,500 lb (4,762 kg)
Average cruise speed: 120 kts (138 mph) 222 km/h
Maximum climb rate: 1,760 ft (536 m) per minute at 10,500 lb (4,762 kg)
Vertical climb rate: 460 ft (140 m) per minute at 10,500 lb (4,762 kg), at sea level static
OGE hovering ceiling: 5,325 ft (1,623 m) ISA
Service ceiling: 16,780 ft (5,115 m) at 10,500 lb (4,762 kg)
Operational radius: 115 naut miles (132 miles) 213 km at sea level static, 10 minutes reserve at maximum duration speed, at 10,500 lb (4,762 kg)
Duration: 2.8 hours

Bell AH-1F HueyCobra

Note: Fuji of Japan produces the helicopter as the AH-1S. However, all US production has ended, with Bell now concentrating on twin-engined models. The description below is, therefore, brief. Planned Romanian production has switched to AH-1W SuperCobra.
First flight: 7 September 1965 as prototype of original AH-1G.
Role: Attack, anti-armour, fire support, fire suppression, and heliborne escort.
Sales: Currently used by the US Army, Bahrain, Israel, Japan (still under construction as the Fuji-built AH-1S), Jordan, South Korea, Pakistan, Thailand and Turkey. Various upgrading programmes for existing helicopters have taken place, including 52 US Army Bell AH-1F HueyCobras having their night combat capability improved with the addition of Hughes Cobra-NITE (or C-NITE) targeting systems installed at Camp Humphries in South Korea (C-NITE has also been adopted by Japan, South Korea, Pakistan and the US Army National Guard for their AH-1F/S types, while Israel has a Tamam Precision Instruments Industries-produced thermal imaging system). C-NITE allows TOW missiles to be launched at night, in adverse weather or through smoke, haze and dust. Other upgrades have taken place under the US Army Cobra Fleet Life Extension and other programmes, but all single-engine HueyCobra production by Bell in the USA has ended.
Crew: 2, in tandem stepped cockpits. Flat-plate anti-glint glazing. Jettisonable doors and windows for emergency escape.
Rotor system: 2-blade, composite, with swept tips.

Details for AH-1F

PRINCIPAL DIMENSIONS:
Rotor diameter (main): 44 ft (13.41 m)
Maximum length, rotors turning: 53 ft 1 ins (16.18 m)
Maximum height: 13 ft 5 ins (4.09 m) to above rotor head
Wing span: 10 ft 9 ins (3.28 m)

MAIN ROTOR:
Aerofoil section: Special Kaman
Blade chord: 2 ft 6 ins (0.76 m)
Blade area: 104.5 sq ft (9.71 m^2)
Rotor disc: 1,520.2 sq ft (141.23 m^2)
Rpm: 746 ft (227 m) per second

TAIL ROTOR:
Diameter: 8 ft 6 ins (2.59 m)

UNDERCARRIAGE:
Type: Twin fixed skids
Skid track: 7 ft (2.13 m)

WEIGHTS:
Empty: 6,600 lb (2,993 kg)
Maximum take-off and landing: 10,000 lb (4,536 kg)

PERFORMANCE:
Maximum speed: 122 kts (141 mph) 227 km/h
Maximum climb rate: 1,620 ft (494 m) per minute
Ceiling: 12,200 ft (3,718 m), HIGE and service
G limits: +2.5, -0.5
Range: 273 naut miles (315 miles) 507 km

Tail rotor characteristics: 2-blade, to starboard.
Safety features: Include blade and airframe tolerance to 23-mm strikes.
Engine: AlliedSignal T53-L-703 turboshaft.
Engine rating: 1,800 shp (1,342 kW).
Fuel system: 980 litres.
Hydraulic system: 2 systems, each 1,500 psi.
Flight avionics/instrumentation: Includes AN/ASN-128 Doppler, HSI, digital fire control computer, laser rangefinder, automatic target tracker, pilot's Kaiser HUD, IFF, Hughes LAAT stabilized sighting system, Cobra-NITE (or C-NITE) targeting systems, and much more.
Self-protection systems: AN/ALQ-144 IR jammer, radar warning, chaff/flare dispensers, and IR reflective paint.
Fixed guns: General Electric Universal Turret System, with M-197 20-mm 3-barrel Gatling type cannon for close range of up to 1.08 naut miles (1.25 miles) 2 km.
Ammunition: 750 rounds.
Number of weapon pylons: 4, under the stub wings.
Expendable weapons and equipment: 8 TOW anti-armour missiles under outer pylons, and rockets or up to 4 AAMs on the inner pylons.

Bell AH-1W SuperCobra and AH-1W (4BW)

First flight: First AH-1W was introduced in March 1986.

Details *(for AH-1W, except under Aircraft variants)*

Role: Attack, anti-armour, fire support, fire suppression, and heliborne escort.
Sales: AH-1Ws currently in production for the US Marine Corps, with the present contract calling for 213; 21 delivered in the last full year (plus 28 canopy modifications). See also H-1 Programme for AH-1W (4BW). Other operators are Taiwan (63 firm/options) and Turkey (10). During Operation Desert Storm, US Marine Corps AH-1Ws accounted for 97 tanks, 104 armoured vehicles, 16 bunkers, and 2 anti-aircraft artillery sites, achieving a 92% mission readiness rate under conditions that reached 57-63° C.
Crew: 2, in tandem stepped and armoured cockpits. Dual controls.
Rotor system: 2-blade, semi-rigid seesaw main rotor, with aluminium alloy blades, and elastomeric and Teflon coated bearings. Rotor brake. A 4-blade rotor, without hinges and of bearingless type, will be fitted to existing USMC AH-1W (4BW) helicopters under the H-1 Programme (which see); has composite blades and 2 composite yokes, and possesses a ballistic tolerance to hits from 23-mm shells.
Tail rotor characteristics: 2-blade, semi-rigid, bonded metal.
Wing surfaces: Similar style to HueyCobra, of NACA 0030/0024 aerofoil section.
Flight control system: Hydraulic.
Fuselage: Ultra-slim fuselage cross-section, as a feature of all HueyCobra/SuperCobra types.
Airframe materials: Metal.
Engines: 2 General Electric T700-GE-401 turboshafts.
Engine rating: Each 1,690 shp (1,260 kW) take off.
Transmission rating: 2,032 shp (1,515 kW) take-off, 1,725 shp (1,286 kW) maximum continuous.
Fuel system: 2 non-suction, crashworthy, self-sealing tanks. 1,162 litres, of which 1,128 litres capacity is usable. 291 or 379 litre auxiliary fuel tanks carried under the stub wings. System survives 23-mm shell hits.
Electrical system: 28 volt single conductor type. 2 × 28 volt 400 amp generators and 2 × 24 volt 40 amp-hour ni-cd batteries. 3 inverters (1,000VA main, 750VA 3-phase, and 365VA for AIM-9s).

↑ **Bell AH-1F HueyCobra operated by Bahrain**

↑ Bell AH-1W SuperCobra operated by the USMC

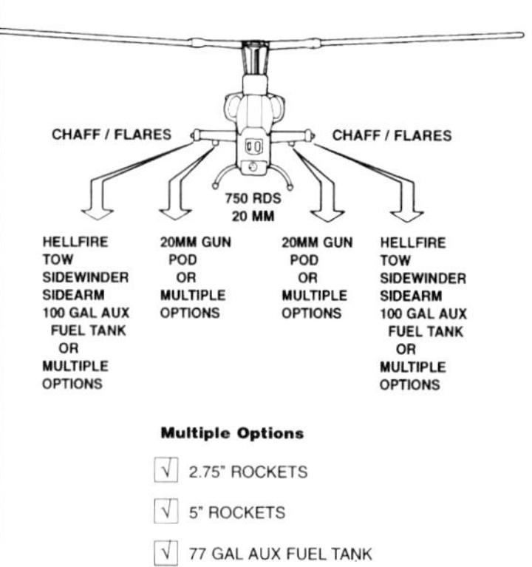

↑ Bell AH-1W SuperCobra armament diagram *(courtesy Bell Helicopter Textron)*

Hydraulic system: Dual, variable delivery, each 3,000 psi.
Flight avionics/instrumentation: Tamam Precision Instruments Industries night targeting system (NTS), first delivered on a US Marine Corps AH-1W in June 1994, integrates the TOW/Hellfire missile systems with FLIR, laser rangefinder/designator, automatic target tracker, TV and video recorder. With NTS, SuperCobra can detect, acquire, track, range, designate and attack targets at night, in adverse weather or limited visibility; NTS can also designate targets for all NATO aircraft that use laser-guided weapons. Kaiser HUD. Helmet-mounted display integrates the NVGs with targeting and navigation cues and also the helmet sight system to control the turret. ADF, Tacan, radar beacon system, radar altimeter, GPS, IFF and much more. For precise target location, the navigation system also includes Teledyne AN/APN-217 Doppler. Airborne Target Handover System can work in conjunction with other helicopters and aeroplanes.
Self-protection systems: Dual radar warning, laser warning, missile warning, IR jammers, dual chaff/flare dispensers, and IR reflective paint.
Fixed guns: General Electric Universal Turret System with 110° azimuth, 18° elevation and 50° depressed angle of tracking, with M-197 20-mm 3-barrel Gatling type cannon for close range of up to 1.08 naut miles (1.25 miles) 2 km. Fired by either crew member, able to be slaved to their helmet-mounted sights. Rate of fire 675 rounds per minute.
Ammunition: 750 rounds of M-50 or 20-mm HEI ammunition.
Number of weapon pylons: 2 under each wing, with 3 planned for new wings . AN/ALE-39 chaff dispenser above each wing.
Expendable weapons and equipment: Dual anti-armour capability, with up to 8 TOW II or Hellfire missiles. Other store options/additions include 2.75-ins rockets with submunition warheads or 5-ins Zuni rockets, CBU-55B fuel air bombs, GPU-2A 20-mm gun pods, M-188 smoke grenade dispenser, SUU-44 flare dispenser, 295 or 378 litre auxiliary fuel tanks, or Maverick air-to-ground, 2 × AIM-9L Sidewinder air-to-air and 2 × AGM-122A Sidearm anti-radiation missiles. See diagram.

Details for AH-1W

PRINCIPAL DIMENSIONS:
Rotor diameter (main): 48 ft (14.63 m)
Maximum length, rotors turning: 58 ft (17.68 m)
Fuselage length: 45 ft 6 ins (13.87 m)
Maximum height: 14 ft 3 ins (4.34 m)
Wing span: 11 ft 7 ins (3.53 m)

MAIN ROTOR:
Aerofoil section: Modified Wortmann FX-083
Blade chord: 2 ft 9 ins (0.84 m)
Blade area: each 66 sq ft (6.13 m^2)
Rotor disc: 1,809.7 sq ft (168.1 m^2)
Rpm: 311

TAIL ROTOR:
Diameter: 9 ft 9 ins (2.97 m)
Rpm: 1,460

UNDERCARRIAGE:
Type: Fixed twin skids. Provision for ground handling wheels
Skid track: 7 ft 4 ins (2.24 m)

WEIGHTS:
Empty: 10,300 lb (4,672 kg)
Maximum take-off: 14,750 lb (6,690 kg)
Useful load: 4,450 lb (2,018 kg)
Payload: 1,661 lb (753 kg) of stores

PERFORMANCE:
Maximum attainable speed: 170 kts (196 mph) 315 km/h
Maximum cruise speed: 152 kts (175 mph) 282 km/h
Climb rate: 2,000 ft (610 m) per minute
Vertical climb rate: 645 ft (196 m) per minute in air-to-aır configuration, mid-mission weight, intermediate rated power
Climb rate, OEI: 800 ft (244 m) with AAMs, ISA
IGE hovering ceiling: 14,750 ft (4,500 m)
OGE hovering ceiling: 3,000 ft (914 m) with 4 TOW and 4 Hellfire missiles, full ammunition and rockets
Service ceiling: 18,000 ft (5,485 m)
G limits: +2.5, -0.5
Range: 317-320 naut miles (365-368 miles) 587-593 km
Duration: 3 hours

Aircraft variants:
AH-1W is the standard in-service version, as described.
AH-1W (4BW) is the designation of SuperCobra after being fitted with a performance-enhancing 4-blade main rotor, offering improved manoeuvrability and agility, reduced vulnerability, greater payload, greater reliability through simplicity of design, 70% reduction in rotor vibration, and easier maintenance. See H-1 Programme entry. Revised tail stabilizer with endplates, moved aft. Prototype has been tested. Offers increases in empty and take-off weights to 12,200 lb (5,534 kg) and 18,500 lb (8,391 kg) respectively, 6,300 lb (2,858 kg) stores load, maximum and cruise speeds of 210 kts (242 mph) 389 km/h and 148 kts (170 mph) 274 km/h respectively, G limit of +3.2, and vertical climb rate of 1,740 ft (530 m) per minute. See Rotor system.
Integrated Weapon System 'glass cockpit' upgrade for USMC AH-1Ws will include an integrated weapon management system, advanced mission computer, digital moving map display, colour multi-function displays, hands on throttle/collective/cyclic (HOTCC), and more.
AH-1Z is the designation of upgraded AH-1W (4BW) helicopters under the H-1 Programme (which see).

Bell OH-58D Kiowa Warrior

First flight: September 1983.
First delivery: December 1985.
Role: Armed reconnaissance with light attack capability. With the multi-purpose light helicopter configuration, the OH-58D can be optionally equipped to perform other important missions by installing equipment kits on existing hardpoints on the outside of the helicopter, including cargo hook operations up to 2,000 lb (907 kg), emergency medevac with 2 litters, 700 lb (318 kg) of supplies carried to an operating radius of 100 naut miles, and insertion of 6 troops for point security or special operations (troops carried outside, 3 per side).

Aims

▪ OH-58D Kiowa programme was initiated as an upgrade of existing US Army OH-58A Kiowas. Modification of OH-58Ds to armed Kiowa Warrior configuration has included some 15 designated 'Prime Chance' and shipped to the Persian Gulf for operations from US Navy vessels, where they accumulated about 7,500 hours NVG flight time. Later, 115 OH-58Ds took part in Desert Shield/Storm, flying nearly 9,000 hours and achieving a 92% full mission capability. All Kiowas are becoming armed Kiowa Warriors.

Development

▪ 21 September 1981. Bell was awarded a US Army helicopter improvement (AHIP) contract, to upgrade OH-58As to OH-58D standard, with redeliveries from 1985. Subsequent further requirements raised the OH-58D Kiowa specification to armed Kiowa Warrior standard.

Details

Sales: Most of the 411 OH-58Ds contracted have been delivered. Taiwan has 26 OH-58Ds, with 13 more ordered.
Crew/passengers: Minimum crew of 2. 6 troops or 2 litters can be carried on the outside of the helicopter (see Role).
Freight, external: Sling load on a 2,000 lb (907 kg) capacity cargo hook.
Rotor system: 4-blade main rotor, with elastomeric bearings, composites yokes and all-composites blades, and able to survive hits from 0.50-ins shells. Rotor folding (MMS detachment) for fast air deployment by transport aircraft, taking 2 persons 10 minutes or 4 persons 7 minutes (2 helicopters can be deployed in a C-130 Hercules).
Tail rotor characteristics: 2 blade, on port side of fin.
Flight control system: Hydraulic.
Engine: Allison 250-C30R or X turboshaft.
Engine rating: 650 shp (484.7 kW).
Transmission rating: 637 shp (475 kW) take-off, 550 shp (410 kW) continuous.
Fuel system: 424 litres.

↑ Bell OH-58D Kiowa Warrior

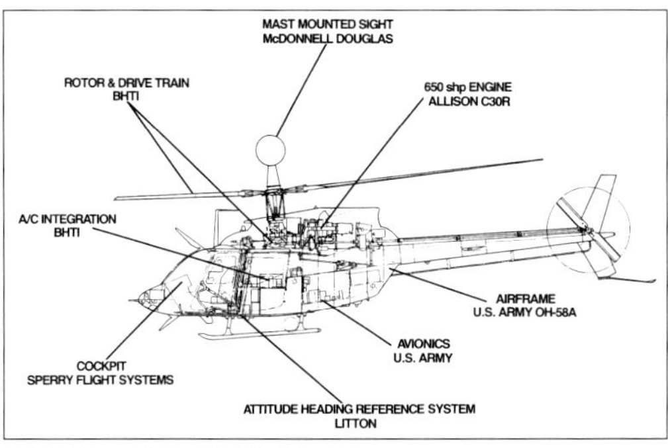

↑ **Bell OH-58D improvements diagram**

Electrical system: AC supply comprises the main 3-phase 120/208 volt, 400 Hz alternator. 28 volt DC supply via the AC supply using a transformer rectifier. Stand-by single-phase 115 volt, 400 Hz AC inverter, and 20 volt DC starter-generator.
Hydraulic system: 2 systems, each 1,000 psi.
Flight avionics/instrumentation: Mast-Mounted Sight (MMS) as a fully-integrated multi-sensor equipment package. It includes a high-resolution and low-light level TV camera, IR thermal imaging sensor for navigation/target acquisition/designation at night or under obscured conditions, laser rangefinder/designator for precise target location/guidance of Hellfire missiles and Copperhead artillery rounds or hand-off to Cobra for TOW engagement, and boresight assembly for quick in-flight sensor alignment. These functions provide the OH-58D with day/night, adverse weather and extended stand-off range reconnaissance, surveillance, intelligence gathering, and threat and target damage assessment capabilities. The MMS has a quick-release capability. Other OH-58D avionics in the 'all glass cockpit' with multi-function displays include (from 1991 redeliveries) video recorder for storing TV and IR imagery from the mission and with cockpit playback capability, data transfer system with data-loading module for pre-mission storing of navigation waypoints and radio frequencies, night vision goggle (NVG) flight reference symbology display, Have-Quick UHF and SINCGARS FM anti-jam radios, and displays to align and fire weapons. Integrated GPS/INS for improved accuracy in navigation. Digitized Kiowa Warrior improves communications, target acquisition/tracking (up to 6 targets at a time), and has overall enhanced capability. 3-axis stability and control augmentation system.
Self-protection systems: Latest standard configuration has IR seeker jammer, pulse and CW radar warning receivers, laser warning detector, and inherent IR suppression.
Number of weapon pylons: 2 Universal weapons pylons.
Expendable weapons and equipment: When armed, can carry 4 Hellfire anti-armour missiles, 4 Stinger AAMs, 2 × 7-round Hydra 70 rocket pods, 2 × 0.5-ins machine-guns, or a mix.

Details for OH-58D

PRINCIPAL DIMENSIONS:
Rotor diameter (main): 35 ft (10.67 m)
Maximum length, rotors turning: 42 ft 2 ins (12.85 m)
Fuselage length: 34 ft 6 ins (10.52 m)
Width, blades folded: 7 ft 10 ins (2.39 m)
Maximum height: 12 ft 11 ins (3.94 m), including MMS

MAIN ROTOR:
Blade chord: 9.5 ins (0.24 m)
Blade area: each 14.83 sq ft (1.38 m^2)
Rotor disc: 962 sq ft (89.37 m^2)
Rpm: 395

TAIL ROTOR:
Diameter: 5 ft 5 ins (1.65 m)
Rpm: 2,381

UNDERCARRIAGE:
Type: Twin fixed skids
Skid track: 7 ft 6 ins (2.29 m)

WEIGHTS:
Empty: 3,289 lb (1,492 kg)
Maximum take-off: 5,500 lb (2,495 kg)
Payload: 2,000 lb (907 kg) sling load

PERFORMANCE:
Never-exceed speed (V_{NE}): 130 kts (150 mph) 241 km/h
Fast cruise speed: 114 kts (131 mph) 211 km/h
Maximum climb rate: 1,600 ft (488 m) per minute, at sea level, ISA
IGE hovering ceiling: 10,000 ft (3,050 m), ISA
OGE hovering ceiling: 6,900 ft (2,100 m), ISA
Service ceiling: 15,000 ft (4,570 m)
Range: 223 naut miles (257 miles) 414 km
Duration: 3.1 hours.

Bell (Agusta) BA 609

First flight: Expected late 1999.
Certification: Expected in the year 2000, under FAR 25 for fixed-wing and FAR 29 for helicopters. Will be certified for IFR all-weather flight into known icing conditions. 2-pilot IFR, but will be capable of single pilot IFR. Category A performance.
Role: Basically a civil tiltrotor transport, combining the speed and comfort of a turboprop aeroplane with the vertical take-off/landing capability of a helicopter; typically operates as a turboprop aeroplane 95% of the flight. Other civil/government applications may include natural resource exploration, medical transportation, search and rescue, law enforcement, maritime surveillance, and training.

Aims

- Designed for low maintenance and maximum operational flexibility. Lower operating cost than helicopters.
- Low external nose signature. Variable approach profiles to minimize nose footprint.

Development

- 1995-97. Market research and engineering development period.
- 18 November 1996. Announcement of a joint venture between Bell and Boeing. See 1 March 1998.
- 1997. Customer interface period; ongoing.
- 1 March 1998. Bell Helicopter Textron assumed Boeing's 49% interest in what had been previously the Bell Boeing 609 civil tilt-rotor, with management of the programme from Fort Worth. Agusta of Italy has become a partner (see Foreword).
- 2001. Anticipated first delivery.

Details

Sales: Completion of the first of 4 prototypes in 1998, with the remainder in 1998-99. 61 sales commitments to 36 customers by 24 February 1998, as Mitsui of Japan (3), Textron Inc, Austin Jet, Bristow of the UK (2), United Industries of South Korea, Lider of Brazil (3), Northern Mountain Helicopters of Canada, CHC (2), Helitech of Australia, Lloyd's Investments of Poland, Massachusetts Mutual, Hillwood Development, Petroleum Helicopters, AeroVals of Andorra (2), Helicopter Services of Norway (2), Petroleum Tiltrotors of Dubai (2), and several individuals including Greg Norman. 1998 quoted price of US$8 to 10 million.
Crew/passengers: Crew of 1 or 2 plus 9 passengers (180 lb, 81.6 kg each) in a pressurized cabin, or other layouts according to role including 6-passenger VIP/executive, 12 passenger high-density and 2 litter medical/SAR with 3 seated patients/

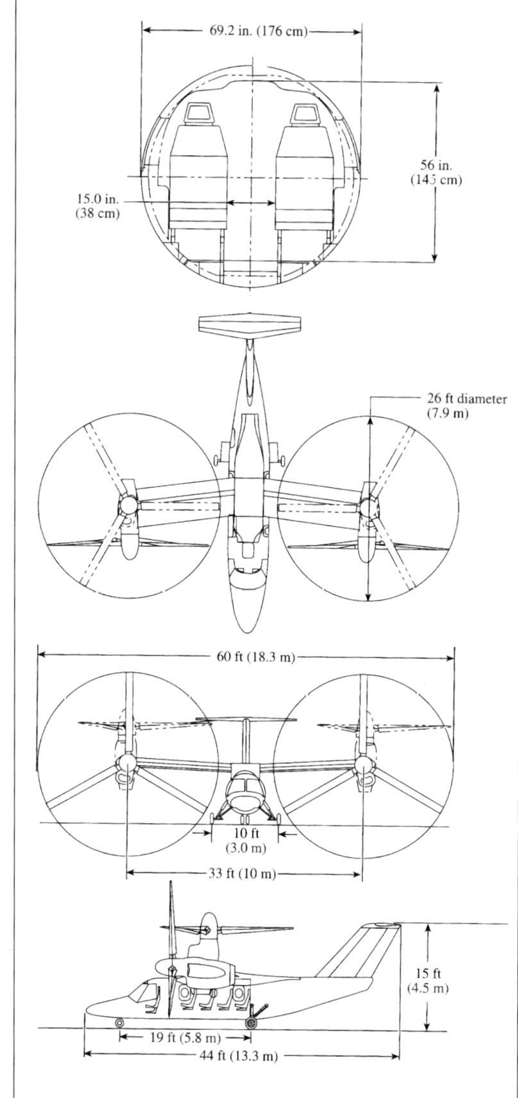

↑ **Bell (Agusta) BA 609 tiltrotor general arrangement and cabin cross section *(top)*** *(courtesy Bell Helicopter Textron)*

↑ **Bell (Agusta) BA 609 tiltrotor**

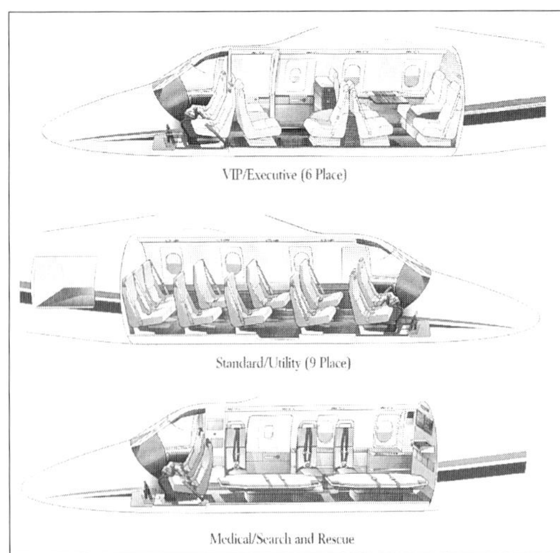

↑ **Bell (Agusta) BA 609 tiltrotor interiors, with 6-passenger VIP/executive *(top)*, 9-passenger standard/utility *(centre)* and medical/SAR** *(courtesy Bell Helicopter Textron)*

attendants. In the 12-passenger high-density layout and the SAR/medical layouts, cabin seats mostly face inward. A 22-passenger variant has been proposed as the Model 620, but this will not be developed until the beginning of the 21st century.
Cabin: Pressurized, with maximum differential of 5.5 psi.
Freight, internal: 55 cu ft (1.56 m^3) baggage compartment aft of the main cabin, with starboard side external door; 40 lb (18 kg) allowance per passenger in 9 passenger layout.
Cabin access: Door on starboard side of fuselage, of 30 ins (0.76 m) width.
Rotor system: 3-blade composite proprotors.
Wings: Forward swept dihedral wings of constant chord, with trailing-edge flaperons.
Tail surfaces: Sweptback T-tail, with the horizontal stabilizer with elevator mounted outside the proprotor wake to reduce pitching moment during transitions between vertical/horizontal flight.
Flight control system: Lear Astronics triplex (dual primary plus secondary) digital fly-by-wire and Lear Astronics computers flight control system; the system provides pitch, roll, yaw, tilt and rotor speed and thrust control. Dowty Aerospace actuators (15).
Airframe: Composite fibre-skinned pressurized fuselage, with aluminium internal structure. Composites wing. Toray of Japan is contracted to supply composite subassemblies.

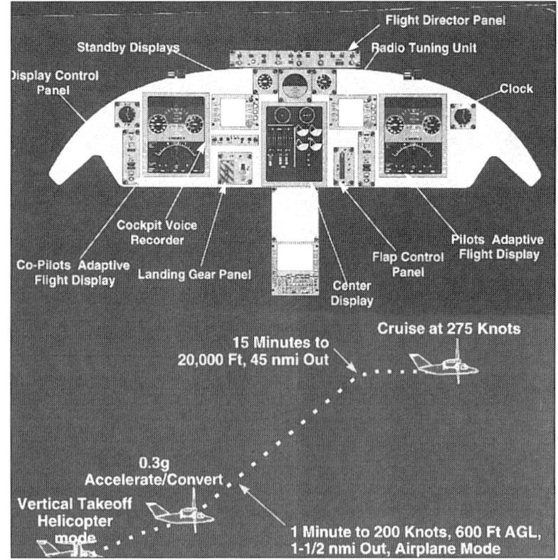

↑ **Bell (Agusta) BA 609 flight deck with Rockwell Collins Pro Line 21 suite *(top)* and Bell (Agusta) BA 609 take-off profile *(bottom)*** *(courtesy Bell Helicopter Textron)*

Engines: 2 Pratt & Whitney Canada PT6C-67A turboshafts (choice announced in November 1996). Complete propulsion assemblies at the wingtips tilt from horizontal to vertical attitude for vertical, transitional and horizontal flight (see V-22 entry for general principle). Oil system modified, with 2 pumps, to maintain required pressure when in vertical and transitional modes of flight.
Engine rating: Each 1,850 shp (1,380 kW).
Transmission: Modified to provide direct drive. Cross-shafting to drive both proprotors should either engine become inoperable; manual backup to tilt proprotors into helicopter mode in an emergency.
Fuel system: Standard tanks in wings, plus optional auxiliary tanks.
Radar: Optional Rockwell Collins WXR-800 solid-state weather radar.
Flight avionics/instrumentation: Rockwell Collins Pro Line 21 2-pilot IFR equipped advanced 'glass' cockpit, with pilot and co-pilot liquid crystal adaptive active matrix primary flight displays and central multifunction display (total of 3, each 8 × 10 ins, 20 × 25.4 cm), standby displays, flight director panel and more (see diagram). Primary flight displays provide attitude, heading, airspeed, altitude, vertical speed, flight control annunciations, nacelle tilt and rotor pitch status and navigational data. The multi-function display provides primary and secondary engine information, crew alert information and other aircraft system information such as hydraulic pressure and undercarriage and flap positions. Lear Astronics flight control computer, air data system, AHRS and magnetic reference sensor. GPS. Health and usage monitoring system (HUMS). Equipped with a complete Pro Line radio sensor package, including dual RTU-4200 radio tuning units that integrate all communication, navigation and surveillance radio sensor operations into a centralized control point. The units control VHF com, VHF nav, DME, ADF and Mode S transponder capabilities, and allow growth for TCAS and Satcom. Pro Line system can be customized for government/military operations with Tacan and UHF com and direction finding capabilities. Optional ALT-4000 radio altimeter.

Details for BA 609

PRINCIPAL DIMENSIONS:
Proprotor diameter: Each 26 ft (7.92 m)
Length overall: 44 ft (13.41 m)
Width, overall: 60 ft (18.29 m)
Width between proprotor hubs: 33 ft (10.06 m)
Height: 15 ft (4.57 m) to top of fin

CABIN:
Width: 5 ft 9.2 ins (1.76 m)
Height: 4 ft 8 ins (1.42 m)

MAIN ROTOR:
Rotor disc: 530 sq ft (49.24 m^2)

UNDERCARRIAGE:
Type: Messier-Dowty retractable nosewheel type, with twin nosewheels
Wheel base: 19 ft (5.79 m)
Wheel track: 10 ft (3.05 m)

WEIGHTS:
Empty, equipped: 10,500 lb (4,763 kg)
Maximum take-off: 16,000 lb (7,257 kg)
Useful load: 5,500 lb (2,495 kg)

PERFORMANCE:
Maximum cruise speed: 275 kts (317 mph) 510 km/h
Long-range cruise speed: 250 kts (288 mph) 463 km/h
Operational ceiling: 25,000 ft (7,620 m)
Range: 750 naut miles (864 miles) 1,390 km
Range with auxiliary fuel: 1,000 naut miles (1,151 miles) 1,853 km

Bell Helicopter Textron Inc and The Boeing Company — USA

Corporate address:
See Combat section for Boeing company details and above for Bell Helicopter Textron.

Bell Boeing V-22 Osprey

First flight: Aircraft No 1 flew on 19 March 1989. This began the FSD programme, and was followed by 5 more FSD aircraft (aircraft No 6 as non-flying airframe). In December 1996 (according to Bell) the first EMD aircraft flew (official first flight 5 February 1997), followed by 3 more EMD aircraft for flight tests at NAS Patuxent River, Maryland.
First delivery (production): Expected mid-1999 for MV-22A.
Role: Vertical-lift tilt-rotor transport and multi-purpose aircraft, combining the flying attributes of a helicopter and aeroplane.

Development

- December 1981. Development initiated by the US Department of Defense, with Bell and Boeing receiving a preliminary design contract in April 1983 under the joint services tiltrotor or JVX programme.
- 9 August 1989. First flight of No 2 FSD, followed by No 4 on 21 December 1989, No 3 on 9 May 1990, and No 5 on 11 June 1991.
- 6 May 1990. First cross-country flight by AC No 2, covering 1,210 naut miles (1,393 miles) 2,241 km between Dallas and Wilmington (Del).
- 4-7 December 1990. AC Nos 3 and 4 undertook the first sea trials on board USS *Wasp*.
- 7 June 1992. Completion of 4 months of climatic trials, subjecting AC No 4 to weather extremes that included temperatures from –54° to +49° C.
- 13 December 1994. Critical Design Review. Minor modifications recommended.

↑ **Bell Boeing V-22 Osprey in latest EMD form, with proprotors in cruise flight attitude, plus lower views of the proprotors in transition**

▪ 15 March 1997. First EMD for tests at NAS Patuxent River.
▪ 23 August 1997. First flight of the second EMD aircraft.
▪ 30 January 1998. Fourth and final V-22 EMD was flown to Patuxent River. Used for avionics testing, formation and night flying.
▪ April-July 1998. Fourth EMD flown by operational evaluation pilots and then undertook a 6-day operational trial.
▪ 20 August 1998. Set unofficial rotorcraft record, by achieving 221 kts with 10,000 lb load.
▪ Mid-1999. First USMC MV-22A delivery expected.
▪ 2001. Anticipated initial operational capability with MV-22A.
▪ 2003. First CV-22 delivery to the USAF.

Details

Sales: Current DoD procurement stands at 523 aircraft, with the US Marine Corps purchasing 425, USAF 50 and US Navy 48. The low rate Initial Production contract has been issued and the first production aircraft are under construction; low-rate initial production to last until after Lot 4 deliveries in 2003. FY98 defence budget covered the purchase of 7 more Ospreys, instead of the expected 5, indicating a required increase in production rate; some 30 MV-22s for the USMC were under contract at the time of writing.
Crew/passengers: 2 flight crew. 24 troops or 12 litters plus attendants, depending on role. Crashworthy seats.
Cockpit/cabin: Over-pressurized to permit operation in NBC contaminated areas.
Freight, external: 10,000 lb (4,536 kg) on single cargo hook, 15,000 lb (6,804 kg) on dual hooks.
Cabin access: Ramp/door under the upswept rear fuselage. Starboard-side fuselage door.
Rotor system: 2 × 3-blade high-twist proprotors mounted with engines and transmissions at the tips of the wings, the proprotors turning in opposite directions (direction of rotation prevents impact of disintegrating parts in an accident from striking the cockpit/cabin). Proprotor tip speed 661.9 ft (201.75 m) per second. Complete propulsion assemblies tilt from horizontal to vertical attitude (through 90° plus a further 7° 30' aft rotation) for vertical, transitional and horizontal flight. Cyclic control swashplates are controlled asymmetrically for yaw and symmetrically for forward/rearward flight in hovering mode, making sideways flight possible. Elastomeric bearings. Proprotors are interconnected by shafts through the wing, to allow both to function in the event of an engine failure. Blades of graphite/glassfibre construction. Automatic, powered blade folding/stowing (takes some 84 seconds) and blade de-icing.
Wing/tail surfaces: High-mounted and slightly forward-swept wings, with ailerons and single-slotted flaperons that droop during hovering mode. Wings designed to separate from the fuselage under extreme crash loads, so that the inertia of the engines and transmissions are instantly relieved. Twin fin/rudder tail unit, with elevator.
Flight control system: Triple computer and MIL-STD-1553B databus-controlled digital fly-by-wire system (triple redundant), with triple self-monitored primary and automatic processors. Shielded from EMI, EMP and directed energy weapons. Automatic flight envelope protection features.

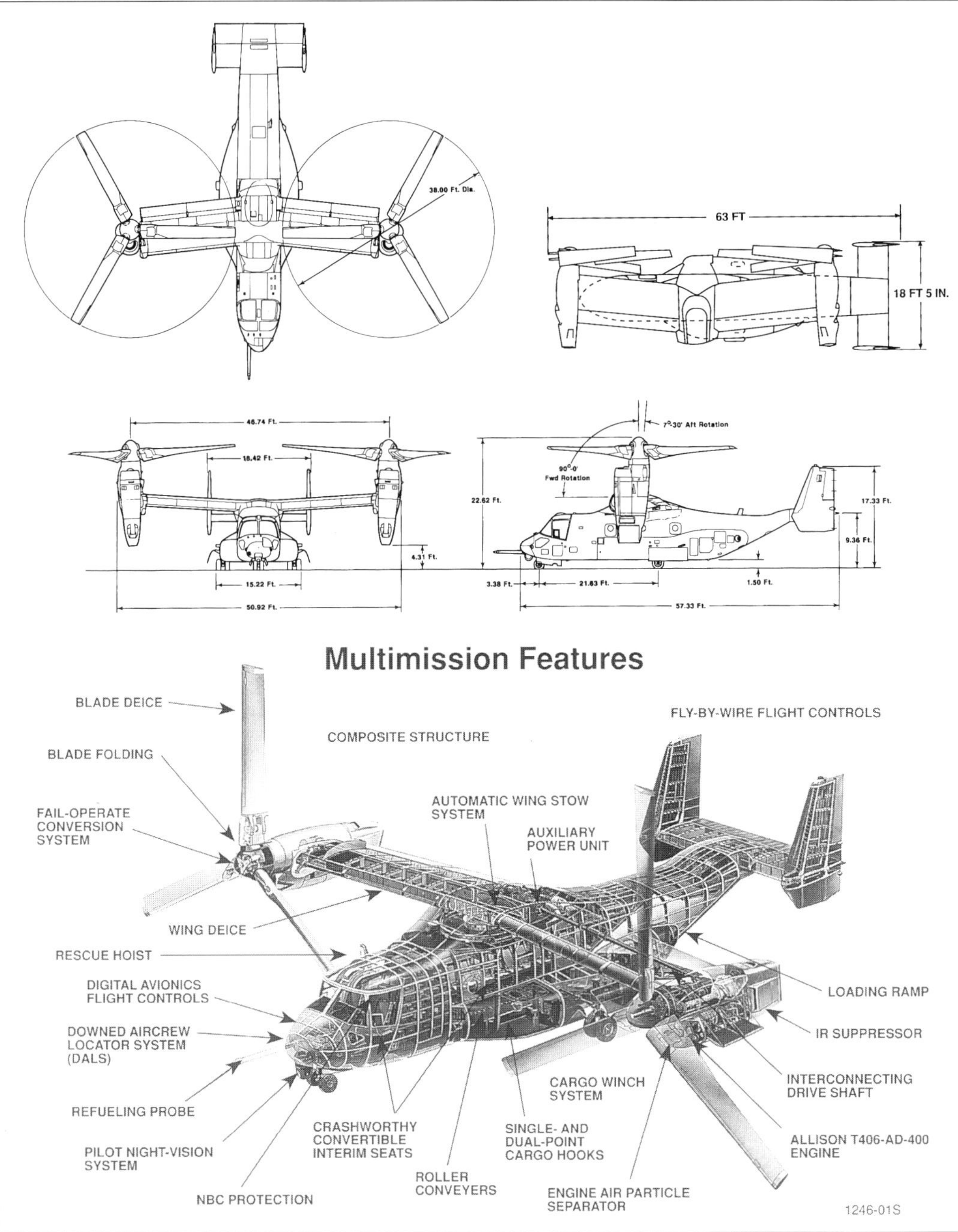

↑ **Bell Boeing V-22 Osprey general arrangements, including stowed with blades folded and wings rotated to stow over fuselage *(top, right)***
(courtesy Bell Boeing)

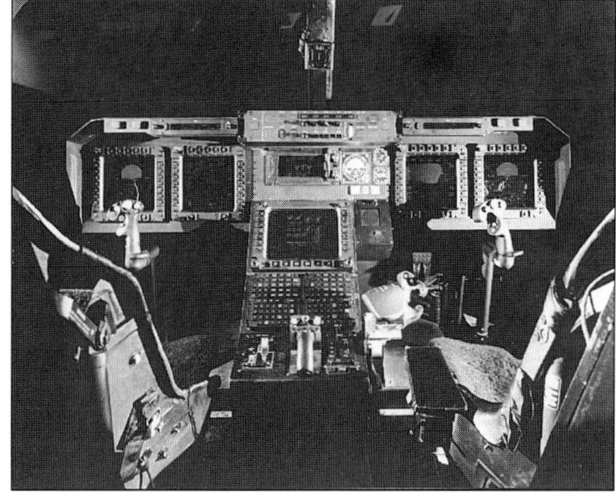

↑ **Bell Boeing V-22 Osprey cockpit in the current configuration**

Airframe: An optimum mix of metal and advanced graphite/epoxy materials constitute the fuselage construction.
Safety features: All critical systems are triple redundant and separated, some designed to withstand ballistic impact or are armour protected. Extensive built-in fire protection, and nitrogen inerting to prevent explosion (see Fuel system). Forward fuselage constructed to preclude crumpling into the cockpit or digging into the earth in an accident.
Engines: 2 Allison T406-AD-400 turboshafts. APU. Spraymat type inlet ice protection.
Engine rating: Each 6,150 shp (4,586 kW).
Transmission rating: 4,750 shp (3,542 kW) take-off for MV-22A and 4,970 shp (3,706 kW) for HV-22A/CV-22A. 5,920 shp (4,414 kW) emergency OEI.
Fuel system: 4,649 litres in the sponsons and 2,979 litres in the wings. 9,221 litres of auxiliary fuel for self deployment. 7,949 litres capacity for CV-22. OBIGGS for tanks.

Details for Osprey

PRINCIPAL DIMENSIONS:
Proprotor diameter: Each 38 ft (11.58 m)
Fuselage length: 57 ft 4 ins (17.48 m), excluding nose probe
Fuselage length stowed, wing fore and aft: 62 ft 7 ins (19.08 m)
Width, proprotors turning: 84 ft 7 ins (25.78 m)
Width, blades folded: 18 ft 5 ins (5.61 m)
Maximum height: 22 ft 7 ins (6.88 m)
Height to top of fins: 17 ft 8 ins (5.38 m) overall, or 17 ft 4 ins (5.28 m) to top of actual surface
Height when stowed: 18 ft 1 ins (5.51 m)

CABIN:
Length: 24 ft 2 ins (7.37 m)
Width: 5 ft 11 ins (1.8 m)
Height: 6 ft (1.83 m)
Volume: 858 cu ft (24.3 m^3) usable

MAIN ROTOR:
Blade chord: 2 ft 11.5 ins (0.9 m) root, 1 ft 10 ins (0.56 m) tip
Blade area: 261.52 sq ft (24.3 m^2)
Rotor disc: 2,268 sq ft (210.7 m^2)

UNDERCARRIAGE:
Type: Retractable, with steerable nosewheels. Twin wheels on each unit. Maximum 14.7 ft (4.5 m) per second impact
Wheel base: 21 ft 7.5 ins (6.59 m)
Wheel track: 15 ft 2.6 ins (4.63 m) over outer wheels

WEIGHTS:
Empty: 33,140 lb (15,032 kg)
Maximum take-off: 47,500 lb (21,545 kg) for normal vertical take-off, 55,000 lb (24,948 kg) STOL, and 60,500 lb (27,442 kg) self-deployment
Payload: 20,000 lb (9,072 kg) internal (see Freight, external)

PERFORMANCE:
Maximum speed: 377 kts (434 mph) 699 km/h TAS demonstrated in August 1997
Maximum cruise speed: 275 kts (317 mph) 510 km/h in horizontal flight at sea level or 313 kts (361 mph) 581 km/h at best height, and 100 kts (115 mph) 185 km/h in helicopter attitude at sea level
Maximum climb rate: 2,320 ft (707 m) per minute
Vertical climb rate: 1,090 ft (332 m) per minute
OGE hovering ceiling: 14,200 ft (4,328 m)
Service ceiling: 26,000 ft (7,925 m)
Ceiling, OEI: 11,300 ft (3,444 m)
Range: 515 naut miles (593 miles) 954 km, amphibious assault
Self-deployment range: 2,100 naut miles (2,418 miles) 3,892 km

Flight refuelling probe: Detachable probe in the starboard side of the nose.
Electrical system: AC supply via 2 × 40 kVA generators. DC supply via 50/80 kVA variable-frequency generators and rectifiers. 15 amp-hour lead-acid battery.
Hydraulic system: 2 principal and 1 back-up systems, each 5,000 psi.
Braking system: Multi-disc carbon.
Oxygen system: On-board oxygen generating system.
Radar: Raytheon Systems AN/APQ-174D in offset nose radome (not on MV-22).
Flight avionics/instrumentation: Advanced digital cockpit, with 4 MFDs (2 for each flight crew member) and a central active matrix liquid crystal Control Display Unit/EICAS, with a flight director control panel above the CDU/EICAS. NVG compatible. 2 mission computers, AHRS, VOR/ILS, Tacan, Elbit digital moving map, radar altimeter and more. Pilot night vision and integrated helmet display systems. FLIR for MV-22A and TF/TA for CV-22B.
Self-protection systems: IR and radar warning receivers, missile threat detectors, and chaff/flare dispensers. Up to 75% lower acoustic signature than a helicopter.

Aircraft variants:
CV-22 for long-range special operations missions, insertion and extraction of special forces teams and equipment at a mission radius in excess of 500 naut miles with the US Air Force.
HV-22 for strike rescue, delivery and retrieval of special warfare teams and logistics transportation in support of the fleet with the US Navy.
MV-22 for amphibious combat assault and assault support with the US Marine Corps (from assault ships and land bases); and medevac, special operations, long-range combat logistics support, combat air support and low intensity conflict support with the US Army.
Other possible roles include ASW with the US Navy, flight refuelling tanker and possessing the ability to hover over a supply ship to replenish for further operations, airborne early warning, and medical evacuation.

The Boeing Company — USA

Corporate address:
See Combat section for company details.

ACTIVITIES

▪ On 4 August 1997, Boeing began operations as a single reorganized company, having merged with McDonnell Douglas. Former McDonnell Douglas helicopters thus became Boeing types.
▪ On 25 February 1998 the Board of Directors of Textron Inc approved a plan to purchase a substantial portion of the commercial helicopter business of The Boeing Company. Under the terms of the proposed sale, Bell Helicopter Textron was to acquire the Boeing (former McDonnell Douglas) MD 500 and MD 600 series product lines. The agreement was to include spare parts and support for Boeing's MD Explorer helicopter, though this was not being purchased by Bell and continues at the present time as a Boeing product. However, the purchase had (at the time of writing) still to clear US Federal review, and until then the helicopters remain Boeing products. In addition, Bell Helicopter Textron has taken over Boeing's 49% interest in the Bell Boeing 609 civil tilt-rotor, as of 1 March 1998.
▪ Boeing collaborates with Bell Helicopter Textron on the V-22 Osprey, and with Sikorsky on the RAH-66 Comanche.
▪ Factory activities also include production of composite and composite/aluminium wing sub-assemblies for Boeing 737, 747, 757 and 767 transports, and the design and production of fixed leading-edges for the 777.
▪ In April 1992 Boeing received a contract for 242 H-46 Sea Knight night-vision goggle kits, followed in December by a contract for 442 engine condition control system kits, all delivered by Spring 1994. Additionally, on 29 July 1992 Boeing received a contract to design, test, verify and validate flight test improved dynamic components for the H-46. In April 1993, it received a contract for 114 dynamic component upgrade production kits, later increased to 298, for completion by 1998. These upgrades followed earlier increased fuel capacity and emergency flotation kits.

Boeing MD 500E, MD 530F and Defender

First flight: 28 January 1982 (MD 500E) and 22 October 1982 (MD 530F).
Role: MD 500E and MD 530F are light utility helicopters, used for executive transportation, cargo lifting, law enforcement, patrol and other roles. Defender is a military and paramilitary member of the same family, with more specialized equipment, armament and crashworthy fuselage structure.
Sales: About 4,650 of all civil and military versions (including past and present MD 500 and 530 variants and military/paramilitary Defenders). Military users of currently-available Defender variants include Colombia, the Philippines and the US Army (AH-6 and MH-6 types).

↑ Philippine Air Force Boeing MD 520 MG Defender with gun and rocket pods, photographed at Sangley Point in 1997 and operated by the 17th Strike Squadron of the 15th Strike Wing *(Denis Hughes)*

Details *(for MD 500E and MD 530F, as appropriate, except under Aircraft variants)*

Crew/passengers: Pilot plus up to 4 passengers. 270° potential visibility from the cockpit, due to extensive glazing. Optional 4-seat executive, litter or other layouts, including cargo carrying in the aft compartment.
Freight, external: Cargo hook with a 2,000 lb (907 kg) capacity.
Cabin access: 2 doors each side of the fuselage.
Optional equipment: Includes dual controls, searchlight, wire strike kit, cargo hook or underfuselage cargo pod.
Rotor system: Fully articulated 5-blade type, of metal. Fail-safe main rotor and steel strap rotor retention system. Manual folding.
Tail rotor characteristics: Metal, 2-blade standard, with optional 4-blade Quiet Tail Rotor for MD 500E.
Tail surfaces: Ventral and dorsal fins, with T-mounted horizontal stabilizer with endplate fins of 5 ft 5 ins (1.65 m) span.
Flight control system: Mechanical.
Airframe materials: Metal.
Engine: *MD 500E* has an Allison 250-C20B or C-20R turboshaft of 420 shp (313.3 kW) but derated to 375 shp (280 kW) for take-off and 350 shp (261 kW) continuous. *MD 530F* has an Allison 250-C30 turboshaft of 650 shp (485 kW) but derated to 425 shp (317 kW) for take-off up to 50 kts, 375 shp (280 kW) above 50 kts and 350 shp (261 kW) maximum continuous.
Engine rating: See above.
Transmission rating: 350 shp (261 kW) maximum continuous.
Fuel system: 242 litres usable, weighing 403 lb (183 kg). Self-sealing tanks and 79 litre auxiliary tank optional.
Flight avionics/instrumentation: Standard VFR. Optional avionics to customer requirements, and include radar, FLIR, air communications system and scanner/alert system.

Aircraft variants:
MD 500E is the standard lower-powered version, with a choice of 250-C20B or R engines.
MD 530F is the hot-day/high-altitude version with more engine power, increased diameter rotors for extra thrust and directional control at high altitudes, and 8 ins (0.2 m) extended tailboom.
MG Defender is offered in paramilitary and fully-militarized versions. Paramilitary is for law enforcement, patrol and similar missions and can be lightly armed. The fully militarized versions, again based on the MD 500E and MD 530F, are for day/night and adverse weather operations, capable of nap-of-the-earth anti-armour, armed support, day/night surveillance and other specialized missions in addition to utility work. Fully militarized models each have a fully integrated cockpit using 1553B digital databus inter-facing, with multi-function displays, data transfer unit with ground loader, and hands on lever and stick control (incorporating weapon firing). Autopilot, AHRS, Doppler navigator, ADF/VOR, radar altimeter, transponder and optional ground proximity warning system. Other options include a TOW sighting system for use with TOW 2 anti-armour missiles, FLIR, laser ranger, IFF, and radar warning receiver. NATO standard pylons on outriggers. Other weapon choices are launchers for 2.75-ins rockets, 7.62-mm machine-gun pods or Stinger AAMs.
TOW Defender specializes in an anti-armour role, with 4 TOW 2 missiles and a sighting system. Any choice of MD 500E/530F engine.
Nightfox is a variant of either fully militarized MG Defender, specializing in night operations and using FLIR and NVG.

Boeing MD 520N and MD 520N Defender

First flight: 1 May 1990 (prototype, following trials with a modified OH-6A NOTAR from 17 December 1981).
Certification: 30 September 1991.
First delivery: October 1991.
Role: MD 520N is a light utility helicopter, used for executive transportation, cargo lifting, law enforcement, patrol and other roles. Defender is a military and paramilitary member of the same family, with more specialized equipment, armament and crashworthy fuselage structure.

Details for MD 500E, *with MD 530F in italics*

PRINCIPAL DIMENSIONS:
Rotor diameter (main): 26 ft 5 ins (8.05 m), *27 ft 5 ins (8.36 m)*
Maximum length, rotors turning: 30 ft 10 ins (9.35 m), *32 ft 7 ins (9.93 m)*
Fuselage length: 24 ft 7 ins (7.49 m), *the same*
Fuselage width: 4 ft 7 ins (1.4 m)
Maximum height: 8 ft 9.5 ins (2.69 m), or 9 ft 9.5 ins (3 m) with extended undercarriage, *the same*

CABIN:
Length: 8 ft (2.44 m)
Width: 4 ft 3.5 ins (1.31 m)

MAIN ROTOR:
Blade chord: 6.75 ins (0.17 m)
Blade area: each 6.67 sq ft (0.62 m^2), *6.96 sq ft (0.647 m^2)*
Rotor disc: 547.81 sq ft (50.89 m^2), *587.5 sq ft (54.58 m^2)*
Rpm: 492, *477*

TAIL ROTOR:
Diameter: 4 ft 7 ins (1.4 m), *4 ft 10 ins (1.47 m)*
Rpm: 2,933, *2,848*

UNDERCARRIAGE:
Type: Fixed skids, with extended gear optional, *the same*. Optional floats or emergency buoyancy floats. Can land on a 20 ° slope
Skid track: 6 ft 3.5 ins (1.92 m), *the same*

WEIGHTS:
Empty: 1,481 lb (672 kg) standard, 1,417 lb (643 kg) industrial, *1,591 lb (722 kg) standard*
Maximum take-off: 3,000 lb (1,361 kg), *3,100 lb (1,406 kg)*
Maximum take-off, external load: 3,550 lb (1,610 kg), *3,750 lb (1,700 kg)*
Useful load: 1,519 lb (689 kg) normal category, or 2,069 lb (938 kg) external load operations, *1,509 lb (684 kg) normal, or 2,159 lb (979 kg) external load operations*

PERFORMANCE (MD 500E with C20B engine, *MD 530F with C30*):
Never-exceed speed (V_{NE}): 152 kts (175 mph) 281 km/h at sea level, *the same*
Maximum cruise speed: 135 kts (155 mph) 249 km/h at sea level or 133 kts (153 mph) 246 km/h at 5,000 ft (1,525 m), *134 kts (154 mph) 247 km/h at sea level or 135 kts (155 mph) 249 km/h at 5,000 ft (1,525 m)*
Maximum climb rate: 1,770 ft (539 m) per minute at sea level and ISA, 1,776 ft (541 m) per minute ISA + 20° C, *2,069 ft (630 m) per minute sea level and ISA, 2,061 ft (628 m) per minute ISA + 20° C*
IGE hovering ceiling: 8,500 ft (2,590 m) ISA, 6,000 ft (1,830 m) ISA + 20° C, *14,300 ft (4,360 m) ISA, or 12,000 ft (3,660 m) ISA + 20° C*
OGE hovering ceiling: 6,000 ft (1,830 m) ISA, 3,100 ft (945 m) ISA + 20° C, *12,000 ft (3,660 m) ISA or 9,750 ft (2,970 m) ISA + 20° C*
Service ceiling: 16,000 ft (4,875 m) certified limit, *the same*
Range: 239 naut miles (275 miles) 442 km at sea level or 264 naut miles (304 miles) 489 km at 5,000 ft (1,525 m), *206 naut miles (237 miles) 381 km at sea level or 232 naut miles (267 miles) 430 km at 5,000 ft (1,525 m)*
Duration: 2.7 hours at sea level, *2 hours at sea level*

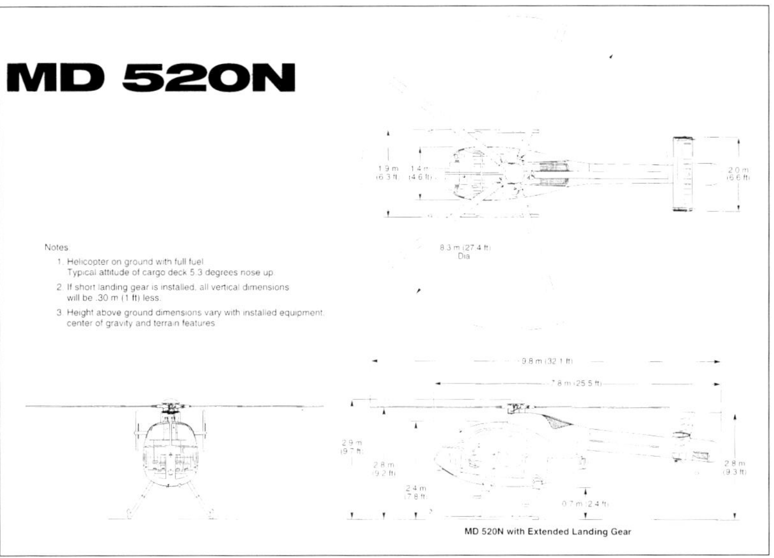

↑ Boeing MD 520N general arrangement *(courtesy Boeing)*

↑ Boeing MD 520N of the Los Angeles County Sheriff's Department, flying alongside an MD 500E

Sales: Nearly half delivered of a total of more than 200 firm orders/options at the time of writing. In addition, some US Army special operations AH-6s and MH-6s have been converted to NOTAR.
Crew/passengers: Pilot and up to 4 passengers for MD 520N, with optional VIP interior.
Freight, external: Optional cargo hook of 2,000 lb (907 kg) capacity.
Optional equipment: As for MD 500E/530F.
Rotor system: Fully articulated 5-blade type, of metal. Fail-safe main rotor and steel strap rotor retention system (see MD 600N for details). Manual folding. Static mast-hub support system, with a static mast rigidly attached to the fuselage. All dynamic loads are transmitted through this mast, rather than through the transmission. A separate, inner drive shaft transmits engine torque to the main rotor hub. This feature is said to offer improved flight control integrity and helps retain rotor system components in the event of a main blade strike.

Details for MD 520N, *with Defender in italics where different*

PRINCIPAL DIMENSIONS:
Rotor diameter: 27 ft 5 ins (8.36 m)
Maximum length, rotors turning: 32 ft 1 ins (9.78 m)
Fuselage length: 25 ft 6 ins (7.77 m)
Fuselage width: 4 ft 7 ins (1.4 m)
Maximum height: 9 ft 8 ins (2.95 m)

CABIN: Similar to MD 500E/530F but with a lowered mid-cabin divider and some other changes to enhance visibility

UNDERCARRIAGE:
Type: Fixed skids with replaceable shoes, with extended gear optional, *the same.* Optional floats or emergency buoyancy floats
Skid track: 6 ft 3.5 ins (1.92 m)

WEIGHTS:
Empty: 1,586 lb (719 kg) standard, 1,486 lb (674 kg) industrial
Maximum take-off: 3,350 lb (1,520 kg) normal category
Maximum take-off, external load: 3,850 lb (1,746 kg)
Useful load: 1,764 lb (800 kg) standard or 1,864 lb (845 kg) industrial for normal category, or 2,364 lb (1,072 kg) standard and industrial with external load

PERFORMANCE (MTOW, normal category)**:**
Never-exceed speed (V_{NE}): 152 kts (175 mph) 281 km/h
Cruise speed: 125 kts (144 mph) 232 km/h at sea level, 120 kts (138 mph) 222 km/h at 5,000 ft (1,525 m), *125 kts (144 mph) 232 km/h at sea level, 120 kts (138 mph) 222 km/h at 5,000 ft (1,525 m)*
Maximum climb rate: 1,546 ft (471 m) per minute at sea level, ISA, or 1,280 ft (390 m) ISA + 20° C
IGE hovering ceiling: 9,300 ft (2,835 m) ISA, 5,100 ft (1,554 m) ISA + 20° C
OGE hovering ceiling: 5,600 ft (1,705 m) ISA, 1,400 ft (427 m) ISA + 20° C
Service ceiling: 20,000 ft (6,100 m)
Range: 202 naut miles (233 miles) 375 km at sea level, or 210 naut miles (242 miles) 389 km at 5,000 ft (1,525 m), *202 naut miles (233 miles) 375 km at sea level, or 210 naut miles (242 miles) 389 km at 5,000 ft (1,525 m)*
Duration: 2.2 hours

Anti-torque system: NOTAR (no tail rotor) anti-torque system consists of an enclosed variable-pitch fan (with 13 thermoplastic blades) driven from the main transmission, a circulation control tailboom, direct-jet thruster and vertical stabilizers mounted at the tips of a horizontal aerofoil tailplane. The port stabilizer is controlled by the anti-torque pedals, the starboard being servo operated. In operation, fan-created low air pressure is forced through 2 circulation control slots in the boom, causing the main rotor downwash to "hug" the contour of the boom, providing the majority of the anti-torque force required in a hover by creating a lateral lift that counteracts main rotor torque. Remaining anti-torque and directional control are provided by the direct-jet thruster, which uses part of the fan-created air pressure, controlled by anti-torque pedal input. The NOTAR system permits greater manoeuvrability, precise directional control even in extreme crosswinds, increases safety both in the air and on the ground, and gives considerable noise reduction. Static mast hub support. NOTAR is said to be 60% less vulnerable to ballistic damage from small arms fire.
Tail surfaces: See Anti-torque system.
Flight control system: Mechanical push tube type, without hydraulic boost. See MD 600N.
Airframe materials: Similar to MD 530F but with a new NOTAR lightweight carbon composite tailboom, with a horizontal stabilizer of carbon composite and Kevlar. Vertical stabilizers are of glassfibre. See MD 600N for more details.
Safety features: Defender has crashworthy structure.
Engine: Allison 250-C20R turboshaft.
Engine rating: 450 shp (313 kW), derated to 425 shp (317 kW) for take-off and 375 shp (280 kW) maximum continuous.
Fuel system: 242 litres.
Flight avionics/instrumentation: As for MD 500E/530F.

Aircraft variants:
MD 520N is the civil version.
MD 520N Defender is the military version, similar in role and equipment options to the MD 500 series Defender.

Boeing MD 600N

First flight: 22 November 1994.
Certification: 26 May 1997.
First delivery: July 1997 to AirStar Helicopters.
Role: Stretched version of the MD 520N, for utility, electronic news gathering, air medical transport, offshore work, VIP transport, law enforcement and tour operators. Military version is envisaged.

Development

■ Prototype based on the MD 520N but with a 2 ft 6 ins (0.76 m) cabin plug and a 2 ft 4 ins (0.71 m) tailboom plug, plus replacement of an underseat fuel tank with a below cabin floor tank, to achieve the required dimensions and cabin volume.

Details

Sales: 150-180 expected to be ordered before the turn of the century.
Crew/passengers: Pilot and 7 passengers. Reversible forward bench seat in cabin. In medical role, offers 2 configurations: dual litter kit, or single litter kit capable of advanced cardiac life support (ACLS) level of care; both configurations give the nurse/doctor full access to the feet and head, along with space for life support equipment.
Cabin access: Double centre-opening doors on each side of the fuselage, of 5 ft 2 ins (1.57 m) width, allowing easy passenger and cargo loading. Separate front-hinged cockpit doors. Aft cabin has a 6 ft (1.83 m) flat floor for cargo carrying. Authorized to fly with doors off, as may be required for law enforcement or similar roles.
Freight, external: 3,000 lb (1,361 kg) external hook capacity for outsized, bulky loads. Helicopter certified to lift a 2,727 lb (1,237 kg) load.
Optional equipment: Large range of options, including heater/defogger, dual flight controls, particle separator, heated pitot tube, extended undercarriage, tundra pads, cargo hook, rotor brake, airframe fuel filter, main rotor and NOTAR balance

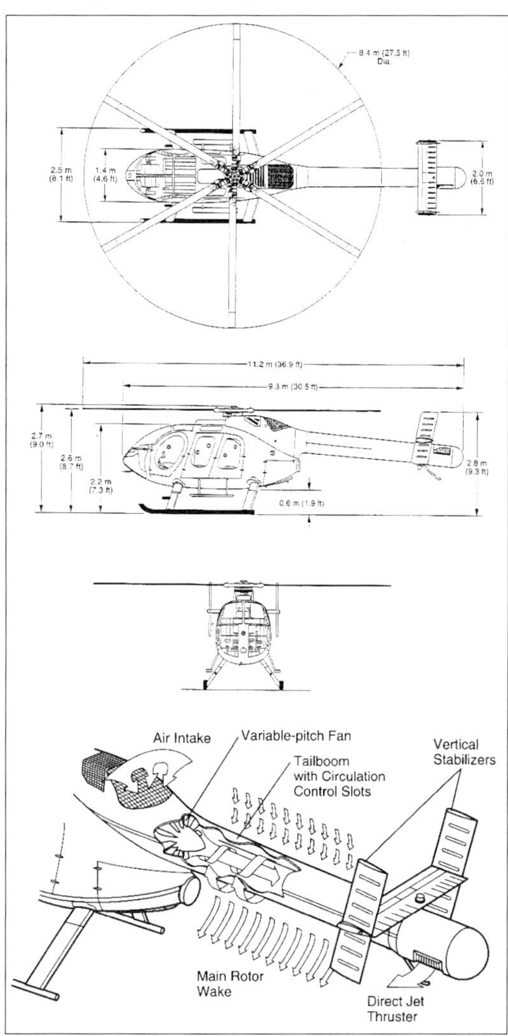

↑ Boeing MD 600N general arrangement, with NOTAR diagram at bottom *(courtesy Boeing)*

↑ Boeing MD 600N delivery to AirStar

kit, air conditioning, custom soundproofing, sliding windows, wire strike, VHF/UHF/FM/AM transceivers, intercommunications systems, and a wide range of instruments and avionics, including encoding altimeter, PA system, radar altimeter, transceiver, transponder, GPS receiver, emergency locator transmitter, turn and bank indicator, instantaneous vertical speed indicator, altitude gyro, directional gyro and more.
Rotor system: 6-blade (metal, utilizing nickel abrasion strips to minimize the effects of erosion) fully articulated main rotor. Blades retained by an exclusive steel strap pack system that accommodates blade flapping and feathering; system has redundant load paths for added safety. Blade retention system has no grease fittings. Blades are secured to the hub with quick-release lever-type pins. Elastomeric lead/lag dampers are standard on the MD 600N main rotor system. Static mast-hub support system, with a static mast rigidly attached to the fuselage. All dynamic loads are transmitted through this mast, rather than through the transmission. A separate, inner drive shaft transmits engine torque to the main rotor hub. This feature is said to offer improved flight control integrity and helps retain rotor system components in the event of a main blade strike. Transient load factors for the rotor system of +3.5g and - 0.5g are attainable.
Anti-torque system: NOTAR (see MD 520N).
Flight control system: Mechanical push tube type, without hydraulic boost. No grease fittings. Anti-torque pedals control the vertical stabilizer and rotating thruster motion using a combination of push pods and push-pull cables. Adjustable friction devices are incorporated in the cyclic, collective and throttle controls. In addition, electrical cyclic trim actuators allow flight loads to be trimmed out.
Airframe: Fuselage is a semi-monocoque aluminium structure. Crew and passenger compartments are protected by a rigid, 3-dimensional A-frame truss that also acts as an integral seat structure. The aircraft forward belly is a double-walled keel beam that supports the front undercarriage struts and provides energy absorption in the event of a hard landing. The aft cabin belly is also double walled, providing space for a newly-designed, 2-cell, crash-resistant fuel tank. NOTAR tailboom is a carbon composite structure, with a horizontal stabilizer of carbon composite and Kevlar. Vertical stabilizers are of glassfibre.
Engine: Allison 250-C47M turboshaft, with FADEC. Hydro-mechanical manual system for back-up to FADEC.
Engine rating: 808 shp (603 kW), derated to 600 shp (447 kW) take-off and 530 shp (395 kW) maximum continuous.
Transmission: 600 shp (447 kW) rated for take-off and 530 shp (395 kW) continuous main transmission, with only 4 gears and 2 gear meshes. Designed for 3,000 hours TBO. A single mechanic can change the transmission without removing any other component on the rotor head. Main rotor transmission, through a second drive shaft, drives a gearbox for the NOTAR fan. An overrunning clutch between the engine and the main rotor transmission permits freewheeling of the rotor system during autorotation. All drive shafts are fitted with fail-safe couplings at both ends.
Fuel system: 435 litres in a 2-cell, baffled, crash-resistant (designed to FAR Pt 27 criteria) fuel bladder tank under the floor (see Airframe). Puncture-resistant bladders and frangible, breakaway connections are incorporated to prevent fuel spillage. Does not require boost fuel pumps; an engine suction-type fuel pump is used for fuel transfer to the engine.
Electrical system: Standard system is 28 volt DC, via a 200 amp heavy duty starter generator. Rated at 140 amps maximum continuous power. 28 volt, 17 amp, ni-cd heavy duty battery as a standard auxiliary power receptacle.
Flight avionics/instrumentation: T-configuration instrument panel, providing space for engine and flight instruments in the upper portion and for avionics/communications in the lower portion. Flight and engine instruments are airspeed indicator, barometric altimeter, magnetic compass, outside air temperature indicator, digital chronometer, dial tachometers, digital/analog engine torque meter, digital/analog turbine outlet temperature, dual indicator with engine oil and oil pressure, fuel quantity indicator, dual volt/ampere meter, and running time meter. Annunciator panel has warning lights and caution lights. Many options (see Optional equipment).

Details for MD 600N

PRINCIPAL DIMENSIONS:
Rotor diameter: 27 ft 5 ins (8.36 m)
Maximum length, rotors turning: 36 ft 9 ins (11.2 m)
Fuselage length: 30 ft 6 ins (9.3 m)
Width, blades folded: 6 ft 6 ins (1.98 m)
Maximum height: 9 ft 8 ins (2.95 m)

CABIN:
Length: 6 ft (1.83 m)
Width: 4 ft (1.22 m)
Height: 4 ft (1.22 m)

UNDERCARRIAGE:
Type: Fixed skids with replaceable shoes, with extended gear optional. Articulated, for slope landing. New, heavy duty, nitrogen-charged dampers, of large piston diameter, embedded in the fuselage belly section, acting as shock absorbers and providing ground resonance stability. Optional floats or emergency buoyancy floats
Skid track: 6 ft 3.5 ins (1.92 m)

WEIGHTS:
Empty: 2,101 lb (953 kg)
Maximum take-off: 4,100 lb (1,860 kg)
Maximum take-off, external load: 4,700 lb (2,131 kg)
Maximum certified useful load: 2,120 lb (961 kg) internal, 2,720 lb (1,233 kg) external
Payload: 2,120 lb (961 kg) internal, and 2,727 lb (1,237 kg) external

PERFORMANCE (at MTOW)**:**
Never-exceed speed (V_{NE}): 135 kts (155 mph) 250 km/h
Maximum cruise speed: 136 kts (157 mph) 248 km/h at 3,000 ft (914 m), or 132 kts (152 mph) 245 km/h at sea level
Sideways/rearward speed: more than 30 kts (35 mph) 56 km/h
Maximum climb rate: 1,775 ft (541 m) per minute at sea level and ISA, or 1,750 ft (533 m) per minute at ISA + 20° C
IGE hovering ceiling: 11,500 ft (3,505 m) ISA, or 7,400 ft (2,255 m) at ISA + 20° C
OGE hovering ceiling: 6,800 ft (2,070 m) ISA, or 4,000 ft (1,219 m) ISA + 20° C
Operating ceiling: 20,000 ft (6,100 m)
Range: 330 naut miles (380 miles) 611 km at sea level, or 380 naut miles (437 miles) 704 km at 6,000 ft (1,829 m)
Duration: 3.5 hours at sea level, or 3.8 hours at 5,000 ft (1,524 m)
Operating temperature range: -25° C to +45° C
Slope landing angle: up to 20°

Boeing MD 900 and MD 902 Explorer and Combat Explorer

Comments: Reports in mid-1998 suggested negotiations were underway to sell Explorer to Belgium.
First flight: 18 December 1992 (first MD 900 prototype), 17 September 1993 (second MD 900), 16 December 1993 (third MD 900) and 3 August 1994 (fourth MD 900).
Certification: FAA 2 December 1994 for MD 900. IFR and UK certification 1995 for MD 900. 11 February 1998 for MD 902 to Category A.
First delivery: 16 December 1994 (first of 5 for Petroleum Helicopters), followed by an air ambulance version for Rocky Mountain Helicopters.
Role: Commercial and military light helicopters.
Sales: Well over 100 firm orders and a large number of options, the former including 17 for 3 Japanese customers. Production rate of 48 per year. MD 902 has now become the standard production version, taking over from the MD 900.
Crew/passengers: 8 seats, including crew of 1 or 2.
Freight, internal: 51.4 cu ft (1.46 m^3) baggage compartment, if closed off.
Cabin access: Sliding cabin door each side, 4 ft 2 ins (1.27 m) wide, large enough to allow loading of a standard 4 ft (1.22 m) pallet with a forklift vehicle. Opening 4 ft 4 ins (1.32 m) if door removed.
Rotor system: 5-blade bearingless composite rotor, with titanium leading-edge abrasion strip and carbonfibre flexbeam blade retention straps. Detachable swept tips with balance-tracking-weights.
Anti-torque system: NOTAR (see MD 520N and MD 600N). MD 902 has improved NOTAR, with improved inlet screen design/tip sealing.
Flight control system: Hydraulic actuators. More powerful stabilizer control on MD 902.
Airframe materials: Typical light alloy A-frame structure, with composites skin, fairings and access doors. Deep keel beams that extend the full length of the helicopter for added safety. Tailplane span 9 ft 4 ins (2.84 m)

↑ Boeing MD Explorer operated by St. Alphonsus Regional Medical Center's Life Flight air medical services unit

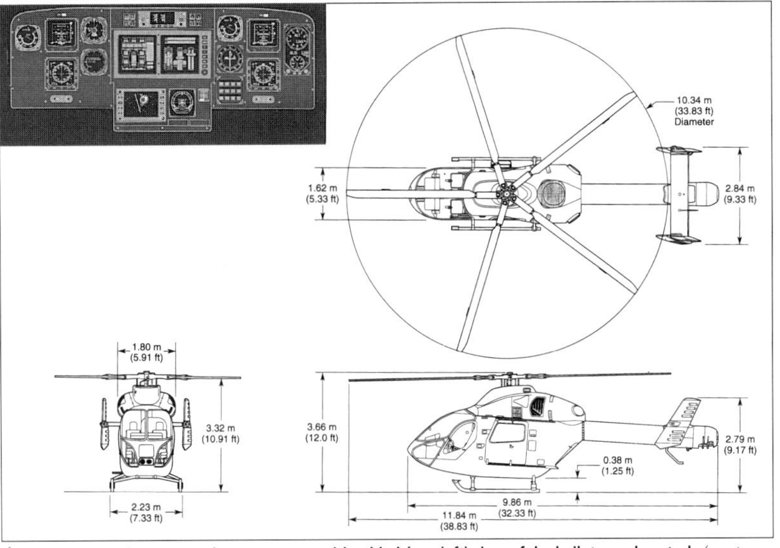

↑ **Boeing MD Explorer general arrangement, with added *(top-left)* view of dual pilot panel controls** *(courtesy Boeing)*

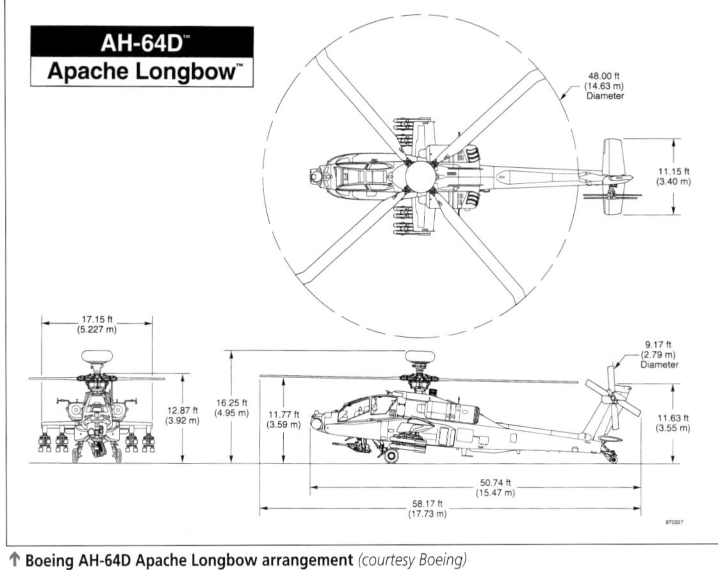

↑ **Boeing AH-64D Apache Longbow arrangement** *(courtesy Boeing)*

Safety features: Energy-absorbing crew seats (16 g forward and 20 g downward).
Engines: Initially 2 × 650 shp (485 kW) Pratt & Whitney Canada PW206A turboshafts for MD 900, offering 690 shp (514.5 kW) for 2.5 minutes OEI; later PW206Bs. Alternatively, 2 × 641 shp (478 kW) Turbomeca Arrius 2C turboshafts. Single-engine operation capability. 2 × PW206Es for MD 902 of same take-off rating, but with 732 shp (546 kW) for 2.5 minutes OEI. MD 902 also has improved NACA air inlets (offering greater air flow at speeds above 40 kts) and engine compartment fire suppression.
Transmission rating: Planetary transmission. 900 shp (671 kW) continuous, 1,000 shp (746 kW) for 5 minutes, and 575 shp (429 kW) for 2.5 minutes OEI for MD 900. Upgraded transmission for MD 902 that can run dry for 30 minutes at 50% power. 5,000 hours TBO.
Fuel system: 602 litres usable for MD 900. Self-sealing fuel lines. Provision for 666 litre tank. MD 902 has improved fuel system of 708 litres, with extra tank under baggage compartment floor.
Electrical system: Dual DC starter-generators. Battery.
Flight avionics/instrumentation: Advanced avionics. Dual pilot or single-pilot operation. Integrated Instrument Display System (IIDS) with colour liquid crystal displays for engine, rotor track and balance data, and records engine exceedences and allows maintainers to automatically monitor engine trend analysis, giving advanced warning of potential problems. Improved IIDS software for MD 902 and standard gyro.

Aircraft variants:
MD 900 Explorer was the initial civil version, with PW206A/B turboshafts as standard.
MD 902 Explorer is the improved version, with PW206E turboshafts and many other changes as detailed.
Combat Explorer is the military version. NightHawk electro-optical surveillance and targeting multi-sensor system, with daylight and infra-red sighting, laser ranging and laser designation capabilities, also useful in navigation and search/seizure operations as well as threat location and identification; can use co-ordinates supplied by radar or GPS. FLIR. Armament includes Hellfire anti-armour missiles, 2.75-ins rocket launchers and guns. Integrated display system, with weather radar, VOR/ADF/GPS navigation, IFF, VHF/UHF/HF communications, and RWR. Operational weight 6,900 lb (3,130 kg), maximum permitted speed 150 kts (172 mph) 278 km/h, maximum duration 3 to 3.35 hours, hovering OGE 10,700 ft (3,261 m) and IGE 12,600 ft (3,840 m), ISA.

Details for MD 902 Explorer

PRINCIPAL DIMENSIONS:
Rotor diameter: 33 ft 10 ins (10.31 m)
Maximum length, rotors turning: 38 ft 10 ins (11.84 m)
Fuselage length: 32 ft 4 ins (9.86 m)
Fuselage width: 5 ft 4 ins (1.62 m) at nose, 5 ft 11 ins (1.8 m) at engine nacelles
Maximum height: 12 ft (3.66 m)

CABIN:
Length: 12 ft 11 ins (3.94 m) to instrument panel, including baggage compartment. 6 ft 3 ins (1.91 m) main cabin alone. 14 ft (4.26 m) flat floor space
Width: 4 ft 9 ins (1.45 m)
Height: 4 ft 1 ins (1.24 m)
Volume: 172.5 cu ft (4.88 m^3) main cabin

MAIN ROTOR:
Rotor disc: 899.04 sq ft (83.52 m^2)

UNDERCARRIAGE:
Type: Fixed skids, mounted on dampers
Skid track: 7 ft 4 ins (2.24 m)

WEIGHTS:
Empty: 3,265 lb (1,480 kg), standard configuration
Maximum take-off: 6,250 lb (2,835 kg)
Maximum take-off, external load: 6,740 lb (3,057 kg)
Useful load: 2,807 lb (1,273 kg) standard configuration
Payload: 3,000 lb (1,360 kg) externally

PERFORMANCE:
Never-exceed speed (V_{NE}): 160 kts (184 mph) 296 km/h at sea level
Maximum cruise speed: 145 kts (167 mph) 268 km/h at sea level
Maximum climb rate: 2,800 ft (853 m) per minute
Vertical climb rate: 1,350 ft (411 m) per minute
Climb rate, OEI: 1,000 ft (305 m) per minute
IGE hovering ceiling: 12,800 ft (3,900 m) ISA, 9,550 ft (2,910 m) ISA + 20 °C
OGE hovering ceiling: 11,300 ft (3,445 m) ISA, 7,100 ft (2,165 m) ISA + 20 °C
Ceiling: 18,000 ft (5,485 m), or 10,500 ft (3,200 m) OEI
Range: 300 naut miles (345 miles) 556 km
Duration: 3.5 hours, at 5,000 ft (1,525 m), ISA

PERFORMANCES FOR MD 900 EXPLORER ACHIEVED DURING CERTIFICATION/TESTING:
Forward flight: 177 kts (204 mph) 328 km/h
Sideways flight: 40 kts (46 mph) 74 km/h
G loading: +3
Banked turns: 60°
Climb rate: 2,800 ft (853 m) per minute
Descent rate: 2,000 ft (610 m) per minute
Autorotational descent: 4,600 ft (1,402 m) per minute/148 kts
Sideslips: ±16° at 100 kts

Boeing AH-64D Apache Longbow

First flight: 15 April 1992 for first AH-64D prototype without radar. 29 September 1995 for first preproduction AH-64D. Original YAH-64 prototype flew on 30 September 1975.
Role: Day/night and adverse weather attack helicopter, designed to survive in a mid-to-high intensity battlefield and be self-deployable. Also suited to air combat, coastal defence, air defence suppression, deep strike, joint air attack, armed reconnaissance, fire support and more.

Development

■ 4 prototypes appeared in 1992-93, followed in 1994 by 2 prototypes of the anticipated AH-64C version with many AH-64D features but minus the Longbow radar and upgraded engines. That same year the US Army abandoned the AH-64C designation, deciding instead to designate all modernized Apaches as AH-64Ds whether or not fitted with Longbow radar. The AH-64Cs became the fifth and sixth AH-64D prototypes.
■ 13 November 1992. First flight of the second Apache Longbow prototype (then known as Longbow Apache), followed by the third on 30 June 1993, fourth on 4 October 1993, fifth on 19 January 1994, and sixth on 4 March 1994.
■ 21 March 1997. Roll out of the first production AH-64D at the Boeing plant as Mesa, Arizona.
■ 1998. Early elements of an Apache upgrade announced, with Boeing receiving a 4-year US Army contract for design and testing of a composite mid-fuselage section. DARPA contracted development of the "Drive Train 2000" transmission, while further upgrades might include a 5-blade rotor and new engines.
■ 29 May 1998. First flight of AH-64D with RTM322 engines.
■ June 1998. IOC by 1-227th Aviation Regiment of the US Army at Fort Hood (TX) with Apache Longbow.

Details

Sales: All remaining active US Army, US Army National Guard and US Army Reserve AH-64As (from 821 production helicopters delivered) are being upgraded to the current AH-64D standard, the programme starting in 1996 and not expected to be completed until the year 2010. Whilst all 750 or thereabouts helicopters will thereafter adopt the name Apache Longbow, only 227 will receive the Longbow radar itself, although installation on a non-equipped helicopter is possible in a few hours. In addition, new or ex-US Army AH-64As were ordered by Egypt (24 + 12), Greece (20), Israel (42, with current intentions to upgrade to Apache Longbow standard from the year 2001), Kuwait (16 Apache Longbows requested, together with 384 Hellfire missiles), Saudi Arabia (12) and the United Arab Emirates (30). 30 AH-64Ds were ordered by the Netherlands on 7 April 1995, for delivery from 1998, with 12 US Army AH-64As on loan since 1996 until these arrive. On 13 July 1995 the British Government ordered 67 AH-64Ds for the British Army Air Corps, all but 8 being assembled from Boeing-supplied kits by GKN Westland; an additional 20 may be required to compensate for the reduction in British Army tanks; ground-based training (including simulators) for British Army ground and air crews was selected in 1998 to be a joint venture between Boeing and GKN Westland, based at Dishforth, Middle Wallop, Wattisham and the Royal Electrical and Mechanical Engineers base at Arborfield. Singapore has short-listed the AH-64D for its attack helicopter requirement.
Crew: 2 in tandem, the pilot to the rear in a 1 ft 7 ins (0.48 m) upward-stepped cockpit to improve forward vision. Fragmentation protection barrier between the cockpits. Boron armour protection against 12.7-mm hits.
Rotor system: 4-blade main rotor with swept tips. Metal/composites blades that fold, with tolerance to 23-mm hits. Electric blade de-icing. Steel blade/hub retention straps with elastomeric bearings.
Tail rotor characteristics: 2 teetering 2-blade rotors, with 55° separation in "scissors" configuration, on the port side of the fin.
Tail surfaces: Horizontal stabilizer with automatically adjusting incidence, for optimum position during hover and all other flying modes (span 11 ft 2 ins, 3.4 m).
Flight control system: Principal redundant hydraulic system, with Honeywell fly-by-wire back-up.
Safety features: Can survive 12.7-mm gunfire hits for a minimum of 30 minutes continued flight, and some components can survive 23-mm strikes.

MULTI-MISSION FLEXIBILITY / PERFORMANCE

Mission	Wingtip	Starboard wing	Cannon	Port wing	Wingtip	Average ingress flight speed (VMCP)	Average egress flight speed (VMCP)	Mission duration	Mission range
COMBAT MISSION	2 ATAM	4 Hellfire	320 Rounds 30mm	4 Hellfire	2 ATAM	141 KNOTS	148 KNOTS	3.27 HR	269 NM
MULTI-ROLE MISSION	2 ATAM	4 Hellfire 19 FFAR	1,200 Rounds 30mm	4 Hellfire 19 FFAR	2 ATAM	134 KNOTS	145 KNOTS	3.08 HR	251 NM
CLOSE-SUPPORT MISSION	2 ATAM	8 Hellfire	1,200 Rounds 30mm	8 Hellfire	2 ATAM	132 KNOTS	143 KNOTS	3.06 HR	247 NM
GROUND-SUPPRESSION	2 ATAM	38 FFAR	1,200 Rounds 30mm	38 FFAR	2 ATAM	136 KNOTS	148 KNOTS	3.10 HR	258 NM

MULTI-MISSION FLEXIBILITY / PERFORMANCE

Mission	Starboard wing	Cannon	Port wing	Average ingress flight speed (VMCP)	Average egress flight speed (VMCP)	Mission duration	Mission range
COMBAT MISSION	4 Hellfire	320 Rounds 30mm	4 Hellfire	152 KNOTS	158 KNOTS	3.56 HR	307 NM
MULTI-ROLE MISSION	4 Hellfire 19 FFAR	1,200 Rounds 30mm	4 Hellfire 19 FFAR	145 KNOTS	155 KNOTS	3.40 HR	288 NM
CLOSE-SUPPORT MISSION	8 Hellfire	1,200 Rounds 30mm	8 Hellfire	143 KNOTS	153 KNOTS	3.38 HR	282 NM
	38 FFAR	1,200 Rounds 30mm	38 FFAR	148 KNOTS	158 KNOTS	3.42 HR	297 NM

↑ **Weapon loads and performance data for various missions, with AH-64D Apache Longbow at top and AH-64A below. Note that speeds and missions at 2,000 ft (610 m) and 21° C conditions; ingress speeds maintain weapon load, egress speeds are with self-defence weapons only (33% initial rounds for both, plus 2 ATAMs for Apache Longbow only); range and duration missions flown with full weapons for ingress and 33% initial rounds (plus 2 ATAMs for Apache Longbow) for egress; 20 minutes fuel reserve** *(courtesy Boeing)*

Details for AH-64D Apache Longbow, *with AH-64A in italics*

PRINCIPAL DIMENSIONS:
Rotor diameter (main): 48 ft (14.63 m), *the same*
Maximum length, rotors turning: 58 ft 2 ins (17.73 m), *the same*
Fuselage length: 50 ft 9 ins (15.47 m) from TADS/PNVS nose to the turning tail rotor, *the same*
Width, over wings: 17 ft 2 ins (5.227 m), *the same*
Maximum height: 16 ft 3 ins (4.95 m) to top of Longbow radar, 12 ft 10 ins (3.92 m) to top of rotor head, 11 ft 7.5 ins (3.55 m) to top of fin, *height overall 15 ft 2.9 ins (4.64 m)*

MAIN ROTOR:
Blade chord: 1 ft 9 ins (0.53 m), *the same*
Rotor disc: 1,809.5 sq ft (168.11 m^2), *the same*

TAIL ROTOR:
Diameter: 9 ft 2 ins (2.79 m), *the same*

UNDERCARRIAGE:
Type: Fixed, with castoring and self-centring tailwheel. Main units can 'kneel' to lower height for air transportation. Can sustain landings at 42 ft (12.8 m) per second, *the same*
Main wheel tyre size: 8.50-10
Tail wheel tyre size: 5.00-4
Wheel base: 34 ft 9 ins (10.59 m)
Wheel track: 6 ft 8 ins (2.03 m)

WEIGHTS:
Empty: 11,800 lb (5,352 kg), *11,387 lb (5,165 kg)*
Primary mission take-off: 16,601 lb (7,530 kg), *15,075 lb (6,838 kg)*
Maximum take-off, for ferrying: 22,283 lb (10,107 kg)

PERFORMANCE (baseline, primary mission weight)**:**
Never-exceed speed (V_{NE}): 197 kts (227 mph) 364 km/h
Maximum speed: 141 kts (162 mph) 261 km/h at sea level and ISA (transmission limit), or 143 kts (165 mph) 265 km/h at 2,000 ft (610 m) and 21° C; *150 kts (173 mph) 278 km/h at sea level and ISA, 153 kts (176 mph) 284 km/h at 2,000 ft (610 m) and 21° C*
Cruise speed: 141 kts (162 mph) 261 km/h at sea level and ISA (transmission limit), or 143 kts (165 mph) 265 km/h at 2,000 ft (610 m) and 21° C, MRP; *150 kts (173 mph) 278 km/h at sea level and ISA, 153 kts (176 mph) 284 km/h at 2,000 ft (610 m) and 21° C*
Also, see Chart for multi-mission performance
Maximum climb rate: 2,415 ft (736 m) per minute at sea level and ISA, or 2,370 ft (722 m) per minute at 2,000 ft (610 m) and 21° C, IRP; *2,915 ft (889 m) per minute at sea level and ISA, 2,890 ft (881 m) per minute at 2,000 ft (610 m) and 21° C, IRP*
Vertical climb rate: 1,475 ft (450 m) per minute at sea level and ISA, or 1,255 ft (383 m) per minute at 2,000 ft (610 m) and 21° C, MRP; *2,175 ft (663 m) per minute at sea level and ISA, 2,050 ft (625 m) per minute at 2,000 ft (610 m) and 21° C, MRP*
IGE hovering ceiling: 13,690 ft (4,172 m) ISA, or 12,290 ft (3,745 m) ISA at 15° C, MRP; *15,895 ft (4,845 m) ISA, or 14,845 ft (4,525 m) ISA at 15° C, MRP*
OGE hovering ceiling: 9,480 ft (2,889 m) ISA, 7,960 ft (2,426 m) ISA at 15° C, MRP; *12,685 ft (3,866 m) ISA, or 11,215 ft (3,418 m) ISA at 15° C, MRP*
Range with internal fuel: 220 naut miles (253 miles) 407 km at sea level and ISA, or 234 naut miles (269 miles) 433 km at 4,000 ft (1,220 m) and 35° C, both with 30 minutes reserve
Duration: Design mission 1.83 hours. Maximum 3.2 hours at sea level and ISA or 3.3 hours at 4,000 ft (1,220 m) and 35° C

Engines: 2 General Electric T700-GE-701C turboshafts. IR suppression (Black Hole), and particle separators. AlliedSignal 36-155 (BH) APU for engine start-up. See Development.
Engine rating: Each 1,890 shp (1,409 kW) take-off and 1,662 shp (1,239.4 kW) maximum continuous. Emergency OEI contingency rating of 1,940 shp (1,447 kW).
Transmission: Can continue without oil for 60 minutes.
Fuel system: 1,420 litres weighing 2,442 lb (1,108 kg) maximum internal in 2 fuselage cells. 5,980 lb (2,712 kg) maximum external auxiliary via 4 × 870 litre non-ballistic tolerant tanks under the stub wings. Qualification testing in 1998 of a new Robertson Aviation 492 litre crash survivable, self-sealing and ballistic tolerant auxiliary tank that can be installed internally in place of the 30-mm ammunition magazine in 30 minutes. Although replacing ammunition, it permits all stub-wing pylons to carry weapons.
Electrical system: Increased AC power on AH-64D by use of 2 × 70 kVA (instead of 35 kVA) engine-driven generators. 2 transformer rectifiers for DC supply. Back-up battery.
Hydraulic system: Twin Parker Bertea, at 3,000 psi.
Braking system: Mainwheel hydraulic.
Radar: Mast-mounted Longbow fire control radar (360°). In under 30 seconds the crew unmasks the radar dome for a single radar scan, then remasks. As the scan is completed, onboard processors have *detected* the precise location, speed and direction of movement of up to 256 targets, *classified* the targets as tracked or wheeled, air defence, helicopters or aeroplanes, *prioritized* the most dangerous or priority targets in the target array, and *displayed* the target information and indicated the highest threat targets. All target information, plus its own identification/location/time, are then transmitted to command elements via digital data burst through the improved data modem. The battle area is then divided, and priority fire zones and attack teams assigned.
Flight avionics/instrumentation: Integrated GPS, HF radio, target acquisition and designation sight (TADS) and pilot night vision sensor (PNVS), inertial navigation, radar frequency interferometer, and Longbow fire control radar. TADS in a turret able to rotate ±120° in azimuth and +30°/-60° in elevation provides the co-pilot/gunner with the capabilities for target search, detection, recognition, and laser spot tracking and designation by means of direct-view optics (4° or 18° field of view), TV (0° 50′ or 4° field of view) and FLIR (3° 6′, 10° 6′ and 50° field of view) sensors that may be used individually or in combination. PNVS provides thermal imaging capabilities that enable nap-of-the-earth (NOE) flight and is installed in a turret able to rotate ±90° in azimuth and +20°/-45° in elevation. TADS/PNVS are carried at the nose, and AH-64D introduces reliability improvements. Terrain profiling/avoidance. Airborne target handover system (ATHS). AN/ASN-157 Doppler navigation, with AHRS; AH-64Ds have inertial navigation/GPS. SINCGARS radio and GPS were first deployed in AH-64As of the 5-501st Aviation Regiment, in 1993. 2 AlliedSignal colour active matrix multi-function displays (MFDs) of 6 ins (15 cm) square in each cockpit from Lot 2 AH-64D upgrades (monochrome CRTs for first 24 upgrades of Lot 1), and crew integrated helmet and display sighting system (IHADSS); AH-64D has some 200 cockpit switches, about one-sixth the number for AH-64A. AH-64D also features enhanced fire control computer, and antennae relocation to improve NOE communication and improve IFF. Fault detection and location system (FDLS). All systems are integrated through a MIL-STD-1553B multiplex databus system with ADA language and 32-bit processors. The AH-64D upgrade introduces improved data modem, manprint crewstation (provides increased crew effectiveness partly through the MFDs, ease of maintenance, automated data transfer with the DTU in rear cockpit, and enhanced situation awareness), new weapons processor, and mission planning console. AFCS, with autohover (see Tail surfaces). DTU has a cartridge able to store updated information covering 10 flight directions with up to 99 waypoints each, up to 50 known targets, 15 boundary lines, 12 areas of engagement, plus fire and no-fire zones, while another use is to store maintenance information.
Self-protection systems: Radar (AN/APR-39) and laser (AN/AVR-2) warning, radar (AN/ALQ-136) and infra-red (AN/ALQ-144) jammers, and chaff dispensers.
Fixed guns: Flexible-firing 30-mm M230 Chain Gun automatic cannon, with reliability upgrade and side loader.

↑ Boeing AH-64D Apache Longbow

Ammunition: 1,200 rounds (see Fuel system).
Number of weapon pylons: 4 under the stub wings, plus dual AAM launchers on both tips.
Expendable weapons and equipment: 16 Hellfire anti-tank missiles or 76 × 2.75-ins rockets typically. 4 AIM-92 Stinger AAMs on wingtip launchers, or alternatively 2 Sidewinders or 4 Mistrals; Starstreak in operational trials. AAMs can also be carried on the main pylons. Maverick is among other possible weapon choices. See weapon diagrams.

Aircraft variants:
AH-64A Apache was the original production version, as delivered to the US Army and all foreign customers prior to the Netherlands and the UK. Will remain the principal version with the US Army while upgrading to AH-64D takes place. T700-GE-701 engines of 1,570 shp (1,170.7 kW) maximum continuous and 1,723 shp (1,285 kW) maximum contingency ratings.
AH-64C, see Development.
AH-64D Apache Longbow is the current version, either by conversion of AH-64As or newly built (as for the Netherlands and UK). Features Longbow radar and more powerful engines, as detailed. Improved electrical, navigation and vapour cooling systems, plus EMI hardening. Said to be 700% more survivable and 400% more lethal than the AH-64A Apache.
GKN Westland WAH-64D Apache Longbow is the version for the British Army Air Corps (67 ordered), featuring RTM322 engines. Laser-based infra-red defence aid suite. Performance generally similar, as the GKN Westland-built transmission will be the same type as that in the US Apache.
JAH-64 applies to non-operational test AH-64s with the US Army.

Boeing H-47 Chinook

First flight: 21 September 1961 (YHC-1B/YCH-47A prototype).
Certification: 19 June 1981 for Commercial Chinook.
First delivery: 16 August 1962.
Role: Heavy-lift transport helicopter, primarily for the movement of troops, artillery, ammunition, fuel, water, barrier materials, equipment and supplies on the battlefield, with secondary medevac, aircraft recovery, firefighting, paratroop drop, heavy construction, civil development, SAR and disaster relief.
Sales: Boeing-produced military Chinooks operate with the US Army, US Army National Guard, US Army Reserve and 10 other nations (Argentina, Australia, Canada, Japan, Netherlands, Singapore, South Korea, Spain, Thailand and the UK), the latter including HC Mks 1, 2 and 3 purchased for the RAF (Mk 3s including 8 new special forces examples, with deliveries up to 1999, making a total RAF procurement of 58 Chinooks); Singapore, having received 6 Chinooks, is understood to have ordered a further 6, with 4 options, for delivery in 2000-2001. Other Chinooks built by Agusta in Italy and Kawasaki in Japan operate with 7 nations; Egypt, as a recipient of 15 Agusta-built Chinooks, is expected to receive 4 more from the USA. A further 13 Chinooks went to commercial operators. Current CH-47Ds and MH-47Es with US forces were produced by upgrade of earlier versions, first flown on 11 May 1979 and first delivered to the 101st Airborne Division at Fort Campbell, Ky, on 28 February 1983, with IOC by the 159th Aviation Assault Battalion on 28 February 1984. All US CH-47D/MH-47Es had been delivered by November 1995, totalling 481.

Details *(principally CH-47D, except as indicated)*

Crew/passengers: 2 pilots plus provision for a combat commander. 33 to 55 troops, or 24 litters and 2 attendants.
Freight, internal: Weapon systems, freight or vehicles instead of troops.
Freight, external: Forward and aft cargo hooks, each 17,000 lb (7,711 kg) capacity, and centre hook of 26,000 lb (11,793 kg) capacity.
Cabin access: Rear ramp/door, 6 ft 6 ins high × 7 ft 7 ins wide (1.98 m × 2.31 m). Door can be open in flight or removed. Door each side of the fuselage, the larger starboard door of 5 ft 6 ins × 3 ft (1.68 × 0.91 m).
Rotor system: 2 contra-rotating and intermeshing 3-blade rotors in tandem, with flapping and drag hinges. Blades of glassfibre construction. Manual blade folding. Tolerance to hits from 23-mm shells.
Flight control system: Hydraulic.
Fuselage: Watertight underfloor area for buoyancy.
Engines: 2 × AlliedSignal T55-L-714s turboshafts currently for International standard and ICH, otherwise T55-L-712s.
Engine rating: Each 4,867 shp (3,629 kW) maximum and 4,168 shp (3,108 kW) continuous for T55-L-714s, or 3,750 shp (2,796 kW) maximum and 3,000 shp (2,237 kW) continuous for T55-L-712s. APU.
Transmission rating: Maximum 7,500 shp (5,593 kW).
Fuel system: 3,899 litres in fuselage pods. Optional 3 × 3,028 litre auxiliary tanks in the cabin.
Electrical system: Includes 2 × 40 kVA transmission-mounted alternators.
Hydraulic system: Principal system for controls, at 3,000 psi. Utility supply at 3,350 psi.
Braking system: Hydraulic disc.
Flight avionics/instrumentation: IFR equipped. Includes AFCS with autostabilization and hold, gyromagnetic compass, Tacan, ADF, VOR/glideslope/marker beacon receiver, ADF, IFF, radar altimeter, and more. RAF Chinooks have Racal Super TANS INS with GPS. Chinook International modernizations for the Netherlands were the first with 'glass' cockpit displays, as offered on new Internationals.
Self-protection systems: Chaff/flare dispensers, IR jammers, radar and/or missile approach warning receivers are available, as adopted by the UK.
Fixed guns: Can carry cabin-mounted machine-guns. See MH-47E.

Aircraft variants:
CH-47D is the main current version, as detailed.
CH-47D International is the 'new-build' export equivalent of the US Army CH-47D, built in Japan as the ***Kawasaki CH-47J***. Also available in MH-47E type. Lengthened fuselage, at 52 ft 1 ins (15.88 m), and available with advanced digital cockpit with multi-function displays and electronic flight instruments. Typical accommodation for 44 troops or 24 litters. 28,000 lb (12,700 kg) payload. T55-L-712-SSB engines of 4,400 shp (3,281 kW) initially, but now standardized on T55-L-714As of 4,867 shp (3,629 kW) maximum and 4,168 shp (3,108 kW) continuous ratings. 30 new CH-47D Internationals delivered to East Asian forces, 3 to the UK and 6 to the Netherlands.

Details for CH-47D, *with MH-47E in italics*

PRINCIPAL DIMENSIONS:
Rotor diameter: Each 60 ft (18.29 m)
Maximum length, rotors turning: 99 ft (30.18 m)
Fuselage length: 51 ft (15.54 m), *52 ft 1 ins (15.88 m) plus 16 ft 6 ins (5.03 m) for the refuelling probe*
Width, blades folded: 12 ft 5 ins (3.78 m)
Maximum height: 18 ft 11.5 ins (5.78 m) to top of aft hub

CABIN:
Length: 30 ft 6 ins (9.3 m)
Width: 7 ft 6 ins (2.29 m)
Height: 6 ft 6 ins (1.98 m)
Volume: 1,474 cu ft (41.74 m^3)

MAIN ROTOR:
Aerofoil section: VR7/8
Blade chord: 2 ft 8 ins (0.81 m)
Blade area: each 80 sq ft (7.43 m^2)
Rotor disc: each 2,827.5 sq ft (262.68 m^2)
Rpm: 225

UNDERCARRIAGE:
Type: Fixed, with 4 units, forward units having twin wheels. Castoring rear wheels, the starboard steerable. Fuselage inclined upwards by 1.56 ° from tail to nose when on the ground
Wheel base: 22 ft 6 ins (6.86 m)
Wheel track: 11 ft 11 ins (3.63 m) to outside of wheels

WEIGHTS:
Empty: 23,401 lb (10,614 kg), *26,918 lb (12,210 kg)*
Maximum take-off: 50,000 lb (22,680 kg), *54,000 lb (24,494 kg)*
Useful load: 26,599 lb (12.065 kg)

PERFORMANCE (at 50,000 lb)**:**
Maximum speed (VMCP): 145 kts (167 mph) 269 km/h
Cruise speed: 143 kts (165 mph) 265 km/h at sea level, *140 kts (161 mph) 259 km/h*
Maximum climb rate: 1,522 ft (464 m) per minute, *1,841 ft (561 m) per minute, sea level*
IGE hovering ceiling: 8,200 ft (2,499 m) ISA, or 4,350 ft (1,326 m) at ISA + 20° C, *9,800 ft (2,987 m) ISA*
OGE hovering ceiling: 4,950 ft (1,509 m) ISA, or 500 ft (152 m) ISA + 20° C, *5,500 ft (1,676 m) ISA*
Service ceiling: 8,450 ft (2,575 m), *10,150 ft (3,094 m)*
Range: 230 naut miles (265 miles) 426 km, sea level, ISA
Self-deployment range: *1,260 naut miles (1,451 miles) 2,333 km*
ODA team extraction radius: *505 naut miles (581 miles) 935 km*

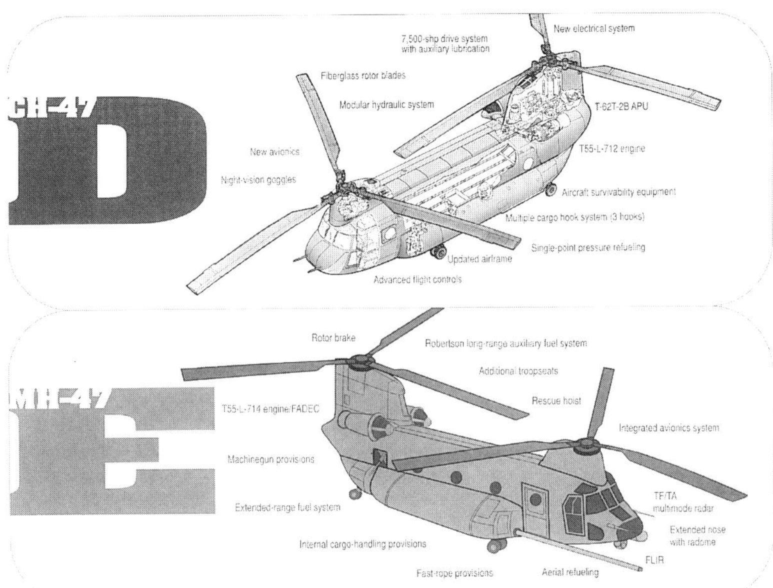

↑ **Boeing CH-47D and MH-47E upgrade features** *(courtesy Boeing)*

↑ **Boeing CH-47D International Chinook** *(courtesy Boeing)*

CH-47 International Chinook modernization covers the modernizing of nearly 60 early model Chinooks of Greece (9 Agusta-built CH-47Cs, modernized 1993-95), the Netherlands (7 ex-Canadian CH-47Cs, the first handed over in September 1994), Spain (9 CH-47Cs, modernized 1991-93) and the UK (over 30 Chinook HC Mk 1s to HC Mk 2 standard, modernized 1993-95) to US Army CH-47D configuration. Netherlands first incorporated the new advanced 'glass' cockpit.

MH-47D became an early US Special Operations Chinook for the 160th SOAR, preceding the MH-47E and featuring AlliedSignal Bendix/King RDR-1300 radar, upgraded com/nav systems, thermal image system, flight refuelling probe, and provision for 7.62-mm Miniguns. 11 completed from CH-47Ds.

MH-47E became the principal US Special Operations Chinook, with the prototype delivered in May 1991. The total procurement (including 1 prototype) was restricted to 25 (delivered by 1995) to perform clandestine long-range airlift insertion/extraction missions into hostile territory. Same dimensions as the CH-47D International, additional troop seats, rescue hoist, T55-L-714 engines, extended range fuel system, internal auxiliary tanks, inflight refuelling capability, internal cargo handling system, OBOGS, rotor brake, provision for 0.50-ins machine-guns, and an integrated avionics system with mission management system, multi-function controls and displays, avionics processing, FLIR, TF/TA radar, global communications and navigation, and aircraft survivability equipment. Can complete a 5 hour 30 minute covert mission over a 300 naut mile (345 mile) 555 km radius at low level, day or night, in adverse weather, over any terrain. 7,828 litres of fuel standard, with 3 × 3,028 litre auxiliary tanks optional.

CH-47 Improved Cargo Helicopter is the programme name for US Army CH-47Ds to be upgraded to allow them to remain operational until at least 2022. In late 1996, the US Army approved a funding plan to modernize 300 Chinooks to ICH configuration, with first deliveries slated for 2002. The programme has 3 main elements, namely vibration reduction, engine improvements and preparing for digital battlefield. Boeing is investigating lower vibration levels using 2 approaches that can be used in tandem or independently: first is the development of an Active Vibration Suppressor (AVS), which will monitor aircraft vibration levels and actively suppress multiple harmonic frequencies transmitted throughout the fuselage from the rotor system; the other is the evaluation of ways to reduce structural loading through dynamic tuning, or selective stiffening of specific aircraft structures. Engine improvement will see the adoption of T55-L-714 engines with FADEC (separate ECP), with advantages including operations closer to the helicopter's 50,000 lb (22,680 kg) gross weight in high altitude/hot temperature (4,000 ft, 1,219 m and 35° C) conditions to carry standard loads without reducing fuel, range or duration. Preparing for the digital battlefield means that efforts will involve improved situation awareness and command & control, including GPS and Doppler integration and development of HUD capability for NVGs; long-range communications may also be upgraded; MIL-STD-1553B databus, CDUs and electronic cockpit displays; Rockwell Collins selected in 1998 as 'glass' cockpit supplier. Remanufactured airframe.

The Boeing Company and Sikorsky Aircraft USA

Corporate address:
See Combat section for Boeing company details and Sikorsky later in this section.

Boeing Sikorsky RAH-66 Comanche

First flight: 4 January 1996 (36 minute flight).
Role: All-weather multi-role battlefield helicopter, with primary mission of armed reconnaissance. Can be configured for air combat and light attack.

Aims

- To provide the US Army with an armed reconnaissance helicopter of low observability, combined with speed and agility, intended to replace the AH-1 and OH-58. To provide the capabilities demanded of a smaller force structure, including improved mobility, increased survivability and much reduced operation and support costs. Simple remove-and-replace maintenance.
- A Comanche can be transported by C-130, 3 by C-141, 4 by C-17 and 8 by C-5. Can be loaded on or off a C-130 in 22 minutes.

Development

- 21 June 1988. Demonstration/validation phase was initiated by a request for proposals for the LHX (Light Helicopter Experimental). Boeing and Sikorsky teamed against competing Bell and McDonnell Douglas.
- 5 April 1991. Dem/val contract go-ahead for prototypes went to the Boeing and Sikorsky team. Dem/val programme to prove all critical components, including mission equipment avionics and a growth version of the T800 engine.
- January 1992. Weapon systems preliminary design review.
- October 1993. Critical design review.
- 25 May 1995. Roll out of the first of 2 YRAH-66 prototypes.
- 20 September 1996. Chief Warrant Officer John Armbrust became the first US Army pilot to fly Comanche.
- 25 February 1997. First flight of the prototype with undercarriage retracted.
- April 1997. First 40 flying hours accumulated by the first prototype.
- September 1998. First flight of the second prototype (MEP), to join the test programme.
- 1999. Installation of the T800-LHT-801 growth engine.
- 1999. First reconnaissance MEP flight anticipated.
- 2001. 6 EOC aircraft with reconnaissance MEP to be completed for evaluation, without armament (see Sales)
- 30 September 2002. End of Phase III programme, to have included 6 EOC helicopters (see Sales).
- 2003. Production decision.
- November 2004. Low rate initial production.
- December 2006. Initial operational capability with 6 Comanches.

Details

Sales: 2 flying (second base-MEP equipped) and 2 static test prototypes. US$2.1 billion funding for fiscal years 1991-97 for dem/val prototype programme; US$1.699 billion Phase III funding awarded on 31 December 1996 for continued dem/val,

↑ **Boeing Sikorsky RAH-66 Comanche prototype with undercarriage retracted**

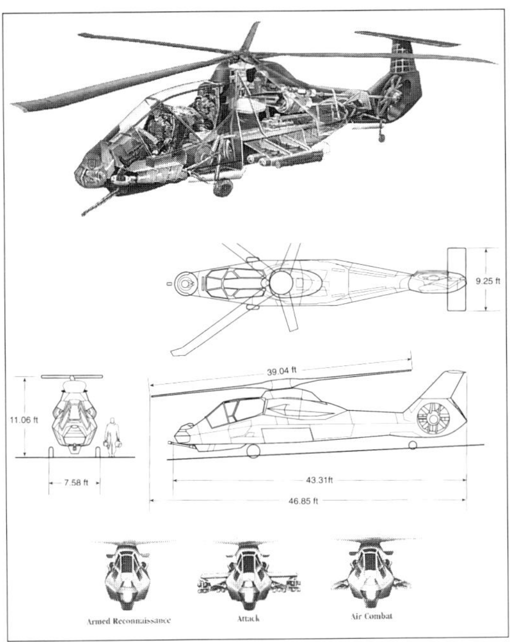

↑ **Boeing Sikorsky RAH-66 Comanche general arrangements *(top and centre)*, with front views *(bottom)* showing Comanche in internally armed configuration for reconnaissance *(left)*, with full attack armament *(middle)*, and with anhedral stub wings for air combat *(right)*** *(courtesy Boeing Sikorsky)*

to be completed by 30 September 2002 and including 6 early operational capability (EOC) Comanches to be manufactured in 2001 for operational evaluation with a specially formed US Army unit; these will not carry weapons but will have the reconnaissance mission equipment package (MEP). Following evaluation they will be given more powerful processors and armament, and redelivered for full operational use. Army requirement for 1,292 Comanches, with low-rate production beginning in about 2004 and IOC in December 2006.
Crew: 2 in tandem, the rear WSO raised, in sealed and pressurized cockpits. Sidestick cyclic pitch controllers (4 axes). Conventional collective controls.
Rotor system: 5-blade main rotor with flexbeam bearingless hub, having composite blades with swept tips. Pitch change via carbonfibre cuff fairings on the torque tubes.
Tail rotor characteristics: 8-blade Fantail rotor system of composite construction, with capacity of 600 shp (447 kW) for snap turns. Tolerance to 12.7-mm hits. Can operate for 30 minutes on 7 blades.
Tail surfaces: T-tail of composites, with horizontal stabilizer above the fin (span 9 ft 3 ins, 2.82 m). 3° increase in stabilizer incidence during the initial flight test phase has reduced tail symmetric loads, providing 7° incidence; small temporary metal strip trailing-edge Gurney flaps fitted to the first prototype have prevented roll due to asymmetric loads, the port flap at 90° down and the starboard at 90° up.
Flight control system: Lear Astronics dual triplex redundant fly-by-wire.
Airframe: Composites crashworthy structure, incorporating composites box beam, ballistically tolerant up to 23-mm gunfire.
Safety features: Crashworthy crew seats can withstand 38 ft (11.6 m) per second vertical impact.
Engines: 2 LHTEC T800-LHT-801 turboshafts (prototype flying prior to 1999 with non-growth T800).
Engine rating: Each 1,031.8 shp (769.4 kW) at 4,000 ft (1,220 m), 35° C.
Transmission: Split torque type, of 2,198 shp (1,639 kW) maximum rating. Gearbox was modified during early trials, with an elastomeric-damper plate attached to the gear web to prevent resonance; modified transmission now fitted to the prototype is reportedly expected to allow 107% rotor rpm in high-g manoeuvring.
Fuel system: 1,416 litres internally, but with 3,407 litres with external fuel tanks for self-deployment.
Electrical system: Triple.
Hydraulic system: Triple.
Radar: Longbow fire-control radar in one-third of the helicopters, with provision in the remainder.
Flight avionics/instrumentation: Provides real-time reconnaissance information. Advanced cockpit management system organizes and displays intelligence and allows rapid digital transmission of critical battlefield information to the tactical field commander. Passive long-range, high-resolution sensors. Targeting by second-generation focal-plane-array FLIR, low-light-level TV, laser rangefinder/designator, and aided target detection/classification. Night vision/adverse weather pilotage system with the FLIR and image intensifiers. Mission equipment has some commonality with the F-22A, and adopts a highly refined version of the digital map system used on the F-117A; Harris fibre-optic databus, 3D digital map, controls and multi-function liquid crystal displays (6 × 8 ins, 15 × 20 cm – two in each cockpit for tactical/map information), and a smaller LCD for weapons and fuel data. MIL-STD-1553B and additional databus, as well as the fibre-optic databus previously mentioned. Hamilton Standard flight control computer, air vehicle interface computer, and 35° × 52° field of view helmet-integrated display and sighting system (also a Kaiser system). On-board diagnostic system and self-healing digital mission electronics. Navigation system has inputs from GPS, Litton AHRS, radar altimeter and more. IFF. Anti-jam communications, including Have Quick.
Self-protection systems: Integrated IR suppression, low acoustic/visual signatures, and reduced cross section. "A breakthrough" heat-suppression system minimizes threats from heat-seeking missiles. Protection against blowing sand, high temperatures, electromagnetic interference, and NBC (nuclear, biological and chemical) agents.
Fixed guns: Northrop Grumman stowable turreted 3-barrel 20-mm Gatling-type gun. Rates of fire are 750 or 1,500 rounds per minute.
Ammunition: 320 rounds basic and 500 rounds maximum.
Number of weapon pylons: Removable anhedral stub wings for an air combat role, with added larger stub wings to carry anti-armour missiles or other weapons in attack configuration (see diagram).
Expendable weapons and equipment: Internal 4 Hellfire anti-armour and 2 Stinger air-to-air missiles. Internal plus external weapons total 14 Hellfires or 28 Stingers, or 56 × 2.75-ins rockets.

Details for Comanche

PRINCIPAL DIMENSIONS:
Rotor diameter (main): 39 ft 0.5 ins (11.9 m)
Maximum length, rotors turning: 46 ft 10 ins (14.28 m)
Fuselage length: 43 ft 3.75 ins (13.2 m)
Maximum height: 11 ft 1.5 ins (3.39 m)

MAIN ROTOR:
Aerofoil section: Boeing VR12 to 85% of length, becoming Sikorsky SSCA 09 from 92% of length to tip
Blade chord: 1 ft 3 ins (0.381 m)
Blade area: 16.15 sq ft (1.5 m^2)
Rotor disc: 1,197.04 sq ft (111.2 m^2)
Rpm: 359

TAIL ROTOR:
Diameter: 4 ft 6 ins (1.37 m)
Blade chord: 6.6 ins (16.8 cm)

UNDERCARRIAGE:
Type: Retractable tailwheel type. Main units can 'kneel' to lower height for transportation by freighter
Wheel track: 7 ft 7 ins (2.31 m)

WEIGHTS:
Empty: 8,690 lb (3,942 kg)
Maximum take-off: 17,222 lb (7,812 kg) for self-deployment
Primary mission gross: 10,597 lb (4,806.8 kg)
Useful load at primary mission gross: 2,832 lb (1,284.6 kg)
Useful load at maximum alternate gross: 5,062 lb (2,296.1 kg)

PERFORMANCE (at 4,000 ft, 1,220 m, 35° C):
Dash speed: >175 kts (202 mph) 324 km/h
Cruise speed: 165 kts (190 mph) 306 km/h
Sideways/backwards speed: 45 kts (52 mph) 83 km/h
Vertical climb rate: 1,418 ft (432 m) per minute
Masking: 1.6 seconds
180° hover turn to target: 4.7 seconds
Snap turn to target at 80 kts: 4.5 seconds
G limits: +3.5, -1
Range for self-deployment: 1,260 naut miles (1,451 miles) 2,334 km

Ken Brock Manufacturing Inc — USA

Corporate address:
11852 Western Avenue, Stanton, CA 90680.
Telephone: +1 714 898 4366
Facsimile: +1 714 894 0811

Ken Brock KB-2 Freedom Machine

Role: Single-seat autogyro.
Sales: Sold in kit form, each kit requiring approximately 20-30 hours to assemble (detailing such as painting, polishing, etc is not included in the estimated assembly time). Price for the kit, including engine, was approximately US$12,000 at the time of writing.

↑ **Ken Brock Manufacturing KB-2 Freedom Machine**

Rotor system: 2-blade.
Airframe materials: Aluminium alloy, but can have a wooden tail unit.
Engine: McCulloch or Volkswagen piston engine.
Engine rating: Typically 90 hp (67 kW).
Fuel system: 34 litres.

Details for KB-2

PRINCIPAL DIMENSIONS:
Rotor diameter: 22 ft (6.71 m)
Fuselage length: 11 ft 3 ins (3.43 m)
Maximum height: 6 ft 8 ins (2.03 m)

MAIN ROTOR:
Aerofoil section: Clark Y
Rotor disc: 380 sq ft (35.3 m^2)

WEIGHTS:
Empty: 240 lb (109 kg)
Maximum take-off: 650 lb (295 kg)

PERFORMANCE:
Maximum speed: 78-82 kts (90-95 mph) 145-153 km/h
Cruise speed: 52-61 kts (60-70 mph) 97-113 km/h
Take-off distance: 220 ft (67 m)
Landing distance: 15 ft (5 m)
Maximum climb rate: 1,200 ft (366 m) per minute
Ceiling: 12,000 ft (3,660 m)
Range: 130 naut miles (150 miles) 241 km
Duration: 2 hours

Ken Brock KB-3

Role: Single-seat ultralight autogyro.
Sales: As for KB-2.
Rotor system: 2-blade rotor.
Engine: Rotax 582 piston engine.
Engine rating: 64.4 hp (48 kW).
Fuel system: 19 litres.

Details for KB-3

PRINCIPAL DIMENSIONS:
Rotor diameter: 22 ft (6.71 m)
Fuselage length: 11 ft (3.35 m)
Maximum height: 7 ft 7 ins (2.31 m)

MAIN ROTOR:
Rotor disc: 380 sq ft (35.3 m^2)

WEIGHTS:
Empty: 250 lb (113 kg)
Maximum take-off: 600 lb (272 kg)

PERFORMANCE:
Maximum speed: 55 kts (63 mph) 101 km/h
Cruise speed: 52 kts (60 mph) 97 km/h
Maximum climb rate: 700 ft (213 m) per minute
Ceiling: 12,000 ft (3,660 m)
Range: 87 naut miles (100 miles) 161 km

B W Rotor Company Inc — USA

Comments: Details of the Sky Cycle can be found in the 1996-97 edition of *WA&SD*, page 346.

Craft Aerotech — USA

Comments: Details of the Craft Aerotech 200 can be found in the 1996-97 edition of *WA&SD*, page 347.

Eagle's Perch Inc — USA

Corporate address:
15268 Carrollton Blvd, Carrollton, VA 23314.

Telephone: +1 757 238 8148
Facsimile: +1 757 238 2018

Founded: December 1995.

Information:
Emitt Wallace (CEO and President).

ACTIVITIES

- Produces co-axial helicopters.
- R&D for helicopter UAVs; current UAV based on the Eagle's Perch general layout has a new airframe, similar vertical tail surfaces on a modified tailboom, blades shortened to 9 ft 10 ins (3 m) diameter, and a MTOW of 525 lb (238 kg). Hydraulic actuator used to move all control surfaces (rotor head and tail turning control flaps).
- Wind tunnel models.

Eagle's Perch

First flight: 1994 (originally as the Perch Nolan 51-HJ).
First delivery: 1995.
Role: Single-seat homebuilt helicopter. Can be used for agricultural spraying and other roles.
Sales: Kit costing US$17,995 without engine, instruments and avionics. Typically 250 working hours to assemble. Helicopter is easily trailerable and can be garaged in a 15 ft (4.57 m) length.
Optional equipment: 113.5 litre capacity chemical tank and spray-booms (latter foldable and detachable in minutes), spotlights, lightweight hoist, camera, sensors, carrying cases and FLIR.
Rotor system: 2 co-axial, contra-rotating, pendulum type, with gimbal control for pitch/yaw. Aluminium blades of modern aerofoil, asymmetrical type.

↑ Eagle's Perch single-seat homebuilt helicopter

Tail surfaces: Horizontal stabilizer on a high boom, with endplates and large tabs.
Airframe: Main structure is welded steel tubing.
Engines: 2 Rotax 503 or Hirth 2706 piston engines. Can fly with 1 engine.
Engine rating: Each 49.6 hp (37 kW) for Rotax or 65 hp (48.5 kW) for Hirth.
Fuel system: 38 litres in 2 tanks. 76 and 151 litre tanks available.

Details for Eagle's Perch

PRINCIPAL DIMENSIONS:
Rotor diameter: Each 14 ft (4.27 m)
Fuselage length: 14 ft 3 ins (4.34 m)
Maximum length, rotors turning: 14 ft 11 ins (4.55 m)
Height: 8 ft 1 ins (2.46 m)

UNDERCARRIAGE:
Type: Twin fixed skids

WEIGHTS:
Empty: 565 lb (256 kg)
Maximum take-off: 1,000 lb (454 kg)
Useful load: 431 lb (195 kg)

PERFORMANCE:
Maximum speed: 87 kts (100 mph) 161 km/h
Cruise speed: 61 kts (70 mph) 113 km/h
Climb rate: 3,000 ft (914 m) per minute
Ceiling: 10,000 ft (3,048 m)

The Enstrom Helicopter Company — USA

Corporate address:
PO Box 490, 2209 22nd Street, Twin County Airport, Menominee, MI 49858.

Telephone: +1 906 863 1200
Facsimile: +1 906 863 6821
E-mail: enstrom@cybrzn.com

Founded: 1959.

Employees: 90.

Information:
Robert Cleand (Vice President, Marketing Services).

ACTIVITIES

- Manufactures the F28F, 280FX, 480 and TH-28 helicopters, and provides overhaul capability for major components.
- Enstrom has signed an agreement with Wuhan Helicopter Corporation of China to allow licence production of up to 100 helicopters of all models a year.

Enstrom F28F and 280FX

First flight: 1962 for the original F28. F28F certified on 31 December 1980.
Role: Light helicopters, mainly for civil use but suited to tours, external cargo, military, police patrol, power and pipeline patrol, training, agricultural and other roles.
Sales: Total number of piston-engined models produced by 1998 was 945, including a fleet of 15 used by the Chilean Army, 10 used by the Peruvian Army and 12 by the Colombian Air Force; the military fleets are used as primary helicopter trainers (the F28F and 280FX are rugged helicopters designed for repeated autorotations in the training environment).
Crew/passengers: Pilot and 2 passengers, with optional dual controls.
Freight, internal: 6.3 cu ft (0.178 m^3) baggage compartment, capacity of 108 lb (49 kg).
Optional equipment: Includes agricultural equipment, exhaust silencer, cargo hook, and fixed floats.
Rotor system: 3-blade, metal, high inertia, fully articulated main rotor. Low tip speed and low disc loading. Fail safe rotor hub featuring closed cycle hydraulic dampers, and total protection from mast bumping. Rotating controls are inside the fuselage. V belt drive from engine to transmission; transmission chip detectors.
Tail rotor characteristics: 2-blade, teetering, to port side of tailboom.
Tail surfaces: Vertical fin on each end of the horizontal stabilizer on both F28F and 280FX.
Fuselage: Kick-in access steps.
Airframe materials: Steel tube main structure, aluminium alloy and glassfibre cabin area skins, and aluminium alloy stressed skin tailboom.
Engine: Textron Lycoming HIO-360-F1AD turbocharged piston engine. Starter motor.
Engine rating: 225 hp (168 kW).
Fuel system: 159 litres. Optional 49 litre auxiliary tank in the baggage compartment.
Electrical system: F28F has a 12 volt engine-driven alternator. 280FX has a 24 volt supply, which is optional for F28F.
Flight avionics/instrumentation: Customer choice of avionics. Full range of standard instruments, including airspeed indicator, compass, altimeter, turn/bank indicator, tachometer and much more.

Aircraft variants:
F28F is the standard version.
F28F-P Sentinel is the police variant, offered with police communication equipment, optional searchlight to the starboard side of the fuselage, and optional FLIR.
280FX became available in 1985, based on the F28F but with various cabin and airframe refinements, most obviously a reshaped air intake above the cabin, endplate fins to the tail stabilizer, and faired skids.

Details for F28F, *with 280FX in italics where different*

PRINCIPAL DIMENSIONS:
Rotor diameter (main): 32 ft (9.75 m)
Maximum length, rotors turning: 29 ft 3 ins (8.91 m)
Maximum height: 9 ft (2.74 m)

MAIN ROTOR:
Aerofoil section: NACA 0013.5
Blade chord: 9.5 ins (0.24 m)
Rotor disc: 804 sq ft (74.69 m^2)

TAIL ROTOR:
Diameter: 4 ft 8 ins (1.42 m)

UNDERCARRIAGE:
Type: Fixed, high energy-absorbing twin skids, with retractable ground handling wheels. Optional floats
Skid track: 7 ft 3 ins (2.21 m)

WEIGHTS:
Empty: 1,570 lb (712 kg), *1,585 lb (719 kg)*
Maximum take-off: 2,600 lb (1,179 kg)
Useful load: 1,030 lb (467 kg), *1,015 lb (460 kg)*

PERFORMANCE:
Maximum cruise speed: 97 kts (112 mph) 180 km/h, *102 kts (117 mph) 188 km/h*
Economic cruise speed: 89 kts (102 mph) 164 km/h, *93 kts (107 mph) 172 km/h*
Maximum climb rate: 1,450 ft (442 m) per minute at 2,350 lb (1,066 kg) weight, or 1,150 ft (350 m) per minute at MTOW
IGE hovering ceiling: 13,200 ft (4,023 m) at 2,350 lb (1,066 kg), or 7,700 ft (2,347 m) at MTOW
OGE hovering ceiling: 8,700 ft (2,650 m) at 2,350 lb (1,066 kg)
Ceiling: 12,000 ft (3,660 m) maximum approved
Range with full fuel: 241 naut miles (277 miles) 446 km, *261 naut miles (300 miles) 483 km, no reserve*
Duration: 3 hours 30 minutes

↑ Enstrom 280FX light helicopter

↑ Enstrom 480

Enstrom 480 Turbine

First flight: October 1989.
Certification: June 1993.
First delivery: July 1993.
Role: Turboshaft-powered light helicopter, suited also to utility, law enforcement, patrol, training and more.
Sales: 34 sold by March 1998.
Crew/passengers: Pilot and 4 passengers, pilot and 3 passengers in executive layout with more leg room (front starboard seat removed), 2 pilots for training (starboard seat moved outboard and dual controls fitted) plus 1 passenger, or the pilot plus cargo when the starboard front seat is removed and the rear seat folded. Front seats are adjustable, as are the pedals.
Rotor system: Similar to 280FX. Main rotor hub and blades weigh over 300 lb (136 kg).
Safety features: Crashworthy features, including seats, fuel system and skids.
Engine: Allison 250-C20W turboshaft.
Engine rating: 420 shp (335.6 kW), derated to 289 shp (215.5 kW) maximum for 5 minutes and 269 shp (200.5 kW) continuous. Derating allows full take-off power to above 13,000 ft (3,960 m) or over 49° C. Standard Pall Land Marine particle separator which removes 93% of dust, sand or foreign objects in the air inlet.

Details for 480 Turbine

PRINCIPAL DIMENSIONS:
Rotor diameter (main): 32 ft (9.75 m)
Fuselage length: 29 ft 10 ins (9.09 m)
Fuselage width: 5 ft 10 ins (1.78 m)
Maximum height: 8 ft 6 ins (2.59 m) to top of tail rotor

TAIL ROTOR:
Diameter: 5 ft 0.5 ins (1.53 m)

UNDERCARRIAGE:
Type: Similar to 280FX but much larger and heavier to stand rigours of training
Skid track: 8 ft 6 ins (2.59 m)

WEIGHTS:
Empty: 1,675 lb (760 kg), with standard equipment
Maximum take-off: 2,850 lb (1,293 kg)
Useful load: 1,175 lb (533 kg)

PERFORMANCE:
Never-exceed speed (V_{NE}): 125 kts (144 mph) 232 km/h
Cruise speed: 114 kts (131 mph) 211 km/h at 2,500 lb (1,134 kg) weight, or 106 kts (122 mph) 196 km/h at 2,850 lb (1,293 kg), both at 3,000 ft (915 m)
Maximum climb rate: 1,580 ft (482 m) per minute at 2,500 lb (1,134 kg) weight, 1,450 ft (442 m) at 2,850 lb (1,293 kg) weight
IGE hovering ceiling: 14,000 ft (4,267 m) at 2,500 lb (1,134 kg) weight, or 10,000 ft (3,050 m) at 2,850 lb (1,293 kg) weight
OGE hovering ceiling: 12,000 ft (3,660 m) at 2,500 lb (1,134 kg) weight, or 6,900 ft (2,103 m) at 2,850 lb (1,293 kg) weight
Service ceiling: 13,000 ft (3,960 m)
Range: 412 naut miles (475 miles) 764 km at 2,500 lb (1,134 kg), or 382 naut miles (440 miles) 708 km at 2,850 lb (1,293 kg), no reserve, at sea level
Duration: 5 hours at 2,500 lb (1,134 kg), or 4.7 hours at 2,850 lb (1,293 kg), no reserve, at sea level

Fuel system: 341 litres in 2 interconnected tanks.
Flight avionics/instrumentation: VFR or IFR.

Aircraft variants:
480 Turbine is the standard model, as detailed.
TH-28 is the designation of a 3-seat military version with crashworthy features. Intended mainly for training and patrol. Crashworthy seats, fuel cells, and a wide instrument panel that can be configured for IFR training, with full dual instrumentation.

Erickson Air-Crane Co LLC — USA

Corporate address:
3100 Willow Springs Road, Central Point, OR 97502.
Telephone: +1 541 664 5544
Facsimile: +1 541 664 2312
Founded: 1972.
Information:
Lee Ramage (Director, Marketing and Sales – *telephone* +1 541 664 7615, *facsimile* +1 541 664 7613) and Dennis Hubbard (Media Services).

ACTIVITIES

▪ Operates a fleet of 15 Sikorsky S-64E and F heavy lift helicopters, used for many tasks including construction work, logging and firefighting; Erickson has developed and certified the **Helitanker** system for firefighting. The 15th helicopter was built by Erickson and joined the fleet in July 1997, and a 16th will be completed in 1998. The S-64E is certified for a 20,000 lb (9,071 kg) external load and the S-64F is certified for a 25,000 lb (11,340 kg) external load. Erickson originally operated 4 S-64Es purchased from Sikorsky.
▪ Erickson Air-Crane purchased the Type Certificate and manufacturing rights for the S-64 from Sikorsky in 1992 and owns all tooling, enabling the company to manufacture new examples, with a capacity to construct 2 per year. The helicopter is now known as the **Erickson S-64 Aircrane**.
▪ Erickson Air-Crane has developed modification programmes for the S-64 featuring a stronger tailboom, new engine mounts and increased main rotor blade life among other upgrades. This enables ex-US Army CH-54 Tarhes to be brought up to the new Aircrane standard.
▪ Helitanker conversion, first flown in 1992, consists of a pilot controlled, variable flow rate, multiple drop capable 9,464 litre tank attached to the fuselage. The tank can be hover filled in approximately 40 seconds from any water source 18 ins (0.46 m) or more in depth. US Forestry Service trials in 1995. Helitanker was deployed to Victoria, Australia in December 1997, to assist the Department of Natural Resources and Environment fight bushfires, with the first mission in January 1998. Other firefighting work has since followed.
▪ An Emergency Response Vehicle prototype container has also been constructed by Erickson, intended to assist in the evacuation of persons from high building fires.

↑ Erickson Air-Crane S-64 Helitanker firefighting helicopter taking water while hovering

Farrington Aircraft Corporation USA

Corporate address:
4460 Shemwell Road, Paducah, KY 42003.

Telephone: +1 502 898 2403
Facsimile: +1 502 898 8691
E-mail: fac@farringtonacft.com
Web site: www.farringtonacft.com

Information:
J. T. Potter.

ACTIVITIES

▪ The Farrington Heliplane is an upgrade of the original Air & Space Model 18-A autogyro, that is no longer marketed (68 Model 18-As built in the mid-1960s at Muncie, Indiana).
▪ Conducts rotorcraft flight training, and represents Robinson Helicopter.

Farrington 20A Heliplane

Certification: Model 20A recently certified (according to correspondence of April 1998).
Role: Certified tandem 2-seat autogyro, with possible roles including photographic and patrol.

Aims

▪ Modernized derivative of the Air & Space Model 18-A, which attained pre-production certification in the early 1960s.
▪ Take-off and land with little or no ground roll.

Details

Sales: Basic price US$129,995. Optional equipment available.
Freight, internal: 100 lb (45.4 kg) baggage capacity.
Rotor system: 3-blade rotor.

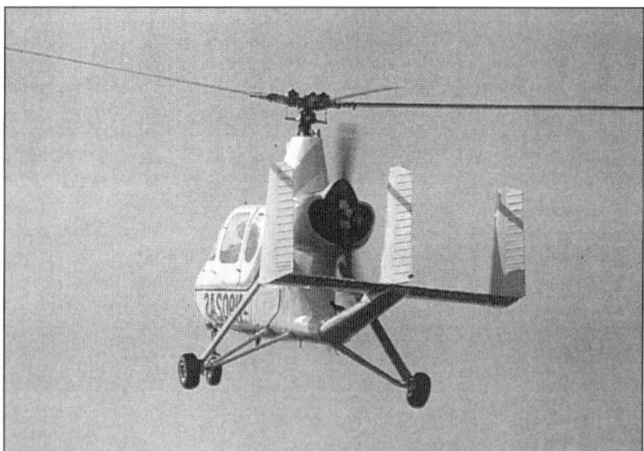

↑ **Farrington Heliplane** *(courtesy Farrington Aircraft)*

Engine: Recently uprated to a 200 hp (149 kW) fuel-injected Textron Lycoming IO-360-C1C engine with a Hartzell constant-speed propeller to allow 2 persons and full fuel (Model 20A form), and 260 hp (194 kW) Textron Lycoming O-540 to carry the tank, pump and booms required for agricultural work.
Fuel system: 106 litres.

Aircraft variants:
Model 20A with an IO-320 engine. Certified.
Ag version was in the flight test stage in April 1998, with an O-540 engine.

Details for 20A

PRINCIPAL DIMENSIONS:
Rotor diameter: 35 ft (10.67 m)
Maximum length: 19 ft 10 ins (6.05 m)
Width: 9 ft 2 ins (2.79 m)
Maximum height: 9 ft 8 ins (2.95 m)

UNDERCARRIAGE:
Type: Fixed nosewheel type

WEIGHTS:
Maximum take-off: about 2,000 lb (907 kg)

PERFORMANCE:
Never-exceed speed: 100 kts (115 mph) 185 km/h
Cruise speed: 80 kts (92 mph) 148 km/h
Minimum flight speed: 25 kts (29 mph) 47 km/h
Take-off distance: 0-200 ft (0-61 m)
Landing distance: under 100 ft (31 m)
Range: about 173 naut miles (200 miles) 322 km
Duration: 3 hours

Farrington Twinstarr

First flight: 1991.
Role: Simplified tandem 2-seat sporting autogyro (with dual controls) for recreational use, also for dual instruction with trainee in front seat (same seat for solo flying).
Sales: Kits for US$20,000 to US$25,000 (1998 cost, complete, various options), taking typically 250 hours to assemble. 10 built at the time of writing, with the production of kits being accelerated to meet demand.
Optional equipment: Includes a new full cockpit enclosure (heated for Winter flying) as a replacement for the standard partial enclosure, other rotor blades (McCutcheon Sky Wheels, RAF, etc), electric or hydraulic pre-starter, engine cooling baffles, 15 amp lightweight alternator with regulator, flight instruments, radios and transponders, Cleveland wheels, wheel and leg fairings, spinner, rotor brake and more.
Rotor system: Farrington 2 blade rotor, with blades constructed using aluminium D-section spars, foam cores and composite covering. Farrington hub and blade bar, constructed using all needle bearings in the hub and control linkage.
Airframe materials: Welded 4130 steel tube structure, with composites fairing and tail unit.
Engine: Textron Lycoming O-320 piston engine, with Sensenich fixed-pitch propeller. New options of a Mazda or 135 hp (100.6 kW) Subaru engine.
Engine rating: 150-160 hp (112-119 kW).
Fuel system: 76 litres

Details for Twinstarr

PRINCIPAL DIMENSIONS:
Rotor diameter: 27-30 ft (8.23-9.14 m)
Fuselage length: 13 ft (3.96 m)
Maximum height: 8 ft 6 ins (2.59 m) for flight, 5 ft 8 ins (1.73 m) for storage

UNDERCARRIAGE:
Type: Fixed nosewheel type, with spring steel legs. Matco 5.00 × 5 wheels, castoring nosewheel and dual hydraulic toe brakes
Wheel track: 7 ft 1 ins (2.16 m)

WEIGHTS:
Empty: 700 lb (318 kg)
Maximum take-off: 1,200 lb (544 kg)
Useful load: 550 lb (249 kg)

PERFORMANCE:
Maximum speed: 77 kts (89 mph) 143 km/h
Cruise speed: 56 kts (65 mph) 105 km/h
Minimum flight speed: 20 kts (23 mph) 37 km/h
Take-off distance: under 500 ft (152 m), reduced to 50-150 ft (15-46 m) using hydraulic pre-rotator
Landing distance: under 50 ft (15 m)
Maximum climb rate: 700-1,000 ft (213-305 m) per minute
Ceiling: 10,000 ft (3,050 m)
Range: about 112 naut miles (130 miles) 209 km

↑ **Farrington Twinstarr** *(courtesy Farrington Aircraft)*

Global Helicopter Technology, Inc (GHTI) USA

Corporate address:
5070 South Collins, Suite 206, Arlington, TX 76018.

Telephone: +1 817 557 3391
Facsimile: +1 817 557 3392
E-mail: ghti@why.net

Founded: February 1987.

Employees: 14 full time.

Information:
Charles Cole (Director, Business Development).

ACTIVITIES

▪ Developing, testing and certifying aircraft modifications and products that reduce costs and improve performance. Works with operators, both industry and government, and with OEMs and aftermarket manufacturers.
▪ Offers the **Huey800** retrofit kit for the Bell UH-1H, requiring no expensive tooling and as little as 200 working hours to install. Based principally on the installation of a LHTEC T801 turboshaft engine, the conversion kit offers over 50% better duration and range. Pilot workload is significantly reduced through automatic starting, automatic engine and aircraft limit protection, and simplified emergency procedures afforded by the engine FADEC. The US Border Patrol recently conducted a 1 year test evaluation of 5 Huey800s, operating along the Southern US border. Also, the US Army and Army National Guard are planning to utilize the T801 engine in 130 National Guard Light Utility Helicopters.
▪ Design and FAA certification of a Vibration Reduction System for Bell 205 and 206 helicopters.
▪ Design, test and FAA certification of various helicopter wheeled landing gear.
▪ Analysis, flight test and FAA certification of firefighting waterbomber tank installations for various helicopters.
▪ Design, analysis, instrumentation and test of a proprietary automated weight and balance measurement system for commercial airlines.

↑ **Global Helicopter Technology Huey800 during a 1 year evaluation by the US Border Patrol**

Groen Brothers Aviation, Inc (GBA) USA

Corporate address:
2320 W California Avenue, Suite A, Salt Lake City, Utah 84104.

Telephone: +1 801 973 0177
Facsimile: +1 801 973 4027
E-mail: cyndiu@netquest.net
Web site: http://www.groenbros.com

Information:
Cyndi Upthegrove (Marketing Manager – marketing office address 18000 Pacific Hwy, S, Suite 408, Seattle, WA 98188, *telephone* +1 206 241 8116, *facsimile* +1 206 241 8117).

DIVISION

NGA INDUSTRIAL, LTD

HQ address:
140 Guang Zhou Road, Suite 22D, Nanjing, China 210024.

Telephone: +86 25 360 5073
Facsimile: +86 25 360 4953

Activities:
- Handles sales and support in China.

↑ Groen Brothers Aviation H2X gyroplane with patented collective pitch control

Groen Brothers Hawk III, Hawk V, Hawk VIII and Commuter Hawk

Details *(apply to the production Hawk III, except under Development and Aircraft variants)*

First flight: 5 February 1997 (H2X prototype of Hawk III). 18 June 1997 for first vertical (jump) take-off.
Certification: Initial certification sought in the US/Canada and China.
Role: Gyroplane, with uses including transport, utility, survey, aerial photography, flight training, agricultural, military/law enforcement, ground attack, unmanned surveillance and more.
Chief designer: Mark Woolsey, P.E.

Aims

- Vertical (jump) take-off, with no ground roll. Take-off and landing distances to clear a 50 ft (15 m) obstacle of 50 ft (15 m). Rotor system of Hawk series designed to achieve high speed; composite rotor blade aerofoils designed for maximum efficiency. Patented collective pitch control enhances vertical take-offs as well as high speed.

Development

- Development of the Hawk series of gyroplanes has been continuous since 1986. A proof-of-concept prototype was flown in 1986, followed by the proof-of-design single-seat prototype (Hawk I) in 1993. The production prototype (H2X) was undergoing flight tests at the time of writing. Upon completion of the flight tests, demonstrator aircraft will be used for evaluation and certification (see Certification). Further development is in progress on the next prototype in the Hawk series, the Hawk V, which is a 5-seat turboprop version of the aircraft.

Details

Sales: GBA has received an order for 200 Hawk IIIs from the Shanghai Energy and Chemical Company (SECC), which plans to use them for corporate transport and air taxi roles. Additional orders are expected from the US Public Use (law enforcement) community. Hawk III was priced at US$270,000 at the time of writing; price can vary depending on the avionics and other options chosen. SECC also ordered up to 100 Hawk Vs and 100 Hawk VIIIs in mid-1998.
Crew/passengers: Pilot and 2 passengers in the enclosed cabin.
Cockpit/cabin: Offers unrestricted visibility. Shoulder room is standard 4 ft 6 ins (1.37 m). Floor area of 7 ft 4 ins × 3 ft 10 ins (2.24 × 1.17 m) and supports a 21 cu ft (0.59 m^3), 1,020 lb (463 kg) useful load. Main stick controls pitch and roll, and pitch control. Rudder pedals for yaw control.
Cabin access: Port and starboard doors.
Rotor system: 2-blade teetering rotor with swashplate control. Composite proprietary rotor blades. Engine-driven pre-rotation drive.
Tail surfaces: Fins area 396 sq ins (2,555 cm^2); rudder 1,100 sq ins (7,097 cm^2); and tailplane 1,673 sq ins (10,794 cm^2). Tailplane span 11 ft 4 ins (3.45 m).
Airframe: Aluminium fuselage (stressed skin monocoque), tail surfaces, hub structure and propeller. Glassfibre nose cone, engine cowlings and wingtips.
Engine: Teledyne Continental TSIOL-550 turbo-supercharged, fuel-injected piston engine.
Engine rating: 350 hp (261 kW) maximum, 220 hp (164 kW) continuous.
Transmission: To supply power to pre-rotate the rotor for vertical take-off only.
Fuel system: 284 litres in a bladder tank contained within the fuel cell compartment located aft of the passenger compartment and forward of the engine compartment.
Electrical system: 24 volt and magnetos ignition.
Hydraulic system: 4 independent systems, comprising undercarriage extension/retraction, clutch pre-rotation, rotor brake, and wheel brakes.
Braking system: Cleveland toe brakes on rudder pedals; differential main gear braking for steering.
Flight avionics/instrumentation: Basic IFR instrumentation. Customer may select an EFIS and moving map (GPS) option. Communications avionics comprise AlliedSignal Bendix/King KT 71 and KX 155 radios.

Aircraft variants:
Hawk III 3-seater, as detailed.
Hawk V is a projected 5-seater; mock-up built; primary engineering in hand.
Hawk VIII is a projected 8-seater; preliminary studies and engineering underway.
Commuter Hawk is a projected 30+ seater; marketing and competitive assessment is underway.

Details for Hawk III

PRINCIPAL DIMENSIONS:
Rotor diameter: 42 ft (12.8 m)
Maximum length, rotors turning: 42 ft (12.8 m)
Fuselage length: 21 ft 9 ins (6.63 m)

CABIN:
Length: 7 ft 4 ins (2.24 m)
Width: 3 ft 10 ins (1.17 m)

ROTOR:
Blade chord: 1 ft 1 ins (0.33 m)
Rotor disc: 1,385 sq ft (128.7 m^2)

UNDERCARRIAGE:
Type: Retractable, with castoring nosewheel. Differential braking for steering
Nose wheel size: Cleveland wheels, 500 × 5
Main wheel size: Cleveland wheels, 600 × 6
Wheel base: 7 ft 9.5 ins (2.38 m)
Wheel track: 9 ft (2.74 m)

WEIGHTS:
Empty, equipped: 1,700 lb (771 kg)
Maximum take-off: 2,720 lb (1,234 kg)
Payload: 1,020 lb (462 kg), including fuel

PERFORMANCE:
Never-exceed speed (V_{NE}): 156 kts (180 mph) 290 km/h
Maximum operating speed: 139 kts (160 mph) 257 km/h
Typical cruise and low level speed: 122 kts (140 mph) 225 km/h
Minimum speed: 17.5 kts (20 mph) 32 km/h
Take-off/landing distance over a 50 ft (15 m) obstacle: 50 ft (15 m)
Maximum climb rate: 1,500 ft (457 m) per minute
Autorotational descent rate, power off: 1,600 ft (488 m) per minute
G limit: 4
Service ceiling: 16,000 ft (4,875 m)
Range with maximum fuel: 521 naut miles (600 miles) 966 km at 113 kts

Hillberg Helicopters USA

Corporate address:
PO Box 8974, Fountain Valley, CA 92728-8974.

Telephone: +1 909 279 5678

Information:
Don Hillberg.

ACTIVITIES

- Maintains a fleet of helicopters of varied types.
- Maintenance, modification, consulting, construction and testing with helicopters.

Hillberg RotorMouse EH 1-01 and EH 1-02, and RotorMouse (Baby Huey)

Role: Light Experimental category kit helicopters, with turbine power.

↑ Hillberg RotorMouse EH 1-01 prototype

Aircraft variants:
RotorMouse EH 1-01 is a single-seat Experimental category kit turbine helicopter in combat style, for sport and utility uses. First flown in August 1993. Prototype has a 145 shp (108 kW) AiResearch 36-55-C turboshaft APU from an AH-64A Apache helicopter, and a 20 ft (6.1 m) diameter 2-blade, non-foldable, semi-rigid main rotor (main rotor rpm 510 ±20); all-aluminium semi-monocoque airframe structures, using 2024-T3 aluminium skin, bulkheads and keel; stainless steel firewall and engine deck; crash-resistant fuel cell, with 124.5 litres usable capacity; R-22 transmission and swashplate, tail rotor gearbox and sprag blades off the QH-50 drone helicopter; stick grip from an F-86; pro-seal full service electrical system. Empty weight 625 lb (283 kg), gross weight 1,300-1,370 lb (590-621 kg), average weight for maximum performance 990 lb (449 kg), cruise speed over 139 kts (160 mph) 257 km/h, sideways speed 39 kts (45 mph) 72 km/h, climb rate 4,700 ft (1,433 m) per minute at 52 kts (60 mph) 97 km/h, vertical climb rate 2,700 ft (823 m) per minute, and 3 hours duration at typical cruise speed of 113 kts (130 mph) 209 km/h, providing a range of 338 naut miles (390 miles) 627 km.
RotorMouse EH 1-02 is a tandem 2-seat Experimental category kit turbine helicopter in combat style, based on the EH 1-01. Useful load of ±900 lb (408 kg) comprises the pilot and co-pilot of 250 lb (113 kg) maximum weight each, 100 lb (45.4 kg) of baggage and 300 lb (136 kg) of fuel for 3 hours duration. 17 sold by March 1998. Single or twin turbine engines. Fuselage length 26 ft 9 ins (8.16 m). Empty weight ±900 lb (408 kg), and gross weight ±1,800-2,000 lb (816-907 kg). Estimated cruise speed 126 kts (145 mph) 233 km/h, and climb rate 2,500 ft (762 m) per minute.
RotorMouse (Baby Huey) is a 4-seat design derived from the E 1-02, with styling that is reminiscent of a UH-1. 2,500 lb (1,134 kg) gross weight.

Hillberg Turbine Exec

First flight: August 1997.
Role: Re-engined RotorWay Exec, with turbine power.

Aims

▪ Retrofit kit reduces the empty weight by 170 lb (77 kg), increases useful load, provides improved hot and high performance, and offers low maintenance.

Details

Sales: Not a full kit, but a retrofit kit for the replacement of the Exec's normal piston engine, drive belts, fan radiator, oil bath, water pump, chain drive and more, with a turbine engine, gear reducer clutch, tail rotor shaft and gearbox, main gearbox, hangar bearings and fuel cell.
Engine: Solar T62 T32 turbine engine, offering 150 shp (112 kW).
Fuel system: 230 lb (104 kg).

↑ Hillberg Turbine Exec

Details for Turbine Exec

PRINCIPAL DIMENSIONS:
Same as RotorWay Exec

WEIGHTS:
Empty: ±750 lb (340 kg)
Maximum take-off: ±1,485 lb (674 kg)
Useful load: ±735 lb (333 kg)

Hillberg T-4 Turbine

Comments: Designated T-4 in March 1998 but unnamed, this is a 4-seat turbine helicopter that first flew some years ago. Production pending final financing. Length 28 ft (8.53 m). Cabin 9 ft (2.74 m) long and 4 ft 6 ins (1.37 m) wide.

Hinchman Aircraft Company — USA

Corporate address:
14 South Water Street, Monrovia, IN 46157.
Telephone: +1 317 996 3157
Facsimile: +1 317 996 3148

Hinchman H-1 Racer

First flight: 1987 in original form. Details and photograph apply to the latest configuration.
Role: Single-seat autogyro.
Sales: Plans and kits, former US$150 and latter US$13,000, taking typically 150 working hours to assemble from a kit.

Details for H-1 Racer

PRINCIPAL DIMENSIONS:
Rotor diameter: 25 ft (7.62 m)
Airframe length: 12 ft 7 ins (3.28 m)
Width: 5 ft (1.52 m)
Maximum height: 8 ft (2.44 m)

ROTOR:
Blade chord: 9 ins (0.23 m)
Disc area: 490 sq ft (45.52 m^2)

UNDERCARRIAGE:
Type: Fixed nosewheel type, with self-aligning nosewheel mechanism and 5 ins (13 cm) suspension travel. Main legs constructed of single formed piece of 2024-T4 aluminium; cable between struts for additional strength on hard landings. Wheel fairings. Pedal in centre of foot pedals for hydraulic disc brakes

WEIGHTS:
Empty: 380 lb (172 kg)
Payload: 250 lb (113.4 kg)

PERFORMANCE:
Maximum speed: 87 kts (100 mph) 161 km/h
Cruise speed: 56 kts (65 mph) 105 km/h
Minimum speed: 26 kts (30 mph) 48 km/h
Take-off distance: 0-500 ft (0-152 m)
Landing distance: 0-10 ft (0-3 m)
Maximum climb rate: 800 ft (244 m) per minute

Rotor system: 2-blade (McCutcheon Sky Wheels), constructed with an aluminium spar and Kevlar composites, and bolted to the hub. Gimble rotor head. Mechanical pre-rotator to turn blades to 300 rpm, with drive shaft from the pre-rotator directly behind the mast.
Tail surfaces: Fin and rudder, with 4130 steel tube structure covered with Stits fabric.
Airframe: 6063-T6 aluminium tube structure, with 5 piece body (front and rear tops, bottom section and 2 rear bottom sections) weighing just 12 lb (5.44 kg) fitted in 1996 and constructed of 70% Kevlar and 30% carbonfibre with a one-eighth thick honeycomb for stiffness.
Engine: Rotax 503, with 2.58:1 reduction gear. 5 ft (1.52 m) Warp Drive ground adjustable 3-blade pusher propeller.
Engine rating: 52 hp (38.8 kW).
Transmission: Right-angle 2-stage gearbox using helical gears with a 2:1 reduction. First stage slip clutch to spin blades.
Fuel system: 19 litres. Approximately 38 litre capacity seat tank to be an option.

↑ Hinchman H-1 Racer in latest form

Hiller Aircraft Corporation USA

Corporate address:
3200 Imjin Road, Marina, CA 93933-501.

Telephone: +1 408 384 4550
Facsimile: +1 408 384 3100

Founded:
Original Hiller Aircraft Division of Hiller Industries was founded in 1942, becoming Hiller Helicopters in 1948. The present company was established in 1994 at Newark, California, after Jeffrey Hiller (son of the founder) led an investment consortium to purchase back the assets from Rogerson Hiller Corporation. Current location active since 1996, with a majority of the company owned through Thai investment.

Information:
Craig Smith.

Hiller UH-12E3 and E3T, and UH-12E5 and E5T

First flight: 1958 for original UH-12E. 2 June 1995 for the first new-production UH-12E3 (N101BX); January 1995 for UH-12E5 (E4 conversion).
Role: Utility helicopters, with uses including transport, agricultural spraying and dusting, forestry work, construction, law enforcement and training.
Sales: Initial production began with an order for 20 UH-12E3/5s for a Thai investment group. Only E3 and E3T in low rate production at the time of writing. Spare part production for over 1,000 older UH-12s still flying began in September 1994, supplementing spares bought from Rogerson Hiller.
Crew/passengers: 3 or 5 seats, according to version (see Aircraft variants). Optional internal or external litter.
Standard equipment: Long list includes a cargo hook hard point.
Optional equipment: Long list includes dual controls, quick-release cargo hook, cyclic control grip, spray system, spreader system, night lighting equipment, loudspeaker, remote searchlight, cargo racks, hydraulic drive kit (turbine only), auto re-ignition kit (turbine only), and particle separator (turbine only).
Rotor system: 2-blade main rotor, with a retention bolt and drag link attaching blade to rotor head. Electrically controlled trim system.
Tail rotor characteristics: 2 blades.
Engine: See Aircraft variants.
Fuel system: 174 litres standard, plus 1 or 2 × 76 litre auxiliary tanks.
Electrical system: Lead-acid battery. Optional ni-cd battery with monitor. Alternator. External power receptacle.
Flight avionics/instrumentation: Optional radio, ADF, transponder, instantaneous vertical speed indicator, and artificial horizon.

Aircraft variants:
UH-12E3 is the basic 3-seat utility helicopter, with a 345 hp (257 kW) Textron Lycoming VO-540-C2A piston engine derated to 305 hp (227 kW). In production.
UH-12E3T is the turbine version of the 3-seater, with a 420 shp (313 kW) Allison 250-C20B turboshaft derated to 301 shp (224 kW). In production.
UH-12E5 is a 5-seater. Not thought to be in production. Same engine as E3. Specifications can be found in the 1996-97 edition of *WA&SD*, page 350.
UH-12E5T is a 5-seat turbine version, with the same engine as the E3T.

↑ Hiller UH-12E3

Details for UH-12E3T

PRINCIPAL DIMENSIONS:
Rotor diameter (main): 35 ft 5 ins (10.79 m)
Maximum length, rotors turning: 40 ft 8.5 ins (12.41 m)
Fuselage length: 28 ft 6 ins (8.69 m)
Maximum height: 10 ft 1 ins (3.08 m) to above rotor hub

TAIL ROTOR:
Diameter: 5 ft 6 ins (1.68 m)

UNDERCARRIAGE:
Type: Fixed twin skids. Standard ground handling wheels. Optional amphibious gear
Skid track: 7 ft 6 ins (2.29 m)

WEIGHTS:
Empty: 1,640 lb (744 kg)
Maximum take-off: 3,100 lb (1,406 kg)
Payload: 1,460 lb (662 kg)

PERFORMANCE:
Never-exceed speed (V_{NE}): 83 kts (96 mph) 154 km/h
Maximum cruise speed: 78 kts (90 mph) 145 km/h
Maximum climb rate: 1,518 ft (463 m) per minute
Vertical climb rate: 967 ft (295 m) per minute
IGE hovering ceiling: 11,300 ft (3,444 m) at 2,800 lb (1,270 kg) weight, or 8,600 ft (2,621 m) at MTOW
OGE hovering ceiling: 8,700 ft (2,652 m) at 2,800 lb (1,270 kg) weight or 5,600 ft (1,707 m) at MTOW
Service ceiling: 14,000 ft (4,267 m) at 2,800 lb (1,270 kg) weight
Range at maximum cruise speed: 149 naut miles (171.9 miles) 276 km with standard fuel or 227 naut miles (319 miles) 513 km with auxiliary fuel
Duration at maximum cruise speed: 1.91 hours with standard fuel or 3.54 hours with auxiliary fuel

Kaman Aerospace Corporation USA

Corporate address:
PO Box 2, Bloomfield, CT 06002.

Telephone: +1 860 243 7547, 8311
Facsimile: +1 860 243 7514
Web site: http://www.kaman.com

Founded:
December 1945 as Kaman Aircraft Corporation.

Employees:
1,200, at its Bloomfield, Moosup (CT), Jacksonville (FL) and Tucson (AZ) facilities.

Information:
J. Kenneth Nasshan (Vice President, Public Relations – *telephone* +1 860 243 7319); David M. Long (Public Relations Manager – *telephone* +1 860 243 6319, *facsimile* +1 860 243 6365, *E-mail* dml-corp@kaman.com).

ACTIVITIES

▪ Subsidiary of Kaman Corporation. In addition to its own helicopters, Kaman is a major components subcontractor for military aircraft that include the F-14, AH-1, F-22, Comanche, C-17 and V-22, while its commercial subcontracting includes wing structures and other components for Boeing aircraft. It also manufactures fairings and thrust reversers for commercial jets and components for the Space Shuttle.

Kaman SH-2G Super Seasprite

First flight: 28 December 1989 (first SH-2G was a modified SH-2F used for development as the sole YSH-2G). First actual SH-2G was delivered to the US Navy on 21 March 1989.
Role: Anti-submarine and anti-shipping helicopter, with other roles including over-the-horizon warning/targeting, SAR, surveillance, mine-countermeasures, medevac, vertrep and utility roles.

Development

▪ Upgraded version of the SH-2F Seasprite, with more advanced and powerful engines and enhanced mission equipment. New engines, wiring and connectors, fuel and hydraulic lines, transmission systems, on-board acoustic processor, flight control rods, suction fuel system, generators, APU and data bus, plus zero-time structure.

Details

Sales: Royal Australian Navy contracted for 11 SH-2G(A) helicopters on 26 June 1997, with deliveries scheduled to begin in early 2001 and to be completed by mid-2002, for deployment from 8 Anzac class frigates; for surveillance/over-the-horizon warning/targeting, anti-ship, anti-submarine, SAR, medevac and Vertrep. Royal New Zealand Navy contracted for 4 SH-2Gs on 25 June 1997, for delivery from the year 2000; for deployment on Anzac and Leander class frigates and armed with Maverick; RNZN first flew the first of 4 temporary SH-2Fs on 24 February 1998, pending arrival of 'G's. Egypt ordered 10 SH-2G(E)s in 1995, delivered from 1997 as remanufactured ex-US Navy SH-2Fs with engineering configuration changes and installation of dipping sonar for ASW. SH-2G is also operational with the US Navy Reserve Squadrons HSL-84 at North Island, San Diego, and HSL-94 at Willow Grove, Pennsylvania, first taken by HSL-84 on 25 February 1993. Thailand offered ex-USN SH-2Fs.
Crew/passengers: 3 crew plus room for 1 passenger. Removal of the sonobuoy launcher allows for 4 passengers or 2 litters. Can be configured for multi-place troop layout.
Optional equipment: Includes 4,000 lb (1,814 kg) cargo hook and 600 lb (272 kg) capacity rescue hoist.
Rotor system: 4-blade main rotor with titanium hub and retention straps. Blades have a light alloy D-section leading-edge spar, honeycomb trailing-edge pocket and glassfibre skin. Each blade incorporates a Kaman servo flap. Manual blade folding.
Tail rotor characteristics: 4-blade.
Tail surfaces: Fixed incidence tailplane.

Details for SH-2G

PRINCIPAL DIMENSIONS:
Rotor diameter (main): 44 ft (13.41 m)
Maximum length, rotors turning: 52 ft 6 ins (16 m)
Fuselage length: 40 ft 2 ins (12.24 m), or 38 ft 4 ins (11.68 m) folded
Width, blades folded: 12 ft 3 ins (3.73 m)
Maximum height: 15 ft 1 ins (4.6 m), or 13 ft 7 ins (4.14 m) folded

MAIN ROTOR:
Rotor disc: 1,521.11 sq ft (141.32 m^2)

TAIL ROTOR:
Diameter: 8 ft 1 ins (2.46 m)

UNDERCARRIAGE:
Type: Retractable main units, fixed tailwheel
Wheel base: 16 ft 9 ins (5.11 m)
Wheel track: 10 ft (3.05 m)

WEIGHTS:
Empty: 8,430 lb (3,824 kg)
Maximum take-off: 13,500 lb (6,123 kg)
Useful load: 5,070 lb (2,300 kg)

PERFORMANCE:
Maximum speed: 141 kts (162 mph) 261 km/h at 5,000 ft (1,525 m)
Maximum climb rate: 2,070 ft (631 m) per minute at sea level
Climb rate, OEI: 1,305 ft (398 m) per minute at sea level
IGE hovering ceiling: 17,600 ft (5,365 m)
OGE hovering ceiling: 14,600 ft (4,450 m)
Service ceiling: 20,400 ft (6,220 m), or 12,080 ft (3,680 m) OEI
Range: 540 naut miles (622 miles) 1,000 km, at 5,000 ft (1,524 m), with 3 auxiliary tanks, 20 minutes reserve
Duration: 5.3 hours, at 5,000 ft (1,524 m), with 3 auxiliary tanks, 20 minutes reserve

↑ Kaman SH-2G(A) Seasprite in Royal Australian Navy configuration, with Penguin missiles

↑ Kaman K-MAX undertaking construction work with Helog of Switzerland

Airframe: Conventional monocoque structure. Zero-time remanufacture.
Engines: 2 General Electric T700-GE-401 turboshafts.
Engine rating: Each 1,437 shp (1,072 kW) maximum continuous, 1,690 shp (1,260 kW) 30-minute maximum, and 1,723 shp (1,285 kW) contingency.
Fuel system: 1,779 litres. 1 to 4 × 378 litre auxiliary fuel tanks.
Electrical system: Includes T-62 APU and dual 30 kVA alternators.
Radar: LN-66 HP for ASW, or LN-66 HP Enhanced, Seaspray or APS-143 for surveillance role.
Flight avionics/instrumentation: Integrated cockpit with 1553B databus. Royal Australian Navy and Royal New Zealand Navy helicopters having Litton glass cockpits with 4 colour MFDs. Communications comprise AN/APX-72 IFF/SIF, intercom, AN/ARC-159 radios and KY-58 secure voice; optional AN/ARC-182 radio. Instruments comprise K884059 attitude and K884058 HSI. Navigation comprises AN/ASN-50 AHRS, AN/APN-217(V)3 Doppler, AN/APQ-107 Radalt warning system, AN/APN-171 radar altimeter, MB-1 stand-by compass, AN/ARN-118 Tacan, AN/ASN-150 Tacnav and DF-301E UHF/VHF-DF. Standard mission equipment comprises AN/ALE-39 ECM, AN/ALR-66 ESM, and K884100 interface converter unit. Optional mission equipment comprises AN/AAQ-22 or AAQ-16 passive imaging device (PID) for surveillance role, AN/AAQ-16 FLIR, AN/ALQ-144 IR countermeasures, AN/ARR-47 missile detectors, AN/ALE-39 chaff/flare dispensers, and AQH-11 mission tape recorder. AN/ASN-150 tactical management system. ASW equipment comprises AN/UYS-503 acoustic data processor, AN/AQS-18A dipping sonar, AN/ASQ-81(V)2 MAD, AN/AKT-22 data-link, AN/ARN-146 on-top position indicator, K682770 sonobuoy launcher, AN/ARR-84 sonobuoy receiver, AN/ASQ-188 torpedo presetter and AN/AKT-22(V)6 Xmtr/multiplexer. For mine-countermeasures role, can have Kaman Magic Lantern laser mine detection system plus Term and RAMECS mine destruction systems; Magic Lantern deployed on some USN Reserve helicopters. Standard mission equipment for all US Navy SH-2Gs. Optional mission equipment on some US Navy SH-2Gs. Export SH-2Gs may have both standard and optional equipment, according to governmental approval.
Fixed guns: Can have a 7.62-mm gun in each cabin door.
Number of weapon pylons: 2, plus 2 auxiliary fuel tank stations (or all 4 can carry tanks).
Expendable weapons and equipment: 1 or 2 Mk 50 or Mk 46 torpedoes, or 2 Maverick or Sea Skua missiles, 8 marine markers, and DIFAR and DICASS sonobuoys. Penguin Mk 2 Mod 7 anti-ship missiles for Royal Australian Navy. Hellfire is another offered missile option. Small arms mounting for M-60, 0.50-ins calibre, or 2.75-ins rockets.

Kaman K-MAX "Aerial Truck"

First flight: 23 December 1991.
Certification: 30 August 1994 for FAA certification.
Role: Designed for the repetitive lift and torque loading requirements of external load operations, including logging, firefighting, agricultural, construction, reforestation and oil/mineral exploration.
Sales: Mountain West Helicopters of Utah (2), Woody Contracting of Oregon, Cariboo Chilcotin of Canada, ROTEX Helicopter AG of Liechtenstein, Helog AG of Switzerland (2, with 1 operated by Heli Air Zagel Lufftransport AG), Midwest Helicopters Ltd of Canada (2), Kachina Forest Products Inc of Idaho, Superior Helicopter LLC of Oregon, Rainier Helicopter Logging Inc of Washington, Japan Royal Helicopter Company Ltd of Tokyo (2), Central Copters Inc of Montana, Grizzly Mountain Aviation of Oregon, and Kimberly-Clark Inc of Alabama (long-term lease). The US Navy's Military Sealift Command (MSC) has undertaken 2 VERTREP demonstrations with K-MAX, under the Pacific Fleet Operational Evaluation, to evaluate the concept of a commercial helicopter under charter/lease arrangements being used for the vertical replenishment of ships at sea; the second 180-day evaluation saw deployment of 2 helicopters from USNS *Niagara Falls* after a pre-deployment work-up from Anderson Air Force Base and ships around Guam, embarking for the Arabian Gulf on 3 June 1996.
Crew: Pilot only, on an energy absorbing seat designed for 20 g downward and 16 g forward impact; energy absorbing cyclic stick for added safety. An external 'Class A' seat has been developed for attachment to either side of the helicopter, allowing an extra person to be ferried to remote locations during deployments.
Freight, external: 5,000 lb (2,268 kg) can be lifted to 8,000 ft (2,440 m) out of ground effect, and 6,000 lb (2,722 kg) to lower altitudes. Spray rig for agricultural work and a 2,500 litre bambi-bucket for firefighting.
Rotor system: 2 side-by-side intermeshing, contra-rotating rotors (Synchro-lift), with composite blades, with electrical servo-flap control that eliminates the need for hydraulic boost systems or artificial stability augmentation. Bearingless rotors are specifically designed for infinite life and ruggedness. Blades can be folded by removal of drag damper pins. Single transmission for both rotors.
Tail rotor characteristics: Not fitted.
Tail surfaces: Horizontal stabilizer with endplates mounted at mid-fuselage, and vertical fin with inset rudder.
Airframe materials: Light alloy. Removable tailcone.
Engine: AlliedSignal T5317A-1 turboshaft, with particle separator.
Engine rating: 1,800 shp (1,342 kW) design rating, but derated to 1,500 shp (1,118.6 kW).
Transmission rating: 1,500 shp (1,118.6 kW).
Fuel system: 863 litres.
Braking system: Mainwheels.

Details for K-MAX

PRINCIPAL DIMENSIONS:
Rotor diameter: Each 48 ft 4 ins (14.73 m)
Maximum length, rotors turning: 52 ft (15.9 m)

MAIN ROTOR:
Rpm: Normally 270 maximum

UNDERCARRIAGE:
Type: Fixed nosewheel type, with a plate at each wheel for landing on soft ground
Wheel base: 13 ft 6 ins (4.11 m)
Wheel track: 11 ft 8 ins (3.56 m)

WEIGHTS:
Empty: 4,800 lb (2,177 kg)
Maximum take-off: 11,500 lb (5,216 kg)
Typical mission weight: 10,694 lb (4,850 kg), with pilot, 1.5 hours of fuel and 5,000 lb (2,268 kg) hook load
Payload: up to 6,000 lb (2,722 kg). See Freight, external

PERFORMANCE:
Never-exceed speed (V_{NE}): 100 kts (115 mph) 185 km/h without an external load, or 80 kts (92 mph) 148 km/h with an external load
Maximum climb rate: 2,500 ft (762 m) per minute
OGE hovering ceiling: 25,000 ft (7,620 m) estimated, with 6,000 lb (2,722 kg) load, ISA

Little Wing Autogyros, Inc — USA

Corporate address:
746 Hwy 89 North, Mayflower, AR 72106.
Telephone: +1 501 470 7444
Information: Ron Herron.

ACTIVITIES

▪ Has constructed the **Roto-Pup** cabin kit autogyro, based on a Piper Cub Special fuselage. Bensen rotor head. 4 versions, the single-seat Ultralight possibly using a nose-mounted Rotax 503 engine, the LW-2, tandem 2-seat LW-2+2 with a Hirth F30 engine among choices, and LW-3 with a VW engine.

Piasecki Aircraft Corporation — USA

Comments: Activities include marketing rights for the PZL-Świdnik W-3A in the Americas and Pacific rim and vectored thrust ducted propeller work for the US Army. See the 1996-97 edition of *WA&SD*, page 355 for further details.

Revolution Helicopter Corp Inc (RHCI) USA

Corporate address:
1905 West Jesse James Road, Excelsior Springs, MO 64024.

Telephone: +1 816 637 2800
Facsimile: +1 816 637 7936
E-mail: sales@revolutionhelicopter.com
Web site: http://www.revolutionhelicopter.com

Founded: January 1990.

Employees: 40.

Information:
Lee Sarouhan (Customer Service Representative) and Erica Hupp (Public Relations Co-ordinator).

Revolution Mini-500 Bravo

First flight: 1992.
Role: Single-seat kit helicopter, used for a variety of private, business and utility applications.
Sales: Over 400 Mini-500s and latest Mini-500 Bravos (otherwise designated Mini-500B) had been delivered to customers in the USA and more than 24 other countries at the time of writing. Current Mini-500 Bravo sells at US$24,500 in the USA, Mexico and Canada, and internationally for US$26,500.
Crew: Pilot only, up to 250 lb (113 kg) weight. Can accommodate pilots over 6 ft (1.83 m) tall.
Standard equipment: Includes full flight and engine instrumentation, landing and navigation lights, and ground handling wheels.
Optional equipment: Includes chip detector for the main transmission and tail rotor gearbox.
Rotor system: 2-blade semi-rigid, teetering. Blades of composite construction, with solid aluminium leading-edge, foam core and Kevlar skins. Yoke control system, which eliminates the conventional swashplate. 2.25-ins chromoly steel drive shaft (nickel plated), with control rods inside. Sprag clutch to allow immediate autorotation in the event of engine failure. Spiral-bevel ring and pinion drive line to main rotor, with 4.857:1 speed reducing ratio. Bravo has an improved rotor head, with improved bearings and minor configuration changes to improve stability and reduce vibration levels.
Tail rotor characteristics: 2-blade, free to teeter, rigid interplane. Aluminium alloy blades. Precone angle 2°. Spiral-bevel gears drive line to tail rotor. Bravo has introduced new lighter replaceable tail rotor tips, making the system quieter while maintaining full tail rotor pedal authority.
Tail surfaces: Dorsal/ventral fin, with T-mounted horizontal stabilizer with endplates.
Flight control system: Conventional mechanical.
Airframe: Tubular 4130 chromoly steel fuselage structure, with foam/composite cabin. Bravo airframe has been strengthened in several areas, increasing overall durability and allowing the helicopter to better withstand rough terrain operations.
Engine: Rotax 582 piston engine.
Engine rating: 67 hp (50 kW).
Transmission: 2 Kevlar belt-drives from engine to transmission. New Bravo improvements include a lighter yet stronger main transmission housing with an improved bearing/gearing system providing greater durability, longer life and reduced maintenance; stronger, lighter tail rotor gearbox case, plus improved internal gearing for quieter, cooler and longer-lasting operation; and dynamically balanced centrifugal clutch spin balanced to 100% rpm, significantly reducing unwanted vibrations.
Fuel system: 55.6 litres.
Electrical system: For engine starting, clutch engagement, instruments, lighting and com/nav systems.
Flight avionics/instrumentation: Airspeed indicator, hourmeter, magnetic compass, vertical speed indicator, altimeter, dual rotor and engine tachometer, and engine coolant temperature gauge. Optional AlliedSignal Bendix/King Crown KLX 135 GPS/com and KT 76A transponder.
Expendable weapons and equipment: Mini-500 in military paint scheme has been shown with dummy rocket launchers on undercarriage outriggers.

Details for Mini-500

PRINCIPAL DIMENSIONS:
Rotor diameter (main): 19 ft 2 ins (5.84 m)
Maximum length, rotors turning: 22 ft 6 ins (6.86 m)
Fuselage length: 18 ft (5.49 m)
Fuselage width: 3 ft (0.91 m)
Maximum height: 8 ft 3 ins (2.51 m)

CABIN:
Length: 4 ft 3 ins (1.3 m)
Width: almost 3 ft (0.91 m)
Height: 4 ft 5 ins (1.35 m)

MAIN ROTOR:
Blade chord: 8 ins (0.2 m)
Rpm: 550

TAIL ROTOR:
Diameter: 3 ft 10 ins (1.17 m)
Rpm: 2,671

UNDERCARRIAGE:
Type: Fixed twin skids
Skid track: 5 ft 3 ins (1.6 m)

WEIGHTS:
Empty: 485 lb (220 kg)
Maximum take-off: 840 lb (381 kg)
Useful load: 355 lb (161 kg)

PERFORMANCE:
Never-exceed speed (V_{NE}): 104 kts (120 mph) 193 km/h
Maximum speed: 100 kts (115 mph) 185 km/h
Maximum cruise speed: 65 kts (75 mph) 121 km/h
Maximum climb rate: 1,100 ft (335 m) per minute
IGE hovering ceiling: 7,000 ft (2,133 m)
OGE hovering ceiling: 7,000 ft (2,133 m)
Service ceiling: 10,000 ft (3,050 m)
Range: 196 naut miles (225 miles) 361 km, no reserve
Duration: 3 hours maximum, no reserve

↑ Revolution currently offers the improved Mini-500 Bravo single-seat helicopter

Revolution Voyager-500

Comments: Unveiled at Sun 'n Fun air show in Lakeland on 19 April 1998, the new Voyager-500 is a 2-seat helicopter powered by a US Air Power H1300 165 hp (123 kW) specially developed engine, derated to 138 hp (103 kW) and further derated by limiting the helicopter's gross weight to 1,170 lb (531 kg) where a maximum of only 106.3 hp (79.3 kW) is required. Projected service ceiling is 14,000 ft (4,267 m), payload 560 lb (254 kg) at sea level, 82 kts (95 mph) 153 km/h cruise speed, and direct operating costs as low as US$20 per hour. Quick-build kit requires 150-200 working hours to assemble, at an introductory cost of US$48,500 (exclusive of paint and avionics).

↑ Revolution Voyager-500 fuselage assembly

Robinson Helicopter Company USA

Corporate address:
2901 Airport Drive, Torrance, CA 90505.

Telephone: +1 310 539 0508
Facsimile: +1 310 539 5198

Founded: 1971.

Employees: Over 500.

Information:
Tim A. Goetz (Director of Marketing).

Robinson R22 series (including Beta II and Mariner II)

First flight: 28 August 1975 for R22. 31 January 1996 for latest Beta II.
Certification: 26 March 1979 by the FAA.
First delivery: October 1979.
Role: Lightweight helicopter for transport and pleasure, flight training, aerial photography, law enforcement, agriculture and more.

Aims

■ Originally designed as a low-cost and inexpensive-to-operate helicopter for mainly personal owner-operator use but with many other potential applications.

↑ Robinson R22 Beta II

↑ Robinson R44 Newscopter with FSI UltraMedia camera system, delivered in 1998 to WLBT Channel 3

Details *(based on the latest Beta II, except where stated)*

Sales: More than 2,700 sold. Basic price at time of writing about US$139,000 for Beta II, US$148,000 for Mariner II or police configuration, and US$163,090 for IFR Trainer with recommended avionics (otherwise basic as for Beta II).
Crew/passengers: Pilot and passenger. Dual controls standard (T-bar cyclic), but passenger controls are removable. Throttle synchronizer.
Freight, internal: Baggage stowed in a compartment under each seat, with total volume 2.5 cu ft (0.07 m^3).
Freight, external: Belly hardpoint optional for 400 lb (181 kg) capacity hook.
Optional equipment: Apollo DTM-3 spray gear, with 24 ft (7.32 m) sprayboom and 151 litre undercarriage-attached chemical hopper.
Rotor system: 2-blade teetering type (elastomeric teeter stop limits blade teetering during start-up and shut down on windy days), with tri-hinge rotor head that eliminates lag hinges, dampers and hydraulic struts. Flexures, teflon-lined bearings and sealed ball bearings eliminate need for grease fittings. Maintenance-free flex couplings are used in place of universal joints and gear couplings in the main and tail drive system. Automatic clutch engagement simplifies and shortens start-up procedure and reduces chances of overspeed. Balanced control forces eliminates the need for the pilot to manipulate an electric trim system and allows the pilot to remove his/her hand from the collective without applying friction. Each blade has a hardened stainless steel spar and leading edge (latter for erosion protection), and an aft portion of light alloy honeycomb and bonded aluminium alloy skin. Rotor brake standard. Standard rpm governor. Sprag clutch. An advanced Carb Heat Assist device can be engaged to automatically add carburettor heat when the collective is lowered and reduce carburettor heat when the collective is raised, simplifying procedures and enhancing safety during approaches and practice autorotations.
Tail rotor characteristics: 2-blade, metal.
Tail surfaces: Fin, with a small horizontal stabilizer on the starboard side.
Flight control system: Push-pull tubes and bell cranks.
Airframe: Primary structure of welded steel tubing and riveted aluminium alloy. Aluminium alloy monocoque tailboom. Glassfibre and thermoplastics used for secondary structures.
Engine: Textron Lycoming O-360-J2A piston engine. New electronic throttle governor based on the R44 governor (sensing only engine rpm; previous governor sensed rotor rpm and applied both collective and throttle inputs to control rpm) incorporated on all new helicopters from s/n 2520 and offered as a retrofit kit.
Engine rating: Derated to 131 hp (97.7 kW) at 2,652 rpm.
Transmission: 131 hp (97.7 kW) take-off, 124 hp (92.5 kW) continuous. V-belts drive from engine, with sprag clutch. Main gearbox chip and temperature, and tail gearbox chip warning lights.
Fuel system: 72 litres standard. 42 litre auxiliary tank. Gravity flow fuel system.
Electrical system: 12 volt DC supply with starter-generator.
Flight avionics/instrumentation: Includes as standard a clock, magnetic compass, digital OAT gauge, hourmeter, carb air temperature gauge, fuel quantity gauge, cylinder head gauge, oil temperature and pressure gauges, ammeter, AlliedSignal Bendix/King KY 197 com transceiver, intercom, rate-of-climb indicator, airspeed indicator, dual rotor and engine tachometer, altimeter, and manifold pressure gauge. Warning lights for low fuel, main gearbox temperature and chip, tail gearbox chip, low oil pressure, low voltage alternator, rotor rpm (and horn warning) and rotor brake engaged. Options include transponder, remote altitude encoder, nav/com, headsets, digital clock, GPS, artificial horizon, directional gyro, vertical compass, and millibar altimeter. See also Aircraft variants (particularly IFR Trainer).

Aircraft variants:
R22 was the initial production version, with 150 hp (112 kW) Textron Lycoming O-320-A2C engine.
R22 Alpha superseded R22, introducing a 160 hp (119.3 kW) O-320-B2C engine. 124 hp (92.5 kW) take-off and continuous transmission rating.
R22 Beta followed Alpha as the standard version, as detailed in the 1996-97 edition of *WA&SD*. Same engine but with higher transmission rating for take off.
R22 Beta II is the current standard version, with a Textron Lycoming O-360-J2A engine that provides nearly 13% more power at altitude. Throttle governor as standard instead of optional, carb heat assist, improved CAT probe, high-capacity oil cooler, more comfortable cyclic grip, governor-off warning light, vernier mixture control and more. 2,000 hour approved TBO for engine and airframe.
R22 Mariner was the first version to be equipped with utility floats. Was given corrosion proofing throughout, special handling wheels, and gauge/nozzle for checking float pressure. Floats installation added about 33 lb (15 kg) to empty weight. V_{NE} 95 kts (109 mph) 176 km/h. Optional equipment included alternative aft battery provision (for operations without floats), belly tie-down ring, main rotor blade supports, wind deflectors, 2-man life-raft, I-Com IC-M56 marine radio, I-Com IC 3230 radio, and single pilot multiple radio control panel.
R22 Mariner II is the current float version, with a Textron Lycoming O-540-F1B5 engine. Transmission rated at 225 hp (168 kW) take-off and 205 hp (153 kW) continuous. Standard fuel 121 litres, with 68 litres of auxiliary fuel. MTOW 2,400 lb (1,089 lb). V_{NE} 130 kts (150 mph) 241 km/h and economic cruise speed 110 kts (127 mph) 204 km/h. Range similar to Beta II. VFR certified 10 December 1992.
R22 IFR Trainer configuration was conceived for instrument flight training, and includes an artificial horizon, encoding altimeter, turn co-ordinator, HSI, digital clock, ADF, nav/com, transponder and marker beacon. DME optional. Designed for instrument training but not approved for actual IFR operations.
R22 law enforcement configuration optionally adds a dual searchlight with up to 12 million candlepower, public address speaker and siren, 70 amp alternator (exchange) for use with the searchlight, and single pilot multiple radio control panel and dual pilot combinations to the basic R22 Beta II.
R22 agricultural has an Apollo Helicopter Services DTM-3 spraying system and 151.4 litre chemical tank.

Details for R22 Beta II

PRINCIPAL DIMENSIONS:
Rotor diameter (main): 25 ft 2 ins (7.67 m)
Maximum length, rotors turning: 28 ft 9 ins (8.76 m)
Fuselage length: 20 ft 8 ins (6.3 m)
Cabin width: 3 ft 8 ins (1.12 m)
Maximum height: 8 ft 11 ins (2.72 m) to top of rotor hub

CABIN:
Length: 4 ft 3.5 ins (1.3 m)
Width: 3 ft 7 ins (1.09 m)
Height: 4 ft (1.22 m)

MAIN ROTOR:
Aerofoil section: NACA 63-015
Blade chord: 7.2 ins (0.18 m)
Rotor disc: 497.4 sq ft (46.21 m^2)
Rpm: 530 normal

TAIL ROTOR:
Diameter: 3 ft 6 ins (1.07 m)
Blade chord: 4 ins (10 cm)
Rpm: 3,396 normal

UNDERCARRIAGE:
Type: Fixed twin skids, with ground handling wheels
Skid track: 6 ft 4 ins (1.93 m)

WEIGHTS:
Empty, equipped: 845 lb (383 kg)
Maximum take-off: 1,370 lb (621 kg)
Useful load: 516 lb (234 kg)
Useful load with full fuel: 338 lb (153 kg)

PERFORMANCE:
Never-exceed speed (V_{NE}): 102 kts (118 mph) 190 km/h
Economic cruise speed: 96 kts (110 mph) 177 km/h
Maximum climb rate: 1,000 ft (305 m) at sea level
IGE hovering ceiling, ISA: 9,500 ft (2,896 m)
IGE hovering ceiling, ISA + 20° C: 8,300 ft (2,530 m)
Service ceiling: 14,000 ft (4,265 m)
Range: 182 naut miles (210 miles) 337 km
Range with auxiliary fuel: 275 naut miles (317 miles) 510 km, no reserve
Duration: 2.2 hours, no reserve, standard fuel

Robinson R44 series (including Astro, Clipper and Newscopter)

First flight: 30 March 1990.
Certification: 10 December 1992 for R44 Astro. 17 July 1996 for R44 Clipper.
First delivery: May 1993.
Role: Light civil helicopter, with other applications including law enforcement, air taxi, sightseeing, aerial photography, reporting, construction support and agricultural spraying. Basically a 4-seat development of the R22.
Sales: Some 360 operating in over 30 countries. US deliveries started in July 1995. Seven Newscopters delivered by July 1998. Basic price for R44 Astro at time of writing was US$265,000, for Clipper US$281,000, for IFR Trainer US$286,370 with recommended avionics (otherwise basic price as for Astro), for Newscopter US$495,000, and for Police Helicopter US$440,000-485,000 (depending on IR/camera selected). R44 became the first piston helicopter to be flown around the world, between 10 May and 15 August 1997.

Details *(based on R44 Astro, except where stated; similar to R22, except as described)*

Crew/passengers: 2+2, including pilot. Lap belt and shoulder strap restraints are designed for high forward g loads.

Flight control system: New hydraulic system optional from 1999.
Engine: Textron Lycoming O-540-F1B5 piston engine.
Engine rating: 260 hp (194 kW), derated to 225 hp (168 kW) for take-off and 205 hp (153 kW) continuous.
Transmission: Rated at 225 hp (168 kW) take-off and 205 hp (153 kW) continuous.
Fuel system: 121 litres standard. Auxiliary tank of 68 litres.
Flight avionics/instrumentation: Includes as standard a clock, artificial horizon, magnetic compass, digital OAT gauge, hourmeter, cylinder head gauge, oil temperature and pressure gauges, ammeter, AlliedSignal Bendix/King KY 197 com transceiver, intercom, rate-of-climb indicator, airspeed indicator, dual rotor and engine tachometer, altimeter, and manifold pressure gauge. Warning lights for low fuel, main gearbox temperature and chip, tail gearbox chip, low oil pressure, low voltage alternator, rotor rpm (and horn warning), voltage, and rotor brake and starter engaged. Optional are Jet Electronics 305-1AL artificial horizon or artificial horizon w/slip skid indicator (exchange – required for Part 135 air taxi operation), turn co-ordinator, Jet Electronics 205-1AL directional gyro (required for Part 135 air taxi operation), PAI-700 vertical compass (exchange), LC-2 digital clock (exchange), millibar altimeter (replaces standard in-Hg), AlliedSignal Bendix/King KT 76A transponder and KT 70 Mode S transponder (latter required for Part 135 air taxi operation), remote altitude encoder (used with KT 76A and required for Part 135 air taxi operation), GPS, AlliedSignal Bendix/King nav/com (KX 155 with KI 203 indicator), AlliedSignal Bendix/King ADF, Pointer 3000 or 4000 ELT and more.

Aircraft variants:
R44 Astro, as detailed.
R44 Clipper is the twin float version, with similar engine and MTOW to Astro, 1,470 lb (667 kg) empty weight, similar range, V_{NE} of 120 kts (138 mph) 222 km/h, and economic cruise speed of 100 kts (115 mph) 185 km/h.
R44 IFR Trainer configuration was conceived for instrument flight training. Wide range of recommended and optional avionics.
R44 Newscopter is equipped with FSI UltraMedia RS, 750 Line 3 CCD camera with 5-axes gyrostabilized gimbal and laptop control console; 6 ins (15 cm) Sony FDL-X600 flat screen colour monitor, 3 × 4 ins (10 cm) flat screen colour monitors,

Details for R44 Astro

PRINCIPAL DIMENSIONS:
Rotor diameter (main): 33 ft (10.06 m)
Maximum length, rotors turning: 38 ft 7 ins (11.76 m)
Fuselage length: 29 ft 9 ins (9.07 m) to end of tail rotor guard
Fuselage width: 4 ft 2.5 ins (1.28 m)
Maximum height: 10 ft 9 ins (3.28 m) to top of rotor hub

MAIN ROTOR:
Blade chord: 10 ins (25.4 cm)
Rotor disc: 855.3 sq ft (79.46 m^2)
Rpm: 404

TAIL ROTOR:
Diameter: 4 ft 10 ins (1.47 m)
Blade chord: 5 ins (12.7 cm)
Rpm: 2,403

UNDERCARRIAGE:
Type: Crashworthy gear
Skid track: 7 ft 2 ins (2.18 m)

WEIGHTS:
Empty: 1,420 lb (644 kg)
Maximum take-off: 2,400 lb (1,088 kg)
Useful load: 980 lb (445 kg)
Useful load with full fuel: 687 lb (312 kg)

PERFORMANCE:
Never-exceed speed (V_{NE}): 130 kts (150 mph) 241 km/h
Economic cruise speed: 110 kts (127 mph) 204 km/h
Maximum climb rate: 1,000 ft (305 m) per minute
IGE hovering ceiling: 6,400 ft (1,950 m) at MTOW
IGE hovering ceiling, ISA + 20° C: 4,800 ft (1,463 m)
Service ceiling: 14,000 ft (4,265 m)
Range: 348 naut miles (401 miles) 645 km
Duration: 3.3 hours with standard fuel, no reserve

cameras in the cockpit and on the tail, 5 position vertical interval video switcher, Geneva audio system, Sony on-air tuner, 2 FM radios, GPS and second com, video recorder, microwave transmitter, microwave omnidirectional antenna, and 24 or 28 volt electrical system. Several items of optional equipment.

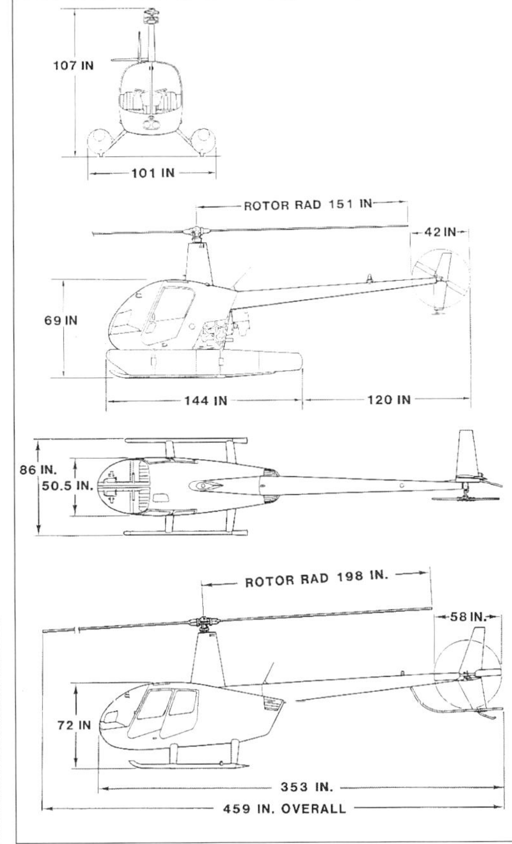

↑ **Robinson R22 Mariner II general arrangement *(top)* with R44 Astro *(below)*** *(courtesy Robinson)*

R44 Police Helicopter is equipped with an Inframetrics 445G-MkII infra-red sensor and 7 × zoom colour TV camera or Wescam 12DS infra-red sensor and 14 × zoom colour TV camera on a gyrostabilized nose gimbal. Certified January 1997.

RotorWay International — USA

Corporate address:
4140 West Mercury Way, Chandler, AZ 85226.
Telephone: +1 602 961 1001
Facsimile: +1 602 961 1514
Web site: www.rotorway.com
E-mail: rotorway@primenet.com
Founded: 1 June 1990 (present company).
Information:
Susie Bell (Marketing Director).

ACTIVITIES

■ The current Exec 162F has been available since August 1994, replacing the former Exec 90 kit helicopter. See also Engine section.

RotorWay Exec 162F

Role: 2-seat, light, kit-built helicopter.

Aims

■ In comparison with the Exec 90, Exec 162F has a redesigned and more comfortable cabin, adding 2 cu ft (0.0565 m^3) of volume, providing more leg room. Door apertures are widened to improve accessibility (door can be removed). The current version of the engine introduces dual electronic ignition, electronic fuel injection, and FADEC.

Details

Sales: More than 500 kits of the Exec 90 and later Exec 162F shipped since 1990. Current Exec 162F became available in kit form from August 1994. Kit (US$62,350 at time of writing) comes complete (including RotorWay engine and many prefabricated components), requiring only paint and avionics. Marketed in the USA and over 44 foreign countries. Production rate increased to 12 kits per month for 1998.
Crew/passengers: 2, side-by-side, with dual controls.
Optional equipment: Includes Helipac cargo hold.
Rotor system: 2-blade. The blades have asymmetric aerofoil section and are of aluminium alloy construction, attached to an aluminium alloy teetering hub by retention straps. Elastomeric bearings.
Tail rotor characteristics: 2-blade, each with steel spar and aluminium alloy skins.
Tail surfaces: Revised design dorsal/ventral fin. Small horizontal stabilizer with endplates mounted mid-way along the boom.
Flight control system: Dual push-pull cable controlled swashplate for cyclic pitch control.
Airframe materials: Welded 4130 chromoly tubular steel tube structure, with wrap-round non-structural glassfibre cabin enclosure. Aluminium alloy monocoque tailboom.
Engine: RotorWay RI 162F piston engine.
Engine rating: 150 hp (112 kW).
Fuel system: 64.4 litres.
Flight avionics/instrumentation: Kit comes with the instrument panel, digital display monitor, engine instruments, rotor tachometer, and flight instruments. Avionics optional.

↑ **RotorWay Exec 162F**

Details for Exec 162F

PRINCIPAL DIMENSIONS:
Rotor diameter (main): 25 ft (7.62 m)
Fuselage length: 22 ft (6.71 m)
Maximum height: 8 ft (2.44 m)

CABIN:
Width: 3 ft 8 ins (1.12 m)

TAIL ROTOR:
Diameter: 4 ft (1.22 m)

UNDERCARRIAGE:
Type: Twin fixed skids. Ground handling wheels. Optional Full Lotus floats
Skid track: 5 ft 5 ins (1.65 m)

WEIGHTS:
Empty: 975 lb (442 kg)
Maximum take-off: 1,500 lb (680 kg)
Crew: 425 lb (193 kg)
Equipped useful load: 525 lb (238 kg)

PERFORMANCE:
Maximum speed: 100 kts (115 mph) 185 km/h at sea level, ISA
Cruise speed: 82 kts (95 mph) 153 km/h
Maximum climb rate: 1,000 ft (305 m) per minute
IGE hovering ceiling: 7,000 ft (2,135 m)
OGE hovering ceiling: 5,000 ft (1,525 m)
Service ceiling: 10,000 ft (3,050 m)
Range: 156 naut miles (180 miles) 290 km, cruise speed
Duration: 2 hours with maximum fuel, cruise speed

B. J. Schramm (Eagle Research and Development) USA

Corporate address:
2203 South 10th Avenue, Caldwell, ID 83605.
Facsimile: +1 208 466 1385
Information:
B. J. Schramm.

Schramm Helicycle

Role: Kit-built single-seat helicopter, also able to become a compound helicopter (see Engines). In ultralight form, has no cabin enclosure or stub wings/pusher engines.

Aims

▪ High speed helicopter with good high altitude performance and low operating costs. Maximum speed more than 104 kts (120 mph) 193 km/h in compound form.

Details

Crew/passengers: Pilot only in a heavily glazed enclosed cabin.
Rotor system: 2-blade, semi-rigid teetering type, with blades constructed using a 2024-T351 aluminium spar and bonded aluminium skin. Asymmetrical aerofoil section, with reflected trailing edge. No blade twist. Swashplate for pitch change. Elastomeric bearings on the machined rotor head.
Tail rotor characteristics: 2-blade, shaft driven, constructed of 4130 steel spar and aluminium skins and bolted to the pitch-change shaft.
Wings: Stub wings attached in compound layout, of aerofoil section to generate lift and with integral fuel tanks, mounting the engines (see Engines). Removing wings takes about 5 minutes.
Tail surfaces: Sweptback dorsal/ventral fin with tailguard, and port stabilizer.
Flight control system: Push-pull cable for tail rotor pitch change, actuating slider mechanism.
Airframe: Welded 4130 steel tubular structure, with glassfibre cabin enclosure optional.
Engines: Single Rotax 618 piston engine in helicopter form, derated to 60 hp (44.7 kW) and with optional turbocharging or nitrous oxide injection. Optional Rotax 503 in ultralight form. When flown as a compound aircraft, small stub wings are attached immediately aft of the cabin, with a fan-cooled 10 hp (7.5 kW) engine enclosed in a glassfibre pod at each tip and each driving a 2-blade wooden pusher propeller with spinner, adding some 70 lb (31.8 kg) to the weight of the airframe. Prototype uses McCulloch engines on the stub wings, but other types are being investigated.
Transmission: Oil-filled, 356-T6 aluminium cast main rotor transmission, with 5 V-belts and a combined overrunning clutch and cooling fan, the latter forcing cool air through the radiator plenum. Oil-filled bevel gear tail rotor gearbox, with drive shaft extending from the plenum.
Fuel system: Main tank located aft of the cabin structure, ahead of the engine. Additional fuel in the stub wings when fitted.

Schweizer Aircraft Corporation USA

Corporate address:
See Reconnaissance section for company details.

ACTIVITIES

▪ In addition to the helicopters below and the aeroplanes in the Reconnaissance section, Schweizer supports Hughes Model 269 series helicopters (predecessor of the Model 300) operating with about 75 different US agencies.

Schweizer Model 300C series

First flight: June 1984. Originally flown in August 1969 as the Hughes 300C, itself developed from the Hughes 300 of 1964.

Details *(principally for Model 300C)*

Role: Civil and military light utility helicopter.
Sales: Well over 3,550 Model 300 types built by Hughes and Schweizer, with the latter producing more than 750 since 1984 as the licence holder.
Crew/passengers: 3 persons side-by-side, with optional dual controls. 100 lb (45 kg) of baggage. Can be configured for litter carrying.
Freight, external: 900 lb (408 kg) sling load, or alternative 200 lb (91 kg) capacity freight racks.
Optional equipment: Simplex agricultural equipment for liquid or dry chemicals.
Rotor system: 3-blade (metal) fully articulated main rotor, with elastomeric dampers.
Tail rotor characteristics: 2-blade (metal spar, glassfibre skin), teetering.
Tail surfaces: Ventral fin and starboard dihedral stabilizer.
Flight control system: Mechanical, with electric cyclic trimming system.
Airframe: Steel tubing structure, with metal enclosure.
Safety features: Energy absorbing skids, crushable sub-floor, and yielding seat structure.
Engine: Textron Lycoming HIO-360-D1A piston engine.
Engine rating: 190 hp (141.6 kW).
Transmission: Electrically tensioned multi-belt and pulley reduction drive from engine.
Fuel system: 113.6 litres standard capacity, raised to 185.5 litres with auxiliary fuel tank.
Electrical system: 24 volt supply via an alternator and battery.
Flight avionics/instrumentation: Can include ADF, transponders and transceiver.

Aircraft variants:
Model 300C is the basic version, as detailed.
Model 300C Sky Knight is a police version, with optional night flying equipment, dual controls, searchlight, IR sensor, loudspeaker and siren, police communications, exhaust muffler, 28 volt electrical system to power the equipment, and much more.
Model 300CB is a training version, the first going to Helicopter Adventures. FAA certified in August 1995. Offers lower operating costs due to extended times on the life-limited components, standard right-hand pilot-in-command, and a 180 hp (134 kW) HO-360-C1A carburettor engine. 132 litres of fuel. 1,750 lb (794 kg) gross weight.
TH-300C is a military dual-control trainer, as used by Thailand.
RoboCopter 300 has been developed by Schweizer and its Japanese distributor Kawada Industries as a multi-purpose UAV (unmanned) version, suited to reconnaissance, pipeline patrol, agricultural, flying crane and other roles. First flown in 1996 and based on the Model 300CB. Automatic 3-axes gyrostabilization and rotor auto-engage system. Future plans envisage a derated engine version, to use auto fuel.

Details for Model 300C

PRINCIPAL DIMENSIONS:
Rotor diameter (main): 26 ft 10 ins (8.18 m)
Maximum length, rotors turning: 30 ft 10 ins (9.4 m)
Fuselage length: 22 ft 2.2 ins (6.76 m) from tip of skids to tailskid
Fuselage width: 4 ft 3 ins (1.3 m)
Maximum height: 8 ft 8.5 ins (2.65 m)

MAIN ROTOR:
Aerofoil section: NACA 0015
Blade chord: 6.75 ins (0.17 m)
Blade area: each 7.55 sq ft (0.702 m^2)
Rotor disc: 565.5 sq ft (52.54 m^2)

TAIL ROTOR:
Diameter: 4 ft 3 ins (1.3 m)

UNDERCARRIAGE:
Type: Energy absorbing fixed twin skids. Provision for ground handling wheels and floats
Skid base: 8 ft 3 ins (2.51 m)
Skid track: 6 ft 6.5 ins (1.99 m)

WEIGHTS:
Empty: 1,100 lb (499 kg)
Maximum take-off: 2,050 lb (930 kg) normal category
Typical operating weight: 1,700 lb (771 kg)
Maximum take-off, external load: 2,150 lb (975 kg)
Useful load: 950 lb (431 kg) normal category, 1,050 lb (476 kg) external load operations

PERFORMANCE:
Never-exceed speed (V_{NE}): 91 kts (105 mph) 168 km/h at sea level
Maximum cruise speed: 86 kts (99 mph) 159 km/h at sea level and typical operating weight, or 79 kts (91 mph) 146 km/h at sea level and MTOW
Maximum climb rate: 1,305 ft (398 m) per minute at typical operating weight, 750 ft (229 m) per minute at MTOW
IGE hovering ceiling: 10,800 ft (3,292 m) at typical operating weight, or 5,800 ft (1,768 m) at MTOW
OGE hovering ceiling: 8,600 ft (2,621 m) at typical operating weight, or 2,750 ft (838 m) at MTOW
Ceiling: 10,200 ft (3,108 m)
Range: 224 naut miles (258 miles) 415 km at typical operating weight, or 195 naut miles (224 miles) 361 km at MTOW, both at 4,000 ft (1,220 m), no reserve, standard fuel
Duration: 3.8 hours at typical operating weight, or 3.4 hours at MTOW, no reserve, standard fuel

Schweizer Model 330 and 330SP

First flight: June 1988 for Model 330.
Certification: 1992 for Model 330 and 1997 for Model 330SP.
First delivery: 1993. First law enforcement Model 330, to the West Palm Beach Police Department, delivered in 1996. First military sale of the Model 330 to the Netherlands (Navy) in 1996 for training.
Role: Light utility and training helicopter, with good hot-and-high performance. Other roles similar to Model 300C, including law enforcement and agricultural.
Crew/passengers: 3 seats for training and 4 for utility. Dual or 3 sets of controls are available for training.
Rotor system: 3-blade, fully articulated main rotor, with elastomeric dampers.
Tail rotor characteristics: 2-blade (metal spar, glassfibre skin), teetering.
Tail surfaces: Horizontal stabilizer with endplates on boom, and tall ventral and smaller dorsal fins.

↑ Schweizer Model 300Cs delivered to the Argentine Coast Guard in 1996

↑ New Schweizer Model 330SP turbine helicopter, first operated by the West Palm Beach Police Department

Engine: Allison 250-C20W turboshaft.
Engine rating: 420 shp (313.3 kW), derated to 235 shp (175 kW) take-off for 5 minutes, 220 shp (164 kW) maximum continuous.
Transmission: 235 shp (175 kW) take-off and 220 shp (164 kW) maximum continuous.
Fuel system: 227 litres.

Aircraft variants:
Model 330 was the original version.
Model 330SP is the latest version, offering increased area main rotor blades, high stance undercarriage and a larger main rotor hub, resulting in significant improvements in performance (see table). Performance improvements include a 13% increase in maximum cruise speed, 17% increase in maximum specific range, 7% in maximum specific duration, 10% in controllability margins, and 42% in rotor roughness speed from 88 to 125 kts, plus decreased auto descent rates, more confortable cruise attitude, greater inertia and efficiency of the rotor system, and a 12 ins (0.305 m) increase in ground clearance for infra-red and camera equipment and for off-site landings. Improvements can be retrofitted to existing Model 330s or delivered as features of new helicopters.

Details for Model 330, *with 330SP in italics where different*

PRINCIPAL DIMENSIONS:
Rotor diameter (main): 26 ft 10 ins (8.18 m)
Maximum length, rotors turning: 30 ft 10 ins (9.4 m), *31 ft 0.5 ins (9.46 m)*
Fuselage length: 22 ft 4.5 ins (6.82 m) from nose to ventral fin
Fuselage width: 5 ft 8 ins (1.72 m)
Maximum height: 9 ft 6.5 ins (2.91 m)

CABIN:
Width: 5 ft 7 ins (1.7 m)
Height: 4 ft 5 ins (1.35 m)

MAIN ROTOR:
Rpm: 471

UNDERCARRIAGE:
Type: Fixed twin skids with streamline legs; *skid height increased to 2 ft 7 ins (0.79 m)*
Skid track: 6 ft 10 ins (2.08 m)

WEIGHTS:
Empty: 1,120 lb (508 kg), *1,140 lb (517 kg)*
Typical operating weight: 1,900 lb (862 kg)
Maximum take-off: 2,230 lb (1,012 kg), *2,260 lb (1,025 kg)*
Useful load: 1,110 lb (503 kg), *1,120 lb (508 kg)*

PERFORMANCE:
Never-exceed speed (V_{NE}): 108 kts (124 mph) 200 km/h at sea level
Vr at 2,230 lb (1,012 kg), 2,000 ft (610 m) HD: *125 kts (144 mph) 232 km/h*
Maximum cruise speed: *100 kts (115 mph) 185 km/h at 2,230 lb (1,012 kg) or 104 kts (120 mph) 193 km/h at 2,000 lb (907 kg), both sea level*
Typical cruise speed: 100 kts (115 mph) 185 km/h at typical operating weight, 94 kts (108 mph) 174 km/h at MTOW
Climb rate: 1,380 ft (421 m) per minute at sea level
IGE hovering ceiling: 14,000 ft (4,267 m) at typical operating weight, 8,200 ft (2,500 m) at MTOW, zero winds; *8,300 ft (2,530 m) at MTOW or 13,600 ft (4,145 m) at 2,000 lb (907 kg)*
OGE hovering ceiling: 11,300 ft (3,444 m) at typical operating weight, 5,900 ft (1,798 m) at MTOW; *6,000 ft (1,829 m) at MTOW, or 11,200 ft (3,415 m) at 2,000 lb (907 kg)*
Ceiling: 12,000 ft (3,660 m) pressure altitude
Range: 269 naut miles (310 miles) 498 km at typical operating weight or 252 naut miles (290 miles) 467 km at MTOW, both with no reserve; *300 naut miles (345 miles) 556 km at 1,500 ft (457 m) or 319 naut miles (367 miles) 591 km at 4,000 ft (1,220 m), both ISA*
Duration: 3.6 hours at typical operating weight, 3.4 hours at MTOW, both with no reserve; *4 hours at 1,500 ft (457 m), or 4.19 hours at 4,000 ft (1,220 m), both ISA*

Sikorsky Aircraft USA

Corporate address:
6900 Main Street, PO Box 9729, Stratford, CT 06497-9129.

Telephone: +1 203 386 4000
Facsimile: +1 203 386 7300
Web site: http://www.sikorsky.com

Founded:
Foundations in the Sikorsky Aero Engineering Corporation of 1923. Sikorsky Aviation Corporation founded on 3 October 1928, becoming a division of United Technologies Corporation in 1929 (and remaining a division to this day).

Employees: 11,500.

Information:
William Tuttle (Manager, Public Relations – *telephone* +1 203 386 5261).

ACTIVITIES

- Specializes in the development and manufacture of intermediate to heavy helicopters (9,900-70,400 lb, 4,500-32,000 kg), used by all 5 branches of the US armed forces and civil/military operators worldwide.
- Licensing agreements established production lines for Sikorsky-based helicopters in the UK (GKN Westland), Italy (Agusta), Japan (Mitsubishi) and South Korea (Korean Air for H-60 Black Hawk).
- Developing the RAH-66 Comanche with Boeing (see Boeing Sikorsky).
- Sikorsky leads an international team developing S-92 Helibus.
- During the last full year (at the time of writing), Sikorsky delivered 101 helicopters and 12 kits.

Sikorsky S-70A/C, H-60 Black Hawk series and derivatives

First flight: 17 October 1974.
Role: UH-60 is principally for troop assault and redeployment, artillery support, medevac, logistic and utility. Use of ESSS (see Number of weapon pylons) provides substantial attack and suppression capability. Specialized variants of H-60 include those for search/rescue and electronic warfare.

Development

- 23 December 1976. UH-60A selected for production against the competing Boeing UH-61A, to meet the US Army Utility Tactical Transport Aircraft System (UTTAS) requirement.

Details *(principally for the UH-60L, unless stated)*

Sales: Approaching 1,700 H-60s of all versions ordered at the time of writing for the US Army and USAF alone, with deliveries to the US Army continuing. 1,908 S-70/H-60 series helicopters delivered by June 1998, including 72 in 1997 and 31 during January-June 1998, not including SH-60B/F/Js of the Seahawk general type. The 2,000th H-60 series helicopter was rolled out by Sikorsky in May 1994, a figure which included all US Army, US Air Force, US Navy, Coast Guard and export variants described in this and the SH-60 entry. Exported Black Hawk variants serving, or on order, with 23 governments, including those of Argentina, Australia, Bahrain, Brazil, Brunei, Colombia, Egypt, Greece, Hong Kong, Israel, Japan, Jordan, Malaysia, Mexico, Morocco, People's Republic of China, Philippines, South Korea, Saudi Arabia, Spain, Taiwan, Thailand and Turkey.
Crew/passengers: 2 flight crew on armour-protected and crashworthy seats (optional gunner in the cabin) and a fully-equipped 11-person infantry squad (14 possible), able to be airlifted in demanding 4,000 ft (1,220 m) elevations and 35°C temperatures or in desert and arctic climates. Alternatively, 4 or 6 litters or internal/external freight.
Freight, external: 9,000 lb (4,082 kg) sling load.
Size of main loading doors: 5 ft 9 ins × 4 ft 6 ins (1.75 × 1.37 m).
Optional equipment: 600 lb (272 kg) capacity rescue hoist.
Rotor system: 4-blade main rotor, with 3° forward tilt. Each blade has a 20° swept tip and comprises a titanium spar, Nomex honeycomb core and composites trailing edge and skins, with titanium/nickel leading-edge anti-erosion strip. 18° blade twist. Bifilar vibration damper over rotor head. Blade de-icing. New 16% wider-chord blades with 20° drooped tips became available from 1997, to enhance hovering. Monobloc titanium rotor head with elastomeric bearings and hydraulic drag dampers.
Tail rotor characteristics: Cross-beam layout, with 2 separate superimposed 2-blade composite rotors set at 90°. 20° inward cant to widen CG range and offer some lift.
Tail surfaces: Electrically controlled 14 ft 4.6 ins (4.39 m) variable-incidence tailplane, set at 34° in hover in concert with the rotor downwash. Fin area permits a controlled emergency landing in the event of tail rotor failure or loss.
Flight control system: Hydraulic.
Airframe materials: Metal, but with composite floors, doors, fairings and other non-structural components.
Safety features: Built-in tolerance to small arms fire and most

↑ Royal Brunei Air Force Sikorsky S-70A Black Hawk with radar, FLIR and auxiliary tanks

↑ Newly available 'glass' cockpit and digital avionics for the Black Hawk

medium-calibre high-explosive projectiles, as well as specially designed airframe and undercarriage features, for a high degree of battlefield survivability. Wire strike protection. Can survive a 38 ft (11.6 m) per second vertical impact rate, or a simultaneous 20g longitudinal/10g vertical impact.
Engines: 2 General Electric T700-GE-701C turboshafts. APU.
Engine rating: Each 1,870 shp (1,394 kW) maximum, 1,620 shp (1,208 kW) continuous, and 1,940 shp (1,447 kW) contingency.
Transmission rating: 3,400 shp (2,535 kW).
Fuel system: 1,363 litres usable. 2 × 700 litre internal or 2 × 871 litre ESSS-carried auxiliary fuel tanks.
Electrical system: 2 AlliedSignal generators, plus a 17 amp-hour ni-cd battery.
Radar: See Aircraft variants.
Flight avionics/instrumentation: Automatic flight control system, with digital 3-axis autopilot and autostabilization (see MH-60K). Navigation equipment includes AN/ASN-128 Doppler, radar altimeter, ADF, VOR/marker beacon/glideslope, and gyro compass; some have AN/ARN-148 Omega. Wide range of communication equipment. 'Glass' cockpit and digital automated flight computer system are now available for S-70 Black Hawks to simplify pilot workload. Among options is an EFIS to provide primary pilotage and navigation displays for the aircrew.
Self-protection systems: IR jammer, radar warning and chaff/flare.
Fixed guns: 2 pintle-mounted 7.62-mm M134 Miniguns in the cabin, or 0.50-ins guns.
Number of weapon pylons: External Stores Support System (ESSS), consisting of removable stub wings that attach to the fuselage sides (above the cabin), have 2 pylons each for auxiliary fuel tanks, weapons or other stores. ESSS attachment is built into the airframe structure.
Expendable weapons and equipment: Using ESSS (External Stores Support System), can carry over 10,000 lb (4,536 kg) of stores, including auxiliary fuel tanks, ECM pods, up to 16 Hellfire anti-armour missiles (with 16 more carried internally for reload), guns, and mine dispensers.

Aircraft variants:
AH-60L is a 4-crew heavily-armed special operations helicopter (few prepared by modification of former MH-60Ls), used to escort the MH-60K. Operated during Desert Storm. Typically 4 Hellfires, rocket pods, 2 × 30-mm cannon and 2 × 7.62-mm Miniguns, with provision for grenade launchers and Stinger AAMs. AlliedSignal RDR-1400C weather radar, Stormscope, GEC-Marconi HUD, AN/AAQ-16 FLIR and laser designator. GPS, satcom, secure communications and much more. Flight refuelling probe.
CH-60, see Seahawk.
EH-60A is the designation of 66 UH-60As modified for electronic warfare with the US Army and Army National Guard under the Special Electronics Mission Aircraft programme. Fitted with the AN/ALQ-151(V)2 Quick Fix IIB airborne ECM surveillance and detection/jamming suite, installed by Tracor's Flight Systems division at Mojave. 2 dipole antennae on each tailboom side and a large underfuselage whip aerial. Capable of locating AM/FM, continuous wave and single sideband signals. Has transmitters to jam VHF emissions and radar signals. Data link to down link with command or interface with other EH-60s. 2 equipment operators in the main cabin. 32 now being upgraded with Advanced Quick Fit and other changes including T700-GE-701C engines. Hover infra-red suppressor. Self-protection with missile and radar warning, infra-red jammer, and chaff/flare dispensers. Funding being requested for a command and control variant with AN/ASC-15B(V)1 communications equipment.
HH-60G Pave Hawk combat rescue helicopter (see MH-60G) for long-range SAR. AN/AAQ-16B infra-red imaging system.
MH-60G Pave Hawk is a special operations version for the USAF. Based on the UH-60 but with aerial refuelling capability and internal auxiliary fuel, mission-unique communication and navigation equipment (including AN/APN-239 radar, Doppler, inertial navigation, Tacan, map display, secure HF and satellite communications), fast rope system, 7.62-mm and 0.50-ins calibre armament, and tow plates to facilitate air transportability. Empty weight 12,330 lb (5,593 kg), maximum take-off/landing

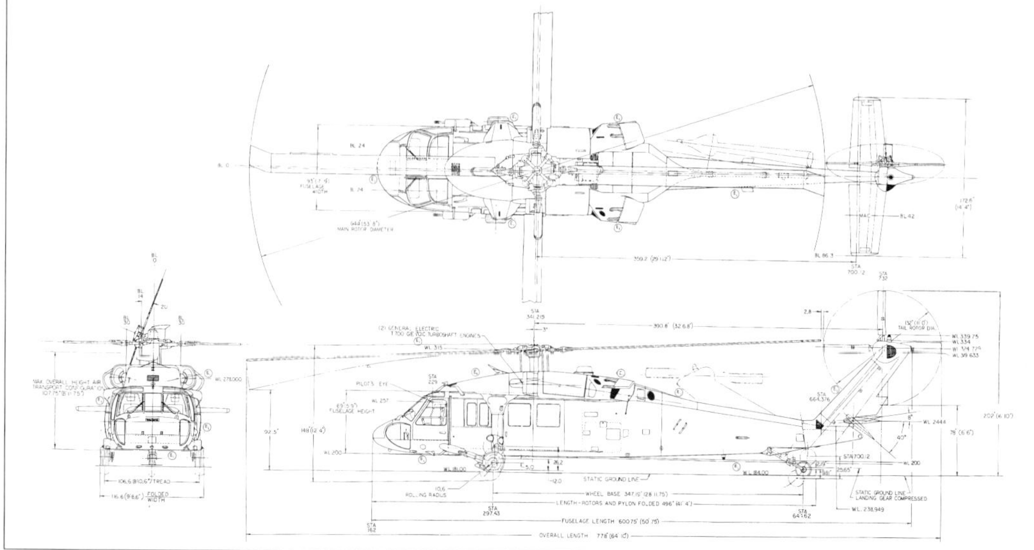
↑ Sikorsky UH-60L Black Hawk general arrangement

Details for UH-60L Black Hawk

PRINCIPAL DIMENSIONS:
Rotor diameter (main): 53 ft 8 ins (16.36 m)
Maximum length, rotors turning: 64 ft 10 ins (19.76 kg)
Fuselage length: 50 ft 0.75 ins (15.26 m)
Length, rotors and pylon folded: 41 ft 4 ins (12.6 m)
Fuselage width: 7 ft 9 ins (2.36 m)
Maximum height: 16 ft 10 ins (5.13 m)
Air-transportable height: 8 ft 11.75 ins (2.74 m)

CABIN:
Length: 12 ft 7 ins (3.84 m)
Width: 6 ft 2 ins (1.88 m)
Height: 4 ft 6 ins (1.37 m)
Volume: 410 cu ft (11.6 m^3)

MAIN ROTOR:
Blade chord: 1 ft 8.75 ins (0.53 m)
Blade area: each 46.7 sq ft (4.34 m^2)
Rotor disc: 2,262 sq ft (210.147 m^2)

TAIL ROTOR:
Diameter: 11 ft (3.35 m)
Cant angle: 20 ° inward

UNDERCARRIAGE:
Type: Fixed tailwheel type. Some are ski equipped
Main wheel tyre size: 26 × 10.0-11
Tail wheel tyre size: 15 × 6.0-6
Wheel base: 28 ft 11.75 ins (8.83 m)
Wheel track: 8 ft 10.6 ins (2.7 m)

WEIGHTS:
Empty: 11,605 lb (5,263 kg)
Mission gross weight: 17,527 lb (7,950 kg)
Maximum alternate gross weight: 22,000 lb (9,979 kg)
Maximum alternate gross weight, external load above 8,000 lb (3,629 kg): 23,500 lb (10,659 kg)
Maximum take-off, ferry flight: 24,500 lb (11,113 kg)
Payload: 9,000 lb (4,082 kg) external sling load

PERFORMANCE:
Never-exceed speed (V_{NE}): 195 kts (225 mph) 361 km/h
Maximum cruise speed: 153 kts (176 mph) 283 km/h at 4,000 ft (1,220 m) and 35° C, or 159 kts (183 mph) 294 km/h at 2,000 ft (610 m) and 21° C, or 155 kts (178 mph) 287 km/h at sea level
Cruise speed, OEI: 112 kts (129 mph) 207 km/h
Vertical climb rate: 963 ft (293 m) per minute at 95% IRP, or 1,440 ft (439 m) per minute at 95% MRP at 4,000 ft (1,220 m) and 35° C, or 2,750 ft (838 m) per minute at 2,000 ft (610 m) and 21° C, or over 3,000 ft (915 m) per minute at sea level
IGE hovering ceiling: 9,500 ft (2,895 m) at 35° C
OGE hovering ceiling: 7,650 ft (2,332 m) at 35° C, or 9,375 ft (2,858 m) at 21° C, or 11,125 ft (3,390 m) ISA
Service ceiling: 19,150 ft (5,837 m), ISA
Self-deployment range: 1,150 naut miles (1,324 miles) 2,130 km
Duration: 2.3 hours

weight 22,000 lb (9,979 kg), and ferry weight 24,500 lb (11,113 kg). $V_{MCP}/V_{BR}/V_{BE}$ 150/135/79 kts respectively, service ceiling 14,200 ft (4,328 m), and hovering ceiling OGE 4,000 ft (1,220 m) at 35°C and mid-mission point or 4,300 ft (1,310 m) ISA. Maximum range 504 naut miles. 103 produced for dual combat search and rescue and special operations, but 82 were later redesignated HH-60Gs for combat rescue.

MH-60K special operations helicopter for the US Army has a useful load of 10,000 lb (4,536 kg), 1,363-2,271 litres of internal and 1,741 litres of external fuel, a 130 kts maximum cruise speed, 120 kts best range speed, and range without refuelling of 755 naut miles. Superseded the MH-60A with the 160th Special Operations Aviation Regiment. 4 crew plus 12 troops with no internal auxiliary fuel or 7 troops with internal auxiliary fuel. Based on the UH-60A, but with UH-60L-type engines/transmission. Fully integrated cockpits and avionics, night/all-weather capability, precise navigation, aerial refuelling, digital automatic flight control computer with coupled automatic approach/depart/hover functions, and electromagnetic environment protection compatible with shipborne operations. AN/APQ-174A radar. FLIR. Full self-protection systems, including missile and laser warning, infra-red and radio jammers, chaff/flare dispensers, 0.50-ins calibre guns, and can mount Stinger AAMs.

MH-60L special operations version, see AH-60L.

UH-60A Black Hawk was the original US Army assault transport version, with 1,560 shp (1,163 kW) T700-GE-700 engines. Maximum gross weight 20,250 lb (9,185 kg) , but with a 24,500 lb (11,113 kg) maximum weight for ferrying. Same roles as noted for UH-60L.

UH-60C is a US Army command and control version under evaluation, following the modification of earlier UH-60As for a similar role as **UH-60A(C)s**.

UH-60J is a Japanese (Mitsubishi built) combat search and rescue helicopter for the Air and Maritime Self Defence forces. Variant of the S-70A but with T700-IHI-401C turboshafts.

UH-60L Black Hawk is the current US Army assault transport helicopter, having superseded the UH-60A in production in 1989. As detailed. 24% more power and new gearbox. Can carry a fully equipped 11-man infantry squad in 4,000 ft (1,220 m) elevations and 35° C temperatures and operate in climates from the desert to arctic.

UH-60P is the South Korean assembled (Korean Air) equivalent of UH-60L. Variant of the S-70A.

UH-60Q (Dustoff – Dedicated Unhesitating Service To Our Fighting Forces) is a required US Army medevac version (6 litters and medical equipment) with a high standard of navigation equipment including Doppler with embedded GPS, stormscope, and inertial navigation. Litton smart multi-function displays in the 'glass' cockpit. Other equipment includes SINCGARS radio subsystem, FLIR, searchlight and self-protection systems. Prototype evaluated 1993-94. Up to 87 conversions from UH-60As required, with a contract of February 1996 covering the first 2 and 2 more ordered thereafter for qualification trials.

VH-60N White Hawk Presidential transport; 9 VIP transports with the US Marine Corps.

Firehawk is a new aerial firefighting version being developed in co-operation with the US Army and Army National Guard.

↑ USAF Sikorsky HH-60G Pave Hawk, featuring in-flight refuelling probe, increased internal fuel, fuel management panel, upgraded navigation systems and colour weather/mapping radar

↑ Royal Thai Navy S-70B-7, operating from the offshore patrol helicopter carrier *Chakkrinruebet*

Demonstrator being produced in 1998 by converting a UH-60L. Removable 3,785 litre water or retardant tank being fitted, fabricated by Aero Union Corp. Extended undercarriage for increased ground clearance.

S-70A is the international variant of the UH-60. Design gross weight 16,825 lb (7,632 kg), and maximum gross weight 22,000 lb (9,979 kg). T700-GE-701A engines.

S-70C is similar to the S-70A/UH-60 but commercially certified and offered for both civil and military use. 24 went to China as S-70C-2s but were withdrawn from use through lack of spares. 14 went to Taiwan as utility helicopters for the Air Force. S-70C(M)-1s have also gone to Taiwan (Navy) as Thunderhawks for ASW, with APS-128 radar, dipping sonar and ESM. General Electric CT7-2 engines. 2 delivered to the UK (to GKN Westland as WS-70L and Rolls-Royce), with the GKN-Westland helicopter transferred to Bahrain.

Sikorsky S-70B and SH-60B Seahawk and derivatives

First flight: 12 December 1979.

Role: All-weather, autonomous anti-submarine (ASW) and anti-surface surveillance and targeting (ASST) for Seahawk, with secondary vertrep, SAR, communications relay and medevac. See Aircraft variants for roles of derivatives.

Development

■ Derivative of the Army UH-60 Black Hawk, to meet the US Navy LAMPS III requirement for a shipborne light multi-purpose helicopter. 5 prototypes.

Details *(SH-60B Seahawk, except under Sales and Aircraft variants)*

Sales: To US Navy and Coast Guard, Spain, Australia, Japan, Taiwan, Greece, Thailand and Turkey; see Aircraft variants. Total SH-60B, F and J deliveries by June 1998 were 310, including 7 during 1997 and 2 in 1998 (by June). Total deliveries of HH-60H and J by 1998 were 84, with 9 in 1996 and none in 1997.

Crew: 3, as the pilot and co-pilot/airborne tactical officer in the cockpit, and sensor operator in the main cabin. No seat armour. Dual controls.

Cabin access: Starboard sliding door to main cabin.

Standard equipment: 6,000 lb (2,721 kg) capacity cargo hook, and 600 lb (272 kg) capacity rescue hoist. RAST (recovery assist, secure and traverse) system for assisted landing and stowage on deck.

Rotor system: Similar to Black Hawk. Electric blade folding and rotor brake.

Airframe materials: Similar to Black Hawk but with anti-corrosion features compatible with seaborne operations. Tail folds for stowage.

Engines: 2 General Electric T700-GE-401C turboshafts.

Engine rating: Each 1,870 shp (1,394 kW) maximum, 1,620 shp (1,208 kW) continuous, and 1,940 shp (1,447 kW) contingency.

Transmission rating: 3,400 shp (2,535 kW).

Fuel system: 2,233 litres standard. 2 × 454 litre auxiliary tanks. Capable of hover refuelling.

Radar: Raytheon Systems AN/APS-124 search radar with undernose radome.

Flight avionics/instrumentation: Communications include AN/ARC-159(V)2 UHF and AN/ARC-174(V)2 HF radio, Sierra Research AN/ARQ-44 data link for tactical link with the parent ship's ATACO (the ship can operate the helicopter's radar and acoustic processor, relaying data back to the helicopter via the 2-way data link), and IFF transponders. Navigation systems include AN/ARN-118(V) Tacan, AN/APN-217 Doppler radar, AN/ARA-50 UHF/DF, radar altimeter and provision for GPS. Raytheon Systems radar (see above) and AN/ASQ-81(V)2 MAD bird carried on a tailboom pylon, launchers on port side of fuselage for 25 passive or active sonobuoys of several types, Rospatch AN/AAR-94 99-channel receiver, AN/UYS-2 acoustic processor (with selectable full-band, quarter-band and eighth-band verniers), AN/ALQ-142 ESM in corner-nose pods (offers passive surface contacts), and magnetic tape memory unit. Some have AN/AAS-44 forward-looking infra-red sensors with laser designators (compatible with Hellfire) or other FLIR. See Aircraft variants for avionics/equipment of other variants. See also Black Hawk entry for new 'glass' cockpit.

Expendable weapons and equipment: Up to 3 × Mk 46 or Mk 50 torpedoes, or Penguin AGM-119B (Mk 2 Mod 7) anti-ship missiles interfacing with the MIL-STD-1553B digital databus architecture. Hellfire anti-armour missiles integrated from 1996 for small targets (trials conducted with an M299 launcher at Patuxent River test centre).

Aircraft variants:

CH-60 is a US Navy fleet combat support helicopter, based on a UH-60L airframe but featuring SH-60F dynamics, AFCS, and blade and tail folding. First flown as a modified UH-60L demonstrator on 6 October 1997. Up to 250 required for vertrep, special warfare, combat SAR and utility to supersede older helicopters including the Sea King and Sea Knight , with 42 ordered under fiscal years 1999-2001.

HH-60H is a combat search and rescue/special warfare support helicopter, entering US Navy service in 1989. Primary mission for special warfare support is a 200 naut mile radius of action with 8 troops, mid-mission hover at 3,000 ft (915 m) at 35° C and 147 kts cruise. Primary mission for combat SAR (strike recovery) is 250 naut miles radius, 4 survivors, and same hover/cruise. Communications are dual UHF/VHF/FM radios, HF radio, IFF and VHF/UHF/HF/IFF crypto computers. Navigation and tactical data systems as for SH-60F. Mission subsystems are 6,000 lb (2,721 kg) cargo hook, NVG compatible lighting, rescue hoist, 2 × M60D 7.62-mm machine-guns, and automatic approach, coupled hover and automatic departure. Survivability systems are IR jammer, 2 chaff/flare dispensers, radar and laser warning receivers, missile plume detector, AN/ARD-6 emergency locator, and hover IR suppressor system (HIRSS). New increase in armament includes

↑ The latest Sikorsky CH-60 US Navy fleet combat support helicopter, during vertrep evaluation

Hellfire anti-armour missiles on M299 launchers, 2.75-ins rocket launchers, and gun pods. 42 delivered.
HH-60J Jayhawk is a medium range recovery (MMR) multi-mission helicopter for the US Coast Guard, for offshore SAR, law enforcement, drug interdiction, logistics, aids to navigation, marine environment protection and military readiness. 4 crew and 6 survivors for SAR. Compatible with helicopter decks of Hamilton and Bear class cutters. Navigation systems include AlliedSignal RDR-1300C search/weather radar, Doppler radar, AHRS, VHF/UHF ADF, Tacan, Tacnav, radar altimeter, VOR/ILS, LF/ADF and GPS. Mission data systems comprise dual redundant mission computers, MIL-STD-1553B digital data bus architecture, multi-function keypad access, and cockpit video displays. Same communications as HH-60H. Mission subsystems comprise rescue hoist, automatic approach/coupled hover/automatic departure, and third external pylon station for fuel. Triple redundant hydraulic and electrical systems. 300 naut mile radius of action. First flown 8 August 1989 and delivered from March 1990. 42 delivered.

Details for SH-60B Seahawk, *unless stated*

PRINCIPAL DIMENSIONS:
Rotor diameter (main): 53 ft 8 ins (16.36 m)
Maximum length, rotors turning: 64 ft 10 ins (19.76 m)
Fuselage length: 50 ft 0.75 ins (15.26 m)
Length, folded: 41 ft 0.6 ins (12.5 m)
Width, folded: 10 ft 9 ins (3.28 m)
Maximum height: 17 ft 2 ins (5.23 m) over tail rotor
Height, folded: 13 ft 3 ins (4.04 m)

CABIN: See Black Hawk

TAIL ROTOR:
Diameter: 11 ft (3.35 m)

UNDERCARRIAGE:
Type: Similar to Black Hawk, but with twin tailwheels moved forward towards cabin. Emergency flotation gear
Wheel base: 15 ft 10 ins (4.83 m)
Wheel track: 8 ft 10.6 ins (2.7 m)

WEIGHTS:
Empty, operating: 13,648 lb (6,190 kg)
Mission maximum take-off: 21,110 lb (9,575 kg) for ASW, 19,226 lb (8,721 kg) ASST
Maximum take-off: 21,884 lb (9,927 kg)
Payload: 4,100 lb (1,860 kg) internal, 6,000 lb (2,721 kg) external

PERFORMANCE:
Dash speed: 145 kts (167 mph) 268 km/h
Cruise speed (HH-60J): 146 kts (168 mph) 270 km/h
Vertical climb rate: 700 ft (213 m) per minute at sea level, 32 °C
Vertical climb rate, OEI: 450 ft (137 m) per minute at sea level, 32 °C
Radius of action (HH-60J): 300 naut miles (345 miles) 555 km
Duration: 3.5 to 6 hours
On-station time (HH-60J): 1 hour 30 minutes at 300 naut mile radius for interdiction role, or 45 minutes for MRR role

SH-60B Seahawk was the first production version for the US Navy, first flying in LAMPS III production form on 11 February 1983, with the initial delivery on 24 March that year to HSL-41. Equipment integration by IBM (becoming Loral Federal Systems Division). Eventual upgrading to SH-60R anticipated. 188 delivered. As detailed.
SH-60F is a CV Helo variant of Seahawk for the US Navy, intended for close-quarter (inner zone) ASW protection for aircraft carrier battle groups. Deployed from 1991. Primary mission is with 4 crew, 1 internal and 1 external auxiliary fuel tank and 2 × Mk 50 torpedoes (can carry 3), at 21,800 lb (9,888 kg) take-off, offering a dash speed of 133 kts and a 4.2 hour endurance at sea level, tropical day. Mission equipment comprises AN/AQS-13F dipping sonar with AN/UYS-2 digital acoustic processing and 1,500 ft (457 m) depth capability, sonobuoy launcher and storage carousel, 99-channel sonobuoy receiver, on-board sonobuoy processing, and mission tape recorder system. Mission subsystems are rescue hoist, automatic approach, coupled hover and automatic departure. Communications are dual UHF/VHF/FM radios, HF radio and tactical data link. Navigation systems comprise Tacan, Tacnav, Doppler radar, radar altimeter and provision for GPS. Tactical data systems are dual redundant AN/ASN-150 mission computers, MIL-STD-1553B digital databus architecture, multi-function keypad access and cockpit video displays. 74 helicopters. To be withdrawn over coming years and converted into SH-60Rs and extra HH-60Hs.
SH-60J is the Mitsubishi-built S-70B-3 with T700-IHI-401C engines, for ship- (Yukikaze class destroyers) and shore-based ASW with the JMSDF. RAST equipped. Production continuing.
SH-60R is the combined designation of SH-60Bs and Fs after upgrade starting 1998 into a single new variant for LAMPS and CV Helo operations, featuring Raytheon and Thomson Sintra developed AN/AQS-22 Airborne Low Frequency Sonar (ALFS) dipping sonar system with high-speed reel, Raytheon transmitter/receiver and AN/UYS-2 acoustic processor, interfacing through a MIL-STD-1553B databus with colour high-resolution displays. AN/APS-147 radar, AN/AAS-44 FLIR/laser ranger, AN/AYK-14 computer and new ESM are among other changes. 7.62-mm gun. IOC in the year 2002.
S-70B is the international variant of Seahawk, as the S-70B-1 with AQS-13F dipping sonar for the Spanish Navy (6, designated HS.23); S-70B-2 with role adaptable weapon system (RAWS) for the Royal Australian Navy and fitted with Racal Super Searcher radar and a full range of other avionics including internal ASQ–504(V) MAD and DHS-901 data link (16, half built in Australia; being upgraded with FLIR and ESM); S-70B-6 Aegean Hawk for the Hellenic Navy (6 plus 2 more ordered) with APS-143(V)3 radar, AQS-18(V)3 dipping sonar and ESM ; S-70B-7 for the Royal Thai Navy for maritime patrol and SAR (6 for the Navy as shipborne helicopters tailored to its own definition of sea control, initially for SAR, maritime patrol and coastal surveillance); and S-70B-28 for the Turkish Navy (4 ordered, delivery in the year 2000, with 4 more under negotiation at the time of writing; total eventual requirement reportedly for 28). Fairey Hydraulics Decklock system is under trial for the S-70B.
Aegean Hawk, see S-70B-6 above.
S-70C(M)1 Thunderhawk is the Taiwanese Navy ASW variant with APS-128PC radar, AQS-18(V) dipping sonar and AN/ALR-66(V)2 ESM. 10 built, with at least 2 modified for sigint.

Sikorsky S-76 series

First flight: 13 March 1977 for S-76A.
Certification: November 1978 for S-76A to FAR 29. 1996 for S-76C+.
First delivery: 1979 for S-76A. 23 July 1996 for latest S-76C+, to Norsk Helikopter.
Role: Civil/military passenger and utility transport, offshore work, medevac, search and rescue, and training.
Sales: 473 of all versions delivered by June 1998, including 18 in 1997 and 7 in 1998 (1996 deliveries included 6 S-76Bs to the Royal Thai Navy). S-76C+ selected in 1998 to replace Wessex HCC.Mk 4s for the British Royal Household, now operated by Air Hanson under a 10-year lease arrangement. Users of the S-76C include several commercial operators, the former Royal Hong Kong Auxiliary Air Force (2), Spanish Air Force (8 for IFR pilot training) and the Japan Maritime Safety Agency (2 in 1994-95 for SAR). Lloyd Helicopter Group operates 5 S-76s with SPZ-7600 for SAR on behalf of the RAAF.

Details *(for the S-76C+)*

Crew/passengers: 1 (for VFR configuration) or 2 (for IFR) crew plus 12-13 passengers (14 persons in total) or 4 or more in executive/business layouts, or 2 litters and 4 seats. 4 crew in SAR configuration.
Freight, internal: Baggage compartment area 38 cu ft (1.08 m^3).
Cabin access: Optional sliding cabin doors (instead of normal hinged) can be opened in flight up to 125 kts.
Optional equipment: Includes dual controls, external cargo hook, SX-16 Nightsun 360° searchlight, 600 lb (272 kg) capacity and 200 ft (61 m) long rescue hoist.
Rotor system: 4-blade fully-articulated main rotor. Each blade has a 30° swept tip and comprises a titanium spar, Nomex honeycomb core and composites trailing edge and skins, with titanium/nickel leading-edge anti-erosion strip. High twist. Bifilar vibration damper system over rotor head. Blade de-icing. Monobloc titanium rotor head with elastomeric bearings and hydraulic drag dampers. Optional manual blade folding and rotor brake.

↑ Sikorsky S-76C+, the latest version of the S-76 series, with Arriel 2S1 engines

Tail rotor characteristics: Cross-beam layout, with 2 separate superimposed 2-blade composite rotors set at 90°.
Tail surfaces: 10 ft (3.05 m) span horizontal stabilizer.
Flight control system: Hydraulic.
Airframe materials: Metal, but with many composite non-structural components.
Engines: 2 Turbomeca Arriel 2S1 turboshafts. Optional particle separators.
Engine rating: Each 980 shp (731 kW) for 30 seconds emergency OEI at sea level, 889 shp (663 kW) for 2 minutes OEI at sea level, 856 shp (638 kW) take-off at sea level, and 794 shp (592 kW) maximum continuous and maximum cruise.
Transmission rating: 1,600 shp (1,193 kW) take-off and maximum continuous.
Fuel system: 1,064 litres standard. 208 litre auxiliary tank available.
Electrical system: DC supply via a transmission-driven 7.5 kVA generator and AC via a static inverter for IFR-equipped helicopters when more electrical power is required. 2 × 200 amp starter-generators when VFR equipped. 17 amp-hour ni-cd battery standard, with optional 34 amp-hour.
Hydraulic system: 3,000 psi.
Radar: At customer's request. For SAR is typically a Honeywell Primus 700/701 radar with precision surface mapping, weather detection and beacon mode.
Flight avionics/instrumentation: VFR or IFR (Cat A IFR for FAR Part 29 requirements). Available avionics include Honeywell SPZ-7600 dual digital AFCS with fully coupled autopilot, automatic search/mark on target and approach to hover, and Doppler coupled hover (also controllable by a hoist operator for SAR); EFIS complete flight profile and multi-faceted display system; Racal R-Nav-2; and FLIR for search and rescue. Other choices, at customer's request, include different AFCS, DME, ADF, radar altimeter, and so on. New GEC-Marconi Health and Usage Monitoring System (HUMS) installation for S-76+ was certified in October 1997 by the British and Norwegian civil aviation authorities, as an adaptation of HUMS installed in S-76A+ and S-76C, and first delivered on an S-76C+ to Norsk Helikopter AS of Sola, Norway.
Expendable weapons and equipment: See H-76 Eagle (below).

Details for S-76C+

PRINCIPAL DIMENSIONS:
Rotor diameter (main): 44 ft (13.41 m)
Maximum length, rotors turning: 52 ft 6 ins (16 m)
Fuselage length: 43 ft 4 ins (13.22 m)
Fuselage width: 7 ft (2.13 m)
Width, including horizontal stabilizer: 10 ft (3.05 m)
Maximum height: 14 ft 6 ins (4.42 m) over tail rotor, or 11 ft 9 ins (3.58 m) over main rotor hub

CABIN:
Length: 8 ft 1 ins (2.46 m)
Width: 6 ft 4 ins (1.93 m)
Height: 4 ft 5 ins (1.35 m)
Floor area: 45 sq ft (4.18 m^2)
Volume: 204 cu ft (5.78 m^3)

MAIN ROTOR:
Blade chord: 1 ft 3.5 ins (0.39 m)
Rotor disc: 1,520.53 sq ft (141.262 m^2)

TAIL ROTOR:
Diameter: 8 ft (2.44 m)

UNDERCARRIAGE:
Type: Retractable, with nosewheel. Optional low pressure tyres and emergency flotation gear
Main wheel tyre size: 14.5 × 5.5-6
Nose wheel tyre size: 13 × 5.0-4
Wheel base: 16 ft 5 ins (5 m)
Wheel track: 8 ft (2.44 m)

WEIGHTS:
Empty, Deluxe executive configuration: 8,138 lb (3,691 kg)
Maximum take-off: 11,700 lb (5,307 kg)
Useful load: 3,562 lb (1,616 kg)

PERFORMANCE:
Never-exceed speed (V_{NE}) and maximum cruise: 155 kts (178 mph) 287 km/h
Long-range cruise speed: 140 kts (161 mph) 259 km/h
Best climb rate: 1,625 ft (495 m) per minute at sea level
IGE hovering ceiling: 5,650 ft (1,722 m)
OGE hovering ceiling: 1,800 ft (549 m)
Service ceiling: 12,700 ft (3,871 m)
Service ceiling, OEI: 3,200 ft (975 m), 30 minute power
Range: 439 naut miles (506 miles) 813 km at 140 kts and 4,000 ft (1,220 m), standard fuel, ISA, no reserve, or 385 naut miles (443 miles) 713 km at the same speed and altitude, with 30 minutes reserve

Aircraft variants:
H-76 Eagle appeared in 1985 in armed multi-role and naval versions as a military variant of the S-76B. Wide range of specialized mission avionics available, including mast or roof mounted sighting system with laser rangefinder, FLIR, HUD, and self-protection warning, jamming and other systems. Provision for armoured crew seats and self-sealing fuel tanks. Multi-purpose pylon system (MPPS) for the carriage of TOW or Hellfire anti-armour missiles, anti-ship missiles and torpedoes, Stinger AAMs, rockets, guns and mine dispensers and more. No known purchasers.
S-76A was the initial production model with 650 shp (484.7 kW) Allison 250-C30 turboshaft engines. Variants included the Mark II with detail changes that included those to improve maintenance and provide slightly higher engine and transmission ratings, and the Utility. Subsequent Arriel turboshaft retrofits to existing S-76s produced the S-76A+. Out of production.
S-76B has Pratt & Whitney Canada PT6B-36A turboshafts, each 981 shp (731.5 kW) at take-off, for better performance and payload in hot-and-high applications. Can use Honeywell SPZ-7000 digital AFCS with EFIS or similar.
S-76C introduced French Arriel 1S1 engines, offering greater payload and enhanced reliability without sacrificing range. Retains the increased structural gross weight capability and uprated drive train of the S-76B.
S-76C+ is the latest version, said to be able to carry more payload over longer distances and at faster speeds, while using less fuel than other intermediate-class helicopters. Arriel 2S1 engines.
S-76N is the naval equivalent of the H-76, based on the S-76B. Sikorsky refers to Royal Thai S-76Ns as S-76Bs.

Sikorsky S-80, CH-53E Super Stallion and MH-53E Sea Dragon

First flight: 1 March 1974 for Super Stallion.
First delivery: CH-53Es from 16 June 1981.
Role: Heavy-lift transport, amphibious assault and vertical on-board delivery (VOD) for Super Stallion, and principally mine countermeasures for Sea Dragon.
Sales: 232 CH-53E and MH-53E types delivered by June 1998, including 4 in 1997 and 1 CH-53E in 1998, mostly to the US Marine Corps and Navy, but with 11 S-80Ms delivered to Japan from 1989-1994.

Details *(CH-53E Super Stallion, except where indicated)*

Crew/passengers: 3 crew and 55 troops for all models, including Sea Dragon if required. Alternative payloads include freight internally or sling loads including crippled aircraft for deck-clearing or recovery.
Freight, external: 36,000 lb (16,329 kg) cargo hook.
Cabin access: Hydraulic rear ramp/door for straight-in loading/unloading.
Rotor system: 7-blade fully-articulated main rotor. Blades, with 14° twist, have titanium spar, Nomex honeycomb core and composites skins. Steel/titanium rotor head. Rotor brake. Hydraulic blade folding. "Blade inspection method" spar-cracking detection system.
Tail rotor characteristics: 4-blade rotor, mounted on the port side of a 20° outward-canted large fin. Aluminium alloy blades. Rotor position provides lift as well as anti-torque forces, and increases the CG range.
Tail surfaces: Composites fin. Strut-braced, tapering horizontal stabilizer to starboard. Stabilizer is cranked to allow for the angle of the fin. Area of the fin would permit controlled landing in the event of tail rotor loss or failure.
Flight control system: Hydraulic.
Fuselage: Sealed, to allow flotation in an emergency alighting. Hydraulic tail folding for ship stowage.
Airframe materials: Principally metal, but with composites cockpit area and fairings.
Engines: 3 General Electric T64-GE-416 turboshafts. 4,750 shp (3,542 kW) T64-GE-419s are expected to be installed in a CH/MH retrofit programme. APU.
Engine rating: Each 4,380 shp (3,266 kW).
Transmission rating: 13,140 shp (9,798 kW).
Fuel system: 3,850 litres. Provision for 2 × 2,460 litre auxiliary tanks on the sponsons. In-flight refuelling and hover refuelling to extend range and self deploy.
Flight refuelling probe: 21 ft 11.5 ins (6.7 m), retracting to 10 ft 6 ins (3.2 m).
Electrical system: 115 volt AC supply via 3 alternators, at 400 Hz. 28 volt DC supply via 2 × 200 amp transformer rectifiers.
Hydraulic system: 3,000 psi; 4,000 psi for engine start-up system.
Flight avionics/instrumentation: AFCS with 4-axis autopilot and dual digital automatic flight control system computers, complete with automatic approach and departure from a coupled hover features. Some retrofitted with AN/APN-217 Doppler, FLIR and GPS. Future upgrades might include colour displays, AHRS, Omega and ground proximity warning system.

↑ Sikorsky CH-53E Super Stallion operated by the USMC

Self-protection systems: Expected to receive missile warning and chaff/flare systems.
Fixed guns: See Aircraft variants.
Expendable weapons and equipment: Sidewinder AAMs have been tested for self protection.

Aircraft variants:
CH-53E Super Stallion is the US Marine Corps/US Navy heavy-lift transport version, as detailed.

Details for CH-53E, *with MH-53E in italics where different*

PRINCIPAL DIMENSIONS:
Rotor diameter (main): 79 ft (24.08 m)
Maximum length, rotors turning: 99 ft 0.5 ins (30.18 m)
Length, folded: 60 ft 6 ins (18.44 m)
Fuselage length: 73 ft 4 ins (22.35 m)
Fuselage width: 8 ft 10 ins (2.69 m)
Maximum width (excluding rotors): 23 ft 11 ins (7.29 m), *27 ft 7 ins (8.41 m)*
Width, folded: 28 ft 5 ins (8.66 m)
Maximum height: 28 ft 4 ins (8.64 m)
Height, folded: 18 ft 7 ins (5.66 m)

CABIN:
Length: 30 ft (9.14 m)
Width: 7 ft 6 ins (2.29 m)
Height: 6 ft 6 ins (1.98 m)

MAIN ROTOR:
Blade chord: 2 ft 6 ins (0.76 m)
Rotor disc: 4,901.7 sq ft (455.383 m^2)

TAIL ROTOR:
Diameter: 20 ft (6.1 m)
Cant angle: 20°

UNDERCARRIAGE:
Type: Retractable, with castoring nosewheels. Twin wheels on each unit
Wheel base: 27 ft 3 ins (8.31 m)
Wheel track: 13 ft (3.96 m)

WEIGHTS:
Empty: 33,373 lb (15,138 kg), *36,336 lb (16,482 kg)*
Maximum take-off: 69,750 lb (31,638 kg)
Maximum take-off, external load: 73,500 lb (33,339 kg)
Payload: 32,000 lb (14,515 kg) basic mission
Useful load (MH-53E): *26,000 lb (11,793 kg) influence sweep mission*

PERFORMANCE:
Maximum speed: 170 kts (196 mph) 315 km/h at sea level
Cruise speed: 150 kts (173 mph) 278 km/h at sea level
Maximum climb rate: 2,500 ft (762 m) per minute with a 25,000 lb (11,340 kg) payload
IGE hovering ceiling: 11,550 ft (3,520 m)
OGE hovering ceiling: 9,500 ft (2,896 m)
Ceiling: 18,500 ft (5,659 m)

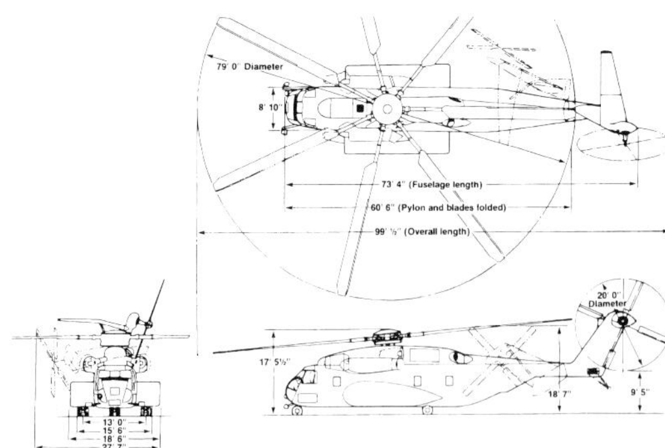

↑ Sikorsky MH-53E Sea Dragon general arrangement *(courtesy Sikorsky)*

MH-53E Sea Dragon is a US Navy airborne mine countermeasures (AMCM) helicopter based on the CH-53E, primarily to sweep mined areas to free a shipping lane. Has extra large composites sponsons, each holding 6,056 litres of fuel to permit a 4-hour towing mission, plus reserve. Internal range extension tanks (7 × 1,136 litre) are available. To increase response time and offer self-deployment, a flight refuelling probe is provided. Internal 30,000 lb (13,600 kg) tension tow boom and hydraulic winch for deployment of minesweeping systems. Specialized electrical, hydraulic (additional hydraulic system for AMCM gear) and environmental control systems, and dual digital automatic flight control system computers, complete with automatic tow-tension and skew-angle hold while under tow, and automatic approach and departure from a coupled hover features. Can tow mechanical, acoustic and magnetic hydrofoil sweeping gear through the water. Folding blades and tail pylon. Can also perform vertical on-board delivery (VOD). Can carry a cabin gun. Upgrade has begun to retrofit GPS, 2 horizontal situation colour displays and mission data loader. Delivered from 26 June 1986 and initially operated by HM-14. First sea deployment began on 9 December 1989.
S-80E is the international export version of CH-53E.
S-80M is the international export version of MH-53E.

Sikorsky S-92 Helibus

First flight: 1998 at West Palm Beach Development Flight Center.
Certification: 2000 to FAR/JAR 29.
First delivery: 2001.
Role: Civil and military medium passenger and cargo transport, aeromedical, offshore, search and rescue, resource development support and utility helicopter.

Development

■ 12 June 1995. Full-scale development launched. Sikorsky responsible for design, and manufacture of the dynamic systems, plus final assembly, flight test and certification. Risk-sharing partners are Jingdezhen Helicopters Corporation of China/CATIC (2%, responsible for the tail unit), Mitsubishi of Japan (7.5%, responsible for the centre fuselage), and AIDC of Taiwan (6.5%, responsible for the cockpit including windows, electrical harnesses and hydraulic lines, equipment cooling and environmental ducts), Embraer of Brazil (4%, providing the sponsons with fuel cells, gauging systems and undercarriage), and Gamesa of Spain (7%, providing the aft transition tailcones and strongback composite structures as sliding pylons and upper deck fairings, complete with supporting hardware and the titanium and aluminium supporting structures).
■ February 1998. First 3 of 5 Helibus prototypes in final assembly.
■ 15 February 1998. Sikorsky announced it was launching business discussions with prospective customers.
■ 9-11 June 1998. First prototype transported to Florida for ground testing.

Details

Sales: 3 S-92A and 2 S-92A International prototypes. Expected price about US$12.5-$13 million. Anticipated market for 240 S-92s in the near term, both civil and military. Offered to Canada as a possible SAR helicopter. Potential customers include Hong Kong, Denmark, Finland, Norway and Sweden. Sikorsky expects to deliver about 6 helicopters in 2001, followed by up to 48 per year thereafter.
Crew/passengers: 2 flight crew and 19-22 passengers (3 abreast) with 30 ins (76.2 cm) seat pitch, with 7 cabin windows per side. Martin Baker crashworthy/energy-absorbing seats for crew and passengers. Alternatively, 12 or 16 litters in medical layout. See Freight, internal.
Optional equipment: Includes Lucas Aerospace rescue hoist.
Cabin/cabin access: Active vibration control. Military/utility version with rear ramp/door loading and only 2 cabin windows per side.
Freight, internal: Square-section cabin, large enough for 3 LD3 standard containers or 2 LD3s and 4 standard pallets in the S-92A International. Door plates can be turned over to provide rollers for freight loading in S-92A International.
Freight, external: 10,000 lb (4,536 kg) sling load for the S-92A International and military versions.
Rotor system: 4-blade main rotor, with shaft tilted 5°. New blades have advanced aerofoils, 30° and 20° tip-droop, and were first tested on a Black Hawk in December 1993. Blades have graphite spars and glassfibre skins, with graphite fittings. Titanium yoke rotorhead, with elastomeric bearings; expected 50,000 hour service life. Damping at mid-span.
Tail rotor characteristics: Fully articulated, developed from the Black Hawk rotor. Inward-canted rotor position provides lift as well as anti-torque forces, and increases the CG range. New intermediate gearbox and high-speed shafts. Tail rotor system can run dry for 30 minutes.
Tail surfaces: Tall integral fin and port strut-braced stabilizer.
Airframe: 40% by weight composites, including fuselage nose and roof, part of the pylon, stabilizer, sponsons and fairings. Semi-monocoque tailcone of aluminium construction, with composite fairings.
Engines: 2 General Electric CT7-6D turboshafts for the first 2 prototypes and CT7-8s for the remaining 3 prototypes, the latter being the certification configuration engines.
Engine rating: Each 1,750 shp (1,305 kW) for CT7-6Ds. For CT7-8s, ratings are 2,400 shp (1,790 kW) twin-engined take-off, 2,050 shp (1,529 kW) maximum continuous, and 2,500 shp (1,864 kW) OEI, all at sea level and ISA; or 1,900 shp (1,417 kW) twin-engined take-off, 1,450 shp (1,081 kW) maximum continuous, and 2,000 shp (1,491 kW) OEI for 30 seconds at 4,000 ft (1,219 m) and 35° C.
Transmission: New 4,170 shp (3,110 kW) 4-stage planetary gearbox, derated to 3,850 shp (2,871 kW) or 2,150 shp (1,603 kW) for 30 seconds OEI in S-92A form and 2,000 shp (1,491 kW) in International form. Lucas Aerospace couplings, comprising 2 high-speed input-drive, 5 tailrotor drive and a single flexible tailrotor driveshaft.
Fuel system: 2,196 litres, housed in crashworthy Aerazur self-sealing cells in the breakaway sponsons. Suction fuel system. Internal auxiliary tanks optional. International can also have bolt-on 870 litre external tanks.
Electrical system: Dual. AlliedSignal 36-150 APU to provide electrical and pneumatic power while on the ground or in flight, coupled to a generator.
Hydraulic system: Dual.
Flight avionics/instrumentation: Open/flexible avionics architecture, with integrated avionics via a MIL-STD-1553B data bus or ARINC 429 or other interface, with IFR. Hamilton Standard AFCS. 'Glass cockpit', incorporating Sanders (a Lockheed Martin Company) EFIS with 4 or optional 5 (when required for special missions) 6 ins × 8 ins (15.25 × 20.3 cm) colour active matrix liquid crystal multi-function displays, with 5 bezel soft-keys under displays, similar to that found on the C-130J. Hamilton Standard flight control computer/AFCS. GEC-Marconi HUMS (health usage monitoring system).

Details for S-92A, *unless stated, provisional/estimated*

PRINCIPAL DIMENSIONS:
Rotor diameter (main): 56 ft 4 ins (17.17 m)
Maximum length, rotors turning: 68 ft 5 ins (20.85 m)
Fuselage length: 56 ft 10 ins (17.32 m)
Fuselage width: 7 ft 1 ins (2.16 m)
Width over sponsons: 12 ft 9 ins (3.89 m)
Maximum height: 21 ft 2 ins (6.45 m)

CABIN:
Length: 18 ft 7 ins (5.67 m)
Width: 6 ft 7 ins (2 m)
Height: 6 ft (1.83 m)
Volume: 596 cu ft (16.877 m^3)
Baggage volume: 110 cu ft (3.1 m^3)

TAIL ROTOR:
Diameter: 11 ft (3.35 m)

UNDERCARRIAGE:
Type: Messier-Bugatti wheels and brakes. Retractable type, with twin wheels on each unit
Wheel base: 19 ft (5.79 m)
Wheel track: 11 ft 5 ins (3.48 m)

WEIGHTS:
Empty: 15,500 lb (7,030 kg) civil transport, or 15,200 lb (6,894 kg) international utility
Maximum take-off: 25,200 lb (11,430 kg) with internal load, with alternate gross weight of 26,500 lb (12,020 kg) with external load
Fuel: 4,000 lb (1,814 kg)
Payload: About 8,500 lb (3,855 lb) internal, 10,000 lb (4,536 kg) external

PERFORMANCE (provisional):
Cruise speed: 155 kts (178 mph) 287 km/h
Best range speed: 140 kts (161 mph) 259 km/h
G limits: +2.95, -1
IGE hovering ceiling: 11,600 ft (3,535 m)
OGE hovering ceiling: 7,300 ft (2,225 m)
Service ceiling: 15,000 ft (4,572 m)
Range: 490 naut miles (564 miles) 908 km with CT7-8 engines, with reserve

Aircraft variants:
S-92A (formerly S-92C) is the basic civil version, with CT7-8 engines in production form. Baggage volume 110 cu ft (3.1 m^3).
S-92A International (formerly S-92IU) is the basic utility version, with CT7-8 engines in production form. Civil certified, with military options including IR suppressors, ballistic protection and more.

↑ Sikorsky S-92As and S-92A Internationals under construction

SnoBird Aircraft Inc — USA

Comments: Details of the Adventurer 636D-4, Charger 582S, Exciter 503S and Stealth Charger 582SE can be found in the 1996-97 edition of *WA&SD*, page 364.

Sport Copter Inc — USA

Corporate address:
34012 North Honeyman Road, Scappoose, OR 97056.

Telephone: +1 503 543 7000
Facsimile: +1 503 543 7041
Web site: www.sportcopter.com

Sport Copter Lightning, Sport Copter II and Vortex

First flight: October 1993.
First delivery: November 1996.

Details *(Vortex, except under Sales and Aircraft variants)*

Role: Single-seat autogyro, with pilot on a composite Cyber seat. Room aft of seat for cargo/equipment.
Sales: Vortex kit costs US$15,400 (at the time of writing), requiring an estimated 120 working hours to assemble. Lightning kit costs US$10,495, requiring an estimated 50 hours to assemble. Sport Copter II costs US$27,500.
Rotor system: McCutchen Sky Wheels 2-blade, with steel spar, wooden core and aluminium alloy skins. Shock-mounted rotorhead. Standard pre-rotator. Optional rotor brake.
Tail surfaces: Large fin and rudder, and small horizontal stabilizer with endplates.
Airframe materials: Triangulated aluminium tubing structure, with glassfibre cockpit fairing.
Engine: Standard Rotax 582, or other engine including Rotax 618 or Subaru. 3-blade adjustable propeller.

↑ Sport Copter Vortex single-seat autogyro

Engine rating: 64.4 hp (48 kW) for standard engine.
Fuel system: 38 litres.
Flight instrumentation: Full instrumentation is available.

Aircraft variants:
Lightning is a single-seat ultralight autogyro with a Rotax 503 engine and 3:1 reduction gearbox. 19 litres of fuel. Similar general appearance to Vortex. Cyber seat. Weight 252 lb (114.3 kg). Maximum speed 55 kts (63 mph) 101 km/h, and range 69-87 naut miles (80-100 miles) 129-161 km.
Sport Copter II is a new 2-seat autogyro of very streamlined appearance, with a shock-absorbing undercarriage and a Subaru 2,200 cc converted automobile engine of 160 hp (119.3 kW). Maximum weight 1,300 lb (590 kg). Maximum speed 113 kts (130 mph) 209 km/h, and range 269 naut miles (310 miles) 499 km.
Vortex is a single-seat autogyro, as detailed. Optional rough-field package, floats and detachable folding mast.

Details for Vortex

PRINCIPAL DIMENSIONS:
Rotor diameter: 25 ft (7.62 m)
Fuselage length: 12 ft (3.66 m)
Width: 5 ft 11 ins (1.8 m)
Maximum height: 8 ft 4 ins (2.54 m)

MAIN ROTOR:
Rotor disc: 490.8 sq ft (45.6 m^2)

UNDERCARRIAGE:
Type: Fixed nosewheel type, with swing-arm nosewheel suspension. Toe-operated differential hydraulic disc brakes. Optional Lotus floats

WEIGHTS:
Empty: 325 lb (147.5 kg)
Maximum take-off: 760 lb (345 kg)

PERFORMANCE:
Maximum speed: 87 kts (100 mph) 115 km/h
Cruise speed: 69 kts (80 mph) 129 km/h
Minimum speed: 4.5-9 kts (5-10 mph) 8-16 km/h
Take-off distance: 10-200 ft (3-61 m)
Landing distance: 0-10 ft (0.3 m)
Maximum climb rate: 1,200 ft (366 m) per minute
Service ceiling: 13,000 ft (3,960 m)
Range: 147 naut miles (170 miles) 275 km

Star Aviation Inc — USA

Comments: Star Aviation is no longer in business. Details of the Lonestar Sport Helicopter can be found in the 1996-97 edition of *WA&SD*, page 365.

Tridair Helicopters, Inc — USA

Corporate address:
3000 Airway Avenue, Suite 300, Costa Mesa, CA 92626.

Telephone: +1 714 540 3000
Facsimile: +1 714 540 1042

Founded: 1980.

Employees: 3.

Information:
Douglas D. Daigle (President).

ACTIVITIES

- Modification of the Bell 206L-1, L-3 and L-4 into Category A/Performance Class One light twin-engined helicopters.
- Has applied to the FAA for approval to install the Gemini twin-engined conversion into the Bell 407.

Tridair Gemini ST

First flight: 16 January 1991.
Certification: November 1993.
First delivery: January 1994.
Role: Major modification of the Bell LongRanger, meeting FAA Pt 29 standards. With the latest FAA approval, the Gemini ST conversion can now be carried out to the 206L-1, L-3 and L-4 models of LongRanger. Certified to FAA Part 27, 36 and 29 Cat A operation.

Development

- November 1993. Received its first FAA certification (STC) as a conventional twin-engined helicopter.
- 12 September 1994. Gemini ST received FAA certification to operate 1 or both engines in all phases of flight, validating it as the world's first single/twin aircraft.

Details *(main modifications to the LongRanger are detailed below)*

Sales: 18 at the time of writing.
Cockpit: 2 throttles are mounted on each collective. Electric throttle releases allow throttles to be advanced above the start position or retarded below idle or cutoff. N2 governor switches allow adjustments, up or down, of both engines independently or simultaneously. The start switch is located on the pilot cyclic, allowing engine start without removing hands from the primary flight controls. Heating and air conditioning kit.
Rotor system: K-flex driveshaft, with 5,000 hours TBO. Rotor brake.
Tail surfaces: Horizontal stabilizer is extended about 3 ins (8 cm) on each side and the port vertical fin is toed inward. The stabilizer has a doubler bonded on the underside to strengthen it for the increased load factor.
Airframe materials: Cowls have been changed and are of fire-resistant carbonfibre wafer material.

↑ Tridair Helicopters Gemini ST twin-engined conversion of the LongRanger

Details for Gemini ST

WEIGHTS:
Empty, operating: 2,640 lb (1,197 kg)
Normal and maximum take-off: 4,550 lb (2,064 kg)
Useful load: 1,610 lb (730 kg) standard configuration
Maximum external load: 2,000 lb (907 kg)

PERFORMANCE:
Long-range cruise speed: 112 kts (129 mph) 207 km/h at MTOW, 118 kts (136 mph) 219 km/h at 3,600 lb (1,633 kg), both at 5,000 ft (1,525 m)
Maximum continuous cruise speed: 101 kts (116 mph) 187 km/h at MTOW, 116 kts (134 mph) 215 km/h at 3,600 lb (1,633 kg)
IGE/OGE hovering ceiling: 10,000 ft (3,050 ft) at MTOW, 15,000 ft (4,575 m) at 3,600 lb (1,633 kg), both ISA and ISA +20° C
Ceiling: 10,000 ft (3,050 m) at MTOW, 20,000 ft (6,100 m) at 4,000 lb (1,814 kg)
Range: 246 naut miles (283 miles) 455 km at MTOW, 280 naut miles (322 miles) 518 km at 3,600 lb (1,633 kg), both sea level, long-range cruise speed, no reserve

Engines: 2 Allison 250-C20R turboshafts. Standard particle separators. Standard engine fire loops for each engine. Engine fire suppression is available as an approved kit. Each engine inlet has an anti-ice system, selectable in the cockpit.
Engine rating: Each 450 shp (335.6 kW) take-off, 380 shp (283 kW) maximum continuous.
Transmission rating: 435 shp (324 kW) take-off (5 minutes), and 370 shp (276 kW) maximum continuous. Soloy combining gearbox, with 2 independent, gear-driven oil pumps to provide oil during operation of either engine. 2 independent oil systems. 2 electric oil-cooling fans. Freewheeling clutches are mounted on the output shaft.
Fuel system: 427 litres. Modified system. Rupture resistant fuel cells.
Electrical system: Battery compartment is enlarged to allow either a 24 amp hour Marathon TSP-9117A ni-cd or Gill G639E lead-acid battery. These heavier batteries eliminate the need for ballast plates. Dual independent electrical systems provide redundant power for the equipment. 2 × 30 VDC 150 amp starter-generators provide power through 2 generator control units to 5 buses, to a 28 volt system.
Flight avionics/instrumentation: Flight instruments remain unchanged. Engine, fuel and electric instruments are of all new technology, provided by Transicoil. Caution and warning annunciator light panel is only slightly larger than the original.

Vertical Aviation Technologies Inc — USA

Corporate address:
PO Box 2527, Sanford, FL 32772-2527.

Telephone: +1 407 322 9488
Facsimile: +1 407 330 2647

Founded: 1988.

Employees: 20.

Information:
Bradley G. Clark (President).

ACTIVITIES

▪ FAA approved repair station for Sikorsky and Orlando Helicopter Airways helicopters. Also engine work and accessories.
▪ Various programmes include the *Elite* upgrade of the Sikorsky S-55 with an AlliedSignal TPE331-3 turboshaft engine, and other S-55 (and ex-military H-19) modifications to produce the agricultural *Bearcat*, AT-55 *Defender* assault and utility military transport, external-lift *Heavy Lift*, *Heli-Camper* with sleeping accommodation for 4, *Nite-Writer* with a computerized aerial advertising system, *Vistaplane* for passenger or medevac roles, and the *Aggressor*. The latter, offered in piloted and unmanned forms, has been reconfigured to represent a Russian-built Mil Mi-24 *Hind-E*.

Vertical Aviation Technologies Hummingbird

Role: 4-seat, kit-built modernized and improved development of the Sikorsky S-52-3.

Development

▪ Improvements include a new nose design, engine conversion, fairings and cowlings, electric cyclic trim, instrument panel, and pressurized main rotor blades.

↑ **Vertical Aviation Technologies Hummingbird in camouflage** *(courtesy Vertical Aviation Technologies)*

▪ Variant has been marketed by the Danubian Aircraft Co in Hungary.

Details

Sales: Kit for US$140,500 with engine, or 14 smaller kits for purchasing in stages. Typical assembly time is 1,000-1,500 working hours.
Rotor system: 3-blade fully articulated main rotor. Pressurized blades, hydraulic fan drive and dual ignition. Rotor brake. Flight control trim system.
Tail rotor characteristics: 2-blade.
Tail surfaces: 2 anhedral stabilizers, with tailguard.
Flight control system: Mechanical, with cables.
Airframe: Semi-monocoque of mainly aluminium, with newly constructed airframe (including a new glassfibre nose design), tail cone and components using original Sikorsky drawings and engineering reports.
Engine: Aluminium V-8 liquid-cooled, fuel-injected piston engine. Other engines are under consideration, including an Allison turboshaft.
Engine rating: 260 hp (194 kW).
Transmission: System comprises a coupling between the engine and main gearbox, a main drive shaft extending from the top of the main gearbox to the main rotor head, and a take-off drive from the main gearbox which drives the tail rotor driveshaft, intermediate gearbox and tail rotor head.
Fuel system: 216 litres in a tank beneath the cabin.

Details for Hummingbird

PRINCIPAL DIMENSIONS:
Rotor diameter (main): 33 ft (10.06 m)
Maximum length, rotors turning: 39 ft 9 ins (12.12 m)
Fuselage length: 30 ft 6 ins (9.3 m)
Fuselage width: 5 ft (1.52 m)
Maximum height: 8 ft 7 ins (2.62 m) to top of rotor head, or 9 ft 8 ins (2.95 m) over tail rotor

MAIN ROTOR:
Rotor disc: 855.3 sq ft (79.46 m^2)

TAIL ROTOR:
Diameter: 5 ft 9 ins (1.75 m)

UNDERCARRIAGE:
Type: Fixed quadricycle, with hydraulic brakes
Wheel base: 6 ft 2 ins (1.88 m)
Wheel track: 6 ft (1.83 m) front wheels, 8 ft 2 ins (2.49 m) rear wheels

WEIGHTS:
Empty: 1,800 lb (816 kg)
Maximum take-off: 2,700 lb (1,225 kg)
Payload: 900 lb (408 kg)

PERFORMANCE:
Never-exceed speed (V_{NE}): 96 kts (110 mph) 177 km/h
Normal cruise speed: 78 kts (90 mph) 145 km/h
Maximum climb rate: 1,250 ft (381 m) per minute at 2,300 lb (1,043 kg), or 950 ft (290 m) per minute at MTOW
Ceiling: 11,000 ft (3,350 m)
Range: 347 naut miles (400 miles) 644 km

Vertech — USA

Comments: Details of the Vortech G-1B, Kestrel, MEG-2XH, Shadow and Skylark I range of ultralight, pressure-jet and strap-on helicopters, and autogyro, can be found in the 1996-97 edition of *WA&SD*, page 366.

Multi-national

Eurocopter Group — France/Germany

Corporate address:
10, avenue Marcel-Cachin, B.P. 107, 93123 La Courneuve Cedex, France.

Telephone: +33 1 49 34 45 00
Facsimile: +33 1 49 34 45 30
Web site: www.eurocopter.com

Founded: 16 January 1992

Employees:
Stated as 9,709 at the time of writing, but reduced to 9,500 according to final update information.

Information:
Jean Louis Espes (Press and Information Senior Manager – address Aéroport International Marseille-Provence, 13725 Marignane Cedex, France; *telephone* +33 4 42 85 95 55, *facsimile* +33 4 42 85 95 64).

ACTIVITIES

▪ The capital of Eurocopter had been shared, until 1997, on 2 levels; Eurocopter Holding S.A. had been owned by Aerospatiale of France (60%) and Daimler-Benz Aerospace of Germany (40%), which in turn had a 75% share in Eurocopter S.A. Since 1997, Eurocopter France, International and Participants have been brought together into what is claimed to be the first integrated European aeronautical company, with only Eurocopter Deutschland remaining as a 100% subsidiary. American Eurocopter Corp, Eurocopter Canada Ltd, Eurocopter International Japan, Eurocopter Service Japan, Eurocopter International Pacific, Eurocopter Southern Africa and Eurocopter Tiger GmbH (see the 1996-97 edition of *WA&SD*, page 367) are among the related organizations that are merged into the new company organization.
▪ On 25 April 1997, Eurocopter and Denel of South Africa formed a strategic alliance to collaborate on the Rooivalk and Oryx programmes, focusing on development, production and customer support of these products.
▪ On 15 May 1997, Eurocopter signed an agreement with China National Helicopter Corp (CHC) and CATIC, covering the joint development of rotor systems for helicopters in the 5-6 tonne class, applicable to new helicopters being developed and built by AVIC in China.
▪ In the last complete year (at the time of writing), Eurocopter received orders for 303 helicopters (compared with 228 for 1996 and 105 for 1995, not including the EC 120) and delivered 210 new helicopters and 55 used. Company turnover of about 10,100 million FF equated to about 55% for the civil and semi-public sector and 45% for the military sector, with 58% overall for export. 1998 deliveries were expected to be increased to about 250.
▪ See also Euromil and NHIndustries.

SUBSIDIARY

EUROCOPTER DEUTSCHLAND

HQ address:
Postfach 9801140, Munich 80, Germany.

Telephone: +49 89 60 00-64 88
Facsimile: +49 89 60 00-44 37

Activities:
▪ Tasked with development and production of helicopters of German origin. Research projects include those to reduce the noise levels, weights, fuel consumption and operating costs of next-generation helicopters, while also increasing cruise speed. The **Hubschrauber 2010** was one of many designs published as artist's impressions and detailed in the press but, according to Eurocopter Deutschland, does not relate to any genuine helicopter. Main plants at Donauwörth and Ottobrunn.

Eurocopter Super Puma AS 332 Mks 1 and 2, Cougar AS 532 Mks 1 and 2, Cougar 100, and Horizon AS 532UL

First flight: 13 September 1978.
Role: Twin-engined, medium civil transport (Super Puma AS 332), military multi-role (Cougar AS 532), and battlefield surveillance (Horizon).
Sales: 539 Super Pumas and Cougars ordered by 1998, including 43 in 1997 alone, of which 453 had been delivered. First operator of the AS 332 L2 Super Puma Mk 2 was Helikopter Service A/S, for oil exploration support over the North Sea. 4 Horizons to the French Army 1996-98.

Details *(Super Puma AS 332 L2, unless stated. Cougar 100 entry under Aircraft variants, plus details in table, provide an overview of the Super Puma Mk 1)*

Crew/passengers: 2-3 crew and 19-24 passengers. 2 pilots are required for IFR flying, but single-pilot VFR is allowable under DGAC Cat B conditions. Alternative layouts for 12 litters plus 4 seats, and 8-12 VIPs.
Freight, external: 9,921 lb (4,500 kg).
Cabin access: Sliding door each side, size 4 ft 3 ins × 4 ft 5 ins (1.3 × 1.35 m).
Optional equipment: Includes rescue winch, cable cutter, bubble observation windows, APU, and automatic transition and hover modes.
Rotor system: 4-blade main rotor with a Spheriflex rotor head, elastomeric bearings and Kevlar retention straps. Composites blades with parabolic tips.
Tail rotor characteristics: 4-blade, to starboard. Similar type of rotor head to main rotor, and composite blades.
Tail surfaces: Port-side horizontal stabilizer, with leading-edge inverted slot.
Flight control system: Hydraulic.
Fuselage: Side sponsons can house auxiliary fuel, emergency floats, life rafts, etc.
Airframe materials: Crashworthy structure incorporating composite materials.
Engines: 2 Turbomeca Makila 1A2 turboshafts.
Engine rating: Each 2,109 shp (1,572 kW) maximum contingency and 1,845 shp (1,375 kW) maximum take-off.
Transmission: 3,232 shp (2,410 kW), or 2,234 shp (1,666 kW) OEI.
Fuel system: Crash-proof fuel system. 2,020 litres standard. Auxiliary fuel in sponsons (each 325 litres), cabin tank (600 litres) and central crashworthy tank (320 litres). For ferrying, up to 5 × 475 litre tanks can be carried in the cabin.
Electrical system: AS 532 U2 Cougar has 2 × 30/40 kVA, 115/200 volt, 400 Hz alternators for AC supply, and 2 × 26 volt transformer rectifiers for DC. 43 amp-hour ni-cd battery. 4 hour stand-by battery. Hydraulically powered emergency supply.

↑ **Eurocopter Cougar 100 AS 532 UB with fixed undercarriage** *(courtesy Eurocopter)*

↑ **Eurocopter Cougar AS 532 A2 in combat SAR configuration, with weapons, flotation gear, refuelling probe and FLIR**

Hydraulic system: 2 independent systems with stand-by electric pumps.
Radar: Optional weather radar, including AlliedSignal RDR-1400 or -1500 for SAR.
Flight avionics/instrumentation: SFIM 165 dual-redundant 4-axis digital autopilot. Integrated digital avionics with EFIS. Optional GPS. HUMS.
Expendable weapons and equipment: See Aircraft variants.

Aircraft variants:
Super Puma AS 332 L1 is a Mk 1 civil version, still marketed. Articulated main rotor of 51 ft 2 ins (15.6 m) diameter, and fuselage length 53 ft 5.5 ins (16.29 m) when including the standard 5-blade tail rotor. Makila 1A1 engines, each 1,877 shp (1,400 kW) maximum contingency, 1,819 shp (1,357 kW) take-off, 1,783 shp (1,330 kW) intermediate emergency power, and 1,589 shp (1,185 kW) maximum continuous power. Normal accommodation for 2 crew and 10-12 passengers, with 20-24 in high density layout.
Super Puma AS 332 L2 is the later Mk 2 (lengthened fuselage of 55 ft 1 ins, 16.79 m including 4-blade tail rotor) civil version, integrating modern technologies, with a composites fuselage plug to increase cabin length. New and larger main rotor and 4-blade tail rotor, both with Spheriflex heads. Makila 1A2 engines, new transmission, and integrated digital avionics with EFIS. First helicopter with a certified 'super-contingency' operation capability.
Super Puma AS 332 L2 VIP for 8 to 15 VIP passengers, depending on internal furnishing and outfitting. Also available in Cougar military form.
Cougar 100 AS 532 AB is a military armed version of UB, with cannon and rockets. Fixed undercarriage and no sponsons. Fuselage length 50 ft 11.5 ins (15.53 m) including 5-blade tail rotor.
Cougar AS 532 AC is a military armed Mk 1 short version, with cannon and rockets. Fuselage length 50 ft 11.5 ins (15.53 m) including 5-blade tail rotor.
Cougar AS 532 AL is the armed variant of UL (long version), with cannon and rockets. Fuselage length 53 ft 5.5 ins (16.29 m) when including the standard 5-blade tail rotor.
Cougar AS 532 SC is an armed naval short version, with 2 AM39 Exocet missiles or 2 torpedoes. Foldable tail (all Super Pumas also have folding main rotor). Variable immersion sonar. Deck secure system. Fuselage length 50 ft 11.5 ins (15.53 m) including 5-blade tail rotor.
Cougar 100 AS 532 UB is a reduced cost military utility Mk 1 short-fuselage version, with fixed undercarriage and no sponsons. See table for dimensions, weights and performance. VFR with 1 pilot and 1 qualified crewman, and IFR with 2 crew. 20 troops or 6 litters and 6 seated persons. Cabin fitted with 13 cargo tie-down floor rings, 2 sliding plug doors of 4 ft 3 ins (1.3 m) width and 4 ft 5 ins (1.35 m) height, 10 jettisonable

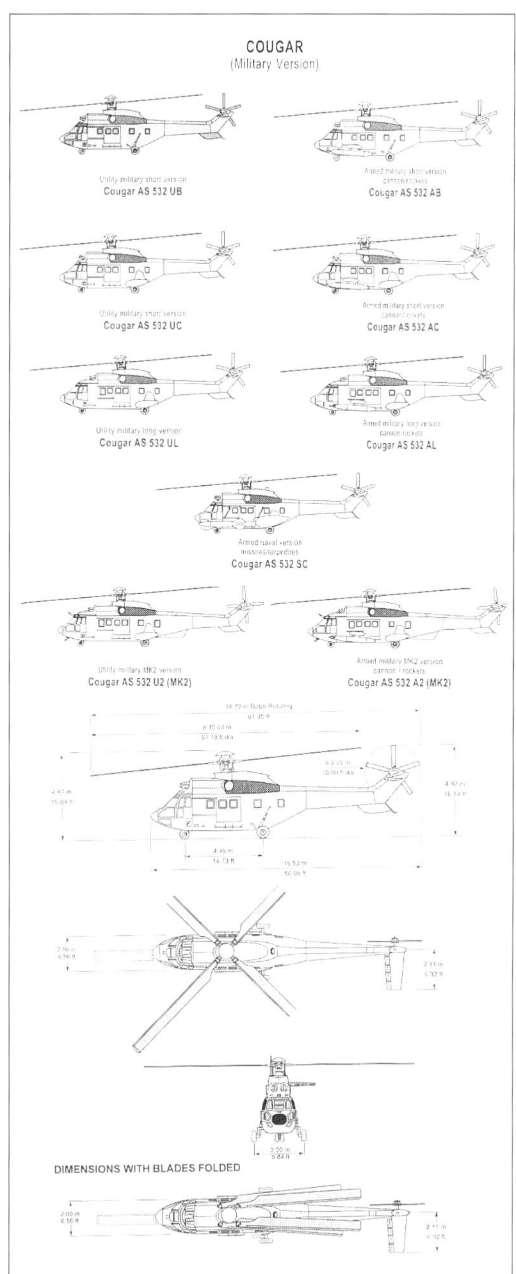

↑ **Eurocopter Cougar AS 532 family, with *(lower)* Cougar 100 AS 532 UB general arrangement** *(courtesy Eurocopter)*

windows (including 4 in sliding doors), and removable rear panel. 2 Makila 1A1 engines, each 1,877 shp (1,400 kW) maximum contingency, 1,819 shp (1,357 kW) take-off, 1,783 shp (1,330 kW) intermediate emergency power, and 1,589 shp (1,185 kW) maximum continuous power. 1,533 litres of fuel standard, with optional 324 litre auxiliary central tank and 1 to 4 optional 475 litre ferrying tanks. Main rotor has 4 composite blades with gust and droop stops and 5-blade (composites) tail rotor as typically for Mk 1 versions; flying control system fitted with 4 dual-body servo units (3 on the cyclic and collective pitch channels and 1 on the anti-torque pitch control channel) with a single chamber per body; duplex autopilot associated with 2 vertical gyro units and 1 baroanemometric module. Electrical system has 2 × 20/30 kVA, 115/200 V, 400 Hz alternators; 43 amp-hour ni-cd battery, 2 × 150 amp transformer-rectifiers, stand-by battery, and 2 × 26 V, 400 Hz transformers. 2 independent hydraulic systems, left system feeding 1 of the servo-unit bodies, the autopilot and wheel brakes, the right system feeding the other body of the servo units; 1 DC auxiliary electropump on stand-by for the left-hand system. Standard radio kit comprises Chelton 805-1 UHF, Chelton 905-2 VHF/AM, AlliedSignal Bendix/King KNR 634 A VOR, Bendix/King KDF 806 ADF, Bendix/King KTU 709 Tacan, Bendix/King KXP 756 transponder, Bendix/King KRA 405 B radio altimeter, Trimble TNL 2101 NVG GPS, and NAT N 301 (2 CP) ICS. Many options.

Cougar AS 532 UC is a military utility Mk 1 short version for 2 crew and 21 troops or other loads. Fuselage length 50 ft 11.5 ins (15.53 m) including 5-blade tail rotor.

Cougar AS 532 UL is a utility military long version (fuselage length 53 ft 5.5 ins, 16.29 m, when including the standard 5-blade tail rotor) for 2 flight crew and 25 troops. Armour protection. RWR, chaff/flare dispensers and infra-red suppressors for self protection. Crashworthy fuel system.

Cougar AS 532 A2 (Mk 2) is an armed military Mk 2 version (lengthened fuselage of 55 ft 1 ins, 16.79 m including 4-blade tail rotor), offered with FN Herstal 621 gun pods or other guns/cannon, rocket launchers, and cabin-mounted 12.7-mm guns. In combat SAR form, offered with personal locator system (PLS) developed specifically for recovery in hostile territory, and accurate autonomous navigation by means of a Sextant Avionique Nadir Mk 2 computer capable of interfacing with GPS, INS, Doppler, VOR, Tacan and DME. For night missions, third-generation NVG, with compatible lighting in cockpit and cabin. SFIM 165 dual-redundant 4-axis digital autopilot. FLIR, searchlight, rescue hoist and self-protection suite. Up to 500 naut mile radius of action at alternate 25,000 lb (11,340 kg) MTOW.

Cougar AS 532 U2 (Mk 2) is the military utility equivalent of the L2 Super Puma Mk 2 (lengthened fuselage of 55 ft 1 ins, 16.79 m including 4-blade tail rotor). Up to 29 troops/commandos.

Cougar AS 532 UL Horizon is the battlefield surveillance and intelligence gathering version, which has superseded the earlier Orchidée programme. Based on AS 532 UL but with an underfuselage Horizon pulse Doppler radar antenna (and datalink transmitter/receiver) that rotates at 2° 24' or 8° per second to provide a 108 naut mile scanning range. First delivery to the French Army 24 June 1996 and all 4 delivered by 1998 from the 1992 development contract. An Horizon system consists of a fully equipped truck-mounted ground station (complete with 2 consoles and a data link terminal) and 2 Cougar helicopters equipped with the multi-mode radar, a digital processing unit, an operator's console for on-board processing, navigation and communication equipment, and a secure data link.

↑ Eurocopter Cougar AS 532 UL Horizon helicopter and ground station

Details for AS 332 L2 Super Puma, *with new Cougar 100 AS 532 UB in italics*

PRINCIPAL DIMENSIONS:
Rotor diameter (main): 53 ft 2 ins (16.2 m), *51 ft 2 ins (15.6 m)*
Maximum length, rotors turning: 63 ft 11.75 ins (19.5 m), *61 ft 4 ins (18.7 m)*
Fuselage length: 55 ft 1 ins (16.79 m), *50 ft 11.5 ins (15.53 m)*, both including tail rotor
Width, blades folded: 12 ft 8 ins (3.86 m)
Fuselage width: *6 ft 7 ins (2 m)*
Maximum height: 16 ft 4 ins (4.97 m), *16 ft 2 ins (4.92 m) over tailrotor, 15 ft 1 ins (4.6 m) over rotor head*

CABIN:
Length: 25 ft 10 ins (7.87 m), *19 ft 10 ins (6.05 m)*
Width: 5 ft 11 ins (1.8 m), *the same*, maximum
Height: 4 ft 9 ins (1.45 m), *4 ft 10 ins to 5 ft 1 ins (1.47 to 1.55 m)*

MAIN ROTOR:
Rotor disc: 2,217.36 sq ft (206 m^2)

TAIL ROTOR:
Diameter: 10 ft 4 ins (3.15 m), *10 ft (3.05 m)*

UNDERCARRIAGE:
Type: Retractable, with twin self-centring nosewheels. Optional emergency flotation gear for offshore operations, housed in the sponsons
Wheel base: 17 ft 4 ins (5.28 m), *14 ft 9 ins (4.49 m)*
Wheel track: 9 ft 10 ins (3 m), *the same*

WEIGHTS:
Empty: 10,274 lb (4,660 kg), *9,590 lb (4,350 kg)*
Normal maximum take-off: 20,503 lb (9,300 kg)
Maximum take-off: *19,840 lb (9,000 kg)*
Maximum operational, with sling load: 20,613 lb (9,350 kg)
Useful load: 10,229 lb (4,640 kg), *10,250 lb (4,650 kg)*
Maximum sling load: *9,920 lb (4,500 kg)*

PERFORMANCE:
Never-exceed speed (V_{NE}): 170 kts (195 mph) 315 km/h, *150 kts (173 mph) 278 km/h*
Cruise speed: 151 kts (174 mph) 280 km/h at sea level, *134 kts (154 mph) 249 km/h, pitch limited to 16°*
Economic cruise speed: *129 kts (148 mph) 239 km/h*
Maximum climb rate: 1,299 ft (396 m) per minute at sea level, *1,417 ft (432 m) per minute at 70 kts*
IGE hovering ceiling, ISA: 10,761 ft (3,280 m), *9,186 ft (2,800 m)*
IGE hovering ceiling, ISA + 20°: 5,906 ft (1,800 m)
OGE hovering ceiling, ISA: 6,922 ft (2,110 m), *5,413 ft (1,650 m) at 20,613 lb (9,350 kg)*
OGE hovering ceiling, ISA + 20°: *2,789 ft (850 m)*
Service ceiling: 17,000 ft (5,180 m), *11,319 ft (3,450 m)*
Range with standard fuel: 448 naut miles (515 miles) 830 km, *310 naut miles (357 miles) 573 km, no reserve*
Range with auxiliary tanks: 648 naut miles (745 miles) 1,200 km, *380 naut miles (437 miles) 704 km with central auxiliary fuel tank, no reserve*

Eurocopter Ecureuil AS 350, AStar and Fennec AS 550

First flight: 27 June 1974.
Role: Light multi-role civil helicopter (Ecureuil and Astar) and armed/unarmed military helicopter (Fennec).
Sales: 2,084 ordered by 1998, including 102 in 1997 alone, with 2,055 delivered. Ecureuil has also been built by Helibras.

Details *(Ecureuil AS 350 B2 and B3, except where stated and under Aircraft variants)*

Crew/passengers: Pilot plus 5 passengers. Alternatively, pilot plus 4 passengers in a 'comfort' layout, pilot plus 6 passengers in a high-density layout, or pilot, doctor, medical attendant and 1 or 2 litters in a casualty evacuation layout; some of the medical equipment can be carried in the 3 baggage compartments.
Baggage compartments: Left compartment of 8.29 cu ft (0.235 m^3), right compartment of 7.06 cu ft (0.2 m^3), and rear compartment of 18.717 cu ft (0.53 m^3).
Freight, external: 2,557 lb (1,160 kg) sling load for B2 and 3,086 lb (1,400 kg) for B3. 2,000 lb (907 kg) sling load for AS 350 BA.
Optional equipment: Very wide range of options, including dual controls with fuel flow twist grip, extra glazing, windshield wiper/s, cabin heating, adaptation for night missions with NVG, wire strike protection system, fuel tank self sealing, emergency flotation gear, life rafts installation, skis, sand filter, reinforced sand erosion blade protection strips, cargo sling, Bambi Bucket firefighting installation, Conair and Isolair firefighting installations, EMS kit, rear sliding doors, electric hoist, searchlights, hailers, crop-spraying gear, observation systems, and more.
Rotor system: 3-blade (manually folding) main rotor, with Starflex head fitted with spherical thrust bearings. Hydraulic servo units. Blade construction of stainless steel spar with strip foam filler, rovings and glassfibre skin.
Tail rotor characteristics: Composites 2 blade (same construction as main blades) type, to starboard. Hydraulic servo unit and a load compensator.
Tail surfaces: Dorsal and ventral fins, and horizontal stabilizer with inverted aerofoil section (8 ft 3.5 ins, 2.53 m span).
Airframe materials: Light alloy, but with extensive use of composites for the cabin area, cowlings and rotors.
Engine: Turbomeca Arriel 1D1 turboshaft in AS 350 B2, and Arriel 2B in AS 350 B3.
Engine rating: 732 shp (546 kW) maximum for Arriel 1D1. Arriel 2B has 847 shp (632 kW) take-off power and 728 shp (543 kW) maximum continuous power.

↑ Eurocopter Fennec AS 550 A3 in fire-support form, with 20-mm gun, rocket launcher and roof sighting system

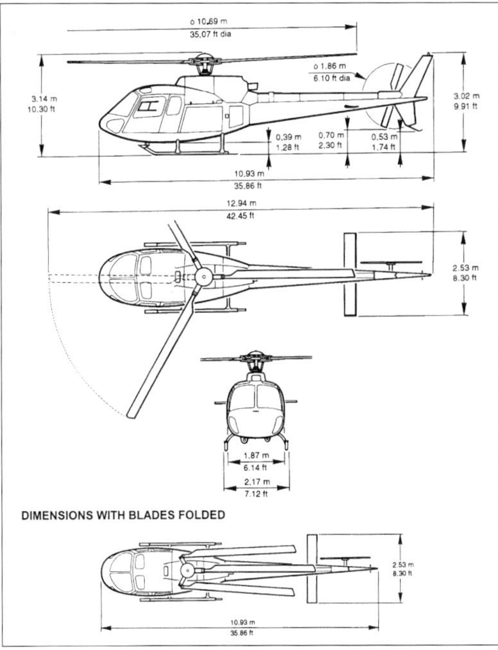

↑ **Eurocopter Ecureuil AS 350 B3 general arrangement** *(courtesy Eurocopter)*

↑ **Eurocopter Fennec AS 555 UN**

Transmission: 590 shp (440 kW) for AS 350 B2. Transmission as given for AS 350 B3 has main gearbox (with epicycloidal reduction gear, bevel gear and castings), anti-vibration mounted, with oil sight gauge, chip detector, oil temperature and pressure switches, port for endoscope and self-sealing valve for oil sampling and draining. Engine to main gearbox coupling shaft, rotor brake, and main rotor rpm sensor and high and low rpm warning device. Tail drive carried by 5 anti-friction bearings. Tail gearbox with oil sight gauge, chip detector and port for endoscopic inspection.
Fuel system: 539 litres, with optional 475 litre ferry tank.
Electrical system: 4.5 kW, 28 volt DC starter-generator. 15 amp-hour ni-cd battery. Ground power receptacle.
Hydraulic system: 580 psi.
Flight avionics/instrumentation: Instruments for AS 350 B3 comprise airspeed indicator, altimeter, rate of climb indicator, rotor and free turbine tachometer dual indicator, clock, warning panel, magnetic compass, heated pitot head, ICS connection to aural warning issued from VEMD, and LCD dual screen vehicle and engine multifunction display (VEMD) providing the following information: first limitation indicator (FLI), torquemeter, exhaust gas temperature, gas generation tachometer, engine oil temperature/pressure, fuel quantity and fuel flow and estimated remaining time to fly, ammeter and voltmeter, outside air temperature, enhanced usage monitoring functions (IGE/OGE performance calculations, engine cycle counting, engine power check and overlimits display), and VEMD and peripheral maintenance information. Wide range of optional avionics and equipment, including 3-axis autopilot with failure passivation unit (2-axis autopilot without failure passivation unit being studied), gyro instruments and Euronav III GPS moving map. Radio communication and radio navigation equipment for minimal installations for General Aviation day VFR operations comprise AIM 505-2B gyro-horizon plus AIM 200-DC gyro-directional, AlliedSignal Bendix/King KLX 135 A VHF/AM/GPS, and Team TB 27 ICS. Equipment can be added depending upon operating needs or requirements of national authorities.

Aircraft variants:
Ecureuil AS 350 BA is the base version of the range, with a Turbomeca Arriel 1B engine of 640 shp (447 kW). Hinged or optional sliding cabin doors. Empty weight 2,526 lb (1,146 kg), maximum weight 4,630 lb (2,100 kg), and maximum weight with sling load 4,960 lb (2,250 kg). Cruise speed is 126 kts.
Ecureuil AS 350 B2 has a more powerful 732 shp (546 kW) Arriel 1D1 engine and upgraded transmission, as detailed. Referred to as SuperStar in America.
Ecureuil AS 350 B3 is a new variant and the most advanced of the single-engine Ecureuil range, featuring an 847 shp (632 kW) Arriel 2B turboshaft, digital engine control system and new tail rotor of wider chord. Centralized LCD screen display. First flown 4 March 1997, with certification November 1997.
AS 350D AStar is the name for Ecureuil marketed in America, with an AlliedSignal LTS101-600A-3 of 615 shp (458.6 kW).
Fennec AS 550 A2 is the military armed version, with Arriel 1D1 engine and self-sealing fuel tanks. Dimensionally similar to Ecureuil, except all versions of Fennec are 10 ft 11.5 ins (3.34 m) high due to taller undercarriage skids. Can be equipped with multi-purpose weapon beams for rockets, missiles and 20-mm gun pods. Provision for 20-mm axial cannon. Standard sliding doors. Optional cannon or machine-gun mounted in door opening. Instrument panel adapted to tactical flight, and internal/external provision for flight using night vision goggles. Optional day/night sighting system. Can still carry 5 troops or a sling load. Armed with a mix of 20-mm cannon and rocket launcher, it can perform a tactical mission of 2 hours 45 minutes in NOE flight with 20 minutes reserve. With rocket launchers or cannon configuration, mission time becomes 3 hours. Fennecs have low infra-red reflection paint, seal-sealing fuel tanks, main gearbox with 45 minute dry-run capability, impact-resistant main blades and hub, and armour-plated seats.
Fennec AS 550 A3 is the latest military armed version, fitted with Arriel 2B engine. Empty weight 2,696 lb (1,223 kg), maximum take-off weight 4,960 lb (2,250 kg), useful load 2,264 lb (1,027 kg), maximum cargo sling load 3,086 lb (1,400 kg), maximum operational weight with external load 6,062 lb (2,750 kg), and maximum operational weight with jettisonable external weapons 5,400 lb (2,450 kg). Fast cruise speed 133 kts (153 mph) 246 km/h. Similar armament choices to AS 550 A2.
Fennec AS 550 C2 is the armed military missile version. Can be equipped with 4 missiles and can still carry 5 troops or a sling load. HeliTOW sighting system and TOW missiles for anti-armour. Can have a night vision system. Armed with 4 anti-tank missiles, it can perform day/night missions lasting 2 hours 45 minutes in NOE flight with 20 minutes reserve. In air-to-air configuration with 4 Mistral missiles, it can undertake a 3 hour mission in NOE flight with 20 minutes reserve. Arriel 1D1.
AS 550 C3 Fennec is the latest armed military missile version, fitted with Arriel 2B engine. Weapons and mission times as for AS 550 C2.
AS 550 U2 Fennec is the utility military version, also suited to reconnaissance/observation and training tasks. Arriel 1D1.
AS 550 U3 Fennec is the latest utility version, fitted with Arriel 2B engine. Empty weight 2,661 lb (1,207 kg), maximum take-off weight 4,960 lb (2,250 kg), useful load 2,299 lb (1,043 kg), maximum cargo sling load 3,086 lb (1,400 kg), and maximum operational weight with external load 6,062 lb (2,750 kg). Fast cruise speed 133 kts (153 mph) 246 km/h.

Details for AS 350 B2, *with B3 in italics where different*

PRINCIPAL DIMENSIONS:
Rotor diameter (main): 35 ft 1 ins (10.69 m)
Maximum length, rotors turning: 42 ft 5.5 ins (12.94 m)
Fuselage length: 35 ft 10.5 ins (10.93 m), including tailfin
Width, blades folded: 8 ft 4 ins (2.53 m)
Maximum height: 10 ft 3.5 ins (3.14 m) over rotor head, 9 ft 11 ins (3.02 m) over tail

CABIN:
Length: 7 ft 11 ins (2.42 m)
Width: 5 ft 5 ins (1.65 m) maximum
Height: 4 ft 3 ins (1.3 m)
Volume: 105.943 cu ft (3 m^3)

MAIN ROTOR:
Blade chord: 1 ft 1.8 ins (0.35 m)
Rotor disc: 966.06 sq ft (89.75 m^2)
Rpm: 394

TAIL ROTOR:
Diameter: 6 ft 1 ins (1.86 m)

UNDERCARRIAGE:
Type: Fixed twin skids. Emergency flotation gear on the skids
Skid track: 7 ft 1.5 ins (2.17 m)

WEIGHTS:
Empty: 2,542 lb (1,153 kg), *2,588 lb (1,174 kg)*
Normal maximum take-off: 4,960 lb (2,250 kg), *the same*
Maximum take-off, external load: 5,511 lb (2,500 kg), *6,172 lb (2,800 kg)*
Useful load: *2,372 lb (1,076 kg)*

PERFORMANCE:
Never-exceed speed (V_{NE}): 155 kts (178 mph) 287 km/h, *the same*
Cruise speed: 133 kts (153 mph) 246 km/h at sea level, *132 kts (152 mph) 245 km/h*
Recommended cruise speed: *123 kts (143 mph) 230 km/h*
Maximum climb rate: 1,675 ft (510 m) per minute, *1,830 ft (558 m) per minute*
IGE hovering ceiling, ISA: 9,840 ft (3,000 m), *13,385 ft (4,080 m)*
IGE hovering ceiling, ISA + 20° C: *10,660 ft (3,250 m)*
OGE hovering ceiling, ISA: 7,545 ft (2,300 m), *11,155 ft (3,400 m)*
OGE hovering ceiling, ISA+ 20° C: *8,530 ft (2,600 m)*
Service ceiling: 15,100 ft (4,600 m), *>15,750 ft (4,800 m)*
Range: 360 naut miles (416 miles) 670 km, *357 naut miles (411 miles) 662 km,* no reserve
Duration: *4.1 hours, at 54 kts, no reserve*
Operating limits: ISA + 35° C to -40° C

Eurocopter Ecureuil AS 355, TwinStar and Fennec AS 555

First flight: 28 September 1979.
Role: Twin-engined version of the AS 350/550.

Aims

▪ Particularly suited to missions requiring high performance with OEI, such as rooftop take-off, harbour pilot drop-off, work on power lines and pylons, and offshore connections (sea rescue).

Details *(Ecureuil AS 355 N, except for Sales and Aircraft variants)*

Sales: 629 ordered by 1998, with 617 delivered.
Crew/passengers: Pilot plus 5 passengers. Other layouts similar to single-engined Ecureuil versions.

↑ Eurocopter Ecureuil AS 555 N in 5-seat layout *(courtesy Eurocopter)*

Freight, external: 2,500 lb (1,134 kg) sling load.
Rotor system: 3-blade (manually folding) composites main rotor, with Starflex bearingless rotor head. Combiner gearbox, with freewheels.
Tail rotor characteristics: Similar to Ecureuil.
Tail surfaces: Similar to Ecureuil.
Airframe materials: Similar to Ecureuil.
Engines: 2 Turbomeca Arrius 1A (TM 319) turboshafts with FADEC.
Engine rating: Each 456 shp (340 kW) take off, and 520 shp (388 kW) OEI max contingency,
Fuel system: 730 litres usable.
Electrical system: 2 starter-generators.
Flight avionics/instrumentation: Rockwell Collins, Honeywell or SFIM autopilot. Avionics to customer's requirements for VFR or IFR flying.

Aircraft variants:
Ecureuil AS 355 F2 is a twin-engined version of Ecureuil, differing from the AS 355 N in having 2 Allison 250-C20F turboshafts (each 420 shp, 313 kW). Known in America as the TwinStar. Particularly suited to performing offshore liaisons, flying over built-up areas and in inhospitable zones.
Ecureuil AS 355 N is the principal civil version, with Arrius 1A engines. As detailed. Also known as TwinStar in America.
Fennec AS 555 AN is a twin Arrius 1A-engined version of Fennec AS 550 A2 armed military helicopter. Armed with a 20-mm cannon and rocket launcher, it can perform a tactical mission out to 27 naut miles (31 miles) 50 km, loiter for 1 hour and 30 minutes, and return with 20 minutes fuel reserve.
Fennec AS 555 MN is a twin Arrius 1A-engined unarmed naval helicopter. Suited to small-tonnage vessel operations. Can be used for maritime patrol, SAR (with hoist), and OTH targeting.
Fennec AS 555 SN is a twin Arrius 1A-engined version of the AS 550 S2 Fennec armed naval helicopter. Capable of operating from low-tonnage vessels. Can perform (at low cost) maritime surveillance, OTH targeting, submarine attack and sea support missions. Weapons can include a lightweight torpedo. AlliedSignal RDR-1500B radar, Doppler, 3-axis autopilot and more. Recommended cruise speed 110 kts (127 mph) 204 km/h, radius of action 150 naut miles (173 miles) 278 km, and maximum endurance 4 hours.
Fennec AS 555 UN is a twin Arrius 1A-engined version of AS 550 U2 Fennec for utility military missions, capable also of reconnaissance/observation, and IFR training. Basically an unarmed AS 555 AN.

Details for Ecureuil AS 355 N

PRINCIPAL DIMENSIONS: Similar to Ecureuil

CABIN: Similar to Ecureuil

MAIN ROTOR: Similar to Ecureuil

TAIL ROTOR: Similar to Ecureuil

UNDERCARRIAGE: Similar to Ecureuil

WEIGHTS:
Empty: 3,045 lb (1,381 kg)
Normal maximum take-off: 5,600 lb (2,540 kg)
Maximum take-off, external load: 5,732 lb (2,600 kg)
Useful load: 2,566 lb (1,164 kg) maximum

PERFORMANCE (ISA):
Never-exceed speed (V_{NE}): 150 kts (172 mph) 278 km/h
Fast cruise speed: 121 kts (139 mph) 224 km/h at sea level
Maximum climb rate: 1,355 ft (414 m) per minute at sea level
IGE hovering ceiling: 8,530 ft (2,600 m)
OGE hovering ceiling: 5,085 ft (1,550 m)
Ceiling: 13,125 ft (4,000 m)
Range: 389 naut miles (448 miles) 721 km with standard fuel

↑ Eurocopter Panther AS 565 SB firing an AS 15TT missile

Eurocopter Dauphin AS 365 N and Panther AS 565

First flight: 29 February 1984 (Panther AS 365 M prototype).
Role: Multi-purpose civil passenger, offshore liaison, VIP, freight and aerial photography (Dauphin 2) and armed/unarmed military and naval (Panther) helicopters.
Sales: 628 by 1998, including 16 in 1997, with 608 delivered (including out-of-production models of the SA/AS 365/565/366). Also built in China by Harbin, currently in Z-9B form.

Details *(principally for Dauphin AS 365 N2 and latest N3, unless stated)*

Crew/passengers: Pilot plus 12 passengers, or 5, 8 or 11 passengers in VIP and business layouts. For EMS, 1, 2 or 4 litters plus attendants.
Cabin access: Each door 3 ft 9.5 ins (1.16 m) high. Pilot door 1 ft 9 ins (0.53 m) wide, front cabin door 3 ft 9 ins (1.14 m) wide, and rear cabin door 4 ft 2 ins (1.27 m) wide when including the door extension.
Freight, external: 3,527 lb (1,600 kg) sling load.
Optional equipment: Very wide range of options includes rescue hoist, icing detector, de-icing of front cockpit glazing, regulated heating system, mechanically driven or other air conditioning system, crew crashworthy seats, nosewheel castor lock, wire strike protection system, sliding windows on enlarged and bubble sided doors, emergency flotation gear, life raft installation, sand filters, reinforced sand erosion main blade protection strips, skis, ferry tanks, fuel jettison system, cargo sling, firefighting equipment, Drip tub sea rescue equipment, searchlight, hailer with siren system, observation systems, and more.
Rotor system: 4 glassfibre/carbonfibre blades with Starflex head fitted with gust and droop stops; mast fitted with rotor rpm phonic-wheel. Flying control system fitted with 3 dual-chamber/dual body main servo units (on cyclic and collective pitch channels) and 1 dual-chamber/dual body rear servo unit on tail rotor pitch control channel.
Tail rotor characteristics: Fenestron fan-in-fin composites tail rotor. 11 blades. See Rotor system.
Tail surfaces: Large fin. Horizontal stabilizer, with endplates toed to port by 10° (span 10 ft 8 ins, 3.25 m).
Flight control system: Hydraulic.
Airframe materials: Principally alloy or alloy/Nomex composite sandwich construction, but with all-composites fenestron, fin, fairings and nose.
Engines: 2 Turbomeca Arriel 1C2 turboshafts for AS 365 N2. 2 Arriel 2Cs for AS 365 N3.
Engine rating: Each 763 shp (569 kW) maximum contingency and 737 shp (550 kW) maximum take-off for Arriel 1C2. Each 851 shp (635 kW) take-off, 800 shp (597 kW) maximum continuous power, 977 shp (729 kW) OEI for 30 seconds, 879 shp (656 kW) OEI for 2 minutes, and 851 shp (635 kW) OEI continuous for Arriel 2C.
Transmission: AS 365 N3 main gearbox, anti-vibration mounted, with oil gauge, magnetic plug, oil pressure and temperature pick-up, lubrication system, thermal switch, rotor tachometer drive and holes for endoscope and oil sampling. Free wheels integral with main gearbox. Engine/main gearbox coupling shafts. Tail gearbox with oil sight gauge and magnetic plug. rotor brake.
Fuel system: 1,135 litres standard. 180 litre auxiliary tank in hold. 460 litre ferry tank can be positioned in the cabin, replacing the aft seating. All figures are usable capacities.
Electrical system: 2 × 250VA, 115/26 V, 400 Hz single-phase static inverters, 2 × 4.8 kW starter-generators, 27 amp-hour ni-cd battery with temperature detector, and external DC power receptacle. Optional equipment includes 10 kVA AC alternator and 43 amp-hour battery.
Hydraulic system: Dual independent systems feeding servo units, undercarriage actuation system and assisted brakes, each 870 psi. Self-sealing hydraulic ground coupling. Stand-by hydraulic system with electro-pump for actuating undercarriage and providing hydraulic assistance on the ground with the rotor stopped.
Braking system: Hydraulic disc.
Radar: Optional. See below.
Flight avionics/instrumentation: Standard instruments for N3 are 2 airspeed indicators with digital speed displays, 2 altimeters, 2 rate of climb indicators with provisions for rate of climb pre-set on pilot's side, 2 gyro-horizons, 2 gyro-compasses, 2 × 4 ins (10 cm) HSIs, selector switch for gyro-compasses, RMI, stand-by gyro-horizon, 2 heated pitot heads, dual torquemeter, 2 tailpipe temperature indicators, 2 engine oil pressure and temperature indicators, 2 fuel pressure indicators, main gearbox oil pressure and temperature indicator, 2 hydraulic pressure gauges, voltmeter, ammeter, dual fuel contents gauge, fuel circuit control and inspection panel, electrical control panel, undercarriage position selector and indicator, 2 stop watches, 1 triple tachometer for rotor and engines rpm, rotor tachometer, 2 DNG indicators with OEI lights, stand-by magnetic compass, outside air temperature indicator, warning panel and various warning lights. 2 pilot IFR. SFIM 155 D duplex autopilot, with optional coupler. Minimum radio communication and radio navigation equipment for VFR operation comprises Rockwell Collins VHF 22A VHF/AM Nos 1 and 2, VIR 32 VOR/ILS, ADF 60 ADF, TDR 90 (or TDR 94 if Mode S is necessary) transponder, Shadin 8800 T altitude encoder, and Team TB 31 ICS. Alternative AlliedSignal Bendix/King suite with KTR 908 Nos 1 and 2, KNR 634 A, KDF 806 and KXP 756 (or MST 67-A if Mode S is necessary) replacing the Rockwell Collins equipment respectively. Minimum equipment for IFR operation adds Thomson CNI

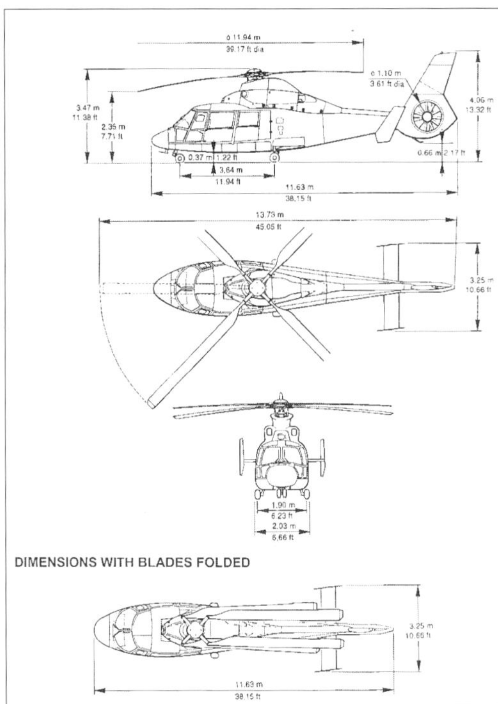

↑ Eurocopter Dauphin AS 365 N3 general arrangement *(courtesy Eurocopter)*

AHV 16 radio altimeters. Wide range of optional avionics, including AlliedSignal Bendix/King EFIS, EHSI, flight director coupler, AlliedSignal RDR-1400C or RDR-2000 weather radar, B.F. Goodrich WX 1000 stormscope, Trimble TNL 2101 GPS, and more.

Aircraft variants:
Dauphin AS 365 N2 is a current civil transport version, as detailed. Certified for VFR operations in 1989.
Dauphin AS 365 N3 is the latest civil transport version, as also detailed.
AS 366 G1 variant was delivered to the US Coast Guard between November 1984 and April 1989 as a short-range recovery helicopter. See the 1996-97 edition of *WA&SD*, page 369.
Panther AS 565AB is the armed military helicopter and air-to-air version. Armament can include 2 × Giat M621 20-mm cannon pods (180 rounds of ammunition each), 2 × 68-mm or 2.75-ins rocket launchers, or up to 8 Mistral AAMs. All currently available Panthers use 2 × Arriel 2C turboshafts, each 851 shp (635 kW) at take-off, 800 shp (597 kW) maximum continuous, and 977 shp (729 kW) OEI rating for 30 seconds, and have crashworthy fuel systems and equipment choices that include self-protection systems.
Panther AS 565 MB is the unarmed naval version. Can be used for many roles including maritime patrol and surveillance (with radar), SAR (with hoist), and OTH targeting. Arriel 2Cs.
Panther AS 565 SB is the armed naval version and can perform maritime surveillance, OTH targeting, submarine detection and attack, anti-ship, SAR and sea support missions. For ASW, the principal detection system is either a Thomson Sintra ASM HS 312 sonar or Sextant Avionique MAD, with 2 torpedoes for attack. Agrion 15 radar and 4 × AS 15TT missiles for ASV. Typically AlliedSignal Bendix/King RDR-1500 or Omera ORB 32 surveillance radar for search and rescue. Arriel 2Cs. See data table.
Panther AS 565 UB is the military utility version for unarmed reconnaissance/observation, transporting commandos or sling loads, SAR, litter-carrying, and IFR training. Other roles can include conversion for electronic missions. Arriel 2Cs.

Eurocopter EC 155

First flight: 17 June 1997.
Certification: JAR Pt 29 expected October 1998.
First delivery: Originally expected November 1998, initially to launch customer Helikopter Service Group.
Role: New generation, 'widebody' medium-twin helicopter, formerly known as the Dauphin AS 365 N4.

Aims

- Larger main rotor compared with Dauphin AS 365 N.
- Noise level of about 4dB below the latest ICAO standards.
- Substantially enlarged cabin compared with Dauphin AS 365 N, designed to provide 40% more internal space, with 7 ins (18 cm) higher ceiling and 11.8 ins (30 cm) extra length.
- Corporate and VIP interior featuring enhanced soundproofing, low vibration level, efficient air conditioning system, and hinged door with specific foldable boarding step.

Details

Sales: First orders for 13 for the German Border Guard for transport (for delivery 1998-2001 – plus 2 options) and 6 (plus 6 options) for Helikopter Service Group of Norway.

↑ Eurocopter EC 155 first prototype *(courtesy Eurocopter)*

Details for Dauphin AS 365 N3, *with Panther AS 565 SB in italics*

PRINCIPAL DIMENSIONS:
Rotor diameter (main): 39 ft 2 ins (11.94 m), *the same*
Maximum length, rotors turning: 45 ft 0.5 ins (13.73 m), *the same*
Fuselage length: 38 ft 2 ins (11.63 m), *39 ft 7.5 ins (12.08 m)*
Width, blades folded: 10 ft 8 ins (3.25 m), *the same*
Maximum height: 11 ft 5 ins (3.47 m) over rotor head, 13 ft 4 ins (4.06 m) over tail, *the same*

CABIN:
Length: 7 ft 3 ins (2.2 m), *the same*
Width: 6 ft 3.5 ins (1.92 m) maximum, *the same*
Height: 4 ft 7 ins (1.4 m), *the same*
Volume: 176.57 cu ft (5 m^3), plus 38.84 cu ft (1.1 m^3) in the baggage hold, *the same*

MAIN ROTOR:
Blade chord: 1 ft 3 ins (0.385 m), *the same*
Rotor disc: 1,204.48 sq ft (111.9 m^2), *the same*

TAIL ROTOR:
Diameter: 3 ft 7.25 ins (1.1 m), *the same*

UNDERCARRIAGE:
Type: Retractable, with twin self-centring nosewheels. Emergency flotation gear for offshore missions, *the same*
Main wheel tyre size: 15 × 6.00
Wheel base: 11 ft 11 ins (3.64 m), *the same*
Wheel track: 6 ft 3 ins (1.9 m), *the same*

WEIGHTS:
Empty: 5,073 lb (2,301 kg), *5,097 lb (2,312 kg)*
Maximum take-off: 9,480 lb (4,300 kg), *9,369 lb (4,250 kg)*
Maximum take-off with external load: 9,480 lb (4,300 kg), *9,369 lb (4,250 kg)*
Useful load: 4,407 lb (1,999 kg), *4,272 lb (1,938 kg)*

PERFORMANCE:
Never-exceed speed (V_{NE}): 155 kts (178 mph) 287 km/h, *the same*
Fast cruise speed: 148 kts (171 mph) 275 km/h, *147 kts (170 mph) 273 km/h*, both at sea level
Recommended cruise speed: 148 kts (171 mph) 275 km/h, *144 kts (165 mph) 266 km/h*, both at sea level
Maximum climb rate: 1,338 ft (408 m) per minute, *the same*, both at sea level
IGE hovering ceiling, ISA: 8,612 ft (2,625 m), *6,233 ft (1,900 m)*
IGE hovering ceiling, ISA + 20° C: 5,962 ft (1,817 m), *3,937 ft (1,200 m)*
OGE hovering ceiling, ISA: 3,781 ft (1,153 m), *5,085 ft (1,550 m)*
OGE hovering ceiling, ISA+ 20° C: 1,020 ft (311 m), *2,789 ft (850 m)*
Service ceiling: >15,332 ft (4,673 m), *>13,780 ft (4,200 m)*
Range: 440 naut miles (506 miles) 814 km at sea level, *435 naut miles (500 miles) 805 km*, both with standard fuel
Range with auxiliary tanks: 512 naut miles (589 miles) 948 km, *503 naut miles (579 miles) 932 km*
Duration: 4.1 hours, *4 hours*; or 4.8 hours, *4.6 hours* with auxiliary tanks

Details for EC 155

PRINCIPAL DIMENSIONS:
Rotor diameter (main): 41 ft 4 ins (12.6 m)
Maximum length, rotors turning: 46 ft 11 ins (14.3 m)
Fuselage length: 41 ft 9 ins (12.73 m)
Maximum height: 11 ft 11.25 ins (3.64 m) to top of rotor head, 14 ft 3 ins (4.35 m) over tail

CABIN:
Volume: 235 cu ft (6.7 m^3) usable

UNDERCARRIAGE:
Type: Retractable, with twin nosewheels
Wheel base: 12 ft 10 ins (3.91 m)
Wheel track: 6 ft 3 ins (1.90 m)

WEIGHTS:
Maximum take-off: 10,582 lb (4,800 kg)
Maximum take-off with external load: 11,023 lb (5,000 kg)

PERFORMANCE:
Fast cruise speed: 145 kts (167 mph) 268 km/h
Recommended cruise speed: 140 kts (161 mph) 260 km/h
Maximum range: 480 naut miles (553 miles) 890 km

Crew/passengers: 1 or 2 pilots plus up to 12 passengers as a passenger transport. Alternative accommodation for 13 passengers in public services and utility forms, various VIP configurations (typically 5 to 8 passengers), or 6 litters and 2 attendants in casualty evacuation layout.
Freight, internal: 88 cu ft (2.5 m^3) cargo compartment, with separate access on both sides.
Cabin access: 2 front doors, plus 2 rear sliding doors.
Rotor system: 5-blade, Spheriflex main rotor system. Provides low external noise signature and lower vibration level; introduction of automatically variable rotor rpm results in quieter hovering, take-offs and landings.
Tail rotor characteristics: Fenestron tail rotor system with 10 unequally spaced composite blades. Provides low external noise signature, with a gain in noise reduction of about 8 to 10dB.
Tail surfaces: Large fin. Horizontal stabilizer, with endplates (not toed to port as for Dauphin).
Engines: 2 Turbomeca Arriel 2C1 turboshaft engines, with FADEC.
Engine rating: Each 977 shp (729 kW) for 30 seconds.
Flight avionics/instrumentation: Avionique Nouvelle integrated flight and display system for improved in-flight safety, reduced crew workload, and ease of maintenance. Pilot and co-pilot have active-matrix LCD displays in a redesigned instrument panel. German Border Guard helicopters are IFR equipped.

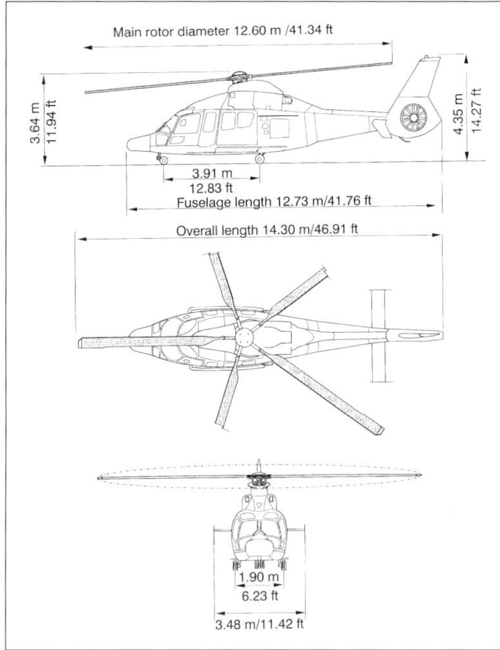

↑ Eurocopter EC 155 general arrangement *(courtesy Eurocopter)*

Eurocopter BO 105 and EC Super Five

First flight: 16 February 1967 for BO 105.
Role: Civil and military light helicopters, with armed versions. Mainly used for rescue, offshore, law enforcement, emergency medical, executive/utility and SAR applications, but with other possibilities including firefighting.

Sales: 1,378 BO 105s and EC Super Fives by 1998 (none ordered in 1997), with 1,365 delivered, mainly BO 105 variants but including 2 EC Super Fives to Bahrain (navy, for SAR), to Brazil, 2 to EMERCOM of Russia for EMS and SAR, 17 to the Federal German Ministry of the Interior (delivered 1996-97 for rescue and civil defence), the Hellenic Police, and a German motoring organization. Military operators include the German Army, whose BO 105 PAH-1s were upgraded with new blades and other improvements (take-off weight increased to 5,511 lb, 2,500 kg); many have digital avionics and Hot 2 anti-armour missiles on light launchers, but plans to retrofit roof sights for night operations were cancelled. 28 Spanish BO 105ATHs received new blades, NVG cockpits, GPS and Hot missiles to enhance their anti-armour capabilities, plus either radar and infra-red warning receivers or chaff/flare dispensers.

Details *(generally applicable to all versions, as indicated)*

Crew/passengers: Pilot plus 4-5 passengers. Rear bench seat is removable for cargo or to allow 1 or 2 litters.
Freight, external: 1,984 lb (900 kg) for EC Super Five, and 2,205 lb (1,000 kg) for LSA-3 and Super Lifter.
Cabin access: Rear clamshell doors for internal cargo, with complete access to the cabin, able to accept long loads projecting out under the boom. 2 hinged doors to the cockpit. 2 sliding doors to the main passenger compartment.
Optional equipment: Dual controls (standard on EC Super Five). Steerable searchlight for SAR, or FLIR, IR searchlight and loudspeaker for law enforcement, and firefighting equipment. Many other options.
Rotor system: 4-blade (manually foldable) hingeless rigid main rotor (System Bölkow), with a single-piece drop-forged titanium rotor head with 4 titanium inner sleeves to which the fibre composites blades are bolted. Lead-lag and flapping motions are absorbed by the inherent elasticity of the blades. The inner sleeves are retained within the rotor head by flexible tension-torsion straps attached to 2 quadruple retaining nuts located in the head centre to take up the centrifugal forces. Pendulum absorbers, acting as vibration dampers, are fixed to the blade roots. LSA-3 blades have drooped leading and reflexed trailing edges, and 8° linear twist. Super Lifter and EC Super Five blades taper towards tip at 0.8 radius and are constructed of hard foam filler, with spar (rovings), balancing lead rod, fibre reinforced composites skin and nickel leading-edge anti-erosion strip.
Tail rotor characteristics: 2-blade, mounted to port. Same construction as the main blades, but with stainless steel anti-erosion leading edges. See Aircraft variants for different types.
Tail surfaces: Small horizontal stabilizer with endplate fins towards the rear of the tailboom.
Flight control system: Hydraulic.
Airframe materials: Mainly metal, with some secondary structures of composites.

↑ **Eurocopter EC Super Five** *(courtesy Eurocopter)*

Safety features: Crashworthy structure, with realistic survivability in an impact of 26 ft (8 m) per second sink rate and 49 ft (15 m) per second forward speed.
Engines: 2 Allison 250-C20B turboshafts for CBS and EC Super Five. LSA-3 and Super Lifter offered with Allison 250-C28Cs, each 500 shp (373 kW) take-off and 550 shp (410 kW) OEI rating.
Engine rating: Each 420 shp (313.2 kW) take-off for C20Bs, with 440 shp (328 kW) OEI rating.
Transmission rating: Separate and independent drive shaft for each engine up to the main transmission.
Fuel system: 1,005 lb (456 kg) standard for CBS, EC Super Five and LSA-3; 570 litres usable. Fully separated feed to each engine. Auxiliary tanks can be carried in the cargo compartment.
Electrical system: Dual 28 volt DC supply via starter-generators. 25 amp-hour ni-cd battery.
Hydraulic system: Dual hydraulic boost system containing 2 independent modules. 1,500 psi.
Radar: Optional weather radar.
Flight avionics/instrumentation: Stability Augmentation System (pitch and roll axis) is standard. VFR/IFR instrumentation to customer's choice.
Expendable weapons and equipment: See Sales.

Aircraft variants:
BO 105 CBS basic version. Out of production. Allison 250-C20B turboshafts.
BO 105 LSA-3 is more powerful than the EC Super Five (see below), having 500 shp (373 kW) Allison 250-C28C engines for improved hot-and-high performance.
BO 105 LSA-3 Super Lifter is a variant of the BO 105 LSA-3, certified in 1995. It has EC Super Five blades and a new tail rotor developed from the BK 117 C-1. Intended primarily for external lift and sling load work. Allison 250-C28Cs.
EC Super Five is the latest production version, quoted as "the new BO 105 CBS-5", offering improved main rotor blades, upgraded main transmission over earlier similarly powered (Allison 250-C20B) versions of BO 105 for increased OEI performance, and additional equipment including standard dual controls. New rotor blades provide up to 330 lb (150 kg) more thrust, lower vibration level and reduced fuel consumption. Additional equipment package weighs 37.6 lb (17 kg). Certified for IFR flights.

Details for BO 105 CBS, LSA-3 and EC Super Five, unless specified

PRINCIPAL DIMENSIONS:
Rotor diameter (main): 32 ft 3.5 ins (9.84 m)
Maximum length, rotors turning: 38 ft 11 ins (11.86 m)
Fuselage length: 28 ft 11 ins (8.81 m), tail rotor vertical
Width, blades folded: 8 ft 3.5 ins (2.53 m)
Maximum height: 9 ft 10 ins (3 m)

CABIN:
Width: 4 ft 7 ins (1.4 m)
Height: 4 ft 1.25 ins (1.25 m)
Useful volume: about 127.13 cu ft (3.6 m^3)

MAIN ROTOR:
Aerofoil section: NACA 23012 for CBS and LSA-3, and DM-H4/H3 for Super Lifter and EC Super Five
Blade chord: 10.63 ins (0.27 m)
Rotor disc: 818.59 sq ft (76.05 m^2)
Rpm: 424 for CBS

TAIL ROTOR:
Diameter: 6 ft 3 ins (1.9 m)
Rpm: 2,220 for CBS

UNDERCARRIAGE:
Type: Fixed skids. Crashworthiness by the ability to absorb energy by elastic and plastic deformation

WEIGHTS:
Empty: 2,868 lb (1,301 kg) for CBS, 2,910 lb (1,320 kg) for EC Super Five, and 3,153 lb (1,430 kg) for LSA-3
Normal maximum take-off: 5,511 lb (2,500 kg) for CBS and EC Super Five, and 5,732 lb (2,600 kg) for LSA-3 and Super Lifter
Maximum take-off weight with external load: 6,283 lb (2,850 kg) for Super Lifter
Useful load: 2,580 lb (1,170 kg) for LSA-3 and 3,241 lb (1,470 kg) for Super Lifter
External payload: 1,984 lb (900 kg) for EC Super Five, and 2,205 lb (1,000 kg) for LSA-3

PERFORMANCE:
Never-exceed speed (V_{NE}): 131 kts (150 mph) 242 km/h for CBS, 145 kts (168 mph) 270 km/h for EC Super Five, 129.5 kts (149 mph) 240 km/h for LSA-3
Maximum cruise speed: 130 kts (149 mph) 240 km/h for CBS, 131 kts (151 mph) 243 km/h for EC Super Five, and 129 kts (149 mph) 239 km/h for LSA-3, all at sea level
Maximum climb rate: 1,457 ft (444 m) per minute for CBS, 1,614 ft (492 m) per minute for EC Super Five, and 1,810 ft (552 m) per minute for LSA-3, all at sea level
Vertical climb rate: 512 ft (156 m) per minute for EC Super Five
IGE hovering ceiling: 5,000 ft (1,524 m) for CBS, 7,800 ft (2,378 m) for Super Five, and 11,500 ft (3,500 m) for LSA-3
OGE hovering ceiling: 5,340 ft (1,628 m) for EC Super Five, 8,365 ft (2,550 m) for LSA-3
Service ceiling/maximum operating altitude: 10,000 ft (3,050 m) for CBS, 17,000 ft (5,182 m) for EC Super Five, and 20,000 ft (6,100 m) for LSA-3
Service ceiling, OEI: 3,000 ft (915 m) for EC Super Five
Range: 299 naut miles (345 miles) 555 km for CBS, 305 naut miles (350 miles) 564 km for EC Super Five, and 278 naut miles (320 miles) 515 km for LSA-3, all at sea level with standard fuel
Ferry range: 527 naut miles (606 miles) 976 km for EC Super Five with maximum standard fuel plus 2 × 200 litre long-range auxiliary tanks
Duration: 3.4 hours for CBS, 3.5 hours for EC Super Five and 3 hours for LSA-3, all at sea level with standard fuel

Eurocopter EC 135 and EC 635

First flight: 15 February 1994 (EC 135 S-01); second pre-production EC 135 (S-02) first flew on 16 April 1994; third pre-production EC 135 (S-03) flew on 28 November 1994.
Certification: 14 June 1996 by German LBA to JAR Pt 27, 2 July 1996 for French DGAC, 31 July 1996 for FAA to FAR Pt 27 (all VFR, including engine isolation and systems redundancy requirements according to Pt 29 for EC 135), and 1998 for CAA.
First delivery: 31 July 1996 to Deutsche Rettungsflugwacht eV, in EMS form.
Role: Light multi-purpose helicopter (EC 135) and military variant (EC 635).

Aims

▪ EC 135 meets current and new transport category operating regulations, with certification to JAR Part 27 (LBA/DGAC) and FAA Part 27, including the requirement for systems segregation and Cat A requirements of Appdx C. Low noise level, 6 dB lower than the new ICAO limit in Annex 16. Can operate in -30° C to +54° C conditions. Main objectives were to make the helicopter more economical by simplifying maintenance procedures and reduce direct operating and life cycle costs, whilst increasing performance.

Details *(for EC 135, except under Aircraft variants)*

Sales: Over 120 EC 135s ordered by July 1998, including 58 in 1997 alone. Production rate increased to 50 per year from 1998. Anticipated sales of 900 over many years.
Crew/passengers: 1 or 2 pilots plus 5/6 passengers standard, with alternative arrangements of 4/5 passengers in VIP layout or 6/7 passengers in high density layout. Casualty evacuation arrangements comprise the pilot, 1 litter and 3 seats (second litter in stowed position possible); pilot, 2 litters and 2 seats; 2 pilots, 1 litter and 3 seats (second litter in stowed position possible); or 2 pilots, 2 litters and 2 seats. Crash-resistant seats for crew and passengers. Ram-air and electrical 3-stage ventilating system for cockpit and single-stage system for the cabin.

↑ Eurocopter EC 135 equipped for law enforcement *(courtesy Eurocopter)*

Cabin access: 2 hinged cockpit doors (with sliding window and map case in pilot's door). 2 wide passenger sliding doors. 2 large and removable rear clamshell doors for rear loading capability and carrying long items.
Freight, external: 2,645 lb (1,200 kg).
Optional equipment: Large range of equipment options for the cockpit, cabin and cargo compartment, for heating and ventilation, undercarriage, landing and searchlights (including illumination), FLIR, stabilized camera systems, general mission, and handling and picketing.
Rotor system: Bearingless main rotor system, comprising rotor head/mast in a single piece, and 4 fibre-reinforced main rotor blades with anti-erosion strips, control cuff, elastomeric lead-lag dampers and special blade tip painting. Provisions for in-flight main rotor track and balance system. Flight control system has dual hydraulic boost. Electric trim system. Yaw-SAS (Stability Augmentation System). Rotor tilted forward by 5°. Rotor brake.
Tail rotor characteristics: Fenestron anti-torque system with 10 metal-blade rotor with asymmetric blade spacing and stator.
Tail surfaces: Horizontal stabilizer, with swept endplate fins toed to starboard.
Flight control system: Hydraulic, with electric SAS servos (see Rotor system).
Airframe: Crashworthy design. Extensive use of Kevlar/carbonfibre in the structure. Upper deck with fittings for main gearbox, engines, hydraulics and cooling systems. Main frame reinforced for wire-strike protection system.

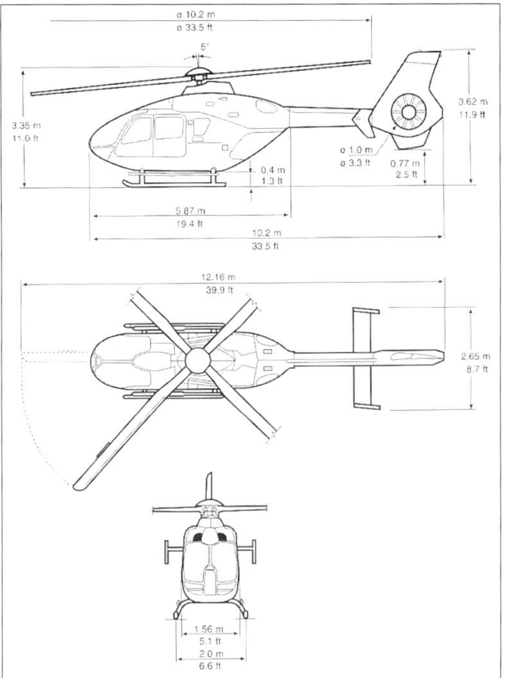

↑ Eurocopter EC 135 general arrangement *(courtesy Eurocopter)*

Engine: 2 Turbomeca Arrius 2B1 or Pratt & Whitney Canada PW206B turboshafts. Each has FADEC. S-01 had the Arrius engines fitted, S-02 the PW206Bs.
Engine rating: Arrius 2B1: 583 shp (435 kW) take-off, 559 shp (417 kW) maximum continuous, 696 shp (519 kW) OEI for 2.5 minutes, and 634 shp (473 kW) OEI maximum continuous. PW206B: 621 shp (463 kW) take-off, 562 shp (419 kW) maximum continuous, 732 shp (546 kW) OEI for 2.5 minutes, and 671 shp (500 kW) OEI maximum continuous.
Transmission: 2 × 413 shp (308 kW) take-off, 2 × 380 shp (283 kW) maximum continuous, 1 × 551 shp (411 kW) OEI for 2.5 minutes, and 1 × 473 shp (353 kW) OEI maximum continuous. Flat-shaped main gearbox with 2 stages, electrical chip detector system with check capability (main/fenestron gearbox), independent oil cooling and lubrication system, main gearbox attachment with Anti Resonance Isolation System (ARIS), free wheel assemblies in the engine input drive, tail rotor drive shaft, and tail gearbox with splash lubrication and oil level sight gauge.
Fuel system: 1,269.9 lb (576 kg) main and supply total capacity, of which 1,253.1 lb (568.4 kg) is usable.
Electrical system: Power generation system with 2 × 160A, 28 volt DC starter-generators for Arrius 2B, or 2 × 200A, 28 volt DC starter-generators for PW206B. 24 volt, 17 amp-hour ni-cd battery for Arrius 2B, or 24 volt, 25 amp-hour ni-cd battery for PW206B. External power connector. Power distribution system has 2 primary busbars, 2 shedding busbars, 2 essential busbars, 2 high load busbars (80 A) for optional equipment only, 2 high power busbars (160 A or 200 A), and battery bus.
Hydraulic system: Dual, redundant.
Radar: Optional weather radar.
Flight avionics/instrumentation: Cockpit display system (CDS) with digital indication for torque, engine parameters, dual ammeter (generator/battery), dual voltmeter, outside air temperature, fuel quantity, engine cycles, caution lights, advisory lights, engine failure trouble shooting, and optional equipment (such as load on the hook, cable length, radar altitude, mast moment). Airspeed indicator, encoding altimeter, vertical speed indicator, magnetic compass, clock, ambient air thermometer sensor, dual torque indicator, triple tachometer, dual tachometer for engines, 3 indicators for oil pressure and temperature (transmission and engines), dual turbine outlet temperature indicator, warning unit, DC power control/engine control (FADEC), main switch panel, pitot static system (electrically heated), and static pressure crossover system. Minimum items of communication and navigation equipment for dual pilot VFR operation with AlliedSignal Bendix/King Silver Crown package comprises JET AIM 510-1G 3 ins (7.6 cm) artificial horizon with slip indicator, KCS 55A/KI 525A gyro magnetic heading system with HSI, KX 165 VHF nav/com system, Becker AS 3100-12 com control system, and KT 71 transponder. If pitch and roll-SAS is installed, a 4 ins (10 cm) GH14-391 artificial horizon is installed in place of the 3 ins plus an AC system is required. Additional equipment for single pilot VFR operation comprises GPS navigation, CDI for GPS, VHF-AM com system (second system), marker beacon, HF com, com control system (second station), IC amplifier, ADF with RMI, radio magnetic indicator, DME, radar altimeter, emergency locator transmitter, Mode S transponder, stormscope, RDR-2000 colour weather radar, moving map, radio master switches and tactical FM radio. Alternative AlliedSignal Bendix/King Gold Crown for VFR operation. For IFR operation, Silver Crown/Gold Crown and conventional instrumentation, Rockwell Collins Pro Line II and conventional instrumentation, EFS 40 with Gold Crown, EFS 40 with Pro Line II (ARINC version), and EFS 40 with Gold Crown.

Aircraft variants:
EC 135P1 is civil helicopter with Pratt & Whitney Canada engines.
EC 135T1 is civil helicopter with Turbomeca engines.
EC 635 light utility helicopter is the military version of EC 135, suited to military and paramilitary roles such as utility, training, troop transport, reconnaissance and SAR. Either engine option.

Details for EC 135

PRINCIPAL DIMENSIONS:
Rotor diameter (main): 33 ft 5.5 ins (10.2 m)
Maximum length, rotors turning: 39 ft 11 ins (12.16 m)
Fuselage length: 33 ft 6 ins (10.2 m)
Width, without rotors: 8 ft 8 ins (2.65 m)
Maximum height: 11 ft (3.35 m) over rotor head, 11 ft 10 ins (3.62 m) over tailfin

CABIN:
Length: 13 ft 6 ins (4.11 m) including baggage area, 10 ft 0.5 ins (3.06 m) without baggage area
Width: 4 ft 11 ins (1.5 m) for the cockpit and first passenger seats, becoming 4 ft 0.5 ins (1.23 m) at rear of cabin
Height: 4 ft 1.5 ins (1.26 m) maximum
Volume: 134.2 cu ft (3.8 m^3) cabin, 38.8 cu ft (1.1 m^3) for baggage compartment

TAIL ROTOR:
Diameter: 3 ft 3.5 ins (1 m)

UNDERCARRIAGE:
Type: Fixed twin skids with protectors, capable of taking ground-handling wheels
Skid track: 6 ft 7 ins (2 m)

WEIGHTS:
Empty, basic version, wet: 3,148 lb (1,428 kg) with Turbomeca engines, 3,181 lb (1,443 kg) with P&WCs
Maximum take-off: 5,798 lb (2,630 kg), with either engine type
Useful load: 2,474 lb (1,122 kg) with Turbomeca engines, 2,441 lb (1,107 kg) with P&WCs
Maximum take-off, external load: 6,393 lb (2,900 kg), with either engine type

PERFORMANCE:
Never-exceed speed (V_{NE}): 155 kts (178 mph) 287 km/h, with either engine type
Maximum cruise speed: 139 kts (160 mph) 257 km/h at sea level
Recommended cruise speed: 120 kts (138 mph) 222 km/h with P&WCs, 125 kts (144 mph) 231 km/h with Turbomecas
Maximum climb rate: 1,752 ft (534 m) per minute at sea level, with either engine type
IGE hovering ceiling, ISA: 14,600 ft (4,450 m) with P&WCs, 14,200 ft (4,330 m) with Turbomecas
IGE hovering ceiling, ISA + 20° C: 10,600 ft (3,230 m) with P&WCs, 10,200 ft (3,110 m) with Turbomecas
OGE hovering ceiling, ISA: 11,800 ft (3,600 m) with P&WCs, 11,400 ft (3,475 m) with Turbomecas
OGE hovering ceiling, ISA+ 20° C: 6,900 ft (2,100 m) with P&WCs, 6,500 ft (1,980 m) with Turbomecas
Service ceiling: 20,000 ft (6,100 m), with either engine type
Service ceiling, OEI: 11,600 ft (3,540 m) with P&WCs, 11,400 ft (3,470 m) with Turbomecas
Cat A clear heliport, OEI: 10,100 ft (3,080 m) with P&WCs, 9,850 ft (3,000 m) with Turbomecas
Range: 365 naut miles (420 miles) 676 km with P&WCs, 360 naut miles (413 miles) 665 km with Turbomecas, both with standard tanks and no reserve
Duration: 3 hours 55 minutes with P&WCs, and 3 hours 44 minutes with Turbomecas, standard tanks and no reserve

Eurocopter SA 342 Gazelle

Comments: First flown on 7 April 1967, this light utility, anti-armour, air-to-air and training helicopter was last produced in SA 342M form for the French Army. Details and a photograph can be found in the 1996-97 edition of *WA&SD*, page 371.

↑ Eurocopter Tiger in HAP configuration for the French Army, with 30-mm cannon, 68-mm rockets and Mistral AAMs *(Gérôme Deulin)*

↑ Eurocopter Tiger in German Army UHT configuration, equipped with Trigat anti-tank missiles

Eurocopter Tiger (Tigre)

First flight: 27 April 1991 (PT1 first prototype).
Role: Anti-armour and combat support (HAC/UHT) and escort/support (HAP).

Aims

▪ Can operate in NBC conditions and continue flying after a nuclear electromagnetic pulse.

Development

▪ Programme has been funded by France and Germany to meet the requirements of their armies.
▪ 22 April 1993. First flight of the second prototype (PT2), becoming PT2R in 1996 when given HAP systems for testing.
▪ 19 November 1993. First flight of the third prototype (PT3), featuring the 'core' avionics suite. Became PT3R in 1997 when given UHT systems for continued testing.
▪ 15 December 1994. First flight of the fourth prototype (PT4) in HAP configuration, used for weapon trials (see below). Undertook cold weather testing in Sweden in early 1997 but was lost in February 1998 during demonstrations in Australia.
▪ 30 June 1995. The bi-national Memorandum of Understanding for the industrialization phase of the Tiger programme and its Trigat weapon system was signed.
▪ 21 September-December 1995. First series of in-flight firing tests completed by the fourth prototype (PT4), firing its cannon and Mistral self-protection missiles.
▪ 21 February 1996. First flight of the fifth and final prototype (PT5) in German Army configuration, used later for weapons trials for the UHT configuration, including Stinger, unguided rockets, Hot 2, Trigat and 12.7-mm gun pod (see below).
▪ April 1997. 5 Stinger eject test vehicle (EGV) air-to-air missiles were launched from prototype PT5.
▪ May-June 1997. 6 Hot 2 missiles were launched from prototype PT5 at Meppan in Germany using the Osiris mast-mounted sight for guidance. Also, PT4 undertook the first launch of a heat-seeking Mistral AAM from the Landes proving ground at Cazaux in France against a flying target, and also tested cannon fire with an active fire control system.
▪ 20 June 1997. Long awaited production investment contract was signed by the Federal German Agency for Military Technology and Procurement.
▪ February 1998. PT4 HAP prototype crashed near the Townsville base in North East Australia during an experimental night flight for the Australian Army. The helicopter was destroyed but the crew escaped uninjured. Tiger has been shortlisted to meet the Australian Air 87 requirement.
▪ 20 May 1998. MoU signed by Germany and France covering series production.
▪ 2001. Production deliveries will start with 2 UHTs to Germany. See Sales.
▪ 2003. Production deliveries to France will start with 2 HAPs.
▪ 2011. Production deliveries of the HAC version to France.

Details

Sales: Original requirement was for 427 for the French and German forces, comprising 140 HACs and 75 HAPs for France, and 212 for Germany as PAH-2s (later UHTs). French plans altered in 1994 to encompass 100 HACs and 115 HAPs, but still with the possibility of further downsizing. Following the signing of the production investment contract in June 1997, in May 1998 80 helicopters for each country were ordered, with production and final assembly at Donauwörth in Germany and Marignane in France. At the time of writing, because of budget restraints and delays, it was expected that France would receive only 25 helicopters between 2003 and 2005, while Germany would receive the first production helicopters in 2001, with 50 in service within 5 years and all 212 to eventually be delivered from German production lines. Export interest has come from Australia (HAP for Air 87 requirement), and Spain. HAP is derived from Eurocopter's HCP (Hélicoptère de Combat Polyvalent), while HAC and UHT derive from U Tiger.
Crew: 2 in tandem and stepped cockpits, with the pilot forward. Crash-resistant and armoured seats. Dual controls, with each crew member able to fly the helicopter and fire the weapons (except for the anti-armour missiles, which can only be fired from the rear cockpit).
Cockpit: Virtually flat glass windscreens to prevent sun glint.
Rotor system: 4-blade main hingeless, failsafe, rotor. Based on a rigid, soft in plane rotor concept. Fibre composites blades, hub with titanium centrepiece and lower/upper fibre composites plates, conical/radial elastomeric bearings, and viscoelastic lead-lag dampers. SARIB vibration suppressor. Blades have ballistic tolerance.
Tail rotor characteristics: 3-blade Spheriflex type, to starboard. Composites blades.
Wing/tail surfaces: Small stub wings with anhedral outer panels for weapon/fuel carriage. Horizontal stabilizer towards the rear of the boom, with endplate fins toed to port.
Fuselage: Lower fuselage structure of crash-dedicated design and materials to enhance survivability.
Airframe materials: 80% carbon/carbon or carbon/Kevlar composites, with 11% aluminium, 6% titanium and the remainder other materials. Frames and beams are Kevlar and carbon laminates. Panels are self-stabilized sandwich structures, comprising carbon and Kevlar skins filled with Nomex honeycomb. Fabrics are impregnated with epoxy resins. Low IR reflection paint. Wings have aluminium spars, the remainder of carbonfibre.
Safety features: 90% protection in crashes in MIL-STD-1290. Crew will survive 34 ft (10.5 m) per second vertical, 26 ft (8 m) per second lateral, and 39 ft (12 m) per second longitudinal impact.
Engines: 2 MTU/Turbomeca/Rolls-Royce MTR 390 turboshafts, with FADEC. IR suppressor in which exhaust gas is diluted with cold air and diverted upwards. Armour plate between engines.
Engine rating: Each 1,285 shp (958 kW) take-off, 1,170 shp (872.5 kW) maximum continuous and 1,555 shp (1,160 kW) super contingency.
Transmission: Main gearbox can dry run for 30 minutes.
Fuel system: 1,354 litres usable as standard. Self-sealing tanks, self-sealing breaking zones in the fuel lines. 2 auxiliary tanks available, carried on the 'wet' inner wing pylons. Maximum internal and external fuel is 3,472 lb (1,575 kg).
Electrical system: AC supply via 2 × 20 kVA alternators (30 kVA optional). DC supply via 2 × 300 amp, 28 volt transformer rectifiers and 2 × 23 amp-hour ni-cd batteries.
Hydraulic system: 2 autonomous and 1 auxiliary systems.
Flight avionics/instrumentation: Dual redundant MIL-STD-1553B databus architecture. 5 on-board computers by Sextant Avionique working with VDO-L and Litef, as the ACSG (armament computer symbol generator), MCSG (mission computer symbol generator), BCSG (bus computer symbol generator), RTU (remote terminal unit) and the CDD mission data concentrator. Sextant Avionique/Nord Micro AFCSs comprises 2 redundant digital computers controlling the 4 axes (pitch, roll, yaw and collective). Rhode & Schwarz CDU (control and display unit) at each crew station for communications, navigation, radio navigation and systems status. The operating radio frequencies are displayed on a liquid crystal radio frequency indicator (RFI). A removable data insertion device (DID) is inserted in the CDU, allowing mission preparation at a ground station. Radio communication equipment is controlled either directly via the databus or via remote terminal units (depending on type). Information from/to radio communications

Details for Tiger

PRINCIPAL DIMENSIONS:
Rotor diameter (main): 42 ft 8 ins (13 m)
Maximum length, rotors turning: 51 ft 10 ins (15.8 m)
Fuselage length: 46 ft 2 ins (14.08 m) for HAC/UHT, 49 ft 2.5 ins (15 m) for HAP
Width over wings: 14 ft 10 ins (4.52 m)
Maximum height: 12 ft 6 ins (3.81 m) to above rotor head

MAIN ROTOR:
Rotor disc: 1,428.4 sq ft (132.7 m^2)

TAIL ROTOR:
Diameter: 8 ft 10 ins (2.7 m)

UNDERCARRIAGE:
Type: High energy absorbing fixed tailwheel type
Wheel base: 25 ft 1.25 ins (7.65 m)
Wheel track: 7 ft 10.5 ins (2.4 m)

WEIGHTS:
Empty: 7,275 lb (3,300 kg) basic
Design mission: 11,905 lb (5,400 kg)
Maximum weight: 13,062 lb (5,925 kg)
Alternative gross: 13,228 lb (6,000 kg) with external load
Overload gross: 13,448 lb (6,100 kg)
Maximum useful load: 3,968 lb (1,800 kg) for HAP with roof sight, 3,638 lb (1,650 kg) for HAC/UHT with mast sight, including mission fuel

PERFORMANCE (sea level, ISA at design mission weight):
Design limit speed: 161 kts (185 mph) 298 km/h for HAC/UHT, 174 kts (200 mph) 322 km/h for HAP
Fast cruise speed: 150 kts (173 mph) 280 mph for HAP with roof sight, 140 kts (161 mph) 260 km/h for HAC/UHT with mast sight
Armed flight speed: 145 kts (167 mph) 269 km/h for HAC, 155 kts (178 mph) 287 km/h for HAP
Maximum climb rate: 2,106 ft (642 m) per minute for HAC, 2,264 ft (690 m) per minute for HAP
Vertical climb rate: 1,023 ft (312 m) per minute for HAC, 1,260 ft (384 m) per minute for HAP
Yaw rate: 40° per second
OGE hovering ceiling: 10,500 ft (3,200 m) for HAC, 11,480 ft (3,500 m) for HAP
Maximum range, internal fuel: 432 naut miles (497 miles) 800 km for HAC/UHT and HAP
Design mission duration: 2 hours 50 minutes for HAC/UHT and HAP
Maximum duration, internal fuel: 3 hours 25 minutes for HAC/UHT and HAP

and utility systems such as engines, electrical systems, hydraulics and fuel systems are collated by 2 remote terminal units, permitting monitoring by the crew during the mission. Anomalies of any sub-system are detected, and recorded in the removable mission data transfer systems for postflight evaluation and maintenance purposes; the crew may be informed immediately. Interfacing with the basic helicopter bus, the dual redundant mission computers serve also as bus controllers for the specific redundant MIL-STD-1553B interfacing the sights and weapons. Navigation subsystem was developed by Sextant Avionique in co-operation with Teldix and DASA, featuring a hybrid design (Pixyz, with 2 identical strap-down navigation units with 3-axis ring laser gyros and silicon accelerometers, 2 magnetometers, 2 air data modules, radio altimeter, Teldix/Canadian Marconi CMA 2012 4-beam Doppler radar), GPS, and low air speed sensors. Dornier/VDO-L digital map, with Eurogrid map generator. 2 Sextant Avionique/VDO-L colour liquid-crystal multi-function displays (6 × 6 ins, 15 × 15 cm) with function keys and a helmet sight/display for each crew member (Sextant Avionique Topowl for HAP/HAC and GEC-Marconi for UHT); Sextant Avionique HUD for HAP/HAC pilot, and HAP can have an automatic air surveillance and warning system (DAV) based on a pulse Doppler radar. HAC and UHT have a Euromep Osiris mast-mounted sight with IRCCD infra-red channel, CCD TV camera and laser rangefinder (flight tested on a Panther), and nose-mounted FLIR with 40° × 30° field of view. HAP has a Stryx gyrostabilized roof-mounted sight with thermographic, TV, direct optical channels, and laser rangefinder. Thomson-CSF TSC 2000 IFF.
Self-protection systems: Radar/laser warning receivers for HAP. Radar, laser and missile launch/approach warning receivers, plus chaff/flares for HAC/UHT. Optional infra-red jammer for HAC/UHT.
Fixed guns: Turreted Giat 30-781 30-mm gun for HAP. Air-to-air and air-to-ground fire control system, with ±90° azimuth and ±30° elevation.
Ammunition: 150-450 rounds.

↑ **Eurocopter Tiger pilot's *(left)* and gunner's *(right)* cockpits** *(courtesy Eurocopter)*

Number of weapon pylons: 4, 2 under each stub wing.
Expendable weapons and equipment: Mission configurations for HAC/UHT are 8 Hot 3 plus 4 Mistral or Stinger missiles, 8 Trigat plus 4 Mistral or Stinger missiles, 4 Trigat plus 4 Hot 3 and 4 Mistral or Stinger missiles, or 2 ferry tanks on the inner pylons. Mission configurations for HAP are the turreted gun with up to 450 rounds of ammunition, gun plus 4 Mistrals, gun plus 44 × 68-mm SNEB rockets in 2 pods and 4 Mistrals, gun plus 68 rockets in 4 pods, or 2 ferry tanks.

Aircraft variants:
HAC (Hélicoptère Anti-Char) is the French anti-tank/combat support version with the same equipment as UHT, designed as a highly mobile and survivable weapon system, fitted with fire-and-forget anti-armour missiles for use by day or night and in adverse weather. Requirements include to identify and engage ground targets by day and night at up to 2.7 naut miles (3.1 miles) 5 km or more; low detectability, with use of a mast-mounted sight; and self-defence with 4 AAMs.
HAP (Hélicoptère d'Appui et de Protection) is the French escort/support version, intended to offer day and night protection to anti-armour helicopters against enemy helicopters and light armoured vehicles using the short-range 30-mm wide angle turreted gun, and engage medium/long-range air threats with Mistrals. In combat support, it uses its short-range gun and medium/long-range 68-mm rockets. Fourth Tiger prototype was HAP configured.
UHT is the multi-role anti-tank//combat support version for Germany, which has been substituted for the former PAH-2 version. Similar to HAC.

Eurocopter/CATIC/ST Aero — France/Germany/China/Singapore

Corporate address:
See Combat section for details of CATIC and Singapore Technologies Aerospace.

Colibri EC 120 B

First flight: 9 June 1995 in EC 130 prototype form with Arrius 1F engine.
Certification: 1997.
First delivery: 1997.
Role: Light civil helicopter, suited to passenger/cargo transport, law enforcement, training/liaison, utility and air medical uses.

Aims

- First helicopter in its class (1.6 tonne) to comply with JAR 27 requirements.
- Quiet operation (6.6 dB below ICAO limit).

Development

- 20 October 1992. Development contract was signed, enabling the development phase to begin in January 1993. Joint multi-national team was established at Marignane (Eurocopter 61%, CATIC 24% and ST Aero 15%).
- February 1997. Marketing began.

Details

Sales: 100 ordered by 1998, of which orders for 68 had been received in 1997 alone.
Crew/passengers: Pilot and 4 passengers, or 2 pilots and 3 passengers, or 1 pilot, 1 litter and 1 or 2 medical attendants.
Cabin: Ventilation/demisting/heating (optional air conditioning) ducts, shut-off valve, rotor brake controls and cabin lighting circuit in the ceiling.
Cabin access: 5 ft 7.3 ins (1.71 m) door opening on the port side (with front door and rear sliding door), 3 ft 9.25 ins (1.15 m) on the starboard side (larger front door only).
Baggage compartment: 4 ft 3.5 ins (1.31 m) length aft of the main cabin, equipped with tie-down rings. Starboard lateral hinged cargo door, and rear hinged access cargo door.
Standard equipment: Airborne kit includes pitot head cover, static port stoppers, engine exhaust pipe cover, air intake plug (over cabin), ground handling wheels, mooring rings, main-blade socks, document holder and airborne kit storage bag. The kit is not included in the standard empty weight of the helicopter.
Optional equipment: Includes wire strike protection system, windshield wiper, cabin fan, very cold weather starting kit, extreme weather starting kit, air conditioning system, ground power receptacle, night vision goggles, enhanced stability augmentation system (ESAS 2-axes), emergency flotation gear, skis, sand prevention filter, electric hoist, agricultural spraying system, executive interior and lighting, main blade folding, many items of communication/navigation equipment, and more.
Rotor system: Spheriflex 3-blade main rotor with droop stops. Composite blades, with roving spar, carbon rib, foam fillers, counterweight, carbon leading-edge torsion box, glass/carbon skin, and erosion and lightning protection. Flight control set assisted by 3 main rotor servo units.
Tail rotor characteristics: Shrouded 8-blade fenestron type, with composites blades.
Tail surfaces: Small horizontal stabilizer under the tailboom (8 ft 6.5 ins, 2.6 m span). Fin.
Safety features: Crash-resistant fuel system and pilot/passenger seats.
Airframe materials: Extensive use of composites. CATIC/Harbin, which have a 24% share in the programme, are responsible for design and production of the complete fuselage structure, fully equipped, including fuel and hydraulic systems. Singapore Technologies Aerospace, with a 15% share, is responsible for the tailboom, the composites structure for the fenestron tail rotor, and cabin doors. Eurocopter, as 61% share team leader, is in overall charge of overall design, ground and flight testing, including design and production of the drive trains, avionics suite, electrical systems, overall integration, final assembly and certification.
Engine: Turbomeca Arrius 2F turboshaft. See also Optional equipment.
Engine rating: 504 shp (376 kW) take-off, 449 shp (335 kW) maximum continuous power.
Transmission: Main gearbox with oil sight gauge, electrical chip detector, oil temperature and pressure switches, ports for

↑ **Eurocopter/CATIC/ST Aero Colibri EC 120 B in training configuration** *(courtesy Eurocopter)*

↑ Eurocopter/CATIC/ST Aero Colibri EC 120 B instrument panel and Spheriflex rotor head *(courtesy Eurocopter)*

Details for EC 120 B

PRINCIPAL DIMENSIONS:
Rotor diameter (main): 32 ft 10 ins (10 m)
Maximum length, rotors turning: 37 ft 9.5 ins (11.52 m)
Fuselage length: 31 ft 6 ins (9.6 m)
Fuselage width: 4 ft 11 ins (1.5 m)
Maximum height: 11 ft 2 ins (3.4 m) over tailfin, 10 ft 1 ins (3.08 m) over rotor head

CABIN:
Length: 7 ft 6.5 ins (2.3 m), plus 4 ft 3.5 ins (1.31 m) of aft baggage length
Width: 4 ft 5 ins (1.35 m)
Height: 4 ft 1 ins (1.25 m)
Volume: 103.82 cu ft (2.94 m^3) of useful cabin and cargo hold volume, excluding single pilot area

MAIN ROTOR:
Blade chord: 10.24 ins (0.26 m)

TAIL ROTOR:
Diameter: 2 ft 5.5 ins (0.75 m)

UNDERCARRIAGE:
Type: Fixed twin skids. See also Optional equipment
Skid track: 6 ft 9.5 ins (2.07 m)

WEIGHTS:
Empty: 2,095 lb (950 kg) standard, including engine oil and non-usable fuel
Maximum: 3,748 lb (1,700 kg)
Maximum take-off, external load: 3,902 lb (1,770 kg)
Useful load: 1,653 lb (750 kg)
Maximum cargo sling load: 1,543 lb (700 kg)

PERFORMANCE (at 3,704 lb, 1,680 kg take-off weight):
Never-exceed speed (V_{NE}): 150 kts (173 mph) 278 km/h
High cruise speed: 123 kts (142 mph) 228 km/h
Economic cruise speed: 103 kts (119 mph) 191 km/h
Climb rate: 1,325 ft (404 m) per minute
IGE hovering ceiling, ISA: 10,000 ft (3,048 m)
IGE hovering ceiling, ISA + 20° C: 4,500 ft (1,372 m)
OGE hovering ceiling, ISA: 8,300 ft (2,530 m)
OGE hovering ceiling, ISA+ 20° C: 2,500 ft (762 m)
Service ceiling: 17,600 ft (5,364 m)
Range: 395 naut miles (455 miles) 732 km, at 103 kts, no reserve
Duration: 4.18 hours, at 65 kts, no reserve
Operating temperatures: ISA + 30° C (objective at ISA + 35° C limited to +50° C mid-1998), and 25° C (objective at -40°C beginning 1999)

boroscope, and self-sealing valve for oil sampling and draining. Engine to main gearbox coupling shaft, rotor brake, and main rotor high and low rpm warning device. Rear tail drive with low maintenance level, and tail gearbox with oil sight gauge, electrical chip detector and port for boroscopic inspection.
Fuel system: 416 litres in 2 tanks, with 411.5 litres standard usable. Optional 80 litre ferry tank.
Electrical system: 4.5 kW, 28 volt DC starter-generator. Ni-cd battery.
Flight avionics/instrumentation: Airspeed indicator, altimeter, self-powered rotor and free turbine tachometer dual indicator, warning panel, stand-by magnetic compass, heated pitot head, external side slip indicator, control box for light and electrical generation, cockpit breaker panel, cargo circuit breaker panel, and LCD dual screen vehicle and engine multifunction display (VEMD) providing the following information: first limitation indicator (FLI), torquemeter, exhaust gas temperature, gas generation tachometer, engine oil temperature/pressure, fuel quantity, ammeter and voltmeter, battery temperature, outside air temperature, enhanced usage monitoring functions (IGE/OGE performance calculations, engine cycle counting, engine power check and overlimits display), and VEMD and peripheral maintenance information. Radio and navigation equipment and mission equipment are detailed within the 5 individual configurations under Aircraft variants. See also Optional equipment.

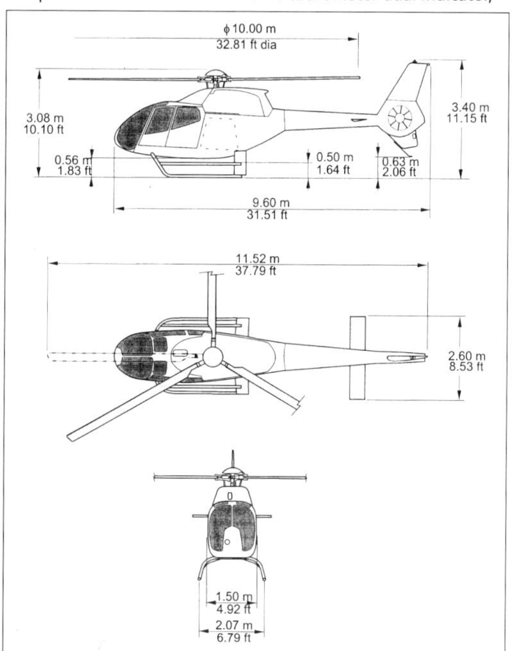

↑ Eurocopter/CATIC/ST Aero Colibri EC 120 B general arrangement *(courtesy Eurocopter)*

Aircraft variants:
Passenger transport configuration has dual controls, cabin fan and comfortable cabin layout as mission equipment. Radio com/nav equipment encompasses gyro instruments (AIM 510-22A drum-type gyro horizon and AIM 205 gyro directional indicator), AlliedSignal Bendix/King KX 165 VOR-VHF/AM No 1 (combined) with frequencies selector, TEAM SIB 120 ICS and passenger interphone, chronometer, Aerosonic 35-020-011-05 vertical speed indicator, Bendix/King KY 196A VHF-AM No 2, Trimble TNL 2000 App GPS, Jolliet JE2 NG emergency locator transmitter, and Bendix/King KT 76A transponder.
Law enforcement configuration has dual controls, cabin fan, camera, public address system, searchlight, etc as mission equipment. Radio com/nav equipment is similar to Passenger transport configuration, but without KY 196A VHF-AM No 2. Optional equipment includes infra-red camera, loudspeakers, searchlight, and more. Missions include patrol, search, pursuit, drug deterrence, firefighting support, crowd control, anti-terrorist operation and medevac.
Training configuration has dual controls and cabin fan as mission equipment. Radio com/nav equipment is similar to Passenger transport but without Trimble TNL 2000 App GPS.
Utility configuration has cabin fan, cargo sling and rear view mirror as mission equipment. Radio com/nav equipment is similar to Passenger transport but without KY 196A VHF-AM No 2, TNL 2000 App GPS, and KT 76A transponder.
Air medical transport configuration has cabin fan and structural capability for medical installation (possibility of backwards-facing front seat, foldable stretcher and single rear seat) as mission equipment. Radio com/nav equipment is similar to Passenger transport but without KY 196A VHF-AM No 2 and TNL 2000 App GPS.

Eurocopter/Kawasaki — Germany/Japan

Corporate address:
See Combat section for Kawasaki company details.

Eurocopter/Kawasaki BK 117

First flight: 13 June 1979.
Certification: To FAR Pt 29 Cat A, including Cat A standard take-off and landing procedures; qualifies for new JAR-OPS 3 Class 1 performance definition requirements.
Role: Light multi-purpose helicopter used for passenger and freight transport, VIP transport, law enforcement, SAR, EMS, firefighting and more.
Sales: 270 ordered from Eurocopter by 1998, of which 262 delivered. Well over 100 delivered separately by Kawasaki. Also has been licence-built by IPTN in Indonesia and assembled from Kawasaki kits in South Korea. Assembly lines in Germany and Japan.

Details *(principally for the BK 117 B-2)*

Crew/passengers: Pilot and 7-10 passengers or 2 litters in an EMS role.
Freight, external: 3,307 lb (1,500 kg).
Cabin access: Sliding door on each side of the fuselage and rear clamshell doors.
Optional equipment: Includes dual controls. Kawasaki now offers a certified active vibration reduction system for its newly built helicopters and for retrofit.
Rotor system: 4-blade hingeless rigid main rotor (System Bölkow), with fibre composites blades. Optional manual blade folding. See BO 105 for a detailed description of the System Bölkow rotor system. Separate and independent main transmission drive shaft for each engine. Rotor brake in German-built BK 117s, otherwise optional.
Tail rotor characteristics: 2-blade, mounted to port. Fibre composites blades.
Tail surfaces: Horizontal stabilizer towards rear of tailboom, with large swept endplate fins toed to starboard (span 8 ft 10 ins, 2.7 m).
Flight control system: Hydraulic. Fly-by-wire system has been test flown.
Airframe materials: High percentage of composites for the secondary structure, including cabin doors, nose access door, some of the lower fuselage shells, hydraulic/main transmission/engine cowlings, horizontal stabilizer and endplates.
Safety features: Crashworthy structure, able to survive a 26 ft (8 m) per second vertical and 49 ft (15 m) per second forward speed.
Engines: 2 AlliedSignal LTS101-750 B-1 turboshafts.
Engine rating: Each 684 shp (510 kW) maximum take-off, 550 shp (410 kW) maximum continuous , and 735 shp (548 kW) OEI maximum rating.
Transmission rating: 987 shp (736 kW) for take-off and 847 shp (632 kW) maximum continuous. 770 shp (574 kW) emergency OEI rating for 2.5 minutes.

↑ Eurocopter/Kawasaki BK 117 C-1

Fuel system: 710 litres, weighing 1,230 lb (558 kg). Auxiliary fuel tank raises capacity by 353 lb (160 kg). Fully separated system for each engine.
Electrical system: Dual 28 volt DC supply via 2 × 150 amp engine-driven starter-generators. 1 or 2 inverters for AC supply. 25 amp-hour ni-cd battery.
Hydraulic system: Dual system with 2 independent modes. 1,500 psi.
Radar: See below.
Flight avionics/instrumentation: Space for a variety of different communication, navigation and instrument fits of conventional or electronic types, for both VFR and IFR operations. Different types of radar, a fully-digitalized AFCS with or without coupled flight director and flight management systems can be fitted, as well as VFR/IFR instrumentation. Kawasaki and Furono also now offer a combined GPS and 3-dimensional moving map display.

Aircraft variants:
BK 117 B-2 is the current LTS101-engined version, as detailed. Certified 17 January 1992.
BK 117 C-1 is a later version with Turbomeca Arriel 1E2 engines with automatic speed control, first flown on 6 April 1990 and delivered from 1993. 738 shp (550 kW) maximum take-off, 692 shp (516 kW) maximum continuous, and 770 shp (574 kW) OEI rating according to Eurocopter data. Better hot-and-high performance, and 10,000 ft (3,050 m) IGE hover ceiling. Enhancement programme has been conducted, affecting mainly the tail rotor and to increase engine and transmission OEI ratings.

Details for BK 117 B-2, *with C-1 in italics*

PRINCIPAL DIMENSIONS:
Rotor diameter (main): 36 ft 1 ins (11 m)
Maximum length, rotors turning: 42 ft 8 ins (13 m)
Fuselage length: 32 ft 6 ins (9.91 m) tail rotor vertical
Width, blades folded: 8 ft 10 ins (2.7 m)
Maximum height: 11 ft 0.25 ins (3.36 m) to top of rotor head, 12 ft 7.5 ins (3.85 m) to top of turning tail rotor

CABIN:
Length: 9 ft 11 ins (3.02 m)
Width: 4 ft 10.75 ins (1.49 m) maximum
Height: 4 ft 2 ins (1.28 m) maximum
Volume: 176.57 cu ft (5 m^3)

MAIN ROTOR:
Blade chord: 12.6 ins (0.32 m)
Rotor disc: 1,022.89 sq ft (95.03 m^2)

TAIL ROTOR:
Diameter: 6 ft 5 ins (1.956 m)

UNDERCARRIAGE:
Type: Fixed twin skids. Crashworthiness through energy absorption by elastic or plastic deformation. Ground handling wheels. Optional emergency flotation gear, skis or skid plates
Skid track: 7 ft 10.5 ins (2.4 m)

WEIGHTS:
Empty: 3,818 lb (1,732 kg), *3,889 lb (1,764 kg)*
Maximum take-off: 7,385 lb (3,350 kg), *the same*
Maximum take-off weight with external load: 7,716 lb (3,500 kg), *the same*
Maximum useful load: 3,516 lb (1,595 kg), *3,494 lb (1,585 kg)*

PERFORMANCE (MTOW, ISA)**:**
Never-exceed speed (V_{NE}): 150 kts (172 mph) 278 km/h, *the same*
Fast cruise speed: 133 kts (153 mph) 247 km/h at sea level, *the same*
Maximum climb rate: 1,770 ft (540 m) per minute at sea level
IGE hovering ceiling: 8,200 ft (2,500 m), *10,000 ft (3,050 m) at 7,054 lb (3,200 kg) weight and 8,400 ft (2,560 m) at MTOW*
OGE hovering ceiling: 4,200 ft (1,280 m), *9,480 ft (2,890 m) at 7,054 lb (3,200 kg) weight and 4,495 ft (1,370 m) at MTOW*
Maximum certified altitude: 10,000 ft (3,050 m), *15,000 ft (4,570 m)*
Ceiling, OEI: 4,200 ft (1,280 m)
Range, standard fuel: 294 naut miles (338 miles) 545 km, *292 naut miles (336 miles) 540 km*, at sea level
Range with auxiliary fuel: *501 naut miles (576 miles) 927 km*
Duration: 2.9 hours, *3 hours*, with standard fuel, at sea level

European Future Advanced Rotorcraft (Eurofar) — France/Germany/UK

Comments: A programme to develop a passenger-carrying twin-turboshaft tilt-rotor transport was launched in 1987, with the feasibility study completed 4 years later. Agusta of Italy and CASA of Spain withdrew from the next phase of the programme, leaving further work in the hands of Dassault, Eurocopter and GKN Westland. In 1997, work restarted at the CEAT S4 windtunnel in Toulouse to define the final configuration, with testing of a one-sixth scale model continuing into 1998. Sales prospects for the Eurofar, which is not expected to fly until 2004, may be affected by faster progress in the USA with civil tilt-rotors, and until further progress is made on the Eurofar project and a final design selected, no further details will be carried. As currently envisaged, Eurofar will carry 2 pilots and 30 passengers.

Euromil — France/Germany/Russia

Corporate address: 2 Sokolnichesky Val, 107113 Moscow, Russia.
Telephone: +7 095 264 9274 **Facsimile:** +7 095 264 5341
Information: Vladimir Yablokov (General Director).

ACTIVITIES

▪ On 18 December 1992, an initial agreement was signed between Mil, Kazan, the Klimov/St Petersburg engine bureau and Eurocopter for joint development, manufacturing and marketing of the Mi-38. Each organization has a 25% shareholding. The co-operation was formalized in October 1994 when the Euromil joint venture was established.

Euromil Mi-38

First flight: Planned for 1998-99.
First delivery: 2001.
Role: Medium multi-purpose helicopter, to replace the Mi-8/17 family, with roles including passenger/troop and cargo transport, medevac, rescue, photogrammetry and ecological.

Aims

▪ Delivery of an 11,023 lb (5,000 kg) payload over a 270 naut mile (311 mile) 500 km range.
▪ To carry 30 passengers or 12 VIPs over a 432 naut mile (497 mile) 800 km range.
▪ 2 or 3 times more cost efficient than the Mi-8/-17, easier to maintain and greater reliability.
▪ All weather, day or night operation.
▪ Built according to Russian AP-29 and European JAR 29 standards. Engine meets AP-33 and JAR E regulations. Primary certification in Russia is expected, followed by JAA.

Development

▪ 30 July 1981. Governmental order for Mi-8 replacement, initially designated Mi-8M, with TV7-117 turboshaft engines.
▪ 1983. Original project considerably altered and redesignated Mi-38, under development by the Kazan division of the Mil Design Bureau.
▪ 1985. Shown on Soviet television in model form.
▪ January 1990. Work restarted, with new requirements. Development moved from Kazan to Mil in Moscow.
▪ August 1991. Full-scale mock-up accepted, shown in Summer 1992.

Details

Sales: 5 prototypes are being built at Kazan. First prototype to fly in 1998-99, followed by the second and third at 6 month intervals, used to develop the basic helicopter. Fourth and fifth prototypes will help to develop the customized Russian version. Demand for more than 300 helicopters expected during 15 years for the civil market, plus military examples.
Crew/passengers: 2 pilots and 1 other crew member, plus up to 30 passengers, 12 VIPs or 16 litters in medical layout. Possible pilot only for cargo carrying.
Freight, internal: 11,023 lb (5,000 kg).
Freight, external: 13,228 lb (6,000 kg).
Cabin access: Clamshell rear doors with ramp width of 5 ft 11 ins (1.8 m), and front fuselage side door of 5 ft 6 ins × 4 ft 9 ins (1.68 × 1.45 m). Hatch in cabin floor for sling load or air-drop operations.
Loading facilities: Optional cabin floor roller system and cargo hoist. Optional closed circuit TV system for remote viewing of external loads and handling.
Optional equipment: Includes emergency floats, rescue hoist and cargo handling equipment.
Rotor system: 6-blade composites main rotor, with spherical elastomeric bearings and hydraulic drag dampers. Titanium rotor head. Elecric leading-edge de-icing.
Tail rotor characteristics: 2 × 2-blade composite rotors, in scissors configuration. Electric de-icing.
Tail surfaces: Horizontal stabilizer with inset tabs.
Airframe: Central structure of aluminium, secondary structure and fairings of composites. Firewalls of titanium. Undercarriage of high resistance steel.
Engines: 2 Klimov/St Petersburg TVA-3000 turboshafts or Pratt & Whitney PW127s. FADEC, with mechanical back-up. Dust filters standard.
Engine rating: Each 2,500 shp (1,864 kW) for take-off (at zero altitude and ISA + 25° C), with 3,750 shp (2,796 kW) OEI

Details for Mi-38

PRINCIPAL DIMENSIONS:
Rotor diameter (main): 69 ft 3 ins (21.1 m)
Maximum length, rotors turning: 82 ft 8 ins (25.2 m)
Fuselage length: 65 ft 5 ins (19.95 m)
Fuselage width: 7 ft 10.5 ins (2.4 m)
Maximum width: 16 ft 1 ins (4.9 m)
Maximum height: 15 ft 8 ins (4.78 m) to above rotor head

CABIN:
Length: 22 ft 4 ins (6.8 m) excluding ramp
Width: 7 ft 8 ins (2.34 m) maximum, 7 ft 3 ins (2.2 m) at floor
Height: 5 ft 11 ins to 6 ft 1 ins (1.8 to 1.85 m)
Volume: 1,041.8 cu ft (29.5 m^3)

MAIN ROTOR:
Blade chord: 1 ft 8.5 ins (0.52 m)
Rotor disc: 3,764 sq ft (349.67 m^2)
Rpm: 195

TAIL ROTOR:
Diameter: 12 ft 7 ins (3.84 m)
Blade chord: 11 ins (0.28 m)

UNDERCARRIAGE:
Type: Fixed, with twin nosewheels. Optional emergency inflatable floats
Wheel base: 17 ft (5.17 m)
Wheel track: 14 ft 9 ins (4.5 m)
Static ground clearance: 2 ft (0.6 m)

WEIGHTS:
Empty: 18,298 lb (8,300 kg)
Normal take-off: 31,306 lb (14,200 kg)
Maximum take-off: 34,392 lb (15,600 kg)
Payload: 11,023 lb (5,000 kg) internal, 13,228 lb (6,000 kg) external

PERFORMANCE:
Maximum cruise speed: 148 kts (171 mph) 275 km/h
Cruise speed: 135 kts (155 mph) 250 km/h
OGE hovering ceiling: 9,185 ft (2,800 m)
Service ceiling: 17,060 ft (5,200 m)
Range with full internal fuel: 432 naut miles (497 miles) 800 km, with a 7,716 lb (3,500 kg) payload, 30 minutes reserve
Range with 11,023 lb (5,000 kg) payload: 175 naut miles (202 miles) 325 km, 30 minutes reserve
Range with auxiliary fuel: 702 naut miles (808 miles) 1,300 km, with a 3,968 lb (1,800 kg) payload, 30 minutes reserve

↑ **Euromil Mi-38** *(Piotr Butowski)*

emergency rating for 30 seconds. VD-100 APU.
Transmission: 4-stage main gearbox, ratio 80.5:1, with input rating of 5,000 shp (3,729 kW).
Fuel system: 3,796 litres in 6 underfloor bag tanks. Optional auxiliary tanks inside the cabin.
Electrical system: DC supply via 3 generators. AC supply from DC via transformer rectifiers. 2 batteries.
Hydraulic system: 3 systems, with redundancy.
Radar: Weather/navigation radar.
Flight avionics/instrumentation: Advanced flight deck with 6 colour CRT displays (each 6 ins, 15.25 cm). Integrated digital flight/navigation systems. System architecture is based on ARINC 429. Autopilot, with autostabilization, autohover and auto-landing. Navigation equipment includes Doppler, GPS, ILS and radio compass. Equipment health monitoring and warning system.

E. H. Industries Ltd (EHI) — Italy/UK

Corporate address:
Pyramid House, Solatron Road, Farnborough, Hampshire GU14 7QL, England.
Telephone: +44 1252 372121
Facsimile: +44 1252 386480
Founded: 1980.

ACTIVITIES

- Jointly and equally owned by Agusta of Italy and GKN Westland of the UK to develop and produce the EH 101.
- E.H. Industries Inc (1735 Jefferson Davis Highway, Suite 805, Arlington, VA 22202, USA – *telephone* +1 703 412 8000, *facsimile* +1 703 412 8010) is a US subsidiary.

E.H. Industries EH 101

First flight: 9 October 1987 for Westland-assembled PP1, 26 November 1987 for Agusta-assembled PP2.
Certification: 24 November 1994 for Civil.
First delivery: 1998, a Civil Mk 510 to the Tokyo Police.
Role: Medium multi-role with Naval, Utility, SAR and Civil variants.

Development

- July 1990. Deck operating trials by PP2 on *N Grecale* and *Maestrale* ships.
- 30 September 1988. First flight of Westland-assembled PP3 in Civil form, followed by Naval PP4 on 15 June 1989.
- 26 April 1989. Italian Naval PP6 first flew, and undertook trials on board *Giuseppe Garibaldi* and *Andrea Doria* in 1991.
- 24 October 1989. First flight of Naval PP5, in Royal Navy Merlin configuration. Undertook trials on board HMS *Norfolk* and HMS *Iron Duke* 1991-92.
- 18 December 1989. First flight of the Agusta-assembled PP7 Military Utility helicopter, followed on 24 April 1990 by Westland-assembled Civil PP8 and on 16 January 1991 by the Agusta-assembled Civil PP9.
- 6 December 1995. First flight of a production Merlin HM Mk 1, used initially for operational performance trials; following 6 examples also used for various pre-service trials.
- 27 May 1997. First fully operational Merlin HM Mk 1 was handed over to the Royal Navy.
- 28 May 1997. First production Civil variant was rolled out by Agusta and first flown on 17 June, later delivered to the Tokyo Police in 1998. In September 1997 the second Civil EH 101 flew.

Details

Sales: 22 Series 411s for the RAF as Merlin HC Mk 3s, with provision for flight refuelling probes and FLIR, and with self-protection equipment including GEC-Marconi Sky Guardian 2000 RWR and Hughes Danbury AVR-2A(V) laser device, to be delivered from September 1999; to be operational with Nos 28 and 72 Squadrons from the year 2002. 44 Series 111s for the Royal Navy as Merlin HM Mk 1s to replace Sea Kings on Invincible-class carriers from the year 2000 (first on HMS *Ark Royal)*, to be operated from other ships including frigates, and from shore; may be upgraded to HM Mk 2s from about the year 2005 with improvements to the sensors and processors, higher-rated transmission compatible with new variants of the RTM332 engine, and the necessary equipment/weapons to allow expansion into anti-ship/anti-surface warfare roles. Merlin project costs according to the UK Government's National Audit Office had risen to over £4.2 billion, which may put the prospect of a further 20 Merlins for the Royal Navy in doubt. Italian Navy confirmed an order for 16 in October 1995 for ship and shore use, including 8 Series 110s for anti-submarine/anti-surface vessel deployment, 4 Series 410s with rear ramps for utility use and 4 Series 112 'Enhanced Radar Aircraft' or ASVW/Es for airborne early warning (Eliradar HEW-784 surveillance radar); a further 8 expected to be ordered later; all have FLIR. The Royal Navy is also in need of a new AEW variant (see Aircraft variants). Saudi Arabia is a likely early export customer (Naval). 15 AW320 Cormorants (Series 500s with rear ramps) ordered by the Canadian Government as a naval/SAR helicopter based on the Civil. First actual Civil ordered by the Tokyo Police (Mk 510) and delivered 1998.
Crew/passengers: Flight crew of 2, plus an observer and systems operators for ASW. Naval version can carry 8 litters and 10 seated casualties over extended ranges in a SAR role. Military transport version will accommodate 30 equipped to 45 troops (latter without seating; 55 passenger capacity has been demonstrated as an emergency evacuation capability) or 16 litters plus attendants, or a light strike vehicle and crew. The civil Heliliner accommodates 30 passengers (4 abreast) or has a VIP interior.
Freight, internal: 9,500 lb (4,309 kg) for Utility; NATO pallets can be loaded via the side door, or vehicle, trailer, guns, ammunition, etc via the ramp.
Freight, external: 12,000 lb (5,443 kg) capacity cargo hook; 10,000 lb (4,535 kg) load for Utility.
Cabin access: Forward, port passenger door of 5 ft 7 ins × 3 ft (1.7 × 0.91 m). Sliding cargo door on starboard side of 5 ft 1 ins × 6 ft (1.55 × 1.82 m). Utility/Military Utility and SAR versions have hydraulically-operated rear ramp/door, of 6 ft 11 ins × 5 ft 11 ins (2.1 × 1.8 m).
Loading facilities: Reinforced floor for cargo use. Roller strips and ball matting can be installed in the Utility versions to ease loading. Active Control of Structural Response (ACSR) vibration suppression system in at least Civil version.
Standard equipment: Deck lock.
Optional equipment: Hydraulic hoist, electric standby hoist, searchlight, emergency flotation system, wire strike protection and more. Optional toilet and galley for Civil. Full ice protection system optional. Armoured seats for Military Utility. See Aircraft variants for more.
Rotor system: 5-blade main rotor system using both composites and metal components; elastomeric bearings. Rotor head assembly incorporates multiple load paths for both lift and centrifugal loads. Ballistically tolerant composite blades. Active control structural response (ACSR) system to control rotor-induced vibration. Heated blade de-icing. Automatic blade folding. Main rotor negative pitch facility.
Tail rotor characteristics: 4-blade tail rotor to port. Ballistically tolerant composite blades. Manual or automatic blade folding is optional.
Fuselage: Modular construction, comprising forward fuselage, main cabin, sponsons, rear ramp when fitted, rear fuselage, tail unit and upper deck structure. Naval variant has automatic tail folding. Reconfigured rear fuselage and boom for ramp-equipped Utility and SAR versions.
Airframe: Extensive use of composites, including the tail unit made of carbon epoxy and Kevlar epoxy skinned sandwich panels over a central skeleton of aluminium-lithium light metal alloy or foam cored composite ribs and longerons, with a Kevlar/Nomex/Kevlar sandwich forward fairing and leading edge.
Safety features: Major systems are duplicated or triplicated. Damage tolerant airframe structure and rotating components.
Engines: 3 General Electric CT7-6 turboshafts standard for Heliliner and civil utility helicopters, with a combined 6,000 shp (4,474 kW) at take-off and 5,160 shp (3,848 kW) maximum continuous. 3 Rolls-Royce Turbomeca RTM322-01/8s for Merlin HM Mk 1s, with a combined 6,304 shp (4,700 kW) take-off and 5,529 shp (4,123 kW) maximum continuous. 3 General Electric/Alfa Romeo Avio/FiatAvio T700/T6As for Italian naval helicopters, with combined rating of 6,000 shp (4,474 kW) at take-off and 5,537 shp (4,129 kW) maximum continuous. Military Utility has option of

↑ **Royal Navy E.H. Industries EH 101 Merlin HM Mk 1**

T700/T6As with a combined rating of 6,000 shp (4,474 kW) at take-off and 5,537 shp (4,129 kW) maximum continuous, or RTM322-02/8s (for Merlin HC Mk 3s) with a maximum 6,722 shp (5,013 kW) or 5,589 shp (4,168 kW) maximum continuous.
Engine rating: See above.
Transmission: 4-stage, load-sharing design, with dual lubrication circuits in main gearbox, plus a 30 minute run-dry capability. Main rotor gearbox mounted via 8 struts to 4 points on the airframe. Ratings of 5,304 shp (3,956 kW) maximum take-off for 5 minutes and 4,983 shp (3,715 kW) maximum continuous for Civil and Naval. 5,580 shp (4,161 kW) maximum at take-off for 2.5 minutes and 4,982 shp (3,715 kW) maximum continuous for Military Utility. OEI maximum continuous rating for Civil, Naval and Military Utility is 3,713 shp (2,769 kW).
Fuel system: 3,137 litres standard in 3 tanks. 1,514 litre or 3,028 litre auxiliary tank for self-ferry. Crashworthy. Fuel tank inerting and dry bay protection can be fitted.
Flight refuelling probe: Bolt-on (4 hours) air-to-air refuelling package is available. Range can also be extended by hover-in-flight refuelling.
Electrical system: 2 twin-channel 90 kVA generators, either able to supply all helicopter and mission systems. APU-driven 25 kVA generator can maintain power to essential flight systems.
Hydraulic system: 3 independent supplies for flight control servos, able to operate independently in an emergency. 3,000 psi.
Braking system: Hydraulic.
Radar: 360° search and tracking radar for naval roles and SAR. Merlin has GEC-Marconi Blue Kestrel. AlliedSignal weather radar for civil versions. For EEZ patrol, radar can scan 30,000 sq miles (77,700 sq km) per hour. See Sales for Eliradar HEW-784.
Flight avionics/instrumentation: Avionics system is integrated through digital MIL-STD-1553B databuses on military variants and ARINC 429 on Civil. Digital AFCS incorporates dual architecture and provides automatic stabilization; heading, hold and trim; turn co-ordination; and autotrim; plus autopilot facilities, allowing both single pilot VFR and IFR operation. EFIS cockpit with 6 high-definition colour CRTs. Autonomous and integrated navigation system, with Doppler, GPS and INS. Optional digital maps. Health and usage monitoring (HUMS). NVG compatible (optional). See also Aircraft variants for specific equipment and Sales.
Self-protection systems: Provision on Military Utility for IR jammers, missile approach warning, radar warning receivers, chaff/flare dispensers, and laser detection and warning.
Fixed guns: Machine-guns can be pintle-mounted at the cabin doors or fixed externally for suppressive fire.
Expendable weapons and equipment: Naval version can carry 4 homing torpedoes or depth charges, mines, or 2 anti-ship missiles including Harpoon, Sea Eagle, Exocet and Marte Mk 2. Military utility can have AAMs, rocket pods and a chin turret for a steerable 12.7-mm gun.

Details for EH 101, *all versions, with differences as indicated*

PRINCIPAL DIMENSIONS:
Rotor diameter (main): 61 ft (18.59 m)
Maximum length, rotors turning: 74 ft 9 ins (22.8 m)
Fuselage length: 64 ft 1 ins (19.53 m), except 63 ft 9 ins (19.43 m) for Military Utility
Fuselage length, folded (Naval): 51 ft 8 ins (15.75 m)
Cabin width: 9 ft 2 ins (2.8 m)
Width over sponsons: 14 ft 11 ins (4.55 m) for Civil, 15 ft 1.5 ins (4.61 m) Naval/SAR/Military Utility
Fuselage width, folded (Naval): 17 ft 5.5 ins (5.32 m)
Maximum height: 21 ft 9 ins (6.62 m)
Maximum height, folded (Naval): 17 ft 1 ins (5.2 m)

CABIN:
Length: 21 ft 4 ins (6.5 m) Civil/Utility/SAR, or 23 ft 3 ins (7.09 m) Naval
Width: 7 ft 5 ins (2.25 m) at floor, 8 ft 2 ins (2.5 m) maximum
Height: 6 ft 2 ins (1.88 m)
Volume: 970 cu ft (27.47 m^3) Civil, 1,024 cu ft (29 m^3) Naval, 1,112 sq ft (31.5 m^3) Utility
Baggage bay (Civil): 135 cu ft (3.82 m^3)

MAIN ROTOR:
Rotor disc: 2,923 sq ft (271.56 m^2)

TAIL ROTOR:
Diameter: 13 ft 2 ins (4 m)
Rotor disc: 135 sq ft (12.6 m^2)

UNDERCARRIAGE:
Type: Retractable, with twin steerable nosewheels. Twin wheels on main units of Military Utility and SAR versions, otherwise single but with option of twin for Civil offshore and soft ground operations. Allows landings of 12 ft (3.7 m) per second without deformation. Optional emergency flotation gear
Wheel base: 22 ft 11 ins (7 m)

WEIGHTS:
Maximum take-off: 32,187 lb (14,600 kg), with 34,172 lb (15,500 kg) demonstrated
Useful load: 12,170 lb (5,520 kg) for Naval, 13,228 lb (6,000 kg) for Civil, 12,544 lb (5,690 kg) for Military Utility
Payload: up to 11,023 lb (5,000 kg) for Naval and SAR
Payload, external sling: 10,000 lb (4,536 kg) for Military Utility

PERFORMANCE (typical):
Never-exceed speed (V_{NE}): 167 kts (192 mph) 309 km/h, also quoted as a dash speed for the SAR variant
Cruise speed: 150 kts (173 mph) 278 km/h
Best range cruise speed: 142 kts (163 mph) 263 km/h
G limit: 3, for at least Military Utility
Service ceiling: 15,000 ft (4,575 m)
Radius of action (Military Utility): 320 naut miles (368 miles) 593 km with 18 troops, or 190 naut miles (219 miles) 352 km with 30 troops
Radius of action (Civil offshore support): 180 naut miles (207 miles) 333 km
Range (Civil and Military Utility): over 400 naut miles (460 miles) 740 km with 30 passengers
Range (Heliliner) with 4 internal tanks: 610 naut miles (702 miles) 1,130 km
Range (SAR), with 5 internal tanks: 750 naut miles (863 miles) 1,390 km
Ferry range (Utility): 864 naut miles (994 miles) 1,600 km with auxiliary fuel tanks
Duration: over 4 hours for Civil, 5 hours for Naval, and up to 9 hours for SAR

Aircraft variants:
Civil variant is offered in EH 101-500 ***Utility*** with rear ramp and EH 101-300 ***Heliliner*** passenger versions. CT7-6 engines. A VIP layout has 4 armchairs in the forward cabin and 2 sofas in the aft. Heliliner complies to JAROPS 3, Class 1 for offshore take-off. Baggage volume 135 cu ft (3.82 m^3). Optional toilet and galley. Single main wheels standard, with twin wheels optional for offshore or soft ground operation. Advanced flight management, advanced electronic displays, dual flight controls, GPS navigation, high-energy absorbing undercarriage, compatible with existing offshore platforms, optional multiple window exists, optional external life rafts, optional rotor ice protection system, optional flotation gear, HUMS, crashworthy fuel tanks, and weather radar.
Naval variant offers fully autonomous, all-weather and day/night capability, and can operate from shore or 3,500 tonne frigates with winds of up to 50 kts in any direction. Automatic main rotor and tail section folding for compact stowage. T700/T6A or RTM322-01/8 engines (former selected by Italian Navy and latter selected by Royal Navy). Single or optional twin wheels on each undercarriage unit. Possible naval missions include ASW/ASUW, EEZ protection, ASST, OTH targeting and surveillance, electronic warfare, airborne early warning, mine-countermeasures/ deployment, SAR, amphibious assault/troop transport and vertrep. Known as Merlin to the Royal Navy. Features include optional FLIR, 360° radar, mission console with 4 full-colour display screens, ESM, solid state data transfer device for tactical and maintenance information/data link, optional digital map display, optional mission recorder, retractable rescue hoist, sonobuoy dispensers, and weapons. Thomson Marconi Sonar/Thomson Sintra FLASH/AQS-950 dipping sonar and advanced sonobuoy processing system for Merlin. Normalair-AlliedSignal sonobuoy dispenser with 10 sonobuoy capacity, MAD and ESM/ECCM. Normalair-AlliedSignal mission recording system. Automated stores management. NVG compatible (optional). For maritime patrol and EEZ protection, can search an area of 45,000 sq naut miles per sortie. Cargo hook for underslung loads.
SAR variant can carry 4 crew and 28 seated survivors, or 4 litters and 4 seated survivors plus 2,205 lb (1,000 kg) of specialized equipment. Can also be configured for 16 litters and a medical team for casevac, or as a transport carrying a 20-strong search team in Arctic clothing. Hydraulic hoist plus electric standby hoist. Rear ramp. Doppler hover and automatic search modes. Winchman hover trim control. Optional flight refuelling probe. All-weather operational capability, from arctic (-40° C) to tropical (+50° C). Alert to take-off time under 5 minutes. Optional wire strike protection, optional secondary rescue hoist, SAR communications, optional NVG compatibility, optional defensive aids, search/weather radar, optional FLIR, crashworthy pilots' seats, and optional air-to-air refuelling.

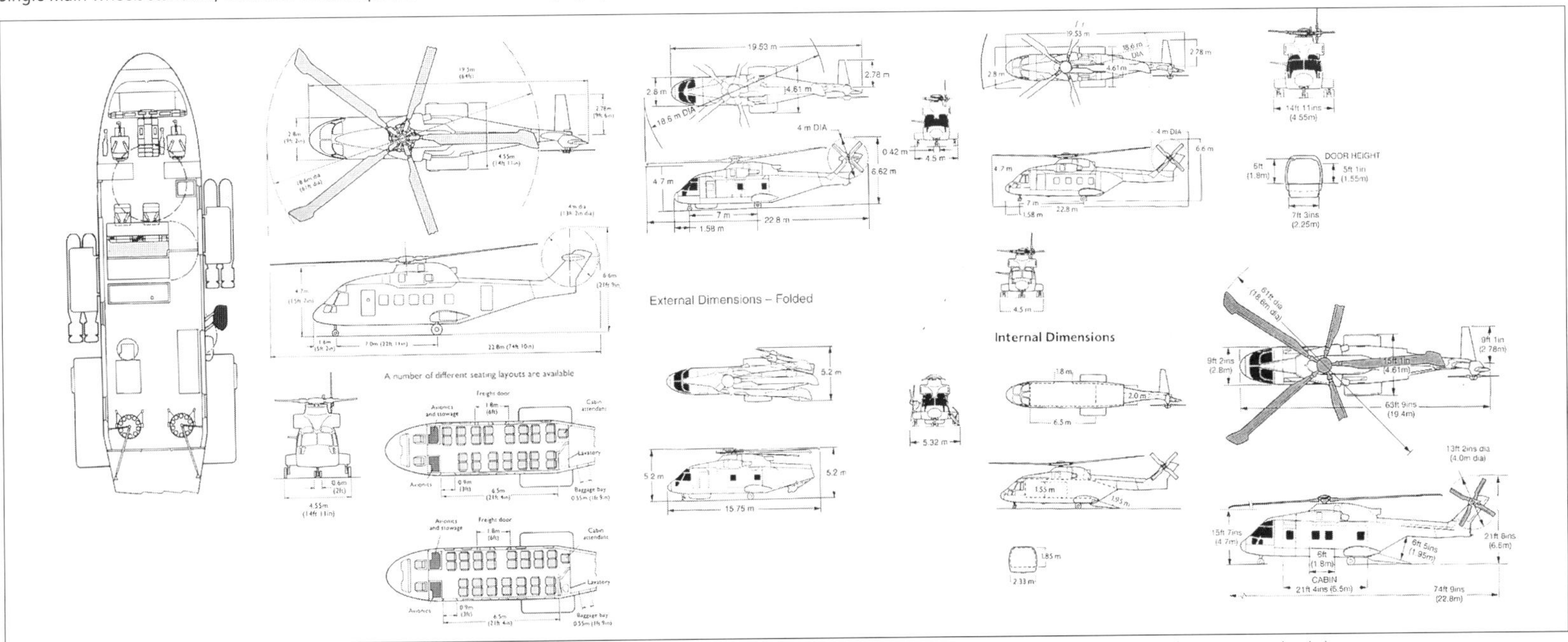

↑ E.H. Industries EH 101, showing a typical Naval cabin configuration *(far left)*, plus general arrangements for *(left to right)* Civil, Naval, SAR and Military Utility versions *(courtesy E.H. Industries)*

Military Utility version, like SAR, has a rear ramp. T700/T6A or RTM322-02/8 engines (latter as chosen for RAF). See Self-protection systems. Optional window and door gun positions. Optional armour and armoured crew seats. Side-mounted troop seats (optionally crashworthy) and optional centre troop row and rear crew seats. Large siding door. Optional heavy duty cabin floor and ramp with flush tie-down points; NVG compatible; 4 self-sealing (optionally crashworthy) fuel tanks; selective pressure refuel, defuel, jettison and buddy-buddy refuelling; optional rapid role fit flight refuelling probe; optional empty bay fire suppression; optional ferry tanks; optional armoured fuel manifold; optional cargo winch for non-self-loading freight; optional conveyor for palleted freight, optional bubble windows for rear crew all-round visibility; twin-wheel undercarriage with high-flotation tyres; optional wire strike protection system; optional rotors ice protection; main rotor negative pitch facility; optional automatically deployable emergency locator transmitter; optional accident data recorder; optional cockpit voice recorder; underfloor stowage for role equipment, with optional strops, nets and servicing kit; optional 12,000 lb (5,443 kg) underslung load hook, with permanent fitting in large access/vision hatch (load measurement displayed in cockpit); optional rescue hoist and hover trim controller at the cargo door; and optional fast roping/abseiling facility. Military utility missions include tactical troop lift, logistic support, combat search and rescue, casualty evacuation, and command and control. Day/night and NOE operation. Optional FLIR display and digital maps.

CH-148 Petrel and ***CH-149 Chimo*** were versions ordered by Canada, 35 and 15 respectively. Cancelled by the Canadian Government in 1993.

AW320 Cormorant is a lower-cost naval/SAR model based on the Civil and offered to Canada to replace CH-113 Labradors. 15 ordered with Computing Devices Canada Helicopter Acoustic Processing System (HAPS) that encompasses GEC-Marconi Cormorant dipping sonar.

Compound-lift variant of Merlin has been proposed by GKN Westland to meet the Royal Navy's Future Organic Airborne Early Warning (FOAEW) requirement. A competing suggestion has come from British Aerospace for a fixed-wing aircraft with wingtip Sidetrack synthetic aperture radar. If approved, the Merlin would feature anhedral stub wings above the cabin, improved engines and a flight refuelling probe to provide higher performances and duration.

NHIndustries (NHI) — France/Germany/Italy/Netherlands

Corporate address:
Le Quatuor, Bâtiment C, 42 Route de Galice, 13082 Aix-en-Provence Cedex 2, France.

Telephone: +33 42 95 97 00
Facsimile: +33 42 95 97 49
E-mail: nhi@aix.pacwan.net

Founded: August 1992.

Information:
Alain Gauthier (Commercial Department Manager – *telephone* +33 42 95 97 02).

ACTIVITIES

▪ NHIndustries is prime contractor for design and development, industrialization, production and logistic support of the NH90 helicopter, and is responsible for marketing and sales. The 4 contributing companies to this international programme are Agusta (26.9%), Eurocopter Deutschland (24%), Eurocopter (42.4%) and Fokker (6.7%).

▪ An international programme office, representing the 4 participating governments, was founded in February 1992 as NAHEMA (NAto HElicopter Management Agency).

NHIndustries NH90

First flight: 18 December 1995.
Role: Tactical transport helicopter (TTH) and multi-role NATO frigate helicopter (NFH).

Aims

▪ To meet the needs of the navies of France, Germany, Italy and the Netherlands, the armies of France, Germany and Italy, and the air forces of Germany and Italy.

Development

▪ Following studies by a NATO Industrial Advisory Group (NIAG SG14) during 1983-84, and feasibility and pre-definition studies thereafter, the governments of the participating nations signed a memorandum of understanding in December 1990 for full development of a Naval/Tactical helicopter. NHI was founded to manage this joint venture.
▪ March 1992. Signature of the Intercompany Agreement by Agusta (28.2% of Design and Development), Eurocopter Deutschland (23.7%), Eurocopter France (41.6%) and Fokker (6.5%).
▪ 28 September 1995. The ground test vehicle made its first run at Cascina.
▪ 29 September 1995. Roll-out PT1 first prototype, with the first flight on 18 December.
▪ 19 March 1997. First flight of the PT2 second prototype, following its roll-out the previous November.
▪ 2 July 1997. PT2 successfully flown with the fly-by-wire primary control system.
▪ 1998. Production go-head anticipated.
▪ 2003. Production deliveries to start, initially to the Netherlands Navy.

Details

Sales: Programme included the production of a ground test vehicle, 3 prototypes in a common basic configuration (PT1-3), a TTH (Tactical Transport) with full mission systems (PT4), and an NFH (PT5) with specific naval mission systems. PT1-PT3 assembled and tested by Eurocopter, with Eurocopter Deutschland producing PT4 and Agusta producing the ground test vehicle and PT5. Planned procurement of 149 NFHs (France 27, Germany 38, Italy 64 and the Netherlands 20) and 498 TTHs (France 133 proposed but possibly to be reduced to 68, Germany 205 and Italy 160). Export potential for 500-700 worldwide.
Crew/passengers: Can be pilot only for VFR and IFR operations. More typically, NFH has a crew of 3 comprising the pilot, tactical co-ordinator (in co-pilot position) and systems operator (Senso). Fourth crew station optional, allowing for 2 pilots and a separate Tacco position next to the Senso. 2 crew for the TTH. 14-20 troops or up to 12 litters, or a light vehicle and its 3 crew in TTH.
Cockpit: Side-stick controllers.
Freight, internal: Maximum >5,512 lb (2,500 kg) of cargo, or a light tactical vehicle with crew.
Cabin access: Large sliding door each side of 5 ft 3 ins (1.6 m) width and 4 ft 1 ins (1.5 m) height, plus a rear ramp/door of 5 ft 10 ins (1.78 m) width and 5 ft 2 ins 1.58 m) length.
Standard equipment: Rescue hoist.
Rotor system: Advanced 4-blade main rotor is of maintenance free, 'hinged' spheriflex type. Each damage tolerant blade is hinged on a single elastomeric spherical thrust bearing secured to the titanium main rotor hub. Blades, of composite type with multi-box structure and mixed glass-carbon skin, are equipped with heating mats which can be activated when the ice protection kit is installed. Dynamic system has 30 minutes dry running capability. NFH has auto blade folding.
Tail rotor characteristics: 4-blade (composites), hinged spheriflex type, designed for low noise and easy setting.
Tail surfaces: Horizontal stabilizer mounted to starboard under the tail rotor pylon and fin.
Flight control system: Multi-redundant fly-by-wire, with no mechanical back-up, with 4 independent lines for data transfer with 4 control processing units (digital and analog).
Airframe: Carbonfibre all-composites crashworthy fuselage, with low IR signature.
Safety features: See Fuel system. Shock-absorbing seats and energy absorbing undercarriage ensure crew survivability in vertical landings of up to 36 ft (11 m) per second (according to MIL-STD-1290 – 85 percentile).
Engines: 2 RTM322-01/9 turboshafts in each of the first prototypes and for production helicopters from Turbomeca, Rolls-Royce, MTU, Piaggio and Topps. Alternatively, General Electric/Alfa Romeo Avio T700/T6Es for NFHs and TTHs, as selected by Italy. APU for engine start and ECS ground operation. IR suppressor and sand filters on TTH.
Engine rating: Each 2,234 shp (1,666 kW) maximum for 30 minutes, 2,092 shp (1,560 kW) maximum continuous power, 2,250 shp (1,678 kW) OEI continuous, 2,506 shp (1,869 kW) OEI maximum contingency, and 2,784 shp (2,076 kW) OEI for 30 seconds emergency.
Transmission: 3,084 shp (2,400 kW). Modular main gearbox features an integrated lubrication system, an innovative monitoring and diagnostic system, and 2 accessory gearboxes. Dynamic system has 30 minute dry running time capability. On the ground, the APU drives the remote accessory gearbox, to provide electrical and hydraulic power and air conditioning.
Fuel system: Comprises high capacity, crash-resistant, self-sealing tank cells in the cabin floor. Fuel inert gas system. Pressure refuelling port, hover-in-flight refuelling and dumping capability. 4,193 lb (1,902 kg) of usable fuel standard in NFH.
Electrical system: Includes 3 alternators, 2 driven by the main gearbox and 1 driven by the remote accessory gearbox. In addition to the DC provided by 2 batteries, an emergency DC generator is driven by the RAGB.
Hydraulic system: Redundant flight control hydraulic system features 2 main separated and independent circuits. In addition, an independent Utility System provides hydraulic power for the undercarriage and ancillary operations. In case of failure, one circuit can be powered by a back-up electrically-driven pump, while the other circuit is permanently supplied in parallel by an accessory gearbox driven pump of the Utility System.
Radar: NFH has a 360°, track-while-scan, target recognition radar; not selected at the time of writing but one proposal is the SeaFalcon from a European and US consortium known as HEART (Helicopter Euro-American Radar Team). TTH has weather radar. See also Aircraft variants.
Flight avionics/instrumentation: Avionics system integration based on 2 independent dual-redundancy MIL-STD-1553B digital databuses, 1 supporting the core avionics system and 1 the mission system. The core avionics system, common to both TTH and NFH versions of the helicopter, is designed for the management of the multi-function Sextant Avionique control and display units, basic communications, navigation and guidance functions, and for monitoring and check-out of avionic and vehicle systems. Crew commands are directly inserted through display and keyboard units (DKU). The NVG-compatible control and display system consists of 4 Sextant Avionique SMD 88 type 8 × 8 ins (20 × 20 cm) colour liquid crystal smart multi-function displays (MFD) for flight and mission functions in the TTH version of the helicopter and 5 in the NFH version (plus a further 3 or 6 MFDs in the cabin stations of NFH), a central warning system, 2 remote frequency indicators (RFI) and a set of conventional back-up instruments. The navigation element of the core system comprises an inertial reference system (IRS) with GPS, Doppler velocity sensor (DVS), radar altimeter, air data system (ADS), microwave landing system (MLS), and distance measuring equipment (DME-P). The communication and identification elements of the core system comprise ICS, 2 V/UHF radios, 1 V/UHF direction finder/homer, 1 HF/SBB, and an IFF transponder plus Mode S. A special Helicopter Performance Computation function of the core system can provide the crew at any time with information on how the helicopter is operating or it can predict how it may operate in a given situation, supporting the crew in its mission-oriented decision making. The interface between the core bus and the mission bus is provided through the Mission Tactical Computer. *Dedicated Mission System in NFH* comprises a tactical control system (TCS), data link 11, radar (see above), IFF interrogator, dipping sonar and sonobuoys, MAD, ESM, chaff/flare dispensers, tactical FLIR, stores management system, and data recording system. The NFH's TCS integrates all mission sensors, communication and navigation data, and air vehicle information; it also supports the crew in performing the attack phase (direct or indirect by OTHT) of the mission. A dedicated video network is used within the NFH mission system architechure to distribute the information generated in video format to all cockpit and cabin MFDs. NFH has a complex audio distribution network to distribute voice

↑ **NHIndustries NH90 large sliding door arrangement** *(G. Deulin for NHI)*

↑ NHIndustries NH90 second prototype *(G. Deulin for NHI)*

Details for NH90, *with differences between TTH and NFH where indicated*

PRINCIPAL DIMENSIONS:
Rotor diameter (main): 53 ft 6 ins (16.3 m)
Maximum length, rotors turning: 64 ft 2.25 ins (19.563 m)
Fuselage length: 52 ft 5 ins (15.97 m)
Width: 15 ft 2 ins (4.618 m) without main rotor
Width over sponsons: 11 ft 11 ins (3.633 m)
Maximum height: 17 ft 10 ins (5.44 m)

CABIN:
Length: 13 ft 2 ins (4 m) without ramp, 15 ft 9 ins (4.8 m) with ramp, usable
Width: 6 ft 7 ins (2 m)
Height: 5 ft 2 ins (1.58 m)

MAIN ROTOR:
Blade chord: 2 ft 1.5 ins (0.65 m)
Rotor disc: 2,246.1 sq ft (208.67 m^2)
Rpm: 256.6

TAIL ROTOR:
Diameter: 10 ft 6 ins (3.2 m)
Rpm: 1,235.4

UNDERCARRIAGE:
Type: Retractable, with twin nosewheels. Crashworthy. Emergency flotation gear
Wheel base: 19 ft 11 ins (6.083 m)

WEIGHTS:
Empty, operating: 14,171 lb (6,428 kg)
Mission gross: 20,062 lb (9,100 kg) for NFH, 19,180 lb (8,700 kg) for TTH
Mission payload: >5,512 lb (2,500 kg) for TTH
Maximum payload: 10,140 lb (4,600 kg)

PERFORMANCE:
Dash speed: 162 kts (186 mph) 300 km/h at sea level and ISA + 10° C for NFH, and same for TTH at 3,280 ft (1,000 m) and ISA + 15° C
Maximum cruise speed: 157 kts (181 mph) 291 km/h for NFH at sea level and ISA + 10° C, and 161 kts (185 mph) 298 km/h for TTH at 3,280 ft (1,000 m) and ISA + 15° C
Economic cruise speed: 140 kts (162 mph) 260 km/h for NFH at sea level and ISA + 10° C, and 141 kts (163 mph) 262 km/h for TTH at 3,280 ft (1,000 m) and ISA + 15° C
Climb rate: 2,264 ft (690 m) per minute for NFH at sea level and ISA + 10° C, and 2,165 ft (660 m) per minute for TTH at 3,280 ft (1,000 m) and ISA + 15° C
IGE hovering ceiling: >10,825 ft (3,300 m) for NFH, and >11,483 ft (3,500 m) for TTH, both ISA
OGE hovering ceiling: 8,530 ft (2,600 m) for NFH, 9,514 ft (2,900 m) for TTH, both ISA
Maximum operating ceiling: 19,685 ft (6,000 m) at ISA + 15° C for TTH or ISA + 10° C for NFH
Radius of action: > 135 naut miles (155 miles) 250 km for TTH with a 4,409 lb (2,000 kg) payload at 3,280 ft (1,000 m) and ISA + 15° C
Maximum range: >513 naut miles (590 miles) 950 km for NFH at sea level and ISA + 10 ° C, and >475 naut miles (547 miles) 880 km for TTH at 6,560 ft (2,000 m) and ISA + 20° C
Ferry range: >647 naut miles (745 miles) 1,200 km for NFH at sea level and ISA + 10° C, and >620 naut miles (715 miles) 1,150 km for TTH at 6,560 ft (2,000 m) and ISA + 20° C
Duration: 5 hours for NFH at sea level and ISA + 10° C, and 4.5 hours for TTH at 6,560 ft (2,000 m) and ISA + 20° C
Operating time, at 50 naut miles from base: 3.3 hours with 20 minutes reserve for NFH at sea level and ISA + 10° C

messages, warning tones and audio information (Data Link 11 messages). Specific mission related audio features include Underwater communication (UWT) for voice communication between co-operating units. *Dedicated Mission Systems in TTH* comprise the tactical control system (TCS) that interfaces with the core system via the core databus, video lines and dedicated lines to generate the tactical situation and record and up/down load the tactical/mission data; the electronic warfare system (EWS – see Aircraft variants); the dedicated mission flight aids (MFA – see Aircraft variants); and the tactical communication system (TCOM) that allows all communication with the ground forces to be undertaken in the most accurate and secure way (predefined radio silence period, frequency hopping, secure voice, etc). Crew has access to the mission system via the DKUs and MFDs. Autopilot. Automatic monitoring and diagnostic system. See Aircraft variants for Mission flight aids.
Self-protection systems: TTH has an electronic warfare system comprising missile launch detector, radar warning receiver, laser warning receiver, chaff/flares and IR jammer.
Expendable weapons and equipment: See Aircraft variants.

Aircraft variants:
NFH is the NATO Frigate Helicopter naval variant, primarily for autonomous ASW and ASUW but with additional roles including anti-air warfare support, vertrep, SAR, troop transport and minelaying. Designed for day and night/adverse weather/severe ship motion environment operations, with the capability to launch and recover from small ships in extreme adverse weather conditions. Equipped with a fully integrated flight control/basic and mission avionics system, it can undertake its mission autonomously with a crew of 3 (optionally 4). Operationally it can detect, classify, identify by type, track and attack submarines and surface targets, including over-the-horizon, and by day and night. Equipment includes sonobuoys or dipping sonar, AQS-950 acoustic processor, tactical radar, MAD, tactical FLIR, electronic warfare systems, and ASW/ASV weapons such as missiles and torpedoes (see Avionics). The NFH Helo-Ship Interface capabilities allow effective and safe on-deck operations in the most severe environment: Harpoon deck-lock system, automatic main rotor blade and tail boom folding (in under 3 minutes), telebriefing (protected communication between the NFH crew and the tactical operations centre on the parent ship), and data umbilical link (transfer of Link 11 information from the ship to the helicopter for quick mission preparation).
TTH is the Tactical Transport Helicopter version, primarily for carrying 14-20 troops or material (more than 5,511 lb, 2,500 kg), heliborne operations and SAR/combat SAR, but with additional applications including medevac, special operations, electronic warfare, airborne command post, parachuting, VIP transport and training. Large sliding doors, rescue hoist, and cargo hook. Optimized for low signatures (acoustic, radar and infra-red) and is equipped with mission flight aids comprising a night vision system (FLIR, NVG, and Sextant Avionique Topowl helmet mounted sight and display), weather radar, Sextant Avionique digital map, Obstacle Warning System, and optional VHF/FM data link. Other equipment comprises fuselage-side weapon carriers, cable cutters, armoured pilots' seats, defensive weapons suite, passive and active countermeasures and, as an option, a rear-mounted ramp/door to allow loading of a light vehicle. Also designed for high manoeuvrability and survivability in Nap of the Earth (NOE) operations near the forward edge of the battlefield area. Crashworthiness to MIL-STD-1290 (85% potential survivability). Single pilot IFR/IMC. NBC, EMI and laser protection. Optional fuselage side weapon carriers.

General Aviation

(incorporating Business, Agricultural, Light Transport & piston-engined Training aircraft)

Aero Boero S.A.

Argentina

Corporate address:
Plant 1: Brasil y Alem, 2421 Morteros (Córdoba). *Plant 2:* Av.9 de Julio 1101, 2400 San Francisco (Córdoba). Also Rua André Cavalcante, 13A Rio de Janeiro, RJ, Brazil.

Telephone:
Plant 1: +54 562 22121 or 22690. *Plant 2:* +54 564 22972 or 24118. *Brazil:* +55 21 224 0450

Facsimile:
Plant 1: +54 562 22121. *Brazil:* + 55 21 224 2933

Founded:
1959.

Information:
Hector A. Boero (President).

Aero Boero AB 115 and AB 115/150

First flight: February 1973.
Role: Training, agricultural (AB 115/150) and recreational.
Crew/passengers: 3.
Baggage capacity: *AB 115:* 7.42 cu ft (0.21 m^3); *AB 115/150:* 7.06 cu ft (0.2 m^3)
Chemical tank/hopper: *AB 115/150:* 280 litres of insecticide in an underfuselage pod.
Wing characteristics: High-wing monoplane with bracing struts. Conventional controls.
Construction materials: All duralumin wing and spar, and reinforced SAE 4130 steel tube fuselage structure with Dacron fabric skin.
Engine: *AB 115:* Textron Lycoming O-235-C2A, *AB 115/150:* O-320-A2B.
Engine rating: *AB 115:* 115 hp (85.75 kW) at 2,800 rpm; *AB 115/150:* 150 hp (112 kW) at 2,700 rpm.
Fuel system: 2 × 57 litre tanks.
Flight avionics/instrumentation: Ready to fit any radio, navigation or IFR instruments.

Details for AB 115, with AB 115/150 as indicated

PRINCIPAL DIMENSIONS:
Wing span: 35 ft 9 ins (10.9 m)
Maximum length: 23 ft 3 ins (7.08 m)
Maximum height: 6 ft 11 ins (2.1 m) *at rest*, 9 ft 9 ins (2.98 m) *flying attitude*

WINGS:
Aerofoil section: NACA 23012
Area: 186 sq ft (17.28 m^2)
Aspect ratio: 6.87

UNDERCARRIAGE:
Type: Fixed, with tailwheel

WEIGHTS:
Empty: 1,226 lb (556 kg)
Maximum take-off: 1,768 lb (802 kg)
Payload: 542 lb (246 kg)

PERFORMANCE:
Maximum speed: 119 kts (137 mph) 220 km/h
Cruise speed: 92 kts (106 mph) 170 km/h *for AB 115*, 97 kts (112 mph) 180 km/h *for AB 115/150*
Stall speed: 46 kts (53 mph) 85 km/h *clean*, 38 kts (44 mph) 70 km/h *with flaps*. Electrical stall warning
Landing speed: 42 kts (48 mph) 77 km/h
Take-off distance: 328-427 ft (100-130 m) *for AB 115*, 279-328 ft (85-100 m) for *AB 115/150*
Landing distance: 263 ft (80 m) for *AB 115*, 246 ft (75 m) for *AB 115/150*
Maximum climb rate: 670 ft (204 m) per minute *for AB 115*, 787 ft (240 m) per minute for *AB 115/150*

↑ Aero Boero AB 180 PSA 2-seater for a military preselection role

Aircraft variants:
AB 115 is the basic model, not used for agricultural work.
AB 115/150 is the higher powered model, suitable also for agricultural work.

Aero Boero AB 180 AG, PSA and RVR

Role: Agricultural (*AB 180 AG*), glider-towing (*RVR*), military preselection (*PSA*) and recreational. AB 180 RVR can climb at 590 ft (180 m) per minute towing a Standard class glider, or 394 ft (120 m) per minute towing a 2-seater.
Details: Similar to AB 115, except as quoted.
Crew/passengers: Up to 3 (*AG/RVR*), with PSA having 2 in tandem.
Baggage capacity: 7.42 cu ft (0.21 m^3). *AB 180 PSA* has 7.35 cu ft (0.208 m^3) or 55 lb (25 kg).
Chemical tank/hopper: *AB 180 AG* has 320 litres of insecticide in an underfuselage pod.
Wing control surfaces: AB 180 RVR is fitted with extra large flaps.
Engine: Textron Lycoming O-360-A1A.
Engine rating: 180 hp (134.3 kW) at 2,700 rpm.
Fuel system: 2 × 88 litre tanks.

Aero Boero AB 260 AG

First flight: 23 December 1972.
Role: Agricultural aircraft.
Crew/passengers: Pilot only normally; second person can be carried.
Baggage capacity: 7.42 cu ft (0.21 m^3)
Chemical tank/hopper: 550 litres of insecticide.
Dispersal equipment: Wing-installed spraybars, with underwing atomizers.
Wing characteristics: Low monoplane wings with upper bracing struts, wing fences and down-turned wingtips.
Construction materials: Duralumin wings. SAE 4130 steel fuselage structure, with duralumin and composites skins.
Engine: Textron Lycoming O-540-H2B5D.
Engine rating: 260 hp (194 kW) at 2,700 rpm.
Fuel system: 2 × 120 litre tanks.

Details for AB 180

PRINCIPAL DIMENSIONS: As for AB 115 except:
Wing span: 35 ft 4.5 ins (10.78 m) *for AB 180 PSA*

UNDERCARRIAGE:
Wheel track: 5 ft 11 ins (1.8 m)

WEIGHTS:
Empty: 1,415 lb (642 kg) *for AB 180 AG*, 1,327 lb (602 kg) *for RVR*
Maximum take-off: 2,209 lb (1,002 kg) *for AB 180 AG*, 1,861 lb (844 kg) *for PSA*, 1,962 lb (890 kg) *for RVR*
Payload: 794 lb (360 kg) *for AB 180 AG*, 635 lb (288 kg) *for RVR*, 534 lb (242 kg) *for PSA*

PERFORMANCE:
Maximum speed: 113 kts (130 mph) 210 km/h *for AB 180 AG*, 132 kts (152 mph) 245 km/h *for PSA* and *RVR*
Cruise speed: 89 kts (103 mph) 165 km/h *for AB 180 AG*, 114 kts (131 mph) 211 km/h *for PSA*, 107 kts (123 mph) 198 km/h *for RVR*
Stall speed, clean: 46 kts (53 mph) 85 km/h *for AB 180 AG*, 43.5 kts (50 mph) 80 km/h *for PSA*, 44.5 kts (51 mph) 82 km/h *for RVR*
Stall speed, with flaps: 43 kts (49 mph) 79 km/h *for AB 180 AG* and *RVR*, 42 kts (48 mph) 77 km/h *for PSA*. Electrical stall warning
Landing speed: 48 kts (55 mph) 88 km/h *for AB 180 AG*, 45 kts (52 mph) 84 km/h *for RVR*
Take-off distance: 492-820 ft (150-250 m) *for AB 180 AG*, 378 ft (115 m) light *for PSA*, 279-394 ft (85-120 m) *for RVR*
Landing distance: 394 ft (120 m) *for AB 180 AG*, 279 ft (85 m) *for PSA*, 289 ft (88 m) *for RVR*
Maximum climb rate: 453 ft (138 m) per minute *for AB 180 AG*, 1,024 ft (312 m) per minute *for PSA* and *RVR*
G limits: +4.4, -1.9 *for AB 180 PSA*
Ceiling: 23,000 ft (7,000 m) *for AB 180 RVR*
Range: 541 naut miles (623 miles) 1,002 km *for AB 180 PSA*
Duration: 4 to 4 hours 45 minutes

↑ Aero Boero AB 260 AG agricultural aircraft

Details for AB 260 AG

PRINCIPAL DIMENSIONS:
Wing span: 35 ft 9 ins (10.9 m)
Maximum length: 23 ft 11.5 ins (7.3 m)
Maximum height: 6 ft 5.5 ins (1.97 m)

WINGS:
Aerofoil section: NACA 23012
Area: 186 sq ft (17.28 m^2)
Aspect ratio: 6.87

UNDERCARRIAGE:
Type: Fixed, with tailwheel

WEIGHTS:
Empty: 1,521 lb (690 kg)
Maximum take-off: 2,976 lb (1,350 kg)
Payload: 1,455 lb (660 kg)

PERFORMANCE:
Maximum speed: 135 kts (155 mph) 250 km/h
Cruise speed: : 119 kts (137 mph) 220 km/h
Stall speed: : 49 kts (56 mph) 90 km/h *clean*, 43.5 kts (50 mph) 80 km/h *with flaps*. Electrical stall warning
Landing speed: 49 kts (56 mph) 90 km/h
Take-off distance: 591-886 ft (180-270 m)
Landing distance: 492 ft (150 m)
Maximum climb rate: 984 ft (300 m) per minute

AEA Research Pty Ltd — Australia

Corporate address:
Building 1C Eagle Drive, Jandakot Airport, Western Australia 6164. *Mailing address:* PO Box 238, Willetton, Western Australia 6955.

Telephone: +61 8 9414 7011
Facsimile: +61 8 9414 7022
E-mail: aea@icenet.com.au

Founded:
1992.

Information:
Julie Swannell.

ACTIVITIES

- Formed as a research subsidiary of Aeronautical Engineers Australia for the purpose of developing aeronautical products.
- Affiliated companies are Aeronautical Engineers Australia, aircraft consulting and design specialists and aircraft weight control authority, and Airline Technical Services Pty Ltd, an engineering group working with regional airlines in Australia.

AEA Explorer 350 and 500 family

Details: For Explorer 350R, except under Aircraft variants.
First flight: 23 January 1998.
Certification: Proof of concept aircraft was issued a certificate of airworthiness on 27 April 1998. Joint CASA and FAA certification for the Explorer 350R expected mid-2001. Designed to FAR 23 Amdt 52.
First delivery: Last quarter 2001.
Role: 8-passenger light aircraft.
Sales: Plans underway to take Explorer 350R and a number of additional aircraft designs in the Explorer family through to certification and on to production. POC aircraft had accumulated 82 flying hours of testing by the end of April 1998.
Crew/passengers: 8 passengers. Flat cabin floor allows flexible seating arrangement. Large cargo door and crew doors for freight loading.
Baggage capacity: 400 lb (181 kg). Forward and aft cargo compartments.
Wing characteristics: Braced, high mounted, with constant-chord centre section and tapering outer panels.
Wing control surfaces: Ailerons and flaps.
Tail control surfaces: Horn-balanced elevators (starboard tab) and horn-balanced tall rudder. Tailplane span 16 ft 8 ins (5.08 m).
Construction materials: Carbonfibre for fuselage shell; a provisional patent has been granted for a newly devised construction method which minimizes both construction and assembly time. Remainder of primary structure is of high-grade aluminium alloy.
Engine: Teledyne Continental TSIO-550-E3B piston engine, with 6 ft 4 ins (1.93 m) diameter Hartzell HC-C3YF-1RF/F8468A-8R propeller.
Engine rating: 350 hp (261 kW).
Fuel system: 610 litres.

Aircraft variants:
Explorer 350R is the 8-seat initial version of the Explorer family, detailed here.
Explorer 350F uses the same airframe as 350R but has a fixed undercarriage.
Explorer 500R is a larger 10-seat turboprop variant, with retractable undercarriage.
Explorer 500F is similar to 500R but with fixed undercarriage.

↑ AEA Explorer 350R

Details for Explorer 350R

PRINCIPAL DIMENSIONS:
Wing span: 47 ft 4 ins (14.41 m)
Maximum length: 31 ft 9 ins (9.69 m)
Maximum height: 15 ft 6 ins (4.72 m)

CABIN:
Length: 11 ft (3.35 m)
Width: 5 ft 1 ins (1.55 m)
Height: 4 ft 5 ins (1.35 m)
Volume: 250 cu ft (7 m^3)
Cargo door: 4 ft 2 ins (1.27 m) width and 4 ft 1 ins (1.24 m) height

WINGS:
Area: 197.6 sq ft (18.36 m^2)
Aspect ratio: 11.3
Chord: 4 ft 9.5 ins (1.46 m) root, 2 ft (0.61 m) tip

UNDERCARRIAGE:
Type: Retractable nosewheel type, with unique retraction system which enables the wheels to be retracted into streamline pods without encroaching on the cabin floor area. Suited to unpaved runways
Wheel base: 10 ft 4 ins (3.16 m)
Wheel track: 11 ft 9 ins (3.6 m)

WEIGHTS:
Empty: 3,000 lb (1,360 kg)
Maximum ramp weight: 4,835 lb (2,193 kg)
Maximum take-off: 4,800 lb (2,177 kg)
Payload: 1,800 lb (816 kg)

PERFORMANCE:
Never-exceed speed (V_{NE}): 207 kts (238 mph) 383 km/h
Cruise speed: 150-155 kts (173-178 mph) 278-287 km/h
Stall speed: 65 kts (75 mph) 121 km/h *clean*, 52 kts (60 mph) 97 km/h *with flaps*
Take-off distance: 1,110 ft (338 m)
Take-off and landing distance over a 50 ft (15 m) obstacle: 1,480 ft (450 m)
Landing distance: 696 ft (211 m)
Maximum climb rate: 800 ft (244 m) per minute at sea level
Ceiling: 30,000 ft (9,145 m), service
Maximum operating altitude: 30,000 ft (9,145 m)
Range with full fuel: 1,100 naut miles (1,266 miles) 2,038 km, cruise power, with allowances for start, taxi and reserve

AeroSPORT Pty Ltd — Australia

Corporate address:
PO Box 630, Oakbank, South Australia 5243.

Telephone: +61 8 8388 4349, 4747
Facsimile: +61 8 8388 4644

Information:
John Cotton (Managing Director).

AeroSPORT Supa Pup 4

First flight: 1994, with a Mosler engine.
Certification: In May 1998, was 90% through the process of obtaining Australian certification to CAO 101.55 (undergoing CASA approval). Will also comply with US Primary Category regulations.
Role: Single-seat light/ultralight cabin monoplane.
Sales: Fully assembled, and also available in 3-stage kit form (approximately 250 hours building time). As of May 1998, the company had everything in place to start production, and had started sub-contracting components and purchasing materials. Orders already received. In May 1998, basic kit without engine and instruments $14,500. Rotax kit $19,500. Fully assembled aircraft add $5,000.
Crew/passengers: Can accommodate a 6 ft 4 ins (1.93 m) pilot.
Wing characteristics: Strut-braced high-wing monoplane. Simple and quick folding wing mechanism using 2 pins.
Control surfaces: Conventional.
Engine: Prototype initially fitted with a 40 hp (29.8 kW) Mosler engine. 48 hp (35.8 kW) Rotax 503 engine fitted thereafter, followed by a 54 hp (40.3 kW) Jabiru. All 3 engines available for production/kit aircraft.
Fuel system: 44 litres (64 lb, 29 kg).

↑ AeroSPORT Supa Pup 4

Details for Supa Pup 4

PRINCIPAL DIMENSIONS:
Wing span: 25 ft 10 ins (7.88 m)
Maximum length: 18 ft 9 ins (5.7 m)

CABIN:
Width: 1 ft 11 ins (0.584 m) at shoulder height
Height: 3 ft 1 ins (0.94 m) seat to roof

WINGS:
Area: 105.5 sq ft (9.8 m^2)
Aspect ratio: 6.4
Chord: 4 ft 1 ins (1.243 m)
Dihedral: 2°

UNDERCARRIAGE:
Type: Fixed, with tailwheel

WEIGHTS:
Empty: 397-441 lb (180-200 kg)
Maximum take-off: 661-750 lb (300-340 kg)

PERFORMANCE:
Maximum speed: 100 kts (115 mph) 185 km/h
Cruise speed: over 90 kts (104 mph) 167 km/h
Stall speed: 35 kts (41 mph) 66 km/h
Take-off distance over a 50 ft (15 m) obstacle: 657 ft (200 m)
Maximum climb rate: 450 ft (137 m) per minute with Mosler, 1,100 ft (335 m) per minute with Rotax, and 1,000 ft (305 m) per minute with Jabiru
Duration: 5.3 hours with Mosler, and 3.8 hours with Rotax/Jabiru

Eagle Aircraft Pty Ltd — Australia

Corporate address: PO Box 586, Fremantle, Western Australia 6160.
Sales & marketing: 24 Compass Road, Jandakot Airport, Western Australia 6164.
Telephone: +61 8 9414 1174 **Facsimile:** +61 8 9414 1175
Founded: 1985.
Information: Ron Scherpenzeel (Manager, Sales and Marketing).

ACTIVITIES

▪ Eagle Aircraft is owned by Eagle Aircraft (Malaysia) Sdn Bhd of Suite 19-14-3, Level 14, UOA Centre 19, Jalan Pinang 50450 Kuala Lumpur, Malaysia – *telephone* +60 3 264 5099, *facsimile* +60 3 264 5093.
▪ The original production Eagle X-TS was assembled in Australia. The latest Eagle 150 is factory produced in Malaysia and Australia and certified to international standards.

Eagle Aircraft Eagle 150

First flight: March 1988 as a 2-seater with an Aeropower engine. Pre-production Eagle X-TS with a Teledyne Continental engine had been first flown on 6 November 1992.
Certification: 21 September 1993 by the CAA of Australia.
Role: Recreation, ab-initio training, and fire spotting and surveillance.
Sales: By May 1998, in addition to the original X-TS pre-production prototype (*VH-XEG*) and the production prototype (*VH-XEP*), 22 aircraft have been ordered. These include 10 examples of the original X-TS production model, now known as Series 100s, of which 5 have since been converted to Series 150s (plus *VH-XEP*, which has also been converted to a Series 150). Of the 12 Series 150s ordered, 5 had been delivered by May 1998, including single aircraft to CTRM Malaysia and the Melacca Flying Club in Malaysia, 2 to Phoenix Aviation and 1 to CAA. Some aircraft are leased.
Crew/passengers: 2, side-by-side.
Cockpit: The cockpit area is specially strengthened with Kevlar to become a high-strength capsule with good penetration resistance. Optional dual controls.
Baggage capacity: 66 lb (30 kg).
Wing characteristics: Straight, with no anhedral/dihedral and raised wingtips. Overwing fences and 8 small turbulators. Stall strips on leading edges. Removable for storage and transport.
Wing control surfaces: Slotted ailerons and flaps.
Tail control surfaces: Elevators and rudder, with tabs. Tailplane removable for storage and transport.
Canard: Has a higher angle of incidence than the mainplane. As the aircraft approaches a stall, the canard stalls first, resulting in a loss of lift forward of the centre of gravity. This causes the nose to drop and the aircraft to enter a shallow dive, which allows the airspeed to increase. If the pilot takes no corrective action, the aircraft enters into a phugoid flight on a smooth glide ratio which should enable the aircraft to be landed safely. In addition, because the canard stalls ahead of the mainplane, the ailerons are still effective in the stall and there is no noticeable wing drop. Also, said to be exceptionally spin resistant. Full-width single-slotted flaps.
Flight control system: Push rods, except for cable operated rudder and electrically actuated flaps and electric pitch trim tab on starboard elevator.
Construction materials: Carbon cloth, Kevlar, Nomex honeycomb and special vinylester resins for resistance to corrosion and fatigue. See also Cockpit.
Engine: Teledyne Continental IO-240-A or B, with a 5 ft 11 ins (1.8 m) McCauley 2-blade metal propeller.
Engine rating: 125 hp (93.2 kW) at 2,800 rpm.
Fuel system: 100 litres. Fuel consumption 23 litres per hour at cruise speed.
Electrical system: 12 volt DC incorporating 60 amp alternator.
Braking system: Cleveland discs on main units.
Flight avionics/instrumentation: Modern avionics system. Full range of flight and engine instruments. Standard options include navigation systems (GPS, ADF), gyro instruments (DG, AH and T&B). VHF radio is standard, and an ATC transponder is an option.

Aircraft variants:
Eagle 150A and ***B***, according to engine model.

↑ Eagle Aircraft Eagle 150, clearly showing the overwing fences and turbulators

Details for Eagle 150

PRINCIPAL DIMENSIONS:
Wing span: 23 ft 6 ins (7.16 m)
Maximum length: 21 ft 2 ins (6.45 m)
Maximum height: 7 ft 7 ins (2.31 m)

WINGS:
Aerofoil section: Roncz
Area: 56 sq ft (5.2 m^2)
Aspect ratio: 9.86

CANARD:
Span: 16 ft (4.88 m)

UNDERCARRIAGE:
Type: Fixed, with steerable (17°) nosewheel. Glassfibre/epoxy mainwheel spring legs
Turning circle: 17 ft 1 ins (5.21 m)

WEIGHTS:
Empty: 941 lb (427 kg)
Maximum take-off: 1,411 lb (640 kg)
Payload: 470 lb (213 kg)

PERFORMANCE:
Never-exceed speed (V_{NE}): 165 kts (190 mph) 305 km/h CAS
Maximum speed: 130 kts (150 mph) 240 km/h TAS
Cruise speed: 115 kts (132 mph) 213 km/h TAS, at 75% power
Stall speed: 45 kts (52 mph) 83 km/h *full flaps*, 55 kts (64 mph) 101 km/h *clean*
Take-off distance over a 50 ft (15 m) obstacle: 1,280 ft (390 m)
Landing distance over a 50 ft (15 m) obstacle: 1,198 ft (365 m)
Maximum climb rate: 1,037 ft (316 m) per minute at sea level
G limits: +3.8, -1.9 limit; +8.55, -4.27 ultimate
Ceiling: 15,000 ft (4,570 m)
Range: 540 naut miles (621 miles) 1,000 km at 75% power
Duration: 5 hours at 60% power

Gippsland Aeronautics Pty Ltd — Australia

Corporate address:
PO Box 881, Latrobe Valley Airfield, Morwell 3840, Victoria.

Telephone: +61 351 74 3086
Facsimile: +61 351 74 0956

Founded:
1971.

Information:
George Morgan and Peter Furlong (Managing Director/Director).

ACTIVITIES

- CAA approved manufacture and maintenance facility.
- Aircraft design, modification and manufacture. Modification programmes have covered a wide variety of aircraft, from wooden homebuilts to pressurized turboprops.

Gippsland GA-8 Airvan

First flight: 3 March 1995. Second flight test prototype (003) flown 31 August 1996, featuring fuel injected engine, larger passenger windows and minor aerodynamic and structural modifications including a revised fin and rudder layout. Structural tests conducted on airframe 001 and further airframes constructed for the certification programme.
Certification: Designed to FAR Pt 23.
Role: General purpose utility, capable of operating from unprepared and short airstrips. Designed for quick change between 8-seat passenger and cargo, medevac (2 litters and 3 seats, including pilot) and other layouts.
Crew/passengers: Pilot plus 7/8 passengers. Pilot on left with all controls, instruments, selectors and switches. Optional set of flight controls and instruments to the right, in dual control layout. Locker provided aft of the passenger cabin, in which up to 5 passenger seats can be stowed.
Cabin access: Forward-hinged door each side for access to the cockpit. Large sliding door on port side for access to the main cabin, size 3 ft 6.5 ins × 3 ft 6 ins (1.09 × 1.07 m).
Wing characteristics: Based on the GA-200 wing but high mounted with streamlined strut each side.
Wing control surfaces: Conventional ailerons and flaps.
Tail control surfaces: Variable incidence tailplane to provide a wide trim range with maximum aerodynamic efficiency. Constant-chord elevators. Half-span rudder located on the lower part of the fin.
Construction materials: All-metal stressed skin construction, fully corrosion protected. Floor of passenger cabin provided with a quick release system to allow rapid conversion from freight to passenger or combi configurations. Engine cowlings of composite materials and feature large, easily removable access panels.
Engine: Textron Lycoming IO-540-K piston engine, with Hartzell 2-blade constant-speed metal propeller. Optional 3-blade constant-speed propeller. Project to install an IO-580X engine was underway at time of writing.
Engine rating: 300 hp (224 kW).
Fuel system: 340 litres total, carried in a single integral tank in each wing, between the fuselage and strut.
Flight avionics/instrumentation: See Crew/passengers. Centrally located control pedestal, radio stack and overhead switch accessible from either front seat.

Details for Airvan

PRINCIPAL DIMENSIONS:
Wing span: 40 ft 8 ins (12.412 m)
Maximum length: 28 ft 9 ins (8.76 m)
Maximum height: 12 ft (3.66 m)

CABIN:
Length: 13 ft 2 ins (4.01 m)
Width: 4 ft 2 ins (1.27 m)
Height: 3 ft 11 ins (1.19 m)
Area: 54 sq ft (5 m^2) floor area, with 37 sq ft (3.44 m^2) of floor space available for cargo
Volume: 180 cu ft (5.1 m^3)
Height to sill: 2 ft 10 ins (0.86 m)

WINGS:
Aerofoil section: Modified USA 35-B
Area: 207.8 sq ft (19.305 m^2)
Aspect ratio: 7.981
Dihedral: 2.5°
Incidence: 3.3° at root
Washout: 1.7°

UNDERCARRIAGE:
Type: Fixed, with nosewheel or twin floats
Wheel base: 7 ft 6.5 ins (2.299 m)
Wheel track: 9 ft 2 ins (2.794 m)

WEIGHTS:
Empty: 2,000 lb (907 kg)
Maximum take-off: 4,000 lb (1,814 kg)

PERFORMANCE:
Never-exceed speed (V_{NE}): 185 kts (213 mph) 343 km/h
Maximum structural cruise speed (V_{NO}): 146 kts (168 mph) 270 km/h
Cruise speed: 120 kts (138 mph) 222 km/h, at 10,000 ft (3,050 m)
Stall speed: 59 kts (68 mph) 110 km/h *clean*, 53 kts (61 mph) 98 km/h *with 38° flaps*
Take-off distance over a 50 ft (15 m) obstacle: 1,500 ft (457 m), ISA, at sea level
Landing distance over a 50 ft (15 m) obstacle: 1,300 ft (396 m), ISA, at sea level
Climb rate: 550 ft (168 m) per minute
Range: 720 naut miles (829 miles) 1,334 km at 1 litre/min fuel burn and 120 kts cruise
Duration: 6 hours at 67% power, no reserve

Gippsland GA-200 Fatman and AG-Trainer

Certification: 1 March 1991, on the basis of Australian CAO 101.16 and 101.22, incorporating FAR 23 Amendment 23.36, making certification in both normal and agricultural categories. FAA certification to FAR 23 in restricted category recently gained, with plans to obtain normal category.
Role: Agricultural, and dual-control agricultural trainer (AG-Trainer).
Sales: Approximately 50 sold. Aircraft operating in Australia, China and New Zealand.
Crew: Pilot. Second seat for the loader driver or to allow aerial viewing by the farmer. Side by side seating arrangement to minimize centre of gravity shift with the cockpit load and to utilize the wide fuselage width.
Cockpit: Dual controls in AG-Trainer.
Baggage capacity: Storage compartment under the passenger seat.
Chemical hopper: 800 litres. Transparent rear face, to allow the pilot to view the contents. Constructed of glassfibre and Derakane 411 chemically resistant vinylester resin. Gippsland multi-role door/hopper outlet, suitable for operation with both solids and liquids. AG-Trainer has 750 litres capacity (see Aircraft variants). See Aircraft variants for 1,000 litre version.
Safety equipment: Crashworthy structure, to provide a "good fly-on" capability following an obstacle strike. The forward fuselage has been optimized to "progressively crumple" in a sudden forward deceleration, protecting the cockpit. "Pilot behind load" configuration. Upward opening doors, preventing the opening edge from jamming in a closed position in the event of an overturn.
Wing characteristics: Low mounted, with strut bracing to save approximately 100 lb (45 kg) weight over a cantilever spar design. Wingtip shape evolved to provide the best possible swath width without compromising aircraft performance.
Wing control surfaces: Gap-sealed ailerons. Single-slotted flaps. Take-off flap setting 15°; landing flap (max) setting 38°. Flaps can be used in normal operations and significantly reduce turn radius with fully loaded aircraft. With flaps extended, there is said to be no noticeable change in pitch trim, due to the incorporation of a simple interconnect system which applies bias to the elevator trim spring at such times.
Tail control surfaces: Horn-balanced elevators and rudder.
Construction materials: All metal wings with full-depth laminated fail-safe spars; the outboard section is joined to the inner section at the strut intersections by load distribution doublers. This allows the relatively easy replacement of the outer wing panels. All of the aircraft's components are corrosion proofed and leading edges consist of replaceable segments to minimize "down time" due to bird strikes or other minor impacts. The wingtips are also removable. Welded SAE 4130 chromium molybdenum steel tube fuselage assembly, with metal side panels attached by half-turn Druz fasteners from the engine bay back to the rear of the cockpit. The rear fuselage upper turtledeck is easily opened for inspection, maintenance and cleaning.
Engine: Textron Lycoming O-540-H2A5 or optional O-540-A1D5, with 7 ft (2.13 m) McCauley 1A200/FA 84 52 fixed-pitch, 2-blade, metal propeller.
Engine rating: 260 hp (194 kW) for H2A5, limited to 250 hp (186.4 kW) at 2,575 rpm for noise considerations. 250 hp (186.4 kW) for A1D5.
Fuel system: 200 litres (usable) of premium grade auto fuel or Avgas carried in 2 wing tanks plus a 12 litre header tank.
Electrical system: 14 volt, 55 amp auto alternator with internal voltage regulation supplies an auto or R-35 aviation battery.

↑ Gippsland GA-8 Airvan in latest modified form, with larger passenger windows and minor aerodynamic/structural modifications including a revised fin and rudder layout

↑ Gippsland GA-200 agricultural aircraft, showing its easily detachable panels

A 28 volt night working light system is available, which is virtually independent of the electrical system, consisting of 2 retractable underwing 600 watt lights powered by a separate 28 volt, 55 amp auto alternator mounted on the engine rear accessory case.
Braking system: Cleveland disc. Hydraulic "lock off" parking brake.
Flight avionics/instrumentation: Arranged in a small panel in front of the pilot.

Aircraft variants:
GA-200 Fatman is the standard agricultural aircraft, as detailed.
1,000 litre hopper capacity version of GA-200 is under development, with a 300 hp (224 kW) engine and constant-speed propeller.
AG-Trainer is a dedicated dual-control trainer variant, used in the "Spray Safe" agricultural training programme. Used as a conventional agricultural aircraft between training. 50 litres less hopper capacity due to the second set of rudder pedals.

Details for GA-200

PRINCIPAL DIMENSIONS:
Wing span: 39 ft 4 ins (11.984 m)
Maximum length: 24 ft 6.5 ins (7.48 m)
Maximum height: 7 ft 7.7 ins (2.33 m)

WINGS:
Area: 211 sq ft (19.6 m^2)
Aspect ratio: 7.33
Dihedral: 7°

UNDERCARRIAGE:
Type: Fixed, with steerable and castoring tailwheel

WEIGHTS:
Empty, operating: 1,698 lb (770 kg), include oil and usable fuel
Maximum take-off: 2,900 lb (1,315 kg) certified
Typical agricultural take-off: 3,750 lb (1,700 kg)

PERFORMANCE:
Ferry cruise speed: 100 kts (115 mph) 185 km/h at MTOW, *clean*, 1,000 ft (305 m) altitude, ISA, at 2,420 engine rpm
Stall speed at MTOW: 54 kts (62 mph) 100 km/h *clean*; 49 kts (57 mph) 91 km/h *with 38° flaps*
Stall speed at typical landing weight: 45 kts (52 mph) 84 km/h *clean*, 41 kts (47 mph) 76 km/h *with 38° flaps*
Landing speed: 50-55 kts (58-63 mph) 93-102 km/h *with full flaps*
Take-off distance: 1,395 ft (425 m), with full hopper, zero wind and 15° C at sea level
Landing distance: 650 ft (200 m) approximately, with full flaps and light weight
Maximum climb rate: 970 ft (296 m) per minute at MTOW, *clean*, sea level, ISA
Roll rate: 2 seconds from 45° bank through 45° bank the other way at normal working airspeeds

Jabiru Aircraft Pty Ltd — Australia

Corporate address:
PO Box 5186, Airport Drive, Bundaberg West 4670, Queensland.
Telephone: +61 7 4155 1778
Facsimile: +61 7 4155 2669
E-mail: info@jabiru.net.au
Information:
Phillip Ainsworth (Joint Managing Director).

ACTIVITIES

▪ Produces the Jabiru 2200 engine (see Engine section), in addition to the Jabiru LSA (Australian ultralight), SK and ST light aircraft. UK distributor is ST Aviation.

↑ Jabiru ST lightplane used by an aero club

Jabiru Aircraft Jabiru LSA, SK and ST

First flight: 1989 in original LSA form.
Certification: 1 October 1991 under CAO 101.55. Conforms to BCAR Section S.
Role: General aviation lightplane and kitplane (SK and ST) and Australian ultralight (LSA).
Crew/passengers: 2, side-by-side, with dual controls.
Wing control surfaces: Ailerons and slotted flaps.
Tail control surfaces: Elevators and inset rudder.
Construction materials: Glassfibre, with metal bracing struts.
Engine: 60 hp (44.7 kW) Jabiru 1600 with dual ignition, with a 54 ins (1.37 m) wooden propeller, originally for first LSA version. More powerful Jabiru 2200 standard for currently available Jabiru aircraft.
Engine rating: 80 hp (59.7 kW) at 3,300 rpm for Jabiru 2200.
Fuel system: 65 litres, with fuel consumption at cruise of 14-15 litres per hour for Jabiru 2200.
Flight control system: Mechanical, with cables. Adjustable pitch trim.
Electrical system: 12 volt DC/120 watt and 20 amp-hour battery.
Braking system: Hydraulic disc on main units.
Flight avionics/instrumentation: VFR.

Aircraft variants:
LSA is the ultralight version, principally for Australian operators.
SK is the latest assembled/kit version, with ST Aviation in the UK receiving the first example in 1996. Jabiru 2200 engine.
ST is the general aviation model, available to the Australian and export markets since 1994. Ready built, but can be purchased as a kit requiring about 600 working hours to assemble. Jabiru 2200 engine.

Details for Jabiru ST with Jabiru 2200 engine, wheel fairings and 1 pilot

PRINCIPAL DIMENSIONS:
Wing span: 26 ft 4 ins (8.034 m)
Maximum length: 16 ft 5 ins (5.004 m)
Maximum height: 6 ft 7 ins (2.013 m)

WINGS:
Aerofoil section: NACA 4412
Area: 85 sq ft (7.9 m^2)
Aspect ratio: 8.16
Dihedral: 1° 15′
Incidence: 2° 30′

UNDERCARRIAGE:
Type: Fixed, with steerable (15°) nosewheel

WEIGHTS:
Empty: 517 lb (235 kg)
Maximum take-off: 946 lb (430 kg)

PERFORMANCE:
Never-exceed speed (V_{NE}): 116 kts (133 mph) 215 km/h
Maximum speed: 115 kts (132 mph) 213 km/h
Cruise speed: 100 kts (115 mph) 185 km/h at 75% power
Stall speed: 40 kts (46 mph) 74 km/h with *full flaps*, 45 kts (52 mph) 84 km/h *clean*
Take-off distance: 656 ft (200 m)
Landing distance: 525 ft (160 m)
Maximum climb rate: 1,000 ft (305 m) per minute
G limits: +6.6. -3.3 ultimate
Ceiling: 15,000 ft (4,570 m)
Range: 400 naut miles (460 miles) 741 km
Duration: 4 hours

Seabird Aviation Australia Pty Ltd — Australia

Corporate address:
Hervey Bay Airport, PO Box 618, Pialba 4655, Queensland.
Telephone: +61 71 25 3144
Facsimile: +61 71 25 3123
E-mail: seabird@ozemail.com.au
International representation:
AeroSystems Corporation Pty Ltd, South Brisbane 4101, Queensland.
Information:
Don Adams (Managing Director).

Seabird Seeker SB7L

First flight: 1 October 1989 (as SB5 prototype).
Certification: 24 January 1994 to CAA FAR 23 standards.
Role: Multi-role, including agriculture, border patrol, customs and security surveillance, drug control, survey, fire spotting, game park observation, news gathering, medevac, photographic, pipe and power line patrol, search and rescue, tourism and training.
Sales: Available since 1994.

Details for SB7L

PRINCIPAL DIMENSIONS:
Wing span: 36 ft 4 ins (11.07 m)
Maximum length: 23 ft (7.01 m)
Maximum height: 8 ft 2 ins (2.49 m)

CABIN:
Length: 7 ft 3 ins (2.21 m)
Width: 3 ft 8 ins (1.12 m)
Height: 3 ft 7 ins (1.09 m)

WINGS:
Aerofoil section: 63_2215 modified
Area: 141 sq ft (13.1 m^2)
Aspect ratio: 9.36

UNDERCARRIAGE:
Type: Fixed, with tailwheel. Floats were put under development
Turning circle: 15 ft 1 ins (4.6 m)

WEIGHTS:
Empty, operating: 1,332 lb (604 kg) prototype, 1,301 lb (590 kg) production aircraft (approximately)
Maximum take-off: 1,977 lb (897 kg); analysis undertaken to increase AUW to 2,039 lb (925 kg)
Disposable load with maximum fuel: 392 lb (178 kg) prototype
Maximum disposable load: 646 lb (293 kg) prototype, 670 lb (304 kg) production aircraft, increasing to 732 lb (332 kg) at 2,039 lb (925 kg) AUW (see MTO)
Crew weight range (total): 176-423 lb (80-192 kg)

PERFORMANCE:
Cruise speed: 112 kts (129 mph) 207 km/h, 75% power
Patrol speed: 65 kts (75 mph) 120 km/h CAS
Stall speed: 58 kts (67 mph) 108 km/h *clean*; changes being introduced to the flaps will further improve the stall speed
Take-off distance (ISA): 867 ft (264 m) at sea level, 1,016 ft (310 m) at 2,000 ft altitude, 1,194 ft (364 m) at 4,000 ft (1,220 m) altitude, 1,407 ft (429 m) at 6,000 ft (1,830 m) altitude
Landing distance: 650 ft (198 m)
Maximum climb rate (ISA): 944 ft (288 m) per minute at sea level, 813 ft (248 m) per minute at 2,000 ft (610 m), 688 ft (210 m) per minute at 4,000 ft (1,220 m), 567 ft (173 m) per minute at 6,000 ft (1,830 m)
G limits: +3.8, -1.52
Range: 394 naut miles (453 miles) 730 km at 75% power (with reserve), or 449 naut miles (517 miles) 832 km at patrol power (with reserve)
Duration: 3.55 hours at 75% power, 6.9 hours at patrol power

Crew: 2 normally. 3-seat arrangement was put under development. Can carry litter in a single pilot layout.
Cockpit: Dual controls. Removable 'gullwing' doors, and removable right-hand seat and controls for installing special mission equipment, 100 litre agricultural spray tank or a litter.
Baggage capacity: 15 cu ft (0.42 m^3). Total load behind seats and in compartment 96 lb (43 kg).
Wing characteristics: Braced high-mounted, with stall strips and vortex generators. 2 underwing hard points for attaching a total of 264 lb (120 kg) of stores.
Wing control surfaces: Slotted ailerons and slotted flaps (20°, 40°).
Tail control surfaces: Single-piece elevator (with trim tab) and rudder (with tab).
Construction materials: Aluminium alloy wings, boom and tail, with FRP wingtips. Roll cage (of chromoly tubular steel) cabin structure, with FRP non-load bearing skins. FRP dorsal and ventral finlets.
Engine: Textron Lycoming O-360-B2C, with a 5 ft 10 ins (1.78 m) Bishton BB-177 wood/epoxy fixed-pitch 2-blade pusher propeller or electric constant-speed 3-blade propeller.
Engine rating: 160 hp (119.3 kW).
Fuel system: 160 litres, of which 148 are usable. Analysis undertaken in 1994 to increase fuel to 182 litres, with 170 usable by increasing MTOW (see table). Fuel flow 40 litres per hour at 75% power, or 22 litres per hour at patrol power of 68 hp (50.7 kW).
Flight control system: Mechanical, with push/pull rods.
Electrical system: 28 volt, with 70 amp alternator and 18 amp-hour battery.
Braking system: Cleveland toe brakes.
Flight avionics/instrumentation: VFR standard, including AlliedSignal Bendix/King KY 97A VHF communications and KT 76A transponder. Options include IFR instrumentation and avionics, Garmin GPS/moving map, KX 15/K1208 nav/com, KR 87 ADF/KI 227 ADF and more. FLIR is an option for surveillance, among other equipment. Emergency locator transponder (ELT) in fin.

Aircraft variants:
SB7L is the current standard version, with noise certification that meets US and European standards. Wide range of features and options, including camera/store drop hatch, vertical and oblique camera mounts, wing hard points, medevac conversion, low-volume sprayer, and searchlight/loudspeaker.

↑ Seabird Seeker SB7L multi-purpose aircraft, offering the cockpit visibility of a helicopter

Skyfox Aviation Ltd — Australia

Corporate address:
PO Box 3561, Pathfinder Drive, Caloundra, Queensland 4551.

Telephone: +61 7 5491 5355
Facsimile: +61 7 5491 8237
E-mail: skyfoxpl@ozemail.com.au
Web site: http://www.ozemail.com.au/~skyfoxpl/

Founded:
Hedaro International Pty Ltd began manufacturing light aircraft in Australia under the trading name Skyfox in 1991. In 1996 the company became an unlisted public company under the new name Skyfox Aviation Ltd.

Employees: 18.

Information:
Sales & Marketing department.

Skyfox Aviation Skyfox series

First flight: 6 September 1989.
Certification: 1991 under Ultralight 101.55; 1993 under General Aviation JAR-VLA; 1994 JAR-VLA validated in Switzerland; 1997 JAR-VLA validated in the UK; was seeking US validation at time of writing.
Role: STOL leisure, ab-initio training, surveillance, and more.
Sales: Total sales of 180 aircraft at the time of writing. CA25N production began September 1995, accounting for 71 units.
Crew/passengers: 2 persons, with dual controls.
Baggage capacity: Compartment aft of the cabin, with outside access.
Wing control surfaces: All-flying ailerons carried behind and slightly below the wings.
Tail control surfaces: Elevators and rudder.
Construction materials: Fuselage of welded 4130 chrome molybdenum steel tubing, skinned with Stits Polyfibre fabric. Wings have fabric-covered 6061-T6 aluminium spars (2) and plywood ribs, and moulded downturned glassfibre wingtips. Wings fold in line with the fuselage (4 minutes by 1 person).
Engine: Rotax 912A piston engine.
Engine rating: 81 hp (60.4 kW) maximum output.
Fuel system: 48 litres usable.
Braking system: Hydraulic, dual toe, disc type.
Electrical system: 12 volt, maintenance free battery. CDI ignition.
Flight avionics/instrumentation: Full VFR panel of instruments and a 760-channel VHF radio.

Aircraft variants:
CA21 production ended in 1991. VW Aeropower engine.
CA22 is a current production ultralight, certified under Australian Civil Aviation Order 101.55. Rotax 912 engine. See Recreational section.
CA25 is the general aviation version, certified under JAR-VLA.
CA25N is a new nosewheel undercarriage variant, also JAR-VLA certified.

Details for CA25N

PRINCIPAL DIMENSIONS:
Wing span: 31 ft 3 ins (9.52 m)
Maximum length: 18 ft 4.5 ins (5.6 m), or 21 ft 6.5 ins (6.57 m) folded
Maximum height: 6 ft 1.5 ins (1.87 m)

CABIN:
Width: 3 ft 4 ins (1.02 m)

WINGS:
Chord, including ailerons: 4 ft 2.75 ins (1.29 m)
Area: 124.6 sq ft (11.58 m^2)
Aspect ratio: 7.84

UNDERCARRIAGE:
Type: Fixed nosewheel type. Blain strut nose leg and cross bond system (CBS) main gear suspension

WEIGHTS:
Empty: 705 lb (320 kg)
Maximum take-off: 1,150 lb (522 kg)

PERFORMANCE:
Maximum speed: 95 kts (109 mph) 176 km/h at 5,000 ft (1,525 m)
Cruise speed: 85 kts (98 mph) 157 km/h, 75% power
Loiter speed: 50 kts (58 mph) 93 km/h
Stall speed: 43 kts (50 mph) 80 km/h
Take-off and landing distance: 400 ft (122 m)
Maximum climb rate: 800 ft (244 m) per minute
Ceiling: 10,000 ft (3,050 m), service
Range: approximately 300 naut miles (345 miles) 556 km, 70% power
Duration: approximately 3.75 hours, 70% power

↑ Skyfox Aviation CA25N JAR-VLA certified general aviation version of the Skyfox

Diamond Aircraft Industries GmbH — Austria

Corporate address:
N.A. Otto-Strasse 5, A-2700 Wiener Neustadt.

Telephone: +43 2622 26 700
Facsimile: +43 2622 26 780
E-mail: sales@diamond-ac-ind.co.at

Founded:
1981 as Hoffmann Flugzeugbau-Friesach GesmbH, becoming HOAC-Austria, Flugzeugwerk Wiener Neustadt Gesellschaft mhH after a management buy-out in 1989. Name changed to Diamond Aircraft Industries on 1 March 1996, to conform with the Canadian subsidiary and present a uniform name to the world market.

Employees: 60.

Information:
Michael Feinig (Sales Department).

ACTIVITIES

- Diamond Aircraft produces the HK 36 Super Dimona motorglider that is available in 4 different versions (TS, TC, TTS and TTC) and is built in Austria. Details can be found in the Glider section. The name HK 36 Katana Xtreme is only used for the American market.
- The DV 20 Katana 2-seat lightplane was developed and built in Austria, but production there has been stopped and it is now built only by the related Canadian company as the DA 20 Katana.
- See below for the DV 22 Speed Katana.
- The DA 40 Katana is the company's latest product (see below).

DIVISION

DIAMOND AIRCRAFT INDUSTRIES CANADA

HQ Address: London, Ontario, Canada.

Founded: June 1993.

Employees: 250.

Activities
- Founded as a subsidiary to produce aircraft for the North American market. Production of the DA 20 version of the DV 20 began 29 June 1994.

Diamond Aircraft Industries Canada DA 20 Katana

Comments: The DV 20 Katana is no longer built in Austria. The only current production version is the DA 20 Katana derivative produced by the related Canadian company.
First flight: 16 March 1991 (as Austrian HOAC LF 2000).
17 December 1992 first flight of the Austrian DV 20 Katana prototype.
Certification: 26 April 1993 in Austria.
Role: Recreational and training lightplane, developed to JAR-VLA using experience gained from production of the Dimona and Super Dimona motorgliders.
Sales: Some 500 Katanas of all Austrian (DV 20) and Canadian versions have been built, with production continuing only in Canada as the DA 20. Production of the DA 20 began on 29 June 1994 and the current production rate is 1.1 aircraft per working day (over 330 DA 20A1s built by March 1998). Cost US$106,785 ex-works Canada.
Crew: 2, side-by-side.
Cockpit: Entry via the single-piece upward/backward hinging canopy.
Baggage capacity: Baggage shelf in the cockpit.
Wing characteristics: Upswept wingtips. Optional folding wings to help storage and transport.
Wing control surfaces: Ailerons and flaps (15°, 40°).
Tail control surfaces: T-tail with elevator (with tab) and large rudder. Small ventral tailfin.
Construction materials: Composites, including a carbonfibre I-beam main spar.
Engine: Rotax 912 F3, with a constant-speed composites propeller for A1 version. See Aircraft variants for A2 and C1.
Engine rating: 81 hp (60.4 kW).
Fuel system: 76 litres.
Flight control system: Mechanical, with electrically-operated flaps.
Electrical system: 12 volt system, with 40 amp alternator and 12 volt battery.
Braking system: Dual hydraulic disc, toe operated. Parking brake.

↑ Diamond Aircraft Industries DA 20 Katana *(Heinz Zeggl)*

Flight avionics/instrumentation: Standard equipment includes altimeter, magnetic compass, attitude and directional gyros (3 ins, 7.6 cm display), airspeed indicator, turn co-ordinator indicator, speed indicator, dual push-to-talk switch, AlliedSignal Bendix/King KX 125 transceiver, KLN 35A GPS and KT 76A transponder, SSD 120 blind altitude encoder, PM 501 voice activated intercom, and emergency locator transmitter. Several optional avionics/equipment packages.

Aircraft variants:
DA 20A1, as detailed, with 81 hp (60.4 kW) Rotax engine.
DA 20A2 is the latest Rotax 912 version, of 100 hp (75 kW).
DA 20C1 first flew in 1997 with a 125 hp (93.2 kW) Teledyne Continental IO-240-B piston engine driving a 5 ft 9 ins (1.75 m) Hoffmann HO-14HM-175-15 wood/composites propeller. Empty weight 1,166 lb (529 kg) and MTOW 1,650 lb (748 kg). Maximum cruise speed 134 kts (154 mph) 248 km/h. Entered production in Spring 1998.

Details for DA 20A1 Katana

PRINCIPAL DIMENSIONS:
Wing span: 35 ft 4 ins (10.8 m)
Maximum length: 23 ft 6 ins (7.2 m)
Maximum height: 6 ft 11 ins (2.1 m)

COCKPIT:
Width: 3 ft 7 ins (1.1 m)

WINGS:
Aerofoil section: Wortmann FX 63-137 modified, laminar flow
Area: 124.86 sq ft (11.6 m^2)
Aspect ratio: 10.06

UNDERCARRIAGE:
Type: Fixed, with nosewheel. Wheel fairings are optional
Turning circle: 16 ft 9 ins (5.1 m)

WEIGHTS:
Empty: 1,090 lb (494 kg)
Maximum take-off: 1,610 lb (730 kg)
Useful load: 520 lb (236 kg)

PERFORMANCE:
Never-exceed speed (V_{NE}): 161 kts (185 mph) 298 km/h
Cruise speed: 119 kts (137 mph) 220 km/h at 75% power
Stall speed: 50 kts (58 mph) 93 km/h *clean*, 44 kts (51 mph) 81 km/h *with flaps*
Take-off distance over a 50 ft (15 m) obstacle: 1,600 ft (454 m)
Landing distance over a 50 ft (15 m) obstacle: 1,490 ft (244 m)
Maximum climb rate: 730 ft (223 m) per minute at sea level
Ceiling: 14,000 ft (4,267 m), service
Range: 523 naut miles (602 miles) 969 km at 75% power, with reserve
Noise emission: 65.2 dB maximum at take-off

Diamond Aircraft DA 22 Speed Katana

Comments: Only 2 prototypes of this aircraft were built, and series production will not take place.

Diamond Aircraft DA 40 Katana

First flight: 1998.
Certification: Will be certified for VFR and IFR operations in the USA, Canada, Austria, Germany, Switzerland, France, the

↑ Diamond Aircraft DA 40 Katana, first flown in 1998

Netherlands, Portugal, Italy, UK, Russia, Denmark, Czech Republic, Turkey and South Africa.
First delivery: To start in 1999 for Rotax and Teledyne Continental powered models, and some months later for Textron Lycoming powered model.
Role: 4-seater, intended principally for IFR flight training. Design is very similar to DA 20 Katana.
Sales: 2 prototypes built and were presented at the ILA in Berlin. Prices for the first 50 aircraft ordered, ex-factory and with standard equipment are DM 199,900 net with Rotax 914 or Teledyne Continental IO-240 engine, and DM 230,000 net with a Textron Lycoming IO-360 engine, rising to DM 220,000 and DM 250,000 respectively from the 51st aircraft.
Crew/passengers: 4 persons in the enclosed cabin. Upward and forward tilting canopy for unrestricted access to the front seats, and port-side door for access to the rear seats.
Baggage capacity: Compartment aft of the seats, with baggage secured with a fabric net.
Wing control surfaces: Half-span flaps, electrically actuated via mechanical linkages that also provide synchronization. Ailerons actuated via steel control tubes and aluminium bellcranks.
Tail control surfaces: GRP laminate rudder, cable actuated. Tailplane and elevator of GRP/foam/GRP sandwich construction, with elevator actuated by steel control tubes. Centring and increased control forces are provided by 2 compression coil springs mounted concentrically to the vertical push-pull tube of the elevator control system. The common spring base can be moved by an electric actuator which provides elevator trimming function.
Flight control system: See above.
Construction materials: Fuselage of glass reinforced plastic (GRP) construction, with local carbon reinforced plastic (CRP) reinforcement in areas of high stress. Stressed fuselage skin is primarily made of single GRP laminate with local GRP/PVC foam/GRP sandwich construction to increase stiffness and reduce noise. 2 fuselage shells (halves) are bonded together along the joint flange in the vertical plane. Internal structure consists of the firewall, a number of transverse bulkheads, a longitudinal bulkhead in the tailcone, and a main bulkhead (spar bridge) that receives the wing spar stubs. Vertical stabilizer is integrated with the fuselage. Wing skins of CRP/foam/CRP sandwich construction. 2 composite constructed I-section spars in each wing, and ribs to provide mounting surfaces for control tube guides and support for control bellcranks. See Wing and Tail control surfaces.
Engine: Choice of Rotax 914 piston engine with constant-speed propeller, Teledyne Continental IO-240 with fixed variable propeller, and Textron Lycoming IO-360 with constant-speed propeller.
Engine rating: 121 hp (90 kW) at 5,800 rpm, 125 hp (93.2 kW) at 2,800 rpm, and 165 hp (123 kW) at 2,400 rpm respectively.
Fuel system: Tank integrated into the wings. 115 litres capacity except for IO-360-engined version, which has 160 litres.
Electrical system: 14 volt DC, with an alternator with self-contained rectifier and regulator. 12V/35 amp-hour battery for engine starting.
Flight avionics/instrumentation: In addition to standard equipment, an optional VFR package (DM 19,900) comprises AlliedSignal Bendix/King KX 125 com/nav, XPDR KT 76 transponder including blindencoder, artificial horizon, directional gyro, turn co-ordinator, outside air temperature gauge, ACL, position lights and landing light. IFR packages, 2-axis autopilot and GPS are to be offered as options.

Details for DA 40 with Rotax 914, *with IO-360 in italics where different*

PRINCIPAL DIMENSIONS:
Wing span: 38 ft 10 ins (11.84 m)
Maximum length: 25 ft 6 ins (7.77 m)
Height: 6 ft 8.25 ins (2.04 m)

WINGS:
Aerofoil section: Wortmann FX 63-137/20 DAI laminar flow
Area: 137.78 sq ft (12.8 m^2)
Aspect ratio: 10.95

UNDERCARRIAGE:
Type: Fixed, nosewheel type, with steel tube nose strut sprung via an elastomeric spring pack. Steering by differential braking of main wheels and friction damped castoring nosewheel

WEIGHTS:
Empty: 1,300 lb (590 kg), *1,499 lb (680 kg)*
Maximum take-off: 2,094 lb (950 kg), *2,425 lb (1,100 kg)*
Payload: 794 lb (360 kg), *926 lb (420 kg)*

PERFORMANCE:
Maximum speed: 114 kts (131 mph) 211 km/h, *141 kts (162 mph) 261 km/h*
Cruise speed at 7,500 ft (2,285 m): 123 kts (142 mph) 228 km/h, *138 kts (159 mph) 256 km/h*
Cruise speed at 14,000 ft (4,265 m): 130 kts (150 mph) 241 km/h, *129 kts (149 mph) 239 km/h*
Take-off distance over a 50 ft (15 m) obstacle: 1,654 ft (504 m), *1,496 ft (456 m)*
Maximum climb rate at sea level: 736 ft (224 m) per minute, *1,000 ft (306 m) per minute*
Maximum climb rate at 10,000 ft (3,050 m): 501 ft (153 m) per minute, *515 ft (157 m) per minute*

Soko Holding Co — Bosnia-Herzegovina

Comments: Holding organization for various Soko companies, including Soko Air Ltd. See Activities under Soko Air Ltd.

Soko Air Ltd — Bosnia-Herzegovina

Corporate address:
Rodoč bb, 88000 Mostar.
Telephone: +387 88 350-070
Facsimile: +387 88 350-081
E-mail: soko.zrakoplovna@laus.hr
Founded: 1950.
Information:
Miroslav Coric (Director of Soko Air) and Valentina Marincic (Director, Marketing).

ACTIVITIES

▪ As of 1998, Soko has been restructured, divided into several companies according to their activities and shareholder structures, though retaining a common identity under Soko Holding Co and operating from the former Soko company's Mostar-Rodoč facilities. Under this reorganization, Soko's current aviation activities are carried out by Soko Air Ltd.
▪ Current programmes include industrial co-operation with international civil aircraft manufacturers for component production.
▪ Design and manufacture of various support equipment for civil aviation, such as air cargo containers and pallets, airport cargo and baggage transport dollies, and aircraft servicing vehicles for toilets, water, etc.
▪ Design and manufacture of light aircraft, including the Soko 2, the **LH-1** light piston-engined utility helicopter in an advanced stage of engineering design, and a family of **2**, **4** and **6 seat** light aircraft in the initial design stage.
▪ Industrial co-operation in non-aviation areas using aerospace production technologies.
Note: Soko wished to point out that it never went out of business, but had to cease work for short periods of the order of a couple of months. Even during the Fall of 1992, between 2 surges of conflict in the area, Soko completed deliveries of aircraft components to Eurocopter, SOCEA/SOGERMA, Latécoère, IAI-Malkam, Deutche Airbus and Dornier.

(Best known former recent programmes were the Super Galeb jet trainer and Orao attack aircraft, both of which were detailed in the 1996-97 edition of *WA&SD*, the former under the UTVA heading on page 106 and the latter in the multi-national section on page 170.)

Soko Air Soko 2

First flight: November 1996.
Certification: Designed to JAR-VLA, and should be certified in the Utility category as a landplane, and Normal category as a floatplane.

Development

▪ Design was initiated in 1992, immediately after the cessation of hostilities in the area. Following new conflicts, activities on the programme resumed in 1994. The prototype was flown in 1996, and after about 6 hours of initial flight testing, the aircraft was returned to the factory for minor modification and improvements, including the installation of redesigned and enlarged winglets, new main wheels with hydraulic disc brakes of improved efficiency, redesigned engine cowling, exhaust noise damper, cabin heating system, wider and more comfortable seats, and an optional BRS-5 parachute recovery system. These updates had been completed by the end of 1997, when another prototype, configured as the **Soko 2H floatplane**, had been built. Flight testing was to resume in 1998, pending the resolution of administrative difficulties arising from Bosnia-Herzegovina having no flight test establishment.

Details

Role: 2-seat very light personal and club aircraft. Optional BRS-5 rocket-assisted parachute recovery system, though not available with floatplane due to weight limitations.

↑ **Soko Air Soko 2** *(courtesy Soko Air)*

Details for Soko 2 landplane with BRS-5, *with 2H floatplane in italics for weights*

PRINCIPAL DIMENSIONS:
Wing span: 31 ft 10 ins (9.7 m)
Maximum length: 26 ft (7.918 m)
Width, wings folded: 7 ft 10.5 ins (2.4 m)
Maximum height: 6 ft 2 ins (1.88 m)
Height with wings folded: 8 ft 5 ins (2.56 m)

WINGS:
Aerofoil section: NACA 23018
Area: 156.61 sq ft (14.55 m^2)
Chord: 4 ft 11 ins (1.5 m)
Aspect ratio: 6.47
Dihedral: 1° from roots
Incidence: 14° root, 12° 30' tip

UNDERCARRIAGE:
Type: Fixed, with steerable tailwheel on leaf-spring leg and connected by springs to rudder actuating horns. Cantilever main legs with drag-brace struts, attached to fuselage and swivelling on longitudinal axes, provided with Soko rubber-in-compression shock absorbers. Can be reconfigured as a floatplane, using Soko GFRP-laminate floats (tailwheel assembly also removed)
Main wheel tyre size: 5.00-5/6PR
Wheel base: 17 ft 11 ins (5.46 m)
Wheel track: 5 ft 11 ins (1.8 m)

WEIGHTS:
Empty: 800 lb (363 kg), *866 lb (393 kg)*
Maximum take-off: 1,168 lb (530 kg) utility and 1,290 lb (585 kg) Normal, *1,290 lb (585 kg)*

PERFORMANCE (estimated, at 1,036 lb, 470 kg AUW)**:**
Never-exceed speed (V_{NE}): 100 kts (115 mph) 185 km/h
Maximum speed: 78 kts (90 mph) 145 km/h
Cruise speed: 67 kts (78 mph) 125 km/h, at 75% power
Stalling speed: 40.5 kts (47 mph) 75 km/h
Take-off distance: 417 ft (127 m)
Landing distance: 328 ft (100 m)
Maximum climb rate: 902 ft (275 m) per minute
Time to 11,480 ft (3,500 m): 18 minutes 30 seconds
Ceiling: 18,110 ft (5,520 m)
Duration: 5 hours 30 minutes

Crew/passengers: 2 persons in tandem, under an upward-opening canopy hinged on centre-line cabin roof beam. Dual controls with adjustable propellers. Cabin heated and ventilated.
Wing characteristics: Braced high-wing monoplane. Wing panels fold backwards along the fuselage sides.
Wing control surfaces: Ailerons, with ground-adjustable tab. No flaps.
Tail control surfaces: T-tail, with all-moving tailplane fitted with combined trim/anti-tab. Rudder.
Construction materials: Wings have a 3 piece, single spar, fabric-covered light alloy structure, with tubular oblique auxiliary spar extending aft from the main spar/wing brace strut junction. Metal strip leading- and trailing-edge reinforcements. Single-spar metal/fabric ailerons. Winglets of glassfibre reinforced plastics/foam sandwich construction. Pod and boom fuselage of conventional semi-monocoque light alloy construction. Single-spar fin of all-metal stressed skin construction, single-spar fabric-covered rudder, and tailplane with metal-skinned leading-edge torsion boxes and trailing-edge reinforcement strips.
Engine: Limbach L.2000 EC1 carried behind wing centre section, with 4 ft 11 ins (1.5 m) diameter MS Propeller fixed-pitch, 2-blade, wooden pusher propeller with spinner.
Engine rating: 80 hp (59.7 kW).
Fuel system: 50 litres, in wing centre-section tank.
Electrical system: 12 volt DC, with engine-driven alternator and 30 amp-hour battery.
Braking system: Hydraulic disc brakes, actuated by hand lever on control grip.
Flight avionics/instrumentation: Standard basic instruments. Optional instruments up to full IFR and night-flying equipment. Optional avionics to customer's requirements. Prototype fitted with AlliedSignal Bendix/King KX 99 760-channel VHF com, Dualcom BT-101 intercom, Garmin 100AVD GPS and AlliedSignal Bendix/King KT 76A ATC transponder.

Aircraft variants:
Soko 2 is the landplane.
Soko 2H is the floatplane.

Indústria Aeronáutica Neiva S.A. — Brazil

Corporate address:
Rua Nossa Senhora de Fátima 360, Caixa Postal 10, 18608-900 Botocatu (SP).
Telephone: +55 149 21 2122 and 5077
Facsimile: +55 149 22 1285 and 21 2110
Founded:
12 October 1954 (see Activities).
Information:
Adriano Bruder di Creddo (Technical publications).

ACTIVITIES

- Sub-contracted by Embraer in 1975 to build the single- and twin-engined light aircraft licensed from Piper of the USA.
- Incorporated by Embraer in March 1980, when all engineering and production tooling for the Embraer/Piper line and for the Ipanema agricultural aircraft were transferred to Botucatu.
- A total of 3,251 aircraft of all types had been built by Neiva between 1956 and May 1998, including 781 Ipanemas, 21 Urupema gliders, 288 Cariocas, 477 Coriscos, 145 Tupis, 294 Minuanos, 206 Sertanejos, 868 Senecas/Cuestas, 132 Navajos and 39 Carajas.

Embraer/Neiva EMB-202 Ipanema

First flight: 30 July 1970 (as EMB-200 prototype).
Certification: 14 December 1971 for the original EMB-200 version.
Role: Single-seat agricultural aircraft.
Sales: Production of all models stood at 781 by May 1998 (first 10 delivered in 1972, and high point production was 1975, when 81 were delivered; 401 EMB-201As were built up to 1992).
Chemical hopper: 950 litres, 1,653 lb (750 kg).
Dispersal equipment: Micronair atomizers, or spreader/dusting or spray booms. Atomizers and booms near the wing trailing edges, dusting equipment below the fuselage. Various options including ram air pressure generator for the liquid application equipment and lightweight applicators including the Micronair AU5000 with rotary atomizers.
Wing characteristics: Low-mounted cantilever, with substantial dihedral and down-turned wingtips. Leading edges and wingtips are detachable for quick replacement if damaged.
Wing control surfaces: Frise ailerons and slotted flaps.
Tail control surfaces: Elevators (starboard tab) and rudder.
Construction materials: Welded steel tube structure and mainly metal (some glassfibre) skins.
Engine: Textron Lycoming IO-540-K1J5D or Teledyne Continental IO-550, with a 7 ft (2.13 m) constant-speed propeller.
Engine rating: 300 hp (224 kW).
Fuel system: 292 litres, of which 264 litres are usable. Consumption 69 litres per hour at 75% power, 6,000 ft (1,830 m) altitude.
Flight control system: Mechanical/manual.
Electrical system: 28 volt DC, with a 28 volt/35 amp alternator and 2 × 43 amp-hour batteries.
Braking system: Hydraulically operated disc.
Flight avionics/instrumentation: VFR (ADF and VHF). Can be fitted optionally with AlliedSignal Bendix/King KX 99 transceiver and Garmin 55 AVD GPS.

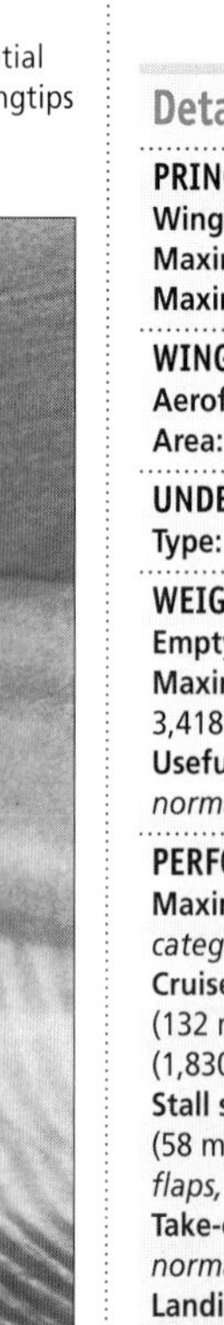

↑ Embraer/Neiva EMB-202 Ipanema with spray booms

Details for EMB-202 Ipanema

PRINCIPAL DIMENSIONS:
Wing span: 38 ft 4 ins (11.69 m)
Maximum length: 24 ft 3.5 ins (7.43 m)
Maximum height: 7 ft 3.5 ins (2.22 m)

WINGS:
Aerofoil section: NACA 23015 modified
Area: 214.6 sq ft (19.94 m^2)

UNDERCARRIAGE:
Type: Fixed, with tailwheel

WEIGHTS:
Empty, equipped: 2,249 lb (1,020 kg)
Maximum take-off: 3,968 lb (1,800 kg) *restricted category*, 3,418 lb (1,550 kg) *normal*
Useful load: 1,720 lb (780 kg) *restricted*, 1,168 lb (530 kg) *normal*

PERFORMANCE:
Maximum speed: 121 kts (139 mph) 224 km/h *restricted category*, 124 kts (143 mph) 230 km/h *normal*
Cruise speed: 111 kts (128 mph) 206 km/h *restricted*, 115 kts (132 mph) 213 km/h *normal*, at 75% power and 6,000 ft (1,830 m)
Stall speed: 55 kts (64 mph) 102 km/h *clean, restricted;* 50 kts (58 mph) 93 km/h *clean, normal;* 53 kts (61 mph) 99 km/h *30° flaps, restricted;* 50 kts (58 mph) 93 km/h *30° flaps, normal*
Take-off distance: 1,162 ft (354 m) *restricted*, 656 ft (200 m) *normal*, both sea level, ISA
Landing distance: 558 ft (170 m) *restricted*, 502 ft (153 m) *normal*, both sea level, ISA
Maximum climb rate: 928 ft (283 m) per minute *normal*
Ceiling: 11,400 ft (3,470 m) *restricted*
Range: 506 naut miles (583 miles) 939 km

Details for EMB-720D Minuano

PRINCIPAL DIMENSIONS:
Wing span: 36 ft 2 ins (11.02 m)
Maximum length: 27 ft 8 ins (8.43 m)
Maximum height: 8 ft 2 ins (2.49 m)

WEIGHTS:
Empty: 2,095 lb (950 kg)
Maximum take-off: 3,600 lb (1,633 kg)

PERFORMANCE:
Maximum speed: 147 kts (169 mph) 272 km/h
Cruise speed: 123 kts (142 mph) 228 km/h at 55% best power
Stall speed: 58 kts (67 mph) 108 km/h *with flaps*
Range: up to 890 naut miles (1,024 miles) 1,650 km at 55% best economy power

Embraer/Neiva EMB-720D Minuano

Role: 6/7-seat lightplane, based on the Piper PA-32-301 Saratoga.
Sales: 294 sold by May 1998 in all versions, past and present, including several to air taxi operators. First 12 delivered in 1975.
Engine: Textron Lycoming IO-540-K1G5.
Engine rating: 300 hp (224 kW).

Embraer/Neiva EMB-810D Cuesta (Seneca)

Role: 6 passenger lightplane, based on the Piper PA-34-220T Seneca III.
Sales: Some 868 Cuestas sold by May 1998 in all versions, past and present
Engines: 2 Teledyne Continental L/TSIO-360KBs.
Engine rating: Each 220 hp (164 kW).

Details for EMB-810D Cuesta

PRINCIPAL DIMENSIONS:
Wing span: 38 ft 11 ins (11.86 m)
Maximum length: 28 ft 7 ins (8.72 m)
Maximum height: 9 ft 11 ins (3.02 m)

WEIGHTS:
Empty: 3,197 lb (1,447 kg)
Maximum take-off: 4,751 lb (2,155 kg)

PERFORMANCE:
Maximum speed: 196 kts (226 mph) 363 km/h
Cruise speed: 180 kts (207 mph) 334 km/h at 55% power
Stall speed: 64 kts (74 mph) 118 km/h
Range: 920 naut miles (1,059 miles) 1,705 km at 55% power

Airtech Canada Aviation Services Ltd — Canada

Corporate address:
PO Box 415, Suite 103, Peterborough, Ontario K9J 6Z3.

Telephone: +1 705 743 9483
Facsimile: +1 705 749 0841
E-mail: airtechcanada@ptbo.igs.net

Founded: 1977.

Information:
Bernard J. LaFrance (General Manager).

↑ 15th Airtech Canada DHC/1000 hp Otter conversion, for Katmai Air, with engine on its initial run-up, cowls off, in June 1998

ACTIVITIES

- Design, engineering, assembly, manufacture and marketing of aircraft and aviation products.
- Principal products/services are the conversion/completion of fixed and rotary wing aircraft for medevac uses, re-engining the DHC-2 Beaver and DHC-3 Otter, repair/maintenance/overhaul of small aircraft, and design/manufacture/testing/installation of specialized aircraft and aviation modifications, parts and assemblies.
- Holds Canadian STA and US STC for the DHC-2 Beaver/600 hp conversion and the DHC-3 Otter/1000 hp conversion. The conversions can be undertaken by Airtech or by a third party using an Airtech kit, with authorized installers in Canada being Selkirk Air of Manitoba and Victoria Air Maintenance of Sidney, BC.
- For the medevac role, has developed or custom engineered and installed a number of portable and semi-dedicated and dedicated air ambulance interiors and patient restraint systems.

Airtech Canada DHC/1000 hp Otter

Certification: Received the STA in 1983.
Role: Re-engined Otter, offering enhanced short take-off, landing and climb capability on wheels, skis or floats, and extends its operational life into the 21st century.
Sales: Conversion marketed since 1983. 15 completed by June 1998, operated in Canada, the USA and Peru; 13th conversion went to Green Airways of Ontario (its second example), and the most recent deliveries went to Blue Water Aviation of Canada (second example) and Katmai Air of Alaska, USA.
Engine: WSK PZL-Kalisz ASz-62IR-M18/DHC-3 radial piston engine.
Engine rating: 967 hp (721 kW).

Details for DHC/1000 hp Otter

PRINCIPAL DIMENSIONS:
Wing span: 58 ft (17.68 m)
Maximum length: 42 ft (12.8 m)
Maximum height: 12 ft 7 ins (3.84 m) *landplane*, 15 ft (4.57 m) *seaplane*

WEIGHTS:
Empty: 4,925 lb (2,234 kg) *landplane*, 5,300 lb (2,404 kg) *seaplane*
Maximum take-off: 8,000 lb (3,629 kg)

PERFORMANCE:
Never-exceed speed (V_{NE}): 157 kts (181 mph) 291 km/h IAS *landplane*, 146 kts (168 mph) 270 km/h IAS *seaplane*
Maximum normal speed (V_{NO}): 125 kts (144 mph) 233 km/h IAS *landplane*, 116 kts (134 mph) 216 km/h IAS *seaplane*
Take-off distance: 440 ft (134 m) *landplane*, 478 ft (146 m) *seaplane*, at sea level
Maximum climb rate: 1,680 ft (512 m) per minute *landplane*, 1,570 ft (478 m) per minute *seaplane*, at sea level
Ceiling: 17,500 ft (5,335 m) *landplane*, 15,700 ft (4,785 m) *seaplane*, service
Range: 677 naut miles (780 miles) 1,255 km at 112 kts and 10,000 ft (3,050 m), 405 bhp (302 kW), *landplane*

Alberta Aerospace Corporation — Canada

Corporate address:
10201 Southport Road, SW, Suite 1130, Calgary, Alberta T2W 4X9

Telephone: +1 403 255 2810
Facsimile: +1 403 640 4024

Information:
C. Raymond Johnson (President and CEO).

↑ Alberta Aerospace Phoenix FanJet in 4-seat personal transport layout

ACTIVITIES

- In 1995, Promavia of Belgium licensed Alberta Aerospace to enable the company to develop the Jet Squalus for *ab initio* pilot training, to be certified according to FAR-23 and JAR-23 under the new name **Phoenix FanJet** in early 1999. The Jet Squalus flying prototype was also sold and Alberta Aerospace subsequently purchased the remaining assets of interest for the production of the aircraft in Canada. Changes introduced to the FanJet include use of a 1,600 lbf (7.1 kN) Williams-Rolls FJ44 engine in a modified airframe, enlarged flaps and ailerons, deletion of the dual underfuselage airbrakes, and revision of the systems. Options will include a Honeywell Primus 1000 'glass' cockpit. Cost of a Phoenix FanJet at the time of writing was expected to be $1.575 million. A Phoenix FanJet 4-seat, pressurized (4.67 psi), higher-powered (1,900 lbf, 8.45 kN) personal transport variant is also being developed, for certification in late 1999 and expected to cost about $1.9 million.

Details for Phoenix FanJet 2-seat trainer, *with data for the Phoenix FanJet 4-seater in italics*

PRINCIPAL DIMENSIONS:
Wing span: 33 ft 8 ins (10.26 m), *the same*
Maximum length: 30 ft 8.25 ins (9.35 m)
Maximum height: 11 ft 9.5 ins (3.59 m)

WINGS:
Area: 162 sq ft (15.05 m^2)
Aspect ratio: 6.99

UNDERCARRIAGE:
Type: Retractable trailing arm type, with steerable nosewheel
Wheel base: 11 ft 9 ins (3.58 m)
Wheel track: 11 ft 9.5 ins (3.59 m)

WEIGHTS (provisional):
Empty, equipped: 3,408 lb (1,546 kg), *3,808 lb (1,727 kg)*
Maximum take-off: 5,100 lb (2,313 kg), *6,300 lb (2,857 kg)*
Useful load: 1,692 lb (767 kg), *2,492 lb (1,130 kg)*
Fuel capacity: 700 litres, *1,060 litres*

PERFORMANCE (provisional):
Maximum cruise speed: 315 kts (363 mph) 584 km/h at 20,000 ft (6,100 m), 345 kts (397 mph) 639 km/h at 25,000 ft (7,620 m)
Economic cruise speed: 261 kts (301 mph) 484 km/h, *273 kts (314 mph) 506 km/h*
Stall speed: 61 kts (70 mph) 113 km/h, *the same*
Take-off distance over a 50 ft (15 m) obstacle: 2,300 ft (701 m), *3,000 ft (915 m)*
Landing distance over a 50 ft (15 m) obstacle: 2,400 ft (732 m), *3,000 ft (915 m)*
Maximum climb rate: 2,360 ft (719 m) per minute, *2,630 ft (802 m) per minute*
G limits: +6, -3; *+3.6, -1.6*
Ceiling: 25,000 ft (7,620 m), service
Range: 715 naut miles (823 miles) 1,325 km, *1,179 naut miles (1,357 miles) 2,185 km*, both at 25,000 ft (7,620 m)

Canada Air R.V. Inc — Canada

Corporate address:
Suite 1380, 194-3803 Calgary Trail South, Edmonton, Alberta T6J 5M8.

Telephone: +1 403 944 9210
Facsimile: +1 403 461 0584
E-mail: 75767.54@compuserve.com

Founded:
3 November 1988.

Information:
Dale Alton (Marketing Manager).

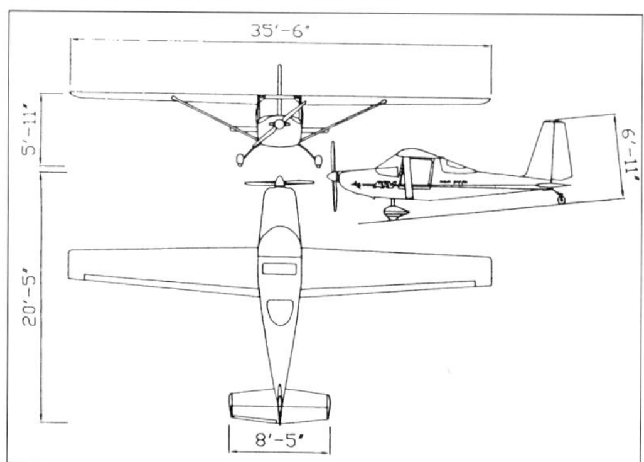

↑ Canada ARV Griffin 2-seat cabin lightplane *(courtesy Canada Air R.V.)*

Canada ARV Griffin

Role: Side-by-side 2-seat lightplane, with dual controls. Available for home construction.
Baggage capacity: 200 lb (91 kg).
Wing control surfaces: Near full-span flaperons.
Tail control surfaces: Tapered elevators (port tab) and rudder.
Construction materials: All-metal structure but with composite wingtips. Wing designed for superior slow flight fuel efficiency, docile stall characteristics, good glide ratio, responsive flaperon control, high lift coefficient, and good power to speed ratio.
Engine: Designed to accommodate engines of 110-275 lb (50-125 kg), including Teledyne Continental O-200A, 118 hp (88 kW) Subaru EA-81 and Suzuki Turbo.
Fuel system: 181.7 litres.

Details for ARV Griffin with Subaru engine

PRINCIPAL DIMENSIONS:
Wing span: 35 ft 6 ins (10.82 m)
Maximum length: 20 ft 5 ins (6.22 m)
Maximum height: 6 ft 11 ins (2.11 m)

WINGS:
Aerofoil section: Laminar flow UA-2
Area: 115 sq ft (10.68 m^2)
Aspect ratio: 10.96

UNDERCARRIAGE:
Type: Steerable Nosewheel or tailwheel type, with hydraulic disc brakes. Adaptable to floats or skis

WEIGHTS:
Empty: 720 lb (327 kg)
Maximum take-off: 1,500 lb (680 kg)

PERFORMANCE:
Maximum speed: 122 kts (141 mph) 227 km/h
Cruise speed: 111 kts (128 mph) 206 km/h, 75% power at sea level
Stall speed: 44 kts (50 mph) 81 km/h
Take-off distance: 250 ft (77 m), from grass
Landing distance: 450 ft (137 m)
Maximum climb rate: 954 ft (291 m) per minute
G limit: 6.6 ultimate
Ceiling: 13,000 ft (3,960 m), service
Range: 781 naut miles (900 miles) 1,448 km, 75% power at 7,000 ft (2,134 m), 45 minutes reserve

Conair Aviation Ltd — Canada

Corporate address:
PO Box 220, Abbotsford, British Columbia V2S 4NY.

Telephone: +1 604 855 1171
Facsimile: +1 604 855 1017

Information:
Lorna Thomassen.

ACTIVITIES

▪ Converts aeroplanes and helicopters mainly for firefighting duties, but also for insect and oil control, and other roles involving spraying and aerial discharge. In addition to those for customers, it operates its own fleet of aircraft.
▪ Conversion can involve structural inspection and modification, systems replacement, upgraded avionics and (in the case of Turbo Firecat) replacement of original radial engines with turboprops.
▪ Systems have been fitted to aircraft as diverse as the DC-6B and C-130. Principal products are the Firecat, a firefighting modification of the Grumman Tracker former ASW aircraft, with a cabin retardant tank and optional foam injection system; and the Turbo Firecat, introducing P&WC PT6A-67AF turboprops and with a similar compartmentalized tank for 3,456 litres of retardant. The F27 Firefighter is a conversion of the Fokker Friendship, also suited to fire detection, spraying and other activities. For helicopters, Conair produces the Helitanker, a belly retardant tank that is installed beneath the fuselage, refilled via a tank in the main cabin or on the ground, or while hovering.

Found Aircraft Canada Inc — Canada

Corporate address:
300 Jones Road, Gravenhurst, Ontario P1P 1A1.

Telephone: +1 705 687 6167, or 378 0530 for hangar
Facsimile: +1 705 687 0923, or 378 0594 for hangar

Information:
N. K. 'Bud' Found.

ACTIVITIES

▪ Developing the Model 2E Bush Hawk as an improved version of the Found FBA-2C, in response to requests to place the FBA-2C back into production. Airframe structural test programme for proof of engineering was proceeding and several tests had been successfully completed by April 1998.

Found FBA-2E Bush Hawk

Certification: Programme for reinstating the Type Certificate of the FBA-2C in Canada and the USA was progressing at the time of writing (see company introduction). Original FBA-2C was certified to FAA CAR 3 in Canada and the USA, to operate on wheels, skis, floats, retractable wheel skis and wheel floats.
Role: 5-seat passenger or freight/utility aircraft, particularly suited to operations in undeveloped regions.
Sales: 27 original FBA-2Cs were manufactured in Toronto from the 1960s and 9 remain flying. Orders and options for 6 FBA-2E Bush Hawks were under advanced negotiation in April 1998.
Crew/passengers: 5 persons. See Cabin access. Roll-up hammock style rear bush seat stows in top rear cabin.
Cabin access: 4 large doors (larger rear doors on the Model 2E than earlier 2C) help loading of passengers, bulky items of equipment or freight (such as 45 Imp gallon drums rolled in; rear cabin can accommodate 2 such drums), or a litter with patient.
Engine: Textron Lycoming IO-540-D4A5 piston engine. 2- and 3-blade propellers being tested.
Engine rating: 260 hp (194 kW).

↑ Found FBA-2 on floats in British Columbia

Details for FBA-2E Bush Hawk

PRINCIPAL DIMENSIONS:
Wing span: 36 ft (10.97 m)
Maximum length: 25 ft 6 ins (7.77 m)

CABIN:
Length: 11 ft 6 ins (3.51 m)
Width: 3 ft 6 ins (1.07 m)
Volume: 120 cu ft (3.4 m^3), including open baggage compartment; rear cabin volume 87 cu ft (2.46 m^3)

WINGS:
Area: 180 sq ft (16.72 m^2)
Aspect ratio: 7.2

UNDERCARRIAGE:
Type: Fixed tailwheel type on the first Model 2E, with nosewheel type available on subsequent aircraft. Optional Edo 2960 floats, or Edo 2790 amphibious floats, or Federal C-3200 retractable wheel/skis
Main wheel tyre size: 8.00 × 6

WEIGHTS:
Maximum take-off: 3,200 lb (1,451.5 kg), except 3,100 lb (1,406 kg) with Edo 2790s
Useful load: 1,450 lb (658 kg) with wheel undercarriage, 1,200 lb (544 kg) with Edo 2960s, 900 lb (408 kg) with Edo 2790s, and 1,335 lb (605.5 kg) with Federal wheel/skis

PERFORMANCE:
Cruise speed: 105 kts (120 mph) 193 km/h typically with floats
Maximum climb rate: 900 ft (274 m) per minute at sea level, with floats, at MTOW*
Take-off time: 25-30 seconds at sea level, with floats, at MTOW*
Climb from 830 ft to 10,000 ft (253 to 3,050 m): 13 minutes with wheels, at MTOW*
Range: over 521 naut miles (600 miles) 965 km at economic cruise speed, at 5,000 ft (1,525 m)
Duration: over 6 hours

* Preliminary data from testing development aircraft

Zenair Ltd — Canada

Corporate address:
Huronia Airport, Midland, Ontario L4R 4K8.

Telephone: +1 705 526 2871
Facsimile: +1 705 526 8022

Founded: 1974.

Information:
Mathieu Heintz (Vice President).

ACTIVITIES

▪ In addition to the certified CH 2000, Zenair offers a range of experimental aircraft for home construction (see Recreational section).

LICENSEE

ZENITH AIRCRAFT COMPANY

HQ address:
Mexico Memorial Airport, Mexico, MO 65265-0650, USA.

Telephone: +1 314 581 9000
Facsimile: +1 314 581 0011

Activities:
▪ Zenair Aircraft has established a joint venture with the Czech Aircraft Works, to manufacture and market the CH-601 and CH.701 in kit and assembled forms for the European market. See Recreational section.

↑ Zenair Zenith CH 2000

Zenair Zenith CH 2000

First flight: 26 June 1993.
Certification: 26 July 1994 (Canadian), 31 July 1994 (FAA); JAR/VLA.
Role: 2-seat training (dual controls), business and pleasure. Approved for spins.
Sales: Deliveries began in September 1994.
Wing control surfaces: Ailerons and flaps.
Tail control surfaces: All moving type, with elevator trim control.
Flight control system: Mechanical, but electric flaps.
Construction materials: Metal.
Engine: Textron Lycoming O-235-N2C piston engine, with a 6 ft (1.83 m) Sensenich 2-blade metal propeller.
Engine rating: 116 hp (86.5 kW).
Fuel system: 106 litres. Optional 2 × 53 litre wing tanks in place of fuselage tank.
Electrical system: 12 volt, 60 amp, with heavy duty battery.
Braking system: Cleveland wheels and hydraulic disc toebrakes.
Flight avionics/instrumentation: AlliedSignal Bendix/King com transceiver and transponder, encoder, airspeed indicator, altimeter, fluid magnetic compass, static air source, hour meter and more. Stall warning system. Options include gyro package, GPS, audio/marker panel, nav receiver with or without glideslope and tri-nav indicator, and ADF. Optional IFR, Trainer or Cross-Country packages.

Details for Zenith CH 2000

PRINCIPAL DIMENSIONS:
Wing span: 28 ft 10 ins (8.79 m)
Maximum length: 23 ft (7.01 m)
Maximum height: 6 ft 10 ins (2.08 m)

CABIN:
Width: 3 ft 10 ins (1.17 m)

WINGS:
Aerofoil section: LS(1)-0417 mod
Area: 137 sq ft (12.73 m^2)
Aspect ratio: 6

UNDERCARRIAGE:
Type: Fixed, with steerable nosewheel. Optional wheel fairings

WEIGHTS:
Empty: 1,000 lb (454 kg) standard
Maximum take-off: 1,550 lb (703 kg)
Useful load: 550 lb (249 kg)

PERFORMANCE:
Never-exceed speed (V_{NE}): 147 kts (170 mph) 273 km/h
Cruise speed: 100 kts (115 mph) 185 km/h, at 75% power
Stall speed: 44 kts (50 mph) 81 km/h
Take-off distance over a 50 ft (15 m) obstacle: 1,550 ft (473 m)
Landing distance over a 50 ft (15 m) obstacle: 1,300 ft (396 m)
Maximum climb rate: 820 ft (250 m) per minute
G limits: +4.4, -2.2
Range: 434 naut miles (500 miles) 804 km, 75% power, no reserve

Empresa Nacional de Aeronáutica (ENAER) — Chile

Corporate address:
See Combat section for company details.

ENAER T-35 Pillán

Comments: Details of this military and civil basic flying, aerobatic and instrument trainer, first flown on 6 March 1981 but no longer in production, can be found in the 1996-97 edition of *WA&SD*, page 385. See Combat section for Pillán 2000.

ENAER Ñamcu and EuroENAER Eaglet

First flight: April 1989 for Ñamcu, 8 May 1998 for Eaglet.
Certification: Meets FAR Pt 23, and JAR 23 for Eaglet.
Role: Aerobatic lightplane, club trainer and utility aircraft. Also offered in homebuilt kit form.
Sales: Production in Chile began in 1995. Also being assembled from 1998 as the Eaglet in the Netherlands by EuroENAER at its Den-Helder factory, using main assemblies constructed in Chile. Up to 10 Eaglets were expected to be built in 1998, following certification.
Crew/passengers: 2 persons.
Cockpit: Dual controls. 2 upward-hinging doors form the centre section of the canopy.
Baggage capacity: 22 lb (10 kg) behind seats.
Wing control surfaces: Ailerons and flaps.
Tail control surfaces: Elevators (starboard tab) and rudder.
Construction materials: Glassfibre, carbonfibre and foam composites.
Engine: Textron Lycoming O-235-N2C piston engine, with a

↑ ENAER Ñamcu, now also assembled in the Netherlands as the EuroENAER Eaglet *(Denis Hughes)*

5 ft 10 ins (1.78 m) 2-blade fixed-pitch propeller. EuroENAER Eaglet has a Textron Lycoming O-320-D2A, derated to 148 hp (110 kW).
Engine rating: 116 hp (86.5 kW) for O-235-N2C.
Fuel system: 100 litres.
Electrical system: 12 volt 70 amp alternator and 12 volt 35 amp-hour lead acid battery.
Braking system: Cleveland hydraulic disc on main units.
Flight avionics/instrumentation: VFR. Optional upgrade to IFR.

Aircraft variants:
Ñamcu is the original Chilean version, as detailed.

Details for Ñamcu

PRINCIPAL DIMENSIONS:
Wing span: 27 ft 3 ins (8.31 m)
Maximum length: 23 ft 1.5 ins (7.05 m)
Maximum height: 7 ft 11 ins (2.42 m)

WINGS:
Aerofoil section: NACA 63_2415
Area: 107.746 sq ft (10.01 m^2)

UNDERCARRIAGE:
Type: Fixed, with steerable nosewheel

WEIGHTS:
Empty: 1,203 lb (546 kg)
Maximum take-off and landing: 1,764 lb (800 kg)

PERFORMANCE:
Maximum permissible speed: 177 kts (203 mph) 328 km/h
Maximum speed: 127 kts (146 mph) 235 km/h, or 140 kts (161 mph) 260 km/h for Eaglet
Cruise speed: 103 kts (118 mph) 191 km/h, at 75% power
Stall speed: 50 kts (58 mph) 93 km/h *with flaps*, 56 kts (65 mph) 104 km/h *clean*; reduced stall speed for Eaglet
Take-off distance: 1,000 ft (304 m)
Landing distance: 580 ft (177 m)
Maximum climb rate: 970 ft (295 m) per minute
G limits: +4.4, -2.2
Ceiling: 14,010 ft (4,270 m)
Range with full fuel: 500 naut miles (575 miles) 926 km at cruise speed
Duration: 3.6 hours

Eaglet is the EuroENAER variant for the European market, with a derated O-320-D2A engine. Modified flaps and elevators, cockpit upgrades, crashproof seats, wheel spats and more

Beijing Keyuan Light Aircraft Industrial Co Ltd — China

Corporate address:
No 7 Zhong Guan Cun South Road, Haidian, Beijing 100080.
Telephone: +86 10 257 2822, 255 7943
Facsimile: +86 10 257 2922

ACTIVITIES

▪ AD-200 was designed by the Nanjing University of Aeronautics and Astronautics, and said to have a special lifesaving system to safely land the pilot and aircraft at the same time.

Beijing Keyuan AD-200 Blue Eagle

First flight: 1 September 1988 in AD-200A form with a Rotax 447 engine.
Certification: 26 December 1995 in AD-200A form. Designed and manufactured according to CCAR-23.
Role: STOL light general-purpose aircraft, with uses including touring, training, sports and patrol. In AD-200N modified form, can also be used for agricultural, aerial photography, exploration, delivery and other special roles.
Sales: At least 30 ordered of all types, with more than 20 delivered.
Crew/passengers: 2, in tandem, under a sideways hinged (to starboard) single-piece canopy.
Wing control surfaces: Rear-mounted slightly sweptback wings, with ailerons. Endplate sweptback winglet/fins and horn-balanced rudders.
Canard: Nose-mounted, constant chord, with full-span elevators.
Construction materials: Glassfibre reinforced plastic. Quick assembly/disassembly for storage and transportation.
Engine: Rotax 582/2V piston engine, with a 5 ft 8 ins (1.73 m) diameter 2-blade pusher propeller.
Engine rating: 64 hp (47.7 kW).
Fuel system: 88 lb (40 kg)
Flight avionics/instrumentation: Equipped with a compass, airspeed indicator and altimeter. Can be equipped with an engine tachometer and a cylinder head temperature indicator.

Aircraft variants:
AD-200A was the initial production version, with a Rotax 447 engine. No longer marketed.
AD-200B first flew in March 1996 and is in production. Rotax 582/2V.
AD-200N first flew in October 1995 and is in production (thought to be aimed at special uses – see Role). Increased empty weight. Rotax 582/2V. See table for spraying performance.

↑ Beijing Keyuan AD-200 Blue Eagle *(Sebastian Zacharias)*

Details for AD-200B, *with AD-200N in italics where different*

PRINCIPAL DIMENSIONS:
Wing span: 30 ft 10.5 ins (9.408 m)
Maximum length: 20 ft 7.5 ins (6.29 m)
Maximum height: 6 ft 7 ins (2.01 m)

WINGS:
Area: 121.48 sq ft (11.286 m^2)

UNDERCARRIAGE:
Type: Fixed, nosewheel type
Wheel base: 8 ft (2.436 m)
Wheel track: 5 ft 4.5 ins (1.64 m)

WEIGHTS:
Empty: 628 lb (285 kg), *738 lb (335 kg)*
Maximum take-off: 1,212 lb (550 kg)

PERFORMANCE:
Maximum speed: 81 kts (93 mph) 150 km/h
Cruise speed: 57 kts (65 mph) 105 km/h
Stall speed: 37 kts (43 mph) 68 km/h
Take-off and landing distance: under 328 ft (100 m)
Maximum climb rate: 590 ft (180 m) per minute
G limit: +3.8, -1.9
Ceiling: 9,840 ft (3,000 m)
Range: 216 naut miles (248 miles) 400 km

SPRAYING PERFORMANCE FOR AD-200N:
Spraying speed: *59-65 kts (68-75 mph) 110-120 km/h*
Spraying height: *>10-16 ft (3-5 m)*
Spraying width: *72-98 ft (22-30 m)*
Spraying time: *6.67 to 16.67 minutes with a 265 lb (120 kg) chemical payload, depending on a flow rate of 18 to 7.2 kg per minute pro rata*

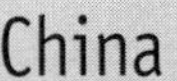

Harbin Aircraft Manufacturing Corporation — China

Corporate address:
See Combat section for company details.

Harbin Y11B1

First flight: 25 December 1990.
Certification: 1993 (CAAC). Designed to FAR Pt 23.
Role: Light general-purpose transport, suited to short-haul passenger and cargo operations, agricultural, forestry and geological survey roles.
Sales: Over 40 of the earlier Y11 model were completed. Very small number of the 'B' version delivered.
Crew/passengers: 1 or 2 pilots plus 7 passengers.
Wing control surfaces: Ailerons (starboard tab) and double-slotted flaps.
Tail control surfaces: Elevators and rudder, with tabs.
Engines: 2 Teledyne Continental TSIO-550 piston engines, with 7 ft 10 ins (2.4 m) Hartzell PHC-C3YF-2KUF/FC 3-blade propellers.
Engine rating: Each 350 hp (261 kW).
Fuel system: 992 lb (450 kg).
Flight avionics/instrumentation: AlliedSignal Bendix/King VFR and IFR nav/com.

↑ **Harbin Y11B1** *(Sebastian Zacharias)*

Details for Y11B1

PRINCIPAL DIMENSIONS:
Wing span: 56 ft 0.5 ins (17.08 m)
Maximum length: 39 ft 5 ins (12.017 m)
Maximum height: 17 ft 7 ins (5.356 m)

WINGS:
Aerofoil section: NACA 4412
Area: 367.69 sq ft (34.16 m^2)
Aspect ratio: 8.54

UNDERCARRIAGE:
Type: Fixed, with self-centring nosewheel. Twin mainwheels

WEIGHTS:
Empty: 5,520 lb (2,504 kg)
Normal take-off: 7,716 lb (3,500 kg), overload 8,598 lb (3,900 kg)
Maximum landing: 7,716 lb (3,500 kg)
Payload: 1,984-2,645 lb (900-1,200 kg)

PERFORMANCE:
Maximum speed: 143 kts (165 mph) 265 km/h at 9,840 ft (3,000 m), MCP
Maximum cruise speed: 127 kts (146 mph) 235 km/h at 9,840 ft (3,000 m), MCP
Take-off distance: 1,427 ft (435 m), with 656 ft (200 m) roll
Landing distance: 1,739 ft (530 m), with 902 ft (275 m) roll
Maximum climb rate: 1,102 ft (336 m) per minute at sea level, MCP
Climb rate, OEI: 108 ft (33 m) per minute at sea level
Ceiling: 19,685 ft (6,000 m)
Ceiling, OEI: 6,890 ft (2,100 m)
Range with full fuel: 583 naut miles (671 miles) 1,080 km, at 9,840 ft (3,000 m), optimum cruise speed
Range with full payload: 162 naut miles (186 miles) 300 km, at 9,840 ft (3,000 m), optimum cruise speed

Hongdu Aviation Industry (Group) Corporation Ltd — China

Corporate address:
See Combat section for company details.

Hongdu CJ-6A

First flight: 27 August 1958.
Role: Primary piston-engined trainer.
Sales: Over 1,500 serving with the Air Force of the People's Liberation Army, and exported (sometimes as the PT-6A) to Albania, Bangladesh, Cambodia, North Korea, Tanzania and Zambia. Thought to remain in low-rate production.

Details for CJ-6A

PRINCIPAL DIMENSIONS:
Wing span: 33 ft 6 ins (10.22 m)
Maximum length: 27 ft 9 ins (8.46 m)
Maximum height: 10 ft 8 ins (3.25 m)

UNDERCARRIAGE:
Type: Retractable, with nosewheel

WEIGHTS:
Empty: 2,414 lb (1,095 kg)
Maximum take-off: 3,086 lb (1,400 kg)

PERFORMANCE:
Maximum speed: 160 kts (184 mph) 297 km/h
Take-off distance: 919 ft (280 m)
Maximum climb rate: 1,245 ft (380 m) per minute
Ceiling: 20,500 ft (6,250 m)
Duration: 3.6 hours

↑ **Hongdu (formerly Nanchang) CJ-6As in Chinese military service**

↑ **Hongdu (formerly Nanchang) N-5A during a dusting demonstration** *(Sebastian Zacharias)*

Crew: Instructor and student in tandem. Rear seat is not raised.
Construction materials: Metal.
Engine: South Aero Engine Company HS6A radial piston engine.
Engine rating: 285 hp (212.5 kW).
Fuel system: 100 litres.

Hongdu N-5A

First flight: 26 December 1989.
Certification: 12 August 1992.
Role: Agricultural spraying and dusting.
Sales: In production, with those operated in China under purchase or lease arrangements including 5 used by Longken General Aviation services. Under an agreement with the Canadian Aerospace Group, up to 240 may be 'final assembled' in Canada for sale in North America; the first 2 airframes were to be dispatched in May 1998.
Crew/passengers: Pilot, with a tandem seat to the rear for ferrying a support operative as required.
Pressurization system: Cockpit has a low level of pressurization to prevent chemicals entering during operations.
Chemical tank/hopper: In the forward fuselage, with a maximum 2,116 lb (960 kg) load of liquid or dry chemicals. Contents can be dumped in 5 seconds in an emergency.
Dispersal equipment: Full-span spraybars to the rear of the wing trailing edges, with low-to-high settings for liquids.

Details for N-5A

PRINCIPAL DIMENSIONS:
Wing span: 44 ft (13.418 m)
Maximum length: 34 ft 5 ins (10.487 m)
Maximum height: 12 ft 3 ins (3.733 m)

WINGS:
Aerofoil section: Modified LS(1)-0417
Area: 279.9 sq ft (26 m^2)
Aspect ratio: 6.92

UNDERCARRIAGE:
Type: Retractable, with nosewheel

WEIGHTS:
Empty: 2,927 lb (1,328 kg)
Maximum take-off: 4,960 lb (2,250 kg) normal, 5,400 lb (2,450 kg) overload

PERFORMANCE:
Maximum speed: 111 kts (127 mph) 205 km/h
Spray speed: 92 kts (106 mph) 170 km/h typically
Stall speed: 57 kts (65 mph) 105 km/h *clean*, 47 kts (53 mph) 86 km/h *with flaps*
Take-off distance: 994 ft (303 m)
Landing distance: 807 ft (246 m)
Maximum climb rate: 843 ft (257 m) per minute
Ceiling: 12,300 ft (3,750 m), service
Range with full payload: 135 naut miles (155 miles) 250 km, with 45 minutes reserve
Duration: 1.8 hours

Safety equipment: Wire cutter on the nosewheel leg and ahead of the windshield. Wire deflector from the windshield to the fin. Crashworthy fuselage.
Wing control surfaces: Ailerons (with tabs) and single-slotted flaps.
Tail control surfaces: Elevators and rudder, all with tabs.
Flight control system: Mechanical, except for electrically actuated flaps and elevator tabs.
Construction materials: Metal, except for glassfibre hopper.
Engine: Textron Lycoming IO-720-D1B piston engine. An N-5A development is using a South Aero Engine Company HS6K radial of 400 hp (298.3 kW).
Engine rating: 400 hp (298 kW).
Fuel system: 315 litres.
Electrical system: AC generator and 30 amp-hour battery.
Braking system: Mainwheel hydraulic discs.
Flight avionics/instrumentation: AlliedSignal Bendix/King KY 96A VHF transceiver, with optional KHF 950 HF/SSB. Stall warning system. Other equipment is available upon request.

Shenyang Sailplane and Lightplane Co Ltd — China

Corporate address:
Shcnliao Dong 17 Tiexi District, Shenyang 110021.
Telephone: +86 24 5894217
Facsimile: +86 24 5892397
Information:
Lin Jia Ru (General Manager).

Shenyang Sailplane and Lightplane Co HY 650C (HU2C) and HY 650D (HU2D)

First flight: 1996.
Role: 3-seat (HU2C) and 4-seat (HU2D) light aircraft.
Sales: Replaced HY 650B (HU2B) in production from 1997.
Wing control surfaces: Strut-braced high-wing monoplane with ailerons.
Tail control surfaces: Conventional tail unit, with horn-balanced rudder and elevators.
Construction materials: Wooden structure.
Engine: 115 hp (85.75 kW) Rotax 914F2 piston engine for HU2C, 136 hp (101.4 kW) Limbach 2400 EFC for HU2D.
Fuel system: 57 litres for HU2C.

↑ Shenyang Sailplane and Lightplane Co HY 650C (HU2C) *(J Ewald)*

Details for HU2C and D

PRINCIPAL DIMENSIONS:
Wing span: 48 ft 11.5 ins (14.902 m) for HU2C, 49 ft 0.5 ins (14.95 m) for HU2D
Maximum length: 25 ft 1 ins (7.64 m) for HU2C, 25 ft 3 ins (7.7 m) for HU2D
Maximum height: 7 ft (2.14 m) for HU2C, 7 ft 3 ins (2.2 m) for HU2D

WINGS:
Aerofoil section: Göttingen Gö 535
Area: 211.26 sq ft (19.627 m^2) for HU2C, 211.3 sq ft (19.63 m^2) for HU2D
Aspect ratio: 11.3 for HU2C, 11.4 for HU2D

UNDERCARRIAGE:
Type: Fixed tailwheel type. Optional floats as HU2CS and presumably HU2DS
Main wheel tyre size: 500 × 500 mm for HU2D

WEIGHTS:
Empty: 1,146 lb (520 kg) for HU2C, 1,257 lb (570 kg) for HU2D
Maximum take-off: 1,874 lb (850 kg) for HU2C, 2,205 lb (1,000 kg) for HU2D

PERFORMANCE:
Maximum allowable speed: 108 kts (124 mph) 200 km/h for HU2D
Maximum speed: 86 kts (99 mph) 160 km/h for HU2C, 97 kts (112 mph) 180 km/h for HU2D
Cruise speed: 65 kts (75 mph) 120 km/h, 81 kts (93 mph) 150 km/h for HU2D
Stall speed: 41 kts (47.5 mph) 76 km/h for HU2C, 46 kts (53 mph) 85 km/h for HU2D
Maximum climb rate: 689 ft (210 m) per minute for HU2D
Ceiling: 11,480 ft (3,500 m) for HU2D
Range: over 539 naut miles (621 miles) 1,000 km for HU2D
Duration: 6.5 hours for HU2D

Shijiazhuang Aircraft Manufacturing Corporation — China

Corporate address:
25 Beihuanxi Road, Shijiazhuang, Hebei 050062.
Telephone: +86 311 7754251
Facsimile: +86 311 7752993
Telex: 26236 HBJXC-CN
Founded: 1970.

ACTIVITIES

- In addition to the Y5B, Shijiazhuang produces the W5A, W5B and W6 light aircraft.

Shijiazhuang Y5B and Y5C

First flight: 2 June 1989 for the Y5B, although other Y5 models of this licence-built Antonov An-2 have been built since 1957.
Certification: 20 May 1989 for Supplemental Type Certificate. Conforms to CCAR 23.
Role: Agricultural spraying and spreading biplane, designated Y5B. Can easily be modified for 12 passengers with agri-forest

Details for Y5B

PRINCIPAL DIMENSIONS:
Wing span: 59 ft 7.5 ins (18.176 m) upper, 46 ft 9 ins (14.236 m) lower
Maximum length: 41 ft 7.5 ins (12.688 m)
Maximum height: 20 ft (6.097 m)

WINGS:
Aerofoil section: P-II-C 14%
Area: 468.72 sq ft (43.546 m^2) upper, 301.17 sq ft (27.98 m^2) lower
Aspect ratio: 7.7 upper wing, 7.25 lower wing

UNDERCARRIAGE:
Type: Fixed, with tailwheel
Main wheel tyre size: 800 × 260 mm
Tail wheel tyre size: 360 × 150 mm

WEIGHTS:
Empty: 7,339 lb (3,329 kg) for spreading, 7,385 lb (3,350 kg) for spraying
Normal take-off: 11,574 lb (5,250 kg)
Payload: 3,307 lb (1,500 kg)

PERFORMANCE (at normal take-off weight)**:**
Maximum speed at 5,575 ft (1,700 m): 138 kts (159 mph) 256 km/h *clean*, 119 kts (137 mph) 220 km/h *with spreading gear*, 116 kts (134 mph) 215 km/h *with spray gear*
Maximum speed at sea level: 129 kts (149 mph) 239 km/h *clean*, 111 kts (128 mph) 205 km/h *with spreading gear*, 108 kts (125 mph) 200 km/h *with spray gear*
Stall speed: 52 kts (59 mph) 95 km/h
Take-off distance: 502 ft (153 m) *clean*, 564 ft (172 m) *with spreading gear*, 600 ft (183 m) *with spray gear*
Landing distance: 574 ft (175 m) *clean*, 525 ft (160 m) *with spreader gear*, 515 ft (157 m) *with spray gear*, with brakes
Spraying height: 16 to 23 ft (5 to 7 m)
Spraying swath width: 197 ft (60 m) ultra-low volume, 131-164 ft (40-50 m) low volume and high volume
Maximum climb rate: 590 ft (180 m) per minute *clean*, 394 ft (120 m) per minute *with spreading gear*, 374 ft (114 m) per minute *with spray gear*, all at sea level
Ceiling: 14,765 ft (4,500 m) *clean*, 11,350 ft (3,460 m) *with spreading gear*, 10,660 ft (3,250 m) *with spray gear*, all service
Turning radius: 1,150 ft (350 m)
Technical range: 456 naut miles (525 miles) 845 km *clean*, at 3,280 ft (1,000 m), fuel consumption 1,102 lb (500 kg)

↑ Shijiazhuang Y5C, newly delivered to the PLA Air Force as a paratroop transport

equipment removed, 10 paratroops, for touring, ambulance and other roles. The multi-role version has the subdesignation Y5BD, while dedicated passenger and paratroop versions are Y5BK and Y-5C respectively.
Details: For Y5B.
Crew: 1 or 2.
Chemical tank/hopper: 3,307 lb (1,500 kg) load of liquid or dry chemicals.
Spray equipment: Full span spraybars below the trailing-edges of the lower wings.
Safety equipment: Cable cutter above the cockpit.
Wing characteristics: Wire-braced biplane.
Engine: WSK Kalisz ASz-62IR-16 radial piston engine, or a licence-built version as the South Aero Engine Company HS5.
Engine rating: 967 hp (721 kW).
Hydraulic system: None.
Flight avionics/instrumentation: AlliedSignal Bendix/King com radios, ADF and more.

Aircraft variants:
Y5B and subvariants, see Role and as detailed.
Y5C is the latest paratroop version, first flown in 1996 and operated by the PLA Air Force. New features include triple wingtip vanes. Weights similar to Y5B.

Shijiazhuang (W6) Dragonfly-6

Role: Single-seat light agri-forest aircraft with spreading and spraying equipment. With simple refit, is suited to forest patrol and aerial photographic work. 3-axis control.
Hopper capacity: 309 lb (140 kg).
Wing control surfaces: Strut-braced mid-set wings, with ailerons.
Tail control surfaces: Twin fins and rudders and high-set tailplane.
Construction materials: Riveted aluminium alloy fuselage, with GRP cockpit pod. Leading-edge of the wing is glued and riveted aluminium alloy, with a non-metal structure of hard polyurethane core and GRP skin used for the rear section of the wing and ailerons. Riveted aluminium alloy thin skin is used for the tail.
Engine: Limbach L 2400 ECIB piston engine.
Engine rating: 83 hp (62 kW) at 3,200 rpm.
Flight avionics/instrumentation: Magnetic compass, airspeed indicator, altimeter, rate-of-climb indicator, current meter, voltmeter and engine meters.

Details for W6

PRINCIPAL DIMENSIONS:
Wing span: 32 ft 2 ins (9.8 m)
Maximum length: 21 ft 11 ins (6.68 m)
Maximum height: 5 ft 8.5 ins (1.74 m)

UNDERCARRIAGE:
Type: Fixed nosewheel type

WEIGHTS:
Empty: 705 lb (320 kg)

PERFORMANCE:
Cruise speed: 49-51 kts (56-59 mph) 91-95 km/h
Take-off distance: 460 ft (140 m)
Landing distance: 404 ft (123 m)
Ceiling: 8,200 ft (2,500 m), service
Range: 115 naut miles (133 miles) 214 km
Duration: 2.35 hours

↑ Shijiazhuang (W6) Dragonfly-6 *(courtesy Shijiazhuang)*

Xiamen AD Light Aircraft Company — China

Corporate address:
1st Light Steel Building, Huli District, Xiamen.
Telephone: +86 592 6034048, 6021518
Facsimile: +86 592 6021518

ACTIVITIES

■ Designed and developed in association with the Nanjing University of Aeronautics and Astronautics (NUAA).

Xiamen AD-100 and NUAA FT-300

Role: Single/2-seat lightplane (AD-100) and 3-seat lightplane (FT-300).
Details: AD-100, except under Aircraft variants.
Crew/passengers: Pilot only in AD-100 and AD-100S, under a sideways hinged (to starboard) canopy. 2 seats, side-by-side, in AD-100T, with centre-hinged and upward lifting canopy sections.
Wing control surfaces: Slightly sweptback high-mounted rear wings, with ailerons, endplate fins and rudders.
Canard: Low-mounted constant-chord canard at nose, with elevators.
Construction materials: Principally glassfibre reinforced plastics construction.
Engine: 27 hp (20.1 kW) Rotax 277 for AD-100 and AD-100S, and 52 hp (38.8 kW) Rotax 462 for AD-100T.
Fuel system: 19 litres in AD-100 and AD-100S, 45.4 litres in AD-100T.
Aircraft variants:
AD-100 is the single-seat nosewheel version.
AD-100S is similar to AD-100 but has twin floats.

↑ Xiamen AD-100 (*nearest*), with 2-seat AD-100T (*rear*) *(Sebastian Zacharias)*

AD-100T is a 2-seat version with nosewheel undercarriage, with a redesigned cockpit and canopy area.

FT-300 is a 3-seat derivative of the AD-100T, first flown in 1994 and available with either nosewheel or floats undercarriage. 80 hp (59.7 kW) engine. Empty weight 661-772 lb (300-350 kg), MTOW 1,367 lb (620 kg), and maximum speed 81 kts (93 mph) 150 km/h.

Details for AD-100 versions, as specified

PRINCIPAL DIMENSIONS:
Wing span with endplates: 29 ft 2.5 ins (8.9 m) for AD-100 and S, 31 ft 2 ins (9.5 m) for AD-100T
Wing span: 28 ft 6 ins (8.68 m) for AD-100 and S, 30 ft 5.5 ins (9.28 m) for AD-100T
Canard span: 11 ft 6 ins (3.5 m) for AD-100 and S, 13 ft 3 ins (4.04 m) for AD-100T
Maximum length: 16 ft 5.5 ins (5.02 m) for AD-100 and S, 16 ft 9.5 ins (5.12 m) for AD-100T
Maximum height: 5 ft 10.5 ins (1.79 m) for AD-100, 7 ft 1 ins (2.16 m) for AD-100S, and 6 ft 4 ins (1.93 m) for AD-100T

WINGS:
Area: 114.4 sq ft (10.63 m^2) for AD-100 and AD-100S, 124.1 sq ft (11.53 m^2) for AD-100T
Canard area: 30.03 sq ft (2.79 m^2) for AD-100 and S, 34.77 sq ft (3.23 m^2) for AD-100T

UNDERCARRIAGE:
Type: Fixed nosewheel type for AD-100 and AD-100T, and twin floats for AD-100S
Wheel/float track: 4 ft 7 ins (1.4 m) for AD-100, 5 ft 1 ins (1.54 m) for AD-100S, and 5 ft 3 ins (1.6 m) for AD-100T

WEIGHTS:
Empty: 331 lb (150 kg) for AD-100, 397 lb (180 kg) for AD-100S, and 573 lb (260 kg) for AD-100T
Maximum take-off: 639 lb (290 kg) for AD-100 and S, 1,102 lb (500 kg) for AD-100T

PERFORMANCE:
Maximum speed: 76 kts (87 mph) 140 km/h for AD-100, 56 kts (65 mph) 104 km/h for AD-100S, and 73 kts (85 mph) 136 km/h for AD-100T
Cruise speed: 47 kts (55 mph) 88 km/h for AD-100, 42 kts (48 mph) 77 km/h for AD-100S, and 49 kts (56 mph) 90 km/h for AD-100T
Canard stall speed: 26 kts (30 mph) 48 km/h for AD-100, 29 kts (34 mph) 54 km/h for AD-100S, and 31.5 kts (36 mph) 58 km/h for AD-100T
Take-off distance: 164 ft (50 m) for AD-100, 296 ft (90 m) for AD-100S, and 197 ft (60 m) for AD-100T
Landing distance: 197 ft (60 m) for AD-100, 132 ft (40 m) for AD-100S, and 214 ft (65 m) for AD-100T
Maximum climb rate: 590 ft (180 m) per minute for AD-100 and T, 394 ft (120 m) per minute for AD-100S
Ceiling: 11,155 ft (3,400 m) for AD-100, 6,560 ft (2,000 m) for AD-100S, and 9,840 ft (3,000 m) for AD-100T
Range: 189 naut miles (217 miles) 350 km for AD-100, 108 naut miles (124 miles) 200 km for AD-100S, and 211 naut miles (244 miles) 392 km for AD-100T
Duration: 4 hours for AD-100, 2.5 hours for AD-100S, and 4.4 hours for AD-100T

Aviones de Colombia S.A. — Colombia

Corporate address:
Entrada 1, Aeropuerto Eldorado, Bogatá.
Telephone: +57 1 413 8300
Facsimile: +57 1 413 8075

ACTIVITIES

▪ Has assembled and marketed particular Cessna aircraft. Developed a side-by-side 2-seat agricultural training version of the Cessna AgTruck, as the AgTrainer, and began production in 1992 of its own single-seat agricultural aircraft as the AC-05 Pijao (Teledyne Continental IO-520-D engine and 1,060 litre hopper).

El Gavilán S.A. — Colombia

Corporate address:
Apartado Aéreo 6781, Carrera 3 No 56-19, Santafé de Bogatá, DC.
Telephone: +57 1 676 1101, 1198
Facsimile: +57 1 676 0290, 0650
E-mail: gavilan/@trauco.colomsat.net.co
Web site: //ourworld.compuserve.com/homepages/gavilan358
Founded: 1991.
Information:
Omar Porras (Marketing Manager) and Eric C. Leaver (General Manager - *E-mail* leaver@andinet.lat.net).

ACTIVITIES

▪ The Gavilán project has been sponsored by the Leaver Group which, apart from El Gavilán S.A. consists of 4 more companies, all dedicated to different areas of General Aviation and that employ over 500 people. These companies are Aero-Mercantil S.A. (founded 45 years ago) representing several aircraft and component manufacturers in Colombia, among them New Piper, Boeing, Textron Lycoming, Teledyne Continental and AlliedSignal; Aero Industrias Leaver y Cia S.A. with over 40 years experience in maintenance and repair of aircraft and aviation components; Aeroexpreso Bogotá providing support to the oil industry by supplying aircraft and helicopters; and Aerocentro de Colombia Ltda flying school.

▪ Other partners in the El Gavilán project are the Inter-American Investment Corporation and the Instituto de Fomento Industrial (the latter owned by the Colombian Government to promote new industry). From the outset, the project has used the services of General Aviation Technical Services of the USA.

El Gavilán Gavilán 358

First flight: 27 April 1990. First prototype was subsequently lost in an accident due to engine failure after the crankshaft broke. 29 May 1996 for second prototype. 7 August 1997 for the first production line aircraft.
Certification: Conforms to FAR 23, Amendment 45 and FAR 36.
First delivery: 1998.
Role: Single-engine utility, suitable for operations from short unprepared runways. Passenger, cargo, aerial photography and patrol missions, or air ambulance.
Sales: Colombian Air Force has confirmed the purchase of 12 for patrol, logistic support and transport missions. In addition, 5 others sold to customers in Colombia, 1 in Guatemala and 1 in Ecuador at the time of writing. Many letters of intention to purchase received from customers in various countries. Price at time of writing US$332,000 with standard equipment.
Crew/passengers: Pilot and co-pilot (dual controls) or passenger plus 6 other passengers, 4 litters and an attendant in air ambulance layout, parachutists or freight.
Cabin access: 3 doors, 2 to the cockpit and a large double door for cargo on the port side of the fuselage (cargo capacity 17 cu ft, 0.48 m^3; 200 lb, 90.7 kg). Flat cabin floor, parallel to the ceiling.
Wing control surfaces: Ailerons and 3-position electrically-actuated single-slotted flaps (15°, 30° and 40°).
Tail control surfaces: Fixed tailplane (15 ft 4.25 ins, 4.68 m), interchangeable port and starboard. Horn-balanced elevators and rudder. Starboard elevator has a trim tab with indicator; rudder trim with indicator.
Flight control system: Cables and pushrods.
Construction materials: Tubular steel truss fuselage structure, with aluminium alloy skins. 2-spar wings of aluminium alloy (strut braced) and aluminium alloy tail unit.
Engine: Textron Lycoming TIO-540-W2A piston engine, with a 7 ft (2.13 m) Hartzell 3-blade constant-speed propeller.
Engine rating: 350 hp (261 kW).
Fuel system: 454 litres in rubber cell type tanks in the wings, with 447 litres usable.
Electrical system: 28 volt, 70 amp alternator. 24 volt, 10 amp-hour battery.
Braking system: Cleveland hydraulic dual mainwheel brakes. Parking brake.
Flight avionics/instrumentation: Standard flight instruments comprise airspeed indicator, attitude indicator, altimeter, turn co-ordinator, air-driven directional gyro, rate-of-climb indicator, magnetic compass, outside temperature gauge, clock, gyro pressure, heated pitot tube, and static pressure sources. Engine, electric, fuel and other instruments. Annunciator panel (with press to test). Standard avionics comprise AlliedSignal Bendix/King KLX 135A nav/com-GPS and Ameri-King AK 450 emergency locator transmitter.

↑ **El Gavilán Gavilán 358** *(courtesy El Gavilán)*

Details for Gavilán 358

PRINCIPAL DIMENSIONS:
Wing span: 42 ft (12.8 m)
Maximum length: 31 ft 5 ins (9.58 m)
Maximum height: 12 ft 3.125 ins (3.74 m)

WINGS:
Aerofoil section: NACA 4412
Area: 204 sq ft (18.95 m^2)
Aspect ratio: 8.65

UNDERCARRIAGE:
Type: Fixed, with trailing-link type castoring nosewheel. Nose and main gear have Keoprene elastomeric shock absorbers requiring no gas or oil chambers
Main wheel tyre size: 7:00 × 6
Nose wheel tyre size: 6:00 × 6
Wheel track: 11 ft (3.35 m)

WEIGHTS:
Empty: 2,800 lb (1,270 kg) standard VFR equipped
Maximum take-off and landing: 4,500 lb (2,041 kg)
Useful load: 1,700 lb (771 kg)
Payload: 980 lb (444.5 kg) with full fuel

PERFORMANCE:
Design maximum diving speed: 203 kts (233 mph) 376 km/h CAS
Cruise speed at 10,000 ft (3,050 m): 135 kts (155 mph) 250 km/h at 75% power, 130 kts (150 mph) 241 km/h at 65% power, 126 kts (145 mph) 233 km/h at 55% power, all CAS
Best climb speed: 85 kts (98 mph) 157 km/h
Stall speed: 69 kts (80 mph) 128 km/h *clean*, 58 kts (67 mph) 108 km/h *with 40 ° flaps*, CAS
Take-off distance: 1,022 ft (310 m) with 15 ° flaps
Take-off distance over a 50 ft (15 m) obstacle: 1,880 ft (573 m)
Landing distance: 640 ft (195 m)
Landing distance over a 50 ft (15 m) obstacle: 1,588 ft (484 m)
Maximum climb rate: 885 ft (270 m) per minute
Ceiling: 12,500 ft (3,810 m) without high altitude kit, 22,500 ft (6,860 m) with high altitude kit, both service
Range: 770 naut miles (885 miles) 1,425 km at 75% power, 820 naut miles (943 miles) 1,518 km at 65% power, 945 naut miles (1,088 miles) 1,750 km at 55% power, all with 30 minutes reserve

Aerotechnik CZ sro — Czech Republic

Corporate address:
Airport Kunovice, CZ 686 04 Kunovice.

Telephone: +420 632 537111
Facsimile: +420 632 537900
E-mail: *For Evektor:* evektor@brn.pvtnet.cz
Web site: *For Evektor:* www.pvtnet-www-evektor

Information:
E. Laendler (for Aerotechnik).

ACTIVITIES

■ Eurostar, detailed below, was developed in association with **Evektor Ltd** of the same address. Other Aerotechnik produced very light aircraft/ultralights are the P 220 UL and the Czech/Slovakian Fox. The L-13 Vivat/Super Vivat motorgliders, detailed in the 1996-97 edition of *WA&SD*, are out of production (confirmed May 1998).

Aerotechnik EV-97 Eurostar

Certification: Conforms with Czech UL-2, Slovak P-ULL-1 and German BFU standards.
Role: Very light/ultralight aircraft, with dual controls.
Sales: In addition to sales from Aerotechnik, Ikarusflug in Germany is an agent (DM 98,850 in 1998).
Crew/passenger: 2 seats, side by side, under a forward-hinged Plexiglas canopy. 22 lb (10 kg) of baggage aft of seats.

↑ **Aerotechnik EV-97 Eurostar, as marketed by German agent Ikarusflug** *(Ikarusflug)*

Wing control surfaces: Low-mounted foldable wings, with ailerons and 3-position split flaps over 70% of span (0°, 15° and 50°). Upturned wingtips.
Tail control surfaces: Rudder and elevators (with trim tab).
Flight control system: Mechanical, with rods and bell cranks.
Construction materials: Mostly metal, except for glassfibre wingtips and mainwheel legs.
Engine: Rotax 912 A or UL piston engine, with V230C 2-blade wooden fixed-pitch propeller or optional 5 ft 7 ins (1.7 m) 3-blade propeller.
Engine rating: 80 hp (59.7 kW).
Fuel system: 50 litres.
Electrical system: Single-phase generator integrated to engine and 12 volt battery.
Flight avionics/instrumentation: Similar to Fox, which see.

Details for Eurostar

PRINCIPAL DIMENSIONS:
Wing span: 25 ft 11 ins (7.9 m)
Maximum length: 20 ft 2 ins (6.15 m)
Maximum height: 5 ft 9 ins (1.75 m)
Width, wings folded: 8 ft 2.5 ins (2.5 m)

CABIN:
Width: 3 ft 5 ins (1.04 m)

WINGS:
Aerofoil section: NACA 2315
Area: 109.79 sq ft (10.2 m^2)
Aspect ratio: 6.12

UNDERCARRIAGE:
Type: Fixed nosewheel type, with castoring or optionally steerable nosewheel. Glassfibre cantilever spring mainwheel legs. Hydraulic brakes. Wheel fairings optional
Main wheel tyre size: 350 × 140 mm
Nose wheel tyre size: 300 × 100 mm

WEIGHTS:
Empty: 606 lb (275 kg)
Maximum take-off: 992 lb (450 kg)
Useful load: 386 lb (175 kg)

PERFORMANCE:
Never-exceed speed (V_{NE}): 116 kts (133 mph) 215 km/h IAS
Maximum speed: 100 kts (115 mph) 185 km/h IAS
Cruise speed: 73 kts (84 mph) 135 km/h IAS
Best climb speed: 65 kts (75 mph) 120 km/h IAS
Stall speed: 42 kts (49 mph) 78 km/h *clean*, 35 kts (41 mph) 65 km/h *with full flaps*, both IAS
Design manoeuvring speed: 86 kts (99 mph) 160 km/h IAS
Maximum flap extended speed: 67 kts (77 mph) 124 km/h IAS
Maximum climb rate: 886 ft (270 m) per minute at 2,000 ft (610 m)
Ceiling: 19,685 ft (6,000 m)

Aerotechnik P 220 UL

Role: Very light/ultralight sports monoplane.
Sales: Available also as a kit. ULR version is DM 70,800, ULM DM 70,100 in 1998.
Crew/passenger: 2 seats, side by side, under a large canopy.
Wing control surfaces: Cantilever low-mounted, with upturned wingtips. Ailerons and flaps.
Tail control surfaces: Slab tailplane with wide-chord balance/trim tab. Swept fin and large-area rudder.
Flight control system: Mechanical.
Construction materials: All metal, except for glassfibre wingtips.
Engine: 80 hp (59.7 kW) Rotax 912 UL or Mikron IIIB piston engine, with 2-blade propeller.
Flight avionics/instrumentation: Similar to Fox, which see.

↑ **Aerotechnik P 220 UL** *(courtesy Aerotechnik)*

Details for P 220 UL

PRINCIPAL DIMENSIONS:
Wing span: 25 ft 9.5 ins (7.86 m)
Maximum length: 19 ft 10 ins (6.05 m) with Rotax, 20 ft (6.1 m) with Mikron

WINGS:
Area: 105.81 sq ft (9.83 m^2)

UNDERCARRIAGE:
Type: Fixed nosewheel type. Wheel fairings. Hydraulic disc brakes
Main wheel tyre size: SAWA 14 × 4

WEIGHTS:
Empty: 584 lb (265 kg) with Rotax, 602 lb (273 kg) with Mikron
Maximum take-off: 992 lb (450 kg) to UL-2 regulations (calculation up to 1,058 lb, 480 kg)

PERFORMANCE:
Never-exceed speed (V_{NE}): 116 kts (133 mph) 215 km/h IAS
Cruise speed: 65-97 kts (75-112 mph) 120-180 km/h with Rotax, 65-92 kts (75-106 mph) 120-170 km/h with Mikron
Minimum speed with flaps: 35 kts (41 mph) 65 km/h at MTOW
Maximum climb rate: 886 ft (270 m) per minute with Rotax, 591 ft (180 m) per minute with Mikron
G limits: +4, -2
Duration: 5 hours with Rotax, 4 hours 30 minutes with Mikron

Aerotechnik Aeropro/Evektor Fox

Role: Light/ultralight sport cabin monoplane, of similar configuration to a Piper Cub. Can be towed or trailored. Wide range of optional equipment to customers' requirements.
Crew/passenger: 2 seats in an enclosed cabin with upward opening doors. Dual stick control.
Wing control surfaces: Strut-braced, high-mounted, folding wings with wide-span flaperons (Junkers flap).

Details for Fox

PRINCIPAL DIMENSIONS:
Wing span: 30 ft 2 ins (9.2 m)
Maximum length: 19 ft 8 ins (6 m)
Height: 5 ft 11 ins (1.8 m)

WINGS:
Aerofoil section: NACA 4412
Area: 123.78 sq ft (11.5 m^2)
Aspect ratio: 7.36

UNDERCARRIAGE:
Type: Fixed, with steerable tailwheel. Hydraulic disc brakes
Main wheel tyre size: 420 × 150 mm

WEIGHTS:
Empty: 496 lb (225 kg) for Fox 503, 540 lb (245 kg) for Fox 582, and 584 lb (265 kg) for Fox 912
Crew weight: 2 × 198 lb (90 kg)
Maximum take-off: 992 lb (450 kg)

PERFORMANCE:
Never-exceed speed (V_{NE}): 100 kts (115 mph) 185 km/h
Maximum speed: 84 kts (96 mph) 155 km/h for Fox 503, 89 kts (103 mph) 165 km/h for Fox 582, and 94 kts (109 mph) 175 km/h for Fox 912
Cruise speed: 59-94 kts (68-109 mph) 110-175 km/h
Stall speed: 35 kts (40 mph) 64 km/h, *with flaps*
Maximum climb rate: 590 ft (180 m) per minute for Fox 503, 985 ft (300 m) per minute for Fox 582, and 1,280 ft (390 m) per minute for Fox 912
Duration: 5 hours for Fox 503 and 582, and 6 hours for Fox 912, at economic speed

↑ **Aerotechnik Aeropro/Evektor Fox** *(courtesy Aerotechnik)*

Tail control surfaces: Conventional strut-braced tailplane with elevators (with trim tab), and fin with rudder.
Flight control system: Rods and cables.
Construction materials: Chrome molybdenum steel tube fuselage frame structure, with engine nacelle and forward skins of glassfibre, the remainder fabric covered. Lexan F5006 glazing. Wings have 2 spar tubes of aluminium alloy, a system of diagonal steel tube struts and a system of 14 ribs and 13 auxiliary ribs supporting the fabric skin, with a glassfibre leading-edge structure bonded in front of the spar tube and an aluminium alloy shaped trailing-edge batten. Flaperons each have an aluminium alloy tube and laminate sandwich structure (foam, epoxy resin and glassfibre). Welded steel tube tail unit, fabric covered.
Engine: See Aircraft variants.
Fuel system: 2 × 25 litre wing tanks plus a 5 litre equalizing tank in the fuselage.
Flight avionics/instrumentation: Wide range of options, including AlliedSignal Bendix/King KY 97A com transceiver, KT 76A transponder, Terra AT 3000 altitude encoder and Garmin GPS 95XL.

Aircraft variants:
Fox 503 has a 48 hp (36 kW) Rotax 503 CB 2-stroke engine with 3-blade composite ground-adjustable propeller, and mechanical starter. 1998 cost DM 43,600.
Fox 582 has a 64 hp (47.7 kW) Rotax 582 DCDI 2-stroke engine with similar composite propeller, and electric starter. 1998 cost DM 48,070 (standard).
Fox 912 has an 80 hp (59.7 kW) Rotax 912 UL 4-stroke engine with 2-blade fixed-pitch wooden propeller, and electric starter. 1998 cost DM 60,130 (standard).

Aero Vodochody Ltd — Czech Republic

Corporate address:
See Combat section for details.

Comments: Aero Vodochody and AIDC of Taiwan have set up a 50/50% joint venture for the Aero Vodochody-designed Ae 270 as Ibis Aerospace Ltd, following the signing of an agreement on 15 March 1997, enabling development, production and marketing in both countries (for the Asian and rest of the world markets).

Ibis Aerospace Ltd — Czech Republic/Taiwan

Corporate address:
See Aero Vodochody above and Aero Vodochody and AIDC in the Combat section.

Ibis Aerospace Ae 270 Ibis

First flight: 1999.
Certification: Planned for 2001; FAR 23 for Ae 270 P.
First delivery: Planned for 2001.
Noise levels: Conforms to FAR 36.
Role: Short-haul transport and general utility.
Chief designer: Jan Mikula.
Sales: 5 prototypes (3 flying and 2 static/fatigue). Production lines in Czech Republic and Taiwan.
Crew/passengers: 2 crew and 8 passengers in the corporate version, pilot plus 2,645 lb (1,200 kg) of cargo (passenger/cargo door 4 ft 1 ins, 1.25 m square), combi or other interiors including 4-passenger executive.
Wing control surfaces: Ailerons, single-slotted Fowler flaps, and roll-control spoilers.
Tail control surfaces: Elevators and rudder (with trim tab). Floatplane has finlets on the tailplane.
Construction materials: Metal, stressed skin.
Engine: See Aircraft variants.
Fuel system: 1,146 litres.
Electrical system: 28 volt DC, via a 250 amp engine-driven starter-generator. 37 amp-hour battery.
Hydraulic system: 2,175 psi.
De-icing system: Wing and tail leading edges, windshield, engine air intake, propeller blades, pitot static system and stall warning sensor.
Flight avionics/instrumentation: Standard flight, navigation and engine instrumentation and cockpit arrangement complies with FAR Pt 23. Optional equipment for VFR and IFR. Autopilot will become an option for single-pilot IFR.

Aircraft variants:
Ae 270 P has an 850 shp (634 kW) Pratt & Whitney Canada PT6A-42 turboprop engine, retractable nosewheel undercarriage, pressurization, and AlliedSignal Bendix/King avionics.
Ae 270 FP is an amphibious floatplane version of Ae 270 P.
Ae 270 W has a 778 shp (580 kW) Walter M601 F turboprop, fixed undercarriage and is not pressurized.
Ae 270 FW is an amphibious floatplane version of Ae 270 W.

↑ **Ibis Aerospace Ae 270 Ibis general arrangement and cabin layouts** *(courtesy Aero Vodochody)*

Details for Ae 270 P

PRINCIPAL DIMENSIONS:
Wing span: 45 ft 3 ins (13.8 m)
Maximum length: 40 ft 2 ins (12.24 m)
Maximum height: 15 ft 9 ins (4.79 m)

CABIN:
Length: 16 ft 4 ins (4.98 m)
Width: 4 ft 9 ins (1.44 m)
Height: 4 ft 5.5 ins (1.36 m)
Volume: 264.9 cu ft (7.5 m^3)
Passenger/cargo door size: 4 ft 1 ins × 4 ft 1 ins (1.25 × 1.25 m)

WINGS:
Area: 226 sq ft (21 m^2)
Aspect ratio: 9.07
Dihedral: 6°
Incidence: 3°

UNDERCARRIAGE:
Type: See Aircraft variants
Wheel base: 11 ft 7 ins (3.53 m)
Wheel track: 9 ft 3 ins (2.83 m)

WEIGHTS:
Empty: 3,942 lb (1,788 kg)
Maximum take-off: 7,275 lb (3,300 kg)

PERFORMANCE:
Cruise speed: 206 kts (237 mph) 381 km/h at sea level, 220 kts (254 mph) 408 km/h at 13,125 ft (4,000 m)
Stall speed: 80 kts (92 mph) 148 km/h *clean*, 61 kts (71 mph) 113 km/h *with flaps*
Take-off distance over a 50 ft (15 m) obstacle: 1,637 ft (499 m)
Landing distance over a 50 ft (15 m) obstacle: 2,799 ft (853 m)
Maximum climb rate: 1,614 ft (492 m) per minute
Ceiling: 31,825 ft (9,700 m), service
Range: 1,230 naut miles (1,416 miles) 2,280 km at 19,685 ft (6,000 m), with 45 minutes reserve

The following were received too late for full entries — Czech Republic

↑ Aerotrade Racak 2 in June 1998 *(Aviation Picture Library)*

Aerotrade sro (Novodvorská 994, 142 21 Praha 4 – *telephone* +420 2 4404 2389, *facsimile* +420 2 4404 2832). Produces the **Racak 2** composites ultralight, with a Rotax 912 UL engine. Wing span 35 ft 5 ins (10.8 m), length 21 ft 4 ins (6.5 m), empty weight 606 lb (275 kg), MTOW 992 lb (450 kg), maximum speed 87 kts (101 mph) 162 km/h, climb rate 984 ft (300 m) per minute, and g limits +4, -2.
ATEC vos (Opolanská 171, 289 07 Libice nad Cidlinou – *telephone* +420 324 77371, *facsimile* +420 324 3002). Produces the **Zephyr** 2-seat low-wing ultralight of mixed construction (wood, composites and PES fabric), with Rotax 503, 582 or 912 engine. Wing span 34 ft 9 ins (10.6 m), length 20 ft 4 ins (6.2 m), empty weight 540-628 lb (245-285 kg), MTOW 992 lb (450 kg), maximum speed (with Rotax 912 UL) 119 kts (137 mph) 220 km/h, climb rate 984 ft (300 m) per minute, take-off distance 394 ft (120 m), landing distance 657 ft (200 m), range 431 naut miles (497 miles) 800 km, and g limits +4, -2.
Automedia sro (Okružní 5, Brno). Produces the single-seat **JK-1**, with twin booms and a Rotax 582 engine. Wing span 34 ft 9 ins (10.6 m), length 19 ft 4 ins (5.9 m), MTOW 992 lb (450 kg), and maximum speed 92 kts (106 mph) 170 km/h.
Firma BVL (Jeronýmova, Lomnice nad Popelkou – *telephone/facsimile* +420 431 672 016). Produces the **Qualt 200L** 2-seat low-wing monoplane, with Limbach 2000 engine (alternative Rotax, VW, JPX, etc). Wing span 30 ft 2 ins (9.2 m), length 19 ft 4 ins (5.9 m), empty weight (Limbach engine) 628 lb (285 kg), MTOW 992 lb (450 kg), maximum speed 130 kts (149 mph) 240 km/h, and range 350 naut miles (403 miles) 650 km.

BTA Top-Air sro — Czech Republic

Corporate address:
Drátovenská 361, 735 51 Bohumín.
Telephone: +420 69 603 1152
Facsimile: +420 69 603 1100

ACTIVITIES

▪ Formerly known as the Swing spol sro Swing.

BTA Top-Air BTA-4 Tango

Role: Very light monoplane.
Sales: Initially sold only in the Czech Republic.

↑ BTA Top-Air BTA-4 Tango *(MFG via Martin Salajka and Aviation Picture Library)*

Details for Tango

PRINCIPAL DIMENSIONS:
Wing span: 33 ft 5.5 ins (10.2 m)
Maximum length: 20 ft 8 ins (6.29 m)
Maximum height: 7 ft 10.5 ins (2.4 m)

CABIN:
Width: 4 ft 3.5 ins (1.31 m)
Height: 3 ft 8 ins (1.12 m)

WINGS:
Area: 138.85 sq ft (12.9 m^2)
Aspect ratio: 8.065
Dihedral: 3°

UNDERCARRIAGE:
Type: Fixed steerable nosewheel type, with cantilever composites spring main gear legs. Optional wheel fairings, and tailwheel undercarriage

WEIGHTS:
Empty: 608 lb (276 kg)
Maximum take-off: 992 lb (450 kg)

PERFORMANCE:
Never-exceed speed (V_{NE}): 129.5 kts (149 mph) 240 km/h
Maximum speed: 108 kts (124 mph) 200 km/h
Cruise speed: 97 kts (112 mph) 180 km/h at 85% power, or 78 kts (90 mph) 145 km/h at 65% power
Stall speed: 33 kts (38 mph) 60 km/h
Take-off distance: 230 ft (70 m)
Landing distance: 460 ft (140 m)
Maximum climb rate: 1,375 ft (420 m) per minute
Ceiling: 17,390 ft (5,300 m)
Range: 539 naut miles (621 miles) 1,000 km

Crew/passenger: 2 seats, side by side, in an enclosed cabin with bulged Perspex doors. Dual controls. USH-520 parachute system.
Wing control surfaces: Strut-braced, folding/detachable, high-mounted wings with ailerons and 3-position plain flaps (0°, 20° and 40°).
Tail control surfaces: Slab tailplane with trim tab.
Flight control system: Mechanical, with push/pull rods, except for electrically actuated trim tab.
Construction materials: Principally composites, of glassfibre reinforced plastics sandwich construction, with the wings and tail unit having rigid leading-edges and Ceconite skins.
Engine: Rotax 912UL piston engine, with Junkers Profly 1700 Maxi 2-blade composites, ground-adjustable propeller, with spinner. Alternative Rotax 582UL engine.
Engine rating: 80 hp (59.7 kW) for Rotax 912UL.
Fuel system: 75 litres.
Braking system: Optional hydraulic disc brakes instead of standard mechanical drum type.

Letov a.s. — Czech Republic

Corporate address:
Beranovych 65, 199 02 Prague 9 - Letňany.
Telephone: +420 2 6611 3112, 2298
Facsimile: +420 2 859 0553, 826 546

ACTIVITIES

▪ See also the Recreational section for Letov LK-2 Sluka, LK-3 Nova and ST-4 Aztek.
▪ According to correspondence of 18 May 1998, the Letov company has been unable to complete development of the L-11, and has become bankrupt. It was then seeking an interested party to continue development and begin production.

Letov L-11

First flight: 22 May 1997, with official roll-out and first flight on 3 June 1997.
Certification: Civil Airworthiness Certificate in Special category on 7 May 1997, after ground and structural tests. Regular certification with definitive engine type had not been gained at the time of writing.
Role: Basic trainer and glider towing.
Crew/passenger: 2 seats, side by side, under upward hinging canopy. Dual controls standard. Cabin ventilated via small sliding windows but not heated.
Baggage capacity: Space aft of seats, capacity 88 lb (40 kg).
Wing control surfaces: Forward swept (6°) wings with statically balanced, differentially operated ailerons (20° down, 25° up) and 3-position split flaps (20° for take-off, 35° landing).
Tail control surfaces: Variable-incidence tailplane (0° to -4°), with mass-balanced elevators (33° up, 27° 30′ down). Rudder (30° movement) with ground-adjustable tab.
Flight control system: Mechanical, with control rods for ailerons, flaps and elevators, and cables for rudder. Hand-operated tailplane incidence (0° to -5°) for longitudinal control trimming.
Construction materials: Braced duralumin wings, each with 1 main spar, 1 auxiliary rear spar, 16 ribs and riveted skins. Welded aluminium fuel tank, bolted between ribs 2 and 7 and forming an integral part of the wing. Bracing struts are constructed of formed duralumin sheet. Ailerons are of glassfibre reinforced plastics (GFRP) and rigid foam. Split flaps have sandwich structure with bonded aluminium honeycomb core and duralumin skins, and are suspended by piano hinges to the lower fuselage flange of the rear wing spar. GFRP wing tips. Semi-monocoque duralumin fuselage structure with 7 frames, longerons and riveted stressed skin. Duralumin 2-spar tail structure.
Engine: Teledyne Continental O-200-A-48 piston engine for initial flight tests, with 5 ft 11 ins (1.8 m) VZLÚ V236A propeller or 5 ft 9 ins (1.76 m) McCauley 1A101HCM 6948 propeller. More powerful engine was to follow, allowing glider towing. Full flight performance tests had not been performed by mid-May 1998, because of the poor condition of the existing engine.
Engine rating: 100 hp (74.6 kW).
Fuel system: 100 litres in 2 interconnected wing tanks placed between the main and rear spars and ribs Nos 2 and 6. Tanks, removable from above, create upper wing contour. Hand-operated pump for engine start-up only, and electric (double) fuel quantity indicator.
Electrical system: Engine-driven generator and 12 volt, 35 amp-hour battery.
Flight avionics/instrumentation: Full VFR instrumentation eventually, including VHF radio, but prototype has simple equipment. Electrically heated pitot tube.

↑ Letov L-11 *(Martin Salajka, via Aviation Picture Library)*

Details for L-11

PRINCIPAL DIMENSIONS:
Wing span: 31 ft 2 ins (9.5 m)
Maximum length: 21 ft 8 ins (6.6 m)
Maximum height: 9 ft 6 ins (2.9 m)

CABIN:
Width: 3 ft 6.5 ins (1.08 m)
Height: 3 ft 9 ins (1.15 m)

WINGS:
Aerofoil section: MS1/-0313/1675
Area: 115.71 sq ft (10.75 m^2)
Aspect ratio: 8.4
Dihedral: 1° 30'
Thickness/chord ratio: 17%

UNDERCARRIAGE:
Type: Fixed with steerable nosewheel. Steel nosewheel leg with shock absorber and cantilever spring composite main legs. Cable-operated drum brakes
Wheel base: 5 ft 11 ins (1.8 m)
Wheel track: 7 ft 11 ins (2.41 m)

WEIGHTS:
Empty, equipped: 974 lb (442 kg), dry
Maximum take-off: 1,477 lb (670 kg) ± 10 kg

PERFORMANCE:
Never-exceed speed (V_{NE}): 147 kts (169 mph) 272 km/h, approved
Maximum speed: 132 kts (152 mph) 245 km/h
Stall speed: 51 kts (59 mph) 95 km/h *clean*, 47 kts (54 mph) 86 km/h *with 35° flaps*
Take-off distance over a 50 ft (15 m) obstacle: 689 ft (210 m)
Landing distance over a 50 ft (15 m) obstacle: 820 ft (250 m)
Maximum climb rate: 1,329 ft (405 m) per minute
Ceiling: 22,150 ft (6,750 m), service
G limits: +4.08, -2.08
*Flight tests were interrupted after about 50 flight tests (13 flying hours) because of the condition of the engine.

Moravan Inc — Czech Republic

Corporate address:
765 81 Otrokovice.

Telephone: +420 67 767 1111
Facsimile: +420 67 7922103, 7922148

Founded:
1934 as Zlinská Letecká Akciová Spolecnost, its name changing to Moravan in 1949. Products continue to be known as Zlins.

Information:
Valerij Osokin (Zlin Sales).

Moravan Zlin Z-50

Comments: First flown on 18 July 1975 in original Zlin Z 50 L form, the final Z 50 LS single-seat basic and advanced aerobatics version was detailed and illustrated in the 1996-97 edition of *WA&SD*, page 388.

Moravan Zlin Z-137 T

Comments: First flown on 6 September 1981 in prototype Z-37 form, the final Z-137 T version of this agricultural and firefighting monoplane was detailed and illustrated in the 1996-97 edition of *WA&SD*, page 389.

Moravan Zlin Z-142 and Z-242

First flight: 29 December 1978 for Z-142.
Details: Principally Z-142 C and Z-242 L.
Role: 2-seat basic and advanced civil and military training, aerobatics, night and IFR training, glider and banner towing, observation and patrol. Can be operated in Aerobatic, Normal and Utility categories.
Sales: Z-142 C was put into production in 1992 (10 built), following construction of more than 750 Z-42, Z-142 and Z-43 types; a Z-142 C demonstrator was flown in Canada in Canadian Armed Forces colours. 8 Z-142CAFs for the Czech Air Force. Production of the Z-242 L began in 1992.
Baggage capacity: 44 lb (20 kg).
Wing characteristics: Slightly swept-forward wings (4° 20') for Z-142 C and straight wings for Z-242 L.
Wing control surfaces: Slotted flaps and ailerons, latter with ground adjustable tabs.
Tail control surfaces: Horn-balanced single-piece elevator with trim tabs, and rudder with ground adjustable tab.
Flight control system: Ailerons and elevator are rod controlled, rudder rod/cable.
Construction materials: Metal structure, with metal skins except for composite mid-fuselage panels. Guaranteed technical airframe service life of 3,500 hours.
Engine: 206.5 hp (154 kW) LOM Prague M 337 AK piston engine, with a 6 ft 7 ins (2 m) Avia Hamilton Standard V 500 A propeller, in Z-142 C. 200 hp (149 kW) Textron Lycoming AEIO-360-A1B6 in Z-242 L, with a 6 ft 2 ins (1.88 m) Mühlbauer MTV-9-B-C/C-188-18a constant-speed 3-blade propeller.
Fuel system: 2 × 60 litres in wings. 2 × 50 litre wingtip auxiliary tanks in Z-142 C and 55 litre in Z-242 L. 5 litre aerobatic tank in the centre fuselage. 90 seconds inverted flight limit for Z-142 C, 60 seconds for Z-242 L.
Electrical system: 28 volt DC, via engine-driven 600 W dynamo, plus auxiliary 25 amp-hour lead-acid battery for Z-142 C. Z-242 L has 1.6 kW generator and 19 amp-hour battery for electrical power.
Braking system: Mainwheel hydraulic disc brakes.
Flight avionics/instrumentation: 7 optional approved packages based on AlliedSignal Silver Crown equipment.

Aircraft variants:
Z-142 C entered production in 1992, with a LOM Prague engine.
Z-142 CAF is the Czech Air Force training version.
Z-242 L is basically a Textron Lycoming engined version of the Z 142 C, though featuring other substantial changes including redesigned engine cowling, straight wings of increased span with rounded wingtips and larger wingroot fairings, high capacity wingtip tanks, taller vertical tail, modified and rounded horizontal tail, and modified electrical system. Weights are the same but performance is slightly higher. Currently the most important version for foreign armed forces.

Details for Z 142C, *with Z-242 L in italics*

PRINCIPAL DIMENSIONS:
Wing span: 30 ft 0.5 ins (9.16 m), *30 ft 8 ins (9.34 m)*
Maximum length: 24 ft 0.5 ins (7.33 m), *22 ft 9.5 ins (6.94 m)*
Maximum height: 9 ft 0.25 ins (2.75 m), *9 ft 8.25 ins (2.95 m)*

WINGS:
Aerofoil section: NACA $63_2416.5$
Area: 141.55 sq ft (13.15 m^2), *148.11 sq ft (13.76 m^2)*
Aspect ratio: 6.38, *6.34*

UNDERCARRIAGE:
Type: Fixed, with steerable (±38°) nosewheel. Optional wheel fairings, *the same*

WEIGHTS:
Empty: 1,609 lb (730 kg), *the same*
Maximum take-off: 2,138 lb (970 kg) Aerobatic, 2,403 lb (1,090 kg) Normal, *the same*

PERFORMANCE (Normal category)**:**
Maximum speed: 123 kts (142 mph) 228 km/h at 1,640 ft (500 m), ISA, *124 kts (143 mph) 230 km/h CAS*
Maximum cruise speed: 109 kts (126 mph) 202 km/h, 75% power, at 1,640 ft (500 m), ISA, *114 kts (132 mph) 212 km/h at 1,640 ft (500 m), CAS*
Economic cruise speed: 100 kts (115 mph) 186 km/h, 65% power, at 1,640 ft (500 m), ISA
Stall speed: 65 kts (75 mph) 120 km/h *clean*, 56 kts (64 mph) 103 km/h, *with flaps*; *64 kts (74 mph) 118 km/h clean, 54 kts (62 mph) 100 km/h with flaps*
Take-off distance: 827 ft (252 m), *873 ft (266 m)*
Landing distance: 722 ft (220 m)
Maximum climb rate: 826 ft (252 m) per minute, *885 ft (270 m) per minute*, both at sea level
G limits: +6, -3.5 Aerobatic, +3.8, -1.5 Normal; *the same*
Ceiling: 14,175 ft (4,320 m), service
Range: 413-522 naut miles (475-601 miles) 765-967 km, according to cruise speed, at 1,640 ft (500 m), *570 naut miles (656 miles) 1,056 km*

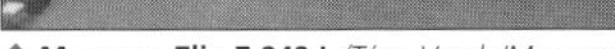
↑ Moravan Zlin Z-242 L *(Tána Vesela/Moravan)*

↑ Moravan Zlin Z-143 Ls *(Tána Vesela/Moravan)*

Z-242 LA is a new low-power version, with a 180 hp (134 kW) Textron Lycoming O-360-A1A engine and 6 ft 2 ins (1.88 m) McCauley B3D36C424/74SA-O 3-blade propeller. Empty weight 1,532 lb (695 kg) and MTOW 2,138 lb (970 kg) in Utility category with load factors +4.4, -1.76 or 2,248 lb (1,020 kg) in Normal category with load factors +3.8, -1.52. Maximum speed 122 kts (140 mph) 226 km/h, and range 289 naut miles (332 miles) 536 km at 3,280 ft (1,000 m) in Utility category.

Moravan Zlin Z-143 L

First flight: 24 April 1992.
Certification: 1994.
Role: 4-seater, based on the Z 242 L. Similar roles but also including air taxi, tourist, light business and family flying.
Sales: In production.
Baggage capacity: 132 lb (60 kg).
Engine: Textron Lycoming O-540-J3A5 piston engine, with a 6 ft 5 ins (1.96 m) MTV-9-B/195-45a 3-blade propeller.
An Avia M 337 AK engined version is anticipated.
Engine rating: 235 hp (175 kW).
Fuel system: 2 × 60 litre wing tanks. 2 × 50 litre auxiliary tiptanks.
Electrical system: As for Z-242 L.

Details for Z-143 L

PRINCIPAL DIMENSIONS:
Wing span: 33 ft 3 ins (10.136 m)
Maximum length: 24 ft 10 ins (7.577 m)
Maximum height: 9 ft 6.5 ins (2.91 m)

WINGS:
Area: 159 sq ft (14.776 m^2)
Aspect ratio: 6.953

WEIGHTS:
Empty: 1,830 lb (830 kg)
Maximum take-off: 2,976 lb (1,350 kg) Normal, 2,380 lb (1,080 kg) Aerobatic

PERFORMANCE (Utility category)**:**
Maximum speed: 144 kts (166 mph) 267 km/h at sea level
Cruise speed: 127 kts (146 mph) 235 km/h at 75% power, 117 kts (134 mph) 216 km/h at 60% power, at sea level
Stall speed: 54 kts (62 mph) 100 km/h
Take-off distance: 558 ft (170 m)
Landing distance: 1,000 ft (305 m)
Maximum climb rate: 1,457 ft (444 m) per minute
G limits: +4.4, -1.76 Aerobatic; +3.8, -1.5 Normal
Ceiling: 18,700 ft (5,700 m)
Range: 259 naut miles (298 miles) 480 km at 65% power, 295 naut miles (340 miles) 548 km at 58% power, both at 10,000 ft (3,050 m)

Aircraft variants:
Z-143 L is the current production version, as detailed.
Z-143 is a projected version with a LOM Prague M 337 AK engine.

MSP Air spol sro — Czech Republic

Corporate address:
Pavla Hanuse 299, Hradec Králové 500 02.
Telephone: +420 49 40160, 38392
Facsimile: +420 49 38162
Information:
Lubomír Valásek.

MSP Air WK 94

First flight: 25 March 1995.
Role: Side-by-side 2-seat lightplane.
Sales: US$33,333 to US$36,364 at time of writing.
Wing characteristics: Forward swept, dihedral wings. Conventional flight controls.
Construction materials: Duralumin riveted wings. Welded fuselage structure of chromium-molybdenum tubing, with fabric skin.

↑ MSP Air WK 94

Engine: Rotax 532 piston engine in the prototype.
Engine rating: 64.4 hp (48 kW).
Braking system: Mechanical.

Details for WK 94

PRINCIPAL DIMENSIONS:
Wing span: 42 ft (12.8 m)
Maximum length: 29 ft 6 ins (9 m)

WEIGHTS:
Empty: 547 lb (248 kg)
Maximum take-off: 992 lb (450 kg)

PERFORMANCE:
Maximum speed: 86 kts (99 mph) 160 km/h
Cruise speed: 49-70 kts (56-81 mph) 90-130 km/h
Minimum speed: 34 kts (39 mph) 62 km/h
Take-off distance: 328 ft (100 m)
Landing distance: 361 ft (110 m)
Maximum climb rate: 787 ft (240 m) per minute
G limits: +4, –2
Duration: 3 hours

Arab Organization for Industrialization (AOI) — Egypt

Corporate address:
See Combat section for details.

AOI Helwan 2

Certification: Tested and approved to civil aviation regulations.
Role: 2-seat multi-purpose, including sporting, light cargo, reconnaissance, aerial photography, survey, patrol, law enforcement, and agricultural.
Engine: 80 hp (59.7 kW) piston engine.
Flight avionics/instrumentation: VHF transceiver, magnetic compass, altimeter, airspeed indicator, artificial horizon, and ambient temperature indicator. Options include G meter, rate of climb/descent indicator, turn/bank indicator, turn/slip indicator, GPS, fuel gauge, tachometer and more.

Details for Helwan 2

PRINCIPAL DIMENSIONS:
Wing span: 32 ft 10 ins (10 m)
Maximum length: 19 ft 8 ins (6 m)
Maximum height: 7 ft 3 ins (2.2 m)

WEIGHTS:
Empty: 727 lb (330 kg)
Maximum take-off: 1,146 lb (520 kg)

PERFORMANCE:
Maximum speed: 97 kts (112 mph) 180 km/h
Cruise speed: 76 kts (87 mph) 140 km/h
Landing distance: 263 ft (80 m)
Ceiling: 9,840 ft (3,000 m)
Range: 324 naut miles (373 miles) 600 km

AOI Helwan 3

Certification: Tested and approved to civil aviation regulations; certified by the ECAA.

↑ AOI Helwan 2 *(courtesy AOI)*

Role: Multi-purpose, including sporting, light cargo, reconnaissance and contamination detection, aerial photography, survey, patrol, law enforcement and agricultural.
Crew/passenger: 2 seats, side by side. Dual controls.
Engine: Textron Lycoming O-320-A2B piston engine.
Engine rating: 150 hp (112 kW).
Fuel system: 120 litres.
Flight avionics/instrumentation: VHF transceiver, magnetic compass, altimeter, airspeed indicator, engine indicators, fuel gauge, and ambient temperature indicator. Options include G meter, rate of climb/descent indicator, turn/bank indicator, artificial horizon, GPS and more.

→ AOI Helwan 3 *(courtesy AOI)*

Details for Helwan 3

PRINCIPAL DIMENSIONS:
Wing span: 36 ft 8 ins (11.17 m)
Maximum length: 22 ft (6.7 m)

WINGS:
Area: 185.14 sq ft (17.2 m^2)
Aspect ratio: 7.25

WEIGHTS:
Empty: 1,257 lb (570 kg)
Maximum take-off: 1,720 lb (780 kg)

PERFORMANCE:
Maximum speed: 135 kts (155 mph) 250 km/h
Economic cruise speed: 89 kts (103 mph) 165 km/h
Minimum speed: 46 kts (53 mph) 85 km/h
Glide ratio: 15:1
G limits: +4, -2
Ceiling: 9,840 ft (3,000 m)
Range: 324 naut miles (373 miles) 600 km
Duration: 4 hours

Ethiopian Airlines S.C. — Ethiopia

Corporate address:
PO Box 1755, Addis Ababa.

Telephone: +251 1 186746
Facsimile: +251 1 611474
Telex: 21012
Cable: ETHAIR

Information:
Tilahun Kassa (Division Manager, Agro Aircraft Manufacturing)

ACTIVITIES

■ Its Agro Aircraft Manufacturing plant is constructing the Ag-Cat Corporation Ag-Cat G164B Turbine as the **Eshet**, for domestic use and for sale to other African countries with the exception of Algeria, South Africa and Tunisia. The plan is to produce about 120 over 10 years, though current production is 6 per year; the first 12 all went to Admas Air Services, a charter and cargo service organization in Ethiopia which subsequently became part of Ethiopian Airlines. Pratt & Whitney Canada 680 shp (507 kW) PT6-15AG, 750 shp (559.3 kW) PT6-34AG or 550 shp (410 kW) PT6-20B turboprop engine, with 435 litres of fuel standard and 1,514 litres for ferrying. Same 1,514 litre hopper, 3,150 lb (1,429 kg) empty weight and 7,020 lb (3,184 kg) MTOW (CAM 8) as Ag-Cat Turbine according to the latest brochure. See Ag-Cat Corporation for further details of the Ag-Cat Turbine.

↑ **Ethiopean Airlines Eshet** *(courtesy Ethiopean Airlines)*

Aero Kuhlmann — France

Corporate address:
Aérodrome de Cerny, 91590 Cerny.

Telephone & facsimile: +33 1 69 90 17 80
E-mail: aerokuhlmann@magic.fr
Web site: http://www.magic.fr/avianet

Aero Kuhlmann Scub

First flight: 5 May 1996.
Certification: Conforms to JAR-VLA.
Role: Tandem 2-seat, dual control, braced high-wing monoplane.

Details for Scub

PRINCIPAL DIMENSIONS:
Wing span: 36 ft 1 ins (11 m)
Maximum length: 23 ft (7 m)
Maximum height: 5 ft 11 ins (1.8 m)

WINGS:
Aerofoil section: LS1 Mod 0417
Area: 153.92 sq ft (14.3 m^2)
Aspect ratio: 8.46

UNDERCARRIAGE:
Type: Fixed tailwheel type, with drum brakes. Optonal twin floats

WEIGHTS:
Empty: 551 lb (250 kg)
Maximum take-off: 992 lb (450 kg)

PERFORMANCE:
Never-exceed speed (V_{NE}): 92 kts (105 mph) 170 km/h
Cruise speed: 81 kts (93 mph) 150 km/h
Stall speed: 32,5 kts (37.5 mph) 60 km/h
Take-off distance: 230 ft (70 m)
Landing distance: 230 ft (70 m)
Range: 539 naut miles (621 miles) 1,000 km

Sales: Price FFr 290,000 plus tax in basic wheel undercarriage form, at time of writing.
Wing control surfaces: Ailerons.
Tail control surfaces: Elevators (with starboard trim tab) and rudder.
Construction materials: Welded steel tube fuselage, and carbon spar and plywood wing, all fabric covered.
Engine: JPX 4TX75A piston engine, with 2-blade wooden propeller.
Engine rating: 75 hp (56 kW).
Fuel system: 78 litres.

↑ **Aero Kuhlmann Scub, with one wing folded and optional twin floats beside standard tailwheel undercarriage** *(Aviation Picture Library)*

AkroTech Europe — France

Corporate address:
9 rue de l'Aviation, Aérodrome, 21121 Darois.

Telephone: +33 3 80 35 65 10
Facsimile: +33 3 80 35 65 15
E-mail: aeroland@micronet.fr

Information:
Dominique Roland (CEO).

ACTIVITIES

■ AkroTech Europe is a subsidiary of Aeronautical Service (AES), the former having been founded to put into production the CAP 222, a series-built version of the US AkroTech Giles G-202 kitplane (see Recreational section) and designed by Richard Giles.

■ AkroTech Europe has purchased the assets of Avions Mudry et Cie, with the intention of continuing production of the Mudry CAP 10B and CAP 232 (the CAP 231 EX is out of production). Former Mudry aircraft will be produced under the AkroTech name, with production facilities in both Darois and Bernay. In total, Mudry received orders for some 370 CAP 10s, CAP 231s and CAP 232s, including 12 in 1997, and by 1998 a total of 358 had been delivered by Mudry/AkroTech.

AkroTech CAP 10B

First flight: 1968.
Certification: 4 September 1970, with VFR 1974. Certification recognized in 19 countries.
Role: Aerobatic, training, aeroclub flying and private use.
Sales: Some 370 CAP 10s built for customers in more than 20 countries, accumulating over 500,000 flying hours. May 1998 price FFr 750,000.
Crew/passenger: 2 seats, side by side, with dual controls. Rear sliding (jettisonable) bubble canopy.
Baggage capacity: 44 lb (20 kg) aft of seats.
Wing control surfaces: Semi-elliptical wing trailing-edges and wingtips. Slotted ailerons and plain flaps.
Tail control surfaces: Ground adjustable stabilizer incidence. Horn-balanced elevators (with trim tabs) and horn-balanced rudder (with balance tab).
Construction materials: Wooden structure, with Okoumé plywood skins and polyester fabric covering.
Engine: Textron Lycoming AEIO-360-B2F piston engine, with fixed-pitch propeller.
Engine rating: 180 hp (134 kW).
Fuel system: 72 litres, with optional 75 litre fuselage auxiliary tank. Inverted fuel system; Christen inverted oil system.
Electrical system: 12 volt ni-cd battery.
Braking system: Hydraulic disc brakes on main wheels. Parking brake.
Flight avionics/instrumentation: AlliedSignal Bendix/King avionics.

Details for CAP 10B

PRINCIPAL DIMENSIONS:
Wing span: 26 ft 5.5 ins (8.06 m)
Maximum length: 23 ft 6 ins (7.16 m)
Maximum height: 8 ft 4.5 ins (2.55 m)

WINGS:
Aerofoil section: NACA 23012
Area: 116.79 sq ft (10.85 m^2)
Aspect ratio: 5.99
Dihedral: 5°
Incidence: 0°

UNDERCARRIAGE:
Type: Fixed tailwheel type, with steerable tailwheel (can be disconnected for castoring on the ground). Fairings over alloy main legs and oleo-pneumatic shock absorbers, and streamline fairings over 380 × 150 mm main wheels

WEIGHTS:
Empty: 1,212 lb (550 kg)
Maximum take-off: 1,830 lb (830 kg) Normal category, or 1,675 lb (760 kg) Aerobatic category
Useful load: 630 lb (285 kg)

PERFORMANCE:
Never-exceed speed (V_{NE}): 184 kts (211 mph) 340 km/h
Maximum cruise speed: 148 kts (170 mph) 274 km/h
Cruise speed: 135 kts (155 mph) 250 km/h, at 75% power
Stall speed: 51 kts (59 mph) 95 km/h *clean*, 43.5 kts (50 mph) 80 km/h *with flaps*, IAS
Take-off distance: 1,149 ft (350 m)
Landing distance: 1,182 ft (360 m)
Maximum climb rate: 1,575 ft (480 m) per minute
Ceiling: 16,400 ft (5,000 m), service
G limits: +6, -4.5
Range: 540 naut miles (621 miles) 1,000 km

Aircraft variants:
CAP 10B was the final Mudry version, upon which the AkroTech CAP 10B details are based.
CAP 10R became the glider tug version. Not marketed.

AkroTech CAP 222

First flight: 12 June 1997.
Certification: Designed to meet JAR 23.
Role: High performance aerobatic competition aircraft and high-performance trainer. See also AkroTech Giles G-202 in Recreational section.
Sales: Production rate expected to be about 20 per year. Price US$170,000 for certified CAP 222 in May 1998.
Crew/passenger: 2 in tandem. 6 ins (15 cm) rudder pedal adjustment.
Wing control surfaces: Low-mounted straight-tapered wings, with full-span ailerons with spades (9.96 sq ft, 0.925 m^2; deflection ±22°). No flaps.
Tail control surfaces: Horn-balanced elevators and horn-balanced rudder. Trim tab; servo tab deflection 30° up, 1° down.
Flight control system: Mechanical. Electrically-operated elevator trim tab.
Construction materials: All carbonfibre airframe.
Engine: Textron Lycoming AEIO-360-A1E piston engine, with an MT 3-blade constant-speed propeller.
Engine rating: 200 hp (149 kW).
Fuel system: 68 litres main, plus 155 litres wing tanks.
Electrical system: 14 volt DC, via engine-driven 40 amp alternator and 12 volt, 17 amp-hour sealed lead acid battery.
Flight avionics/instrumentation: Vision VM 1000 for engine control. To have Rocky Mountain Instrument micro encoder, providing altitude, air speed, encoder and low altitude alarm.

Details for CAP 222

PRINCIPAL DIMENSIONS:
Wing span: 22 ft (6.71 m)
Maximum length: 20 ft (6.1 m)
Maximum height: 5 ft 7 ins (1.7 m)

CABIN:
Width: 2 ft 4 ins (0.71 m) front cockpit, 1 ft 11 ins (0.58 m) rear cockpit

WINGS:
Aerofoil section: Same as CAP 232
Chord: 5 ft (1.52 m) at root, 3 ft (0.91 m) at tip
Area: 90 sq ft (8.36 m^2)

UNDERCARRIAGE:
Type: Fixed tailwheel type, with main wheel fairings

WEIGHTS:
Empty: 1,000 lb (454 kg)
Maximum take-off: 1,600 lb (726 kg)

PERFORMANCE:
Never-exceed speed (V_{NE}): 220 kts (253 mph) 407 km/h IAS
Cruise speed: 170 kts (196 mph) 315 km/h, at 75% power
Stall speed: 57 kts (66 mph) 106 km/h
Take-off distance over a 50 ft (15 m) obstacle: 1,080 ft (330 m)
Landing distance over a 50 ft (15 m) obstacle: 1,210 ft (369 m)
Maximum climb rate: 2,000 ft (610 m) per minute
Ceiling: 20,800 ft (6,340 m), service
Roll rate: 500° per second
G limits: ±10 at 1,350 lb (612 kg)
Range: 900 naut miles (1,036 miles) 1,667 km at 46% power and 9,500 ft (2,895 m), with 45 minutes reserve
Duration: 6.04 hours at 46% power

↑ AkroTech CAP 232

AkroTech CAP 232

First flight: 7 July 1994.
Certification: Compliant with FAA FAR 23 and certified in every country into which the aircraft is exported.
Role: Single-seat aerobatic competition monoplane, capable of cross-country and ferry flights.
Sales: Production rate expected to be 10 per year. Price FFr 1,250,000 in May 1998.
Crew: Pilot only under a single-piece bubble canopy. Custom-made moulded seat. Ergonomic throttle. Elbow supports. 7 ins (18 cm) of stick travel. Rudder pedals with footrests, with 6 ins (15 cm) of adjustment.
Wing control surfaces: Low-mounted wing has 15% thickness/chord ratio at root and 12.5% at tip, with wide-span ailerons.
Tail control surfaces: Horn-balanced elevators with port geared tab, and rudder.
Flight control system: Push/pull rods.
Construction materials: High-performance wing of pre-impregnated carbonfibre and structural resin, cured at high temperature under high pressure (autoclave system).
Engine: Textron Lycoming AEIO-540-L1B5D piston engine, with 4-blade MT-Propeller MTV-14-B-C/C190-17 propeller. Inverted fuel system. Christen inverted oil system.
Engine rating: 300 hp (223.7 kW).
Fuel system: 208 litres usable.
Flight avionics/instrumentation: Factory installed navigation panels allow room for a GPS, nav/com and Mode C transponder for cross-country flights.

Details for CAP 232

PRINCIPAL DIMENSIONS:
Wing span: 24 ft 3.5 ins (7.4 m)
Maximum length: 22 ft 2 ins (6.75 m)
Maximum height: 6 ft 3 ins (1.9 m)

WINGS:
Aerofoil section: 232.14.5 at root, 232.12 at tip
Area: 109.8 sq ft (10.2 m^2)
Aspect ratio: 5.37

UNDERCARRIAGE:
Type: Fixed tailwheel type, with glassfibre main gear legs. Streamline wheel fairings

WEIGHTS:
Empty: 1,290 lb (585 kg)
Maximum take-off: 1,808 lb (820 kg) normal category, or 1,609 lb (730 kg) aerobatic category

PERFORMANCE:
Never-exceed speed (V_{NE}): 219 kts (252 mph) 405 km/h
Maximum speed: 189 kts (217 mph) 350 km/h
Cruise speed: 178 kts (205 mph) 330 km/h, 75% power
Manoeuvring speed: 170 kts (195 mph) 315 km/h
Stall speed: 57 kts (65 mph) 105 km/h
Maximum climb rate: 3,290 ft (1,003 m) per minute
Roll rate: 420° per second at 170 kts
G limits: ±10
Range: 647 naut miles (745 miles) 1,200 km, 45% power

Arc Atlantique Aviation — France

Corporate address:
Tours St Symphorien Airport, 37100, Tours.

Telephone: +33 47 51 25 64
Facsimile: +33 47 54 29 49

Information:
André Daout.

Arc Atlantique (Fournier) RF 47

First flight: 9 April 1993.
Certification: To meet JAR/VLA.
Role: 2-seat lightplane.
Sales: Price about FFr 600,000 at time of writing.
Baggage capacity: Compartment for 44 lb (20 kg).
Wing control surfaces: Ailerons and slotted flaps.
Tail control surfaces: Elevators with trim tab, and rudder.
Construction materials: Principally plywood, but with some composites and fabric.
Engine: Limbach L 2400 EB1 piston engine, with an MT 155 105-1A 2-blade propeller.
Engine rating: 86 hp (64 kW).
Fuel system: 84 litres, of which 80 are usable.

Electrical system: 25 amp alternator and 27 amp-hour battery.
Flight avionics/instrumentation: AlliedSignal Bendix/King KX 125 nav/com 760 channel transceiver, 200 channel nav receiver (OBS optional), and optional KX 155-KLX 135. Other options are Becker or Narco equipment, GPS and intercom.

Details for RF 47

PRINCIPAL DIMENSIONS:
Wing span: 32 ft 10 ins (10 m)
Maximum length: 21 ft 1.5 ins (6.44 m)
Maximum height: 7 ft 3.5 ins (2.22 m)

WINGS:
Area: 117.65 sq ft (10.93 m^2)
Aspect ratio: 9.15

UNDERCARRIAGE:
Type: Fixed, with nosewheel

WEIGHTS:
Empty: 870 lb (395 kg)
Maximum take-off: 1,367 lb (620 kg)

PERFORMANCE:
Never-exceed speed (V_{NE}): 125 kts (143 mph) 230 km/h
Maximum speed: 108 kts (124 mph) 200 km/h
Cruise speed: 97 kts (112 mph) 180 km/h
Stall speed: 46 kts (53 mph) 85 km/h *clean*, 42 kts (49 mph) 78 km/h *with 30° full flaps*
Take-off distance over a 50 ft (15 m) obstacle: 1,495 ft (455 m)
Landing distance over a 50 ft (15 m) obstacle: 1,362 ft (415 m)
Maximum climb rate: 787 ft (240 m) per minute
Ceiling: 16,400 ft (5,000 m)
Duration: 5-6 hours

↑ **Arc Atlantique RF 47** *(courtesy Arc Atlantique)*

Aviasud Industries — France

Corporate address:
Rue Rudolf Diesel, 83600 Fréjus Cedex.

Founded:
Aviasud has been building aircraft since 1980.

Information:
Bernard Collin (President).

ACTIVITIES

▪ In addition to the aircraft detailed below, the Mistral has been licence-built in Brazil by Ultraleger for the Brazilian domestic market. A new side-by-side (staggered) 2-seat Cessna-type cabin monoplane was to be launched featuring a nosewheel undercarriage and folding wings, while the designation **AE 210 Alizé** was applied to a proposed JAR-VLA variant of Albatros.

Aviasud AE 206 Mistral and AE 207 Mistral Twin

First flight: 1985.
Role: Ultralight for pilot training, aerial photography, surveillance, agricultural spraying, and banner towing.
Sales: Some 250 delivered, including about 30 Mistral Twins (available to order only). See introduction for Brazilian Mistral construction.
Crew/passengers: 2 seats, side by side.

Details for AE 206

PRINCIPAL DIMENSIONS:
Wing span: 30 ft 10 ins (9.4 m)
Maximum length: 19 ft 4.5 ins (5.9 m)
Maximum height: 7 ft 4.5 ins (2.25 m)

WINGS:
Aerofoil section: NACA 23012
Area: 176.53 sq ft (16.4 m^2)
Aspect ratio: 5.39

WEIGHTS:
Empty: 452 lb (205 kg)
Maximum take-off: 860 lb (390 kg)

PERFORMANCE:
Cruise speed: 70 kts (81 mph) 130 km/h
Minimum speed: 30 kts (34.5 mph) 55 km/h
Take-off distance: 263 ft (80 m)
Maximum climb rate: 787 ft (240 m) per minute
Ceiling: 15,000 ft (4,575 m)
Range: 286 naut miles (329 miles) 530 km

Control surfaces: All moving bottom wings act as large size ailerons. Slab tailplane with tab and rudder. Manual control.
Construction materials: Mostly composites, but with wooden wing ribs.
Engine: 64.4 hp (48 kW) Rotax 582.
Fuel system: 60 litres.

Aircraft variants:
AE 206 Mistral is the standard version, as described.
AE 206 US was produced as an "Ultra Silent" version, with 3.48:1 reduction gear and a larger propeller.
AE 207 Mistral Twin is a twin-engined version, mainly for aerial work such as surveillance and advertising. Rotax 503 mounted as a pusher on the upper wing, to supplement the existing Rotax 582. Maximum take-off weight 992 lb (450 kg).

Aviasud AE 209 Albatros

First flight: 1991.
Role: Ultralight monoplane.
Sales: Production aircraft No 102 was being assembled when the last information was received.
Crew/passengers: 2 seats, side-by-side, slightly offset to provide more shoulder room.
Baggage capacity: 15.89 cu ft (0.45 m^3) behind seats.
Wing characteristics: Can be folded for stowage and transportation by 1 person in under a minute.
Control surfaces: 3-axis, with slab tailplane.
Flight control system: Manual.
Construction materials: Composites (including carbonfibre and Tedlar, and with vacuum or pressure lamination) as well as traditional building methods.
Engine: See Aircraft variants.
Fuel system: 60 litres.

↑ **Aviasud AE 206 Mistral**

↑ **Aviasud AE 209 Albatros**

Aircraft variants:
AE 209-50 has a 49.6 hp (37 kW) Rotax 503 engine.
AE 209-64 has a Rotax 64.4 hp (48 kW) 582 engine.
AE 209-80 has a 77.8 hp (58 kW) Rotax 912 engine.

Details for AE 209

PRINCIPAL DIMENSIONS:
Wing span: 31 ft 10 ins (9.7 m)
Maximum length: 24 ft 2 ins (7.36 m)
Maximum height: 7 ft (2.13 m)

WINGS:
Area: 166.84 sq ft (15.5 m^2)
Aspect ratio: 6.07

UNDERCARRIAGE:
Type: Fixed, with tailwheel. Optional skis. Nosewheel undercarriage version is to be offered

WEIGHTS:
Empty: 452 lb (205 kg) with Rotax 503, 507 lb (230 kg) with Rotax 582, and 573 lb (260 kg) with Rotax 912
Maximum take-off: 904 lb (410 kg) with Rotax 503, and 992 lb (450 kg) with Rotax 582 and Rotax 912

PERFORMANCE:
Maximum speed: 76 kts (87 mph) 140 km/h with Rotax 503, 86 kts (99 mph) 160 km/h with Rotax 582, and 94 kts (109 mph) 175 km/h with Rotax 912
Take-off distance: 246 ft (75 m) with Rotax 582
Landing distance: 213 ft (65 m) with Rotax 582
Maximum climb rate: 659 ft (201 m) per minute with Rotax 503, 827 ft (252 m) per minute with Rotax 582, and 1,083 ft (330 m) per minute with Rotax 912
Ceiling: 15,000 ft (4,575 m) with Rotax 582
Range: 281 naut miles (323 miles) 520 km with Rotax 582

Avions Automobiles Philippe Moniot — France

Corporate address:
Issoire Aviation, Rex Composites, Zone Industrielle, BP1, 63501 Issoire Cedex.

Telephone: +33 4 73 89 01 54
Facsimile: +33 4 73 89 54 59

Information:
Philippe Moniot.

Avions Automobiles Philippe Moniot APM-20-1 Lionceau

First flight: 21 November 1995.
Certification: Conforms to JAR-VLA.

↑ Avions Automobiles Philippe Moniot APM-20-1 Lionceau *(courtesy Philippe Moniot)*

Details for APM-20-1 Lionceau

PRINCIPAL DIMENSIONS:
Wing span: 27 ft 7 ins (8.4 m)
Maximum length: 21 ft 4 ins (6.5 m)
Maximum height: 7 ft 10.5 ins (2.4 m)

WINGS:
Aerofoil section: NACA 63618
Area: 96.88 sq ft (9 m^2)
Aspect ratio: 7.84
Dihedral: 3°
Incidence: 2°

UNDERCARRIAGE:
Type: Fixed nosewheel type. Optional wheel fairings
Wheel track: 6 ft 3.5 ins (1.92 m)

WEIGHTS:
Empty, standard equipment: 794 lb (360 kg)
Crew weight: 379 lb (172 kg)
Maximum take-off: 1,367 lb (620 kg)
Maximum landing: 1,344 lb (610 kg)

PERFORMANCE:
Never-exceed speed (V_{NE}): 140 kts (161 mph) 260 km/h
Maximum cruise speed/normal operating limit speed (V_{NO}): 126 kts (145 mph) 234 km/h
Cruise speed at 75% power: 112 kts (129 mph) 208 km/h
Stall speed: 45 kts (52 mph) 83 km/h
Take-off distance: 492 ft (150 m)
Take-off distance over a 50 ft (15 m) obstacle: 1,313 ft (400 m)
Landing distance: 492 ft (150 m)
Landing distance over a 50 ft (15 m) obstacle: 821 ft (250 m)
Maximum climb rate: 492 ft (150 m) per minute at MTOW
Ceiling: 14,765 ft (4,500 m), service
Range: 593 naut miles (683 miles) 1,100 km, with 102 litres of usable fuel, 30 minutes reserve; or 378 naut miles (435 miles) 700 km, with 70 litres of usable fuel, 30 minutes reserve

Role: Light training aircraft, with other uses including proficiency, blind flying, mountain flying, aerial photography, light freight carrying, etc.
Crew/passengers: 2 seats, side-by-side, under a rear-sliding bubble canopy.
Baggage capacity: 59.5 lb (27 kg), aft of seats.
Wing control surfaces: Ailerons and slotted flaps.
Tail control surfaces: Single-piece elevator with central spring tab for pitch trimming, and rudder.
Flight control system: Mechanical, except for electrically actuated flaps.
Construction materials: Carbonfibre/epoxy composites, using a new process perfected by Rex Composites and its subsidiaries, allowing much lighter structures, increased mechanical strength and optimized construction.
Engine: 80 hp (59.7 kW) Rotax 912 piston engine, with 120 hp (89.5 kW) Textron Lycoming engine available. 5 ft 7 ins (1.7 m) diameter EVRA 2-blade fixed-pitch propeller constructed of beech wood with glassfibre/epoxy coating, or Duquesne AL1 propeller.
Fuel system: 70 litres standard (68 litres usable); 108 lb (49 kg) weight. Optional 104 litres (102 litres usable).
Flight avionics/instrumentation: Standard VFR.

Dassault Aviation — France

Corporate address:
See Combat section for company details.

ACTIVITIES

▪ By 1998, a total of 573 Falcon jets of the currently available versions had been ordered, including 98 orders placed in 1997 alone and 12 in 1998 up to the time of writing, of which 508 had then been delivered. It was anticipated that 50-60 Falcons would be ordered in 1998, with production stepped up from 55 to 70 per year. In terms of overall cumulative figures for all Falcon jets (including those models no longer available), the latest figures supplied indicate that Dassault had then delivered 1,246 Falcons. These comprised 226 Falcon 10s and 100s, 512 Falcon 20s and 200s, 267 Falcon 50/50EXs, 189 Falcon 900/900EXs, and 52 Falcon 2000s. In addition to passenger transport, Falcons have been used for medevac, maritime surveillance (including F20Gs as HU-25A/B/C Guardians with the US Coast Guard, F20s as Gardians with the French Navy and F900s with Japan), photogrammetry, navaid calibration, cargo, electronic monitoring (Canada, Norway and Pakistan), scientific research, military training and more. All newly built Falcons have certification extended to operation in RSVM (Reduced Vertical Separation) areas.

Dassault Falcon 50 and 50EX

First flight: 7 November 1976 for Falcon 50. 10 April 1996 for Falcon 50EX.
Certification: 27 February 1979 for French DGAC and 7 March 1979 for FAA for Falcon 50. 15 November 1996 for French DGAC and 20 December 1996 for FAA for Falcon 50EX. All new Falcons received FAA/JAA certification for operation in compliance with the new RSVM air control norms.
First delivery: July 1979 for Falcon 50, and February 1997 for Falcon 50EX.
Role: 3-turbofan transcontinental, medium-sized business jet. Successor to the Falcon 20.
Sales: 267 Falcon 50s and 50EXs delivered at the time of writing. Initial production batch of Falcon 50EXs covers 40 aircraft.
Crew/passengers: Crew of 2 (flight), plus a third cockpit seat, and typically 8 or 9 passengers; 4-seat and 2 fold-out table front lounge and a rear lounge with 2 seats plus a 3-seat sofa. 2 galleys at front of cabin (1 with oven) and rear toilet. Up to 12 passengers with wardrobe and galleys removed; front or rear toilet. Maximum cabin pressure differential 8.85 psi.
Baggage capacity: Pressurized compartment of 90 cu ft (2.55 m^3), for up to 2,205 lb (1,000 kg).
Wing control surfaces: Aileron, double-slotted flaps, leading-edge slat, and 3 spoiler/air brakes per wing.
Tail control surfaces: Variable-incidence tailplane, elevators and inset rudder.
Construction materials: Metal, except for carbonfibre ailerons.
Engines: 3 AlliedSignal TFE731-3-1C turbofans for Falcon 50, each 3,700 lbf (16.46 kN). Falcon 50EX has AlliedSignal TFE731-40 turbofans, each rated at 3,700 lbf (16.46 kN) at take-off at sea level, ISA + 17° C, for which thrust has been increased by 10% during climb and 24% during cruise (at 40,000 ft, 12,190 m and Mach 0.8) but specific fuel consumption reduced by 7%.
Fuel system: 15,520 lb (7,040 kg).
Radar: Honeywell Primus 400 weather radar.
Flight avionics/instrumentation: For Falcon 50, Rockwell Collins 86C EFIS and 80F autopilot and choice of long-range navigation and avionic equipment, including satellite communications. For Falcon 50EX, Rockwell Collins Pro Line 4, with 4 large flat-panel EFIS-4000 7.25 × 7.25 ins (18.5 × 18.5 cm) displays, and 3 Sextant Avionique liquid-crystal engine-control instruments (EIED). Falcon 50EX avionics thereby comprise APS-4000 Cat II autopilot, 2 flight directors with 4-display EFIS, 2 ADC-850C air data systems, 2 AlliedSignal GNS-XES FMS with integrated GPS receiver, 2 Honeywell Laseref III laser gyro IRS, and dedicated maintenance computer.

Aircraft variants:
Falcon 50 is the standard version with AlliedSignal TFE731-3-1C turbofans.
Falcon 50 retrofit sees Falcon 50 operators worldwide upgrading the flight decks of their aircraft by retrofitting the Rockwell Collins Pro Line 4 to provide the advanced avionics capabilities of the Falcon 50EX (see below).
Falcon 50EX (extended performance) version was launched on 26 April 1995 and first flew on 10 April 1996, with deliveries from 1997. AlliedSignal TFE731-40 turbofans, offering improvement in performance, giving an increased level of initial cruise (from FL390 to FL410) and either increased range (extra 200 naut miles at Mach 0.75 or 400 naut miles at Mach 0.8) or

Details for Falcon 50, with Falcon 50EX where stated to be different

PRINCIPAL DIMENSIONS:
Wing span: 61 ft 10.5 ins (18.86 m)
Maximum length: 60 ft 9 ins (18.52 m)
Maximum height: 22 ft 10.5 ins (6.975 m)
Fuselage diameter: 6 ft 8 ins (2.03 m)

CABIN:
Length: 23 ft 6 ins (7.16 m)
Width: 6 ft 1.1 ins (1.86 m), or 5 ft 3 ins (1.59 m) at floor
Height: 5 ft 10.87 ins (1.8 m)
Volume: 530 cu ft (15 m^3)

WINGS:
Area: 503.75 sq ft (46.8 m^2)
Aspect ratio: 7.6

UNDERCARRIAGE:
Type: Retractable, with steerable (±60° taxi, ±180° tow) nosewheels. Twin wheels on each unit
Main wheel tyre size: 26 × 6.6-14 ins
Nose wheel tyre size: 14.5 × 5.5-6 ins
Wheel base: 23 ft 9 ins (7.24 m)
Wheel track: 13 ft 1 ins (3.98 m)

WEIGHTS:
Empty, equipped: 20,200 lb (9,163 kg), and 21,175 lb (9,605 kg) for Falcon 50EX
Maximum take-off: 38,800 lb (17,600 kg), and 39,705 lb (18,010 kg) for Falcon 50EX
Maximum landing: 35,715 lb (16,200 kg)
Payload: 4,750 lb (2,155 kg), 3,770 lb (1,710 kg) for Falcon 50EX

PERFORMANCE:
Maximum permitted operating speed (V_{MO}): 351-370 kts (403-425 mph) 650-685 km/h IAS; same for Falcon 50EX
Maximum operating Mach number (M_{MO}): Mach 0.86
Maximum cruise speed: Mach 0.82 at 35,000 ft (10,650 m), or 470 kts (541 mph) 870 km/h at 31,000 ft (9,450 m)
Long-range cruise speed: Mach 0.75, or Mach 0.8 for Falcon 50EX
Landing speed: 123 kts (142 mph) 228 km/h at MLW, or 102 kts (117 mph) 189 km/h with 8 passengers and NBAA IFR reserves, both CAS
Balanced field length: 4,700 ft (1,430 m) at MTOW, or 4,462 ft (1,360 m) with 8 passengers and maximum fuel, both at sea level and ISA, and 4,710 ft (1,435 m) with 8 passengers and maximum fuel for Falcon 50EX
Landing field length: 4,922 ft (1,500 m) at MLW, or 3,560 ft (1,085 m) with 8 passengers and NBAA IFR reserves, and 3,675 ft (1,120 m) with 8 passengers and NBAA IFR reserves for Falcon 50EX
Time to climb to 39,000 ft (11,890 m): 30 minutes, and 23 minutes for Falcon 50EX
Maximum certified altitude: 45,000 ft (13,715 m), and 49,000 ft (14,935 m) for Falcon 50EX
Range with 8 passengers: 3,148 naut miles (3,622 miles) 5,830 km with NBAA IFR reserves, or 3,510 naut miles (4,039 miles) 6,500 km with 45 minutes LR reserves
Range for Falcon 50EX: 3,250 naut miles (3,742 miles) 6,023 km at Mach 0.75, or 3,025 naut miles (3,483 miles) 5,605 km at Mach 0.8, with reserves

↑ **Dassault Falcon 50 Evasan operated by Tyrolean Air Ambulance** *(courtesy Dassault)*

increased cruise speed. Rockwell Collins Pro Line 4 EFIS and 3 Sextant Avionique liquid crystal engine indicators. Some 100 other modifications and complete re-organization of manufacturing, the former including use of digital computer for engine thrust and bleed air control.
Falcon 50 Evasan is the Falcon 50/50EX fitted with medical evacuation modules, including electrical power for connecting medical equipment, lighting, alarms, etc. Units are removable, and installation requires no modification to the structure. Modules are installed on rails (via interface adapters) and can be partly equipped or fully fitted out to become a true resusitation units (see Falcon Multirole). Changeover from VIP cabin to medevac facility takes under 2 hours. Can accommodate 1 or more litters, allowing up to 10 light casualties or 4 medically assisted patients to be carried simultaneously. Satellite communications can be installed, offering 2-way communications with hospitals. First Falcon 50EX with medevac module delivered 21 February 1997.
Falcon 50 Surmar is a maritime surveillance and SAR variant (see Falcon multirole) for the French Navy, as 4 Falcon 50s, for delivery between April 1999 and February 2000. Thomson-CSF/RCM Ocean Master 100 radar and Thomson-TTD Chlio FLIR, jettisonable floor hatch, 8 SAR chains each with capacity of 25, 2 domed observation windows, and additional nav/com equipment including 2 Rockwell Collins V/UHF ARC 210, 2 Honeywell FMS/MMMS, and 2 Honeywell GPIRS (GPS coupled with the IRS). Can be retrofitted with Falcon 50EX avionics.
Falcon 50 sigint, see Falcon Multirole.

Dassault Falcon 900B, 900C and 900EX

First flight: 21 September 1984. Falcon 900EX first flew on 1 June 1995.
Certification: March 1986. 31 May 1996 for French DGAC and July 1996 for FAA for 900EX. All new Falcons received FAA/JAA certification for operation in compliance with the new RSVM air control norms.
Role: 3-turbofan intercontinental, medium-sized, widebody business jet.
Sales: 166 Falcon 900Bs and 23 EXs delivered at the time of writing.
Details: Principally for Falcon 900B, with 900EX generally similar except where stated.
Crew/passengers: 2 flight crew. Up to 19 passengers. Cabin may be divided into 3 sections, with toilets at each end, allowing the rear lounge to have a sofa that can easily be converted into a bed. Maximum cabin pressure differential 9.28 psi.
Baggage capacity: 127.13 cu ft (3.6 m^3).
Wing control surfaces: Aileron, double-slotted flaps, leading-edge slat, and 3 spoiler/air brakes per wing. A laminar-flow wing was tested on a Falcon 900 in 1994.

↑ **Dassault Falcon 900EX** *(courtesy Francois Robineau - Dassault/Aviaplans)*

↑ **Dassault Falcon 900EX typical cabin arrangement** *(courtesy Dassault)*

Tail control surfaces: Variable-incidence tailplane, elevators and inset rudder.
Construction materials: Greater use of composites than Falcon 50.
Engines: 3 AlliedSignal TFE731-5BR-1C turbofans, each 4,750 lbf (21.13 kN), for Falcon 900B. AlliedSignal TFE731-60 turbofans, each 5,000 lbf (22.24 kN), for 900EX.
Fuel system: 19,158 lb (8,690 kg), or 20,825 lb (9,446 kg) for Falcon 900EX.
Radar: Honeywell Primus 870 colour weather radar.
Flight avionics/instrumentation: Avionics suite of Falcon 900B built around a Honeywell SPZ 8000 system with a dual multiplexed digital databus linking the 2 Honeywell SPZ 800 autopilots to 2 flight directors with EFIS displays, 2 FMZ 800 flight management systems with advanced databases, and 2 (or optionally 3) Laseref II ring laser inertial reference systems that provide heading and attitude reference. Dual AZ 810 air data computers. FMS may also drive the digital Rockwell Collins Pro Line 2 com and radio-nav units. Falcon 900EX has Honeywell Primus 2000 avionics with 5 displays, each 8 × 7 ins (20 × 18 cm) and made up of 4 multi-function EFIS displays and a Sextant Avionique engine indication electronic display (EIED), 2 FMZ-2000 FMSs (with an optional third), integrated avionics computer, automatic flight director and autothrottle. Optional Flight Dynamics HGS-2850 HUD for Cat IIIa all-weather landings available to 900EX.

Aircraft variants:
Falcon 900B is the standard version, as detailed.
Falcon 900C is the latest variant, to replace 900B, with 900EX avionics. Honeywell Primus 2000 suite with 5 EFIS displays. Certification expected mid-1999, with deliveries from 2000.

Details for Falcon 900B, with 900EX where stated to be different

PRINCIPAL DIMENSIONS:
Wing span: 63 ft 5 ins (19.33 m)
Maximum length: 66 ft 4 ins (20.21 m)
Maximum height: 24 ft 9.5 ins (7.55 m)

CABIN:
Length: 39 ft (11.9 m)
Width: 7 ft 8.1 ins (2.34 m), or 6 ft 1.2 ins (1.86 m) at floor
Height: 6 ft 1.6 ins (1.87 m)
Volume: 1,267.8 cu ft (35.9 m^3)

WINGS:
Area: 527.43 sq ft (49 m^2)
Aspect ratio: 7.63

UNDERCARRIAGE:
Type: Retractable, with steerable (±60° taxi, ±180° tow) nosewheels. Twin wheels on each unit
Main wheel tyre size: 29 × 7.7-15 ins
Nose wheel tyre size: 17.5 × 5.75-8 ins
Wheel base: 25 ft 11 ins (7.9 m)
Wheel track: 14 ft 7 ins (4.45 m)

WEIGHTS:
Empty, equipped: 22,608 lb (10,255 kg), and 23,876 lb (10,830 kg) for 900EX
Maximum take-off: 45,503 lb (20,640 kg), and 48,303 lb (21,910 kg) for 900EX
Maximum landing: 42,000 lb (19,050 kg)
Payload: 4,784 lb (2,170 kg), and 6,162 lb (2,795 kg) for 900EX

PERFORMANCE:
Maximum permitted operating speed (V_{MO}): 351-370 kts (403-425 mph) 650-685 km/h IAS, and same for 900EX
Maximum operating Mach number (M_{MO}): Mach 0.84-87
Maximum cruise speed: Mach 0.85 or 513 kts (590 mph) 950 km/h at 36,000 ft (10,970 m)
Stall speed: 85 kts (98 mph) 158 km/h, wheels and flaps down for 900B and 900EX
Landing speed: 132 kts (152 mph) 244 km/h at MLW, or 106 kts (122 mph) 196 km/h with 8 passengers and NBAA IFR reserves, both CAS
Balanced field length: 4,955 ft (1,510 m) at MTOW, or 4,675 ft (1,425 m) with 8 passengers and maximum fuel, and 5,035 ft (1,535 m) with 8 passengers and maximum fuel for 900EX, all at sea level and ISA
Landing field length: 5,840 ft (1,780 m) at MLW, or 3,800 ft (1,160 m) with 8 passengers and NBAA IFR reserves, and 3,970 ft (1,210 m) with 8 passengers and NBAA IFR reserves for 900EX
Initial cruise altitude: 39,370 ft (12,000 m) for Falcon 900EX
Maximum certified altitude: 51,000 ft (15,550 m) for 900B and 900EX
Range with 8 passengers: 3,995 naut miles (4,598 miles) 7,400 km with NBAA IFR reserves
Range with 8 passengers for Falcon 900EX: 4,500 naut miles (5,182 miles) 8,340 km at Mach 0.84

Falcon 900EX is the extended performance version, delivered from October 1996. Can carry 8 passengers with the regulation NBAA-IFR reserves over a range of 4,500 naut miles. AlliedSignal TFE731-60 turbofans, and the latest Honeywell Primus 2000 avionics. HUD optional for Cat IIIa all-weather landings. Increased fuel capacity. 20% of the total investment from Alenia, AlliedSignal, Hellenic Aircraft Industries, Honeywell, Latécoère and Sabca.
Falcon 900B/EX Evasan is fitted with medical evacuation modules (see Falcon 50 for general features). Can accommodate up to 10 litters plus 4 seats or other arrangements typically from 2 litters upwards. Can also have an operating unit 'trauma room' arrangement for on-site treatment. Satellite communications can be installed, offering 2-way communications with hospitals.
Falcon 900 Multirole sales include 2 operated by the Japan Maritime Safety Agency. See Falcon Multirole.

Dassault Falcon 2000

First flight: 4 March 1993.

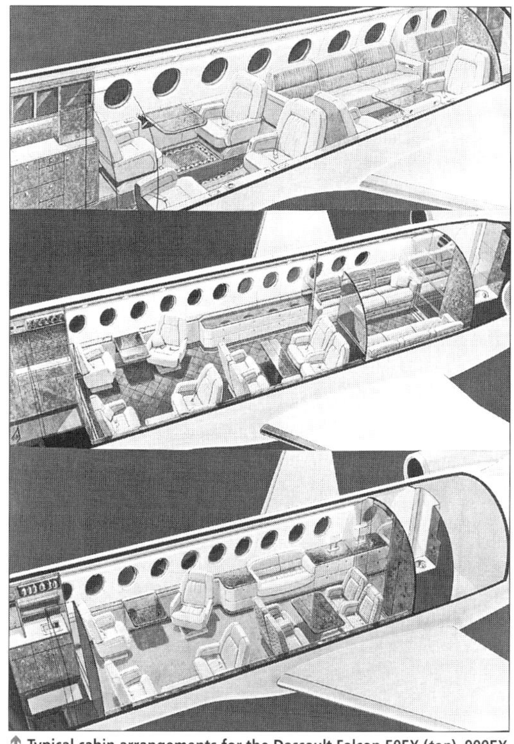

↑ **Typical cabin arrangements for the Dassault Falcon 50EX (*top*), 900EX (*centre*) and 2000 (*bottom*)** *(courtesy Dassault)*

Certification: 30 November 1994 for JAR 25, 2 February 1995 for FAA. All new Falcons received FAA/JAA certification for operation in compliance with the new RSVM air control norms.
First delivery: 16 February 1995.
Role: Twin-turbofan, transcontinental, widebody business jet; combines Falcon 50 economy with Falcon 900 comfort. Alenia has 25% share interest in Falcon 2000.
Sales: First operated by Flicape of South Africa. 52 delivered at the time of writing.
Crew/passengers: 2 flight crew (plus a third crew member on a jump seat) and up to 19 passengers. Basic layout is with a forward lounge with 4 seats and 2 tables and a rear lounge with 2 seats, a table and a 3-person sofa which is convertible to a couch. Other layouts include a "two and a half" lounge arrangement.

Details for Falcon 2000

PRINCIPAL DIMENSIONS:
Wing span: 63 ft 5 ins (19.33 m)
Maximum length: 66 ft 4.5 ins (20.23 m)
Maximum height: 23 ft 2 ins (7.06 m)

CABIN:
Length: 31 ft 0.5 ins (9.46 m)
Width: 7 ft 8 ins (2.34 m), maximum
Height: 6 ft 2 ins (1.87 m)
Volume: 1,024 cu ft (29 m^3)

WINGS:
Area: 527.4 sq ft (49 m^2)
Aspect ratio: 7.625

UNDERCARRIAGE:
Type: Retractable, with steerable (±60° taxi, ±180° tow) nosewheels. Twin wheels on each unit
Wheel base: 24 ft 3 ins (7.39 m)
Wheel track: 14 ft 7 ins (4.45 m)

WEIGHTS:
Empty, equipped: 20,735 lb (9,405 kg)
Maximum take-off: 35,803 lb (16,240 kg)
Maximum landing: 33,000 lb (14,968 kg)
Payload: 7,209 lb (3,270 kg)

PERFORMANCE:
Maximum operating Mach number (M_{MO}): Mach 0.85
Cruise speed: Mach 0.8 to Mach 0.85
Balanced field length: 5,250 ft (1,600 m) with 8 passengers, full fuel, sea level
Landing distance: 4,233 ft (1,290 m) with 8 passengers, sea level, FAR 121
Initial cruise altitude: 41,000 ft (12,500 m)
Maximum certified altitude: 47,000 ft (14,330 m)
Range: 3,000 naut miles (3,455 miles) 5,560 km with 8 passengers, NBAA-IFR reserves, at Mach 0.8

↑ **Dassault Falcon 2000** *(courtesy Francois Robineau - Dassault/Aviaplans)*

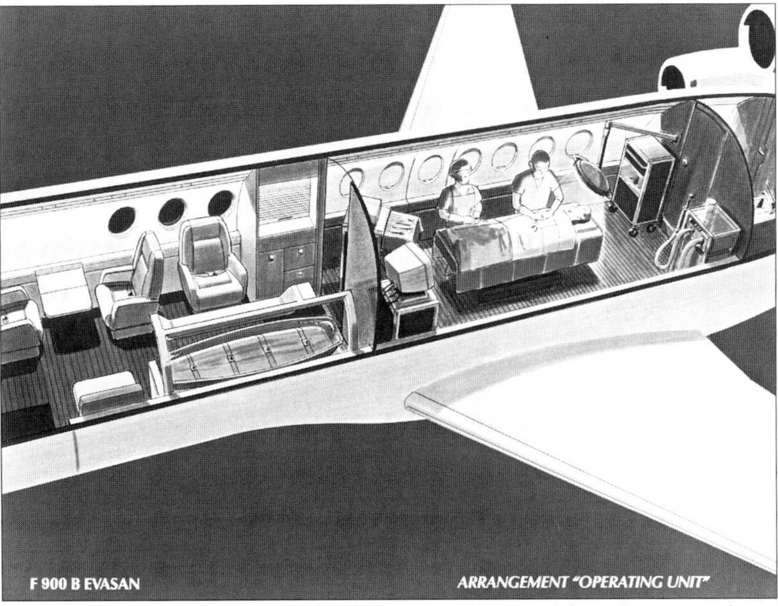

↑ Dassault Falcon 900 series in Evasan layout, with trauma room operating unit for on-site treatment plus a litter/equipment module in the forward cabin *(courtesy Dassault)*

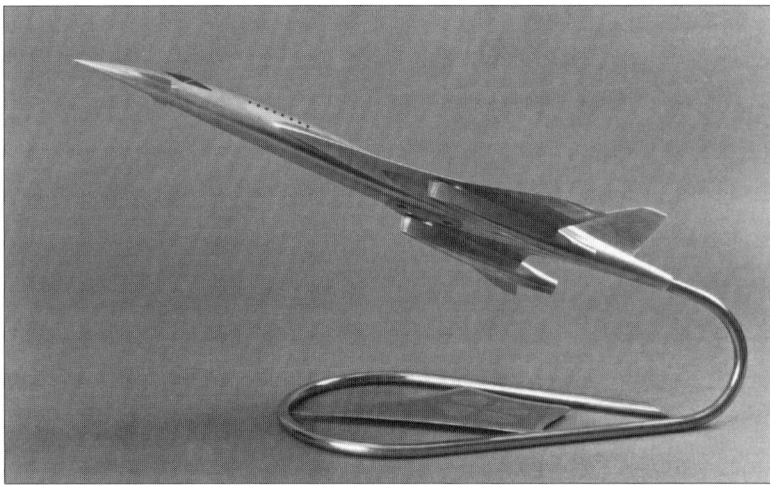

↑ Dassault supersonic Falcon: on 19 May 1998 Dassault's Chairman, Serge Dassault, and Executive Vice-President Bruno Revellin-Falcoz, presented the company's design concept for a 2 crew and 8 passenger supersonic Falcon business jet, capable of a non-stop range of 4,000 naut miles at Mach 1.8 cruise speed. Transonic cruise speed would be Mach 0.95. Having 3 non-afterburning engines derived from the General Electric F414 or Snecma M88, it is 106 ft 4 ins (32.42 m) long, has a wing span of 55 ft 7 ins (16.95 m), wing area of 1,400 sq ft (130 m^2), empty weight of 37,600 lb (17,050 kg), MTOW of 85,826 lb (38,930 kg), and fuel capacity of 45,800 lb (20,775 kg). Operating altitude would be about 60,000 ft (18,300 m). It is expected to have a 'smart' undercarriage, with 4-wheel bogies that tilt hydraulically to prevent the need for taller legs. No programme launch decision has yet been made *(courtesy Dassault/Aviaplans J.P. Soton)*

Baggage capacity: 134.2 cu ft (3.8 m^3), with the option of a further 49.4 cu ft (1.4 m^3) unpressurized volume.
Airframe: Falcon 900 forward fuselage and undercarriage, with wings that only slightly differ from those of the Falcon 50/900 (revised leading-edge slats).
Engines: 2 CFE Company CFE738-1-1B turbofans, with FADEC.
Engine rating: Each 5,725 lbf (24.47 kN).
Fuel system: 6,865 litres, weighing 12,155 lb (5,513 kg).
Radar: Weather radar.
Flight avionics/instrumentation: Rockwell Collins Pro Line 4, with 7.25 ins (18 cm) EFIS (4 screens) and multimode autopilot, dual com/nav, AHRS, ADS, ADF, DME and radio altimeter. 3 Sextant Avionique liquid crystal EIED reconfigurable engine indicators. Honeywell FMZ-2000 FMS. Optional Flight Dynamics HGS 2850 HUD for Cat IIIa all-weather landing, and TCAS.

Aircraft variants:
Falcon 2000, as detailed.
Falcon 2000 Evasan is the medical evacuation version, with typically 4 litters plus 5 seats.

Dassault Falcon Multirole

Role: Generic term for any version of Falcon when equipped for special roles other than passenger transport, including aerial photography, medevac, calibration (using Fanfis Normac NM 3625B system), maritime surveillance, target towing, aerial survey, weapon systems training, crew training, electronic warfare, etc. Special systems can also be applied to transport versions for partial or complementary special functions, such as infra-red surveillance, light cargo transport, etc. Some fitting-out arrangements may be mixed (calibration plus VIP transportation, SAR plus medevac, for example). Falcon 50/50EX can also be used for sigint, to detect radio signals and pinpoint their sources. Some roles can be operated with a single pilot. Almost 20% of Falcons sold are regularly used for specific utility missions.

Nogatec International — France

Corporate address:
2 Villa Ghis, 92400 Courbevoie.
Telephone: +33 1 47 89 05 77
Facsimile: +33 1 46 91 02 27
E-mail: nogatec@planete.net
Information:
Ien Nio Bourelly.

ACTIVITIES

▪ Fior Concept, a division of Nogaro Technologies, designed the WAF 96 light aircraft to be marketed by Nogatec International. This has 2 tandem seats under a very large canopy and a 180 hp (134 kW) Textron Lycoming O-360 piston engine. Although construction of the prototype was begun in 1997, allowing the first flight and certification under JAR-VLA in 1998, in May 1998 the editor was informed by Nogatec that the programme had been placed on hold.

Reims Aviation S.A. — France

Corporate address:
See Reconnaissance section for company details and the Vigilant series. Plans to reintroduce single-engined Cessna lightplanes into production in France were abandoned in 1998.

Reims F 406 Caravan II

First flight: 22 September 1983.
Certification: 21 December 1984.

↑ Reims F 406 Caravan IIs *(courtesy Reims Aviation)*

Role: Unpressurized utility, commuter, executive, cargo, ambulance, skydiving, target-towing and pilot training.
Sales: Production deliveries started in 1985 and continued in 1998. At the time of writing, 79 F 406s had been delivered to 46 customers in 23 countries, with 14 orders then outstanding (6 aircraft ordered in last full year).
Crew/passengers: 2 crew plus 12 passengers, 6 VIPs, litters or other loads depending on role.
Cargo capacity: Up to a 3,445 lb (1,563 kg) load. Optional large cargo door. Underfuselage cargo pod is available of 45.9 cu ft (1.3 m^3) capacity.
Wing control surfaces: Ailerons (port trim tab) and Fowler flaps.

Details for F 406

PRINCIPAL DIMENSIONS:
Wing span: 49 ft 5.5 ins (15.08 m)
Maximum length: 39 ft 0.25 ins (11.893 m)
Maximum height: 13 ft 2 ins (4.01 m)

CABIN:
Length: 18 ft 9 ins (5.71 m) with cockpit
Width: 4 ft 8 ins (1.42 m)
Height: 4 ft 3.5 ins (1.31 m)

WINGS:
Aerofoil section: NACA 23018, 23012 (root/tip)
Area: 252.74 sq ft (23.48 m^2)
Aspect ratio: 9.685

UNDERCARRIAGE:
Type: Retractable, with nosewheel
Main wheel tyre size: 22 × 7.75-10, of 95 psi
Nose wheel tyre size: 6.00 × 6, of 50 psi

WEIGHTS:
Empty: 5,423 lb (2,460 kg)
Maximum take-off and landing: 9,850 lb (4,468 kg)
Useful load: 4,892 lb (2,219 kg) maximum
Payload: 3,445 lb (1,563 kg)

PERFORMANCE:
Maximum operating speed (V_{MO}): 230 kts (265 mph) 426 km/h, IAS
Maximum cruise speed: 246 kts (283 mph) 455 km/h, at 15,000 ft (4,570 m)
Stall speed: 94 kts (108 mph) 174 km/h *clean*, 81 kts (93 mph) 150 km/h *landing configuration*, both IAS
Take-off distance: 1,726 ft (526 m)
Take-off distance over a 50 ft (15 m) obstacle: 2,635 ft (803 m)
Maximum climb rate: 1,850 ft (564 m) per minute
Ceiling: 30,000 ft (9,145 m), service
G limits: +3.6, -1.44, design
Range with full fuel: 1,153 naut miles (1,327 miles) 2,137 km, with 45 minutes reserve

Tail control surfaces: Horn-balanced elevators and rudder, with tabs.
Engines: 2 Pratt & Whitney Canada PT6A-112 turboprops, with 7 ft 9 ins (2.36 m) propellers.
Engine rating: Each 500 shp (373 kW).
Fuel system: 1,823 litres, of which 1,798 litres are usable, weighing 3,183 lb (1,444 kg).
Electrical system: 28 volt, with 2 engine-driven starter generators and a 39 amp-hour battery.
Hydraulic system: Flind Power manufactured, for wing flaps and undercarriage actuation. 1,740 psi.
Braking system: Hydraulic disc.
Oxygen system: 114.9 cu ft (3.25 m^3) bottle located in the nose compartment. 13 hours at 30,000 ft (9,145 m).
Radar: AlliedSignal Bendix/King RDS 82 weather radar optional. Similar make 1500 radar on French customs aircraft, and GEC-Marconi Seaspray 2000 on Scottish Fishery Protection Agency aircraft (see Vigilant in Reconnaissance section).
Flight avionics/instrumentation: AlliedSignal Bendix/King Silver Crown, with optional Gold Crown. Other options, including IFR.

Avions Robin — France

Corporate address: 1 route de Troyes, 21121 Darois.
Telephone: +33 3 80 44 20 50 **Facsimile:** +33 3 80 35 60 80 **E-mail:** avions@avions-robin.fr
Founded: 1957.
Information: Jacques Bigenwald.

ACTIVITIES

- A subsidiary of Aeronautical Service (AES).

Robin 200

First flight: 1971 for HR 200/120 B, on which Robin 200 is based.
Role: 2-seat lightplane and trainer.
Sales: Production was reinstated in mid-1993. Some 160 delivered by 1998.
Cockpit: Entrance via steps and a forward-sliding canopy. Dual controls.
Wing control surfaces: Ailerons and slotted flaps.

Details for Robin 200

PRINCIPAL DIMENSIONS:
Wing span: 27 ft 4 ins (8.33 m)
Maximum length: 21 ft 9.5 ins (6.64 m)
Maximum height: 6 ft 4.5 ins (1.94 m)

CABIN:
Width: 3 ft 7 ins (1.1 m) at elbow level

WINGS:
Area: 134.55 sq ft (12.5 m^2)
Aspect ratio: 5.55

UNDERCARRIAGE:
Type: Fixed, with steerable nosewheel. Wheel fairings

WEIGHTS:
Empty: 1,157 lb (525 kg)
Maximum take-off: 1,719 lb (780 kg)

PERFORMANCE:
Cruise speed: 120 kts (139 mph) 223 km/h at 75% power, best altitude
Take-off distance over a 50 ft (15 m) obstacle: 1,674 ft (510 m)
Landing distance over a 50 ft (15 m) obstacle: 1,460 ft (445 m)
Maximum climb rate: 768 ft (234 m) per minute
Ceiling: 12,800 ft (3,900 m), service
Range: 567 naut miles (652 miles) 1,050 km at 75% power, best altitude, no reserve

Tail control surfaces: Slab tailplane with tabs and rudder.
Flight control system: Manual, except electric flaps.
Construction materials: All metal.
Engine: Textron Lycoming O-235-L2A piston engine.
Engine rating: 118 hp (88 kW).
Fuel system: 120 litres.
Braking system: Disc brakes.
Flight avionics/instrumentation: Can be equipped with a comprehensive set of navaids and blind-flying instruments. VFR night-time illumination is standard.

Robin DR 400 series

First flight: May 1972.
Certification: 1977.
Role: 2, or 2+2 or 4-seat lightplanes.
Sales: Some 1,678 aircraft of the series delivered by 1998, used by aero clubs, flying schools and private pilots.
Cockpit: Entrance via a forward-sliding canopy. Dual controls. From mid-1993, third window on the rear fuselage was deleted from the /120 and /140 B models.
Baggage capacity: Accessible from the outside on Major and Regent. Capacity 88 lb (40 kg) for Dauphins and Major, and 132 lb (60 kg) for Regent and Remos.
Wing control surfaces: Ailerons, flaps and ventral airbrakes.
Tail control surfaces: Slab tailplane with tabs and horn-balanced rudder.
Flight control system: Manual, except for electric flaps.
Construction materials: Wooden airframe, with some composite parts. Wings covered with Dacron fabric.
Engine: See Aircraft variants. New engine cowling from mid-1993.
Fuel system: Optional auxiliary tank is available to the Dauphin 4, Major, Regent and Remo, to increase range by almost 30% without reducing cabin space.
Electrical system: 12 volt, 60 amp alternator. 12 volt, 32 amp-hour battery.
Braking system: Toe-operated hydraulic disc brakes on both sides.
Flight avionics/instrumentation: Instrument panel designed to integrate a large choice of optional equipment.

Aircraft variants:
DR 400/100 Cadet was produced in the early 1980s (only 14 built) as the 2-seater, powered by a 112 hp (83.5 kW) Textron Lycoming O-235 piston engine. See 1996-97 edition of WA&SD, page 395 for details.
DR 400/120 Dauphin 2+2 has 2+2 seating. It is powered by a 118 hp (88 kW) Textron Lycoming O-235-L2A piston engine, with 2-blade fixed-pitch propeller, and has 110 litres of fuel. Wing span 28 ft 7 ins (8.72 m) and length 22 ft 10 ins (6.96 m). Wing area 146.4 sq ft (13.6 m^2). Empty weight 1,212 lb (550 kg), gross weight 1,984 lb (900 kg), maximum speed 130 kts (150 mph) 241 km/h, stalling speed 44 kts (51 mph) 82 km/h, climb rate 590 ft (180 m) per minute, and range 500 naut miles (576 miles) 928 km.
DR 400/140 B Dauphin 4 is a full 4-seater, as detailed in the main data box. 160 hp (119.3 kW) O-320-D engine, 2-blade fixed-pitch propeller, and 110 litres of fuel standard and 160 litres with auxiliary tankage.
DR 400/160 Major is a 4-seater, powered by a 160 hp (119.3 kW) Textron Lycoming O-320-D piston engine with 2-blade fixed-pitch propeller. 190 litres of fuel standard and 240 litres with auxiliary tankage. Same dimensions as Dauphin. Wing area 152.85 sq ft (14.2 m^2). Empty weight 1,318 lb (598 kg), gross weight 2,315 lb (1,050 kg), maximum speed 146 kts (168 mph) 271 km/h, stalling speed 50 kts (58 mph) 93 km/h, climb rate 836 ft (255 m) per minute, and range 826 naut miles (950 miles) 1,530 km on standard fuel and 1,026 naut miles (1,180 miles) 1,900 km with auxiliary fuel.

Details for DR 400/140 B Dauphin 4, *with Remo 200 in italics*

PRINCIPAL DIMENSIONS:
Wing span: 28 ft 7 ins (8.72 m), *the same*
Maximum length: 22 ft 10 ins (6.96 m), *23 ft 8 ins (7.22 m)*
Maximum height: 7 ft 4 ins (2.23 m), *the same*

CABIN:
Width: 3 ft 7.33 ins (1.1 m) at elbow level, *the same*

WINGS:
Aerofoil section: NACA 43012 modified
Area: 146.4 sq ft (13.6 m^2), *the same*
Aspect ratio: 5.59

WEIGHTS:
Empty: 1,278 lb (580 kg), *1,433 lb (650 kg)*
Maximum take-off: 2,204 lb (1,000 kg), *2,425 lb (1,100 kg)*
Useful load: 926 lb (420 kg), *992 lb (450 kg)*

PERFORMANCE:
Maximum speed: 143 kts (165 mph) 265 km/h, *146 kts (168 mph) 270 km/h*
Maximum cruise speed: 117 kts (133 mph) 215 km/h, *135 kts (155 mph) 250 km/h*
Stall speed: 47 kts (54 mph) 87 km/h, *49 kts (57 mph) 91 km/h*
Take-off distance over a 50 ft (15 m) obstacle: 1,591 ft (485 m), *1,313 ft (400 m)*
Landing distance over a 50 ft (15 m) obstacle: 1,541 ft (470 m), *1,362 ft (415 m)*
Maximum climb rate: 865 ft (264 m) per minute, *1,024 ft (312 m) per minute*
Ceiling: 14,000 ft (4,265 m), service
Range: 464 naut miles (534 miles) 860 km with standard fuel, 740 naut miles (851 miles) 1,370 km with auxiliary fuel, *408 naut miles (470 miles) 756 km with standard fuel, 598 naut miles (688 miles) 1,108 km with auxiliary fuel*

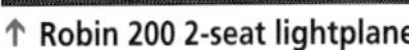
↑ Robin 200 2-seat lightplane

↑ Robin DR400/180 Regent 4-seat lightplane

DR 400/180 Regent is a 4-seater, powered by a 180 hp (134 kW) Textron Lycoming O-360-A piston engine, with 2-blade fixed-pitch propeller. 190 litres of fuel standard and 240 litres with auxiliary tankage. Same dimensions as Dauphin. Wing area 152.85 sq ft (14.2 m^2). Empty weight 1,345 lb (610 kg), gross weight 2,425 lb (1,100 kg), maximum speed 150 kts (173 mph) 278 km/h, stalling speed 51 kts (59 mph) 95 km/h, climb rate 826 ft (252 m) per minute, and range 785 naut miles (904 miles) 1,455 km on standard fuel and 975 naut miles (1,121 miles) 1,805 km with auxiliary fuel.
DR 400/180 R Remo 180 is a 4-seater suited also to glider towing, powered by a 180 hp (134 kW) Textron Lycoming O-360-A piston engine, with 2-blade fixed-pitch propeller. 110 litres of fuel standard and 160 litres with auxiliary tankage. Same dimensions as Dauphin. Wing area 146.4 sq ft (13.6 m^2). Empty weight 1,305 lb (592 kg), gross weight 2,205 lb (1,000 kg), maximum speed 146 kts (168 mph) 270 km/h, stalling speed 47 kts (54 mph) 87 km/h, climb rate 1,102 ft (336 m) per minute, and range 426 naut miles (491 miles) 790 km on standard fuel and 610 naut miles (702 miles) 1,130 km with auxiliary fuel. For glider towing, stall speed 45 kts (52 mph) 84 km/h, climb rate 689 ft (210 m) per minute, and noise level 72.1 dB(A).
DR 400/200 R Remo 200 is a 4-seater suited also to glider towing, powered by a 200 hp (149 kW) Textron Lycoming IO-360 piston engine, with 2-blade constant-speed propeller. 110 litres of fuel standard and 160 litres with auxiliary tankage. For glider towing, stall speed 45 kts (52 mph) 84 km/h, climb rate 846 ft (258 m) per minute, and noise level 65.6 dB(A). See main data box.
DR400/200i President, see separate entry.

↑ Robin DR400/200i President

Robin DR400/200i President

Role: New model of the DR400 series, with a larger fuselage for increased headroom and more cabin width.

Details for DR400/200i President

PRINCIPAL DIMENSIONS:
Wing span: 28 ft 7 ins (8.72 m)
Maximum length: 23 ft 1.5 ins (7.05 m)
Maximum height: 7 ft 4 ins (2.23 m)

CABIN:
Width: 3 ft 11.25 ins (1.2 m) at elbow level

WEIGHTS:
Maximum take-off: 2,535 lb (1,150 kg)
Useful load: 1,102 lb (500 kg)

PERFORMANCE:
Maximum speed: 147 kts (169 mph) 273 km/h
Cruise speed: 137 kts (158 mph) 253 km/h at 8,500 ft (2,590 m), 75% power
Take-off distance over a 50 ft (15 m) obstacle: 1,477 ft (450 m)
Maximum climb rate: 1,000 ft (305 m) per minute
Range: 993 naut miles (1,143 miles) 1,840 km at 75% power, 1,092 naut miles (1,258 miles) 2,025 km at 65% power, both with no reserve

Crew/passengers: 4+1 seating.
Baggage capacity: 132 lb (60 kg).
Wing control surfaces: Ailerons, flaps and ventral airbrakes.
Tail control surfaces: Slab tailplane with tabs and horn-balanced rudder. Electric rudder trim system.
Flight control system: Manual, except for electric flaps.
Engine: Textron Lycoming IO-360-A1B6 piston engine, with Hartzell 2-blade constant-speed propeller.
Engine rating: 200 hp (149 kW).
Fuel system: 275 litres usable in 4 tanks.
Flight avionics/instrumentation: Standard equipment includes gyro horizon, directional gyro, turn rate indicator, rate of climb indicator, altimeter, outside air temperature gauge, intercom, avionics master switch, heated pitot head, and more.

Robin 1180 Aiglon II

Comments: The original R 1180 Aiglon first flew in 1976 and was certified in 1978 as a 4-seat lightplane of metal construction, with a 180 hp (134 kW) Textron Lycoming O-360-A3A engine. Restarting production of an updated version with a similar engine as the Aiglon II was considered in 1997 and announced in the UK, but Robin confirmed in May 1998 that this project has not progressed.

Robin 2160

Certification: 1978. Certified to FAR Pt 23 Aerobatic category in 1982.
Role: 2-seat aerobatic lightplane, also suited to basic training and cross-country flying.
Sales: Production reinstated in December 1993. Some 120 delivered by 1998.
Cockpit: Entrance via a forward-sliding (jettisonable) canopy. Dual controls.
Wing control surfaces: Ailerons and slotted flaps.
Tail control surfaces: Slab tailplane with tabs and horn-balanced rudder.
Flight control system: Manual, except for electric flap control.
Construction materials: Aluminium alloy, semi-monocoque structure.
Engine: Textron Lycoming O-320-D2A piston engine, with a Sensenich 74DM6S5-2-64 propeller.
Engine rating: 160 hp (119 kW).
Fuel system: 120 litres, or optional 160 litre tank.
Electrical system: 12 volt, 24 amp-hour battery.
Braking system: Cleveland discs.
Flight avionics/instrumentation: Standard equipment includes airspeed indicator, altimeter, stall warning horn, ball-type slip

↑ Robin 2160 2-seat lightplane

Details for 2160

PRINCIPAL DIMENSIONS:
Wing span: 27 ft 4 ins (8.33 m)
Maximum length: 23 ft 3.5 ins (7.1 m)
Maximum height: 7 ft (2.13 m)

WINGS:
Area: 140 sq ft (13 m^2)
Aspect ratio: 5.34

UNDERCARRIAGE:
Type: Fixed, with steerable and auto-centring nosewheel. Wheel fairings

WEIGHTS:
Empty: 1,213 lb (550 kg)
Maximum take-off: 1,764 lb (800 kg) Aerobatic, 1,984 lb (900 kg) Utility

PERFORMANCE (Aerobatic category):
Maximum cruise speed: 131 kts (150 mph) 242 km/h at 75% power and 8,500 ft (2,590 m)
Stall speed: 46 kts (53 mph) 85 km/h, *with flaps*
Take-off distance over a 50 ft (15 m) obstacle: 1,345 ft (410 m)
Maximum climb rate: 1,023 ft (312 m) per minute
G limits: +6, -3
Ceiling: 15,000 ft (4,575 m), service
Range: 514 naut miles (592 miles) 952 km at 65% power and 11,000 ft (3,350 m), or 459 naut miles (528 miles) 850 km at 75% power and 8,500 ft (2,590 m), both with standard fuel and no reserve

indicator, magnetic compass and tachometer, with optional equipment including accelerometer, AlliedSignal Bendix/King KX 155-38 VHF/VOR, KI 208 VOR indicator, KT 76A transponder, ACK 30 alticoder, GPS, JE2 emergency locator transmitter and more.

Robin 3000

First flight: 1988 in current R 3000/160 form.
Role: 4-seat lightplane.
Sales: 76 delivered by 1998.

Details for R 3000

PRINCIPAL DIMENSIONS:
Wing span: 32 ft 2.25 ins (9.81 m)
Maximum length: 24 ft 7.75 ins (7.51 m)
Maximum height: 8 ft 8.75 ins (2.66 m)

WINGS:
Aerofoil section: NACA 43012
Area: 155.75 sq ft (14.47 m^2)
Aspect ratio: 6.65

UNDERCARRIAGE:
Type: Fixed, with steerable and auto-centring nosewheel

WEIGHTS:
Empty: 1,433 lb (650 kg)
Maximum take-off: 2,535 lb (1,150 kg)
Useful load: 1,102 lb (500 kg)

PERFORMANCE:
Maximum speed: 146 kts (168 mph) 270 km/h at sea level
Maximum cruise speed: 138 kts (158 mph) 255 km/h at 75% power and optimum height
Economic cruise speed: 129 kts (148 mph) 238 km/h at 65% power
Stall speed: 49 kts (57 mph) 91 km/h, *with flaps*
Take-off distance over a 50 ft (15 m) obstacle: 1,854 ft (565 m)
Landing distance over a 50 ft (15 m) obstacle: 1,772 ft (540 m)
Maximum climb rate: 875 ft (267 m) per minute, at sea level
G limits: +4.4, -2.2
Ceiling: 15,000 ft (4,575 m), service
Range: 869 naut miles (1,000 miles) 1,610 km at 65% power, and 805 naut miles (926 miles) 1,490 km

↑ Robin 3000 4-seat lightplane

Cockpit: Entrance via retractable step and a forward-sliding jettisonable canopy. Dual controls. 2 storage boxes under the panel.
Baggage capacity: 15.2 cu ft (0.43 m^3), for 88 lb (40 kg).
Wing characteristics: Winglets to minimize induced drag.
Wing control surfaces: Ailerons and slotted flaps.
Tail control surfaces: T-tail with elevator and tabs, and rudder.
Flight control system: Manual, except for electric flaps.
Construction materials: Aluminium alloy.
Engine: Textron Lycoming O-360-A2A piston engine, with 2-blade fixed-pitch propeller.
Engine rating: 160-180 hp (119-134 kW).
Fuel system: 225 litres.
Electrical system: 12 volt, 60 amp alternator, and 12 volt battery.
Braking system: Hydraulic disc.

Flight avionics/instrumentation: Standard and optional equipment includes airspeed indicator, altimeter, stall warning horn, ball-type slip indicator, magnetic compass, tachometer, and more. Annunciator panel with push to test, pitot heat, flaps down, starter engaged, alternator inoperative, fuel level low, selector off, fuel pressure low and oil pressure low.

Robin X-4 and New 4-seater

Comments: Programmes terminated. No production planned at present. Details can be found in the 1996-97 edition of *WA&SD*, page 396.

Socata Groupe Aerospatiale France

Corporate address:
See Reconnaissance section for company details.

Socata TB 30 Epsilon and TB 31 Omega

Comments: The TB 30 Epsilon piston-engined trainer and the TB 31 Omega turboprop trainer continue to be promoted in Socata brochures received for this edition of the book. However, no new production has been undertaken for some years, nor have Epsilons been upgraded to Omega standard as offered as an alternative to new production. Full descriptions can be found in the 1996-97 edition of *WA&SD*, pages 42-43 and 396. See Epsilon Mk2.

Socata Rallye 235 F

Comments: Details of this 4-seat training, glider and banner towing, liaison and observation lightplane can be found in the 1996-97 edition of *WA&SD*, pages 396-397.

Socata TB9C Tampico Club, TB10 Tobago and TB200 Tobago XL

First flight: 9 March 1979 (TB9), 23 February 1977 (TB10) and 27 March 1991 (TB200).
Certification: FAR Pt 23, with Amendments 1-16, 26 April 1979 (TB10).
Role: Ab initio, basic and instrument flying, proficiency training, pleasure, cross-country and liaison, for operation in the normal category.
Details: Principally for TB200 Tobago XL.

Crew/passengers: 4 or 5 persons. Entry via 2 large access doors. Rear windows kick out for emergency exits. Rear bench seat removable for cargo carrying. Dual yoke controls.
Baggage capacity: 143 lb (65 kg), accessible from inside cabin and via outside door.

Wing control surfaces: Ailerons with tabs, and flaps.
Tail control surfaces: Slab tailplane with anti-balance tab, and rudder with ground-adjustable tab.
Flight control system: Push-pull rods and cables, manual trim actuated by cables and electrically actuated flaps.

↑ Socata TB9C Tampico Club

Details for TB200 Tobago XL

PRINCIPAL DIMENSIONS:
Wing span: 32 ft 0.5 ins (9.77 m)
Maximum length: 25 ft 3 ins (7.7 m)
Maximum height: 9 ft 11 ins (3.02 m)

CABIN:
Length: 8 ft 3.5 ins (2.53 m)
Width: 4 ft 2.5 ins (1.28 m)
Height: 3 ft 8 ins (1.12 m)

WINGS:
Area: 128.09 sq ft (11.9 m^2)
Aspect ratio: 8.02

UNDERCARRIAGE:
Type: Fixed of trailing link type, with steerable nosewheel. Wheel fairings
Wheel base: 6 ft 5 ins (1.96 m)
Wheel track: 7 ft 8 ins (2.33 m)

WEIGHTS:
Empty: 1,576 lb (715 kg) average
Maximum take-off and landing: 2,535 lb (1,150 kg)
Useful load: 959 lb (435 kg)

PERFORMANCE:
Maximum speed: 140 kts (161 mph) 259 km/h
Maximum cruise speed: 130 kts (149 mph) 240 km/h at 8,500 ft (2,590 m)
Best economy cruise speed: 115 kts (132 mph) 213 km/h at 8,500 ft (2,590 m)
Stall speed: 53 kts (61 mph) 98 km/h, *with flaps*
Take-off distance over a 50 ft (15 m) obstacle: 1,558 ft (475 m)
Landing distance over a 50 ft (15 m) obstacle: 1,474 ft (449 m)
Maximum climb rate: 940 ft (286 m) per minute
Climb to 8,500 ft (2,590 m): 12 minutes 30 seconds
Ceiling: 16,000 ft (4,875 m), certified
Range: 636 naut miles (732 miles) 1,179 km

Construction materials: Metal, semi-monocoque.
Engine: Textron Lycoming IO-360-A1B6 piston engine, with a 6 ft 2 ins (1.88 m) Hartzell 2-blade constant-speed propeller.
Engine rating: 200 hp (149 kW).
Fuel system: 210 litres, of which 204 litres are usable.
Electrical system: 28 volt, 70 amp alternator. 24 volt, 10 amp-hour ni-cd battery. VHF-VOR feeder. VHF antenna.
Flight avionics/instrumentation: VFR or IFR, according to equipment.

Aircraft variants:
TB9C Tampico Club is the low power model, having a 160 hp (119 kW) Textron Lycoming O-320-D2A engine and 158 litres of fuel (152 litres usable). Same dimensions as TB200, and same 4/5 persons and baggage. Average empty weight 1,426 lb (647 kg) and MTOW 2,337 lb (1,060 kg). Maximum cruise speed 107 kts (123 mph) 198 km/h.
TB10 Tobago has a 180 hp (134 kW) O-360-A1AD engine and 210 litres of fuel (204 litres usable). Same dimensions as TB200. Average empty weight 1,543 lb (700 kg) and MTOW 2,535 lb (1,150 kg). Maximum cruise speed 127 kts (146 mph) 235 km/h.
TB200 Tobago XL is the highest powered version, as detailed.

Socata TB20 Trinidad and TB21 Trinidad TC

First flight: 14 November 1980 (TB20).
Certification: 18 December 1981 to FAR Pt 23, Amendments 1-16.
Role: Advanced instrument training, IFR training, pleasure flights, surveillance missions, and high-speed long-distance liaison missions. For use in Normal category.
Sales: 129 delivered by 1998.
Details: Principally for TB20.
Baggage capacity: 143 lb (65 kg), accessible from inside the cabin and via outside door.
Control surfaces: Generally as for Tobago.
Construction materials: Metal, semi-monocoque.
Engine: Textron Lycoming IO-540-C4D5D piston engine, with 6 ft 8 ins (2.03 m) Hartzell 2-blade constant-speed propeller.
Engine rating: 250 hp (186.4 kW).
Fuel system: 336 litres, of which 326 are usable.
Electrical system: Similar to Tobago.
De-icing system: TB20 and TB21 can be equipped with a total glycol de-icing system, allowing flying into known icing conditions (in countries in which the option is certified).
Flight avionics/instrumentation: VFR and IFR, according to equipment. Can be equipped with single AlliedSignal Bendix/King EHSI 40 EFIS, as certified on 22 April 1996.

Details for TB20 Trinidad

PRINCIPAL DIMENSIONS:
Wing span: 32 ft 0.5 ins (9.77 m)
Maximum length: 25 ft 3.5 ins (7.71 m)
Maximum height: 9 ft 4 ins (2.85 m)

CABIN: As for Tobago

WINGS:
Area: 128.09 sq ft (11.9 m^2)
Aspect ratio: 8.02

UNDERCARRIAGE:
Type: Retractable trailing link type, with steerable nosewheel

WEIGHTS:
Empty: 1,764 lb (800 kg) average
Maximum take-off and landing: 3.086 lb (1,400 kg)
Useful load: 1,323 lb (600 kg)

PERFORMANCE:
Maximum speed: 167 kts (192 mph) 309 km/h
Maximum cruise speed: 163 kts (188 mph) 301 km/h at 8,500 ft (2,590 m)
Best economy cruise speed: 157 kts (181 mph) 290 km/h at 8,500 ft (2,590 m)
Stall speed: 70 kts (81 mph) 130 km/h *clean*, 59 kts (68 mph) 110 km/h *in landing configuration*
Take-off distance over a 50 ft (15 m) obstacle: 2,150 ft (655 m), ISA
Landing distance over a 50 ft (15 m) obstacle: 1,750 ft (533 m), ISA
Maximum climb rate: 1,200 ft (366 m) per minute
Climb to 8,000 ft (2,440 m): 9 minutes, ISA
Ceiling: 20,000 ft (6,100 m), certified
Range: 1,108 naut miles (1,275 miles) 2,053 km, maximum

Aircraft variants:
TB20 Trinidad has a fuel-injected engine. As detailed.
TB21 Trinidad TC is similar to TB20 but has a turbocharged TIO-540-AB1AD engine. Average empty weight 1,860 lb (844 kg) and MTOW 3,086 lb (1,400 kg). Maximum cruise speed 186 kts (214 mph) 344 km/h.

Socata TBM 700

First flight: 14 July 1988
Certification: 31 January 1990. Part 23 Amdt 34 certified for IFR into known icing conditions.
Role: Pressurized business aircraft, and multi-mission aircraft for liaison, training, aerial photography, medevac, target towing, ECM, freight carrying, patrol and law enforcement, NBC spraying simulation, navaid calibration, anti-hail rocket launching, and coast watch.
Details: TBM 700, except under Aircraft variants.
Crew/passengers: 6 or 7 including pilot/s.
Cabin: Environmental control system provided by engine bleed-air and bootstrap system. Pressure differential 6.2 psi.
3 emergency oxygen bottles under the seats. Pilot masks with microphone and 4/5 passenger masks.
Baggage capacity: 110 lb (50 kg) in the unpressurized nose compartment, 220 lb (100 kg) in the pressurized aft compartment.
Wing control surfaces: Ailerons (port trim tab), single-slotted Fowler flaps and spoilers.
Tail control surfaces: Balanced elevators and rudder, with trim tabs.
Flight control system: Push-pull rods and cables, except for electric flaps and trim tabs.
Construction materials: Mostly metal, with Nomex honeycomb used in the construction of the tail and control surfaces. Composites wing leading edges and tips, and undercarriage doors.
Engine: Pratt & Whitney Canada PT6A-64 turboprop, with a 7 ft 7 ins (2.31 m) Hartzell HC-E4N-3/E9083S(K) 4-blade constant-speed, reverse control, metal propeller. Foreign object damage (FOD) protection with inertial separator.
Engine rating: 1,570 shp (1,171 kW), derated to 700 shp (522 kW).
Fuel system: 1,100 litres, of which 1,066 litres are usable.
Electrical system: Bus distribution, 28 volt system with a 5.6 kW starter-generator and auxiliary alternator. 40 amp-hour ni-cd battery.
Braking system: Hydraulic disc type.

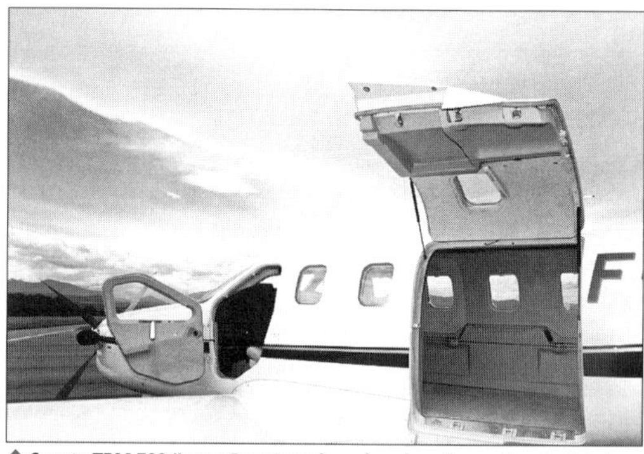
↑ Socata TBM 700 'Large Door' version, showing also optional pilot door

↑ Socata Trinidad with wheels retracted

↑ Socata TBM 700 pressurized business and multi-mission aircraft

Details for TBM 700

PRINCIPAL DIMENSIONS:
Wing span: 41 ft 7 ins (12.68 m)
Maximum length: 34 ft 11 ins (10.645 m)
Maximum height: 14 ft 3.5 ins (4.355 m)

CABIN:
Length: 13 ft 3.5 ins (4.05 m)
Width: 3 ft 11.5 ins (1.21 m)
Height: 4 ft (1.22 m)

WINGS:
Area: 193.75 sq ft (18 m^2)
Aspect ratio: 8.93

UNDERCARRIAGE:
Type: Retractable, with steerable nosewheel
Wheel base: 9 ft 6.7 ins (2.914 m)
Wheel track: 12 ft 8.5 ins (3.874 m)

WEIGHTS:
Empty: 4,100 lb (1,860 kg) average
Maximum take-off: 6,579 lb (2,984 kg)
Maximum landing: 6,250 lb (2,835 kg)
Useful load: 2,513 lb (1,140 kg)

PERFORMANCE:
Maximum cruise speed: 300 kts (345 mph) 555 km/h at 26,000 ft (7,925 m)
Economic cruise speed: 243 kts (280 mph) 450 km/h at 30,000 ft (9,145 m)
Stall speed: 61 kts (71 mph) 113 km/h
Required runway length over a 50 ft (15 m) obstacle: 2,133 ft (650 m)
Required landing distance over a 50 ft (15 m) obstacle, with reserve: 1,640 ft (500 m), ISA
Maximum climb rate: 1,875 ft (572 m) per minute at sea level
Climb to 20,000 ft (6,100 m): 11 minutes 45 seconds, ISA
Climb to 30,000 ft (9,145 m): 20 minutes 30 seconds, ISA
Ceiling: 30,000 ft (9,145 m) certified
Range: 1,350 naut miles (1,553 miles) 2,500 km at 300 kts, 1,550 naut miles (1,783 miles) 2,870 km at 243 kts, both with maximum fuel; or 900 naut miles (1,036 miles) 1,667 km at 300 kts, 1,080 naut miles (1,243 miles) 2,000 km at 243 kts, both with 6 passengers plus baggage

De-icing system: Pneumatic for wing, tailplane and fin leading edges. Electric for propeller, pitots and windshield. Hot gas for engine air inlets.
Radar: See Aircraft variants and Avionics.
Flight avionics/instrumentation: Variety of avionics suites from Sextant Avionique, AlliedSignal Bendix/King, Magnavox, RCA and Rockwell Collins, according to requirements and role. Options include VHF, UHF, V/UHF, HF, VOR/ILS, Tacan, GPS, Loran, ADF and GNS com/nav. EFIS. Transponder and IFF. HF and INMARSAT-C. AlliedSignal Bendix/King KFC 275 autopilot and KAS 297C vertical speed/altitude preselector.

Aircraft variants:
TBM 700, as detailed. For aerial photography, it can have a vertically-mounted Leica/Wild or Zeiss camera in the cabin and vertical viewfinder; for freight carrying the floor is reinforced with bonded metal doublers, and tie-down points are available in the 63.57 cu ft (1.8 m^3) volume cabin; hard point for an Alkan 6170 B pylon is available under the fuselage for target towing equipment or an ECM unit; a gyrostabilized underfuselage turret can be carried housing an infra-red camera and a video camera for patrol and law enforcement, with an operator's station in the cabin; AlliedSignal RDR 1500 B radar and other equipment (including rescue) for coast watch; etc.
TBM 700 'Large Door' increases possibilities of usage within the multi-mission role, while a pilot door is a proposed option to further add to the versatility of use. Allows a maximum freight volume of 123.6 cu ft (3.5 m^3). Door sizes 3 ft 11 ins × 3 ft 6.5 ins (1.19 × 1.08 m). Optional pilot door 3 ft 4 ins × 2 ft 7 ins (1.02 m × 0.78 m). MTOW 6,578 lb (2,984 kg). Maximum payload 1,764 lb (800 kg). Conversion to passenger configuration available for cross-country flying, with quick change capability. Metal reinforced floor and tie-down points in floor rails customized according to type of freight.
TBM 700S was a proposed stretched version for 2 additional passengers or a 3,417 lb (1,550 kg) useful load. Programme ended.

Socata TB360 Tangara

First flight: 24 February 1997.
Certification: FAR Pt 23 Amendment 14, for VFR and IFR.
First delivery: 1998.

↑ Socata TB360 Tangara

Details for Tangara

PRINCIPAL DIMENSIONS:
Wing span: 36 ft 10 ins (11.23 m)
Maximum length: 29 ft 10 ins (9.09 m)
Maximum height: 10 ft 4.5 ins (3.16 m)

CABIN:
Length: 9 ft 6.25 ins (2.9 m)
Width: 3 ft 9 ins (1.14 m)
Height: 4 ft 1.25 ins (1.25 m) maximum

WINGS:
Aerofoil section: NACA 63A-415 mod
Area: 183.96 sq ft (17.09 m^2)
Aspect ratio: 7.38
Dihedral: 5°

UNDERCARRIAGE:
Type: Retractable, with steerable nosewheel
Wheel base: 6 ft 8 ins (2.03 m)
Wheel track: 10 ft 10 ins (3.3 m)

WEIGHTS:
Empty: 2,588 lb (1,174 kg), average
Maximum take-off and landing: 3,800 lb (1,725 kg)
Useful load: 1,212 lb (550 kg), maximum

PERFORMANCE:
Maximum cruise speed: 174 kts (200 mph) 322 km/h at sea level
Cruise speed at 75% power: 165 kts (190 mph) 306 km/h at 8,500 ft (2,590 m)
Cruise speed at 45% power: 120 kts (138 mph) 222 km/h at 8,500 ft (2,590 m)
Take-off distance over a 50 ft (15 m) obstacle: 1,670 ft (509 m)
Landing distance over a 50 ft (15 m) obstacle: 1,330 ft (405 m)
Maximum climb rate: 1,400 ft (427 m) per minute, at sea level
Climb rate, OEI: 310 ft (94 m) per minute
Ceiling: 20,000 ft (6,100 m), certified
Ceiling, OEI: 5,500 ft (1,675 m), certified
Range at 75% power: 800 naut miles (921 miles) 1,480 km, at 8,500 ft (2,590 m), full fuel
Range at 45% power: 1,140 naut miles (1,312 miles) 2,110 km, at 8,500 ft (2,590 m), full fuel

Role: Advanced training, multi-engine type rating, IFR training, pleasure, surveillance, and high-speed long-distance liaison flights. For use in Normal category. Based on the US Gulfstream American GA-7 Cougar, for which Socata received the rights in 1995.
Crew/passengers: 4 persons. Dual controls.
Baggage capacity: Maximum capacity in compartments 250 lb (113 kg).
Wing control surfaces: Ailerons with trim tabs and Fowler flaps.
Tail control surfaces: Horn-balanced rudder and elevators, with trim tabs.
Flight control system: Push-pull rods and cables, except for electrically actuated flaps.
Construction materials: Metal, semi-monocoque.
Engines: 2 Textron Lycoming O-360-A1G6 piston engines, with 6 ft 1 ins (1.85 m) Hartzell 2-blade, constant-speed propellers with feathering.
Engine rating: Each 180 hp (134 kW).
Fuel system: 447 litres, with 431.5 litres usable. One structural fuel tank per wing and a feeder tank, 2 engine-driven fuel pumps and 2 electric auxiliary fuel pumps.
Electrical system: 2 × 28 volt, 70 amp alternators. 24 volt, 36 amp-hour battery.
Hydraulic system: For undercarriage and brakes.
Flight avionics/instrumentation: AlliedSignal Bendix/King avionics.

Socata MS series

Comments: On 3 March 1998 a 200 hp (149 kW) Morane Renault engine mounted on a Socata TB20 Trinidad flew for the first time at Tarbes Ossun, France, the flight lasting 50 minutes. The engine has been developed by Société de Motorisations Aéronautiques (SMA), a subsidiary of Socata and Renault Sport. 3 differently-rated SMA engines are to be fitted to a new range of Socata aircraft, namely the engines MR 180, MR 250 and MR 300 (see Engine section), the MR 250 having been introduced to the public at the 1997 Paris Air Show. However, the Trinidad will continue to flight test the MS engine, and appearance of actual Morane and Epsilon Mk2 aircraft with MR engines will not take place until the year 2000. The following aircraft types are to be available from the year 2000:

Socata MS 180 Morane and MS 250 Morane

First flight: Year 2000.
Certification: To be certified to FAR Pt 23 Amendments 1 to 16.
Role: 4/5-seat light aircraft with dual yoke controls, for basic training, VFR and IFR training, cross-country flights and liaison. MS 250 also suited to surveillance and long-distance fast liaisons.
Baggage capacity: 143 lb (65 kg).
Flight control system: Push-pull rods, manual elevator trim actuated by cables, and electrically-actuated flaps. MS 250 also has manual rudder trim.
Construction materials: Metal.
Engine: 180 hp (134 kW) SMA MR 180 turbocharged piston engine in MS 180, driving a 6 ft 2 ins (1.88 m) diameter Hartzell 3-blade constant-speed propeller. 250 hp (186.4 kW) MR 250 engine in MS 250, driving a 6 ft 8 ins (2.03 m) Hartzell 3-blade constant-speed propeller. Computer-aided engine controls.
Fuel system: 210 litres (204 usable) in 2 wing tanks for MS 180, and 336 litres (326 usable) for MS 250.

↑ Socata MS 180 and MS 250 Moranes, to first fly in the year 2000

Electrical system: Electrical system of 28 volt, 80 amp alternator with regulator and 24 volt, 15 amp-hour battery. MS 250 has 24 volt, 20 amp-hour battery.

Aircraft variants:
MS 180 Morane has a 180 hp (134 kW) engine and fixed undercarriage.
MS 250 Morane has a 250 hp (186.4 kW) engine and retractable undercarriage.

Details for MS 180 Morane, *with MS 250 Morane in italics*

PRINCIPAL DIMENSIONS:
Wing span: 32 ft 0.5 ins (9.77 m), *the same*
Maximum length: 25 ft 3 ins (7.7 m), *25 ft 3.5 ins (7.71 m)*
Maximum height: 9 ft 11 ins (3.02 m), *9 ft 3.5 ins (2.85 m)*

CABIN:
Length: 8 ft 3.5 ins (2.53 m), *the same*
Width: 4 ft 2.5 ins (1.28 m), *the same*
Height: 3 ft 8 ins (1.12 m), *the same*

WINGS:
Area: 128.09 sq ft (11.9 m^2), *the same*
Aspect ratio: 8.02, *the same*

UNDERCARRIAGE:
Type: Fixed, with steerable nosewheel (main gear of trailing link type), *retractable, with steerable nosewheel (main gear of trailing link type)*
Wheel base: 6 ft 5 ins (1.96 m), *6 ft 3 ins (1.91 m)*

WEIGHTS:
Empty: 1,543 lb (700 kg), *1,764 lb (800 kg)*, both average
Maximum take-off and landing: 2,535 lb (1,150 kg), *3,086 lb (1,400 kg)*
Useful load: 992 lb (450 kg), *1,323 lb (600 kg)*

PERFORMANCE:
Maximum cruise speed: 134 kts (154 mph) 248 km/h at 10,000 ft (3,050 m), *189 kts (218 mph) 350 km/h at 15,000 ft (4,575 m)*
Take-off distance over a 50 ft (15 m) obstacle: 1,657 ft (505 m), *2,150 ft (655 m)*
Landing distance over a 50 ft (15 m) obstacle: 1,509 ft (460 m), *1,750 ft (533 m)*
Climb to 8,500 ft (2,590 m): 14 minutes 50 seconds
Climb to 8,000 ft (2,440 m): *7 minutes 10 seconds*
Climb to 12,000 ft (3,660 m): 23 minutes 30 seconds, *10 minutes 50 seconds*
Ceiling: 17,000 ft (5,180 m), *23,000 ft (7,010 m)*, service
Range: 996 naut miles (1,147 miles) 1,845 km, *1,433 naut miles (1,650 miles) 2,655 km*
Duration: 7 hours at 15,000 ft (4,570 m), *8 hours 10 minutes at 20,000 ft (6,100 m)*, both maximum speed

↑ Socata TB20 Trinidad first flown on 3 March 1998 with a 200 hp (149 kW) Morane Renault engine, as the engine development testbed for the new Socata Morane lightplane

Socata MS 300 Epsilon Mk2

First flight: Year 2000.
Role: Basic and primary military training, including full aerobatic capability, plus screening.
Crew: Tandem 2-seater, with dual controls. Detonating microchord canopy jettisoning.
Flight control system: Push-pull rods, manual trims actuated by cables, and electrically actuated flaps.
Construction materials: Metal.
Engine: SMA MR 300 turbocharged piston engine, driving a 6 ft 6 ins (1.98 m) diameter Hartzell 3-blade constant-speed propeller. Computer-aided engine controls. 2 minutes inverted flight duration.
Engine rating: 300 hp (224 kW).
Fuel system: 210 litres of Jet A1 fuel in 2 structural tanks in the wing leading edges. Feed tank to supply engine during inverted flight. Inverted flight duration 2 minutes. Engine-driven injection pump. Electric auxiliary fuel pump.
Electrical system: Distribution via bus bars. 28 volt, 80 amp alternator. 24 volt, 20 amp-hour ni-cd battery.

Details for MS 300 Epsilon Mk2

PRINCIPAL DIMENSIONS:
Wing span: 26 ft (7.92 m)
Maximum length: 24 ft 11 ins (7.59 m)
Maximum height: 8 ft 7.5 ins (2.63 m)

UNDERCARRIAGE:
Type: Electrohydraulically actuated retractable nosewheel type, with trailing-link main gear

WEIGHTS:
Empty, equipped: 2,046 lb (928 kg) average
Maximum take-off and landing: 2,866 lb (1,300 kg)

PERFORMANCE:
Never-exceed speed (V_{NE}): 281 kts (323 mph) 520 km/h
Maximum cruise speed: 206 kts (237 mph) 381 km/h at sea level, ISA, or 223 kts (257 mph) 413 km/h at 10,000 ft (3,050 m)
Maximum flap extended speed: 130 kts (149 mph) 240 km/h
Maximum undercarriage extended speed: 130 kts (149 mph) 240 km/h
Stalling speed: 63 kts (73 mph) 116 km/h, CAS, landing configuration
Take-off distance over a 50 ft (15 m) obstacle: 2,100 ft (640 m)
Landing distance over a 50 ft (15 m) obstacle: 2,264 ft (690 m)
Climb to 10,000 ft (3,050 m): 5 minutes 20 seconds
Climb rate: 1,860 ft (567 m) per minute at 10,000 ft (3,050 m), 1,445 ft (440 m) per minute at 15,000 ft (4,575 m)
G limits: +6.7, -3.35
Sustained load factor: 2.5 at 10,000 ft (3,050 m); 2.2 at 15,000 ft (4,575 m)
Range: 830 naut miles (955 miles) 1,538 km at 15,000 ft (4,575 m) and 222 kts

↑ Socata MS 300 Epsilon Mk2 military trainer

Extra Flugzeugbau GmbH

Germany

Corporate address:
Flugplatz Dinslaken Schwarze Heide 21, 46569 Hünxe.

Telephone: +49 2858 91370
Facsimile: +49 2858 913730

Employees:
60.

Information:
Wolfgang Lukas.

ACTIVITIES

- In 1994 the 100th Extra aerobatic monoplane was delivered to a customer.
- In 1995 a new manufacturing facility was completed, raising factory floor area from the initial 2,153 sq ft (200 m^2) to 48,437 sq ft (4,500 m^2).

Extra 200

First flight: 2 April 1996.
Certification: Same standards as Extra 300.
Role: Reduced cost 2-seat aerobatic competition and aerobatic training aircraft.
Engine: Textron Lycoming AEIO-360-A1E piston engine, with an MT 2-blade constant-speed propeller (3-blade optional).
Engine rating: 200 hp (149 kW).
Fuel system: 116 litres standard (114 usable), and 154 litres long-range tank (151 usable).

Details for Extra 200

PRINCIPAL DIMENSIONS:
Wing span: 24 ft 7 ins (7.5 m)
Maximum length: 22 ft 4 ins (6.81 m)
Maximum height: 8 ft 5 ins (2.57 m)

WINGS:
Area: 111.9 sq ft (10.4 m^2)
Aspect ratio: 5.41

UNDERCARRIAGE:
Type: Fixed, with steerable tailwheel. Mainwheel fairings

WEIGHTS:
Empty: 1,199 lb (544 kg)
Maximum take-off: 1,914 lb (868 kg) Normal category, 1,848 lb (838 kg) 2 crew Aerobatic, and 1,340 lb (608 kg) pilot only Aerobatic

PERFORMANCE:
Never-exceed speed (V_{NE}): 220 kts (253 mph) 407 km/h
Cruise speed: 150 kts (173 mph) 278 km/h, at 75% power
Manoeuvre speed: 158 kts (182 mph) 292 km/h
Stall speed: 52 kts (60 mph) 97 km/h at 1,540 lb (698 kg), or 56 kts (65 mph) 104 km/h at Normal category MTOW
Maximum climb rate: 2,250 ft (685 m) per minute at 1,540 lb (698 kg), or 1,600 ft (488 m) per minute at Normal category MTOW
Ceiling: 15,000 ft (4,575 m), service
G limits: ±10 with pilot only
Range: 450 naut miles (518 miles) 834 km at 150 kts and 8,000 ft (2,440 m), 45 minutes reserve
Range with long-range tanks: 600 naut miles (691 miles) 1,112 km at 150 kts and 8,000 ft (2,440 m), 45 minutes reserve

↑ Extra 200 lower-cost 2-seat aerobatic competition and aerobatic training aircraft

Extra 300 series

First flight: 6 May 1988.
Certification: 16 May 1990.
Role: Pilot only (Extra 300 S) or tandem 2-seat unlimited aerobatic competition monoplane, with 2-seaters suited also to training and cross-country flying.
Details: Principally for the Extra 300, except where indicated and in data box.
Wing control surfaces: Ailerons.
Tail control surfaces: Elevators (starboard trim tab) and horn-balanced rudder.
Flight control system: Push-pull rods and cables.
Construction materials: Composites wings and tail unit. Steel tube fuselage structure, with aluminium and fabric skins.
Engine: Textron Lycoming AEIO-540-L1B5 piston engine, with an MTV-9-B-C/C200-15 3-blade constant-speed propeller.
Engine rating: 300 hp (224 kW).
Fuel system: 158 litres usable for Extra 300. Standard fuel for Extra 300L is 171 litres (169 litres usable), with 208 litres in long-range tank (206 usable).
Electrical system: 12 volt generator. Battery.

↑ Rear pilot's cockpit on an Extra 300L

↑ Extra 300L

Details for Extra 300, *with Extra 300L in italics*

PRINCIPAL DIMENSIONS:
Wing span: 26 ft 3 ins (8 m), *25 ft 3 ins (7.7 m)*
Maximum length: 23 ft 4.5 ins (7.12 m), *22 ft 10 ins (6.96 m)*
Maximum height: 8 ft 7 ins (2.62 m), *the same*

WINGS:
Aerofoil section: MA-15/MA-12 (root/tip)
Area: 115.17 sq ft (10.7 m^2), *the same*
Aspect ratio 5.981, *5.541*

UNDERCARRIAGE:
Type: Fixed, with steerable tailwheel. Mainwheel fairings

WEIGHTS:
Empty: 1,470 lb (666 kg), *1,440 lb (653 kg) standard*
Maximum take-off and landing: 2,094 lb (950 kg) Normal category, *the same*, or 1,918 lb (870 kg) Aerobatic

PERFORMANCE:
Never-exceed speed (V_{NE}): 220 kts (253 mph) 407 km/h, *the same*
Maximum speed: 185 kts (213 mph) 343 km/h
Maximum cruise speed: 178 kts (205 mph) 330 km/h
Cruise speed at 45% power: 170 kts (196 mph) 315 km/h, *the same*, at 8,000 ft (2,440 m)
Maximum manoeuvre speed: 158 kts (182 mph) 292 km/h, *the same*
Stall speed: 55 kts (63.5 mph) 102 km/h at 1,800 lb (816 kg), 60 kts (69 mph) 111 km/h at MTOW, *the same*
Maximum climb rate: 3,200 ft (975 m) per minute, *the same*
Roll rate: 340° per second, *400° per second*
Ceiling: 16,000 ft (4,875 m), *the same*
G limits: ±8 with 2 crew at 1,918 lb (870 kg) MTOW, or ±10 with pilot only at 1,810 lb (821 kg) MTOW, or +6, -3 Normal category, *the same*
Range: 415 naut miles (478 miles) 768 km at 45% power, with 45 minutes reserve, *the same*, standard tanks
Range with long-range tanks: 510 naut miles (587 miles) 945 km at 45% power, with 45 minutes reserve, *the same*
Duration: 2 hours 30 minutes

Aircraft variants:
Extra 300 2 -seater, as detailed.
Extra 300L is a low-wing monoplane (instead of mid-wing), although wing area remains similar. Deeper ailerons. Fuselage shortened by some 10-12 ins (25-30 cm). Many other small changes, including carbon seats, electric rear-seat adjustment, etc. Roll rate increased. Increased fuel.
Extra 300 S is a single-seat variant of the Extra 300, with 24 ft 7 ins (7.5 m) wing span and new ailerons, wing area 112.38 sq ft (10.44 m^2), length 21 ft 10 ins (6.65 m), standard empty weight 1,343 lb (609 kg), MTOW 2,094 lb (950 kg), aerobatic weight 1,810 lb (821 kg), 160 litres of fuel, V_{NE} 220 kts (253 mph) 407 km/h, and maximum cruise speed 185 kts (213 mph) 343 km/h. Roll rate 380° per second.

Extra 330

Comments: Slightly modified version of the Extra 300, powered by a Textron Lycoming AEIO-580 engine.

Extra 400

Comments: In 1998 the Extra 400 was still undergoing improvement. The data provided was received in April 1998 and was the most up-to-date then available.
First flight: 4 April 1996.
Certification: 23 April 1997 (LBA to FAR Pt 23). Certified for pressurized IFR flights, and flights into known icing conditions.
Role: Pressurized touring high-wing monoplane.
Sales: DM 1.3 million plus 15% VAT (US$764,700 approximately) at time of writing.
Crew/passengers: 6 seats in pressurized cabin, with leather interior and air conditioning.
Pressurization: 5.5 psi differential.
Wing control surfaces: Ailerons and Fowler flaps. Tested with both upturned and downturned wingtips.
Tail control surfaces: T-tail with rudder and horn-balanced elevators.
Flight control system: Mechanical flaps.
Construction materials: Composites structure of carbonfibre, with lightning protection.
Engine: Teledyne Continental TSIOL-550-A engine, with a 6 ft 3 ins (1.9 m) diameter Mühlbauer MTV-14-D/190-17 3- or 4-blade constant-speed propeller.
Engine rating: 350 hp (261 kW).
Fuel system: 2 wing tanks, with total of about 680 litres.
Electrical system: 2 alternators (1 × 100 amp and 1 × 85 amp), plus 24 volt, 17 amp-hour battery.
De-icing system: Pneumatic rubber (Teflon) boots in wing and stabilizer, electrically heated propeller, pitot tubes and lift detector. Hot air windshield defroster or electrically heated windshield. Wing ice detection light.
Flight avionics/instrumentation: Complete pilot/co-pilot instrumentation standard, with stormscope WX1000 plus central display system and CDS. AlliedSignal Bendix/King Silver Crown avionics with KMA 24 audio panel and marker receiver, 2 KX 155-43 (KX 165) com/nav, KN 63 DME, KR 87 ADF, 2 KT 71 or KT 76A (Mode S in USA) transponders, KLN 90B GPS, KEA 130A encoding altimeter, ED 461 EHSI EFIS, ED 462 EADI EFIS, KAS 297-B altitude/vertical speed select, PM 1000 intercom, and S-TEC 55 autopilot.

↑ Extra 400 with 4-blade propeller

Details for Extra 400

PRINCIPAL DIMENSIONS:
Wing span: 34 ft 5.5 ins (11.5 m)
Maximum length: 30 ft 10 ins (9.39 m)
Maximum height: 10 ft 2 ins (3.09 m)

CABIN:
Length: 13 ft 6 ins (4.125 m), front to rear bulkhead
Width: 4 ft 7 ins (1.39 m)
Height: 4 ft 1 ins (1.24 m)
Passenger door: 2 ft 3 ins (0.68 m) width, 3 ft 9.25 ins (1.15 m) height

WINGS:
Wing area: 153.43 sq ft (14.254 m^2)
Aspect ratio: 9.28

UNDERCARRIAGE:
Type: Retractable nosewheel type, hydraulically retracted while the strut and the lower main strut of the main gear are shortened
Wheel track: 8 ft 5 ins (2.56 m)

WEIGHTS:
Empty, operating: 2,659 lb (1,206 kg)
Maximum take-off and landing: 4,300 lb (1,950 kg)
Mid-cruise: 3,858 lb (1,750 kg)
Payload: 1,217 lb (552 kg)

PERFORMANCE:
Maximum speed: 259 kts (298 mph) 480 km/h, at 20,000 ft (6,100 m), mid-cruise weight
Maximum cruise speed: 243 kts (280 mph) 450 km/h at 25,000 ft (7,620 m), 75% power, mid-cruise weight
Economic cruise speed: 229 kts (264 mph) 424 km/h at 25,000 ft (7,620 m), 65% power, mid-cruise weight
Stall speed: 60 kts (69 mph) 111 km/h *with full flaps*
Maximum operating altitude: 25,000 ft (7,620 m)
Range: 918 naut miles (1,057 miles) 1,700 km with 6 persons, or 1,404 naut miles (1,616 miles) 2,600 km with 5 persons, both 80% power at climb, maximum operating altitude at approximately 65% and 45 minutes hold at 55% power

Flight Design GmbH — Germany

Corporate address:
Sielmingerstrasse 65, D-70771 L.-Echterdingen.
Telephone: +49 711 90287 0
Facsimile: +49 711 90287 99
Web site: http//www.flightdesign.com
Information:
Matthias Betsch.

ACTIVITIES

▪ Flight Design produces rigid-wing hang gliders and paragliders. Its subsidiary manufacturing plant in the Ukraine, known as Ost-West-Consulting, produces components for Flight Design's new CT composites lightplane, produced in association with Albert Schulze-Oechterding from ASO Flugsport.

Flight Design CT

First flight: 1996.
Certification: June 1997 under German ultralight regulations.
Role: Light/ultralight monoplane.
Sales: Approximately 35 sold by May 1998. Initial 4 aircraft built per month, using assemblies produced by Ost-West-Consulting in the Ukraine, expected to rise to 20 per month by the end of 1998. Price in May 1998 DM 85,200 without tax.

↑ Flight Design CT 2-seat composites monoplane

Crew/passenger: 2 crew, side by side, with adjustable seats (leg length and back angle). 4-point security belts. Large cabin doors.
Baggage capacity: 2 baggage lockers, with outside access. 2 storage areas in cabin.
Wing control surfaces: Cantilever, high-mounted wing with mass balanced ailerons and plain flaps (-8° to +30°).
Tail control surfaces: Mass balanced slab tailplane (span 7 ft 10 ins, 2.38 m) with trim tab. Fin with rudder and manual pendulum rudder trim. Ventral fin.
Flight control system: Manual.
Construction materials: Carbonfibre and carbon/aramid sandwich, with glassfibre around the cockpit area to protect the crew.
Engine: Rotax 912 UL2 piston engine, with 5 ft 8 ins (1.73 m) Neuform 2-blade adjustable-pitch propeller.
Engine rating: 80 hp (59.7 kW).
Fuel system: 100 litres in 2 wing tanks.
Braking system: Single hydraulic mainwheel brakes.
Flight avionics/instrumentation: Instrumentation comprises speedometer, altimeter, magnetic compass with deviation table, RPM meter, oil pressure gauge, oil temperature gauge, CHT gauge, and emergency rescue system (only in German basic version).

Details for CT

PRINCIPAL DIMENSIONS:
Wing span: 30 ft 6.5 ins (9.31 m)
Maximum length: 20 ft 4.75 ins (6.214 m)
Maximum height: 7 ft 1.25 ins (2.165 m)

CABIN:
Width: 4 ft 1 ins (1.24 m)

WINGS:
Area: 116.25 sq ft (10.8 m^2)
Aspect ratio: 8
Dihedral: 1° 30'

UNDERCARRIAGE:
Type: Fixed nosewheel type with large wheels, with castoring nosewheel. All forward-canted legs of steel tubing. Optional wheel fairings
Wheel base: 5 ft 1.5 ins (1.56 m)

WEIGHTS:
Empty: 628 lb (285 kg)
Maximum take-off: 992-1,190 lb (450-540 kg) according to differing certification rules
Minimum payload: 132 lb (60 kg) pilot on 1 seat

PERFORMANCE (ISA, with wheel fairings)**:**
Never-exceed speed (V_{NE}): 145 kts (167 mph) 270 km/h
Maximum speed: 130 kts (149 mph) 240 km/h
Cruise speed at 75% power: 121 kts (140 mph) 225 km/h
Cruise speed at 55% power: 103 kts (118 mph) 190 km/h
Take-off speed: 40.5 kts (47 mph) 75 km/h with 15° flaps
Manoeuvre speed: 80 kts (92 mph) 148 km/h
Maximum speed with flaps: 65 kts (74 mph) 120 km/h
Stall speed: 42 kts (49 mph) 78 km/h *clean*, 35 kts (41 mph) 65 km/h *with 26° flaps*, 46 kts (53 mph) 85 km/h *with -8° flaps*
Take-off distance: 296 ft (90 m)
Take-off distance over a 50 ft (15 m) obstacle: 525 ft (160 m)
Maximum climb rate: 748 ft (228 m) per minute at 5,030 rpm and 78 kts
G limits: 8.8 at 992 lb (450 kg), 7.3 at 1,190 lb (540 kg), ultimate
Range: 809 naut miles (932 miles) 1,500 km, with 30 minutes reserve

Burkhart Grob Luft-und Raumfahrt GmbH & Co KG — Germany

Corporate address:
See Reconnaissance section for company details

Grob G 115 series

First flight: November 1985.
Certification: 22 March 1987, to FAR Pt 23 for day and night IFR operations.
Role: Lightplanes, trainers and aerobatic (not G 115C or C/2 IFR) aircraft, with training suited to civil flying schools, commercial flying colleges and military pilot screening/training establishments.
Details: G 115TA except under Aircraft variants.
Crew/passengers: 2 seats, side by side. Control sticks.
Wing control surfaces: Ailerons and flaps.
Tail control surfaces: Balanced elevators (port trim tab) and rudder.
Flight control system: Manual, except for electric flaps.
Construction materials: Composites.
Engine: Textron Lycoming AEIO-540-D4D5 piston engine, with a 3-blade Hartzell constant-speed propeller.
Engine rating: 260 hp (194 kW).
Fuel system: 190 litres usable.
Flight avionics/instrumentation: Customer choice. Can be IFR equipped.

↑ Grob G 115C (*nearest*), G 115D (*centre*) and G 115TA

Aircraft variants:
G115C is the utility version, not intended for aerobatic training. 160 hp (119 kW) Textron Lycoming O-320-D1A with a Sensenich 2-blade fixed-pitch propeller. Fixed nosewheel undercarriage. Control wheels, with sticks optional. MTOW 2,182 lb (990 kg), maximum speed 125 kts (144 mph) 231 km/h and range 556 naut miles (640 miles) 1,030 km at 45% power, 5,000 ft (1,525 m) and 45 minutes reserve. Climb rate 1,020 ft (310 m) per minute. Wing span 32 ft 10 in (10 m), length 24 ft 8.5 ins (7.53 m), height 7 ft 11 ins (2.4 m) and 143 litres of fuel. Airframe limits +4.4, –1.76 g. Time between major inspections of airframe 12,000 flying hours.
G 115C/1-Acro is a version of G 115C but suited to aerobatics. MTOW 2,182 lb (990 kg) utility and 2,028 lb (920 kg) aerobatic. Same maximum speed, climb rate, range, dimensions, fuel and engine/propeller. Airframe limits +6, –3 g.
G 115C/2 IFR has IFR instruments as standard and a 180 hp (134 kW) Textron Lycoming O-360-A1F6 engine with a 2-blade constant-speed propeller. Not intended for aerobatic training. Same utility weights as G 115C. Maximum speed 133 kts (153 mph) 246 km/h, climb rate 1,100 ft (335 m) per minute, range 560 naut miles (644 miles) 1,037 km at 45% power, 5,000 ft (1,525 m) and 45 minutes reserve. Same dimensions, fuel and g limits as G 115C. Fixed nosewheel undercarriage.
G 115D is an aerobatic and utility version. Fuel injected 180 hp (134 kW) Textron Lycoming AEIO-360-B1F engine with a Hoffmann 3-blade constant-speed propeller and inverted fuel/oil systems. Fixed nosewheel undercarriage. Control sticks. Same dimensions and fuel as G 115C, and same weights and g limits as G 115C/1-Acro. Maximum speed 132 kts (152 mph) 244 km/h, climb rate 1,020 ft (310 m) per minute, and range 410 naut miles (472 miles) 760 km. Time between major inspections of airframe reduced to 4,000 hours for aerobatic versions.
G 115D/2 is similar to G 115D but with a fuel injected 160 hp (119 kW) AEIO-320-D1B engine and 2-blade fixed-pitch propeller. Same dimensions, weights, fuel, maximum speed and g limits. Climb rate 1,000 ft (305 m) per minute and range 540 naut miles (621 miles) 1,000 km. Longest take-off distance of any G 115 version, at 1,050 ft (320 m) or 1,800 ft (548 m) over a 50 ft (15 m) obstacle.
G 115TA is an aerobatic and utility version, designed to meet the special requirements of commercial flying schools or military training establishments. Fully IFR equipped, and with retractable undercarriage and constant-speed propeller. Has been tested to limits exceeding ±12g and is certified to +6, –4 g. Time between major inspections of 15,000 hours for airframe. First delivered to UAE in 1996 (with air conditioning for desert conditions), which ordered 12 plus 12 options for a ground-attack training role.

Details for Grob G 115TA

PRINCIPAL DIMENSIONS:
Wing span: 33 ft 5 ins (10.188 m)
Maximum length: 26 ft 5.5 ins (8.065 m)
Maximum height: 8 ft 5 ins (2.57 m)

WINGS:
Aerofoil section: Eppler 696
Area: 141 sq ft (13.1 m^2)
Aspect ratio: 7.92

UNDERCARRIAGE:
Type: Retractable, with steerable nosewheel

WEIGHTS:
Empty: 1,874-1,962 lb (850-890 kg)
Maximum take-off: 2,976 lb (1,350 kg) aerobatic, 3,175 lb (1,440 kg) utility
Useful load: 805 lb (365 kg) aerobatic, 1,003 lb (455 kg) utility

PERFORMANCE:
Maximum speed: 173 kts (199 mph) 320 km/h
Cruise speed: 171 kts (197 mph) 317 km/h, 70% power at 8,000 ft (2,440 m), ISA
Stall speed: 53 kts (61 mph) 98 km/h aerobatic, 55 kts (64 mph) 103 km/h utility
Take-off and landing distance: 1,100 ft (336 m), sea level, ISA
Take-off and landing distance over a 50 ft (15 m) obstacle: 2,000 ft (610 m)
Maximum climb rate: 1,500 ft (457 m) per minute aerobatic, 1,200 ft (366 m) per minute utility, sea level, ISA
G limits: +6, –4 aerobatic, +4.4, –1.76 utility
Range: 707 naut miles (814 miles) 1,310 km at 45% power and 5,000 ft (1,525 m), ISA, 45 minutes reserve

Grob GF 200, GF 250, GF 300 and GF 350

Details: For GF 200, except under Aircraft variants.
First flight: 26 November 1991.
Certification: Complies to FAR Pt 23.
Role: Pressurized lightplane.
Sales: Over 300 interested buyers at time of writing.
Crew/passengers: Pilot plus 3 or 4 passengers.
Baggage capacity: 110 lb (50 kg).
Wing characteristics: Multi-curvature leading edge and straight trailing edge, with upturned wingtips.
Wing control surfaces: Fowler flaps.
Tail control surfaces: T-tail, with variable incidence tailplane and elevators. Dorsal and ventral fins, with a ventral rudder only in production form.
Construction materials: Composites.
Engine: Teledyne Continental Voyager TSIOL-550, with Bauer-MT V-9-D/CLD190-B009 3-blade constant-speed propeller.
Engine rating: 310 hp (231 kW).
Fuel system: 350 litres.
Electrical system: 28 volt, 70 amp.

Aircraft variants:
GF 200 is the initial production version, as detailed.
GF 250 is an intended 6-seat version of GF 200, with a 350 hp (261 kW) piston engine.
GF 300 is an intended 6-seat turboshaft version, with a 420 shp (313 kW) Allison engine. Pressurization and a de-icing system. Cruise speed 243 kts (280 mph) 450 km/h.
GF 350 is an intended 6/8-seat version, with twin Allison turboshafts and a cruise speed of 302 kts (348 mph) 560 km/h.

Details for Grob GF 200

PRINCIPAL DIMENSIONS:
Wing span: 36 ft 1 ins (11 m)
Maximum length: 28 ft 6.5 ins (8.7 m)
Maximum height: 11 ft 3 ins (3.42 m)

WINGS:
Area: 134.55 sq ft (12.5 m²)
Aspect ratio: 9.68

UNDERCARRIAGE:
Type: Retractable, with nosewheel

WEIGHTS:
Maximum take-off: 3,748 lb (1,700 kg)
Maximum useful load: 1,323 lb (600 kg)

PERFORMANCE:
Maximum cruise speed: 235 kts (270 mph) 435 km/h at 20,000 ft (6,100 m)
Cruise speed, 75% power: 200 kts (230 mph) 370 km/h at 22,000 ft (6,700 m)
Stall speed: 54 kts (61 mph) 98 km/h
Take-off distance: 1,188 ft (362 m)
Take-off distance over a 50 ft (15 m) obstacle: 2,363 ft (720 m)
Landing distance: 984 ft (300 m)
Landing distance over a 50 ft (15 m) obstacle: 2,300 ft (700 m)
Maximum climb rate: 1,221 ft (366 m) per minute
G limits: +3.8, –1.52
Range at 45% power: 1,272 naut miles (1,464 miles) 2,356 km at 13,000 ft (3,960 m), or 1,244 naut miles (1,431 miles) 2,304 km at 22,000 ft (6,700 m), both with 45 minutes reserve

→ Grob GF 200 proof-of-concept aircraft

HK Aircraft Technology AG I.G. — Germany

Corporate address:
Bahnhofstrasse 5, D-86928 Greifenberg.
Telephone: +49 8192 7858 or 7572 712013/5 (Mengen)
Facsimile: +49 8192 7858 or 7572 712014 (Mengen)

ACTIVITIES

▪ Wega project is promoted by the Bavarian Ministry of Economics, Transport and Technology, and the European Union. Reportedly derived from the US Skystar Pulsar kit-built aircraft.

HK Aircraft Wega

Certification: JAR-VLA.
First flight: 9 April 1998.
First delivery: 1998.
Role: 2-seat very light sport aircraft. Seats reclined at 35°. Central control stick.
Sales: Expected price DM 150,000 (May 1998) with standard instruments.
Wing control surfaces: Ailerons and flaps.
Tail control surfaces: Tailplane of 8 ft (2.44 m) span, with horn-balanced elevators. Rudder on sweptback tailfin.
Flight control system: Mechanical.
Construction materials: Composites sandwich, except for reinforced areas with embedded fibre compound-sheets of aluminium.
Engine: Rotax 914 Turbo piston engine, with Mühlbauer 3-blade propeller.
Engine rating: 114 hp (85 kW).
Fuel system: 2 × 52 litre tanks.
Flight avionics/instrumentation: Engine information instrumentation, warning systems, and com and transponder.

Details for Wega

PRINCIPAL DIMENSIONS:
Wing span: 25 ft (7.62 m)
Maximum length: 20 ft 4 ins (6.2 m)
Maximum height: 6 ft 7 ins (2 m)

CABIN:
Length: 4 ft 3 ins (1.29 m)
Width: 3 ft 6 ins (1.06 m) at elbow height
Height: 3 ft 7 ins (1.10 m)

WINGS:
Chord at tip: 2 ft 1.5 ins (0.65 m)

UNDERCARRIAGE:
Type: Fixed nosewheel type, with wheel fairings. Cleveland hydraulic brakes
Wheel base: 4 ft 7 ins (1.4 m)

WEIGHTS:
Empty: 705 lb (320 kg)
Maximum take-off: 1,411 lb (640 kg)

PERFORMANCE:
Never-exceed speed (V_{NE}): 180 kts (207 mph) 333 km/h
Cruise speed: 170 kts (196 mph) 315 km/h
Speed at best rate of climb: 65 kts (75 mph) 120 km/h
Speed for best angle of climb (V_X): 62 kts (71 mph) 115 km/h
Stall speed: 45 kts (52 mph) 84 km/h, *with 35° flaps*
Take-off distance over a 50 ft (15 m) obstacle: 1,149 ft (350 m)
Landing distance over a 50 ft (15 m) obstacle: 1,247 ft (380 m)
Maximum climb rate: 2,500 ft (762 m) per minute at sea level
G limits: +3.8, -2
Ceiling: 20,000 ft (6,100 m), service
Range: 809 naut miles (932 miles) 1,500 km

↑ HK Aircraft Technology Wega after its first flight in April 1998
(courtesy HK Aircraft Technology)

Ikarusflug Gbr Leichtflugzeugbau — Germany

Corporate address:
Mennwangerstrasse 3, D-88682 Salem.
Telephone: +49 75 53 17 70
Facsimile: +49 75 53 6 05 38

ACTIVITIES

▪ In addition to the Eurofox detailed below, Ikarusflug is the German agent for the Czech EV-97 Eurostar. Eurofox is believed to have been based on the US Skystar Kitfox, with changes introduced by Evektor in the Czech Republic (see Aerotechnik) including a new wing section, longer fuselage, undercarriage changes, new wing control surface and roomier cabin. A Czech marketed version is known as the Aerotechnik Aeropro/Evektor Fox (Aeropro of Slovakia manufacturing Fox/Eurofox airframes). The details here are for the German-marketed Eurofox model.

Ikarusflug Eurofox

Certification: 1996 to German and Czech JAR-VLA requirements for Eurofox Basic.
Role: STOL very light monoplane.
Sales: Eurofox Basic priced at DM 71,900 in 1998, and Eurofox Pro at DM 76,650. Also available in kit form.
Crew/passenger: 2 seats, side by side in the enclosed cabin. USH 520 or BRS-5UL4 ballistic parachute system available.

Details for Eurofox and Eurofox Pro

PRINCIPAL DIMENSIONS:
Wing span: 30 ft 2 ins (9.2 m)
Maximum length: 18 ft 10.5 ins (5.75 m)
Maximum height: 5 ft 11 ins (1.8 m) for Eurofox and 6 ft 10 ins (2.08 m) for Eurofox Pro
Length/width, wings folded: 20 ft/7 ft 10.5 ins (6.1/2.4 m)

CABIN:
Width: 3 ft 6 ins (1.06 m)

WINGS:
Aerofoil section: NACA 4412 mod
Chord: 4 ft 3 ins (1.3 m)
Area: 123.78 sq ft (11.5 m²)
Aspect ratio: 7.36

UNDERCARRIAGE:
Type: Eurofox has a fixed tailwheel undercarriage. Eurofox Pro has a fixed nosewheel undercarriage, with castoring nosewheel and optional wheel fairings
Main wheel tyre size: 420 × 150 mm for Eurofox, 380 × 150 mm for Eurofox Pro
Nose/tail wheel tyre size: 210 × 65 mm tailwheel for Eurofox, 300 × 100 mm nosewheel for Eurofox Pro
Wheel base: 4 ft 1 ins (1.25 m) for Eurofox Pro
Wheel track: 6 ft 1 ins (1.85 m) for Eurofox Pro

WEIGHTS:
Empty: 573 lb (260 kg) for Eurofox, 595 lb (270 kg) for Eurofox Pro
Maximum take-off: 992 lb (450 kg)

PERFORMANCE:
Never-exceed speed (V_{NE}): 100 kts (115 mph) 185 km/h
Cruise speed: 86 kts (99 mph) 160 km/h, 75% power for Eurofox and Eurofox Pro
Take-off distance: 197 ft (60 m) for Eurofox Pro
Maximum climb rate: 885-1,083 ft (270-330 m) per minute for Eurofox, and 945 ft (288 m) for Eurofox Pro at MTOW
Range: 378 naut miles (435 miles) 700 km

Wing control surfaces: Strut-braced, high-mounted, folding wings with wide-span ailerons that also function as flaps (20° maximum deflection).
Tail control surfaces: Conventional strut-braced tailplane (span 7 ft 7.5 ins, 2.32 m) with elevators, and fin with rudder.
Construction materials: Wings constructed using 2 aluminium alloy tube spars and aluminium alloy ribs, with glassfibre reinforced plastics wingtips and Ceconite skin. Aileron/flap of glassfibre sandwich construction. Fuselage of welded steel tubing, Ceconite covered, except for glassfibre nose cowling.
Engine: Rotax 912 UL piston engine, with 1:2.273 reduction gear to a 5 ft 11 ins (1.8 m) 2-blade SR30 or 5 ft 9 ins (1.75 m) 3-blade fixed-pitch propeller for Eurofox and 5 ft 4 ins (1.62 m) 2-blade propeller for Eurofox Pro.
Engine rating: 80 hp (59.7 kW).
Fuel system: 58 litres in 2 × 25 litre tanks plus a 6 litre tank.
Electrical system: DC system via a 250 W generator. 16 amp-hour battery.
Braking system: Hydraulic disc type.

Aircraft variants:
Eurofox Basic is the tailwheel version.
Eurofox Pro is the nosewheel version. Slightly heavier empty weight.

↑ Ikarusflug Eurofox Pro

Kaiser Flugzeugbau — Germany

Corporate address:
Flugplatz Schönhagen, D-14959 Schönhagen.
Telephone: +49 3329 629 40
Facsimile: +49 3329 629 41

Comments: Seen at the ILA Berlin convention in May 1998, the **Kaiser Magic** is a single-seat biplane, powered by either a 200 hp (149 kW) PZL-Franklin 6A-350C1R or 125 hp (93 kW) 4A-235B4 piston engine, the former with a 9-D-C/C188-18a propeller. Wing span 22 ft 4 ins (6.8 m), length 21 ft 4 ins (6.5 m), height 7 ft 3 ins (2.2 m), MTOW 1,653 lb (750 kg), V_{NE} 188 kts (217 mph) 350 km/h and climb rate 2,950 ft (900 m) per minute with larger engine. Price DM 160,000 or DM 130,000, depending on engine.

→ Kaiser Magic at ILA Berlin in May 1998 *(courtesy Aviation Picture Library)*

Mylius Flugzeugwerk GmbH & Co KG — Germany

Corporate address:
Gebäude 422, Flugplatz, D-54634 Bitburg.
Telephone: +49 6561 95 05 0
Facsimile: +49 6561 95 05 50
Information:
Albert Mylius, Heinz Heller, and Sabine Palzer.

Mylius MY-102, MY-103 and MY-104

Certification: Designed to conform to European JAA standards, with US FAR Pt 23 to follow.
Role: 3 separate aircraft in single, 2 and 4 seats versions, based on a common modular design, suited to education, training, aerobatics, glider/banner towing, touring and more (see Aircraft variants).
Sales: 2 MY-102s and 1 MY-103 flying by mid 1998.
Crew/passengers: Pilot only in MY-102, 2 persons side by side in MY-103 and 4 persons in MY-104. Dual controls in multi-seat versions, with conventional centre sticks and pedals. All versions heated.
Wing control surfaces: Ailerons and flaps.
Tail control surfaces: All-moving balanced tailplane with trimmable anti-servo tab, and fin. Tail surfaces (and flaps) are identical in all versions.
Flight control system: Except for the all-moving balanced tailplane which is cable operated, all control surfaces and flaps are pushrod operated, with the flaps having electric actuation. Controls to the nosewheel are uncoupled when retracted on aircraft with retractable gear.
Construction materials: Integral aluminium alloy spar-stringer design. MY-102, MY-103 and MY-104 have modular, interchangeable substructures. All aircraft have identical tapered and detachable wings with single main spar, connected to the fuselage centre bridge by 2 main bolts and an auxiliary bolt. Wing end caps for MY-103 and MY-104 to increase span. Flaps and ailerons hinged to an auxiliary spar. Integral fuel tanks. Moderately rectangular fuselage is a stringer design covered with aluminium alloy sheets. Firewall of 0.6-mm stainless steel. Engine cowling of glassfibre. Long fin-root extension carries the sliding canopy and improves the spin behaviour of the aircraft.
Engine: Textron Lycoming engines in the 160-200 hp (119.3-149 kW) range. MY-102/200 has a 200 hp (149 kW) AEIO-360 engine with a Mühlbauer MTV 3-blade constant-speed propeller. MY-103/160 Standard has a 160 hp (119.3 kW) O-320 engine with a 3-blade constant-speed propeller. MY-103/200 Basic Trainer has an AEIO-360 with 4-blade constant-speed propeller. MY-104/200 has an IO-360 with a 3-blade constant-speed propeller. For aerobatics, inverted oil system available. Depending on mission and engine power, variable-pitch 2, 3 or 4-blade propellers can be used. Anti-noise blankets in the cowling and Liese noise attenuators.
Fuel system: 197 litres for MY-102 and MY-103, and 276 litres for MY-104.
Undercarriage: Fixed nosewheel type for MY-102 and MY-103, with option of a retractable nose unit; fixed main gear has spring steel shock absorption. Wheels are faired and have brakes. Undercarriage of MY-104 is electrically retractable, with main gear retracting into the wing bridge outside the centre portion of the fuselage.
Electrical system: Standard version has 12 volt system with a 40 amp-hour battery.
Flight avionics/instrumentation: Modular instrument panel to shorten time for repair and maintenance. Instruments range from simple VFR to IFR.

Aircraft variants:
MY-102 is an affordable single-seat aerobatics and glider/banner towing aircraft.
MY-103 is a 2-seater for education, training and club use, available in Standard and Basic Trainer versions. Can be used for education up to PPL and aerobatics licence, allowing systematic training thereafter in an MY-102. Full aerobatic capability, with optional inverted oil system. Large payload, and good range and speed. 200 hp (149 kW) version is ideal for banner/glider towing. Basic Trainer version has enlarged canopy for increased visual angle and helmet clearance according to MIL-STD-1333B resp 33547B. Can be used for ab-initio training of military and commercial pilots.
MY-104 is a 4-seater for uses including IFR training (equipped with the appropriate avionics panel), long-range touring, and charters. Fully retractable undercarriage and the ruggedness of the utility class.

↑ Mylius MY-102s

↑ Mylius MY-103/200 Basic Trainer cockpit layout

	MY-102/200	MY-103/160 Standard	MY-103/200 Basic Trainer	MY-104/200
Wing span	25 ft 7 ins (7.8 m)	27 ft 7 ins (8.4 m)	27 ft 7 ins (8.4 m)	34 ft 1 ins (10.4 m)
Length	21 ft (6.4 m)	21 ft 4 ins (6.5 m)	21 ft 4 ins (6.5 m)	24 ft 7 ins (7.5 m)
Height	7 ft 7 ins (2.32 m)	7 ft 7 ins (2.32 m)	7 ft 7 ins (2.32 m)	7 ft 10 ins (2.38 m)
Wing area sq ft (m^2)	101.2 (9.4)	111 (10.31)	111 (10.31)	145 (13.47)
Aspect ratio	6.6	6.85	6.85	8
Weight empty lb (kg)	1,058 (480)	1,235 (560)	1,270 (576)	1,498 (680)
Maximum take-off weight lb (kg)	2,050 (930)	2,050 (930)	2,050 (930)	2,772 (1,257)
Payload lb (kg)	992 (450)	815 (370)	780 (354)	1,274 (578)
Payload with maximum fuel lb (kg)	680 (308)	508 (230)	468 (212)	833 (378)
Never-exceed speed (V_{NE}) kts (mph) km/h	216 (248) 400	216 (248) 400	216 (248) 400	216 (248) 400
Normal cruise speed kts (mph) km/h	159 (183) 295	138 (159) 256	148 (170) 274	148 (170) 274
Manoeuvring speed kts (mph) km/h	133 (153) 246	146 (168) 270	146 (168) 270	135 (155) 250
Stall speed, flaps and undercarriage down kts (mph) km/h	52 (60) 97		54 (62.5) 100	
Landing speed kts (mph) km/h	58 (67) 107	57 (66) 106	57 (66) 106	57 (66) 106
Take-off distance over a 50 ft (15 m) obstacle ft (m)	788 (240)		821 (250)	
Climb rate at sea level ft (m) per minute	1,811 (552)	1,024 (312)	1,417 (432)	1,142 (348)
Service ceiling ft (m)	20,000 (6,100)	18,000 (5,500)	22,000 (6,700)	18,000 (5,500)
Range, with 15 minutes reserve naut miles (miles) km	677 (780) 1,255	836 (963) 1,550	664 (765) 1,231	985 (1,135) 1,826
Duration, at 65% power	4.5 hours	6.3 hours	4.5 hours	7 hours

Remos Aircraft GmbH — Germany

Corporate address:
Waldweg 1, D-85283 Eschelbach.

Telephone: +49 8442 967777
Facsimile: +49 8442 967796

Founded:
1987.

ACTIVITIES

▪ Production of the Mirage. The earlier Rotax 582-powered **Gemini Ultra** is available only to special order, taking 6 months for delivery.

Remos G-3 Mirage

First flight: 1997.

↑ **Remos G-3 Mirage** *(L. Kreitmayr)*

Role: Very light monoplane, with ballistic parachute for added safety.
Wing control surfaces: Ailerons and flaps.
Tail control surfaces: Slab elevator, with trim tab, and rudder.
Flight control system: Mechanical/manual, except for electrically actuated flaps and trim tab.
Construction materials: Composites used for the tapering fuselage. Folding strut-braced wings with composites leading edges and wingtips, the rest fabric covered.
Engine: Rotax 912 UL, with 3-blade propeller.
Engine rating: 80 hp (59.7 kW).
Fuel system: 70 litres.

Details for Mirage

PRINCIPAL DIMENSIONS:
Wing span: 32 ft 2 ins (9.8 m)
Maximum length: 21 ft 3 ins (6.47 m)
Maximum height: 5 ft 7 ins (1.7 m)
Wing area: 129.6 sq ft (12.04 m^2)

UNDERCARRIAGE:
Type: Fixed nosewheel type, with rubber-in-compression shock absorption on nosewheel leg

WEIGHTS:
Empty: 626 lb (284 kg)
Maximum take-off: 992 lb (450 kg)

PERFORMANCE:
Never-exceed speed (V_{NE}): 118 kts (136 mph) 220 km/h
Cruise speed: 105 kts (121 mph) 195 km/h
Stall speed: 34 kts (39 mph) 63 km/h
Take-off distance over a 50 ft (15 m) obstacle: 591 ft (180 m)
Landing distance over a 50 ft (15 m) obstacle: 657 ft (200 m)
Maximum climb rate: 1,142 ft (348 m) per minute
G limits: +4, -2
Range: 485 naut miles (559 miles) 900 km
Duration: 6 hours

Ruschmeyer Aircraft Production KG — Germany

Corporate address:
Segelfliegerweg 41, D-49324 Melle-Flugplatz.

Telephone: +49 54 22 46737 (airfield) or 57 31 4233
Facsimile: +49 57 31 41529

Founded:
1987.

ACTIVITIES

▪ Ruschmeyer stopped R90 production in 1997 and moved to a new facility at the same address. The German facility is to become only a development centre. A production facility is being sought in the USA, but by May 1998 no location had been found. Production is unlikely to restart until about the year 2000.

Ruschmeyer R90 series

First flight: 1991 for R90-230 RG.
Certification: June 1992 (LBA), 24 June 1994 (FAA) for R90-230 RG. Certified to FAR/JAR Pt 23 Amdt 24.
Details: Principally for R90-230 RG.
Role: Touring lightplane and basic IFR trainer for private and commercial pilots.

Details for Ruschmeyer R90-230 RG

PRINCIPAL DIMENSIONS:
Wing span: 31 ft 2 ins (9.5 m)
Maximum length: 26 ft (7.93 m)
Maximum height: 8 ft 11.5 ins (2.73 m)

CABIN:
Length: 9 ft 4.5 ins (2.86 m)
Width: 3 ft 9 ins (1.14 m)
Height: 4 ft 1 ins (1.24 m)

WINGS:
Aerofoil section: Wortmann laminar flow
Area: 139.28 sq ft (12.94 m^2)
Aspect ratio: 6.97

UNDERCARRIAGE:
Type: Retractable, with nosewheel. Trailing link type, with electrohydraulic actuation
Turning radius: 20 ft 6 ins (6.24 m)

WEIGHTS:
Empty: 1,980 lb (898 kg)
Maximum take-off and landing: 2,976 lb (1,350 kg)
Useful load: 996 lb (452 kg)

PERFORMANCE:
Maximum speed: 175 kts (201 mph) 324 km/h
Cruise speed: 168 kts (193 mph) 311 km/h at 6,000 ft (1,830 m) and 85% power, or 144 kts (166 mph) 267 km/h at 9,000 ft (2,740 m) and 55% power, or 110 kts (126 mph) 204 km/h at 3,000 ft (915 m) at 38% power
Stall speed: 67 kts (77 mph) 124 km/h *clean*, 58 kts (67 mph) 107 km/h *in landing configuration*
Take-off distance over a 50 ft (15 m) obstacle: 1,706 ft (520 m)
Landing distance over a 50 ft (15 m) obstacle: 1,575 ft (480 m)
Maximum climb rate: 1,140 ft (347 m) per minute at MTOW
Climb to 10,000 ft (3,050 m): 12 minutes at MTOW
G limits: +3.8, –1.52 certified; +9 design
Ceiling: 16,000 ft (4,875 m) at MTOW, 20,000 ft (6,100 m) at 2,425 lb (1,100 kg) AUW
Range: 870 naut miles (1,001 miles) 1,611 km, with 45 minutes reserve
Duration: 7.8 hours

Crew/passengers: 4 persons. Dual controls.
Cockpit: Gull-wing doors.
Baggage capacity: 28.25 cu ft (0.8 m^3) for 110 lb (50 kg). Accessible from outside.
Wing characteristics: Low mounted, with leading-edge stall strips and upturned wingtips for improved lateral stability.
Wing control surfaces: Ailerons with some differential movement, and 3-position Fowler flaps (port tab).
Tail control surfaces: Elevators (port trim/anti-servo tab) and rudder.

↑ Ruschmeyer R90-230 RG

Flight control system: Push-pull rods. Electric flaps.
Construction materials: BASF Palatal A430 resin fibre composites material (RFCM), even for primary structures. Ruschmeyer claims for RFCM include durability up to 72° C, improved material strength, and structural field repair without special tools. Airframe structure is certified for 18,000 flight hours, while tests have simulated 54,000 hours without structural fatigue.
Engine: Textron Lycoming IO-540-C4D5 piston engine, with 4-blade constant-speed propeller. By flat rating the engine to 2,400 rpm, by employing a special acoustically high damping exhaust system, and by use of the MTV-14-B propeller, noise levels are 8.1 dB below ICAO Annex 16 Chapter 6 and 10.2 dB below ICAO Annex 16 Chapter 10 limits.
Engine rating: Flat-rated to 230 hp (171.5 kW).
Fuel system: 250 litres, of which 236 litres are usable.

Aircraft variants:
R90-180 RG is a 4-seater with a 180 hp (134 kW) O-360 engine and retractable undercarriage. Gross weight 2,535 lb (1,150 kg). Maximum speed 130 kts (150 mph) 240 km/h. Under development (confirmed May 1998).
R90-230 FG is a fixed undercarriage version of the R90-230 RG. Empty weight 1,874 lb (850 kg). 90% ready for certification by May 1998.
R90-230 RG is a retractable gear version of FG. Is the basic version of the R90 family, as detailed.
R90-300 T-RG is under development, with a supercharged 300 hp (224 kW) engine and 400 litres of fuel. Gross weight 3,417 lb (1,550 kg). Maximum speed 240 kts (276 mph) 445 km/h.
R90-420 AT is a 4-seat turboprop proof-of-concept version, first flown on 2 November 1993 and used as a 'fun' aircraft by Ruschmeyer. Not intended for production at present. 420 shp (313 kW) Allison 250-B20 turboprop engine. Gross weight 3,197 lb (1,450 kg). Maximum cruise speed 243 kts (280 mph) 450 km/h. Noise level 14 dB(A) below ICAO limit.

Ruschmeyer R95

Comments: Development of this 5-seat pressurized aircraft has ended. Details can be found in the 1996-97 edition of *WA&SD*, page 400.

Scheibe-Flugzeugbau GmbH — Germany

Corporate address:
August-Pfaltz-Strasse 23, D-85221 Dachau.
Telephone: +49 8131 720834
Facsimile: +49 8131 736985

ACTIVITIES

■ See also the Glider section.

Scheibe SF 40

First flight: 1994.
Role: Very light monoplane. SF 40-C has flight test permission to tow a glider up to a maximum weight of 882 lb (400 kg) and banner tow, while SF 40-A and -B can banner tow.
Sales: SF 40-C-Allround costs DM 100,000–110,000, plus 16% tax.
Details: SF 40-C-Allround.
Crew/passenger: 2 seats, side by side, under a forward-hinged single-piece canopy.
Baggage capacity: 3.88 cu ft (0.11 m^3).
Wing control surfaces: Conventional ailerons.
Tail control surfaces: Conventional elevator and rudder.
Flight control system: Manual.
Construction materials: Mainly glassfibre wings, and fabric-covered tubular fuselage structure.
Engine: Rotax 912 piston engine, with a 2-blade propeller with spinner.
Engine rating: 80 hp (59.7 kW).
Fuel system: 55 litres.
Electrical system: Engine-driven alternator and 12 volt/18 amp-hour battery.
Flight avionics/instrumentation: Standard, plus optional.

Aircraft variants:
SF 40-A and -B were the first versions, each with a tailwheel undercarriage, powered by a 60 hp (44.7 kW) Sauer-Motor engine and with a 32 litre fuel tank. Wing span 35 ft 5 ins (10.8 m). MTOW 882/992 lb (400/450 kg). Maximum cruise speed 81 kts (93 mph) 150 km/h. Range 269 naut miles (310 miles) 500 km. 5 built.
SF 40-C-Allround is the latest version with a nosewheel undercarriage and Rotax engine, as detailed.

↑ Scheibe SF 40-C-Allround *(J. Ewald)*

Details for SF 40-C-Allround

PRINCIPAL DIMENSIONS:
Wing span: 31 ft 2 ins (9.5 m)
Maximum length: 19 ft 10 ins (6.05 m)
Maximum height: 7 ft 5.5 ins (2.27 m)

CABIN:
Length: 4 ft 6 ins (1.37 m)
Width: 3 ft 3.75 ins (1.01 m)
Height: 3 ft 4.25 ins (1.02 m)
Volume: 33.9 cu ft (0.96 m^3), plus baggage area

WINGS:
Area: 129.17 sq ft (12 m^2)
Aspect ratio: 7.52

UNDERCARRIAGE:
Type: Fixed nosewheel type, with streamline fairings
Wheel track: 4 ft 11 ins (1.5 m)

WEIGHTS:
Empty: 639 lb (290 kg)
Maximum take-off and landing: <992 lb (450 kg)
Payload: 353 lb (160 kg)

PERFORMANCE:
Never-exceed speed (V_{NE}): 116 kts (134 mph) 216 km/h
Maximum cruise speed: 103-108 kts (118-124 mph) 190-200 km/h
Cruise speed: 84 kts (96 mph) 155 km/h
Take-off and landing distance: 279 ft (85 m)
Take-off distance over a 50 ft (15 m) obstacle: 607 ft (185 m)
Maximum climb rate: 885/950 ft (270/290 m) per minute
Range: 377 naut miles (435 miles) 700 km

GanzAVIA Kft — Hungary

Corporate address:
PO Box 62, H-1475 Budapest.

Telephone: +36 1 210 1150
Facsimile: +36 1 334 0364

Works:
Köbányai út 21, H-1087 Budapest.

Information:
Pál Michelberger (Managing Director).

ACTIVITIES

▪ GanzAVIA was founded by the Ganz Machinery Works Holding Ltd to develop the Dino. By 1998, the prototype Dino had accumulated some 200 flying hours and 400 take-offs. However, due to a lack of orders and capital, the design and manufacturing of the second modified aircraft stopped in January 1996. When restarted, this will have a more comfortable cabin, wing tanks for about 120 litres of fuel, and a new braking system. A later concept is for a 4-seat version. See Sales.

GanzAVIA GAK-22 Dino

↑ GanzAVIA GAK-22 Dino

First flight: October 1993.
Certification: 19 April 1995 for Hungarian Civil Aviation Inspectorate certificate of airworthiness.
Role: 2-seat light multi-purpose and aerobatic/sporting biplane, with dual controls. Suited to private, aerial photography, training, agricultural, light transport and glider towing.
Sales: Prototype was re-registered *HA-YACT* following certification. Basic aircraft cost DEM 148,000. Production aircraft can be delivered with Hungarian certification. Delivery period is 8 months. In 1998, the company had the capacity to deliver 6 aircraft.
Baggage capacity: Space aft of seats.
Wing characteristics: Negative stepped 'back staggered' biplane, with cantilever surfaces and raked-back wingtips. Intended to avoid spinning.
Wing control surfaces: Flaperons on lower wings only, interconnected to elevator.
Tail control surfaces: One-piece horn-balanced elevator with port tab and a horn-balanced rudder.
Flight control system: Push rods. Interconnected control system between the flaperons and elevator, resulting in the flaperons being lowered when the elevator is raised.
Construction materials: Fuselage has a welded steel tube structure, with duralumin skins for the cabin area, fabric at the rear and a glassfibre engine cowling. Wings have 3 ft 7 ins (1.09 m) negative stagger and are single-spar structures of aluminium alloy, with glassfibre wingtips. Tail surfaces are of similar construction to the wings, though the moving surfaces have glassfibre tips.
Engine: Textron Lycoming O-235-H2C piston engine, with a 5 ft 11 ins (1.8 m) Mühlbauer 2-blade fixed-pitch propeller. 180 hp (134 kW) engine of AEIO-360-B1F or similar type optional, with a variable-pitch propeller for Aerobatics.
Engine rating: 115 hp (85.75 kW).
Fuel system: 80 litres in single tank.
Flight avionics/instrumentation: To customer's requirements. Standard equipment includes speedometer, altimeter, variometer, turn indicator, magnetic compass, directional gyro, nav/com radio station, artificial horizon and more.

Aircraft variants:
GAK-22 Dino is the 2-seater, as detailed.
4-seat version was expected to fly in prototype form in the latter part of 1995 but did not.

Details for GAK-22 Dino 115 hp prototype

PRINCIPAL DIMENSIONS:
Wing span: 25 ft 3 ins (7.7 m)
Maximum length: 20 ft 2 ins (6.1 m)
Maximum height: 8 ft 6.5 ins (2.6 m)

WINGS:
Aerofoil section: NACA 23018/23012 at root/tip
Area: 151.125 sq ft (14.04 m^2)
Incidence: 4° upper wing, 3° lower wing
Washout: 1°12' both wings

UNDERCARRIAGE:
Type: Fixed, with nosewheel. Cantilever spring main legs. Wheel fairings optional. Drum brakes

WEIGHTS:
Empty: 948 lb (430 kg)
Maximum take-off: 1,587 lb (720 kg)

PERFORMANCE:
Never-exceed speed (V_{NE}): 135 kts (155 mph) 250 km/h
Maximum speed: 105 kts (121 mph) 195 km/h
Cruise speed: 97 kts (112 mph) 180 km/h
Stall speed: 43.5 kts (50 mph) 80 km/h
Take-off distance: 657 ft (200 m)
Ceiling: 10,500 ft (3,200 m), service
Range: 378 naut miles (435 miles) 700 km

Bharat Heavy Electricals Ltd — India

Corporate address:
Heavy Electrical Equipment Plant, Ranipur (Hardwar) 249 403 U.P.

Telephone: +91 133 426457, 427350-427359
Facsimile: +91 133 426462, 426254

Information:
H.W. Bhatnagar (General Manager – Aviation).

BHEL LT-IIM Swati

↑ Bharat (BHEL) LT-IIM Swati

First flight: 17 November 1990 (with a Rolls-Royce Continental O-240-A engine and tailwheel undercarriage).
Certification: January 1992. Designed to comply with FAR Pt 23 Utility and Normal categories.
Role: 2-seat lightplane, suited also to training and other uses. Designed by the Technical Centre of Directorate General of civil aviation in India.
Details: Production version.
Wing control surfaces: Ailerons and plain flaps.
Tail control surfaces: Elevators and rudder.

Flight control system: Manual.
Construction materials: Fuselage of chromoly steel tube, with fabric covering aft and metal and composites forward. Metal tail surfaces. Wooden wings.
Engine: Textron Lycoming O-235-N2C piston engine, with a 5 ft 10 ins (1.78 m) Hoffmann HO 14-178115 fixed-pitch, 2-blade, wood/composites propeller.
Engine rating: 116 hp (86.5 kW).
Fuel system: 90 litres.
Braking system: Hydraulic mainwheel brakes.
Flight avionics/instrumentation: VFR instrumentation. Optional radio.

Details for Swati in Utility category

PRINCIPAL DIMENSIONS:
Wing span: 30 ft 3 ins (9.2 m)
Maximum length: 23 ft 8 ins (7.21 m)
Maximum height: 9 ft 1.5 ins (2.78 m)

WINGS:
Aerofoil section: NASA GA(W)-1
Area: 128.74 sq ft (11.96 m^2)
Aspect ratio: 7.077

UNDERCARRIAGE:
Type: Fixed, with steerable nosewheel

WEIGHTS:
Empty: 1,168 lb (530 kg)
Maximum take-off: 1,698 lb (770 kg)

PERFORMANCE:
Never-exceed speed (V_{NE}): 145 kts (167 mph) 268 km/h
Maximum and cruise speed: 105 kts (121 mph) 195 km/h
Stall speed: 41 kts (48 mph) 76 km/h
Take-off distance: 850 ft (259 m)
Landing distance: 660 ft (201 m)
Maximum climb rate: 670 ft (204 m) per minute
G limits: +4.4, –1.76
Ceiling: 10,000 ft (3,050 m), service
Range: 245 naut miles (282 miles) 453 km
Duration: 2 hours 45 minutes

Hindustan Aeronautics Limited (HAL) — India

Corporate address:
See Combat section for company details.

HAL HPT-32 Deepak

First flight: 6 January 1977.
Certification: 25 November 1991. Designed to meet FAR Pt 23.
Fatigue life: 6,500 hours.
Role: 2-seat ab initio and basic trainer, designed to replace the HT-2. Also capable of instrument, navigation, night and formation flying, observation, liaison, and sport. Utility roles include towing.
Sales: 134 produced for the Indian Air Force and 8 for the Indian Navy.
Wing control surfaces: Ailerons (with geared and ground tabs) and plain flaps.
Tail control surfaces: Single-piece elevator (with geared and trim tabs) and rudder (with trim tab).
Flight control system: Mechanical, except for electric flap control and rudder trim. Electric booster pump.
Construction materials: Metal, with semi-monocoque fuselage structure.
Engine: Textron Lycoming AEIO-540-D4B5 piston engine, with a 6 ft 8 ins (2.03 m) diameter Hartzell 2-blade propeller.
Engine rating: 260 hp (194 kW).
Fuel system: 228 litres, including a small collector tank (210 litres usable).
Electrical system: 24 volt DC supply, with 70 amp alternator. 16 amp-hour ni-cd battery.
Braking system: Hydraulic discs.
Flight avionics/instrumentation: 4-channel UHF main and 4-channel VHF standby R/Ts with built-in intercom facility (twin VHF optional), ASI, altimeter, TSI, directional gyro, artificial horizon and magnetic standby compass, audio stall warning and more.

↑ HAL HPT-32 Deepak in Indian military service

Details for HPT-32 Deepak

PRINCIPAL DIMENSIONS:
Wing span: 31 ft 2 ins (9.5 m)
Maximum length: 25 ft 4 ins (7.72 m)
Maximum height: 9 ft 5 ins (2.88 m)

WINGS:
Area: 161.46 sq ft (15 m^2)
Aspect ratio: 6.017
Dihedral: 5°

UNDERCARRIAGE:
Type: Fixed, with nosewheel
Wheel track: 11 ft 4 ins (3.45 m)

WEIGHTS:
Empty: 1,962 lb (890 kg)
Maximum take-off and landing: 2,755 lb (1,250 kg)

PERFORMANCE:
Maximum speed: 143 kts (165 mph) 265 km/h at sea level
Maximum cruise speed: 115 kts (132 mph) 213 km/h at 10,000 ft (3,050 m)
Stall speed: 62 kts (72 mph) 115 km/h *clean*, 60 kts (68 mph) 110 km/h *with flaps*
Take-off distance: 1,352 ft (412 m)
Landing distance: 745 ft (227 m)
Maximum climb rate: 1,100 ft (335 m) per minute at sea level
Time to 9,840 ft (3,000 m): 15 minutes 24 seconds
G limits: +6, –3
Ceiling: 16,400 ft (5,000 m)
Range: 437 naut miles (503 miles) 810 km at 9,840 ft (3,000 m)
Duration: 4 hours 42 minutes, with 20 litres reserve
* ISA + 20° C for field performance and ISA + 15° C for altitude performance

National Aerospace Laboratories — India

Corporate address:
PO Bag 1779, Kodihalli, Bangalore 560 017.
Telephone: +91 80 573351

ACTIVITIES

■ Include the development of the Hansa, now produced by Taneja, and development of the Saras.

National Aerospace Laboratories Saras

First flight: Initially planned for 1996 but now programme delayed, with first flight expected in April 1999.
Certification: To conform to FAR Pt 25 and Pt 121.
Role: Multi-purpose, as a regional transport, for business or cargo, or configured for patrol, ambulance, aerial photography, environmental monitoring and other specialized missions.

Aims

■ For hot-and-high operations (quoted as airfields at 6,560 ft, 2,000 m and up to 45° C), with concrete or unpaved runways.

Development

■ Programme managed by NAL's Centre for Civil Aircraft Design and Development.
■ 1993. Agreement signed between Myasishchev and NAL for joint development of a regional transport, following earlier individual programmes of similar type. Development programme was to be funded on a 50/50 basis between Russia and India, but Russian share was small.
■ 1997. Russia (MAPO "Myasishchev") reportedly withdrew from programme. Its Duet version is no longer progressing.
■ 1997. Reported $15.27 million funding received for prototype development, with $5.5 million reportedly coming from India's Kumran Industries and Taneja aerospace.
Sales: Originally to be 3 M-102 prototypes, 2 (including 1 static) built at Smolensk, Russia, and 1 in Nasik, India (assembled from parts supplied by Smolensk factory). Sokol plant at Nizhny Novgorod had planned to be the Russian manufacturer.
Manufacture now to be in India by Kumran and Taneja as risk-sharing partners. Price estimated at less than US$4 million each. Break-even point on costs reached after 106 delivered.

Details

Crew/passengers: 1 or 2 pilots. Maximum of 14 passengers in the main cabin, at 30 ins (76.2 cm) seat pitch. Business version could carry 8/9 passengers, with additional amenities including tables, galley, etc. Combi layout for 7 passengers and cargo. 6 litters and 2 seated attendants in ambulance layout. Normalair environmental control system.
Baggage capacity: 38.85 cu ft (1.1 m^3).
Pressurization system: 8 psi cabin differential.
Wing control surfaces: Ailerons (with tabs), single-slotted Fowler flaps, and spoilers.
Tail control surfaces: Elevators (starboard tab) and rudder (with tab).
Flight control system: Mechanical/manual but with electric flaps and tabs.
Construction materials: Aluminium alloy, except for composites ailerons, flaps, wingtips, wing-root fairings, tail unit, nosecone

Details for Saras

PRINCIPAL DIMENSIONS:
Wing span: 48 ft 3 ins (14.7 m)
Maximum length: 49 ft 3.5 ins (15.02 m)
Maximum height: 17 ft 3 ins (5.26 m)

CABIN:
Length: 21 ft 10.5 ins (6.66 m)
Width: 5 ft 11 ins (1.8 m)
Height: 5 ft 8 ins (1.72 m)
Volume: 565 cu ft (16 m^3)

UNDERCARRIAGE:
Type: Retractable, with twin steerable (± 53°C) nosewheels

WEIGHTS:
Empty, equipped: 9,073 lb (4,116 kg)
Maximum take-off and landing: 13,450 lb (6,100 kg)
Payload: 2,716 lb (1,232 kg)

PERFORMANCE:
Maximum level speed: 323 kts (372 mph) 600 km/h
Cruise speed: 297 kts (342 mph) 550 km/h
Stall speed: 88 kts (102 mph) 163 km/h *clean*, 72 kts (82 mph) 132 km/h *with flaps*
Take-off distance: 1,410 ft (430 m), ISA
Landing distance: 1,122 ft (342 m), ISA
Take-off distance over a 50 ft (15 m) obstacle: 1,739 ft (530 m), ISA
Landing distance over a 50 ft (15 m) obstacle: 1,985 ft (605 m), ISA
Maximum climb rate: 2,428 ft (740 m) per minute
Operating ceiling: 29,525 ft (9,000 m)
Range: More than 640 naut miles (736 miles) 1,185 km with 14 passengers, 1,330 naut miles (1,531 miles) 2,465 km with 8 passengers, and 1,510 naut miles (1,740 miles) 2,800 km with full fuel

↑ Russian-produced mock-up of the Saras *(Piotr Butowski)*

and engine cowls. Fuselage and undercarriage were to be built in Russia, wings and tail unit in India; present manufacturing arrangements in India. 20,000 flying hours or 20 years life.
Engines: Pratt & Whitney Canada PT6A-66 engines, flat rated at 850 shp (634 kW) up to 25,000 ft (7,620 m), with 7 ft 1 ins (2.16 m) Hartzell 6-blade handed constant-speed pusher propellers.
Fuel system: 1,595 litres (usable) in wing tanks. System by Secondo Mona of Italy.
Electrical system: 28 volt DC supply, with 2 x 400 amp starter-generators and emergency 43 amp-hour ni-cd battery. 115 volt/400Hz AC supply, with 2 inverters.
Hydraulic system: 3,000 psi.
De-icing system: Electrical.
Radar: Weather type.
Flight avionics/instrumentation: IFR, using an integrated digital system (ARINC 429). Includes 4-screen EFIS displays, flight control computer, and GPS navigation. Conventional back-up instruments. The expected supplier of avionics will be either AlliedSignal Bendix/King or Rockwell Collins.

Taneja Aerospace and Aviation Ltd (TAAL) — India

Corporate address:
1010 Tenth Floor, Prestige Meridian-I, 29 M G Road, Bangalore 560001.
Telephone: +91 80 555 0609, 0610, 0944
Facsimile: +91 80 555 0955
Email: taal@giasvg01.vsnl.net.in
Founded:
Subsidiary of The Indian Seamless Metal Tubes Ltd company, and the first private sector company in India to venture into aircraft manufacturing, starting its manufacturing activities in April 1993 and flying its first aircraft (a licence-built Partenavia P 68 Observer 2) on 17 March 1994.
Information:
Vinod Singel.

FACILITIES

▪ Production plant at Hosur in Tamilnadu.

ACTIVITIES

▪ In addition to aircraft manufacturing, maintenance and servicing, TAAL has started a Flying Training Academy to train aircraft maintenance engineers and civil pilots.
▪ Licenced by the former Partenavia of Italy to initially assemble from kits and more recently to manufacture in India the P 68-C, P 68 C-TC, P 68 Observer and AP 68TP-600 Viator. Following the assembly of 5 aircraft from Italian supplied kits (P 68 Observer 2 first flown on 17 March 1994, Viator, 2 P 68-Cs and a P 68 C-TC), in January 1997 TAAL began further manufacture of P 68s using more indigenously produced assemblies. The first had been scheduled for roll-out in September 1997, when some 5 aircraft were on order (3 for TAAL's Netair programme). However, following VulcanAir's purchase of Partenavia's aircraft in March 1998, a new licence was being negotiated to permit continued production. For details of the P 68, see VulcanAir under Italy.
▪ TAAL is manufacturing the Hansa, developed by NAL with TAAL participation.

↑ TAAL (NAL) Hansa 3 production prototype *(courtesy TAAL)*

TAAL (NAL) Hansa 3

First flight: 17 November 1993 for original prototype, 26 January 1996 for Hansa 2RE, 26 November 1996 for Hansa 3 with IO-240 engine, and 11 May 1998 for Rotax engined Hansa 3.
Certification: JAR-VLA Normal category, with FAA FAR Pt 23 expected in 1998.
Role: 2-seat lightplane and ab initio trainer, with dual controls.
Sales: Prototypes at the time of writing, as the original O-200B-engined Hansa, later re-engined with an IO-240 (as 2RE,

Details for TAAL Hansa 3

PRINCIPAL DIMENSIONS:
Wing span: 34 ft 4 ins (10.47 m)
Maximum length: 23 ft 7.5 ins (7.2 m)
Maximum height: 8 ft 6 ins (2.6 m)

WINGS:
Aerofoil section: NASA LS(1)0415 root, with LS(1)0413 for tapering outer sections
Area: 134.23 sq ft (12.47 m^2)
Aspect ratio: 8.79
Dihedral: 4°

UNDERCARRIAGE:
Type: Fixed, with steerable (±33°) nosewheel. Hydraulic disc brakes

WEIGHTS:
Empty: 1,069 lb (485 kg)
Maximum take-off: 1,653 lb (750 kg)

PERFORMANCE:
Maximum cruise speed: 116 kts (134 mph) 215 km/h at 10,000 ft (3,050 m)
Stall speed: 44 kts (51 mph) 82 km/h *clean*
Take-off distance over a 50 ft (15 m) obstacle: 985 ft (300 m)
Landing distance over a 50 ft (15 m) obstacle: 1,510 ft (460 m)
Maximum climb rate: 853 ft (260 m) per minute at sea level
Ceiling: 17,700 ft (5,400 m), service
Range: 455 naut miles (524 miles) 843 km

featuring also increases in wing span and flaps), and the Hansa 3 production prototype, most recently with a Rotax 914 F3 engine. Production for 1998.
Wing control surfaces: Mass balanced Frise-type ailerons and single-slotted Fowler flaps.
Tail control surfaces: Horn-balanced elevators (port trim tab) and rudder.
Flight control system: Push-pull rods, except for electrically activated trim tab.
Construction materials: Composites, using carbonfibre, glassfibre, epoxy and PVC foam to form moulded sandwich shells for the wings, tail and fuselage. Wings are 3 spar and tail 2-spar types.
Engine: Originally 125 hp (93.2 kW) Teledyne Continental IO-240B piston engine, with 5 ft 8 ins (1.73 m) diameter Sensenich 2-blade fixed-pitch wooden propeller. Currently Rotax 914 F3, with variable pitch propeller.
Fuel system: 100 litres capacity (95 usable).
Electrical system: 15 volt, 60 amp generator and 12 volt, 18 amp-hour battery.
Flight avionics/instrumentation: VFR instrumentation. AlliedSignal Bendix/King KX 125 VHF/VOR com/nav.

→ **Taneja-built P 68 C-TC** *(Simon Watson)*

Aviation Industries of Iran (AII) — Iran

Corporate address:
See Helicopter section for company details.

Information:
Dr S. Pourtakdoust. A. Sardari (Commercial Director).

ACTIVITIES

▪ AII is a company affiliated to the Iranian Ministry of Industries, Iran Industrial Development and Renovation Organization (IDRO), established for the production of various types of powered aeroplanes, other air vehicles, gliders, kites, balloons and parachutes, ground and air facilities, and the repair and maintenance of light and medium weight aircraft. It has based its activities on setting up the infrastructure industries for manufacturing aircraft and promoting aviation. Established in April 1993, it relies on domestic experts, researchers and industrialists.

▪ In addition to the aircraft detailed in the Helicopter and Glider sections, AII has been developing 2-seat training aircraft (including the 160 hp, 119 kW Textron Lycoming powered all-metal low-wing monoplane reportedly called the IR-02), and a 10/12-seat STOL high-wing transport reportedly known as the IR-12, with 2 × 500 shp (373 kW) turboprops. None are as yet known to have flown, except for the glider on 30 May 1996, though the modern composites construction of the glider clearly indicates that the expertise exists to produce such powered aircraft.

▪ Affiliated organizations are the Iran Arvand Aero Club, Iran Aviation Travel Agency, Aviation Research Centre and Iran Have Aviation Commercial services.

H.F. Dorna Co — Iran

Corporate address:
No 20 6th Sarvestan Street, Pasdaran Avenue, Zarabkhaneh, Tehran 16619.

Telephone: +98 21 8084827
Facsimile: +98 21 231831

Founded: 1989.

Chief Engineer:
Farid Najmabadi.

Information:
Y. Antesary (Managing Director).

H.F. Dorna Blue Bird

First flight: 1997.
Certification: JAR-VLA requirements in 1998.
Role: 2-seat composites touring lightplane.
Wing characteristics: Low-wing monoplane, with constant chord.
Wing control surfaces: Ailerons and plain flaps.
Tail control surfaces: Elevators (with trim) and rudder.
Flight control system: Pushrod and cables, except for electric trim and possibly flaps.
Engine: Rotax 914 F3 turbocharged piston engine, with an MT Propeller fixed- or variable-pitch 2-blade propeller.
Engine rating: 115 hp (85.75 kW).
Fuel system: About 130 litres.
Electrical system: 12 volt DC supply, via 2 × 40 amp alternators and 12 volt, 35 amp-hour battery.
Hydraulic system: None.
Braking system: Mainwheel brakes.
Flight avionics/instrumentation: Conventional VFR.

↑ **H.F. Dorna Blue Bird** *(courtesy Dorna)*

Details for H.F. Dorna Blue Bird

PRINCIPAL DIMENSIONS:
Wing span: 30 ft 6 ins (9.3 m)
Maximum length: 19 ft 9 ins (6.017 m)
Maximum height: 6 ft 5 ins (1.96 m)

WINGS:
Aerofoil section: NACA 63_2-215
Area: 117.11 sq ft (10.88 m^2)
Aspect ratio: 7.949

UNDERCARRIAGE:
Type: Fixed, with nosewheel. Cantilever mixed construction legs, with composites wheel fairings

WEIGHTS:
Empty: 877 lb (398 kg)
Maximum take-off and landing: 1,451 lb (658 kg)

PERFORMANCE:
Never-exceed speed (V_{NE}): 217 kts (249 mph) 402 km/h
Maximum speed: 174 kts (200 mph) 322 km/h at 12,000 ft (3,660 m)
Long-range cruise speed: 122 kts (140 mph) 225 km/h
Stall speed: 46 kts (53 mph) 84 km/h *with flaps*
Take-off distance: 703 ft (214 m)
Landing distance: 800 ft (244 m)
Maximum climb rate: 1,699 ft (518 m) per minute at sea level
Ceiling: 14,000 ft (4,270 m)
Range with full fuel: 781 naut miles (899 miles) 1,448 km

Israel Aircraft Industries Ltd (IAI) — Israel

Corporate address:
See Combat section for company details.

Note: The Astra SPX is among the product lines being promoted by Galaxy Aerospace, a privately-held US Corporation which is also fitting-out, marketing and supporting the **Galaxy** widebody business jet developed at IAI's Tel Aviv facilities. IAI is a shareholder in Galaxy Aerospace. Details of Galaxy can be found in the US part of this section.

IAI 1125 Astra SP and SPX

First flight: 19 March 1984 (original Astra), 16 August 1994 for latest Astra SPX.
Certification: 29 August 1985 to FAR Pt 25 through Amdt 54 and Pt 36 for original Astra. 8 January 1996 for SPX for FAA.
Role: Business jets.
Noise levels: FAR 36 noise levels 79.1 take-off, 89.5 sideline and 91.9 approach, all EPNdB for SPX.
Sales: Deliveries of the Astra SP started in 1990. Deliveries of Astra SPX began in 1996, initially to Hewlett-Packard. 2 Astra SPXs joined the 201st Airlift Squadron, US Air National Guard as C-38As.
Details: Astra SP and SPX, as specified.
Crew/passengers: 2 crew (with dual controls) plus 6 to 9 passengers.
Baggage capacity: 55 cu ft (1.5 m^3), for 1,102 lb (500 kg).
Pressurization system: 8.9 psi cabin differential.
Wing characteristics: Tapered wings, with inboard sections of 34° sweepback and outer sections of 25° sweepback. SPX has increased span, with winglets.
Wing control surfaces: Ailerons, flight/ground airbrakes on upper surfaces, slotted flaps (inboard and outboard) and leading-edge slats (latter deploying to 25° automatically with the flaps or under certain height, angle of attack and/or speed conditions). Leading-edge pneumatic de-icing boots.
Tail control surfaces: Variable-incidence tailplane. Elevators and rudder, with tabs. Tailplane de-icing.
Flight control system: Push-pull rods and bell cranks (hydraulically boosted ailerons), except for electric flaps and slats.
Construction materials: Metal, but with considerable use of composites for parts of the wings and tail, wing/body fairings, most control surfaces, tailcone, and several panels and access doors. GAMESA of Spain responsible for the fuselage and wing sections. SPX uses Kevlar, Nomex, graphite, epoxy and foam in its secondary structures and comprise about 6% of aircraft basic weight; titanium in high temperature areas.
Engines: 2 AlliedSignal TFE731-3A-200G turbofans with target thrust reversers for Astra SP, or TFE731-40R-200Gs with Dee Howard thrust reversers for SPX.

↑ IAI 1125 Astra SPX *(Paul Bowen)*

Engine rating: Each 3,700 lbf (16.46 kN) for Astra SP and 4,250 lbf (18.9 kN) for SPX at ISA + 9° C.
Fuel system: 4,900 litres usable, with 378 litres available in a removable auxiliary tank that does not reduce cabin volume. 9,365 lb (4,248 kg) by weight usable fuel with auxiliary tank.
Electrical system: 28 volt DC supply via 2 × 300 amp engine-driven starter-generators. AC supply from DC via 2 single-phase 850 VA inverters. 2 × 24 volt, 24 amp-hour ni-cd batteries, used partly for engine starting.
Hydraulic system: Dual systems, each 3,000 psi.
Braking system: Multi disc, with Goodyear anti-skid.
Radar: Rockwell Collins WXR-850 colour weather radar.
Flight avionics/instrumentation: Astra SP has electronic and mechanical, including 5-screen (6 ins, 15 cm) Rockwell Collins EFIS 86C, APS 85 digital autopilot, air data system, dual AHS 85 AHRS and more. Astra SPX has Rockwell Collins Pro Line 4 flight instrumentation, 2 ADC-850C air data computers, FCC-4000 autopilot/FDS, 2 AHC-85E AHRS, 2 VHF-422A coms, 2 VIR-432 nav (including GS and MKR), ADF-462, 2 DME-442, 2 TDR-94 Mode S transponder, ALT-50B radio altimeter, provision for a cockpit voice recorder, 2 Baker M1135 cockpit voice recorders and 1 Baker M1050 cabin audio. 4 EFD-4077 7.25 ins (18.4 cm) square CRT displays.

Aircraft variants:
Astra SP followed original Astra version, with aerodynamic, avionics and cabin upgrades.
Astra SPX first flew on 16 August 1994. Certified 1996. Rockwell Collins Pro Line 4 avionics. AlliedSignal TFE731-40R-200G turbofans with Dee Howard thrust reversers and FADEC. Revised wings with winglets to reduce drag, increase lateral stability and provide superior roll response. Prototype attained Mach 0.92. Greater weights. See table for more details.

Details for Astra SP, *with SPX in italics*

PRINCIPAL DIMENSIONS:
Wing span: 52 ft 8 ins (16.05 m), *54 ft 7 ins (16.64 m)*
Maximum height: 55 ft 7 ins (16.94 m), *the same*
Maximum height: 18 ft 2 ins (5.54 m), *the same*

CABIN:
Length: 22 ft 6 ins (6.86 m) including cockpit, 17 ft 2 ins (5.21 m) without, *the same*
Width: 4 ft 11 ins (1.5 m), *4 ft 9 ins (1.45 m)*
Height: 5 ft 7 ins (1.7 m), *the same*

WINGS:
Aerofoil section: Sigma 2
Area: 316.6 sq ft (29.42 m^2), *the same*
Aspect ratio: 8.759, *9.41*
Sweepback: *34° inboard, 25° outboard for SPX*

UNDERCARRIAGE:
Type: Retractable, with steerable nosewheels. Twin wheels on each unit. Trailing link main gear
Wheel base: 24 ft 1 ins (7.34 m)
Wheel track: 9 ft 1 ins (2.77 m)

WEIGHTS:
Empty: 13,225 lb (6,000 kg), *13,700 lb (6,213 kg)*, basic operating
Maximum take-off: 23,500 lb (10,660 kg), *24,645 lb (11,179 kg)*
Maximum landing: 20,695 lb (9,387 kg), *the same*
Useful load: 10,425 lb (4,728 kg), *11,100 lb (5,034 kg)*
Payload: 2,775 lb (1,258 kg), *3,300 lb (1,496 kg)*

PERFORMANCE:
Maximum operating Mach number: Mach 0.855, *Mach 0.875*
Maximum cruise speed: Mach 0.8 or 455 kts (524 mph) 842 km/h at 19,000 lb (8,618 kg) cruise weight, or 463 kts (533 mph) 857 km/h at 16,000 lb (7,257 kg) cruise weight, both at 35,000 ft (10,670 m); *Mach 0.82 or 470 kts (541 mph) 867 km/h at 41,000 ft (12,500 m) typically*
Long range cruise speed: *432 kts (497 mph) 800 km/h*
Stall speed: 132 kts (152 mph) 244 km/h clean IAS, or 97 kts (112 mph) 180 km/h landing configuration IAS
Balanced field length: 5,250 ft (1,600 m), *5,395 ft (1,644 m)*
Landing distance over a 50 ft (15 m) obstacle: 2,720 ft (829 m), *2,920 ft (890 m)*
Maximum climb rate: 3,700 ft (1,128 m) per minute, *3,800 ft (1,160 m) per minute*, both at sea level
Climb rate, OEI: 1,010 ft (308 m) per minute, *1,349 ft (411 m) per minute*
Maximum operating altitude: 45,000 ft (13,715 m), *the same*
Range: 3,202 naut miles (3,687 miles) 5,930 km, ISA, VFR reserves; *3,256 naut miles (3,749 miles) 6,034 km VFR, or 2,949 naut miles (3,396 miles) 5,465 km IFR*

Israviation Ltd — Israel

Comments: In November 1996, new US$8 million production facilities were inaugurated for the ST-50. However, in September 1997 Israviation was placed into receivership and the workforce was reduced to 63 while a new investor was sought. By October 1997 no new investor had been found and the various assets of Israviation were later sold (confirmed September 1998).
A subsidiary was Euraviation in Switzerland.

Israviation ST-50

First flight: 7 December 1994 for proof-of-concept prototype.
Certification: Had been expected in 1998 to FAR Pt 23 Amdt 45 Normal category, and CAAI regulations, for single-pilot operation in all weather conditions.
Role: Pressurized business and private aircraft.

Development

- ST-50 programme was financed by Euraviation Holding and by the Israeli Government.
- Cirrus Design Corporation of Duluth, Minnesota, USA, provided the initial technology know-how, with the aerodynamic concept based on the Cirrus VK-30. Cirrus became a major sub-contractor to Israviation, producing the proof-of-concept prototype. Core engineering was conducted at Duluth, where both companies' engineering teams combined their efforts, later transferred to Israel.

Sales: Price US$1,250,000 when final communication received.
Crew/passengers: 5 persons, 2 in front and bench seat at rear.
Baggage capacity: 300 lb (136 kg), with internal access. Volume 26 cu ft (0.74 m^3).
Pressurization system: 6 psi cabin differential.
Wing control surfaces: Ailerons, Fowler flaps and trim tab.
Tail control surfaces: Tailplane (span 21 ft 2 ins, 6.45 m) with elevators and pitch trim system. Dorsal and ventral fins, with rudder. Ventral fin serves to protect propeller from the ground (propeller ground clearance 2 ft 11 ins, 0.89 m).
Construction materials: Entirely composites. Wing with 2 'C' section main spars and rear spar for the undercarriage loads. Semi-monocoque fuselage structure of prepreg glass and carbon fibres. Pressure vessel is contained between the forward and aft pressure bulkheads. Fireproof engine compartment is used to retain structural integrity in the event of an engine fire.
Engine: Pratt & Whitney Canada PT6A-135B turboprop, driving a 7 ft 4 ins (2.24 m) MTV-9-E-C-F-R 3-blade pusher constant-speed propeller through a Kamatics driveshaft equipped with flexible couplings.
Engine rating: 810 shp (608 kW), derated to 500 shp (373 kW).
Fuel system: 662 litres in wings and fuselage, of which 643 litres are usable.
Electrical system: Engine-driven starter-generator (230 amp), 130 amp secondary alternator, and 24 volt, 43 amp-hour lead-acid battery.

↑ **Israviation ST-50 pressurized 5-seater** *(courtesy Israviation)*

Oxygen system: Individual emergency oxygen mask for each passenger.
De-icing: Complete de-icing/anti-icing system.
Radar: Weather radar, with AlliedSignal Bendix/King antenna.
Flight avionics/instrumentation: ARNAV ICDS 2000 integrated avionics SmartSuite, with 4 flat-panel colour liquid crystal displays for primary flight information, multi-function (with WxLink weather graphics) and EICAS displays for engine, navigation, flight planning, weather radar and communications information. Back-up conventional gauges. Fully integrated flight management system, with AHRS, computers and including IFR certified Loran and GPS receiver. ICDS 2000 uses the ARNAV high speed communications bus and ARINC 429 databus. AlliedSignal Bendix/King dual KX 165-21 transceivers with glideslope, and KT 70 transponder. Options include ARNAV System 6 DataLink flight following/air traffic management system, and satcom.

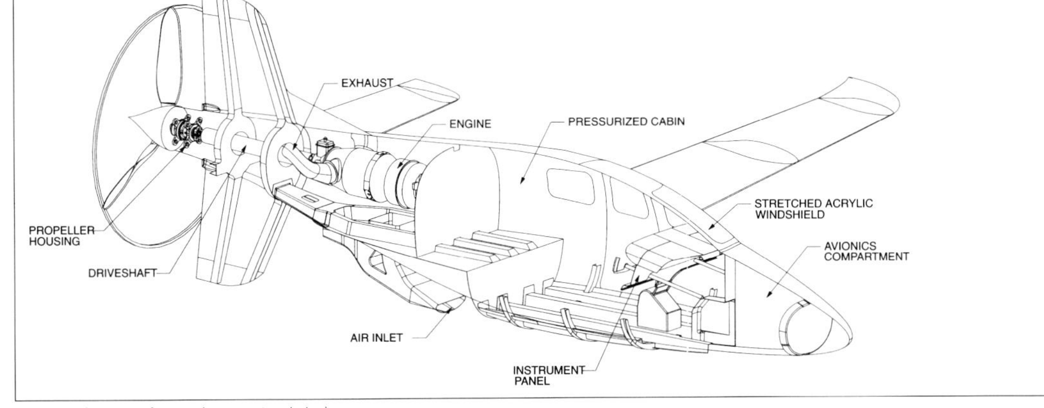

↑ **Israviation ST-50 layout** *(courtesy Israviation)*

Details for ST-50

PRINCIPAL DIMENSIONS:
Wing span: 39 ft 2 ins (11.94 m)
Maximum length: 27 ft 10 ins (8.48 m)
Maximum height: 11 ft (3.35 m)

CABIN:
Length: 10 ft 5 ins (3.18 m)
Width: 5 ft (1.52 m)
Height: 4 ft 4 ins (1.32 m)

WINGS:
Area: 165 sq ft (15.33 m^2)
Aspect ratio: 9.3
Sweepback: 0°
Dihedral: 4° 30'

UNDERCARRIAGE:
Type: Retractable, with nosewheel. Trailing-link main gear
Wheel track: 11 ft (3.35 m)

WEIGHTS:
Empty: 3,250 lb (1,474 kg)
Maximum take-off/ramp: 5,250 lb (2,381 kg)
Useful load: 1,950 lb (884 kg)

PERFORMANCE:
Cruise speed: 280 kts (322 mph) 518 km/h at 30,000 ft (9,150 m)
Stall speed: 61 kts (71 mph) 113 km/h, *with flaps*, EAS
Take-off distance: 1,400 ft (427 m)
Landing distance: 1,200 ft (366 m)
Maximum climb rate: 1,800 ft (549 m) per minute at sea level
G limits: +3.8, −1.9 clean
Ceiling: 31,000 ft (9,450 m), service
Range: 1,100 naut miles (1,266 miles), 2,037 km, with 45 minutes reserve

Eurospace Aeronautical Constructions — Italy

Corporate address:
Viale Cesare Pavese 77, 00144 Rome.
Telephone: +39 06 502 0554, 501 1759, 500 5760
Facsimile: +39 06 501 6994
Information:
Costantino Panvini Rosati (Marketing Manager).

Eurospace F-15-F and F-15-F 300 Excalibur, and F-15-F 300 Excalibur Military

First flight: October 1994.
Certification: To FAR Pt 23. Exceeds ICAO noise requirements.
First delivery: From December 1998 for F-15-F, January 1999 for F-15-F 300 and December 1999 for F-15-F 300 Excalibur Military.
Role: Civil and military training (utility configuration performs all basic aerobatic manoeuvres) and touring, and can be IFR equipped.
Sales: Price for F-15-F with standard equipment US$175,000 (ex works). Price for F-15-F 300 with standard equipment US$225,000 (ex works). Price for F-15-F 300 Excalibur Military with standard equipment US$250,000 (ex works).
Crew/passengers: 4 persons, under a high-visibility sliding canopy. Muffler with air exchanger for cabin heating. Ventilation system.
Baggage capacity: Rear baggage door with lock.
Wing control surfaces: Ailerons and flaps.
Tail control surfaces: Elevators (with trim tab) and rudder (with fixed trim).
Flight control system: Electric flaps.
Construction materials: All metal, with a few glassfibre components.
Engine: 200 hp (149 kW) Textron Lycoming AEIO-360-A1B6 piston engine in F-15-F, 300 hp (224 kW) Teledyne Continental

↑ **Eurospace F-15-F Excalibur** *(courtesy Aviation Picture Library)*

Details for F-15-F, *with F-15-F 300 in italics*

PRINCIPAL DIMENSIONS:
Wing span: 33 ft 9 ins (10.28 m), *the same*
Maximum length: 23 ft 11 ins (7.29 m), *the same*
Maximum height: 10 ft 2 ins (3.1 m), *the same*

WINGS:
Area: 145.31 sq ft (13.5 m^2)
Aspect ratio: 7.83

UNDERCARRIAGE:
Type: Retractable, with steerable nosewheel. Electrically operated through mechanical linkage, with battery as back-up and manual as emergency extension system

WEIGHTS:
Empty: 1,720 lb (780 kg), *1,900 lb (862 kg)*
Maximum take-off: 2,700 lb (1,225 kg), *3,002 lb (1,361 kg)*
Payload: 981 lb (445 kg), *1,210 lb (549 kg)*

PERFORMANCE:
Never-exceed speed (V_{NE}): 200 kts (230 mph) 370 km/h, *the same*
Maximum speed: 152 kts (175 mph) 281 km/h, *183 kts (211 mph) 339 km/h*
Cruise speed: 148 kts (170 mph) 274 km/h, *177 kts (204 mph) 328 km/h*, both at 75% power, 6,500 ft (1,980 m)
Stall speed: 56 kts (65 mph) 104 km/h, *58 kts (67 mph) 107 km/h*
Take-off distance: 1,182 ft (360 m), *the same*
Maximum climb rate: 1,160 ft (354 m) per minute, *1,500 ft (456 m) per minute*, both at sea level
Ceiling: above 15,000 ft (4,570 m), *above 20,075 ft (6,120 m)*, both service
Range: 725 naut miles (835 miles) 1,343 km, *750 naut miles (863 miles) 1,390 km*, both at 65% power
Duration: 5 hours 30 minutes at 65% power, *the same*

IO-550-F piston engine in F-15-F 300, and 300 hp (224 kW) Textron Lycoming AEIO-540-D4A5 in Excalibur Military, each with an MT 3-blade constant-speed variable-pitch propeller.
Electrical system: AC generator and 24 volt battery. External power receptacle.
Braking system: Hydraulically actuated disc on each main wheel. Manually operated parking brake.
Flight avionics/instrumentation: Standard avionics include AlliedSignal Bendix/King KX 155-34 com/nav/ISO/AA, KI 208 VOR/Loc converter/indicator plus com/nav antennae, KT 76A transponder and emergency locator transmitter. 2 option packages: Option 1 with KX 155-35 com/nav/ISO/AA, KI 209 VOR/Loc/GS and nav/com/GS antennae, KR 87 ADF, KI 227 indicator and loop/sense antenna, KN 63 DME, KDI 572 indicator, KMA 24 audio control console with integral marker beacon receiver, and KEA 130 encoding altimeter; and Option 2 with KX 155-35, KN 72 VOR/Loc/GS converter and nav/com/GS antennae, KR 87, KI 227, RMI KI 229, KN 63, KDI 572, KMA 24 with integral marker beacon receiver, KEA 130, and KCS 55-01 HSI. Co-pilot's instrumentation is gyro horizon, airspeed indicator, rate of climb indicator, altimeter and directional gyro.

Aircraft variants:
F-15-F Excalibur is the AEIO-360-A1B6-powered version, for delivery from December 1998.
F-15-F 300 Excalibur is the more-powerful IO-550-F-engined version, for delivery from early 1999.
F-15-F 300 Excalibur Military has an AEIO-540-D4A5 engine, for delivery from December 1999.

General Avia Costruzioni Aeronautiche srl — Italy

Corporate address:
Viale Roma 25, 06065, Passignano s/T (PG).
Telephone: +39 075 829444
Facsimile: +39 075 829442
E-mail: generalavia@econet.it
Information:
Massimo Piva (Sales Manager).

General Avia F.22 Pinguino series and F.220 Airone

First flight: 13 June 1989 (F.22/A prototype).
Certification: 4 May 1993 for F.22A, 17 December 1993 for F.22B, 13 May 1994 for F.22R and C, and 18 July 1997 for F.22 Bupp.
Details: Principally F.22C, except under Aircraft variants.
Role: 2-seat aerobatics light aircraft and trainer.

↑ General Avia F.22 Pinguino

↑ General Avia's new F.220 Airone 4-seat development of the F.22C

Wing control surfaces: Ailerons and flaps.
Tail control surfaces: Horn-balanced elevators (port trim tab) and rudder.
Flight control system: Manual, except for electric flaps.
Construction materials: Metal.
Engine: Textron Lycoming IO-360-A1A piston engine.
Engine rating: 180 hp (134 kW).
Fuel system: 160 litres. Provision for auxiliary fuel.
Flight avionics/instrumentation: AlliedSignal Bendix/King Silver Crown.

Aircraft variants:
F.22A Pinguino has a 116 hp (86.5 kW) Textron Lycoming O-235-N2C engine and 105 litres of fuel. Optional retractable undercarriage.
F.22B Pinguino has a 160 hp (119 kW) Textron Lycoming O-320-D2A engine and 135 litres of fuel. Optional retractable undercarriage.
F.22 Bupp is the latest version with a 160 hp (119 kW) O-320-D2A engine with variable-pitch propeller and fixed undercarriage.
F.22C Pinguino is the high-powered version, as detailed.
F.22R Pinguino-Sprint has a 160 hp (119 kW) O-320-D1A as standard and features a constant-speed propeller and retractable undercarriage.
F.220 Airone is basically a 4-seat development of the F.22C, with a cabin-type fuselage and doors replacing the sliding canopy. 200 hp (149 kW) IO-360-A1A engine and 245 litres of fuel. Retractable undercarriage.

Details for F.22C

PRINCIPAL DIMENSIONS:
Wing span: 27 ft 11 ins (8.5 m)
Maximum length: 24 ft 3 ins (7.4 m)
Maximum height: 9 ft 4 ins (2.84 m)

WINGS:
Aerofoil section: NACA laminar
Area: 116.47 sq ft (10.82 m^2)
Aspect ratio: 6.677

UNDERCARRIAGE:
Type: Fixed, with steerable nosewheel. Optional retractable undercarriage

WEIGHTS:
Empty: 1,411 lb (640 kg)
Maximum take-off: 1,984 lb (900 kg)

PERFORMANCE:
Maximum speed: 165 kts (190 mph) 305 km/h
Stall speed: 54 kts (62 mph) 100 km/h, *with flaps*
Take-off distance: 656 ft (200 m)
Landing distance: 788 ft (240 m)
Maximum climb rate: 1,476 ft (450 m) per minute
Ceiling: 19,000 ft (5,800 m), service
G limits: +6, -3
Range: 702 naut miles (808 miles) 1,400 km, with standard fuel

Partenavia Costruzioni Aeronautiche SpA — Italy

Comments: Partenavia aircraft can now be found under the VulcanAir entry. See also Taneja Aerospace and Aviation Ltd (TAAL) of India. Details and illustrations of the projected PD 90 Tapete Air Truck transport and PD 93 Idea lightplane can be found in the 1996-97 edition of *WA&SD*, pages 216-217 and 405-406 respectively.

Rinaldo Piaggio — Italy

Corporate address:
See the Reconnaissance section for company details. Tushav, a Turkish holding company, took a 51% shareholding in Piaggio in mid-1998.

Piaggio P.180 Avanti (and Jet version)

First flight: 23 September 1986.
Certification: 7 March 1990 (RAI/FAA Pt 23).
Role: Turboprop business aircraft.
Sales: By May 1998 a total of 43 production Avantis had been ordered (not including the original prototype and 2 test airframes). Recent orders and deliveries have been 3 delivered to the Italian Army, 2 delivered to the civil protection department in 1998, and 12 ordered for the Italian Air Force. Price in May 1998 was US$4.5 million, a reduction made possible by the replacement of some composite components produced in the USA by Italian-manufactured metal parts.
Crew/passengers: 1 or 2 pilots, plus 9 passengers. Alternative layouts include a 5-VIP arrangement.
Pressurization system: 9 psi maximum cabin differential.
Baggage compartment: 44.14 cu ft (1.25 m^3).
Wing control surfaces: Ailerons (starboard trim tab), and co-ordinated flaps on both the wings and canards.
Tail control surfaces: Variable-incidence tailplane, with elevators (with tabs). Rudder with trim tab.
Flight control system: Mechanical, except electric flaps and trim.
Construction materials: Metals and composites, with carbonfibre or Kevlar and epoxy used in the construction of the tail and tailcone, nose and canards, outer wing flaps, undercarriage doors and engine fairings (see Sales).
Engines: 2 Pratt & Whitney Canada PT6A-66 turboprops, with 7 ft 1 ins (2.16 m) Hartzell 5-blade constant-speed pusher propellers. A stretched turbofan version is to be developed.
Engine rating: Each flat-rated to 850 shp (633.8 kW).
Fuel system: 1,600 litres.
Electrical system: 2 starter-generators (400 amp, 28 volt), 38 amp-hour ni-cd battery.
Radar: Rockwell Collins WXR-840 weather radar.
Flight avionics/instrumentation: Rockwell Collins suite with 3-screen EFIS-85B, APS-65A autopilot, dual VHF-22A transceivers, dual VIP-32 VOR/LOC/GLS/MKR receivers, marker beacons, ADF-462 ADF, glideslope, dual DME-42, dual TDR-90

transponders, ALT-55B radio altimeter, dual MCS-65 compasses, dual RMI-3337s, and ADS-85 air data system.

Aircraft variants:
A stretched turbofan derivative of Avanti is to be developed.

↑ **Piaggio P.180 Avanti**

Details for Avanti

PRINCIPAL DIMENSIONS:
Wing span: 46 ft 0.5 ins (14.03 m)
Maximum length: 47 ft 3.5 ins (14.41 m)
Maximum height: 13 ft 0.75 ins (3.97 m)

CABIN:
Length: 14 ft 7.2 ins (4.45 m)
Width: 6 ft 0.8 ins (1.85 m)
Height: 5 ft 8.9 ins (1.75 m)
Volume: 375.04 cu ft (10.62 m^3)

WINGS:
Area: 172.22 sq ft (16 m^2)
Aspect ratio: 12.303

UNDERCARRIAGE:
Type: Retractable, with twin steerable nosewheels

WEIGHTS:
Empty: 7,500 lb (3,402 kg)
Maximum take-off: 11,550 lb (5,239 kg)
Maximum landing: 10,946 lb (4,965 kg)
Useful load: 4,100 lb (1,860 kg)
Payload: 2,000 lb (907 kg)

PERFORMANCE:
Maximum operating Mach number (M_{MO}): Mach 0.67
Maximum speed: 395 kts (455 mph) 732 km/h at high altitude
Stall speed: 109 kts (126 mph) 202 km/h *clean*, 93 kts (107 mph) 173 km/h *landing configuration*
Take-off over a 50 ft (15 m) obstacle: 2,850 ft (870 m)
Landing over a 50 ft (15 m) obstacle: 2,860 ft (872 m)
Maximum climb rate: 2,950 ft (900 m) per minute, at sea level
Ceiling: 41,000 ft (12,500 m)
Range: 1,400 naut miles (1,612 miles) 2,592 km, at 39,000 ft (11,900 m) with reserves

Sivel Srl — Italy

Corporate address:
Via G. Cesare, 33, 21040 Venegono Superiore (Varese).

Telephone and facsimile: +39 0331 864 856
E-mail: ernvalto@tin.it

Founded:
1990.

Information:
Ernesto Valtorta.

ACTIVITIES

▪ Information received in May 1998 stated that Sivel was then working on other aviation programmes and that production of general aviation aircraft was to start that year.

Sivel SD-27 Corriedale

First flight: 1992.
Certification: Certified under JAR-VLA.
Role: 2-seat touring, private, aero club and training aircraft.
Sales: As of May 1998, intentions were to produce 5 SD-27s before the end of 1998.
Baggage capacity: Shelf area aft of seats.
Wing control surfaces: Constant-chord wings with ailerons and flaps.
Tail control surfaces: Horn-balanced single-piece elevator with central tab, and horn-balanced rudder.
Construction materials: Welded chromoly steel tubing for the main cabin area structure, with a composites shell, with an aluminium alloy monocoque tailcone and tail unit.

↑ **Sivel SD-27 Corriedale** *(courtesy Sivel)*

Details for Sivel SD-27

PRINCIPAL DIMENSIONS:
Wing span: 32 ft 10 ins (10 m)
Maximum length: 23 ft 4 ins (7.1 m)
Maximum height: 9 ft 1 ins (2.76 m)

CABIN:
Width: 3 ft 7.3 ins (1.1 m)

WINGS:
Area: 134.55 sq ft (12.5 m^2)
Aspect ratio: 8

UNDERCARRIAGE:
Type: Fixed, with swivelling nosewheel. Designed to operate from unprepared airstrips

WEIGHTS:
Empty: 882 lb (400 kg)
Maximum take-off: 1,367 lb (620 kg)

PERFORMANCE:
Never-exceed speed (V_{NE}): 132 kts (152 mph) 245 km/h
Maximum speed: 105 kts (121 mph) 195 km/h
Cruise speed: 97 kts (112 mph) 180 km/h at 75% power and 8,000 ft (2,440 m)
Best rate of climb speed: 65 kts (75 mph) 120 km/h
Stall speed: 43 kts (49 mph) 79 km/h *with flaps*, 50 kts (57 mph) 92 km/h *clean*
Take-off distance: 460 ft (140 m)
Landing distance: 361 ft (110 m)
Maximum climb rate: 925 ft (282 m) per minute at sea level
Ceiling: 13,125 ft (4,000 m), service
G limits: +4.4, -1.76
Range: 540 naut miles (621 miles) 1,000 km
Duration: 6 hours

Engine: Rotax 912 piston engine, with a 5 ft 7 ins (1.7 m) MT 2-blade fixed-pitch propeller or optional MT constant-speed propeller.
Engine rating: 80 hp (59.7 kW).
Fuel system: 80 litres usable.

Aircraft variants:
SD-27 is the standard initial production version, as detailed.
Aerobatic version first flew in 1995 with a 160 hp (119 kW) engine.
4-seat touring version is anticipated.
Future version could have a 125 hp (93.2 kW) Teledyne Continental IO-240 engine.

Sivel SD-28 Trittico/Lincoln

First flight: Scheduled for February 1999.
Role: Side-by-side 2-seat aerobatic and sporting aircraft.
Sales: As of May 1998, intentions were to complete the prototype SV-28, allowing its first flight in February 1999.
Crew/passengers: 2 persons, side by side. Dual controls. Baggage area aft of seats.
Wing characteristics: Low-mounted, constant-chord, with upturned wingtips that have some sweepback. Dihedral 7°.
Wing control surfaces: Ailerons and flaps.
Tail control surfaces: Horn-balanced single-piece elevator with central tab, and horn-balanced rudder.
Flight control system: Mechanical.
Construction materials: Metal, generally similar to SD-27.
Engine: Textron Lycoming AEIO-320-D piston engine, with an MT-Propeller MTV-12C/180-17 3-blade hydraulically variable-pitch propeller. Fuel/oil systems suited to inverted flight.
Engine rating: 160 hp (119.3 kW).
Fuel system: 160 litres in 4 wing tanks.
Electrical system: 12 volt, 30 amp-hour battery.
Flight avionics/instrumentation: VFR. To customer's requirements.

Details for SD-28

PRINCIPAL DIMENSIONS:
Wing span: 26 ft 3 ins (8 m)
Maximum length: 21 ft 4 ins (6.5 m)
Maximum height: 9 ft 1 ins (2.76 m)

WINGS:
Aerofoil section: NACA 641415 modified
Area: 107.6 sq ft (10 m^2)
Aspect ratio: 6.4
Dihedral: 4° 30′

UNDERCARRIAGE:
Type: Fixed, with nosewheel
Wheel base: 5 ft 6 ins (1.67 m)
Wheel track: 7 ft 7 ins (2.31 m)

WEIGHTS:
Empty: 1,168 lb (530 kg)
Maximum take-off: 1,764 lb (800 kg)

PERFORMANCE:
Maximum speed: 140 kts (161 mph) 259 km/h IAS
Cruise speed: 130 kts (150 mph) 241 km/h at 75% power, IAS
Range with full fuel: 540 naut miles (622 miles) 1,000 km at cruise speed

Costruzioni Aeronautiche Tecnam srl — Italy

Corporate address:
1ª Traversa via G. Pascoli, I-80026 Casoria (NA).

Telephone: +39 081 7583210, 7588854, 7588751
Facsimile: +39 081 7584528

Founded:
1986. Member of the Associazione Italiana Costruttori Aerodine da Diporto e Sportive (AICA).

Information:
Dott. Giovanni Pascale Langer (Managing Director).

ACTIVITIES

▪ Other work includes manufacture of ATR 42-72 stabilizers and other parts, Boeing MD 80/90/717 fuselage panels, and parts for Agusta A109 and EH 101 helicopters. Workshops qualified to RAI and NATO AQAP-4.

↑ Tecnam P92 Echo

↑ Tecnam P96 Golf

Tecnam P92 and P92-J Echo

First flight: 13 March 1993.
Certification: P92-J certified version (JAR-VLA) became available in April 1995.
Role: 2-seat JAR-VLA certified or kit-built ultralight monoplane, with dual controls.
Sales: Over 300 sold at time of writing, with production rate of 8/9 per month.
Baggage capacity: Aft of seats.
Wing control surfaces: Frise ailerons and half-span flaps (0-35°).
Tail control surfaces: Slab tailplane (span 9 ft 6 ins, 2.9 m) with trim/anti-balance tab.
Flight control system: Manual, except for electric flaps and trim.
Construction materials: Metal frames, torsion box, spars, ribs and skins, except for glassfibre wing leading edges, lower part of engine cowl (partly metal upper section) and wing/fin tips, and Dacron fabric on the tailplane aft of the alloy spar to minimize mass-balancing, ailerons and flaps.
Engine: 80 hp (59.7 kW) Rotax 912 standard, with 5 ft 5 ins (1.65 m) 2-blade wooden propeller. Optional 80 hp (59.7 kW) Limbach L 2000.
Engine rating: See above.
Fuel system: 2 × 30 litre tanks in the composite wing leading edges.
Electrical system: 100 W, 12 volt alternator. 15 amp-hour battery.
Braking system: Hydraulic disc brakes with cockpit brake lever. Parking brake.
Flight avionics/instrumentation: Airspeed indicator, altimeter, magnetic compass, bank indicator, engine speed indicator and temperature gauge. Wide instrument panel allows for extra equipment up to IFR.

Aircraft variants:
P92 complies to Italian ULM regulations.
P92-J is certified to JAR-VLA and has a MTOW of 1,180 lb (535 kg).

Details for P92 Echo with Rotax 912 engine

PRINCIPAL DIMENSIONS:
Wing span: 31 ft 6 ins (9.6 m)
Maximum length: 20 ft 8 ins (6.3 m)
Maximum height: 7 ft 6.5 ins (2.3 m)

WINGS:
Area: 142.08 sq ft (13.2 m^2)
Aspect ratio: 6.98
Dihedral: 1° 30'

UNDERCARRIAGE:
Type: Fixed, with steerable nosewheel. Wheel fairings
Main and nose wheel tyre size: 5.00-5
Wheel track: 5 ft 11 ins (1.8 m)

WEIGHTS:
Empty: 622 lb (282 kg)
Maximum take-off: 992 lb (450 kg)

PERFORMANCE:
Maximum speed: 112 kts (129 mph) 208 km/h
Cruise speed: 89 kts (103 mph) 165 km/h at 65% power, 84 kts (96 mph) 155 km/h at 55% power
Stall speed: 37 kts (42 mph) 67 km/h *clean*, 34 kts (39 mph) 63 km/h *with flaps*
Take-off distance: 296 ft (90 m)
Landing distance: 300 ft (92 m)
Maximum climb rate: 1,083 ft (330 m) per minute at 59 kts, sea level
Duration: 4.5 hours

Tecnam P96 Golf

First flight: February 1997.
Role: Very light low-wing monoplane.
Crew/passenger: 2 persons, side by side, in an enclosed cabin. Dual controls. Canopy slides backwards on guiderails and can be opened during flight.
Baggage capacity: Aft of seats.
Wing control surfaces: Constant-chord wings (except at roots) with considerable dihedral and upturned wingtips, with differential Frise ailerons and half-span flaps.
Tail control surfaces: Slab tailplane (span 9 ft 6 ins, 2.9 m) with trim/anti-balance tab. Vertical tail is similar to that of P92.
Flight control system: Manual, except for electrically actuated flaps and trim.
Construction materials: According to Tecnam, the fuselage features a composites top-deck fairing from aft of the canopy to the tail, "keeping wetted area to a minimum while allowing for good pressure recovery aft of the cabin canopy". The main fuselage area permits cockpit entry for tall persons while still keeping the cross-section minimal to reduce aerodynamic drag, achieved by lowering the height of the carry-through structures.
Engine: Rotax 912 piston engine, with 1:2.27 reduction gear to a 5 ft 5.5 ins (1.66 m) 2-blade wooden propeller.
Engine rating: 80 hp (59.7 kW).
Fuel system: 2 × 35 litre tanks in wing leading-edges.
Braking system: Hand-lever operated hydraulic disc brakes.
Flight avionics/instrumentation: Panel can accommodate blind-flying instrumentation and com/nav radio.

Details for Golf

PRINCIPAL DIMENSIONS:
Wing span: 28 ft 6.5 ins (8.7 m)
Maximum length: 20 ft 4 ins (6.2 m)
Maximum height: 7 ft 4.5 ins (2.25 m)

WINGS:
Area: 131.32 sq ft (12.2 m^2)
Aspect ratio: 6.2

UNDERCARRIAGE:
Type: Fixed, with steerable nosewheel. Main legs of steel alloy leaf-spring type, and rubber-in-compression shock absorption for nosewheel. Wheel fairings. Suited to rough ground operation. Tail guard
Nose and main wheel tyre size: 5.00-5
Wheel base: 5 ft 3 ins (1.6 m)
Wheel track: 6 ft 3 ins (1.9 m)

WEIGHTS:
Empty: 617 lb (280 kg) basic
Maximum take-off: 992 lb (450 kg)

PERFORMANCE:
Maximum speed: 119 kts (137 mph) 220 km/h
Cruise speed: 94 kts (109 mph) 175 km/h at 65% power, 88 kts (101 mph) 163 km/h at 55% power
Stall speed: 37.5 kts (43 mph) 69 km/h *clean*, 35 kts (40 mph) 64 km/h *with flaps*
Take-off distance: 322 ft (98 m)
Landing distance: 584 ft (178 m)
Maximum climb rate: 1,000 ft (305 m) per minute at 59 kts, sea level
Duration: 4 hours 30 minutes

Pietro Terzi srl — Italy

Corporate address:
20154 Milano, P. Le A Baiamonti 1.

Telephone: +39 02 3360 9080
Facsimile:+39 02 3360 7996

Information:
Dr Ing Pietro Terzi

ACTIVITIES

▪ Also produces the T30C, E and SL Katana (see Recreational Aircraft section) and the Windspider partially inflatable sailing craft.

Terzi T-9 Stiletto

First flight: 1990.
Certification: Conforms to FAR Pt 23 and JAR-VLA.
Role: Lightplane suited to civil/military training, club use, personal use, surveillance, civil protection, forest patrol, traffic control and more.
Crew/passenger: 2 seats, side by side, under an upward opening rear-hinged canopy. Can taxi with canopy up.

↑ Pietro Terzi T-9 Stiletto

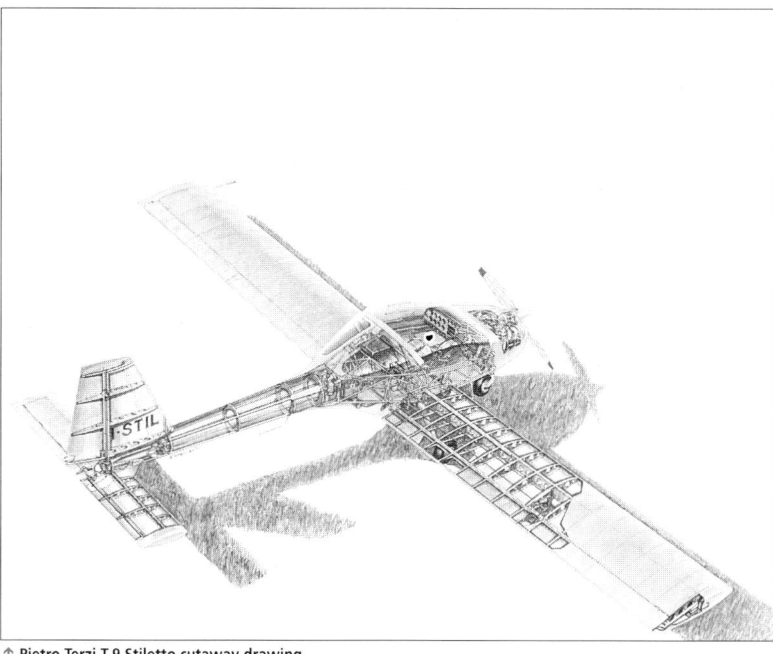

↑ Pietro Terzi T-9 Stiletto cutaway drawing

Baggage capacity: Aft of seats.
Wing control surfaces: Mass-balanced ailerons and 2-position flaps. Wings are detachable.
Tail control surfaces: Slab tailplane with combined anti-servo/trim tab and rudder.
Flight control system: Manual, with ailerons actuated by pushrods in the fuselage and cables in the wings. Similar arrangement for tailplane, with pushrods in the fuselage and cables in the tailboom. Rudder is cable actuated. Manual flaps.
Construction materials: All metal. Fuselage comprises 2 parts, the crash resistant steel tube framework cockpit area and a detachable aluminium alloy tailboom carrying the tail unit. Glassfibre cabin enclosure and cantilever undercarriage legs. Wings have 2024 T3 metal structure, with main spar, forward and rear auxiliary spars, and rivetted aluminium alloy skins. Aluminium alloy tail unit.
Engine: Rotax 912A piston engine, with integrated reduction gear and a 2-blade fixed-pitch wooden propeller.
Engine rating: 80 hp (59.7 kW).
Fuel system: 80 litres in a single tank on the baggage area floor of the prototype; beneath floor on production models.
Electrical system: 12/14 volt, including alternator as main source plus a battery. External power socket for engine starting.
Braking system: Hydraulic differential disc brakes.
Flight avionics/instrumentation: Large instrument panel allows for nav/com, ADF, transponder and GPS.

↑ Pietro Terzi T30C Katana (see Recreational section)

Details for T-9 Stiletto

PRINCIPAL DIMENSIONS:
Wing span: 33 ft 8 ins (10.26 m)
Maximum length: 22 ft 6 ins (6.85 m)
Maximum height: 7 ft 6.5 ins (2.3 m)

WINGS:
Aerofoil section: Wortmann FX67-K-150/17
Area: 132.5 sq ft (12.31 m^2)
Aspect ratio: 8.551

UNDERCARRIAGE:
Type: Fixed, with castoring nosewheel. Main wheel legs are glassfibre flat spring type. Cantilever spring steel nosewheel leg

WEIGHTS:
Empty: 837.5 lb (380 kg)
Maximum take-off: 1,433 lb (650 kg)
Useful load: 595 lb (270 kg)

PERFORMANCE:
Maximum cruise speed: over 108 kts (124 mph) 200 km/h at sea level
Stall speed: 43.5 kts (50 mph) 80 km/h *clean*, 40 kts (46 mph) 74 km/h *with flaps*, both IAS
Take-off distance: 328 ft (100 m)
Take-off distance over a 50 ft (15 m) obstacle: 624 ft (190 m)
Landing distance over a 50 ft (15 m) obstacle: 575 ft (175 m)
Climb rate: over 800 ft (244 m) per minute at sea level, at IAS of 65/67 kts
Ceiling: 13,780 ft (4,200 m), service
G limits: 4.4
Range: 399 naut miles (460 miles) 740 km, at sea level, 30 minutes reserve

VulcanAir SpA — Italy

Corporate address:
Via G.Pascoli 7, 80026 Casoria (NA).
Telephone: +39 081 591 8237, 8105, 8173, 8111
Facsimile: +39 081 591 8172
Founded:
1989.
Information:
Lucille Fyfe (Assistant to the President).

ACTIVITIES

■ VulcanAir is situated on an area of 645,835 sq ft (60,000 m^2) in the proximity of Capodichino Airport in Naples. The company was incorporated in 1989 by the Finmeccanica Group, and in 1996 was acquired by the private group 'Neapolitana Holding' with the intention of developing aircraft manufacture, maintenance (holding JAR 145 certification as a major aircraft repair and maintenance station), aerial work (including aerial photogrammetry, patrol, surveillance, reconnaissance and aerial survey missions), passenger and cargo transport, and a flying school for commercial pilots. VulcanAir has taken over the SF600A Canguro from the former SIAI-Marchetti, and on 4 March 1998 won an auction to take over Partenavia's P 68 series of aircraft, including jigs, tooling, aircraft, parts and manufacture, with the intention of restarting production in late 1998 or soon thereafter.

VulcanAir P 68 C, P 68 C-TC and Observer 2

First flight: 25 May 1970 in original P 68 Victor form.
Role: Twin piston-engined transport for private and commercial use. Observer 2 for observation, patrol and similar roles.
Details: For P 68 C-TC, except under Aircraft variants.
Sales: Some 400 P 68s are flying worldwide
Crew/passengers: 6 or 7 persons, with seats quickly removable for cargo carrying. Options include club seating with folding table and refreshment unit, litters for an air ambulance role, parachutist modifications, photogrammetry camera and tracking hatches, etc.
Baggage capacity: 19.78 cu ft (0.56 m^3) for 400 lb (181 kg), with a large baggage/freight door (also used as an emergency exit).
Wing control surfaces: Ailerons and single-slotted flaps.
Tail control surfaces: Slab tailplane and rudder, both with tabs.
Flight control system: Rod and cable, except for electric flaps.
Construction materials: Principally metal, with glassfibre wing/body fairings.
Engines: 2 Textron Lycoming TIO-360-C1A6D turbocharged piston engines, with Hartzell constant-speed propellers.
Engine rating: Each 210 hp (156.6 kW).
Fuel system: 538 litres, of which 520 litres are usable.
De-icing system: Standard.
Radar: See avionics.
Flight avionics/instrumentation: Instrument panel, with annunciator panel warning light system, accommodates sophisticated avionics packages including autopilot/flight directors, weather radar, HF, etc. VFR/IFR, with options including AlliedSignal Bendix/King Silver Crown or Rockwell Collins suite.

Aircraft variants:
P 68 C has a 200 hp (149 kW) IO-360-A1B6 engine. Empty operating weight 2,800 lb (1,270 kg), MTOW 4,387 lb (1,990 kg), maximum speed 172 kts (198 mph) 318 km/h, service ceiling 18,535 ft (5,650 m), and OEI ceiling 7,000 ft (2,150 m).
P 68 C-TC is a turbocharged variant of the P 68 C, as detailed. Offers improved hot-and-high performance. OEI ceiling of 12,600 ft (3,850 m).
P 68 Observer 2 is an observation and patrol variant of P 68 C, with a unique highly-glazed plexiglas cabin for good forward and downward visibility. Can carry weather radar, FLIR, SLAR and more, the standard transparent nose giving way to a thimble fairing when a nose sensor is carried. Upturned wingtips to

improve minimum control and stalling speeds, and offer better OEI handling. Empty weight 2,910 lb (1,320 kg), MTOW 4,594 lb (2,084 kg), maximum speed 174 kts (200 mph) 322 km/h, and service ceiling 18,000 ft (5,500 m).
P 68 Observer 2-TC is the turbocharged variant.
AP 68 TP-300 Spartacus is a 8/9-seat variant with Allison 250-B17C turboprops.

↑ VulcanAir P 68 C-TC

Details for P 68 C-TC

PRINCIPAL DIMENSIONS:
Wing span: 39 ft 4.5 ins (12 m)
Maximum length: 31 ft 3.5 ins (9.54 m)
Maximum height: 11 ft 2 ins (3.4 m)

WINGS
Aerofoil section: NACA 63-3515
Area: 200.21 sq ft (18.6 m^2)
Aspect ratio: 7.74
Dihedral: 1°

UNDERCARRIAGE:
Type: Fixed, with steerable nosewheel. Wheel fairings
Wheel track: 7 ft 10.5 ins (2.4 m)

WEIGHTS:
Empty: 2,866 lb (1,300 kg)
Maximum take-off: 4,387 lb (1,990 kg)
Maximum landing: 4,365 lb (1,980 kg)
Useful load: 1,521 lb (690 kg)

PERFORMANCE:
Maximum speed: 174 kts (200 mph) 322 km/h at sea level
Cruise speed: 170 kts (196 mph) 315 km/h at 75% power, or 149 kts (172 mph) 276 km/h at 55% power
Minimum control speed: 60 kts (69 mph) 111 km/h
Stall speed: 65 kts (75 mph) 120 km/h *clean*, 57 kts (66 mph) 106 km/h *with full flaps*
Take-off distance: 755 ft (230 m)
Landing distance: 788 ft (240 m)
Maximum climb rate: 1,520 ft (462 m) per minute at sea level
Climb rate, OEI: 295 ft (90 m) per minute at sea level
Ceiling: over 25,000 ft (7,620 m)
Range: 830 naut miles (955 miles) 1,540 km at 75% power, or 1,055 naut miles (1,215 miles), 1,955 km at 55% power, both at 12,000 ft (3,660 m), 45 minutes reserve

VulcanAir AP 68 TP-600 Viator

First flight: 29 March 1985.
Role: Unpressurized small commuter, charter and utility transport, also suited to air ambulance, surveillance and maritime patrol, photogrammetry, remote sensing (2 belly openings are available for photographic or sensor equipment), paratrooping and multi-engine training.
Crew/passengers: 2 pilots plus 9 passengers.
Wing control surfaces: Ailerons (with trim tabs) and single-slotted flaps. Leading-edge stall strips.
Tail control surfaces: Elevators with vortex generators and rudder, all with trim tabs.
Flight control system: Rod and cable, except for electric flaps.
Construction materials: Metal.
Engines: 2 Allison 250-B17C turboprops, with Hartzell 3-blade constant-speed propellers.
Engine rating: Each flat-rated at 328 shp (245 kW).
Fuel system: 840 litres; 1,488 lb (675 kg) useful fuel by weight.
Electrical system: 28 volt DC supply via 2 starter-generators. 24 volt, 29 amp-hour battery.
De-icing system: For flying surfaces and engines.
Radar: Colour weather radar.
Flight avionics/instrumentation: Standard IFR avionics, 3-axis autopilot, instrument panel with annunciator panel warning light system, HF, etc.

Details for Viator

PRINCIPAL DIMENSIONS:
Wing span: 39 ft 4.5 ins (12 m)
Maximum length: 37 ft (11.27 m)
Maximum height: 11 ft 11 ins (3.63 m)

CABIN:
Length: 17 ft 4 ins (5.29 m)
Width: 3 ft 8.5 ins (1.13 m)
Height: 4 ft 1.5 ins (1.265 m)
Volume: 229.55 cu ft (6.5 m^3)

WINGS
Aerofoil section: NACA 63-3515
Area: 200.21 sq ft (18.6 m^2)
Aspect ratio: 7.74

UNDERCARRIAGE:
Type: Retractable, with nosewheel

WEIGHTS:
Empty: 3,571 lb (1,620 kg)
Maximum take-off: 6,614 lb (3,000 kg)
Maximum landing: 6,283 lb (2,850 kg)
Payload: 1,918 lb (870 kg)

PERFORMANCE:
Maximum speed: 220 kts (254 mph) 409 km/h at 12,000 ft (3,660 m)
Maximum-range cruise speed: 180 kts (207 mph) 334 km/h at 12,000 ft (3,660 m)
Stall speed: 80 kts (92 mph) 148 km/h *clean*, 65 kts (75 mph) 121 km/h *with flaps*
Take-off distance: 1,313 ft (400 m)
Landing distance: 1,050 ft (320 m)
Maximum climb rate: 1,650 ft (503 m) per minute
Ceiling: 26,000 ft (7,925 m) service, or 11,400 ft (3,475 m) OEI
Range: 899 naut miles (1,034 miles) 1,665 km at 12,000 ft (3,660 m), 178 kts, with 1,200 lb (545 kg) payload and 45 minutes fuel reserve

↑ VulcanAir AP 68 TP-600 Viator

VulcanAir SF600A Canguro

First flight: 30 December 1978.
Certification: FAR Pt 23.
Role: Multi-purpose transport.
Crew/passengers: 1 or 2 pilots (dual controls). 9 folding passenger seats in the main cabin, or room for 10 troops or paratroops, or 2 litters and attendants in ambulance configuration.
Wing control surfaces: Ailerons and double-slotted flaps.
Tail control surfaces: Elevators (electric and manual trim) and rudder (manual trim).
Flight control system: Cable, but with electric aileron and elevator trim, and electric flaps.
Engines: 2 Allison 250-B17F1 turboprops, with Hartzell 3-blade propellers.
Engine rating: Each 450 shp (335.6 kW).
Fuel system: 1,024 litres.
De-icing system: Optional.
Radar: Optional weather radar. See Aircraft variants.
Flight avionics/instrumentation: Instrument panel offers space for double instruments, and options include autopilot.

↑ VulcanAir SF600A Canguro

Aircraft variants:
SF600A roles, in addition to transport, can include photogrammetry with 1 or 2 Wild or Zeiss cameras and high precision navigation systems, and maritime early warning and surveillance with a 360° scanning radar or SLAR and FLAR.

Details for SF600A

PRINCIPAL DIMENSIONS:
Wing span: 49 ft 2 ins (15 m)
Maximum length: 40 ft 1 ins (12.21 m)
Maximum height: 14 ft 1 ins (4.3 m)

CABIN:
Length: 16 ft 8.5 ins (5.09 m)
Width: 3 ft 11 ins (1.2 m)
Height: 4 ft 1 ins (1.25 m)
Volume: 279 cu ft (7.9 m^3)
Cargo door size: Sliding door 4 ft 10.5 ins × 3 ft 8.5 ins (1.48 × 1.12 m), openable in flight

WINGS:
Area: 258.33 sq ft (24 m^2)
Aspect ratio: 9.375

UNDERCARRIAGE:
Type: Fixed, with steerable nosewheel

WEIGHTS:
Empty: 4,674 lb (2,210 kg), operating (cargo)
Maximum take-off: 7,947 lb (3,605 kg)

PERFORMANCE:
Maximum speed: 173 kts (199 mph) 320 km/h at 5,000 ft (1,525 m)
Cruise speed: 165 kts (190 mph) 306 km/h
Stall speed: 67 kts (77 mph) 124 km/h, *with flaps*
Take-off distance: 1,444 ft (440 m)
Landing distance: 984 ft (300 m)
Maximum climb rate: 1,260 ft (384 m) per minute
G limits: +3.5, –1.4
Ceiling: 20,000 ft (6,100 m), service
Range: 930 naut miles (1,070 miles) 1,722 km

Korean Air — South Korea

Corporate address:
See Helicopter section for company details.

Korean Air Chang-Gong 91

First flight: 22 November 1991.
Certification: 31 August 1993.
Role: 4-seat lightplane.
Crew/passengers: Pilot and 3 passengers, with a fifth rear seat suited to a child.

↑ Korean Air Chang-Gong 91

Details for Chang-Gong 91

PRINCIPAL DIMENSIONS:
Wing span: 33 ft 5 ins (10.2 m)
Maximum length: 25 ft 5 ins (7.74 m)
Maximum height: 8 ft 10 ins (2.7 m)

CABIN:
Length: 10 ft (3.05 m)
Width: 3 ft 10 ins (1.17 m)

WINGS:
Aerofoil section: NACA 63_2-415
Area: 160 sq ft (14.86 m^2)
Aspect ratio: 7

UNDERCARRIAGE:
Type: Fixed, with steerable nosewheel. Prototype has been flown with wheel fairings

WEIGHTS:
Empty: 1,850 lb (839 kg)
Maximum take-off and landing: 2,700 lb (1,225 kg)

PERFORMANCE:
Maximum speed: 183 kts (210 mph) 339 km/h at sea level
Cruise speed: 102-118 kts (117-136 mph) 189-220 km/h at 5,000 ft (1,525 m)
Stall speed: 63 kts (73 mph) 117 km/h *clean*, 54 kts (62 mph) 100 km/h with *full flaps*
Take-off distance: 2,050 ft (625 m)
Landing distance: 411 ft (125 m)
Maximum climb rate: 738 ft (225 m) per minute at sea level
Ceiling: 16,500 ft (5,025 m)
Range: 810 naut miles (932 miles) 1,500 km

Baggage capacity: 100 lb (45 kg) aft of the seats.
Wing control surfaces: Frise ailerons (with tabs) and slotted flaps (0-40°).
Tail control surfaces: Slab tailplane with geared tab, and rudder.
Construction materials: Principally metal, but with composites in the tail unit.
Engine: Textron Lycoming IO-360-A1B6 piston engine, with a Hartzell 2-blade constant-speed propeller.
Engine rating: 200 hp (149 kW).
Fuel system: 212 litres.
Electrical system: 14 volt DC supply via an engine-driven alternator.
Braking system: Disc brakes.
Flight avionics/instrumentation: AlliedSignal Bendix/King suite, with KX 155 com/nav, ADF, DME, transponder, marker beacon receiver and more.

Aeroplastika — Lithuania

Corporate address:
J. Bakanavsko 29, 3019 Kaunas.
Telephone: +370 7 708446
Facsimile: +370 7 705733

ACTIVITIES
- Developed the LAK-X, manufactured by Avia Baltika.

Avia Baltika Aviation Ltd — Lithuania

Corporate address:
7c-24 Draugystes Street, 3036 Kaunas.
Telephone: +370 7 710457, 541230
Facsimile: +370 7 710405
Information:
Josif Legenzov (General Manager), Kestas Leonavicius (Chief Designer).
Production and maintenance:
Address: 86a Vilniaus Street, Karmelava, 4301 Kaunas.
Founded:
1991 (incorporated) on the basis of the Kaunas helicopter service and repair factory.

ACTIVITIES
- Production of the LAK-X.
- Supply and maintenance of aviation equipment and spare parts anywhere in the world.
- Overhaul of Mi-8 helicopters.
- Overhaul of aviation equipment, units and components.
- Completion and improvement of aviation equipment, research and more.
- Aircraft leasing and provision of helicopters.
- Transportation (cargo and passengers) in the Baltic States region, and rescue work for the public sector. Company owns 4 Mil helicopters, including an Mi-8VIP used for Government representatives, businessmen and tourists as required.

Note: The LAK-X is produced at Kaunas by Avia Baltika but was developed by **Aeroplastika**.

Avia Baltika (Aeroplastika) LAK-X

First flight: 2 August 1992.
Role: Composites primary and sport lightplane.
Sales: Also available as a kitplane.
Crew/passengers: 2 persons side-by-side under a forward-hinged bubble canopy.
Baggage capacity: 66 lb (30 kg).
Wing control surfaces: Ailerons (10° down for landing). Flaps deflected 3° up for maximum speed, 0° for cruise, 15° take-off and 40° landing.
Tail control surfaces: Elevators (with trim) and rudder.
Flight control system: Rods/levers for ailerons and elevators, cables for rudder, and electrically actuated flaps and trim.
Construction materials: All composites, principally glassfibre and foam sandwich construction but also with spar caps and undercarriage legs of unidirectional glassfibre/epoxy.

↑ Avia Baltika (Aeroplastika) LAK-X *(courtesy Avia Baltika)*

Details for LAK-XA

PRINCIPAL DIMENSIONS:
Wing span: 35 ft 0.5 ins (10.68 m)
Maximum length: 23 ft (7 m)
Maximum height: 7 ft 6.5 ins (2.3 m)

WINGS:
Aerofoil section: NACA 64 series
Area: 108.18 sq ft (10.05 m^2)
Aspect ratio: 11.35
Dihedral: 6°
Incidence: 4°
Twist: 2°

UNDERCARRIAGE:
Type: Fixed, with nosewheel. Streamline wheel fairings

WEIGHTS:
Empty: 970 lb (440 kg)
Maximum take-off: 1,587 lb (720 kg)

PERFORMANCE:
Maximum speed: 135 kts (155 mph) 250 km/h
Maximum cruise speed: 119 kts (137 mph) 220 km/h
Economic cruise speed: 108 kts (124 mph) 200 km/h
Stall speed: 44.5 kts (51 mph) 82 km/h, *with flaps*
Take-off and landing distance: 492 ft (150 m)
Maximum climb rate: 984 ft (300 m) per minute at sea level
G limits: +4, –2
Range: 459 naut miles (528 miles) 850 km

Engine: 5 piston engine options, the LAK-XE having either an 80 hp (59.7 kW) Rotax 912, 100 hp (74.5 kW) Rotax 914 or 93 hp (69.4 kW) Limbach L 2400 and Mühlbauer MTV-1 composite 2-blade propeller; the LAK-XA having a 114 hp (85 kW) PZL-Rzeszów PZL-F.4A235B31 or 125 hp (93.2 kW) Teledyne Continental IO-240-A and McCauley metal 2-blade propeller.
Engine rating: See above.
Fuel system: 2 wing tanks, each 55 litres, with 100 litres maximum usable fuel.
Electrical system: 12 volt alternator and battery for flaps, trim, cockpit heating, lights, avionics and engine starting.
Braking system: Wheel brakes.
Flight avionics/instrumentation: AlliedSignal Bendix/King KX 125 com/nav, KLN 35A GPS, and KT 76A transponder. Conventional flight instrumentation.

Aircraft variants:
LAK-XA (for America) has a larger engine, greater fuel capacity and heavier weights, as detailed in the table.
LAK-XE (for Europe) has a Rotax or Limbach engine, and an empty, fuel and gross weight of 882 lb (400 kg), 110 lb (50 kg) and 1,433 lb (650 kg) respectively. G limits +5, –2.5.

SME Aviation Sdn Bhd (SMEAv) — Malaysia

Corporate address:
Lot No 14101, Pangkalan TUDM, Subang, PO Box 7547, 40718 Shah Alam, Selangor Darul Ehsan.

Telephone: +60 3 746 8577
Facsimile: +60 3 746 8566

Founded:
September 1993, as a subsidiary of SME Technologies Sdn Bhd (SMET). SME Aerospace Sdn Bhd (SMEA) is another subsidiary of SMET, having begun operations in 1992 as an aircraft parts manufacturer.

Information:
Prabhakaran Nair (General Manager).

SUBSIDIARY

SME AERO

Activities:
▪ This Florida-based company in the USA in a joint venture between SME and Aero Associates, to market the AeroTiga in North America.

↑ SME MD3-160 AeroTiga

SME MD3-160 AeroTiga

First flight: 12 August 1983 as Swiss prototype. 25 May 1995 for first SME-produced aircraft.
Certification: 22 January 1991 (Swiss FOCA) and 2 September 1992 by the FAA to FAR Pt 21.29. 29 August 1997 for Type Certification by the Malaysian DCA.
Role: Leisure, and basic and aerobatic training.
Sales: 5 manufactured by MDB Flugtechnik AG of Switzerland (the designer and developer), of which 2 have been operated in Malaysia and 1 in the USA. 40 being built in Malaysia under current orders, all for delivery by early 1999, as 20 for the Royal Malaysian Air Force and 20 for the Indonesian Ministry of Communications. Following early deliveries to the RMAF (from December 1995), Indonesia received its first batch of 5 in October 1997. Being marketed also in the USA by SME Aero, with anticipated sales of 20 per year from 1999.
Crew/passengers: 2 persons, side by side. Forward sliding, jettisonable canopy. Cabin heating and ventilation.
Wing characteristics: Entire wing consists of only 5 different modules, which are interchangeable left and right wings.
Wing control surfaces: Single-slotted mass-balanced ailerons (with balance tabs) and flaps.

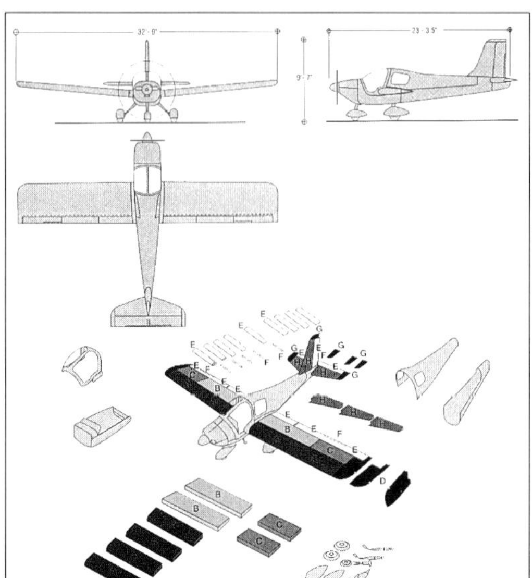
↑ SME MD3-160 AeroTiga general arrangement, plus airframe component interchangeability diagram *(courtesy SME)*

Details for MD3-160

PRINCIPAL DIMENSIONS:
Wing span: 32 ft 9.6 ins (10 m)
Maximum length: 23 ft 3.6 ins (7.1 m)
Maximum height: 9 ft 7.2 ins (2.92 m)

WINGS:
Aerofoil section: NACA $64_2$15-414 modified
Area: 161.46 sq ft (15 m^2)
Aspect ratio: 6.67
Dihedral: 5° 30'
Thickness/chord ratio: 14%

UNDERCARRIAGE:
Type: Fixed, with steerable (30° port, 44° starboard) nosewheel. Optional glassfibre fairings
Wheel base: 5 ft 1 ins (1.55 m)
Wheel track: 6 ft 9 ins (2.05 m)

WEIGHTS:
Empty: 1,477 lb (670 kg)
Maximum take-off: 2,028 lb (920 kg) utility, 1,852 lb (840 kg) aerobatic
Maximum landing: 1,964 lb (891 kg)

PERFORMANCE:
Never-exceed speed (V_{NE}): 158 kts (182 mph) 293 km/h utility, 175 kts (201 mph) 324 km/h aerobatic
Design cruise speed: 123 kts (142 mph) 228 km/h utility, 138 kts (159 mph) 256 km/h aerobatic
Maximum cruise speed: 137 kts (158 mph) 254 km/h at sea level
Maximum range cruise speed: 104 kts (120 mph) 193 km/h aerobatic
Manoeuvring speed (V_A): 110 kts (127 mph) 204 km/h utility, 121 kts (139 mph) 224 km/h aerobatic
Maximum speed, flaps extended: 90 kts (104 mph) 166 km/h
Stall speed: 56 kts (65 mph) 104 km/h *clean*, 47 kts (54 mph) 87 km/h *with flaps*, both with idle power
Take-off distance: 541 ft (165 m)
Landing distance: 568 ft (173 m)
Maximum climb rate: 985 ft (300 m) per minute at sea level and 453 ft (138 m) per minute at 10,000 ft (3,050 m)
G limits: +4.4, -2.2 utility, +6, -3 aerobatic
Range: 472 naut miles (543.5 miles) 875 km at sea level, 496 naut miles (571 miles) 919 km at 10,000 ft (3,050 m), both still air
Duration: 4 hours 9.6 minutes at sea level, 4 hours at 10,000 ft (3,050 m)

Tail control surfaces: Tailplane (span 9 ft 10 ins, 3 m) with mass-balanced single-piece elevator with trim tab. Mass-balanced rudder with balance tab. Rudder and elevator are the same modules as the flaps and ailerons. Left and right sections of tailplane are the same modules as the fin. Elevator tips are same modules as rudder tip.
Flight control system: Manually operated, through mechanical cable and rod linkage, for ailerons, elevator and rudder. Electrically operated flaps. Elevator trim tab controlled by wheel on centre console.
Construction materials: Primary structure of aluminium alloy, with aluminium skin covering an internal structure of pressed parts and extrusions. Other structural members (such as frames, ribs, stringers, reinforcements, rigid hinges and skin panels) share structural loads. Wings built with bonded aluminium honeycomb, with a single main spar. Fuselage has semi-monocoque metal structure, split into upper and lower halves, with streamlining achieved through use of glassfibre fairings; glassfibre used for wingtips, and fin and wheel fairings, while carbonfibre is used for engine cowling. Stainless steel firewall. 2-spar tailplane and fin structures. Modular construction, with interchangeable airframe parts. Airframe is built by SMEA (see Founded).
Engine: Textron Lycoming O-320-D2A piston engine, with a 6 ft 2 ins (1.88 m) Sensenich 74DM658-0-62 2-blade fixed-pitch propeller with glassfibre spinner, or McCauley Type 1-C 172-AGM-7462 propeller. Optional 160 hp (119 kW) AEIO-320-D2B or 116 hp (86.5 kW) O-235-N2A.
Engine rating: 160 hp (119 kW).
Fuel system: 148 litres in 2 wing tanks, with 144 litres usable.
Electrical system: 28 volt DC supply via a belt-driven 70 amp alternator and 24 volt battery.
Flight avionics/instrumentation: Certified for VFR. Communications avionics are audio control panel, nav/com and VHF com. Navigation avionics are VOR/Loc/glideslope, transponder and encoding altimeter. Optional avionics are available. Full range of standard instruments, including directional gyro, artificial horizon, airspeed indicator, altimeter, vertical speed indicator, and turn and bank indicator.

JSC Aviatehnologie — Moldova

Corporate address:
MD2062, 49/6 Dacia Street, Chisinau.
Telephone: +373 2 55 10 22, 55 43 71 and 52 39 40
Facsimile: +373 2 55 19 34
Chairman:
Bondarenco Vladimir.

ACTIVITIES

- Recently privatized joint stock company, with the state owning 60% and private shareholders 40%.
- Construction of ultralight aircraft, design and production of air accident prevention equipment, production of fuel equipment for aeroplanes and helicopters, production of airport ground service equipment, and more.

Aviatehnologie Favorit

First flight: 1996.
Role: Very light monoplane. A 2-seat basic training version is under study.
Sales: 2 prototypes at time of writing, the second displayed at the Paris Air Show in 1997.
Crew: Pilot only under a single-piece hinged canopy.
Wing control surfaces: Ailerons only on mid-mounted tapering wings.
Tail control surfaces: T-tail, with full-width elevator and tall rudder.

Details for Favorit

PRINCIPAL DIMENSIONS:
Wing span: 33 ft 2 ins (10.1 m)
Maximum length: 20 ft (6.1 m)

UNDERCARRIAGE:
Type: Fixed tailwheel type. Faired main wheels carried on cantilever spring main legs. Small faired tailwheel

PERFORMANCE:
Maximum speed: 70 kts (80.5 mph) 130 km/h
Cruise speed: 59 kts (68.5 mph) 110 km/h
Take-off distance: 657 ft (200 m)
G limits: +6, -4.5

Construction materials: Pod and boom fuselage. Airframe of composites construction.
Engine: Hirth F 23A 2-stroke piston engine, with a 3-blade fixed-pitch propeller with small spinner.
Engine rating: 39.6 hp (29.5 kW).
Fuel system: Fuel consumption 9 litres per hour.

↑ **Aviatehnologie Favorit single-seat very light aircraft** *(Aviation Picture Library)*

Delta-V srl — Moldova

Corporate address:
See the Helicopter section for details of the company and the AK-21 autogyro.

Delta-V/Technoavia Ronata

First flight: 1998?
Certification: Conforms to AP-23.
Role: 4-seat 'ekranoplan' wing-in-ground effect aircraft, being developed with JSC Technoavia in Russia.
Wing characteristics: Blended anhedral wing/rear fuselage of reversed delta planform, with sweptforward leading-edges and straight dihedral outer panels carrying control surfaces. Between the main wing and outer panels are integral float pods.
Tail control surfaces: T-tail, with constant-chord tailplane mounted above a fin and rudder.
Construction materials: Aluminium alloy.
Engine: Above-wing pylon-mounted Textron Lycoming O-320-A piston engine, with a 2-blade pusher propeller.
Engine rating: 140 hp (104 kW).
Fuel system: 330.5 lb (150 kg).

Details for Ronata

PRINCIPAL DIMENSIONS:
Wing span: 30 ft 10 ins (9.4 m)
Maximum length: 31 ft 6 ins (9.6 m)
Maximum height: 9 ft 2 ins (2.8 m)

WEIGHTS:
Empty, equipped: 1,984 lb (900 kg)
Maximum take-off: 2,976 lb (1,350 kg)
Useful load: 661 lb (300 lb)

PERFORMANCE:
Maximum speed: 108 kts (124 mph) 200 km/h
Take-off speed: 43 kts (50 mph) 80 km/h
Range: 540-647 naut miles (621-745 miles) 1,000-1,200 km

↑ **Delta-V Ronata 4-seat wing-in-ground-effect lightplane** *(courtesy Delta-V)*

Pacific Aerospace Corporation Ltd (PAC) — New Zealand

Corporate address:
Hamilton Airport, Private Bag HN3027, Hamilton.
Telephone: +64 7 843 6144
Facsimile: +64 7 843 6134
E-mail: pacific@aerospace.co.nz
Founded: 1982.
Employees: 110.
Information:
John McWilliam (Marketing Manager).

ACTIVITIES

- Much of PAC's business is concerned with manufacture of details and structural components and the manufacture of its own aircraft.
- Approved to manufacture details and/or assemblies for the Boeing 747, 777, MD-11 and Hornet, Airbus A330 and A340, and more.

PAC CT/4E Airtrainer

First flight: 23 February 1972; 14 December 1991 for the latest CT/4E.
Certification: CT/4 was originally designed to meet FAR Pt 23, for aerobatic aircraft, and also to meet British AvP970. 8 May 1992 for the CT/4E, under FAR Pt 23 Amdt 36.
Role: 2/3-seat trainer.
Sales: Marketing is centred on the CT/4E. 114 CT/4As and Bs were produced for the RTAF, RAAF, RNZAF and Ansett/BAe Flying Training School at Tamworth, Australia (30, 51, 19 and 12 respectively, plus the 2 prototypes). Further 2 built in 1997. Cs and Es offered to RTAF, following earlier purchase of A/Bs.
Baggage capacity: 170 lb (77 kg).
Wing control surfaces: Ailerons (16.5° up, 10.5° down) and single-slotted flaps (30° maximum deflection).
Tail control surfaces: Shielded horn-balanced elevator (25° up, 15° down) and rudder, both with trims.

↑ PAC CT/4E Airtrainer

↑ PAC CR-750 Cresco

Flight control system: Pushrods and cables.
Construction materials: All metal, except for Kevlar wing root fairings.
Engine: Textron Lycoming AEIO-540-L1B5 piston engine, with a 6 ft 4 ins (1.93 m) Hartzell 3-blade propeller.
Engine rating: 300 hp (224 kW).
Fuel system: 205 litres usable. Optional long-range wingtip tanks (2 × 77 litres).
Electrical system: 28 volt DC.
Flight avionics/instrumentation: Engine and electrical monitoring instruments, flight instruments and radio equipment. Duplicated instruments are altimeter, airspeed indicator, turn and bank indicator, and vertical speed indicator.

Aircraft variants:
CT/4B has a 210 hp (156.6 kW) Teledyne Continental IO-360-H piston engine.
CT/4C turboprop version has an Allison 250-B17D engine with McCauley 3-blade constant-speed propeller. Prototype retained fixed undercarriage. Interest from RTAF.
CT/4E is the current piston-engined version, essentially similar to the original CT/4A but with a single-piece carry-through structure and the wing moved 2.5 ins (6.4 cm) further forward. Higher performance than the previous CT/4B.

Details for CT/4E

PRINCIPAL DIMENSIONS:
Wing span: 26 ft (7.92 m)
Maximum length: 23 ft 5.75 ins (7.16 m)
Maximum height: 8 ft 6 ins (2.59 m)

CABIN:
Length: 8 ft 11 ins (2.72 m)
Width: 3 ft 7.5 ins (1.1 m)
Height: 4 ft 6.7 ins (1.38 m)

WINGS:
Aerofoil section: NACA 23008 (modified) root, NACA 4412 tip
Area: 129 sq ft (11.98 m^2)
Aspect ratio: 5.24

UNDERCARRIAGE:
Type: Fixed, with steerable nosewheel
Wheel base: 5 ft 5.5 ins (1.66 m)
Wheel track: 9 ft 9 ins (2.97 m)

WEIGHTS:
Empty: 1,675 lb (760 kg)
Maximum take-off and landing: 2,600 lb (1,179 kg)

PERFORMANCE:
Maximum speed: 163 kts (188 mph) 302 km/h
Cruise speed: 152 kts (175 mph) 281 km/h at 75% power
Stall speed: 44 kts (51 mph) 82 km/h, *with full flaps*
Take-off distance: 612 ft (187 m)
Landing distance: 552 ft (169 m)
Maximum climb rate: 1,830 ft (558 m) per minute
G limits: +6, –3
Ceiling: 18,200 ft (5,550 m)
Range: 520 naut miles (598 miles) 963 km at 75% power

PAC CR-750 Cresco

First flight: 28 February 1979 for prototype Cresco.
Certification: 9 April 1984 for the earlier Cresco 08-600.
Role: Multi-role, for agricultural, firebombing, casevac, utility, passenger, cargo and rainmaking roles. Design and construction follows closely that of the FU24.
Sales: 20 produced for users in New Zealand and 3 exported to Bangladesh. Current version is the CR-750.
Crew/passengers: 6 seats civil, 8 military, using an optional passenger kit. 2 litters and 2 attendants, or 2 litters, 3 sitting casualties and an attendant in an air ambulance role.
Chemical tank/hopper: 4,976 lb (2,257 kg) dry chemical payload, or 2,000 litres liquids. Hopper removable in 4 man-hours by experienced personnel, to offer a cargo area.
Dispersal equipment: Micronair spray equipment with wind-driven rotary atomizer or Transland boom and nozzle equipment for higher application rates (up to 1,272 litres per minute). Transland Swathmaster for very high application rates. Also aerial spreading of solids via a range of dispersal equipment, including the high application Easton hopper outlet (clamshell type). Controllable fire bombing door with minimum discharge time of 3 seconds.
Safety equipment: Wire cutter and deflector cable.
Engine: Pratt & Whitney PT6A-34AG turboprop, with a 3-blade metal constant-speed propeller.
Engine rating: 750 shp (559 kW).
Fuel system: 544 litres, of which 520 litres are usable.
Electrical system: 28 volt, 150 amp generator, and 2 × 12 volt lead-acid batteries.
Braking system: Hydraulic. Parking brake.
Flight avionics/instrumentation: Instruments include an altimeter, magnetic compass, airspeed indicator, turn and slip indicator and much more. Optional avionics in basic and advanced Narco and AlliedSignal Bendix/King suites.

PAC FU24-954 Fletcher

First flight: 1954 for original US prototype.
Certification: 1955. Meets FAR Pt 23.
Role: Agricultural, firebombing, rainmaking, utility, aerial survey, photography and more.
Sales: 307 built.
Crew/passengers: 6 seats civil, 8 military, using an optional passenger kit. 2 litters and 2 attendants, or 2 litters, 3 sitting casualties and an attendant in an air ambulance role. Dual controls.
Chemical tank/hopper: 1,294 litres of liquid chemicals or up to 2,343 lb (1,063 kg) of dry chemicals.
Dispersal equipment: Micronair ultra-low volume spray equipment with wind-driven rotary atomizer units for typically up to 160 litres per minute application rate, or low volume spray equipment. Also aerial spreading of solids via a range of dispersal equipment, including the ultra high application Easton hopper outlet (clamshell type), the high volume Transland solid spreader with gate box and agitator, and the medium volume Transland Swathmaster with gate box and agitator. Controllable fire bombing door with minumum discharge time of 3 seconds.
Safety equipment: Seat collapse point of 25g. Optional wire cutter and deflector cable.
Wing control surfaces: Plain ailerons (25° up, 10° down) and single-slotted flaps (4 position, 40° maximum deflection).
Tail control surfaces: Slab tailplane (20° up, 5° down) with trim and anti-balance tab. Unbalanced rudder.

Details for CR-750 Cresco

PRINCIPAL DIMENSIONS:
Wing span: 42 ft (12.8 m)
Maximum length: 36 ft 4.25 ins (11.08 m)
Maximum height: 11 ft 11 ins (3.63 m)

CABIN CARGO AREA:
Length: 11 ft 10 ins (3.61 m)
Width: 3 ft 6 ins (1.07 m)
Height: 4 ft 2.5 ins (1.28 m)
Rear access door size: 39 × 38 ins (99 × 94 cm)

WINGS:
Area: 294 sq ft (27.31 m^2)
Aspect ratio: 6

WEIGHTS:
Empty: 2,850 lb (1,293 kg)
Maximum take-off: 8,250 lb (3,742 kg) Agricultural category/Restricted and rainmaking roles, or 6,450 lb (2,926 kg) Normal category for utility cargo and passengers
Useful load: 5,400 lb (2,449 kg) agricultural and rainmaking roles, or 3,430 lb (1,555 kg) utility cargo and passengers

PERFORMANCE:
Maximum cruise speed: 157 kts (181 mph) 291 km/h at sea level, ISA
Cruise speed (75% power): 148 kts (170 mph) 274 km/h
Stall speed: 61.3 kts (70.6 mph) 114 km/h *with full flaps* at MTOW, 36.5 kts (42 mph) 68 km/h *with full flaps* at 3,000 lb (1,360 kg) landing weight
Take-off distance: 750 ft (229 m) unstick at utility weight, 1,305 ft (398 m) unstick at MTOW, both ISA
Landing distance: 805 ft (245 m) ground roll with a 6,450 lb (2,926 kg) load and reverse propeller
Maximum climb rate: 1,658 ft (505 m) per minute at Normal category MTOW, 1,090 ft (332 m) per minute at Agricultural MTOW
Ceiling: 29,000 ft (8,840 m) clean, or 25,900 ft (7,900 m) with spraygear, both at 6,450 lb (2,926 kg), absolute
Range: 364 naut miles (420 miles) 676 km at 75% power, 7,000 lb (3,175 kg) weight with spraygear
Ferry range: 2,040 naut miles (2,350 miles) 3,782 km
Duration: 3 hours 5 minutes at 60% power
Typical load performance: 24,545 litres of liquid chemicals per hour (1,800 litres per trip), or 30 tonnes of dry chemicals per hour (2.2 tonnes per trip), using an airstrip 3.5 to 8.1 naut miles (4 to 9.3 miles) 6.5 to 15 km from the drop zone, at sea level

Flight control system: Mechanical, except for elevator trim.
Construction materials: Metal, stressed skin.
Engine: Textron Lycoming IO-720-A1A or A1B piston engine, with a 7 ft 2 ins (2.18 m) Hartzell 3-blade constant-speed propeller. AlliedSignal TFE331-450 turboprop has been under consideration.
Engine rating: 400 hp (298 kW).
Fuel system: 259 litres, of which 242 litres are usable. Optional integral tanks of 282 litres, of which 263 litres are usable. Optional methanol fuelled conversion kit.
Electrical system: 28 volt, 70 amp alternator and 2 × 12 volt batteries.
Flight avionics/instrumentation: Similar to Cresco.

Details for FU24-954

PRINCIPAL DIMENSIONS:
Wing span: 42 ft (12.8 m)
Maximum length: 32 ft 8.75 ins (9.98 m)
Maximum height: 9 ft 4 ins (2.84 m)

CABIN CARGO AREA:
Length: 10 ft (3.05 m)
Width: 4 ft (1.22 m)
Height: 4 ft 3 ins (1.3 m)
Cargo door size: As for Cresco

WINGS:
Aerofoil section: NACA 4415
Area: 294 sq ft (27.31m^2)
Aspect ratio: 6

UNDERCARRIAGE:
Type: Fixed, with steerable nosewheel

WEIGHTS:
Empty: 2,662 lb (1,207 kg)
Maximum take-off: 5,430 lb (2,463 kg) Agricultural, 4,860 lb (2,204 kg) Normal
Payload: 2,126 lb (964 kg) Agricultural, 1,556 lb (705 kg) Normal, both with full fuel

PERFORMANCE:
Never-exceed speed (V_{NE}): 143 kts (164 mph) 265 km/h
Maximum speed: 126 kts (145 mph) 233 km/h at sea level
Maximum cruise speed: 113 kts (130 mph) 209 km/h at 75% power
Spray speed: 90-115 kts (104-132 mph) 167-212 km/h
Swath width: 70-80 ft (21-24 m) liquid, 25-50 ft (7.5-15 m) dry
Stall speed: 55 kts (64 mph) 102 km/h *clean*, 49 kts (57 mph) 91 km/h *with flaps*
Take-off distance: 800 ft (244 m)
Landing distance: 680 ft (207 m)
Maximum climb rate: 920 ft (280 m) per minute at sea level
G limits: +3.8, -1.5
Ceiling: 16,000 ft (4,875 m), service
Range: 305 naut miles (351 miles) 565 km at MTOW and sea level, 60% power, clean
Duration: 3.77 hours at MTOW and 5,000 ft (1,525 m), 60% power, clean

Aeronautical Industrial Engineering and Project Management Company Ltd — Nigeria

Corporate address:
General Aviation Service Centre, PO Box 5662, Old Kaduna Airport, Kaduna.

Telephone: +234 62 236676
Facsimile: +234 62 237325

Founded:
1979.

ACTIVITIES

▪ AIEP received 60 kits from the USA to assemble under licence a variant of the Van's RV-6A, known as the Air Beetle (see Recreational section). T18 basic version (as built for the Nigerian Air Force as a trainer) has a 180 hp (134 kW) Textron Lycoming O-360-A1A engine.

Pakistan Aeronautical Complex (PAC) — Pakistan

Corporate address:
See Combat section (under Pakistan and Multi-national) for company details. The Mushshak and Super Mushshak are products of the Aircraft Manufacturing Factory.

PAC Mushshak and Super Mushshak

Note: In 1998 the Chief Editor of *WA&SD* was informed by AMF that the weapon-carrying capability of Mushshak is optional under the design, but that under the licence agreement for manufacture between Saab and AMF this capability is not being offered.
Certification: Saab Safari/Supporter (Mushshak) certified to Swedish Civil Aviation on 1 February 1965. Meets FAR Pt 23 in Normal, Utility and Aerobatic categories.
Role: Multi-purpose civil/military lightplanes, capable of several roles including training (basic, instrument, aerobatic, night flying, navigation and formation), crop spraying, army co-operation, observation, border patrol, and forward area support with droppable containers. Licence-built Saab versions of the Saab Safari and Supporter (see Aircraft variants).
Sales: Large number built, including some 268 Mushshaks for the Pakistan armed forces. In late 1994, 3 were given to Oman and 6 to Syria.
Details: Principally for Mushshak, except under Aircraft variants.
Crew/passengers: 2 crew, side by side, under an upward-hinged canopy. Large baggage compartment in the rear of the cabin can be used instead to accommodate a third person.
Wing control surfaces: Ailerons (starboard servo tab) and flaps.
Tail control surfaces: Slab tailplane with trim/anti-servo tab, and rudder with tab.
Flight control system: Mechanical, except for electric flaps.

↑ Pakistan Aeronautical Complex Super Mushshak

Details for Mushshak

PRINCIPAL DIMENSIONS:
Wing span: 29 ft (8.84 m)
Maximum length: 23 ft (7.01 m)
Maximum height: 8 ft 6.5 ins (2.6 m)

WINGS:
Aerofoil section: NASA 0125 cambered
Area: 128.1 sq ft (11.9 m^2)
Aspect ratio: 6.57

UNDERCARRIAGE:
Type: Fixed, with nosewheel

WEIGHTS:
Empty: 1,424 lb (646 kg)
Maximum take-off: 2,645 lb (1,200 kg) Normal, 2,480 lb (1,125 kg) Utility, and 1,980 lb (898 kg) Aerobatic

PERFORMANCE (Normal category):
Never-exceed speed (V_{NE}): 197 kts (226 mph) 364 km/h
Maximum speed: 125 kts (144 mph) 232 km/h
Cruise speed: 110 kts (127 mph) 204 km/h at 75% power, sea level
Stall speed: 66 kts (76 mph) 122 km/h *clean* and engine idling, 60 kts (69 mph) 111 km/h *with 38° flaps* and zero thrust
Take-off distance: 850 ft (259 m) *with 10° flaps*
Landing distance: 530 ft (162 m) including 1 second delay before braking
Maximum climb rate: 710 ft (216 m) per minute at sea level
Time to 6,000 ft (1,830 m): 11.5 minutes
G limits: +4.8, -2.4, or +6, -3 for Aerobatic category
Ceiling: 10,400 ft (3,170 m), or 18,800 ft (5,730 m) for Aerobatic category
Duration: 5 hours 10 minutes at 65% power, with reserve

Construction materials: Principally metal, but with some use of glassfibre. 8,300 hour structural life.
Engine: Textron Lycoming IO-360-A1B6 piston engine, with a 6 ft 2 ins (1.88 m) Hartzell 2-blade constant-speed propeller.
Engine rating: 200 hp (149 kW).
Fuel system: 182 litres.
Braking system: Hydraulically operated disc brakes.
Flight avionics/instrumentation: Typically VHF, UHF and ADF.
Expendable equipment: See 'Note' at the start of this entry. If ever offered, the weapon capability would be up to 661 lb (300 kg) of external stores (including pylons) at 6 stations (inner stressed for 330 lb, 150 kg; the remainder for 220 lb, 100 kg), including machine-gun or rocket pods, light missiles or relief containers.

Aircraft variants:
Mushshak is the main military production version, developed from the Saab Safari/Supporter, but can undertake civil roles. Textron Lycoming engine. As detailed.
Shahbaz was developed as an upgraded version of Mushshak, with a 210 hp (156.6 kW) Teledyne Continental TSIO-360-MB piston engine and a McCauley 2-blade metal propeller. 6 underwing stations. Length 23 ft 6 ins (7.16 m). 4 produced. No longer offered.
Super Mushshak has been introduced by AMF at Kamra as an upgraded version of the Saab MFI-17, launched with a 260 hp (194 kW) Textron Lycoming IO-540-V4A5 engine (rating at 2,700 rpm). Conforms to US FAR Pt 23 Normal, Utility and Aerobatic categories. Features are capability to carry external loads, optional environmental control system, heavy-duty undercarriage, good short/rough field performance, and operation with only a small demand on logistic support due to simple and robust construction for high availability and easy maintenance. Certified to carry out the following basic manoeuvres: stall and spin, steep turns, roll (barrel, slow 4 point roll), hammer head stall, inverted flying and loop. Meets the requirements of modern primary flying training syllabus and is seen as an ideal primary trainer. Also suited to a wide range of army co-operation missions including low-level surveillance, forward control, and forward area support with droppable supply control. Features optional electric trims, electrically operated instruments, and 20-30% increase in performance parameters due to more powerful engine.

Western Pacific Aviation Corporation — Philippines

Corporate address:
RPMCI Hangar, Manila Domestic Airport, PO Box 7633, Airport Airmail Exchange Office, Domestic Road, Pasay City.

Telephone: +63 2 832 3375, 2777
Facsimile: +63 2 833 0605

Information:
R. P. Moscardon.

ACTIVITIES

■ WPAC produces the Skyfox, which is similar in most respects to the Skystar Kitfox (originally licensed to Philippine Aircraft Company Inc by Denny Aerocraft in 1987). The original Rotax 532-engined **Skyfox 1** was superseded by the Rotax 582-engined **Skyfox 2** which, in the current form, has a Rotax 912 engine. WPAC has the capability to produce quantities to order, but the number produced has been modest.

Agrolot Foundation — Poland

Corporate address:
Aleja Krakowska 110-114, 00-971 Warszawa.

Telephone: +48 22 8460031, ext 586
Facsimile: +48 22 8462701

Information:
Andrzej Słociński (President).

Agrolot Foundation PZL-126P Mrówka (Ant)

First flight: 20 April 1990 for the PZL-126 prototype.
Certification: Conforms to FAR Pt 23.
Role: Very small and light, low-volume agricultural aircraft, also suited to pest and disease control, forest and pipe/power line patrol, survey and more.
Sales: First prototype had a PZL-Franklin 2A-120C1 piston engine of 52 hp (39 kW) and made only 16 flights before being abandoned in 1996. Second prototype, redesignated PZL-126P (poprawiony, adjusted) was built from 1997.
Details: PZL-126P.

Details for PZL-126P

PRINCIPAL DIMENSIONS:
Wing span: 25 ft 1.5 ins (7.66 m), or 27 ft 9 ins (8.46 m) with wingtip tanks
Maximum length: 17 ft 3 ins (5.25 m)
Maximum height: 9 ft 2 ins (2.8 m)

WINGS:
Aerofoil section: NACA GA(W)-1
Area: 74 sq ft (6.9 m^2)
Aspect ratio: 8.5

UNDERCARRIAGE:
Type: Fixed, with castoring nosewheel. Cantilever spring mainwheel legs of duralumin
Main and nose wheel tyre size: 350 × 135 mm

WEIGHT:
Maximum take-off: 1,268 lb (575 kg)

PERFORMANCE:
Design maximum cruise speed: 105 kts (121 mph) 195 km/h
Spray speed: 75 kts (87 mph) 140 km/h

↑ **Agrolot Foundation PZL-126 Mrówka (Ant) with wingtip spraytanks removed** *(Agrolot)*

Crew: Pilot only under a single-piece side-hinged canopy with small port-side sliding panel. 'Air bag' seat adjustment.
Dispersal equipment: When required, 2 × 35 litre wingtip chemical spraytanks with atomizers can be attached to the wingtips via fast-locks, each with 2 tip-vanes, an electric power socket and a control valve to regulate delivery rate. Typical liquid chemical flow rate is 2 litres per hectare. An additional spraytank can be carried under the fuselage. For non-chemical biological pest control, a spreader can be used to 'seed' Trichrogramma wasp eggs.
Wing characteristics: Constant-chord, single-spar, dihedral wings with wingtip chemical spraytanks with tip vanes. Wings detachable for towing.
Wing control surfaces: Flaps and flaperons.
Tail control surfaces: Full-width, single-piece elevator with trim tab, and forward-canted rudder with balance tab.
Flight control system: Pushrods, except for cable-operated rudder.
Construction materials: Metal, except for glassfibre/epoxy wingtips and engine cowling. Equipment bay, with access panel, in bottom of semi-monocoque fuselage.
Engine: Teledyne Continental O-200-A piston engine, with a 5 ft 9 ins (1.75 m) McCauley 1A100MCM6950 2-blade metal propeller.
Engine rating: 100 hp (74.6 kW).
Fuel system: 200 litres in 2 wing tanks.
Electrical system: 24 volt.
Hydraulic system: For differential disc brakes.
Flight avionics/instrumentation: IFR capable. VOR/GS, transponder, GPS, and 720-channel UHF com radio. Lightweight electronic engine instrumentation. Easily removable instrument panel. Specialized equipment for particular missions can include camera and thermal systems.

East European Markets Ltd — Poland

Corporate address:
12 Widok Street, 00-023 Warsaw.

Telephone: +48 22 8274858
Facsimile: +48 22 8277788, 428506

ACTIVITIES

■ Markets the J-5 Marco light aircraft/motorglider currently owned by Aviation Farm Ltd (see Recreational section). In addition to the standard single-seat version offered with a KFM-107ER MAX or Rotax 447UL-SCDJ engine and with a retractable tailwheel undercarriage, a version with twin fixed and faired main wheels became available in 1998, with laminated legs.

Instytut Lotnictwa

Poland

Corporate address:
See Combat section for company details.

ACTIVITIES

▪ In addition to the I-23 detailed below, the company is developing a 2-seat braced high-wing monoplane for training, glider towing and patrol as the **AS-2**, with a MTOW of 1,653 lb (750 kg).

Instytut Lotnictwa PZL I-23

First flight: Ground trials began late September 1998, allowing first flight in October 1998.
Certification: Designed to conform fo JAR 23, Normal and Utility.
Role: 4-seat lightplane for private use, flying clubs, training (basic navigation, performing), sightseeing and business.
Sales: Deliveries from 1999/2000, with expected production rate of 100 per year.
Wing control surfaces: Ailerons and single-slotted flaps.
Tail control surfaces: Elevators (port tab) and 2-section rudder (with tab).
Flight control system: Mechanical.
Construction materials: Principally glassfibre, carbonfibre and epoxy.

↑ **Instytut Lotnictwa PZL I-23 4-seat lightplane** *(J. Grzegorzewski)*

Engine: Textron Lycoming O-360 piston engine. Other engines in the 115-180 hp (85.75-134 kW) range.
Engine rating: 180 hp (134 kW).
Fuel system: 150 litres (291 lb, 132 kg).
Electrical system: 12 volt, with alternator and 32 amp-hour battery.
Flight avionics/instrumentation: AlliedSignal Bendix/King VFR suite. Options include IFR suite, 2-axis autopilot, GPS and DME.

Details for I-23

PRINCIPAL DIMENSIONS:
Wing span: 29 ft 4 ins (8.94 m)
Maximum length: 23 ft 1 ins (7.04 m)
Maximum height: 8 ft (2.44 m)

WINGS
Area: 107.64 sq ft (10 m^2)
Aspect ratio: 7.992

UNDERCARRIAGE:
Type: Retractable or optional fixed, with nosewheel

WEIGHTS
Empty: 1,318 lb (598 kg), zero fuel
Maximum take-off: 476 lb (1,050 kg)

PERFORMANCE:
Maximum speed: 159 kts (183 mph) 295 km/h
Stall speed: 62 kts (72 mph) 115 km/h *clean*, 52 kts (60 mph) 96 km/h *with flaps*
Take-off distance: 541 ft (165 m)
Landing distance: 400 ft (122 m)
Maximum climb rate: 1,000 ft (306 m) per minute
Ceiling: 14,425 ft (4,400 m), service
Range with full fuel: 771 naut miles (888 miles) 1,430 km

WSK "PZL-Mielec" S.A.

Poland

Corporate address:
See Combat section for company details.

PZL-Mielec An-2 (NATO name *Colt*)

First flight: 31 August 1947 in Novosibirsk, Russia. 6 September 1949 for first production aircraft in Kiev. 23 October 1960 for first aircraft of Polish manufacture. See also Y-5 under China.
Role: Single-engined general-purpose biplane, with uses including agricultural, passenger and cargo transport, paradropping, photogrammetry and more.
Airframe life: 16,000 flying hours for agricultural version, 20,000 hours for cargo version.
Sales: Designed by Antonov. Series manufactured at factory No 473 at Kiev (3,167 built between 1949-62), factory No 464 at Dolgoprudnyi in Russia (429 An-2Ms built between 1964-1965), PZL-Mielec in Poland (nearly 12,000 built since 1960), and in China at Nanchang (727 built between 1957-68) and Shijiazhuang (which see). 10,605 Polish-built An-2s delivered to the USSR/Russia/CIS, with 468 remaining in Poland, and others to 18 further countries including Bulgaria (222), Romania (132), Hungary (119), North Korea (115), former Yugoslavia (63), Czech Republic and Slovakia (as Czechoslovakia, 49), and former East Germany (20).
Crew/passengers: 2 flight crew and 12 passengers or up to 3,307 lb (1,500 kg) of cargo, 6 litters in the ambulance version, or 3,527 lb (1,600 kg) of chemicals in the agricultural version.
Wing control surfaces: Automatic slats, ailerons (port trim tab) and trailing-edge flaps on upper wing; full-span trailing-edge flaps on lower wings.
Tail control surfaces: Conventional elevators (port trim tab) and rudder (trim tab).
Flight control system: Cable/pushrod, except for electric flaps and trim tabs.
Construction materials: Metal, partly fabric skinned.
Engine: WSK-Kalisz ASz-62IR radial piston engine.
Engine rating: 967 hp (721 kW).
Fuel system: 1,200 litres in 6 upper wing tanks.
Braking system: Pneumatic.
Flight avionics/instrumentation: RV-UM radio altimeter, ARK-19 radio compass, R-842 and R-860 com radios.

Aircraft variants (in order of production quantity):
An-2R (rolniczy, agricultural) is the most popular Polish-built version (7,833 built). Differing spray and spreading equipment, but used also as a utility aircraft with equipment removed.

↑ **PZL-Mielec An-2R agricultural aircraft** *(Piotr Butowski)*

Details for An-2TD/TP

PRINCIPAL DIMENSIONS:
Wing span: 59 ft 7.5 ins (18.176 m) upper, 46 ft 9 ins (14.236 m) lower
Maximum length: 41 ft 9 ins (12.735 m) tail up, 40 ft 8 ins (12.4 m) tail down
Maximum height: 13 ft 2 ins (4.013 m) tail down

CABIN:
Length: 13 ft 5 ins (4.1 m)
Width: 5 ft 3 ins (1.6 m)
Height: 5 ft 11 ins (1.8 m)
Volume: 423.78 cu ft (12 m^3)
Main door size: 5 ft high × 4 ft 9.5 ins wide (1.53 × 1.46 m)

WINGS:
Aerofoil section: RPS-14% upper, RIIS-14% lower
Area: 468.72 sq ft (43.546 m^2) upper, 301.17 sq ft (27.96 m^2) lower
Dihedral: 3° upper, 4° lower
Incidence: 3° upper, 1° lower

UNDERCARRIAGE:
Type: Fixed, with tailwheel
Main wheel tyre size: 800 × 260 mm
Tail wheel tyre size: 470 × 210 mm
Wheel base: 26 ft 10.5 ins (8.19 m)
Wheel track: 11 ft 4 ins (3.454 m)

WEIGHTS:
Empty: 7,595 lb (3,445 kg)
Normal take-off and landing: 11,574 lb (5,250 kg)
Maximum take-off: 12,125 lb (5,500 kg)
Payload: 3,307 lb (1,500 kg)

PERFORMANCE:
Maximum speed at sea level: 124 kts (143 mph) 230 km/h
Maximum speed at 5,250 ft (1,600 m): 137 kts (157 mph) 253 km/h
Cruise speed: 103 kts (118 mph) 190 km/h at 2,625 ft (800 m)
Approach speed: 49 kts (56 mph) 90 km/h
Take-off distance: 591-722 ft (180-220 m)
Landing distance: 689-739 ft (210-225 m)
Maximum climb rate: 710 ft (216 m) per minute at sea level
Ceiling: 13,650 ft (4,160 m), service
Range: 750 naut miles (863 miles) 1,390 km

↑ PZL-Mielec M18 Dromader *(Piotr Butowski)*

↑ PZL-Mielec M20 Mewa *(Piotr Butowski)*

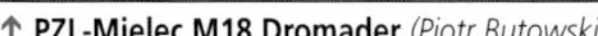

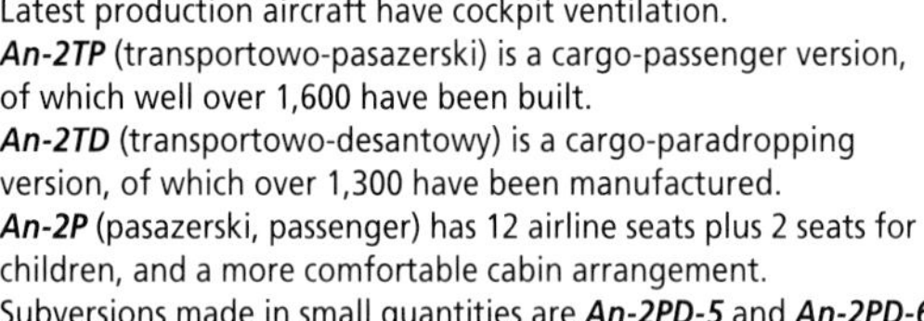

Latest production aircraft have cockpit ventilation.
An-2TP (transportowo-pasazerski) is a cargo-passenger version, of which well over 1,600 have been built.
An-2TD (transportowo-desantowy) is a cargo-paradropping version, of which over 1,300 have been manufactured.
An-2P (pasazerski, passenger) has 12 airline seats plus 2 seats for children, and a more comfortable cabin arrangement.
Subversions made in small quantities are ***An-2PD-5*** and ***An-2PD-6*** VIP versions for 5 and 6 passengers respectively. 862 built.

PZL-Mielec M18 Dromader series

First flight: 27 August 1976 (piloted by T. Gołębiowski). November 1997 for 'BS' model.
Certification: FAR Pt 23, with certification in 14 countries including Poland, Canada and the USA. In addition, many US distributors and companies possess Supplemental Type Certificates allowing installation of enlarged fuel tanks, PW&C PT6A-45AG turboprop engine and a 2-seat training cockpit. M18B received the revised Polish BB-120 Type Certificate in February 1994.
Airframe life: 6,000 hours.
Role: Agricultural and forestry work. Latter can include firefighting, fire patrol, neutralizing contaminated soil, and spraying against diseases and pests.
Sales: Some 700 built at time of writing, 90% for export to 23 countries. First 2 M18BS ordered in 1998. On 2 July 1997, an assembly line was opened in Brazil, with 15 planned for assembly in that year and 40 in 1998.
Crew/passenger: Pilot in a sealed cockpit to prevent chemical ingress. Small cabin aft for a passenger (opposite facing).
Chemical tank/hopper: 2,500 litres of liquid chemical or up to 2,976 lb (1,350 kg) of dry chemicals.
Dispersal equipment: 58 ft 1 ins (17.7 m) sprayboom. Alternative atomizer, spreader, or water-bombing equipment. Water bombing dump time (2,500 litres) is 2.5 seconds.
Safety equipment: Cockpit can withstand a 40g impact. Cable cutters.
Wing control surfaces: Slotted ailerons (port with balance tab, and starboard with trim tab) and 2-section slotted flaps (10° for take-off, 15° for landing – see also M18B).
Tail control surfaces: Elevators and rudder, with trim tabs.
Flight control system: Pushrod and cable, except for hydraulic flaps and electric trim tabs.
Construction materials: Metal, with some use of corrugated skins.
Engine: WSK Kalisz ASz-62IR-M18 radial piston engine, with a 10 ft 10 ins (3.3 m) 4-blade AW-2-30 propeller.
Engine rating: 967 hp (721 kW).
Fuel system: 400 or 720 litres in outer wings.
Electrical system: 100 amp generator and 25 amp-hour ni-cd battery.
Hydraulic system: Up to 1,987 psi for the agricultural equipment, brakes and flaps.
Braking system: Hydraulic disc. Parking brake.

Aircraft variants:
M18 was the initial version, series manufactured from 1979.
M18A became the main production version from 1984, with second seat for ground personnel member (for ferrying flights). As detailed.
M18AS is a 2-seat training version of M18A, fitted with an instructor's cockpit in the front of the cabin area. Reduced capacity hopper. First flown 31 March 1988. Several built.
M18B has been the main production model since 1995, but designed for firefighting at up to 11,684 lb (5,300 kg) AUW. Primary changes are a modified tailplane and elevator control system, incorporation of elastic interconnection between the ailerons and rudder control systems, and wing flap deflection increased for landing (30°) and take-off (15°). All these modifications result in enhanced lateral stability, improved manoeuvring, steeper landing descent path, landing distance reduced by about 200 m, ability to take-off with a 4,853 lb (2,200 kg) payload, and reduced need to use elevator trim.
M18BS is a 2-seat trainer version of M-18B.
M18C and ***D*** are new models with 1,200 hp (895 kW) K-9AA engine and larger diameter propeller.
Dromader Super Turbo was a turboprop version (with Russian TVD-20 engine) proposed in the 1980s but never realized. Similar modification was later accomplished in the USA (Melex T-45 Turbine Dromader).
In the 1980s a series of prototypes based on Dromader was conceived, including M21 Dromader Mini of 1982, M24 Dromader Super of 1987 and M-25 Dromader Micro (project only).

Details for M18A Dromader

PRINCIPAL DIMENSIONS:
Wing span: 58 ft 1 ins (17.7 m)
Maximum length: 31 ft 1 ins (9.47 m)
Maximum height: 12 ft 2 ins (3.7 m)

WINGS:
Aerofoil section: NACA 4416/4412 (root/tip)
Area: 430.6 sq ft (40 m^2)
Aspect ratio: 7.83

UNDERCARRIAGE:
Type: Fixed, with castoring and lockable tailwheel
Main wheel tyre size: 800 × 260 mm
Tail wheel tyre size: 380 × 150 mm

WEIGHTS:
Empty: about 5,977 lb (2,710 kg)
Maximum take-off: 9,260 lb (4,200 kg) Normal FAR Pt 23, 10,362 lb (4,700 kg) Restricted, and 11,684 b (5,300 kg) Cam 8 max

PERFORMANCE (with dry chemical equipment)**:**
Maximum speed: 128 kts (147 mph) 237 km/h
Work speed: 92 kts (106 mph) 170 km/h
Stall speed: 65 kts (74 mph) 119 km/h *clean*, 59 kts (68 mph) 109 km/h *with flaps*
Take-off distance: 624 ft (190 m) at 9,300 lb (4,218 kg) weight, or 1,503 ft (458 m) with 5,600 lb (2,540 kg) hopper load
Landing distance: 985 ft (300 m)
Maximum climb rate: 1,358 ft (414 m) per minute without equipment, at 9,300 lb (4,218 kg) weight
G limits: +3.4, -1.4 to FAR Pt 23
Ceiling: 21,300 ft (6,500 m)
Range with full fuel: 524 naut miles (603 miles) 970 km

PZL-Mielec M20 Mewa (Seagull) and M32

First flight: 25 July 1979, prototype M20.00 assembled from parts delivered from the USA.
Certification: Polish certificates according to FAR Pt 23 (22 September 1983 with PZL-Franklin engines, and 12 December 1988 with Teledyne Continentals), followed by US, Australian, German and Lithuanian.
Role: Passenger, air taxi, executive, light cargo, ambulance and reconnaissance/patrol. Developed from the Piper PA-34-200T Seneca II.
Sales: 33 built by end of 1998, including 5 delivered that year. 4 used by Polish air ambulance service, 1 delivered in 1996 to Polish Ministry of the Interior forces, and many sold to individuals in Poland, Germany, the USA and elsewhere.
Crew/passengers: See Aircraft variants. Additional seat for a seventh person is optional. Dual controls.
Baggage capacity: Compartments in the nose and the cabin behind the seats. See Aircraft variants.
Wing control surfaces: Frise ailerons and single-slotted flaps.
Tail control surfaces: Slab tailplane with trim tab, and balanced rudder with anti-servo tab.
Flight control system: Manual, cable type.
Construction materials: Metal.
Engines: 2 Teledyne Continental TSIO/LTSIO-360-KB piston engines, with Hartzell 2-blade constant-speed propellers. Optional APU for special missions.
Engine rating: Each 220 hp (164 kW).
Fuel system: 371 litres standard, of which 352 litres are usable. Optional long-range auxiliary tanks to increase capacity to 484 litres, of which 465 litres are usable. Extra long-range wingtip tanks.
Electrical system: 24 volt, with alternators and battery.
Hydraulic system: 2 systems, at 2,233 psi for the undercarriage and 1,500 psi for brakes.
Braking system: Disc brakes. Parking brake.
De-icing system: Fitted.
Radar: Optional weather radar.
Flight avionics/instrumentation: Current model offered with AlliedSignal Bendix/King Silver Crown suite. ELT. Options include GPS, area navigation and autopilot, but not all options (these and others including air conditioning) can be carried with 6 passengers on board; the new M20 04 remedies this by having a higher MTOW.

Aircraft variants:
M20 00 was the first prototype, with PZL-Franklin F6A350 engines. Constructed from US parts.
M20 01 was the Polish-built prototype, first flown on 22 September 1982.
M20 02 was a prototype with changes to systems. First flown on 10 October 1985.
M20 03 is a production version with Teledyne Continental engines. Prototype first flew 13 October 1988. First 4 bought by Polish air ambulance service. Current models based on M20 03 are as follows:
Passenger/air taxi has seating for the pilot, 5 forward-facing passengers and 88 lb (40 kg) of baggage in 17.66 cu ft (0.5 m^3) of space.
Service/light cargo version carries the pilot, 1 passenger and 750 lb (340 kg) of cargo in 141 cu ft (4 m^3) of space.
Club/executive version has the pilot and 5 opposite-facing seats, table, fold-down armrests and refreshment console.

Details for the current M20 03 Mewa

PRINCIPAL DIMENSIONS:
Wing span: 38 ft 11 ins (11.86 m)
Maximum length: 27 ft 7 ins (8.72 m)
Maximum height: 9 ft 11 ins (3.02 m)

CABIN:
Length: 10 ft 5 ins (3.17 m) from instrument panel to rear wall
Width: 4 ft 1 ins (1.24 m)
Height: 3 ft 6 ins (1.07 m)

WINGS:
Aerofoil section: NACA 652-415
Area: 206.45 sq ft (19.18 m²)
Aspect ratio: 7.33
Dihedral: 7°
Incidence: 2°

UNDERCARRIAGE:
Type: Retractable, with steerable nosewheel
Wheel base: 7 ft (2.13 m)
Wheel track: 11 ft 1 ins (3.39 m)

WEIGHTS:
Empty: 2,910 lb (1,320 kg)
Maximum take-off: 4,563 lb (2,070 kg)
Maximum landing: 4,343 lb (1,970 kg)
Payload: 1,080 lb (490 kg)

PERFORMANCE:
Maximum speed: 194 kts (224 mph) 360 km/h
Cruise speed: 168 kts (193 mph) 311 km/h at 45% power, at 24,800 ft (7,560 m)
Stall speed: 67 kts (77 mph) 124 km/h *clean*, 61 kts (70 mph) 112 km/h *with landing flaps*
Take-off distance over a 50 ft (15 m) obstacle: 1,457 ft (444 m)
Landing distance over a 50 ft (15 m) obstacle: 2,150 ft (655 m)
Maximum climb rate: 1,500 ft (456 m) per minute near ground
Ceiling: 25,000 ft (7,620 m)
Range: 669 naut miles (770 miles) 1,240 km with standard fuel, 989 naut miles (1,139 miles) 1,833 km with optional fuel, 45% power, 45 minutes reserve

Ambulance version carries the pilot plus 1 litter or an incubator and 2 attendants, and attachment fittings and supply system for in-flight-usable medical equipment. Special arrangement of the doctor's seat.
Reconnaissance/patrol version has various configurations for maritime/border patrol, police work, SAR, and environmental pollution control. Special optional equipment includes external radio/radar/FLIR/UV detectors, aerial camera, high-power searchlight and loudspeakers.
M20 04 is a new version that first flew in 1995. Maximum take-off weight is 4,750 lb (2,155 kg). Strengthened main spar and fuselage structure, and 28 volt electrical system. Can carry the full range of options with full passenger load.
M32 is a projected pilot plus 7 seats development of Mewa, with 2 × 420 hp (313 kW) engines, wing span of 45 ft 11 ins (14 m), length of 31 ft 6 ins (9.6 m), take-off weight of 7,055 lb (3,200 kg), payload of 1,190 lb (540 kg), speed of 232 kts (267 mph) 430 km/h, and range of 1,349 naut miles (1,553 miles) 2,500 km.

PZL-Mielec M26 Iskierka (Little Spark; Air Wolf for export)

First flight: 15 July 1986 for M26 00 prototype with PZL-Franklin 6A-35D engine, and 24 June 1987 for M26 01 prototype with Textron Lycoming engine.
Certification: 26 October 1991 (Polish). Meets FAR Pt 23 requirements.
Role: Civil and military basic (VFR and IFR), professional licence, preliminary, navigation and aerobatic trainer.
Sales: Programme suspended when, in the late 1980s, the Polish Air Force selected the PZL-130 Orlik as a propeller-driven trainer. Production reinstated in 1995, when distributor Melex of the USA ordered an initial 12 aircraft for US sales (deliveries began July 1996 and the first 3 received by Spring 1997). Very large number ordered by Melex for sales in August 1996, possibly connected to interest in the trainer from 3 central American nations. 1 aircraft in Polish military pilot school in Deblin.
Crew: 2, in tandem, with the instructor in the raised rear cockpit.
Baggage capacity: Behind rear seat.
Wing control surfaces: Frise ailerons and single-slotted flaps.
Tail control surfaces: Elevators (with starboard trim tab) and rudder.
Construction materials: Metal. Uses M20 Mewa assemblies, such as parts of the wings, vertical tail, fuselage, undercarriage and many systems.
Engine: Textron Lycoming AEIO-540-L1B5D piston engine, with a 6 ft 3 ins (1.9 m) 3-blade propeller.
Engine rating: 300 hp (224 kW).
Fuel system: 2 wing fuel tanks (each 90 litres) and a header tank (9 litres) in the fuselage, offering a usable 172 litres. Optionally, 2 extra wing tanks can be fitted, increasing total fuel to 352 litres.
Electrical system: 100 amp alternator and 25 amp-hour battery.
Hydraulic system: As for Mewa.
Braking system: Mainwheel hydraulic discs. Parking brake.
Flight avionics/instrumentation: AlliedSignal Bendix/King suite now standard. Provision for gunsight, gun camera and armament control system.
Expendable weapons and equipment: 2 pylons for light bombs or weapon pods.

↑ **PZL-Mielec M26 Iskierka and cockpit** *(courtesy WSK "PZL-Mielec")*

Details for M26 Iskierka

PRINCIPAL DIMENSIONS:
Wing span: 28 ft 2.5 ins (8.6 m)
Maximum length: 27 ft 3 ins (8.295 m)
Maximum height: 9 ft 8.5 ins (2.96 m)

WINGS:
Aerofoil section: NACA 652-415
Area: 150.69 sq ft (14 m²)
Aspect ratio: 5.28
Dihedral: 7°
Incidence: 2°

UNDERCARRIAGE:
Type: Retractable, with nosewheel
Main and nose wheel tyre size: 436 × 155 m
Wheel base: 6 ft 1.5 ins (1.867 m)
Wheel track: 9 ft 7 ins (2.927 m)

WEIGHTS:
Empty: 2,315 lb (1,050 kg)
Maximum take-off: 3,086 lb (1,400 kg) utility, 2,756 lb (1,250 kg) aerobatic

PERFORMANCE:
Never-exceed speed (V_{NE}): 207 kts (239 mph) 385 km/h aerobatic, 200 kts (230 mph) 371 km/h utility
Maximum speed: 178 kts (205 mph) 330 km/h aerobatic, 173 kts (199 mph) 321 km/h utility
Stall speed: 60 kts (69 mph) 110 km/h, *with flaps*
Take-off distance over a 50 ft (15 m) obstacle: 1,706 ft (520 m) aerobatic, 2,050 ft (625 m) utility
Landing distance over a 50 ft (15 m) obstacle: 2,087 ft (636 m) aerobatic, 2,248 ft (685 m) utility
Maximum climb rate: 1,772 ft (540 m) per minute aerobatic, 1,181 ft (360 m) per minute utility
G limits: +4, -1.72 at MTOW
Range: 760 naut miles (876 miles) 1,410 km utility, with 30 minutes reserve

PZL "Warszawa-Okëcie" — Poland

Corporate address: See Combat section for company details.

Note: The Chief Editor was informed in May 1998 that the **PZL-140 Orlik 2000** turboprop business aircraft, using PZL-130 TC-1 components was merely a 'paper project' that had progressed no further than mock-ups, and should not be detailed in the book.

PZL Warszawa-Okëcie PZL-104 Wilga series

First flight: 24 June 1962.
Role: Multi-purpose short take-off lightplane, including passenger, ambulance, agricultural, patrol, survey and aerial towing. Also special missions variant, including armed for COIN/border patrol.
Sales: 1,000 built and exported to 32 countries. Licence built in Indonesia as PZL-104 **Gelatik**. As of May 1998, 8 Wilgas were to be delivered in 1998 to the domestic market, including 5 to the Polish border guard in Wilga 2000 form.
Crew/passengers: Pilot and 3 passengers or other layouts.
Details: Principally for Wilga 35 and 80.
Wing control surfaces: Slotted ailerons (starboard tab), slotted flaps and leading-edge slats. Ailerons can droop for landing.
Tail control surfaces: Single-piece elevator with tab and rudder.
Flight control system: Manual/mechanical.
Engine: WSK-Kalisz AI-14RA radial piston engine in Wilga 35, and AI-14RA-KAF with repositioned carburettor in Wilga 80. PZL 2-blade wooden propeller.
Engine rating: 260 hp (194 kW).
Fuel system: 195 litres. 90 litre auxiliary tank can be fitted in the cabin, in place of the rear seats.
Electrical system: DC supply via a generator and ni-cd battery.
Hydraulic system: 565 psi for brakes.
Flight avionics/instrumentation: Polish or AlliedSignal Bendix/King nav/com.
Expendable weapons and equipment: Patrol and COIN aircraft can carry UB-16 rocket pod and Strela-2M AAM launchers on 2 underwing pylons. Believed to have been offered to domestic market and Thailand. Surveillance version as Wilga 80-S, developed by Terra-Scan in the USA in 1995, has Wescam IR system.

Aircraft variants:
Wilga 35 became the basic version, manufactured 1968-79, meeting BCAR certification standards. Wilga 35A (aeroclub) is equipped for towing up to 3 gliders, Wilga 35H has Airtech twin floats, Wilga 35R is for agricultural use, and Wilga 35P is for passenger-liaison use. Standard metal construction.
Wilga 35M, with a much more powerful 360 hp (268 kW) Aerostar M-14P engine and PZL-144 propeller, has been terminated.
Wilga 80 is similar to Wilga 35 except for the carburettor and slightly differing dimensions. First flew 30 May 1979. FAR Pt 23.
Wilga 80-550 is a version of the Wilga 80 with a 300 hp (224 kW) Teledyne Continental IO-550 horizontally-opposed engine (instead of radial) and other changes, to improve general performance. Developed and marketed by Melex in the USA, it is also produced by PZL using Melex kits.
PZL-104M Wilga 2000 flew for the first time on 20 August 1996 and is a refined version powered by a Textron Lycoming IO-540 engine of 300 hp (224 kW), with AlliedSignal Bendix/King avionics, as well as slightly changed wings, new fuel tanks, opływowe undercarriage, and take-off weight 3,086 lb (1,400 kg). In September 1997, 5 ordered by Polish border guard

↑ **Cockpit of Wilga 2000** *(Piotr Butowski)*

↑ PZL Warszawa-Okëcie PZL-104 Wilga 80 in special mission version form, with UB-16 unguided rocket pod and 2 Strela-2M AAMs under port wing *(Cezary Piotrowski)*

↑ PZL Warszawa-Okëcie PZL-104M Wilga-2000 *(Piotr Butowski)*

Details for Wilga 35A, *with Wilga 2000 in italics*

PRINCIPAL DIMENSIONS:
Wing span: 36 ft 6 ins (11.12 m), *37 ft (11.28 m)*
Maximum length: 26 ft 7 ins (8.1 m), *27 ft 9 ins (8.46 m)*
Maximum height: 9 ft 8.5 ins (2.96 m)

WINGS:
Aerofoil section: NACA 2415
Area: 166.84 sq ft (15.5 m^2), *the same*
Aspect ratio: 7.98, *8.21*

UNDERCARRIAGE:
Type: Fixed, with steerable tailwheel. Tall, pivoted, main legs. Low pressure main tyres. Optional floats or skis

WEIGHTS:
Empty: 1,984 lb (900 kg), *2,205 lb (1,000 kg)*
Maximum take-off and landing: 2,866 lb (1,300 kg), *3,086 lb (1,400 kg)*

PERFORMANCE:
Never-exceed speed (V_{NE}): 150 kts (173 mph) 279 km/h
Maximum speed: 105 kts (121 mph) 195 km/h, *the same*
Cruise speed: 85 kts (98 mph) 157 km/h, at 75% power
Stall speed: 30.5 kts (35 mph) 56 km/h, *with flaps*
Minimum speed (Wilga 2000): *approx 33 kts (38 mph) 60 km/h*
Take-off distance: 397 ft (121 m) on grass, *893 ft (272 m)*
Landing distance: 348 ft (106 m) on grass, *542 ft (165 m)*
Climb rate: 906 ft (276 m), *965 ft (294 m)*, per minute at sea level
Ceiling: 13,125 ft (4,000 m), service
Range: 302 naut miles (348 miles) 560 km, with 30 minutes reserve, *755 naut miles (870 miles) 1,400 km at 175 km/h*

equipped with FLIR, delivered 1998. Others ordered.
Wilga floatplane with PZL floats is to be available in Summer of 1999.

PZL Warszawa-Okëcie PZL-105L Flaming

Comments: First flown on 19 December 1989, the Flaming was conceived as a multi-purpose lightplane to replace Wilga, offering a larger cabin for 6 persons and improved performance. However, in May 1998 the Chief Editor was informed by PZL Warszawa-Okëcie that the Flaming programme had been halted while development of Wilga 2000 and other programmes progressed. Doubt was expressed whether Flaming would be put back into development at a later date. For full details and a photograph, see the 1996-97 edition of *WA&SD*, page 414.

PZL Warszawa-Okëcie PZL-106BT Turbo-Kruk (Raven) and New Variant

First flight: 17 April 1973 for Textron Lycoming IO-720A1B powered prototype. 18 September 1985 for current PZL-106BT.
Role: Agricultural and firefighting.
Details: PZL-106BT, unless stated.
Sales: All production of the piston-engined Kruk (PZL-106A; AS certified to BCAR and 146 built; B with new wing, plus BS and BR subversions with ASz-62IR and PZL-3SR engines respectively) and turboprop-engined Kruk was halted in about 1991-92. Production of the turbine Kruk only restarted in 1994, offering a new larger 1,500 litre chemical hopper. Total Kruk production by May 1998 stood at 350 piston engined aircraft and 30 turbine engined PZL-106BTs. 5 for delivery in 1998, with negotiations then underway for delivery of 10-12 to South America in 1999.
Crew: Pilot, with jump-seat to transport a mechanic to site. For training, a second dual control cockpit can be fitted ahead of the standard cockpit and a small training hopper installed. Cockpit sealed to prevent chemical ingress. Cockpit heated and ventilated. Optional cockpit air flow filtering system.
Chemical tank/hopper: Glassfibre, with 1,400 litre liquid capacity or 2,866 lb (1,300 kg) of dry chemicals standard, with option of 1,600 litre tank or 3,307 lb (1,500 kg) chemical load.
Dispersal equipment: Spraybars for liquids, with nozzles and fan-driven pump. Alternative 6 atomizers and fan-driven pump, or tunnel spreader for dry chemicals. Optional pneumatically controlled hopper lid and hopper hydraulic balance.
Load dump time is about 5 seconds. Swath width 82 ft (25 m) with tunnel spreader, 147 ft (45 m) with atomizer, 98 ft (30 m) with nozzles. Fastening elements for transportation of equipment optional.
Safety equipment: Designed to allow the pilot to survive a 40g impact. Steel roll-over cage, and cable cutters on the undercarriage and windshield. Cable deflector from the windshield cutter to the tail.
Wing control surfaces: Full-span fixed slats, slotted flaps and ailerons.
Tail control surfaces: Elevators and inset rudder with tab.
Construction materials: All-metal 2-spar wing structure, braced with short struts. Flaps and ailerons trailing edges covered with canvas. Welded steel tube fuselage structure. Pilot's cockpit with additional mechanic's seat attached to the truss. Elevators and rudder trailing edges covered with canvas.
Engine: Walter M601D turboprop, with an 8 ft 2 ins (2.5 m) Avia

Details for PZL-106BT Turbo-Kruk

PRINCIPAL DIMENSIONS:
Wing span: 49 ft 3 ins (15 m)
Maximum length: 33 ft 11 ins (10.34 m)
Maximum height: 14 ft 3 ins (4.34 m)

WINGS:
Aerofoil section: NACA 2415
Area: 341.1 sq ft (31.69 m^2)
Aspect ratio: 7.19
Sweepback: 6°

UNDERCARRIAGE:
Type: Fixed, with steerable tailwheel
Wheel track: 10 ft 2 ins (3.1 m)

WEIGHTS:
Empty: 3,703 lb (1,680 kg)
Maximum take-off: 7,716 lb (3,500 kg) overloaded or restricted categories, or 6,614 lb (3,000 kg) non-aerobatic category

PERFORMANCE (equipped with tunnel spreader, unless stated; 6,614 lb, 3,000 kg weight, ISA)**:**
Maximum speed: 116 kts (133 mph) 215 km/h
Maximum speed, clean: 129 kts (149 mph) 240 km/h
Cruise speed: 113 kts (130 mph) 210 km/h, *clean*
Operating flight speed: 76-92 kts (87-106 mph) 140-170 km/h
Minimum speed: 54 kts (62 mph) 100 km/h at 3,000 kg with tunnel spreader, throttled engine, or 62 kts (72 mph) 115 km/h
Take-off distance: 1,067 ft (325 m) at MTOW, or 886 ft (270 m) at 3,000 kg weight
Landing distance: 985 ft (300 m) at MTOW, or 886 ft (270 m) at 3,000 kg weight
Climb rate: 1,083 ft (330 m) per minute, or 886 ft (270 m) per minute with agricultural equipment
Maximum range: 716.6 naut miles (825 miles) 1,328 km, clean

↑ PZL Warszawa-Okëcie PZL-106BT Turbo-Kruk *(Piotr Butowski)*

V508D constant-speed 3-blade propeller.
Engine rating: 724 shp (540 kW).
Fuel system: 560 litres. Integral tanks in torque box between spars. Ferry fuel can be carried in the hopper.

Aircraft variants:
PZL-106BT Turbo-Kruk, as detailed.
P&WC PT6A-34AG powered version has been under test since Summer 1998 (SP-PPW), featuring airframe improvements to reduce drag, modified cockpit, improved electrical system, and more. With possible export potential, it is also helping in the 'Larger Kruk' programme.

PZL Warszawa-Okëcie PZL-110 and PZL–111 Koliber

First flight: 18 April 1978 (original low-powered PZL-Rzeszów PZL-F.4A-engined version).
Certification: FAR 23 in Normal and Utility categories.
Role: Pleasure, training, aerial towing and more, originally based on the Socata Rallye.
Sales: By May 1998, a total of 70 Kolibers had been delivered. At that time, 25 Koliber 160s and 10 Koliber 235As were on order for export.
Crew/passengers: 4 persons. Dual controls. Entrance via a sliding canopy. 110 lb (50 kg) baggage capacity for 235A.
Wing control surfaces: Balanced ailerons (with ground adjustable tabs), Fowler flaps and automatic leading-edge slats.
Tail control surfaces: Balanced elevator (with tab) and rudder (with ground adjustable tab).
Flight control system: Mechanical, except for electric flaps.
Construction materials: Metal, with corrugated skins for the elevator, flaps and rudder.
Engine: See Aircraft variants.
Fuel system: 105 litres basic for PZL-110, but with the option of 177 litres. 161 basic for the Koliber 235A, with option of 290 litres.
Electrical system: 12 volt for all versions except Koliber 150A, which is 24 volt. Supply via an alternator and battery.
Hydraulic system: For brakes only.
Braking system: Hydraulic disc.
Flight avionics/instrumentation: Include ADF, VOR, turn and bank indicator, attitude and direction gyros, and UHF transceiver. Koliber 150A has a higher standard of avionics and can undertake IFR and night flying. Koliber 235A has Narco or AlliedSignal Bendix/King radio-nav, including GPS.

Aircraft variants:
PZL-110 Koliber was the initial production version, powered by a PZL-Franklin 4A-235B3 engine. 32 built.
PZL-110 Koliber 150 has a 150 hp (112 kW) Textron Lycoming O-320-E2A piston engine, with a 5 ft 10 ins (1.78 m) Sensenich 74DM6 2-blade constant-speed propeller. Production includes 3 Kolibers upgraded to this standard.
PZL-110 Koliber 150A of 1993 appearance has a higher-standard of avionics and uprated electrical system, as required for IFR. FAR Pt 23 Amdt 23 certified. Sold in North America as the Koliber II by Cadmus Corporation.

↑ PZL Warszawa-Okëcie PZL-111 Koliber 235A prototype

PZL-110 Koliber 160A is a new version, with a 160 hp (119 kW) Textron Lycoming O-320-D2A engine, with Sensenich 74DM6-0-58 (56,56) propeller. Already achieved export success. Empty weight 1,338 lb (607 kg), MTOW 1,874 lb (850 kg) Normal and 1,697 lb (770 kg) Utility, 161 litres of fuel, same dimensions as 150A, maximum cruise speed 102 kts (117 mph) 189 km/h, climb rate 669 ft (204 m) per minute, and maximum range 463 naut miles.
PZL-111 Koliber 235A has a 235 hp (175 kW) Textron Lycoming O-540-B4B5 piston engine, with option of 3-blade McCauley or 2-blade Hartzell constant-speed propeller. Strengthened structure, suited to glider/banner towing. Additional small windows in rear of cockpit and extended dorsal fin. Prototype unofficially named ***Senior*** first flown 13 September 1995. Versions with 160 hp (119.3 kW), 180 hp (134 kW) and 200 hp (149 kW) engines offered but not known to have been built.

Details for the Koliber 150A, *with 235A in italics*

PRINCIPAL DIMENSIONS:
Wing span: 31 ft 11.5 ins (9.74 m), *the same*
Maximum length: 24 ft 2 ins (7.37 m), *24 ft 8 ins (7.52 m)*
Maximum height: 9 ft 2 ins (2.8 m), *the same*

WINGS:
Aerofoil section: Modified NACA 63A-416, *the same*
Area: 136.49 sq ft (12.68 m^2), *the same*
Aspect ratio: 7.497, *the same*

UNDERCARRIAGE:
Type: Fixed, with castoring nosewheel

WEIGHTS:
Empty: 1,208 lb (548 kg), *1,554 lb (705 kg)*
Maximum take-off: 1,874 lb (850 kg), *2,094 lb (950 kg) Utility, 2,535 lb (1,150 kg) Normal*
Maximum landing: *2,535 lb (1,150 kg) for 235A*

PERFORMANCE:
Never-exceed speed (V_{NE}): 145 kts (167 mph) 270 km/h
Cruise speed: 104 kts (119 mph) 192 km/h, *130 kts (149 mph) 240 km/h*, both 75% power
Stall speed: 48 kts (56 mph) 89 km/h *clean*, 43 kts (49 mph) 79 km/h *with flaps*, IAS
Take-off distance: *443 ft (135 m) for 235A*
Landing distance: *561 ft (171 m) for 235A*
Take-off over a 50 ft (15 m) obstacle: 1,132 ft (345 m)
Landing over a 50 ft (15 m) obstacle: 998 ft (304 m)
Maximum climb rate: 709 ft (216 m), *1,220 ft (372 m)*, per minute at sea level
G limits: +4.4, -1.5 normal
Ceiling: 13,400 ft (4,085 m), service
Range with full fuel: 525 naut miles (605 miles) 974 km, no reserve, *895 naut miles (1,031 miles) 1,660 km with optional fuel*

PZL Warszawa-Okëcie PZL-112 Koliber Junior

In May 1998 the Chief Editor was informed by PZL Warszawa-Okëcie that a new side-by-side 2-seat trainer was being developed, of similar layout to the Koliber 150A but powered by a Rotax 914 F-4 engine with Hoffmann constant-speed propeller or, alternatively, a Limbach L2400EF with Hoffmann variable-pitch propeller. To be certified to FAR 23 for IFR and VFR use. Empty weight 992 lb (450 kg), MTOW and MLW 1,543 lb (700 kg). Wing span 28 ft 10.5 ins (8.8 m), length 22 ft (6.7 m), height 9 ft 10 ins (3 m) and wing area 111.94 sq ft (10.4 m^2). Maximum speed 113 kts (130 mph) 210 km/h, cruise speed 97 kts (112 mph) 180 km/h, stall speed 43 kts (50 mph) 80 km/h, climb rate 787 ft (240 m) per minute, G limits +4.4 and -1.8, take-off distance over a 50 ft (15 m) obstacle 1,313 ft (400 m), landing distance over a 50 ft (15 m) obstacle 1,149 ft (350 m), and maximum range 593 naut miles (683 miles) 1,100 km. First flight is expected in 1999.

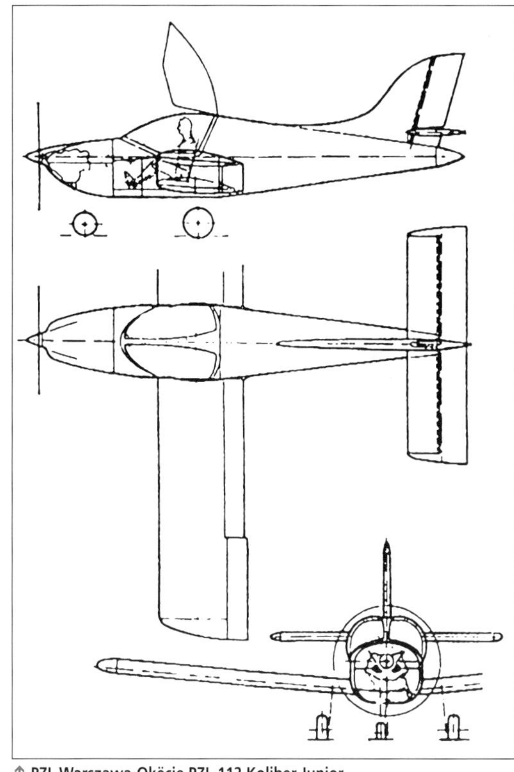
↑ PZL Warszawa-Okëcie PZL-112 Koliber Junior

PZL Warszawa-Okëcie PZL-240 Pelikan

Comments: Under development as a specialized firefighting biplane (load drop 1.5 seconds), capable also of forest spraying and agricultural work. Cabin, rear fuselage with control surfaces, and wings come from the Kruk. Can carry 6,100 litres (8,818 lb, 4,000 kg) of fire extinguishing agents for a 1.5 hour mission, or 6,614 lb (3,000 kg) for 5 hours. Reinforced stainless steel 4-chamber hopper (212 cu ft, 6 m^3) comprises the central main assembly of the airframe structure, to which other assemblies attach. 2,000 shp (1,491 kW) P&WC PW120 turboprop, with 12 ft 6 ins (3.8 m) Hamilton Standard propeller. Fuel capacity 1,150 litres. Wing span 50 ft 10 ins (15.5 m), wing area 699.65 sq ft (65 m^2), length 36 ft 1 ins (11 m), and height 16 ft 9 ins (5.1 m). Empty weight 6,614 lb (3,000 kg), and MTOW 16,535 lb (7,500 kg) Restricted and 12,125 lb (5,500 kg) Normal. Maximum speed 124 kts (143 mph) 230 km/h, operational speed 92 kts (106 mph) 170 km/h, stall speed 43 kts (50 mph) 80 km/h, take-off distance on grass 886 ft (270 m) and landing distance 821 ft (250 m), all at Restricted weight, sea level, ISA.

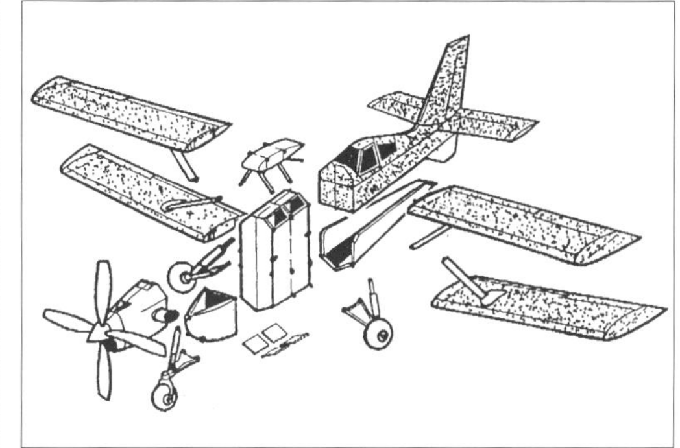
↑ PZL-240 Pelikan biplane layout and manufacturing sections

Aerostar S.A. — Romania

Corporate address:
See Combat section for details.

Aerostar Yak-52

First flight: May 1978.
Role: Fully aerobatic military and civil trainer, built under Yakovlev licence.
Sales: More than 1,700 in use worldwide. Still offered and manufactured.
Crew: 2 in tandem, with dual controls. No rear-instructor elevation.
Delivered with: Towing bars (for hand and car towing), false undercarriage (used for transportation), anchor devices and cables, cockpit lock, cover, spare parts, manuals, tools and wooden transport box. Warranty covers 300 flying hours in 15 months, with no more than 3 months in the producer's wooden box.
Wing control surfaces: Slotted ailerons (with ground-adjustable tabs) and split flaps.
Tail control surfaces: Elevators (port trim tab) and rudder (ground-adjustable tab).
Flight control system: Pushrod and cables, except for pneumatic flaps.
Construction materials: Aluminium alloy and steel, but with fabric covering for the ailerons, elevators and rudder. Airframe life of 5,000 flying hours or 20 years.
Engine: Aerostar M-14P radial supercharged piston engine, with

a 7 ft 10 ins (2.4 m) V-530TA-D35 2-blade variable-pitch propeller. Engine life of 2,250 flying hours, propeller life of 800 flying hours or 12 years.
Engine rating: 360 hp (268 kW).
Fuel system: 122 litres (220 lb, 100 kg). Collector tank for inverted flight.
Electrical system: 27 volt DC supply, via an engine-driven 3 kW generator. 12 volt battery. 36 volt, 400 Hz AC supply via 2 inverters.
Braking system: Pneumatic brakes.
Flight avionics/instrumentation: Gyro and radio compasses, VHF com and more.

↑ **For German partner Air Light, Aerostar manufactures the Wild Thing ultralight, first delivered in 1997 (see Recreational section – Ultraleight Wild Thing)**

↑ **Aerostar Yak-52** *(courtesy Aerostar)*

Details for Aerostar Yak-52

PRINCIPAL DIMENSIONS:
Wing span: 30 ft 6 ins (9.3 m)
Maximum length: 25 ft 5 ins (7.745 m)
Maximum height: 8 ft 10 ins (2.7 m)

COCKPIT:
Width: 2 ft 5 ins (0.73 m)
Height: 3 ft 8 ins (1.12 m)

WINGS:
Area: 161.46 sq ft (15 m^2)
Aspect ratio: 5.766

UNDERCARRIAGE:
Type: Retractable, with nosewheel. Mainwheel legs retract forward and nosewheel aft, leaving all 3 wheels exposed to prevent serious damage in a wheels-up landing. Optional skis
Wheel base: 6 ft 1 ins (1.86 m)
Wheel track: 8 ft 11 ins (2.71 m)

WEIGHTS:
Empty, equipped: 2,238 lb (1,015 kg)
Maximum take-off: 2,877 lb (1,305 kg)

PERFORMANCE:
Never-exceed speed (V_{NE}): 194 kts (223 mph) 360 km/h
Maximum speed: 154 kts (177 mph) 285 km/h at sea level, 146 kts (168 mph) 270 km/h at 3,280 ft (1,000 m)
Cruise speed: 103 kts (118 mph) 190 km/h at 3,280 ft (1,000 m)
Landing speed: 59 kts (68 mph) 110 km/h
Stall speed: about 48 kts (56 mph) 90 km/h *with flaps*, engine idling
Take-off distance: 560 ft (170 m)
Landing distance: 985 ft (300 m)
Maximum climb rate: 1,378 ft (420 m) per minute at sea level
G limits: +7, -5
Ceiling: 13,125 ft (4,000 m), service
Range with full fuel: 297 naut miles (341 miles) 550 km

CPCA S.A. (Centrul de Projiectare Si Consulting Pentru Aviatie S.A.) Romania

Corporate address:
I. Maiorescu Nr. 10, 1100 Craiova, Dolj.
Telephone and facsimile: +40 51 412482
E-mail: adccv@topedge.com
Founded: 1991.
Information:
Valeriu Bâlbâie (General Manager).

ACTIVITIES

■ Research into military, light/ultralight aircraft and helicopters. See also Helicopter section for ADC-H1.
■ Ultralight production.

CPCA DK-10 Dracula

First flight: 1998.

↑ **CPCA DK-10 Dracula** *(courtesy CPCA)*

Certification: To meet FAR Pt 23 standards.
Role: 2-seat lightplane and trainer, with sliding canopy.
Baggage capacity: 0.17 cu ft (6 m^3) aft of the seats.
Wing control surfaces: Ailerons (port trim tab) and slotted flaps.
Tail control surfaces: Horn-balanced elevators and rudder, all with trim.
Flight control system: Mechanical, except for hydraulic flaps and electric trim.
Construction materials: Metal.
Engine: Textron Lycoming O-320-A1A piston engine, with a 2-blade constant-speed propeller.
Engine rating: 150 hp (112 kW).
Fuel system: 92 litres.
Electrical system: DC supply via a 28 volt engine-driven starter-generator. 24 volt battery.
Hydraulic system: 3,046 psi.
Braking system: Mainwheel hydraulic.
Flight avionics/instrumentation: AlliedSignal Bendix/King DME, VOR/ILS, marker beacon receiver, VHF com and transponder.

CPCA ADC-XO

First flight: 1997.
Certification: Conforms to JAR-VLA standards.
Role: 2-seat ultralight monoplane.
Wing control surfaces: Strut-braced high-wing monoplane, with ailerons and flaps.
Tail control surfaces: Elevators and rudder.
Flight control system: Mechanical.
Construction materials: Metal, fabric and glassfibre.
Engine: Rotax 582 piston engine, with 2-blade fixed-pitch propeller.
Engine rating: 65 hp (48.5 kW).
Fuel system: 50 litres.
Electrical system: DC supply via a 12 volt engine-magneto-generator and 12 volt battery.
Flight avionics/instrumentation: AlliedSignal Bendix/King hand-held nav/com transceiver.

Details for DK-10 Dracula

PRINCIPAL DIMENSIONS:
Wing span: 27 ft 6 ins (8.38 m)
Maximum length: 22 ft 11 ins (6.98 m)
Maximum height: 6 ft 11 ins (2.1 m)

WINGS:
Aerofoil section: NACA 23-023/23-012 (root/tip)
Area: 107.64 sq ft (10 m^2)
Aspect ratio: 7.022
Dihedral: 5°

UNDERCARRIAGE:
Type: Retractable, with steerable nosewheel
Wheel base: 5 ft 11 ins (1.805 m)
Wheel track: 9 ft (2.728 m)

WEIGHTS:
Empty: 1,389 lb (630 kg)
Maximum take-off and landing: 2,050 lb (930 kg)
Payload: 496 lb (225 kg)

PERFORMANCE (provisional):
Maximum speed: 173 kts (199 mph) 320 km/h
Stall speed: 58 kts (66 mph) 107 km/h *clean*, 52 kts (59 mph) 96 km/h *with flaps*
Take-off distance: 591 ft (180 m)
Landing distance: 558 ft (170 m)
Maximum climb rate: 750 ft (228 m) per minute at sea level
Ceiling: 23,300 ft (7,100 m)
Range with full fuel: 593 naut miles (683 miles) 1,100 km

Details for ADC-XO

PRINCIPAL DIMENSIONS:
Wing span: 31 ft 6.5 ins (9.61 m)
Maximum length: 20 ft 6 ins (6.25 m)
Maximum height: 6 ft 7 ins (2 m)

WINGS:
Aerofoil section: NACA 4412
Area: 138.64 sq ft (12.88 m^2)
Aspect ratio: 7.17

UNDERCARRIAGE:
Type: Fixed, with tailwheel

WEIGHTS:
Empty: 507 lb (230 kg)
Maximum take-off and landing: 992 lb (450 kg)

PERFORMANCE (provisional)**:**
Maximum speed: 86 kts (99 mph) 160 km/h
Cruise speed: 71 kts (82 mph) 132 km/h
Stall speed: 40 kts (46 mph) 73.5 km/h
Take-off and landing distance: 328 ft (100 m)
Maximum climb rate: 1,180 ft (360 m) per minute
Ceiling: 9,840 ft (3,000 m)
Range: 172.5 naut miles (199 miles) 320 km

↑ **CPCA ADC-XO 2-seat ultralight** *(courtesy CPCA)*

IAR-SA Brasov — Romania

Corporate address:
See IAR-SA Brasov in the Helicopter section for company details. See also Gliders/Motorgliders.

IAR 46

First flight: 1993.
Role: 2-seat lightplane for private use.
Certification: Conforms to JAR-VLA.
Wing control surfaces: Ailerons and plain flaps.
Tail control surfaces: T-tail with elevators (with tabs) and large rudder.
Flight control system: Mechanical.
Construction materials: Principally metal, but with fabric covering the elevators and rudder, and glassfibre fairings.
Engine: Rotax 912 F3/A3 piston engine, with a 5 ft 7 ins (1.7 m) Hoffmann HO-V352F/170FQ 2-blade variable-pitch composites propeller.
Engine rating: 77.8 hp (58 kW).
Fuel system: 78 litres.
Flight avionics/instrumentation: VFR instrumentation. Options at customer's request.

Details for IAR 46

PRINCIPAL DIMENSIONS:
Wing span: 37 ft 6 ins (11.42 m)
Maximum length: 25 ft 9 ins (7.85 m)
Maximum height: 7 ft 1 ins (2.15 m)

WINGS:
Area: 149.29 sq ft (13.87 m^2)
Aspect ratio: 9.403

UNDERCARRIAGE:
Type: Retracting main wheels, fixed tailwheel

WEIGHTS:
Empty: 1,168 lb (530 kg) ±5 kg
Maximum take-off: 1,653 lb (750 kg)

PERFORMANCE:
Never-exceed speed (V_{NE}): 151 kts (174 mph) 280 km/h
Maximum speed: 116 kts (133 mph) 215 km/h
Maximum cruise speed: 103 kts (118 mph) 190 km/h
Economic cruise speed: 92 kts (106 mph) 170 km/h
Minimum control speed: 49 kts (56.5 mph) 91 km/h at $\beta = 0°$, 44 kts (50.5 mph) 81 km/h at $\beta = 45°$
Stall speed: 42 kts (48 mph) 78 km/h
Take-off distance over a 50 ft (15 m) obstacle: 1,477 ft (450 m)
Landing distance: 330 ft (100 m)
Maximum climb rate: 846 ft (258 m) per minute at sea level
Ceiling: 16,400 ft (5,000 m), service
G limits: +4.4, -2.2
Range: 431 naut miles (497 miles) 800 km, no reserve

↑ **IAR-SA Brasov IAR 46** *(courtesy IAR-SA Brasov)*

IAR Noga VI

Comments: Development of this business jet has been terminated. For details and an illustration, see the 1996-97 edition of *WA&SD*, page 417.

Aero-M JSC — Russia

Corporate address:
32 Varshavskoye shosse, MRTI RAN building, 113519 Moscow.
Facsimile: +7 095 314 1053
Information:
Nikolai Florov (General Manager).

Aero-M A-209

First flight: Had been expected in 1998.
Certification: Planned according to AP-23 standards.
Role: 9-seat passenger and utility aircraft.
Sales: Production is being prepared at the Saratov aircraft plant. Expected price US$600,000.
Crew/passengers: Standard 2 crew plus 9 passengers; mixed passenger/cargo, cargo, ambulance and VIP versions planned.
Wing control surfaces: High-mounted monoplane wings, with flaps and ailerons (port trim tab).
Tail control surfaces: Elevators and rudder (each with trim tab).
Construction materials: Metal.
Engines: 2 OKBM/Voronezh M25-01 piston engines, each a supercharged version of M-14, with 3-blade propellers.
Engine rating: 450 hp (335.6 kW).
Fuel system: 992 lb (450 kg).
Radar: Weather.
Flight avionics/instrumentation: IFR, GPS.

Aircraft variants:
A-209 (209 for 2 engines and 9 passengers) is the basic version with M25-01 engines, as described.
A-209AL is a projected 12-passenger version with 2 AL-34 turboprops of 760 shp (567 kW) each.
A-209E is a projected western version with Pratt & Whitney Canada PT6A or AlliedSignal TPE331 engines and AlliedSignal Bendix-King avionics.

Details for A-209

PRINCIPAL DIMENSIONS:
Wing span: 52 ft 6 ins (16 m)
Maximum length: 39 ft 10 ins (12.14 m)
Maximum height: 15 ft (4.57 m)

UNDERCARRIAGE:
Type: Retractable, with nosewheel. Optional wheel/skis

WEIGHTS:
Empty, operating: 6,393 lb (2,900 kg)
Maximum take-off: 8,598 lb (3,900 kg)
Useful load: 2,205 lb (1,000 kg)
Payload: 1,852 lb (840 kg)

PERFORMANCE:
Maximum operating speed: 200 kts (230 mph) 370 km/h
Cruise speed: 129.5 kts (149 mph) 240 km/h
Landing speed: 130 kts (96 mph) 155 km/h
Take-off distance: 1,312 ft (400 m)
Landing distance: 1,050 ft (320 m)
Maximum climb rate: 1,300 ft (396 m) per minute, at sea level
Cruise altitude: 9,845 ft (3,000 m)
Range with maximum fuel and 992 lb (450 kg) payload: 836 naut miles (963 miles) 1,550 km
Range with 1,631 lb (740 kg) payload and 353 lb (160 kg) fuel: 210 naut miles (242 miles) 390 km

↑ **Model of the Aero-M A-209** *(Piotr Butowski)*

Aeropract

Russia

Corporate address:
PO Box 9863, Samara 443008

Telephone: +7 8462 638291, 638250
Facsimile: +7 8462 271568, 325166, 271566

ACTIVITIES

▪ See also Recreational section for Flirt microlight. Aeroprakt is a Ukrainian company (which see) based in Kiev.

Aeropract A-21 and A-21M Solo

Role: Small and light single-seat private low-wing monoplane, with potential for other uses including aeroclub, agricultural and forest/pipeline patrol.
Control surfaces: Conventional.
Engine: See Aircraft variants.
Fuel system: 119 lb (54 kg) for A-21, 48.5 lb (22 kg) for A-21M.
Aircraft variants:
A-21 has a Russian RMZ-640 piston engine of 36 hp (27 kW).
A-21M is a more powerful 45.6 hp (34 kW) Rotax engined version, with a 2-blade propeller with spinner.

Details for A-21M Solo, *with A-21 weights and performance data in italics*

PRINCIPAL DIMENSIONS:
Wing span: 21 ft 10 ins (6.65 m)
Maximum length: 15 ft 6 ins (4.73 m)
Maximum height: 5 ft 10.5 ins (1.794 m)

WINGS:
Area: 64.58 sq ft (6 m^2)
Aspect ratio: 7.37

UNDERCARRIAGE:
Type: Fixed, with a steerable nosewheel

WEIGHTS:
Maximum take-off: 617 lb (280 kg), *595 lb (270 kg)*

PERFORMANCE:
Maximum speed: 103 kts (118 mph) 190 km/h, *86 kts (99 mph) 160 km/h*
Minimum control speed: 43 kts (50 mph) 80 km/h, *41 kts (47 mph) 75 km/h*
Maximum climb rate: 984 ft (300 m) per minute, *590 ft (180 m) per minute*
G limits: +6, -3, *the same*
Range with full fuel: 116 naut miles (133.5 miles) 215 km, *251 naut miles (289 miles) 466 km*

Aeropract A-23M

First flight: 8 January 1993 for prototype with 2 RMZ-640 engines.
Role: Tandem 2-seat lightplane, possibly available in assembled and kit forms.
Airframe: Similar pod and boom layout to A-20 (see Ukraine), except with larger boom, low-mounted tailplane and nosewheel undercarriage.
Wing control surfaces: Ailerons on constant-chord wings.
Tail control surfaces: Elevators and rudder.
Flight control system: Manual.
Construction materials: Wood and foam/composites materials.
Engine: Single Rotax 582 piston engine, with 2-blade fixed-pitch pusher propeller.
Engine rating: 64 hp (47.7 kW).
Fuel system: 84 lb (38 kg) in tank aft of seats.

Details for A-23 prototype with RMZ-640 engines

PRINCIPAL DIMENSIONS:
Wing span: 32 ft 10 ins (10 m)
Maximum length: 24 ft 3 ins (7.4 m)
Maximum height: 7 ft 10 ins (2.4 m)

WINGS:
Aerofoil section: R-IIIA-15.5
Area: 145.31 sq ft (13.5 m^2)
Aspect ratio: 7.41
Dihedral: 1° 30′

UNDERCARRIAGE:
Type: Fixed, with a steerable (±15°) nosewheel. Can have wheel/skis

WEIGHTS:
Empty: 723 lb (328 kg)
Maximum take-off: 1,169 lb (530 kg)

PERFORMANCE:
Maximum speed: 78 kts (90 mph) 145 km/h
Cruise speed: 70 kts (81 mph) 130 km/h
Stall speed: 40.5 kts (47 mph) 75 km/h
Climb rate: 660 ft (200 m) per minute
Range with full fuel: 194 naut miles (224 miles) 360 km

Aeropract A-25 Breeze

First flight: 9 November 1994.
Certification: Conforms to AP-23 (FAR Pt 23) regulations.
Role: 4-seat amphibian, the roles to include passenger and cargo transport, ambulance, patrol and training. Dual controls.
Sales: Approximately US$120,000.
Wing characteristics: Cantilever constant-chord mid-mounted wings with down-turned wingtips to perform as outer floats.
Wing control surfaces: Ailerons and flaps.
Tail control surfaces: Sweptback fin and rudder, with mid-mounted constant-chord tailplane with elevators (with starboard trim).
Flight control system: Manual, except for electric flaps and trim.
Construction materials: Mainly glassfibre reinforced plastics sandwich construction.
Engine: LOM M-337 6-cylinder piston engine (optional Wankel rotary type), with 5 ft 11 ins (1.8 m) 2-blade fixed-pitch pusher propeller.
Engine rating: 210 hp (157 kW).
Fuel system: 421 lb (191 kg) in 2 wing tanks.

Details for A-25

PRINCIPAL DIMENSIONS:
Wing span: 34 ft 9.5 ins (10.6 m)
Maximum length: 26 ft 1 ins (7.95 m)
Maximum height: 9 ft 8.5 ins (2.96 m)

WINGS:
Aerofoil section: NACA $63_2$417 mod
Area: 158.22 sq ft (14.7 m^2)
Aspect ratio: 7.64
Dihedral: 3°
Incidence: 3°

UNDERCARRIAGE:
Type: Retractable, with a steerable (±15°) nosewheel
Wheel base: 9 ft 4.5 ins (2.86 m)
Wheel track: 9 ft 5.5 ins (2.88 m)

WEIGHTS:
Empty: 1,389 lb (630 kg)
Maximum take-off: 2,700 lb (1,225 kg)
Payload: 882 lb (400 kg)

PERFORMANCE:
Maximum speed: 140 kts (162 mph) 260 km/h
Cruise speed: 108 kts (124 mph) 200 km/h
Take-off speed: 56 kts (65 mph) 104 km/h
Landing speed: 51 kts (59 mph) 95 km/h
Take-off distance: 952 ft (290 m) from ground, 1,640 ft (500 m) from water
Landing distance: 378 ft (115 m)
Climb rate: 885 ft (270 m) per minute
G limits: +3.8, -2
Range with full fuel: 539 naut miles (621 miles) 1,000 km

Aeropract A-27

First flight: June 1998.
Comments: Under test on Volga river near Samara. 95 hp (71 kW) Hirth F30 engine. Maximum speed 70-76 kts (81-87 mph) 130-140 km/h with floats. MTOW 1,323 lb (600 kg).

↑**Aeropract A-27, first flown in June 1998** *(Piotr Butowski)*

↑ **Aeropract A-21M Solo** *(Piotr Butowski)*

↑**Aeropract A-25 Breeze** *(Piotr Butowski)*

Aeroprogress Inc/Khrunichev State Space Research Center — Russia

Comments: See Combat section for a general overview of these closely affiliated organizations. Also see the 1996-97 edition of *WA&SD* for various projects no longer listed here.
Note: Copyright for all projects belongs to Aeroprogress except for T-411, T-417, T-420, T-422, T-430 and T-440.

ACTIVITIES

■ Undertakes the design and construction of a wide range of different types of aircraft, from military to commuter and wing-in-ground-effect, many of which are still in the development stage. Of several dozens of Aeroprogress/Khrunichev projects only the general purpose aircraft are being continued. See respective sections of previous edition for projects of combat aircraft and airliners, as well as for other general purpose projects. Extensively described below are the T-101 and T-411 aircraft which are under test. Remaining projects currently marketed by Aeroprogress/Khrunichev are presented in shortened form. According to the designers, the most promising of these are T-417 and T-701/705.
■ Associated with Aeroprogress is Washington Aeroprogress Inc in the USA (initially offering kits of the T-411 Wolverine – which see).
■ Member of the Business Aviation Association, an important grouping of production facilities in Russia to co-operate over civil production. The BAA includes among many facilities those of Myasishchev, Yakovlev and MAPO "MiG", the latter where most Aeroprogress manufacture takes place. Orders total hundreds of aircraft.

AEROPROGRESS INC
Corporate address: 65A Volokolamskoye Highway, Moscow 123424.
Telephone: +7 095 1459890, 1458044 **Facsimile:** +7 095 1459477
Founded: 1990.
Information: Evgeny P. Grunin (President and General Designer).

KHRUNICHEV STATE SPACE RESEARCH CENTER
Corporate address: 18 Novozavodskaya Street, Moscow 121309.
Telephone: +7 095 1458343, 1459085, 1458044 **Facsimile:** +7 095 1459477
Founded: 1994 for the Aviation Department.
Information: Evgeny P. Grunin (Chief Designer Aviation Department).

↑ **Aeroprogress T-101 Gratch** *(Piotr Butowski)*

Aeroprogress T-101 Gratch series

Details: For T-101 Gratch, except under Aircraft variants.
First flight: 7 December 1994 at Lukhovitsy, piloted by Viktor Zabolotsky.
Role: Military and civil STOL passenger and cargo transport, with other uses including agricultural, firefighting, air ambulance, survey and photographic.
Sales: Production by MAPO "MiG". Aeroprogress stated intentions for 275 T-101s by early 1995, including 200 utility and airborne troop transports for air forces, 25 for the Russian Ministry of Emergencies and 50 for agricultural work. Up to the time of writing, some 30 aircraft completed (including 2 for static/fatigue tests) or in different stages of production, but work has practically halted due to a lack of firm orders (also, further versions are not being continued). MAPO "MiG" is ready to build 40-50 aircraft a year. In 1998, MAPO "MiG" reportedly intended to commit to seeing through the certification process.
Crew/passengers: Up to 10 persons, including 1 or 2 pilots. Typical cabin arrangement has 9 passenger seats (at 27.2 ins, 69 cm pitch) and a compartment for 1,102 lb (500 kg) of cargo. Other layouts are available.
Cabin access: Upwards opening hatch 5 ft 3 ins (1.6 m) wide and 5 ft 11 ins (1.8 m) high installed in the port side of the rear fuselage. Usually, a smaller passenger door is built into the hatch. Cockpit has door each side.
Wing control surfaces: Drooped ailerons (30° up, 14° down – port trim tab), 4-section slotted flaps (40° landing) and 2-section automatic leading-edge slats.
Tail control surfaces: Elevators (port trim tab) and rudder (with tab).
Flight control system: Pushrod and cables, except for electric flaps and slats.
Construction materials: Metal.
Engine: OMKB/OMSK TVD-10B turboprop, with AV-24AN 3-blade constant-speed propeller of 9 ft 2 ins (2.8 m) diameter.
Engine rating: 1,011 shp (754 kW).
Fuel system: 1,200 litres in 6 wing tanks between the spars.
Electrical system: 120/208 volt AC supply, at 400 Hz, via an alternator. DC supply. 24 volt ni-cd battery.
Hydraulic system: 2,132 psi, for braking system only.
Braking system: Mainwheel hydraulic brakes and anti-skid devices.
Flight avionics/instrumentation: VFR or IFR. Includes AP-93 autopilot, ADF marker beacon receiver, radio altimeter and back-up VBM-1PB altimeter, A-723 radio and Grom satellite navigation, ELT, digital air data system, gyro horizon, and compass.

Aircraft variants:
T-101 is the standard transport with a TVD-10B engine, as detailed.
T-101E is a more powerful model, with Pratt & Whitney Canada PT6A-65AR, Saturn/Moscow AL-34, OMKB/OMSK TVD-20, AlliedSignal TPE331-14A or other 1,400 shp (1,044 kW) class turboprop. MTOW 12,500 lb (5,670 kg).
T-101L (lyzhnyi) has skid undercarriage for take-off and landing on snow of thickness exceeding 14 ins (35 cm).
T-101P (pozharnyi) is a firefighting floatplane, with water carried in the floats.
T-101Skh was a highly modified low-wing agricultural aircraft, powered by a TVD-20. Later renamed ***T-203 Pchela*** (Bee), but now terminated.
T-101S (special) was an armed military assault transport, with weapons/stores carried on 4 underwing pylons and possibly on new stub-wings (latter each have a wingtip and pylon station). Later transformed into ***T-204 Condor*** with 2 PT6A-34 or M-601E engines (750-805 shp, 559-600 kW each) installed on outriggers on the sides of the fuselage instead of the single TVD-10B engine in the fuselage nose. These changes were ordered by the Federal Frontier Guard of the Russian Federation which wanted a twin-engined patrol aircraft. Retractable undercarriage. Now terminated.
T-101V (vodnyi, water) is a more powerful floatplane version, with 1,380 shp (1,029 kW) TVD-20 turboprop. US amphibious floats, expected to be licence built in Russia. Wing span increased to 60 ft 8 ins (18.5 m), MTOW 12,599 lb (5,715 kg) and maximum speed 151 kts (174 mph) 280 km/h.
T-102 was similar to T-101 but with a nosewheel. Sometimes named ***T-105***, but now terminated.
T-201 Aist was a project of the T-101 series, with a wing span increased to 65 ft 7 ins (20 m).
T-202 was a project with wing span of 72 ft 2 ins (22 m).

Details for T-101

PRINCIPAL DIMENSIONS:
Wing span: 59 ft 8 ins (18.18 m)
Maximum length: 49 ft 4 ins (15.04 m)
Maximum height: 21 ft 11 ins (6.67 m)

CABIN:
Length: 13 ft 9 ins (4.2 m)
Width: 5 ft 3 ins (1.6 m)
Height: 5 ft 11 ins (1.8 m)

WINGS:
Aerofoil section: P-II-14
Area: 470.17 sq ft (43.68 m^2)
Aspect ratio: 7.57

UNDERCARRIAGE:
Type: Fixed, with tailwheel. Optional floats, amphibious floats, or skis
Main wheel tyre size: 720 × 320 mm
Tail wheel tyre size: 480 × 200 mm
Wheel base: 27 ft 3 ins (8.30 m)
Wheel track: 11 ft (3.36 m)

WEIGHTS:
Empty: 7,341 lb (3,330 kg)
Maximum take-off and landing: 11,574 lb (5,250 kg)
Payload: 3,086 lb (1,400 kg) (design payload is 4,409 lb, 2,000 kg)

PERFORMANCE:
Maximum speed: 162 kts (186 mph) 300 km/h
Cruise speed: 135 kts (155 mph) 250 km/h
Stall speed: 49 kts (56 mph) 90 km/h
Maximum climb rate: 925 ft (282 m) per minute
Take-off distance: 1,149 ft (350 m)
Take-off distance over a 50 ft (15 m) obstacle: 1,641 ft (500 m)
Landing distance: 657 ft (200 m)
Landing distance over a 50 ft (15 m) obstacle: 1,018 ft (310 m)
Ceiling: 13,125 ft (4,000 m), service
Range with maximum payload: 377 naut miles (435 miles) 700 km at 9,840 ft (3,000 m) and 135 kts, with reserve for 45 minutes
Range with full fuel: 755 naut miles (870 miles) 1,400 km at 9,840 ft (3,000 m) and 135 kts, with reserve for 45 minutes (1,187 naut miles, 1,367 miles, 2,200 km range is expected with additional fuel)

Aeroprogress/Khrunichev T-411 Aist and T-421

First flight: 10 November 1993 as the Aeroprogress T-411.
Role: STOL-capable multi-purpose lightplane. Designed to be simple, reliable, relatively inexpensive and efficient.
Sales: This Aeroprogress design was taken over by Khrunichev and is also produced in the USA by Washington Aeroprogress as the Wolverine. Prototype made by Aeroprogress now in the USA, first pre-production aircraft made by Khrunichev flew on 15 August 1997 (pilot Viktor Zabolotsky) and was shown at MAKS'97 in Zhukovsky. Series of 5 was expected to be built in 1998. Price US$120,000-130,000, or about US$50,000-70,000 in kit form.
Crew/passengers: Pilot plus 4 passengers or 661 lb (300 kg) of cargo. Spacious baggage hold. 2 passengers and baggage with maximum fuel. Starboard front seat and rear bench seat can be folded or removed to allow other roles such as ambulance and patrol.
Wing control surfaces: Ailerons (with tabs), slotted flaps and fixed leading-edge slats.
Tail control surfaces: Elevators with trim tabs and rudder.
Flight control system: Mechanical, but with electric trim tabs and trailing-edge flaps.

Details for T-411 Aist

PRINCIPAL DIMENSIONS:
Wing span: 42 ft 9 ins (13.02 m)
Maximum length: 31 ft (9.45 m)
Maximum height: 8 ft 3.5 ins (2.53 m)

CABIN:
Length: 13 ft 6 ins (4.1 m)
Width: 4 ft 2 ins (1.27 m)
Height: 4 ft 3 ins (1.3 m)
Cargo door size: 4 ft × 2 ft 1.5 ins (1.22 × 0.65 m)

WINGS:
Aerofoil section: NACA 23011

UNDERCARRIAGE:
Type: Fixed, with steerable and lockable tailwheel. Optional floats
Main wheel tyre size: 600 × 180 mm
Tail wheel tyre size: 300 × 135 mm

WEIGHTS:
Maximum take-off: 3,527 lb (1,600 kg)

PERFORMANCE:
Maximum cruise speed: 108 kts (124 mph) 200 km/h
Stall speed: 43 kts (50 mph) 80 km/h
Take-off distance: 443 ft (135 m)
Take-off distance over a 50 ft (15 m) obstacle: 787 ft (240 m)
Landing distance: 476 ft (145 m)
Landing distance over a 50 ft (15 m) obstacle: 821 ft (250 m)
Ceiling: 9,840 ft (3,000 m)
Range with full fuel: 377 naut miles (435 miles) 700 km or 647 naut miles (745 miles) 1,200 km with normal or maximum fuel respectively

↑ Production Aeroprogress/Khrunichev T-411 Aist at Zhukovsky *(Piotr Butowski)*

Construction materials: Metal structure, with metal and Dacron fabric covering.
Engine: AOOT OKBM/Voronezh M-14P 9-cylinder radial piston engine and MTV-9 3-blade variable-pitch propeller (2-blade V530TA-D35 propeller for the prototype).
Engine rating: 360 hp (268 kW).
Fuel system: 573 lb (260 kg).
Electrical system: 27 volt DC supply via an engine-driven generator. 25 amp-hour battery.
Flight avionics/instrumentation: VFR. Instrumentation includes speed indicator, altimeter, magnetic compass, gyro horizon, automatic direction finder, marker beacon receiver and more. GPS. Optional AlliedSignal Bendix/King nav/com for IFR.

Aircraft variants:
Aeroprogress T-411 Aist-2 (Stork) was the prototype of 1993.
T-411 Aist is a production version with M-14P engine. Reconfigured undercarriage, cabin glazing and oil radiator compared with the prototype. Slightly larger wing (span of 42 ft 9 ins, 13.02 m rather than 41 ft 9 ins, 12.73 m), and new 3-blade propeller.
Wolverine is the name for a derivative produced in the USA.
T-421 is a version with Teledyne Continental TSIO-550B engine (350 hp, 261 kW).

Other T-series aircraft

T-311 Kolibri (Hummingbird): Simple and cheap kitplane. High-wing monoplane with fixed undercarriage and STOL features.
T-315 Mukha (Fly) and T-317 Mukha-2: Light STOL aircraft. Frame-type structure. Airframe may be easily disassembled and containerized for transportation. T-317 is made of lower-quality steel to reduce cost.
T-407 Skvorets (Starling): Passenger and cargo aircraft of simple technology, allowing manufacture at repair works. All-metal construction. Provision for Textron Lycoming or Teledyne Continental engine, as well as AlliedSignal Bendix/King avionics. Full-scale mock-up built.
T-415 Snegir' (Bullfinch): STOL lightplane. Fuselage, wing and tail unit covered with Stits synthetic fabric. Wings may be detached for transportation. Can perform aerobatics when payload limited to 661 lb (300 kg); g limits +5, -1.5.
T-417 Pegas (Pegasus): Developed from T-407 against an order from Peru, for operation in regions of high humidity. Construction of stainless steel and specially-prepared aluminium.
T-420 Strizh (Swift): High-wing monoplane with fixed nosewheel undercarriage. Upwards opening rear cabin door. Considered as a core model for other versions. Provision for Allison 250-B17C turboprop engines and retractable undercarriage.
T-421 Bober (Beaver): Considered as a possible replacement for the DHC-2 Beaver and developed against an order from the See-Land company of Canada. STOL features from unpaved airstrips, while also ski and float undercarriages possible. Fail-safe structure.
T-422 Yastreb (Hawk): Transport aircraft designed for Russian Federal Border Guard Service. Possible retractable undercarriage, as well as ski and float variants. Features include low clearance for easy loading/maintenance. ***T-422A*** is a version with Allison 250-C20 turboprop engines, whereas ***T-422M*** will have Russian M-14Ps.

↑ T-315 Mukha *(Piotr Butowski)*

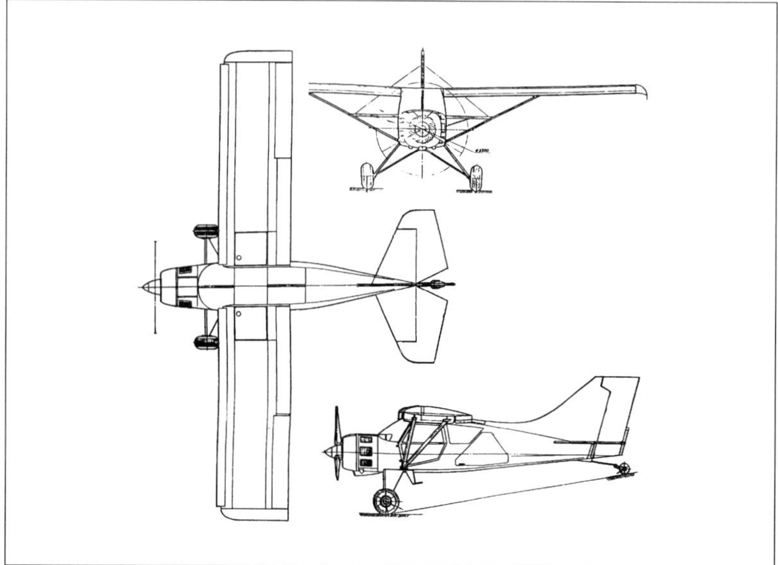

↑ T-415 Snegir'

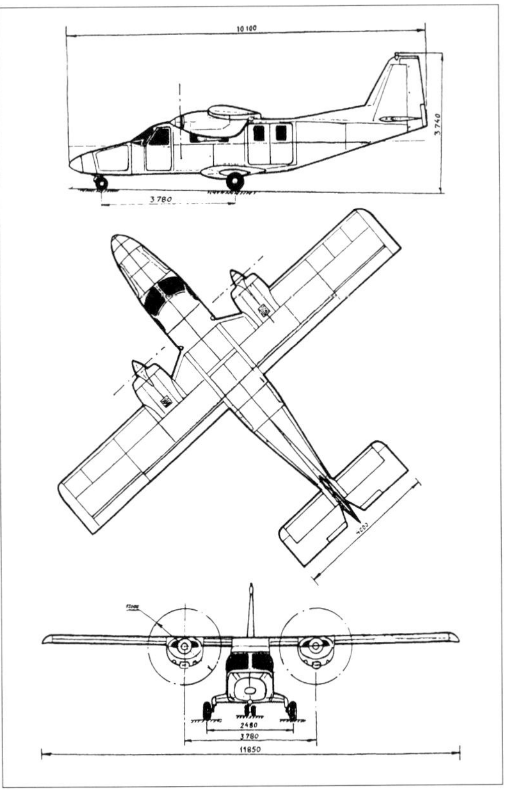

↑ T-422 Yastreb

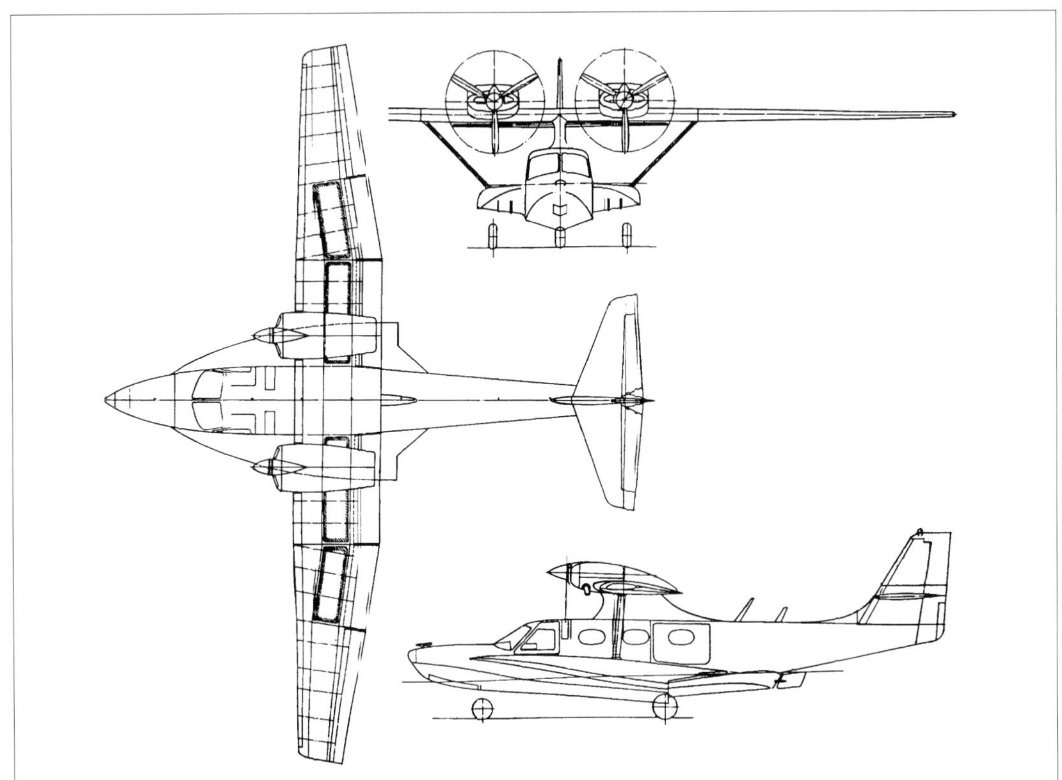

↑ T-474 Brigantine

T-425 Zhavoronok-2 (Lark): STOL aircraft developed for forest service. Automatic slats.

T-427 Bulldog: Designed to the requirements of the Russian Ministry of Emergencies. Able to land on short unprepared strips with descending rate of 787 ft (240 m) per minute. Fixed slats. Large hatch for cargo or casualties. Allison 250-B17C turboprop powered version under consideration.

T-430 Sprinter: Business low-wing monoplane with retractable undercarriage. IFR.

T-431 Korsar (Corsair): Patrol and rescue boat-type seaplane/amphibian for fishery services. Fuselage hull made of stainless steel, with remainder of fuselage of composite construction.

T-431-2 Korsar-2: Seaplane developed for Border Guard and Ministry of Emergencies. Side float of T-101V Gratch, wings and tail unit of T-411. De-icing system enables use in northern regions. Provision for Allison 250-B17C turboprop engine.

T-435 Korvet (Corvette): Seaplane/amphibian with composite hull. Wing of An-2.

T-440 Mercury: Business turboprop with a 1,726 naut mile (1,988 mile) 3,200 km range and 296 kts (341 mph) 550 km/h cruise speed. Full-scale mock-up shown at MAKS'97 in Zhukovsky.

Details for Aeroprogress/Khrunichev T-series aircraft

	T-311 Kolibri	T-315 Mukha	T-317 Mukha-2	T-407 Skvorets	T-415 Snegir'	T-417 Pegas	T-420 Strizh	T-421 Bober	T-422 Yastreb	T-425 Zhavoronok-2
Engine	Teledyne Continental IO-360ES	AOOT/Voronezh M-14P	AOOT/Voronezh M-14P	AOOT/Voronezh M-14P	AOOT/Voronezh M-14X	Teledyne Continental TSIO-550	Teledyne Continental IO-360ES	Allison 250-B17C	Teledyne Continental TSIO-550B	Textron Lycoming IO-720
Power, hp (kW)	1 × 210 (156)	1 × 360 (268)	1 × 360 (268)	1 × 360 (268)	1 × 360 (268)	1 × 350 (261)	1 × 210 (156)	1 × 420 (313)	2 × 350 (261)	1 × 400 (298)
Seats	4	5	5	7	6	6	7	6	9 (10)	6
Take-off weight lb (kg)	2,425 (1,100)	3,307 (1,500)	3,638 (1,650)	4,585 (2,080)	3,351 (1,520)	4,365 (1,980)	4,387 (1,990)	4,630 (2,100)	6,856 (3,110)	4,674 (2,120)
Payload lb (kg)	705 (320)	882 (400)	772 (350)	1,323 (600)	794 (360)	1,323 (600)	992 (450)	1,433 (650)	1,763 (800)	1,433 (650)
Fuel lb (kg)	392 (178)	353 (160)	353 (160)	661 (300)	529 (240)	661 (300)	948 (430)	595 (270)	1,543 (700)	529 (240)
Cruise speed kts (mph) km/h	146 (168) 270	108 (124) 200	100 (115) 185	116 (134) 215	135 (155) 250	130 (149) 240	162 (186) 300	156 (180) 290	151 (174) 280	130 (149) 240
Range naut miles (miles) km	593 (683) 1,100	539 (621) 1,000	459 (528) 850	960 (1,106) 1,780	669 (770) 1,240	1,074 (1,236) 1,990	1,090 (1,255) 2,020	701 (807) 1,300	1,241 (1,429) 2,300	685 (789) 1,270
Take-off distance ft (m)	657 (200)	788 (240)	1,313 (400)	1,969 (600)	706 (215)	1,116 (340)	1,477 (450)	952 (290)	1,477 (450)	689 (210)
Landing distance ft (m)	657 (200)	1,050 (320)	1,378 (420)	1,346 (410)	1,083 (330)	1,313 (400)	1,969 (600)	1,050 (320)	1,559 (475)	886 (270)

↑ **T-421 Bober** *(Piotr Butowski)*

↑ **T-430 Sprinter** *(Piotr Butowski)*

↑ **T-435 Korvet** *(Piotr Butowski)*

↑ **T-417 Pegas** *(Piotr Butowski)*

↑ **T-420 Strizh** *(Piotr Butowski)*

T-451 Zhavoronok (Skylark): STOL kitplane designed against an order of AJV company of New York, USA. Wing with automatic slats.
T-455 Aist-3 (Stork): Version of T-411 Aist but with nosewheel undercarriage.
T-471 Korvet-2: Amphibious seaplane developed from T-420 Strizh.
T-474 Brigantine: Seaplane developed with use of components from T-420. Retractable undercarriage. Model tested in TsAGI hydrodynamics tunnel.
T-505 Strekoza (Dragonfly): STOL aircraft designed against an order from Moscow's Mayor for city police, mainly for traffic control. Preliminary order for 10 aircraft reported. Wing of An-2 aircraft and undercarriage of Mi-2 helicopter.
T-509 Mustang: Low-cost STOL aircraft. Variants include **T-509A** with nosewheel and **T-509V** amphibian.
T-515 Mustang-3: STOL aircraft for use from unprepared strips including these in mountain regions, developed for Kirgizia.
T-521 Mustang-2: Built in T-101 layout but with reduced size. Ordered by Russian Ministry of Emergencies.
T-527 Mustang-4: Light military STOL transport aircraft. May be armed with machine-guns. Fuel tanks are filled with polyurethane foam, cockpit and engine compartments are armoured, and control system pushrods can withstand 7.62-mm gun fire.
T-612 Korshun-2 (Vulture): STOL aircraft developed for Border Guard Service. Possible use of 450 shp (336 kW) turboprop engine.
T-618 Korshun-3: Developed against an order of Border Guard Service. Wing and tailplane of Czech Zlin Z-137T agricultural aircraft.
T-620 Korshun: Business aircraft based on T-602 Oriol (see 1996-97 edition of *WA&SD*).
T-701 Condor: Unrefined STOL aircraft constructed with maximum use of An-2 components (some 90%, whereas about 70% of An-2 parts are used in T-101 Gratch).
T-705 Orlan: As T-701 but with nosewheel.

	T-427 Bulldog	T-430 Sprinter	T-431 Korsar	T-431-2 Korsar-2	T-435 Korvet	T-440 Mercury	T-451 Zhavoronok	T-455 Aist-3	T-471 Korvet-2	T-474 Brigantine
Engine	AOOT/Voronezh M-25	Teledyne Continental TSIO-360KB	AOOT/Voronezh M-14P	AOOT/Voronezh M-14P	AOOT/Voronezh M-25	Pratt & Whitney Canada PT6A-135	AOOT/Voronezh M-14X	Textron Lycoming TSIO-540	Allison 250-B17C	Teledyne Continental TSIO-520
Power hp (kW)	1 × 450 (336)	2 × 200 (149)	1 × 360 (268)	1 × 360 (268)	1 × 450 (336)	2 × 750 (559)	1 × 360 (268)	1 × 350 (261)	1 × 420 (313)	2 × 310 (231)
Seats	6	6	5	5	6	6-10	6	6	7	7
Take-off weight lb (kg)	3,748 (1,700)	4,630 (2,100)	4,189 (1,900)	4,299 (1,950)	4,850 (2,200)	9,259 (4,200)	3,307 (1,500)	3,638 (1,650)	4,740 (2,150)	5,578 (2,530)
Payload lb (kg)	1,102 (500)	1,102 (500)	816 (370)	838 (380)	882 (400)	2,435 (1,100)	882 (400)	750 (340)	992 (450)	1,543 (700)
Fuel lb (kg)	529 (240)	871 (395)	529 (240)	529 (240)	529 (240)	2,645 (1,200)	529 (240)	529 (240)	948 (430)	1,058 (480)
Cruise speed kts (mph) km/h	146 (168) 270	194 (224) 360	119 (137) 220	116 (134) 215	130 (149) 240	297 (342) 550	111 (127) 205	130 (149) 240	162 (186) 300	146 (168) 270
Range naut miles (miles) km	782 (901) 1,450	1,063 (1,224) 1,970	593 (683) 1,100	566 (652) 1,050	539 (621) 1,000	1,726 (1,988) 3,200	809 (932) 1,500	755 (870) 1,400	982 (1,131) 1,820	1,122 (1,292) 2,080
Take-off distance ft (m)	493 (150)	1,477 (450)	1,378 (420)	1,395 (425)	1,313 (400)	1,411 (430)	853 (260)	821 (250)	1,346 (410)	1,312 (400)
Landing distance ft (m)	821 (250)	1,969 (600)	1,067 (325)	1,083 (330)	1,115 (340)	1,969 (600)	1,149 (350)	1,280 (390)	1,116 (340)	1,149 (350)

↑ **T-440 Mercury** *(Piotr Butowski)*

↑ **T-527 Mustang-4**

	T-505 Strekoza	T-509 Mustang	T-515 Mustang-3	T-521 Mustang-2	T-527 Mustang-4	T-612 Korshun-2	T-618 Koshun-3	T-620 Korshun	T-701E Condor	T-705 Orlan
Engine	Pratt & Whitney Canada PT6A-114	Walter M-601E	Walter M-601E	Walter M-601E	Pratt & Whitney Canada PT6A-114	AOOT/Voronezh M-25	AOOT/Voronezh M-14P	Allison 250-B17C	P&W/Klimov PK6A-67	P&W/Klimov PK6A-67
Power hp (kW)	1 × 600 (447)	1 × 720 (537)	1 × 720 (537)	1 × 720 (537)	1 × 600 (447)	2 × 450 (336)	2 × 360 (268)	2 × 420 (313)	1 × 1,341 (1,000)	1 × 1,341 (1,000)
Seats	8	9 (14)	8	9 (11)	8	10	8	9	9 (12)	9 (12)
Take-off weight lb (kg)	6,173 (2,800)	7,077 (3,210)	5,952 (2,700)	6,834 (3,100)	6,173 (2,800)	7,055 (3,200)	6,614 (3,000)	7,055 (3,200)	11,574 (5,250)	11,684 (5,300)
Payload lb (kg)	1,984 (900)	2,491 (1,130)	1,543 (700)	2,094 (950)	1,984 (900)	2,205 (1,000)	1,940 (880)	2,116 (960)	3,307 (1,500)	3,307 (1,500)
Fuel lb (kg)	1,433 (650)	1,984 (900)	904 (410)	1,323 (600)	1,433 (650)	1,102 (500)	1,014 (460)	1,543 (700)	2,116 (960)	2,116 (960)
Cruise speed kts (mph) km/h	130 (149) 240	173 (199) 320	173 (199) 320	167 (193) 310	130 (149) 240	167 (193) 310	146 (168) 270	213 (245) 395	167 (193) 310	167 (193) 310
Range naut miles (miles) km	539 (621) 1,000	777 (894) 1,440	512 (590) 950	593 (683) 1,100	539 (621) 1,000	755 (870) 1,400	755 (870) 1,400	955 (1,100) 1,770	647 (745) 1,200	647 (745) 1,200
Take-off distance ft (m)	1,362 (415)	1,362 (415)	1,247 (380)	1,395 (425)	1,362 (415)	1,477 (450)	1,559 (475)	1,575 (480)	1,969 (600)	1,969 (600)
Landing distance ft (m)	1,083 (330)	1,182 (360)	1,083 (330)	1,116 (340)	1,083 (330)	1,707 (520)	1,640 (500)	1,706 (520)	2,133 (650)	2,133 (650)

Aeroric Science and Production Enterprise — Russia

Corporate address:
ul. Chaadayeva, 1, d. 86, Nizhny Novgorod 603035.

Telephone: +7 8312 466763, 293095
Facsimile: +7 8312 466763

Information:
Victor Morozov (Manager and Chief Designer).

Aeroric Dingo

First flight: See Sales.
Role: Light passenger/cargo amphibious lightplane of unusual layout, able to operate from virtually any type of surface due to its air cushion landing system. Suited also to ambulance/SAR, patrol, fire survey and ecological monitoring.
Sales: Full-scale mock-up shown 1992, first (incomplete) prototype shown 1995. A series of 5 aircraft (plus 1 airframe for static tests) was put under construction at the Sokol Joint Stock Company at Nizhny Novgorod. 3 airframes (including 1 for static tests) had been almost completed by Summer 1997, and engines were thereafter installed onto the first flight prototype, intended to permit flight testing in 1998.
Crew/passengers: Pilot and 7-8 passengers or 1,653 lb (750 kg) of cargo.
Wing characteristics: Low-mounted, with short and wide centre section limited by side cigar-shaped inflatable floats, plus long unswept outer panels.
Wing control surfaces: Front and rear flaps on wing centre section to create (together with side floats) a closed box for air cushion. Slats, flaps and ailerons at outer wing panels.
Tail control surfaces: T-type carried on twin tailbooms with single elevator and 2 rudders.
Construction materials: All metal.
Engine: 1,100 shp (820.3 kW) Pratt & Whitney Canada PT6A-65B turboprop, with Hartzell pusher propeller (9 ft 3 ins, 2.82 m diameter) as cruise engine, plus 250 shp (186.4 kW) TVA-200 auxiliary engine for the air cushion.
Fuel system: 1,323 lb (600 kg) standard, 2,204 lb (1,000 kg) maximum.

Details for Dingo

PRINCIPAL DIMENSIONS:
Wing span: 46 ft 9 ins (14.25 m)
Maximum length: 42 ft 6 ins (12.95 m)
Maximum height: 11 ft 3 ins (3.42 m)

CABIN:
Length: 13 ft 5 ins (4.1 m)
Width: 4 ft 2.5 ins (1.28 m)
Height: 4 ft 6 ins (1.38 m)

UNDERCARRIAGE:
Type: Twin wing-root floats

WEIGHTS:
Empty, operational: 4,938 lb (2,240 kg)
Nominal take-off: 8,157 lb (3,700 kg)
Payload: 1,653 lb (750 kg)

PERFORMANCE:
Maximum speed: 189 kts (217 mph) 350 km/h
Cruise speed: 148-162 kts (171-186 mph) 275-300 km/h
Take-off distance: 1,149 ft (350 m) from water, 935 ft (285 m) from shore
Landing distance: 985 ft (300 m)
Ceiling: 11,480 ft (3,500 m)
Allowable wave height: 1.15 ft (0.35 m)
Range with full fuel: 809 naut miles (932 miles) 1,500 km
Range with full payload: 458 naut miles (528 miles) 850 km

↑ Aeroric Dingo *(Piotr Butowski)*

AKS-Invest — Russia

Corporate address:
Nizhny Novgorod.

Founded: 1990.

Employees: 70.

Information:
Vladimir Latyshenko (General Manager).

AKS-Invest MiG-TA4

First flight: MiG-TA4 is a project. See Sales.
Role: General purpose aircraft with air-cushion undercarriage. TA4 means Transportnyi Alternativnyj (alternative transport) 4-seats.
Sales: In 1994, a full-size mock-up was constructed and detailed design started. Work stopped in 1995 due to a lack of fundings. In order to develop the aircraft's air cushion system, an SVP-500 (sredstvo na vozdushnoi podushke, air-cushion vehicle, payload 1,102 lb, 500 kg) was built. It became an independent programme and 8 SVP-500s were sold and a further 10 were ordered by Ministry of Emergencies. Manufacturing of MiG-TA4 is expected at Sokol plant in Nizhny Novgorod.

↑ Poisk-01A is a single-seat technology demonstrator for the MiG-TA4 programme *(Piotr Butowski)*

Crew/passengers: 1+3.
Engines: Single Teledyne Continental IO-550-C piston cruise engine (300 hp, 224 kW) plus single Nelson N-63CP (48 hp, 35.75 kW) piston engine to generate the air cushion.

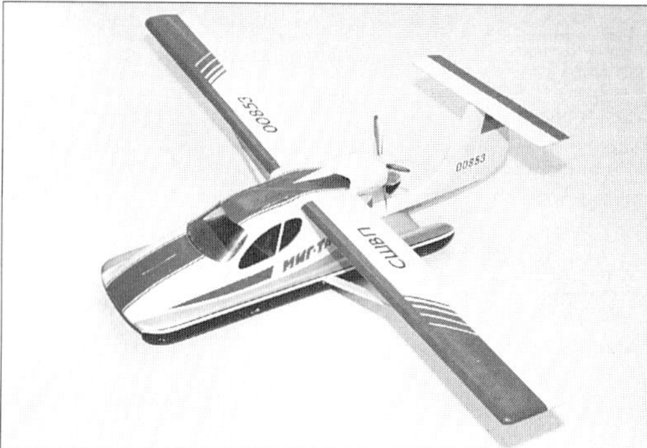

↑ AKS-Invest MiG-TA4 *(Piotr Butowski)*

Details for MiG-TA4

PRINCIPAL DIMENSIONS:
Wing span: 40 ft 8 ins (12.4 m)
Maximum length: 29 ft 8 ins (9.05 m)
Maximum height: 9 ft 1 ins (2.77 m)
Fuselage width: 7 ft 5 ins (2.26 m)

UNDERCARRIAGE:
Type: Air-cushion

WEIGHTS:
Maximum take-off: 3,836 lb (1,740 kg)
Payload: 661 lb (300 kg)

PERFORMANCE:
Maximum speed: 145 kts (168 mph) 270 km/h
Cruise speed: 97-108 kts (112-124 mph) 180-200 km/h
Take-off speed: 54 kts (62 mph) 100 km/h
Take-off distance: 673 ft (205 m)
Landing distance: 837 ft (255 m)
Ceiling: 13,125 ft (4,000 m)
Range with 3 passengers and 286 kg (130 kg) fuel: 539 naut miles (621 miles) 1,000 km, at 9,840 ft (3,000 m) altitude, with 30 minutes reserve
Ferry range with additional fuel: 1,079 naut miles (1,242 miles) 2,000 km

NPP Alpha-M — Russia

Corporate address:
140160 Zhukovsky, PO Box 74.

Telephone: +7 095 5565467
Facsimile: +7 095 5565583

Founded:
1992, as a subsidiary of the Myasishchev design bureau.

Information:
Victor Koldiayev (Manager).

ACTIVITIES

▪ Another aircraft is the 4-seat **A-111** with a single 210 hp (157 kW) engine, 2,755 lb (1,250 kg) take-off weight, 143 kts (165 mph) 265 km/h maximum speed and 1,365 naut miles (1,572 miles) 2,530 km maximum range. Project only.

Alpha-M SL-A and A-211

First flight: 1993.
Role: 2/4-seat lightplane (see Baggage), suited to private use and also offered as a kit. Fully aerobatic when flown in the utility category.
Sales: Based on SL-90 Leshiy components (see under Interavia I-1) delivered to NPP Alpha-M by Lukhovitsy aircraft plant as payment for design support during preparation for SL-90's production (10 sets of parts delivered). First 6 aircraft completed in 1997, of which 2 sold to the USA and 3 in Russia, including 2 with aerial photographic cameras and used by a geophysical company in Astrakhan. See Aircraft variants for No 8 as first A-211. Contract for delivery of 150 aircraft to the USA failed because of a lack of cash flow.
Baggage/cargo capacity: 331 lb (150 kg), with provision in the plans for an aft facing jump seat making the aircraft a 2+2 seating arrangement.
Wing characteristics: High-mounted, unswept, with slight dihedral.
Wing control surfaces: The wing now features a slotted flap with increased flap span to reduce the stall speed to 32.5 kts (37.5 mph) 60 km/h. To increase roll response at slow speed, Alpha has redesigned the ailerons from a simple top-hinged flap to a fully-balanced centre pivot design.

↑ NPP Alpha-M SL-A *(Piotr Butowski)*

Tail control surfaces: Elevators and rudder (with tab).
Flight control system: Mechanical.
Construction materials: Metal and fabric.
Engine: LOM M332A piston engine in current aircraft. M332A engine provides adequate performance for weights up to 1,874 lb (850 kg). Wide choice of engines is available within the recommended power range of 125-160 hp (93-119 kW), with maximum acceptable power of 210 hp (157 kW).
Engine rating: 140 hp (104.4 kW).
Fuel system: 2 wing tanks for a total of 100 litres.
Flight avionics/instrumentation: Customer choice.

Aircraft variants:
SL-A is an Alpha-M derivative of the SL-90 lightplane (which see under Interavia). Offered in 2 versions: ***SL-A (V)*** powered by LOM M332A and ***SL-A (D)*** with Teledyne Continental IO-240-A1B. Name ***Gzhelka*** applied to aircraft No 4 bought by the manager of the Gzhel company (marketing Russian handicrafts, therefore given a special paint finish), later sold to the USA but damaged.
A-211 will be a version certified according to JAR VLA standards. Airframe No 8 was assigned to be the first completed according to these specifications.
A-211K (kit) is a kit version of A-211.

Details for SL-A

PRINCIPAL DIMENSIONS:
Wing span: 32 ft 10 ins (10 m)
Maximum length: 21 ft (6.4 m)
Maximum height: 9 ft 2 ins (2.8 m)

WINGS:
Aerofoil section: P-IIIP
Area: 135.63 sq ft (12.6 m^2)
Aspect ratio: 7.94
Thickness/chord ratio: 15%

UNDERCARRIAGE:
Type: Fixed, with tailwheel. Skis and floats offered

WEIGHTS:
Empty: about 1,102 lb (500 kg)
Maximum take-off: 1,653 lb (750 kg)

PERFORMANCE:
Maximum speed: 86 kts (99 mph) 160 km/h
Cruise speed: 76 kts (87 mph) 140 km/h
Stall speed: 40.5 kts (47 mph) 75 km/h
Landing speed: 46 kts (53 mph) 85 km/h
Take-off and landing distance: 493 ft (150 m)
Ceiling: 6,560 ft (2,000 m), service
Range with full fuel: 405 naut miles (466 miles) 750 km
Range with full payload: 200 naut miles (230 miles) 370 km

Avgur Aerostat Centre — Russia

Corporate address:
See Buoyant Aircraft section.

ACTIVITIES

■ Although airships are its main activities, Avgur has joined the Moscow Aviation Institute to propose the lightweight Krechet multi-role VTOL aircraft.

Avgur/MAI Krechet

First flight: Project announced Summer 1997. Experimental thrust (flow) vectoring system (ducted propeller and airfoil cascade of 4 ft 10 ins, 1.47 m diameter) has been tested on Aerostatika-01 and Aerostatika-02 airships (see Buoyant Aircraft section for photograph). Flyable test bed of the power plant system (without wings and with ski undercarriage) was put under construction.

Aims

■ Ability to operate from virtually any type of surface due to low pressure of exhaust stream.
■ Low IR-visibility due to low temperature of exhaust gases.
■ Increased load when adopting short take-off instead of VTOL.

Details

Role: Lightweight multi-role VTOL aircraft for both military (air-to-ground, anti-helicopter, assault, transport, liaison and training) and civil uses.
Crew: 2, side-by-side.
Passengers/freight: 6-8 airborne troops can be accommodated in a cabin behind the cockpit. Alternatively, 4 litters, freight or special equipment.
Cockpit/cabin access: Rear loading ramp.
Expendable weapons and equipment: Possible.
Wing characteristics: Wide centre section and swept long outer panels.
Wing control surfaces: Multi-section flaps, ailerons and interceptors.
Tail control surfaces: Twin wingtip endplates with rudders and no tailplane.
Canard: Unswept, constant chord, with elevons.
Flight control system: By engine flow vectoring at near zero speed, and usual aerodynamic controls during high-speed flight.
Engines: 2 turboprop engines driving 3 ducted fans. All 3 fans are of the same construction and size. First of them (lift only) is installed in the nose of the fuselage with slighty forwards (from vertical) inclined axis. 2 other fans (lift-cruise) are carried on the fuselage sides beneath the wing centre section, with horizontal axis. Each fan has flow vectoring system formed by airfoil cascade behind the nozzle.
Engine rating: Each 1,440 hp (1,074 kW).

Details for Krechet

PRINCIPAL DIMENSIONS:
Wing span: 39 ft 4 ins (11.98 m)
Canard span: 19 ft 8 ins (6 m)
Maximum length: 30 ft 11 ins (9.43 m)

UNDERCARRIAGE:
Type: Retractable, with nosewheel
Wheel track: 10 ft 6 ins (3.2 m)

WEIGHTS:
Normal take-off: 7,418 lb (3,365 kg)
Payload: 1,323 lb (600 kg)

PERFORMANCE:
Cruise speed: 208 kts (239 mph) 385 km/h
Range: 647 naut miles (745 miles) 1,200 km

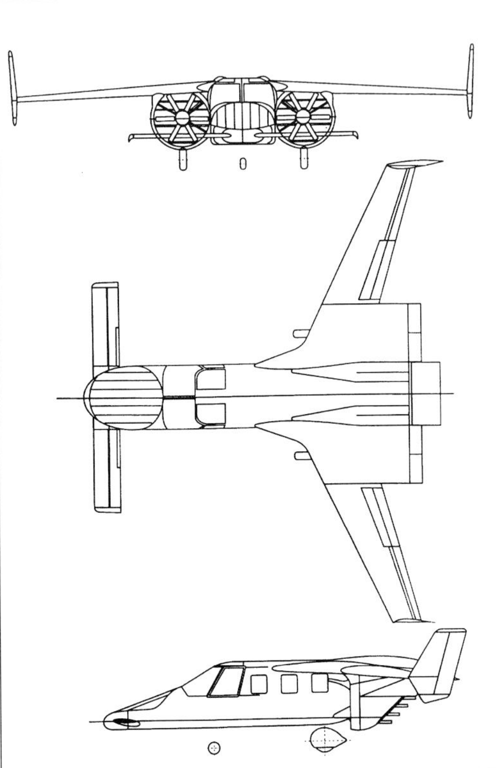

↑ **Avgur/MAI Krechet multi-purpose VTOL aircraft** *(courtesy Avgur)*

Avia Ltd — Russia

Corporate address:
ul. Kominterna, 13/4, Moscow 129327.
Telephone: +7 095 1844377
Facsimile: +7 095 1844377
Email: avia@glasnet.ru
Founded:
March 1991.
Information:
Alexander Loshkarev (Director General).

Avia Accord-201 (Akkord-201)

First flight: April 1994 for Accord prototype and 20 August 1997 for Accord-201 production model (pilot Aleksei Zemyanoi).
Certification: Designed to FAR Pt 23 standards.
Role: Land, float or amphibious lightplane for passengers, cargo and air ambulance work.
Sales: Produced by Sokol at Nizhny Novgorod, with final assembly probably at Baranovichi (Belarus) repair plant. Accord prototype was built in 1994; at time of writing, 3 production Accord-201s completed or under construction. Contract for 2 aircraft for Almazy-Yakutia-Sakha company reported in November 1997, for geological monitoring.
Details: For Accord-201.
Crew/passengers: Pilot and 6 passengers. Baggage compartment aft of the rear seats.
Engines: 2 Teledyne Continental IO-360-ES piston engines.
Engine rating: Each 210 hp (156.6 kW).
Fuel system: 650 litres.

↑ **Avia Accord-201 production version** *(Piotr Butowski)*

Flight avionics/instrumentation: Wide choice of avionics, including EFIS and GPS.

Aircraft variants:
Accord was the 5-seat prototype, powered by 2 × 150 hp (112 kW) VAZ-4133A rotary piston engines. Described in previous edition of *WA&SD*.
Accord-201 is an enlarged 7-seat production version with more powerful engines, as well as modern avionics. First flown 20 August 1997. As detailed.

Avia Accord-Jet

Comments: Another project under development is the **Accord-Jet** 4-seat business jet. Length 32 ft 10 ins (10.0 m), wing span 36 ft 1 ins (11.0 m), height 10 ft 10 ins (3.3 m), cruise speed 389 kts (447 mph) 720 km/h. take-off weight 5,952 lb (2,700 kg), and range with 4 passengers 2,158 naut miles (2,485 miles) 4,000 km.

Details for Accord-201

PRINCIPAL DIMENSIONS:
Wing span: 44 ft 7.5 ins (13.6 m)
Maximum length: 26 ft 2 ins (7.974 m) with wheels only, 27 ft (8.22 m) amphibious
Maximum height: 9 ft 10 ins (3.0 m) wheels, 10 ft 10 ins (3.3 m) amphibious

UNDERCARRIAGE:
Type: Fixed, with nosewheel. Optional twin floats. Provision for adding electrically-lowering twin floats outside the mainwheels, allowing amphibious operations

WEIGHTS:
Maximum take-off: 4,409 lb (2,000 kg)
Payload: 1,653 lb (750 kg) wheels only, 1,323 lb (600 kg) amphibious

PERFORMANCE:
Maximum speed: 162 kts (186 mph) 300 km/h wheels only, 151 kts (174 mph) 280 km/h amphibious, at sea level
Cruise speed: 154 kts (177 mph) 285 km/h wheels only, 143 kts (165 mph) 265 km/h amphibious, at 6,560 ft (2,000 m)
Economic cruise speed: 113 kts (130 mph) 210 km/h wheels only, 111 kts (127 mph) 205 km/h amphibious, at 9,840 ft (3,000 m)
Take-off distance: 788 ft (240 m) land, 1,116 ft (340 m) water
Landing distance: 640 ft (195 m) land
G limits: +3.8, -1.6
Range with full fuel: 1,915 naut miles (2,206 miles) 3,550 km at economic cruise speed

Aviacor International Aircraft Corporation JSC — Russia

Corporate address:
32 Pskovskaya ul., 443052 Samara; Moscow representative at 6 Novoposelkovaya, Moscow 123459.

Telephone: +7 8462 294151; Moscow representative: +7 095 4935053, 4928412
Facsimile: +7 8462 270691; Moscow representative: +7 095 4929371, 4934388

Aviacor M-12 Kasatik

First flight: 1995.
Role: 3-seat sporting, training and utility aircraft.
Sales: First prototype accumulated some 150 flying hours. Second aircraft crashed on 14 October 1997 in Samara during its maiden flight. Third aircraft constructed. Preparation for production was underway at time of writing
Crew/passengers: Pilot plus 2 passengers.
Wing characteristics: Braced, high-mounted.
Construction materials: All-metal, module-type. Can be easily dismantled for transportation.
Engine: Originally 2 Russian-built Vikhr-30 piston engines with pusher propellers of 5 ft 3 ins (1.6 m) diameter. In Autumn 1997, replaced by 2 Rotax 462 engines.
Engine rating: 35 hp (26 kW).
Fuel system: 54 litres.

↑ **Aviacor M-12 Kasatik** *(courtesy Aviacor)*

Details for M-12 Kasatik

PRINCIPAL DIMENSIONS:
Wing span: 32 ft 10 ins (10 m)
Maximum length: 20 ft 4 ins (6.2 m)
Maximum height: 6 ft 5 ins (1.95 m)

UNDERCARRIAGE:
Type: Fixed, with nosewheel. Single wheel at each unit. Optional skis or floats
Main wheel tyre size: 300 × 120 mm
Wheel track: 5 ft 3 ins (1.6 m)

WEIGHTS:
Empty: 551 lb (250 kg)
Maximum take-off: 1,146 lb (520 kg)
Payload: 485 lb (220 kg), including pilot

PERFORMANCE:
Cruise speed: 67 kts (78 mph) 125 km/h
Required runway length: 493 ft (150 m)
Climb rate: 590 ft (180 m) per minute
Ceiling: 9,840 ft (3,000 m), service
G limits: +4.4, -2.2
Range with maximum payload: 216 naut miles (248 miles) 400 km
Duration: 5 hours

Aviakompleks JSC — Russia

Corporate address:
140160 Zhukovsky, Moskovskoi obl., Box 931.

Telephone: +7 095 5564398, 5567905
Facsimile: +7 095 5564398

Founded:
1989.

Information:
Valeri Tkach (General Manager).

Aviakompleks AS-2

First flight: 1991 (piloted by Viktor Zabolotsky).
Certification: Built to meet JAR-VLA requirements.
Role: 2-seat recreational aircraft, suited also for training, patrol, and agricultural work.
Sales: First 3 built were 1 for static tests, 1 AS-2 and 1 AS-2K.
Crew/passengers: 2.
Wing characteristics: Braced high-wing monoplane.
Construction materials: Aluminium alloys, with steel in critical elements. Glassfibre wing leading-edges and cabin. Fabric skins for wing.
Engine: Rotax 582 piston engine above the cockpit. Other engines over 50 hp (37.3 kW) possible.
Engine rating: 65 hp (48.5 kW).

Aircraft variants:
AS-2 is the initial version.
AS-2K has cockpit canopy.

↑ **Aviakompleks AS-2K** *(Piotr Butowski)*

Details for AS-2

PRINCIPAL DIMENSIONS:
Wing span: 31 ft 6 ins (9.6 m)
Maximum length: 19 ft 0.5 ins (5.8 m)
Maximum height: 8 ft 6 ins (2.6 m)

WINGS:
Area: 131.32 sq ft (12.2 m^2)
Aspect ratio: 7.55

UNDERCARRIAGE:
Type: Fixed with nosewheel. Possible skis or floats
Wheel base: 5 ft 1.5 ins (1.56 m)
Wheel track: 5 ft 3 ins (1.6 m)

WEIGHTS:
Empty: 507 lb (230 kg)
Maximum take-off: 992 lb (450 kg)

PERFORMANCE:
Maximum speed: 76 kts (87 mph) 140 km/h
Cruise speed: 65 kts (75 mph) 120 km/h
Stall speed: 27 kts (31 mph) 50 km/h
Take-off distance: 164 ft (50 m)
Landing distance: 214 ft (65 m)
Maximum climb rate: 1,180 ft (360 m) per minute
G limits: +4.5, -3
Range with maximum payload: 243 naut miles (279 miles) 450 km
Ferry range with auxiliary tank: 539 naut miles (621 miles) 1,000 km

Aviatika – see KB MAI

Aviaton

Russia

Corporate address:
143991 Moskovskaya obl., p/o Chernoe.

Telephone: +7 095 2528221, 5229066
Facsimile: +7 095 1916827, 2156274, 2889596

Information:
Avtangil Khachapuridze (General Manager).

↑ **Aviaton Merkury 4-seat lightplane** *(Piotr Butowski)*

Aviaton Merkury

First flight: Prototype was shown at MAKS'97 in Zhukovsky in August 1997 and the first flight was soon after.
Role: 4-seat lightplane for passengers, cargo, training, surveillance and air ambulance work.
Sales: Series of 5 aircraft started at MAPO in Moscow at the time of writing, including the first aircraft ready for flight, second nearly completed.
Crew/passengers: Pilot and 3 passengers.
Baggage compartment: Aft of the rear seats.
Engines: 2 LOM M332A piston engines.
Engine rating: Each 140 hp (104.4 kW).
Fuel system: 794 lb (360 kg).

Details for Merkury

PRINCIPAL DIMENSIONS:
Wing span: 33 ft 1.5 ins (10.12 m)
Maximum length: 21 ft 9.5 ins (6.646 m)
Maximum height: 10 ft 4 ins (3.15 m)

WINGS:
Area: 136.16 sq ft (12.65 m^2)
Aspect ratio: 8.1

UNDERCARRIAGE:
Type: Fixed, with nosewheel
Wheel base: 5 ft 10 ins (1.785 m)
Wheel track: 6 ft 11 ins (2.10 m)

WEIGHTS:
Empty: 1,984 lb (900 kg)
Maximum take-off: 3,307 lb (1,500 kg)
Payload: 661 lb (300 kg)

PERFORMANCE:
Maximum speed: 189 kts (217 mph) 350 km/h
Cruise speed: 140 kts (162 mph) 260 km/h
Stall speed: 54 kts (62.5 mph) 100 km/h
Take-off speed: 62 kts (71.5 mph) 115 km/h
Landing speed: 59 kts (68 mph) 110 km/h
Take-off distance: 411 ft (125 m)
Landing distance: 657 ft (200 m)
Climb rate: 1,180 ft (360 m) per minute
Ceiling: 13,125 ft (4,000 m)
G limits: +4, -3
Range with full fuel: 809 naut miles (932 miles) 1,500 km

Beriev Taganrog Aviation Complex

Russia

Corporate address:
See Combat section for company details.

Beriev Be-103

First flight: 15 July 1997 at Taganrog (from land, piloted by Vladimir Ulyanov). 19 April 1998 for first take-off from water.
Certification: Designed to meet Russian AP-23 and US FAR Pt 23.
Role: Light passenger/cargo amphibian, also suited to urgent medical care, tourism, business, fire survey and ecological monitoring. Also taken as a technology demonstrator for ultra-heavy amphibian of similar layout (see Be-1200 and Be-2500 in Airliner section).
Sales: First batch of 4 aircraft under construction in Komsomolsk-on-Amur at time of writing. On 18 August 1997, first prototype (*RA-37019*) crashed in Zhukovsky, killing the pilot (V. Ulyanov). Second prototype delivered from Komsomolsk to Taganrog in September 1997, and began flight tests on 17 November piloted by Vladimir Dubenetsky; 6 flights made by May 1998.
Crew/passengers: Pilot and 5 passengers. Alternatively, pilot and passenger plus 849 lb (385 kg) of cargo, pilot and 3 seats for casualties/attendant plus a litter in ambulance configuration, or pilot and 3 other crew in patrol layout.
Wing characteristics: Low-mounted, almost delta-planform wings with water-displacing characteristics for amphibious operations. Floats not required.
Wing control surfaces: Ailerons only.
Tail control surfaces: Slab mid-mounted tailplane (span 12 ft 10 ins, 3.9 m) with starboard tab, plus rudder with tab.
Flight control system: Manual (pushrods and cables), with electric tab.
Construction materials: All metal.
Engines: Prototype fitted with 2 Teledyne Continental IO-360ES4 piston engines, each 210 hp (156.6 kW), carried on fuselage-mounted pylons, with 3-blade variable-pitch tractor propellers. AOOT OKBM/Voronezh M-17F turbo-supercharged and fuel-injected piston engines planned for Russian market, each 200 hp (149 kW) at take-off.
Fuel system: 450 litres.
Hydraulic system: 2 independent systems, 1 for undercarriage retracting/extension and other for wheel brakes.

Details for Be 103

PRINCIPAL DIMENSIONS:
Wing span: 41 ft 9 ins (12.72 m)
Maximum length: 34 ft 11 ins (10.65 m)
Maximum height: 12 ft 2.5 ins (3.72 m)

CABIN:
Length: 12 ft (3.65 m)
Width: 3 ft 11 ins (1.2 m)
Height: 4 ft 1 ins (1.25 m)
Volume: 148.32 cu ft (4.2 m^3)

WINGS:
Aerofoil section: NACA 2412M
Area: 270.17 sq ft (25.1 m^2)
Aspect ratio: 6.46
Sweepback: 16.74°
Dihedral: 6.36° at outer panels

UNDERCARRIAGE:
Type: Retractable, with steerable nosewheel (originally designed with a tailwheel undercarriage)
Main wheel tyre size: 476 × 168 mm
Nose wheel tyre size: 400 × 150 mm
Wheel base: 13 ft 4 ins (4.055 m)
Wheel track: 7 ft 5.5 ins (2.27 m)

WEIGHTS:
Empty, operational: 3,395 lb (1,540 kg)
Maximum take-off: 4,519 lb (2,050 kg)

PERFORMANCE:
Maximum speed: 154 kts (177 mph) 285 km/h
Cruise speed: 124 kts (143 mph) 230 km/h
Stall speed: 54 kts (62 mph) 100 km/h
Take-off distance: 1,280 ft (390 m) from water, 706 ft (215 m) from shore
Landing distance: 1,149 ft (350 m) to water, 624 ft (190 m) to shore
Maximum climb rate: 1,279 ft (390 m) per minute
Range with full fuel: 690 naut miles (795 miles) 1,280 km
Range with full payload: 270 naut miles (311 miles) 500 km

Beriev Be-103 light amphibian *(courtesy Beriev)*

↑ **Beriev Be-103 cockpit** *(Piotr Butowski)*

Electrical system: 27 volt DC system and 36 volt/400 Hz AC system, with generators, rectifiers and a 25 amp-hour battery.
Pneumatic system: 710 psi.
Braking system: On main units.
Radar: Optional AlliedSignal RDR-2000 weather radar.
Flight avionics/instrumentation: AlliedSignal Bendix/King digital flight control/navigation system. Optional KFC 150 autopilot.

Central Hydrofoil Design Bureau JSC named after "R.E. Alekseev" — Russia

Corporate address:
51 Svoboda Street, Nizhny Novgorod 603003.
Telephone: +7 8312 251037
Facsimile: +7 8312 251909

Note: Volga-2 is a further development of hydrofoil boats and static air cushion vehicles. Although details of wing-in-ground-effect vehicles 'ekranoplans' are not usually carried in *WA&SD*, an exception has been made in this case due to 20 having been ordered in 1997 by the Russian city of Syktyvkar for passenger-carrying use while operating from lakes, making the Volga-2 the first Russian WIGE to enter proper series production.

Alekseev Volga-2

Role: Amphibious wing-in-ground-effect vehicle for passenger and cargo carrying.
Sales: 20 ordered by Syktyvkar. Manufactured by Sokol at Nizhny Novgorod.

↑ Alekseev Volga-2 *(courtesy CHDB)*

Crew/passengers: Pilot seated centrally in the cockpit, with 8 passengers aft.
Engines: 2 × 140 hp (104 kW) VAZ-413s, driving (via shafts) 2 shrouded tractor propellers. Control vanes in propeller slipstream.

Details for Volga-2

PRINCIPAL DIMENSIONS:
Maximum length: 37 ft 6 ins (11.43 m)
Beam: 25 ft 0.5 ins (7.63 m)
Maximum height: 10 ft 11 ins (3.32 m)
Draft: 10 ins (0.25 m)

WEIGHTS:
Empty: 3,527 lb (1,600 kg)
Maximum take-off: 5,516 lb (2,500 kg)

PERFORMANCE:
Cruise speed: 65 kts (75 mph) 120 km/h
Range: 270 naut miles (310 miles) 500 km
Wave height: 1 ft 8 ins (0.5 m)
Amphibious capability: Roughness 1 ft 8 ins (0.5 m), gradient 10°

Dubna Machinebuilding Plant JSC — Russia

Corporate address:
141980 Dubna, Moskovskaya obl., ul. Zhukovskogo, 2.
Telephone: +7 096 21 25567, 51414, 51613
Facsimile: +7 096 21 23524
Information:
Alexander Zalyubovsky (Chief designer).

ACTIVITIES

▪ Light recreational and general purpose aircraft designed by the Typhoon Design Bureau. Many projects offered, initially named Z-1 Shmel (now Dubna-1), **Z-2 Selena**, Z-3 Osa (now Dubna-2), **Z-6 Duet**, **Z-7 Bekas**, and **Z-8 Stayer**, of which only the Dubnas were built; Z-2 etc were early projects, later terminated. Typhoon now incorporated into Dubna Machinebuilding Plant (Dubnensky Mashinostroitelnyi Zavod, DMZ) and the aircraft formerly named DMZ are now Dubna.

Dubna Machinebuilding Plant/Typhoon Dubna-1

First flight: 21 May 1994 (as Z-1 Shmel), piloted by Boris Kelazev.
Certification: Planned according to JAR-VLA and JAR-22 (Chapters H and J).
Role: Single-seat recreational and agricultural aircraft.
Sales: Originally a homebuilt aircraft by Alexander Zalyubovsky, but thereafter built in series by Dubna Machinebuilding Plant. 5 aircraft built; series production now terminated.
Crew/passengers: 1.

Details for Dubna-1

PRINCIPAL DIMENSIONS:
Wing span: 30 ft 11 ins (9.42 m)
Maximum length: 16 ft 7.5 ins (5.065 m)

WINGS:
Aerofoil section: TsAGI/Typhoon R2-14M2
Area: 111.54 sq ft (10.362 m²)
Aspect ratio: 8.56

UNDERCARRIAGE:
Type: Possible wheel, ski and float gear

WEIGHTS:
Empty: 441 lb (200 kg)
Maximum take-off: 992 lb (450 kg)

PERFORMANCE:
Cruise speed: 59 kts (68 mph) 110 km/h
Take-off speed: 38 kts (43 mph) 70 km/h
Landing speed: 35 kts (40 mph) 65 km/h
Maximum climb rate: 886 ft (270 m) per minute
G-limits: +4.5, -3

Wing characteristics: Braced high-wing monoplane.
Wing control surfaces: Single-slotted trailing-edge flaps and ailerons (starboard trim tab).
Tail control surfaces: Elevators (trim tab) and rudder (ground-adjustable tab).
Engine: Single Rotax 582 piston engine with pusher propeller. Russian made AOOT OKBM/Voronezh M-18-01 on prototype.
Engine rating: 65 hp (48.5 kW).

Aircraft variants:
Dubna-1 was originally named ***Z-1 Shmel*** (Bumble-bee), later ***DMZ-1*** before a further change of name.

Dubna Machinebuilding Plant/Typhoon Dubna-2

First flight: May 1996, piloted by Boris Kelazev.
Certification: Planned according to JAR-VLA and JAR-22 (Chapter H and J).
Role: 2-seat derivative of Dubna-1, used also as a trainer.
Sales: 35 expected to be completed before the end of 1998.
Crew/passengers: 2, plus 66 lb (30 kg) of cargo.
Wing characteristics: Braced high-wing monoplane.
Wing control surfaces: Single-slotted trailing-edge flaps, and ailerons (starboard trim tab).
Tail control surfaces: Elevators (trim tab) and rudder (ground-adjustable tab).
Engine: Single Rotax 912UL piston engine with pusher propeller.
Engine rating: 80 hp (59.7 kW).
Fuel system: 70 litres.

Aircraft variants:
Dubna-2 was originally named ***Z-3 Osa*** (Wasp), later ***DMZ-2***. Development started by Typhoon Design Bureau, completed jointly with Dubna Machinebuilding Plant.

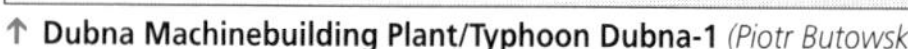

↑ Dubna Machinebuilding Plant/Typhoon Dubna-1 *(Piotr Butowski)*

↑ Dubna Machinebuilding Plant/Typhoon Dubna-2 *(Piotr Butowski)*

Details for Dubna-2

PRINCIPAL DIMENSIONS:
Wing span: 32 ft 6.5 ins (9.92 m)
Maximum length: 19 ft 7 ins (5.965 m)
Maximum height: 9 ft 6 ins (2.906 m)

WINGS:
Area: 117.54 sq ft (10.92 m^2)
Aspect ratio: 9.01

UNDERCARRIAGE:
Type: Fixed nosewheel type, with option of ski and float gear
Wheel base: 6 ft 3 ins (1.90 m)
Wheel track: 3 ft 11 ins (1.20 m)

WEIGHTS:
Empty, operating: 653 lb (296 kg)
Maximum take-off: 1,270 lb (576 kg)

PERFORMANCE:
Maximum speed: 89 kts (103 mph) 165 km/h
Cruise speed: 62 kts (71 mph) 115 km/h
Take-off speed: 46 kts (53 mph) 85 km/h
Landing speed: 40.5 kts (47 mph) 75 km/h
Take-off distance: 394 ft (120 m)
Maximum climb rate: 492 ft (150 m) per minute
Ceiling: 13,125 ft (4,000 m), service
G-limits: +4, -2.5
Range with maximum fuel: 270 naut miles (311 miles) 500 km

Gidroplan Ltd — Russia

Corporate address:
443056 Samara, Moskovskoye shosse, 4-6.

Telephone: +7 8462 347655
Facsimile: +7 8462 347655

Founded:
1992 as Redan, with current name since 1995.

Information:
Yelena Balandina.

ACTIVITIES

■ Designing and manufacturing of light aircraft. In addition to the Che-20, Che-22 and Ch-25, the 4-seat ***Che-40*** amphibian made its maiden flight in June 1997, while the ***Tsykada*** light agricultural aircraft has also appeared.

↑ **Gidroplan Tsykada** *(courtesy Gidroplan)*

Gidroplan Che-20, Che-22 and Che-25

First flight: 1989 for Che-20 (piloted by Boris Chernov), 1992 for Che-22 (Boris Chernov and Yevgeniy Yungerov), and June 1996 for Che-25.
Certification: Che-22 built according to JAR-VLA and FAR Pt 23 regulations
Role: Light passenger, tourist and training amphibian/flying-boat, also suited to fire survey and ecological monitoring.
Sales: Single Che-20 built by Boris Chernov as a homebuilt aircraft. Improved Che-22 has been manufactured by Gidroplan in Samara since 1993, with 12 sold including 10 in Russia, 1 to China and 1 to the Philippines. Single Che-25 prototype built.
Details: Che-22.
Crew/passengers: Pilot plus 2 passengers (seat pitch 23.6 ins, 60 cm) under a light, detachable canopy. Parachute aircraft rescue system in the container fitted above the wing centre section.
Baggage compartment: 4 compartments, total of 33 cu ft (0.94 m^3) for light cargo.

↑ **Gidroplan Che-22** *(Piotr Butowski)*

Wing control surfaces: Full-span slotted flaperon (9° to 17°).
Tail control surfaces: Horn-balanced rudder (±25°) and elevator.
Flight control system: Mechanical.
Construction materials: Glassfibre, D-18T aluminium and 30KhGSA steel.
Engine/s: 6 different engine arrangements can be fitted, including single- and twin-engined configurations: single Rotax 912 (80 hp, 59.7 kW), single Rotax 582 (64 hp, 47.7 kW), 2 Rotax 582s, 2 Rotax-503s (each 49 hp, 36.5 kW), 2 Rotax 447s (each 41.6 hp, 31 kW), or 2 Rotax 462s (each 51 hp, 38 kW).
Fuel system: 2 wing centre-section tanks; total of 80 litres.
Hydraulic system: None.
Electrical system: To supply engine starter and radio.
Braking system: None.
Flight avionics/instrumentation: Single radio, 118 through 136 MHz.

Aircraft variants:
Che-20 was a 2-seat homebuilt prototype, tested between 1989-1992. Open cockpit, removable undercarriage. 2 Vikhr-30M piston engines, each 35 hp (26 kW). Improved during tests and redesignated ***Che-20M***.
Che-22 is the production version with cockpit canopy and retractable undercarriage (introduced in 1996), and built according to JAR-VLA and FAR Pt 23 regulations. Originally proposed in 3 subversions: ***Che-22D*** with single Rotax 912, ***Che-22R*** with single Rotax 582, and ***Che-22R-2*** with 2 Rotax 503 engines. Currently, 6 differently-engined variants proposed, all named Che-22.
Che-25 is a 4-seat development, with the fuselage lengthened by 17.7 ins (45 cm) and the hull configuration changed. 2 Rotax 582 engines. Take-off weight 1,874 lb (850 kg). Has not entered production because of poorer flight handling characteristics. See Activities for later 4-seater.

Details for Che-22

PRINCIPAL DIMENSIONS:
Wing span: 38 ft 5 ins (11.7 m)
Maximum length: 22 ft (6.7 m)
Maximum height: 7 ft 3 ins (2.2 m)

CABIN:
Length: 4 ft 11 ins (1.5 m)
Width: 3 ft 7 ins (1.1 m)
Height: 3 ft 7 ins (1.1 m)

WINGS:
Aerofoil section: TsAGI P III A-15
Area: 169 sq ft (15.7 m^2), gross
Aspect ratio: 8.72
Sweepback: 0°
Thickness/chord ratio: 15%
Dihedral: 0° 30′
Twist: 0°

UNDERCARRIAGE:
Type: Retractable introduced in 1996; removable undercarriage before 1996. Fixed tail guard
Main wheel tyre size: 300 × 150 mm
Wheel track: 5 ft 3 ins (1.6 m)

WEIGHTS:
Empty, operating: 882 lb (400 kg)
Normal take-off: 1,433 lb (650 kg)
Maximum take-off and landing: 1,653 lb (750 kg)

PERFORMANCE:
Maximum operating speed: 92 kts (106 mph) 170 km/h
Cruise speed: 70 kts (81 mph) 130 km/h
Stall speed: 33 kts (38 mph) 60 km/h
Take-off and landing distance: 328 ft (100 m)
Maximum climb rate: 984 ft (300 m) per minute, at sea level
Ceiling: 9,840 ft (3,000 m), service
Range with full fuel: 270 naut miles (310 miles) 500 km

Ilyushin Aviation Complex — Russia

Corporate address:
See Combat section for company details.

Ilyushin Il-103

First flight: 17 May 1994 (piloted by Igor Gudkov).
Certification: 15 February 1996 issued by Interstate Air Register, FAR 23 and AP-23 requirements, and Chapter 3 Appendix 16 ICAO noise limits.
Role: Private, business, training, and coast guard/law enforcement patrol.
Sales: Manufactured at MAPO "MiG" factory at Lukhovitsy. First production Il-103 flew on 30 January 1995, piloted by Igor Gudkov. First 2 production series, 6 aircraft each, have been completed. Sales at the time of writing include 1 to Bulgaria (in September 1997) and others to Tatarstan National Flying Club, Air Transport Academy in St Petersburg, and Ministry of Ecology. Next series of about 40 aircraft was put under construction. Expected sales of 1,000 in the CIS and 500 in the west (partnered with Fairchild Dornier USA). Price

Details for Il-103 (utility)

PRINCIPAL DIMENSIONS:
Wing span: 34 ft 8 ins (10.56 m)
Maximum length: 26 ft 3 ins (8 m)
Maximum height: 10 ft 3 ins (3.13 m)

CABIN:
Length: 8 ft 8 ins (2.65 m)
Width: 4 ft 3 ins (1.3 m)
Height: 4 ft 2 ins (1.27 m)

WINGS:
Area: 158.34 sq ft (14.71 m^2)
Aspect ratio: 7.581

UNDERCARRIAGE:
Type: Fixed, with castoring nosewheel and shimmy damper. Float and ski gear optional
Wheel base: 6 ft 9 ins (2.05 m)
Wheel track: 7 ft 10.5 ins (2.4 m)

WEIGHTS:
Empty: 1,687 lb (765 kg)
Maximum take-off: 2,888 lb (1,310 kg)
Payload: 871 lb (395 kg)

PERFORMANCE:
Maximum speed: 135 kts (155 mph) 250 km/h utility
Cruise speed: 121.5 kts (140 mph) 225 km/h
Stall speed: 63 kts (73 mph) 117 km/h *clean*, 60 kts (69 mph) 110 km/h *with flaps*
Take-off distance over a 50 ft (15 m) obstacle: 1,706 ft (520 m)
Landing distance over a 50 ft (15 m) obstacle: 1,575 ft (480 m)
Maximum climb rate: 984 ft (300 m) per minute, at sea level
Ceiling: 9,840 ft (3,000 m)
G limits: +4.4, –2.2
Range with full fuel: 577 naut miles (665 miles) 1,070 km, with 45 minutes reserve

by Ilyushin is US$156,500 in standard specification.
Crew/passengers: 2 folding front seats and a rear bench for 2 or 3 more passengers. Gullwing doors. Unrestricted access to the baggage hold for fast loading/unloading. Accommodation for 485 lb (220 kg) of cargo with the rear seats taken out.
Wing control surfaces: Ailerons and single-slotted flaps.
Tail control surfaces: Single-piece horn-balanced elevator with trim tab, and horn-balanced rudder.
Flight control system: Pushrod and cables, except for electric tab.
Construction materials: Metal, except for glassfibre wing, tail tips and tab.
Engine: Teledyne Continental IO-360-ES piston engine, with a 6 ft 4 ins (1.93 m) Hartzell 2-blade variable-pitch propeller.
Engine rating: 210 hp (157.6 kW).
Fuel system: 200 litres. Capable of inverted flight.
Electrical system: 27 volt DC supply, via an 1,800 kW generator. 25 amp-hour battery.
Hydraulic system: For the brakes.
Braking system: Hydraulic multi-disc type.
Flight avionics/instrumentation: IFR. Flight/navigation equipment for precise navigation and landing approach under ICAO Cat I. Can be equipped with western avionics at the customer's request. 2 such avionics versions are being prepared, the first with an AlliedSignal Bendix/King avionics suite and the second with a mixture of instruments from various manufacturers. Among other equipment, these 2 versions carry GPS, ILS and ADF. First aircraft with AlliedSignal avionics (*RA-10323*, *c/n 0203*) was shown at the Paris Air Show in June 1997.

Ilyushin Il-104

Comments: Twin-engined derivative of Il-103.

↑ **Ilyushin Il-103** *(Piotr Butowski)*

Interavia JSC — Russia

Corporate address:
141352 Moskovskaya oblast, Sergiyevoposadsky rayon, p/o Abramtsevo, pos. Repikhovo.
Facsimile: +7 095 258 4050

ACTIVITIES

■ Develops light general purpose aircraft. First aircraft was the SL-90 Leshiy, later developed into the I-1 at Interavia, SL-A and A-211 that can be found under NPP Alpha-M, and SL-39VM-1 (see MAPO). Aerobatic I-3 has been continued by Interavia, as well as by Technoavia (as SP-91, which see). The I-5 project is currently being continued under the designation SM-92 Finist by Technoavia (which see) and also as the I-12 by Interavia.

Interavia I-1 (with SL-1 and SL-90)

First flight: February 1991 for SL-90 (piloted by Viktor Zabolotskiy), March 1992 for I-1R, and August 1994 for I-1L (piloted by Vladimir Yegorov).
Certification: Expected 1998 for I-1L.

↑ **Interavia I-1L** *(Piotr Butowski)*

Role: 2-seat lightplane, suited to private use, training, cargo carrying, ecological monitoring and survey, photography, SAR, agricultural and patrol.
Sales: In production at the MAPO plant at Lukhovitsy, and marketed by MiG "MAPO-M". Some 75 SL-90s/I-1s built, including 12 I-1Rs and 5 I-1Ls. 10 airframes delivered to NPP Alpha-M.
Crew/passengers: 2, with possible third seat instead of baggage compartment.
Baggage/cargo capacity: 35.31 cu ft (1 m^3)
Wing characteristics: Forward-swept wings, with slight dihedral.
Wing control surfaces: Ailerons and plain flaps.
Tail control surfaces: Elevators (starboard tab) and rudder.
Flight control system: Mechanical.
Construction materials: Metal and fabric.
Engine: Textron Lycoming O-320-E2A piston engine, with 6 ft 1 ins (1.86 m) diameter Hoffmann (or Mühlbauer) 2-blade fixed-pitch propeller.
Engine rating: 140 hp (104.4 kW).
Flight avionics/instrumentation: Customer's choice.

Aircraft variants (in order of appearance):
SL-1 (SL for samolot logkiy, light aircraft) was built at Myasishchev's prototype workshop in Zhukovsky (2 examples).
SL-90 Leshiy was a version of 1990, built against an order from the forestry service for a patrol aircraft (Leshiy is a mythical woodland spirit). For a period it was developed by the Russian/Bulgarian Aviotechnica joint venture. Powered by an OKBM/Voronezh M-3 piston engine of only 110 hp (82 kW), instead of the expected 140 hp (104.4 kW). 2-blade wooden fixed-pitch VM-3-08 propeller. Because of the lack of engine power, the wing span had to be extended from the original 32 ft 10 ins (10.0 m) to 38 ft 1 ins (11.6 m) and performance thereby decreased. MTOW 1,698 lb (770 kg), and maximum speed 124 kts (143 mph) 230 km/h. Manufactured at Lukhovitsy in 1992.
I-1 became a version of the SL-90 with slight wing forward sweep. Same M-3 engine.
I-1R uses a VAZ 4133-10A engine (140 hp, 104.4 kW), allowing wing span to be reduced to 33 ft 2 ins (10.1 m). Forward wing sweep retained.
Izdelye 23 was an intermediate prototype, featuring the airframe of the I-1R and a Textron Lycoming engine.
I-1L is the current production version, powered by a Textron Lycoming O-320-E2A engine. See general description.
SL-39WM-1 is a derivative by Lukhovitsy Machinebuilding Plant, which see.
SL-A and ***A-211*** are derivatives by NPP Alpha-M, which see.

Details for I-1L

PRINCIPAL DIMENSIONS:
Wing span: 32 ft 10 ins (10 m)
Maximum length: 22 ft (6.7 m)
Maximum height: 9 ft 10 ins (3 m) in flying configuration

UNDERCARRIAGE:
Type: Fixed, with tailwheel
Main wheel tyre size: 400 × 150 mm
Wheel track: 8 ft 9.5 ins (2.68 m), parked

WEIGHTS:
Maximum take-off: 1,940 lb (880 kg)
Payload: 384 lb (174 kg)

PERFORMANCE:
Maximum speed: 135 kts (155 mph) 250 km/h
Cruise speed: 81 kts (93 mph) 150 km/h
Landing speed: 46 kts (53 mph) 85 km/h
Take-off distance: 919 ft (280 m) grass
Landing distance: 722 ft (220 m) grass
Ceiling: 9,840 ft (3,000 m), service
G limits: +6, –3
Range with full fuel: 324 naut miles (373 miles) 600 km

Interavia I-3 and E-3

First flight: 10 August 1993 (piloted by Viktor Zabolotsky).
Role: Unlimited aerobatic aircraft, suited also to training.
Sales: Manufactured by Tushino Machine Built Plant in Moscow; initial batch of 48 put in hand. 6 delivered to the USA, distributed by Shadetree Aviation, 600 Clipper Hill Road, Danvill, CA 94526 (*telephone*: +1 510 743 1786, *facsimile* +1 510 743 9807 – also an authorized distributor for the Yakovlev Yak-55M).
Crew/passengers: Pilot under a small bubble canopy, but capable of being converted into a 2-seater with full flight and engine instruments and controls in under 1 hour using an interchangeable modular unit.
Wing control surfaces: Drooping ailerons (with tabs).
Tail control surfaces: Horn-balanced elevators and rudder (ground-adjustable tab on rudder).
Flight control system: Probably mechanical.
Construction materials: All-metal construction, using electro-chemical coating for good corrosion prevention.
Engine: AOOT OKBM/Voronezh M-14P radial piston engine, with a 3-blade MT-3 or MT-9 propeller. Possible use of a 2-blade V-530TA-D35 propeller.
Engine rating: 360 hp (268.5 kW).

Details for I-3

PRINCIPAL DIMENSIONS:
Wing span: 26 ft 7 ins (8.1 m)
Maximum length: 22 ft (6.7 m)
Maximum height: 7 ft 3 ins (2.2 m), parked

WINGS:
Aerofoil section: Symmetrical
Area: 124.22 sq ft (11.54 m^2)
Aspect ratio: 5.69

UNDERCARRIAGE:
Type: Fixed, with tailwheel. Cantilever spring main legs
Main wheel tyre size: 400 × 150 mm
Tail wheel tyre size: 200 × 80 mm
Wheel track: 8 ft 6.5 ins (2.6 m), parked

WEIGHTS:
Empty: 1,609-1,695 lb (730-769 kg)
Maximum take-off: 2,335 lb (1,059 kg)

PERFORMANCE:
Never-exceed speed (V_{NE}): 248 kts (286 mph) 460 km/h
Maximum speed: 189 kts (217 mph) 350 km/h
Stall speed: 54 kts (62 mph) 100 km/h
Take-off distance: 860 ft (262 m) grass
Landing distance: 1,565 ft (477 m) grass
Maximum climb rate: 2,953 ft (900 m) per minute
G limits: +12, −10 pilot only; +11, −9 as a 2-seater
Range: 377 naut miles (435 miles) 700 km

↑ Interavia I-3 in 2-seat configuration, with single-seat canopy removed and seen under rear fuselage *(Piotr Butowski)*

Aircraft variants:
I-3 is the current production version, as detailed.
E-3 is the export version of the I-3.
I-3M is a projected version with the airframe lightened by 154 lb (70 kg) and with a more comfortable cockpit.
SP-91 is a version developed by Technoavia company (which see). (Vyacheslav Kondratyev, owner of Technoavia, worked at Interavia before 1992.)

KB MAI (Design Bureau of Moscow Aviation Institute) — Russia

Telephone: +7 095 1584468
Founded: 1977 (see Activities).
Information: Kazimir Mikhailovich Zhidovetsky (Chief Designer).

ACTIVITIES

▪ 7 projects undertaken in the 1990s, the 890, 890A, 890SKh, 890U, 900, 910 (960) and 920 (the latter a single-seat glider), of which 3 are in production (890, 890SKh and 890U). Others, including the **Aviatika-MAI-950** business jet, remained paper projects.

▪ Between 1991 and 1997 the projects were undertaken under the company Aviatika, founded to unite a number of enterprises specializing in aviation and related fields. It began when the Moscow Dementyev Aviation Production Association (producing MiG fighters), Gromov Flight Research Institute (major testing facility) and the Moscow Aviation Institute (leading university) united to produce civil light aircraft in accordance with Russia's conversion programme. On 17 February 1993, Aviatika (as the first Russian commercially operated aircraft building company) received a Russian State Certificate as a designer of light civil aircraft. In 1997 Aviatika withdrew and thereafter all projects came under the KB MAI name.

Aviatika-MAI-890 and -920

Details: Aviatika-MAI-890, except under Aircraft variants (unless stated).
First flight: MAI Junior, a pre-prototype for the MAI-89, first flew July 1987. Summer 1990 for MAI-89 prototype (piloted by Mikhail Markov). Michail Markov established a world time-to-climb to 3,000 m record for this category of aircraft in August 1990 with the MAI-89 prototype.
Certification: Meets JAR-VLA and FAR Pt 23 regulations.
Role: Light multi-purpose sporting, training, ecological monitoring, survey and agricultural biplane. Aviatika-MAI-890A is an autogyro variant by application of a conversion kit. Aviatika-MAI-920 is a glider.
Sales: At least 350 built at the time of writing, including approximately 200 single-seaters and 150 2-seaters. Of these, 270 (150 single-seaters and 120 2-seaters) sold to customers in more than 15 countries. During 1996 and 1997, production was practically halted because of many unsold aircraft held at the factory. However, in 1997 production resumed and 50 more were put in hand.
Crew/passengers: Pilot only in the Aviatika-MAI-890; 2 persons in the Aviatika-MAI-890U.
Cockpit: Optional side doors, 1 jettisonable in flight. Seat is adapted for use of a backpack parachute, but a BRS ballistic parachute system can be mounted on the central post.
External equipment: 265 lb (120 kg) payload as external stores carried on 4 attachment points as: under the engine mounts (132 lb, 60 kg), under the belly (220 lb, 100 kg), and lower wingtips (each 99 lb, 45 kg).
Wing control surfaces: Full-width, lower-wing ailerons.
Tail control surfaces: Small tailplane and fin, large elevators (with ground-adjustable tab) and rudder (with similar tab).
Construction materials: Aluminium alloy, steel and titanium, with fabric-covered flying surfaces. Glassfibre cockpit fairing. All essential components of the airframe (fittings, control linkages, etc) are located externally for easy inspection.
Engine: 64.4 hp (48 kW) Rotax 582 or 77.8 hp (58 kW) Rotax 912 piston engine, with a 2-blade pusher propeller.
Fuel system: 50 litres (81.5 lb, 37 kg). Optional 55 litre auxiliary tank installed on the under-engine mounts (see External equipment above).
Flight avionics/instrumentation: Flight and engine instruments. VHF transceiver at customer's request.

Aircraft variants:
MAI-89 was the first prototype.
Aviatika-MAI-890 is the single-seat multi-purpose version, as detailed.

↑ Aviatika-MAI-890 *(Piotr Butowski)*

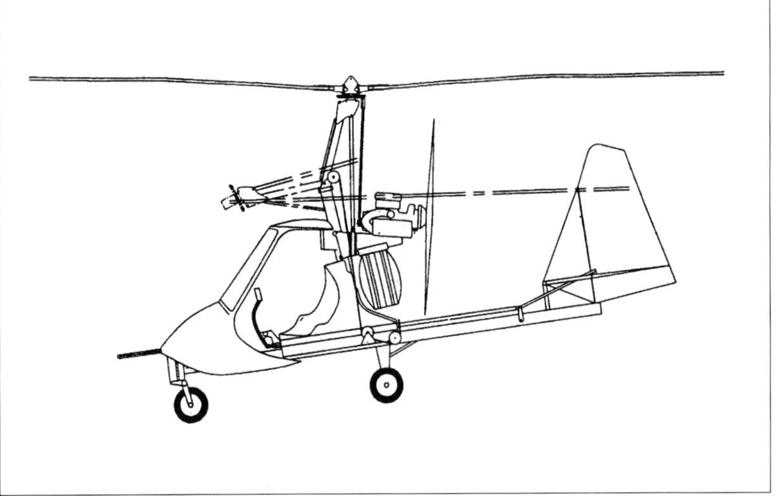
↑ Aviatika-MAI-890A autogyro

Details for Aviatika-MAI-890 with Rotax 582, unless stated

PRINCIPAL DIMENSIONS:
Wing span: 26 ft 7 ins (8.11 m) upper wing
Maximum length: 17 ft 5.5 ins (5.32 m), including pitot
Maximum height: 7 ft 5 ins (2.25 m)

WINGS:
Area: 153.82 sq ft (14.29 m²)

UNDERCARRIAGE:
Type: Fixed, with nosewheel. Provision for floats or skis

WEIGHTS:
Empty: 567 lb (257 kg)
Empty for 890U: 657 lb (298 kg)
Maximum take-off: 838 lb (380 kg)
Maximum take-off for 890U: 1,135 lb (515 kg)
Maximum take-off for 890-912SKh: 1,190 lb (540 kg)

PERFORMANCE (at MTOW):
Maximum speed: 76 kts (87 mph) 140 km/h
Maximum speed for 890U: 65 kts (75 mph) 120 km/h
Cruise speed: 49-70 kts (56-81 mph) 90-130 km/h
Stall speed: 35 kts (41 mph) 65 km/h
Take-off distance: 181 ft (55 m)
Take-off distance for 890U: 312 ft (95 m)
Take-off distance for 890-912SKh: 378 ft (115 m)
Maximum climb rate: 965 ft (294 m) per minute
Ceiling: 16,400 ft (5,000 m), service
G limits: +7.5, -3.75 at 694 lb (315 kg), or +6, -4 ultimate; +5, -2.5 or +4, -2 limit (same conditions)
Duration: 3.5 hours

Aviatika-MAI-890-912SKh is an agricultural version used for the protection of arable, green and forest plantations from pests and disease. Ultra-low-volume and biological Micronair AU-7000 atomizer system uses only 3.3 lb (1.5 kg) of chemical per pass, or more when required. Swath width 46 ft (14 m). Features a cockpit canopy, 220 lb (100 kg) chemical tank, and Rotax 912 engine. More than 15 built and sold (only to Russian customers).
Aviatika-MAI-890U is the side-by-side 2-seat version. MAI-89U prototype with Rotax 582 first flew August 1991. Aviatika-MAI-890U production aircraft first flew 15 July 1992. Aviatika-MAI-890U with Rotax 912 first flew 16 September 1992.
Aviatika-MAI-890A is an autogyro version, either sold as such or produced by conversion of a standard 890 using a gyro assembly unit. Similar roles to 890. Rotax 912 engine. 23 ft 7.5 ins (7.2 m) 2-blade rotor. Empty weight 430 lb (195 kg), and MTOW 794 lb (360 kg). Most important feature is its aeroplane-like control system (not typical for autogyros). Prototype flew in 1994.
Aviatika-MAI-920 is a simple training glider, using 90% Aviatika-890 components. See Glider section. First flown 15 September 1992.

Aviatika-MAI-900 Acrobat

First flight: 22 February 1993, piloted by Leonid Lobas.
Role: Single-seat aerobatic competition monoplane.
Sales: Available; prototype only built at the time of writing.
Wing control surfaces: Ailerons (port ground-adjustable tab), and manoeuvre flaps used for longitudinal control (direct lift control).
Tail control surfaces: Horn-balanced elevators (starboard ground-adjustable tab) and rudder (similar tab).
Construction materials: All metal. Cantilever wings and strut-braced tailplane.
Engine: AOOT OKBM/Voronezh M-14P radial piston engine.
Engine rating: 360 hp (268.5 kW).

Details for Aviatika-900

PRINCIPAL DIMENSIONS:
Wing span: 23 ft 5.5 ins (7.15 m)
Maximum length: 18 ft 8.5 ins (5.7 m)
Maximum height: 9 ft 10 ins (3 m)

WINGS:
Aerofoil section: Symmetrical
Area: 107.64 sq ft (10 m²)
Aspect ratio: 5.11

UNDERCARRIAGE:
Type: Fixed, with steerable tailwheel. Cantilever spring-type main legs

WEIGHTS:
Empty: 1,301 lb (590 kg)
Maximum take-off and landing: 1,576 lb (715 kg)

PERFORMANCE:
Maximum speed: 170 kts (196 mph) 315 km/h
Take-off and landing speed: 59 kts (68 mph) 110 km/h
Stall speed: 58 kts (67 mph) 107 km/h
Take-off distance: 220 ft (66 m)
Landing distance: 394 ft (120 m)
Maximum climb rate: 4,530 ft (1,380 m) per minute, at sea level
G limits: ±11

↑ **Aviatika-MAI-900 Acrobat** *(Piotr Butowski)*

Aviatika-MAI-910 and 960

First flight: 18 June 1995 for 910.
Certification: Developed to comply with JAR-VLA.
Role: Sporting, training and utility monoplane.
Sales: Prototype only at the time of writing.
Crew/passengers: 2 persons side-by-side. Seat can be reclined and 1 of the dual controls removed, providing space for a litter or long item of cargo.
Cockpit: Jettisonable sliding doors, and side hatches for access to the cargo compartment.
Baggage/cargo capacity: Large cargo compartment, equipped with a retractable floor to allow use of camera and video equipment as required.
Wing characteristics: Braced, high-mounted. Folding. Higher aspect ratio than Aviatika-MAI-890 wing.
Wing control surfaces: Wide-span flaperon.
Tail control surfaces: As for Aviatika-MAI-890.
Construction materials: Wings have a spar constructed of large diameter tubing, with ribs and leading/trailing-edges of stamped metal sheet. Identical tail unit to the Aviatika-MAI-890. Large diameter tube tailboom. Glassfibre engine cowling. Outer parts of the wings, flaperons and tail covered with cotton fabric.
Engine: Rotax 912 piston engine. Optionally Rotax 914 (100 hp; 74.6 kW).
Engine rating: 77.8 hp (58 kW).

Aircraft variants:
Aviatika-MAI-910 is the basic version, as detailed.
Aviatika-MAI-960 has a thick tailboom (can be replaced in 15 minutes).

↑ **Aviatika-MAI-910** *(courtesy KB MAI)*

Details for Aviatika-MAI-960

PRINCIPAL DIMENSIONS:
Wing span: 35 ft 3 ins (10.73 m)
Maximum length: 17 ft 3 ins (5.26 m)
Maximum height: 8 ft 7 ins (2.49 m)

WINGS:
Area: 120.56 sq ft (11.2 m²)

UNDERCARRIAGE:
Type: Fixed, easily converted between nosewheel and tailwheel in the field

WEIGHTS:
Empty: 838 lb (380 kg)
Maximum take-off: 1,367 lb (620 kg)

PERFORMANCE:
Maximum speed: 84 kts (96 mph) 155 km/h
Cruise speed: 70 kts (81 mph) 130 km/h
Take-off speed: 43 kts (50 mph) 80 km/h
Landing speed: 42 kts (48 mph) 78 km/h
Stall speed: 41 kts (48 mph) 76 km/h
Take-off distance: 493 ft (150 m)
Landing distance: 476 ft (145 m)
Climb rate: 689 ft (210 m) per minute
Ceiling: 9,840 ft (3,000 m)
G limits: +4, -2
Range: 216 naut miles (248 miles) 400 km

OKB Krilya — Russia

Corporate address:
123480 Moscow, ul. Vilisa Latsisa, 21-3-206.

Telephone: +7 095 4968017
Facsimile: +7 095 3943621

Information:
Alexander Revo (General Manager).

ACTIVITIES

▪ In addition to the Yrbis, the **Orka** 2-seat turboprop aircraft is under development, but at a very early stage.

Krilya Yrbis

First flight: Project.
Role: 6-seat executive aircraft.
Development: During 1993-1994, a 1:5-scale model was fully tested in TsAGI's T-102 wind tunnel. In February 1995 the project was taken over by Tupolev and designated ***Tu-44***, but in mid-1996 it was taken back by OKB Krilya because of a reported lack of support from Tupolev.
Crew/passengers: Pilot plus 5 passengers, plus 220 lb (100 kg) of baggage.
Wing control surfaces: Trailing-edge flaps and ailerons (port trim tab).
Tail control surfaces: T-type swept tail with trim tabs in port elevator and rudder.

↑ **Model of the Krilya Yrbis** *(Piotr Butowski)*

Flight control system: Mechanical, rigid.
Construction materials: Mainly D-16 aluminium alloy.
Engine: Single nose-mounted piston or turboprop engine.
3 versions planned: ***Yrbis-L*** with Textron Lycoming IO-720-A1B (400 hp, 298 kW) piston engine, ***Yrbis-C*** with Teledyne Continental IO-550-G (325 hp, 242 kW) piston engine, and ***Yrbis-T*** with Pratt & Whitney Canada PT6A-27 (550 shp, 410 kW) turboprop. Hartzell 3-blade propeller.
Flight system avionics/instrumentation: AlliedSignal Bendix/King Silver Crown.

Details for Yrbis-T, *with Yrbis-L in italics where different*

PRINCIPAL DIMENSIONS:
Wing span: 43 ft 8 ins (13.3 m)
Maximum length: 34 ft 9 ins (10.6 m), *33 ft 9.5 ins (10.3 m)*

WINGS:
Area: 191.6 sq ft (17.8 m^2), gross
Aspect ratio: 9.94

UNDERCARRIAGE:
Type: Retractable, with nosewheel

WEIGHTS:
Empty, operating: 2,690 lb (1,220 kg), *2,557 lb (1,160 kg)*
Take-off: 4,960 lb (2,250 kg), *4,321 lb (1,960 kg)*

PERFORMANCE:
Maximum speed: 254 kts (292 mph) 470 km/h, *205 kts (236 mph) 380 km/h*, both at 9,840 ft (3,000 m)
Cruise speed: 238 kts (273 mph) 440 km/h, *184 kts (211 mph) 340 km/h*
Take-off distance: 722 ft (220 m), *853 ft (260 m)*
Landing distance: 656 ft (200 m)
Range with full fuel: 1,295 naut miles (1,491 miles) 2,400 km
Range with full payload: 755 naut miles (870 miles) 1,400 km

Lukhovitsy Machinebuilding Plant — Russia

Corporate address:
140500, Lukhovitsy, Moskovskaya oblast.

Telephone: +7 096 63 11376
Facsimile: +7 096 63 11180, 11376

ACTIVITIES

▪ Established in 1953 as a division of GAZ-30 plant (now MAPO), since 1968 also undertaking final assembly of aircraft. SL-39WM is the only original design of Lukhovitsy, although the factory is manufacturing also the MiG-29, Il-103, I-1L, T-101 Gratch and others.

Lukhovitsy SL-39WM

First flight: 1994 (piloted by Viktor Zabolotsky).
Role: 2-seat lightplane, suited to private use, training, cargo carrying, ecological monitoring and survey, photography, SAR, agricultural and patrol.
Sales: 5 SL-39WM-1s assembled at Lukhovitsy from the remaining parts of Interavia I-1s when Lukhovitsy plant switched production from the I-1 to the I-1L.
Crew/passengers: 2.
Baggage/cargo capacity: 28.25 cu ft (0.8 m^3).
Wing characteristics: Forward-swept wings, with slight dihedral.
Wing control surfaces: Ailerons and plain flaps.
Tail control surfaces: Elevators (starboard tab) and rudder.
Flight control system: Mechanical.
Construction materials: Metal and fabric.
Engine: Walter LOM M332A piston engine, with VM-3-08 2-blade propeller.
Engine rating: 140 hp (104.4 kW).
Fuel system: 120 litres.
Flight avionics/instrumentation: Conventional. Optional GPS.

Aircraft variants:
SL-39WM-1, nicknamed Terminator, as described. Designation stands for Samolet Logkiy (light aircraft), assembled in workshop 39, with Walter Minor engine.
SL-39WM-2 is a reported project with nosewheel undercarriage.

↑ **Lukhovitsy SL-39WM-1** *(Piotr Butowski)*

Details for SL-39WM-1

PRINCIPAL DIMENSIONS:
Wing span: 32 ft 10 ins (10 m)
Maximum length: 23 ft 7.5 ins (7.2 m)

UNDERCARRIAGE:
Type: Fixed, with tailwheel
Main wheel tyre size: 400 × 150 mm
Wheel track: 8 ft 9.5 ins (2.68 m), parked

WEIGHTS:
Maximum take-off: 1,720 lb (780 kg)
Payload: 331 lb (150 kg)

PERFORMANCE:
Maximum speed: 102.5 kts (118 mph) 190 km/h
Cruise speed: 86 kts (99 mph) 160 km/h
Landing speed: 43 kts (50 mph) 80 km/h
Maximum climb rate: 886 ft (270 m) per minute
Take-off distance: 656 ft (200 m) grass
Landing distance: 328 ft (100 m) grass
G limits: +3.5, -1.5
Ceiling: 4,920 ft (1,500 m), service
Range with full fuel: 324 naut miles (373 miles) 600 km

MAPO "MiG" — Russia

Corporate address:
See Combat section for company details.

MAPO "MiG" MiG-115

First flight: Project only.
Role: Light general-purpose tandem biplane designed to replace An-2.
Certification: Built according to AP-23 (FAR-23) standards.
Sales: Development started in 1994, with preliminary design completed in Summer 1996. In May 1996 model tested in TsAGI wind tunnel. Series production expected at Moscow MAPO plant. Demand estimated at 700-800 aircraft.
Crew: 1-2.
Passengers: 15 passengers on airline-type seats, or 18 paratroops on folding seats, or mixed payload of 9 passengers and 1,102 lb (500 kg) cargo, or 3,307 lb (1,500 kg) of cargo only.

Details for MiG-115

PRINCIPAL DIMENSIONS:
Front wing span: 40 ft (12.2 m)
Rear wing span: 52 ft 3.5 ins (15.94 m)
Maximum length: 48 ft 1 ins (14.66 m)
Maximum height: 19 ft 10 ins (6.04 m)

CABIN:
Length: 16 ft 9 ins (5.1 m)
Width: 6 ft 5 ins (1.96 m) maximum, 6 ft (1.82 m) at floor
Height: 5 ft 11 ins (1.8 m)

TAIL UNIT:
Tailplane span: 21 ft (6.4 m)

UNDERCARRIAGE:
Type: Fixed, with nosewheel
Wheel base: 15 ft 10 ins (4.83 m)
Wheel track: 13 ft 10.5 ins (4.23 m)

WEIGHTS:
Empty: 7,346 lb (3,332 kg)
Maximum take-off: 12,566 lb (5,700 kg)
Payload: 3,307 lb (1,500 kg)

PERFORMANCE:
Maximum speed: 221 kts (255 mph) 410 km/h
Economic speed: 183 kts (211 mph) 340 km/h
Approach speed: 62 kts (71 mph) 114 km/h
Take-off distance: 1,214 ft (370 m)
Landing distance: 804 ft (245 m)
Ceiling: 22,965 ft (7,000 m), or 9,840 ft (3,000 m) with passengers
Climb rate: 1,770 ft (540 m) per minute
G-limits: +3.2, -1.3
Range with full fuel: 1,996 naut miles (2,299 miles) 3,700 km
Range with full payload: 809 naut miles (932 miles) 1,500 km, with 45 minutes reserve

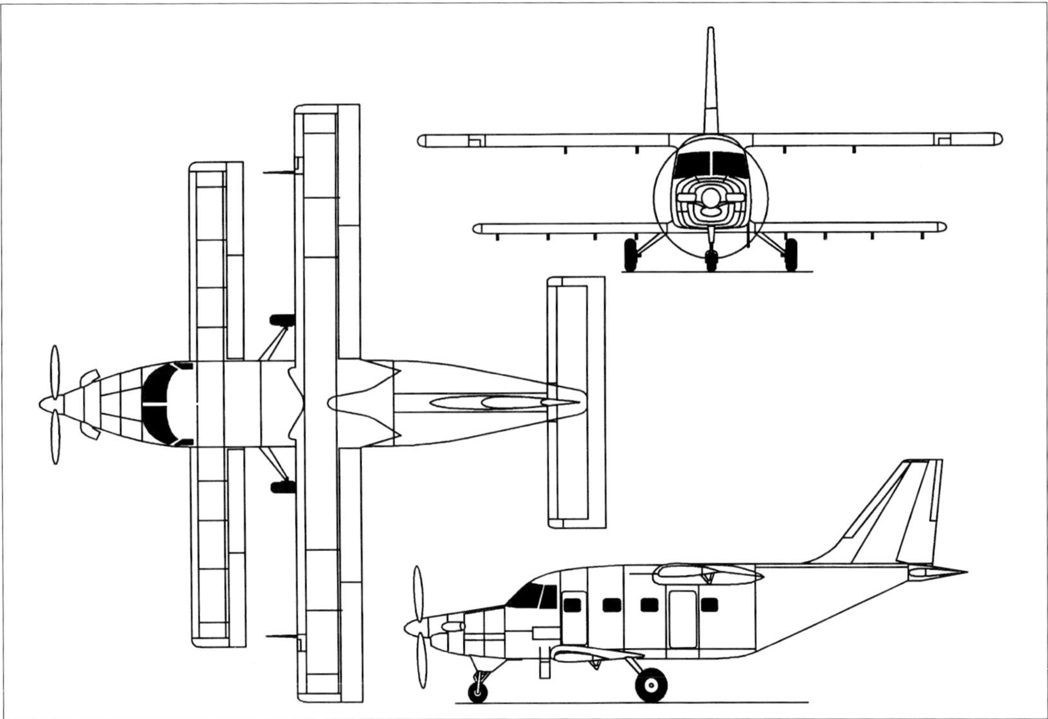

↑ MAPO "MiG" MiG-115 *(Piotr Butowski)*

Freight hold capacity: Up to 3,307 lb (1,500 kg), including a LD-3 container, or light car, or bulk freight.
Freight hold access: Rear ramp. Side door for crew and passengers located in port side of the forward fuselage.
Wing characteristics: Tandem biplane with low-mounted front wing and high-mounted rear wing, both unswept. No anhedral/dihedral.
Wing control surfaces: Trailing-edge flaps and ailerons on upper wing, full-span flaps on lower wing.
Tail control surfaces: Single horn-balanced elevator, and rudder with tab.
Engine: Pratt & Whitney Canada PT6A-67 turboprop, with 6-blade 9 ft 10 ins (3 m) diameter propeller. Also OKBM/Omsk TVD-20M (1,400 shp, 1,044 kW) is under consideration.
Engine rating: 1,300 shp (969 kW).
Fuel system: Maximum 3,748 lb (1,700 kg), or nominal 1,918 lb (870 kg).

MAPO "MiG" MiG-125

First flight: Project, announced 1997.
Role: Business jet, targeted at the domestic Russian market and featuring moderate price, long range, and high cruise speed.
Crew/passengers: Pilot plus 5-7 passengers when 4,000 km range required.
Tail control surfaces: Mid-mounted swept tailplane with elevators, and rudder.
Engines: 2 Williams Rolls FJ44-2 turbofans.
Engine rating: Each 2,300 lbf (10.23 kN).
Fuel system: 4,100 lb (1,860 kg).

Details for MiG-125

PRINCIPAL DIMENSIONS:
Wing span: 39 ft 1 ins (11 m)
Maximum length: 39 ft 8 ins (12.1 m)
Maximum height: 15 ft 1 ins (4.6 m)

CABIN:
Length: 11 ft 4 ins (3.45 m)
Width: 5 ft 6 ins (1.67 m)
Height: 5 ft 5 ins (1.65 m)

UNDERCARRIAGE:
Type: Retractable, with nosewheel

WEIGHTS:
Maximum take-off: 12,225 lb (5,545 kg)
Payload: 805 lb (365 kg) with maximum fuel

PERFORMANCE:
Maximum cruise speed: 469 kts (541 mph) 870 km/h
Take-off distance: 3,216 ft (980 m)
Cruise altitude: 45,000 ft (13,720 m)
Range: 2,142 naut miles (2,467 miles) 3,970 km with 4 passengers, 45 minutes

NPO Molniya — Russia

Corporate address:
For company details, see Airliners section.

Molniya-1 and Molniya-3

First flight: 18 December 1992 (piloted by Nikolai Generalov).
Fatigue life: 3,000 hours or 6,000 cycles.
Role: Light general-purpose transport, including passenger, ambulance and dual-control training.
Sales: Production started in 1993 at the Samara plant. Small number completed at the time of writing, with others in final assembly.
Crew/passengers: 6 persons, including the pilot. Other layouts include 4-person business, and a litter and 2 medical attendants in an ambulance role.
Wing characteristics: Low-mounted, to the rear of the cabin. Wings foldable or detachable.
Control surfaces: On each of the canards, wings, twin vertical and adjoining tailplane.

↑ Molniya-1 *(Piotr Butowski)*

Engine: AOOT OKBM/Voronezh M-14PM-1 radial piston engine mounted in the rear of the fuselage pod, with a 3-blade MTV-9 pusher propeller. Alternative Teledyne Continental TSIOL-550-B piston engine of 350 hp (261 kW). Allison 250-B17F turboprop under consideration for Molniya-3.
Engine rating: 360 hp (268.5 kW).

Details for Molniya-1

PRINCIPAL DIMENSIONS:
Wing span: 27 ft 11 ins (8.5 m)
Maximum length: 25 ft 9.5 ins (7.86 m)
Width, with wings folded or detached: 11 ft 10 ins (3.6 m)
Maximum height: 7 ft 7 ins (2.3 m)

CABIN:
Length: 9 ft (2.75 m)
Width: 4 ft 1.5 ins (1.25 m)
Height: 4 ft 1 ins (1.24 m)
Door size: 3 ft 1.5 ins × 3 ft 11 ins (0.95 × 1.19 m)

WINGS:
Area: 123.78 sq ft (11.5 m^2)
Aspect ratio: 6.28

UNDERCARRIAGE:
Type: Fixed, with nosewheel. Optional skis
Wheel base: 11 ft 2 ins (3.398 m)
Wheel track: 9 ft 11 ins (3.02 m)

WEIGHTS:
Maximum take-off: 3,836 lb (1,740 kg)
Payload: 1,113 lb (505 kg)

PERFORMANCE:
Maximum speed: 173 kts (199 mph) 320 km/h
Cruise speed: 121.5-154 kts (140-177 mph) 225-285 km/h at 4,920 ft (1,500 m) altitude
Landing speed: 70 kts (81 mph) 130 km/h
Take-off distance: 1,477 ft (450 m)
Landing distance: 1,149 ft (350 m)
Climb rate at sea level: 787 ft (240 m) per minute
Range with full fuel: 539 naut miles (621 miles) 1,000 km
Range with full payload: 270 naut miles (310 miles) 500 km

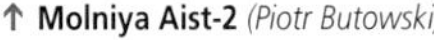
↑ Molniya Aist-2 *(Piotr Butowski)*

↑ Molniya Lagoda *(Piotr Butowski)*

Fuel system: 2 wing tanks with a total of 344 litres of fuel (551 lb, 250 kg).

Aircraft variants:
Molniya-1 is the piston-engined version, as detailed.
Molniya-3 is a proposed derivative powered by an Allison 250-B17F turboprop and with AlliedSignal Bendix/King avionics suite. Expected price is $380,000 (rather than $200,000 for Molniya-1). Russian engines (such as the Saturn AL-34 and Granit TVD-400) are being considered, but these are not yet available.

Other Molniya programmes (also see Airliner section):

Molniya Aist is a project for a conventional general-purpose low-cost aircraft with 2 piston engines carried on the high-mounted wing and with a fixed tailwheel type undercarriage. The 2 versions proposed are: the smaller **Aist-2** accommodating a pilot plus 5 passengers, with a MTOW of 4,518 lb (2,050 kg), 2 automobile-type APD-2300 engines (each 210 hp, 157 kW), wing span 38 ft 8 ins (11.8 m), length 29 ft 6 ins (9 m), maximum speed 173 kts (199 mph) 320 km/h, and range 1,511 naut miles (1,740 miles) 2,800 km with full fuel and 728 naut miles (839 miles) 1,350 km with full payload; and the larger **Aist-4** of the same layout but accommodating a pilot and 8 passengers plus 1,102 lb (500 kg) of cargo (or pilot plus 2,425 lb, 1,100 kg of cargo) at MTOW of 7,936 lb (3,600 kg), powered by APD-7000 automobile-type engines (each 425 hp, 317 kW), with a wing span of 49 ft 3 ins (15 m), length 37 ft 1 ins (11.3 m), maximum speed 173 kts (199 mph) 320 km/h, and range 971 naut miles (1,118 miles) 1,800 km. However, at the time of writing development of Aist had been stopped because of lack of funding.
Lagoda is a 10-seat amphibian with 2 pusher 720 shp (537 kW) turboprops. Patrol and medevac versions are envisaged. Maximum take-off weight 9,259 lb (4,200 kg), payload 1,984 lb (900 kg), cruising speed 189 kts (217 mph) 350 km/h, range 431 naut miles (497 miles) 800 km with full payload, range 809 naut miles (932 miles) 1,500 km with full fuel and 1,102 lb (500 kg) of payload, and allowable wave height 20-24 ins (50-60 cm). Another version is **Ladoga-9** with tractor propellers.
Molniya-100 is a projected multi-purpose transport, with a pilot and 15-19 passengers or 8 business passengers, or 4 litters and 2 attendants in an air ambulance role. All cabin seating can be removed for freight carrying. Wing span 46 ft 11 ins (14.3 m), length 41 ft (12.48 m), MTOW 9,480 lb (4,300 kg), payload 3,307 lb (1,500 kg), and maximum speed 216 kts (249 mph) 400 km/h on the power of 2 pusher-mounted 435 hp (324 kW) Teledyne Continental GTSIO-520-K piston engines. Range is 324 naut miles (373 miles) 600 km with full payload and 1,079 naut miles (1,243 miles) 2,000 km with full fuel, both at cruising speed of 175-205 kts (202-236 mph) 325-380 km/h.
Molniya-300 is a high-performance business and commuter aircraft, with 2 crew and 15 commuter passengers or 6 business passengers. Wing span 44 ft 1 ins (13.44 m), length 43 ft 4 ins (13.2 m), MTOW 14,990 lb (6,800 kg), payload 2,976 lb (1,350 kg), maximum speed 502 kts (578 mph) 930 km/h, and range 1,565-2,755 naut miles (1,800-3,170 miles) 2,900-5,100 km on the power of 2 Russian 2,700 lbf (12 kN) turbofans or US Allisons.

↑ Molniya-100 *(Piotr Butowski)*

↑ Molniya-300 *(Piotr Butowski)*

MAPO "Myasishchev" — Russia

Corporate address:
See Combat section for company details.

Myasishchev M-101 Gzhel and M-201 Sokol

Details: M-101T, except under Aircraft variants.
First flight: 31 March 1995 at Nizhny Novgorod (piloted by Viktor Vasenkov).
Certification: To conform to local AP-23 and US FAR Pt 23 certification requirements. Russian certificate had been expected in 1998, and US for M-101PW thereafter.
Role: Pressurized passenger, passenger/cargo, cargo or ambulance light transport. 4-seat VIP version under development.
Sales: Production started at Sokol plant in Nizhny Novgorod. First 4 built before Summer 1997 included 1 for static testing. Total of about 28 were to be built by the end of 1998.
Crew/passengers: 8 persons, including 1 or 2 pilots.
Wing control surfaces: Ailerons (with tabs) and flaps (45° deflection).
Tail control surfaces: Elevators and rudder, with tabs.
Engine: Walter M 601F turboprop, with a 7 ft 6 ins (2.3 m) AV-510 5-blade propeller.
Engine rating: 760 shp (567 kW) at take-off, 670.5 shp (500 kW) cruise.
Fuel system: 992 lb (450 kg).
Flight avionics/instrumentation: AlliedSignal Bendix/King suite.

Aircraft variants:
M-101T Gzhel has as standard a Walter engine, but a P&WC PT6A may be offered later. (Gzhel is an old village famous for its original majolica, faience and blue-and-white porcelain pottery, situated close to the town of Zhukovsky. It is also the name of a company marketing Russian country handicraft which sponsored a part of the work on M-101.) Initially, at project stage, the aircraft was also called ***Combi*** or Nelly.
M-101PW is a version powered by a P&WC PT6A-64 and developed by General Aviation joint venture formed by Myasishchev and General Aircraft USA and several other US investors (Myasishchev 25%). Expected initial sales in the USA

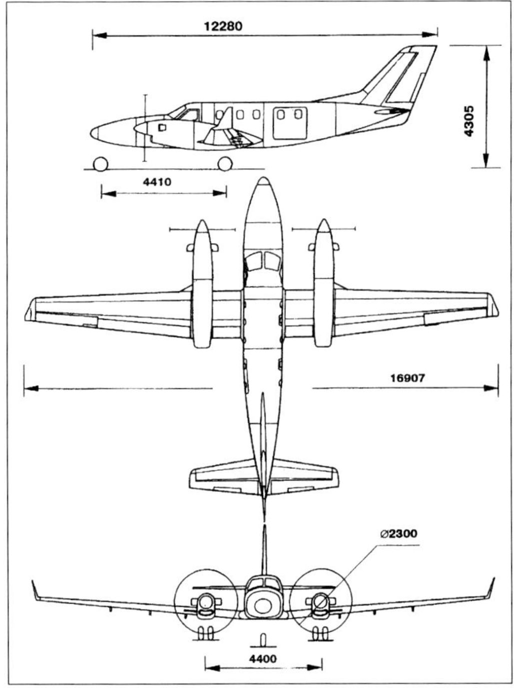

↑ **Myasishchev M-201 Sokol** *(courtesy MAPO "Myasishchev")*

are 25 aircraft, priced US$1.3 million each.
M-201 Sokol (Falcon), previously known as ***M-103***, is a projected twin-engined derivative of the M-101T for 1-2 pilots and 10 passengers. 2 M-601F engines. Wing span 55 ft 6 ins (16.907 m), length 40 ft 3.5 ins (12.28 m), height 14 ft 1 ins (4.3 m), maximum take-off weight 10,362 lb (4,700 kg), and payload 1,984 lb (900 kg). Maximum cruise speed will be 297 kts (342 mph) 550 km/h, range with maximum payload 1,079 naut miles (1,243 miles) 2,000 km, and maximum range 1,943 naut miles (2,237 miles) 3,600 km. ***M-201PW*** will have P&WC PT6A turboprops, and is a version developed by General Aircraft.

Details for M-101T Gzhel

PRINCIPAL DIMENSIONS:
Wing span: 42 ft 8 ins (13 m)
Maximum length: 32 ft 9 ins (9.975 m)
Maximum height: 12 ft 2.5 ins (3.72 m)

CABIN:
Length: 14 ft 11.5 ins (4.56 m)
Width: 4 ft 4 ins (1.32 m)
Height: 4 ft 2 ins (1.26 m)
Volume: 266 cu ft (7.53 m^3)
Cabin door: 4 ft 0.5 ins × 3 ft 9 ins (1.23 × 1.15 m)

WINGS:
Area: 183.63 sq ft (17.06 m^2)
Aspect ratio: 9.906

UNDERCARRIAGE:
Type: Retractable, with nosewheel. Can operate from prepared or unprepared airstrips
Wheel base: 9 ft 3 ins (2.826 m)
Wheel track: 9 ft 10 ins (3 m)

WEIGHTS:
Empty: 4,445 lb (2,016 kg)
Maximum take-off: 6,614 lb (3,000 kg)
Payload: 1,190 lb (540 kg)

PERFORMANCE:
Maximum speed: 283 kts (326 mph) 525 km/h
Cruise speed: 194-243 kts (224-280 mph) 360-450 km/h
Stall speed: 61-68 kts (70-78 mph) 112-125 km/h
Landing speed: 78-81 kts (90-93 mph) 145-150 km/h, *45° flaps*
Required runway length: 1,641-1,969 ft (500-600 m) unimproved
Take-off distance: 1,050 ft (320 m)
Landing distance: 919 ft (280 m) with thrust reverse
Time to 24,935 ft (7,600 m): 25 minutes
Cruise altitude: 24,935 ft (7,600 m)
Range: 761 naut miles (876 miles), 1,410 km, with 45 minutes reserve

Myasishchev M-202PW Olen (Deer)

First flight: Project only.
Role: Multi-purpose. Larger-size development of the Indian M-102 Saras, designed solely by Myasishchev with no Indian participation. To be assembled in the USA by General Aviation joint venture formed by Myasishchev and General Aircraft USA and several other US investors (Myasishchev 25%).
Crew/passengers: 2 pilots plus a maximum of 19 passengers. Business version for fewer passengers, with additional cabin features including tables, galley, and so on.
Wing characteristics: Low mounted and slightly swept.
Wing control surfaces: Ailerons and flaps.
Tail control surfaces: Elevators (with tab) and rudder (with tab).
Flight control system: Mechanical/manual, except for electric flaps and tabs.
Engines: 2 Pratt & Whitney Canada PT6A-67R turboprops with 7 ft 6 ins (2.3 m) diameter pusher propellers.
Engine rating: Each in 1,400 shp (1,044 kW) class.
Radar: Weather.

↑ **Myasishchev M-101T Gzhel** *(Piotr Butowski)*

Details for M-202PW

PRINCIPAL DIMENSIONS:
Wing span: 59 ft 1 ins (18 m)
Maximum length: 51 ft 10 ins (15.8 m)
Maximum height: 18 ft 4.5 ins (5.6 m)

UNDERCARRIAGE:
Type: Retractable, with single steerable nosewheel

WEIGHTS:
Maximum take-off: 16,314 lb (7,400 kg)
Payload: 3,968 lb (1,800 kg)

PERFORMANCE:
Cruise speed: 302 kts (348 mph) 560 km/h
Operating ceiling: 29,525 ft (9,000 m)
Range with full fuel: 1,727 naut miles (1,988 miles) 3,200 km
Range with full payload: 1,133 naut miles (1,305 miles) 2,100 km

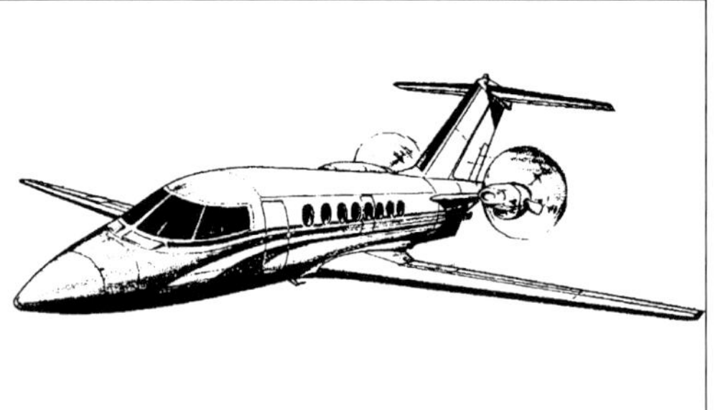
↑ **Myasishchev M-202PW Olen** *(courtesy MAPO "Myasishchev")*

Myasishchev M-203PW Barsuk (Badger)

First flight: Project started in 1996.

Details for M-203PW

PRINCIPAL DIMENSIONS:
Wing span: 47 ft 11 ins (14.6 m)
Maximum length: 30 ft 1 ins (9.17 m) flight line
Maximum height: 10 ft 11.5 ins (3.34 m) parked

UNDERCARRIAGE:
Type: Fixed, with tailwheel

WEIGHTS:
Maximum take-off: 6,173 lb (2,800 kg)
Payload: 1,984 lb (900 kg)

PERFORMANCE:
Maximum speed: 151 kts (174 mph) 280 km/h
Cruise altitude: 9,840 ft (3,000 m)
Take-off distance over a 50 ft (15 m) obstacle: 853 ft (260 m)
Landing distance over a 50 ft (15 m) obstacle: 821 ft (250 m)
Range with full fuel: 809 naut miles (932 miles) 1,500 km
Range with full payload: 539 naut miles (621 miles) 1,000 km

Aims

- Simple structure and easy maintenance.
- Operation from small unpaved airstrips due to large wing and strong spring undercarriage.

Details

Role: General purpose aircraft, mainly suited to passenger and cargo carrying flights but also for agricultural work, patrol, ambulance and aerial photography. Project developed by General Aviation joint venture.
Crew/passengers: 10, including 1-2 pilots.
Cabin access: Large sliding door on port side of fuselage.
Wing characteristics: Braced, high mounted, tapering wings with slight dihedral.
Wing control surfaces: Ailerons (starboard trim) and flaps.
Tail control surfaces: Balanced elevators and rudder (with tab).

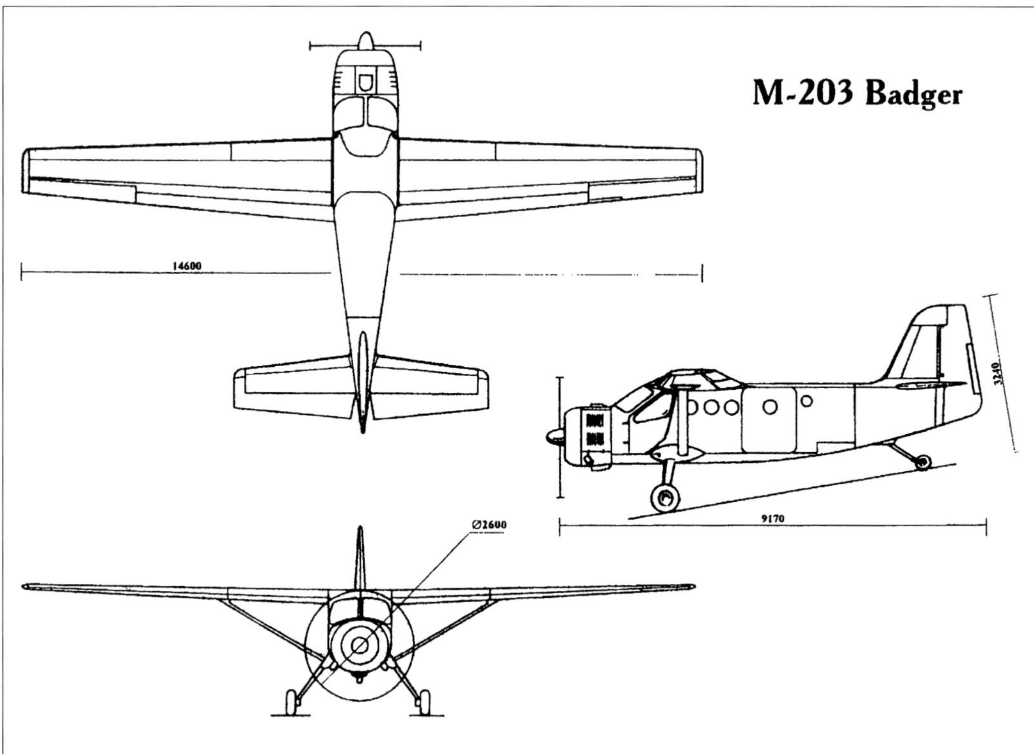

↑ **Myasishchev M-203PW Barsuk (Badger)** *(courtesy MAPO "Myasishchev")*

Engine: Single Pratt & Whitney R-985 radial piston engine.
Engine rating: 450 hp (335.6 kW)
Flight avionics/instrumentation: VFR or IFR.

Myasishchev M-500

First flight: Not flown at time of writing. Full-scale mock-up shown in 1995.

Aims:

- 67.8 hectares per flight hour productivity in an agricultural role. Up to 48% cost reduction per hectare in comparison with the An-2.
- Recoup of capital investment is estimated at 2.11 years at 540 flying hours per year, or 1.87 years at 1,000 flying hours per year.
- 5,000 flying hours airframe life.

Role: Agricultural and forestry, with variants suited to cargo carrying, air mail, patrol, ambulance, aerial photography, primary pilot training and business flights.
Sales: Proposed for a competition for modern agricultural aircraft, opened in early 1990s by Russia's ministry of agriculture. Later competition cancelled, but Myasishchev continues the programme at a low rate.
Crew/passengers: Pilot plus 7 for passenger version.
Chemical tank/hopper capacity: 2,094 lb (950 kg), loaded through the top of the fuselage, aft of the cockpit.
Spray equipment: Carried at the trailing-edge of the wings.
Wing characteristics: Straight, low mounted, with dihedral. Winglets.
Wing control surfaces: Ailerons and flaps.
Tail control surfaces: Continuous elevator and balanced rudder, with tabs.

Details for M-500 with M-14NTK engine

PRINCIPAL DIMENSIONS:
Wing span: 49 ft 2.5 ins (15 m)
Maximum length: 34 ft 4.5 ins (10.48 m)
Maximum height: 11 ft 10.5 ins (3.62 m)

WINGS:
Aerofoil section: P4-15M
Area: 290.625 sq ft (27 m^2)
Aspect ratio: 8.33

UNDERCARRIAGE:
Type: Fixed, with tailwheel
Wheel base: 23 ft 8 ins (7.22 m)
Wheel track: 9 ft 2 ins (2.8 m)

WEIGHTS:
Empty: 2,925 lb (1,327 kg)
Normal take-off: 5,291 lb (2,400 kg)
Allowable take-off: 6,393 lb (2,900 kg)
Payload: 2,094 lb (950 kg)

PERFORMANCE:
Spray speed: 65-113 kts (75-130 mph) 120-210 km/h
Take-off distance: 1,477 ft (450 m) from unpaved airfield, 1,411 ft (430 m) from concrete, 30° C temperature
Landing distance: 1,592 ft (485 m) unpaved or paved, 30° C temperature
Operating altitude for spraying: 3.2 to 98 ft (1 to 30 m)
Ferry range: 539 naut miles (621 miles) 1,000 km, or 809 naut miles (932 miles) 1,500 km with TDA-450 engine, with reserve
Duration: 2 hours, with reserve

Engine: Single AOOT OKBM/Voronezh M-14NTK radial piston engine uprated to 430 hp (321 kW). A Motor/Ufa TDA-450 turbo Diesel engine rated at 450 shp (336 kW) is being considered.
Fuel system: 214 lb (97 kg). Consumption in ACO, 190 g/hp per hour.

↑ **Mock-up of the Myasishchev M-500** *(Piotr Butowski)*

Pegas — Russia

Corporate address:
140160 Zhukovsky, Moskovskaya ob., LII im. Gromova.
Telephone: +7 095 5567860
Facsimile: +7 095 5565334
Founded:
1991.
Information:
E. Sabadash (Chief Designer).

Pegas Chirok (Teal)

First flight: Project launched in October 1991, with first flight originally planned for 1997. Full-scale mock-up built at the time of writing in 1998.

↑ **Pegas Chirok (Teal)** *(Piotr Butowski)*

Role: Light passenger/cargo amphibian, with patrol, ambulance and tourist roles.
Crew/passengers: Pilot plus 2 persons.
Wing characteristics: Low-mounted, with blended fuselage/wing centre section and unswept outer panels.
Wing control surfaces: Full-span flaps and interceptors at outer panels.
Tail control surfaces: Inverted V-type (tailplane span 9 ft 1 ins, 2.76 m). Rudders in line with propellers.
Construction materials: All composites (carbonfibre). Airframe life 5,000 flight hours.
Engines: 2 Rotax 582UL piston engines, with 4 blade ducted pusher propellers. Additionally, AOOT OKBM/Voronezh M18-02 (55 hp, 41 kW) piston engine to drive 2 centrifugal fans creating an air cushion.
Engine rating: 64.4 hp (48 kW).
Fuel system: Total of 250 litres in 2 tanks.
Flight avionics/instrumentation: See Aircraft variants.

Aircraft variants:
Chirok-V (visual) will have only simple instrumentation to operate according to VFR.
Chirok-P (polnyi, full) will receive new-generation Lilia (Lily) integrated avionics suite, for IFR.

Details for Chirok

PRINCIPAL DIMENSIONS:
Wing span: 32 ft 10 ins (10.01 m)
Maximum length: 19 ft 4 ins (5.89 m)
Maximum height: 7 ft 4.5 ins (2.25 m)

CABIN:
Length: 7 ft 3 ins (2.2 m)
Width: 4 ft 1 ins (1.24 m)
Height: 4 ft 1 ins (1.24 m)

WINGS:
Aerofoil section: GA(W)-1
Area: 106.13 sq ft (9.86 m^2)
Aspect ratio: 10.16
Thickness/chord ratio: 17%
Dihedral: 5° on outer panels
Incidence: +3°

UNDERCARRIAGE:
Type: Combined, with (basic) 7 ft 3 ins to 8 ft 2 ins (2.2 to 2.5 m) wide and 14 ft 9 ins (4.5 m) long air-cushion formed between underfuselage inflatables, and (auxiliary) retractable nosewheel (300 × 125 mm) and single rear ski

WEIGHTS:
Empty, operational: 816 lb (370 kg)
Normal take-off: 1,411 lb (640 kg)
Maximum take-off: 1,543 lb (700 kg)
Payload: 463 lb (210 kg)

PERFORMANCE:
Maximum speed: 135 kts (155 mph) 250 km/h
Cruise speed: 108 kts (124 mph) 200 km/h
Stall speed: 38 kts (44 mph) 70 km/h
Take-off distance: 230 ft (70 m)
Ceiling: 13,125 ft (4,000 m)
Range with full payload: 216 naut miles (248 miles) 400 km
Ferry range: 1,079 naut miles (1,243 miles) 2,000 km

REDA-MDT Ltd

Russia

Corporate address:
Matrosskaya Tishina, d.23/7, korp. 5, Moscow 107076.

Telephone: +7 095 268 4664
Facsimile: +7 095 268 0036

Founded:
1991.

ACTIVITIES

■ The twin-engined and 4-seat **Prize** is under development, based on the Pony technology demonstrator, though not built at the time of writing; take-off weight 4,409 lb (2,000 kg) and with 2 ducted Teledyne Continental IO-240 or Textron Lycoming O-235 piston engines.

REDA-MDT Pony

First flight: First near-ground flights of Pony performed on 19 December 1994 on the lake near Astrakhan (pilot Viktor Zabolotsky). After being rebuilt (including soft wing skins replaced by metal skins), in September 1995 full-scale test flights at Dubna began.
Role: 2-seat amphibian.
Sales: 4 airframes (including 1 for static tests) built by Pony JSC, established by REDA-MDT in 1993.

↑ **REDA-MDT Pony** *(Piotr Butowski)*

Details for Pony

PRINCIPAL DIMENSIONS:
Wing span: 37 ft 9 ins (11.5 m)
Maximum length: 31 ft 2 ins (9.5 m)

UNDERCARRIAGE:
Type: Retractable, with nosewheel. Permanent floats

WEIGHTS:
Maximum take-off: 2,050 lb (930 kg)
Payload: 220 lb (100 kg)

PERFORMANCE:
Maximum speed: 97 kts (112 mph) 180 km/h
Take-off distance: 394 ft (120 m) land, 985 ft (300 m) water
Landing distance: 263 ft (80 m) land, 394 ft (120 m) water
Range: 270-323 naut miles (310-373 miles) 500-600 km
Duration: 3.5 hours

Engines: Originally, Pony had a single 77.8 hp (58 kW) Rotax 912A, later replaced by a 140 hp (104 kW) LOM M-332AR.

SAU Scientific-Production Corporation

Russia

Corporate address:
103062 Moscow; ul. Zhukovskogo, 8.

Telephone: +7 095 9162973, 9213359
Facsimile: +7 095 9163068
E-mail: sau@tayfi.msk.ru

Founded:
1993 to design and manufacture the R-50 Robert amphibian.

Information:
Yuri Usoltsev (Chief Designer).

FACILITIES

■ SAU (Samoloty-Amfibii Universalnye, Universal Amphibian Aircraft) is a corporation with Amokom of Moscow (financial support), LAT of Taganrog (design), TsAGI of Moscow (scientific leadership), Dubnenski Mashinostroitelnyi Zavod of Dubna (manufacturing) and Raduga of Dubna (certification tests) shareholders.
■ R-50 Robert amphibian has been designed by LAT (Lyogkaya Aviatsia Taganroga, Taganrog's Light Aircraft), 347900 Taganrog, ul. Chekhova, 2, GSP-85; *telephone* and *facsimile* +7 86344 60474.
■ Series production will be undertaken by Dubna Machinebuilding Plant (which see).

SAU R-50 Robert, and R-01 and R-02 technology demonstrators

First flight: 17 May 1989 for R-01, piloted by Yevgeni Lakhmastov, and 20 September 1996 for R-02. R-50 Robert had originally been expected to fly in 1997.
Certification: Designed to meet AP-23 (FAR Pt 23) standards.
Airframe life: 10,000 flying hours or 10,000 cycles (including 2,500 on water).

↑ **SAU R-02 technology demonstrator for the R-50 Robert** *(Piotr Butowski)*

Development

■ 1989. Design started at Taganrog.
■ December 1995. Mock-up of R-50 accepted by state commission.

Details (R-50 Robert, unless stated)

Role: Light amphibian, suited to passenger, cargo, training, surveillance, medevac and firefighting.
Sales: After R-01 and R-02 technology demonstrators, a series of 6 R-50s were to be built at Dubna Machinebuilding Plant. Approximate price US $280,000. Manufacturer expects to sell 230-520 aircraft in Russia plus 250-330 abroad (mainly Latin America and South-East Asia).
Crew/passengers: Pilot plus 5 passengers, or litter and 2 attendants. Air conditioned cabin.
Wing characteristics: Mid-mounted, unswept, with wide and fattened root sections producing the hydrodynamic force during take-off and alighting.
Wing control surfaces: Ailerons; no flaps.
Tail control surfaces: Conventional, with elevators (port trim tab) and rudder (trim tab). Tailplane span 14 ft 0.5 ins (4.28 m).
Fuselage: Double-stepped, V-shaped hull. 5 watertight bulkheads. Special shape of hull ensures dynamic stability during take-off and alighting; underwing floats are not needed.
Construction materials: Aluminium-alloy structure with mainly composite skins.
Engines: 2 LOM M337AR piston engines mounted on pylons on the wing roots. 3-blade V546a pusher propellers, each with a diameter of 6 ft 3 ins (1.9 m).
Engine rating: Each 210 hp (157 kW).

↑ **SAU R-50 Robert impression** *(courtesy SAU Scientific-Production Corporation)*

Details for R-50 Robert

PRINCIPAL DIMENSIONS:
Wing span: 50 ft 6 ins (15.4 m)
Maximum length: 37 ft 5 ins (11.4 m)
Maximum height: 13 ft 3 ins (4.04 m)

CABIN:
Length: 10 ft 4 ins (3.14 m)
Width: 4 ft 5 ins (1.35 m)
Height: 4 ft 1 ins (1.25 m)
Volume: 162.4 cu ft (4.6 m^3)

WINGS:
Area, gross: 310.22 sq ft (28.82 m^2)
Aspect ratio: 8.23
Dihedral/anhedral: 3.1° anhedral at leading edge of wing root section; no anhedral/dihedral at trailing edge; considerable dihedral on outer panels

UNDERCARRIAGE:
Type: Retractable, with nosewheel
Main wheel tyre size: 500 × 150 mm
Nose wheel tyre size: 400 × 150 mm
Wheel track: 14 ft 0.5 ins (4.28 m)

WEIGHTS:
Empty: 3,113 lb (1,412 kg)
Maximum take-off: 5,071-5,291 lb (2,300-2,400 kg)
Payload: 948 lb (430 kg)

PERFORMANCE:
Maximum operating speed: 140 kts (161 mph) 260 km/h
Cruise speed: 119 kts (137 mph) 220 km/h
Stall speed: 53 kts (61 mph) 97 km/h, *with flaps*
Landing speed: 61 kts (70 mph) 112 km/h
Take-off distance: 1,247 ft (380 m) from water, 886 ft (270 m) from land
Landing distance: 886 ft (270 m) water, 821 ft (250 m) land
Ceiling: 9,840 ft (3,000 m), service
G limits: +3.8, -1.62
Range with full fuel: 809 naut miles (932 miles) 1,500 km with 419 lb (190 kg) payload
Range with full payload: 270 naut miles (310 miles) 500 km
Maximum duration: 8 hours
Maximum allowable wave height: 1 ft 8 ins (0.5 m)
Required water depth: 3 ft 11 ins (1.2 m)

Fuel system: 416 litres (794 lb, 360 kg) in 2 tanks inside leading-edge areas of wing roots.
Hydraulic system: For undercarriage.
Braking system: Disc brakes on main wheels.
Radar: Weather radar optional.
Flight system avionics/instrumentation: VOR/ILS, GPS, and autopilot.

Aircraft variants:
R-01 is the single-seat technology demonstrator. Take-off weight 970 lb (440 kg). Single 44 hp (33 kW) Robin 44EC piston engine with pusher propeller of 4 ft 8 ins (1.43 m) diameter.
R-02 is the second demonstrator (named ***R-01M*** at project stage), this time a 2-seater. It is also considered suitable for training. Maximum take-off weight 1,235 lb (560 kg), Rotax 912A3 piston engine (79 hp, 59 kW), maximum cruise speed 86 kts (99 mph) 160 km/h, take-off distance 1,969 ft (600 m), landing distance 1,641 ft (500 m), service ceiling 9,840 ft (3,000 m), range 270 naut miles (310 miles) 500 km, ferry range 458 naut miles (528 miles) 850 km, and maximum wave height 1 ft (0.3 m).
R-50 (named ***Robert*** in memory of Robert Bartini, an Italian aircraft designer working in the Soviet Union, particularly in Taganrog) is the resulting 5-seat general-purpose amphibian, as described.
R-50AML (aero-mobilnaya laboratoriya) or ***R-50GF*** (geo-fizicheskiy) is an ecological-monitoring version.
R-50P (pozharnyi) is a firefighting version, mainly for fire patrol, but can also take up 700 litres of water during the take-off run, or 400 litres when filled at an airfield.
R-50M is a planned further development with the cabin lengthened by 2 ft 6 ins (75 cm), maximum take-off weight 5,952 lb (2,700 kg), and range 324 naut miles (373 miles) 600 km with a 1,235 lb (560 kg) payload when using current engines, or 405 naut miles (466 miles) 750 km with 1,433 lb (650 kg) payload when new 240 hp (179 kW) engines have been fitted.

SAVIAT JSC — Russia

Full name: Spetsialnye AVAIAtsionnye Tekhonologii, Special Aviation Technologies.	
Corporate address: 123424 Moscow, Volokolamskoye shosse, d. 73 komn. 327.	
Telephone: +7 095 490 0772 **Facsimile:** +7 095 490 0615	
Founded: 1990.	
Employees: 20.	
Information: Vladimir S. Savinich.	

ACTIVITIES

▪ Development of light aircraft made from composite materials. From the E-1 (described below), a 16-seat version known as **E-5** of similar configuration is being prepared. E-5 design data includes a wing span of 32 ft 10 ins (10 m), length of 35 ft 5 ins (10.8 m), and a maximum take-off weight of 9,590 lb (4,350 kg).

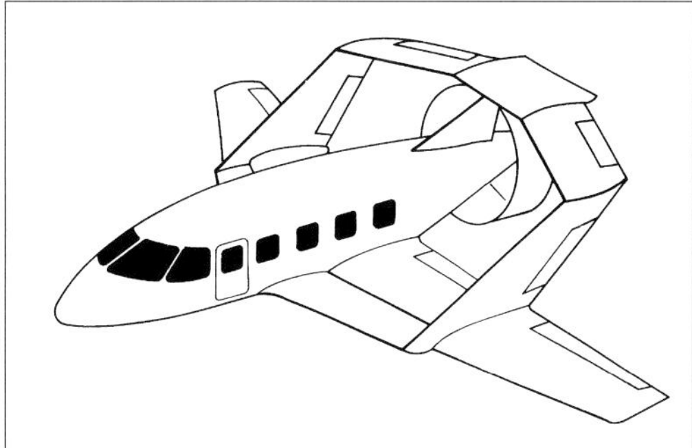

↑ **Proposed SAVIAT E-5**

SAVIAT E-1

Details for SAVIAT E-1

PRINCIPAL DIMENSIONS:
Wing span: 23 ft 3 ins (7.08 m)
Maximum length: 19 ft 8 ins (6 m)
Maximum height: 10 ft 4 ins (3.14 m)

CABIN:
Length: 8 ft 10 ins (2.7 m)
Width: 4 ft 6.5 ins (1.38 m)
Height: 4 ft 2.5 ins (1.28 m)
Volume: 97.1 cu ft (2.75 m^3)
Main door size: 3 ft 7 ins × 3 ft 9.5 ins (1.1 × 1.15 m)

WINGS:
Aerofoil section: P-351
Area: 129.3 sq ft (12.01 m^2), gross
Chord at root: lower wing 3 ft 11 ins (1.2 m), upper wing 3 ft 3 ins (1.0 m)
Chord at tip: 2 ft (0.6 m)
Thickness/chord ratio: 15%
Dihedral/anhedral: lower wing 9° dihedral, upper wing 6° anhedral

CANARDS:
Span: 13 ft 9 ins (4.2 m)
Area: 38.6 sq ft (3.59 m^2)
Sweepback: 30°

TAIL UNIT:
Fin height: 4 ft 5 ins (1.35 m)

UNDERCARRIAGE:
Type: Retractable, with nosewheel
Main wheel tyre size: 400 × 150 mm
Nose wheel tyre size: 310 × 135 mm
Wheel base: 7 ft 10 ins (2.38 m)
Wheel track: 7 ft 3 ins (2.2 m)
Turning radius: 10 ft 10 ins (3.3 m)

WEIGHTS:
Empty, operating: 1,764 lb (800 kg)
Normal take-off: 2,866 lb (1,300 kg)
Maximum take-off: 2,998 lb (1,360 kg)
Maximum landing: 2,888 lb (1,310 kg)
Payload, normal: 771 lb (350 kg)

PERFORMANCE:
Maximum operating speed: 172 kts (199 mph) 320 km/h
Cruise speed: 162 kts (186 mph) 300 km/h
Stall speed: 65 kts (75 mph) 120 km/h
Take-off distance: 755 ft (230 m)
Landing distance: 689 ft (210 m)
Maximum climb rate: 1,575 ft (480 m) per minute, at sea level
Ceiling: 18,865 ft (5,750 m), service
Range with full fuel: 755 naut miles (870 miles) 1,400 km
Range with full payload: 323 naut miles (373 miles) 600 km

First flight: Not flown at time of writing. Development began in 1991, and in 1992 a model (1:3.725 scale) was tested in the TsAGI wind tunnel. In the following year a mock-up was built of composite materials, but in 1995 further development was frozen because of a lack of funding, though restarted in September 1996 with participation by MIG "MAPO-M".
Certification: Designed to meet FAR-23 standards.
Role: Light passenger, training, ambulance or cargo aircraft. Has parachute emergency landing system.
Sales: Full-size mock-up only at the time of writing. In 1997, it was reported that talks with a Malaysian company about joint manufacturing of E-1 took place.
Crew/passengers: Pilot plus 3 or 4 passengers (seat pitch 37.4 ins, 95 cm), or a litter and a medical attendant in ambulance role, or up to 992 lb (450 kg) of cargo.
Baggage compartment: 11.3 cu ft (0.32 m^3) volume.
Wing characteristics: Rhomboidal-like biplane box, consisting of upper and lower wings connected at tips by vertical posts. Lower wings swept 24.25°, upper wings with negative sweep angle -5°.
Wing control surfaces: Slotted flaps (deflection 30°) on lower wings. Upper wings have elevators (±20°) at root, elevons (+20°, -30°) in the centre and ailerons (±20°) near the wing tips.
Tail control surfaces: Swept tailplane with 2-section rudder (±25°).
Canard surfaces: Canard with an elevator (+20°, -10°).
Flight control system: Includes manual/mechanical and automatic fly-by-wire systems. Manual system for canards, elevons, lower section of rudder, and flaps. Automatic system for elevators, ailerons, and upper section of rudder. Automatic control system provides flight stabilization only (yaw, roll, pitch, heading and height). Dual controls for training version.
Fuselage: Monocoque.
Construction materials: Mainly laminated glassfibre reinforced plastics, with some use of carbonfibre plastics, and limited use of aluminium and titanium.
Engine: Textron Lycoming IO-540-D4A5 piston engine, with ducted AV-83TG 4-blade controllable-pitch pusher propeller. Use of VAZ-430-4 rotary piston engine is planned for the Russian market.
Engine rating: 260 hp (194 kW) at 2700 rpm.
Fuel system: 210 litres.
Hydraulic system: Used for undercarriage.
Electrical system: 24V, and 115V/400Hz AC.
De-icing system: Electric, fitted to leading edges of canard, wing and propeller blades.
Fire system: Extinguisher in engine compartment; fuel cut-off valve.
Radar: None.
Flight system avionics/instrumentation: KX 165 navigation system, GPS, KT 76A transponder, marker, KY 196A com radio.

↑ **Full-scale mock-up of SAVIAT E-1** *(courtesy SAVIAT)*

SibNIA named after Chaplygin — Russia

Corporate address:
See Combat section for company details.

SibNIA Dzhinn

First flight: Originally expected in 1997. Not flown at time of writing.
Role: 2-seat lightplane, suited to training, patrol, agricultural and other work.
Crew/passengers: 2 side-by-side in heated cockpit, with baggage compartment at rear.
Wing control surfaces: Ailerons and plain flaps.
Tail control surfaces: Elevators on a 9 ft 6 ins (2.9 m) span tailplane, and rudder.
Flight control system: Mechanical.
Construction materials: Metal and wood.
Engine: LOM M332 piston engine, with 5 ft 11 ins (1.8 m) 2-blade propeller. Rotax 912 is an option.
Engine rating: 140 hp (104.4 kW).
Fuel system: 50 litres.
Flight avionics/instrumentation: VFR or customer's choice.

Details for Dzhinn

PRINCIPAL DIMENSIONS:
Wing span: 30 ft 7.5 ins (9.334 m)
Maximum length: 22 ft 4 ins (6.8 m)
Maximum height: 8 ft 2.5 ins (2.5 m)

UNDERCARRIAGE:
Type: Fixed, with nosewheel

WEIGHTS:
Empty: 926 lb (420 kg)
Maximum take-off: 1,411 lb (640 kg)
Take-off with single pilot: 1,234 lb (560 kg)

PERFORMANCE:
Maximum speed: 119 kts (137 mph) 220 km/h
Cruise speed: 81 kts (93 mph) 150 km/h
Stall speed: 40 kts (46 mph) 74 km/h
Take-off distance: 378 ft (115 m), from concrete
Landing distance: 361 ft (110 m), on concrete
Climb rate: 1,180 ft (360 m) per minute
G limit: +4 at MTOW
Range with full fuel: 270 naut miles (310 miles) 500 km

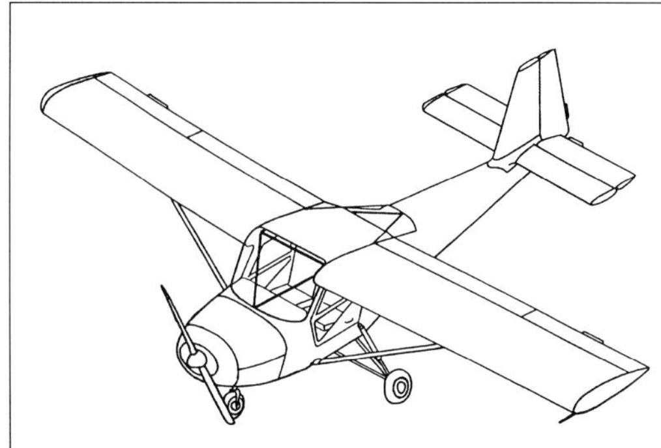
↑ SibNIA Dzhinn 2-seat lightplane

Students Design Bureau SKB at Samara State Aerospace University — Russia

Corporate address:
443086 Samara, Moskovskoe Street, 34, korp. 3, kv 1.
Telephone: +7 8462 357281
Founded:
1955.
Information:
Dmitri Suslakov.

SKB Samara Che-15

Comments: 2-seat lightplane with float undercarriage (optional wheels or skis), powered by a Rotax 582 engine. Cruise speed 54 kts (62 mph) 100 km/h and range 189 naut miles (217 miles) 350 km.

↑ **SKB Samara Che-15** *(Piotr Butowski)*

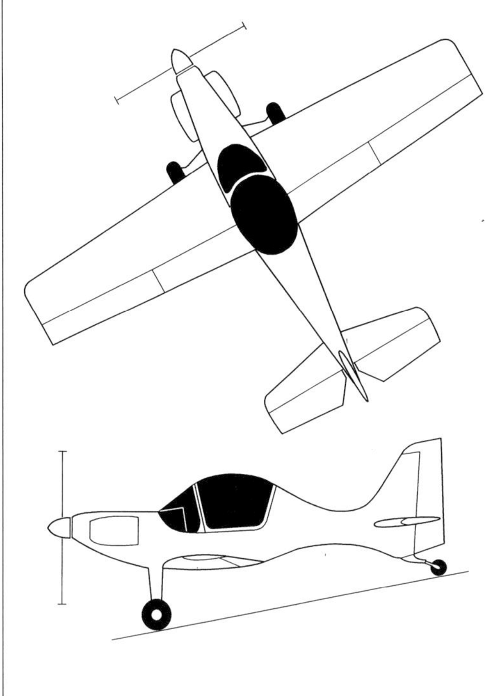
↑ **SKB Samara A-16** *(Piotr Butowski)*

↑ **SKB Samara S-202K** *(Pascal K. Anjou)*

SKB Samara A-16

First flight: Virtually complete airframe was displayed at MAK"97; was to fly within a few months of engine availability.
Role: Single-seat aerobatic and recreational low-wing monoplane.
Construction materials: Fully glassfibre composites, except for Cast-V fabric covering the wings.
Engine: Hirth F30 piston engine.
Engine rating: 95 hp (71 kW).

Details for A-16

PRINCIPAL DIMENSIONS:
Wing span: 18 ft 0.5 ins (5.5 m)
Maximum length: 14 ft 9 ins (4.5 m)

UNDERCARRIAGE:
Type: Fixed, with tailwheel

WEIGHTS:
Empty: 441 lb (200 kg)
Maximum take-off: 661 lb (300 kg)

PERFORMANCE:
Maximum diving speed: 194 kts (224 mph) 360 km/h
Maximum speed: 140 kts (162 mph) 260 km/h, level
Approach speed: 51 kts (59 mph) 95 km/h
G limit: +11
Range: 135 naut miles (155 miles) 250 km
Ferry range: 323 naut miles (373 miles) 600 km

SKB Samara S-202, and S-302 and S-400 projects

Details: S-202, except under Aircraft variants.
First flight: 19 June 1994 (accumulated some 200 flying hours at time of writing).
Certification: Built to meet JAR-VLA regulations.
Role: 2-seat flying-boat/amphibian, with roles including recreational, patrol and training.
Control surfaces: Conventional 3-axis.
Engine: 2 piston engines, with 2-blade pusher propellers, installed on above-fuselage pylons. Original Russian Vikhr-30s replaced by RMZ-640s (each 30 hp, 22.4 kW). Proposed engines include Rotax 503s or a single Hirth F30.

Aircraft variants:
S-202 is an amphibious lightplane, as detailed. 2 built. Named ***S-202K*** (kolesnyi, wheel) when fitted with a wheel undercarriage, or S-202L (lyzhnyi, ski) when fitted with a ski undercarriage.
S-302 is a development of the S-202 with new wing. Prototype under construction at time of writing.
S-400 is an enlarged 4-seat version of S-202, powered by 2 Hirth F30 engines. Fully retractable undercarriage, and new wing with GA(W)-1 aerofoil section and slotted flaps. Prototype under construction at time of writing.

Details for S-202 with RMZ-640 engines

PRINCIPAL DIMENSIONS:
Wing span: 39 ft 0.5 ins (11.9 m)
Maximum length: 23 ft (7 m)

WINGS:
Aerofoil section: P-IIIA-15

UNDERCARRIAGE:
Type: Removable fixed wheel or ski type

WEIGHTS:
Empty: 728 lb (330 kg)
Maximum take-off: 1,212 lb (550 kg)

PERFORMANCE:
Maximum speed: 73 kts (84 mph) 135 km/h
Cruise speed: 59 kts (68 mph) 110 km/h
Approach speed: 32 kts (37 mph) 60 km/h
Take-off distance: 493 ft (150 m) from ground, 821 ft (250 m) from water, with maximum load
G limits: +4.5, -2.25
Range: 243 naut miles (279 miles) 450 km, maximum
Range with 2 crew: 135 naut miles (155 miles) 250 km

Sukhoi Design Bureau — Russia

Corporate address:
See Combat section for company details.

Sukhoi S-16

First flight: Project only.
Role: Light general-purpose transport, including passenger, cargo and ambulance.

Details for Sukhoi S-16 with PT6A-135 engines, *with weights and performance for TDA-450F engines in italics*

PRINCIPAL DIMENSIONS:
Wing span: 46 ft 3 ins (14.1 m)
Maximum length: 43 ft (13.1 m)
Maximum height: 12 ft 9.5 ins (3.9 m)

CABIN:
Length: 16 ft 9.5 ins (5.12 m)
Width: 5 ft 1 ins (1.54 m)
Height: 4 ft 7 ins (1.4 m)

WINGS:
Area: 237.9 sq ft (22.1 m^2), gross
Aspect ratio: 9

WEIGHTS:
Empty, operating: 6,151 lb (2,790 kg), *5,842 lb (2,650 kg)*
Maximum take-off: 10,582 lb (4,800 kg), *10,251 lb (4,650 kg)*

PERFORMANCE:
Cruise speed: 281 kts (323 mph) 520 km/h, *216 kts (249 mph) 400 km/h*
Required runway length: 2,133 ft (650 m), *1,610 ft (500 m)*
Range with full fuel: 755 naut miles (870 miles) 1,400 km, *1,295 naut miles (1,491 miles) 2,400 km*
Range with full payload: 270 naut miles (310 miles) 500 km, *453 naut miles (522 miles) 840 km*

↑ Model of the Sukhoi S-16 *(Piotr Butowski)*

Sales: Production expected at Tbilisi, Georgia. Price $2.3 million.
Crew/passengers: 1-2 crew plus 16 passengers, or 8 passengers and 2,205 lb (1,000 kg) of cargo, or 4,409 lb (2,000 kg) of cargo.
Engines: 2 Pratt & Whitney Canada PT6A-135 turboprops, with advanced pusher propellers. A variant with Russian TDA-450F engines (each 450 hp, 335.6 kW) is under consideration.
Engine rating: Each 680 shp (507 kW).

Sukhoi S-21

First flight: Project only.

Development

▪ 1989. Work started, possibly based on a former military project for a future interceptor. Association with Gulfstream Aerospace on the project ended in 1992.
▪ 1993. Detailed design started, but soon stopped due to lack of funding. See Sales.

Details for S-21 (subject to change)

PRINCIPAL DIMENSIONS:
Wing span: 65 ft 4 ins (19.92 m)
Maximum length: 120 ft 9 ins (36.8 m)
Maximum height: 31 ft 4 ins (9.55 m)

CABIN:
Length: 16 ft 10 ins (5.125 m)
Width: 6 ft 7 ins (2 m)
Height: 6 ft 1 ins (1.86 m)

WEIGHTS:
Empty: 54,167 lb (24,570 kg)
Maximum take-off: 114,199 lb (51,800 kg)
Payload: 2,006 lb (910 kg)

PERFORMANCE:
Supersonic cruise speed: 1,147 kts (1,320 mph) 2,125 km/h, or Mach 2
Subsonic cruise speed: 548 kts (631 mph) 1,015 km/h, or Mach 0.95
Required runway length: 6,496 ft (1,980 m)
Range: 3,993 naut miles (4,598 miles) 7,400 km

↑ Model of the Sukhoi S-21, with Su-49 above *(Piotr Butowski)*

Details

Role: Supersonic business jet.
Airport limits: To comply with all emission/noise requirements.
Sales: Project still mentioned by Sukhoi as a priority programme, while another supersonic business jet project, the **S-51 for 68 passengers**, has been terminated.
Crew/passengers: 2 flight crew and 6-10 passengers.
Wing characteristics: Canard layout, with cranked delta main wings.
Engines: 3 Aviadvigatel/Perm D-21A1 turbofans, developed from the MiG-31's D-30F-6 engine.
Engine rating: 16,525 lbf (73.5 kN).
Fuel system: Maximum 58,466 lb (26,520 kg).
Flight avionics/instrumentation: Honeywell navigation.

Sukhoi S-96

First flight: Project only.
Role: Executive aircraft (ICAO II landings).
Sales: Production planned at Tbilisi, Georgia.
Crew/passengers: 1-2 crew plus 4-8 passengers.
Engines: 2 Soyuz/Moscow TV128-100 propfans, with 2 ft 11 ins (0.9 m) diameter propellers.
Engine rating: Each 1,300 shp (969.4 kW).
Fuel system: 2,646 lb (1,200 kg)

↑ Model of the Sukhoi S-96 *(Piotr Butowski)*

Details for Sukhoi S-96

PRINCIPAL DIMENSIONS:
Wing span: 38 ft 8.5 ins (11.8 m)
Maximum length: 42 ft (12.8 m)
Maximum height: 11 ft 8 ins (3.55 m)

CABIN:
Length: 12 ft 7 ins (3.83 m)
Width: 4 ft 9.5 ins (1.46 m)
Height: 4 ft 9 ins (1.45 m)

WINGS:
Area: 177.6 sq ft (16.5 m^2), gross
Sweepback: 17° at quarter chord

UNDERCARRIAGE:
Wheel base: 17 ft 2 ins (5.24 m)
Wheel track: 7 ft 6 ins (2.28 m)

WEIGHTS:
Empty, operating: 6,248 lb (2,834 kg)
Maximum take-off: 9,766 lb (4,430 kg)
Payload: 1,640 lb (744 kg)
Payload with maximum fuel: 820 lb (372 kg)

PERFORMANCE:
Maximum cruise speed: 459 kts (528 mph) 850 km/h
Cruise speed: 410 kts (472 mph) 760 km/h
Required runway length: 2,953 ft (900 m)
Cruise altitude: 41,000 ft (12,500 m)
Range with maximum fuel: 2,374-2,698 naut miles (2,734-3,107 miles) 4,400-5,000 km
Range with maximum payload: 1,457-1,619 naut miles (1,678-1,864 miles) 2,700-3,000 km

Sukhoi Su-26, Su-29 and Su-31

First flight: 30 June 1984 for original Su-26 piloted by Yevgeniy Frolov; 9 August 1991 for Su-29 2-seater piloted by Yevgeniy Frolov; June 1992 for Su-31 (Su-29T) piloted by Jurgis Kairys.
Role: Competition aerobatics and training.
Programme manager: Boris Rakitin.
Sales: Under production by Sukhoi Advanced Technologies in Moscow (plus 7 Su-29s manufactured by Dubna Machinebuilding Plant); total of 145 of all versions built at time of writing, including some 130 for export, mainly to the USA, but also to the UK, Spain, Switzerland, France, Italy, South Africa, Australia, Indonesia, UAE, Lithuania and Ukraine. On 5 March 1997, Argentine Air Force signed an order for 8 Su-29 trainers. In current production are Su-29s (about 50) and Su-31s (about 20, including 5 Su-31Ms). In 1997, a declaration of intent was signed covering assembly of the Su-29 and Su-31 in China. Some 30 Su-29s and Su-31Ms were to be built during 1998.
Wing control surfaces: Wide-span ailerons (each with a ground-adjustable tab and 2 hanging balance tabs).
Tail control surfaces: Horn-balanced elevator and rudder, each with a ground-adjustable tab.
Flight control system: Pushrods and cables.
Construction materials: Over 50% composites for Su-26M, 60% for Su-29 and 70% for Su-31.
Engine: 360 hp (268.5 kW) AOOT OKBM/Voronezh M-14P radial piston engine for Su-26 and Su-29. Su-31 has an uprated 400 hp (298 kW) M-14PF.

Aircraft variants:
Su-26 is a single-seat competition aircraft; small-batch production.
Su-26M was the first true production version (manufactured from 1988), with some upgrades in the wing and tail manufacturing technology, allowing structural weight to be reduced by 220 lb (100 kg), plus refinement of the aerodynamics. M-14P engine with a Muhlbauer 3-blade variable-pitch propeller (some aircraft with Russian-made 2-blade V-530TAD-35 propeller) and 60 litres of fuel. Pilot seat reclined by 45°.
Su-26M2 has provision for 139.5 litre centreline-mounted external tank for ferry flights. Smoke tank located in the starboard wing.
Su-26MX is an export derivative of Su-26M, with step to climb into the cockpit, controllable trim tabs and 2 wing fuel tanks (each 110 litres) used for ferry flights; range extended to 647 naut miles (745 miles) 1,200 km. In 1989, it became the first new Soviet aircraft delivered to the USA.
Su-29 is a 2-seat aerobatic trainer, also suited to competition. Extended wing span. Same M-14P engine but with an MTV-3-8-S/L250-21 propeller and 290 litres of fuel (70 litres in a fuselage tank for competition flying, plus 2 × 110 litre wing tanks for ferry flights). Shown at Paris in June 1991, before its first flight. Series production started in Spring 1992 at Sukhoi and in 1993 at Dubna, with first deliveries in May 1992. Russian certificate received in June 1994. Optional Bekker and AlliedSignal Bendix/King avionics; GPS.
Su-29KS or ***LL*** is an experimental version for testing the Zvezda KS-38 (SKS-94) lightweight ejection seat. Also used for training and maintaining military/civil pilot skills. MTOW 2,601 lb (1,180 kg). Never-exceed speed 237 kts (273 mph) 440 km/h. G limit of 7.5. The KS-38 ejection seat can be used during take-off at a minimum speed of 27-32 kts (31-37 mph) 50-60 km/h, as well as in flight at altitudes of over 33 ft (10 m), or 131 ft (40 m) inverted flight. Maximum speed for ejection is 216 kts (248 mph) 400 km/h, and maximum altitude 16,400 ft (5,000 m).
Su-29M is a production version of the Su-29, featuring the KS-38 ejection seats as standard instead of parachutes.
Su-29U was a projected 2-seat trainer version with a retractable undercarriage, now developed into Su-49, which see in a separate entry.
Su-31 (sometimes named ***Su-31T***, prototype ***Su-29T***, T standing for turnirnyi, competition) is a single-seat competition version derived from the Su-29 but considerably improved. Uprated M-14PF engine with an MTV-9 propeller. Further refined aerodynamics, reduced structural weight, and more precise flying qualities. Pilot seat reclined by 35°, and bulged canopy for better visibility. New main undercarriage with titanium spring legs and hydraulic disc brakes. 2 baggage compartments added. 70 litres of standard fuel for competition flying, with 220 litres in the wings for ferry flights in the export ***Su-31X*** version or 140 litres in an underbelly tank in Russian Su-31s.
Su-31M is similar to the basic Su-31 but with a KS-38 ejection seat and local aerodynamic improvements. First flew in May 1995 piloted by Yevgeniy Frolov.
Su-31U is the only version to feature a retractable undercarriage. Project only.

↑ Sukhoi Su-31 (bottom), with 2 Su-29s flown with 1 and 2 crew *(courtesy Sukhoi)*

Sukhoi Su-38

First flight: Not flown at time of writing.
Project manager: Alexander Zudilov.
Role: Specialized agricultural aircraft. Possible use as a waterbomber/patrol or for aerial photography.
Crew: Pilot in a sealed cockpit to prevent chemical ingress (originally designed with available tandem seat for passenger for ferrying if no internal chemical hooper was carried).
Chemical tank/hopper: 1,050 litres of liquid or dry chemicals.
Dispersal equipment: Adapted to use a sprayboom, atomizer or spreader from various manufacturers.
Safety equipment: Cockpit fitted into a forced frame to withstand a heavy impact.
Wing control surfaces: Constant-chord wings with winglets have ailerons and flaps.
Tail control surfaces: Horn-balanced elevators (starboard with a trim tab) and rudder (with a ground adjustable tab).
Flight control system: Mechanical.
Construction materials: Much use of composites, as for Sukhoi aerobatics aircraft. Service life 10,000 hours.
Engine: AOOT OKBM/Voronezh M-14P radial piston engine, with a 3-blade MTV-3 propeller.

Details for Su-26M, Su-29 and Su-31

	Su-26M	Su-29	Su-31
Engine	M-14P	M-14P	M-14PF
Engine rating	360 hp (268.5 kW)	360 hp (268.5 kW)	400 hp (298 kW)
Wing span	25 ft 7 ins (7.8 m)	26 ft 11 in (8.2 m)	25 ft 7 ins (7.8 m)
Wing area	127.3 sq ft (11.83 m^2)	131.4 sq ft (12.203 m^2)	127 sq ft (11.8 m^2)
Length	22 ft 5 ins (6.827 m)	24 ft (7.32 m)	22 ft 8 ins (6.9 m)
Height	9 ft 1.5 ins (2.78 m)	9 ft 5.5 ins (2.885 m)	9 ft 1 ins (2.76 m)
Empty weight	1,499 lb (680 kg)	1,697 lb (770 kg)	1,433 lb (650 kg)
Normal TOW	1,841 lb (835 kg)	1,900 lb (862 kg)*	1,720 lb (780 kg)
Never-exceed speed (V_{NE})	243 kts (280 mph) 450 km/h	243 kts (280 mph) 450 km/h	243 kts (280 mph) 450 km/h
Maximum speed	167 kts (193 mph) 310 km/h	175.5 kts (202 mph) 325 km/h	178 kts (205 mph) 330 km/h
Take-off speed	65 kts (75 mph) 120 km/h		59 kts (68 mph) 110 km/h
Landing speed	62 kts (71.5 mph) 115 km/h	65 kts (75 mph) 120 km/h	62 kts (71.5 mph) 115 km/h
Stall speed			61 kts (71 mph) 113 km/h
Take-off distance	525 ft (160 m)		361 ft (110 m)
Landing distance	820 ft (250 m)		985 ft (300 m)
Climb rate at sea level	3,543 ft (1,080 m) per minute	3,150 ft (960 m) per minute	4,725 ft (1,440 m) per minute
Roll rate	345° per second	345° per second	400° per second
G limits	+12, -10	+12, -10, or +9, -7 with 2 pilots	+12, -10
Ferry range	431 naut miles (497 miles) 800 km	647 naut miles (745 miles) 1,200 km	647 naut miles (745 miles) 1,200 km

* Weight in aerobatic version with single pilot. Maximum take-off weight of Su-29 is 2,646 lb (1,200 kg).

↑ Sukhoi Su-38 model

Engine rating: 360 hp (268.5 kW).
Fuel system: 200 litres.
Electrical system: 28.5 volt; 28 amp-hour battery.

Aircraft variants:
Early design announced May 1994 and based directly on the Su-29 aerobatic trainer and competition aircraft, but with larger high-lift wing and sealed cockpit.
Current design (as described) was created between December 1994 and February 1995, as the result of consultations with the US NAAA (National Agricultural Aviation Association), which showed that the original design did not meet the basic demands for modern agricultural aircraft.

Details for Su-38

PRINCIPAL DIMENSIONS:
Wing span: 36 ft 7 ins (11.15 m)
Maximum length: 25 ft 0.5 ins (7.63 m)
Maximum height: 7 ft 6.5 ins (2.3 m)

WINGS:
Aerofoil section: CAHI P-31Y
Dihedral: 3°
Incidence: 2°

UNDERCARRIAGE:
Type: Fixed with tailwheel
Wheel base: 17 ft 1 ins (5.20 m)
Wheel track: 7 ft 6.5 ins (2.30 m)

WEIGHTS:
Empty, operating: 2,315 lb (1,050 kg)
Maximum take-off: 4,630 lb (2,100 kg)

PERFORMANCE:
Maximum speed: 162 kts (186 mph) 300 km/h at sea level
Maximum speed with dispersal equipment: 119 kts (136 mph) 220 km/h
Required runway length: 984 ft (300 m)
G limits: +4.4, -1.9
Range with full fuel: 431 naut miles (497 miles) 800 km

Sukhoi Su-49

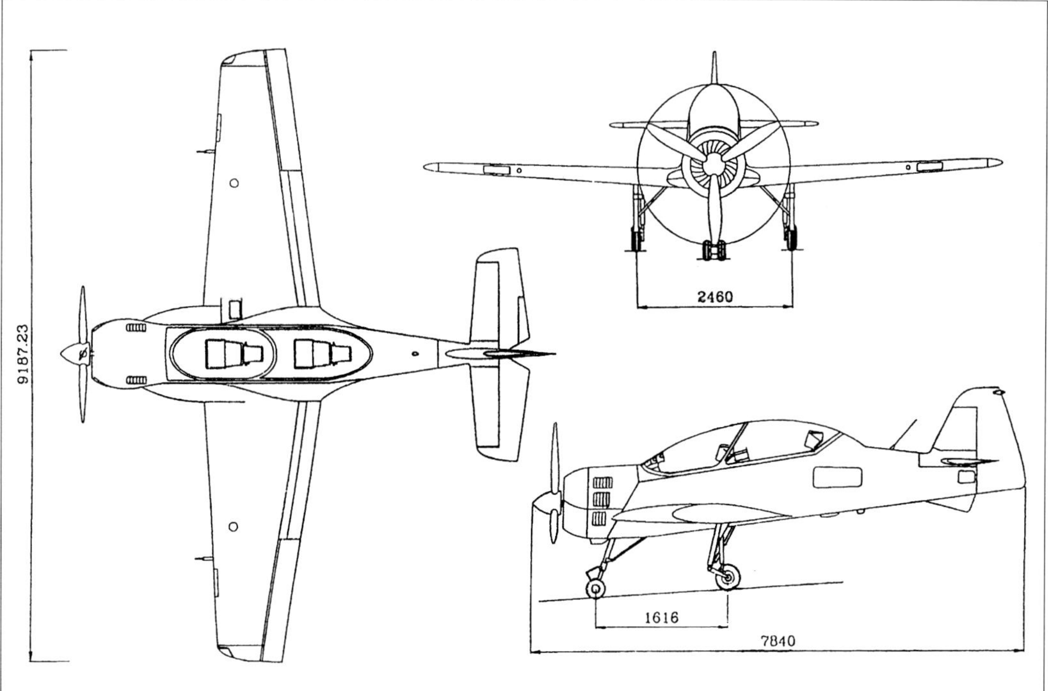

↑ Sukhoi Su-49 *(courtesy Sukhoi)*

First flight: Possibly 1998.
Role: Single piston or turboprop engined primary trainer, developed from the Su-26 and Su-29 series. First announced 1992 with the designation Su-29U, later redesignated Su-32 and then Su-39 (under this designation in the previous edition), but since Summer 1996 known as Su-49.
Sales: Proposed as a replacement for the Yakovlev Yak-52 basic trainer. Sales expected for 1,500 aircraft, mainly for Russian armed forces. Approximate cost US$500,000.
Crew: 2 in tandem cockpits (instructor at rear).
Crew escape: Lightweight Zvezda/Sukhoi KS-38 (SKS-94) ejection seats.
Expendable weapons and equipment: Gun packs, bombs and rockets suspended on 2 underwing pylons. Provision for podded radar, as well as radar and IR warning receivers.
Engine: 400 hp (298 kW) AOOT OKBM/Voronezh M-14PF radial piston engine, with an MTV-9 propeller. Other piston engines have been under consideration.
Fuel system: 320 litres of internal fuel, with provision for 2 × 100 litre drop tanks.
Braking system: Mainwheel hydraulic brakes.

Aircraft variants:
2 versions developed, with different avionics suites: ***basic trainer*** and ***advanced trainer/combat*** aircraft. First will have VFR systems including KDF 806 ILS/VOR and conventional cockpit, while the more advanced version will have an integrated flight/navigation/ aiming system, 'glass' cockpit and weapons. Service life 10,000 hours.

Details for Su-49 with M-14PF engine

PRINCIPAL DIMENSIONS
Wing span: 30 ft 2 ins (9.187 m)
Maximum length: 25 ft 9 ins (7.84 m)
Maximum height: 8 ft 6.5 ins (2.6 m)

WINGS:
Aerofoil section: NACA 23012
Area: 131.32 sq ft (12.20 m^2)
Aspect ratio: 5.92
Chord at root: 6 ft 2 ins (1.88 m)
Chord at tip: 2 ft 11 ins (0.885 m)
Sweepback at leading edge: 5° 30'
Dihedral: 1° 30'

TAIL UNIT:
Tailplane span: 9 ft 6 ins (2.9 m)

UNDERCARRIAGE:
Type: Pneumatically retractable, with nosewheel
Main and nose wheel tyre size: 400 × 140-150 mm
Wheel base: 5 ft 3.5 ins (1.616 m)
Wheel track: 8 ft 1 ins (2.46 m)

WEIGHTS:
Empty, operating: 2,315 lb (1,050 kg)
Nominal take-off: 2,954 lb (1,340 kg)
Maximum take-off: 3,307 lb (1,500 kg)

PERFORMANCE:
Never-exceed speed (V_{NE}): 270 kts (310 mph) 500 km/h
Maximum speed: 189 kts (217 mph) 350 km/h at sea level
Maximum cruise speed: 178 kts (205 mph) 330 km/h
Landing speed: 59 kts (68 mph) 110 km/h
Take-off distance: 755 ft (230 m)
Landing distance: 1,148 ft (350 m)
Maximum climb rate: 2,660 ft (810 m) per minute at sea level
G limits: +11, -8
Ceiling: 13,125 ft (4,000 m)
Range: 809 naut miles (932 miles) 1,500 km, internal fuel

SCF Technoavia — Russia

Full name: Scientific-Commercial Firm "Technoavia".
Corporate address: Kronshtadsky Bvld 7a, Moscow 125212.
Telephone: +7 095 452 5822, 5603 **Facsimile:** +7 095 452 5694
Founded: 1991.
Employees: 25.
Information: Vyacheslav Petrovich Kondratiev (General Director) and Khalide Khusyainova Makagonova.

ACTIVITIES

■ Development, test and sale of general purpose aircraft; flight training for amateur pilots. In 1992 Technoavia restarted production of the Yakovlev Yak-18T 4-seat general purpose aircraft at the Smolensk aircraft factory and, in 1994, proposed a 6-seat derivative as the SM-94. In addition to the aircraft detailed later, under development are the **SM-95** twin-engined patrol modification of Finist for border guard use; the **Miniakro** ultralight aerobatic aircraft (take-off weight 970 lb, 440 kg; empty 441 lb, 200 kg; maximum speed 146 kts,168 mph, 270 km/h with Rotax engine), and the 4-seat **Ronata** wing-in-ground-effect craft.

Technoavia SM-92 Finist

First flight: 28 December 1993 (piloted by Mikhail Molchanyuk).
Certification: Meets AP-23 (FAR Pt 23) standards.
Role: STOL light transport, agricultural, survey and other work.
Sales: 8 SM-92s (7 in operation, including 1 in UK and 1 in Belgium) and 1 SM-92P built by Smolensk aircraft factory at time of writing. Next 16 SM-92Ps (including 2 prototypes) ordered by Russian Federal Border Guard Service (FBGS) at the beginning of 1996. The intention of FBGS was to eventually order 300 Finists for service in several tens of detachments stationed at small unpaved airstrips along the frontiers. A typical Flight would consist of 4 aircraft, though in some important areas the Flights would be strengthened to 6–8 aircraft. The first 4 armed Finists

were expected to be stationed at the frontiers with Baltic states, 2 other Flights sent to Stavropol (Caucasus) and Chita (near the border with China), and the last 2 aircraft used at the training centre for the border service at Kurgan (former Air Force training centre). In 1996, however, the Smolensk factory went bankrupt before any aircraft had been built. In spite of these troubles, the SM-92P remains a priority programme for FBGS, which is looking for another manufacturing plant. After unsuccessful talks with the Sokol factory at Nizhny Novgorod, the Technoavia company entered into a contract with Aerostar of Romania; the aircraft will be adapted for military needs (i.e. converted from SM-92 into SM-92P) in Russia. In October 1997, the Government of Yakutia ordered 14 Finists.
Details: SM-92, unless stated.
Crew/passengers: Pilot plus 6 passengers, or 2 litters and a medical attendant in an air ambulance role, or 7 paratroops when passenger seats removed, or 1,323 lb (600 kg) of cargo. SM-92P carries 2 pilots plus a gunner-observer. Passenger seat pitch 29.1 ins (74 cm) in transport role.
Baggage compartment: 2 ft 7.5 ins × 1 ft 8 ins × 2 ft 5.5 ins (0.8 × 0.5 × 0.75 m).
Wing characteristics: Braced high-wing monoplane.
Wing control surfaces: Frise ailerons (+10°/–25°) and 3-position (0° in flight, 20° for take-off, 40° for landing) 2-section Fowler flaps.
Tail control surfaces: Horn-balanced elevators (+22°/–17°; starboard trim tab) and rudder (±25°, with ground adjustable tab).
Flight control system: Mechanical, except for electric flaps.
Construction materials: Mainly aluminium and steel, with some use of titanium and composite materials.
Engine: AOOT OKBM/Voronezh M-14P radial piston engine. MT-Propeller MTV-3 3-blade controllable-pitch propeller of 8 ft 2 ins (2.5 m).
Engine rating: 360 hp (268.5 kW).

↑ Technoavia SM-92P Finist with rocket launchers

Details for SM-92 and SM-92P

PRINCIPAL DIMENSIONS:
Wing span: 47 ft 11 ins (14.6 m)
Maximum length: 29 ft 11.5 ins (9.13 m)
Maximum height: 10 ft 1 ins (3.08 m)

CABIN:
Length: 11 ft 2 ins (3.4 m)
Width: 4 ft 6.5 ins (1.38 m)
Height: 4 ft 6.5 ins (1.38 m)
Volume: 181.87 cu ft (5.15 m^3)
Main door size: 4 ft 5 ins × 3 ft 8 ins (1.35 m × 1.12 m)

WINGS:
Aerofoil section: P-301M
Aspect ratio: 10.43
Area: 220 sq ft (20.44 m^2)
Chord: 4 ft 7 ins (1.4 m)
Twist: -2°

TAIL UNIT:
Span: 18 ft 2 ins (5.53 m)

UNDERCARRIAGE:
Type: Fixed, with steerable/castoring tailwheel. Optional skis or floats
Main wheel tyre size: 600 × 180 mm
Tail wheel tyre size: 255 × 110 mm
Wheel base: 21 ft 7.5 ins (6.588 m)
Wheel track: 9 ft 8 ins (2.95 m)

WEIGHTS:
Empty, operating: 3,153 lb (1,430 kg)
Empty, operating, SM-92P: 3,042 lb (1,380 kg)
Normal take-off: 5,181 lb (2,350 kg)
Maximum take-off and landing: 5,181 lb (2,350 kg)
Payload: 1,323 lb (600 kg)
Payload with maximum fuel: 1,213 lb (550 kg)
Maximum weapon load, SM-92P: 1,257 lb (570 kg)
Weapon load with maximum fuel, SM-92P: 1,146 lb (520 kg)
Fuel with maximum payload/weapons: 507 lb (230 kg)

PERFORMANCE (SM-92 and SM-92P without external stores):
Maximum diving speed: 156 kts (180 mph) 290 km/h
Maximum operating speed: 124 kts (143 mph) 230 km/h
Cruise speed: 108 kts (124 mph) 200 km/h
Stall speed: 54 kts (62 mph) 100 km/h *with flaps*, or 62 kts (72 mph) 115 km/h *clean*
Ceiling: 9,840 ft (3,000 m), service
Take-off and landing: 821 ft (250 m) (roll)
Maximum climb rate: 984 ft (300 m) per minute at sea level
Range with full fuel: 744 naut miles (857 miles) 1,380 km with 40 minutes reserve
Range with full payload, SM-92: 593 naut miles (683 miles) 1,100 km, with 40 minutes reserve

Fuel capacity: 370 litres in 2 wing tanks (617 lb, 280 kg).
Electrical system: 27 volt.
Braking system: Disc-type brakes.
De-icing system: Optional pneumatic Goodrich de-icing system for wings and electric system on propeller.
Oxygen system: Optional.
Fire system: Fire-resistant partition between the engine and cockpit; fuel cut-off valve.
Flight avionics/instrumentation: Russian-made speedometer, altimeter, variometer, clock, magnetic compass, artificial horizon, and critical angle-of-attack indicator. AlliedSignal Bendix/King KR 87 ADF, KT 76A transponder, turn and slide indicator, Garmin GPS-150, KA 134 intercom, and 2 KY 96A VHF radio stations.
Armament: SM-92P is armed with 3 × 7.62-mm machine-guns (2 fixed PKTs attached to fuselage sides and 1 movable PKS machine-gun inside cabin, shooting through the opened cabin door) and 2 × B8V7 launchers, each with 7 × S-8 unguided 80-mm rockets. 2 × 100 kg bombs can be carried under the fuselage (illuminating bombs for night actions).

Aircraft variants:
SM-92 is a basic utility version.
SM-92P is an armed patrol version ordered by the Russian Federal Border Guard Service. First flown 18 August 1995 (pilot Viktor Barchenkov), with flight tests completed in September 1996.
Turbine-powered derivative of SM-92 is being considered.

Technoavia SM-94

First flight: 22 December 1994 for first SM-94-1 prototype, piloted by Mikhail Molchanyuk and Viktor Barchenkov.
Role: Light multi-purpose derivative of Yak-18T (which see), with further uses including patrol and fire-support.
Sales: SM-94-1 prototype completed only at the time of writing. Under consideration by Russian Federal Border Guard Service.

↑ Technoavia SM-94-1 6-seat derivative of the Yak-18T

Production originally planned at Smolensk Aircraft Plant.
Crew/passengers: Pilot plus 5 passengers.
Wing control surfaces: Slotted ailerons (22° up, 15° down, with tabs) and split flaps (50°).
Tail control surfaces: Elevators (±25°, with tabs) and rudder (27°).
Flight control system: Pushrod/cable.
Engine: AOOT OKBM/Voronezh M-14P radial piston engine, with 3 blade MTV-3 propeller.
Engine rating: 360 hp (268.5 kW).
Fuel system: 360 litres.
Braking system: Pneumatic on mainwheels.
Expendable weapons and equipment: Unguided rocket pods, gun pods and small bombs on 2 underwing pylons.
Flight avionics/instrumentation: Standard Russian instrumentation plus KLX 135 GPS, and KR 87 radio-compass.

Aircraft variants:
SM-94-1 is the first prototype with only some of the upgrades introduced, including 6-seat cockpit, additional AlliedSignal avionics and new propeller.
SM-94 will be the production version with reshaped tailfin and weapon pylons added under the wings. As described.

Details for SM-94, as for Yak-18T except as follows

PRINCIPAL DIMENSIONS:
Maximum length: 27 ft 9 ins (8.45 m)

WEIGHTS:
Empty: 2,425 lb (1,100 kg)
Maximum take-off: 4,122 lb (1,870 kg)

PERFORMANCE:
Maximum speed: 151 kts (174 mph) 280 km/h
Maximum climb rate: 886 ft (270 m) per minute
Range with full fuel: 728 naut miles (839 miles) 1,350 km

Technoavia SP-91 and SP-95

First flight: 6 February 1995 for SP-91 (piloted by Vladimir Makagonov).
Role: Interchangeable single- or 2-seat aerobatic competition and training aircraft. SP-95 is the follow-on version to SP-91. The aim was to produce an aerobatic aircraft with Su-26's capabilities at one-third the price.
Sales: 5 SP-91s operating in the USA and 1 used by Technoavia.
Details: Both SP-91 and SP-95, unless stated.
Crew/passengers: 1 or 2 pilots.
Wing characteristics: Low-wing monoplane, with all-metal twin-spar wing.

↑ Technoavia SP-91 aerobatic aircraft

Wing control surfaces: Near full-span drooping ailerons (±25° deflection; drooped -5°, 0°, 5°, 10° or 15°).
Tail control surfaces: Braced tailplane (span 9 ft 2 ins, 2.8 m for SP-91 and 10 ft 6 ins, 3.2 m for SP-95) with horn-balanced elevators (with ground adjustable tab) and rudder; both elevator and rudder deflected ±25°.
Construction materials: All-metal, mainly aluminium and steel.
Engine: AOOT OKBM/Voronezh M-14P radial piston engine. German MT-Propeller MTV-3 3-blade controllable-pitch propeller of 7 ft 10.5 ins (2.4 m) diameter (8 ft 2.5 ins, 2.5 m for SP-95). Pneumatic engine starting.
Engine rating: 360 hp (268.5 kW).
Fuel capacity: 2 fuel tanks in the wings, total capacity 110 litres (181 lb, 82 kg for SP-91) or 330 litres (543 lb, 246 kg for SP-95).
Electrical system: 27 volt.
Braking system: Disc-type brakes.
Fire system: Fire-resistant partition between the engine and cockpit; fuel cut-off valve.
Flight avionics/instrumentation: Altimeter, speedometer, clock, accelerometer, and magnetic compass. VHF radio system and intercom.

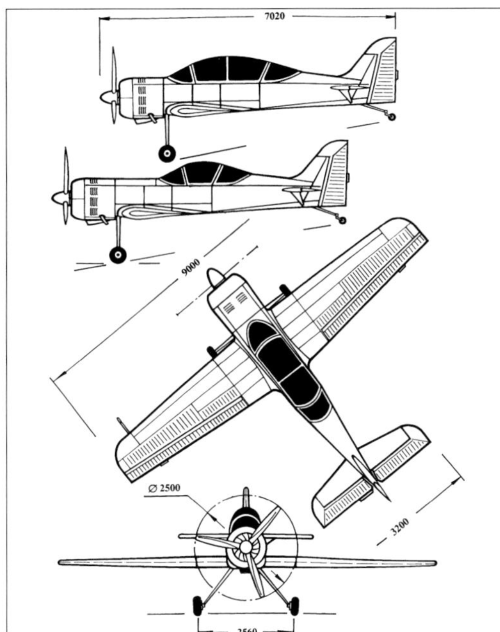

↑ Technoavia SP-95 *(courtesy Technoavia)*

Aircraft variants:
SP-91 refers to the initial prototype and pre-production aircraft.
SP-95 is the production version of increased dimensions. Manufacturing originally assigned to the Smolensk aircraft factory.

Details for SP-91, *with SP-95 in italics*

PRINCIPAL DIMENSIONS:
Wing span: 26 ft 7 ins (8.1 m), *29 ft 6.5 ins (9 m)*
Maximum length: 22 ft (6.7 m), *23 ft 0.5 ins (7.02 m)*
Maximum height: 7 ft 3 ins (2.2 m)

WINGS:
Area: 124.2 sq ft (11.54 m^2), *118.4 sq ft (11.0 m^2)*, gross
Chord at root: 6 ft 11 ins (2.1 m), *5 ft 3 ins (1.6 m)*
Chord at tip: 3 ft 1.5 ins (0.95 m), *2 ft 10 ins (0.86 m)*
Aspect ratio: 5.68, *7.36*
Sweepback: 0° at 25% chord
Thickness/chord ratio: 15.5% *(SP-95 16%)* at root, 12% *(the same)* at tip
Dihedral/anhedral: None
Twist: 0°

UNDERCARRIAGE:
Type: Fixed, with tailwheel
Main wheel tyre size: 400 × 150 mm
Tail wheel tyre size: 200 × 80 mm
Wheel base: 17 ft 4 ins (5.28 m), *17 ft 10 ins (5.43 m)*
Wheel track: 7 ft 9 ins (2.354 m), *the same*

WEIGHTS:
Empty, operating: 1,764 lb (800 kg)
Normal take-off for SP-95 with pilot only: *2,083 lb (945 kg)*
Maximum take-off and landing: 2,381 lb (1,080 kg)
Maximum landing: 2,381 lb (1,080 kg)

PERFORMANCE:
Never-exceed speed (V_{NE}): 242 kts (279 mph) 450 km/h
Maximum speed: 162 kts (186 mph) 300 km/h
Stall speed: 57 kts (65.5 mph) 105 km/h *clean*, 51.5 kts (59 mph) 95 km/h *with drooped ailerons*
Take-off distance: 230 ft (70 m) (roll)
Landing distance: 492 ft (150 m) (roll)
Maximum climb rate (pilot only): 3,150 ft (960 m) per minute, *3,347 ft (1,020 m) per minute*, both at sea level
G limits with pilot: +12, -10
G limits with 2 crew: +11, -9
Range with full fuel: 378 naut miles (435 miles) 700 km, *809 naut miles (932 miles) 1,500 km*

Technoavia SS-98

Comments: This new project, as Selsko-khozyaistvennyi samolet (agricultural aircraft project of 1998), is for a low-wing monoplane suited to agricultural, firefighting, patrol and training purposes but otherwise externally similar in many ways to SM-92 Finist. To be built at Voronezh, it will have a crew of 1 or 2, a 1,000 litre chemical tank, working speed of 57-108 kts (65-124 mph) 105-200 km/h, take-off distance of 820-1,542 ft (250-470 m), landing distance of 820 ft (250 m), and a duration of 6 hours.

↑ Technoavia SS-98 agricultural and other purpose monoplane

Tupolev Joint-Stock Company — Russia

Corporate address:
See Combat section for company details. See also Airliners and Reconnaissance sections.

Tupolev Tu-24

First flight: Project; full scale mock-up displayed in 1993.
Programme manager: Daniil Gapeyev.
Role: Multi-purpose lightplane with agricultural version (Tu-24SKh) as basic, plus versions for patrol, communications and law enforcement (F), fisheries/wildlife protection and survey (R), air ambulance (S), general passenger/parachutist/cargo transport (T), and training (U).
Sales: Developed for an agricultural aircraft competition announced by the Russian ministry of agriculture in the early 1990s. Competition was to be judged by the end of 1994 but was halted due to financial restraints. Further details can be found in 1996–97 edition of *WA&SD*, pages 428–429.

Tupolev Tu-34

First flight: Had been expected late 1998.
Certification: Designed to meet AP-23 (FAR 23) requirements.

Development

▪ 1992. Development began. Original design for a low-wing monoplane with small canards. Details below refer to the modified current version.
Role: Pressurized, 7-seat STOL multi-purpose transport. Ambulance, patrol and training versions are expected.
Sales: To be built at the Kyrgyzstan-Russian factory near Bishkek (former naval equipment factory) according to Kyrgyz Government resolution No 613 of 20 December 1996. Tu-34 is the most important project of Tupolev's small aircraft programme.

↑ Tupolev Tu-34 *(Piotr Butowski)*

Crew/passengers: Pilot plus 6 passengers or 1,543 lb (700 kg) of cargo.
Wing characteristics: High-wing monoplane with slightly forward-swept wings.
Wing control surfaces: Slats, interceptors, flaps and ailerons. Port aileron has trim tab.
Tail control surfaces: T-type conventional tail with adjustable tailplane. Trim tabs on elevator and rudder.
Flight control system: Fly-by-wire control of tailplane, interceptors, slats, flaps and trim tabs.
Construction materials: Mainly aluminium alloys (front fuselage and wings) and glassfibre composite materials (rear fuselage, tail, wing high-lift devices and nose cone). Rear fuselage additionally strengthened by carbonfibre reinforced plastics.
Engines: 2 turboprop engines with 4-blade controllable-pitch pusher propellers: Turbomeca TP319 Arrius 1D (each 420 shp, 313.2 kW) or modified version of Allison 250-20C with added reduction gear (each 420 shp, 313.2 kW). Initially, TSIO-360-KB (220 hp, 164 kW) piston engines and RKBM/Rybinsk DN-250 (each 240 hp, 179 kW) diesel engines were considered.
Fuel system: Total of 770 litres (1,235 lb, 560 kg) of fuel in 2 torsion-box tanks inside the wings. 2 additional fuel tanks can be suspended under the wings, each of 280 litres.

Aircraft variants:
Initially 3 versions were considered, as the 5-seat ***Tu-34-100*** with 2 TSIO-360-KBs, 5-seat ***Tu-34-200*** with DN-250s, and 7-seat ***Tu-34-300*** with TP319ARs. Last version only selected for production, becoming simply ***Tu-34***.

Details for Tu-34

PRINCIPAL DIMENSIONS:
Wing span: 44 ft (13.4 m)
Maximum length: 32 ft 10 ins (10 m)
Maximum height: 10 ft 4 ins (3.16 m)

CABIN:
Length: 12 ft 7.5 ins (3.85 m)
Width: 5 ft (1.52 m)
Height: 4 ft 5 ins (1.34 m)
Main door size: 2 ft 10 ins × 4 ft 1 ins (0.86 × 1.245 m)

WINGS:
Area: 187.3 sq ft (17.4 m^2), gross
Aspect ratio: 10.32

UNDERCARRIAGE:
Type: Retractable, with steerable nosewheel
Wheel base: 11 ft 3 ins (3.425 m)
Wheel track: 7 ft 10.5 ins (2.4 m)

WEIGHTS:
Empty, operating: 3,188 lb (1,446 kg)
Maximum take-off: 5,556 lb (2,520 kg)
Maximum landing: 5,512 lb (2,500 kg)
Maximum payload: 1,543 lb (700 kg)

PERFORMANCE:
Maximum operating speed: 254 kts (292 mph) 470 km/h at 19,685 ft (6,000 m), or 189 kts (217.5 mph) 350 km/h at sea level
Maximum cruise speed: 243 kts (280 mph) 450 km/h at altitude
Economic cruise speed: 216 kts (248.5 mph) 400 km/h at 19,685-24,935 ft (6,000-7,600 m)
Required runway length: 1,640 ft (500 m)
Take-off distance: 919 ft (280 m)
Landing distance: 739 ft (225 m)
Maximum climb rate: 2,559 ft (780 m) per minute, at sea level
Ceiling: 19,685-24,935 ft (6,000-7,600 m), service
Absolute ceiling: 36,090 ft (11,000 m)
Range with full fuel: 1,127 naut miles (1,299 miles) 2,090 km with 882 lb (400 kg) of payload, at economic speed, 45 minutes reserve
Range with full payload: 323 naut miles (373 miles) 600 km

Tupolev Tu-54 or Voronezh VSKhS

First flight: Project; full-scale mock-up shown 1993.
Role: Agricultural aircraft; compared with the An-2, the treatment of 1 hectare is expected to be 46% less expensive, and the Tu-54 itself will be about one-third the price.
Development: Originally developed as **VSKhS** (*Voronezhski Selsko-Khozyaistvennyi Samoyot*, Voronezh Agricultural Aircraft) by the Voronezh division of Tupolev, later taked over by Tupolev JSC and renamed **Tu-54**. Designed for a competition announced in the early 1990s by Russian ministry of agriculture.
Sales: Initial batch of 5 aircraft was under construction by Voronezh production plant before financial support stopped in 1994. Manufacturing transferred to Kyrgyzstan and according to Kyrgyz Government resolution No 613 of 20 December 1996, Tu-54 (together with Tu-34) will be built at the Kyrgyzstan-Russian factory in Dastan near Bishkek.
Crew: Pilot only in raised cockpit located above the chemical hopper.
Wing characteristics: Strut-braced low-wing monoplane.
Wing control surfaces: Fowler flaps and ailerons.
Tail control surfaces: Elevators with ground adjustable tabs. Horn balanced rudder, also with ground adjustable tab.
Construction materials: Metal.
Engine: AOOT OKBM/Voronezh M-14P radial piston engine, with VISh-9 controllable-pitch 3-blade propeller of 8 ft 6 ins (2.6 m) diameter.
Engine rating: 360 hp (268.5 kW).
Fuel system: 200 litres. Cruise fuel consumption 40 litres per hour.

Details for Tu-54

PRINCIPAL DIMENSIONS:
Wing span: 41 ft 4 ins (12.59 m)
Maximum length: 28 ft 2 ins (8.577 m)
Maximum height: 9 ft 6 ins (2.9 m)

WINGS:
Area: 242.2 sq ft (22.5 m^2), gross
Aspect ratio: 7.04

UNDERCARRIAGE:
Type: Fixed, with tailwheel
Main wheel tyre size: 700 × 250 mm
Tail wheel tyre size: 300 × 125 mm
Wheel track: 9 ft 2 ins (2.8 m)

WEIGHTS:
Empty, operating: 2,712 lb (1,230 kg)
Maximum take-off: 4,828 lb (2,190 kg)
Chemical payload: 1,764 lb (800 kg)

PERFORMANCE:
Maximum speed: 151 kts (174 mph) 280 km/h
Operating speed: 65-86 kts (75-99 mph) 120-160 km/h
Stall speed: 47.5 kts (55 mph) 88 km/h, landing configuration
Take-off distance: 1,001 ft (305 m), concrete runway
Landing distance: 870 ft (265 m)
Maximum climb rate: 827 ft (252 m) per minute
Range with full fuel: 459 naut miles (528 miles) 850 km

↑ **Tupolev Tu-54** *(Piotr Butowski)*

Tupolev Tu-400

Role: 8/10-seat business jet; regional transport version also planned.

Development

■ Design stage. Design first presented in 1992 as the ***Tu-2000*** and later as the ***Tu-20*** regional transport for 19 passengers, then powered by 2 turboprops (Pratt & Whitney Canada PT6A-67A or AlliedSignal TPE331-20) with pusher propellers. Since 1995, the design has been modified as the Tu-400, to have 2 turbofans.

Details

Crew/passengers: 2 pilots plus 6-8 passengers or 3,307 lb (1,500 kg) of cargo.
Wing characteristics: Low-mounted, with moderate sweep and dihedral.
Wing control surfaces: Slats, interceptors, flaps and ailerons.
Tail control surfaces: T-type conventional tail.
Engines: 2 Pratt & Whitney Canada PW305 turbofans.
Engine rating: Each 5,290 lbf (23.53 kN).

Details for Tu-400

PRINCIPAL DIMENSIONS:
Wing span: 53 ft 10 ins (16.4 m)
Maximum length: 58 ft (17.67 m)
Maximum height: 17 ft 3 ins (5.25 m)
Fuselage diameter: 6 ft 7 ins (2 m)

CABIN:
Length: 21 ft 3 ins (6.47 m)
Width: 5 ft 11 ins (1.8 m)
Height: 5 ft 10 ins (1.78 m)

WEIGHTS:
Maximum take-off: 28,219 lb (12,800 kg)
Payload: 3,307 lb (1,500 kg)

PERFORMANCE:
Cruise speed: 432 kts (497 mph) 800 km/h
Required runway length: 5,250 ft (1,600 m)
Range with full fuel: 3,777 naut miles (4,350 miles) 7,000 km with 6 passengers

Tupolev Tu-4x4

Role: Business aircraft at the project stage. Same configuration as Tu-324, Tu-400 and Tu-414, but smallest size of this series.
Passengers: 4 to 7.
Engines: 2 Soyuz/Moscow R127-300 turbofans.
Engine rating: 1,764 lbf (7.84 kN)
Fuel system: 2,646 lb (1,200 kg)

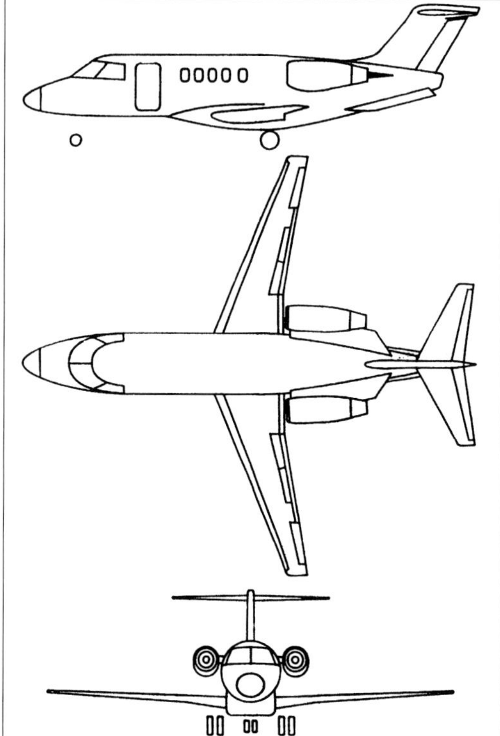

↑ **Tupolev Tu-4x4** *(courtesy Tupolev)*

Details for Tu-4x4

PRINCIPAL DIMENSIONS:
Wing span: 38 ft 1.5 ins (11.62 m)
Maximum length: 42 ft 7 ins (12.97 m)
Maximum height: 12 ft 9.5 ins (3.9 m)

WEIGHTS:
Empty, operating: 6,548 lb (2,970 kg)
Maximum take-off: 9,965 lb (4,520 kg)
Payload: 1,764 lb (800 kg)

PERFORMANCE:
Cruise speed: 405-453 kts (466-522 mph) 750-840 km/h
Required runway length: 3,839 ft (1,170 m)
Cruise altitude: 41,339-44,619 ft (12,600-13,600 m)
Range with full payload: 890 naut miles (1,025 miles) 1,650 km
Range with full fuel: 1,781 naut miles (2,050 miles) 3,300 km with 4 passengers

Unikomtrans — Russia

Corporate address:
Samara.

Telephone: +7 8462 270834

Information:
Oleg Nikolayevich Voronkov.

↑ Unikomtrans 11 amphibian, with wingtips/stabilizers folded *(Piotr Butowski)*

Unikomtrans 11

First flight: Shown at Zhukovsky in 1995 but not yet flown.
Role: Light passenger, tourist and training amphibian/flying-boat.
Crew/passengers: 2-4 persons (rear seats rearward facing). Upward opening cockpit canopy. Dual controls.
Baggage compartment: 331 lb (150 kg) when rear seats removed.
Wing characteristics: Strut and pylon braced parasol-type wing, of constant chord and slight dihedral. Fold-down wingtips/stabilizers (see Undercarriage).
Wing control surfaces: 2 ailerons, meeting in centre and extending fully to folding outer wing panels.
Tail control surfaces: Constant-chord tailplane with elevators, and slightly swept fin and rudder.
Construction materials: Metal, with 2-step hull.
Engines: 2 × 45 hp (33.6 kW) AK-94 piston engines with 2-blade tractor propellers, mounted on the wing leading edge.

Details for Unikomtrans 11

PRINCIPAL DIMENSIONS:
Wing span: 32 ft 10 ins (10 m)
Maximum length: 21 ft 4 ins (6.5 m)

UNDERCARRIAGE:
Type: Mainwheels on cantilever bowed legs carried just ahead of the wing strut, used for amphibious operations. Wheels can be swivelled up for water operations or can be removed. Fixed tail guard/support with very small tailwheel. 3 ft 5 ins (1.04 m) long wingtips fold down as stabilizing floats when operating from/to water
Main wheel tyre size: 300 × 125 mm

WEIGHTS:
Empty, operating: 661 lb (300 kg)
Normal take-off: 1,058 lb (480 kg)
Maximum take-off: 1,323 lb (600 kg)

PERFORMANCE:
Maximum operating speed: 92 kts (106 mph) 170 km/h
Take-off and landing distance: 197 ft (60 m)
Maximum climb rate: 590 ft (180 m) per minute
Duration: 3 hours with full fuel

Yakovlev Joint Stock Company – A.S. Yakovlev Design Bureau — Russia

Corporate address:
See Combat section for all company details.

Yakovlev Yak-18T

First flight: 1967 (a development of the Yak-18 tandem 2-seat trainer of 1946 first appearance).
Fatigue life: 5,000 flying hours.
Role: Light multi-purpose, including passengers, light cargo, ambulance and training.
Sales: 537 built during 1973–1982 by Smolensk aircraft factory. 1993–1995 production restarted and 54 aircraft built. See under Technoavia for SM-94 upgraded version.
Crew/passengers: 4 persons, or 2 persons plus light cargo, or the pilot, an attendant and 1 litter in ambulance layout (using the baggage door to load the patient).
Cockpit: Dual controls.
Baggage hold: To the rear of the seats, with its own loading door.
Wing control surfaces: Slotted ailerons (with tabs) and split flaps.
Tail control surfaces: Elevators (with tabs) and rudder.
Construction materials: Mostly metal, with fabric covering for the outer wings, ailerons, and all of the wire-braced tail.
Engine: AOOT OKBM/Voronezh M-14P radial, with 2-blade V530TA-D35 propeller.
Engine rating: 360 hp (268.5 kW).
Fuel system: 208 litres (308 lb, 140 kg) maximum, or 220 lb (100 kg) normal.
Flight control system: Mechanical, with hydraulic flap actuation.
Braking system: Pneumatic on mainwheels.
Flight avionics/instrumentation: VFR.

↑ Yakovlev Yak-18T *(Piotr Butowski)*

Details for Yak-18T

PRINCIPAL DIMENSIONS:
Wing span: 36 ft 7.5 ins (11.16 m)
Maximum length: 27 ft 6 ins (8.39 m)
Maximum height: 11 ft 2 ins (3.4 m)

WINGS:
Aerofoil section: Clark YH
Aspect ratio: 6.62
Area: 202.36 sq ft (18.8 m^2)

UNDERCARRIAGE:
Type: Retractable, with non-steerable nosewheel
Wheel base: 6 ft 5 ins (1.955 m)
Wheel track: 10 ft 3 ins (3.12 m)

WEIGHTS:
Empty: 2,683 lb (1,217 kg)
Maximum take-off: 3,638 lb (1,650 kg)
Payload: 961 lb (436 kg)

PERFORMANCE:
Never-exceed speed (V_{NE}): 248 kts (286 mph) 460 km/h
Maximum speed: 159 kts (183 mph) 295 km/h
Cruise speed: 135 kts (155 mph) 250 km/h
Take-off distance: 1,329 ft (405 m)
Landing distance: 1,477 ft (450 m)
Maximum climb rate: 984 ft (300 m) per minute
Ceiling: 18,050 ft (5,500 m)
Range with normal fuel: 324 naut miles (373 miles) 600 km
Range with full fuel: 485 naut miles (559 miles) 900 km

↑ Yakovlev Yak-48 *(Piotr Butowski)*

Yakovlev Yak-48

First flight: Project reportedly developed from the Israeli-developed Galaxy (Yakovlev became a subcontractor).
Certification: To comply with FAR/JAR Pt 25.
Role: Long-range executive/business transport and small regional airliner. Project supported by Governmental resolution of 20 February 1995.
Crew/passengers: 2 crew on VIP version, 3 otherwise. For passengers, see Aircraft variants.
Galley: Galley and toilet standard.
Wing control surfaces: Ailerons, slats, trailing-edge flaps and multi-section spoilers.
Tail control surfaces: Rudder and mid-mounted swept tailplane with elevators.
Engines: 2 CFE738-2 turbofans, each 6,430 lbf (28.6 kN), or Ivchenko PROGRESS/Zaporozhye AI-22-1s, each 7,710 lbf (34.3 kN).
Flight avionics/instrumentation: From Leninets of St Petersburg in co-operation with Finmecanica of Italy. Also Rockwell Collins being considered.

Aircraft variants:
4/8-passenger VIP version, with CFE738-2 turbofans.
18-seat regional airliner, with same engines.
27-seat variant, with same engines. Fuselage lengthened by 8 ft 8 ins (2.65 m).
33-seat variant with AI-22-1 engines. Fuselage lengthened by 8 ft 8 ins (2.65 m).

Details for Yak-48, applying to all variants except as stated

PRINCIPAL DIMENSIONS:
Wing span: 62 ft 6.5 ins (19.06 m)
Maximum length: 63 ft 3.5 ins (19.291 m), or 72 ft 0.5 ins (21.956 m) for 27 and 33 seat variants
Maximum height: 20 ft 11 ins (6.37 m)

CABIN:
Length: 24 ft 7 ins (7.5 m), or 33 ft 3.5 ins (10.15 m) for 27 and 33 seat variants
Width: 7 ft 2 ins (2.186 m) maximum
Height: 6 ft 2 ins (1.87 m) maximum

WINGS:
Area: 344.4 sq ft (32 m^2)

WEIGHTS:
Empty: 20,922 lb (9,490 kg) VIP variant, or 23,479 lb (10,650 kg) 33 seat variant
Maximum take-off: 34,612 lb (15,700 kg) with CFE engines, or 37,478 lb (17,000 kg) with AI-22-1 engines

PERFORMANCE:
Maximum cruise speed: 469 kts (540 mph) 870 km/h
Required runway length: 5,906 ft (1,800 m) for VIP variant, 6,562 ft (2,000 m) for 33 seat variant
Cruise altitude: 44,950 ft (13,700 m) for VIP version, or 39,370-39,700 ft (12,000-12,100 m) for other variants
Range: 2,968 naut miles (3,417 miles) 5,500 km for VIP variant, 1,969 naut miles (2,268 miles) 3,650 km for 18 seat variant, 1,160 naut miles (1,336 miles) 2,150 km for 27 seat variant, and 998 naut miles (1,149 miles) 1,850 km for 33 seat variant

Yakovlev Yak-52

Comments: In 1978, the Yak-52 entered production at Intreprinderea de Avioane (now Aerostar S.A.) in Bacau, Romania. 500th aircraft built in 1983, 1,000th in 1987, 1,500th in 1990. More than 1,700 built at time of writing (large-scale production ended in 1992 due to lack of orders from Russia). In use in CIS, Romania, USA (about 180), UK, Hungary, Canada, Italy, Denmark, and Vietnam. See Aerostar.

Yakovlev Yak-54

First flight: 23 December 1993 (pilot Sh. Khamidulin).
Role: Aerobatic trainer and sports competition, as a 2-seat development of the Yak-55M.
Sales: Production at Saratov. First 10 aircraft built as 4 by design bureau, 2 in Saratov, and 4 in USA. In February 1997, 2 Yak-54s were presented in Seattle, USA. Orders for 48 reported from US dealer (Mitch Travis) with expected further sales of 300. Price US$160,000.
Crew: 2, or pilot only for competition flying.
Cockpit: Tandem, under a single bubble canopy.
Wing characteristics: Mid-wing monoplane with no anhedral/dihedral.
Wing control surfaces: Large horn-balanced ailerons only, with hanging balance tabs.
Tail control surfaces: Horn-balanced elevators and rudder (with tab).
Construction materials: Metal.
Engine: AOOT OKBM/Voronezh M-14P radial, with a 3-blade variable-pitch propeller.
Engine rating: 360 hp (268.5 kW).

Details for Yak-54

PRINCIPAL DIMENSIONS:
Wing span: 26 ft 9 ins (8.16 m)
Maximum length: 22 ft 8 ins (6.91 m)

WINGS:
Aerofoil section: Symmetrical
Area: 138.75 sq ft (12.89 m^2)

UNDERCARRIAGE:
Type: Fixed, with tailwheel

WEIGHTS:
Empty: 1,653 lb (750 kg)
Normal take-off: 2,183 lb (990 kg), or 1,874 lb (850 kg) as a single-seater for competitions
Maximum take-off: 2,425 lb (1,100 kg)

PERFORMANCE:
Never-exceed speed (V_{NE}): 243 kts (280 mph) 450 km/h
Maximum speed: 167 kts (193 mph) 310 km/h
Stall speed: 60 kts (169 mph) 110 km/h
Maximum climb rate: 2,955 ft (900 m) per minute
Roll rate: 6 rad per second, 360° per second
G limits: +9, -7
Ceiling: 13,125 ft (4,000 m)
Ferry range: 378 naut miles (435 miles) 700 km

Yakovlev Yak-55M

First flight: 28 May 1981 (pilot Oleg Bulygin) for Yak-55, and 5 May 1989 (pilot Nikolai Nikityuk) for Yak-55M.
Role: Aerobatics/aerobatics trainer.
Sales: Manufactured at Arsenyev plant; 108 Yak-55s built during 1986-1991 plus 106 improved Yak-55Ms from 1991. Some 50 Yak-55/55Ms sold to the USA. Often used as a trainer, as its performance is inferior to some other competition aircraft and price is much lower due to its conventional metal construction.
Crew: Pilot only.
Wing control surfaces: Drooping ailerons (±25°), with ground-adjustable tabs.
Tail control surfaces: Elevators (±25°), and rudder (27°), all surfaces with ground-adjustable tabs.
Flight control system: Pushrod and cables.
Construction materials: Metal.
Engine: AOOT OMKB/Voronezh M-14P piston engine, with V350TA-D35 2-blade controllable-pitch propeller (optionally 3-blade Hoffmann propeller).
Fuel system: 190 litres maximum.

Details for Yak-55M

PRINCIPAL DIMENSIONS:
Wing span: 26 ft 7 ins (8.1 m)
Maximum length: 23 ft 11 ins (7.29 m)
Maximum height: 9 ft 2 ins (2.8 m)

WINGS:
Aerofoil section: Symmetrical
Area: 137.78 sq ft (12.8 m^2)
Aspect ratio: 5.13

UNDERCARRIAGE:
Type: Fixed, with tailwheel
Main wheel tyre size: 400 × 150 mm
Wheel track: 7 ft 10.5 ins (2.4 m)
Wheel base: 18 ft 9 ins (5.71 m)

WEIGHTS:
Maximum take-off: 1,885 lb (855 kg) for aerobatics, 2,149 lb (975 kg) for ferry flight

PERFORMANCE:
Never-exceed speed (V_{NE}): 243 kts (280 mph) 450 km/h
Maximum level speed: 165 kts (190 mph) 305 km/h
Stall speed: 54-57 kts (62-66 mph) 100-105 km/h
Stall speed in inverted flight: 57-62 kts (66-72 mph) 105-115 km/h
Take-off distance: 493 ft (150 m)
Landing distance: 1,526 ft (465 m)
Maximum climb rate: 3,050 ft (930 m) per minute
G limits: +9, -6
Roll rate: 6 rad per second, 345° per second
Ferry range: 380 naut miles (438 miles) 705 km, with 10% reserve

↑ Yakovlev Yak-54 *(Piotr Butowski)*

↑ Yakovlev Yak-55M *(Piotr Butowski)*

Aircraft variants:
Yak-55 was the initial production version, with wing span of 29 ft 6 ins (9 m) and area of 159.36 sq ft (14.805 m^2).
Yak-55M was conceived to provide higher roll rate and distinctly marked rotation points. Due to shorter wing, roll rate increased by 50% (from 4 to 6 rad per second) and maximum level speed by 8 kts (9 mph) 15 km/h. Higher wing loading was compensated by drooping ailerons (instead of slotted ailerons for Yak-55). Pilot's seat was reclined 28°. New wheels and new hydraulic (rather than mechanical) wheel brakes were introduced.

Yakovlev Yak-56

First flight: Expected late 1998 or early 1999.
Role: Piston-engined primary trainer, as a development of the Yak-54 aerobatics trainer (initially known as Yak-54M).
Crew: 2 in tandem cockpits (instructor at rear).
Crew escape: Lightweight Zvezda/Sukhoi KS-38 ejection seats.
Expendable weapons and equipment: Gun packs, bombs and rockets suspended on 2 underwing pylons.
Engine: 400 hp (298 kW) AOOT OKBM/Voronezh M-14PF radial piston engine.
Undercarriage: Retractable, with nosewheel.

Yakovlev Yak-57

Comments: Project for a new single-seat competition aerobatics aircraft, with a piston engine.

Yakovlev Yak-58

First flight: 17 April 1994 in Tbilisi (pilot Alexander Vyatkin); originally believed to have flown on 26 December 1993.
Certification: Testing started in December 1997.
Role: Business and executive transport, air-taxi, light cargo carrying, training, liaison, patrol of forests/gas and oil pipelines, EEZ/fishery survey, and ecological work. Cabin allows future modification to ambulance and other roles. A radio surveillance version was shown at the Paris Air Show in 1997 with Thomson-CSF Communications system enabling detection of emergency calls, illegal activities and other radio communications signals; operator console with a computer and display in the cabin.
Sales: Manufactured at Tbilisi, Georgia (no prototypes built by Yakovlev). At time of writing, 2 at Zhukovsky test centre and some 20 in assembly or completed at Tbilisi. An order for 12 from Alakon Russian-Kazakh joint venture reported, as well as options for 100. Large number of options to buy received.
Crew/passengers: Seats for 6 in the all-passenger cabin layout.
Wing characteristics: Low mounted and constant chord, with down-turned wingtips. Supports the tail booms.
Wing control surfaces: Ailerons and flaps.
Tail control surfaces: Tall twin boom unit, with twin inward-toed fins/rudders and a joining tailplane with elevator.
Canards: Small fixed canards added on production aircraft, fitted to the cabin doors.
Fuselage: Central nacelle type, with rear-mounted engine. Large doors.
Engine: Shrouded AOOT OKBM/Voronezh M-14PT radial, with a 3-blade variable-pitch pusher propeller. Allison turboprop-powered version is being proposed.
Engine rating: 360 hp (268.5 kW); planned increase to 400 hp (298 kW).
Flight control system: Mechanical, except hydraulic flaps.
Flight avionics/instrumentation: VFR.

Details for Yak-58

PRINCIPAL DIMENSIONS:
Wing span: 41 ft 8 ins (12.7 m)
Maximum length: 28 ft 1 ins (8.55 m)
Maximum height: 10 ft 4.5 ins (3.16 m)

WINGS:
Area: 215.28 sq ft (20 m^2)

UNDERCARRIAGE:
Type: Retractable, with nosewheel

WEIGHTS:
Empty: 2,800 lb (1,270 kg)
Maximum take-off: 4,685 lb (2,125 kg)
Payload: 992 lb (450 kg)

PERFORMANCE:
Maximum cruise speed: 162 kts (186 mph) 300 km/h
Long-range cruise speed: 154 kts (177 mph) 285 km/h
Take-off distance: 2,001 ft (610 m)
Landing distance: 1,969 ft (600 m)
Ceiling: 13,125 ft (4,000 m)
Range with full payload: 539 naut miles (621 miles) 1,000 km, with 45 minutes reserve

Aircraft variants:
Yak-58, as detailed.
Radio surveillance version (with Thomson-CSF Communications system) for real-time processing of signals from voice communications to digital data transmissions. Main task to provide interception, direction finding, homing, transmission location, listening, analysis, decoding and recording of signals. System can also integrate and merge other data from optical and infra-red sensors, replay mission with onboard observation camera, and more. Frequency range 20–500 MHz (upgradable) for direction finding and 2–500 MHz (upgradable) for listening. Precision of direction finding antenna <1.5° RMS. Scanning rate 40 MHz/s to 2,000 MHz/s. Operational sensitivity 3μV/m typical (10 mW at 180 km).

Yakovlev Yak-112

First flight: 20 October 1992 of Smolensk-built aircraft (pilot Vladimir Yakimov); 19 October 1993 of Irkutsk-built aircraft (sometimes known as Yak-112I), both with Teledyne Continental IO-360-ES engines. 15 December 1995 with Textron Lycoming IO-540-ES engine. 23 April 1997 with Teledyne Continental IO-550M engine.
Role: Passenger carrying, light cargo and mail carrying, glider towing, powerline/forest patrol, air ambulance, fish reserve survey, and agricultural.
Sales: Series manufacturing was launched at Smolensk, but currently production at Irkutsk aircraft plant only (no prototypes built by Yakovlev). At least 6 aircraft were flying at the time of writing. Many hundreds of 'soft' orders reported.

↑ Yakovlev Yak-58 shown in radio surveillance version. Note the underfuselage direction finding antennae *(Piotr Butowski)*

↑ Yakovlev Yak-112 *(Piotr Butowski)*

Crew/passengers: Pilot plus 3.
Wing characteristics: Strut-braced, high wing with down-turned tips.
Wing control surfaces: Ailerons.
Tail control surfaces: Horn-balanced elevators and rudder.
Construction materials: Much use of composites.
Engine: Textron Lycoming IO-540 or Teledyne Continental IO-550M (260 hp, 194 kW), with 6 ft 9 ins (2.05 m) diameter Hartzell 3-blade propeller for production aircraft. Originally, Teledyne Continental IO-360-ES on the prototype. 2 Russian-made engines were also considered for Yak-112, AOOT OKBM/Voronezh M-17 and RKBM/Rybinsk DN-200, but both were halted.
Fuel system: 260 lb (120 kg).
Flight avionics/instrumentation: Export aircraft have AlliedSignal Bendix/King radio communications (KY 196A-30, KT 76A), flight control (KAP-150) and navigation (KC 55A, KNS 81-10, KX 165, KP 87) systems for all-weather, day and night flying. Modern Russian MIKBO-3 (malogabaritnyi integrirovannyi kompleks bortovogo oborudovanya, small-size integrated airborne instrument system) was under development, but now terminated.

Details for Yak-112

PRINCIPAL DIMENSIONS:
Wing span: 33 ft 7.5 ins (10.25 m)
Maximum length: 22 ft 10 ins (6.96 m)
Maximum height: 9 ft 6 ins (2.9 m)

WINGS:
Area: 182.6 sq ft (16.96 m^2)
Aspect ratio: 6.19

UNDERCARRIAGE:
Type: Fixed, with nosewheel

WEIGHTS:
Empty: 2,072 lb (940 kg)
Maximum take-off: 3,053 lb (1,385 kg)
Payload: 798 lb (362 kg)

PERFORMANCE:
Maximum cruise speed: 124 kts (143 mph) 230 km/h
Long-range cruise speed: 113 kts (130 mph) 210 km/h
Landing speed: 65 kts (75 mph) 120 km/h
Take-off distance: 853 ft (260 m)
Landing distance: 1,115 ft (340 m)
Ceiling: 13,125 ft (4,000 m)
Range with full fuel: 523 naut miles (602 miles) 970 km
Range with full payload: 216 naut miles (248 miles) 400 km

Aircraft variants:
First aircraft with 210 hp (156.6 kW) engine was underpowered and had to be radically upgraded.
Current aircraft have 260 hp (194 kW) engine with new propeller (formerly 2-blade of 6 ft 4 ins, 1.93 m diameter) and lowered structural weight, as well as new engine cowling and mount, new fuel system, modified undercarriage springs and reshaped wheel fairings, deleted wingtips, and added wing-root fillets. As described.

Aerotek — South Africa

Full name: Manufacturing and Aeronautical Systems Technology.
Corporate address: PO Box 395, Pretoria 0001.
Telephone: +27 12 841 2780, 4866 **Facsimile:** +27 12 349 1158
Information: Derick Knoll (Marketing Manager).

↑ **Aerotek Hummingbird** *(courtesy Aerotek)*

Aerotek Hummingbird

First flight: 8 May 1993.
Certification: Meets FAR Pt 23 requirements.
Role: Light aircraft, designed as a very stable, observation platform, capable of low-speed flight.
Crew/passengers: 2 seats, with possibility for a third seat in the payload area in an emergency. 4-seat version is envisaged.
Wing control surfaces: Plain ailerons (25% chord) and split flaps (25% chord).
Tail control surfaces: Single elevator and rudder. Tailplane, elevator and rudder are removable for transportation.
Flight control system: Pushrod and cables.
Construction materials: Glassfibre and Nomex.
Engine: Textron Lycoming O-360-A3A piston engine, with a 2-blade fixed-pitch pusher propeller.
Engine rating: 180 hp (134 kW).
Fuel system: 80 litres in 2 wing tanks.
Braking system: Mainwheels brake independently.
Flight avionics/instrumentation: VFR, with various options.

Details for Hummingbird

PRINCIPAL DIMENSIONS:
Wing span: 37 ft 9 ins (11.5 m)
Maximum length: 22 ft (6.7 m)
Maximum height: 7 ft 10.5 ins (2.4 m)

CABIN:
Width: 4 ft 2 ins (1.27 m) maximum

WINGS:
Aerofoil section: NASA GAW-1
Area: 185.67 sq ft (17.25 m^2)
Aspect ratio: 7.67

UNDERCARRIAGE:
Type: Fixed, with steerable nosewheel

WEIGHTS:
Empty: 1,433 lb (650 kg)
Maximum take-off: 2,425 lb (1,100 kg)
Useful load: 992 lb (450 kg)

PERFORMANCE:
Maximum speed: 120 kts (138 mph) 222 km/h
Cruise speed: 100 kts (115 mph) 185 km/h at 70% power
Stall speed: 38 kts (44 mph) 71 km/h *with flaps*
Take-off and landing distance: <820 ft (250 m)
Maximum climb rate: >1,000 ft (305 m) per minute
Ceiling: 15,000 ft (4,575 m)
Duration: 4.5 hours at cruise speed

FFA Flugzeugwerke Altenrhein A.G. — Switzerland

Corporate address: CH-9423 Altenrhein.
Telephone: +41 71 858 51 11 **Facsimile:** +41 71 858 53 30
Founded: 1948.
Information: Bruno Widmer (*telephone*: +41 71 85 85 325, *facsimile:* +41 71 85 85 331).

↑ **FFA AS 202/18A4 Bravo** *(courtesy FFA)*

FFA AS 202 Bravo series

First flight: 7 March 1969 (for AS 202/15 prototype).
Certification: 12 December 1975 for AS 202/18A and December 1995 for AS 202/32TP.
Role: Light private, training and towing aircraft. AS 202/32TP also suited to liaison, patrol and surveillance. AS 202/18A4 and AS 202/32TP are capable of aerobatics.
Sales: As of May 1998, the AS 202/18A remained available. Only a single AS 202/26A was built. A single AS 202/32TP has been built, but this version is available for purchase also.
Crew/passengers: 2 persons side-by-side with dual controls, with the capability of a third person in non-aerobatic form.
Baggage capacity: 220.5 lb (100 kg) of baggage.
Wing control surfaces: Ailerons (with ground adjustable tabs) and single-slotted flaps.
Tail control surfaces: Elevators (starboard trim tab) and balanced rudder (with tab).
Flight control system: Mechanical, except for electric tabs on the AS 202/18A4.
Construction materials: Metal, but with glassfibre used in the construction of the engine cowls and fairings.

Engine: See Aircraft variants.
Fuel system: 170 litres. AS 202/32TP adds 2 × 57 litre wingtip tanks.
Electrical system: Standard 12 volt supply, via an engine-driven alternator, though all models have the option of a 28 volt supply.
Braking system: Mainwheel hydraulic disc brakes.
Flight avionics/instrumentation: Customer's choice, with options including autopilot and blind-flying equipment.

Aircraft variants:
AS 202/18A4 is the current piston-engined version. 180 hp (134 kW) Textron Lycoming AEIO-360-B1F piston engine, with a Hartzell 2 blade constant-speed or Hoffmann 3-blade propeller.
AS 202/26A1 appeared in 1978. Has 260 hp (194 kW) Textron Lycoming AEIO-540-D4B5 and other improvements. Better hot and high performance.
AS 202/32TP Turbine Bravo was certified in 1995 for utility roles, though it is also aerobatic capable. Main differences are the use of a 420 shp (313.3 kW) Allison 250-B17D turboprop engine (flat rated to 332 shp, 248 kW), with a 6 ft 10 ins (2.08 m) diameter Hartzell HC-B3TF-7A/10173N-19R 3-blade constant-speed propeller, and the adoption of wingtip tanks, raising empty weight and performance.

Details for AS 202/18A4, *with AS 202/32TP in italics*

PRINCIPAL DIMENSIONS:
Wing span: 32 ft 1 ins (9.78 m), *32 ft 8 ins (9.95 m)*
Maximum length: 24 ft 7 ins (7.5 m), *25 ft 6 ins (7.78 m)*
Maximum height: 9 ft 2.5 ins (2.81 m), *the same*

WINGS
Aerofoil section: Modified NACA $63_2618/63_2415$, *the same*
Area: 149.19 sq ft (13.86 m^2), *151.34 sq ft (14.06 m^2)*
Aspect ratio: 6.901, *7.04*

UNDERCARRIAGE:
Type: Fixed, with steerable nosewheel, *the same*
Wheel track: 7 ft 5 ins (2.26 m)

WEIGHTS:
Empty: 1,598 lb (725 kg), *1,653 lb (750 kg)*
Maximum take-off: 2,381 lb (1,080 kg), *the same*, utility; or 2,315 lb (1,050 kg) aerobatic
Landing weight: 2,315 lb (1,050 kg), *the same*

PERFORMANCE:
Maximum speed: 175 kts (201 mph) 324 km/h, *214 kts (246 mph) 396 km/h*, both IAS
Cruise speed: 130 kts (150 mph) 241 km/h, *150 kts (173 mph) 278 km/h*
Stall speed: 58 kts (67 mph) 108 km/h, *62 kts (72 mph) 115 km/h*, both *clean*; 47 kts (54 mph) 87 km/h, *53 kts (61 mph) 98 km/h*, both *with flaps*
Take-off distance: 706 ft (215 m), *509 ft (155 m)*
Landing distance: 689 ft (210 m), *the same*
Maximum climb rate: 890 ft (271 m) per minute, *1,900 ft (580 m) per minute*, both at sea level
Normal acceleration: +6, -3 g, *+4, -2.2*
Maximum range: 500 naut miles (575 miles) 926 km
Duration: 5 hours

Pilatus Aircraft Ltd — Switzerland

Corporate address:
See Combat section for company details

Pilatus PC-6/B2-H4 Turbo Porter

First flight: 4 May 1959 for PC-6 piston-engined prototype.
Certification: Complies with US CAR Part 3 category Normal. Swiss Type Certificate F56-10. Aerial work (agricultural, firefighting, etc) certified under CAR 8. Certified noise level to ICAO Annex 16 is 75.3 dB(A).
Role: Super-STOL utility aircraft, with varied roles including passenger/cargo transport, photogrammetry, air ambulance, liaison, survey, SAR, supply dropping, parachuting, firefighting, cloud seeding, towing and agricultural.
Sales: Over 500 in civil and military use in over 50 countries.
Crew/passengers: Pilot and 7-10 passengers or 10 parachutists or litters.
Agricultural/firefighting equipment: Any Turbo Porter can be temporarily converted for an agricultural role in a few hours. Ag version is available: self-contained system uses 2 underwing Micronair spray pods of 189 litres each and Micronair AU 4000 atomizers with variable output of 0-30 litres per minute. For firefighting, each water load dropped can extinguish an area of fire measuring 66 ft (20 m) wide and 200-390 ft (60-120 m) long, depending on the altitude of flight.
Other equipment: Vertically (through floor hatch) or horizontally (through the sliding door) mounted camera for a photogrammetric role, with conversion from standard transport configuration taking 1 man-hour. For a relief role, supplies weighing up to 661 lb (300 kg) can be air-dropped through the floor hatch.
Wing control surfaces: Ailerons (with geared tabs) and double-slotted flaps.

Details for Turbo Porter

PRINCIPAL DIMENSIONS:
Wing span: 52 ft 1 ins (15.87 m)
Maximum length: 35 ft 9 ins (10.9 m)
Maximum height: 10 ft 6 ins (3.2 m)

CABIN:
Length: 7 ft 7 ins (2.3 m)
Width: 3 ft 10 ins (1.16 m)
Height: 4 ft 2.5 ins (1.28 m)

WINGS:
Aerofoil section: NACA 64-514
Area: 324.53 sq ft (30.15 m^2)
Aspect ratio: 8.35

UNDERCARRIAGE:
Type: Fixed, with steerable and lockable tailwheel. Optional wheel/skis or floats

WEIGHTS:
Empty: 2,800 lb (1,270 kg), standard configuration, with usable fuel, without passenger seats or radio
Maximum take-off: 6,173 lb (2,800 kg), or 5,732 lb (2,600 kg) with wheel/ski undercarriage
Maximum landing: 5,864 lb (2,660 kg)
Payload: 2,083 lb (945 kg) excluding options

PERFORMANCE:
Never-exceed speed (V_{NE}): 151 kts (174 mph) 279 km/h CAS
Maximum cruise speed: 125 kts (144 mph) 232 km/h at sea level
Manoeuvring speed: As for cruise
Stall speed: 58 kts (67 mph) 108 km/h *clean*, 52 kts (60 mph) 97 km/h *with flaps*, CAS
Take-off distance: 646 ft (197 m) at sea level
Landing distance: 417 ft (127 m) at sea level
Maximum climb rate: 1,010 ft (308 m) per minute at sea level
G limits: +3.58, -1.43
Ceiling: 29,000 ft (8,840 m), service
Range: 500 naut miles (575 miles) 926 km at 10,000 ft (3,050 m), optimum cruise speed, no reserve
Range with 2 underwing tanks: 870 naut miles (1,001 miles) 1,611 km
Duration: 4 hours 20 minutes, or 7 hours 35 minutes with underwing tanks

Tail control surfaces: Variable-incidence tailplane, elevator (with Flettner tabs) and rudder.
Flight control system: Mechanical, except for electric tailplane and flaps.
Construction materials: All components are corrosion protected. Aluminium parts (including skin) are Alodine treated and other metals are cadmium-plated or coated with baked enamel.
Engine: Pratt & Whitney Canada PT6A-27 turboprop, with an 8 ft 5 ins (2.57 m) Hartzell HC-B3TN-3D reversing constant-speed 3-blade propeller.
Engine rating: 680 shp (507 kW), flat rated to 550 shp (410 kW).
Fuel system: 644 litres standard, 2 × 243.5 litre underwing tanks optional.
Electrical system: 30 volt starter-generator. 24 volt, 34 or 40 amp-hour ni-cd battery.
Flight avionics/instrumentation: Customer's choice. VFR or IFR. Basic instrumentation includes altimeter, airspeed indicator, vertical speed indicator, and magnetic compass.

↑ Pilatus PC-6/B2-H4 Turbo Porter floatplane

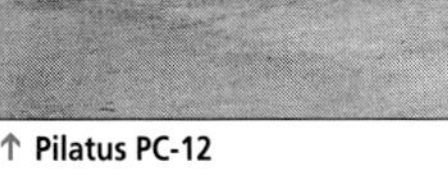

↑ Pilatus PC-12

Pilatus PC-12

First flight: 31 May 1991.
Certification: 30 March 1994 (FAR Pt 23 Normal category to Amdt 42).
Role: Pressurized utility and business aircraft.
Sales: Over 80 delivered at time of writing.
Crew/passengers: 9 or 10 (6 in business configuration), including 1 or 2 pilots respectively. See Aircraft variants for other layouts. Also a litter and attendants in air ambulance role. Dual controls.
Baggage capacity: 40 cu ft (1.13 m^3).
Pressurization system: 5.8 maximum cabin differential.
Wing control surfaces: Mass-balanced ailerons (with ground-adjustable trim tabs) with sealed aileron/wing gap, and 3-position Fowler flaps (0° up, 15° take-off, 40° landing).
Tail control surfaces: Variable-incidence tailplane, elevators and rudder (with Flettner tab).
Flight control system: Mechanical, except for electric tailplane, flaps and rudder tab.
Construction materials: Principally metal, but with Kevlar/glassfibre winglets, glassfibre/honeycomb sandwich engine cowling, and Kevlar honeycomb and glassfibre dorsal and ventral fin fairings. 20,000 flying hours or 27,000 landings fatigue life.
Engine: Pratt & Whitney Canada PT6A-67B turboprop, with an 8 ft 9 ins (2.67 m) Hartzell HC-E4A-3D/E10477K constant-speed 4-blade aluminium propeller.
Engine rating: 1,605 shp (1,197 kW) thermodynamic power, flat rated at 1,200 shp (894.8 kW).
Fuel system: 1,540 litres, of which 1,522 litres are usable.
Electrical system: 28 volt DC supply via a primary 300 amp starter-generator and back-up 100 amp generator. 24 volt, 40 amp-hour ni-cd battery. 7 DC distribution power buses. 115/26 volt AC supply with 2 power buses, at 400 Hz, via 2 × 150 volt static inverters.
Hydraulic system: 3,000 psi for undercarriage only.
Radar: Optional colour weather radar.
Flight avionics/instrumentation: Can operate under VFR and IFR by day and night, and fly into known icing conditions. Standard equipment (primarily AlliedSignal Bendix/King) is KFC 325 integrated AFCS with EFIS, including KMC 321 mode controller, EFS 40 (4 ins, 10 cm displays for EADI and EHSI), KX 165 com/nav transceivers (2 each), KN 63 DME, KR 87 digital ADF, KNI 582 RMI, KI 204 COI, KR 21 marker receiver and lights, KT 70 modes transponder, KEA 130A encoding altimeter, Narco ELT-910 emergency locator transmitter and more. Full range of flight/engine and other instruments. Wide range of optional avionics.

Aircraft variants:
Basic version is the '4.1 ton', with the '4.5 ton' ***Optional Weight Increase*** available.
PC-12 Corporate Commuter seats up to 9 in airline comfort.
PC-12 Executive has high levels of comfort and convenience for 6 passengers, or 4 passengers in 'conferencing' arrangement.
PC-12 Combi can be either the Corporate Commuter or Executive version, easily converted to a combined passenger/cargo arrangement; typically 4 passengers and 210 cu ft (5.95 m^3) of freight or equipment. Large cargo door is standard on all PC-12s, and the flat heavy-load bearing floor permits oversized equipment to be carried.
PC-12 Freighter is a cargo only version.
PC-12 Eagle was first demonstrated in October 1995 and is a special missions version with an underfuselage pannier for electro-optical mission sensors and a forward FLIR turret, and stations inside the cabin for 2 mission operators. Roles include surveillance, comint/elint, and reconnaissance, but can also be used for passenger/cargo carrying. New wingtips (with optional radar in starboard pod) and changes to tail surfaces.

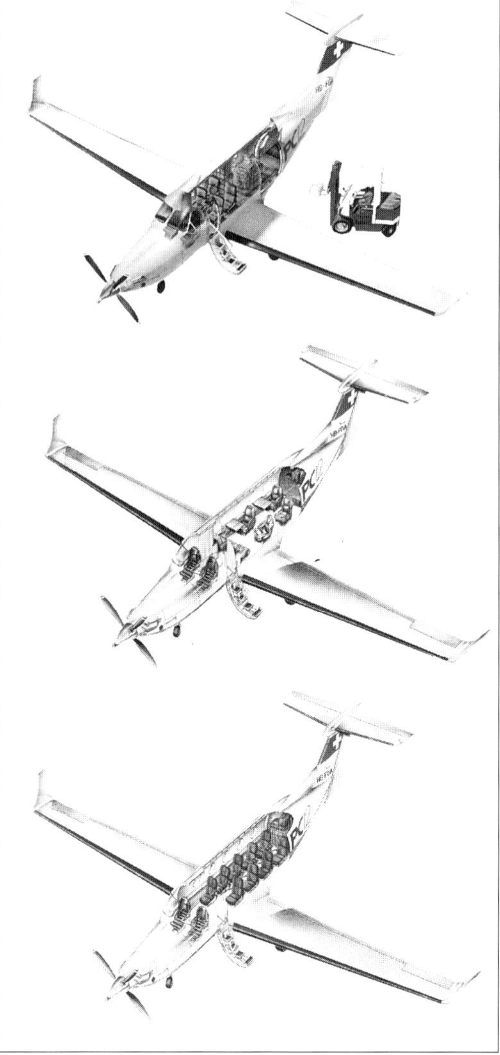

↑ Pilatus PC-12 in Cargo (*top*), Executive and Corporate Commuter layouts *(courtesy Pilatus)*

Details for PC-12

PRINCIPAL DIMENSIONS:
Wing span: 53 ft 3 ins (16.23 m)
Maximum length: 47 ft 3 ins (14.4 m)
Maximum height: 14 ft (4.26 m)

CABIN:
Length: 16 ft 11 ins (5.16 m)
Width: 5 ft (1.53 m)
Height: 4 ft 9 ins (1.45 m)
Cargo area volume: 330 cu ft (9.34 m^3), for up to 3,086 lb (1,400 kg) of cargo
Cargo door size: 4 ft 5 ins × 4 ft 4 ins (1.35 × 1.32 m)

WINGS:
Aerofoil section: LS(1)-417 mod
Area: 277.82 sq ft (25.81 m^2)
Aspect ratio: 10.2

UNDERCARRIAGE:
Type: Retractable, with steerable nosewheel (±12° with pedals, ±60° with differential braking)
Wheel base: 11 ft 7 ins (3.54 m)
Wheel track: 14 ft 10 ins (4.53 m)
Turning radius: 33 ft 6 ins (10.31 m) wingtip, 13 ft 5 ins (4.12 m) nosewheel

WEIGHTS:
Empty: 5,260 lb (2,386 kg) with 11 seats
Maximum take-off and landing: 9,039 lb (4,100 kg), or 9,920 lb (4,500 kg) optional weight increase
Useful load: 3,410 lb (1,547 kg), or 4,233 lb (1,920 kg) optional weight increase
Payload: 2,285 lb (1,036 kg), or 3,108 lb (1,410 kg) optional weight increase

PERFORMANCE:
Maximum cruise speed: 262 kts (301 mph) 485 km/h at 20,000 ft (6,100 m)
Stall speed: 88 kts (101 mph) 163 km/h *clean*, 61 kts (70 mph) 113 km/h *landing configuration*, both at 40° bank angle, at MTOW
Take-off distance: 1,020 ft (310 m) at sea level, ISA, MTOW
Landing distance: 1,395 ft (425 m) at sea level, ISA (roll)
Maximum climb rate: 1,700 ft (518 m) per minute at sea level at 9,920 lb (4,500 kg)
G limits: +3.4, -1.36 *clean*, or +2, -0 *with flaps lowered*
Ceiling: 35,000 ft (10,670 m) service, 30,000 ft (9,150 m) operating altitude
Range: 1,815 naut miles (2,090 miles) 3,363 km, at 204 kts cruise speed and operating altitude
Duration: 8 hours 54 minutes, at 204 kts and operating altitude

Chung Shan Institute of Science and Technology — Taiwan

Comments: The Aeronautical Systems Research division of this Institute has completed preliminary design of a 6/9-seat twin-engined aircraft under the SAP (Small Aircraft Project) programme. Originally expected to have 2 turboprops of Pratt & Whitney Canada PT6A-27 or AlliedSignal TPE331-10U class, a second concept has been displayed in model form showing twin turbofans in the 1,900 lbf (8.45 kN) range, such as the Williams-Rolls FJ44. Maximum take-off weight is said to be about 10,500 lb (4,763 kg), and it is to feature an integrated 'glass' cockpit, with AlliedSignal Bendix/King and Rockwell Collins among contenders. The most striking feature of the SAP is its blended wing/fuselage design, with the inner wing section being of large chord and thickness to increase stability and lift, while the outer panels with winglets are of much reduced chord and thickness. A prototype is anticipated in the year 2000, and partners are being sought.

Aeroprakt Ltd — Ukraine

Corporate address:
ul. Sovkhoznaya 24-39, 252142 Kiev.
Telephone: +380 44 4884055
Facsimile: +380 44 4777835
Information:
Oleg Letovchenko.

ACTIVITIES

▪ Aeroprakt aircraft are marketed by Global Aero Design Centre Pte Ltd, Keppel Distripark, Block 511, Kampong Bahru Road 05-04, Singapore 099447 (*telephone* +65 278 5466, *facsimile* +65 270 9122).

Aeroprakt A-20

Role: Light/ultralight private and multi-purpose monoplane, with latter roles possibly including survey, aerial photography, patrol, training and towing Has performed well in international ultralight competitions. Parachute recovery system.
Sales: Manufactured by Kiev aircraft production plant, and sold to customers in at least 9 countries. Sometimes known by the name Flirt.
First flight: 5 August 1991, and 11 May 1997 for A-20M.
Crew/passengers: 2 persons in tandem, with dual controls.
Wing characteristics: Strut-braced high-wing monoplane, with constant-chord wings.
Wing control surfaces: Flaperon over entire span.
Tail control surfaces: T-tail, with single elevator (with tab) and rudder.
Flight control system: Mechanical, with rods and cables.
Construction materials: Pod and boom type. Mainly aluminium alloy, except for composites (honeycomb) fuselage pod and some use of fabric covering on wings and tail. Can be dismantled for storage/transport.
Engine: See aircraft variants.
Fuel system: 43 litres for A-20-503 and 38 litres for A-20M.

Aircraft variants:
A-20-503 is a basic version powered by a 50 hp (37.3 kW) Rotax 503, with a 3-blade pusher propeller. 43 litres of fuel. Price $20,500.
A-20-582 has a 64 hp (47.7 kW) Rotax 582 engine, providing a cruise speed of 73 kts (84 mph) 135 km/h.

↑ **Aeroprakt A-20** *(Geoffrey P. Jones)*

A-20-912 (or ***A-20M***) is an upgraded 'high-speed' version with an 80 hp (59.7 kW) Rotax 912, 38 litres of fuel, new undercarriage, covered engine, and shorter wing. First flown on 11 May 1997. Price $27,500.

Details for A-20-503, *with A-20-912 in italics*

PRINCIPAL DIMENSIONS:
Wing span: 37 ft 1 ins (11.3 m), *31 ft 2 ins (9.5 m)*
Length: 21 ft 9.5 ins (6.64 m)
Height: 5 ft 10 ins (1.77 m)

WINGS:
Aerofoil section: P-IIIa-15
Area: 165.76 sq ft (15.4 m^2), *143.16 sq ft (13.3 m^2)*
Dihedral: 1° 30'
Incidence: 3° 30'

UNDERCARRIAGE:
Type: Fixed, with tailwheel. Wheel fairing on the mainwheels

WEIGHTS:
Empty: 463 lb (210 kg), *551 lb (250 kg)*
Maximum take-off: 882 lb (400 kg), *992 lb (450 kg)*

PERFORMANCE:
Maximum speed: 81 kts (93 mph) 150 km/h, *113 kts (130 mph) 210 km/h*
Cruise speed: 65 kts (75 mph) 120 km/h, *97 kts (112 mph) 180 km/h*
Take-off and landing distance: 263 ft (80 m)
Maximum climb rate: 787 ft (240 m) per minute, *984 ft (300 m) per minute*
Ceiling: 11,480 ft (3,500 m), service
G limits: +4, -2
Range: 216 naut miles (248 miles) 400 km

↑ **Aeroprakt A-22** *(courtesy Andriej Sowienko via Piotr Butowski)*

A-20S is an ecological survey version, with nose-mounted radiometer.

Aeroprakt A-22

First flight: 21 October 1996 (pilot Yuri Yakovlev).
Certification: Designed to conform to BFU-95.
Role: 2-seat private high-wing cabin monoplane, also suited to towing, survey, aerial photography and other roles.
Sales: Price $33,000.
Wing characteristics: Strut-braced, high-wing monoplane with forward-swept wings.
Wing control surfaces: Slotted flaperons over entire trailing edge of wings.
Tail control surfaces: Conventional rudder and elevators (with tab).
Construction materials: Mainly aluminium alloy, except for some use of fabric covering on wings and tail, and GFRP for engine cowl, tip of fin, wing fillets and elsewhere. Can be dismantled for storage/transport.
Engine: Rotax 912UL piston engine, with 5 ft 3 ins (1.6 m) DUC 30 3-blade ground-adjustable tractor propeller. Optional Rotax 503 and 582.
Engine rating: 80 hp (59.7 kW).
Fuel system: 38 litres.

Aeroprakt A-24

Comments: 2-seat amphibian, powered by a Rotax 582 engine. Reportedly based on the Russian Gidroplan Che-20 (which see), matched with the wings and tail of the Aeroprakt A-20. Design stage at time of writing.

Details for Aeroprakt A-22

PRINCIPAL DIMENSIONS:
Wing span: 32 ft 2 ins (9.8 m)
Length: 20 ft 8 ins (6.3 m)
Height: 7 ft 11 ins (2.41 m)

WINGS:
Aerofoil section: P-IIIa-15
Area: 147.68 sq ft (13.72 m^2)
Aspect ratio: 7
Sweep forward: 2° 30'
Dihedral: 1° 30'
Incidence: 4°

UNDERCARRIAGE:
Type: Fixed, with steerable nosewheel. All wheels with streamlined fairings

WEIGHTS:
Empty: 573 lb (260 kg)
Maximum take-off: 992 lb (450 kg)

PERFORMANCE:
Maximum speed: 92 kts (106 mph) 170 km/h
Cruise speed: 70 kts (81 mph) 130 km/h
Stall speed: 35 kts (41 mph) 65 km/h, *clean*
Landing speed: 38 kts (43.5 mph) 70 km/h
Take-off and landing distance: 296 ft (90 m)
Climb rate: 984 ft (300 m) per minute
Ceiling: 14,760 ft (4,500 m), service
G limits: +4, -2
Range: 243 naut miles (279 miles) 450 km

Antonov ASTC (Aviation Scientific-Technical Complex) — Ukraine

Corporate address:
See Electronic section for company details.

Antonov An-3

First flight: 13 May 1980 (piloted by Sergei Gorbik).
Role: Mid-life upgrade of An-2 with new TVD-20 turboprop engine and modified airframe. According to Antonov, the An-3 is 60% more effective and 30% less expensive in operation than An-2.
Sales: First project for a re-engined An-2 with a turboprop began in 1971 (with TV2-117S engine), and a prototype with a TVD-20 flew in 1980 but did not enter series production. Currently, the re-engining of An-2s to An-3 standard is to take place at Omsk (Russia) and Vinnitsa (Ukraine). Polyot plant at Omsk was ready to convert 70-80 aircraft in 1998 and 200 in 1999. An order for 30 was reported from the Tyumenaviatrans company.
Crew/passengers: 1 or 2 flight crew and 12 passengers or 4,409 lb (2,000 kg) of cargo, or 2,200 litres of chemicals for agricultural work.
Airframe: As for An-2 (which see in Polish section), except separation of the cockpit from the main cabin and effective air conditioning system (in An-2, access to the cockpit is via the main cabin, whereas An-3 has a separate door for the pilot at the port side of the fuselage). Visibility from the cockpit has been improved by moving the cockpit forward by 18 ins (46 cm), though the modification was necessary to balance the lighter weight of the engine. Several small cockpit windows on the starboard side have been replaced by a single large window.

↑ **Antonov An-3. Note the reshaped nose and large cockpit window** *(Piotr Butowski)*

Details for An-3

PRINCIPAL DIMENSIONS: As for An-2 except:
Length: 44 ft 9 ins (13.65 m)

WEIGHTS:
Take-off: 12,786 lb (5,800 kg)
Payload: 4,409 lb (2,000 kg)

PERFORMANCE:
Cruise speed: 119 kts (137 mph) 220 km/h
Take-off distance: 460 ft (140 m)
Landing distance: 345 ft (105 m) with thrust reverse
Range: 415 naut miles (478 miles) 770 km with 3,307 lb (1,500 kg) payload

Engine: OMKB/Omsk TVD-10 turboprop, with 3-blade AV-17 propeller. Also OMKB/Omsk TVD-20, RKBM/Rybinsk TVD-1500 and Pratt & Whitney Canada PT6A-45 are under consideration.
Engine rating: 1,000 shp (746 kW).

Aircraft variants:
An-3T transport.
An-3SKh (selskokhozyaistvennyi) agricultural aircraft.
An-3 'VIP' transport with luxury cabin.

↑ Model of the Antonov An-104 *(Piotr Butowski)*

Antonov An-102 and An-104

Comments: An-102 and An-104 have been projects for specialized agricultural aircraft. An-102 was to have a take-off weight of 12,125 lb (5,500 kg), including 3,968 lb (1,800 kg) of chemicals. Wing span was 66 ft 11 ins (20.4 m) and length 44 ft 7 ins (13.6 m). It was to use a single TVD-1500SKh turboprop engine of 1,300 shp (969 kW), with a 3-blade propeller. Operational speed has been quoted as 81-97 kts (93-112 mph)150-180 km/h, required airfield length 1,641 ft (500 m), flight endurance 6 hours, and ferry range 539 naut miles (621 miles) 1,000 km. According to design calculations, the aircraft would be capable of spraying 160 hectares at a fuel consumption of 1.4 kg per hectare. The main task for the designers of the An-102 was to provide a way of allowing more accurate dosage and spraying of chemical agents, to be achieved by an operating altitude of only 17 ft (5 m) which, in turn, called for improved navigation and flight equipment. Pilot comfort was to be enhanced by the adoption of a ventilated cockpit. Other variants of An-102 would allow forest patrol, cargo carrying and other roles. However, work on An-102 has been halted due to lack of funding, with the An-104 (see photograph) currently the favoured programme. The An-104 retains the general layout of An-102 but is much lighter, with a design take-off weight of 5,512 lb (2,500 kg) and chemical load of 1,764 lb (800 kg). Powered by a TVD-100 turboprop of 600-800 shp (447-597 kW), it will require 1,313 ft (400 m) of runway.

Icar Ltd — Ukraine

Corporate address:
Aviaklub Ikar, 252151 Kiev, pr. Vozdukhoflotskiy, 94A.

Telephone: +380 44 245 9597, 269 0007
Facsimile: +380 44 245 9597, 269 0007

Founded: 1995.

Information:
Vladimir Karpets (Director - *telephone* +380 44 271 0741), and Sergei Orlov (Chief designer - *telephone* +380 44 476 9209).

Details for AP-23M with Rotax 912, *with weights and performance when Rotax 582 fitted in italics*

PRINCIPAL DIMENSIONS:
Wing span: 30 ft 4 ins (9.25 m)
Maximum length: 20 ft 6 ins (6.25 m)
Maximum height: 5 ft 9 ins (1.75 m)

WINGS:
Area: 126.4 sq ft (11.74 m^2)
Aspect ratio: 7.29

UNDERCARRIAGE:
Type: Fixed, with large mainwheels and tailwheel

WEIGHTS:
Empty: 569 lb (258 kg), *529 lb (240 kg)*
Take-off: 992-1,102 lb (450-500 kg)
Payload: Pilot plus 287 lb (130 kg)

PERFORMANCE:
Maximum speed: 108 kts (124 mph) 200 km/h
Cruise speed: 86 kts (99 mph) 160 km/h, *59 kts (68 mph) 110 km/h*
Stall speed: 27 kts (31 mph) 50 km/h
Landing speed: 32 kts (37 mph) 60 km/h
Take-off distance: 230 ft (70 m), *279 ft (85 m)*
Landing distance: 230 ft (70 m)
Maximum climb rate: 984 ft (300 m) per minute, *689 ft (210 m) per minute,* both at sea level
Ceiling: 11,480 ft (3,500 m), service
G limits: +4, -3
Range with full fuel: 539 naut miles (621 miles) 1,000 km, *394 naut miles (453 miles) 730 km*

↑ Icar AP-23 Enei

Icar AP-23 Enei

First flight: 26 November 1995, piloted by Igor Gaponovich.
Certification: Conforms to JAR-VLA.
Role: Light sporting, training and utility aircraft. STOL features, due to large flaps and strong undercarriage.
Sales: Single AP-23 prototype built, with series production of the AP-23M.
Crew/passengers: 2 persons, side-by-side.
Wing characteristics: Braced, high-mounted, single-spar.
Wing control surfaces: Large 4-position flaps and ailerons.
Tail control surfaces: Elevator and rudder.
Construction materials: Fuselage of welded steel tubes. Wing structure of riveted stamped aluminium. Glassfibre for engine cowling and forward fuselage skin, the remainder fabric covered.
Engine: Rotax 912 (80 hp, 59.7 kW) or Rotax 582 (64 hp, 47.7 kW) piston engine, with 3-blade propeller.

Aircraft variants:
AP-23 Enei is the prototype, as described.
AP-23M is the production version with some improvements to the aerodynamics (undercarriage struts, engine cowling) and wider use of composites materials.

Lilienthal JSC — Ukraine

Corporate address:
310108, Kharkov, pr. Kurchatova, 12/72.

Telephone: +380 572 441166, 442467
Facsimile: +380 572 354403

Founded: 1975.

Employees: 40.

Information:
Vladimir Meglinsky, marketing.

ACTIVITIES

▪ Design, production and sale of hang gliders (X-14), motordeltas (X-29, X-35, X-37) and light aircraft (X-32 Bekas), plus pilot training.

Lilienthal X-32 Bekas

First flight: March 1993 (piloted by Konstantin Vasilenko).
Certification: 1995.
Role: Recreational flying (X-32AT), training (X-32UT), and chemical agricultural work (X-32SKh). X-32H is a floatplane variant.
Sales: Series built.
Crew/passengers: 2, in tandem.
Wing characteristics: Braced high-wing monoplane.
Wing control surfaces: Flaps and ailerons.
Tail unit: T-type with elevator and rudder. Ventral fin.
Engine: Standard Rotax 582. Rotax 462 (53 hp, 39.5 kW) or Rotax 618 (75 hp, 56 kW) can be fitted at customer's request. VPSh-2 fixed-pitch 3-blade pusher propeller.
Engine rating: 64 hp (47.7 kW).
Fuel system: 60 litres. Additional 25 litre fuel tank can be fitted in the fuselage.
Flight avionics/instrumentation: VFR.

↑ Lilienthal X-32 Bekas *(Piotr Butowski)*

Details for X-32 Bekas

PRINCIPAL DIMENSIONS:
Wing span: 29 ft 6 ins (9 m)
Maximum length: 21 ft 6 ins (6.56 m)
Maximum height: 6 ft 4.5 ins (1.94 m)

WINGS:
Aerofoil section: NACA 4412
Area: 132.7 sq ft (12.33 m^2), gross
Aspect ratio: 6.57

UNDERCARRIAGE:
Type: Fixed with nosewheel. Main wheels with brakes. Ski and float undercarriage optional
Wheel tyre size: 400 × 90 mm
Wheel base: 6 ft 11 ins (2.1 m)
Wheel track: 5 ft 7 ins (1.7 m)

WEIGHTS:
Empty, operating: 551 lb (250 kg)
Maximum take-off: 992 lb (450 kg)

PERFORMANCE:
Never-exceed speed (V_{NE}): 90 kts (104 mph) 168 km/h
Maximum operating speed: 81 kts (93 mph) 150 km/h
Cruise speed: 67.5 kts (78 mph) 125 km/h
Stall speed: 31 kts (36 mph) 57 km/h *with flaps*
Landing speed: 32 kts (37 mph) 60 km/h
Take-off distance: 164 ft (50 m)
Landing distance: 98 ft (30 m)
Maximum climb rate: 787 ft (240 m) per minute, at sea level
Ceiling: 13,125 ft (4,000 m), service
G limits: +4.28, -2.14
Duration: 5 hours or 6.5 hours with additional fuel tank

Chichester-Miles Consultants Ltd (CMC) — United Kingdom

Corporate address:
4 The Woodford Centre, Lysander Way, Old Sarum, Salisbury, Wiltshire SP4 6BU.
Telephone: +44 1722 328777
Facsimile: +44 1722 335888
Information:
Chris Burleigh MSc, C.Eng, MRAeS (Chief Designer).

ACTIVITIES

■ Has developed the Leopard 4-seat sports executive jet.

CMC Leopard

First flight: 12 December 1988 of first (unpressurized) prototype with Noel Penny Turbines NPT301-3A turbojet engines (flight trials to September 1991). 9 April 1997 for second pre-production prototype (pressurized), with Williams FJX-1 engines.
Certification: Production aircraft to be certified to FAR Pt 23/ JAR Pt 23.
First delivery: Target date for first sales 2002.
Role: 4-seat sports executive jet.
Sales: Maximum selling price at time of writing US$1,350,000 for equipped production aircraft, excluding taxes. By November 1997, Leopard 002 had completed the 16-flight First Phase (low-speed phase, restricted to 260 kts TAS) of its flight trials at Cranfield Airfield in Bedfordshire. The aircraft was thereafter prepared for flutter-clearance, handling and performance trials over a flight envelope exceeding 35,000 ft (10,670 m) and the normal operating speed of 434-452 kts. Leopard 002 is representative of the production design and has an EFIS cockpit, liquid anti-icing system (AS&T system for wings and tailerons), in-built Al-mesh lightning protection and provision for high-altitude (45,000 ft, 13,715 m) pressurization/ECS. See First delivery.
Details: Leopard 002 in latest configuration.
Crew/passengers: 4 persons under an upward-opening canopy. Seats semi-reclined by 35°. Optional dual controls. Vapour-cycle air-conditioning.
Pressurization system: 9.6 psi maximum cabin differential.
Wing control surfaces: Full-span (27° chord) plain flaps/lift dumpers/airbrakes with ±45° deflection and pitch/roll tailerons.
Tail control surfaces: Sweptback tailerons with trim for pitch and roll control, and all-moving fin with trim for yaw control.
Flight control system: Simple manual system and power systems all electric.
Construction materials: All composites, using glass/aramid/ carbon reinforcement. Aluminium alloy engine nacelles.
Engines: Original Leopard concept was built around Williams WR19-3 turbofans; prototype 001 had Noel Penny turbojets (see First flight). Leopard 002 has 2 × 700 lbf (3.11 kN) Williams International FJX-1 turbofans; by 1999-2000 these experimental engines will be replaced by the first examples of the new 950 lbf (4.23 kN) FJX-2 in 002, as required for production aircraft.

↑ CMC Leopard 002 pre-production sports executive jet

Electrical system: 24 volt for undercarriage, flaps, trim and canopy operation.
Flight avionics/instrumentation: Full avionics, with AlliedSignal Bendix/King EFIS and conventional standby.

Details for Leopard in current form

PRINCIPAL DIMENSIONS:
Wing span: 23 ft 6 ins (7.16 m)
Maximum length: 24 ft 10 ins (7.7 m)
Maximum height: 6 ft 9 ins (2.06 m)

WINGS:
Aerofoil section: ARA-designed transonic/laminar flow/supercritical
Area: 62.9 sq ft (5.85 m^2)
Aspect ratio: 8.78

UNDERCARRIAGE:
Type: Retractable, with twin steerable nosewheels, with oleo main legs and rubber-in-compression nose leg
Wheel base: 10 ft 6 ins (3.2 m)
Wheel track: 11 ft 4 ins (3.45 m)

WEIGHTS:
Empty: 2,200 lb (998 kg)
Maximum take-off: 4,000 lb (1,814 kg)

PERFORMANCE (provisional)**:**
Cruise speed: Mach 0.76-0.8 at 45,000-51,000 ft (13,715-15,545 m)
Required field length for take-off: 2,750 ft (838 m) at sea level, ISA
Required field length for landing: 2,450 ft (747 m) at sea level, ISA
Maximum climb rate: 6,430 ft (1,960 m) per minute at sea level
Ceiling: 55,000 ft (16,765 m), service
Range with full payload: 1,500 naut miles (1,725 miles) 2,775 km

FLS Aerospace Limited — United Kingdom

Corporate address:
Long Border Road, Stansted Airport, Essex CM24 1RE.
Telephone: +44 1279 680068
Facsimile: +44 1279 680047
E-mail: sales@flsaerospace.com
Information:
Bryan Southgate.

ACTIVITIES

■ FLS Aerospace is said to be Europe's leading independent aircraft maintenance organization. It offers a range of services, including aircraft engineering and component support for civil operators worldwide. Products range from aircraft heavy maintenance and modification through aircraft coating, overhaul and repair of structural/electrical and hydraulic components, backed by extensive spares holdings, logistical network and airline technical services support. Operates from maintenance centres at London-Stansted, London-Heathrow, Manchester and Copenhagen-Denmark international airports, and a components storage and distribution centre at London-Heathrow. Approvals include CAA, JAA and USA. Quality standards to ISO 9001.
■ FLS's 2 general aviation aircraft projects, **Sprint** and **Optica**, were both for sale at the time of writing in May 1998.

Slingsby Aviation Ltd

United Kingdom

Corporate address:
Kirkbymoorside, York YO6 6EZ.

Telephone: +44 1751 432474
Facsimile: +44 1751 431173
Telex: 57911 SELG
E-mail: SAL1@Slingsby.co.uk

Information:
Chris Holliday (International Sales Executive).

ACTIVITIES

- Member of the ML Holdings PLC group of companies.
- Offers a comprehensive professional pilot training programme in addition to the sale of Firefly aircraft and sub-contract component manufacture.

Slingsby T67 Firefly series

First flight: 15 May 1981 as the T67A, a licence-built Fournier RF6B.
Certification: All current models are certified to FAR 23 Amdt 27, with T67M260 certified to JAR 23 and FAR 23 Amdt 42. Approved to British BCAR Section K, Issue 6, Chapters 2-2 to 2-5.
Role: Civil and military pilot trainer, aerobatic and private aircraft.
Sales: As of May 1998, 255 delivered to military and commercial academies and other customers in 13 countries, including the T67M260 as the new Enhanced Flight Screener (EFS) aircraft for the USAF (delivered from 1994). Under consideration for the UK MoD programme to replace Bulldog used in University Air Squadron and Air Experience Flight operations, via PFI contracts, still to be decided at time of writing in 1998.
Crew/passengers: Side-by-side 2 seats, with dual controls. Fixed windscreen. Backwards sliding canopy incorporating DV windows with fresh-air scoops.
Baggage capacity: 66 lb (30 kg).
Wing control surfaces: Mass-balanced Frise-type ailerons and fixed-hinge flaps (18° take-off, 40° landing).
Tail control surfaces: Fixed incidence tailplane. Mass-balanced elevator (port trim tab).
Flight control system: Manual, except for optional electric (instead of manual) trim tab.
Construction materials: Glassfibre fuselage of conventional frame and top-hat stringer construction, with stainless steel firewall. All glassfibre wings with double skin (inner corrugated), with flaps having Kevlar skins. Glassfibre tail unit. Tailplane incorporates a built-in VOR antenna, the fin a VHF antenna.

Details for T67C, *with T67M260 in italics where different*

PRINCIPAL DIMENSIONS:
Wing span: 34 ft 9 ins (10.59 m)
Maximum length: 24 ft (7.32 m), *24 ft 10 ins (7.55 m)*
Maximum height: 7 ft 9 ins (2.36 m)

WINGS:
Aerofoil section: NACA 23015/23013 (root/tip)
Area: 136 sq ft (12.63 m^2)
Aspect ratio: 8.88
Dihedral: 3° 30'
Incidence: 3°

UNDERCARRIAGE:
Type: Fairey Hydraulics supplied fixed type, with steerable nosewheel
Main wheel tyre size: 6.00-6
Nose wheel tyre size: 5.00-6
Wheel base: 5 ft (1.52 m)
Wheel track: 8 ft (2.44 m)
Turning circle: 31 ft 9 ins (9.68 m) taxying, 27 ft 4 ins (8.33 m) using tow bar

WEIGHTS:
Empty: 1,510 lb (685 kg), *1,750 lb (794 kg)*
Maximum take-off and landing: 2,150 lb (975 kg), *2,550 lb (1,157 kg)*

PERFORMANCE:
Never-exceed speed (V_{NE}): 180 kts (207 mph) 333 km/h, *195 kts (224 mph) 361 km/h*
Maximum speed: 127 kts (146 mph) 235 km/h, *152 kts (175 mph) 281 km/h at sea level*
Cruise speed: 116 kts (134 mph) 215 km/h, *140 kts (161 mph) 259 km/h*, both at 8,000 ft (2,440 m) and 75% power
Stall speed: 49 kts (57 mph) 91 km/h, *54 kts (62 mph) 100 km/h*, with flaps
Take-off distance: 1,100 ft (335 m), *1,095 ft (334 m)*
Landing distance: 1,142 ft (348 m), *1,315 ft (401 m)*
Maximum climb rate: 900 ft (274 m) per minute, *1,380 ft (420 m) per minute*, at sea level
G limits: +6, -3
Range: 554 naut miles (638 miles) 1,026 km, *407 naut miles (468 miles) 753 km*, 60-65% power at 8,000 ft (2,440 m)
Duration: 7 hours 20 minutes, *5 hours 40 minutes*, best economy speed at 8,000 ft (2,440 m)

Engine: See Aircraft variants.
Fuel system: 159 litres (252 lb, 114 kg) in wing tanks, or optionally 113 litres in the fuselage for T67C1/C2 and T67M Mk 2.
Braking system: Parker Hannifin hydraulically operated brakes.
Flight avionics/instrumentation: Colour coded ASI, altimeter, VSI, electric turn co-ordinator, artificial horizon and directional gyro, accelerometer, engine tachometer, compass and more.

Aircraft variants:
T67C is the low cost aerobatic training variant, offering the same airframe and g limits as the other models. 160 hp (119 kW) Textron Lycoming O-320-D2A piston engine, with a 2-blade fixed-pitch metal propeller. Fuel in the fuselage or wings. No inverted fuel/oil systems. Recommended for a flying syllabus of about 70 hours.
T67M Mk 2 is the lowest powered of the M military models, with a 160 hp (119 kW) AEIO-320-D1B piston engine and Hoffmann 2-blade constant-speed propeller. Inverted fuel and oil systems. Recommended for a military flying syllabus of about 80 hours.
T67M200 is broadly similar to the T67M260 but with a 200 hp (149 kW) AEIO-360-A1E engine and Hoffmann 3-blade constant-speed composites propeller. Fuel and oil systems for sustained inverted flight. Recommended for a military flying syllabus of about 100 hours.
T67M260 has a 260 hp (194 kW) AEIO-540-D4A5 piston engine and 3-blade constant-speed composites propeller. Electric trim standard. Known in USAF service as the T-3A.

↑ Slingsby T67M260 (T-3A) Firefly

ST Aviation Ltd

United Kingdom

Corporate address:
Technology House, High Street, Downham Market, Norfolk PE38 9HH.

Telephone: +44 1366 385 558
Facsimile: +44 1366 385 559
Web site: Http://www.jabiru.co.uk

ACTIVITIES

- UK distributor for the Australian Jabiru (see Australia), but only in Jabiru UL (wing span 30 ft 10 ins, 9.398 m) Ultralight and SK (wing span 26 ft 4 ins, 8.034 m) kit-built versions, at £20,000 each (May 1998).

→ ST Aviation marketed Jabiru SK *(left)* and Ultralight

Warrior (Aero-Marine) Ltd

United Kingdom

Corporate address:
IRC House, The Square, Pennington, Lymington, Hampshire SO41 8GN.

Telephone: +44 1582 488336
Facsimile: +44 1582 488447
E-mail: daviddorman@compuserve.com

Information:
David Dorman.

Warrior (Aero-Marine) Centaur

Comments: Unveiled on 7 September 1998 at Farnborough International, the Centaur is a 6-seat light amphibian with a new hull design inspired by the slender hulls of performance yachts, combined with composites construction. With continuous hydrodynamic streamlines, the hull is said to achieve high speeds in displacement mode and does not encounter a drag 'hump' as it starts to plane. This results in a hull with substantial reductions in hydrodynamic shock-loading, structural weight and drag (hydrodynamic and aerodynamic). Other features include wings that fold to within the beam of the sponsons that are mounted on low stub wings, fitting of an 8.8 hp (6.6 kW) waterjet with 360° vectoring (at the stern) for low speed manoeuvring, and stowable passenger seats for freight carrying. AlliedSignal Bendix/King Silver Crown VFR avionics, with options of IFR, 2-axis autopilot, marine HF radio, bow mounted weather radar, and more. 280-310 hp (209-231 kW) Teledyne Continental IO-550 or Textron Lycoming IO-540 engine. Prototype is expected to be built by CMC (see earlier entry). Delivery of the first 10 production aircraft is expected within 4 years if development is fully funded, priced (in 1998) at about US$500,000 to US$575,000. Certification to JAR 23. Wing span 42 ft 2.5 ins (12.86 m), length 36 ft 7 ins (11.15 m), and height 11 ft 6 ins (3.5 m). Equipped weight 2,426 lb (1,100 kg), maximum payload 1,213 lb (550 kg), maximum fuel 780 lb (354 kg), and MTOW 4,000 lb (1,814 kg). Maximum cruise speed with TIO-580-A1A at 10,000 ft (3,050 m) ISA 139 kts (160 mph) 257 km/h at 85% power, and 1,200 naut miles (1,381 miles) 2,224 km range with 620 lb (281 kg) payload.

↑ Warrior (Aero-Marine) Centaur one-fifth scale model under test. Centaur is expected to operate in 80% rougher water than equivalent seaplanes

Advanced Aerodynamics & Structures Inc (AASI) USA

Corporate address:
3501 Lakewood Blvd, Long Beach, CA 90808.

Telephone: +1 562 938 8618
Facsimile: +1 562 938 8620
Web site: www.AASIaircraft.com

Employees:
95.

Information:
Gene Comfort (Executive Vice President and General Manager).

↑ **AASI Jetcruzer-500** *(courtesy AASI)*

AASI Jetcruzer-500 and -600

Details: Jetcruzer-500, except under Aircraft variants.
First flight: 11 January 1989. First production-standard Jetcruzer-450 flew on 2 September 1992. 22 August 1997 for Jetcruzer-500.
Certification: 4 June 1994 to FAR Pt 23 for Jetcruzer-450, with certification for Jetcruzer-500 production version now expected in latter part of 1999.
Role: Business and multi-purpose aircraft, including military, cargo carrying, ambulance and radar-equipped SAR.
Sales: Pressurized third Jetcruzer-500 under final assembly in July 1998, for test flying from October. 150 orders by August 1998, with deliveries from late 1999. Cost US$1.3 million for 6-seat version and US$1.8 million for 12-seat version.
Crew/passengers: 6 persons (including pilot/s), or 5-seat executive layout with toilet, or litter and 2 attendants in a medevac role. New FAA certified 21-26g seating. Dual controls.
Baggage capacity: 25.25 cu ft (0.715 m^3).
Pressurization system: 6.2 psi maximum cabin differential for Jetcruzer-500.
Wing characteristics: Rear-mounted main wings with compound sweep (34° at roots) and winglets. Spin resistant. FAA certification.
Wing control surfaces: Ailerons. No flaps.
Tail control surfaces: Rudders in winglets.
Flight control system: Pushrods, torque tubes and bellcranks.
Construction materials: Metal wings and canards, graphite composite fuselage (cured in nitrogen pressurized autoclave) with embedded copper and aluminium screen lightning protection.
Engine: Pratt & Whitney Canada PT6A-66A turboprop, with a 6 ft 8 ins (2.03 m) Hartzell 5-blade constant-speed pusher propeller.
Engine rating: 1,572 eshp (1,172 ekW).
Fuel system: 946 litres (1,675 lb, 760 kg) for Jetcruzer-500.
Electrical system: Engine-mounted 300 amp starter-generator. 2 × 24 volt batteries.
Braking system: Hydraulic.
Radar: Optional colour weather radar.
Flight avionics/instrumentation: Includes IFR standard package with AlliedSignal Silver Crown equipment including ADI and HSI, dual VHF com CNI, dual nav with VOR/ILS and G/S, GPS, transponder and marker beacon. Optional avionics include single or dual EFIS (4 ins, 10 cm), Loran, radar altimeter, storm scope, DME, fully coupled 3-axis autopilot, and more. Standard flight instruments include ADI, HSI, airspeed indicator, altimeter, turn and bank indicator, and vertical speed indicator. Range of engine/fuel instruments.

Aircraft variants:
Jetcruzer-450 was the unpressurized prototype version, with a 680 shp (507 kW) PT6A-27 turboprop engine. Not available. Stretched into current Jetcruzer-500 model.
Jetcruzer-500 is the standard length model, with standard pressurization.
Jetcruzer-650 is a stretched 12-seat long-range development, with a PT6A-66A engine. Length increased to 34 ft (10.36 m). MTOW 6,500 lb (2,948 kg).

Details for Stratocruzer

PRINCIPAL DIMENSIONS:
Wing span: 46 ft (14.02 m)
Maximum length: 36 ft (10.97 m)
Maximum height: 13 ft 3 ins (4.08 m)

WEIGHTS:
Empty: 5,850 lb (2,653 kg)
Maximum take-off: 12,500 lb (5,670 kg)

PERFORMANCE:
High cruise speed: 418 kts (482 mph) 775 km/h
Stall speed: 81 kts (93 mph) 150 km/h
Take-off distance: 4,100 ft (1,250 m)
Landing distance: 3,650 ft (1,113 m)
Maximum climb rate: 3,650 ft (1,113 m) per minute
Ceiling: 45,000 ft (13,700 m)
Range with full fuel: 3,213 naut miles (3,700 miles) 5,954 km

Details for Jetcruzer-500

PRINCIPAL DIMENSIONS:
Wing span: 42 ft 2 ins (12.85 m)
Maximum length: 30 ft 2 ins (9.21 m)
Maximum height: 10 ft 2 ins (3.1 m)
Canard span: 18 ft 9 ins (5.72 m)

CABIN:
Length: 15 ft 2.5 ins (4.63 m)
Width: 4 ft 2 ins (1.27 m)
Height: 4 ft 4 ins (1.32 m)
Volume: 211.7 cu ft (5.99 m^3)

WINGS:
Aerofoil section: NACA 2412
Area: 193.2 sq ft (17.95 m^2)
Aspect ratio: 9.22

UNDERCARRIAGE:
Type: Retractable, with steerable nosewheel

WEIGHTS:
Empty: 3,200 lb (1,451 kg)
Maximum take-off: 5,500 lb (2,495 kg)
Maximum landing: 5,400 lb (2,449 kg)
Payload: 2,300 lb (1,043 kg)

PERFORMANCE:
Maximum speed: 313 kts (360 mph) 580 km/h*
Maximum cruise speed: 310 kts (357 mph) 574 km/h*
Stall speed: 65 kts (75 mph) 121 km/h
Take-off distance: 1,947 ft (594 m)
Landing distance: 1,705 ft (520 m)
Maximum climb rate: 3,200 ft (975 m) per minute at MTOW
Ceiling: 30,000 ft (9,140 m)
Range with full fuel: 1,421 naut miles (1,636 miles) 2,633 km at economic cruise speed
Duration: 4.4 hours at 320 kts
*320 kts cruise at over 22,000 ft for certification reported.

AASI Stratocruzer-1250

First flight: Prototype was structurally complete by August 1995. Not said to have flown in reply for this edition of *WA&SD*.
Role: 10/13-seat intercontinental business jet. Cost US$3.5 million.
Engines: 2 Williams-Rolls FJ44-2A turbofans.
Engine rating: Each 2,300 lbf (10.23 kN).

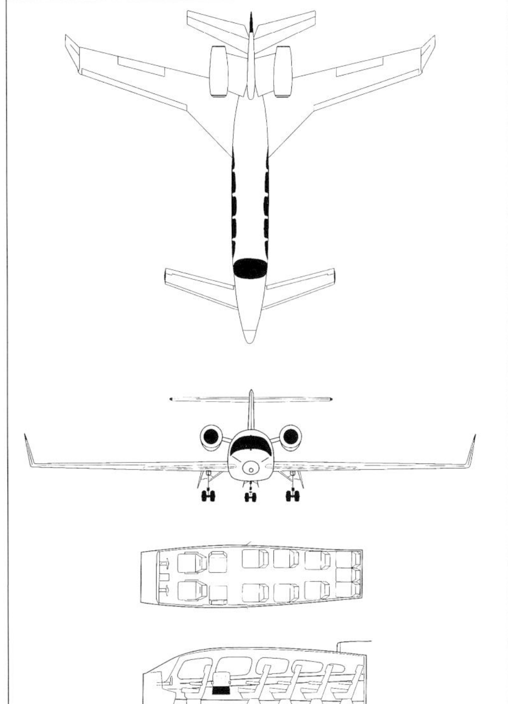

↑ **AASI Stratocruzer-1250 general arrangement** *(courtesy AASI)*

Ag-Cat Corporation USA

Corporate address:
PO Box 351, Malden Industrial Park, Building 167, Malden, MO 63863.

Telephone: +1 573 276 5770
Facsimile: +1 573 276 5776

Founded:
1995 from the previous Malden Ag-Craft Inc.

Information:
Jim Rossiter (Executive Vice-President and COO).

ACTIVITIES

▪ Owner and manufacturer of the former Schweizer Ag-Cat series. At time of writing, the company was undergoing major financial and managerial reorganization.

Ag-Cat Corporation Ag-Cat series

First flight: 27 May 1957 (original Grumman Ag-Cat).
Role: Single-seat piston and turboprop agricultural biplanes, capable also of fire bombing.

Details for Ag-Cat Turbine

PRINCIPAL DIMENSIONS:
Wing span: 42 ft 5 ins (12.93 m) upper
Maximum length: 33 ft 1 ins (10.08 m) (3 point attitude)
Maximum height: 12 ft 1 ins (3.68 m)

WINGS:
Aerofoil section: NACA 4412
Area: 392.7 sq ft (36.48 m^2)

UNDERCARRIAGE:
Type: Fixed, with steerable tailwheel

WEIGHTS:
Empty: 3,150 lb (1,429 kg) standard
Certified gross weight: 5,200 lb (2,359 kg)
Maximum take-off (CAM 8): 7,020 lb (3,184 kg)
Useful load (CAM 8): 3,870 lb (1,755 kg)

PERFORMANCE:
Spray speed: 113 kts (130 mph) 209 km/h
Stall speed: 56 kts (64 mph) 103 km/h
Take-off distance over a 50 ft (15 m) obstacle: 900 ft (274 m) with 680 hp engine at certified gross weight
Landing distance over a 50 ft (15 m) obstacle: 1,333 ft (406 m)
Typical working height: 10 ft (3 m)
Range with full fuel: 172 naut miles (198 miles) 319 km

↑ Ag-Cat Corporation Ag-Cat with a P&W radial engine

Sales: Some 2,600 Ag-Cats of all versions had been built by Grumman and Schweizer since 1958. Now built by Ag-Cat.
Chemical tank/hopper: See Aircraft variants.
Safety equipment: Cockpit strengthened and padded in case of overturn, and pressurized to prevent chemicals entering during spraying operations.
Wing control surfaces: Ailerons on all wings, the lower port having a ground-adjustable tab.
Tail control surfaces: Horn-balanced elevators and rudder, with ground-adjustable tabs.
Flight control system: Mechanical.
Construction materials: Metal, including welded steel-tube fuselage and tail structures and aluminium wings, except for fabric covering on part of the undersurface of the wings and the wire-braced tail unit. Glassfibre wingtips.
Engine: See Aircraft variants.
Electrical system: All have a 24 volt supply. APU external power receptacle.
Braking system: Parker Hannifin hydraulic disc brakes. Parking brake.

Aircraft variants:
Ag-Cat 450B has a 450 hp (335.6 kW) Pratt & Whitney R-985 radial engine and 242 litres of fuel. 43.4 cu ft (1.23 m^3) and 1,230 litres hopper. 25 ins (63.5 cm) wide gate. Solid system controls. Trailing-edge spray system and bottom loader. Other equipment available. Certified gross weight 5,200 lb (2,359 kg), MTOW (CAM 8) 7,020 lb (3,184 kg), maximum useful load (CAM 8) 3,395 lb (1,540 kg), and working speed 100 kts (115 mph) 185 km/h.
Ag-Cat 600B has a 600 hp (447.4 kW) Pratt & Whitney R-1340 radial engine, with 303 litres of fuel. 53.4 cu ft (1.51 m^3) and 1,514 litres hopper. 38 ins (96.5 cm) wide gate. Navigation lights. Trailing-edge spray system and bottom loader. Other equipment available. Weights and speeds as quoted for Ag-Cat 450B except maximum useful load (CAM 8) 3,370 lb (1,529 kg).
Ag-Cat Turbine has either a 680 shp (507 kW) Pratt & Whitney Canada PT6A-15AG or 750 shp (559.3 kW) PT6A-34AG turboprop and 454 litres of fuel. Hopper, gate and spray system as for Ag-Cat 600B.

Air Tractor Inc USA

Corporate address:
PO Box 485, Olney, TX 76374.

Telephone: +1 940 564 5616
Facsimile: +1 940 564 2348

Founded:
1958.

Air Tractor Production to 19 May 1998

Model	No.	Model	No.
AT-250	1	AT-402B	25*
AT-300/301	570	AT-501	9
AT-302/302A	17	AT-502	208
AT-400	72	AT-502A	24*
AT-400A	14	AT-502B	210*
AT-401	198	AT-503	1
AT-401A	1	AT-503A	3*
AT-401B	57*	AT 602	56*
AT-402	67	AT-802	23*
AT-402A	51*	AT-802A	44*

* Still in production

Air Tractor AT-401B, AT-402 series, AT-502 series, AT-503A, AT-602 and AT-802 series

Details: AT-401B, except under Aircraft variants.
Role: Single-seat agricultural aircraft, capable of fire-bombing.
Cockpit: 3-piece windshield optional. Nylon mesh seat cover.
Chemical tank/hopper: Vinylester (Derakane) 1,514 litre hopper, with in-ferry flight hopper rinse system. Window.
Dispersal equipment: 2 ins (5 cm) stainless steel spray system with streamline booms (41 nozzles). Spraybook swath width 80 ft (24.4 m). Transland 2.5 ins (6.4 cm) bottom loading valve. Agrinautics 2 ins (5 cm) spray pump with Transland on-off valve. 5-blade ground-adjustable AT-4300 spray fan, partly to increase fluid flow consistency for more volume per acre. 39 ins (96.5 cm) Transland gate box. Optional 8-unit Micronair mini-atomizer, Transland 22358 extra high volume spreader, Transland 54401 NorCal Swathmaster, 40 extra nozzles for high-volume spraying, Crop Hawk Flowmaster, 3 ins (7.62 cm) spray system, and fire-bombing dump door and vent.
Safety equipment: Energy-absorbing spring undercarriage, burst-resistant fuel tanks, 5,000 lb (2,268 kg) pilot restraint system, heavy wall overturn structure, optimum battery location, ergonomic seat, and flexible fuel line construction. Optional retractable 600 watt landing light.
Wing characteristics: Low-mounted, with Hoerner wingtips to increase span and swath width, and offer faster climb rate and better control. Stall resistant wings, with steel spar caps.
Wing control surfaces: Ailerons (with boost tabs) that droop by 10° when the Fowler high-lift flaps are fully extended.
Tail control surfaces: Horn-balanced elevators and rudder (all with boost tabs).
Flight control system: Mechanical, except for electric flaps.
Construction materials: Metal, except for glassfibre wing/body fairings and wingtips. Reinforced wing leading edges.
Engine: Pratt & Whitney R-1340 radial piston engine, with 2-blade constant-speed propeller. Can be converted to have a new or used turboprop engine.
Engine rating: 600 hp (447.4 kW).
Fuel system: 477 litres. Optional ferry fuel system.
Electrical system: 35 amp alternator.
Braking system: Cleveland 4-piston brakes.
Flight avionics/instrumentation: Options include Narco ELT, AlliedSignal Bendix/King KY 196 com radio and KX 115 nav/com.

Aircraft variants:
AT-401B, as detailed. Useful load 3,725 lb (1,690 kg).
AT-402A became available in 1997 as a lower-powered and lower-cost version of the AT-402, with a 550 shp (410 kW) Pratt & Whitney Canada PT6A-11AG turboprop engine.
AT-402B has a 680 shp (507 kW) Pratt & Whitney PT6A-15AG turboprop engine, with a Hartzell 3-blade constant-speed propeller. Fuel capacity 644 litres standard, with 818 and

↑ **Air Tractor AT-401B** *(courtesy Air Tractor)*

886 litre options. 250 amp starter-generator, and 2 × 24 volt 21 amp-hour batteries. Similar hopper and dispersal equipment to AT-401B. Maximum operating weight (CAM 8) 7,860 lb (3,565 kg) and useful load 4,121 lb (1,869 kg). Similar spray speed. Cruise speed 140 kts (162 mph) 261 km/h at 8,000 ft (2,440 m).
AT-502A is a variant of AT-502 (hopper capacity 1,892 litres), with a 1,100 shp (820 kW) PT6A-45R turboprop and 818 litres of fuel. Wing span 52 ft (15.85 m), providing an 85 ft (26 m) swath width. MTOW 10,480 lb (4,753 kg) and useful load 5,910 lb (2,680 kg). Working speed 104-130 kts (120-150 mph) 193-241 km/h and cruise speed 152 kts (175 mph) 282 km/h using 475 shp at 8,000 ft (2,440 m).
AT-502B has AT-502A's wings combined with a PT6A-15AG engine and 644 litre fuel capacity. MTOW 9,700 lb (4,400 kg). Virtually identical working and cruise speeds to AT-502.
AT-503A is derived from the single AT-503, which was developed as a tandem 2-seater with full cockpit duplication, based on AT-502 with a PT6A-34AG engine. Used for work and ag pilot training.
AT-602 first flew on 1 December 1995, with deliveries from July 1996. Second largest model in the range, with a wing span of 56 ft (17.07 m), wing area 336 sq ft (31.22 m^2), empty weight with spray equipment installed 5,600 lb (2,540 kg), MTOW 12,500 lb (5,670 kg), landing weight 12,000 lb (5,443 kg), useful load 6,900 lb (3,130 kg), and hopper capacity 2,385 litres. Engine is a 1,050 shp (783 kW) Pratt & Whitney Canada PT6A-60AG turboprop, with a 5-blade constant-speed reversing Hartzell HC-B5MP-30/M10876ANS propeller. Fuel capacity 818 litres. Maximum speed 172 kts (198 mph) 318 km/h, cruise speed at 8,000 ft (2,440 m) 158 kts (182 mph) 293 km/h, typical working speed 126 kts (145 mph) 233 km/h, stall speed at MTOW (clean) 86 kts (99 mph) 160 km/h, stall speed at MTOW (with flaps) 72 kts (82 mph) 132 km/h, stall speed as usually landed 52 kts (60 mph) 97 km/h, take-off distance at MTOW with 10° flaps at 35°C (wind 5 mph) on paved runway 1,830 ft (558 m), climb rate at MTOW 650 ft (198 m) per minute, and range at economic cruise speed at 8,000 ft (2,440 m) and 144 kts TAS (no reserve) 521 naut miles (600 miles) 965 km. Has 1.75 ins (44.5 mm) streamline aluminium booms with 44 nozzles, Transland 38 ins (0.97 m) wide gate, 250 amp starter-generator, 3 batteries, air conditioning, cabin heater and hoerner wingtips. Optional equipment includes Transland 22358 high-volume spreader, 8 unit mini atomizer Micronair installation in lieu of standard spray system, non-controllable fire-bombing dump door and vent, and more. Wide range of optional instruments/avionics.
AT-802 first flew in 1990 and is the largest of the Air Tractor range. It is a 2-seater for both agricultural and firefighting roles, the latter having a computerized fire gate and 3,104 litre hopper plus 68 litre foam tank. The agricultural hopper is 3,028 litres. Same MTOW as AT-802A, but useful load of 9,190 lb (4,168 kg) as a fire bomber and 9,540 lb (4,327 kg) for agricultural work. 1,424 shp (1,062 kW) PT6A-67R turboprop, with 961 litres of fuel.
AT-802A is a single-seat version of AT-802, with a 9,330 lb (4,232 kg) useful load as a fire bomber and 9,680 lb (4,391 kg) for agricultural uses. Unchanged hopper capacities. The firefighting version is sometimes referred to as the **AT-802AF**.

↑ **Air Tractor AT-602** *(courtesy Air Tractor)*

Details for AT-401B, *with AT-802A agricultural version in italics*

PRINCIPAL DIMENSIONS:
Wing span: 51 ft 1 ins (15.57 m), *58 ft (17.68 m)*
Maximum length: 27 ft (8.23 m), *35 ft 8 ins (10.87 m)*
Maximum height: 8 ft 6 ins (2.59 m), *11 ft (3.35 m)*

WINGS:
Area: 306 sq ft (28.43 m^2), *391 sq ft (36.33 m^2)*
Aspect ratio: 8.5, *8.6*

UNDERCARRIAGE:
Type: Fixed, with castoring/lockable tailwheel

WEIGHTS:
Empty: 4,244 lb (1,925 kg), *6,320 lb (2,866 kg)*, both with spray equipment
Maximum take-off: 7,860 lb (3,565 kg), *16,000 lb (7,257 kg)*
Maximum landing: 6,000 lb (2,721 kg), *16,000 lb (7,257 kg)*
Useful load: 3,725 lb (1,690 kg), *9,680 lb (4,391 kg)*

PERFORMANCE:
Maximum speed: 135 kts (156 mph) 250 km/h, *182 kts (210 mph) 337 km/h*, both at sea level
Cruise speed: 124 kts (143 mph) 230 km/h at 4,000 ft (1,220 m), *166 kts (191 mph) 307 km/h at 8,000 ft (2,440 m) empty of chemical*
Spray speed: typically 104-122 kts (120-140 mph) 193-226 km/h, *113-139 kts (130-160 mph), 209-257 km/h*
Stall speed: 64 kts (73 mph) 119 km/h clean, 53 kts (61 mph) 98 km/h with flaps, 47 kts (54 mph) 87 km/h as usually landed, all at MLW; *88 kts (101 mph) 163 km/h clean, 76 kts (87 mph) 140 km/h with flaps, 53 kts (61 mph) 99 km/h as usually landed, all at MTOW*
Take-off distance: 1,318 ft (402 m), *1,900 ft (580 m)*, both at MTOW
Maximum climb rate: 1,100 ft (335 m) per minute at sea level, at 6,000 lb weight, *780 ft (238 m) per minute at MTOW and 1,220 shp*
Range: 547 naut miles (630 miles) 1,014 km at 132 mph and 8,000 ft, no reserves, *529 naut miles (610 miles) 981 km/h at economic cruise speed*

Alturair — USA

Corporate address:
See Helicopter section for company details.

Comments: Alturair offers a comprehensive line of custom parts and services for the BD-5 builder, with current developments at Alturair including the GAW wing package (for BD-5G/GR), lightweight rotary engine, drive systems and fast build kit assemblies. BD-5B uses a 90 hp (67 kW) Honda engine, BD-5G a 70 hp (52 kW) Zenoah, BD-5GR a 100+ hp (74.6+ kW) Alturair, and BD-5J a Microturbo turbojet. See Recreational section for more details of Zenoah-powered model.

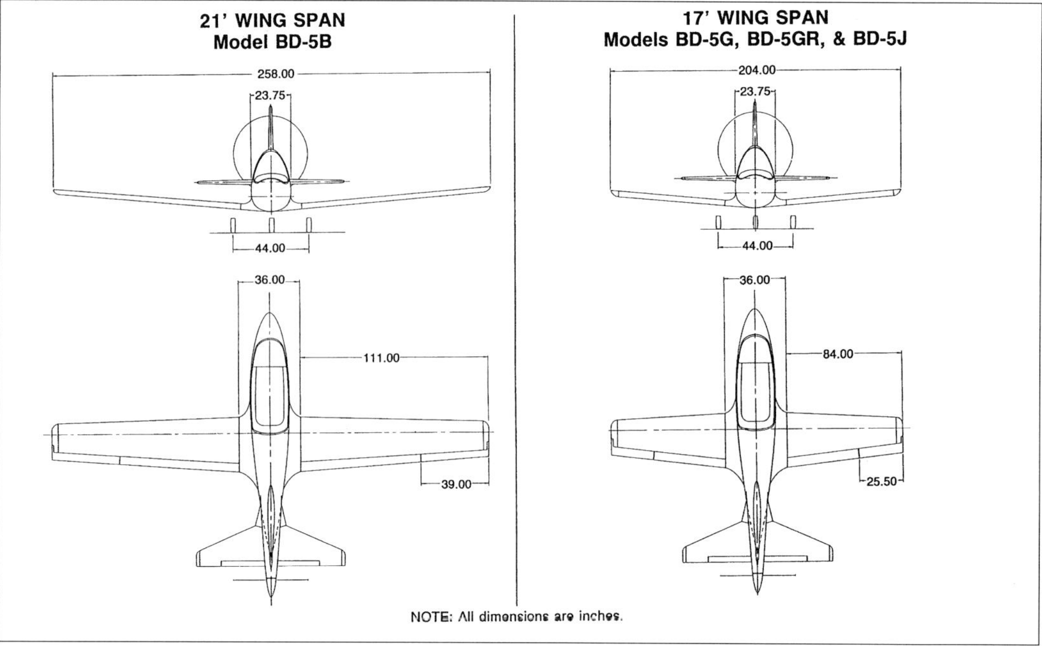

→ **BD-5 general arrangements** *(courtesy Alturair)*

American Champion Aircraft Corporation — USA

Corporate address:
PO Box 37, 32032 Washington Avenue, Highway D, Rochester, WI 53167.

Telephone: +1 414 534 6315
Facsimile: +1 414 534 2395

Information:
Jerry Mehlhaff (President).

ACTIVITIES

▪ Offers a range of Dacron-covered 2-seat high-wing cabin monoplanes, all based on former Bellanca/Champion aircraft. These are the 118 hp (88 kW) Textron Lycoming O-235-K2C-powered Aurora, 160 hp (119.3 kW) Adventure and 160 hp (119.3 kW) O-320-B2B-powered Explorer, all 3 based on the Citabria, and the 180 hp (134 kW) Scout and Super Decathlon with O-360 and AEIO-360 engines respectively. All are approved.

→ **American Champion Aircraft Super Decathlon**

Angel Aircraft Corporation — USA

Corporate address:
Municipal Airport, 1410 Arizona PL SW, Orange City, IA 51041-7453.

Telephone: +1 712 737 3344
Facsimile: +1 712 737 3399
E-mail: angelaircraft@juno.com

ACTIVITIES

▪ This company developed the Model 44 Angel. Designed by Carl Mortenson, a former missionary pilot and mechanic, it was conceived to fit between single-engined STOL lightplanes and STOL twins of Twin Otter type, for missionary and other work in remote areas (operating from unprepared strips), and also for marketing as an executive aircraft and other roles. Certification to FAR Pt 23 for day, night, VFR and IFR in the Normal category was received on 20 October 1992.

Angel Aircraft Model 44 Angel

Role: STOL missionary, utility and executive aircraft (see introduction). Also suited to medevac/rescue, mining/oil/rubber/forestry operations, patrol/observation/surveillance, ranching, and sport.
Crew/passengers: 8, or 6 with reclining seats.

↑ **Angel Aircraft Model 44 Angel** *(courtesy Angel Aircraft)*

Details for Angel

PRINCIPAL DIMENSIONS:
Wing span: 40 ft (12.19 m)
Maximum length: 33 ft 3 ins (10.13 m)
Maximum height: 11 ft 6 ins (3.5 m)

WINGS:
Area: 225.2 sq ft (20.92 m^2)
Aspect ratio: 7.08

UNDERCARRIAGE:
Type: Retractable, with castoring nosewheel, suited to use from rough strips. Electrically-driven hydraulic pumps for undercarriage, with hand pump as back-up and free-fall for emergency
Main wheel tyre size: 8.50-10
Nose wheel tyre size: 8.50-6

WEIGHTS:
Empty: 3,880 lb (1,760 kg)
Maximum take-off: 5,800 lb (2,631 kg)
Useful load: 1,920 lb (871 kg)

PERFORMANCE:
Maximum speed: 180 kts (207 mph) 333 km/h
Cruise speed: 176 kts (203 mph) 326 km/h at 75% power and 9,000 ft (2,745 m), or 158 kts (182 mph) 293 km/h at 55% power and 15,000 ft (4,575 m)
Stall speed: 71 kts (82 mph) 132 km/h *clean and power off*, 51 kts (59 mph) 95 km/h *in landing configuration and power on*
Take-off distance: 658 ft (201 m) minimum roll
Landing distance: 568 ft (174 m) minimum roll with brakes
Maximum climb rate: 1,345 ft (410 m) per minute, or 196 ft (60 m) per minute OEI
Ceiling: 20,500 ft (6,250 m), or 5,178 ft (1,578 m) OEI
Range with full fuel: 1,415 naut miles (1,629 miles) 2,620 km at 55% cruise and 8,000 ft (2,440 m)
Duration: 9.3 hours (range conditions). 13.1 hours for surveillance

Engines: 2 Textron Lycoming IO-540-M1C5 piston engines, with 6 ft 4 ins (1.93 m) Hartzell 3-blade constant-speed pusher propellers.
Engine rating: Each 300 hp (224 kW).
Fuel system: 844 litres.
Electrical system: 12 volt.
Braking system: Cleveland brakes.
Flight avionics/instrumentation: AlliedSignal Bendix/King Silver Crown and Garmin GPS.

Aviat Inc — USA

Corporate address:
PO Box 1240, 672 South Washington, Afton, WY 83111.
Telephone: +1 307 886 3151
Facsimile: +1 307 886 9674

ACTIVITIES

- Markets the A-1 Husky as a metal and fabric, strut-braced and high-wing 2-seat cabin monoplane, with a 180 hp (134 kW) Textron Lycoming O-360-C1G piston engine. A further variant with clipped wings and inverted fuel and oil systems became the Acro-Husky.
- Also markets the Eagle II aerobatic biplane as a kit (see Recreational section), and offers a range of single- and 2-seat Pitts Special aerobatic biplanes.

Avtek Corporation — USA

Corporate address:
555 Airport Way, Camarillo, CA 93010.
Telephone: +1 805 482 2700
Facsimile: +1 805 987 0068
Founded:
1982.
Information:
Peter M. Wanbaugh (Director, Procurement).

Avtek 400A

First flight: 17 September 1984 for proof-of-concept prototype.
Certification: 2000.
Role: Pressurized, all-composites business jetfan.
Sales: 62 ordered at time of writing in 1998. Basic price US$2.2 million IFR equipped.

↑ Avtek 400A

Crew/passengers: Pilot plus 5 or 8 passengers.
Baggage capacity: 22 cu ft (0.62 m^3) in the nose compartment and 44 cu ft (1.24 m^3) aft cabin.
Pressurization system: 7.6 psi maximum cabin differential.
Wing characteristics: Rear-mounted, high aspect ratio, sweptback wings. Thick strakes between the engine nacelles and the fuselage.
Wing control surfaces: 2-section ailerons, with inner sections also used for pitch-axis trim.
Canard control surfaces: Elevators on the canard. The canard contributes to lift, while providing horizontal stability. High position minimizes airflow interference with the main wings at take-off and landing attitudes.
Tail control surfaces: Rudder only.
Flight control system: Mechanical, with pushrods, except for electric trim.
Construction materials: Kevlar and Nomex as the basic airframe materials (72%), with mainly carbonfibre/graphite for the remainder.
Engines: 2 Pratt & Whitney Canada PT6A-3 turboprops, with 6 ft 4 ins (1.93 m) 4-blade Kevlar pusher propellers.
Engine rating: Each 680 shp (507 kW).
Fuel system: 1,003 litres.
Electrical system: 28 volt DC generators.
Hydraulic system: Engine-driven hydraulic pump provides pressure of 2,000 psi for undercarriage actuation (with manual back-up system).
Radar: Optional colour weather radar (see below).
Flight avionics/instrumentation: Wide range of optional avionics by AlliedSignal Bendix/King, Rockwell Collins and Honeywell, including EFIS and EICAS and Honeywell colour weather radar. Full IFR instrumentation optional.
Oxygen system: Capacity of 49 cu ft (1.39 m^3) and pressure 1,850 psi provides constant flow for passengers and demand for pilot.

Aircraft variants:
400A business aircraft, as detailed.

Details for Avtek 400A

PRINCIPAL DIMENSIONS:
Wing span: 35 ft (10.67 m)
Maximum length: 39 ft 4 ins (11.99 m)
Maximum height: 11 ft 4 ins (3.45 m)

CABIN:
Length: 15 ft 1 ins (4.6 m), including cockpit
Width: 4 ft 7 ins (1.4 m)
Height: 4 ft 6 ins (1.37 m)
Main door size: 3 ft 10 ins × 2 ft 6 ins (1.17 × 0.76 m)

WINGS:
Area: 144.2 sq ft (13.4 m^2)
Canard: 48.7 sq ft (4.52 m^2)

UNDERCARRIAGE:
Type: Retractable, with steerable nosewheel

WEIGHTS:
Empty: 3,644 lb (1,653 kg) basic IFR, 3,779 lb (1,714 kg) equipped
Maximum take-off and landing: 6,500 lb (2,948 kg)

PERFORMANCE:
Maximum speed: 363 kts (418 mph) 673 km/h
Stall speed: 72 kts (83 mph) 134 km/h
Take-off distance over a 50 ft (15 m) obstacle: 1,520 ft (464 m)
Landing distance over a 50 ft (15 m) obstacle: 1,280 ft (390 m)
Maximum climb rate: 4,630 ft (1,410 m) per minute
Ceiling: 42,500 ft (12,950 m)
Range with full fuel: 1,921 naut miles (2,213 miles) 3,561 km, with NBAA reserves

419 Express is a projected 19-passenger airliner development, with 1,173 shp (875 kW) PT6A-45 engines.
Explorer is a special mission version proposed by former Valmet of Finland (now Finavitec).

Ayres Corporation — USA

Corporate address:
PO Box 3090, 1 Ayres Way, Albany, GA 31707.
Telephone: +1 912 833 1440
Facsimile: +1 912 439 9790
E-mail: webmaster@ayres-corp.com
Web site: www.ayres-corp.com
Information:
Terry Humphrey.

Ayres S2R-600 400 Gallon Turbo Thrush

Note: This was formerly known as Ayres 600 Thrush, but has been renamed Turbo Thrush despite having an R-1340 radial piston engine.
Role: Agricultural aircraft, with optional fire bomber equipment.
Sales: Operating in over 60 countries.
Crew/passengers: Pilot. Airframe is built with aft compartment, which can be utilized for baggage or a forward facing seat can be mounted with dual controls. Adjustable mesh seating.
Cockpit: Optional aft-of-cockpit bubble windows.
Chemical tank/hopper: 1,514 litres liquid, 53 cu ft (1.5 m^3) dry chemicals, in a clear-vision glassfibre hopper.
Dispersal equipment: Universal spray system with external 2 ins (5 cm) stainless steel plumbing. 2 ins (5 cm) Transland pump, streamline spraybooms with 68 nozzles, and 3 ins (7.6 cm) port-side loader. Optional Micronair AU5000 installation, fire-bomber installation, smoker installation, Crop Hawk flow meter, Weath Aero fan assembly, Micronair application monitor, Transland stainless steel spreader, and more.
Safety equipment: Sealed cockpit. Massive overturn structure. Undercarriage wire cutters. Cockpit wire deflector and deflector cable from canopy to fin.

↑ Ayres S2R-600 400 Gallon Turbo Thrush *(courtesy Ayres)*

Wing control surfaces: Ailerons (with servo tabs) and flaps.
Tail control surfaces: Elevators and rudder.
Flight control system: Mechanical, except for electric flaps.
Construction materials: Metal, with heli-arc welded 4130 chromoly tubular steel fuselage structure and upper/lower steel spar caps. Quick detach Alclad aluminium fuselage skins, and stainless steel bottom fuselage skins. Aerodynamic wing root fairings increase performance and seal wing from chemicals. Glassfibre cockpit canopy.
Engine: Pratt & Whitney R-1340 radial piston engine, with a Hamilton Standard 12D40 constant-speed propeller with EAC AG100-2 blades.
Engine rating: 600 hp (447.4 kW).
Fuel system: 515 litres. Optional 863 litre and ferry fuel systems.
Electrical system: 24 volt, 50 amp alternator and 24 volt battery.
Braking system: Cleveland 4-piston disc brakes.
Flight avionics/instrumentation: See next entry for similar options.

Details for S2R-600 400 Gallon Turbo Thrush

PRINCIPAL DIMENSIONS:
Wing span: 47 ft 6 ins (14.48 m)
Maximum length: 29 ft 4.5 ins (8.95 m)
Maximum height: 9 ft 2 ins (2.79 m)

WINGS:
Area: 350 sq ft (32.516 m^2)
Aspect ratio: 6.45

UNDERCARRIAGE:
Type: Fixed, with steerable/lockable steel spring tailwheel
Tail wheel tyre size: 5.00 × 5
Wheel track: 9 ft (2.74 m)

WEIGHTS:
Empty: 4,250 lb (1,928 kg)
Typical operating: 8,000 lb (3,629 kg)

PERFORMANCE:
Never-exceed speed (V_{NE}): 138 kts (159 mph) 256 km/h
Cruise speed: 113 kts (130 mph) 209 km/h at 70% power and 4,000 ft (1,220 m)
Spray speed: 100-117 kts (115-135 mph) 185-217 km/h
Stall speed: 45 kts (52 mph) 84 km/h in usual landing configuration
Take-off distance: 1,320 ft (402 m) at 7,900 lb (3,583 kg)
Landing distance: 600 ft (183 m) as usually landed
Maximum climb rate: 1,040 ft (317 m) per minute at sea level, at 6,000 lb (2,722 kg) AUW
Ferry range: 350 naut miles (403 miles) 648 km at 70% power

Ayres S2R 510 Gallon Turbo Thrush

Role: Agricultural aircraft, with optional fire bomber equipment. See Aircraft variants.
Details: Similar to S2R-600 400 Gallon Turbo Thrush, except as detailed below.
Chemical tank/hopper: 1,931 litres liquid, 68.2 cu ft (1.93 m^3) dry chemicals, clear-vision glassfibre hopper.
Dispersal equipment: Similar to -600 Thrush, but with 2.5 ins (6.4 cm) port-side loader.
Engine: Pratt & Whitney Canada PT6A or AlliedSignal TPE331 turboprop engine, with Hartzell or McCauley reversing propeller. See Aircraft variants.
Fuel system: 863 litres usable.
Electrical system: 24 volt system, with 200 amp starter-generator and dual 24 volt batteries.
Braking system: Cleveland dual caliper disc brakes.
Flight avionics/instrumentation: Optional AlliedSignal Bendix/King KX 155 nav/com, KI 208 indicator, KR 87 ADF, KT 76A transponder with blind encoder; artificial horizon, directional gyro, turn co-ordinator, heated pitot and VSI.

Aircraft variants:
S2R-T15 510 Gallon Turbo Thrush, with a 1,931 litre hopper and Pratt & Whitney Canada PT6A-15AG turboprop engine of 680 shp (507 kW).
S2R-T34 510 Gallon Turbo Thrush, with 1,931 litre hopper and 750 shp (559 kW) PT6A-34AG engine.
S2R-T65 510 Gallon Turbo Thrush, with 1,931 litre hopper and 1,230 shp (917 kW) PT6A-65AG engine. Used by US State Department as a special missions NEDS (narcotics eradication delivery systems) aircraft; 19 delivered.
S2R-G6 510 Gallon Turbo Thrush, with 1,931 litre hopper and 750 shp (559 kW) AlliedSignal TPE331-6 turboprop engine.
S2R-G10 510 Gallon Turbo Thrush, with 1,931 litre hopper and 900 shp (671 kW) AlliedSignal TPE331-10 turboprop engine.
S2R-600 400 Gallon Turbo Thrush, with a radial piston engine and smaller hopper. See separate entry.
S2R-660 660 Gallon Turbo Thrush, is the latest model, certified in 1998. See separate entry below.
Vigilante is an AlliedSignal TPE331-14GR-engined special surveillance, support and law enforcement version.

↑ Ayres S2R-G6 510 Gallon Turbo Thrush

Details for S2R-T34 and -G6 Turbo Thrush

PRINCIPAL DIMENSIONS:
Wing span: 44 ft 5 ins (13.54 m) short span, 47 ft 6 ins (14.48 m) long span
Maximum length: 33 ft (10.06 m)
Maximum height: 9 ft 2 ins (2.79 m)

WINGS:
Aerofoil section: NACA 4412
Area: 326.6 sq ft (30.34 m^2) short span, 350 sq ft (32.516 m^2) long span

WEIGHTS:
Empty: 4,300 lb (1,950 kg)
Typical operating: 9,700 lb (4,400 kg)

PERFORMANCE:
Never-exceed speed (V_{NE}): 138 kts (159 mph) 256 km/h
Cruise speed: 130 kts (150 mph) 241 km/h at 55% power
Spray speed: 78-130 kts (90-150 mph) 145-241 km/h
Stall speed: 50 kts (57 mph) 92 km/h as usually landed
Take-off distance: 1,200 ft (366 m) at typical operating weight
Landing distance: 600 ft (1,969 m) as usually landed
Maximum climb rate: 1,740 ft (530 m) per minute at 6,000 lb (2,721 kg)
Ferry range: 668 naut miles (770 miles) 1,239 km at 45% power and 7,500 ft (2,285 m)

Ayres S2R-660 660 Gallon Turbo Thrush

Certification: 1998.
Role: Agricultural aircraft, with optional fire bomber equipment.
Details: Similar to other Turbo Thrush versions, except as detailed below.
Chemical hopper/tank: 2,498 litres liquid, 88 cu ft (2.49 m^3) dry chemical, clear-vision glassfibre hopper.
Dispersal equipment: Universal Spray System with 3 ins (7.6 cm) stainless steel plumbing. 3 ins (7.6 cm) Transland pump. Streamlined spray booms with 68 nozzles (70% of boom). 3 ins (7.6 cm) port side loader.
Pressurization system: Pressurized aft fuselage.
Wing control surfaces: Drooped ailerons for shorter take offs.
Construction materials: Longer steel spar caps for added strength and longevity. Superior corrosion protection.
Engine: Choice of 940 shp (701 kW) AlliedSignal TPE331-10, 1,173 shp (875 kW) Pratt & Whitney Canada PT6A-45, 1,050 shp (783 kW) PT6A-60AG, or 1,300 shp (969 kW) PT6A-65AG turboprop.
Fuel system: 863 litres usable.

↑ Ayres S2R-660 660 Gallon Turbo Thrush, certified in 1998. Note the new undercarriage arrangement

Details for S2R-660 660 Gallon Turbo Thrush with PT6A-65AG

PRINCIPAL DIMENSIONS:
Wing span: 50 ft (15.24 m)
Maximum length: 33 ft 6 ins (10.21 m)
Maximum height: 9 ft 2 ins (2.79 m)

WINGS:
Area: 375 sq ft (34.84 m^2)
Aspect ratio: 6.67

UNDERCARRIAGE:
Type: Fixed tailwheel type, with new rugged steel spring main legs
Tail wheel tyre size: 6.00 × 6
Wheel track: 9 ft 6 ins (2.9 m)

WEIGHTS:
Empty: 5,250 lb (2,381 kg)
Typical operating: 12,500 lb (5,670 kg)

PERFORMANCE:
Never-exceed speed (V_{NE}): 173 kts (200 mph) 322 km/h
Cruise speed: 152 kts (175 mph) 281 km/h, at 55% power
Spray speed: 87-152 kts (100-175 mph) 161-282 km/h
Stall speed: 50 kts (57 mph) 92 km/h as usually landed
Take-off distance: 1,500 ft (457 m)
Landing distance: 600 ft (183 m) as usually landed
Climb rate: 1,250 ft (381 m) per minute at 10,500 lb (4,763 kg), or 1,025 ft (312 m) per minute at typical operating weight, both at sea level
Range: 521 naut miles (600 miles) 965 km at 50% power, 143 kts, and 8,500 ft (2,590 m)

Century Aerospace Corporation — USA

Corporate address:
3250 University Blvd, SE Access Road B, Alberquerque, NM 87106.

Telephone: +1 505 246 8200
Facsimile: +1 505 246 8300
Web site: www.centuryaero.com

Information:
Don Coburn (Sales and Marketing – *E-mail* info@centuryaero.com).

Century Aerospace Century Jet CJ-1 and CJ-2

First flight: Expected 2000.
Certification: FAA Pt 23 in 2000.
Role: Light entry level business jet.
Sales: As of May 1998, funding was being sought to construct the first prototype, when deposits for 20 production aircraft had been received. Price US$1.95 million.

Details

Crew/passengers: Pilot plus 5 passengers in heated and air conditioned cabin/cockpit. Optional toilet. Clam-shell cabin door with airstair.
Baggage capacity: 40 cu ft (1.13 m^3), of which 30 cu ft (0.85 m^3) is pressurized.

↑ Century Jet Corporation Century Jet

Pressurization system: 8.5 psi vapour cycle (8,000 ft, 2,440 m cabin altitude at 41,000 ft, 12,495 m).
Wing control surfaces: Ailerons with bungee trim and single-slotted Fowler flaps. Speedbrakes/lift-dumpers.
Tail control surfaces: Horn-balanced elevators with geared trim tabs, and rudder with bungee trim.
Flight control system: Mechanical, with cables, except for electrically actuated flaps.
Construction materials: 2024 and 7075 Al aluminium wings, adhesive bonded with redundant mechanically fastened spar caps (manufactured by DeVore Aviation) and autoclave cured carbonfibre honeycomb sandwich fuselage with internal frames and bulkheads (manufactured by R-Cubed).
Engine: Prototypes and initial CJ-1 production aircraft each have a 1,900 lbf (8.45 kN) Williams-Rolls FJ44-1A turbofan, with later aircraft adopting the more powerful 2,300 lbf (10.23 kN) FJ44-2 as CJ-2s, which can be retrofitted to initial aircraft.
Fuel system: 1,079 litres (1,060 litres usable).
Flight avionics/instrumentation: AlliedSignal Bendix/King KLN 90B GPS, KR 21 marker receiver, KN 63 DME, KR 87 ADF, KFC integrated automatic flight control system, dual KX 165 nav/com, dual KT 70 Mode-S transponder, and KMA 24H audio panel.
Electrical system: 300 amp generator, 100 amp back-up generator, and 28 volt 44 amp-hour battery.
Hydraulic system: 3,000 psi for undercarriage.
De-icing system: Pneumatic boots on wing/tailplane leading edges. Hot air bleed for engine inlet.

Aircraft variants:
CJ-1 with FJ44-1A engine.
CJ-2 with FJ44-2 engine.

Details for Century Jet CJ-1, *with CJ-2 in italics*

PRINCIPAL DIMENSIONS:
Wing span: 39 ft 5 ins (12.01 m), *the same*
Maximum length: 34 ft 9.5 ins (10.6 m), *the same*
Maximum height: 13 ft 2 ins (4.01 m), *the same*

CABIN:
Length: 14 ft 9.5 ins (4.51 m), *the same*
Width: 4 ft 7 ins (1.4 m), *the same*
Height: 4 ft 7 ins (1.4 m), *the same*
Volume: 220 cu ft (6.23 m^3), *the same*

WINGS:
Aerofoil section: OSU SZ(2)-01255 laminar flow at root, CAC SZ(7)-0113 at tip
Area: 158 sq ft (14.68 m^2), *the same*
Aspect ratio: 9.83, *the same*
Sweepback: 5°
Dihedral: 3°
Incidence: 1° 30'
Twist: 2° 24'
Thickness/chord ratio: 15.5% at root, 13% at tip

UNDERCARRIAGE:
Type: Electro-hydraulically retractable, with steerable (±30°) nosewheel
Main wheel tyre size: 17.5 × 5.1 ins, pressure 96 psi
Nose wheel tyre size: 14.2 × 5 ins, pressure 50 psi
Wheel base: 13 ft 3.5 ins (4.05 m)
Wheel track: 7 ft 8.5 ins (2.35 m)
Turning circle: 18 ft 11 ins (5.77 m)

WEIGHTS:
Empty: 3,460 lb (1,569 kg), *3,500 lb (1,588 kg)*
Maximum ramp weight: 6,050 lb (2,744 kg), *the same*
Maximum take-off: 5,950-6,000 lb (2,700-2,721 kg), *the same*
Useful load: 2,490 lb (1,129 kg), *2,550 lb (1,157 kg)*

PERFORMANCE:
Maximum cruise speed: 360 kts (415 mph) 667 km/h, *400 kts (460 mph) 741 km/h*
Long-range cruise speed: 260 kts (299 mph) 482 km/h, *300 kts (345 mph) 556 km/h*
Stall speed: 70 kts (81 mph) 130 km/h with flaps, *the same*
Take-off distance over a 50 ft (15 m) obstacle: 2,750 ft (839 m), *2,500 ft (762 m)*
Landing distance over a 50 ft (15 m) obstacle: 2,200 ft (671 m)
Climb rate: 3,350 ft (1,021 m) per minute at sea level
Maximum altitude: 41,000 ft (12,495 m), *the same*
Range: 1,600 naut miles (1,840 miles) 3,965 km maximum and 1,300 naut miles (1,500 miles) 2,400 km at high cruise speed; and *1,500 naut miles (1,727 miles) 2,780 km*, all with 45 minutes reserve

Cessna Aircraft Company — USA

Corporate address:
One Cessna Boulevard, Wichita, KS 67215 (mailing address: PO Box 7706, Wichita, KS 67277-7706).

Telephone: +1 316 941 6056, from outside the USA; 1-800-4 CESSNA within the USA
Facsimile: +1 316 941 8181
Web site: http://www.cessna.textron.com/

Founded:
18 December 1927.

Information:
Jan McIntire (Director, Corporate Communications – *telephone* +1 316 941 6488, *facsimile:* +1 316 941 7812).

ACTIVITIES

- As announced in 1998, Cessna delivered 618 new aircraft in the last full year, and took orders for over 1,200 aircraft. Of those delivered, 360 were Skyhawks and Skylanes, 78 Caravans and 180 Citations.
- In May 1998 Cessna delivered its 250th Model 525 CitationJet.
- In a ceremony in June 1997, Cessna received ISO9001 certification for quality.
- Cessna Single Engine Piston Facility in Independence, Kansas opened on 3 July 1996 for production of Skyhawk, Skylane and Stationairs.

Cessna deliveries of currently available aircraft, as of May 1998	
172R Skyhawk	402
182S Skylane	147
206 Stationair/Turbo Stationair	*
208 Caravan	939
CitationJet	250
Citation Bravo	31
Citation Ultra	189
Citation Excel	**
Citation VII	84
Citation X	41

* Deliveries started late 1998
** Deliveries began 2 July 1998

Cessna 172R and 172SP Skyhawk

Note: The 172R new and refined version of the Skyhawk differs from previous models in having a fuel-injected IO-360 engine, dual engine-driven vacuum pumps for powering the flight instruments, electric fuel boost pump, standard epoxy corrosion proofing, stainless steel control cables, a new 'junction box' electrical system to consolidate and protect power components to enhance reliability, thicker cabin windows and new acoustic soundproofing.

↑ Cessna 172R Skyhawk

Details for 172R Skyhawk

PRINCIPAL DIMENSIONS:
Wing span: 36 ft 1 ins (11 m)
Maximum length: 26 ft 11 ins (8.2 m)
Maximum height: 8 ft 11 ins (2.72 m)

CABIN:
Length: 11 ft 10 ins (3.61 m) firewall to aft baggage area
Width: 3 ft 3.5 ins (1 m)
Height: 4 ft (1.22 m)

WINGS:
Area: 175.5 sq ft (16.3 m^2)

UNDERCARRIAGE:
Type: Fixed, with steerable nosewheel. Optional wheel fairings
Main wheel tyre size: 6.00 × 6
Nose wheel tyre size: 5.00 × 5

WEIGHTS:
Empty: 1,600 lb (726 kg)
Maximum take-off and landing: 2,450 lb (1,111 kg) Normal, 2,100 lb (952 kg) Utility
Useful load: 857 lb (389 kg) Normal, 507 lb (230 kg) Utility

PERFORMANCE:
Maximum speed: 123 kts (142 mph) 228 km/h at sea level
Cruise speed: 122 kts (140 mph) 226 km/h at 8,000 ft (2,440 m), 80% power
Stall speed: 51 kts (59 mph) 95 km/h *clean*, or 47 kts (54.5 mph) 87 km/h *with flaps*, both power off
Take-off distance: 945 ft (288 m)
Landing distance: 550 ft (168 m)
Maximum climb rate: 720 ft (219 m) per minute at sea level
Ceiling: 13,500 ft (4,115 m), service
Range: 580 naut miles (668 miles) 1,075 km at 8,000 ft (2,440 m) and 80% power, or 687 naut miles (791 miles) 1,273 km at 10,000 ft (3,050 m) and 60% power

Details: For 172R.
First flight: 19 April 1995 for 172 'restart prototype' with a Textron Lycoming IO-360 engine, actually an old repainted 172N Skyhawk used for development testing. First of 3 pre-production 172Rs flew 16 April 1996.
Certification: 21 June 1996 under FAR Pt 23.
First delivery: 18 January 1997 to the Aircraft Owners and Pilots Association membership sweepstakes winner, with first export on 30 January 1997 (Australia).
Role: 4-seat lightplane.
Crew/passengers: 4 persons in a cabin with 360° wraparound windows, 2 large cabin doors, extended-shelf baggage compartment, and multi-level ventilation system. Dual controls.
Baggage capacity: 120 lb (54.4 kg).
Wing control surfaces: Ailerons and preselect single-slotted flaps.
Tail control surfaces: Horn-balanced elevators (starboard trim tab) and rudder.
Flight control system: Stainless steel control cables. Electric preselect flaps.
Construction materials: Light alloy, with composites for nose cowling, wing and tail caps, and wheel fairings.
Engine: 160 hp (119.3 kW) Textron Lycoming IO-360-L2A piston engine, with a 6 ft 3 ins (1.91 m) McCauley 2-blade fixed-pitch metal propeller with spinner.
Fuel system: 212 litres total in 2 tanks, of which 201 litres usable.
Electrical system: 28 volt, 60 amp alternator. 24 volt, 12.75 amp-hour battery (5 hour rate).
Braking system: Toe-operated hydraulic brakes. Parking brake.
Flight avionics/instrumentation: AlliedSignal Bendix/King avionics. Nav/com transceiver, nav indicator, audio panel with marker beacon lights, voice-activated intercom, and Mode-C transponder, plus standard flight instruments (altimeter, digital clock, magnetic compass, attitude and directional gyros, true airspeed indicator, outside air temperature indicator, turn co-ordinator indicator, and vertical speed indicator) and engine instruments, annunciator panel (oil, fuel, vacuum, voltage), strobe lights, supplemental (cold fluorescent) glareshield lighting, new electrical fuel gauges and more. Optional packages, ranging from dual nav/coms, digital ADF and moving map GPS, to single-axis autopilot system.

Aircraft variants:
172R as detailed.
172SP has 180 hp (134 kW) IO-360-L2A. MTOW 2,560 lb (1,160 kg). Useful load 960 lb (435 kg).

Cessna 182S Skylane

First flight: 16 July 1996.
Certification: 3 October 1996 to FAR Pt 23.
First delivery: 24 April 1997.

Details for 182S Skylane

PRINCIPAL DIMENSIONS:
Wing span: 36 ft 1 ins (11 m)
Maximum length: 28 ft (8.53 m)
Maximum height: 9 ft 3 ins (2.82 m)

CABIN:
Length: 11 ft 2 ins (3.4 m) firewall to aft baggage area
Width: 3 ft 6 ins (1.07 m)
Height: 4 ft (1.22 m)

WINGS:
Area: 174 sq ft (16.17 m^2)

UNDERCARRIAGE:
Type: Fixed, with steerable nosewheel. Optional wheel fairings
Main wheel tyre size: 6.00 × 6
Nose wheel tyre size: 5.00 × 5

WEIGHTS:
Empty: 1,882 lb (854 kg)
Maximum take-off: 3,100 lb (1,406 kg)
Maximum landing: 2,900 lb (1,315 kg)
Useful load: 1,228 lb (557 kg)

PERFORMANCE:
Maximum speed: 145 kts (167 mph) 269 km/h at sea level
Cruise speed: 140 kts (161 mph) 259 km/h at 6,000 ft (1,829 m) and 80% power
Stall speed: 54 kts (62.5 mph) 100 km/h *clean*, or 49 kts (57 mph) 91 km/h *with flaps*, both power off
Take-off distance: 795 ft (243 m)
Landing distance: 590 ft (180 m)
Maximum climb rate: 924 ft (282 m) per minute at sea level
Ceiling: 18,100 ft (5,517 m), service
Range: 820 naut miles (944 miles) 1,519 km at 6,500 ft (1,980 m) and 75% power

↑ Cessna 182S Skylane

Role: 4-seat lightplane.
Crew/passengers: 4 persons in a cabin with 360° wraparound windows, 2 large cabin doors, aft baggage area, and multi-level ventilation system. Dual controls.
Baggage capacity: 200 lb (91 kg).
Wing control surfaces: Ailerons and preselect single-slotted flaps.
Tail control surfaces: Horn-balanced elevators (with trim system) and rudder (with trim).
Flight control system: Stainless steel control cables. Electric preselect flaps.
Construction materials: As for Skyhawk.
Engine: 230 hp (171.5 kW) Textron Lycoming IO-540-AB1A5 piston engine, with 6 ft 10 ins (2.08 m) McCauley 2-blade, constant-speed, metal propeller with governor and spinner. Manual cowl flaps.
Fuel system: 348 litres in 2 tanks, with 333 litres usable.
Electrical system: As for Skyhawk.
Braking system: As for Skyhawk.
Flight avionics/instrumentation: Standard package is equipped for full IFR flight, with dual nav/coms, glideslope, VFR moving-map GPS, audio panel with marker beacon, Mode-C transponder with digital encoder, and single-axis autopilot. Optional IFR upgrade package adds a digital KR 87 ADF and exchanges original standard units with a KLN 89B IFR approach-certified GPS, its MD 41-228 GPS/nav selector/annunciator, and a more capable KAP 140 2-axis autopilot with electric trim. Standard flight (same as Skyhawk, which see) and engine instruments.

Cessna 206H Stationair and T206H Turbo Stationair

Note: New and refined versions differ from early-produced Stationairs/Turbo Stationairs in having contoured seats (vertically adjustable and reclining front seats; individual reclining back seats, of 26g energy-absorbing type), a composite headliner and a multi-level ventilation system as well as all-electric engine gauges and a segmented, metal instrument panel with backlit non-glare instruments and back-up cold-fluorescent light system. Also tinted windows, hinged side windows, epoxy corrosion proofing, stainless steel cables, ambient noise reduction soundproofing, 88 US gallon usable fuel capacity, strobe lights, handles and steps to check fuel levels, static wicks, ground power unit (GPU) plug and fire extinguisher. Optional packages include utility interior, electric propeller anti-ice boots, a 16 cu ft (0.453 m^3) cargo pod, floatplane provisions kit, and oversized tyres for rugged terrain.
First flight: 6 November 1996 for prototype of new Model 206 Stationair, and 28 August 1996 for prototype of new Turbo Stationair.
Certification: 9 September 1998.
First delivery: Late 1998.

Details for Stationair, *with Turbo Stationair in italics*

PRINCIPAL DIMENSIONS:
Wing span: 36 ft (10.97 m), *the same*
Maximum length: 28 ft 3 ins (8.61 m), *the same*
Maximum height: 9 ft 3.5 ins (2.83 m), *the same*

CABIN:
Length: 12 ft 1 ins (3.68 m), *the same*
Width: 3 ft 8 ins (1.12 m), *the same*
Height: 4 ft 1.5 ins (1.26 m), *the same*

UNDERCARRIAGE:
Type: Fixed, with nosewheel

WEIGHTS:
Empty: *2,277 lb (1,033 kg) standard*
Maximum ramp: 3,614 lb (1,639 kg), *3,616 lb (1,640 kg)*
Maximum take-off: *3,600 lb (1,633 kg)*
Useful load: 1,400 lb (635 kg), *1,323 lb (600 kg)*

PERFORMANCE (preliminary)**:**
Cruise speed at sea level: 150 kts (173 mph) 278 km/h
Cruise speed at height: 143 kts (165 mph) 265 km/h at 6,500 ft (1,980 m), *165 kts (190 mph) 306 km/h at 20,000 ft (6,100 m)*, both at 75% power, and *170 kts (196 mph) 315 km/h at 17,000 ft (5,180 m)*
Take-off distance: 900 ft (275 m), *835 ft (255 m)*
Maximum climb rate: 920 ft (280 m) per minute, *1,010 ft (308 m) per minute*, both at sea level
Ceiling: 16,000 ft (4,875 m), *27,000 ft (8,230 m)*, both service

↑ **Cessna 206H Stationair** *(courtesy Cessna)*

Role: 6-seat utility aircraft.
Sales: 1998 production sold out by January that year. Fully equipped Stationair US$289,900, and Turbo Stationair US$324,900.
Engine: 300 hp (224 kW) Textron Lycoming IO-540 for Stationair and 310 hp (231 kW) TIO-540 for Turbo Stationair; it was announced in 1998 that the originally planned IO-580-A1A and TIO-580-A1A engines did not meet required serviceability standards after testing during airframe and engine certification programmes. 3-blade, constant-speed McCauley propeller.
Fuel system: 333 litres usable.
Flight avionics/instrumentation: Modern instrumentation is standard on both aircraft, including a digital clock, exhaust gas temperature gauge and hour meter. Included in the standard package are dual nav/com radios, glideslope receiver, an audio panel with marker beacon receiver and a 6-position voice-actuated intercom system, digital transponder with encoder, VFR GPS, and a single-axis autopilot. The nav avionics option upgrades the aircraft with an IFR-certified GPS, adds ADF and upgrades the autopilot to 2-axis control.

Cessna 208 Caravan

First flight: 9 December 1982.
Certification: 1984.
Role: Commuter, business, cargo, bush operations, ambulance, utility, military/government multi-purpose and specialized missions.
Sales: Military and civil/commercial use in many countries. Largest customer is Federal Express, which received 40 Caravans (as Cargomasters) and 260 Super Cargomasters. See earlier listing of sales.
Crew/passengers: See Aircraft variants. 36 ins (91.4 cm) seat pitch in 10-seat commuter layout. Optional air conditioning for Caravan/Grand Caravan.
Wing control surfaces: Ailerons (with trim), single-slotted Fowler flaps over 70% of span and slot-lip spoilers.
Tail control surfaces: Horn-balanced elevators (with trim tabs) and rudder. Tailplane has vortex generators.
Flight control system: Cables, bell cranks and push-pull rods, but with electric flaps.
Construction materials: Metal.
Engine: See Aircraft variants.
Fuel system: 1,268 litres (usable 1,257 litres) except for Grand Caravan at 1,270 litres.
Electrical system: 2 power sources, the primary 200 amp engine-driven starter-generator and a back-up 75 amp alternator. 24 volt lead-acid (45 amp-hour) or optional ni-cd (40 amp-hour) battery.
Hydraulic system: For toe-operated brakes only.
De-icing system: Optional full de-ice package (meeting FAR Pt 25).
Radar: Optional AlliedSignal Bendix/King RDR-2000 (replacing RDS-81 from 1997) colour weather radar in a wing pod.
Flight avionics/instrumentation: AlliedSignal Bendix/King Silver Crown. Typically KR 87 digital ADF, KLN 89B (replaced Trimble 2000A) GPS, KMA 24H audio control console, dual KX 165 nav/com, KFC 150 flight director/autopilot, KT 70 Mode-S transponder, KN 63 DME, and KR 21 marker beacon. To customers' request. Flight and engine instruments, independent pitot static systems on pilot and co-pilot air speed indicators, as well as on VSI and altimeter instruments.

Details for Grand Caravan

PRINCIPAL DIMENSIONS:
Wing span: 52 ft 1 ins (15.88 m)
Maximum length: 41 ft 7 ins (12.67 m)
Maximum height: 15 ft 5.5 ins (4.71 m)

CABIN:
Length: 16 ft 10 ins (5.12 m)
Width: 5 ft 2 ins (1.58 m)
Height: 4 ft 3.5 ins (1.31 m)
Volume: 340 cu ft (9.63 m^3), plus standard use of an external cargo pod of 111.5 cu ft (3.16 m^3), with 1,090 lb (494 kg) capacity
Cabin door size: 4 ft 1 ins × 4 ft 2 ins (1.24 × 1.27 m)

WINGS:
Aerofoil section: NACA 23017.424, 23012 (root/tip)
Area: 279.4 sq ft (25.96 m^2)
Aspect ratio: 9.72

UNDERCARRIAGE:
Type: Fixed, with steerable nosewheel

WEIGHTS:
Empty: 4,285 lb (1,944 kg)
Maximum take-off: 8,750 lb (3,969 kg)
Maximum landing: 8,500 lb (3,856 kg)
Useful load: 4,500 lb (2,041 kg)

PERFORMANCE:
Cruise speed: 184 kts (212 mph) 341 km/h at 10,000 ft (3,050 m)
Stall speed: 61 kts (71 mph) 113 km/h, engine idling
Take-off distance: 1,365 ft (416 m)
Landing distance: 950 ft (290 m)
Maximum climb rate: 975 ft (297 m) per minute at sea level
Ceiling: 23,700 ft (7,224 m), service
Range: 907 naut miles (1,044 miles) 1,680 km at 10,000 ft (3,050 m), with 45 minutes reserve

↑ Cessna Super Cargomaster

Aircraft variants:
Caravan is the basic version, with a 600 shp (447 kW) Pratt & Whitney Canada PT6A-114 turboprop and 3-blade constant-speed, reversible propeller. Length 37 ft 7 ins (11.46 m), maximum height 16 ft 4 ins (4.98 m), standard empty weight 3,973 lb (1,802 kg), maximum take-off weight 8,000 lb (3,629 kg), maximum useful load 4,062 lb (1,842 kg), cruise speed 184 kts (212 mph) 341 km/h at 10,000 ft (3,050 m), and range 960 naut miles (1,105 miles) 1,779 km at 10,000 ft (3,050 m). 12 ft 8 ins (3.86 m) cabin length, with 254 cu ft (7.19 m^3) volume plus optional 82.7 cu ft (2.37 m^3) external cargo pod. Maximum seating for 14, or 10 under FAR Pt 23.
Caravan Amphibian is an amphibious or straight float version of Caravan, with 4,902 lb (2,224 kg) standard empty weight, 8,000 lb (3,629 kg) MTOW, and 3,133 lb (1,421 kg) maximum useful load. No cargo pod, but up to 300 lb (136 kg) of baggage in the floats. Take-off run on water 2,025 ft (617 m). Cruise speed at 10,000 ft (3,050 m) 163 kts (188 mph) 302 km/h and range 855 naut miles (984 miles) 1,584 km at same altitude. Tailplane finlets.
Grand Caravan is the largest version. 675 shp (503 kW) PT6A-114A turboprop. Propeller as Caravan. Seating for 14 persons, or 9 plus 2 crew under FAR Pt 23 regulations when passenger seat pitch is 36 ins (91 cm). Features a quick-change interior, requiring 30 minutes to convert the passenger interior for all cargo. As detailed.
Super Cargomaster (Model 208B) is based on the Grand Caravan but is intended for cargo operations, as required by Federal Express. 2 crew. Standard use of the larger cargo pod.
U-27A is a military version of the Caravan for the US foreign military sales programme. Missions can include troop transport, reconnaissance, medevac, rescue/relief, surveillance and other special roles with appropriate equipment installed in the cabin. Can have a roll-up door.

↑ Cessna Caravan, Grand Caravan, Super Cargomaster and Caravan Amphibian *(courtesy Cessna)*

Cessna Model 525 CitationJet and CJ1

First flight: 29 April 1991 for CitationJet.
Certification: October 1992 to FAR Pt 23, including day, night, VFR, IFR, single pilot and flight into known icing conditions.
First delivery: March 1993; first CJ1 in year 2000.

↑ Cessna CitationJet

↑ Cessna Citation VII

Role: Business jet.
Sales: Successor CJ1 announced October 1998, having Collins Pro Line 21 avionics, 200 lb (91 kg) MTOW increase, and 1,475 naut mile range with pilot + 3 pax.
Wing control surfaces: Wing has natural laminar flow aerofoils. Outboard ailerons (port trim tab), flaps, and upper and lower surface speed brakes.
Tail control surfaces: T-tail, with elevators (trim tabs) and rudder (servo trim tab).
Flight control system: Pushrod, bell crank, sector and stainless steel cable systems to actuate rudder, elevators and ailerons.
Construction materials: Aluminium alloys, steel and other materials. Wing structure is of 3-spar design.
Radar: RDR-2000 weather radar; RTA-800 for CJ1.
Flight avionics/instrumentation: Standard avionics include Honeywell SPZ-5000 integrated digital flight director/autopilot with 2 EFIS screens (5 ins, 12.7 cm square), dual AlliedSignal VHF com transceivers; dual AlliedSignal nav receivers including VOR, localizer and glideslope/marker receiver; radio magnetic indicator (RMI); AlliedSignal DME; dual AlliedSignal Mode-S transponders; AlliedSignal ADF, AlliedSignal KLN 90B GPS; AlliedSignal KI 204 nav indicator (VOR/ILS); dual encoding altimeters; AlliedSignal KCS 55A compass; dual Honeywell VG-14A vertical gyros. Dual 250 VA AC inverters are installed using a split AC bus system feeding the avionics equipment.

Cessna Model 650 Citation VII

First flight: February 1991.
Certification: January 1992 to FAR Pt 25 transport category, day, night, VFR, IFR (including FAR Pt 91 Category II) and flight into known icing conditions.
Noise characteristics: 65.4 dbA take-off with 7° flaps, 81.6 dbA approach with full flaps.
Role: Mid-size business jet.
Wing control surfaces: Wing has advanced supercritical section. Each wing has aileron (with trim tab), 4 panels of spoilers and 3-section flap. Stall strips and stall fence on each wing. Outboard spoiler panel on each wing used to provide additional roll authority after approximately 3° of aileron deflection, while centre 2 panels provide fully-modulated drag control in flight. All 8 spoiler panels available for emergency descent and for lift dumping after touchdown.
Tail control surfaces: T-tail, with variable-incidence tailplane. Elevators with tabs and rudder with trim tab (rudder incorporates boost system to minimize yaw in asymmetric thrust situations).
Flight control system: Pushrod and cable actuation systems for rudder, elevators and ailerons, with hydraulic power for ailerons and spoilers (manual reversion for ailerons if hydraulic power lost). Electrically actuated flaps.
Construction materials: Mainly light alloy. Cabin structure consists of 3 bond assemblies; use of doublers and double-size splices, and a combination of bonding and rivetting. Nose section includes composite radome. Aft fuselage section contains fuselage fuel tank aft of pressure bulkhead. Wings of bonded and rivetted construction, built in 3 sections, outer 2 joined to centre section carry-through. Flaps of Kevlar/graphite composites.
Radar: Primus 870 Doppler colour weather radar.
Flight avionics/instrumentation: Honeywell SPZ-8000 dual digital flight director/autopilot, comprising a duplex autopilot, EFIS with 4 colour screens (5 × 6 ins, 12.7 × 15 cm) and radar; pitch, roll and heading information provided by dual AHZ-600 AHRS. Rockwell Collins ALT-55 radio altimeter, dual Honeywell Primus II RCZ-850 integrated VHF com transceivers, dual Honeywell Primus II RNZ-850 nav receivers, dual Rockwell Collins RMI 36 indicators, and more. Optional Wulfsberg GNS-X flight management system for VOR/DME, Loran-C, GPS, VLF/Omega, and IRS/INS.

Cessna Model 750 Citation X

First flight: 21 December 1993.
Certification: 3 June 1996, with category as for Citation VII.
Role: Long-range business jet.
Sales: See earlier listing.
Wing control surfaces: Supercritical wing, with speed brakes and spoilers optimized for drag control with minimum pitching moments.
Tail control surfaces: Highly swept T-tail, with movable tailplane for trim. Elevators and 2-piece rudder.
Flight control system: Dual hydraulically-powered non-reversible controls for wings, with manual reversion. Elevators and lower portion of rudder hydraulically powered, upper rudder portion electrically powered.
Construction materials: Forward fuselage and cockpit derived from Citation VII. Composites for control surfaces, flaps, spoilers and speed brakes.
Radar: Colour weather radar.
Flight avionics/instrumentation: Honeywell Primus 2000 dual digital autopilot/flight director/EICAS system includes 5 screen (8 × 7 ins, 20 × 18 cm) EFIS display; attitude and heading information by dual AH-800 AHRS; air data information by dual AZ-840 Micro Air Data Computers. Radio altimeter. Honeywell com/nav package with dual RM-855 RMUs, dual RNZ-850 nav units, dual RCZ-850 com units; radio system functions include dual VOR, localizer, glideslope, marker beacon, DME's Mode-S transponder, VHF coms and single ADF. AlliedSignal Bendix/King KHF 950 HF com, dual Honeywell AV-850 Audio Control panels, dual Honeywell FMS and more; back-up instruments.

↑ Cessna Citation X

↑ Cessna Citation Bravo

Cessna Model 550 Citation Bravo

First flight: 25 April 1995.
Certification: April 1996 to FAR Pt 25 transport category, including day, night, VFR, IFR and flights into known icing conditions. Gravel runway operations optional.
Role: Business jet.
Sales: See earlier listing.
Wing control surfaces: Outboard aileron, one flap section, and upper and lower speed brake per wing, the port aileron having a trim tab.
Tail control surfaces: Tailplane incorporates 9° dihedral for minimum sonic fatigue and thrust effects. Elevators with trim tabs and rudder with servo/trim tab.
Flight control system: Pushrod, bellcrank, sector and stainless steel cable systems used to actuate rudder, elevators and ailerons. Trim wheels for mechanical trim for aileron, rudder and elevators. Pitch trim is also electrically powered through a split switch. Speed brakes are electrically controlled and hydraulically activated.
Construction materials: Aluminium alloys, steel and other materials. Wing main spar carry-through consists of 2 halves bonded together, either section capable of carrying fail-safe loads. Wing structure has 2-cell torque box formed by spars, stringers, ribs and skin. Flaps constructed of metal ribs and spar, with glassfibre skin (flap speed set at 8 seconds from fully retracted to fully extended position of 40°).
Radar: Honeywell P-650 colour weather radar.
Flight avionics/instrumentation: Honeywell P-1000 digital flight guidance and display system, with dual PFDs (8 × 7 ins, 20 × 18 cm) and a single multi-function display of similar size, and dual flight directors integrated into a single 3-axis fail passive autopilot; dual Honeywell VG-14A vertical gyros and dual C-14D compass system. AlliedSignal flight management system (FMS), with GPS and IFR approach capability and fuel flow interface. Dual AlliedSignal KY 196A VHF com transceivers, dual AlliedSignal nav receivers (including VOR, localizer, glideslope and marker beacon), dual AlliedSignal DME, dual AlliedSignal Mode-S transponders. AlliedSignal ADF, and more.

Cessna Model 560-XL Citation Excel

First flight: 29 February 1996.
Certification: 22 April 1998 to same requirements as Citation VII.
Role: Business jet.
Sales: Over 200 ordered for delivery by 2001 (as of September 1998). First delivery 2 July 1998. 15 for delivery in 1998 and over 40 in 1999.
Wing control systems: Outboard aileron (port with trim tab), 2-Fowler flap sections, and upper and lower speed brake per wing. Ailerons, flaps and speed brakes gaps are sealed to reduce drag. Infinite positioning of flaps, with detents at take-off (7°), take-off/approach (15°), and landing (35°) positions.
Tail control surfaces: As for Bravo.
Flight control system: Pushrod and cable systems to actuate rudder, elevators and ailerons. Mechanical trim for aileron, rudder and elevators. Pitch trim is also electrically powered through a split switch. Hydraulically actuated flaps.
Construction materials: Aluminium alloys, steel and other materials. Fail-safe principles using multiple load paths, crack stopper bands, low stress levels and small panel size in all primary structure. Design limit load factors +3g, -1.2g, with ultimate loads defined as 1.5 times limit factors. Flaps use graphite composite laminates with titanium tracks.
Radar: Honeywell Primus colour weather radar.
Flight avionics/instrumentation: Honeywell P-1000 digital flight guidance and display system, with dual PFDs (8 × 7 ins, 20 × 18 cm) and a single multi-function display; dual flight directors integrated into single 3-axis fail passive autopilot; dual AHRS. Standby mechanical HSI. Dual Honeywell TR-850 VHF com transceivers; dual Honeywell NV-850 nav receivers contained in the RNZ-851 integrated navigation unit include VOR, localizer, glideslope and marker beacon receivers; dual Honeywell DM-850 transceivers contained in the INU with dual DI-851 indicators; Honeywell HS-852B Mode-S transponders; Primus II radio system; Honeywell DF-850 automatic direction finder (ADF) and more.

Cessna Model 560 Citation Ultra and Ultra Encore

First flight: 9 July 1998 for new Ultra Encore.
Certification: June 1994; late 1999 for Ultra Encore.
Role: Business jet.
Sales: Ultra includes UC-35A transports for US Army and 5 OT-47B tracker aircraft (carrying modified AN/APG-66 radar and WF-360 infra-red trackers). Ultra Encore deliveries from 2000, featuring PW535A engines, Honeywell Primus 1000 avionics, and 2,000 naut mile range.
Wing and tail control surfaces: As for Excel.
Flight control system: Pushrod and cable systems used to actuate rudder, elevators and ailerons. Mechanical trim for aileron and rudder and back-up manual trim for elevator. Primary pitch trim is electrically powered through split switch. Hydraulically actuated flaps. Electrically controlled and hydraulically actuated speed brakes.
Construction materials: Similar to Excel but with +3.8g and -1.52g design limits, and graphite used for ailerons and flaps.
Radar: Honeywell Primus 650 colour weather radar.
Flight avionics/instrumentation: Flight directór/autopilot/EFIS as for Bravo (P-1000). Stand-by indicator and HSI. TR-850 and RNZ-851 (see Excel). Loral/Fairchild A200S cockpit voice recorder, and Artex ELT110-4 ELT.

Cessna CJ2 and Model 680 Citation Sovereign

Comments: Announced at the October 1998 NBAA convention. CJ2 will fly in 1999, for delivery from 2001, as a 2+6 seat larger CitationJet development, with FJ44-2C engines, Pro Line 21 avionics, 400 kts cruise speed, and 1,680 naut mile range. The all-new Citation Sovereign seats 10 passengers in a 24 ft (7.32 m) cabin, uses PW306C engines, will cruise at 444 kts, have a 2,820 naut mile range, and receive certification in 2002.

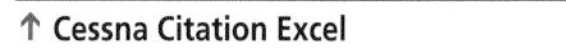
↑ Cessna Citation Excel

↑ Cessna Citation Ultra

(Pax=Passengers)	CitationJet	Citation VII	Citation X	Citation Bravo	Citation Excel	Citation Ultra
Crew + Pax	2 + 4/5	2 + 13	2 + 9/12	2 + 7/10	2 + 6/8	2+ 7/8
Engine × 2	Williams-Rolls FJ44-1A	AlliedSignal TFE731-4R-2S	Allison AE 3007C	P&WC PW530A	P&WC PW545A	P&WC JT15D-5D
Engine rating (each)	1,900 lbf (8.45 kN)	4,080 lbf (18.15 kN)	6,400 lbf (28.47 kN)	2,885 lbf (12.83 kN)	3,785 lbf (16.84 kN)	3,045 lbf (13.55 kN)
Usable fuel	3,220 lb (1,460 kg)	7,385 lb (3,350 kg)	13,000 lb (5,896 kg)	4,860 lb (2,204 kg)	6,590 lb (2,989 kg)	5,775 lb (2,619 kg)
Wing span	46 ft 9 ins (14.26 m)	53 ft 6 ins (16.3 m)	63 ft 11 ins (19.48 m)	52 ft 2 ins (15.9 m)	55 ft 8 ins (16.97 m)	52 ft 2 ins (15.9 m)
Length	42 ft 7 ins (12.98 m)	55 ft 6 ins (16.92 m)	72 ft 2 ins (22.01 m)	47 ft 2 ins (14.39 m)	51 ft 10 ins (15.78 m)	48 ft 11 ins (14.9 m)
Height:	13 ft 9 ins (4.2 m)	16 ft 10 ins (5.13 m)	18 ft 11 ins (5.77 m)	15 ft (4.57 m)	17 ft 2 ins (5.24 m)	15 ft (4.57 m)
Cabin length pressure vessel	15 ft 8 ins (4.79 m)	23 ft 10 ins (7.26 m)	28 ft 6 ins (8.67 m)	20 ft 8 ins (6.3 m)	23 ft (7.01 m)	20 ft 4 ins (6.8 m)
Cabin width	4 ft 10 ins (1.47 m)	5 ft 6 ins (1.67 m)	5 ft 6 ins (1.67 m)	5 ft 6 ins (1.67 m)	4 ft 10 ins (1.47 m)	4 ft 10 ins (1.47 m)
Cabin height	4 ft 9 ins (1.45 m)	5 ft 8 ins (1.73 m)	5 ft 8 ins (1.73 m)	4 ft 8 ins (1.43 m)	5 ft 8 ins (1.73 m)	4 ft 7 ins (1.4 m)
Cabin pressurization differential	8.5 psi	9.3 psi	9.3 psi	8.7 psi	9.3 psi	8.9 psi
Weight empty lb (kg) *VII and X empty weights exclude interior	6,315 (2,864), 6,750 (3,062) basic operating with single pilot	11,770 (5,339)	19,376 (8,788)	8,750 (3,969)	12,310 (5,584)	9,395 (4,261)
Maximum take-off weight lb (kg)	10,400 (4,717)	22,450 (10,183)	35,700 (16,193)	14,800 (6,713)	20,000 (9,072)	16,300 (7,394)
Maximum landing weight lb (kg)	9,700 (4,399)	20,000 (9,072)	31,800 (14,424)	13,500 (6,123)	18,700 (8,482)	15,200 (6,895)
Usable load lb (kg)	4,185 (1,898)	10,880 (4,935)	16,624 (7,541)	6,250 (2,835)	8,090 (3,670)	7,105 (3,223)
M_{MO}	Mach 0.7 at 30,500 ft	Mach 0.83	Mach 0.92	Mach 0.7 at 27,880 ft and above	Mach 0.77 indicated	Mach 0.75 indicated
Maximum cruise speed kts (mph) km/h	383 (441) 710 at 33,000 ft	476 (548) 881 at 37,000 ft	Mach 0.91 at 37,000 ft	401 (462) 743 at 33,000 ft	430 (495) 796 at 35,000 ft	430 (495) 796 at 35,000 ft
Stall speed kts (mph) km/h at MLW	82 (95) 152 in landing configuration	97 (112) 180 CAS in landing configuration		83 (96) 154 CAS	82 (95) 152 in landing configuration	82 (95) 152 with 35° flaps
Maximum climb rate ft (m) per minute	3,311 (1,009)	4,442 (1,354)	3,720 (1,134)	3,195 (974)	3,090 (942)	4,230 (1,290)
Ceiling ft (m)	41,000 (12,500)	51,000 (15,545)	51,000 (15,545)	45,000 (13,715)	45,000 (13,715)	45,000 (13,715)
Take-off runway length MTOW, sea level, ISA ft (m)	3,080 (939)	4,690 (1,430)	5,710 (1,740)	3,600 (1,097)	3,590 (1,095)	3,180 (970)
Landing runway length, MLW ft (m)	2,750 (838)	2,910 (887)	3,820 (1,164)	3,180 (969)	3,180 (970)	2,800 (854)
Range, with 45 minutes reserve naut miles (miles) km	1,485 (1,710) 2,750	2,220 (2,556) 4,111 with 6 pax	3,250 (3,742) 6,023 at 34,500 lb	1,900 (2,188) 3,519 with 4 pax + crew	2,027 (2,334) 3,756 with 4 pax + crew	1,960 (2,257) 3,630 with 5 pax + crew

Cirrus Design Corporation — USA

Corporate address:
4515 Taylor Circle, Duluth, MN 55811.

Telephone: +1 218 727 2737
Facsimile: +1 218 727 2148

Information:
Alan Klapmeier (President).

ACTIVITIES

▪ The Cirrus VK30 turboprop kitplane (first flown in 1988) provided the aerodynamic concept behind the now-halted Israviation ST-50, which see under Israel. Cirrus became a major sub-contractor to Israviation, undertaking core engineering and producing the ST-50 proof-of-concept prototype.

Cirrus SR20

First flight: 21 March 1995 for first prototype. First production prototype flew 28 January 1998, followed by second in June 1998.
Certification: Expected late 1998, under FAR Pt 23.
First delivery: 1999.
Role: 4-seat composites light aircraft, with dual single-handed side control yokes. Parachute recovery system.
Sales: 195 ordered by July 1998. Price US$159,600 at time of writing.
Wing control surfaces: Ailerons (starboard tab) and flaps.
Tail control surfaces: 12 ft 10 ins (3.91 m) span tailplane with horn-balanced elevators; rudder.
Construction materials: Composites. Improved crashworthiness, with energy absorbing structures, special engine mount and firewall structure. Cirrus Airframe Parachute System (CAPS).
Engine: Teledyne Continental IO-360-ES piston engine, with a 6 ft 4 ins (1.93 m) 3-blade constant-speed propeller.
Engine rating: 200 hp (149 kW).
Fuel system: 227 litres usable.
Flight avionics/instrumentation: IFR equipped. Trimble TrimLine avionics suite. GPS for primary navigation. Moving map display. S-Tec System 20 autopilot, with optional System 30. ARNAV ICDS 2000 liquid crystal MFD.

↑ **Cirrus SR20** *(Geoffrey P. Jones)*

Details for SR20

PRINCIPAL DIMENSIONS:
Wing span: 35 ft 7 ins (10.85 m)
Maximum length: 26 ft 3 ins (8 m)
Maximum height: 9 ft 3 ins (2.82 m)

CABIN:
Length: 10 ft 10 ins (3.3 m)
Width: 4 ft 1 ins (1.24 m)
Height: 4 ft 2 ins (1.27 m)

WINGS:
Area: 135 sq ft (12.54 m^2)
Aspect ratio: 9.38
Dihedral: 4° 30'

UNDERCARRIAGE:
Type: Fixed, with nosewheel. Wheel fairings
Wheel base: 7 ft 5 ins (2.26 m)
Wheel track: 9 ft (2.74 m)

WEIGHTS:
Empty: 1,875 lb (850 kg)
Maximum take-off: 2,900 lb (1,315 kg)
Useful load: 1,025 lb (465 kg)

PERFORMANCE:
Never-exceed speed (V_{NE}): 200 kts (230 mph) 370 km/h CAS
Cruise speed: 160 kts (184 mph) 296 km/h at 6,500 ft (1,980 m) and 75% power
Full flap extension speed: 120 kts (138 mph) 222 km/h CAS
Manoeuvring speed: 135 kts (155 mph) 250 km/h CAS
Stall speed: 65 kts (75 mph) 121 km/h *clean*, 57 kts (66 mph) 106 km/h *with flaps*, both IAS
Take-off distance over a 50 ft (15 m) obstacle: 1,865 ft (569 m)
Landing distance over a 50 ft (15 m) obstacle: 1,960 ft (598 m)
Maximum climb rate: 900 ft (274 m) per minute at sea level
Ceiling: 16,000 ft (4,875 m)
G limits: +3.8, -1.9
Range with full fuel: 800 naut miles (921 miles) 1,481 km, with 45 minutes reserve

Classic Aircraft Corporation — USA

Corporate address:
Capital City Airport, MI 48906.

Telephone: +1 517 321 7500
Facsimile: +1 517 321 5845

Information:
D. C. Kettles

ACTIVITIES

■ This company offers the Waco Classic YMF Super biplane, as a modernized development of the 1930s Waco Model F open-cockpit commercial 3-seater. Power is provided by a reworked 275 hp (205 kW) Jacobs R-755-B2 radial piston engine.

Colemill Enterprises Inc — USA

Comments: Details and activities of this aircraft modification company can be found in the 1996-97 edition of *WA&SD*, page 441.

Commander Aircraft Company — USA

Corporate address:
Wiley Post Airport, Hangar 8, 7200 NW 63rd Street, Bethany, OK 73008.

Telephone: +1 405 495 8080
Facsimile: +1 405 495 8383

Founded:
1988.

Commander 114

Certification: 4 May 1992 for Commander 114B.
Role: 4-seat high-performance lightplane and trainer, the latest development of the original Rockwell Commander 112/114 series.

↑ **Commander Aircraft Commander 114AT all-purpose trainer** *(Geoffrey P. Jones)*

Details for Commander 114B

PRINCIPAL DIMENSIONS:
Wing span: 32 ft 9.1 ins (9.99 m)
Maximum length: 24 ft 11 ins (7.59 m)
Maximum height: 8 ft 5 ins (2.57 m)

CABIN:
Length: 6 ft 3 ins (1.91 m)
Width: 3 ft 11 ins (1.19 m)
Height: 4 ft 1 ins (1.24 m)

WINGS:
Aerofoil section: Laminar flow
Area: 152 sq ft (14.12 m^2)
Aspect ratio: 7.06

UNDERCARRIAGE:
Type: Retractable, with steerable and lockable nosewheel
Turning circle: 28 ft 5.5 ins (8.67 m)

WEIGHTS:
Empty: 2,044 lb (927 kg)
Maximum take-off: 3,250 lb (1,474 kg)
Useful load: 1,216 lb (551 kg)

PERFORMANCE:
Maximum speed: 164 kts (189 mph) 304 km/h
Cruise speed: 155 kts (178 mph) 287 km/h at 65% power
Stall speed: 61 kts (71 mph) 113 km/h *clean*, 56 kts (65 mph) 104 km/h *landing configuration*
Take-off distance: 1,040 ft (317 m)
Landing distance: 720 ft (220 m)
Maximum climb rate: 1,070 ft (326 m) per minute at sea level
Ceiling: 16,800 ft (5,120 m)
Cruise range: 725 naut miles (834 miles) 1,342 km at 55% power

Baggage capacity: 200 lb (91 kg).
Wing control surfaces: Ailerons and single-slotted flaps.
Tail control surfaces: Elevators and rudder, both with trim.
Flight control system: Electric flaps.
Engine: Textron Lycoming IO-540-T4B5 piston engine, with a McCauley Black Mac 3-blade constant-speed propeller.
Engine rating: 260 hp (194 kW).
Fuel system: 265 litres.
Electrical system: 28 volt, with 85 amp alternator and battery.
Flight avionics/instrumentation: Can be IFR equipped. Standard avionics include AlliedSignal Bendix/King KMA 24-03 audio panel, KX 155 digital nav/com with GS or LOC indicator, and KT 76 A transponder. Other standard equipment includes Terra AT-3000 altitude encoder and ELT. Large range of optional avionics, including 2-axis AFCS. Full standard flight/engine instruments.

Aircraft variants:
114AT Advanced Trainer, for primary training.
114B, as detailed. Advertized as in "all new streamlined" form by Australian agents in 1998.
Long-range version of 114B was being developed in 1998, reportedly increasing range at 75% power by 255 naut miles.
114TC is a turbocharged version, first flown in 1994. 270 hp (201.3 kW) Textron Lycoming TIO-540-AG1A engine with a McCauley 3-blade constant-speed propeller. Fuel capacity 340.7 litres.

Contender Aircraft Inc — USA

Corporate address:
Reno, NV.

Telephone: +1 702 677 1110
Facsimile: +1 702 677 4580

Information:
Brad and Larry Heuberger.

ACTIVITIES

■ At the 1996 NBAA convention, it was announced that this company intended to develop 3 new and related pressurized business and commuter aircraft, all powered by Williams-Rolls FJ44-1A or -2 turbofan engines. The first version was to be the twin-engined **Contender 202** of 53 ft 8 ins (16.36 m) length and 48 ft 9 ins (14.86 m) wing span, with MTOW of 12,500 lb (5,670 kg) and range of 3,277 naut miles (3,773 miles) 6,073 km, accommodating 2 pilots and 7 to 19 passengers, depending upon cabin layout and role. Price is expected to be US$4.5 million. This will be followed by the triple-engined and stretched **Contender 303** and the largest triple-engined **Contender 606.** In general configuration, all have rear-mounted and slightly swept anhedral wings and low-mounted swept canards.

According to details received on 17 September 1998, finance was expected to be in place by October 1998, allowing start of prototype construction in December 1998, the first flight a year later and certification 18-24 months thereafter.

Aircraft variants:
Contender 202 is the smallest version, with twin 1,900 lbf (8.45 kN) Williams-Rolls FJ44-1A engines. See Activities for passengers, some dimensions and weights.

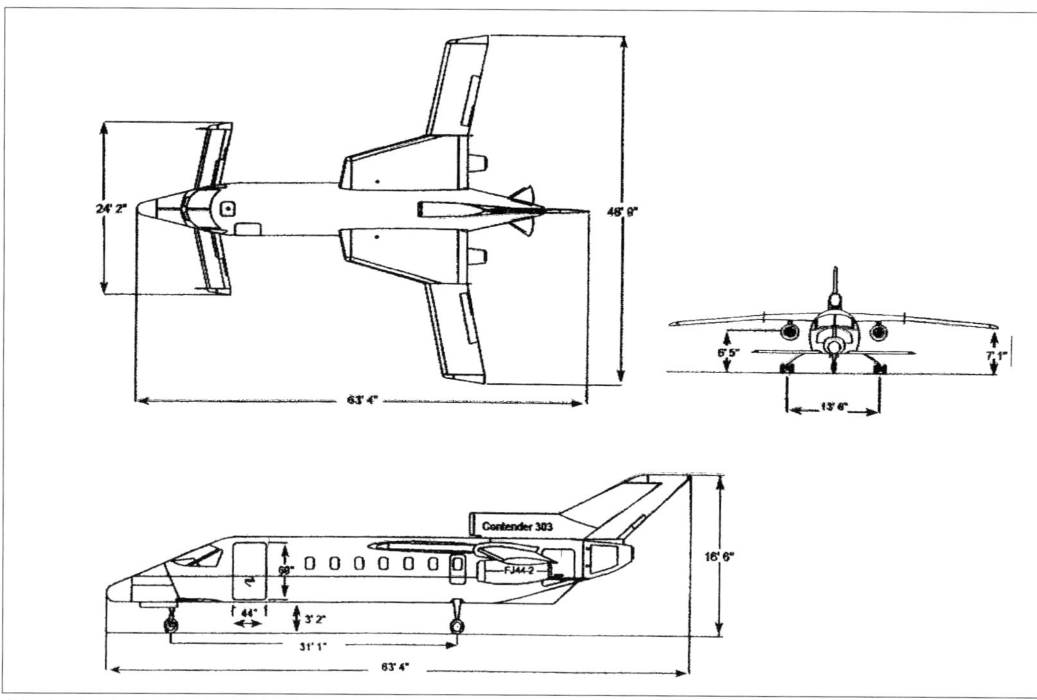

↑ **Contender Aircraft Contender 303** *(courtesy Contender Aircraft)*

Details for Contender 303, *with 606 in italics* (preliminary)

PRINCIPAL DIMENSIONS:
Wing span: 48 ft 9 ins (14.86 m), *50 ft 5 ins (15.37 m)*
Canard span: 24 ft 2 ins (7.37 m), *25 ft 10 ins (7.87 m)*
Maximum length: 63 ft 4 ins (19.3 m), *the same*
Maximum height: 16 ft 6 ins (5.03 m), *16 ft 8 ins (5.08 m)*

CABIN:
Length: 27 ft 11 ins (8.51 m) aft pressure bulkhead to cockpit divider, *the same*
Width: 6 ft 10 ins (2.08 m), *8 ft 6 ins (2.59 m)*
Height: 5 ft 11 ins (1.8 m), *6 ft 2 ins (1.88 m)*
Volume: 962 cu ft (27.24 m^3), *1,210 cu ft (34.26 m^3)*
Baggage capacity: 135 cu ft (3.82 m^3) rear checked volume and 600 lb (272 kg) capacity, 172.4 cu ft (4.88 m^3) checked volume and 900 lb (408 kg) capacity

WINGS:
Wings/Canard lifting area: 446 sq ft (41.43 m^2), *the same*
Sweepback: 12° wing outer panel and canard, *the same*
Fuel strake sweep: 74°, *the same*

UNDERCARRIAGE:
Type: Retractable nosewheel type, with twin wheel main units
Wheel base: 31 ft 1 ins (9.47 m), *the same*
Wheel track: 13 ft 8 ins (4.17 m), *15 ft 4 ins (4.67 m)*

WEIGHTS:
Empty: 6,738 lb (3,056 kg), *7,880 lb (3,574 kg)*
Maximum ramp weight: 15,518 lb (7,039 kg), *19,980 lb (9,063 kg)*
Maximum take-off: 15,418 lb (6,993 kg), *19,780 lb (8,972 kg)*
Maximum landing: 15,318 lb (6,948 kg), *19,680 lb (8,927 kg)*
Maximum payload: 4,036 lb (1,831 kg), *7,256 lb (3,291 kg)* passengers; 4,511 lb (2,046 kg), *8,081 lb (3,665 kg)* cargo

PERFORMANCE (at MTOW)**:**
Maximum cruise speed: Mach 0.78 (450 kts, 518 mph, 833 km/h), *the same*
Long-range cruise speed: Mach 0.73 (420 kts, 484 mph, 778 km/h), *the same*
Balanced field length: 3,380 ft (1,030 m), *3,480 ft (1,061 m),* both sea level and ISA
Landing field length: 2,280 ft (695 m), *2,390 ft (729 m),* both sea level and ISA
Maximum climb rate: 4,600 ft (1,402 m) per minute, *4,300 ft (1,311 m) per minute,* both sea level ISA
Climb rate, OEI: 1,700 ft (518 m) per minute, *1,500 ft (457 m) per minute*
Optimum cruise altitude: 41,000 ft (12,500 m), *the same*
Range: 2,066 naut miles (2,379 miles) 3,828 km, *1,556 naut miles (1,792 miles) 2,883 km,* with maximum passengers, at FL410, IFR reserve

Expected to first fly in late 1999. Price US$4.5 million. ***Contender 303*** carries 2 crew plus 11 passengers as an executive jet and up to 19 for regional/commuter work. Seat pitch 32 ins (81.28 cm). 3 x 2,300 lbf (10.23 kN) Williams-Rolls FJ44-2 engines. Fuel capacity 2,605 litres standard, 2,983 litres optional. Pressurization 8.7 psi. Priced at US$6.3 million.
Contender 606 is the wide-body regional/commuter jet for 3 crew and 29-33 passengers, with 15 passenger executive and all-cargo alternative layouts. Seat pitch 32 ins (81.28 cm). 3 x 2,300 lbf (10.23 kN) Williams-Rolls FJ44-2 engines. Fuel capacity 2,605 litres standard, 2,983 litres optional. Pressurization 8.7 psi. Priced at US$9.9 million.

Galaxy Aerospace Corporation — USA

Corporate address:
One Galaxy Way, Alliance Airport, Fort Worth, TX 76177.
Telephone: +1 817 837 3700
Facsimile: +1 817 837 3723
Founded:
February 1997.
Information:
Jeff Miller (*telephone* +1 817 837 3726, *facsimile* +1 817 837 3862).

ACTIVITIES

▪ Founded to produce, market and support a line of advanced technology business aircraft, encompassing the Astra SPX transcontinental business jet manufactured by Israel Aircraft Industries (which see) and the new Galaxy intercontinental business jet that has been under development at IAI's facilities in Tel Aviv. IAI is a partner in Galaxy Aerospace.

↑ Galaxy Aerospace Galaxy on its second flight on 31 December 1997

Galaxy Aerospace Galaxy

First flight: 25 December 1997.
Certification: Expected late 1998. FAR Pt 25 Transport category (Amdts 1 through 82 scheduled). Also scheduled to meet Stage III noise requirements of FAR 36 (Amdts 1 through 12) and FAR 34 engine emissions and fuel venting. For day and night VFR and IFR (including Cat II IFR approaches).
Service life: 36,000 flight hours or 20,000 flights.
First delivery: 1999.
Role: Wide-body intercontinental business jet.
Sales: Cost of about US$14.5 million at time of writing.
Crew/passengers: 8 passengers with toilet in executive layout is among interior options. Optional ability to allow conversion of the executive layout into an 18 passenger corporate shuttle overnight.
Baggage capacity: 125 cu ft (3.54 m^3), for 2,400 lb (1,089 kg).
Wing characteristics: Double-swept, low-mounted, low-drag/high-lift wing with winglets for drag reduction.
Wing control surfaces: Ailerons, leading-edge slats, Krueger flaps and trailing-edge slotted Fowler flaps. 4 air brakes/lift dumpers on each wing.
Tail control surfaces: Mid-mounted trimmable tailplane (via screw jack actuator driven by 2 independent electric motors) with elevators. Rudder, with trim tab.
Flight control system: Hydraulically actuated ailerons and elevators (both with manual back-up). Manually-operated rudder, with bias system powered by engine bleed air, assists pilot in case of single engine operations. Electrical jack actuator for tailplane. Electric trim tab on rudder. Flaps and slats are each operated by a separate power drive unit. Hydraulically-powered Krueger flaps and air brakes.
Construction materials: Aluminium alloy, with alloy steels and titanium where required.
Engines: 2 Pratt & Whitney Canada PW306A turbofans, with Rohr/Nordam hydraulically-actuated target-type thrust reversers as standard and FADEC.
Engine rating: 5,700 lbf (25.35 kN) at ISA + 10° C.
Fuel system: 8,048 litres, or 14,250 lb (6,464 kg) usable, in 2 wing tanks (with feed tanks), a carry-through structure tank, a forward lower tank and a fuselage tank.
Electrical system: 28 volt DC, supplied via a 28 volt, 400 amp starter-generator on each engine. 2 × 24 volt, 43 amp-hour ni-cd batteries used normally for engine and APU starting. Third battery for emergency power to essential flight instruments and emergency equipment. AlliedSignal GTCP 36-150 APU may be used for electrical power and pressurization in flight, and air conditioning and heating during ground operations; equipped with a 28 volt, 400 amp starter-generator. 28 volt DC external power receptacle. Electrical power distributed via busses. 115 volt AC can be supplied by an optional static inverter.
Hydraulic system: 2 fully independent systems, both operating at 3,000 psi.
Braking system: 2 hydraulically-operated brakes on each undercarriage main gear.
Radar: Standard Rockwell Collins WXR-850 weather radar.
Flight avionics/instrumentation: Rockwell Collins Pro Line 4. Standard equipment and avionics include (all Rockwell Collins, unless stated) 5 EFD-4077 EFIS and EICAS CRT displays (each 7.25 ins, 18.4 cm square) , 2 FCC-4005 autopilot system, 2 AHC-85E AHRS, 2 ADC-850C air data system, 2 VHF-422B coms, 2 VIR-432 nav (with glideslope and marker beacon), ADF-462 ADF, 2 DME-442 DME, 2 TDR-94D transponders, ALT-4000 radio altimeter, ICC-4005 integrated avionics processor subsystem, 2 RTU-4200 radio tuning, and MDC-4000 maintenance diagnostic computer, J.E.T 501-1197-05 standby attitude indicator, FAI 8059-20 standby airspeed indicator, FAI 8047-10 standby altimeter, PAI 700 emergency compass, System TBD flight management system (FMS), and cockpit voice recorder.

Details for Galaxy

PRINCIPAL DIMENSIONS:
Wing span: 58 ft 1 ins (17.71 m) official specification, though sometimes quoted as 58 ft 2 ins (17.72 m)
Maximum length: 62 ft 3 ins (18.97 m)
Maximum height: 21 ft 5 ins (6.53 m)

CABIN:
Length: 24 ft 5 ins (7.44 m) cockpit divider to aft pressure bulkhead
Width: 7 ft 2 ins (2.18 m)
Height: 6 ft 3 ins (1.91 m)
Volume: 868 cu ft (24.56 m^3)

WINGS:
Area: 369 sq ft (34.28 m^2)
Sweepback: 34.5° inboard, 25° outboard

UNDERCARRIAGE:
Type: Retractable, with electro-hydraulic nosewheel steering via 'steer-by-wire' (steering commands from rudder pedals [±10°] and handwheel limited to ±60°; towing angle limited to ±100° without disconnection). Twin wheels on each unit
Wheel base: 24 ft 3 ins (7.39 m)

WEIGHTS:
Manufacturer's bare empty weight: 15,555 lb (7,056 kg), excluding interior furnishings and options
Basic operating weight: 18,100 lb (8,210 kg)
Maximum ramp weight: 33,600 lb (15,241 kg)
Maximum take-off: 33,450 lb (15,173 kg)
Maximum landing: 27,500 lb (12,474 kg)
Useful load: 15,500 lb (7,031 kg)
Payload: 4,900 lb (2,223 kg)

PERFORMANCE (provisional)**:**
Maximum operating Mach number (M_{MO}): 0.85 above 25,000 ft (7,620 m)
Typical cruise speed: Mach 0.82 at 39,000 ft (11,887 m) and 27,000 lb (12,247 kg), 470 kts (541 mph) 871 km/h TAS
Maximum flap extended speeds (V_{FE}): 250 kts (288 mph) 463 km/h CAS with 12° flaps/slats down, 225 kts (259 mph) 417 km/h CAS with 20° flaps/slats down, and 180 kts (207 mph) 334 km/h CAS with 40° flaps/slats down, all ±3%
Manoeuvring speed: 240 kts (276 mph) 448 km/h IAS
Stall speed: 102 kts (118 mph) 189 km/h CAS at MLW, ±3%, CAS
FAA take-off balanced field length: 6,040 ft (1,841 m), at MTOW
FAA landing distance: 3,400 ft (1,036 m) , at MLW
Maximum operating altitude: 45,000 ft (13,716 m)
G limits: +2.65, -1 with flaps and gear up
Range: 3,620 naut miles (4,168 miles) 6,706 km ±5%, at long-range cruise speed of Mach 0.75

Gevers Aircraft Inc — USA

Corporate address:
PO Box 430, Brownsburg, IN 46112.

Telephone: +1 317 852 2735
Facsimile: +1 317 852 2735
E-mail: geversair@iquest.net

Founded:
1988.

Information:
David E. Gevers (President).

ACTIVITIES

■ Developing an innovative 6-seat twin-engined general aviation aircraft known as Genesis. Telescopic wing has 2 telescoping sections which increase span and are completely retractable inside the fixed centre section, providing a near 2:1 span ratio. Multi-configuration undercarriage converts in flight for water, snow, hard surface, and intermittent snow/hard surface, and is retractable. Interconnected propeller drive connects both propellers to both engines. Movable propeller arms raise propellers for landing, providing ground clearance for water spray, debris and loading/unloading. Wings, undercarriage and propeller position are converted in flight to suite mission, condition and environment. Patents issued for all systems.

Details for Genesis

PRINCIPAL DIMENSIONS:
Wing span: 50 ft (15.24 m) extended, 26 ft (7.92 m) retracted
Maximum length: 38 ft (11.58 m)
Maximum height: 12 ft 4 ins (3.76 m)

WINGS:
Area: 308 sq ft (28.6 m^2) extended, 220 sq ft (20.4 m^2) retracted
Chord: 10 ft 8 ins (3.25 m) at fixed root, 6 ft 8 ins (2.03 m) at fixed tip, and constant 3 ft 8 ins (1.12 m) for extension
Aspect ratio: 8.33 extended, 3.1 retracted

UNDERCARRIAGE:
Type: See Activities. Dual main wheels on fuselage centreline, with retractable castoring outriggers mounted on lower half of propeller pivot arm. Outrigger arms rise for water operation and also serve as pontoons. Adjustable-height skis attached to main and nose wheels, serving also as gear doors. All gear positions selected from cockpit in flight via a single control lever
Wheel base: 18 ft 6 ins (5.64 m)
Wheel track: 10 ft 6 ins (3.2 m)

WEIGHTS:
Empty: 3,600 lb (1,633 kg)
Maximum take-off: 6,000 lb (2,721 kg)

PERFORMANCE:
Maximum speed: 267 kts (308 mph) 496 km/h at MTOW
Cruise speed: 243 kts (280 mph) 450 km/h at 75% power, sea level, wings retracted
Stall speed: 95 kts (109 mph) 176 km/h with undercarriage, flaps and wings retracted; or 55 kts (63 mph) 102 km/h with undercarriage, flaps and wings extended
Take-off distance: 720 ft (220 m) hard surface, 1,000 ft (305 m) water
Landing distance: 230 ft (70 m) hard surface, 500 ft (153 m) water
G limits: 3.8 wings extended, 6 wings retracted
Range: 1,910 naut miles (2,200 miles) 3,540 km

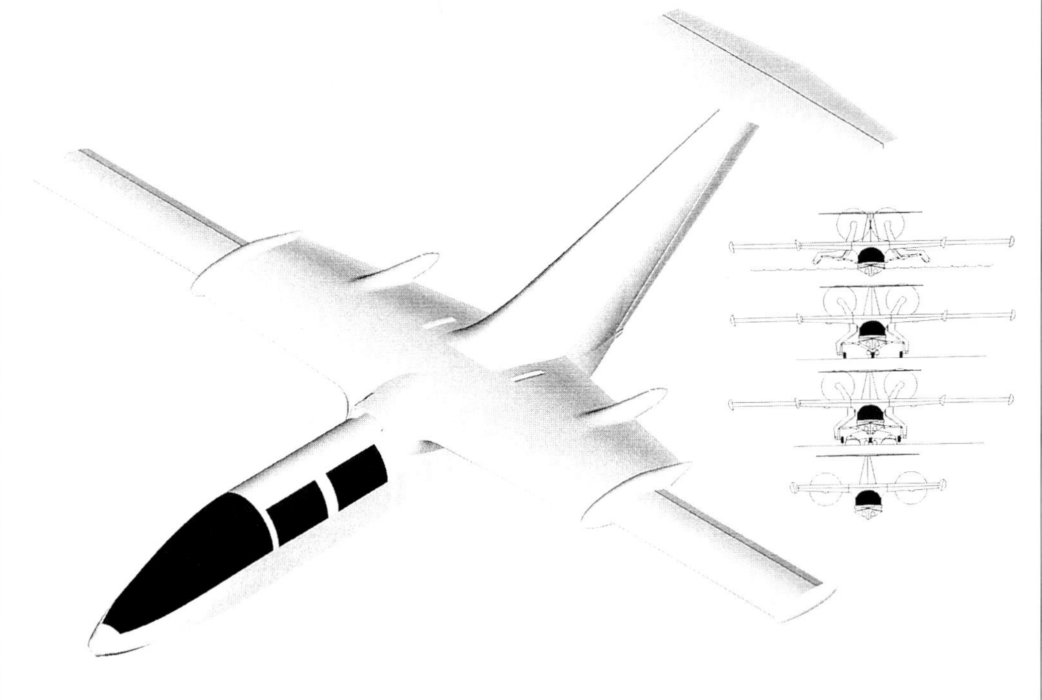

↑ **Gevers Genesis in latest form** *(courtesy Gevers)*

Gevers Genesis

Role: Multiple configurations allow executive, recreational, personal, SAR, bush, seaplane, training, cargo, aerobatic, aerial photography, STOL and other possible roles.
Sales: Prototype construction had begun in 1998. Discussions taking place with potential customers, including for a possible larger version.
Crew/passengers: 6 standard, with 4 or 8 optional.
Wing characteristics: Telescoping wing sections double the span. See Activities.
Wing control surfaces: Ailerons on both fixed wing centre section and telescoping sections, remaining fully operational while retracting/extending wings.
Tail control surfaces: T-tail with elevators and flight-adjustable tailplane incidence.
Flight control system: Manual and electric with manual override.
Construction materials: Single step shock-absorbing hull. Riveted aluminium alloy wings, tail and lower fuselage. Glassfibre cabin compartment.
Engines: 2 Textron Lycoming TIO-540 piston engines, mounted in tandem in the fuselage and driving Hartzell contra-rotating, constant-speed, feathering and reversible-pitch metal pusher propellers. V type engines optional. See Activities.
Engine rating: Each 325 hp (242.4 kW).
Fuel system: 757 litres.
Braking system: Dual hydraulic.
Flight avionics/instrumentation: Dual VFR and IFR instrumentation.

Aircraft variants:
Standard 4-8 seat cabin options, with possible wider cargo version and pressurized versions.

Gulfstream Aerospace Corporation — USA

Corporate address:
PO Box 2206, Savannah, GA 31402-2206.

Telephone: +1 912 965 3000
Facsimile: +1 912 965 3775

Employees: About 7,300.

Information:
Christian H. Flathman (Corporate Communications – *telephone* +1 912 965 3700).

FACILITIES

■ Production facilities at Savannah (Georgia), Oklahoma City (Oklahoma) and Mexicali (Mexico), with service and completion centres in Savannah and Long Beach (California).

Note: See also Lockheed Martin/Gulfstream Aerospace entry.

Gulfstream Aerospace Gulfstream IV series

First flight: 19 September 1985.
Certification: 22 April 1987.
Role: Pressurized, long-range and high-capacity business jet, with special mission military variants.
Sales: 22 IV-SPs delivered during the last full year at time of writing.
Details: For Gulfstream IV-SP, except under Aircraft variants.
Crew/passengers: 2 flight crew plus attendant and typically 13 business passengers, with maximum of 19.
Baggage capacity: 169 cu ft (4.79 m^3), for 2,000 lb (907 kg).
Pressurization system: 9.45 psi maximum cabin differential.
Wing control surfaces: Aileron (port trim tab), single-slotted Fowler flap and 3 spoilers (for aileron assist, lift dumping and speedbrake) per wing. Stall strip and 4 vortillons per wing.
Tail control surfaces: Elevators (with trim tabs) and rudder.
Flight control system: Hydraulic, with manual back-up.
Construction materials: Principally metal, but with composites control surfaces (except flaps) and some other components.
Engines: 2 Rolls-Royce Tay Mk 611-8 turbofans. AlliedSignal GTCP 36-100 APU.
Engine rating: Each 13,850 lbf (61.61 kN).
Fuel system: 29,500 lb (13,381 kg).
Electrical system: 115/200 volt AC supply, at 400 Hz, via 2 alternators. 28 volt DC supply via converters. 2 × 24 volt, 40 amp-hour ni-cd batteries.
Hydraulic system: Dual, each 3,000 psi.
Radar: Colour weather radar.
Flight avionics/instrumentation: Honeywell SPZ-8000 digital avionics package including SPZ-8400 digital AFCS, FMZ-800 Phase II flight management system with six 8 ins (20 cm) square colour CRTs, dual ADCs, dual flight guidance system including autothrottles, dual air data computers, and dual PZ-800 performance computers. Dual laser INS. AHRS. Dual VOR/LOC/GS/marker beacon receivers, dual DME, dual ADF and more. Options include GPS, VLF Omega and TCAS. Optional Honeywell/GEC-Marconi 2020 HUD, already in use and expected to be fitted to about 12 VI-SP/Vs in 1998.

Aircraft variants:
Gulfstream IV was the initial version, replaced by IV-SP from September 1992.
Gulfstream IV-B was a projected longer-range model being studied in association with Textron Aerostructures, as announced at the September 1994 Farnborough Air Show. 4,600 naut mile (5,297 mile) 8,519 km range. Programme on hold.
Gulfstream IV-MPA is a Multi-Purpose Aircraft and the newest available model of the range, offering a quick-change interior for high or low density seating, cargo or combinations. Based on the IV-SP/C-20G. Maximum 26 passengers, or executive layouts, or 4,800 lb (2,177 kg) of cargo. Optional large cargo door.
Gulfstream IV-SP entered service in 1992. As detailed.
SRA-4 is a little used generic term for aircraft modified for special missions (mainly military). Current aircraft are based on IV-SP. See Reconnaissance section.

↑ **Gulfstream IV-SP** *(courtesy Gulfstream)*

↑ **Gulfstream Aerospace Gulfstream V** *(courtesy Gulfstream)*

Details for Gulfstream IV-SP

PRINCIPAL DIMENSIONS:
Wing span: 77 ft 10 ins (23.72 m)
Maximum length: 88 ft 4 ins (26.92 m)
Maximum height: 24 ft 5 ins (7.44 m)

CABIN:
Length: 45 ft 1 ins (13.74 m)
Width: 7 ft 4 ins (2.24 m)
Height: 6 ft 2 ins (1.88 m)
Volume: 1,525 cu ft (43.18 m^3)

WINGS:
Area: 950 sq ft (88.26 m^2)
Aspect ratio: 6.38

UNDERCARRIAGE:
Type: Retractable, with steerable nosewheels. Twin wheels on each unit

WEIGHTS:
Empty: 35,500 lb (16,100 kg)
Maximum take-off: 74,600 kg (33,838 kg)
Maximum landing: 66,000 lb (29,937 kg)
Payload: 6,500 lb (2,948 kg)

PERFORMANCE:
Maximum operating Mach number (M_{MO}): Mach 0.88
Cruise speed: Mach 0.8 normal
Take-off distance: 5,450 ft (1,662 m), sea level, ISA
Landing distance: 3,190 ft (972 m), sea level, ISA, MLW
Maximum climb rate: 4,122 ft (1,256 m) per minute at sea level
Normal cruise altitude: 45,000 ft (13,715 m)
Range: 4,220 naut miles (4,859 miles) 7,815 km with 3 crew and 8 passengers, NBAA IFR reserve
Duration: 9 hours 27 minutes, conditions as for range

Gulfstream Aerospace Gulfstream V

First flight: 28 November 1995.
Certification: 16 December 1996 (provisional) and April 1997 (full).
Role: Pressurized, long-range (global) business jet, as a larger and more powerful development of the Gulfstream IV.
Sales: 29 delivered during the last full year at time of writing.
Crew/passengers: 2 flight crew, attendant plus typically 13-15 business passengers, with 19 maximum.
Baggage capacity: 226 cu ft (6.4 m^3), for 2,500 lb (1,134 kg)
Engines: 2 BMW Rolls-Royce BR710-48 turbofans. AlliedSignal RE220 APU.
Engine rating: Each 14,750 lbf (65.61 kN).
Fuel system: 41,000 lb (18,597 kg).
Flight avionics/instrumentation: Honeywell SPZ-8500 digital avionics package including AFCS, FMS with six 8 ins (20 cm) square colour EFIS/EICAS displays. Honeywell/GEC-Marconi 2020 HUD. AlliedSignal CAS-67A TCAS II, Mk VI GPWS and maintenance-data acquisition system; and Rockwell Collins communications, navigation and transponder suite, incorporating the RT-4220 integrated radio-tuning unit with liquid-crystal display. Has "office in the sky" capability using IBM satellite communications.

Aircraft variants:
Gulfstream V, as detailed.
C-37A is the USAF designation for 2 (plus 4 options) Gulfstream Vs replacing Boeing VC-137s with the 89th Airlift Wing from 1998. First received its preliminary acceptance in September 1997.
ASTOR contender; see Reconnaissance section.

Details for Gulfstream V

PRINCIPAL DIMENSIONS:
Wing span: 93 ft 6 ins (28.5 m)
Maximum length: 96 ft 54 ins (29.39 m)
Maximum height: 25 ft 10 ins (7.87 m)

CABIN:
Length: 50 ft 1 ins (15.27 m)
Width: 7 ft 4 ins (2.24 m)
Height: 6 ft 2 ins (1.88 m)
Volume: 1,669 cu ft (47.26 m^3)

WINGS:
Larger and more efficient than IV-SP's but of basically similar configuration
Area: 1,137 sq ft (105.63 m^2)
Aspect ratio: 7.69

WEIGHTS:
Basic operating weight: 46,800 lb (21,228 kg) with 3 crew
Maximum take-off: 89,000 lb (40,370 kg)
Maximum landing: 72,000 lb (32,658 kg)
Payload: 6,500 lb (2,948 kg)

PERFORMANCE:
Maximum operating Mach number (M_{MO}): Mach 0.9
Cruise speed: Mach 0.87 maximum, 0.8 long-range
Take-off distance: 5,870 ft (1,790 m) sea level, ISA
Landing distance: 2,950 ft (900 m) sea level, ISA, MLW
Maximum climb rate: 4,188 ft (1,276 m) per minute at sea level
Cruise altitude: 41,000 ft (12,500 m) initial, 51,000 ft (15,550 m) final
Range: 6,500 naut miles (7,485 miles) 12,038 km with 8 passengers and 4 crew at Mach 0.8, NBAA IFR reserve
Duration: 14 hours 38 minutes, conditions as for Range

Integrated Systems Aero Engineering Inc (ISAE) — USA

Corporate address:
Hangar FL-7, Logan Airport, Logan, UT 84321.
Telephone: +1 801 753 2218
Facsimile: +1 801 753 9198
Information:
Dave Repko (Sales & Marketing Manager).

↑ **ISAE Omega II** *(courtesy ISAE)*

ISAE Omega II

Certification: Intended FAR Pt 23 Aerobatic category.
Role: Tandem 2-seat aerobatic lightplane, developed from the Streak 90 Palomino.
Sales: Originally offered as a kit with 200 hp (149 kW) AEIO-360-A1E6 engine, but now certified aircraft only.
Baggage capacity: 120 lb (54 kg).

Details for Omega II

PRINCIPAL DIMENSIONS:
Wing span: 28 ft 3 ins (8.6 m)
Maximum length: 25 ft (7.62 m)
Maximum height: 9 ft 6 ins (2.9 m)

WINGS:
Aerofoil section: Laminar flow
Area: 106.8 sq ft (9.92 m^2)
Aspect ratio: 7.47

UNDERCARRIAGE:
Type: Retractable, with steerable nosewheel. Hydraulic actuation, with emergency "fall" into locked position

WEIGHTS:
Empty, operating: 1,500 lb (680 kg)
Maximum take-off: 2,300 lb (1,043 kg)
Useful load: 800 lb (363 kg)

PERFORMANCE:
Maximum speed: 205 kts (236 mph) 380 km/h
Cruise speed: 193 kts (223 mph) 359 km/h at 75% power and 6,000 ft (1,830 m)
Stall speed: 61 kts (70 mph) 113 km/h, *clean*
Take-off distance: 1,100 ft (336 m)
Landing distance: 1,200 ft (366 m), dry pavement, with brakes
Maximum climb rate: 3,000 ft (914 m) per minute at sea level
Roll rate: 130° per second
Range: 651 naut miles (750 miles) 1,207 km

Wing control surfaces: Frise type ailerons and plain flaps (15°, 30° or 40°).
Tail control surfaces: Elevators (with tab) and rudder.
Flight control system: Push-pull rods, torque tubes and cables. Electric tab.
Construction materials: All metal.
Engine: 300 hp (224 kW) Textron Lycoming AEIO-540-L, with Hartzell constant-speed propeller.
Fuel system: 197 litres usable in 2 wing tanks, and with a collector tank and flop-tube pickup for inverted capability.
Electrical system: 24 volt.
Braking system: Disc brakes.

Kestrel Aircraft Company — USA

Corporate address:
1630 Westheimer Drive, Norman, OK 73069.

Telephone: +1 405 573 0090
Facsimile: +1 405 329 8844

Information:
Charles Sallaway (Vice-President, Marketing).

ACTIVITIES

▪ As of May 1998, Kestrel Aircraft is currently involved in the certification of the K-250 model, which has the highest gross weight of the planned family of 4-seat aircraft. In addition to the K-250, the company has begun advanced engineering design on the K-325 6-seater. All models, including the future K-160, K-180 and K-200RG are planned to share the same wing, and all 4-seat models share the same fuselage dimensions, adjusting only in carbon structure for appropriate gross weights of each model.

Kestrel K-160, K-180, K-200R, K-250/M and K-325

First flight: 19 November 1995 for the KL-1A proof of concept prototype. 1998 for K-250.

Details for K-250 (latest May 1998 figures)

PRINCIPAL DIMENSIONS:
Wing span: 36 ft 9 ins (11.2 m)
Maximum length: 26 ft 9 ins (8.15 m)
Maximum height: 8 ft 11.5 ins (2.73 m)

WINGS:
Area: 179.6 sq ft (16.69 m^2)
Aspect ratio: 7.52

UNDERCARRIAGE:
Type: Fixed, with nosewheel. Wheel fairings

WEIGHTS:
Maximum ramp: 3,700 lb (1,678 kg)
Useful load: 1,650 lb (748 kg)

PERFORMANCE:
Maximum speed: 174 kts (200 mph) 322 km/h
Cruise speed: 154 kts (177 mph) 285 km/h, at 75% power at 8,000 ft (2,440 m)
Take-off distance: 862 ft (263 m)
Climb rate: 1,485 ft (453 m) per minute, at sea level
Ceiling: 15,000 ft (4,575 m), service
Range: 920 naut miles (1,059 miles) 1,705 km, at 75% power

↑ **Kestrel Aircraft KL-1A proof of concept prototype for the K-250** *(courtesy Jack Hammett)*

Certification: 1999-2000 to FAR Pt 23 Normal and Utility.
Role: Civil and military high-wing cabin lightplanes.
Sales: Following the POC prototype, 3 flight test and 2 fatigue test K-250s have/are being built for certification purposes. In addition, 4 K-325s will be built for certification.
Details: K-250, except under Aircraft variants.
Crew/passengers: 4 seats in an enclosed cabin.
Construction materials: All Kestrel models are built principally from autoclaved carbonfibre.
Engine: See Aircraft variants.
Fuel system: 329 litres usable.

Aircraft variants:
KL-1A refers to the proof of concept prototype. 160 hp (119.3 kW) Textron Lycoming O-320-D2G engined 4-seater.
K-160 is to be a standard 4-seater with fixed undercarriage. Planned to have the same engine as KL-1A, with 2-blade aluminium propeller, plus avionics. Planned price US$145,000 (1998 dollars).
K-180 is another standard, fixed undercarriage version, but with a 180 hp (134 kW) Textron Lycoming O-360-A4M and 2-blade aluminium propeller, and appropriate avionics. Planned price US$149,500 (1998 dollars).
K-200R is a 4-seat version with retractable undercarriage. Planned 200 hp (149 kW) Teledyne Continental IO-360-ES with 3-blade constant-speed propeller, and appropriate avionics. Planned price US$169,500 (1998 dollars).
K-250 is a 4-seat, fixed undercarriage model for IFR operation. Proposed 250 hp (186.4 kW) Teledyne Continental IO-550-G engine, with 3-blade constant-speed propeller. Avionics at customer's choice. First flown in 1998. Planned price US$189,500 (1998 dollars).
K-250M (Military Trainer) is the base model K-250 modified for military training purposes. Avionics at customer's specifications. Planned price US$199,500 (1998 dollars).
K-325 Utility/Cargo is an IFR 6-seat version with fixed undercarriage, with a 325 hp (242.4 kW) Teledyne Continental TSIO-550-B engine and 3-blade constant-speed propeller. Larger fuselage married to the same wing, engine mount and systems of previous versions. To be offered also in floatplane version for bush operations in Canada and Alaska. Planned price US$249,500 (1998 dollars).

Lake Aircraft Inc — USA

Corporate address:
Laconia Airport, 50 Airport Road, Gilford, NH 03246.

Telephone: +1 603 524 5868
Facsimile: + 1 603 524 5728
E-mail: wolf@amphib.com
Web site: http://www.amphib.com

Founded:
1959.

International marketing:
606 North Dyer Blvd, Kissimmee Airport, Kissimmee, FL 34741.
Telephone: +1 407 847 9000
Facsimile: +1 407 847 4516
Information:
Haig Hogopian (Vice President, International Marketing & Sales).

FACILITIES

▪ Also at Renton Airport, 500 W Perimeter Road, Renton, WA 98055.

ACTIVITIES

▪ Over 1,300 amphibians delivered of all past and current versions.

Lake Renegade, Turbo Renegade, Seawolf, Seafury and Turbo Seafury

Certification: 1983 for the current Renegade.
Role: Civil and military, single-engined, passenger and utility amphibians.
Details: For Turbo Renegade, except under Aircraft variants.
Crew/passengers: 6 persons, including pilot/s.
With passenger seats removed, can carry 2 litters plus pilot and/or attendant/co-pilot.
Baggage capacity: 200 lb (91 kg).
Airframe characteristics: Single-step hull, with a retractable rudder.
Wing control surfaces: Ailerons (with ground-adjustable trim tabs) and single-slotted flaps.
Tail control surfaces: Elevators, and rudder (with tabs). Port elevator is split into 2 sections, the smaller outer section used also for trimming.
Flight control system: Manual except for hydraulic flaps and port elevator trim section.
Construction materials: Metal.
Engine: Textron Lycoming TIO-540-AA2AD, with a 6 ft 4 ins (1.93 m) Hartzell Q-tip pusher propeller.
Engine rating: 270 hp (201 kW).

↑ Lake Seawolf amphibian *(courtesy Lake)*

Details for Turbo Renegade, unless stated

PRINCIPAL DIMENSIONS:
Wing span: 38 ft 4 ins (11.68 m)
Maximum length: 29 ft 8 ins (9.04 m), or 28 ft 4 ins (8.63 m) for Seawolf
Maximum height: 9 ft 11.5 ins (3.03 m)

CABIN:
Length: 10 ft 4 ins (3.15 m)
Width: 3 ft 5 ins (1.04 m)
Height: 3 ft 7 ins (1.09 m)

WINGS:
Aerofoil section: NACA 4415
Area: 164 sq ft (15.24 m^2)
Aspect ratio: 8.96

UNDERCARRIAGE:
Type: Retractable with swivelling nosewheel

WEIGHTS:
Empty: 2,075 lb (941 kg)
Maximum take-off: 3,140 lb (1,424 kg)
Useful load: 1,065 lb (483 kg)

PERFORMANCE:
Cruise speed: 155 kts (178 mph) 287 km/h at 75% power
Stall speed: 55 kts (64 mph) 102 km/h *clean*, 49 kts (57 mph) 91 km/h *landing configuration*
Take-off distance: 880 ft (268 m) *land*, 1,250 ft (381 m) *water*
Landing distance: 475 ft (145 m) *land*, 600 ft (183 m) *water*
Maximum climb rate: 900 ft (274 m) per minute at sea level, MTOW
Ceiling: 23,800 ft (7,255 m) service, or 20,000 ft (6,100 m) certified
Range: 1,120 naut miles (1,290 miles) 2,074 km, or 1,000 naut miles (1,150 miles) 1,853 km for Seawolf on standard fuel
Duration: 8 hours for Seawolf with standard fuel

Fuel system: 288 litres, with 341 litres optional.
Electrical system: 12 volt supply, via an engine-driven alternator and 30 amp-hour battery.
Hydraulic system: 1,250 psi for undercarriage, flaps and elevator trim.
Braking system: Disc brakes.
Flight avionics/instrumentation: Avionics to customer's requirements. Can include full IFR equipment, dual nav/com, RNAV, ADF, autopilot, etc. Full range of engine instruments.

Aircraft variants:
Renegade seats 6 and is powered by a 250 hp (186.4 kW) Textron Lycoming IO-540-C4B5 piston engine.
Turbo Renegade is a 4-seater with a turbocharged engine, as detailed. Planned to be licence-built in China by the Chengdu Asia Water Aircraft Company, following delivery of 11 US-built aircraft to China.
Seafury and ***Turbo Seafury*** are versions of Renegade and Turbo Renegade for salt water operations, also having sea survival equipment.
Seawolf is a military version, equipped with Alkan 6091 underwing NATO standard pylons and stores, designed to meet the special mission needs of government agencies and military organizations. 333 litres of usable fuel, with optional 234 litres in external tanks for 1,500 naut mile range and 12 hours duration. Can carry external cargo pods; weapons such as 200 lb bombs, rocket launchers, cartridge launchers and machine-gun pods; wing-mounted rescue pods; SAR pods and more. IO-540 or turbocharged version of engine. Can be radar equipped. See data table.

Learjet Inc — USA

Corporate address:
One Learjet Way, PO Box 7707, Wichita, KS 67277.

Telephone: +1 316 946 2000, 2450; or 3085 for Public Relations
Facsimile: +1 316 946 2220, 3235

Founded:
1962, becoming a subsidiary of Bombardier in 1990 as part of the Aerospace Group – North America.

Employees:
Over 3,700.

Learjet 31A

First flight: 11 May 1987 (prototype).
Certification: 12 August 1988 to FAR Pt 25 transport category, including day, night, VFR, IFR, FAA FAR Pt 91 Category II and flight into known icing.
Role: Pressurized light corporate jet.
Sales: 152 Learjet 31/31As at time of writing.
Details: For Learjet 31A, except under Aircraft variants.
Wing characteristics: Cambered leading edge. Winglets.
Wing control surfaces: Ailerons (with geared balance tabs plus port electric trim tab), single-slotted flaps and spoilers.
Tail control surfaces: Variable-incidence tailplane. Elevators, and rudder (with trim tab).
Flight control system: Mechanical, except for electrically controlled and hydraulically actuated flaps and spoilers, and electric trim tabs.
Construction materials: Metal.
Electrical system: DC supply via 2 × 30 volt, 400 amp, engine-driven starter-generators. 2 × 24 volt, 40 amp-hour lead-acid batteries for engine starting and emergency bus operation. 3,000 VA AC supply, with 115/26 volt auto-transformers, providing 26 volts.
Hydraulic system: 1,500 psi.
Radar: AlliedSignal Bendix/King RDS 82 VP.
Flight avionics/instrumentation: AlliedSignal Bendix/King KFC 3100 system, with 5 tube EFIS 50, dual digital 3-axis autopilot/flight director, dual Series III VHF transceivers, dual Series III VOR/ILS nav receivers, ADF, Series III DME, dual Mode-S transponder, dual central air data computers with digitally interfaced displays, dual AHRS, and radar altimeter. Universal UNS-1M FMS.

Aircraft variants:
Learjet 31A, as detailed.
Learjet 31A/ER is the extended-range model, with a 20 ft 7 ins (6.27 m) cabin length, 16,500 lb (7,484 kg) MTOW, 4,653 lb (2,111 kg) of usable fuel, and performance differences.

Learjet 35A

Comments: No longer marketed. Details in the 1996-97 edition of *WA&SD*, page 445.

↑ Learjet 31A *(courtesy Learjet)*

Learjet 45

First flight: 7 October 1995.
Certification: 22 September 1997 to FAR Pt 25 transport category, including day, night, VFR, IFR, and flight into known icing. JAA certification received Summer 1998.
First delivery: May 1998.
Role: Mid-size pressurized corporation jet and crew trainer.
Sales: Over 155 ordered at time of writing. 35-40 to be delivered by 31 January 1999
Control surfaces: Similar to Learjet 31A except both ailerons have electric trim tabs.
Undercarriage: Unlike previous Learjets, Learjet 45 has air-oil trailing-link shock-struts and steer-by-wire nosewheel steering (±55%).
Hydraulic system: 3,000 psi, for undercarriage and uplocks, main gear doors, brakes, flaps, thrust reversers and spoilers.
Radar: Honeywell Primus 650 weather radar, with optional Primus 870.
Flight avionics/instrumentation: Honeywell Primus 1000 avionics suite, and dual Primus II nav/com/identification radio pulse package. Primus 1000 includes 4 EFIS screen displays, each 8 × 7 ins (20 × 18 cm), as 2 PFDs, an MFD and EICAS. Heart of Primus 1000 is the integrated avionics computer, combining the EFIS and EICAS processor, flight director and digital autopilot in a single LRU. Primus II includes a liquid-crystal flat display which also provides back-up navigation and engine displays.

Learjet 60

First flight: 18 October 1990 for prototype; 15 June 1992 for first production aircraft.
Certification: 15 January 1993. FAR Pt 25 transport category, including day, night, IFR, and flight into known icing. Complies with new Reduced Vertical Separation Minimum (RVSM) regulations.
Role: Transcontinental corporate jet.
Sales: 119 delivered (since January 1993) at time of writing.
Baggage capacity: 58.7 cu ft (1.66 m^3) for 640 lb (290 kg).
Radar: Rockwell Collins WXR-840 weather radar.
Flight avionics/instrumentation: Rockwell Collins Pro Line 4 digital suite, including integrated 4 CRT screen EFIS, AMS-850 avionics management system to centralize cockpit control (by providing EFIS, radar and TCAS control and radio management as well as flight management capability), dual channel digital

Pax=Passengers	Learjet 31A	Learjet 45	Learjet 60
Crew + Pax	2 + 9	2 + 9	2 + 10
Engine × 2	AlliedSignal TFE731-2-3B turbofans	AlliedSignal TFE731-20 turbofans	Pratt & Whitney Canada PW305A turbofans
Engine rating (each)	3,500 lbf (15.57 kN)	3,500 lbf (15.57 kN)	4,600 lbf (20.46 kN)
Usable fuel lb (kg)	4,124 (1,871)	6,000 (2,722)	7,910 (3,588)
Wing span	43 ft 9.6 ins (13.4 m)	47 ft 9.6 ins (14.58 m)	43 ft 9 ins (13.34 m)
Length	48 ft 8.4 ins (14.83 m)	58 ft (17.68 m)	58 ft 8 ins (17.88 m)
Height	12 ft 3.6 ins (3.75 m)	14 ft 1.2 ins (4.3 m)	14 ft 8 ins (4.47 m)
Wing area sq ft (m^2)	264.51 (24.57)	311.6 (28.95)	264.5 (24.57)
Cabin Length from cockpit divider to end of pressurized compartment	17 ft 1 ins (5.2 m)	19 ft 9 ins (6.02 m)	17 ft 8 ins (5.38 m)
Cabin width	4 ft 11 ins (1.5 m)	5 ft 1 ins (1.55 m)	5 ft 11 ins (1.8 m)
Cabin height	4 ft 5 ins (1.35 m)	4 ft 11 ins (1.5 m)	5 ft 8 ins (1.73 m)
Cabin pressurization differential	9.4 psi	9.4 psi	
Weight empty, basic operating lb (kg)	11,100 (5,035)	12,850 (5,829)	14,640 (6,641)
Maximum take-off weight lb (kg)	16,500 (7,484)	20,200 (9,163)	23,500 (10,660)
Maximum landing weight lb (kg)	15,300 (6,940)	19,200 (8,709)	19,500 (8,845)
Payload with maximum fuel lb (kg)	1,526 (692)	1,600 (726)	1,200 (544)
Maximum cruise speed kts (mph) km/h	463 (533) 858, or Mach 0.81	463 (533) 858, or Mach 0.81	453 (522) 839
Long-range cruise speed kts (mph) km/h	418 (481) 775, or Mach 0.73	434 (500) 804, or Mach 0.76	420 (484) 778, or Mach 0.74
Stall speed kts (mph) km/h	93 (107) 172, landing configuration		
Maximum climb rate ft (m) per minute, MTOW, sea level, ISA	5,480 (1,670)		4,500 (1,372)
Maximum operating altitude ft (m)	51,000 (15,545)	51,000 (15,545)	51,000 (15,545)
Balanced field length ft (m), MTOW, sea level, ISA	3,280 (1,000)	4,580 (1,396)	5,450 (1,661)
Landing distance ft (m), MLW, sea level, ISA	2,767 (843)	2,990 (911)	3,420 (1,042)
Range naut miles (miles) km	1,266 (1,457) 2,345 with NBAA IFR reserve, ISA, and 2 crew + 4 pax	1,710 (1,968) 3,167 with NBAA IFR reserve, ISA, and 2 crew + 4 pax	2,409 (2,773) 4,461 with NBAA IFR reserve, ISA, and 2 crew + 4 pax
Noise levels Take-off, Sideline, Approach EPNdb	81, 92.6, 87		78.9, 83.2, 87.7

↑ **Learjet 45** *(courtesy Learjet)*

fail-passive autopilot, dual flight directors, dual AHRS, dual digital central air data computers and cockpit voice recorder. Universal UNS1-B optional.

↑ **Learjet 60** *(courtesy Learjet)*

Lockheed Martin Corporation (Skunk Works)/Gulfstream Aerospace Corporation — USA

Corporate address:
See Combat section for Lockheed Martin, and earlier in this section for Gulfstream Aerospace.

Comments: In September 1998, at Farnborough, it was announced that these companies had teamed to undertake a joint feasibility study into a **Supersonic Business Jet (SBJ).** They consider advancements in aeronautic science have improved both the technical feasibility and the business case for an SBJ. The globalization of business and emergence of new markets in far-off regions are among other reasons for this latest study. In addition to supersonic cruise capability, it is considered that the SBJ must be able to operate out of key general aviation airports, be able to fly efficiently at subsonic speeds and merge with other air traffic, have an initial cruise altitude capability above other subsonic traffic and be able to fly non-stop between Europe and the central United States. After conceptually exploring the feasibility of designing, manufacturing and marketing a commercially viable SBJ, the companies will then determine whether to proceed with developing and testing a technology demonstration vehicle. It is anticipated that the advancement of the programme towards the introduction into service of an SBJ would take 8 to 10 years.

The defined initial SBJ requirements are a cruise capability of between Mach 1.6 and 2, range of over 4,000 naut miles, stand-up cabin with room for 8 passengers and 3 crew, an outfitting allowance typically associated with Gulfstream aircraft, and take-off noise characteristics compatible with anticipated future community standards.

Maule Air, Inc

USA

Corporate address:
2099 GA Highway, 133 South Moultrie, GA 31768.

Telephone: +1 912 985 2045
Facsimile: +1 912 890 2402

Employees:
Some 100.

Information:
Brent Maule (Sales and Marketing – *telephone* +1 912 985 9628).

Maule M-7, MT-7 and MXT-7 series

Role: STOL-capable 4 or 5-seat leisure and business aircraft, also suited to cargo carrying, glider and banner towing, instruction, law enforcement and more.
Sales: Over 2,000 Maule aircraft have been produced since 1962. 54 aircraft delivered in the last full year at the time of writing.
Details: All current aircraft are strut-braced, high-wing cabin monoplanes. All piston-engined models are 23 ft 6 ins (7.16 m) long, and all turboprop models are 24 ft (7.32 m) long.
Crew/passengers: See Aircraft variants. Dual controls. Standard double cargo door.
Baggage capacity: 250 lb (113 kg).
Equipment options: Large range of options available from Maule, ranging from auxiliary fuel tank to glider tow release kit, plexiglas door, camera hole, float fittings and installation, ski attachments, 78 ins and 80 ins (1.98 m and 2.03 m) McCauley 3-blade propellers, vortex generators and much more. Also, large range of optional avionics, with 3 IFR packages ranging from US$10,990 to US$22,199 (May 1998 figures), and 28 volt system upgrade for IFR packages.
Wing control surfaces: Ailerons and flaps. Flap settings -7°, 0°, 24°, and 40°, with several versions also having a 48° setting.
Tail control surfaces: Elevators (port trim tab) and rudder (servo tab, linked to ailerons).
Construction materials: All aluminium wing. Fuselage and tail group of alloy steel tubing with trusses welding. Ceconite fabric covered.
Engine: See Aircraft variants.
Fuel system: 151 litres of usable fuel in 2 wing tanks. Auxiliary tank raises total fuel capacity to 276 litres, though standard for MX-7-180B, -180C, MXT-7-180, all -235s and -260s.
Electrical system: 60 amp engine-driven alternator and 12 volt battery. 100 amp starter-generator and 24 volt battery on at least M-7-420C.
Braking system: Hydraulic. Parking brakes.
Flight avionics/instrumentation: Standard SP-1 package avionics include AlliedSignal Bendix/King KT 76A transponder and KX 125-01 nav/com, Narco AR-850 remote altitude encoder, and PS Engineering PM1000II crew intercom (4-seaters). Standard package SP-2 replaces nav/com with Bendix/King KLX 135A GPS/com, which SP-3 package has Garmin GNC 250XL GPS/com (requires use of headsets). Optional IFR packages (see Equipment options). Standard instruments include altimeter, airspeed indicator, rate of climb indicator, tachometer and more. Wide range of optional equipment includes S-Tec 2-axis autopilot.

Aircraft variants:
MX-7-160 Sportplane is a 4-seater with a 160 hp (119.3 kW) Textron Lycoming O-320-B2D engine and 32 ft 11 ins (10.03 m) wing span. Wing area 165.6 sq ft (15.38 m^2). Oleo strut tailwheel undercarriage. May 1998 price US$99,069.
MX-7-180A Sportsplane is similar to MX-7-160 but has a 180 hp (134 kW) O-360-C4F engine. May 1998 price US$104,499.
MXT-7-160 Comet is a nosewheel undercarriage version of MX-7-160. Usually flown as 2-seater, but with option for 4 seats. May 1998 price US$108,000.
MXT-7-180A Comet is a nosewheel version of MX-7-180A. Usually flown as 2-seater, but with option for 4 seats. May 1998 price US$113,499.
MX-7-180B Star Rocket is a 4-seat (plus optional jump seat) oleo-strut tailwheel type, with a 180 hp (134 kW) Textron Lycoming O-360-C1F engine. Optional skis and floats. 30 ft 10 ins (9.4 m) wing span and 157.9 sq ft (14.67 m^2) wing area. May 1998 price US$116,435.
MX-7-180C has a spring gear tailwheel undercarriage and O-360-C1F engine. May 1998 price US$121,435.
MXT-7-180 Star Rocket is a 4-seater (plus optional jump seat), with a nosewheel undercarriage. O-360-C1F engine. Optional skis and floats. 32 ft 11 ins (10.03 m) wing span. May 1998 price US$126,888.
M-7-235B Super Rocket is a 5-seat oleo strut tailwheel type, with a 235 hp (175 kW) Textron Lycoming O-540-B4B5 engine. Optional skis and floats. 33 ft 8 ins (10.26 m) wing span. May 1998 price US$129,868. Alternative IO-540-W1A5 engine takes price to US$137,568.
M-7-235C Orion is similar to M-7-235B but has a spring gear

↑ **Maule MXT-7 Comet** *(courtesy Maule)*

tailwheel undercarriage. May 1998 price US$135,706 with O-540-B4B5 engine and US$143,406 with IO-540-W1A5 engine.
MT-7-235 Super Rocket is a 5-seater with nosewheel undercarriage, with a 235 hp (175 kW) Textron Lycoming IO-540-W1A5 engine. 32 ft 11 ins (10.03 m) wing span. May 1998 price US$149,278.
M-7-260 is a new oleo strut tailwheel undercarriage version, with a 260 hp (194 kW) IO-540-V4A5 engine. May 1998 price US$147,568.
M-7-260C is a new version, similar to M-7-260 but with a spring gear tailwheel undercarriage. May 1998 price US$153,988.
MT-7-260 is a new version, similar to M-7-260 but with a nosewheel undercarriage. May 1998 price US$159,278.
M-7-420C is a new spring gear tailwheel 4/5-seater, with a 420 shp (313 kW) Allison 250-B17C turboprop engine. May 1998 price US$450,000.
MT-7-420 is a nosewheel version of the M-7-420. May 1998 price US$470,000.
M-7-420 Amphibian is an amphibious version with Edo floats. May 1998 price US$512,000.

Details for M-7-235B

PRINCIPAL DIMENSIONS:
Wing span: 33 ft 8 ins (10.26 m)
Maximum length: 23 ft 6 ins (7.16 m)
Maximum height: 6 ft 4 ins (1.93 m)

CABIN:
Width: 3 ft 6 ins (1.07 m)

WINGS:
Aerofoil section: USA 35B mod
Area: 177 sq ft (16.44 m^2)
Aspect ratio: 6.4
Dihedral: 1°
Incidence: 0° 30'

WEIGHTS:
Empty: 1,500 lb (680 kg)
Maximum take-off: 2,500 lb (1,134 kg)

PERFORMANCE:
Cruise speed: 139 kts (160 mph) 257 km/h at 75% power
Stall speed: 31 kts (35 mph) 57 km/h
Take-off distance over a 50 ft (15 m) obstacle: 600 ft (183 m)
Landing distance over a 50 ft (15 m) obstacle: 500 ft (153 m)
Maximum climb rate: 2,000 ft (610 m) per minute at sea level, with pilot only and 50% fuel
Ceiling: 20,000 ft (6,100 m)
Range: 760 naut miles (875 miles) 1,408 km

Mid-Continent Aircraft Corporation

USA

Corporate address:
Drawer L, Hayti, MO 63851.

Telephone: +1 314 359 0500
Facsimile: +1 314 359 0538

Founded:
1949.

Information:
Richard Reade (President).

ACTIVITIES

■ Mid-Continent markets the King Cat, a Schweizer/Ag-Cat Corporation Ag-Cat C converted to use a 1,200 hp (895 kW) Wright R radial engine with a new 3-blade propeller. With the 1,893 litre/67 cu ft (1.897 m^3) hopper, it has a working speed of 87-113 kts (100-130 mph) 161-209 km/h. Options include a 38 ins (97 cm) gatebox and wide spreader. In addition, a 2,271 litre hopper is available, and the company also offers AlliedSignal modifications.
■ Authorized distributor of the Ag-Cat, Ayres Turbo Thrush, Cessna and Melex M18 agricultural aircraft. The business is divisionalized into large international aircraft parts sales and FAA approved repair station Class 1, 2 and 3 DFQR172D; insurance brokerage for agricultural aircraft; and refurbishment of the Stearman trainer into MCMD Custom Specials with 220, 300 and 450 hp (164, 224 and 336 kW) engines. It also operates 4 agricultural aircraft.

↑ **Mid-Continent King Cat**

Moller International

USA

Comments: See 1996-97 edition of *WA&SD*, page 447, for details of the Moller VTOL light aircraft and a photograph.

Mooney Aircraft Corporation

USA

Corporate address:
PO Box 72, Louis Schreiner Field, Kerrville, TX 78028.

Telephone: +1 830 896 6000
Facsimile: +1 830 896 7333

Founded:
5 July 1946.

Information:
Susan Harrison (Marketing Manager – *telephone* +1 830 792 2917).

ACTIVITIES

■ Mooney marked production of its 10,000th aircraft in 1994. 86 aircraft of all types delivered in the last full year at the time of writing, 13 more than the previous year.

Mooney Allegro, Bravo, Encore and Ovation

↑ **Mooney Ovation** *(courtesy Mooney)*

First flight: 1976 for the original Mooney 201.
Details: For the Allegro, except under Aircraft variants and table.
Role: 4-seat lightplane. Dual controls.
Sales: 97 aircraft produced of all types in 1998. Production of Allegro ended October 1998 (new longer-fuselage version to be introduced). Encore production probably in batch form only, against accumulated orders.
Baggage capacity: 120 lb (54.4 kg). Also, rear seats can be removed for carrying light cargo.
Wing control surfaces: Ailerons and single-slotted flaps.
Tail control surfaces: Variable incidence tailplane (fin moves with tailplane). Elevators and forward-swept rudder.
Flight control system: Manual, except for electric flaps. Optional electric trimming.
Construction materials: Metal, including tubular steel welded fuselage cabin, and 1-piece single-spar wing.
Engine: Textron Lycoming IO-360-A3B6D piston engine, with a 6 ft 2 ins (1.88 m) McCauley 2-blade constant-speed propeller.
Engine rating: 200 hp (149 kW).
Fuel system: 242 litres usable.
Electrical system: 28 volt, 70 amp alternator and 24 volt battery (10 amp-hour).
Braking system: Hydraulic disc. Parking brake.
Flight avionics/instrumentation: Blind-flying instrumentation. Selection of AlliedSignal Bendix/King avionics packages, with or without DME, RNAV, EFIS and GPS. Other options include flight control system/autopilot, ADF, RMI, Mode-C transponder, radar altimeter, and Goodrich stormscope.

Aircraft variants:
Allegro (M-20J), as detailed above. Formerly known as MSE. Wing span 36 ft 1 ins (11 m), length 24 ft 8 ins (7.52 m) and height 8 ft 4 ins (2.54 m). Empty weight 1,726 lb (783 kg), maximum take-off weight 2,900 lb (1,315 kg). Maximum speed 175 kts (202 mph) 324 km/h at sea level, cruise speed 168 kts (193 mph) 311 km/h at 8,000 ft (2,440 m) at 75% power, and stall speed 62 kts (72 mph) 115 km/h IAS clean or 58 kts (67 mph) 108 km/h in landing configuration. Duration 7 hours.
Encore (M-20K) is a new and upgraded version of the 1980's Mooney 252 4-seater, first flown on 3 March 1997. Supplementary Type Certificate awarded April 1997. New instrument panel and cabin interior, improved soundproofing and Ovation-type strengthened undercarriage, plus other improvements. 210 hp (157 kW) Teledyne Continental TSIO-360-SB with 3-blade constant-speed McCauley propeller. 286.2 litres of fuel. Length 25 ft 5 ins (7.75 m), wing span and height as for Ovation. Empty weight 2,130 lb (966 kg), maximum take-off weight 3,130 lb (1,420 kg), approximate useful load 1,000 lb (454 kg), and payload (typically equipped) 550 lb (249 kg). Never-exceed speed (V_{NE}) 196 kts (225 mph) 363 km/h IAS, climb rate 1,300 ft (396 m) per minute at sea level, and maximum range 1,100 naut miles (1,266 miles) 2,038 km.
Bravo (M-20M) is a 4-seater, with a turbocharged Textron Lycoming TIO-540-AF1A engine, with a 6 ft 3 ins (1.91 m) McCauley 3-blade constant-speed propeller. Formerly known as TLS. First appeared in 1989. Redesigned interior in 1994. Same dimensions as Ovation. Empty weight 2,268 lb (1,029 kg), maximum take-off weight 3,368 lb (1,528 kg), and maximum useful load 1,100 lb (499 kg). 337 litres of usable fuel. Maximum cruise speed 220 kts (253 mph) 408 km/h at 25,000 ft (7,620 m), stall speed 66 kts (76 mph) 123 km/h clean or 59 kts (68 mph) 110 km/h in landing configuration, climb rate 1,230 ft (375 m) per minute at sea level, maximum certified ceiling 25,000 ft (7,620 m), range 1,070 naut miles (1,232 miles) 1,983 km at 13,000 ft (3,960 m) with reserve, and duration 6.7 hours at same altitude.
Ovation (M-20R) was unveiled on 27 April 1994, first flew in May, certified July, and the initial 21 (of 31 ordered) were delivered that year. Combines the Bravo airframe and interior with a 280 hp (209 kW) Teledyne Continental IO-550-G5B engine, with 6 ft 1 ins (1.85 m) McCauley 3-blade constant-speed propeller. Fuel capacity 337 litres usable. Baggage 125 lb (56.7 kg). 2 × 24 volt lead-acid batteries. Composites sandwich cabin side panels to reduce vibration and noise.

Details for M-20R Ovation

PRINCIPAL DIMENSIONS:
Wing span: 36 ft 1 ins (11 m)
Maximum length: 26 ft 9 ins (8.15 m)
Maximum height: 8 ft 4 ins (2.54 m)

WINGS:
Area: 175 sq ft (16.26 m^2)
Aspect ratio: 7.4

UNDERCARRIAGE:
Type: Retractable (electric), with steerable nosewheel

WEIGHTS:
Empty: 2,269 lb (1,029 kg)
Maximum take-off: 3,368 lb (1,527 kg)
Maximum landing weight: 3,200 lb (1,451 kg)
Useful load: 1,143 lb (519 kg)

PERFORMANCE:
Maximum cruise speed: 190 kts (219 mph) 352 km/h at 9,000 ft (2,745 m)
Stall speed: 66 kts (76 mph) 122 km/h *clean*, 59 kts (68 mph) 110 km/h *in landing configuration*, both IAS
Maximum climb rate: 1,200 ft (366 m) per minute at sea level
Ceiling: 20,000 ft (6,100 m), service
Range: 1,129 naut miles (1,300 miles) 2,090 km at 9,000 ft (2,745 m)
Duration: 6.7 hours, with reserve

New Meyers Aircraft Company

USA

Corporate address:
St Lucie County International Airport, Fort Pierce, Florida.

ACTIVITIES

■ Company owned by the Seminole tribe.
■ New Meyers offers 2 aircraft, the 2-seat **SP20** with a 200 hp (149 kW) Textron Lycoming IO-360-C1E6 engine and McCauley 3-blade constant-speed propeller that provide a cruise speed of 165 kts, and the **M300** 4-seat derivative with a 300 hp (224 kW) engine to allow a cruise speed in excess of 200 kts and also featuring S-Tec autopilot and Trimble GPS. The SP20 is an updated version of the original 145 hp (108 kW) Continental-engined Meyers 145A of 1947 certification, featuring also a tubular steel structure for the cabin area, wet wing for 227 litres of fuel, and a sliding cockpit canopy.

Nexus LLC

USA

Corporate address:
822 North Mission, Wichita, KS 67206.

Telephone: +1 316 652 0236
Facsimile: +1 316 686 4014
E-mail: lcesola@aol.com

Information:
Lloyd Hanna.

ACTIVITIES

■ Nexus is developing and will market the 48 ft (14.63 m) span **NAC-100** STOL utility transport in association with APEC Aerospace of Singapore, suited to carrying 8 persons (including pilot/s), or mixed passenger/cargo, all cargo, a litter and 3 attendants plus pilot, or other loads. Intended for both commercial and military uses, it will be powered by a single 750 shp (559 kW) Walter M 601E-11 turboprop engine fitted with a 7 ft 6 ins (2.3 m) diameter Avia-Hamilton Standard 5-blade constant-speed, reversible-pitch propeller. Up to 1,060 litres of fuel will be carried in the cantilever high-mounted wings, providing a range of 800 naut miles (921 miles) 1,480 km with full fuel or 500 naut miles (575 miles) 926 km with full payload. Maximum cruise speed is expected to be 160 kts (184 mph) 296 km/h. The near square-section cabin has a width of 4 ft 5 ins (1.35 m), height of 4 ft 2 ins (1.28 m) and length of 12 ft 7 ins (3.84 m), with access via a side door and a rear ramp. An unusual design feature is its twin outward-canted vertical tails.

In late May 1998, the Chief Editor was informed that construction of the prototype had not yet begun. Eventual production is expected to take place in Singapore.

The New Piper Aircraft, Inc

USA

Corporate address:
2926 Piper Drive, Vero Beach, FL 32960.

Telephone: +1 561 567 4361
Facsimile: +1 561 778 2144
Web site: http://www.newpiper.comm/

Founded:
1936 for the original Piper Aircraft. On 17 July 1997, The New Piper Aircraft, Inc became operational as a subsidiary of Newco Pac Inc and purchased the assets of the Piper Aircraft Corporation.

Employees: 700.

Information:
Kimberley V. Wheeler (Marketing Manager – *telephone* +1 561 567 4361 Ext 2500).

ACTIVITIES

- New Piper delivered 222 aircraft in the last full year at time of writing, 36 more than the previous year.
- New aircraft are the Seneca V that was certified in December 1996 and announced in early 1997, and the turboprop-powered Malibu Meridian also unveiled in 1997 and first flown on 21 August 1998.
- New Piper is considering the possibility of developing a single-engined business jet, possibly using a Williams FJX-2 turbofan
- New Piper offers its 'Step-up Program', whereby if a customer 'trades up' to a new aircraft within 18 months, 100% of the original purchase price, minus a minimal usage fee, is used towards the purchase of the next-in-line up Piper aircraft.

↑ Piper PA28-181 Archer III

Piper PA18-150 Super Cub

Comments: Production of the Super Cub ended in 1995. For details and a photograph, see the 1996-97 edition of *WA&SD*, pages 448-449.

Piper PA28-161 Warrior III

First flight: 27 August 1976 as PA28-161 Warrior II, following the original version of 1972.
Certification: 9 August 1973 for original version.
Role: 4-seat lightplane and trainer.
Sales: US$134,900 at time of writing.
Crew/passengers: 4 persons, with rear bench seat. Heat Muff to provide cabin heat and fresh-air vents.
Baggage capacity: Carpeted baggage compartment with security straps.
Wing control surfaces: 4 position flaps (0°, 10°, 25° and 40°).
Tail control surfaces: Slab tailplane with combined anti-servo/trim tab.
Flight control system: Stainless steel cables. Optional electric trim.
Construction materials: Mainly light alloy metal, but with glassfibre for engine cowling, and wing, tailplane and fin tips.
Fuel system: 2 tanks with 189 litres total capacity (182 litres usable). Engine-driven pump, electric emergency pump, and electric engine primer system.
Electrical system: 28 volt, 60 amp alternator. 24 volt, 10 amp-hour battery. External power receptacle.
Undercarriage: Fixed, with steerable nosewheel. Pilot/co-pilot toe brakes and parking brake. Mainwheels 6.00 × 6 with Michelin tyres. Nosewheel 5.00 × 5 with Michelin tyre.
Flight avionics/instrumentation: Avionics include AlliedSignal Bendix/King KX 155A com/nav, KI 208 VOR/Loc indicator, KT 76C transponder, Narco AR-850 altitude reporter, PMA6000M audio panel, intercom included in PMA6000M (4 positions), and more. Flight instruments and indicators include Piper airspeed indicator, magnetic compass, sensitive altimeter, gyro horizon, directional gyro, turn rate indicator, rate of climb indicator, alternate static source, outside air temperature gauge, digital ammeter, electric clock, annunciator panel, automatic emergency locator transmitter (ELT) and more. An Advanced Training Group of avionics can be exchanged for the standard avionics package at a cost at time of writing of US$11,525, which includes KX 155A with glideslope, KR 87 digital ADF, KLN 89 GPS (VFR) and much more.

Piper PA28-181 Archer III

Role: 4-seat light aircraft.
Sales: US$149,600 at time of writing.
Crew/passengers: 4 persons, the rear on individual seats. Super Quietized soundproofing. Heat Muff to provide cabin heat and fresh-air vents. Optional Piper Aire air conditioning.
Baggage capacity: Carpeted baggage compartment with security straps, volume 26 cu ft (0.74 m^3) and capacity 200 lb (91 kg).
Control surfaces: Similar to Warrior III.
Construction: Similar to Warrior III. Axisymmetric engine cowling.
Fuel system: 2 tanks with 189 litres total capacity (182 litres usable). Engine-driven pump, electric auxiliary pump, and electric engine primer system.
Electrical system: 28 volt, 70 amp alternator. 24 volt, 10 amp-hour battery. External power receptacle.
Undercarriage: Fixed, with steerable nosewheel. Pilot/co-pilot toe brakes and parking brake. All wheels 6.00 × 6 with Michelin tyres.
Flight avionics/instrumentation: Avionics and flight instruments and indicators generally similar to Warrior III but including recording tachometer. Optional avionics package for US$11,800 at time of writing adds second KX 155A, KI 209 VOR/Loc/GS indicator, KR 87 ADF and KLN 89 GPS (VFR), while second optional package at US$18,900 at time of writing adds second KX 155A, KI 209A VOR/Loc/GS indicator with internal GPS switching, KR 87 ADF, KLN 89B GPS (IFR) and KAP 140 single-axis autopilot. Other options available, including KAP 140 autopilot of 2-axis type with altitude hold and electric trim (for use with standard avionics package).

Piper PA28R-201 Arrow

First flight: 16 September 1975.
Role: 4-seat lightplane and trainer.
Sales: Price US$204,700 at time of writing.
Crew/passengers: 4 persons, the rear on individual seats. Heat Muff to provide cabin heat and fresh-air vents.
Baggage capacity: Carpeted baggage compartment with security straps, capacity 200 lb (91 kg).

↑ Piper PA28-161 Warrior III

↑ Piper PA28R-201 Arrow

Control surfaces: Similar to Warrior III.
Fuel system: 291 litres in 2 tanks (272.5 litres usable). Engine-driven pump, and electric auxiliary pump.
Electrical system: 14 volt, 60 amp alternator. 12 volt, 35 amp-hour battery. External power receptacle.
Undercarriage: Electro-hydraulic retractable, with steerable nosewheel. Pilot/co-pilot toe brakes and parking brake. Mainwheels 6.00 × 6 with Michelin tyres. Nosewheel 5.00 × 5 with Michelin tyre.
Flight avionics/instrumentation: Standard AlliedSignal Bendix/King KX 155 com with audio amplifier/broad band antenna, KX 155 nav with VOR antenna, KI 203 VOR/Loc indicator, VOR/Loc converter included in KI 203, KT 76A transponder, Narco AR-850 altitude reporter, Piper avionics master switch, Telex 100T microphone/noise cancelling, and more. Advanced Training Group IFR package for exchange for standard avionics at US$37,445 at time of writing, with many items including KX 155 glideslope receiver and KLN 89B GPS. Flight instruments and indicators generally similar to Archer III but including gear position lights and gear-in-transit/not locked light.

Piper PA28-236 Dakota

Comments: This model is no longer available. For details see the 1996-97 edition of *WA&SD*, page 448.

Piper PA32R-301 Saratoga II HP and PA32R-301T TC

Role: 5/6-seat lightplane and business aircraft.
Sales: Price for Saratoga II HP about US$378,900, and for Saratoga II TC about US$398,200, both for 1998.
Crew/passengers: 5 persons with entertainment/executive console or 6 persons without, with 3/4 passenger seats in club layout. Heat Muff to provide cabin heat and fresh-air vents. Quietized Super soundproofing. Provisions in console for radio/CD player, flight phone, multi-media entertainment system, and lap-top computer station. Optional Piper Aire air conditioning.
Baggage capacity: Compartments with security straps. Rear cabin and hat shelf area 17.3 cu ft (0.49 m^3) for 100 lb (45.4 kg), and fuselage nose 7 cu ft (0.2 m^3) for 100 lb (45.4 kg).
Wing control surfaces: 4 position flaps (0°, 10°, 25° and 40°).
Tail control surfaces: Slab tailplane with combined anti-servo/trim tab. Rudder with trim.
Flight control system: Mechanical, with stainless steel cables, except for electrically operated flaps.
Construction materials: Similar to Warrior III.
Fuel system: 2 interconnected tanks, with 405 litres total capacity (386 litres usable). Engine-driven pump, and electric emergency pump.
Electrical system: 28 volt, 90 amp alternator. 24 volt, 10 amp-hour battery. External power receptacle.
Undercarriage: Electro-hydraulically retractable, with steerable nosewheel. Pilot/co-pilot toe brakes and parking brake. Mainwheels 6.00 × 6 with Michelin tyres. Nosewheel 5.00 × 5 with Michelin tyre.
Flight avionics/instrumentation: Standard new generation AlliedSignal Bendix/King avionics package with dual KX 155A nav/com, KI 525A VOR/Loc GS/HS, KN 72 VOR converter, KI 204 VOR/Loc/GS indicator, KLN 89B GPS, KN 62A DME, PMA-6000 audio selector/intercom panel with MB receiver and lights, KT 76C transponder, Narco AR-850 altitude reporter, KFC 150 flight control system (autopilot), and more. Options include weather avoidance scope, KLN 90B GPS and KR 87 slaved ADF. Flight instruments and indicators include Piper truespeed indicator, illuminated magnetic compass, ADI, HSI, turn rate indicator, rate of climb indicator, AN heated pitot head with dual flush static ports, alternate instrument static source, DVR-300i electric clock with voice recorder, annunciator panel, new engine instrument indicators/monitoring system having digital display monitoring panel with fuel management including GPS interface, temperature reading including OAT, electrical system performance, and exceedence monitoring and recording, and more. Automatic emergency locator beacon (ELT).

↑ Piper PA32R-301T Saratoga II TC cabin *(Scott Wohrman)*

↑ Piper PA32R-301T Saratoga II TC *(Scott Wohrman)*

Aircraft variants:
Saratoga II HP, with fuel-injected IO-540-K1G5 engine.
Saratoga IITC is similar to Saratoga II TC but has a turbocharged TIO-540-AH1A engine. First appeared 1997.

Piper PA34-220T Seneca V

Note: Unveiled on 16 January 1997, replacing previous Seneca IV (see 1996-97 edition of *WA&SD*, page 448 for Seneca IV details). Upgraded turbocharged L/TSIO-360-RB engines provide lower engine speeds for quieter, more fuel-efficient cruising without loss of airspeed or power. Other features include Hartzell 2-blade propellers (instead of Seneca IV's McCauley 3-blade, though the McCauley is optional), an extended life heater and environmentally friendly air-conditioning system. Also has a new instrumentation system featuring state-of-the-art micro-processed digital displays, and a newly designed cockpit which places engine switches in an overhead panel. Executive Console.
Role: 5/6-seat, twin-engined lightplane and trainer.
Sales: Price US$472,900 at time of writing.
Crew/passengers: 5 persons with entertainment/executive console or 6 persons without, with 3/4 passenger seats in club layout. Heating and ventilation. Quietized Super soundproofing. Entertainment/executive console, with provisions for multi-media entertainment system with optional radio/CD/video player (USA only), radio/CD unit, and flight phone system. Optional air conditioning and built-in oxygen system..
Baggage capacity: Compartments with security straps. Rear cabin and hat shelf area 17.3 cu ft (0.49 m^3) for 85 lb (38.6 kg), and fuselage nose 15.3 cu ft (0.433 m^3) for 100 lb (45.4 kg).
Wing control surfaces: Slotted flaps, with 2 ins (5 cm) flap position indicator.
Tail control surfaces: Slab tailplane, with combined anti-balance/trim tab. Rudder, with anti-servo tab.
Flight control system: Mechanical, with stainless steel cables, except for electrically operated flaps.
Construction materials: Light alloy metal, except for glassfibre wingtips.
Fuel system: 6 tanks, with total 484.5 litres capacity (462 litres usable). 2 engine-driven pumps. Electric auxiliary pumps.
Electrical system: 2 × 28 volt, 85 amp alternators. 24 volt, 19 amp-hour battery. External power receptacle.
Undercarriage: Electro-hydraulically retractable, with steerable nosewheel. Pilot/co-pilot toe brakes and parking brake. Wheels 6.00 × 6 with Michelin tyres.

↑ Piper PA34-220T Seneca V

Radar: Provision for radar (RDR 2000).
Flight avionics/instrumentation: Standard AlliedSignal Bendix/King avionics include dual KX 165-25 nav/com, KI 525-07 HSI VOR/Loc GS indicator, VOR/Loc converter included in KX 165-25, dual glideslope receivers included in KX 165-25s, KI 206 VOR/Loc indicator, KLN 90B GPS, KN 62A DME, PS Engineering PM 6000 audio selector panel, KT 71 transponder, Narco AR-850 altitude reporter, KFC 150 flight control system (autopilot) with 2-axis flight director, and more. Automatic emergency locator beacon (ELT). Options include insight strike finder weather avoidance system, dual KR 87 digital ADF with KI 228-01 slaved indicator, KRA 10A radar altimeter, Argus 7000 moving map/flight display system, and KAS 297B altitude preselect with enc altimeter. Flight instruments and indicators include Piper truespeed indicator, illuminated magnetic compass, sensitive altimeter, ADI, HSI, turn rate indicator, rate of climb indicator, DVR-300I-XT digital voice recorder clock, annunciator panel, optional air condition door open, engine hour meter, new engine instrument indicators/monitoring system, digital readout indicator, and more.

Piper PA44-180 Seminole

First flight: 1976.
Role: 4-seat, twin-engined lightplane and trainer.
Sales: Price US$319,600 at time of writing.
Crew/passengers: 4 persons on individual seats. Heating and ventilation. Quietized soundproofing
Baggage capacity: Baggage compartments with security straps. Rear cabin area 24 cu ft (0.68 m^3) for 200 lb (91 kg) plus hat shelf.
Wing control surfaces: Plain ailerons and 4-position flaps (0°, 10°, 25° and 40°).
Tail control surfaces: Slab tailplane with tab. Rudder with anti-servo tab.
Flight control system: Mechanical, with stainless steel cables. Optional S-Tec electric trim.
Construction materials: Light alloy metal.
Fuel system: 2 tanks, with total of 416 litres (409 usable). 2 engine-driven pumps, 2 electric auxiliary pumps, and 2 electric engine primers.
Electrical system: 2 × 14 volt, 70 amp alternators. 12 volt, 35 amp-hour battery. External power receptacle.
Undercarriage: Electro-hydraulically retractable, with steerable nosewheel. Pilot/co-pilot toe brakes and parking brake. Mainwheels 6.00 × 6 with Michelin tyres. Nosewheel 5.00 × 5 with Michelin tyre.
Flight avionics/instrumentation: Standard AlliedSignal Bendix/King avionics package includes KX 155 com with audio amplifier broad band antenna, KX 155 nav with VOR antenna, VOR/Loc indicator and converter included in KI 203s, KT 76A transponder, and Narco AR-850 altitude reporter. Automatic emergency locator transmitter (ELT). Advanced training group IFR package is available as an exchange for standard avionics, costing US$42,205 at time of writing and including KR 87 digital ADF and KLN 89B GPS. Flight instruments and indicators include gyro horizon, turn rate indicator, rate of climb, OAT gauge, electric clock, dual vacuum system with indicator, Piper truespeed indicator, illuminated magnetic compass, sensitive altimeter, dual ammeters, annunciator panel, dual tachometer, engine hour meter, flight time meter, and more.

↑ Piper PA46-350P Malibu Mirage

↑ Piper PA44-180 Seminole

Piper PA46-350P Malibu Mirage and Malibu Meridian

First flight: 1983. New Malibu Meridian 21 August 1998.
Details: For Malibu Mirage, except under Aircraft variants.
Certification: 1983 (July 2000 for Malibu Meridian).
Role: Pressurized 6-seat business aircraft.
Sales: Price US$768,700 at time of writing (US$1.3 million for Malibu Meridian, of which 90 ordered by August 1998).
Crew/passengers: 6 persons on individual seats. Heater Muff cabin heating, supplemental electric heater, ventilation, and air conditioning (refrigerant cycle type). Quietized super soundproofing. Emergency oxygen system. Forward refreshment/entertainment centres.
Baggage capacity: Baggage compartments with security straps. Forward compartment 13 cu ft (0.37 m^3) with capacity 100 lb (45.4 kg), and aft compartment 20 cu ft (0.57 m^3) with capacity 100 lb (45.4 kg). Nose baggage door with (moulded) seal.
Wing control surfaces: Ailerons and flaps (0° to 36°, with preselect feature); wing flap position indicator.
Tail control surfaces: Horn-balanced elevator with trim tab, and horn-balanced rudder.
Flight control system: Mechanical, with stainless steel cables and galvanized aileron cables, except for electric flaps and elevator trim.
Construction materials: Metal.
Fuel system: 462 litres total (usable 454 litres). Engine driven pump, 2 centrifugal type electric pumps and electric emergency pump.
Electrical system: Dual 28 volt, 70 amp alternators. 24 volt, 10 amp-hour battery. 26 volt, 400 Hz AC static inverter. External power receptacle.
De-icing system: De-icing group (flight into known icing) includes PPG pilot's heated glass windscreen.
Undercarriage: Electro-hydraulically retractable, with steerable nosewheel. Pilot/co-pilot toe brakes and parking brake. Mainwheels 6.00 × 6 with Michelin tyres. Nosewheel 5.00 × 5 with Michelin tyre.
Radar: RDR-2000 weather radar.
Flight avionics/instrumentation: AlliedSignal Bendix/King avionics, including dual KX 165-25 nav/com with glideslope, KI 525A-07 HSI VOR/Loc GS indicator, KI 206-04 VOR/Loc indicator, KI 256 AP/FD attitude gyro (AIR) horizontal gyro reference, KCS 55A directional gyro reference slaved compass system/HSI, KLN 90B GPS with moving map, KN 63 DME receiver and indicator with KDI 572 master control, PS Engineering PMA-6000 audio selector panel, KR 87 digital slaved ADF with KI 227-01 slaved indicator and KA 44B antenna, KT 71 digital transponder, KEA 130A encoding altimeter, KAS 297B altitude/vertical speed/alerter altitude preselect/system, KC 291 yaw damper system, and KFC 150 autopilot providing single-cue V-BAR flight director system and KI 256 attitude gyro with auto electric trim, altitude hold, and VOR/Loc/GS coupling. Optional EHI-40 electronic flight instrument system (EFIS) as exchange for Bendix/King standard package, with many features including ED 461 EHSI with ADF-VOR bearing pointer DME display and R/nav/LRN map modes. Many optional avionics. Automatic emergency locator transmitter (ELT). Flight instruments and indicators include engine monitoring instrument system (EMIS) with 10 large full sweep, parallax-free, trend displays (analog indicators and digital indicator); Piper truespeed indicator, magnetic compass, dual pictorial turn rate indicators, 2 rate of climb indicators, PCR 300I electric clock with voice recorder, gyro air filter, vacuum gauge, heated pitot head, overhead switch panel, annunciator panel, 6-channel cylinder head temperature monitoring system with selectable cylinder readout, Hobbs meter (flight time recorder), and alternate static source.

Aircraft variants:
Malibu Mirage, as detailed.
Malibu Meridian is the new turboprop variant of Malibu, first rolled out on 13 August 1998. Pratt & Whitney Canada PT6A-42A engine, derated to 350 shp (261 kW). Fast cruise speed 262 kts (302 mph) 485 km/h, ceiling 30,000 ft (9,145 m), and range 1,070 naut miles (1,232 miles) 1,983 km with 645 litres fuel. Wing root cuff, larger tailplane, glass cockpit with dual Garmin GNS 350 nav/com, Meggit EIDS, and S-Tec 550 autopilot. Deliveries from the year 2,000.

	PA28-161 Warrior III	PA28-181 Archer III	PA28R-201 Arrow	PA32R-301 Saratoga II HP	PA32R-301T Saratoga II TC	PA34-220T Seneca V	PA44-180 Seminole	PA46-350P Malibu Mirage
Role	Lightplane and trainer	Lightplane	Lightplane and trainer	Lightplane and business aircraft	Lightplane and business aircraft	Twin-engined lightplane and trainer	Twin-engined lightplane and trainer	Pressurized business aircraft
Passengers	4	4	4	5/6	5/6	5/6	4	6
Engine/s	Textron Lycoming O-320-D3G	Textron Lycoming O-360-A4M	Textron Lycoming O-360-C1C6	Textron Lycoming IO-540-K1G5	Textron Lycoming TIO-540-AH1H	2 × Teledyne Continental TSIO-360-RB and L/TSIO-360-RB	2 × Textron Lycoming O-360-A1H6/ LO-360-A1H6	Textron Lycoming TIO-540-AE2A
Engine rating	160 hp (119.3 kW)	180 hp (134 kW)	200 hp (149 kW)	300 hp (224 kW)	300 hp (224 kW)	Each 220 hp (164 kW)	Each 180 hp (134 kW)	350 hp (261 kW)
Propeller	6 ft 2 ins (1.88 m) Sensenich 2-blade, fixed-pitch	6 ft 4 ins (1.93 m) Sensenich 2-blade, fixed-pitch	McCauley 2-blade, constant-speed	Hartzell 3-blade, constant-speed	Hartzell 3-blade, constant-speed	6 ft 4 ins (1.93 m) Hartzell 2-blade, constant-speed	6 ft 2 ins (1.88 m) Hartzell 2-blade, constant-speed	6 ft 8 ins (2.03 m) Hartzell 2-blade, constant-speed
Usable fuel	182 litres	182 litres	272.5 litres	386 litres	386 litres	462 litres	409 litres	454 litres
Wing span	35 ft (10.67 m)	35 ft 6 ins (10.8 m)	35 ft 5 ins (10.8 m)	36 ft 2 ins (11.02 m)	36 ft 2 ins (11.02 m)	38 ft 11 ins (11.86 m)	38 ft 7 ins (11.76 m)	43 ft (13.11 m)
Length	23 ft 9.5 ins (7.25 m)	24 ft (7.32 m)	24 ft 8 ins (7.52 m)	27 ft 11 ins (8.5 m)	27 ft 11 ins (8.5 m)	28 ft 7 ins (8.71 m)	27 ft 7 ins (8.41 m)	28 ft 11 ins (8.81 m)
Height	7 ft 4 ins (2.23 m)	7 ft 4 ins (2.23 m)	7 ft 11 ins (2.41 m)	8 ft 6 ins (2.59 m)	8 ft 6 ins (2.59 m)	9 ft 11 ins (3.02 m)	8 ft 6 ins (2.59 m)	11 ft 4 ins (3.45 m)
Wing area sq ft (m^2)	170 (15.79)	170 (15.79)	170 (15.79)	178.3 (16.56)	178.3 (16.56)	208.7 (19.39)	183.8 (17.08)	175 (16.26)
Cabin length	8 ft 2 ins (2.49 m)	8 ft 2 ins (2.49 m)	8 ft 2 ins (2.49 m)	10 ft 4.25 ins (3.16 m)	10 ft 4.25 ins (3.16 m)	10 ft 4.25 ins (3.16 m)	8 ft 1 ins (2.46 m)	12 ft 4 ins (3.759 m)
Cabin width	3 ft 5.25 ins (1.05 m)	3 ft 5.75 ins (1.06 m)	3 ft 5.75 ins (1.06 m)	4 ft 0.75 ins (1.24 m)	4 ft 0.75 ins (1.24 m)	4 ft 0.75 ins (1.24 m)	3 ft 5.5 ins (1.054 m)	4 ft 1.5 ins (1.26 m)
Cabin height	3 ft 8.25 ins (1.12 m)	3 ft 9 ins (1.14 m)	3 ft 8.75 ins (1.137 m)	3 ft 6 ins (1.07 m)	3 ft 6 ins (1.07 m)	3 ft 6 ins (1.07 m)	4 ft 1 ins (1.24 m)	3 ft 11 ins (1.19 m)
Baggage lb (kg)	200 (91)	200 (91)	200 (91)	200 (91)	200 (91)	200 (91)	200 (91)	200 (91)
Cabin pressurization differential	N/A	N/A	N/A	N/A	N/A	N/A	N/A	5.5 psi
Weight empty lb (kg)	1,509 (684)	1,658 (752)	1,766 (801)	2,407 (1,092)	2,464 (1,118)	3,377 (1,532)	2,586 (1,173)	3,080 (1,397)
Maximum take-off weight lb (kg)	2,440 (1,107)	2,550 (1,156)	2,750 (1,247)	3,600 (1,633)	3,600 (1,633)	4,750 (2,154)	3,800 (1,723)	4,300 (1,950)
Average useful load lb (kg)	938 (425)	900 (408)	992 (450)	1,208 (548)	1,151 (522)	1,373 (623)	1,230 (558)	1,238 (562)
Maximum speed kts (mph) km/h	117 (135) 217	133 (153) 246	145 (167) 269	170 (196) 315	192 (221) 356	205 (236) 380	168 (193) 311	232 (267) 430
Normal cruise speed kts (mph) km/h	115 (132) 213	128 (147) 237	137 (158) 254	163 (188) 302	186 (214) 345 at 15,000 ft (4,570 m)	198 (228) 367 at 18,000 ft (5,485 m)	162 (187) 300 at 75% power	215 (248) 398 high speed cruise
Stall speed kts (mph) km/h	50 (58) 93 IAS *clean*, 44 (51) 82 IAS *with full 40° flaps*	50 (58) 93 IAS *clean*, 46 (53) 85 IAS *with full 40° flaps*	60 (69) 111 IAS *clean*, 55 (64) 102 IAS *with full 40° flaps*	65 (75) 120 IAS *clean*, 60 (69) 111 IAS *with full 40° flaps*	60 (69) 111 IAS *with full 40° flaps*	61 (71) 113 IAS *with full 40° flaps*	57 (66) 106 IAS *clean*, 55 (64) 102 IAS *with full 40° flaps*	58 (67) 108 IAS *with full flaps*
Maximum climb rate ft (m) per minute	644 (196)	667 (203)	831 (253)	1,116 (340)	—	1,400 (427)	1,340 (408)	1,218 (371)
Service ceiling ft (m)	11,000 (3,353)	13,236 (4,034)	16,200 (4,938)	15,588 (4,751)	20,000 (6,100)	25,000 (7,620) approved	15,000 (4,572)	25,000 (7,620) approved
Take-off distance, at MTOW ft (m)	1,620 (494) over a 50 ft (15 m) obstacle	1,600 (488) over a 50 ft (15 m) obstacle	1,600 (488) over a 50 ft (15 m) obstacle	1,800 (549) over a 50 ft (15 m) obstacle	1,800 (549) over a 50 ft (15 m) obstacle	1,825 (556) over a 50 ft (15 m) obstacle	2,200 (671) over a 50 ft (15 m) obstacle	2,380 (726) over a 50 ft (15 m) obstacle
Landing distance, at MLW ft (m)	1,160 (354) over a 50 ft (15 m) obstacle	1,400 (427) over a 50 ft (15 m) obstacle	1,520 (463) over a 50 ft (15 m) obstacle	1,520 (463) over a 50 ft (15 m) obstacle	1,520 (463) over a 50 ft (15 m) obstacle	2,700 (823) over a 50 ft (15 m) obstacle	1,490 (454) over a 50 ft (15 m) obstacle	1,950 (595) over a 50 ft (15 m) obstacle
Range naut miles (miles) km	417 (480) 772 at 75% power	499 (574) 924 at 55% power, 6,000 ft (1,830 m) and 45 minutes reserve	658 (757) 1,219 at 75% power, and 45 minutes reserve	740 (852) 1,371, 45 minutes reserve	822 (946) 1,523 at 15,000 ft (4,570 m), 45 minutes reserve	700 (806) 1,297 at 10,000 ft (3,050 m), 45 minutes reserve	610 (702) 1,130 at 75% power, 45 minutes reserve	1,055 (1,215) 1,955, with 45 minutes reserve

Raisbeck Engineering Inc — USA

Corporate address:
4411 South Ryan Way, Seattle, WA 98178.

Telephone: 800 537 7277 (within US, Canada and Mexico), or +1 206 723 2000 (international)
Facsimile: +1 206 723 2884

Founded:
1974.

Information:
Robert P. Steinbach (Vice President Sales/Service) and Thomas L. Halvorson (Vice President Marketing).

ACTIVITIES

■ Raisbeck offers a range of enhancements for Beech King Airs and Super King Airs, and by 1998 had installed well over 5,000 individual systems. These systems are known as Quiet Turbofan Propellers (for all King Airs except B100, 300 and 350), Ram Air Recovery Systems (200/B200), Enhanced Performance Leading Edges (200, B200 series), Composite Exhaust Stack Fairings (all King Airs except B100), Dual Aft Body Strakes (for all King Airs), Fully-Enclosed MLG Doors (200/B200, 100/A100/B100, F90 – when equipped with high flotation main undercarriage), Nacelle Wing Lockers (for all King Airs) and Gross Weight Increase (C90, C90-1, C90A, 100, A100 and E90). In addition, on 31 March 1995 Raisbeck made the first delivery of its Learjet Aft Fuselage Locker, an entirely external fairing to the existing fuselage that begins as a rearward extension of the horizontal fuselage keel beam and rolls into a 17 ins (43 cm) deep ventral fin, replacing the aircraft's current fin. Within the 18 ft (5.49 m) fairing is an 8 ft (2.44 m) drawer which deploys sideways to carry 300 lb (136 kg) of cargo (see 1996-97 edition of *WA&SD*, page 449 for photograph). Has also received FAA certification for a Boeing 727-200 Noise Abatement System kit, to lower noise levels below Stage 3.

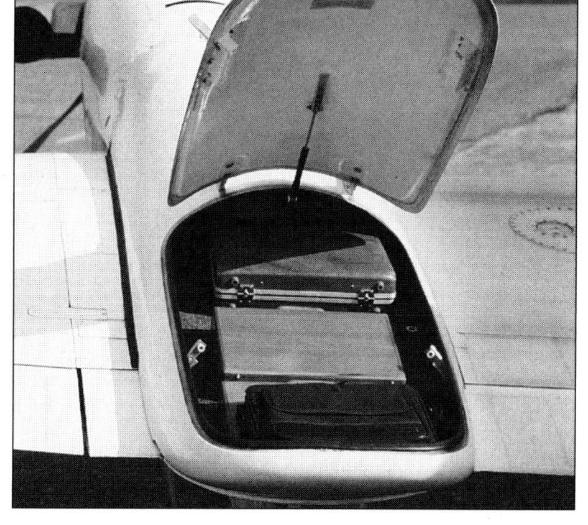

→ Raisbeck-produced Nacelle Wing locker, a modification available to all King Airs

Raytheon Aircraft Company

USA

Corporate address:
See Combat section for company details.

ACTIVITIES

■ Details of the Beech T-6A Texan II can be found in Combat section. Also see Foreword.
■ Details of the Beech 1900D Airliner can be found in the Airliners section.
■ Production of the Beech Starship 2000A 8/9-seat business jetprop ended in 1995 after 53 aircraft.
■ In September 1998 Raytheon awarded a contract to British Aerospace Airbus at Broughton for the manufacture of wings, fuselages and equipment for Hawker business jets. A contract for doors, long-range fuel tanks and flaps went to BAe Prestwick.
■ In September 1998, Raytheon Aerospace received ISO 9002 certification.
■ During the last full year at the time of writing (in 1998) Raytheon delivered 33 Hawker 800XPs, 43 Beechjets, 116 King Airs (30 Super King Air 350s, 45 King Air B200s and 41 King Air C90s), 2 Hawker 1000s, 42 1900D Airliners, 35 Baron 58s, 85 Bonanza A36s and 14 B36TCs, plus 15 military Beechjet 400Ts (Jayhawks) and 1 military King Air B200 (RC-12K), making 370 commercial and 16 military sales. Some 127 King Airs and 50 Hawker 800XPs among 1998 sales, with 200th civilian Beechjet 400A delivered at the October 1998 NBAA convention.

Beech Bonanza A36 and B36TC

First flight: Prototype Bonanza Model 35 first flew on 22 December 1945. Model 33 Debonair first flew in September 1959, from which the F33 later evolved. Model 36 appeared in 1968, followed by the A36 in 1983. B36TC appeared in 1982.
Role: Utility, commercial training and business.
Baggage capacity: 37 cu ft (1.05 m^3) cabin compartment for 400 lb (181 kg), and 10 cu ft (0.28 m^3) for 70 lb (32 kg).
Wing control surfaces: Ailerons (with trim tabs) and 3-position single-slotted flaps. Vortex generators.
Tail control surfaces: Elevators (with trim tabs) and rudder (with ground-adjustable tab).
Flight control system: Mechanical, except for electric flaps.
Construction materials: Metal.
Electrical system: 28 volt, with 60 amp alternator and 15.5 amp-hour battery.
Flight avionics/instrumentation: Standard avionics include AlliedSignal Bendix/King KX 155-39 760-channel com transceiver with audio amplifier, 200-channel nav receiver with KI 208 VOR/Loc converter indicator, microphone, cabin speaker, headset, and nav/com antennae. Many options. Range of engine and flight instruments.

Aircraft variants:
F33A is no longer offered. See 1996-97 edition of *WA&SD*, page 449, for details.
A36, as detailed above and in tables.
A36AT is the commercial training version for airline use, with a Hartzell propeller, engine flat rated to 290 hp (216 kW) and other changes.
B36TC is a turbocharged version of A36, with a 300 hp (224 kW) TSIO-520-UB engine and 6 ft 6 ins (1.98 m) propeller. Maximum speed 213 kts (245 mph) 394 km/h and MTOW 3,850 lb (1,746 kg).

Beech Baron 58

Certification: 1969.
Role: High-performance private and business aircraft.
Baggage capacity: 18 cu ft (0.51 m^3) in nose for 300 lb (136 kg), 12 cu ft (0.34 m^3) centre cabin for 200 lb (91 kg), 37 cu ft (1.05 m^3) rear compartment for 400 lb (181 kg), and 10 cu ft (0.28 m^3) extended rear compartment for 120 lb (54 kg).
Wing control surfaces: Ailerons (port trim tab) and single-slotted flaps.
Tail control surfaces: Elevators and rudder, all with trim tabs.
Flight control system: Manual, except for electric flaps.
Construction materials: Metal.
Electrical system: 28 volt, with 2 × 60 amp alternators and 2 × 12 volt, 25 amp-hour batteries.
Flight avionics/instrumentation: Standard avionics include AlliedSignal Bendix/King KX 155-39 760-channel com transceiver with audio amplifier, 200-channel nav receiver with KI 208 VOR/Loc converter indicator, KR 87 ADF with KI 227-00 indicator and combined loop/sense antenna, microphone, headset, cabin speaker, and nav/com antennae. Many options. Range of flight instruments.

↑ Beech Baron 58

Beech King Air C90B and C90SE

First flight: King Air C90 dates from 1970, with C90B from 1991.
Role: Pressurized business aircraft.
Baggage capacity: 53.5 cu ft (1.51 m^3) aft for 350 lb (158 kg), and 26.8 cu ft (0.76 m^3) with aft toilet.
Electrical system: 3-bus system with automatic load shedding, solid state generator controllers and a 34 amp-hour ni-cd battery. 2 Flite-Tronics 250VA inverters.
Wing control surfaces: Ailerons (port trim tab) and 3-position single-slotted flaps. Aileron cable tension regulator.
Tail control surfaces: Elevators and rudder, all with trim tabs.
Flight control system: Manual, except for electric flaps.
Construction materials: Metal.
Flight avionics/instrumentation: AlliedSignal Bendix/King avionics, including dual KY 196As with dual antennae, single or dual VOR/ILS nav (VHF), ADF, dual Mode-S transponders, DME, encoding altimeter, audio/marker beacon and cockpit voice recorder. Many options, including AlliedSignal package with KFC 250 flight control system.

Aircraft variants:
C90B accommodates a pilot plus 6 or 7 passengers. McCauley 4-blade propellers and Rockwell Collins Pro Line II avionics. Standard WXR-270 colour weather radar and APS-65H flight director/autopilot.
C90SE is the later lower-cost and reduced specification version; see above details and table. First delivery September 1994.

↑ Beech Bonanza B36TC

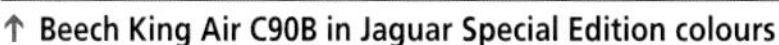

↑ Beech King Air C90B in Jaguar Special Edition colours

↑ Beech Beechjet 400A

Beech Super King Air B200 series

First flight: 1972 for the original Super King Air 200.
Certification: 1981 for B200.
Role: Pressurized business, cargo, and military special mission aircraft.
Sales: 1,500th commercial Super King Air B200 series aircraft was delivered in 1995.
Baggage capacity: 55.3 cu ft (1.57 m^3) aft for 550 lb (249 kg).
Wing control surfaces: Ailerons (port trim tab) and single-slotted flaps. Yaw damper system. Aileron cable tension regulator.
Tail control surfaces: Elevators and rudder, all with trim tabs.
Flight control system: Manual, except for electric flaps.
Construction materials: Metal.
Electrical system: 2 × 28 volt (250 amp) starter-generators and a 24 volt (34 amp-hour) ni-cd battery. AC supply via inverters.
Radar: Rockwell Collins WXR-270 colour weather radar.
Flight avionics/instrumentation: Standard Rockwell Collins Pro Line II suite with 4 ins (10 cm) EFIS-84 flight control system. Includes APS-65H autopilot. Optional Pro Line II with EFIS-85B(14). Other options.

Aircraft variants:
B200 is the standard version, as detailed.
B200C is generally similar but features a large cargo door.
B200CT is a merger of C and T features.
B200SE was certified in mid-1995 as a lower cost version, having 3-blade propellers and WXR-270 radar as an option.
B200T offers removable wingtip tanks for an additional 401 litres of fuel. A *maritime patrol* version with specialized equipment serves with the armed forces or government agencies of Algeria, France, Germany, Japan, Malaysia, Peru, Puerto Rico, and Uruguay.
C-12 is the US armed forces designation for their support transport models. More specialized versions include the US Army's RC-12 Guardrail series of specially-equipped comint aircraft with numerous aerials and antennae. See Reconnaissance section.

Beech Super King Air 350

First flight: 1988.
Role: Pressurized business, cargo, and military special mission aircraft. A noise management system that significantly lowers cabin sound levels was introduced as standard equipment on 1998 models.
Baggage capacity: 55.3 cu ft (1.57 m^3) aft for 550 lb (249 kg).
Wing control surfaces: Ailerons (port trim tab) and single-slotted flaps. Yaw damper system. Aileron cable tension regulator.
Tail control surfaces: Elevators and rudder, all with trim tabs.
Flight control system: Manual, except for electric flaps. Dual pushrod trim tab actuators.
Construction materials: Metal.
Electrical system: 2 × 28 volt (300 amp) starter-generators and a 24 volt (34 amp-hour) ni-cd battery. AC supply via inverters.
Radar: WXR-840 colour weather radar.
Flight avionics/instrumentation: Standard Rockwell Collins Pro Line II suite and including APS-65J autopilot with FIS-85 5 ins (12.7 cm) flight director system. Other options.

Aircraft variants:
350, as detailed above and in table.
350C features a large cargo door with integral airstair door, and dry chemical toilet facing forward.
RC-350 Guardian is a multi-sensor version offering elint/comint, surveillance radar, synthetic aperture radar, FLIR, long-range electro-optical or remote spectroscopy sensors.

Beech Beechjet 400A

First flight: 1986, derived from the Mitsubishi Diamond II. 400A version first flew 22 September 1989.
Role: Pressurized business jet and trainer.
Baggage capacity: Total of 58.4 cu ft (1.65 m^3) in forward, aft and external aft positions, for 950 lb (431 kg).
Wing control surfaces: Ailerons, single- and double-slotted Fowler flaps, and spoilers (for aileron assist, lift-dumping and speed brakes). Dual flap asymmetrical detection system.
Tail control surfaces: Variable-incidence tailplane. Elevators and rudder (with tab).
Flight control system: Mechanical primary surfaces, hydraulic/mechanical spoilers, and electric roll trim, pitch trim and yaw trim. Hydraulic flaps.
Construction materials: Aluminium alloy and steel used for skin and structure.

↑ Beech Super King Air 350

↑ Hawker 800XP, the first in Canadian registration (Canadian certification having been received December 1997)

Electrical system: 28 volt DC supply via 2 × 400 amp starter-generators. 24 volt, 36 amp-hour ni-cd battery. 2 AC inverters (50 VA, 115 and 26 volt).
Radar: Rockwell Collins WXR-840.
Flight avionics/instrumentation: Rockwell Collins Pro Line 4 flight control system with FIS-870 display and FCS-850 flight control system and including APS-850A autopilot. FMS-850 flight management system with data base unit, and VLF/Omega/RNAV. Dual VHF com, single or dual VOR/ILS, ADF, dual marker beacons, dual glideslope, dual DMEs, dual transponders, radio altimeter, etc.

Aircraft variants:
400A, as detailed.
400T is a military training version for the JASDF, with long-range navigation systems and other changes. First deliveries January 1994.
T-1A Jayhawk is the USAF version for training aerial tanker crews. 180 ordered, the last delivered on 23 July 1997, by which time more than 182,000 flight hours had been flown by T-1As and over 680 students had graduated from the programme. GPS being added. See 1996-97 edition of *WA&SD*, page 450, for photograph.

Hawker 800XP

First flight: 1 September 1994.
Certification: 26 July 1995 for CAA, 28 July 1995 for FAA.
Role: Mid-size business jet.
Sales: Further 20 (with 16 additional options) ordered by Executive Jets in September 1998. (The 1,000th Hawker business jet was an 800XP, delivered to the Gainey Corporation in 1998.)
Baggage capacity: 47-65 cu ft (1.33-1.84 m^3), depending on selected cabin interior.
Wing control surfaces: Ailerons (with tabs) and 4-position double-slotted flaps. Upper/lower airbrakes.
Tail control surfaces: Elevators and rudder, all with tabs.
Flight control system: Manual, except for hydraulic flaps and airbrakes.
Construction materials: Metal.
Electrical system: DC supply via 2 × 28 volt starter-generators. 2 × 24 volt, 23 amp-hour ni-cd batteries (lead acid optional). 2 × AC inverters and 1 standby inverter. 2 alternators provide AC power for windshield anti-ice.
Radar: Honeywell Primus 870 weather radar.

Pax=Passengers	**Bonanza A36**	**Baron 58**	**King Air C90B**	**King Air B200**	**King Air 350**	**Beechjet 400A**	**Hawker 800XP**	**Premier I (preliminary)**	**Hawker Horizon (preliminary)**
Crew + Pax	1 + 5	1 + 5	1 + 5/6	1 + 7/8	1 + 9	2 + 7/9	2 + 8/12	1/2 + 6	2 + 8/12
Engine/s	Teledyne Continental IO-550-B	2 × Teledyne Continental IO-550-C	2 × Pratt & Whitney Canada PT6A-21 turboprops	2 × Pratt & Whitney Canada PT6A-42 turboprops	2 × Pratt & Whitney Canada PT6A-60A turboprops	2 × Pratt & Whitney Canada JT15D-5 turbofans	2 × AlliedSignal TFE731-5BR turbofans	2 × Willams-Rolls FJ44-2A turbofans	2 × Pratt & Whitney Canada PW308A
Engine rating	300 hp (224 kW)	Each 300 hp (224 kW)	Each 550 shp (410 kW)	Each 850 shp (633.8 kW)	Each 1,050 shp (783 kW)	Each 2,900 lbf (12.9 kN)	Each 4,660 lbf (20.73 kN)	2,300 lbf (10.23 kN)	6,500 lbf (28.91 kN)
Propeller/s	6 ft 8 ins (2.03 m) McCauley 3-blade constant-speed	6 ft 5 ins (1.96 m) 3-blade constant-speed	7 ft 6 ins (2.29 m) McCauley 4-blade, auto feathering, with synchrophaser	7 ft 9 ins (2.36 m) Hartzell 4-blade, auto feathering with synchrophaser	8 ft 9 ins (2.69 m) Hartzell 4-blade, auto feathering with synchrophaser	N/A	N/A	N/A	N/A
Usable fuel	280 litres	628 litres standard, 734 litres optional	1,454 litres	2,059 litres	2,040 litres	2,774 litres	5,650 litres	—	7,910 litres
Wing span	33 ft 6 ins (10.21 m)	37 ft 10 ins (11.53 m)	50 ft 3 ins (15.32 m)	54 ft 6 ins (16.61 m)	57 ft 11 ins (17.65 m)	43 ft 6 ins (13.26 m)	51 ft 4 ins (15.65 m)	44 ft 6 ins (13.56 m)	61 ft 9 ins (18.82 m)
Length	27 ft 6 ins (8.38 m)	29 ft 10 ins (9.09 m)	35 ft 6 ins (10.82 m)	43 ft 10 ins (13.36 m)	46 ft 8 ins (14.22 m)	48 ft 5 ins (14.76 m)	51 ft 2 ins (15.6 m)	46 ft (14.02 m)	69 ft 2 ins (21.08 m)
Height	8 ft 7 ins (2.62 m)	9 ft 9 ins (2.97 m)	14 ft 3 ins (4.34 m)	14 ft 10 ins (4.52 m)	14 ft 4 ins (4.37 m)	13 ft 11 ins (4.24 m)	18 ft 1 ins (5.51 m)	15 ft 4 ins (4.67 m)	19 ft 8 ins (5.99 m)
Wing area sq ft (m^2)	181 (16.82)	199.2 (18.51)	293.94 (27.31)	303 (28.15)	310 (28.8)	241.4 (22.43)	374 (34.75)	212 (19.7)	531 (49.33)
Cabin length	12 ft 7 ins (3.84 m)	12 ft 7 ins (3.84 m) including rear baggage compartment	12 ft 7 ins (3.84 m) excluding cockpit	16 ft 8 ins (5.08 m) excluding cockpit	19 ft 6 ins (5.94 m) excluding cockpit	15 ft 6 ins (4.72 m) excluding cockpit	21 ft 4 ins (6.5 m)	13 ft 6 ins (4.11 m)	25 ft (7.62 m)
Cabin width	3 ft 6 ins (1.07 m)	3 ft 6 ins (1.07 m)	4 ft 6 ins (1.37 m)	4 ft 6 ins (1.37 m)	4 ft 6 ins (1.37 m)	4 ft 11 ins (1.5 m)	6 ft (1.83 m) maximum	—	—
Cabin height	4 ft 2 ins (1.27 m)	4 ft 2 ins (1.27 m)	4 ft 9 ins (1.45 m)	4 ft 9 ins (1.45 m)	4 ft 9 ins (1.45 m)	4 ft 9 ins (1.45 m)	5 ft 9 ins (1.75 m)	5 ft 5 ins (1.65 m)	6 ft (1.83 m)
Cabin pressurization differential	N/A	N/A	5 psi	6.5 psi	6.5 psi	9 psi	8.55 psi	8.4 psi	—
Weight empty lb (kg)	2,320 (1,052) basic operating	3,600 (1,633) basic operating	6,702 (3,040) basic operating	8,192 (3,716) basic operating	9,110 (4,132) basic operating	10,050 (4,558)	16,145 (7,323) basic operating	—	20,930 (9,494)
Maximum take-off weight lb (kg)	3,650 (1,655)	5,500 (2,494)	10,100 (4,581)	12,500 (5,670)	15,000 (6,804)	16,100 (7,303)	28,000 (12,700)	12,500 (5,670)	36,000 (16,329)
Maximum landing weight lb (kg)	3,650 (1,655)	5,400 (2,449)	9,600 (4,354)	12,500 (5,670)	15,000 (6,804)	15,700 (7,121)	23,350 (10,591)	—	33,500 (15,195)
Useful load lb (kg)	1,330 (603)	1,924 (873)	3,458 (1,569)	4,398 (1,995)	5,990 (2,717)	5,850 (2,653) at ramp weight	11,975 (5,432)	—	15,270 (6,926)
Maximum speed kts (mph) km/h	184 (212) 340	208 (239) 385	249 (286) 461	292 (336) 541	315 (363) 583	468 (539) 866. Mach 0.78 M_{MO}	465 (535) 862	461 (530) 854	484 (557) 897
Maximum cruise speed kts (mph) km/h	176 (202) 326 at 6,000 ft and 3,400 lb	203 (234) 376 at 5,000 ft and 5,200 lb	247 (284) 457 at 16,000 ft	289 (333) 535	311 (358) 576 at 18,000 ft	443 (510) 820 at 23,000 ft	465 (535) 862	461 (530) 854	484 (557) 897
Stall speed kts (mph) km/h	68 (78) 126 IAS *clean*, 59 (68) 110 IAS *with 30° flaps*	84 (97) 156 IAS *clean*, 75 (86) 139 IAS *with flaps*	88 (101) 163 *clean*, 78 (90) 145 *with flaps*	99 (114) 183 IAS *clean*, 75 (86) 139 IAS *with flaps*	96 (111) 178 *clean*, 81 (94) 150 *with flaps*	110 (127) 204 *clean*, 92 (106) 171 *with full flaps*	—	—	—
Maximum climb rate ft (m) per minute	1,208 (368) at MTOW	1,735 (529) at MTOW	2,003 (611) at MTOW	2,448 (746) at MTOW	2,731 (832) at MTOW	3,770 (1,150) at MTOW	—	—	—
Ceiling ft (m)	18,500 (5,640)	20,688 (6,305) at MTOW	28,900 (8,810)	35,000 (10,668)	above 35,000 (10,668)	45,000 (13,715)	41,000 (12,500)	41,000 (12,497)	45,000 (13,715)
Take-off distance ft (m)	971 (296) with 12° flaps, at MTOW (ground roll)	1,400 (427) at MTOW (ground roll)	2,033 (620) at MTOW (ground roll)	1,856 (566) at MTOW (ground roll)	3,300 (1,006) required field length at MTOW	4,290 (1,308) field length at MTOW	5,030 (1,533) at MTOW, sea level	3,000 (915) at MTOW, sea level	5,250 (1,600) at MTOW, sea level
Landing distance ft (m)	920 (281) at MLW (ground roll)	1,425 (435) at MLW (ground roll)	1,401 (427) at MLW (ground roll)	1,760 (537) at MLW (ground roll)	1,448 (442) at MLW (ground roll)	3,514 (1,072) at MLW	2,650 (808) at MLW	—	2,340 (713)
Range naut miles (miles) km	901 (1,037) 1,669 at 12,000 ft	1,313 (1,511) 2,432 at 12,000 ft	1,330 (1,530) 2,463 at 29,000 ft	1,859 (2,139) 3,443 at 31,000 ft	1,813 (2,086) 3,358 at 35,000 ft	1,693 (1,949) 3,135 at 45,000 ft	2,503 (2,882) 4,639 with 6 pax, NBAA IFR	1,500 (1,727) 2,778, with 4 pax and NBAA IFR (with 100 naut mile alternate)	3,400 (3,915) 6,300 with 6 pax, NBAA IFR

↑ Hawker Horizon, Raytheon's latest business jet for certification in the Year 2001

↑ Raytheon Premier I at roll-out on 19 August 1998

Flight avionics/instrumentation: Honeywell SPZ-8000 suite is standard, including dual RNZ-850 integrated navigation unit. AA-300 radio altimeter, dual AHZ-600 AHRS, dual ADZ-810 air data computer, dual EDZ-818 flight director with MDZ-818 multifunction display, digital DFZ-800 AFCS, FMS with dual FMZ-2000 and Honeywell GPS. Options include TCAS and GPWS. Optional Rockwell Collins suite available as an option.

Aircraft variants:
800 production has ended. See 1996-97 edition of *WA&SD*, pages 450-451, for details and photograph, plus C-29A USAF model.
800XP extended performance model appeared in 1995, featuring TFE731-5BR engines, increased useful load and improved environmental system. Current production version.
U-125 is the JASDF designation for its flight inspection Hawker 800s (3).
U-125A is the JASDF designation for its search and rescue variant. First Wichita assembled aircraft flew to Japan in November 1997 for installation of mission equipment and pre-delivery activities, allowing delivery to the JASDF in 1998. 6 earlier U-125As had been assembled in the UK. 14 ordered, of 27 eventually required for delivery through to 2005 (if all ordered).

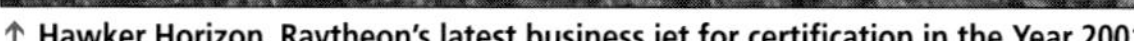

Hawker 1000

Comments: Production of this twin-turbofan business jet has ended, after 52 aircraft had been delivered. Details can be found in the 1996-97 edition of *WA&SD*, page 451.

Hawker Horizon

First flight: Expected fourth quarter of 1999.
Certification: First quarter of 2001 (FAA).
First delivery: 2001.
Role: High-performance 'super mid-size' business jet.
Baggage capacity: 105 cu ft (2.97 m^3).
Wing control surfaces: Ailerons (with tabs) and double-slotted flaps. Wing mounted spoiler panels serve as speed brakes and augment roll control.
Tail control surfaces: Trimmable horizontal stabilizer for pitch trim, with elevators for main pitch control, and large powered rudder.
Flight control system: Manual, except for electrically actuated flaps, hydraulic rudder, roll spoilers and speed brakes.
Construction materials: Carbonfibre/epoxy honeycomb composite fuselage, metal wings and tail surfaces. Manufacture of the first production wing was underway at Fuji Heavy Industries in May 1998, for delivery to Wichita in early 1999.
Electrical system: AC electrical system with power rectified to DC where required. In-flight capable APU provides additional capability as a backup to the normal system.
Flight avionics/instrumentation: The integrated flight control system and avionics are provided by Honeywell. The Honeywell Primus Epic features a 5-display format utilizing 10 × 8 ins (25.4 × 20.32 cm) flat-panel LCD displays. In addition to the primary flight displays and the multifunction displays, the Epic system features EICAS (Engine Instrumentation and Crew Advisory System) with Synoptic.

Raytheon Premier I

First flight: Rolled-out on 19 August 1998 and flown October.
Certification: Summer 1999 (FAA), to FAR Pt 23.
Role: High-performance light entry level business jet.
Sales: Over 140 ordered by October 1998, including 22 from Raytheon Air Travel. Price US$4.1 million. Deliveries from 1999.
Crew/passengers: 1 or 2 crew plus 6 passengers.
Baggage capacity: 60 cu ft (1.7 m^3).
Wing control surfaces: Ailerons with roll spoiler augmentation, flaps and speed brakes.
Tail control surfaces: Movable horizontal stabilizer for pitch trim, with elevators for main pitch control and rudder with trim tab.
Flight control system: Manual, except for hydraulic flaps, roll spoilers and speed brakes.
Construction materials: Carbonfibre/epoxy honeycomb composite fuselage, metal wings and tail surfaces.
Electrical system: DC supply via 2 × 300 amp starter-generators. Main battery supplies 24 volts DC to the aircraft and the starter-generators supply a regulated 28 volts DC.
Flight avionics/instrumentation: Rockwell Collins Pro Line 21 EFIS featuring active matrix colour LCD 10 × 8 ins (25.4 × 20.3 cm) primary flight display and multifunction display units. Features also include new AFC-3000 attitude heading reference system (AHRS) and an advanced flight control system with new fail-passive autopilot. Rockwell Collins Pro Line radio sensor package and solid state weather radar are also standard.

Sherpa Aircraft Manufacturing Company — USA

Corporate address:
SW Shaw Street, Aloha, OR 97007.

Telephone: +1 503 649 8558

Information:
Glen Gordon.

↑ Sherpa Aircraft Sherpa *(courtesy Sherpa)*

ACTIVITIES

■ This company has developed the Sherpa, which was intended for FAA certification.

Sherpa Aircraft Sherpa

First flight: 1994.
Role: 5-seat utility aircraft.
Construction materials: Tubular steel, fabric covered.
Engine: Textron Lycoming IO-720-A1B piston engine, with Hartzell 3-blade constant-speed propeller.
Engine rating: 400 hp (298 kW).
Fuel system: 458 litres.
Flight avionics/instrumentation: Options to include 2-axis autopilot.

Details for Sherpa

PRINCIPAL DIMENSION:
Wing span: 42 ft 7 ins (12.98 m)

WINGS:
Area: 258 sq ft (23.97 m^2), or 300 sq ft (27.87 m^2) with flaps extended

UNDERCARRIAGE:
Type: Fixed, with tailwheel. Optional large Tundra tyres, floats or skis

WEIGHTS:
Empty: 2,585 lb (1,172 kg)
Maximum take-off: 4,750 lb (2,154 kg)
Useful load: 2,165 lb (982 kg)

PERFORMANCE:
Cruise speed: 139 kts (160 mph) 296 km/h
Slow speed: about 39 kts (45 mph) 73 km/h
Take-off distance: 135 ft (41 m) at 3,000 lb AUW
Landing distance: 145 ft (44 m) at 3,000 lb AUW

Sierra Industries, Inc — USA

Corporate address:
PO Box 5184, Uvalde, TX 78802-5184.

Telephone: +1 830 278 4381
Facsimile: +1 830 278 7649
Web Site: www.sierra-industries.com
E-mail: sierra@admin.hilconet.com

Information:
Mark Huffstuter (President).

ACTIVITIES

▪ Offers a series of Cessna Citation enhancement products, including as follows:
Eagle Modification for Citation 500 includes wing root cuff, wing to body fairings, spar mod, increased gross take-off weight to 12,500 lb (5,670 kg), reinforced MLG uplock, replace MLG wheel halves, recalibrated instrumentation, additional electric anti-ice panels with high-tech "J" boxes, modified fuel vent system, flap core seals, Longwing modification, wingtip recognition lights, re-rigged ailerons, de-ice boots, and paint on affected areas.
Eagle Modification for Citation 501SP and Citation 500 with existing Longwing is similar to that above but minus replacement MLG wheel halves, Longwing modification and wingtip recognition lights.
Eagle 400SP Modification is for Citation 500/501SPs and includes the Eagle Modification, Longwing (if Model 500), installation of JT15D-4 engines, reinstallation of existing thrust reversers, increased gross take-off weight to 12,500 lb (5,670 kg), 43,000 ft (13,100 m) service ceiling, spar modification (if due) and exterior paint. Does not include purchase of -4 engines.
Eagle 400 Modification on aircraft with Eagle Modification accomplished includes installation of JT15D-4 engines, reinstallation of existing thrust reversers, 43,000 ft (13,100 m) service ceiling, and full exterior paint. Does not include purchase of -4 engines.
Silver Edition Eagle Modification for Models 500/501SPs includes full Eagle modification, Longwing modification (of Model 500), single-pilot authorization, new wing leading-edge de-ice boots, 12,500 lb (5,670 kg) MTOW authority, exterior paint, wingtip recognition lights, spar modification if due, new heated leading edge panels, and flap seals.
Longwing modification for Model 500 includes 38 ins (97 cm) wingspan increase, Sierra single-pilot authorization, new wing leading-edge de-ice boots, Sierra JT15D-1A engine update, increased gross take-off weight to 12,500 lb (5,670 kg), paint on affected areas and fuel to 3,807 lb (1,727 kg).
Single pilot authorization for the Model 500 for aircraft already equipped with the Eagle or Longwing modifications.
Wingtip mounted recognition lights for Models 500/501SP.
Spar modification for Models 500/501SP to eliminate reoccurring inspections.
JT15D-1A or 1B engine updates to Models 500/501SP.
Citation inlet and exhaust covers for Models 500/501SP.
Baggage compartment modifications.
Citation cockpit enhancements including 4-point crew restraint system, avionics master switch, alternate gear horn mute switch and new cockpit panel segments.
▪ Also offers R/STOL high-lift systems for piston-engined aircraft, and more.

Sino Swearingen Company (SSAC) — USA

Corporate address:
1770 Sky Place Boulevard, San Antonio, TX 78216.

Telephone: +1 210 258 8699
Facsimile: +1 210 258 3973
Web site: http://www.sj30jet.com
E-mail: ssacsj30@aol.com

Founded:
1995.

Employees:
Over 200.

Information:
Mike Potts (Director, Corporate Communications – *telephone* +1 210 258 3992).

ACTIVITIES

▪ Partnership formed between Sino-Aerospace International Incorporated and Swearingen Aircraft Incorporated, to pursue certification, manufacture and marketing of the SJ30-2.
▪ Final assembly, flight test and delivery of SJ30-2s and subsequent Sino-Swearingen products from factory complex in Martinsburg, West Virginia.

Sino Swearingen SJ30-2

First flight: 13 February 1991 in original Swearingen SJ30 form. 8 November 1996 in modified SJ30-2 prototype form. 4 September 1997 with FJ44-2A engines installed, the first aircraft to fly with this new engine.
Certification: Expected late 1999 to FAR Pt 23 commuter category, for day, night, VFR, IFR and flight into known icing conditions, and single pilot operation.
Role: 6 or 7-seat (including pilot/s) light entry level executive business jet.
Sales: Deliveries expected from late 1999. US$3.5 million fully equipped (1995 dollars) quoted in April 1998. In addition to the first prototype, the first of 3 certification prototypes was built in 1998, plus 1 static test and 1 fatigue test airframe. More than 100 ordered by April 1998.
Pressurization system: 12 psi cabin differential, for sea level cabin comfort up to 41,000 ft (12,500 m).
Wing control surfaces: Ailerons (trim tabs), Fowler slotted flaps and leading-edge slats. Airbrakes/lift dumpers.
Tail control surfaces: Variable-incidence tailplane. Elevators and rudder (trim tab). 2 outward-canted ventral fins for yaw damping.
Flight control system: Manual, except for electric tailplane, flaps and trim tabs, hydraulic slats and electro-hydraulic airbrakes/lift dumpers.
Construction materials: Metal. Composites and bonding are not part of any load path.
Engines: 2 Williams-Rolls FJ44-2A turbofans.
Engine rating: Each 2,300 lbf (10.23 kN).
Fuel system: 2,710 litres (4,800 lb, 2,177 kg).
Electrical system: DC supply via 2 × 28 volt 300 amp engine-driven starter-generators. Inverters for AC supply.
Radar: Honeywell Primus WX650 colour weather radar.
Flight avionics/instrumentation: Honeywell Primus 1000 integrated avionics system, with 2 primary flight displays (EFIS) (8 × 7 ins, 20.3 × 17.8 cm), integrated avionics computer, dual AZ-850 air data computer, Primus II integrated com, and 3-axis autopilot/flight director.

↑ Sino Swearingen SJ30-2

Details for SJ30-2 (as of April 1998)

PRINCIPAL DIMENSIONS:
Wing span: 42 ft 4 ins (12.9 m)
Maximum length: 46 ft 11.5 ins (14.32 m)
Maximum height: 14 ft 3 ins (4.34 m)

CABIN:
Length: 12 ft 6 ins (3.81 m)
Width: 4 ft 8 ins (1.43 m)
Height: 4 ft 3.5 ins (1.31 m)
Volume: 330.5 cu ft (9.36 m^3)
Door width: 2 ft 8 ins (0.81 m)

WINGS:
Area: 190.7 sq ft (17.72 m^2)
Aspect ratio: 9.4
Sweepback: 32° 36'
Dihedral: 2° 18'

UNDERCARRIAGE:
Type: Retractable, with steerable (±60°) nosewheel. Twin wheels on each unit
Wheel base: 18 ft 8.5 ins (5.7 m)
Wheel track: 6 ft 10 ins (2.08 m)

WEIGHTS:
Empty, equipped: 7,700 lb (3,493 kg)
Empty, operating: 7,900 lb (3,583 kg)
Maximum ramp: 13,300 lb (6,032 kg)
Maximum take-off: 13,200 lb (5,987 kg)
Maximum landing: 12,540 lb (5,688 kg)
Maximum baggage: 500 lb (227 kg)

PERFORMANCE:
High cruise speed: Above Mach 0.8
Long-range cruise speed: Mach 0.78 or 447 kts (515 mph) 828 km/h
Stall speed: 91 kts (105 mph) 169 km/h CAS
FAA take-off balanced field length: 3,850 ft (1,173 m) or less ±3%
FAA landing distance: 3,420 ft (1,042 m) or less ±3%
Cruise altitude: 49,000 ft (14,935 m)
Climb rate: 5,000 ft (1,525 m) per minute
Climb rate OEI: 1,500 ft (457 m) per minute
VFR range: over 2,550 naut miles (2,936 miles) 4,725 km ±5%, 45 minutes fuel reserve
NBAA IFR range: over 2,500 naut miles (2,879 miles), 4,633 km ±5%, with pilot plus 3 passengers

DESIGN DATA:
Maximum operating Mach number (M_{MO}): Mach 0.83 above 29,000 ft (8,840 m)
Maximum operating speed (V_{MO}): 320 kts (368 mph) 593 km/h CAS, up to 29,000 ft (8,840 m)
Undercarriage operation: 225 kts (259 mph) 417 km/h CAS
Maximum flaps extended speed (V_{FE}): 200 kts (230 mph) 370 km/h CAS, *approach flaps*; or 170 kts (196 mph) 315 km/h CAS, *landing flaps*

Star*Kraft Inc — USA

Corporate address:
2401 Cooper Street, Fort Scott, KS 66701.

Telephone: +1 316 223 5500
Facsimile: +1 316 224 2265

Information:
Roger Kraft (President).

ACTIVITIES

▪ Concept design of the Star*Kraft 700 began in 1992, with prototype assembly starting in 1993. Introduced at the NBAA show in Las Vegas, Nevada in September 1995. In 1998, flight testing had been accelerated. Currently looking for financial partner/s to fund certification and production processes.

Star*Kraft 700, Star*Kraft 1100 and Star*Kraft 500

Details: For Star*Kraft 700, except under aircraft variants.
First flight: December 1994.
Role: 8/9-seat pressurized business aircraft, with 'centreline thrust' twin-engine arrangement. Emergency parachute safety system.
Sales: Projected price in 1998 US$1.6 million.
Crew/passengers: 8/9 seats, comprising 2 in cockpit area, 2 individual seats behind, 3-person bench seat, aft inward-facing stowable seat, and inward-facing seat/toilet.
Baggage capacity: Aft baggage area.
Pressurization system: 8,000 ft (2,440 m) pressure maintained to 30,000 ft (9,145 m) altitude.
Wing control surfaces: Ailerons and Fowler flaps.
Tail control surfaces: Horn-balanced elevators with electrically-actuated trim tabs, dorsal fin with horn-balanced rudder and fixed ventral fin.
Construction materials: All composite/E-glass and carbonfibre. Lightning strike safety system. 'Weeping wing' de-ice system on all critical surfaces.
Engines: 2 × 350 hp (261 kW) Teledyne Continental TSIOL-550-A piston engines, with tractor and pusher 6 ft 8 ins (2.03 m) 3-blade propellers. Alternative 700 hp (522 kW) Orenda 700 engines with 7 ft 6 ins (2.29 m) 3-blade propellers, although 600 hp (447.4 kW) Orenda 600s installed in 1998 for continued test flying. Engines mounted in tandem centreline thrust configuration, with rear engine driving a pusher propeller via a shaft.
Fuel system: Wing tanks for 814 litres with TCM engines, 1,230 litres with Orenda 700s.
Electrical system: 2 × 100 amp alternators. 24 volt battery.

Aircraft variants:
Star*Kraft 700 is the 8-seat version, with either Teledyne Continental or Orenda engines.
Star*Kraft 700-SE is a projected single-engined variant with fixed undercarriage.
Star*Kraft 1100 is a projected stretched 12-seat/cargo version.
Star*Kraft 500 is a projected single-engined aircraft for 5 passengers.

↑ Star*Kraft 700 centreline thrust twin-engined business aircraft *(courtesy Star*Kraft)*

Details for Star*Kraft 700 with Teledyne Continental engines, *with Orenda 700 engines in italics*

PRINCIPAL DIMENSIONS:
Wing span: 42 ft 3.5 ins (12.9 m), *the same*
Maximum length: 36 ft (10.97 m), *the same*
Maximum height: 14 ft 1 ins (4.29 m), *the same*

CABIN:
Length: 14 ft 8 ins (4.47 m), *the same*
Width: 5 ft 3.5 ins (1.61 m), *the same*
Height: 4 ft 9.1 ins (1.45 m), *the same*

WINGS:
Aerofoil section: Laminar
Area: 197 sq ft (18.3 m^2), *the same*
Aspect ratio: 9.08, *the same*

UNDERCARRIAGE:
Type: Retractable, with nosewheel
Wheel base: 12 ft 3 ins (3.73 m), *the same*

WEIGHTS:
Empty: 4,900 lb (2,223 kg), *5,600 lb (2,540 kg)*
Maximum take-off: 7,300 lb (3,311 kg), *9,000 lb (4,082 kg)*
Useful load: 2,400 lb (1,088 kg), *3,400 lb (1,542 kg)*
Payload with full fuel: 1,110 lb (503.5 kg), *1,450 lb (658 kg)*

PERFORMANCE:
Cruise speed: 275 kts (317 mph) 510 km/h, *350 kts (403 mph) 649 km/h*, both at 75% power and 30,000 ft (9,145 m)*
Stall speed: 74 kts (85.5 mph) 137 km/h, *77 kts (89 mph) 143 km/h*, flaps and undercarriage down*
Maximum climb rate: 1,200 ft (366 m) per minute, *3,020 ft (920 m) per minute**
Climb rate, OEI: 400 ft (122 m) per minute, *950 ft (290 m) per minute**
Normal cruise altitude: 30,000 ft (9,145 m), *the same*
Range: *1,320 naut miles (1,520 miles) 2,446 km with full load, or 1,610 naut miles (1,854 miles) 2,983 km with full fuel*, both with 45 minutes reserve
Duration: 5.2 hours, *4.6 hours*, both at 55% power*
*Preliminary, subject to verification

Thurston Aeromarine Corporation — USA

Comments: No recent news of the Teal III and Seafire has been received. See 1996-97 edition of *WA&SD*, page 453, for brief details.

Tradewind Turbines Corporation — USA

Comments: Details and a photograph of the Prop-Jet Bonanza can be found in the 1996-97 edition of *WA&SD*, page 453.

Vazar Aerospace — USA

Comments: Details of the Dash 3 Turbine Otter, and a photograph, can be found in the 1996-97 edition of *WA&SD*, page 453.

VisionAire Corporation — USA

Corporate address:
Spirit of St Louis Airport, 595 Bell Avenue, Chesterfield, MO 63005.

Telephone: +1 314 530 1007
Facsimile: +1 314 530 0005
Web site: http://www.visionaire.com
E-mail: info@visionaire.com

Founded:
1988.

Information:
Douglas L. Herrman (Director, Marketing Communications & Research - *telephone* +1 314 530 6400 ext 3124, *E-mail* doug.herrman@visionaire.com).

ACTIVITIES

▪ Series production of the Vantage (said to be the world's first composite business jet), is at Ames, Iowa, where a 116,000 sq ft (10,777 m^2) factory was opened on 26 May 1998. A second factory is being considered for international markets. The following data is correct to May 1998, by which time the proof of concept aircraft (*N247VA*) had flown on 116 occasions.

VisionAire VA-10 Vantage

First flight: 16 November 1996 for the proof of concept (POC) aircraft constructed by Scaled Composites Inc. First development prototype (VT1) to fly in December 1998, followed by VT2 in February 1999. First flight of the first production aircraft (PT1) expected June 1999.
Certification: To FAR Pt 23 Amdt 51 (single pilot operation) expected November 1999.
First delivery: Expected in the final quarter of 1999.
Role: 6-seat, single-turbofan, all-composite corporate jet. Dual controls.
Sales: POC aircraft is being followed by 2 flying development (VT1 and VT2) and 2 structural test prototypes.
125 production aircraft sold by May 1998 to customers in 39 US states and 8 countries. Anticipated full rate production of 115 aircraft per year. Price US$1.8 million (1998 dollars).
Crew/passengers: Pilot and 5 passengers. Toilet aft of cabin. Electric vapour-cycle air conditioning system.
Baggage capacity: 2 areas, volumes 22.3 cu ft (0.63 m^3) main, 9.5 cu ft (0.269 m^3) rear.
Pressurization system: 8,000 ft (2,440 m) pressure maintained to altitude.
Wing characteristics: Mid-mounted sweptforward wings to reduce drag.
Wing control surfaces: Aerodynamically-balanced ailerons. Single-slotted, offset hinged flaps.
Tail control surfaces: Conventional dihedral tailplane, with aerodynamically-balanced elevators. Aerodynamically-balanced rudder.
Flight control system: Mechanical, except for 3-axis electric trim (when AFCS is engaged, automatic trim is accomplished to unload the control surface servo-actuators; when autopilot is not engaged, the manual electric trim system is independent of the KFC 325 automatic trim system). Yaw damper. Forward main undercarriage gear doors act as independent air brakes.
Construction materials: Pre-preg carbon-graphite construction. Main wing spar passes aft of cabin. Overfuselage ram-air scoops.
Engine: Single Pratt & Whitney Canada JT15D-5 turbofan.
Engine rating: 2,900 lbf (12.9 kN).
Fuel system: 2 wing tanks, with 908 litres total capacity in prototype and 1,412 litres in production aircraft.
Electrical system: 28 volt system.
Braking system: Hydraulic.
Radar: RDR-2000 colour weather radar.
Flight avionics/instrumentation: Dual IFR, with EFIS. VisionAire Vantage/AlliedSignal control panel is a 2 tube EFIS 50 system; CRTs within system driven by a single symbol generator, switching between various peripheral subsystems such as VHF navigation, GPS, long-range nav, automatic direction finder (ADF), KFC 325 automatic flight control system (AFCS), weather radar, BF Goodrich Stormscope 1000E, angle of attack, radar altitude, marker beacon, and DME. Compass gyro system, vertical gyro system and yaw rate gyro system. Future autopilot configurations will incorporate an air data computer and AHRS to comply with Reduced Vertical Separation Minimums. Primary navigation via dual KX 165A nav/coms. Secondary navigation by DME and ADF. KLN 900 GPS for long-range navigation. GPS receiver provides a moving waypoint display on the EHSI, depicting VORS, airports and waypoints. Dual Mode-S transponders. Radio panel consists of a voice-activated intercom and telephone capabilities among others (teamed with Iowa State University to develop voice control system, to also control navigation/landing lights and temperature).

↑ VisionAire VA-10 Vantage proof of concept aircraft

Details for Vantage

PRINCIPAL DIMENSIONS:
Wing span: 47 ft 6 ins (14.48 m)
Maximum length: 40 ft 9.5 ins (12.43 m)

CABIN (not including cockpit area)**:**
Length: 10 ft 10 ins (3.3 m)
Width: 5 ft 2 ins (1.57 m)
Height: 5 ft (1.52 m)
Volume: 312 cu ft (8.83 m^3)

WINGS:
Area: 222 sq ft (20.62 m^2)
Aspect ratio: 10.16
Sweep forward: -8°
Dihedral: 3° 54′
Thickness/chord ratio: 14.7%

UNDERCARRIAGE:
Type: Hydraulically retractable, with single nosewheel and mainwheels
Wheel base: 17 ft (5.18 m)
Wheel track: 8 ft (2.44 m)

WEIGHTS:
Empty: 4,500 lb (2,041 kg)
Maximum take-off and landing: 7,800 lb (3,538 kg)
Payload: 1,230 lb (558 kg)

PERFORMANCE:
Maximum operating Mach number (M_{MO}): Mach 0.65
Maximum cruise speed: 350 kts (403 mph) 649 km/h, at 41,000 ft (12,495 m)
Economic cruise speed: 250 kts (288 mph) 463 km/h, at 35,000 ft (10,670 m)
Stall speed: 70 kts (81 mph) 130 km/h, *with flaps, power off*
Take-off distance over a 50 ft (15 m) obstacle: 2,000 ft (610 m)
Landing distance over a 50 ft (15 m) obstacle: 2,500 ft (762 m)
Maximum climb rate: 4,000 ft (1,219 m) per minute at sea level
Maximum altitude: 41,000 ft (12,495 m) certified
G limits: +4.75, -2.5
Range: 1,575 naut miles (1,813 miles) 2,918 km with pilot and 1 passenger, to 1,000 naut miles (1,151 miles) 1,853 km with pilot and 5 passengers

Vortex Aircraft Company, LLC — USA

Corporate address:
500 Harbor Drive West, Suite 1310, San Diego, CA 92101.

Telephone: +1 619 234 5387 (JETS)
Facsimile: +1 619 338 9963
E-mail: vortexjet@aol.com

Founded:
1997.

Information:
Gary J. Kauffman (CEO).

ACTIVITIES

▪ In July 1997, Vortex Aircraft acquired all the assets of the Bede Jet Corporation of Chesterfield, Missouri. Vortex intends to certify, manufacture and market several versions of the BD-10 design, which has been renamed Vortex PhoenixJet. The only asset not acquired was the single remaining BD-10 prototype. Vortex is re-engineering the original design intended by Bede as a supersonic kit aircraft, with the aim of certifying it under FAR Pt 23 as a subsonic aircraft, and no kits will be offered. Initially, however, funding for production of an interim non-certified version has also been sought, allowing a production aircraft to be delivered in approximately one year to meet immediate demand for certain military applications as well as general aviation niches (perhaps 200 as experimental aircraft).

Vortex PhoenixJet-TJ

Note: The Chief Editor was informed by Mr Kauffman in May 1998 that Vortex was still undertaking considerable design review for the proposed certified aircraft version, which could eventually affect some of the details given below.
First flight: 8 July 1992 for BD-10 prototype, 11 November 1994 for the Peregrine PJ-1 and 21 June 1995 for the PJ-2 prototypes (Peregrine Flight International formerly acquired rights in the BD-10 programme).
Certification: To be certified under FAR Pt 23.
Role: Military primary jet and electronics warfare training, with the capability of serving also as a weapons systems platform,

↑ Vortex PhoenixJet-TJ

target training and being used as an advanced pilot proficiency trainer. Also civil aircraft for the sport, aerobatic competition and other general aviation markets.
Sales: Initially focusing primarily on military sales. See Activities. Expected price US$995,000. Estimated sales of over 2,000 PhoenixJets worldwide is thought possible.
Crew/passenger: 2 persons in tandem, with available ejection seats. Pressurized and climate controlled cockpit. Dual HOTAS controls with floor-mounted sticks. Starboard hinged canopy. Oxygen system.
Baggage capacity: 100 lb (45.4 kg) aft of seats.
Pressurization system: 9 psi maximum differential, using engine bleed air.
Wing characteristics: The BD-10 supersonic wing being replaced by a new simpler, less costly to manufacture wing designed for the subsonic flight envelope, with improved structural integrity and greater fuel capacity. Optional pylons on hard points.

Details for PhoenixJet-TJ; latest figures provided in May 1998

PRINCIPAL DIMENSIONS:
Wing span: 21 ft 6 ins (6.55 m)
Maximum length: 27 ft 6.5 ins (8.4 m)
Maximum height: 8 ft 1 ins (2.46 m)

CABIN:
Length: 9 ft 5 ins (2.87 m)
Width: 2 ft 8 ins (0.81 m)
Height: 4 ft 1.25 ins (1.25 m)

WINGS:
Aerofoil section: Supercritical (custom design)
Area: 101 sq ft (9.38 m^2)
Aspect ratio: 4.58
Sweepback: 27°
Dihedral: 0°
Incidence: 0°
Thickness/chord ratio: 9%

UNDERCARRIAGE:
Type: Electro-mechanically retractable, with castoring nosewheel (differential braking steering)
Wheel base: 15 ft 6 ins (4.72 m)
Wheel track: 8 ft 5 ins (2.57 m)

WEIGHTS (estimated)**:**
Empty: 2,680 lb (1,216 kg)
Crew weight: 380 lb (172 kg)
Maximum take-off: 4,850 lb (2,200 kg)

PERFORMANCE (estimated)**:**
Cruise speed: Mach 0.81 or 465 kts (535 mph) 862 km/h
Stall speed: 73 kts (84 mph) 135 km/h EAS, take-off weight, in landing configuration
Take-off distance over a 50 ft (15 m) obstacle: 1,230 ft (375 m)
Landing distance over a 50 ft (15 m) obstacle: 1,520 ft (464 m)
Maximum climb rate: 7,100 ft (2,165 m) per minute at sea level
Ceiling: 46,000 ft (14,020 m)
Cruise altitude: 40,000 ft (12,190 m)
Cruise range: 920 naut miles (1,060 miles) 1,706 km, or 981 naut miles (1,130 miles) 1,818 km at economic cruise speed, both with 45 minutes reserve

Wing control surfaces: Ailerons with trim tab and single-slotted flaps.
Tail control surfaces: Redesigned tail unit with variable incidence tailplane (trimmable 4° up, 14° down). Elevators. Twin fins with rudder. 2 ventral fins.
Flight control system: Mechanical, with push-pull tubes (not boosted), except for electric tailplane trim and tab. Twin airbrakes under the air inlets.
Construction materials: Airframe is 70% aluminium alloy and 30% glassfibre reinforced plastics sandwich construction. Wings and tail unit are all metal, the wings and tailplane having aluminium alloy honeycomb skins and the 2-spar fins having sheet skins.
Engine: 2,950 lbf (13.12 kN) General Electric CJ-610/J-85 turbojet; a new 'state-of-the-art engine' will be more fuel efficient and further increase range.
Fuel system: 5 interconnected fuselage cells, for 852 litres of fuel (1,690 lb, 766.6 kg).
Electrical system: Engine-driven generator, plus battery.
Braking system: Cleveland mainwheel brakes.
De-icing system: Hot air for windscreen, and electric for leading edges of wings, tailplane, fins and inlets.
Radar: Weather radar.
Flight avionics/instrumentation: IFR. New technology 'glass' cockpit and its associated avionics as standard equipment. Autopilot.

Weatherly Aviation Company, Inc — USA

Corporate address:
2100 Flightline Drive, PO Box 68, Lincoln, CA 95648.
Telephone: +1 916 645 9080
Facsimile: +1 916 645 1816

ACTIVITIES

- Markets the piston-engined 620 and the turboprop-engined 620 BTG.

Weatherly 620 and 620 BTG

Role: Single-seat agricultural aircraft.
Details: For 620 BTG, except under Aircraft variants.
Sales: Price US$185,000 plus engine in 1998.
Crew: Pilot, on a 4-way adjustable seat with open nylon mesh covering. Tinted turning windows in canopy top. Adjustable rudder pedals. Cabin forced fresh air system. Bleed air heater. Optional air conditioner and windshield washer. Baggage compartment.
Chemical tank/hopper: Heavy duty glassfibre hopper with upper and lower windows of 47.5 cu ft (1.345 m^3) and capacity 1,344 litres. Optional hopper rinse out system.
Dispersal equipment: Standard equipment includes Weath-Aero fan (blades feather during ferrying); 2 ins (5 cm) SS bottom load tube, less valve; 2 ins (5 cm) Agrinautics spray pump and 3-way valve; 2 ins (5 cm) spray system and pylon mounted drop boom (full length or two-thirds length) with one-eighth NPT holes every 6 ins (15.24 cm) including 40 nozzles; and 25 ins (63.5 cm) Transland gate box. Optional equipment includes Transland stainless steel spray system, pneumatic boom system, smoker, Crop Hawk aluminium flow meter with extra cartridge, and nickel plated flow meter with extra cartridge.
Safety equipment: Main gear and cockpit wire deflectors. Wire deflector cable (canopy to vertical fin).
Wing control surfaces: High lift to drag ratio wings, with tip vanes to diffuse normal formation of the wing tip vortex, creating a strong downwash outboard of the tip, introducing smaller vortices in the tip area; this results in both a delay in the formation of the trailing vortex and a decrease in its intensity.
Flight control system: Aerodynamically balanced, ball bearing mounted control surfaces. Stainless steel rudder cables.
Construction materials: All metal airframe and control surfaces, but with glassfibre tail fairings. Fuselage of monocoque construction to reduce airframe weight; large openings and

↑ **Weatherly Model 620 BTG** *(courtesy Weatherly Aviation Company)*

removable panels for easy inspection and maintenance. Wing leading edges attached with piano hinges so the wing is easily inspected.
Engine: AlliedSignal TPE331-1-151A turboprop, with new McCauley 3GFR34C602/100LA-2 3-blade propeller with spinner.
Fuel system: 492 litres total, with 439 litres usable.
Electrical system: 24 volt, with 250 amp starter-generator. External APU plug.
Flight avionics/instrumentation: Ball slip indicator. Electronic outside air temperature gauge.

Aircraft variants:
620 is the piston-engined version with a 450 hp (335.7 kW) Pratt & Whitney R-985-AN-1, -3 or -14B engine and new Hartzell 3-blade propeller with a HC-B3R30-4B hub and R10152-5 1/2R blades. Fuel capacity 369 litres (341 litres usable). 24 volt electrical system with 50 amp Jasco alternator. Similar hopper to 620 BTG, but has a 2.5 ins (6.35 cm) bottom load tube, less valve. Same wing span as BTG, length 26 ft 9 ins (8.15 m) and height 8 ft (2.44 m).
620 BTG is the turboprop version, as detailed.

Details for 620 BTG

PRINCIPAL DIMENSIONS:
Wing span: 46 ft 8 ins (14.22 m)
Maximum length: 29 ft 8 ins (9.04 m)
Maximum height: 9 ft 6 ins (2.9 m)

WINGS:
Area: 277 sq ft (25.73 m^2)
Thickness/chord ratio: 15%

UNDERCARRIAGE:
Type: Fixed tailwheel type, with oleo suspension pinned at the spar so that landing loads are transmitted to the spar in a way that avoids twisting stresses. Trailing strut carries forward and aft loads during landing. Spring tailwheel assembly with full swivel locking wheel. 3 piston Cleveland brakes
Main wheel tyre size: 8.5 × 10
Tail wheel tyre size: 12.5 × 4.5
Wheel track: 10 ft 6 ins (3.2 m)

WEIGHTS:
Empty: 3,030 lb (1,374 kg) with standard equipment
Typical Part 8 operating: 6,000 lb (2,722 kg)

PERFORMANCE:
Maximum speed: 153 kts (176 mph) 283 km/h
Typical ferry speed: 122 kts (140 mph) 225 km/h
Stall speed: 52.5 kts (60 mph) 96.5 km/h at 4,300 lb gross or 62 kts (71 mph) 114 km/h at 6,000 lb gross, both standard equipment
Take-off distance: 940 ft (287 m) at 6,000 lb gross
Climb rate: 1,400 ft (427 m) per minute at sea level, at 6,000 lb gross
Ceiling: 15,000 ft (4,572 m), service

Williams International USA

Corporate address:
2280 West Maple Road, PO Box 200, Walled Lake, MI 48390-0200.

Telephone: +1 810 624 5200

Information:
Ron Schwedland (Director, business development - *telephone* +1 248 960 2468, *facsimile* +1 248 624 5345, *E-mail* RSCHWEDLAND@WILLIAMS-INT.COM).

ACTIVITIES

■ See also engine section for Williams-Rolls FJ44 series engines, the latest FJ44-2A now flying on the Sino Swearingen SJ30-2 business jet and on the Raytheon Premier I. See also Williams International in the Engine section.

Williams V-Jet II

Note: The V-Jet II is an engine demonstration special aircraft, detail designed and manufactured by Scaled Composites. It was conceived as a result of a competitive procurement programme among jet engine companies by NASA, when in 1996 Williams International was selected to join NASA in a US$100 million co-operative General Aviation Propulsion Program to revitalize the US light aircraft industry through small turbofan engine technology. Under the programme, Williams and its industry team members provide 60% of the resources and NASA 40% for the initial engine demonstration phase. The new Williams engine is designated FJX-2, and the intention is to demonstrate how old piston-engined light aircraft can be replaced by all new, 4 or 6 seat twin-turbofan aircraft. V-Jet II is not intended for production, and is the culmination of several V-Jets designed in the past years by Dr Williams, with 3 full-scale mock-ups and at least a dozen small models studied prior to the present V-Jet II.
First flight: 13 April 1997.
Role: Engine demonstration special aircraft, to demonstrate new Williams engines over a range of flight speeds and altitudes expected to be required for future turbofan-powered light aircraft. To be pressurized.
Sales: Not intended for production.
Crew/passengers: 5 seats as currently arranged. Airstair door.
Wing characteristics: Mid-mounted, high aspect ratio, forward-swept wings.
Tail control surfaces: Y-tail, with twin outward-canted fins with inset rudders and tabs, and fixed ventral fin.
Construction materials: All composites. Wing spar carry-through structure aft of cabin.
Engines: 2 × 550 lbf (2.45 kN) Williams FJX-1 low-bypass ratio turbofans currently installed, with 700 lbf (3.11 kN) high-bypass ratio FJX-2s intended to be fitted during the fourth year of the NASA/Williams programme (in the year 2000).

↑ **Williams V-Jet II engine demonstration special aircraft**

Details for V-Jet II

PRINCIPAL DIMENSIONS:
Wing span: 35 ft 4 ins (10.76 m)

WINGS:
Area: 118 sq ft (10.96 m^2)

UNDERCARRIAGE:
Type: Retractable, with twin nosewheels

WEIGHTS:
Maximum take-off: 3,800 lb (1,723 kg)

PERFORMANCE:
Demonstrated speed: 295 kts (340 mph) 547 km/h at time of writing
Demonstrated altitude: 30,000 ft (9,145 m) at time of writing

Wipaire Inc USA

Comments: Brief details of Wipline floats and aircraft modifications offered by this company can be found in the 1996-97 edition of *WA&SD*, page 454.

→ **By October 1998 the British company, Europa Aviation, had sold 525 kits of its Europa lightplane (see Recreational Aircraft section). In the same month it was announced that in 1999 an Europa XS would be test flown with a new British 'next generation' 120 hp (89.5 kW) Wilksch Airmotive 3-cylinder diesel engine, currently in an advanced stage of development (at time of writing). Shown here is an Europa XS (nearest), with a standard fixed undercarriage Europa to its rear**
(courtesy Wilksch Airmotive)

Recreational Aircraft

This section details aircraft available for amateur construction and ultralights/microlights. A number of the aircraft are also available in ready-assembled form from the manufacturer and can be used for training, patrol, agricultural and other professional roles. Some aircraft originally produced as "homebuilts" but now certificated can be found in the General Aviation section. Helicopters and autogyros available for amateur construction are detailed in the main Helicopter section. Addresses and Telephone/Facsimile numbers are given for the first entry of each company.

Argentina

Alfonso Libelus

Address:
Valentin Guillermo Alfonso, Av. Congreso 5449, 1431 Capital Federal, Buenos Aires.

Telephone: +54 1 755 7958

Type: Single-seat, mid-wing ultralight motorglider with pusher engine and fixed nosewheel undercarriage.
Construction: Carbonfibre and metal.
Wing span: 49 ft (14.9 m)
Length: 20 ft (6.1 m)
Empty weight: 452 lb (205 kg)
Gross weight: 696 lb (316 kg)
Recommended engine: 32 hp (23.9 kW) half-Volkswagen, designed by Mory Hummel.
Maximum speed: 81 kts (93 mph) 151 km/h
Cruise speed: 65 kts (75 mph) 121 km/h
Stall speed: 28 kts (33 mph) 52 km/h
Best glide ratio: 30:1
Take-off distance: 400 ft (122 m)
Availability: Complete kits, with engine.
Comments: Kit costs about US$18,000. Developed from an aluminium prototype 1982-95.

Schoepf MS0.1

Address:
569 Jose Ingenieros, 2900 San Nicholas.

Type: Side-by-side 2-seat, low-wing, cabin monoplane with fixed tailwheel undercarriage.
Construction: Wood and fabric.
Wing span: 28 ft 8 ins (8.75 m)
Length: 22 ft 8 ins (6.9 m)
Empty weight: 880 lb (400 kg)
Gross weight: 1,452 lb (660 kg)
Recommended engine: 90 hp (67 kW) Teledyne Continental C90-12F.
Maximum speed: 121 kts (139 mph) 225 km/h
Cruise speed: 107 kts (124 mph) 200 km/h
Stall speed: 38 kts (44 mph) 70 km/h
Take-off distance: 600 ft (183 m)
Climb rate: 690 ft (210 m) per minute
Range: 483 naut miles (559 miles) 900 km
Availability: Plans.
Comments: First flew 11 April 1990.

Australia

AAW Aerolite 1+1

Address:
Australian Aviation Works, 5 Utrecht Court, Donvale, W. Australia 3111.

Telephone: +61 3 8423132
Facsimile: +61 3 8418177

Type: Single-seat, high-wing cabin monoplane, with fixed nosewheel undercarriage.
Construction: Wood, metal tube and fabric.
Wing span: 30 ft (9.14 m)
Length: 17 ft 6 ins (5.33 m)
Empty weight: 350 lb (159 kg)
Gross weight: 680 lb (308 kg)
Recommended engine: 49.6 hp (37 kW) Rotax 503, 64.4 hp (48 kW) Rotax 532, 65 hp (48.5 kW) Rotax 582 or 73.8 hp (55 kW) Rotax 618.
Maximum speed: 87 kts (100 mph) 161 km/h
Cruise speed: 65 kts (75 mph) 121 km/h
Take-off distance: 300 ft (92 m)
Climb rate: 900 ft (274 m) per minute
Range: 208 naut miles (240 miles) 386 km
Availability: Plans and kits.
Comments: Microlight or homebuilt, with option of a second seat.

AAW Aeromax 1700 Sport

Type: Single-seat, open cockpit, strut-braced parasol monoplane, with fixed tail-dragger undercarriage.
Construction: Wood, metal tube and fabric.
Wing span: 30 ft (9.14 m)
Length: 17 ft 6 ins (5.33 m)
Empty weight: 350 lb (159 kg)
Gross weight: 680 lb (308 kg)
Recommended engine: 50-100 hp (37.3-74.6 kW)
Maximum speed: 87 kts (100 mph) 161 km/h
Cruise speed: 65 kts (75 mph) 121 km/h
Stall speed: 34 kts (39 mph) 63 km/h
Take-off distance: 300 ft (92 m)
Climb rate: 900 ft (274 m) per minute
Range: 208 naut miles (240 miles) 386 km
Availability: Plans.
Comments: Modified Australian version of the PFA Luton LA-4 Minor (see UK).

AAW Karatoo C Model

Type: Side-by-side 2-seat high-wing cabin monoplane, with fixed tailwheel undercarriage.
Construction: Wood, metal tube and fabric.
Wing span: 33 ft (10.06 m)
Length: 20 ft 6 ins (6.25 m)
Empty weight: 700 lb (318 kg)
Gross weight: 1,300 lb (590 kg)
Recommended engine: 105 hp (78.3 kW)
Maximum speed: 96 kts (110 mph) 177 km/h
Cruise speed: 83 kts (95 mph) 153 km/h
Take-off distance: 300 ft (92 m)
Climb rate: 1,000 ft (305 m) per minute
Range: 434 naut miles (500 miles) 804 km
Availability: Plans.
Comments: Australian version of Jesse Anglin's Karatoo. Partial kits for wings and ailerons available.

↑ **Australian Aviation Works (AAW) Karatoo C Model** *(Geoffrey P. Jones)*

AAW Spacewalker I

Type: Single-seat, open cockpit low-wing monoplane, with fixed tailwheel undercarriage.
Construction: Wood, tube and fabric.
Wing span: 26 ft (7.92 m)
Length: 17 ft 3 ins (5.26 m)
Empty weight: 540 lb (245 kg)
Gross weight: 850 lb (386 kg)
Recommended engine: 65 hp (48.5 kW) Teledyne Continental.
Maximum speed: 109 kts (125 mph) 201 km/h
Cruise speed: 97 kts (112 mph) 180 km/h
Stall speed: 33 kts (38 mph) 61 km/h
Take-off distance: 300 ft (92 m)
Climb rate: 850 ft (259 m) per minute
Range: 260 naut miles (300 miles) 482 km
Availability: Plans.
Comments: Jesse Anglin's design from the USA. Also available is the tandem-seat **Spacewalker II**. See also Warner Revolution I and II under USA.

↑ **Australian Aviation Works Spacewalker I** *(Geoffrey P. Jones)*

Austflight Drifter

Address:
Austflight ULA Pty. Ltd, PO Box 84, Boonah, Queensland 4310.

Telephone: +61 7 5463 2755
Facsimile: +61 7 5463 2987

Type: Tandem 2-seat, open-cockpit, high-wing microlight, with pusher engine and option of fixed tailwheel undercarriage or floats/skis.
Construction: Steel tube and fabric.
Wing span: 30 ft (9.14 m)
Length: 19 ft 6 ins (5.94 m)
Empty weight: 550 lb (249 kg)
Gross weight: 1,100 lb (499 kg)
Recommended engine: 65 hp (48.5 kW) Rotax 582 or 74 hp (55.2 kW) Rotax 618
Cruise speed: 64 kts (74 mph) 119 km/h
Take-off distance: 350 ft (107 m)
Climb rate: 800 ft (244 m) per minute
Range: 195 naut miles (225 miles) 362 km
Availability: Complete aircraft only, certified to Australian CAO 101.55.
Comments: Considerably modified version of the former Maxair Drifter (see also Lockwood Aviation Supply in USA). 490 sold in Australia.

↑ **Austflight Drifter SB on floats** *(Geoffrey P. Jones)*

Australian Light Wing PR

Address:
Howard Hughes Engineering Pty. Ltd, PO Box 89, Ballina, NSW 2478.

Telephone: +61 66 86 8658
Facsimile: +61 66 86 8343

Type: Tandem 2-seat, braced high-wing, cabin monoplane, with a fixed tail-dragger or float undercarriage.
Construction: Steel tube, alloy and fabric.
Wing span: 31 ft 10 ins (9.7 m)
Length: 19 ft 1 ins (5.82 m)
Empty weight: 476 lb (216 kg), 584 lb (265 kg) with floats.
Gross weight: 881 lb (400 kg), 992 lb (450 kg) with floats.
Recommended engine: 65 hp (48.5 kW) Rotax 532
Maximum speed: 80 kts (92 mph) 148 km/h
Cruise speed: 65 kts (75 mph) 120 km/h
Stall speed: 29 kts (34 mph) 54 km/h
Take-off distance over a 50 ft obstacle: 1,000 ft (305 m)
Climb rate: 900 ft (274 m) per minute
Range: 149 naut miles (172 miles) 276 km
Availability: Kits and factory complete.
Comments: Prototype Light Wing first flew in June 1986.

Australian Light Wing GR-912

Type: Side-by-side 2-seat, high-wing, cabin monoplane, with fixed tailwheel undercarriage.
Construction: Steel tube, alloy and fabric.
Wing span: 31 ft 2 ins (9.5 m)
Length: 18 ft 4 ins (5.6 m)
Empty weight: 551 lb (250 kg)
Gross weight: 992 lb (450 kg)
Recommended engine: 77.8 hp (58 kW) Rotax 912
Maximum speed: 105 kts (121 mph) 194 km/h
Cruise speed: 70 kts (81 mph) 130 km/h
Stall speed: 38 kts (44 mph) 71 km/h
Take-off distance: 328 ft (100 m)
Climb rate: 750 ft (230 m) per minute
Range: 300 naut miles (345 miles) 555 km
Availability: Kits and factory complete.
Comments: Optional flaps. A further and similar version, the GA-55, is also produced.

Corby/CSN Starlet CJ-1

Address:
John C. Corby, 34 Coronet Court, North Rocks, Sydney, NSW 2151 (*also* USA: CSN, 510 NW 46th Terrace, Fort Lauderdale, FL 33317-2044).
Telephone: USA: +1 954 581 8835
E-mail: USA: corbystarlet@juno.com

Type: Single-seat, low-wing monoplane, with fixed tail-dragger or tailwheel undercarriage.
Construction: Wood.
Wing span: 18 ft 6 ins (5.64 m)
Length: 14 ft 9 ins (4.5 m)
Empty weight: 465 lb (211 kg) in Utility category with 1-piece spar
Gross weight: 700 lb (318 kg)
Recommended engine: 60 hp (44.7 kW) Volkswagen (options for 45-75 hp, 33.6-56 kW)
Maximum speed: 139 kts (160 mph) 257 km/h
Cruise speed: 113 kts (130 mph) 209 km/h
Stall speed: 31 kts (35 mph) 57 km/h
Take-off distance over a 50 ft obstacle: 1,000-1,100 ft (305-335 m)
Climb rate: 1,100 ft (335 m) per minute
Range: 231 naut miles (266 miles) 428 km
Availability: Plans, sold in 23 countries and 40 US states.
Comments: Designed by Australian John Corby. Plans also available in the USA.

↑ **New Zealand-built Corby Starlets** *(Geoffrey P. Jones)*

Fisher/Sadler Vampire

Address:
Ron Fisher, 32 Aquilla Ave, Torquay 3228.
Telephone & Facsimile: +61 352 614916

Type: Side-by-side 2-seat, mid-wing, cabin monoplane, with twin-booms and fixed nosewheel undercarriage.
Construction: Metal and composites.
Wing span: 28 ft (8.53 m)
Length: 19 ft 6 ins (5.94 m)
Gross weight: 1,200 lb (544 kg)
Recommended engine: 80 hp (59.7 kW) Jabiru or Limbach L2000
Cruise speed: 100 kts (115 mph) 185 km/h
Availability: Kits.
Comments: Revival of the Sadler Vampire from the USA. Possible future certification in the Primary Category in the USA.

Kimberley Sky-Rider

Address:
Gareth J. Kimberley, 211 Fowler Road, Illawong, NSW 2234.
Telephone: +61 2 543 2348

Type: Single-seat, high-wing, open microlight, with a fixed tailwheel undercarriage.
Construction: Steel and alloy tube, and fabric.
Wing span: 32 ft 4 ins (9.86 m)
Length: 19 ft 6 ins (5.94 m)
Empty weight: 195 lb (88.5 kg)
Gross weight: 400 lb (181 kg)
Recommended engine: 20 hp (15 kW) Fuji-Robin or Rotax of equivalent size
Maximum speed: 43 kts (50 mph) 80 km/h
Cruise speed: 39 kts (45 mph) 72 km/h
Stall speed: 19 kts (21 mph) 34 km/h
Take-off distance: 246 ft (75 m)
Climb rate: 300 ft (92 m) per minute
Range: 70 naut miles (80 miles) 129 km
Availability: Plans.
Comments: Designed in 1977. Plans sold in 20 countries worldwide. Prototype now in the Powerhouse Museum, Sydney.

↑ **Kimberley Sky-Rider**

Moyes Dragonfly

Address:
Moyes Microlightes Pty. Ltd, 2-4 Taylor Street, Waverley, NSW 2024 (*also* 1805 Dean Still Road, Davenport, FL 33837, USA).
Telephone: +61 2 387 5114 (USA: +1 813 424 0070)
Facsimile: +61 2 387 4472 (USA: +1 813 424 0070)

Type: Tandem 2-seat, high-wing microlight, with fixed tailwheel undercarriage.
Construction: Alloy tube and fabric.
Wing span: 34 ft 8 ins (10.57 m)
Length: 20 ft (6.1 m)
Empty weight: 330 lb (150 kg)
Gross weight: 800 lb (363 kg)
Recommended engine: 65 hp (48.5 kW) Rotax 582
Maximum speed: 65 kts (75 mph) 121 km/h
Cruise speed: 52 kts (60 mph) 97 km/h
Take-off distance: 50 ft (15 m)
Climb rate: 1,400 ft (427 m) per minute
Range: 87 naut miles (100 miles) 161 km
Availability: Kits.
Comments: Built to tow unpowered microlights and hang-gliders. Also available in the USA.

Skybound Skybat

Address:
C/o Andrew Richards or Ray Hill.
Telephone: +61 3 5281 7468 or 5796 2229

Type: Single-seat, mid-wing, aerobatic cabin microlight, with fixed tailwheel undercarriage.
Construction: Steel tube, fabric and composites.
Wing span: 20 ft (6.1 m)
Empty weight: 251 lb (114 kg)
Gross weight: 592 lb (269 kg)
Recommended engine: 65 hp (48.5 kW) Hirth 2706
Maximum speed: 110 kts (127 mph) 204 km/h
Cruise speed: 90 kts (104 mph) 167 km/h
Stall speed: 39 kts (44 mph) 71 km/h
Take-off distance: 246 ft (75 m)
Climb rate: 1,000 ft (305 m) per minute
Range: 182 naut miles (210 miles) 338 km
Availability: Kits.
Comments: Ultralight under Australian CAO-95-10 regulations. First flown November 1996. Kits without engine and instruments A$13,000. Construction time about 300 working hours.

Skyfox Aviation CA-22 Skyfox

Address:
Skyfox Aviation, P O Box 910, Caloundra, Queensland 4551.
Telephone: +61 74 91 5355
Facsimile: +61 74 91 8237

Type: Side-by-side 2-seat, high-wing cabin microlight, with fixed tailwheel undercarriage.
Construction: Steel, alloy and fabric.
Wing span: 31 ft 3 ins (9.53 m)
Length: 18 ft 5 ins (5.61 m)
Empty weight: 640 lb (290 kg)
Gross weight: 992 lb (450 kg)
Recommended engine: 77.8 hp (58 kW) Rotax 912
Maximum speed: 95 kts (109 mph) 176 km/h
Cruise speed: 85 kts (98 mph) 157 km/h
Stall speed: 40 kts (46 mph) 74 km/h
Take-off distance: 400 ft (122 m)
Climb rate: 940 ft (287 m) per minute
Range: 288 naut miles (331 miles) 533 km
Availability: Factory complete aircraft.
Comments: Microlight version of the CA-25, which is certificated under JAR/VLA.

Slepcev Storch

Address:
Nestor Slepcev, VRBAS, Beechwood, NSW 2446.
Facsimile: +61 65 85 6458

Type: Tandem 2-seat, high-wing cabin monoplane, with fixed tailwheel undercarriage.
Construction: Metal, steel tube and fabric.
Wing span: 33 ft 8 ins (10.26 m)
Length: 31 ft 4 ins (10.39 m)
Empty weight: 618 lb (280 kg)
Gross weight: 996 lb (452 kg)
Recommended engine: 73.8 hp (55 kW) Rotax 618 (other options)
Maximum speed: 68 kts (78 mph) 126 km/h
Cruise speed: 56 kts (65 mph) 105 km/h
Stall speed: 16 kts (18 mph) 29 km/h
Climb rate: 1,200 ft (366 m) per minute
Range: 87 naut miles (100 miles) 161 km
Availability: Kits.
Comments: 75% replica of the WWII Fieseler Storch.

↑ **Slepcev Storch, available as a kitplane, at Sun 'n Fun '97**

Austria

HB Flugtechnik HB-207 Alfa

Address: H. Brditschka Flugtechnik GmbH, Dr Adolf-Scharf Strasse 42, A-4053 HAID-Ansfelden.
Telephone: +43 72 29 791 04 or 791 17 **Facsimile:** +43 72 29 791 04 15 or 791 17 15

Type: Side-by-side 2-seat, low-wing cabin monoplane, with retractable or fixed nosewheel undercarriage.
Construction: Aluminium and composites.
Wing span: 29 ft 6 ins (9 m)
Length: 19 ft 6 ins (5.95 m)
Empty weight: 948 lb (430 kg)
Gross weight: 1,411 lb (640 kg)
Recommended engine: 110 hp (80 kW) Porsche Austria (options are Limbach, Rotax and Textron Lycoming)
Maximum speed: 166 kts (191 mph) 308 km/h
Cruise speed: 130 kts (149 mph) 240 km/h
Stall speed: 49 kts (56 mph) 90 km/h *clean*
Take-off distance: 624 ft (190 m)
Climb rate: 1,080 ft (330 m) per minute
Range: 485 naut miles (559 miles) 900 km
Availability: Complete kits.
Comments: First flown March 1995. At least 32 sold. Latest project by Austrian motorglider manufacturer Brditschka.

↑ **Prototype HB Flugtechnik HB-207 Alfa**

Ultraleichtflug Apollo Racer GT

Address: Ultraleichtflug-Austria, Scubertgasse 1, A-8055 Graz.
Telephone & Facsimile: +43 316 29 14 74

Type: Single-seat powered trike, rogallo-wing microlight.
Construction: Alloy tube, composites and fabric.
Wing span: 32 ft 10 ins (10 m)
Length: 8 ft 2 ins (2.5 m)
Empty weight: 119 lb (54 kg)
Gross weight: 419 lb (190 kg)
Recommended engine: 49.6 hp (37 kW) Rotax 503, with Rotax 582 optional
Maximum speed: 65 kts (75 mph) 120 km/h
Cruise speed: 54 kts (62 mph) 100 km/h
Stall speed: 22 kts (25 mph) 40 km/h
Climb rate: 785 ft (240 m) per minute
Availability: Kits or complete aircraft.
Comments: One of several variants manufactured by the company.

Belgium

Lambert Mission M212-100

Address: Lambert Aircraft Engineering, Lupinestraat 5, B-8500 Kortrijk.
Telephone & Facsimile: +32 56 213347

Type: Side-by-side 2-seat, low-wing, cabin monoplane, with fixed nosewheel undercarriage.
Construction: Composites.
Wing span: 32 ft 2 ins (9.8 m)
Length: 24 ft 3 ins (7.4 m)
Empty weight: 981 lb (445 kg)
Gross weight: 1,653 lb (750 kg)
Recommended engine: 150 hp (112 kW) Zoche ZO-01A
Maximum speed: 138 kts (159 mph) 256 km/h
Cruise speed: 121 kts (140 mph) 225 km/h
Stall speed: 45 kts (52 mph) 83 km/h
Take-off distance: 575 ft (175 m)
Climb rate: 1,240 ft (378 m) per minute
Range: 755 naut miles (870 miles) 1,400 km, at 60% power
Availability: Kits. Complete aircraft to FAR-23 probable for the future.
Comments: Winning design at the recent Royal Aeronautical Society Light Aircraft Design Competition, by Filip Lambert. 2+2-seat and 4-seat versions planned.

Ultracraft Calypso

Address: Ultracraft, St Quirinusstraat 72, B-3550 Heusden-Zoloer.
Telephone & Facsimile: +32 11 436678

Type: Single-seat, parasol-wing monoplane, with fixed tail-dragger undercarriage.
Construction: Wood and fabric.
Wing span: 28 ft 4 ins (8.65 m)
Length: 20 ft (6.1 m)
Empty weight: 331 lb (150 kg)
Gross weight: 650 lb (295 kg)
Recommended engine: 39.6 hp (29.5 kW) Rotax 447
Maximum speed: 84 kts (96 mph) 155 km/h
Cruise speed: 57 kts (65 mph) 105 km/h
Stall speed: 27 kts (31 mph) 50 km/h
Climb rate: 590 ft (180 m) per minute
Availability: Complete aircraft.
Comments: Prototype first flew in 1995.

↑ **Ultracraft Calypso** *(Geoffrey P. Jones)*

Brazil

Altair Coelho AC-10

Address: Av. Martinho Poeta 2130, 9299-180 Eldorado do Sul, RS (Ilha da Pintada).

Type: Side-by-side 2-seat, parasol-wing amphibian, with fixed tailwheel undercarriage.
Construction: Steel tube, wood and composites.
Wing span: 29 ft 6 ins (9 m)
Length: 18 ft 8 ins (5.7 m)
Empty weight: 591 lb (268 kg)
Gross weight: 1,102 lb (500 kg)
Recommended engine: 65 hp (48.5 kW) Franklin
Maximum speed: 81 kts (93 mph) 150 km/h
Cruise speed: 73 kts (84 mph) 135 km/h
Stall speed: 41 kts (47 mph) 75 km/h
Take-off distance: 492 ft (150 m) land, 656 ft (200 m) water
Climb rate: 490 ft (150 m) per minute
Availability: Plans.
Comments: One of Altair Coelho's many and diverse designs.

↑ **Altair Coelho AC-10 amphibian** *(Leonardo Andrade)*

Altair Coelho AC-11

Type: Side-by-side 2-seat, strut-braced low-wing monoplane, with either fixed tailwheel or nosewheel undercarriage.
Construction: Steel tube and wood.
Wing span: 25 ft 7 ins (7.8 m)
Length: 18 ft 10 ins (5.75 m)
Empty weight: 639 lb (290 kg)
Gross weight: 1,234 lb (560 kg)
Recommended engine: 180 hp (134 kW) turbocharged VW2000 with reduction drive
Maximum speed: 81 kts (93 mph) 150 km/h
Cruise speed: 76 kts (87 mph) 140 km/h
Stall speed: 38 kts (44 mph) 70 km/h
Take-off distance: 656 ft (200 m)
Climb rate: 945 ft (288 m) per minute
Availability: Plans.
Comments: Developed from the AC-8 Vega. 5 under construction in Brazil in both undercarriage configurations.

↑ **Altair Coelho AC-11 prototype** *(Leonardo Andrade)*

Vector Fox V5

Address: Vector Ultralight SA, Rua Bruno Sebra 60, BR-20971 Rio de Janeiro.

Type: Tandem 2-seat, high-wing microlight, with pusher engine and fixed nosewheel undercarriage.
Construction: Alloy tube and fabric.
Wing span: 31 ft 8 ins (9.66 m)
Empty weight: 397 lb (180 kg)
Gross weight: 884 lb (401 kg)
Recommended engine: 49.6 hp (37 kW) Rotax 503
Maximum speed: 67 kts (78 mph) 125 km/h
Cruise speed: 62 kts (71 mph) 115 km/h
Stall speed: 27 kts (31 mph) 50 km/h
Climb rate: 985 ft (300 m) per minute
Availability: Complete aircraft.
Comments: Also available in side-by-side 2-seat form.

Canada

Aces High Cuby 1 and Cuby II

Address: Aces High Light Aircraft Ltd, RR #1, London, Ontario, N6A 4B5.
Telephone & Facsimile: +1 519 652 3020

Details: Cuby 1, except under Engine, Comments and photograph.
Type: Single-seat, high-wing cabin microlight, with fixed tailwheel undercarriage.
Construction: Steel tube and fabric.
Wing span: 33 ft 6 ins (10.21 m)
Length: 18 ft 3 ins (5.56 m)
Empty weight: 250 lb (113 kg)
Gross weight: 850 lb (386 kg)
Recommended engine: 26 hp (19 kW) Rotax 277 (50 hp, 37.3 kW Rotax 503 for larger 2-seat Cuby II)
Maximum speed: 83 kts (95 mph) 153 km/h
Cruise speed: 48 kts (55 mph) 89 km/h
Stall speed: 25 kts (28 mph) 45 km/h
Take-off distance: 150 ft (46 m)
Climb rate: 700 ft (213 m) per minute
Range: 174 naut miles (200 miles) 322 km
Availability: Kits.
Comments: Engine options for Cuby 1. Side-by-side 2-seat Cuby II is similar. Both have float and ski gear options.

↑ Aces High Cuby II built in the UK *(Geoffrey P. Jones)*

ASAP Beaver RX-550

Address:
OK Landing Road, Vernon, British Columbia.

Type: Tandem 2-seat, open cockpit, high-wing microlight, with fixed nosewheel undercarriage.
Construction: Steel tube and fabric.
Wing span: 35 ft (10.67 m)
Length: 21 ft (6.4 m)
Empty weight: 450 lb (204 kg)
Gross weight: 1,110 lb (503 kg)
Recommended engine: 65 hp (48.5 kW) Rotax 582
Maximum speed: 70 kts (80 mph) 129 km/h
Cruise speed: 56 kts (65 mph) 105 km/h
Stall speed: 26 kts (29 mph) 47 km/h
Take-off distance: 400 ft (122 m)
Climb rate: 800 ft (244 m) per minute
Range: 104 naut miles (120 miles) 193 km
Availability: Kits.
Comments: Variant of the Spectrum Beaver RX-550, a 2-seat training version of the Beaver RX-28. Some 2,000 completed and flown.

ASAP Chinook Plus 2

Type: Tandem 2-seat, high-wing microlight, with fixed tailwheel undercarriage.
Construction: Steel tube and fabric.
Wing span: 32 ft (9.75 m)
Length: 17 ft 8 ins (5.38 m)
Empty weight: 380 lb (172 kg)
Gross weight: 900 lb (408 kg)
Recommended engine: 65 hp (48.5 kW) Rotax 582
Maximum speed: 83 kts (95 mph) 153 km/h
Cruise speed: 72 kts (83 mph) 134 km/h
Take-off distance: 250 ft (77 m)
Climb rate: 1,200 ft (366 m) per minute
Range: 259 naut miles (298 miles) 479 km
Availability: Kits.
Comments: Smaller Rotax 503 engine optional. Over 650 estimated to have been completed and flown.

Avionnerie Cyclone

Address:
Avionnerie Lac St-Jean Inc, 373 de la Friche, Dolbeau, Quebec, G8L 2T3.

Telephone: +1 418 276 7903
Facsimile: +1 418 276 9079

Type: 4-seat, high-wing cabin monoplane based on a Cessna 185, with options for nosewheel, tailwheel or float undercarriage.
Construction: Metal.
Wing span: 38 ft (11.58 m)
Length: 26 ft (7.92 m)
Empty weight: 1,700 lb (771 kg)
Gross weight: 3,000 lb (1,361 kg)
Recommended engine: 230 hp (171.5 kW) Teledyne Continental
Maximum speed: 148 kts (170 mph) 274 km/h
Cruise speed: 137 kts (158 mph) 254 km/h
Stall speed: 51 kts (58 mph) 94 km/h
Take-off distance: 750 ft (229 m)
Climb rate: 1,300 ft (396 m) per minute
Range: 756 naut miles (870 miles) 1,400 km
Availability: Partial kits.
Comments: Cessna-type fuselage with redesigned wings. Engine options from 145 to 350 hp (108-261 kW).

Back Forty Developments Tundra

Address:
Back Forty Developments Ltd, RR 4, Campbellford, Ontario K0L 1L0.

Telephone: +1 705 653 2219

Type: Tandem 2-seat, open high-wing microlight, with fixed tail-dragger undercarriage.
Construction: Metal, steel tube and fabric.
Wing span: 32 ft (9.75 m)
Length: 19 ft (5.79 m)
Empty weight: 385 lb (175 kg)
Gross weight: 850 lb (386 kg)
Recommended engine: 64 hp (47.7 kW) Rotax 532
Maximum speed: 83 kts (95 mph) 153 km/h
Cruise speed: 61 kts (70 mph) 113 km/h
Take-off distance: 200 ft (61 m)
Climb rate: 800 ft (244 m) per minute
Range: 121 naut miles (140 miles) 225 km
Availability: Kits.

Circa Reproductions Nieuport 11

Address:
Circa Reproductions, Graham Lee, General Delivery, Lamont, Alberta T0B 2R0.

Telephone: +1 403 895 2975

Type: Single-seat biplane replica, with fixed tail-dragger undercarriage.
Construction: Metal, steel tube and fabric.
Wing span: 21 ft 6 ins (6.55 m)
Length: 16 ft 4 ins (4.98 m)
Empty weight: 350 lb (159 kg)
Gross weight: 675 lb (306 kg)
Recommended engine: 46 hp (34.3 kW) Rotax
Maximum speed: 82 kts (94 mph) 151 km/h
Cruise speed: 70 kts (80 mph) 129 km/h
Stall speed: 23 kts (26 mph) 42 km/h
Take-off distance: 125 ft (38 m)
Climb rate: 850 ft (259 m) per minute
Range: 173 naut miles (200 miles) 322 km
Availability: Plans and kits.
Comments: 87% scale replica. Lighter microlight version for 40 hp (30 kW) Rotax available (Nieuport 11UL). Also 87% scale Nieuport 12.

Custom Flight Bright Star

Address:
Custom Flight Components Ltd, RR1, Perkinsfield, Ontario L0L 2J0.

Telephone: +1 705 526 9626
Facsimile: +1 705 526 2529

Type: Tandem 2-seat, high-wing monoplane, with fixed tailwheel or nosewheel undercarriage.
Construction: Steel tube, metal and fabric.
Wing span: 36 ft (11.97 m)
Length: 23 ft 6 ins (7.16 m)
Empty weight: 1,000 lb (454 kg)
Gross weight: 1,800 lb (816 kg)
Recommended engine: 108 hp (80.5 kW) Textron Lycoming (other options of 100-180 hp, 74.6-134 kW)

↑ Custom Flight Bright Star *(Geoffrey P. Jones)*

Maximum speed: 100 kts (115 mph) 185 km/h
Cruise speed: 87 kts (100 mph) 161 km/h
Stall speed: 31 kts (35 mph) 57 km/h
Take-off distance: 225 ft (69 m)
Climb rate: 1,000 ft (305 m) per minute
Availability: Kits.
Comments: Introduced in 1996 as a minimal Piper Super Cub representation, with spring steel undercarriage and no flaps.

Custom Flight North Star

Type: Tandem 2-seat, high-wing cabin monoplane based on the Piper Super Cub, with fixed tailwheel or float undercarriage.
Construction: Metal, steel tube and fabric.
Wing span: 36 ft 4 ins (11.07 m)
Length: 22 ft 6 ins (6.86 m)
Empty weight: 1,170 lb (531 kg)
Gross weight: 2,200 lb (998 kg)
Recommended engine: 150 hp (112 kW) Textron Lycoming
Maximum speed: 122 kts (140 mph) 225 km/h
Cruise speed: 100 kts (115 mph) 185 km/h
Stall speed: 30 kts (35 mph) 56 km/h
Take-off distance: 280 ft (86 m)
Climb rate: 1,100 ft (335 m) per minute
Range: 521 naut miles (600 miles) 965 km
Availability: Kits.
Comments: Piper PA-18 Super Cub lookalike, built with more modern techniques.

Elmwood Aviation Christavia Mk.1

Address:
R.B. Mason, RR4, Elmwood Drive, Belleville, Ontario K8N 4Z4.

Telephone: +1 613 967 1853

Type: Tandem 2-seat, strut-braced high-wing, cabin monoplane, with fixed tailwheel undercarriage.
Construction: Alloy tube and wood.
Wing span: 32 ft 6 ins (9.9 m)
Length: 20 ft 8 ins (6.3 m)
Empty weight: 745 lb (338 kg)
Gross weight: 1,300 lb (590 kg)
Recommended engine: 65 hp (48.5 kW) Teledyne Continental A65
Maximum speed: 104 kts (120 mph) 193 km/h
Cruise speed: 87 kts (100 mph) 161 km/h
Stall speed: 31 kts (35 mph) 57 km/h
Take-off distance: 350 ft (107 m)
Climb rate: 850 ft (259 m) per minute
Range: 304 naut miles (350 miles) 563 km
Availability: Plans and kits.
Comments: First flown 3 October 1981. Over 130 known to be flying. Several built for work in the mission field.

Elmwood Aviation Christavia Mk.4

Type: 4-seat, strut-braced high-wing, cabin monoplane, with fixed tailwheel undercarriage.
Construction: Alloy tube and wood.
Wing span: 35 ft 6 ins (10.82 m)
Length: 23 ft (7 m)
Empty weight: 1,100 lb (500 kg)
Gross weight: 2,150 lb (975 kg)
Recommended engine: 150 hp (112 kW) Textron Lycoming O-320
Maximum speed: 111 kts (128 mph) 206 km/h
Cruise speed: 102 kts (118 mph) 190 km/h
Stall speed: 34 kts (39 mph) 63 km/h
Take-off distance: 450 ft (137 m)
Climb rate: 800 ft (244 m) per minute
Range: 347 naut miles (400 miles) 643 km
Availability: Plans and kits.
Comments: 4-seat development of Christavia Mk.1. First flown 3 January 1986. For missionary work.

Falconar/Mignet HM.293

Address:
Falconar Air Engineering, 7739 81st Avenue, Edmonton, Alberta, T6C OV4.

Telephone: +1 403 465 2024
Facsimile: +1 403 465 2029

Type: Single-seat, tandem-wing homebuilt with open cockpit, with fixed tailwheel or tail-dragger undercarriage.
Construction: Wood and fabric.
Wing span: 20 ft (6.1 m)
Length: 13 ft (3.96 m)
Empty weight: 350 lb (159 kg)
Gross weight: 600 lb (272 kg)
Recommended engine: 60 hp (44.7 kW) Volkswagen
Maximum speed: 96 kts (110 mph) 177 km/h
Cruise speed: 78 kts (90 mph) 145 km/h
Stall speed: Does not stall.
Take-off distance: 150 ft (46 m)
Climb rate: 1,400 ft (427 m) per minute
Range: 260 naut miles (300 miles) 483 km
Availability: Plans and some kit components.
Comments: Larger version of the HM.290 single-seater. Plans for both redrawn from originals by Henri Mignet in the 1940s. Folding wings. See Grunberg/Mignet HM.293.

Falconar/Mignet HM.360

Type: Single-seat, tandem-wing, homebuilt version of the Pou-du-Ciel, with fixed tailwheel undercarriage.
Construction: Wood.
Wing span: 21 ft (6.4 m)
Length: 13 ft (3.96 m)
Empty weight: 390 lb (177 kg)
Gross weight: 700 lb (318 kg)
Recommended engine: 100 hp (74.6 kW) Teledyne Continental
Maximum speed: 109 kts (125 mph) 200 km/h
Cruise speed: 83 kts (95 mph) 153 km/h
Stall speed: Does not stall.
Take-off distance: 130 ft (40 m)
Climb rate: 1,500 ft (457 m) per minute
Range: 286 naut miles (330 miles) 530 km
Availability: Plans and some components.
Comments: Largest single-seat version of the Pou-du-Ciel. 2-seat development is the **HM.380**.

↑ **Falconar/Mignet HM.360 with a McCulloch engine and enclosed cockpit, built by Jack McWhorter in Florida** *(Geoffrey P. Jones)*

Falconar Cubmajor

Type: Tandem 2-seat, strut-braced and high-wing, cabin monoplane, with fixed tailwheel or -dragger undercarriage.
Construction: Wood.
Wing span: 35 ft (10.67 m)
Length: 23 ft 10 ins (7.26 m)
Empty weight: 900 lb (408 kg)
Gross weight: 1,400 lb (635 kg)
Recommended engine: Teledyne Continental C-85
Maximum speed: 100 kts (116 mph) 187 km/h
Cruise speed: 91 kts (105 mph) 169 km/h
Stall speed: 44 kts (50 mph) 81 km/h
Take-off distance: 250 ft (77 m)
Climb rate: 860 ft (262 m) per minute
Range: 239 naut miles (275 miles) 442 km
Availability: Plans and kit components.
Comments: Version of the Luton L.5 Major that dates from 1939. Several built in Britain from Phoenix-supplied plans.

Falconar Jodel F.9

Type: Single-seat, low-wing, open cockpit monoplane, with fixed tailwheel or tail-dragger undercarriage.
Construction: Wood.
Wing span: 23 ft (7.01 m)
Length: 17 ft 11 ins (5.46 m)
Empty weight: 402 lb (182 kg)
Gross weight: 660 lb (300 kg)
Recommended engine: 60 hp (44.7 kW) Volkswagen
Maximum speed: 122 kts (140 mph) 225 km/h
Cruise speed: 87 kts (100 mph) 161 km/h
Stall speed: 26 kts (30 mph) 49 km/h
Take-off distance: 320 ft (98 m)
Climb rate: 600 ft (183 m) per minute
Range: 365 naut miles (420 miles) 676 km
Availability: Plans and kit components.
Comments: Canadian version of the classic Jodel D.9 (see France). A more streamlined and larger-engined version is the **Falconar F.10**.

Falconar F.12A Cruiser

Type: Side-by-side 2-seat (optional third child seat), low-wing, cabin monoplane, with fixed tailwheel undercarriage.
Construction: Wood.
Wing span: 28 ft (8.53 m)
Length: 22 ft 6 ins (6.86 m)
Empty weight: 898 lb (407 kg)
Gross weight: 1,800 lb (816 kg)
Recommended engine: 150 hp (112 kW) Textron Lycoming O-320
Maximum speed: 161 kts (185 mph) 298 km/h
Cruise speed: 139 kts (160 mph) 257 km/h
Stall speed: 37 kts (42 mph) 68 km/h
Take-off distance: 300 ft (92 m)
Climb rate: 1,100 ft (335 m) per minute
Range: 486 naut miles (560 miles) 900 km
Availability: Plans and some kit components.
Comments: Design based on the Jodel D.11 (see France).

Falconar Golden Hawk ARV-1L (1996)

Type: Tandem 2-seat, high-wing canard type, with pusher engine and fixed nosewheel undercarriage.
Construction: Composites, metal and wood.
Wing span: 34 ft (10.36 m)
Length: 14 ft (4.27 m)
Empty weight: 500 lb (227 kg)
Gross weight: 890 lb (404 kg)
Recommended engine: 55 hp (41 kW) Hirth 2704
Maximum speed: 113 kts (130 mph) 209 km/h
Cruise speed: 87 kts (100 mph) 101 km/h
Stall speed: 35 kts (40 mph) 65 km/h
Take-off distance: 250 ft (77 m)
Climb rate: 1,000 ft (305 m) per minute
Range: 217 naut miles (250 miles) 402 km
Availability: Kits.

Freedom Lite SkyWatch SS-11

Address:
Freedom Lite Inc, Box 51, Walton, Ontario N0K 1Z0.
Telephone: +1 519 887 9966
Facsimile: +1 519 887 6465

Type: Tandem 2-seat, high-wing microlight, with pusher engine and fixed nosewheel undercarriage.
Construction: Steel tube, metal and fabric.
Wing span: 33 ft (10.06 m)
Length: 21 ft 6 ins (6.55 m)
Empty weight: 420 lb (190 kg)
Gross weight: 950 lb (431 kg)
Recommended engine: 50 hp (37.3 kW) Rotax 503
Maximum speed: 87 kts (100 mph) 161 km/h
Cruise speed: 61-78 kts (70-90 mph) 112-145 km/h
Stall speed: 25 kts (29 mph) 47 km/h
Take-off distance: 200 ft (61 m)
Climb rate: 700 ft (213 m) per minute
Range: 217 naut miles (250 miles) 402 km
Availability: Kits.
Comments: First flew Summer 1995. Accommodates large people. 9 sold in Canada. 300 hour assembly. Float option with Rotax 618 engine.

↑ **Freedom Lite SkyWatch SS-11** *(Geoffrey P. Jones)*

Murphy Aircraft Maverick

Address:
Murphy Aircraft Mfg. Ltd, Unit 1, 8155 Aitken Road, Chilliwack, British Columbia V2R 4H5.
Telephone: +1 604 792 5855
Facsimile: +1 604 792 7006
E-mail: mursales@murphyair.com

Type: Side-by-side 2-seat, high-wing, cabin microlight/homebuilt, with fixed tailwheel undercarriage.
Construction: Metal.
Wing span: 29 ft 6 ins (8.99 m) (standard wing)
Length: 20 ft 8 ins (6.3 m)
Empty weight: 395 lb (179 kg)
Gross weight: 950 lb (431 kg)
Recommended engine: 53 hp (39.5 kW) Rotax 503 (as for details) or 65 hp (48.5 kW) Rotax 582
Maximum speed: 104 kts (120 mph) 193 km/h
Cruise speed: 70 kts (80 mph) 129 km/h
Stall speed: 28 kts (32 mph) 52 km/h
Take-off distance: 150 ft (46 m)
Climb rate: over 600 ft (183 m) per minute
Range: 191 naut miles (220 miles) 354 km
Availability: Kits.
Comments: Introduced in 1993. Microlight category in some countries.

Murphy Aircraft Rebel and Rebel Elite

Details: Apply to Rebel, except under Comments.
Type: 3-seat, high-wing, STOL cabin monoplane, with fixed tailwheel, float or ski undercarriage.
Construction: Semi-monocoque alloy.
Wing span: 30 ft (9.14 m)
Length: 21 ft 6 ins (6.55 m)
Empty weight: 650-900 lb (295-408 kg)
Gross weight: 1,057-1,650 lb (479-748 kg)
Recommended engine: 80 hp (59.7 kW) Rotax 912 or other engines up to a 160 hp (119.3 kW) Textron Lycoming (as for details)
Maximum speed: 131 kts (151 mph) 243 km/h
Cruise speed: 104 kts (120 mph) 193 km/h
Stall speed: 35 kts (40 mph) 65 km/h
Take-off distance: 300 ft (92 m)
Climb rate: 1,200 ft (366 m) per minute
Range: 691 naut miles (796 miles) 1,281 km
Availability: Kits.
Comments: First flown in 1990. STOL bush aeroplane with engine options. **Rebel Elite** with tricycle undercarriage available from 1997.

↑ **Murphy Rebel** *(Geoffrey P. Jones)*

Murphy Aircraft Renegade II

Type: Tandem 2-seat, open cockpit microlight biplane, with fixed tailwheel undercarriage.
Construction: Sheet alloy, tubing, composites and wood.
Wing span: 21 ft 4 ins (6.50 m)
Length: 18 ft 6 ins (5.64 m)
Empty weight: 375-425 lb (170-193 kg)
Gross weight: 850 lb (385 kg)
Recommended engine: 53 hp (39.5 kW) Rotax 503
Maximum speed: 104 kts (120 mph) 193 km/h
Cruise speed: 61 kts (70 mph) 113 km/h
Stall speed: 32 kts (36 mph) 58 km/h
Take-off distance: 150 ft (46 m) (solo)
Climb rate: 700 ft (213 m) per minute
Range: 213 naut miles (245 miles) 394 km
Availability: Kits and plans.
Comments: First flown in May 1985. Lighter version of the Renegade Spirit, complying with Canadian microlight regulations.

Murphy Aircraft Renegade Spirit

Type: Tandem 2-seat, open cockpit biplane, with fixed tailwheel undercarriage.
Construction: Sheet alloy, tubing, composites and wood.
Wing span: 21 ft 4 ins (6.50 m)
Length: 18 ft 6 ins (5.64 m)
Empty weight: 460 lb (209 kg)
Gross weight: 950 lb (431 kg)
Recommended engine: 80 hp (59.7 kW) Rotax 912 (as for details given) or 64 hp (47.7 kW) Rotax 582
Maximum speed: 104 kts (120 mph) 193 km/h
Cruise speed: 74 kts (85 mph) 137 km/h
Stall speed: 32 kts (36 mph) 58 km/h
Take-off distance: 100 ft (31 m) solo
Climb rate: 900 ft (274 m) per minute
Range: 206 naut miles (237 miles) 381 km
Availability: Kits and plans.
Comments: First flown 6 May 1987. Darryl Murphy's most successful homebuilt to date, with an estimated 500 completed.

↑ **Murphy Renegade Spirit with radial-type cowling** *(Geoffrey P. Jones)*

Murphy Aircraft SR-2500 Super Rebel

Type: 4-seat, high-wing, cabin monoplane, with fixed tricycle undercarriage.
Construction: Metal.
Wing span: 36 ft (10.97 m)
Length: 24 ft (7.32 m)
Empty weight: 1,450 lb (658 kg)
Gross weight: 3,000 lb (1,361 kg)
Recommended engine: 250 hp (186 kW) Textron Lycoming IO-540 (options for O-320 and O-360).
Maximum speed: 139 kts (160 mph) 257 km/h
Cruise speed: 126 kts (145 mph) 233 km/h
Stall speed: 38 kts (43 mph) 70 km/h
Take-off distance: 600 ft (183 m)
Climb rate: 1,000 ft (305 m) per minute
Range: 538 naut miles (620 miles) 998 km
Availability: Kits.
Comments: 4-seat development of Rebel. First flew 1996. Over 100 ordered.

Norman Aviation Karatoo J-6

Address: Norman Aviation, CP 61032, Levis, Quebec G6V 8X3.
Telephone: +1 418 833 4337 **Facsimile:** +1 418 833 7057

Type: Side-by-side 2-seat, high-wing, cabin monoplane, with fixed tail-dragger undercarriage or floats.
Construction: Wood, alloy tube and fabric.
Wing span: 33 ft 8 ins (10.26 m)
Length: 19 ft (5.79 m)
Empty weight: 620 lb (281 kg)
Gross weight: 1,058 lb (480 kg)
Recommended engine: 71 or 90 hp (53 or 67 kW) Subaru
Maximum speed: 113 kts (130 mph) 210 km/h
Cruise speed: 78 kts (90 mph) 145 km/h
Stall speed: 33 kts (38 mph) 61 km/h
Take-off distance: 200 ft (61 m)
Climb rate: 500 ft (152 m) per minute
Range: 347 naut miles (400 miles) 643 km
Availability: Kits.
Comments: Modified version of Jesse Anglin's Karatoo.

Norman Aviation Nordic II

Type: Side-by-side 2-seat, high-wing, cabin monoplane, with fixed tailwheel undercarriage.
Construction: Alloy tube and fabric.
Wing span: 33 ft 8 ins (10.26 m)
Length: 19 ft (5.79 m)
Empty weight: 600 lb (272 kg)
Gross weight: 1,058 lb (480 kg)
Recommended engine: 71 hp (53 kW) Subaru EA 81
Maximum speed: 113 kts (130 mph) 209 km/h
Cruise speed: 70 kts (80 mph) 129 km/h
Stall speed: 31 kts (35 mph) 57 km/h
Take-off distance: 150 ft (46 m)
Climb rate: 600 ft (183 m) per minute
Range: 347 naut miles (400 miles) 643 km
Availability: Kits and plans.
Comments: Very similar to the Nordic VI, the ready-to-fly version. Over 400 Nordic aircraft now flying, including some in Bolivia and Australia.

Norman Aviation Nordic VI-912

Type: Side-by-side 2-seat, high-wing, cabin monoplane, with fixed tailwheel undercarriage.
Construction: Alloy tube, wood and fabric.
Wing span: 30 ft (9.14 m)
Length: 19 ft (5.79 m)
Empty weight: 620 lb (281 kg)
Gross weight: 1,058 lb (480 kg)
Recommended engine: 80 hp (59.6 kW) Rotax 912, or 71-100 hp (53-74.6 kW) Subaru
Maximum speed: 87 kts (100 mph) 161 km/h
Cruise speed: 78 kts (90 mph) 145 km/h
Stall speed: 33 kts (38 mph) 61 km/h
Take-off distance: 200 ft (61 m)
Climb rate: 600 ft (183 m) per minute
Range: 347 naut miles (400 miles) 644 km
Availability: Kits.
Comments: Latest design, originally only offered ready assembled. 422 Norman kits and completed aircraft sold.

↑ **Norman Aviation Nordic VI-912**

Norman Aviation Nordic VII

Type: Single-seat, high-wing, cabin monoplane, with fixed tailwheel undercarriage.
Construction: Alloy tube and fabric.
Wing span: 30 ft (9.14 m)
Length: 16 ft 6 ins (5.03 m)
Empty weight: 270 lb (122 kg)
Gross weight: 800 lb (363 kg)
Recommended engine: 65 hp (48.5 kW) Rotax 582
Maximum speed: 91 kts (105 mph) 169 km/h
Cruise speed: 78 kts (90 mph) 145 km/h
Take-off distance: 70 ft (22 m)
Climb rate: 1,600 ft (487 m) per minute
Range: 260 naut miles (300 miles) 482 km
Availability: Kits.
Comments: Norman Aviation's first single-seater.

Paxman's Aerocraft Viper

Address: Paxman's Northern Lite, PO Box 1155, Glenwood, Alberta T0K 2R0.
Telephone: +1 403 626 3490 **Facsimile:** +1 403 626 3490

Type: Side-by-side 2-seat, low-wing, cabin monoplane, with fixed tail-dragger undercarriage.
Construction: Wood and fabric.
Wing span: 27 ft (8.23 m)
Length: 20 ft 6 ins (6.25 m)
Empty weight: 585 lb (265 kg)
Gross weight: 1,050 lb (476 kg)
Recommended engine: 100 hp (74.6 kW) Suzuki-Turbo
Maximum speed: 109 kts (125 mph) 200 km/h
Cruise speed: 96 kts (110 mph) 177 km/h
Stall speed: 42 kts (48 mph) 78 km/h
Take-off distance: 300 ft (92 m)
Climb rate: 1,500 ft (457 m) per minute
Range: 508 naut miles (585 miles) 941 km
Availability: Plans and kits.
Comments: Prototype first flew in 1994.

Pegazaire-100 STOL

Address: Pegase Aero Enr, 173 Rg3 Worktele, Ferme-Neuve, Quebec J0W 1C0.
Telephone & Facsimile: +1 819 587 3218

Type: Side-by-side 2-seat, STOL high-wing, cabin monoplane, with fixed tail-dragger undercarriage.
Construction: Steel tube, aluminium and fabric.
Wing span: 29 ft 6 ins (9 m)
Length: 22 ft 6 ins (6.86 m)
Empty weight: 795 lb (360 kg)
Gross weight: 1,350 lb (612 kg)
Recommended engine: 100 hp (74.6 kW) CAM-100 (also Rotax 912 or Teledyne Continental A65)
Maximum speed: 106 kts (122 mph) 196 km/h
Cruise speed: 91 kts (105 mph) 169 km/h
Stall speed: 16 kts (18 mph) 29 km/h
Climb rate: 1,350 ft (411 m) per minute
Range: 382 naut miles (440 miles) 708 km
Availability: Kits and plans.
Comments: Wide cabin and leading-edge slats. Different engine/airframe combinations meet both Canadian ultralight and homebuilt requirements.

↑ **Pegazaire-100 STOL with CAM-100 engine** *(Geoffrey P. Jones)*

Replica Plans SE.5A

Address: Replica Plans, PO Box 346, Yarrow, British Colombia V0X 2A0.
Telephone: +1 604 823 6428 **Facsimile:** +1 604 532 9822

Type: 85% replica World War 1 biplane, with fixed tailwheel or tail-dragger undercarriage.
Construction: Wood and fabric.
Wing span: 23 ft 4 ins (7.11 m)
Length: 18 ft 2 ins (5.54 m)
Empty weight: 750 lb (340 kg)
Gross weight: 1,150 lb (522 kg)
Recommended engine: Teledyne Continental C85
Maximum speed: 96 kts (110 mph) 177 km/h
Cruise speed: 74 kts (85 mph) 137 km/h
Stall speed: 31 kts (35 mph) 57 km/h
Take-off distance: 400 ft (122 m)
Climb rate: 600 ft (183 m) per minute
Availability: Plans.
Comments: First flown in the 1970s. Also suitable for engines of 65-115 hp (48.5-85.75 kW).

Streamline Welding 10-200 Ultimate Competitor and 10-300 Ultimate Winner

Address: Streamline Welding, 296 Homewood Avenue, Hamilton, Ontario L8P 2M9.
Telephone & Facsimile: +1 905 526 9990

Details: For Ultimate Competitor, except under Comments.
Type: Single-seat, competition/aerobatic biplane, with fixed tailwheel undercarriage.
Construction: Steel tube, alloy and wood.
Wing span: 16 ft (4.88 m)
Length: 17 ft 4 ins (5.28 m)
Empty weight: 925 lb (420 kg)
Gross weight: 1,350 lb (612 kg)
Recommended engine: Textron Lycoming IO-360
Maximum speed: 191 kts (220 mph) 354 km/h
Cruise speed: 148 kts (170 mph) 273 km/h
Stall speed: 52 kts (60 mph) 97 km/h
Take-off distance: 450 ft (137 m)
Climb rate: 2,000 ft (610 m) per minute
Range: 434 naut miles (500 miles) 804 km
Availability: Kits.
Comments: Basic Ultimate 10 Dash 100 first flew on 6 October 1985 with a 100 hp (74.6 kW) Teledyne Continental. Other version is the 10-300 Ultimate Winner for engines of up to 350 hp (261 kW).

↑ **Streamline Welding 10-200 Ultimate Competitor** *(Geoffrey P. Jones)*

Streamline Welding 20-300 Ultimate Companion

Type: Tandem 2-seat, competition/aerobatic biplane, with fixed tailwheel undercarriage.
Construction: Steel tube, alloy and wood.
Wing span: 19 ft 6 ins (5.94 m)
Length: 21 ft (6.4 m)
Empty weight: 1,200 lb (544 kg)
Gross weight: 2,000 lb (907 kg)
Recommended engine: 300 or 350 hp (224 or 261 kW) Textron Lycoming
Maximum speed: 217 kts (250 mph) 402 km/h
Cruise speed: 165 kts (190 mph) 306 km/h
Stall speed: 46 kts (53 mph) 86 km/h
Take-off distance: 600 ft (183 m)
Climb rate: 3,000 ft (914 m) per minute
Range: 434 naut miles (500 miles) 804 km
Availability: Kits.
Comments: Available as 20-300E (exhibition) and 20-300T (Trainer).

Ultravia Pelican Club S

Address:
Ultravia Aero Inc, 300-D Airport Road, Mascouche, Quebec J7K 3C1.
Telephone: +1 514 953 1491
Facsimile: +1 514 966 6299

Type: Side-by-side 2-seat, high-wing, cabin monoplane, with fixed tailwheel or nosewheel undercarriage.
Construction: Composites and sheet alloy.
Wing span: 34 ft 5 ins (10.49 m)
Length: 19 ft 6 ins (5.94 m)
Empty weight: 500 lb (227 kg)
Gross weight: 1,000 lb (453 kg)
Recommended engine: 64.4 hp (48 kW) Rotax 582 for the S and 80 hp (59.6 kW) Rotax 912 for the GS model (see Comments).
Maximum speed: 100 kts (115 mph) 185 km/h
Cruise speed: 87 kts (100 mph) 161 km/h
Stall speed: 29 kts (33 mph) 53 km/h
Take-off distance: 300 ft (92 m)
Climb rate: 800 ft (244 m) per minute
Range: 434 naut miles (500 miles) 804 km
Availability: Kits.
Comments: First flown in May 1982. One of 5 versions. Similar Pelican Club VS with 52 hp (38.8 kW) Rotax 503 has gross weight of 950 lb (431 kg), and Pelican Club GS has 1,200 lb (544 kg) gross weight.

Ultravia Pelican Club PL-912 and PL-914

Type: Side-by-side 2-seat, high-wing cabin monoplane, with fixed nosewheel undercarriage. Tailwheel and float options.
Construction: Composites and sheet alloy.
Details: PL-912, except where stated.
Wing span: 29 ft 6 ins (8.99 m)
Length: 19 ft 6 ins (5.94 m)
Empty weight: 700 lb (318 kg)
Gross weight: 1,250 lb (567 kg)
Recommended engine: 80 hp (59.6 kW) Rotax 912 for PL-912 model, and 100 hp (74.6 kW) Rotax 914 for new PL-914
Maximum speed: 117 kts (135 mph) 217 km/h
Cruise speed: 107 kts (123 mph) 198 km/h, at 60% power and 6,000 ft (1,830 m)
Stall speed: 38 kts (43 mph) 70 km/h, with full flaps
Take-off distance: 450 ft (137 m)
Climb rate: 950 ft (290 m) per minute
Range: 521 naut miles (600 miles) 965 km
Availability: Kits.
Comments: Nosewheel undercarriage version suitable for pilot training. PL-914 is faster but heavier.

↑ **Ultravia Pelican Club PL-914 with fixed nosewheel undercarriage** *(Geoffrey P. Jones)*

Western Aircraft PGK-1 Hirondelle

Address:
Western Aircraft Supplies, 623 Markerville Road North East, Calgary, Alberta T2E 5X1.
Telephone: +1 403 275 3513
Facsimile: +1 403 276 3087

Type: Side-by-side 2-seat, low-wing, cabin monoplane, with fixed tail-dragger undercarriage.
Construction: Wood and fabric.
Wing span: 26 ft (7.92 m)
Length: 20 ft 8 ins (6.3 m)
Empty weight: 944 lb (428 kg)
Gross weight: 1,475 lb (700 kg)
Recommended engine: 115 hp (85.75 kW) Textron Lycoming
Maximum speed: 123 kts (142 mph) 229 km/h
Cruise speed: 117 kts (135 mph) 217 km/h
Stall speed: 48 kts (55 mph) 89 km/h
Take-off distance: 750 ft (230 m)
Climb rate: 1,000 ft (305 m) per minute
Range: 521 naut miles (600 miles) 965 km
Availability: Plans and some components.
Comments: First flown on 27 June 1976. Examples mainly in North America but first European example was flown in France in 1994.

↑ **PGK-1 Hirondelle (Swallow) built by Yves Denoual at Avranches, France** *(Geoffrey P. Jones)*

Zenair Zenith CH-200

Address:
Zenair Ltd, Huronia Airport, Midland, Ontario L4R 4K8 (or USA: Zenith Aircraft Co, Box 650, Mexico, MO 65265-0650).
Telephone: +1 705 526 2871 (USA: +1 573 581 9000)
Facsimile: +1 705 526 8022 (USA: +1 573 581 0011)

Type: Side-by-side 2-seat, low-wing, cabin monoplane, with fixed nosewheel or tailwheel undercarriage.
Construction: Metal.
Wing span: 23 ft (7 m)
Length: 19 ft 8 ins (5.99 m)
Empty weight: 970 lb (440 kg)
Gross weight: 1,500 lb (680 kg)
Recommended engine: 100-150 hp (74.6-112 kW) Textron Lycoming
Maximum speed: 145 kts (167 mph) 269 km/h
Cruise speed: 132 kts (152 mph) 245 km/h
Stall speed: 47 kts (54 mph) 87 km/h
Take-off distance: 600 ft (183 m)
Climb rate: 1,700 ft (518 m) per minute
Range: 347 naut miles (400 miles) 643 km
Availability: Plans.
Comments: Prototype designed by Chris Heintz and first flown on 22 March 1970. Hundreds flying worldwide. Other variants include the CH-250 long-range version, the single-seat CH-100, and the Acro CH-150 and CH-180 aerobatic versions.

↑ **Zenair Zenith CH-200** *(Geoffrey P. Jones)*

Zenair Zenith CH-300 (Tri-Z)

Type: 3/4-seat, low-wing, cabin monoplane, with fixed nosewheel undercarriage.
Construction: Metal.
Wing span: 26 ft 7 ins (8.1 m)
Length: 22 ft 6 ins (6.86 m)
Empty weight: 1,140 lb (517 kg)
Gross weight: 1,850 lb (859 kg)
Recommended engine: 125-180 hp (93.2-134 kW) Textron Lycoming
Maximum speed: 130 kts (150 mph) 241 km/h
Cruise speed: 109 kts (125 mph) 201 km/h
Stall speed: 45 kts (51 mph) 82 km/h
Take-off distance: 650 ft (198 m)
Climb rate: 800 ft (244 m) per minute
Range: 521 naut miles (600 miles) 965 km
Availability: Plans and custom ordered kits. Commercially built version is the Zenair CH-2000.

Chile

Details of the **ENAER Ñamcu** can be found in the General Aviation section. Now also built in the Netherlands as the EuroENAER Eaglet.

China

Beijing University Mifeng-11

Address:
Beijing University of Aeronautics and Astronautics, PO Box 85, 37 Xue Yuan Road, Haidian District, Beijing 100083.

Type: 2/3-seat, high-wing, utility microlight, with pusher engine and fixed nosewheel undercarriage.
Construction: Steel tube, metal and composites.
Wing span: 28 ft 6 ins (8.69 m)
Length: 19 ft 10 ins (6.05 m)
Empty weight: 397 lb (180 kg)
Recommended engine: 62 hp (46.2 kW) Rotax 532
Maximum speed: 90 kts (103 mph) 166 km/h
Range: 474 naut miles (546 miles) 878 km with auxiliary tank.
Availability: not known.
Comments: First flown in May 1991. The Mifeng-11 (Bee-11) is one of a succession of Mifeng microlights by Beijing University that commenced in the early 1980s.

HAMC HFY-5

Details of this 2-seat "propulsive wing" microlight can be found in the 1996-97 edition of *WA&SD*.

Colombia

Agrocopteros MXP-740

Address:
Agrocopteros Ltda, Apartado Aereo 1789, Calle 20 N8A-18, Cali.
Telephone: +57 3 825110 and 833519
Facsimile: +57 3 842002

Type: Side-by-side 2-seat, high-wing cabin monoplane, with fixed nosewheel undercarriage.
Construction: Metal.
Wing span: 29 ft 6 ins (9 m)
Length: 21 ft 3 ins (6.5 m)
Empty weight: 616 lb (280 kg)
Gross weight: 1,200 lb (544 kg)
Recommended engine: 80 hp (59.6 kW) Rotax 912
Maximum speed: 83 kts (95 mph) 153 km/h
Cruise speed: 74 kts (85 mph) 137 km/h
Stall speed: 31 kts (35 mph) 57 km/h
Take-off distance: 100 ft (31 m)
Climb rate: 1,000 ft (305 m) per minute
Range: 369 naut miles (425 miles) 684 km
Availability: Kits and complete aircraft.
Comments: Version of the Zenair CH-701 STOL. Also available is the **MXP-640** (a version of the Zenair CH-601 Zodiac). Also produced in Slovakia as the **Ekoflug MXP-740** (Address: Ekoflug sro, PO Box G-19, 043 49 Kosice 1).

Czech Republic

Bohemia Air Bohem 3

Address:
Bohemia Air sro, Podhorska 7, 466 01 Jablonec nad Nisou.

Type: Side-by-side 2-seat, low-wing, cabin microlight, with folding wings and fixed nosewheel undercarriage.
Construction: Steel tube, metal and fabric.
Wing span: 29 ft 6 ins (9 m)
Length: 18 ft 9 ins (5.72 m)
Empty weight: 595 lb (270 kg)
Gross weight: 992 lb (450 kg)
Recommended engine: 78 hp (58 kW) Verner SVS140 or 80 hp (59.6 kW) Rotax 912
Maximum speed: 124 kts (143 mph) 230 km/h
Cruise speed: 97 kts (112 mph) 180 km/h
Stall speed: 34 kts (39 mph) 63 km/h, flaps down
Range: 485 naut miles (559 miles) 900 km
Availability: Kits and complete aircraft.
Comments: Steerable nosewheel. Undercarriage suited for operation from rough or smooth landing strips.

↑ Bohemia Air Bohem 3

CRO Metallica LG2

Address:
CRO holding spol sro, Louky 351, budova IMC, 762 51 Zlin.
Telephone: +420 67 7631 333
Facsimile: +420 67 7631 356
E-mail: cross@zl.inext.cz

Type: Tandem 2-seat, mid-wing microlight, with pusher engine and fixed nosewheel undercarriage. Larger wing span motorglider version is also available.
Construction: Metal.
Wing span: 30 ft 10 ins (9.4 m), or 39 ft 4 ins (12 m) for motorglider
Length: 21 ft 8 ins (6.6 m)
Gross weight: 992 lb (450 kg)
Recommended engine: Hirth, Rotax or Skoda
Cruise speed: 76 kts (87 mph) 140 km/h, or 54 kts (62 mph) 100 km/h for motorglider
Stall speed: 34 kts (39 mph) 63 km/h, or 32.5 kts (37.5 mph) 60 km/h for motorglider
Climb rate: 690 ft (210 m) per minute
Range: 216 naut miles (248 miles) 400 km
Availability: Assembled.
Comments: Riveted duralumin sheet construction. Good visibility.

↑ Prototype CRO Metallica LG2

Fantasy Air Cora

Address:
Fantasy Air, Kollarova 511, 397 01 Pisek.
Telephone: +420 362 210246
Facsimile: +420 362 214457

Type: Side-by-side 2-seat, semi-enclosed, high-wing microlight/homebuilt, with fixed nosewheel undercarriage.
Construction: Composites and wood.
Wing span: 35 ft 5 ins (10.8 m)
Length: 24 ft 7 ins (7.5 m)
Empty weight: 441 lb (200 kg)
Gross weight: 926 lb (420 kg)
Recommended engine: 50 hp (37 kW) Rotax 503
Maximum speed: 89 kts (103 mph) 165 km/h
Cruise speed: 43-84 kts (50-96 mph) 80-155 km/h
Stall speed: 25 kts (28 mph) 45 km/h
Take-off distance: 164 ft (50 m)
Climb rate: 590 ft (180 m) per minute
Range: 216 naut miles (248 miles) 400 km
Availability: Kits.
Comments: Originally the Jora, now built by Fantasy Air. Said to have good low-speed handling.

↑ Fantasy Air Cora

Inteco VM-23 Variant

Address:
Inteco, Velkomoravska 1469, Stare Mesto, CS-686 03 Uherske Hrasdiste.

Type: 2+2-seat, high-wing, cabin monoplane, with fixed tailwheel undercarriage.
Construction: Steel tube, metal and fabric.
Wing span: 35 ft 5 ins (10.8 m)
Length: 24 ft 5 ins (7.45 m)
Empty weight: 992 lb (450 kg)
Gross weight: 1,984 lb (900 kg)
Recommended engine: 140 hp (104.4 kW) LOM M.332
Maximum speed: 108 kts (124 mph) 200 km/h
Cruise speed: 86 kts (99 mph) 160 km/h
Take-off distance: 590 ft (180 m)
Climb rate: 728 ft (222 m) per minute
Range: 400 naut miles (460 miles) 740 km
Availability: Prototype only to date - possible commercial production.
Comments: By glider designer and manufacturer Jiri Valny. Inteco hopes to obtain FAR 23 certification.

Interplane Skyboy

Address:
Interplane sro, Airport Zbraslavice, 285 21 Zbraslavice.
Telephone: +420 327 4892
Facsimile: +420 327 3550

Type: Side-by-side 2-seat, high-wing microlight, with pusher engine and fixed nosewheel undercarriage.
Construction: Composites and fabric.
Wing span: 34 ft 5 ins (10.5 m)
Length: 20 ft 11 ins (6.37 m)
Empty weight: 447 lb (203 kg)
Gross weight: 992 lb (450 kg)
Recommended engine: 50 hp (37.3 kW) Rotax
Never-exceed speed (V_{NE}): 89 kts (102 mph) 165 km/h
Cruise speed: 65 kts (75 mph) 120 km/h
Stall speed: 30 kts (34 mph) 55 km/h
Take-off distance: 263 ft (80 m)
Availability: Kits and complete aircraft.
Comments: Wings can be folded in 15 minutes by 2 persons.

↑ Interplane Skyboy *(Geoffrey P. Jones)*

TL Ultralight TL-32 Typhoon and TL-96 Star

Address:
Dobrovského 734, 500 02 Hradec Králové.
Telephone: +420 49 613378

Type: Side-by-side 2-seat, high-wing microlight/homebuilt, with fixed nosewheel undercarriage.
Construction: Steel tube and composites.
Wing span: 35 ft 1 ins (10.7 m)
Length:19 ft 4 ins (5.9 m)
Empty weight: 430 lb (195 kg)
Gross weight: 882 lb (400 kg)
Recommended engine: 40 hp (30 kW) Rotax 447
Maximum speed: 59 kts (68 mph) 110 km/h
Cruise speed: 49 kts (56 mph) 90 km/h
Stall speed: 25 kts (28 mph) 45 km/h
Take-off distance: 164 ft (50 m)
Climb rate: 400 ft (122 m) per minute (gross)
Range: 189 naut miles (217 miles) 350 km
Availability: Kits or assembled.
Comments: Above details for Typhoon. 2-seat low-wing Star has Rotax 912 and 992 lb (450 kg) MTOW.

TL Ultralight TL-132 and TL-232 Condor

Type: Side-by-side 2-seat, high-wing microlight/homebuilt, with fixed tailwheel undercarriage. TL-232 has tandem seats.
Construction: Steel tube and fabric.
Wing span: 34 ft 9 ins (10.6 m)
Length: 16 ft 11 ins (5.16 m)
Recommended engine: 45.6 hp (34 kW) Rotax 503 for microlight version (option of Rotax 912 or Hirth F30).
Maximum speed: 97 kts (112 mph) 180 km/h
Cruise speed: 73 kts (84 mph) 135 km/h
Stall speed: 30 kts (34 mph) 55 km/h
Climb rate: 395 ft (120 m) per minute
Availability: Kits or assembled.
Comments: Also **TL-532 Fresh** 2-seater (flown 1995) has Rotax 582.

Kappa KP-2U Sova (Owl)

Address:
Kappa spol sro, Brtnicka 21, CZ-586 01 Jihlava.
Telephone: +420 66 28121
Facsimile: +420 66 28122

Type: Side-by-side 2-seat, low-wing microlight, with retractable nosewheel undercarriage.
Construction: Metal, with special riveting technology.
Wing span: 32 ft 6 ins (9.9 m)
Length: 23 ft 7 ins (7.2 m)
Empty weight: 573 lb (260 kg)
Gross weight: 992 lb (450 kg)
Recommended engine: 73.8 hp (55 kW) Rotax 618 UL (optional Rotax 912)
Maximum speed: 129 kts (149 mph) 240 km/h
Cruise speed: 100 kts (115 mph) 185 km/h
Stall speed: 26 kts (30 mph) 48 km/h
Climb rate: 1,280 ft (390 m) per minute
Range: 539 naut miles (621 miles) 1,000 km
Availability: Complete aircraft.
Comments: Fowler flaps, electrically retractable undercarriage and special winglets.

↑ Prototype Kappa KP-2U Sova

Let Mont Tulak

Address:
Let Mont sro, Nr226, G7 788 13 Vikyiovice.
Telephone: +420 649 216043 or 214081
Facsimile: +420 649 214085 or 213877

Type: Side-by-side 2-seat, high-wing, cabin monoplane, with fixed tailwheel undercarriage.
Construction: Steel tube and fabric.
Wing span: 30 ft 10 ins (9.4 m)
Length: 19 ft 11 ins (6.08 m)
Empty weight: 551 lb (250 kg)
Gross weight: 992 lb (450 kg)
Recommended engine: 45.6 hp (34 kW) Rotax 503
Maximum speed: 86 kts (99 mph) 160 km/h
Cruise speed: 65 kts (75 mph) 120 km/h
Stall speed: 34 kts (39 mph) 62 km/h
Take-off distance: 213 ft (65 m)
Climb rate: 490 ft (150 m) per minute
Availability: Complete aircraft and kits.
Comments: Designed by O. Klier H. Podesva. Similar design, the **Piper UL**, is also available.

Letov LK-2 Sluka

Address:
Letov a.s., Division LETOV AIR, Beranovych 65, 199 02 Prague 9 - Letnany.
Telephone: +420 2 6611 3051
Facsimile: +420 2 858 7175

Type: Single-seat, open cockpit, high-wing microlight, with fixed nosewheel undercarriage.
Construction: Aluminium and steel tube, composites and fabric.
Wing span: 30 ft 2 ins (9.2 m)
Length:16 ft 10 ins (5.12 m)
Empty weight: 331 lb (150 kg)
Gross weight: 551 lb (250 kg)
Recommended engine: 41.6 hp (31 kW) Rotax 447
Maximum speed: 54 kts (62 mph) 100 km/h
Cruise speed: 38 kts (43 mph) 70 km/h
Stall speed: 24 kts (27 mph) 43 km/h
Take-off distance: 164 ft (50 m)
Climb rate: 690 ft (210 m) per minute
Range: 129 naut miles (149 miles) 240 km
Availability: Kits or assembled.
Comments: Prototype first flew in February 1991.

Letov LK-3 Nova

Type: Side-by-side 2-seat, semi-enclosed, high-wing microlight/homebuilt, with fixed nosewheel undercarriage.
Construction: Alloy and steel tube, composites and fabric.
Wing span: 34 ft 5 ins (10.5 m)
Length: 19 ft 3 ins (5.9 m)
Empty weight: 441 lb (200 kg)
Gross weight: 860 lb (390 kg)
Recommended engine: 64.4 hp (48 kW) Rotax 582
Maximum speed: 59 kts (68 mph) 110 km/h
Cruise speed: 43 kts (50 mph) 80 km/h
Stall speed: 26 kts (30 mph) 48 km/h
Take-off distance: 197 ft (60 m)
Climb rate: 787 ft (240 m) per minute
Range: 94 naut miles (108 miles) 175 km
Availability: Kits and assembled.
Comments: Prototype first flew in 1993.

Letov ST-4 Aztek

Type: Side-by-side 2-seat, semi-enclosed cockpit microlight, with fixed nosewheel undercarriage and folding wings.
Construction: Alloy and steel tube, composites and fabric.
Wing span: 34 ft 1 ins (10.4 m)
Length: 19 ft 4 ins (5.9 m)
Empty weight: 485 lb (220 kg)
Gross weight: 992 lb (450 kg)
Recommended engine: 64.4 hp (48 kW) Rotax 582 (or Rotax 503, Rotax 912 or Walter M202)
Maximum speed: 70 kts (81 mph) 130 km/h
Cruise speed: 54 kts (62 mph) 100 km/h
Stall speed: 27 kts (30 mph) 49 km/h
Take-off distance: 197 ft (60 m)
Climb rate: 690 ft (210 m) per minute
Availability: Kits and assembled.
Comments: 1996 model.

Motorlet Praha M-7

Address:
J. Vycital, Motorlet Praha, clen Aeroklubu Havlickuv Brod, Soucasne.

Type: Side-by-side 2-seat, high-wing, microlight/homebuilt, with fixed nosewheel undercarriage.
Construction: Metal and composites.
Recommended engine: 64.4 hp (48 kW) Walter M202
Comments: First flown in September 1994. No other information available.

OK Fly Lesus

Address:
OK Fly s.r.o., PO Box 60, 261 05 Pribram 5.
Telephone & Facsimile: +420 42 306 27 229

Type: Side-by-side 2-seat, high-wing monoplane, with fixed nosewheel undercarriage.
Construction: Composites.
Wing span: 32 ft 2 ins (9.8 m)
Length: 20 ft 4 ins (6.2 m)
Empty weight: 617 lb (280 kg)
Gross weight: 992 lb (450 kg)
Recommended engine: 50 hp (37 kW) Rotax 503 (optional other Rotax and Hirth engines)
Maximum speed: 108 kts (124 mph) 200 km/h
Cruise speed: 86 kts (99 mph) 160 km/h
Stall speed: 34 kts (39 mph) 63 km/h
Take-off distance: 590 ft (180 m)
Climb rate: 590 ft (180 m) per minute
Range: 324 naut miles (373 miles) 600 km
Availability: Commercial production planned.
Comments: OK Fly has specialized in hang-glider skin and wind-surf sail production for 15 years.

TIB Caprice 21

Address:
TIB, Zibohlavy u Kolina, TCH-28000 Kolin.
Telephone: +420 321 20 459
Facsimile: +420 321 20 458

Type: Tandem 2-seat, high-wing monoplane, with pusher engine and fixed nosewheel undercarriage.
Construction: Alloy, steel tube and fabric.
Wing span: 36 ft 3 ins (11.05 m)
Empty weight: 386 lb (175 kg)
Gross weight: 992 lb (450 kg)
Recommended engine: 66 hp (49 kW) Arrow GP 530 AC
Maximum speed: 70 kts (81 mph) 130 km/h
Cruise speed: 51 kts (59 mph) 95 km/h
Stall speed: 30 kts (34 mph) 55 km/h
Climb rate: 690 ft (210 m) per minute
Availability: Complete aircraft.
Comments: Promoted as a training aircraft with rugged construction and safe handling.

↑ TIB Caprice 21 *(Geoffrey P. Jones)*

Urban UFM 11 and UFM 13 Lambáda

Address:
Urban Aviation sro, Libchavy (German agent: Aircraft Trading CS, c/o Cestmir Sebesta, Am Moselstausee 21, D-56858 St Aldegund).
Telephone: (Germany: +49 6542 900076)
Facsimile: (Germany: +49 6542 900077)

Details: UFM 13, except under Comments.
Type: Side-by-side 2-seat, mid-wing, cabin monoplane, with fixed nosewheel undercarriage.
Construction: Composites.
Wing span: 42 ft 8 ins (13 m)
Length: 21 ft 8 ins (6.6 m)
Gross weight: 992 lb (450 kg)
Recommended engine: 41.6 hp (31 kW) Rotax 447 or BMW 800
Maximum speed: 108 kts (124 mph) 200 km/h
Cruise speed: 92 kts (106 mph) 170 km/h
Stall speed: 35 kts (41 mph) 65 km/h
Climb rate: 217 ft (66 m) per minute
Availability: Complete aircraft and kits.
Comments: Designed by Pavel Urban and first flown in 1996. Easily detachable wings. UFM 11 model also available, with 38 ft 9 ins (11.8 m) wings and faster cruise.

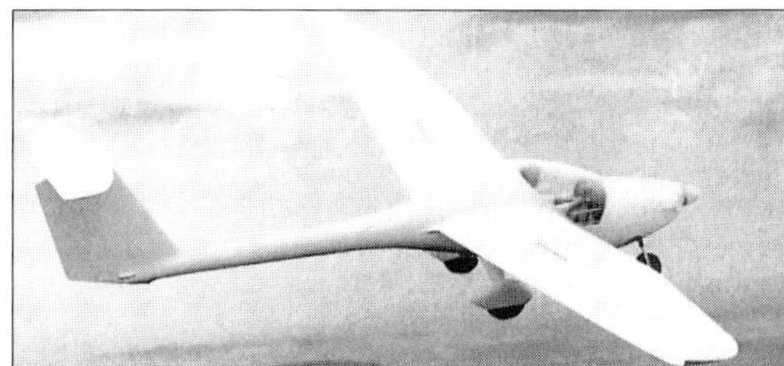
↑ Urban UFM 13 Lambáda

France

Adam RA.14 Loisirs/Maranda

Address:
Designed by Roger Adam in France, but marketed by Falconar Air Engineering in Canada (which see).

Type: 2/3-seat, high-wing, cabin monoplane, with fixed tail-dragger undercarriage.
Construction: Wood.
Wing span: 31 ft 9 ins (9.68 m)
Length: 22 ft (6.71 m)
Empty weight: 1,100 lb (500 kg)
Gross weight: 1,850 lb (840 kg)
Recommended engine: 150 hp (112 kW) Textron Lycoming O-320
Maximum speed: 113 kts (130 mph) 200 km/h
Cruise speed: 100 kts (115 mph) 185 km/h
Stall speed: 39 kts (45 mph) 73 km/h
Take-off distance: 100 ft (30 m)
Climb rate: 1,300 ft (395 m) per minute
Availability: Kits and plans.

Air Creation SX GTE582 S Clipper

Address:
Air Creation, Aerodrome de Lanas, 07200 Aubenas.

Telephone: +33 4 75 93 66 66
Facsimile: +33 4 75 35 04 00

Type: Tandem 2-seat, microlight with Rogallo wing and trike.
Construction: Alloy tube and fabric.
Wing span: 33 ft 2 ins (10.1 m)
Length: 9 ft 10 ins (3.0 m)
Empty weight: 287 lb (130 kg)
Gross weight: 882 lb (400 kg)
Recommended engine: 64.4 hp (48 kW) Rotax 582
Maximum speed: 73 kts (84 mph) 136 km/h
Cruise speed: 48 kts (55 mph) 89 km/h
Minimum speed: 29 kts (33 mph) 53 km/h
Climb rate: 1,045 ft (318 m) per minute
Range: 162 naut miles (186 miles) 300 km
Availability: Commercially built or as kits.
Comments: 1 of 4 Clipper single- and tandem-seat microlights, some with optional fuselage pods. Over 1,000 of all types sold.

Air Creation Racer and Twin

Type: Single-seat and tandem 2-seat (respectively), microlights with Rogallo-wings and trikes.
Details: Single-seat XP Racer 503.
Construction: Alloy tube and fabric.
Wing span: 30 ft 2 ins (9.2 m)
Empty weight: 170 lb (77 kg)
Gross weight: 567 lb (257 kg)
Recommended engine: 49.6 hp (37 kW) Rotax 503
Maximum speed: 73 kts (84 mph) 135 km/h
Cruise speed: 54 kts (62 mph) 100 km/h
Minimum speed: 25 kts (28 mph) 45 km/h
Climb rate: 1,380 ft (420 m) per minute
Availability: Commercially built or as kits.
Comments: 1 of 6 Racer and Twin models.

↑ **Air Creation XP Racer 503**

Air Est Goeland

Address:
Air Est Services, 37 rue Saint-Michel, 57155 Marly.

Telephone: +33 3 87 50 39 66
Facsimile: +33 3 87 63 91 48

Type: Single-seat, high-wing microlight/motorglider, with pusher engine and fixed nosewheel undercarriage.
Construction: Wood and composites.
Wing span: 49 ft 2 ins (15 m)
Length: 20 ft 2 ins (6.15 m)
Empty weight: 410 lb (186 kg)
Gross weight: 661 lb (300 kg)
Recommended engine: 24 hp (17.9 kW) König SC.430
Maximum speed: 70 kts (81 mph) 130 km/h
Cruise speed: 59 kts (68 mph) 110 km/h
Stall speed: 30 kts (34 mph) 55 km/h
Availability: Kits.
Comments: Designed by Robert Clave.

Ameur Aviation Balbuzard II

Address:
Ameur Aviation Technologie, Lotissement Pasqualini, Baleone, 20167 Sarrola Carcopino.

Telephone: +33 4 95 20 77 14
Facsimile: +33 4 95 20 76 21

Type: Side-by-side 2-seat, cabin monoplane, with pusher engine, V-tail and retractable nosewheel undercarriage.
Construction: Composites.
Wing span: 25 ft 5 ins (7.74 m)
Length: 17 ft 7 ins (5.35 m)
Empty weight: 507 lb (230 kg)
Gross weight: 1,069 lb (485 kg)
Recommended engine: 118 hp (88 kW) Textron Lycoming O-235
Maximum speed: 228 kts (263 mph) 423 km/h
Cruise speed: 162 kts (186 mph) 300 km/h
Stall speed: 54 kts (62 mph) 99 km/h
Climb rate: 1,378 ft (420 m) per minute
Range: 228 naut miles (262 miles) 423 km
Availability: Kits.
Comments: Completely redesigned and re-engined from original Rotax-powered prototype. First flew with O-235 in July 1996.

↑ **Ameur Aviation Balbuzard II**

Arno Chéreau Aéronautique J-300 Srs 2

Address:
Arno Chereau Aeronautique, La Tiercerie, 37110 Morand.

Telephone: +33 2 47 29 66 66
Facsimile: +33 2 47 56 96 03

Type: Side-by-side 2-seat, high-wing microlight, with fixed tailwheel undercarriage.
Construction: Alloy tube, wood and fabric.
Wing span: 33 ft 5 ins (10.2 m)
Length: 17 ft 3 ins (5.26 m)
Empty weight: 384 lb (174 kg)
Gross weight: 992 lb (450 kg)
Recommended engine: 80 hp (59.6 kW) Rotax 912 (options include BMW, JPX and Limbach)
Maximum speed: 103 kts (118 mph) 190 km/h
Cruise speed: 65 kts (75 mph) 120 km/h
Stall speed: 32 kts (36 mph) 58 km/h
Take-off distance: 296 ft (90 m)
Climb rate: 945 ft (288 m) per minute
Range: 874 naut miles (1,006 miles) 1,620 km
Availability: Kits and complete aircraft.
Comments: Formerly the JCC Aviation J.300. Used for crop dusting and aerial surveillance, and a military version has been on trial with the Armée de Terre.

↑ **Arno Chéreau Aéronautique J-300 Srs 2 with crop spraying gear** *(Geoffrey P. Jones)*

Blavier GB.8C2

Address:
Gerrard Blavier, 2 sente du Buisson, 78470 Milon-le-Chapelle.

Type: Side-by-side 2-seat, low-wing monoplane, with nosewheel undercarriage (nosewheel alone retracts).
Construction: Wood.
Gross weight: 1,764 lb (800 kg)
Recommended engine: 160 hp (119 kW) Textron Lycoming O-320
Maximum speed: 150 kts (173 mph) 279 km/h
Cruise speed: 141 kts (162 mph) 261 km/h
Stall speed: 55 kts (64 mph) 102 km/h
Range: 493 naut miles (568 miles) 914 km
Availability: Plans.
Comments: First flown September 1996.

↑ **Blavier GB.8C2 prototype** *(Geoffrey P. Jones)*

Buse'Air 150

Address:
Chantier Djicat, ZA Leucate Village, 11370 Leucate.

Telephone: +33 4 68 40 01 41
Facsimile: +33 4 68 40 09 96

Type: Side-by-side 2-seat, high-wing, cabin monoplane, with fixed nosewheel undercarriage.
Construction: Composites.
Wing span: 34 ft (10.36 m)
Length: 21 ft (6.4 m)
Empty weight: 485 lb (220 kg)
Gross weight: 992 lb (450 kg)
Recommended engine: 64.4 hp (48 kW) Rotax 582 (also Hirth F.30 or Limbach 2000)
Maximum speed: 92 kts (106 mph) 170 km/h
Cruise speed: 76 kts (87 mph) 140 km/h
Stall speed: 33 kts (38 mph) 60 km/h
Climb rate: 846 ft (258 m) per minute
Range: 260 naut miles (300 miles) 483 km
Availability: Kits.
Comments: 5 partial kits. Microlight version available, as is a version with larger engines in the JAR/VLA category. Folding wings.

C.A.C. Choucas

Address:
Construction Aéronautique Choucas, Aeropole, 05130 Tallard.

Telephone and Facsimile: +33 4 92 54 00 99

Type: Side-by-side 2-seat, cabin monoplane/motorglider, with fixed tailwheel undercarriage.
Construction: Composite and wood.
Wing span: 47 ft 1 ins (14.35 m)
Length: 17 ft 5 ins (5.3 m)
Recommended engine: 50 hp (37.3 kW) Rotax 503
Maximum speed: 89 kts (103 mph) 165 km/h
Cruise speed: 70 kts (81 mph) 130 km/h
Stall speed: 33 kts (38 mph) 60 km/h
Glide ratio: 22:1 at 46 kts (53 mph) 85 km/h
Climb rate: 785 ft (240 m) per minute
Availability: Kits.
Comments: Designed by Claude Noin and Charly Baum. Said to be spin-proof.

↑ **C.A.C. Choucas** *(Geoffrey P. Jones)*

Campana Aviation Campana

Address:
Campana Aviation, Aeroport de Tarbes-Ossun-Lourdes, Pyrene Aeropole, 65290 Louey.

Telephone: +33 5 62 32 73 67
Facsimile: +33 5 62 32 73 69

Type: Side-by-side 2-seat, low-wing monoplane, with fixed nosewheel undercarriage.
Construction: Composites.
Wing span: 36 ft 4 ins (11.08 m)

Length: 22 ft 4 ins (6.8 m)
Empty weight: 772 lb (350 kg)
Gross weight: 1,323 lb (600 kg)
Recommended engine: 77.8 hp (58 kW) Rotax 912
Maximum speed: 113 kts (130 mph) 210 km/h
Cruise speed: 97 kts (112 mph) 180 km/h
Stall speed: 38 kts (44 mph) 70 km/h
Take-off distance: 165 ft (50 m)
Climb rate: 1,375 ft (420 m) per minute
Range: 917 naut miles (1,056 miles) 1,700 km
Availability: Kit or complete aircraft.
Comments: First flown November 1994. Suitable for commercial and military uses.

↑ **Campana flown by designer Bela Nogrady** *(Geoffrey P. Jones)*

CATA LMK.1 Oryx

Details can be found in the 1996-97 edition of *WA&SD*.

C.L.7 Speed

Address:
Centre National RSA, Aerodrome Montauban, 82000 Montauban.

Type: High performance, side-by-side 2-seat, low-wing monoplane, with retractable tailwheel undercarriage.
Construction: Wood.
Wing span: 23 ft 11 ins (7.3 m)
Length: 19 ft 8 ins (6 m)
Empty weight: 882-937 lb (400-425 kg)
Gross weight: 1,543-1,587 lb (700-720 kg)
Recommended engine: 160 or 180 hp (119.3-134 kW) Textron Lycoming
Maximum speed: 194-205 kts (224-236 mph) 360-380 km/h
Cruise speed: 162-173 kts (186-199 mph) 300-320 km/h
Stall speed: 54 kts (62 mph) 100 km/h
Range: 648 naut miles (745 miles) 1,200 km
Availability: Plans eventually.
Comments: A French homebuilt for touring.

C.L.8 RSA Club

Address:
Centre National RSA (address as above).

Type: Side-by-side 2-seat, low-wing monoplane, with fixed nosewheel undercarriage.
Construction: Wood.
Wing span: 26 ft 11 ins (8.2 m)
Length: 19 ft 8 ins (6 m)
Empty weight: 992 lb (450 kg)
Gross weight: 1,543 lb (700 kg)
Recommended engine: 115 hp (85.75 kW) Textron Lycoming O-235
Maximum speed: 148 kts (171 mph) 275 km/h
Cruise speed: 124 kts (143 mph) 230 km/h
Stall speed: 49 kts (56 mph) 90 km/h
Range: 486 naut miles (559 miles) 900 km
Availability: Plans.
Comments: Designed by Louis Cariou against a joint FNA/RSA requirement for a new French flying club trainer complying with FAR 23. First flown 1996.

CQR.1 Roitelet (Wren)

Address:
RSA Centre Regional Quercy-Rouergue des Constructeurs Amateurs (address as above).

Type: Single-seat, parasol-wing microlight/homebuilt, with fixed tail-dragger undercarriage.
Construction: Wood.
Recommended engine: 25 hp (19 kW) Rotax 277, or 332 or 447
Availability: Plans.
Comments: Designed by Charles Roussoulieres at Montauban and first flown in June 1991.

Colomban MC 15 CriCri

Address:
Michel Colomban, 37bis rue Lakanal, 92500 Rueil-Malmaison.
Telephone: +33 2 47 51 88 76

Type: Single-seat, twin-engined, aerobatic monoplane, with fixed nosewheel undercarriage.
Construction: Light alloy.
Wing span: 16 ft 1 ins (4.9 m)
Length: 12 ft 10 ins (3.91m)
Recommended engines: 2 x 15 hp (11.2 kW) JPX PUL 212
Maximum speed: 159 kts (183 mph) 295 km/h
Cruise speed: 108 kts (124 mph) 200 km/h
Stall speed: 39 kts (45 mph) 72 km/h
Take off distance: 328 ft (100 m)
Climb rate: 1,280 ft (390 m) per minute
Range: 216 naut miles (248 miles) 400 km
Availability: Plans.
Comments: Nearly 600 sets of plans sold, with about 100 flying.

↑ **Colomban MC 15 CriCri built in the Netherlands** *(Geoffrey P. Jones)*

Colomban MC-100 Banbi

Type: Side-by-side 2-seat, low-wing monoplane, with fixed nosewheel undercarriage.
Construction: Metal.
Wing span: 21 ft 9 ins (6.63 m)
Length: 17 ft 9 ins (5.4 m)
Empty weight: 518 lb (235 kg)
Gross weight: 992 lb (450 kg)
Recommended engine: 80 hp (59.6 kW) Rotax 912
Maximum speed: 162 kts (186 mph) 300 km/h
Cruise speed: 135 kts (155 mph) 250 km/h
Stall speed: 43 kts (50 mph) 80 km/h
Take-off distance: 575 ft (175 m)
Climb rate: 1,378 ft (420 m) per minute
Range: 567 naut miles (652 miles) 1,050 km
Availability: Plans plus some components (see Dyn'Aero MCR-01)
Comments: Prototype first flew 15 July 1994. Detatchable wings.

Croses EC-3 Pouplume

Address:
Avions Croses, 120 rue du Glacel, 73500 Modane.
Telephone: +33 4 79 05 19 38

Type: Single-seat, tandem-wing Pou-du-Ciel type, with fixed tailwheel undercarriage.
Construction: Wood.
Wing span: 25 ft 7 ins (7.8 m)
Length: 9 ft 10 ins (3 m)
Empty weight: 243-309 lb (110-140 kg)
Gross weight: 485-573 lb (220-260 kg)
Recommended engine: Converted 2-stroke motorcycle engine of 10.5-18 hp (8-13.4 kW), but more recently small Rotax types.
Maximum speed: 38 kts (44 mph) 70 km/h
Cruise speed: 27 kts (31 mph) 50 km/h
Stall speed: Will not stall.
Availability: Plans.
Comments: One of the first practical modern microlights, first flown in June 1961. Fixed rear wing and pivoting forward wing.

Croses EC-6 Criquet (Locust)

Type: Side-by-side 2-seat, tandem-wing homebuilt (also microlight version as the EC-6L Legère), with fixed tailwheel undercarriage.
Construction: Wood.
Wing span: 25 ft 7 ins (7.8 m)
Length: 15 ft 3 ins (4.65 m)
Empty weight: 639 lb (290 kg)
Gross weight: 1,213 lb (550 kg)
Recommended engine: 90 hp (67 kW) Teledyne Continental or Rotax 503 for microlight version.
Maximum speed: 115 kts (132 mph) 213 km/h
Cruise speed: 86 kts (99 mph) 160 km/h
Stall speed: Will not stall.
Climb rate: 1,000 ft (305 m) per minute
Availability: Plans.
Comments: Prototype first flew on 6 July 1965. Very popular Pou-du-Ciel type, with at least 30 completed and flown in France. Developed into the EC-8 Tourisme and EC-9 Paras Cargo.

↑ **Croses EC-6 Criquet at Marennes in France** *(Geoffrey P. Jones)*

Croses Airplume

Address:
Yves Croses, 35 avenue de Saxe, 69006 Lyon.

Type: Tandem 2-seat, open cockpit Pou-du-Ciel type, with fixed tailwheel undercarriage.
Construction: Composites and wood.
Wing span: 25 ft 11 ins (7.9 m)
Length: 17 ft 1 ins (5.2 m)
Empty weight: 383 lb (174 kg)
Recommended engine: 35 hp (26 kW) Cuyuna, Limbach or Rectimo
Maximum speed: 70 kts (81 mph) 130 km/h
Range: 239 naut miles (275 miles) 442 km
Availability: Kits and plans.
Comments: Developed by Emilien Croses' son. Utilized for aerial crop dusting.

Denise RD.20/150 Raid Driver

Address:
Robert Denize, 17 rue de l'Abbe Borreau, 78400 Chatou.

Type: 2-seat, low-wing, cabin monoplane, with tailwheel undercarriage.
Construction: Wood and fabric.
Wing span: 27 ft 11 ins (8.5 m)
Length: 22 ft 8 ins (6.9 m)
Empty weight: 1,102 lb (500 kg)
Gross weight: 1,631 lb (740 kg)
Recommended engine: 150 hp (112 kW) Textron Lycoming IO-320
Maximum speed: 151 kts (174 mph) 280 km/h
Cruise speed: 108 kts (124 mph) 200 km/h
Range: 324 naut miles (373 miles) 600 km
Availability: Plans.
Comments: Developed from the RD.105 and built between 1986 and 1989.

↑ **Denise RD.20/150 Raid Driver prototype** *(Geoffrey P. Jones)*

Druine D.5 Turbi

Address:
Avions Roger Druine, 10 avenue Aristide Briand, 94100 St Maur.

Type: Tandem 2-seat, open-cockpit, low-wing monoplane, with fixed tailwheel or tail-dragger undercarriage.
Construction: Wood.
Wing span: 28 ft 6 ins (8.7 m)
Length: 22 ft 6 ins (6.86 m)
Empty weight: 617 lb (280 kg)
Gross weight: 1,091 lb (495 kg)
Recommended engine: 65 hp (48.5 kW) Teledyne Continental or Walter Mikron
Maximum speed: 84 kts (96 mph) 155 km/h
Cruise speed: 65 kts (75 mph) 120 km/h
Range: 345 naut miles (397 miles) 640 km
Availability: Plans.
Comments: 2-seat development of the Turbulent, first flown on 20 December 1951.

Druine D.31 Turbulent

Type: Single-seat, open-cockpit, low-wing monoplane, with fixed tail-dragger undercarriage.
Construction: Wood.
Wing span: 21 ft 7 in (6.58 m)
Length: 17 ft 6 in (5.33 m)
Empty weight: 395 lb (179 kg)
Gross weight: 619 lb (281 kg)
Take-off distance: 310 ft (95 m)
Recommended engine: Volkswagen conversions
Maximum speed: 109 kts (126 mph) 202 km/h
Cruise speed: 76 kts (88 mph) 141 km/h
Stall speed: 39 kts (44 mph) 71 km/h
Climb rate: 450 ft (137 m) per minute
Range: 216 naut miles (248 miles) 400 km
Availability: Plans.
Comments: Classic homebuilt also commercially produced in Britain by Rollason.

↑ **Druine D.31 Turbulent at Cranfield in July 1997** *(Geoffrey P. Jones)*

Druine D.60 Condor

Type: Side-by-side 2-seat, low-wing, cabin monoplane, with fixed tailwheel undercarriage.
Construction: Wood.
Wing span: 30 ft 2 ins (9.2 m)
Length: 21 ft 6 ins (6.55 m)
Empty weight: 664 lb (301 kg)
Gross weight: 1,102 lb (500 kg)
Recommended engine: 90 or 100 hp (67 or 74.6 kW) Teledyne Continental
Maximum speed: 97 kts (112 mph) 180 km/h
Cruise speed: 86 kts (99 mph) 160 km/h
Range: 351 naut miles (404 miles) 650 km
Availability: Plans.
Comments: First flown November 1954. Most Condors were commercially built by Rollason in Britain.

Duruble RD-03 Edelweiss 150

Address:
Roland Duruble, 40 rue de Paradis, Les Essarts, 76530 Grand-Couronne.
Telephone: +33 2 35 32 20 63

Type: 2/4-seat low-wing cabin monoplane, with retractable nosewheel undercarriage.
Construction: Duralumin.
Wing span: 28 ft 11 ins (8.82 m)
Length: 22 ft 7 ins (6.88 m)
Empty weight: 1,124 lb (510 kg)
Gross weight: 2,227 lb (1,010 kg)
Recommended engine: 150 hp (112 kW) Textron Lycoming
Maximum speed: 148 kts (171 mph) 275 km/h
Cruise speed: 128 kts (148 mph) 238 km/h
Stall speed: 57 kts (66 mph) 105 km/h
Take-off distance over a 50 ft obstacle: 1,675 ft (510 m)
Climb rate: 1,160 ft (354 m) per minute
Range: 593 naut miles (685 miles) 1,100 km
Availability: Plans.
Comments: Developed from the 2-seat RD-02 and designed to FAR 23 standard. Prototype first flew in 1982.

Dyn'Aero CR.100

Address:
Dyn'Aero SA, 19 rue de l'Aviation, 21121 Darois.
Telephone: +33 3 80 35 60 62
Facsimile: +33 3 80 35 60 63

Type: Side-by-side 2-seat, aerobatic, low-wing monoplane, with fixed tailwheel undercarriage.
Construction: Wood and fabric.
Wing span: 27 ft 11 ins (8.5 m)
Length: 23 ft 4 ins (7.1 m)
Empty weight: 1,213 lb (550 kg)
Gross weight: 1,874 lb (850 kg), 1,675 lb (760 kg) for aerobatics
Recommended engine: 180 hp (134 kW) Textron Lycoming AEIO-360
Maximum speed: 205 kts (236 mph) 380 km/h
Cruise speed: 165 kts (190 mph) 306 km/h
Take-off distance: 492 ft (150 m)
Climb rate: 1,575 ft (480 m) per minute
Availability: Kits.
Comments: Designed by Chris Robin and first flown on 27 August 1992. Many sold, including 2 to French Army.

Dyn'Aero MCR-01 Banbi

Type: Side-by-side 2-seat, low-wing monoplane, with fixed nosewheel undercarriage.
Construction: Composites.
Wing span: 21 ft 9 ins (6.63 m)
Length: 17 ft 9 ins (5.4 m)
Empty weight: 507 lb (230 kg)
Gross weight: 992 lb (450 kg)
Recommended engine: 80 hp (59.7 kW) Rotax 912 (optional Rotax 912 or JPX 4T.75)
Maximum speed: 173 kts (199 mph) 320 km/h
Cruise speed: 121 kts (140 mph) 225 km/h
Stall speed: 47 kts (54 mph) 87 km/h
Climb rate: 1,378 ft (420 m) per minute
Range: 567 naut miles (652 miles) 1,050 km
Availability: kits
Comments: Kit version of the Colomban MC-100.

↑ **Dyn'Aero MCR-01 Banbi prototype** *(Geoffrey P. Jones)*

Dyn'Aero MCR.01 ULM

Type: Side-by-side 2-seat, low-wing monoplane, with fixed nosewheel undercarriage.
Construction: Composites.
Wing span: 27 ft 2 ins (8.28 m)
Length: 18 ft 5 ins (5.62 m)
Empty weight: 529 lb (240 kg)
Gross weight: 992 lb (450 kg)
Recommended engine: 80 hp (59.6 kW) Rotax 912 (optional Rotax 914 and JPX 4T.75)
Maximum speed: 146 kts (168 mph) 270 km/h
Cruise speed: 96 kts (111 mph) 178 km/h
Stall speed: 34 kts (39 mph) 63 km/h
Availability: Kits.
Comments: ULM/microlight version of Banbi, with greater wing and tail spans, reduced stall speed and wing loading.

Grinvalds G.801 Orion

Address:
Club Orion, c/o Michel Suire, 9 rue des Hirondelles, 91210 Draveil (now also available in Spain from Advanced Technology in Aviation, Pla de Terol, s/n E-03520 Polop [Alicante]).

Type: 4-seat, cabin monoplane, with pusher engine and retractable nosewheel undercarriage.
Construction: Composites.
Wing span: 29 ft 6 ins (9 m)
Length: 21 ft 10 ins (6.65 m)
Empty weight: 1,340 lb (608 kg)
Gross weight: 2,310 lb (1,048 kg)
Recommended engine: 200 hp (149 kW) Textron Lycoming IO-360
Maximum speed: 178 kts (205 mph) 330 km/h
Cruise speed: 162 kts (186 mph) 300 km/h
Stall speed: 60 kts (69 mph) 111 km/h
Take-off distance over a 50 ft obstacle: 1,800 ft (548 m)
Climb rate: 885 ft (270 m) per minute
Range: 1,618 naut miles (1,864 miles) 3,000 km, with auxiliary tanks fitted
Availability: Plans.
Comments: G-801 plans and access to moulds are still available via Club Orion and ATA in Spain, who are strengthening existing fuselages with carbonfibre. ATA telephone +34 6 689 6122.

↑ **Grinvalds G-801 Orion** *(Geoffrey P. Jones)*

Grunberg/Mignet HM.293

Address:
Rodolphe Grunberg, Association des Amateurs Pouducielistes, 47310 Roquefort, or Rodolphe Grunberg Sarl, 105 Arcades du Gravier, 47000 Agen.
Telephone: +33 5 53 96 77 90
Facsimile: +33 5 53 47 05 89

Type: Single-seat, tandem-wing microlight, with fixed tailwheel undercarriage.
Construction: Wood and fabric.
Wing span: 20 ft (6.1 m) and 15 ft 9 ins (4.8 m)
Length: 12 ft 7.5 ins (3.85 m)
Empty weight: 265 lb (120 kg)
Gross weight: 485 lb (220 kg)
Recommended engine: 40 hp (29.8 kW) Rotax 447 (optional Hirth)
Maximum speed: 70 kts (81 mph) 130 km/h
Cruise speed: 51 kts (59 mph) 95 km/h
Minimum speed: 16.5 kts (19 mph) 30 km/h
Take-off distance: 164 ft (50 m)
Climb rate: 394 ft (120 m) per minute
Range: 215 naut miles (248 miles) 400 km
Availability: Plans and some components.
Comments: Redesign of Henri Mignet's HM.293. 22 flying and 60 under construction at time of writing.

↑ **Grunberg/Mignet HM.293 at the 1997 RSA Rally** *(Geoffrey P. Jones)*

Humbert Moto-du-Ciel

Address:
Ets Humbert, rue du Menil, 88160 Ramonchamps.
Telephone: +33 3 29 25 05 75
Facsimile: +33 3 29 25 98 97

Type: Tandem-seat, open-framework, high-wing microlight, with fixed nosewheel undercarriage. Optional cabin.
Construction: Steel tube, wood and composites.
Wing span: 37 ft 1 ins (11.3 m)
Length: 21 ft 4 ins (6.5 m)
Empty weight: 381 lb (173 kg)
Gross weight: 866 lb (393 kg)
Recommended engine: 1,600cc Volkeswagen
Maximum speed: 59 kts (68 mph) 110 km/h
Cruise speed: 52 kts (60 mph) 96 km/h
Stall speed: 27 kts (31 mph) 50 km/h
Climb rate: 590 ft (180 m) per minute
Range: 378 naut miles (435 miles) 700 km
Availability: Plans and kits.
Comments: First flown in March 1985. Also now available with Rotax engines and optional cockpit pod.

Humbert Le Tetras

Type: Side-by-side 2-seat, high-wing, cabin monoplane, with fixed tailwheel undercarriage. Microlight or homebuilt.
Construction: Steel tube, metal and composites.
Wing span: 37 ft 1 ins (11.3 m)
Length: 21 ft 4 ins (6.5 m)
Empty weight: 529 lb (240 kg)
Gross weight: 992 lb (450 kg)
Recommended engine: 72 hp (53.7 kW) HW2000 for microlight, or 80 hp (59.7 kW) Rotax 912
Maximum speed: 86 kts (99 mph) 160 km/h
Cruise speed: 65 kts (75 mph) 120 km/h
Stall speed: 35 kts (41 mph) 65 km/h
Take-off distance: 246 ft (75 m)
Climb rate: 395 ft (120 m) per second
Availability: Kits.

↑ **Humbert Le Tetras** *(Geoffrey P. Jones)*

Jacques Coupe JC-01

Address:
Avions Jacques Coupe, La Trute, Azay-le-Cher, 37270 Montlouis-sur-Loire.
Telephone: +33 2 47 50 41 84

Type: Side-by-side 2-seat, low-wing, cabin monoplane, with fixed tailwheel undercarriage.
Construction: Wood and fabric.
Wing span: 27 ft 5 ins (8.35 m)
Length: 21 ft (6.4 m)
Empty weight: 728 lb (330 kg)
Gross weight: 1,279 lb (580 kg)
Recommended engine: 65 hp (48.5 kW) Teledyne Continental A65-8F
Maximum speed: 108 kts (124 mph) 200 km/h
Cruise speed: 76 kts (87 mph) 140 km/h

↑ **Jacques Coupe JC-01** *(Geoffrey P. Jones)*

Stall speed: 25 kts (28 mph) 45 km/h
Take-off distance: 295 ft (90 m)
Availability: Plans.
Comments: Prototype first flew on 16 March 1976 (see JC-200 nosewheel version).

Jacques Coupe JC-200

Type: Side-by-side 2-seat, low-wing, cabin monoplane, with fixed nosewheel undercarriage.
Construction: Wood and fabric.
Wing span: 27 ft 5 ins (8.35 m)
Length: 21 ft (6.4 m)
Empty weight: 1,102 lb (500 kg)
Gross weight: 1,653 lb (750 kg)
Recommended engine: 100 hp (74.5 kW) Teledyne Continental
Maximum speed: 108 kts (124 mph) 200 km/h
Cruise speed: 86 kts (99 mph) 160 km/h
Stall speed: 24 kts (28 mph) 45 km/h
Take-off distance: 328 ft (100 m)
Availability: Plans and possibly kits.
Comments: Prototype JC-2 first flew in May 1981. Several JC-200s completed since.

Jodel D.9 Bebe

Address:
SAB, Aerodrome Beaune Challanges, 21200 Beaune (also from Falconar Air Engineering in Canada).
Telephone: +33 3 80 22 01 51
Facsimile: +33 3 80 24 19 43

Type: Single-seat, low-wing monoplane, with fixed tail-dragger (some have nosewheel) undercarriage.
Construction: Wood and fabric.
Wing span: 23 ft (7 m)
Length: 17 ft 11 ins (5.45 m)
Empty weight: 419 lb (190 kg)
Gross weight: 705 lb (320 kg)
Recommended engine: 40 hp (30 kW) Volkeswagen
Maximum speed: 87 kts (100 mph) 160 km/h
Cruise speed: 74 kts (85 mph) 137 km/h
Stall speed: 35 kts (41 mph) 65 km/h
Take-off distance: 360 ft (110 m)
Climb rate: 750 ft (230 m) per minute
Range: 216 naut miles (248 miles) 400 km
Availability: Plans and kits.
Comments: Original Jodel design of Joly and Delemontez first flew in January 1948. Canadian version is the Falconar F-9. Some have spring steel or nosewheel undercarriages and enclosed cockpits instead of open.

Jodel D.11

Type: Side-by-side 2-seat, low-wing, cabin monoplane, with fixed tailwheel undercarriage.
Construction: Wood and fabric.
Wing span: 27 ft (8.23 m)
Length: 17 ft 11 ins (5.45 m)
Empty weight: 750 lb (340 kg)
Gross weight: 1,239 lb (562 kg)
Recommended engine: 65-90 hp (48.5-67 kW) Teledyne Continental
Maximum speed: 93 kts (107 mph) 173 km/h
Cruise speed: 87 kts (100 mph) 161 km/h
Stall speed: 43 kts (50 mph) 80 km/h
Take-off distance: 500 ft (152 m)
Climb rate: 500 ft (152 m) per minute
Range: 260 naut miles (299 miles) 482 km
Availability: Kits and plans.
Comments: Developed for commercial production by several companies. Canadian versions: Falconar F-11 (2 seats) and F-12 (3 seats).

Jodel D.18 and D.19

Type: Side-by-side 2-seat, low-wing, cabin monoplane, with fixed tailwheel undercarriage. D.19 has nosewheel undercarriage.
Details: For D.18, except where stated.
Construction: Wood and fabric.
Wing span: 24 ft 7 ins (7.5 m)
Length: 18 ft 8 ins (5.7 m)
Empty weight: 551 lb (250 kg)
Gross weight: 1,014 lb (460 kg)
Recommended engine: 1,600cc Volkswagen or Limbach
Maximum speed: 135 kts (155 mph) 250 km/h
Cruise speed: 92 kts (106 mph) 170 km/h
Stall speed: 39 kts (45 mph) 72 km/h
Take-off distance over a 50 ft obstacle: 590 ft (180 m)
Climb rate: 590 ft (180 m) per minute
Range: 459 naut miles (528 miles) 850 km
Availability: Plans and some components
Comments: Developed from the Delemontez-Cauchy DC-01 and first flown on 21 May 1984. Extremely popular homebuilt in France. Nosewheel undercarriage version is the D.19.

Jodel D.20 Jubilee

Type: Side-by-side 2-seat, low-wing, cabin monoplane, with fixed nosewheel undrcarriage.
Construction: Wood and fabric.
Wing span: 24 ft 7 ins (7.5 m)
Length: 19 ft (5.8 m)
Empty weight: 551-573 lb (250-260 kg)
Gross weight: 1,256 lb (570 kg)
Recommended engine: 85 hp (63.4 kW) JPX 4TX.75
Maximum speed: 130 kts (149 mph) 240 km/h
Cruise speed: 108 kts (124 mph) 200 km/h
Stall speed: 33 kts (38 mph) 60 km/h
Range: 809 naut miles (932 miles) 1,500 km
Availability: Kits.
Comments: First flown 3 March 1997. SAB's first complete kitplane.

↑ **Jodel D.20 Jubilee**

Jodel D.150 Mascaret

Type: Side-by-side 2-seat, low-wing, sport touring monoplane, with fixed tailwheel undercarriage.
Construction: Wood and fabric.
Wing span: 20 ft 8 ins (6.3 m)
Length: 20 ft 8 ins (6.3 m)
Empty weight: 750 lb (340 kg)
Gross weight: 1,587 lb (720 kg)
Recommended engine: 100-115 hp (74.6-85.75 kW)
Cruise speed: 117 kts (135 mph) 217 km/h
Climb rate: 630 ft (190 m) per minute
Range: 521 naut miles (600 miles) 965 km
Availability: Plans and some components.
Comments: 61 aircraft originally built commercially by SAN at Bernay, France.

Jonathan Souricette (Mousetrap)

Address:
Michel Barry,
171 Avenue du Général le Clerc, 91190 Gif/Yvette.

Type: Single-seat, open cockpit, shoulder-wing microlight, with fixed tail-dragger undercarriage.
Construction: Wood and styrofoam.
Wing span: 29 ft 6 ins (9 m)
Length: 18 ft 8 ins (5.7 m)
Empty weight: 220 lb (100 kg)
Gross weight: 441 kg (200 kg)
Recommended engine: 22 hp (16.4 kW) JPX PUL 425
Maximum speed: 65 kts (75 mph) 120 km/h
Cruise speed: 54 kts (62 mph) 100 km/h
Stall speed: 23 kts (26 mph) 42 km/h
Take-off distance: 328 ft (100 m)
Climb rate: 225-490 ft (70-150 m) per minute
Range: 270 naut miles (310 miles) 500 km
Availability: Plans and kits.
Comments: Easy to build microlight designed by Michel Barry.

↑ Lightweight Souricette being man-handled *(Geoffrey P. Jones)*

JP Marie JPM.01 Medoc

Address:
Didier Marie, 35 rue de Caumont, Residence l'Aigiliere, 76520 Quevreville-la-Poterie.

Type: Side-by-side 2-seat, low-wing monoplane, with fixed nosewheel undercarriage.
Construction: Wood.
Wing span: 24 ft 7 ins (7.5 m)
Length: 20 ft 4 ins (6.2 m)
Empty weight: 462 lb (210 kg)
Gross weight: 1,014 lb (460 kg)
Recommended engine: 68 hp (50.7 kW) Limbach 1700
Maximum speed: 103 kts (118 mph) 190 km/h
Cruise speed: 92 kts (106 mph) 170 km/h
Stall speed: 43 kts (50 mph) 80 km/h
Climb rate: 787 ft (240 m) per minute
Range: 367 naut miles (422 miles) 680 km
Availability: Plans.
Comments: First flown in 1991. Several engine options.

Junqua RJ.03 Ibis

Address:
Junqua-Diffusion Internationale, c/o SCAM, 69 rue Garibaldi, 94100 Saint-Maur.
Telephone: +33 1 42 83 45 79
Facsimile: +33 1 42 83 00 65

Type: Tandem 2-seat, monoplane with canard. Fixed nosewheel undercarriage.
Construction: Wood and foam.
Wing span: 20 ft 5 ins (6.22 m)
Length: 16 ft 1 ins (4.9 m)
Empty weight: 573 lb (260 kg)
Gross weight: 1,036 lb (470 kg)
Recommended engine: 2,000cc Volkswagen or Limbach
Maximum speed: 140 kts (161 mph) 259 km/h
Cruise speed: 110 kts (127 mph) 204 km/h
Stall speed: 52 kts (60 mph) 96 km/h
Take-off distance: 1,706 ft (520 m)
Climb rate: 617 ft (188 m) per minute
Range: 432 naut miles (497 miles) 800 km
Availability: Plans.
Comments: Developed from the RJ.02 Volucelle. Prototype Ibis first flew on 25 May 1991.

↑ Junqua RJ.03 Ibis *(Geoffrey P. Jones)*

Jurca MJ.2 Tempete

Address:
3 allées des Bordes, 94430 Chevennevieres (also from the USA: Ken Heit, 1733 Kansas, Flint, MI 48506).
Telephone: +33 1 45 94 01 38 (USA: +1 313 232 5395)

Type: Single-seat, aerobatic, low-wing monoplane, with fixed tail-dragger undercarriage.
Construction: Wood and fabric.
Wing span: 19 ft 8 ins (6 m)
Length: 19 ft (5.8 m)
Empty weight: 639 lb (290 kg)
Gross weight: 948 lb (430 kg)
Recommended engine: 65 hp (48.5 kW) Teledyne Continental. Variety of other engine options up to 180 hp (134 kW).
Maximum speed: 104 kts (120 mph) 193 km/h
Cruise speed: 89 kts (102 mph) 165 km/h
Stall speed: 48 kts (55 mph) 90 km/h
Take-off distance: 820 ft (250 m)
Climb rate: 558 ft (170 m) per minute
Range: 269 naut miles (310 miles) 500 km
Availability: Plans.
Comments: Prototype first flew on 27 June 1956.

Jurca MJ.5 Sirocco

Type: Tandem 2-seat, low-wing, aerobatic monoplane, with fixed or retractable tail-dragger undercarriage.
Construction: Wood and fabric.
Wing span: 23 ft (7 m)
Length: 20 ft 2 ins (6.15 m)
Empty weight: 948 lb (430 kg)
Gross weight: 1,499 lb (680 kg)
Take-off distance: 820 ft (250 m)
Recommended engine: 115 hp (85.75 kW) Textron Lycoming. Variety of other engine options up to 200 hp (149 kW).
Maximum speed: 127 kts (146 mph) 235 km/h
Cruise speed: 116 kts (134 mph) 215 km/h
Stall speed: 43 kts (50 mph) 80 km/h
Climb rate: 820 ft (250 m) per minute
Range: 477 naut miles (550 miles) 1,018 km
Availability: Plans.
Comments: Developed from the MJ.2 and first flown on 3 August 1962.

Jurca MJ.10 Spitfire

Type: 75% scale Spitfire replica.
Construction: Wood.
Wing span: 27 ft 8 ins (8.43 m)
Length: 23 ft 5 ins (7.14 m)
Empty weight: 1,450 lb (658 kg)
Gross weight: 2,860 lb (1,297 kg)
Recommended engine: 105 hp (78.5 kW) Teledyne Continental
Maximum speed: 124 kts (143 mph) 230 km/h
Cruise speed: 113 kts (130 mph) 210 km/h
Stall speed: 60 kts (69 mph) 110 km/h
Range: 432 naut miles (497 miles) 800 km
Availability: Plans.
Comments: One of Jurca's many World War II fighter replicas. Also available in 75% scale are the **MJ.8** (Fw-190), **MJ.9** (Bf-109) and **MJ.12** (P-40).

Jurca MJ.53 Autan

Type: Side-by-side 2-seat, aerobatic, low-wing monoplane. with retractable tailwheel undercarriage.
Construction: Wood.
Wing span: 24 ft 11 ins (7.6 m)
Length: 21 ft 4 ins (6.5 m)
Empty weight: 1,323 lb (600 kg)
Gross weight: 1,860 lb (844 kg)
Recommended engine: 180 hp (134 kW) Textron Lycoming
Cruise speed: 130 kts (149 mph) 240 km/h
Stall speed: 49-54 kts (56-62 mph) 90-100 km/h
Climb rate: 985 ft (300 m) per minute
Range: 521 naut miles (600 miles) 965 km
Availability: Plans.
Comments: Developed from the MJ.5 Sirocco. First flew 20 December 1991.

↑ Jurca MJ.53 Autan built by F. Melani at Salon, France *(Geoffrey P. Jones)*

Jurca MJ.77 Gnatsum (Mustang)

Type: 75% scale P.51 Mustang replica.
Construction: Wood.
Wing span: 27 ft 10 ins (8.48 m)
Length: 21 ft 6 ins (6.55 m)
Empty weight: 2,200 lb (998 kg)
Gross weight: 2,860 lb (1,297 kg)
Recommended engine: 200-360 hp (149-268.5 kW) Geschwender
Cruise speed: 151 kts (175 mph) 280 km/h
Climb rate: 1,500 ft (457 m) per minute
Availability: Plans.
Comments: See also MJ.10 Spitfire.

↑ Jurca MJ.77 Gnatsum completed in France by Alain Anziani *(Geoffrey P. Jones)*

Jurca MJ.100 Spitfire

Type: Full-scale homebuilt Spitfire replica.
Construction: Wood or metal tube.
Wing span: 36 ft (10.97 m)
Length: 29 ft 11 ins (9.12 m)
Empty weight: 3,900 lb (1,769 kg)
Gross weight: 5,060 lb (2,295 kg)
Recommended engine: 690 hp (514.5 kW) Hispano Suiza V.12 or V-12 Allison
Maximum speed: 308 kts (355 mph) 571 km/h
Cruise speed: 261 kts (300 mph) 483 km/h
Climb rate: 3,500 ft (1,065 m) per minute
Range: 434 naut miles (500 miles) 804 km
Availability: Plans.
Comments: One of Marcel Jurca's full-scale World War II fighter replicas that include the **MJ.80** (Fw-190) and **MJ.90** (Bf-109).

Kieger AK.1

Address:
André Kieger, 85 route de Bischwiller, 67500 Hagenau.
Telephone and Facsimile: +33 3 88 93 55 81
E-mail: kieger@cit.enscm.fr

Type: Side-by-side 2-seat, low-wing cabin monoplane, with fixed tailwheel undercarriage.
Construction: Wood and fabric.
Wing span: 27 ft 5 ins (8.35 m)
Length: 20 ft 5 ins (6.22 m)
Empty weight: 932 lb (423 kg)
Gross weight: 1,464 lb (664 kg)
Recommended engine: 115 hp (85.7 kW) Limbach L2000
Cruise speed: 108 kts (124 mph) 200 km/h
Stall speed: 41 kts (47 mph) 75 km/h
Climb rate: 985 ft (300 m) per minute
Range: 475 naut miles (546 miles) 880 km
Availability: Plans.
Comments: First flown on 17 March 1989.

↑ Kieger AK.1 prototypes built by André Kieger *(Geoffrey P. Jones)*

Kieger AK.2

Type: Side-by-side 2-seat, low-wing glider tug, with fixed nosewheel undercarriage.
Construction: Wood and fabric.
Wing span: 31 ft (9.45 m)
Empty weight: 1,102 lb (500 kg)
Gross weight: 1,653 lb (750 kg)
Recommended engine: 180 hp (134 kW) Textron Lycoming O-360
Cruise speed: 81-89 kts (93-103 mph) 150-165 km/h
Towing speed: 62-75 kts (71-87 mph) 115-140 km/h
Stall speed: 38 kts (44 mph) 70 km/h

Climb rate: 640 ft (195 m) per minute, with 500 kg glider
Availability: Plans.
Comments: Towing development of AK.1, with strengthened fuselage.

↑ Kieger AK.2 under construction

Kitair/Aviakit Helios-5-TR

Address:
Kitair, ZA St.Pouange, 10120 St André.
Telephone: +33 3 25 41 90 34 **Facsimile:** +33 3 25 41 71 11

Type: Side-by-side 2-seat, high-wing monoplane, with fixed nosewheel undercarriage.
Construction: Wood and composites.
Wing span: 36 ft 1 ins (11 m)
Length: 19 ft 8 ins (6 m)
Empty weight: 340 lb (154 kg)
Gross weight: 992 lb (450 kg)
Recommended engine: 50 hp (37.3 kW) Rotax 503 or 64.4 hp (48 kW) Rotax 582
Maximum speed: 81 kts (93 mph) 150 km/h
Cruise speed: 65 kts (75 mph) 120 km/h
Stall speed: 27 kts (31 mph) 50 km/h
Availability: Kits.
Comments: Detatchable wings to facilitate road transportation.

Kitair/Aviakit Hermes

Type: Side-by-side 2-seat, low-wing, cabin monoplane, with fixed nosewheel undercarriage.
Construction: Wood and composites.
Wing span: 32 ft 10 ins (10 m)
Length: 23 ft (7 m)
Empty weight: 474 lb (215 kg)
Gross weight: 992 lb (450 kg)
Recommended engine: 77.8 hp (58 kW) Rotax 912 (optional Rotax 582)
Maximum speed: 100 kts (115 mph) 185 km/h
Cruise speed: 89 kts (103 mph) 165 km/h
Stall speed: 33 kts (38 mph) 60 km/h
Availability: Kits.
Comments: Introduced in 1996.

↑ Kitair/Aviakit Hermes, first displayed at Epinal in July 1996 *(Geoffrey P. Jones)*

Koenig AK.09 Faucon and Junkers Ultima

Details: Apply to AK.09, except under Comments.

Address:
Koenig Engineering, 49 route du Mont St Odile, 67220 Breitenbach.
Telephone: +33 88 58 95 78 **Facsimile:** +33 88 58 95 77

Type: Side-by-side 2-seat, low-wing, cabin monoplane, with fixed nosewheel undercarriage.
Construction: Composites.
Wing span: 27 ft 3 ins (8.3 m)
Length: 19 ft 8 ins (6 m)
Empty weight: 551 lb (250 kg)
Gross weight: 992 lb (450 kg)
Recommended engine: 50 hp (37.3 kW) Rotax 503 or 64.4 hp (48 kW) 582 for microlight version, or 77.8 hp (58 kW) Rotax 912 for JAR/VLA version.
Maximum speed: 140 kts (162 mph) 260 km/h
Cruise speed: 124 kts (143 mph) 230 km/h
Stall speed: 35 kts (41 mph) 65 km/h
Climb rate: 1,220 ft (372 m) per minute
Range: 431 naut miles (497 miles) 800 km
Availability: Kits.
Comments: First flown in 1993. Also available from a German supplier as the Ultima (Junkers Flugzeugbau, Bavariaring 38, D-80336 München; telephone +49 89 767 00057; facsimile +49 89 767 00058).

La Mouette Ghost 12, 14 and 16

Address:
La Mouette, 1 rue de la Petite-Fin, 21121 Fontain-les-Dijon.
Telephone: +33 3 80 56 66 47 **Facsimile:** +33 3 80 55 42 01

Type: Single- or 2-seat, Rogallo-wing only for other microlights, with trike and pusher engine.
Details: For Ghost 12. See Comments.
Construction: Alloy tube and fabric.
Wing span: 31 ft 6 ins (9.6 m)
Weight: 92.5 lb (42 kg)
Availability: Commercially manufactured.
Comments: Also available are the larger Ghost 14 (47 ft 7 ins, 14.5 m) and Ghost 16 (51 ft 2 ins, 15.6 m). Also, separate La Mouette Topless is a 33 ft 2 ins (10.12 m) span hang glider.

La Mouette Paramotor SR.210

Type: Single-seat, ram-air parachute, with shrouded engine and propeller attached to the pilot.
Construction: Alloy tube and fabric.
Empty weight: 44 lb (20 kg)
Gross weight: 220 lb (100 kg)
Recommended engine: Solo 210
Climb rate: 275 ft (84 m) per minute
Availability: Commercially built by La Mouette.
Comments: First flown on 8 October 1993 and over 70 built. Also the Paramotor SR.210GH, ZR.250 with Zenoah 250 engine and ZR.250BI.

La Mouette/ULM Cosmos Phase II

Type: Tandem 2-seat, Rogallo-wing microlight, with trike and pusher engine.
Construction: Alloy tube and fabric.
Wing span: 34 ft 9 ins (10.6 m)
Empty weight: 309 lb (140 kg)
Gross weight: 772 lb (350 kg)
Recommended engine: 50 hp (37.3 kW) Rotax
Maximum speed: 70 kts (81 mph) 130 km/h
Cruise speed: 41 kts (47 mph) 75 km/h
Stall speed: 25 kts (28 mph) 45 km/h
Climb rate: 985 ft (300 m) per minute
Range: 113 naut miles (130 miles) 210 km
Availability: Commercially manufactured.
Comments: First flown in March 1991. Hundreds sold.

↑ ULM Cosmos Phase II *(Geoffrey P. Jones)*

Lascaud Bifly

Address:
Ets D. Lascaud, 41 rue de Crussol, 07500 Granges-les-Valence.
Telephone: +33 4 75 44 47 02

Type: Single-seat, tandem-wing microlight.
Construction: Wood.
Wing span: 20 ft 4 ins (6.19 m)
Length: 10 ft 8 ins (3.25 m)
Empty weight: 143 lb (65 kg)
Gross weight: 353 lb (160 kg)
Recommended engine: 22 hp (16.4 kW) JPX PUL 425
Maximum speed: 65 kts (75 mph) 120 km/h
Cruise speed: 38 kts (43 mph) 70 km/h
Stall speed: 16.5 kts (19 mph) 30 km/h
Take-off distance: 131 ft (40 m)
Climb rate: 590 ft (180 m) per minute
Range: 89 naut miles (102 miles) 165 km
Availability: Kits.
Comments: Microlight version of the classic Henri Mignet Pou-du-Ciel formula.

Lefebvre MP.205 Busard

Address:
Robert Lefebvre, 393 rue Pierre Cardinal, La Paillade, 34100 Montpellier.

Type: Single-seat, low-wing, racing monoplane, with fixed tailwheel undercarriage.
Construction: Wood.
Wing span: 19 ft 8 ins (6 m)
Length: 17 ft 7 ins (5.35 m)
Empty weight: 527 lb (239 kg)
Gross weight: 760 lb (345 kg)
Recommended engine: 90 hp (67 kW) Teledyne Continental
Maximum speed: 156 kts (180 mph) 290 km/h
Stall speed: 40 kts (45 mph) 74 km/h
Range: 242 naut miles (279 miles) 450 km
Availability: Plans.
Comments: Original Max Plan MP.204 first flew on 5 June 1952. First MP.205 built by M. Lefebvre flew in 1975. Other versions with different engines.

Lucas L.5

Address:
Emile Lucas, 7 allée des Acacias, 60330 Lagny-le-Sec.
Telephone: +33 3 44 60 87 45 **Facsimile:** +33 3 44 60 04 81

Type: Side-by-side 2-seat (also 3 or 4 seat), low-wing, cabin monoplane, with either fixed nosewheel or retractable tailwheel undercarriage.
Construction: Metal.
Wing span: 30 ft 2 ins (9.2 m)
Length: 20 ft 8 ins (6.3 m)
Empty weight: 1,036 lb (470 kg)
Gross weight: 1,587 lb (720 kg)
Recommended engine: 115 hp (85.75 kW) Textron Lycoming O-235
Maximum speed: 146 kts (168 mph) 270 km/h with retractable gear
Cruise speed: 138 kts (158 mph) 255 km/h
Stall speed: 51 kts (59 mph) 95 km/h
Take-off distance: 920 ft (280 m)
Climb rate: 985 ft (300 m) per minute
Range: 499 naut miles (575 miles) 925 km
Availability: Plans and some components.
Comments: Prototype first flew on 13 August 1976. Many versions built with different capacity engines.

↑ Lucas L.5 built by M. Devicq with 4 seats and 180 hp (134 kW) Textron Lycoming engine *(Geoffrey P. Jones)*

Lucas L.6

Type: Tandem 2-seat, low-wing, cabin monoplane, with either retractable tailwheel or nosewheel undercarriage. Suitable for use as a motorglider with wingtip extensions.
Construction: Metal.

Wing span: 31 ft 2 ins (9.5 m)
Length: 23 ft (7 m)
Empty weight: 992 lb (450 kg)
Gross weight: 1,499 lb (680 kg)
Recommended engine: 80 hp (59.7 kW) Limbach
Maximum speed: 108 kts (124 mph) 200 km/h
Cruise speed: 86 kts (99 mph) 160 km/h
Take-off distance: 985 ft (300 m)
Range: 540 naut miles (621 miles) 1,000 km
Availability: Plans and some components.
Comments: First flown 4 September 1991. Suitable for other engines.

Lucas L.7 and L.8

Details: L.7, except under Comments.
Type: 3-seat, high-wing, cabin monoplane, with fixed nosewheel undercarriage.
Construction: Metal.
Wing span: 34 ft 5 ins (10.5 m)
Empty weight: 1,146 lb (520 kg)
Gross weight: 1,742 lb (790 kg)
Recommended engine: 108 hp (80.5 kW) Textron Lycoming O-235
Maximum speed: 113 kts (130 mph) 210 km/h
Cruise speed: 105 kts (121 mph) 195 km/h
Stall speed: 46 kts (53 mph) 85 km/h
Climb rate: 787 ft (240 m) per minute
Availability: Plans.
Comments: First flown in 1997. Can carry 220 lb (100 kg) of baggage or parachutist. Tail-dragger version is Lucas L.8.

Mecavia Onyx Biplace

Address:
Mecavia, 2 rue des Naudinieres, 37270 Larcay.
Telephone: +33 2 47 27 60 65
Facsimile: +33 2 47 27 61 60

Type: Tandem 2-seat, canard monoplane with winglets, pusher engine and fixed nosewheel undercarriage.
Construction: Composites and wood.
Wing span: 30 ft 2 ins (9.2 m)
Empty weight: 485 lb (220 kg)
Gross weight: 970 lb (440 kg)
Recommended engine: 50 hp (37.3 kW) Rotax 503, 65 hp (48.5 kW) Rotax 582 or 80 hp (59.7 kW) Hirth F.30
Maximum speed: 100 kts (115 mph) 185 km/h
Cruise speed: 81 kts (93 mph) 150 km/h
Stall speed: 35 kts (40 mph) 64 km/h
Climb rate: 985 ft (300 m) per minute
Availability: Kits.
Comments: Developed from the single-seat Piel CP.150 Onyx. First flown 1994.

↑ **Mecavia Onyx** *(Geoffrey P. Jones)*

Mignet HM.1000 Balerit

Address:
Avions Henri Mignet, 14 rue Henri Mignet, St Romain-de-Benêt, 17600 Saujon.
Telephone: +33 5 46 02 26 00
Facsimile: +33 5 46 02 85 85

Type: Tandem-wing, 2-seat, Pou-du-Ciel type microlight, with fixed nosewheel undercarriage.
Wing span: 23 ft 11 ins (7.3 m)
Length: 16 ft 5 ins (5 m)
Empty weight: 386 lb (175 kg)
Gross weight: 628 lb (285 kg)
Recommended engine: 46 hp (34 kW) Rotax 503
Maximum speed: 78 kts (90 mph) 145 km/h
Cruise speed: 70 kts (81 mph) 130 km/h
Stall speed: Does not stall.
Take-off distance: 300 ft (91 m)
Climb rate: 1,230 ft (376 m) per minute
Range: 216 naut miles (248 miles) 400 km
Availability: Complete aircraft and kits.
Comments: Sold in large numbers in France (130+) for sporting use and air work including surveillance by the Armée de l'Air.

Mignet HM.1100 Cordouan

Type: Side-by-side 2-seat, tandem-wing microlight, with fixed nosewheel undercarriage.
Construction: Composites and metal.
Wing span: 24 ft (7.3 m) and 21 ft 4 ins (6.5 m)
Length: 16 ft 8 ins (5.07 m)
Empty weight: 573 lb (260 kg)
Gross weight: 992 lb (450 kg)
Recommended engine: 80 hp (59.6 kW) Rotax 912
Maximum speed: 103 kts (118 mph) 190 km/h
Cruise speed: 81 kts (93 mph) 150 km/h
Stall speed: Does not stall.
Take-off distance: 262 ft (80 m)
Climb rate: 885 ft (270 m) per minute
Range: 296 naut miles (341 miles) 550 km
Availability: Complete aircraft.
Comments: First flown 1997. Folding wings and 3-axis control.

↑ **Mignet HM.1100 Cordouan** *(Geoffrey P. Jones)*

Morin M.81 Butterfly

Address:
André Morin, 20 avenue Leon Renault, 92700 Colombes.
Telephone: +33 2 47 82 47 00

Type: Side-by-side 2-seat, high-wing microlight, with fixed nosewheel undercarriage.
Construction: Steel tube, aluminium, wood and fabric.
Wing span: 37 ft 4 ins (11.38 m)
Length: 20 ft (6.08 m)
Empty weight: 529 lb (240 kg)
Gross weight: 992 lb (450 kg)
Recommended engine: 64 hp (47.7 kW) Rotax 582
Maximum speed: 73 kts (84 mph) 135 km/h
Cruise speed: 65 kts (75 mph) 120 km/h
Stall speed: 33 kts (38 mph) 60 km/h
Climb rate: 690 ft (210 m) per minute
Range: 270 naut miles (310 miles) 500 km
Availability: Plans.
Comments: One of 4 Morin designs since 1982. 15 under construction in France.

↑ **Morin M.81 Butterfly prototype** *(Geoffrey P. Jones)*

Nickel & Foucard Asterix

Address:
Rudy Nickel, 106 avenue Chateau-Fleury, 26100 Romans.

Type: Tandem 2-seat, monoplane with pivoting wing, pusher propeller and fixed tailwheel undercarriage.
Construction: Wood and fabric.
Wing span: 24 ft 7 ins (7.5 m)
Length: 16 ft 11 ins (5.15 m)
Empty weight: 441 lb (200 kg)
Gross weight: 824 lb (374 kg)
Recommended engine: 45 hp (33.6 kW) Citroen Visa converted motorcar engine.
Maximum speed: 78 kts (90 mph) 145 km/h
Cruise speed: 70 kts (81 mph) 130 km/h
Stall speed: 33 kts (38 mph) 60 km/h
Take-off distance: 492 ft (150 m)
Climb rate: 492 ft (150 m) per minute
Range: 189 naut miles (217 miles) 350 km
Availability: Plans.
Comments: Prototype built by Rudy Nickel and Joseph Foucard first flew in 1987. Several completed in France.

Nicollier HN.433 Menestrel

Address:
Avions H. Nicollier, 13 rue de Verdun, 25000 Besançon.
Telephone: +33 3 81 53 57 01

Type: Single-seat, low-wing monoplane, with fixed tailwheel undercarriage.
Construction: Wood and fabric.
Wing span: 23 ft (7 m)
Length: 17 ft 5 ins (5.3 m)
Empty weight: 443 lb (201 kg)
Gross weight: 727 lb (330 kg)
Recommended engine: 39 hp (29 kW) Rectimo-VW (also other 30-50 hp, 22.4-37.3 kW engines)
Maximum speed: 103 kts (118 mph) 190 km/h
Cruise speed: 92 kts (106 mph) 170 km/h
Stall speed: 26 kts (30 mph) 48 km/h
Take-off distance: 395 ft (120 m)
Climb rate: 590 ft (180 m) per minute
Range: 278 naut miles (320 miles) 515 km
Availability: Plans and some components.
Comments: Prototype first flew on 25 November 1962. Redesigned version, HN.434, also available.

Nicollier HN.500 Bengali

Type: Side-by-side 2-seat, low-wing, cabin monoplane, with fixed nosewheel undercarriage.
Construction: Wood.
Wing span: 27 ft 6 ins (8.39 m)
Length: 20 ft 4 ins (6.2 m)
Recommended engine: 100 hp (74.6 kW) Teledyne Continental O-200
Cruise speed: 105 kts (121 mph) 195 km/h
Availability: Plans.
Comments: First flown on 9 June 1988.

Nicollier HN.700 Menestrel II

Type: 2-seat, low-wing monoplane, with fixed tailwheel undercarriage.
Construction: Wood and fabric.
Wing span: 25 ft 7 ins (7.8 m)
Length: 17 ft 5 ins (5.3 m)
Empty weight: 622 lb (282 kg)
Gross weight: 1,102 lb (500 kg)
Recommended engine: 80 hp (59.7 kW) Limbach
Maximum speed: 101 kts (116 mph) 187 km/h
Cruise speed: 95 kts (109 mph) 176 km/h
Stall speed: 43 kts (50 mph) 80 km/h
Take-off distance: 600 ft (183 m)
Climb rate: 1,280 ft (390 m) per minute (2 persons)
Range: 540 naut miles (621 miles) 1,000 km
Availability: Plans and some components.
Comments: 2-seat development of the HN.433 and 434.

↑ **Nicollier HN.700 Menestrel II** *(Geoffrey P. Jones)*

Nogaro Midour

Address:
Aero Club de Bas Armagnac, Aerodrom BP.17, 32110 Nogaro.
Telephone: +33 5 62 09 00 69 Facsimile: +33 5 62 09 01 32

Type: Tandem 2-seat, low-wing monoplane trainer and glider tug, with fixed nosewheel undercarriage.
Construction: Wood and composites.
Wing span: 28 ft 7 ins (8.72 m)
Length: 22 ft 4 ins (6.8 m)
Empty weight: 1,213 lb (550 kg)
Gross weight: 1,742 lb (790 kg)
Recommended engine: 180 hp (134 kW) Textron Lycoming O-360
Maximum speed: 162 kts (186 mph) 300 km/h
Cruise speed: 103 kts (118 mph) 190 km/h
Take-off distance: 460 ft (140 m)
Climb rate: 730 ft (220 m) per minute
Availability: Plans.
Comments: Designed at Nogaro by members of the Aero Club de Bas Armagnac, utilizing some Robin components. Specially silenced engine with 4-blade Hoffmann propeller.

Ollivier Collivier

Address:
Charles Ollivier, 85450 Chaille-les-Marais.

Type: 4-seat, low-wing, cabin monoplane, with retractable tailwheel undercarriage.
Construction: Wood and fabric.
Wing span: 28 ft 7 ins (8.72 m)
Length: 22 ft 10 ins (6.96 m)
Empty weight: 1,433 lb (650 kg)
Gross weight: 2,425 lb (1100 kg)
Recommended engine: 180 hp (134 kW) Textron Lycoming O-320
Maximum speed: 170 kts (196 mph) 315 km/h
Cruise speed: 150 kts (173 mph) 278 km/h
Stall speed: 57 kts (66 mph) 105 km/h
Range: 783 naut miles (900 miles) 1,450 km
Availability: Plans.
Comments: Based on the Robin DR.400 with retractable undercarriage. First flown 10 May 1989.

Paumier MP.2 Baladin

Address:
Norbert Parent, 500 route d'Ox, 31800 Seysses.

Type: Side-by-side 2-seat, low-wing monoplane, with retractable nosewheel undercarriage.
Construction: Wood and fabric.
Empty weight: 869 lb (394 kg)
Recommended engine: 90 hp (67 kW) Teledyne Continental C90-8F
Cruise speed: 124 kts (143 mph) 230 km/h
Availability: Plans.
Comments: First flown March 1961.

Pena Bilouis 01

Address:
Louis Pena, Les Hts de Saubagnacq, 6 imp Grand Piton, 40100 Dax.
Telephone: +33 5 58 90 00 71

Type: Tandem 2-seat, low-wing aerobatic monoplane, with retractable tailwheel undercarriage.
Construction: Steel tube, wood and fabric.
Wing span: 27 ft 7 ins (8.4 m)
Length: 21 ft 2 ins (6.45 m)
Empty weight: 1,279 lb (580 kg)
Gross weight: 1,896 lb (860 kg)
Recommended engine: 200 hp (149 kW) Textron Lycoming
Maximum speed: 167 kts (192 mph) 310 km/h
Cruise speed: 151 kts (174 mph) 280 km/h
Stall speed: 52 kts (59 mph) 95 km/h
Climb rate: 2,360 ft (720 m) per minute
Range: 458 naut miles (528 miles) 850 km
Availability: Plans.
Comments: 2-seat development of the Capena, stressed to +8/-6g and first flown at Dax in June 1991.

Pena Bilouis Dahu

Type: 4-seat, low-wing, mountain tourer, with fixed tailwheel undercarriage.
Construction: Wood.
Wing span: 29 ft 6 ins (9 m)
Length: 23 ft 9 ins (7.25 m)
Empty weight: 1,190-1,345 lb (540-610 kg)
Gross weight: 1,984-2,645 lb (900-1,200 kg)
Recommended engine: 180 hp (134 kW) Textron Lycoming
Maximum speed: 156 kts (180 mph) 290 km/h
Cruise speed: 108 kts (124 mph) 200 km/h
Stall speed: 49 kts (56 mph) 90 km/h
Take-off distance: 558 ft (170 m)
Range: 539 naut miles (621 miles) 1,000 km
Availability: Plans, plus those for fixed nosewheel and 2-seat variants.

↑ **Pena Bilouis Dahu prototype** *(Geoffrey P. Jones)*

Pena Capena 01

Type: Single-seat, low-wing, aerobatic monoplane, with fixed tailwheel undercarriage.
Construction: Wood.
Wing span: 22 ft 4 ins (6.8 m)
Length: 17 ft 8 ins (5.39 m)
Empty weight: 970 lb (440 kg)
Gross weight: 1,213 lb (550 kg)
Recommended engine: 108-160 hp (80.5-119 kW) Textron Lycoming, with possible 200 hp (149 kW)
Maximum speed: 199 kts (230 mph) 370 km/h
Cruise speed: 148 kts (170 mph) 275 km/h
Stall speed: 43 kts (50 mph) 80 km/h
Climb rate: 1,970 ft (600 m) per minute
Availability: Plans.
Comments: Designed by French aerobatic pilot Louis Pena. First flown in 1985.

Piel CP.80 Zef (Zephyr)

Address:
Avions Claude Piel, Le Mas de Darnetz, 19300 Egletons (*also* from Gene's Aircraft, 118 Notre-Dame, Le Gardeur, Quebec J5Z 3C3, Canada).
Telephone: +33 5 55 93 09 79 (Canada: +1 514 585 4059)

Type: Single-seat, low-wing, racing monoplane, with fixed tailwheel undercarriage.
Construction: Wood, with polyester wingtips.
Wing span: 19 ft 8 ins (6 m)
Length: 17 ft 5 ins (5.3 m)
Empty weight: 573 lb (260 kg)
Gross weight: 838 lb (380 kg)
Recommended engine: 90 hp (67 kW) Teledyne Continental C90
Maximum speed: 174 kts (200 mph) 322 km/h
Cruise speed: 135 kts (155 mph) 249 km/h
Stall speed: 52 kts (59 mph) 95 km/h
Take-off distance: 655 ft (200 m)
Climb rate: 2,360 ft (720 m) per minute
Range: 243 naut miles (280 miles) 450 km
Availability: Plans.
Comments: Used for Formula One air racing.

Piel CP.90 Pinocchio

Type: Single-seat, low-wing monoplane, with fixed tailwheel undercarriage.
Construction: Wood and fabric.
Wing span: 23 ft 7 ins (7.2 m)
Length: 19 ft 8 ins (6 m)
Empty weight: 738 lb (335 kg)
Gross weight: 1,102 lb (500 kg)
Recommended engine: 100 hp (74.6 kW) Teledyne Continental O-200
Maximum speed: 140 kts (162 mph) 260 km/h
Cruise speed: 124 kts (143 mph) 230 km/h
Stall speed: 41 kts (47 mph) 75 km/h
Take-off distance: 590 ft (180 m)
Climb rate: 1,575 ft (480 m) per minute
Range: 297 naut miles (341 miles) 550 km
Availability: Plans.
Comments: Smaller, single-seat version of the Emeraude, suitable for aerobatics.

Piel CP.328 Super Emeraude

Type: Side-by-side 2-seat, low-wing, cabin monoplane, with fixed tailwheel undercarriage.
Construction: Wood and fabric.
Wing span: 26 ft 5 ins (8.04 m)
Length: 21 ft 2 ins (6.45 m)
Empty weight: 904 lb (410 kg)
Gross weight: 1,543 lb (700 kg)
Recommended engine: 100-115 hp (74.6-85.75 kW) Teledyne Teledyne Continental
Maximum speed: 124 kts (143 mph) 230 km/h
Cruise speed: 111 kts (127 mph) 205 km/h
Stall speed: 53 kts (61 mph) 97 km/h
Take-off distance: 755 ft (230 m)
Climb rate: 787 ft (240 m) per minute
Range: 540 naut miles (621 miles) 1,000 km
Availability: Plans.
Comments: Developed from the Emeraude. Hundreds flying worldwide, including commercially built variants.

↑ **Piel CP.328 Super Emeraude** *(Geoffrey P. Jones)*

Piel CP.402 Donald

Type: Single-seat, high-wing, cabin monoplane, with fixed tailwheel or tail-dragger undercarriage.
Construction: Wood and fabric.
Wing span: 24 ft 6 ins (7.47 m)
Length: 16 ft 5 ins (5 m)
Empty weight: 309 lb (140 kg)
Gross weight: 551 lb (250 kg)
Recommended engine: 45 hp (33.6 kW) Volkswagen or 65 hp (48.5 kW) Teledyne Continental
Maximum speed: 70 kts (81 mph) 130 km/h
Cruise speed: 59 kts (68 mph) 110 km/h
Stall speed: 30 kts (34 mph) 55 km/h
Availability: Plans.
Comments: First flown on 16 June 1953. Examples still being built in France.

↑ **Piel CP.402 Donald built by Claude Fouissac** *(Geoffrey P. Jones)*

Piel CP.605 Diamant

Type: 3/4-seat, low-wing, cabin monoplane, with fixed or retractable (CP.605B) nosewheel undercarriage.
Construction: Wood and fabric.
Wing span: 30 ft 2 ins (9.2 m)
Length: 23 ft (7 m)
Empty weight: 1,146 lb (520 kg)
Gross weight: 1,874 lb (850 kg)
Recommended engine: 160 hp (119.3 kW) Textron Lycoming IO-320

Maximum speed: 140 kts (162 mph) 260 km/h
Cruise speed: 124 kts (143 mph) 230 km/h
Stall speed: 45 kts (51 mph) 82 km/h
Take-off distance: 525 ft (160 m)
Climb rate: 1,080 ft (330 m) per minute
Range: 621 naut miles (714 miles) 1,150 km
Availability: Plans.
Comments: Development of Emeraude. CP.604 prototype first flew in 1964. CP.605 is certificated for commercial production.

Piel CP.751 Beryl

Type: Tandem 2-seat, low-wing monoplane, with fixed tailwheel undercarriage.
Construction: Wood.
Wing span: 26 ft 5 ins (8.04 m)
Length: 22 ft 8 ins (6.9 m)
Empty weight: 1,058 lb (480 kg)
Gross weight: 1,675 lb (760 kg)
Recommended engine: 180 hp (134 kW) Textron Lycoming O-360
Maximum speed: 151 kts (174 mph) 280 km/h
Cruise speed: 135 kts (155 mph) 250 km/h
Stall speed: 54 kts (62 mph) 100 km/h
Take-off distance: 623 ft (190 m)
Climb rate: 1,280 ft (390 m) per minute
Range: 593 naut miles (683 miles) 1,100 km
Availability: Plans.
Comments: Uses the Emeraude wing, and is suitable for aerobatics. Several CP.70 variants, including retractable nosewheel undercarriage version and with different engines.

Piel CP.1320 Saphir

Type: 3-seat, low-wing monoplane, with retractable tailwheel undercarriage.
Construction: Wood.
Wing span: 27 ft 11 ins (8.5 m)
Length: 22 ft (6.7 m)
Empty weight: 1,426 lb (647 kg)
Gross weight: 1,852 lb (840 kg)
Recommended engine: 160 hp (119 kW) Textron Lycoming
Maximum speed: 162 kts (186 mph) 300 km/h
Cruise speed: 146 kts (168 mph) 270 km/h
Stall speed: 46 kts (53 mph) 85 km/h
Take-off distance: 1,180 ft (360 m)
Range: 1,080 naut miles (1,242 miles) 2,000 km
Availability: Plans.
Comments: Combines features of the Super Emeraude with 3-seats of the Super Diamant. Aerobatic with 2 occupants, stressed to +5, –2.5g.

Pottier P.50 Bouvreuil (Bullfinch)

Address: Jean Pottier, 4 rue de Poissy, 78130 Les Mureaux.
Telephone: +33 1 30 91 96 43 **Facsimile:** +33 1 34 92 97 26

Type: Single-seat, low-wing monoplane, with retractable or non-retractable tail-dragger undercarriage.
Construction: Wood.
Wing span: 20 ft 4 ins (6.2 m)
Length: 18 ft 6 ins (5.65 m)
Empty weight: 595 lb (270 kg)
Gross weight: 882 lb (400 kg)
Recommended engine: 100 hp (74.6 kW) Teledyne Continental
Maximum speed: 167 kts (192 mph) 310 km/h
Cruise speed: 151 kts (174 mph) 280 km/h
Stall speed: 43 kts (50 mph) 80 km/h
Availability: Plans.
Comments: First example built by Michel Sugnaux in Switzerland with a retractable undercarriage. First flown 27 July 1979.

Pottier P.60 Minacro

Type: Single-seat, aerobatic biplane, with fixed tailwheel undercarriage.
Construction: Wood and fabric.
Wing span: 16 ft 5 ins (5 m)
Length: 15 ft 1 ins (4.6 m)
Empty weight: 617 lb (280 kg)
Gross weight: 937 lb (425 kg)
Recommended engine: 90 hp (67 kW) Teledyne Continental C90F
Maximum speed: 113 kts (130 mph) 210 km/h
Cruise speed: 103 kts (118 mph) 190 km/h
Stall speed: 46 kts (53 mph) 85 km/h
Take-off distance: 328 ft (100 m)
Climb rate: 1,312 ft (400 m) per minute
Range: 308 naut miles (354 miles) 570 km
Availability: Plans.
Comments: First example completed in Austria by M. Auboeck.

↑ **Pottier P.60 built by George Caminade at Sarlat, France** *(Geoffrey P. Jones)*

Pottier P.70S

Type: Single-seat, mid-wing monoplane, with either nosewheel or tailwheel undercarriage.
Construction: Metal.
Wing span: 19 ft 2 ins (5.85 m)
Length: 16 ft 11 ins (5.15 m)
Empty weight: 474 lb (215 kg)
Gross weight: 794 lb (360 kg)
Recommended engine: 40-60 hp (30-44.7 kW) Volkswagen
Maximum speed: 111 kts (127 mph) 205 km/h
Cruise speed: 97 kts (112 mph) 180 km/h
Stall speed: 38 kts (44 mph) 70 km/h
Take-off distance: 755 ft (230 m)
Climb rate: 490 ft (150 m) per minute
Range: 216 naut miles (248 miles) 400 km
Availability: Plans and some components.

↑ **Pottier P.70S built by G Mallett at Meaux, France** *(Geoffrey P. Jones)*

Pottier P.80S

Type: Single seat, low-wing monoplane, with fixed nosewheel or tailwheel undercarriage.
Construction: Metal.
Wing span: 19 ft 2 ins (5.85 m)
Length: 16 ft 11 ins (5.15 m)
Empty weight: 441 lb (200 kg)
Gross weight: 794 lb (360 kg)
Recommended engine: 40-70 hp (30-52.2 kW) Volkswagen
Maximum speed: 116 kts (134 mph) 215 km/h
Cruise speed: 97 kts (112 mph) 180 km/h
Stall speed: 38 kts (44 mph) 70 km/h
Take-off distance: 755 ft (230 m)
Climb rate: 490 ft (150 m) per minute
Range: 216 naut miles (248 miles) 400 km
Availability: Plans and some components.

Pottier P.100TS and P.110TS

Details: P.100TS, exept under Comments.
Type: 2/3 seat, high-wing, cabin monoplane, with fixed nosewheel undercarriage.
Construction: Metal.
Wing span: 22 ft 6 ins (6.85 m)
Length: 21 ft 4 ins (6.5 m)
Empty weight: 959 lb (435 kg)
Gross weight: 1,499 lb (680 kg)
Recommended engine: 100 hp (74.6 kW) Teledyne Continental
Maximum speed: 135 kts (155 mph) 250 km/h
Cruise speed: 127 kts (146 mph) 235 km/h
Stall speed: 43 kts (50 mph) 80 km/h
Take-off distance: 755 ft (230 m)
Climb rate: 1,220 ft (370 m) per minute
Range: 351 naut miles (404 miles) 650 km
Availability: Plans.
Comments: Prototype first flew on 16 October 1980. Full 3-seat version is the P.110TS, for engines up to 150 hp (112 kW).

Pottier P.170S

Type: Tandem 2-seat, mid-wing monoplane, with fixed or retractable nosewheel undercarriage.
Construction: Metal.
Wing span: 19 ft 8 ins (6 m)
Length: 18 ft 8 ins (5.7 m)
Empty weight: 507 lb (230 kg)
Gross weight: 981 lb (445 kg)
Recommended engine: 70 hp (52.2 kW) Volkswagen
Maximum speed: 111 kts (127 mph) 205 km/h
Cruise speed: 100 kts (115 mph) 185 km/h
Stall speed: 43 kts (50 mph) 80 km/h
Take-off distance: 920 ft (280 m)
Climb rate: 985 ft (300 m) per minute
Range: 216 naut miles (248 miles) 400 km
Availability: Plans and some components.

Pottier P.180S

Type: Side-by-side 2-seat, low-wing monoplane, with fixed nosewheel undercarriage.
Construction: Metal.
Wing span: 21 ft 4 ins (6.5 m)
Length: 17 ft 7 ins (5.35 m)
Empty weight: 529 lb (240 kg)
Gross weight: 1,268 lb (575 kg)
Recommended engine: 70 hp (52.2 kW) Volkswagen
Maximum speed: 108 kts (124 mph) 200 km/h
Cruise speed: 97 kts (112 mph) 180 km/h
Stall speed: 46 kts (53 mph) 85 km/h
Take-off distance: 820 ft (250 m)
Climb rate: 550 ft (168 m) per minute
Range: 324 naut miles (373 miles) 600 km
Availability: Plans and some components.
Comments: One of France's most popular homebuilt designs.

Pottier P.190S Castor

Type: Side-by-side 2-seat, low-wing monoplane, with fixed nosewheel undercarriage.
Construction: Wood and fabric.
Wing span: 21 ft 4 ins (6.5 m)
Length: 17 ft 7 ins (5.35 m)
Recommended engine: 55-90 hp (41-67 kW)
Availability: Plans.
Comments: Wooden version of the P.180S.

Pottier P.210S Coati and P.220S Koala

Details: P.220S Koala, except under Comments.
Type: Side-by-side 2-seat, low-wing monoplane, with fixed nosewheel undercarriage.
Construction: Metal.
Wing span: 21 ft 4 ins (6.5 m)
Length: 18 ft 2 ins (5.54 m)
Empty weight: 595 lb (270 kg)
Gross weight: 1,058 lb (480 kg)
Recommended engine: 75 hp (56 kW) Volkswagen
Maximum speed: 113 kts (130 mph) 210 km/h
Cruise speed: 103 kts (118 mph) 190 km/h
Stall speed: 43 kts (50 mph) 80 km/h
Take-off distance: 623 ft (190 m)
Range: 378 naut miles (435 miles) 700 km
Availability: Plans.
Comments: 2-seat and nosewheel version of the similar single-seat Pottier P.210S Coati tail-dragger.

Pottier P.230S Panda

Type: 3-seat, low-wing, cabin monoplane, with fixed nosewheel undercarriage.
Construction: Metal.

Wing span: 26 ft 7 ins (8.1 m)
Length: 20 ft 10 ins (6.35 m)
Empty weight: 838 lb (380 kg)
Gross weight: 1,543 lb (700 kg)
Recommended engine: 100 hp (74.6 kW) Teledyne Continental
Maximum speed: 121 kts (140 mph) 225 km/h
Cruise speed: 113 kts (130 mph) 210 km/h
Stall speed: 49 kts (56 mph) 90 km/h
Take-off distance: 690 ft (210 m)
Climb rate: 788 ft (240 m) per minute
Range: 405 naut miles (466 miles) 750 km
Availability: Plans and some components.
Comments: Prototype built by Charles Bire and first flown in 1990. 4 seat version is the P.240S Saiga for 150-180 hp (112-134 kW) engines. See also SG Aviation in Italy.

↑ **Pottier P.230S Panda** *(Geoffrey P. Jones)*

Pottier P.300 Ara

Type: 3-seat, low-wing monoplane, with a V-tail, pusher engine and retractable nosewheel undercarriage.
Construction: Composites.
Wing span: 22 ft 8 ins (6.9 m)
Length: 15 ft 9 ins (4.8 m)
Recommended engine: 120 hp (89.5 kW) Limbach
Cruise speed: 175 kts (202 mph) 325 km/h
Stall speed: 58 kts (66 mph) 106 km/h *clean*, 48 kts (56 mph) 89 km/h *with flaps*
Range: 540 naut miles (621 miles) 1,000 km
Availability: Prototype was still under construction at the time of writing. Kits are expected.
Comments: Prototype under construction by Charles Bire.

Quaissard GQ-01 Monogast

Address:
Gaston Quaissard, 4 rue Boileau, 01000 Bourg-en-Bresse.

Type: Single-seat, high-wing, cabin monoplane, with fixed tailwheel undercarriage.
Construction: Wood and fabric.
Wing span: 24 ft 1 ins (7.33 m)
Length: 18 ft 4 ins (5.58 m)
Recommended engine: 47 hp (35 kW) Volkswagen 1,600cc
Maximum speed: 81 kts (93 mph) 150 km/h
Cruise speed: 70 kts (81 mph) 130 km/h
Stall speed: 35 kts (41 mph) 65 km/h
Availability: Plans.
Comments: Prototype first flew on 15 November 1983.

↑ **Quaissard GQ-01 Monogast built by Daniel Labrusie** *(Geoffrey P. Jones)*

SMAN Petrel

Details can be found in the 1996-97 edition of *WA&SD*.

Stern/Mallick SM-01 Vega

Address:
René Stern, 10 rue du Château, 57730 Folscherville
(*also* from Gene's Aircraft, 118 Notre-Dame, Le Gardeur, Quebec J5Z 3C3, Canada).
Telephone: +33 3 87 92 25 49 (Canada: +1 514 585 4059)

Type: Side-by-side 2-seat, low-wing monoplane, with fixed tailwheel undercarriage.
Construction: Wood and fabric.
Wing span: 24 ft 11 ins (7.6 m)
Length: 19 ft 4 ins (5.9 m)
Empty weight: 1,014 lbg (460 kg)
Gross weight: 1,499 lb (680 kg)
Recommended engine: 115 hp (85.75 kW) Textron Lycoming O-235
Maximum speed: 140 kts (162 mph) 260 km/h
Cruise speed: 113 kts (130 mph) 210 km/h
Stall speed: 45 kts (51 mph) 82 km/h
Take-off distance: 600 ft (183 m)
Climb rate: 900 ft (274 m) per minute
Range: 521 naut miles (600 miles) 965 km
Availability: Plans.
Comments: Developed from the Stern ST-87 with the assistance of Richard Mallick. First flown in 1992.

↑ **Stern/Mallick SM-01 Vega prototype** *(Geoffrey P. Jones)*

Stern ST-87 Europlane

Type: Side-by-side 2-seat, low-wing monoplane, with fixed nosewheel undercarriage.
Construction: Wood and fabric.
Wing span: 24 ft 11 ins (7.6 m)
Length: 19 ft 4 ins (5.9 m)
Empty weight: 842 lb (382 kg)
Gross weight: 1,323 lb (600 kg)
Recommended engine: 80 hp (59.7 kW) Limbach
Maximum speed: 135 kts (155 mph) 250 km/h
Cruise speed: 103 kts (118 mph) 190 km/h
Stall speed: 43 kts (50 mph) 80 km/h
Range: 499 naut miles (575 miles) 975 km
Availability: Plans.
Comments: Developed from the single-seat ST-80 Balade. First flown on 7 June 1991.

Synairgie SkyRanger, Skylight and Jet Ranger

Address:
Synairgie, 19 avenue de la Gare, 76340 Blangy sur Bresle.
Telephone: +33 2 35 93 63 50
Facsimile: +33 2 35 94 25 05

Details: SkyRanger, except under Comments.
Type: Side-by-side 2-seat, high-wing microlight, with fixed nosewheel undercarriage.
Construction: Steel tube and fabric.
Wing span: 31 ft 2 ins (9.5 m)
Empty weight: 467 lb (212 kg)
Gross weight: 992 lb (450 kg)
Recommended engine: 80 hp (59.6 kW) Rotax 912

↑ **Synairgie SkyRanger** *(Geoffrey P. Jones)*

Maximum speed: 86 kts (99 mph) 160 km/h
Cruise speed: 76 kts (87 mph) 140 km/h
Stall speed: 35 kts (41 mph) 65 km/h
Climb rate: 985 ft (300 m) per minute
Availability: Kits.
Comments: Synairgie Skylight is a light Rotax 503-powered version with no flaps, and Jet Ranger is a tandem 2-seat version with a Rotax 582.

Tech'Aero TR.200 (Cobra)

Address:
Tech'Aero, le Bois d'Oissel, 27190 Glisolles.
Telephone: +33 2 32 37 60 01
Facsimile: +33 2 32 37 00 14

Type: Tandem 2-seat, competition/aerobatic monoplane, with fixed tailwheel undercarriage.
Construction: Steel tube, wood and fabric.
Wing span: 26 ft 3 ins (8 m)
Length: 21 ft (6.4 m)
Empty weight: 1,237 lb (561 kg)
Gross weight: 1,920 lb (871 kg)
Recommended engine: 200 hp (149 kW) Textron Lycoming AEIO-360A1B
Maximum speed: 169 kts (194 mph) 313 km/h
Cruise speed: 158 kts (181 mph) 292 km/h
Stall speed: 53 kts (61 mph) 97 km/h
Take-off distance over a 35 ft (11 m) obstacle: 1,300 ft (396 m)
Climb rate: 2,200 ft (670 m) per minute
Range: 700 naut miles (810 miles) 1,304 km, at 55% power
Availability: Kits.
Comments: Designed by Gerard Feugray. More than 10 flying. Stressed to +10/-9g.

↑ **Tech'Aero TR.200, known as the Cobra** *(Geoffrey P. Jones)*

Germany

B & L BL.1 Kéa

Address:
B & L Hinz, Bei der Kirche 17, D-70794 Filderstadt.
Telephone: +49 7158 65441

Type: Side-by-side 2-seat, low-wing monoplane, with single retractable main wheel, outriggers under wings, and tailwheel.
Construction: Composites.
Wing span: 32 ft 10 ins (10 m)
Empty weight: 970 lb (440 kg)
Gross weight: 1,587 lb (720 kg)
Recommended engine: 90 hp (67 kW) Limbach L2400
Maximum speed: 145 kts (168 mph) 270 km/h
Cruise speed: 132 kts (152 mph) 245 km/h
Stall speed: 46 kts (53 mph) 85 km/h
Climb rate: 985 ft (300 m) per minute
Availability: Plans.
Comments: Detachable wings and tail. High-performance version, the BL.2 Ara, is under development.

↑ **B & L BL.1 Kéa** *(Geoffrey P. Jones)*

Cosy Europe Cozy Classic

Address:
Uli Wolter, Cosy Europe, Ahornstrasse 10, D-86510 Ried.
Telephone: +49 8233 60594
Facsimile: +49 8233 20150

Type: 2/3-seat canard type, with a pusher engine, and retractable nose gear and fixed main wheels.
Construction: Mostly composites.
Wing span: 26 ft 4 ins (8.03 m)
Length: 17 ft 9 ins (5.4 m)
Empty weight: 960 lb (435 kg)
Gross weight: 1,750 lb (794 kg)
Recommended engine: 160 hp (119 kW) Textron Lycoming IO-320
Maximum speed: 195 kts (225 mph) 362 km/h
Cruise speed: 162 kts (187 mph) 301 km/h
Stall speed: 58 kts (67 mph) 108 km/h
Take-off distance: 1,476 ft (450 m)
Climb rate: 1,500 ft (457 m) per minute
Range: 868 naut miles (1,000 miles) 1,609 km
Availability: Plans and kits.
Comments: Cosy Europe purchased the design rights to the Cozy from Nat Puffer in 1987. Original US Cozy first flew on 19 July 1982. French kits are available from Stratifies Composites Aeronautiques of Bourges.

Dallach Sunrise II

Address:
W.D. Flugzeugleichtbau GmbH, Foststrasse 15, 73529 Schwäb Gmünd Strassdorf.
Telephone: +49 71 71 48 04
Facsimile: +49 71 71 4 41 98

Type: Tandem 2-seat, open-cockpit microlight, with fixed tailwheel undercarriage, available as low-wing monoplane or biplane.
Construction: Steel tube, wood and fabric.
Wing span: 42 ft 11 ins (13.08 m)
Length: 17 ft 5 ins (5.31 m)
Empty weight: 331 lb (150 kg)
Gross weight: 728 lb (330 kg)
Recommended engine: 40 hp (30 kW) KKHD
Maximum speed: 81 kts (93 mph) 150 km/h
Cruise speed: 65 kts (75 mph) 121 km/h
Stall speed: 22 kts (25 mph) 41 mph
Climb rate: 570 ft (175 m) per minute
Availability: Kits and assembled.
Comments: Biplane version has a shorter wing span.

Dallach D.3 Sunwheel

Type: Tandem 2-seat, open-cockpit biplane, with fixed tailwheel undercarriage.
Construction: Steel tube, wood and fabric.
Wing span: 23 ft (7 m)
Length: 18 ft 8 ins (5.7 m)
Empty weight: 485 lb (220 kg)
Gross weight: 882 lb (400 kg)
Recommended engine: 65 hp (48.5 kW) Sauer ULM 2000 (optional Rotax 912 UL)
Maximum speed: 78 kts (90 mph) 145 km/h
Cruise speed: 70 kts (81 mph) 130 km/h
Stall speed: 30 kts (34 mph) 55 km/h
Take-off distance: 230 ft (70 m)
Climb rate: 690 ft (210 m) per minute
Range: 161 naut miles (186 miles) 300 km
Availability: Kits.
Comments: Capable of limited aerobatics and stressed to +8/-4.5g.

↑ **Dallach D.3 Sunwheel built in France** *(Geoffrey P. Jones)*

Dallach D.4 Fascination

Address:
See Sunrise entry. US agents: Siggi's Airplane Works Inc, 372 Briarwood Road, Venice, FL 34293.
Telephone: USA: +1 941 484 9100
Facsimile: USA: +1 941 493 0230

Type: Side-by-side 2-seat, low-wing, cabin monoplane, with retractable nosewheel undercarriage. Tailwheel version is available.
Construction: Steel tube, metal and composites.
Wing span: 29 ft 5 ins (8.97 m)
Length: 20 ft 5 ins (6.22 m)
Empty weight: 551 lb (250 kg)
Gross weight: 1,202 lb (545 kg)
Recommended engine: 80 hp (59.6 kW) Rotax 912 (future options for Rotax 914)
Maximum speed: 166 kts (191 mph) 308 km/h
Cruise speed: 140 kts (161 mph) 259 km/h
Stall speed: 35 kts (41 mph) 65 km/h
Take-off distance: 230 ft (70 m)
Climb rate: 1,100 ft (335 m) per minute
Range: 524 naut miles (604 miles) 972 km, increased with optional wingtip tanks
Availability: Kits.
Comments: First 2 German-built examples flew in 1996. Launched in the USA in 1997.

↑ **Dallach D.4 Fascination at RSA Epinal rally** *(Geoffrey P. Jones)*

Delta Dart II

Address:
Delta Dart Flugzeugbau, Mühlenstrasse 26, D-39435 Egeln.
Telephone: +49 39 268 92200
Facsimile: +49 39 268 92202

Type: Tandem 2-seat, pusher-engined homebuilt, with rear delta wings and endplate fins/rudders, forward canard and retractable nosewheel undercarriage.
Construction: Composites.
Wing span: 20 ft 6 ins (6.25 m)
Length: 18 ft 2 ins (5.54 m)
Empty weight: 551 lb (250 kg)
Gross weight: 992 lb (450 kg)
Recommended engine: 75 hp (56 kW) Wankel
Maximum speed: 135 kts (155 mph) 250 km/h
Range: 755 naut miles (870 miles) 1,400 km
Comments: First flew in 1992. Example completed in South Africa.

Funk FK.6

Address:
B & F Technik Vertriebs GmbH, Am Neuen Rheinhafen 10, D-67346 Speyer/Rhein.
Telephone: +49 62 32 72076 or 72077
Facsimile: +49 62 32 72078

Type: Single-seat, high-wing monoplane, with a pusher engine, V-tail and fixed tail-dragger undercarriage.
Construction: Metal, composites and fabric.
Wing span: 36 ft 1 ins (11 m)
Length: 17 ft 9 ins (5.41 m)
Empty weight: 331 lb (150 kg)
Gross weight: 551 lb (250 kg)
Recommended engine: 22 hp (16.4 kW) Hirth 263-A
Maximum speed: 81 kts (93 mph) 150 km/h
Cruise speed: 65 kts (75 mph) 121 km/h
Take-off distance: 230 ft (70 m)
Climb rate: 700 ft (213 m) per minute
Range: 404 naut miles (466 miles) 750 km
Availability: Plans.
Comments: Built as a private project at former MBB's Speyer factory and first flown in early 1985.

Funk FK.9

Type: Side-by-side 2-seat, high-wing monoplane, with a tail-dragger undercarriage (see Comments).
Construction: Steel tube and fabric; some wood and foam.
Wing span: 32 ft 2 ins (9.8 m)
Length: 19 ft 2 ins (5.85 m)
Empty weight: 441 lb (200 kg)/507 lb (230 kg) (Rotax 503/912)
Gross weight: 992 lb (450 kg)
Engine: 46 hp (34.3 kW) Rotax 503 DCDI or 80 hp (59.7 kW) Rotax 912 UL
Maximum speed: 89 kts (103 mph) 165 km/h
Cruise speed: 86 kts (99 mph) 160 km/h
Take-off distance: 328 ft (100 m)
Climb rate: 1,365 ft (415 m) per minute
Range: 341 naut miles (393 miles) 633 km
Availability: Kits, without engine, instruments, seats.
Comments: Folding wings. In production since 1991. Also available with fixed nosewheel undercarriage as FK.9TG. Manufactured by Central School of Aviation Technology at Krosno, Poland. 80+ delivered at time of writing.

↑ **Funk FK.9TG with nosewheel undercarriage** *(Geoffrey P. Jones)*

Funk FK.9 Mark 3

Type: Side-by-side 2-seat, high-wing monoplane, with fixed nosewheel undercarriage.
Construction: Steel tube and composites.
Wing span: 32 ft 4 ins (9.85 m)
Length: 19 ft 2 ins (5.85 m)
Empty weight: 595 lb (270 kg)
Recommended engine: 77.8 hp (58 kW) Rotax 912
Maximum speed: 130 kts (149 mph) 240 km/h
Availability: Kits.
Comments: Unveilled at Aero '97 in Friedrichschafen.

Funk FK.12 Comet

Type: Tandem 2-seat, open-cockpit, microlight biplane, with fixed tailwheel undercarriage.
Construction: Steel tube, metal and fabric.
Wing span: 22 ft (6.7 m)
Length: 17 ft 5 ins (5.3 m)
Empty weight: 529 lb (240 kg)
Gross weight: 992 lb (450 kg)
Recommended engine: 80 hp (59.6 kW) Rotax 912 (optional Rotax 914)
Maximum speed: 119 kts (137 mph) 220 km/h
Cruise speed: 100 kts (116 mph) 186 km/h
Stall speed: 35 kts (41 mph) 65 km/h
Availability: Kits.
Comments: First flown in 1997.

↑ **Funk FK.12 Comet prototype**

Hepp HX.300 Surprise

Address:
August Hepp, Schienenhof 4, D-88427 Bad Schussenried.
Telephone: +49 7392 18184
Facsimile: +49 7392 150424

Type: Side-by-side 2-seat, low-wing, cabin monoplane, with fixed nosewheel undercarriage.
Construction: Composites.
Wing span: 23 ft 4 ins (7.1 m)
Length: 16 ft 9 ins (5.1 m)
Empty weight: 551 lb (250 kg)
Gross weight: 992 lb (450 kg)

Recommended engine: 80 hp (59.6 kW) Rotax 912
Availability: Kits.

↑ **Hepp HX.300 Surprise in unfinished form** *(Geoffrey P. Jones)*

Ikarus C.22

Address: Ikarus Comco, Flugplatz Mengen, Am Flugplatz 11, D-88367 Hohentengen.
Telephone: +49 70 344082

Type: Side-by-side 2-seat, high-wing microlight, with fixed nosewheel undercarriage.
Construction: Alloy tube and fabric.
Wing span: 34 ft 1 ins (10.4 m)
Empty weight: 408 lb (185 kg)
Gross weight: 882 lb (400 kg)
Recommended engine: 64 hp (47.7 kW)
Maximum speed: 78 kts (90 mph) 145 km/h
Cruise speed: 70 kts (81 mph) 130 km/h
Stall speed: 30 kts (34 mph) 55 km/h
Climb rate: 985 ft (300 m) per minute
Availability: Complete aircraft.
Comments: Designed by Swiss engineer Hans Gygax. More than 1,000 built and flown since 1982. Ikarus C.42 Cyclone, developed from C.22, is now manufactured in US by Flightstar.

↑ **Ikarus C.22** *(Geoffrey P. Jones)*

Leichtflugzeug Sky Walker

Address: Leichtflugzeug GmbH & Co KG, Osemundstrasse 22, D-5982 Neuenrade.
Telephone: +49 2392 6309

Type: Tandem 2-seat, open-cockpit, high-wing microlight/homebuilt, with pusher engine and fixed nosewheel undercarriage or floats.
Construction: Steel tube and fabric.
Wing span: 33 ft 3 ins (10.13 m)
Length: 18 ft 8 ins (5.69 m)
Empty weight: 392 lb (178 kg)
Gross weight: 833 lb (378 kg)
Recommended engine: 50 hp (37.3 kW) Rotax 503 (option for Rotax 582 or Sauer UL2100)
Maximum speed: 65 kts (75 mph) 121 km/h
Stall speed: 31 kts (35 mph) 57 km/h
Climb rate: 590 ft (180 m) per minute
Range: 247 naut miles (285 miles) 458 km
Availability: Kits and assembled.
Comments: Used by the Helmond Police in the Netherlands.

LO-Fluggerätebau LO-120

Address: LO-Fluggerätebau GmbH, Aspachstrasse 14, D-88276 Effishofen.
Telephone: +49 751 55 1014 **Facsimile:** +49 751 55 1032

Type: Tandem 2-seat, open-cockpit, high-wing homebuilt/microlight, with pusher engine, twin tail booms and inverted V tail unit. Fixed nosewheel undercarriage.
Wing span: 50 ft 10 ins (15.5 m)
Length: 24 ft 3 ins (7.4 m)
Gross weight: 990 lb (450 kg)
Recommended engine: 39.6 hp (29.5 kW) Hirth 2704, or Rotax 447 or Rotax 503
Maximum speed: 81 kts (93 mph) 150 km/h
Cruise speed: 62 kts (71 mph) 115 km/h
Stall speed: 27 kts (31 mph) 50 km/h
Climb rate: 690 ft (210 m) per minute
Range: 377 naut miles (435 miles) 700 km
Availability: Kits.
Comments: Version is the **LO-120 Bausatz I**, which has a shorter wing span (39 ft 4 ins, 12 m) and reduced length (22 ft 11 ins, 7 m).

Panek/Mattlener PUL 10

See under Aerdelta, Italy.

Platzer Kiebitz and P.4 Motte

Address: Michael Platzer, Am Rohleiber 20, 34302 Elleuberg.
Telephone: +49 5665 2820

Details: Kiebitz, except under Comments and photograph/caption.
Type: Tandem 2-seat, microlight biplane, with fixed tailwheel undercarriage.
Construction: Steel tube fuselage and wood/composite wings.
Empty weight: 463 lb (210 kg)
Gross weight: 882 lb (400 kg)
Recommended engine: 74 hp (55.2 kW) Sauer VW UL2100
Cruise speed: 59 kts (68 mph) 110 km/h
Stall speed: 35 kts (41 mph) 65 km/h
Availability: Plans and kits.
Comments: Designed by Michael Platzer and approximately based on the Fw Stieglitz. Also available is a parasol-wing monoplane version as the P.4 Motte, with a 100 hp (74.6 kW) Mid-West rotary or other engine.

↑ **Platzer P.4 Motte with a Nissan Micra engine** *(Geoffrey P. Jones)*

PC Flight Pretty Flight

Address: Calin Gologan, Dr. Herrmannstrasse 4, D-87710 Mindelheim, or Peter Maderitsch, Panorama Strasse 6, D-88450 Berkheim.
Telephone: +49 8261 6215 or 8395 2986 **Facsimile:** +49 8261 20455 or 8395 2986 **E-mail:** calin.gologan@t-online.de

Type: Side-by-side 2-seat, high-wing, cabin microlight, with fixed nosewheel undercarriage.
Construction: Metal and fabric.
Wing span: 32 ft 10 ins (10 m)
Empty weight: 595 lb (270 kg)
Gross weight: 992 lb (450 kg)
Recommended engine: 80 hp (59.6 kW) Rotax 912 UL
Maximum speed: 113 kts (130 mph) 210 km/h
Cruise speed: 105 kts (121 mph) 195 km/h
Stall speed: 34 kts (39 mph) 62 km/h
Take-off distance: 328 ft (100 m)
Climb rate: 1,080 ft (330 m) per minute
Availability: Kits.
Comments: Designed by Calin Gologan and first flown in 1997. Special wingtip design for improved low-speed control.

↑ **PC Flight Pretty Flight**

Tandem Aircraft Sunny

Address: Tandem Aircraft KG, Am Flugplatz, D-88348 Saulgau.
Telephone: +49 7581 8479 **Facsimile:** +49 7581 8169

Type: 2-seat, positive-stagger, biplane microlight of interlinked box-wing configuration, with pusher engine and fixed undercarriage (single-seat version also available).
Construction: Alloy tube, stainless steel and fabric.
Wing span: 22 ft (7 m)
Length: 12 ft 5 ins (3.8 m)
Empty weight: 414 lb (188 kg)
Gross weight: 881 lb (400 kg)
Recommended engine: 64 hp (47.7 kW). Also suitable for Rotax engines of 60-80 hp (44.7-59.7 kW).
Maximum speed: 81 kts (93 mph) 150 km/h
Cruise speed: 70 kts (81 mph) 130 km/h
Stall speed: Claimed not to stall but minimum speed of 30 kts (34 mph) 55 km/h
Climb rate: 1,020 ft (310 m) per minute
Range: 173 naut miles (200 miles) 321 km
Availability: Commercially built but kits of the single-seat version have been made available.
Comments: First flown in 1990. Over 100 sold in Germany and France.

↑ **Tandem Aircraft Sunny in 2-seat form** *(Geoffrey P. Jones)*

Ultraleicht Wild Thing

Address: Air-light GmbH-Süd, Hauptstrasse 98, D-90562 Heroldsberg.
Telephone: +49 911 518 8803 **Facsimile:** +49 911 518 7319

Type: Side-by-side 2-seat, high-wing, cabin monoplane, with fixed tailwheel undercarriage.
Construction: Metal.
Wing span: 30 ft 2 ins (9.2 m)
Length: 22 ft 8 ins (6.9 m)
Empty weight: 602 lb (273 kg)
Gross weight: 992 lb (450 kg)
Recommended engine: 80 hp (59.7 kW) Jabiru (optional 94 hp, 70 kW Hirth F30)
Maximum speed: 116 kts (134 mph) 215 km/h

↑ **Ultraleicht Wild Thing**

Cruise speed: 92 kts (106 mph) 170 km/h
Stall speed: 31 kts (35 mph) 56 km/h
Climb rate: 985 ft (300 m) per minute
Range: 485 naut miles (559 miles) 900 km
Availability: Kits.
Comments: Bush-plane type in microlight category. Plexiglas doors.

India

Raj Hamsa X'Air

Address:
Raj Hamsa Altralights Pvt Ltd, 301 Shah sultan, 17 Cunningham Road, 560052 Bangalore.
Telephone: +91 80 2258134 or 2258741
Facsimile: +91 80 2259696

Type: Side-by-side 2-seat, high-wing microlight, with fixed nosewheel undercarriage.
Construction: Steel and alloy tube, and fabric.
Wing span: 32 ft 2 ins (9.8 m)
Empty weight: 507 lb (230 kg)
Gross weight: 992 lb (450 kg)
Recommended engine: 52 hp (38.8 kW) Rotax 503.2V
Maximum speed: 59 kts (68 mph) 110 km/h
Cruise speed: 46 kts (53 mph) 85 km/h
Stall speed: 26 kts (30 mph) 48 km/h
Climb rate: 590 ft (180 m) per minute
Availability: Kits.
Comments: Version of US-designed Weedhopper.

↑ **Raj Hamsa X'Air** *(Geoffrey P. Jones)*

Italy

Euroala Jet Fox JF 97

Address:
Euroala, L.go Mosciano, 28 64046 Montorio al Vomano (TE).
Telephone: +39 0348 3395009
Facsimile: +39 0861 870979

Type: Side-by-side 2-seat, high-wing microlight, with fixed nosewheel undercarriage.
Construction: Metal, composites and fabric.
Wing span: 31 ft 10 ins (9.7 m)
Length: 19 ft (5.78 m)
Empty weight: 419 lb (190 kg)
Gross weight: 992 lb (450 kg)
Recommended engine: 64.4 hp (48 kW) Rotax 582 or 77.8 hp (58 kW) Rotax 912 (data for Rotax 912 version)
Maximum speed: 92 kts (106 mph) 170 km/h
Cruise speed: 73 kts (84 mph) 135 km/h
Stall speed: 33 kts (38 mph) 60 km/h
Climb rate: 885 ft (270 m) per minute
Availability: Factory complete.
Comments: Developed from JF 91 microlight. JF 97 certified in Germany, France, Belgium and Luxembourg.

↑ **Euroala Jet Fox JF 97**

Eurofly FireFox and BasicFox

Address:
Eurofly, Via Ca' Onorai 50, 35015 Galliera Veneta (PD).
Telephone: +39 049 596 5464

Details: Refer to FireFox, except under Comments.
Type: Tandem 2-seat, high-wing microlight, with pusher engine and fixed nosewheel undercarriage.
Construction: Alloy tube and fabric.
Wing span: 28 ft 3 ins (9.6 m)
Length: 20 ft 4 ins (6.2 m)
Empty weight: 331 lb (150 kg)
Gross weight: 794 lb (360 kg)
Recommended engine: 48 hp (35.8 kW) Rotax 503
Maximum speed: 70 kts (81 mph) 130 km/h
Cruise speed: 57 kts (65 mph) 105 km/h
Stall speed: 22 kts (25 mph) 40 km/h
Climb rate: 787 ft (240 m) per minute
Range: 113 naut miles (130 miles) 210 km
Availability: Factory produced.
Comments: Simplified version of the FireFox is the BasicFox.

Ferrari ULM Olimpios

Address:
Ferrari ULM, via Garibaldi, 104/A, 35040 Castelbaldo (PD).
Telephone: +39 0425 57316
Facsimile: +39 0425 546422

Type: Side-by-side 2-seat, high-wing, cabin monoplane, with fixed nosewheel undercarriage.
Construction: Metal or composites.
Wing span: 32 ft 10 ins (10 m)
Length: 20 ft 8 ins (6.3 m)
Empty weight: 595 lb (270 kg)
Gross weight: 992 lb (450 kg)
Recommended engine: 64 hp (47.7 kW) Rotax 582
Maximum speed: 162 kts (186 mph) 300 km/h
Cruise speed: 108 kts (124 mph) 200 km/h
Stall speed: 33 kts (38 mph) 60 km/h
Climb rate: 787 ft (240 m) per minute
Range: 324 naut miles (372 miles) 600 km
Availability: Kits and complete aircraft.

Ferrari ULM Tucano

Type: Single-seat, high-wing microlight, with fuselage pod, tail-boom, pusher engine and fixed nosewheel undercarriage.
Construction: Metal and fabric.
Wing span: 33 ft 4 ins (10.17 m)
Length: 19 ft (5.8 m)
Empty weight: 441 lb (200 kg)
Gross weight: 838 lb (380 kg)
Recommended engine: 64 hp (47.7 kW) Rotax 582
Maximum speed: 92 kts (106 mph) 170 km/h
Cruise speed: 76 kts (87 mph) 140 km/h
Stall speed: 33 kts (38 mph) 60 km/h
Climb rate: 885 ft (270 m) per minute
Range: 151 naut miles (174 miles) 280 km
Availability: Kits and complete aircraft.
Comments: Over 150 sold.

III Sky Arrow 450T and 650T/TC

Address:
Iniziative Industriali Italiane SpA, Corso Trieste, 150-00198 Rome.
Telephone: +39 06 8415821 or 8541164
Facsimile: +39 06 8557162

Details: Refer to Sky Arrow 450T, except under Comments and photograph/caption.
Type: Tandem 2-seat, high-wing microlight, with pusher engine and either fixed nosewheel or float undercarriage (see Comments).
Construction: Composites.
Wing span: 31 ft 6 ins (9.6 m)
Length: 24 ft 11 ins (7.6 m)
Empty weight: 628 lb (285 kg)
Gross weight: 992 lb (450 kg)
Recommended engine: 77.8 hp (58 kW) Rotax 912
Maximum speed: 109 kts (126 mph) 202 km/h
Cruise speed: 94 kts (109 mph) 175 km/h
Stall speed: 33 kts (38 mph) 60 km/h
Take-off distance: 351 ft (107 m)
Climb rate: 1,000 ft (305 m) per minute
Range: 377 naut miles (435 miles) 700 km
Availability: Easy-build kit or completed.
Comments: Also available as Sky Arrow 650T/TC certified light aircraft. See also Pacific Aerosystem in USA.

↑ **III Sky Arrow 650 TC**

Lucchini Speedy

Address:
Lucchini & c, Via le Valeggio 2, 46100 Mantova.
Telephone: +39 0376 328569 or 220661

Type: Single-seat, high-wing microlight, with pusher engine and fixed nosewheel undercarriage.
Construction: Metal.
Wing span: 25 ft 11 ins (7.9 m)
Length: 19 ft 8 ins (6 m)
Empty weight: 397 lb (180 kg)
Gross weight: 661 lb (300 kg)
Recommended engine: 52 hp (38.8 kW) Rotax 462 or 64 hp (47.7 kW) Rotax 582
Maximum speed: 113 kts (130 mph) 210 km/h
Cruise speed: 86 kts (99 mph) 160 km/h
Stall speed: 28 kts (33 mph) 52 km/h
Climb rate: 885 ft (270 m) per minute
Availability: Kits and complete aircraft.
Comments: 2-seat version under development.

Maefin TopFun

Address:
Maefin, Luigi Muciarelli, Pozzuolo Umbro (PG).
Telephone: +39 075 957134 or 0376 800235 (North Italy)

Type: Side-by-side 2-seat, high-wing monoplane, with fixed nosewheel undercarriage.
Construction: Metal, composites and fabric.
Wing span: 30 ft 4 ins (9.24 m)
Length: 18 ft 11 ins (5.77 m)
Empty weight: 540 lb (245 kg)
Gross weight: 992 lb (450 kg)
Recommended engine: 64.4 hp (48 kW) Rotax 582 or 77.8 hp (58 kW) Rotax 912
Maximum speed: 86 kts (99 mph) 160 km/h
Cruise speed: 76 kts (87 mph) 140 km/h
Stall speed: 22 kts (25 mph) 40 km/h
Climb rate: 1,180 ft (360 m) per minute
Range: 162 naut miles (186 miles) 300 km
Availability: Kits.
Comments: Quick-build kit.

Panek/Mattlener Aerdelta PUL 10*

*The former Italian Nike Aerdelta PUL 10 is now the Panek/Mattlener PUL10 (see Germany).
Type: Side-by-side 2-seat, flying-wing monoplane, with pusher engine and retractable nosewheel undercarriage.
Construction: Steel tube and composites.
Wing span: 32 ft 10 ins (10 m)
Length: 13 ft (3.95 m)
Empty weight: 540 lb (245 kg)
Gross weight: 992 lb (450 kg)
Recommended engine: 80 hp (59.7 kW) Rotax 912, driving a Newform 2-blade propeller.

Maximum speed: over 108 kts (124 mph) 200 km/h
Cruise speed: 84 kts (96 mph) 155 km/h
Stall speed: 33 kts (38 mph) 60 km/h
Take-off distance: 493 ft (150 m)
Range: 650 naut miles (748 miles) 1,204 km
Availability: Kits.
Comments: Derived from the Canadian Ultraflight Lazair microlight and the PUL 9, PUL 10 first flew in May 1997. Also suitable for military use and unmanned operations. Manufactured by Nurflügel in Germany.

↑ **Panek/Mattlener PUL 10** *(Geoffrey P. Jones)*

Rodaro Flysynthesis Storch

Address:
Flysynthesis Srl, via Gorizia 63, I-33050 Gonars (Udine).
Telephone: +39 0432 992482 **Facsimile:** +39 0432 993557

Type: Single or side-by-side 2-seat, high-wing, cabin microlight, with fixed nosewheel undercarriage.
Construction: Metal and composites.
Wing span: 33 ft 2 ins (10.1 m)
Length: 20 ft (6.1 m)
Recommended engine: 52 hp (38.8 kW) Rotax 503 (optional Jabiru)
Maximum speed: 78 kts (90 mph) 145 km/h
Cruise speed: 62 kts (71 mph) 115 km/h
Stall speed: 30 kts (34 mph) 55 km/h
Availability: Complete aircraft and kits.
Comments: Low-wing, Rotax 912-powered **Texan** also available.

↑ **Rodaro Flysynthesis Storch microlight** *(Geoffrey P. Jones)*

SG Aviation Storm 280SI, 320E and Storm 400TI

Address:
SG Aviation (Industria Aeronautica Italiana), via Degli Artiglieri snc, 04016 Sabaudia-Latina.
Telephone: +39 0336 765 541 or 773 515 216 **Facsimile:** +33 0773 511 407

Details: Storm 320E, except under Comments.
Type: Side-by-side 2-seat, low-wing, cabin monoplane, with fixed nosewheel undercarriage.
Construction: Metal.
Wing span: 28 ft 3 ins (8.6 m)
Length: 21 ft 6 ins (6.55 m)
Empty weight: 705 lb (320 kg)
Gross weight: 1,146 lb (520 kg)
Recommended engine: 100 hp (74.6 kW) Teledyne Continental
Maximum speed: 135 kts (155 mph) 250 km/h
Cruise speed: 128 kts (148 mph) 238 km/h
Stall speed: 35 kts (41 mph) 65 km/h
Climb rate: 1,200 ft (366 m) per minute
Range: 539 naut miles (621 miles) 1,000 km
Availability: Complete aircraft and kits.
Comments: Meets JAR/VLA specifications. 3-seat version is Storm 400TI, with 116 hp (86.5 kW) Textron Lycoming O-235-N2C. Rotax 912 powers smaller Storm 280SI.

Terzi T30C, T30E and T30SL Katana

Address:
Pietro Terzi srl, 20154 Milano, P.LE A. Baiamonti 1.
Telephone: +39 02 33609080 **Facsimile:** +39 02 33607996

Details: T30E, except under Recommended engine and Comments.
Type: Single-seat, mid-wing, competition/aerobatic monoplane, with fixed tailwheel undercarriage.
Construction: Alloy wings and tail, with steel tube fuselage covered with removable composite shells.
Wing span: 25 ft 6 ins (7.77 m)
Length: 22 ft (6.7 m)
Empty weight: 1,450 lb (658 kg)
Gross weight: 1,940 lb (880 kg)
Recommended engine: 400 hp (298 kW) Textron Lycoming IO-720 (T30C has 300 hp, 224 kW Textron Lycoming IO-540)
Never-exceed speed (VNE): 273 kts (314 mph) 505 km/h
Maximum and cruise speed: 194 kts (224 mph) 360 km/h
Stall speed: 53 kts (61 mph) 98 km/h
Climb rate: 4,525 ft (1,380 m) per minute
Range: 217 naut miles (250 miles) 402 km
Availability: Ready to fly.
Comments: First flown on 16 January, 1991. The new T30SL is structurally simplified, has an IO-720 engine, MTOW 2,160 lb (980 kg), and performance similar to 'E'. G limits ±12 and roll rate 400° per second. See also General Aviation section for photograph.

Lithuania

Address:
V. Kensgaila Aircraft Enterprize, Roziu 87, Panevezys 5306.
Telephone: +7 1254 60774

Kensgaila VK-8 Ausra

Type: Side-by-side 2-seat, agricultural monoplane, with fixed tailwheel undercarriage.
Construction: Metal and composites.
Wing span: 48 ft 8 ins (14.83 m)
Length: 32 ft 10 ins (10 m)
Empty weight: 2,513 lb (1,140 kg)
Gross weight: 4,850 lb (2,200 kg)
Recommended engine: 360 hp (268 kW) M-14P radial
Maximum speed: 119 kts (137 mph) 220 km/h
Cruise speed: 97 kts (112 mph) 180 km/h
Stall speed: 39 kts (44 mph) 71 km/h
Climb rate: 985 ft (300 m) per minute
Range: 258 naut miles (298 miles) 480 km
Comments: First flown in 1989. First seen at the 5th National Homebuilt Convention at Riga in 1989.

Poland

Aviation Farm Ltd J-5 Marco

Address:
Marketed through East European Markets Ltd, 12 Widok Street, 00-023, Warsaw.
Telephone: +48 22 8274858 **Facsimile:** +48 22 8277788, 428506

Type: Single-seat light aircraft/motorglider, with monoplane wings, pusher engine, tailboom and V-tail. Option of retractable single main wheel with wingtip outriggers, or fixed tailwheel undercarriage.
Construction: Glassfibre.
Wing span: 26 ft 7 ins (8.1 m)
Length: 15 ft 3 ins (4.65 m)
Empty weight: 393 lb (178 kg)
Gross weight: 622 lb (282 kg)
Recommended engine: 30 hp (22.4 kW) KFM-107 ER MAX or 41.6 hp (31 kW) Rotax 447UL-SCDJ
Maximum and cruise speed: 108 kts (124 mph) 200 km/h
Stall speed: 30 kts (34.5 mph) 55 km/h
Take-off distance: 814 ft (248 m) on grass *with 10° flaps*, 735 ft (224 m) on concrete
Climb rate: 418 ft (127 m) per minute
Range: 245 naut miles (282 miles) 455 km
Comments: Former Alpha (Janowski) design, purchased in 1990s by Aviation Farm. Above data received May 1998. See General Aviation section.

↑ **Marco J-5 built in Germany** *(Geoffrey P. Jones)*

Antoniewski AT-1

Details can be found in the 1996-97 edition of *WA&SD*.

Orlinski RO-7 Orlik

Address:
Roman Orlinski, ul Lesna 4, PL-82-200 Malbork.

Type: Single-seat, low-wing, cabin monoplane, with fixed tailwheel undercarriage.
Construction: Steel tube and wood.
Wing span: 24 ft 11 ins (7.6 m)
Length: 18 ft (5.5 m)
Empty weight: 485 lb (220 kg)
Gross weight: 705 lb (320 kg)
Recommended engine: 65 hp (48.5 kW) Walter Mikron III
Maximum speed: 81 kts (93 mph) 150 km/h
Cruise speed: 49 kts (56 mph) 90 km/h
Stall speed: 39 kts (45 mph) 73 km/h
Take-off distance: 328 ft (100 m)
Climb rate: 984 ft (300 m) per minute
Range: 215 naut miles (248 miles) 400 km
Availability: Plans and some components.

Radwan KR-2PM Swift Mk II and Mk III

Address:
Radwan Ltd, PO Box 23, 00-958 Warsaw 66.
Telephone: +48 90 28 24 26 **Facsimile:** +48 22 38 15 74

Type: Side-by-side 2-seat, low-wing monoplane, with fixed nosewheel undercarriage.
Construction: Laminated wood (optional metal wings).
Details: Refer to Mk II, except under Comments.
Wing span: 21 ft (6.4 m)
Length: 15 ft 11 ins (4.85 m)
Empty weight: 551 lb (250 kg)
Gross weight: 992 lb (450 kg)
Recommended engine: 80 hp (59.7 kW) Limbach L2000 EA2
Maximum speed: 146 kts (168 mph) 270 km/h
Cruise speed: 119 kts (137 mph) 220 km/h
Stall speed: 35 kts (41 mph) 65 km/h
Climb rate: 690 ft (210 m) per minute
Availability: Complete aircraft.
Comments: Company founded in 1989. Swift has dual controls and VFR panel. Wider cockpit version (3 ft 10 ins, 1.16 m) with 103 hp (76.8 kW) L2400 EFI engine is Swift Mk III.

↑ **Radwan KR-2PM Swift** *(Geoffrey P. Jones)*

Remos Aircraft Gemini and Gemini Ultra (and Micro-Viper)

Address:
German distributor: Remos Aircraft GmbH, Waldweg 1, D-85283 Eschelbach. US distributor of similar Micro-Viper: Akro-Viper Inc, 2781 Marden Court, Northbrook, IL 60062.

Telephone: German distributor: +49 8442 9677 77.
US distributor: +1 708 498 1164
Facsimile: US distributor: +1 708 498 1064

Type: Side-by-side 2-seat, high-wing monoplane, with fixed nosewheel undercarriage.
Construction: Composites and fabric.
Wing span: 35 ft 5 ins (10.8 m)
Length: 21 ft 8 ins (6.6 m)
Empty weight: 527 lb (240 kg)
Gross weight: 992 lb (450 kg)
Recommended engine: 64.4 hp (48 kW) Rotax 582, or Rotax 912 for Gemini Ultra
Maximum speed: 79 kts (91 mph) 146 km/h
Cruise speed: 70 kts (81 mph) 130 km/h
Stall speed: 27 kts (31 mph) 50 km/h
Climb rate: 690 ft (210 m) per minute
Availability: To special order.
Comments: Designed in Poland by Adam Kurbiel. Certified in Germany and Poland. See Remos under Germany in General Aviation section for later **G-3 Mirage**.

↑ German Remos Gemini

Russia

Russian light/recreational aircraft

Note: The following light aircraft of Russian origin are detailed in the General Aviation section (which see), only a few of which are available in self-assembly form as an option to ready assembled.

Aeropract A-21 Solo
Aeropract A-23M
Aeropract A-25
Aeropract A-27
Alpha-M SL-A and A-211
Avgur/MAI Krechet
Avia Accord
Aviacor M-12 Kasatik
Aviakompleks AS-2
Dubna-1 and Dubna-2
KB MAI Aviatika-MAI-890 and -920
KB MAI Avlatlka-MAI-900 Acrobat
KB MAI Aviatika-MAI-910 and -960
Interavia I-1
Lukhovitsy SL-39WM
SKB Samara A-16
SKB Samara S-202, S-302 and S-400

In addition, see **Aeroprakt, Icar and Lillienthal** under Ukraine.

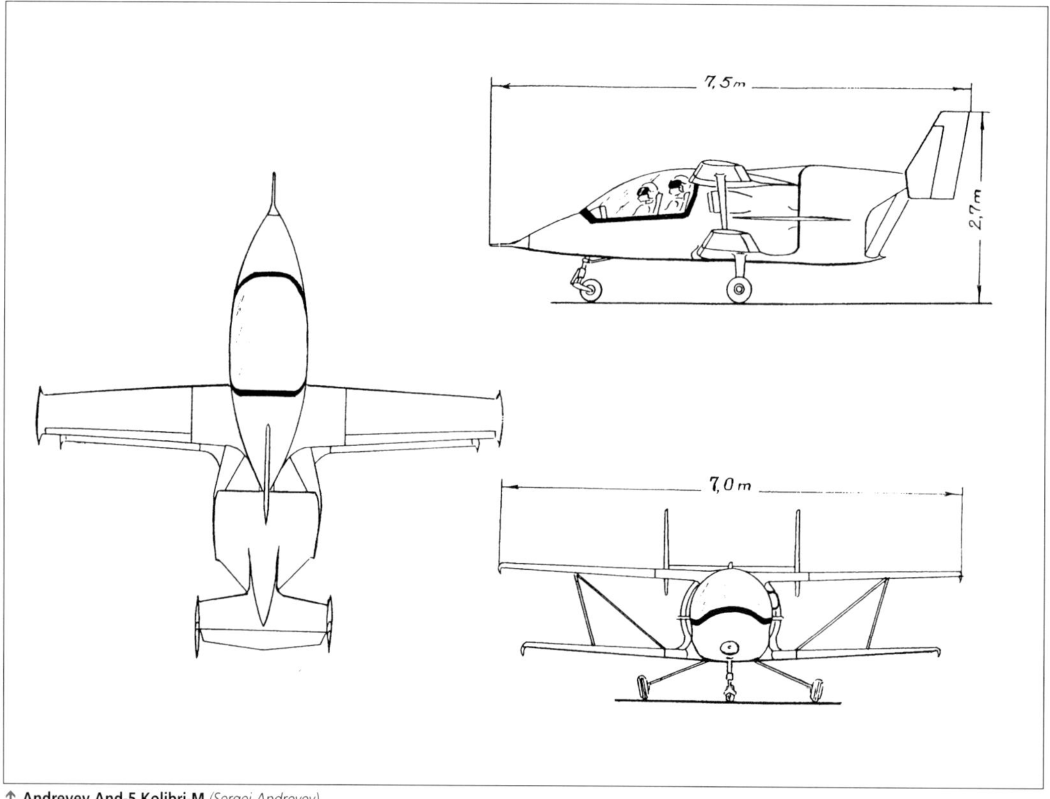

↑ **Andreyev And-5 Kolibri-M** *(Sergei Andreyev)*

Andreyev And-4 Kolibri and And-5 Kolibri-M

Address:
Sergei Andreyev, ul. Ordzhonikidze, 11-29, Komsomolsk-na-Amure, 16.

Telephone: +7 42172 42808

Details: And-4 Kolibri, except under Comments.
Type: Single-seat biplane, with pusher engine and fixed nosewheel undercarriage.
Wing span: 19 ft 3 ins (5.87 m)
Length: 14 ft 6 ins (4.42 m)
Empty weight: 422 lb (191.5 kg)
Gross weight: 650 lb (295 kg)
Recommended engine: 20 hp (14.9 kW) RMZ-640 Buran
Maximum speed: 67 kts (78 mph) 125 km/h
Cruise speed: 62 kts (71 mph) 115 km/h
Stall speed: 42 kts (48 mph) 77 km/h
Take-off distance: 493 ft (150 m)
Range: 189 naut miles (217 miles) 350 km
Comments: First flown 6 July 1994. Work on And-5 Kolibri-M 2-seater is underway, with Rotax 912; wing span 23 ft (7 m), length 24 ft 7 ins (7.5 m), gross weight 1,433 lb (650 kg) and cruise speed 118-135 kts (137-155 mph) 220-250 km/h.

Type: 2-seat, open-cockpit monoplane, with fixed nosewheel undercarriage.
Construction: Aluminium tube and fabric.
Wing span: 33 ft 5.5 ins (10.2 m)
Empty weight: 496 lb (225 kg)
Gross weight: 1,036 lb (470 kg)
Recommended engine: 64 hp (47.7 kW) Rotax 532
Maximum speed: 59 kts (68 mph) 110 km/h
Cruise speed: 49 kts (56 mph) 90 km/h
Stall speed: 33 kts (38 mph) 60 km/h
Take-off distance: 230 ft (70 m)
Climb rate: 453 ft (138 m) per minute
Range: 81 naut miles (93 miles) 150 km

Aviator M-9 Marathon

Address:
Aviator Scientific-Production Enterprise, pr. Budennogo 14, 105118 Moscow.

Telephone: +7 095 369 8959
Facsimile: +7 095 276 2941 (Interaero distributor)

↑ **Aviator M-9 Marathon** *(Piotr Butowski)*

Boulgakov Boulg-2 Gorizont

Address:
Valeri Boulgakov, ul. Levchenko, 12-36, 140160 Zhukovsky, Moskovskoi oblasti.

Telephone: +7 096 903 5649
Facsimile: +7 095 253 7475

Type: Single-seat, tandem swept-wing biplane, with fixed nosewheel undercarriage.
Wing span: 18 ft 8 ins (5.7 m)
Length: 19 ft (5.8 m) front wing, 20 ft (6.1 m) rear wing
Empty weight: 734 lb (333 kg)
Gross weight: 1,124 lb (510 kg)
Recommended engines: 2 uprated TS-10 jets, with total thrust of about 337 lbf (1.5 kN)
Comments: Built in 1992.

↑ **Boulgakov Boulg-2 Gorizont** *(Piotr Butowski)*

Slovenia

Flight Team Sinus

Address:
German agent: Flight Team (Peter Gotzner), Lessingstrasse 6, D-97072 Würzburg.

Telephone: German agent: +49 9339 1297
Facsimile: German agent: +49 9339 99851
E-mail: flight.team@t-online.de

Type: Side-by-side 2-seat, high-wing, cabin microlight/motorglider, with T-tail and fixed tailwheel undercarriage.
Construction: Composites.
Wing span: 49 ft (14.95 m)
Length: 21 ft 8 ins (6.61 m)
Empty weight: 496 lb (225 kg)
Gross weight: 992 lb (450 kg)
Recommended engine: 53 hp (49.6 kW) Rotax 503 UL
Maximum speed: 100 kts (116 mph) 186 km/h
Cruise speed: 87 kts (102 mph) 164 km/h
Stall speed: 32 kts (36 mph) 58 km/h
Take-off distance: 397 ft (121 m)
Climb rate: 407 ft (124 m) per minute
Availability: Complete aircraft.
Comments: Designed and built in Slovenia but distributed through Germany. 3 models, as Economy, Standard and Executive. Schempp-Hirth airbrakes.

Spain

Aero-Jean AJ.1/RF-5 Serrania

Address:
Aero-Jean SA, PO Box 40, 23280 Beas de Seguria (or France: Avions Rene Fournier, 37270 Athée-Nitray).

Telephone: (France: +33 47 50 68 30)
Facsimile: (France: +33 47 50 24 22)

Type: Tandem 2-seat, low-wing, monoplane motorglider, with retractable single main-wheel undercarriage and outriggers.
Construction: Wood.
Wing span: 45 ft (13.72 m), 28 ft (8.53 m) with wingtips folded
Length: 29 ft (8.84 m)
Empty weight: 925 lb (420 kg)
Gross weight: 1,431 lb (650 kg)
Recommended engine: Limbach L2000 E01
Maximum speed: 135 kts (155 mph) 250 km/h
Cruise speed: 113 kts (130 mph) 210 km/h
Stall speed: 42 kts (49 mph) 78 km/h
Take-off distance: 656 ft (200 m)
Climb rate: 630 ft (192 m) per minute
Range: 485 naut miles (558 miles) 900 km
Availability: Kits.
Comments: Kit version of the French Fournier RF-5 produced under licence in Spain.

Bücker Prado Jungmann

Address:
Bücker Prado S. L., PO Box 1239, Albacete (*also* USA: Krybus Aviation, PO Box 14, Santa Paula, CA 93060).

Telephone: +34 67 210581 or 67 245180 (USA: +1 805 525 8764)
Facsimile: +34 67 67 210581 (USA: +1 805 525 1147)

Type: Tandem 2-seat, aerobatic biplane, with fixed tailwheel undercarriage.
Construction: Steel tube, wood and fabric.
Wing span: 24 ft 3 ins (7.4 m)
Length: 22 ft 1 ins (6.73 m)
Empty weight: 992 lb (450 kg)
Gross weight: 1,587 lb (720 kg)
Recommended engine: 125-150 hp (93.2-112 kW) Tigre G-IV, Textron Lycoming O-360 or LOM M-332AK (Czech engine from Krybus)
Maximum speed: 104 kts (120 mph) 193 km/h
Cruise speed: 96 kts (111 mph) 179 km/h
Stall speed: 39 kts (45 mph) 73 km/h
Climb rate: 1,705 ft (520 m) per minute
Range: 193 naut miles (222 miles) 357 km
Availability: Kits.
Comments: Kits fabricated using original jigs for Bücker/CASA Bu.131.

↑ **Krybus Aviation Bü-131 Jungmann with O-360 engine** *(Krybus Aviation)*

Bücker Prado Jungmeister

Type: Single-seat, aerobatic biplane, with fixed tailwheel undercarriage.
Construction: Steel tube, wood and fabric.
Wing span: 21 ft 8 ins (6.6 m)
Length: 19 ft 9 ins (6 m)
Empty weight: 925 lb (420 kg)
Gross weight: 1,342 lb (609 kg)
Recommended engine: Scarab or Textron Lycoming O-360
Maximum speed: 117 kts (135 mph) 217 km/h
Cruise speed: 107 kts (123 mph) 198 km/h
Stall speed: 44 kts (50 mph) 80 km/h
Climb rate: 2,100 ft (640 m) per minute
Range: 260 naut miles (300 miles) 482 km
Availability: Kits.
Comments: Classic pre-war aerobatic aircraft now available again in kit form.

↑ **Bü-133 Jungmeister with Krybus O-360 installation** *(Krybus Aviation)*

Sweden

Andreasson BA-4B

Address:
Bjorn Andreasson, Collins Vag 22B, S-23600 Hollviksnas.

Type: Single-seat, open or enclosed cockpit, aerobatic biplane, with fixed tailwheel undercarriage.
Construction: Metal, with optional wood wings.
Wing span: 17 ft 7 ins (5.34 m)
Length: 15 ft (4.6 m)
Empty weight: 600 lb (272 kg)
Gross weight: 827 lb (375 kg)
Recommended engine: 100 hp (74.6 kW) Rolls-Royce Continental O-200-A or other type
Maximum speed: 122 kts (140 mph) 225 km/h
Cruise speed: 104 kts (120 mph) 193 km/h
Stall speed: 33 kts (38 mph) 61 km/h
Climb rate: 2,000 ft (610 m) per minute
Range: 152 naut miles (175 miles) 281 km
Availability: Plans.
Comments: Several built in the UK, including by Crosby Aircraft.

Switzerland

Brändli BX-2 Cherry

Address:
BX-Aviation, c/o Max Brändli, Hoeweg 2, CH-2553 Safnern.

Telephone and Facsimile: +41 32 55 18 23

Type: Side-by-side 2-seat, low-wing monoplane, with retractable nosewheel undercarriage.
Construction: Wood and foam composites.
Wing span: 22 ft 11 ins (7 m)
Length: 17 ft 5 ins (5.3 m)
Empty weight: 700 lb (318 kg)
Gross weight: 1,213 lb (550 kg)
Recommended engine: 90 hp (67 kW) Teledyne Continental A65 or Rotax 912
Maximum speed: 141 kts (162 mph) 260 km/h
Cruise speed: 109 kts (125 mph) 200 km/h
Stall speed: 45 kts (52 mph) 84 km/h
Take-off distance: 985 ft (300 m)
Climb rate: 590 ft (180 m) per minute
Range: 500 naut miles (575 miles) 805 km
Availability: Plans and some components.
Comments: Prototype first flew on 24 April 1982. Quickly detachable wings and tail for trailering.

↑ **Brändli BX-2 Cherry built by Hans Brandstatter in Austria with a Rotax 912 engine** *(Geoffrey P. Jones)*

Brügger MB-2 Colibri 2

Address:
Max Brügger, CH-1724 Zenauva.

Telephone: +41 37 33 29 20

Type: Single-seat, low-wing monoplane, with fixed tailwheel undercarriage.
Construction: Wood and fabric.
Wing span: 19 ft 8 ins (6 m)
Length: 15 ft 9 ins (4.8 m)
Empty weight: 474 lb (215 kg)
Gross weight: 727 lb (330 kg)
Recommended engine: 40 hp (30 kW) 1,600cc Volkswagen
Maximum speed: 96 kts (111 mph) 180 km/h
Cruise speed: 86 kts (99 mph) 160 km/h
Stall speed: 33 kts (38 mph) 60 km/h
Take-off distance: 656 ft (200 m)
Climb rate: 590 ft (180 m) per minute
Range: 269 naut miles (310 miles) 500 km
Availability: Plans.
Comments: Prototype first flew on 1 May 1970. An all-metal Colibri 3 was built but not continued. Over 280 Colibri 2s are under construction or flying in Europe.

Tschechnia

Wenn TL232 Condor

Address:
TL Ultralight, Dobrovskeho 734, Hradec Kralove 50002. (German agent: Martin Wezel, Erlenbachstrasse 38, D-72768 Reutlingen.)

Telephone: (German agent: +49 7121 68408)
Facsimile: (German agent: +49 7121 677238)

Type: Side-by-side 2-seat, high-wing, cabin monoplane, with fixed nosewheel undercarriage.
Construction: Steel tube, metal and fabric.

Wing span: 34 ft 9 ins (10.6 m)
Length: 19 ft 11 ins (6.08 m)
Empty weight: 584-617 lb (265-280 kg)
Gross weight: 992 lb (450 kg)
Recommended engine: 64.4 hp (48 kW) Rotax 582, or Rotax 912
Maximum speed: 97 kts (112 mph) 180 km/h
Cruise speed: 70 kts (81 mph) 130 km/h with Rotax 582, or 81 kts (93 mph) 150 km/h with Rotax 912
Climb rate: 610 ft (186 m) per minute with Rotax 582, or 905 ft (276 m) with Rotax 912
Range: 302 naut miles (348 miles) 560 km
Availability: Kits or complete aircraft.
Comments: Developed from TL132 Condor designed by Jiri Tlusty in 1993.

↑ German registered Wenn TL232 Condor

UK

Aviation Enterprises Chevvron 2-32C

Address:
Aviation Enterprises, Membury Airfield, Lambourne, Berkshire RG16 7TJ.
Telephone and Facsimile: +44 1488 72224

Type: Side-by-side 2-seat, low-wing microlight-trainer, with fixed nosewheel undercarriage. Floats available outside of UK.
Construction: Composites.
Wing span: 44 ft (13.41 m)
Length: 23 ft (7.01 m)
Empty weight: 408 lb (185 kg)
Gross weight: 860 lb (390 kg)
Recommended engine: 32 hp (24 kW) König
Maximum speed: 65 kts (75 mph) 121 km/h
Cruise speed: 55 kts (63 mph) 101 km/h
Stall speed: 31 kts (35 mph) 57 km/h
Take-off distance: 300 ft (92 m)
Climb rate: 375-500 ft (114-152 m) per minute
Range: 200 naut miles (230 miles) 370 km
Availability: Factory built.
Comments: Prototype Chevvron first flew in 1983. Over 40 Chevvron 2-32Cs built. Super Chevvron 2-45CS remains under development.

↑ Aviation Enterprises Chevvron 2-32C *(Geoffrey P. Jones)*

Bell Aeromarine Flitzer

Address:
153 Parker Drive, Leicester LE4 0JP.
Telephone: +44 116 234 0088
Facsimile: +44 116 234 0295

Type: Single-seat, open-cockpit biplane, with fixed tail-dragger undercarriage.
Construction: Wood and fabric.
Wing span: 18 ft (5.49 m)
Length: 14 ft 9 ins (4.5 m)
Empty weight: 480 lb (218 kg)
Gross weight: 750 lb (340 kg)
Recommended engine: 1,834cc Volkswagen
Maximum speed: 76 kts (88 mph) 142 km/h
Cruise speed: 63 kts (72 mph) 116 km/h
Stall speed: 37 kts (42 mph) 68 km/h
Take-off distance: 390 ft (119 m)
Climb rate: 700 ft (213 m) per minute
Availability: Kits and plans.
Comments: Designed by Lynn Williams and first flown in Spring 1995.

↑ Bell Aeromarine Flitzer at Cranfield in July 1996 *(Ed Hicks)*

CFM Streak Shadow and Star Streak

Address:
CFM Aircraft Ltd, Unit 2D, Eastlands Industrial Estate, Leiston, Suffolk IP16 4LL.
Telephone: +44 1728 832353
Facsimile: +44 1728 832944
E-mail: 101534.302@CompuServe.com

Details: Refer to Streak Shadow, except under Recommended engine.
Type: Tandem 2-seat, high-wing monoplane, with pusher engine and fixed nosewheel undercarriage.
Construction: Composites, wood and metal.
Wing span: 28 ft (8.53 m)
Length: 21 ft (6.4 m)
Empty weight: 438 lb (199 kg)
Gross weight: 900 lb (408 kg)
Recommended engine: 64.4 hp (48 kW) Rotax 582 (Rotax 618 for Star Streak)
Maximum speed: 105 kts (121 mph) 195 km/h
Cruise speed: 87 kts (100 mph) 161 km/h
Stall speed: 37 kts (42 mph) 68 km/h
Take-off distance over a 50 ft (15 m) obstacle: 426 ft (130 m)
Climb rate: 950 ft (290 m) per minute
Range: 260 naut miles (300 miles) 482 km
Availability: Kits.
Comments: See Laron Aviation Technologies for US built versions of CFM Shadow range. Prototype first flew in 1983. Company recently reformed from previous CFM Metal-Fax.

↑ Designer David Cook with a CFM Streak Shadow

DM Aerospace Thorpe T-211 AeroSport

Address:
DM Aerospace Ltd, 16 Hilton Square, Pendlebury, Swinton, Manchester M27 4DB.
Telephone: +44 161 727 3200
Facsimile: +44 161 727 3379

Type: Side-by-side 2-seat, low-wing monoplane, with fixed nosewheel undercarriage.
Construction: Metal.
Wing span: 25 ft (7.62 m)
Length: 18 ft (5.49 m)
Empty weight: 780 lb (354 kg)
Gross weight: 1,270 lb (576 kg)
Recommended engine: 100 hp (74.6 kW) Teledyne Continental O-200 or similarly rated Jabiru
Maximum speed: 137 kts (158 mph) 254 km/h
Cruise speed: 104 kts (120 mph) 193 km/h
Stall speed: 39 kts (45 mph) 73 km/h
Take-off distance: 450 ft (137 m)
Climb rate: 750 ft (229 m) per minute
Range: 412 naut miles (475 miles) 764 km
Availability: Complete aircraft and kits.
Comments: Company importing both production aircraft and kits, the latter selling for about £15,000 without engine.

↑ DM Aerospace Thorpe T-211 AeroSport

Europa Aviation Europa

Address:
Europa Aviation Ltd, Unit 2A, Dove Way, Kirby Mills Industrial Estate, Kirbymoorside, N. Yorks YO6 6NR (USA: Europa Aviation Inc, 3400 Airfield Drive West, Lakeland, FL 33811).
Telephone: +44 1751 431773 (USA: +1 941 647 5355)
Facsimile: +44 1751 431706 (USA: +1 941 646 2877)
E-mail: europa-aviation,co.uk (USA: europa@gate.net)

Type: Side-by-side 2-seat, cabin monoplane, with retractable single main wheel and wingtip outriggers. Fixed nosewheel version available.
Construction: Composites.
Wing span: 26 ft (7.92 m)
Length: 19 ft 3 ins (5.87 m)
Empty weight: 730 lb (331 kg)
Gross weight: 1,300 lb (590 kg)
Recommended engine: 80 hp (59.7 kW) Rotax 912. Other options include Teledyne Continental O-200, Subaru EA18, 80 hp (59.6 kW) Jabiru, Mid-West AE100R rotary, and BMW 1100RS
Maximum speed: 144 kts (166 mph) 267 km/h
Cruise speed: 120-129 kts (138-149 mph) 222-240 km/h
Stall speed: 39 kts (45 mph) 73 km/h
Take-off distance: 600 ft (183 m)
Climb rate: 800 ft (244 m) per minute
Range: 649 naut miles (747 miles) 1,202 km
Availability: Kits.
Comments: First flown in September 1992. Some 525 kits sold. New motorglider version also available, with interchangeable 43 ft (13.11 m) wing span.

↑ Europa with AE100R engine and fixed nosewheel undercarriage

Europa Aviation Europa XS

Type: Side-by-side 2-seat (possibility of rear child seat) monoplane, with retractable single main wheel and wingtip outriggers. Fixed nosewheel version available.
Construction: Composites.
Wing span: 26 ft (7.92 m)
Length: 19 ft 2 ins (5.84 m)
Empty weight: 710 lb (322 kg)
Gross weight: 1,370 lb (621 kg)
Recommended engine: 100 hp (74.6 kW) turbocharged Rotax 914
Maximum speed: 174 kts (200 mph) 322 km/h
Cruise speed: 130 kts (149 mph) 240 km/h
Stall speed: 39 kts (45 mph) 73 km/h
Range: 1,000 naut miles (1,150 miles) 1,850 km
Availability: Kits.
Comments: Launched at Oshkosh '97. 70 lb (31.7 kg) increase in AUW. New non-direct steering tailwheel.

Isaacs Fury II

Address:
John O. Isaacs, 23 Linden Grove, Chandlers Ford, Eastleigh, Hants SO5 1LE.
Telephone: +44 1703 260885

Type: Single-seat, 70% scale representation of a Hawker Fury biplane, with fixed tail-dragger undercarriage.
Construction: Wood and fabric.
Wing span: 21 ft (6.4 m)
Length: 19 ft 3 ins (5.87 m)
Empty weight: 710 lb (322 kg)
Gross weight: 1,000 lb (454 kg)
Recommended engine: 125 hp (93.2 kW) Textron Lycoming O-290
Maximum speed: 100 kts (115 mph) 185 km/h
Cruise speed: 87 kts (100 mph) 161 km/h
Stall speed: 33 kts (38 mph) 61 km/h
Take-off distance: 400 ft (122 m)
Climb rate: 1,600 ft (488 m) per minute
Range: 173 naut miles (200 miles) 321 km
Availability: Plans.
Comments: Designed by John Isaacs. First flown 30 August 1963. About 30 completed and flown worldwide.

↑ **Isaacs Fury built by Graham Jones, in Persian AF colours** *(Geoffrey P. Jones)*

Isaacs Spitfire

Type: 60% scale representation of the Spitfire, with fixed tailwheel undercarriage.
Construction: Wood and fabric.
Wing span: 22 ft 1 ins (6.75 m)
Length: 19 ft 3 ins (5.87 m)
Empty weight: 805 lb (365 kg)
Gross weight: 1,100 lb (499 kg)
Recommended engine: 100 hp (74.6 kW) Teledyne Continental
Maximum speed: 130 kts (150 mph) 241 km/h
Cruise speed: 116 kts (134 mph) 216 km/h
Stall speed: 45 kts (52 mph) 84 km/h
Take-off distance: 600 ft (183 m)
Climb rate: 1,100 ft (335 m) per minute
Range: 174 naut miles (200 miles) 321 km
Availability: Plans.
Comments: First flown on 5 May 1975.

Mainair Blade 503 and 582

Address:
Mainair Sports Ltd, Unit 2, Alma Industrial Estate, Regent Street, Rochdale, Lancashire OL12 0HQ.
Telephone: +44 1706 55134
Facsimile: +44 1706 31561

Type: Tandem 2-seat, flex-wing microlight, with pusher engine and fixed nosewheel undercarriage.

↑ **Mainair Blade 2-seater** *(Paul Tomlin)*

Construction: Alloy tube and fabric.
Wing span: 34 ft 6 ins (10.52 m)
Length: 9 ft 2 ins (2.8 m)
Empty weight: 463 lb (210 kg)
Gross weight: 860 lb (390 kg)
Recommended engine: 50 hp (37.3 kW) Rotax 503 or 64.4 hp (48 kW) Rotax 582-2V
Maximum speed: 91 kts (105 mph) 169 km/h
Cruise speed: 43-61 kts (50-70 mph) 80-113 km/h
Stall speed: 25 kts (28 mph) 45 km/h
Availability: Completed aircraft.
Comments: In-flight trimmer and aerodynamic fins on the wheel spats give the Blade good handling in turbulent air.

Mainair Mercury

Type: Single-seat or tandem 2-seat, flex-wing monoplane, with pusher engine and fixed nosewheel undercarriage.
Construction: Alloy tube and fabric.
Wing span: 34 ft 9 ins (10.6 m)
Length: 11 ft 4 ins (3.46 m)
Empty weight: 328 lb (149 kg)
Gross weight: 728 lb (330 kg)
Recommended engine: 51 hp (38 kW) Rotax 462, 50 hp (37.3 kW) Rotax 503 or 64.4 hp (48 kW) Rotax 582
Maximum speed: 77 kts (89 mph) 143 km/h
Cruise speed: 43-52 kts (50-60 mph) 80-97 km/h
Stall speed: 25 kts (28 mph) 45 km/h
Climb rate: 490 ft (150 m) per minute (dual)
Range: 434 naut miles (500 miles) 804 km with long-range tank
Availability: Kit or ready built.
Comments: Aerodynamic fuselage pod can be fitted to the trike unit.

Mainair Rapier

Type: Tandem 2-seat, flex-wing microlight, with pusher engine and fixed nosewheel undercarriage.
Construction: Alloy tube and fabric.
Wing span: 34 ft 6 ins (10.52 m)
Length: 9 ft 2 ins (2.79 m)
Empty weight: 334 lb (151 kg)
Gross weight: 814 lb (369 kg)
Recommended engine: Rotax 462. Optional Rotax 503.
Maximum speed: 71 kts (82 mph) 132 km/h
Cruise speed: 39-56 kts (45-65 mph) 72-105 km/h
Stall speed: 26 kts (30 mph) 49 km/h
Climb rate: 600 ft (183 m) per minute
Availability: Complete aircraft and kits.
Comments: New 1997 model combining Blade wing and Mercury trike.

Nipper Kits Nipper Mk.III

Address:
Nipper Kits & Components Ltd, Foxley, Blackness Lane, Keston, Kent BR2 6HL.
Telephone & Facsimile: +44 1689 858351

Type: Single-seat, mid-wing, aerobatic homebuilt, with fixed nosewheel undercarriage.
Construction: Steel tube, wood and fabric.
Wing span: 19 ft 8 ins (6 m)
Length: 15 ft (4.57 m)
Empty weight: 465 lb (211 kg)
Gross weight: 750 lb (340 kg), 685 lb (311 kg) for aerobatics
Recommended engine: 60 hp (44.7 kW) 1,834cc Volkswagen. Other engines now available.
Maximum speed: 100 kts (115 mph) 185 km/h
Cruise speed: 78 kts (90 mph) 145 km/h
Stall speed: 34 kts (39 mph) 63 km/h
Take-off distance: 280 ft (86 m)

↑ **Nipper with tip-tanks** *(Geoffrey P. Jones)*

Climb rate: 650 ft (198 m) per minute
Range: 139 naut miles (160 miles) 257 km, or 304 naut miles (350 miles) 563 km with tip tanks
Availability: Plans and some components.
Comments: Developed from the Avions Fairey Tipsy Nipper.

Pegasus AX2000

Address:
Pegasus Aviation, Elm Tree Park, Manton, Marlborough, Wiltshire SN8 1PS.
Telephone: +44 1672 861578
Facsimile: +44 1672 861550
E-mail: pegasus@cccp.net
Web Site: http://www.avnet.co.uk/pegasus/pegasus.htm

Type: Side-by-side 2-seat, monoplane, with nosewheel undercarriage.
Details: For Rotax 582 model.
Construction: Glassfibre and Ultralam fabric.
Wing span: 30 ft 10 ins (9.4 m)
Length: 18 ft 4 ins (5.6 m)
Empty weight: 443 lb (201 kg)
Gross weight: 992 lb (450 kg)
Recommended engine: 52 hp (38.8 kW) Rotax 503TC/DI with 2.58:1 reduction or 64.4 hp (48 kW) Rotax 582 with 3.47:1 reduction
Never-exceed speed (V_{NE}): 78 kts (90 mph) 145 km/h
Maximum speed: 69 kts (80 mph) 129 km/h
Stall speed: 31 kts (35 mph) 56 km/h at MTOW
Take-off distance over a 50 ft (15 m) obstacle: 185 ft (57 m)
Climb rate: 555 ft (169 m) per minute at MTOW
Availability: Factory built.
Comments: 3-axis control type. Latest AX2000 designed to meet 450 kg European Ultralight standards. Said to have outstanding STOL and rough field performance. Suited to touring, training, or use as a light sailplane/hang glider tug. Maximum/minimum crew weight 397/121 lb (180/55 kg).

↑ **Pegasus AX2000**

Pegasus Chaser-S

Type: Single-seat, flex-wing microlight, with nosewheel trike.
Construction: Alloy tube, fabric and composites.
Wing span: 26 ft 7 ins (8.1 m)
Length: 16 ft 1 ins (4.9 m) wing bag
Empty weight: 220 lb (100 kg)
Gross weight: 485 lb (220 kg)
Recommended engine: 35 hp (26 kW) Rotax 337, or 40 hp (30 kW) Rotax 447 or 508
Maximum speed: 80-82 kts (92-95 mph) 148-153 km/h
Cruise speed: 48-61 kts (55-70 mph) 89-113 km/h, depending on engine
Stall speed: 30 kts (34 mph) 55 km/h
Take-off distance over a 50 ft (15 m) obstacle: 285-312 ft (87-95 m)
Availability: Factory built.

Pegasus Quantum Sport and Supersport

Type: 2-seat, flex-wing microlight, with nosewheel trike.
Construction: Alloy tube, Trilam and Kevlar fabric, and composites.
Details: For Supersport 912 version, with Rotax 912 engine.
Wing span: Q2 wing of 33 ft 10 ins (10.3 m)
Length: 9 ft 2 ins (2.8 m) trike
Gross weight: 860 lb (390 kg)
Recommended engine: 80 hp (59.6 kW) Rotax 912, with 2.2:1 reduction. Also offered with Rotax 582, 462 and 503.

Never-exceed speed (V_{NE}): 78 kts (90 mph) 145 km/h
Maximum speed: 76 kts (88 mph) 141 km/h
Stall speed: 26 kts (30 mph) 48 km/h
Take-off distance over a 50 ft (15 m) obstacle: 492 ft (150 m)
Climb rate: 1,100 ft (335 m) per minute at MTOW
Availability: Factory built, or kit for export only.
Comments: Quantum Supersport 912 is top-of-the-range version of Quantum Sport and Supersport series. Sport has instrument binnacle instead of full aerodynamic pod. Maximum pilot/passenger weight 379 lb (172 kg); minimum pilot weight 121 lb (55 kg). G limits +6/-3 ultimate.

↑ Pegasus Supersport

Pegasus Quantum LITE Basic 503TC

Type: 2-seat, flex-wing microlight/light aircraft, with nosewheel trike.
Construction: Alloy tube, Trilam and Kevlar fabric, and composites.
Wing: As for Quantum Supersport.
Recommended engine: 50 hp (37.3 kW) Rotax 503TC
Availability: Factory built.
Comments: New budget version of Quantum range, by standardisation of specifications and colours, and by building on a production line basis with no factory fit options (available options are purchased as kits).

Pegasus Quasar

Type: 2-seat, flex-wing microlight/light aircraft, with nosewheel trike.
Construction: Alloy tube, Trilam or Mylar and Kevlar fabric, and composites.
Wing span: 34 ft (10.35 m)
Length: 9 ft 3 ins (2.82 m) for trike
Empty weight: 385 lb (175 kg)
Gross weight: 858 lb (390 kg)
Recommended engine: 54 hp (40 kW) Rotax 582
Maximum speed: 69 kts (80 mph) 129 km/h
Cruise speed: 52 kts (60 mph) 97 km/h
Stall speed: 23 kts (26 mph) 42 km/h
Take-off distance over a 50 ft (15 m) obstacle: 575 ft (175 m)
Climb rate: 666 ft (203 m) per minute
Availability: Factory built.

PFA Currie Wot

Address:
Popular Flying Association, Terminal Building, Shoreham Airport, Shoreham-by-Sea, Sussex BN43 5FF.
Telephone: +44 1273 461616
Facsimile: +44 1273 463390

Type: Single-seat biplane, with fixed tail-dragger undercarriage.
Construction: Wood and fabric.
Wing span: 22 ft 1 ins (6.73 m)
Length: 18 ft 4 ins (5.59 m)
Empty weight: 550 lb (249 kg)
Gross weight: 900 lb (408 kg)
Recommended engine: 65 hp (48.5 kW) Walter Mikron or 90 hp (67 kW) Teledyne Continental C90
Maximum speed: 83 kts (95 mph) 153 km/h
Cruise speed: 70 kts (80 mph) 129 km/h
Stall speed: 35 kts (40 mph) 65 km/h
Take-off distance: 500 ft (152 m)
Climb rate: 600 ft (183 m) per minute
Range: 208 naut miles (240 miles) 386 km
Availability: Plans.
Comments: Designed by Mr J. R. Currie in 1937. Plans sold via the PFA.

PFA/Luton LA.4 Minor

Type: Single-seat, parasol-winged monoplane, with fixed tailwheel undercarriage.
Construction: Wood and fabric.
Wing span: 25 ft (7.62 m)
Length: 20 ft 9 ins (6.32 m)
Empty weight: 480 lb (218 kg)
Gross weight: 750 lb (340 kg)
Recommended engine: Volkswagen, Teledyne Continental or Textron Lycoming, between 40 and 65 hp (30 and 48.5 kW)
Maximum speed: 65 kts (75 mph) 121 km/h
Cruise speed: 60 kts (69 mph) 111 km/h
Stall speed: 25 kts (28 mph) 45 km/h
Take-off distance: 300 ft (92 m)
Climb rate: 350 ft (107 m) per minute
Range: 173 naut miles (200 miles) 321 km
Availability: Plans.
Comments: Classic homebuilt design from 1936. See also Falconar Cubmajor (Canada).

↑ PFA/Luton LA.4 Minor with Textron Lycoming O-145 engine *(Geoffrey P. Jones)*

Sherwood Ranger ST

Address:
TCD Ltd, Larkfield, Retford Road, Mattersey, Doncaster, S. Yorkshire DN10 5HG (USA: Sherwood America Aviation, which see).
Telephone: +44 1777 817975
Facsimile: +44 1302 752643

Type: Single/tandem-seat, open-cockpit biplane, with fixed tailwheel undercarriage.
Construction: Wood, tube and fabric.
Wing span: 23 ft (7.01 m)
Length: 20 ft (6.1 m)
Empty weight: 500 lb (227 kg)
Gross weight: 1,000 lb (454 kg)
Recommended engine: 64.4 hp (48 kW) Rotax 582 (Rotax 503 for lighter "LW" series).
Maximum speed: 83 kts (95 mph) 153 km/h
Cruise speed: 78 kts (90 mph) 145 km/h
Stall speed: 33-37 kts (38-42 mph) 61-68 km/h
Take-off distance: 700 ft (214 m)
Climb rate: 1,200 ft (366 m) per minute
Range: 182 naut miles (210 miles) 338 km
Availability: Kits.
Comments: First flown in October 1992. Folding wings, and also available as the LW microlight.

Smith Acro Advanced

Address:
Barry Smith, 2 Wrentree Close, Redcar, Cleveland TS10 4SB.
Telephone: +44 1642 475631 or 470322

Type: Single-seat, aerobatic monoplane, with fixed tailwheel undercarriage.
Construction: Steel tube, wood and composites.
Wing span: 19 ft 10 ins (6.05 m)
Length: 15 ft 11 ins (4.85 m)
Empty weight: 490 lb (222 kg)
Gross weight: 750 lb (340 kg)
Recommended engine: 68 hp (50.7 kW) 2.1 litre Acro Aerobatic Volkswagen conversion
Never-exceed speed (V_{NE}): 174 kts (200 mph) 322 km/h
Cruise speed: 113-122 kts (130-140 mph) 209-225 km/h
Stall speed: 42 kts (48 mph) 78 km/h
Take-off distance: 656 ft (200 m)
Climb rate: 1,500 ft (457 m) per minute
Range: 391 naut miles (450 miles) 724 km
Availability: Prototype only.
Comments: Intended for affordable competition aerobatics up to advanced level. Designed by Barry Smith.

↑ Smith Acro Advanced *(Geoffrey P. Jones)*

Speedtwin Developments Speedtwin Mk.I and II

Address:
Speedtwin Developments Ltd, Upper Cae Garw Farm, Monmouth, Gwent NP5 4PJ.
Telephone: +44 1600 860165
Facsimile: +44 1600 860813

Details: Speedtwin Mk I, except under comments.
Type: Tandem 2-seat, aerobatic monoplane, with twin engines and fixed tailwheel undercarriage.
Construction: Metal.
Wing span: 26 ft (7.92 m)
Length: 22 ft 10 ins (6.96 m)
Empty weight: 1,750 lb (794 kg)
Gross weight: 2,250 lb (1,020 kg) or 2,000 lb (907 kg) for aerobatics
Recommended engines: 2 × 100 hp (74.6 kW) Teledyne Continental O-200s
Maximum speed: 155 kts (178 mph) 286 km/h
Cruise speed: 139 kts (160 mph) 257 km/h
Stall speed: 59 kts (68 mph) 110 km/h
Take-off distance: 540 ft (165 m)
Climb rate: 1,200 ft (366 m) per minute
Range: 1,129 naut miles (1,300 miles) 2,092 km
Availability: Kits.
Comments: First flown in 1992. G limits +4.4/-2.2. Speedtwin Mk.II has 2 × 160 hp (119.3 kW) Textron Lycoming IO-320s (174 kts, 200 mph, 322 km/h maximum speed and stressed to +6/-3). Agents in Australia and USA.

Taylor JT.1 Monoplane

Address:
79 Springwater Road, Leigh-on-Sea, Essex SS9 5BW.
Telephone: +44 1702 521484

Type: Single-seat, open or enclosed cockpit, low-wing monoplane, with fixed tailwheel undercarriage.
Construction: Wood and fabric.
Wing span: 21 ft (6.4 m)
Length: 15 ft (4.57 m)
Empty weight: 430 lb (195 kg)
Gross weight: 660 lb (299 kg)
Recommended engine: 40 hp (30 kW) 1,500cc Volkswagen. Engines in the 40-60 hp (30-44.7 kW) range are suitable.
Maximum speed: 100 kts (115 mph) 185 km/h
Cruise speed: 87 kts (100 mph) 161 km/h
Stall speed: 35 kts (40 mph) 65 km/h, *clean*
Take-off distance: 600 ft (183 m) from grass, 350 ft (107 m) paved
Climb rate: 1,000 ft (305 m) per minute
Range: 252 naut miles (290 miles) 466 km
Availability: Plans.
Comments: First flight 4 July 1959. Many completed and flown worldwide.

Taylor JT.2 Titch

Type: Single-seat, racing monoplane, with fixed tailwheel undercarriage.
Construction: Wood and fabric.
Wing span: 18 ft 11 ins (5.77 m)
Length: 16 ft 2 ins (4.93 m)

Empty weight: 505 lb (229 kg)
Gross weight: 760 lb (345 kg)
Recommended engine: 85 hp (63.4 kW) Teledyne Continental C85 (also suitable for 105 hp, 78.3 kW Textron Lycoming)
Maximum speed: 174 kts (200 mph) 322 km/h
Cruise speed: 139 kts (160 mph) 257 km/h
Stall speed: 52 kts (59 mph) 95 km/h
Take-off distance: 600 ft (183 m) from grass, 350 ft (107 m) paved
Climb rate: 1,600-2,000 ft (488-610 m) per minute
Range: 330 naut miles (380 miles) 611 km
Availability: Plans.
Comments: Prototype first flew on 4 January 1967. Used for Formula One air racing and by Vic Davies for European city-to-city records. Many completed worldwide.

↑ **Taylor Titch built in the USA**

Thruster Aircraft T.300

Address:
Thruster Aircraft Services Ltd, Malt House, Ginge, nr Wantage, Oxon OX12 8QS.
Telephone: +44 1235 833305
Facsimile: +44 1235 833390

Type: Side-by-side 2-seat, open, high-wing microlight, with fixed tail-dragger undercarriage.
Construction: Alloy, tube and fabric.
Wing span: 31 ft 6 ins (9.6 m)
Length: 18 ft (5.49 m)
Empty weight: 396 lb (180 kg)
Gross weight: 516 lb (234 kg)
Maximum speed: 70 kts (81 mph) 130 km/h
Cruise speed: 59 kts (68 mph) 109 km/h
Range: 196 naut miles (226 miles) 363 km
Availability: Kits or factory complete aircraft.
Comments: T.500 version with enclosed rear fuselage also available, both a development of the Thruster Gemini. Originally an Australian company, though some Thrusters are still built there.

Thruster Aircraft T.600 Nova

Type: Side-by-side 2-seat, high-wing microlight, with fixed tail-dragger or nosewheel undercarriage.
Construction: Alloy, tube and fabric.
Wing span: 31 ft 6 ins (9.6 m)
Length: 19 ft (5.8 m)
Empty weight: 434 lb (197 kg) for T.600N, 412 lb (187 kg) for T.600T
Gross weight: 860 lb (390 kg)
Recommended engine: 49.6 hp (37 kW) Rotax 503.2V
Maximum speed: 71 kts (82 mph) 132 km/h
Cruise speed: 55 kts (63 mph) 101 km/h
Stall speed: 35 kts (40 mph) 65 km/h
Climb rate: 460 ft (140 m) per minute
Range: 196 naut miles (226 miles) 364 km
Availability: Kits or factory complete.
Comments: Development of older T.300.

↑ **Thruster T.600N Nova** *(Geoffrey P. Jones)*

Whittaker MW.5 Sorcerer

Address:
Mike Whittaker, Appletree Cottage, Churchfield Road, Clayton, Doncaster, South Yorkshire, DN5 7BZ.
Telephone: +44 1977 643508

Type: Single-seat, high-wing monoplane, with tail-dragger undercarriage.
Construction: Steel tube, wood and fabric.
Wing span: 28 ft (8.53 m)
Length: 15 ft 9 ins (4.8 m)
Empty weight: 308 lb (140 kg)
Gross weight: 528 lb (239 kg)
Recommended engine: 50 hp (37.3 kW) Fuji-Robin
Maximum speed: 85 kts (98 mph) 158 km/h
Cruise speed: 61 kts (70 mph) 113 km/h
Range: 149 naut miles (172 miles) 276 km
Availability: Plans.
Comments: Microlight or homebuilt category. Rotax 503 and 532 engines optional. Several completed and flown.

Whittaker MW.6 Merlin

Type: Tandem 2-seat, high-wing monoplane, with fixed nosewheel undercarriage.
Construction: Alloy tube and fabric.
Wing span: 32 ft (9.75 m)
Length: 17 ft 6 ins (5.33 m)
Empty weight: 400 lb (181 kg)
Gross weight: 800 lb (363 kg)
Recommended engine: 50 hp (37.3 kW) Robin, 50 hp (37.3 kW) Rotax 503 or 64.4 hp (48 kW) Rotax 532
Maximum speed: 100 kts (115 mph) 185 km/h
Cruise speed: 70 kts (80 mph) 129 km/h
Range: 104 naut miles (120 miles) 193 km
Availability: Plans.
Comments: Development of MW.5. Over 25 completed and flown.

Whittaker MW.7

Type: Single-seat, aerobatic monoplane, with fixed tail-dragger undercarriage.
Construction: Alloy tube and fabric.
Wing span: 22 ft (6.71 m)
Length: 15 ft (4.57 m)
Empty weight: 320 lb (145 kg)
Gross weight: 540 lb (245 kg)
Recommended engine: 64 hp (47.7 kW) Rotax 532
Maximum speed: 100 kts (115 mph) 185 km/h
Cruise speed: 78 kts (90 mph) 145 km/h
Range: 220 naut miles (253 miles) 407 km
Availability: Plans.
Comments: First flown in August 1988. One of the few available aerobatic microlights.

↑ **Whittaker MW.7 built by Kim Wilcox** *(Geoffrey P. Jones)*

Whittaker MW.8

Type: Single-seat, enclosed-cockpit monoplane, with pusher engine and fixed nosewheel undercarriage.
Construction: Alloy tube, wood and fabric.
Wing span: 29 ft 6 ins (8.99 m)
Length: 18 ft 4 ins (5.59 m)
Empty weight: 400 lb (181 kg)
Gross weight: 680 lb (308 kg)
Recommended engine: 42.9 hp (32 kW) Rotax 508
Availability: Plans.
Comments: Suitable for precision flying competitions, with good cockpit visibility, good fuel economy, and flaps for spot landings. First flown in 1993.

USA

Ace Aircraft Baby Ace D

Address:
Ace Aircraft Co, 05-134th Street, Chesapeake, WV 25315.
Telephone: +1 304 949 3098

Type: Single-seat, open-cockpit, parasol-wing monoplane, with fixed tailwheel undercarriage.
Construction: Steel tube, wood and fabric.
Wing span: 26 ft 5 ins (8.05 m)
Length: 17 ft 9 ins (5.41 m)
Empty weight: 575 lb (261 kg)
Gross weight: 950 lb (431 kg)
Recommended engine: Teledyne Continental A65 or other engines of 65 or 85 hp (48.5 or 63.4 kW)
Maximum speed: 96 kts (110 mph) 177 km/h
Cruise speed: 87 kts (100 mph) 161 km/h
Stall speed: 30 kts (34 mph) 55 km/h
Take-off distance: 250 ft (77 m)
Climb rate: 1,200 ft (366 m) per minute
Range: 304 naut miles (350 miles) 563 km
Availability: Plans and kits.
Comments: Originally designed by "Ace" Corben in the 1930s, and updated to Model D form (first flying in 1956). Over 350 completed.

↑ **Ace Aircraft Baby Ace Model D with 80 hp (59.6 kW) engine** *(Geoffrey P. Jones)*

Ace Aircraft Junior Ace E

Type: Side-by-side 2-seat version of the Baby Ace Model D, with parasol wing and fixed tailwheel undercarriage.
Construction: Steel tube, wood and fabric.
Wing span: 26 ft (7.92 m)
Length: 18 ft (5.49 m)
Empty weight: 809 lb (367 kg)
Gross weight: 1,335 lb (606 kg)
Recommended engine: 85 hp (63.4 kW) Teledyne Continental C85
Maximum speed: 113 kts (130 mph) 209 km/h
Cruise speed: 91 kts (105 mph) 169 km/h
Stall speed: 39 kts (44 mph) 71 km/h
Take-off distance: 400 ft (122 m)
Climb rate: 500 ft (153 m) per minute
Range: 304 naut miles (350 miles) 563 km
Availability: Plans and kits.

Acro Sport Acro-Sport I and Super Acro Sport

Address:
Acro Sport Inc, P O Box 462, Hales Corner, WI 53130.
Telephone: +1 414 529 2609

Type: Single-seat, competition/aerobatic biplane, with fixed tailwheel undercarriage.
Details: Acro-Sport I, except under Comments.
Construction: Steel tube, wood and fabric.
Wing span: 19 ft 7 ins (5.97 m)
Length: 17 ft 6 ins (5.33 m)
Empty weight: 733 lb (332 kg)
Gross weight: 1,350 lb (612 kg)
Recommended engine: 180 hp (134 kW) Textron Lycoming IO-360
Maximum speed: 132 kts (152 mph) 245 km/h
Cruise speed: 113 kts (130 mph) 209 km/h

Stall speed: 44 kts (50 mph) 81 km/h
Take-off distance: 150 ft (46 m)
Climb rate: 1,800-3,500 ft (549-1,067 m) per minute
Range: 304 naut miles (350 miles) 563 km
Availability: Plans and components.
Comments: Designed for construction by school students. First flown on 11 January 1972. Super Acro Sport, suitable for unlimited international level aerobatics, is generally similar but with a different wing section.

↑ **Acro Sport I built in the UK with an IO-360 engine** *(Geoffrey P. Jones)*

Acro Sport Acro-Sport II

Type: Tandem 2-seat, aerobatic biplane, with fixed tailwheel undercarriage.
Construction: Steel tube, wood and fabric.
Wing span: 21 ft 8 ins (6.6 m)
Length: 18 ft 10 ins (5.74 m)
Empty weight: 875 lb (397 kg)
Gross weight: 1,520 lb (689 kg)
Recommended engine: 180 hp (134 kW) Textron Lycoming IO-360-A4B or similar
Maximum speed: 124 kts (143 mph) 230 km/h
Cruise speed: 107 kts (123 mph) 198 km/h
Stall speed: 46 kts (53 mph) 86 km/h
Take-off distance: 300 ft (92 m)
Climb rate: 1,500 ft (457 m) per minute
Range: 260 naut miles (300 miles) 483 km
Availability: Plans and components.
Comments: 2-seat development of the Acro Sport I. First flown on 9 July 1978. Over 70 believed to be completed and flown.

Acro Sport Pober Junior Ace

Type: Side-by-side 2-seat, parasol-wing monoplane, with fixed tail-dragger undercarriage.
Construction: Steel tube, wood and fabric.
Wing span: 34 ft (10.36 m)
Length: 20 ft (6.1 m)
Empty weight: 750 lb (340 kg)
Gross weight: 1,320 lb (599 kg)
Recommended engine: Teledyne Continental C65, A/C85 or other type
Maximum speed: 113 kts (130 mph) 209 km/h
Cruise speed: 70 kts (80 mph) 129 km/h
Stall speed: 39 kts (45 mph) 73 km/h
Take-off distance: 350 ft (107 m)
Climb rate: 500 ft (152 m) per minute
Range: 217 naut miles (250 miles) 402 km
Availability: Plans and components.
Comments: Updated version of the 1930s design by "Ace" Corben (see Ace Aircraft Co).

Acro Sport Pober Pixie

Type: Single-seat, open cockpit, parasol-wing monoplane, with fixed tailwheel undercarriage.
Construction: Steel tube, wood and fabric.
Wing span: 29 ft 10 ins (9.09 m)
Length: 17 ft 3 ins (5.26 m)
Empty weight: 543 lb (246 kg)
Gross weight: 900 lb (408 kg)
Recommended engine: 60 hp (44.7 kW) Limbach SL1700, other Volkswagens or Teledyne Continental A/C65
Maximum speed: 90 kts (103 mph) 166 km/h
Cruise speed: 72 kts (83 mph) 134 km/h
Stall speed: 26 kts (30 mph) 49 km/h
Take-off distance: 300 ft (92 m)
Climb rate: 500 ft (152 m) per minute
Range: 252 naut miles (290 miles) 466 km
Availability: Plans and components.
Comments: Designed by ex-EAA President Paul Poberezny. First flown in July 1974.

Acro Sport Pober Super Ace

Type: Single-seat, parasol-wing monoplane, with fixed tailwheel undercarriage.
Construction: Steel tube, wood and fabric.
Wing span: 27 ft 4 ins (8.32 m)
Length: 18 ft 5 ins (5.61 m)
Empty weight: 685 lb (311 kg)
Gross weight: 1,030 lb (467 kg)
Take-off distance: 350 ft (107 m)
Recommended engine: 85 hp (63.4 kW) Teledyne Continental A/C85
Maximum speed: 139 kts (160 mph) 257 km/h
Cruise speed: 96 kts (110 mph) 177 km/h
Stall speed: 33 kts (38 mph) 61 km/h
Take-off distance: 350 ft (107 m)
Climb rate: 500 ft (152 m) per minute
Range: 217 naut miles (250 miles) 402 km
Availability: Plans and components.

Acro Sport Nesmith Cougar I

Type: Side-by-side 2-seat, high-wing, cabin monoplane, with fixed tailwheel undercarriage.
Construction: Sheet metal, steel tube, wood and fabric.
Wing span: 20 ft 6 ins (6.25 m)
Length: 18 ft 11 ins (5.77 m)
Empty weight: 624 lb (283 kg)
Gross weight: 1,250 lb (567 kg)
Recommended engine: Teledyne Continental A/C85
Maximum speed: 152 kts (175 mph) 282 km/h
Cruise speed: 104 kts (120 mph) 193 km/h
Stall speed: 46 kts (53 mph) 86 km/h
Take-off distance: 800 ft (244 m)
Climb rate: 1,300 ft (396 m) per minute
Range: 521 naut miles (600 miles) 965 km
Availability: Plans and components.
Comments: Over 100 completed, mainly in North America.

↑ **Acro Sport Nesmith Cougar built by Ken Dannenburg** *(Geoffrey P. Jones)*

Advanced Aeromarine Mallard

Address:
152 East Eighth Street, Apopka, FL 32703.
Telephone: +1 407 877 7871
Facsimile: +1 407 293 1533

Type: Side-by-side 2-seat, high-wing, amphibious monoplane, with retractable tail-dragger undercarriage.
Construction: Composites, metal and fabric.
Wing span: 29 ft 7 ins (9.02 m)
Length: 22 ft 4 ins (6.83 m)
Empty weight: 775 lb (352 kg)
Gross weight: 1,250 lb (567 kg)
Recommended engine: 80 hp (59.6 kW) Rotax 912
Maximum speed: 87 kts (100 mph) 161 km/h
Cruise speed: 69 kts (80 mph) 129 km/h
Stall speed: 31 kts (35 mph) 57 km/h
Take-off distance: 350 ft (107 m)
Climb rate: 750 ft (229 m) per minute
Range: 278 naut miles (320 miles) 515 km
Availability: Kits.
Comments: Revised version of the Keuthan Buccaneer. Also available as a Buccaneer conversion. Other aircraft available.

Adventure Air 2 + 2 Amphibian, Super Adventurer and Adventurer 4-Place

Address:
Adventure Air, Carroll County Airport, PO Box 368, Berryville, AR 72616-0368.
Telephone: +1 501 423 5350
Facsimile: +1 501 423 5366

Details: 2 + 2 Amphibian.
Type: 2 + 2-seat, amphibious monoplane, with pusher engine mounted above the wing and retractable tailwheel undercarriage.
Construction: Composites.
Wing span: 35 ft (10.67 m)
Length: 24 ft (7.32 m)
Empty weight: 1,800 lb (816 kg)
Gross weight: 3,000 lb (1,361 kg)
Recommended engine: 200 hp (149 kW) Textron Lycoming
Maximum speed: 137 kts (158 mph) 254 km/h
Cruise speed: 113 kts (130 mph) 209 km/h
Stall speed: 47 kts (54 mph) 87 km/h
Take-off distance: 700 ft (214 m) land, 1,000 ft (305 m) water
Climb rate: 800 ft (244 m) per minute
Range: 1,390 naut miles (1,600 miles) 2,575 km, with optional 189 litre wing tanks
Availability: Kits.
Comments: First flown in 1993. Other available models include the Super Adventurer and Adventurer 4-Place. Engine options include 210 hp (156.6 kW) Teledyne Continental, 220 hp (164 kW) Ford V.8 and 230 hp (171.5 kW) Chevrolet 4.3L.

↑ **Adventure Air 2 + 2 Amphibian** *(Geoffrey P. Jones)*

Adventure Air Adventurer 333

Type: Side-by-side seated, shoulder-wing, amphibious monoplane, with pusher engine and retractable tailwheel undercarriage.
Construction: Composites and chromoly.
Wing span: 35 ft 10 ins (10.92 m)
Length: 24 ft 6 ins (7.47 m)
Empty weight: 2,000 lb (907 kg)
Gross weight: 3,333 lb (1,512 kg)
Recommended engine: 333 hp (248 kW) Chevrolet 5.7L-350CI
Maximum speed: 137 kts (158 mph) 254 km/h
Cruise speed: 122 kts (140 mph) 225 km/h
Stall speed: 53 kts (61 mph) 99 km/h
Take-off distance: 600 ft (183 m) land, 800 ft (244 m) water
Range: 1,389 naut miles (1,600 miles) 2,575 km, with optional 454 litre tanks
Availability: Kits.
Comments: Has sleeping bunk or 60 cu ft (1.7 m^3) cargo capacity.

AeroCad AeroCanard RG, FG and SB

Address:
AeroCad Inc, PO Box 1988, Fort Pierce-Florida Airport, Fort Pierce, FL 34954.
Telephone: +1 561 460 8020
E-mail: Jeff@aerocad.com
Web Site: http://www.aerocad.com

Details: AeroCanard RG, except under Type and Comments.
Type: 4-seat, cabin monoplane with canards, winglets, pusher engine, and retractable undercarriage. Also fixed gear version (FG) with retractable nosewheel and fixed main units.
Construction: Composites.
Wing span: 28 ft 1 ins (8.56 m)
Length: 16 ft 9 ins (5.11 m)
Empty weight: 1,300 lb (590 kg)
Gross weight: 2,150 lb (975 kg)
Recommended engine: 200 hp (149 kW) Textron Lycoming IO-360
Maximum speed: 196 kts (225 mph) 362 km/h
Cruise speed: 182 kts (210 mph) 338 km/h
Stall speed: approx 61 kts (70 mph) 113 km/h
Take-off distance: 800 ft (244 m)
Climb rate: 1,900 ft (580 m) per minute
Range: 869 naut miles (1,000 miles) 1,609 km
Availability: Kits.
Comments: Prototype first flew in 1996. AeroCanard SB (Short Body) also available.

↑ AeroCad AeroCanard FG at Sun 'n Fun '97 *(Geoffrey P. Jones)*

Aerocar Coot-A

Address:
Dr Richard A. Steeves, 6958 Applewood Drive, Madison, WI 53719.
Telephone: +1 608 833 5586
Facsimile: +1 608 263 9167
E-mail: rsteeves@facstaff.wise.edu

Type: Side-by-side 2-seat, amphibious monoplane, with retractable nosewheel undercarriage.
Construction: Metal, composites and wood.
Wing span: 36 ft (10.97 m)
Length: 22 ft (6.71 m)
Empty weight: 1,300 lb (590 kg)
Gross weight: 1,900 lb (862 kg)
Take-off distance: 200 ft (61 m) land, 600 ft (183 m) water
Recommended engine: 180 hp or 220 hp (134 or 164 kW) Franklin
Maximum speed: 122 kts (140 mph) 225 km/h
Cruise speed: 104 kts (120 mph) 193 km/h
Climb rate: 1,000-1,250 ft (305-381 m) per minute
Range: 434 naut miles (500 miles) 804 km
Availability: Plans.
Comments: Prototype first flew in February 1971, designed by the late 'Molt' Taylor. Richard Steeves has taken over sales.

↑ Aerocar Coot-A built by Richard Steeves *(Geoffrey P. Jones)*

Aerocar Mini-Imp

Address:
Aerocar Associates, Box 1171, Longview, WA 98632.

Type: Single-seat, high-wing monoplane, with engine in mid-fuselage and tail-mounted pusher propeller, inverted V-tail and retractable nosewheel undercarriage.
Construction: Metal and composites.
Wing span: 25 ft (7.62 m)
Length: 16 ft (4.88 m)
Empty weight: 500 lb (227 kg)
Gross weight: 850 lb (386 kg)
Recommended engine: 100 hp (74.6 kW) Teledyne Continental O-200
Maximum speed: 174 kts (200 mph) 322 km/h
Cruise speed: 152 kts (175 mph) 282 km/h
Stall speed: 48 kts (55 mph) 89 km/h
Take-off distance: 600 ft (183 m)
Climb rate: 1,500 ft (457 m) per minute
Range: 434 naut miles (500 miles) 805 km
Availability: Plans.
Comments: Designed by the late Moulton 'Molt' Taylor. Similar version constructed of Taylor Paper Glass became the **Micro-Imp**. Current status uncertain.

Aerocomp CompAir 6

Address:
Aerocomp Inc, 2335 Newfound Harbor Drive, Merritt Island, FL 32952.
Telephone and Facsimile: +1 407 453 6641

Type: 6-seat, high-wing, cabin monoplane, with fixed tailwheel undercarriage.
Construction: Composites.
Wing span: 34 ft 6 ins (10.52 m)
Length: 25 ft (7.62 m)
Empty weight: 1,490 lb (676 kg)
Gross weight: 2,850 lb (1,293 kg)
Recommended engine: 205 hp (153 kW) Franklin
Maximum speed: 135 kts (156 mph) 251 km/h
Cruise speed: 126 kts (145 mph) 233 km/h
Stall speed: 38 kts (43 mph) 70 km/h
Take-off distance: 350 ft (107 m)
Climb rate: 1,700 ft (518 m) per minute
Range: 851 naut miles (980 miles) 1,577 km
Availability: Kits.
Comments: Development of CompMonster. Many kits sold, including to South Africa.

↑ Aerocomp CompAir 6 *(Geoffrey P. Jones)*

Aerocomp CompAir Trainer

Type: Side-by-side 2-seat, high-wing, cabin monoplane, with fixed nosewheel undercarriage.
Construction: Composites.
Recommended engine: 120 hp (89.5 kW) Franklin
Maximum speed: 104 kts (120 mph) 193 km/h
Cruise speed: 87 kts (100 mph) 161 km/h
Availability: Kits.
Comments: First shown in 1997. Can carry 2 persons, full fuel and 50 lb (22.7 kg) baggage.

Aerocomp CompMonster

Type: 4-seat, high-wing, cabin monoplane, with fixed tailwheel or float undercarriage.
Construction: Composites.
Wing span: 35 ft (10.67 m)
Length: 26 ft (7.92 m)
Empty weight: 1,350 lb (612 kg)
Gross weight: 2,750 lb (1,247 kg)
Recommended engine: 180 hp (134 kW) Textron Lycoming IO-360. Prototype has 110 hp (82 kW) Hirth 95
Maximum speed: 123 kts (142 mph) 229 km/h
Cruise speed: 115 kts (132 mph) 212 km/h
Stall speed: 37 kts (42 mph) 68 km/h
Take-off distance: 400 ft (122 m)
Climb rate: 1,200 ft (366 m) per minute
Range: 573 naut miles (660 miles) 1,062 km
Availability: Kits.
Comments: First flown 3 April 1995.

↑ Aerocomp CompMonster on Aerocomp floats *(Geoffrey P. Jones)*

See also – Merlin Aircraft

Aerolites AeroMaster AG

Address:
Aerolites Inc, 12104 David Road, Welsh, LA 70591.
Telephone and Facsimile: +1 318 734 3865
E-mail: aerolites@centuryinter.net

Type: Single-seat, low-wing monoplane for agricultural spraying, with fixed tailwheel undercarriage.
Construction: Composites, steel tube and fabric.
Wing span: 28 ft 8 ins (8.74 m)
Length: 18 ft 6 ins (5.64 m)
Empty weight: 425 lb (193 kg)
Gross weight: 1,000 lb (454 kg)
Recommended engine: 64.4 hp (48 kW) Rotax 582
Maximum speed: 96 kts (110 mph) 177 km/h
Cruise speed: 52 kts (60 mph) 97 km/h
Stall speed: 28 kts (32 mph) 52 km/h
Take-off distance: 500 ft (153 m)
Climb rate: 800 ft (244 m) per minute
Range: 130 naut miles (150 miles) 241 km
Availability: Kits.
Comments: Kit includes Spray Miser CDA ag system. 56 kts (65 mph) 105 km/h spray speed - 113.5 litre tank covers up to 120 acres.

↑ Aerolites AeroMaster AG with spray gear *(Geoffrey P. Jones)*

Aerolites AG Bearcat

Details can be found in the 1996-97 edition of *WA&SD*.

Aerolites Aeroskiff

Type: Side-by-side 2-seat, high-wing, amphibious monoplane, with retractable tailwheel undercarriage.
Construction: Metal, composites and fabric.
Wing span: 29 ft 8 ins (9.04 m)
Length: 22 ft 4 ins (6.81 m)
Empty weight: 565 lb (256 kg)
Gross weight: 1,125 lb (510 kg)
Recommended engine: 64.4 hp (48 kW) Rotax 582 (optional 73.8 hp, 55 kW) Rotax 618
Maximum speed: 82 kts (95 mph) 153 km/h
Cruise speed: 56 kts (65 mph) 105 km/h
Stall speed: 33 kts (38 mph) 62 km/h
Take-off distance: 400 ft (122 m) land, 550 ft (168 m) water
Climb rate: 600 ft (183 m) per minute
Availability: Kits.
Comments: Wings detach in 30 minutes.

↑ Aerolites Aeroskiff

Aerolites Bearcat

Type: Single-seat, parasol wing monoplane, with fixed tail-dragger undercarriage.
Construction: Steel tube, aluminium and fabric.
Wing span: 30 ft (9.14 m)
Length: 17 ft 6 ins (5.33 m)
Empty weight: 275 lb (125 kg)
Gross weight: 700 lb (318 kg)
Recommended engine: 42 hp (31.3 kW) Rotax 447
Maximum speed: 61 kts (70 mph) 113 km/h
Cruise speed: 48 kts (55 mph) 89 km/h
Stall speed: 24 kts (27 mph) 44 km/h
Take-off distance: 150 ft (46 m)
Climb rate: 750-1,200 ft (229-366 m) per minute
Range: 104 naut miles (120 miles) 193 km
Availability: Kits.
Comments: 3-axis control microlight representation of the 1930s Corben Baby Ace. Stated 100 hour build time.

Aero-Systems Cadet STF

Address:
Aero-Systems, 9031 Suncrest Street, Wichita, KS 67212.
Telephone: +1 316 722 2494

Type: Side-by-side 2-seat, replica of the 1941 Culver Cadet monoplane, with retractable tailwheel undercarriage.
Construction: Steel tube, wood and fabric.

Wing span: 27 ft (8.23 m)
Length: 18 ft (5.49 m)
Empty weight: 785 lb (356 kg)
Gross weight: 1,350 lb (612 kg)
Recommended engine: 90 hp (67 kW) Teledyne Continental
Maximum speed: 152 kts (175 mph) 282 km/h
Cruise speed: 113 kts (130 mph) 209 km/h
Stall speed: 47 kts (54 mph) 87 km/h
Take-off distance: 800 ft (244 m)
Climb rate: 800 ft (244 m) per minute
Range: 452 naut miles (520 miles) 836 km
Availability: Plans.

Aero Wood Avocet 1-A

Address:
Aero Wood Specialities Inc, 4950 County Road 1510, Pomona, MO 65789.
Telephone: +1 417 257 2422
Facsimile: +1 417 257 2239

Type: 4-seat, amphibious monoplane, with pusher engine and retractable nosewheel undercarriage.
Construction: Metal and composites.
Wing span: 39 ft (11.89 m)
Length: 26 ft 3 ins (8 m)
Empty weight: 1,960 lb (889 kg)
Gross weight: 3,520 lb (1,597 kg)
Recommended engine: 300 hp (224 kW) Textron Lycoming IO-540
Maximum speed: 143 kts (165 mph) 265 km/h
Cruise speed: 135 kts (155 mph) 249 km/h
Take-off distance: 700 ft (214 m)
Climb rate: 1,200 ft (366 m) per minute
Range: 782 naut miles (900 miles) 1,448 km
Availability: Kits.
Comments: Designed in 1993 to have exceptional visibility and large payload capacity.

Aerovant Acroduster 1

Address:
Aerovant Aircraft Corp, 2342 Jonquil Place, Rockford, IL 61107.
Telephone: +1 815 877 4508

Type: Single-seat, aerobatic biplane, with fixed tailwheel undercarriage.
Construction: Steel tube, wood and fabric.
Wing span: 19 ft (5.79 m)
Length: 15 ft 9 ins (4.8 m)
Empty weight: 740 lb (336 kg)
Gross weight: 1,190 lb (540 kg)
Recommended engine: 200 hp (149 kW) Textron Lycoming
Maximum speed: 156 kts (180 mph) 290 km/h
Cruise speed: 143 kts (165 mph) 266 km/h
Stall speed: 61 kts (70 mph) 113 km/h
Climb rate: 3,000 ft (915 m) per minute
Range: 260 naut miles (300 miles) 482 km
Availability: Plans.
Comments: Formerly the Stolp SA-700 Acroduster. Rights purchased by Walt Peters of Aerovant in April 1990. 20 built.

↑ Aerovant Acroduster 1

AFI Prescott Pusher II

Address:
Tom Prescott, Aviation Franchising International (AFI), San Antonio, TX.

Type: 4-seat, cabin monoplane, with pusher engine, T-tail and retractable nosewheel undercarriage.
Construction: Steel tube and metal.
Wing span: 29 ft 4 ins (8.94 m)
Length: 20 ft 3 ins (6.17 m)
Empty weight: 1,400 lb (635 kg)
Gross weight: 2,400 lb (1,089 kg)
Recommended engine: 180 hp (134 kW) Textron Lycoming
Maximum speed: 207 kts (238 mph) 383 km/h
Cruise speed: 156 kts (180 mph) 290 km/h
Stall speed: 64 kts (73 mph) 118 km/h
Take-off distance over a 50 ft (15 m) obstacle: 1,725 ft (526 m)
Climb rate: 950 ft (290 m) per minute
Range: 869 naut miles (1,000 miles) 1,609 km
Comments: Revised version of the Pusher. May be produced commercially and certificated but no new information.

Air Magic Spitfire

Address:
Air Magic Ultralights, Hangar 594, Ellington Airfield, Houston, TX 77034.
Telephone: +1 713 482 8124
Facsimile: +1 713 484 0005

Type: Single-seat, open-cockpit microlight, with fixed nosewheel undercarriage.
Construction: Steel tube and fabric.
Wing span: 30 ft (9.14 m)
Length: 17 ft 11 ins (5.46 m)
Empty weight: 252 lb (114 kg)
Gross weight: 550 lb (249 kg)
Recommended engine: 40 hp (30 kW) Rotax 447
Maximum speed: 56 kts (65 mph) 105 km/h
Cruise speed: 48 kts (55 mph) 89 km/h
Climb rate: 700 ft (213 m) per minute
Range: 104 naut miles (120 miles) 193 km
Availability: Factory built microlight and kit.
Comments: Air Magic also sells the faster **Spitfire Super Sport**, 2-seat **Spitfire II** and **Spitfire II Elite**.

Aircraft Designs Stallion

Address:
Aircraft Designs Inc, 5 Harris Court Building S, Monterey, CA 93940.
Telephone: +1 408 649 6212
Facsimile: +1 408 649 5738

Type: 4-seat, high-wing monoplane, with retractable nosewheel undercarriage.
Construction: Welded steel frame and composites.
Wing span: 35 ft (10.67 m)
Length: 25 ft (7.62 m)
Empty weight: 2,200 lb (998 kg)
Gross weight: 3,800 lb (1,724 kg)
Recommended engine: 230 hp (171.5 kW) Teledyne Continental IO-550-G
Maximum speed: 225 kts (260 mph) 418 km/h
Cruise speed: 195 kts (224 mph) 360 km/h
Stall speed: 60 kts (69 mph) 111 km/h
Take-off distance: 1,200 ft (366 m)
Climb rate: 1,600 ft (488 m) per minute
Range: 2,258 naut miles (2,600 miles) 4,184 km
Availability: Kits.
Comments: Designed by Martin Hollmann. First flown 1994. Uses wings and undercarriage from Lancair IV. 6-seat version also available as the **Super Stallion**.

↑ Aircraft Designs 4-seat Stallion

Aircraft Spruce & Speciality One Design DR.107

Address:
Aircraft Spruce & Speciality Inc, PO Box 424, Fullerton, CA 92632.
Telephone: +1 800 824 1930 or 714 870 7551
Facsimile: +1 714 871 7289

Type: Single-seat, low-wing, aerobatic monoplane, with fixed tailwheel undercarriage.
Construction: Steel tube, metal, composites and fabric.
Wing span: 19 ft 4 ins (5.89 m)
Length: 17 ft (5.18 m)
Empty weight: 740 lb (336 kg)
Gross weight: 1,140 lb (517 kg)
Recommended engine: 180 hp (134 kW) Textron Lycoming AEIO-360
Maximum speed: 169 kts (195 mph) 314 km/h
Cruise speed: 139 kts (160 mph) 257 km/h
Stall speed: 55 kts (63 mph) 102 km/h
Take-off distance: 250 ft (77 m)
Climb rate: 2,000 ft (610 m) per minute
Range: 304 naut miles (350 miles) 563 km
Availability: Plans and kits.
Comments: First flown in 1994. Designed for single-class aerobatic competition utilizing a common engine and standard aircraft construction, by Dan Rihn.

↑ Aircraft Spruce & Speciality One Design DR.107 prototype *(Geoffrey P. Jones)*

Aircraft Spruce & Speciality Rihn DR.109

Type: Tandem 2-seat, low-wing, aerobatic monoplane, with fixed tailwheel undercarriage.
Construction: Steel tube, wood and fabric.
Wing span: 24 ft (7.32 m)
Length: 22 ft (6.71 m)
Empty weight: 1,260 lb (572 kg)
Gross weight: 1,950 lb (885 kg)
Recommended engine: 200 hp (149 kW) Textron Lycoming IO-360
Maximum speed: 167 kts (192 mph) 309 km/h
Cruise speed: 146 kts (168 mph) 270 km/h
Stall speed: 51 kts (58 mph) 94 km/h
Take-off distance: 600 ft (183 m)
Range: 434 naut miles (500 miles) 805 km
Availability: Kits.
Comments: 2-seat version of One Design DR.107.

Aircraft Spruce & Speciality Wittman W.10 Tailwind

Type: Side-by-side 2-seat, high-wing, cabin monoplane, with fixed tail-dragger undercarriage.
Construction: Steel tube, wood and fabric.
Wing span: 24 ft (7.32 m)

Length: 19 ft 7 ins (5.97 m)
Empty weight: 876 lb (397 kg)
Gross weight: 1,425 lb (646 kg)
Recommended engine: 145 hp (108 kW) Teledyne Continental O-300
Maximum speed: 174 kts (200 mph) 322 km/h
Cruise speed: 156 kts (180 mph) 290 km/h
Take-off distance: 750 ft (229 m)
Climb rate: 1,200 ft (366 m) per minute
Range: 521 naut miles (600 miles) 965 km
Availability: Plans.
Comments: Designed by Steve Wittman in 1953. Rights acquired in 1995.

Aircraft Spruce & Speciality Breezy

Type: Tandem 2-seat, open-frame, high-wing monoplane, with fixed nosewheel undercarriage.
Construction: Steel tube, wood and fabric.
Wing span: 33 ft (10.06 m)
Length: 22 ft 6 ins (6.86 m)
Empty weight: 700 lb (318 kg)
Gross weight: 1,200 lb (544 kg)
Recommended engine: 90 hp (67 kW) Teledyne Continental C90
Maximum speed: 91 kts (105 mph) 169 km/h
Cruise speed: 65 kts (75 mph) 121 km/h
Range: 217 naut miles (250 miles) 402 km
Availability: Plans and some components.
Comments: Designed in 1964. Utilizes components from other aircraft, including PA-18 Super Cub wings.

Aircraft Spruce & Speciality Baby Lakes, Super Baby Lakes and Buddy Baby Lakes

Details: Refer to Baby Lakes, except under Comments.
Type: Single-seat, open-cockpit biplane, with fixed tailwheel undercarriage.
Construction: Metal, wood and fabric.
Wing span: 16 ft 8 ins (5.08 m)
Length: 13 ft 10 ins (4.22 m)
Empty weight: 480 lb (218 kg)
Gross weight: 850 lb (386 kg)
Recommended engine: 85 hp (63.4 kW) Teledyne Continental O-85
Maximum speed: 117 kts (135 mph) 217 km/h
Cruise speed: 103 kts (118 mph) 190 km/h
Stall speed: 48 kts (55 mph) 89 km/h
Take-off distance: 300 ft (92 m)
Climb rate: 2,000 ft (610 m) per minute
Range: 217 naut miles (250 miles) 402 km
Availability: Plans and kits.
Comments: Scale representation of the Great Lakes Biplane of the 1930s. Designed by Barney Oldfield. Also available are the 108 hp (80.5 kW) Textron Lycoming-powered single-seat **Super Baby Lakes** and the slightly larger and similarly powered 2-seat **Buddy Baby Lakes**.

Aircraft Spruce & Speciality Acrolite

Type: Single-seat, 'entry level' aerobatic biplane, with fixed tailwheel undercarriage.
Construction: Steel tube, metal and wood.
Wing span: 20 ft (6.1 m)
Length: 17 ft (5.18 m)
Empty weight: 495 lb (225 kg)
Gross weight: 750 lb (340 kg)
Recommended engine: 80 hp (59.6 kW) Rotax 912
Maximum speed: 113 kts (130 mph) 209 km/h
Cruise speed: 96 kts (110 mph) 177 km/h
Take-off distance: 500 ft (152 m)
Range: 217 naut miles (250 miles) 402 km
Availability: Plans and components.
Comments: Introduced in 1996. Optional wood or metal wings.

Aircraft Technologies Acro I

Address:
Aircraft Technologies Inc, 4265 Lilburn Industrial Way, Lilburn, GA 30247.
Telephone: +1 770 806 9098

Type: Single-seat, low-wing, aerobatic monoplane, with fixed tailwheel undercarriage.
Construction: Composites.
Wing span: 19 ft 4 ins (5.89 m)
Length: 17 ft (5.18 m)
Empty weight: 750 lb (340 kg)
Gross weight: 1,222 lb (554 kg)
Recommended engine: 200 hp (149 kW) Textron Lycoming IO-360
Maximum speed: 243 kts (280 mph) 451 km/h
Cruise speed: 222 kts (255 mph) 410 km/h
Stall speed: 48 kts (55 mph) 89 km/h
Climb rate: 2,700 ft (823 m) per minute
Range: 868 naut miles (1,000 miles) 1,609 km
Availability: Plans and kits.
Comments: Developed for the International Aerobatic Club "One Design" competition. In full production.

↑ **Aircraft Technologies Acro I** *(Geoffrey P. Jones)*

Aircraft Technologies Atlantis

Type: Side-by-side 2-seat, low-wing, aerobatic monoplane, with fixed tailwheel undercarriage.
Construction: Steel tube, metal and composites.
Wing span: 24 ft 6 ins (7.47 m)
Length: 20 ft (6.1 m)
Empty weight: 1,000 lb (454 kg)
Gross weight: 1,750 lb (794 kg)
Recommended engine: 210 hp (157 kW) Textron Lycoming IO-360
Maximum speed: 221 kts (255 mph) 410 km/h
Cruise speed: 156 kts (180 mph) 290 km/h
Stall speed: 57 kts (65 mph) 105 km/h
Climb rate: 1,500 ft (457 m) per minute
Range: 868 naut miles (1,000 miles) 1,609 km
Availability: Plans and kits.
Comments: 2-seat development of Acro I. Stressed to ±15g.

↑ **Aircraft Technologies Atlantis prototype under construction** *(Geoffrey P. Jones)*

Airight SX300 and SX200

Address:
Airight Inc, 1445 South Sierra Drive, Wichita, KS 67209.
Telephone: +1 316 943 5752

Details: SX300, except under Comments.
Type: Side-by-side 2-seat, low-wing monoplane, with retractable nosewheel undercarriage.
Construction. Metal.
Wing span: 24 ft 4 ins (7.42 m)
Length: 21 ft 1 ins (6.43 m)
Empty weight: 1,600 lb (725 kg)
Gross weight: 2,400 lb (1,089 kg)

↑ **Airight SX300** *(Geoffrey P. Jones)*

Recommended engine: 300 hp (224 kW) Textron Lycoming IO-540
Maximum speed: 247 kts (285 mph) 459 km/h
Cruise speed: 230 kts (265 mph) 426 km/h
Stall speed: 78 kts (90 mph) 145 km/h
Take-off distance: 1,100 ft (335 m)
Climb rate: 2,400 ft (732 m) per minute
Range: 999 naut miles (1,151 miles) 1,852 km
Availability: Kits.
Comments: Jim Ryan of Airight acquired rights in SX300 from Ed Swearingen. Kits built in lots of 25. Certified version with larger wing to meet FAA's 61 kts stall criterion is the SX200, nearing completion at time of writing.

AkroTech Giles G-200

Address:
AkroTech Aviation Inc, 53774 Airport Road, Scappoose, OR 97056, or AkroTech Europe, Aerodrome, 21121 Darois, France.
Telephone: +1 503 543 7960 (France: +33 3 80 44 20 71)
Facsimile: +1 503 543 7964
E-mail: info@akrotech.com (France: aeroland@micronet.fr)

Type: Single-seat, low-wing, aerobatic monoplane, with fixed tailwheel undercarriage.
Construction: Composites
Wing span: 20 ft (6.1 m)
Length: 18 ft (5.49 m)
Empty weight: 750 lb (340 kg)
Gross weight: 1,150 lb (522 kg)
Recommended engine: 200 hp (149 kW) Textron Lycoming AEIO-360
Maximum speed: 220 kts (253 mph) 407 km/h
Cruise speed: 184 kts (212 mph) 341 km/h
Stall speed: 48 kts (55 mph) 89 km/h
Take-off distance: 300 ft (92 m)
Climb rate: 3,550 ft (1,082 m) per minute
Range: 868 naut miles (1,000 miles) 1,609 km
Climb rate: 3,500 ft (1,080 m) per minute
Availability: Kits.
Comments: First flew 1992.

↑ **AkroTech Giles G-202** *(Geoffrey P. Jones)*

AkroTech Giles G-202

Type: Tandem 2-seat, aerobatic monoplane, with fixed tailwheel undercarriage.
Construction: Composites.
Wing span: 22 ft (6.71 m)
Length: 19 ft 10 ins (6.05 m)
Empty weight: 950 lb (431 kg)
Gross weight: 1,600 lb (726 kg)
Recommended engine: 200 hp (149 kW) Textron Lycoming IO-360
Maximum speed: 220 kts (253 mph) 407 km/h
Cruise speed: 176 kts (203 mph) 327 km/h
Stall speed: 51 kts (58 mph) 94 km/h
Take-off distance: 400 ft (122 m)
Climb rate: 2,500 ft (762 m) per minute
Range: 781 naut miles (900 miles) 1,448 km
Availability: Kits.
Comments: 2-seat version of G-200. First flew December 1995.

Alturair BD-5

Address:
Alturair, 1405 North Johnson, El Cajon, CA 92020.
Telephone: +1 619 449 1570
Facsimile: +1 619 442 0481

Type: Single-seat, low-wing monoplane, with pusher engine and retractable nosewheel undercarriage.
Construction: Metal.
Wing span: 17 ft (5.18 m)
Length: 13 ft 7 ins (4.14 m)
Empty weight: 355 lb (161 kg)
Gross weight: 660 lb (299 kg)
Recommended engine: 70 hp (52.2 kW) Zenoah
Maximum speed: 202 kts (232 mph) 373 km/h
Cruise speed: 199 kts (229 mph) 369 km/h
Stall speed: 62 kts (71 mph) 114 km/h
Take-off distance: 600 ft (183 m)
Climb rate: 1,900 ft (579 m) per minute
Range: 499 naut miles (575 miles) 925 km
Availability: Re-worked original Bede kits.
Comments: Support company for Jim Bede's homebuilt project of the 1970s.

American Homebuilts' John Doe STOL Aircraft

Address:
American Homebuilts', 10419 Vander Karr Road, Hebron, IL 60034.
Telephone: +1 815 648 4617

Type: Tandem 2-seat, high-wing monoplane, with fixed tailwheel undercarriage.
Construction: Steel tube, metal and fabric.
Wing span: 30 ft 7 ins (9.32 m)
Length: 20 ft 9 ins (6.32 m)
Empty weight: 878 lb (398 kg)
Gross weight: 1,400 lb (635 kg)
Recommended engine: 125 hp (93.2 kW) Teledyne Continental IO-240
Maximum speed: 139 kts (160 mph) 257 km/h
Cruise speed: 102 kts (117 mph) 188 km/h
Stall speed: 26 kts (30 mph) 49 km/h
Take-off distance: 200 ft (61 m)
Climb rate: 1,000 ft (305 m) per minute
Availability: Kits.
Comments: Proof-of-concept prototype flew 1994. Patented control system. STOL bush plane.

↑ **American Homebuilts' John Doe STOL Aircraft** *(Geoffrey P. Jones)*

Arnet Pereyra Aventura UL and HP

Address:
Arnet Pereyra Inc, 3795 Fly Park Drive, Rockledge, FL 32955.
Telephone: +1 407 635 8005
Facsimile: +1 407 639 8557

Details: Aventura UL, except under Comments.
Type: Single-seat, amphibious monoplane, with pusher engine and retractable tailwheel undercarriage.
Construction: Composites, aluminium tube and fabric.
Wing span: 27 ft 8 ins (8.43 m)
Length: 20 ft 6 ins (6.25 m)
Empty weight: 254 lb (115 kg)
Gross weight: 580 lb (263 kg)
Recommended engine: 40 hp (30 kW) Rotax 447 (optional Rotax 277)
Maximum speed: 55 kts (63 mph) 101 km/h
Cruise speed: 48 kts (55 mph) 89 km/h
Stall speed: 25 kts (28 mph) 45 km/h
Take-off distance: 150 ft (46 m)
Climb rate: 500 ft (152 m) per minute
Range: 87 naut miles (100 miles) 161 km
Availability: Kits.
Comments: Part 103 ultralight. More powerful version is Aventura HP with Rotax 582.

↑ **Arnet Pereyra Aventura UL**

Arnet Pereyra Aventura II

Type: Side-by-side 2-seat, amphibious monoplane, with pusher engine and retractable tailwheel undercarriage.
Construction: Composites, aluminium tube and fabric.
Wing span: 30 ft 8 ins (9.35 m)
Length: 23 ft (7.01 m)
Empty weight: 550 lb (249 kg)
Gross weight: 1,100 lb (499 kg)
Recommended engine: 80 hp (59.6 kW) Rotax 912
Maximum speed: 78 kts (90 mph) 145 km/h
Cruise speed: 65 kts (75 mph) 121 km/h
Stall speed: 39 kts (45 mph) 73 km/h
Take-off distance: 150 ft (46 m)
Climb rate: 700 ft (213 m) per minute
Range: 260 naut miles (300 miles) 483 km
Availability: Kits.

Associate Air Liberty 181

Address:
Associate Air, 582 Niemi Road, Woodland, WA 98674.
Telephone: +1 360 225 7093

Type: 4-seat, high-wing, cabin monoplane, with fixed tailwheel undercarriage.
Construction: Metal and composites.
Wing span: 39 ft 6 ins (12.04 m)
Length: 24 ft 6 ins (7.47 m)
Empty weight: 1,900 lb (862 kg)
Gross weight: 3,200 lb (1,451 kg)
Recommended engine: 230 hp (171.5 kW) Teledyne Continental O-470
Maximum speed: 122 kts (140 mph) 225 km/h
Cruise speed: 117 kts (135 mph) 217 km/h
Stall speed: 26 kts (30 mph) 49 km/h
Take-off distance: 200 ft (61 m)
Climb rate: 2,000 ft (610 m) per minute
Range: 956 naut miles (1,100 miles) 1,770 km
Availability: Kits.
Comments: First flown 1996. Estimated build time 2,000 working hours.

↑ **Associate Air Liberty 181**

AviaBellanca SkyRocket III

Address:
AviaBellanca Aircraft Corporation, 11800 Sunrise Valley Drive, Suite 322, Reston, VA 20191.
Telephone: +1 703 860 3823
Facsimile: +1 703 860 9144
E-mail: avbellanca@aol.com

Type: 6-seat, low-wing, cabin monoplane, with retractable nosewheel undrcarriage.
Construction: Composites.
Wing span: 35 ft (10.67 m)
Length: 37 ft (11.28 m)
Empty weight: 2,490 lb (1,129 kg)
Gross weight: 4,200 lb (1,905 kg)
Recommended engine: 435 hp (324 kW) Teledyne Continental GTSIO-520F
Maximum speed: 295 kts (340 mph) 547 km/h
Cruise speed: 245 kts (282 mph) 454 km/h, at 75% power and 10,000 ft (3,050 m)
Stall speed: 59 kts (68 mph) 110 km/h
Take-off distance: 680 ft (208 m)
Climb rate: 2,080 ft (634 m) per minute
Range: 586-1,563 naut miles (675-1,800 miles) 1,086-2,897 km
Availability: Kits. Certified aircraft to FAR Pt 23 to follow.
Comments: Prototype SkyRocket II flew 1995. Chairman/Chief Design Engineer is August Bellanca, son of Guiseppe Mario Bellanca who formed original Bellanca Aircraft Corp in 1927.

↑ **AviaBellanca SkyRocket III kitplane**

Aviat Eagle II

Address:
Aviat Inc, PO Box 1240, 672 South Washington, Afton, WY 83111.
Telephone: +1 307 886 3151
Facsimile: +1 307 886 9674

Type: Tandem 2-seat, aerobatic biplane, with fixed tailwheel undercarriage.
Construction: Steel tube, wood and fabric.
Wing span: 19 ft 11 ins (6.07 m)
Length: 18 ft 6 ins (5.64 m)
Empty weight: 1,025 lb (465 kg)
Gross weight: 1,578 lb (716 kg)
Recommended engine: 200 hp (149 kW) Textron Lycoming AEIO-360AID
Maximum speed: 160 kts (184 mph) 296 km/h
Cruise speed: 143 kts (165 mph) 266 km/h
Stall speed: 55 kts (63 mph) 102 km/h
Take-off distance: 800 ft (244 m)
Climb rate: 2,100 ft (640 m) per minute
Range: 330 naut miles (380 miles) 611 km
Availability: Kits.
Comments: Formerly Christen Industries Christen Eagle. Eagle II first flew in February 1977.

↑ **Aviat Eagle II built by Arnold Timmerman in Germany** *(Geoffrey P. Jones)*

Aviat Pitts S-1S and S-2B

Details: S-1S, except under Comments.
Type: Single-seat, aerobatic biplane, with fixed tail-dragger undercarriage.
Construction: Steel tube, wood and fabric.
Wing span: 17 ft 4 ins (5.28 m)
Length: 15 ft (4.57 m)
Empty weight: 761 lb (345 kg)
Gross weight: 1,150 lb (522 kg)
Recommended engine: 180 hp (134 kW) Textron Lycoming AEIO-360-B4A
Maximum speed: 120 kts (138 mph) 222 km/h
Cruise speed: 105 kts (121 mph) 195 km/h
Stall speed: 54 kts (62 mph) 100 km/h

Take-off distance: 600 ft (183 m)
Climb rate: 2,500 ft (762 m) per minute
Range: 292 naut miles (337 miles) 542 km
Comments: Complete certified aircraft (or plans), including 2-seat S-2B.

Avid Bandit and Freedom

Address:
Avid Aircraft Inc, PO Box 728, Caldwell, ID 83606.
Telephone: +1 208 454 2600
Facsimile: +1 208 454 8608
E-mail: avidair@primenet.com

Details: Bandit, except under Comments.
Type: Side-by-side 2-seat, high-wing, cabin monoplane, with fixed nosewheel or tailwheel undercarriage.
Construction: Steel tube and fabric.
Wing span: 29 ft 9 ins (9.07 m)
Length: 17 ft (5.18 m)
Empty weight: 425 lb (193 kg)
Gross weight: 1,000 lb (454 kg)
Recommended engine: 50 hp (37.3 kW) Rotax 503 or 64.4 hp (48 kW) Rotax 582
Maximum speed: 82 kts (95 mph) 153 km/h
Cruise speed: 69 kts (80 mph) 129 km/h
Stall speed: 26 kts (30 mph) 49 km/h
Take-off distance: 150 ft (46 m) grass
Climb rate: 550 ft (168 m) per minute
Range: 304 naut miles (350 miles) 563 km
Availability: Kits.
Comments: Microlight version of the Avid Mark IV. Single-seat, Rotax 277-powered Avid Freedom followed.

Avid Catalina

Type: 3-seat amphibian, with pusher engine and retractable tailwheel undercarriage.
Construction: Steel tube and fabric.
Wing span: 36 ft (10.97 m)
Length: 19 ft 5 ins (5.92 m)
Empty weight: 600 lb (272 kg)
Gross weight: 1,200 lb (544 kg)
Recommended engine: 65 hp (48.5 kW) Rotax 582 or 100 hp (74.6 kW) AMW
Maximum speed: 78 kts (90 mph) 145 km/h
Cruise speed: 65 kts (75 mph) 121 km/h
Stall speed: 32 kts (36 mph) 58 km/h
Take-off distance: 300 ft (92 m) land, 756 ft (230 m) water.
Climb rate: 750 ft (229 m) per minute
Range: 316 naut miles (364 miles) 585 km
Availability: Kits.
Comments: Developed from the Avid Amphibian, which first flew on 12 July 1985.

↑ **Avid Catalina**

Avid Magnum

Type: Side-by-side 2-seat, or 2+1, high-wing, cabin monoplane, with fixed nosewheel or tailwheel undercarriage.
Construction: Steel tube and fabric.
Wing span: 33 ft (10.06 m)
Length: 21 ft (6.4 m)

↑ **Avid Magnum with nosewheel undercarriage** *(Geoffrey P. Jones)*

Empty weight: 950 lb (431 kg)
Gross weight: 1,750 lb (794 kg)
Recommended engine: 160 hp (119.3 kW) Textron Lycoming O-320
Maximum speed: 130 kts (150 mph) 241 km/h
Cruise speed: 113 kts (130 mph) 209 km/h
Stall speed: 32 kts (36 mph) 58 km/h
Take-off distance: 150 ft (46 m)
Climb rate: 1,350 ft (411 m) per minute
Range: 434 naut miles (500 miles) 804 km
Availability: Kits.
Comments: Suitable for floats and skis.

Avid Mark IV Speedwing

Type: Side-by-side 2-seat, high-wing, cabin monoplane with aerobatic capabilities, with fixed nosewheel or tailwheel undercarriage.
Construction: Steel tube and fabric.
Wing span: 23 ft 11 ins (7.3 m)
Length: 17 ft 11 ins (5.46 m)
Empty weight: 510 lb (231 kg)
Gross weight: 1,050 lb (476 kg)
Recommended engine: 64.4 hp (48 kW) Rotax 582. Rotax 912 or Subaru are options.
Maximum speed: 130 kts (150 mph) 241 km/h
Cruise speed: 96 kts (110 mph) 177 km/h
Stall speed: 40 kts (46 mph) 74 km/h
Take-off distance: 300 ft (92 m)
Climb rate: 850 ft (259 m) per minute
Range: 492 naut miles (566 miles) 911 km
Availability: Kits.
Comments: STOL version of Mark IV also available with 29 ft 11 ins (9.12 m) wing span and higher gross weight.

Bede Aircraft BD-4 and BD-6

Address:
BD-4 Aircraft, 732 Crown Industrial Blvd, Chesterfield, MO 63005.
Telephone: +1 314 537 2333
Facsimile: +1 314 536 2822

Details: Refer to BD-4, except under Comments.
Type: 4-seat, high-wing, cabin monoplane, with fixed nosewheel or tailwheel undercarriage.
Construction: Metal.
Wing span: 25 ft (7.62 m)
Length: 21 ft 6 ins (6.55 m)
Empty weight: 1,140 lb (517 kg)
Gross weight: 2,500 lb (1,134 kg)
Recommended engine: 180 hp (134 kW) Textron Lycoming IO-360
Maximum speed: 179 kts (206 mph) 332 km/h
Cruise speed: 152 kts (175 mph) 282 km/h
Stall speed: 49 kts (56 mph) 190 km/h
Take-off distance: 450 ft (138 m)
Climb rate: 1,800 ft (549 m) per minute
Range: 679 naut miles (782 miles) 1,258 km
Availability: Plans and kits.
Comments: First flown in the early 1970s. Hundreds now flying. Single-seat BD-6 also available.

↑ **Bede BD-4** *(Geoffrey P. Jones)*

Bede BD-5

Address:
BD Micro-Technologies Inc, 1260 Wade Road, Siletz, OR 97380.
Telephone: +1 503 444 1343

Type: Single-seat, low-wing monoplane, with pusher engine and retractable nosewheel undercarriage.
Construction: Metal.
Wing span: 17 or 21 ft (5.18 or 6.4 m)
Length: 12 ft (3.66 m)
Empty weight: 510 lb (231 kg)
Gross weight: 890 lb (404 lb)
Recommended engine: 95 hp (70.8 kW)
Maximum speed: 209 kts (240 mph) 386 km/h
Cruise speed: 174 kts (200 mph) 322 km/h
Stall speed: 68 kts (78 mph) 126 km/h
Take-off distance: 1,250 ft (381 m)
Climb rate: 1,900 ft (579 m) per minute
Range: 825 naut miles (950 miles) 1,529 km
Availability: Partial kits and plans.
Comments: Set up by Ed "Skeeter" Karnes to cater for existing BD-5 builders and provide new kit components.

↑ **Bede BD-5** *(Geoffrey P. Jones)*

Bede Aircraft BD-12C and BD-14

Address:
Bede Aircraft Corporation, 732 Crown Industrial Blvd, Chesterfield, MO 63005
Telephone: +1 314 537 2333
Facsimile: +1 314 536 2822

Details: For BD-12C, except under Comments.
Type: Tandem 2-seat, low-wing monoplane, with pusher engine and retractable nosewheel undercarriage.
Construction: Metal and composites.
Wing span: 22 ft (6.71 m)
Length: 19 ft 6 ins (5.94 m)
Empty weight: 590 lb (268 kg)
Gross weight: 1,220 lb (553 kg)
Recommended engine: 80-100 hp (59.6-74.6 kW) range
Maximum speed: 160 kts (184 mph) 296 km/h
Cruise speed: 149 kts (172 mph) 277 km/h
Take-off distance: 850 ft (259 m)
Climb rate: 1,110 ft (338 m) per minute
Range: 816 naut miles (940 miles) 1,512 km
Availability: Kits.
Comments: 1994 development of the BD-5. A larger 4-seat development, the BD-14A with 150 hp (112 kW) engine, is also under development.

Bounsall Super Prospector

Address:
Bounsall Aircraft, PO Box 506, Mesquite, NV 89024.

Type: Single-seat, parasol-wing, STOL monoplane, with fixed tail-dragger undercarriage.
Construction: Steel tube, wood and fabric.
Wing span: 29 ft 8 ins (9.04 m)
Length: 19 ft 4 ins (5.89 m)
Empty weight: 470 lb (213 kg)
Gross weight: 860 lb (390 kg)
Recommended engine: 60 hp (44.7 kW) HAPI
Maximum speed: 87 kts (100 mph) 161 km/h
Cruise speed: 78 kts (90 mph) 145 km/h
Stall speed: 31 kts (35 mph) 57 km/h
Take-off distance: 300 ft (92 m)
Climb rate: 800 ft (244 m) per minute
Range: 260 naut miles (300 miles) 482 km
Availability: Plans and kits.
Comments: Cheap to purchase STOL bush-plane.

Bowdler Aviation Supercat

Address:
Bowdler Aviation Inc, PO Box 132, Monroe, MI 48161-0132.

Type: Single-seat, low-wing microlight, with fixed tailwheel undercarriage.
Construction: Mostly wood.
Wing span: 27 ft 4 ins (8.33 m)
Length: 15 ft 10 ins (4.83 m)

Empty weight: 325 lb (147 kg)
Gross weight: 650 lb (295 kg)
Recommended engine: 40 hp (30 kW) Rotax 447
Maximum speed: 74 kts (85 mph) 137 km/h
Cruise speed: 61 kts (70 mph) 113 km/h
Stall speed: 28 kts (32 mph) 52 km/h
Take-off distance: 150 ft (46 m)
Climb rate: 900 ft (274 m) per minute
Range: 121 naut miles (140 miles) 225 km
Availability: Plans and kits.
Comments: First flown in May 1984 and originally marketed by First Strike of Piggott, Arkansas, before Bowdler took over.

↑ **Bowdler Aviation Supercat** *(Geoffrey P. Jones)*

Bowers Fly Baby 1-A

Address:
Peter M. Bowers, 10458 18th Avenue South, Seattle, WA 98168.
Telephone: +1 206 242 2582

Type: Single-seat, open-cockpit, low-wing monoplane, with fixed tailwheel or tail-dragger undercarriage.
Construction: Wood and fabric.
Wing span: 28 ft (8.53 m)
Length: 18 ft 11 ins (5.77 m)
Empty weight: 605 lb (274 kg)
Gross weight: 925 lb (420 kg)
Recommended engine: 85 hp (63.4 kW) Teledyne Continental C85
Maximum speed: 104 kts (120 mph) 193 km/h
Cruise speed: 87 kts (100 mph) 161 km/h
Take-off distance: 350 ft (107 m)
Climb rate: 1,050 ft (320 m) per minute
Range: 208 naut miles (240 miles) 386 km
Availability: Plans.
Comments: First flown 27 July 1960, later winning an EAA design contest. Biplane version, the **Fly Baby 1-B**, also available.

↑ **Bowers Fly Baby 1-B built in the UK with a C90 engine** *(Geoffrey P. Jones)*

Bradley Aerobat

Address:
Bradley Aerospace, 960 Muir Avenue, Chico, CA 95926.
Telephone: +1 916 899 7918
Facsimile: +1 916 899 2942

Type: Single-seat, low-wing, aerobatic monoplane, with fixed nosewheel undercarriage (see Comments).
Construction: Metal.
Wing span: 18 ft (5.49 m)
Length: 13 ft 6 ins (4.11 m)
Empty weight: 300 lb (136 kg)
Gross weight: 540 lb (245 kg)
Recommended engine: 95 hp (71 kW) Rotax
Maximum speed: 171 kts (197 mph) 317 km/h
Cruise speed: 122 kts (140 mph) 225 km/h
Take-off distance: 150 ft (46 m)
Climb rate: 1,300 ft (396 m) per minute
Range: 173 naut miles (200 miles) 322 km
Availability: Kits.
Comments: Third generation aerobatic design, refined in 1994. STOL and tail-dragger options.

Bronson Ultralight

Address:
Bill Bronson, 2540 Hillcrest Drive, High Ridge, MO 63049.
Telephone: +1 314 677 4047

Type: Single-seat, high-wing monoplane, with fixed tail-dragger undercarriage.
Construction: Steel tube and fabric.
Recommended engine: Bronson half Volkswagen engine.
Availability: Plans
Comments: Instructions on engine and microlight aircraft construction.

Brutsche Freedom 40

Address:
Brutsche Aircraft Corporation, 475 E. 900 S, Ste 108, m/s 67, Salt Lake City, UT 84111.
Telephone: +1 801 355 8060
Facsimile: +1 801 328 2060

Type: Single-seat, high-wing, cabin monoplane, with fixed tailwheel undercarriage.
Construction: Metal
Wing span: 28 ft (8.53 m)
Length: 18 ft (5.49 m)
Empty weight: 330 lb (150 kg)
Gross weight: 600 lb (272 kg)
Recommended engine: 40 hp (30 kW) Hirth 2702 or Rotax 447
Maximum speed: 76 kts (87 mph) 140 km/h
Cruise speed: 73 kts (84 mph) 135 km/h
Stall speed: 25 kts (29 mph) 47 km/h
Take-off distance: 150 ft (46 m)
Climb rate: 1,040 ft (317 m) per minute
Range: 120 naut miles (138 miles) 222 km
Availability: Plans and partial kit.
Comments: 15 sold at time of writing.

Brutsche Freedom Sport Utility

Type: 4-seat, high-wing, cabin monoplane, with fixed tailwheel undercarriage.
Construction: Metal.
Wing span: 31 ft (9.45 m)
Length: 24 ft 6 ins (7.47 m)
Empty weight: 1,175 lb (533 kg) for 160 hp, 1,225 lb (556 kg) for 180 hp, 1,250 lb (567 kg) for 210 hp
Gross weight: 2,150 lb (975 kg) for 160 hp, 2,200 lb (998 kg) for 180 hp, 2,250 lb (1,020 kg) for 210 hp
Recommended engine: 160 hp (119 kW), or 180 hp (134 kW) Textron Lycoming O-360, or 210 hp (157 kW) Teledyne Continental
Maximum speed: 162 kts (187 mph) 301 km/h, for 160 hp
Cruise speed: 159 kts (183 mph) 295 km/h at 8,000 ft (2,440 m), for 160 hp at 75% power
Stall speed: 41 kts (47 mph) 76 km/h, for 160 hp
Climb rate: 1,225 ft (373 m) per minute, for 160 hp
Range: 1,094 naut miles (1,260 miles) 2,027 km, for 160 hp at 55% power
Availability: Kits.
Comments: STOL utility aircraft with slotted track flaps. To conform to FAR Part 23 Utility Category.

Buckeye Eagle 447

Address:
Buckeye Powered Parachute Inc, 16111 Linden Road, Argos, IN 46501.
Telephone & Facsimile: +1 219 892 5566

Type: Single-seat, open-frame trike, with pusher engine and ram-air parachute.
Construction: Steel tube, composites and fabric.
Wing span: 35 ft 6 ins (10.82 m)
Length: 8 ft 9 ins (2.67 m)
Empty weight: 220 lb (100 kg)
Gross weight: 500 lb (227 kg)
Recommended engine: 40 hp (30 kW) Rotax 447. Alternative Rotax 503
Maximum and cruise speed: 23 kts (26 mph) 42 km/h
Take-off distance: 150 ft (46 m)
Climb rate: 500 ft (152 m) per minute
Range: 43 naut miles (50 miles) 80 km
Availability: Kits.
Comments: 2-seat Buckeye **Dream Machine 503** and **582** also available.

↑ **Buckeye Eagle 447** *(Geoffrey P. Jones)*

Buethe Barracuda

Address:
Buethe Enterprises Inc, PO Box 486, Cathedral City, CA 92234.
Telephone: +1 619 324 9455

Type: Side-by-side 2-seat, low-wing monoplane, with retractable nosewheel undercarriage.
Construction: Mostly wood.
Wing span: 24 ft 10 ins (7.57 m)
Length: 21 ft 6 ins (6.55 m)
Empty weight: 1,540 lb (699 kg)
Gross weight: 2,300 lb (1,043 kg)
Recommended engine: 250 hp (186.4 kW) Textron Lycoming IO-540
Maximum speed: 181 kts (208 mph) 335 km/h
Cruise speed: 143 kts (165 mph) 266 km/h
Stall speed: 56 kts (64 mph) 103 km/h
Take-off distance: 800 ft (244 m)
Climb rate: 2,500 ft (762 m) per minute
Range: 695 naut miles (800 miles) 1,287 km
Availability: Plans and kits.
Comments: Designed by Dr William Buethe and first flown on 29 June 1975.

↑ **Buethe Barracuda** *(Geoffrey P. Jones)*

Butterfly Banty

Address:
Butterfly Aero, 1333 Garrard Creek Road, Oakville, WA 98568.
Telephone: +1 360 273 9202
Facsimile: +1 360 273 5083

Type: Single-seat, parasol-wing microlight, with fixed tail-dragger undercarriage.
Construction: Wood and fabric.
Wing span: 32 ft (9.75 m)
Length: 18 ft 10 ins (5.74 m)
Empty weight: 237 lb (108 kg)
Gross weight: 500 lb (227 kg)
Recommended engine: 25 hp (19 kW) Rotax 277
Maximum speed: 48 kts (55 mph) 89 km/h
Cruise speed: 43 kts (50 mph) 80 km/h

Stall speed: 20 kts (23 mph) 37 km/h
Take-off distance: 220 ft (67 m)
Climb rate: 400 ft (122 m) per minute
Range: 78 naut miles (90 miles) 145 km
Availability: Plans.
Comments: Mike Kimbrel's design for an easy to build microlight. Wings fold in 4 minutes.

↑ **Butterfly Banty**

CADI 2001

Address:
Composite Aircraft Design Inc, 5085 South Arville Street, Las Vegas, NV 89118.
Telephone: +1 702 876 4352

Type: 4-seat, low-wing monoplane, with tail-mounted propeller, T-tail, winglets and a retractable nosewheel undercarriage.
Construction: Composites.
Wing span: 27 ft (8.23 m)
Length: 24 ft (7.32 m)
Empty weight: 1,800 lb (816 kg)
Gross weight: 3,000 lb (1,361 kg)
Recommended engine: 300 hp (224 kW) Textron Lycoming IO-540
Maximum speed: 261 kts (300 mph) 483 km/h
Cruise speed: 217 kts (250 mph) 402 km/h
Take-off distance: 2,000 ft (610 m)
Range: 869 naut miles (1,000 miles) 1,609 km
Availability: Kits.

Capella Aircraft Capella

Address:
Capella Aircraft Corporation, 4211-C Todd Lane, Austin, TX 78744.
Telephone: +1 512 441 8844
Facsimile: +1 512 441 1997

Type: Single-seat, high-wing monoplane, with fixed tailwheel or nosewheel undercarriage.
Construction: Metal, tube and fabric.
Wing span: 27 ft 6 ins (8.38 m)
Length: 17 ft 4 ins (5.28 m)
Empty weight: 360 lb (163 kg)
Gross weight: 625 lb (283 kg)
Recommended engine: 49.6 hp (37 kW) Rotax 503
Maximum speed: 80 kts (92 mph) 148 km/h
Cruise speed: 71 kts (82 mph) 132 km/h
Stall speed: 33 kts (38 mph) 61 km/h
Take-off distance: 130 ft (40 m)
Climb rate: 830 ft (253 m) per minute
Range: 137 naut miles (158 miles) 254 km
Availability: Kits, using "match hole" assembly.
Comments: Company formerly Flightworks.

↑ **Capella Aircraft Capella** *(Geoffrey P. Jones)*

Capella Aircraft Capella XS and XLS

Type: Side-by-side 2-seat, high-wing monoplane, with fixed tailwheel or nosewheel undercarriage.
Details: Refer to XS, except under Comments.
Construction: Metal, tube and fabric.
Wing span: 28 ft 6 ins (8.69 m)
Length: 18 ft 5 ins (5.61 m)
Empty weight: 490 lb (222 kg)
Gross weight: 1,100 lb (499 kg)
Recommended engine: 64.4 hp (48 kW) Rotax 582
Maximum speed: 93 kts (107 mph) 172 km/h
Cruise speed: 83 kts (95 mph) 153 km/h
Stall speed: 32 kts (37 mph) 60 km/h
Take-off distance: 230 ft (71 m)
Climb rate: 930 ft (283 m) per minute
Range: 413 naut miles (476 miles) 766 km
Availability: Kits.
Comments: Similar Rotax 912 version is the Capella XLS.

Carlson Sparrow Ultralight

Address:
Carlson Aircraft Inc, 50643 S.R. 14, PO Box 88, East Palestine, OH 44413-0088.
Telephone: +1 330 426 3934
Facsimile: +1 330 426 1144

Type: Single-seat, high-wing microlight, with fixed nosewheel undercarriage.
Construction: Steel tube and fabric.
Wing span: 30 ft 2 ins (9.19 m)
Length: 16 ft 9 ins (5.11 m)
Empty weight: 254 lb (115 kg)
Gross weight: 504 lb (229 kg)
Recommended engine: 25 hp (19 kW) Rotax 277
Maximum speed: 55 kts (63 mph) 101 km/h
Cruise speed: 50 kts (58 mph) 93 km/h
Stall speed: 23 kts (26 mph) 42 km/h
Take-off distance: 140 ft (43 m)
Climb rate: 750 ft (229 m) per minute
Range: 173 naut miles (200 miles) 322 km
Availability: Kits.
Comments: **Sparrow Sport Special** is similar but is a full homebuilt with larger engine (50 hp, 37 kW Rotax 503), with higher weights and performance, and tailwheel undercarriage.

↑ **Carlson Sparrow Sport Special** *(Geoffrey P. Jones)*

Carlson Sparrow II and Sparrow-ette

Details: Sparrow II, except under Comments.
Type: Side-by-side 2-seat, high-wing monoplane, with fixed nosewheel undercarriage.
Construction: Steel tube and fabric.
Wing span: 31 ft 2 ins (9.5 m)
Length: 18 ft (5.49 m)
Empty weight: 510 lb (231 kg)
Gross weight: 1,050 lb (476 kg)
Recommended engine: 64.4 hp (48 kW) Rotax 582
Maximum speed: 113 kts (130 mph) 209 km/h
Cruise speed: 82 kts (95 mph) 153 km/h
Stall speed: 31 kts (36 mph) 58 km/h
Take-off distance: 100 ft (31 m)
Climb rate: 1,750 ft (533 m) per minute
Range: 260 naut miles (300 miles) 483 km
Availability: Kits.
Comments: Enlarged 2-seat version of the Sparrow Ultralight. Also similar is the Sparrow-ette with Rotax 582, shorter span and lower gross weight.

Carlson Sparrow II XTC

Type: Side-by-side 2-seat, high-wing monoplane, with fixed nosewheel undercarriage.
Construction: Steel tube and fabric.
Wing span: 31 ft 2 ins (9.5 m)
Length: 18 ft (5.49 m)
Empty weight: 600 lb (272 kg)
Gross weight: 1,250 lb (567 kg)
Recommended engine: 80 hp (59.6 kW) Rotax 912 or 100 hp (74.6 kW) Teledyne Continental. Tests with 100 hp (74.6 kW) Subaru in progress.
Maximum speed: 113 kts (130 mph) 209 km/h
Cruise speed: 96 kts (110 mph) 177 km/h
Stall speed: 34 kts (39 mph) 63 km/h
Take-off distance: 150 ft (46 m)
Climb rate: 1,100 ft (335 m) per minute
Range: 347 naut miles (400 miles) 643 km
Availability: Kits.

Carlson Skycycle

Type: Single-seat, low-wing monoplane, with fixed tailwheel undercarriage.
Construction: Metal, steel tube, wood and fabric.
Wing span: 20 ft (6.1 m)
Length: 15 ft (4.57 m)
Empty weight: 500 lb (227 kg)
Gross weight: 800 lb (363 kg)
Recommended engine: 65 hp (48.5 kW) Teledyne Continental O-145-B2
Maximum speed: 121 kts (139 mph) 224 km/h
Cruise speed: 87 kts (100 mph) 161 km/h
Stall speed: 50 kts (57 mph) 92 km/h
Take-off distance: 350 ft (107 m)
Climb rate: 875 ft (267 m) per minute
Range: 173 naut miles (200 miles) 322 km
Availability: Kits.
Comments: Adaptation of the 1945 Skycycle design. 800 kit options placed at time of writing.

↑ **Carlson Skycycle** *(Geoffrey P. Jones)*

Cassagneres Ryan STA

Address:
Ev Cassagneres, 430 Budding Ridge, Cheshire, CT 06410.
Telephone: +1 203 272 2127

Type: Tandem 2-seat, open-cockpit, low-wing monoplane, with fixed tailwheel undercarriage.
Construction: Metal and fabric.
Wing span: 30 ft (9.14 m)
Length: 21 ft 6 ins (6.55 m)
Empty weight: 1,023 lb (464 kg)
Gross weight: 1,575 lb (714 kg)
Recommended engine: 125 hp (93.2 kW) Menasco C-4
Maximum speed: 122 kts (140 mph) 225 km/h
Cruise speed: 104 kts (120 mph) 193 km/h
Stall speed: 37 kts (42 mph) 68 km/h
Take-off distance: 525 ft (160 m)
Climb rate: 850 ft (259 m) per minute
Range: 304 naut miles (350 miles) 563 km
Availability: Plans.
Comments: Representation of the classic 1930's design. Engine option includes the CASA Tigre.

CEI Free Spirit Mk.II

Address:
CEI, 345 Woodside Way, Auburn, CA 95603.
Telephone: +1 916 878 6867
Facsimile: +1 916 878 6967

Type: Side-by-side 2-seat, or 2+1, low-wing monoplane, with retractable nosewheel undercarriage.
Construction: Composites.
Wing span: 29 ft 6 ins (8.99 m)
Length: 20 ft 8 ins (6.3 m)
Empty weight: 950 lb (431 kg)
Gross weight: 1,850 lb (839 kg)
Recommended engine: 210 hp (156.6 kW) Teledyne Continental IO-360
Maximum speed: 230 kts (265 mph) 426 km/h
Cruise speed: 191 kts (220 mph) 354 km/h
Stall speed: 55 kts (63 mph) 102 km/h
Take-off distance: 600 ft (183 m)

Climb rate: 2,000 ft (610 m) per minute
Range: 1,216 naut miles (1,400 miles) 2,253 km
Availability: Kits.
Comments: Prototype Cabrinha Free Spirit Mk I first flew in July 1986 with a 150 hp (112 kW) Textron Lycoming. Mk II first flew in 1991. Ordered by Pakistan for pilot training. Airframe components manufactured in Asia.

CGS Hawk Classic

Address:
CGS Aviation Inc, PO Box 470635, Broadview Hts, OH 44147.
Telephone: +1 216 632 1424
Facsimile: +1 216 632 1207

Type: Single-seat, high-wing monoplane, with pusher engine and fixed tailwheel or optional nosewheel undercarriage.
Construction: Steel tube and fabric.
Wing span: 28 ft 10 ins (8.79 m)
Length: 20 ft 8 ins (6.3 m)
Empty weight: 254 lb (115 kg)
Gross weight: 650 lb (295 kg)
Recommended engine: 41.6 hp (31 kW) Rotax 447. Larger engine optional.
Maximum speed: 78 kts (90 mph) 145 km/h
Maximum cruise speed: 65 kts (75 mph) 121 km/h
Stall speed: 26 kts (30 mph) 49 km/h
Take-off distance: 100 ft (31 m)
Climb rate: 800 ft (244 m) per minute
Range: 130 naut miles (150 miles) 241 km
Availability: Kits.

CGS Hawk II Classic

Type: Tandem 2-seat, high-wing microlight, with pusher engine and nosewheel or optional tailwheel undercarriage.
Construction: Steel tube and fabric.
Wing span: 34 ft (10.36 m)
Length: 21 ft 5 ins (6.53 m)
Empty weight: 395 lb (179 kg)
Gross weight: 950 lb (431 kg)
Recommended engine: 50 hp (37.3 kW) Rotax 503
Maximum speed: 78 kts (90 mph) 145 km/h
Maximum cruise speed: 65 kts (75 mph) 121 km/h
Stall speed: 31 kts (35 mph) 57 km/h
Take-off distance: 200 ft (61 m)
Climb rate: 600 ft (183 m) per minute
Range: 152 naut miles (175 miles) 281 km
Availability: Kits.
Comments: Suitable for flight training.

CGS Hawk Arrow

Type: Single-seat, high-wing microlight, with pusher engine and fixed nosewheel undercarriage.
Construction: Steel tube and fabric.
Wing span: 28 ft 10 ins (8.79 m)
Length: 21 ft 3 ins (6.48 m)
Empty weight: 282 lb (128 kg)
Gross weight: 650 lb (295 kg)
Recommended engine: 40 hp (30 kW) Rotax 447
Maximum speed: 78 kts (90 mph) 145 km/h
Cruise speed: 65 kts (75 mph) 121 km/h maximum
Stall speed: 26 kts (30 mph) 49 km/h
Take-off distance: 125 ft (38 m)
Climb rate: 800 ft (244 m) per minute
Availability: Kits.
Comments: Other engine options and larger fuel tank. Convertible to **Ag-Hawk** for crop-spraying.

↑ CGS Hawk Arrow

CGS Hawk II Arrow

Type: Tandem 2-seat, high-wing microlight, with pusher engine and fixed nosewheel or optional tailwheel undercarriage.
Construction: Steel tube and fabric.
Wing span: 34 ft (10.36 m)
Length: 22 ft 2 ins (6.76 m)
Empty weight: 395 lb (179 kg)
Gross weight: 950 lb (431 kg)
Recommended engine: 49.6 hp (37 kW) Rotax 503
Maximum speed: 78 kts (90 mph) 145 km/h
Maximum cruise speed: 65 kts (75 mph) 121 km/h
Stall speed: 31 kts (35 mph) 57 km/h
Take-off distance: 200 ft (61 m)
Climb rate: 600 ft (183 m) per minute
Range: 130 naut miles (150 miles) 241 km
Availability: Kits.
Comments: In production since 1990.

Classic Aero Enterprises H-2 Honey Bee

Address:
Classic Aero Enterprises, 343 Wrexham Court, No 107, Hampton, VA 23669.
Telephone: +1 757 851 2856

Type: Single-seat, open-cockpit biplane, with fixed tailwheel undercarriage.
Construction: Steel tube, wood and fabric.
Wing span: 19 ft (5.79 m)
Length: 15 ft 9 ins (4.8 m)
Empty weight: 335-495 lb (152-225 kg)
Gross weight: 550-700 lb (249-317.5 kg)
Recommended engine: 40 or 95 hp (30 or 70.8 kW)
Maximum speed: 59-69 kts (68-80 mph) 109-129 km/h
Cruise speed: 48-59 kts (55-68 mph) 89-109 km/h
Stall speed: 21-30.5 kts (24-35 mph) 39-57 km/h
Take-off distance: 125-200 ft (38-61 m)
Climb rate: 400-850 ft (122-259 m) per minute
Range: 156 naut miles (180 miles) 289 km
Availability: Plans.
Comments: Stressed to +8, -6g. Former Howland type.

↑ **Classic Aero Enterprises H-2 Honey-Bee** *(Geoffrey P. Jones)*

Classic Aero Enterprises H-3 Pegasus

Type: Single-seat, open-cockpit, low-wing microlight, with fixed tail-dragger undercarriage.
Construction: Steel tube, wood and fabric.
Wing span: 25 ft (7.62 m)
Length: 15 ft (4.57 m)
Empty weight: 252-345 lb (114-156.5 kg)
Gross weight: 500-595 lb (227-270 kg)
Recommended engine: 28-55 hp (21-41 kW) Hirth 263
Maximum speed: 69-82 kts (80-95 mph) 129-153 km/h
Cruise speed: 56-69 kts (65-80 mph) 105-129 km/h
Stall speed: 26-36 kts (30-41 mph) 48.5-66 km/h
Take-off distance: 200 ft (61 m)
Climb rate: 500-700 ft (153-214 m) per minute
Range: 156 naut miles (180 miles) 289 km
Availability: Plans (see below).
Comments: Construction from a kit takes 250+ hours. Drawings available to modify the H-3 into the **HP-40 Warhawk** design, see 1996-97 edition of *WA&SD* for illustration.

Clutton Fred

Address:
Eric Clutton, 913 Cedar Lane, Tullahoma, TN 37388.

Type: Single-seat, parasol-wing monoplane, with fixed tail-dragger undercarriage.
Construction: Wood, aluminium and fabric.
Wing span: 22 ft 6 ins (6.86 m)
Length: 16 ft (4.88 m)
Empty weight: 550 lb (249 kg)
Gross weight: 800 lb (363 kg)
Recommended engine: 65 hp (48.5 kW) Teledyne Continental or Volkswagen
Maximum speed: 74 kts (85 mph) 137 km/h
Cruise speed: 61 kts (70 mph) 113 km/h
Take-off distance: 900 ft (275 m)
Climb rate: 500 ft (152 m) per minute
Range: 173 naut miles (200 miles) 322 km
Availability: Plans.
Comments: Designed in the UK by Eric Clutton (now resides in USA). Fred stands for "Flying Run-about Experimental Design". First flown on 3 November 1963. Series I, II & III versions.

Collins Dipper Amphibian

Address:
Collins Aero, 238 Fairville Road, RD1, Chadds Ford, PA 19317.
Telephone: +1 215 388 2393

Type: Side-by-side 2-seat, high-wing amphibian, with pylon mounted pusher engine and retractable nosewheel undercarriage.
Construction: Metal and glassfibre.
Wing span: 33 ft 4 ins (10.16 m)
Length: 25 ft 4 ins (7.72 m)
Empty weight: 1,060 lb (481 kg)
Gross weight: 1,760 lb (798 kg)
Take-off distance: 600 ft (183 m)
Recommended engine: 150 or 180 hp (112 or 134 kW) Textron Lycoming
Maximum speed: 108 kts (124 mph) 200 km/h
Cruise speed: 100 kts (115 mph) 185 km/h
Stall speed: 39 kts (45 mph) 73 km/h
Range: 499 naut miles (575 miles) 925 km
Climb rate: 1,400 ft (427 m) per minute
Availability: Plans.
Comments: Prototype first flew on 24 August 1982. Cessna 150 part fuselage and tail utilized.

Cosmos Echo 12, Magnum 21 Bidlum and Chronos 16 BiPhase II

Address:
Cosmos, 8710 Carefree Highway, Peoria, AZ 85382.
Telephone: +1 602 931 4991

Details: Echo 12, except under Comments.
Type: Single-seat, open trike microlight, with pusher engine and pivoting Rogallo wing.
Construction: Steel tube and fabric.
Wing span: 32 ft (9.75 m)
Length: 8 ft (2.44 m)
Empty weight: 246 lb (112 kg)
Gross weight: 600 lb (272 kg)
Recommended engine: 40 hp (30 kW) Rotax 447
Maximum speed: 76 kts (87 mph) 140 km/h
Cruise speed: 39 kts (45 mph) 73 km/h
Take-off distance: 100 ft (31 m)
Climb rate: 1,000 ft (305 m) per minute
Range: 130 naut miles (150 miles) 241 km
Availability: Kits and factory complete aircraft.
Comments: Also available are the similar tandem 2-seat Magnum 21 Bidlum and Chronos 16 BiPhase II, both Rotax 503 powered.

Co-Z Mark III and Mark IV

Address:
Co-Z Development Corporation, 2046 N. 63rd Place, Mesa, AZ 85205.
Telephone: +1 602 981 6401

Details: Cozy Mark IV, except under Comments.
Type: 4-seat, canard monoplane, with pusher engine and nosewheel undercarriage (retractable nosewheel).
Construction: Composites.
Wing span: 28 ft 2 ins (8.59 m)

Length: 16 ft 11 ins (5.16 m)
Empty weight: 1,050 lb (476 kg)
Gross weight: 2,050 lb (930 kg)
Recommended engine: 180 hp (134 kW) Textron Lycoming O-360
Maximum speed: 200 kts (230 mph) 370 km/h
Cruise speed: 191 kts (220 mph) 354 km/h
Take-off distance: 1,700 ft (519 m), at MTOW
Climb rate: 1,200 ft (366 m) per minute, at MTOW
Range: 869 naut miles (1,000 miles) 1,609 km
Availability: Plans and kit components.
Comments: Nathan Puffer's design developed from his Cosy Classic, which in turn was a side-by-side 2-seat development of the Rutan Long-EZ. Cozy III also available as a lower-powered 2+1 version. (See Cosy Classic under Germany.)

Craft 200 FW

Address:
Craft Aerotech, 1843 S. 14th Street West, Missoula, MT 59801.
Telephone: +1 406 543 8133

Type: Side-by-side 2-seat, high-wing monoplane, with twin pusher engines and fixed nosewheel undercarriage.
Construction: Composites, metal and fabric.
Wing span: 30 ft 6 ins (9.3 m)
Length: 18 ft (5.49 m)
Empty weight: 700 lb (318 kg)
Gross weight: 1,200 lb (544 kg)
Recommended engines: 2 x 49.6 hp (37 kW) Rotax 503s
Maximum speed: 122 kts (140 mph) 225 km/h
Cruise speed: 104 kts (120 mph) 193 km/h
Stall speed: 44 kts (50 mph) 81 km/h
Take-off distance: 650 ft (198 m)
Climb rate: 1,000 ft (305 m) per minute
Range: 608 naut miles (700 miles) 1,126 km
Availability: Kits.

Culp Special

Address:
Culp Specialities, PO Box 7542, Shreveport, LA 71137.
Telephone: +1 318 222 0850

Type: Tandem 2-seat, open-cockpit biplane, with fixed tail-dragger undercarriage.
Construction: Steel tube, wood and fabric.
Wing span: 24 ft (7.32 m)
Length: 21 ft (6.4 m)
Empty weight: 1,478 lb (670 kg)
Gross weight: 2,100 lb (953 kg)
Recommended engine: 360 hp (268 kW) Vedenyev M-14P radial
Maximum speed: 191 kts (220 mph) 354 km/h
Cruise speed: 130 kts (150 mph) 241 km/h
Stall speed: 61 kts (70 mph) 113 km/h
Take-off distance: 400 ft (122 m)
Climb rate: 3,500 ft (1,067 m) per minute
Range: 521 naut miles (600 miles) 965 km
Availability: Plans and kits.
Comments: Designed to be reminiscent of 1930's sport biplanes (Lairds).

Cvjetkovic CA-61 Mini-Ace and CA-65 Skyfly

Address:
Anton Cvjetkovic, 5324 W. 121 Street, Hawthorne, CA 90250.
Telephone: +1 310 643 6931

Details: CA-65, except under Comments.
Type: Side-by-side 2-seat, low-wing monoplane, with retractable tailwheel undercarriage.
Construction: Wood and fabric.
Wing span: 25 ft (7.62 m)
Length: 19 ft (5.79 m)
Empty weight: 900 lb (408 kg)
Gross weight: 1,500 lb (680 kg)
Recommended engine: 125 hp (93.2 kW) Textron Lycoming O-290
Maximum speed: 156 kts (180 mph) 290 km/h
Cruise speed: 135 kts (155 mph) 249 km/h
Stall speed: 48 kts (55 mph) 89 km/h
Take-off distance: 450 ft (137 m)
Climb rate: 1,000 ft (305 m) per minute
Range: 434 naut miles (500 miles) 804 km
Availability: Plans.
Comments: The CA-65 first flew July 1965. An all-metal version is optional. A single-seater from Anton Cvjetkovic is the CA-61 Mini-Ace.

↑ Cvjetkovic CA-65 Skyfly

D'Apuzzo D-201 Sportwing

Address:
Nick d'Apuzzo Airplane Designs, 1029 Blue Rock Ln, Blue Bell, PA 19422.
Telephone: +1 215 646 8122

Type: Tandem 2-seat, open-cockpit, sport biplane, with fixed tailwheel undercarriage.
Construction: Steel tube and fabric.
Wing span: 27 ft (8.23 m)
Length: 21 ft 10 ins (6.65 m)
Empty weight: 1,295 lb (587 kg)
Gross weight: 1,900 lb (862 kg)
Recommended engine: 160 hp (119.3 kW) Textron Lycoming IO-360
Maximum speed: 115 kts (132 mph) 212 km/h
Cruise speed: 106 kts (122 mph) 196 km/h
Stall speed: 41 kts (47 mph) 76 km/h
Take-off distance: 420 ft (128 m)
Climb rate: 1,050 ft (320 m) per minute
Range: 312 naut miles (360 miles) 579 km
Availability: Plans and components.
Comments: Developed from the earlier PJ-260 Senior Aero Sport.

Desert Aviation Staggerlite

Address:
Desert Aviation, 4704 West Knollside Street, Tuscon, AZ 85741.
Telephone: +1 602 744 7595

Type: Single-seat, forward-stagger, biplane representation of the Beechcraft Staggerwing, with fixed tailwheel undercarriage.
Construction: Wood and fabric.
Wing span: 18 ft (5.49 m)
Length: 15 ft (4.57 m)
Empty weight: 250 lb (113 kg)
Gross weight: 500 lb (227 kg)
Recommended engine: 30 hp (22.4 kW) Kawasaki 440
Maximum speed: 55 kts (63 mph) 101 km/h
Cruise speed: 52 kts (60 mph) 97 km/h
Stall speed: 23 kts (26 mph) 42 km/h
Take-off distance: 150 ft (46 m)
Climb rate: 800 ft (244 m) per minute
Availability: Plans or kits.
Comments: Prototype appeared 1997.

DFE Ascender III-A, B and C

Address:
DFE Ultralights, RD 1, Box 185, Vanderbilt, PA 15486.
Telephone: +1 412 529 0450
Facsimile: +1 412 529 0596

Details: Ascender III-A, except under Comments.
Type: Single-seat, open microlight, with trike and canard.
Construction: Steel tube and fabric.
Wing span: 33 ft (10.06 m)
Length: 12 ft 4 ins (3.76 m)
Empty weight: 165 lb (75 kg)
Gross weight: 425 lb (193 kg)
Recommended engine: 22 hp (16.4 kW) Zenoah G25 (see Comments).
Maximum speed: 48 kts (55 mph) 89 km/h
Cruise speed: 35 kts (40 mph) 64 km/h
Stall speed: 18 kts (20 mph) 32 km/h
Take-off distance: 125 ft (38 m)
Climb rate: 400 ft (122 m) per minute
Range: 130 naut miles (150 miles) 241 km
Availability: Kits.
Comments: Also available with the 35 hp (26 kW) Cuyuna 430 in the Ascender III-B and III-C versions.

DFL Tango

Address:
DFL Holdings, Inc, 3001 NE 20th Way, Gainsville FL 32609.
Telephone: +1 352 377 4146
Facsimile: +1 352 377 2033

Type: Side-by-side 2-seat, composites-built, low-wing monoplane, with fixed nosewheel undercarriage.
Recommended engine: 180 hp (134 kW) Textron Lycoming
Comments: Kits. First shown at Sun 'n Fun 1997.

Dickey E-Racer

Address:
Shirl Dickey Enterprises, 8631 W. College Drive, Phoenix, AZ 85037.
Telephone: +1 602 691 0515
Facsimile: +1 602 804 8090

Type: 2-seat, canard monoplane, with pusher engine and retractable nosewheel undercarriage.
Construction: Composites.
Wing span: 26 ft 2 ins (7.98 m)
Length: 17 ft (5.18 m)
Empty weight: 1,000 lb (454 kg)
Gross weight: 1,800 lb (816 kg)
Recommended engine: 240 hp (179 kW) Buick V-8 converted motorcar engine
Maximum speed: 209 kts (240 mph) 386 km/h
Cruise speed: 191 kts (220 mph) 354 km/h
Take-off distance: 1,200 ft (366 m)
Climb rate: 2,500 ft (762 m) per minute
Range: 869 naut miles (1, 000 miles) 1,609 km
Availability: Plans.
Comments: Several examples completed and flown.

Dyke Delta JD-2

Address:
Dyke Aircraft, 2840 Old Yellow Springs Road, Fairborn, OH 45324.
Telephone: +1 513 878 9832

Type: 4-seat, delta wing monoplane, with retractable nosewheel undercarriage.
Construction: Steel tube, composites and fabric.
Wing span: 22 ft 2 ins (6.76 m)
Length: 19 ft (5.79 m)
Empty weight: 1,080 lb (490 kg)
Gross weight: 1,950 lb (885 kg)
Recommended engine: 180 hp (134 kW) Textron Lycoming O-360
Maximum speed: 182 kts (210 mph) 322 km/h
Cruise speed: 156 kts (180 mph) 338 km/h
Take-off distance: 700 ft (214 m)
Climb rate: 2,000 ft (610 m) per minute
Range: 550 naut miles (633 miles) 1,018 km

↑ Dyke Delta JD.II built in France *(Geoffrey P. Jones)*

Availability: Plans and partial kits.
Comments: Developed from the JD-1 flying wing. First flown in July 1966. An estimated 40 examples completed and flown.

Early Bird Jenny

Address: Early Bird Aircraft Co, 125 Stearman Court, Erie, CO 80516.
Telephone: +1 303 665 5169

Type: Tandem 2-seat, 67% Curtiss JN biplane representation, with fixed tail-dragger undercarriage.
Construction: Steel tube and fabric.
Wing span: 27 ft 6 ins (8.38 m)
Length: 18 ft 4 ins (5.59 m)
Empty weight: 419 lb (190 kg)
Gross weight: 800 lb (363 kg)
Recommended engine: 45.6 hp (34 kW) Rotax 503 (also 60 hp, 44.7 kW Geo Metro auto conversion or Rotax 582)
Maximum speed: 61 kts (70 mph) 113 km/h
Cruise speed: 52 kts (60 mph) 97 km/h
Stall speed: 31 kts (35 mph) 57 km/h
Take-off distance: 100 ft (31 m)
Climb rate: 800 ft (244 m) per minute
Range: 260 naut miles (300 miles) 483 km
Availability: Plans and kits.
Comments: Over 530 sets of plans sold. Kits available from Falconar (see under Canada).

↑ Early Bird Jenny

Early Bird SPAD XIII

Type: Single-seat, 80% SPAD XIII biplane representation, with fixed tail-dragger undercarriage.
Construction: Steel tube, composites and fabric.
Wing span: 20 ft 2 ins (6.15 m)
Length: 16 ft 3 ins (4.95 m)
Empty weight: 550 lb (249 kg)
Gross weight: 800 lb (363 kg)
Recommended engine: 85 hp (63.4 kW) converted Geo Tracker auto conversion
Maximum speed: 78 kts (90 mph) 145 km/h
Cruise speed: 70 kts (80 mph) 129 km/h
Stall speed: 39 kts (45 mph) 73 km/h
Take-off distance: 250 ft (77 m)
Climb rate: 800 ft (244 m) per minute
Range: 208 naut miles (240 miles) 386 km
Availability: Plans and kits (latter from Leading Edge Air Foils Inc - Raisner Airport Depot).
Comments: Appeared 1996. 35 sets of plans sold.

↑ Early Bird SPAD XIII

Earthstar Thunder Gull J

Address: Earthstar Aircraft Inc, Star Route 313, Santa Margarita, CA 93453.
Telephone: +1 805 438 5235

Type: Single-seat, high-wing monoplane, with pusher engine and fixed nosewheel undercarriage.
Construction: Metal and fabric.
Wing span: 20 ft (6.1 m)
Length: 17 ft 3 ins (5.26 m)
Empty weight: 252 lb (114 kg)
Gross weight: 550 lb (249 kg)
Recommended engine: 25 hp (19 kW) Rotax 277 (optional Rotax 447 or 503)
Maximum speed: 104 kts (120 mph) 193 km/h
Cruise speed: 65 kts (75 mph) 121 km/h
Stall speed: 23 kts (26 mph) 42 km/h
Take-off distance: 125 ft (39 m)
Climb rate: 700 ft (213 m) per minute
Range: 104 naut miles (120 miles) 193 km
Availability: Kits.
Comments: Wings fold for trailering.

Earthstar Thunder Gull JT2, Thunder Gull Odyssey and Soaring Gull

Details: Thunder Gull JT2, except under Comments.
Type: Tandem 2-seat, high-wing monoplane, with pusher engine and fixed nosewheel undercarriage.
Construction: Metal and fabric.
Wing span: 24 ft (7.32 m)
Length: 17 ft (5.18 m)
Empty weight: 392 lb (178 kg)
Gross weight: 850 lb (386 kg)
Recommended engine: 49.6 hp (37 kW) Rotax 503 (option for Rotax 447)
Maximum speed: 104 kts (120 mph) 193 km/h
Cruise speed: 74 kts (85 mph) 137 km/h
Stall speed: 32 kts (37 mph) 60 km/h
Take-off distance: 200 ft (610 m)
Climb rate: 800 ft (244 m) per minute
Range: 278 naut miles (320 miles) 515 km
Availability: Kits.
Comments: Suitable for pilot training and stressed to +6/-4g. Also available is Thunder Gull Odyssey with greater wing span and higher gross weight, and single-seat Soaring Gull.

Eklund Thorpe T-18

Address: Eklund Engineering, PO Box 1510, Lockeford, CA 95237.
Telephone: +1 209 727 0318 **Facsimile:** +1 209 727 0873

Type: Single-seat, low-wing monoplane, with fixed tailwheel undercarriage.
Construction: Sheet metal.
Wing span: 20 ft 10 ins (6.35 m)
Length: 18 ft 11 ins (5.77 m)
Empty weight: 923 lb (419 kg)
Gross weight: 1,500 lb (680 kg)
Recommended engine: 150 hp (112 kW) Textron Lycoming
Maximum speed: 159 kts (183 mph) 294 km/h
Cruise speed: 156 kts (180 mph) 290 km/h
Stall speed: 52 kts (60 mph) 97 km/h
Take-off distance: 1,000 ft (305 m)
Climb rate: 1,200 ft (366 m) per minute
Range: 460 naut miles (530 miles) 853 km
Availability: Plans.
Comments: The late John Thorpe's classic all-metal homebuilt design that first flew on 12 May 1964. Some parts available - see Sport Aircraft T-18.

↑ Eklund Engineering Thorpe T-18 *(Geoffrey P. Jones)*

Erospace Technologies Aurora

Address: John Harvey, Erospace Technologies Inc, 288 Watercrest Street, Sebastian, FL 32958.
Telephone and Facsimile: +1 407 388 0966

Type: Up to 7-seat, mid-wing, cabin monoplane, with twin pusher engines and retractable nosewheel undercarriage.
Construction: Composites (carbon).
Wing span: 31 ft 4 ins (9.55 m)
Empty weight: 2,550 lb (1,157 kg)
Gross weight: 4,266 lb (1,935 kg)
Recommended engines: 2 × Universal Tech V-4 diesels
Maximum speed: 291 kts (335 mph) 540 km/h
Cruise speed: 252 kts (290 mph) 467 km/h
Availability: Kits proposed.
Comments: Prototype under construction at time of writing.

Erospace Technologies Darling

Type: Single-seat, low-wing monoplane, with fixed nosewheel undercarriage.
Construction: Metal.
Wing span: 20 ft (6.1 m)
Length: 16 ft (4.88 m)
Empty weight: 340 lb (154 kg)
Gross weight: 620 lb (281 kg)
Recommended engine: 40 hp (30 kW) Rotax (other engines in 40-100 hp, 30-74.6 kW range)
Maximum speed: 118 kts (136 mph) 219 km/h
Cruise speed: 107 kts (123 mph) 198 km/h
Stall speed: 45 kts (52 mph) 84 km/h
Take-off distance: 528 ft (161 m)
Climb rate: 1,100 ft (335 m) per minute
Range: 351 naut miles (404 miles) 650 km, no reserves
Availability: Kits.
Comments: First flown 28 September 1996.

Evans VP-1 and VP-2

Address: Evans Aircraft, Box 744, La Jolla, CA 92038.

Details: VP-1, except under Comments.
Type: Single-seat, open-cockpit, low-wing monoplane, with fixed tailwheel undercarriage.
Construction: Wood and fabric.
Wing span: 24 ft (7.32 m)
Length: 18 ft (5.49 m)
Empty weight: 475 lb (215.5 kg)
Gross weight: 685 lb (311 kg)
Recommended engine: 50 hp (37.3 kW) Volkswagen
Maximum speed: 83 kts (95 mph) 153 km/h
Cruise speed: 65 kts (75 mph) 121 km/h
Stall speed: 35 kts (40 mph) 65 km/h
Take-off distance: 500 ft (153 m)
Climb rate: 600 ft (183 m) per minute
Range: 173 naut miles (200 miles) 322 km
Availability: Plans.
Comments: Designed for easy building and flying. Originally called Volksplane. Plans for the 2-seat VP-2 are also available.

↑ Evans VP-1 built by John Penney, the first completed in the UK *(Geoffrey P. Jones)*

Express Aircraft Express FT

Address: 5845 193rd Avenue, Rochester, WA 98579.
Telephone: +1 360 273 8907, **Facsimile:** +1 360 273 9780

Type: 4-seat, low-wing, cabin monoplane, with fixed nosewheel undercarriage.
Construction: Composites.
Wing span: 31 ft 6 ins (9.6 m)
Length: 26 ft (7.92 m)
Empty weight: 1,700 lb (771 kg)
Gross weight: 2,850 lb (1,293 kg)

Recommended engine: 200 hp (149 kW) Textron Lycoming IO-360, or other engines including the LPE TIIV-600
Maximum speed: 174 kts (200 mph) 322 km/h
Cruise speed: 169 kts (195 mph) 314 km/h
Stall speed: 55 kts (63 mph) 102 km/h
Take-off distance: 700 ft (214 m)
Climb rate: 1,200 ft (366 m) per minute
Range: 1,303 naut miles (1,500 miles) 2,414 km
Availability: Kits.
Comments: Formerly the Wheeler, then Express Design, then Experimental Aircraft Technologies Express. Larry Olsen reformed Express Aircraft in 1997.

Express Aircraft Loadmaster, Express CT, Srs 90 and Auriga

Details: Loadmaster, except under Comments.
Type: 6-seat, low-wing monoplane, with under-fuselage cargo pod and fixed nosewheel undercarriage.
Construction: Composites.
Wing span: 31 ft (9.45 m)
Length: 26 ft (7.92 m)
Empty weight: 1,825 lb (828 kg)
Gross weight: 3,200 lb (1,451 kg)
Recommended engine: 260 hp (194 kW) Textron Lycoming IO-540
Maximum speed: 196 kts (225 mph) 362 km/h
Cruise speed: 187 kts (215 mph) 346 km/h
Stall speed: 68 kts (78 mph) 126 km/h
Take-off distance: 700 ft (214 m)
Climb rate: 1,250 ft (381 m) per minute
Range: 1,216 naut miles (1,400 miles) 2,253 km
Availability: Kits.
Comments: Prototype first flew in 1993. Also available are the Express CT, Srs 90 and Auriga.

Explorer Ellipse

Address:
Explorer Aviation, 120 E South 6th, Grangeville, ID 83530.
Telephone: +1 208 983 2423
Facsimile: +1 208 983 3767

Type: 4-seat, high-wing, cabin monoplane, with fixed tailwheel undercarriage.
Construction: Wood, steel tube, composites and fabric.
Wing span: 36 ft 10 ins (11.23 m)
Length: 26 ft (7.92 m) with wings folded
Empty weight: 1,177 lb (534 kg)
Gross weight: 2,200 lb (998 kg)
Recommended engine: 150 hp (112 kW) Textron Lycoming O-320 (other optional engines of 125-200 hp, 93.2-149 kW)
Maximum speed: over 191 kts (220 mph) 354 km/h
Cruise speed: 130 kts (150 mph) 241 km/h at 75% power and 8,000 ft (2,440 m)
Stall speed: 57 kts (65 mph) 105 km/h *clean*, 44 kts (50 mph) 81 km/h *with flaps*
Take-off distance over 50 ft (15 m) obstacle: 1,500 ft (458 m)
Climb rate: 1,500 ft (458 m) per minute
Availability: Kits.
Comments: First flown Spring 1997. Estimated 1,000 hour build time. Also available from Euro Fly Aéro of France.

Ferguson F-2

Address:
Ferguson Aircraft Inc, 2431 Ferguson Pl, Dallas, GA 30132.
Telephone: +1 404 443 2747

Type: 2-seat, high-wing monoplane, with pusher engine and fixed tailwheel undercarriage.
Construction: Steel tube and fabric.
Wing span: 30 ft (9.14 m)
Length: 21 ft 3 ins (6.48 m)
Empty weight: 430 lb (195 kg)
Gross weight: 900 lb (408 kg)
Recommended engine: 65 hp (48.5 kW) AMW
Maximum speed: 78 kts (90 mph) 145 km/h
Cruise speed: 61 kts (70 mph) 113 km/h
Take-off distance: 200 ft (61 m)
Climb rate: 1,300 ft (396 m) per minute
Range: 174 naut miles (200 miles) 322 km
Availability: Kits.

Fighter Escort Wings P-51

Address:
Fighter Escort Wings, Ardmore Airpark, #206 Gene Autry, OK 73436-0206.
Telephone: +1 405 389 5452
Facsimile: +1 405 389 5451

Type: 1+1-seat, low-wing fighter representation, with retractable tailwheel undercarriage.
Construction: Composites.
Wing span: 25 ft 5 ins (7.75 m)
Length: 21 ft 3 ins (6.48 m)
Empty weight: 1,200 lb (544 kg)
Gross weight: 2,000 lb (907 kg)
Recommended engine: 160-300 hp (119.3-224 kW) liquid cooled V-6 or V-8
Maximum speed: 217 kts (250 mph) 402 km/h
Cruise speed: 182 kts (210 mph) 338 km/h
Stall speed: 48 kts (55 mph) 89 km/h
Take-off distance: 900 ft (275 m)
Climb rate: 1,000 ft (305 m) per minute
Range: 651 naut miles (750 miles) 1,207 km
Availability: Kits.
Comments: Two-thirds scale P-51 Mustang representation designed by Ron Renzelman. First flown in 1992. Two-thirds scale Corsair also available.

Fisher Avenger

Address:
Fisher Aero Corp, 7118 State Route 335, Portsmouth, OH 45662.
Telephone and Facsimile: +1 614 820 2219

Type: Single-seat, low-wing monoplane, with fixed tailwheel undercarriage.
Construction: Wood and fabric.
Wing span: 27 ft (8.23 m)
Length: 16 ft 3 ins (4.95 m)
Empty weight: 270 lb (122 kg)
Gross weight: 550 lb (249 kg)
Recommended engine: 48 hp (35.8 kW) Rotax 503 (optional VW in Avenger V or Subaru)
Maximum speed: 78 kts (90 mph) 145 km/h
Cruise speed: 70 kts (80 mph) 129 km/h
Take-off distance: 100 ft (31 m)
Climb rate: 900 ft (274 m) per minute
Range: 130 naut miles (150 miles) 241 km
Availability: Plans and kits.
Comments: Unveilled in 1994.

↑ **Fisher Avenger** *(Geoffrey P. Jones)*

Fisher Celebrity

Type: Tandem 2-seat, open-cockpit biplane, with fixed tailwheel undercarriage.
Construction: Wood, steel tube and fabric.
Wing span: 22 ft (6.71 m)
Length: 17 ft (5.18 m)
Empty weight: 600 lb (272 kg)
Gross weight: 1,250 lb (567 kg)
Recommended engine: 100 hp (74.6 kW) Teledyne Continental O-200
Maximum speed: 100 kts (115 mph) 185 km/h
Cruise speed: 87 kts (100 mph) 161 km/h
Stall speed: 35 kts (40 mph) 65 km/h
Take-off distance: 300 ft (92 m)
Climb rate: 1,200 ft (366 m) per minute
Range: 173 naut miles (200 miles) 322 km
Availability: Kits.
Comments: Quick-build and partial kits available. Prefabricated components also include J-3 Cub type cowling.

Fisher Culex

Type: Tandem 2-seat, mid-wing monoplane, with fixed tailwheel undercarriage.
Construction: Wood.
Wing span: 30 ft (9.14 m)
Length: 20 ft 4 ins (6.2 m)
Empty weight: 950 lb (431 kg)
Gross weight: 1,750 lb (794 kg)
Recommended engines: 2 × 80 hp (59.7 kW) Limbach 2000
Maximum speed: 130 kts (150 mph) 241 km/h
Cruise speed: 113 kts (130 mph) 209 km/h
Stall speed: 52 kts (60 mph) 97 km/h
Take-off distance: 250 ft (77 m)
Climb rate: 1,500 ft (457 m) per minute
Range: 677 naut miles (780 miles) 1,255 km
Availability: Plans and kits.

Fisher Horizon 2

Type: Tandem 2-seat, high-wing monoplane, with fixed tail-dragger undercarriage.
Construction: Wood, steel tube and fabric.
Wing span: 26 ft (7.92 m)
Length: 19 ft 8 ins (5.99 m)
Empty weight: 570 lb (259 kg)
Gross weight: 1,050 lb (476 kg)
Recommended engine: 80 hp (59.7 kW) Limbach
Maximum speed: 96 kts (110 mph) 177 km/h
Cruise speed: 83 kts (95 mph) 153 km/h
Stall speed: 31 kts (35 mph) 57 km/h
Take-off distance: 250 ft (77 m)
Climb rate: 900 ft (274 m) per minute
Range: 217 naut miles (250 miles) 402 km
Availability: Plans and kits.
Comments: Development of the Horizon 1. Has slotted flaps and ailerons for greater control with less drag, a lower stall and faster cruise speeds.

Fisher Mariah

Type: Tandem 2-seat, low-wing monoplane, with fixed nosewheel undercarriage.
Construction: Wood and fabric.
Wing span: 25 ft (7.62 m)
Length: 20 ft (6.1 m)
Empty weight: 800 lb (363 kg)
Gross weight: 1,300 lb (590 kg)
Recommended engine: 85 hp (63.4 kW) Teledyne Continental
Maximum speed: 130 kts (150 mph) 241 km/h
Cruise speed: 113 kts (130 mph) 209 km/h
Take-off distance: 400 ft (122 m)
Climb rate: 1,200 ft (366 m) per minute
Range: 339 naut miles (390 miles) 627 km
Availability: Plans and kits.
Comments: First flown 1993.

Fisher Youngster

Type: Single-seat biplane, with fixed tail-dragger undercarriage.
Construction: Steel tube and fabric.
Wing span: 18 ft (5.49 m)
Length: 15 ft 6 ins (4.72 m)
Empty weight: 370 lb (168 kg)
Gross weight: 650 lb (295 kg)
Recommended engine: 45.6 hp (34 kW) Rotax 503
Maximum speed: 87 kts (100 mph) 161 km/h
Cruise speed: 74 kts (85 mph) 137 km/h
Take-off distance: 200 ft (61 m)
Climb rate: 750 ft (229 m) per minute
Availability: Plans and kits.
Comments: Strengthened, 65 hp (48.5 kW) VW model is the Youngster V.

Fisher Flying Products FP-303

Address:
Fisher Flying Products, PO Box 468, Edgeley, ND 58433.
Telephone: +1 701 493 2286
Facsimile: +1 701 493 2539

Type: Single-seat, low-wing microlight, with fixed tail-dragger undercarriage.
Construction: Wood, tube and fabric.
Wing span: 27 ft 8 ins (8.43 m)
Length: 16 ft 6 ins (5.03 m)
Empty weight: 235 lb (107 kg)
Gross weight: 450 lb (204 kg)
Recommended engine: 25 hp (19 kW) Rotax 277
Maximum speed: 52 kts (60 mph) 97 km/h
Cruise speed: 39-52 kts (45-60 mph) 72-97 km/h
Stall speed: 22 kts (25 mph) 41 km/h
Take-off distance: 125 ft (38 m)
Climb rate: 750 ft (229 m) per minute
Range: 78 naut miles (90 miles) 145 km
Availability: Kits.
Comments: Estimated 250 hours build time.

Fisher Flying Products FP-505 Skeeter

Type: Single-seat, parasol-wing microlight, with fixed tail-dragger undercarriage.
Construction: Wood, tube and fabric.
Wing span: 28 ft (8.53 m)
Length: 16 ft 6 ins (5.03 m)
Empty weight: 250 lb (113.4 kg)
Gross weight: 500 lb (227 kg)
Recommended engine: 25 hp (19 kW) Rotax 277
Maximum speed: 54 kts (62 mph) 100 km/h
Cruise speed: 48 kts (55 mph) 89 km/h
Stall speed: 23 kts (26 mph) 42 km/h
Take-off distance: 150 ft (46 m)
Climb rate: 750 ft (229 m) per minute
Range: 156 naut miles (180 miles) 289 km
Availability: Kits.
Comments: Rotax 447 or 503 engine also suitable.

Fisher Flying Products FP-606 Sky Baby

Type: Single-seat, parasol-wing microlight, with fixed nosewheel undercarriage.
Construction: Wood and fabric.
Wing span: 28 ft 10 ins (8.79 m)
Length: 17 ft 4 ins (5.28 m)
Empty weight: 250 lb (113.4 kg)
Gross weight: 500 lb (227 kg)
Recommended engine: 25 hp (19 kW) Rotax 277
Maximum speed: 74 kts (85 mph) 137 km/h
Cruise speed: 65 kts (75 mph) 121 km/h
Stall speed: 23 kts (26 mph) 42 km/h
Take-off distance: 150 ft (46 m)
Climb rate: 700 ft (213 m) per minute
Range: 95 naut miles (110 miles) 177 km
Availability: Kits.
Comments: Introduced in 1987. An average builder should be able to complete an FP-606 in 500 hours – option for a quick-build kit for 300 hour build time.

↑ **Fisher Flying Products FP-606 Sky Baby** *(Geoffrey P. Jones)*

Fisher Flying Products Classic

Type: Tandem 2-seat biplane, with fixed tailwheel undercarriage.
Construction: Wood and fabric.
Wing span: 22 ft (6.71 m)
Length: 16 ft 9 ins (5.11 m)
Empty weight: 400 lb (181 kg)
Gross weight: 850 lb (386 kg)
Recommended engine: 64.4 hp (48 kW) Rotax 582
Maximum speed: 87 kts (100 mph) 161 km/h
Cruise speed: 74 kts (85 mph) 136 km/h
Stall speed: 34 kts (39 mph) 63 km/h
Take-off distance: 200 ft (61 m)
Climb rate: 900 ft (274 m) per minute
Range: 195 naut miles (225 miles) 362 km
Availability: Kits.
Comments: Development of the single-seat FP-404 EXP. Classic first flew on 25 March 1987.

Fisher Flying Products Dakota Hawk

Type: Side-by-side 2-seat, cabin monoplane, with fixed tailwheel undercarriage.
Construction: Wood.
Wing span: 28 ft 6 ins (8.69 m)
Length: 19 ft (5.79 m)
Empty weight: 600 lb (272 kg)
Gross weight: 1,150 lb (522 kg)
Recommended engine: 77.8 hp (58 kW) Rotax 912 (option for Teledyne Continental 65 or 85 or Subaru conversion)
Maximum speed: 87 kts (100 mph) 161 km/h
Cruise speed: 78 kts (90 mph) 145 km/h
Stall speed: 31 kts (35 mph) 57 km/h
Take-off distance: 350 ft (107 m)
Climb rate: 850 ft (259 m) per minute
Range: 217 naut miles (250 miles) 402 km
Availability: Kits.
Comments: Introduced in 1992. Folding wings.

↑ **Fisher Flying Products Dakota Hawk** *(Geoffrey P. Jones)*

Fisher Flying Products R-80 Tiger Moth

Type: Tandem 2-seat, open cockpit, 80%-scale representation of a DH.82 Tiger Moth, with fixed tailwheel undercarriage.
Construction: Wood, composites and fabric.
Wing span: 23 ft (7.01 m)
Length: 19 ft (5.79 m)
Empty weight: 560 lb (254 kg)
Gross weight: 1,150 lb (522 kg)
Recommended engine: 100 hp (74.6 kW) Mid-West AE100R (see Comments)
Maximum speed: 96 kts (110 mph) 177 km/h
Cruise speed: 78 kts (90 mph) 145 km/h
Take-off distance: 300 ft (92 m)
Climb rate: 800 ft (244 m) per minute
Range: 217 naut miles (250 miles) 402 km
Availability: Kits.
Comments: Unveilled in 1994. Rotax or Subaru engine options.

↑ **Fisher Flying Products R-80 Tiger Moth** *(Geoffrey P. Jones)*

Fisher Flying Products Super Koala

Type: Side-by-side 2-seat, high-wing monoplane, with fixed tailwheel undercarriage.
Construction: Wood and fabric (see Comments).
Wing span: 31 ft (9.45 m)
Length: 18 ft 1 ins (5.51 m)
Empty weight: 400 lb (181 kg)
Gross weight: 830 lb (376 kg)
Recommended engine: 64.4 hp (48 kW) Rotax 582 (option for Rotax 503)
Maximum speed: 74 kts (85 mph) 137 km/h
Cruise speed: 70 kts (80 mph) 129 km/h
Stall speed: 28 kts (32 mph) 52 km/h
Take-off distance: 150 ft (46 m)
Climb rate: 1,100 ft (335 m) per minute
Range: 195 naut miles (225 miles) 362 km
Availability: Kits.
Comments: Geodetic wooden structure, with option for steel tube fuselage structure. Development of the single-seat **FP-202 Koala** microlight.

Flightstar II

Address:
Flightstar Inc, Ellington Airport, PO Box 760, Ellington, CT 06029.
Telephone: +1 203 875 8185
Facsimile: +1 203 870 5499

Type: Side-by-side 2-seat, high-wing microlight, with fixed nosewheel or floats undercarriage.
Construction: Steel tube, fabric and composites.
Wing span: 32 ft 6 ins (9.91 m)
Length: 19 ft (5.79 m)
Empty weight: 420 lb (191 kg)
Gross weight: 970 lb (440 kg)
Recommended engine: 49.6 hp (37 kW) Rotax 503 (option for Rotax 582)
Maximum speed: 87 kts (100 mph) 161 km/h
Cruise speed: 56 kts (65 mph) 105 km/h
Stall speed: 32 kts (36 mph) 58 km/h
Take-off distance: 200 ft (61 m)
Climb rate: 700 ft (213 m) per minute
Range: 156 naut miles (180 miles) 289 km
Availability: Kits.
Comments: Tom Peghiny's design supersedes the Aviastar II (see Flightstar Spyder). Rotax 582 recommended for float flying and heavier gross weights. See Ikarus C.22 (Germany).

↑ **Flightstar Inc Flightstar II**

Flightstar C-42 Cyclone

Type: Side-by-side 2-seat, high-wing monoplane, with fixed nosewheel undercarriage.
Construction: Composites, metal and fabric.
Wing span: 31 ft (9.45 m)
Length: 20 ft 4 ins (6.2 m)
Empty weight: 540 lb (245 kg)
Gross weight: 992 lb (450 kg)
Recommended engine: 80 hp (59.6 kW) Rotax 912 UL
Maximum speed: 96 kts (110 mph) 177 km/h
Cruise speed: 91 kts (105 mph) 169 km/h
Stall speed: 34 kts (39 mph) 63 km/h
Take-off distance: 258 ft (79 m)
Climb rate: 960 ft (293 m) per minute
Range: 260 naut miles (300 miles) 483 km
Availability: Kits and production aircraft.
Comments: Certified to US Primary Category. 70 sold in Germany alone.

↑ **Flightstar C-42 Cyclone** *(Geoffrey P. Jones)*

Flightstar Spyder and Formula

Details: Spyder, except under Comments.

Type: Single-seat, high-wing microlight, with fixed tail-dragger undercarriage.
Construction: Composites, tube and fabric.
Wing span: 30 ft (9.14 m)
Length: 16 ft 6 ins (5.03 m)
Empty weight: 280 lb (127 kg)
Gross weight: 650 lb (295 kg)
Recommended engine: 41.6 hp (31 kW) Rotax 447
Maximum speed: 87 kts (100 mph) 161 km/h
Cruise speed: 52 kts (60 mph) 97 km/h
Stall speed: 23 kts (26 mph) 42 km/h
Take-off distance: 180 ft (55 m)
Climb rate: 1,000 ft (305 m) per minute
Range: 173 naut miles (200 miles) 322 km
Availability: Kits.
Comments: Flightstar ultralight was introduced in 1982. In the mid-1980s it was manufactured under licence by Pampas Bull in Argentina as the Aviastar. More powerful version is the Rotax 503-powered Flightstar Formula.

Flying K Enterprises Sky Raider

Address:
Flying K Enterprises Inc, 3403 Arthur Street, Caldwell, ID 83605.
Telephone: +1 208 455 7529

Type: Single-seat, high-wing monoplane, with fixed tailwheel undercarriage.
Construction: Steel tube and fabric.
Wing span: 26 ft 3 ins (8 m)
Length: 17 ft (5.18 m)
Empty weight: 250 lb (113 kg)
Gross weight: 550 lb (249 kg)
Recommended engine: 28 hp (20.9 kW) Rotax
Maximum and cruise speed: 55 kts (63 mph) 101 km/h
Stall speed: 24 kts (27 mph) 44 km/h
Take-off distance: 75 ft (23 m)
Climb rate: 600 ft (183 m) per minute
Range: 104 naut miles (120 miles) 193 km
Availability: Kits.
Comments: First shown July 1996. Flight controls do not need disconnecting to fold wings. 25 sold at time of writing.

↑ **Flying K Sky Raider at Sun 'n Fun '97** *(Geoffrey P. Jones)*

Freebird Sport Aircraft Freebird

Address:
Freebird Sport Aircraft, 260 Airport Road, Lake Wales, FL 33853.
Telephone: +1 941 326 9616

Type: Side-by-side 2-seat, high-wing microlight, with fixed nosewheel undercarriage.
Construction: Composites, steel tube and fabric.
Wing span: 28 ft (8.53 m)
Length: 17 ft 8 ins (5.38 m)
Empty weight: 385 lb (175 kg)
Gross weight: 970 lb (440 kg)
Recommended engine: 52 hp (38.8 kW) Rotax 503
Maximum speed: 78 kts (90 mph) 145 km/h
Cruise speed: 74 kts (85 mph) 137 km/h, at 75% power, with doors
Stall speed: 28 kts (32 mph) 52 km/h
Take-off distance: 125 ft (38 m)

↑ **Freebird Sport Aircraft Freebird** *(Geoffrey P. Jones)*

Range: 147 naut miles (170 miles) 274 km
Availability: Kits.
Comments: Removable wings.

Freewing Freebird Mk.V

Address:
Freewing Aircraft, Technical Advance Program, Building 340-1300, University of Maryland, College Park, MD 20742.
Telephone: +1 301 314 7794
Facsimile: +1 301 314 9592

Type: Side-by-side 2-seat, high-wing monoplane, with fixed tailwheel undercarriage.
Construction: Steel tube, composites and fabric.
Wing span: 33 ft 4 ins (10.16 m)
Empty weight: 670 lb (304 kg)
Maximum weight: 1,050 lb (476 kg)
Recommended engine: 100 hp (74.6 kW) Mid-West AE100R rotary
Maximum speed: 69 kts (80 mph) 129 km/h
Cruise speed: 61 kts (70 mph) 113 km/h
Stall speed: 26 kts (30 mph) 49 km/h
Take-off distance: 200 ft (61 m)
Range: 112 naut miles (130 miles) 209 km
Availability: Plans.
Comments: Developed from other experimental light aircraft with pivoting main wing, helping to give a smooth ride in turbulence. Earlier open-frame Freebird Mk IV has a 100 hp (74.6 kW) pusher engine and 65 kts (75 mph) 121 km/h maximum speed.

Frontier Aircraft MD-11

Address:
Frontier Aircraft, 225 Wall Street, Vail, CO 81657.
Telephone: +1 970 476 9300
Facsimile: +1 970 476 6232

Type: Side-by-side 2-seat, high-wing, cabin monoplane, with fixed tailwheel undercarriage.
Construction: Metal.
Wing span: 29 ft 6 ins (8.99 m)
Length: 27 ft 6 ins (8.38 m)
Empty weight: 1,150 lb (522 kg)
Gross weight: 2,000 lb (907 kg)
Recommended engine: 140 hp (104 kW) Walter LOM M332
Maximum speed: 174 kts (200 mph) 322 km/h
Cruise speed: 130 kts (150 mph) 241 km/h
Stall speed: 31 kts (35 mph) 57 km/h
Take-off distance: 500 ft (152 m)
Climb rate: 1,000 ft (305 m) per minute
Range: 607 naut miles (700 miles) 1,126 km
Availability: Kits.
Comments: Introduced in 1995.

Glassic Composites SQ.2000

Address:
Glassic Composites LLC, 15425 Dayton Pike, Sale Creek, TN 37373.
Telephone: +1 423 332 8300
Facsimile: +1 423 332 4080
E-mail: GlassicComp@aol.com

Type: 4-seat, cabin, canard monoplane, with pusher engine and retractable nosewheel undercarriage.
Construction: Composites.
Recommended engine: Textron Lycoming IO-360-C1A
Availability: Kits.
Comments: Designed by Kurt Thompson. Introduced 1997.

↑ **Glassic Composites SQ.2000** *(Geoffrey P. Jones)*

Several versions, including SQ.2000ES with fixed undercarriage and SQ.2000XP with fast-build wings.

Golden Circle T-Bird I

Address:
Golden Circle Air Inc, 10 Ellison Drive, DeSoto, IA 50069.
Telephone: +1 515 834 2225
Facsimile: +1 515 834 2152

Type: Single-seat, high-wing microlight, with pusher engine and fixed tailwheel undercarriage.
Construction: Steel tube and fabric.
Wing span: 31 ft 9 ins (9.68 m)
Length: 18 ft (5.49 m)
Empty weight: 272 lb (123 kg)
Gross weight: 572 lb (259 kg)
Recommended engine: 49.6 hp (37 kW) Rotax 503
Maximum speed: 78 kts (90 mph) 145 km/h
Cruise speed: 56 kts (65 mph) 105 km/h
Stall speed: 26 kts (30 mph) 49 km/h
Take-off distance: 70 ft (22 m)
Climb rate: 900 ft (274 m) per minute
Range: 87 naut miles (100 miles) 161 km
Availability: Kits.
Comments: Successor to the Teratorn Tierra microlight. Also available are the 2-seat T-Bird Side-by-Side, the T-Bird Tandem and 3-seat T-Bird III, all with Rotax 582 engines.

Great Plains Sonerai I

Address:
Great Plains Aircraft, PO Box 545, Boys Town, NE 68010.
Telephone: +1 402 493 6507
Facsimile: +1 402 333 7750

Type: Single-seat, mid-wing monoplane, with fixed tailwheel undercarriage.
Construction: Metal and fabric (glassfibre engine cowls).
Wing span: 16 ft 8 ins (5.08 m)
Length: 16 ft 8 ins (5.08 m)
Empty weight: 440 lb (200 kg)
Gross weight: 700 lb (318 kg)
Recommended engine: 60 hp (44.7 kW) Volkswagen or larger
Maximum speed: 148 kts (170 mph) 274 km/h
Cruise speed: 130 kts (150 mph) 241 km/h
Stall speed: 39 kts (45 mph) 73 km/h
Take-off distance: 600 ft (183 m)
Climb rate: 1,000 ft (305 m) per minute
Range: 260 naut miles (300 miles) 483 km, with 45 minutes reserves
Availability: Plans and kits.
Comments: Designed by John Monnett and first flown in July 1971.

Great Plains Sonerai II

Type: Tandem 2-seat, mid-wing monoplane, with fixed tailwheel or nosewheel undercarriage.
Construction: Metal and fabric (glassfibre engine cowls).
Wing span: 18 ft 8 ins (5.69 m)
Length: 18 ft 10 ins (5.74 m)
Empty weight: 520 lb (236 kg)
Gross weight: 950 lb (431 kg)
Recommended engine: 60-82 hp (44.7-61 kW) Volkswagen
Maximum speed: 152 kts (175 mph) 282 km/h
Cruise speed: 122 kts (140 mph) 225 km/h
Stall speed: 39 kts (45 mph) 73 km/h
Take-off distance: 900 ft (274 m)
Climb rate: 500 ft (152 m) per minute
Range: 213 naut miles (245 miles) 394 km
Availability: Plans and kits.
Comments: 2-seat development of the Sonerai I. Also available are 4 further 2-seat versions, as the low-wing L, lengthened LS

↑ **Great Plains Sonerai II built in Belgium** *(Geoffery P. Jones)*

(20 ft 4 ins, 6.2 m), LT with a standard 2,180 cc VW, and lengthened LTS with the 2,180 cc engine.

Green Sky Micro Mong

Address:
Green Sky Adventures Inc, 2395 Cream Ridge Road, Orwell, OH 44076.
Telephone: +1 216 293 6624
Facsimile: +1 216 293 6321

Type: Single-seat biplane, with fixed tail-dragger undercarriage.
Construction: Metal and fabric.
Wing span: 19 ft 6 ins (5.94 m)
Length: 14 ft (4.26 m)
Empty weight: 320 lb (145 kg)
Gross weight: 650 lb (295 kg)
Take-off distance: 200 ft (61 m)
Recommended engine: 49.6 hp (37 kW) Rotax 503
Maximum speed: 96 kts (110 mph) 177 km/h
Cruise speed: 74 kts (85 mph) 137 km/h
Stall speed: 39 kts (45 mph) 73 km/h
Climb rate: 1,000 ft (305 m) per minute
Range: 173 naut miles (200 miles) 322 km
Availability: Plans and kits.

Green Sky Zippy Sport

Type: Single-seat, high-wing monoplane, with fixed tail-dragger undercarriage.
Construction: Metal, wood and fabric.
Wing span: 26 ft 4 ins (8.03 m)
Length: 17 ft 10 ins (5.44 m)
Empty weight: 421 lb (191 kg)
Gross weight: 680 lb (308 kg)
Recommended engine: 49.6 hp (37 kW) Rotax 503
Maximum speed: 104 kts (120 mph) 193 km/h
Cruise speed: 87 kts (100 mph) 161 km/h
Stall speed: 35 kts (40 mph) 65 km/h
Take-off distance: 350 ft (107 m)
Climb rate: 700 ft (213 m) per minute
Range: 260 naut miles (300 miles) 483 km
Availability: Plans.
Comments: Introduced by Gerald Olenik in 1992 to appeal to homebuilders who like mixed construction.

Grega GN-1 Aircamper

Address:
John W. Grega, 255 Grand Blvd, Bedford, OH 44146-2146.
Telephone: +1 216 232 5790

Type: Tandem 2-seat, parasol-wing monoplane, with fixed tailwheel undercarriage.
Construction: Steel tube and wood.
Wing span: 29 ft (8.84 m)
Length: 18 ft 2 ins (5.54 m)
Empty weight: 650 lb (295 kg)
Gross weight: 1,100 lb (499 kg)
Take-off distance: 300-400 ft (92-122 m)
Recommended engine: 65 hp (48.5 kW) Teledyne Continental
Maximum speed: 100 kts (115 mph) 185 km/h
Cruise speed: 76 kts (87 mph) 140 km/h
Stall speed: 22 kts (25 mph) 41 km/h
Take-off distance: 300 ft (92 m)
Climb rate: 500 ft (152 m) per minute
Range: 304 naut miles (350 miles) 563 km
Availability: Plans plus some components.
Comments: Revised version of the Pietenpol Aircamper of 1920s origin. First flown in 1963, with an estimated 500 examples completed.

↑ **Grega GN-1 Aircamper 2-seater** *(Geoffrey P. Jones)*

Griffon Lionheart

Address:
Griffon Aerospace Inc, 920 Yarbrough Road, Harvest, AL 35749.
Telephone: +1 205 721 9055
Facsimile: +1 205 831 1694

Type: 7-seat, reverse-stagger, cabin biplane kitplane, with retractable tailwheel undercarriage. Composites. First flew Summer 1997.

Halsted Saffire

Address:
Barry Halsted, 17542 Briarwood Street, Fountain Valley, CA 92708.
Telephone: +1 714 962 9921

Type: Tandem 2-seat, low-wing monoplane, with retractable nosewheel undercarriage.
Construction: Metal.
Wing span: 28 ft (8.53 m)
Length: 25 ft (7.62 m)
Empty weight: 1,625 lb (737 kg)
Gross weight: 2,350 lb (1,066 kg)
Recommended engine: Teledyne Continental IO-360C
Maximum speed: 183 kts (211 mph) 339 km/h
Cruise speed: 178 kts (205 mph) 330 km/h
Stall speed: 60 kts (69 mph) 111 km/h
Take-off distance over a 50 ft (15 m) obstacle: 1,600 ft (488 m)
Climb rate: 1,200 ft (366 m) per minute
Range: 700 naut miles (806 miles) 1,296 km
Availability: Plans.
Comments: Prototype first flew on 24 November 1990. Won "Plans-Built Champion" award at EAA Oshkosh 1991.

Harmon Rocket

Address:
D & J Harmon Co, Inc, 2000 S Union Avenue, Bakersfield, CA 93307.
Telephone: +1 905 836 1028

Type: Tandem 2-seat, low-wing monoplane, with fixed tailwheel undercarriage.
Construction: Metal.
Wing span: 22 ft (6.71 m)
Length: 20 ft 4 ins (6.2 m)
Empty weight: 1,200 lb (544 kg)
Gross weight: 1,960 lb (889 kg)
Recommended engine: 250 hp (186 kW) Textron Lycoming IO-540
Maximum speed: about 261 kts (300 mph) 483 km/h
Cruise speed: 195 kts (225 mph) 362 km/h
Stall speed: 52 kts (60 mph) 97 km/h
Climb rate: 3,000 ft (915 m) per minute
Availability: Parts to convert Van's RV-4.
Comments: High-performance conversion of the Van's RV-4. At time of writing, 18 Rockets were flying and over 90 were under construction.

↑ **Harmon Rocket built by Carl Wright at Ventura, CA** *(Geoffrey P. Jones)*

Higher Planes Mitchell Wing A-10 and T-10

Address:
Higher Planes Inc, Box 4, Dover, KS 66420.
Telephone: +1 913 256 6029

Details: A-10, except under Comments.
Type: Single-seat, high-wing microlight, with winglets, pusher engine and fixed nosewheel undercarriage.
Construction: Metal, steel tube and fabric.
Wing span: 34 ft 4 ins (10.47 m)
Length: 9 ft 4 ins (2.84 m)
Empty weight: 280 lb (127 kg)
Gross weight: 553 lb (251 kg)
Recommended engine: 26 hp (19.4 kW) Rotax 277
Maximum speed: 61 kts (70 mph) 113 km/h
Cruise speed: 48 kts (55 mph) 89 km/h
Stall speed: 25 kts (28 mph) 45 km/h
Take-off distance: 200 ft (61 m)
Climb rate: 800 ft (244 m) per minute
Range: 173 naut miles (200 miles) 322 km
Availability: Kits.
Comments: Also available is 49.6 hp (37 kW) Rotax 503-powered T-10 2-seater.

Highlander Aircraft Highlander

Address:
Highlander Aircraft Corporation, 2255 Orkla Drive, Golden Valley, MN 55427.
Telephone: +1 612 783 7018
Facsimile: +1 612 525 1566

Type: Side-by-side 2-seat monoplane, with fixed nosewheel undercarriage.
Construction: Metal.
Wing span: 29 ft 6 ins (8.99 m)
Length: 18 ft (5.49 m)
Empty weight: 715 lb (324 kg)
Gross weight: 1,165 lb (528 kg)
Recommended engine: 80 hp (59.6 kW) Rotax 912
Maximum speed: 97 kts (112 mph) 180 km/h
Cruise speed: 90 kts (104 mph) 167 km/h
Stall speed: 54 kts (62 mph) 100 km/h *clean*, 48 kts (55 mph) 88 km/h *with flaps*
Take-off distance: 600 ft (183 m)
Climb rate: 800 ft (244 m) per minute
Range: 370 naut miles (426 miles) 685 km
Availability: Kits
Comments: UK design by Richard Noble as the ARV Super2, later the Aviation Scotland ARV-1 Super2. Now built in conjunction with Sweden, where it is certificated as the Opus 280.

Hipp's Superbird J-3 Kitten and J-5 Super Kitten

Address:
Hipp's Superbird Inc, PO Box 266, Saluda, NC 28773.
Telephone: +1 704 749 3986
Facsimile: +1 704 749 5803

Details: J-3 Kitten, except under Comments.
Type: Single-seat, high-wing microlight, with fixed tailwheel undercarriage.
Construction: Steel tube, composites, wood and fabric.
Wing span: 30 ft (9.14 m)
Length: 16 ft 4 ins (4.98 m)
Empty weight: 254 lb (115 kg)
Gross weight: 500 lb (227 kg)
Recommended engine: 28 hp (20.9 kW) Rotax 277
Maximum speed: 55 kts (63 mph) 101 km/h
Cruise speed: 51 kts (59 mph) 95 km/h
Stall speed: 26 kts (30 mph) 49 km/h
Climb rate: 800 ft (244 m) per minute
Range: 104 naut miles (120 miles) 193 km
Availability: Plans and kits.
Comments: Introduced in 1984. Also available is the J-5 Super Kitten with 39.6 hp (29.5 kW) Rotax 447.

Hipp's Superbird J-4 Sportster and Super Sportster

Details: Sportster, except under Comments and photograph.
Type: Single-seat, parasol-wing microlight, with fixed tailwheel undercarriage.
Construction: Composites, wood, steel tube and fabric.
Wing span: 28 ft (8.53 m)
Length: 16 ft 4 ins (4.98 m)
Empty weight: 240 lb (109 kg)
Gross weight: 500 lb (227 kg)

↑ Hipp's Superbird Super Sportster *(Geoffrey P. Jones)*

Recommended engine: 25 hp (19 kW) Rotax 277
Maximum speed: 55 kts (63 mph) 101 km/h
Cruise speed: 51 kts (59 mph) 95 km/h
Stall speed: 21 kts (24 mph) 39 km/h
Climb rate: 800 ft (244 m) per minute
Range: 104 naut miles (120 miles) 193 km
Availability: Plans and kits.
Comments: Smaller and more basic development of the J-3 Kitten. Also available is the Super Sportster with wheel spats, faired turtle-deck and a Rotax 447 engine.

Hipp's Superbirds Reliant and Reliant SX

Details: Reliant, except under Comments.
Type: Single-seat, high-wing microlight, with fixed tailwheel undercarriage.
Construction: Composites, wood, steel tube and fabric.
Wing span: 30 ft (9.14 m)
Length: 16 ft 4 ins (4.98 m)
Empty weight: 254 lb (115 kg)
Gross weight: 500 lb (227 kg)
Recommended engine: 28 hp (20.9 kW) Rotax 277
Maximum speed: 55 kts (63 mph) 101 km/h
Cruise speed: 52 kts (60 mph) 97 km/h
Climb rate: 800 ft (244 m) per minute
Range: 104 naut miles (120 miles) 193 km
Availability: Kits.
Comments: More refined version of the J-3 Kitten, introduced in 1987. Also available is the Reliant SX with a Rotax 447 engine.

Hirt Trio

Address:
Hirt Aircraft, PO Box 2134, Hemet, CA 92546-2134.
Telephone: +1 909 925 3404

Type: Side-by-side 2-seat, forward-swept-wing monoplane, with canard and fixed nosewheel undercarriage.
Construction: Composites.
Wing span: 30 ft (9.14 m)
Length: 21 ft 6 ins (6.55 m)
Empty weight: 1,050 lb (476 kg)
Gross weight: 1,650 lb (748 kg)
Recommended engine: 160 hp (119.3 kW) Textron Lycoming
Maximum speed: 156 kts (180 mph) 290 km/h
Cruise speed: 150 kts (173 mph) 278 km/h
Stall speed: 48 kts (55 mph) 89 km/h
Take-off distance: 950 ft (290 m)
Climb rate: 1,000 ft (305 m) per minute
Range: 695 naut miles (800 miles) 1,287 km
Availability: Plans and kits anticipated.
Comments: Prototype first flew in 1994. Twin control yokes.

Historical Aircraft P-51D

Address:
Historical Aircraft Corporation, 536 Star Lane South, St. Paul, MN 55075.
Telephone: +1 612 451 3283

Type: Single-seat, scale fighter representation, with retractable tailwheel undercarriage.
Construction: Steel tube and composites.
Wing span: 24 ft (7.32 m)
Length: 20 ft 8 ins (6.3 m)
Empty weight: 1,354 lb (614 kg)
Gross weight: 1,960 lb (889 kg)
Recommended engine: 230 hp (171.5 kW) Ford V-8 conversion
Maximum speed: 222 kts (255 mph) 410 km/h
Cruise speed: 187 kts (215 mph) 346 km/h
Take-off distance: 1,800 ft (550 m)
Climb rate: 2,300 ft (700 m) per minute
Range: 608 naut miles (700 miles) 1,126 km
Availability: Kits.
Comments: Other 60%-scale representations include the **AU-1 Corsair**, **P-40 Tomahawk** and **PZL P.11c**. Also 85%-scale **Ryan STA**.

Hummel Bird

Address:
Morry Hummel, 509 E. Butler Street, Bryan, OH 43506-0880.
Telephone: +1 419 636 3390

Type: Single-seat, low-wing monoplane, with fixed tailwheel or nosewheel undercarriage.
Construction: Metal.
Wing span: 21 ft (6.4 m)
Length: 13 ft 4 ins (4.06 m)
Empty weight: 270 lb (122.5 kg)
Gross weight: 540 lb (245 kg)
Recommended engine: 30 hp (22.4 kW) half Volkswagen
Maximum speed: 104 kts (120 mph) 193 km/h
Cruise speed: 90 kts (104 mph) 167 km/h
Stall speed: 35 kts (40 mph) 65 km/h
Take-off distance: 500 ft (153 m)
Climb rate: 700 ft (213 m) per minute
Range: 172 naut miles (200 miles) 322 km
Availability: Plans, engines and engine conversion components.
Comments: Diminutive single-seater modified from the Watson Windwagon. First flown in June 1981.

↑ Hummel Bird *(Geoffrey P. Jones)*

Hummel CA-2

Type: Single-seat, open-cockpit microlight, with fixed tailwheel undercarriage.
Construction: Metal.
Wing span: 26 ft (7.92 m)
Length: 16 ft 6 ins (5.03 m)
Empty weight: 250 lb (113 kg)
Gross weight: 500 lb (227 kg)
Recommended engine: Rotax 277 (optional Rotax 447 or Half VW)
Maximum speed: 55 kts (63 mph) 101 km/h
Cruise speed: 43 kts (50 mph) 80 km/h
Stall speed: 23 kts (26 mph) 42 km/h, *with flaps*
Range: 108 naut miles (125 miles) 201 km
Availability: Plans.

Hy-Tek Hurricane, Ultra 103, Clipwing and Hauler

Address:
Hy-Tek (Mike Kern), 23055 Airport Road, North-East, No 1, Aurora, OR 97002.
Telephone: +1 503 678 5740
Facsimile: +1 503 678 2771

Details: Hurricane, except under Comments.
Type: Single-seat, high-wing microlight, with fixed nosewheel undercarriage.
Construction: Aluminium, chromoly steel and fabric.
Wing span: 28 ft (8.53 m)
Empty weight: 254 lb (115 kg)
Gross weight: 525 lb (238 kg)
Recommended engine: 39.6 hp (29.5 kW) Rotax 447
Maximum speed: 87 kts (100 mph) 161 km/h

↑ Hy-Tek Hurricane *(Geoffrey P. Jones)*

Cruise speed: 55 kts (63 mph) 101 km/h
Stall speed: 24 kts (27 mph) 44 km/h
Take-off distance: 100 ft (31 m)
Climb rate: 800 ft (244 m) per minute
Availability: Kits.
Comments: Several other models available, including Ultra 103, Clipwing and Hauler.

Innovation Genesis

Address:
Innovation Engineering Inc, 8970 Harrison Street, Davenport, IA 52804.
Telephone: +1 319 386 6966
Facsimile: +1 319 386 4569

Type: Side-by-side 2-seat, high-wing microlight, with pusher engine and fixed nosewheel undercarriage.
Construction: Composites, steel tube and fabric.
Wing span: 26 ft 8 ins (8.13 m)
Length: 18 ft 6 ins (5.64 m)
Empty weight: 450 lb (204 kg)
Gross weight: 1,000 lb (454 kg)
Recommended engine: 53 hp (39.5 kW) Rotax 503 (other variants installed with Rotax 582, 618 or 912 engines)
Maximum speed: 104 kts (120 mph) 193 km/h
Cruise speed: 69 kts (80 mph) 129 km/h
Stall speed: 35 kts (40 mph) 65 km/h, dual
Take-off distance: 300 ft (92 m), dual
Climb rate: 500 ft (152 m) per minute, dual
Range: 543 naut miles (625 miles) 1,005 km
Availability: Kits.
Comments: Fast-build kit, with 3 ft 7 ins (1.09 m) wide cabin.

Innovation Skyquest

Type: Side-by-side 2-seat, high-wing monoplane, with twin pusher engines and fixed nosewheel undercarriage.
Construction: Composites, steel tube and fabric.
Wing span: 30 ft 8 ins (9.35 m)
Length: 19 ft 4 ins (5.89 m)
Empty weight: 820 lb (372 kg)
Gross weight: 1,400 lb (635 kg)
Recommended engine: 2 × 49.6 hp (37 kW) Rotax 503s
Maximum speed: 87 kts (100 mph) 161 km/h
Cruise speed: 74-87 kts (85-100 mph) 137-161 km/h
Stall speed: 39 kts (45 mph) 73 km/h, power off
Take-off distance: under 300 ft (92 m)
Climb rate: 1,200 ft (366 m) per minute
Range: 330 naut miles (380 miles) 611 km, with auxiliary tank
Availability: Kits.
Comments: Twin-engined development of Genesis. Launched at Oshkosh 1997.

↑ Innovation Skyquest

Javelin Wichawk

Address:
Javelin Aircraft Co Inc, 662 South Governour, Wichita, KS 67207.
Telephone: +1 316 686 8500

Type: Side-by-side 2-seat (optional third seat) biplane, with fixed tailwheel undercarriage.
Construction: Metal, composites, wood and fabric.
Wing span: 24 ft (7.01 m)
Length: 19 ft (5.79 m)
Empty weight: 1,281 lb (581 kg)
Gross weight: 2,400 lb (1,088 kg)
Recommended engine: 180 hp (134 kW) Textron Lycoming O-360
Maximum speed: 122 kts (140 mph) 225 km/h
Cruise speed: 110 kts (127 mph) 204 km/h
Stall speed: 50 kts (57 mph) 92 km/h
Take-off distance: 150 ft (46 m)
Climb rate: 1,700 ft (518 m) per minute
Range: 434 naut miles (500 miles) 804 km

Availability: Plans.
Comments: Prototype first flew on 24 May 1971. Hundreds under construction or flying.

↑ Javelin Wichawk built by Don Goodman *(Geoffrey P. Jones)*

Javelin V6 STOL

Type: 4-seat, high-wing, cabin monoplane, with fixed tailwheel undercarriage.
Construction: Metal tubing, metal sheet and fabric.
Wing span: 32 ft (9.75 m)
Length: 22 ft 4 ins (6.81 m)
Empty weight: 1,250 lb (567 kg)
Gross weight: 2,200 lb (998 kg)
Recommended engine: 230 hp (171.5 kW) Ford converted auto engine
Maximum speed: 122 kts (140 mph) 225 km/h
Cruise speed: 113 kts (130 mph) 209 km/h
Stall speed: 45 kts (52 mph) 84 km/h
Take-off distance: 150 ft (46 m)
Climb rate: 1,700 ft (518 m) per minute
Range: 564 naut miles (650 miles) 1,046 km
Availability: Plans.
Comments: Utilises Piper PA-22 Tri-Pacer parts.

Kelly-D

Address:
Dudley R. Kelly, Rt. 4, Box 194, Versailles, KY 40383.
Telephone: +1 606 873 5253

Type: Tandem 2-seat, open-cockpit biplane, with fixed tailwheel undercarriage.
Construction: Wood, steel tube and fabric.
Wing span: 26 ft 4 ins (8.03 m)
Length: 19 ft 3 ins (5.87 m)
Empty weight: 950 lb (431 kg)
Gross weight: 1,500 lb (680 kg)
Recommended engine: 115 hp (85.75 kW) Textron Lycoming O-235
Maximum speed: 91 kts (105 mph) 169 km/h
Cruise speed: 78 kts (90 mph) 145 km/h
Stall speed: 39 kts (45 mph) 73 km/h
Take-off distance: 400 ft (122 m)
Climb rate: 800 ft (244 m) per minute
Range: 234 naut miles (270 miles) 434 km
Availability: Plans.

Kelly Hatz CB-1

Type: Tandem 2-seat, open-cockpit biplane, with fixed tailwheel undercarriage.
Construction: Wood, steel tube and fabric.
Wing span: 25 ft 4 ins (7.72 m)
Length: 19 ft (5.79 m)
Empty weight: 850 lb (386 kg)
Gross weight: 1,400 lb (635 kg)
Recommended engine: 100 hp (74.6 kW) Teledyne Continental O-200. Other optional inline and radial engines.
Maximum speed: 91 kts (105 mph) 169 km/h
Cruise speed: 74 kts (85 mph) 137 km/h
Stall speed: 35 kts (40 mph) 65 km/h
Take-off distance: 400 ft (122 m)

↑ Kelly Hatz CB-1 built by Petr Iser in Germany *(Geoffrey P. Jones)*

Climb rate: 750 ft (229 m) per minute
Range: 174 naut miles (200 miles) 322 km
Availability: Plans.
Comments: Designed by John D. Hatz and first flown on 19 April 1968.

Kemmeries Tukan

Address:
Kemmeries Aviation, Ultralight Flight Center, Pleasant Valley Airport, 8710 West Carefree Hwy, Peoria, AZ 85382.
Telephone: +1 602 566 8026
Facsimile: +1 602 561 2287

Type: Single-seat trike (with option for 1+1 seating) microlight, with pusher engine and pivoting Rogallo wing.
Construction: Steel tube and fabric.
Wing span: 35 ft (10.67 m)
Length: 8 ft (2.44 m)
Empty weight: 254 lb (115 kg)
Gross weight: 769 lb (349 kg)
Recommended engine: 41.6 hp (31 kW) Rotax 447
Maximum speed: 61 kts (70 mph) 113 km/h
Cruise speed: 24-53 kts (28-61 mph) 45-98 km/h
Stall speed: 20 kts (23 mph) 37 km/h
Take-off distance: 50 ft (15.5 m)
Climb rate: 750 ft (229 m) per minute
Range: 61 naut miles (70 miles) 112 km
Availability: Plans and kits.
Comments: In production since 1987. Also agents for the French Air Creation and Cosmos/La Mouette microlights.

Keuthan Buccaneer II and SX

Address:
Keuthan Aircraft, 910 Airport Road, Merritt Island, FL 32952.
Telephone: +1 407 452 3200
Facsimile: +1 407 452 7111

Details: Buccaneer II, except under Comments.
Type: Side-by-side 2-seat, high-wing amphibian, with retractable tailwheel undercarriage.
Construction: Composites, steel tube and fabric.
Wing span: 29 ft 8 ins (9.04 m)
Length: 22 ft 4 ins (6.81 m)
Empty weight: 575 lb (261 kg)
Gross weight: 1,150 lb (522 kg)
Take-off distance: 275 ft (84 m) land, 300 ft (92 m) water
Recommended engine: 64.4 hp (48 kW) Rotax 582 (Rotax 618 and 912 optional)
Maximum speed: 78 kts (90 mph) 145 km/h
Cruise speed: 63 kts (73 mph) 117 km/h
Stall speed: 37 kts (42 mph) 68 km/h
Climb rate: 650 ft (198 m) per minute
Range: 217 naut miles (250 miles) 402 km
Availability: Kits.
Comments: Also available is the single-seat Buccaneer SX with either Rotax 503 or 582 engine.

↑ Keuthan Buccaneer II with wheels retracted

Keuthan Sabre I and II

Details: For Sabre I, except under Comments.
Type: Single-seat, high-wing, pusher-engined monoplane, with fixed undercarriage of nosewheel, tailwheel or float types.
Construction: Steel tube and fabric.
Wing span: 29 ft 8 ins (9.04 m)
Length: 20 ft 1 ins (6.12 m)
Empty weight: 345 lb (156 kg)
Gross weight: 755 lb (342 kg)
Recommended engine: 49.6 hp (37 kW) Rotax 503 (Rotax 447 and 582 options)
Maximum speed: 78 kts (90 mph) 145 km/h
Cruise speed: 56 kts (65 mph) 105 km/h
Stall speed: 26 kts (29 mph) 47 km/h
Take-off distance: 125 ft (39 m) from land
Climb rate: 1,100 ft (335 m) per minute
Range: 217 naut miles (250 miles) 402 km
Availability: Kits.
Comments: Also available is the similar side-by-side 2-seat Sabre II, suitable for Rotax 582, 618 or 912 engines.

Keuthan Zephyr II

Type: Tandem 2-seat, high-wing monoplane, with fixed tail-dragger undercarriage.
Construction: Steel tube and fabric.
Wing span: 29 ft 8 ins (9.04 m)
Length: 22 ft 6 ins (6.86 m)
Empty weight: 475 lb (215 kg)
Gross weight: 1,100 lb (499 kg)
Recommended engine: 64.4 hp (48 kW) Rotax 582 (options are the Rotax 618 and 912)
Maximum speed: 78 kts (90 mph) 145 km/h
Cruise speed: 63 kts (73 mph) 117 km/h
Stall speed: 29 kts (33 mph) 53 km/h
Take-off distance: 125 ft (39 m)
Climb rate: 1,100 ft (335 m) per minute
Range: 217 naut miles (250 miles) 402 km
Availability: Kits.
Comments: Wings are easily detachable.

Kimball/Pitts Model 12

Address:
Jim Kimball Enterprises Inc, PO Box 849, 5354 Cemetary Road, Zellwood, FL 32798-0849 and Scott Randale, Mid-America Aircraft, 528 South Belmont, Wichita, KS 67218.
Telephone: +1 407 889 3451
Facsimile: +1 407 889 7168
E-mail: JWKimball@AOL.com

Type: Tandem 2-seat, enclosed-cockpit, sport biplane, with fixed tailwheel undercarriage.
Construction: Steel tube, wood and fabric.
Wing span: 23 ft (7.01 m)
Length: 19 ft 6 ins (5.94 m)
Empty weight: 1,500 lb (680 kg)
Recommended engine: 360 hp (268 kW) Vedenyev M-14P radial
Maximum speed: 174 kts (200 mph) 322 km/h
Cruise speed: 148 kts (170 mph) 274 km/h
Stall speed: approx 65 kts (75 mph) 121 km/h
Climb rate: 3,000 ft (915 m) per minute
Range: 456 naut miles (525 miles) 845 km
Availability: Plans and kits.
Comments: Curtis Pitts' 12th design, sometimes called Macho Stinker.

↑ Kimball/Pitts Model 12 *(Geoffrey P. Jones)*

Kolb Firestar I, Firestar II and STOL Mark III

Address:
Kolb Company Inc, RD. 3, Box 38, Phoenixville, PA 19460.
Telephone: +1 616 948 4136
Facsimile: +1 610 948 6727

Details: Firestar I, except under Comments.
Type: Single-seat, high-wing microlight, with pusher engine and fixed tailwheel undercarriage.
Construction: Steel tube and fabric.
Wing span: 27 ft 6 ins (8.38 m)
Length: 21 ft 3 ins (6.48 m)
Empty weight: 275 lb (125 kg)
Gross weight: 550 lb (250 kg)

Recommended engine: 39.6 hp (29.5 kW) Rotax 447
Maximum speed: 55 kts (63 mph) 101 km/h
Cruise speed: 48 kts (55 mph) 89 km/h
Stall speed: 26 kts (29 mph) 47 km/h
Take-off distance: 125 ft (39 m)
Climb rate: 1,000 ft (305 m) per minute
Availability: Kits.
Comments: Also available are the tandem 2-seat Firestar II and the STOL Mark III 2-seater with larger wings and Rotax 582 engine.

Kolb Slingshot

Type: Single-seat, high-wing microlight, with pusher engine and fixed tailwheel undercarriage.
Construction: Steel tube and fabric.
Wing span: 22 ft (6.71 m)
Length: 19 ft (5.79 m)
Empty weight: 345 lb (156 kg)
Gross weight: 850 lb (386 kg)
Recommended engine: 64.4 hp (48 kW) Rotax 582
Maximum speed: 87 kts (100 mph) 161 km/h
Cruise speed: 76 kts (87 mph) 140 km/h
Stall speed: 34 kts (39 mph) 63 km/h
Take-off distance: 100 ft (31 m)
Climb rate: 1,300 ft (396 m) per minute
Availability: Kits.
Comments: Introduced 1996.

↑ **Kolb Slingshot** *(Geoffrey P. Jones)*

Kolb Flyer

Type: Single-seat, high-wing microlight, with pusher engine and fixed nosewheel undercarriage.
Construction: Steel tube and fabric.
Availability: Kits.
Comments: Introduced 1997. Minimum aircraft with 3-axis control.

↑ **Kolb Flyer** *(Geoffrey P. Jones)*

Lancair 320 Mk.II

Address: Lancair International Inc, 2244 Airport Way, Redmond, OR 97756.
Telephone: +1 541 923 2244 **Facsimile:** +1 541 923 2255

Type: Side-by-side 2-seat, low-wing monoplane, with retractable nosewheel undercarriage.
Construction: Composites.
Wing span: 23 ft 6 ins (7.16 m)
Length: 21 ft (6.4 m)
Empty weight: 1,090 lb (494 kg)
Gross weight: 1,685 lb (764 kg)
Recommended engine: 180 hp (134 kW) Textron Lycoming IO-360 (optional 160 hp, 119.3 kW O-320)
Maximum speed: 222 kts (255 mph) 410 km/h
Cruise speed: 200 kts (230 mph) 370 km/h
Stall speed: 55 kts (63 mph) 102 km/h
Take-off distance: 690 ft (210 m)
Climb rate: 1,750 ft (533 m) per minute
Range: 990 naut miles (1,140 miles) 1,834 km
Availability: Kits.
Comments: Designed by Lance Niebaur. Prototype Lancair 200 first flew in June 1984; Lancair 360 Mk II developed from earlier Lancair 320. Kits sold in many countries.

Lancair IV, IVP and Tigress

Details: For IV except under Comments.
Type: 4-seat, low-wing monoplane, with retractable nosewheel undercarriage and optional pressurised cabin (IVP).
Construction: Composites.
Wing span: 30 ft 3 ins (9.22 m)
Length: 25 ft (7.62 m)
Empty weight: 1,900 lb (862 kg)
Gross weight: 3,200 lb (1,451 kg)
Recommended engine: 350 hp (261 kW) Teledyne Continental TSIO-550-B
Maximum speed: 274 kts (315 mph) 507 km/h
Cruise speed: 260 kts (300 mph) 483 km/h
Stall speed: 65 kts (75 mph) 121 km/h
Take-off distance: 1,200 ft (366 m)
Climb rate: 2,600 ft (792 m) per minute
Range: 1,259 naut miles (1,450 miles) 2,333 km
Availability: Kits.
Comments: First flown in 1990. New 2-seat kit version of IVP is Tigress, with larger wing and fuselage, 600 hp (447 kW) V-8 Orenda engine, and 352 kts cruise at 20,000 ft (6,100 m).

Lancair Super ES and Columbia 300

Type: 4-seat, low-wing, cabin monoplane, with fixed nosewheel undercarriage.
Construction: Composites.
Wing span: 35 ft 6 ins (10.82 m)
Length: 25 ft (7.62 m)
Empty weight: 1,900 lb (862 kg)
Gross weight: 3,000 lb (1,361 kg)
Recommended engine: 300 hp (224 kW) Teledyne Continental IO-550G
Maximum speed: 203 kts (234 mph) 377 km/h
Cruise speed: 195 kts (225 mph) 362 km/h
Stall speed: 50 kts (57 mph) 92 km/h
Climb rate: 2,000 ft (610 m) per minute
Range: 1,042 naut miles (1,200 miles) 1,931 km
Availability: Kits.
Comments: A joint venture company has been formed between Lancair and a Malaysian organization to gain FAR Pt 23 certification for a new Lancair to be called the Columbia 300. Production-assembled examples will be built at a new plant at Bend Municipal Airport, Oregon.

↑ **Lancair Super ES with fixed undercarriage introduced in 1993** *(Geoffrey P. Jones)*

Laron Aviation Shadow & Streak Shadow

Address: Laron Aviation Technologies Inc, PO Box 5026, Borger, TX 79008-5026.
Telephone: +1 806 273 8513 **Facsimile:** +1 806 273 8375 **E-mail:** laron@arn.net

Type: Tandem 2-seat, high-wing monoplane, with pusher engine and fixed nosewheel undercarriage.
Construction: Composites, wood and metal.
Details: Shadow (A), Streak Shadow (B).
Wing span: (A) 32 ft 11 ins (10.03 m), (B) 28 ft (8.53 m)
Length: (A) and (B) 21 ft (6.4 m)
Empty weight: (A) 349 lb (158 kg), (B) 388 lb (176 kg)
Gross weight: (A) 824 lb (374 kg), (B) 900 lb (408 kg)
Recommended engine: (A) 45.6 hp (34 kW) Rotax 503, (B) 64.4 hp (48 kW) Rotax 583
Maximum speed: (A) 89 kts (102 mph) 164 km/h, (B) 105 kts (121 mph) 195 km/h
Cruise speed: (A) 78 kts (90 mph) 145 km/h, (B) 87 kts (100 mph) 161 km/h
Stall speed: (A) 22 kts (25 mph) 41 km/h, (B) 27 kts (31 mph) 50 km/h
Take-off distance: (A) and (B) 100 ft (31 m)
Climb rate: (A) 700 ft (213 m), (B) 1,100 ft (335 m) per minute
Range: (A) 169 naut miles (195 miles) 313 km, (B) 279 naut miles (322 miles) 518 km
Availability: Kits.
Comments: Manufactured under licence from CFM of UK.

Laron Aviation Star Streak

Type: Tandem 2-seat, high-wing monoplane, with pusher engine and fixed nosewheel undercarriage.
Construction: Composites, wood and metal.
Wing span: 30 ft (9.14 m)
Length: 21 ft (6.4 m)
Empty weight: 400 lb (181 kg)
Gross weight: 900 lb (408 kg)
Recommended engine: 85 hp (63.4 kW) Hirth F-30
Maximum speed: 123 kts (141 mph) 227 km/h
Cruise speed: 106 kts (122 mph) 196 km/h
Stall speed: 31 kts (35 mph) 57 km/h
Take-off distance: 50-100 ft (15.5-31 m)
Climb rate: 2,100 ft (640 m) per minute
Range: 269 naut miles (310 miles) 499 km
Availability: Kits.
Comments: First flown 1990.

Laron Aviation 1/2 Tun

Type: Single-seat, high-wing microlight, with pusher engine and fixed tail-dragger undercarriage.
Construction: Metal and fabric.
Wing span: 26 ft (7.92 m)
Length: 21 ft (6.4 m)
Empty weight: 250 lb (113 kg)
Gross weight: 550 lb (249 kg)
Recommended engine: 41.6 hp (31 kW) Rotax 447
Maximum speed: 55 kts (63 mph) 101 km/h
Cruise speed: 48 kts (55 mph) 89 km/h
Minimum speed: 22 kts (25 mph) 41 km/h
Take-off distance: 150 ft (46 m)
Climb rate: 1,000 ft (305 m) per minute
Range: 95 naut miles (110 miles) 177 km
Availability: Kits.
Comments: Single-seat version of Tundra, introduced 1997.

↑ **Laron Aviation 1/2 Tun** *(Geoffrey P. Jones)*

Laron Aviation Tundra

Type: Tandem 2-seat, high-wing monoplane, with fixed nosewheel undercarriage.
Construction: Metal and fabric.
Wing span: 32 ft (9.75 m)
Length: 21 ft (6.4 m)
Empty weight: 400 lb (181 kg)
Gross weight: 900 lb (408 kg)
Recommended engine: 49.6 hp (37 kW) Rotax 582 DC (see Comments)
Maximum speed: 87 kts (100 mph) 161 km/h
Cruise speed: 65-74 kts (75-85 mph) 121-137 km/h
Stall speed: 31 kts (35 mph) 57 km/h
Take-off distance: 100 ft (31 m)
Climb rate: 800 ft (244 m) per minute
Range: 202 naut miles (233 miles) 375 km
Availability: Kits.
Comments: 3-stage kit, with option for Rotax 503 or 912.

Laron Aviation Wizard

Type: Side-by-side 2-seat, high-wing microlight/homebuilt, with pusher engine, twin tails and fixed nosewheel undercarriage.
Construction: Steel tube, composites, wood and fabric.
Wing span: 30 ft 8 ins (9.35 m)
Length: 19 ft 8 ins (5.99 m)
Empty weight: 462 lb (210 kg)
Gross weight: 924 lb (419 kg)
Recommended engine: 64.4 hp (48 kW) Rotax 582
Maximum speed: 104 kts (120 mph) 193 km/h

Cruise speed: 78 kts (90 mph) 145 km/h
Take-off distance: 164 ft (50 m)
Climb rate: 1,350 ft (411 m) per minute
Range: 234 naut miles (270 miles) 434 km
Availability: Kits.
Comments: Formerly Dong In Wizard.

↑ **Laron Aviation Wizard** *(H.S. Park)*

Lexicon Aviation RS-1 Shrike

Address:
Richard Cox, Lexicon Aviation, 6250 Royal Pines Drive, Clover, SC 29710.
Telephone: +1 803 631 4810
Facsimile: +1 803 631 4652

Type: Single-seat, low-wing, jet-powered monoplane, with retractable nosewheel undercarriage.
Construction: Metal and composites.
Wing span: 22 ft (6.71 m)
Length: 16 ft (4.88 m)
Gross weight: 900 lb (408 kg)
Recommended engine: TRJ-300C with afterburner
Availability: Possibility of kits eventually.
Comments: Prototype shown at Oshkosh '96. Built in conjunction with Bob Clark of Custom Built Aircraft of Chattanooga, TN.

Leza Lockwood Air Cam

Address:
Leza Lockwood, 1 Leza Drive, Sebring, FL 33870.
Telephone: +1 941 655 4242
Facsimile: +1 941 655 0310
E-mail: aircam@ct.net

Type: Tandem 2-seat, high-wing monoplane, with twin pusher engines and fixed tailwheel undercarriage.
Construction: Metal and fabric.
Wing span: 32 ft 4 ins (9.86 m)
Length: 21 ft (6.4 m)
Empty weight: 740 lb (336 kg)
Gross weight: 1,300 lb (590 kg)
Recommended engines: 2 × 64.4 hp (48 kW) Rotax 582 (as for details) or 75 hp (56 kW) Rotax 618s
Maximum speed: 78 kts (90 mph) 145 km/h
Cruise speed: 39-65 kts (45-75 mph) 72-121 km/h
Take-off distance: 250 ft (77 m)
Climb rate: 1,000 ft (305 m) per minute
Range: 130 naut miles (150 miles) 241 km
Availability: Kits.
Comments: Designed for National Geographic aerial photography. Flies at gross on one engine.

↑ **Leza Lockwood Air Cam** *(Geoffrey P. Jones)*

Light Miniature LM-1 and LM-2 variants

Address:
Light Miniature Aircraft, 19695 NW 80th Drive, Okeechobee, FL 34972.
Telephone: +1 813 467 9033

Details: Refer to LM-1A, except under Comments.
Type: Single-seat, high-wing monoplane, with fixed tail-dragger undercarriage.
Construction: Wood and fabric.
Wing span: 27 ft (8.23 m)
Length: 17 ft 8 ins (5.38 m)
Empty weight: 335 lb (152 kg)
Gross weight: 600 lb (272 kg)
Recommended engine: 39.6 hp (29.5 kW) Rotax 447, or others including the 45 hp (33.6 kW) Zenoah
Maximum speed: 56 kts (65 mph) 105 km/h
Stall speed: 21 kts (24 mph) 39 km/h
Take-off distance: 200 ft (61 m)
Climb rate: 600 ft (183 m) per minute
Range: 139 naut miles (160 miles) 257 km
Availability: Plans and kits.
Comments: LM-1A and LM-1X are scale representations of the Piper J-3, with differing spans. The LM-2X is a 75% Taylorcraft representation and the LM-2X-2P is a 2-seater.

↑ **Light Miniature LM-2X 75% scale Taylorcraft representation** *(Geoffrey P. Jones)*

Light Miniature LM-3X and LM-5X Super Cub

Details: Refer to LM-3X, except under Comments.
Type: Single-seat, high-wing monoplane, with fixed tail-dragger undercarriage.
Construction: Steel tube and fabric.
Wing span: 30 ft (9.14 m)
Length: 17 ft 6 ins (5.33 m)
Empty weight: 325 lb (147 kg)
Gross weight: 600 lb (272 kg)
Recommended engine: 39.6 hp (29.5 kW) Rotax 447
Maximum speed: 65 kts (75 mph) 121 km/h
Cruise speed: 56 kts (65 mph) 105 km/h
Stall speed: 24 kts (27 mph) 44 km/h
Take-off distance: 100 ft (31 m)
Climb rate: 600 ft (183 m) per minute
Range: 95 naut miles (110 miles) 177 km
Availability: Plans and kits.
Comments: 75% scale Aeronca representation. Also available is the LM-5X Super Cub representation with either 100 hp (74.6 kW) engine or 65 hp (48.5 kW) Rotax 582.

(RFW) Lightning Bug

Address:
c/o Reflex Fibreglass Works Inc, PO Box 497, Walterboro, SC 29488.

Type: Single-seat, low-wing monoplane, with fixed tailwheel or nosewheel undercarriage.
Construction: Composites.
Wing span: 17 ft 10 ins (5.44 m)
Length: 17 ft 5 ins (5.31 m)
Empty weight: 475 lb (215 kg)
Gross weight: 800 lb (363 kg)
Recommended engine: 90 hp (67 kW) AMW 750
Maximum speed: 217 kts (250 mph) 402 km/h
Cruise speed: 196 kts (225 mph) 362 km/h
Stall speed: 74 kts (85 mph) 137 km/h
Take-off distance: 800 ft (244 m)
Climb rate: 1,200 ft (366 m) per minute
Range: 764 naut miles (880 miles) 1,416 km
Availability: Kits.
Comments: Capable of aerobatics.

Lockwood Aviation Supply Drifter

Address:
Lockwood Aviation Supply Inc, 280 Hendricks Way, Suite A, Sebring, FL 33870.
Telephone: +1 941 655 5100
Facsimile: +1 941 655 6225

Type: Tandem 2-seat, open-cockpit, high-wing microlight, with pusher engine and fixed tailwheel or float undercarriage (see Comments).
Construction: Steel and alloy tube, and fabric.
Wing span: 30 ft (9.14 m)
Length: 21 ft (6.4 m) with nose fairing
Empty weight: 385 lb (175 kg)
Gross weight: 785 lb (356 kg)
Recommended engine: Rotax XP505 (optional Rotax 447 or 582)
Maximum speed: 65 kts (75 mph) 121 km/h
Cruise speed: 52 kts (60 mph) 97 km/h
Stall speed: 32 kts (36 mph) 58 km/h
Availability: Kits.
Comments: Reworked former Maxair Drifter. DR447 is single-seat version. Certified in Australia, Israel, Japan and Canada. See also Austflight Drifter under Australia.

↑ **Lockwood Aviation Supply Drifter with nose fairing and floats**

Loehle P-40

Address:
Loehle Aircraft Corporation, Shipmans Creek Road, Wartrace, TN 37183.
Telephone: +1 615 857 3419
Facsimile: +1 615 857 3908

Type: Single-seat, low-wing monoplane, with retractable tailwheel undercarriage.
Construction: Wood and fabric.
Wing span: 28 ft 8 ins (8.74 m)
Length: 22 ft 10 ins (6.96 m)
Empty weight: 550-600 lb (249-272 kg)
Gross weight: 900 lb (408 kg)
Recommended engine: 64.4 hp (48 kW) Rotax 582
Maximum speed: 87 kts (100 mph) 161 km/h
Cruise speed: 65-74 kts (75-85 mph) 121-137 km/h
Stall speed: 28 kts (32 mph) 52 km/h
Take-off distance: 150 ft (46 m)
Climb rate: 1,200 ft (366 m) per minute
Range: 273 naut miles (315 miles) 507 km
Availability: Kits.
Comments: Option for fixed undercarriage. Curtiss P-40 representation, based on the Loehle 5151 fuselage.

↑ **Loehle P-40** *(Geoffrey P. Jones)*

Loehle 5151 RG Mustang

Type: Single-seat, low-wing monoplane, with retractable tailwheel undercarriage.
Construction: Wood and fabric.
Wing span: 27 ft 5 ins (8.36 m)
Length: 22 ft 10 ins (6.96 m)
Empty weight: 513-600 lb (233-273 kg)
Gross weight: 900 lb (408 kg)
Recommended engine: 64.4 hp (48 kW) Rotax 582

Maximum speed: 87 kts (100 mph) 161 km/h
Cruise speed: 65-74 kts (75-85 mph) 121-137 km/h
Stall speed: 26 kts (30 mph) 49 km/h
Take-off distance: 150 ft (46 m)
Climb rate: 1,200 ft (366 m) per minute
Range: 273 naut miles (315 miles) 507 km
Availability: Kits.
Comments: Developed from the fixed undercarriage Loehle 5151 Mustang, an approximate 75% scale Mustang representation which first flew on 30 January 1986. 250 kits sold at time of writing.

Loehle SPAD XIII, Fokker D.VII and SE.5a

Type: Single-seat, open-cockpit, microlight/homebuilt biplane, with fixed tail-dragger undercarriage.
Construction: Aluminium and fabric.
Details: Refer to SPAD XIII, except under Comments.
Wing span: 24 ft (7.32 m)
Length: 16 ft 6 ins (5.03 m)
Empty weight: 250 lb (113 kg)
Gross weight: 525 lb (238 kg)
Recommended engine: 28 hp (20.9 kW) Rotax 277 for Pt 103 ultralights (details below for this) or 45.6 hp (34 kW) Rotax 503 for Experimental category aircraft
Maximum speed: 55 kts (63 mph) 102 km/h
Cruise speed: 46 kts (53 mph) 86 km/h
Stall speed: 18 kts (20 mph) 32 km/h
Take-off distance: 80 ft (25 m)
Climb rate: 600 ft (183 m) per minute
Range: 69 naut miles (80 miles) 129 km
Availability: Kits.
Comments: Formerly Squadron Aviation type, acquired in 1994. Other similar types include Fokker D.VII and SE.5a.

↑ **Loehle SPAD XIII representation** *(Geoffrey P. Jones)*

Loehle Sport Parasol

Type: Single-seat, parasol-wing microlight, with fixed tailwheel undercarriage.
Construction: Wood and fabric.
Wing span: 25 ft 6 ins (7.77 m)
Length: 18 ft 5 ins (5.61 m)
Empty weight: 252-300 lb (114-136 kg)
Gross weight: 600 lb (273 kg)
Recommended engine: 49.6 hp (37 kW) Rotax 503
Maximum speed: 74 kts (85 mph) 137 km/h
Cruise speed: 56 kts (65 mph) 105 km/h
Stall speed: 19 kts (22 mph) 36 km/h
Take-off distance: 100 ft (31 m)
Climb rate: 750 ft (229 m) per minute
Range: 174 naut miles (200 miles) 322 km
Availability: Kits.
Comments: Introduced into the Loehle range in 1992 as a cheap to purchase, simple to build and easy to fly microlight. 100 kits sold at time of writing.

Marquart MA-5 Charger

Address:
Ed Marquart, Box 3032, Riverside, CA 92519-3032.
Telephone: +1 909 683 9582

Type: Tandem 2-seat, aerobatic biplane, with fixed tailwheel undercarriage.
Construction: Steel tube and fabric.
Wing span: 24 ft (7.32 m)
Length: 20 ft (6.1 m)
Empty weight: 1,000 lb (454 kg)
Gross weight: 1,550 lb (703 kg)
Recommended engine: 125 hp (93.2 kW) Textron Lycoming
Maximum speed: 109 kts (125 mph) 201 km/h
Cruise speed: 101 kts (116 mph) 187 km/h
Stall speed: 37 kts (42 mph) 68 km/h
Take-off distance: 600 ft (183 m)
Climb rate: 1,000 ft (305 m) per minute
Range: 347 naut miles (400 miles) 643 km
Availability: Plans.
Comments: Classic sport biplane design of Edward Marquart.

Aerocomp (ex-Merlin Aircraft) GT-582

Address:
See Aerocomp.

Type: Side-by-side 2-seat, high-wing monoplane, with fixed tailwheel undercarriage.
Construction: Steel tube and fabric.
Wing span: 30 ft (9.14 m)
Length: 20 ft (6.1 m)
Empty weight: 480 lb (218 kg)
Gross weight: 1,300 lb (590 kg)
Recommended engine: 64.4 hp (48 kW) Rotax 582
Maximum speed: 96 kts (110 mph) 177 km/h
Cruise speed: 74 kts (85 mph) 137 km/h
Stall speed: 32 kts (36 mph) 58 km/h
Take-off distance: 85 ft (26 m)
Climb rate: 1,200 ft (366 m) per minute
Range: 289 naut miles (333 miles) 536 km
Availability: Kits.
Comments: Originally the Canadian Macair Merlin, later a Merlin Aircraft type. Available in STOL configuration with 25 kts (28 mph) 45 km/h stall speed. Also available are **CAM 100** and other Rotax powered versions with varying designations.

Aerocomp (ex-Merlin Aircraft) Explorer

Type: 4-seat, high-wing, cabin monoplane, with fixed tail-dragger undercarriage.
Construction: Steel tube and fabric.
Wing span: 39 ft (11.89 m)
Length: 22 ft (6.71 m)
Empty weight: 1,480 lb (671 kg)
Gross weight: 3,000 lb (1,361 kg)
Recommended engine: 180 hp (134 kW) Textron Lycoming IO-360 or 250 hp (186 kW) Mazda rotary
Maximum speed: 117 kts (135 mph) 219 km/h
Cruise speed: 102 kts (118 mph) 191 km/h
Stall speed: 31 kts (35 mph) 57 km/h
Take-off distance: 400 ft (122 m)
Climb rate: 1,500 ft (457 m) per minute
Availability: Kits.
Comments: Introduced in 1995.

Mirage Celerity and Marathon

Address:
Eldon and Karen Helmer, 1091 W Sahara Palms Drive, Tucson, AZ 85704.
Telephone: +1 520 797 2161

Details: Celerity, except under Comments.
Type: Side-by-side 2-seat, low-wing, cabin monoplane, with retractable tailwheel undercarriage.
Construction: Composites and wood.
Wing span: 25 ft (7.62 m)
Length: 22 ft 10 ins (6.96 m)
Empty weight: 1,169 lb (530 kg)
Gross weight: 1,800 lb (816 kg)
Recommended engine: 160 hp (119.3 kW) Textron Lycoming O-320-B1A
Maximum speed: 191 kts (220 mph) 354 km/h
Cruise speed: 178 kts (205 mph) 330 km/h
Stall speed: 46 kts (53 mph) 86 km/h
Take-off distance: 800 ft (244 m)
Climb rate: 1,800 ft (549 m) per minute
Range: 869 naut miles (1,000 miles) 1,609 km
Availability: Plans and some components.
Comments: Designed by Larry Burton and first flown on 18 May 1985. Former Mirage Aircraft assets purchased by Eldon and Karen Helmer. **Mirage Marathon** is under development as a fixed nosewheel gear version.

↑ **Mirage Celerity built by the late Larry Burton** *(Geoffrey P. Jones)*

Monnett Sonex

Address:
John Monnett, 955 Grace, Eglin, IL 60120.

Type: Side-by-side 2-seat, low-wing monoplane, with fixed nosewheel or tailwheel undercarriage.
Construction: Metal.
Wing span: 22 ft (6.71 m)
Length: 17 ft 8 ins (5.38 m)
Empty weight: 510 lb (231 kg)
Gross weight: 910 lb (413 kg)
Recommended engine: Various types in 60-100 hp (44.7-74.6 kW) range. Performance figures based on 70 hp (52.2 kW) Volkswagen
Maximum speed: 130 kts (150 mph) 241 km/h
Stall speed: 35 kts (40 mph) 65 km/h
Availability: Kits.

Montana Coyote Mountain Eagle

Address:
Montana Coyote Inc, 3302 Airport Road, Helena, MT 59601.
Telephone: +1 406 449 3556

Type: Side-by-side 2-seat, high-wing, cabin monoplane, with fixed tailwheel undercarriage.
Construction: Wood, steel tube, composites and fabric.
Wing span: 37 ft (11.28 m)
Length: 25 ft (7.62 m)
Empty weight: 1,100 lb (499 kg)
Gross weight: 2,000 lb (907 kg)
Recommended engine: 150 hp (112 kW) Textron Lycoming O-320
Maximum speed: 109 kts (125 mph) 201 km/h
Cruise speed: 91 kts (105 mph) 169 km/h
Stall speed: 31 kts (35 mph) 57 km/h
Take-off distance: 350 ft (107 m)
Climb rate: 1,250 ft (381 m) per minute
Range: 391 naut miles (450 miles) 724 km
Availability: Kits.
Comments: First flown in Spring 1991 with 125 hp (93.2 kW) Honda Prelude engine. New variant in 1994 named the Mountain Eagle.

Morrisey 2000

Address:
Morrisey Aircraft Co, PO Box 27889, Las Vegas, NV 89126.
Telephone: +1 702 735 6553

Type: Tandem 2-seat, low-wing monoplane, with fixed nosewheel undercarriage.
Construction: Metal.
Wing span: 30 ft (9.14 m)
Length: 20 ft (6.1 m)
Empty weight: 975 lb (442 kg)
Gross weight: 1,600 lb (726 kg)
Recommended engine: 115 hp (85.75 kW) Textron Lycoming O-235

↑ **Morrisey 2000/Varga Kachina** *(Geoffrey P. Jones)*

Maximum speed: 115 kts (132 mph) 212 km/h
Cruise speed: 109 kts (125 mph) 201 km/h
Stall speed: 37 kts (42 mph) 68 km/h
Take-off distance: 500 ft (153 m)
Climb rate: 1,000 ft (305 m) per minute
Range: 304 naut miles (350 miles) 563 km
Availability: Kits and certificated assembled aircraft.
Comments: Original Morrisey 1000C Nifty first flew in 1948. Many subsequent modifications and commercial builders, including Varga which built the Kachina.

Mountaineer Dual 175 and Mite Lite

Address:
Mountain Trikes, PO Box 557, Finkle Road, Millerton, NY 12546.
Telephone: +1 518 789 6550
Facsimile: +1 518 789 6775

Details: Dual 175, except under Comments.
Type: Tandem 2-seat, trike microlight, with pusher engine and shift Rogallo wing.
Construction: Alloy tube and fabric.
Wing span: 33 ft 4 ins (10.16 m)
Length: 11 ft (3.35 m)
Empty weight: 250 lb (113 kg)
Gross weight: 750 lb (340 kg)
Recommended engine: 49.6 hp (37 kW) Rotax 503 UL-DC
Maximum speed: 58 kts (67 mph) 108 km/h
Cruise speed: 43 kts (50 mph) 80 km/h
Take-off distance: 250 ft (77 m)
Climb rate: 900 ft (274 m) per minute
Availability: Kits.
Comments: Also available in a single-seat Rotax 277-powered version, as the Mountaineer Mite Lite.

Mustang Aeronautics Midget Mustang

Address:
Mustang Aeronautics, 1470 Temple City, Troy, MI 48084.
Telephone: +1 248 589 9277
Facsimile: +1 248 588 6788

Type: Single-seat, low-wing monoplane, with fixed tailwheel undercarriage.
Construction: Metal.
Wing span: 18 ft 6 ins (5.64 m)
Length: 16 ft 5 ins (5 m)
Empty weight: 680 lb (308 kg)
Gross weight: 1,000 lb (454 kg)
Recommended engine: 150 hp (112 kW) Textron Lycoming O-320 (option for 100 hp, 74.5 kW O-200)
Maximum speed: 200 kts (230 mph) 370 km/h
Cruise speed: 187 kts (215 mph) 346 km/h
Stall speed: 54 kts (62 mph) 100 km/h
Take-off distance: 450 ft (138 m)
Climb rate: 2,200 ft (670 m) per minute
Range: 347 naut miles (400 miles) 643 km
Availability: Plans and kits.
Comments: Originally designed by David Long in the 1940s and updated for sale as a homebuilt in the 1950s by Robert Bushby.

↑ **Mustang Aeronautics Midget Mustang built by Kit Sodergren of Sacramento** *(Geoffrey P. Jones)*

Mustang Aeronautics Mustang II

Type: Side-by-side 2-seat, low-wing monoplane, with fixed tailwheel undercarriage.
Construction: Metal.
Wing span: 24 ft 4 ins (7.42 m)
Length: 19 ft 6 ins (5.94 m)
Empty weight: 1,100 lb (499 kg)
Gross weight: 1,600 lb (726 kg)
Recommended engine: 180 hp (134 kW) Textron Lycoming IO-360 (option for 160 hp, 119.3 kW O-320)
Maximum speed: 191 kts (220 mph) 354 km/h
Cruise speed: 182 kts (210 mph) 338 km/h
Stall speed: 54 kts (62 mph) 100 km/h
Take-off distance: 470 ft (144 m)
Climb rate: 1,800 ft (549 m) per minute
Range: 456 naut miles (525 miles) 845 km
Availability: Plans and kits.
Comments: 2-seat development of the Midget Mustang, first flown on 9 July 1966. Also examples with retractable nosewheel undercarriage.

National Aeronautics Cassutt IIIM

Address:
National Aeronautics Co, 5611 Kendall Court, #4, Arvada, CO 80002.
Telephone & Facsimile: +1 303 940 8442

Type: Single-seat, mid-wing, monoplane racer, with fixed tailwheel undercarriage.
Construction: Wood, steel tube and fabric.
Wing span: 15 ft (4.57 m)
Length: 16 ft (4.88 m)
Empty weight: 500 lb (227 kg)
Gross weight: 850 lb (386 kg)
Recommended engine: Teledyne Continental C85 or O-200
Maximum speed: 200 kts (230 mph) 370 km/h
Cruise speed: 165 kts (190 mph) 306 km/h
Stall speed: 59 kts (67 mph) 108 km/h
Take-off distance: 450 ft (138 m)
Climb rate: 1,500 ft (457 m) per minute
Range: 391 naut miles (450 miles) 724 km
Availability: Plans and kits.
Comments: Prototype designed and built by Capt Tom Cassutt in 1954 for air racing. Examples built in UK by Airmark Ltd. Aerobatic, and regularly raced at Reno.

O'Neill Magnum V8

Address:
O'Neill Airplane Co, 791 Livingston, Carlyle, IL 62231.
Telephone: +1 618 594 2681

Type: 6-seat, high-wing, cabin monoplane, with unusual 4-wheel fixed undercarriage.
Construction: Metal.
Wing span: 36 ft (10.97 m)
Length: 25 ft 10 ins (7.87 m)
Empty weight: 1,900 lb (862 kg)
Gross weight: 3,800 lb (1,724 kg)
Recommended engine: 380 hp (283.4 kW) O'Neill Ford V8 conversion
Maximum speed: 161 kts (185 mph) 298 km/h
Cruise speed: 122 kts (140 mph) 225 km/h
Take-off distance: 1,000 ft (305 m)
Climb rate: 1,500 ft (457 m) per minute
Range: 347 naut miles (400 miles) 643 km
Availability: Plans and some kit components.
Comments: Large cargo-carrying homebuilt with swing-tail for loading out-sized items.

Osprey Aircraft Osprey 2

Address:
Osprey Aircraft, 3741 El Ricon Way, Sacramento, CA 95864.
Telephone: +1 916 483 3004

Type: Side-by-side 2-seat, mid-wing amphibian, with pylon mounted pusher engine and retractable nosewheel undercarriage.
Construction: Composites and wood.
Wing span: 26 ft (7.92 m)
Length: 21 ft (6.4 m)
Empty weight: 970 lb (440 kg)
Gross weight: 1,560 lb (707 kg)
Recommended engine: 150 hp (112 kW) Textron Lycoming O-320
Maximum speed: 122 kts (140 mph) 225 km/h
Cruise speed: 113 kts (130 mph) 209 km/h
Stall speed: 55 kts (63 mph) 102 km/h
Take-off distance: 400 ft (122 m) land, 530 ft (162 m) water
Climb rate: 800 ft (244 m) per minute, at MTOW
Range: 477 naut miles (550 miles) 885 km
Availability: Plans and kits.
Comments: Designed by George Pereira and developed from the Osprey I. Prototype Osprey II first flew from water in April 1973.

↑ **Osprey II built in the USA** *(Geoffrey P. Jones)*

Osprey Aircraft Osprey GP-4

Type: Side-by-side 2-seat, low-wing, cabin monoplane, with retractable nosewheel undercarriage.
Construction: Wood.
Wing span: 24 ft 8 ins (7.52 m)
Length: 21 ft 6 ins (6.55 m)
Empty weight: 1,248 lb (566 kg)
Gross weight: 1,985 lb (900 kg)
Recommended engine: 200 hp (149 kW) Textron Lycoming IO-360-A1A
Maximum speed: 217 kts (250 mph) 402 km/h
Cruise speed: 209 kts (240 mph) 386 km/h
Stall speed: 57 kts (65 mph) 105 km/h
Take-off distance: 300 ft (92 m)
Climb rate: 1,500 ft (457 m) per minute, at MTOW
Range: 955 naut miles (1,100 miles) 1,770 km
Availability: Plans and kits.
Comments: First flown in 1984.

↑ **Osprey Aircraft Osprey GP-4**

Pacific Aerosystem Sky Arrow 1450L

Address:
Pacific Aerosystem Inc, 5760 Chesapeake Ct, San Diego, CA 92123.
Telephone: +1 619 571 1441
Facsimile: +1 619 571 0803

Type: Tandem 2-seat, high-wing monoplane, with pusher engine and either fixed nosewheel undercarriage or floats.
Construction: Composites.
Wing span: 31 ft 6 ins (9.6 m)
Length: 24 ft 11 ins (7.59 m)
Empty weight: 770 lb (349 kg)
Gross weight: 1,450 lb (658 kg)
Recommended engine: 80 hp (59.6 kW) Rotax 912
Maximum speed: 80 kts (92 mph) 148 km/h
Cruise speed: 68 kts (78 mph) 126 km/h
Take-off distance: 500 ft (153 m)
Climb rate: 800 ft (244 m) per minute
Range: 304 naut miles (350 miles) 563 km
Availability: Kits.
Comments: Also the 1450A with 920 lb (417 kg) empty weight. See III Sky Arrow under Italy.

Papa 51 Thunder Mustang

Address:
Papa 51 Inc, 102 North Kings Road, Nampa, ID 83687.
Telephone: +1 208 466 5204
Facsimile: +1 208 466 1385

Type: Tandem 2-seat, three-quarter-scale representation of a North American P-51 Mustang, with retractable tailwheel undercarriage.
Construction: Composites and metal.
Wing span: 23 ft 10 ins (7.26 m)
Length: 24 ft 3 ins (7.39 m)
Empty weight: 2,000 lb (907 kg)
Gross weight: 3,000 lb (1,361 kg)
Recommended engine: 640 hp (477 kW) Falconer V-12
Maximum speed: 330 kts (380 mph) 612 km/h
Cruise speed: 270 kts (311 mph) 501 km/h
Stall speed: 77 kts (88 mph) 142 km/h
Take-off distance: 1,200 ft (366 m)
Climb rate: 5,900 ft (1,800 m) per minute
Range: 1,042 naut miles (1,200 miles) 1,931 km
Availability: Kits.
Comments: First flown 16 November 1996.

↑ **Papa 51 Thunder Mustang** *(Geoffrey P. Jones)*

ParaPlane PSE-2 and PM-2

Address:
ParaPlane Corp, 68 Stacey Haines Road, Medford, NJ 08055.
Telephone: +1 609 261 1234
Facsimile: +1 609 261 9116

Details: PSE-2, except under Comments.
Type: Single-seat, powered parachute, with fixed nosewheel trike.
Construction: Metal and fabric.
Wing span: 30 ft 6 ins (9.3 m)
Length: 6 ft 6 ins (1.98 m)
Empty weight: 235 lb (107 kg)
Gross weight: 554 lb (251 kg)
Recommended engine: 45.6 hp (34 kW) Rotax 503
Maximum and cruise speed: 24 kts (28 mph) 45 km/h
Take-off distance: 100 ft (31 m)
Climb rate: 650 ft (198 m) per minute
Range: 21.7 naut miles (25 miles) 40 km
Availability: Kits.
Comments: Another ParaPlane variant is the PM-2, powered by twin 15 hp (11.2 kW) Solo engines.

Parascender 1-447

Address:
Parascender Technologies Inc, 1040 E. Carroll Street, Kissimmee, FL 34744.
Telephone: +1 407 935 0775
Facsimile: +1 407 935 0778
E-mail: para@iag.net

Type: Single-seat, powered parachute, with fixed nosewheel undercarriage trike.
Construction: Steel tube and fabric.
Wing span: 36 ft 6 ins (11.13 m)
Length: 8 ft 9 ins (2.67 m)
Empty weight: 205 lb (93 kg)
Gross weight: 455 lb (206 kg)
Take-off distance: 100 ft (31 m)
Recommended engine: 39.6 hp (29.5 kW) Rotax 447 (see Comments)
Maximum and cruise speed: 23 kts (26 mph) 42 km/h
Climb rate: 450 ft (137 m) per minute
Availability: Kits.
Comments: Other single-seat and 2-seat variants are Rotax 503 powered, plus the Para-Ag agricultural model for spray applications.

Parker Teenie Two

Address:
Calvin Parker, Box 2092, Harker Heights, TX 76543.
Telephone: +1 817 698 3283
Facsimile: +1 817 698 1207

Type: Single-seat, low-wing monoplane, with fixed nosewheel undercarriage.
Construction: Metal.
Wing span: 18 ft (5.49 m)
Length: 12 ft 10 ins (3.91 m)
Empty weight: 320 lb (145 kg)
Gross weight: 585 lb (265 kg)
Recommended engine: 60 hp (44.7 kW) Volkswagen
Maximum speed: 122 kts (140 mph) 225 km/h
Cruise speed: 104 kts (120 mph) 193 km/h
Take-off distance: 600 ft (183 m)
Climb rate: 1,000 ft (305 m) per minute
Range: 347 naut miles (400 miles) 643 km
Availability: Plans and kits of raw materials.

Pazmany PL-2

Address:
Pazmany Aircraft Corporation, PO Box 80051, San Diego, CA 92138.
Telephone: +1 619 224 7330

Type: Side-by-side 2-seat, low-wing, cabin monoplane, with fixed nosewheel undercarriage.
Construction: Metal.
Wing span: 27 ft 10 ins (8.48 m)
Length: 19 ft 4 ins (5.89 m)
Empty weight: 875 lb (397 kg)
Gross weight: 1,416 lb (642 kg)
Recommended engine: 108 hp (80.5 kW) Textron Lycoming O-235
Maximum speed: 125 kts (144 mph) 232 km/h
Cruise speed: 111 kts (128 mph) 206 km/h
Stall speed: 47 kts (54 mph) 87 km/h
Take-off distance: 700 ft (214 m)
Climb rate: 1,200 ft (366 m) per minute
Range: 331 naut miles (381 miles) 613 km
Availability: Plans.
Comments: Developed from the single-seat PL-1 and first flown on 4 April 1969. As well as over 100 homebuilt examples flying, PL-2s have been built by the air forces of Vietnam, Thailand and Korea.

↑ **Pazmany PL-2 built by the Republic of Korea Air Force**

Pazmany PL-4A

Type: Single-seat, low-wing monoplane, with T-tail and fixed tailwheel undercarriage.
Construction: Metal.
Wing span: 26 ft 8 ins (8.13 m)
Length: 16 ft 6 ins (5.03 m)
Empty weight: 578 lb (262 kg)
Gross weight: 850 lb (386 kg)
Recommended engine: 50 hp (37.3 kW) Volkswagen
Maximum speed: 96 kts (110 mph) 177 km/h
Cruise speed: 87 kts (100 mph) 161 km/h
Stall speed: 42 kts (48 mph) 78 km/h
Take-off distance: 560 ft (171 m)
Climb rate: 650 ft (198 m) per minute
Range: 243 naut miles (280 miles) 450 km
Availability: Plans.
Comments: Prototype first flew on 12 July 1972. Examples built by air cadets in Argentina and Canada.

Pazmany PL-9 Stork

Type: Tandem 2-seat, high-wing monoplane, with fixed tailwheel undercarriage.
Construction: Metal and fabric.
Wing span: 36 ft (10.97 m)
Length: 24 ft 4 ins (7.42 m)
Empty weight: 1,132 lb (513 kg)
Gross weight: 1,673 lb (759 kg)
Recommended engine: 150 hp (112 kW)
Maximum speed: 101 kts (116 mph) 187 km/h
Cruise speed: 83 kts (95 mph) 153 km/h
Take-off distance: 250 ft (77 m)
Climb rate: 1,400 ft (427 m) per minute
Range: 288 naut miles (332 miles) 534 km
Availability: Plans.
Comments: Representation of a German WW2 Fieseler Storch.

Performance Aircraft Legend

Address:
12901 West 151 Street, Ste. C, Olathe, KS 66062.
Telephone: +1 913 780 9140
Facsimile: +1 913 782 1092

Type: Tandem 2-seat, low-wing monoplane, with retractable nosewheel undercarriage.
Construction: Composites.
Wing span: 25 ft 4 ins (7.72 m)
Length: 25 ft (7.62 m)
Empty weight: 2,000 lb (907 kg)
Gross weight: 3,000 lb (1,361 kg)
Recommended engine: 575 hp (429 kW) V-8
Maximum speed: 322 kts (371 mph) 597 km/h
Cruise speed: 234 kts (270 mph) 435 km/h
Stall speed: 67 kts (77 mph) 124 km/h
Take-off distance: 900 ft (274 m)
Climb rate: 5,825 ft (1,775 m) per minute
Range: 1,302 naut miles (1,500 miles) 2,414 km
Availability: Kits.
Comments: First flown 1996.

↑ **Performance Aircraft Legend** *(Geoffrey P. Jones)*

Performance Mountain Goat

Address:
Performance Engineering, 4970 Owens Drive, #612, Pleasanton, CA 94588.
Telephone: +1 415 373 9396

Type: 2-seat, high-wing, cabin monoplane, with fixed tailwheel undercarriage.
Construction: Steel tube, composites and fabric.
Wing span: 36 ft (10.97 m)
Length: 22 ft 6 ins (6.86 m)
Empty weight: 1,070 lb (485 kg)
Gross weight: 2,170 lb (984 kg)
Recommended engine: 160 hp (119.3 kW) Textron Lycoming O-320
Maximum speed: 132 kts (152 mph) 245 km/h
Cruise speed: 115 kts (132 mph) 212 km/h
Stall speed: 31 kts (35 mph) 57 km/h
Take-off distance: 120 ft (37 m)
Climb rate: 1,700 ft (518 m) per minute
Range: 869 naut miles (1,000 miles) 1,609 km
Availability: Kits.
Comments: Bush plane with good high- and low-speed performance.

Peris JN-1

Address:
Nancy Peris, 149 South Eastland Drive, Lancaster, PA 17602.
Telephone: +1 717 393 5928

Type: Single-seat, high-wing microlight, with fixed tail-dragger undercarriage.
Construction: Composites, steel tube and wood.
Wing span: 30 ft (9.14 m)
Length: 17 ft 4 ins (5.28 m)
Empty weight: 320 lb (145 kg)
Gross weight: 600 lb (272 kg)
Recommended engine: 38 hp (28.3 kW) Kawasaki 440
Maximum speed: 56 kts (65 mph) 105 km/h
Cruise speed: 52 kts (60 mph) 97 km/h
Take-off distance: 250 ft (77 m)
Climb rate: 600 ft (183 m) per minute
Range: 96 naut miles (110 miles) 177 km
Availability: Plans.
Comments: Conventional single-seat microlight.

Phantom Sport Airplane Phantom X1 and X2

Address:
Phantom Sport Airplane Corporation, PO Box 1684, Carthage, NC 28327.
Telephone: +1 910 947 4744
Facsimile: +1 910 944 7449

Details: Refer to X1, except under Comments.
Type: Single-seat, high-wing microlight, with fixed nosewheel undercarriage.
Construction: Steel tube and fabric.
Wing span: 28 ft 6 ins (8.69 m)
Length: 16 ft 9 ins (5.11 m)
Empty weight: 250 lb (113 kg)
Gross weight: 510 lb (231 kg)
Recommended engine: 39.6 hp (29.5 kW) Rotax 447
Maximum speed: 53 kts (61 mph) 98 km/h
Cruise speed: 48 kts (55 mph) 89 km/h
Take-off distance: 100 ft (31 m)
Climb rate: 800 ft (244 m) per minute
Availability: Kits.
Comments: Phantom X2 is a 2-seat version with a Rotax 503 engine, 30 ft (9.14 m) span and 950 lb (431 kg) gross weight.

Pietenpol Sky Scout

Address:
Don Pietenpol, 1604 Meadow Circle SE, Rochester, MN 55904-5251.
Telephone: +1 507 289 2436

Type: Single-seat, parasol-wing monoplane, with fixed tail-dragger undercarriage.
Construction: Wood and fabric.
Wing span: 27 ft 3 ins (8.31 m)
Length: 16 ft 2 ins (4.93 m)
Empty weight: 320 lb (145 kg)
Gross weight: 520 lb (236 kg)
Recommended engine: 20 hp (14.9 kW)
Maximum speed: 54 kts (62 mph) 100 km/h
Cruise speed: 48 kts (55 mph) 89 km/h
Take-off distance: 150 ft (46 m)
Climb rate: 200 ft (61 m) per minute
Range: 87 naut miles (100 miles) 161 km
Availability: Plans.
Comments: Designed shortly after the famous Pietenpol Aircamper in the 1930s. Plans for the separate 2-seat Aircamper also available (see also Grega Aircamper).

Pop's Props Cloudster, Pinocchio and Zing

Address:
Pop's Props, RR1, Box 98, Cooksville, IL 61730.
Telephone: +1 309 725 3237
Facsimile: +1 309 725 3239

Details: Cloudster, except under Comments.
Type: Single-seat, parasol-wing microlight, with fixed tail-dragger undercarriage.
Construction: Wood and fabric.
Wing span: 30 ft (9.14 m)
Length: 16 ft 6 ins (5.03 m)
Empty weight: 250 lb (113 kg)
Gross weight: 500 lb (227 kg)
Recommended engine: 35 hp (26 kW) Pop's Props half Volkswagen
Maximum speed: 52 kts (60 mph) 97 km/h
Cruise speed: 43 kts (50 mph) 80 km/h
Stall speed: 19 kts (22 mph) 36 km/h
Take-off distance: 200 ft (61 m)
Climb rate: 650 ft (198 m) per minute
Range: 65 naut miles (75 miles) 120 km
Availability: Kits.
Comments: Also available are Pinocchio and Zing.

Preceptor N-3 Pup and Sport

Address:
Preceptor Aircraft Corporation, 1230 Shepard Street, Hendersonville, NC 28792.
Telephone: +1 704 697 8284
Facsimile: +1 704 696 3739

Details: Refer to Pup, except under Comments.
Type: Single-seat, high-wing microlight, with fixed tailwheel undercarriage.
Construction: Steel tube and fabric
Wing span: 30 ft 6 ins (9.3 m)
Length: 16 ft 6 ins (5.03 m)
Empty weight: 254 lb (115 kg)
Gross weight: 535 lb (243 kg)
Recommended engine: 40 hp (30 kW) 2-cylinder 1083 Defiant built by TEC
Maximum speed: 55 kts (63 mph) 101 km/h
Cruise speed: 52 kts (60 mph) 97 km/h
Stall speed: 24 kts (27 mph) 44 km/h
Take-off distance: 150 ft (48 m)
Climb rate: 600 ft (183 m) per minute
Range: 130 naut miles (150 miles) 241 km
Availability: Plans and kits.
Comments: Representation of a Piper Cub. Preceptor Sport is a lighter 25 hp (18.6 kW) version.

↑ **Preceptor N-3 Pup built by Eugene Berry of Modesto, California** *(Geoffrey P. Jones)*

Preceptor N-3/L-4 Super Pup

Type: Single-seat, high-wing monoplane, with fixed tailwheel undercarriage.
Construction: Steel tube and fabric.
Wing span: 26 ft (7.92 m)
Length: 16 ft 6 ins (5.03 m)
Empty weight: 330 lb (150 kg)
Gross weight: 630 lb (286 kg)
Recommended engine: 50 hp (37.3 kW)
Maximum speed: 88 kts (101 mph) 163 km/h
Cruise speed: 74 kts (85 mph) 137 km/h
Stall speed: 31 kts (35 mph) 57 km/h
Take-off distance: 300 ft (92 m)
Climb rate: 800 ft (244 m) per minute
Range: 260 naut miles (300 miles) 482 km
Availability: Plans and kits.
Comments: More powerful version of the N-3 Pup. Also as a representation of a Piper liaison aircraft.

Preceptor Stinger

Type: Single-seat, parasol-wing monoplane, with fixed tailwheel undercarriage.
Construction: Steel tube, wood and fabric.
Wing span: 30 ft 6 ins (9.3 m)
Length: 17 ft (5.18 m)
Empty weight: 350 lb (159 kg)
Gross weight: 650 lb (295 kg)
Recommended engine: 50 hp (37.3 kW) TEC
Maximum speed: 78 kts (90 mph) 145 km/h
Cruise speed: 69 kts (80 mph) 129 km/h
Stall speed: 24 kts (27 mph) 44 km/h
Take-off distance: 100 ft (31 m)
Climb rate: 1,000 ft (305 m) per minute
Range: 260 naut miles (300 miles) 483 km
Availability: Kits.
Comments: First flown 1995. Fuselage based on N-3 Pup. Designed to resemble a 1930's racer.

↑ **Preceptor Stinger**

Preceptor Ultra Pup

Type: Tandem 2-seat, high-wing monoplane, with fixed tailwheel undercarriage.
Construction: Steel tube and fabric.
Wing span: 30 ft 6 ins (9.3 m)
Length: 17 ft 3 ins (5.26 m)
Empty weight: 450 lb (204 kg)
Gross weight: 1,050 lb (476 kg)
Recommended engine: 60 hp (44.7 kW) Preceptor Gold built by TEC
Maximum speed: 96 kts (110 mph) 177 km/h
Cruise speed: 78 kts (90 mph) 145 km/h
Stall speed: 31 kts (35 mph) 57 km/h
Take-off distance: 300 ft (92 m)
Climb rate: 1,500 ft (457 m) per minute
Range: 304 naut miles (350 miles) 563 km
Availability: Plans and kits.
Comments: Folding wings. Can also be configured as a microlight trainer.

Preceptor Storch Replica

See Slepcev Storch in Australia.

Progressive SeaRey and Sting Ray

Address:
Progressive Aerodyne Inc, 520 Clifton Street, Orlando, FL 32808.
Telephone: +1 407 292 3700
Facsimile: +1 407 292 5555

Details: SeaRey, except under Comments.
Type: Side-by-side 2-seat, high-wing amphibian, with pusher engine and retractable tailwheel undercarriage.
Construction: Steel tube, composites and fabric.
Wing span: 29 ft 10 ins (9.09 m)
Length: 22 ft 5 ins (6.83 m)
Empty weight: 640 lb (290 kg)
Gross weight: 1,200 lb (544 kg)
Take-off distance: 175 ft (54 m)
Recommended engine: 64.4 hp (48 kW) Rotax 582
Maximum speed: 91 kts (105 mph) 169 km/h (optional Rotax 912)
Cruise speed: 74 kts (85 mph) 137 km/h
Stall speed: 32 kts (37 mph) 60 km/h
Take-off distance: 175 ft (54 m) from land or water
Climb rate: 650 ft (198 m) per minute
Availability: Kits.
Comments: Sting Ray is a single-seat version with a Rotax 447 engine.

↑ **Progressive SeaRey** *(Geoffrey P. Jones)*

Prostar PT.2C

Address:
Prostar Aircraft Inc, PO Box 760, Beeville, TX 78104.

Telephone: +1 512 358 7670
Facsimile: +1 512 358 8128

Type: Side-by-side 2-seat, high-wing, cabin monoplane, with fixed tail-dragger undercarriage.
Construction: Metal, composites and fabric.
Wing span: 32 ft 6 ins (9.91 m)
Length: 22 ft (6.71 m)
Empty weight: 800 lb (363 kg)
Gross weight: 1,550 lb (703 kg)
Take-off distance: 300 ft (92 m)
Recommended engine: 150 hp (112 kW) Textron Lycoming O-320
Maximum speed: 113 kts (130 mph) 209 km/h
Cruise speed: 100 kts (115 mph) 185 km/h
Climb rate: 1,200 ft (344 m) per minute
Range: 260 naut miles (300 miles) 482 km
Availability: Kits.

Prowler Jaguar

Address:
Prowler Aviation Inc, 3777A Meadow View Drive, No 800, Redding, CA 96002.

Telephone: +1 916 365 4524
Facsimile: +1 916 365 4570

Type: Tandem 2-seat, low-wing monoplane, with retractable tailwheel undercarriage.
Construction: Metal.
Wing span: 25 ft 5 ins (7.75 m)
Length: 21 ft (6.4 m)
Empty weight: 1,560 lb (708 kg)
Gross weight: 2,500 lb (1,134 kg)
Recommended engine: 350 hp (261 kW) Rodeck V8 conversion
Maximum speed: 261 kts (300 mph) 483 km/h
Cruise speed: 217 kts (250 mph) 402 km/h
Stall speed: 52 kts (60 mph) 97 km/h
Take-off distance: 1,100 ft (336 m)
Climb rate: 2,500 ft (762 m) per minute
Range: 1,042 naut miles (1,200 miles) 1,931 km
Availability: Kits.
Comments: Developed from George Morse's Prowler, which first flew in 1985.

Quad City Challenger II Special and variants

Address:
Quad City Aircraft Corporation, PO Box 370, 3810 34th Street, Moline, IL 61266-0370.

Telephone: +1 309 764 3515
Facsimile: +1 309 762 3920
E-mail: daveatqcu@aol.com

Details: Challenger II Special, except under Comments.
Type: Tandem 2-seat, high-wing monoplane, with pusher engine and fixed nosewheel undercarriage.
Construction: Steel tube and fabric.
Wing span: 26 ft (7.92 m)
Length: 20 ft (6.1 m)
Empty weight: 350 lb (159 kg)
Gross weight: 850 lb (386 kg)
Recommended engine: 49.6 hp (37 kW) Rotax 503
Maximum speed: 87 kts (100 mph) 161 km/h

↑ **Quad City Challenger II Special** *(Geoffrey P. Jones)*

Cruise speed: 74 kts (85 mph) 137 km/h
Stall speed: 32 kts (37 mph) 60 km/h, at MTOW
Take-off distance: 250 ft (77 m), at MTOW
Climb rate: 700 ft (213 m) per minute, at MTOW
Range: 191 naut miles (220 miles) 354 km
Availability: Kits.
Comments: Other Challenger models are the single-seat Challenger UL (Rotax 277), Challenger Special (Rotax 447) and the 2-seat Challenger II (Rotax 447).

Quicksilver GT 400 and GT 500

Address:
Quicksilver Manufacturing, 42214 Sarah Way, Temecula, CA 92590.

Telephone: +1 909 506 0061
Facsimile: +1 909 506 1589

Details: GT 400, except under Comments.
Type: Single-seat, high-wing microlight, with fixed nosewheel undercarriage.
Construction: Steel tube and fabric.
Wing span: 30 ft (9.14 m)
Length: 19 ft 9 ins (6.02 m)
Empty weight: 276 lb (125 kg)
Gross weight: 570 lb (258 kg)
Recommended engine: 49.6 hp (37 kW) Rotax 503
Maximum speed: 57 kts (66 mph) 106 km/h
Cruise speed: 54 kts (62 mph) 100 km/h
Stall speed: 24 kts (27 mph) 44 km/h
Take-off distance: 60 ft (19 m)
Climb rate: 1,540 ft (470 m) per minute
Range: 67 naut miles (78 miles) 125 km
Availability: Kits.
Comments: 2-seat version is the Quicksilver GT 500, the first homebuilt design to be certificated in the USA under new FAA regulations.

Quicksilver MX Sport, MX Sprint, MX.II Sprint and MXL.II Sprint

Details: MX Sprint, except under Comments.
Type: Single-seat, open trike microlight, with pusher engine.
Construction: Steel tube and fabric.
Wing span: 28 ft (8.53 m)
Length: 18 ft 2 ins (5.54 m)
Empty weight: 250 lb (113 kg)
Gross weight: 525 lb (238 kg)
Recommended engine: 39.6 hp (29.5 kW) Rotax 447
Maximum speed: 47 kts (54 mph) 87 km/h
Cruise speed: 43 kts (50 mph) 80 km/h
Stall speed: 21 kts (24 mph) 39 km/h
Take-off distance: 65 ft (20 m)
Climb rate: 900 ft (274 m) per minute
Range: 73 naut miles (84 miles) 135 km
Availability: Kits.
Comments: Successor to Eipper. Other similar single-seater is the MX Sport with spats and fuselage pod. 2-seat versions are the MX.II Sprint and MXL.II Sprint, both with Rotax 503 engines.

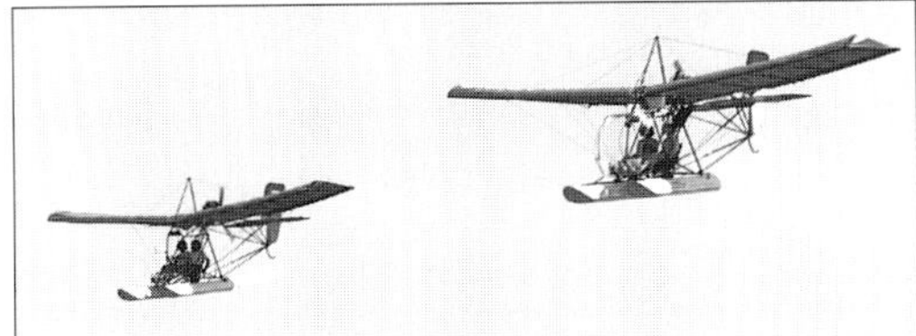

↑ **Quicksilver MX.II Sprints** *(Geoffrey P. Jones)*

Quikkit Glass Goose

Address:
Quikkit Division of Rainbow Flyers Inc, 9002 Summer Glen, Dallas, TX 75243-7445.

Telephone and Facsimile: +1 214 349 0462
E-mail: quikkit@airmail.net

Type: Side-by-side 2-seat, biplane amphibian, with pusher engine and retractable nosewheel undercarriage.
Construction: Composites.
Wing span: 27 ft (8.23 m)
Length: 19 ft 6 ins (5.94 m)
Empty weight: 950 lb (431 kg)
Gross weight: 1,800 lb (816 kg)
Recommended engine: 160 hp (119.3 kW) Textron Lycoming O-320 (optional 185 hp, 138 kW Subaru)
Maximum speed: 139 kts (160 mph) 257 km/h
Cruise speed: 122 kts (140 mph) 225 km/h
Stall speed: 37 kts (42 mph) 68 km/h
Take-off distance: 800 ft (244 m)
Climb rate: 1,200 ft (366 m) per minute
Range: 955 naut miles (1,100 miles) 1,770 km
Availability: Kits.
Comments: Improved derivative of the Aero Composites Sea Hawker which first flew in 1982. Introduced in 1992.

↑ **Quikkit Glass Goose amphibian**

R & B Aircraft Bearhawk

Address:
R & B Aircraft Co, 7590 Breckinridge Mill Road, Fincastle, VA 24090.

Telephone and Facsimile: +1 540 473 3661

Type: 4-seat, high-wing, cabin monoplane, with fixed tailwheel undercarriage.
Construction: Metal and fabric.
Wing span: 33 ft (10.06 m)
Length: 23 ft 6 ins (7.16 m)
Empty weight: 1,150 lb (522 kg)
Gross weight: 2,500 lb (1,134 kg)
Recommended engine: 170 hp (127 kW) Textron Lycoming O-360
Maximum speed: 152 kts (175 mph) 282 km/h
Cruise speed: 104-130 kts (120-150 mph) 193-241 km/h
Stall speed: 35 kts (40 mph) 65 km/h
Take-off distance: 600 ft (183 m), at MTOW
Climb rate: 1,500 ft (457 m) per minute
Range: 694 naut miles (800 miles) 1,287 km
Availability: Plans.
Comments: First flown 1995. Suitable for larger engines. Estimated 1,500-2,000 hours build time.

↑ **R & B Aircraft Bearhawk**

Raceair Skylite

Address:
Raceair, 2331 Dodgeville Road, Rome, OH 44085.

Telephone: +1 216 563 3387

Type: Single-seat, parasol-wing microlight, with fixed tailwheel undercarriage.
Construction: Steel tube and fabric.
Wing span: 29 ft 2 ins (8.89 m)
Length: 17 ft 6 ins (5.33 m)
Empty weight: 240 lb (109 kg)
Gross weight: 520 lb (236 kg)
Recommended engine: 28 hp (20.9 kW) Rotax 277
Maximum speed: 52 kts (60 mph) 97 km/h
Cruise speed: 41 kts (47 mph) 76 km/h
Stall speed: 22 kts (25 mph) 41 km/h
Take-off distance: 400 ft (122 m)
Climb rate: 400 ft (122 m) per minute
Range: 78 naut miles (90 miles) 144 km
Availability: Plans.
Comments: Easy to build microlight.

RagWing RW.2 Special

Address: RagWing Aviation, Box 39, Tokeena Air Park, Townville, SC 29689.
Telephone and Facsimile: +1 864 972 5606

Type: Single-seat biplane, with fixed tail-dragger undercarriage.
Construction: Wood and fabric.
Wing span: 18 ft (5.49 m)
Length: 14 ft 11 ins (4.55 m)
Empty weight: 278 lb (126 kg)
Gross weight: 550 lb (249 kg)
Recommended engine: 38 hp (28.3 kW) Kawasaki 440
Never-exceed speed (VNE): 108 kts (125 mph) 201 km/h
Cruise speed: 61 kts (70 mph) 113 km/h
Stall speed: 26 kts (30 mph) 49 km/h
Take-off distance: 200 ft (61 m)
Climb rate: 750 ft (229 m) per minute
Range: 108 naut miles (125 miles) 201 km
Availability: Plans and kits.
Comments: Available as a microlight or experimental homebuilt.

RagWing RW.3 Trainer PT2T and other RagWing types

Details: Refer to RW.3, except under Comments.
Type: Tandem 2-seat, parasol-wing monoplane, with fixed tail-dragger undercarriage.
Construction: Wood and fabric.
Wing span: 28 ft 6 ins (8.69 m)
Length: 17 ft (5.18 m)
Empty weight: 450 lb (204 kg)
Gross weight: 900 lb (408 kg)
Recommended engine: 52 hp (38.8 kW) Rotax 503
Maximum speed: 91 kts (105 mph) 169 km/h
Cruise speed: 70 kts (80 mph) 129 km/h
Stall speed: 32 kts (36 mph) 58 km/h
Take-off distance: 200 ft (61 m)
Climb rate: 650 ft (198 m) per minute
Range: 226 naut miles (260 miles) 418 km
Availability: Plans and kits.
Comments: Designed as a representation of the Pietenpol Aircamper and to complement the single-seat 35 hp (26 kW) Kawasaki-powered **RagWing RW.1 Ultra-Piet**. Other designs include the **RW.4** to **RW.11**.

Rand-Robinson KR-1

Address: Rand-Robinson Engineering Inc, 15641 Product Lane, Ste A5, Huntington Beach, CA 92649.
Telephone: +1 714 898 3811 Facsimile: +1 714 890 1658

Type: Single-seat, low-wing monoplane, with either fixed or retractable tailwheel undercarriage.
Construction: Composites and wood.
Wing span: 17 ft (5.18 m)
Length: 12 ft 11 ins (3.94 m)
Empty weight: 375 lb (170 kg)
Gross weight: 750 lb (340 kg)
Recommended engine: 90 hp (67 kW) Volkswagen
Maximum speed: 191 kts (220 mph) 354 km/h
Cruise speed: 130 kts (150 mph) 241 km/h
Stall speed: 39 kts (45 mph) 73 km/h
Take-off distance: 350 ft (107 m)
Climb rate: 1,500 ft (457 m) per minute
Range: 1,216 naut miles (1,400 miles) 2,253 km
Availability: Plans and kits.
Comments: Designed by Ken Rand and Stuart Robinson and first flown in February 1972. One of the first homebuilts to make extensive use of composite construction.

↑ **Rand-Robinson KR-1 built by Richard Shirley** *(Geoffrey P. Jones)*

Rand-Robinson KR-2 and KR-2S

Details: KR-2, except under Comments.
Type: Side-by-side 2-seat, low-wing monoplane, with either fixed or retractable nosewheel or tailwheel undercarriage.
Construction: Composites and wood.
Wing span: 20 ft 10 ins (6.35 m)
Length: 14 ft 8 ins (4.47 m)
Empty weight: 480 lb (217 kg)
Gross weight: 900 lb (408 kg)
Recommended engine: 2,100cc Volkswagen
Maximum speed: 174 kts (200 mph) 322 km/h
Cruise speed: 156 kts (180 mph) 290 km/h
Stall speed: 39 kts (45 mph) 73 km/h
Take-off distance: 350 ft (107 m)
Climb rate: 1,000 ft (305 m) per minute
Range: 1,390 naut miles (1,600 miles) 2,575 km
Availability: Plans and kits.
Comments: First flown in July 1974. Newer version is the KR-2S with longer fuselage, higher canopy, 23 ft (7 m) wing span and suitable for 76 hp (56.7 kW) Volkswagen engine.

RANS S-4 and S-5 Coyote

Address: Rans Co, 4600 Highway 183 Alternate, Hays, KS 67601.
Telephone: +1 913 625 6346 Facsimile: +1 913 625 2795

Type: Single-seat, high-wing monoplane, with fixed tailwheel (S-4) or nosewheel (S-5) undercarriage.
Construction: Steel tube and fabric
Wing span: 29 ft 6 ins (8.99 m)
Length: 17 ft (5.18 m)
Empty weight: 290 lb (131.5 kg)
Gross weight: 587 lb (266 kg)
Recommended engine: 41.6 hp (31 kW) Rotax 447 (optional Rotax 503)
Maximum speed: 83 kts (95 mph) 153 km/h
Cruise speed: 48 kts (55 mph) 89 km/h
Stall speed: 24 kts (27 mph) 44 km/h
Take-off distance: 60 ft (18.5 m)
Climb rate: 800 ft (244 m) per minute
Range: 74 naut miles (85 miles) 136 km
Availability: Kits
Comments: Designed by Randy Schlitter, now company President.

Rans S-6 Coyote II

Type: Side-by-side 2-seat, high-wing monoplane, with fixed nosewheel or tailwheel undercarriage.
Construction: Steel tube and fabric.
Wing span: 34 ft 6 ins (10.52 m)
Length: 20 ft (6.1 m)
Empty weight: 440 lb (200 kg)
Gross weight: 930 lb (422 kg)
Recommended engine: 64.4 hp (48 kW) Rotax 582 (options for Rotax 503 and 912)
Maximum speed: 104 kts (120 mph) 193 km/h
Cruise speed: 78 kts (90 mph) 145 km/h
Stall speed: 33 kts (38 mph) 61 km/h
Take-off distance: 145 ft (45 m)
Climb rate: 1,000 ft (305 m) per minute
Range: 191 naut miles (220 miles) 354 km
Availability: Kits.
Comments: Available in microlight or homebuilt/experimental category.

Rans S-7 Courier

Type: Tandem 2-seat, high-wing monoplane, with fixed tailwheel undercarriage.
Construction: Steel tube and fabric.
Wing span: 29 ft 3 ins (8.92 m)
Length: 21 ft (6.4 m)
Empty weight: 520 lb (236 kg)
Gross weight: 1,025 lb (465 kg)
Recommended engine: 64.4 hp (48 kW) Rotax 582
Maximum speed: 104 kts (120 mph) 193 km/h
Cruise speed: 70 kts (80 mph) 129 km/h
Stall speed: 31 kts (35 mph) 57 km/h
Take-off distance: 175 ft (54 m)
Climb rate: 750 ft (229 m) per minute
Range: 208 naut miles (240 miles) 386 km
Availability: Kits.
Comments: Prototype first flew in October 1985.

↑ **Rans S-7 Courier built by Mike Turnbull in the UK** *(Geoffrey P. Jones)*

Rans S-9 Chaos and S-10 Sakota

Details: S-9 Chaos, except under Comments and photograph.
Type: Single-seat, mid-wing monoplane, with fixed tailwheel undercarriage.
Construction: Steel tube and fabric.
Wing span: 22 ft (6.71 m)
Length: 15 ft 8 ins (4.78 m)
Empty weight: 320 lb (145 kg)
Gross weight: 670 lb (304 kg)
Recommended engine: 52 hp (38.8 kW) Rotax 503SC
Maximum speed: 113 kts (130 mph) 209 km/h
Cruise speed: 74 kts (85 mph) 137 km/h
Stall speed: 26 kts (29 mph) 47 km/h
Take-off distance: 200 ft (61 m)
Climb rate: 800 ft (244 m) per minute
Range: 147 naut miles (170 miles) 273 km
Availability: Kits.
Comments: 2-seat Rans S-10 Sakota is available with a Rotax 582, 960 lb (435 kg) gross weight and 24 ft (7.32 m) wing span.

↑ **Rans S-10 Sakota built in Belgium** *(Geoffrey P. Jones)*

Rans S-12 and S-14 Airaile

Details: S-12, except under Comments.
Type: Side-by-side 2-seat, high-wing monoplane, with pusher engine and fixed nosewheel undercarriage.
Construction: Steel tube and fabric.
Wing span: 31 ft (9.45 m)
Length: 20 ft 4 ins (6.2 m)
Empty weight: 410 lb (186 kg)
Gross weight: 920 lb (417 kg)
Recommended engine: 52 hp (38.8 kW) Rotax 503SC
Maximum speed: 87 kts (100 mph) 161 km/h
Cruise speed: 56 kts (65 mph) 105 km/h
Stall speed: 26 kts (30 mph) 49 km/h
Take-off distance: 275 ft (84 m)
Climb rate: 500 ft (152 m) per minute
Range: 226 naut miles (260 miles) 418 km
Availability: Kits.
Comments: Introduced in 1991. The single-seat Rans S-14 Airaile has smaller dimensions and a Rotax 447 engine.

↑ **Rans S-12 Airaile** *(Geoffrey P. Jones)*

Rans S-16 Shekari

Type: Side-by-side 2-seat, mid-wing, aerobatic monoplane, with fixed tailwheel undercarriage.
Construction: Composites, steel tube and fabric.
Wing span: 25 ft (7.62 m)
Length: 19 ft 11 ins (6.07 m)
Empty weight: 590 lb (268 kg)
Gross weight: 1,200 lb (544 kg)

Recommended engine: 80 hp (59.6 kW) Rotax 912 or 115 hp (86 kW) Teledyne Continental IO-240B
Maximum speed: 148 kts (170 mph) 274 km/h
Cruise speed: 122 kts (140 mph) 225 km/h
Stall speed: 50 kts (57 mph) 92 km/h *clean*
Take-off distance: 325 ft (99 m)
Climb rate: 500 ft (152 m) per minute
Range: 334 naut miles (385 miles) 619 km
Availability: Kits.
Comments: First flown March 1997. Similar in appearance to Rans S-10 but stressed for aerobatics. Spatted undercarriage.

Redfern Fokker DR.1

Address:
Walter Redfern, S-211 Spenser, Post Falls, ID 83854.
Telephone: +1 208 773 8280

Type: Single-seat, triplane replica, with fixed tailwheel undercarriage.
Construction: Wood, steel tube and fabric.
Wing span: 23 ft 8 ins (7.21 m)
Length: 19 ft (5.79 m)
Empty weight: 1,112 lb (504 kg)
Gross weight: 1,455 lb (660 kg)
Recommended engine: 145 hp (108 kW) Warner radial
Maximum speed: 104 kts (120 mph) 193 km/h
Cruise speed: 87 kts (100 mph) 161 km/h
Take-off distance: 100 ft (31 m)
Climb rate: 2,000 ft (610 m) per minute
Range: 260 naut miles (300 miles) 482 km
Availability: Plans.
Comments: Over 5,000 sets of plans sold. One of 4 Walter Redfern replicas of World War I aircraft. Others are the **Nieuport 17, Nieuport 24** and **DH-2**.

↑ **Redfern Fokker DR.1 built by Ned and James Butler** *(Geoffrey P. Jones)*

Renaissance Composites Berkut

Address:
Renaissance Composites, 3025 Airport Avenue, Santa Monica, CA 90405.
Telephone: +1 310 391 1943

Type: Tandem 2-seat, canard monoplane, with pusher engine and retractable nosewheel undercarriage.
Construction: Composites.
Wing span: 26 ft 8 ins (8.13 m)
Length: 18 ft 6 ins (5.64 m)
Empty weight: 1,035 lb (469 kg)
Gross weight: 2,000 lb (907 kg)
Recommended engine: 205 hp (153 kW) Textron Lycoming IO-360B1A. Optional 260 hp (194 kW) IO-540
Maximum speed: 215 kts (248 mph) 399 km/h
Cruise speed: 191 kts (220 mph) 354 km/h
Stall speed: 61 kts (70 mph) 113 km/h
Take-off distance: 1,000 ft (305 m)
Climb rate: 2,000 ft (610 m) per minute
Range: 1,066 naut miles (1,228 miles) 1,976 km
Availability: Kits.
Comments: Former Experimental Aircraft Berkut, designed by Dave Ronneberg. First flown on 11 July 1991. Solid foam-core wings of first 50 kits now replaced by carbonfibre wings with separate skins and ribs.

Repeat Aircraft DH.88 Comet

Details can be found in the 1996-97 edition of *WA&SD*.

↑ **Repeat Aircraft DH.88 Comet replica** *(Geoffrey P. Jones)*

Rotor-Wings Flaglor Scooter

Address:
Rotor-Wings & Flying Machines, 10405 Button Quail, Austin, TX 78758-5032.
Telephone: +1 512 837 8041

Type: Single-seat, high-wing monoplane, with fixed tail-dragger undercarriage.
Construction: Wood.
Wing span: 28 ft (8.53 m)
Length: 15 ft 6 ins (4.72 m)
Empty weight: 346 lb (157 kg)
Gross weight: 650 lb (295 kg)
Recommended engine: 40 hp (30 kW) Volkswagen
Maximum speed: 78 kts (90 mph) 145 km/h
Cruise speed: 65 kts (75 mph) 121 km/h
Stall speed: 31 kts (35 mph) 57 km/h
Climb rate: 600 ft (183 m) per minute
Range: 152 naut miles (175 miles) 281 km
Availability: Plans.
Comments: Prototype first flew in June 1967.

Sabre Aircraft Sabre

Address:
Sabre Aircraft Inc, 1001 W. Monona Drive, Phoenix, AZ 85027.
Telephone: +1 602 582 6308
Facsimile: +1 602 925 6688

Type: Single- or 2-seat, open-framed trike, with pusher engine and shift Rogallo wing.
Construction: Steel tube and fabric.
Wing span: 34 ft (10.36 m)
Length: 10 ft (3.05 m)
Empty weight: 205 lb (93 kg)
Gross weight: 600 lb (272 kg)
Recommended engine: 32 hp (23.9 kW) Kawasaki. Optional Rotax 447 or 503
Maximum speed: 43 kts (50 mph) 80 km/h
Cruise speed: 40 kts (46 mph) 74 km/h
Take-off distance: 100 ft (31 m)
Climb rate: 1,000 ft (305 m) per minute
Range: 87 naut miles (100 miles) 161 km
Availability: Kits.

St.Croix Pietenpol Aerial

Address:
St Croix Aircraft, 1139 State Highway 148, Corning, IA 50841.
Telephone: +1 515 322 4041

Type: Tandem 2-seat biplane, with fixed tail-dragger undercarriage.
Construction: Wood, steel tube and fabric.
Wing span: 29 ft 6 ins (8.99 m)
Length: 19 ft 6 ins (5.94 m)
Empty weight: 900 lb (408 kg)
Gross weight: 1,400 lb (635 kg)
Recommended engine: 145 hp (108 kW) Teledyne Continental O-300
Maximum speed: 91 kts (105 mph) 169 km/h
Cruise speed: 74 kts (85 mph) 137 km/h
Take-off distance: 250 ft (77 m)
Climb rate: 1,000 ft (305 m) per minute
Range: 130 naut miles (150 miles) 241 km
Availability: Plans.
Comments: Biplane development of the Pietenpol Aircamper. Latter aircraft also available in plans form from St.Croix. Other St.Croix aircraft are the single-seat **Excelsior Ultralight** and a **Sopwith Triplane** replica.

Ron Sands Fokker DR-1

Address:
Ron Sands, 89 Forrest Road, Mertztown, PA 19539.
Telephone and Facsimile: +1 610 682 6788

Type: Single-seat, replica triplane, with fixed tailwheel undercarriage.
Construction: Metal, wood and fabric.
Wing span: 23 ft 8 ins (7.21 m)
Length: 19 ft (5.79 m)
Empty weight: 1,150 lb (522 kg)
Gross weight: 1,600 lb (726 kg)
Recommended engine: 110 hp (82 kW) Le Rhône. Suitable for Warner and Textron Lycoming radials
Maximum speed: 104 kts (120 mph) 193 km/h
Cruise speed: 96 kts (110 mph) 177 km/h
Take-off distance: 300 ft (92 m)
Climb rate: 1,800 ft (549 m) per minute
Range: 217 naut miles (250 miles) 402 km
Availability: Plans.
Comments: Full-scale replica of the WWI Fokker DR-1 Triplane. Other Ron Sands replicas are the Fokker D-VIII and 1929 Primary Glider.

Seawind 3000

Address:
Seawind/S.N.A. Inc, PO Box 607, Kimberton, PA 19442-0607 (in Europe: Tony Irwin, Seawind Europe, Normanton on Soar, Nr Loughborough, Leicestershire LE12 5HB, UK).
Telephone: +1 610 983 3377 (UK: +44 1509 842 231)
Facsimile: +1 610 983 3335 (UK: +44 1509 842 201)
E-mail: UK: seawind.europe@ndirect.co.uk

Type: 4-seat amphibian, with tail-mounted engine and retractable nosewheel undercarriage.
Construction: Composites.
Wing span: 35 ft (10.67 m)
Length: 27 ft 2 ins (8.28 m)
Empty weight: 2,300 lb (1,043 kg)
Gross weight: 3,400 lb (1,542 kg)
Recommended engine: 300 hp (224 kW) Textron Lycoming IO-540 (optional engines between 200-410 hp, 149-306 kW, plus a 420 shp, 313 kW Allison turboprop)
Maximum speed: above 174 kts (200 mph) 322 km/h
Cruise speed: 166 kts (191 mph) 307 km/h
Stall speed: 50 kts (57 mph) 92 km/h, flaps and undercarriage down
Take-off distance: 820 ft (250 m) land, 1,100 ft (336 m) water
Climb rate: 1,250 ft (381 m) per minute
Range: 1,268 naut miles (1,460 miles) 2,349 km
Availability: Kits.
Comments: Development of the Canadian Seawind 2000. Production prototype first flew on 23 August 1982. 120 kits sold and 15 flying at time of writing.

↑ **Seawind 3000 with canopy raised**

Sequoia F.8L Falco and 300 Sequoia

Address:
Sequoia Aircraft Corporation, 2000 Tomlynn Street, PO Box 6861, Richmond, VA 23230.
Telephone: +1 804 353 1713
Facsimile: +1 804 359 2618

Details: Falco, except under Comments.
Type: Side-by-side 2-seat, low-wing monoplane, with retractable nosewheel undercarriage.
Construction: Wood.
Wing span: 26 ft 3 ins (8 m)
Length: 21 ft 9 ins (6.63 m)
Empty weight: 1,212 lb (550 kg), equipped

Gross weight: 1,880 lb (853 kg)
Recommended engine: 160 hp (119.3 kW) Textron Lycoming IO-320-B1A (180 hp, 134 kW IO-360-B1E also fitted)
Maximum speed: 184 kts (212 mph) 341 km/h
Cruise speed: 165 kts (190 mph) 306 km/h
Stall speed: 54 kts (62 mph) 100 km/h, flaps and undercarriage down
Take-off distance: 570 ft (174 m)
Climb rate: 1,140 ft (347 m) per minute
Range: 869 naut miles (1,000 miles) 1,609 km
Availability: Plans and kits.
Comments: Homebuilt version of Stelio Frati's Italian production aircraft. Also available is the all-metal 300 hp (224 kW) **300 Sequoia**.

Six-Chuter Skye-Ryder Aerochute and Aerochute 2

Address:
Six-Chuter Inc, PO Box 8331, Yakima, WA 98908.
Telephone: +1 509 966 8211
Facsimile: +1 509 966 4284

Details: Aerochute, except under Comments.
Type: Single- or 2-seat, open-framed trike, with fixed undercarriage, pusher engine and ram-air parachute.
Construction: Composites, steel tube and fabric.
Wing span: 36 ft 6 ins (11.13 m)
Length: 12 ft 4 ins (3.76 m)
Empty weight: 231 lb (105 kg)
Gross weight: 420 lb (191 kg)
Recommended engine: 39.6 hp (29.5 kW) Rotax 447 or 49.6 hp (37 kW) Rotax 503
Maximum and cruise speed: 23 kts (26 mph) 42 km/h
Stall speed: Stall resistant
Take-off distance: 50-100 ft (15.5-31 m)
Climb rate: 700 ft (213 m) per minute
Range: 45 naut miles (52 miles) 83 km
Availability: Kits.
Comments: Designed by Larry Neiborsky in 1991. 2-seater is the Aerochute 2.

Sherwood America Sherwood Ranger XP

Address:
Sherwood America Aviation, 904 Silver Spur Road, Ste. 333, Rolling Hills Estate, CA 90274.
Telephone: +1 310 325 3422
Facsimile: +1 310 378 7685

Comments: More details under Sherwood Ranger in UK.

↑ **Sherwood America Sherwood Ranger XP built in the USA** *(Geoffrey P. Jones)*

Skystar Kitfox Classic IV

Address:
Skystar Aircraft Corporation, Inc, 100K North Kings Road, Nampa, ID 83687.
Telephone: +1 208 466 1711
Facsimile: +1 208 466 8703

Type: Side-by-side 2-seat, high wing cabin monoplane, with fixed tailwheel undercarriage.
Construction: Steel tube and fabric.
Wing span: 32 ft (9.75 m)
Length: 18 ft 5 ins (5.61 m)
Empty weight: 495 lb (225 kg)
Gross weight: 1,200 lb (544 kg)
Recommended engine: 80 hp (59.6 kW) Rotax 912 (options for engines in 50-100 hp, 37.3-74.6 kW range)
Maximum speed: 97 kts (112 mph) 180 km/h
Cruise speed: 96 kts (110 mph) 177 km/h
Stall speed: 28 kts (32 mph) 52 km/h
Take-off distance: 200 ft (61 m)
Climb rate: 840 ft (256 m) per minute
Range: 147 naut miles (170 miles) 273 km
Availability: Kits.
Comments: Latest version of the original Denney Kitfox series. Prototype Kitfox first flew on 7 May 1984. Kitfox IV introduced in mid-1991 and previously sold as the Kitfox XL.

Skystar Kitfox Series 5 and Speedster

Details: Kitfox Series 5, except under Comments.
Type: Side-by-side 2-seat, high-wing, cabin monoplane, with fixed tailwheel undercarriage.
Construction: Steel tube and fabric.
Wing span: 29 ft (8.84 m)
Length: 20 ft 7 ins (6.27 m)
Empty weight: 705 lb (320 kg)
Gross weight: 1,550 lb (703 kg)
Recommended engine: 80 hp (59.6 kW) Teledyne Continental O-200 (optional Rotax 618, 912 and 918, and new 125 hp, 93.2 kW IO-240B)
Maximum speed: 107 kts (123 mph) 198 km/h
Cruise speed: 96 kts (110 mph) 177 km/h
Stall speed: 31 kts (35 mph) 57 km/h
Take-off distance: 185 ft (57 m)
Climb rate: 750 ft (229 m) per minute
Range: 525 naut miles (605 miles) 973 km
Availability: Kits.
Comments: Long-wing version also available, as is the Kitfox Speedster.

↑ **Skystar Kitfox Series 5 built by George Crenshaw of Florida** *(Geoffrey P. Jones)*

Skystar Kitfox Vixen

Type: Side-by-side 2-seat, high-wing, cabin monoplane, with fixed nosewheel undercarriage.
Construction: Steel tube and fabric.
Wing span: 29 ft (8.84 m) short-wing, 32 ft (9.75 m) long-wing
Length: 20 ft 4 ins (6.2 m)
Empty weight: 725 lb (329 kg)
Gross weight: 1,550 lb (703 kg)
Recommended engine: 125 hp (93.2 kW) Teledyne Continental IO-240 (optional Rotax 912 or other engines in 80-125 hp, 59.6-93.2 kW range)
Maximum speed: 126 kts (145 mph) 233 km/h
Cruise speed: 120 kts (138 mph) 222 km/h
Stall speed: 39 kts (44 mph) 71 km/h
Take-off distance: 230 ft (70 m)
Climb rate: 1,200 ft (366 m) per minute
Range: 536 naut miles (618 miles) 994 km
Availability: Kits.
Comments: Developed for Skystar by Harry Riblett, becoming the first nosewheel undercarriage version of Kitfox.

↑ **Skystar Kitfox Vixen** *(Geoffrey P. Jones)*

Skystar Pulsar II

Type: Side-by-side 2-seat, low-wing monoplane, with fixed nosewheel or tailwheel undercarriage.
Construction: Composites.
Wing span: 25 ft (7.62 m)
Length: 19 ft 6 ins (5.94 m)
Empty weight: 460 lb (209 kg)
Gross weight: 900 lb (408 kg)
Recommended engine: 64.4 hp (48 kW) Rotax 582
Maximum speed: 122 kts (140 mph) 225 km/h
Cruise speed: 113 kts (130 mph) 209 km/h
Stall speed: 39 kts (45 mph) 73 km/h
Take-off distance: 800 ft (244 m)
Climb rate: 1,000 ft (305 m) per minute
Range: 434 naut miles (500 miles) 804 km
Availability: Kits.
Comments: 2-seat version of the Star-Lite, designed by Mark Brown, which is no longer available. Prototype Pulsar first flew on 3 April 1988. Formerly marketed by Aero Designs.

Skystar Pulsar XP

Type: Side-by-side 2-seat, low-wing monoplane, with fixed nosewheel or tailwheel undercarriage.
Construction: Composites.
Wing span: 25 ft (7.62 m)
Length: 19 ft 6 ins (5.94 m)
Empty weight: 510 lb (231 kg)
Gross weight: 960 lb (435 kg)
Recommended engine: 80 hp (59.7 kW) Rotax 912
Maximum speed: 139 kts (160 mph) 257 km/h
Cruise speed: 122 kts (140 mph) 225 km/h
Stall speed: 40 kts (46 mph) 74 km/h
Take-off distance: 800 ft (244 m)
Climb rate: 1,200 ft (366 m) per minute
Range: 521 naut miles (600 miles) 965 km
Availability: Kits.
Comments: More powerful version of the Pulsar II. Quick-build kits available.

↑ **Skystar Pulsar XP** *(Geoffrey P. Jones)*

Sky Technology Sky Car

Address:
Kenneth G. Wernicke, Sky Technology Vehicle Design & Development Company, Fort Worth, TX.

Type: 4-seat, low-wing monoplane, with stub wings and endplates, twin fins, and fixed nosewheel undercarriage. Designed to operate as an automobile or aircraft.
Construction: Composites.
Wing span: 8 ft 6 ins (2.59 m)
Length: 21 ft (6.4 m)
Gross weight: 1,400 lb (635 kg)
Recommended engine: 180 hp (134 kW) Mazda rotary in proof-of-concept version and 475 hp (354 kW) in production type
Maximum speed: 189 kts (217 mph) 349 km/h
Cruise speed: 152 kts (175 mph) 282 km/h
Take-off distance: 980 ft (299 m)
Range: 521 naut miles (600 miles) 965 km
Availability: Proof-of-concept prototype under construction.
Comments: Project under development - current project status uncertain.

Sorrell SNS-7 Hiperbipe

Address:
Sorrell Aircraft Co Ltd, 16525 Tilley Road South, Tenino, WA 98589.
Telephone: +1 206 264 2866
Facsimile: +1 206 264 2154

Type: Side-by-side 2-seat, reverse stagger, aerobatic, cabin biplane, with aerofoil-shaped fuselage and fixed tailwheel undercarriage.
Construction: Metal and fabric.
Wing span: 22 ft 10 ins (6.96 m)
Length: 20 ft 10 ins (6.35 m)
Empty weight: 1,236 lb (561 kg)

Gross weight: 1,911 lb (867 kg)
Recommended engine: 180 hp (134 kW) Teledyne Continental IO-360-B1E
Maximum speed: 148 kts (170 mph) 274 km/h
Cruise speed: 139 kts (160 mph) 257 km/h
Stall speed: 43 kts (49 mph) 79 km/h *clean*
Take-off distance: 400 ft (122 m)
Climb rate: 1,500 ft (457 m) per minute
Range: 436 naut miles (502 miles) 807 km
Availability: Kits.

↑ **Sorrell SNS-7 Hiperbipe** *(Geoffrey P. Jones)*

Spencer Amphibian Air Car

Address: Spencer Aircraft Inc, PO Box 327, Kansas, IL 61933.
Telephone and Facsimile: +1 217 948 5505

Type: 4-seat, high-wing amphibian, with pusher engine, fixed wing floats and retractable nosewheel undercarriage.
Construction: Wood, steel tube, composites and fabric.
Wing span: 37 ft 4 ins (11.38 m)
Length: 26 ft 5 ins (8.05 m)
Empty weight: 2,150 lb (975 kg)
Gross weight: 3,200 lb (1,451 kg)
Recommended engine: 300 hp (224 kW) Teledyne Continental IO-520
Maximum speed: 135 kts (155 mph) 249 km/h
Cruise speed: 117 kts (135 mph) 217 km/h
Stall speed: 38 kts (43 mph) 70 km/h
Take-off distance: 700 ft (214 m)
Climb rate: 1,000 ft (305 m) per minute
Range: 651 naut miles (750 miles) 1,207 km
Availability: Plans and kits.
Comments: Original Air Car patent received in January 1950. Spencer Amphibian Air Car Inc was sold to Robert F. Kerans on 15 July 1988. At least 37 are flying.

↑ **Spencer Amphibian Air Car** *(Geoffrey P. Jones)*

Sport Aircraft (Sunderland) S-18

Address: Sport Aircraft Inc, 44211 Yucca, Unit A, Lancaster, CA 93535.
Telephone: +1 805 949 2312 or 945 2366

Type: Side-by-side 2-seat, low-wing monoplane, with fixed tailwheel undercarriage.
Construction: Metal.
Wing span: 20 ft 10 ins (6.35 m)
Length: 19 ft 4 ins (5.89 m)
Empty weight: 923 lb (419 kg)
Gross weight: 1,600 lb (726 kg)
Recommended engine: 150 hp (112 kW) Textron Lycoming
Maximum speed: 159 kts (183 mph) 295 km/h
Cruise speed: 143 kts (165 mph) 266 km/h
Stall speed: 55 kts (63 mph) 101 km/h
Take-off distance: 900 ft (275 m)
Climb rate: 1,200 ft (366 m) per minute
Range: 460 naut miles (530 miles) 853 km
Availability: Plans and kits.
Comments: Sport Aircraft took over the sale of plans and kits of the classic Thorpe T-18 Tiger from Sunderland Aircraft, who had developed a modified version as the S-18. See also Eklund Engineering Thorpe T-18 (USA).

Sport Racer

Address: Sport Racer Inc, 14 Hawthorne Road, Valley Center, KS 67147.
Telephone: +1 316 755 0659

Type: Tandem 2-seat, mid-wing monoplane, with fixed tailwheel undercarriage.
Construction: Metal, composites and wood.
Wing span: 22 ft (6.71 m)
Length: 21 ft (6.4 m)
Empty weight: 1,175 lb (533 kg)
Gross weight: 1,825 lb (828 kg)
Recommended engine: 230 hp (171.5 kW) Javelin Ford auto conversion
Maximum speed: 200 kts (230 mph) 370 km/h
Cruise speed: 152 kts (175 mph) 282 km/h
Take-off distance: 1,600 ft (488 m)
Climb rate: 900 ft (274 m) per minute
Range: 456 naut miles (525 miles) 845 km
Availability: Plans.
Comments: Suitable for racing and aerobatics. Several examples completed and flown.

Stallings Air Master

Address: Jerry Stallings, 7822 Gulfton, Houston, TX 77036.
Telephone & Facsimile: +1 713 780 1123

Type: Side-by-side 2-seat, low-wing monoplane, with retractable nosewheel undercarriage.
Construction: Composites.
Wing span: 26 ft 6 ins (8.08 m)
Length: 21 ft (6.4 m)
Gross weight: 1,885 lb (855 kg)
Recommended engine: 150 hp (112 kW) Textron Lycoming O-320
Maximum speed: 207 kts (238 mph) 383 km/h
Cruise speed: 174 kts (200 mph) 322 km/h
Climb rate: 2,000 ft (610 m) per minute
Range: 868 naut miles (1,000 miles) 1,609 km
Availability: Plans.
Comments: Also known as the Airplane Builders Air Master. First flown in 1994. Designed by the late Jerry Stallings. Current status unclear.

Starfire Firebolt

Address: Starfire Aviation Inc, 907 South Hohokam Drive, Tempe, AZ 85281.
Telephone: +1 602 731 9419

Type: Tandem 2-seat, aerobatic biplane, with fixed tailwheel undercarriage.
Construction: Steel tube, wood and fabric.
Wing span: 24 ft (7.32 m)
Length: 21 ft (6.4 m)
Empty weight: 1,354 lb (614 kg)
Gross weight: 2,000 lb (907 kg)
Recommended engine: 340 hp (254 kW) Textron Lycoming IO-540-K1AS modified
Maximum speed: 186 kts (214 mph) 344 km/h
Cruise speed: 176 kts (202 mph) 325 km/h
Take-off distance: 400 ft (122 m)
Climb rate: 4,000 ft (1,220 m) per minute
Range: 521 naut miles (600 miles) 965 km
Availability: Plans.
Comments: Highly modified Skybolt with good cross-country performance. Enclosed cockpit option.

Starlight Engineering Warp 1-A

Address: Starlight Engineering, PO Box 90241, Dayton, OH 45490.
Telephone: +1 513 836 9228

Type: Single-seat, mid-wing monoplane, with pusher engine and fixed nosewheel undercarriage.
Construction: Alloy tube and composites.
Wing span: 24 ft 6 ins (7.47 m)
Length: 19 ft 6 ins (5.94 m)
Empty weight: 250 lb (113 kg)
Gross weight: 575 lb (261 kg)
Recommended engine: 45.6 hp (34 kW) Rotax 503 (options include Zenoah, and 40-100 hp, 30-74.6 kW Cuyana)
Maximum speed: 87 kts (100 mph) 161 km/h
Cruise speed: 48-61 kts (55-70 mph) 89-113 km/h
Stall speed: 19 kts (22 mph) 36 km/h
Take-off distance: 50 ft (16 m)
Climb rate: 900 ft (274 m) per minute
Range: 87 naut miles (100 miles) 161 km
Availability: Kits.
Comments: First flown 1997. Clark "Y" partial laminar-flow wing section gives high speed on low power.

↑ **Starlight Engineering Warp 1-A at Sun 'n Fun 1997** *(Geoffrey P. Jones)*

Steen Skybolt and Knight Twister

Address: Steen Aero Lab, 1210 Airport Road, Marion, NC 28752.
Telephone and Facsimile: +1 704 652 7382

Details: Skybolt, except under Comments.
Type: Tandem 2-seat, open-cockpit, sport biplane, with fixed tailwheel undercarriage.
Construction: Wood, steel tube and fabric.
Wing span: 24 ft (7.32 m)
Length: 19 ft (5.79 m)
Empty weight: 1,250 lb (567 kg)
Gross weight: 1,800 lb (816 kg)
Recommended engine: 260 hp (194 kW) Textron Lycoming IO-540-D4A5
Maximum speed: 156 kts (180 mph) 290 km/h
Cruise speed: 139 kts (160 mph) 257 km/h
Stall speed: 52 kts (60 mph) 97 km/h
Take-off distance: 300 ft (92 m)
Climb rate: 3,500 ft (1,067 m) per minute
Range: 391 naut miles (450 miles) 724 km
Availability: Plans.
Comments: Designed by Lamar Steen and first flown in October 1970. Design rights purchased by Hale Wallace in 1990. Aeropac SA of Mendoza, Argentina, now building the Skybolt and Pitts S.1. Also available from Steen are plans for the Knight Twister sport biplane.

Steen Pitts S1-C Special

Type: Single-seat, open or enclosed cockpit, sport biplane, with fixed tail-dragger undercarriage.
Wing span: 17 ft 4 ins (5.28 m)
Length: 15 ft 6 ins (4.72 m)
Empty weight: 830 lb (376 kg)
Gross weight: 1,150 lb (522 kg)
Take-off distance: 300 ft (92 m)
Recommended engine: 200 hp (149 kW) Textron Lycoming AEIO-360
Maximum speed: 161 kts (185 mph) 298 km/h
Cruise speed: 152 kts (175 mph) 282 km/h
Stall speed: 56 kts (64 mph) 103 km/h
Climb rate: 2,800 ft (853 m) per minute
Range: 268 naut miles (309 miles) 497 km
Availability: Plans.
Comments: Rights to homebuilt/experimental versions of Curtis Pitts' famous 1944 design were taken over by Steen Aero Lab in December 1994. Certified versions manufactured by Aviat. Steen offers the S1-C and S1-SS (symmetrical wing but with Super Stinker aileron aerofoil technology).

Stewart S-51D Mustang

Address:
Stewart 51 Inc, 3120 Airport West Drive, Vero Beach, FL 32960.
Telephone and Facsimile: +1 407 778 0051

Type: Tandem 2-seat, low-wing monoplane representing a 70%-scale P-51 Mustang, with retractable tail-dragger undercarriage.
Construction: Metal.
Wing span: 26 ft (7.92 m)
Length: 22 ft (6.71 m)
Empty weight: 2,200 lb (998 kg)
Gross weight: 2,960 lb (1,343 kg)
Recommended engine: 400 hp (298 kW) V-8
Maximum speed: 230 kts (265 mph) 426 km/h
Cruise speed: 204 kts (235 mph) 378 km/h
Stall speed: 57 kts (65 mph) 105 km/h
Take-off distance: 1,370 ft (418 m)
Climb rate: 2,380 ft (725 m) per minute
Range: 573 naut miles (660 miles) 1,062 km
Availability: Kits.
Comments: First flown in May 1985.

Stoddard-Hamilton Glasair Super IIFT and TD

Address:
Stoddard-Hamilton Aircraft Inc, 18701 58th Avenue NE, Arlington, WA 98223.
Telephone: +1 206 435 8533
Facsimile: +1 206 435 9525
E-mail: glasair@stoddard-hamilton.com

Type: Side-by-side 2-seat, low-wing, cabin monoplane, with fixed nosewheel (FT) or fixed tailwheel (TD) undercarriage.
Construction: Composites.
Details: Principally for TD.
Wing span: 23 ft 4 ins (7.11 m)
Length: 20 ft 9 ins (6.32 m)
Empty weight: 1,200 lb (544 kg)
Gross weight: 2,100 lb (953 kg)
Recommended engine: 180 hp (134 kW) Textron Lycoming
Maximum speed: 202 kts (232 mph) 373 km/h
Cruise speed: 195 kts (224 mph) 360 km/h
Stall speed: 44 kts (50 mph) 81 km/h
Take-off distance: 350 ft (107 m)
Climb rate: 2,700 ft (823 m) per minute
Range: 1,303 naut miles (1,500 miles) 2,414 km
Availability: Kits.
Comments: Prototype first flew in 1979. Claimed as the first pre-moulded composite kitplane. Prototype in EAA Museum.

Stoddard-Hamilton Glasair Super IIRG

Type: Side-by-side 2-seat, low-wing, cabin monoplane, with retractable nosewheel undercarriage.
Construction: Composites.
Wing span: 23 ft 4 ins (7.11 m)
Length: 20 ft 9 ins (6.32 m)
Empty weight: 1,325 lb (601 kg)
Gross weight: 2,200 lb (998 kg)
Recommended engine: 180 hp (134 kW) Textron Lycoming
Maximum speed: 217 kts (250 mph) 402 km/h
Cruise speed: 204 kts (235 mph) 378 km/h
Stall speed: 47 kts (54 mph) 87 km/h
Take-off distance: 800 ft (244 m)
Climb rate: 2,700 ft (823 m) per minute
Range: 1,390 naut miles (1,600 miles) 2,575 km
Availability: Kits.
Comments: Stretched version of the Glasair II, introduced in 1993. RG = retractable gear.

↑ **Stoddard-Hamilton Glasair Super IIRG** *(Geoffrey P. Jones)*

Stoddard-Hamilton Glasair III

Type: Side-by-side 2-seat, low-wing, cabin monoplane, with retractable nosewheel undercarriage.
Construction: Composites.
Wing span: 23 ft 3 ins (7.09 m)
Length: 21 ft 4 ins (6.5 m)
Empty weight: 1,625 lb (737 kg)
Gross weight: 2,500 lb (1,134 kg)
Recommended engine: 300 hp (224 kW) Textron Lycoming (turbocharged Textron Lycoming TIO-540 optional)
Maximum speed: 252 kts (290 mph) 467 km/h
Cruise speed: 239 kts (275 mph) 443 km/h
Stall speed: 65 kts (74 mph) 119 km/h
Take-off distance: 900 ft (275 m)
Climb rate: 2,400 ft (732 m) per minute
Range: 1,113 naut miles (1,281 miles) 2,061 km
Availability: Kits.
Comments: Introduced in 1987, offering higher performance. Wingtip extensions available. Fully aerobatic.

Stoddard-Hamilton GlaStar

Type: Side-by-side 2-seat, high-wing, cabin monoplane, with fixed nosewheel or tailwheel undercarriage.
Construction: Metal and composites.
Wing span: 35 ft (10.67 m)
Fuselage: 22 ft (6.71 m)
Empty weight: 1,100 lb (499 kg)
Gross weight: 1,950 lb (885 kg)
Recommended engine: 125 hp (93.2 kW) Teledyne Continental IO-240 (options in 100-180 hp, 74.6-134 kW range)
Maximum speed: 148 kts (170 mph) 274 km/h
Cruise speed: 130 kts (150 mph) 225 km/h
Stall speed: 39 kts (45 mph) 73 km/h
Take-off distance: 230 ft (70 m)
Climb rate: 1,500 ft (457 m) per minute
Range: 651 naut miles (750 miles) 1,207 km
Availability: Kits.
Comments: First flown on 29 November 1994. 500 kits sold at time of writing. 20 per month being produced.

↑ **Stoddard-Hamilton GlaStar** *(Geoffrey P. Jones)*

Stoddard-Hamilton Turbine 250/III

Details can be found in the 1996-97 edition of *WA&SD*.

Stolp SA-300 Starduster Too

Address:
Stolp Starduster Corporation, 4301 Twining Street, Riverside, CA 95209.
Telephone: +1 800 833 9102
Facsimile: +1 909 784 0072

Type: Tandem 2-seat, open-cockpit biplane, with fixed tailwheel undercarriage.
Construction: Wood, steel tube and fabric.
Wing span: 24 ft (7.32 m)
Length: 21 ft 9 ins (6.63 m)
Empty weight: 1,139 lb (517 kg)
Gross weight: 2,000 lb (907 kg)
Recommended engine: 180 hp (134 kW) Textron Lycoming O-360
Maximum speed: 174 kts (200 mph) 322 km/h
Cruise speed: 100 kts (115 mph) 185 km/h
Stall speed: 51 kts (58 mph) 94 km/h
Take-off distance: 700 ft (214 m)
Climb rate: 1,800 ft (549 m) per minute
Range: 521 naut miles (600 miles) 965 km
Availability: Plans and kits.
Comments: Louis Stolp design, first flown in November 1957. Derived from the original SA-100 single-seat Starduster (now the **SA-101**, plans for which are still available).

Stolp SA-500 Starlet

Type: Single-seat, high-wing monoplane, with fixed tailwheel undercarriage.
Construction: Wood, steel tube and fabric.
Wing span: 25 ft (7.62 m)
Length: 17 ft (5.18 m)
Empty weight: 700 lb (318 kg)
Gross weight: 1,058 lb (480 kg)
Recommended engine: 85-125 hp (63.4-93.2 kW), typically Volkswagen 1,500cc or 108 hp (80.5 kW) Textron Lycoming
Maximum speed: 113 kts (130 mph) 209 km/h
Cruise speed: 78 kts (90 mph) 145 km/h
Stall speed: 42 kts (48 mph) 78 km/h
Take-off distance: 400 ft (122 m)
Climb rate: 1,000 ft (305 m) per minute
Range: 521 naut miles (600 miles) 965 km
Availability: Plans and kits.
Comments: Prototype first flew on 1 June 1969.

↑ **Stolp SA-500 Starlet built in UK in the early 1970s** *(Geoffrey P. Jones)*

Stolp SA-750 Acroduster Too

Type: Tandem 2-seat, enclosed or open cockpit, aerobatic biplane, with fixed tailwheel undercarriage.
Construction: Wood, steel tube and fabric.
Wing span: 21 ft 5 ins (6.53 m)
Length: 18 ft 6 ins (5.64 m)
Empty weight: 1,050 lb (476 kg)
Gross weight: 1,950 lb (885 kg)
Recommended engine: 200 hp (149 kW) Textron Lycoming IO-360
Maximum speed: 161 kts (185 mph) 298 km/h
Cruise speed: 135 kts (155 mph) 249 km/h
Stall speed: 48 kts (55 mph) 89 km/h
Take-off distance: 700 ft (214 m)
Climb rate: 2,300 ft (701 m) per minute
Availability: Plans and kits.
Comments: Developed from the **Stolp SA-700 Acroduster** single-seater first flown in 1973.

↑ **Stolp SA-750 Acroduster Too built in France** *(Geoffrey P. Jones)*

Stolp SA-900 V-Star

Type: Single-seat, open cockpit, aerobatic biplane, with fixed tailwheel undercarriage.
Construction: Wood, steel tube and fabric.
Wing span: 23 ft (7.01 m)
Length: 17 ft 1 ins (5.21 m)
Empty weight: 700 lb (318 kg)
Gross weight: 1,000 lb (454 kg)
Recommended engine: 60-150 hp (44.7-112 kW) Teledyne Continental
Maximum speed: 78 kts (90 mph) 145 km/h
Cruise speed: 65 kts (75 mph) 121 km/h
Stall speed: 31 kts (35 mph) 57 km/h
Take-off distance: 400 ft (122 m)
Climb rate: 600 ft (183 m) per minute
Range: 239 naut miles (275 miles) 442 km
Availability: Plans and kits.
Comments: Low cost, low power, aerobatic design, as a biplane version of the SA-500 Starlet.

Sunrise SNS-8 and SNS-9 Hiperlight

Address:
Sunrise Aircraft Corporation, Sheridan Airport, 21821 SW Rock Creek Road, Sheridan, OR 97378.

Telephone: +1 503 843 3616
Facsimile: +1 503 843 4361

Details: SNS-8, except under Comments.
Type: Single-seat, reverse-stagger biplane microlight, with fixed tail-dragger undercarriage.
Construction: Steel tube and fabric
Wing span: 22 ft (6.71 m)
Length: 15 ft 8 ins (4.78 m)
Empty weight: 247 lb (112 kg)
Gross weight: 500 lb (227 kg)
Recommended engine: 28 hp (20.9 kW) Rotax 277
Maximum speed: 82 kts (95 mph) 153 km/h
Cruise speed: 48 kts (55 mph) 89 km/h
Stall speed: 24 kts (27 mph) 44 km/h
Take-off distance: 150 ft (46 m), grass
Climb rate: 700 ft (213 m) per minute
Range: 173 naut miles (200 miles) 321 km
Availability: Kits.
Comments: Formerly the Sorrell Hiperlight, taken over in April 1997. Other single-seat versions are the **SNS-8 EXP** (Rotax 447) and the **SNS-2 Guppy** (Rotax 377). 2-seat version is the **SNS-9 EXP II** (Rotax 503).

↑ **Sunrise SNS-8 Hiperlight EXP**

Superdrone Henderson Little Bear

Address:
Superdrone Aviation Inc, Sky Manor Road, RD 2, Box 52, Pittstown, NJ 08867.

Telephone: +1 908 996 7916
Facsimile: +1 908 996 7964

Type: Tandem 2-seat, high-wing monoplane, with fixed tailwheel undercarriage.
Construction: Steel tube and fabric.
Wing span: 35 ft 3 ins (10.74 m)
Length: 22 ft 4 ins (6.81 m)
Empty weight: 649 lb (294 m)
Gross weight: 1,220 lb (553 kg)
Recommended engine: 65 hp (48.5 kW) Teledyne Continental
Maximum speed: 74 kts (85 mph) 137 km/h
Cruise speed: 61 kts (70 mph) 113 km/h
Stall speed: 28 kts (32 mph) 52 km/h
Take-off distance: 400 ft (122 m)
Climb rate: 800 ft (244 m) per minute
Range: 295 naut miles (340 miles) 547 km
Availability: Kits.
Comments: Piper Cub representation.

Super Stinker

Details can be found in the 1996-97 edition of *WA&SD*.

Swick T and Jungmeister Special

Address:
Swick Aircraft, Rt.1, Box 203, McKinney, TX 75070.

Telephone: +1 214 347 2596

Details: Refer to Swick T, except under Comments.
Type: Side-by-side 2-seat, high-wing, cabin monoplane, with fixed tailwheel undercarriage.
Construction: Wood and steel tube.
Wing span: 27 ft 6 ins (8.38 m)
Length: 22 ft 3 ins (6.78 m)
Empty weight: 900 lb (408 kg)
Gross weight: 1,280 lb (581 kg)
Recommended engine: 180 hp (134 kW)
Maximum speed: 122 kts (140 mph) 225 km/h
Cruise speed: 113 kts (130 mph) 209 km/h
Take-off distance: 400 ft (122 m)
Climb rate: 1,800 ft (549 m) per minute
Range: 339 naut miles (390 miles) 627 km
Availability: Plans.
Comments: Swick T is a 'beefed-up' Taylorcraft type, now also approved for homebuilder construction. Also available from Jim Swick is the 2-seat, 360 hp (268 kW) Vedeynev M-14-powered Jungmeister Special, several of which have been produced.

↑ **Swick Jungmeister Special** *(Geoffrey P. Jones)*

TEAM Air-Bike and Air-Bike Tandem

Address:
TEAM Aircraft Inc, 10790 Ivy Bluff Road, Bradyville, TN 37026.

Telephone: +1 615 765 5397
Facsimile: +1 615 765 7234
E-mail: teneng@aol.com

Details: Refer to Air Bike, except under Comments.
Type: Single-seat, high-wing microlight, with fixed tailwheel undercarriage.
Construction: Wood, steel tube and fabric.
Wing span: 26 ft (7.92 m)
Length: 16 ft (4.88 m)
Empty weight: 225 lb (102 kg)
Gross weight: 440 lb (200 kg)
Recommended engine: 22 hp (16.4 kW) Zenoah G-25
Maximum speed: 70 kts (80 mph) 129 km/h
Cruise speed: 42 kts (48 mph) 77 km/h
Stall speed: 31 kts (35 mph) 57 km/h
Take-off distance: 160 ft (49 m)
Climb rate: 550 ft (168 m) per minute
Range: 130 naut miles (150 miles) 241 km
Availability: Kits.
Comments: Basic open framed, sit-astride microlight. New 2-seat version is the Air-Bike Tandem, introduced in 1997 and featuring a Rotax 503, 31 ft 4 ins (9.55 m) wing span and 900 lb (408 kg) gross weight.

↑ **TEAM Air-Bike Tandem** *(Geoffrey P. Jones)*

TEAM Hi-MAX

Type: Single-seat, high-wing monoplane, with fixed tailwheel undercarriage.
Construction: Wood and fabric.
Wing span: 25 ft (7.62 m)
Length: 16 ft (4.88 m)
Empty weight: 323 lb (147 kg)
Gross weight: 560 lb (254 kg)
Recommended engine: 42 hp (31.3 kW) Zenoah G-50 in 1400Z Hi-MAX (Rotax 447 in 1700R Hi-MAX)
Maximum speed: 87 kts (100 mph) 161 km/h
Cruise speed: 61 kts (70 mph) 113 km/h
Stall speed: 26 kts (30 mph) 49 km/h
Take-off distance: 100 ft (31 m)
Climb rate: 1,200 ft (366 m) per minute
Range: 104 naut miles (120 miles) 193 km
Availability: Plans and kits.
Comments: Common components with the miniMAX series. Introduced in 1987. Other designs from TEAM include **1650 Eros**.

↑ **TEAM Hi-MAX** *(Geoffrey P. Jones)*

TEAM miniMAX

Type: Single-seat, mid-wing monoplane, with either open or enclosed cockpit and fixed tailwheel undercarriage.
Construction: Wood and fabric.
Wing span: 25 ft (7.62 m)
Length: 16 ft (4.88 m)
Empty weight: 300 lb (136 kg) according to version
Gross weight: 600 lb (272 kg) according to version
Recommended engine: Typical options for 7 different models of the miniMax basic design are:
1030R Max 103UL - 28 hp (20.9 kW) Rotax 277
1100R miniMax - 41.6 hp (31 kW) Rotax 447
1200Z Open Cockpit – 42 hp (31.6 kW) Zenoah G-50
1300Z Enclosed Cockpit – 42 hp (31.6 kW) Zenoah G-50
1500R Open Cockpit –42 hp (31.6 kW) Zenoah G-50
1550V V-Max – 50 hp (37.3 kW) Volkswagen 1,600cc modified auto engine
1600R Enclosed Cockpit – 41.6 hp (31 kW) Rotax 447
Maximum speed: 87 kts (100 mph) 161 km/h
Cruise speed: 65 kts (75 mph) 121 km/h
Stall speed: 23 kts (26 mph) 42 km/h
Take-off distance: 150 ft (46 m)
Climb rate: 650-1,200 ft (198-366 m) per minute
Range: 104-173 naut miles (120-200 miles) 193-322 km
Availability: Plans and kits.
Comments: Tennessee Engineering and Manufacturing (TEAM) flew Wayne Ison's miniMAX prototype in February 1985.

↑ **TEAM miniMAX built in the UK by Christopher Nice** *(Rod Kenward)*

Theiss Aviation Speedster

Address:
Theiss Aviation, PO Box 1086, Salem, OH 44460.

Telephone: +1 330 332 2031

Type: Single-seat, open-cockpit biplane, with fixed tailwheel undercarriage.
Construction: Wood and fabric.
Wing span: 17 ft 6 ins (5.33 m)
Length: 13 ft 2 ins (4.01 m)
Empty weight: 252 lb (114 kg)
Gross weight: 477 lb (216 kg)
Recommended engine: 40 hp (30 kW) Kawasaki 440A
Maximum speed: 54 kts (62 mph) 100 km/h
Cruise speed: 49 kts (56 mph) 91 km/h
Stall speed: 24 kts (28 mph) 45 km/h
Take-off distance: 150 ft (46 m)
Climb rate: 750 ft (229 m) per minute
Range: 108 naut miles (125 miles) 201 km
Availability: Kits.
Comments: Intended to represent a 1930's racer.

↑ Theiss Aviation Speedster prototype *(Geoffrey P. Jones)*

Time Warp Mk V Spitfire

Address:
Time Warp Inc, Lakeland, FL 33811.
Telephone: +1 941 647 3487

Type: Spitfire representation.

Titan Tornado Sport

Address:
Titan Aircraft, 2730 Walter Main Road, Geneva, OH 44041.
Telephone: +1 216 466 0602 **Facsimile:** +1 216 466 7550

Type: Single-seat, high-wing monoplane, with pusher engine and fixed nosewheel undercarriage.
Construction: Metal, composites and fabric.
Wing span: 20 ft (6.1 m)
Length: 18 ft 6 ins (5.64 m)
Empty weight: 325 lb (147 kg)
Gross weight: 700 lb (318 kg)
Recommended engine: 41.6 hp (31 kW) Rotax 447 (option for 28 hp, 20.9 kW Rotax 277 for microlight version)
Maximum speed: 91 kts (105 mph) 169 km/h
Cruise speed: 70 kts (80 mph) 129 km/h
Take-off distance: 200 ft (61 m)
Climb rate: 1,200 ft (366 m) per minute
Range: 217 naut miles (250 miles) 402 km
Availability: Kits.
Comments: Microlight version, the **Tornado UL 103**, also available.

Titan Tornado II Trainer

Type: Tandem 2-seat, high-wing monoplane, with fixed nosewheel undercarriage.
Construction: Metal, composites and fabric.
Wing span: 23 ft 6 ins (7.16 m)
Length: 19 ft (5.79 m)
Empty weight: 440 lb (200 kg)
Gross weight: 900 lb (408 kg)
Recommended engine: 49.6 hp (37 kW) Rotax 503 (optional Rotax 582)
Maximum speed: 104 kts (120 mph) 193 km/h
Cruise speed: 74 kts (85 mph) 137 mph
Take-off distance: 250 ft (76.5 m)
Climb rate: 1,400 ft (427 m) per minute
Range: 217 naut miles (250 miles) 402 km
Availability: Kits.
Comments: Titan Tornado II with 64.4 hp (48 kW) Rotax 582 has higher gross weight and cruise speed. Many examples of both types are flying.

Tri-R KIS and KIS TD

Address:
Tri-R Technologies Inc, 1114 E. 5th Street, Oxnard, CA 93030.
Telephone: +1 805 385 3680 **Facsimile:** +1 805 385 3682

Details: KIS, except under Comments.
Type: Side-by-side 2-seat, low-wing, cabin monoplane, with fixed nosewheel undercarriage.
Construction: Composites.
Wing span: 23 ft (7.01 m)
Length: 22 ft (6.71 m)
Empty weight: 680 lb (308 kg)
Gross weight: 1,200 lb (544 kg)
Recommended engine: 125 hp (93.2 kW) Teledyne Continental IO-240 (optional 80 hp, 59.7 kW Limbach L2000 or 100 hp, 74.6 kW CAM-100)
Maximum speed: 169 kts (195 mph) 314 km/h
Cruise speed: 139 kts (160 mph) 257 km/h
Stall speed: 48 kts (55 mph) 89 km/h
Take-off distance: 1,200 ft (366 m)
Climb rate: 1,000 ft (305 m) per minute
Range: 651 naut miles (750 miles) 1,207 km
Availability: Kits.
Comments: Designed by Rich Trickel and first flown in 1991. Keep It Simple = KIS. Tri-R KIS TD is tailwheel (TD=tail-dragger) version.

↑ Tri-R KIS built in the UK by Adrian Caple, with IO-240 engine *(Geoffrey P. Jones)*

Tri-R KIS TR-4 Cruiser

Type: 4-seat, low-wing, monoplane, with fixed nosewheel undercarriage.
Construction: Composites.
Wing span: 29 ft (8.84 m)
Length: 25 ft (7.62 m)
Empty weight: 1,200 lb (544 kg)
Gross weight: 2,400 lb (1,089 kg)
Recommended engine: 180 hp (134 kW) Textron Lycoming O-360
Maximum speed: 165 kts (190 mph) 306 km/h
Cruise speed: 152 kts (175 mph) 282 km/h
Stall speed: 44 kts (50 mph) 81 km/h
Take-off distance: 1,200 ft (366 m)
Climb rate: 1,100 ft (335 m) per minute
Range: 803 naut miles (925 miles) 1,488 km
Availability: Kits.
Comments: First flown in 1994. Kit parts manufactured by High Tech Composites.

↑ Tri-R KIS TR-4 Cruiser *(Geoffrey P. Jones)*

Turner T-40A and Super T-40

Address:
Turner Aircraft Inc, Rt 4, Box 115AB3, Grandview, TX 76050.
Telephone: +1 817 783 5350

Details: T-40A, except under Comments.
Type: Side-by-side 2-seat, low-wing monoplane, with fixed tailwheel or nosewheel undercarriage.
Construction: Wood.
Wing span: 27 ft 8 ins (8.43 m)
Length: 20 ft (6.1 m)
Empty weight: 1,050 lb (476 kg)
Gross weight: 1,600 lb (726 kg)
Recommended engine: 125 hp (93.2 kW) Textron Lycoming
Maximum speed: 148 kts (170 mph) 274 km/h
Cruise speed: 128 kts (147 mph) 237 km/h
Stall speed: 49 kts (56 mph) 90 km/h
Take-off distance: 1,250 ft (381 m)
Climb rate: 850 ft (259 m) per minute
Range: 412 naut miles (475 miles) 764 km
Availability: Plans.
Comments: Single-seat Turner T-40 first flew in April 1961. 2-seat T-40A first flew in July 1966. Also available is Super T-40 with increased wing span, higher gross weight and 150 hp (112 kW) engine.

↑ Turner T-40A built by Dean Meadows at La Mesa, CA *(Geoffrey P. Jones)*

Two Wings Mariner UL and EXP

Address:
Two Wings Aviation, 6821 167th Avenue, Forest Lake, MN 55025.
Telephone: +1 612 464 2099

Details: Mariner UL, except under Comments.
Type: Single- (optional 2-) seat, amphibious biplane, with pusher engine and retractable tail-dragger undercarriage.
Construction: Metal and fabric.
Wing span: 28 ft 6 ins (8.69 m)
Length: 18 ft 9 ins (5.72 m)
Empty weight: 304 lb (138 kg)
Gross weight: 950 lb (431 kg)
Recommended engine: 39.6 hp (29.5 kW) Rotax 447 or other type
Maximum speed: 54 kts (62 mph) 100 km/h
Cruise speed: 48 kts (55 mph) 89 km/h
Stall speed: 26 kts (30 mph) 49 km/h
Take-off distance: 150 ft (46 m)
Climb rate: 800 ft (244 m) per minute
Range: 65 naut miles (75 miles) 120 km
Availability: Kits.
Comments: Also available is the Mariner EXP with a 60 hp (44.7 kW) Subaru engine.

↑ Two Wings Mariner UL with 65 hp (48.5 kW) Rotax 583, built by Dale Fogerty of WI *(Geoffrey P. Jones)*

Two Wings Mariner Mono EXP

Type: Single- (optional 2-) seat, shoulder-wing amphibian, with pylon-mounted pusher engine and retractable tailwheel undercarriage.
Construction: Metal and fabric.
Wing span: 30 ft (9.14 m)
Length: 18 ft 9 ins (5.72 m)
Empty weight: 380 lb (172 kg)
Gross weight: 900 lb (408 kg)
Recommended engine: 60 hp (44.7 kW) Subaru (see Comments)
Maximum speed: 87 kts (100 mph) 161 km/h
Cruise speed: 74 kts (85 mph) 137 km/h
Take-off distance: 200 ft (61 m)
Climb rate: 1,000 ft (305 m) per minute
Range: 347 naut miles (400 miles) 643 km
Availability: Kits.
Comments: Also available as a microlight with a 39.6 hp (29.5 kW) Rotax 447 engine. Designed by Larry Seivert in 1984.

US Aviation Cumulus

Address:
US Aviation, 265 Echo Lane, South St Paul, MN 55075.
Telephone and Facsimile: +1 612 450 0930

Type: Single-seat, open-cockpit, microlight/motorglider, with pusher engine and fixed tail-dragger undercarriage.
Construction: Metal and fabric.
Wing span: 43 ft (13.11 m)
Length: 20 ft (6.1 m)
Empty weight: 360 lb (163 kg)

Gross weight: 640 lb (290 kg)
Recommended engine: 41.6 hp (31 kW) Rotax 447
Maximum speed: 78 kts (90 mph) 145 km/h
Cruise speed: 30-65 kts (35-75 mph) 56-121 km/h
Stall speed: 28 kts (32 mph) 52 km/h
Take-off distance: 170 ft (52 m)
Climb rate: 1,000 ft (305 m) per minute
Range: 173 naut miles (200 miles) 321 km
Availability: Kits.
Comments: Developed from the Cloud Dancer. Also available is the SuperFloater glider kit aircraft.

US Light Aircraft Hornet

Address:
US Light Aircraft Corporation, 27080 Rancho Ballena Lane, Ramona, CA 92065.
Telephone & Facsimile: +1 619 789 8607

Type: Tandem 2-seat, high-wing microlight, with pusher engine and fixed nosewheel undercarriage.
Construction: Metal and fabric.
Wing span: 27 ft 6 ins (8.38 m)
Length: 20 ft (6.1 m)
Empty weight: 475 lb (216 kg)
Gross weight: 1,000 lb (454 kg)
Recommended engine: 55 hp (41 kW) Hirth (optional 65 hp, 48.5 kW Hirth)
Maximum speed: 87 kts (100 mph) 161 km/h
Cruise speed: 70 kts (80 mph) 129 km/h
Stall speed: 39 kts (45 mph) 73 km/h, at MTOW
Take-off distance: 200 ft (61 m)
Climb rate: 800 ft (244 m) per minute
Range: 373 naut miles (430 miles) 692 km
Availability: Kits.
Comments: Introduced by Jim Millett in 1983. Pneumatic suspension, and electrically-actuated flaps.

↑ **US Light Aircraft Hornet** *(Geoffrey P. Jones)*

Van's RV-3

Address:
Van's Aircraft Inc, PO Box 160, North Plains, OR 97133.
Telephone: +1 503 647 5117
Facsimile: +1 503 647 2206

Type: Single-seat, low-wing monoplane, with fixed tail-dragger undercarriage.
Construction: Metal.
Wing span: 19 ft 11 ins (6.07 m)
Length: 19 ft (5.79 m)
Empty weight: 750 lb (340 kg)
Gross weight: 1,100 lb (499 kg)
Recommended engine: 150 hp (112 kW) Textron Lycoming O-320
Maximum speed: 182 kts (210 mph) 338 km/h
Cruise speed: 152 kts (175 mph) 282 km/h
Stall speed: 45 kts (52 mph) 84 km/h
Take-off distance: 250 ft (77 m)
Climb rate: 2,000 ft (610 m) per minute
Range: 445 naut miles (512 miles) 824 km
Availability: Plans and kits.
Comments: Designed by Richard VanGrunsven and first flown in 1972.

Van's RV-4

Type: Tandem 2-seat, low-wing monoplane, with fixed tailwheel undercarriage.
Construction: Metal.
Wing span: 23 ft (7.01 m)
Length: 20 ft 4 ins (6.2 m)
Empty weight: 905 lb (411 kg)
Gross weight: 1,500 lb (680 kg)
Recommended engine: 160 hp (119.3 kW) Textron Lycoming O-320
Maximum speed: 177 kts (204 mph) 328 km/h
Cruise speed: 167 kts (192 mph) 309 km/h
Stall speed: 47 kts (54 mph) 87 km/h
Take-off distance: 425 ft (130 m)
Climb rate: 1,650 ft (503 m) per minute
Range: 565 naut miles (650 miles) 1,046 km
Availability: Plans and kits.
Comments: 2-seat development of the Van's RV-3 and first flown on 21 August 1979. One of the world's most popular homebuilts, with over 500 flying and 1,500 under construction.

Van's RV-6 and RV-6A

Details: RV-6A, except under Comments and photograph.
Type: Side-by-side 2-seat, low-wing monoplane, with fixed nosewheel undercarriage.
Construction: Metal.
Wing span: 23 ft (7.01 m)
Length: 20 ft 2 ins (6.15 m)
Empty weight: 965 lb (438 kg)
Gross weight: 1,600 lb (726 kg)
Recommended engine: 160 hp (119.3 kW) Textron Lycoming O-320
Maximum speed: 174 kts (200 mph) 322 km/h
Cruise speed: 165 kts (190 mph) 306 km/h
Stall speed: 48 kts (55 mph) 89 km/h
Take-off distance: 525 ft (160 m)
Climb rate: 1,500 ft (457 m) per minute
Range: 673 naut miles (775 miles) 1,247 km
Availability: Plans and kits.
Comments: Prototype RV-6 2-seater with tailwheel undercarriage, derived from the RV-4, first flew in June 1986. Nosewheel undercarriage RV-6A first flew in July 1988. Candidate for certification. Built commercially in Nigeria as the **Air Beetle**.

↑ **Van's RV-6 built by Nigel Reddish in the UK** *(Ed Hicks)*

Van's RV-8

Type: Tandem 2-seat, low-wing monoplane, with fixed tailwheel undercarriage.
Construction: Metal.
Wing span: 23 ft (7.01 m)
Length: 21 ft (6.4 m)
Empty weight: 1,067 lb (484 kg)
Gross weight: 1,800 lb (816 kg)
Recommended engine: 200 hp (149 kW) Textron Lycoming IO-360
Maximum speed: 193 kts (222 mph) 357 km/h
Cruise speed: 184 kts (212 mph) 341 km/h
Stall speed: 45 kts (52 mph) 84 km/h
Take-off distance: 250 ft (77 m)
Climb rate: 1,900 ft (579 m) per minute
Range: 694 naut miles (800 miles) 1,287 km
Availability: Kits.
Comments: Introduced in 1995 as a larger fuselage version of the RV-4.

↑ **Van's RV-8** *(Geoffrey P. Jones)*

Velocity Aircraft Velocity and Velocity RG

Address:
Velocity Aircraft, 200 W. Airport Drive, Sebastian, FL 32958.
Telephone: +1 407 589 1860
Facsimile: +1 407 589 1893

Details: Velocity, except under Comments.
Type: 4-seat monoplane with canard, wing-mounted fins, pusher engine and nosewheel undercarriage (fixed main gear and retractable nose wheel).
Construction: Composites.
Wing span: 28 ft 7 ins (8.71 m)
Length: 16 ft 6 ins (5.03 m)
Empty weight: 1,250 lb (567 kg)
Gross weight: 2,250 lb (1,021 kg)
Recommended engine: 200 hp (149 kW) Textron Lycoming IO-360
Maximum speed: 200 kts (230 mph) 370 km/h
Cruise speed: 174 kts (200 mph) 322 km/h
Stall speed: 64 kts (73 mph) 118 km/h
Take-off distance: 850 ft (259 m)
Climb rate: 1,400 ft (427 m) per minute
Range: 1,042 naut miles (1,200 miles) 1,931 km
Availability: Kits.
Comments: Dan Maher design debuted in 1985. Fully-retractable undercarriage variant is the Velocity RG.

Velocity Aircraft Velocity 173, 173 RG and Elite RG

Type: 4-seat monoplane with canard, wing-mounted fins, pusher engine and fixed (173) or retractable (173 RG and Elite RG) nosewheel undercarriage.
Details: Velocity 173, except under Comments and photograph.
Construction: Composites.
Wing span: 31 ft (9.45 m)
Length: 19 ft 3 ins (5.87 m)
Empty weight: 1,300 lb (590 kg)
Gross weight: 2,400 lb (1,089 kg)
Recommended engine: 200 hp (149 kW) Textron Lycoming IO-360
Maximum speed: 171 kts (197 mph) 317 km/h
Cruise speed: 162 kts (187 mph) 301 km/h
Stall speed: 59 kts (67 mph) 108 km/h
Take-off distance: 750 ft (229 m)
Climb rate: 1,000 ft (305 m) per minute
Range: 1,129 naut miles (1,300 miles) 2,092 km
Availability: Kits.
Comments: Fully fixed undercarriage version of the Velocity, but also available in fully retractable form as the Velocity 173 RG. Also Velocity Elite RG with shorter wing span and length.

↑ **Velocity 173 RG built in the Netherlands** *(Geoffrey P. Jones)*

Viking Dragonfly

Address:
Viking Aircraft Ltd, PO Box 646, Elkhorn, WI 53121.
Telephone: +1 414 723 1048
Facsimile: +1 414 723 1049

Type: Side-by-side 2-seat monoplane, with canard and fixed tailwheel undercarriage (main wheels located in wingtip fairings).
Construction: Composites.
Wing span: 22 ft (6.71 m)
Length: 20 ft (6.1 m)
Empty weight: 610 lb (277 kg)
Gross weight: 1,150 lb (522 kg)
Recommended engine: 60 hp (44.7 kW) Volkswagen 1,835cc
Maximum speed: 156 kts (180 mph) 290 km/h
Cruise speed: 126 kts (145 mph) 233 km/h
Stall speed: 42 kts (48 mph) 78 km/h
Take-off distance: 1,200 ft (366 m)
Climb rate: 850 ft (259 m) per minute
Range: 434 naut miles (500 miles) 804 km
Availability: Plans and kits.
Comments: First flown 16 June 1980. 3 versions, the Mk I, Mk II with main undercarriage legs under the inboard section of the wings for operation on narrow taxiways and unprepared strips, and the Mk III with fixed nosewheel gear.

Viking Aircraft Cygnet

Type: Side-by-side 2-seat, shoulder-wing monoplane, with fixed tailwheel undercarriage.

Construction: Metal, wood and fabric.
Wing span: 30 ft (9.14 m)
Length: 19 ft (5.79 m)
Empty weight: 585 lb (265 kg)
Gross weight: 1,100 lb (499 kg)
Recommended engine: 60 hp (44.7 kW) Volkswagen
Maximum speed: 94 kts (108 mph) 174 km/h
Cruise speed: 87 kts (100 mph) 161 km/h
Stall speed: 42 kts (48 mph) 78 km/h
Take-off distance: 700 ft (214 m)
Climb rate: 580 ft (177 m) per minute
Range: 339 naut miles (390 miles) 627 km
Availability: Plans.
Comments: Originally the Sisler SF-2 Whistler and first flown in 1973. Name changed to Cygnet with design modifications soon after. In 1983 HAPI Engines acquired the rights, when also dealer for the Viking Dragonfly.

↑ **Viking Cygnet registered in the UK** *(Geoffrey P. Jones)*

Vintage 75 Stearman

Address:
Vintage 75 Inc, 518S West Street, Raleigh, NC 27601.
Telephone: +1 919 664 8906
E-mail: vin75@ipass.net

Type: Tandem 2-seat, three-quarters scale representation of a Boeing Stearman biplane, with fixed tailwheel undercarriage.
Construction: Metal, wood and composites.
Wing span: 24 ft 4 ins (7.42 m)
Length: 18 ft 9 ins (5.72 m)
Empty weight: 1,000 lb (454 kg)
Gross weight: 1,450 lb (658 kg)
Recommended engine: 160 hp (119 kW) Mazda 13B with reduction unit (optional 120 hp, 89.5 kW 3-cylinder radial)
Availability: Kits and complete aircraft.
Comments: Designed by Jeffrey Schroeder.

↑ **Vintage 75 Stearman representation**

Volmer VJ-22 Sportsman

Address:
Volmer Aircraft, Box 5222, Glendale, CA 91201.
Telephone: +1 818 247 8718

Type: Side-by-side 2-seat, shoulder-wing amphibian, with pylon-mounted pusher engine above the wings and retractable tailwheel undercarriage.
Construction: Wood and fabric.
Wing span: 36 ft 6 ins (11.13 m)
Length: 24 ft (7.32 m)
Empty weight: 1,000 lb (454 kg)
Gross weight: 1,500 lb (680 kg)
Take-off distance: 350 ft (107 m) land, 1,000 ft (305 m) water
Recommended engine: 90 hp (67 kW) Teledyne Continental C90
Maximum speed: 96 kts (110 mph) 177 km/h
Cruise speed: 74 kts (85 mph) 137 km/h
Stall speed: 39 kts (45 mph) 73 km/h
Climb rate: 600 ft (183 m) per minute
Range: 260 naut miles (300 miles) 482 km
Availability: Plans.
Comments: Volmer Jensen's 22nd design (previous types were mostly gliders) and first flown on 22 December 1958. Uses wings from Aeronca Champion or Chief. A single-seat open microlight from Volmer is the **VJ-24W SunFun**.

↑ **Volmer VJ-22 Sportsman prototype**

Wag-Aero Sport Trainer and Acro Trainer

Address:
Wag-Aero Group, 1216 North Road, Box 181, Lyons, WI 53148.
Telephone: +1 414 763 9586
Facsimile: +1 414 763 7595

Details: Sport Trainer, except under Comments.
Type: Tandem 2-seat, high-wing monoplane, with fixed tailwheel undercarriage.
Construction: Steel tube and fabric.
Wing span: 36 ft (10.97 m)
Length: 22 ft 4 ins (6.81 m)
Empty weight: 720 lb (327 kg)
Gross weight: 1,400 lb (635 kg)
Recommended engine: 85 hp (63.4 kW) Teledyne Continental (see Comments)
Maximum speed: 89 kts (102 mph) 164 km/h
Cruise speed: 82 kts (94 mph) 151 km/h
Stall speed: 34 kts (39 mph) 63 km/h
Take-off distance: 208 ft (64 m)
Climb rate: 490 ft (150 m) per minute
Range: 191 naut miles (220 miles) 354 km
Availability: Plans and kits.
Comments: Modern representation of the Piper Cub, also suitable for Franklin or Textron Lycoming engines. Special shortened and strengthened wing for the Acro Trainer aerobatic version.

Wag-Aero Sportsman 2 + 2

Type: 4-seat (2 + 2), high-wing, cabin monoplane, with fixed tailwheel undercarriage.
Construction: Steel tube and fabric.
Wing span: 35 ft 9 ins (10.9 m)
Length: 23 ft 4 ins (7.11 m)
Empty weight: 1,080 lb (490 kg)
Gross weight: 2,200 lb (998 kg)
Recommended engine: 150 hp (112 kW) Textron Lycoming
Maximum speed: 112 kts (129 mph) 208 km/h
Cruise speed: 108 kts (124 mph) 200 km/h
Stall speed: 33 kts (38 mph) 61 km/h
Take-off distance: 361 ft (110 m)
Climb rate: 800 ft (244 m) per minute
Range: 582 naut miles (670 miles) 1,078 km
Availability: Plans and kits.
Comments: Modern representation of the Piper PA-14 Family Cruiser. Optional hinged turtle-deck for loading long items such as a litter.

↑ **Wag-Aero Sportsman 2 + 2 with 190 hp (142 kW) Ford Javelin V6 engine, built by Mike Luckey at Rossville, TX** *(Geoffrey P. Jones)*

Wag-Aero Wag-A-Bond, Classic and Traveler

Details: Wag-A-Bond, except under Comments.
Type: Side-by-side 2-seat, high-wing, cabin monoplane, with fixed tailwheel undercarriage.
Construction: Steel tube and fabric.
Wing span: 29 ft 4 ins (8.94 m)
Length: 18 ft 9 ins (5.72 m)
Empty weight: 725 lb (329 kg)
Gross weight: 1,450 lb (658 kg)
Recommended engine: 115 hp (85.75 kW) Textron Lycoming O-235
Maximum speed: 118 kts (136 mph) 219 km/h
Cruise speed: 108 kts (124 mph) 200 km/h
Stall speed: 39 kts (45 mph) 73 km/h
Take-off distance: 415 ft (127 m)
Climb rate: 850 ft (259 m) per minute
Range: 738 naut miles (850 miles) 1,368 km
Availability: Plans and kits.
Comments: Modern representation of the Piper Vagabond. The Classic model is suitable for 65-100 hp (48.4-74.6 kW) engines and the Traveler for 108-115 hp (80.5-85.75 kW) engines.

WAR Aircraft Focke Wulf 190

Address:
WAR Aircraft Replicas of Florida, PO Box 79007, Tampa, FL 33619.
Telephone: +1 813 620 0631

Type: Single-seat, half-scale representation of a Focke Wulf Fw 190, with retractable tailwheel undercarriage.
Construction: Wood, foam and composites.
Wing span: 20 ft (6.1 m)
Length: 17 ft (5.18 m)
Empty weight: 600 lb (272 kg)
Gross weight: 900 lb (408 kg)
Recommended engine: 100 hp (74.6 kW) Teledyne Continental O-200
Maximum speed: 182 kts (210 mph) 338 km/h
Cruise speed: 117 kts (135 mph) 217 km/h
Stall speed: 48 kts (55 mph) 89 km/h
Take-off distance: 900 ft (275 m)
Climb rate: 700 ft (213 m) per minute
Range: 347 naut miles (400 miles) 643 km
Availability: Plans.
Comments: 1996 revival of Santa Paula, California-based company's designs for half-scale representations of **Fw 190**, **F.4U Corsair**, **Sea Fury** and **Thunderbolt**.

Warner Revolution and Super Sport

Address:
Warner Aerocraft Corp, 9415 Laura Court, Seminole, FL 33776-1625
Telephone and Facsimile: +1 813 595 2382

Details: Revolution I, except under Comments.
Type: Single-seat, low-wing monoplane, with fixed tailwheel undercarriage.
Construction: Wood, steel tube and fabric.
Wing span: 26 ft (7.92 m)
Length: 17 ft (5.18 m)
Empty weight: 500 lb (227 kg)
Gross weight: 750 lb (340 kg)
Recommended engine: 65 hp (48.5 kW) Teledyne Continental
Maximum speed: 100 kts (115 mph) 185 km/h
Cruise speed: 91 kts (105 mph) 169 km/h
Stall speed: 37 kts (42 mph) 68 km/h
Take-off distance: 300 ft (92 m)
Climb rate: 800 ft (244 m) per minute
Range: 260 naut miles (300 miles) 482 km
Availability: Plans and kits.
Comments: Version of the former Country Air Space-Walker. Tandem 2-seat version, the Revolution II, uses a 100 hp (74.6 kW) Textron Lycoming O-235. New aircraft for 1998 is 2-seat Super Sport, with 235 hp (175 kW) engine.

Weedhopper DeLuxe Ultralight

Address:
Weedhopper Inc, PO Box 1377, Clinton, MO 39056.
Telephone: +1 601 924 0806

Type: Single-seat, open-frame, high-wing microlight, with fixed nosewheel undercarriage.
Construction: Steel tube and fabric.
Wing span: 28 ft (8.53 m)

Length: 18 ft 3 ins (5.56 m)
Empty weight: 252 lb (144 kg)
Gross weight: 500 lb (227 kg)
Recommended engine: 39.6 hp (29.5 kW) Rotax 447
Maximum speed: 54 kts (62 mph) 100 km/h
Cruise speed: 43 kts (50 mph) 80 km/h
Stall speed: 25 kts (28 mph) 45 km/h
Take-off distance: 80 ft (25 m)
Climb rate: 900 ft (274 m) per minute
Range: 65 naut miles (75 miles) 120 km
Availability: Kits.
Comments: Developed in 1978. See also Raj Hamsa X'Air.

(RFW) White Lightning WLAC-1

Address:
Reflex Fibreglass Works, PO Box 497, Walterboro, SC 29488-0497.
Telephone and Facsimile: +1 803 549 1800

Type: 4-seat, low-wing monoplane, with retractable nosewheel undercarriage.
Construction: Composites.
Wing span: 27 ft 8 ins (8.43 m)
Length: 23 ft 4 ins (7.11 m)
Empty weight: 1,350 lb (612 kg)
Gross weight: 2,400 lb (1,089 kg)
Recommended engine: 210 hp (156.6 kW) Teledyne Continental IO-360
Maximum speed: 243 kts (280 mph) 451 km/h
Cruise speed: 215 kts (247 mph) 398 km/h
Stall speed: 79 kts (90 mph) 145 km/h *clean*
Take-off distance: 1,200 ft (366 m)
Climb rate: 1,500 ft (457 m) per minute
Range: 1,738 naut miles (2,000 miles) 3,218 km
Availability: Kits.
Comments: Designed by Howell "Nick" Jones and originally named the Jones White Lightning. Prototype first flew on 8 March 1986. 15 examples completed and flown at time of writing.

↑ **(RFW) White Lightning built by Peter Huff of Texas** *(Geoffrey P. Jones)*

Wings Unlimited Kingfisher and Super Kingfisher

Address:
Wings Unlimited, 6230 Rock Island Road, Charlotte, NC 28278.
Telephone and Facsimile: +1 704 588 9249

Details: Kingfisher, except under Comments.
Type: Side-by-side 2-seat, high-wing amphibian, with pylon-mounted engine and retractable tail-dragger undercarriage.
Construction: Mainly wood and fabric.
Wing span: 36 ft 1 ins (11 m)
Length: 23 ft 7 ins (7.19 m)
Empty weight: 1,050 lb (476 kg)
Gross weight: 1,600 lb (726 kg)
Recommended engine: 100 hp (74.5 kW) Teledyne Continental O-200A (other engines can include the 115 hp, 85.75 kW Textron Lycoming O-235)
Maximum speed: 83 kts (95 mph) 153 km/h
Cruise speed: 74 kts (85 mph) 137 km/h
Stall speed: 33 kts (38 mph) 61 km/h
Take-off distance: 1,000 ft (305 m) land, 2,000 ft (610 m) water
Climb rate: 700 ft (214 m) per minute
Range: 243 naut miles (280 miles) 450 km
Availability: Plans.

↑ **Wings Unlimited (Anderson) Kingfisher amphibian** *(Geoffrey P. Jones)*

Comments: Originally the Anderson Kingfisher and first flown on 24 April 1969. Later marketed by Richard Warner Aviation before Wings Unlimited. Super Kingfisher version has a 150 hp (112 kW) Textron Lycoming and much improved performance.

Wolf W-11 Boredom Fighter

Address:
Donald Wolf, 17 Chestnut Street, Huntington, NY 11743.
Telephone: +1 516 427 9678

Type: Single-seat biplane, with fixed tailwheel undercarriage.
Construction: Wood and fabric.
Wing span: 20 ft (6.1 m)
Length: 15 ft 9 ins (4.8 m)
Empty weight: 473 lb (215 kg)
Gross weight: 770 lb (349 kg)
Recommended engine: 65 hp (48.5 kW) Teledyne Continental A65 or others
Maximum speed: 102 kts (118 mph) 190 km/h
Cruise speed: 87 kts (100 mph) 161 km/h
Stall speed: 37 kts (42 mph) 68 km/h
Take-off distance: 250 ft (77 m)
Climb rate: 1,200 ft (366 m) per minute
Range: 382 naut miles (440 miles) 708 km
Availability: Plans.
Comments: Styled like a WWI fighter. First flown 30 August 1979.

↑ **Wolf W-11 Boredom Fighter built in Austin, TX, with 100 hp (74.6 kW) Teledyne Continental engine** *(Geoffrey P. Jones)*

Zenith Aircraft CH-601 Zodiac, CH-601 UL and Super Zodiac CH-601 HDS

Address:
Zenith Aircraft Co, Box 650, Mexico, MO 65265-0650.
Telephone: +1 573 581 9000
Facsimile: +1 573 581 0011
E-mail: zenithair@aol.com

Details: Zodiac, except where indicated and under Comments.
Type: Side-by-side 2-seat, low-wing, cabin monoplane, with fixed nosewheel or tailwheel undercarriage.
Construction: Metal.
Wing span: 27 ft (8.23 m)
Length: 19 ft (5.79 m)
Empty weight: 640 lb (290 kg), or 537 lb (244 kg) for UL
Gross weight: 1,200 lb (544 kg), or 1,047 lb (475 kg) for UL
Recommended engine: 80 hp (59.6 kW) Rotax 912 (optional 65-115 hp, 48.5-85.75 kW)
Maximum speed: 117 kts (135 mph) 217 km/h
Cruise speed: 104 kts (120 mph) 193 km/h
Stall speed: 39 kts (44 mph) 71 km/h
Take-off distance: 450 ft (137 m), or 400 ft (122 m) for UL
Climb rate: 1,200 ft (366 m) per minute
Range: 408 naut miles (470 miles) 756 km, or 312 naut miles (360 miles) 579 km for UL
Availability: Plans or kits.
Comments: Original CH-601 first flew June 1984, and CH-601 HDS flew August 1991. Previously built in Canada. Kits for European market manufactured in Czech Republic. Super Zodiac CH.601 HDS has 23 ft (7 m) wing span.

Zenith Aircraft Zodiac Gemini CH.620

Type: Side-by-side 2-seat, twin-engined, low-wing monoplane, with retractable nosewheel or tailwheel undercarriage.
Construction: Metal.
Wing span: 27 ft 3 ins (8.31 m)
Length: 19 ft 6 ins (5.94 m)
Empty weight: 770 lb (349 kg)
Gross weight: 1,450 lb (658 kg)
Recommended engines: 2 x 80 hp (59.6 kW) Jabiru 2200s
Maximum speed: 135 kts (155 mph) 249 km/h
Cruise speed: 122 kts (140 mph) 225 km/h
Stall speed: 48 kts (55 mph) 89 km/h
Take-off distance: 450 ft (137 m)
Climb rate: 1,280 ft (390 m) per minute
Range: 564 naut miles (650 miles) 1,046 km
Availability: Kits.
Comments: First flew 1996.

↑ **Zenith Aircraft Zodiac Gemini CH.620** *(Geoffrey P. Jones)*

Zenith Aircraft Zenair STOL CH.701

Type: Side-by-side 2-seat, high-wing, utility cabin monoplane, with fixed nosewheel, float or ski undercarriage.
Construction: Metal.
Wing span: 27 ft (8.23 m)
Length: 20 ft (6.1 m)
Empty weight: 460 lb (209 kg)
Gross weight: 960 lb (435 kg)
Recommended engine: 65 or 80 hp (48.5 or 59.6 kW) Rotax
Maximum speed: 74 kts (85 mph) 137 km/h
Cruise speed: 65 kts (75 mph) 121 km/h
Stall speed: 25 kts (28 mph) 45 km/h
Take-off distance: 75-115 ft (23-35 m)
Climb rate: 1,200 ft (366 m) per minute
Range: 234 naut miles (270 miles) 434 km
Availability: Kits and plans.
Comments: Prototype first flew in 1986. Over 500 flying in 40 countries. Type certificated in Israel and Mexico.

Venezuela

VSTOL Aircraft Corp Pairadigm and Super Solution 2000

Address:
US agent: VSTOL Aircraft Corporation, PO Box 7534, Fort Meyers, FL 33911.
Telephone and Facsimile: US agent: +1 941 936 1261

Details: Apply to Pairadigm, except under Comments.
Type: Tandem 2-seat, high-wing monoplane, with twin pusher engines and fixed tailwheel undercarriage.
Construction: Steel tube, composites and fabric.
Wing span: 32 ft (9.75 m)
Length: 22 ft (6.71 m)
Empty weight: 701 lb (318 kg)
Gross weight: 1,402 lb (636 kg)
Recommended engines: 2 x 50 hp (37.3 kW) Rotax
Maximum speed: 87 kts (101 mph) 162 km/h
Cruise speed: 35-70 kts (40-81 mph) 65-130 km/h
Stall speed: 20 kts (23 mph) 36 km/h
Take-off distance: 100 ft (31 m)
Climb rate: 1,200 ft (366 m) per minute
Range: 218 naut miles (251 miles) 405 km
Availability: Kits.
Comments: Developed in Venezuela from earlier XC-280. Used for crop-spraying. 15 flying. Also available is single-engined Super Solution 2000.

↑ **VSTOL Aircraft Corp Pairadigm manufactured in Venezuela** *(Geoffrey P. Jones)*

Gliders and Motorgliders

Designation (Type)	a) Crew b) Materials	a) Aerofoil b) Wing aspect ratio	a) Span ft-ins (m) b) Wing area sq ft (m^2) c) Length ft-ins (m)	Weights lb (kg): a) empty b) maximum c) ballast (max)	Wing loading lb/sq ft (kg/m^2) a) minimum b) maximum	a) Minimum rate of sink ft (m)/sec b) at speed of kts (mph) km/h	a) Best glide ratio b) at speed of kts (mph) km/h	Speeds kts (mph) km/h: a) stalling b) maximum c) cruise	a) Engine b) Fuel capacity in litres	Comments
Under the heading *Type*, the following abbreviations have been used: **G** = Glider; **MGS** = Motorglider, self-launch; **MGN** = Motorglider, no self-launch										
Australia										
Manufacturer: Moyes Microlights Pty Ltd. 2-4 Taylor Street, Waverley 2024, NSW (Telephone: +61 2 387 5114)										
Tempest (G)	a) 1 b) Tubes and fabric	a) - b) 12	a) 42-6 (12.95) b) 150 (13.92) c) 21 (6.4)	a) 220 (100) b) 440 (200) c) -	a) - b) 2.93 (14.32)	a) 2.83 (0.86) b) -	a) - b) -	a) - b) 70 (80) 129 c) -		Kits available.
Austria										
Manufacturer: Diamond Aircraft Industries GmbH., N.A. Otto-Strasse 5, A-2700 Wiener Neustadt (former HOAC) (Telephone: +43 2622 26700, Facsimile: +43 2622 26780, E-mail: sales@diamond-ac-ind.co.at)										
HK 36 Super Dimona TS (MGS)	a) 2 b) Composites	a) FX 63-137 b) 17.43	a) 53-7 (16.33) b) 164.7 (15.3) c) 21 (6.4)	a) 1,190 (540) b) 1,697 (770) c) -	a) - b) 10.3 (50.3)	a) 3.74 (1.14) b)	a) 28 b) -	a) - b) 141 (162) 261 c) 111 (127) 205	a) Front mounted 81 hp (60.4 kW) Rotax 912 A3 b) 77	Production continues. Tailwheel version. Suitable for towing gliders up to 816 lb (370 kg).
HK 36 Super Dimona TC (MGS)	a) 2 b) Composites	a) FX 63-137 b) 17.43	a) 53-7 (16.33) b) 164.7 (15.3) c) 23-11 (7.28)	a) 1,224 (555) b) 1,697 (770) c) -	a) - b) 10.3 (50.3)	a) 3.84 (1.17) b) -	a) 27 b) -	a) - b) 141 (162) 261 c) 108 (124) 200	a) Front mounted 81 hp (60.4 kW) Rotax 912 A3 b) 77	Production continues. Nosewheel version. Suitable for towing gliders up to 816 lb (370 kg).
HK 36 Super Dimona TTS (MGS)	a) 2 b) Composites	a) FX 63-137 b) 17.43	a) 53-7 (16.33) b) 164.7 (15.3) c) 23-11 (7.28)	a) 1,202 (545) b) 1,698 (770) c) -	a) - b) 10.3 (50.3)	a) 3.74 (1.14) b) -	a) 28 b) -	a) - b) 141 (162) 261 c) 121 (140) 225	a) Front mounted 115 hp (85.75 kW) Rotax 914 F3 b) 77	Production continues. Tailwheel version. Suitable for towing gliders up to 1,157 lb (525 kg).
HK 36 Super Dimona TTC (MGS)	a) 2 b) Composites	a) FX 63-137 b) 17.43	a) 53-7 (16.33) b) 164.7 (15.3) c) 23-11 (7.28)	a) 1,235 (560) b) 1,697 (770) c) -	a) - b) 10.3 (50.3)	a) 3.84 (1.17) b) -	a) 27 b) -	a) - b) 141 (162) 261 c) 108 (124) 220	a) Front mounted 115 hp (85.75 kW) Rotax 914 F3 b) 77	Production continues. Nosewheel version. Suitable for towing gliders up to 1,157 lb (525 kg).
Brazil										
Manufacturer: AEROMOT-Industria Mecanico-Metalurgica Ltda., Avenue das Industrias, 1210, PO Box 8031, Porto Alegre - RS 90200-290 (Telephone: +55 51 371 1644, Facsimile: +55 51 371 1655, E-mail: chica@aeromot.com.br)										
AMT 100 Ximango (MGS)	a) 2 b) Glassfibre	a) NACA 64.3.618 b) 16.32	a) 57-4 (17.47) b) 201.3 (18.7) c) 25-10.5 (7.89)	a) 1,323 (600) b) 1,764 (800) c) -	a) 7.39 (36.09) b) 8.76 (42.78)	a) 3.08 (0.94) b) 54 (62) 100	a) 30 b) 59 (69) 110	a) 41 (47) 76 b) 132 (152) 245 c) 103 (118) 190	a) Front mounted 80 hp (59.7 kW) Limbach L 2000 EO1 b) 90	Production continues. Based on French RF-10 design.
AMT 200 Super Ximango (MGS)	a) 2 b) Glassfibre	a) NACA 64.3.618 b) 16.32	a) 57-4 (17.47) b) 201.3 (18.7) c) 26-5 (8.05)	a) 1,334 (605) b) 1,874 (850) c) -	a) 7.39 (36.09) b) 9.31 (45.45)	a) 3.08 (0.94) b) 57 (65) 105	a) 31 b) 59 (69) 110	a) 41 (47) 76 b) 132 (152) 245 c) 111 (127) 205	a) Front mounted 80 hp (59.7 kW) Rotax 912 A2 b) 90	Production continues. Also available with Rotax 912 A3 and hydraulic constant-speed propeller.
AMT 300 Turbo Ximango (MGS)	a) 2 b) Glassfibre/ carbonfibre	a) NACA 64.3.618 mod b) 16.80	a) 58-1 (17.7) b) 62 (18.9) c) 26-5 (8.05)	a) 1,356 (615) b) 1,874 (850) c) -	a) 7.39 (36.09) b) 8.76 (42.78)	a) 3.28 (0.93) b) 54 (62) 100	a) 32.5 b) 59 (69) 110	a) 41 (47) 76 b) 132 (152) 245 c) 124 (143) 230	a) Front mounted 115 hp (85.75 kW) Rotax 914 F b) 90	Prototype first flew July 1997. Rotax 914 F version of AMT 200 with winglets and major aerodynamic refinements.
AMT 300 R Reboque (MGS)	a) 2 b) Glassfibre/ carbonfibre	a) NACA 64.3.618 mod b) 16.80	a) 58-1 (17.7) b) 62 (18.9) c) 26-5 (8.05)	a) 1,367 (620) b) 1,874 (850) c) -	a) 7.58 (37) b) 8.76 (42.78)	a) 3.28 (0.93) b) 54 (62) 100	a) 32.5 b) 59 (69) 110	a) 43 (49) 79 b) 132 (152) 245 c) 124 (143) 230	a) Front mounted 115 hp (85.75 kW) Rotax 914 F b) 90	Prototype first flew July 1997. Towplane version of AMT 300, capable of towing gliders of 1,278 lb (580 kg).
Manufacturer: IPE - Industria Projetos e Estruturas Aéronautics Ltda, CP 7931, BR-80021 Curitiba, Paraná										
IPE-02b Nhapecan II (G)	a) 2 b) Composites	a) b) 16	a) 54-5 (16.6) b) 185.1 (17.2) c) 28 (8.54)	a) 750 (340) b) 1,235 (560) c) -	a) - b) 6.67 (32.56)	a) 2.46 (0.75) b) 38 (43.5) 70	a) 32 b) 48 (55) 88	a) 37 (42.5) 68 b) 108 (124) 200 c) -		Many built, including 80th as prototype IPE-02c Nhapecan III.

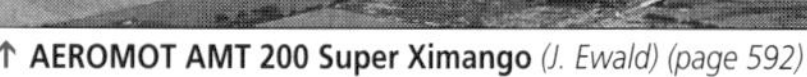
↑ **AEROMOT AMT 200 Super Ximango** *(J. Ewald) (page 592)*

↑ **Aerotechnik L-13 SL Vivat** *(J. Ewald) (page 593)*

Designation (Type)	a) Crew b) Materials	a) Aerofoil b) Wing aspect ratio	a) Span ft-ins (m) b) Wing area sq ft (m²) c) Length ft-ins (m)	Weights lb (kg): a) empty b) maximum c) ballast (max)	Wing loading lb/sq ft (kg/m²) a) minimum b) maximum	a) Minimum rate of sink ft (m)/sec b) at speed of kts (mph) km/h	a) Best glide ratio b) at speed of kts (mph) km/h	Speeds kts (mph) km/h: a) stalling b) maximum c) cruise	a) Engine b) Fuel capacity in litres	Comments
Under the heading *Type*, the following abbreviations have been used: **G** = Glider; **MGS** = Motorglider, self-launch; **MGN** = Motorglider, no self-launch										
China										
Manufacturer: Shenyang Sailplane and Lightplane Co. Ltd., Shenliao Dong 17, Tiexi District, Shenyang 110021 (Telephone: +86 24 589 4217, Facsimile: +86 24 589 4217)										
HU-1 Seagull (MGS)	a) 2 b) Aluminium alloy, wood, glassfibre and fabric	a) Eppler E-603 b) 16.35	a) 55-10 (17) b) 190.3 (17.68) c) 25 (7.62)	a) 1,323 (600) b) 2,315 (1,050) c) -	a) - b) 12.16 (59.39)	a) 4.92 (1.5) b) 43 (50) 80	a) 20 b) -	a) 46 (53) 85 b) 121 (140) 225 c) -	a) Overwing mounted 116 hp (86.5 kW) Textron Lycoming O-235-N2A b) -	Used mainly for aerial photography and survey work.
HU-2 Petrel 650B (MGS)	a) 2 or 3 b) Wood and fabric	a) Göttingen 535 b) 11.34	a) 48-11 (14.92) b) 211.3 (19.63) c) 23 (7.02)	a) 1,069 (485) b) 1,653 (750) c) -	a) - b) 7.82 (38.2)	a) - b) -	a) - b) -	a) 33 (37.5) 60 b) 73 (84) 135 c) 54 (62) 100	a) Front mounted 80 hp (59.7 kW) Limbach L 2000 EO1 b)	Many built since 1990. Resembles a conventional high-wing lightplane.
X-9 Jian Fan (G)	a) 2 b) Aluminium alloy and wood	a) Göttingen 535 b) 11	a) 47-4 (14.42) b) 203.4 (18.9) c) 24-1 (7.34)	a) 507 (230) b) 838 (380) c) -	a) - b) 4.12 (20.1)	a) 3.15 (0.96) b) 32.5 (37) 60	a) 17 b) 36 (42) 67	a) 24.5 (28) 45 b) 81 (93) 150		Training glider, of which many built.
X-10 Qian Jin (G)	a) 1 b) Wood and glassfibre	a) NACA 43012A b) 18.63	a) 52-6 (16) b) 147.9 (13.74) c) 25 (7.63)	a) 556 (252) b) 754 (342) c) -	a) - b) 5.1 (24.9)	a) 2.46 (0.75) b) 37 (42) 68	a) 26 b) 38 (43.5) 70	a) 32.5 (37.5) 60 b) 135 (155) 250		Club glider. Modified version of SZD 8/14 Jaskolka.
Czech Republic										
Manufacturer: Aerotechnik CZ sro, Podnik UV Svarzarmu, CZ -68604 Kunovice (Telephone: +420 632 53 7111, Facsimile: +420 632 53 7900)										
L-13 SEH Vivat (SDM has twin-wheel undercarriage) (MGS)	a) 2 b) Metal	a) NACA 63_2A615 and A612 b) 14	a) 55-1.5 (16.8) b) 217.4 (20.2) c) 27-3 (8.3)	a) 1,102 (500) b) 1,587 (720) c) -	a) - b) 7.29 (35.6)	a) 3.61 (1.1) b) 51 (59) 95	a) 25 b) 54 (62) 100	a) 32.5 (37.5) 60 b) 111 (127) 205 c) 92 (106) 170	a) Front mounted 75 hp (56 kW) Walter Mikron III AE b) 50	Out of production. Single-wheel semi-retractable or twin-wheel fixed undercarriages.
L-13 SL Vivat (SDL has twin-wheel undercarriage) (MGS)	a) 2 b) Metal	a) NACA 63_2A615 and A612 b) 14	a) 55-1.5 (16.8) b) 217.4 (20.2) c) 27-3 (8.3)	a) 1,102 (500) b) 1,587 (720) c) -	a) - b) 7.29 (35.6)	a) 3.61 (1.1) b) 51 (59) 95	a) 25 b) 54 (62) 100	a) 32.5 (37.5) 60 b) 111 (127) 205 c) 92 (106) 170	a) Front mounted 69.7 hp (52 kW) Limbach L 2000 EO1 b) 50	Out of production. Single-wheel semi-retractable or twin-wheel fixed undercarriages.
Manufacturer: HPH Ltd., Karlov 197, PO Box 112, CZ-28401 Kutná Hora (Telephone: +420 327 51 3441, Facsimile: +420 327 51 3441, E-mail hph@mira.cz)										
Glasflügel 304 S (G)	a) 1 b) Composites	a) HQ b) 22.78	a) 49-2.5 (15) b) 106.35 (9.88) c) 21-2 (6.45)	a) - b) - c) -	a) - b) -	a) - b) -	a) - b) -	a) - b) - c) -	a) - b) -	Standard class version of 304 CZ. New for 1999.
Glasflügel 304 CZ (G)	a) 1 b) Composites	a) HQ b) 22.78	a) 49-2.5 (15) b) 106.35 (9.88) c) 21-2 (6.45)	a) 518 (235) b) 992 (450) c) 254 (115)	a) 6.35 (31) b) 9.33 (45.55)	a) 2.26 (0.69) b) 50 (58) 93 at max wing loading	a) 43 b) 63 (72) 116 at max wing loading	a) 40 (46) 73 at max wing loading b) 135 (155) 250 c) -		Trailing-edge flaps/airbrakes. Prototype of new production version with winglets flew June 1997. 70 304s were built 1980/81 by Deutsch-Brasilianische Flug- und Fahrzeugbau GmbH in Germany, followed by 8 304bs at Jastreb, former Yugoslavia.
Manufacturer: Inteco, Velkomoravská 1469, CZ-68604 Uherské Hradisté (Telephone: +420 632 61186, Facsimile: +420 632 61186)										
L-213A (G)	a) 1 b) Metal	a) - b) 12.44	a) 41-3 (12.57) b) 136.7 (12.7) c) 24 (7.31)	a) 507 (230) b) 772 (350) c) -	a) - b) 5.76 (28.14)	a) 3.94 (1.2) b) 48 (55) 88	a) not measured b) achieved at 60 (69) 111	a) 38 (44) 70 b) 189 (217) 350 c) -		Fully aerobatic +8/-6 g. Only prototype built. Not in production.

↑ **HPH Glasflügel 304 CZ** *(J. Ewald) (page 593)*

↑ **LET L 13 AC Blanik** *(Page 594)*

Designation (Type)	a) Crew b) Materials	a) Aerofoil b) Wing aspect ratio	a) Span ft-ins (m) b) Wing area sq ft (m^2) c) Length ft-ins (m)	Weights lb (kg): a) empty b) maximum c) ballast (max)	Wing loading lb/sq ft (kg/m^2) a) minimum b) maximum	a) Minimum rate of sink ft (m)/sec b) at speed of kts (mph) km/h	a) Best glide ratio b) at speed of kts (mph) km/h	Speeds kts (mph) km/h: a) stalling b) maximum c) cruise	a) Engine b) Fuel capacity in litres	Comments
Under the heading *Type*, the following abbreviations have been used: **G** = Glider; **MGS** = Motorglider, self-launch; **MGN** = Motorglider, no self-launch										
Czech Republic										
Manufacturer: LET a.s., Kunovice 1177, CZ-68604 Kunovice (Telephone: +420 632 51 11 11, Facsimile: +420 632 61 352, E-mail: let@let.cz)										
L 13A Blaník (G)	a) 2 b) Metal	a) NACA 63$_2$A615 and A612 b) 13.7	a) 53-2 (16.2) b) 206.1 (19.5) c) 27-7 (8.4)	a) 644 (292) b) 1,102 (500) c) -	a) 4.08 (19.9) b) 5.35 (26.1)	a) 2.79 (0.85) b) 37 (42.5) 68	a) 28 b) 46 (53) 86	a) 32.5 (37.5) 60 b) 129 (149) 240 c) -		Semi aerobatic. Wings incorporate Fowler flaps. About 3,000 L-13s built between 1958 and 1981. L-13A is strengthened version for about 9,000 hour lifetime. 5 built in 1996.
L 13 AC Blaník (G)	a) 2 b) Metal	a) NACA 63$_2$A615 and A612 b) 11.4	a) 46-3 (14.1) b) 57-1.5 (17.41) c) 27-7 (8.4)	a) 675 (306) b) 1,124 (510) c) -	a) 4.71 (23) b) 32.98 (161)	a) - b) -	a) 26 b) -	a) 37 (43) 68 b) 124 (143) 230 c) -		Fully aerobatic dual trainer, with wings and front fuselage of L-23 and tail of L-13. Prototype built in 1997. Wingtips available to increase span to 53 ft 2 ins (16.2 m).
L 23 Super Blaník (G)	a) 2 b) Metal	a) NACA 63$_2$A615 and A612 b) 13.7	a) 53-2 (16.2) b) 206.1 (19.15) c) 27-11 (8.5)	a) 683 (310) b) 1,124 (510) c) 44 (20)	a) 4.5 (22) b) 28.88 (141)	a) 2.69 (0.82) b) 37 (42.5) 68	a) 28 b) 49 (56) 90	a) 32.5 (37.5) 60 b) 124 (143) 230 c) -		Semi aerobatic. In production, with 270 built since 1989.
L 23 Super Blaník (G), with wingtips fitted		b) 16.6	a) 59-8.5 (18.2) b) 215.6 (20.03) c) 27-11 (8.5)	a) 695 (315)	b) 5.22 (25.5)	a) - b) -	a) 32 b) -	a) 29 (34) 54 b) 124 (143) 230 c) -		
L 33 Sólo (G)	a) 1 b) Metal	a) - b) 18.12	a) 46-4 (14.12) b) 118.4 (11) c) 21-9 (6.62)	a) 463 (210) b) 750 (340) c) 44 (20)	a) 5.12 (25) b) 33.59 (164)	a) 2.17 (0.66) b) 37 (42.5) 68	a) 33 b) 49 (56) 90	a) 35 (41) 65 b) 183 (211) 340 c) -		In production. 70 built since 1993.
Manufacturer: Orlican Aircraft, CZ-56537 Chocen										
VSO-10 Gradient (G)	a) 1 b) Glassfibre, wood and metal	a) FX 61-163 b) 18.75	a) 49-2.5 (15) b) 129.2 (12) c) 23 (7)	a) 551 (250) b) 838 (380) c) 123.5 (56)	a) 5.47 (26.7) b) 6.49 (31.7)	a) 2.10 (0.64) b) 39 (45) 73	a) 36 b) 49 (56) 90	a) 37 (42.5) 68 b) 135 (155) 250 c) -		225 built between 1976 and 1989.
Discus CS: see Schempp-Hirth, Germany										
Manufacturer: Profe, Lestinska 811, CZ-54901 Nove Mesto nad Metuji (Telephone: +420 441 72353, Facsimile: +420 441 72353)										
Banjo (G)	a) 1 b) Composites, wood and fabric	a) SM701 - FX 60-126 b) 17	a) 43-8 (13.3) b) 113 (10.5) c) 20-8 (6.3)	a) 227 (103) b) 441 (200) c) -	a) b) 3.89 (19)	a) 2.23 (0.68) b) 35 (40) 65	a) 28 b) 43 (50) 80	a) 27 (31) 50 b) 76 (87) 140 c) -		Microlight glider. In production. MGS version planned.

↑ **LET L 23 Super Blaník** *(Pavel Lukes/LET) (page 594)*

↑ **LET L 33 Sólo** *(Page 594)*

↑ **Orlican VSO-10 Gradient** *(J. Ewald) (page 594)*

↑ **Profe Banjo** *(J. Ewald) (page 594)*

Designation (Type)	a) Crew b) Materials	a) Aerofoil b) Wing aspect ratio	a) Span ft-ins (m) b) Wing area sq ft (m^2) c) Length ft-ins (m)	Weights lb (kg): a) empty b) maximum c) ballast (max)	Wing loading lb/sq ft (kg/m^2) a) minimum b) maximum	a) Minimum rate of sink ft (m)/sec b) at speed of kts (mph) km/h	a) Best glide ratio b) at speed of kts (mph) km/h	Speeds kts (mph) km/h: a) stalling b) maximum c) cruise	a) Engine b) Fuel capacity in litres	Comments
Under the heading *Type*, the following abbreviations have been used: **G** = Glider; **MGS** = Motorglider, self-launch; **MGN** = Motorglider, no self-launch										
France										
Manufacturer: Air Est Services, 37 rue Saint-Michel, F-57155 Marly (Telephone: +33 387 503 966, Facsimile: +33 387 639 148)										
Goeland (MGS)	a) 1 b) Glassfibre, wood and fabric	a) - b) 19	a) 49-2.5 (15) b) 129.17 (12) c) 20-2 (6.15)	a) 397 (180) b) 661 (300) c) -	a) - b) 5.12 (25)	a) 2.46 (0.75) b) 38 (43) 70	a) 27 b) 40 (47) 75	a) 32 (36) 58 b) 86 (99) 160 c) 70 (81) 130	a) 24 hp (17.9 kW) König b) 25	In production. At least 7 built since 1995.
JCD 03 Pelican (G)	a) 1 b) Glassfibre	a) Autostable b) 4.3	a) 23-7.5 (7.2) b) 129.17 (12) c) 10-2 (3.1)	a) 187 (85) b) 419 (190) c) -	a) - b) 3.24 (15.8)	a) - b) -	a) - b) -	a) 22 (25) 40 b) 70 (81) 130 c) -		Microlight glider. Prototype first flew in 1987. Kits available.
JCD 03 Pelican (MGS)	a) 1 b) Glassfibre	a) 17% b) 7	a) 23-7.5 (7.2) b) 129.17 (12) c) 10-2 (3.1)	a) 187 (85) b) 419 (190) c) -	a) 1.43 (7) b) 3.28 (16)	a) - b) -	a) - b) -	a) 22 (25) 40 b) 70 (81) 130 c) 41 (47) 75	a) 12 hp (8.95 kW) Solo 210 or other engines up to 20 hp (15 kW) b) 10-25	Pelican motorglider. Prototype first flew in 1997. Possible kit.
TST-1 Alpin (G/MGN)	a) 1 b) Wood and fabric	a) FX 61-184 b) 15	a) 40-8 (12.4) b) 107.6 (10) c) 19-2 (5.85)	a) 297-320 (135-145) b) 551 (250), or 650 (295) with engine c) -	a) - b) -	a) - b) -	a) - b) -	a) 34 (39) 62 b) 97 (112) 180 c) -	Non-retractable 24 hp (18 kW) UVMV Prague-built M 115 for MG, positioned aft of the cockpit, or other engine types	Strength load factors complies with JAR 22 regulations. Available as a glider or motorglider in plans, kit and ready-to-fly forms.
TST-3 Alpin T (MGN)	a) - b) -	a) FX 61-184 b) 17.1	a) 43-11.5 (13.4) b) 113 (10.5) c) 19-2 (5.85)	a) 287-298 (130-135) b) 573 (260) c) -	a) - b) -	a) - b) -	a) - b) -	a) 35 (41) 65 b) 97 (112) 180 c) -	Retractable 24 hp (18 kW) UVMV Prague-built M 115 for MG, positioned aft of the cockpit, or other engine types	Strength load factors complies with JAR 22 regulations. Available as a glider or motorglider in plans, kit and ready-to-fly forms.
Manufacturer: S.N. Centrair, Z.I. de l'Aérodrome, B.P. 44, F-36300 Le Blanc (Telephone: +33 254 370796, Facsimile: +33 254 374864)										
Alliance 34	a) 2 b) Glassfibre	a) FX 61-184 and FX 60-126 b) 17	a) 51-10 (15.8) b) 159.3 (14.8) c) 24-7 (7.5)	a) 771 (350) b) 1,190 (540) c) -	a) 5.73 (28) b) 7.48 (36.5)	a) 2.3 (0.7) b) 41 (47) 75	a) 35 b) 51 (59) 95	a) 35 (41) 65 b) 135 (155) 250 c) -		New licenced production version of Scheibe SF 34B Delphin.
Marianne	a) 2 b) Composites	a) OAP 1 and OAP 2 b) 20	a) 60-10 (18.54) b) 184.9 (17.18) c) 29-6 (9)	a) 895 (406) b) 1,347 (611) c) -	a) 5.63 (27.5) b) 7.28 (35.56)	a) 2.07 (0.63) b) 46 (53) 85	a) 42 b) 57 (65) 105	a) 40 (46) 73 b) 140 (162) 260 c) -		Built since 1985.
101 Club	a) 1 b) Composites	a) OAP 1 and OAP 2 b) 21.43	a) 49-2.5 (15) b) 113 (10.5) c) 22-4.5 (6.82)	a) 540 (245) b) 1,003 (455) c) -	a) - b) 8.87 (43.3)	a) 2.13 (0.65) b) 39 (45) 72	a) 38 b) 50 (57) 92	a) - b) 135 (155) 250 c) -		Non-retractable monowheel. No water ballast.
Pégase A	a) 1 b) Composites	a) OAP 1 and OAP 2 b) 21.43	a) 49-2.5 (15) b) 113 (10.5) c) 22-4.5 (6.82)	a) 553 (251) b) 1,003 (455) c) -	a) - b) 8.87 (43.3)	a) 2.2 (0.67) b) 43 (50) 80	a) 40 b) 53 (61) 98	a) - b) 135 (155) 250 c) -		Hundreds built. Similar to 101 Club but with retractable wheel.
Pégase B	a) 1 b) Composites	a) OAP 1 and OAP 2 b) 21.43	a) 49-2.5 (15) b) 113 (10.5) c) 22-4.5 (6.82)	a) 564 (256) b) 1,113 (505) c) 160 litres of water	a) 6.35 (31) b) 9.85 (48.1)	a) 2.13 (0.65) b) 45 (52) 83	a) 40 b) 55 (63) 102	a) - b) 135 (155) 250 c) -		Version of Pégase A with water ballast.
Pégase D	a) 1 b) Composites	a) OAP 3 and OAP 2 b) 21.43	a) 49-2.5 (15) b) 113 (10.5) c) 22-4.5 (6.82)	a) 551 (250) b) 1,113 (505) c) 160 litres of water	a) 6.25 (30.5) b) 9.85 (48.1)	a) 1.97 (0.6) b) 47 (54) 87	a) 41 b) 58 (66) 107	a) 39 (45) 72 b) 135 (155) 250 c) -		Based on Pégase B and certified in 1986.

↑ **Air Est Services TST-1 Alpin** *(Geoffrey P. Jones) (page 595)*

↑ **S.N. Centrair Pégase B** *(Peter F. Selinger) (page 595)*

Designation (Type)	a) Crew b) Materials	a) Aerofoil b) Wing aspect ratio	a) Span ft-ins (m) b) Wing area sq ft (m^2) c) Length ft-ins (m)	Weights lb (kg): a) empty b) maximum c) ballast (max)	Wing loading lb/sq ft (kg/m^2) a) minimum b) maximum	a) Minimum rate of sink ft (m)/sec b) at speed of kts (mph) km/h	a) Best glide ratio b) at speed of kts (mph) km/h	Speeds kts (mph) km/h: a) stalling b) maximum c) cruise	a) Engine b) Fuel capacity in litres	Comments
Under the heading *Type*, the following abbreviations have been used: **G** = Glider; **MGS** = Motorglider, self-launch; **MGN** = Motorglider, no self-launch										
Germany										
Manufacturer: Air Energy Entwicklungsgesellschaft mbH & Co KG, Zullamtstrasse 10, D-52064 Aachen (Telephone: +49 241 408681, Facsimile: +49 241 406785)										
Silent AE-1 (MGS)	a) 1 b) Glassfibre	a) - b) 13.98	a) 39-4.5 (12) b) 110.87 (10.3) c) 21 (6.4)	a) 441 (200) b) 661 (300) c) -	a) - b) 5.96 (29.1)	a) 2.46 (0.75) b) 39 (45) 72	a) 31 b) 51 (59) 95	a) 35 (41) 65 b) 97 (112) 180 c) climb only	a) 13 kW electric DC motor drives mid-fuselage folding retractable propeller. b) Ni-cd battery pack for 1 launch to 1,970 ft (600 m)	Electric version of Italian Silent. Flaperons. Prototype first flew on 20 August 1997. Certified May 1998.
Manufacturer: Akademische Fliegergruppe Berlin e.V., Strasse des 17. Juni 135, D-10623 Berlin (Telephone: +49 30 314 24995, Facsimile: +49 30 314 24995, E-mail: akaflieg@tu-berlin.de)										
B 12 (G)	a) 2 b) Glassfibre, carbonfibre and aramid	a) FX 67-K-170 and FX 67-K-150 b) 20	a) 59-1 (18) b) 178.47 (16.58) c) 29-1 (8.86)	a) 967 (438.5) b) 1,367 (620) c) -	a) 6.62 (32.3) b) 7.66 (37.4)	a) 2.23 (0.68) b) 49 (56) 90	a) 40.5 b) 59 (68) 110	a) 39 (45) 72 b) 135 (155) 250 c) -		1 built in 1977. Modified to T-tail in 1987. Janus wings.
B 13 (MGN)	a) 2 b) Glassfibre, carbonfibre and aramid	a) HQ41/14.35 b) 28.5	a) 76-1.5 (23.2) b) 204 (18.95) c) 28-1 (8.55)	a) 1,301 (590) b) 1,764 (800) c) -	a) 7.46 (36.4) b) 8.64 (42.2)	a) 1.9 (0.58) b) 51 (59) 95	a) 46 b) 53 (61) 98	a) 38 (44) 70 b) 135 (155) 250 c) -	a) Mid-fuselage 32 hp (23.9 kW) Rotax 377, with 5-blade Oehler retractable and folding front propeller b) 25	1 built in 1991. Wings modified from Stemme S-10.
Manufacturer: Akademische Fliegergruppe Braunschweig e.V., Flughafen, D-38108 Braunschweig (Telephone: +49 531 2952149 or +49 531 350312, Facsimile: +49 531 355173)										
SB-10 (G)	a) 2 b) Glassfibre, carbonfibre and metal	a) FX 62-K-153, FX 62-K-131 and FX 60-126 b) 36.6	a) 95-2 (29) b) 247 (22.95) c) 34 (10.36)	a) 1,407 (638) b) 1,854 (841) c) 220 (100)	a) 6.55 (32) b) 7.38 (37)	a)1.35 (0.41) b) 40 (47) 75	a) 53 b) 49 (56) 90	a) 35 (41) 65 b) 108 (124) 200 c) -		1 built in 1972. First use of carbonfibre. Still the largest glider flying.
SB-10 (G), without wingtips		a) - b) 31	a) 85-4 (26) b) 234.8 (21.81) c) -	a) 1,400 (635) b) 1,958 (888)	a) 6.76 (33) b) 8.4 (41)	a) 1.41 (0.43)	a) 51	a) 38 (43) 70 b) - c) -		
SB-11 (G)	a) 1 b) Glassfibre and carbonfibre	a) FX 62-K-144/21vg1,25 b) 21.3	a) 49-2.5 (15) b) 113.7 (10.56) c) 24-3.5 (7.4)	a) 650 (295) b) 1,036 (470) c) 231 (105)	a) 7.07 (34.5) b) 9.11 (44.5)	a) 2.3 (0.7) b) 46 (53) 85	a) 41 b) 56 (65) 104	a) 41 (47) 75 or 31.5 (36) 58 with flaps extended b) 143 (165) 265 c) -		1 built in 1978, featuring variable wing geometry (142 sq ft, 13.2 m^2 with flaps extended, providing wing aspect ratio of 17 and best glide ratio of 36.6).
SB-12 (G)	a) 1 b) Glassfibre	a) HQ14/18.43 and HQ15/18.72 b) 22.5	a) 49-2.5 (15) b) 107.9 (10.02) c) 21 (6.4)	a) 525 (238) b) 992 (450) c) 331 (150)	a) 6.35 (31) b) 9.22 (45)	a) 1.97 (0.6) b) 43 (50) 80	a) 41 b) 53 (61) 98	a) 38 (44) 70 b) 135 (155) 250 c) -		1 built in 1980, based on Glasflügel 206 Hornet.
SB-13 (G)	a) 1 b) Glassfibre, carbonfibre and aramid	a) HQ34N/14.83 and HQ36N/15.2 b) 19.4	a) 49-2.5 (15) b) 124.9 (11.6) c) 9-11 (3.02)	a) 580 (263) b) 1,120 (508) c) 298 (135)	a) 5.9 (28.8) b) 7.68 (37.5)	a) 1.9 (0.58) b) 43 (50) 80	a) 41 b) 56 (64) 103	a) 39 (45) 72 b) 108 (124) 200		Flying wing with 15° sweepback and winglets. 3-parachute glider rescue system. 1 built in 1988.
SB-14 (G)	a) 1 b) Glassfibre, carbonfibre and aramid	a) Akaflieg design b) -	a) 59-1 (18) b) - c) 22-10 (6.95)	a) - b) - c) -	a) - b) -	a) - b) -	a) - b) -	a) - b) - c) -		New 18 m glider with flaps. Under construction.
Manufacturer: Akademische Fliegergruppe Darmstadt e.V., Magdalenenstrasse 8, D-64289 Darmstadt (Telephone: +49 6151 24720 and +49 6151 164090, Facsimile: +49 6151 355173)										
D-39b (MGS)	a) 1 b) Glassfibre and wood	a) - b) 22.85	a) 57-5 (17.5) b) 144.24 (13.4) c) 23-2.5 (7.07)	a) 966 (438) b) 1,259 (571) c) -	a) - b) 8.74 (42.7)	a) 2.33 (0.71) b) 47 (55) 88	a) 36 b) 54 (62) 100	a) 40 (46) 74 b) 135 (155) 250 c) 108 (124) 200	a) Front-mounted 68 hp (50.7 kW) Limbach 1700 EI b) 32	1 built in 1979 with 15 m span, later extended to version b.
D-39 HKW (MGS)	a) 1 b) Glassfibre and wood	a) FX 67-K-170 b) 20.28	a) 59-1 (18) b) 172 (15.98) c) 25-11 (7.9)	a) 1,140 (517) b) 1,400 (635) c) -	a) - b) 8.13 (39.7) c) about 2.79 (0.85)	a) about 2.79 (0.85) b) 59 (68) 110	a) about 32 b) 67 (78) 125	a) 40 (46) 73 b) 135 (155) 250 c) 103 (118) 190	a) Front-mounted 80 hp (59.7 kW) Limbach L 2000 EB1B b) 45	18 m version of D-39b with flaps. 1 built by Akaflieg member (H.K. Weinerth). First flight 10 August 1995.

↑ **Air Energy Silent AE-1** *(J. Ewald) (page 596)*

↑ **Akademische Fliegergruppe Berlin B 13** *(J. Ewald) (page 596)*

Designation (Type)	a) Crew b) Materials	a) Aerofoil b) Wing aspect ratio	a) Span ft-ins (m) b) Wing area sq ft (m^2) c) Length ft-ins (m)	Weights lb (kg): a) empty b) maximum c) ballast (max)	Wing loading lb/sq ft (kg/m^2) a) minimum b) maximum	a) Minimum rate of sink ft (m)/sec b) at speed of kts (mph) km/h	a) Best glide ratio b) at speed of kts (mph) km/h	Speeds kts (mph) km/h: a) stalling b) maximum c) cruise	a) Engine b) Fuel capacity in litres	Comments
Under the heading *Type*, the following abbreviations have been used: **G** = Glider; **MGS** = Motorglider, self-launch; **MGN** = Motorglider, no self-launch										
Germany										
Manufacturer: Akademische Fliegergruppe Darmstadt e.V (continued)										
D-40 (G)	a) 1 b) Glassfibre and carbonfibre	a) - b) 23.7 or 19.5 with flaps extended	a) 49-2.5 (15) b) 102.25 (9.5) or 123.8 (11.5) with flaps extended c) 22-2 (6.75)	a) 668 (303) b) 1,102 (500) c) 220 (100)	a) 6.55 (32) b) 10.86 (53)	a) - b) -	a) - b) -	a) - b) 146 (168) 270 c) -	a) - b) -	'Folding knife' wing with Fowler flaps. 1 built in 1986.
D-41 (G)	a) 2 b) Carbonfibre and aramid	a) LS-6, modified at extended root b) 28.6	a) 65-7.5 (20) b) 150.5 (13.98) c) 28-2.5 (8.6)	a) 888 (403) b) 1,433 (650) c) 265 (120)	a) 6.92 (33.8) b) 9.52 (46.5)	a) 1.07 (0.6) b) 46 (53) 85	a) 44 b) 57 (65) 105	a) 41 (47) 75 b) 146 (168) 270 c) -	a) - b) -	Side-by-side 2-seater, with flaps. 1 built in 1993.
D-43 (G)	a) 2 b) Carbonfibre and aramid	a) - b) -	a) - b) -	a) - b) - c) -	a) - b) -	a) - b) -	a) - b) -	a) - b) - c) -	a) - b) -	Trainer without flaps, based on D-41 fuselage design. Under construction.
Manufacturer: Akademische Fliegergruppe an der Universität Hannover e.V., Welfengarten 1, D-30167 Hannover (Telephone: +49 511 73032 or 511 762 6422, Facsimile: +49 511 762 3456, E-mail: AFH@stud.uni-hannover.de)										
AFH 22 (G)	a) 2 b) Glassfibre	a) Eppler 603 b) 17.1	a) 57-5 (17.5) b) 190.5 (17.7) c) 28-9.5 (8.77)	a) 829 (376) b) 1,270 (576) c) -	a) 5.28 (25.8) b) 6.62 (32.3)	a) 2.23 (0.68) b) 52 (60) 96	a) 37 b) -	a) 41 (47) 75 b) 108 (124) 200 c) -		Wings of Twin-Astir prototype. 1 built in 1982.
AFH 24 (G)	a) 1 b) Glassfibre and carbonfibre	a) - b) 21.91	a) 49-2.5 (15) b) 110.9 (10.3) c) 22-11.5 (7)	a) 582 (264) b) 1,058 (480) c) 265 (120)	a) 7.17 (35) b) 9.54 (46.6)	a) - b) -	a) 41 b) -	a) 39 (45) 72 b) 146 (168) 270 c) -		Nosecone & canopy slide forward. 1 built in 1991.
AFH 26 (G)	a) 1 b) Glassfibre, carbonfibre and aramid	a) With flaps b) 27.98	a) 59-1 (18) b) 124.6 (11.58) c) 23-9.5 (7.25)	a) 556 (252) b) 1,213 (550) c) 397 (180)	a) 6.14 (30) b) 9.73 (47.5)	a) - b) -	a) about 50 b) -	a) 42 (48) 77 b) 170 (196) 315 c) -		Prototype under construction.
Manufacturer: Akademische Fliegergruppe Karlsruhe e.V., Kaiserstrasse 12, D-76128 Karlsruhe (Telephone:+49 721 608 2044)										
AK 1 (MGS)	a) 1 b) Steel tube, aluminium and wood	a) FX 61-163 b) 15.7	a) 49-2.5 (15) b) 154.6 (14.36) c) 23-7.5 (7.25)	a) 551 (250) b) 838 (380) c) -	a) 4.71 (23) b) 5.43 (26.5)	a) 2.23 (0.68) b) 38 (43) 70	a) 30 b) 43 (50) 80	a) 30 (34) 55 b) 97 (112) 180 c) -	a) Mid-fuselage, retractable, 28 hp (20.9 kW) Hirth F10A b) 25	1 built in 1971.
AK 5	a) 1 b) Glassfibre	a) HQ21 b) 21.7	a) 49-2.5 (15) b) 110.7 (10.3) c) 22-4 (6.8)	a) 613 (278) b) 1,069 (485) c) 353 (160)	a) 6.76 (33) b) 9.32 (45.5)	a) 2.10 (0.64) b) 46 (53) 85	a) 39.5 b) 57 (65) 105	a) 37 (43) 68 b) 146 (168) 270 c) -		1 built in 1990.
AK 5b	a) 1 b) Glassfibre and carbonfibre	a) HQ21 b) 21.7	a) 49-2.5 (15) b) 110.7 (10.3) c) 22-4 (6.8)	a) 593 (269) b) 1,069 (485) c) 353 (160)	a) 6.55 (32) b) 9.32 (45.5)	a) - b) -	a) - b) -	a) - b) - c) -		1 built in 1996. Optimized version of the AK 5.
Manufacturer: Akademische Fliegergruppe München e.V., Arcisstrasse 21, D-80333 München (Telephone: +49 89 286111, Facsimile: +49 89 286111)										
Mü 27 (G)	a) 2 b) Glassfibre, carbonfibre, aluminium, wood and steel	a) FX 67-VC 170/136 b) 27.5 or 20.2 with flaps extended	a) 72-2 (22) b) 189.44 (17.6) or 257.25 (23.9) with flaps extended c) 33-9.5 (10.3)	a) 1,570 (712) b) 1,984 (900) c) -	a) 7.72 (37.7) with flaps extended b) 10.47 (51.1)	a) 2.49 (0.76)* b) 57 (65) 105*	a) 42* b) 62 (71) 115*	a) 53 (61) 98 or 37 (42) 68 with flaps extended b) 124 (143) 230 or 76 (87) 140 with flaps extended c) -		1 built in 1979. 38% flaps. Heaviest glider flying. *Minimum sink rate 2.26 ft (0.69 m) at 46 kts and best glide ratio 36 at 52 kts, both with flaps extended.
Mü 28 (G)	a) 1 b) Glassfibre	a) FX 71-L-150/20 b) 10.9	a) 39-4.5 (12) b) 142.1 (13.2) c) 22-2 (6.75)	a) 694 (315) b) 937 (425) c) -	a) 5.82 (28.4) b) 6.60 (32.2)	a) 3.28 (1.0) b) 48 (55) 89	a) 27 b) 56 (64) 103	a) 36 (42) 67 b) 205 (236) 380 c) -		Fully aerobatic, with automatic flap setting; ± 10g. 1 built in 1983.

↑ **Akademische Fliegergruppe Darmstadt D-39 HKW** *(J. Ewald) (page 596)*

↑ **Akademische Fliegergruppe Karlsruhe AK 5b** *(J. Ewald) (page 597)*

Designation (Type)	a) Crew b) Materials	a) Aerofoil b) Wing aspect ratio	a) Span ft-ins (m) b) Wing area sq ft (m^2) c) Length ft-ins (m)	Weights lb (kg): a) empty b) maximum c) ballast (max)	Wing loading lb/sq ft (kg/m^2) a) minimum b) maximum	a) Minimum rate of sink ft (m)/sec b) at speed of kts (mph) km/h	a) Best glide ratio b) at speed of kts (mph) km/h	Speeds kts (mph) km/h: a) stalling b) maximum c) cruise	a) Engine b) Fuel capacity in litres	Comments
Under the heading *Type*, the following abbreviations have been used: **G** = Glider; **MGS** = Motorglider, self-launch; **MGN** = Motorglider, no self-launch										
Germany										
Manufacturer: Akademische Fliegergruppe Stuttgart e.V. Pfaffenwaldring 35, D-70569 Stuttgart (Telephone: +49 711 685 2443, Facsimile: +49 711 685 2496, E-mail: akaflieg@akaflieg.lhr.ike.uni-stuttgart.de)										
fs-29 (G)	a) 1 b) Glassfibre, carbonfibre and aluminium alloy	a) FX 73-170 and FX 73-K-170/22 b) 20.67 or 28.54 with wings extended	a) 42-8 (13) or 62-4 (19) with wings extended b) 92.1 (8.56) or 135.2 (12.56) with wings extended c) 23-6 (7.16)	a) 787 (357) b) 992 (450) c) -	a) 7.29 (35.6) with wings extended b) 10.77 (52.6)	a) - b) -	a) - b) -	a) 38 (44) 70 with wings extended b) 135 (155) 250 or 81 (93) 150 with wings extended c) -		Extendable wings. 1 built in 1975.
fs-31 (G)	a) 2 b) Glassfibre, carbonfibre and aramid	a) E 603 b) 17.24	a) 57-5 (17.5) b) 191.2 (17.76) c) 28-11.5 (8.82)	a) 772 (350) b) 1,235 (560) c) 220 (100)	a) 5.06 (24.7) b) 6.45 (32.1)	a) 2.1 (0.64) b) 46 (53) 85	a) 38 b) 54 (62) 100	a) 37 (43) 68 b) 135 (155) 250 c) -		1 built in 1981. Wings of Twin Astir prototype. Fuselage design later used for ASH-25.
fs-32 (G)	a) 1 b) Glassfibre and carbonfibre	a) FX 81-K-144/20 b) 22.64	a) 49-2.5 (15) b) 107 (9.94) c) 21-9 (6.62)	a) 628 (285) b) 1,102 (500) c) 265 (120)	a) 7.27 (35.5) b) 10.3 (50.3)	a) 1.97 (0.6) b) 46 (53) 85	a) 43 b) 57 (65) 105	a) 33 (38) 60 b) 135 (155) 250 c) -		1 built in 1992. Has Fowler flaps.
fs-33 Gavilán (G)	a) 2 b) Carbonfibre, glassfibre and aramid	a) AH 81 K144/17 b) 27.8	a) 65-7.5 (20) b) 155 (14.4) c) 32-9 (9.98)	a) 772 (350) b) 1,411 (640) c) 417 (189)	a) 6.06 (29.6) b) 9.09 (44.4)	a) 1.77 (0.54) b) 46 (53) 85	a) 48 b) 57 (65) 105	a) 41 (47) 75 b) 151 (174) 280 c) -		Fuselage based on fs 31 design. First flew June 1998.
Manufacturer: Christiani Wassertechnik GmbH, Heinrich-Heine-Strasse 15, D-52249 Eschweiler (Telephone: +49 2403 53047, Facsimile: +49 2403 51468)										
Project A 'Aachen' (MGS)	a) 1 b) Wood, steel tube and glassfibre	a) U. Schäfer/ R. Horten b) 10.8	a) 43-1 (13.13) b) 171.9 (15.97) c) 12-9 (3.898)	a) 430 (195) b) 661 (300) c) -	a) - b) 3.92 (19.14)	a) 3.94 (1.2) b) 37 (42) 68	a) 20 b) 38 (43) 70	a) 30 (34) 55 b) 86 (99) 160 c) 65 (75) 120	a) 36 hp (26.8 kW) Hirth 530 cc b) 25	Light flying-wing motorglider, with 27.75° sweepback. BRS rescue system. 1 built in 1995. Production anticipated.
Manufacturer: DG Flugzeugbau GmbH, Im Schollengarten 20, D-76646 Bruchsal-Untergrombach (former Glaser-Dirks Flugzeugbau) (Telephone: +49 7257 8910, Facsimile: +49 7257 8922)										
DG-303 Elan (Acro) (G)	a) 1 b) Glassfibre	a) HQ21 mod b) 21.91	a) 49-2.5 (15) b) 110.5 (10.27) c) 22-4 (6.8)	a) 540 (245) b) 1,157 (525) c) 419 (190)	a) 6.19 (30.2) b) 10.47 (51.1)	a) 1.94 (0.59) b) 42 (48.5) 78	a) 42 b) 66 (76) 122	a) 35 (40.5) 65 b) 146 (168) 270 c) -		Production version of DG-300 with winglets. Produced at Elan, Slovenia. Total of 473 built since 1983. Acro versions are fully aerobatic +7/-5g; Club versions have fixed undercarriage and no ballast.
DG 400 (MGS)	a) 1 b) Glassfibre	a) FX 67-K-170/17 b) 27.24	a) 55-9 (17) b) 113.8 (10.57) c) 22-11.5 (7)	a) 683 (310) b) 1,014 (460) c) 198 (90)	a) 7.46 (36.4) b) 8.91 (43.5)	a) 1.77 (0.54) b) 43 (50) 80	a) 45 b) 59 (68) 110	a) 34 (39.5) 63 b) 146 (168) 270 c) about 70 (81) 130	a) Mid-fuselage, retractable Rotax 505 b) 20	290 built from 1981 to 1992.
DG-400 (MGS), without wingtips		b) 22.5	a) 49-2.5 (15) b) 107.6 (10.0) c) 22-11.5 (7)	a) 675 (306) b) 1,058 (480) c) 198 (90)	a) - b) 9.83 (48)	a) 1.97 (0.6) b) -	a) 42 b) -	a) 35 (41) 65 b) - c) -	a) Mid-fuselage, retractable Rotax 505 b) 20	
DG-505 Elan Orion (G), 20 m wingtips	a) 2 b) Glassfibre and carbonfibre	a) FX 73 K-170/17 b) 22.7	a) 65-8 (20) b) 189.4 (17.6) c) 28-5 (8.66)	a) 904 (410) b) 1,653 (750) c) 353 (160)	a) 5.76 (28.1) b) 8.73 (42.6)	a) 1.8 (0.55) b) 43 (50) 80	a) about 44 b) 59 (68) 110	a) 37 (42.5) 68 b) 146 (168) 270 c) -		Production version of DG-500, produced at Elan, Slovenia. Total of 58 built.
DG-505 Elan Orion (G), 18 m wingtips (Trainer)	a) 2 b) Glassfibre and carbonfibre	b) 19.5	a) 59-1 (18) b) 178.7 (16.6) c) 28-5 (8.66)	a) 882 (400) b) 1,653 (750) c) 353 (160)	a) 5.98 (29.2) b) 9.26 (45.2)	a) 2.13 (0.65) b) 45 (52) 83	a) about 40 b) 62 (71) 114	a) 38 (43) 69 b) 146 (168) 270 c) -		Trainer version with 18 m wings, fixed undercarriage and no ballast.

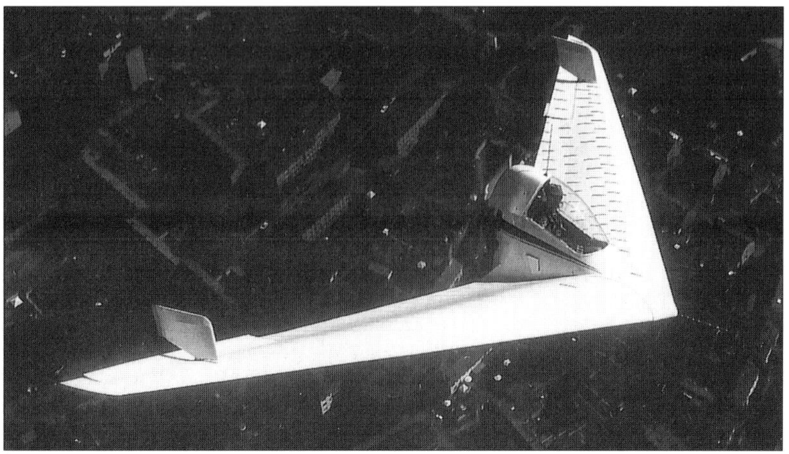

↑ **Christiani Wassertechnik Aachen** *(J. Ewald) (page 598)*

↑ **DG Flugzeugbau DG-400** *(PJ Photo Library) (page 598)*

Designation (Type)	a) Crew b) Materials	a) Aerofoil b) Wing aspect ratio	a) Span ft-ins (m) b) Wing area sq ft (m^2) c) Length ft-ins (m)	Weights lb (kg): a) empty b) maximum c) ballast (max)	Wing loading lb/sq ft (kg/m^2) a) minimum b) maximum	a) Minimum rate of sink ft (m)/sec b) at speed of kts (mph) km/h	a) Best glide ratio b) at speed of kts (mph) km/h	Speeds kts (mph) km/h: a) stalling b) maximum c) cruise	a) Engine b) Fuel capacity in litres	Comments
Under the heading *Type*, the following abbreviations have been used: **G** = Glider; **MGS** = Motorglider, self-launch; **MGN** = Motorglider, no self-launch										
Germany										
Manufacturer: DG Flugzeugbau GmbH (continued)										
DG-505 Elan Orion (G), 17.2 m wings	a) 2 b) Glassfibre and carbonfibre	a) - b) 18.3	a) 56-5 (17.2) b) 174.4 (16.2) c) 28-5 (8.66)	a) 882 (400) b) 1,378 (625) c) 353 (160)	a) 6.12 (29.9) b) 7.91 (38.6)	a) - b) -	a) - b) -	a) 38 (44) 70 b) 146 (168) 270 c) -		Fully aerobatic configuration +7/-5g.
DG-505/20 Elan Winglets (G)	a) 2 b) Glassfibre and carbonfibre	a) FX 73-K-170/17 b) 22.7	a) 65-7.5 (20) b) 189.2 (17.58) c) 28-5 (8.66)	a) 970 (440) b) 1,653 (750) c) 353 (160)	a) 6.14 (30) b) 8.75 (42.7)	a) 1.74 (0.53) b) 43 (50) 80	a) 44 b) 59 (68) 110	a) 31 (36) 57 b) 146 (168) 270 c) -		Production version of DG-500 produced at Elan. 9 built in 20 m form since 1994.
DG-505/22 Elan (G)	a) 2 b) Glassfibre and carbonfibre	b) 26.5	a) 72-2 (22) b) 196.9 (18.29) c) 28-5 (8.66)	a) 981 (445) b) 1,653 (750) c) 353 (160)	a) 5.94 (29) b) 8.4 (41)	a) 1.67 (0.51) b) 43 (50) 80	a) 47 b) 59 (68) 110	a) 32 (36) 58 b) 146 (168) 270 c) -		Another production version of DG-500 produced at Elan. 17 built in 22 m form since 1989.
DG-505 MB/20 (MGS)	a) 2 b) Glassfibre and carbonfibre	a) FX 73-K-170/17 b) 22.7	a) 65-7.5 (20) b) 189.2 (17.58) c) 28-5 (8.66)	a) 1,179 (535) b) 1,819 (825) c) 220 (100)	a) 6.14 (30) b) 8.75 (42.7)	a) 1.74 (0.53) b) 43 (50) 80	a) 44 b) 59 (68) 110	a) 31 (36) 57 b) 145 (168) 270 c) 81 (93) 150	a) Mid-fuselage 65 hp (48.5 kW) Solo 2625 with retractable propeller b) 78	Production version of DG-500 M (which was equipped with 60 hp, 44.7 kW Rotax 535) produced at Elan. Prototype flew in 1992.
DG-505 MB/22 (MGS)	a) 2 b) Glassfibre and carbonfibre	a) FX 73-K-170/17 b) 26.5	a) 72-2 (22) b) 196.9 (18.29) c) 28-5 (8.66)	a) 1,190 (540) b) 1,819 (825) c) 220 (100)	a) 6.86 (33.5) b) 9.24 (45.1)	a) 1.67 (0.51) b) 43 (50) 80	a) 47 b) 59 (68) 110	a) 37 (42.5) 68 b) 146 (168) 270 c) 81 (93) 150	a) Mid-fuselage 65 hp (48.5 kW) Solo 2625 with retractable propeller b) 78	Another production version of DG-500 M. 62 built in 22 m form since 1987.
DG-600 (G)	a) 1 b) Carbonfibre and aramid	a) HQ35 mod and HQ37 b) 20.55	a) 49-2.5 (15) b) 117.9 (10.95) c) 22-5 (6.83)	a) 567 (257) b) 1,157 (525) c) 419 (190)	a) 6 (29.3) b) 9.81 (47.9)	a) 1.84 (0.56) b) -	a) 45 b) -	a) 35 (40) 64 b) 146 (168) 270 c) -		60 of all DG-600 versions built between 1987 and 1993.
DG-600 (G), with 17 m wingtips	a) 1 b) Carbonfibre and aramid	a) HQ35 mod and HQ37 b) 24.94	a) 55-9 (17) b) 124.75 (11.59) c) 22-5 (6.83)	a) 573 (260)	b) 9.28 (45.3)	a) 1.64 (0.5) b) -	a) 49 b) -	a) 33.5 (38.5) 62 b) - c) -		Special winglet wingtips offered by DG and others.
DG-600 (G), with 18 m wingtips	a) 1 b) Carbonfibre and aramid	a) HQ35 mod and HQ37 b) 27.24	a) 59-1 (18) b) 127.1 (11.81)	a) 578 (262) b) 1,058 (480) c) 419 (190)	a) 5.94 (29) b) 8.32 (40.6)	a) 1.61 (0.49) b) -	a) 50 b) 59 (68) 110	a) 33.5 (38.5) 62 b) - c) -		Special winglet wingtips offered by DG and others.
DG-600 M (MGS)	a) 1 b) Carbonfibre and aramid	a) HQ35 mod and HQ37 b) 20.55	a) 49-2.5 (15) b) 117.9 (10.95) c) 22-5 (6.83)	a) 672 (305) b) 1,157 (525) c) 265 (120)	a) 7.21 (35.2) b) 9.81 (47.9)	a) 1.97 (0.6) b) 48 (55) 88	a) 45 b) 65 (75) 120	a) 38.5 (44.5) 71 b) 146 (168) 270 c) 65 (75) 120	a) Mid-fuselage, retractable 24 hp (18 kW) Rotax 275 b) 22	See DG-600 above.
DG-600 M (MGS), with 17 m wingtips	a) 1 b) Carbonfibre and aramid	a) HQ35 mod and HQ37 b) 24.94	a) 55-9 (17) b) 124.75 (11.59) c) 22-5 (6.83)	a) 683 (310) b) - c) -	a) 6.88 (33.6) b) 9.28 (45.3)	a) 1.74 (0.53) b) 45 (52) 84	a) 49 b) 62 (71) 115	a) 37.5 (43) 69 b) - c) -	a) Mid-fuselage, retractable 24 hp (18 kW) Rotax 275 b) 22	Special winglet wingtips offered by DG and others.
DG-600/18M Evolution (MGS)	a) 1 b) Carbonfibre and aramid	a) HQ35 mod and HQ37 b) 27.24	a) 59-1 (18) b) 127.1 (11.81) c) 22-5 (6.83)	a) 699 (317) b) 1,058 (480) c) -	a) 6.88 (33.6) b) 8.32 (40.6)	a) 1.67 (0.51) b) 45 (52) 83	a) 50 b) 59 (68) 110	a) 37 (42.5) 68 b) 146 (168) 270 c) 65 (75) 120	a) Mid-fuselage, retractable 24 hp (18 kW) Rotax 275 b) 22	Special winglet wingtips offered by DG and others.
DG-800 A (MGS)	a) 1 b) Carbonfibre and aramid	a) DU 89-138/14 and DU 92-137/14 b) 27.43	a) 59-1 (18) b) 127.1 (11.81) c) 23-0.5 (7.02)	a) 723 (328) b) 1,157 (525) c) 265 (120)	a) 7.07 (34.5) b) 9.11 (44.5)	a) 1.64 (0.5) b) 41 (47) 76	a) 50 b) 59 (68) 110	a) 37 (42.5) 68 b) 146 (168) 270 c) 81 (93) 150	a) Mid-fuselage, retractable 43 hp (32 kW) Rotax 505 b) 22 + 30	42 built between 1991 and 1996. Replaced in production by DG-800B. New performance improving winglets for 18 m versions available since Autumn 1997.

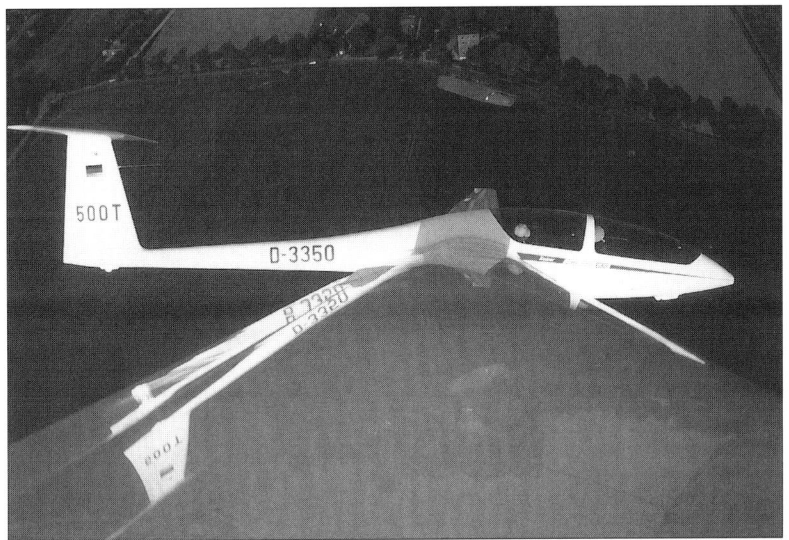

↑ **DG Flugzeugbau DG-500 Trainer/DG-505 Elan Orion** *(J. Ewald) (page 598)*

↑ **DG Flugzeugbau DG-800 B** *(J. Ewald) (page 600)*

Designation (Type)	a) Crew b) Materials	a) Aerofoil b) Wing aspect ratio	a) Span ft-ins (m) b) Wing area sq ft (m^2) c) Length ft-ins (m)	Weights lb (kg): a) empty b) maximum c) ballast (max)	Wing loading lb/sq ft (kg/m^2) a) minimum b) maximum	a) Minimum rate of sink ft (m)/sec b) at speed of kts (mph) km/h	a) Best glide ratio b) at speed of kts (mph) km/h	Speeds kts (mph) km/h: a) stalling b) maximum c) cruise	a) Engine b) Fuel capacity in litres	Comments
Under the heading *Type*, the following abbreviations have been used: **G** = Glider; **MGS** = Motorglider, self-launch; **MGN** = Motorglider, no self-launch										
Germany										
Manufacturer: DG Flugzeugbau GmbH (continued)										
DG-800 A (MGS), with 15 m winglet wingtips	a) 1 b) Carbonfibre and aramid	a) DU 89-138/14 and DU 92-137/14 b) 21.07	a) 49-2.5 (15) b) 115 (10.68) 23-0.5 (7.02)	a) 710 (322)	a) 7.7 (37.6) b) 10.08 (49.2)	a) 1.94 (0.59) b) 43 (50) 80	a) 45 b) 63 (72) 116	a) 39 (45) 72 b) - c) -	a) Mid-fuselage, retractable 43 hp (32 kW) Rotax 505 b) 22 + 30	
DG-800 B (MGS)	a) 1 b) Carbonfibre and aramid	a) DU 89-138/14 and DU 92-137/14 b) 27.43	a) 59-1 (18) b) 127.1 (11.81) c) 23-0.5 (7.02)	a) 745 (338) b) 1,157 (525) c) 220 (100)	a) 7.07 (34.5) b) 9.11 (44.5)	a) 1.64 (0.5) b) 41 (47) 76	a) 50 b) 59 (68) 110	a) 37 (42.5) 68 b) 146 (168) 270 c) 81 (93) 150	a) Mid-fuselage 54 hp (40.3 kW) Solo 2625, with retractable propeller b) 22 + 30	36 DG-800 Bs built since 1994. First 5 prototypes flew with the 50 hp (37.3 kW) MWAE 50 engine. Winglets for 18 m versions available.
DG-800 B (MGS), with 15 m winglet wingtips	a) 1 b) Carbonfibre and aramid	a) DU 89-138/14 and DU 92-137/14 b) 21.07	a) 49-2.5 (15) b) 115 (10.68) c) 23-0.5 (7.02)	a) 736 (334)	a) 7.7 (37.6) b) 10.08 (49.2)	a) 1.94 (0.59) b) 43 (50) 80	a) 45 b) 63 (72) 116	a) 39 (45) 72 b) - c) -	a) Mid-fuselage 54 hp (40.3 kW) Solo 2625, with retractable propeller b) 22 + 30	See above.
DG-800 S (G)	a) 1 b) Carbonfibre and aramid	a) DU 89-138/14 and DU 92-137/14 b) 27.43	a) 59-1 (18) b) 127.1 (11.81) c) 22-6 (6.86)	a) 578 (262) b) 1,157 (525) c) 397 (180)	a) 5.94 (29) b) 9.11 (44.5)	a) 1.54 (0.47) b) 38 (44) 71	a) 50 b) 59 (68) 110	a) 34 (39.5) 63 b) 146 (168) 270 c) -		24 DG-800 Ss built since 1993. New performance improving winglets for 18 m version available since Autumn 1997.
DG-800 S (G), with 15 m winglet wingtips	a) 1 b) Carbonfibre and aramid	a) DU 89-138/14 and DU 92-137/14 b) 21.07	a) 49-2.5 (15) b) 115 (10.68) c) 22-6 (6.86)	a) 564 (256)	a) 6.45 (31.5) b) 10.08 (49.2)	a) 1.8 (0.55) b) 4o (46.5) 75	a) 45 b) 63 (72) 116	a) 36 (41) 66 b) - c) -		
Manufacturer: Flugtechnik & Leichtbau Bürogemeinschaft GbR, R. Kickert & H. L. Meyer, Lilienthalplatz 2A, Gebäude 15, D-38105 Braunschweig (Telephone: +49 531 235 1105, Facsimile: +49 531 235 1107, E-mail: HALU.MEYER@t-online.de)										
ETA (MGS)	a) - b) -	a) HQR b) 51.33	a) 101-2 (30.84) b) 199.45 (18.53) c) 32 (9.75)	a) 1,323 (600) b) 2,028 (920) c) -	a) - b) -	a) - b) -	a) - b) -	a) - b) - c) -	a) Retractable Binder system b) -	To be the world's largest glider. 4 ordered.
Manufacturer: Flugwissenschaftliche Vereinigung Aachen (1920) e.V., Templergraben 55, D-52062 Aachen (Telephone: +49 241 80 6824, Facsimile: +49 241 8888 233)										
FVA-27 'Ente' (G)	a) 1 b) Glassfibre, carbonfibre and aramid	a) Canard: FX 67-K-170. Wing: HQ 21M2/25 b) Canard: 13.9. Wing: 29.2	a) 49-2.5 (15) b) 82.9 (7.7) (wing plus canard: 102.26, 9.5) c) 13-1.5 (4)	a) 573 (260) b) 1,058 (480) c) 220 (100)	a) 7.11 (34.7) b) 10.34 (50.5)	a) - b) -	a) - b) -	a) - b) 151 (174) 280 c) -		Canard glider with pilot rescue system. Under construction. First flight expected in 1999.
Manufacturer: Frank + Waldenberger, An der Kühlweid 3, D-76661 Philippsburg (Telephone: +49 7256 4807)										
H 101 Salto (G)	a) 1 b) Glassfibre	a) FX 66-17-AII-182 b) 20.6	a) 43-8 (13.3) b) 92.35 (8.58) c) 18-8.5 (5.7)	a) 401 (182) b) 617 (280) c) -	a) - b) 6.7 (32.7)	a) - b) -	a) - b) -	a) 38 (44) 70 b) 151 (174) 280 c) -		Originally based on Hütter 30 GfK and first built by Start & Flug. Fully aerobatic with 13.3 m wing.
H 101 Salto (G), with wingtips	a) 1 b) Glassfibre	a) FX 66-17-AII-182 b) 26.4	a) 50-10 (15.5) b) 98 (9.1) c) 18-8.5 (5.7)	a) 412 (187) b) 683 (310)	a) - b) 6.96 (34)	a) 2.3 (0.7) b) 39 (45) 72	a) 35.5 b) 51 (58) 94	a) 33.5 (39) 62 b) 135 (155) 250 c) -		
Manufacturer: Glasfaser-Flugzeug-Service GmbH, Hofener Weg, D-72582 Grabenstätten (Telephone: +49 7382 1032, Facsimile: +49 7382 1629, E-mail: streifly@)aol.com)										
Albatros (G)	a) 1 b) Glassfibre, carbonfibre and aramid	a) DU 91-122 series b) 24.89	a) 49-2.5 (15) b) 97.3 (9.039) c) 22-4 (6.8)	a) 485 (220) b) 992 (450) c) 254 (115)	a) 6.76 (33) b) 10.24 (50)	a) - b) -	a) - b) -	a) - b) 146 (168) 270		First flight had been expected 1998. Safety cockpit, glider rescue system, and semi-electronic flight control.

↑ **Frank + Waldenberger H 101 Salto** *(J. Ewald) (page 600)*

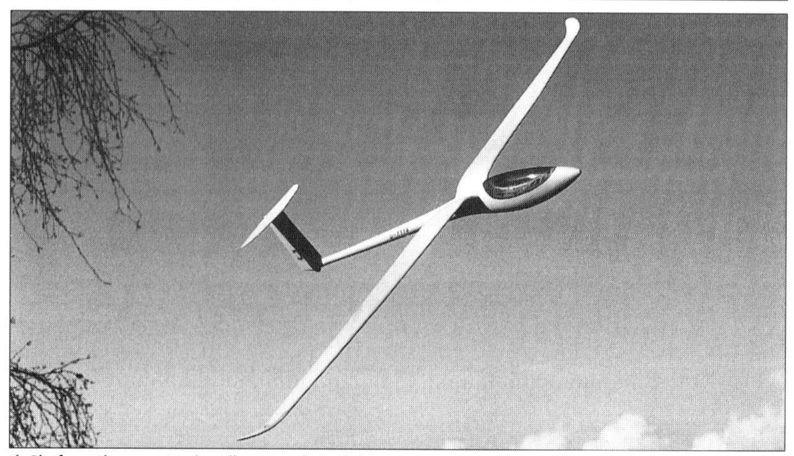
↑ **Glasfaser-Flugzeug-Service Albatros scale model** *(Peter F. Selinger) (page 600)*

Designation (Type)	a) Crew b) Materials	a) Aerofoil b) Wing aspect ratio	a) Span ft-ins (m) b) Wing area sq ft (m^2) c) Length ft-ins (m)	Weights lb (kg): a) empty b) maximum c) ballast (max)	Wing loading lb/sq ft (kg/m^2) a) minimum b) maximum	a) Minimum rate of sink ft (m)/sec b) at speed of kts (mph) km/h	a) Best glide ratio b) at speed of kts (mph) km/h	Speeds kts (mph) km/h: a) stalling b) maximum c) cruise	a) Engine b) Fuel capacity in litres	Comments
Under the heading *Type*, the following abbreviations have been used: **G** = Glider; **MGS** = Motorglider, self-launch; **MGN** = Motorglider, no self-launch										
Germany										
Manufacturer: Gomolzig Flugzeugbau GmbH, Höfen 84a, D-42277 Wuppertal (Telephone: +49 202 660782, Facsimile: +49 202 660782)										
Gomolzig Caproni Calif A 21 S (G)	a) 2 b) Metal	a) FX 67-K-170/ FX 60-126 b) 25.65	a) 67-8 (20.63) b) 174.3 (16.19) c) 25-9 (7.84)	a) 971 (440) b) 1,421 (644) c) -	a) 6.55 (32) b) 8.19 (40)	a) 1.97 (0.6) b) 49 (56) 90	a) 41 b) 57 (65) 105	a) 34 (39) (63) b) 138 (158) 255 c) -		Side-by-side 2-seater, with trailing-edge flaps/airbrakes. Built by Caproni of Italy from 1972 to 1982. 6 Califs newly built from original parts, equipped with winglets. First of these flew 1997.
Manufacturer: Herbert Gomolzig Ingenieurbüro, Höfen 84a, D-42277 Wuppertal (Telephone: +49 202 6481470, Facsimile: +49 202 660578)										
RF-9 ABS (MGS)	a) 2 b) Wood	a) NACA 64_3618 b) 16	a) 56-8.5 (17.28) b) 193.75 (18) c) 27-1 (8.25)	a) 1,168 (530) b) 1,653 (750) c) -	a) - b) 8.89 (43.4)	a) 3.28 (1) b) 58 (66) 107 (at max wing loading)	a) 28 b) 52 (60) 97 (at max wing loading)	a) 38 (44) 70 b) 119 (137) 220 c) 103 (118) 190	a) Front mounted 80 hp (59.7 kW) Rotax 912 A3 b) 80	New version of French RF-9, first proposed by ABS and EIS. Production started 1998.
Manufacturer: Burkhart Grob Luft- und Raumfahrt GmbH & Co KG, Am Flugplatz, D-86874 Tussenhausen-Mattsies (Telephone: +49 8268 9980)										
G 103 C Twin III (Acro) (G)	a) 2 b) Glassfibre	a) HQ32 - E 583 mod b) 18.5	a) 59.1 (18) b) 188.6 (17.52) c) 26-10 (8.18)	a) 838 (380) b) 1,323 (600) c) -	a) 5.26 (25.7) b) 7.03 (34.3)	a) 2.1 (0.64) b) 39 (45.5) 73	a) 38 b) 57 (66) 106	a) 34 (39.5) 63 b) 151 (174) 280 c) -		Versions G-103 A and B (Twin-Astir and Twin II) produced since 1976. Acro versions fully aerobatic. Production ended.
G 103 C Twin III SL (MGS)	a) 2 b) Glassfibre	a) HQ32 - E 583 mod b) 18.5	a) 59.1 (18) b) 188.6 (17.52) c) 26-10 (8.18)	a) 1,014 (460) b) 1,565 (710) c) -	a) - b) 8.3 (40.5)	a) 2.1 (0.64) b) 42 (51) 82	a) 38 b) 59 (68) 109	a) 37 (42.5) 68 b) 151 (174) 280 c) -	a) Mid-fuselage, retractable 43 hp (32 kW) Rotax 505 b)	Powered version of Twin III. Production ended.
G 109 B (MGS)	a) 2 b) Glassfibre	a) - b) 15.9	a) 57-1 (17.4) b) 204.5 (19) c) 26-7 (8.1)	a) 1,367 (620) b) 1,874 (850) c) -	a) - b) 9.16 (44.7)	a) 3.61 (1.1) b) 58 (71) 108	a) 28 b) 62 (71) 115	a) 40 (45.5) 73 b) 130 (149) 240 c) 103 (118) 190	a) Front-mounted 90 hp (67 kW) Grob G 2500 b) -	Earlier version, G 109A with 75 hp (56 kW) Limbach engine, also delivered as Vigilant T.1 for RAF Air Cadet use. Production ended.
Manufacturer: HFBK, c/o Prof. Günter Rochelt, Lerchenfeld 2, D-20081 Hamburg (Telephone: +49 40 2984 0)										
Solair 2 (MGS)	a) 1 b) Carbonfibre, aramid and glassfibre	a) DU 95-136+8 b) 23.5	a) 65-7.5 (20) b) 183 (17) c) 20-1 (6.12)	a) 287 (130) b) 551 (250) c) -	a) - b) 2.77 (13.5)	a) - b) -	a) - b) -	a) - b) - c) -	a) 2 x 4.5 kW DC pusher electric motors; Dino HP 550-100 in V-tail tips b) 4 ni-cd accumulator packs (65V/5.2 Ah)	Second Solar motorglider adaptation of a glider; Solair 1 flew in 1981. 144.67 sq ft (13.44 m^2) of solar panels. First flew May 1998.

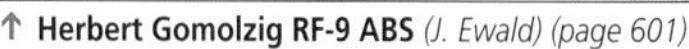

↑ **Herbert Gomolzig RF-9 ABS** *(J. Ewald) (page 601)*

↑ **Burkhart Grob G 103 C Twin III Acro** *(J. Ewald) (page 601)*

↑ **HFBK/Rochelt Solair 2** *(J. Ewald) (page 601)*

↑ **IFB, Universität Stuttgart Icaré 2** *(J. Ewald) (page 602)*

Designation (Type)	a) Crew b) Materials	a) Aerofoil b) Wing aspect ratio	a) Span ft-ins (m) b) Wing area sq ft (m^2) c) Length ft-ins (m)	Weights lb (kg): a) empty b) maximum c) ballast (max)	Wing loading lb/sq ft (kg/m^2) a) minimum b) maximum	a) Minimum rate of sink ft (m)/sec b) at speed of kts (mph) km/h	a) Best glide ratio b) at speed of kts (mph) km/h	Speeds kts (mph) km/h: a) stalling b) maximum c) cruise	a) Engine b) Fuel capacity in litres	Comments
Under the heading *Type*, the following abbreviations have been used: **G** = Glider; **MGS** = Motorglider, self-launch; **MGN** = Motorglider, no self-launch										
Germany										
Manufacturer: IFB, Universität Stuttgart, Pfaffenwaldring 31, D-70550 Stuttgart (Telephone: +49 711 685 3101, Facsimile: +49 711 685 2449, E-mail: rehmet@ifb.uni-stuttgart.de)										
Icaré 2 (MGS)	a) 1 b) Carbonfibre, aramid and glassfibre	a) b) 25	a) 82-0 (25) b) 269 (25) c) -	a) 639 (290) b) 838 (380) c) -	a) - b) 3.11 (15.2)	a) 1.28 (0.39) b) 27 (31) 50	a) 43 b) 34 (39) 63	a) 24 (27.5) 44 b) 65 (75) 120 c) 62 (71) 115	a) 12 kW electric DC pusher motor in tail with folding propeller b) Ni-cd accumulator pack and solar panels	First flew 1996. Horizontal flight possible with average 500 W/m^2.
Manufacturer: Willi Klotz KG, Laufer Weg 22, D-90562 Heroldsberg (Telephone: +49 911 5180364, Facsimile: +49 911 5186843)										
Moka 1 (MGS)	a) 2 b) Glassfibre, carbonfibre and aramid	a) FX 67-K-170/17 b) 23.52	a) 68-3 (20.8) b) 201.82 (18.75) c) 27-2.5 (8.3)	a) 1,168 (530) b) 1,742 (790) c) -	a) 7.168 (35) b) 8.52 (41.6)	a) - b) -	a) c 44 b) -	a) 41 (47.5) 76 b) 131 (151) 243 c) -	a) 2 × 50 hp (37.3 kW) Mid West AE 50R rotary engines with 4-blade folding propellers b) 2 × 45	First flight had been expected in 1998. Light 'observer' version planned as Moka 3.
Manufacturer: Jürgen Lutz, Schillerstrasse 11, D-73265 Dettingen (Telephone: +49 7021 53423)										
Libelle (G)	a) 1 b) Wood and steel tube	a) - b) 7.6	a) 34-5.5 (10.5) b) 156.1 (14.5) c) 23-5.5 (7.15)	a) 148 (67) b) 346 (157) c) -	a) 1.8 (8.8) b) 2.21 (10.8)	a) 2.62 (0.8) b) -	a) 15 b) -	a) 19 (22) 35 b) 49 (56) 90 c) -	a) - b) -	Homebuilt microlight glider.
Manufacturer: Nitsche Flugzeugbau GmbH. Streichenweg 21, D-83246 Unterwössen (Telephone: +49 8641 690026, Facsimile: +49 8641 690027, E-mail: Samburo@t-online.de)										
AVo 68 S Samburo (MGS)	a) 2 b) Wood and steel tube	a) NACA/Gö b) 13.6	a) 54-9 (16.68) b) 222.8 (20.7) c) 26-0.5 (7.94)	a) 1,080 (490) b) 1,510 (685) c) -	a) 5.63 (27.5) b) 6.76 (33)	a) 3.41 (1.04) b) 40 (47) 75	a) 22 b) 49 (56) 90	a) 32.5 (37.5) 60 b) 89 (103) 165 c) 79 (91) 147	a) Front mounted Limbach L 1700 E1 b) 40	29 built from 1976 by Alpla factory in Austria. Project taken over by Nitsche in 1994. 7 already modified to R standard (see below).
AVo 68 R Samburo (MGS)	a) 2 b) Wood and steel tube	a) NACA/Gö b) 13.6	a) 54-9 (16.68) b) 222.8 (20.7) c) 26-5 (8.05)	a) 1,058 (480) b) 1,510 (685) c) -	a) 5.63 (27.5) b) 6.76 (33)	a) 3.38 (1.03) b) 46 (53) 85	a) 27 b) 51.5 (59) 95	a) 28 (32) 51 b) 116 (134) 215 c) 96 (111) 178 or 86 (99) 160 at 65% power	a) Front mounted 80 hp (59.7 kW) Rotax 912 A3 b) 40, optional 60	Production version, suitable for towing gliders up to 1,323 lb (600 kg). 2-wheel undercarriage available.
Manufacturer: Heinz Neumann and Dieter Reich, Anechostrasse 16, D-81827 München (Telephone: +49 89 4306 970)										
ULF-1	a) 1 b) Wood, fabric and glassfibre	a) FX 63-137/18-15 b) 8	a) 34-1.5 (10.4) b) 144.2 (13.4) c) 18-2.5 (5.55)	a) 99 (45) b) 298 (135) c) -	a) - b) 2.05 (10)	a) 2.62 (0.8) b) -	a) 15 b) -	a) 17.5 (20) 32 b) 38 (43) 70 c) -		Microlight glider, also foot-launchable. Drawings available. About 10 built.
Manufacturer: Rolladen-Schneider Flugzeugbau GmbH, Mühlstrasse 10, D-63329 Egelsbach (Telephone: +49 61 032 04126, Facsimile: +49 61 034 5526)										
LS 4-b (G)	a) 1 b) Glassfibre, carbonfibre and aramid	a) Lemke, without flaps b) 21.4	a) 49-2.5 (15) b) 113 (10.5) c) 22-5 (6.83)	a) 529 (240) b) 1,157 (525) c) 375 (170)	a) 6.04 (29.5) b) 10.24 (50)	a) 1.97 (0.6) b) 40.5 (47) 75	a) 41 b) 54 (62) 100	a) 37 (42.5) 68 b) 151 (174) 280 c) -		More than 1,000 of all LS 4 versions built since 1980. Production continues.

↑ **Lutz Libelle** *(Peter F. Selinger) (page 602)*

↑ **Neumann ULF-1** *(Peter F. Selinger) (page 602)*

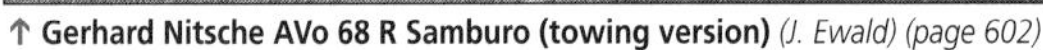

↑ **Gerhard Nitsche AVo 68 R Samburo (towing version)** *(J. Ewald) (page 602)*

↑ **Rolladen-Schneider LS 6** *(Peter F. Selinger) (page 603)*

Designation (Type)	a) Crew b) Materials	a) Aerofoil b) Wing aspect ratio	a) Span ft-ins (m) b) Wing area sq ft (m^2) c) Length ft-ins (m)	Weights lb (kg): a) empty b) maximum c) ballast (max)	Wing loading lb/sq ft (kg/m^2) a) minimum b) maximum	a) Minimum rate of sink ft (m)/sec b) at speed of kts (mph) km/h	a) Best glide ratio b) at speed of kts (mph) km/h	Speeds kts (mph) km/h: a) stalling b) maximum c) cruise	a) Engine b) Fuel capacity in litres	Comments
Under the heading *Type*, the following abbreviations have been used: **G** = Glider; **MGS** = Motorglider, self-launch; **MGN** = Motorglider, no self-launch										
Germany										
Manufacturer: Rolladen Schneider Flugzeugbau GmbH (continued)										
LS 6 (G)	a) 1 b) Glassfibre, carbonfibre and aramid	a) Lemke, with flaps b) 21.4	a) 49-2.5 (15). Also built as 57-5 (17.5) LS 6-b and 59-1 (18) LS 6-c, using wingtips b) 113 (10.5) c) 21-10 (6.66)	a) 551 (250) b) 1,157 (525) c) 353 (160)	a) - b) 10.24 (50)	a) under 1.97 (0.6) b) -	a) 43 b) -	a) 35 (40.5) 65 b) 146 (168) 270		Several versions developed, including LS 6-a with 5.5 litres of ballast in the tailfin; -b and -c have carbonfibre wings and wingtips.
LS 7 (WL) (G)	a) 1 b) Glassfibre, carbonfibre and aramid	a) Lemke, without flaps b) 23.1	a) 49.2.5 (15) b) 104.7 (9.73) c) 21-10 (6.66)	a) 529 (240) b) 1,071 (486) c) 375 (170)	a) 6.55 (32) b) 10.24 (50)	a) - b) -	a) 43 b) -	a) 37 (42.5) 68 b) 146 (168) 270		Production from 1988 until 1994. WL = winglets.
LS 8-a (G)	a) 1 b) Glassfibre, carbonfibre and aramid	a) Lemke LS 6 section but without flaps b) 21.4	a) 49-2.5 (15) b) 113 (10.5) c) 22-0.5 (6.72)	a) 562 (255) b) 1,157 (525) c) 397 (180)	a) 6.46 (31.5) b) 10.24 (50)	a) under 1.97 (0.6) b) 46 (53) 85	a) 43 b) -	a) 36 (41) 66 b) 151 (174) 280		LS 6 wing section without flaps but with winglets. More than 130 built since 1994. Production continues.
LS 8/18 (G), with 18 m wingtips	a) 1 b) Glassfibre, carbonfibre and aramid	b) 29.13	a) 59 (18) b) 122.7 (11.4) c) 22-0.5 (6.72)	a) 584 (265)	a) 6.1 (29.8) b: 9.42 (46)		a) 49 b) -	a) 36 (41) 66		Production continues.
LS 9 (MGS)	a) 1 b) Glassfibre, carbonfibre and aramid	a) Lemke LS 6 section, with flaps b) 28.4	a) 59-1 (18) b) 122.7 (11.4) c) 22-5 (6.83)	a) 827 (375) b) 1,157 (525) c) -	a) - b) 9.42 (46)	a) 1.97 (0.6) b) 51 (59) 95	a) over 47 b) 59 (68) 110	a) 38 (44) 70 b) 146 (168) 270 c) 76 (87) 140	a) Mid-fuselage mounted 55 hp (41 kW) Solo 2625, with retractable propeller b) 23	Prototype flew in 1995 with Rotax engine, then from 1997 with Solo, when production began. Based on LS 4 fuselage and LS 6-c wings.
LS 10 (G)	a) 1 b) -	a) - b) -	a) 49-2.5 (15) b) -	a) - b) - c) -	a) - b) -	a) - b) -	a) - b) -	a) - b) -		New 15 m glider with flaps. Prototype construction started in 1997.
Manufacturer: Scheibe-Flugzeugbau GmbH, August-Pfaltz-Strasse 23, D-85221 Dachau (Telephone: +49 8131 720834, Facsimile: +49 8131 736985)										
SF 25C Falke 2000 (MGS)	a) 2 b) Wood and steel tube	a) Mü b) 13.8	a) 50-2.5 (15.3) b) 195.9 (18.2) c) 24-11 (7.6)	a) 959 (435) b) 1,433 (650) c) -	a) - b) 7.31 (35.7)	a) 3.28 (1) b) -	a) 23 b) -	a) 35 (40.5) 65 b) 103 (118) 190 c) 92 (106) 170	a) Front-mounted 80 hp (59.7 kW) Limbach L-2000 EA b) 55 Note: Ior Avia of Thionville-Yutz, France, modifies SF 25s and SF 28s for aerotowing with Limbach L 2400 EB1 engines.	More than 1,000 SF 25 Falkes of all versions built since 1966. SF 25 B with 45 hp (35.8 kW) Stamo, and SF 25C with 60 hp (44.7 kW) Limbach SL 1700 EA engine. Also SF 25E Superfalke with 59 ft 1 ins (18 m) wing with FX S 02-196 aerofoil. Built in 1, 2 and 3 wheel versions.
SF 25C Rotax-Falke (MGS)	a) 2 b) Wood and steel tube	a) Mü b) 13.8	a) 50-2.5 (15.3) b) 195.9 (18.2) c) 24-11 (7.6)	a) 959 (435) b) 1,433 (650) c) -	a) - b) 7.31 (35.7)	a) 3.28 (1.0) b) -	a) 23 b) -	a) 35 (40.5) 65 b) 103 (118) 190 c) 97 (112) 180	a) Front-mounted 80 hp (59.7 kW) Rotax 912A b) 55	Production version, in 1, 2 or 3 wheel models. Variable pitch propeller. Suitable for towing gliders up to 1,323 lb (600 kg).
SF 28A Tandem-Falke (MGS)	a) 2 b) Wood and steel tube	a) FX S 02-196 b) 14.4	a) 53.6 (16.3) b) 195.9 (18.5) c) 26-7 (8.1)	a) 904 (410) b) 1,345 (610) c) -	a) - b) 6.76 (33)	a) 2.95 (0.9) b) 38 (44) 70	a) 27 b) 51 (59) 95	a) 32.5 (37.5) 60 b) 103 (118) 190 c) -	a) Front mounted 65 hp (48.5 kW) Limbach SL 1700 EA1 b) 40	Tandem seats. No longer in production.
SF 34B Delphin	See France - Centrair Alliance 34									

↑ **Rolladen-Schneider LS 8/18** *(J. Ewald) (page 603)*

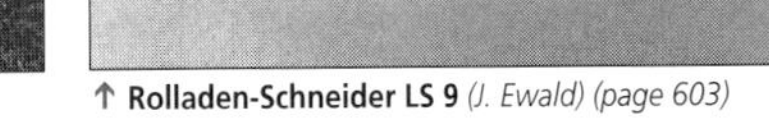

↑ **Rolladen-Schneider LS 9** *(J. Ewald) (page 603)*

Designation (Type)	a) Crew b) Materials	a) Aerofoil b) Wing aspect ratio	a) Span ft-ins (m) b) Wing area sq ft (m^2) c) Length ft-ins (m)	Weights lb (kg): a) empty b) maximum c) ballast (max)	Wing loading lb/sq ft (kg/m^2) a) minimum b) maximum	a) Minimum rate of sink ft (m)/sec b) at speed of kts (mph) km/h	a) Best glide ratio b) at speed of kts (mph) km/h	Speeds kts (mph) km/h: a) stalling b) maximum c) cruise	a) Engine b) Fuel capacity in litres	Comments
Under the heading *Type*, the following abbreviations have been used: **G** = Glider; **MGS** = Motorglider, self-launch; **MGN** = Motorglider, no self-launch										
Germany										
Manufacturer: Scheibe-Flugzeugbau GmbH (continued)										
SF 36 R (MGS)	a) 2 b) Glassfibre	a) FX 61-184 and FX 60-126 b) 17.1	a) 53-6 (16.3) b) 167.9 (15.6) c) 23-7.5 (7.2)	a) 1,135 (515) b) 1,576 (715) c) -	a) - b) 9.35 (45.8)	a) 2.95 (0.9) b) 43 (50) 80	a) 28 b) 51 (59) 95	a) 40.5 (47) 75 b) 113 (130) 210 c) 97 (112) 180	a) Front-mounted 80 hp (59.7 kW) Rotax 912A b) 70	Prototypes built in 1981. 1 and 2 wheel versions with Limbach engines, some converted to Rotax or Sauer engines. Series production now planned in France.
Manufacturer: Schempp-Hirth Flugzeugbau GmbH, Krebenstrasse 25, D-73230 Kirchheim/Teck (Telephone: +49 7021 2441, Facsimile: +49 7021 483809)										
Discus a (G)	a) 1 b) Glassfibre and carbonfibre	a) Horstmann, Quast, Althaus, Holighaus b) 21.3	a) 49-2.5 (15) b) 113.9 (10.58) c) 20-10 (6.35)	a) 496 (225) b) 1,157 (525) c) 370 (168)	a) 5.94 (29) b) 10.16 (49.6)	a) 1.94 (0.59) b) 42 (48) 78	a) 44 b) 54 (62) 100	a) 36 (41) 66 b) 135 (155) 250 c) -		More than 800 Discus of all glider and motorglider versions built since 1984. Production continues. Discus a version has a narrow fuselage.
Discus b and CS (G)	a) 1 b) Glassfibre and carbonfibre	a) Horstmann, Quast, Althaus, Holighaus b) 21.3	a) 49-2.5 (15) b) 113.9 (10.58) c) 21-7 (6.58)	a) 507 (230) b) 1,157 (525) c) 370 (168)	a) 6.04 (29.5) b) 10.16 (49.6)	a) 1.94 (0.59) b) 44 (51) 82	a) 43 b) 52 (60) 97	a) 37.5 (43) 69 b) 135 (155) 250 c) -		CS built by Orlican in Czech Republic.
Discus bM (MGS)	a) 1 b) Glassfibre and carbonfibre	a) Horstmann, Quast, Althaus, Holighaus b) 21.3	a) 49-2.5 (15) b) 113.9 (10.58) c) 21-7 (6.58)	a) 694 (315) b) 1,157 (525) c) 370 (168)	a) 7.56 (36.9) b) 10.16 (49.6)	a) 2.2 (0.67) b) -	a) 42.5 b) -	a) 41 (47.5) 76 b) 135 (155) 250 c) 81 (93) 150	a) Mid-fuselage 48 hp (35.8 kW) Rotax 463, with retractable propeller b) 29	9 built since 1991.
Discus bT (MGN)	a) 1 b) Glassfibre and carbonfibre	a) Horstmann, Quast, Althaus, Holighaus b) 21.3	a) 49-2.5 (15) b) 113.9 (10.58) c) 21-7 (6.58)	a) 606 (265) b) 992 (450) c) 370 (168)	a) 6.96 (34) b) 8.7 (42.5)	a) 2 (0.61) b) 42 (48) 78	a) 43 b) -	a) 39.5 (45) 73 b) 135 (155) 250 c) -	a) Mid-fuselage, retractable 20.8 hp (15.5 kW) Solo b) 29	162 built since 1991. Engine can be taken out to obtain weight data as Discus b.
Discus 2a and b (G)	a) 1 b) glassfibre, carbonfibre and aramid	a) Horstmann Würz 14.5% b) 22.15	a) 49-2.5 (15) b) 109.36 (10.16) c) 20-9 (6.335) for 2a, 22-2.5 (6.77) for 2b	a) 518 (235) for 2a, 529 (240) for 2b b) 1,157 (525) c) -	a) 6.14 (30) for 2a, 6.25 (30.5) for 2b b) 10.58 (51.67)	a) - b) -	a) - b) -	a) 37 (42.5) 68 for 2a, 38 (44) 70 for 2b b) 135 (155) 250		Discus 2a first flown 16 May 1998. 2b without flaps flown 3 April 1998. In production.
Duo-Discus (G)	a) 2 b) Glassfibre, carbonfibre and aramid	a) HQ31-A/XX b) 24.4	a) 65-7.5 (20) b) 176.5 (16.4) c) 28-3.5 (8.62)	a) 904 (410) b) 1,543 (700) c) 441 (200)	a) 6.0 (29.3) b) 8.75 (42.7)	a) 1.97 (0.6) b) 38 (43) 70	a) 45 b) 54 (62) 100	a) 37 (42.5) 68 b) 135 (155) 250 c) -		135 built since 1993. Production continues.
Janus (G)	a) 2 b) Glassfibre	a) FX 67-K-170/150 b) 20	a) 59-8.5 (18.2) b) 178.7 (16.6) c) 28-1.5 (8.57)	a) 838 (380) b) 1,367 (620) c) 529 (240)	a) 5.57 (27.2) b) 7.64 (37.3)	a) 2.3 (0.7) b) 49 (56) 90	a) 39.5 b) 59 (68) 110	a) 38 (43.5) 70 b) 119 (137) 220 c) -		About 300 of all Janus glider and motorglider versions built between 1974 and 1995. Flying T-tail.
Janus B (G)	a) 2 b) Glassfibre	a) FX 67-K-170/150 b) 20	a) 59-8.5 (18.2) b) 178.7 (16.6) c) 28-3.5 (8.62)	a) 816 (370) b) 1,367 (620) c) 529 (240)	a) 5.49 (26.8) b) 7.64 (37.3)	a) 2.3 (0.7) b) 49 (56) 90	a) 39.5 b) 59 (68) 110	a) 38 (43.5) 70 b) 119 (137) 220 c) -		Conventional T-tail.
Janus C (G)	a) 2 b) Glassfibre and carbonfibre	a) FX 67-K-170/150 b) 20	a) 65-7.5 (20) b) 186.2 (17.3) c) 28-3.5 (8.62)	a) 805 (365) b) 1,543 (700) c) 529 (240)	a) 5.2 (25.4) b) 8.3 (40.5)	a) 1.97 (0.6) b) 49 (56) 90	a) 43 b) 59 (68) 110	a) 35 (40.5) 65 b) 135 (155) 250 c) -		Built since 1979.
Janus Ce (G)	a) 2 b) Glassfibre and carbonfibre	a) FX 67-K-170/150 b) 20	a) 65-7.5 (20) b) 186.2 (17.3) c) 28-3.5 (8.62)	a) 893 (405) b) 1,543 (700) c) 529 (240)	a) 5.6 (27.5) b) 8.3 (40.5)	a) 1.97 (0.6) b) 49 (56) 90	a) 43 b) 59 (68) 110	a) 35 (40.5) 65 b) 135 (155) 250		Has larger rudder and retractable main wheel.
Janus CM (MGS)	a) 2 b) Glassfibre and carbonfibre	a) FX 67-K-170/150 b) 20	a) 65-7.5 (20) b) 186.2 (17.3) c) 28-3.5 (8.62)	a) 1,058 (480) b) 1,543 (700) c) -	a) - b) 8.3 (40.5)	a) 2.23 (0.68) b) 52 (60) 97	a) 43.5 b) 61 (70) 113	a) 39.5 (46) 73 b) 135 (155) 250 c) -	a) Mid-fuselage, retractable 59 hp (44 kW) Rotax 535A b) 44	38 built since 1982. See also Wolf Hirth.
Janus CT (MGN)	a) 2 b) Glassfibre and carbonfibre	a) FX 67-K-170/150 b) 20	a) 65-7.5 (20) b) 186.2 (17.3) c) 28-3.5 (8.62)	a) 981 (445) b) 1,543 (700) c) 529 (240)	a) 6.12 (29.9) b) 8.3 (40.5)	a) 2.23 (0.68) b) 52 (60) 97	a) 43.5 b) 61 (70) 113	a) 39.5 (46) 73 b) 135 (155) 250 c) -	a) Mid-fuselage, retractable 26 hp (19.4 kW) Solo 2350 b) 18	17 built since 1983.
Nimbus 3D (G)	a) 2 b) Carbonfibre and glassfibre	a) Wortmann, Althaus, Holighaus b) 36	a) 80-8.5 (24.6) b) 181.4 (16.85) c) 28-3.5 (8.62)	a) 1,069 (485) b) 1,653 (750) c) 370 (168)	a) 6.76 (33) b) 9.11 (44.5)	a) 1.57 (0.48) b) 47 (54) 87	a) 57 b) 57 (65) 105	a) 37 (42.5) 68 b) 148 (171) 275 c) -		13 built between 1986-1993.

↑ **Scheibe SF 36 type with 2-wheel undercarriage** *(Peter F. Selinger) (page 604)*

↑ **Schempp-Hirth Duo-Discus** *(PJ Photo Library) (page 604)*

Designation (Type)	a) Crew b) Materials	a) Aerofoil b) Wing aspect ratio	a) Span ft-ins (m) b) Wing area sq ft (m²) c) Length ft-ins (m)	Weights lb (kg): a) empty b) maximum c) ballast (max)	Wing loading lb/sq ft (kg/m²) a) minimum b) maximum	a) Minimum rate of sink ft (m)/sec b) at speed of kts (mph) km/h	a) Best glide ratio b) at speed of kts (mph) km/h	Speeds kts (mph) km/h: a) stalling b) maximum c) cruise	a) Engine b) Fuel capacity in litres	Comments
Under the heading *Type*, the following abbreviations have been used: **G** = Glider; **MGS** = Motorglider, self-launch; **MGN** = Motorglider, no self-launch										
Germany										
Manufacturer: Schempp-Hirth Flugzeugbau GmbH (continued)										
Nimbus 3DM (MGS)	a) 2 b) Carbonfibre and glassfibre	a) Wortmann, Althaus, Holighaus b) 36	a) 80-8.5 (24.6) b) 181.4 (16.85) c) 28-3.5 (8.62)	a) 1,345 (610) b) 1,808 (820) c) 370 (168)	a) 8.4 (41) b) 9.97 (48.7)	a) 1.57 (0.48) b) 47 (54) 87	a) 57 b) 57 (65) 105	a) 38.5 (44) 71 b) 148 (171) 275 c) -	a) Mid-fuselage, retractable 59 hp (44 kW) Rotax 535C b) 50	27 built between 1986-1993.
Nimbus 3DT (MGN)	a) 2 b) Carbonfibre and glassfibre	a) Wortmann, Althaus, Holighaus b) 36	a) 80-8.5 (24.6) b) 181.4 (16.85) c) 28-3.5 (8.62)	a) 1,168 (530) b) 1,764 (800) c) 370 (168)	a) 7.41 (36.2) b) 9.73 (47.5)	a) 1.57 (0.48) b) 47 (54) 87	a) 57 b) 57 (65) 105	a) 37 (42.5) 68 b) 148 (171) 275 c) -	a) Mid-fuselage, retractable 26 hp (19.4 kW) Solo 2350 b) 18	25 built between 1986-1993.
Nimbus 4 (G)	a) 1 b) Carbonfibre, aramid and glassfibre	a) Wortmann, Althaus, Holighaus b) 39.1	a) 86-7.5 (26.4) b) 191.6 (17.8) c) 25-8 (7.82)	a) 1,058 (480) b) 1,653 (750) c) 714 (324)	a) 6.33 (30.9) b) 8.62 (42.1)	a) 1.38 (0.42) b) 46 (53) 86	a) 60 b) 59 (68) 110	a) 35 (40) 64 b) 154 (177) 285 c) -		8 built since 1990. Production continues.
Nimbus 4D (G)	a) 2 b) Carbonfibre, aramid and glassfibre	a) Wortmann, Althaus, DU, Holighaus b) 39.1	a) 86-11 (26.5) b) 193.3 (17.96) c) 28-7 (8.72)	a) 1,157 (525) b) 1,653 (750) c) 362 (164)	a) 6.84 (33.4) b) 8.56 (41.8)	a) 1.54 (0.47) b) -	a) 60 b) -	a) - b) 154 (177) 285		Built since 1994. DT version available as MGN with mid-fuselage retractable 26 hp (19.6 kW) Solo 2350. Production continues.
Nimbus 4DM (MGS)	a) 2 b) Carbonfibre, aramid and glassfibre	a) Wortmann, Althaus, DU, Holighaus b) 39.1	a) 86-11 (26.5) b) 193.3 (17.96) c) 28-7 (8.72)	a) 1,312 (595) b) 1,808 (820) c) 362 (164)	a) 7.64 (37.3) b) 9.11 (44.5)	a) 1.54 (0.47) b) -	a) 60 b) -	a) - b) 154 (177) 285 c) -	a) Mid-fuselage 59 hp (44 kW) Rotax 535C; since 1997 also with 65 hp (48 kW) Solo 2625, driving a retractable propeller b) 44	Built since 1994. Production continues.
Nimbus 4M (MGS)	a) 1 b) Carbonfibre, aramid and glassfibre	a) Wortmann, Althaus, Holighaus b) 39.1	a) 86-7.5 (26.4) b) 191.6 (17.8) c) 25-8 (7.82)	a) 1,261 (572) b) 1,764 (800) c) 714 (324)	a) 7.43 (36.3) b) 9.2 (44.9)	a) 1.38 (0.42) b) -	a) 60 b) 59 (68) 110	a) 38 (44) 70 b) 154 (177) 285 c) -	a) Mid-fuselage, retractable 43hp (32 kW) Rotax 505A b) -	10 built since 1986. Production continues.
Nimbus 4T (MGN)	a) 1 b) Carbonfibre, aramid and glassfibre	a) Wortmann, Althaus, Holighaus b) 39.1	a) 86-7.5 (26.4) b) 191.6 (17.8) c) 25-8 (7.82)	a) 1,157 (525) b) 1,764 (800) c) 714 (324)	a) 6.9 (33.7) b) 9.2 (44.9)	a) 1.38 (0.42) b) -	a) 60 b) 59 (68) 110	a) 36.5 (42) 67 b) 154 (177) 285 c) -	a) Mid-fuselage, retractable 26 hp (19.6 kW) Solo 2350 b) -	10 built since 1990. Production continues.
Ventus a and b (G)	a) 1 b) Glassfibre and carbonfibre	a) Wortmann, Althaus, Holighaus b) 23.7	a) 49-2.5 (15) b) 102.4 (9.51) c) Ventus a: 20-10 (6.35) Ventus b: 21-7 (6.58)	a) 485 (220) b) 948 (430) c) 370 (168)	a) 6.35 (31) b) 9.26 (45.2)	a) 2.17 (0.66) b) 49 (56) 90	a) 43.5 b) 63 (73) 117	a) 35 (40.5) 65 b) 135 (155) 250 c) -		More than 600 Ventus gliders and motorgliders built between early 1980s to 1994. Trailing-edge airbrakes. Ventus a has a narrow fuselage.
Ventus b/16.6	a) 1 b) Glassfibre and carbonfibre	a) Wortmann, Althaus, Holighaus b) 27.7	a) 54-5.5 (16.6) b) 107.2 (9.96) c) 21-7 (6.58)	a) 503 (228)	a) 6.25 (30.5) b) 8.85 (43.2)	a) 1.84 (0.56) b) 40 (47) 75	a) 46.5 b) 56 (64) 103	a) 32.5 (37.5) 60 b) - c) -		Ventus b with removable wingtips.
Ventus bT (MGN)	a) 1 b) Glassfibre and carbonfibre	a) Wortmann, Althaus, Holighaus b) 27.7	a) 54-5.5 (16.6) b) 107.2 (9.96) c) 21-7 (6.58)	a) 580 (263) b) 948 (430) c) 370 (168)	a) 6.94 (33.9) b) 8.85 (43.2)	a) 1.84 (0.56) b) 40 (47) 75	a) 46.5 b) -	a) 33 (38) 61 b) 135 (155) 250 c) -	a) Mid-fuselage, retractable 26 hp (19.4 kW) Solo 2350 b) -	179 of all Ventus Turbo versions built between 1983 to 1994.
Ventus c (G)	a) 1 b) Glassfibre, carbonfibre and aramid	a) Wortmann, Althaus, Holighaus b) 23.7	a) 49-2.5 (15) b) 102.4 (9.51) c) 21-7 (6.58)	a) - b) - c) -	a) - b) -	a) - b) -	a) - b) -	a) - b) - c) -	a) - b) -	Built from 1986 to 1994, with removable wingtips (see following entries), Schempp-Hirth airbrakes and 5 litre water ballast tank in the fin.

↑ **Schempp-Hirth Janus CM** *(page 604)*

↑ **Schempp-Hirth Nimbus 3D** *(Peter F. Selinger) (page 604)*

Designation (Type)	a) Crew b) Materials	a) Aerofoil b) Wing aspect ratio	a) Span ft-ins (m) b) Wing area sq ft (m^2) c) Length ft-ins (m)	Weights lb (kg): a) empty b) maximum c) ballast (max)	Wing loading lb/sq ft (kg/m^2) a) minimum b) maximum	a) Minimum rate of sink ft (m)/sec b) at speed of kts (mph) km/h	a) Best glide ratio b) at speed of kts (mph) km/h	Speeds kts (mph) km/h: a) stalling b) maximum c) cruise	a) Engine b) Fuel capacity in litres	Comments
Under the heading *Type*, the following abbreviations have been used: **G** = Glider; **MGS** = Motorglider, self-launch; **MGN** = Motorglider, no self-launch										
Germany										
Manufacturer: Schempp-Hirth Flugzeugbau GmbH (continued)										
Ventus c/16.6	a) 1 b) Glassfibre, carbonfibre and aramid	a) Wortmann, Althaus, Holighaus b) 27.7	a) 54-5.5 (16.6) b) 107.2 (9.96) c) 21-7 (6.58)	a) - b) - c) -	a) - b) -	a) - b) -	a) - b) -	a) - b) -		As previous entry.
Ventus c/17.6	a) 1 b) Glassfibre, carbonfibre and aramid	a) Wortmann, Althaus, Holighaus b) 30.2	a) 57-9 (17.6) b) 109.25 (10.15) c) 21-7 (6.58)	a) 538 (244) b) 1,102 (500) c) 370 (168)	a) - b) 10.10 (49.3)	a) 1.77 (0.54) b) 40 (47) 75	a) 48 b) -	a) 31.5 (36) 58 b) 135 (155) 250 c) -		As above.
Ventus cM (MGS)	a) 1 b) Glassfibre, carbonfibre and aramid	a) Wortmann, Althaus, Holighaus b) 30.2	a) 57-9 (17.6) b) 109.25 (10.15) c) 21-7 (6.58)	a) 683 (310) b) 948 (430) c) 370 (168)	a) 7.76 (37.9) b) 8.68 (42.4)	a) - b) -	a) 48 b) -	a) 35 (40) 64 b) 146 (168) 270 c) -	a) Mid-fuselage, retractable 27 hp (20 kW) Solo engine b) -	109 built between 1988 and 1994.
Ventus cT (MGN)	a) 1 b) Glassfibre, carbonfibre and aramid	a) Wortmann, Althaus, Holighaus b) 30.2	a) 57-9 (17.6) b) 109.25 (10.15) c) 21-7 (6.58)	a) 637 (289) b) 948 (430) c) 370 (168)	a) 7.37 (36) b) 8.68 (42.4)	a) - b) -	a) 48 b) -	a) 34 (39.5) 63 b) 146 (168) 270 c) -	a) Mid-fuselage, retractable 20.8 hp (15.5 kW) Solo engine b) -	109 built between 1987 and 1994.
Ventus 2a and b (G)	a) 1 b) Carbonfibre, glassfibre and aramid	a) Wortmann, Althaus, DU, Holighaus b) 23.3	a) 49-2.5 (15) b) 104.4 (9.7) c) Ventus 2a: 20-10 (6.35) Ventus 2b: 21-7 (6.58)	a) Ventus 2a: 496 (225) Ventus 2b: 507 (230) b) 1,157 (525) c) 384 (174)	a) 6.43 (31.4) b) 11.08 (54.1)	a) - b) -	a) - b) -	a) 30 (34) 55 b) 146 (168) 270 c) -		Built since 1994 and production continues. Narrow fuselage. All Ventus 2 performance data not yet measured.
Ventus 2c (G), with 18 m wingtips	a) 1 b) Carbonfibre, glassfibre and aramid	a) Althaus, DU, Holighaus b) 29.5	a) 59-1 (18) b) 118.4 (11) c) 22-3 (6.78)	a) 582 (264) b) 1,157 (525) c) 384 (174)	a) 6.3 (30.8) b) 9.3 (45.5)	a) - b) -	a) - b) -	a) 30 (34) 55 b) 146 (168) 270 c) -		Built since 1995 and production continues. 4-part wing with inner section having 37 ft 3 ins (11.36 m) span.
Ventus 2c (G), with 15 m wingtips	a) 1 b) Carbonfibre, glassfibre and aramid	a) Althaus, DU, Holighaus b) 23.3	a) 49-2.5 (15) b) 104.4 (9.7) c) 22-3 (6.78)	a) 556 (252) b) 1,157 (525) c) 384 (174)	a) 6.9 (33.8) b) 11.1 (54.3)	a) - b) -	a) - b) -			See above.
Ventus 2cM (MGS)	a) 1 b) Carbonfibre, glassfibre and aramid	a) Althaus, DU, Holighaus b) 29.5	a) 59-1 (18) b) 118.4 (11) c) 22-2 (6.78)	a) 772 (350) b) 1,157 (525) c) 384 (174)	a) 7.95 (38.8) b) 9.32 (45.5)	a) - b) -	a) - b) -	a) 32.5 (38) 60 b) 146 (168) 270 c) 73 (84) 135	a) Mid-fuselage mounted 44 hp (32.8 kW) Solo engine, with retractable propeller; 53.6 hp (40 kW) Solo 2625 available from 1998 b) 43	Built since 1995 and production continues. 4-part wing with inner section having 37 ft 3 ins (11.36 m) span. May also be flown with 15 m tips when the engine is removed.
Ventus 2cT (MGN), with 18 m wingtips	a) 1 b) Carbonfibre, glassfibre and aramid	a) Althaus, DU, Holighaus b) 29.5	a) 59-1 (18) b) 118.4 (11) c) 22-2 (6.78)	a) 683 (310) b) 1,157 (525) c) 384 (174)	a) 7.17 (35) b) 9.32 (45.5)	a) - b) -	a) - b) -	a) 32.5 (38) 60 b) 146 (168) 270 c) 70 (81) 130	a) Mid-fuselage, retractable 20.8 hp (15.5 kW) Solo engine b) 25	Built since 1995 and production continues. 4-part wing with inner section having 37 ft 3 ins (11.36 m) span.
Ventus 2cT (MGN), with 15 m wingtips	a) 1 b) Carbonfibre, glassfibre and aramid	a) Althaus, DU, Holighaus b) 23.3	a) 49-2.5 (15) b) 104.4 (9.7) c) 22-2 (6.78)	a) 657 (298) b) 1,157 (525) c) 384 (174)	a) 7.86 (38.4) b) 11.12 (54.3)	a) - b) -	a) - b) -	a) - b) - c) -		
Manufacturer: Alexander Schleicher Segelflugzeugbau GmbH & Co, Huhnrain 1, D-36161 Poppenhausen/Wasserkuppe (Telephone: +49 6658 89 0, Facsimile: +49 6658 89 40 and 23)										
ASH 25 (G)	a) 2 b) Glassfibre, carbonfibre and aramid	a) HQ17-14.38, DU 84-132V3 b) 38.32	a) 82 (25) b) 175.6 (16.31) c) 29-6 (9)	a) 1,036 (470) b) 1,653 (750) c) 265 (120)	a) 6.96 (34) b) 9.42 (46)	a) 1.38 (0.42) b) 40.5 (47) 75	a) 58 b) 51 (59) 95	a) 41 (47) 75 b) 151 (174) 280		105 built since 1986. Production continues.

↑ **Schempp-Hirth Ventus 2cM** *(J. Ewald) (page 606)*

↑ **Schempp-Hirth Ventus 2cT** *(PJ Photo Library) (page 606)*

Designation (Type)	a) Crew b) Materials	a) Aerofoil b) Wing aspect ratio	a) Span ft-ins (m) b) Wing area sq ft (m^2) c) Length ft-ins (m)	Weights lb (kg): a) empty b) maximum c) ballast (max)	Wing loading lb/sq ft (kg/m^2) a) minimum b) maximum	a) Minimum rate of sink ft (m)/sec b) at speed of kts (mph) km/h	a) Best glide ratio b) at speed of kts (mph) km/h	Speeds kts (mph) km/h: a) stalling b) maximum c) cruise	a) Engine b) Fuel capacity in litres	Comments
Under the heading *Type*, the following abbreviations have been used: **G** = Glider; **MGS** = Motorglider, self-launch; **MGN** = Motorglider, no self-launch										
Germany										
Manufacturer: Alexander Schleicher Segelflugzeugbau GmbH & Co (continued)										
ASH 25 (G), with wingtips	a) 2 b) Glassfibre, carbonfibre and aramid	a) HQ17-14.38, DU 84-132V3 b) 39.82	a) 84 (25.6) b) 177.2 (16.46) c) 29-6 (9)	a) 1,049 (476)	a) 8.81 (43) b) 9.34 (45.6)	a) - b) -	a) 60 b) -	a) - b) -		See previous entry.
ASH 25 E (MGN)	a) 2 b) Glassfibre, carbonfibre and aramid	a) HQ17-14.38, DU 84-132V3 b) 38.32	a) 82 (25) b) 175.6 (16.31) c) 29-6 (9)	a) 1,179 (535) b) 1,653 (750) c) 265 (120)	a) 7.37 (36) b) 9.42 (46)	a) 1.48 (0.45) b) 43 (50) 80	a) 58 b) 51 (59) 95	a) 42 (48) 77 b) 151 (174) 280 c) -	a) Mid-fuselage, retractable 24 hp (17.9 kW) Rotax 277 b) -	64 built between 1987 and 1994.
ASH 25 E (MGN), with wingtips	a) 2 b) Glassfibre, carbonfibre and aramid	a) HQ17-14.38, DU 84-132V3 b) 39.82	a) 84 (25.6) b) 177.2 (16.46) c) 29-6 (9)	a) 1,177 (534)	b) 9.34 (45.6)	a) - b) -	a) 60	a) - b) - c) -		See above.
ASH 25 M (MGS)	a) 2 b) Glassfibre, carbonfibre and aramid	a) HQ17-14.38, DU 84-132V3 b) 38.32	a) 82 (25) b) 175.6 (16.31) c) 29-6 (9)	a) 1,246 (565) b) 1,742 (790) c) 309 (140)	a) 8.07 (39.4) b) 9.91 (48.4)	a) 1.61 (0.49) b) 44 (51) 82	a) 57 b) 51 (59) 95	a) 37 (42.5) 68 b) 151 (174) 280 c) -	a) Mid-fuselage, 50 hp (37.3 kW) Mid-West AE 50R rotary engine, driving a retractable propeller b) -	20 built since 1994.
ASH 25 M (MGS), with wingtips	a) 2 b) Glassfibre, carbonfibre and aramid	a) HQ17-14.38, DU 84-132V3 b) 39.82	a) 84 (25.6) b) 177.2 (16.46) c) 29-6 (9)	a) 1,261 (572)	b) 9.83 (48)		a) 60		See above.	See above.
ASH 26 (G)	a) 1 b) Glassfibre, carbonfibre and aramid	a) DU 89-134/14 b) 27.74	a) 59-1 (18) b) 125.7 (11.68) c) 23-1.5 (7.05)	a) 617 (280) b) 1,157 (525) c) 386 (175)	a) 6.14 (30) b) 9.22 (45)	a) 1.57 (0.48) b) 46 (53) 85	a) 50 approx b) 48 (55) 88	a) 33.5 (39) 62 b) 146 (168) 270 c) -		18 built since 1993. Production continues. Modification to ASH 26 E standard possible in factory.
ASH 26 E (MGS)	a) 1 b) Glassfibre, carbonfibre and aramid	a) DU 89-134/14 b) 27.74	a) 59-1 (18) b) 125.7 (11.68) c) 23-1.5 (7.05)	a) 772 (350) b) 1,157 (525) c) 220 (100)	a) 7.54 (36.8) b) 9.22 (45)	a) 1.57 (0.48) b) 46 (53) 85	a) 50 approx b) 52 (60) 96	a) 37 (42.5) 68 b) 146 (168) 270	a) Mid-fuselage, 50 hp (37.3 kW) Mid-West AE 50R rotary engine, driving a retractable propeller b) -	112 built since 1993. Production continues. Engine easily removable.
ASK 13 (G)	a) 2 b) Wood, steel tube and fabric	a) Gö 535/549 mix, Gö 541 b) 14.63	a) 52-6 (16) b) 188.4 (17.5) c) 26-10 (8.18)	a) 653 (296) b) 1,058 (480) c) -	a) 4.44 (21.7) b) 5.61 (27.4)	a) 2.3 (0.7) b) 32.5 (38) 60	a) 27 b) 46 (53) 85	a) 31-33 (36-38) 57-61 b) 108 (124) 200 c) -		600 built from 1966 to 1980, plus 90 produced by JUBI, Oerlinghausen after 1980.
ASK 21 (G)	a) 2 b) Glassfibre	a) FX S02-196, FX 60-126 b) 16.1	a) 55-9 (17) b) 193.2 (17.95) c) 27-5 (8.35)	a) 794 (360) b) 1,323 (600) c) -	a) 4.92 (24) b) 6.84 (33.4)	a) 2.23 (0.68) b) 41 (47) 76	a) 34 b) 49 (56) 90	a) 35-40 (41-46) 65-74 b) 151 (174) 280) c) -		657 built since 1979. Production continues. Fully aerobatic (+6.5/-4g). Called the Vanguard in RAF Air Cadet use.
ASK 23B (G)	a) 1 b) Glassfibre	a) FX 61-168, FX 60-126 b) 17.44	a) 49-2.5 (15) b) 138.9 (12.9) c) 23-1.5 (7.05)	a) 529 (240) b) 838 (380) c) -	a) 4.92 (24) b) 6.03 (29.46)	a) 2.17 (0.66) b) 40 (46) 74	a) 34 b) 49 (56) 90	a) 35 (40) 64 b) 116 (134) 215 c) -		147 ASK 23s and 23Bs built since 1983. Production continues. Semi aerobatic (+5.3/-2.65g).
ASW 20 (G)	a) 1 b) Glassfibre	a) FX 62-K-131 mod, FX 60-126 b) 21.43	a) 49-2.5 (15) b) 113 (10.5) c) 22-4.5 (6.82)	a) 573 (260) b) 1,001 (454) c) 265 (120)	a) 6.55 (32) b) 8.81 (43)	a) 1.94 (0.59) b) 46 (52) 84	a) 42 b) 54 (62) 100	a) 37 (42.5) 68 b) 143 (165) 265 c) -		865 of all ASW 20 versions built from 1977 to 1990. Also built by Centrair/France in different versions.
ASW 20 (G), with wingtips (ASW 20L)	a) 1 b) Glassfibre	a) FX 62-K-131 mod, FX 60-126 b) 24.9	a) 54-5 (16.59) b) 118.9 (11.05) c) 22-4.5 (6.82)	a) 589 (267) b) 838 (380) c) -	a) 6.25 (30.5) b) 7.05 (34.4)	a) 1.8 (0.55) b) 43 (50) 80	a) 45.5 b) 49 (56) 90	a) 35 (40) 64 b) 135 (155) 250		As above.
ASW 22 (G)	a) 1 b) Glassfibre, carbonfibre and aramid	a) HQ17-14.38, FX 60-126 b) 32.47	a) 72-2 (22) b) 160.4 (14.9) c) 26-7 (8.1)	a) 904 (410) b) 1,673 (750) c) 485 (220)	a) 6.55 (32) b) 10.3 (50.3)	a) 1.44 (0.44) b) 40 (47) 75	a) 55 b) 59 (68) 110	a) 36 (41) 66 b) 151 (174) 280		36 built from 1981 to 1986.
ASW 22 (G), with wingtips	a) 1 b) Glassfibre, carbonfibre and aramid	a) HQ17-14.38, FX 60-126 b) 37.19	a) 78-9 (24) b) 166.73 (15.49) c) 26-7 (8.1)	b) 1,433 (650)	a) 6.47 (31.6) b) 8.6 (42)	a) 1.35 (0.41)	a) 57 b) 54 (62) 100			See above.

↑ **Schleicher ASH 25 M** *(Manfred Münch) (page 607)*

↑ **Schleicher ASW 20L** *(PJ Photo Library) (page 607)*

Designation (Type)	a) Crew b) Materials	a) Aerofoil b) Wing aspect ratio	a) Span ft-ins (m) b) Wing area sq ft (m^2) c) Length ft-ins (m)	Weights lb (kg): a) empty b) maximum c) ballast (max)	Wing loading lb/sq ft (kg/m^2) a) minimum b) maximum	a) Minimum rate of sink ft (m)/sec b) at speed of kts (mph) km/h	a) Best glide ratio b) at speed of kts (mph) km/h	Speeds kts (mph) km/h: a) stalling b) maximum c) cruise	a) Engine b) Fuel capacity in litres	Comments
Under the heading *Type*, the following abbreviations have been used: **G** = Glider; **MGS** = Motorglider, self-launch; **MGN** = Motorglider, no self-launch										
Germany										
Manufacturer: Alexander Schleicher Segelflugzeugbau GmbH & Co (continued)										
ASW 22 B (G)	a) 1 b) Glassfibre, carbonfibre and aramid	a) HQ17-14.38, DU 84-123V3 b) 38.32	a) 82 (25) b) 175.6 (16.31) c) 26-7 (8.1)	a) 990 (449) b) 1,653 (750) c) 485 (220)	a) 6.6 (32.2) b) 9.42 (46)	a) 1.31 (0.40) b) 40.5 (47) 75	a) 60 b) 62 (71) 115	a) 36 (41) 66 b) 151 (174) 280 c) -		7 B/BLs built since 1986. Production continues.
ASW 22 BL (G)	a) 1 b) Glassfibre, carbonfibre and aramid	a) HQ17-14.38, DU 84-123V3 b) 41.81	a) 86-7.5 (26.4) b) 179.4 (16.67) c) 26-7 (8.1)	a) 1,003 (455) b) -	a) 6.49 (31.7) b) 9.22 (45)	a) - b) -	a) above 60 b) -	a) - b) - c) -		As above, with wingtips.
ASW 22 BE (MGS)	a) 1 b) Glassfibre, carbonfibre and aramid	a) HQ17-14.38, DU 84-123V3 b) 38.32	a) 82 (25) b) 175.6 (16.31) c) 26-7 (8.1)	a) 1,202 (545) b) 1,786 (810) c) -	a) 7.72 (37.7) b) 10.18 (49.7)	a) 1.41 (0.43) b) 43 (50) 80	a) 60 b) 62 (71) 115	a) 37 (42.5) 68 b) 151 (174) 280 c) 70 (81) 130	a) From 1986 to 1997: Mid-fuselage, retractable 49 hp (36.5 kW) Rotax 505A. From 1997: Mid-fuselage, 50 hp (37.3 kW) Mid-West AE 50R rotary engine, driving a retractable propeller b) -	29 BEs and BLEs built since 1986. Production continues.
ASW 22 BLE (MGS)	a) 1 b) Glassfibre, carbonfibre and aramid	a) HQ17-14.38, DU 84-123V3 b) 41.81	a) 86-7.5 (26.4) b) 179.4 (16.67) c) 26-7 (8.1)	a) 1,210 (549)	a) 7.6 (37.1) b) 9.95 (48.6)	a) - b) -	a) above 60 b) -	a) - b) - c) -	As above.	As above.
ASW 24 (G)	a) 1 b) Glassfibre, carbonfibre and aramid	a) DU 84-158 b) 22.5	a) 49-2.5 (15) b) 107.6 (10) c) 21.6 (6.55)	a) 507 (230) b) 1,102 (500) c) 342 (155)	a) 6.14 (30) b) 10.24 (50)	a) 1.9 (0.58) b) 46.5 (53) 86	a) 43.5 b) 70 (81) 130	a) 38 (44) 70 b) 151 (174) 280 c) -		241 built since 1987. Production continues. ASW 24 B has winglets.
ASW 24 TOP (MGS)	a) 1 b) Glassfibre, carbonfibre and aramid	a) DU 84-158 b) 22.5	a) 49-2.5 (15) b) 107.6 (10) c) 21.6 (6.55)	a) 606 (275) b) 1,102 (500) or 1,014 (460) max for self-launch c) 342 (155)	a) 7.05 (34.4) b) 10.24 (50)	a) 1.9 (0.58) b) 46.5 (53) 86	a) 43.5 b) 70 (81) 130	a) 40.5 (47) 75 b) 151 (174) 280 c) -	a) Removable Fischer & Entwicklungen mid-fuselage pod, with 24 hp (17.9 kW) König SC 430 engine driving a folding propeller b) -	8 ASW 24 modified by Fischer & Entwicklungen, Germany. Production continues.
ASW 24 E (MGS)	a) 1 b) Glassfibre, carbonfibre and aramid	a) DU 84-158 b) 22.5	a) 49-2.5 (15) b) 107.6 (10) c) 21.6 (6.55)	a) 606 (275) b) 1,102 (500) or 1,014 (460) max for self-launch c) 342 (155)	a) 7.05 (34.4) b) 10.24 (50)	a) 1.9 (0.58) b) 46.5 (53) 86	a) 43.5 b) 70 (81) 130	a) 40.5 (47) 75 b) 151 (174) 280 c) -	a) Mid-fuselage retractable 24 hp (17.9 kW) Rotax 275 b) -	54 built from 1988 to 1993.
ASW 27 (G)	a) 1 b) Glassfibre, carbonfibre, aramid and polyethylene fibre	a) DU 89-134/14, DU 92-131/14 mod b) 25	a) 49-2.5 (15) b) 96.9 (9) c) 21-6 (6.55)	a) 496 (225) b) 1,102 (500) c) 397 (180)	a) 6.72 (32.8) b) 11.38 (55.56)	a) 1.71 (0.52) b) -	a) 48 b) 54 (62) 100	a) 38 (44) 70 b) 151 (174) 280 c) -		55 built since 1995. Production continues.
Manufacturer: Fritz Steinlehner, Berliner Strasse 14, D-84524 Neuötting (Telephone: +49 8671 70586)										
Steinlehner/ Huber SH 2H	a) 1 b) Wood and glassfibre	a) FX 71-L-150/20 b) 9.48	a) 34-1.5 (10.4) b) 122.7 (11.4) c) 21-4 (6.5)	a) 529 (240) b) 750 (340) c) -	a) - b) 6.1 (29.8)	a) 2.66 (0.81) b) -	a) 26 b) 46 (53) 85	a) 35 (41) 65 b) 124 (143) 230		1 homebuilt constructed in 1989 by H. Havrda. SH 1S under construction. Fully aerobatic (±8g).

↑ **Schleicher ASW 24 TOP** *(Peter F. Selinger) (page 608)*

↑ **Schleicher ASW 27** *(J. Ewald) (page 608)*

Designation (Type)	a) Crew b) Materials	a) Aerofoil b) Wing aspect ratio	a) Span ft-ins (m) b) Wing area sq ft (m^2) c) Length ft-ins (m)	Weights lb (kg): a) empty b) maximum c) ballast (max)	Wing loading lb/sq ft (kg/m^2) a) minimum b) maximum	a) Minimum rate of sink ft (m)/sec b) at speed of kts (mph) km/h	a) Best glide ratio b) at speed of kts (mph) km/h	Speeds kts (mph) km/h: a) stalling b) maximum c) cruise	a) Engine b) Fuel capacity in litres	Comments
Under the heading *Type*, the following abbreviations have been used: **G** = Glider; **MGS** = Motorglider, self-launch; **MGN** = Motorglider, no self-launch										
Germany										
Manufacturer: Stemme GmbH & Co KG, Flugplatz Strausberg, D-15344 Strausberg (Telephone: +49 3341 31 1170, Facsimile: +49 3341 31 1173)										
S 10 (V) (MGS)	a) 2 b) Composites	a) HQ41/14.35 b) 28.2	a) 75-5.5 (23) b) 201.3 (18.7) c) 27-7.5 (8.42)	a) 1,411 (640) b) 1,874 (850) c) -	a) 7.84 (38.3) b) 9.28 (45.3)	a) 1.84 (0.56) b) 46 (53) 85	a) 50 b) 57 (65) 105	a) 38 (44) 70 b) 146 (168) 270 c) 89 (103) 165 or 121 (140) 225 with variable-pitch propeller	a) Mid-fuselage 93 hp (69.4 kW) Limbach L 2400 ED1D, driving a front folding propeller b) 90 or 120	Over 62 built since 1986 and production continues. 'V' versions have variable-pitch propellers.
S 10 (V)C (MGS)	a) 2 b) Composites	a) HQ41/14.35 b) 28.2	a) 75-5.5 (23) b) 201.3 (18.7) c) 27-7.5 (8.42)	a) 1,477 (670) b) 2,161 (980) c) -	a) 8.32 (40.6) b) 10.73 (52.4)	a) 1.97 (0.6) b) 48 (55) 88	a) 50 b) 59 (68) 109	a) 40.5 (47) 75 b) 146 (168) 270 c) 89 (103) 165 or 121 (140) 225 with variable-pitch propeller	a) Mid-fuselage 93 hp (69.4 kW) Limbach L 2400 ED1D, driving a front folding propeller b) 90 or 120	3 built since 1990; production on request. Used as multi-purpose sensor platform with underwing pods.
S 10 (V)T (MGS)	a) 2 b) Composites	a) HQ41/14.35 b) 28.2	a) 75-5.5 (23) b) 201.3 (18.7) c) 27-7.5 (8.42)	a) 1,422 (645) b) 1,874 (850) c) -	a) 7.84 (38.3) b) 9.28 (45.3)	a) 1.84 (0.56) b) 46 (53) 85	a) 50 b) 57 (65) 105	a) 38 (44) 70 b) 146 (168) 270 c) 127 (146) 235	a) Mid-fuselage 115 hp (85.75 kW) turbocharged Rotax 914 F, driving a front folding propeller b) 90 or 120	Built since 1997 and production continues.
Manufacturer: Technoflug GmbH, Dr.-Kurt-Steim-Strasse 6, D-78713 Schramberg-Sulgen (Telephone: +49 7422 8423, Facsimile: +49 7422 8744)										
Piccolo b (MGS)	a) 1 b) Glassfibre	a) FX 63-137 b) 16.6	a) 43-7.5 (13.3) b) 114.1 (10.6) c) 20-7 (6.28)	a) 397 (180) b) 655 (297) c) -	a) - b) 5.73 (28)	a) 2.95 (0.9) b) -	a) 23 b) 42 (48) 78	a) 29.5 (34) 54 b) 92 (106) 170 c) 65-73 (75-84) 120 -135	a) 23hp (17.15 kW) Solo 2350 BS behind wing with folding 3-blade pusher propeller b) 22.5	Over 100 built since 1986, as the production version of the Neukom AN 20K. Fulfils JAR motorglider and microlight specifications. Strut-braced wings.
TFK-2 Carat	a) 1 b) -	a) - b) 21.27	a) 49-2.5 (15) with or without winglets b) 113.9 (10.58) c) 20-4.5 (6.21)	a) 716.5 (325) b) 1,036 (470) c) -	a) 7.54 (36.8) b) 9.09 (44.4)	a) 2.46 (0.75) b) 49 (56) 90	a) 35 b) 57 (65) 105	a) 43.5 (50) 80 b) 135 (155) 250 c) 108 (124) 200	a) 53.6 hp (40 kW) Sauer b) 54	Retractable undercarriage. To be JAR certified 'semi-aerobatic'. First flown 1997.
Manufacturer: TWI Flugzeuggesellschaft mbH (no longer operating)										
Taifun 17 EII (MGS)	a) 2 b) Glassfibre	a) FX 67-K-170/17 b) 16.4	a) 55-9 (17) b) 189.4 (17.6) c) 25-6 (7.78)	a) 1,345 (610) b) 1,874 (850) c) -	a) - b) 9.89 (48.3)	a) 3.12 (0.95) b) 46 (53) 85	a) 30 b) 62 (71) 115	a) 39 (45) 72 b) 135 (155) 250 c) -	a) Front-mounted 90 hp (67 kW) Limbach L 2400 EB1B b) 90	Was produced by Valentin and later FFB. Retractable 3-wheel undercarriage. Some modified to Rotax 914 and other engines by Korff/Germany.
Kiwi (MGS) and Mistral C (G)	a) 1 b) Glassfibre	a) FX 61-163/FX 60-126 b) 20.4	a) 49-2.5 (15) b) 118.7 (11.03) c) 22-4 (6.8)	a) 452 (205) as glider b) 838 (380) as MGS c) -	a) - b) 7.07 (34.5) as MGS	a) 1.9 (0.58) as glider b) -	a) 37 as glider b) -	a) 33.5 (39) 62 b) 132 (152) 245 c) -	a) as MGS: Removable mid-fuselage Fischer & Entwicklungen pod with 24 hp (17.9 kW) König SC 430 engine, driving a folding propeller	Was produced as the Mistral C glider by Valentin and later FFT. Became the Kiwi motorglider.
Manufacturer: Wolf Hirth Flugzeugbau GmbH, Flugplatz Nabern, Nenestrasse 107, D-73230 Kirchheim/Teck (Telephone: +49 7021 89 3398, Facsimile: +49 7021 89 3399)										
Janus CMH (MGS)	a) 2 b) Glassfibre and carbonfibre	a) FX 67-K-170/150 b) 20	a) 65-7.5 (20) b) 186.2 (17.3) c) 28-3.5 (8.62)	a) 1,058 (480) b) 1,543 (700) c) -	a) - b) 8.3 (40.5)	a) 2.23 (0.68) b) 52 (60) 97	a) 43.5 b) 61 (70) 113	a) 39.5 (46) 73 b) 135 (155) 250 c) -	a) Mid-fuselage 63 hp (47 kW) Rotax 582/40, with retractable shaft-driven propeller b) 14	Prototype for a new propeller-drive concept built in a Janus C in 1995. Available for other engines and gliders.
Hungary										
Manufacturer: Autó-Aeró Közlekedéstechnikai (no longer operating)										
Góbé R-26 SU (G)	a) 2 b) Metal and fabric	a) Göttingen 549 mod b) 10.9	a) 45-11 (14) b) 193.75 (18) c) 29.6 (9)	a) 529 (240) b) 970 (440) c) -	a) - b) 5 (24.4)	a) 3.18 (0.97) b) 40.5 (47) 75	a) 23.2 b) 43.5 (50) 80	a) 33.5 (39) 62 b) 103 (118) 190		Large number built from early 1960s to the mid-1980s.

↑ **Stemme S10 (V)C** *(page 609)*

↑ **Technoflug Piccolo b** *(Peter F. Selinger)* *(page 609)*

Designation (Type)	a) Crew b) Materials	a) Aerofoil b) Wing aspect ratio	a) Span ft-ins (m) b) Wing area sq ft (m^2) c) Length ft-ins (m)	Weights lb (kg): a) empty b) maximum c) ballast (max)	Wing loading lb/sq ft (kg/m^2) a) minimum b) maximum	a) Minimum rate of sink ft (m)/sec b) at speed of kts (mph) km/h	a) Best glide ratio b) at speed of kts (mph) km/h	Speeds kts (mph) km/h: a) stalling b) maximum c) cruise	a) Engine b) Fuel capacity in litres	Comments
Under the heading *Type*, the following abbreviations have been used: **G** = Glider; **MGS** = Motorglider, self-launch; **MGN** = Motorglider, no self-launch										
India										
Manufacturer: Technical Centre, Civil Aviation Department, Nr Safdarjung Airport, New Dehli 110003 (Telephone: +91 133 611504)										
ATS-1 Ardhra	a) 2 b) Wood and fabric	a) FX 61-184 b) 12.46	a) 54-1.5 (16.5) b) 235 (21.83) c) 28.3 (8.61)	a) 723 (328) b) 1,120 (508) c) -	a) - b) 4.77 (23.28)	a) 2.53 (0.77) b) 39 (45) 72	a) 28 b) 49 (56) 90	a) 33 (38) 61 b) 113 (130) 210		Most built by HAL. Production completed.
Iran										
Manufacturer: Aviation Industries of Iran (AII), Ministry of Industries, Building No 2, 56 Gharani Avenue, Tehran 15815 (Telephone: +98 21 817 2570 and 2572, Facsimile: +98 21 889 7658 and 7659)										
IR-G1 Nasim/AVA 101 (G)	a) 2 b) Composites	a) - b) 16	a) 55-9 (17) b) 194 (18.02) c) 27-5 (8.35)	a) 1,014 (460) b) 1,323 (600) c) -	a) 4.71 (23) b) 6.76 (33)	a) 2.3 (0.7) b) -	a) 35 b) 54 (62) 100	a) 38 (43) 70 b) 133 (153) 247 c) -		Iran Hava Commercial Services Co at same address also for sales. Glider first flew 30 May 1996; for JAR 22 certification. Load factor +5.3/-2.65.
Italy										
Manufacturer: Alisport SRL., Via Confaltonieri 22, I-22060 Cremella (LC)										
Silent (G) and (MGS)	a) 1 b) Glassfibre	a) - b) 13.98	a) 39-4.5 (12) b) 110.87 (10.3) c) 21 (6.4)	a) 265 (120) b) 485 (220) c) -	a) - b) 4.37 (21.35)	a) 2.46 (0.75) b) -	a) 31 b) -	a) - b) 108 (124) 200	a) Also powered versions with mid-fuselage mounted engine pod and folding propeller or retractable engine	Equipped with flaperons. Prototypes flying in 1996. Electric-driven version built 1997 in Germany by Air Energy.
Lithuania										
Manufacturer: AB Sportinė Aviacija, Pociúnai, LT-4340 Prienai (ex-Lithuanian Factory of Aviation, LAK) (Telephone: +370 49 51575, Facsimile: +370 49 53039)										
LAK 12 (G)	a) 1 b) Glassfibre and carbonfibre	a) FX 67-K-170/150 b) 28.5	a) 67 (20.42) b) 157.5 (14.63) c) 23-9 (7.23)	a) 794 (360) b) 1,433 (650) c) 419 (190)	a) 6.14 (30) b) 9.1 (44.43)	a) 1.57 (0.48) b) 40.5 (47) 75	a) 48 b) 62 (71) 115	a) 35 (41) 65 b) 135 (155) 250 c) -		Built since 1979. Production continues.
LAK-17 Nida (G)	a) 1 b) Glassfibre and carbonfibre	a) VAG/KTU 92-130 and 150/15 b) 24.83	a) 49-2.5 (15) b) 97.52 (9.06) c) 21-1 (6.42)	a) 461 (209) b) 899 (408) c) 359 (163)	a) 6.14 (30) b) 9.22 (45)	a) 1.74 (0.53) b) 43.5 (50) 80	a) 45 b) 62 (71) 115	a) 38 (44) 70 b) 135 (155) 250 c) -		Built since 1992. Production continues.
LAK-17 A Nida (G)	a) 1 b) Glassfibre and carbonfibre	a) VAG/KTU 92-130, 13 mod, -150/15, KTU 93-147/22 and -148 (tips) b) 24.83	a) 49-2.5 (15) b) 97.52 (9.06) c) 21-1 (6.42)	a) 434 (197) b) 999 (453) c) 410 (186)	a) 5.69 (27.8) b) 10.24 (50)	a) 1.74 (0.53) b) 43.5 (50) 80	a) 44 b) 62 (71) 115	a) 38 (44) 70 b) 135 (155) 250 c) -		First flown 28 May 1998.
LAK-17 A Nida (G), with wingtips	a) 1 b) Glassfibre and carbonfibre	a) - b) 32.99	a) 59-0.5 (18) b) 105.7 (9.82) c) 21-1 (6.42)	a) 448 (203)	a) - b) 9.44 (46.1)	a) - b) -	a) 45 b) -	a) - b) - c) -		

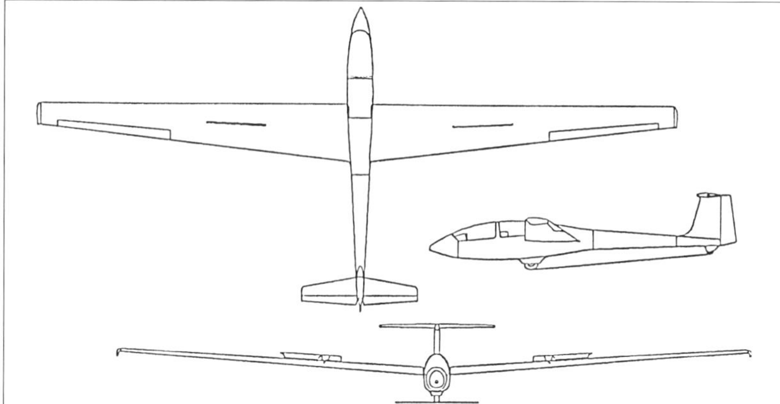
↑ Aviation Industries of Iran IR-G1 Nasim/AVA 101 *(page 610)*

↑ AB Sportinė Aviacija LAK 12 *(page 610)*

↑ AB Sportinė Aviacija LAK 17 Nida *(page 610)*

↑ HB Aviation HB 23/2400 Hobbyliner *(J. Ewald) (page 611)*

Designation (Type)	a) Crew b) Materials	a) Aerofoil b) Wing aspect ratio	a) Span ft-ins (m) b) Wing area sq ft (m^2) c) Length ft-ins (m)	Weights lb (kg): a) empty b) maximum c) ballast (max)	Wing loading lb/sq ft (kg/m^2) a) minimum b) maximum	a) Minimum rate of sink ft (m)/sec b) at speed of kts (mph) km/h	a) Best glide ratio b) at speed of kts (mph) km/h	Speeds kts (mph) km/h: a) stalling b) maximum c) cruise	a) Engine b) Fuel capacity in litres	Comments
Under the heading *Type*, the following abbreviations have been used: **G** = Glider; **MGS** = Motorglider, self-launch; **MGN** = Motorglider, no self-launch										
Netherlands										
Manufacturer: HB Aviation International, Maraboeweg 8, NL-8218 MV Lelystad Airport (Telephone:+31 320 288 30, Facsimile: +31 320 288 148, E-mail: e.evers@pi.net)										
HB 23/2400 Hobbyliner/ Scanliner	a) 2 b) Wood, steel and composites	a) FX 61-184, FX 60-126 b) 14	a) 53-10 (16.41) b) 205.3 (19.07) c) 24-1.5 (7.35)	a) 1,168 (530) or 1,213 (550) b) 1,676 (760) c) -	a) - b) 8.16 (39.85)	a) 4.59 (1.4) b) 60 (69) 111	a) 18 b) 63 (72) 116	a) 40.5 (47) 75 b) 108 (124) 200 c) 93 (107) 172	a) Mid-fuselage 110 hp (82 kW) VW-HB-2400 b) 100	About 60 built and production continues. Scanliner is an observation aircraft with a full glass cockpit. Built in Austria.
Norway										
Manufacturer: Lunds Tekniske, PO Box 463, N-8601 Mo (Telephone: +47 75 152100)										
Silhouette (MGS)	a) 1 b) Composites	a) - b) 13.46 or 18.69 with wing extensions	a) 41 (12.5) with wing extensions b) 90 (8.36) with wing extensions c) 19-3 (5.87)	a) 578 (262) b) 825 (374) c) -	a) - b) 9.16 (44.74) with wing extensions	a) - b) -	a) - b) -	a) 45.5 (52.5) 84 b) 121 (140) 225 c) 104 (120) 193	a) Front mounted 40 hp (29.8 kW) Rotax 447 or 50 hp (37.3 kW) Rotax 503 b) -	Homebuilt light aircraft with standard wings, or motorglider with wing extensions.
Poland										
Manufacturer: DWL KK Ltd. Warsaw (marketed by Solaire North America Ltd., 41 Cottonwood Lane, Hilton Head Island, SC 19926, USA)										
PW-2D Gapa D (G)	a) 1 b) Glassfibre and fabric	a) - b) 9.5	a) 36-1 (11) b) 136.7 (12.7) c) 18-0.5 (5.5)	a) 243 (110) b) 485 (220) c) -	a) - b) 3.55 (17.32)	a) 3.61 (1.1) b) 28 (32) 52	a) 16 b) 38 (43) 70	a) - b) 81 (93) 150 c) -		'Primary' certified to JAR 22 Utility category.
Manufacturer: J and AS Aero Design. ul Nowowiejska 2/29, PL-91 061, Lodz (Telephone: +48 42 323552)										
J6 Fregata (MGS)	a) 1 b) Composites	a) - b) 17.24	a) 41-2 (12.55) b) 98.33 (9.135) c) 16-9 (5.11)	a) 573 (260) b) 904 (410) c) -	a) - b) 9.19 (44.88)	a) 3.3 (1) b) -	a) 23 b) -	a) 41 (47) 75 b) 108 (124) 200 c) 97 (112) 180	a) 52 hp (38.8 kW) J and AS 3PZ-800 b) 60	First flown in 1995. Enlarged development of J5 Marco type.
Manufacturer: Edward Marganski, Poland. Worldwide sales and information: Güntert + Kohlmetz, Bruchsaler Strasse 52, D-76646 Bruchsal (Germany: Telephone: +49 7257 1071, Facsimile: +49 7257 1070)										
MDM-1 Fox (G); MGN version under construction	a) 2 b) Glassfibre and carbonfibre	a) NACA 64.412 b) 15.88	a) 45-11 (14) b) 132.7 (12.33) c) 24-2.5 (7.38)	a) 750 (340) b) 1,157 (525) c) -	a) 6.96 (34) b) 8.7 (42.5)	a) 3.12 (0.95) b) 53 (61) 98	a) 30 b) 67 (78) 125	a) 44.5 (51) 82 b) 152 (175) 282 c) -		25 built since 1993. Fully aerobatic: +7.5/-5.5g with 2 crew, +10/-7.5g with pilot only. Production continues.
Swift S-1 (G)	a) 1 b) Glassfibre	a) NACA $64_1$412 b) 13.8	a) 41-7 (12.68) b) 126.3 (11.73) c) 22-8 (6.91)	a) 639 (290) b) 904 (410) c) -	a) 6.02 (29.4) b) 7.15 (34.9)	a) 3.12 (0.95) b) 46.5 (53) 86	a) 28 b) 68 (78) 126	a) 39 (45) 72 b) 155 (178) 287 c) -		33 built. Production continues. Fully aerobatic: +10/-7.5g.
Manufacturer: Politechnika Warszawska, Institute of Aerodynamics and Applied Mechanics, Nowowiejska 22/24, PL-00-665 Warsaw (Telephone: +48 2 6285748, Facsimile: +48 2 628587)										
PW-4 Pelikan (MGS)	a) 2 b) Glassfibre and fabric	a) - b) 13.95	a) 53-2 (16.2) b) 202.4 (18.8) c) 26-3 (8)	a) 1,102 (500) b) 1,587 (720) c) -	a) - b) 7.84 (38.3)	a) 3.94 (1.2) b) 46.5 (53) 86	a) 20 b) 51 (59) 95	a) 38 (44) 70 b) - c) -	a) Mid-fuselage 80 hp (59.7 kW) Limbach L 2000 EC1 driving a pusher propeller b) 40	Prototype first flew in December 1990.
PW-5 Smyk - see PZL-Swidnik										
PW-6 (G)	a) 2 b) Glassfibre	a) - b) 16.8	a) 52-6 (16) b) 164.15 (15.25) c) 25-9 (7.85)	a) 661 (300) b) 1,146 (520) c) -	a) - b) 6.96 (34)	a) 2.46 (0.75) b) -	a) 34 b) -	a) 37 (42.5) 68 b) 124 (143) 230		2-seat version of the PW-5, under construction in 1997. MGS version also planned.
Manufacturer: PDPS PZL-Bielsko, ul. Cieszynska 325, PL-43-300 Bielsko-Biala (Telephone:+48 33 125021, Facsimile: +48 33 123739)										
SZD-48-3 Jantar Standard 3 (G)	a) 1 b) Glassfibre	a) NN-8 b) 21.1	a) 49-2.5 (15) b) 114.7 (10.66) c) 22-6 (6.85)	a) 573 (260) b) 1,190 (540) c) 331 (150)	a) 6.27 (30.6) b) 10.37 (50.65)	a) 1.97 (0.6) b) 40.5 (47) 75	a) 40 b) 51 (59) 95	a) 38 (44) 70 b) 154 (177) 285 c) -		345 built since 1983. Semi aerobatic.
SZD 50-3 Puchacz (G)	a) 2 b) Glassfibre	a) FX 61-168/ 60-1261 b) 15.3	a) 54-8 (16.67) b) 195.5 (18.16) c) 27-6 (8.38)	a) 794 (360) b) 1,257 (570) c) -	a) 5.02 (24.5) b) 6.43 (31.4)	a) 2.3 (0.7) b) 40.5 (47) 75	a) 30 b) 46 (53) 85	a) 32.5 (37.5) 60 b) 116 (134) 215		Over 286 built since 1979. Production continues. Semi aerobatic.
SZD 51-1 Junior (G)	a) 1 b) Glassfibre	a) FX SO2-196/SO2/1-158 b) 18	a) 49-2.5 (15) b) 134.7 (12.51) c) 21-11 (6.69)	a) 496 (225) b) 838 (380) c) -	a) 4.18 (20.4) b) 6.23 (30.4)	a) 1.77 (0.54) b) 38 (43.5) 70	a) 35 b) 43 (50) (80)	a) 32.5 (37.5) 60 b) 119 (137) 220 c) -		Over 200 built since 1979. Production continues. Semi aerobatic.
SZD-54 Perkoz (G)	a) 2 b) Glassfibre	a) NN-8 b) 18.7	a) 57-5 (17.5) b) 176.1 (16.36) c) 26-3 (8)	a) 805 (365) b) 1,290 (585) c) -	a) - b) 7.32 (35.76)	a) 2.2 (0.67) b) -	a) 35 b) -	a) 32.5 (37.5) 60 b) 146 (168) 270 c) -		Prototype flew in 1991.

↑ **Edward Marganski MDM-1 Fox** *(J. Ewald) (page 611)*

↑ **Politechnika Warszawska PW-4 Pelikan** *(Wojciech Fraczek) (page 611)*

Designation (Type)	a) Crew b) Materials	a) Aerofoil b) Wing aspect ratio	a) Span ft-ins (m) b) Wing area sq ft (m²) c) Length ft-ins (m)	Weights lb (kg): a) empty b) maximum c) ballast (max)	Wing loading lb/sq ft (kg/m²) a) minimum b) maximum	a) Minimum rate of sink ft (m)/sec b) at speed of kts (mph) km/h	a) Best glide ratio b) at speed of kts (mph) km/h	Speeds kts (mph) km/h: a) stalling b) maximum c) cruise	a) Engine b) Fuel capacity in litres	Comments
Under the heading *Type*, the following abbreviations have been used: **G** = Glider; **MGS** = Motorglider, self-launch; **MGN** = Motorglider, no self-launch										
Poland										
Manufacturer: PDPS PZL-Bielsko (continued)										
SZD-55-1 (G)	a) 1 b) Glassfibre	a) NN-27 b) 23.44	a) 49-2.5 (15) b) 103.33 (9.6) c) 22-6 (6.85)	a) 474 (215) b) 1,102 (500) c) 430 (195)	a) 5.84 (28.5) b) 10.67 (52.1)	a) 1.9 (0.58) b) 41 (47) 76	a) 44 b) 64 (74) 119	a) 34 (39.5) 63 b) 138 (158) 255 c) -		Over 63 built since 1988. Production continues. Semi aerobatic.
SZD-56-1 Diana (G)	a) 1 b) Carbonfibre and aramid	a) NN-27-13 b) 27.57	a) 49-2.5 (15) b) 87.83 (8.16) c) 22-7 (6.88)	a) 408 (185) b) 904 (410) c) 353 (160)	a) - b) 10.24 (50)	a) 1.51 (0.46) b) 39 (45) 72	a) 48 b) 60 (70) 112	a) 35 (41) 65 b) 148 (171) 275 c) -		Built since 1990. Production continues.
SZD-59 Acro (G)	a) 1 b) Glassfibre	a) NN-8 b) 17.8	a) 43-4 (13.2) b) 105.5 (9.8) c) 22-6 (6.85)	a) 595 (270) b) 838 (380) c) -	a) 7 (34.2) b) 7.95 (38.8)	a) 2.53 (0.77) b) 52 (60) 97	a) 36 b) 57 (66) 106	a) 44.5 (51) 82 b) 154 (177) 285 c) -		Built since 1991. Production continues. Fully aerobatic +7/-5g.
SZD-59 Acro (G), with wing extensions	a) 1 b) Glassfibre	a) NN-8 b) 21.1	a) 49-2.5 (15) b) 114.7 (10.66)	a) 617 (280) b) 1,190 (540) c) 331 (150)	a) 6.35 (31) b) 10.38 (50.7)	a) 2.17 (0.66) b) 44 (51) 82	a) 40 b) 60 (69) 111	a) 40 (46) 74 b) 143 (165) 265		See above. Semi-aerobatic.
Manufacturer: PZL-Świdnik S.A., Al. Lotników Polskich 1, PL-21-045 Świdnik (Telephone: +48 81 680901, Facsimile: +48 81 680919)										
PW-5 Smyk (G)	a) 1 b) Glassfibre	a) NN 18-17 b) 17.8	a) 44-1 (13.44) b) 109.4 (10.16) c) 20-4 (6.2)	a) under 419 (190) b) 661 (300) c) -	a) - b) 6.04 (29.5)	a) 2.1 (0.64) b) 39.5 (45) 73	a) 33 b) 43 (50) 80	a) 33.5 (39) 62 b) 119 (137) 220 c) -		World class glider. 140 built since 1992. Prototype built by Politechnika Warszawska.
Manufacturer: WSK PZL-Krosno, ul. Zwirki i Wiguri 6, PL- 38-400 Krosno (Telephone: +48 131 680901, Facsimile: +48 131 22911 or 22861)										
KR-03A Puchatek (G)	a) 2 b) Aluminium alloy and fabric	a) FX SO2/1-158 b) 13.7	a) 53-10 (16.4) b) 209.25 (19.44) c) 28-4 (8.63)	a) under 772 (350) b) 1,190 (540) c) -	a) 4.38 (21.39) b) 5.69 (27.77)	a) 2.56 (0.78) b) 41 (47) 75	a) 27 b) 46 (53) 85	a) 32 (37) 59 b) 108 (124) 200 c) -	a) - b) -	Over 51 built since 1986. Production continues. Semi aerobatic.
Romania										
Manufacturer: IAR S.A., 1 Aeroportului Street, PO Box 198, 2200 Brasov (Telephone: +40 68 150014, 150015 or 150597, Facsimile: +40 68 151304 and 150623)										
IAR-35 (G)	a) 1 b) Aluminium alloy	a) NACA 642-015 b) 13.3	a) 39-4 (12) b) 116.25 (10.8) c) 21-4 (6.5)	a) 573 (260) b) 882 (400) c) -	a) - b) 7.21 (35.2)	a) 3.94 (1.2) b) 51 (59) 95	a) 27 b) 54 (62) 100	a) 46 (53) 85 b) 181 (208) 335		Built since 1989. Production continues. Fully aerobatic (±7g)
IS-28B2 (G)	a) 2 b) Aluminum alloy	a) FX 61-163 and FX 60-126 b) 15.84	a) 55-9 (17) b) 196.33 (18.24) c) 27-9 (8.45)	a) 882 (400) b) 1,300 (590) c) -	a) - b) 6.62 (32.3)	a) 2.56 (0.78) b) 46 (53) 85	a) 34 b) 54 (62) 100	a) 38 (44) 70 b) 124 (143) 23 c) -		In production. Single-seat, aerobatic (+6.5/-4g).

↑ **PDPS PZL-Bielsko SZD-48-3 Jantar Standard 3** *(Peter F. Selinger) (page 611)*

↑ **PZL-Świdnik PW-5 Smyk** *(J. Ewald) (page 612)*

↑ **WSK PZL-Krosno KR-03A Puchatek** *(page 612)*

↑ **IAR IS-28B2** *(PJ Photo Library) (page 612)*

Designation (Type)	a) Crew b) Materials	a) Aerofoil b) Wing aspect ratio	a) Span ft-ins (m) b) Wing area sq ft (m^2) c) Length ft-ins (m)	Weights lb (kg): a) empty b) maximum c) ballast (max)	Wing loading lb/sq ft (kg/m^2) a) minimum b) maximum	a) Minimum rate of sink ft (m)/sec b) at speed of kts (mph) km/h	a) Best glide ratio b) at speed of kts (mph) km/h	Speeds kts (mph) km/h: a) stalling b) maximum c) cruise	a) Engine b) Fuel capacity in litres	Comments
Under the heading *Type*, the following abbreviations have been used: **G** = Glider; **MGS** = Motorglider, self-launch; **MGN** = Motorglider, no self-launch										
Romania										
Manufacturer: IAR S.A (continued)										
IS-28 M2A (MGS), Limbach powered	a) 2 b) Aluminium alloy	a) FX 61-163 and FX 60-126 b) 15.84	a) 55-9 (17) b) 196.33 (18.24) c) 24-7 (7.5)	a) 1,235 (560) b) 1,676 (760) c) -	a) - b) 8.54 (41.7)	a) 3.94 (1.2) b) 43 (50) 80	a) 24 b) 54 (62) 100	a) 36 (41) 66 b) 119 (137) 220 c) 92 (106) 170	a) Front-mounted 80 hp (59.7 kW) Limbach L 2000 EO1 b) 40-60	Semi aerobatic. 80 hp (59.7 kW) Limbach-powered prototype version of 68 hp (50.7 kW) IS-28A; built in 1994.
IS-28 M2G (MGS)	a) 2 b) Aluminium alloy	a) FX 61-163 and FX 60-126 b) 15.84	a) 55-9 (17) b) 196.33 (18.24) c) 25-3 (7.7)	a) 1,279 (580) b) 1,720 (780) c) -	a) - b) 8.77 (42.8)	a) 3.77 (1.15) b) 43 (50) 80	a) 24 b) 57 (65) 105	a) - b) 119 (137) 220 c) 97 (112) 180	a) Front-mounted 80 hp (59.7 kW) Limbach L 2000 EO1 b) 40-60	M2G is slightly modified to conform to JAR. Built since 1995 and production continues.
IS-28 M2GR (MGS)	a) 2 b) Aluminium alloy	a) FX 61-163 and FX 60-126 b) 15.84	a) 55-9 (17) b) 196.33 (18.24) c) 25-3 (7.7)	a) 1,279 (580) b) 1,720 (780) c) -	a) - b) 8.77 (42.8)	a) 3.77 (1.15) b) 43 (50) 80	a) 24 b) 57 (65) 105	a) 41 (47) 75 b) 119 (137) 220 c) 103 (118) 190	a) Front-mounted 80 hp (59.7 kW) Rotax 912 A3 b) 60	Rotax-powered version. Prototype built 1997. Production continues.
IS-29 D2 (G)	a) 1 b) Aluminium alloy	a) FX 61-163 and FX 60-126 b) 21.84	a) 49-2.5 (15) b) 110.9 (10.3) c) 24 (7.3)	a) 529 (240) b) 794 (360) c) -	a) - b) 7.15 (34.9)	a) 2 (0.61) b) 42 (48) 78	a) 37 b) 50 (58) 93	a) 41 (47) 75 b) 121 (140) 225 c) -		Production continues.
Russia										
Manufacturer: KB MAI (Design Bureau of Moscow Aviation Institute) (Telephone: +7 095 1584468)										
Aviatika 920 (G)	a) 1 b) Metal, fabric and glassfibre	a) 1-14 b) 9.96	a) 32-10 (10) b) 108.07 (10.04) c) 17-5 (5.3)	a) 227 (103) b) 441 (200) c) -	a) - b) 4.08 (19.9)	a) 3.61 (1.1) b) -	a) 15 b) -	a) 24.5 (28) 45 b) - c) -		Developed from the Aviatika 890 aeroplane.
South Africa										
Manufacturer: Celair Ltd., PO Box 77, Ermelo 2350, Transvaal										
Celstar CG-1 (G)	a) 1 b) Composites	a) FX 71-L-150/25 b) 11.7	a) 36-3 (11.05) b) 110.8 (10.3) c) 21-4 (6.5)	a) 584 (265) b) 826 (375) c) -	a) - b) 7.46 (36.4)	a) 2.95 (0.9) b) -	a) 23 b) -	a) 43.5 (50) 80 b) 175 (201) 324 c) -		Fully aerobatic (±10g).
Sweden										
Manufacturer: AB Radab, Box 92054, S-120 06 Stockholm (Telephone: +46 8 6440610, Facsimile: +46 8 6404436, E-mail: windex@algonet.se)										
Windex 1200 C (MGS)	a) 1 b) Glassfibre and carbonfibre	a) RR-17 b) 19.75	a) 39-8.5 (12.1) b) 79.76 (7.41) c) 16-2 (4.92)	a) 386 (175) b) 683 (310) or 595 (270) aerobatic c) -	a) - b) 8.58 (41.9)	a) 2.13 (0.65) b) 40.5 (47) 75	a) 38 b) 54 (62) 100	a) 38 (41) 70 b) 146 (168) 270 c) 113 (130) 209	a) Tailfin-mounted 24 hp (17.9 kW) König, driving a variable-pitch propeller. b) -	Kit MGS in 3 parts. Fully aerobatic (+9/-7 g) at below 595 lb (270 kg).

↑ **Aviatika 920** *(page 613)*

↑ **Celair Celstar CG-1** *(J. Ewald) (page 613)*

↑ **AB Radab Windex 1200 C** *(J. Ewald) (page 613)*

↑ **Edgley EA.9 Optimist** *(J. Ewald) (page 614)*

Designation (Type)	a) Crew b) Materials	a) Aerofoil b) Wing aspect ratio	a) Span ft-ins (m) b) Wing area sq ft (m^2) c) Length ft-ins (m)	Weights lb (kg): a) empty b) maximum c) ballast (max)	Wing loading lb/sq ft (kg/m^2) a) minimum b) maximum	a) Minimum rate of sink ft (m)/sec b) at speed of kts (mph) km/h	a) Best glide ratio b) at speed of kts (mph) km/h	Speeds kts (mph) km/h: a) stalling b) maximum c) cruise	a) Engine b) Fuel capacity in litres	Comments
Under the heading *Type*, the following abbreviations have been used: **G** = Glider; **MGS** = Motorglider, self-launch; **MGN** = Motorglider, no self-launch										
United Kingdom										
Manufacturer: Edgley Sailplanes Ltd., Unit 1, Fletcher Industrial Estate, Clovelly Road, Bideford, Devon EX39 3EU (Telephone: +44 1237 422251, Facsimile: +44 1237 422253)										
EA.9 Optimist (G)	a) 1 b) Composites and Fibrelam	a) FX 61-184 and FX 60-126 b) 18.85	a) 51-6 (15.7) b) 140.58 (13.06) c) 22-10 (6.95)	a) 476 (216) b) 739 (335) c) -	a) 4.49 (21.9) b) 5.26 (25.7)	a) 1.97 (0.6) b) 35 (40) 65	a) 34 b) 41 (47) 76	a) 32 (37) 60 b) 125 (144) 232 c) -		Prototype built in 1995. Available as a pre-fabricated kit; production of kits started in 1997.
Manufacturer: Kenilworth International Ltd., 17 Thorn Close, Verwood, Dorset BH31 6QG (Telephone: +44 1202 828886 and 0976 817626, Facsimile: +44 1202 828886)										
Mechta Me-7	a) 1 b) Glassfibre	a) FX 61-157 b) 20.6	a) 41-8 (12.7) b) 82.88 (7.7) c) 17-5.5 (5.3)	a) 287 (130) b) 551 (250) c) -	a) 5.06 (24.7) b) 6.64 (32.4)	a) 2.56 (0.78) b) 43.5 (50) 80	a) 32 b) 51 (59) 95	a) 33.5 (39) 62 b) 119 (137) 220 c) -		Production version of Russian Russia 2. Available with tailskid or nosewheel. Production continues. 2-seat version planned.
United States of America										
Manufacturer: Advanced Aeromarine, 152 East Eighth Street, Apoka, FL 32703 (Telephone: +1 407 877 7871, Facsimile: +1 407 293 1533)										
Sierra (G)	a) 1 b) Aluminium tubing, glassfibre and fabric	a) - b) 12.75	a) 42-8 (13) b) 142 (13.2) c) 21 (6.4)	a) 200 (91) b) 450 (204) c) -	a) 3.33 (16.26) b) -	a) 2.5 (0.76) b) -	a) - b) -	a) 23.5 (27) 43.5 b) - c) 36 (42) 68 best glide speed		Lightweight sailplane, offered in kit (construction time about 80-100 hours) and ready-built forms. Spoilers for glide path control.
Manufacturer: Advanced Soaring Concepts Inc., 4730 Calle Quetzal, Camarillo, CA 93012 (Telephone: +1 805 389 3434)										
Falcon (G)	a) 1 b) Glassfibre, carbonfibre, aramid and steel tubes	a) - b) -	a) 49-2.5 (15) b) -	a) 580 (263) b) - c) -	a) - b) -	a) - b) -	a) 44 b) -	a) - b) -		Kit glider, with flaps. Optional 18 m wingtips.
American Spirit (G)	a) 1 b) Glassfibre, carbonfibre and aramid	a) - b) 23.9	a) 49-2.5 (15) b) 101.1 (9.39) c) 21-6 (6.55)	a) 508 (230) b) 1,157 (525) c) -	a) 10.89 (53.19) b) -	a) - b) -	a) 42 b) 61 (70) 113	a) - b) 117 (135) 217 c) -		Kit glider. Prototype of 18 m version (XL) flying with boron fibre main spar.
Manufacturer: Aero Dovron Inc., 8718 150th Court North, Palm Beach Gardens, FL 33418 (Telephone: +1 407 575 1259)										
Mini Straton D-7 (MGS)	a) 1 b) Glassfibre, wood and fabric	a) - b) 11.9	a) 35-5 (10.8) b) 105.5 (9.8) c) 19-8 (5.99)	a) 243 (110) b) 463 (210) c) -	a) - b) 4.45 (21.75)	a) - b) -	a) 14 b) -	a) 24 (28) 44 b) 54 (62) 100 c) 43 (50) 80	a) 24 hp (17.9 kW) Trabant or Rotax 277 engine behind wings, driving a pusher propeller. b) -	Available as a kit. Built in Czech Republic.
Manufacturer: Bright Star Gliders Inc, 48 Barham Avenue, Santa Rosa, CA 95407 (Telephone: +1 707 576 7627)										
Swift (G) + (MGS)	a) 1 b) Metal tube, fabric and glassfibre	a) - b) 11.5	a) 39 (11.89) b) 135 (12.54) c) 10 (3.05)	a) 235 (106.6) b) 450 (204) c) -	a) - b) -	a) 3.35 (1.02) b) -	a) 20 b) -	a) 24 (27) 44 b) 65 (75) 121 c) 46 (52) 84	a) Optional 24 hp (17.9 kW) König SC 430. b) 11.4	Kit glider and/or motorglider.

↑ **Kenilworth Mechta Me-7** *(J. Ewald) (page 614)*

↑ **Advanced Soaring Concepts American Spirit XL** *(Peter F. Selinger) (page 614)*

Designation (Type)	a) Crew b) Materials	a) Aerofoil b) Wing aspect ratio	a) Span ft-ins (m) b) Wing area sq ft (m^2) c) Length ft-ins (m)	Weights lb (kg): a) empty b) maximum c) ballast (max)	Wing loading lb/sq ft (kg/m^2) a) minimum b) maximum	a) Minimum rate of sink ft (m)/sec b) at speed of kts (mph) km/h	a) Best glide ratio b) at speed of kts (mph) km/h	Speeds kts (mph) km/h: a) stalling b) maximum c) cruise	a) Engine b) Fuel capacity in litres	Comments
Under the heading *Type*, the following abbreviations have been used: **G** = Glider; **MGS** = Motorglider, self-launch; **MGN** = Motorglider, no self-launch										
United States of America										
Manufacturer: Contor Composites Inc, Salt Lake City, Utah (Telephone: +1 800 474-GLID, E-mail <sciflyus@aol.com)										
Standard Scimitar I (G)	a) 1 b) Glassfibre, carbonfibre and aramid	a) PM-24/14.4% b) 21.4	a) 49-2.5 (15) b) 113 (10.5) c) -	a) 600 (272) b) 1,125 (510) c) 250 (113)	a) - b) 10.2 (49.8)	a) - b) -	a) 43 b) 60 (69) 111	a) - b) -		1 built, using Ventus fuselage and Discus planform wing with electronic boundary layer control.
Scimitar II (G)	a) 1 b) Glassfibre, carbonfibre and aramid	a) PM-24/14.4% b) -	a) 49-2.5 (15) b) 100.4 (9.33) c) -	a) 463 (210) b) 1,157 (525) c) -	a) - b) -	a) - b) -	a) 45.3 b) -	a) 36 (42) 67 b) 146 (168) 271 c) -		Under construction at time of writing.
Manufacturer: Group Genesis Inc, Marion Municipal Airport, 1530 Pole Lane Road, Marion OH 43302 (Telephone: +1 614 387 9464, Facsimile: +1 614 387 0501, E-mail: groupgen@aol.com)										
Genesis 1 (G)	a) 1 b) Composites	a) Roncz G-745 b) 20.1	a) 49-2.5 (15) b) 120.5 (11.19) c) 13-9 (4.2)	a) 500 (227) b) 1,157 (525) c) -	a) 5.02 (24.5) b) 9.6 (46.8)	a) 1.9 (0.58) b) 45 (52) 83	a) 43 b) 65 (75) 120	a) - b) 157 (180) 290		Prototype built in 1994.
Genesis 2 (G)	a) 1 b) Composites	a) Roncz G-745 b) 20.18	a) 49-2.5 (15) b) 120 (11.15) c) 16 (4.86)	a) 490 (222) b) 1,157 (525) c) -	a) 5.02 (24.5) b) 9.54 (46.6)	a) 1.9 (0.58) b) 46 (53) 85	a) 44 b) 67 (78) 125	a) 37 (43) 68 b) 140 (162) 260		Production version built by Sportiné Aviacija in Lithuania. Production started in 1997.
Manufacturer: Larry Haig										
Minibat (G)	a) 1 b) Foam and glassfibre	a) - b) 10 or 14 with wingtip extensions	a) 25 (7.62), or 32-8 (9.96) with wingtip extensions b) 64.5 (5.99) or 76.5 (7.11) with wingtip extensions c) -	a) 110 (50) or 130 (59) with wingtip extensions b) 325 (147) or 350 (159) with wingtip extensions c) -	a) - b) 5 (24.41) or 4.5 (21.97) with wingtip extensions	a) 1.78 (0.54) b) -	a) 23 or 30 with wingtip extensions b) -	a) - b) - c) -		Flying-wing kit. MGN version possible.
Manufacturer: Fred Hermanspann										
Chinook S (G)	a) 2 b) Aluminium and glassfibre	a) FX 67-K-170/17 b) 22.7	a) 57 (17.37) b) 143 (13.29) c) -	a) 630 (286) b) 1,050 (476) c) -	a) - b) 7.34 (35.84)	a) 2.17 (0.66) b) 42 (48) 77	a) 40 b) 53 (61) 98	a) - b) - c) -		First flown 1996, as improved version of 1993 Chinook. Hydraulically-actuated trailing-edge flaps and main wheel.
Manufacturer: Marske Aircraft Corporation, 975 Loire Valley Drive, Marion, OH 43302										
Monarch F (G)	a) 1 b) Wood, fabric and composites	a) NACA 43012A b) 9.7	a) 42-7 (12.98) b) 186 (17.27) c) 12-6 (3.81)	a) 220 (100) b) 450 (204) c) -	a) - b) 2.42 (11.81)	a) 2.5 (0.76) b) 26 (30) 48	a) 20 b) 35 (40) 64	a) 21 (24) 39 b) 61 (70) 113 c) -		Plans and kits available.
Pioneer II-D (G)	a) 1 b) Wood, fabric and composites	a) NACA 33012/ 33010 mod b) 12.6	a) 42-7 (12.98) b) 144 (13.38) c) 12-6 (3.81)	a) 350 (159) b) 600 (272) c) -	a) - b) 4.17 (20.34)	a) 2.1 (0.64) b) -	a) 35 b) -	a) 31 (35) 57 b) 113 (130) 209 c) 83 (95) 153		Latest version. Plans and kits available.
Manufacturer: Jim Maupin Ltd, 24201 Rowel Court, Tehachapi, CA 93561 (Telephone: +1 805 821 3450, Facsimile: +1 805 821 3450, E-mail: maupin@mtxinu.com)										
Carbon Dragon (G)	a) 1 b) Wood and composites	a) Culver b) 12.9	a) 44 (13.41) b) 150 (13.94) c) 20 (6.1) approx	a) 144 (65.3) b) 335 (152) c) -	a) - b) 2.23 (10.9)	a) 1.67 (0.51) b) -	a) 25 b) -	a) - b) 61 (70) 112 c) -		Plans available. Foot launched.

↑ **Group Genesis Genesis 1** *(page 615)*

↑ **Jim Maupin Woodstock** *(page 616)*

Designation (Type)	a) Crew b) Materials	a) Aerofoil b) Wing aspect ratio	a) Span ft-ins (m) b) Wing area sq ft (m^2) c) Length ft-ins (m)	Weights lb (kg): a) empty b) maximum c) ballast (max)	Wing loading lb/sq ft (kg/m^2) a) minimum b) maximum	a) Minimum rate of sink ft (m)/sec b) at speed of kts (mph) km/h	a) Best glide ratio b) at speed of kts (mph) km/h	Speeds kts (mph) km/h: a) stalling b) maximum c) cruise	a) Engine b) Fuel capacity in litres	Comments
Under the heading *Type*, the following abbreviations have been used: **G** = Glider; **MGS** = Motorglider, self-launch; **MGN** = Motorglider, no self-launch										
United States of America										
Manufacturer: Jim Maupin Ltd (continued)										
Windrose (MGS)	a) 1 b) Wood and composites	a) - b) 17.9	a) 41-6 (12.65) b) 96 (8.92) c) 21-7 (6.58)	a) 512 (232) b) 700 (317.5) c) -	a) - b) 7.29 (35.59)	a) 2.3 (0.7) b) 40 (46) 74	a) 29 b) 45.5 (52) 84	a) - b) 114 (132) 212 c) 87 (100) 161	a) 35 hp (26 kW) Cuyuna UL-II-02 mounted in pod behind cockpit b) 19	Plans available.
Windrose II (MGS)	a) 1 b) Wood and composites	a) - b) 23.7	a) 49-2 (14.98) b) 102 (9.47) c) 21-7 (6.58)	a) 512 (232) b) 740 (336) c) -	a) - b) 7.27 (35.48)	a) - b) -	a) - b) -	a) - b) 114 (132) 212 c) 87 (100) 161	a) 46 hp (34.3 kW) Rotax 503 mounted in pod behind cockpit b) 19	Plans available.
Woodstock (G)	a) 1 b) Wood and fabric	a) IRV Culver b) 14.5	a) 39 (11.89) b) 104.7 (9.73) c) 19 (5.79)	a) 235 (106.6) b) 450 (204) c) -	a) - b) 4.3 (20.98)	a) 2.62 (0.8) b) -	a) 24 b) -	a) 29.5 (34) 54 b) 87 (100) 161		Plans available.
Manufacturer: Rensselaer Polytechnic Institute, Troy, New York										
RP3 (G)	a) 2 b) Composites	a) FX 67-170 b) 17	a) 54 (16.46) b) 180 (16.7) c) 17 (5.18)	a) 650 (295) b) - c) -	a) - b) -	a) 3.05 (0.93) b) 39 (45) 72	a) 33 b) 44.5 (51) 82	a) 37 (42) 68 b) - c) -		Pilot in the centre or crew side-by-side.
Manufacturer: Donald Roberts										
Cygnet (G)	a) 1 b) Steel tube, aluminium and glassfibre	a) - b) 18	a) 42-8 (13) b) 103 (9.57) c) -	a) 364 (165) b) 606 (275) c) -	a) - b) 5.88 (28.71)	a) - b) -	a) - b) -	a) - b) - c) -		1 built in 1992. US entry for World Class design contest.
Manufacturer: Ron Sands, Inc, 89 Forrest Road, Mertztown, PA 19539 (Telephone: +1 610 682 6788, Facsimile: +1 610 682 6788)										
1929 Primary Glider (G)	a) 1 b) Steel tube, wood and fabric	a) Clark Y b) 6.4	a) 32 (9.75) b) 160 (14.86) c) 17-8 (5.38)	a) 175 (79.4) b) 375 (170) c) -	a) - b) 2.34 (11.44)	a) - b) -	a) - b) -	a) 26 (30) 48.5 b) 56 (65) 105		Original 1929 primary design. Plans available, with wooden or steel tube fuselage.
Manufacturer: Schweizer Aircraft Corporation, PO Box 147, Elmira, NY 14902 (Telephone: +1 607 739 3821, Facsimile: +1 607 796 2488)										
SGS 1-36 Sprite (G)	a) 1 b) Aluminium alloy	a) FX 61-163, FX 60-126 b) 15	a) 46-2 (14.07) b) 140.72 (13.07) c) 20-7 (6.27)	a) 475 (216) b) 710 (322) c) -	a) - b) 5.045 (24.63)	a) 2.25 (0.69) b) 36.5 (42) 67.5	a) 31 b) 46 (53) 85	a) 30.5 (35) 56 b) 105 (121) 195 c) -		Out of production, but supported by the company.
SGS 2-33A (G)	a) 2 b) Metal	a) - b) 11.8	a) 51 (15.54) b) 219.5 (20.39) c) 25-9 (7.85)	a) 600 (272) b) 1,040 (471.7) c) -	a) - b) 4.74 (23.14)	a) 3.1 (0.94) b) 36.5 (42) 67.5	a) 22.25 b) 45 (52) 83.5	a) 30.5 (35) 56 b) 85 (98) 157 c) -		Training glider. Out of production, but supported by the company.
SGM 2-37 (MGS)	a) 2 b) Aluminium alloy	a) FX 61-163, FX 60-126 b) 18.1	a) 59-6 (18.14) b) 195.71 (18.18) c) 27-6 (8.38)	a) 1,260 (571.5) b) 1,850 (839) c) -	a) - b) 9.45 (46.15)	a) 3.8 (1.16) b) 52 (60) 96.5	a) 22 b) 54 (62) 100	a) 44 (50) 81 b) 116 (133) 214 gliding c) -	a) Front mounted 112 hp (83.5 kW) Textron Lycoming O-235-L2C, or 150-180 hp (112-134 kW) O-320/O-360 b) -	12 delivered to the USAF's Academy at Colorado Springs as TG-7As.
Manufacturer: US Aviation, 265 Echo Lane, South St Paul, MN 55075 (Telephone: +1 612 450 0930, Facsimile: +1 612 450 0930)										
Super Floater (G)	a) 1 b) Metal tube and fabric	a) - b) 8.44	a) 38 (11.58) b) 168 (15.61) c) 19 (5.79)	a) 179 (81) b) 400 (181) with ballistic parachute c) None	a) - b) 2.38 (11.62)	a) 3 (0.91) b) 23 (27) 43	a) 15 b) 30 (35) 56	a) 23 (27) 43 b) 52 (60) 96 c) -		FAR 103 ultralight sailplane, offer in completed form. Full-span ailerons can be configured as flaperons. See also Recreational section for details of the Cumulus.

↑ US Aviation Super Floater *(page 616)*

↑ New Schempp-Hirth Discus 2b, first flown 3 April 1998 *(J Ewald) (page 604)*

Operational Commercial Satellite Launch Vehicles

The vehicles detailed are being marketed actively for commercial launches of civilian spacecraft, have firm launch committments and also conduct launches for government and other agencies. They do not include vehicles used purely for government purposes, or those being marketed speculatively. Thrust and payload weights vary slightly according to mission objectives.
(GEO=geostationary Earth orbit, GTO=geostationary transfer orbit, LEO=low Earth orbit)

China Great Wall Industry Corporation Long March — China

Corporate address:
22 Fucheng Road, Haidian Qu, 100036 Beijing.
Telephone: +86 10 6837 0285
Facsimile: +86 10 6842 9217

Summary

Long March (LM) boosters are all available for commercial work but only the LM2C, LM2E, LM3, LM3A and LM3B are being marketed actively. Launches are thought to be priced at about US$50-$60 million.

Variants and Specifications

LM2C first stage is powered by 4 YF-20 nitrogen tetroxide-UDMH engines, producing a lift-off thrust of 626,000 lbf (2,785 kN) and a burn time of 132 seconds. The stretched second stage for commercial missions is powered by a similar YF-22 engine with a thust of 171,000 lbf (761 kN) and nominal burn time of 110 seconds on the original version but longer with an additional 19.7 tons (20 tonnes) of propellants on the commercial vehicle. The third stage for commercial GTO launches is provided by a CPKM solid propellant motor or (as in the case of the launches of Iridium satellites) an SD Smart Dispenser using solid motors and liquid thrusters. The LM2C can place 3,175 lb (1,440 kg) into GTO using the CPKM from Xichang or 2,645 lb (1,200 kg) into LEO from Jiuquan. It was first launched in 1975 and has made 19 successful flights. It has been contracted to fly 22 Iridium satellites on 11 launches from Tuiyuan to the year 2002.
LM2E is an uprated version of the LM2C but with 4 liquid strap on boosters each powered by 166,355 lbf (740 kN) thrust nitrogen tetroxide-UDMH YF-20B engines with a burn time of 125 seconds. The uprated YF-20B engines of the stretched first stage have a thrust of 665,650 lbf (2,961 kN) and burn time of 158 seconds. The second stage has 1 YF-22B and 4 YF-23B nitrogen tetroxide-UDMH engines/verniers with the thrust of 177,150 lbf (788 kN) and 300 seconds burn time. This configuration can place 19,400 lb (8,800 kg) into LEO from Xichang, which can be increased to 20,280 lb (9,200 kg) with the addition of a solid propellant EPKM upper stage. GTO launches of payloads weighing 7,628 lb (3,460 kg) are possible with the EPKM or 6,923 lb (3,140 kg) with the Thiokol Star 63F solid propellant upper stage. The LM2E has made 10 flights since 1990, with 7 successes, 2 failures and 1 failure to reach the correct orbit. It has an option to launch 1 satellite.
LM3 is equipped with the same first stage as the LM2C, a second stage with a YF-22 engine and 4 YF-23 verniers firing on nitrogen tetroxide-UDMH, with a thrust of 171,975 lbf (765 kN) and 110 seconds burn time, and a cryogenic LOX-LH third stage with a 9,890 lbf (44 kN) thrust YF-73 engine and a total burn time of 800 seconds in 2 possible burns. It can carry 5,512 lb (2,500 kg) to GTO from Xichang, and has had 7 successful and 3 partially successful launches since 1984. It is manifested to fly 1 Hughes HS-376 communications satellite.
LM3A is uprated and employs the first stage from the LM2E, the second stage from the LM3, and a new restartable cryogenic 35,070 lbf (156 kN) thrust H-18 engine with a 470 second burn time with 2 ignitions. It can place 5,070 lb (2,300 kg) into GTO and has successfully flown 3 times since 1994.
LM3B is an LM3A with the strap-on boosters of the LM2E and can place 10,582 lb (4,800 kg) into GTO. It has experienced 4 successes and 1 failure and is manifested to fly 6 commercial communications satellites, with 5 options.
LM3C is an LM3B with 2 instead of 4 strap-ons. It is also available for launches of 8,157 lb (3,700 kg) to GTO.

Arianespace Ariane — France

Corporate address:
Boulevard de l'Europe, BP 177, F91006 Evry Cedex.
Telephone: +33 1 60876000
Facsimile: +33 1 60876247

Summary

Arianespace operates 6 versions of the Ariane 4 from the Guiana Space Centre, Kourou, French Guiana. The larger models of the Ariane 4 can carry 2 large communications satellites to GTO, a capability not matched by other commercial boosters. Ariane launches began in December 1979, with 29 Ariane 1, 2 and 3 models achieving a record of 25 successes and 4 failures. Arianespace took over commercial operation on the ninth flight in 1984. The Ariane 4 made its debut in June 1988. It will continue to fly until after the year 2002, while the new Ariane 5 begins its commercial operations starting on flight 504 in March 1999. There are 13 Ariane 5s available for Arianespace. A new order of Ariane 5s is expected once the European Space Agency (ESA)-funded Ariane 503 development flight has proved the system, after the loss of the 501 maiden launch vehicle in June 1996. Ariane launches are priced at about US$80-$90 million for a dedicated flight. The cost of a dual-satellite launch is shared by the customers. Arianespace has an order book of 37 satellites, at least 10 of which are firmly manifested on the Ariane 5, plus 8 options for launches from ESA and other government customers. Ariane launches have also been used to deploy small auxiliary piggyback satellites.

Variants and Specifications

Ariane 40 3-stage vehicle comprises a first stage powered by 4 SEP Viking 5 nitrogen tetroxide-UDMH engines with a combined lift-off thrust of 611,000 lbf (2,718 kN) and burn time of 150 seconds. The second stage has a similar Viking 4, with thrust of 179,400 lbf (798 kN) and 125 seconds burn time. The cryogenic 14,600 lbf (65 kN) thrust LOX/LH third stage engine has an available 780 seconds of burn time. It can place 4,630 lb (2,100 kg) to GTO but its primary function is to launch payloads of 6,040 lb (2,740 kg) to Sun-synchronous orbits (SSO). The 40 has achieved 6 successful launches.
Ariane 42L is powered by 2 liquid nitrogen tetroxide-UDMH strap-on PAL boosters with a 169,275 lbf (753 kN) thrust and 142 second burn-time. It places 7,605 lb (3,450 kg) payloads into GTO and has flown successfully 7 times.
Ariane 42P includes thrust augmentation from 2 PAP solid propellant strap-on boosters with a thrust of 140,500 lbf (625 kN) and burn time of 33 seconds. This can carry 6,437 lb (2,920 kg) to GTO. It has flown 10 successful launches, and has experienced 1 failure.
Ariane 44L, with 4 PALs, can place a maximum 10,560 lb (4,790 kg) into GTO and has achieved 27 successful launches and 1 failure. Its SSO capability is 13,558 lb (6,150 kg).
Ariane 44P, with 4 PAP boosters, places 7,452 lb (3,380 kg) into GTO. It has flown 12 successful missions.
Ariane 44LP carries 2 PAPs and 2 PALs and can place 9,193 lb (4,170 kg) into GTO and has a record of 18 successful launches with 1 failure.
Ariane 5 is a 2-stage vehicle with the core stage powered by a SEP Vulcain cryogenic LOX-LH engine of 202,325 lbf (900 kN) thrust and burn time of 580 seconds. Thrust augmentation for the first 132 seconds is provided by 2 solid propellant strap-on boosters with a thrust of 11,575 lbf (51.5 kN). The second stage is powered by a re-startable DASA Aestus 6,180 lbf (27.5 kN) thrust nitrogen tetroxide-MMH engine, with a burn time of 1,100 seconds. The Ariane 5 can carry a maximum of 14,991 lb (6,800 kg) to GTO but is being marketed primarily for 13,007 lb (5,900 kg) 2-satellite launches. An uprated Vulcain Mk 2 is planned, which with other modifications (including a new high energy upper stage) may increase the Ariane 5's performance to 16,535 lb (7,500 kg) to GTO. However, the first flight of any uprated vehicle is unlikely until after the year 2002. Ariane 5's first flight failed in 1996 but next 2 succeeded in 1997-98.

↑ Ariane 44L launch at Kourou

Starsem Soyuz, Molniya and Rus — France/Russia

Corporate address:
33 rue Fernand Forest, 92150 Suresnes, France.
Telephone: +33 1 46 25 03 60
Facsimile: +33 1 45 06 05 62

Summary

Starsem is a joint Aerospatiale-Arianespace-Russian Space Agency-Samara Space Centre venture to market Soyuz variants for LEO and medium Earth orbit missions. Launch prices are thought to be in the region of US$40 million. Soyuz is manifested to fly 24 Globalstar satellites into LEO on 6 launches, plus 8 optional launches and 4 Cluster science satellites on 2 launches. Soyuz is also used to carry piggyback satellites on national launches.

Variants and Specifications

Soyuz U is the current version and comprises a core stage powered by a single 4-chamber LOX-kerosene RD-107 engine, offering 219,860 lbf (978 kN) thrust with 310 seconds burn time. The stage has 4 strap-ons, each with similar engines which burn for 120 seconds. Stage 2 is powered by a 67,000 lbf (298 kN) thrust LOX-kerosene RD-0110 engine, with a burn time of 255 seconds. Soyuz U has flown 726 successful launches with 15 failures, all within the total Soyuz record of 1,062 successful and 30 failure launches since 1966. It can place a maximum of 16,535 lb (7,500 kg) into LEO. Starsem Soyuz also offers a new upper stage called the Ikar, providing a more conservative 7,716 lb (3,500 kg) capability.

Molniya is a current 4-stage vehicle, offered for 4,409 lb (2,000 kg) launches to elliptical orbits.

Rus is a generic name for both the Molniya and Soyuz which are being uprated as part of this family of vehicles. Rus includes the Soyuz 2 which, with a Fregat multiple re-start upper stage that offers a 877 second burn time from its nitrogen tetroxide-UDMH engine, can place 18,739 lb (8,500 kg) into LEO.

Eurockot Rokot — Germany/Russia

Corporate address:
PO Box 286146, Hunefeldstrasse 1-5, D-28 199 Bremen, Germany.
Telephone: +49 421 5396501
Facsimile: +49 421 5396500

Summary

The Rokot is a modified SS-19 strategic missile marketed jointly by Russia's Khrunichev and Germany's DASA. Launches are priced at about US$10 million.

Variants and Specifications

Rokot first stage is powered by a nitrogen tetroxide-UDMH engine, with a thrust of 412,300 lbf (1,834 kN) and 121 seconds burn time. The second stage is powered by a similar engine with 52,830 lbf (235 kN) thrust and 158 seconds burn time. It is equipped with a restartable third Breeze nitrogen tetroxide – UDMH stage with a thrust of 4,496 lbf (20 kN). It can place 4,079 lb (1,850 kg) into LEO and flew once successfully from Baikonur in 1994 on a demonstration flight. It is manifested for 2 commercial launches, and has 1 option to launch 2 satellites. Launches are from Plesetsk, Baikonur and Svobodny.

Rocket Systems Corporation (RSC) H2 — Japan

Corporate address:
Hamamatsucho Central Building, 1-29-6 Hamamatsucho, Minato-Ku, Tokyo 105.
Telephone: +81 3 5470 7900
Facsimile: +81 3 5470 7950

Summary

The National Space Development Agency's H2 is Japan's first indigenously-developed GTO launcher. A lack of commercial market success has been due to its high launch cost of US$120 million, as a result of excessive development costs and delays. A newer low-cost version, the H2A, is being developed for lower-cost commercial launches after the year 2000, marketed by RSC, a consortium of Japanese manufacturers led by Mitsubishi. The H2 is booked for several national launches, while the new H2A has 21 launch commitments, from ESA (1) and 10 each from Hughes and Lockheed Martin.

Variants and Specifications

H2 was first launched from the Tanegashima Space Centre in 1994. The 2-stage H2 has a first stage powered by the LE-5 cryogenic LOX/LH engine with a thrust of 189,500 lbf (843 kN) and burn time of 346 seconds. The stage is augmented by 2 solid propellant strap-on boosters with a thrust of 350,700 lbf (1,560 kN) and 66 seconds burn time. Some H2s can be equipped with 2 additional Solid Sub-Boosters (SSB) with a thrust of 7,870 lbf (35 kN) and 66 seconds burn time. The second stage is equipped with the uprated and restartable 27,200 lbf (121 kN) thrust LE-5A cryogenic engine, with a total burn time of 609 seconds. The H2 has flown 5 successful missions since 1994, including a flight with the SSBs, plus 1 failure to place the payload in the correct orbit. It can carry 8,818 lb (4,000 kg) to GTO.

H2A will duplicate H2 performance but will cost less and will fly in the year 2000. The first version will be based on the H2 but with smaller yet more powerful solid rocket boosters (based on the Thiokol 4A-XL motor) and an uprated LE-7A engine. It is also being marketed for LEO launches of clusters of up to 5 satellites. Further H2A enhancements will have 1 or 2 piggyback "first stage" stages, increasing GTO performance to a maximum of 13,228 lb (6,000 kg).

Polyot Cosmos 3M — Russia

Corporate address:
226 Bogdana Khmelinitskogo Street, 644021 Omsk 21.
Telephone: +7 38112 39 74 32
Facsimile: +7 38112 57 92 00

Summary

Polyot is the manufacturer of the Cosmos 3M. It has agreements with several companies to market the booster for LEO launches, including Assured Access to Space of the USA and Germany's OHB Systems. A joint small satellite and launch service is also offered with the Final Analysis company of the USA. Launch prices are US$10 million.

Variants and Specifications

Cosmos 3M first stage is powered by a 4-chamber RD-216 nitrogen tetroxide-UDMH engine, offering a thrust of 388,000 lbf (1,726 kN). The second stage is powered by a 11D49 nitrogen tetroxide-UDMH motor, of 35,300 lbf (157 kN) thrust and 335 seconds burn time. It can place 3,748 lb (1,700 kg) into LEO from the Plesetsk Cosmodrome or Kapustin Yar and has flown 396 successful missions since 1964, with 5 partial failures and 19 failures. It is manifested to fly 4 commercial satellites.

Komplex Scientific and Technical Centre Start — Russia

Address:
Berjozovaya Alleya, ul. 10/1, 127276 Moscow.
Telephone: +7 095 402 7321
Facsimile: +7 095 402 8229

Summary

Russia's first all-solid propellant satellite launchers, the Start family comprises refurbished SS-18 and SS-20 strategic missiles. Start launchers fly from silos at Plesetsk and the new Svobodny base. Joint-marketing is possible with Sweden, Australia and the Russian Cosmos company.

Variants and Specifications

Start 1 is a 5-stage vehicle and can place 1,102 lb (500 kg) into LEO. It is contracted to carry 3 commercial satellites and has flown 3 successful missions since 1993.

Start 2 is a 6-stage vehicle (the extra stage is a repeat of the second stage) and can place 1,543 lb (700 kg) into LEO. It failed once in 1995.

NPO Yuzhnoye Zenit 2 — Ukraine

Corporate address:
3 Krivorozhskaya Street, 320059, Dnepropetrovsk.
Telephone: +380 56 242 00 23
Facsimile: +380 56 292 50 41

Summary

The Zenit 2 is being marketed by the Ukraine separately from the Zenit 3-based Sea Launch venture (see USA/Ukraine).

Variants and Specifications

Zenit 2 is powered by the RD-171 LOX-kerosene engine, providing 1,631,850 lbf (7,259 kN) thrust and a 144 seconds burn time. The second stage has a similar RD-120 engine, offering 187,260 lbf (833 kN) thrust and a burn time of 1,100 seconds. It can place 30,290 lb (13,740 kg) into LEO from Plesetsk or Baikonur and has made 23 successful flights since 1985, with 7 failures and 1 partial failure. After launching 12 Globestar satellites in 1998, it is likely to gain new contracts.

Boeing Delta 2, 3 and 4 — USA

Corporate address:
See Combat section.

Summary

2 versions of Delta 2, with 2 and 3 stages respectively, are currently available and a new 3-stage Delta 3 was introduced in December 1998. A 2-model fleet of Delta 4s has been selected by the US Air Force for the Evolved Expendable Launch Vehicle (EELV) programme, a contract for which was also awarded to Lockheed Martin in June 1998. The main customers for the Delta 2 fleet are NASA and the US Air Force, primarily for science

spacecraft and Navstar GPS satellites respectively; and Motorola and Loral, the operators of the Iridium and Globalstar satellite systems. NASA's missions are part of a Medium Expendable Launch Vehicle contract and the space agency also awarded McDonnell Douglas (now Boeing) a contract to operate a Med-Lite fleet of Delta 2 versions for its future science missions. The Delta 4 will complement the Delta 3. The Delta 2s are the latest in a family of Thor Delta and Delta boosters first launched in 1960, clocking up 250 launches, including 13 failures and 1 partial failure. Commercial launches on the Delta 2 are priced at about US$60 million.

Variants and Specifications

Delta 2/7920 is a 2-stage vehicle with the first stage powered by a Rocketdyne RS-27A liquid oxygen (LOX)/kerosene engine providing a lift-off thrust of 200,000 lbf (890 kN) and a burn time of 260 seconds. Thrust is augmented by 9 strap-on Alliant graphite epoxy solid propellant motors (GEM), each with a lift-off thrust of 100,250 lbf (446 kN). 6 GEMs ignite at launch and 3 at 65.5 seconds, after burnout of the original 6. It can also fly less powerful missions with 3 or 4 GEMs if required. The second stage is powered by a restartable Aerojet AJ-10 nitrogen tetroxide-Aerozine 50 engine with a thrust of 9,600 lbf (43 kN) and burn-time of 432 seconds. The 7920 can place 11,330 lb (5,139 kg) into low Earth orbit (LEO) from Complex 17 at Cape Canaveral, Florida and 8,590 lb (3,896 kg) into LEO from Complex 2 West at Vandenberg AFB, California. First launch took place in 1995 and it has achieved 15 successful launches and no failures. It is manifested to fly Iridium, Globalstar and a US Air Force satellites in 1998. The vehicle for Globalstar launches will be equipped with 4 GEMS.

Delta 2/7925 is a 7920 plus a Thiokol Star 48B solid propellant third stage with a thrust of 14,840 lbf (66 kN) and burn time of 87 seconds. It can place 3,966 lb (1,799 kg) into geostationary transfer orbit (GTO) and current GPS satellites weighing 4,480 lb (2,032 kg) into hybrid 12,425 mile (20,000 km) circular orbits. As with the 7920, it can carry 3 or 4 GEMs if required. First launched in 1989, it has flown 46 successful missions, with 1 failure and 1 partial failure. It is manifested to fly 1 commercial satellite, 19 GPS 2R satellites and others for the US Air Force and NASA up to the year 2000.

7920/7925 Med Lite version has been allocated 7 NASA launches from 1998 with several others to be determined.

Delta 3 comprises a first stage from the Delta 2 but with an enlarged LOX tank and GEMs lengthened by 4 ft (1.22 m). Its second stage will be powered by a 20,900 lbf (93 kN) thrust Pratt & Whitney RL-10B2 restartable, LOX-liquid hydrogen (LH) cryogenic engine derived from the Centaur upper stage. It will place 8,400 lb (3,810 kg) into GTO and 18,400 lb (8,346 kg) into LEO. 17 firm GTO contracts. First launch failed August 1998.

↑ **Delta 2/7925 launch**

Lockheed Martin Astronautics Athena — USA

Corporate address:
See Combat section.

Summary

The Athena fleet is marketed for launches to LEO and is also contracted by NASA. It was formerly known as the LMLV.

Variants and Specifications

Athena 1 comprises a Thiokol Castor 120 solid propellant first stage with a thrust of 400,150 lbf (1,780 kN) and burn time of 86 seconds, and a second stage using a 43,160 lbf (192 kN) thrust Orbus 21D motor which fires for 154 seconds. The vehicle is also equipped with an orbit adjust module (OAM). It can place 1,763 lb (800 kg) into LEO, from SLC 6 at Vandenberg AFB, California or from Pad 46 at Cape Canaveral, Florida. It has experienced 2 successes and 1 failure. *Athena 1* is manifested to fly 1 commercial satellite.

Athena 2 is equipped with an uprated OAM to increase payload performance to 4,400 lb (2,000 kg). This is contracted to carry 1 commercial and 1 company remote sensing satellites.

Uprated versions with Castor 120 strap on motors are planned.

Orbital Sciences Corporation (OSC) Pegasus and Taurus — USA

Corporate address:
21700 Atlantic Boulevard, Dulles, VA 20166.

Telephone: +1 703 406 5000
Facsimile: +1 703 406 3502

Summary

OSC markets these vehicles for launches to LEO for international commercial and government customers. Pegasus is launched from a NASA B-52 or the OSC TriStar. Prime take-off bases are Cape Canaveral, Florida; Vandenberg and Edwards AFB and Dryden, California; and Wallops Island, Virginia.

Variants and Specifications

Pegasus is the original version, which has flown 8 times since 1990, including 2 partial successes, and can place 882 lb (400 kg) into LEO.

Pegasus XL is the current air-launched stretched version of the original Pegasus, offering 1,047 lb (475 kg) to LEO. The first stage is powered by a solid propellant Orion 50S with a thrust of 134,880 lbf (600 kN) and burn time of 65 seconds. The second stage is a 25,630 lbf (114 kN) thrust Orion 50XL with a 70 seconds burn time. Stage 3 is an Orion 38, with a thust of 11,915 lbf (53 kN) and 64 seconds burn time. An optional fourth stage is the monopropellant Hydrazine Auxiliary Propulsion System. The XL has a launch record of 13 successes, 2 failures and 1 failure to separate payloads, since 1994. It is manifested to carry 35 firm company, commercial, NASA, US Air Force and other payloads, plus opportunities to fly as many as 20 others as a result of small launch vehicle contracts with the US Air Force and NASA. Pegasus also offers piggyback satellite transportation as part of another NASA Ultralight contract.

Taurus is a solid propellant vehicle and uses 2 types of first stage, the Peacekeeper missile first stage for US Air Force launches or the Castor 120 for commercial flights. It can place 3,000 lb (1,360 kg) into LEO, from Pad 46 at Cape Canaveral, Florida and from Vandenberg AFB, California. The Castor has a thrust of 382,840 lbf (1,703 kN) and a burn time of 83 seconds. The second stage is an Orion 50S with a thrust of 105,880 lbf (471 kN) and 72 seconds burn time. Stage 3 is an Orion 38 with a 7,645 lbf (34 kN) thrust and 64 seconds burn time. Taurus has flown 3 successful missions since 1994, and is manifested to fly 7 missions for the US Air Force, NASA (as part of a Med Lite contract), and commercial customers.

Taurus XL will be the Med Lite version, which will use the Castor 120 and the stretch from the Pegasus XL. This can place 3,219 lb (1,460 kg) into LEO.

Taurus XLS will provide a 3,970 lb (1,800 kg) to LEO capability, using Castor 4B strap-on boosters.

ILS International Launch Systems Atlas and Proton — USA/Russia

Corporate address:
101 West Broadway, Suite 2000, San Diego, CA 92101, USA.

Telephone: +1 619 654 6470
Facsimile: +1 619 654 6500

Summary

2 workhorses of the US and Russian space programmes, the Atlas and Proton respectively, are marketed by a Lockheed Martin-Khrunichev-RSC Energia joint company, named ILS and established in 1995. Uprated versions of the Atlas and Proton are planned, including the Atlas 2AR, which could be replaced rapidly by Lockheed Martin's proposed 3-vehicle EELV fleet; the US Air Force will announce the EELV contract winners in June 1998. Launches are offered for about US$60 million-US$70 million. ILS currently operates 2 Atlas and 1 Proton vehicles. The Atlas flies from Complex 36 at Cape Canaveral, Florida, and a new Atlas pad has been built for launches from Vandenberg AFB, California. Proton is launched from the Baikonur Cosmodrome in Kazakhstan and a new pad may be built at the Plesetsk Cosmodrome, Russia.

Variants and Specifications

Atlas 2 was developed for the US Air Force Medium Launch Vehicle programme and will not be used for future commercial launches. This used 2 Rocketdyne RS-27 booster first stage engines of 200,000 lbf (890 kN) thrust each, with a burn time of 160 seconds, and a 60,500 lbf (269 kN) thrust Rocketdyne MA-5A sustainer engine with a burn time of 277 seconds. Both used LOX-kerosene. The second Centaur stage was powered by 2 Pratt & Whitney RL-10A-3-3A LOX-LH engines, with a total 32,825 lbf (146 kN) thrust and burn time of 408 seconds, with 2 available firings. It could carry 6,195 lb (2,810 kg) to GTO and successfully flew 9 times since 1991. It was retired in 1998.

Atlas 2A is an enhanced version of the Atlas 2, with new RL-10A-4 motors for the Centaur stage and other improvements. It can place 6,713 lb (3,045 kg) to GTO and has flown 14 successful launches since 1992. It is manifested to fly 12 satellites and the others for the US Air Force and NASA (under the Intermediate Expendable Launch Vehicle - IELV programme).

Atlas 2AS has been created as the primary commercial vehicle by adding 4 Thiokol Castor 4A solid propellant strap-on boosters to the Atlas 2A. 2 of the boosters ignite on the pad and burn for 54 seconds, while the second pair ignite at T+57 seconds. It also has upgraded RL-10A-4-1 engines and can place 8,223 lb (3,730 kg)

↑ **Atlas 2AS AC-108/Telstar 401 launch**

to GTO. It has made 14 successful flights with no failures since 1993. It is manifested to fly 12 commercial satellites and others for the US Air Force and NASA, whose EOM-1 spacecraft will be the first of this class of Atlas to be launched from the new pad at Vandenberg in 1998.

Atlas 2AR, which will make its debut in 1998 carrying a Loral built satellite (company has an option for a second launch), is a completely new version of the fleet designed to carry 8,906 lb (4,040 kg) into GTO. It comprises a first stage using a Pratt & Whitney/NPO Energomash RD Amross RD-180 LOX-kerosene motor of 95,100 lbf (423 kN) thrust, and Centaur second stage powered by a single uprated and restartable P&W RL-10E cryogenic motor.

Atlas 2ARS is an uprated 2AR, with 2 Thiokol solid-popellant strap-on boosters. GTO capability is increased to 9,390 lb (4,260 kg).

Proton K/SL-12 carries payloads of 3,527 lb (1,600 kg) directly into GEO or 10,582 lb (4,800 kg) to GTO. Its first stage is powered by a 6-nozzled RD-253 nitrogen tetroxide (stored in the core stage)/kerosene (in 6 side tanks, with nozzles) engine, providing 1,978,280 lbf (8,800 kN) of thrust and a burn time of 130 seconds. Similar 4-chamber RD-0210 second stage engines of 534,135 lbf (2,376 kN) thrust burn for 300 seconds, while the single 133,300 lbf (593 kN) thrust RD-0210 fires for 250 seconds on the third stage. The current DM2, LOX/kerosene and restartable fourth stage has a thrust of 19,100 lbf (85 kN).

Proton K first flew in 1967 and has made 196 successful launches (including 7 commercial GEO flights), with 19 failures and 11 partial failures. It is manifested to carry 16 commercial GEO satellites and 7 Iridium LEO satellites (on launches not operated by ILS), as well as national craft.

Proton KM is an uprated version with new cryogenic third stage and Breeze upper stage, and could provide a 9,259 lb (4,200 kg) GEO capability after the year 2000.

Sea Launch — USA/Ukraine/Russia/Norway

Corporate address:
PO Box 3999, MS 8X-57, Seattle, Washington 98124-2499, USA.
Telephone: +1 206 477 5770
Facsimile: +1 206 393 0250

Summary

Boeing of the USA has linked with the Ukraine's NPO Yushnoye and Yuzhmash, Russia's NPO Energia and Kvaerner of Norway to market the Zenit 3 for GTO launches under the joint operator's name Sea Launch.

Variants and Specifications

Sea Launch is a Zenit 3SL vehicle, which is a Zenit 2 (see Ukraine) with the DM stage from the Proton (see USA/Russia). The Sea Launch will place 12,566 lb (5,700 kg) into GTO. Launches will be from an offshore mobile platform called Odyssey, located close to the former Christmas Island in the Pacific Ocean. The operator received options to launch 19 satellites for Hughes and Lockheed Martin (Loral), starting in June 1999, plus 1 firm.

Operational Manned Spacecraft

Russian Space Agency Soyuz TM — Russia

Corporate address:
Shchepkin Street, 129857 Moscow.
Telephone: +7 095 28 89 905
Facsimile: +7 095 25 18 702

Summary

The Soyuz TM is used to ferry 2- and 3-person crews to and from the Mir 1 space station and will be used for flights to and from the ISS. 2 TMs will also serve as the interim Assured Crew Return Vehicles for the operational ISS.

Variants and Specifications

Soyuz TM is an updated version of the original Soyuz which first flew manned in 1967. It comprises a service module with twin solar panels and a multiple-restart primary orbital manoeuvring and retro rocket engine, the latter powered by nitrogen tetroxide-UDMH and offering a thrust of 698 lbf (3.1 kN). The descent module, which contains the crew for launch and re-entry, measures 7.2 ft (2.2 m) high and wide. The orbital module provides space for cargo and living quarters during solo orbital periods, prior to docking with Mir or other space station. The TM has flown 28 missions, the first of which was an unmanned test flight. Launches on the Soyuz booster from Baikonur are regular and routine, taking place in all weather conditions. Soyuz TM is likely to be in service until about the year 2010.

↑ Soyuz TM-20 launched on the Euromir 95 mission *(ESA/P. Aventurier)*

Russian Space Agency Mir 1 — Russia

Corporate address:
see previous entry.

↑ Mir 1 space station before the 1997 collision

Summary

Construction of the Mir 1 space station began in 1986 and was completed (6 years late) with the launch of the Spektr module. Mir could be in service until 2000, providing experiment facilities and space for commercial passengers while the ISS is being built, though technical difficulties in 1997 caused by the collision of a **Progress** tanker craft has put its future in doubt. When it is decommissioned, it will have to be de-orbited for a controlled re-entry over an ocean using the engines of 2 docked unmanned Progress tankers.

Variants and Specifications

Mir 1 comprises a core module, and the Kvant 1, Kvant 2, Kristall, Priroda and Spektr modules, the latter 4 docked to a multiple port adaptor on the core module. Progress tankers dock to the Kvant 1 at the rear of the core module. The Soyuz TM docks at the Kvant 1 or Kvant 2 ports. The Space Shuttle docked with the Kristall module.

United Space Alliance Space Transportation System (Space Shuttle) — USA

Corporate address:
1150 Gemini, Houston, TX 77058-2708.

Telephone: +1 281 212 6369
Facsimile: +1 281 212 6322

Summary

The manned Space Shuttle is likely to remain operational until about the year 2010, although it is expected to be upgraded, particularly with the addition of liquid strap-on boosters to replace the current solid rocket boosters. It has not yet been decided what will replace the Shuttle, although NASA and Lockheed Martin Skunk Works are developing a technological demonstrator of a single-stage-to-orbit reusable space transportation system known as the **X-33 VentureStar**. The 273,000 lb (123,830 kg) wedge-shaped X-33 is expected to fly up to 15 research missions from Edwards AFB from 1999. A full-sized launch vehicle when ready for service is expected to improve reliability and reduce the cost of placing each pound of payload into space from the current US$10,000 to only US$1,000. Another proposed manned vehicle is the X-38, a 6-person re-entry craft to provide emergency return from the International Space Station. A sub-scale prototype has been undergoing unmanned atmospheric glide tests since 1997.
The Space Shuttle itself is now operated by the United Space Alliance (a Boeing-Lockheed Martin partnership) on behalf of NASA. The latest flight (at the time of writing) was STS-89, launched on 23 January 1998 using *Endeavour.*

↑ Space Shuttle views and statistics

Variants and Specifications

Space Shuttle system comprises an Orbiter with 3 reusable Space Shuttle Main Engines (SSMEs) which are supplied with cryogenic LOX/LH propellants from an External Tank. SSME thrust is complemented by 2 Solid Rocket Boosters (SRBs). The operational Orbiter fleet comprises *Columbia*, *Discovery*, *Atlantis* and *Endeavour*. The SSMEs each provide a thrust of 394,300 lbf (1,754 kN) and a burn time of 520 seconds, while the SRBs each provide a thrust of 3,300,000 lbf (14,680 kN). Burn time is 120 seconds. The 7-segment SRBs are recovered at sea and elements are re-used. Total lift-off thrust is some 7,783,000 lbf (34,622 kN). The Shuttle is launched from pads 39A and 39B at the Kennedy Space Centre north of Cape Canaveral, Florida. It can place a nominal maximum payload of 55,000 lb (24,948 kg) into LEO but the actual maximum amount carried has so far been 48,830 lb (22,150 kg) and has more typically been 37,500 lb (17,000 kg). This reduction has been the result of modifications since the *Challenger* accident in 1986. The maximum crew complement has been 8 (STS 61A in 1985). There have been 92 launches, one of which failed (*Challenger*). The latest mission (at time of writing in November 1998) included on board *Discovery* 77 year old John Glenn. *Columbia* has flown the longest mission, lasting 17 days 15 hours. The majority of Space Shuttle missions scheduled after 1997 will be dedicated to the assembly of the International Space Station (ISS). Over 33 dedicated ISS missions will be flown from December 1998 to 2003.

↑ Lockheed Martin X-33 VentureStar

International Space Station — International

Operator:
National Aeronautics and Space Administration (NASA).

Corporate address:
Washington DC 20546, USA.

Telephone: +1 202 358 1000

Summary

A joint programme involving the USA, Russia, Canada, Japan and Europe, the International Space Station (ISS) is expected to be completed in the year 2004 and will comprise 6 laboratories, 2 habitation modules, 2 logistics modules, an array of 8 solar panels providing 110 kW of electricity, a remote manipulator system and other equipment, with a working volume of 43,000 cu ft (1,217.6 m^3). It will have cost US$17 billion to build but, with the costs of earlier work on the Freedom and Alpha designs since 1984, the total cost of the project will be closer to US$60 billion, not including the US$40 million cost of operating it and the cost of the 33 Space Shuttle flights to support its construction. The future and eventual final configuration of the ISS is not certain, as it depends on continuing support from Russia, funding, the continuing reliability of the Space Shuttle, and other factors.

Variants and Specifications

ISS's first element will be the Russian Zarya Functional Energy Block (FGB), scheduled for launch in November 1998. The Space Shuttle was scheduled to make the first NASA flight in December 1998 as STS88, using *Endeavour*, its crew including the Russian Sergei Krikalev, and carrying the Node 1. The first crew to man the station will be launched in January 1999. At this stage the ISS will comprise the FGB, the Node 1, the Russian Service Module (or a US Interim Control Module) and a Soyuz TM.

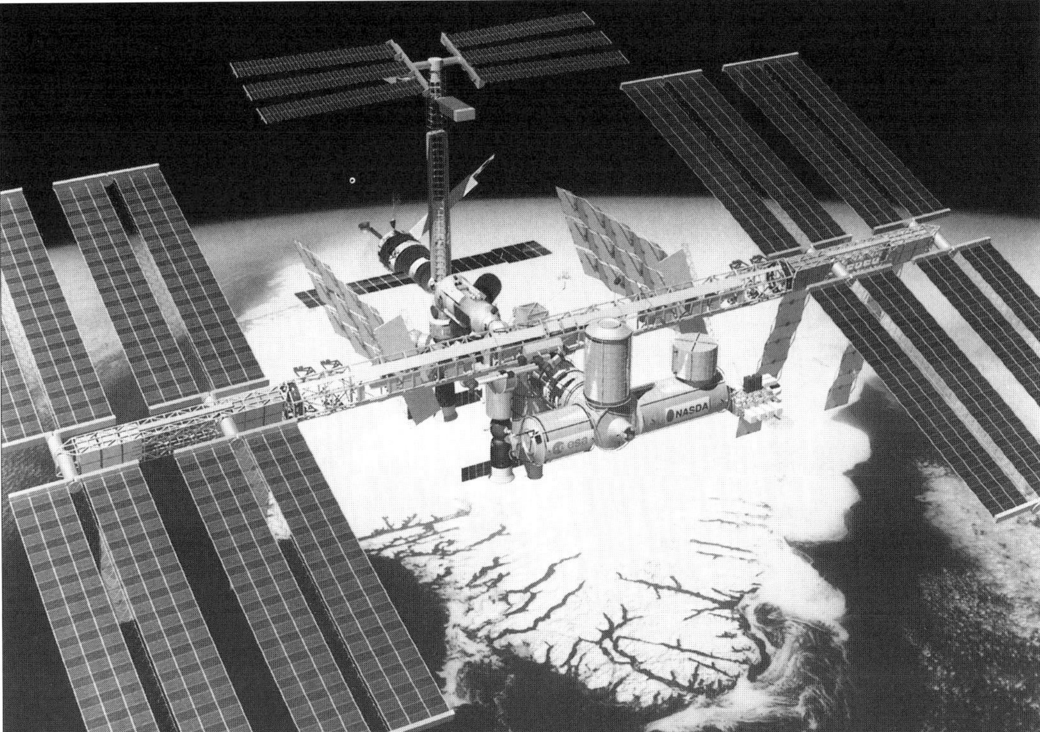

↑ International Space Station computer generated illustration (by NASA), showing it in completed form with elements from the USA, Russia, Europe, Canada and Japan. It wil be about 350 ft (107 m) long and weigh approximately 900, 000 lb (408,200 kg)

Buoyant Aircraft (Airships)

Manufacturers, Designers and Major Operators

The term Buoyant Aircraft is a more up-to-date and meaningful expression for Airships, as many can operate 'heavy'. However, to retain plain and familiar language, the term Airship has been used in the entries.
(note: tons are 2,240 lb; tonnes are 1,000 kg)

The Chief Editor would like to acknowledge The Airship Association Ltd (6 Kings Road, Cheriton, Folkestone, Kent CT20 3LG, England), both in the UK and USA.

Begul Aviation Australia — Australia

Corporate address:
Ballarat 3350, Victoria.

ACTIVITIES

- In February 1997 it was reported that Begul Aviation had patented the design of a hybrid airship known as the Advanced Air Vehicle, which was featured in model form on a display at Ballarat Airport, Victoria. The AAV features dual side-by-side envelopes and a 2-deck gondola suspended between and beneath, the whole connected by high-technology rigid beams of substantial thickness. Each envelope carries horizontal and a dorsal tail fins. With an anticipated load capacity of a Hercules freighter, coupled with a duration of up to 14 days and fuel efficiency approximately double that of a helicopter, it could serve many commercial and military applications, including passenger and cargo carrying, survey and monitoring, surveillance and more besides. The cost of an AAV would be approximately A$25 to 40 million.

LTA-Brasil — Brazil

Corporate address:
Rua da Passagem, 115 – Botafogo – CEP; 22.290-030 Rio de Janeiro RJ.
Telephone: +55 21 275 5981 and 295 0794
Facsimile: +55 21 295 8249
Information:
Dr Sergio B.V. Gomes (Technical Director).

ACTIVITIES

- Established in December 1994, its main activities are airship operations for advertising, photographic work and VIP flights, plus consultancy work in the lighter-than-air field. It operated a leased Lightship A60+ until April 1996, by which time 1,400 hours had been flown while advertising for Pepsi and Petrobras. Operations were thereafter suspended due to a lack of sponsors, but flying was expected to resume in late 1997 with another airship type. Consultancy work for various private and government agencies continues, as interest in using current and future airship designs in Brazil's hinterland is a growing opportunity.

21st Century Airships Inc — Canada

Corporate address:
Box 177, 180 Main Street, Newmarket, Ontario L3Y 4X1 (offices); 110 Pony Drive, Newmarket, Ontario L3Y 4W2 (manufacturing plant).
Telephone: +1 905 898 6274
Facsimile: +1 905 898 7245
Information:
Hokan Colting.

21st Century Airships SPAS 13 Ball of Dreams

First flight: 13 May 1994.
Role: Semi-rigid helium airship demonstrator (C-FRLM).

Aims

- To demonstrate the advantages of a spherical airship, with the crew/passengers seated inside the envelope in a spacious cabin.
- To show the envelope to be extremely helium-tight, and thereby cost efficient.
- Steering and altitude control through varied and deflected thrust, the technology having been developed and patented by the company.

Development

SPAS 13 reinflated 1995 after 112 flights, in improved form and decorated as Ball of Dreams baseball. 40 more flights but since deflated. In store in November 1998.

Details

Crew/Passengers: Pilot and 1 passenger occupying an internal cabin with 96 sq ft (8.92 m^2) of panoramic window area.
2 ground crew required.
Diameter: 43 ft (13.11 m)
Height: 45 ft (13.72 m) including undercarriage.
Envelope: Outside load-bearing envelope made of Spectra fabric, said to be ten times stronger than steel of the same weight. Second inner envelope of Mylar film and reinforced with Kevlar, and containing helium gas. 41,200 cu ft (1,167 m^3).
Take-off weight: 2,403 lb (1,090 lb)
Empty weight: 1,596 lb (724 kg)
Engines: 2 Rotax 503s, each 50 hp (37.3 kW).
Propellers: 2 three-blade, each 6 ft (1.83 m) diameter.
Control vanes: 4 surfaces behind each engine deflect air for ascending/descending.
Maximum airspeed: 26 kts (30 mph) 48 km/h
Cruise speed: 16.5 kts (19 mph) 30 km/h

↑ 21st Century Airships SPAS 13 demonstrator

21st Century Airships SPAS 70

First flight: 5 August 1997.
Role: Advertising and aerial filming.

Aims

- Internal built-in cabin, and envelope/control technologies demonstrated on SPAS 13.

Development

- Developed as a larger spherical airship. Has undergone important design revisions prior to its first flight, including the use of 4 engines instead of 2 and a reduction in passengers from 4 to 3.
- Fly-by-wire used for throttle and main controls (including engine vanes).
- August 1997 – Summer 1999. Certification, using Subaru engines. Certificated Rotax engines being retrofitted. See Crew.

Details

Crew/Passengers: Pilot and 3 passengers in internal cabin.
2 ground crew required. For flight testing for certification, only 2 seats fitted.
Cabin: Usable floor space 700 sq ft (65 m^3). To simplify management of 4 engines, the instrument panels have all engine instruments and controls colour coded. In addition to regular engine monitoring instruments, there are internal pressure gauges, outside/inside and helium temperature gauges, fire warning lights for each engine and the APU, VHF transceivers, transponder, radar altimeter, GPS and stormscope.
Diameter: 56 ft (17.07 m)
Height: 56 ft (17.07 m). No undercarriage fitted.
Envelope: *Volume* 92,000 cu ft (2,605 m^3). Special tie-down arrangement.

↑ 21st Century Airships SPAS 70 cabin, with only 2 seats for trials and panoramic windows

↑ 21st Century Airships SPAS 70, first flown in August 1997, with 4 engines and the envelope decorated as the Earth

↑ Drawing of the cockpit/cabin for the 21st Century Airships Voyage of Dreams 10-passenger glass bottom airship

Take-off weight: 5,512 lb (2,500 kg)
Empty weight: 3,197 lb (1,450 kg)
Engines: 4 Saburu converted motorcar engines, each 100 hp (74.6 kW). 4 Rotax engines retrofitted. Engines mounted in vertically-stacked pairs each side of the envelope, the upper pair 20 ft (6 m) from the ground, and the lower pair 13 ft (4 m) off the ground. Airship can fly on 2 engines but 4 fitted for safety.
Propellers: Fully open (not shrouded).
Control vanes: Steering and altitude control through varied and deflected thrust (see SPAS 13).
Maximum airspeed: 35 kts (40 mph) 65 km/h
Cruise speed: 20 kts (23 mph) 37 km/h
Duration: 12 hours

21st Century Airships SPAS-75 Voyage of Dreams

First flight: Scheduled to be built and certified by Summer of 1999.
Role: Sightseeing passenger rides.

Aims

▪ Internal built-in cabin with partially glass bottom. Offers passengers a high level of comfort, with 360° views through wrap-round windows.

Development

▪ Based on SPAS 13 and 5-seater technology.

Details

Crew/Passengers: Pilot and 10 passengers. 2 ground crew.
Diameter: 75 ft (22.86 m)
Height: 66 ft (20.1 m) including undercarriage.
Envelope: 220,000 cu ft (6,230 m^3).
Engines: 4, each 140 hp (104.4 kW).
Propellers: In shrouds.
Control vanes: Steering and altitude control through varied and deflected thrust (see SPAS 13).
Maximum airspeed: 30 kts (35 mph) 56 km/h
Cruise speed: 22 kts (25 mph) 40 km/h

Pan Atlantic Aerospace Corp — Canada

Corporate address:
PO Box 599, Station B, Ottawa, Ontario K1P 5P7.
Telephone: +1 613 722 1454
Facsimile: +1 613 722 1691
E-mail: LTADRONE @ AOL.com
Information:
Fredrick Ferguson (CEO), Nick Baumberg (Office Manager/Communications).

ACTIVITIES

▪ Pan Atlantic Aerospace Corp is a subsidiary of Av-Intel Inc and is a research company focusing on a number of airship projects. None has yet reached the construction stage, with exception of the one-third scale LESA and the LEAP drones, and the company is engaged in setting up financing. The CAS is likely to be the first project to carry forward, though HASP is a current programme at the conceptual stage.
▪ The company moved location in late 1997. The address quoted applies to this change.

Pan Atlantic Aerospace Cargo Airship System (CAS)

First flight: First pre-production vehicle flights unlikely to be before 1999.
Role: Patented large cargo-carrying airship, aimed at high value, low density cargo markets.

Aims

▪ Segmented pressure airship to provide a net payload of up to 500 tons (508 tonnes) and built in sizes of up to 1,700 ft (518 m) length. Uses LEAP technology (which see).
▪ To operate at costs approximately one-third that of low-cost fixed-wing cargo aircraft.
▪ To operate in all weather conditions and to meet and exceed 35fps gust loads.
▪ Utilise articulation, modern high strength and lightweight materials, and allow effective load transfer throughout the module envelopes.
▪ To maximise volume and payload without building a craft much beyond 200 ft (61 m) height, a long high fineness ratio design is chosen. Although such a design has higher aerodynamic bending moments from flight and gust loads, CAS will take these loads and remain structurally sound through modularization.

Development

▪ Approximately $10m spent in first phase of development, including two 50 ft (15.24 m) scaled flying drones, wind tunnel analyses, final design definition, simulation, market and business feasibility, etc.
▪ A phase covering detailed engineering, conclude market-user commitments, and complete manufacturing contracts probably continues.

Details

Length: 1,500 ft (457.2 m)
Diameter: 200 ft (61 m)
Envelope: 6 modules: front powered control module section and rear tail section 350 ft × 200 ft (106.7 × 61 m) each, and 4 payload modules 200 ft × 200 ft. Total *volume* 39,793,500 cu ft (1,126,825 m^3). Fabric assumed to be Dacron and Tedlar laminate for weight calculations**. Use of Kevlar or Spectra would reduce projected weights.
Fineness ratio: 7.5:1
Drag coefficient: 0.026
Ballonets: 20% of total volume.
Gross buoyancy: 1,965,800 lb (891,671 kg) with all ballonets fully inflated.

↑ Impression of the Pan Atlantic Aerospace CAS airship prototype in its hangar

Empty weight: 420,000 lb (190,500 kg)**
Payload: 1,284,000 lb (582,400 kg) net available payload (containers + cargo).
Engines: 4 Allison GMA 2100 turboprops, each 6,000 shp (4,474 kW).
Fuel: 238,000 lb (107,955 kg) for 4,000 mile range at cruise speed, with 10% fuel reserves.
Maximum airspeed: 82.5 kts (95 mph) 153 km/h
Cruise speed: 66 kts (76 mph) 122 km/h
Range: 3,476 naut miles (4,000 miles) 6,437 km
Duration: 52.6 hours

Pan Atlantic Aerospace High Altitude Satellite Platform (HASP)

First flight: Not yet flown. Conceptual project only.
Role: High altitude robotic platform for surveillance, communications and other equipment payloads.

Aims

▪ 2 HASP airships per system, with one or other operating in 6-week cycles.
▪ LEAP type technology for envelope.
▪ 70,000 ft (21,335 m) operating altitude.

Details

Engines: 4.

Pan Atlantic Aerospace Long Endurance Airship Platform (LEAP)

First flight: 9 December 1990. Completed flight trials.
Role: Long Endurance Articulating Powered (LEAP), remotely piloted, drone airship. Suitable as a platform for TV and motion picture cameras, radar and IR systems, over-the-horizon transmitters, high-intensity lights, pollution probes, geodetic survey equipment, etc.

Aims

▪ On-board stability augmentation to ease piloting fatigue during lengthy operations.
▪ Low cost, energy efficient and environmentally safe surveillance through remotely controlled guidance.

Development

▪ Result of 3 years R&D of pre-production prototypes.

Details

Crew: No on-board crew. 1 ground-based operator. Multiple and redundant radio control transmission and frequencies provide back-up assurance for added flight safety.
Length: 67 ft (20.42 m)
Diameter: 11 ft (3.4 m)
Envelope: Modular design, consisting 3 separate sections, for simplified inflation, ground handling, and increased structural integrity. Total *volume* 5,339 cu ft (151.18 m^3). Carbonfibre stiffeners at nose.
Surface area: 2,655.5 sq ft (246.7 m^2)
Ballonet: Automatic ballonet operation. *Volume* 7.5% of total.
Total lift: 335.3 lb (152.1 kg)
Gross weight: 263.3 lb (119.5 kg)
Payload: 72 lb (32.6 kg), maintained at various altitudes for up to 6 hours.
Engines: 3 remotely-controlled 1.5 hp (1.12 kW) engines mounted on the front section, individually controlled for precise low speed manoeuvrability and hover control.
Fuel: Main fuel cells above side engines.
Canards: Engines and horizontal/ventral canards attached to an aluminium or carbonfibre support yoke. Fixed ventral canard, and vectored horizontal canards.
Tail surfaces: Cruciform fins and active rudders.
Maximum airspeed: 26 kts (30 mph) 48 km/h

Pan Atlantic Aerospace Long Endurance Manned Solar Airship (LEMS)

This programme for a solar-electric powered version of the multi-segmented long fineness ratio airship is on hold. Full details can be found in the 1996-97 edition of *WA&SD*.

Pan Atlantic Aerospace Long Endurance Solar Airship (LESA)

First flight: 8 October 1991.
Role: One-third scale, electric-powered, radio-controlled drone airship, to assist in the LEMS programme (which see).

Development

▪ 1991. Nord-Am initiated design and fabrication.

Details

Length: 48 ft (14.63 m)
Envelope: 6-segment, long fineness ratio.

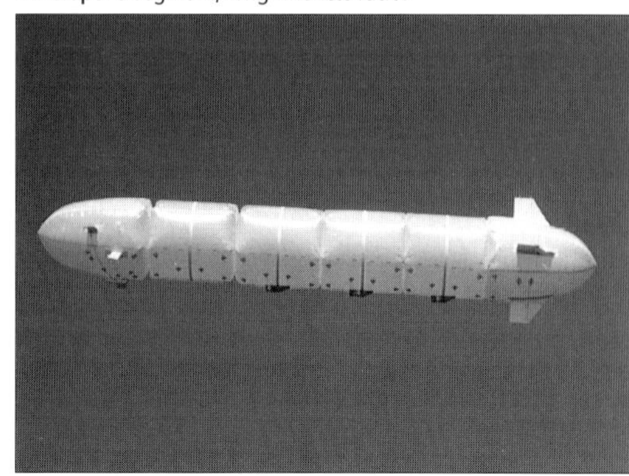

↑ Pan Atlantic Aerospace LESA

Pan Atlantic Aerospace Magnus 60

This programme remains on hold while awaiting financing. Full details appeared in the 1996-97 edition of *WA&SD*. An abbreviated description follows.
Role: Rotating spherical VTOL, low speed, highly manoeuvrable, heavy-lift airship. To be used for low-level aerial animated advertising and capable of precise station keeping.

Aims

▪ Exploit the Magnus effect, which causes lift to be generated by a spherical object that rotates while moving in a horizontal direction.
▪ Does not require mooring masts or large ground crews.
▪ Anticipated to be approximately 50% less expensive than similar size standard airships.
▪ Operate precision hover.
▪ Statically stable in pitch and roll, easy to pilot, good control power in yaw, and precise low speed manoeuvring.

Development

▪ Initially invented and developed during 1979-88 by Mr Ferguson and scale tested during 1981-86.
▪ Pan Atlantic Aerospace subsequently prepared design definition for an advertising version, with an electronic advertising panel on a towed aerostat, joined to Magnus 60 by light aluminium or plastic tubing.

Details

Crew: 2, plus video equipment, etc in enclosed cabin gondola.
Diameter: 60 ft (18.3 m) maximum.
Envelope: *Volume* 113,097 cu ft (3,203 m^3). As forward speed increases, sphere rotation is started and lift is generated by the Magnus effect. The effect lift is sufficient to counteract the 600 lb (272 kg) negative buoyancy that the engines had been lifting and all engine thrust is dedicated to propel the airship forward. Climb and descent is controlled by sphere rotation speed, ballonet volume and engine pitch settings. A safety valve in the envelope allows quick release of helium gas.
Surface area: 11,310 sq ft (1,050.7 m^2)
Ballonet: *Volume* 11,310 cu ft (320.26 m^3)
Lift volume: 101,787 cu ft (2,882.28 m^3)
Gross lift: 6,484 lb (2,941 kg)
Net lift: 1,084 lb (491.7 kg)
Empty weight: Envelope 1,414 lb (641.4 kg). Ballonet 44 lb (20 kg)
Payload: over 1,000 lb (453.6 kg)
Engines: 2 pivoting engines (90°), positioned vertically for take-off, each controlled separately by the pilot using a stick and twist grip.
Cruise speed: 30.5 kts (35 mph) 56 km/h approximately.
Duration: 4.5 hours

↑ Impression of the Pan Atlantic Aerospace Magnus 60 rotating spherical VTOL airship

Beijing Orient Air Service — China

ACTIVITIES

▪ Operates at the time of writing an ABC A-60+ Lightship (No 9), as a joint venture with Thakrai Corporation of Singapore.

Beijing University of Aeronautics and Astronautics — China

Address:
PO Box 85, 37 Xue Yuan Road, Haidian District, Beijing 100083.

Telephone: +86 10 62028347
Facsimile: +86 10 62028356

ACTIVITIES

▪ The BUAA has a small research group that has produced a series of Mifeng (Bee) aircraft, mostly microlights and the Mifeng-6 hot-air airship. The latter first flew on 20 December 1985 and 4 have been constructed, used for aerial photography, power line lifting, research and recreation/sport. However, despite this, it is believed that there is no formal airship manufacturing in China. The Mifeng-6 accommodates 4 persons, is 110 ft (33.7 m) long, has an envelope volume of 105,300 cu ft (2,983 m^3), and the Rotax 447 engine is used not only for power but also to inflate the envelope. Burners provide the heat needed for buoyancy variation.

↑ **BUAA Mifeng-6 hot-air airship**

Hangzhou Airship Research Institute — China

Address:
15-3-102 Li Dong Shan Nong, Hangzhou 310013.

Information:
Zhang Chuhong (Director).

ACTIVITIES

▪ The first airship by Zhang Chuhong first flew in 1984. The latest known craft is the XIHU-5 (West Lake-5).

Hangzhou XIHU-5

First flight: 1994.
Role: Passenger carrying.

Development

▪ 1995. Began trials to gain CAAC certification.
▪ 1996-7. Thought to have undergone retrofit with US Textron Lycoming engines before achieving certification.

Details

Crew/Passengers: Flight crew plus 20 passengers in a fully enclosed 39 ft 4 ins (12 m) length gondola.
Length: 183 ft 9 ins (56 m)
Diameter: 45 ft 11 ins (14 m)
Envelope: *Volume* 213,654 cu ft (6,050 m^3)
Ballonet: *Volume* 55,550 cu ft (1,573 m^3)
Empty weight: 7,288 lb (3,306 kg)
Take-off weight: 12,529 lb (5,683 kg)
Engines: 2 × 160 hp (119.3 kW) Textron Lycoming O-320 thrust-vectoring piston engines believed to be retrofitted, mounted in ducts at the rear of the gondola.
Stabilizers: Cruciform tail surfaces, the ventral surface having a rudder.
Maximum airspeed: 47 kts (54 mph) 87 km/h

↑ **Hangzhou Airship Research Institute XIHU-5**
(courtesy KM Photo Library)

Shanghai Aircraft Research Institute — China

Address:
PO Box 232-003-78, Long Hua Airport Building, Shanghai 200232.

Telephone: +86 21 4390811
Facsimile: +86 21 4390584

Information:
Wu Li Yao (Chief Designer).

ACTIVITIES

▪ This research organisation has built 2 robotic helium airships as the Shen Zhou-1 and -2, flown since 1992. They are each powered by 3 × 2.5 hp (1.9 kW) engines driving shrouded propellers, all attached to the gondola and able to vector for vertical or horizontal control in addition to providing propulsion (Shen Zhou-2 has 2 vectoring and 1 fixed engine). The cruciform tail fins carry movable control surfaces. Envelope volumes of the Shen Zhou-1 and -2 are 1,024 cu ft (29 m^3) and 1,060 cu ft (30 m^3) respectively. Uses, apart from research that may lead to the development of a large airship, could include surveillance.

The Special Vehicle Institute of AVIC — China

Address:
PO Box 307, Jingmen, Hubei 448035.

Telephone: +86 724 2332521
Facsimile: +86 724 2332551

Information:
Xu Zhongxin (Manager, Chief Engineer, lighter-than-air programme).

ACTIVITIES

▪ The former Huahang Airship Development Group was disbanded in 1991 after completion of its first manned airship, the non-rigid helium FK-4 (70,600 cu ft; 2,000 m^3 envelope volume and 2 vectoring Rotax 503 engines with shrouded propellers), first flown in August 1990 and recognised as having been the first passenger-carrying airship of its kind built in China. This was followed by a small robotic airship, known as the FK-6, with a volume of 3,100 cu ft (88 m^3). The head member of this Group, The Special Vehicle Institute of AVIC, inherited the majority of its academic properties and programmes.
▪ The Institute is a subsidiary of Aviation Industries of China, specializing in the R&D of seaplanes and surface-effect craft in addition to airships.
▪ In 1996, the Institute was awarded a Governmental Specific Fund to undertake the FK100 project, aimed at developing a 9-seat modern non-rigid airship.

The Special Vehicle Institute of AVIC FK100

First flight: Planned for mid-1997 but rescheduled to 1998.
Role: Non-rigid helium airship, for sightseeing, short-distance transportation, broadcasting and photography platform, and advertising. Other roles could include coastal patrol, rescue, monitoring, anti-smuggling and drug interdiction work.

Details

Sales: 1 ordered for the domestic market by August 1997.
Crew/Passengers: 9 seats.
Gondola: Length 22 ft 10 ins (6.95 m), width 5 ft 7 ins (1.7 m), height 6 ft 11 ins (2.1 m).
Length: 140 ft 11 ins (42.945 m)
Diameter: 36 ft 8 ins (11.184 m)
Width over tailfins: 40 ft 9 ins (12.428 m)
Height: 48 ft 3 ins (14.706 m)
Envelope: *Volume* 92,984 cu ft (2,633 m^3)
Ballonet: 26% of total volume.
Fineness ratio: 3.8:1
Take-off weight: 5,886 lb (2,670 kg)
Empty weight: 4,012 lb (1,820 kg)
Disposable load: 1,874 lb (850 kg) gross
Engines: 2 Rotax 914F2s, each 100 hp (74.6 kW).
Propellers: 2 shrouded, each 4 ft 3 ins (1.3 m) diameter. Controllable vectored thrust, +90°, -120°.

Tailfins area: 646 sq ft (60 m^2)
Control surfaces: Each tailfin has a trailing-edge control surface with inset tab.
Maximum airspeed: 55 kts (63 mph) 102 km/h
Ceiling: 9,840 ft (3,000 m)
Duration: 11.5 hours

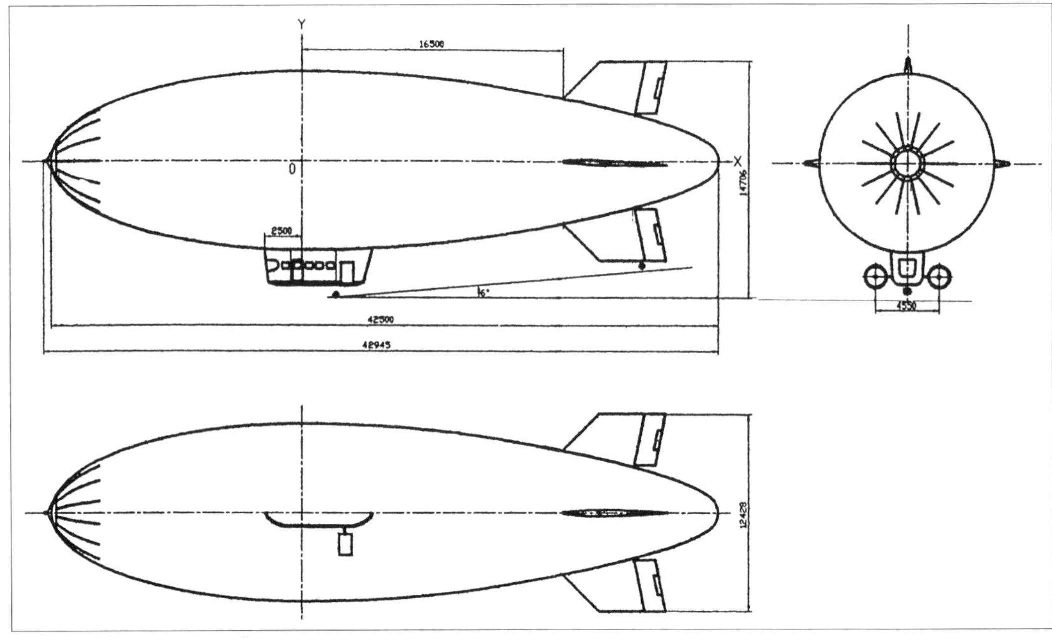

↑ The Special Vehicle Institute of AVIC FK100

Kubicek Ltd — Czech Republic

Corporate address:
Francouzská 81, 602 00 Brno.
Telephone: + 420 5 45 21 19 17
Facsimile: +420 5 45 21 30 74
Information:
Dipl Ing Ales Kubicek (Owner), Michael Suchy (Sales Manager).

ACTIVITIES

▪ Producer of lighter-than-air craft since 1983, the last 8 years as a private company.
▪ Offers some 11 standard types of hot-air balloons and a hot-air airship, plus constructs special shape envelopes and other cool-air inflatables such as tents. Kubicek planned an improved hot-air airship for another customer.

Kubicek AV-1 and Avgur/Kubicek AV-1R

Details: AV-1, except under third Development entry.
First flight: 16 October 1993 (*OK-3040*)
Role: Hot-air airship. Actively marketed in the Czech Republic and Russia.

Development

▪ First modern Czech airship, initially produced for TICO Prague.
▪ September 1994. The first AV-1 had accumulated its first 50 flying hours.
▪ 1997. Version marketed jointly with the Avgur Aerostat Centre in Moscow, Russia, as the AV-1R (which see).

Details

Crew: Pilot and passenger.
Length: 114 ft 10 ins (35 m)
Height of envelope: 39 ft 4 ins (12 m)
Envelope: *Volume* 98,880 cu ft (2,800 m^3)
Weight of envelope: 430 lb (195 kg)
Weight of gondola: 529 lb (240 kg)
Engine: 1 Rotax 503 of 50 hp (37.3 kW).
Propeller: 1 Justra-Stratos 4-blade pusher.
Burners: 2 Kubicek-kovo H3s.
Maximum airspeed: 13.5 kts (15.5 mph) 25 km/h
Duration: 1.5 hours

↑ Kubicek AV-1 produced for TICO

R & P Development — France

Full Name:
Régipa & Partners Development.
Corporate address:
Technoparc 4, voie 5, BP 531, F-31674 Labège-Innopole Cédex.
Telephone: +33 5 61 39 13 43
Facsimile: +33 5 61 39 13 70
Information:
Olivier Regipa (Managing Partner).

ACTIVITIES

▪ Independent and privately owned consulting and contract research corporation. It specializes in the study of advanced structures and dynamic systems (for example, sails, textile architecture and flexible containers) using high-performance non-rigid composites. Especially committed to the invention of new designs and to the improvement of laminates and technology process (weaving, coating, assembling, modelling, etc).
▪ Special attention has been given to balloons and airships. Balloon systems include a wide range of potential products, low-cost tethered aerostats for transmission and data collection, drones and remotely piloted vehicles for detection, surveillance and reconnaissance missions, high performance balloons as tethered hovering cranes, heavy-payload lighter-than-air, and high-altitude long endurance geostationary platforms.
▪ AVEA (Aile Verticale Epaisse Aérostatique) or Buoyant Steerable Thick Wing is an on-going programme lead by R & P Development.

AVEA (Aile Verticale Epaisse Aérostatique)

First flight: Not yet flown in full-size form.
Role: Helium and air filled heavy-lift airship for various tasks, including aerial logging, heavy equipment installation, supplying remote construction sites, mining and oil operations, off-shore exploration support, aerial mapping and surveying, rescue operations, and resource development.

Aims

▪ Modular airship using the structural properties of cylinders as the core of the design (see Envelope).
▪ VTOL precision performance and station-keeping without relative speed, due to aerostatic stability of each module. Vertical steering by rapidly varying the mass of air in the modules.
▪ Said to handle all climatic considerations.
▪ Minimal ground assistance, including no mooring mast or hangarage. In a heavy-lift capacity, the design would allow cargo to be moved directly from containerships to marshalling yards, so eliminating marine craft, handling equipment and ground transportation between sea and shore.
▪ Family of low initial cost and low operating cost AVEAs.

Development

▪ 1983. Original AVEA was conceived by Dr Robert Regipa of the Balloon Division of CNES, a pioneer of high-altitude scientific balloons.
▪ AVEA was the result of researching the limitations of traditional stratospheric lighter-than-air craft, addressing the perceived problem of good performance set against the disadvantage of inability to withstand superpressure and consequently not incorporating the required level of structural integrity.
▪ 1989. Full-size demonstrator of a modulen was fabricated, measuring 76 ft 9 ins (23.4 m) height, 27 ft 7 ins (8.4 m) diameter and 45,909 cu ft (1,300 m^3) volume.
▪ 1991. Following extensive control of its overall superpressure resistance on the ground, the craft was released, successfully performing its mission. Several other scientific prototypes followed.
▪ Over 10 years of engineering and research have covered physical and superpressure testing; tension, static-loading and fatigue testing; wind tunnel testing; scaled proof-of-concept versions and hydraulic analogues.
▪ A partnership, including aircraft manufacturers, venture capitalists and public authorities was being formed at the time of writing in order to finance a full-size demonstrator.
▪ Technology has been independently assessed and endorsed by CNES Balloons Division, Toulouse; DSM, High Performance Fibers, Sittard, The Netherlands; ONERA, Centre d'Etudes et de Recherches de Toulouse; Ecole Nationale Supérieure de d'Aéronautique et de l'Espace, Toulouse; IMA (Institut de Maintenance Aéronautique), Université de Bordeaux; Conseil Général de la Région Nord – Pas de Calais, Lille; ; Conseil Général des Ponts & Chaussées, Paris. In addition, on 15 June 1988 the European Ministers of Research in Copenhagen granted the status of Eurêka to the project.

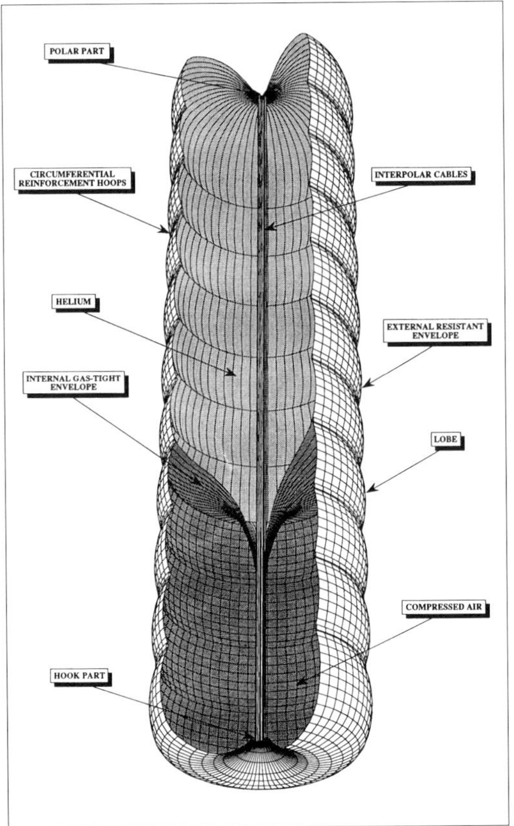

↑ AVEA module construction

Details

Sales: A market study in 1997 co-financed by Nord – Pas de Calais Region and ANVAR (French Innovation Agency) showed the potential for a series of AVEAs in the heavy-lift marketplace, capable of lifting and hovering with net loads of between 100 and 500 tonnes.

↑ Impression of AVEAs working in a heavy-lift capacity at a harbour

Envelope: The AVEA consists of a combination of several modules, proportioned in size and arranged in such a way as to provide aerodynamic characteristics consistent with the best profile and drag coefficient. They are joined side-by-side in vertical form and allowed freedom to move in relationship to each other. By the combination of modules, it is possible to design buoyant aircraft that are equipped for horizontal propulsion (see illustration) and with all necessary auxiliary devices (rudder, vertical fin, etc). A module itself is a vertical cylinder composed of an inner envelope inflated with helium and an outer envelope inflated with air. Helium inflation is possible only on the ground during release of the craft, the upper 'polar part' having a safety valve to allow venting in case the internal pressure rises above the limit. The module can also have its inner envelope inflated and deflated, with the view to increasing flight safety through leakage adjustment, for vertical control in case of an emergency. The basic cylinder module is a "Cartesian diver". Ascent and descent are controlled by releasing or adding air; as the craft rises, air pressure decreases and the volume of the inner envelope increases, whereas the mass of air in the outer envelope decreases, the volume of the entire craft thereby remaining substantially constant. When a module delivers a payload, it needs to take on a counterweight of air or counterballast before releasing it; the lifting of a payload requires the opposite. Opening the air valve provides the necessary lift capacity. For every mission, the parameters of the module are adjusted to optimize the field of stresses to which the envelope is subjected, achieving the best balance of excess pressure and weight.

CargoLifter AG — Germany

Full name: CargoLifter Aktiengesellschaft.
Corporate address: Kreuzberger Ring 21, D-65205 Wiesbaden.
Telephone: +49 611 974 8188 **Facsimile:** +49 611 974 8100 **E-mail:** info@cargolifter.com **Web site:** www.cargolifter.com
Information: Dr Carl v. Gablenz (President & CEO).

ACTIVITIES

- Founded on 1 September 1996 to design, construct and operate a multi-functional large airship.

CargoLifter CL 160

First flight: One-eighth test vehicle named Joey assembled from December 1998, for June 1999 first flight. Full-scale test flights possibly 2001.
Role: Semi-rigid helium airship for the transportation of very heavy and outsized cargoes, plus other shipments and people, in an environmentally friendly manner.

Aims

- Create a procedure and system to permit loading and unloading of cargo ("Airloading") at a particular location while the airship remains in the air, to prevent the need for landing facilities. The procedure and system (patent pending) is based on taking advantage of the inherent lift capability of the airship, its ability to create additional lift, and the capacity of the design to incorporate a loading system which precludes landing. During unloading/loading a cargo, the airship will function as a flying-crane positioned over the loading area by a system of wires. After arriving at the location, 4 wires are dropped from the loading frame to the ground and captured by winches. The lift of the airship is increased by releasing ballast water, which has the effect of tightening the wires (as the wires are attached to the loading frame, the airship above the loading frame can "sail" into the wind and is still manoeuvrable). The winches are activated, which pulls the loading frame and the load exactly into position. The load is removed and replaced with either a new cargo or containers for water ballast. The loading frame and load is then winched into the hovering airship, the wires released from the ground and the airship can depart.
- Land only for major annual maintenance and will moor to a mast.

Development

- Early 2002. Planned start of commercial services.

Details

Sales: Preliminary cost estimate for a CL 160 is approximately 100 million DM. Design freeze 1998.
Crew/Passengers: Maximum of 10 crew.
Gondola: Attached to the keel and forward of the loading bay.

↑ **CargoLifter CL 160** *(CargoLifter AG)*

Length: 794 ft (242 m)
Diameter: 193 ft 7 ins (59 m) maximum
Width over fins: 262 ft 5 ins (80 m)
Height over fins: 279 ft (85 m)
Envelope: Semi-rigid structure with keel and catenary curtain. In-flight access to all main parts of the airship. *Volume* 15,891,615 cu ft (450,000 m^3).
Fineness ratio: 4:1
Gross useful lift: 177 tons (180 tonnes)
Payload: Keel along the bottom of the airship will have in its centre the loading bay, with cargo in a loading frame. Payload weight will be distributed along the keel and throughout the envelope, which will lead to a thicker shape than for traditional long airships. Lifting capacity of the first version will be 157.5 tons (160 tonnes). Loading bay 164 ft (50 m) in length, 26 ft (8 m) width and 26 ft (8 m) height.
Engines: Total of 4-6 main diesels, with 2-3 located along the envelope on both sides; they will be located forward, centre (if 6) and rear. Thrust vectoring. Additional thruster engines in the bow and stern of the envelope for manoeuvrability (see drawing). Total installed engine power 6,973 hp (5,200 kW). Additional ballast water is captured from the engine exhaust to allow the weight of the airship to remain constant as fuel is burned.
Propellers: Tractor propellers. See above for thrusters.
Fuel: Consumption 4.5 litres per km at 54 kts (62 mph) 100 km/h and 6,560 ft (2,000 m) altitude.
Stabilizers: Cruciform tail fins.
Maximum airspeed: 75 kts (87 mph) 140 km/h
Cruise speed: 43 kts (50 mph) 80 km/h
Operating altitude: 6,560 ft (2,000 m) maximum pressure altitude, ASL.
Ceiling: 6,560 ft (2,000 m)
Range: Up to 5,400 naut miles (6,215 miles) 10,000 km with maximum payload.
Maximum range: 8,100 naut miles (9,320 miles) 15,000 km
Duration: 185 hours at maximum range cruise speed in still air, or 125 hours at maximum payload range in still air.

GEFA-FLUG GmbH — Germany

Full name:
Gesellschaft zur Entwicklung und Förderung Aerostatischer Flugsysteme mbH.
Corporate address: Weststrasse 24c, D-52074 Aachen.
Telephone: +49 241 88 90 40 **Facsimile:** +49 241 88 90 420
Information: Michael Taschenmacher.

ACTIVITIES

▪ Manufacturers traditionally-shaped and special shape hot-air balloons, plus hot-air airships, the latter partly government funded. Other products include tethered advertising gas aerostats and miniature display balloons.
▪ Operates a number of hot-air airships and hot-air balloons in Europe.

GEFA-FLUG AS 80 GD

First flight: 1990.
Role: 2-seat hot-air airship for environmental projects and advertising.

Development

▪ Based on the Thunder & Colt AS 80 Mk II.

Details

Crew: 2 in a semi-enclosed gondola.
Length: 118 ft 1.3 ins (36 m)
Diameter: 37 ft 8.8 ins (11.50 m)
Height: 44 ft 9.4 ins (13.65 m)
Envelope: *Volume* 79,460 cu ft (2,250 m^3). *Advertising area* 3,014 sq ft (280 m^2).
Surface area: 10,656 sq ft (990 m^2)
Take-off weight: 1,477 lb (670 kg)

↑ GEFA-FLUG AS 80 GD 2-seat hot-air airship

Empty weight: 419 lb (190 kg) including tail unit.
Engine: 52 hp (38.8 kW) Rotax 462
Cruise speed: 24 kts (28 mph) 45 km/h
Duration: 60 minutes

GEFA-FLUG AS 105 GD

Role: Hot-air airship to be used for environmental research projects and advertising.

Development

▪ 1998. 4 production airships completed to date.

Details

Crew/Passengers: Pilot and 3 passengers.
Length: 134 ft 6 ins (41 m)
Diameter: 41 ft (12.5 m)
Height: 45 ft 11 ins (14 m)
Envelope: *Volume* 105,000 cu ft (3,000 m^3)
Take-off weight: 1,764 lb (800 kg)
Engine: 65 hp (48.5 kW) Rotax 582.
Maximum airspeed: 24 kts (28 mph) 45 km/h
Duration: 4 hours

Institut Für Statik und Dynamik der Luft- und Raumfahrtkonstruktionen - Universität Stuttgart — Germany

Address:
Pfaffenwaldring 27, D-70550 Stuttgart.
Telephone: +49 711 685 3612 **Facsimile:** +49 711 685 3706
Information: Markus Schlenker.

ACTIVITIES

▪ The Project Solar Airship "Lotte" began in 1991, when a group of students, scientists and teachers gathered to design and construct a solar-powered airship.
▪ Believing that solar-powered flight was one possible solution to ecologically safe air traffic, and that airships have the large surface area necessary to be equipped with solar cells, they set about designing and constructing a highly efficient, lightweight propulsion system using a flexible photo-voltaic generator. This system was integrated into a remotely-controlled airship.
▪ After 20 months, Lotte 1 flew at the International Garden Exhibition 1993 in Stuttgart but was destroyed that June when its hangar collapsed during a thunderstorm.
▪ Lotte 1 was followeed by Lotte 2, rolled out with only minor alterations 6 weeks later. It had a new envelope and new fins. In November 1993 it took part in the World Solar Challenge in Australia and flew about 178 naut miles (205 miles) 330 km in 4 days before radio command interference caused it to crash into a tree.
▪ Lotte 3 was constructed from the existing structure and given an advanced radio-control system. Many on-board data acquisition devices are used for scientific research on lighter-than-air vehicles. The propulsion and power-control system is built from modular components. Electronic systems have been redesigned to support commercial observation and advertising operations.
▪ Lotte 3 currently operates under a primary flight permit and underwent final flight testing for a permanent registration in late 1997.

ISD – Universität Stuttgart Lotte 3

Role: Remotely-piloted airship.

Aims

▪ 2 redundant radio circuits on different frequencies control the airship and check operational modes for safe flying. High-performance data acquisitioning and telemetry system informs pilot on the ground of systems' condition. Airship can be controlled by 2 pilots at different locations, to extend range.
▪ On-board tracking system based on satellite navigation receivers is under development.
▪ Fail-safe vital systems.

Details

Crew: Airship is stored on a special truck. 4 people are needed to operate the airship.
Length: 51 ft 2 ins (15.6 m)
Diameter: 13 ft 2 ins (4 m)
Envelope: *Volume* 3,849 cu ft (109 m^3)
Ballonets: 2
Take-off weight: 216 lb (98 kg)
Payload: 26.5 lb (12 kg)
Engines: See Battery/Solar cells.
Propellers: Single propeller mounted at the tail.
Battery/Solar cells: Maximum solar cell area is 6 panels of 12.6 sq ft (1.17 m^2) each. Maximum output of solar generator 1,123 W. Maximum battery capacity 1,080 Wh. Motor rated at 2 hp (1.5 kW). To allow for varying payload and duration requirements, the number of battery and solar cells can be altered.
Maximum airspeed: 24 kts (28 mph) 45 km/h
Operating altitude: 3,280 ft (1,000 m)
Take-off distance: minimum 197 × 197 ft (60 × 60 m)

↑ **ISD – Universität Stuttgart Lotte 3** *(Monika Rüger)*

Ingolf Schäfer — Germany

Address:
Kleinlindener Strasse 42, D-35398 Giessen.

Telephone: +49 6403 75065
Facsimile: +49 6403 75065
E-mail: 100344.1264@compuserve.com

ACTIVITIES

▪ Having been Project Manager for the 3 Universität Stuttgart Lotte solar-powered RPAs, Ingolf Schäfer has developed another such craft, the details of which follow.
▪ Designed to take part in the 1996 World Solar Challenge in Australia. As there were no other participants, it flew presentation flights at several Australian locations. Project has been supported by the cargo airline, Air Foyle.

Lotte-96

First flight: October 1996.
Role: Solar-powered, remotely-piloted, pressurized, helium airship for research and proof-of-concept.

Details

Crew/Passengers: None.
Length: 33 ft 6 ins (10.2 m)
Diameter: 6 ft 11 ins (2.1 m)
Envelope: *Volume* 742 cu ft (21 m^3). Gas loss rate, 1.5 litres per day.
Take-off weight: 44 lb (20 kg)
Solar panel: Series of panels over the upper envelope, more than 70 sq ft (6.5 m^2). Efficiency 15%.
Stabilizers: Dorsal and horizontal surfaces at tail forming an inverted 'Y'.
Maximum airspeed: 35 kts (40 mph) 65 km/h demonstrated; over 43 kts (50 mph) 80 km/h possible.

↑ Ingolf Schäfer's Lotte-96 solar-powered airship

WDL Luftschiffgesellschaft mbH — Germany

Corporate address:
Flughafen, 45470 Mülheim/Ruhr.

Telephone: +49 208 37 80 80
Facsimile: +49 208 3 78 08 33 or 41

Information:
Arnold D. Beier (marketing, sales, operations).

ACTIVITIES

▪ WDL corporate group comprises 7 aviation companies offering:
▪ Development of airships and a shipyard for complete construction (WDL is an official authorized manufacturer of airships).
▪ Airship operation for advertising, promotion and observation tasks.
▪ Advertising from the air with slogans and banners towed by aircraft.
▪ Scheduled flight services for passengers and freight.
▪ Authorized (by LBA) technical department for aircraft up to 20t. All work including major repairs and basic overhauls.
▪ Electronics and instrument service.
▪ Group of inspection engineers.

WDL 1

First flight: Mid-1970s.
Role: Helium airship for advertising.

Details

Crew/Passengers: 8 persons, including pilot.
Length: 190 ft 3 ins (58 m)
Width: 53 ft 9 ins (16.4 m)
Height: 62 ft (18.9 m)
Envelope: Total *volume* 227,038 cu ft (6,429 m^3)
Engines: 2 Teledyne Continental piston engines, each 210 hp (156.6 kW).
Cruise speed: 30-50 kts (35-57 mph) 55-90 km/h
Operating altitude: 1,000-6,000 ft (300-1,800 m)

WDL 1B

First flight: 30 August 1988.
Role: Helium airship for advertising, promotion and observation.

Details

Crew/Passengers: 8 persons, including pilot. Total air/ground crew comprises 20.
Length: 196 ft 10 ins (60 m)
Width: 53 ft 9 ins (16.4 m)
Height: 63 ft 4 ins (19.3 m)
Envelope: Total *volume* 254,266 cu ft (7,200 m^3). Gondola and envelope are painted with customer/corporate colours/logo. Also prepared for advertising lightshows at night, with a 108 × 26 ft (33 × 8 m) screen each side holding a total of approximately 10,000 different coloured bulbs controlled by a computer unit in the airship.
Empty weight: 11,244 lb (5,100 kg)
Payload: 2,600 lb (1,180 kg)
Engines: 2 Teledyne Continental piston engines, each 210 hp (156.6 kW).
Cruise speed: 30-58 kts (35-65 mph) 55-105 km/h
Operating altitude: 1,000-6,000 ft (300-1,800 m)
Duration: 22 hours

↑ WDL 1B 8-seat airship in Asahi markings

Zeppelin Luftschifftechnik GmbH — Germany

Corporate address:
PO Box 25 64, Leutholdstrasse 108, D-88045 Friedrichshafen.

Telephone: +49 7541 202 05
Facsimile: +49 7541 202 516

Information:
Klaus Hagenlocher (*telephone*: +49 7541 202 515).

ACTIVITIES

▪ Founded 1993 for the development and production of New Technology (NT) airships.
▪ Parent company, Luftschiffbau Zeppelin GmbH, originally founded in 1908 and still exists under the auspices of the Zeppelin Foundation. Shareholders in ZLT include ZF Friedrichshafen AG (16%, and has developed a new gear for the NT propeller drive) and its subsidiary Leförder Metallwaren AG (16%), Stuttgarter Hofbräu AG, CSC Microcadam (products used by Zeppelin in the development of the NT), and Linde AG (undertook to fill the envelope with helium and carry out gas rinsing operations).

Zeppelin NT series LZ N 07

First flight: 8 August 1997.
Role: Rigid helium airship for commuter and tourist passenger carrying; freighting; monitoring/control/surveillance operations for environmental protection, fishery surveillance, maritime patrol, coastal/border patrol and more; atmospheric and marine chemistry, atmospheric physics, gravimetric measurements and other research tasks; TV; traffic control; advertising and other missions (see Sales).

Aims

▪ Based on the rigid airframe principle. Majority of the static and dynamic loads are carried by the rigid structure. Thereby, the airship remains fully manoeuvrable even if internal pressure drops.
▪ Safety by redundant configuration of structure, envelope and systems.
▪ Improved performance, especially maximum speed.
▪ All year availability due to all-weather capability.
▪ Environmentally friendly, with low noise level and low pollutants emission due to economic fuel consumption.
▪ High manoeuvrability and simplified take-off and landing procedures, resulting in reduced ground crew requirements.
▪ Cabin and cockpit free from noise and vibration.
▪ Engine arrangement substantially reduces effects of lateral gusts during slow approach, ensuring a controlled and accurate landing. Engines and fuel tanks installed well away from the cabin.

Development

▪ LZ N 07 was conceived as the demonstration model for the NT series, though production versions are being built (see Sales).
▪ May 1995. Assembly of the prototype began.
▪ 1997. A gigantic assembly hangar at Friedrichshafen Airport was built, measuring 361 ft length by 226 ft width by 105 ft height (110 × 69 × 32 m), for assembly and maintenance of 3 N 07 airships.
▪ 6 August 1997. Roll-out of the prototype N 07.
▪ 1999. Production to start. The prototype to begin tourism and advertising flights following end of test flying.

Details

Sales: Preliminary contracts signed in 1997 with 4 customers for 5 N 07 airships: airship 1 will be acquired by Skyship Cruise Ltd of Switzerland for exclusive tourist cruises, advertising and promotional purposes, to be delivered by the end of 1999; airship 2 will be German based (at Bonn-Hangelar airport) with RLBG Rheinsche Luftschiffbetreibergesellschaft mbH and used mainly for scientific and technical purposes with special external systems to accommodate measuring instruments, to be delivered early 2000; airship 3 will go in Spring 2000 to Kurt Ernsting's Zeppelin GmbH & Co KG and based at Münster/Osnabrück airport for passenger services to the Hannover trade fair or to the North Sea islands as well as for advertising; and airships 4 and 5 will be operated by Munich-based TransATLANTISche

Luftschiffahrtgesellschaft mbH for tourist cruises, advertising and 'happenings', delivered in Spring and late 2000 respectively. Production capacity is thereby full until the year 2001 but it is stated that there remains a sustained demand for more airships from Europe and overseas, with advanced negotiations underway with various South American countries for airships for environmental observation work.
Crew/Passengers: 2 crew plus 12 passengers (in 35 ft 1 ins, 10.7 m long and 7 ft 6 ins, 2.3 m wide cabin). *Volume* of cabin 918 cu ft (26 m^3). Cabin avionics include AMLCD system and EFIS, with provision for weather radar, monitor for displaying mission parameters, and stormscope. Pilot side-stick controllers. Galley and wardrobe.
Length: 246 ft 1 ins (75 m)
Diameter: 46 ft 7 ins (14.2 m) maximum
Width over winglets: 63 ft 11 ins (19.5 m)
Height: 56 ft 5 ins (17.2 m)
Envelope and Structure: Total *volume* 290,463 cu ft (8,225 m^3). Multi-layer laminate envelope (attached continuously to the longerons) of Dacron, Mylar and Tedlar. By injecting air into the air chamber, it is possible to stiffen the outer envelope because of the effect of the membrane (for descending). All aerodynamic loads exerted on the envelope are transferred to the primary structure. 3 gas cells each consist of a cylindrical section of the outer envelope and an integrated lifting-gas cell together with a corresponding section of the air chamber, which passes through the lower region of the airship. Rigid and continuous primary structure extends over the entire length, and all major assemblies (such as engines, tail units and gondola) are attached to it. The triangular frames and 3 rows of longerons are braced with diagonal ties to form a rigid spatial framework and are principally of carbonfibre and aluminium alloy respectively.
Ballonet/s: *Volume* 63,743 cu ft (1,805 m^3)
Maximum gross weight: 17,416 lb (7,900 kg)
Payload: 4,078 lb (1,850 kg) for 1,000 m cruise altitude
Engines: 3 Textron Lycoming IO-360 engines of 200 hp (149 kW) each: 2 mounted as vectored thrust units, and a similar stern-mounted unit with twin 3-blade propellers capable of delivering lateral thrust together with vectored/horizontal thrust for exact pitch and yaw control. Fly-by-wire control.
Stabilizers: Controlled using fly-by-wire systems.
Maximum airspeed: 70 kts (81 mph) 130 km/h
Cruise speed: 62 kts (71 mph) 115 km/h
Maximum altitude: 8,200 ft (2,500 m)
Range: 485 naut miles (559 miles) 900 km with a 1,000 kg payload, ISA, 90 km/h, and 45 minutes reserve.
Duration: 14 hours at 70 km/h, or 28 hours at 70 km/h with reduced payload.

↑ Zeppelin LZ N 07 rear pivoting engine unit assembly, with a propeller acting at right-angles to the longitudinal axis, for enhanced lateral control

↑ Zeppelin LZ N 07 prototype demonstrator

↑ Zeppelin LZ N 07 cockpit

↑ Zeppelin LZ N 07 passenger cabin

Zeppelin NT series LZ N 30

First flight: Not yet flown.
Role: Passenger carrying.

Development

▪ As the company has concentrated all its resources on the LZ N 07 programme, it has not yet proceeded with the LZ N 30 project.

Details

Crew/Passengers: 2 crew plus 84 passengers.
Length: 361 ft (110 m)
Diameter: 74 ft (22.5 m) maximum
Envelope: Total *volume* 1,060,400 cu ft (30,000 m^3)
Maximum gross weight: 66,140 lb (30,000 kg)
Payload: 33,069 lb (15,000 kg)
Engines: 3, type not yet defined.
Maximum airspeed: 76 kts (87 mph) 140 km/h
Cruise speed: 67 kts (78 mph) 125 km/h
Maximum altitude: 9,800 ft (3,000 m)
Duration: 23 hours at 70 km/h, or 82 hours at 70 km/h with reduced payload.

Szolcsák Airships Hungary — Hungary

Corporate address:
H-3231 Gyöngyössolymos, Virág ut 35.
Telephone: +36 37 370 480
Facsimile: +36 37 370 480
Information:
Gyula Szolcsák.

ACTIVITIES

▪ Has produced a small remotely-controlled electric airship as the SG-05, first flown in 1994 and described and illustrated in the 1996-97 edition of *WA&SD*. More recently, has produced 2 new electric flat-bodied drone airships as the SV-03 and SV-04. Under development is a manned hybrid airship as the SV-05.

Szolcsák Airships Hungary SV-03

First flight: 16 May 1996.
Role: Experimental, flat-bodied, remotely-controlled, hybrid airship.

↑ Szolcsák SV-03 remotely-controlled electric airship

Details

Crew: None.
Length: 20 ft 6 ins (6.24 m)
Width: 10 ft 6 ins (3.19 m)
Height: 4 ft 9 ins (1.45 m)
Envelope: *Volume* 372.9 cu ft (10.558 m^3)
Engines: 4 Mabuchi RS 540 electric motors.

Szolcsák Airships Hungary SV-04

First flight: 4 May 1997.
Role: Experimental, flat-bodied, remotely-controlled, hybrid airship.

Details

Crew: None

↑ Szolcsák SV-04 remotely-controlled electric airship

Length: 18 ft 9 ins (5.72 m)
Width: 6 ft 5 ins (1.95 m)
Height: 2 ft 10 ins (0.86 m)
Envelope: *Volume* 164.2 cu ft (4.65 m^3)
Engine: Single 4.5 hp (3.35 kW) MOKI 30.

Szolcsák Airships Hungary SV-05

First flight: Not yet flown.
Role: Experimental, flat-bodied, hybrid airship.

Development

- Under development in 1998.

Details

Crew/passengers: 2
Length: 66 ft 11 ins (20.4 m)

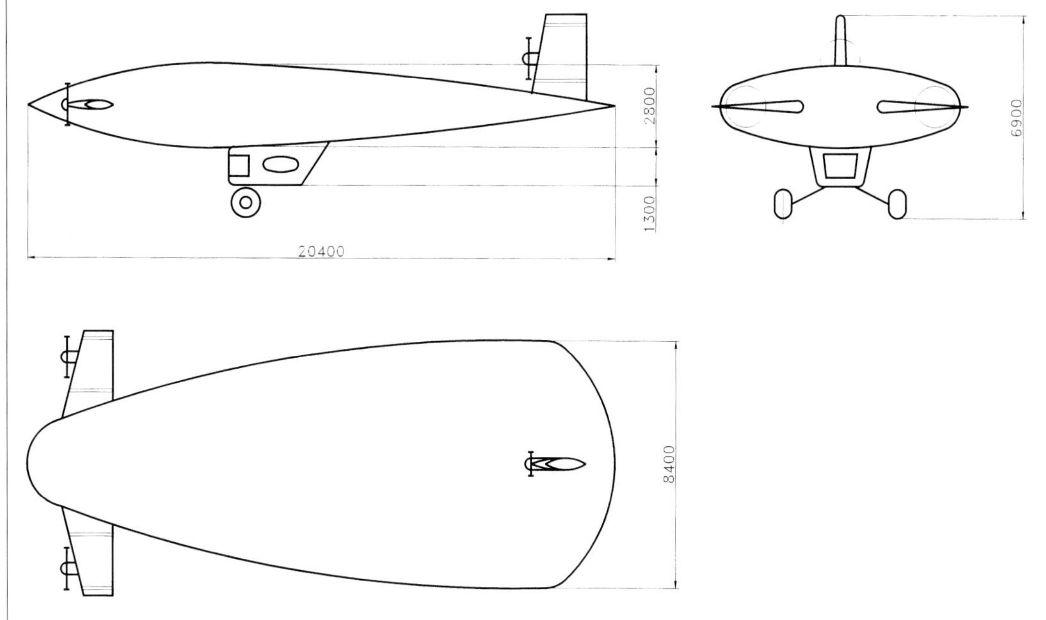

↑ Szolcsák SV-05 projected passenger airship

Width: 27 ft 7 ins (8.4 m)
Height: 9 ft 2 ins (2.8 m) for envelope, 22 ft 8 ins (6.9 m) overall.
Engine: 3 engines, each 20 hp (15 kW).

Skypia Co Ltd — Japan

Corporate address:
LTA development division, 1-7-15, Uehara 1-chome, Shibuya-ku, Tokyo 151.

Telephone: +81 3 3469 8600
Facsimile: +81 3 3469 8601
E-mail: PDF02776@niftyserve.or.jp
Web site: http://www.mmjp.or.jp/skypia/home/skypia.html

Information:
Tairo Kusagaya (LTA [Airship] Development Manager).

ACTIVITIES

- Skypia was founded on 1 March 1990 by Hayashi Tatsuo (company President), to develop hi-tech airships.
- Products include both manned and remotely-piloted airships.

Skypia Mambow 3 and Mambow 3 Plus (MoonFish 3 and 3 Plus or M-3 and M-3 Plus)

First flight: 8 June 1995.
Role: Helium remotely-piloted airship (Mambow 3) and piloted airship (Mambow 3 Plus). Uses include remote sensing.

Aims

- Low-speed stability and the ability to take-off/land in a narrow garden.
- Needs for remote-sensing-survey were pitch/roll of under 1.03° per second, yaw less than 0.803° per second, and a ground speed/sensing altitude of under 0.393 m per second at 100 ft (30 m) altitude and 3.93 m per second at 1,000 ft (300 m) altitude.

Development

- Development of Mambow 3 by Kusagaya began as a remotely-piloted airship for remote sensing (see dates below). However, in mid-development emphasis moved to an experimental single-seat manned variant, suitable for sky-sports and local cross-country flying. The latter proved capable of good manoeuvrability, including flying backwards in no-wind conditions and of taking-off/landing in an area just 4-times the length of the envelope. The National Institute of Agro-Environmental Science (Ministry of Agriculture, Forestry and Fisheries) bought the manned airship, which can be hangared or moored to a mast without deflation.
- 28 June 1993. Start of development.
- 14 March 1994. Hangar constructed.
- 14 November 1994. Roll-out.
- 8 June 1995. First flight of Mambow 3 Plus, lasting 64 minutes.
- 14 March 1996. First remotely-piloted flight, lasting 49 minutes.
- 17 October 1996. Operational study completed.
- Cost of developing Mambow 3 Plus over 3 years was Yen150 million (about £750,000).

Details (generally apply to the Mambow 3 Plus, unless stated)

Sales: Cost Yen45 million (about £225,000). Ground support mast car Yen4.5 million (about £22,500). Hangar Yen10 million (about £50,000). Weather observation tower Yen10 million (about £50,000). Original Mambow 3 Plus bought by NIAES (see Development).
Crew/Passengers: Pilot. 7 ground crew for moving airship in/out of hangar, mast mooring and take-off/landing.
Gondola: Open duralumin frame, with external suspension from envelope.
Length: 70 ft 6 ins (21.5 m)
Width: 20 ft 4 ins (6.2 m)
Height: 25 ft 11 ins (7.9 m)
Envelope: Fabric of TPU/Ethylen Vinylalchol Copolymer/VECTRAN Cloth/TPU 200g/m^2. 20 gores and high-frequency melt seal. *Volume* 13,949 cu ft (395 m^3). Pressure control via 2 electric blowers. 2 valves for ballonet and gas envelope. Duralumin nose cone frame with 10 battens, 2 yaw lines and a nose wire.
Ballonet: 1, in centre. *Volume* 3,284 cu ft (93 m^3). TPU/Ethylen Vinylalchol Copolymer/TPU 120g/m^2.
Ballast: 20 litres of water and sand bags.
Payload: 220 lb (100 kg)
Engine: 1 air-cooled, 2-stroke 375 cc, rated at 30 hp (22.4 kW).
Propellers: 2 wooden, variable-pitch, ducted 2-blade propellers, turning at 3,000 rpm. Vertical vectoring, -90° and +120°. See Stabilizers.
Fuel: 28 litres.
Batteries: 3V, 6V and 12V.
Stabilizers: Cruciform tail fins with control surfaces. Vertical and horizontal area rudders, elevators, differential control thrust and thrust vectoring controlled by fly-by-wire.
Vertical tailfin area: 90 sq ft (8.4 m^2)
Horizontal tailfin area: 95 sq ft (8.8 m^2)
Maximum airspeed: 32 kts (37 mph) 60 km/h

↑ Skypia Mambow 3 Plus

↑ Skypia Mambow 3 Plus showing the hangar and ground support mast car

Cruise speed: 24 kts (28 mph) 45 km/h
Sinking speed: 262 ft (80 m) per minute
Operating altitude: 1,770 ft (540 m) above ground level in radio-controlled RPA form.
Duration: 3 hours

Skypia Mambow 4 (MoonFish 4 or M-4)

↑ Skypia Mambow 4 during indoor exhibition flying

Role: Helium remotely-piloted airship. Originally intended as scale test vehicle for Mambow 3. Now indoor display airship for advertising and exhibition.

Development

▪ Probably first displayed on 26 October 1995.

Details

Sales: Cost Yen3.5 million (about £17,500). Japan Tent-Sheet Industry association was first customer.
Length: 16 ft 5 ins (5 m)
Diameter: 8 ft 2 ins (2.5 m)
Width: 9 ft 10 ins (3 m)
Height: 9 ft 10 ins (3 m)
Envelope: *Volume* 635.7 cu ft (18 m^3)
Ballonet: *Volume* 105.9 cu ft (3 m^3)
Ballast: Small lead.
Take-off weight: 35.3 lb (16 kg), including battery.
Payload: 1.1 lb (0.5 kg)
Engines: 4 electric motors, with 4 vectoring ducted fans.
Stabilizers: Cruciform, with 2 rudders and 2 elevators.
Maximum airspeed: 10 ft (3 m) per second
Cruise speed: up to 1.6 ft (0.5 m) per second
Turning radius: 0 ft (0 m) with no wind.
Duration: 10-20 minutes for experienced user, or 5 minutes for beginner.

Rigid® Airship Design, MARO BV — Netherlands

Corporate address:
Franse Kampweg 7, 1243 JC 's-Graveland.
Telephone: +31 35 656 48 77
Facsimile: +31 35 656 30 07
Information:
I. Alexander (Project Leader), J. Williams (Administration/Marketing).

ACTIVITIES

▪ In 1995, the company began work on the design of a prototype and a series of classic rigid airships, in association with major Dutch industrial partners and Government agencies.
▪ Design work is undertaken at 's-Graveland, where application for design approval had been made to the certifying RLD authority in December 1996.
▪ First airship, the *Holland Millennium Navigator*, is intended to take part in the Dutch millennium celebrations.

Rigid® Airship Design *Navigator*

First flight: Not yet flown.
Role: Rigid, multi-cellular, unpressurized helium airship for large-capacity scheduled/tourist passenger carrying, long-endurance surveillance, and low-density/high volume cargo operations.

Aims

▪ Technological advances incorporated mainly in the outer cover, gas cell material, engines, gearboxes, propellers, low speed control and water recovery systems.
▪ 'Stretch' capability has been incorporated into the design, allowing the possibility of an increase in useful lift to 49.2 tons (50 tonnes).

Development

▪ Mooring system is being developed requiring a ground crew no greater than for a comparable aeroplane.

Details

Sales: First of the Navigator airships will be the *Holland Millennium Navigator*.
Crew/Passengers: Maximum 230 passengers for short-haul flights, accommodated within the hull.
Length: 570 ft 10 ins (174 m)
Diameter: 95 ft 2 ins (29 m)
Envelope: *Volume* 2,648,600 cu ft (75,000 m^3)
Gross useful lift: 34.45 tons (35 tonnes)
Engines: 6 diesel engines with vectoring propellers, each 550 hp (410 kW). Water recovery system to maintain equilibrium.
Maximum airspeed: 80 kts (92 mph) 148 km/h
Duration: 22 days

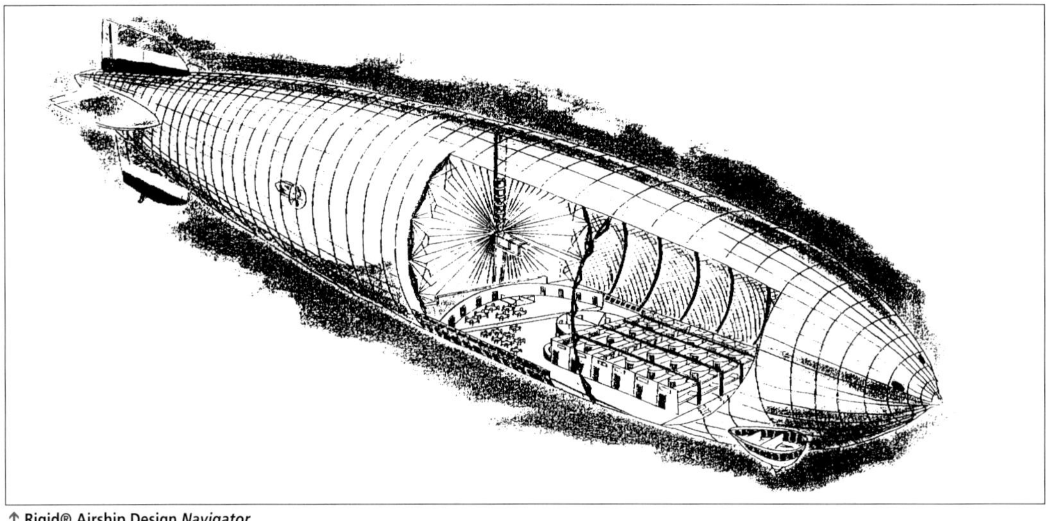

↑ **Rigid® Airship Design *Navigator***

Firma Aerostatika – Scientific & Industrial Enterprise — Russia

Corporate address:
31-1-315 Krylatiskaya Street, 121614 Moscow.
Telephone: +7 095 158 48 18
Facsimile: +7 095 415 26 30
Information:
Dr Alexander Kirilin (President).

Aerostatika 01

First flight: 12 August 1994.
Role: Multi-functional, small-volume, non-rigid helium airship for manned, remotely controlled and tethered aerostat uses. Can be viewed as a scale prototype for the Aerostatika 02.

Development

▪ Assisted by MAI (Moscow Aviation Institute).
▪ First flown at Kubinka, with 20 flights before the end of that year.
▪ Intended for continued use in RPA role from 1996, under a Defence Ministry (Russian) funded programme.

Details

Crew: Pilot only, with up to a 154 lb (70 kg) payload (see Payload).
Gondola: Forward fuselage of an Aviatika-890 sporting aircraft. Avionics include GPS.
Length: 75 ft (22.88 m)
Height: 25 ft 2 ins (7.68 m)
Envelope: Constructed of diagonally-plied Kapron/polyethylene film, 9 layers of rubber and 3 of rubberised aluminium offering low gas permeability, with cold-sealed self-vulcanizing adhesive/hermetic tape seams. 4 gores of Lavsan to strengthen gondola-carrying area of envelope. *Volume* 13,066 cu ft (370 m^3). Emergency helium gas valve and ballast release system.
Ballonet: 1, in centre of envelope, *volume* 1,589 cu ft (45 m^3), with electric-powered compressor to maintain inflation in an emergency.
Fineness ratio: 4:1
Payload: 154 lb (70 kg) with a pilot, 220 lb (100 kg) in remotely-controlled form, or 330 lb (150 kg) as a tethered and unmanned aerostat.
Engines: 2 RM2-640 piston engines, each 28 hp (20.9 kW) and driving 4-blade propellers in an elongated duct, each with 5 lever-controlled thrust-vectoring vanes in the exhaust.
Stabilizers: 8 wire-braced 2-spar tail fins, the 4 cruciform fins with electro-mechanically-controlled movable rudders/elevators.
Maximum airspeed: 40-46 kts (47-53 mph) 75-85 km/h
Cruise speed: 38 kts (43.5 mph) 70 km/h
Operating altitude: 3,280 ft (1,000 m)
Duration: up to 2 hours

Aerostatika 02

First flight: *01507* seen flying at the August 1995 Moscow Airshow.
Role: Multi-functional non-rigid helium airship, said to be suited to aerial advertising and promotional work, surveying and monitoring, as a camera platform, and for military patrol and reconnaissance. Used also as a test vehicle for the vectoring thrust lift system to be used on the Avgur Krechet multi-purpose aeroplane (see General Aviation section).

↑ **Aerostatika 02 showing Aviatika-890 gondola and thrust system tested for the Krechet aeroplane** *(PJ Photo Library)*

Development

- Larger development of the Aerostatika 01, offering much greater envelope volume and improved thrust/weight ratio.
- Certified by the Russian Federation as an experimental airship. US certification sought.
- Remained flying in Russia in 1997, possibly on commercial activities, as the only known Russian airship in continued service.

Details

Crew: Pilot.
Gondola: Forward fuselage of an Aviatika-890 sporting aircraft. Avionics include GPS.
Length: 90 ft 8 ins (27.64 m)
Diameter: 22 ft 8 ins (6.9 m)
Height: 31 ft 2 ins (9.5 m)
Envelope: *Volume* 22,990 cu ft (651 m^3), constructed as a sandwich of Russian rubberized diagonally-plied fabric, combining KTM-1/Lavsan, rubber and an outer rubberized aluminium coating.
Fineness ratio: 4:1
Payload: 220 lb (100 kg) with a pilot.
Engines: 2 Rotax 582 piston engines, each 64 hp (48 kW), with thrust vectoring, plus a retrofitted tail-thruster.
Stabilizers: Similar to 01.
Maximum airspeed: 49 kts (56 mph) 90 km/h
Cruise speed: 40 kts (47 mph) 75 km/h
Operating altitude: 8,200 ft (2,500 m)
Duration: Approximately 4 hours at cruise.

Aerostatika 200 and 300

The third of 4 Aerostatika airships planned, the 200 is a much larger 4/5-seat non-rigid type of 77,690 cu ft (2,200 m^3) intended for commercial passenger operations. The 8-seat Aerostatika 300 has a 165 ft 8 ins (50.5 m) long envelope, of 141,000 cu ft (3,993 m^3) volume, and 2 Rotax 914 and 1 M337 engines. To fly in the year 2000.

Vozdukhoplavatelnyi Tsentr 'Avgur' – Avgur Aerostat Centre — Russia

Corporate address: Raskovoi per 17-19, 125124 Moscow.
Telephone and Facsimile: +7 095 214 7965
Information: Smanislav V. Fedorov.

ACTIVITIES

- Avgur has produced, and continues to develop, a growing series of airships for both manned and unmanned applications. An early small tethered aerostat for advertising use was known as the Avgur 6.
- Kubicek of the Czech Republic has joined Avgur in the promotion of the AV-1R, a variant of the Czech AV-1 (which see).

The following is a summary of several Avgur programmes:

Avgur/Kubicek AV-1R

Role: 2-seat hot-air airship for recreational, advertising and training purposes.

Development

- Manufactured and marketed jointly by Avgur and Kubicek of the Czech Republic (which see).
- The basic 1997 price was US$85,000, and an AV-1R can be delivered in 4 months of the order.

Details

Crew: Pilot and passenger. 3-5 ground crew.
Length: 113 ft 3 ins (34.5 m)
Diameter: 41 ft (12.5 m)
Height: 47 ft 9 ins (14.55 m)
Envelope: *Volume* 98,880 cu ft (2,800 m^3)
Empty weight: 1,014 lb (460 kg)
Gross weight: 1,653 lb (750 kg)
Standard temperature: 60-100° C; maximum allowable 130° C
Engine: 1 Rotax 503 UL-2V of 50 hp (37.3 kW).
Burners: 2 Kubicek-kovo H3s.
Maximum airspeed: 14.5 kts (17 mph) 27 km/h
Cruise speed: 11 kts (12.5 mph) 20 km/h
Cruise altitude: 2,625 ft (800 m)
Duration: 1.5-2 hours

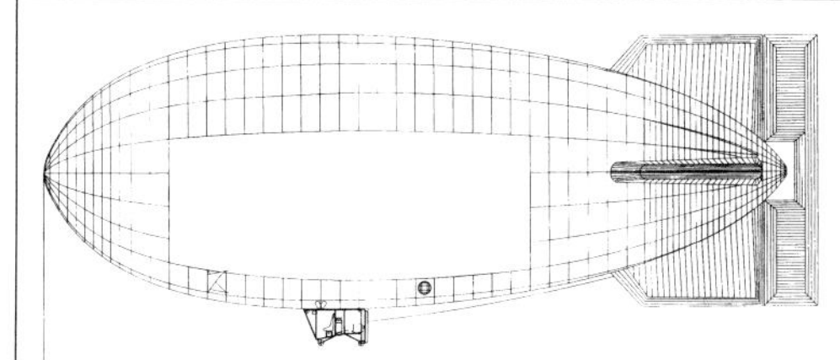

↑ **Avgur/Kubicek AV-1R** *(Avgur)*

Avgur DEP-140

Role: Semi-rigid, helium airship for survey, patrol, ecological and other uses.

Development

- In preliminary design stage.

Details

Crew: 5 persons, including 1 or 2 crew.
Length: 93 ft 6 ins (28.5 m)
Diameter: 33 ft 2 ins (10.1 m)
Height: 42 ft 8 ins (13 m)
Envelope: *Volume* 49,441 cu ft (1,400 m^3)
Ballonet: 20% of envelope volume
Empty weight: 1,830 lb (830 kg)
Gross weight: 3,197 lb (1,450 kg)
Payload: 948 lb (430 kg)
Engine: 74 hp (55.5 kW), gas fuelled.
Maximum airspeed: 48 kts (56 mph) 90 km/h
Cruise speed: 32 kts (37 mph) 60 km/h
Ceiling: 6,560 ft (2,000 m)
Range: 539 naut miles (621 miles) 1,000 km
Duration: 10-18 hours

Avgur DPD-5000

Role: Semi-rigid, helium, long-range patrol airship (Dalnyi Patrulnyi Dirizhabl), suited also to other roles (see Development).

Development

- In preliminary design stage. Hydraulic controls.
- Can be installed with a radar, with a 98 ft (30 m) antenna; or infra-red, video equipment and more for surveillance; or mine-sweeping equipment; or rescue gear; or weapons.

Details

Crew: 12.
Length: 420 ft (61 m)
Diameter: 92 ft 6 ins (28.2 m)
Height: 105 ft (32 m)
Envelope: *Volume* 1,771,032 cu ft (50,150 m^3)
Ballonet: 25% of envelope volume
Empty weight: 49,050 lb (22,250 kg)
Gross weight: 95,240 lb (43,200 kg)
Payload: 33,500 lb (15,200 kg)
Engines: 2 turbo-diesel types for cruise, each 2,070 hp (1,544 kW), and a 100 hp (74.6 kW) turbo-diesel control engine.
Maximum airspeed: 81 kts (93 mph) 150 km/h
Cruise speed: 59 kts (68 mph) 110 km/h
Ceiling: 10,500 ft (3,200 m)
Range: 4,695 naut miles (5,405 miles) 8,700 km
Duration: 20-98 hours

Avgur MA-55 and AASR-1600

Details: MA-55, except under Development.
Role: Motorised (motorizovannyi aerostat), helium airship for recreational, advertising, training and rescue roles.

Development

- Prototype believed to be completed in 1998, with a second airship also reportedly built.
- Basic price of a production example is expected to be US$185,000.
- Also seen as a scale prototype for the AASR-1600 3/4-seat patrol airship ordered in 1995 by the Russian Government.

Details

Crew: 1. Ground crew 4-6.
Length: 83 ft 8 ins (25.5 m)
Diameter: 21 ft 1.5 ins (6.44 m)
Height: 26 ft 9 ins (8.15 m)
Envelope: *Volume* 19,423 cu ft (550 m^3)
Ballonet: *Volume* 2,825 cu ft (80 m^3)
Empty weight: 882 lb (400 kg)
Gross weight: 1,322 lb (600 kg)
Payload: 110 lb (50 kg)
Engine: 1 VAZ-1111 converted motorcar engine, producing 28 hp (21 kW). 2.5 kW Elektrodvigatel EPU-2500 control engine.
Maximum airspeed: 46 kts (53 mph) 85 km/h
Cruise speed: 32 kts (37 mph) 60 km/h
Cruise altitude: 2,625 ft (800 m)
Pressure ceiling: 4,920 ft (1,500 m)
Range: 324-350 naut miles (373-404 miles) 600-650 km
Duration: 10-24 hours

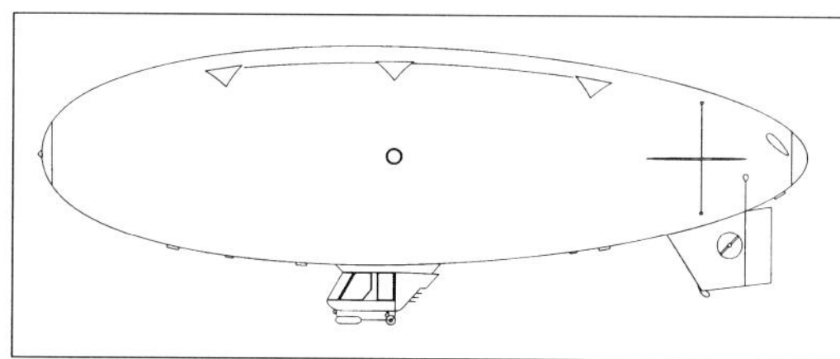

↑ **Avgur MA-55** *(Avgur)*

Avgur MD-900

Role: Semi-rigid, helium, modular-type airship (Modulnyi Dirizhabl). See Crew and Gondola for uses.

Development

- At preliminary design stage.

Details

Crew and Gondola: Possibly 3 crew. Standard modules of 32 ft 10 ins × 9 ft 10 ins × 8 ft 2 ins (10 × 3 × 2.5 m), for 12 tourist passengers, radar for surveillance, ecological monitoring equipment, medical equipment, hermetic medevac layout for 24 persons, energy production (containing electric generators), and more.
Length: 200 ft (61 m)
Diameter: 56 ft (17.1 m)
Height: 72 ft 2 ins (22 m)
Envelope: *Volume* 317,830 cu ft (9,000 m^3)
Ballonet: Approximately 20% of envelope volume
Empty weight: 10,320 lb (4,680 kg)
Gross weight: 19,025 lb (8,630 kg)
Payload: 6,890 lb (3,170 kg)
Engines: 2 turbo-diesel for cruise, each 375 hp (280 kW), plus 1 turbo-diesel of 50 hp (37.3 kW) for control.
Maximum airspeed: 65 kts (75 mph) 120 km/h
Cruise speed: 46 kts (53 mph) 85 km/h
Ceiling: 6,560 ft (2,000 m)
Range: 1,619 naut miles (1,865 miles) 3,000 km
Duration: 20-50 hours

Avgur PD-160

Role: Semi-rigid, helium patrol airship (Patrulnyi Dirizhabl), suited also to surveillance. Equipment can include video, loudspeakers, etc.

Development

- In technical design phase in 1997.

Details

Crew: 2-4. Ground crew 4-6.
Length: 118 ft 5 ins (36.1 m)
Diameter: 30 ft 9 ins (9.37 m)
Height: 39 ft 4 ins (12 m)
Envelope: *Volume* 56,500 cu ft (1,600 m^3)

Ballonet: 20% of envelope volume
Empty weight: 1,764 lb (800 kg)
Gross weight: 3,307 lb (1,500 kg)
Engine: 100 hp (74.6 kW) Teledyne Continental O-200B for cruise. 2.5 kW Elektrodvigatel EPU-2500 control engine.
Maximum airspeed: 54 kts (62 mph) 100 km/h
Cruise speed: 32 kts (37 mph) 60 km/h
Pressure ceiling: 6,560 ft (2,000 m)

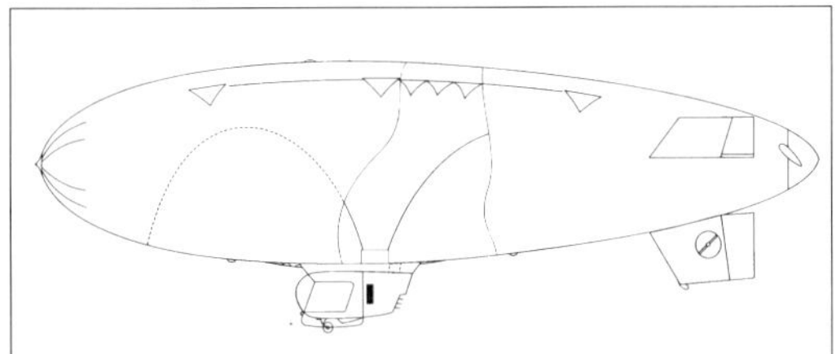

↑ **Avgur PD-160** *(Avgur)*

Cruise altitude: 3,280 ft (1,000 m)
Range: up to 755 naut miles (870 miles) 1,400 km
Duration: 12-48 hours

Avgur RD-1.5

Role: Unmanned, experimental, remotely-controlled, semi-rigid, helium airship. Reports suggest possible target use, perhaps by helicopters.

Development

▪ Prototype under flight trials in 1997.

Details

Length: 19 ft 10 ins (6.05 m)
Diameter: 5 ft 10 ins (1.79 m)
Height: 6 ft 6 ins (1.98 m)
Envelope: *Volume* 318.15 cu ft (9.009 m^3)
Empty weight: 13.7 lb (6.2 kg)
Engines: 2 × 80 W Robby Power 600s
Maximum airspeed: 39 ft (12 m) per second
Cruise speed: 25 ft (7.5 m) per second
Duration: 30 minutes to 1.5 hours

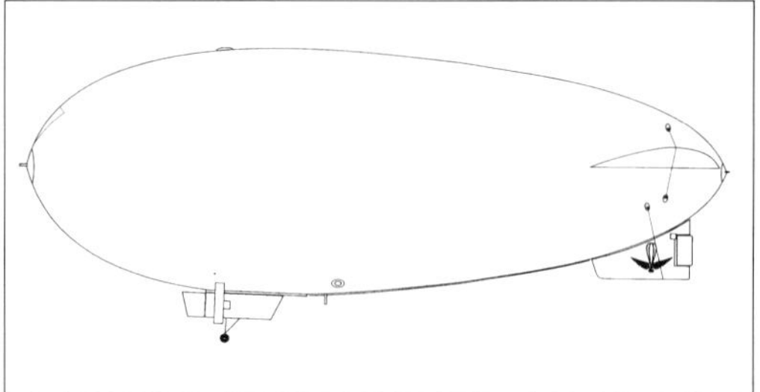

↑ **Avgur RD-1.5** *(Avgur)*

Dolgoprudny Automation Systems Design Bureau — Russia

Corporate address:
1 Letnaya Street, 141700 Dolgoprudny, Moscow Region.
Telephone: +7 095 408 89 09
Facsimile: +7 095 408 75 11
Information:
Petr P. Dementyev (Chief Designer).

Dolgoprudny Automation (DKBA) DP-800 Ecology

First Flight: Intended to take place in 1995-96 but further delayed.
Role: Experimental, semi-rigid, helium airship, designed as a part of a technical programme for the Aviation Department in accordance with a Government decision. Myasishchev (see next entry) has participated in the programme. Many possible roles, including search and rescue, surveillance, mapping, promotional, tourism, environmental protection, broadcasting, traffic control, fishery protection, fire-watch and fire-fighting.

Aims

▪ Zero take-off and landing runs, though short runs are optional; reportedly initially expected to require a take-off/landing operating area of 4.1 million sq ft (385,000 m^2). The airship is towed to the take-off field using a special collapsible mooring mast on a tractor chassis.
▪ Aerostatic balancing.
▪ Flight without relying on lifting gas.
▪ Management of propeller thrust vectoring and control surfaces.
▪ Use of modern materials and on-board equipment.
▪ Conforms to British Standards of Airworthiness for airships; its manoeuvrability is said to be similar to that of non-aerobatic aeroplanes.
▪ Day and night flights in accordance with Level 1 category ICAO.

Development

▪ This programme covers a wide range of tasks, including the validation/testing of new technical decisions, technologies and materials; manuals for the designers; norms of airworthiness and other documents, which are necessary for the creation and legal certification of airships in Russia; the development of methods and programmes for testing, demands for the testing of airship ports, and technical tasks for designing and constructing support buildings; creation of a training centre for simulating the flight dynamics and for aircrew training; the construction of 2 experimental airships with load-carrying capacity of up to 3 tonnes.
▪ Project has been approved, and all scientific and research work is complete. A mock-up of the cockpit has been built, all technical documents printed, the test stand is ready, and the development of technological processes for attachments was virtually finished by early 1995.

Details

Crew/Passengers/Gondola: All-metal semi-monocoque gondola of 32 ft 10 ins (10 m) length, divided into 6 separate compartments: cockpit for 2 pilots, under-cockpit accessory compartment, the cabin for 12 passengers, under-cabin 3-section ballast tank, engine bay and tail compartments. Ground crew of 3-5, excluding truck drivers.
Length: 205 ft (62.5 m) – some sources say 62 m.
Diameter: 51 ft 8 ins (15.75 m)
Height: 72 ft 2 ins (22 m) overall
Envelope: Russian rubberized diagonally-plied fabric (2-ply) of Kapron type with aluminium coating, offering gas permeability of up to 3 l/m^2 per day. *Volume* 283,895 cu ft (8,039 m^3). Calculated lifetime is 16,000 hours under gas over 5 years (including 2 years in storage), with further usage in accordance with technical conditions. The single leg undercarriage beneath the gondola is from an Mi-24 helicopter.
Ballonet/s: 26% of envelope volume
Fineness ratio: Believed to be 3.95:1
Take-off weight: 18,520 lb (8,400 kg)
Empty weight: 11,354 lb (5,150 kg)
Maximum load: 6,619 lb (3,000 kg) including fuel and ballast.
Engines: 2 M-14V-26 radial piston engines from a Ka-26 helicopter, each 325 hp (242.4 kW), giving 275 hp (205 kW) for cruise. Engine power is transmitted through side pylons to the 2 propellers.
Propellers: 2 shrouded AV-83 4-blade, reversible/variable-pitch propellers, of 4 ft 11 ins (1.5 m) diameter. Propellers can be vectored ±120°.
Fuel: 2,205 lb (1,000 kg), of minimum 91 octane (B-91/115, Oil-100 and OM-270).
Stabilizers: Cruciform tail, with metal framework covered with fabric. Operation of the elevators and rudders is mechanical, accomplished from the control-wheel column in the gondola cockpit, with no pedal operation. Remote control can be installed if required by customers.

↑ **Model of the Dolgoprudny Automation DP-800 Ecology**

Maximum airspeed: 62.5 kts (71 mph) 115 km/h
Cruise speed: 43 kts (50 mph) 80 km/h
Maximum climb rate: 1,970 ft (600 m) per minute
Ceiling: 8,850 ft (2,700 m)
Range: 723.5 naut miles (832.5 miles) 1,340 km
Duration: 44.7 hours at 70 km/h

Dolgoprudny Automation (DKBA) DP-6000 Vityaz

Role: Very large passenger and/or cargo airship. Can be adapted for various military roles, including AEW housing phased-array radars, airborne communications and relay, intelligence, search and rescue, and more.

Aims

▪ Projected very large airship with a 20-tonne carrying capacity, using experience gained from building the DP-800.

Development

▪ Development started in 1993. Not thought to have flown.

Details

Crew/Passengers: 2-deck gondola of 106 ft 7 ins (32.5 m) length, accommodating 144 passengers in the commercial or military transport models, or 84 passengers and cargo in the mixed-load layout, or all cargo. Gondola appears to have a detachable lower/central portion, able to accept a passenger or cargo pod or have a heavy cargo platform attached for outsized loads including long vehicles in a flying-crane configuration. The gondola also houses a modern cockpit, crew utility and rest areas, toilets, passenger galley and bar, power unit, and a ballast bay.
Length: 411 ft 7 ins (125.46 m)
Envelope: 4 gas compartments.
Engines: 2 diesel engines of 800 hp (597 kW) or 1,000 hp (746 kW) each, driving 2 shrouded and vectoring propellers on the rear cabin sides, plus 1 or 2 TV7-117 turboshaft engines of 2,500 shp (1,864 kW) driving a shrouded cruise propeller/s from the rear of the gondola.
Propellers: See Engines.
Stabilizers: Cruciform tail fins with electrically-powered elevators and rudders.
Cruise speed: 54 kts (62 mph) 100 km/h with a 20-tonne payload.
Ceiling: 9,850 ft (3,000 m) with a 12-tonne payload.
Range: 1,890 naut miles (2,175 miles) 3,500 km at 3,280 ft (1,000 m) altitude.

Myasishchev Design Bureau — Russia

Corporate address:
See Combat section.

ACTIVITIES

▪ In addition to participating in the DP-800 Ecology programme, Myasishchev has designed the KRUI-3.

Myasishchev KRUI-3

Role: Helium, semi-rigid, hybrid, passenger-carrying airship.

Aims

▪ To carry 28 passengers over a distance of 1,000 km, at a speed of 110 km/h and at 1,000-2,000 m altitude.
▪ Low cabin noise and environmentally safe cruising.
▪ Requires a 1,150 ft (350 m) diameter operating site.
▪ Envelope service life 8 years.

Details

Crew/Passengers: 6 crew plus 28 passengers, with 4 passengers

in each compartment equipped with luxury seats, air conditioning and table. Galley for hot food. Platform with bar and television, used also for sightseeing and recreation.
Gondola: Total passenger area is 70 ft 6 ins (21.5 m) long, 16 ft 5 ins (5 m) wide and 7 ft 6 ins (2.3 m) high.
Length: 278 ft 11 ins (85 m)
Diameter: 65 ft 7 ins (20 m)
Envelope: *Volume* 706,295 cu ft (20,000 m^3)
Take-off weight: 30,865 lb (14,000 kg)
Engines: 2 TVD-100 turboprops, each 960 hp (716 kW).
Propellers: 2 vectoring, in shrouds.
Maximum airspeed: 65 kts (74 mph) 120 km/h
Duration: up to 12 hours

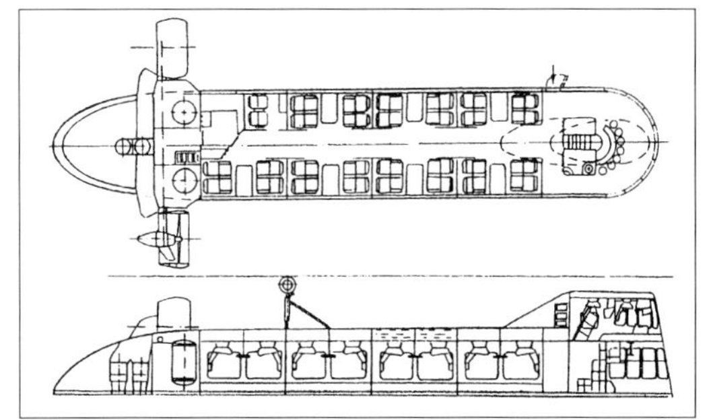

↑ **Myasishchev KRUI-3 gondola layout** *(Myasishchev)*

The Themoplane Design Bureau, Moscow Aviation Institute — Russia

Corporate address:
4 Volokolamskoe Shosse, 125871 Moscow.
Telephone: +7 095 158 79 16 or 158 41 27
Facsimile: + 7 095 158 29 77
Telex: 411746 Sokol SU
Information:
Dr Leon P. Poniaev (Deputy General Director).

Thermoplane ALA-40

First flight: 1993.
Role: One-fifth scale test and proof-of-concept model of the ALA-600. Also itself proposed for aerial inspection of above-ground oil, gas and heating pipelines, road traffic control, pollution control, TV and radio broadcasting, medical and police services, rescue, and tourism. Advertising space offered on the lower envelope skin.

Aims

▪ To prove the design concept, leading eventually to the production of very large Thermoplanes capable of carrying many passengers or bulky/heavy freight (including harvested produce, vehicles, building sections and generators) in difficult weather conditions (as found in Siberia, the far North and far East regions of Russia), in areas of sparse population and few, if any, roads or railways. These regions often have high-velocity winds with substantial changes in direction, and long periods of very low temperatures with freezing fog, snow and ice. However, they are remote areas rich in mineral resources including oil, gas, gold, diamonds, forests and more.
▪ An unballasted airship with the ability to operate on an ecologically friendly basis, without the need for the usual complex of ground bases, hangars and mooring posts.
▪ To show the *wheel* or *disc* configuration offers smaller, lighter and stronger airships, compared to conventional types, with improved distribution of stress loads. Designers claim a 200 m diameter Thermoplane could carry a 500 tonnes load, which they say would require a conventional airship length of approximately 700 m.
▪ Dual gas system (see Envelope). The recyclable nature of the engine gas is to provide ecologically clean operations.
▪ Very smooth aerodynamic surface minimises turbulence and drag and allows a new system of adaptive blowing flow control to improve aerodynamic qualities, dampening stress loads and distortion.

Development

▪ 1980. Russian LTA Thermoplane Design Bureau formed. LTA-Dirigible Programme was initially headed by Professor S. Eger but subsequently lead by Professor Yuri Ryzhov. Programme funded from the outset by a consortium that includes the oil and gas company Ritek, the Energy Resource Fund, the gold and diamond company Nika, Aviastar, and the Moscow Aviation Institute.
▪ 1989. Design work completed.

↑ **Thermoplane ALA-40 *(4001)***

▪ End-1991. Construction of the first of 3 ALA-40s *(4001)* neared completion at the Aviastar Industrial Complex plant.
▪ Mid-1992. Full ground test programme began, the static and dynamic tests at the Flight Test Control Aero Centre.
▪ 1994. Second ALA-40 *(4002)* completed at Ulyanovsk, for ground and flight tests in 1995.

Details

Crew: Occupy a gondola fabricated from a converted Mi-2 helicopter.
Envelope diameter: 131 ft 3 ins (40 m)
Envelope height: 52 ft 6 ins (16 m)
Envelope: Total *volume* 376,450 cu ft (10,660 m^3), of which 204,800 cu ft (5,800 m^3) is helium/hydrogen. Centre section holds the helium (or hydrogen) in spherical cells to give lift equal to the empty weight of the vehicle. Remaining volume filled with high-temperature gas from the propulsive engines, providing the additional lift needed to carry the payload.
Payload: 4,410-7,715 lb (2,000-3,500 kg)
Engines: 2 engines mounted with the gondola for propulsion, plus another on the forward envelope to assist stability.
Propellers: 2 propulsive propellers plus a series of 4 small horizontally-mounted propellers around the envelope for extra lift and control.
Stabilizer: Large tailplane-type surface at rear, plus 2 twin vertical rudders and a series of other fins and elevators on the undersurface.
Maximum airspeed: 59 kts (68 mph) 110 km/h
Ceiling: 6,550 ft (2,000 m)

Thermoplane ALA-600

First flight: Not known to have been completed. Full details can be found in the 1996-97 edition of *WA&SD*.
Role: Passenger or heavy-lift freight carrying. To carry a 600 tonnes load over 5,000 km.

Airship Arabia — Saudi Arabia

Airship Arabia has reportedly purchased the Skyship 600-06, formerly owned by Airship Japan. The airship has been given a new envelope. Airship Management Services, Inc (AMS) of the USA (which see) is providing technical and operational support.

The Hamilton Airship Company Ltd – THAC — South Africa

Corporate address:
PO Box 67492, Bryanston 2021, Johannesburg.
Telephone: +27 11 706 2047
Facsimile: +27 11 706 2303
Information:
Annemarie Roux (Marketing & Communications Director); Ben Naude (Project Manager).

ACTIVITIES

▪ The patented Hamilton airship was designed by Jonathan Hamilton (Managing Director). A major aviation company has been subcontracted to refine the design and manufacture the prototype.
▪ THAC was founded in 1995 for the design, development, manufacture and leasing of new technology airships. It has recently become a public company, with 40% of the shares being purchased by a US bank.

Hamilton HA 132

First flight: Anticipated for 1998-99.
Role: Rigid, helium airship for passenger and other operations (see Aims).

Aims

▪ Intended to be the first of a product line of airships for commercial and military use. Uses include eco-tourism, game viewing, shuttle services, exclusive luxury travel, humanitarian aid, flying hospital and aerial surveillance.
▪ 3 engines at the tail ensures redundancy.
▪ Neutral buoyancy, and improved manoeuvrability due to special features.
▪ Dual fly-by-wire control system.
▪ Fixed wheels forward of the gondola and at the rear. Requires no external mooring mast. Has self-docking and mooring system to reduce operating costs.
▪ Avionics include weather radar, Doppler radar, GPS and radio navigation system; stormscope; multiple channel digital health monitoring system (HUMS); collision avoidance system; LCD EFIS and MFDs, with conventional back-up instruments.

Development

▪ Design began in 1995, with refinement of the design completed by early 1997.
▪ June 1997. Construction began.
▪ 1998-99. Completion and certification anticipated.

Details

Crew/Passengers: 2 crew and 120 passengers for daily trips or 40 passengers in luxury cabins.
Gondola: 2,906 sq ft (270 m^2), on 3 decks.
Length: 433 ft (132 m)
Diameter: 64 ft (19.5 m)

Envelope: Patented internal central spine of carbonfibre and composites, with external ribs of aluminium cross-braced with Kevlar cables. 23 helium cells. Separate envelope of high-strength, multi-layer laminate (polyester and Tedlar), with low permeability (allows airship to be moored in the open permanently). *Volume* 282,520 cu ft (8,000 m^3).
Payload: 12.5 tons (12.7 tonnes) , excluding fuel, ballast and crew.
Engines: 3 Chevrolet V8s mounted on the tail, each 530 hp (395 kW). Thrust vectoring.
Propellers: 3 fixed-pitch, driven via a reversible belt-driven gearbox.
Maximum airspeed: 86 kts (99 mph) 160 km/h
Cruise speed: 65 kts (75 mph) 120 km/h
Range: 216 naut miles (248 miles) 400 km on full power, 971 naut miles (1,118 miles) 1,800 km on cruise power.

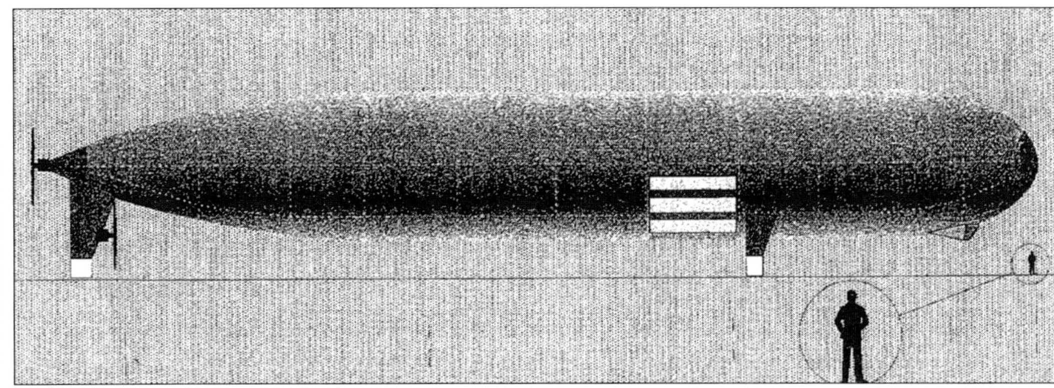
↑ Hamilton HA 132

Hamilton HA 140, 156, 158 and 360

Comments: HA 140 expected to fly about 1999 for passenger (6 crew + 48 pax) or SAR roles; length 459 ft (140 m) and volume 1,952,903 cu ft (55,300 m^3). HA 156 planned as 50 ton cargo airship. HA 158 and HA 360 planned at 518 ft (158 m) and 1,181 ft (360 m) length respectively.

Airspeed Airships — UK

Airspeed Airships has ceased trading. See the 1996-97 edition of *WA&SD* for details of the AS 400.

Airship Technologies Group — UK

Corporate address:
Airship Technologies (Services) Ltd, Sixth Floor, Town Hall, St Paul's Square, Bedford MK40 1SJ.
Telephone: +44 1234 221802
Facsimile: +44 1234 221801
Information:
J. Roger Munk (Technical Director).

ACTIVITIES

▪ Following Westinghouse's 1995 decision to withdraw from defence contracting, Airship Technologies Group was formed to facilitate the continuation and development of the airship design team under the leadership of J. Roger Munk and to return to the UK the manufacture of the new-era high-technology airships initiated by Munk at Cardington in the 1970s.

Airship Technologies Model 04 (AT-04)

First flight: Not yet flown.
Role: Non-rigid airship. Passenger and cargo transport, patrol, surveillance, AEW, mine-countermeasures and anti-submarine roles are possible.

Aims

▪ Military roles (see above and Disposable load) can include installation of an eliptical radar antennae up to 30 ft (9.14 m) wide and deep in the envelope.
▪ Fly-by-light control system, with autopilot.
▪ Trans-Atlantic ferry range on internal fuel and can deploy completely self-contained with its own docking mast, mission equipment and spares to a green field site.
▪ Patrols lasting up to 5 days are possible.
▪ Direct operating costs are one-fortieth those of helicopters with comparable lift.
▪ Could be equipped with defensive and offensive weapons.
▪ Claimed by the company to be the first truly cost-effective, multi-purpose airship ever designed, and to sell at a lower cost per seat than any other airship.
▪ IFR avionics include EFIS and GPS.

Details

Crew/Passengers: 2 flight crew, 2 cabin crew and 52 passengers in the gondola. See Engines.
Gondola: Kevlar, with honeycomb centre section. Length 56 ft 9 ins (17.3 m), 8 ft (2.45 m) width and 6 ft 4 ins (1.93 m) height.
Length: 261 ft 4 ins (79.65 m)
Width: 58 ft 9 ins (17.9 m)
Height: 68 ft 11 ins (21 m)
Envelope: Laminated fabric, with heat-sealed seams. *Volume* 501,470 cu ft (14,200 m^3).
Ballonet/s: 27% of envelope volume.
Lift/Drag ratio: 4.45
Gross weight: 30,865 lb (14,000 kg)

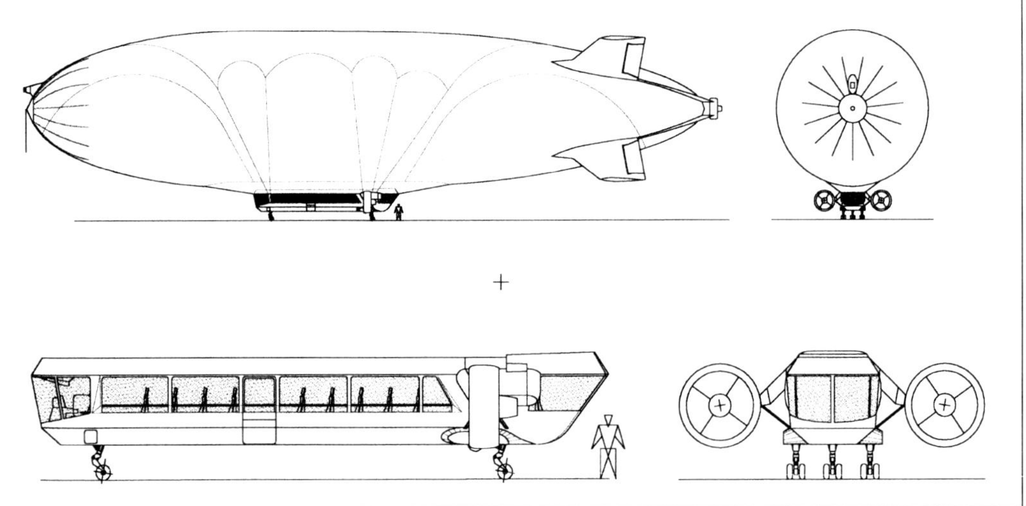
↑ Airship Technologies AT-04 general layout

Empty weight: 15,510 lb (7,035 kg)
Disposable load: Up to 6.5 tons (6.6 tonnes) in a military role, and is fitted with a rear ramp to the gondola which provides in-flight access to a load-carrying beam able to carry up to 2.5 tons (2.54 tonnes).
Engines: 3 Zoche ZO-02A air-cooled radial diesel engines, each 350 hp (261 kW). 2 engines drive vectoring ducted propulsors on the gondola and the third is a fixed installation at the rear. Each engine has a 50 kVA starter/generator. The combination of vectoring engines and bow thruster give the AT airships both a hovering capability and the ability to deck with only 3 or less groundcrew.
Propellers: See Engines.

↑ Airship Technologies AT-04 in military form, with Double Eagle mine-countermeasures equipment in the gondola. Note the stern thruster

Fuel: Avtur, or diesel in an emergency. 2,728 litres of usable fuel in 2 internal tanks.
Electrical system: Total of 150 kVA (see Engines), 115V AC.
Maximum airspeed: 70 kts (81 mph) 130 km/h
Continuous speed: 62 kts (71 mph) 115 km/h
Maximum climb rate: 2,500 ft (762 m) per minute
Minimum turn radius: 470 ft (144 m)

Airship Technologies Model 05 (AT-05)

Role: Will be certified for 24 passengers, with 2 flight and 2 cabin crew.

↑ Airship Technologies AT-04 gondola in military form, with a retractable air-defense missile launcher

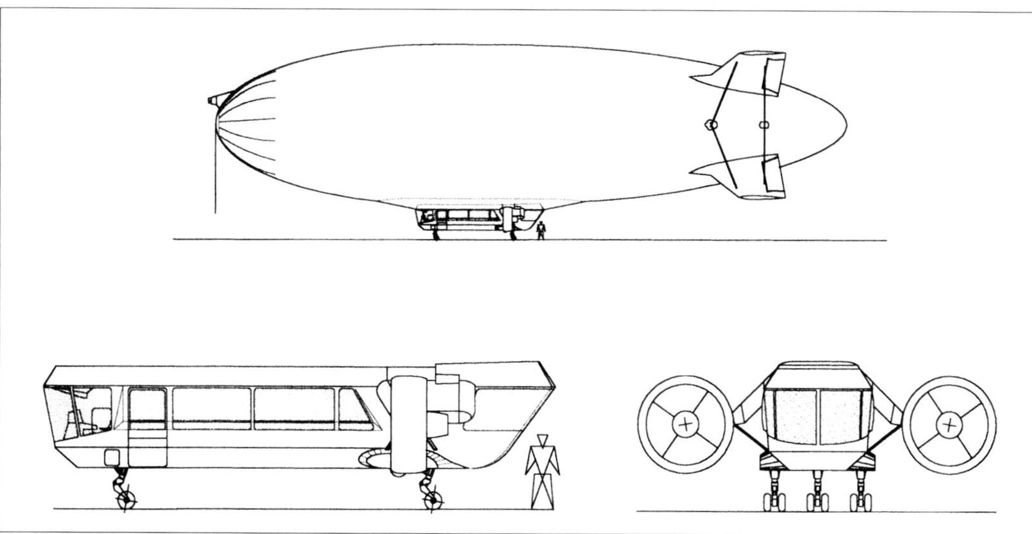

↑ **Airship Technologies AT-05 general layout**

Aims

▪ Shortened version of AT-04, with a 12 ft (3.66 m) section removed and fitted with a 335,490 cu ft (9,500 m^3) envelope.
▪ Powered by 2 Zoche diesels, driving vectoring propulsors, each with a 50 kVA starter-generator. Will have a bow thruster.

Airship Technologies Model 06 (AT-06)

Role: Combined passenger/freight role (if compared to AT-04 and 5, AT-06 would carry 450 passengers).

Aims

▪ 2,966,430 cu ft (84,000 m^3) envelope.
▪ Design 80% complete and is on hold pending market interest.

Airship Technologies Model 07 (AT-07)

Role: Heavy-lift airship to support operations in areas with little ground infrastructure.

Aims

▪ Advances in modern material technology permit the design and construction of a 984.2 ton (1,000 tonne) lift capacity airship.
▪ Design has started.
▪ One possible use being investigated is the shipment of natural gas.

Airship Technologies Model 08 (AT-08)

Role: Remotely-controlled stratospheric design (80,000 ft, 24,385 m altitude flying) aimed at the communications market.

Aims

▪ Design studies are underway.

Cameron Balloons Ltd — UK

Corporate address:
St John's Street, Bedminster, Bristol BS3 4NH

Telephone: +44 117 9637216
Facsimile: +44 117 9661168
Telex: 444825 GASBAG

Information:
Alan Noble

ACTIVITIES

▪ Cameron Balloons took over Thunder & Colt in late 1994 and made it a division, though it retains its own name for marketing purposes.
▪ Constructed the helium gas/hot-air balloon *Solar Spirit*, in which American Steve Fossett attempted the first round-the-world balloon flight in January 1997, establishing instead a world distance record for balloons.
▪ The **DP60** and **DP70** are no longer offered (see the 1996-97 *WA&SD* for details). The DG-14 helium airship is also offered in 2-seat form from 1998.

Cameron DG-14

First flight: 1989.
Role: Non-rigid, for advertising, photographic, surveillance and recreational use.

Aims

▪ To offer significantly better cost/performance ratio than other helium airships.
▪ Low purchase cost and minimal running costs.
▪ Though normally moored to a portable mast when not in flight, its low height allows it to enter a standard aircraft hangar without deflation for maintenance or protection, preserving helium.

Development

▪ 20 February 1991. Received BCAR 31 certification.

Details

Crew: Pilot (see Payload) plus 2 ground crew. Low-cost, 2-seat model now also offered.
Length: 62 ft 2 ins (18.95 m)
Diameter: 22 ft 7 ins (6.88 m) maximum
Height: 26 ft 4 ins (8.03 m) including gondola/car.
Envelope: Double laminated nylon. *Volume* 12,000 cu ft (340 m^3). Manual and automatic gas valves. Main and overpressure rip panels.
Ballonets: Main and tail.
Payload/ballast: Lifting capacity at 15° C at sea level is the pilot of 180 lb (81.6 kg) weight plus 90 lb (41 kg) of disposable ballast.
Engine: 570 cc König 2-stroke piston engine, with electric start. Vertical vectoring of the fan for control, which reduces the take-off roll to a few feet and cushions landing.

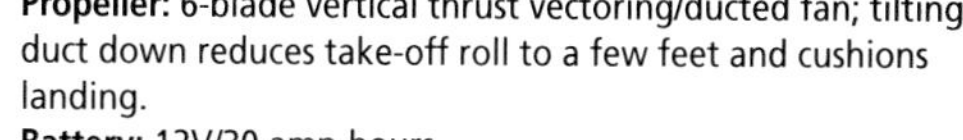

Propeller: 6-blade vertical thrust vectoring/ducted fan; tilting duct down reduces take-off roll to a few feet and cushions landing.
Battery: 12V/30 amp-hours
Fuel: 23 litres, as 40:1 petrol/oil mix.
Maximum airspeed: 26 kts (30 mph) 48 km/h
Operating ceiling: 2,800 ft (850 m)
Duration: 2 hours

↑ **Cameron DG-14 helium airship**

Cameron DP80 and DP90

First flight: 1986 for general type.
Role: Hot-air airships for recreation and advertising. (DP60 and DP70 are no longer offered.)

Details

Crew/Passengers: Pilot or pilot and passenger. Aluminium gondola with a full-height polycarbonate windscreen. Intercom system is standard.
Length: *DP80* 111 ft (33.83 m), *DP90* 115 ft (35.05 m)
Width: *DP80* 40 ft (12.19 m), *DP90* 42 ft (12.80 m)
Height: *DP80* 50 ft (15.24 m), *DP90* 51 ft (15.54 m)
Envelope: Lower and centre sections of high tenacity ripstop nylon, upper third of Hyperlast. *Volumes: DP80* 80,000 cu ft (2,265 m^3), *DP90* 90,000 cu ft (2,548 m^3). Each side of the envelope can have an advertising display of approximately: *DP80* 990 sq ft (91.97 m^2), *DP90* 1,066 sq ft (99.03 m^2).
Engine: Rotax 582UL with hush kit is standard on the *DP80* and *DP90*.
Propeller: 3-blade pusher in a shroud.
Propane tanks: Choice covers 2 Worthingtons containing 77 litres, 2 Cameron 599s containing 85 litres, or 2 Cameron 426s containing 108 litres.
Maximum airspeed: 15 kts (17 mph) 27 km/h

↑ **Cameron DP80 hot-air airship**

Lindstrand Balloons Ltd

UK

Corporate address:
Maesbury Road, Oswestry, Shropshire SY10 8ZZ.

Telephone: +44 1691 671717
Facsimile: +44 1691 671122

Information:
Per Lindstrand (Managing Director – *facsimile* +44 1691 671345).

ACTIVITIES

▪ Among other work, Lindstrand Balloons constructed the 1.1 million cu ft (31,148 m^3) combined helium gas and hot-air balloon *Virgin Global Challenger* for the January 1997 round-the-world attempt.
▪ Future projects may include resurrecting 2 previous helium craft designs, and various special projects that could include constructing envelopes for satellite/stratosphere applications.

Lindstrand AS 300

First flight: 5 February 1993.
Role: Pressurized, non-rigid hot-air airship.

Aims

▪ Can be operated in winds up to 10 kts with an experienced crew.
▪ Designed to carry a 1,653 lb (750 kg) raft slung beneath it from 6 points on the envelope.
▪ Largest hot-air airship built at the time of its appearance.
▪ New envelope shape (see Development) to give better aerodynamics (less drag and leaves fins protruding further into the airflow, and on a longer torque arm, resulting in improved turn performance).
▪ New fin geometry resulting in a much stiffer fin without increased weight or the use of non-fabric stiffeners.
▪ New air distributing system for the tailplane to ensure constant fin buoyancy during flight and less air loss.
▪ A new catenary load curtain developed using finite element analysis programme, which could simulate flight motions. This enables the elimination of pitch instability.
▪ Precise control by thrust reverser (see Engine).

Development

▪ AS 300 created for *Operation Canopée*, to undertake botanic research of rainforests.
▪ Follows on from the AS 261 which flew 260 hours and performed excellent work in South America and Africa.
▪ 1992. Lindstrand Balloons received the order to build the new AS 300 envelope and update the gondola.
▪ 1993. Delivery. Used for its intended purpose in Summer 1993 in Borneo but political difficulties prevented plans for its use elsewhere. Thereafter based in France, and made an appearance (non-competitive) at the 1994 World Airship Championships.

Details

Crew/Passengers: 7 persons, including pilot. Stainless steel spaceframe gondola, capable of being split into 5 sections for airlift by Twin Otter.
Length: 167 ft 2 ins (50.96 m)
Diameter: 59 ft 9 ins (18.2 m) maximum
Width: 67 ft 3 ins (20.5 m) maximum
Height: 68 ft 10 ins (20.98 m)
Envelope: *Volume* 300,960 cu ft (8,522.2 m^3). The main hull of the envelope is pressurised using a 5 hp (3.7 kW) Honda engine driving a multi-blade fan. Pressure is regulated by 2 fabric pressure relief valves forward of the gondola. Hull shape is maintained using a Kevlar catenary system to distribute the loads from the gondola into the top of the envelope. Fins have a separate pressurization system fed by a multi-blade fan, belt-driven off the propulsion system. Fin shape is maintained by multiple internal formers. Stability of the fins by using a large footprint at the base of the fins, attaching all the internal formers to the main hull and by a tip tube giving longitudinal stiffness at the fin tip. Rigging lines facility to secure the fin tips to the main hull. Entire envelope is manufactured from HTN 90. An emergency 5 hp (3.7 kW) electric fan can supply either the main hull or fins.
Fineness ratio: 2.8:1
Total lift: 5,952 lb (2,700 kg) maximum
Weights: Envelope 904 lb (410 kg). Gondola 1,173 lb (532 kg) dry. Propane capacity 849 lb (385 kg). Avgas 99.2 lb (45 kg).
Engine: 100 hp (74.6 kW) Teledyne Continental O-200 piston engine. (See also Envelope.) Thrust reverser installed behind the pusher propeller, consisting of 2 air vanes that swing into the propwash by lever control. This results in a 60% effective reverse thrust which can also make the airship go backwards.
Propeller: 4-blade Hoffmann.
Fuel: See Weights.
Maximum airspeed: over 20 kts (23 mph) 37 km/h

↑ Lindstrand AS 300 hot-air airship

Lindstrand HS 110

First flight: 1 May 1995.
Role: Non-rigid, hot-air airship solely for advertising purposes.

Aims

▪ Optimised for low maintenance and ease of handling in the air and transportation on the ground.
▪ Set-up time from the transport trailer is under 30 minutes.
▪ Refuelling without envelope deflation.
▪ Can be tethered. 10 kts surface windspeed limit for free flying.

Details

Crew/Passengers: 2 persons side-by-side. Controls between the seats.
Gondola: Glassfibre, tubular stainless steel triangular framework and aluminium floors; 1 person only when extra propane is carried or when single pilot flight is desired. 2 ground crew.
Length: 111 ft 7 ins (34 m)
Diameter: 42 ft 8 ins (13 m)
Width: 48 ft 6 ins (14.78 m) over fins
Height: 51 ft 10 ins (15.8 m) overall
Envelope: Manufactured from high-tenacity polyamide fabric coated with a high temperature silicon elastomer; jointing technique is a double-fell twin needle seam reinforced with load tape. *Volume* 110,358 cu ft (3,125 m^3). Twin catenary load curtain ensures a non-distorting shape, even in turbulence. 2 pressure relief valves in front of the gondola prevent accidental over-pressurization. Advertising can be directly on the hull or on 2 side banners of 67 ft (20 m) length and 1 under the chin of 18.4 ft × 11.2 ft (5.6 m × 3.4 m) and with an area of 150 sq ft (14 m^2). Banners can be changed in under 1 hour using Velcro and back-up straps and have a weight penalty of 66 lb (30 kg). Fast deflation time using 2 rip panels situated either side of the uppermost fin; in addition, numerous small deflation slots are provided in the fin assembly.
Surface area: 1,500 sq ft (139.4 m^2)
Fineness ratio: 2.575:1
Empty weight: 441 lb (200 kg)
Engine: 64 hp (47.7 kW) Rotax 582UL 2-stroke engine, with reduction gearbox.
Propeller: 4-blade composites type.
Fuel: 35 litres for the engine in a removable, translucent plastic tank. 176 lb (80 kg) of propane gas in 2 cylinder tanks for envelope inflation; further 88 lb (40 kg) can be carried instead of the passenger.
Burners: Twin burners of modified JetStream type and can be fired individually or as a pair to give more longitudinal control (see Fuel). Activated from the sitting position by a specially designed hydraulic system.
Electrical system: 12V, 155W alternator and stored in a 24 Ah high-capacity battery. Night flying kit has an extra 230W alternator.
Stabilizer: 4 fins, inflated via a 5 hp (3.73 kW) pressurizing engine and multi-blade fan at the gondola, have much higher air pressure than the hull and thereby stay rigid even under full turns.
Maximum airspeed: 20 kts (23 mph) 37 km/h
Advertising cruise speed: 10-12 kts (11.5-14 mph) 19-22 km/h
Duration: up to 2 hours on standard fuel; almost 3.5 hours with extra propane.

↑ Lindstrand HS 110 2-seat hot-air airship

Promotional Ideas Group — UK

Corporate address:
14 Perry Way, Lightwater, Surrey GU18 5LB.

Telephone: +44 1276 473870 or 1628 34290
Facsimile: +44 1276 473870
E-mail: pig@netcomuk.co.uk
Web site: http://netcomuk.co.uk/~pig/home.htm

Information:
Doug Smith (Partner).

ACTIVITIES

▪ Founded in 1993, primarily to design and build an RPA (Remote Piloted Airship) for aerial advertising and filming.
▪ Involvement in late 1997 in a surveillance project in Borneo, in conjuction with the Orangutan Foundation International and JPL NASA. PIG3 was expected to be used, but a tailor-made **PIG4** was under construction in the late Summer of 1997. The mission proposal was a validation study of the use of a Quantum Well Infrared Photodetector (QWIP) camera to survey Orangutan populations.

Promotional Ideas Group PIG3

First flight: July 1994 (PIG1 first prototype), July 1995 (PIG2 second prototype).
Role: Non-rigid helium RPA (Remote Piloted Airship) for use as an advertising and filming platform. Can be tethered at nose for long-term events (topped up with helium periodically).

Aims

▪ PIG3 is a 9% larger redesigned/re-engineered version of PIG2, combining increased power with overall weight loss, making it capable of flying in average UK wind conditions by offering a higher power to weight ratio.

Development

▪ PIG3 is available for commercial flying. Assembly from scratch, including inflation, takes approximately 2 hours.
▪ Petrol driven version of PIG3 is to be made available for reconnaissance, surveying and other applications, with 33 lb (15 kg) payload and 5.4 naut miles (6.2 miles) 10 km range.

Details

Length: 28 ft 9 ins (8.75 m)
Diameter: 8 ft 4 ins (2.55 m)
Envelope: *Volume* 992 cu ft (28.1 m^3). Dual skin comprising lightweight re-enforced nylon outer shell with a lightweight helium retaining inner envelope. Advertising banners are attached to the outer shell and are interchangeable.
Gross lift: 66.4 lb (30.1 kg)
Take-off weight: 62 lb (28 kg)
Payload (free): 4.4 to 8.8 lb (2 to 4 kg), as CCD colour camera and microwave link for filming.
Engines: 2 × 2.75 hp (2 kW) high-powered electric motors. Motors rotate through ±90° to the horizontal to aid climb and descent, and can each run independently in forward or reverse.
Propellers: 1 ft 2 ins (0.36 m)
Batteries: 2 × 31.2 V ni-cd, requiring 3 minutes to change per pit stop.
Control surfaces: Remote radio control via a 7-channel PCM unit: computer channel mixing has been used for rudder, elevator and engine thrust vector control; 1 channel has been configured to operate an emergency dump valve.
Maximum airspeed: 26-30 kts (30-35 mph) 48-56 km/h
Cruise speed: 8.5 kts (10 mph) 16 km/h
Ceiling: 400 ft (122 m), under CAA regulations; maximum operating height 1,640 ft (500 m).
Range: Normally within 4,920 ft (1,500 m) of pilot.
Duration: 20 minutes at maximum speed, 1 hour at cruise speed, 2-3 hours at ideal conditions, per battery set.

↑ Promotional Ideas Group PIG3 RPA

SkyShips Limited — UK

Corporate address:
Leighs Lodge, Great Leighs, Chelmsford, Essex CM3 1QJ.

Telephone: +44 1245 362980
Facsimile: +44 1245 362981
E-mail: ives@skyships.co.uk
Web site: www.skyships.demon.co.uk

Information:
William Ives.

ACTIVITIES

▪ Production, sale and hire of Cirrus 840 and 1000 unmanned airships.
▪ Research and development of unmanned remotely-piloted airships.
▪ Development of advanced avionics (autopilots/telemetry links, etc) for UAVs.
▪ Consultancy and management of balloon and airship technology-based products.

SkyShips Cirrus 840

First flight: 18 January 1997, in the Cardington airship shed.
Role: Unmanned RPA (remote or autonomous control) for advertising, camera platform, surveillance, surveying, etc.

Aims

▪ Computerized control and navigation system.
▪ 35MHz PCM radio control.

Development

▪ August 1996. Received a UK Department of Trade and Industry (DTI) innovation award to assist development.
▪ 25 January 1997. First outside flight. Currently undergoing a 200 hour test programme.

Details

Length: 27 ft (8.5 m)
Diameter: 8 ft 3 ins (2.5 m)
Height: 9 ft 6 ins (2.9 m) overall
Envelope: Polyurethane-coated nylon. 8 gores. *Volume* 840 cu ft (23.8 m^3). Heligas or similar gas. Overpressure and manual valves.
Ballonet: 10% of volume
Surface area: 538 sq ft (50 m^2)
Fineness ratio: 3.4:1
Take-off weight: 55 lb (25 kg)
Payload: 11 lb (5 kg)
Engines: 2 electric motors, with +90/-10° vectoring.
Propellers: 1 ft 4 ins (0.4 m) 3-blade ducted.
Batteries: Twin 24V plus 12V. Optional battery supply for payload and fluorescent tubes for illumination.
Stabilizers: X-form composite fins.
Maximum airspeed: 30 kts (35 mph) 55 km/h
Cruise speed: 10 kts (12 mph) 19 km/h
Operating altitude: 400 ft (122 m) in accordance with CAA regulations; possible 1,000 ft (305 m)

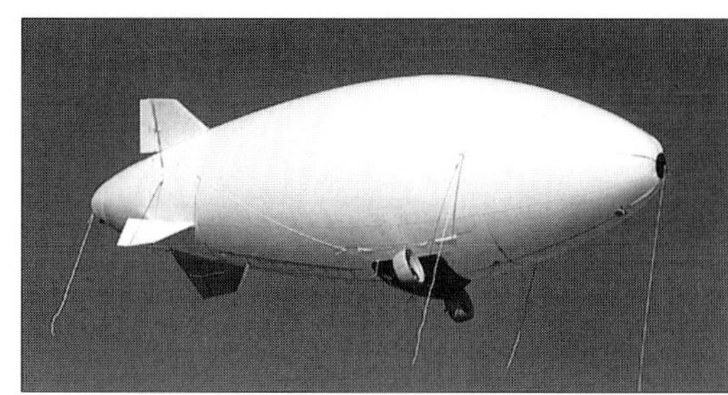

↑ SkyShips Cirrus 840 prototype

Range: 0.54 naut miles (0.62 miles) 1 km of pilot when flown manually.
Duration: 1 hour typically; up to 3 hours dependent upon battery configuration.

SkyShips Cirrus 1000

Role: Generally similar to Cirrus 840, with similar motors and performance. Differences are detailed below.
Length: 31 ft 2 ins (9.5 m)
Envelope: *Volume* 1,025 cu ft (29 m^3)
Ballonet: 10% of volume
Surface area: 624 sq ft (58 m^2)
Fineness ratio: 3.8:1
Take-off weight: 66 lb (30 kg)
Payload: 22 lb (10 kg)

The Lightship Group — UK

Corporate address:
1, Stafford Park 12, Telford, Shropshire TF3 3BJ.

Telephone: +44 1952 292 360
Facsimile: +44 1952 201 657
E-mail: BruceofTLG@aol.com
Web site: www.lightships.com

Information:
Bruce Renny (Marketing Director).

USA:
Corporate address:
5728 Major Boulevard, Suite 314, Orlando, Florida 32819.

Telephone: +1 407 363 7777
Facsimile: +1 407 363 0962

ACTIVITIES

▪ Formed in February 1995 as a partnership between Virgin Lightships (part of the Virgin Group) and Lightship America (part of the American Blimp Corporation – the manufacturer of the Lightship). Some 150 employees.
▪ The world's largest airship operator, with a fleet of 11 A-60+ Lightship airships worldwide in an advertising and promotional capacity on behalf of Anheuser-Busch, Blockbuster Video, the RAC, Mazda Cars, Virgin Atlantic, Russell Stover Candies, Pepsi-Cola and Sanyo. Those Lightships flying in the USA are operated as an air carrier under FAR Part 135. In addition, the Lightship Group received in July 1997 certification for the first of the new 10-seat A-150 Lightship airships, and the company plans to field a fleet of 12 A-150s within 5 years.

↑ The Lightship Group's A-60+ Lightship with RAC logo

Thunder & Colt — UK

Corporate address:
St John's Street, Bedminster, Bristol BS3 4NH.

Telephone: +44 1179 532 772
Facsimile: +44 1179 663 638

Information:
Alan Noble.

ACTIVITIES

- Manufactures an expanding range of hot-air airships. The AS 105 Mk II is now the primary airship, with the first AS 120 under construction at the time of writing.

Thunder & Colt AS 80GD

First flight: 1988 in original form.
Role: Recreational and advertising pressurised hot-air airship.

Details

Crew/Passengers: Pilot or pilot and passenger. Stainless steel and aluminium gondola, with polycarbonate windscreen.
Gondola: Stainless steel spaceframe and aluminium panels. Length 12 ft 7 ins (3.84 m), width 5 ft 9 ins (1.75 m) maximum, and height 5 ft 11 ins (1.8 m). Weight 463 lb (210 kg).
Length: 121 ft 5 ins (37 m)
Diameter: 37 ft 9 ins (11.5 m) maximum
Envelope: *Volume* 80,000 cu ft (2,265 m^3). Twin catenary system to distribute loads from the gondola and engine to the envelope. Envelope constructed of Longlife fabric. Envelope pressurised via an electric fan and air scoop aft of the propeller. Pressure relief valve. Rip panel for deflation.
Fineness ratio: 3.2:1
Weights: Envelope 419 lb (190 kg). Gondola 463 lb (210 kg) dry. Propane 242 lb (110 kg) maximum.
Engine: 52 hp (38.8 kW) Rotax 462 piston engine on AS 80 Mk II.
Propeller: 2-blade pusher type on AS 80 Mk II.
Maximum airspeed: 20 kts (23 mph) 37 km/h for AS 80 Mk II
Duration: 2.5 hours for AS 80 Mk II

↑ Thunder & Colt AS 105 Mk II

Thunder & Colt AS 105 Mk II

Role: Recreational and advertising pressurised hot-air airship.

Details

Crew/Passengers: Pilot or pilot and passenger. Stainless steel and aluminium gondola, with polycarbonate windscreen.
Gondola: As for AS 80GD.
Length: 111 ft 7 ins (34 m)
Diameter: 41 ft (12.4 m) maximum
Envelope: *Volume* 105,000 cu ft (3,000 m^3). Twin catenary system to distribute loads from the gondola and engine to the envelope. Envelope constructed of Longlife fabric. Envelope pressurised via an electric fan and air scoop aft of the propeller. Pressure relief valve. Rip panel for deflation.
Fineness ratio: 2.5:1
Weights: Envelope 495 lb (225 kg). Gondola 463 lb (210 kg) dry. Propane 242 lb (110 kg) maximum.
Engine: 52 hp (38.8 kW) Rotax 462 piston engine.
Propeller: 3-blade pusher type.
Maximum airspeed: 20 kts (23 mph) 37 km/h
Duration: 2.5 hours

Thunder & Colt AS 105GD

Role: As for AS 105 Mk II.

Aims

- Similar envelope; overall length 134 ft 6 ins (41 m); diameter 41 ft (12.5 m); and weight 441 lb (200 kg).

Thunder & Colt AS 120 Mk II

Role: Recreational and advertising pressurised hot-air airship.

Aims

- Generally similar to other airships. Envelope volume 120,000 cu ft (3,400 m^3); overall length 116 ft (35.5 m); diameter 43 ft (13 m); and weight 540 lb (245 kg).

Advanced HYBRID Aircraft — USA

Corporate address:
PO Box 144, Eugene, Oregon 97440.

Telephone: +1 541 344 5323
Facsimile: +1 541 344 5323
Web site: http://www.ahausa.com

Manager:
Bruce N. Blake P.Eng, MRAeS, C.Eng, BE(Aero), LAME (Manager and Director).

AHA Albatross RPMB

First flight: 1987.
Role: Non-rigid fully functioning, remotely piloted mini blimp (RPMB), 80% scale proof-of-concept vehicle assisting in the Hornet programme. Has operated at more than 25% heaviness.

Aims

- To prove that the combination of aerostatic and aerodynamic lift generation is viable.
- To show the airship will operate stably and under full control from very low to maximum speeds.
- To prove the airship can taxi on the field, with little need for ground crew.

Development

- The prospects of increased productivity for hybrid buoyant airships is stated by AHA to be good, with the expectation of increased speed and greater disposable load for a given helium volume over EQ (equilibrium) airships and minimal ground crew.

↑ Advanced HYBRID Aircraft Albatross RPMB

AHA Gnat mtkb-1

First flight: Not yet flown.
Role: Modern version of the manned, tethered, kite balloon for observation, wildlife spotting and other similar uses.

Aims

- Features a typical airship-shaped envelope with ballonet, a blower, 4 tail stabilizers in X form, and main tether and pitch cables.

Details

Sales: Interest shown from Algeria and South Africa, apparently for wildlife spotting and photography.
Crew/Passengers: Pilot only in an under-envelope gondola.
Length: 30 ft (9.14 m)
Diameter: 20 ft (6.1 m)
Envelope: *Volume* 6,600 cu ft (186.9 m^3)
Gross aerostatic lift: 410 lb (186 kg)
Payload: 160 lb (72.6 kg)

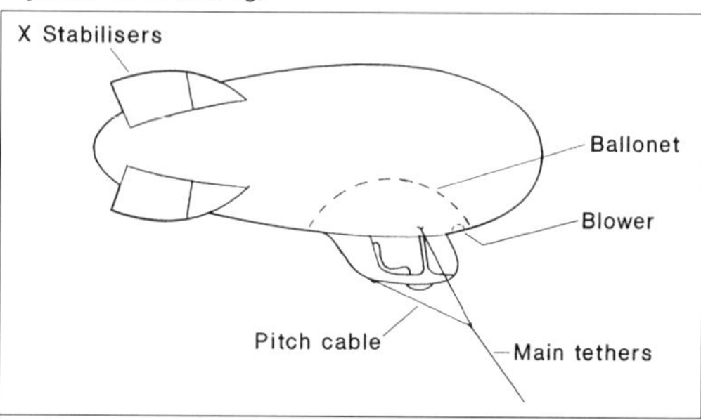

↑ Advanced HYBRID Aircraft Gnat mtkb-1

AHA Hornet Hybrid RPV

Role: Non-rigid, non-EQ, hybrid airship developed as a Combat Aerial Delivery Aircraft, to operate from an offshore base, delivering supplies into an unprepared site by remote control.

Aims

- Incorporated 'voice control' into the airship flight control system design.
- MIL-STD certification to be determined.
- Flight control: Ground-based unit with microcomputer, 17 ins (0.43 m) or larger CRT, laser printer, joystick control, headset

with microphone, uninterruptable power supply, telemetry transceiver, linear power amplifier, parabolic reflector antenna, 9-channel PCM controller (flight), 6-channel PCM controller (video), downlink monitoring software, and telemetry monitoring software/OS. Airborne system with Honeywell autopilot, 3-axis vertical gyro, telemetry transceiver, PCM controller/demodulator, 40W linear power amplifier, integrated GPS system, video camera(s)/mount, servo drive controller, flight data recorder, FCS servos, and instruments and sensors.
▪ Robust, gas-filled bumpers.

Development

▪ Design solicited by the US Navy Contracts Office at Port Hueneme, California. Project is titled Combat Service Aerial Delivery Aircraft (see Role).
▪ AHA is one of two companies shortlisted for the contract.

Details

Sales: Possibly US Navy eventually.
Length: 135 ft (41.14 m)
Diameter: 30 ft (9.14 m)
Width over winglets: 53 ft (16.15 m)
Wing chord: 7 ft 6 ins (2.29 m)
Envelope: *Volume* 68,900 cu ft (1,951 m^3)
Ballonet: Maximum 25% of envelope volume
Gross buoyancy: 3,700 lb (1,678 kg)
Take-off weight: 7,500 lb (3,402 kg)
Heaviness: 51% of MTOW, at 3,800 lb (1,723 kg)
Payload: 2,500 lb (1,134 kg). Payload container at CG: an example size stated at 20 × 8 × 8 ft (6.1 × 2.44 × 2.44 m).
Engines: 4 Mid-West AE100R rotary engines, each 100 hp (74.6 kW). 0° to +45° vectoring angle.
Propellers: 4 vectoring, ducted propulsors.
Maximum airspeed: 81 kts (93 mph) 150 km/h
Operating altitude: 9,000 ft (2,740 m) maximum
Range: 600 naut miles (690 miles) 1,110 km

AHA Hornet LV

First flight: Not yet flown, but the programme was said to have received venture capital at the time of writing.
Role: Non-rigid, hybrid, leisure/sports airship (LV – leisure variant).

Aims

▪ To operate at 50% heaviness, with only half of the total lift provided by the helium filled envelope.
▪ At take-off, with the wings vectored at +30°, aerodynamic lift boosted by the vectored thrust will allow a very short ground run and a steep climb.

Development

▪ A market study estimates the sale of 60 LV units in kit form per year, primarily in the USA and EU. The company's business plan is to raise capital for commercialisation of this airship.

Details

Crew: Pilot in small enclosed gondola.
Length: 50 ft (15.24 m)
Width over winglets: 22 ft 6 ins (6.86 m)
Height: 16 ft (4.88 m)
Envelope: *Volume* 4,300 cu ft (121.76 m^3). *Advertising area* 730 sq ft (67.8 m^2).
Surface area: 1,570 sq ft (145.86 m^2)
Ballonet/s: *Volume* 430 cu ft (12.18 m^3)
Gross aerostatic lift: 270 lb (122.5 kg) at 5% ballonets inflation.
Take-off weight: 540 lb (245 kg) maximum
Empty weight: 336 lb (152.4 kg)
Empty weight (heaviness) at mast: 66 lb (29.94 kg)
Maximum normal heaviness: 270 lb (122.5 kg)
Disposable load: 204 lb (92.53 kg)
Engines: 2 Konig SC 430 pistons.
Fuel: Fuel in the strut-tank assembly.
Propellers: 2, each 4 ft 6 ins (1.37 m) diameter.
Stabilizers/winglets: 4 stabilizers at tail. 2 winglet assemblies carrying engines, able to vector engine thrust by +30° for steep climb.
Maximum airspeed: 51 kts (59 mph) 94 km/h
Minimum airspeed: 23 kts (26 mph) 43 km/h
Maximum climb rate: 2,000 ft (610 m) per minute

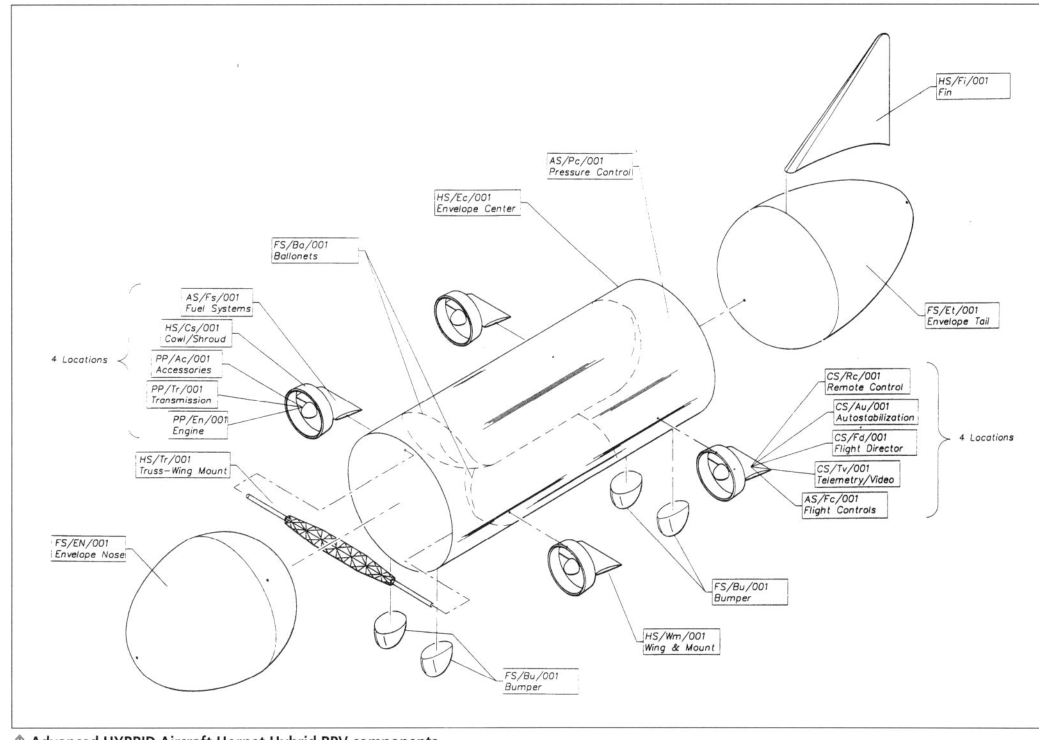

↑ **Advanced HYBRID Aircraft Hornet Hybrid RPV components**

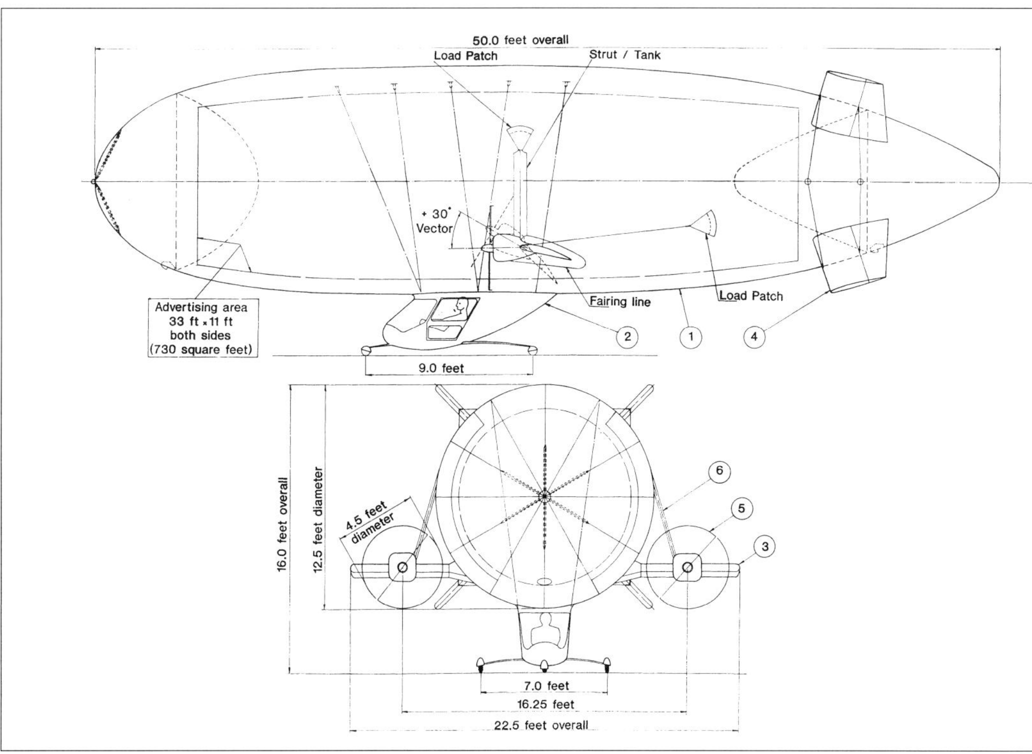

↑ **Advanced HYBRID Aircraft Hornet LV, showing: 1 Envelope assembly, 2 Gondola, 3 Winglet, 4 Stabilizer, 5 Propeller, 6 Strut-tank assembly**

AHA Hornet LV 2-seater

First flight: Not yet flown. However, first sale was imminent in 1998.
Role: Non-rigid, hybrid advertising airship.

Aims

▪ 2-seat and larger version of the LV.
▪ To gain FAA P-8110-2 certification.
▪ See LV entry.

Details

Length: 68 ft (20.73 m)
Diameter: 17 ft (5.18 m)
Width over winglets 30 ft 6 ins (9.30 m)
Winglet chord: 4 ft 6 ins (1.37 m)
Envelope: *Volume* 10,750 cu ft (304.4 m^3)
Ballonet/s: 15% of envelope volume
Take-off weight: 1,350 lb (612.3 kg)
Heaviness: Maximum of 50% of take-off weight
Buoyancy: 675 lb (306 kg)
Disposable load: 510 lb (231.3 kg)
Engines: 2 Mid-West AE100R rotary engines, each 100 hp (74.6 kW). +30° vectoring through tilt of winglets.
Maximum airspeed: 72 kts (83 mph) 133 km/h
Minimum airspeed: 29 kts (33.5 mph) 54 km/h
Operating altitude: 5,000 ft (1,525 m)

AHA Hornet AW

First flight: Not yet flown.
Role: Non-rigid, hybrid airship. Applications for the AW (aerial work) commercial version of Hornet may include aerial survey, mapping, surveillance, and electronic news gathering, where at present small to medium sized fixed and rotary winged aircraft are used. It can also fulfil advertising and promotion roles.

Aims

▪ To offer a wide speed range, and lower acquisition and operating costs than helicopters.
▪ Quieter and with longer endurance than helicopters.
▪ Multi-engine reliability, permitting low altitude operations over built-up areas.
▪ Increased thrust vectoring compared to LV (see Engines).
▪ To gain BCAR Q or FAA P-8110-2 certification.

Details

Length: 100 ft (30.48 m)
Diameter: 20 ft (6.10 m)
Width over winglets: 30 ft 2 ins (9.19 m)
Winglet chord: 4 ft 1 ins (1.24 m)
Envelope: *Volume* 22,000 cu ft (623 m^3)
Ballonet/s: 20% of envelope volume
Take-off weight: 2,822 lb (1,280 kg)
Heaviness: Maximum 56% of take-off weight
Buoyancy: 1,235 lb (560 kg)
Disposable load: 941 lb (427 kg)
Engines: 4 Mid-West AE100R rotary engines, each 100 hp (74.6 kW). +45° vectoring through tilt of wings.
Maximum airspeed: 81 kts (93 mph) 150 km/h
Minimum airspeed: 33 kts (38 mph) 61 km/h
Operating altitude: 7,000 ft (2,135 m)

AHA 1200 Light Utility

First flight: Not yet flown, but the programme was said to have received venture capital at time of writing.
Role: Non-rigid, hybrid airship, specially designed for use in the general aviation field and for light cargo carrying, where low maintenance and low operational costs are paramount. A medium lift, robust and short take-off airship could access unprepared airfields in Third World countries, and in disaster areas. Also advertising and surveillance.

Aims

- Provision for the carriage of unusual cargoes, by the structural design of the spine of the tricycle assembly.
- Carriage of internal and external loads.
- To gain BCAR Q or FAA P-8110-2 certification.

Details

Length: 98 ft 6 ins (30.02 m)
Diameter: 24 ft 6 ins (7.47 m)
Width over winglets: 19 ft 5 ins (5.92 m)
Winglet chord: 4 ft 8 ins (1.42 m)
Envelope: *Volume* 42,400 cu ft (1,200 m^3)
Ballonet/s: 25% of envelope volume
Take-off weight: 3,166 lb (1,436 kg)
Heaviness: Maximum 25% of take-off weight
Buoyancy: 2,381 lb (1,080 kg) at 10% ballonet inflation
Disposable load: 950 lb (431 kg)
Engines: 2 Mid-West AE100R rotary engines, each 100 hp (74.6 kW).

↑ Advanced HYBRID Aircraft Wasp, showing completed prototype. Note the surveillance pod and engine arrangement

Maximum airspeed: 41 kts (47 mph) 76 km/h
Minimum airspeed: 19 kts (22 mph) 35 km/h
Operating altitude: 9,000 ft (2,745 m)

AHA Wasp

First flight: Airship completed in November 1997, with first flight in December 1997.
Role: Remotely piloted 'blimp' airship for aerial surveillance and other uses.

Details

Sales: First delivery to a customer in South Korea, whom has indicated a requirement for as many as 100 for surveillance.
Crew/Passengers: None.
Surveillance pod: *Volume* 3.5 cu ft (0.1 m^3)
Length: 33 ft (10 m)
Diameter: 8 ft 2 ins (2.5 m)
Wheelbase: 8 ft 2 ins (2.5 m)
Wheel track: 5 ft 11 ins (1.8 m)
Height: 11 ft (3.3 m)
Envelope: *Volume* 1,235 cu ft (35 m^3)
Gross aerostatic lift: 75 lb (34 kg)
Engines: 2 air cooled, each 2.4 hp (1.8 kW)
Propellers: 2, each 2-blade of 2 ft × 7 ins (0.61 × 0.18 m)

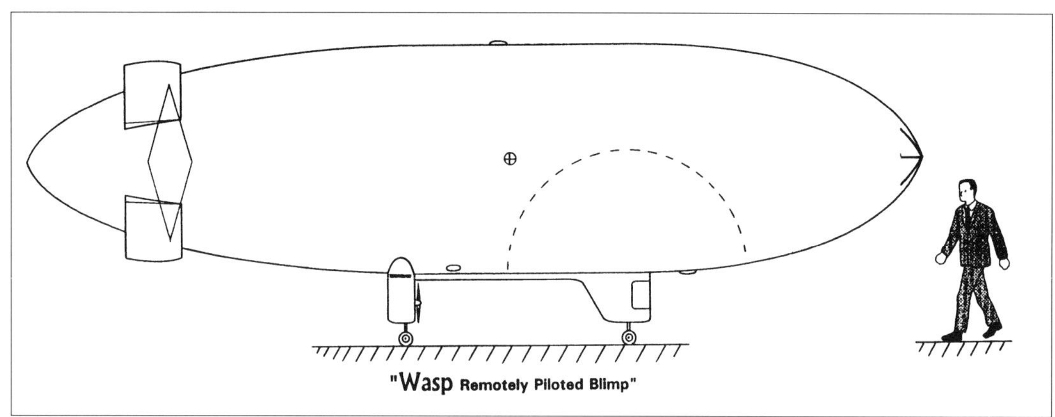

↑ Advanced HYBRID Aircraft Wasp drone blimp

Airship International Ltd — USA

Corporate address:
7380 Sand Lake Road, Suite 200, Orlando, Florida 32819.

Telephone: +1 407 351 0011
Facsimile: +1 407 345 0888

Information:
Scott Bennett (Director of Public Relations).

ACTIVITIES

- Public company trading in the Over-the-Counter NASDAQ under the symbol "BLMP".
- Founded in 1982 by Chairman/President Louis J. Pearlman, it owns and operates Skyship series airships for day and night aerial advertising and promotional purposes of Fortune 500 companies. It has operated in the USA, Europe and Japan, promoting McDonald's Corporation, Metropolitan Life Insurance Corporation, TDK Electronics Corporation and many other companies. It also provides a gyroscopic-mounted camera for aerial media work that locks onto images from as high as 1,000 ft (305 m).
- Airship International has developed the NightSign™ system, said to be the world's largest full colour aerial display, which comprises 2 computerized electronic display boards mounted on the sides of the Skyship. The NightSign™ dimensions are 118 ft (36 m) length and 29 ft (8.8 m) high, with a total of 8,500 multi-colour blue, green, red and yellow lamps designed to graphically depict logos, messages, animation, cartoons, etc, all operated at night by an on-board computer.

Airship Management Services, Inc – AMS — USA

Corporate address:
Two Soundview Drive, Greenwich, CT 06830.

Telephone: +1 203 625 0071
Facsimile: +1 203 625 0065

Information:
Sarah L. Keena.

UK
Address:
11 Linton House, Holland Park Avenue, London W11 3RL.

Telephone: +44 171 221 4122
Facsimile: +44 171 727 3863

Japan
Address:
c/o Nissho Iwai Corporation (Aircraft Dept), 4-5 Akasaka 2-Chome, Minato-ku, Tokyo 107.

Telephone: +81 3 3588 2726
Facsimile: +81 3 3588 4234

ACTIVITIES

- Said to be the most experienced company in operating some of the world's largest airships, AMS owns and operates airships and, through associated companies in the US, UK and Japan, provides technical and operational support to airships worldwide. Also has recently begun supporting Airship Arabia (see Saudi Arabia).
- AMS is a private company with associate offices in London, Athens, Riyadh and Tokyo. It grew out of the demise of Airship Industries (UK) Ltd in 1990 and was founded by George Spyrou.
- The principal client in the USA is Fuji Photo Film (USA) Inc. Apart from advertising/promotional work, the company supports broadcasting, photography and other applications for companies and government bodies, including training UK Ministry of Defence pilots and mechanics after being actively involved in the sale of a Skyship 600 to the MoD in June 1993, sensor testing for US companies and forces, and in 1996 being awarded a contract to provide an airship for the Atlanta Police Department for security surveillance over the Olympics.

↑ Airship Management Services, Inc Skyship 600 in Fuji Film colours

American Blimp Corporation USA

Corporate address:
Suite 5, 1900 N-E 25th Avenue, Hillsboro, OR 97124.
Telephone: +1 503 693 1611
Facsimile: +1 503 681 0906
Information:
E. Judson Brandreth, Jr (Vice-President, Marketing).
Marketing Office for applications in government missions and civil aid:
Address:
302 Ritchie Hwy, Severna Park, MD 21146.
Telephone: +1 410 544 6507
Facsimile: +1 410 544 6509
Web site: www.americanblimp.com

ACTIVITIES

■ Founded by Mr James Thiele and commenced operations in 1987. ABC had built 16 airships by August 1997. The A-60+ is the world's most operated airship type. Lightships are flown in Australia, China, Brazil, South Africa, Europe and North America, and Type Certificated in Canada, Italy, Brazil, Australia and the USA.
■ Some 40 employees at Hillsboro headquarters, where airships are designed and constructed in a 29,000 sq ft (2,694 m^2) facility, adequate for producing about 6-8 airships per year.
■ A wholly owned subsidiary is Lightship America, a 50% partner in The Lightship Group (which see under UK).
■ In 1995 ABC announced the introduction of a new series of airships, the SPECTOR™ Series, in answer to the increasing demand for airships for airborne surveillance by military, police and civil aid agencies, with other possible roles including border security, law enforcement, maritime and EEZ protection, disaster relief and VIP security. The larger of these new airships feature a gondola capable of carrying the pilot and up to 9 passengers (or 2 pilots plus 8), have a duration of more than 24 hours, and are offered with 3 alternative envelopes and 2 gondolas, depending upon the mission requirements for lift. As Lightships they will be produced with internal lights and translucent envelopes.
■ ABC and The Lightship Group are collaborating on the 35-passenger, 500,000 cu ft (14,158 m^3) **Millennia** airship, to undertake a round-the-world flight, starting from Edinburgh Castle, Scotland, on 31 December 1999.

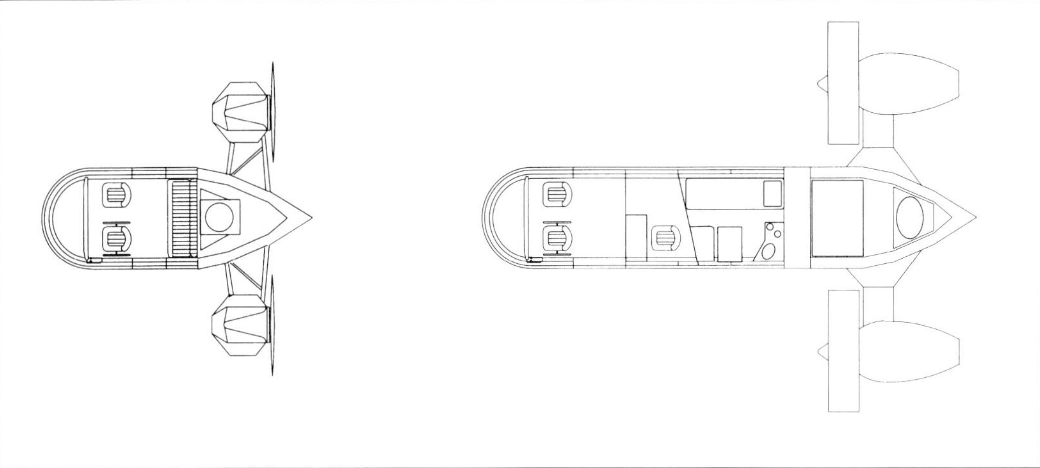

↑ Gondolas of the SPECTOR™ range: *left* for SPECTOR™ 19, *right* for SPECTOR™ 36, 42 and 48 *(American Blimp Corporation)*

ABC A-60+ Lightship and SPECTOR™ 19

First flight: 9 April 1988 (prototype designated A-50).
Role: Non-rigid helium airship. As A-60+ principally for aerial advertising but including transportation. Has gyrostabilized camera mounting and real-time datalink for broadcasting work. See Activities for SPECTOR™.

Development

■ November 1989. First flight of a production A-60, delivered to Virgin Lightships 1990.
■ 1991. FAA certification for the A-60+, with an 8,000 cu ft (226.5 m^3) increase in envelope volume for improved hot and high performance.
■ 1993. A-60 fleet modified to A-60+ standard to offer additional disposable load.
■ Approved for single-pilot operation.

Details

Sales: See Activities, plus The Lightship Group and Beijing Orient Air Service entries. 2 A-60+s also with High Degree (ICARUS) in the USA. 14th airship was inflated in April 1997 at Lakehurst, USA; No 15 and No 16 have since been built.
Crew/Passengers: Pilot and 3 or 4 passengers for A-60+. 1 or 2 pilots (optional dual controls) plus 3 other persons for SPECTOR™ 19. 7 ground crew for routine operations.
Gondola: Enclosed, of aluminium and fabric covered steel. Internal sizes: length 8 ft 10 ins (2.7 m) overall, average width 5 ft (1.52 m), height 6 ft 4 ins (1.93 m). Single pilot controls. King Silver Crown avionics in SPECTOR™ 19, including Apollo 820 GPS. Options include stormscope, ADF and APU. Mission equipment for SPECTOR™ 19 includes possible maritime surface search radar, FLIR and more.
Length: 128 ft (39 m)
Diameter: 33 ft (10.1 m) envelope
Width overall: 36 ft (11 m)
Height: 44 ft (13.4 m)
Envelope: Laminate of polyester material, mylar film, and proprietary urethane films and adhesives, with a Tedlar film™ to provide good UV protection. Heat-bonded seams. Unique external catenary suspension system that eliminates need for a complex internal suspension system and expensive gas tight fittings and bellow sleeves. It also enables the airship to be deflated and reinflated with relative ease for quick operations deployment. Twin pressure relief helium valves on lower envelope to prevent overpressure in an emergency. Top-mounted manoeuvring valve is provided for use in the event of a free ballooning condition. *Volume* 68,000 cu ft (1,926 m^3). Internal illumination of banner signs; an A-60+ has flown with a computer-controlled lightbulb lightsign. 2 side advertising banners 90 ft × 22 ft (27.43 m × 6.7 m) each, plus a belly banner 20 ft × 20 ft (6.1 m × 6.1 m). Minimum airship operating area, approximately a circle 6 ship lengths in diameter.
Ballonet: Single, centre-mounted. 20% of envelope volume, at 13,600 cu ft (385 m^3). Airflow to ballonet established by conventional means via air scoops, plenum chamber and ballonet. Airflow controlled with damper check valves and pressure is regulated by pre-set valve.
Ballast: Small compartment in nose dish, usually for 25 lb (11 kg) in normal conditions to establish the optimum angle of -2°.
Fineness ratio: 3.8:1
Gross buoyancy: 4,144 lb (1,880 kg) for A-60+
Maximum static heaviness/lightness: both 250 lb (113.4 kg)
Gross useful lift: 1,364 lb (618.7 kg) standard, at 2,500 ft (760 m) for A-60+. 1,500 lb (680 kg) for SPECTOR™ 19.
Maximum gross weight: 4,394 lb (1,993 kg)
Empty weight: 2,935 lb (1,331 kg) operating
Payload: 425 lb (193 kg) with pilot, 8 hours fuel, at 3,280 ft (1,000 m), 35° C for SPECTOR™ 19.
Engines: 2 Limbach L 2000 piston engines, each 80 hp (59.6 kW), mounted on outriggers from the gondola; no vectoring.
Propellers: 4 ft 11 ins (1.49 m) diameter MT 2-blade fixed-pitch pusher propellers.
Fuel: 280 litres
Electrical system: 2 alternators, each 28 V, 35 amp.
Stabilizers: Cruciform tail fins with elevators and rudders. Fabric-covered aluminium. For SPECTOR™ 19, rotational clearance at take-off is 9°.
Maximum airspeed: 46 kts (53 mph) 85 km/h
Cruise speed: 35 kts (40 mph) 64 km/h
Maximum climb rate: 1,660 ft (506 m) per minute for A-60+, 1,600 ft (488 m) per minute for SPECTOR™ 19.
Maximum rate of descent: 1,400 ft (427 m) per minute
Ceiling: 10,000 ft (3,050 m) service

↑ American Blimp Corporation A-60+ Lightship No 11 operated by The Lightship Group *(Lightship Group)*

Take-off distance: 366 ft (112 m) or more
Range: 521 naut miles (600 miles) 966 km at 35 kts for SPECTOR™ 19.
Duration: 15 hours at 25 kts

ABC A-130 Lightship and SPECTOR™ 36

First flight: 1996 for A-130.
Role: Non-rigid helium airship. General uses similar to those for A-60+ and SPECTOR™ 19 but with greater accommodation from use of larger gondola.

Details (mainly based on SPECTOR™ 36 data)

Crew/Passengers: Pilot and 9 passengers (or 2 pilots plus 8) in a lengthened version of the A-60+ gondola, with identical pilot station. SPECTOR™ 36 can have a crew of 3 to 9. 11 ground crew for routine operations.
Gondola: Fabric-covered steel. Internal sizes: length 15 ft 8 ins (4.8 m), average width 5 ft (1.5 m), height 6 ft 4 ins (1.93 m). Mission equipment for SPECTOR™ includes possible maritime surface search radar, weather radar, autopilot, FLIR and more.
Length: 158 ft (48.2 m)
Diameter: 41 ft (12.5 m) envelope
Width overall: 45 ft (13.7 m)
Height: 54 ft (16.45 m)
Envelope: Construction as given for A-60+. *Volume* 130,000 cu ft (3,681 m^3).
Ballonet: Single, centre-mounted. 26% of envelope volume.
Fineness ratio: 3.8:1
Maximum gross weight: 8,397 lb (3,809 kg)
Weight empty: 5,388 lb (2,444 kg) total
Payload: 1,406 lb (638 kg) at 1,640 ft (500 m), 25° C
Engines: 2 Textron Lycoming IO-360 piston engines, each 180 hp (134 kW).
Propellers: 5 ft 6 ins (1.68 m) diameter MT 5-blade constant-speed, reversible pitch tractor propellers.
Fuel: 568 litres.
Electrical system: 2 alternators, each 28 V, 90 amp. More alternators may be added.
Maximum airspeed: 52 kts (60 mph) 96 km/h
Maximum climb rate: 1,600 ft (488 m) per minute
Maximum rate of descent: 1,400 ft (427 m) per minute
Ceiling: 10,000 ft (3,050 m) service
Range: 565 naut miles (650 miles) 1,046 km at 35 kts
Duration: 16 hours at 25 kts

ABC A-150 Lightship and SPECTOR™ 42

First flight: 8 January 1997. FAA certification received 3 October 1997.
Role: Non-rigid helium airship. General uses similar to those for A-130 and SPECTOR™ 36.

Details

Sales: The Lightship Group (see UK) received in July 1997 provisional certification for the first of the new A-150 Lightship airships, and plans to field a fleet of 12 A-150s within 5 years.
Details: Mainly based on SPECTOR™ 42 data. Details generally similar to A-130/ SPECTOR™ 36 except as follows.

Length: 165 ft (50.3 m)
Diameter: 43 ft (13.1 m) envelope
Width overall: 46 ft (14 m)
Height: 55 ft (16.76 m)
Envelope: *Volume* 148,300 cu ft (4,200 m^3)
Ballonet: Single, centre-mounted. 26% of envelope volume, as 38,558 cu ft (1,092 m^3).
Ballast: Water trim system, pumping water from the main gondola tank to the nose tank.
Fineness ratio: 3.8:1
Maximum static heaviness/lightness: 750/450 lb (340/204 kg)
Maximum gross weight: 9,689 lb (4,395 kg)
Weight empty: 5,532 lb (2,509 kg) total, 5,852 lb (2,654 kg) operating
Payload: 2,242 lb (1,017 kg) at 1,640 ft (500 m), 25° C
Range: 534 naut miles (615 miles) 988 km at 35 kts
Duration: 15 hours at 25 kts

ABC A-170 Lightship and SPECTOR™ 48

Role: Non-rigid helium airship. General uses similar to those for A-130 and SPECTOR™ 36.

Details
(mainly based on SPECTOR™ 48. Details generally similar to A-150/ SPECTOR™ 42 except as follows.)

Length: 172 ft (52.5 m)
Diameter: 45 ft (13.7 m) envelope
Width overall: 48 ft (14.63 m)
Height: 57 ft (17.4 m)
Envelope: *Volume* 170,000 cu ft (4,814 m^3)
Maximum gross weight: 10,981 lb (4,981 kg)
Weight empty: 5,670 lb (2,572 kg) total
Payload: 3,486 lb (1,581 kg) at 1,640 ft (500 m), 25° C
Maximum climb rate: 1,600 ft (488 m) per minute
Range: 504 naut miles (580 miles) 933 km at 35 kts
Duration: 14 hours at 25 kts

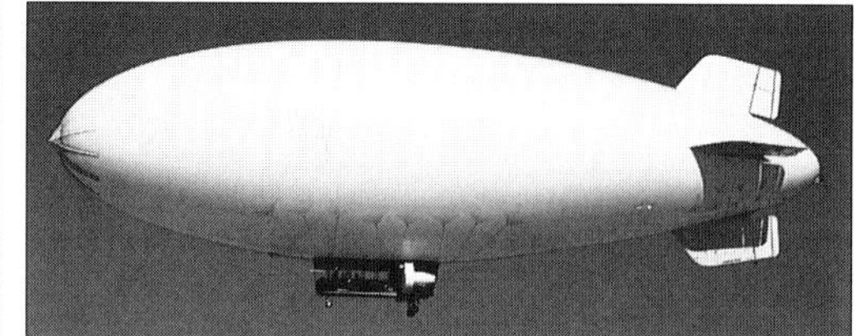

↑ American Blimp Corporation A-150 Lightship during its first flight in 1997

↑ American Blimp Corporation A-150 Lightship interior

Arizona Skyboat — USA

Corporate address: Withheld on request.
Information: Jörg Bracher.

ACTIVITIES

■ Currently (at the time of writing) in the construction phase of a small experimental, rigid, helium airship for 2 persons. Building began in September 1997 and completion is expected in 1999. A suitable engine is being sought.

Barnes Airships — USA

Corporate address: Route 2, Box 86, Statesville, NC 28677.
Telephone: +1 704 876 2378 **Facsimile:** +1 704 876 1251
Information: Tracy Barnes (Director).

Barnes Whispership

First flight: 1991.
Role: Non-rigid, experimental airship.

Aims

■ Low noise and low power requirement.

Details

Crew/Passengers: Pilot and passenger in a gondola with a float.
Length: 56 ft (17.1 m)
Diameter: 19 ft (5.8 m)
Height: 23 ft (7 m) overall
Envelope: 12,000 cu ft (340 m^3)
Fineness ratio: 2.94:1
Gross lift: 603 lb (273.5 kg)
Empty weight: 304 lb (138 kg)
Engine: 5 hp (3.7 kW) piston engine.
Fuel: Standard capacity can be increased to extend duration.
Maximum airspeed: 28 kts (32 mph) 51.5 km/h
Cruise speed: 22 kts (25 mph) 40 km/h
Ceiling: 3,000 ft (914 m)
Duration: 10 hours normal at cruise speed.

Bosch Aerospace, Inc – Airship Group — USA

Corporate address: 7501 South Memorial Parkway, Suite 207, Huntsville, AL 35802-2226.
Telephone: +1 205 882 9394 **Facsimile:** +1 205 883 2951 **E-mail:** jboschma@delphi.com
Information: Jack Randel or James H. Boschma (Technical Director).

ACTIVITIES

■ Headquartered near the Marshall Space Flight Center. Engaged in the research, design, development, testing and manufacture of a wide range of aircraft and products related to aircraft and space flight.
■ Corporate capabilities include projects and products related to fixed-wing aircraft, helicopters, lighter-than-air vehicles, space flight and unmanned air and ground vehicles.
■ Bosch Aerospace Airship Group designs, develops, tests and manufactures manned and unmanned lighter-than-air craft. Primary products are SASS LITE class blimp and the AutoBlimp™.

Bosch Aerospace SASS LITE class

Role: Unmanned remotely-piloted airship, to provide a stable platform for cameras, infrared detectors, radar and other surveillance devices. Said to be ideal for a variety of military, police, disaster, border surveillance, and search & rescue applications.

Aims

■ Typical lengths range from 50 to 100 ft (15.25 to 30.5 m) and a payload capacity of 500 lb (227 kg) or more.
■ Controlled via military hardened data links. All monitoring and flight control equipment is either placed in a mobile vehicle or communication shelter.
■ Range of mounting points may be used to accommodate multiple still and gyro-stabilized video cameras. Easy payload change.
■ Can provide long-duration day or night flights.
■ Capable of autonomous or radio-controlled flight with a non-relay control range of 54 naut miles (62 miles) 100 km. Digital autopilot offers autonomous flight, 100 GPS waypoints, programmable climb and descent rates, and automated switching for hand-off to backup data links in the event of lost communications.
■ 6,000 ft (1,830 m) ceiling, low IR, radar and noise signature provide covert surveillance.
■ Easily transported.
■ Uses lightweight mooring mast with a special articulated coupler. Secure mooring in winds up to 50 mph.
■ Can be internally illuminated for high visibility, serving to deter smugglers, criminals and others.

Development

■ Under development since 1988 with the US armed forces.

Details

Crew: 5 ground crew.
Gondola: Length 7 ft (2.13 m)
Length: 82 ft (25 m) typical

↑ Bosch SASS-LITE RPA

Diameter: 22 ft (6.7 m)
Envelope: *Volume* 22,000 cu ft (623 m^3)
Payload: 380 lb (172.3 kg)
Engine: 40 hp (30 kW) 4-stroke
Fuel: 57 litres
Maximum airspeed: 30 kts (35 mph) 56 km/h
Ceiling: 6,000 ft (1,830 m) above ground level
Duration: 8 hours at cruise

Bosch Aerospace AutoBlimp™

Role: Non-rigid, unmanned, remotely-piloted, helium airship, primarily to provide a stable camera platform for broadcasting.

Also suitable for advertising, public relations and other purposes.

Aims

- Lower operating costs than manned airships. Collapsible for relocation, and can be shipped by truck or air.
- Day or night operations.
- Control by a sophisticated and military hardened uplink.
- Interior lighting for advertising and promotional work.
- Capable of carrying the WESCAM range of gyro-stabilized broadcasting cameras, controlled via a microwave R/F link for live broadcasts.

Development

- Originally designed for the US armed forces.

Details

Gondola: Length 7 ft (2.13 m)
Length: 96 ft (29.26 m)
Diameter: 25 ft (7.62 m)
Envelope: *Volume* 30,282 cu ft (857.5 m^3). 2 advertising banners, each 21 ft × 61 ft (6.4 × 18.6 m).
Payload: 450 lb (204 kg)
Engine: 65 hp (48.5 kW) 4-stroke
Fuel: 136 litres
Maximum airspeed: 39 kts (45 mph) 72 km/h
Duration: 12 hours at cruise

Buoyant Copter, Inc (BCI) — USA

Corporate address:
1013 Talcon Drive, Wilmington, Delaware 19804.
Telephone: +1 302 421 9860
Facsimile: +1 302 421 9864
Information:
Mark J. Connor.

ACTIVITIES

- Buoyant Copter, Inc was established in 1991 to develop a hybrid airship, based upon a patented concept of company Vice-President, Robert L. Caufman. A small-scale 'proof-of-concept' demonstrator is under construction as the Model 18 (18 ft, 5.5 m diameter), while any future full-size craft could fulfil many roles, including heavy lift with a payload exceeding 100 tons.

The patented concept is based upon a mainly spherical helium aerostat, which provides sufficient lift to carry the entire craft and the majority of the slung payload. Around the circumference of the aerostat is carried a large horizontal 'ring', on which is mounted 4 sets of wings, fins and engines. The ring is braced to the extremities of a vertical mast that passes through the aerostat. A ventral gondola is also suspended from the mast. The wings have cyclic and collective movement and the fins have cyclic movement. When under power of the engines, the ring is free to rotate about the axis of the aerostat at approximately 80 revolutions per minute, combining with the aerodynamic effect of the surfaces to provide the remainder of the lift and directional control.

Funding was being sought at the time of writing to continue development; BCI wishes no further information to be published at the present time.

Global Skyship Industries, Inc – GSI — USA

Corporate address:
1001 Armstrong Blvd, Unit A, Kissimmee, Florida 34741.
Telephone: +1 407 932 3779
Facsimile: +1 407 932 2916
Information:
Gary Burns.

ACTIVITIES

- On 12 December 1996, Aviation Support Group Ltd purchased Westinghouse Airships, Inc, and Westinghouse Surveillance Systems, Ltd, from Westinghouse Electric Corporation. These companies were renamed Global Skyship Industries, Inc, and Global Skyship Industries, Ltd.
- Today Global Skyship Industries is the Type Certificate holder of the Skyship 500HL, 600 and 600B, Sentinel S1000 and Sentinel S1240.
- Global Skyship Industries, and its sister company, Airship Operations, Inc, own and operate airships for commercial advertising, military and government applications.

Global Skyship Industries Skyship 500HL

First flight: 30 July 1987.
Role: Non-rigid helium airship.

Aims

- Greater lift capability than Skyship 500.

Development

- 2 airships, based on the former Airship Industries Skyship 500 but modified to incorporate the larger Skyship 600 envelope to increase load under hot and high conditions, and also with gondola changes.

Details

Crew/Passengers: 1 or 2 pilots in an enclosed composites gondola.
Length: 193 ft 7 ins (59 m)
Diameter: 49 ft 10 ins (15.2 m)
Height: 66 ft 7 ins (20.3 m) overall
Envelope: Aerazur-manufactured envelope of 1-ply polyester fabric, with a polyurethane/titanium dioxide outer coating against UL deterioration, and with a polyvinylidene chloride inner film attached with polyurethane. *Volume* 235,000 cu ft (6,654 m^3). Composites nose dome with mooring attachments.
Ballonets: 2, 26% of envelope volume.
Ballast: Water ballast in tanks and non-disposable ballast beneath seats in containers.
Disposable load: 3,120 lb (1,415 kg) maximum structural. An extra 1,191 lb (540 kg) can be carried (envelope mounted only). Typical disposable load comprises crew and basics 1,000 lb (453.5 kg), mission avionics 1,570 lb (712 kg), and fuel 550 lb (249.5 kg) at cruise altitude.
Engines: 2 Porsche 930/10 piston engines, each 204 hp (152.1 kW).
Propellers: 5-blade propulsors in shrouds, able to vector vertically for near V/STOL and hovering flight.
Fuel: 842 lb (382 kg) maximum usable capacity.
Electrical load: 10 kW
Stabilizers: Cruciform tail with elevators and rudders, of composites construction.
Maximum airspeed: 55 kts (63 mph) 102 km/h
Cruise speed: 35 kts (40 mph) 65 km/h, economical
Cruise altitude: 3,000-5,000 ft (915-1,525 m)
Ceiling: 8,000 ft (2,440 m)
Duration: 8 hours without reballasting or refuelling, allowing 20% reserves.

Global Skyship Industries Skyship 600 and 600B

First Flight: 6 March 1984 for 600, and June 1996 for 600B (certification with TCOM Tedlar laminate envelope).
Role: Non-rigid helium airship for surveillance, border patrol, interdiction, crowd control, police, training, and limited military tasks including command/control/communications.

Development

- 1 September 1984. CAA Certificate of Airworthiness gained.
- 8 January 1987. C of A for passenger carrying gained.
- 1987-88. Skycruise sight-seeing flights undertaken in Europe, Australia and USA.
- 1989. FAA type certificate gained in the USA, the first ever for a commercial airship.
- 15 September 1993. First flight of the first Skyship 600 in UK military service (*ZH762*) after receiving a new envelope.
- August 1994. *ZH762* (see above) handed to UK MoD's Flight Test Evaluation Centre at Boscombe Down.

Details

Crew/Passengers: 2 pilots plus up to 13 passengers in an enclosed composites gondola or mission equipment.
Gondola: Length overall 38 ft 4 ins (11.68 m), width overall 8 ft 5 ins (2.56 m), main cabin length 22 ft 7 ins (6.88 m), main cabin headroom 6 ft 4 ins (1.92 m).
Length: 193 ft 7 ins (59 m)
Diameter: 49 ft 10 ins (15.2 m)
Height: 66 ft 7 ins (20.3 m) overall
Tailspan: 63 ft (19.2 m)
Envelope: Skyship 600: Aerazur-manufactured envelope of 1-ply polyester fabric, with a polyurethane/titanium dioxide outer coating against UL deterioration, and with a polyvinylidene chloride inner film attached with polyurethane. Skyship 600B: Tedlar laminate envelope. *Volume* 235,400 cu ft (6,666 m^3). Composites nose dome with mooring attachments.
Ballonets: 2, 26% of envelope volume.
Ballast: Water ballast in tanks and non-disposable ballast beneath seats in containers.
Lift/Drag ratio: 3.88
Disposable load: 3,625 lb (1,644 kg) maximum structural. Typical disposable load is 3,195 lb (1,449 kg), comprising 1,150 lb (521.5 kg) crew and basics, 1,200 lb (544 kg) mission avionics and 845 lb (383.5 kg) fuel at cruise altitude.
Engines: 2 Porsche 930/67 piston engines, each 255 hp (190.2 kW).
Propellers: 5-blade propulsors in shrouds, able to vector -90° and +120° vertically for near V/STOL and hovering flight.
Fuel: 1,067 lb (484 kg) maximum usable capacity.
Electrical load: 10 kW.
Stabilizers: 4 tail surfaces with elevators and rudders, of composites construction.
Maximum airspeed: 55 kts (63 mph) 102 km/h
Cruise speed: 35 kts (40 mph) 65 km/h, economical
Cruise altitude: 5,000 ft (1,525 m)
Duration: 10 hours without reballasting or refuelling, allowing 20% reserves.

↑ **GSI Skyship 600-01 over Cardington** *(A.W.L. Nayler)*

Global Skyship Industries Sentinel S1000

Note: The Sentinel S1000 was the world's largest airship when first flown on 26 June 1991, and was a one-half linear scale model of the Sentinel S5000. It was fitted with a GEC-Marconi fly-by-light (fibre optic) system to reduce potential electromagnetic influence to a minimum, thereby eliminating envelope wires and uncommanded control inputs caused by

electromagnetic interference. However, on 5 August 1995 it was destroyed in a hangar fire. Global is the Type Certificate holder for the S1000 and retains the design and manufacturing rights and could presumably construct further examples if required. An expanded description of the S1000 can be found in the 1996-97 edition of *WA&SD*.
Role: Non-rigid helium airship for airborne early warning, anti-air warfare (AAW), anti-surface warfare (ASUW) with highly sophisticated surface radars including inverse synthetic array systems, mine countermeasures, naval blockade, maritime patrol, fisheries protection, surveillance, policing, drug interdiction, command/control/communications, disaster communications, fire-watch patrol, and more. Commercial applications can include advertising and transportation.

Details

Crew: Total of 25 air/ground crew, including 2 pilots, mechanics, riggers, electricians and ground crew. Pilots operate the flight controls with modern side-stick controllers, and the autopilot provides full instrument flight capability.
Gondola: Length 38 ft 4 ins (11.68 m), width 8 ft 5 ins (2.57 m), headroom 6 ft 4 ins (1.93 m).
Length: 222 ft (67.67 m)
Diameter: 54 ft 9 ins (16.69 m)
Height: 66 ft 3 ins (20.16 m) overall
Envelope: Polyester synthetic with Tedlar outer film, impervious to UV radiation. Heat bonded seaming. *Volume* 353,146 cu ft (10,000 m^3).
Ballonets: Approximately 24% of envelope volume.
Disposable load: 8,715 lb (3,953 kg) maximum structural. Typical disposable load is 5,962 lb (2,704 kg).
Engines: 2 Porsche 930/67 piston engines, each 300 hp (224 kW).
Propellers: 5-blade propulsors in shrouds, able to vector -90° and +120° vertically for near V/STOL and hovering flight.
Fuel: AvGas 100LL. 2,498 lb (1,133 kg) maximum usable capacity.
Maximum airspeed: 60 kts (69 mph) 111 km/h
Cruise speed: 54 kts (62 mph) 100 km/h
Cruise altitude: 8,000 ft (2,440 m) maximum. Typical cruise altitude is 1,000-4,000 ft (305-1,220 m).
Duration: 18 hours without reballasting or refuelling, allowing 20% reserves. Easily capable of a 24 hour mission with auxiliary fuel.

Global Skyship Industries Sentinel S1240

First flight: Not yet flown.
Role: Similar to S1000 but with greater load capability.
Length: 238 ft (72.54 m)
Diameter: 59 ft (18 m)
Height: 70 ft 10 ins (21.6 m)
Envelope: *Volume* 438,000 cu ft (12,400 m^3)
Ballonets: 30% of envelope volume.
Disposable load: 12,282 lb (5,571 kg) maximum structural. Typical disposable load 7,501 lb (3,402 kg), comprising 1,150 lb (521.5 kg) crew and basics, 4,808 lb (2,180.5 kg) mission avionics and 1,543 lb (700 kg) fuel.
Engines: 2 Porsche 930 type piston engines, each 315 hp (235 kW), or possibly 300 hp (223.7 kW) Zoche diesel engines.
Propellers: Possibly 5-blade propulsors in shrouds, able to vector -90° and +120° vertically for near V/STOL and hovering flight.
Fuel: 2,498 lb (1,133 kg) maximum usable capacity.
Electrical load: 20 kW.
Maximum airspeed: 55 kts (63 mph) 102 km/h
Cruise speed: 35 kts (40 mph) 65 km/h, economical
Cruise altitude: 10,000 ft (3,050 m) maximum. Typical cruise altitude 8,000 ft (2,440 m).
Duration: 18 hours without reballasting or refuelling, allowing 20% reserves. Possible 32 hours with auxiliary fuel.

Global Skyship Industries Sentinel S5000

Note: The US Navy's Sentinel S5000 programme has been ended before completion of the prototype, though the technologies developed can be resurrected at any time should the need arise. The design review had been completed by 1994, whilst a Westinghouse programme. Global states that the first flight could be achieved 12 months from receipt of an order.
A full description and illustration of this non-rigid helium airship for AEW (military designation YEZ-2A) can be found in the 1996-97 edition of *WA&SD*.

Global Skyship Industries Sentinel/US Navy Projection

Development

▪ A US Navy design study projected a 25,000 lb (11,340 kg) airship (compared to 12,500 lb/5,670 kg for S5000) with a 3 million cu ft envelope capacity. No further progress at the present time.

Goodyear Airship Operations USA

Corporate address:
841 Wingfoot Lake Road, Mogadore, OH 44260.
Telephone: +1 330 796 7920 or 4100
Facsimile: +1 330 796 8399
Information:
Michael Wittman.

ACTIVITIES

▪ Goodyear airships are primarily for marketing and sales promotions for its parent Tire & Rubber Company. The organization continues to use its original and historically important airship hangar.
▪ Operates 3 airships: *Spirit of Akron* based near the corporate headquarters in Ohio; *Stars & Stripes* based at Pompano Beach, Florida; and *Eagle* based in Carson, California.
▪ The last airship designed and engineered by Goodyear (but completed by Loral Defense Systems – Akron) was the turboprop-powered GZ-22 *Spirit of Akron*, launched in 1989. However, Goodyear has not been in the airship manufacturing business since the latter 1980s, having sold its rights to Loral Defense Systems – Akron in 1987 (now Lockheed Martin). Goodyear continues to carry out repair and rebuild work, and was in late 1997 in the process of fitting a new envelope (prepared at Engineered Fabrics in Georgia) to *Stars & Stripes*, which is also to have a new car and fins (a name change is thereafter possible but unconfirmed). The other 2 airships are rebuilt GZ-20s.

Lockheed Martin USA

Corporate address:
See Combat section.
Information:
Ron Browning.

ACTIVITIES

▪ Lockheed Martin now holds the Type Certificates to former Goodyear airships.

Lockheed Martin GZ-22

First flight: 1989.
Role: Helium airship for advertising, promotional and broadcasting work.

Development

▪ See Goodyear entry.

Details

Crew/Passengers: Pilot and 6 passengers in a steel framed and composites skinned (honeycomb-shaped non-metallic aramid paper/resin and impregnated aramid fibre woven cloth) gondola, with a retractable undercarriage.
Length: 205 ft 6 ins (62.64 m)
Width: 47 ft (14.33 m)
Height: 60 ft 2 ins (18.34 m)
Envelope: Neoprene-impregnated polyester 2-ply fabric. *Volume* 247,800 cu ft (7,017 m^3). 8,064 Night Sign lights.
Gross weight: 15,000 lb (6,804 kg) maximum
Engines: 2 Allison 250-B17C turboprops, each 420 shp (313.2 kW).
Propellers: 2 Hartzell 3-blade propellers, each 5 ft 10 ins (1.78 m), vectorable +75° and -30°.
Stabilizers: X configuration. Aluminium alloy structure covered with heat shrinkable polyester fabric and coated with polyurethane paint.
Maximum airspeed: 56 kts (65 mph) 105 km/h
Cruise speed: 26-35 kts (30-40 mph) 48-64 km/h
Ceiling: 10,000 ft (3,050 m)
Operating altitude: 1,000-3,000 ft (305-915 m)

Interface Airships Inc USA

Corporate address:
PO Box 317, 780 Terra Ceia Road, Terra Ceia, FL 34250.
Telephone: +1 941 723 0955
Information:
Brad Weigle.

ACTIVITIES

▪ Developed for oceanographic research off the coast of Florida, in association with the Florida Institute of Oceanography. Carried GIS, video, GPS and other equipment.

Interface Airships EcoBlimp (*N9243S*)

Role: Helium airship for oceanographic research.

Aims

▪ Concept of design, etc.

Development

▪ Reportedly developed from 1994 and flown for about 100 hours before being deflated, pending a decision on its future.

Details

Crew: 1 pilot and 1 passenger.
Length: 87 ft (26.52 m)
Diameter: 24 ft (7.32 m)
Envelope: Constructed of 6.5 oz urethane/HT nylon, with titanium dioxide/urethane UV protection. *Volume* 28,000 cu ft (792.9 m^3).
Payload: 850 lb (386 kg)
Engines: 2 Konig SC 430 engines, each 23 hp (17.2 kW).
Maximum airspeed: 43 kts (50 mph) 80 km/h
Cruise speed: 26 kts (30 mph) 48 km/h
Duration: 8 hours

L.T.A.S. Corp

USA

Corporate address:
2700 Royal Court, North Las Vegas, NV 89030.
Telephone: +1 702 642 1847
Web site:
http://www.nevada.edu/home/8/walden/NEWHOME.HTML
Information:
Michael K. Walden (CEO).

ACTIVITIES

■ First developments initiated in 1967, beginning with the exploration Scout Craft using gas-filled wing technologies.
■ Mr Walden holds a number of patents in the LTA field, including the Density Control Buoyancy unit that allows an LTA vehicle to land and take-off without venting gas or carrying ballast, and to remain on the ground without ground crew or mooring mast.
■ Continues to design and develop revolutionary airships, with monocoque geodesically ribbed rigid hulls and of lenticular design. Primarily solar powered for extended range and with silent electric thruster propulsion system.
■ In addition to the 30-XB (detailed below) and the Tourer-90, other designs include the 80 ft (24.4 m) diameter 80-AV audio/video (multimedia) unit with a 6,000 lb (2,721 kg) gross lift, and the L.T.A.S. 222 patrol ship. The Tourer-90 differs from the patrol ship (and its larger related cargo carrier and logger counterparts) in that its Density Control System (DCS or DCB) is designed around a large low pressure tank that permits the use of standard high volume compressors which allow the hull system to run on zero super pressure. This permits a thinner hull. The craft will use the company's patented geodesic panel construction.
■ Patented "L.T.A.S. type airships and major systems" were classified by the US DoD after a demonstration of the XEM-1 model rigid-hull airship's capabilities at Nellis AFB in August 1977.
■ In addition to line and remote control models, L.T.A.S. has designed, built and flown since 1989 a series of full-scale manned craft, in co-operation with SPACIAL of Mexico.
■ In 1997, under the "Canopy Trek" programme, Stanford University constructed under license a set of 6 small ultralight craft for use in an expedition over the Brazilian rainforests. The first test craft was demonstrated on 20 September 1997.
■ Patents also cover the "Ionic airflow engine" and more "exotic" versions of the craft. Extreme altitude and speed are possible with these technologies.
■ In addition to commercial applications, uses for the technologies include the Sub Orbital Solar collector and Communications Station (SOSCS) for geostationary positioning, having a 600-900 ft (183-274 m) diameter and 10-20 year operational life, the Sub Orbital Launch Device (SOLD), and a hypersonic SSTO design. The SOSCS Alpha unit handles 1,000,000 calls simultaneously, and Beta 10,000,000. Uses 10 megawatt photovoltaic arrays.

L.T.A.S. Corp 30-XB

First flight: Not thought to have flown at the time of writing.
Role: Proof-of-concept production prototype, solar-powered rigid airship. After trials, could be used for advertising, patrol, as a monitoring station, for fire spotting, resource management using multimedia pod with cameras and microphones, and more.

Aims

■ To demonstrate all patented design features.
■ Incorporates the latest off-the-shelf composite materials and component parts.
■ To prove itself at minimum cost, by limiting payload to 800 lb.
■ Full multi-axis-control vectored thrust (using electric motors and large diameter, slow turning prop fans), eliminating the need for fins or other aerodynamic surfaces. Landing and take-off can safely be made in winds of up to about 80% of cruise speed.
■ Pitch, yaw and roll actively controlled by the vectoring propellers/motor units. Pitch and roll are also dampened by incorporating 'pendulum' stability, accomplished by mounting almost 50% of the airship's weight at a third of the span below the centre of buoyancy.
■ Online Internet weather system and GPS navigation.

Development

■ 1995. Designed to take part in the Airborne Solar Challenge Solar Airship race.

Details

Crew/Passengers: 2 or 3 persons.
Cockpit: 10 ft (3.05 m) diameter, 7 ft (2.13 m) height
Diameter: 45-50 ft (13.72-15.24 m)
Height: 28-32 ft (8.53-9.75 m)
Envelope: Hull construction panels are light, strong and rigid, allowing constant volume during changes in atmospheric conditions, DCB pressure and/or the percentage of helium fill.
Ballonet/s: *Volume* 60% of hull.
Gross buoyancy: 3,600 lb (1,633 kg) at 10,000 ft
Empty weight: 2,800 lb (1,270 kg)
Payload: 600-800 lb (272-363 kg)
Maximum airspeed: 33-35 kts (38-40 mph) 61-64 km/h
Design altitude: 10,000 ft (3,050 m)
Range: Unlimited

L.T.A.S. Corp Tourer-90

Role: 120 ft (36.6 m) diameter, 350,000 cu ft (9,910 m^3), sightseeing airship based on 30-XB technologies, with an 8,000 lb (3,628 kg) payload.

Aims

■ Designed at a customer's request.
■ Intended to be the first man rated version of the company's craft built in the USA.
■ 24 passengers, 12 ft (3.66 m) high cabin ceilings and 360° viewing. Top speed 69 kts (80 mph) 129 km/h.
■ 2 × 300 hp (224 kW) and 4 × 100 hp (74.6 kW) engines.
■ Total cost of the Tourer-90 scaling demonstrator programme is said to be US$5.5 million.

↑ L.T.A.S. Corp 30-XB solar, rigid airship

SkyRider Airships, Inc

USA

Corporate address:
505 Stacy Court, Lafayette, CO 80026-2799.
Telephone: +1 303 644 1122
Facsimile: +1 303 664 1133
E-mail: rider@boulderblimp.com
Information:
Frank E. Rider (President).

ACTIVITIES

■ Has 20 years experience in the design, manufacture and operation of small helium airships in several countries. Currently available for consultancy in the construction or purchase of airships, set-up and management of airship operations, and pilot training.
■ Related organization, Boulder Blimp Company, manufactures giant inflatables for advertising and promotion.

Sky Station International, Inc

USA

Corporate address:
1824 R Street, NW Washington, DC 20009-1604.
Telephone: +1 202 518 0900
Facsimile: +1 202 518 0802
Web site: http://www.skystation.com/news/FCC-STS.htm
Information:
Liza C. Kupczak.

ACTIVITIES

■ Recently formed to implement a revolutionary stratospheric telecommunications service, using geostationary lighter-than-air platforms located in the stratosphere instead of satellite relays. The platforms will form the mainstay of a global broadband Internet transmission system. The company is funding the technical regulation and business implementation of such platforms using proprietary technologies it has developed. Communications payloads are being produced by Alenia of Italy.

TCOM LP

USA

Corporate address:
7115 Thomas Edison Drive, Columbia, Maryland 21046.
Telephone: +1 410 312 2300
Facsimile: +1 410 312 2455
Information:
Eric Schwartz (Marketing).

ACTIVITIES

■ Builds non-rigid, helium-filled aerostats used mainly as tethered radar or camera platforms for airborne tracking and surveillance. A principal operator is the US Customs Service, while South Korea has been an important overseas customer. The Israeli Air Force has used a TCOM AEW aerostat carrying a Westinghouse radar for long-range surveillance. Deployment in southern Israel began in 1991.
■ TCOM's range includes the 71M® of 233 ft (71 m) length and approximately 365,000 cu ft (10,336 m^3) volume, capable of carrying payloads of 3,500 lb (1,600 kg) to an altitude of 15,000 ft (4,600 m); the 32M® of 105 ft (32 m) length and 60,000 cu ft (1,700 m^3) volume, capable of a 880 lb (400 kg) maximum payload or half this to an altitude of 4,500 ft (1,400 m); and the smaller 49 ft (15 m) length 15M™ of approximately 10,000 cu ft (285 m^3) volume, capable of a 154 lb (70 kg) payload and for

deployment in some 1.5 hours to an operating altitude of about 1,000 ft (300 m). The smaller aerostats are transportable, and can be operated from land vehicles, ships and other platforms.

↑ TCOM 32M® aerostat in a sea-based configuration

James Thompson — USA

Address:
854 Starks Building, Louisville, KY 40202.

Telephone: +1 502 582 9391
Facsimile: +1 502 582 9390

James Thompson *N99TW*

First flight: 20 August 1995 at Tillamook, OR.
Role: Non-rigid helium airship, built as a one-off homebuilt.

Development

- First inflated at Tillamook, Oregon, on 30 June 1994.
- First few flying hours have found the airship responsive and nimble, easy and fun to fly.

Details

Crew/Passengers: 2 persons in a steel tube and composites, cable-suspended, gondola.
Length: 82 ft (25 m)
Diameter: 26 ft (7.92 m)
Envelope: *Volume* 28,000 cu ft (792.87 m^3), including ballonets.
Fineness ratio: 3.15:1
Ballonets: 2, each 2,000 cu ft (56.63 m^3) air capacity, providing pitch trim. Maximum combined capacity 3,456 cu ft (97.86 m^3).
Take-off weight: 1,534 lb (695.8 kg) estimated
Ballast: 180 lb (81.65 kg) of lead shot or sand.
Engine: 1,200 cc Honda liquid-cooled piston engine, with belt reduction drive.
Propeller: Fixed-pitch wooden propeller in a shroud.
Stabilizers: 3 aluminium alloy tube/fabric fins, in inverted Y configuration, each with a movable control surface.
Maximum airspeed: 35 kts (40 mph) 65 km/h expected
Ceiling: 4,000 ft (1,220 m) expected

↑ James Thompson *N99TW* helium homebuilt airship

Ulita Industries Inc — USA

Corporate address:
PO Box 512, Sheboygan, WI 53082-0412.

Information:
Mark Forss (President).

ACTIVITIES

- Has designed and manufactured balloons, the UM10-23 Cloud Cruiser airship and fabrics.
- Details of Cloud Cruiser can be found in the 1996-97 edition of *WA&SD*.

University of Virginia — USA

Address:
UVA Solar Airship Program, University of Virginia, Thornton Hall, Charlottesville, VA 22903-7426.

Telephone: +1 804 924 4425
Facsimile: +1 804 982 2037
E-mail: nlm8f@virginia.edu

Information:
Nayana Mallikarjun (Business Team Representative).

ACTIVITIES

- On 5 May 1996, students at the University of Virginia flew their helium remotely-piloted airship *Dunkin*, 32 ft 10 ins (10 m) in length, 13 ft (3.96 m) wide and 8 ft (2.44 m) high, powered by 2 Astro Cobalt 60 electric motors using 3 12V/17 amp-hour lead-acid batteries. This was the first and smallest of several planned radio-controlled airships to be completed in the quest to develop a solar-powered airship for 24-hour and autonomous flying.
- *Aztec* is the second development airship, this time having solar power. It is 59 ft (18 m) in length. A much smaller solar-powered craft is *Inca* of 1997 completion.
- The next airship, an 82 ft (25 m) craft named *Sunjammer*, will appear in 1999.
- Technical and sponsor assistance has come from many companies and organizations, including Bosch Aerospace, Lockheed Martin and TCOM LP.

↑ University of Virginia *Dunkin*

UPship Corporation — USA

Corporate address:
Rt 2, Box 53-4, Elba, AL 36323.

Telephone: +1 334 897 6132
Facsimile: +1 334 897 3434

Information:
Jesse Blenn (President and Chief Designer).

UPship 100

First flight: Not expected until 2000.
Role: Semi-rigid, helium homebuilt airship, intended to become a commercial venture.

Aims

- Advanced design stressing aerodynamic efficiency, full control at all speeds, and passenger comfort.
- Shape of minimum resistance, with propulsion engines in inverted 'V' tail fins and nose mounted thruster for control at all speeds.
- Ease of maintenance, with reduced dependence on internal pressure.
- No-ground-crew mooring capability.
- Test bed for innovations in later airships of all sizes.
- To be the most economical and useful airship available, priced at US$300,000 or less for the certified version.

Development

- Design began in 1989 and has been completed.
- Company Incorporated in 1996.
- Land clearing for landing area and access road underway in 1997.
- 2 US patents pending; others to follow on design innovations.
- Construction of the UPship 100-001 prototype is expected to start in 1998 and take 2 years.
- Venture capital is being sought.

Details

Crew/Passengers: Pilot and 1 passenger, in tandem.
Gondola: Cabin length 16 ft 5 ins (5 m) and width 3 ft 3 ins (1 m).
Length: 105 ft (32 m)
Diameter: 21 ft (6.4 m)
Height: 26 ft 3 ins (8 m)
Envelope: Minimal full-length lower framework; envelope of rip-stop laminate, with 3 helium cells; and internal suspension. *Volume* over 22,250 cu ft (630 m^3). Helium fill at 87.3% is 19,425 cu ft (550 m^3).
Ballonet: 2, comprising 28.6% of envelope volume, at 6,300 cu ft (180 m^3).
Gross lift: 1,213 lb (550 kg)
Empty weight: 728 lb (330 kg)
Useful lift: 485 lb (220 kg)
Additional thruster lift: 165 lb (75 kg)
Engines: 3 Konig SC 430 2-stroke piston engines, each 24 hp (17.9 kW), with reduction drive; 2 operate at the tail and 1 the bow thruster. See Stabilizers.
Propellers: 4 ft 11 ins (1.5 m) diameter
Fuel: 91 litres
Stabilizers: Inverted V twin fins with active control surfaces. Carbonfibre/balsawood construction, with polyester skins. Stick-operated pitch and yaw control by variable-camber ruddervators in the propeller slipstream, with aerodynamic assist; foot pedal control of bow thruster for low speed control and heavy lifting. Tail fin area 215.3 sq ft (20 m^2).
Maximum airspeed: 60 kts (69 mph) 111 km/h
Cruise speed: 47 kts (54.5 mph) 88 km/h at 50% power, 37 kts (43 mph) 69 km/h at 25% power.
Ceiling: 3,280 ft (1,000 m) normal, 9,840 ft (3,000 m) maximum.
Range: 284 naut miles (327 miles) 526 km normal, 448 naut miles (516 miles) 830 km extended.
Duration: 6 hours normal, 12 hours extended.

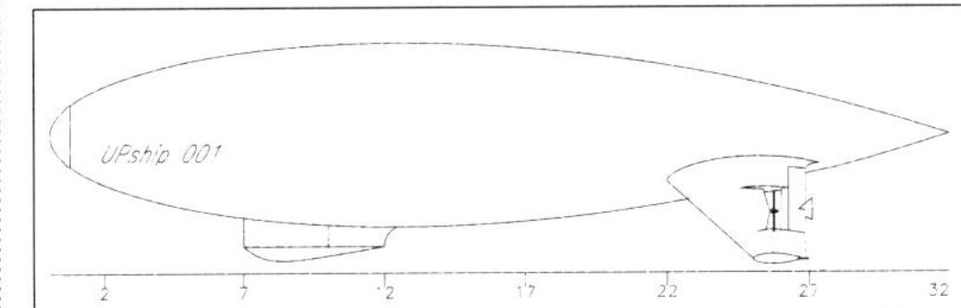

↑ General arrangement of the UPship 100-001 2-seat airship

US-LTA Corporation — USA

Corporate address (US):
750 Commercial Street, Eugene, OR 97402.

Telephone: +1 541 343 1334
Facsimile: +1 541 342 3806
E-mail: jolma@inwavecorp.com

Information:
Joe Olma (Vice-President).

Facilities

- US-LTA is a Canadian owned company, registered as a US corporation. The Corporate office is at 1160 Skana Drive, Delta, BC, V4M 2L4, Canada. It is a division of Aerotech U.S. Inc.
- Engineering and Manufacturing is at Eugene.
- The airship is hangared and operated from Tillamook, OR.

ACTIVITIES

- Design, manufacture and operation of airships for commercial, civil and scientific uses worldwide.
- A longer version of 138-S for 9 persons was proposed as the **185-M**. Not yet built.

US-LTA 138-S

First flight: 28 October 1987.
Role: Non-rigid helium airship for advertising, research and pollution monitoring.

Development

- 24 July 1990. Certified by the FAA under Type Certificate AS2NM.
- Summer 1992. Prototype used for oceanographic research under short-term contract from the Naval Research Laboratory (NRL), with missions including suspending a 700 lb (317 kg) sled carrying research equipment while off the Pacific coast. Success led to further contracts from 1993 onwards.
- Further production undertaken.

Details

Crew/Passengers: Pilot and 5 passengers in a steel tube and composites gondola.
Gondola: Outer shell of glassfibre/foam laminate, attached to a welded tubular steel truss. Maximum gondola weight 5,356 lb (2,429 kg). Cabin length 13 ft 5 ins (4.09 m), maximum width 5 ft 10 ins (1.78 m), headroom 6 ft 4 ins (1.9 m). Single stick hydraulic boost flight controls. Day/night VFR.
Length: 160 ft (48.8 m)
Width: 41 ft 7 ins (12.67 m)
Height: 56 ft 8 ins (17.3 m) overall
Envelope: Advanced composite laminate envelope, of Dacron/polyurethane outer skin bonded with an internal non-woven material. Constructed of 41 individual fabric panels in each of 16 gores. *Volume* 138,000 cu ft (3,907.7 m^3). Internal and external catenary systems, the former supporting about 85% of the weight of the gondola. Air duct and electric blower, 2 inlet air valves and 2 outlet air valves. 22 ft × 60 ft (6.7 × 18.3 m) fibre optic nightsign.
Surface area: 16,787 sq ft (1,560 m^2).
Ballonets : 2 fore and aft, 26% of envelope volume.
Fineness ratio: 3.8:1
Ballast: 206 litres of water, or 1,000 lb (454 kg) of solid.
Operating ambient temperature: 49° maximum; 1° minimum using water ballast.
Maximum design gross weight: 9,300 lb (4,218 kg)
Maximum take-off weight: 8,900 lb (4,037 kg)
Empty weight: 5,900 lb (2,676 kg)
Maximum static heaviness: 400 lb (181 kg)
Maximum static lightness: 200 lb (91 kg)
Maximum useful load: 3,017 lb (1,368 kg) disposable
Maximum landing weight: 8,900 lb (4,037 kg)
Engine: 300 hp (224 kW) Textron Lycoming IO-540-K2A5 piston engine.
Propeller: Hartzell HC-E3YR-7LF 3-blade, Q-tip, reversible-pitch, pusher propeller in a shroud.
Fuel: 401 litres, of which 378 litres are usable.
Electrical system: 28 V, 100 amp negative ground type, powered by an engine-driven 100 amp alternator regulated to 80 amp continuous power. 24 V lead-acid battery for engine starting and emergency operation of essential equipment.
Stabilizers: 3 tailfins of aluminium/fabric, each with a ruddervator and tab, as an inverted 'Y', with 15° ground clearance. Total fin area 649.5 sq ft (60.3 m^2). Total ruddervator area 278.1 sq ft (25.8 m^2).
Pitch attitude: 30° maximum nose up/minimum nose down.
Maximum operating limit airspeed: 47 kts (54 mph) 87 km/h IAS
Maximim speed for water ballast drop: 30 kts (35 mph) 56 km/h IAS
Cruise speed: 30 kts (35 mph) 56 km/h, economical
Maximum climb rate: 1,800 ft (549 m) per minute
Maximum rate of descent: 2,000 ft (610 m) per minute
Operating altitude: 9,000 ft (2,750 m) maximum
Maximum range: 400 naut miles (460 miles) 741 km at 35 kts, estimated
Duration: 16 hours at 19 kts, estimated.

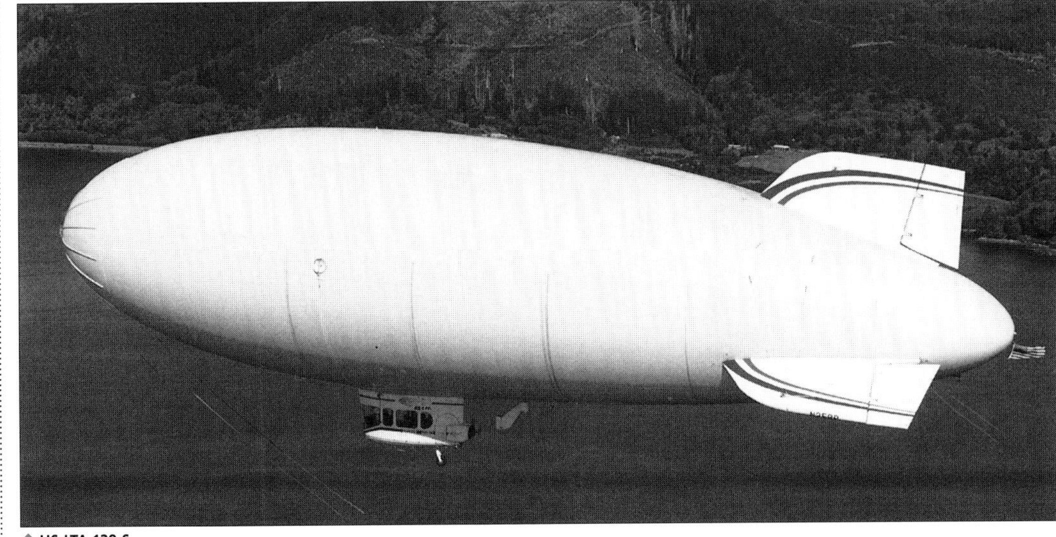

↑ US-LTA 138-S

Worldwide Aeros Corporation — USA

Corporate address:
9617 Canoga Avenue, Chatsworth, CA 91311.

Telephone: +1 818 993 5533
Facsimile: +1 818 993 9435

Information:
Igor Pasternak.

ACTIVITIES

- Designer and manufacturer of lighter-than-air craft.
- Producer of tethered aerostats used for advertising, ecological monitoring and surveillance.
- Developed tethered modular airborne air pollution control stations and systems for radiation monitoring, known as Guard. Used for transboundary air pollution monitoring at the border of Poland and the Ukraine and for radiation monitoring after the Chernobyl nuclear accident.
- Has branches in 6 countries and over 300 employees.
- **Aeros-20** and **Aeros-500** are no longer under development. The single **Aeros-50** is still thought to be flying (see the 1996-97 edition of *WA&SD* for details and a photograph). The D1 and D4 programmes are still under active development.
- Aeros-40 B and Aeros-40 C are in serial production.

↑ Aeros-25 M tethered aerostat system

Aeros-40 B

Role: Non-rigid, helium airship.

Aims

- Fly-by-wire control.

Details (apply to 40B-02)

Sales: First 2 production craft delivered to China.
Crew/Passengers: 2 persons.
Gondola: Enclosed, with reinforced frame of tubing.
Length: 122 ft 3 ins (37.25 m) overall, 120 ft 4 ins (36.7 m) envelope
Width over fins: 30 ft 9 ins (9.37 m)
Diameter: 31 ft 2 ins (9.487 m) envelope
Height: 38 ft 2 ins (11.625 m) overall
Envelope: Constructed of heat-sealed nylon-based fabric. Life of at least 4 years. 16 gores. *Volume* 60,035 cu ft (1,700 m^3). Pressurization system has disk valve with automatic action; forced manual opening and opening pressure adjustment possible; activation for open and lock pressure actuators. 2 helium valves. Nose cone for mooring.
Surface area: 9,381 sq ft (871.5 m^2).
Ballonets: 2 of air chamber type, fore and aft, representing 25% of envelope volume. *Volume* 7,487 cu ft (212 m^3) each. 4 air valves (2 each).
Ballast: water, 44-220 lb (20-100 kg).
Fineness ratio: 3.868:1
Engines: 2 Limbach L1700s, each 68 hp (50 kW).
Propellers: 2, each 4 ft 11 ins (1.5 m) 3-blade pusher.
Fuel: 87 litres basic model; 260 litres maximum fuel reserve.
Stabilizers: Rigid X-form. Fins each constructed as a 3-dimensional frame of alloy tubing, covered by waterproof fabric. Elevators and rudders have flat alloy tubing frame with similar covering. Root rib profile Göttingen 409.
Maximum airspeed: 40 kts (47 mph) 75 km/h

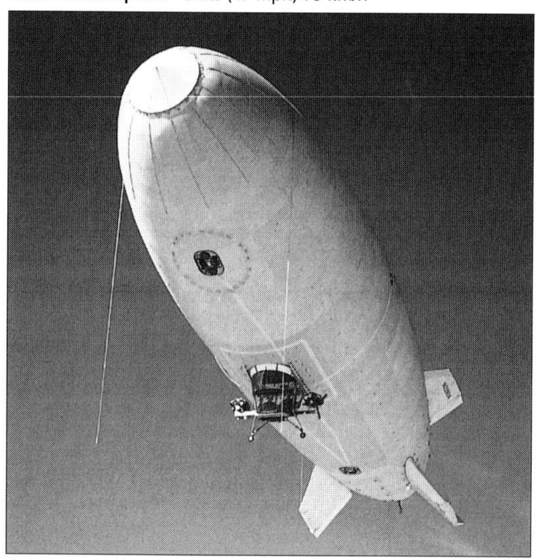

↑ Aeros-40 B

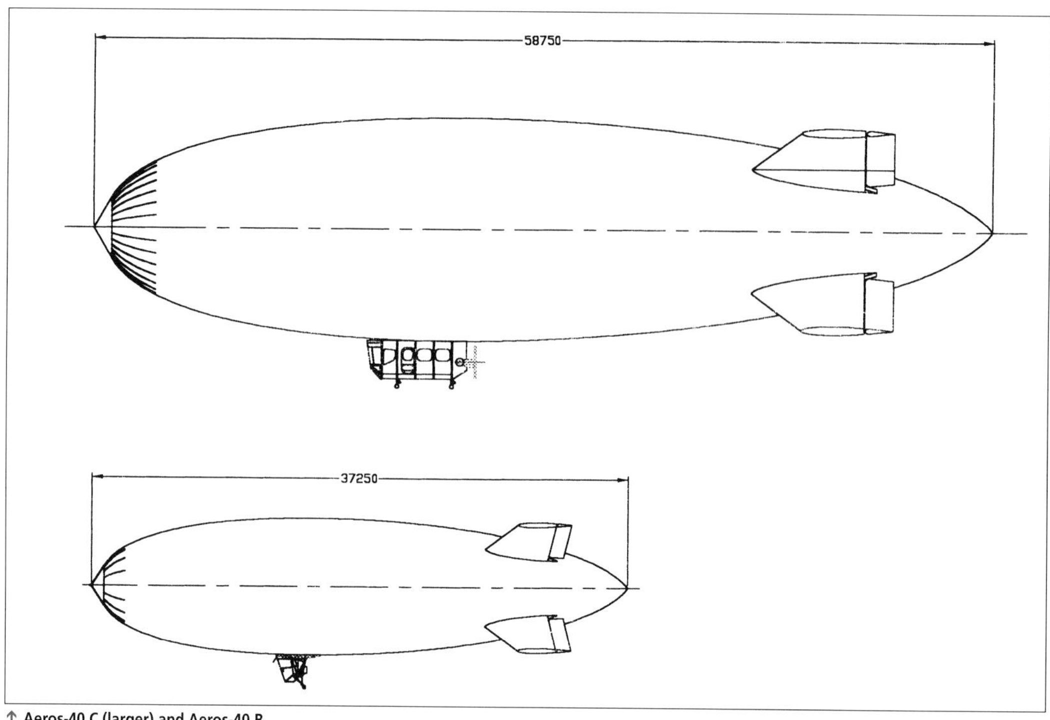

↑ Aeros-40 C (larger) and Aeros-40 B

Cruise speed: 27 kts (31 mph) 50 km/h
Maximum climb rate: 1,200 ft (366 m) per minute
Maximum rate of descent: 1,500 ft (457 m) per minute
Operating altitude: up to 8,200 ft (2,500 m)
Duration: 8 hours average, 16 maximum.

Aeros-40 C

Role: Non-rigid, helium airship.

Aims

- Fly-by-wire control.
- Electric winch.
- Replaceable ballonets.
- System of static balancing.
- Temperature control system.
- Laminated tail profile.

Details

Crew/Passengers: Pilot, 2 other crew and 9 passengers.
Gondola: Enclosed, with reinforced frame of tubing.
Length: 192 ft 9 ins (58.750 m) overall, envelope 181 ft 11 ins (55.44 m).
Diameter: 44 ft 4 ins (13.5 m) envelope
Width over fins: 45 ft 1 ins (13.749 m)
Height: 56 ft 8 ins (17.264 m)
Envelope: Constructed of heat-sealed nylon-based fabric. Life at least 6 years. 24 gores. *Volume* 183,635 cu ft (5,200 m^3). Pressurization system has disk valve with automatic action; forced manual opening and opening pressure adjustment possible; activation for open and lock pressure actuators. 1 helium valve. Nose cone for mooring.
Surface area: 20,107 sq ft (1,868 m^2)
Ballonets: 2 of air chamber type, fore and aft, representing 35% of envelope volume. *Volume* 32,136 cu ft (910 m^3) each. 4 air valves (2 each).
Ballast: Water and lead shot.
Fineness ratio: 4:1
Engines: 2 Textron Lycoming IO-540-K2A5 pistons, each 300 hp (224 kW), on a vectoring thrust frame. Second stability control system via 4 blow thrust engines.
Propellers: 5-blade, constant-speed, reversible pitch, each 6 ft 8 ins (2.03 m) diameter.
Fuel: 681 litres basic model; 1,893 litres maximum fuel reserve.
Stabilizers: Rigid X-form. Fins each constructed as a 3-dimensional frame of alloy tubing, covered by waterproof polyfibre fabric. Elevators and rudders have flat alloy tubing frame with similar covering. Root rib profile Göttingen 409.
Maximum operating airspeed (V_{MO}): 60 kts (69 mph) 111 km/h
Rough air speed: 55 kts (63 mph) 102 km/h
Maximum climb rate: 1,300 ft (400 m) per minute
Maximum rate of descent: 1,510 ft (460 m) per minute
Operating altitude: up to 11,500 ft (3,500 m)
Duration: 8 hours average; 24 hours maximum.

Worldwide Aeros Corporation/Aeroplast — USA/Ukraine

Corporate address:
See Worldwide Aeros Corporation.

Worldwide Aeros-Aeroplast D1 and D4

Role: Rigid, helium, multi-purpose cargo carrier, flying crane, ship escort, tourism and other work airships.

Aims

- No weather, wind speed or visibility restrictions to flying.
- Mooring to the rotating platform of the tower, followed by automatic mast-mooring.
- 60,000 flight hours or 20 years life.

Development

- Programmes initiated in the former USSR in the 1970s.
- Construction of the prototype D1 began October 1995.

Details

Crew/Passengers/Load: 3-level gondola, the bottom level housing the undercarriage equipment. Compartment above is for the pilots, navigator, flight engineer and cargo platform operator, with stairs leading to the crew living compartment and an auxiliary compartment. Cargo carried in a container either fixed in the cargo compartment or mounted on the cargo suspension platform, or without a container on the platform, or carried as a slung load. Cargo compartment 52 ft 6 ins × 20 ft 4 ins × 10 ft 10 ins (16 × 6.2 × 3.3 m) for D1, 164 ft × 52 ft 6 ins × 11 ft 6 ins (50 × 16 × 3.5 m) for D4. Cargo compartment *volume* 11,560 cu ft (327.34 m^3) for D1. Cargo carrying facilitated by an undercarriage with a wheel track and wheel base of (respectively) 20 ft 4 ins and 65 ft 9 ins (8.2 and 20.05 m) for the D1, and 78 ft 9 ins and 170 ft 7 ins (24 and 52 m) for the D4.
Length of envelope: 275 ft 7 ins (84 m) for D1, 551 ft 2 ins (168 m) for D4.
Length overall: 311 ft 8 ins (95 m) for D1
Diameter: 82 ft (25 m) for D1, 164 ft (50 m) for D4
Height overall: 108 ft 3 ins (33 m) for D1
Envelope: Semi-monocoque, with active rigid hull made of 3-ply carbonplastic panels. *Volume* 971,155 cu ft (27,500 m^3) for D1, 7,769,230 cu ft (220,000 m^3) for D4.
Surface area: 57,800 sq ft (5,370 m^2) for D1
Ballonets: Constructed of Vectran base cloth/adhesive/ethylene-vynalalcohol-Copolmere 15/protective agent sandwich.
Payload (fuel and cargo): 27,558 lb (12,500 kg) for D1, 275,580 lb (125,000 kg) for D4.
Engines: 3,600 shp (2,685 kW) General Electric T64 turboprop engine at the tail and 2 × 300 hp (224 kW) Zoche ZO 02A side engines in vectoring shrouds (+120°, -90°) for D1; 6,000 hp (4,474 kW) aft engine and 2 × 1,000 hp (746 kW) side engines for D4.
Stabilizers/wings: Large T-tail, incorporating elevators and a rudder. Canards towards the nose of the hull.
Vertical tailfin area: 1,722 sq ft (160 m^2) for D1
Horizontal tailfin area: 1,076 sq ft (100 m^2) for D1
Maximum airspeed: 151 kts (174 mph) 280 km/h
Cruise speed: 124 kts (143 mph) 230 km/h
Mooring speed: 10-16.5 ft (3-5 m) per second horizontal, 1.6-3.3 ft (0.5-1 m) per second vertical.
Ceiling: 11,800 ft (3,600 m) for D1, 19,700 ft (6,000 m) for D4.
Range: Approximately 540 naut miles (621 miles) 1,000 km with a 10,000 kg payload, or 2,160 naut miles (2,485 miles) 4,000 km with a 2,000 kg payload for the D1.

Engines (Civil and Military)

Designation (type of engine)	Power output (normally take-off rating for piston, turboprop and turboshaft, unless stated)	Specific fuel consumption (S F C)	a) Max RPM b) Pressure or Compression ratio	a) EGT (unless stated to be MGT, TET, TGT or TIT) b) Primary fuel type or Octane rating	Dry weight lb (kg)	a) Length ins (mm) b) Width ins (mm) c) Height ins (mm)	Current aircraft users, and comments
Australia							
Jabiru Aircraft Pty Ltd., PO Box 5186, Airport Drive, Bundaberg West 4670, Queensland (Telephone: +61 74 155 1778, Facsimile: +61 74 155 2669)							
Jabiru 1600 (4-cyl, air-cooled, direct-drive piston)	60 hp (44.7 kW)	0.46 lb/hp/hr (280 g/kW/hr)	a) 3,300 b) 9.5:1	a) 600-680° C b) Avgas 100 LL or Mogas	124 (56)	a) 20.94 (532) b) 22.6 (574) c) 18.58 (472)	Aircraft up to 1,100 lb (499 kg) gross. No longer produced.
Jabiru 2200 (4-cyl, air-cooled, direct-drive piston)	80 hp (59.7 kW)	15 litres per hour at 75% power	a) 3,300 b) 8.5:1	a) 600-680° C b) Avgas 100 LL or Mogas	123.5 (56)	a) 21.3 (541) b) 23.46 (596) c) 17.2 (437)	Aircraft up to 1,250 lb (567 kg) gross. Dual transistorized magneto ignition. Integral AC generator. Electric starter. Displacement 2,200 cc; bore 3.84 ins (97.5 mm); stroke 2.91 ins (74 mm).
Austria							
Bombardier-Rotax GmbH. Welserstrasse 32, (Postfach 5) A-4623 Gunskirchen (Telephone: +43 7246 6101, Facsimile: +43 7246 6370)							
447 UL-SCDI 1V (2-cyl, 2-stroke, fan-cooled piston)	39.6 hp (29.5 kW) at 6,500 rpm	0.84 lb/hp/hr (510 g/kW/hr) at 6,800 rpm	a) 6,800 b) 9.6:1 th; 6.3:1 ef	a) 460-650° C b) MON 83, RON 91	71.9 (32.6)*	a) 21.38 (543) b) 20.59 (523) c) 16.38 (416)	For experimental and ultralight uncertified aircraft. Not certified. *With carburettor and exhaust. Bore 2.66 ins (67.5 mm); stroke 2.4 ins (61 mm). Current production engine.
447 UL-SCDI 2V (2-cyl, 2-stroke, fan-cooled piston)	41.6 hp (31.0 kW) at 6,500 rpm	0.82 lb/hp/hr (500 g/kW/hr) at 6,800 rpm	a) 6,800 b) 9.6:1 th; 6.3:1 ef	a) 460-650° C b) MON 83, RON 91	72.75 (33)*	a) 21.38 (543) b) 20.59 (523) c) 16.38 (416)	For experimental and ultralight uncertified aircraft. Not certified. *With carburettor and exhaust. Bore 2.66 ins (67.5 mm); stroke 2.4 ins (61 mm). Current production engine.
503 UL-DCDI 1V (2-cyl, 2-stroke, fan-cooled piston)	45.6 hp (34.0 kW) at 6,500 rpm	0.84 lb/hp/hr (510 g/kW/hr) at 6,800 rpm	a) 6,800 b) 10.8:1 th	a) 460-650° C b) MON 83, RON 91	84.4 (38.3)*	a) 21.89-22.2 (556-564) b) 20.2 (513) c) 16.77 (426)	For experimental and ultralight uncertified aircraft. Not certified. *With carburettors and exhaust. Bore 2.84 ins (72 mm); stroke 2.4 ins. (61 mm). Current production engine.
503 UL-DCDI 2V (2-cyl, 2-stroke, fan-cooled piston)	49.6 hp (37.0 kW) at 6,500 rpm	0.82 lb/hp/hr (500 g/kW/hr) at 6,800 rpm	a) 6,800 b) 10.8:1 th	a) 460-650° C b) MON 83, RON 91	84.4 (38.3)*	a) 21.89-22.2 (556-564) b) 20.2 (513) c) 16.77 (426)	For experimental and ultralight uncertified aircraft. Not certified. *With carburettors and exhaust. Bore 2.84 ins (72 mm); stroke 2.4 ins (61 mm). Current production engine.
582 UL-DCDI (2-cyl, 2-stroke, liquid-cooled piston, with rotary valve inlet)	64.4 hp (48 kW) at 6,500 rpm, 53.6 hp (40 kW) at 6,000 rpm	0.67 lb/hp/hr (410 g/kW/hr) at 6,800 rpm	a) 6,800 b) 11.5:1 th	a) 500-650° C b) MON 83, RON 91	75.6 (34.3)*	a) 22.91-23.27 (582-591) b) 17.2 (437) c) 17.32 (440)	For experimental and ultralight uncertified aircraft. Not certified. *With carburettors and exhaust. Bore 2.99 ins (76 mm); stroke 2.52 ins (64 mm). Current production engine.
618 UL-DCDI (2-cyl, 2-stroke liquid-cooled piston, with rotary valve inlet)	73.8 hp (55 kW) at 6,750 rpm, 54 hp (40 kW) at 5,300 rpm	0.65 lb/hp/hr (400 g/kW/hr) at 7,000 rpm	a) 7,000 b) 11.5:1 th; 5.95:1 ef	a) 500-650° C b) MON 85, RON 95	87.5 (39.7)*	a) 23.9-28.27 (607-718) b) 22.6 (574) c) 17.72 (450)	For experimental and ultralight uncertified aircraft. Not certified. *With carburettors and exhaust. Bore 2.99 ins (76 mm); stroke 2.68 ins (68 mm). Current production engine.
912 UL-DCDI (4-cyl, 4-stroke, liquid/air-cooled piston)	77.8 hp (58 kW) at 5,500 rpm, 80 hp (59.6 kW) at 5,800 rpm for 5 minutes	0.44 lb/hp/hr (270 g/kW/hr) at 5,800 rpm	a) 5,800 for 5 minutes; 2,550 propeller rpm (2.27 m) or 2,385 rpm (2.49 m) maximum b) 9.0:1	a) 850° C maximum b) RON 90 unleaded or AKI 87 minimum, Avgas 100 LL	121.3 (55.0) with gearbox	a) 22.79 (579) b) 22.68 (576) c) 14.82 (376.5)	For experimental and ultralight uncertified aircraft. Not certified. Bore 3.13 ins (79.5 mm); stroke 2.4 ins (61 mm). Current production engine.
912 A2/3/4 (4-cyl, 4-stroke, liquid/air-cooled piston)	77.8 hp (58 kW), 80 hp (59.6 kW) for 5 minutes	0.44 lb/hp/hr (270 g/kW/hr) at 5,800 rpm	a) 5,800 for 5 minutes b) 9.0:1	a) 850° C maximum b) RON 90 unleaded or AKI 87 minimum, Avgas 100 LL	125.7 (57.0)	a) 22.79 (579) b) 22.68 (576) c) 14.82 (376.5)	912 A2/3/4 certified to JAR-22. Bore 3.13 ins (79.5 mm); stroke 2.4 ins (61 mm). Current production engine.
912 F2/3/4 (4-cyl, 4-stroke liquid/air-cooled piston)	77.8 hp (58 kW), 80 hp (59.6 kW) for 5 minutes	0.44 lb/hp/hr (270 g/kW/hr) at 5,800 rpm	a) 5,800 for 5 minutes b) 9.0:1	a) 850° C maximum b) RON 90 unleaded or AKI 87 minimum, Avgas 100 LL	125.7 (57.0)	a) 22.79 (579) b) 22.68 (576) c) 14.82 (376.5)	Certified to FAR-33. Bore 3.13 ins (79.5 mm); stroke 2.4 ins (61 mm). Current production engine.
912S (as above)	100 hp (74.6 kW)					a) 22.79 (579) b) 22.68 (576) c) 14.82 (376.5)	New version without turbocharger, first flown in August 1998 on the Scheibe-Rotaxfalke motorglider.
914 UL-DCDI (4-cyl, 4-stroke, liquid/air-cooled piston)	100 hp (74.6 kW) at 5,500 rpm, 115 hp (85.7 kW) at 5,800 rpm for 5 minutes	0.45 lb/hp/hr (276 g/kW/hr)	a) 5,800 for 5 minutes; 2,385 propeller rpm (2.49 m) maximum b) 9.0:1	a) 800° C maximum b) MON 85, RON 95, Avgas 100 LL	153.4 (69.6)*	a) 26.18 (665) b) 22.68 (576) c) 20.91 (531)	For experimental and ultralight uncertified aircraft. Not certified. Production began 1995. *With gearbox, intake silencer and exhaust. Bore 3.13 ins (79.5 mm); stroke 2.4 ins (61 mm).
914 F2/3/4 (4-cyl, 4-stroke liquid/air-cooled piston)	100 hp (74.6 kW) at 5,500 rpm, 115 hp (85.7 kW) at 5,800 rpm for 5 minutes	0.45 lb/hp/hr (276 g/kW/hr)	a) 5,800 for 5 minutes b) 9.0:1	b) MON 85, RON 95, Avgas 100 LL	164.7 (74.7)	a) 26.18 (665) b) 22.68 (576) c) 20.91 (531)	FAR-33 and JAR-E certified. *With gearbox, intake silencer and exhaust. Current production engine.
Out of production Rotax engines	277 (1-cyl, 2-stroke, air-cooled piston of 25.5 hp, 19 kW at 6,100 rpm)	377 (2-cyl, 2-stroke, air-cooled piston of 34.9 hp, 26 kW)	462 (2-cyl, 2-stroke, liquid-cooled piston of 51 hp, 38 kW)	503 (single ignition contact breaker version, 1V, of 46.9 hp, 35 kW)	508 (2-cyl, 4-stroke, air-cooled piston of 42.9 hp, 32 kW)	532 (2-cyl, 2-stroke, liquid-cooled piston of 63 hp, 47 kW)	All non-certified, for experimental and ultralight aircraft only.
Belgium							
Techspace Aero SA. B-4041 Herstal (Milmort) (Telephone: +32 4 278 8602, Facsimile: +32 4 278 80 25)							
Produces components for CFM56, TM333, Tyne, GE and P&W engines, and assemblies.							Share capital held by SNECMA (51%), Pratt & Whitney (19%) and Walloon Region of Belgium (30%). Activities include turbojet engine maintenance, repair and test services to commercial and military end user customers, amounting to 32% of total company sales in last full year; on 21 December 1994 Techspace Aero received FAR-145 for maintenance, repair and testing of commercial engines.

Designation (type of engine)	Power output (normally take-off rating for piston, turboprop and turboshaft, unless stated)	Specific fuel consumption (S F C)	a) Max RPM b) Pressure or Compression ratio	a) EGT (unless stated to be MGT, TET, TGT or TIT) b) Primary fuel type or Octane rating	Dry weight lb (kg)	a) Length ins (mm) b) Width ins (mm) c) Height ins (mm)	Current aircraft users, and comments
Brazil							
Celma-Cia Electromecanica. Rua Alice Hervê 356, Bingen, Caixa Postal 90341, CEP 25669-900, Petrópolis, RJ (Telephone: +55 242 237 4962)							
RB168 Spey Mk 807 (twin-shaft turbofan)	11,030 lbf (49.06 kN)	0.659 lb/lbf/hr (18.67 g/kNs)	b) 16.8:1	a) 585° C maximum EGT, 1,107° C maximum MGT b) JP-1, JP-4 and JP-5	2,417 (1,096)	a) 96.7 (2,456) b) 32.5 (826)	Builds the Spey under licence from Rolls-Royce for the Embraer AMX with FiatAvio co-operation. Celma overhauls various General Electric, Pratt & Whitney and CFM engines.
Indústria Mecânica E Aeronáutica Ltda (IMAER). 18600 Botucatú, SP							
IMAER 1000 (2-cyl, air-cooled, piston)	40 hp (29.8 kW)				86 (39)	a) 14.6 (370) b) 30.1 (764) c) 16.14 (410)	Light and very light aircraft. Offered with either electronic or magneto ignition.
IMAER 2000 (4-cyl, air-cooled piston)	80 hp (59.66 kW)				up to 178.5 (81)	a) 23.2 (590) b) 30.1 (764) c) 17.6 (447)	Light and very light aircraft. Offered with either or both electronic and magneto ignition. Certificated.
Canada							
Fire Wall Forward. 9755 West Saanich Road, Sydney, BC V8L 3S1 (Telephone: +1 250 656 4774, Facsimile: +1 250 656 8007)							
CAM 100 (4-cyl, 4-stroke piston, with reduction gear)*	100 hp (74.6 kW)	0.41 lb/hp/hr (249 g/kW/hr)	b) 9.2:1	b) Minimum 90 Octane (unleaded)	203 (92.1)	a) 32 (813) b) 20.47 (520) c) 25.2 (641)	*Modified from a 1,488 cc Honda Civic motorcar engine. Available in converted form. Originally a Canadian Airmotive Inc product.
Orenda Recip Inc. 3160 Derry Road East, Mississauga, Ontario L4T 1A9 (Telephone: +1 905 677 3250, Facsimile: +1 905 673 4049, Web site: www.orenda.com)							
OE 600A (V-8, turbocharged, liquid-cooled piston, with reduction)	600 hp (447.4 kW) take-off, 500 hp (373 kW) continuous	0.45 lb/hp/hr (274 g/kW/hr)	a) 4,400 crankshaft, 2,057 propeller b) 8:1	a) 844° C b) 100 LL	692 (313.9)	a) 37.8 (960) or 59.5 (1,511) with spinner b) 25.5 (648) or 32 (813) overall c) 24.2 (615) or 32.5 (826) overall	Formerly Thunder Engines Thunder. To have FADEC and to be certified. Fuel injected and dual turbochargers. Displacement 495 cc; bore 4.433 ins (112.6 mm); stroke 4 ins (101.6 mm). Reduction gearbox 0.4675:1. King Air 90, Cessna 400 series, Beaver, Star★Kraft, Twin Commander and Ag-Cat.
Pratt & Whitney Canada Inc. 1000 Marie-Victorin, Longueuil, Quebec J4G 1A1 (Telephone: +1 514 647 7677, Facsimile: +1 514 647 4105)							
JT15D-1 (twin-shaft turbofan) See Comments for D-1A/B	2,200 lbf (9.79 kN) take-off	0.54 lb/lbf/hr (15.3 g/kNs)	b) 10:1	a) 960° C MGT b) JP-1, JP4, JP-5	514 (233.1)	a) 56.6 (1,438) b) 27 (693)	Citation/Citation I. D-1 certified in 1971. D-1B introduced 1983. D-1A /D-1B have dry weight of 519 lb (235.4 kg) and length of 59.3 ins (1,506 mm). Out of production.
JT15D-4 (twin-shaft turbofan) See Comments for D-4B/C/D	2,500 lbf (11.12 kN) take-off	0.562 lb/lbf/hr (15.92 g/kNs)	b) 10:1		557 (252.7)	a) 60.4 (1,534) b) 27.3 (693)	D-4 engines on Corvette, Citation II and Mitsubishi Diamond. Similar but heavier (568 lb, 257.6 kg) and longer (63.3 ins, 1,608 mm) D-4B on Citation SII; D-4C for prolonged inverted flight and with electronic fuel control (575 lb, 260.8 kg dry weight and 60.4 ins, 1,534 mm length) on Agusta S.211; and D-4D hot and high version (560 lb, 254 kg) on Diamond 1A. In production in D-4/4C models.
JT15D-5/-5A (twin-shaft turbofan) See Comments for D-5B	2,900 lbf (12.9 kN) to 26.7° C	0.551 lb/lbf/hr (15.61 g/kNs)			632 (286.7)	a) 60.4 (1,534) b) 27 (686)	D-5 on Beech Beechjet 400A, Cessna T-47A and VisionAire Vantage. D-5A on Citation V. Similar but heavier (643 lb, 292 kg) and slightly longer (27.3 ins, 693 mm) D-5B on Beech T-1A Jayhawk. In production.
JT15D-5C (twin-shaft turbofan)	3,190 lbf (14.19 kN) take-off	0.573 lb/lbf/hr (16.23 g/kNs)			665 (301.6)	a) 60.4 (1,534) b) 27.3 (693)	Agusta S.211A and former Rockwell/DASA Ranger 2000. In production.
JT15D-5D (twin-shaft turbofan)	3,045 lbf (13.55 kN) to 26.7° C	0.56 lb/lbf/hr (15.86 g/kNs) take-off			627 (284.4)	a) 63 (1,600) b) 27 (686)	Citation Ultra. In production.
JT15D-5F (twin-shaft turbofan)	2,900 lbf (12.90 kN) to 26.7° C	0.551 lb/lbf/hr (15.61 g/kNs) take-off			635 (288)	a) 60.4 (1,534) b) 27 (686)	In production.
PT6A-11 (free-turbine turboprop with 3 axial and 1 centrifugal stages)	500 shp (373 kW) at 2,200 rpm	0.647 lb/shp/hr (394 g/kW/hr)	a) 2,200		328 (148.8)	a) 62 (1,575) approx b) 19 (483) approx c) 21 (533) approx	Piper Cheyenne 1/1A and T-1040. Single stage compressor turbine; single stage power turbine (as for those engines detailed below until indicated).
PT6A-11AG (free-turbine turboprop with 3 axlal and 1 centrifugal stages)	500 shp (373 kW) at 2,200 rpm	0.647 lb/shp/hr (394 g/kW/hr)	a) 2,200	b) Includes diesel	330 (149.7)	a) 62 (1,575) b) 19 (483) c) 21 (533)	Ayres Turbo Thrush, Ag-Cat Turbine, Weatherly 620TB.
PT6A-15AG (free-turbine turboprop with 3 axial and 1 centrifugal stages)	680 shp (507 kW) take-off, 620 shp (462.3 kW) cruise at 2,200 rpm	0.602 lb/shp/hr (366 g/kW/hr)	a) 2,200	b) Includes diesel	328 (148.8)	a) 62 (1,575) b) 21.5 (546) c) 21 (533)	Air Tractor AT-400, Ayres S2R-T15 Turbo Thrush, Ag-Cat Turbine.
PT6A-21 (free-turbine turboprop with 3 axial and 1 centrifugal stages)	550 shp (410 kW) at 2,200 rpm	0.630 lb/shp/hr (383 g/kW/hr)	a) 2,200		328 (148.8)	a) 62 (1,575) b) 21.5 (546) c) 21 (533)	Beech King Air C90.

Designation (type of engine)	Power output (normally take-off rating for piston, turboprop and turboshaft, unless stated)	Specific fuel consumption (S F C)	a) Max RPM b) Pressure or Compression ratio	a) EGT (unless stated to be MGT, TET, TGT or TIT) b) Primary fuel type or Octane rating	Dry weight lb (kg)	a) Length ins (mm) b) Width ins (mm) c) Height ins (mm)	Current aircraft users, and comments
Canada							
Pratt & Whitney Canada Inc. (continued)							
PT6A-25 (free-turbine turboprop with 3 axial and 1 centrifugal stages)	560 shp (417.6 kW) take-off, 550 shp (410 kW) cruise at 2,200 rpm	0.630 lb/shp/hr (383 g/kW/hr)	a) 2,200		341 (154.7)	a) 62 (1,575) approx b) 21.5 (546) approx c) 24.8 (630) approx	Beech T-34C and PZL-130TE Orlik.
PT6A-25A (free-turbine turboprop with 3 axial and 1 centrifugal stages)	560 shp (417.6 kW) take-off, 550 shp (410 kW) cruise at 2,200 rpm	0.630 lb/shp/hr (383 g/kW/hr)	a) 2,200		343 (155.6)	a) 62 (1,575) b) 21.5 (546) c) 24.8 (630)	Beech T-34C-1, Pilatus PC-7, PZL-130T Orlik Turbo and Daewoo KTX-1. Identical to PT6A-25 except some castings of different alloy, hence weight difference.
PT6A-25C (free-turbine turboprop with 3 axial and 1 centrifugal stages)	750 shp (559.3 kW) take-off, 700 shp (522 kW) cruise at 2,200 rpm	0.595 lb/shp/hr (362 g/kW/hr)	a) 2,200		346 (156.9)	a) 62 (1,575) b) 21.5 (546) c) 24.8 (630)	EMB-312 Tucano, PZL-130TD Orlik, former Atlas Ace and Pilatus PC-7 Mk II (M).
PT6A-27 (free-turbine turboprop with 3 axial and 1 centrifugal stages)	680 shp (507 kW) take-off, 620 shp (462.3 kW) cruise at 2,200 rpm	0.602 lb/shp/hr (366 g/kW/hr)	a) 2,200 b) 6.7:1		328 (148.8)	a) 62 (1,575) b) 21.5 (546) c) 21 (533.4)	Beech 99A and B99, DHC-6 Twin Otter Series 300, EMB-110, Frakes Mallard, Harbin Y-12 II, Let L-410A, Turbo Porter PC-6/B2-H2, Viking Air Turbo Beaver, and Jetcruzer. US military designation T74.
PT6A-34AG (free-turbine turboprop with 3 axial and 1 centrifugal stages)	750 shp (559.3 kW) take-off, 700 shp (522 kW) cruise at 2,200 rpm	0.595 lb/shp/hr (362 g/kW/hr)	a) 2,200		331 (150.1)	a) 62 (1,575) b) 21.5 (546) c) 21 (533.4)	Air Tractor AT-402/AT-502, Ayres S2R-T34 Turbo Thrush, Frakes Turbo Cat A/C, Fieldmaster, Pacific Aero Cresco, Ag-Cat. PT6A-34 for Twin Panda. Similarly rated PT6A-34B was for Beech T-44A, with all magnesium alloy castings replaced by aluminium alloy castings.
PT6A-41 (free-turbine turboprop with 3 axial and 1 centrifugal stages)	850 shp (633.8 kW) at 2,000 rpm	0.591 lb/shp/hr (359.5 g/kW/hr)	a) 2,000		403 (182.8)	a) 67 (1,702) b) 19.4 (493) c) 22.1 (561.3)	Beech Super King Air 200, Piper Cheyenne III. Single stage compressor turbine; two stage power turbine (as for those engines detailed below until indicated). Similar PT6A-41AG used on Frakes Turbo Cat, with dry weight of 412 lb (186.9 kg).
PT6A-42 (free-turbine turboprop with 3 axial and 1 centrifugal stages)	850 shp (633.8 kW) at 2,000 rpm	0.601 lb/shp/hr (365.6 g/kW/hr)	a) 2,000		403 (182.8)	a) 67 (1,702) b) 19.4 (493) c) 22.1 (561.3)	Beech Super King Air B200, Ibis Ae 270 Ibis, and Jetcruzer.
PT6A-45R (free-turbine turboprop with 3 axial and 1 centrifugal stages) See Comments	1,197 shp (892.6 kW) at 1,700 rpm, 956 shp (713 kW) cruise at 1,425 rpm	0.553 lb/shp/hr (336 g/kW/hr)	a) 1,700		448 (203.2)	a) 71.9 (1,826) b) 19.4 (493) c) 22.1 (561.3)	Air Tractor AT-503, Shorts 330/C-23A Sherpa, USAC Turbo Express (DC-3 conversion). Hot end upgrade. Water/methanol removed. Earlier and lighter 1,173 shp (874.7 kW) at 1,700 rpm PT6A-45A/B used by Frakes Mohawk 298 and Shorts 330; PT6A-45B has increased water/methanol injection for take-off. PT6A-45 used by Ayres S2R-660.
PT6A-60A (free-turbine turboprop with 3 axial and 1 centrifugal stages) PT6A-60AG – see Comments	1,050 shp (783 kW) take-off, 1,000 shp (745.7 kW) cruise at 1,700 rpm	0.548 lb/shp/hr (333.3 g/kW/hr)	a) 1,700	b) Jet A, Jet A-1, Jet B, Wide-cut or JP-4	475 (215.5)	a) 72 (1,829) b) 19 (483) c) 22 (559)	Beech King Air 300 and King Air 350. PT6A-60AG for Air Tractor 602 and Ayres S2R-660.
PT6A-61 (free-turbine turboprop with 3 axial and 1 centrifugal stages)	850 shp (633.8 kW) at 2,000 rpm	0.591 lb/shp/hr (359.5 g/kW/hr)	a) 2,000	b) Jet A, Jet A-1, Jet B, Wide-cut or JP-4	429 (194.6)	a) 67.5 (1,715) b) 19 (483) c) 22 (559)	Piper Cheyenne IIIA.
PT6A-62 (free-turbine turboprop with 3 axial and 1 centrifugal stages)	950 shp (708.4 kW) take-off, 900 shp (671 kW) cruise at 2,000 rpm	0.567 lb/shp/hr (345 g/kW/hr)	a) 2,000	b) Jet A, Jet A-1, Jet B, Wide-cut or JP-4	456 (206.8)	a) 70.5 (1,791) b) 19 (483) c) 20.5 (521)	Pilatus PC-9 (M), PZL-130TC Orlik, HTT-35, and Daewoo KTX-1 with PT6A-62A.
PT6A-64 (free-turbine turboprop with 4 axial and 1 centrifugal stages)	700 shp (522 kW) at 2,000 rpm	0.703 lb/shp/hr (428 g/kW/hr)	a) 2,000		456 (206.8)	a) 70 (1,778) b) 19 (483) c) 22 (559)	TBM 700.
PT6A-65AG (free-turbine turboprop with 4 axial and 1 centrifugal stages)	1,300 shp (969.4 kW) at 1,700 rpm, 956 shp (712.9 kW) cruise at 1,425 rpm	0.516 lb/shp/hr (314 g/kW/hr)	a) 1,700		486 (220.4)	a) 75 (1,905) b) 19 (483) c) 22 (559)	Ayres S2R-T65 Turbo Thrush and Croplease Firemaster.
PT6A-65B (free-turbine turboprop with 4 axial and 1 centrifugal stages)	1,100 shp (820.3 kW) take-off, 1,000 shp (745.7 kW) cruise at 1,700 rpm	0.536 lb/shp/hr (326 g/kW/hr)	a) 1,700 b) 10:1	b) Jet A, Jet A-1, Jet B, Wide-cut or JP-4	481 (218.2)	a) 75 (1,905) b) 19 (483) c) 22.5 (571.5)	Beech 1900 Airliner and C-12J, PZL M28 Skytruck, Aeroic Dingo and Beriev Be-32. 1,376 shp (1,026 kW) PT6A-65R used by Shorts 360.
PT6A-65AR (free-turbine turboprop with 4 axial and 1 centrifugal stages)	1,424 shp (1,062 kW) at 1,700 rpm, 956 shp (712.9 kW) at 1,425 rpm	0.509 lb/shp/hr (310 g/kW/hr)	a) 1,700	b) Jet A, Jet A-1, Jet B, Wide-cut or JP-4	486 (220.4)	a) 75 (1,905) b) 19 (483) c) 22 (559)	AMI Cargo Master (DC-3 conversion), Shorts 360, C-23B, and Aeroprogress T-101 Gratch.

Designation (type of engine)	Power output (normally take-off rating for piston, turboprop and turboshaft, unless stated)	Specific fuel consumption (S F C)	a) Max RPM b) Pressure or Compression ratio	a) EGT (unless stated to be MGT, TET, TGT or TIT) b) Primary fuel type or Octane rating	Dry weight lb (kg)	a) Length ins (mm) b) Width ins (mm) c) Height ins (mm)	Current aircraft users, and comments
Canada							
Pratt & Whitney Canada Inc. (continued)							
PT6A-66 (free-turbine turboprop with 4 axial and 1 centrifugal stages)	1,485 shp (1,107 kW) flat-rated to 850 shp (633.8 kW) at 2,000 rpm	0.642 lb/shp/hr (390.5 g/kW/hr)	a) 2,000		456 (206.8) standard rotation, 470 (213.2) reverse rotation	a) 70 (1,778) b) 19.4 (493) c) 22.5 (571.5)	Avanti, Saras.
PT6A-67/-67A (free-turbine turboprop with 4 axial and 1 centrifugal stages)	1,200 shp (894.8 kW) take-off, 1,000 shp (745.7 kW) cruise at 1,700 rpm	0.547 lb/shp/hr (333 g/kW/hr)	a) 1,700		506 (229.5)	a) 74 (1,880) b) 19 (483) c) 22 (559)	Beech RC-12K and Tupolev C-Prop for PT6A-67. Beech Starship 1 used PT6A-67A.
PT6A-67AG (free-turbine turboprop with 4 axial and 1 centrifugal stages) See Comments	1,350 shp (1,006.7 kW) take-off, 1,220 shp (909.75 kW) cruise at 1,700 rpm	0.528 lb/shp/hr (321 g/kW/hr)	a) 1,700		520 (235.9)	a) 76 (1,930) b) 19 (483) c) 22 (559)	Version of PT6A-67A series. Single stage compressor turbine; single stage power turbine. Previous 1,424 shp (1,062 kW) PT6A-67AF for Conair Turbo Firecat.
PT6A-67B (free-turbine turboprop with 4 axial and 1 centrifugal stages)	1,200 shp (894.8 kW) take-off, 1,000 shp (745.7 kW) cruise at 1,700 rpm	0.552 lb/shp/hr (335.8 g/kW/hr)	a) 1,700		515 (233.6)	a) 76 (1,930) b) 19 (483) c) 22 (559)	Pilatus PC-12. Single stage compressor turbine; two stage power turbine (as for engines detailed below until indicated).
PT6A-67D (free-turbine turboprop with 4 axial and 1 centrifugal stages)	1,279 shp (953.75 kW) take-off, 1,106 shp (824.7 kW) cruise at 1,700 rpm	0.530 lb/shp/hr (322.4 g/kW/hr)	a) 1,700		515 (233.6)	a) 74 (1,880) b) 19 (483) c) 22 (559)	Beech 1900D Airliner.
PT6A-67R (free-turbine turboprop with 4 axial and 1 centrifugal stages)	1,424 shp (1,062 kW) at 1,700 rpm, 1,020 shp (760.6 kW) cruise at 1,425 rpm	0.520 lb/shp/hr (316.3 g/kW/hr)	a) 1,700		515 (233.6)	a) 76 (1,930) b) 19 (483) c) 22 (559)	Basler Turbo-67 (DC-3 conversion), Shorts 360-300.
PT6A-68/-68-1/-68-3 (free-turbine turboprop with 4 axial and 1 centrifugal stages)	1,700 shp (1,268 kW) at 2,000 rpm, flat rated to 1,100 shp (820 kW) for PT6A-68 on Texan II	0.540 lb/shp/hr (328.5 g/kW/hr) for PT6A-68 (see Comments)	a) 2,000		572 (259.5)	a) 72.2 (1,834) b) 19 (483) c) 22.5 (571.5)	PT6A-68 for Beech T-6A Texan II/PC-9 Mk II. 1,250 shp (932 kW) PT6A-68-1 for Embraer EMB-314 Super Tucano or 1,600 shp (1,193 kW) PT6A-68-3 (see EMB-314 entry). 1,600 shp (1,193 kW) rating for PT6A-68 used by ALX.
PT6A-112 (free-turbine turboprop with 3 axial and 1 centrifugal stages) See Comments	500 shp (372.9 kW)	0.637 lb/shp/hr (387.5 g/kW/hr)	a) 1,900		326 (147.9)	a) 62 (1,575) b) 21.5 (546) c) 21 (533).	Cessna Conquest I, Reims F 406 Caravan II. Single stage compressor turbine; single stage power turbine. Engine related to the PT6A-11 series
PT6A-114 (free-turbine turboprop with 3 axial and 1 centrifugal stages)	600 shp (447.4 kW) at 1,900 rpm	0.640 lb/shp/hr (389 g/kW/hr)	a) 1,900		345 (156.5)	a) 62 (1,575) b) 21.5 (546) c) 21 (533)	Cessna 208/208B Caravan I. Single stage compressor turbine; single stage power turbine. Engine related to the PT6A-11 series.
PT6A-114A (free-turbine turboprop with 3 axial and 1 centrifugal stages)	675 shp (503.3 kW) at 1,900 rpm	0.616 lb/shp/hr (375 g/kW/hr)	a) 1,900		350 (158.8)	a) 62 (1,575) b) 21.5 (546) c) 21 (533)	Single stage compressor turbine; single stage power turbine. Engine related to the PT6A-11 series.
PT6A-135 (free-turbine turboprop with 3 axial and 1 centrifugal stages)	750 shp (559.3 kW) take-off, 700 shp (522 kW) cruise at 1,900 rpm	0.585 lb/shp/hr (356 g/kW/hr)	a) 1,900		338 (153.3)	a) 62 (1,575) b) 21.5 (546) c) 21 (533)	Embraer EMB-121 Xingu A1, Piper Cheyenne IIXL, Schafer Comanchero, Vardax Resources Turbo Otter. Single stage compressor turbine; single stage power turbine. Engine related to PT6A-34 series.
PT6A-135A (free-turbine turboprop with 3 axial and 1 centrifugal stages)	750 shp (559.3 kW) take-off, 700 shp (522 kW) cruise at 1,900 rpm	0.585 lb/shp/hr (356 g/kW/hr)	a) 1,900		338 (153.3)	a) 62 (1,575) b) 21.5 (546) c) 21 (533)	Beech King Air F90-1, Dornier Seastar, Vazer Dash 3 Turbine Otter. Comments as above.
PT6A-135B (as above)	810 shp (608 kW), derated for ST-50 to 500 shp (373 kW)		a) 1,900			a) 62 (1,575) b) 21.5 (546) c) 21 (533)	Former Israviation ST-50.
PT6B-36A/B (free-turbine turboshaft)	981 shp (731.5 kW) take-off at 6,409 rpm, 887 shp (661.4 kW) max continuous	0.581 lb/shp/hr (353 g/kW/hr) take-off	a) 6,409 shaft	b) JP-4	384 (174) for 36A, 386 (175) for 36B	a) 59.2 (1,504) b) 19.5 (495)	Sikorsky S-76B.
PT6B-37 (free-turbine turboshaft)	1,002 shp (747 kW) take-off, 872 shp (650 kW) max continuous						Agusta A119 Koala. Certified in 1997.
PT6C-67A (turboshaft)	1,850 shp (1,380 kW)		a) 30,000 for direct drive to proprotor				Bell (Agusta) BA 609.

Designation (type of engine)	Power output (normally take-off rating for piston, turboprop and turboshaft, unless stated)	Specific fuel consumption (S F C)	a) Max RPM b) Pressure or Compression ratio	a) EGT (unless stated to be MGT, TET, TGT or TIT) b) Primary fuel type or Octane rating	Dry weight lb (kg)	a) Length ins (mm) b) Width ins (mm) c) Height ins (mm)	Current aircraft users, and comments
Canada							
Pratt & Whitney Canada Inc. (continued)							
PT6C-67B							PZL Swidnik Sokol.
PT6T-3 Twin-Pac® (twinned free-turbine turboshafts – see Comments)	1,800 shp (1,342 kW) take-off at 6,600 rpm, 1,600 shp (1,193 kW) max continuous	0.595 lb/shp/hr (362 g/kW/hr)	a) 6,600 shaft	b) JP-4	648 (294)	a) 65.8 (1,671) b) 43.5 (1,105) c) 32.6 (828)	Bell UH-1N, CUH-1N, VH-1N, AH-1J and AH-1T; Bell and Agusta-Bell 212; Sikorsky S-58T. Twinned free-turbine turboshafts driving a single output shaft through identical geartrains in a common reduction gearbox. PT6T US military designation is T400.
PT6T-3B Twin-Pac® (as above)	1,800 shp (1,342 kW) take-off at 6,600 rpm, 1,600 shp (1,193 kW) max continuous	0.600 lb/shp/hr (365 g/kW/hr)	a) 6,600 shaft	b) JP-4	660 (299.4)	a) 65.8 (1,671) b) 43.5 (1,105) c) 32.6 (828)	Bell/Agusta-Bell 212, 412, 412SP.
PT6T-3BE (as above)	1,800 shp (1,342 kW) take-off, 1,600 shp (1,193 kW) max continuous	0.600 lb/shp/hr (365 g/kW/hr)	a) 6,600 shaft	b) JP-4	665 (301.6)	a) 65.8 (1,671) b) 43.5 (1,105) c) 32.6 (828)	Bell/Agusta-Bell 412/412HP.
PT6T-3D/DE/DF (as above)	1,800 shp (1,342 kW) take-off at 6,600 rpm, 1,700 shp (1,268 kW) max continuous	0.595 lb/shp/hr (362 g/kW/hr)	a) 6,600 shaft	b) JP-4	679 (308)	a) 65.8 (1,671) b) 43.5 (1,105) c) 32.6 (828)	Bell and Agusta-Bell 412HP/EP. PT6T-3D continuous OEI at 970 shp (723.3 kW); PT6T-3DE 30 minutes OEI at 1,025 shp (764.3 kW); PT6T-3DF 30 minutes OEI at 1,060 shp (790.4 kW).
PT6T-6 (as above)	1,970 shp (1,469 kW) take-off at 6,600 rpm, 1,745 shp (1,301 kW) max continuous	0.591 lb/shp/hr (359 g/kW/hr)	a) 6,600 shaft	b) JP-4	660 (299.4)	a) 65.8 (1,671) b) 43.5 (1,105) c) 32.6 (828)	Agusta-Bell 212/412, S-58T.
PT6T-6B (as above)	1,970 shp (1,469 kW) take-off at 6,600 rpm, 1,745 shp (1,301 kW) max continuous	0.591 lb/shp/hr (359 g/kW/hr)	a) 6,600 shaft	b) JP-4	665 (301.6)	a) 65.8 (1,671) b) 43.5 (1,105) c) 32.6 (828)	Agusta-Bell 412HP.
PW118 (free-turbine turboprop)	1,800 shp (1,342.3 kW) take-off, 1,512 shp (1,127.5 kW) at 1,300 rpm	0.523 lb/shp/hr (318 g/kW/hr) take-off	a) 1,300 b) 11.8:1	b) Conforming to CPW204	861 (390.5)	a) 81 (2,057) approx b) 25 (635) approx c) 31 (787) approx	EMB-120RT, EMB-120ER Advanced.
PW118A (free-turbine turboprop)	1,800 shp (1,342.3 kW) take-off, 1,512 shp (1,127.5 kW) at 1,300 rpm	0.528 lb/shp/hr (321 g/kW/hr) take-off	a) 1,300 b) 11.8:1	b) Conforming to CPW204	866 (393)	a) 81 (2,057) approx b) 25 (635) approx c) 31 (787) approx	EMB-120ER Advanced.
PW118B (free-turbine turboprop)	1,800 shp (1,342.3 kW) take-off		a) 1,300	b) Conforming to CPW204		a) 81 (2,057) approx b) 25 (635) approx c) 31 (787) approx	Hot and high improvements for EMB-120ER Advanced.
PW119B and C (free-turbine turboprop) Data for PW119C (see Comments)	2,180 shp (1,626 kW) take-off, 1,734 shp (1,293 kW) cruise at 1,300 rpm	0.513 lb/shp/hr (312 g/kW/hr) at maximum take-off	a) 1,300 b) 11.8:1	b) Conforming to CPW204	916 (415.5)	a) 81 (2,057) approx b) 25 (635) approx c) 33 (838) approx	Fairchild Dornier 328. PW119C offers 5% extra thermodynamic power for the Fairchild Dornier 328-120.
PW120 (free-turbine turboprop)	2,000 shp (1,491.4 kW) take-off, 1,619 shp (1,207 kW) cruise at 1,200 rpm	0.509 lb/shp/hr (310 g/kW/hr) at take-off	a) 1,200 b) 11.8:1	b) Conforming to CPW204	921 (417.75)	a) 84 (2,134) approx b) 25 (635) approx c) 31 (787) approx	ATR 42.
PW120A (free-turbine turboprop)	2,000 shp (1,491.4 kW) take-off, 1,651 shp (1,231 kW) cruise at 1,200 rpm	0.509 lb/shp/hr (310 g/kW/hr) at take-off	a) 1,200 b) 11.8:1	b) Conforming to CPW204	933 (423.2)	a) 84 (2,134) approx b) 25 (635) approx c) 31 (787) approx	de Havilland Dash 8Q Series 100.
PW121 (free-turbine turboprop)	2,150 shp (1,603.25 kW) take-off, 1,700 shp (1,267.7 kW) cruise at 1,200 rpm	0.500 lb/shp/hr (304 g/kW/hr) at take-off	a) 1,200 b) 11.8:1	b) Conforming to CPW204	936 (424.6)	a) 84 (2,134) approx b) 25 (635) approx c) 31 (787) approx	ATR 42-200 and -320, and de Havilland Dash 8Q Series 100B.
PW121A (free-turbine turboprop)	2,200 shp (1,640.5 kW) take-off, 1,700 shp (1,267.7 kW) cruise at 1,200 rpm	0.496 lb/shp/hr (302 g/kW/hr) at take-off	a) 1,200 b) 11.8:1	b) Conforming to CPW204	957 (434)	a) 84 (2,134) approx b) 25 (635) approx c) 31 (787) approx	ATR 42-400.
PW123 (free-turbine turboprop)	2,380 shp (1,775 kW) take-off, 2,030 shp (1,514 kW) cruise at 1,200 rpm	0.494 lb/shp/hr (300.5 g/kW/hr) at take-off	a) 1,200 b) 14.4:1	b) Conforming to CPW204	992 (450)	a) 84 (2,134) approx b) 26 (660.4) approx c) 33 (838) approx	de Havilland Dash 8Q Series 311.

Designation (type of engine)	Power output (normally take-off rating for piston, turboprop and turboshaft, unless stated)	Specific fuel consumption (S F C)	a) Max RPM b) Pressure or Compression ratio	a) EGT (unless stated to be MGT, TET, TGT or TIT) b) Primary fuel type or Octane rating	Dry weight lb (kg)	a) Length ins (mm) b) Width ins (mm) c) Height ins (mm)	Current aircraft users, and comments
Canada							
Pratt & Whitney Canada Inc. (continued)							
PW123AF (free-turbine turboprop)	2,380 shp (1,775 kW) take-off, 2,030 shp (1,514 kW) cruise at 1,200 rpm	0.494 lb/shp/hr (300.5 g/kW/hr) at take-off	a) 1,200 b) 14.4:1	b) Conforming to CPW204	992 (450)	a) 84 (2,134) approx b) 26 (660.4) approx c) 33 (838) approx	Canadair CL-215T, CL-415.
PW123B (free-turbine turboprop)	2,500 shp (1,864.25 kW) take-off, 2,030 shp (1,514 kW) cruise at 1,200 rpm		a) 1,200	b) Conforming to CPW204	992 (450)	a) 84 (2,134) approx b) 26 (660.4) approx c) 33 (838) approx	de Havilland Dash 8Q Series 300B.
PW123C (free-turbine turboprop)	2,150 shp (1,603.25 kW) take-off, 1,950 shp (1,454 kW) cruise at 1,200 rpm	0.508 lb/shp/hr (309 g/kW/hr)	a) 1,200	b) Conforming to CPW204	992 (450)	a) 84 (2,134) approx b) 26 (660.4) approx c) 33 (838) approx	de Havilland Dash 8Q Series 200A.
PW123D (free-turbine turboprop)	2,150 shp (1,603.25 kW) take-off, 1,950 shp (1,454 kW) cruise at 1,200 rpm	0.508 lb/shp/hr (309 g/kW/hr)	a) 1,200	b) Conforming to CPW204	992 (450)	a) 84 (2,134) approx b) 26 (660.4) approx c) 33 (838) approx	de Havilland Dash 8Q Series 200B.
PW123E (free-turbine turboprop)	2,380 shp (1,775 kW)	0.494 lb/shp/hr (300 g/kW/hr)	a) 1,200	b) Conforming to CPW204	992 (450)	a) 84 (2,134) approx b) 26 (660.4) approx c) 33 (838) approx	de Havilland Dash 8Q Series 300A and E.
PW124B (free-turbine turboprop)	2,400 shp (1,790 kW) take-off, 2,088 shp (1,557 kW) cruise at 1,200 rpm	0.492 lb/shp/hr (299 g/kW/hr) at take-off	a) 1,200 b) 14.4:1	b) Conforming to CPW204	1,060 (480.8)	a) 84 (2,134) approx b) 26 (660.4) approx c) 33 (838) approx	ATR 72-200.
PW125B (free-turbine turboprop)	2,500 shp (1,864.25 kW) take-off, 2,030 shp (1,514 kW) cruise at 1,200 rpm	0.486 lb/shp/hr (296 g/kW/hr) at take-off	a) 1,200 b) 14.4:1	b) Conforming to CPW204	1,060 (480.8)	a) 84 (2,134) approx b) 26 (660.4) approx c) 33 (838) approx	Fokker 50-100.
PW126A (free-turbine turboprop)	2,662 shp (1,985 kW) take-off, 2,081 shp (1,552 kW) cruise at 1,200 rpm	0.484 lb/shp/hr (294.4 g/kW/hr) at take-off	a) 1,200 b) 14.7:1	b) Conforming to CPW204	1,060 (480.8)	a) 84 (2,134) approx b) 26 (660.4) approx c) 33 (838) approx	Jetstream ATP. Earlier PW126 of 2,653 shp (1,978.3 kW) take-off and 2,083 shp (1,553.3 kW) cruise also for ATP.
PW127 (free-turbine turboprop) PW127A – see Comments	2,750 shp (2,050.7 kW) take-off, 2,132 shp (1,590 kW) cruise at 1,200 rpm	0.481 lb/shp/hr (292.6 g/kW/hr) at take-off	a) 1,200	b) Conforming to CPW204	1,060 (480.8)	a) 84 (2,134) approx b) 26 (660.4) approx c) 33 (838) approx	ATR 52C and 72-210. PW127A has rating of 2,470 shp (1,842 kW).
PW127B (free-turbine turboprop)	2,750 shp (2,050.7 kW) take-off, 2,132 shp (1,590 kW) cruise at 1,200 rpm	0.481 lb/shp/hr (292.6 g/kW/hr) at take-off	a) 1,200	b) Conforming to CPW204	1,060 (480.8)	a) 84 (2,134) approx b) 26 (660.4) approx c) 33 (838) approx	Fokker 50-300, Fokker 60 Utility.
PW127C (free-turbine turboprop)	2,750 shp (2,050.7 kW) take-off, 2,132 shp (1,590 kW) cruise at 1,200 rpm	0.481 lb/shp/hr (292.6 g/kW/hr) at take-off	a) 1,200	b) Conforming to CPW204	1,060 (480.8)	a) 84 (2,134) approx b) 26 (660.4) approx c) 33 (838) approx	Xi'an Y7-200A, Ilyushin Il-114 and Socata HALE. For information only, the similarly rated PW127D was intended for Jetstream 61 (see entry).
PW127E (free-turbine turboprop)	2,400 shp (1,789.7 kW) take-off, 2,132 shp (1,590 kW) cruise at 1,200 rpm	0.497 lb/shp/hr (302 g/kW/hr)	a) 1,200	b) Conforming to CPW204	1,060 (480.8)	a) 84 (2,134) approx b) 26 (660.4) approx c) 33 (838) approx	ATR 42-500.
PW127F (free-turbine turboprop)	2,750 shp (2,050.7 kW) take-off, 2,132 shp (1,590 kW) cruise at 1,200 rpm	0.481 lb/shp/hr (292.6 g/kW/hr) at take-off	a) 1,200	b) Conforming to CPW204	1,060 (480.8)	a) 84 (2,134) approx b) 26 (660.4) approx c) 33 (838) approx	ATR 72-210A, Il-114PC.
PW127G (free-turbine turboprop)	2,645 shp (1,972 kW) take-off		a) 1,200	b) Conforming to CPW204	1,060 (480.8)	a) 84 (2,134) approx b) 26 (660.4) approx c) 33 (838) approx	Airtech C295.
PW150A (turboprop)	5,071 shp (3,781 kW) take-off, 3,947 shp (2,943 kW) cruise		a) 1,020	b) Conforming to CPW204	1,521 (690)	a) 95.4 (2,423) b) 30.22 (767.6) c) 44.65 (1,134)	de Havilland Dash 8Q Series 400, Tu-136. Three-stage LP, axial-flow compressor driven by second-stage HP turbine, centrifugal HP compressor driven by first-stage HP turbine, and high power/low speed gearbox.
PW200/9 (turboshaft)	615 shp (459 kW)						PZL-Świdnik SW-4 high-performance version.

Designation (type of engine)	Power output (normally take-off rating for piston, turboprop and turboshaft, unless stated)	Specific fuel consumption (S F C)	a) Max RPM b) Pressure or Compression ratio	a) EGT (unless stated to be MGT, TET, TGT or TIT) b) Primary fuel type or Octane rating	Dry weight lb (kg)	a) Length ins (mm) b) Width ins (mm) c) Height ins (mm)	Current aircraft users, and comments
Canada							
Pratt & Whitney Canada Inc. (continued)							
PW206A/E (free-turbine turboshaft)	640 shp (477.25 kW) take-off at 6,000 rpm	not available	a) 6,000 shaft	b) JP-4	237 (107.5)	a) 35.9 (912) b) 19.7 (500) c) 22.3 (566)	MD 900/902 Explorer. Possibly Inalet-8 and -32. PW206A offers 2.5 minutes OEI at 690 shp (514.5 kW). PW206E offers 2.5 minutes OEI at 732 shp (546 kW).
PW206B (free-turbine turboshaft)	621 shp (463 kW) at 5,898 rpm	not available	a) 5,898 shaft	b) JP-4	246.7 (111.9)	a) 41 (1,041) b) 19.7 (500) c) 24.7 (627)	EC 135, MD Explorer.
PW206C and D (free-turbine turboshaft)	640 shp (477.3 kW) for take-off for 5 minutes for 'C'	not available	a) 6,000 shaft for 'C'	b) JP-4 for 'C'	237 (107.5) for 'C'	a) 35.9 (912) b) 19.7 (500) c) 22.3 (566)	Kazan Ansat and Agusta A 109 Power for PW206C. Bell 427 for PW206D.
PW207 (free-turbine turboshaft)	710 shp (529 kW)						Alternative engine for Kazan Ansat.
PW305A (twin-shaft turbofan)	4,679 lbf (20.81 kN) to 33.9° C	0.388 lb/lbf/hr (10.99 g/kNs) take-off	b) 12.9:1	b) JP-1, JP-4, JP-5. Conforms to CPW204	993 (450.4)	a) 65 (1,651) b) 34.3 (871) c) 43.8 (1,113)	Learjet 60. Certified December 1992. Development and production collaboration between P&WC and MTU of Germany.
PW305B (twin-shaft turbofan)	5,266 lbf (23.42 kN) to 23.5° C	0.391 lb/lbf/hr (11.075 g/kNs) maximum take-off	b) 12.9:1	b) JP-1, JP-4, JP-5. Conforms to CPW204	993 (450.4)	a) 65 (1,651) b) 34.3 (871) c) 43.8 (1,113)	Raytheon Hawker 1000. Certified January 1993.
PW306A (twin-shaft turbofan)	6,040 lbf (26.87 kN) to 31° C		b) 12.7:1	b) JP-1, JP-4, JP-5. Conforms to CPW204	1,049 (475.8)	a) 75.7 (1,923) b) 36.5 (927) c) 45.2 (1,148)	Galaxy Aerospace Galaxy. Larger fan and other changes to PW305 models. Certification 1998.
PW306B (PW306/9) (twin-shaft turbofan)	6,050 lbf (26.91 kN) flat rated to 25° C	0.641 lb/lbf/hr (18.16 g/kNs)	b) 14.9:1		1,057 (479.4)	a) 75.7 (1,923) b) 36.5 (927) c) 45.2 (1,148)	Fairchild Dornier 328JET in PW306/9 form. Certification was anticipated for September 1998. Bypass ratio 4.5:1.
PW308A (twin-shaft turbofan)	6,575 lbf (29.25 kN) flat rated to 37°C				1,317 (597.4)	a) 95.85 (2,435) b) 37.03 (941)	Raytheon Hawker Horizon and 428JET. Certification anticipated March 2000.
PW530A (advanced high bypass ratio twin-shaft turbofan)	2,750 lbf (12.23 kN) flat rated to 23° C				617 (279.9)	a) 60 (1,524) b) 27.6 (701) c) 34.4 (874)	Cessna Citation Bravo. Certified December 1995.
PW545A (as above)	3,786 lbf (16.84 kN) flat rated to 28° C				805 (365)	a) 68 (1,727) b) 38.4 (975)	Cessna Excel. Certified February 1997, with deliveries that year.
China (People's Republic of)							
Beijing University of Aeronautics and Astronautics. PO Box 85, 37 Xue Yuan Road, Haidian District, Beijing 100083 (Telephone: +86 10 62028347, Facsimile: +86 106202 8356)							
WP11 (single-shaft turbojet)	1,875 lbf (8.34 kN)	1.1 lb/lbf/hr (31.1 g/kNs)	a) 22,000 b) 5.47:1	a) 740° C b) Daging Nos 1 and 2	421 (191)	b) 23.3 (593) approx	Aircraft and UAVs. Based on the French Turbomeca Marboré but with a higher rating.
Changzhou Lan Xiang Machinery Works. PO Box 37, 568 Tongjiang Avenue, Changzhou, Jiangsu 213002 (Telephone: +86 519 510 5131, Facsimile: +86 519 510 5064)							
WZ6 (free-turbine turboshaft)	2,897 shp (2,160 kW), 1,550 shp (1,156 kW) OEI rating	0.584 lb/shp/hr (355 g/kW/hr)			694 (315)	a) 78 (1,980) approx b) 28.2 (717) approx	Z-8. 20% power reserve at sea level. 3 turbine and 11 compressor stages.
China National South Aero Engine Company (CNSAC). Zhuzhou, Hunan 412002 (Telephone: +86 733 8551591, Facsimile: +86 733 8580611)							
HS5 (9-cyl, 4-stroke, air-cooled, radial piston)	967 hp (721 kW) take-off at 2,200 rpm, 792.5 hp (591 kW) cruise	0.671 lb/hp/hr (408 g/kW/hr) minimum at take-off, 0.626-0.671 lb/hp/hr (381-408 g/kW/hr) cruise	a) 1,511 propeller b) 6.4:1		1,276.5 (579)	a) 52.28 (1,328) b) 54.33 (1,380)	Shijiazhuang Y-5. Chinese-built ASz-62IR-16.
HS6 (9-cyl, 4-stroke, air-cooled, radial piston)	285-400 hp (212.5-298.3)		a) 1,849 propeller rpm estimated b) 5.9:1 estimated		441 (200)	a) 37.64 (956) b) 38.78 (985)	CJ-6A, Haiyan, Y-11 and was to be used on an N-5A development in the most powerful HS6K form.
WJ6 (turboprop)	4,250 eshp (3,167 kW)				2,646 (1,200) ±2% kg	a) 122 (3,099) ±2 mm b) 35.12 (892) ±1 mm c) 46.22 (1,174) ±1 mm	Shannxi Y8/Y8C. WJ6A rated at 4,550 eshp (3,393 ekW). Oil capacity 105 litres; max oil consumption rate 0.8 litres per hour.
WJ9 (turboprop)	680 shp (507.1 kW)						Reportedly intended for a Y-12 variant and other working aircraft.
WZ-8 (turboshaft)	669 shp (499 kW) take-off for WZ-8A and 684 shp (510 kW) for WZ-8D						WZ-8A used in Z-9 helicopters, and WZ-8D in Z-11 helicopters. Licence built Turbomeca Arriel.
Dongan Engine Manufacturing Company. PO Box 51, Harbin, Heilongjiang 150066 (Telephone: +86 451 802 120, Facsimile: +86 451 802 266)							
WJ5A-1 (single-shaft turboprop)	2,900 ehp (2,162.5 ekW) ±3% take-off at 15,600 rpm ±150	not more than 1,715 lb (778 kg) per hour max rating	a) 15,600 ±150 or 14,050 ±225 idling		1,323 (600) net, 1,587 (720) including accessories		Y7-100 and Y7H-500. Derived from the Ivchenko PROGRESS AI-24.
WJ5A-1G (single-shaft turboprop)	2,856 shp (2,130 kW)	9% fuel reduction			1,587.3 (720)	a) 93.74 (2,381) b) 30.31 (770)	Y7-200B. Air flow rate 32.19 lb (14.6 kg) per second.
WJ5A-1(M) (single-shaft turboprop)	2,790 shp (2,080.5 kW)					a) 93.74 (2,381) b) 30.31 (770)	Y7H.

Designation (type of engine)	Power output (normally take-off rating for piston, turboprop and turboshaft, unless stated)	Specific fuel consumption (S F C)	a) Max RPM b) Pressure or Compression ratio	a) EGT (unless stated to be MGT, TET, TGT or TIT) b) Primary fuel type or Octane rating	Dry weight lb (kg)	a) Length ins (mm) b) Width ins (mm) c) Height ins (mm)	Current aircraft users, and comments
China (People's Republic of)							
Dongan Engine Manufacturing Company. (continued)							
WJ5E (single-shaft turboprop)	3,050 eshp (2,275 ekW)	0.584 lb/shp/hr (355 g/kW/hr)				a) 93.74 (2,381) b) 30.31 (770)	Y7H-500.
Liming Engine Manufacturing Corporation. 6 Dongta Street, Dadong District, Shenyang, Liaoning 110043 (Telephone: +86 24 443139, Facsimile: +86 24 732221)							
WP6/6A/6B (turbojet)	5,400 lbf (24.03 kN) and 5,512 lbf (24.52 kN) typical dry ratings for WP6A and B respectively, 8,267 lbf (36.776 kN) and 8,930 lbf (39.72 kN) with afterburning for WP6A and B respectively	1.6 lb/lbf/hr (45.24 g/kNs) with afterburning and 0.97 lb/lbf/hr (27.48 g/kNs) typical dry rating for WP6A	b) 7.44:1		1,599 (725)	a) 215.87 (5,483) b) 26.3 (668) c) 37.4 (950)	J-6/JJ-6 and Q-5, plus CK1C (ChangKong 1C) supersonic target UAV. Based on Russian Tumansky RD-9.
WP7C (twin-shaft turbojet)	9,590 lbf (42.66 kN) dry, 13,625 lbf (60.6 kN) with afterburning			b) RP-1, RP-2		a) 181.1 (4,600) c) 42.72 (1,085)	J-7/J-7 II.
WP7F (twin-shaft turbojet)	9,920 lbf (44.13 kN) dry, 14,330 lbf (63.75 kN) with afterburning			b) RP-1, RP-2		a) 181.1 (4,600) c) 42.72 (1,085)	J-7E.
WS6 (twin-shaft turbofan)	15,983 lbf (71.1 kN) dry, 27,448 lbf (122.1 kN) with afterburning	0.62 lb/lbf/hr (17.56 g/kNs) dry, 2.26 lb/lbf/hr (64 g/kNs) with afterburning	b) 14.44:1	a) 1,177° C (TIT)	4,629 (2,100)	a) 183.23 (4,654) b) 53.94 (1,370) nozzle diameter	No known current applications.
Liyang Machinery Corporation. PO Box 5, Pingba, Guizhou 561102 (Telephone: +86 34 523311)							
WP7B and M batch (twin-shaft turbojet)	9,689 lbf (43.1 kN) dry, 13,443 lbf (59.8 kN) with afterburning	1.01 lb/lbf/hr (28.61 g/kNs) dry, 2.00 lb/lbf/hr (56.67 g/kNs) with afterburning	b) 8.85:1	a) 1,800° C b) RP-1, RP-2	2,447 (1,110)	a) 181.1 (4,600) c) 42.72 (1,085)	Chengdu J-7/F-7A, and J-7/F-7B for M batch. Power to weight ratio 5.5.
WP7B (BM) (twin-shaft turbojet)	9,689 lbf (43.1 kN) dry, 13,443 lbf (59.8 kN) with afterburning	1.01 lb/lbf/hr (28.61 g/kNs) dry, 2.00 lb/lbf/hr (56.67 g/kNs) with afterburning	b) 8.85:1	a) 1,800° C b) RP-1, RP-2	2,409.6 (1,093)	a) 181.1 (4,600) c) 42.72 (1,085)	Chengdu J-7/F-7L and F-7M, and Guizhou JJ-7. Power to weight ratio 5.6.
WP13 (twin-spool turbojet)	9,037 lbf (40.2 kN) dry, 14,815 lbf (65.9 kN) with afterburning	0.961 lb/lbf/hr (27.22 g/kNs) dry, 2.245 lb/lbf/hr (63.61 g/kNs) with afterburning	b) 8.9:1	a) 1,900° C b) RP-1, RP-2	2,496 (1,132)	a) 181.1 (4,600) c) 42.72 (1,085)	Chengdu J-7/F-7III. Power to weight ratio 5.9.
WP13A II (twin-spool turbojet) See Comments for WP13A III or WP13B	9,600 lbf (42.7 kN) dry, 14,815 lbf (65.9 kN) with afterburning	0.99 lb/lbf/hr (28.06 g/kNs) dry, 2.196 lb/lbf/hr (62.22 g/kNs) with afterburning	b) 8.9:1	a) 1,900° C b) RP-1, RP-2	2,648.6 (1,201.4)	a) 202.76 (5,150) b) 35.71 (907) c) 42.72 (1,085)	Chengdu J-8 II/F-8 II. Power to weight ratio 5.6. 10,580 lbf (47.07 kN) dry and 15,437 lbf (68.67 kN) with afterburning WP13B (WP13A III) in F-8 IIM, weighing 2,821 lb (1,280 kg).
WP13F (twin-spool turbojet – new version)	9,690 lbf (43.1 kN) dry, 14,815 lbf (65.9 kN) with afterburning	0.99 lb/lbf/hr (28.06 g/kNs) dry, 2.05 lb/lbf/hr (58.06 g/kNs) with afterburning	b) 9.0:1	a) 1,870° C b) RP-1, RP-2	2,413 (1,094.5)	a) 181.1 (4,600) c) 42.72 (1,085)	Chengdu J-7/F-7M/F-7MG, F-7 III. Power to weight ratio 6.
Xi'an Aero-Engine Corporation. PO Box 13, Xi'an, Shaanxi 710021 (Telephone: +86 29 6613411, Facsimile: +86 29 6614019)							
WP8 (turbojet)	20,945 lbf (93.167 kN)				6,907 (3,133)		Xi'an H-6.
WS9 (twin-shaft turbofan)	12,550 lbf (55.83 kN) dry, 20,515 lbf (91.26 kN) with afterburning	0.675 lb/lbf/hr (19.12 g/kNs) dry, 2.03 lb/lbf/hr (57.5 g/kNs) with afterburning	a) 12,640 b) 20:1	a) 1,167° C MGT, 634-726 ° C EGT b) Kerosene	4,061 (1,842)	a) 205 (5,205) b) 32.45 (824.23) c) 43.0 (1,093.32)	Xi'an JH-7. Based on the Rolls-Royce Spey 202.
Czech Republic							
Aerotechnik CZ. sro. Letište, 68604, Kunovice (Telephone: +420 632 537111 and 537316, Facsimile: +420 632 537900)							
Mikron IIIS (4-cyl, inverted piston)	Up to 75 hp (55.5 kW) take-off		a) 2,600		up to 154.3 (70)		L-13SEH/SDM Vivat in Mikron IIIS AE form with electric starter/alternator. Bore and stroke 3.54 ins (90 mm).
LOM Praha (Prague). 270 Černokostelecká Street, 100 38 Prague 10-Malešice (Telephone: +420 2 701 166 and 702 148, Facsimile: +420 2 706 523)							
M 132 A (4-cyl, inverted, inline piston). Basic version without supercharger (see Comments)	120.7 hp (90 kW) at 2,700 rpm, 94 hp (70 kW) cruise at 2,500 rpm. (Power ±2.5%)	0.46 lb/hp/hr (280 g/kW/hr)	a) 2,700 b) 6.3:1	b) min 78	231.5 (105) ±2%	a) 41.42 (1,052) b) 16.73 (425) c) 27.1 (688)	For light sports aerobatic aircraft (single or multi-engined). Flick rolls forbidden. A and AL refer to basic engines, capable of basic aerobatics with 5 secs of inverted flight. AR for basic aerobatics/5 secs inverted flight. AK with oil system adapted for full aerobatic inverted flight. AK1/2/3 similar to AK except 1.7 kW alternator instead of dynamo.

Designation (type of engine)	Power output (normally take-off rating for piston, turboprop and turboshaft, unless stated)	Specific fuel consumption (S F C)	a) Max RPM b) Pressure or Compression ratio	a) EGT (unless stated to be MGT, TET, TGT, TIT or ITT) b) Primary fuel type or Octane rating	Dry weight lb (kg)	a) Length ins (mm) b) Width ins (mm) c) Height ins (mm)	Current aircraft users, and comments
Czech Republic							
LOM Praha (Prague). (continued)							
M 137 A (6-cyl, inverted, inline piston). Basic version without supercharger (see Comments)	177.7 hp (132.5 kW) at 2,750 rpm, 138 hp (103 kW) at 2,580 rpm. (Power ±2.5%)	0.492 lb/hp/hr (299 g/kW/hr)	a) 2,750 b) 6.3:1	b) min 78	312 (141.5) ±2.5%	a) 52.91 (1,344) b) 17.44 (443) c) 24.8 (630)	For light sports aerobatic aircraft. Flick rolls allowed. A, AL and AZ types, for full aerobatics and inverted flight. AZ has specially adapted crankshaft and other changes.
M 332 AK (4-cyl, inverted, inline piston). Aerobatic modification (see Comments)	138.1 hp (103 kW) at 2,700 rpm, 98.6 hp (73.5 kW) at 2,400 rpm. (Power ±2.5%)	0.457 lb/hp/hr (278 g/kW/hr)	a) 2,700 b) 6.3:1	b) min 78	227 (103) ±2%	a) 43.39 (1,102) b) 16.73 (425) c) 25.79 (655)	For light sports aircraft. Inverted flight allowed. Flick rolls forbidden. A, AR and AK types. AR supplied without 600W dynamo/adapted drive for a 3 kW alternator.
M 337 AK.1 (6-cyl, inverted, inline piston). Aerobatic modification (see Comments)	206.5 hp (154 kW) at 2,750 rpm, 138.8 hp (103.5 kW) at 2,400 rpm. (Power ±2.5%)	0.48 lb/hp/hr (292 g/kW/hr)	a) 2,700 b) 6.3:1	b) min 78	337.3 (153)	a) 55.51 (1,410) b) 17.48 (444) c) 24.72 (628)	For light sports aircraft. Inverted flight allowed. Flick rolls forbidden. A, AK, AK1/2/3 types (see M 132 A for meaning). Users include Moravan Zlin Z-142/-242.
Walter as. Jinonická 329, 158 01 Praha 5 – Jinonice (Telephone: +420 2 52 96 20 01/03, Facsimile: +420 2 52 60 60, E-mail: marketing@walter.cz, Web site: http//www.pressline/com/cz/walter_AS)							
Walter M202 (2-cyl, 2-stroke, air-cooled piston, with reduction gear)	64.4 hp (48 kW) for 5 minutes, 55 hp (41 kW) maximum continuous	0.715 lb/hp/hr (435 g/kW/hr) cruise	a) 2,350 propeller b) 8.4:1 effective	b) min 96 Octane	94.8 (43) without exhaust	a) 16.69 (424) b) 22.28 (566) c) 16.77 (426)	Light and ultralight aircraft. In production since 1994. Certified to L8/S and JAR-22H regulations. Bore 3.23 ins (82 mm); stroke 2.52 ins (64 mm).
Walter M601D (free-turbine turboprop)	724 shp (540 kW), 657 shp (490 kW) maximum continuous	0.648 lb/shp/hr (394 g/kW/hr) take-off	a) 2,080 propeller ±20 b) 6.55:1	a) 568° C b) Aviation kerosene	425.5 (193) ±2%	a) 65.94 (1,675) b) 23.23 (590) with exhaust nozzle c) 25.59 (650)	L-410UVP. In production since 1983. More than 4,450 engines in the M601 series have been produced, installed in over 1,000 aircraft. TBO 1,500 hours.
Walter M601D-1 (free-turbine turboprop)	724 shp (540 kW), 657 shp (490 kW) maximum continuous	0.648 lb/shp/hr (394 g/kW/hr) take-off	a) 2,080 propeller ±20	a) 710-735° C inter-stage turbine temperature (ITT) at take-off b) Aviation kerosene			Slightly modified version of M601D, for PZL-106BT-601 Turbo-Kruk. Certified to FAR 33 in 1994.
Walter M601D-2 (free-turbine turboprop)	536 shp (400 kW) take-off						Derated for take-off. Intended for the Dornier Do-28-G92 STOL, and had been under evaluation in 1997.
Walter M601E (free-turbine turboprop)	751 shp (560 kW), 657 shp (490 kW) maximum continuous	0.649 lb/shp/hr (395 g/kW/hr) take-off	a) 2,080 propeller ±20 b) 6.65:1	a) 572° C b) Aviation kerosene	445.3 (202) ±2%	a) 65.94 (1,675) b) 23.23 (590) with exhaust nozzle c) 25.59 (650)	L-410UVP-E and possibly T-130 Fregat and T-610 Voyage. In production since 1985. Developed for increased take-off power and TBO of 2,000 hours. Electric alternator of 5 kW for de-icing. Avia Hamilton propeller.
Walter M601E-11 (free-turbine turboprop)	751 shp (560 kW), 657 shp (490 kW) maximum continuous	0.649 lb/shp/hr (395 g/kW/hr) take-off	a) 1,800-1,900 propeller	a) 710-735° C ITT at take-off b) Aviation kerosene	445.3 (202) ±2%	a) 65.94 (1,675) b) 23.23 (590) c) 25.59 (650)	Slightly modified version of M601E, first installed on Ayres S2R Turbo Thrush. Certified by FAA in 1995. Also powers Air Tractor, Ag-Cat and Beech King Air 90.
Walter M601E-21 (F-31) (free-turbine turboprop)	751 shp (560 kW), 657 shp (490 kW) maximum continuous	0.639 lb/shp/hr (389 g/kW/hr) take-off	a) 2,080 propeller ±20	a) 690-735° C ITT at take-off b) Aviation kerosene			L-410UVP-E. Developed in 1994, intended for hot climates. Certified by CAI in compliance with JAR-E in 1994.
Walter M601F (F-21) (free-turbine turboprop)	778 shp (580 kW), 670.5 shp (500 kW) maximum continuous	0.633 lb/shp/hr (385 g/kW/hr) take-off	a) 2,080 propeller ±20 b) 6.65:1	a) 567° C b) Aviation kerosene	445.3 (202) ±2%	a) 65.94 (1,675) b) 23.23 (590) with exhaust nozzle c) 25.59 (650)	L-420, Ibis Ae 270 Ibis. Certified in 1993. Derived from M601E and T, with take-off power increased by lower pressure loss exhaust duct. TBO 3,000 hours.
Walter M601F-22 (F-32) (free-turbine turboprop)	751 shp (560 kW), 657 shp (490 kW) cruise and maximum continuous	0.679 lb/shp/hr (413 g/kW/hr) take-off	a) 2,080 propeller ±20	a) 705-735° C ITT at take-off b) Aviation kerosene			Myasishchev M-101T Gzhel. Increased air bleed for cabin pressurization. First flown 1995.
Walter M601F-33 (free-turbine turboprop)				b) Aviation kerosene			PZL-106BT-601 Turbo-Kruk.
Walter M601F-34 (free turbine turboprop)	778 shp (580 kW), 670.5 shp (500 kW) maximum continuous	0.633 lb/shp/hr (385 g/kW/hr) take-off	a) 2,080 propeller ±20	a) 710-735° C ITT at take-off b) Aviation kerosene			Ibis Ae 270 Ibis.
Walter M601T (free-turbine turboprop for aerobatic aircraft)	751 shp (560 kW), 657 shp (490 kW) maximum continuous	0.649 lb/shp/hr (395 g/kW/hr) take-off	a) 2,080 propeller ±20 b) 6.65:1	a) 572° C b) Aviation kerosene	445.3 (202) ±2%	a) 65.94 (1,675) b) 23.23 (590) with exhaust nozzle c) 25.59 (650)	PZL-130TB and TC Orlik. In production since 1993. Derived from M601E. TBO 1,000 hours. Certified 1993.
Walter M601Z (free-turbine turboprop)	512.3 shp (382 kW), 328.5 shp (245 kW) maximum continuous	0.781 lb/shp/hr (475 g/kW/hr) take-off	a) 1,900 propeller b) 6.08:1	a) 524° C b) Aviation kerosene	434.3 (197) ±2%	a) 65.94 (1,675) b) 23.23 (590) with exhaust nozzle c) 25 (635)	In production since 1984. Derived from M601D, for specific conditions of the Z137T agricultural aircraft. TBO 1,500 hours. Engine equipped with a mechanical drive for agricultural devices and the accessory gearbox is modified for small piston compressor installation.
Walter M602B (coaxial, triple-shaft free-turbine turboprop)	2,012 shp (1,500 kW) take-off and maximum continuous	0.498 lb/shp/hr (303 g/kW/hr)	a) 1,200 propeller b) 12.4:1	a) 511° C b) Aviation kerosene	1,080 (490)	a) 89.96 (2,285) b) 29.65 (753) c) 33.54 (852)	L-610. Derived from M602A. 2-shaft gas generator comprises 2-stage radial-flow compressor, annular combustion chamber, 1-stage HP turbine and 1-stage intermediate pressure turbine. Nozzle guide vanes and blades of HP turbine internally cooled.

Designation (type of engine)	Power output (normally take-off rating for piston, turboprop and turboshaft, unless stated)	Specific fuel consumption (S F C)	a) Max RPM b) Pressure or Compression ratio	a) EGT (unless stated to be MGT, TET, TGT or TIT) b) Primary fuel type or Octane rating	Dry weight lb (kg)	a) Length ins (mm) b) Width ins (mm) c) Height ins (mm)	Current aircraft users, and comments
Czech Republic							
Walter as. (continued)							
Walter M701c-500 (turbojet)	1,963 lbf (8.731 kN), 1,577 lbf (7.014 kN) cruise	1.14 lb/lbf/hr (32.29 g/kNs)	a) 15,400 gas generator b) 4.34:1	a) 680° C b) Aviation kerosene	738.5 (335) ±2.5%	a) 83.19 (2,113) b) 35.0 (890) c) 38.58 (980)	L-29. Manufactured 1960-1995.
PDS Kovovyroba sro. Veleslavinská 26, 160 00 Praha 6							
See Comments							Manufactures engines for paragliders.
Ústav pro vyzkum motorovych vozidel. Lihovarská 12, 190 00 Praha 9							
M-115 and M-125 aircraft engines							Manufacturer of these engines.
Egypt							
ABECO (Arab British Engine Company). PO Box 71, Helwan, Cairo (Telephone +20 2 783329, 783563, Facsimile: +20 2 789652, Telex 23185, 93790 ABECO UN)							
Offers overhaul and repair to Astazou XIVH (and IVH1), TV2-117A, Gnome H-1400, VO-540-C2A							Facilities to repair parts using modern technological methods such as plasma spraying, anti-corrosion painting and dynamic balancing for rotating parts.
Arab Organization for Industrialization (AOI). Engine Factory, PO Box 12, Helwan, Cairo (Telephone: +20 2 5546092/5546093, Facsimile: +20 2 781286)							
See Comments.							Production of gas turbine components, assembly/test/overhaul of aero engines and industrial turbines, and assembly of Larzac 04 and PT6A-25E engines. Overhaul and repair of PT6A-25E, Atar 09C and CT-64.
PT6A-25E (free-turbine, triple-stage, axial and centrifugal turboprop)	750 shp (559.3 kW) max continuous at 2,200 rpm (31° C), 700 shp (522 kW) max cruise (29° C)	0.595 lb/shp/hr (362 g/kW/hr)	b) 6.7:1				Tucano. Assembly, testing, overhaul and repair under licence from P&WC.
France							
Sarl JPX. ZI Nord, BP13, 72320 Vibraye (Telephone +33 2 43 93 61 74, Facsimile: +33 2 43 93 62 71)							
4T 60A (4-cyl, air-cooled piston)	65 hp (48.5 kW)		a) 3,200 b) 8.2:1	b) 100 LL or auto fuel	161 (73)	a) 25.59 (650) b) 31.69 (805)	ATL and Jodel types. A lighter version is the 4T 60AES. Converted Volkswagen auto engine.
4TX 75 (4-cyl, air-cooled piston)	75 hp (56 kW)		a) 2,800 b) 8.7:1	b) 100 LL or auto fuel	165.3 (75)		Light aircraft.
PUL 212 (1-cyl, 2-stroke piston)	18 hp (13.42 kW)		a) 6,000		17.4 (7.9)		Experimental category homebuilt aircraft.
PUL 425 (2-cyl, 2-stroke piston)	22 hp (16.4 kW)		a) 4,600		46.3 (21) with reduction gear		Experimental category homebuilt aircraft.
T620 (single-shaft turbojet)	44 lbf (0.196 kN)				13.67 (6.2) minus fuel control system		Light aircraft.
Microturbo S.A. Chemin du pont de Rupé, BP 2089-31019 Toulouse Cedex (Telephone: +33 5 61 37 55 00, Facsimile: +33 5 61 70 74 45)							
TRS 18 (single-shaft turbojet)	225 lbf (1.00 kN) at sea level	1.22 lb/lbf/hr (34.6 g/kNs)	a) 48,750 b) 4.5:1	a) 860° C b) JP-8	81.5 (37) less tailpipe	a) 22.7 (576) b) 12.05 (306) c) 13.7 (348)	Lexicon RS-1 Shrike (or alternative TRJ-300), Scaled NGT, Bede BD-5J, A21SJ glider, C22J, NASA AD-1, Microjet 200B. Other TRS 18 versions (more powerful) for UAVs.
Rectimo Aviation SA. Aeroport de Chambery - Aix les Bains, F-73420 Viviers du Lac (Telephone: +33 4 79 52 00 00, Facsimile: +33 4 79 54 45 27)							
4 AR-1200 (4-cyl, 4-stroke, air-cooled piston)	37.5 hp (28 kW) at 3,600 rpm, 27 hp (20 kW) cruise at 3,200 rpm	0.59 lb/hp/hr (360 g/kW/hr)	a) 3,600 b) 7:1	b) 80 Octane	134.5 (61)	a) 14.17 (360) b) 29.53 (750) c) 21.65 (550)	Light aircraft and motorgliders. Often quoted 4 AR-1600 follow-up engine was never commercialized.
SMA - Société de Motorisations Aeronautiques. 1 avenue du Président Kennedy, 97170 Viry-Châtillon (Telephone: +33 1 69 12 58 00, Facsimile: +33 1 69 12 58 17)							
Morane Renault MR 180 (4-cyl, 4-stroke, horizontally opposed piston, with fuel injection and supercharging)	180 hp (134.2 kW)		a) 2,000 propeller	b) Jet A1			For certification in November 1998. Company formed by Socata and Renault-Sport. TBO 3,000 hours. Air and oil cooling. No reduction gear.
Morane Renault MR 250 (4-cyl, 4-stroke, horizontally opposed piston, with fuel injection and supercharging)	250 hp (186.4 kW)		a) 2,000 propeller	b) Jet A1			Certification in 1998. Reduction gear, ratio 3.2:1. Cooling as above.
Morane Renault MR 300 (4-cyl, 4-stroke, horizontally opposed piston, with fuel injection and supercharging)	300 hp (224 kW)		a) 2,000 propeller	b) Jet A1			Epsilon Mk2. For certification in August 1998. Reduction gear, ratio 3.2:1. Cooling as above.

Designation (type of engine)	**Power output** (normally take-off rating for piston, turboprop and turboshaft, unless stated)	**Specific fuel consumption** (S F C)	**a) Max RPM** **b) Pressure or Compression ratio**	**a) EGT** (unless stated to be MGT, TET, TGT or TIT) **b) Primary fuel type or Octane rating**	**Dry weight** lb (kg)	**a) Length** ins (mm) **b) Width** ins (mm) **c) Height** ins (mm)	**Current aircraft users, and comments**
France							
SNECMA–Société Nationale d'Étude et de Construction de Moteurs d'Aviation. 2 boulevard du Général Martial Valin, 75724 Paris Cedex 15 (Telephone: +33 1 40 60 84 64, Facsimile: +33 1 40 60 84 87)							
Atar 08K50 (single-shaft turbojet)	11,023 lbf (49 kN)	0.97 lb/lbf/hr (27.48 g/kNs)		b) TR0, TR4	2,546 (1,155)	a) 15.51 (3,950) b) 43.86 (1,114) master cross section	Super Etendard.
Atar 09C (single-shaft turbojet)	9,702 lbf (43.16 kN) dry, 13,672 lbf (60.82 kN) with afterburning	1.00 lb/lbf/hr (28.33 g/kNs) dry, 2.01 lb/lbf/hr (57.03 g/kNs) with afterburning	b) 4.5:1	a) 890° C TIT b) TR0/AG or AIR 3405, TR4/AG or AIR 3407	3,197 (1,450)	a) 234 (5,944) forward flange to exhaust nozzle b) 44.09 (1,120) master cross section	Mirage III and V.
Atar 09K50 (single-shaft turbojet)	11,060 lbf (49.2 kN) dry, 15,846 lbf (70.49 kN) with afterburning	0.98 lb/lbf/hr (27.76 g/kNs) dry, 1.967 lb/lbf/hr (55.72 g/kNs) with afterburning	b) 6.15:1	a) 930° C TIT, 930° C TET b) TR0/AG or AIR 3405, TR4/AG or AIR 3407	3,488 (1,582)	a) 234.02 (5,944) forward to aft flanges b) 40.47 (1,028) master cross section	Mirage III and V upgrades, Mirage F1, Mirage 50, Kfir and Cheetah. 9-stage compressor connected to an uncooled 2-stage turbine. Hydromechanical control completed by an electronic computer. TBO 1,200 hours. Overspeed is automatically released at >Mach 1.4, which allows thrust to be increased.
M53-5 (single-shaft turbofan)	12,235 lbf (54.43 kN) dry, 19,840 lbf (88.26 kN) with afterburning	0.87 lb/lbf/hr (24.64 g/kNs) dry	b) 9.8:1	b) TR0	3,241 (1,470)	b) 41.53 (1,055)	Early production Mirage 2000.
M53-P2 (single-shaft turbofan)	14,400 lbf (64.05 kN) dry, 21,400 lbf (95.19 kN) with afterburning	0.90 lb/lbf/hr (25.49 g/kNs) dry, 2.08 lb/lbf/hr (58.92 g/kNs) with afterburning	b) 9.8:1	a) 862° C EGT, 1,327° C TIT b) TR0	3,340 (1,515)	a) 191.3 (4,859) b) 31.89 (810) c) 41.5 (1,054)	Mirage 2000 built after 1985. 3-stage LP compressor, 5-stage HP compressor, annular combustion chamber, and cooled 2-stage turbine.
M88-2 and M88-3 (twin-shaft turbofan) Details for M88-2 (see Comments)	11,250 lbf (50.04 kN) dry, 16,860 lbf (75 kN) with afterburning	0.8 lb/lbf/hr (22.66 g/kNs) dry, 1.8 lb/lbf/hr (51 g/kNs) with afterburning	b) 24.5:1	a) 1,577° C TIT b) TR0	1,977 (896.75)	a) 139.29 (3,538) b) 32.7 (831), 27.4 (696) inlet diameter	Rafale. Power/weight ratio 8.5:1. 3-stage LP compressor with inlet guide vanes, 6-stage HP compressor with variable vanes, annular combustion chamber, cooled single-stage HP and LP turbines, radial afterburner and convergent nozzle. M88-3 for production Rafales of 19,560 lbf (87 kN) with afterburning. Possibly M88-2K for Samsung KTX-2.
M138 (turbopropulsor)	8,000–12,000 shp (5,966–8,948 kW)	Low fuel consumption					High-speed advanced turbopropulsor, proposed for the Airbus Military Corporation (AMC) FLA. European collaboration between SNECMA, MTU, ITP and FiatAvio. Based on SNECMA's M88 military core engine. 8-blade 17 ft (5.18 m) propeller, inline high-power reduction gearbox, 4-stage low-pressure compressor with variable stator vanes, 3-stage low-pressure turbine designed using 3D Aerodynamic codes, FADEC and on condition engine operation. Optimized for high-speed cruise of Mach 0.68–0.72. Growth potential.
Turbomeca. 64511 Bordes Cedex (Telephone: +33 5 59 12 50 00, Facsimile: +33 5 59 53 15 12)							
Arriel 1 (free-turbine turboshaft) See Comments	641 shp (478 kW) take-off, 590 shp (440 kW) maximum continuous for Arriel 1B	0.63 lb/shp/hr (383 g/kW/hr) at 350 kW for Arriel 1B and 1S1; 0.633 lb/shp/hr (385 g/kW/hr) at 350 kW for Arriel 1C2, 1E2 and 1K1.	a) 6,000 shaft for Arriel 1A and 1B b) 9:1 for Arriel 1A and 1B		264.5 (120) including accessories for Arriel 1A and 1B	a) 42.91 (1,090) for Arriel 1A and 1B b) 16.93 (430) for Arriel 1A and 1B c) 22.4 (569) for Arriel 1A and 1B	AS 350 and AS 365C (Arriel 1A/B), AS 365N (640 shp, 477 kW Arriel 1C), AS 365, A 109K and S-76A+ (700 shp, 522 kW Arriel 1C1, 1K, 1M and 1S), AS 365N2 (737 shp, 550 kW Arriel 1C2), AS 350 (684 shp, 510 kW Arriel 1D), AS 350B2, AS 550 Fennec and Kamov Ka-128 (732 shp, 546 kW Arriel 1D1), BK 117 C-1 (738 shp, 550 kW Arriel 1E2), A 109K2 (738 shp, 550 kW Arriel 1K1), AS 565 Panther (748 shp, 558 kW Arriel 1M1), and S-76A+/C (725 shp, 541 kW Arriel 1S1). Offered as replacement engine for AStar AS 350D. TBO 3,000 hours. Well over 3,900 Arriel engines have been produced, totalling over 8 million flight hours.
Arriel 2 (free-turbine turboshaft) See Comments	848 shp (632 kW) for Arriel 2B, 839 shp (626 kW) for Arriel 2C, 856 shp (638 kW) for Arriel 2S1 take-off/continuous OEI ratings.	0.618 lb/shp/hr (376 g/kW/hr) at 400 kW	a) 6,000 shaft				AS 350 B3 (Arriel 2B), AS 365 N3 (Arriel 2C), EC 155 (Arriel 2C1), and Sikorsky S-76C+ (Arriel 2S1). Integrated single crystal blades for higher power levels. Equipped with FADEC. First flown on an S-76C on 30 June 1994 at the subsidiary CGTM. TBO 3,000 flight hours.
Arrius 1/1A1 (free-turbine turboshaft)	479 shp (357 kW) take-off, 547 shp (408 kW) OEI for 2.5 minutes	0.641 lb/shp/hr (390 g/kW/hr) at 221 kW	a) 6,000 shaft		191.8 (87)	a) 30.79 (782) b) 14.17 (360) c) 21.26 (540)	AS 355/555. Has FADEC.
Arrius 1D (turboprop variant of the Arrius turboshaft)	488 shp (364 kW), flat rated for Omega to 360 shp (268 kW)		a) 6,000 shaft		244.7 (111)	a) 32.52 (826) b) 18.74 (476) c) 23.23 (590)	TB 31 Omega. Previously known as the Arrius 1A2. Has FADEC. Several hundred Arrius engines of all versions produced.
Arrius 1F (free-turbine turboshaft)	500 shp (373 kW)		a) 6,000 shaft			a) 30.79 (782) b) 14.17 (360) c) 21.26 (540)	EC 120. Single engine application, with hydromechanical control. Development began in 1993.
Arrius 1M (free-turbine turboshaft)	479 shp (357 kW) take-off		a) 6,000 shaft		191.8 (87)	a) 30.79 (782) b) 14.17 (360) c) 21.26 (540)	AS 555 Fennec. Military version of Arrius 1, in service with the French Air Force and French Army's ALAT.

Designation (type of engine)	Power output (normally take-off rating for piston, turboprop and turboshaft, unless stated)	Specific fuel consumption (S F C)	a) Max RPM b) Pressure or Compression ratio	a) EGT (unless stated to be MGT, TET, TGT or TIT) b) Primary fuel type or Octane rating	Dry weight lb (kg)	a) Length ins (mm) b) Width ins (mm) c) Height ins (mm)	Current aircraft users, and comments
France							
Turbomeca. (continued)							
Arrius 2B (free-turbine turboshaft) See Comments for Arrius 2B1	583 shp (435 kW) take-off, 696 shp (519 kW) OEI for 2.5 minutes	0.608 lb/shp/hr (370 g/kW/hr) at 300 kW	a) 6,000 shaft b) 9:1		244.7 (111)	a) 37.3 (947) b) 15.9 (404) c) 27.2 (692)	EC 135 and EC 635. First flight on 15 February 1994. Arrius 2B1 version has same dimensions, 670.5 shp (500 kW) take-off and 751 shp (560 kW) OEI for 2.5 minutes ratings, and a SFC of 0.615 lb/shp/hr (374 g/kW/hr). TBO 1,300 hours. Some structure as Arrius 1, with 2 modules (reduction gearbox with an output shaft tilted at 28° and a gas generator module including the gas generator turbine with single crystal blades).
Arrius 2C (free-turbine turboshaft)	668 shp (498 kW) take-off, 696 shp (519 kW) OEI for 2.5 minutes)	0.608 lb/shp/hr (370 g/kW/hr) at 300 kW	a) 6,000 shaft		233.7 (106)	a) 38.1 (968) b) 18.5 (470) c) 26.4 (670)	Alternative engine for the MD 900 Explorer. First flown in an Ecureuil test-bed in February 1993. TBO 3,000 hours. Straight output shaft.
Arrius 2D (free-turbine turboshaft)	600 shp (447 kW)		a) 6,000 shaft	b) Jet JP-1, JP-4 and Jet B			Final engine for Omega.
Arrius 2F (free-turbine turboshaft)	504 shp (376 kW) take-off, 449 shp (335 kW) maximum continuous	0.674 lb/shp/hr (410 g/kW/hr) at 200 kW	a) 6,000 shaft		227.1 (103) with equipment	a) 37.2 (945) b) 18.1 (459) c) 27.4 (696)	EC 120 B.
Arrius 2K1 (free-turbine turboshaft)	670.5 shp (500 kW) take-off, 751 shp (560 kW) OEI for 2.5 minutes	0.615 lb/shp/hr (374 g/kW/hr) at 300 kW	a) 6,000 shaft		253.5 (115) with equipment	a) 38.1 (968) b) 18.5 (470) c) 26.4 (670)	A109 Power. Digital Engine Controller. Straight output shaft. TBO 3,000 hours.
Astazou III (single-shaft, single-stage axial and single-stage centrifugal turboshaft)	523-591 shp (390-441 kW) max continuous	0.643-0.65 lb/shp/hr (391-395 g/kW/hr) maximum			324-331 (147-150)	a) 56.42 (1,433) b) 18.11 (460) c) 18.11 (460)	SA 341 Gazelle. SA 341F2 variant uses a 643.7 shp (480 kW) Astazou IIIPA, the maximum rating for an Astazou III type.
Astazou XIVH (single-shaft, two-stage axial and single-stage centrifugal turboshaft)	591.4 shp (441 kW) in SA 341, flat-rated to 55° C, 872 shp (650 kW) in SA 342 maximum power and flat-rated to transmission				352.7 (160)	a) 57.87 (1,470) b) 18.11 (460) c) 18.11 (460)	SA 341 and SA 342J/K/L Gazelle. Flat-rated to transmission limitations on SA 342.
Astazou XIVM1 and M2 (single-shaft, two-stage axial and single-stage centrifugal turboshaft)	858.25 shp (640 kW) maximum power, 592 shp (441 kW) take-off					a) 57.87 (1,470) b) 18.11 (460) c) 18.11 (460)	SA 342L2 Gazelle.
Astazou XVI (single-shaft turboprop)	965 shp (720 kW) in XVIG form	0.525 lb/shp/hr (319 g/kW/hr) in XVIG form	a) 43,000		503 (228) equipped in XVIG form	a) 80.59 (2,047) incl propeller b) 21.5 (546) intake	Pucará (XVIG), early Jetstream and others. XVIG capable of inverted flight.
Artouste III (single-shaft turboshaft)	590 shp (440 kW), flat-rated to 55° C in IIID form	0.747 lb/shp/hr (454 g/kW/hr)	b) 5.2:1		392.4 (178)	a) 71.46 (1,815) b) 19.96 (507) c) 24.68 (627)	SA 315 Lama and SA 316B and C Alouette III (401 lb, 182 kg and 563.2 shp, 420 kW Artouste IIIB for HAL Cheetah and Chetak), and SA 316C Alouette III (IIID).
Makila (free-turbine turboshaft)	1,820 shp (1,357 kW) take-off and 1,877 shp (1,400 kW) OEI for 2.5 minutes for Makila 1A1, 1,845 shp (1,376 kW) take-off and 2,109 shp (1,573 kW) OEI for 30 seconds for Makila 1A2 and 1K2	0.562 lb/shp/hr (342 g/kW/hr) for Makila 1A1, 0.551 lb/shp/hr (335 g/kW/hr) for Makila 1A2, 0.559 lb/shp/hr (340 g/kW/hr) for Makila 1K2, all at 700 kW	a) 23,000 shaft		463 (210)	a) 54.92 (1,395) b) 20.24 (514)	SA 330, AS 332 Super Puma and AS 532 Cougar for Makila 1A1, AS 332 and AS 532 Mk 2 for Makila 1A2, and Rooivalk for Makila 1K2. 1A2 offers increased performance and a super contingency power rating due to the Electronic Engine Control Unit over Makila 1A1. Makila 1A2 is an adaptation of the 1A2. TBO 3,000 hours. Well over 1,300 Makila engines have been produced, totalling over 3 million flight hours.
TM 333 (free-turbine turboshaft) (data for TM 333 2B)	994 shp (741 kW) take-off and continuous OEI, 1,155 shp (861 kW) OEI for 30 seconds	0.585 lb/shp/hr (356 g/kW/hr) at 60% take-off power	a) 6,000 shaft		368.2 (167)	a) 41.14 (1,045) b) 17.72 (450) c) 29.33 (745)	TM 333-1A is the base variant, with the TM 333-1M for the AS 565 Panther military helicopter. TM 333-2B selected for the Indian HAL Advanced Light Helicopter. TM 333-2E has been evolved from the 2B, offering about 9% more power and a dual-channel Digital Engine Control Unit.
Groupement Turbomeca-SNECMA. 2 boulevard du Général Martial Valin, 75724 Paris Cedex 15 (Telephone/Facsimile: see SNECMA)							
Larzac 04-6 (twin-shaft turbofan)	2,965 lbf (13.19 kN)	0.716 lb/lbf/hr (20.28 g/kNs)	a) 22,570 b) 10.53:1	a) 1,130° C TET b) TR0, TR4, TR5	650.4 (295) basic	a) 46.73 (1,187) fwd to aft flanges b) 17.78 (451.6); overall diameter 23.7 (602) c) 30.39 (772)	Alpha Jet. 2-stage LP axial compressor, 4-stage HP axial compressor, annular combustion chamber, 1-stage HP turbine, 1-stage LP turbine, and electronic control.
Larzac 04-20 (twin-shaft turbofan)	3,174 lbf (14.12 kN)	0.745 lb/lbf/hr (21.11 g/kNs)	a) 23,330 b) 11.13:1	a) 1,160° C TET b) TR0, TR4, TR5	650.4 (295) basic	a) 46.73 (1,187) fwd to aft flanges b) 17.78 (451.6); overall diameter 23.7 (602) c) 30.39 (772)	Alpha Jet (C20), MiG-AT or UTS export version (R20, with different nozzle and fuel control and interface). 2-stage LP axial compressor, 4-stage HP axial compressor, annular combustion chamber, 1-stage HP turbine, 1-stage LP turbine, and electronic control.

Designation (type of engine)	Power output (normally take-off rating for piston, turboprop and turboshaft, unless stated)	Specific fuel consumption (S F C)	a) Max RPM b) Pressure or Compression ratio	a) EGT (unless stated to be MGT, TET, TGT or TIT) b) Primary fuel type or Octane rating	Dry weight lb (kg)	a) Length ins (mm) b) Width ins (mm) c) Height ins (mm)	Current aircraft users, and comments
Germany							
Göbler-Hirthmotoren KG. Max-Eyth-strasse 10, 71726 Benningen (Telephone: +49 71 44 60 74 or 60 75, Facsimile: +49 71 44 54 15)							
Hirth F-23A (2-cyl, 2-stroke, horizontally opposed, fan-cooled piston)	39.6 hp (29.5 kW) at 5,500 rpm		a) 6,500 b) 9.3:1	a) 732° C b) 95 ROZ, 85 MOZ unleaded	52.9 (24)	a) 12.78 (324.5) b) 22.91 (582) c) 13.82 (351)	Ultralights, Experimental category aircraft.
Hirth F-30/2c (4-cyl, 2-stroke, horizontally opposed piston, with optional twin fan-cooling)	110 hp (82 kW) at 6,200 rpm		a) 6,500 b) 9.5:1	a) 732° C b) 95 ROZ, 85 MOZ unleaded	129 (58.5) with reduction unit, electric start, exhaust system	a) 17.72 (450) b) 22.91 (582) c) 14.72 (374)	Ultralights, ultralight helicopters and Experimental category aircraft. Displacement 1,042 cc; bore 2.83 ins (72 mm); stroke 2.52 ins (64 mm). Dual ignition. 12 volt DC starter standard. Gearboxes or belt drives optional. Choice of dampener or centrifugal clutch drive couplings. Dual integral pumper style carburetion.
Hirth F-30/4c (4-cyl, 2-stroke, horizontally opposed piston, with optional twin cooling fans)	120 hp (89.5 kW) at 6,200 rpm		a) 6,500 b) 9.5:1	a) 732° C b) 95 ROZ, 85 MOZ unleaded	135 (61.2) with reduction unit, electric start, exhaust system	a) 17.72 (450) b) 22.91 (582) c) 14.72 (374)	As for F-30/2c, except quad integral pumper style carburetion and higher output.
Hirth F-33 (1 cyl, 2-stroke, air-cooled piston)	22 hp (16.4 kW) at 5,200 rpm		b) 9.5:1		35 (26) with exhaust system	a) 11.79 (299.5) b) – c) 14.96 (380)	Displacement 321 cc; bore 2.99 ins (76 mm); stroke 2.72 ins (69 mm). Single 1.34 ins (34 mm) slide type carburettor. Recoil starter. Multi-groove belts reduction unit. New engine to Hirth range.
Hirth F-263 R53 (2-cyl, 2-stroke, inline piston)	27.6 hp (20.6 kW) at 6,000 rpm		a) 6,500 b) 9.5:1	a) 732° C b) 95 ROZ, 85 MOZ unleaded	59.5 (27)	a) 15.16 (385) b) 17.8 (452) c) 13.9 (353)	Ultralights.
Hirth 2702 R 55 (2-cyl, 2-stroke, fan-cooled, inline piston)	39.4 hp (29.4 kW) at 5,700 rpm		a) 6,500 b) 9.3:1	a) 732° C b) 95 ROZ, 85 MOZ unleaded	72.75 (33)	a) 14.84 (377) b) 21.81 (554) c) 14.8 (376)	Ultralights, Experimental category aircraft.
Hirth 2703 R 35 (2-cyl, 2-stroke, fan-cooled, inline piston)	54.2 hp (40.4 kW) at 6,200 rpm		a) 6,500 b) 9.3:1	a) 732° C b) 95 ROZ, 85 MOZ unleaded	72.75 (33)	a) 14.84 (377) b) 21.81 (554) c) 14.8 (376)	Ultralights, ultralight helicopters and Experimental category aircraft.
Hirth 2704 R05 (2-cyl, 2-stroke, fan-cooled, inline piston)	39.6 hp (29.5 kW) at 4,700 rpm		a) 6,500 b) 9.2:1	a) 732° C b) 95 ROZ, 85 MOZ unleaded	66.1 (30)	a) 16.22 (412) b) 22.68 (576) c) 15.1 (383)	Ultralights, Experimental category aircraft.
Hirth 2706 R05 (2-cyl, 2-stroke, fan-cooled, inline piston)	61.7 hp (46 kW) at 6,300 rpm		a) 6,500 b) 9.3:1	a) 732° C b) 95 ROZ, 85 MOZ unleaded	66.6 (30.2)	a) 16.22 (412) b) 21.93 (557) c) 15.1 (383)	Ultralights, Experimental category aircraft.
Dieter König GmbH & Co Motorenbau KG. Friedrich-Olbricht-Damm 72, D-13627 Berlin (Telephone: +49 30 344 30 71, Facsimile: +49 30 344 15 95)							
SC 430 (3-cyl, 2-stroke radial piston with direct or reduction drive)	24 hp (17.9 kW) at 4,000-4,200 rpm	10.8 litres/hr	a) 4,300 b) 7.4:1	a) 150° C b) 100 LL or Super gasoline with Pb	35.3 (16) with exhaust collector, mounts, carburettor and fuel pump	a) 11.42 (290) b) 18.1 (480)	Ultralights and powered parachutes. Displacement 430 cc; bore 2.60 ins (66 mm); stroke 1.65 ins (42 mm). 12 volt electric starter.
SD 570 (4-cyl, 2-stroke radial piston)	28 hp (20.9 kW) at 4,000-4,200 rpm	12 litres/hr	a) 4,300 b) 7.4:1	a) 150° C b) 100 LL or Super gasoline with Pb	40.8 (18.5) with exhaust collector, mounts, carburettor and fuel pump	a) 13.78 (350) b) 18.11 (460)	Ultralights. Displacement 570 cc; bore 2.60 ins (66 mm); stroke 1.65 ins (42 mm). 12 volt electric starter. Optional Powergrip reduction belt, ratio 1.75:1.
FC 500 (4-cyl, 2-stroke, horizontally opposed, water-cooled piston, with belt reduction)	54 hp (40.27 kW) at 6,000 rpm	26 litres/hr full power, 7 litres/hr at 3,800 rpm	a) 6,000		86 (39) without radiator	a) 15.47 (393) b) 15.75 (400)	Displacement 500 cc; bore 2.13 ins (54 mm); stroke 2.13 ins (54 mm). Poly-V-belt reduction, ratio 2.8:1.
Limbach Flugmotoren GmbH & Co KG. Kotthausenerstrasse 5, D-53639 Königswinter – Sassenberg (Telephone: +49 2244 920126, Facsimile: +49 2244 920130)							
L 275E (2-cyl, 2-stroke, horizontally opposed, air-cooled piston)	24 hp (18 kW)		a) 7,300	b) 90 Octane	16.53 (7.5)	a) 8.9 (226) b) 5.4 (390) c) 7.4 (187)	Ultralights.
L 550E (4-cyl, 2-stroke, horizontally opposed piston)	50 hp (37.3 kW)		a) 7,500	b) 90 Octane	34 (15.4)		Lightplanes and ultralights.
SL 1700 series (4-cyl, 4-stroke, horizontally opposed, air-cooled piston)	typically 64 hp (51 kW) take-off		b) 8:1	b) 90 Octane	161 (73)	a) 24.33 (618) b) 30.1 (764) c) 14.49 (368)	Lightplanes and motorgliders. Certified (to JAR-22/H) and non-certified models.
L 1800 series (4-cyl, 4-stroke, horizontally opposed, air-cooled piston)	typically 66 hp (49 kW) take-off		b) 7.5:1	b) Mogas and 100 LL	154.5 (70) approx	a) 24.33 (618) b) 30.1 (764)	Lightplanes, motorgliders and Experimental category aircraft.

Designation (type of engine)	Power output (normally take-off rating for piston, turboprop and turboshaft, unless stated)	Specific fuel consumption (S F C)	a) Max RPM b) Pressure or Compression ratio	a) EGT (unless stated to be MGT, TET, TGT or TIT) b) Primary fuel type or Octane rating	Dry weight lb (kg)	a) Length ins (mm) b) Width ins (mm) c) Height ins (mm)	Current aircraft users, and comments
Germany							
Limbach Flugmotoren GmbH & Co KG. (continued)							
L 2000 series (4-cyl, 4-stroke, horizontally opposed, air-cooled piston)	80 hp (59.7 kW) at 3,400 rpm take-off, 70 hp (52.2 kW) at 3,000 rpm maximum continuous)	12 litres/hr approx	b) 8.4:1	b) Mogas and 100 LL	163.1 (74)	a) 24.33 (618) b) 30.1 (764)	Lightplanes and many motorgliders, including the Fournier RF-5 in L 2000EO 1 form. Also Experimental category aircraft. Certified to JAR-22/H. EO 1 for variable-pitch propeller, EC 1 for variable-pitch pusher, EO 2 for fixed-pitch, EC 2 for fixed-pitch pusher, EO 3 for fixed-pitch (SAE No 1), and EC 3 for fixed-pitch pusher (SAE No 1). Bore 3.54 ins (90 mm); stroke 3.09 ins (78.4 mm). Displacement 1,994 cc.
L 2400 series (4-cyl, 4-stroke, horizontally opposed piston)	typically 93-130 hp (69.4-97 kW)		b) 8.5:1	b) RON 96 minimum. Latest L 2400EFI uses unleaded auto fuel	typically 181 (82) for EB models, or 187.5 (88) for L 2400EFI		Lightplanes and motorgliders, the many types including the Stemme S10 and Arc RF47. Certified JAR-22. Series of at least 9 models, the latest being the 100 hp (74.6 kW) L 2400EFI with electronic fuel injection and solid state ignition, certified under JAR-VLA. Anticipated future derivatives of the EFI could include a turbocharged, geared 160 hp (119.4 kW) model.
MTU-Motoren- und Turbinen-Union München GmbH. Postfach 50 06 40, 80976 München (Telephone: +49 89 1489-0, Facsimile: +49 89 150 26 21, E-mail: YAV1105@dbmail.debis.de)							
See Comments							Part of Daimler-Benz Aerospace. Partner in several multi-national programmes, including Eurojet, International Aero Engines, MTR and Turbo-Union. Also participates in Allison, General Electric, Pratt & Whitney, and Pratt & Whitney Canada programmes, including 12.5% share of engine in PW4000 Growth, CF6 (8-9.6%), PW2000 (21.2%), V2500 (11%), JT8D-200 (12.5%), EJ200 (33%), RB199 (40%), J79 (40%), PW300 (25%), PW500 (25%), Larzac (23%), Tyne (28%), T64 (30%), T700 (15%), MTR390 (40%), and 250-C20 (40%).
Sauer Motorenbau GmbH. 55270 Ober-Olm, Nieder-Olmer-Str 16 (Telephone: +49 61 36 893 77, Facsimile: +49 61 36 854 66)							
SE 1800 E1S (4-cyl, horizontally opposed, air-cooled, direct drive piston)	54 hp (40.3 kW) at 3,000 rpm, 44 hp (32.8 kW) cruise at 2,600 rpm	0.506 lb/hp/hr (308 g/kW/hr)	a) 3,200 b) 8.8:1	a) 600° C b) 93 Octane	139.6 (63.3)	a) 21.65 (550) b) 30.1 (765) c) 11.18 (284)	Fournier RF4, Scheibe SF 25, Stark-Turbulent Jodel Bebe, Tipsy Nipper.
SF 2500 H1S (4-cyl, horizontally opposed, air-cooled, shaft drive piston)	103 hp (76.7 kW) at 3,200 rpm, 80 hp (59.7 kW) cruise	0.506 lb/hp/hr (308 g/kW/hr)	a) 3,400 b) 9.5:1	a) 650° C b) 97 Octane	176.4 (80)	a) 23.62 (600) b) 30.71 (780) c) 10.24 (260)	Stemme S10.
SS 2100 H1S (4-cyl, horizontally opposed, air-cooled, direct drive piston)	80 hp (59.7 kW) at 3,000 rpm, 65 hp (48.5 kW) cruise at 2,700 rpm	0.496 lb/hp/hr (302 g/kW/hr)	a) 3,200 b) 9.5:1	a) 650° C b) 95 Octane	167.6 (76)	a) 23.62 (600) b) 31.1 (790) c) 11.61 (295)	Fournier RF, Scheibe SF 25, Jodel D18.
ST 2500 H1S (4-cyl, horizontally opposed, air-cooled, direct drive piston)	92 hp (68.6 kW) at 3,000 rpm, 75 hp (56 kW) cruise at 2,700 rpm	0.496 lb/hp/hr (302 g/kW/hr)	a) 3,200 b) 9.5:1	a) 650° C b) 95 Octane	174.2 (79)	a) 23.62 (600) b) 30.71 (780) c) 11.61 (295)	Bölkow Junior, Fournier RF, Jodel D18, Valentin TL17.
Michael Zoche Antriebstechnik. Keferstrasse 13, 80802 München (Telephone: +49 89 344 591, Facsimile: +49 89 342 451, E-mail: 101613.444@compuserve.com, Web site: http://ourworld.compuserve.com/homepages/AOSOFT/zoche.htm)							
ZO 01A (4-cyl piston in radial form)	147.5 hp (110 kW)	0.37 lb/hp/hr (225 g/kW/hr) max power, 0.362 lb/hp/hr (220 g/kW/hr) 70% cruise	a) 2,500 b) 17:1	a) 550° C inlet temperature b) Diesel 2, JP-4, JP-5, JP-8 or Jet A	185.2 (84)	a) 32.04 (814) b) 25.35 (644) c) 21.85 (555)	Compact aero diesel engine incorporating the latest cylinder technology as well as refinements such as tungsten counterweights and full aerobatic pressure lubrication. Bore 3.74 ins (95 mm); stroke 3.70 ins (94 mm).
ZO 02A (8-cyl piston in radial form)	295 hp (220 kW)	0.37 lb/hp/hr (225 g/kW/hr) max power, 0.362 lb/hp/hr (220 g/kW/hr) 70% cruise	a) 2,500 b) 17:1	a) 550° C inlet temperature b) Diesel 2, JP-4, JP–5, JP-8 or Jet A	271 (123)	a) 36.38 (924) b) 25.35 (644) c) 25.35 (644)	Compact aero diesel engine incorporating the latest cylinder technology as well as refinements such as tungsten counterweights and full aerobatic pressure lubrication. Bore 3.74 ins (95 mm); stroke 3.70 ins (94 mm).
ZO 03A (2-cyl piston)	68 hp (51 kW)	0.386 lb/hp/hr (235 g/kW/hr) max power, 0.378 lb/hp/hr (230 g/kW/hr) 75% cruise	a) 2,500 b) 17:1	a) 550° C inlet temperature b) Diesel 2, JP-4, JP–5, JP-8 or Jet A	121.25 (55)	a) 29.53 (750) b) 21.85 (555) c) 15.94 (405)	Compact aero diesel engine incorporating the latest cylinder technology as well as refinements such as tungsten counterweights and full aerobatic pressure lubrication. Bore 3.74 ins (95 mm); stroke 3.70 ins (94 mm).
India							
Gas Turbine Research Establishment. Suranjan Das Road, CV Raman Nagar, Bangalore 560 093 (Telephone: +91 80 580 698, Facsimile: +91 80 581 507)							
Kaveri (turbofan)	11,530 lbf (51.3 kN) dry, 18,750 lbf (83.4 kN) with afterburning approximately, flat rated to 20° C		b) 22:1	a) 1,427° C TET			For production examples of the Indian LCA. 6-stage HP compressor, 3-stage LP compressor, single-stage HP and LP turbines, and annular combustor. FADEC engine control.

Designation (type of engine)	Power output (normally take-off rating for piston, turboprop and turboshaft, unless stated)	Specific fuel consumption (S F C)	a) Max RPM b) Pressure or Compression ratio	a) EGT (unless stated to be MGT, TET, TGT or TIT) b) Primary fuel type or Octane rating	Dry weight lb (kg)	a) Length ins (mm) b) Width ins (mm) c) Height ins (mm)	Current aircraft users, and comments
Italy							
Arrow Engineering Srl. Via Badiaschi 25, 29100 Piacenza							
AE 270 AC (1-cyl, 2-stroke, air-cooled piston)	35 hp (26.07 kW) at 6,800 rpm	6-8 litres per hour	a) 6,800		79.4 (36)	a) 18.11 (460) b) 14.88 (378) c) 14.96 (380)	Experimental category homebuilts and ultralights. 267 cc. Bore 2.94 ins (74.6 mm); stroke 2.4 ins (61 mm). Planetary reduction gear ratio 0.321.
AE 430 (2-cyl piston)	28 hp (21 kW) at 6,500 rpm				24.25 (11)		For UAVs.
AE 530 AC (2-cyl, 2-stroke, air-cooled piston)	68 hp (50.7 kW) at 6,800 rpm	8-12 litres per hour	a) 6,800		110.23 (50)	a) 18.94 (481) b) 19.29 (490) c) 18.23 (463)	Experimental category homebuilts and ultralights. 533 cc. Planetary reduction gear ratio 0.361.
AE 1070 AC (4 cyl, piston)	120 hp (89.5 kW) at 6,800 rpm	8-14 litres per hour	a) 6,800		143.3 (119)	a) 20.51 (521) b) 19.3 (490) c) 18.03 (458)	Experimental category homebuilts. 1,066 cc. Helical reduction gear ratio 0.327.
GP250 (1-cyl, 2-stroke, air-cooled piston)	34 hp (25 kW) max power	up to 6 litres per hour	a) 6,800		57.32 (26)	a) 18.11 (460) b) 14.57 (370) c) 14.96 (380)	Experimental category homebuilts and ultralights.
GP500 (2-cyl, 2-stroke, air-cooled piston)	65 hp (48.5 kW)	up to 10 litres per hour	a) 6,800		79.4 (36)	a) 19.69 (500) b) 19.69 (500) c) 17.76 (451)	Experimental category homebuilts and ultralights.
GP654 (2-cyl, 4-stroke, air-cooled V piston)	55 hp (41 kW)	up to 6 litres per hour	a) 6,500		132.3 (60)	a) 27.64 (702) b) 16.97 (431) c) 18.11 (460)	Experimental category homebuilts and ultralights.
GP1000 (4-cyl, air-cooled piston)	120 hp (89.5 kW)	up to 14 litres per hour	a) 6,800		143.3 (65)	a) 20.51 (521) b) 19.3 (490) c) 18.03 (458)	Experimental category homebuilts and ultralights.
GP1500 (6-cyl, air-cooled piston)	180 hp (134 kW)	up to 14 litres per hour	a) 6,800		193 (87.5)	a) 32.3 (821) b) 19.3 (490) c) 18.03 (458)	Experimental category homebuilts and ultralights.
CRM. Via Manzoni 12, 20121 Milan							
CRM 18D/SS (18-cyl, 4-stroke, liquid-cooled, turbocharged diesel)	1,850-2,400 hp (1,380-1,790 kW)				4,000 (1,814)	a) 132.7 (3,370) b) 53.15 (1,350) c) 51.34 (1,304)	Had been proposed for the Sentinel 5000 buoyant aircraft programme.
FiatAvio. Via Nizza 312, 10127 Turin (Telephone: +39 011 68 58 007, Facsimile: +39 011 68 58 945)							
See Comments							Partner in several multi-national programmes, including Eurojet, International Aero Engines and Turbo-Union. Also participates in GE and P&W programmes.
IAME. Engine production ended in 1993							
KFM 107 MAXI (2-cyl, 2-stroke piston)	30 hp (22.4 kW)	8.3 litres per hour at 6,080 rpm	a) 6,300		42-50 (19-11.5)	a) 17.12 (435) b) 17.3 (440) c) 10 (253)	Experimental category homebuilt aircraft and ultralights. Out of production.
KFM 112 (4-cyl, 4-stroke piston)	60 hp (44.7 kW)	11-16 litres per hour	a) 3,200		119 (54)	a) 23 (583) b) 23.7 (603) c) 15 (380)	Experimental category homebuilt aircraft and ultralights. Out of production.
Industrie Aeronautiche E Meccaniche Rinaldo Piaggio SpA. Via Cibrario 4, 16154 Genoa (Telephone: +39 010 64811, Facsimile: +39 010 6520160)							
See Comments							Produces Rolls-Royce Gem, Spey and Viper, and AlliedSignal T53 and T55 engines under licence, and has a share in the RTM 322.
VM Motori SpA, Via Ferrarese 29, 44042 Cento (Fe)							
TPJ 1304HF, 1306HF and 1308HF (4, 6 and 8-cyl, 4-stroke, liquid-cooled, turbocharged pistons)	207, 315 and 423.75 hp (154, 235 and 316 kW)		a) 2,640 b) 18:1	b) JP-4, JP-5, JP-8, Jet A or others	408, 535.7 and 657 (185, 243 and 298)		All versions bore 5.12 ins (130 mm) and stroke 4.33 ins (110 mm).
Japan							
Ishikawajima-Harima Heavy Industries Co Ltd. Shin Ohtemachi Building, 2-1, Ohtemachi 2-chome, Chiyoda-ku, Tokyo 100 (Telephone: +81 3 3244 5333, Facsimile: +81 3 3244 5398, E-mail: eiichi_terada@ihi.co.jp)							
Produces under licence the P&W F100 for the F-15J, Allison T56 for the P-3C, GE T700 for the H-60J, and is a partner in the GE90, IAE V2500, PW4000 and RJ500.							IHI produced 610 GE J79s for F-104/F-4s to 1980, 391 GE T64s for the P-2J and PS/US-1 to 1982, GE T58s for HSS-2/S-61/V-107 helicopters, and 426 TF40 turbofans for F-1/T-2s to 1987. The FJR710 5-tonne class high bypass ratio turbofan development project was completed in 1982, and 4 were fitted to the experimental NAL STOL aircraft.
F3-IHI-30 (twin-shaft turbofan)	3,682 lbf (16.38 kN) take-off	0.7 lb/lbf/hr (19.83 g/kNs)	b) 11:1		749.5 (340)	a) 79.61 (2,022) overall b) 22.05 (560)	T-4. Developed as an R&D project of the Japan Defence Agency. Series production began in 1987.
J3-IHI-7D (turbojet)	3,417 lbf (15.2 kN)				838 (380)	a) 81.89 (2,080) overall b) 24.8 (630) c) 37.87 (962)	P-2J and T1B. 247 delivered to 1980.

Designation (type of engine)	Power output (normally take-off rating for piston, turboprop and turboshaft, unless stated)	Specific fuel consumption (S F C)	a) Max RPM b) Pressure or Compression ratio	a) EGT (unless stated to be MGT, TET, TGT or TIT) b) Primary fuel type or Octane rating	Dry weight lb (kg)	a) Length ins (mm) b) Width ins (mm) c) Height ins (mm)	Current aircraft users, and comments
Japan							
Kawasaki Heavy Industries Ltd. World Trade Center Building, 4-1, 2-chome Hamamatsucho, Minato-ku, Tokyo 105 (Telephone: +81 3 3435 2111, Facsimile: +81 3 3578 3519)							
See Comments							In addition to producing parts for the F100, PW4000, RB211-524/Trent and V2500, Kawasaki builds versions of the AlliedSignal T53 and T-55. Also produces Spey/Olympus/Tyne gas generators.
KT5311A (free-turbine turboshaft)	1,100 shp (820.3 kW)					a) 47.6 (1,209) b) 23 (584.2) c) 24.33 (618)	UH-1B and Fuji-Bell 204B. Production began in 1967 and has ended.
T53-K-13B and KT5313B (free-turbine turboshaft)	1,400 shp (1,044 kW)				551 (250)	a) 47.6 (1,209) b) 23 (584.2) c) 26.1 (663)	UH-1H (T53) and Fuji-Bell 204B-2 (KT53). Production began in 1973.
T53-K-703 (free-turbine turboshaft)	1,800 shp (1,342 kW) take-off, 1,485 shp (1,107 kW) max continuous				544.5 (247)	a) 47.6 (1,209) b) 23 (584.2) c) 26.1 (663)	AH-1S and UH-1J.
T55-K-712 (free-turbine turboshaft)	4,626 shp (3,450 kW) OEI rating, 3,149 shp (2,348 kW) continuous				750 (340)	a) 47.09 (1,196) b) 24.25 (615.9)	CH-47J. Production began in 1984.
Ramjet, as part of Combined Cycle Engine (See Comments)							Experimental ramjet tested in 1995, following tests of a 2.4 ins (60 mm) diameter scale model ramjet combustor at Pratt & Whitney by the Japanese Hypersonic Transport Propulsion Research System Corp. The R&D programme will eventually develop a combined ramjet and turbojet to form a Combined Cycle Engine suited to a Mach 5 hypersonic transport.
Mitsubishi Heavy Industries Ltd. 5-1 Marunouchi 2-chome, Chiyoda-ku, Tokyo 100 (Telephone: +81 3 3212 3111, Facsimile: +81 3 3212 9865)							
Takes part in the PW4000, RJ500 and V2500 multi-national programmes. See comments for TSI-10 and MG5-110.							Produced CT63-M-5A/250-218A turboshaft engines under licence from Allison from 1967-77 (still produces parts for 250 series engines) and P&W JT8D-M-9 turbofans for the C-1 from 1971-81 (still produces parts for the JT8D). Developing TSI-10 turboshaft for OH-1, of 885 shp (660 kW). MG5-110 turboshaft for MH2000, of 876 shp (653 kW), using same core as TSI-10; single-stage compressor type, with electronic control.
Toyota. 1 Toyota-cho, Toyota City, Aichi Prefecture 471-71							
FV2400-2TC (turbocharged piston)	360 hp (268.5 kW)						Developed with Hamilton Standard. FAA approved. Based on Lexus motorcar engine.
Poland							
ILot – Instytut Lotnictwa. Aleja Krakowska 110/114, 02-256 Warszawa (Telephone: +48 22 846 00 11 or 09 93, Facsimile: +48 22 846 44 32, E-mail: ilot@ilot.edu.pl)							
D-18A (twin-shaft turbofan)	3,970 lbf (17.65 kN)	0.74 lb/lbf/hr (20.96 g/kNs)	b) 8.09:1	b) Jet A-1	838 (380)	a) 76.38 (1,940) b) 29.53 (750) c) 35.43 (900)	
K-15 Kaszub (axial-flow turbojet)	3,307 lbf (14.72 kN)	1.007 lb/lbf/hr (28.52 g/kNs)	b) 5.3:1	a) 730° C b) Jet A-1, TS-1, PSM-2	772 (350)	a) 61.42 (1,560) b) 28.54 (725) c) 35.12 (892)	M-93 and M-96 Iryda. Also produced by PZL-Rzeszów.
K-16 (turbojet)	3,527 lbf (15.69 kN)						Put under development for Iryda types.
PZL Kalisz - see WSK "PZL-Kalisz" SA							
WSK "PZL-Rzeszów" SA - Wytwórnia Sprzętu Komunikacy Jnego (Transport Equipment Enterprise), "PZL-Rzeszów" SA Spólka Akcyjna. ul. Hetmańska 120, 35-078 Rzeszów, PO Box 340 (Telephone: +48 17 85 46 100 or 46 200, Facsimile: +48 17 620 750)							
GTD-350W (free-turbine turboshaft)	419.7 shp (313 kW) at 43,200 gas generator rpm, 281.6 shp (210 kW) at 39,375 gas generator rpm	0.816 lb/shp/hr (496 g/kW/hr) at take-off	a) 43,650 b) 6.05:1 at take-off	a) 940° C TIT b) Jet A-1 (DERD 2494), PSM-2 (PN-86/c-96026), RT (GOST10227-86)	307 (139.3)	a) 53.15 (1,350) b) 20.55 (522) c) 26.77 (680)	Mi-2, built by PZL-Świdnik. Being manufactured.
PZL-10W (free-turbine turboshaft)	887.7 shp (662 kW) at 29,156 gas generator rpm, 690.6 shp (515 kW) cruise at 27,865 gas generator rpm	0.60 lb/shp/hr (365 g/kW/hr)	a) 29,156 b) 7.3:1	a) 650° C PTIT b) Jet A-1 (DERD 2494), PSM-2 (PN-86/c-96026), RT (GOST10227-86)	317.5 (144)	a) 73.82 (1,875) b) 29.13 (740) left-hand version, 30.12 (765) right hand version c) 23.43 (595)	PZL-Świdnik W-3 Sokól built by PZL-Świdnik. Being manufactured.
SO-3W (single-shaft turbojet)	2,425 lbf (10.8 kN)	1.1 lb/lbf/hr (31.16 g/kNs)	a) 15,600 b) 5.0:1	a) 720° C EGT b) Jet A-1 (DERD 2494), PSM-2 (PN-86/c-96026), RT (GOST10227-86)	771.6 (350) max	a) 83.15 (2,112) b) 29.92 (760) c) 30.67 (779)	TS-11 Iskra. Being manufactured.
TWD-10B (free-turbine turboprop)	946.7 shp (706 kW) at 29,600 gas generator rpm, 770 shp (574 kW) cruise at 28,400 gas generator rpm	0.613 lb/shp/hr (373 g/kW/hr)	a) 29,600 b) 7.4:1	a) 670° C PTIT b) Jet A-1 (DERD 2494), PSM-2 (PN-86/c-96026), RT (GOST10227-86)	507 (230)	a) 81.10 (2,060) b) 21.85 (555) c) 35.43 (900)	PZL-Mielec M-28/An-28. Being manufactured.

Designation (type of engine)	Power output (normally take-off rating for piston, turboprop and turboshaft, unless stated)	Specific fuel consumption (S F C)	a) Max RPM b) Pressure or Compression ratio	a) EGT (unless stated to be MGT, TET, TGT or TIT) b) Primary fuel type or Octane rating	Dry weight lb (kg)	a) Length ins (mm) b) Width ins (mm) c) Height ins (mm)	Current aircraft users, and comments
Poland							
PZL-Rzeszów manufactured US Franklin engines.							
Franklin engines are manufactured in accordance to original documentation of former Franklin Engines Company, Inc.							
4A235B31 4A235B4 (4-cyl, horizontally opposed, air-cooled piston)	116 hp (86.5 kW) and 125 hp (93.2 kW) respectively	0.513 lb/hp/hr (312 g/kW/hr)	a) 2,880 b) 8.5:1	a) 200° C b) 100/130 grade aviation gasoline (e.g. MIL-G-5572E)	227 (103)	a) 29.21 (742) b) 31.26 (794) c) 26.89 (683)	Includes PZL-110 Koliber. Being manufactured.
6A350C1L (6-cyl, horizontally opposed, air-cooled piston)	205 hp (153 kW)	0.436 lb/hp/hr (265 g/kW/hr)	a) 2,800 b) 10.0:1	a) 200° C b) 100/130 grade aviation gasoline (e.g. MIL-G-5572E)	330.7 (150)	a) 37.80 (960) b) 31.26 (794) c) 24.57 (624)	Includes M-20 Mewa. Being manufactured.
WSK "PZL-Kalisz" SA – Wytwórnia Sprzętu Komunikacyjnego "PZL-Kalisz" SA. ul. Częstochowska 140, 62-800 Kalisz (Telephone: +48 62 765 6100, Facsimile: +48 62 766 30 84)							
AI-14RA (9-cyl, 4-stroke, air-cooled, radial piston with pneumatic starting)	251.3 hp (187.4 kW) take-off at 2,350 rpm, 212.7 hp (158.6 kW) cruise at 2,050 rpm	0.57-0.625 lb/hp/hr (347-380 g/kW/hr) take-off, 0.536-0.582 lb/hp/hr (326-354 g/kW/hr) cruise	a) 1,849 propeller rpm b) 5.9:1	b) min 91 Octane with tetraethyl lead (max 2.5 g/1 kg of fuel); B-91/115 and 100 L	441 (200)	a) 37.64 (956) b) 38.78 (985)	Wilga 35 and Gawron; suitable for ambulance, tourist, and other aircraft.
AI-14RA-KAF (9-cyl, 4-stroke, air-cooled, radial piston with pneumatic starting)	251.3 hp (187.4 kW) take-off at 2,350 rpm, 212.7 hp (158.6 kW) cruise at 2,050 rpm	0.57-0.625 lb/hp/hr (347-380 g/kW/hr) take-off, 0.536-0.582 lb/hp/hr (326-354 g/kW/hr) cruise	a) 1,849 propeller rpm b) 5.9:1	b) min 91 Octane with tetraethyl lead (max 2.5 g/1 kg of fuel); B-91/115 and 100 L	441 (200)	a) 37.64 (956) b) 38.78 (985)	Wilga 80; suitable for ambulance, tourist, and other aircraft. Identical to AI-14RA but with repositioned carburettor.
AI-14RC (9-cyl, 4-stroke, air-cooled, radial piston with electric starting)	251.3 hp (187.4 kW) take-off at 2,350 rpm, 212.7 hp (158.6 kW) cruise at 2,050 rpm	0.57-0.625 lb/hp/hr (347-380 g/kW/hr) take-off, 0.536-0.582 lb/hp/hr (326-354 g/kW/hr) cruise	a) 1,849 propeller rpm b) 5.9:1	b) min 91 Octane with tetraethyl lead (max 2.5 g/1 kg of fuel); B-91/115 and 100 L	441 (200) + 2%	a) 37.64 (956) b) 38.78 (985)	For ambulance, tourist, and other aircraft. Similar to RA but has electric starting.
AI-14RD (9-cyl, 4-stroke, air-cooled, radial piston with electric starting)	273.2 hp (203.7 kW) take-off at 2,400 rpm, 234.7 hp (175 kW) cruise at 2,100 rpm	0.582-0.625 lb/hp/hr (354-380 g/kW/hr) take-off, 0.559-0.603 lb/hp/hr (340-367 g/kW/hr) cruise	a) 1,888 propeller b) 5.9:1	b) min 91 Octane with tetraethyl lead (max 2.5 g/1 kg of fuel); B-91/115 and 100 L	441 (200)	a) 37.64 (956) b) 38.78 (985)	Wilga; suitable for ambulance, tourist, agricultural and other aircraft.
AI-14RDP (9-cyl, 4-stroke, air-cooled, radial piston with pneumatic starting)	273.2 hp (203.7 kW) take-off at 2,400 rpm, 234.7 hp (175 kW) cruise at 2,100 rpm	0.582-0.625 lb/hp/hr (354-380 g/kW/hr) take-off, 0.559-0.603 lb/hp/hr (340-367 g/kW/hr) cruise	a) 1,888 propeller b) 5.9:1	b) min 91 Octane with tetraethyl lead (max 2.5 g/1 kg of fuel); B-91/115 and 100 L	441 (200)	a) 37.64 (956) b) 38.78 (985)	Wilga; suitable for ambulance, tourist, agricultural and other aircraft.
ASz-62IR-16 (9-cyl, 4-stroke, air-cooled, radial piston)	967 hp (721 kW) take-off at 2,200 rpm, 792.5 hp (591 kW) cruise	0.671 lb/hp/hr (408 g/kW/hr) minimum at take-off, 0.626-0.671 lb/hp/hr (381-408 g/kW/hr) cruise	a) 1,511 propeller b) 6.4:1	b) min 91 Octane with tetraethyl lead (max 3.3 g/1 kg of fuel); B-91/115 and 100 LL	1,276.5 (579)	a) 52.28 (1,328) b) 54.33 (1,380)	An-2 and Y-5B. Based on Russian ASh-62.
ASz-62IR-M18 (9-cyl, 4-stroke, air-cooled, radial piston)	967 hp (721 kW) take-off at 2,200 rpm, 792.5 hp (591 kW) cruise	0.671 lb/hp/hr (408 g/kW/hr) minimum at take-off, 0.626-0.671 lb/hp/hr (381-408 g/kW/hr) cruise	a) 1,511 propeller b) 6.4:1	b) min 91 Octane with tetraethyl lead (max 3.3 g/1 kg of fuel); B-91/115 and 100 LL	1,250 (567)	a) 44.49 (1,130) b) 54.33 (1,380)	M-18 Dromader. Version for retrofitting to the DHC-3 Otter has a vacuum pump. WSK "PZL-Kalisz" has not applied any special designation to this version beyond "ASz-62IR-M18 for DHC-3 Otter".
K8-AA (9-cyl, 4-stroke, radial piston with direct drive and pneumatic starting)	273.2 hp (203.7 kW) take-off at 2,400 rpm, 234.7 hp (175 kW) cruise at 2,100 rpm	0.582-0.625 lb/hp/hr (354-380 g/kW/hr) take-off, 0.559-0.603 lb/hp/hr (340-367 g/kW/hr) cruise	a) 2,400 propeller b) 5.9:1	b) min 91 Octane with tetraethyl lead (max 2.5 g/1 kg of fuel); B-91/115 and 100 L	441 (200)	a) 39.15 (994.5) b) 38.78 (985)	Adjusted for aerobatics. Version of the AI-14R.
K9-AA (9-cyl, 4-stroke, air-cooled, radial piston with electric starting)	1,153 hp (860 kW) take-off at 2,300 rpm, 936.3 hp (698.2 kW) cruise at 2,150 rpm	0.694 lb/hp/hr (422 g/kW/hr) minimum at take-off, 0.649-0.694 lb/hp/hr (395-422 g/kW/hr) cruise	a) 1,580 propeller b) 6.4:1	b) min 91 Octane with tetraethyl lead (max 3.3 g/1 kg of fuel); B-91/115 and 100 LL	1,257 (570)	a) 44.49 (1,130) b) 54.33 (1,380)	M-24 Super Dromader; suitable for tourist and ambulance aircraft. Version of the ASz-62R developed by WSK "PZL-Kalisz".
K9-BA (9-cyl, 4-stroke, air-cooled, radial piston with electric starting)	1,153 hp (860 kW) take-off at 2,300 rpm, 936.3 hp (698.2 kW) cruise at 2,150 rpm	0.694 lb/hp/hr (422 g/kW/hr) minimum at take-off, 0.649-0.694 lb/hp/hr (395-422 g/kW/hr) cruise	a) 1,580 propeller b) 6.4:1	b) min 91 Octane with tetraethyl lead (max 3.3 g/1 kg of fuel); B-91/115 and 100 LL	1,257 (570)	a) 44.49 (1,130) b) 54.33 (1,380)	DC-3 conversions and suitable for tourist and ambulance aircraft. Hydraulic and vacuum pumps. Can use feathering propeller.
K9-BB (9-cyl, 4-stroke, air-cooled, radial piston with electric starting)	1,153 hp (860 kW) take-off at 2,300 rpm, 936.3 hp (698.2 kW) cruise at 2,150 rpm	0.694 lb/hp/hr (422 g/kW/hr) minimum at take-off, 0.649-0.694 lb/hp/hr (395-422 g/kW/hr) cruise	a) 1,477 propeller b) 6.4:1	b) min 91 Octane with tetraethyl lead (max 3.3 g/1 kg of fuel); B-91/115 and 100 LL	1,257 (570)	a) 44.49 (1,130) b) 54.33 (1,380)	M-24 Super Dromader and suitable for tourist and ambulance aircraft.

Designation (type of engine)	Power output (normally take-off rating for piston, turboprop and turboshaft, unless stated)	Specific fuel consumption (S F C)	a) Max RPM b) Pressure or Compression ratio	a) EGT (unless stated to be MGT, TET, TGT or TIT) b) Primary fuel type or Octane rating	Dry weight lb (kg)	a) Length ins (mm) b) Width ins (mm) c) Height ins (mm)	Current aircraft users, and comments
Poland							
WSK "PZL-Kalisz" SA – Wytwórnia Sprzętu Komunikacyjnego "PZL-Kalisz" SA. (continued)							
K9-BC (9-cyl, 4-stroke, air-cooled, radial piston with electric starting)	1,153 hp (860 kW) take-off at 2,300 rpm, 936.3 hp (698.2 kW) cruise at 2,150 rpm	0.694 lb/hp/hr (422 g/kW/hr) minimum at take-off, 0.649-0.694 lb/hp/hr (395-422 g/kW/hr) cruise	a) 1,580 propeller b) 6.4:1	b) min 91 Octane with tetraethyl lead (max 3.3 g/1 kg of fuel); B-91/115 and 100 LL	1,257 (570)	a) 44.49 (1,130) b) 54.33 (1,380)	An-2 and Kruk.
WZL Nr 4 – Wojskowe Zaklady Lotnicze Nr 4. ul. Księcia Janusza, 01-133 Warszawa 42 (Telephone: +48 22 685 23 01, Facsimile: +48 22 364 521)							
See Comments							Overhauls R-11F, R-13 and R-25 jet engines, GTD-350 and AI-9W turboshafts as main programmes.
Romania							
Aerostar S.A. Grup Industrial Aeronautic Bacau. Str. Condorilor nr. 9, cod 5500, Bacau (Telephone: +40 34 175070, Facsimile: +40 34 172023)							
M-14P (9-cyl, air-cooled radial piston)	360 hp (268 kW) at 2,900 rpm, 180 hp (134 kW) at 1,850 rpm cruise	0.386 lb/hp/hr (235 g/kW/hr) maximum, 0.258 lb/hp/hr (157 g/kW/hr) minimum	a) 2,900 b) 6.3:1	b) B-91/115 (91 Octane)	471.8 (214)	a) 36.38 (924) b) 38.78 (985) c) 38.78 (985)	AG 6, SM-92 Finist, Su-26, Su-29, Su-31, Yak-18T, Yak-50, Yak-52, Yak-53, Yak-54, Yak-55M and Wilga 35M.
M-14V26 (9-cyl, air-cooled radial piston)	325 hp (242 kW) at 2,800 rpm, 190 hp (142 kW) at 2,350 rpm cruise	0.38 lb/hp/hr (231 g/kW/hr)	a) 2,850 b) 6.3:1 (±0.1%)	b) B-91/115 (91 Octane)	560 (254)	a) 43.39 (1,102) b) 38.78 (985) c) 38.78 (985)	Ka-26, Mi-34.
Russia							
AOOT OKBM. Voroshilov Street 22, 394086 Voronezh (Telephone: +7 0732 57 11 94, Facsimile: +7 0732 33 41 37)							
M-14PF (9-cyl, 4-stroke, air-cooled, radial piston driving a tractor propeller)	390 hp (291 kW) take-off at 2,900 rpm, 310 hp (231.2 kW) cruise at 2,400 rpm	0.474 lb/hp/hr (288 g/kW/hr)	a) 1,975 propeller minimum b) 6.3:1 (±0.1%)	b) B-91/115 of 91 Octane	472 (214)	a) 36.38 (924) ±3 mm b) 38.78 (985) ±3 mm	Su-26M, Su-29, Su-31, Su-38, Yak-54, Yak-55, Yak-56 and others.
M-14PM-1 (9-cyl, 4-stroke, air-cooled, radial piston with an updated gearbox and a pusher propeller)	360 hp (268.5 kW) take-off at 2,900 rpm, 290 hp (216.25 kW) cruise at 2,400 rpm	0.463 lb/hp/hr (282 g/kW/hr)	a) 2,600 propeller minimum b) 6.3:1 (±0.1%)	b) B-91/115 of 91 Octane	472 (214)	a) 39.92 (1,014) b) 38.78 (985)	Molniya-1; Aeroprogress T-401 for M-14PR model and T-411 Aist.
M-14PT (9-cyl, 4-stroke, air-cooled, radial piston driving a pusher propeller)	360 hp (268.5 kW) take-off at 2,900 rpm, 290 hp (216.25 kW) cruise at 2,400 rpm	0.463 lb/hp/hr (282 g/kW/hr)	a) 1,900 propeller minimum b) 6.3:1 (±0.1%)	b) B-91/115 of 91 Octane	472 (214)	a) 38.19 (970) b) 38.78 (985)	Yak-58; Tu-34 uses M-14PS. Generator up to 8 hp/6 kW, and up to an additional 6.7 hp/5 kW power take-off drive to conditioning system compressor.
M-14V (9-cyl, 4-stroke, air-cooled, radial piston with planetary gearbox, centrifugal blower and forced cylinder cooling fan)	370 hp (276 kW) take-off at 2,950 rpm, 190 hp (141.7 kW) cruise at 2,620 rpm	0.496-0.54 lb/hp/hr (302-328 g/kW/hr)	a) 865 output shaft rpm b) 6.3:1 (±0.1%)	b) A76 of 76 Octane	577.6 (262)	a) 43.39 (1,102) b) 38.78 (985)	Airships, and an amphibious motorboat on an air cushion "Bars". M-14V26 for Mi-34 of 325 hp (242.4 kW); new versions developed at 375 and 410 hp (280 and 306 kW).
M-17 (4-cyl, 4-stroke, air-cooled, horizontally opposed piston with turbo-supercharger and low-pressure fuel injection)	175 hp (130.5 kW) take-off at 2,950 rpm, 160 hp (119.3 kW) cruise at 2,880 rpm; power can be boosted to 200 hp (149 kW)	0.386 lb/hp/hr (235 g/kW/hr)	a) 2,950 propeller minimum	b) B-91/115 of 91 Octane	242.5 (110)	a) 39.37 (1,000) b) 32.68 (830) c) 21.65 (550)	Be-103, Il-103 and Yak-112.
M-17F (4-cyl, 4-stroke, air-cooled, horizontally opposed piston with turbo-supercharger and low-pressure fuel injection and an electric starter)	200 hp (149 kW) take-off at 2,450 rpm, 150 hp (112 kW) nominal rating at 2,270 rpm	0.408 lb/hp/hr (248 g/kW/hr)	a) 2,450 propeller minimum	b) B-91/115 of 91 Octane	286.6 (130)	a) 41.34 (1,050) b) 32.68 (830) c) 21.65 (550)	Be-103, Il-103, RT-6, Tu-34 and Yak-112.
M-18-02 (2-cyl, 2-stroke, air-cooled piston with hand or electric starter)	55 hp (41 kW) take-off at 2,500 rpm, 37 hp (27.6 kW) nominal rating at 2,100 rpm	0.772 lb/hp/hr (469 g/kW/hr)	a) 2,200 output shaft rpm b) 7.2:1	b) AN 93 of 93 Octane, with MC 20 oil	61.73 (28)	a) 13.78 (350) b) 19.69 (500) c) 19.69 (500)	Ultralight aircraft and powered gliders.
M-25-01 (9-cyl, 4-stroke, air-cooled, radial piston, with fuel injection, turbo-supercharger and automatic control system (see Comments)	430 hp (320.7 kW) take-off at 2,900 rpm, 300 hp (223.7 kW) nominal rating at 2,460 rpm	0.408 lb/hp/hr (248 g/kW/hr)	a) 1,900 propeller minimum b) 6.3:1 (±0.1%)	b) A 76 of 76 Octane	485 (220)	a) 45.28 (1,150) b) 38.78 (985)	Molniya, Su-26, T-401 Sokol, M-500, Yak-18T, Yak-54, Yak-55M, Yak-58 and A-209. Turbo-supercharger to maintain engine power up to the design flight altitude. Electric or compressed air starting. May be equipped with 4 hp or 8 hp (3 kW or 6 kW) generator.

Designation (type of engine)	Power output (normally take-off rating for piston, turboprop and turboshaft, unless stated)	Specific fuel consumption (S F C)	a) Max RPM b) Pressure or Compression ratio	a) EGT (unless stated to be MGT, TET, TGT or TIT) b) Primary fuel type or Octane rating	Dry weight lb (kg)	a) Length ins (mm) b) Width ins (mm) c) Height ins (mm)	Current aircraft users, and comments
Russia							
AOOT OKBM. (continued)							
M-25 (9-cyl, 4-stroke, air-cooled, radial piston, with fuel injection and automatic control system (see Comments)	430 hp (320.7 kW) take-off at 2,900 rpm, 360 hp (268.5 kW) nominal rating at 2,460 rpm	0.408 lb/hp/hr (248 g/kW/hr)	a) 1,900 propeller minimum b) 6.3:1 (±0.1%)	b) A 76 of 76 Octane	485 (220)	a) 45.28 (1,150) b) 38.78 (985)	Finist, Molniya, Su-26, T-401 Sokol, M-500, Yak-18T, Yak-54, Yak-55M and Yak-58. Electric or compressed air starting. May be equipped with 4 hp or 8 hp (3 kW or 6 kW) generator.
M-29 (4-cyl, 2-stroke, horizontally opposed, air-cooled piston)	74 hp (55.18 kW)	0.77 lb/hp/hr (468 g/kW/hr)	a) 2,500		77.16 (35)	a) 22.44 (570) b) 17.72 (450) c) 17.72 (450)	Aviatika-890 variant.
Joint Stock Company "Aviadvigatel", JSC Perm Motors. 93 Komsomolsky Prospect, GSP-624, Perm, 614600 (Telephone: +7 3422 45 81 41, Facsimile: +7 3422 45 97 77 or 67 44)							
Note: See Rybinsk Motors JSC for changes to the company. Engines by Rybinsk Motors JSC from D-30KP (previously listed under the general "Aviadvigatel" heading) can now be found under the merged Rybinsk Motors JSC heading.							
D-25V (free-turbine turboshaft)	5,500 shp (4,100 kW) take-off (-2%) at 9,950 rpm (+150/-100), up to ISA +15° C	0.65 lb/shp/hr (396 g/kW/hr)	a) 10,580 b) 5.6:1 (±0.2)	a) 555° C b) TC-1, T-1 and T-2 PP	2,738 (1,242) + 2%	a) 107.76 (2,737) without transmission, 217.99 (5,537) with transmission b) 42.76 (1,086) c) 45.59 (5,537)	Mi-6, Mi-6A, Mi-10, Mi-10K, Mi-22.
D-30 (twin-shaft turbofan)	14,991 lbf (66.69 kN) take-off (-2%) at 11,600 rpm (+50/-100), up to ISA +15° C	0.62 lb/lbf/hr (17.56 g/kNs) maximum	a) 11,650 b) 18.4:1 (±0.2)	a) 620° C b) T-1, TC-1	3,417 (1,550) + 2%	a) 156.81 (3,983) ±10 mm b) 41.34 (1,050)	Mid-range Tu-134.
D-30V (twin-shaft turbofan)	9,921 lbf (44.13 kN) at sea level						M-17RM/M-55. Non-afterburning engine.
D-30 II (twin-shaft turbofan with thrust reverser)	14,991 lbf (66.69 kN) take-off (-2%) at 11,550 rpm (+50/-100), up to ISA +15° C	0.62 lb/lbf/hr (17.56 g/kNs) maximum	a) 11,600 b) 18.4:1 (±0.2)	a) 620° C b) T-1, TC-1	3,891 (1,765) + 2%	a) 186.36 (4,733.5) ±10 mm b) 41.34 (1,050)	Mid-range Tu-134A and Tu-134B.
D-30 III (twin-shaft turbofan with thrust reverser)	14,991 lbf (66.69 kN) take-off (-2%) at 11,500 rpm (+50/-100), up to ISA +15° C	0.625 lb/lbf/hr (17.7 g/kNs) maximum	a) 11,550 b) 19.8:1 (±0.2)	a) 600° C b) T-1, PT	3,990 (1,810) + 2%	a) 186.36 (4,733.5) ±10 mm b) 41.34 (1,050)	Mid-range Tu-134A3 and Tu-134B3.
D-30F-6 (twin-shaft turbofan with afterburner) (See Comments for D-30F-6M)	20,944 lbf (93.17 kN) dry, 34,172 lbf (152 kN) with afterburning	0.72 lb/lbf/hr (20.39 g/kNs)	a) 11,200 b) 21.3:1	a) 840° C b) T-6	5,353 (2,428) +2%	a) 279 (7,087) b) 60.63 (1,540)	MiG-31, Sukhoi S-37 prototype. D-30F-6M of 38,580 lbf (171.62 kN) with afterburning on MiG-31M.
D-215 (turboshaft)	7,600 shp (5,667 kW)						Mi-46.
PS-90A or D-90A (twin-shaft turbofan with fan reverser)	35,274-35,583 lbf (156.9-158.3 kN) take-off, to 30° C, 7,716 lbf (34.32 kN) cruise, at 11,000 m altitude and Mach 0.8	0.595 lb/lbf/hr (16.85 g/kNs) cruise	a) 12,400 b) 35.5:1	a) 1,367° C b) TS-1, RT	6,504 (2,950)	a) 195.43 (4,964) b) 74.8 (1,900)	Il-86 re-engined, Il-96-300, Il-96MR, Molniya-400, Molniya-1000 prototype, Tu-154M2, and Tu-204/Tu-214. PS-90AT for Tu-330 and PS-90A76 for Il-76MF.
PS-90A12 (twin-shaft turbofan with fan reverser)	26,455 lbf (117.68 kN) take-off, to +30° C, 5,070 lbf (22.56 kN) cruise, at 11,000 m and Mach 0.8	0.582 lb/lbf/hr (16.485 g/kNs) cruise	a) 11,800 b) 25:1	a) 1,285° C b) TS-1, RT	5,070 (2,300)	a) 187.24 (4,756) b) 65.75 (1,670)	Il-76 upgrade (as Il-76TD-90) and Yak-242.
PS-90P See Multi-national section							
Enterprise named after "V. Chernyshov". 7 Vishnevaya Str., 123362 Moscow.							
See Comments							One of the leading aircraft engine manufacturing plants in Russia, producing the Klimov RD-33 and TV7.
Klimov Corporation. 13 Kantemirovskaya Street, 194100 St Petersburg (Telephone: +7 812 2451586, Facsimile: +7 812 2454329)							
TV2-117A/AG (free-turbine turboshaft) (See Comments)	1,500-1,700 shp (1,120-1,270 kW), 1,000 shp (746 kW) cruise for A	0.683 lb/shp/hr (415 g/kW/hr) cruise	a) 12,000 shaft b) 6.6:1		745.2 (338)	a) 111.6 (2,835) b) 21.54 (547) c) 29.33 (745)	Mi-8. TV2-117TG of similar output used by Mi-8TG and Mi-38, able to use liquefied petroleum gas or kerosene. TG can also use diesel, butane/propane gas or other fuels. Mi-8FT has TV2-117Fs. Mi-9. Prototype Mi-14.

Designation (type of engine)	Power output (normally take-off rating for piston, turboprop and turboshaft, unless stated)	Specific fuel consumption (S F C)	a) Max RPM b) Pressure or Compression ratio	a) EGT (unless stated to be MGT, TET, TGT or TIT) b) Primary fuel type or Octane rating	Dry weight lb (kg)	a) Length ins (mm) b) Width ins (mm) c) Height ins (mm)	Current aircraft users, and comments
Russia							
Klimov Corporation. (continued)							
TV3-117 (free-turbine turboshaft)	1,900 shp (1,417 kW) for TV3-117MT and 2,200 shp (1,640 kW) take off for TV3-117VMA Series 2, 2,400 shp (1,790 kW) contingency for TV3-117VMA Series 2	0.57 lb/shp/hr (347 g/kW/hr) for TV3-117V/VK and 0.507 lb/shp/hr (308 g/kW/hr) for TV3-117VMA Series 2	b) 9.4:1 pressure ratio for TV3-117VMA Series 2	a) 920-990° C TIT for TV3-117VMA Series 2	628.3 (285) for TV3-117MT, 648.2 (294) for TV3-117VMA Series 2	a) 82.09 (2,085) for TV3-117MT, and 80.91 (2,055) for TV3-117VMA Series 2 b) 25.2 (640) for TV3-117MT c) 28.54 (725) for TV3-117MT, and 28.66 (728) for TV3-117VMA Series 2	Ka-27 and Ka-28 (TV3-117KM for Ka-27 and -117VK for late Ka-27s and Ka-28s, of 2,225 shp, 1,659 kW). Mi-8, Mi-14, Mi-17 and Mi-24 (TV3-117MT). Ka-32 (TV3-117V of 2,190 shp, 1,633 kW or VMA). Ka-29 and Ka-31 (TV3-117VK of 2,225 shp, 1,659 kW). Mi-17M, Mi-17V, Mi-24, Mi-25, Mi-28, Mi-35, Mi-40, Mi-171 and Mi-172 (TV3-117VM of 2,225 shp, 1,659 kW). Ka-32A and M, Ka-50, Ka-52, Mi-58 and late Mi-24s (TV3-117VMA). Inalet-18. Air flow rate of 19 lb (8.7 kg) per second minimum for TV3-117VMA Series 2. See also Zaporozhye JSC Motor Sich under Ukraine for further variants of TV3-117.
TV7-117 (free-turbine turboprop)	2,500 shp (1,864 kW) take-off to 35° C, 1,799.6 shp (1,342 kW) cruise for TV7-117-3 version	0.397 lb/shp/hr (241.5 g/kW/hr) for TV7-117-3 version	b) 16:1	a) 1,242° C TET for TV7-117-3 version	1,146.4 (520) for TV7-117-3 version	a) 84.37 (2,143) for TV7-117-3 version b) 34.8 (886) for TV7-117-3 version c) 37 (940) for TV7-117-3 version	An-140, MiG-110, Myasishchev M-150, Il-112, Tu-130 and Il-114 for TV7-117-3 version (formerly TV7-117S). Engine features low fuel consumption and electronic automatic control system. A version said to be intended to replace Chinese WJ5s is the L-3000. TV7-117M2 version is rated at 2,800 shp (2,088 kW).
TVA-3000 (turboshaft)	2,500 shp (1,864 kW), 3,750 shp (2,796 kW) OEI						Ka-40 and Mi-38. Formerly known as the TV7-117V.
RD-33 (twin-shaft turbojet)	11,100 lbf (49.42 kN) dry, 18,300 lbf (81.4 kN) with afterburning	0.77 lb/lbf/hr (21.81 g/kNs) dry, 2.1 lb/lbf/hr (59.48 g/kNs) with afterburning	b) 20:1	a) 1,397° C TET	2,326 (1,055)	a) 166.54 (4,230) b) 39.37 (1,000)	MiG-29, Chengdu Super 7, and South African Mirage F1-Cs and Cheetahs as SMR95s in association with Aerosud. Possibly for MiG-21 upgrade. Air flow approximately 166 lb (75.7 kg) per second. RD-33AS booster for Be-40/42.
RD-33K (twin-shaft turbojet)	19,400 lbf (86.3 kN) with afterburning						MiG-29K, MiG-29M and MiG-33. 22,050 lbf (98.07 kN) with afterburning version tested. Current Series 2 engines have TBO of 700 hours and service life of 1,400 hours. Possible future licensed production in Iran?
RD-33 "Third Series" (see Comments). Engine is believed to be known as the RD-33-191.	11,100 lbf (42.42 kN) dry, 18,300 lbf (81.4 kN) with afterburning						Modernized, with several design features introduced to allow 1,000 hours (instead of 700 hours) between overhauls, improved reliability and lower maintenance costs. Service life 2,000 hours. The fan rotor, centre HP compressor drum and three-stage labyrinth seals of the combustion chamber have been strengthened, and some bearings have also been strengthened. Users include J-10 and MiG-29.
RD-35 (turbofan)							Yak-130. Developed from DV-2S. See Povazské Strojárne under Slovakia.
RD-93 (turbofan)	17,985 lbf (80 kN)						Developed from the RD-33 and built by Liyang in China for the FC-1.
RD-133 (twin-shaft turbojet, with vectored thrust)	18,300 lbf (81.4 kN)			a) 1,407° C TET			For MiG-29 upgrade. Air flow 170 lb (77 kg) per second. Service life 2,000 hours. 3-D thrust vectoring.
RD-331 (non-afterburning turbofan)	11,573 lbf (51.48 kN)						Eurasia Integral as Klimov/Sarkisov RD-331, with single and (for Integral-2010) 2 nozzles.
RD-333 or RD-43 (with thrust vectoring)	22,053 lbf (98.1 kN) with afterburning			a) 1,527° C TET			For MiG-29SMT and MiG-35. Air flow 187.4 lb (85 kg) per second. Service life 2,000 hours. Thrust vectoring.
MKB Granit. 105118 Moscow, pr Budennogo, 16 (Telephone +7 095 369 8013, Facsimile: +7 095 366 1010)							
TVD-150 (turboprop/ turboshaft)	150 shp (112 kW)	1.06 lb/shp/hr (645 g/kW/hr)			115 (52)	b) 10.24 (260) diameter	MKB Granit bureau specialized in producing small turbojet engines for UAVs, including the 132 lbf (0.588 kN) thrust MD-45 and 265 lbf (1.177 kN) thrust MD-120. Current TVD-150 is based on MD-45's gas generator, under development for light aircraft and helicopters.
TVD-450 (turboprop/ turboshaft)	450 shp (335.6 kW)	0.617 lb/shp/hr (375 g/kW/hr)			211.6 (96)	a) 32.28 (820) b) 11.02 (280) diameter	Based on MD-120 gas generator (see above), for light aircraft and helicopters.
OMSK Aircraft Engine Design Bureau "Mars". 644021 Omsk 21 (Telephone: +7 3812 33 4981)							
Glushenkov GTD-3F and 3M (free-turbine turboshafts)	900 shp (671 kW) for 3F and 1,000 shp (746 kW) for 3M		b) 7.3:1 estimated		311 (141) approx	a) 73.82 (1,857) b) 21.13 (740) c) 23.43 (545)	Ka-25 (early models 3F, later 3M). See also PZL-Rzeszów PZL-10W.
Glushenkov TVD-10B/BA (free-turbine turboprop)	1,011 shp (754 kW) as TVD-10B, 1,059 shp (790 kW) as TVD-10BA		b) 7.4:1 estimated		507 (230) approx for TVD-10B	a) 81.1 (2,060) b) 21.85 (555) c) 35.34 (900)	T-101 Gratch, T-501 and possibly T-106. See also PZL-Rzeszów TWD-10B.
Glushenkov TVD-20 (turboprop)	1,380 shp (1,029 kW) take-off	0.506 lb/shp/hr (308 g/kW/hr)			628.3 (285)	a) 69.68 (1,770) b) 33.46 (850) c) 33.27 (845)	T-101V and T-201 Aist, T-203 Pchel and T-282, and NIAT-2.5ST Freighty. TVD-20Bs for An-38-200.
Kobchyenko TV-O-100 (free-turbine turboshaft) (See Comments for TVD-100 turboprop)	700 shp (522 kW)	0.646 lb/shp/hr (393 g/kW/hr)	a) 6,000 shaft b) 9.2:1	a) 1,027° C TET	352.7 (160)	a) 50.2 (1,275) b) 30.71 (780) c) 28.94 (735)	Ka-126 and T-282. One of three choices for production T-610 Voyage and possibly S-86, both in TVD-100 turboprop form. Engine associated also with Soyuz.

Designation (type of engine)	Power output (normally take-off rating for piston, turboprop and turboshaft, unless stated)	Specific fuel consumption (S F C)	a) Max RPM b) Pressure or Compression ratio	a) EGT (unless stated to be MGT, TET, TGT or TIT) b) Primary fuel type or Octane rating	Dry weight lb (kg)	a) Length ins (mm) b) Width ins (mm) c) Height ins (mm)	Current aircraft users, and comments
Russia							
RKBM – Rybinsk Motors JSC, 163 Lenin Avenue, Rybinsk, Yaroslavl reg, 152903 (Telephone: +7 0855 243 100, Facsimile: +7 0855 262 398, 211 605)							
Note: In 1997 RKBM JSC joined with Rybinsk Motors JSC (RM JSC), now trading under the latter name. The company continues to manufacture in series and deliver to operators the D-30KU, D-30KP, D-30KU-154 engines originally developed by the Perm Motor-Building Design Bureau, while the new D-30KU-154 series III engine modification has been developed by Rybinsk Motors JSC and underwent flight testing in late 1997/1998.							
D-30KP (twin-shaft turbofan)	26,455 lbf (117.68 kN) take-off, up to ISA +15° C, 6,062 lbf (26.97 kN) cruise, at 11,000 m altitude and Mach 0.8	0.7 lb/lbf/hr (19.83 g/kNs) cruise	a) 10,620 b) 18.44:1	a) 1,154° C take-off b) TC-1, T-1, PT	5.088 (2,308)	a) 214.49 (5,448) b) 57.28 (1,455)	Il-76M/T.
D-30KP II (twin-shaft turbofan) D-30KP III – see Comments	26,455 lbf (117.68 kN) take-off, to ISA+ 23° C, 6,062 lbf (26.97 kN) cruise, at 11,000 m altitude and Mach 0.8	0.7 lb/lbf/hr (19.83 g/kNs) cruise	a) 10,710 b) 19.2:1	a) 1,123° C cruise b) TC-1, T-1, PT	5,110 (2,318)	a) 214.49 (5,448) b) 57.28 (1,455)	Il-76MD and Il-78. D-30KP II is in production. D-30KP III is higher thrust variant proposed for Il-76TD-90.
D-30KPV (twin-shaft turbofan)	26,455 lbf (117.68 kN) take-off, to ISA+ 23° C, 6,062 lbf (26.97 kN) cruise, at 11,000 m and Mach 0.8	0.7 lb/lbf/hr (19.83 g/kNs) cruise	a) 10,710 b) 20.1:1	a) 1,123° C cruise b) TC-1, T-1, PT	5,090 (2,309)	a) 214.49 (5,448) b) 57.28 (1,455)	Beriev A-40/Be-40.
D-30KU (twin-shaft turbofan)	24,250 lbf (107.88 kN) take-off, to ISA + 21° C, 6,062 lbf (26.97 kN) cruise, at 11,000 m altitude and Mach 0.8	0.7 lb/lbf/hr (19.83 g/kNs) cruise	a) 10,470 b) 17.2:1	a) 1,113° C at take-off b) TC-1, T-1, PT	5,088 (2,308)	a) 224.33 (5,698) b) 57.28 (1,455)	Long-range Il-62M. In production.
D-30KU II (twin-shaft turbofan)	24,250 lbf (107.88 kN) take-off, to ISA + 30° C, 6,062 lbf (26.97 kN) cruise, at 11,000 m altitude and Mach 0.8	0.7 lb/lbf/hr (19.83 g/kNs) cruise	a) 10,550 b) 17.82:1	a) 1,084° C b) TC-1, T-1, PT	5,110 (2,318)	a) 224.33 (5,698) b) 57.28 (1,455)	Long-range Il-62M.
D-30KU-154 II (twin-shaft turbofan)	23,149 lbf (103 kN) take-off, 6,062 lbf (26.97 kN) cruise, to ISA + 30° C	0.7 lb/lbf/hr (19.83 g/kNs) cruise	a) 10,420 b) 17.22:1	a) 1,065° C b) TC-1, T-1, PT	5,082 (2,305)	a) 224.33 (5,698) b) 57.28 (1,455) diameter	Tu-154M. In production.
D-30KU-154 III (twin-shaft turbofan)	23,149 lbf (103 kN) take-off, 6,062 lbf (26.97 kN)	0.472 lb/lbf/hr (13.37 g/kNs) take-off, 0.676 lb/lbf/hr (19.15 g/kNs) cruise at 11,000 m altitude and 800 km/h	a) 10,420 b) 18:1	a) 1,043° C TIT b) T-1 and TC-1	5,086 (2,307), 5,902 (2,677) reversal	a) 212.44 (5,396) b) 57.28 (1,455) fan diameter	Tu-154M. First run 1995 and flight tested in 1997. Air flow 584 lb (265 kg) per second.
D-100 (twin-shaft turbofan)	41,888 lbf (186.33 kN) take-off	0.544 lb/lbf/hr (15.41 g/kNs) cruise at 11,000 m altitude and Mach 0.8	b) 36.7:1 climb	a) 547° C b) Kerosene	7,385-7,716 (3,350-3,500)	a) 163.78 (4,160) b) 92.52 (2,350) fan	Advanced aircraft, including Il-106.
D-110B (twin-shaft propfan with a contra-rotating fan gearbox drive)	44,092 lbf (196.14 kN) take-off	0.52 lb/lbf/hr (14.73 g/kNs) cruise at 11,000 m altitude and Mach 0.8	b) 31.4:1 climb .	a) 548° C b) Kerosene	7,760 (3,520)	a) 161.42 (4,100) b) 105.12 (2,670) fan	Advanced aircraft.
D-112 (reverse-flow propfan with contra-rotating fan direct drive)	46,297 lbf (205.95 kN) take-off	0.51 lb/lbf/hr (14.45 g/kNs) cruise at 11,000 m altitude and Mach 0.8)	b) 36.1:1 climb	a) 548° C b) Kerosene	7,937 (3,600)	b) 113 (2,870) fan	Advanced aircraft.
D-200 (twin-rotor piston with liquid cooling)	220 hp (164 kW) at 2,700 rpm	0.507 lb/hp/hr (308 g/kW/hr)	a) 2,835 b) 9.4:1	b) 91 Octane minimum	352.7 (160)	a) 39 (990) b) 24.53 (623) c) 27.17 (690)	Yak-112 I.
DN-200 (3-cyl, 2-stroke, turbo-supercharged diesel with liquid cooling)	200 hp (149 kW) take-off at 4,700 rpm, 130 hp (97 kW) cruise	0.375 lb/hp/hr (228 g/kW/hr)	a) 2,700 maximum, 1,350 minimum	b) Kerosene, TS-1, diesel, DL, DZ	319.7 (145)	a) 31.5 (800) b) 26.38 (670) c) 16.34 (415)	Yak-112. Possible applications include sport aircraft and helicopters.
Kolesov RD-36-51V (high-altitude turbojet)	15,432 lbf (68.65 kN)	0.88 lb/lbf/hr (24.93 g/kNs) take-off	a) 5,200 b) 15.4:1	a) 627° C TIT b) T-8B	8,510 (3,860)	a) 196.81 (4,999) b) 58.5 (1,486) diameter	M-17. First run in 1974 and flight tested in 1977. Air flow rate 386 lb (175 kg) per second.
Novikov RD-38A (also referred to as RD-38K) (single-shaft turbojet)	6,581 lbf (29.27 kN)	0.413 lb/lbf/hr (11.7 g/kNs) take-off, 1.5 lb/lbf/hr (42.5 g/kNs) cruise	a) 12,200 b) 5:1	a) 1,012° C TIT b) T-1 and TC-1	491.6 (223)	a) 63.11 (1,603) b) 23.23 (590) diameter of inlet	An-71, and A-40 booster. Air flow rate 98.1 lb (44.5 kg) per second. First flight tested in 1986.

Designation (type of engine)	Power output (normally take-off rating for piston, turboprop and turboshaft, unless stated)	Specific fuel consumption (S F C)	a) Max RPM b) Pressure or Compression ratio	a) EGT (unless stated to be MGT, TET, TGT or TIT) b) Primary fuel type or Octane rating	Dry weight lb (kg)	a) Length ins (mm) b) Width ins (mm) c) Height ins (mm)	Current aircraft users, and comments
Russia							
Rybinsk Motors JSC. (continued)							
RD-600V (free-turbine turboshaft)	1,124 shp (838 kW) maximum, 1,300-1,400 shp (969.4-1,044 kW) contingency, 1,000 shp (745.7 kW) maximum continuous	0.50 lb/shp/hr (304 g/kW/hr)	a) 41,800 b) 14.4:1	a) 1,257° C TIT b) Kerosene, T-1 and TC-1	485 (220)	a) 62.91 (1,598) b) 28.74 (730) c) 29.53 (750)	Ka-60, Ka-62 and Yamal. Air flow 9.7 lb (4.4 kg) per second.
TVD-1500V (free-turbine turboprop)	1,300-1,400 shp (969.4-1.044 kW) take-off, 1,000 shp (745.7 kW) maximum cruise at 1,500 rpm, 3000 m altitude and 400 km/h	0.455 lb/shp/hr (277 g/kW/hr) at 3,000 altitude and Mach 0.34	a) 41,800 b) 14.4:1	a) 1,257° C TIT b) Kerosene, T-1 and TC-1	529 (240)	a) 77.36 (1,965) b) 27.56 (700) c) 29.92 (760)	An-38, Khrunichev T-701 Grach, and Sukhoi S-80. 3 axial stages and single centrifugal. Spur and planetary reduction unit. Air flow 9.7 lb (4.4 kg) per second. First run as TVD-1500 in 1992.
TVD-1500V (free-turbine turboshaft)	1,550 shp (1,156 kW) contingency	0.374 lb/shp/hr (228 g/kW/hr) cruise	b) 14.4:1	a) 1,257° C TIT	485 (220)	a) 49.21 (1,250) b) 24.41 (620) c) 29.92 (760)	Kamov helicopters. Uses same core as TVD-1500B.
Salut MMPO Joint-Stock Company. 105118 Moscow (Telephone: +7 095 369 80 01, Facsimile: +7 095 369 12 21)							
Manufacturer of engines from other bureaux (including Ukrainian D-436)							
Joint-Stock Company Samara Scientific-Technical Complex "NK Engines". 2a, S Laso Street, 443026 Samara (Telephone: +7 8462 50 0228, Facsimile: +7 8462 50 1211)							
Note: NK Engines and Kazan formed a joint venture organization in 1997 as the NK Engines FPG or Finance-Industrial group, incorporating also other companies including Motorostroitel and Kuznetsov bureau)							
NK-8 (twin-shaft turbofan)	20,945 lbf (93.17 kN)	0.62 lb/lbf/hr (17.56 g/kNs)	a) 7,050 HP spool and 5,170 LP spool b) 10.25:1	a) 927° C TIT b) Kerosene (Hu, 10250 kcal/kg)	5,115 (2,320)	a) 222.78 (5,658) b) 53.35 (1,355) fan, 56.77 (1,442) engine	Il-62.
NK-8-2 (twin-shaft turbofan)	20,945 lbf (93.17 kN)	0.59 lb/lbf/hr (16.71 g/kNs)	a) 6,820 HP spool and 5,165 LP spool b) 9.6:1	a) 927° C TIT b) Kerosene (Hu, 10250 kcal/kg)	4,740 (2,150)	a) 222.78 (5,658.5) b) 53.35 (1,355) fan, 56.77 (1,442) engine	Tu-154.
NK-8-2U (twin-shaft turbofan)	23,145 lbf (102.97 kN)	0.58 lb/lbf/hr (16.43 g/kNs)	a) 7,060 HP spool and 5,390 LP spool b) 10.7:1	a) 982° C TIT, 308° C EGT b) Kerosene (Hu, 10250 kcal/kg)	4,784 (2,170)	a) 208.19 (5,288) incl thrust reverser b) 53.35 (1,355) fan, 56.77 (1,442) engine	Tu-154.
NK-8-4 (twin-shaft turbofan)	23,145 lbf (102.97 kN)	0.59 lb/lbf/hr (16.71 g/kNs)	a) 6,940 HP spool and 5,380 LP spool b) 10.3:1	a) 982° C TIT, 335.5° C EGT b) Kerosene (Hu, 10250 kcal/kg)	4,938 (2,240)	a) 200.83 (5,101) b) 53.35 (1,355) fan, 56.77 (1,442) engine	Il-62 and Tu-154.
NK-8-4K (twin-shaft turbofan)	23,145 lbf (102.97 kN)	0.61 lb/lbf/hr (17.28 g/kNs)	b) 10.3:1	a) 971° C TIT b) Kerosene (Hu, 10250 kcal/kg)	4,850 (2,200)	b) 53.35 (1,355) fan, 56.77 (1,442) engine	Orlyonok (Eaglet) ground effect Ekranoplan.
NK-15A (turbofan)	33,720 lbf (150 kN)						Cruise engine for EKIP.
NK-22 (twin-shaft turbofan)	28,660 lbf (127.49 kN) dry, 44,090 lbf (196.14 kN) with afterburning	0.69-1.8 lb/lbf/hr (19.54-50.99 g/kNs)	a) 7,670 HP spool and 5,400 LP spool b) 14.75:1	a) 1,117° C TIT b) Kerosene	7,804 (3,540)	a) 293.54 (7,456) b) 53.35 (1,355) fan, 65.75 (1,670) engine	Tu-22M.
NK-25 (turbofan)	31,526 lbf (140.2 kN) dry, 55,155 lbf (245.18 kN) with afterburning					b) 53 (1,348)	Tu-22M3.
NK-32 and NK-321 (triple-shaft turbofan)	30,865 lbf (137.3 kN) dry, 55,115 lbf (245.18 kN) with afterburning		b) 28.4:1	a) 1,357° C TET	7,495 (3,400) approx	a) 236.22 (6,000) approx b) 57.48 (1,460) inlet	Tu-144LL, Tu-160 (NK-321) and Yak-43. 3-stage LP, 5-stage IP and 7-stage HP compressors; single-stage HP, single-stage IP and 2-stage LP turbines, and annular combustor.
NK-44 (triple-shaft turbofan)	97,000 lbf (431.51 kN)	0.302 lb/lbf/hr (8.554 g/kNs)	a) 9,012 HP spool and 6,323 LP spool b) 36.5:1	a) 1,340° C TIT and 449° C EGT b) Kerosene (Hu, 10250 kcal/kg)	18,519 (8,400)	a) 153.54 (3,900) b) 129.92 (3,300)	Molniya-1000, Tu-304.
NK-62M (unducted propfan)	55,100 lbf (245.2 kN)						Myasishchev MGS-6 and MGS-8
NK-63 (ducted propfan)	66,140 lbf (294.2 kN)						Myasishchev MGS-6 and MGS-8
NK-86 (twin-shaft turbofan)	29,320 lbf (130.43 kN)	0.53 lb/lbf/hr (15.01 g/kNs)	a) 7,270 HP spool and 5,510 LP spool b) 13.4:1	a) 987° C TIT b) Kerosene (Hu, 10250 kcal/kg)	4,828 (2,190)	a) 250.28 (6,357) b) 57.28 (1,455) fan, 62.99 (1,600) engine	Il-86.
NK-88 and NK-89 (turbofans)	23,150 lbf (102.97 kN) at take-off for NK-89			b) LNG and Kerosene			Tu-155 (NK-88) and Tu-156 (NK-89), to use LNG fuel. Based on NK-8-2U.
NK-92 (triple-shaft turbofan)	39,685 lbf (176.53 kN)						Il-106. Proposed for Il-96MR.

Designation (type of engine)	Power output (normally take-off rating for piston, turboprop and turboshaft, unless stated)	Specific fuel consumption (S F C)	a) Max RPM b) Pressure or Compression ratio	a) EGT (unless stated to be MGT, TET, TGT or TIT) b) Primary fuel type or Octane rating	Dry weight lb (kg)	a) Length ins (mm) b) Width ins (mm) c) Height ins (mm)	Current aircraft users, and comments
Russia							
Joint-Stock Company Samara Scientific-Technical Complex "NK Engines". (continued)							
NK-93 (triple-shaft geared propfan). NK-94 – see Comments	39,678 lbf (176.5 kN) take-off	0.49 lb/lbf/hr (13.89 g/kNs) at 11,000 m and Mach 0.75	b) 37:1		8,046 (3,650)	a) 216.54 (5,500) approx b) 124.02 (3,150) c) 124.02 (3,150)	An-70T-200, Il-96MK. Another version of the same engine is designated NK-92 as a turbofan (which see). NK-94 is a liquid gas fuelled engine for Tu-156M2 and Tu-338.
NK-116 (turbofan)	231,485 lbf (1,030 kN)						Proposed for Be-2500.
Samara Machine-Building Design Bureau							
NK-12MA (single-shaft turboprop)	14,805 eshp (11,040 ekW) take-off at 8,300 rpm, 12,337 eshp (9,200 ekW) cruise	0.448 lb/eshp/hr (272.5 g/ekW/hr) take-off, 0.355 lb/eshp/hr (216 g/ekW/hr) cruise	a) 8,300 b) 9.5-12.5:1	a) 927° C MGT, 515° C EGT b) T-1, TS-1, T-2, RT	6,757 (3,065)	a) 303.82 (7,717) b) 54.13 (1,375) c) 59.06 (1,500)	An-22.
NK-12MK (single-shaft turboprop)	13,818 eshp (10,304 ekW) take-off at 8,400 rpm, 12,337 eshp (9,200 ekW) cruise	0.456 lb/eshp/hr (277 g/ekW/hr) take-off, 0.485 lb/eshp/hr (295 g/ekW/hr) cruise	a) 8,400 b) 9.7-11:1	a) 905° C MGT, 552° C EGT b) T-1, TS-1, T-2, RT	6,757 (3,065)	a) 303.82 (7,717) b) 54.13 (1,375) c) 59.06 (1,500)	Orlyonok (Eaglet) ground effect Ekranoplan.
NK-12MP (single-shaft turboprop)	15,000 eshp (11,185 ekW) take-off at 8,300 rpm, 9,870 eshp (7,360 ekW) cruise						Final version of NK-12M series, used by Tu-95MS and Tu-142M series.
NK-12MV (single-shaft turboprop)	14,805 eshp (11,040 ekW) take-off at 8,300 rpm, 9,870 eshp (7,360 ekW) cruise	0.448 lb/eshp/hr (272.5 g/ekW/hr) take-off, 0.355 lb/eshp/hr (216 g/ekW/hr) cruise	a) 8,300 b) 9.5-13:1	a) 927° C MGT, 515° C EGT b) T-1, TS-1, T-2, RT	6,680 (3,030)	a) 308.35 (7,832) b) 54.13 (1,375) c) 59.06 (1,500)	Tu-95/Tu-142, Tu-114 and Tu-126.
P-032MR (2-cyl, 2-stroke, air-cooled piston with reduction gearbox and silencer)	31.5 hp (23.5 kW) take-off at 7,000 crankshaft rpm, 22.93 hp (17.1 kW) cruise at 6,300 crankshaft rpm	0.806 lb/hp/hr (490 g/kW/hr)	a) 7,300 crankshaft b) 7.24:1	b) 82 Octane	57.3 (26)	a) 19.88 (505) without silencer b) 17.99 (457) without silencer c) 14.69 (373) without silencer	Lightplanes and microlights.
P-065 (4-cyl, 2-stroke, air-cooled piston with reduction gearbox and silencer)	63 hp (47 kW) take-off at 7,000 crankshaft rpm, 45.9 hp (34.2 kW) cruise at 6,300 crankshaft rpm	0.806 lb/hp/hr (490 g/kW/hr)	a) 7,300 crankshaft b) 7.24:1	b) 82 Octane	125.7 (57)	a) 27.17 (690) without silencer b) 27.36 (695) without silencer c) 19.09 (485) without silencer	Light aircraft.
NPO Saturn. 13 Kasatkin Street, 129301 Moscow (Telephone: +7 095 283 9493, Facsimile: +7 095 283 2863)							
Lyulka AL-21F-3/3A (izdelye 89) (single-shaft turbojet)	17,196 lbf (76.49 kN) dry, 24,692 lbf (109.84 kN) with afterburning	0.76 lb/lbf/hr (21.53 g/kNs) dry, 1.86 lb/lbf/hr (52.68 g/kNs)	b) 14.8:1	a) 1,112° C TET	4,420 (2,005)	a) 203.15 (5,160) b) 34.84 (885)	MiG-23B, Su-17, Su-20, Su-22UM3K and Su-24.
Lyulka AL-31F/FM (izdelye 99V) (twin-shaft turbofan)	16,755 lbf (74.53 kN) dry, 27,560 lbf (122.59 kN) with afterburning for 'F'	0.67 lb/lbf/hr (18.98 g/kNs) dry for 'F'	b) 23:1 for 'F'	a) 1,392° C TET for 'F'	3,373 (1,530) for 'F'	a) 194.88 (4,950) b) 48.03 (1,220) for 'F'	Su-27, Su-30, Su-32FN, Su-34 (initially) and Su-35 (initially). AL-31FM has increased fan diameter, higher TET, 30,865 lbf (137.3 kN) with afterburning, and 0.685 lb/lbf/hr (19.4 g/kNs) SFC.
Lyulka AL-31FP (vectored thrust version of AL-31F)	27,560 lbf (122.59 kN) with afterburning					a) 196.46 (4,990) b) 48.03 (1,220)	Su-30MKI, Su-37 (as AL-37FU), and S-54/55. Early version has 2-D thrust vectoring, but current version for Su-30MKI has 3-D vectoring.
Lyulka AL-31K (turbofan)	29,320 lbf (130.42 kN) with afterburning						Su-33 (Su-27K).
Lyulka AL-32 (turboshaft)	770 shp (574 kW)						
AL-34 (pusher turboprop)	variously rated at 542-700 shp (404-522 kW)						Possibly for the EKIP, Sukhoi S-86, Aeroprogress T-205 and T-610 Voyage, and other Russian light transports. Molniya Vityaz to use 2AL-34 of 1,400 shp (1,044 kW).
AL-35F (twin-shaft turbofan)	30,865 lbf (137.3 kN)						Su-34 and Su-35. Also known as AL-31FM.
AL-37FU (turbofan with thrust vectoring)	30,866 lbf (137.3 kN)	0.70 lb/lbf/hr (19.83 g/kNs)		a) increased TET over AL-31F	3,494-3,527 (1,585-1,600)	b) 36.61 (930) fan diameter approx	Intended main engine type for Su-30MKI and Su-37 in production form. 3-D thrust vectoring. MTBO 1,000 hours. Possibly S-37.
AL-41F (advanced turbofan)	39,678 lbf (176.5 kN)	low consumption			low weight, possibly about 3,307 (1,500)		Mikoyan 1-42. Possibly S-37. To have vectoring nozzles.
Soyuz. Luzhnetskaya nab 2/4, 119270 Moscow (Telephone: +7 095 242 9468 and 2862, Facsimile: +7 095 242 5702)							
GTE-400 (turboshaft)	400 shp (298 kW)						May be fitted to a new Kamov helicopter.

Designation (type of engine)	Power output (normally take-off rating for piston, turboprop and turboshaft, unless stated)	Specific fuel consumption (S F C)	a) Max RPM b) Pressure or Compression ratio	a) EGT (unless stated to be MGT, TET, TGT or TIT) b) Primary fuel type or Octane rating	Dry weight lb (kg)	a) Length ins (mm) b) Width ins (mm) c) Height ins (mm)	Current aircraft users, and comments
Russia							
Soyuz. (continued)							
Tumansky R-11F-300, R-11F2-300 and R-11F2S-300/ F2SK300 (twin-shaft turbojet)	12,676 lbf (56.39 kN), 13,614 lbf (60.56 kN) and 13,614 lbf (60.56 kN) with afterburning respectively					a) 181.1 (4,600) c) 42.72 (1,085)	MiG-21.
Gavrilov R-13-300 (twin-spool turbojet)	9,370 lbf (41.68 kN) dry, 14,308 lbf (63.65 kN) with afterburning						MiG-21MF and SM.
Tumansky R-15BD-300	24,692 lbf (109.84 kN) with afterburning						MiG-25.
Gavrilov R-25-300 (twin-spool turbojet)	9,039 lbf (40.21 kN) dry, 15,100 lbf (67.18 kN) with afterburning		b) 9.55:1				MiG-21bis (izdelye 75 and 75P versions) and MiG-21-93. As the result of short duration increase of rpm to 106% and with second afterburner, the ground level thrust at near sonic speed increases to 21,825 lbf (97.09 kN) for several seconds.
Khachaturov R-27F2M-300 (twin-shaft turbojet) See Comments	14,330 lbf (63.75 kN) dry, 22,046 lbf (98.07 kN) with afterburning				3,307 (1,500)	a) 190.94 (4,850) b) 41.73 (1,060)	MiG-23MS, S and UB. R-27V-300 was the non-afterburning and vectoring-thrust derivative produced for the Yak-36M/38, of smaller dimensions but increased unaugmented thrust.
Khachaturov R-29-300 (turbojet)	18,298 lbf (81.4 kN) dry, 28,660 lbf (127.5 kN) with afterburning		a) 8,800 HP turbine b) 13.1:1		4,145 (1,880)	a) 195.3 (4,960) b) 35.91 (912)	MiG-23M, MF and BN. Air flow 243 lb (110 kg) per second.
Khachaturov R-29B-300 and BS-300 (turbojet)	17,637 lbf (78.46 kN) dry, 25,353 lbf (112.78 kN) with afterburning		a) 8,800 HP turbine b) 12.4:1		3,880 (1,760)		MiG-27, export MiG-23BN and Su-22 (see below). Developed for optimum low-altitude performance, with two nozzle settings only. R-29BS-300 powers the Su-22UM3. Air flow 243 lb (110 kg) per second.
Khachaturov R-35-300 (turbojet)	18,850 lbf (83.85 kN) dry, 28,660 lbf (127.5 kN) with afterburning		b) 13.1:1		3,890 (1,765)	a) 194.88 (4,950) b) 35.91 (912)	MiG-23ML, MLA, MLD, P and PD. Derived from the R-29-300. Air flow 243 lb (110 kg) per second.
Kobchyenko R-79M (twin-shaft turbofan with thrust vectoring)	39,680 lbf (176.5 kN)	0.64 lb/lbf/hr (18.13 g/kNs)			c. 6,060 (c. 2,750)	a) 216.54 (5,500) b) 44.8 (1,138) inlet diameter	Higher-thrust variant of former R-79V-300 (intended for Yak-141), with conventional nozzle replacing any VTOL type. See Sukhoi S-37.
Gavrilov R-95Sh (non-afterburning variant of R-13-300)	9,039 lbf (40.21 kN)						Su-25. Replaced on Su-25BM by R-195s offering lower IR signature and increased thrust.
R-123-300 (twin-shaft turbofan)	3,152 lbf (14.02 kN) class						Bypass ratio c. 6. 2 axial and single centrifugal compressor stages, single HP and LP turbines, and annular reverse-flow combustor.
R-126-300 (twin-shaft turbofan)	8,812 lbf (39.2 kN)						5 axial and single centrifugal compressor stages, 2-stage HP and 3-stage LP turbines, and annular reverse-flow combustor.
R-127-300 (twin-shaft turbofan)	1,985 lbf (8.83 kN)						For bizjets. 2-stage compressor, 2-stage HP and LP turbines, and annular reverse-flow combustor. Bypass ratio 4.8.
Gavrilov R-195 (twin-shaft turbojet)	9,921 lbf (44.13 kN)			b) MT, kerosene and diesel	2,182.5 (990)	a) 129.92 (3,300) b) 35.98 (914)	Su-25BM (upgraded) and last series Su-25UB, and Su-39. 3-stage LP compressor, 5-stage HP compressor, single-stage HP and LP turbines, and canannular combustor.
Gavrilov R-195FS (twin-shaft turbojet with afterburning)	9,259 lbf (41.19 kN) dry, 13,669 lbf (60.8 kN) with afterburning					a) 129.92 (3,300) b) 35.98 (914)	Sukhoi S-54. Afterburning variant of the R-195.
RD-1700							For MiG-AT, to replace Larzac. First flight expected in 1999.
New 135-kN class turbofan	30,350 lbf (135 kN) approx						Being developed for Sukhoi S-54 fighter.
TV116-300 (single-shaft turboprop or turboshaft)	1,080 shp (805 kW)				330.7 (150)	a) 31.5 (800) b) 16.5 (420)	No known applications.
TVD-450 (turboprop)	450 shp (335.6 kW)						One candidate for the Sukhoi S-86. Could be built by Mars?
UMPO Joint-Stock Company. 450039 Ufa (Telephone: +7 3472 38 36 54, Facsimile: +7 3472 38 37 44)							
See Comments							Manufacturer of engines from other design bureaux (including Ukrainian D-436).
Slovakia							
Považské Strojárne a.s. 017 34 Považská Bystrica (Telephone: +42 822 230 78 or 37, Facsimile: +42 822 237 78 or 255 61							
DV-2 (twin-shaft mixed flow turbofan)	4,851 lbf (21.58 kN) take-off, 2,866 lbf (12.75 kN) at 6,000 m and 378 kts	0.61 lb/lbf/hr (17.28 g/kNs)	b) 18.3:1	a) 1,110° C MGT b) Jet A-1	1,045 (474)	a) 67.76 (1,721) without jetpipe b) 39.13 (994) c) 40.83 (1,037)	L-39 MS, L-59 and M-99 Orkan. Company co-operated with Ivchenko PROGRESS ZMKB in DV-2 development from 1980-89. Total air mass flow 109.1 lb (49.5 kg) per second. Bypass ratio 1.46. Single-stage fan, 2-stage axial LPC, 7-stage axial HPC, annular combustor, single-stage air-cooled HPT, 2-stage air-cooled LPT, and electronic-hydromechanical fuel control system.

Designation (type of engine)	Power output (normally take-off rating for piston, turboprop and turboshaft, unless stated)	Specific fuel consumption (S F C)	a) Max RPM b) Pressure or Compression ratio	a) EGT (unless stated to be MGT, TET, TGT or TIT) b) Primary fuel type or Octane rating	Dry weight lb (kg)	a) Length ins (mm) b) Width ins (mm) c) Height ins (mm)	Current aircraft users, and comments
Slovakia							
Považské Strojárne a.s. (continued)							
DV-2A (twin-shaft mixed flow turbofan)	5,510 lbf (24.51 kN)	0.593 lb/lbf/hr (16.81 g/kNs)	b) 15.49:1	a) 1,115° C MGT b) Jet A-1	992 (450)	a) 67.76 (1,721) without jetpipe b) 39.13 (994) c) 40.83 (1,037)	L-159 and PZL-Mielec M-99 Orkan.
DV-2S (military RD-35) (twin-shaft mixed flow turbofan)	4,851 lbf (21.58 kN)	0.586 lb/lbf/hr (16.61 g/kNs)	b) 14.28:1	a) 1,064° C MGT	992 (450)	a) 88.11 (2,238) b) 32.28 (820) c) 41.34 (1,050)	Yak/Aem-130 and Yak-131.
Spain							
ITP – Industria de Turbo Propulsores SA. Parque Tecnologico, n° 300, 48016 Zamudio (Vizcaya) (Telephone: +34 4 489 2248, Facsimile: +34 4 489 2190)							
Partner in the EJ200 and M138 programmes							
Sweden							
Turbomin AB. Författarvägen 19, S-161 40 Bromma (Telephone: +46 8 704 1710, Facsimile: +46 8 704 1898)							
TN 300 (single-shaft turbojet)	65 lbf (0.29 kN) dry, 78 lbf (0.347 kN) with afterburning	1.4 lb/lbf/hr (39.7 g/kNs) dry, 2.8 lb/lbf/hr (79.3 g/kNs) with afterburning	b) 3.5:1	a) 800° C b) Jet A/A-1, JP-5, JP-8, diesel Class 1	13.2 (6)	a) 19.7 (500), 27.6 (700) with afterburner b) 6.5 (165) c) 6.5 (165)	Gliders, UAVs and target drones. Other Turbomin engines include the 17 lbf (0.075kN) TN 75 turbojet for ultra small UAVs and target drones.
Volvo Aero Corporation. S-46181 Trollhättan (Telephone: +46 520 940 00, Facsimile: +46 520 340 10)							
RM6C (Avon Mk 60) (Single spool turbojet)	12,450 lbf (55.4 kN) dry, 17,085 lbf (76 kN) with afterburning	0.93 lb/lbf/hr (26.3 g/kNs) dry, 1.85 lb/lbf/hr (52.4 g/kNs) with afterburning	b) 8.25:1	a) 770° C b) JP-8	3,946 (1,790)	a) 320.5 (8,140)	J35J Draken.
RM8A (twin-shaft turbofan)	14,750 lbf (65.61 kN) dry, 26,000 lbf (115.7 kN) with afterburning	0.62 lb/lbf/hr (17.7 g/kNs) dry, 2.47 lb/lbf/hr (70 g/kNs) with afterburning	b) 16.5:1	b) JP-4, JP-5	4,630 (2,100)	a) 242.2 (6,153) b) 40.6 (1,030) inlet c) 49.61 (1,260)	AJS37 Viggen.
RM8B (twin-shaft turbofan)	16,200 lbf (72.06 kN) dry, 28,110 lbf (125.04 kN) with afterburning	0.64 lb/lbf/hr (18.13 g/kNs) dry, 2.52 lb/lbf/hr (71.4 g/kNs) with afterburning	b) 16.5:1	b) JP-4, JP-5	4,895 (2,220)	a) 245.0 (6,223) b) 40.6 (1,030) inlet c) 49.61 (1,260)	JA37 Viggen.
RM12 (twin-shaft turbofan)	12,141 lbf (54 kN) dry, 18,105 lbf (80.54 kN) with afterburning	0.842 lb/lbf/hr (23.85 g/kNs)	b) 27.2:1	a) 867° C b) MIL-T-5624 grade JP-5	2,325 (1,055)	a) 159.1 (4,040) b) 33.46 (850) c) 43.31 (1,100)	JAS 39 Gripen. F404 type.
Turkey							
Tusas Engine Industries Inc (TEI). P.K. 610 Eskisehir							
F110-GE-100 (twin-shaft turbofan)	16,760 lbf (74.55 kN) dry, 28,000 lbf (124.55 kN) with afterburning		b) 30.4:1	a) 935° C b) MIL-T-5624 grade JP-4, JP-5, JP-8	3,911 (1,774)	a) 182.3 (4,630) max envelope b) 46.5 (1,181) max envelope	F-15, F-16. Joint venture company between GE Aircraft Engines of USA and Turkish shareholders.
F110-GE-129 (twin-shaft turbofan)	17,155 lbf (76.31 kN) dry, 29,000 lbf (129.0 kN) with afterburning		b) 30.7:1	a) 980° C b) As for F110-GE-100	As for F110-GE-100	a) As for F110-GE-100 b) As for F110-GE-100	F-15E, F-16C/D.
Ukraine							
Ivchenko PROGRESS ZMKB. 2 Ivanova Street, 330068 Zaporozhye (Telephone: +380 612 65 03 27 or 65 33 82, Facsimile: +380 612 65 46 97)							
AI-20D series 4 (single-shaft turboprop)	5,180 eshp (3,863 ekW) take-off at 12,300 rpm, 2,990 eshp (2,230 ekW) cruise at 8,000 m altitude and 630 km/h	0.443 lb/eshp/hr (270 g/ekW/hr)	a) 12,300 +90 b) 7.36:1	a) 952° C MGT b) Kerosene RT, TC-1, T-1	2,381 (1,080)	a) 121.89 (3,096) b) 33.15 (842) c) 46.46 (1,180)	An-8, Be-12.
AI-20D series 5E (single-shaft turboprop) (see Comments for AI-20A and K)	5,180 eshp (3,863 ekW) take-off at 12,300 rpm, 2,850 eshp (2,125 ekW) cruise at 8,000 m altitude and 540 km/h	0.511 lb/eshp/hr (311 g/ekW/hr) take-off, 0.439 lb/eshp/hr (267 g/ekW/hr) cruise	a) 12,300 +90 b) 9.45:1	a) 927° C TIT b) Kerosene RT, TC-1, T-1	2,293 (1,040)	a) 121.89 (3,096) b) 33.15 (842) c) 46.46 (1,180)	An-32. Air flow rate 44.97 lb (20.4 kg) per second. The older AI-20A used on the An-10, An-12 and Il-18, and the AI-20K used on the An-12 and Il-18, are each of 4,000 shp (2,983 kW).
AI-20M (single-shaft turboprop)	4,250 eshp (3,169 ekW) take-off at 12,300 rpm, 2,700 eshp (2,013 ekW) cruise at 8,400 m altitude and 630 km/h	0.434 lb/eshp/hr (264 g/ekW/hr)	a) 12,300 b) 7.62:1	a) 900° C MGT b) Kerosene RT, TC-1, T-1	2,293 (1,040)	a) 121.89 (3,096) b) 33.15 (842) c) 46.46 (1,180)	An-12, Il-18D and Il-38. The 5,180 shp (3,863 kW) AI-20DM was installed in the An-8 and Be-12.

Designation (type of engine)	Power output (normally take-off rating for piston, turboprop and turboshaft, unless stated)	Specific fuel consumption (S F C)	a) Max RPM b) Pressure or Compression ratio	a) EGT (unless stated to be MGT, TET, TGT or TIT) b) Primary fuel type or Octane rating	Dry weight lb (kg)	a) Length ins (mm) b) Width ins (mm) c) Height ins (mm)	Current aircraft users, and comments
Ukraine							
Ivchenko PROGRESS ZMKB. (continued)							
AI-24 (single-shaft turboprop)	2,550 eshp (1,902 ekW) take-off at 15,100 rpm, 1,650 eshp (1,230 ekW) cruise at 6,000 m altitude and 504 km/h	0.509 lb/eshp/hr (310 g/ekW/hr)	a) 15,100 b) 6.4:1	a) 877° C MGT b) Kerosene RT, TC-1, T-1	1,323 (600)	a) 92.36 (2,346) b) 26.65 (677) c) 42.32 (1,075)	An-24. Mean time in operation 14,500 hours.
AI-24T (single-shaft turboprop)	2,820 eshp (2,103 ekW) take-off at 15,800 rpm, 1,650 eshp (1,230 ekW) cruise at 6,000 m altitude and 504 km/h	0.518 lb/eshp/hr (315 g/ekW/hr)	a) 15,800 b) 7.05:1	a) 877° C MGT b) Kerosene RT, TC-1, T-1	1,323 (600)	a) 92.36 (2,346) b) 26.65 (677) c) 42.32 (1,075)	An-24, An-26 and An-30.
AI-24VT (single-shaft turboprop)	2,820 eshp (2,103 ekW) take-off at 15,800 rpm, 1,650 eshp (1,230 ekW) cruise at 6,000 m altitude and 360 km/h, ISA + 15° C	0.564 lb/eshp/hr (343 g/ekW/hr) at take-off, 0.527 lb/eshp/hr (321 g/ekW/hr) cruise	a) 15,800 ±150 b) 7.65:1	a) 797° C TIT b) Kerosene RT, TC-1, T-1	1,323 (600)	a) 92.36 (2,346) b) 26.65 (677) c) 42.32 (1,075)	An-24, An-26 and An-30. Air flow rate 31.75 lb (14.4 kg) per second.
AI-25 series 2E (twin-shaft turbofan)	3,307 lbf (14.71 kN) take-off, 443 lbf (1.97 kN) cruise at 6,000 m and 550 km/h, ISA	0.564 lb/lbf/hr (15.97 g/kNs) take-off, 0.795 lb/lbf/hr (22.52 g/kNs) cruise	b) 8.0:1	a) 872° C TIT b) Kerosene RT, TC-1, T-1	767 (348)	a) 78.46 (1,993) b) 32.28 (820) c) 35.28 (896)	Yak-40. Bypass ratio 2.2. Air flow rate 98.8 lb (44.81 kg) per second.
AI-25TL (twin-shaft turbofan)	3,792 lbf (16.87 kN) take-off, 1,135 lbf (5.05 kN) cruise at 8,000 m altitude and 550 km/h, ISA	0.590 lb/lbf/hr (16.71 g/kNs) take-off, 0.815 lb/lbf/hr (23.08 g/kNs) cruise	b) 9.5:1	a) 957° C TIT b) Kerosene RT, TC-1, T-1	772 (350)	a) 132.2 (3,358) b) 38.78 (985) c) 37.72 (958)	L-39 and K-8J. Bypass ratio 1.98. Air flow rate 103.18 lb (46.8 kg) per second.
AI-450 (turboshaft)	450 eshp (335 ekW)						Ka-226 and Ka-228. Compact engine for light aircraft and helicopters.
D-18T series 1 (triple-shaft turbofan)	51,654 lbf (229.78 kN) ideal take-off, to 30° C, 10,714 lbf (47.66 kN) ideal cruise at 11,000 m altitude and Mach 0.75, ISA	0.57 lb/lbf/hr (16.145 g/kNs)	b) 27.5:1	a) 1,122° C TIT	9,001 (4,083)	a) 212.6 (5,400) b) 109.92 (2,792) c) 115.63 (2,937)	An-124 and An-225. Bypass ratio 5.7.
D-18T series 3 (triple-shaft turbofan)	51,654 lbf (229.78 kN) ideal take-off, to 30° C, 10,714 lbf (47.66 kN) ideal cruise at 11,000 m altitude and Mach 0.8, ISA	0.57 lb/lbf/hr (16.145 g/kNs)	b) 25:1	a) 1,337° C MGT b) Kerosene RT, TC-1, T-1	9,039 (4,100)	a) 212.6 (5,400) b) 109.92 (2,792) c) 115.63 (2,937)	An-124 and An-225. Also projected for EKIP. Volga-Dnepr cargo airline funded from 1994 an engine life extension programme, increasing service hours from 1,000 to 4,000.
D-18T1 (triple-shaft turbofan)	57,320 lbf (254.98 kN) max contingency (OEI), 48,149 lbf (214.18 kN) take-off, to 30° C, 11,596 lbf (51.58 kN) cruise at 11,000 m altitude and Mach 0.8, ISA + 10° C	0.615 lb/lbf/hr (17.42 g/kNs)	b) 29.6:1 max contingency, 25:1 normal	a) 1,477° C max contingency, 1,337° C MGT b) Kerosene RT, TC-1, T-1	9,039 (4,100)	a) 212.6 (5,400) b) 109.92 (2,792) c) 116.22 (2,952)	An-218.
D-18TM (triple-shaft turbofan)	55,775 lbf (248 kN) at take-off to 30° C, 11,575 lbf (51.5 kN) cruise at 11,000 m altitude and Mach 0.8, ISA	0.585 lb/lbf/hr (16.57 g/kNs)	b) 28.8:1	a) 1,322° C b) Kerosene RT, TC-1, T-1	10,472 (4,750)	a) 224.41 (5,700) b) 117.4 (2,982) c) 117.56 (2,986)	An-218.
D-18TR (triple-shaft turbofan)	60,627 lbf (269.7 kN) at take-off to 30° C, 12,015 lbf (53.45 kN) cruise at 11,000 m altitude and Mach 0.8, ISA	0.585 lb/lbf/hr (16.57 g/kNs)	b) 30.3:1	a) 1,337° C b) Kerosene RT, TC-1, T-1	10,472 (4,750)	a) 224.41 (5,700) b) 117.4 (2,982) c) 117.56 (2,986)	An-218.

Designation (type of engine)	Power output (normally take-off rating for piston, turboprop and turboshaft, unless stated)	Specific fuel consumption (S F C)	a) Max RPM b) Pressure or Compression ratio	a) EGT (unless stated to be MGT, TET, TGT or TIT) b) Primary fuel type or Octane rating	Dry weight lb (kg)	a) Length ins (mm) b) Width ins (mm) c) Height ins (mm)	Current aircraft users, and comments
Ukraine							
Ivchenko PROGRESS ZMKB. (continued)							
D-27 and D-27M (propfans)	14,000 eshp (10,440 ekW) take-off at 8,394 rpm, to 30° C for D-27, and 16,000 eshp (11,930 ekW) for D-27M, 6,750 eshp (5,033 ekW) cruise at 7,135 rpm at 11,000 m altitude and Mach 0.7, ISA for D-27	0.287 lb/eshp/hr (175 g/ekW/hr) for D-27	a) 8,394 for D-27 b) 22.15:1 for D-27	a) 1,397° C MGT for D-27 b) Kerosene RT, TC-1, T-1 for D-27	3,638 (1,650) for D-27	a) 165.531 (4,204.5) for D-27 b) 49.57 (1,259) for D-27 c) 53.82 (1,367) for D-27	An-70/An-70T, An-180, Be-42 and Yak-46-20. D-27M is a modified version of the D-27 with uprated power.
D-36 series 1 (triple-shaft turbofan)	14,330 lbf (63.745 kN) ideal take-off, ISA, 3,527 lbf (15.69 kN) ideal cruise at 8,000 m altitude and Mach 0.75, ISA	0.65 lb/lbf/hr (18.41 g/kNs)	b) 20:1	a) 1,237° C MGT b) Kerosene RT, TC-1, T-1	2,438 (1,106)	a) 136.594 (3,470) b) 60.67 (1,541) c) 67.382 (1,711.5)	Yak-42, An-72 and An-74. First 3-shaft turbofan with high bypass ratio to come from former USSR.
D-127 (free-turbine turboshaft)	14,500 eshp (10,813 ekW) take-off at 8,314 rpm, 7,250 eshp (5,406 ekW) cruise at 7,135 rpm	0.401 lb/eshp/hr (244 g/ekW/hr)	a) 8,314 b) 24.3:1	a) 1,366° C MGT b) Kerosene RT, TC-1, T-1	2,866 (1,300)	a) 143.94 (3,656) b) 24.65 (626) intake	Project engine.
D-136 (free-turbine turboshaft)	11,400 eshp (8,500 ekW) take-off at 8,300 rpm, 6,100 eshp (4,549 ekW) cruise	0.432 lb/shp/hr (263 g/kW/hr) take-off	a) 8,700 b) 18.3:1	a) 1,205° C TIT b) Kerosene RT, TC-1, T-1	2,315 (1,050)	a) 146.26 (3,715) b) 54.41 (1,382) c) 44.61 (1,133)	Mil Mi-26 and Mi-26T. Air flow rate 79.37 lb (36 kg) per second.
D-227 and D-236 (propfans)	10,850 shp (8,090 kW) for D-236						D-236 geared propfan tested on a Yak-42E-LL. D-227 propfan intended for Yak-46-2.
D-436K (triple-shaft turbofan)	16,535 lbf (73.55 kN)						An-71 *Madcap*.
D-436T1 (triple-shaft turbofan)	16,865 lbf (75 kN) ideal take-off, to 30° C, 3,307 lbf (14.71 kN) cruise at 11,000 m altitude and Mach 0.75, ISA	0.608 lb/lbf/hr (17.22 g/kNs)	b) 23.2:1	a) 1,249° C MGT b) Kerosene RT, TC-1, T-1	3,197 (1,450)	a) 164.13 (4,169) b) 71.73 (1,822) c) 77.13 (1,959)	Tu-134M, Tu-334-100, Tu-414 and Yak-142M. D-436 type for TKS-25 projected transport and EKIP.
D-436T2 (triple-shaft turbofan)	18,078 lbf (80.42 kN) ideal take-off, to 30° C, 3,527 lbf (15.69 kN) cruise at 11,000 m and Mach 0.75, ISA	0.61 lb/lbf/hr (17.28 g/kNs)	b) 24.2	a) 1,277° C MGT b) Kerosene RT, TC-1, T-1	3,197 (1,450)	a) 164.13 (4,169) b) 71.73 (1,822) c) 77.13 (1,959)	Tu-230, Tu-334-100D/-200/Tu-354.
D-436TP (triple-shaft turbofan)	16,865 lbf (75 kN) ideal take-off, to 30° C, 4,375 lbf (19.46 kN) maximum cruise at 8,000 m and Mach 0.6, ISA	0.565 lb/lbf/hr (16.0 g/kNs) at maximum cruise (conditions as before), 0.631 lb/lbf/hr (17.87 g/kNs) cruise at 450 m and Mach 0.35			3,197 (1,450)	a) 164.13 (4,169) b) 71.73 (1,822), and 53.54 (1,360) for fan c) 77.13 (1,959)	Be-200. Low SFC and low specific mass. Built by Motor Sich JSC in the Ukraine, and UMPO JSC and Salut MMPO JSC in Russia.
D-727M (triple-shaft turbofan)	24,990 lbf (111.17 kN) max contingency (OEI), to 30° C, 25,353 lbf (112.78 kN) take-off, to 30° C, 5,070 lbf (22.56 kN) cruise at 11,000 m altitude and Mach 0.8, ISA	0.534 lb/lbf/hr (15.13 g/kNs)	b) 34:1 max contingency, 30:1 normal	a) 1,444° C max contingency, 1,372° C MGT b) Kerosene RT, TC-1, T-1	5,732 (2,600)	a) 196.85 (5,000) b) 85.94 (2,183) intake	Yak-46. Ultra high bypass ratio. High fuel economy combined with proven design. At design stage.
DV-2 (twin-shaft turbofan)	4,850 lbf (21.58 kN) take-off at 15° C, 1,852 lbf (8.24 kN) cruise at 6,000 m altitude and Mach 0.5, ISA	0.78 lb/lbf/hr (22.1 g/kNs)	b) 13.5:1	a) 1,183° C MGT b) Kerosene RT, TC-1, T-1	992 (450)	a) 141.73 (3,600) b) 39.13 (994) c) 40.83 (1,037)	L-59, K-8 Karakorum, and Yak-130. Manufactured in Slovakia.
DV-2F (twin-shaft turbofan)	4,850 lbf (21.58 kN) dry, at <24° C, 8,113 lbf (36.1 kN) with afterburning at <24° C	0.63 lb/lbf/hr (17.84 g/kNs)	b) 13.5:1	a) 1,147° C MGT b) Kerosene RT, TC-1, T-1	1,389 (630)	a) 123.23 (3,130) b) 39.13 (994) intake c) 40.83 (1,037)	Project engine. Afterburning provides supersonic possibilities.

Designation (type of engine)	Power output (normally take-off rating for piston, turboprop and turboshaft, unless stated)	Specific fuel consumption (S F C)	a) Max RPM b) Pressure or Compression ratio	a) EGT (unless stated to be MGT, TET, TGT or TIT) b) Primary fuel type or Octane rating	Dry weight lb (kg)	a) Length ins (mm) b) Width ins (mm) c) Height ins (mm)	Current aircraft users, and comments
Ukraine							
Ivchenko PROGRESS ZMKB. (continued)							
DV-12 (free-turbine turboshaft)	7,500 eshp (5,592.75 ekW) take-off at 11,440 rpm, to 28° C, 3,750 eshp (2,796 ekW) cruise at ISA	0.498 lb/eshp/hr (303 g/ekW/hr)	a) 11,440 b) 15.3:1	a) 1,147° C MGT b) Kerosene RT, TC-1, T-1	1,488 (675)	a) 98.43 (2,500) b) 18.9 (480) intake	Project engine.
DV-22 or AI-22 (twin-shaft turbofan)	8,532 lbf (37.95 kN) take-off, 1,720 lbf (7.65 kN) cruise at 11,000 m altitude and Mach 0.8	0.66 lb/lbf/hr (18.69 g/kNs)	b) 18:1	a) 1,147° C MGT b) Kerosene RT, TC-1, T-1	1,543 (700)	a) 94.49 (2,400) b) 40.16 (1,020) intake	Project engine, possibly for Il-108 and Tu-324.
Zaporozhye JSC Motor Sich. 330068 Zaporozhye (Telephone: +380 612 61 47 77 or 61 44 25, Facsimile: +380 612 65 60 07 or 65 58 85)							
Manufacturer of Ivchenko PROGRESS engines.							
TV3-117VMA-SB2 (free-turbine turboprop)	2,500 eshp (1,864 ekW) take-off to 28° C, 2,800 eshp (2,088 ekW) emergency to 25° C	0.473 lb/eshp/hr (288 g/ekW/hr) at take-off			1,235 (560)		Turboprop engine for An-140, Il-112, Il-114, Tu-130, MiG-110. PROGRESS developed and built by Motor Sich, as versions of the Klimov TV3-117.
TV3-117VMA-SB3 (free-turbine turboshaft)	2,500 eshp (1,864 ekW) take-off to 30° C, 2,800 eshp (2,088 ekW) emergency to 25° C	0.463 lb/eshp/hr (282 g/ekW/hr) at take-off			683 (310)		Turboshaft engine for Ka-50N, final uprated version of Ka-50, Ka-52, Mi-28N, Mi-24M, Ka-32. Development as above.
TV3-117VMA-SBM (free-turbine turboprop)	2,400 eshp (1,790 ekW) take-off to 36° C, 2,500 eshp (1,864 ekW) contingency to 42° C	0.473 lb/eshp/hr (288 g/ekW/hr) at take-off			1,080 (490)		Derivative of the TV3-117VMA-SB2 for An-140.
United Kingdom							
Mid-West Engines Ltd. Hangar SE 38, Gloucestershire Airport, Staverton, Gloucestershire GL51 6SR (Telephone: +44 1452 857456, Facsimile: +44 1452 856519, E-mail: midwestengines@avnet.co.uk, Web site: http://www.avnet.co.uk/midwestengines)							
AE50 Harrier (single-rotor rotary), also known as GAE50 with gearbox fitted	50 hp (37.3 kW) take-off at propeller shaft	9 litres per hour average	a) 7,500, or 6,700 max cruise	a) 950° C maximum b) Avgas 100 LL or RON 92 unleaded	72.75 (33), excluding radiator, silencer, etc.	a) 23 (585) b) 10 (256) across mounting plate c) 11.4 (290) including gearbox	Certified JAR-22. 294 cc Wankel-type rotary, spark ignition. Cooling system with liquid (water/glycol mix) and air (belt driven centrifugal fan). 14 volt, 18 amp alternator with electric starter. Reduction gear ratio 1:3.225, with torsion vibration damper.
AE100 Hawk (twin-rotor rotary), also known as GAE100 with gearbox fitted	95 hp (71 kW) take-off at propeller shaft	18 litres per hour average	a) 7,500, or 6,900 max cruise	a) 950° C b) Avgas 100 LL or RON 92 unleaded	117 (53), excluding radiator, silencer, etc.	a) 28.35 (720) approx b) 18.9 (480) approx c) 16.14 (410) approx	Certified under JAR-E. 588 cc (2 x 294 cc) Wankel type, with cooling as for AE50. 14 volt, 26 amp alternator with electric start. Reduction gear ratio 1:2.968, with torsion vibration damper.
AE110 Hawk (twin-rotor rotary, with fuel injection as Flytronic), also known as GAE110 with gearbox fitted	105 hp (75 kW) take-off at propeller shaft		a) 7,500, or 7,100 max cruise	b) Avgas 100 LL or RON 92 unleaded	122 (55.3), excluding radiator, silencer, etc	a) 28.35 (720) approx b) 18.9 (480) approx c) 16.14 (410) approx	For certification in 1999. 588 cc engine (2 x 294 cc) with Flytronic fuel injection system with automatic altitude compensation. Cooling as for AE50. 14 volt 26 amp alternator with electric starter. Reduction gear ratio 1:2.964, with torsion vibration damper.
Rolls-Royce plc. 65 Buckingham Gate, London SW1E 6AT (Telephone: +44 171 222 9020, Facsimile: +44 171 227 9178, Web site: www.rolls-royce.com)							
RB211-524G and G/H-T (see Comments) (triple-shaft turbofan)	58,000 lbf (258.0 kN) flat rated at 30° C. G/H-T rated at 58,000-60,000 lbf (258-266.9 kN)	0.57 lb/lbf/hr (16.145 g/kNs) cruise	b) 33.0:1		9,670 (4,386)	a) 125 (3,175) b) 86.3 (2,192) fan	B747-400 and B767-300. Single-stage wide-chord fan, 7-stage IP compressor, 6-stage HP compressor, single annular combustor with 18 fuel burners, single-stage IP turbine and HP turbine, and 3-stage LP turbine. Latest standard of RB211 is G/H-T, which was certified in May 1997 and first selected for SAA 747-400s in June 1997; first entered service on Cathay Pacific 747-400 on 20 April 1998. G/H-T incorporates complete high-pressure system of the Trent 700, offering a 2% improvement in fuel consumption.
RB211-524H (triple-shaft turbofan)	60,600 lbf (269.57 kN) flat rated at 30° C	0.57 lb/lbf/hr (16.145 g/kNs)	b) 33.0:1		9,670 (4,386)	a) 125 (3,175) b) 86.3 (2,192) fan	B747-400, B767-300. Single-stage wide-chord fan, 7-stage IP compressor, 6-stage HP compressor, single annular combustor with 18 fuel burners, single-stage IP turbine and HP turbine, and 3-stage LP turbine.
RB211-535C (triple-shaft turbofan)	37,400 lbf (166.37 kN) flat rated at 29° C	0.646 lb/lbf/hr (18.3 g/kNs) cruise	b) 21.1:1		7,294 (3,308)	a) 118.5 (3,010) b) 73.2 (1,859) inlet	B757-200. Similar to -524G/H but with 6-stage IP compressor.
RB211-535E4/E4-B (triple-shaft turbofan)	40,100-43,100 lbf (178.38-191.72 kN) flat rated at 29° C	0.598 lb/lbf/hr (16.94 g/kNs) cruise	b) 25.8:1		7,264 (3,295)	a) 117.9 (2,994) b) 74.5 (1,892) inlet	B757-200, B757-300 and Tu-204. Similar to -524G/H but with 6-stage IP compressor.
Gem 2 (free-turbine turboshaft)	900 shp (671.1 kW) max contingency, 750 shp (559.3 kW) max continuous	0.65 lb/shp/hr (396 g/kW/hr)	b) 12.0:1		330 (149.7)	a) 43.2 (1,097) b) 22.6 (574) c) 23.5 (597)	Naval and multi-role Lynx. Out of production. Includes Mk 1001. Entered service 1976.

Designation (type of engine)	Power output (normally take-off rating for piston, turboprop and turboshaft, unless stated)	Specific fuel consumption (S F C)	a) Max RPM b) Pressure or Compression ratio	a) EGT (unless stated to be MGT, TET, TGT or TIT) b) Primary fuel type or Octane rating	Dry weight lb (kg)	a) Length ins (mm) b) Width ins (mm) c) Height ins (mm)	Current aircraft users, and comments
United Kingdom							
Rolls-Royce plc. (continued)							
RR 1004 (free-turbine turboshaft)	944 shp (704 kW) max contingency, 881 shp (657 kW) take-off, 825 shp (615.2 kW) max continuous	0.525 lb/shp/hr (319 g/kW/hr)	a) 27,000 output speed b) 10.8:1		360 (163.3)	a) 42 (1,067) b) 22.6 (574) c) 23.5 (597)	Agusta A129 Mangusta. Produced under licence by Rinaldo Piaggio in Italy. Direct drive engine. Digital Electronic Fuel Control system.
Gem 41–2 (free-turbine turboshaft)	1,120 shp (835 kW) max contingency, 1,000 shp (745.7 kW) take-off, 890 shp (663.7 kW) max continuous	0.51 lb/shp/hr (310 g/kW/hr)	b) 12.02:1		404 (183.25)	a) 43.2 (1,097) b) 22.6 (574) c) 23.5 (597)	Naval Lynx. Out of production. Entered service 1978.
Gem 42 (free-turbine turboshaft)	1,120 shp (835 kW) max contingency, 1,000 shp (745.7 kW) take-off, 890 shp (663.7 kW) max continuous	0.51 lb/shp/hr (310 g/kW/hr)	a) 6,164 output speed b) 12.02:1		404 (183.25)	a) 42 (1,067) b) 22.6 (574) c) 23.5 (597)	Current production standard for all Lynx applications, including Super Lynx and Battlefield Lynx. UK MoD and French programme to update in-service Gem 2s and 41s to this standard. Entered service 1987. 3-shaft type with 4-stage LP compressor driven by a single-stage LP gas generator turbine, HP centrifugal compressor driven by a single-stage HP gas generator turbine, and 2-stage power turbine driving output shaft. Reverse flow annular combustor, and drive is via reduction gearbox.
Gnome H.1400-1T (free-turbine turboshaft)	1,535 shp (1,145 kW) max contingency at ISA + 30° C, 1,050 shp (783 kW) max continuous	0.627 lb/shp/hr (381 g/kW/hr)	a) 19,500 output speed b) 8.6:1		332 (150.6)	a) 54.8 (1,392) b) 22.7 (577) c) 21.6 (549)	Advanced versions of Westland Sea King and Commando. Optimized for hot-weather operations. Current production model. New deliveries to RAF started in 1994 ensure Gnome service until at least 2020.
Pegasus 11 (twin-shaft, vectored thrust turbofan)	21,000 lbf (93.41 kN) nominal with normal hover bleed	Details not available	b) 14.6:1		3,113 (1,412), 3,179 (1,442) naval versions, minus nozzles	a) 98.83 (2,510) minus nozzles b) 48.05 (1,220) over fan casing	RAF two-seat Harriers, AV-8A Harrier and naval Sea Harriers. Weight 3,734 lb (1,694 kg) installed. See Pegasus 11-61 for length with nozzles. Entered service in 1974. Pegasus (series) is a vectored-thrust turbofan of 2-shaft design, with 3 LP and 8 HP compressor stages driven by 2 LP and 2 HP turbine stages respectively. Combustor is annular and has vaporisers.
Pegasus 11-21 (twin-shaft, vectored thrust turbofan) See Comments for Mks 105, 106 and 152-42	21,450, 21,550 or 21,750 lbf (95.42, 95.86 or 96.75 kN), with a nominal 22,000 lbf (97.86 kN) output	Details not available	b) 15.3:1		3,240 (1,470), minus nozzles, 3,960 lb (1,796 kg) installed	a) 98.83 (2,510) minus nozzles b) 48.05 (1,220) over fan casing	Harrier II/AV-8B. RAF uses Mk 105 of 21,550 lbf. Naval Mk 106 for F/A Mk 2 and Spanish Mk 152-42 of similar power. Early USMC AV-8Bs and some Italian aircraft given 21,450 lbf F402-RR-406A version. Entered service in 1984.
Pegasus 11-61 (twin-shaft, vectored thrust turbofan)	23,800 lbf (105.89 kN) at sea level, ISA conditions	Details not available	b) 16.3:1		4,180 (1,896), 4,260 (1,932) installed	a) 137.2 (3,485) with nozzles b) 48.05 (1,220) intake	USMC AV-8Bs delivered from late 1990 and Italian AV-8Bs, Spanish Matador IIs and Harrier II Plus. US military designation F402-RR-408A. FADEC controlled.
RB163 Spey Mk 511-8/F113-RR-100 (twin-shaft turbofan)	11,400 lbf (50.71 kN) flat rated at 23.5° C	0.8 lb/lbf/hr (22.66g/kNs)	b) 18.4:1		2,483 (1,126)	a) 109.6 (2,784) b) 32.5 (826) fan	Gulfstream II/III/SMA-3. US military designation F113-RR-100. Civil Spey.
RB163 Spey Mk 512-14DW (twin-shaft turbofan)	12,550 lbf (55.83 kN) wet, flat-rated at 25° C	0.82 lb/lbf/hr (23.23 g/kNs)	b) 21.2:1		2,609 (1,183)	a) 109.6 (2,784) b) 37.1 (942)	BAC One-Eleven Series 475 and 500, Romaero Rombac 1-11.
RB168 Spey Mk 202 (twin-shaft turbofan)	12,250 lbf (54.49 kN) dry, 20,515 lbf (91.26 kN) with afterburning				4,093 (1,856)	a) 204.9 (5,204) b) 32.5 (826)	Military Spey. Entered service in 1968.
RB168 Spey Mk 250/251 (twin-shaft turbofan)	11,995 lbf (53.36 kN) dry, 21,995 lbf (97.84 kN) with afterburning				2,740 (1,243)	a) 117 (2,972) b) 32.5 (826)	Nimrod MR (Mk 250) for maritime operations, Nimrod R (Mk 251) for high altitude operations.
RB168 Spey Mk 807 (twin-shaft turbofan)	11,030 lbf (49.06 kN)	0.659 lb/lbf/hr (18.67 g/kNs) take-off maximum	b) 16.8:1	a) 585° C maximum EGT, 1,107° C maximum MGT b) JP-1, JP-4 and JP-5	2,417 (1,096)	a) 96.7 (2,456) b) 32.5 (826)	Variant of Spey for the AMX, built under licence by FiatAvio in Italy and Celma-Cia in Brazil. Entered service in 1989. 4-stage LP and 12-stage HP compressor driven by 2-stage LP and 2-stage HP turbines respectively. Turbo-annular combustor.
Tay 611 (twin-shaft turbofan)	13,850 lbf (61.61 kN) flat-rated at 30° C	0.69 lb/lbf/hr (19.54 g/kNs)	b) 15.8:1		2,951 (1,339)	a) 94.7 (2,405) b) 44 (1,118) fan	Gulfstream IV/IV-SP. Tay designed around core and external gearbox of RB183 Mk 555. Entered service in 1987. 3-stage LP compressor to the rear, 12-stage HP compressor, cannular combustion system consisting of 10 combustors, 2-stage high-pressure turbine and 3-stage LP turbine. Forced mixer to the rear of the LP turbine.
Tay 620 (twin-shaft turbofan)	13,850 lbf (61.61 kN) take-off, 2,550 lbf (11.34 kN) cruise at 35,000 ft and Mach 0.8	0.69 lb/lbf/hr (19.54 g/kNs)	b) 15.8:1		3,185 (1,445)	a) 94.7 (2,405) b) 44 (1,118) fan	Fokker 70 and Fokker 100, latter service entry from late 1994. Entered service in 1988.
Tay 650 (twin-shaft turbofan)	15,100 lbf (67.17 kN) take-off, 2,950 lbf (13.12 kN) cruise at 35,000 ft and Mach 0.8	0.69 lb/lbf/hr (19.54 g/kNs)	b) 16.2:1		3,340 (1,515)	a) 94.8 (2,408) b) 44.8 (1,138) fan	Fokker 100. Tay 650-14 was to re-engine BAC One-Eleven and for Romaero Airstar 2500. Entered service in 1989.

Designation (type of engine)	Power output (normally take-off rating for piston, turboprop and turboshaft, unless stated)	Specific fuel consumption (S F C)	a) Max RPM b) Pressure or Compression ratio	a) EGT (unless stated to be MGT, TET, TGT or TIT) b) Primary fuel type or Octane rating	Dry weight lb (kg)	a) Length ins (mm) b) Width ins (mm) c) Height ins (mm)	Current aircraft users, and comments
United Kingdom							
Rolls-Royce plc. (continued)							
Tay 651 (twin-shaft turbofan) See Comments for Tay 670	15,400 lbf (68.50 kN), flat rated at 28° C	As Tay 650, at higher altitude and speed	b) 16.6:1		3,380 (1,533)	a) 94.8 (2,408) b) 44.8 (1,138) fan	Re-engined B727-100. Service entry December 1992. Tay 670 for re-engined DC-9.
Trent 553 (triple-shaft turbofan)	53,000 lbf (235.76 kN)		b) 35.1:1		10,400 (4,717) basic engine weight	a) 154 (3,912) b) 97.4 (2,474) fan	Trent 500 and 600 being defined for A340-500/-600, and B747 developments respectively.
Trent 556 (triple-shaft turbofan)	56,000 lbf (249.1 kN)	0.5682 lb/lbf/hr (16.09 g/kNs)	b) 36.7:1		10,400 (4,717) basic engine weight	a) 154 (3,912) b) 97.4 (2,474) fan	
Trent 600	65,000 lbf (289.14 kN)		b) 39.4:1			a) 154 (3,912) b) 97.4 (2,474) fan	
Trent 768 (triple-shaft turbofan)	67,500 lbf (300.26 kN), flat rated at 30° C	0.584 lb/lbf/hr (16.54 g/kNs)	b) 33.7:1		10,550 (4,785) basic engine weight	a) 154 (3,912) b) 97.4 (2,474) fan	Airbus A330-300. Service entry 1996. Trent has 8-stage IP compressor, 6-stage HP compressor, single annular combustor with 24 fuel injectors, single-stage HP turbine and IP turbine, 4-stage LP turbine. FADEC.
Trent 772 (triple-shaft turbofan)	71,100 lbf (316.27 kN), flat rated at 30° C	0.584 lb/lbf/hr (16.54 g/kNs)	b) 35.5:1		10,550 (4,785) basic engine weight	a) 154 (3,912) b) 97.4 (2,474) fan	Airbus A330-300. Gained 90 minutes ETOPS clearance by the JAR in February 1995, ahead of airline operations that year.
Trent 775 (triple-shaft turbofan)	75,150 lbf (334.29 kN), flat rated at 30° C	0.565 lb/lbf/hr (16.0 g/kNs)	b) 39.03		10,550 (4,785) basic engine weight	a) 154 (3,912) b) 97.4 (2,474) fan	Airbus A330.
Trent 875 (triple-shaft turbofan)	77,900 lbf (346.52 kN), flat rated at 30° C	0.575 lb/lbf/hr (16.29 g/kNs)	b) 34.9:1		13,100 (5,942) basic engine weight	a) 172 (4,369) b) 110 (2,794)	B777-200. First delivery to Boeing February 1995. Derated thrust model to suit customers' requirements. Trent 800 series has 5-stage LP turbine. Service entry 1996. Approved for 180 minutes ETOPs on 11 October 1996.
Trent 877 (triple-shaft turbofan)	80,270 lbf (357.07 kN), flat rated at 38° C	0.575 lb/lbf/hr (16.29 g/kNs)	b) 35.9:1		13,100 (5,942) basic engine weight	a) 172 (4,369) b) 110 (2,794)	Boeing 777-200 at high MTOW. Service entry 1996.
Trent 884 (triple-shaft turbofan)	86,910 lbf (386.6 kN), flat rated at 30° C	0.575 lb/lbf/hr (16.29 g/kNs)	b) 38.8:1		13,100 (5,942) basic engine weight	a) 172 (4,369) b) 110 (2,794)	B777-200IGW and Tu-304.
Trent 890 (triple-shaft turbofan)	90,000 lbf (400.35 kN)					a) 172 (4,369) b) 110 (2,794)	B777-300 at high MTOW.
Trent 892 (triple-shaft turbofan)	91,450 lbf (406.8 kN), flat rated at 30° C	0.575 lb/lbf/hr (16.29 g/kNs)	b) 40.8:1		13,100 (5,942) basic engine weight	a) 172 (4,369) b) 110 (2,794)	B777-200IGW. Certification of Trent 800 at 90,000 lbf (400.35kN) gained January 1995. First flown on a B747 on 29 March 1995. Service entry 1997.
Trent 895 (triple-shaft turbofan)	95,000 lbf (424.8 kN)				18,086 (8,204)	a) 172 (4,369) b) 110 (2,794)	B777-300.
Trent 900 (triple-shaft turbofan)	80,000 lbf (355.86 kN)		b) 41:1		12,900 (5,851) basic engine weight	a) 172 (4,369) b) 110 (2,794)	Airbus A3XX. Service entry 2003. Bypass ratio 8:1.
Trent 8104 (triple-shaft turbofan)	104,000 lbf (462.62 kN) at 21° C	0.573 lb/lbf/hr (16.12 g/kNs)	b) 45:1		14,400 (6,532) basic engine weight	a) 172 (4,369) b) 110 (2,794)	B777-200X and -300X. Service entry 2001.
Tyne RTy 20 Mk 21 (twin-shaft turboprop)	6,100 eshp (4,549 ekW)	0.439 lb/eshp/hr (267 g/ekW/hr)	b) 13.6:1		2,394 (1,086)	a) 115 (2,920) b) 55 (1,397)	6-stage LP compressor, 9-stage HP compressor, combustion chamber with 10 flame tubes, 1-stage HP turbine with cooled hollow blades, and 3-stage LP turbine. Air flow 46 lb (21 kg) per second. Atlantic/Atlantique. Produced internationally in Europe. In production.
Viper 600 Mk 632 (single-shaft turbojet)	3,970 lbf (17.66 kN)	0.97 lb/lbf/hr (27.48 g/kNs)	b) 5.95:1		830 (376.4)	a) 71.1 (1,806) b) 29 (737) c) 35.5 (902)	Orao and IAR 93A (632-41), IAR 99 Soim (632-41M), MB-326K and MB-339 (632-43), and G-4 Super Galeb (632-46).
Viper 600 Mk 633 (single-shaft turbojet)	5,030 lbf (22.37 kN), with afterburning					a) 71.1 (1,806) b) 29 (737) c) 35.5 (902)	Mk 632 with afterburning. Orao (633-41) and IAR 93B (633-47).
Viper 600 Mk 680-43 (single-shaft turbojet)	4,360 lbf (19.39 kN)	0.98 lb/lbf/hr (27.76 g/kNs)	b) 6.75:1		836 (379.2)	a) 71.1 (1,806) b) 29 (737) c) 35.5 (902)	MB-339C. Mk 680 also for MB-339B demonstrator.
Viper 600 Mk 680-582 (single-shaft turbojet)	4,000 lbf (17.79 kN)		b) 6.75:1		836 (379.2)	a) 71.1 (1,806) b) 29 (737) c) 35.5 (902)	TBO 4,500 hrs. Improved maintainability.
Wilksch Airmotive Limited. 12 Pattison Lane, Woolstone, Milton Keynes MK18 0AX (Telephone: +44 1908 392003, Facsimile: +44 1908 691619)							
Wilksch diesel (3-cyl, 2-stroke)	120 hp (89.5 kW). 140 hp (104 kW) 4-cyl version under development		a) 2,700 approx b) 20:1	b) Diesel/autur	Estimated at 25 (115)	a) 32 (813) b) 24 (610) c) 26 (660) all preliminary	By October 1998, completed over 250 hours of bench tests and some flights in a Piper Cub. Considered for Europa, Cessna 152, Long-E2.
United States of America							
Alliance – see GE - P&W -- The Engine Alliance							

Designation (type of engine)	Power output (normally take-off rating for piston, turboprop and turboshaft, unless stated)	Specific fuel consumption (S F C)	a) Max RPM b) Pressure or Compression ratio	a) EGT (unless stated to be MGT, TET, TGT or TIT) b) Primary fuel type or Octane rating	Dry weight lb (kg)	a) Length ins (mm) b) Width ins (mm) c) Height ins (mm)	Current aircraft users, and comments
United States of America							
AlliedSignal Engines. 1944 East Sky Harbor Circle (85034), PO Box 29003, Phoenix, AZ 85038-9003 (Telephone: +1 602 365 2055, Facsimile: +1 602 365 2029, Web site: http://www.alliedsignal.com/aerospace)							
500 Series Common Core (compact, lightweight family of engines in turboprop, turboshaft and turbofan forms)	7,500 eshp (5,593 ekW) as turboprop and turboshaft, with growth variants to 11,000 eshp (8,203 ekW) being studied. Up to 18,000 lbf (80 kN) as turbofan						Turboprop for a new generation of high-speed regional aircraft. Turboshaft for large cargo and transport helicopters. Turbofan for regional jetliners. Derived from ALF502/LF507.
ALF502L (twin-shaft turbofan)	7,500 lbf (33.362 kN) take-off	0.414-0.428 lb/lbf/hr (11.73-12.12 g/kNs)	b) 13.6:1		1,311 (594.7)	a) 58.56 (1,487) b) 41.7 (1,059)	Canadair 600 Challenger.
ALF502R-3A/5 (twin-shaft turbofan)	6,970 lbf (31 kN) take-off	0.408 lb/lbf/hr (11.56 g/kNs)	b) 11.6 to 12:1		1,336 (606)	a) 56.8 (1,443) b) 41.7 (1,059)	BAe 146. Previous R-3 models all converted to R-3As. R-4 model was never produced.
ALF502R-6 (twin-shaft turbofan)	7,500 lbf (33.36 kN) take-off	0.415 lb/lbf/hr (11.75 g/kNs)	b) 13.6:1		1,336 (606)	a) 58.6 (1,487) b) 41.7 (1,059)	BAe 146.
AS812F (turboprop)							Proposed for FLA. Uses TFE1042 turbofan core.
AS900 family (turbofan)	Initially 7,500 lbf (33.36 kN)						For first test run in July 1999 and certification in 2001. Possible Avro RJ series engine replacement.
F124 see TFE1042-70 and F124-GA-100 after							
LF507-1F (turbofan)	7,000 lbf (31.14 kN) to 23.3° C	0.406 lb/lbf/hr (11.5 g/kNs)	b) 13.8:1		1,385 (628.2)	a) 58.6 (1,487) b) 41.7 (1,059)	Avro RJ70, RJ85 and RJ100. F for FADEC controlled. For Cat III capable regional jets.
LF507-1H (turbofan)	7,000 lbf (31.14 kN) to 23.3° C	0.406 lb/lbf/hr (11.5 g/kNs)	b) 13.8:1		1,375 (623.7)	a) 58.6 (1,487) b) 41.7 (1,059)	BAe 146. H for Hydromechanical controlled, certified in October 1991.
LTP101-700A-1A (free-turbine turboprop)	700 eshp (522 ekW)	0.55 lb/eshp/hr (335 g/ekW/hr) take-off	a) up to 1,950 output		335 (152)	a) 36 (914.4) b) 21 (533.4)	Piaggio P.166-DL3, PAC Cresco, and various re-engined aircraft. Lower rated but otherwise similar 620 eshp (462.3 ekW) LTP101-600A-1A also for P.166-DL3.
LTS101-600A-2 (turboshaft version of the LTP 101)	615 shp (458.6 kW) take-off	0.571 lb/shp/hr (347 g/kW/hr)	a) 6,000		253 (114.75)	a) 30.9 (785) b) 23.6 (599.4)	AS 350D AStar. Plus I and Plus II variants of the LTS101 range incorporate component upgrades.
LTS101-600A-3 (turboshaft version of the LTP 101)	615 shp (458.6 kW) take-off	0.582 lb/shp/hr (354 g/kW/hr)	a) 6,000		253 (114.8)	a) 30.9 (785) b) 22.4 (569)	AS 350D AStar.
LTS101-750B-1 (turboshaft version of the LTP 101)	727 shp (542 kW) take-off	0.577 lb/shp/hr (351 g/kW/hr)	a) 6,000		271 (122.9)	a) 31.0 (787) b) 25.4 (645)	BK 117 B-2.
LTS101-750B-2 (turboshaft version of the LTP 101)	742 shp (553 kW) take-off	0.57 lb/shp/hr (347 g/kW/hr)	a) 6,000		268 (121.6)	a) 32.36 (822) b) 24.7 (627.4)	HH-65A Dolphin.
T53-L-13B/T5313B (free-turbine turboshaft)	1,400 shp (1,044 kW) take-off	0.58 lb/shp/hr (353 g/kW/hr)			540 (245)	a) 47.6 (1,209) b) 23 (584)	UH-1/CH-118 and AH-1 in military T53 form. Bell 205A.
T5317A/A-1 (free-turbine turboshaft)	1,500 shp (1,118.6 kW) take-off	0.59 lb/shp/hr (359 g/kW/hr)			545 (247)	a) 47.6 (1,209) b) 23-(584)	Kaman K-MAX. Commercial version of T53-L-703.
T53-L-701 (turboprop)	1,400 shp (1,044 kW)	0.6 lb/shp/hr (365 g/kW/hr)			693 (314.4)	a) 59.4 (1,508) b) 23 (584)	OV-1 Mohawk.
T53-L-703/T5317A/B (free-turbine turboshaft)	1,800 shp (1,342.3 kW) take-off	0.568 lb/shp/hr (345.5 g/kW/hr)			545 (247.2)	a) 47.6 (1,209) b) 23 (584)	AH-1, UH-1, and Fuji-Bell 205B. K-MAX for T5317A-1. See also Kawasaki.
T55-L-712 and 712-SSB (free-turbine turboshaft)	3,750 shp (2,796 kW) normal maximum for 712, 4,400 shp (3,281 kW) for SSB	0.53 lb/shp/hr (322 g/kW/hr)		b) JP-4, JP-5, JP-8 and CITE	750 (340.2)	a) 48.5 (1,231) b) 28.7 (729)	CH-47D/J Chinook.
T55-L-712E (free-turbine turboshaft)	3,750 shp (2,796 kW) See comments	0.53 lb/shp/hr (322 g/kW/hr)	b) 8.2:1	b) JP-4, JP-5 and CITE	710 (322)	a) 46.5 (1,181) b) 24.25 (616)	CH-47C Chinook. 3,400 shp (2,535 kW) military for 30 minutes, 3,000 shp (2,237 kW) max continuous.
AL5512 (free-turbine turboshaft)	4,075 shp (3,039 kW) take-off	0.53 lb/shp/hr (322 g/kW/hr)			780 (354)	a) 44 (1,118) b) 24.25 (616)	Commercial Chinook. Civil derivative of T55-L-712.
T55-L-714 (free-turbine turboshaft)	5,000 shp (3,729 kW) max contingency	0.503 lb/shp/hr (306 g/kW/hr)	b) 9.3:1	b) JP-4, JP-5, JP-8 and CITE	832 (377.4)	a) 46.5 (1,181) b) 24.25 (616)	MH-47E.

Designation (type of engine)	Power output (normally take-off rating for piston, turboprop and turboshaft, unless stated)	Specific fuel consumption (S F C)	a) Max RPM b) Pressure or Compression ratio	a) EGT (unless stated to be MGT, TET, TGT or TIT) b) Primary fuel type or Octane rating	Dry weight lb (kg)	a) Length ins (mm) b) Width ins (mm) c) Height ins (mm)	Current aircraft users, and comments
United States of America							
AlliedSignal Engines. (continued)							
T55-L-714A (free-turbine turboshaft)	5,000 shp (3,729 kW)			b) JP-4, JP-5, JP-8 and CITE		a) 46.5 (1,181) b) 24.25 (616)	CH-47D Chinook. Selected by Boeing for all new CH-47D sales internationally. Features elimination of magnesium for better operation in salt-water environments, improved torque measurement system, improved FADEC and longer life rotating components.
TFE731-2/2A/2B/2J/2L/2N (twin-shaft turbofan)	3,500 lbf (15.57 kN) take-off to 22.2° C, 755 lbf (3.36 kN) cruise at 40,000 ft and Mach 0.8	0.815 lb/lbf/hr (23.1 g/kNs) cruise	b) 14:1		743 (337)	a) 59.83 (1,519) b) 34.2 (869) c) 39.36 (1,000)	AT-3 Tzu-Chiang, C-101EB, K-8 Karakorum, Learjet 31A/35A/36A/C-21, and IA.63 Pampa.
TFE731-3/3A/3B/3J (twin-shaft turbofan)	up to 3,700 lbf (16.46 kN) to 24.4° C take-off, up to 844 lbf (3.75 kN) cruise (as before)	0.816-0.835 lb/lbf/hr (23.1-23.65 g/kNs) cruise	b) 14.6:1		754-775 (342-351.5)	a) 59.7 (1,516) b) 34.2 (869) c) 39.36 (1,000)	BAe 125-700, C-101BB, Citation III/VI, Falcon 50, JetStar II, Learjet 55/56, Sabreliner 65A and Westwind/1125 Astra SP.
TFE731-3C and -3D (twin-shaft turbofan conversions)							Conversions of earlier -3 engines, with major maintenance periodic inspection intervals extended in 1997 from 1,400 hours to 2,100 hours. Over 400 -3C conversions since 1993 and over 100 -3Ds since 1996. -3Cs power Citation IIIs and VIs, and IAI Astras among others, while -3Ds are used by Falcon 50s, Hawker 400/600/700s, Sabre 65, Jetstar and Westwind.
TFE731-4 (twin-shaft turbofan)	4,000 lbf (17.8 kN) take-off, 929 lbf (4.13 kN) cruise (as before)	0.796 lb/lbf/hr (22.54 g/kNs) cruise			822 (373)	a) 58.15 (1,477) b) 34.2 (869) c) 39.36 (1,000)	Citation VII and G-5 Super Galeb. TFE731-4-1T in L-139, rated at 4,080 lbf (18.15 kN), and with dry weight of 822 lb (373 kg) and 0.518 lb/lbf/hr (14.67 g/kNs) TFC.
TFE731-5/5A/5B/BR/5J (twin-shaft turbofan)	4,300-4,750 lbf (19.13-21.13 kN) take-off, up to 1,052 lbf (4.68 kN) cruise (as above)	0.756-0.802 lb/lbf/hr (21.414-22.72 g/kNs) cruise			852-899 (386-408)	a) 65.54 (1,665) for TFE731-5 b) 33.79 (858) c) 40.52 (1,029)	C-101CC/DD, Citation Ultra, re-engined Falcon 20, Falcon 900/900B, and Raytheon Hawker 800. 4,660 lbf (20.72 kN) TFE731-5BR in Hawker 800XP.
TFE731-20 (twin-shaft turbofan)	3,500 lbf (15.57 kN) take-off to 33.9° C, 876 lbf (3.9 kN) cruise (as above)	0.728 lb/lbf/hr (20.62 g/kNs)	b) 14.3:1		836 (379.2)	a) 59.65 (1,515) b) 34.2 (869) c) 39.36 (1,000)	Learjet 45.
TFE731-40 (twin-shaft turbofan)	4,250 lbf (18.9 kN) take-off to 24.4°C, 1,010 lbf (4.49 kN) cruise (as above)	0.457 lb/lbf/hr (12.94 g/kNs)	b) 22:1 cycle pressure ratio		885 (401)	a) 51.03 (1,296) without spinner c) 28.2 (716) fan housing, 22.37 (568) from centre of spinner to bottom of accessory case.	Falcon 50EX and Astra SPX. Certified in 1995. 24% increase in cruise altitude thrust and 7% reduction in cruise TSFC relative to TFE731-3. N1 control full authority digital control with hydromechanical back-up with integral synchronization and APR. ARINC 429 glass cockpit interface.
TFE731-60 (twin-shaft turbofan)	5,000 lbf (22.24 kN) take-off to 32.2°C, 1,120 lbf (4.98 kN) cruise (as above)	0.405 lb/lbf/hr (11.47 g/kNs)	b) 22:1 cycle pressure ratio		928 (421)	a) 82.2 (2,089) b) 30.3 (770) fan c) 32.68 (830) fan housing, 24.18 (614) from centre of spinner to bottom of accessory case.	Falcon 900EX. Certified in 1995. Utilizes a larger wide-chord damperless fan (geared). 17% increase in cruise altitude thrust and 12% reduction in TSFC relative to TFE731-5. N1 control as for TFE731-40. Bypass ratio 4.1:1.
ITEC TFE1042-70 (F125-GA-100) (twin-shaft turbofan)	6,300 lbf (28 kN) dry, 9,250 lbf (41.1 kN) with afterburning	0.8 lb/lbf/hr (22.7 g/kNs) dry, 2.06 lb/lbf/hr (58.35 g/kNs) with afterburning	b) 18.45:1	a) 1,372° C TIT	1,360 (616.9)	a) 140.2 (3,561) b) 30.8 (782) nozzle c) 33.4 (848)	AIDC/Han Hsiang Ching-Kuo. Forms the core of the proposed AS812F turboprop for FLA. ITEC is a joint venture company with AIDC/Han Hsiang of Taiwan.
F124-GA-100 (twin-shaft turbofan)	6,300 lbf (28.02 kN) dry	0.81 lb/lbf/hr (22.94 g/kNs) typical	b) 19.4:1	a) 1,366° C TIT	1,100 lb (499 kg) approx	a) 66.8 (1,697) b) 30 (762) c) 36 (914)	L-159 and potentially T-45A. Qualified to MIL-E-87231, MIL-STD-1783. Bypass ratio 0.474. Inlet air flow 93.75 lb (42.52 kg) per second. Dual FADEC.
F124X, F124XX, F125X and F125XX (twin-shaft turbofans)							All asked to be deleted by AlliedSignal. See 1996-97 edition of *WA&SD*.
TPE331-5/5A/6 series (single-shaft turboprop)	840 shp (626.4 kW) take-off, with 776 shp (578.66 kW) gearbox limit	0.56 lb/shp/hr (340.6 g/kW/hr)	b) 10.37:1	a) 1,005° C TIT	360 (163.3)	b) 21 (533) c) 26 (660)	Includes Ayres S2R-G6 Turbo Thrush, C-212 and Do 228.
TPE331-8 (single-shaft turboprop)	715 shp (533.2 kW) flat rated to 36° C	0.572 lb/shp/hr (348 g/kW/hr)	b) 10.37:1	a) 1,005° C TIT	370 (168)	b) 21 (533) c) 26 (660)	Cessna Conquest and Conquest II.
TPE331-10/10R/10U (single-shaft turboprop)	1,000 shp (745.7 kW) take-off, with 900 shp (671 kW) gearbox limit	0.558 lb/shp/hr (339 g/kW/hr)	b) 10.37:1	a) 1,065° C TIT	375 (170)	b) 21 (533) c) 26 (660)	Ayres S2R-G10 and S2R-660 Turbo Thrush, C-212 (10R-513C for Series 300), Jetstream 31, Merlin III and other types.
TPE331-11U (single-shaft turboprop)	1,000 shp (745.7 kW) take-off, with 1,100 shp (820.3 kW) gearbox limit	0.558 lb/shp/hr (339 g/kW/hr)	b) 10.37:1	a) 1,065° C TIT	405 (183.7)	b) 21 (533) c) 26 (660)	Merlin 23, Metro 23 and Expediter.

Designation (type of engine)	Power output (normally take-off rating for piston, turboprop and turboshaft, unless stated)	Specific fuel consumption (S F C)	a) Max RPM b) Pressure or Compression ratio	a) EGT (unless stated to be MGT, TET, TGT or TIT) b) Primary fuel type or Octane rating	Dry weight lb (kg)	a) Length ins (mm) b) Width ins (mm) c) Height ins (mm)	Current aircraft users, and comments
United States of America							
AlliedSignal Engines. (continued)							
TPE331-12U/12JR (single-shaft turboprop)	1,100 shp (820.3 kW) take-off	0.547 lb/shp/hr (332.7 g/kW/hr)	b) 10.7:1	a) 1,100° C TIT	407 (184.6)	b) 21 (533) c) 26 (660)	C-212-400 (TPE331-12JR-701C), Metro 23, C-26, Jetstream Super 31, and RAF Tucano. TPE331-12D variant on HTT-35.
TPE331-14A/B and -15 (single-shaft turboprop)	1,645 shp (1,227 kW)	0.502 lb/shp/hr (305 g/kW/hr)	b) 10.8:1	a) 1,100° C TIT	620 (281.2)	b) 23 (584) c) 36 (914)	PA-42-1000 Cheyenne 400 and upgraded S-2 Tracker.
TPE331-14F-801L (single-shaft turboprop)	Derated 750 shp (559.3 kW)						Grob G-520 Strato 1.
TPE331-14GR/HR (single-shaft turboprop)	1,650 shp (1,230 kW)	0.502 lb/shp/hr (305 g/kW/hr)	b) 11.0:1	a) 1,100° C TIT	620 (281.2)	b) 23 (584) c) 36 (914)	An-38, Ayres Vigilante and Jetstream 41, plus upgraded S-2 water bomber. Certification of TPE331-14GR/HR on the An-38 received from the IAC in Russia in September 1996.
TPE331-25/61 and 71 (single-shaft turboprop)	575 shp (428.8 kW) take-off, 445 shp (332 kW) cruise	0.66 lb/shp/hr (401.5 g/kW/hr)	b) 8:1	a) 987° C TIT	335 (152)	b) 21 (533) c) 26 (660)	MU-2B and other early models, and various re-engined aircraft.
Allison Engine Company. PO Box 420, Speed Code U10C, Indianapolis, IN 46206-0420 (Telephone: +1 317 230 5716, Facsimile: +1 317 230 6763, Web site: www.allison.com)							
Rolls-Royce plc of the UK agreed to purchase the Allison Engine Company in November 1994. Allison continues to operate under its own name as a member of Rolls-Royce's Aerospace Group. Allison established the Allison Advanced Development Co to undertake US classified or restricted access programmes.							
250-B17C (free-turbine turboprop)	420 shp (313.2 kW) take-off, 369 shp (275 kW) normal cruise, sea level static	0.657 lb/shp/hr (400 g/kW/hr)	b) 7.2:1	a) 810° C MGT b) Jet	195 (88.5)	a) 45 (1,143) b) 19.4 (493) c) 22.6 (574)	Nomad, Turbine Islander, Turbostar, Viator and more.
250-B17D (free-turbine turboprop)	420 shp (313.3 kW) take-off, 369 shp (275 kW) normal cruise, sea level static	0.657 lb/shp/hr (400 g/kW/hr)	b) 7.2:1	a) 810° C MGT b) Jet	198 (89.8)	a) 45 (1,143) b) 19.4 (493) c) 22.6 (574)	Fuji T-5, SF.260TP, AS 202/32TP Turbine Brave, Turbo Pillán and more. In production. Allison Series II engine.
250-B17F (free-turbine turboprop)	450 shp (335.6 kW) take-off, 380 shp (283.4 kW) normal cruise, sea level static	0.613 lb/shp/hr (373 g/kW/hr)	b) 7.91:1	a) 810° C MGT b) Jet	205 (93)	a) 45 (1,143) b) 19.4 (493) c) 22.6 (574)	Beech A36, Cessna P210, Nomad, Canguro, RediGO, SF.260TP, Ruschmeyer 90-420 AT, Turbine Islander and Defender 4000. In production. Allison Series II engine.
250-C20B/F/J/W (free-turbine turboshaft)	420 shp (313.3 kW) take-off, 370 shp (276 kW) normal cruise, sea level static	0.650 lb/shp/hr (395 g/kW/hr)	b) 7.1:1	a) 810° C MGT b) Jet	161 (73)	a) 38.8 (985) b) 19.4 (493) c) 23.2 (589)	A 109A, AS 355, Bell 47G re-engined, BO 105CBS, Fantrainer 400, Hiller UH-12E3T and UH-12E5T, JetRanger, Ka-226, Kania, LongRanger, MD 500/Defender, EC Super Five. In production. Allison Series II engines. Military designation T63-A-720 for Allison engine in OH-58C. 250-C20W for Enstrom 480 and Schweizer 330.
250-C20R (free-turbine turboshaft)	450 shp (335.6 kW) take-off, 380 shp (283 kW) normal cruise, sea level static	0.608 lb/shp/hr (370 g/kW/hr)	a) 810° C MGT b) 7.9:1	a) 810° C MGT b) Jet	173 (78.5)	a) 38.8 (985) b) 19.4 (493) c) 23.2 (589)	A 109C/CM, AB-206B, MD 500E/Defender, MD 520N, PZL-Świdnik SW-4, Ka-226/228, Inalet-4, Tridair Gemini ST conversions, TwinRanger. In production. Allison Series II engine.
250-C20R/9 (free-turbine turboshaft)	550 shp (410 kW) 30 seconds OEI, 465 shp (346.75 kW) take-off, 400 shp (298 kW) max continuous, sea level static		b) 8.4:1	b) Jet	195 (88.5)	a) 38.8 (985) b) 19.4 (493) c) 23.2 (589)	Has FADEC. In production. Allison Series II engine.
250-C22B (free-turbine turboshaft)	490 shp (365 kW) take-off, 430 shp (320 kW) continuous						
250-C28B/C (free-turbine turboshaft)	500 shp (373 kW) take-off, 494 shp (368.4 kW) normal cruise, sea level static	0.606 lb/shp/hr (369 g/kW/hr)	b) 8.4:1	b) Jet	233 (105.7)	a) 47.3 (1,201) b) 21.9 (557) c) 25.1 (638)	BO 105LSA-3 and Super Lifter, LongRanger. In production. Allison Series III engines.
250-C30G (free-turbine turboshaft)	650 shp (484.7 kW) take-off	0.592 lb/shp/hr (360 g/kW/hr)	b) 8.6:1	b) Jet	240 (109)	a) 41 (1,041) b) 21.9 (557) c) 25.1 (638)	Bell 230, MD 530, S-76.
250-C30M/P/R/S/X (free-turbine turboshaft)	650 shp (484.7 kW) take-off, 600 shp (447.4 kW) normal cruise, sea level static	0.592 lb/shp/hr (360 g/kW/hr)	b) 8.6:1	b) Jet	250 (113.4) C30M, 245 (111) C30P 251 (114) C30S,	a) 41 (1,041) b) 21.9 (557) c) 25.1 (638)	MD 530F, MD Defender, LongRanger III/IV. In production. C30R or X used on Bell 406/OH-58 (military designation T703-AD-700). C30S has lower cruise ratings (for example, 418 shp/312 kW at 75% power, compared to 450 shp/335.5 kW for C30M/P). Allison Series IV engines.
250-C30R/3 (free-turbine turboshaft)			a) 6,016 output shaft				OH-58D Kiowa Warrior. Certified June 1997 by FAA. FADEC. Derived from C47. Compressor (single-stage centrifugal design) is directly coupled to the 2-stage turbine and incorporates a new high-flow impeller and diffuser that provide increases in surge margin. Other improvements.

Designation (type of engine)	Power output (normally take-off rating for piston, turboprop and turboshaft, unless stated)	Specific fuel consumption (S F C)	a) Max RPM b) Pressure or Compression ratio	a) EGT (unless stated to be MGT, TET, TGT or TIT) b) Primary fuel type or Octane rating	Dry weight lb (kg)	a) Length ins (mm) b) Width ins (mm) c) Height ins (mm)	Current aircraft users, and comments
United States of America							
Allison Engine Company. (continued)							
250-C40/47 (as above)	808 shp (602.5 kW) for -C40, 813 shp (606.25 kW) for -C47 take-off and 5 minutes		b) 9.2:1	b) Jet	280 (127)		Bell 407 (C47B) and 430, and MD 600. In production. Growth derivatives of C20R/9, with FADEC. Allison Series IV+ engines.
AE 2100A (free-turbine turboprop)	4,152 shp (3,096 kW) at 1,100 propeller rpm	0.416 lb/shp/hr (253 g/kW/hr) take-off	a) 15,375 (1,100 propeller) b) 16.6:1	a) 852° C MGT b) Jet A/A-1	1,578 (715.8)	a) 115.68 (2,938) b) 30.9 (785) c) 52.52 (1,334)	Saab 2000. Entered service in 1994. 2-shaft, with 14-stage compressor driven by a 2-stage HP turbine, and the 2-stage IP turbine drives the compound planetary reduction gearbox. Annular combustor. FADEC controlled.
AE 2100C (free-turbine turboprop)	3,600 shp (2,685 kW)	0.430 lb/shp/hr (262 g/kW/hr)	a) 15,375 (1,100 propeller) b) 16.6:1	a) 831° C MGT b) ASTM D 1655 JET A/A-1	1,578 (715.8)	a) 115.68 (2,938) b) 32.69 (830) c) 47.41 (1,204)	N-250-100. Entered service in 1997.
AE 2100D3 (free-turbine turboprop)	4,591 shp (3,424 kW)	0.426 lb/shp/hr (259 g/kW/hr)	a) 14,268 (1,021 propeller) b) 16.6:1	a) 852° C MGT b) Jet A/A-1	1,655 (750.7)	a) 115.65 (2,938) b) 25.4 (645) c) 46.4 (1,1/9)	C-130J, L-100F, and C-27J at 4,200 shp (3,132 kW).
AE 3007A/A1/A3 (twin-shaft turbofan) Details for A, except where stated	7,580 lbf (33.72 kN) flat rated to 30° C (uninstalled), derated in A3 form for ERJ135	0.386 lb/lbf/hr (10.92 g/kNs) uninstalled	b) 23:1	a) 888° C MGT b) Jet A	1,608 (729)	a) 115.08 (2,923) b) 46.14 (1,172) c) 55.7 (1,415)	Embraer RJ135 and RJ145. Entered service 1996. High bypass (5:1), 2-spool, axial-flow engine. Single stage fully-ducted LP direct-drive fan, 14-stage axial-flow compressor with inlet guide vanes and 5 variable-geometry stator stages, full annular type combustion liner with 16 fuel nozzles and 2 high tension igniters, 2-stage HP turbine to drive compressor, 3-stage LP turbine to drive fan, and dual FADECs. A1 for ERJ145LR with increased thermodynamic thrust for improved 'hot and high' cruise, and derated A3 for ERJ135.
AE 3007C (twin-shaft turbofan)	6,495 lbf (28.89 kN)	0.378 lb/lbf/hr (10.735 g/kNs)	b) 23:1	a) 888° C MGT b) Jet A	1,588 (720.3)	a) 115.08 (2,923) b) 46.14 (1,172) c) 55.7 (1,415)	Citation X.
AE 3007H (single-stage direct-drive turbofan)	8,290 lbf (36.88 kN)		b) 23:1		1,581 (717)	a) 115.08 (2,923) b) 43.5 (1,105) diameter c) 55.7 (1,415)	Teledyne-Ryan Global Hawk UAV.
AE 301X (AE 3012) (twin-shaft turbofan)	12,000-14,000 lbf (53.38-62.28 kN)					b) 44 (1,118) fan	Active growth programme for 70-90 seat regional airliners and medium/large business jets. AE 3012 proposed for 728JET.
501-D13, A, D and H (turboprop)	3,750 eshp (2,796 ekW)	0.522 lb/eshp/hr (318 g/ekW/hr)	a) 13,820	a) 971° C b) Jet A, A1, JP-4, JP-5	1,756 (796.5)	a) 146.1 (3,711) b) 27.2 (691) c) 39 (991)	L-188 Electra (D13, D13A) and CV-580 (D13D, D13H).
501-D22 (civil) and T56-A-7/-10WA (military) (axial flow, single-shaft turboprop)	4,050 eshp (3,020 ekW) at 13,820 rpm, 2,390 eshp (1,782 ekW) at 84%	0.522 lb/eshp/hr (318 g/ekW/hr) take-off	a) 13,820 (1,020 propeller) b) 9.5:1	a) 971° C TIT b) Jet A/A-1, JP-4, JP-5, JP-8	1,835 (832)	a) 146.1 (3,711) b) 27.2 (691) c) 39 (991), 42 (1,067) for T56-A-10WA	C-130B/E/F (T56-A-7), L-100 Commercial Hercules (501-D22), P-3A Orion (T56-A-10WA). Series II engines.
501-D22A/C/G (civil) and T56-A-14/-15/ -16/-423/-425 (military) (axial flow, single-shaft turboprop)	4,910 eshp (3,661 ekW) at 13,820 rpm, 3,275 eshp (2,442 ekW) at 75%	0.501 lb/eshp/hr (305 g/ekW/hr) take-off	a) 13,820 (1,020 propeller, except 1,106 for E-2C and C-2A) b) 9.5:1	a) 1,077° C TIT b) MIL-T-5624 grades JP-4, JP-5, JP-8	1,820 (825.5)	a) 146.9 (3,731) b) 27.2 (691) c) 39 (991), 42 (1,067) for T56-A-14 and 501-D22C/G	Convair 580A (501-D22G), CV5800 (501-D22G), C-2 Greyhound (T56-A-425), E-2C Hawkeye (T56-A-425), C-130H/H-30 (T56-A-15), C-130F/T and EC-130Q (T56-A-16/-423), L-100-20/-30 (501-D22A), Tracor Super Guppy-201. In addition, T56-A-422s on E-2C/C-2As were designated T56-A-425s, and T56-A-426s on E-2A/Bs and C-2As are retired or modified to other configurations. T56-A-14LFE/ALFE for CP-140 Aurora are commercially improved versions of military T56-A-14 as used on P-3C. T56-A-15LFE is latest production and commercially improved version of military 4,591 shp (3,424 kW) T56-A-15LFE for C-130H/H-30. Series III engine.
T56-A-427 (military), Allison Model 501-M71D but no civil equivalent (axial flow, single-shaft turboprop)	5,250 eshp (3,915 ekW) at 14,239 rpm, 4,062 eshp (3,029 ekW) at 75%	0.473 lb/eshp/hr (288 g/ekW/hr) take-off	a) 14,239 (1,106 propeller) b) 14.1:1	a) 813° C max compensated turbine temperature b) JP-4, JP-5, JP-8	1,940 (880)	a) 146.8 (3,729) b) 27.2 (691) c) 39 (991)	E-2C and Hawkeye 2000. Series IV engine. Entered service 1997. T56/501 are single-shaft engines, each with 14-stage axial flow compressor driven by a 4-stage turbine unit. 2-stage reduction gearbox. Canannular combustor.
T406-AD-400 (twin-shaft turboshaft)	6,150 shp (4,586 kW) at 15,000 rpm, 3,600 shp (2,684 kW) at 12,750 rpm	0.405 lb/shp/hr (246 g/kW/hr)	a) 15,000 b) 16.6:1	a) 1,204° C MGT b) JP-5	970.5 (440.2)	a) 77.94 (1,980) b) 24.5 (622) c) 33.35 (847)	Bell-Boeing V-22 Osprey. Allison Model 501-M80C. To enter service in 1999. Has 14-stage compressor driven by a 2-stage gas generator turbine. Power shaft is driven by a 2-stage power turbine. Includes an infusion cooled annular combustor. FADEC controlled.
'World Engine' (core for new family of turboprops and turboshafts)	Initially 750-850 shp (559-634 kW) range, later taking in 300-1,100 shp (224-820 kW)						To replace 250 series. To incorporate ceramic materials.
Allison-AlliedSignal Partnership (LHTEC) – see also LHTEC							
CTP800-4T (turboprop) See Comments for CTP800-50	2,700 shp (2,013 kW) at 1,200 rpm	0.465 lb/shp/hr (283 g/kW/hr)	a) 22,540 (1,200 propeller) b) 14.0:1	a) 862° C MGT b) JP-4, JP-5, JP-8	1,203 (545.7) without propeller	a) 68.99 (1,752) b) 49.75 (1,263.5) c) 28.82 (732)	Ayres Loadmaster LM200. 3,200 shp (2,386 kW) CTP800-50 for Loadmaster LM250. Air flow 7.3 lb (3.3 kg) per second for CTP800-4T.

Designation (type of engine)	Power output (normally take-off rating for piston, turboprop and turboshaft, unless stated)	Specific fuel consumption (S F C)	a) Max RPM b) Pressure or Compression ratio	a) EGT (unless stated to be MGT, TET, TGT or TIT) b) Primary fuel type or Octane rating	Dry weight lb (kg)	a) Length ins (mm) b) Width ins (mm) c) Height ins (mm)	Current aircraft users, and comments
United States of America							
Allison-AlliedSignal Partnership (LHTEC). (continued)							
CTS800-2 (free-turbine turboshaft)	1,374 shp (1024.6 kW)	0.461 lb/shp/hr (280 g/kW/hr)	a) 23,000				For certification in 1999.
CTS800-4N (free-turbine turboshaft)	1,362 shp (1,015.6 kW) or 1,620 shp (1,208 kW) for Super Lynx	0.45 lb/shp/hr (274 g/kW/hr)	a) 23,000 b) 14.0:1	a) 603° C EGT, 868° C MGT b) JP-4, JP-5	310 (140.6)	a) 31.5 (800) b) 21.7 (551) c) 26.1 (663)	HAL ALH, Westland Super Lynx, HH-65 and Panther. Commercial version of the T800. CTS800/CTP800/T800 each have dual shafts, 2 centrifugal stage compressor, annular combustor, 2-stage HP and 2-stage LP turbines. Turboshaft models equipped with inlet particle separator module. Some versions have speed reduction gearbox. FADEC controlled.
CTS800-54 (free-turbine turboshaft)	1,656 shp (1,235 kW) take-off, 1,553 shp (1,158 kW) max continuous	0.45 lb/shp/hr (274 g/kW/hr)	a) 23,000 b) 14.0:1	a) 603° C EGT, 868° C MGT b) JP-4, JP-5	310 (140.6)	a) 31.5 (800) b) 21.7 (551) c) 26.1 (663)	Commercial version of the T800. HAL ALH, Westland Super Lynx and UH-1H.
T800-LHT-800 (free-turbine turboshaft)	1,334 shp (994.8 kW) at 23,000 rpm, 1,038 shp (774 kW) continuous	0.45 lb/shp/hr (274 g/kW/hr)	a) 23,000 b) 14.0:1	a) 603° C EGT, 868° C MGT b) JP-4. JP-5	310 (140.6)	a) 31.5 (800) b) 21.7 (551) c) 26.1 (663)	RAH-66, A 129 International. Entered service 1996.
T800-LHT-801 (free-turbine turboshaft)	1,563 shp (1,165 kW) at 23,000 rpm, 1,218 shp (908 kW) cruise at similar rpm	0.46 lb/shp/hr (280 g/kW/hr)	a) 23,000 b) 14.0:1	a) 618° C b) JP-4, JP-5	330 (149.7)	a) 32 (813) b) 22.3 (566) c) 26.8 (681)	RAH-66. To enter service in 2000.
Alturdyne. 8050 Armour Street, San Diego, CA 92111-3720 (Telephone: +1 619 565 2131, Facsimile: +1 619 279 4296, E-mail: alturdyne@worldnet.att.net)							
A650 series (rotary piston)	250 hp (186.4 kW) at 6,000 rpm	0.551 lb/hp/hr (335 g/kW/hr)	a) 2,700 propeller b) 10.0:1	b) Gasoline 100 Octane	188 (85.3)	a) 26.5 (673) b) 15 (381) c) 26 (660)	
AT62 (military T62) (turboshaft)	200 shp (149 kW) at 6,000 rpm		a) 6,000 b) 5.0:1	a) 649° C b) Aviation kerosene	100 (45.4)	a) 24 (610) b) 12 (305)	Suitable for helicopters, in addition to ground and industrial applications.
Amtec Corporation. 500 Wynn Drive, Suite 314, Huntsville, AL 35816-3429 (Telephone: +1 205 722 7200, Facsimile: +1 205 722 7212)							
Buddy Twin (1,250 cc, 4-stroke piston with direct drive)	40 hp (29.8 kW) normally aspirated		a) 2,900 b) 7.5:1		69 (31.3)	b) 33 (838) c) 10 (254)	First of 3 engine designs to be developed. Symmetrical crank, needing no counterbalance weights. Journal bearings are twice the diameter and half width of more conventional bearings, said to result in higher torsional stiffness pound-for-pound. Bore 3.7 ins (94 mm); stroke 3.54 ins (90 mm). Dry sump. Normal/supercharged induction.
CFE Company. 111 South 34th Street, PO Box 62332, Phoenix, AZ 85082-2332 (Telephone/Facsimile: – see AlliedSignal)							
CFE738-1-1B (high bypass, twin spool turbofan) CFE738-2 – see Comments	5,725 lbf (25.47 kN) to 30° C take-off, 1,464 lbf (6.514 kN) cruise	0.38 lb/lbf/hr (10.76 g/kNs) at 5,725 lbf SLS. 0.642 lb/lbf/hr (18.13 g/kNs) at 1,464 lbf	b) 35:1	b) Aviation kerosene	1,325 (601)	a) 99.24 (2,520) b) 43 (1,092) c) 47.3 (1,201)	Dassault Falcon 2000. CFE738-2 has 6,430 lbf (28.6 kN) rating.
Dyna-Cam Aero Engine Corporation. PO Box 1159, Torrance, CA 90505-0159 (Telephone: +1 310 791 4642)							
DC/375 (12-cyl piston)	200 hp (149 kW) at 2,000 rpm	0.43 lb/hp/hr (262 g/kW/hr) take-off, 0.40 lb/hp/hr (243 g/kW/hr)	a) 2,000 b) 8.0:1	a) 732° C b) 80 Octane Avgas or auto fuel	265 (120.2)	a) 40 (1,016) b) 15 (381)	Small 4-seat lightplanes, kit aircraft and helicopters.
General Electric Aircraft Engines. One Neumann Way, Cincinnati, OH 45215-6301 (Telephone: +1 513 243 2000, Facsimile: +1 513 243 9160, Web site: http://www.ge.com/geae/)							
GE90 (twin-shaft turbofan)	78,700 lbf (350.08 kN) for GE90-75B, 76,400 lbf (339.9 kN) for GE90-76B flat rated to 32.8° C, 77,000 lbf (342.52 kN) for GE90-77B, 84,700 lbf (376.77 kN) for GE90-85B flat rated to 30° C, and 92,100 lbf (409.67 kN) for GE90-90B, all at maximum take-off	0.52 lb/lbf/hr (14.73 g/kNs) for GE90-77B cruise (Bucket), 0.53 lb/lbf/hr (15.01 g/kNs) for GE90-90B cruise (Bucket)	b) >45:1		16,658 (7,556) for GE90-90B	a) 193 (4,902) flange to flange b) 123 (3,124) fan	Launched in 1990, with partners SNECMA, FiatAvio and IHI. Entered service 1995 on Boeing 777. GE90-75B for 777-200, or GE90-76B at high MTOW, GE90-85B for 777-200IGW, or GE90-90B at high MTOW. GE90-98B for 777-300. Growth engines planned, including 102,000 lbf (453.73 kN) version when required by market. Advanced GE90 compressor tested in 1998. GE90-77B flat rate temperature 32.8° C, or 30° C for GE90-90B. Bypass ratio 8.4/9. GE90-92B certified 1996, with service entry 1997, and GE90-100B for certification 1999.
CF6-80A and A1 (twin-shaft turbofan)	48,000 lbf (213.52 kN), 10,320 lbf (45.91 kN) cruise (as above)	0.344 lb/lbf/hr (9.74 g/kNs)	b) 28:1	a) 1,330° C	8,496 (3,854)	a) 157.4 (3,998) c) 105.3 (2,674.5)	A310 and 767.
CF6-80A2 and A3 (twin-shaft turbofan)	50,000 lbf (222.42 kN)		b) 29:1	a) 1,330° C	8,420-8,496 (3,819-3,854)	a) 157.4 (3,998) c) 105.3 (2,674.5)	A310 and 767.

Designation (type of engine)	Power output (normally take-off rating for piston, turboprop and turboshaft, unless stated)	Specific fuel consumption (S F C)	a) Max RPM b) Pressure or Compression ratio	a) EGT (unless stated to be MGT, TET, TGT or TIT) b) Primary fuel type or Octane rating	Dry weight lb (kg)	a) Length ins (mm) b) Width ins (mm) c) Height ins (mm)	Current aircraft users, and comments
United States of America							
General Electric Aircraft Engines. (continued)							
CF6-80C2A series (twin-shaft turbofan)	52,600-61,500 lbf (234.87-273.57 kN)	0.329 lb/lbf/hr (9.32 g/kNs) approx	b) 30.4:1		8,946 (4,058)	a) 160.9 (4,087) b) 93 (2,362) fan diameter	A300, A310 and A300-600ST. Air flow 1,781 lb (808 kg) per second. Bypass ratio 5.0 in-flight performance (installed) at 35,000 ft and Mach 0.8, ISA. SFC at cruise (Bucket) 0.574 lb/lbf/hr (16.26 g/kNs). SNECMA is 10% partner in total volume production.
CF6-80C2B series (twin-shaft turbofan)	51,570-59,750 lbf (229.4-265.79 kN)	0.329 lb/lbf/hr (9.32 g/kNs) approx	b) 30.4:1		9,135 (4,144) approx	a) 160.9 (4,087)	An-218, 747 and 767. F103-GE-102, equivalent to the CF6-80C2B1. New modified turbine available (of Rene 88), prior to new higher-thrust CF6 variant, available from May 2000.
CF6-80C2D1F (twin-shaft turbofan)	60,960 lbf (271.17 kN) at 30° C	0.34 lb/lbf/hr (9.63 g/kNs)	b) 30.4:1			a) 160.9 (4,087)	767 AWACS and MD-11.
CF6-80E1A2 (twin-shaft turbofan)	67,500 lbf (300.26 kN)	0.327 lb/lbf/hr (9.262 g/kNs)	b) 32.6:1		10,627 (4,820)	a) 164.3 (4,173) b) 962 (2,443) fan diameter	A330. Entered service January 1994. CF6-80E1 received 180 minute ETOPS approval February 1995. Air flow 1,913 lb (868 kg) per second. Bypass ratio 5.3. SFC at cruise (Bucket) 0.578 lb/lbf/hr (16.37 g/kNs). SNECMA is 20% partner in total volume production.
CF6-80E1A3 (twin-shaft turbofan)	72,000 lbf (320.28 kN)	0.34 lb/lbf/hr (9.63 g/kNs)	b) 34.6:1		10,627 (4,820)	a) 173.5 (4,407)	A330. A 70,000 lbf (311.38 kN) version has been defined for A330 growth requirements.
CF6-80E1A4 (twin-shaft turbofan)	68,100 lbf (302.93 kN)	0.338 lb/lbf/hr (9.57 g/kNs)	b) 33.7:1		10,726 (4,865)		
CF6-90 (turbofan)							Molniya-1000 in VH form.
CF34-1A (twin-shaft turbofan)	8,650 lbf (38.48 kN), flat rated to 15° C	0.36 lb/lbf/hr (10.20 g/kNs) take-off, 0.712 lb/lbf/hr (20.17 g/kNs) cruise	a) 7,300 fan, 17,710 core b) 14:1	a) 857° C TIT approx	1,625 (737)	a) 103 (2,616) b) 49 (1,245) maximum diameter	Challenger 601-1A and Inalet-60. Take-off Automatic Power Reserve of 9,140 lbf (40.66 kN). Certification August 1982. Out of production.
CF34-3A (twin-shaft turbofan)	8,729 lbf (38.83 kN) normal take-off, flat rated to 21.1° C	0.357 lb/lbf/hr (10.11 g/kNs) take-off, 0.704 lb/lbf/hr (19.94 g/kNs) cruise	a) 7,300 fan, 17,710 core b) 14:1	a) 871.1° C TIT	1,625 (737)	a) 103 (2,616) c) 49 (1,245) maximum diameter	Challenger 601-3A. Air flow 34 lb (15.4 kg) per second. 14-stage compressor. Take-off Automatic Power Reserve of 9,220 lbf (41.0 kN). Certification 1986. Out of production.
CF34-3A1 (twin-shaft turbofan)	8,729 lbf (38.83 kN) normal take-off, flat rated to 21.1° C	0.357 lb/lbf/hr (10.11 g/kNs) take-off, 0.704 lb/lbf/hr (19.94 g/kNs) cruise	a) 7,300 fan, 17,710 core b) 14:1	a) 899° C TIT approx	1,655 (750.7)	a) 103 (2,616) b) 49 (1,245) maximum diameter	Canadair Regional Jet. Challenger 601-3R and Canadair Special Edition. Dispatch reliability rate of 99.99%. Take-off Automatic Power Reserve of 9,220 lbf (41.0 kN). Certification July 1991.
CF34-3B (twin-shaft turbofan)	8,729 lbf (38.83 kN) normal take-off, flat rated to 30° C	0.346 lb/lbf/hr (9.8 g/kNs) take-off, 0.689 lb/lbf/hr (19.52 g/kNs) cruise	a) 7,300 fan, 17,710 core b) 14:1	a) 899° C TIT approx	1,670 (757.5)	a) 103 (2,616) b) 49 (1,245) maximum diameter	Challenger 604. Certification May 1995. Incorporating 3B1 improvements. Take-off Automatic Power Reserve of 9,220 lbf (41.0 kN).
CF34-3B1 (twin-shaft turbofan) See Comments for -3VB1	8,729 lbf (38.83 kN) normal take-off, flat rated to 30° C.	0.346 lb/lbf/hr (9.8 g/kNs) take-off, 0.689 lb/lbf/hr (19.52 g/kNs) cruise	a) 7,300 fan, 17,710 core b) 14:1	a) 899° C TIT approx		a) 103 (2,616) b) 49 (1,245) maximum diameter	Canadair Regional Jet. CF34-3VB1s for Tu-324. May 1995 certification. New stage 1 compressor rotor design. Increased hot-day ratings and top climb thrust over CF34-3A1 version. Take-off Automatic Power Reserve of 9,220 lbf (41.0 kN), flat rated to 22.8° C.
CF34-8C1 (twin-shaft turbofan)	12,670 lbf (56.36 kN) take-off, or 13,790 lbf (61.34 kN) with APR	0.70 lb/lbf/hr (19.83 g/kNs) cruise approx	b) 27:1 overall pressure ratio		2,160 (980)	a) 128.5 (3,264) b) 52 (1,321) maximum diameter, 46 (1,170) fan	Canadair Regional Jet series 700. Fan flow 440 lb (200 kg) per second for original CF34-8C. Bypass ratio 5. Thrust/weight ratio 6.2. FADEC.
CF34-8D/-8D1/-8XX (twin-shaft turbofan)	10,500 lbf (46.71 kN) for -8D, 13,300 lbf (59.16 kN) for -8D1, and 14,040 lbf (62.45 kN) for -8XX					a) 128.5 (3,264)? b) 52 (1,321) maximum diameter?	Possibly 528JET for -8D (derated), 728JET for -8D1, and 928JET for -8XX.
CJ610 (turbojet)	2,850-3,100 lbf (12.68-13.79 kN) take-off	0.97-0.99 lb/lbf/hr (27.48-28.04 g/kNs)			399-421 (181-191)	a) 45.4-51.1 (1,153-1,298) b) 17.7 (450) flange	Learjet 24/25 series, Vortex PhoenixJet-TJ, and 1123 Westwind.
CT7-2A/C (turboshaft)	1,625 shp (1,212 kW) take-off	0.473 lb/shp/hr (288 g/kW/hr)			442 (200.5)	a) 47 (1,194) b) 26 (660.4) max envelope	Bell 214ST (2A) and S-70C (2C).
CT7-2D/2D1 (turboshaft)	1,625 shp (1,212 kW) take-off	0.473 lb/shp/hr (288 g/kW/hr)			442-466 (200.5-211.4)	a) 47 (1,194) b) 26 (660.4) max envelope	Kamov Ka-62G and S-70C.
CT7-5A (turboprop)	1,735 shp (1,294 kW) take-off, 1,312 shp (978.4 kW) cruise	0.476 lb/shp/hr (290 g/kW/hr) take-off, 0.433 lb/shp/hr (263 g/kW/hr) maximum cruise at 15,000 ft	a) 1,384 propeller, 45,000 core b) 18:1	a) 927° C TIT approx	783 (355)	a) 96 (2,438) b) 29 (736.7) diameter	Saab 340. Certified August 1983. 5-stage axial, single-stage centrifugal compressor; straight-through annular combustor; 2-stage gas generator turbine with advanced blade and vane cooling design; 2-stage LP turbine; analog engine control for -5/-7 models of CT7. No longer in production.
CT7-6/6A/6D (turboshaft)	2,000 shp (1,491.4 kW) take-off and OEI for 2.5 minutes, 1,718 shp (1,281 kW) maximum continuous	0.457 lb/shp/hr (278 g/kW/hr) max continuous to 15° C	b) 18:1		485 (220)	a) 46 (1,168) b) 15.6 (396) nominal diameter	Commercial EH 101 and S-92 (CT7-6D). FADEC and provision for bolt-on particle separator (see T700).

Designation (type of engine)	Power output (normally take-off rating for piston, turboprop and turboshaft, unless stated)	Specific fuel consumption (S F C)	a) Max RPM b) Pressure or Compression ratio	a) EGT (unless stated to be MGT, TET, TGT or TIT) b) Primary fuel type or Octane rating	Dry weight lb (kg)	a) Length ins (mm) b) Width ins (mm) c) Height ins (mm)	Current aircraft users, and comments
United States of America							
General Electric Aircraft Engines. (continued)							
CT7-7A (turboprop)	1,700 shp (1,267.7 kW) take-off, 1,312 shp (978.4 kW) cruise	0.474 lb/shp/hr (288.3 g/kW/hr) take-off, 0.429 lb/shp/hr (261 g/kW/hr) maximum cruise at 15,000 ft	a) 1,384 propeller, 45,000 core b) 18:1	a) 927° C TIT approx	783 (355)	a) 96 (2,438) b) 29 (736.7) diameter	CN 235. Out of production.
CT7-8 and -11 (turboshaft and turboprop respectively) See T700/T6E	1,900 shp (1,417 kW) for CT7-8						S-92 for CT7-8. CN 235, L 610 and Saab 340 as possible users of the CT7-11 turboprop.
CT7-9 series (turboprop)	1,750 shp (1,305 kW) take-off, 1,411-1,499 shp (1,052-1,118 kW) cruise (see Comments)	0.455 lb/shp/hr (277 g/kW/hr) take-off for CT7-9B; 0.461 lb/shp/hr (280 g/kW/hr) for -9C and -9D. 0.413 lb/shp/hr (251 g/kW/hr) maximum cruise at 15,000 ft for CT7-9B and -9D; 0.411 lb/shp/hr (250 g/kW/hr) for -9C.	a) 1,384 propeller, 45,000 core b) 18:1	a) 949° C TIT approx	805 (365.1)	a) 96 (2,438) b) 29 (736.7) diameter	CT7-9B for Saab 340 and Sukhoi S-80 of 1,870 shp (1,394.5 kW) maximum. CT7-9C for CN 235. CT7-9D for L 610G; has an Automatic Power Reserve of 1,940 shp (1,446.7 kW), greater than for the 9B/9C. CT7-9B/-9C certified June 1988, CT7-9D June 1992. Digital Electronic Control for CT7-9 series.
F101-GE-102 (turbofan with afterburning)	30,780 lbf (136.92 kN)				4,460 (2,023)	a) 180.7 (4,590) b) 552 (1,402)	B-1B. 2.76 unscheduled engine-caused shop visits per 1,000 flight hours over a 12-month rolling average.
F103-GE-100/101 (twin-shaft turbofan)	52,500 lbf (233.54 kN) to 26° C	0.376 lb/lbf/hr (10.65 g/kNs)	b) 30.1:1	a) 1,330° C	8,490 (3,851)	a) 173 (4,394) c) 105.3 (2,674.5)	767 AWACS, E-4B and KC-10. Military version of the CF6-50E. 0.163 unscheduled engine-caused shop visits per 1,000 flight hours over a 12-month rolling average.
F103-GE-102 (twin-shaft turbofan)	56,700 lbf (252.22 kN)		b) 30.1:1	a) 1,330° C		a) 173 (4,394) c) 105.3 (2,674.5)	VC-25A. Equivalent to the CF6-80C2B1.
F110-GE-100 (twin-shaft turbofan)	17,530 lbf (78 kN) dry, 27,600 lbf (122.77 kN) with afterburning		b) 30.4:1		3,289 (1,492)	a) 181.9 (4,620) b) 46.5 (1,181)	F-16C/D and F-16N. Air flow 250 lb (113.4 kg) per second. 9-stage HP compressor, single-stage HP turbine, 2-stage LP turbine and annular combustor. -100A has Israeli modification to improve low-level contingency thrust, and -100B has FADEC plus other improvements.
F110-GE-129 (twin-shaft turbofan) see Comments for F110-GE-129EFE	17,000 lbf (75.62 kN) dry, 31,600 lbf (140.57 kN) with afterburning		b) 31:1 approx		3,940 (1,787)	a) 181.9 (4,620) b) 46.5 (1,181)	F-16C/D and F-2 (at 29,600 lbf, 131.67 kN with afterburning) and tested on F-15E. 1.99 unscheduled engine-caused shop visits per 1,000 flight hours over a 12-month rolling average. Air flow 270 lb (122.5 kg) per second. EFE (enhanced fighter engine) is an upgrade for F-15Es and F-16C/Ds. Initially 34,000 lbf (151.24 kN), with growth to 36,000 lbf (160.14 kN). EFE features include wide-chord bladed-disk fan, advanced radial afterburner with 25% less parts, reduced-drag nozzle, and optional axisymmetric thrust-vectoring nozzle.
F110-GE-400 (twin-shaft turbofan)	16,000 lbf (71.17 kN) dry, 27,000 lbf (120.1 kN) with afterburning				3,525 (1,599)	a) 181.9 (4,620) b) 46.5 (1,181)	F-14B/D. 1.11 unscheduled engine-caused shop visits per 1,000 flight hours over a 12-month rolling average. Air flow 250 lb (113.4 kg) per second.
F118-GE-100 (twin-shaft turbofan)	17,300-19,000 lbf (76.96-84.518 kN)		b) 27:1		3,200 (1,451.5) for GE-100	a) 100.5 (2,553) b) 46.5 (1,181)	B-2A for GE-100 and U-2S for GE-101.
F120 and F120-FX (turbofan)							F120-FX as alternate main engine for Boeing and Lockheed-Martin JSFs. GE teamed with Rolls-Royce and Allison. 2-D thrust vectoring. Reportedly has larger core than F119 main engine for JSF, with greater air flow. Bidirectional tapered roller bearings, counter-rotating turbine section with no vanes between single-stage high pressure and low pressure turbines, high-pressure compressor, lamilloy combustor and turbine vanes, advanced augmentor, and Rolls-Royce developed fan module.
F404-GE-400 (twin-shaft turbofan)	11,000 lbf (48.93 kN) dry, 16,000 lbf (71.17 kN) with afterburning				2,180 (988.83)	a) 158.8 (4,034) b) 34.8 (884)	F/A-18, X-29, X-31A EFM, Super Skyhawk (in non-afterburning 100D form) and Gripen in RM12 form. Air flow 142 lb (64.41 kg) per second. F404-GE-100D has 11,000 lbf (48.93 kN) rating and no afterburning.
F404-GE-402 (twin-shaft turbofan)	11,900 lbf (53 kN) dry, 17,700 lbf (78.73 kN) with afterburning		b) 26:1		2,282 (1,035)	a) 158.8 (4,034) b) 34.8 (884)	F/A-18. 0.8 unscheduled engine-caused shop visits per 1,000 flight hours for the whole of the F404 series of engines over a 12-month rolling average. F404 for Samsung KTX-2?
F404-GE-F1D2 (twin-shaft turbojet)	10,800 lbf (48.04 kN). No afterburning		b) 24:1		1,730 (785)	a) 89 (2,260) b) 34.8 (884)	F-117A. Turbojet variant of F404. Air flow 143 lb (64.86 kg) per second.

Designation (type of engine)	Power output (normally take-off rating for piston, turboprop and turboshaft, unless stated)	Specific fuel consumption (S F C)	a) Max RPM b) Pressure or Compression ratio	a) EGT (unless stated to be MGT, TET, TGT or TIT) b) Primary fuel type or Octane rating	Dry weight lb (kg)	a) Length ins (mm) b) Width ins (mm) c) Height ins (mm)	Current aircraft users, and comments
United States of America							
General Electric Aircraft Engines. (continued)							
F404-GE-F2J3 (twin-shaft turbofan)	18,100 lbf (80.51 kN) with afterburning					a) 158.8 (4,034) b) 34.8 (884)	Indian LCA technology demonstrators.
F414-GE-400 (twin-shaft turbofan)	15,000 lbf (66.72 kN) dry, 22,000 lbf (97.86 kN) with afterburning					a) 154 (3,912) b) 30.7 (780) fan	F/A-18E/F, and possibly CASA ATX in lower thrust variant. Delivery of first flight-test engines to US Navy in mid-1995, with the first flight late that year. US Navy awarded Limited Production Qualification status in April 1997. F414 fan provides 16% increased air flow over F404, and the core is based on the F412 turbine design. 9:1 thrust-to-weight ratio.
J79-GE-19 (single-shaft turbojet)	11,870 lbf (52.8 kN) dry, 17,900 lbf (79.62 kN) with afterburning	1.98 lb/lbf/hr (55.8 g/kNs) take-off		b) JP-4 and JP-5	3,847 (1,745)	a) 208.69 (5,300) b) 39.06 (992) compressor	Aeritalia F-104S.
J85-GE-5 (single-shaft turbojet)	2,680 lbf (11.92 kN) dry, 3,850 lbf (17.13 kN) with afterburning	1.03 lb/lbf/hr (29.17 g/kNs) dry, 2.2 lb/lbf/hr (62.32 g/kNs) with afterburning			584 (264.9)	a) 104.6 (2,657) Incl afterburner b) 21 (533)	T-38 Talon.
J85-GE-21 series (single-shaft turbojet)	3,500 lbf (15.57 kN) dry, 5,000 lbf (22.24 kN) with afterburning	1 lb/lbf/hr (28.325 g/kNs) dry, 2.13 lb/lbf/hr (60.33 g/kNs) with afterburning	b) 8.3:1	a) 977° C TIT	684 (310.25)	a) 112.5 (2,858) incl afterburner b) 21 (533)	F-5E/F and RF-5E.
T64-GE-7A (axial-flow turboshaft with direct drive)	3,936 shp (2,935 kW)	0.466 lb/shp/hr (283 g/kW/hr) maximum	12.5:1		720 (326.6)	a) 79 (2,007) b) 20 (508) max envelope c) 32.5 (825.5)	H-53. Being improved to T64-GE-100 standard.
T64-GE-10 (free-turbine turboprop)	2,970 shp (2,215 kW)	0.5 lb/shp/hr (304 g/kW/hr)	12.5:1		1,167 (529.3)	a) 113 (2,870) c) 46 (1,168)	P-2J and PS/US-1 as the T64-IHI-10 built by Ishikawajima.
T64-GE-100 (axial-flow turboshaft)	4,330 shp (3,229 kW) max at 28° C, military rated at 4,090 shp (3,050 kW)	0.487 lb/shp/hr (296 g/kW/hr) maximum	14:1		720 (326.6)	a) 79 (2,007) b) 20 (508) c) 32.5 (825.5)	CH-53C and MH-53J.
T64-GE-413 (axial-flow turboshaft)	3,925 shp (2,927 kW)	0.466 lb/shp/hr (283 g/kW/hr) maximum	14:1		720 (326.6)	a) 79 (2,007) b) 20 (508) c) 32.5 (825.5)	CH-53D.
T64-GE-415/416/A (axial-flow turboshaft)	4,380 shp (3,266 kW) max at 15° C, military rated at 4,110 shp (3,065 kW)	0.466 lb/shp/hr (283 g/kW/hr) maximum	14:1		720 (326.6)	a) 79 (2,007) b) 20 (508) max envelope c) 32.5 (825.5)	H-53E and RH-53D.
T64-GE-419 (axial-flow turboshaft)	4,750 shp (3,542 kW) max at 15° C, military rated at 4,560 shp (3,400 kW)	0.474 lb/shp/hr (288 g/kW/hr)	14:1		755 (342.5) self-contained lube cooler	a) 79 (2,007) b) 20 (508) max envelope c) 32.5 (825.5)	H-53E retrofit.
T64-P4D (free-turbine turboprop)	3,400 shp (2,535 kW) max take-off, flat rated to 45° C, 2,745 shp (2,047 kW) max continuous	0.484 lb/shp/hr (294 g/kW/hr) take-off	a) 1,260 propeller		1,188 (539)	a) 110.14 (2,798) b) 20.1 (510.5) c) 46 (1,168.5)	G222/C-27A. Power to weight ratio 2.86. Similar to the CT64, which see, and the T64 series of turboshafts.
T700-GE-401 (free-turbine turboshaft)	1,723 shp (1,285 kW) max contingency for OEI 2.5 minutes, 1,437 shp (1,071.5 kW) max continuous	0.471 lb/shp/hr (287 g/kW/hr) max continuous	a) 21,000 output b) 15:1		443 (201)	a) 46 (1,168) b) 25 (635), 15.6 (396) nominal diameter c) 23 (584)	AH-1W and Z, SH-2G and early SH-60B.
T700-GE-401C (free-turbine turboshaft)	1,940 shp (1,447 kW) max contingency for OEI 2.5 minutes, 1,662 shp (1,239 kW) max continuous	0.459 lb/shp/hr (279 g/kW/hr) max continuous	a) 21,000 output b) 15:1		458 (207.75)	a) 46 (1,168) b) 25 (635), 15.6 (396) nominal diameter c) 23 (584)	SH-60B, HH-60H and HH-60J Jayhawk.
T700-GE-700 (free-turbine turboshaft)	1,560 shp (1,163 kW), 1,324 shp (987.3 kW) max continuous	0.47 lb/shp/hr (286 g/kW/hr) max continuous	a) 21,000 output b) 15:1		437 (198.2)	a) 46 (1,168) b) 25 (635) c) 23 (584)	UH-60A.
T700-GE-701 (free-turbine turboshaft) For 701A, see Comments	1,723 shp (1,285 kW) max contingency, 1,570 shp (1,170.7 kW) max continuous	0.466 lb/shp/hr (283.5 g/kW/hr) max continuous	a) 21,000 output b) 15:1			a) 46 (1,168) b) 25 (635) c) 23 (584)	AH-64. T700-GE-701A is an alternative for export S-70A.
T700-GE-701C (free-turbine turboshaft)	1,940 shp (1,447 kW) max contingency for OEI 2.5 minutes, 1,662 shp (1,239 kW) max continuous	0.459 lb/shp/hr (279 g/kW/hr) max continuous	a) 21,000 output b) 15:1		456 (207)	a) 46 (1,168) b) 25 (635), 15.6 (396) nominal diameter c) 23 (584)	H-60/WS-70L and AH-64D.
T700/T6A (free-turbine turboshaft)	2,040 shp (1,521 kW) max take-off, 1,807 shp (1,348 kW) max continuous	0.45 lb/shp/hr (274 g/kW/hr)	b) 18:1		485 (220)	a) 47 (1,194) b) 25 (635)	Italian Navy EH 101. Developed by GE, Alfa Romeo Avio and FiatAvio of Italy.

Designation (type of engine)	Power output (normally take-off rating for piston, turboprop and turboshaft, unless stated)	Specific fuel consumption (S F C)	a) Max RPM b) Pressure or Compression ratio	a) EGT (unless stated to be MGT, TET, TGT or TIT) b) Primary fuel type or Octane rating	Dry weight lb (kg)	a) Length ins (mm) b) Width ins (mm) c) Height ins (mm)	Current aircraft users, and comments
United States of America							
General Electric Aircraft Engines. (continued)							
T700/T6E (free-turbine turboshaft)	2,500 shp (1,864 kW)	0.442 lb/shp/hr (269 g/kW/hr)	b) 19:1		531 (241)	a) 48.4 (1,230) b) 25 (635) fan	NH90. Developed by GE, Alfa Romeo Avio and FiatAvio of Italy, with participation of EGT (UK) and Hamilton Standard (USA). MTU of Germany participates in production. Flight tests from 1997. Has larger compressor, increasing engine air flow by about 10%. FADEC. Future derivatives could power potential growth versions of the Apache, EH 101, Black Hawk and S-92. Commercial version is the CT7-8 delivered to Sikorsky from 1998. A proposed commercial turboprop derivative is the CT7-11, with possible application in the CN 235, L 610 and Saab 340.
TF34-GE-100 (twin-shaft turbofan)	9,065 lbf (40.32 kN)		0.37 lb/lbf/hr (10.48 g/kNs)		b) 21:1		A-10A.
TF34-GE-400 (twin-shaft turbofan)	9,275 lbf (41.26 kN)		0.363 lb/lbf/hr (10.28 g/kNs)	b) 21:1	a) 1,225° C EGT b) JP-4 and JP-5	1,478 (670.4)	S-3B, EA-3A, US-3A.
TF39-GE-1C (turbofan)	43,000 lbf (191.28 kN)		b) 26:1	a) 871° C LP TIT	7,900 (3,583)	a) 271 (6,883) b) 100 (2,540)	C-5A and C-5B. Powered 104 aircraft by June 1994. 0.166 unscheduled engine-caused shop visits per 1,000 flight hours over a 12-month rolling average.
GE - P&W – The Engine Alliance (joint company of General Electric Aircraft Engines and Pratt & Whitney – Web site: www.enginealliance.com)							
GP7167 (turbofan)	67,000 lbf (298 kN)	TSFC -6% vs 747-400	b) 43:1		11,500 (5,216) bare engine weight	a) 169 (4,293) b) 99 (2,515) fan	To power 747-400Y. Common core with GP7200 series, with 9-stage HPC, SAC comb and 2-stage HPT. 3-stage LPC and 4-stage LPT. Bypass ratio 7. Fan has lightweight titanium hollow shroudless wide-chord blades. High efficiency, high-pressure ratio core, 3-D compressor and turbine aerodynamics. Close coupled, high efficiency LP turbine dynamics. Low emissions dual annular combustor. FADEC. SVR goal of less than 0.08.
GP7267/GP7275 (turbofans)	67,000 lbf (298 kN) for GP7267, and 75,000 lbf (333.62 kN) for GP7275	TSFC -9% vs 747-400	b) 46:1		13,300 (6,033)	a) 179 (4,547) b) 110 (2,794) fan	For Airbus A3XX. Start of detail design in 1999, allowing first engine test in 2001, FAR 33 certification in 2002, first flight in 2003 and service entry 2004. Bypass ratio 8. 4-stage LPC and 5-stage LPT.
HCI Aviation Inc. 3461 Dissen Road, New Haven, MO 63068 (Telephone: +1 573 237 3605, Facsimile: +1 573 237 3605, E-mail: paige@is.usmo.com, Web site: http://is.usmo.com/~hci/)							
HCI R180 (5-cyl, 4-stroke, radial piston with direct drive)	75 hp (56 kW)	13.25 litres per hour approx at 75% power	a) 2,150 b) 7.5:1	a) 327° C approx preliminary b) 100 LL and 87 RON	122 (55.3)		Initially experimental aircraft. Prototype engine on Fly Baby. Supercharged.
In-Tech International Inc. 7500 West Park Drive, Spokane, WA 99204-5726							
TDIL 210 (3-cyl, 2-stroke, liquid-cooled, diesel, inline piston)	650 hp (484.7 kW) at 4,800 rpm, 450 hp (335.6 kW) cruise at 3,800 rpm	0.36 lb/hp/hr (219 g/kW/hr)	a) 2,060 propeller b) 15.3:1	a) 816° C b) Jet A, JP-4, diesel	580 (263.1)	a) 50.5 (1,283) b) 18 (457) c) 25.5 (648)	Formerly known as Merlyn.
LHTEC (Light Helicopter Turbine Engine Company). Paragon Building, 12400 Olive Blvd, St Louis, MO 63141 (Telephone: +1 317 230 6515, Facsimile: +1 317 230 3410 or 3562, E-mail: fred.w.dickens@Allison.com) see Allison-AlliedSignal partnership							
Light Power Engine Corporation. PO Drawer 3350, Morgantown, WV 26503 (Telephone: +1 304 291 3843, Facsimile: +1 304 292 1902)							
ZM 200 Series III-200 (inverted, fuel injected, inline piston, with direct drive)	150 hp (112 kW) at 2,700 rpm				229 (103.9)	a) 39 (991) b) 10 (254) c) 23 (584)	Turbocharged version is the 175 hp (130.5 kW) at 2,700 rpm ZM 200 Series TIII-200, weighing 246 lb (111.6 kg). TBO for ZM engines 2,200 hours.
ZM 400 Series IVG-400 (fuel injected, V piston, with gear reduction drive)	420 hp (313.2 kW) at 4,300 rpm				430 (195)	a) 42 (1,067) b) 21 (533) c) 22 (559)	Inverted, direct drive versions of same dimensions but 400 lb (181.4 kg) weight are the 230 hp (171.5 kW) at 2,700 rpm ZM 400 Series IIV-400A and ZM 400 Series IIV-400B with an output of 250 hp (186.4 kW) at 2,700 rpm.
ZM 500 Series IIV-500 (inverted V8, liquid-cooled piston, with direct drive)	320 hp (238.6 kW) at 2,700 rpm, 240 hp (179 kW) cruise at 2,400 rpm	0.39 lb/hp/hr (237 g/kW/hr)	a) 2,750 b) 10.2:1	b) 100 LL	480 (217.7)	a) 43.8 (1,113) b) 24 (610) c) 24 (610)	Turbocharged version is the TIIV-500, weighing 568 lb (257.6 kg) dry, with height of 27 ins (686 mm) and offering 320 hp (238.6 kW) at 2,700 rpm.
ZM 500 Series IVG-500A (fuel injected, V piston, with gear reduction drive)	450 hp (335.6 kW) at 4,300 rpm				550 (249.5)	a) 43.8 (1,113) b) 23 (584) c) 24 (610)	Similar IVG-500B offers 500 hp (373 kW) at 4,500 rpm.
ZM 500 Series TIVG-500 (turbocharged, fuel injected, V piston, with gear reduction drive)	500 hp (373 kW) at 4,300 rpm				550 (249.5)	a) 53 (1,346) b) 23 (584) c) 24 (610)	
ZM 500 Series IIV-560 (inverted, fuel injected, V piston, with direct drive)	350 hp (261 kW) at 2,700 rpm				513 (232.7)	a) 43.8 (1,113) b) 24 (610) c) 24 (610)	

Designation (type of engine)	Power output (normally take-off rating for piston, turboprop and turboshaft, unless stated)	Specific fuel consumption (S F C)	a) Max RPM b) Pressure or Compression ratio	a) EGT (unless stated to be MGT, TET, TGT or TIT) b) Primary fuel type or Octane rating	Dry weight lb (kg)	a) Length ins (mm) b) Width ins (mm) c) Height ins (mm)	Current aircraft users, and comments
United States of America							
Light Power Engine Corporation. (continued)							
ZM 500 Series IVG-560 (fuel injected, V piston, with gear reduction drive)	560 hp (417.6 kW) at 4,500 rpm				560 (254)	a) 43.8 (1,113) b) 23 (584) c) 24 (610)	
ZM 600 Series IVG-600 (fuel injected, V piston, with gear reduction drive)	600 hp (447.4 kW) at 4,500 rpm				562 (255)	a) 43.8 (1,113) b) 23 (584) c) 24 (610)	The turbocharged variant is the TIVG-600, of similar power output, 580 lb (263 kg) weight, and 53 ins (1,346 mm) length.
ZM 600 Series TIIV-600 (turbocharged, inverted, fuel injected, liquid-cooled, V8 piston, with direct drive)	380 hp (283.4 kW) at 2,700 rpm, 285 hp (212.5 kW) cruise at 2,400 rpm		a) 2,750 b) 10.2:1	b) 100 LL	578 (262.2)	a) 43.8 (1,113) b) 25 (635) c) 27 (686)	Express. The non-turbocharged version is the IIV-600 of 380 hp (283.4 kW) at 2,700 rpm, with dry weight of 517 lb (234.5 kg) and height of 24 ins (610 mm).
ZM 600 Series TIIV-650 (turbocharged, inverted, fuel injected, liquid-cooled, V8 piston, with direct drive)	500 hp (373 kW) at 2,700 rpm, 375 hp (279.6 kW) cruise at 2,400 rpm	0.39 lb/hp/hr (237 g/kW/hr)	a) 2,750 rated hp, 3,200 max b) 10.2:1	b) 100 LL	596 (270.3)	a) 43.8 (1,113) b) 25 (635) c) 27 (686)	Lancair IV, Cirrus, Glasair III. Non-turbocharged version is the IIV-650 of 450 hp (335.6 kW) at 2,700 rpm, with dry weight of 531 lb (240.9 kg).
Moller International. 1222 Research Park Drive, Davis, CA 95616 (Telephone: +1 916 756 5086, Facsimile: +1 916 767 5179)							
MR 530 PA and PL (single rotor, piston)	75 hp (55.9 kW)	0.6 lb/hp/hr (365 g/kW/hr)	a) 7,500 b) 8.9:1		78 (35.4) for 530 PA and 52 (23.6) for 530 PL	a) 11 (279) b) 11 (279) for 530 PA and 10 (254) for 530 PL c) 10 (254) for 530 PA and 9 (229) for 530 PL	530 cc. PA is air cooled, PL is liquid cooled.
MR 1060 PL (twin rotor, liquid-cooled, piston)	160 hp (119 kW)	0.6 lb/hp/hr (365 g/kW/hr)	a) 7,500 b) 8.9:1		74 (33.6)	a) 15 (381) b) 10 (254) c) 9 (229)	Moller Skycar. Produces more than 1.5 hp per pound weight. Ducted fan VTOL application. Round shape and small size allow it to be placed in the centre of the duct behind the fan hub where it directly drives the fan without a gearbox.
Mosler Motors Inc. 140 Ashwood Road, Hendersonville, NC 28739							
Range of piston engines (4-stroke and air-cooled)	40-82 hp (29.8-61 kW)						Users include Kitfox with a 65 hp (48.5 kW) Mosler 65X.
Nelson engines – see Sport Plane Products Inc							
NSI Propulsion Systems LLC. 19132 59th Drive NE, Arlington, WA 98223 (Telephone: +1 360 435 1055)							
NSI/Suber EA81-98-TBI (1,800 cc, 4-cyl, 4-stroke, water/ ethylene glycol-cooled piston, based on Subaru EA81 auto engine)	98 hp (73 kW) at 5,200 rpm continuous	0.49 lb/hp/hr (298 g/kW/hr) at 5,043 rpm continuous		b) all auto and aviation grades	212 (96.2)*	a) 23 (584) mount to prop flange b) 27 (686) c) 15.5 (394) minus exhaust	Approved for Kitfox Models III/IV, Speedster, Vixen, Murphy Rebel, Glastar, Cessna 120/140/150/152, and Zodiac 601/90. Components available for DIY conversion of Subaru engines. Not certified. *Includes exhaust muffler and tailpipes, mounts, wiring harness and more.
NSI/Suber EA81-118-TBI (as above)	118 hp (88 kW) at 5,800 rpm	0.51 lb/hp/hr (310 g/kW/hr) continuous at 5,800 rpm		b) auto unleaded premium or aviation 90 or 100 LL	214 (97.1)*	a) 23 (584) mount to prop flange b) 27 (686) c) 15.5 (394) minus exhaust	Aircraft and other details as above*. Not certified.
NSI/Suber Turbo EA81-120-EFI (as above, based on Turbo Subaru EA81)	120 hp (89.5 kW) at 4,800 rpm continuous	0.44 lb/hp/hr (268 g/kW/hr) cruise at 3,800 rpm, estimated		b) all auto and aviation grades	222 (100.7)*	a) 23 (584) b) 27 (686) c) 20 (508)	Aircraft as above. Not certified. *Includes stainless steel exhaust pipe, mounts, wiring harness and more.
NSI/Suber EJ22-160-EFI (2,200 cc, 4-cyl, 4-stroke, water/ ethylene glycol-cooled piston, based on Subaru EJ22)	160 hp (119.3 kW) at 5,500 rpm	0.4 lb/hp/hr (243 g/kW/hr) cruise at 4,200 rpm estimated		b) all auto and aviation grades	272 (123.4)*	a) 25 (635) b) 29 (737) c) 16.5 (419) minus muffler	Aircraft as above. Not certified. *Includes exhaust muffler and tailpipes, mounts, wiring harness and more. Production engines shipped from February 1995.
NSI/Suber Turbo EJ22-200-EFI (as above, with turbocharger)	200 hp (149 kW) at 5,200 rpm and 6,000 ft above sea level	0.4 lb/hp/hr (243 g/kW/hr) cruise at 3,800 rpm estimated		b) all auto and aviation grades	284 (128.8)*	a) 25 (635) b) 29 (737) c) 17.75 (451)	Aircraft as above. Not certified. *Includes stainless steel exhaust pipe, mounts, wiring harness and more. Production engines shipped from April 1995.
Pop's Props. RR1, Box 98, Cooksville, IL 61730 (Telephone: +1 309 725 3237, Facsimile: +1 309 725 3239)							
Volkswagen conversion (2-cyl opposed)	35 hp (26 kW)	5.7 litres per hour	a) 3,450 b) 7.1:1	b) 92 Octane	86 (39)	a) 16 (406) b) 30 (762) c) 14 (356)	For light and ultralight aircraft. Plans built only (plans US$19.95).

Designation (type of engine)	Power output (normally take-off rating for piston, turboprop and turboshaft, unless stated)	Specific fuel consumption (S F C)	a) Max RPM b) Pressure or Compression ratio	a) EGT (unless stated to be MGT, TET, TGT or TIT) b) Primary fuel type or Octane rating	Dry weight lb (kg)	a) Length ins (mm) b) Width ins (mm) c) Height ins (mm)	Current aircraft users, and comments
United States of America							
Pop's Props. (continued)							
Kawasaki 340 conversion (water-cooled, oil injected)	35 hp (26 kW)	7.6 litres per hour	a) 6,200 b) 7.0:1	b) 88 Octane	80 (36.3)	a) 15 (381) b) 9 (229) c) 12.5 (318)	For ultralight/microlight aircraft. Complete packages under US$2,000, including reduction unit (belt or gearbox).
Pratt & Whitney. 400 Main Street, East Hartford, CT 06108 (Telephone: +1 860 565 4321, Facsimile: +1 860 565 8896, Web site: www.pweh.com)							
F100-PW-100 (twin-shaft turbofan)	14,670 lbf (65.26 kN) dry, 23,450 lbf (104.31 kN) with afterburning		b) 24.8:1	a) 1,399° C MGT	3,055 (1,386)	a) 191.2 (4,855) without spinner b) 46.5 (1,181)	F-15. Original P&W designation JTF22.
F100-PW-200 (twin-shaft turbofan)	14,590 lbf (64.9 kN) dry, 23,770 lbf (105.74 kN) with afterburning	2.17 lb/lbf/hr (61.47 g/kNs) max power	b) 24.8:1	a) 1,399° C MGT b) JP-4, JP-5, JP-8, Jet A	3,108 (1,410)	a) 191.2 (4,855) without spinner b) 46.5 (1,181) c) 46.5 (1,181)	F-16.
F100-PW-220 (twin-shaft turbofan)	14,590 lbf (64.9 kN) dry, 23,830 lbf (106.0 kN) with afterburning		b) 24.8:1	a) 1,399° C MGT b) JP-4, JP-5, JP-8, Jet A	3,179 (1,442)	a) 191.2 (4,855) without spinner b) 46.5 (1,181) c) 46.5 (1,181)	F-15 and F-16.
F100-PW-220E (twin-shaft turbofan)	14,590 lbf (64.9 kN) dry, 23,770 lbf (105.74 kN) with afterburning		b) 24.8:1	b) JP-4, JP-5, JP-8, Jet A	3,151 (1,429)	a) 191.2 (4,855) without spinner b) 46.5 (1,181) c) 46.5 (1,181)	First of two improvement programmes by retrofit for existing USAF F100-PW-100 and 200 engines to bring them to F100-PW-220 standard.
F100-PW-220P (twin-shaft turbofan)	16,700 lbf (74.287 kN) dry, 27,000 lbf (120.1 kN) with afterburning			b) JP-4, JP-5, JP-8, Jet A	3,365 (1,526.33)	a) 191.2 (4,855) without spinner b) 46.5 (1,181) c) 46.5 (1,181)	Further upgrade version introducing F100-PW-229 features.
F100-PW-229 (twin-shaft turbofan)	17,800 lbf (79.18 kN) dry, 29,000 lbf (129 kN) with afterburning	2.05 lb/lbf/hr (58.07 g/kNs)	b) 32:1	b) JP-4, JP-5, JP-8, Jet A	3,650 (1,656)	a) 191.2 (4,855) without spinner b) 46.5 (1,181) c) 46.5 (1,181)	F-15 and F-16.
F100-PW-229A (twin-shaft turbofan)	37,150 lbf (165.25 kN) with afterburning					Similar overall dimensions to -129	F-15E and F-16C/D in 21st century. Advanced version of F100-PW-229, featuring 25-mm larger fan and new inlet. Fan reportedly increases bypass ratio by 10%. Maximum air flow 275 lb (125 kg) per second.
F117-PW-100 (twin-spool turbofan)	41,700 lbf (185.5 kN) take-off, flat rated to 30.6° C, 35,330 lbf (157.16 kN) max continuous, 8,250 lbf (36.7 kN) cruise at ISA+10° C	0.5998 lb/lbf/hr (16.99 g/kNs)	b) 28:1	a) 1,425° C combustor exit temperature	7,100 (3,221)	a) 141.4 (3,592) flange to flange, 146.8 (3,729) spinner tip to flange b) 84.8 (2,154) c) 84.8 (2,154)	C-5 and C-17. Military variant of the PW2040. Bypass ratio 5.9.
New F117 (provisionally PW2643 commercial designation)	43,000 lbf (191.28 kN)						
F119-PW-100 (twin-spool, counter-rotating, low-bypass ratio, axial-flow turbofan)	Dry rating classified, 35,000 lbf (155.69 kN) class with afterburning	classified	classified	a) classified b) JP-8	classified	a) classified b) classified c) classified	F-22, and also Boeing JSF in SE614 form (see SE614) and Lockheed Martin JSF in SE611 form (see SE611). Fitted with 2-D convergent/divergent exhaust nozzles (±20°) with independent throat and exit area actuation and pitch-axis thrust vectoring. Offers high supersonic speed without afterburning.
J52-P-408/408A (twin-spool turbojet)	11,200 lbf (49.82 kN)				2,318 (1,051)	a) 118.9 (3,020) b) 32.06 (814)	EA-6B Prowler and A-4 Skyhawk respectively.
J52-P-409 (twin-spool turbojet)	12,000 lbf (53.38 kN)						EA-6B Prowler re-engined under the ADVCAP improvement programme. This engine is still offered.
JT3D-3/3B (turbofan variant of J57)	18,000 lbf (80.07 kN)	0.535 lb/lbf/hr (15.15 g/kNs)	b) 13:1		4,340 (1,969)	a) 137 (3,479) b) 53.14 (1,350)	DC-8-50, Super 61/62, and E-8C.
JT8D-209 (twin-spool turbofan)	18,500 lbf (82.29 kN) to 25° C take-off, 4,945 lbf (22 kN) cruise at 35,000 ft and Mach 0.8	0.501 lb/lbf/hr (14.19 g/kNs)	b) 17.4:1		4,435 lb (2,012)	a) 154.2 (3,917) b) 49.2 (1,250)	DC-9 Super 81 and MD-81/-82. Derived from the previous JT8D-9 but with advanced low-pressure compressor features. OEI rating 19,250 lbf (85.63 kN).
JT8D-217/217A (twin-spool turbofan)	20,000 lbf (88.97 kN) normal take-off, rated up to 25° C for -217 and 29° C for -217A, 18,000 lbf (80 kN) max continuous	0.51 lb/lbf/hr (14.45 g/kNs) take-off	b) 18.6:1		4,470 (2,028)	a) 154.2 (3,917) b) 49.2 (1,250)	DC-9 Super 82, MD-82 and MD-87. JT8D-217A take-off power up to 29° C or 5,000 ft. OEI rating of 20,850 lbf (92.75 kN) to 28.9° C. Cruise rating of 5,240 lbf (23.31 kN) at 35,000 ft and Mach 0.8.

Designation (type of engine)	Power output (normally take-off rating for piston, turboprop and turboshaft, unless stated)	Specific fuel consumption (S F C)	a) Max RPM b) Pressure or Compression ratio	a) EGT (unless stated to be MGT, TET, TGT or TIT) b) Primary fuel type or Octane rating	Dry weight lb (kg)	a) Length ins (mm) b) Width ins (mm) c) Height ins (mm)	Current aircraft users, and comments
United States of America							
Pratt & Whitney. (continued)							
JT8D-217C (twin-spool turbofan)	20,000 lbf (88.97 kN) take-off, 5,240 lbf (23.31 kN) cruise at 35,000 ft and Mach 0.8	0.5 lb/lbf/hr (14.16 g/kNs)	b) 18.6:1		4,515 (2,048)	a) 154.2 (3,917) b) 49.2 (1,250) fan tip	MD-82, MD-83, MD-87 and MD-88. OEI rating of 20,850 lbf (92.75 kN).
JT8D-219 (twin-spool turbofan)	21,000 lbf (93.41 kN)	0.519 lb/lbf/hr (14.7 g/kNs)	b) 19.2:1		4,515 (2,048)	a) 154.2 (3,917) b) 49.2 (1,250) fan tip	MD-82, MD-83, MD-87 and MD-88. OEI rating 21,700 lbf (96.53 kN). 2% reduction in fuel burn than JT8D-217A. Used in the **Super 27** re-engining programme for the B727-200 by P&W and Rohr.
JT9D-7R4 series (twin-shaft turbofan)	48,000-56,000 lbf (213.52-249.1 kN) take-off without water injection, 11,250-12,250 lbf (50.04-54.49 kN) cruise at above conditions	0.34-0.364 lb/lbf/hr (9.63-10.31 g/kNs)	b) 23.4-26.7	a) up to 1,300° C TIT	8,905-9,140 (4,039-4,146)	a) 132.7 (3,370) b) 97 (2,464)	JT9D-7R4D/D1 on 767-200 and A310-200; E/E1 on 767, A310-200/300; E3/E4 on 767 and A310-200/300; G2 on 747-200/300; H1 on A300-600.
JT9D-70A series (twin-shaft turbofan) For JT9D-20 and -59A – see Comments	53,000 lbf (235.76 kN) take-off to 30° C without water injection, 11,950 lbf (53.16 kN) cruise at above conditions	0.375 lb/lbf/hr (10.62 g/kNs)	b) 24.5:1	a) up to 1,370° C	9,155 (4,152)	a) 132.2 (3,357) b) 97 (2,464)	B747. Also JT9D-20 of 46,300 lbf (206 kN) on DC-10-40, and JT9D-59A of 53,000 lbf (235.76 kN) on DC-10-40 and A300.
PW2037 (twin-shaft turbofan)	38,250 lbf (170.1 kN) take-off, flat-rated to 30.6° C, 35,330 lbf (157.16 kN) max continuous, 8,250 lbf (36.7 kN) cruise at ISA +10° C	0.342 lb/lbf/hr (9.69 g/kNs) take off (sea level static TSFC)	b) 27:1	a) 1,405° C combustor exit temperature	7,300 (3,311)	a) 141.4 (3,592) flange to flange, 146.8 (3,729) spinner tip to flange b) 78.5 (1,994) fan tip, 84.8 (2,154) fan inlet case flange	B757-200. Introduced FADEC technology to commercial aviation. New performance improvement configuration was the first to use second-generation single crystal turbine blades. Approved for 180 minutes ETOPS. Original certification 1983, allowing service entry 1984.
PW2040 (twin-shaft turbofan) PW2043 – see Comments	41,700 lbf (185.5 kN) take-off, flat rated to 30.6° C, 35,330 lbf (157.16 kN) max continuous, 8,250 lbf (36.7 kN) cruise at ISA +10° C	0.352 lb/lbf/hr (9.97 g/kNs) (sea level static TSFC)	b) 28:1	a) 1,425° C combustor exit temperature	7,300 (3,311)	a) 141.4 (3,592) flange to flange, 146.8 (3,729) spinner tip to flange b) 78.5 (1,994) fan tip, 84.8 (2,154) fan inlet case flange	B757-200/200F. Certification 1987, with service entry the same year. 43,850 lbf (195.06 kN) PW2043s as option for 757-300.
PW2337 (twin-shaft turbofan)	38,250 lbf (170.1 kN) take-off	0.565 lb/lbf/hr (15.95 g/kNs)	b) 27.6-31.8	a) 1,405° C combustor exit temperature	7,300 (3,311)	a) 141.4 (3,592) flange to flange b) 78.5 (1,994) fan tip	Il-96M, Il-96-300D and possibly Il-96-550. Length 146.8 ins (3,729 mm) spinner tip to flange, and width 84.8 ins (2,154 mm) fan inlet case flange.
PW2643 (twin-shaft turbofan)	43,000 lbf (191.28 kN)						New military F117 engine.
PW4050 (twin-spool turbofan)	50,000 lbf (222.42 kN) take-off, 48,120 lbf (214.05 kN) max continuous	0.348 lb/lbf/hr (9.86 g/kNs) take-off (sea level static TSFC)	b) 26.3:1		9,213 (4,179)	a) 132.7 (3,371) b) 96.98 (2,463)	767-200/200ER and 300. PW4000 series is 180 minutes ETOPS approved with FADEC for 767, A300 and A310. Basic dispatch reliability for PW4000 series is 99.88%.
PW4052 (twin-spool turbofan)	52,200 lbf (232.2 kN) to 33.3° C, 49,820 lbf (221.61 kN) max continuous	0.351 lb/lbf/hr (9.94 g/kNs) take-off (sea level static TSFC)	b) 27.5:1		9,213 (4,179)	a) 132.7 (3,371) b) 96.98 (2,463), 94 (2,388) fan	B767-200/200ER/300. Bypass ratio 5. Fan pressure ratio 1.65.
PW4056 (twin-spool turbofan)	56,750 lbf (252.4 kN) take-off, flat rated to 33.3° C in the B747, 56,000 lbf (249.1 kN) take-off in the B767	0.359 lb/lbf/hr (10.17 g/kNs) take-off (sea level static TSFC)	b) 29.7:1		9,213 (4,179)	a) 132.7 (3,371) b) 96.98 (2,463)	B747-400, B767-200ER/300/300ER/400ER. Bypass ratio 4.9. Fan pressure ratio 1.71.
PW4060 (twin-spool turbofan)	60,000 lbf (266.9 kN) take-off, flat rated to 33.3° C, 50,250 lbf (223.53 kN) max continuous	0.365 lb/lbf/hr (10.34 g/kNs) take-off (sea level static TSFC)	b) 31.2:1		9,213 (4,179)	a) 132.7 (3,371) b) 96.98 (2,463), 94 (2,388) fan	B747-400 and B767-300ER/400ER. Bypass ratio 4.8. Fan pressure ratio 1.74.
PW4062 (twin-spool turbofan)	62,000 lbf (275.8 kN) take-off, flat rated to 30° C	0.365 lb/lbf/hr (10.34 g/kNs)	b) 32.3:1		9,213 (4,179)	a) 132.7 (3,371) flange to flange b) 96.98 (2,463)	B747-400 and B767-200ER/300ER/400ER. Bypass ratio 4.8. Fan pressure ratio 1.76.
PW4074 (twin-spool turbofan)	74,000 lbf (329.17 kN), flat rated to 30° C		b) 34.2:1			a) 191.7 (4,869) b) 112 (2,845) fan	B777-200.

Designation (type of engine)	Power output (normally take-off rating for piston, turboprop and turboshaft, unless stated)	Specific fuel consumption (S F C)	a) Max RPM b) Pressure or Compression ratio	a) EGT (unless stated to be MGT, TET, TGT or TIT) b) Primary fuel type or Octane rating	Dry weight lb (kg)	a) Length ins (mm) b) Width ins (mm) c) Height ins (mm)	Current aircraft users, and comments
United States of America							
Pratt & Whitney. (continued)							
PW4077 (twin-spool turbofan)	77,000 lbf (342.52 kN)		b) 34.2:1			a) 191.7 (4,869) b) 112 (2,845) fan	B777-200 at high MTOW.
PW4084 (twin-spool turbofan)	84,600 lbf (376.33 kN), flat rated to 30° C	0.329 lb/lbf/hr (9.32 g/kNs)	b) 34.4:1		14,920 (6,768)	a) 191.6 (4,867) b) 118.5 (3,010)	B777-200IGW. Certified April 1994 and launch engine for B777, entering service in June 1995, then 180-minute ETOPS qualified. Bypass ratio 6.4. Fan pressure ratio 1.70.
PW4090 (twin-spool turbofan)	91,790 lbf (408.31 kN) take-off, flat rated to 30° C		b) 38.6:1		15,585 (7,069)	a) 191.6 (4,867) b) 118.5 (3,010)	B777-200IGW at high MTOW from 1997. Certified 28 June 1996 and first flown August 1996. Bypass ratio 6.3. Fan pressure ratio 1.74.
PW4098 (twin-spool turbofan)	98,000 lbf (435.93 kN) take-off, flat rated to 30° C		b) 42.8:1		16,500 (7,484)	a) 194.7 (4,945) b) 119.5 (3,035)	First flown on 777-300 on 4 February 1998. Bypass ratio 5.8. Fan pressure ratio 1.8.
PW4152 (twin-spool turbofan)	52,000 lbf (231.3 kN) take-off, flat rated to 42.2° C, 49,200 lbf (218.86 kN) max continuous	0.348 lb/lbf/hr (9.86 g/kNs) take-off (sea level static TSFC)	b) 27.1:1		9,332 (4,233)	a) 132.7 (3,371) flange to flange b) 97 (2,464)	A310-200/300. Bypass ratio 5. Fan pressure ratio 1.65.
PW4156/A (twin-spool turbofan)	56,000 lbf (249.1 kN) take-off, flat rated to 33.3° C, 50,000 lbf (222.45 kN) max continuous	0.359 lb/lbf/hr (10.17 g/kNs) take-off (sea level static TSFC)	b) 29.7:1		9,332 (4,233)	a) 132.7 (3,371) flange to flange b) 97 (2,464)	A300-600 and A310-300. Bypass ratio 4.9. Fan pressure ratio 1.71.
PW4158 (twin-spool turbofan)	58,000 lbf (258 kN) take-off, flat rated to 30° C, 50,000 lbf (222.45 kN) max continuous	0.365 lb/lbf/hr (10.34 g/kNs) take-off (sea level static TSFC)	b) 31:1		9,332 (4,233)	a) 132.7 (3,371) flange to flange b) 97 (2,464)	A300-600/600R. Bypass ratio 4.8. Fan pressure ratio 1.73.
PW4164 (twin-spool turbofan)	64,000 lbf (284.7 kN)						A330. Derated version of PW4168.
PW4168 (twin-spool turbofan)	68,000 lbf (302.48 kN), flat rated to 30° C		b) 32.8:1		14,100 (6,396)	a) 163.0 (4,140) b) 106.9 (2,715)	A330. Incorporates Floatwall™ combustor and FADEC of other PW4000 derivative engines. Entered service in December 1994. 180 minute ETOPS approved July 1995. Bypass ratio 5.1. Fan pressure ratio 1.75.
PW4460 (twin-spool turbofan)	60,000 lbf (266.9 kN) take-off, flat rated to 30° C, 50,300 lbf (223.75 kN) max continuous	0.37 lb/lbf/hr (10.48 g/kNs)	b) 31.2:1		9,332 (4,233)	a) 132.7 (3,371) flange to flange b) 97 (2,464)	MD-11. Bypass ratio 4.8. Fan pressure ratio 1.74.
PW4462 (twin-spool turbofan)	62,000 lbf (275.8 kN) take-off, flat rated to 30° C	0.378 lb/lbf/hr (10.71 g/kNs)	b) 32.3:1		9,332 (4,233)	a) 132.7 (3,371) flange to flange b) 97 (2,464)	MD-11. Bypass ratio 4.8. Fan pressure ratio 1.8.
PW6000 series (turbofan)	16,000-23,000 lbf (71.17-102.31 kN)				4.100 (1,860)	a) 99 (2,515) b) 60 (1,524) diameter	Bypass ratio 5.2. A318. Proposed for AE316/317 and other aircraft in the 80+ passenger range. Possibly for N2130. Participation by Northrop Grumman, Hispano-Suiza and AVIC of China. Possible service entry in year 2002.
PW7000/XTE-66 (turbofans)							XTE-66 Joint Technology Demonstrator Engine, also becoming prototype for PW7000 fighter engine. Both use XTC-66 core.
PW8000 (high and low spool, geared turbofan)	25,000-35,000 lbf (111.2-155.7 kN)					a) 124 (3,150) b) 76 (1,930) fan diameter	Under development since early 1998, as extension of PW6000 family, for 120-180 passenger transports. To test run in 1999. Certification about 2001 and service entry 2002. 17 ins (43 cm) reduction gearbox (32,000 shp, 23,860 kW). Bypass ratio 11. To reduce operating costs by up to 10%, fuel burn by 9%, maintenance by nearly 30%, and noise levels by 30 decibels. 40% fewer stages (13) than same-size conventional turbofan, and 52% fewer compressor and turbine airfoils.
SE611 and SE614 (F-119 derivative turbofans)	35,000 lbf (155.7 kN) class						Incorporate larger fan for increased air flow, offering bypass ratio of about 0.6. Increased TET. See F-119, and JSF entries in Combat section.
TF33-P-3 (military designation of the JT3D-2 turbofan)	17,000 lbf (75.62 kN)	0.52 lb/lbf/hr (14.73 g/kNs)	b) 13:1		3,900 (1,769)	a) 136.3 (3,462) b) 53.14 (1,350)	B-52H. Also, P-5/P-9 on EC-135B/C-135B and P-7/P-7A on C-141.
TF33-PW-100/100A (military designation of the JT3D-8B turbofan)	21,000 lbf (93.41 kN)	0.56 lb/lbf/hr (15.86 g/kNs)	b) 15.6:1		4,790 (2,173)	a) 142.2 (3,612) b) 54.06 (1,373)	E-3A/B/C Sentry. Also, 18,000 lbf (80 kN) PW-102 on KC-135E.
RotorWay International. 4140 West Mercury Way, Chandler, AZ 85226 (Telephone: +1 602 961 1001, Facsimile: +1 602 961 1514, Web site: www.rotorway.com)							
RI 162F (4-cyl horizontally opposed piston)	150 hp (111.9 kW) at 4,250 rpm	32.18 litres per hour	a) 4,500 b) 9.4:1	b) 92 Octane premium unleaded auto fuel	180 (81.6)	a) 30 (762) b) 21 (533) c) 21 (533)	Exec 162F. Incorporates FADEC.

Designation (type of engine)	Power output (normally take-off rating for piston, turboprop and turboshaft, unless stated)	Specific fuel consumption (S F C)	a) Max RPM b) Pressure or Compression ratio	a) EGT (unless stated to be MGT, TET, TGT or TIT) b) Primary fuel type or Octane rating	Dry weight lb (kg)	a) Length ins (mm) b) Width ins (mm) c) Height ins (mm)	Current aircraft users, and comments
United States of America							
Sport Plane Products Inc. 420 Harbor Drive, Naples, FL 33940							
Nelson H63C (4-cyl, 2-stroke, air-cooled piston)	43 hp (32 kW) take-off and cruise (2 hp, 1.49 kW used by cooling fan)	17 litres per hour	a) 4,000 b) 8:1		83 (37.6)*	a) 20 (508) b) 23.8 (604.5) c) 14.8 (376)	Light helicopter. *With Kevlar and carbon shrouds, saving 3 lb (1.36 kg) weight. Sport Plane Products Inc is the exclusive distributer of Nelson Engines.
Nelson H63CP (4-cyl, 2-stroke, air-cooled piston)	48 hp (36 kW) take-off, 45 hp (33.6 kW) cruise	23.5 litres per hour maximum power, 16 litres per hour cruise	a) 4,400 take-off, 4,000 cruise b) 8:1		68 (31)		Light aeroplane version of the previous engine.
Nelson H63CP twin installation (see Comments)	96 hp (71.6 kW) take-off, 90 hp (67 kW) cruise		a) 2,400 take-off for propeller shaft	b) 80-90 Octane lead-free auto fuel	200 (91)* including adjustable-pitch propeller		Twin engine installation driving a single propeller, to fit or be adapted to standard engine cowlings for up to 125 hp (93.2 kW) installations. Initial installation in a Glastar. *Including adjustable-pitch propeller.
Teledyne Continental Motors. PO Box 90, Mobile, Alabama 36601 (Telephone: +1 334 438 3411, Facsimile: +1 334 432 7352)							
O-200 (4-cyl, horizontally opposed, air-cooled piston with direct drive)	100 hp (74.6 kW) at 2,750 rpm max continuous		b) 7.0:1	b) 80/87	188 (85.3)	a) 28.5 (724) b) 31.56 (802) c) 23.18 (589)	Cessna 150, Champion Lancer, Taylorcraft F19 and others. Bore 4.06 ins (103.1 mm); stroke 3.87 ins (98.3 mm).
IO-240-A (4-cyl, horizontally opposed, air-cooled piston with direct drive)	125 hp (93.2 kW) take-off at 2,800 rpm (+5%, -0%), 94 hp (70.1 kW) recommended cruise at 2,550 rpm		b) 8.5:1	b) 100/100 LL	246 (111.6) with standard equipment	a) 30.3 (770) b) 31.4 (798) c) 23.5 (597)	Bore 4.44 ins (112.8 mm); stroke 3.87 ins (98.3 mm); displacement 240 cu ins. Dual magnetos ignition.
O-300-A/C/D (6-cyl, horizontally opposed piston with direct drive)	145 hp (108 kW) at 2,700 rpm max continuous		b) 7.0:1	b) 80/87	270 (122.5) for A/C and 272 (123.4) for D	a) 39.75 (1,010) for A/C b) 31.5 (800) c) 23.25 (591) for A/C	Bore 4.06 ins (103.1 mm); stroke 3.87 ins (98.3 mm). Length for O-300-D is 36 ins (914 mm) and height is 27 ins (686 mm).
IO-360-A/AB/C/CB/D/DB (6-cyl, horizontally opposed, air-cooled piston with direct drive)	210 hp (156.6 kW) at 2,800 rpm max continuous		b) 8.5:1	b) 100/100 LL	294 (133.4)	a) 34.6 (879) b) 31.4 (798) c) 24.33 (618)	Cessna 337 and Cessna 172 XP for IO-360 series. Bore 4.44 ins (112.8 mm); stroke 3.87 ins (98.3 mm).
IO-360-ES (6-cyl, horizontally opposed, air-cooled piston with direct drive)	210 hp (156.6 kW) take-off at 2,800 rpm (+5%, -0%), 157 hp (117 kW) recommended cruise at 2,500 rpm		b) 8.5:1	b) 100/100 LL	330 (149.7) with standard equipment	a) 36.32 (922.5) b) 33.05 (839.5) c) 26.22 (666)	Bore 4.44 ins (112.8 mm); stroke 3.87 ins (98.3 mm); displacement 360 cu ins. TCM dual magnetos ignition.
IO-360-G/GB/H/HB/J/JB/K/KB (6-cyl, horizontally opposed, air-cooled piston with direct drive)	210 hp (156.6 kW) take-off at 2,800 rpm, 195 hp (145.4 kW) at 2,600 rpm max continuous		b) 8.5:1	b) 100/100 LL	294 (133.4)	a) 34.6 (879) b) 31.4 (798) c) 24.33 (618)	Bore 4.44 ins (112.8 mm); stroke 3.87 ins (98.3 mm).
TSIO-360-A/AB (6-cyl, horizontally opposed, air-cooled, turbocharged piston with direct drive)	210 hp (156.6 kW) at 2,800 rpm max continuous		b) 7.5:1	b) 100/100 LL	300 (136)	a) 35.84 (910) b) 33.03 (839) c) 23.75 (603)	Cessna T337, Mooney 231/252, Piper Seneca and Turbo Arrow for TSIO-360 series. Bore 4.44 ins (112.8 mm); stroke 3.87 ins (98.3 mm).
TSIO-360-C/CB (as above)	225 hp (167.8 kW) at 2,800 rpm max continuous		b) 7.5:1	b) 100/100 LL	300 (136)	a) 35.84 (910) b) 33.03 (839) c) 23.75 (603)	Bore 4.44 ins (112.8 mm); stroke 3.87 ins (98.3 mm).
TSIO-360-D/DB (6-cyl, horizontally opposed, air-cooled, turbocharged piston with direct drive)	225 hp (167.8 kW) at 2,800 rpm max continuous		b) 7.5:1	b) 100/100 LL	278 (126)	a) 34.6 (879) b) 31.4 (798) c) 24.33 (618)	Bore 4.44 ins (112.8 mm); stroke 3.87 ins (98.3 mm).
L/TSIO-360-E/EB (as above)	200 hp (149 kW) at 2,575 rpm max continuous		b) 7.5:1	b) 100/100 LL	352 (159.7)	a) 56.58 (1,437) b) 31.4 (798) c) 26.44 (672)	Bore 4.44 ins (112.8 mm); stroke 3.87 ins (98.3 mm).
TSIO-360-F/FB (as above)	200 hp (149 kW) at 2,575 rpm max continuous		b) 7.5:1	b) 100/100 LL	359 (162.8)	a) 56.58 (1,437) b) 31.3 (795) c) 26.44 (672)	Bore 4.44 ins (112.8 mm); stroke 3.87 ins (98.3 mm).
TSIO-360-GB/LB (as above)	210 hp (156.6 kW) at 2,700 rpm max continuous		b) 7.5:1	b) 100/100 LL	354 (160.6)	a) 33.57 (853) b) 33.88 (861) c) 31.9 (810)	Bore 4.44 ins (112.8 mm); stroke 3.87 ins (98.3 mm).
TSIO-360-MB (as above)	210 hp (156.6 kW) at 2,700 rpm max continuous		b) 7.5:1	b) 100/100 LL	412 (186.9)	a) 42.78 (1,087) b) 35.78 (909) c) 32.93 (836)	Bore 4.44 ins (112.8 mm); stroke 3.87 ins (98.3 mm).
TSIO-360-H/HB (as above)	210 hp (156.6 kW) at 2,800 rpm max continuous		b) 7.5:1	b) 100/100 LL	313 (142)	a) 35.34 (898) b) 31.38 (797) c) 22.43 (570)	Bore 4.44 ins (112.8 mm); stroke 3.87 ins (98.3 mm).

Designation (type of engine)	Power output (normally take-off rating for piston, turboprop and turboshaft, unless stated)	Specific fuel consumption (S F C)	a) Max RPM b) Pressure or Compression ratio	a) EGT (unless stated to be MGT, TET, TGT or TIT) b) Primary fuel type or Octane rating	Dry weight lb (kg)	a) Length ins (mm) b) Width ins (mm) c) Height ins (mm)	Current aircraft users, and comments
United States of America							
Teledyne Continental Motors. (continued)							
L/TSIO-360-KB (as above)	220 hp (164 kW) at 2,800 rpm max continuous		b) 7.5:1	b) 100/100 LL	359 (162.8)	a) 56.58 (1,437) b) 31.3 (795) c) 26.44 (672)	Bore 4.44 ins (112.8 mm); stroke 3.87 ins (98.3 mm).
O-470-G (6-cyl, horizontally opposed piston with direct drive)	240 hp (179 kW) at 2,600 rpm max continuous		b) 8.0:1	b) 91/96	431 (195.5)	a) 37.56 (954) b) 33.58 (853) c) 26.69 (678)	Bore 5 ins (127 mm); stroke 4 ins (102 mm).
O-470-J (as above)	225 hp (167.8 kW) at 2,550 rpm max continuous		b) 7.0:1	b) 80/87	380 (172.4)	a) 36.03 (915) b) 33.32 (846) c) 27.75 (705)	Bore 5 ins (127 mm); stroke 4 ins (102 mm).
O-470-K/L (as above)	230 hp (171.5 kW) at 2,600 rpm max continuous		b) 7.0:1	b) 80/87	404 (183.25)	a) 36.03 (915) b) 33.56 (852) c) 27.75 (705)	Bore 5 ins (127 mm); stroke 4 ins (102 mm).
O-470-M (as above)	240 hp (179 kW) at 2,600 rpm max continuous		b) 8.0:1	b) 91/96	409 (185.5)	a) 43.31 (1,100) b) 33.56 (852) c) 19.62 (498)	Bore 5 ins (127 mm); stroke 4 ins (102 mm).
O-470-R (as above)	230 hp (171.5 kW) at 2,600 rpm max continuous		b) 7.0:1	b) 80/87	401 (181.9)	a) 36.03 (915) b) 33.56 (852) c) 28.42 (722)	Bore 5 ins (127 mm); stroke 4 ins (102 mm).
O-470-S (as above)	230 hp (171.5 kW) at 2,600 rpm max continuous		b) 7.0:1	b) 100/100 LL	412 (186.9)	a) 36.03 (915) b) 33.56 (852) c) 28.42 (722)	Bore 5 ins (127 mm); stroke 4 ins (102 mm).
O-470-U (as above)	230 hp (171.5 kW) at 2,400 rpm max continuous		b) 8.6:1	b) 100/100 LL	412 (186.9)	a) 36.03 (915) b) 33.56 (852) c) 28.42 (722)	Bore 5 ins (127 mm); stroke 4 ins (102 mm).
IO-470-C (as above)	250 hp (186.4 kW) at 2,600 rpm max continuous		b) 8.0:1	b) 91/61	431 (195.5)	a) 37.93 (963) b) 33.58 (853) c) 26.81 (681)	Bore 5 ins (127 mm); stroke 4 ins (102 mm).
IO-470-D/E (as above)	260 hp (194 kW) at 2,625 rpm max continuous		b) 8.6:1	b) 100/100 LL	426 (193.2)	a) 43.31 (1,100) b) 33.56 (852) c) 19.75 (502)	Bore 5 ins (127 mm); stroke 4 ins (102 mm).
IO-470-F (as above)	260 hp (194 kW) at 2,625 rpm max continuous		b) 8.6:1	b) 100/100 LL	426 (193.2)	a) 37.22 (945) b) 33.56 (852) c) 23.79 (604)	Bore 5 ins (127 mm); stroke 4 ins (102 mm).
IO-470-H (as above)	260 hp (194 kW) at 2,625 rpm max continuous		b) 8.6:1	b) 100/100 LL	431 (195.5)	a) 38.14 (969) b) 33.58 (853) c) 26.81 (681)	Bore 5 ins (127 mm); stroke 4 ins (102 mm).
IO-470-J/K (as above)	225 hp (167.8 kW) at 2,600 rpm max continuous		b) 7.0:1	b) 80/87	401 (181.9)	a) 38.14 (969) b) 33.39 (848) c) 26.81 (681)	Bore 5 ins (127 mm); stroke 4 ins (102 mm).
IO-470-L (as above)	260 hp (194 kW) at 2,625 rpm max continuous		b) 8.6:1	b) 100/100 LL	430 (195)	a) 43.17 (1,097) b) 33.56 (852) c) 19.75 (502)	Bore 5 ins (127 mm); stroke 4 ins (102 mm).
IO-470-M (as above)	260 hp (194 kW) at 2,625 rpm max continuous		b) 8.6:1	b) 100/100 LL	430 (195)	a) 47.16 (1,198) b) 33.56 (852) c) 19.75 (502)	Bore 5 ins (127 mm); stroke 4 ins (102 mm).
IO-470-N (as above)	260 hp (194 kW) at 2,625 rpm max continuous		b) 8.6:1	b) 100/100 LL	433 (196.4)	a) 38.14 (969) b) 33.58 (853) c) 26.81 (681)	Bore 5 ins (127 mm); stroke 4 ins (102 mm).
IO-470-S (as above)	260 hp (194 kW) at 2,625 rpm max continuous		b) 8.6:1	b) 100/100 LL	426 (193.2)	a) 41.41 (1,052) b) 33.56 (852) c) 19.75 (502)	Bore 5 ins (127 mm); stroke 4 ins (102 mm).
IO-470-U (as above)	260 hp (194 kW) at 2,625 rpm max continuous		b) 8.6:1	b) 100/100 LL	423 (191.9)	a) 44.14 (1,121) b) 33.86 (860) c) 19.75 (502)	Bore 5 ins (127 mm); stroke 4 ins (102 mm).
IO-470-V/VO (as above)	260 hp (194 kW) at 2,625 rpm max continuous		b) 8.6:1	b) 100/100 LL	423 (191.9)	a) 43.69 (1,110) b) 33.56 (852) c) 19.75 (502)	Bore 5 ins (127 mm); stroke 4 ins (102 mm).
IO-520-A/J (as above)	285 hp (212.5 kW) at 2,700 rpm max continuous		b) 8.5:1	b) 100/100 LL	431 (195.5)	a) 41.41 (1,052) b) 33.56 (852) c) 19.75 (502)	Aero Commander 500, Cessna 185/188/206/207/210/310, Beech Baron 55/58, Beech Bonanza 33/35/36, Bellanca Viking 300, and Navion for IO-520 series. Bore 5.25 ins (133 mm); stroke 4 ins (102 mm).
IO-520-B/BA/BB (as above)	285 hp (212.5 kW) at 2,700 rpm max continuous		b) 8.5:1	b) 100/100 LL	422 (191.4)	a) 39.71 (1,009) b) 33.58 (853) c) 26.71 (678)	Bore 5.25 ins (133 mm); stroke 4 ins (102 mm).
IO-520-C/CB (as above)	285 hp (212.5 kW) at 2,700 rpm max continuous		b) 8.5:1	b) 100/100 LL	415 (188.2)	a) 42.88 (1,089) b) 33.56 (852) c) 19.75 (502)	Bore 5.25 ins (133 mm); stroke 4 ins (102 mm).
IO-520-D (as above)	300 hp (223.7 kW) take-off at 2,850 rpm, 285 hp (212.5 kW) at 2,700 rpm max continuous		b) 8.5:1	b) 100/100 LL	430 (195)	a) 37.36 (949) b) 35.46 (901) c) 23.79 (604)	Bore 5.25 ins (133 mm); stroke 4 ins (102 mm).

Designation (type of engine)	Power output (normally take-off rating for piston, turboprop and turboshaft, unless stated)	Specific fuel consumption (S F C)	a) Max RPM b) Pressure or Compression ratio	a) EGT (unless stated to be MGT, TET, TGT or TIT) b) Primary fuel type or Octane rating	Dry weight lb (kg)	a) Length ins (mm) b) Width ins (mm) c) Height ins (mm)	Current aircraft users, and comments
United States of America							
Teledyne Continental Motors. (continued)							
IO-520-E (as above)	300 hp (223.7 kW) take-off at 2,850 rpm, 285 hp (212.5 kW) at 2,700 rpm max continuous		b) 8.5:1	b) 100/100 LL	427 (193.7)	a) 47.66 (1,211) b) 33.56 (852) c) 19.75 (502)	Bore 5.25 ins (133 mm); stroke 4 ins (102 mm).
IO-520-F (as above)	300 hp (223.7 kW) take-off at 2,850 rpm, 285 hp (212.5 kW) at 2,700 rpm max continuous		b) 8.5:1	b) 100/100 LL	430 (195)	a) 41.41 (1,052) b) 35.91 (912) c) 19.75 (502)	Bore 5.25 ins (133 mm); stroke 4 ins (102 mm).
IO-520-K (as above)	300 hp (223.7 kW) take-off at 2,850 rpm, 285 hp (212.5 kW) at 2,700 rpm max continuous		b) 8.5:1	b) 100/100 LL	428 (194)	a) 40.91 (1,039) b) 33.56 (852) c) 19.75 (502)	Bore 5.25 ins (133 mm); stroke 4 ins (102 mm).
IO-520-L (as above)	300 hp (223.7 kW) take-off at 2,850 rpm, 285 hp (212.5 kW) at 2,700 rpm max continuous		b) 8.5:1	b) 100/100 LL	431 (195.5)	a) 40.91 (1,039) b) 33.56 (852) c) 23.25 (591)	Bore 5.25 ins (133 mm); stroke 4 ins (102 mm).
IO-520-M/MB (as above)	285 hp (212.5 kW) at 2,700 rpm max continuous		b) 8.5:1	b) 100/100 LL	413 (187.3)	a) 46.8 (1,189) b) 33.56 (852) c) 20.41 (518)	Bore 5.25 ins (133 mm); stroke 4 ins (102 mm).
TSIO-520-B/BB/BE (6-cyl, horizontally opposed, turbo-charged piston with direct drive)	285 hp (212.5 kW) at 2,700 rpm max continuous for BB, 310 hp (231 kW) for BE		b) 7.5:1 for B/BB	b) 100/100 LL for B/BB	423 (191.9) for B/BB, 491 (222.7) for BE	a) 39.75 (1,010) b) 33.56 (852) c) 20.32 (516) for B/BE	Beech Bonanza V35TC, Baron 58TC and 58P, Cessna T206/P210/303/T310/340/401/402/414 for TSIO-520 series. Bore 5.25 ins (133 mm); stroke 4 ins (102 mm).
TSIO-520-C/H (as above)	285 hp (212.5 kW) at 2,700 rpm max continuous		b) 7.5:1	b) 100/100 LL	433 (196.4)	a) 40.91 (1,039) b) 33.56 (852) c) 20.04 (509)	Bore 5.25 ins (133 mm); stroke 4 ins (102 mm).
TSIO-520-D/DB (as above)	285 hp (212.5 kW) at 2,700 rpm max continuous		b) 7.5:1	b) 100/100 LL	423 (191.9)	a) 43.25 (1,099) b) 33.58 (853) c) 22.34 (567)	Bore 5.25 ins (133 mm); stroke 4 ins (102 mm).
TSIO-520-E/EB (as above)	300 hp (223.7 kW) at 2,700 rpm, max continuous		b) 7.5:1	b) 100/100 LL	421 (191)	a) 39.75 (1,010) b) 33.56 (852) c) 20.32 (516)	Bore 5.24 ins (133 mm); stroke 4 ins (102 mm).
TSIO-520-G (as above)	300 hp (223.7 kW) take-off at 2,700 rpm, 285 hp (212.5 kW) at 2,600 rpm max continuous		b) 7.5:1	b) 100/100 LL	433 (196.4)	a) 40.91 (1,039) b) 33.56 (852) c) 20.04 (509)	Bore 5.24 ins (133 mm); stroke 4 ins (102 mm).
TSIO-520-J/JB/N/NB (as above)	310 hp (231 kW) at 2,700 rpm max continuous		b) 7.5:1	b) 100/100 LL	412 (186.9)	a) 54.36 (1,381) b) 33.56 (852) c) 22.5 (572)	Bore 5.24 ins (133 mm); stroke 4 ins (102 mm).
TSIO-520-K/KB (as above)	285 hp (212.5 kW) at 2,700 rpm max continuous		b) 7.5:1	b) 100/100 LL	412 (186.9)	a) 54.36 (1,381) b) 33.56 (852) c) 20.32 (516)	Bore 5.24 ins (133 mm); stroke 4 ins (102 mm).
TSIO-520-L/LB (as above)	310 hp (231 kW) at 2,700 rpm max continuous		b) 7.5:1	b) 100/100 LL	540 (244.9)	a) 50.62 (1,286) b) 33.56 (852) c) 20.02 (509)	Bore 5.25 ins (133 mm); stroke 4 ins (102 mm).
TSIO-520-M/P (as above)	310 hp (231 kW) take-off at 2,700 rpm, 285 hp (212.5 kW) at 2,600 rpm max continuous		b) 7.5:1	b) 100/100 LL	436 (197.8)	a) 40.91 (1,039) b) 33.56 (852) c) 20.04 (509)	Bore 5.25 ins (133 mm); stroke 4 ins (102 mm).
TSIO-520-R (as above)	310 hp (231 kW) take-off at 2,700 rpm, 285 hp (212.5 kW) at 2,600 rpm max continuous		b) 7.5:1	b) 100/100 LL	436 (197.8)	a) 40.91 (1,039) b) 33.56 (852) c) 23.54 (598)	Bore 5.25 ins (133 mm); stroke 4 ins (102 mm).
TSIO-520-T (as above)	310 hp (231 kW) at 2,700 rpm max continuous		b) 7.5:1	b) 100/100 LL	426 (193.2)	a) 38.2 (970) b) 33.56 (852) c) 32.26 (819)	Bore 5.25 ins (133 mm); stroke 4 ins (102 mm).
TSIO-520-UB (as above)	300 hp (223.7 kW) at 2,700 rpm max continuous		b) 7.5:1	b) 100/100 LL	536 (243)	a) 44.73 (1,136) b) 33.56 (852) c) 28.86 (733)	Bore 5.25 ins (133 mm); stroke 4 ins (102 mm).

Designation (type of engine)	Power output (normally take-off rating for piston, turboprop and turboshaft, unless stated)	Specific fuel consumption (S F C)	a) Max RPM b) Pressure or Compression ratio	a) EGT (unless stated to be MGT, TET, TGT or TIT) b) Primary fuel type or Octane rating	Dry weight lb (kg)	a) Length ins (mm) b) Width ins (mm) c) Height ins (mm)	Current aircraft users, and comments
United States of America							
Teledyne Continental Motors. (continued)							
TSIO-520-VB (as above)	325 hp (242.4 kW) at 2,700 rpm max continuous		b) 7.5:1	b) 100/100 LL	456 (206.8)	a) 39.25 (997) b) 33.56 (852) c) 20.41 (518)	Bore 5.25 ins (133 mm); stroke 4 ins (102 mm).
TSIO-520-WB (as above)	325 hp (242.4 kW) at 2,700 rpm max continuous		b) 7.5:1	b) 100/100 LL	539 (244.5)	a) 50.62 (1,286) b) 33.56 (852) c) 20.02 (509)	Bore 5.25 ins (133 mm); stroke 4 ins (102 mm).
L/TSIO-520-AE (as above)	250 hp (186.4 kW) at 2,400 rpm max continuous		b) 8.5:1	b) 100/100 LL	365 (165.6)	a) 38.07 (967) b) 33.29 (846) c) 21.38 (543)	Bore 5.25 ins (133 mm); stroke 4 ins (102 mm).
TSIO-520-AF (as above)	310 hp (231.2 kW) take-off at 2,600 rpm, 285 hp (212.5 kW) at 2,600 rpm max continuous		b) 7.5:1	b) 100/100 LL	418 (189.6)	a) 40.31 (1,024) b) 33.56 (852) c) 23.45 (596)	Bore 5.25 ins (133 mm); stroke 4 ins (102 mm).
TSIO-520-BE (as above)	310 hp (231.2 kW) at 2,600 rpm max continuous		b) 7.5:1	b) 100/100 LL	442 (200.5)	a) 42.64 (1,083) b) 42.5 (1,080) c) 33.5 (851)	Bore 5.25 ins (133 mm); stroke 4 ins (102 mm).
TSIO-520-CE (as above)	325 hp (242.4 kW) at 2,700 rpm max continuous		b) 7.5:1	b) 100/100 LL	527 (239)	a) 41 (1,041) b) 34 (864) c) 25 (635)	Bore 5.25 ins (133 mm); stroke 4 ins (102 mm).
GTSIO-520-C (6-cyl, horizontally opposed, turbocharged piston with geared drive)	340 hp (253.5 kW) at 3,200 rpm max continuous		b) 7.5:1	b) 100/100 LL	481 (218.2)	a) 42.56 (1,081) b) 34.04 (865) c) 23.1 (587)	Aero Commander 685, Cessna 404/421A/421B/421C for GTSIO-520 series. Bore 5.25 ins (133 mm); stroke 4 ins (102 mm).
GTSIO-520-D/H (as above)	375 hp (279.6 kW) at 3,400 rpm max continuous		b) 7.5:1	b) 100/100 LL	508 (230.4)	a) 42.56 (1,081) b) 34.04 (865) c) 26.78 (680)	Bore 5.25 ins (133 mm); stroke 4 ins (102 mm).
GTSIO-520-K (as above)	435 hp (324.4 kW) at 3,400 rpm max continuous		b) 7.5:1	b) 100/100 LL	600 (272.2)	a) 56.25 (1,429) b) 34.04 (865) c) 26.18 (665)	Bore 5.25 ins (133 mm); stroke 4 ins (102 mm).
GTSIO-520-L/N (as above)	375 hp (279.6 kW) at 3,350 rpm max continuous		b) 7.5:1	b) 100/100 LL	557 (252.7)	a) 43.87 (1,114) b) 34.04 (865) c) 26.41 (671)	Bore 5.25 ins (133 mm); stroke 4 ins (102 mm).
GTSIO-520-M (as above)	375 hp (279.6 kW) at 3,350 rpm max continuous		b) 7.5:1	b) 100/100 LL	545 (247.2)	a) 43.87 (1,114) b) 34.04 (865) c) 26.8 (681)	Bore 5.25 ins (133 mm); stroke 4 ins (102 mm).
IO-550-A (6-cyl, horizontally opposed, air-cooled piston with direct drive)	300 hp (223.7 kW) at 2,700 rpm max continuous		b) 7.5:1	b) 100/100 LL	414 (187.8)	a) 46.8 (1,189) b) 33.56 (852) c) 20.41 (518)	Beech Baron 58 and Bonanza A36 for IO-550 series. Bore 5.25 ins (133 mm); stroke 4.25 ins (108 mm).
IO-550-B (as above)	300 hp (223.7 kW) at 2,700 rpm max continuous		b) 8.5:1	b) 100/100 LL	422 (191.4)	a) 37.97 (964) b) 33.56 (852) c) 27.32 (694)	Bore 5.25 ins (133 mm); stroke 4.25 ins (108 mm).
IO-550-C (as above)	300 hp (223.7 kW) at 2,700 rpm max continuous		b) 8.5:1	b) 100/100 LL	433 (196.4)	a) 43.31 (1,100) b) 33.56 (852) c) 19.78 (502)	Bore 5.25 ins (133 mm); stroke 4.25 ins (108 mm).
IO-550-D (as above)	300 hp (223.7 kW) at 2,700 rpm max continuous		b) 7.5:1	b) 100/100 LL	422 (191.4)	a) 36.74 (933) b) 33.56 (852) c) 23.79 (604)	Bore 5.25 ins (133 mm); stroke 4.25 ins (108 mm).
IO-550-E (as above)	300 hp (223.7 kW) at 2,700 rpm max continuous		b) 7.5:1	b) 100/100 LL	426 (193.2)	a) 43.91 (1,115) b) 33.56 (852) c) 19.75 (502)	Bore 5.25 ins (133 mm); stroke 4.25 ins (108 mm).
IO-550-F (as above)	300 hp (223.7 kW) at 2,700 rpm max continuous		b) 7.5:1	b) 100/100 LL	423 (191.9)	a) 40.91 (1,039) b) 33.56 (852) c) 19.75 (502)	Bore 5.25 ins (133 mm); stroke 4.25 ins (108 mm).
IO-550-G (as above)	280 hp (208.8 kW) take-off at 2,500 rpm, 210 hp (156.6 kW) cruise at 75% power (2,300 rpm)		b) 7.5:1	b) 100/100 LL	465 (210.9)*	a) 46.8 (1,189) b) 33.56 (852) c) 20.41 (518.4)	Bore 5.25 ins (133 mm); stroke 4.25 ins (108 mm). Dual magnetos ignition. *With standard equipment (may vary with specification).
IO-550-L (as above)	300 hp (223.7 kW) at 2,700 rpm max continuous		b) 7.5:1	b) 100/100 LL	423 (191.9)	a) 40.91 (1,039) b) 33.56 (852) c) 23.25 (591)	Bore 5.25 ins (133 mm); stroke 4.25 ins (108 mm).
TSIO-550-A (6-cyl, horizontally opposed, air-cooled, turbocharged piston with direct drive)	360 hp (268.5 kW) at 2,600 rpm max continuous		b) 7.5:1	b) 100/100 LL	425 (192.8)	a) 42.64 (1,083) b) 42.5 (1,080) c) 33.5 (851)	Bore 5.25 ins (133 mm); stroke 4.25 ins (108 mm).

Designation (type of engine)	Power output (normally take-off rating for piston, turboprop and turboshaft, unless stated)	Specific fuel consumption (S F C)	a) Max RPM b) Pressure or Compression ratio	a) EGT (unless stated to be MGT, TET, TGT or TIT) b) Primary fuel type or Octane rating	Dry weight lb (kg)	a) Length ins (mm) b) Width ins (mm) c) Height ins (mm)	Current aircraft users, and comments
United States of America							
Teledyne Continental Motors. (continued)							
TSIOL-550-A (as above)	350 hp (261 kW) at 2,700 rpm max continuous		b) 7.5:1	b) 100/100 LL	402 (182.3)	a) 42.65 (1,083) b) 42.5 (1,080) c) 33.5 (851)	Users include new Extra 400, and Grob Strato 2 at 402 hp (300 kW). Bore 5.25 ins (133 mm); stroke 4.25 ins (108 mm).
TSIO-550-B (as above)	350 hp (261 kW) at 2,700 rpm		b) 7.5:1	b) 100/100 LL	566 (256.7)	a) 42.75 (1,086) b) 42.2 (1,072) c) 33.6 (853)	Bore 5.25 ins (133 mm); stroke 4.25 ins (108 mm).
Voyager 550 (6-cyl, horizontally opposed, liquid-cooled piston with direct drive)	350 hp (261 kW) at 2,700 rpm		b) 7.5:1	b) 100/100 LL	504 (228.6)		Bore 5.25 ins (133 mm); stroke 4.25 ins (108 mm). Fuel-injected.
Voyager T-550 (6-cyl, horizontally opposed, liquid-cooled piston with direct drive)	300 hp (223.7 kW) at 2,500 rpm		b) 7.5:1	b) 100 LL	450 (204.1)		Beech Bonanza modification. Bore 5.25 ins (133 mm); stroke 4.25 ins (108 mm). Turbocharged and fuel-injected.
Voyager GT-550 (as above, but geared drive)	400 hp (298.3 kW)		b) 7.5:1	b) 100 LL	550 (249.5)		Piper Chieftain modification. Bore 5.25 ins (133 mm); stroke 4.25 ins (108 mm).
Teledyne CAE, 1330 Laskey Road, Toledo, OH 43612-0971							
J69-T-25A (single-shaft turbojet)	1,025 lbf (4.56 kN)	1.14 lb/lbf/hr (32.3 g/kNs)	a) 21,730		364 (165.1)	a) 35.39 (900) b) 22.3 (566)	Cessna T-37B. Based on French Turbomeca Marboré.
Textron Lycoming Williamsport Division. 652 Oliver Street, Williamsport, PA 17701 (Telephone: +1 717 323 6181, Facsimile: +1 717 327 7066, Web site: www.lycoming.textron.com)							
O-235-C (4-cyl, 4-stroke, horizontally opposed piston, with direct drive)	100/108/115 hp (74.6/80.5/85.75 kW)		a) 2,400/2,600/2,800 b) 6.75:1	b) 80 Octane	213 (96.6)	a) 29.56 (751) b) 32 (813) c) 22.4 (569)	Recommended TBO 2,400 hours maximum. Carburettor.
O-235-L and M (4-cyl, 4-stroke, horizontally opposed piston, with direct drive)	105/112/118 hp (78.3/83.5/88 kW)		a) 2,400/2,600/2,800 b) 8.5:1	b) 100/100 LL	218 (98.9)	a) 29.05 (738) b) 32 (813) c) 22.4 (569)	Recommended TBO 2,400 hours maximum. Carburettor.
O-235-N and P (4-cyl, 4-stroke, horizontally opposed piston, with direct drive)	103/110/116 hp (76.8/82/86.5 kW)		a) 2,400/2,600/2,800 b) 8.1:1	b) 100/100 LL	218 (98.9)	a) 29.05 (738) b) 32 (813) c) 22.4 (569)	Recommended TBO 2,400 hours maximum. Carburettor.
O-320-A and E (4-cyl, 4-stroke, horizontally opposed piston, with direct drive)	140/150 hp (104.4/112 kW)		a) 2,450/2,700 b) 7.0:1	b) 80 Octane	244 (110.7)	a) 29.56 (751) b) 32.24 (819) c) 22.99 (584)	Recommended TBO 2,000 hours maximum.
O-320-B and D (4-cyl, 4-stroke, horizontally opposed piston, with direct drive)	160 hp (119.3 kW)		a) 2,700 b) 8.5:1	b) 100/100 LL	255 (115.7)	a) 29.56 (751) b) 32.24 (819) c) 22.99 (584)	Recommended TBO 2,000 hours maximum.
O-320-B2C (4-cyl, 4-stroke, horizontally opposed piston, with direct drive)	160 hp (119.3 kW)		a) 2,700 b) 8.5:1	b) 100/100 LL	255 (115.7)	a) 29.56 (751) b) 32.24 (819) c) 22.99 (584)	Helicopter engine. Recommended TBO 2,000 hours maximum.
IO-320-B and C (4-cyl, 4-stroke, horizontally opposed piston, with fuel injection and direct drive)	160 hp (119.3 kW)		a) 2,700 b) 8.5:1	b) 100/100 LL	259 (117.5)	a) 33.59 (853) b) 32.24 (819) c) 19.22 (488)	Fuel injected.
LIO-320-B and C (4-cyl, 4-stroke, horizontally opposed piston, with fuel injection and direct drive)	160 hp (119.3 kW)		a) 2,700 b) 8.5:1	b) 100/100 LL	259 (117.5)	a) 33.59 (853) b) 32.24 (819) c) 19.22 (488)	Left hand rotation crankshaft.
AEIO-320-D (4-cyl, 4-stroke, horizontally opposed piston, with fuel injection and direct drive)	160 hp (119.3 kW)		a) 2,700 b) 8.5:1	b) 100/100 LL	271 (123)	a) 30.7 (780) b) 32.24 (819) c) 23.18 (589)	Aerobatic, fuel injected engine. Variants are D1B and D2B of 301 lb (136.5 kg) weight. Recommended TBO of 1,600 hours maximum.

Designation (type of engine)	Power output (normally take-off rating for piston, turboprop and turboshaft, unless stated)	Specific fuel consumption (S F C)	a) Max RPM b) Pressure or Compression ratio	a) EGT (unless stated to be MGT, TET, TGT or TIT) b) Primary fuel type or Octane rating	Dry weight lb (kg)	a) Length ins (mm) b) Width ins (mm) c) Height ins (mm)	Current aircraft users, and comments
United States of America							
Textron Lycoming Williamsport Division. (continued)							
AEIO-320-E (4-cyl, 4-stroke, horizontally opposed piston, with fuel injection and direct drive)	150 hp (112 kW)		a) 2,700 b) 7.0:1	b) 80 Octane	258 (117)	a) 29.05 (738) b) 32.24 (819) c) 23.18 (589)	Aerobatic, fuel injected engine. Variants are E1A, E1B, E2A and E2B, weighing up to 292 lb (132.5 kg). Recommended TBO of 1,600 hours maximum.
(L)O-360-A (4-cyl, 4-stroke, horizontally opposed piston, with direct drive)	180 hp (134.2 kW)		a) 2,700 b) 8.5:1	b) 100/100 LL	265 (120.2)	a) 29.56 (751) b) 33.37 (848) c) 24.56 (624)	Recommended TBO 2,000 hours maximum.
IO-360-A and C (4-cyl, 4-stroke, horizontally opposed piston, with fuel injection and direct drive)	200 hp (149 kW)		a) 2,700 b) 8.7:1	b) 100/100 LL	293 (132.9)	a) 29.81 (757) b) 34.25 (870) c) 19.35 (491.5)	Fuel injected.
AEIO-360-A (4-cyl, 4-stroke, horizontally opposed piston, with fuel injection and direct drive)	200 hp (149 kW)		a) 2,700 b) 8.7:1	b) 100/100 LL	299 (135.6)	a) 29.81 (757) b) 34.25 (870) c) 19.35 (491.5)	Aerobatic, fuel injected engine. Recommended TBO 1,600 hours maximum. Variants are A1A, A1B, A1B6, A1C, A1D, A1E, A1E6, A2A, A2B and A2C, weighing up to 479 lb (217.3 kg).
IO-360-B (4-cyl, 4-stroke, horizontally opposed piston, with fuel injection and direct drive)	180 hp (134.2 kW)		a) 2,700 b) 8.5:1	b) 100/100 LL	270 (122.5)	a) 29.81 (757) b) 33.37 (848) c) 24.84 (631)	Fuel injected.
AEIO-360-B (4-cyl, 4-stroke, horizontally opposed piston, with fuel injection and direct drive)	180 hp (134.2 kW)		a) 2,700 b) 8.5:1	b) 100/100 LL		a) 29.81 (757) b) 33.37 (848) c) 24.84 (631)	Aerobatic, fuel injected engine. Recommended TBO 1,600 hours maximum. Variants are B1B, B1D, B1F, B1F6, B1G6, B2F, B2F6 and B4A, weighing between 384-595 lb (174.2-270 kg).
HO-360-B1A (4-cyl, 4-stroke, horizontally opposed piston, with direct drive)	180 hp (134.2 kW)		a) 2,900 b) 8.5:1	b) 80 Octane	290 (131.5)	a) 32.09 (815) b) 33.37 (848) c) 19.38 (492)	Helicopter engine. Fuel injected. Recommended TBO 2,000 hours maximum.
HO-360-C1A (4-cyl, 4-stroke, horizontally opposed piston, with direct drive)	180 hp (134.2 kW)		a) 2,700 b) 8.5:1	b) 100/100 LL	288 (130.6)	a) 31.82 (808) b) 33.37 (848) c) 19.22 (488)	Helicopter engine. Recommended TBO 2,000 hours maximum.
LIO-360-C (4-cyl, 4-stroke, horizontally opposed piston, with fuel injection and direct drive)	200 hp (149 kW)		a) 2,700 b) 8.7:1	b) 100/100 LL	306 (138.8)	a) 33.65 (855) b) 34.25 (870) c) 19.48 (495)	Fuel injected. Left hand rotation crankshaft.
TO-360-C (4-cyl, 4-stroke, horizontally opposed, turbocharged piston, with direct drive)	210 hp (156.6 kW)		a) 2,575 b) 7.3:1	b) 100/100 LL	343 (155.6)	a) 34.5 (876) b) 36.25 (921) c) 21.02 (534)	Turbocharged.
TIO-360-C (4-cyl, 4-stroke, horizontally opposed, turbocharged and fuel injected piston, with direct drive)	210 hp (156.6 kW)		a) 2,575 b) 7.3:1	b) 100/100 LL	348 (157.9)	a) 35.82 (910) b) 36.25 (921) c) 21.65 (550)	Turbocharged and fuel injected.
HO-360-D1A (4-cyl, 4-stroke, horizontally opposed piston, with direct drive)	190 hp (141.7 kW)		a) 3,200 b) 10.0:1	b) 100/100 LL	321 (145.6)	a) 35.62 (905) b) 35.25 (895) c) 19.48 (495)	Helicopter engine. Fuel injected. Recommended TBO 2,000 hours maximum.
0-360-F (4-cyl, 4-stroke, horizontally opposed piston, with direct drive)	180 hp (134.2 kW)		a) 2,700 b) 8.5:1	b) 100/100 LL	270 (122.5)	a) 31.83 (808) b) 33.37 (848) c) 19.96 (507)	Recommended TBO 2,000 hours maximum.

Designation (type of engine)	Power output (normally take-off rating for piston, turboprop and turboshaft, unless stated)	Specific fuel consumption (S F C)	a) Max RPM b) Pressure or Compression ratio	a) EGT (unless stated to be MGT, TET, TGT or TIT) b) Primary fuel type or Octane rating	Dry weight lb (kg)	a) Length ins (mm) b) Width ins (mm) c) Height ins (mm)	Current aircraft users, and comments
United States of America							
Textron Lycoming Williamsport Division. (continued)							
HO-360-F1AD (4-cyl, 4-stroke, horizontally opposed piston, with direct drive)	190 hp (141.7 kW)		a) 3,050 b) 8.0:1	b) 100/100 LL	293 (132.9)	a) 31.36 (796.5) b) 34.25 (870) c) 19.97 (507)	Helicopter engine. Fuel injected. Recommended TBO 2,000 hours maximum.
TO-360-F (4-cyl, 4-stroke, horizontally opposed, turbocharged piston, with direct drive)	210 hp (156.6 kW)		a) 2,575 b) 7.3:1	b) 100/100 LL	343 (155.6)	a) 34.5 (876) b) 36.25 (921) c) 21.02 (534)	Turbocharged.
AEIO-360-H1A (4-cyl, 4-stroke, horizontally opposed piston, with fuel injection and direct drive)	180 hp (134.2 kW)		a) 2,700 b) 8.5:1	b) 100/100 LL	456 (206.8)	a) 40.38 (1,026) b) 33.37 (848) c) 30.33 (770)	Aerobatic, fuel injected engine. Recommended TBO 1,600 hours maximum.
O-540-A (6-cyl, horizontally opposed piston with direct drive)	250 hp (186.4 kW)		a) 2,575 b) 8.5:1	b) 100/100 LL	356 (161.5)	a) 38.42 (976) b) 33.37 (848) c) 24.56 (624)	Recommended TBO 2,000 hours maximum. Intercooling available for the 540 cu ins engine series.
TIO-540-A (6-cyl, horizontally opposed, turbocharged piston with fuel injection and direct drive)	310 hp (231 kW)		a) 2,575 b) 7.3:1	b) 100/100 LL	511 (231.8)	a) 51.34 (1,304) b) 34.25 (870) c) 22.71 (577)	Turbocharged and fuel injected.
IO-540-AA1A5 (6-cyl, horizontally opposed, turbocharged piston with fuel injection and direct drive)	270 hp (201.3 kW)		a) 2,700 b) 7.3:1	b) 100/100 LL	479 (217.3)	a) 39.24 (997) b) 34.25 (870) c) 19.6 (498)	Fuel injected.
TIO-540-AA1AD (6-cyl, horizontally opposed, turbocharged piston with fuel injection and direct drive)	270 hp (201.3 kW)		a) 2,575 b) 8.0:1	b) 100/100 LL	484 (219.5)	a) 48.57 (1,234) b) 33.37 (848) c) 21.48 (545.5)	Turbocharged and fuel injected.
TIO-540-AB1AD (6-cyl, horizontally opposed, turbocharged piston with fuel injection and direct drive)	250 hp (186.4 kW)		a) 2,575 b) 8.0:1	b) 100/100 LL	474 (215)	a) 39.36 (1,000) b) 33.37 (848) c) 30.06 (764)	Turbocharged and fuel injected.
TIO-540-AE2A (6-cyl, horizontally opposed, turbocharged piston with fuel injection and direct drive)	350 hp (261 kW)		a) 2,500 b) 7.3:1	b) 100/100 LL	595 (270)	a) 42.02 (1,067) b) 46.52 (1,182) c) 27.75 (705)	Turbocharged and fuel injected.
TIO-540-AF1A (6-cyl, horizontally opposed, turbocharged piston with fuel injection and direct drive)	270 hp (201.3 kW)		a) 2,575 b) 8.0:1	b) 100/100 LL	491 (222.7)	a) 40.24 (1,022) b) 33.38 (848) c) 28.62 (727)	Turbocharged and fuel injected.
O-540-B (6-cyl, horizontally opposed piston with direct drive)	235 hp (175.2 kW)		a) 2,575 b) 7.2:1	b) 80 Octane	372 (168.7)	a) 37.22 (945) b) 33.37 (848) c) 24.56 (624)	Recommended TBO 2,000 hours maximum.
IO-540-C (6-cyl, horizontally opposed piston with fuel injection and direct drive)	250 hp (186.4 kW)		a) 2,575 b) 8.5:1	b) 100/100 LL	375 (170)	a) 38.42 (976) b) 33.37 (848) c) 24.46 (621)	Fuel injected.
TIO-540-C (6-cyl, horizontally opposed, turbocharged piston with fuel injection and direct drive)	250 hp (186.4 kW)		a) 2,575 b) 7.2:1	b) 100/100 LL	456 (207)	a) 40.38 (1,026) b) 33.37 (848) c) 30.33 (770)	Turbocharged and fuel injected.
IO-540-D (6-cyl, horizontally opposed piston with fuel injection and direct drive)	260 hp (194 kW)		a) 2,700 b) 8.5:1	b) 100/100 LL	381 (173)	a) 39.34 (999) b) 33.37 (848) c) 24.46 (621)	Aerobatic, fuel injected engine.

Designation (type of engine)	Power output (normally take-off rating for piston, turboprop and turboshaft, unless stated)	Specific fuel consumption (S F C)	a) Max RPM b) Pressure or Compression ratio	a) EGT (unless stated to be MGT, TET, TGT or TIT) b) Primary fuel type or Octane rating	Dry weight lb (kg)	a) Length ins (mm) b) Width ins (mm) c) Height ins (mm)	Current aircraft users, and comments
United States of America							
Textron Lycoming Williamsport Division. (continued)							
AEIO-540-D (6-cyl, horizontally opposed piston with fuel injection and direct drive)	260 hp (194 kW)		a) 2,700 b) 8.5:1	b) 100/100 LL	384 (174.2)	a) 39.34 (999) b) 33.37 (848) c) 24.46 (621)	Aerobatic engine, with fuel injection. Variants are D4A5, D4B5 and D4C5, of lighter weights.
O-540-E (6-cyl, horizontally opposed piston with direct drive)	260 hp (194 kW)		a) 2,700 b) 8.5:1	b) 100/100 LL	375 (170)	a) 37.22 (945) b) 33.37 (848) c) 24.56 (624)	Recommended TBO 2,000 hours maximum.
(L)TIO-540-F (6-cyl, horizontally opposed, turbocharged piston with fuel injection and direct drive)	325 hp (242.4 kW)		a) 2,525 b) 7.3:1	b) 100/100 LL	514 (233.1)	a) 51.34 (1,304) b) 34.25 (870) c) 22.42 (569)	Turbocharged and fuel injected. Left hand rotation crankshaft.
O-540-F1B5 (6-cyl, 4-stroke, horizontally opposed piston, with direct drive)	260 hp (194 kW)		a) 2,800 b) 8.5:1	b) 100/100 LL	369 (167.4)	a) 37.22 (945) b) 33.37 (848) c) 24.56 (624)	Helicopter engine. Recommended TBO 2,000 hours maximum.
O-540-J (6-cyl, horizontally opposed piston with direct drive)	235 hp (175.2 kW)		a) 2,400 b) 8.5:1	b) 100/100 LL	356 (161.5)	a) 38.93 (989) b) 33.37 (848) c) 24.56 (624)	Recommended TBO 2,000 hours maximum.
(L)TIO-540-J (6-cyl, horizontally opposed, turbocharged piston with fuel injection and direct drive)	350 hp (261 kW)		a) 2,525 b) 7.3:1	b) 100/100 LL	518 (235)	a) 51.5 (1,308) b) 34.25 (870) c) 22.56 (573)	Turbocharged and fuel injected. Left hand rotation crankshaft.
IO-540-K (6-cyl, horizontally opposed piston with fuel injection and direct drive)	300 hp (224 kW)		a) 2,700 b) 8.7:1	b) 100/100 LL	438 (198.7)	a) 38.93 (989) b) 34.25 (870) c) 19.6 (498)	Fuel injected.
O-540-L (6-cyl, horizontally opposed piston with direct drive)	235 hp (175.2 kW)		a) 2,400 b) 8.5:1	b) 100/100 LL	369 (167.4)	a) 38.93 (989) b) 33.37 (848) c) 20.43 (519)	Recommended TBO 2,000 hours maximum.
AEIO-540-L (6-cyl, horizontally opposed piston with fuel injection and direct drive)	300 hp (224 kW)		a) 2,700 b) 8.7:1	b) 100/100 LL	445 (201.8)	a) 38.93 (989) b) 34.25 (870) c) 24.46 (621)	Aerobatic engine, with fuel injection. Variant is L1B5 of 356 lb (161.5 kg) weight.
IO-540-S (6-cyl, horizontally opposed piston with fuel injection and direct drive)	300 hp (224 kW)		a) 2,700 b) 8.7:1	b) 100/100 LL	444 (201.4)	a) 39.24 (997) b) 34.25 (870) c) 19.6 (498)	Fuel injected.
TIO-540-S (6-cyl, horizontally opposed, turbocharged piston with fuel injection and direct drive)	300 hp (224 kW)		a) 2,700 b) 7.3:1	b) 100/100 LL	502 (227.7)	a) 39.56 (1,005) b) 36.02 (915) c) 26.28 (667.5)	Turbocharged and fuel injected.
IO-540-T4B5 (6-cyl, horizontally opposed piston with fuel injection and direct drive)	260 hp (194 kW)		a) 2,700 b) 8.5:1	b) 100/100 LL	412 (186.9)	a) 38.93 (989) b) 33.37 (848) c) 21.5 (546)	Fuel injected.
(L)TIO-540-U (6-cyl, horizontally opposed, turbocharged piston with fuel injection and direct drive)	350 hp (261 kW)		a) 2,500 b) 7.3:1	b) 100/100 LL	547 (248.1)	a) 47.4 (1,204) b) 34.25 (870) c) 22.59 (574)	Turbocharged and fuel injected. Left hand rotation crankshaft.
IO-540-W1A5 (6-cyl, horizontally opposed piston with fuel injection and direct drive)	235 hp (175.2 kW)		a) 2,400 b) 8.5:1	b) 100/100 LL	400 (181.4)	a) 38.93 (989) b) 33.37 (848) c) 19.35 (491.5)	Fuel injected.
IO-580-A1A (6-cyl, horizontally opposed piston with fuel injection and direct drive)	300 hp (224 kW)		a) 2,500 b) 7.0:1		244 (110.7)	a) 29.56 (751) b) 32.24 (819) c) 22.99 (584)	Fuel injected. Recommended TBO 2,000 hours maximum. Right and left rotation and intercooling available.

Designation (type of engine)	Power output (normally take-off rating for piston, turboprop and turboshaft, unless stated)	Specific fuel consumption (S F C)	a) Max RPM b) Pressure or Compression ratio	a) EGT (unless stated to be MGT, TET, TGT or TIT) b) Primary fuel type or Octane rating	Dry weight lb (kg)	a) Length ins (mm) b) Width ins (mm) c) Height ins (mm)	Current aircraft users, and comments
United States of America							
Textron Lycoming Williamsport Division. (continued)							
TIO-580-A1A (6-cyl, horizontally opposed, turbocharged piston with fuel injection and direct drive)	310 hp (231.2 kW)		a) 2,500 b) 7.0:1		258 (117)	a) 29.05 (738) b) 32.24 (819) c) 23.18 (589)	Turbocharged and fuel injected.
IO-720-A, B and D (8-cyl, horizontally opposed piston with fuel injection and direct drive)	375/400 hp (280/298 kW)		a) 2,500/2,650 b) 8.7:1	b) 100/100 LL	568 (257.6)	a) 46.08 (1,170) b) 34.25 (870) c) 22.53 (572)	Fuel injected. Recommended TBO 1,800 hours maximum.
Thermo-Jet Standard Inc. PO Box 55976, Houston, TX 77055 – see 1996-97 *WA&SD*, page 607							
U.S. Air Power Inc.							
H1300 (helicopter piston engine)	165 hp (123 kW)						Revolution Voyager 500.
Williams International. 2280 West Maple Road, PO Box 200, Walled Lake, MI 48390-0200 (Telephone: +1 810 624 5200, Facsimile: +1 810 669 3790) – see also Williams-Rolls Inc							
FJX-1 and FJX-2 (turbofans)	550-700 lbf (2.45-3.11 kN) for FJX-1, and 700-950 lbf (3.11-4.23 kN) for FJX-2						CMC Leopard and Williams V-Jet II. FJX-1 is low-bypass ratio type, FJX-2 is high-bypass ratio type.
F112 (turbofan)	700 lbf (3.1 kN)						Boeing X-36.
Multi-national							
SMR95 (South Africa/Russia) – see Klimov RD-33							
Joint Stock Company "Aviadvigatel", Pratt & Whitney and MTU.							
PS-90P and PS-95 (twin-shaft turbofans with fan reverser) Details for PS-90P	38,830 lbf (172.6 kN) take-off, to +30° C, 7,716 lbf (34.32 kN) cruise at 11,000 m altitude and Mach 0.8	0.574 lb/lbf/hr (16.26 g/kNs) cruise	a) 12,400 b) 38.8:1	a) 1,354° C b) IS-1, RT	6,504 (2,950)	a) 195.43 (4,964) b) 75.59 (1,920)	Suited to the Il-76, Il-96M, Tu-204, Tu-234 and Tu-330. New PS-95 under consideration for Il-96-300.
BMW Rolls-Royce GmbH. Hohemarkstrasse 60-70, D-61440 Oberursel, Germany (Telephone: +49 61 71 90 66 96, Facsimile: +49 61 71 90 77 88, E-mail: Caroline.Harris@brr.de for International Communications, Web site: www.netmbx.de/brr/welcome/html)							
BR700-TP (twin-shaft turboprop)	9,000-12,000 shp (6,711-8,948 kW)						Proposed for Future Large Aircraft (FLA). Uses BR710 core.
BR710-48 (twin-shaft turbofan)	14,000-17,000 lbf (62.28-75.62 kN); 14,750 lbf (65.61 kN) flat rated at ISA +20° C for Gulfstream V, 14,750 lbf (65.61 kN) flat rated to ISA +20° C for Bombardier Global Express, and 15,500 lbf (68.95 kN) flat rated to ISA +10° C for Nimrod 2000	0.65 lb/lbf/hr (18.41 g/kNs) cruise	b) 24:1		3,520 (1,597) dressed engine	a) 134 (3,409) b) 51.6 (1,312) c) 62 (1,572) dressed engine	First engine run September 1994. First flight November 1995. Gulfstream V and Global Express engines fully certified since April 1997, with JAA certification August 1996, FAA September 1996 and TCA April 1997. Entry into service for Gulfstream V July 1997, Global Express 1998 and Nimrod December 2001 (selected for Nimrod 25 July 1996). Tu-334-120 and Tu-414.
BR715-58 (twin-shaft turbofan) See Comments for BR715-55	17,000-23,000 lbf (75.62-102.31 kN) growth potential; 18,500-22,000 lbf (82.29-97.86 kN) flat rated to ISA +10° C for Boeing 717	0.61 lb/lbf/hr (17.28 g/kNs)	b) 30-35:1		4,545 (2,062) dressed engine	a) 142 (3,599) b) 62.2 (1,580) c) 72.2 (1,833) dressed engine	First engine run April 1997, with certification 1998 and service entry June 1999. Further installation variants of BR715 proposed for future short-haul aircraft projects; BR715-55 for Tu-334-120D/220. Possibly for AE31X, N2130 and alternative engine for Be-200. Boeing 717.
CFM International SA. 2 Blvd du Général Martial Valin, F-75015 Paris, France (Telephone: +33 1 40 60 81 90, Facsimile: +33 1 40 60 81 47); CFM International Inc. 111 Merchant Street, Cincinnati, OH 45215 (PO Box 15514), USA (Telephone: +1 513 552 3300, Facsimile: +1 513 552 3306)							
CFM56-2 series (twin-shaft turbofan)	22,000 lbf (97.86 kN) take-off for CFM56-2B/-2C1/-2C3/-2C5/-2C6, 24,000 lbf (106.76 kN) take-off for CFM56-2A. 5,760 lbf (25.62 kN) maximum cruise (installed) for CFM56-2A, 4,970 lbf (22.11 kN) for CFM56-2B, and 4,980 lbf (22.15 kN) for CFM56-2C series	0.651-0.661 lb/lbf/hr (18.44-18.72 g/kNs) engine installed, cruise, at 35,000 ft, ISA, Mach 0.8	a) 5,280 fan, 15,183 core b) 30.5:1 to 31.8:1 (-2A) overall pressure ratio at maximum climb thrust	a) 905° C for -2B and -2C series, 930° C for -2A, EGT	4,820 (2,186) for CFM56-2A, 4,671 (2,119) for -2B, 4,635 (2,102) for CFM56-2C1/C3/C5/C6	a) 95.7 (2,430) b) 68.3 (1,735) fan	CFM56-2C series powers DC-8 Super 71, 72 and 73 with a dispatch reliability of 99.95%. First high bypass engine in the 10-tonne class, certified in November 1979 and introduced into commercial service in April 1982. Single-stage HP turbine, same technology applied to all CFM56 engines. Current engine-caused shop visit rate (-2C series) of 0.136 (yearly rolling average). CFM56-2A and -2B power strategic military aircraft: KC-135R (USA), C-135FR (FAF), KE-3A (export), AWACS E-3 (export, RAF & FAF), RC-135R (USAF) and E-6 (US Navy); US military designation F108. 100% dispatch reliability for the CFM56-2A at time of writing. Some 477 military aircraft in service (selected by USAF for RC-135 re-engining programme April 1997).

Designation (type of engine)	Power output (normally take-off rating for piston, turboprop and turboshaft, unless stated)	Specific fuel consumption (S F C)	a) Max RPM b) Pressure or Compression ratio	a) EGT (unless stated to be MGT, TET, TGT or TIT) b) Primary fuel type or Octane rating	Dry weight lb (kg)	a) Length ins (mm) b) Width ins (mm) c) Height ins (mm)	Current aircraft users, and comments
Multi-national							
CFM International SA. (continued)							
CFM56-3B series (twin-shaft turbofan)	18,500-22,000 lbf (82.29-97.86 kN) take-off, flat rated to 30° C. 4,650 lbf (20.68 kN) maximum cruise (installed) for CFM56-3B1, 5,040 lbf (22.42 kN) for CFM56-3B2	0.655 lb/lbf/hr (18.55 g/kNs) engine installed, cruise, at 35,000 ft, ISA, Mach 0.8	a) 5,490 fan, 15,183 core b) 27.5:1 to 28.8:1 overall pressure ratio at maximum climb thrust	a) 930° C	4,276 (1,940) for -3B1, 4,301 (1,951) for -3B-22B	a) 93 (2,362) b) 60 (1,524) fan	Powers the second generation Boeing 737-300, -400 and -500. Entered service in December 1984. Common core and low pressure turbine (LPT) with CFM56-2 models. First run life averaging 14,000 hours and 10,000 cycles, with 99.97% dispatch reliability. Engine-caused shop visit rate 0.070 (yearly rolling average). CFM56-3s have set new industry standard for reliability; 20,000 cycles (first engine run) achieved with Braathens Airlines by 1997 (Norway) as a world record. One engine close to 30,000 hours without shop visit at time of writing, with Germania Flug. -3s also on some E-3 AWACS.
CFM56-3C1 (twin-shaft turbofan)	18,500-23,500 lbf (82.29-104.54 kN) take-off, flat rated to 30° C, 5,370 lbf (23.89 kN) maximum cruise (installed)	0.655 lb/lbf/hr (18.55 g/kNs) cruise (engine installed)	a) 5,490 fan, 15,183 core b) 30.6:1 overall pressure ratio at maximum climb	a) 930° C	4,301 (1,951)	a) 93 (2,362) b) 60 (1,524) fan	Current version offered for all 737-300, -400 and -500 models. For all CFM56-3 versions, 1,953 aircraft serving with more than 150 customers used these engines at time of writing, expected to log 100 million flight hours by 1999. Offered for Tu-230.
CFM56-5A series (twin-shaft turbofan)	25,000 lbf (111.21 kN) take-off, flat rated to 30° C for CFM56-5A1; 26,500 lbf (117.88 kN) T-O/30° C for CFM56-5A3; 22,000 lbf (97.86 kN) take-off, flat rated to 45° C for CFM56-5A4; and 23,500 lbf (104.54 kN) take-off, flat rated to 37.2° C for CFM56-5A5. 5,000 lbf (22.24 kN) maximum cruise (installed) for -5A1 and -5A3, and 4,355 lbf (19.37 kN) for -5A5	0.596 lb/lbf/hr (16.88 g/kNs) cruise (engine installed)	a) 5,280 fan, 15,183 core b) 31.3:1 overall pressure ratio at maximum climb thrust	a) 890° C to 915° C for -5A1, -5A4 and -5A5. 915° C for -5A3	4,995 (2,266)	a) 95.4 (2,423) b) 68.3 (1,735) fan	Powers the Airbus A319, A320 and A340-8000. First ETOPS on A320, certified in August 1987. First use of a Full Authority Digital electronic Engine Control (FADEC) on CFM56 engines. Entered service in April 1988. Some 360 aircraft in service worldwide have logged 10 million flight hours. 20 million are planned by year 2000. CFM56-5A series show a reliability level on the trend of the CFM56-3 fleet. Engine-caused shop visit rate is of 0.073 (yearly rolling average).
CFM56-5B series (twin-shaft turbofan)	30,000 lbf (133.45 kN) for CFM56-5B1 take-off, flat rated to 30° C; 31,000 lbf (137.9 kN) T-O/30° C for CFM56-5B2; 33,000 lbf (146.79 kN) T-O/30° C for CFM56-5B3 (equivalent thrust at Mach 0,25); 27,000 lbf (120.1 kN) take-off, flat rated to 43.9° C for CFM56-5B4; 22,000 lbf (97.86 kN) take-off, flat rated to 45° C for CFM56-5B5; and 23,500 lbf (104.54 kN) T-O/45° C for CFM56-5B6. 5,480 lbf (24.38 kN) maximum cruise (installed) for -5B4, -5B5 and -5B6, 5,840 lbf (25.98 kN) maximum cruise (installed) for -5B1, -5B2 and -5B3.	0.596 lb/lbf/hr (16.88 g/kNs) cruise (engine installed)	a) 5,200 fan, 15,183 core b) 34.4:1 for -5B1, -5B2 and -5B3; 32.6:1 for -5B4, -5B5 and -5B6.	a) 950° C	5,250 (2,381)	a) 102.4 (2,601) b) 68.3 (1,735) fan	The CFM56-5B powers all the A320 family (A319, A320 and A321). First use of a low emissions combustor (DAC: Dual Annular Combustor) in commercial service to reduce oxides of nitrogen by more than 40% vs conventional CFM56 combustor. 450,000 flight hours logged at time of writing, with zero in-flight shut down. 3D-Aero technology incorporated* throughout the last CFM56-5B models, providing the CFM56-5B/P with much improved fan efficiency and an SFC improvement of 3%. The improved CFM-56B/P serves as the core for the CFM56-7 and CFM56-9. *Optimized high pressure compressor, high and low pressure turbines.

Designation (type of engine)	Power output (normally take-off rating for piston, turboprop and turboshaft, unless stated)	Specific fuel consumption (S F C)	a) Max RPM b) Pressure or Compression ratio	a) EGT (unless stated to be MGT, TET, TGT or TIT) b) Primary fuel type or Octane rating	Dry weight lb (kg)	a) Length ins (mm) b) Width ins (mm) c) Height ins (mm)	Current aircraft users, and comments
Multi-national							
CFM International SA. (continued)							
CFM56-5C series (twin-shaft turbofan)	31,200 lbf (138.79 kN) for CFM56-5C2; 32,500 lbf (144.57 kN) for CFM56-5C3; and 34,000 lbf (151.24 kN) for CFM56-5C4, all take-off and flat rated to 30° C. 6,910 lbf (30.74 kN) maximum cruise (installed) for -5C2 and -5C3, 7,416 lbf (32.99 kN) for -5C4	0.567 lb/lbf/hr (16.06 g/kNs) (engine installed)	a) 4,800 fan for -5C2 and -5C3, 4,985 for -5C4. 15,183 core b) 38.3:1 for -5C2 and -5C3, 39.2:1 for -5C4	a) 950° C to 975° C	8,796 (3,990) propulsion system with fluids	a) 103 (2,616) b) 72.3 (1,836) fan	Powers the long-range Airbus A340. Lowest SFC of the CFM56 family and quietest engine in its class, featuring a long duct mixed flow nacelle (to optimize long-range performance and noise). 3D-Aero design on fan and booster offer better efficiency. Optional take-off thrust bump enhances A340 take-off performance. Long engine life capability. A340-300 powered by CFM56-5C4. 4 million flight hours logged since entry into service at time of writing. CFM56-5C4s proposed for An-70T-300 and -400.
CFM56-7 series (twin-shaft turbofan)	19,500 lbf (86.74 kN) for CFM56-7B18; 20,600 lbf (91.63 kN) for CFM56-7B20; 22,700 lbf (100.98 kN) for CFM56-7B22; 24,200 lbf (107.65 kN) for CFM56-7B24; 26,300 lbf (116.99 kN) for CFM56-7B26; and 27,300 lbf (121.44 kN) for CFM56-7B27, all take-off and flat rated to 30° C. 5,420 lbf (24.11 kN) maximum cruise thrust (engine installed) for -7B18, 5,450 lbf (24.24 kN) for -7B20 and -7B22, 5,480 lbf (24.38 kN) for -7B24 and -7B26, and 5,500 lbf (24.47 kN) for -7B27	8% SFC improvement vs CFM56-3 (5% improvement on fuel burn on typical mission vs CFM56-3)	a) 5,380 fan, 15,183 core b) 32.8:1 overall pressure ratio at maximum climb thrust	a) Improved EGT margins for all next-generation 737 models (over 50° C vs CFM56-3C1 at 23,500 lbf)	5,205 (2,361)	a) 103.1 (2,619) b) 61 (1,549) fan	Powers the Next-generation 737-600/-700 and -800. A common engine for 3 A/C application. New solid wide-chord fan blades for higher thrust (vs -3 model) and greater durability. Retains the CFM-56B/P core. 3D-Aero throughout the engine. More EGT margin for longer on wing life. DAC (Dual Annular Combustor) as an option – emissions below current and proposed ICAO standards. Optimized procedure maintenance to significantly reduce operating costs; engine replacement within one shift time. Certified in December 1996; first 737-700 flight in February 1997; Boeing 737-700 certification and service entry 1997, followed by 737-800 and 737-600 in 1998. CFM56-7B27 also offered for the 737-900 and Business Jet.
CFM56-9 (twin-shaft turbofan)	18,000-22,000 lbf (80.07-97.86 kN) take-off, flat rated to 30° C. 4,960 lbf (22.06 kN) maximum cruise thrust (engine installed) for 22,000 lbf model	0.38 lb/lbf/hr (10.76 g/kNs)	a) 6,055 fan, 15,183 core b) 24.1:1 to 28:1 overall pressure ratio at maximum climb thrust	a) 900° C	4,252 (1,929)	a) 91.7 (2,329) b) 56 (1,422) fan tip diameter	Design work underway, allowing certification within 3 years of launch of the proposed AE316/317. Shares common core with CFM56-7 and improved performance CFM56-5B/P. Solid titanium wide-chord fan. Fan/booster/compressor stages 1/2/9. HPT/LPT 1/3. Bypass ratio 5.1. Air flow above 591 lb (268 kg) per second. Separate flow with a cascade thrust reverser system. Designed for cost efficient balance of technology and reliability. Possibly for N2130.
Eurojet Turbo GmbH. Inselkammerstrasse 5, D-82008 Unterhaching, Germany (Telephone: +49 89 666 92 0, Facsimile: +49 89 666 92 139 or 162)							
EJ200 (two-spool turbofan)	13,500 lbf (60 kN) dry, 20,250 lbf (90 kN) with afterburning, rising to 23,000 lbf (102.31 kN)	0.74-0.81 lb/lbf/hr (20.96-22.94 g/kNs) dry, 1.66-1.73 lb/lbf/hr (47-49 g/kNs) with afterburning	b) 26:1	a) about 1,527° C	2,180-2,280 (989-1,034)	a) 157 (3,988) b) 29 (737) inlet	Eurofighter (RAF Typhoon), AT-2000 and possibly CASA ATX. Company is a consortium of Rolls-Royce (UK), MTU (Germany), FiatAvio (Italy), and ITP (Spain). First EJ200 flown 1994. Completion of Initial Certification Testing 1998. Anticipated November 1999 certification. Production deliveries 2000. Has 3 fan (LP) and 5 HP compressor stages, powered by 2 single-stage turbines (LP and HP). Annular combustor with airspray injectors. Reheat system has convergent/divergent nozzle and engine control is by FADEC.
IAE – International Aero Engines AG. 400 Main Street, M/S 121-10, East Hartford, CT 06108, USA (Telephone: +1 860 565 1773, Facsimile: +1 860 565 0600, E-mail: ushsdsbd@ibmmail.com, Web site: http://www.v2500.com)							
V2500-A1 (twin-shaft turbofan)	25,000 lbf (111.21 kN)	0.581 lb/lbf/hr (16.46 g/kNs)	b) 29.4:1		5,074 (2,302)	a) 126 (3,200) b) 63 (1,600) fan	A320-231. IAE is a collaborative venture of Rolls-Royce, MTU, Pratt & Whitney and JAEC. Dispatch reliability 99.92%.
V2522-A5 (twin-shaft turbofan)	22,000 lbf (97.86 kN)	0.575 lb/lbf/hr (16.29 g/kNs) cruise	b) 25.4:1		5,139 (2,331)	a) 126 (3,200) b) 63.5 (1,613) fan	A319-131. Dispatch reliability 99.95%.
V2524-A5 (twin-shaft turbofan)	24,000 lbf (106.76 kN), flat rated to 55° C	0.547 lb/lbf/hr (16.26 g/kNs)	b) 27.1:1		5,139 (2,331)	a) 126 (3,200) b) 63.5 (1,613) fan	A319-132. Dispatch reliability 99.95%.
V2525-D5 (twin-shaft turbofan)	25,000 lbf (111.21 kN), flat rated to 30° C	0.574 lb/lbf/hr (16.287 g/kNs) cruise	b) 27.7:1		5,252 (2,382)	a) 126 (3,200) b) 63.5 (1,613) fan	MD-90-30; B717? Dispatch reliability 99.88%.

Designation (type of engine)	Power output (normally take-off rating for piston, turboprop and turboshaft, unless stated)	Specific fuel consumption (S F C)	a) Max RPM b) Pressure or Compression ratio	a) EGT (unless stated to be MGT, TET, TGT or TIT) b) Primary fuel type or Octane rating	Dry weight lb (kg)	a) Length ins (mm) b) Width ins (mm) c) Height ins (mm)	Current aircraft users, and comments
Multi-national							
IAE – International Aero Engines AG. (continued)							
V2527-A5 (twin-shaft turbofan)	26,500 lbf (117.88 kN), flat rated to 46° C	0.574 lb/lbf/hr (16.287 g/kNs)	b) 27.7:1		5,139 (2,331)	a) 126 (3,200) b) 63.5 (1,613) fan	A320-200. Dispatch reliability 99.95%.
V2528-D5 (twin-shaft turbofan)	28,000 lbf (124.55 kN), flat rated at 30° C	0.574 lb/lbf/hr (16.287 g/kNs)	b) 30.4:1		5,252 (2,382)	a) 126 (3,200) b) 63.5 (1,613) fan	MD-90-55. Dispatch reliability 99.88%.
V2530-A5 (twin-shaft turbofan)	31,400 lbf (139.68 kN), flat rated 30° C	0.574 lb/lbf/hr (16.287 g/kNs)	b) 31.4:1		5,139 (2,331)	a) 126 (3,200) b) 63.5 (1,613) fan	A321-131. Dispatch reliability 99.95%.
V2533-A5 (twin-shaft turbofan)	33,000 lbf (146.79 kN)				5,139 (2,331)	a) 126 (3,200) b) 63.5 (1,613) fan	A321-231 growth derivative. Dispatch reliability 99.95%.
ITEC (International Turbine Engine Corporation) -Joint venture by AlliedSignal (which see) and AIDC/Han Hsiang of Taiwan							
MTFE – Mid Thrust Family Engine – joint venture by MTU of Germany and Pratt & Whitney of USA (which see)							
MTFE (twin-shaft turbofan)	20,000 lbf (88.97 kN) approximately		b) 27:1		3,900 (1,769)	a) 99 (2,515) b) 55 (1,397) fan	6-stage compressor, single-stage HP and 3-stage LP turbines, and annular combustor. FADEC.
MTR – MTU Turbomeca Rolls-Royce GmbH. Inselkammerstrasse 5, D-82008 Unterhaching, Germany (Telephone: +49 89 61 44 94-0, Facsimile: +49 89 614 95 26)							
MTR 390 (free-turbine turboshaft)	1,285-1,556 shp (958-1,160 kW), 1,170 shp (872.5 kW) max continuous	0.46 lb/shp/hr (280 g/kW/hr)	a) 27,000 direct drive output, 8,000 with reduction gearbox b) 14:1		372.6 (169)	a) 42.44 (1,078) b) 29.1 (739) envelope diameter c) 26.85 (682)	Eurocopter Tiger, HAP and Panther. Developed for helicopters in 5-7 tonne weight class (MTOW). Received military certification in May 1996 and civil certification in June 1997. MTR started preparation phase for production in 1997/98, with launch customers France and Germany. Service entry 2001. Twin centrifugal compressor driven by a single-stage gas generator turbine. Reverse flow annular combustor and 2-stage power turbine drives output shaft. Direct or reduction gearbox drive. FADEC controlled.
Rolls-Royce Turbomeca Ltd. 4-5 Grosvenor Place, London SW1X 7HH, England (Telephone: +44 171 235 3641, Facsimile: +44 171 245 6385)							
Adour 102 (twin-shaft turbofan)	5,240 lbf (23.31 kN) dry, 7,305 lbf (32.5 kN) with afterburning	0.74 lb/lbf/hr (20.96 g/kNs)			1,552 (704)	a) 117 (2,970) b) 30 (762) c) 41 (1,041)	Jaguar (French, UK). 2-stage LP and 5-stage HP compressor, driven by 2 single-stage turbines (LP and HP), and an annular combustor.
Adour 104 (twin-shaft turbofan) See Comments for Adour 106	5,270 lbf (23.44 kN) dry, 7,900 lbf (35.14 kN) with afterburning*				1,572 (713)	a) 117 (2,970) b) 30 (762) c) 41 (1,041)	Jaguar (UK). *Turbine gas temperature modification can increase power to 5,350 lbf (23.8 kN), 8,249 lbf (36.69 kN) with afterburning as Adour 106.
Adour 151 (twin-shaft turbofan without afterburning)	5,240 lbf (23.31 kN)		b) 11.0:1		1,220 (533.4)	a) 77 (1,956) b) 30 (762) c) 41 (1,041)	BAe Hawk T.Mk 1/1A.
Adour 801A (twin-shaft turbofan with afterburning)	7,305 lbf (32.5 kN) with afterburning				1,552 (704)	a) 117 (2,970) b) 30 (762) c) 41 (1,041)	Built in Japan by IHI as TF40 to power Mitsubishi F-1/T-2.
Adour 804 (twin-shaft turbofan with afterburning)	8,040 lbf (35.76 kN) with afterburning				1,572 (713)	a) 117 (2,970) b) 30 (762) c) 41 (1,041)	Jaguar International (Ecuador, India and Oman).
Adour 811 (twin-shaft turbofan with afterburning)	5,620 lbf (25 kN) dry, 8,400 lbf (37.37 kN) with afterburning		b) 11.3:1		1,633 (741)	a) 117 (2,970) b) 30 (762) c) 41 (1,041)	Jaguar International (as assembled by HAL in India).
Adour 815 (twin-shaft turbofan with afterburning)	8,400 lbf (37.37 kN) with afterburning				1,627 (738)	a) 117 (2,970) b) 30 (762) c) 41 (1,041)	Jaguar International (Nigeria and Oman).
Adour 851 (twin-shaft turbofan without afterburning)	5,240 lbf (23.31 kN)				1,252 (568)	a) 77 (1,956) b) 30 (762) c) 41 (1,041)	Hawk Mk 50 (Finland, Indonesia and Kenya).
Adour 861/861A (twin-shaft turbofan without afterburning)	5,710 lbf (25.4 kN)	0.74 lb/lbf/hr (20.96 g/kNs)	b)11.3:1		1,272 (577), or 1,240 (562) basic engine weight	a) 77 (1,956) b) 30 (762) c) 41 (1,041)	Hawk Mk 60. Mk 861A has addition of fuel dip for weapons firing. Fan diameter 22.3 ins (566 mm).
Adour 871 (twin-shaft turbofan without afterburning)	5,730 lbf (25.5 kN)	078 lb/lbf/hr (22.09 g/kNs)	b) 11.3:1		1,299 (589)	a) 77 (1,956) b) 30 (762) c) 41 (1,041)	Hawk Mk 100 and Mk 200. Also PZL-Mielec M-99 Orkan. Matched to give more thrust at high speeds/low level and on hot day conditions. DS high-pressure turbine blades and single crystal low-pressure turbine blades. Growth version identified to provide 6,300 lbf (28.02 kN).
Adour 900 (twin-shaft turbofan)	5,990 lbf (26.65 kN)					a) 77 (1,956) b) 30 (762) c) 41 (1,041)	Announced in June 1997, to embody the most modern technologies. To be certified in year 2000. New HP compressor drum, long-life combustion chamber and latest single-crystal blade technology in both rotating and static aerofoils. FADEC. For Australian Hawk Mk 127s.

Designation (type of engine)	Power output (normally take-off rating for piston, turboprop and turboshaft, unless stated)	Specific fuel consumption (S F C)	a) Max RPM b) Pressure or Compression ratio	a) EGT (unless stated to be MGT, TET, TGT or TIT) b) Primary fuel type or Octane rating	Dry weight lb (kg)	a) Length ins (mm) b) Width ins (mm) c) Height ins (mm)	Current aircraft users, and comments
Multi-national							
Rolls-Royce Turbomeca Ltd. (continued)							
F405-RR-400/401 (twin-shaft turbofan without afterburning)	5,450 lbf (24.24 kN) for Mk 400, 5,845 lbf (26 kN) for Mk 401					a) 77 (1,956) b) 30 (762) c) 41 (1,041)	T-45 Goshawk production aircraft, with aircraft carrier capability. Modified Mk 871. US military designation. Goshawk prototype used F405-RR-400 (Adour 861-49) of 5,450 lbf (24.24 kN). DS high-pressure turbine blades and single crystal low-pressure turbine blades.
RTM322 (twin-shaft turboshaft)	2,100-3,000 shp (1,566-2,237 kW) take-off, 1,892 shp (1,411 kW) max continuous	0.48 lb/shp/hr (292 g/kW/hr)	b) 14.7:1		529 (240) civil	a) 46.1 (1,171) b) 23.8 (604)	EH 101, NH90, S-92, and Westland Apache. Also collaborating in programme are Rinaldo Piaggio of Italy and MTU of Germany. Lucas FADEC fitted in 1994. Civil version has max continuous SFC of 0.453 lb/shp/hr (276 g/kW/hr) and military 0.449 lb/shp/hr (273 g/kW/hr). Military dry weight is 539 lb (244 kg). Envelope diameter 25.9 ins (658 mm). 2-spool type, with 3-stage axial and close-coupled centrifugal compressor driven by a 2-stage gas generator turbine. Reverse-flow annular combustion system of large volume, with vaporisers. 2-stage power turbine drives coaxial shaft. FADEC controlled.
SPW – SNECMA and Pratt & Whitney Canada Joint Company (see France and Canada for addresses, Telephone and Facsimile numbers)							
SPW 14 (turbofan)	12,000-16,000 lbf (53.38-71.17 kN) maximum take-off				c. 3,000 (1,360.8)	a) 100 (2,540) b) 50 (1,270) diameter c) 45.1 (1,146) fan diameter	50%/50% collaboration to develop engines for 58-90 passenger regional aircraft, through joint company. FOD tolerant. Wide chord blades. 2-stage HP turbine. 3-stage LP turbine. 4 axial (1 centrifugal) HP compressor. Low pollutant emission combustor with high-altitude relight capability. Long duct mix flow nacelle, with low noise technology and high reverser efficiency. Scheduled first flight on Boeing 720. Chosen by ATR for its projected Airjet regional transports and possibly for Fairchild Dornier 728JET.
Turbo-Union Ltd. PO Box 3, Filton, Bristol BS12 7QE, England (Telephone: +44 0117 979 1234, Facsimile: +44 0117 979 7575)							
RB199 Mk 101 (three-shaft turbofan)	8,000 lbf (35.59 kN) dry, 15,500 lbf (68.95 kN) with afterburning		a) 18,000 HP shaft b) 23.1:1 approx	a) 1,327° C TET	1,980 (898)	a) 127 (3,226) b) 34.25 (870)	Initial Tornado IDS deliveries to European air forces. Entered service in 1980. RB199 is 3-spool type, with 3 LP, 3 IP and 6 HP compressor stages, powered by 3 single-stage turbines (LP, IP and HP). Annular vaporising combustion system. FADEC. Integral thrust reverser (except Mk 104E).
RB199 Mk 103 (three-shaft turbofan)	9,100 lbf (40.5 kN) dry, 16,000 lbf (71.2 kN) with afterburning	0.649 lb/lbf/hr (18.38 g/kNs)	b) 23.5:1	a) 1,327° C TET	2,103 (954) without thrust reverser	a) 126 (3,200) to nozzle exit b) 37 (940)	Tornado IDS.
RB199 Mk 104 (three-shaft turbofan)	9,100 lbf (40.5 kN) dry, 16,410 lbf (73 kN) with afterburning	0.649 lb/lbf/hr (18.38 g/kNs)	b) 23.5:1	a) 1,327° C TET	2,151 (976) without thrust reverser	a) 142 (3,607) incl longer jetpipe b) 37 (940)	Tornado ADV. Derivative Mk 104D used on BAe EAP and Mk 104E used on Eurofighter prototypes as RB199-122s. Entered service in 1985.
RB199 Mk 105 (three-shaft turbofan)	9,550 lbf (42.5 kN) dry, 16,700 lbf (74.3 kN) with afterburning	0.65 lb/lbf/hr (18.41 g/kNs)	b) 24.5:1		2,183 (990) with thrust reverser	a) 130 (3,302) b) 29.6 (752) intake	Tornado ECR. Available for the Tornado IDS.
Williams-Rolls Inc. 2280 West Maple Road, PO Box 200, Walled Lake, MI 48390-0200, USA (Telephone: +1 810 624 5200, Facsimile: +1 810 669 3790, E-mail: RSCHWEDLAND@WILLIAMS-INT.COM)							
FJ44-1 (twin-shaft turbofan)	1,900 lbf (8.45 kN) for FJ44-1A and 1D, 1,800 lbf (8 kN) for FJ44-1C. 506 lbf (2.251 kN) max cruise for -1A/1D	0.758 lb/lbf/hr (21.47 g/kNs) max cruise			447 (202.75)	a) 40.3 (1,024) b) 23.7 (602)	CitationJet and Century Jet CJ-1 for FJ44-1A, Saab Sk 60W re-engine for -1C, and FJ44-1D for Lockheed Martin Darkstar UAV. Also Phoenix Fanjet. Company is a partnership between Williams International of USA and Rolls-Royce of UK. Over 800 delivered by May 1998.
FJ44-2A (twin-shaft turbofan)	2,300 lbf (10.23 kN)						Raytheon Premier 1, Sino-Swearingen SJ30-2, Century Jet CJ-2, and Scaled Composites Proteus. Single-stage fan with integral single-stage LP axial compressor and centrifugal HP compressor, driven by a 2-stage LP and single-stage HP turbine respectively. Single annular combustion system. Certified 7 July 1997.
F129 (military version of FJ44, as above)	1,500 lbf (6.672 kN)	0.48 lb/lbf/hr (13.6 g/kNs)					Derated FJ44, used first in former Cessna 526 JPATS trainer.
See also Williams International under USA for FJX-1 and FJX-2							

↑ Bombardier-Rotax 912 4-cylinder piston engine (see page 651)

↑ Pratt & Whitney Canada PW306 series turbofan (see page 657)

↑ Walter M202 2-cylinder piston engine (see page 659)

↑ Pratt & Whitney Canada PW150A turboprop (see page 656)

↑ Xi'an WS9 turbofan (see page 658)

↑ Pratt & Whitney Canada PW206C turboshaft (see page 657)

↑ Walter M601E-11 turboprop cutaway (see page 659)

↑ SMA Morane Renault MR 180 (see page 660)

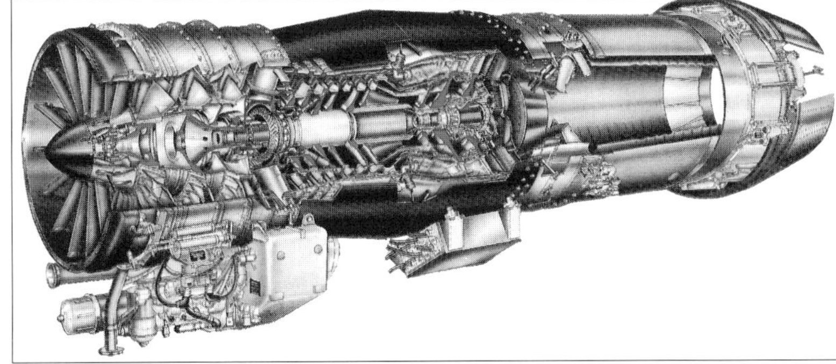
↑ SNECMA M88-2 turbofan cutaway (see page 661)

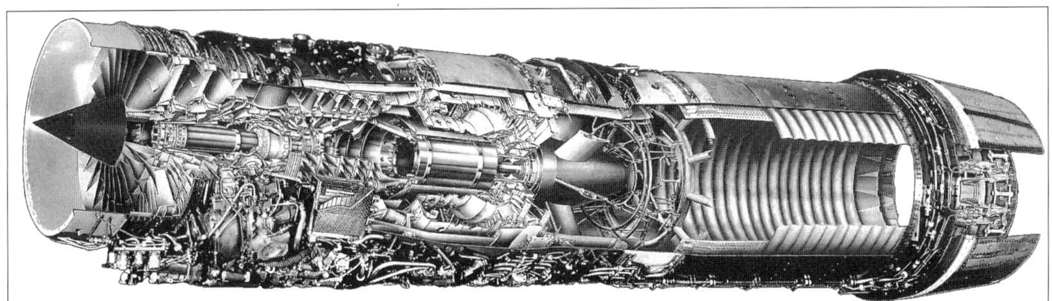
↑ SNECMA M53-P2 turbofan cutaway (see page 661)

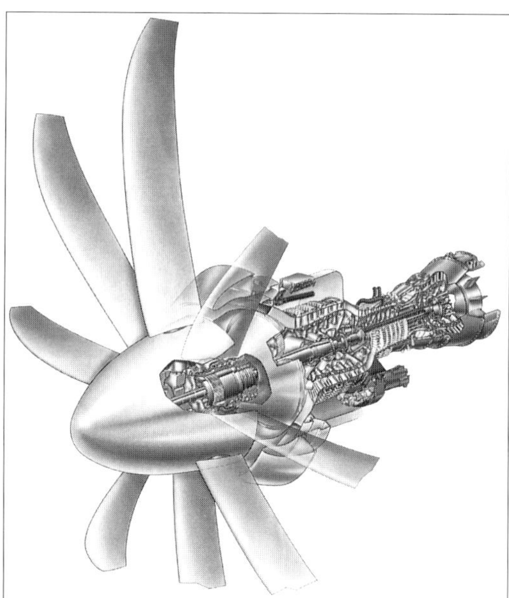

↑ SNECMA, DASA/MTU, ITP and FiatAvio M138 turbopropulsor cutaway (see page 661)

↑ Turbomeca Arrius 2F turboshaft (courtesy Photothéque Turbomeca) (see page 662)

↑ Göbler-Hirthmotoren F33 single-cylinder piston engine (see page 663)

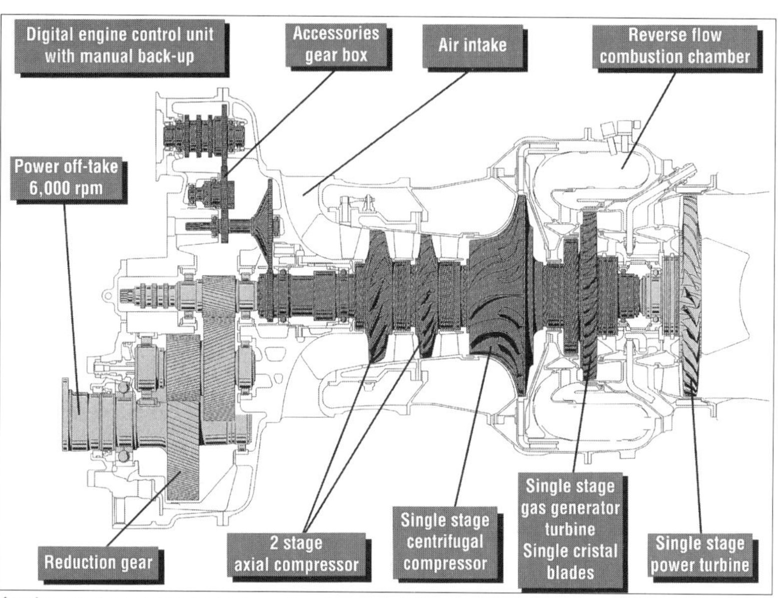

↑ Turbomeca TM 333 turboshaft cutaway (courtesy Photothéque Turbomeca) (see page 662)

↑ Groupement Turbomeca-SNECMA Larzac 04 cutaway (see page 662)

↑ König SD 570 4-cylinder piston engine (see page 663)

↑ Limbach L 2400EF 4-cylinder piston engine (see page 664)

↑ WSK 'PZL-Rzeszów' GTD-350W turboshaft (see page 666)

↑ Zoche ZO 01A 4-cylinder piston engine (see page 664)

↑ ILot – Instytut Lotnictwa D-18A turbofan (see page 666)

↑ WSK 'PZL-Rzeszów" TWD-10B turboprop (see page 666)

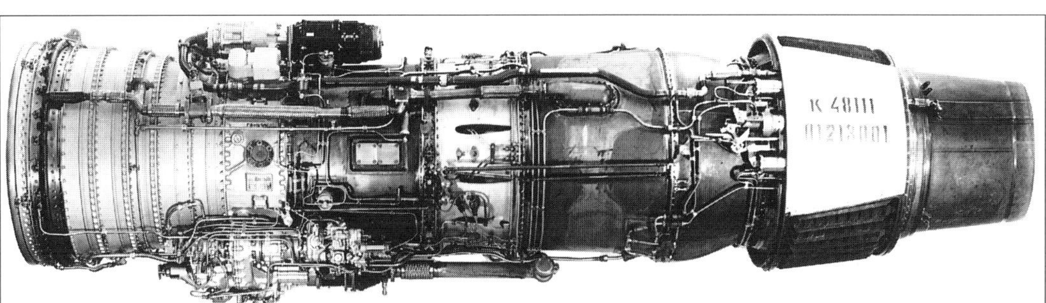
↑ JSC 'Aviadvigatel' D-30 III turboshaft (see page 669)

↑ WSK 'PZL-Rzeszów' built Franklin 4A235B4 piston engine (see page 667)

↑ Klimov RD-33 turbojet (Piotr Butowski) (see page 670)

↑ JSC 'Aviadvigatel' PS-90A turbofan (see page 669)

↑ RKBM – Rybinsk Motors JSC RD-600V turboshaft cutaway (see page 672)

↑ RKBM – Rybinsk Motors JSC D-30KU-154 II turbofan (see page 671)

↑ JSC Samara 'NK Engines' NK-22 turbofan (see page 672)

↑ RKBM – Rybinsk Motors JSC Novikov RD-38A (or K) turbojet (Piotr Butowski) (see page 671)

↑ NPO Saturn AL-31F turbofan (Piotr Butowski) (see page 673)

↑ Volvo RM12 turbofan (see page 675)

↑ Samara Machine-Building Design Bureau NK-12MV turboprop (see page 673)

↑ JSC Samara 'NK Engines' NK-86 turbofan (see page 672)

↑ Povazské Strojárne DV-2 turbofan seen from starboard side (see page 674)

↑ Ivchenko PROGRESS D-18T turbofan (see page 676)

↑ Ivchenko PROGRESS D-436T1 turbofan (see page 677)

↑ Mid-West Engines AE110/GAE110 Hawk with Flytronic fuel injection (see page 678)

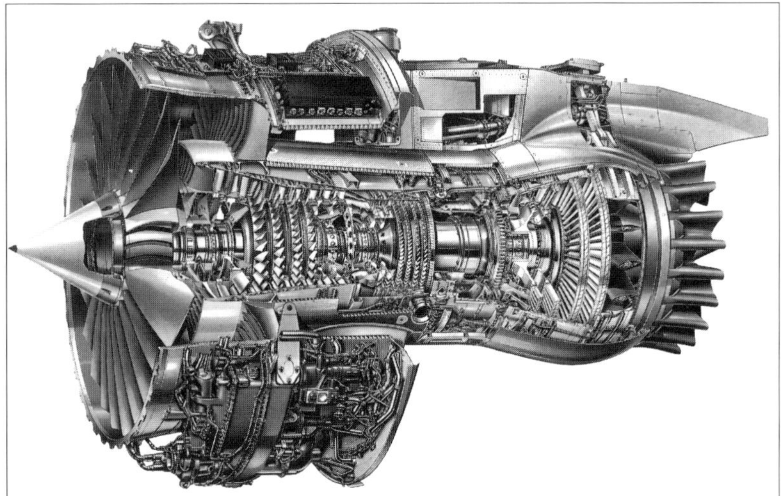

↑ Rolls-Royce RB211-524H turbofan cutaway (see page 678)

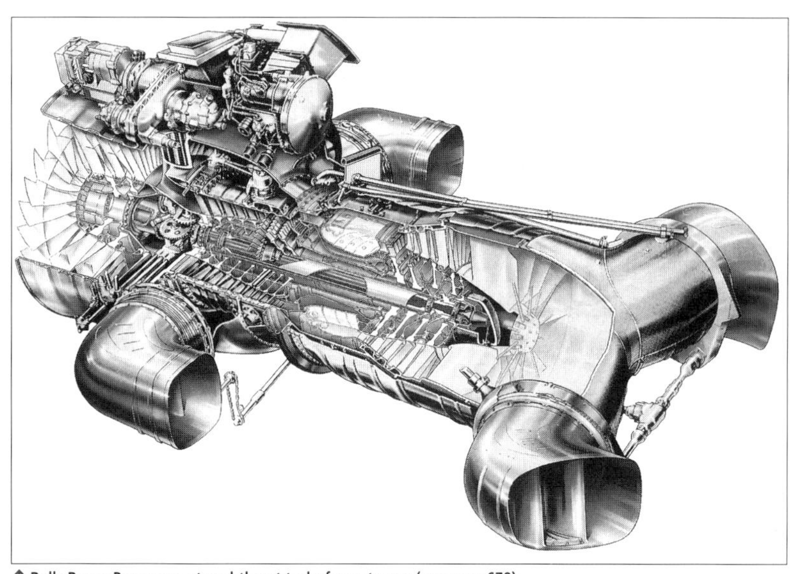

↑ Rolls-Royce Pegasus vectored-thrust turbofan cutaway (see page 679)

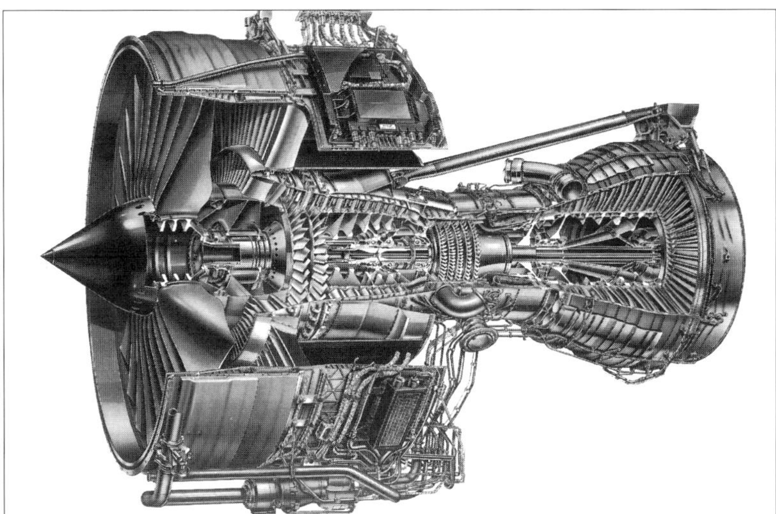

↑ Rolls-Royce Trent 800 series turbofan cutaway (see page 680)

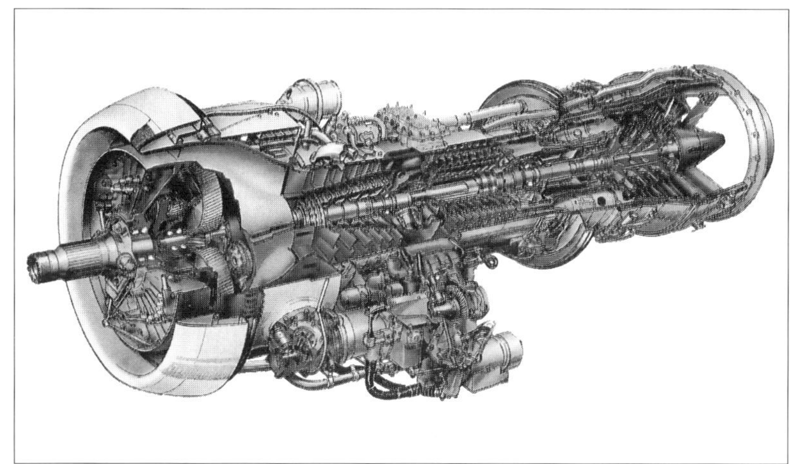

↑ Rolls-Royce Tyne RTy 20 Mk 21 turboprop cutaway (see page 680)

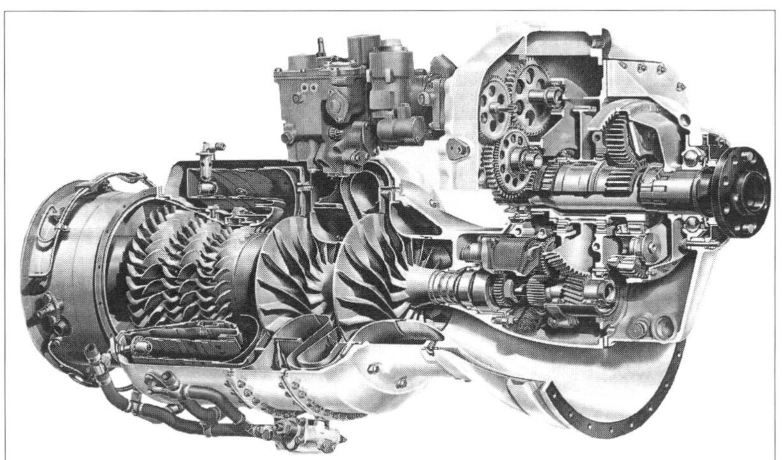

↑ AlliedSignal TPE331-5/-5A turboprop cutaway (see page 682)

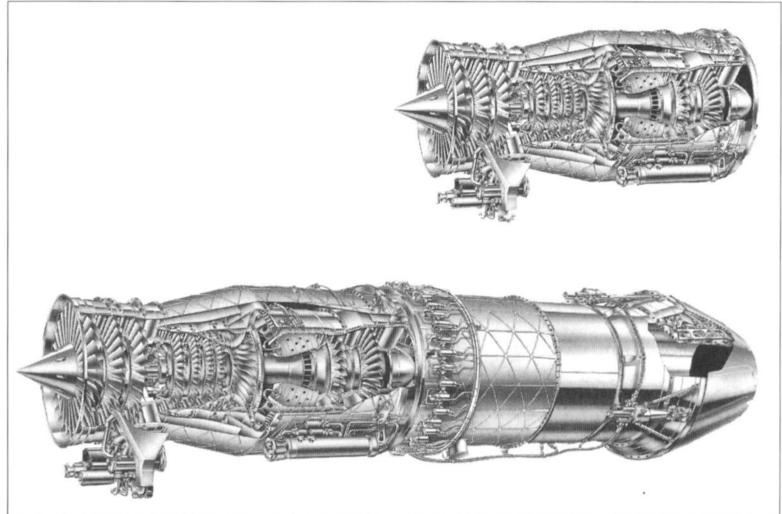

↑ AlliedSignal F124 and F125 turbofan cutaways (see page 682)

↑ LHTEC T800-LHT-801 turboshaft (see page 685)

↑ Allison AE 3007 series turbofan (see page 684)

↑ Amtec Buddy Twin piston engine (see page 685)

↑ CFE Company CFE738 turbofan (see page 685)

↑ General Electric CF34 series turbofan (see page 686)

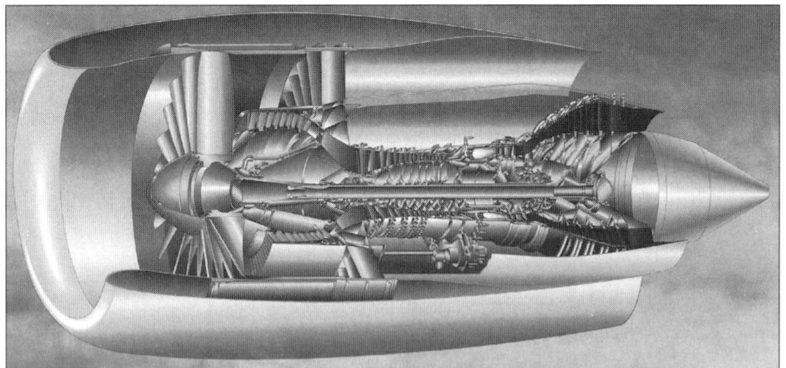

↑ GE-P&W – The Engine Alliance GP7200 series turbofan cutaway (courtesy GE-P&W) (see page 689)

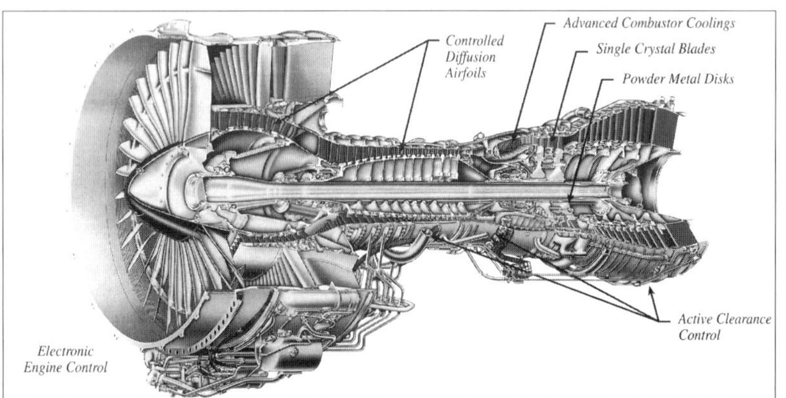

↑ Pratt & Whitney F117-PW-100 turbofan cutaway (see page 691)

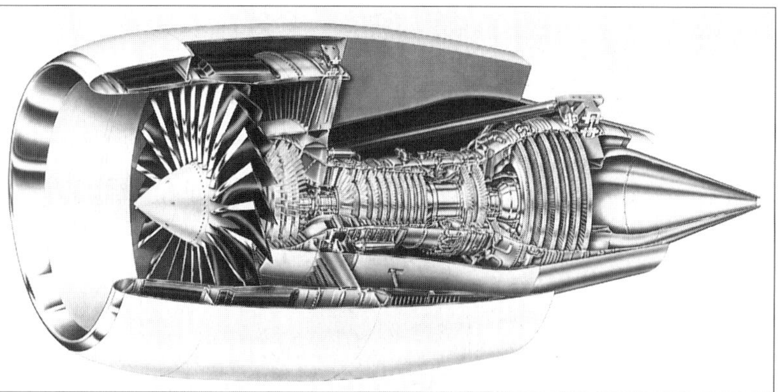

↑ General Electric GE90 turbofan cutaway (see page 685)

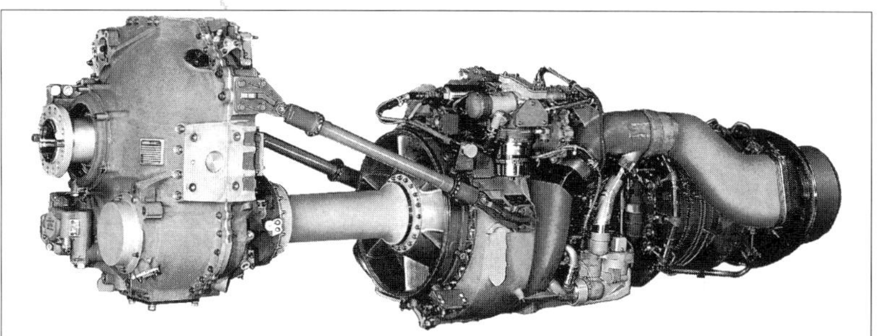

↑ General Electric CT7 series turboprop (see pages 686-687)

↑ General Electric F414 turbofan (see page 688)

↑ Pop's Props Kawasaki 340 conversion (see page 691)

↑ Pratt & Whitney PW2037 turbofan at an MTU München test facility (see page 692)

↑ Teledyne Continental IO-360-ES 6-cylinder piston engine (see page 694)

↑ Textron Lycoming 580 cubic inch series 6-cylinder engine (see pages 701-702)

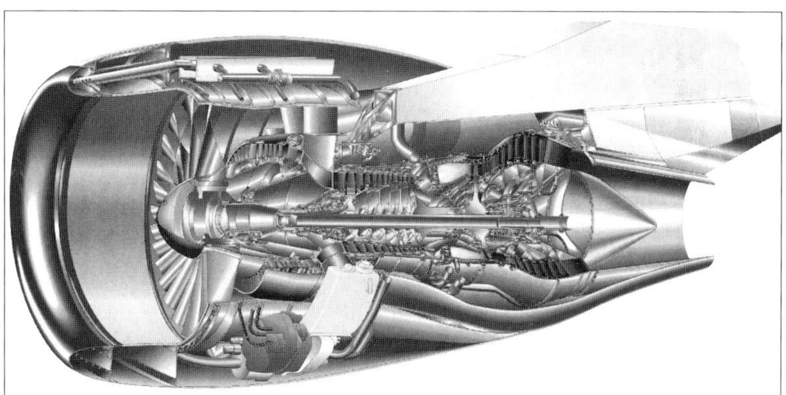
↑ Pratt & Whitney PW6000 series engine cutaway (see page 693)

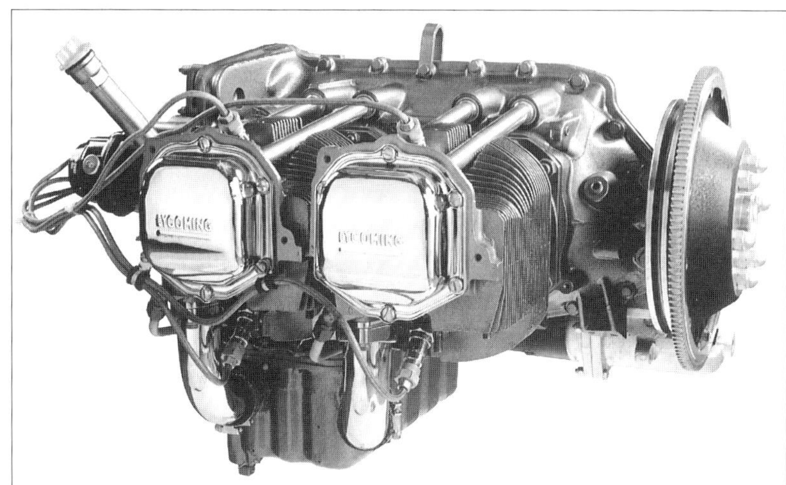
↑ Textron Lycoming 320 cubic inch series 4-cylinder engine (see pages 698-699)

↑ Textron Lycoming 720 cubic inch series 8-cylinder engine (see page 702)

↑ CFM International CFM56-7 at Seattle, prior to installation on the Boeing Next-Generation 737-700 (see page 704)

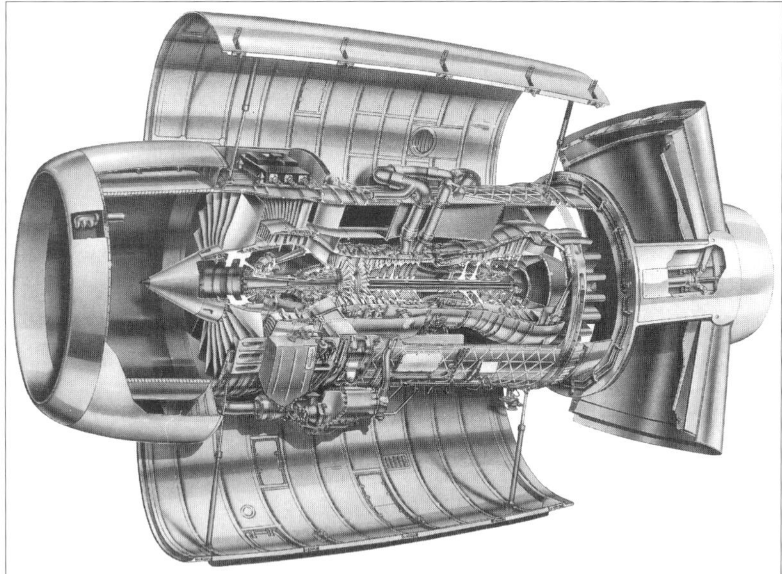

↑ BMW Rolls-Royce BR715 turbofan cutaway (see page 702)

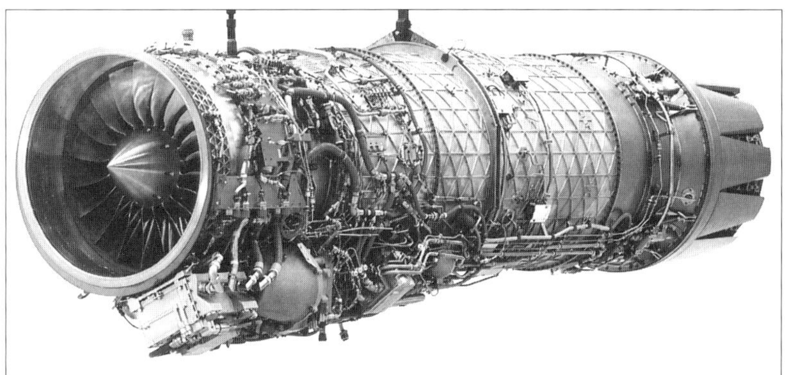

↑ Eurojet EJ200 turbofan (see page 704)

↑ MTR 390 turboshaft flight engine (see page 705)

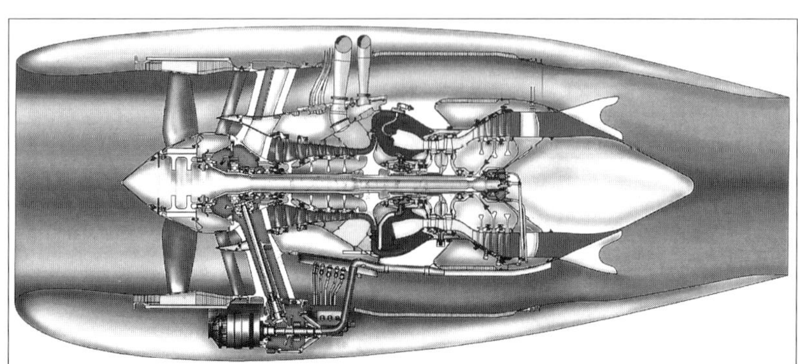

↑ SPW 14 turbofan drawing (see page 706)

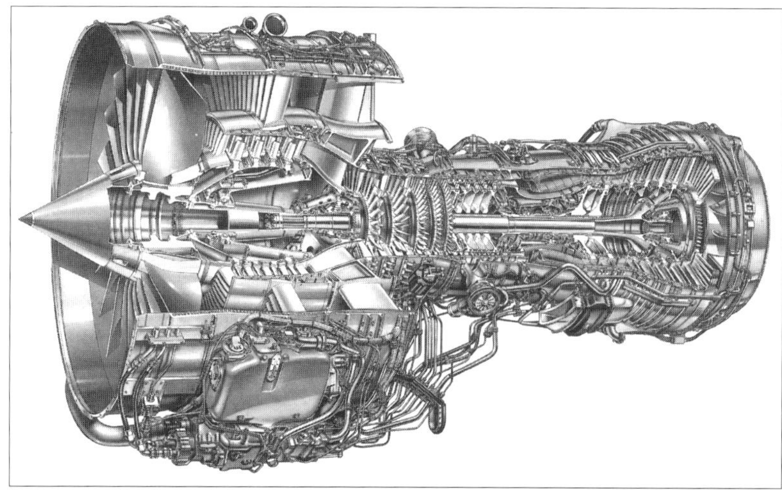

↑ IAE – International Aero Engines V2500-A5 series turbofan cutaway (see pages 704-705)

↑ Rolls-Royce Turbomeca RTM322 turboshaft for the NH90 (see page 706)

↑ Turbo-Union RB199 turbofan cutaway (see page 706)

↑ US Air Power H1300 for the Revolution Voyager-500 helicopter (see page 702)

Missiles

Missiles are listed by nation, then alphabetically by designation. Drawings are reproduced with the kind permission of Air International/Key Publishing. An asterisk (*) by a drawing indicates a missile no longer in first-line service, whereby details can be found in the 1996-97 edition of *WA&SD*.

Air-to-surface

Manufacturer	Designation	a) Length ins (m) b) Span ins (cm)	a) Diameter ins (cm) b) Weight lb (kg)	Range naut miles (km)	Speed	Control	Propulsion	Guidance	a) Warhead lb (kg) b) Fuzing	Comments and Platform(s)
Argentina										
Instituto de Investigaciones Cientificas y Tecnicas de las Fuerzas Armadas (CITEFA) Zufriategui 4380, 1603 Villa Martelli, Buenos Aires Telephone: +54 1 331 2351 Facsimile: +54 1 331 6982	Martin Pescador (MP-1000 – see platforms)	a) 115.8 (2.94) b) 28.7 (73.0)	a) 8.6 (21.9) b) 308.6 (140.0)	1.35 – 4.85 (2.5 – 9.0)	Mach 1+ at impact	Moving canard fins	Solid-propellant rocket	Radio command	a) 88 (40) HE (HE = high explosive)	A-4, A 109 and Pucará. MP-1000 is wire-guided, with 3.2 naut miles (6 km) range
Brazil										
Avibrás Industria Aerospacial Antiga Estrada de Paraibuna km 118, PO Box 229, 12201-970 São José dos Campos SP	MAS-1 Carcara	a) 47.2 (1.20) b) 16.5 (42.0)	a) 4.9 (12.5) b) 99.2 (45.0)				Solid-propellant rocket	Television	a) HE	
China										
Unknown	Cruise missile				Supersonic?		Turbojet?			Under development for H-6?
France										
Aerospatiale Missiles 2 rue Beranger, F-92322, Chatillon-sous-Bagneux Telephone: +33 1 47 46 21 21 Facsimile: +33 1 47 46 33 19	AASM				Subsonic		Solid-propellant rocket	Inertial + GPS, or inertial + semi-active laser, IIR, or radar homing	a) 551 (250) or 2,205 (1,000) unitary warhead or submunitions	Modular, to convert bombs into precision-guided weapons. Confirmed as an on-going programme in September 1998
Matra BAe Dynamics 37 avenue Louis-Breguet, F-78146 Vélizy-Villacoublay Cedex Telephone: +33 1 34 88 30 00 Facsimile: +33 1 34 65 12 15	AASM	a) 118.1 (3) b) 22.8 (58)	b) 661 (300)	Precise to over 8.1 (15)			Propulsion may be used for low-level firing	Inertial with GPS correction + homing	a) HE bomb	Future modular fire-and-forget weapon, comprising smooth autonomous steering kit
Matra BAe Dynamics 37 avenue Louis-Breguet, F-78146 Vélizy-Villacoublay Cedex Telephone: +33 1 34 88 30 00 Facsimile: +33 1 34 65 12 15	Anti-Radar Futur (ARF)		b) 395? (180?)	c.54 (c.100)	Supersonic		Integrated rocket/ramjet (boosted by self-moduled ramjet)	Passive radar homing	a) HE	Future anti-radar missile. Development with Onera.
Matra BAe Dynamics 37 avenue Louis-Breguet, F-78146 Vélizy-Villacoublay Cedex Telephone: +33 1 34 88 30 00 Facsimile: +33 1 34 65 12 15	Apache AP & MAW (and Apache-AI – see Comments)	a) 200.8 (5.10) b) 111.8 (284)	a) 24.8 (63) b) 2,712 (1,230)	75.6 (140)	Mach 0.8	Tail surfaces	Turbojet	Inertial + radar images correlation + altimetric correlation	a) 10 Kriss submunitions 115 (52) b) Variable time delays	Stealth anti-runway stand-off. IOC 1998. Apache-AI has GPS + IIR guidance for much longer range. Mirage F1, Mirage 2000, Rafale, Tornado, Harrier, etc (German, as MAW-Apache)
Matra BAe Dynamics 37 avenue Louis-Breguet, F-78146 Vélizy-Villacoublay Cedex Telephone: +33 1 34 88 30 00 Facsimile: +33 1 34 65 12 15	Apache Interdiction (aerial denied ammunition)	Similar to Apache	b) 2,756 (1,250)	75.6 (140)	Subsonic	Tail surfaces	Turbojet	Inertial + radar images correlation + altimetric correlation	a) Various submunitions	Full-scale development began 1997, for service from 2001
Matra BAe Dynamics 37 avenue Louis-Breguet, F-78146 Vélizy-Villacoublay Cedex Telephone: +33 1 34 88 30 00 Facsimile: +33 1 34 65 12 15	Armat	a) 163 (4.15) b) 47.2 (120.0)	a) 15.8 (40.0) b) 1,213 (550)	21.5 – 65 (40 – 120)		Moving tail fins	Solid-propellant rocket	Passive radar homing	a) 331 (150) HE	Long-range, anti-radar (successor to Martel). Mirage III, Mirage F1, Mirage 2000, Jaguar, Atlantique
Aerospatiale Missiles 2 rue Beranger, F-92322, Chatillon-sous-Bagneux Telephone: +33 1 47 46 21 21 Facsimile: +33 1 47 46 33 19	AS.30 Laser (AS.30L)	a) 143.7 (3.65) b) 39.4 (100.0)	a) 13.5 (34.2) b) 1,146 (520)	5.4 (10)	Mach 1.4		Two-stage solid-propellant rocket	Semi-active laser homing	a) 529 (240) HE or SAP b) Contact & delayed action fuzes	Mirage F1, Mirage 2000, Super Etendard, Jaguar, F-16, Rafale
Aerospatiale Missiles 2 rue Beranger, F-92322, Chatillon-sous-Bagneux Telephone: +33 1 47 46 21 21 Facsimile: +33 1 47 46 33 19	ASMP & ASMP+ (see Range and Comments)	a) 211.8 (5.38) b) 37.8 (96.0)	a) 15.0 (38.0) b) 1,896 (860)	135 (250) or c.270 (c.500) for ASMP+	Mach 3.0	Cruciform moving tail fins	Liquid propellant ramjet with integral solid-propellant rocket booster	Inertial + terrain mapping	a) 300kT nuclear	Mirage 2000D & N, Super Etendard, Rafale. ASMP+ has replaced other programmes (including ASLP) as a follow-on to ASMP from about the year 2005, to cruise at Mach 2.5 during LO-HI-LO flight profile
Matra BAe Dynamics 37 avenue Louis-Breguet, F-78146 Vélizy-Villacoublay Cedex Telephone: +33 1 34 88 30 00 Facsimile: +33 1 34 65 12 15	250kg BGL	a) 142.1 (3.61) b) 56.3 (143.0)	a) 12.8 (32.4) b) 551 (250)			Moving canards	None	Semi-active laser homing	a) HE	Forward guidance kit and rear wings (unfolding) are adapted to standard bombs. Mirage F1, Mirage 2000, Jaguar

Manufacturer	Designation	a) Length ins (m) b) Span ins (cm)	a) Diameter ins (cm) b) Weight lb (kg)	Range naut miles (km)	Speed	Control	Propulsion	Guidance	a) Warhead lb (kg) b) Fuzing	Comments and Platform(s)
France (continued)										
Matra BAe Dynamics 37 avenue Louis-Breguet, F-78146 Vélizy-Villacoublay Cedex Telephone: +33 1 34 88 30 00 Facsimile: +33 1 34 65 12 15	400kg BGL	a) 139.4 (3.54) b) 56.3 (143.0)	a) 15.9 (40.3) b) 1,036 (470)			Moving canards	None	Semi-active laser homing	a) HE	Mirage F1, Mirage 2000, Jaguar
Matra BAe Dynamics 37 avenue Louis-Breguet, F-78146 Vélizy-Villacoublay Cedex Telephone: +33 1 34 88 30 00 Facsimile: +33 1 34 65 12 i5	400kg PE BGL	a) 143.3 (3.64) b) 56.3 (143.0)	a) 15.4 (39.1) b) 992 (450)			Moving canards	None	Semi-active laser homing	a) HE penetrating	Mirage F1, Mirage 2000, Jaguar
Matra BAe Dynamics 37 avenue Louis-Breguet, F-78146 Vélizy-Villacoublay Cedex Telephone: +33 1 34 88 30 00 Facsimile: +33 1 34 65 12 15	Arcole (1,000 kg BGL)	a) 172.1 (4.37) b) 67.7 (172.0)	a) 18.0 (45.7) b) 2,138 (970)	c. 5.4 (c. 10)		Moving canards	None	Semi-active laser homing	a) HE penetrating	Mirage F1, Mirage 2000, Jaguar. Specially suited to destroying bridge piers and other hardened targets
Société des Ateliers Mecaniques de Pont-sur-Sambre (SAMP) 37 Grand Rue, F-59138 Pont-sur-Sambre Telephone: +33 3 27 53 62 62 Facsimile: +33 3 27 67 36 31	MP 22 Excalibur	a) 98.4 (2.50) b) 20.3 (51.6)	a) 10.8 (27.3) b) 697 (316)	c. 6.5 (c. 12)		Moving canard fins	Solid-propellant rocket	Inertial	a) BL EU2 551 (250) general-purpose bomb	Mirage family?
Matra BAe Dynamics 37 avenue Louis-Breguet, F-78146 Vélizy-Villacoublay Cedex Telephone: +33 1 34 88 30 00 Facsimile: +33 1 34 65 12 15	SCALP EG/ Storm Shadow	a) 201 (5.1) b) 118 (300)	a) 24.8 x 20 (63 x 51) b) 2,866 (1,300)	over 135 (250)	540 kts (1,000 km/h)	Tail surfaces	Specially designed turbojet	Inertial with updates via GPS & TERPROM + IIR terminal homing & automatic target recognition	a) 2-stage HE penetrator (precursor charge and penetrator bomb)	Under development as long-range precision stealth cruise missile. Fully autonomous. For French and UK air forces. For Tornado, Eurofighter, Harrier GR7, Mirage 2000, Rafale, etc from year 2001. Range (less than quoted elsewhere) was confirmed September 1998
Germany										
Bodenseewerke-Gerätetechnik GmbH PO Box 101155, D-88641 Überlingen Telephone: +49 7551 896114 Facsimile: +49 7551 896274	Aramis		b) 419? (190?)	54? (100?)	Supersonic		Solid-propellant rocket/ramjet	Combined passive radar/ passive IR homing	a) HE	Anti-radiation type, formerly an Aerospatiale/Daimler-Benz Aerospace programme
Daimler-Benz Aerospace/LFK PO Box 801109, D-81663 Munich Telephone: +49 89 6 07-0 Facsimile: +49 89 6 07 26481	DWS 24 (see Comments for unrelated ASS 500)	a) 138 (3.5) b) 39.3 (100)	a) 24.8 x 12.6 (63 x 32) b) 1,323 (600)	5.4 (10)	Subsonic		None	Inertial	a) 49 submunitions (KB-44 armour-piercing, MIFF anti-tank, MUSA fragmentation or MUSPA anti-runway	Industrial partner Bofors. The ASS 500 is a totally unrelated project to develop a hypersonic bunker penetrating cruise missile for service from 2015. ASS 500 could be launched at 270 naut mile (500 km) range, fly at Mach 2.5-4, use combined INS/IR/phased array radar guidance, and attack with a 1,102 lb (500 kg) kinetic energy warhead
Daimler-Benz Aerospace/LFK PO Box 801109, D-81663 Munich Telephone: +49 89 6 07-0 Facsimile: +49 89 6 07 26481	DWS 39	a) 138 (3.5) b) 39.3 (100)	a) 24.8 x 12.6 (63 x 32) b) 1,323 (600)	4.3 (8) with low level release	Subsonic		None	Inertial (IMU) with GPS	a) As DWS 24 + Bofors MJ-1 fragmentation or MJ-2 anti-tank	Gliding submunition dispenser. Gripen, Viggen. Industrial partner Bofors
Daimler-Benz Aerospace/LFK PO Box 801109, D-81663 Munich Telephone: +49 89 6 07-0 Facsimile: +49 89 6 07 26481	DWS 39-R & MW2-R			8.1 – 16.2 (15 – 30)			Increased range with rocket sustainer			Based on AFDS/MW2. Designed to meet Swedish Air Force requirements (DWS 39-R), and for Tornado and AMX applications (MW2-R)
Daimler-Benz Aerospace/LFK PO Box 801109, D-81663 Munich Telephone: +49 89 6 07-0 Facsimile: +49 89 6 07 26481	AFDS & MW2 (Autonomous Free-flight Dispenser System)	a) 147 (3.74) b) c. 39.3 (100)	b) 1,323 (600)	above 10.8 (20)	Subsonic		None	Inertial + Integrated GPS (autonomous navigation on earth co-ordinates)	a) Submunitions	Variant of DWS 39, adapted for F-16 (AFDS) and Tornado (as MW2). Possible F-4, F/A-18
India										
Aeronautical Development Agency PO Box 1718, Vimanapura Post Office, Bangalore 560017 Telephone: +91 80 5233060 Facsimile: +91 80 5238493	Cruise missile			c. 324 (c.600)	Supersonic		Integrated rocket/ramjet	GPS with radar or IR terminal homing?	a) c.990 (c.450)	Possibly developed from the Lakshya UAV target programme
Iran										
Not known	Karus?				Probably high subsonic		Turbojet?	Inertial with GPS + terminal seeker?		Cruise missile, reportedly under development since mid-1990s

Manufacturer	Designation	a) Length ins (m) b) Span ins (cm)	a) Diameter ins (cm) b) Weight lb (kg)	Range naut miles (km)	Speed	Control	Propulsion	Guidance	a) Warhead lb (kg) b) Fuzing	Comments and Platform(s)
Iraq										
Not known	Ababil	a) 236 (6)	b) 2,205 (1,000)	270 (500)						
Israel										
Rafael Armament Development Authority, Missile Division PO Box 2250/30, Haifa 31021 Telephone: +972 4 990 8503 Facsimile: + 972 4 990 6257 and Lockheed Martin Electronics & Missiles. Joint venture name: PGSUS	AGM-142 Have Nap/ Popeye	a) 191 (4.85) b) 69 (175)	a) 21.0 (53.3) b) 2,998 (1,360)	50+ (92+)	Subsonic?	Moving tail fins	Solid-propellant rocket	Mid-course inertial + datalink, + inter-changeable TV or imaging IR seeker	a) 750 (340) HE blast fragmentation or penetrator	F-4, F-15, F-16, Kfir, B-52H. Selected by South Korea, USA, Australia and Israel. For the RAAF, advanced version has 8-12 micron thermal imaging seeker with wide and narrow fields of view (PEP-3 programme)
Rafael Armament Development Authority, Missile Division PO Box 2250/30, Haifa 31021 Telephone: +972 4 990 8503 Facsimile: + 972 4 990 6257 (see above)	AGM-142B Have Lite/ Popeye 2 (see Comments for C and D)	a) 157.5 (4.0)	a) 21.0 (53.3) b) 2,458 (1,115)	40.5 (75)	Subsonic?	Moving tails	Solid-propellant rocket	Mid-course inertial + datalink, + inter-changeable TV or IIR seeker	a) 800 (363) HE	F-4, F-15, F-16, Kfir & B-52H. Rafael confirmed in 1998 that there was no Popeye 3 Turbo under development. C and D versions are believed to have inertial/TV and IIR respectively
Israel Aircraft Industries Elta Electronic Industries division PO Box 330, Ashdod 77102 Telephone: +972 8 8572312 Facsimile: +972 8 8564568	Griffin			5.4 (10)		Moving canard fins	None	Semi-active laser homing	a) Mk82, Mk83, or Mk84 bomb	Kfir
Israel Aircraft Industries Elta Electronic Industries division PO Box 330, Ashdod 77102 Telephone: +972 8 8572312 Facsimile: +972 8 8564568	Guillotine			16 (30)		Moving canard fins	None	Semi-active laser homing	a) Mk82 or Mk83 bomb	Kfir
Israel Aircraft Industries Elta Electronic Industries division PO Box 330, Ashdod 77102 Telephone: +972 8 8572312 Facsimile: +972 8 8564568	Nimrod	a) 111.8 (2.84) b) 19.7 (50)	a) 8.27 (21.0) b) 220 (100)	13.5 (25)	Subsonic?	Moving tail fins?	Solid-propellant rocket ?	Inertial semi-active laser homing	a) 33 (15) HE	
Elbit Advanced Technology Center PO Box 539, Haifa 31053 Telephone: +972 4 8315315 Facsimile: +972 4 8550002, 8551623	Opher	a) 132.3 (3.36) b) 27.5 (70.0)	a) 10.8 (27.3) b) 300 (661)	3.8+ (7+)		Cold gas; bang bang operation	None	Imaging infra-red seeker (IIRS) in 8-12 μ spectrum	a) Mk82 bomb	Kfir, F-4E
Rafael Armament Development Authority, Missile Division PO Box 2250/30, Haifa 31021 Telephone: +972 4 990 8503 Facsimile: + 972 4 990 6257	Pyramid	a) 109.1 (2.77) b) 46.5 (118.0)	a) 11.4 (29.0) b) 800 (363)		Mach 0.8 average	Aerodynamic	None	TV homing	a) 230kg HE	
Israel Military Industries – TAAS, PO Box 1044, Ramat Hasharon 47100 Telephone: +972 3 548 5222	Star-1	a) 106.6 (2.71) b) 45.3 (115)	a) 13 (33) b) 401 (182)		Mach 0.8	Moving tail fins	Turbojet	GPS + passive radar homing via broad-band seeker	a) HE	Anti-radiation missile
Israel Military Industries – TAAS, PO Box 1044, Ramat Hasharon 47100 Telephone: +972 3 548 5222	Cruise missile	b) 45.3? (115?)	a) 13? (33?)	Over 220 (407)	High subsonic	Moving tail fins	Turbojet?	Inertial with GPS + terminal seeker?	a) HE	Cruise missile, derived from Delilah UAV. Not thought to be in service
Italy										
Consorzio Armamenti Spendibili Multi-Uso (CASMU) Via della Quattro Fontane 21A, I-00 184, Roma Telephone: +39 06 592 3568	Skyshark (rocket-powered, unless stated)	a) 187.0 (4.76) b) 59.0 (150)	b) c.2,579 (c.1,170)	13.5 – 32 (25 – 60)	Subsonic		Solid-propellant rocket	Inertial & GPS + passive IR seeker & datalink	a) c.1,653 (c.750) of submunitions	Tornado, Eurofighter
Consorzio Armamenti Spendibili Multi-Uso (CASMU) Via della Quattro Fontane 21A, I-00 184, Roma Telephone: +39 06 592 3568	Skyshark (turbojet-powered)	a) 187.0 (4.76) b) 59.0 (150)	b) c.3,527 (c.1,600)	135+ (250+)	Subsonic		Turbojet	Unpowered version has 3.2 – 6.4 (6 – 12)	a) 1,985 (900) of submunitions	Tornado, Eurofighter
Japan										
Mitsubishi Electric/ Japan Technical Research & Development Institute 5–1, Marunouchi 2-chome, Chiyoda-ku, Tokyo 100 Telephone: +81 3 3212 3111 Facsimile: +81 3 3212 9865	GCS-1 (Guidance Control Set 1)				Subsonic		None	Passive IIR homing	a) 500 (227) or 1,000 (454) bomb	F-2
Russia										
GNPP Region 13A Kashirskoye Shosse, 115201 Moscow Telephone: +7 095 111 4152 Facsimile: +7 095 111 3055	KAB-500L	a) 120.0 (3.05) b) 29.5 (75.0)	a) 13.8 (35.0) b) 1,177 (534)			Moving surfaces on tail fins	None	Semi-active laser homing	a) Contains 882 (400) HE	Fighter/attack aircraft

Manufacturer	Designation	a) Length ins (m) b) Span ins (cm)	a) Diameter ins (cm) b) Weight lb (kg)	Range naut miles (km)	Speed	Control	Propulsion	Guidance	a) Warhead lb (kg) b) Fuzing	Comments and Platform(s)
Russia (continued)										
GNPP Region 13A Kashirskoye Shosse, 115201 Moscow Telephone: +7 095 111 4152 Facsimile: +7 095 111 3055	KAB-500Kr	a) 120.0 (3.05) b) 29.5 (75.0)	a) 13.8 (35.0) b) 1,157 (525)			Moving surfaces on tail fins	None	TV homing	a) Contains c.838 (c.400) HE	Fighter/attack aircraft
GNPP Region 13A Kashirskoye Shosse, 115201 Moscow Telephone: +7 095 111 4152 Facsimile: +7 095 111 3055	KAB-1500L-F	a) 181.0 (4.60) b) 51.2 (130.0)	a) 22.8 (58.0) b) 3,440 (1,560)			Moving surfaces on tail fins	None	Semi-active laser homing	a) Contains 2,600 (1,180) HE blast	Fighter/attack aircraft
GNPP Region 13A Kashirskoye Shosse, 115201 Moscow Telephone: +7 095 111 4152 Facsimile: +7 095 111 3055	KAB-1500L-Pr	a) 181.0 (4.60) b) 51.2 (130.0)	a) 22.8 (58.0) b) 3,307 (1,500)			Moving surfaces on tail fins	None	Semi-active laser homing	a) Contains 2,425 (1,100) HE penetrating	Fighter/attack aircraft
GNPP Region 13A Kashirskoye Shosse, 115201 Moscow Telephone: +7 095 111 4152 Facsimile: +7 095 111 3055	KAB-1500Kr	a) 183 (4.65) b) 51.2 (130.0)	a) 22.8 (58.0) b) 3,439 (1,560)			Moving surfaces on tail fins	None	TV homing	a) 2601 (1,180) HE	Fighter/attack aircraft
GNPP Region 13A Kashirskoye Shosse, 115201 Moscow Telephone: +7 095 111 4152 Facsimile: +7 095 111 3055	KAB-1500-TK	a) 183 (4.65) b) 51.2 (130.0)	a) 22.8 (58.0)			Moving surfaces on tail fins	None	TV homing	a) HE	Fighter and attack aircraft. Older type of TV guidance
MKB Raduga 2a Zhukovsky Street, Dubna, Moscow Region 141980 Telephone: +7 096 21 24647 Facsimile: +7 096 21 23528	Kh-15P (AS-16 Kickback)	a) c.188.2 (c.4.78) b) 36.2 (92.0)	a) 17.9 (45.5) b) 2,425 (1,100)	135 (250)	Mach 5	Moving tail fins	Solid-propellant rocket	Inertial + passive radar seeker	a) 364 (165) HE	Tu-22M, Tu-160
MKB Raduga 2a Zhukovsky Street, Dubna, Moscow Region 141980 Telephone: +7 096 21 24647 Facsimile: +7 096 21 23528	Kh-22MA/NA (AS-4 Kitchen) (see Comments for Kh-22M and N)	a) 458.7 (11.65) b) 118.1 (300.0)	a) 36.2 (92.0) b) 13,007 (5,900)	275 (510)	1,943 kts (3,600 km/h)	Moving tail fins	Liquid-propellant rocket	Inertial	a) Nuclear	Tu-22M, Tu-95K-22. Kh-22M and N are anti-ship variants (which see)
Zvezda Design Bureau Zvezda-Strela, 7 Ilyicha Street, Kaliningrad, Moscow Region, 141070 Telephone: +7 095 519 5501 Facsimile: +7 095 519 4722	Kh-25ML (AS-10 Karen)	a) 146.06 (3.71) b) 30.9 (78.5)	a) 10.8 (27.5) b) 660 (300)	5.4 (10)	2,790 ft/sec (850 m/sec)	Moving canards	Solid-propellant rocket	Semi-active laser homing	a) 198 (90) blast fragmentation	MiG-27, MiG-29M, Su-17, Su-24, Su-25, Su-39, Ka-50, Ka-52
Zvezda Design Bureau (Address, etc, as above)	Kh-25MP (AS-12 Kegler)	a) 172.0 (4.4) b) 30.9 (78.5)	a) 10.8 (27.5) b) 706 (320)	13.5 – 32.5 (25 – 60)	2,953 ft/sec (900 m/sec)	Moving canards	Solid-propellant rocket	Inertial + passive radar seeker	a) 198 (90) blast fragmentation	MiG-21-93, MiG-23, MiG-27, Su-17, Su-24, Su-27 (sometimes referred to as PD), Ka-50, Ka-52
Zvezda Design Bureau (Address, etc, as above)	Kh-25MPU (AS-12 Kegler)	a) 172.0 (4.4) b) 30.9 (78.5)	a) 10.8 (27.5) b) 706 (320)	13.5 – 32.5 (25 – 60)	2,953 ft/sec (900 m/sec)	Moving canards, with autopilot	Solid-propellant rocket	Inertial + passive radar homing	a) 198 (90) blast fragmentation	Version of Kh-25MP with improved seeker and control system. Platforms as for Kh-25MP
Zvezda Design Bureau (Address, etc, as above)	Kh-25MR (& Kh-25MTP – see Comments) (AS-10 Karen)	a) 145.28 (3.69) b) 30.9 (78.5)	a) 10.8 (27.5) b) 660 (300)	5.4 (10)	2,822 ft/sec (860 m/sec)	Moving canards	Solid-propellant rocket	Radio command (see Comments)	a) 198 (90) blast fragmentation	MiG-23BN, MiG-27, Su-17/20/22, Su-24. Kh-25MTP is an imaging infra-red (IIR) version of Kh-25M
Zvezda Design Bureau (Address, etc, as above)	Kh-28 izdelye 93 (AS-9 Kyle)	a) 236.2 (6.0) b) 55.1 (140.0)	a) 17 (43) b) 1,576 (715)	46 (85)	Mach 0.8		Liquid-propellant rocket	Passive radar homing	a) 245 (111) HE	Su-24. Anti-radiation missile on *Fencer-A/B/C*
GMKB Vympel 90 Volokolamskoye Shosse, Moscow, 123424 Telephone: +7 095 491 0239 Facsimile: +7 095 490 2222	Kh-29TD (AS-14 Kedge)	a) 153.5 (3.90) b) 43.3 (110.0)	a) 15.8 (40.0) b) c.1,521 (c.690)	1.6 – 6.5 (3 – 12)			Solid-propellant rocket	Passive imaging IR homing	a) 699 (317) HE	MiG-27, MiG-29, Su-17, Su-24, Su-25, Mirage F1
GMKB Vympel 90 Volokolamskoye Shosse, Moscow, 123424 Telephone: +7 095 491 0239 Facsimile: +7 095 490 2222	Kh-29L (AS-14 Kedge)	a) 152.8 (3.88) b) 43.3 (110.0)	a) 15.0 (38.0) b) 1,448 (657)	1.1 – 4.3 (2 – 8)	2,625 ft/sec (800 m/sec)	Moving canards & tail surfaces	Solid-propellant rocket	Semi-active laser homing	a) 699 (317) HE	MiG-27, Su-17, Su-24, Su-25, Su-30, Su-32/34, Su-33, Su-39
GMKB Vympel 90 Volokolamskoye Shosse, Moscow, 123424 Telephone: +7 095 491 0239 Facsimile: +7 095 490 2222	Kh-29T & Kh-29TE (see Comments) (AS-14 Kedge)	a) 152.8 (3.88) b) 43.3 (110.0)	a) 15.0 (38.0) b) 1,499 (680)	1.6 – 6.5 (3 – 12)	2,625 ft/sec (800 m/sec)	Moving canards & tail surfaces	Solid-propellant rocket	TV homing	a) 699 (317) HE	MiG-27, MiG-29, Su-17, Su-24, Su-25, Su-30, Su-32/34, Su-39, S-80PT, Mirage F1. Kh-29TE is an extended range version (16 naut miles, 30 km), weighing 1,543 lb (700 kg)
Zvezda Design Bureau Zvezda-Strela, 7 Ilyicha Street, Kaliningrad, Moscow Region, 141070 Telephone: +7 095 519 5501 Facsimile: +7 095 519 4722	Kh-31P (AS-17 Krypton)	a) 185.0 (4.70) b) 45.3 (115) for Kh-31P-1 a) 206.0 (5.23) b) 44.3 (112.5) for Kh-31P-2	a) 14.2 (36.0) b) 1,323 (600)	59.4 – 81 (110 – 150) for Kh-31P-1 & 108 naut miles (200 km) for P-2	3,280 ft/sec (1,000 m/sec)	Moving tail fins	Integrated rocket-ramjet	Inertial + passive radar homing	a) 198 (90) HE b) Impact & proximity fuzes?	MiG-21-93, MiG-29M, MiG-29SM, MiG-35, Su-24, Su-27, Su-30MK, Su-32FN, Su-35/37, Su-39, and J-8II? X-31 export model has interested China and India for Su-27/30s, with co-operation of Boeing. X-31 is being offered to US Navy as a target (Ma-31) , and France is also a potential target customer

Manufacturer	Designation	a) Length ins (m) b) Span ins (cm)	a) Diameter ins (cm) b) Weight lb (kg)	Range naut miles (km)	Speed	Control	Propulsion	Guidance	a) Warhead lb (kg) b) Fuzing	Comments and Platform(s)
Russia (continued)										
Zvezda Design Bureau Zvezda-Strela, 7 Ilyicha Street, Kaliningrad, Moscow Region, 141070 Telephone: +7 095 519 5501 Facsimile: +7 095 519 4722	Kh-38									New generation ASM, to replace Kh-25M. Users include MiG-35
MKB Raduga 2a Zhukovsky Street, Dubna, Moscow Region 141980 Telephone: +7 096 21 24647 Facsimile: +7 096 21 23528	Kh-55 (AS-15 Kent)	a) 237.8 (6.04) b) 122.0 (310)	a) 20.2 (51.4) or 30.3 (77) with auxiliary conformal tanks b) 2,668 (1,210) or 3,307 (1,500) with auxiliary fuel	1,350 (2,500) or 1,619 (3,000) with auxiliary fuel	Subsonic	Moving tail fins	Turbofan	Inertial + terrain matching	a) 200kT nuclear	Tu-95, Tu-160
MKB Raduga 2a Zhukovsky Street, Dubna, Moscow Region 141980 Telephone: +7 096 21 24647 Facsimile: +7 096 21 23528	Kh-58U/ Kh-58E (AS-11 Kilter)	a) 189.5 (4.813) b) 46.1 (117.0)	a) 15.0 (38.0) b) 1,411 (640)	64.75 (120) or 108 (200) when launched by MiG-25BM at Mach 2	3,280 ft/sec (1,000 m/sec) or Mach 4	Moving tail fins	Dual thrust solid-propellant rocket	Autopilot + passive radar homing	a) 328 (149) HE blast fragmentation, with possible nuclear option	MiG-25BM, Su-24, Su-17/22, Su-39. E is export version
MKB Raduga 2a Zhukovsky Street, Dubna, Moscow Region 141980 Telephone: +7 096 21 24647 Facsimile: +7 096 21 23528	Kh-59 Ovod (AS-13 Kingbolt)	a) 211.4 (5.37) b) 49.6 (126.0)	a) 15.0 (38.0) b) 1,676 (760)	21.6 – 86 (40 – 160) depending on launch altitude	3,609 ft/sec (1,100 m/sec)	Moving canards	Two-stage solid-propellant booster & sustainer	TV + datalink	a) 324 (147) HE	MiG-27, MiG-35, Su-17, Su-22, Su-24
MKB Raduga 2a Zhukovsky Street, Dubna, Moscow Region 141980 Telephone: +7 096 21 24647 Facsimile: +7 096 21 23528	Kh-59M Ovod-M (AS-18 Kazoo)	a) 224.0 (5.69) b) 49.6 (126.0)	a) 15.0 (38.0) b) 2,050 (930)	62 (115)	3,280 ft/sec (1,000 m/sec)	Moving canards	Turbofan mounted below fuselage + solid-propellant rocket booster	TV + datalink	a) 694 (315) with 617 (280) of submunitions	Su-24, Su-30MK, Su-32FN, Su-35/37
MKB Raduga 2a Zhukovsky Street, Dubna, Moscow Region 141980 Telephone: +7 096 21 24647 Facsimile: +7 096 21 23528	Kh-65 (Kh-SD)	a) 237.8 (6.04) b) 122.0 (310.0)	a) 20.2 (51.4) b) 2,755 (1,250)	270 – 324 (500 – 600)	886 ft/sec (270 m/sec)	Moving tail fins	Turbofan mounted below rear fuselage		a) 904 (410) HE	Tu-95 Bear-H, Tu-160, Su-32FN, Su-35/37
MKB Raduga 2a Zhukovsky Street, Dubna, Moscow Region 141980 Telephone: +7 096 21 24647 Facsimile: +7 096 21 23528	Kh-101	a) 293.3 (7.45)	b) 4,850 – 5,291 (2,200 – 2,400)	1,500 (2,778)	853 ft/sec (260 m/sec)		Turbojet or turbofan	Inertial + terrain matching + electro-optic terminal phase	a) 882 (400) HE	Tu-95 Bear-H, Tu-22M3, Tu-160. Likely replacement for cancelled Kh-90 cruise missile
KB Tochmash Moscow	S-25L	a) 141.7 (3.60) b) 46.1 (117)	a) 10.47 – 13.4 (26.6 – 34) b) c.838 (c.380)		1,804 ft/sec (550 m/sec)	Moving canards	Solid-propellant rocket	Semi-active laser homing	a) 331 (150) HE	
United Kingdom										
GEC-Marconi Dynamics Warren Lane, Stanmore, Middlesex HA7 4LY Telephone: +44 181 954 2311 Facsimile: +44 181 420 3990	PGM-500		Up to 27 (50) high level launch; 10.7 (20) low level	c.27 (c.50)		Moving wings	Externally-mounted solid-propellant rocket	Semi-active laser homing	a) 500 (227) HE blast fragmentation b) Selectable proximity or impact. Intelligent fuze available for delay, airburst, etc	Smart weapon in Laser, TV and Hawk versions. Interchangeable laser and TV seekers. Laser requires target designation; TV requires data link pod. Mirage 2000, F-4, Harrier GR.7?, Hawk?
GEC-Marconi Dynamics Warren Lane, Stanmore, Middlesex HA7 4LY Telephone: +44 181 954 2311 Facsimile: +44 181 420 3990	PGM-2000			c.27 (c.50)		Moving wings	Two externally-mounted solid-propellant rockets	Semi-active laser homing	a) 2,000 (907) HE blast fragmentation b) Selectable proximity or impact. Intelligent fuze available for delay, airburst, etc	Available in Laser, TV and high-energy Penetrator variants. See above. Mirage 2000, F-4, Harrier GR.7?, Tornado
Matra BAe Dynamics PO Box 19, Six Hills Way, Stevenage, Hertfordshire SG1 2DA Telephone: +44 1438 312422 Facsimile: +44 1438 753377	ALARM	a) 169 (4.30) b) 28.4 (72.0)	a) 8.8 (22.4) b) 584.2 (265)	24.3 (45)		Cruciform moving tail fins	Solid-propellant rocket	Passive radar homing	a) HE blast fragmentation b) Forward-looking range finder	Anti-radar. Tornado, Rafale, Sea Harrier, Eurofighter. 2 user countries to date (UK and Saudi Arabia)
United States of America										
Raytheon Systems Company 2501 South Highway 121, PO Box 405, MS 3500, Lewisville, TX 75067-8127 Telephone: +1 972 462 6500 Facsimile: +1 972 462 6508	AGM-45A Shrike	a) 120.0 (3.05) b) 36.0 (91.4)	a) 8.0 (20.3) b) 390 (177)	15.6 – 21.6 (29 – 40)	Mach 2	Moving wings	Solid-propellant rocket	Passive radar homing	a) 145 (66) fragmentation	Still used? F-16 & others

Manufacturer	Designation	a) Length ins (m) b) Span ins (cm)	a) Diameter ins (cm) b) Weight lb (kg)	Range naut miles (km)	Speed	Control	Propulsion	Guidance	a) Warhead lb (kg) b) Fuzing	Comments and Platform(s)
United States of America (continued)										
Raytheon Systems Company 1151 East Hermans Road, PO Box 11337, Tucson, AZ 85734 Telephone: +1 520 794 3000 Facsimile: +1 520 794 1315	AGM-65A/B Maverick	a) 98.0 (2.49) b) 28.4 (72.0)	a) 12 (30.5) b) 462 (210)	0.5 – 12 (0.9 – 22)	Subsonic	Moving tail fins	Dual-thrust solid-propellant rocket	TV homing (B with scene magnification)	a) 125 (57) HEAT b) Impact	F-4, F-5, F-15, F-16, F/A-18, A-4, A-7, Harrier II, A-10, Viggen, Orao, Super Galeb. Gripen is Maverick user (as Rb 75) and AH-1W but versions unclear
Raytheon Systems Company 1151 East Hermans Road, PO Box 11337, Tucson, AZ 85734 Telephone: +1 520 794 3000 Facsimile: +1 520 794 1315	AGM-65D Maverick	a) 98.0 (2.49) b) 28.4 (72.0)	a) 12 (30.5) b) 485 (220)	10.8 (20)	Subsonic	Moving tail fins	Dual-thrust solid-propellant rocket	Imaging IR seeker (allowing day/night use)	a) 125 (57) HEAT b) Impact	F-4, F-5, F-15, F-16, A-7, Harrier II, A-10, Tornado, P-3C-III, and others
Raytheon Systems Company 1151 East Hermans Road, PO Box 11337, Tucson, AZ 85734 Telephone: +1 520 794 3000 Facsimile: +1 520 794 1315	AGM-65E Maverick	a) 98.0 (2.49) b) 28.4 (72.0)	a) 12 (30.5) b) 646 (293)	10.8 (20)	Subsonic	Moving tail fins	Dual-thrust solid-propellant rocket	Semi-active laser homing	a) 298 (135) blast-penetrator b) Impact	F-4, F/A-18, A-7, Harrier II, F-117?
Raytheon Systems Company 1151 East Hermans Road, PO Box 11337, Tucson, AZ 85734 Telephone: +1 520 794 3000 Facsimile: +1 520 794 1315	AGM-65F Maverick	a) 98.0 (2.49) b) 28.4 (72.0)	a) 12 (30.5) b) 677 (307)	13.5 (25)	Subsonic	Moving tail fins	Dual-thrust solid-propellant rocket	Imaging IR	a) 298 (135) blast-penetrator b) Impact	F/A-18, A-7, AV-8, Harrier II
Raytheon Systems Company 1151 East Hermans Road, PO Box 11337, Tucson, AZ 85734 Telephone: +1 520 794 3000 Facsimile: +1 520 794 1315	AGM-65G Maverick	a) 98.0 (2.49) b) 28.4 (72.0)	a) 12 (30.5) b) 677 (307)	13.5 (25)	Subsonic	Moving tail fins	Dual-thrust solid-propellant rocket	Imaging IR	a) 298 (135) blast penetrator/ fragmentation b) Impact	F-15, F-16, F-117? Digital autopilot and pneumatic (instead of hydraulic) control system
Raytheon Systems Company 1151 East Hermans Road, PO Box 11337, Tucson, AZ 85734 Telephone: +1 520 794 3000 Facsimile: +1 520 794 1315	AGM-65H Maverick	a) 102.4 (2.60) b) 28.4 (72.0)	a) 12 (30.5) b) 672 (305)	13.5 (25)	Subsonic	Moving tail fins	Dual-thrust solid-propellant rocket	Improved TV homing	a) 298 (135) blast-penetrator b) Impact	Introduced performance and reliability improvements
Boeing Aircraft and Missile Systems PO Box 516, St. Louis, MO 63166-0516 Telephone: +1 314 232 2800 Facsimile: +1 314 234 8296	AGM-84E SLAM	a) 175.2 (4.45) b) 35.8 (91.0)	a) 13.5 (34.3) b) 1,366 (620)	54 (100)	Mach 0.85	Cruciform moving tail fins	Turbojet	Cruise: inertial + radar altimeter + GPS; Attack: imaging infra-red + datalink	a) 485 (220) HE penetration blast b) Contact (with time delay) + proximity fuzes	F/A-18, B-52, S-3B. Standoff Land Attack Missile
Boeing Aircraft and Missile Systems PO Box 516, St. Louis, MO 63166-0516 Telephone: +1 314 232 2800 Facsimile: +1 314 234 8296	AGM-84 SLAM ER (Expanded Response)	a) 172.0 (4.37) b) 95.6 (242.8)	a) 13.5 (34.3) b) 1,600 (725.7)	75+ (139+)	Mach 0.85	Cruciform moving tail fins	Turbojet	Cruise: inertial + radar altimeter + GPS; Attack: imaging infra-red + datalink	a) Improved HE penetrator, based on Tomahawk Block III titanium design with shaped nose b) Contact (with time delay) + proximity fuzes	F/A-18, B-52. Guidance Navigation Unit integrates mission computer, inertial measurement, GPS receiver processor and air data system functions into single unit. Weapon data link modified to increase aircraft stand-off control range by 50%
Boeing Aircraft and Missile Systems PO Box 516, St. Louis, MO 63166-0516 Telephone: +1 314 232 2800 Facsimile: +1 314 234 8296	AGM-86B ALCM & AGM-86C CALCM	a) 248.8 (6.32) b) 144.0 (366.0)	a) 24.5 (62.2) b) 3,197 (1,450); 3,300?(1,497?) for AGM-86C	1,350 (2,503) AGM-86B; 1,080 (2,000) for AGM-86C	Mach 0.6	Elevons	Turbofan	Inertial + tercom for AGM-86B; inertial + GPS for AGM-86C	a) 271 (123) W-80-1 200kT thermonuclear; or 1,000 (454) HE blast/ fragmentation for AGM-86C	B-52H, B-1B. Uses 600 lbf (2.67 kN) Williams/Teledyne CAE F107-WR-10 turbofan. AGM-86C CALCM is conventionally armed ALCM
Raytheon Systems Company 2501 South Highway 121, PO Box 405, MS 3500, Lewisville, TX 75067-8127 Telephone: +1 972 462 6500 Facsimile: + 1 972 462 6508	AGM-88A, B & C HARM (data A)	a) 164.2 (4.17) b) 44.5 (113.0)	a) 10 (25.4) b) 794 (360), & 807 (366) for C	10 (18.5)	Mach 2+	Cruciform moving tail fins	Dual-thrust solid-propellant rocket	Passive radar homing	a) 145 (65.8) modified Shrike HE fragmentation b) Motorola proximity fuze	F-15, F-16, F/A-18, F-22, F-117A, EA-6B, Rafale, Tornado. Current production version is AGM-88C, featuring tungsten alloy (not steel) warhead and improved AGM-88C-1 seeker (latter being retrofitted to Bs)
Motorola 8220 East Roosevelt Street, Scottsdale, AZ 85252 Telephone: +1 441 30 33	AGM-122 Sidearm	a) 118.1 (3.00) b) 24.8 (63.0)	a) 5.0 (12.7) b) 201 (91)	4.3 (8)		Cruciform moving canard fins	Solid-propellant rocket	Passive radar homing	a) 22.5 (10.2) HE blast b) Active laser/impact	F/A-18, A-4, Harrier II, AH-64, AH-1
Electronics & Space Corporation	AGM-123 Skipper II	a) 170.5 (4.33) b) 63.0 (160)	a) 14.0 (35.6) b) 1,283 (582)	3.8 (7)		Cruciform moving canard fins	Solid-propellant rocket	Semi-active laser homing	a) Mk83 bomb	F/A-18
Raytheon Systems Company/ Boeing Aircraft and Missile Systems	AGM-129A Advanced Cruise Missile	a) 250.0 (6.35) b) 122.0 (310.0)	a) 25.1 – 27.7 (64 – 70.4) b) 3,709 (1,682)	1,620 (3,000)	Subsonic	Moving fins	Turbofan	Inertial +tercom + laser radar	a) W-80-1 200kT nuclear	Incorporates low-observable technology. B-52H, B-1B, B-2. Williams F112-WR-100 turbofan

Manufacturer	Designation	a) Length ins (m) b) Span ins (cm)	a) Diameter ins (cm) b) Weight lb (kg)	Range naut miles (km)	Speed	Control	Propulsion	Guidance	a) Warhead lb (kg) b) Fuzing	Comments and Platform(s)
United States of America (continued)										
Boeing Aircraft and Missile Systems PO Box 516, St. Louis, MO 63166-0516 Telephone: +1 314 232 2800 Facsimile: +1 314 234 8296	AGM-130A & C	a) 154.5 (3.92), 155.5 (3.95) for C b) 59.0 (150.0)	a) 18.0 (45.7) b) 2,917 (1,323)	13 – 24.3 (24 – 45)	Subsonic	Moving fins	Solid-propellant rocket	INS/GPS + imaging IR or TV seeker, or DME transponder	a) Mk84 (for A), or BLU-109/B (for C) b) Impact (A), impact delay (C)	F-4, F-15E Powered versions of GBU-15, with improved control systems
Raytheon Systems Company 2501 South Highway 121, PO Box 405, MS 3500, Lewisville, TX 75067-8127 Telephone: +1 972 462 6500 Facsimile: + 1 972 462 6508	AGM-154A/B/C Joint Stand-Off Weapon (JSOW)	a) 160.0 (4.06) for A/B, 158 (4.01) for C	a) 20.9 x 23.6 (53 x 60) b) 1,065-1,500 (483-680)	15 – 40 (28 – 74)			None. Test of powered version of C undertaken	AGM-154A and B/JSOW INS/GPS, AGM-154C/ JSOW with unitary INS/GPS midcourse + IIR terminal with datalink	a) 145 BLU-97B combined effect bomblets (shaped charge, blast & incendiary) for AGM-154A, 6 Textron BLU-108/B Sensor Fuzed Weapon Submunitions for AGM-154B & 500-800 lb BLU-111 HE Unitary for AGM-154C	F-15E, F-16, F/A-18, F-117?, B-1B?, B-2, B-52H? and possibly Harrier, Jaguar, Tornado. IOC with USN 1998 and USAF 2000
Northrop Grumman and Raytheon (Northrop Grumman 1840 Century Park East, Los Angeles, CA 90067-2199 Telephone: +1 310 553 6262 Facsimile: +1 310 533 2076)	GAM					Moving tail fins	None	Inertial + GPS	a) 2,000 (907) Mk84	GPS-Aided Munitions, as interim JDAM type using Mk84 bomb and INS/GPS tail kit. Used by B-2. 128 delivered from 1996
Raytheon Systems Company 2501 South Highway 121, PO Box 405, MS 3500, Lewisville, TX 75067-8127 Telephone: +1 972 462 6500 Facsimile: + 1 972 462 6508	GBU-10C, D, E & F Paveway II	a) 170.1 (4.32) b) 66 (168)	a) 18.1 (46.0) b) c.1,985 (c.900)			Moving canard fins	None	Semi-active laser homing	a) Mk84 bomb	Includes F-15E, F-117
Raytheon Systems Company 2501 South Highway 121, PO Box 405, MS 3500, Lewisville, TX 75067-8127 Telephone: +1 972 462 6500 Facsimile: + 1 972 462 6508	GBU-10G, H & J Paveway II	a) 167.7 (4.26) b) 66 (168)	a) 14.6 (37.0) b) c.1,985 (c.900)			Moving canard fins	None	Semi-active laser homing	a) BLU-109/B	Includes F-15E, F-117
Raytheon Systems Company 2501 South Highway 121, PO Box 405, MS 3500, Lewisville, TX 75067-8127 Telephone: +1 972 462 6500 Facsimile: + 1 972 462 6508	GBU-12B, C & D Paveway II	a) 131.1 (3.33) b) 52.75 (134)	a) 10.75 (27.3) b) 603 (225)			Moving canard fins	None	Semi-active laser homing	a) Mk82 bomb	Includes F-15E, F-117
Boeing Aircraft and Missile Systems PO Box 516, St. Louis, MO 63166-0516 Telephone: +1 314 232 2800 Facsimile: +1 314 234 8296	GBU-15	a) 154.5 (3.92) b) 59.0 (149.0)	a) 18.0 (46.0) b) 2,450 (1,111)	0.8 – 44 (1.5 – 82)	Subsonic	Moving canard fins	None	IIR or TV seeker + datalink	a) Mk84, CBU-75 or BLU-109/B bomb	F-4, F-15E, F-16
Raytheon Systems Company 2501 South Highway 121, PO Box 405, MS 3500, Lewisville, TX 75067-8127 Telephone: +1 972 462 6500 Facsimile: + 1 972 462 6508	GBU-16A & B	a) 144.9 (3.68) b) 66 (168)	a) 13.8 (35.0) b) c.1,000 (c.454)			Moving canard fins	None	Semi-active laser homing	a) Mk83 bomb	
Raytheon Systems Company 2501 South Highway 121, PO Box 405, MS 3500, Lewisville, TX 75067-8127 Telephone: +1 972 462 6500 Facsimile: + 1 972 462 6508	GBU-24A/B Paveway III	a) 170 (4.32) b) 79 (2.0)	a) 14.6 (37.0) b) 2,350 (1,066)			Moving canard fins	None	Semi-active laser homing	a) BLU-109 bomb	F-15E, F-16, F-22, FOA
Raytheon Systems Company 2501 South Highway 121, PO Box 405, MS 3500, Lewisville, TX 75067-8127 Telephone: +1 972 462 6500 Facsimile: + 1 972 462 6508	GBU-27B	a) 166.9 (4.24) b) 66.15 (168.0)	a) 14.5 (37) b) 2,169 (984)			Moving fins	None	Semi-active laser homing	a) Penetrator with 529 (240) HE core	F-117A
Raytheon Systems Company 2501 South Highway 121, PO Box 405, MS 3500, Lewisville, TX 75067-8127 Telephone: +1 972 462 6500 Facsimile: + 1 972 462 6508	GBU-28B	a) 230 (5.84) b) 66.15 (168.0)	a) 14.6 (37.0) b) 5,707 (2,130)			Moving fins	None	Modified GBU-27 system	a) 675 (306) HE penetrator based on BLU-109/B	B-1B and B-2? All being upgraded with improved guidance and fuze

Manufacturer	Designation	a) Length ins (m) b) Span ins (cm)	a) Diameter ins (cm) b) Weight lb (kg)	Range naut miles (km)	Speed	Control	Propulsion	Guidance	a) Warhead lb (kg) b) Fuzing	Comments and Platform(s)
United States of America (continued)										
Boeing Aircraft and Missile Systems PO Box 516, St. Louis, MO 63166-0516 Telephone: +1 314 232 2800 Facsimile: +1 314 234 8296	GBU-31 JDAM (Joint Direct Attack Munition)	a) 152.7 (3.88) with Mk84, 148.6 (3.77) with BLU-109	b) 2,036 – 2,056 (924 – 933) with Mk84, 2,115 – 2,135 (959 – 968) with BLU-109	13+ (24+)		Moving tail fins	None	Inertial + GPS	a) 2,000 (907) Mk84 or BLU-109 penetrator bomb	Low-cost guidance kit for bombs, adding tail section containing INS/GPS. 617 kits delivered for EMD; 128 JDAMs for early operational capability with B-2. Other potential platforms include B-1B, B-52, F-14, F-15E, F-16, F/A-18, F-22, F-117A, Harrier, JSF, P-3
Boeing Aircraft and Missile Systems PO Box 516, St. Louis, MO 63166-0516 Telephone: +1 314 232 2800 Facsimile: +1 314 234 8296	GBU-32 JDAM (Joint Direct Attack Munition)	a) 119.5 (3.04)	b) 1,013 – 1,028 (459 – 466)	13+ (24+)		Moving tail fins	None	Inertial + GPS	a) 1,000 (454) Mk83 or BLU-110 penetrator bomb	Platforms as for GBU-31 JDAM. US forces expected to receive 87,496 JDAMs over a decade from 1998. CEP accuracy of under 15 metres, with improvements to achieve 10 metres. Gets target information from aircraft prior to release via a MIL-STD-1760 databus
Unknown	Have Slick	a) c.180 (c.4.60)	a) 27.5 (70) b) c.3,100 (c.1,400)	19 (35)			None?	Imaging IR or active radar homing	a) c. 2,000 (c.900) of stores – warhead or submunitions	Proposed for B-2, F-117A, F-22
Lockheed Martin Electronics & Missiles 5600 Sand Lake Road, Orlando, FL 32819-8907 Telephone: +1 407 356 2000 Facsimile: +1 407 356 2080	JASSM			over 100 (185)			Teledyne J402-CA-400 engine	GPS/IMU inertial	a) Unitary for use against high-value targets in 1,000 lb class (J-1000)	Joint Air-to-Surface Standoff Missile for USAF and US Navy. Anticipated 2,400 missiles for USAF. Contract awarded April 1998. Initial low rate production in year 2000. For B-1B, B-2, B-52H, F-15E, F-16C/D, F/A-18E/F, F-117A, P-3C and S-3B
Lockheed Martin Electronics & Missiles 5600 Sand Lake Road, Orlando, FL 32819-8907 Telephone: +1 407 356 2000 Facsimile: +1 407 356 2080	Wind Corrected Munitions Dispenser (WCMD)			7 (12.9)		Moving tail fins	None	INS	a) Tactical munitions dispenser using BLU-108/B SFW submunitions, GEM or GATOR cluster munitions	B-1B, B-2, B-52H, F-15E, F-16, F-22, F-117A. MIL-STD-1760. Tailkit for CBU-87, 89 or 97 dispenser weapons. First flown 1996
Multinational										
Taurus Systems (subsidiary of Daimler-Benz Aerospace/LFK of Germany and Bofors Celsius of Sweden)	KEPD 350	a) 196.9 (5.0)	b) 3,086 (1,400)	189+ (350+)	Mach 0.8		Turbojet	Tri-Tec system of GPS/INS/ TERNAV + IR homing	a) TDW Mephisto 1,102 (500) dual stage penetrator b) Tandem smart type	Highly modular cruise missile proposed for Tornado, Harrier II, Eurofighter. Ordered by Luftwaffe. Kinetic Energy Penetration Destroyer (KEPD). Reportedly developed from DWS 39. Designed with RCS and IR stealth requirements. Matra BAe Dynamics and Daimler-Benz Aerospace have proposed derivative using Apache technology.
Taurus Systems (subsidiary of Daimler-Benz Aerospace/LFK of Germany and Bofors Celsius of Sweden)	KEPD 50 & KEPD 150	a) 177.2 (4.5) for KEPD 150	b) 2,337 (1,060) for KEPD 150	27 – 81 (50 – 150)	Mach 0.8+		High-power Williams or Microturbo turbojet	Tri-Tec system of GPS/INS/ TERNAV + IR homing	a) TDW Mephisto dual stage area & penetrator (effector) with or without pre-charge	Smaller variants of KEPD 350 have been proposed as medium and long-range weapons, including KEPD 150 for Gripen. Adapted to Tornado, Eurofighter and later Gripen, AMX, F-16, F/A-18. Other platforms could include Mirage, Rafale. Designed with RCS and IR stealth requirements. First captive flight trial of a KEPD 150 mock-up took place on 27 August 1998, from a Gripen
Taurus Systems (subsidiary of Daimler-Benz Aerospace/LFK of Germany and Bofors Celsius of Sweden)	Taurus (PDWS) Data for PDWS 2000, unless stated otherwise	a) 192.9 (4.90) for Taurus 350 A/P	b) under 2,204 (1,000), or 2,403 – 2,734 (1,090 – 1,240) for Taurus 350 A/P	54+ (100+), or 108 – 162+ (200 – 300+) for Taurus 350 A/P	Mach 0.8		Turbojet	Tri-Tec system of GPS/INS/ TERNAV + IR homing	a) Different versions with penetrator or dispenser warheads	Precision Distance Weapon Systems (PDWS) family of stand-off missiles, for possible service from the year 2000. Modular, based on KEPD 350 but reduced version. Possible for international requirements in JASSM class

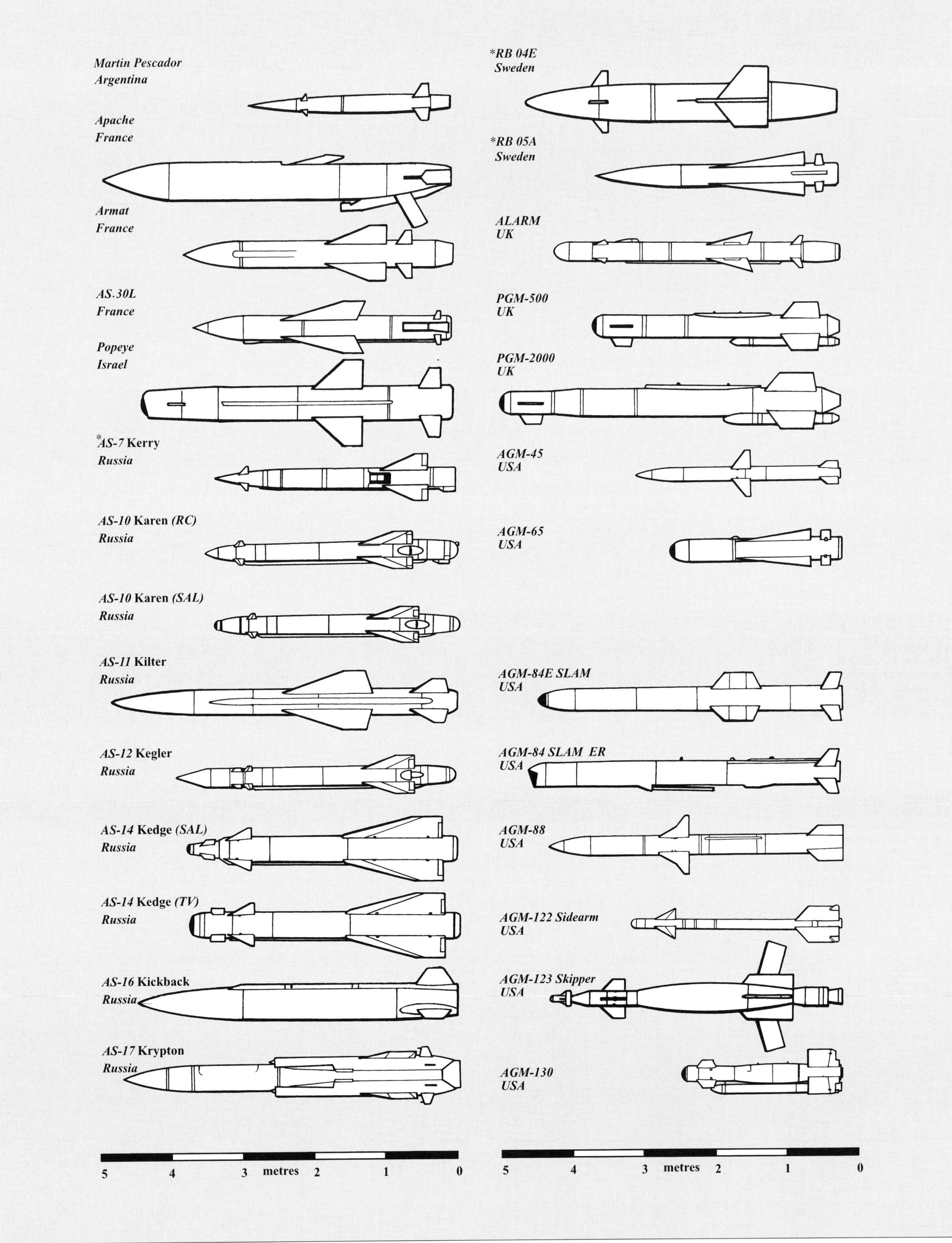
Martin Pescador
Argentina
Apache
France
Armat
France
AS.30L
France
Popeye
Israel
*AS-7 Kerry
Russia
AS-10 Karen (RC)
Russia
AS-10 Karen (SAL)
Russia
AS-11 Kilter
Russia
AS-12 Kegler
Russia
AS-14 Kedge (SAL)
Russia
AS-14 Kedge (TV)
Russia
AS-16 Kickback
Russia
AS-17 Krypton
Russia
5 4 3 metres 2 1 0
*RB 04E
Sweden
*RB 05A
Sweden
ALARM
UK
PGM-500
UK
PGM-2000
UK
AGM-45
USA
AGM-65
USA
AGM-84E SLAM
USA
AGM-84 SLAM ER
USA
AGM-88
USA
AGM-122 Sidearm
USA
AGM-123 Skipper
USA
AGM-130
USA
5 4 3 metres 2 1 0

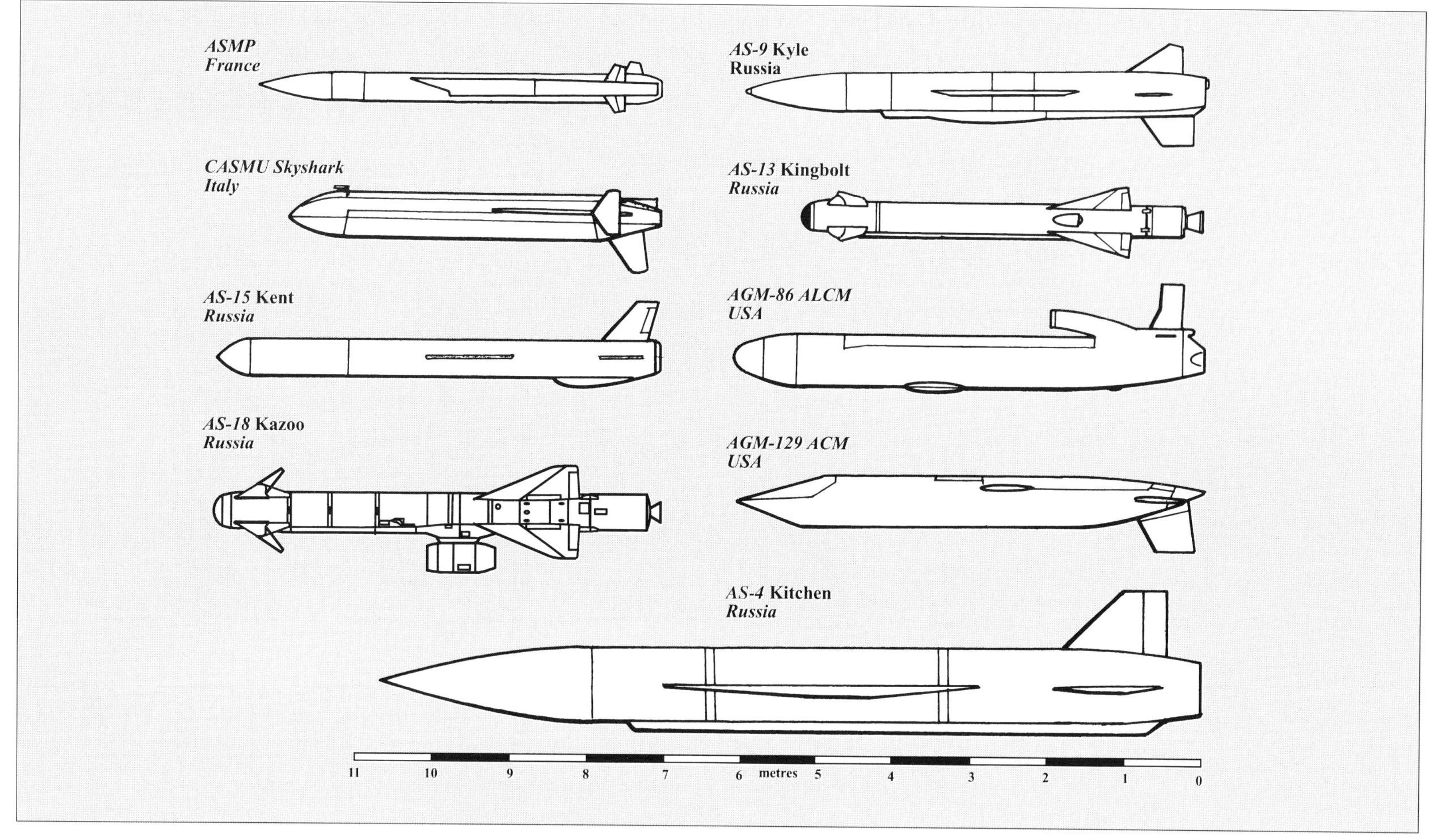

Air-to-air

Manufacturer	Designation	a) Length ins (m) b) Span ins (cm)	a) Diameter ins (cm) b) Weight lb (kg)	Range naut miles (km)	Speed	Control	Propulsion	Guidance	a) Warhead lb (kg) b) Fuzing	Comments and Platform(s)
Brazil										
Mectron Engenharia Industria e Comercio Ltda	MAA-1 Mol (formerly known as Piranha)	a) 111.0 (2.82) b) 25.6 (65.0)	a) 6.0 (15.2) b) 198.4 (90.0)	5.4 (10)	Mach 2+	Moving canard fins	Single-stage solid-propellant rocket	Passive IR homing	a) 26.5 (12.0) HE fragmentation b) Laser proximity fuze	AMX, ALX, Mirage III, F-5. First air launched from a Xavante in 1996. Production begun
China										
China National Aero-Technology Import and Export Corporation (CATIC) CATIC Plaza, 18 Beichen Dong Lu, Chaoyang District, Beijing 100101 Telephone: +86 10 6494 1090 Facsimile: +86 10 6494 1088	PL-2B	a) 117.7 (2.99) b) 20.8 (52.8)	a) 5.0 (12.7) b) 167.6 (76.0)	1.6 (3)		Moving canard fins	Solid-propellant rocket	IR homing	a) 24.9 (11.3) blast fragmentation b) IR proximity fuze	J-5, J-6, J-7, JJ-7, J-8II, A-5
China National Aero-Technology Import and Export Corporation (CATIC) CATIC Plaza, 18 Beichen Dong Lu, Chaoyang District, Beijing 100101 Telephone: +86 10 6494 1090 Facsimile: +86 10 6494 1088	PL-3	a) 117.7 (2.99) b) 20.8 (52.8)	a) 5.0 (12.7) b) 180.8 (82.0)	1.6 (3)		Moving canard fins	Solid-propellant rocket	IR homing	a) 29.7 (13.5) HE blast fragmentation b) IR proximity fuze	J-5, J-6, J-7
China National Aero-Technology Import and Export Corporation (CATIC) CATIC Plaza, 18 Beichen Dong Lu, Chaoyang District, Beijing 100101 Telephone: +86 10 6494 1090 Facsimile: +86 10 6494 1088	PL-5, PL-5B & PL-5E	a) 113.8 (2.89) b) 25.9 (65.7)	a) 5.0 (12.7) b) 187.4 (85.0)	8.6 (16). PL-5E said to have range of 1,640 ft (500 m) to 7.5 naut miles (14 km)		Moving canard fins	Solid-propellant rocket	Passive IR homing. PL-5E seeker has all-aspect capability, with off borcsight ±25° prior to launch at ±40° in flight	a) 19.8 (9.0) continuous-rod or HE blast fragmentation b) IR or radio proximity fuze. Improved on PL-5B	J-5, J-7, JH-7, A-5. PL-5E accelerates at 40g
China National Aero-Technology Import and Export Corporation (CATIC) CATIC Plaza, 18 Beichen Dong Lu, Chaoyang District, Beijing 100101 Telephone: +86 10 6494 1090 Facsimile: +86 10 6494 1088	PL-7 & PL-7B	a) 108.3 (2.75) b) 26.0 (66.0)	a) 6.2 (15.8) b) 198.4 (90.0)			Moving canard fins	Solid-propellant rocket	Passive IR homing	a) 28.6 (13.0) HE fragmentation b) IR proximity fuze	J-7, J-8II, A-5, K-8

Manufacturer	Designation	a) Length ins (m) b) Span ins (cm)	a) Diameter ins (cm) b) Weight lb (kg)	Range naut miles (km)	Speed	Control	Propulsion	Guidance	a) Warhead lb (kg) b) fuzing	Comments and Platform(s)
China (continued)										
Unknown	PL-8	a) 118.1 (3.00) b) 33.9 (86.0)	a) 6.3 (16.0) b) 264.6 (120.0)	2.7 (5)		Moving canard fins	Solid-propellant rocket	Passive IR homing	a) 24.2 (11.0) HE fragmentation b) Laser proximity fuze	J-7
China National Aero-Technology Import and Export Corporation (CATIC) CATIC Plaza, 18 Beichen Dong Lu, Chaoyang District, Beijing 100101 Telephone: +86 10 6494 1090 Facsimile: +86 10 6494 1088	PL-9	a) 117.7 (2.99) b) 31.9 (81.0)	a) 6.3 (16.0) b) 264.6 (120.0)	2.7 (5)		Moving canard fins	Solid-propellant rocket	Passive IR homing	a) 22.0 (10.0) HE b) Laser proximity fuze	J-7, J-8II
China National Aero-Technology Import and Export Corporation (CATIC) CATIC Plaza, 18 Beichen Dong Lu, Chaoyang District, Beijing 100101 Telephone: +86 10 6494 1090 Facsimile: +86 10 6494 1088	PL-10	a) 157.1 (3.99) b) 46.1 (117.0)	a) 11.3 (28.6) b) 661.4 (300.0)	8.1 (15)	Mach 3	Moving wings	Single-stage solid-propellant rocket	Semi-active radar homing	a) HE fragmentation b) RF proximity fuze	J-7, J-8?
China Precision Machinery Import Export Corporation (CPMIEC) 17 Wenchang Hutong, Xidan, PO Box 845, Beijing *or* 18F International Trading Building, Shenzen 518014 Telephone: +86 755 225 1659 Facsimile: +86 755 222 1387	PL-11 (see Comments for QW-1)	a) 153.1 (3.89) b) 26.8 (68)	a) 8.2 (20.8) b) 485 (220)	13.5 (25)	Mach 3+	Cruciform mid-mounted surfaces	Dual-thrust solid-propellant rocket	Semi-active/ passive radar homing	a) HE blast fragmentation	FC-1 and other fighters. The totally unrelated QW-1 from CPMIEC is a short-range (2.7 naut mile, 5 km) IR self-defence AAM of 60.2 ins (1.53 m) length, 2.75 ins (7 cm) diameter, and 36.4 lb (16.5 kg) weight
France										
Aerospatiale Missiles F-92322 Chatillon-sous-Bagneux Telephone: +33 1 47 46 21 21 Facsimile: +33 1 47 46 33 19	ASMP-R	a) 211.8 (5.38) b) 37.8 (96.0)	a) 15.0 (38.0) b) 1,896 (860)	135 (250)	Mach 3.0	Moving tail fins	Liquid-propellant ramjet with integral solid propellant rocket booster	Passive radar homing	a) c.441 (c.200) HE	Projected anti-AEW weapon. Mirage 2000?, Rafale?
Matra BAe Dynamics 37 avenue Louis-Breguet, F-78146 Vélizy-Villacoublay Cedex Telephone: +33 1 34 88 30 00 Facsimile: +33 1 34 65 12 15	Meteor	a) 142 (3.6) b) 22.28 (56.6)	a) 6.7 (17)	Beyond visual range		4 rear fins	Ramrocket	Update data link + active radar seeker	a) HE, blast fragmentation b) Proximity & impact	Projected medium/beyond-visual range air-to-air missile. BVRAAM type, in co-operation with Alenia, DASA/LFK, GEC-Marconi and Saab. Mirage 2000?, Gripen?, Eurofighter?, Rafale?
Matra BAe Dynamics 37 avenue Louis-Breguet, F-78146 Vélizy-Villacoublay Cedex Telephone: +33 1 34 88 30 00 Facsimile: +33 1 34 65 12 15	MICA EM & IR	a) 122.1 (3.10) b) 22.1 (56.0)	a) 6.3 (16.0) b) 247 (112)	Hundreds of metres to 32+ (60+)		Moving tail fins + thrust vectoring	Solid-propellant rocket	Inertial with datalink up-dating + active radar homing (EM) or passive IR imagery terminal guidance (IR) interchange-able with active radar head	a) 26.5 (12) HE blast fragmentation b) Active radar proximity fuze & impact	Long-range interception, combat and self-defence missile with multi-target capability. MICA IR in development stage. Mirage 2000, Rafale, Gripen. 3 user countries at time of writing
Matra BAe Dynamics 37 avenue Louis-Breguet, F-78146 Vélizy-Villacoublay Cedex Telephone: +33 1 34 88 30 00 Facsimile: +33 1 34 65 12 15	Mistral ATAM	a) 73.2 (1.86) b) 7.5 (19.0)	a) 3.5 (9.0) b) 43 (19.5)	0.16 – 2.7+ (0.3 – 5+)	Mach 2.5	Moving canard fins	Solid-propellant rocket	Passive IR homing	a) 6.6 (3.0) fragmentation b) Contact & active laser proximity fuzes	For helicopters, for very short-range combat against helicopters and aircraft. AS 565 Panther, A129, Gazelle, Tigre, AH-64
Matra BAe Dynamics 37 avenue Louis-Breguet, F-78146 Vélizy-Villacoublay Cedex Telephone: +33 1 34 88 30 00 Facsimile: +33 1 34 65 12 15	R.550 Magic 1	a) 107.1 (2.72) b) 26.0 (66.0)	a) 6.2 (15.7) b) 196 (89)	0.15 – 5+ (0.3 – 10+)	Mach 2+	Moving canard fins	Solid-propellant rocket	Passive IR homing	a) 27.5 (12.5) HE fragmentation b) Contact & IR proximity fuzes	Mirage III, Mirage 5, Mirage F1, Mirage 2000, Jaguar, Shamsher, Super Etendard, Alpha Jet, Sea Harrier, MiG-21, MiG-23, Harrier II, A-5, C-101, MB-339, BAe Hawk, F-16, J-7, Atlantique
Matra BAe Dynamics 37 avenue Louis-Breguet, F-78146 Vélizy-Villacoublay Cedex Telephone: +33 1 34 88 30 00 Facsimile: +33 1 34 65 12 15	R.550 Magic 2 Mk 2	a) 108.3 (2.75) b) 26.0 (66.0)	a) 6.3 (16.0) b) 196.2 (89)	0.27 – 10.8+ (0.5 – 20+)	Mach 2+	Moving canard fins 3-axis control	Solid-propellant rocket	Passive IR homing/ optical scanning	a) 27.5 (12.5) pre-fragmented b) Contact & RF proximity fuzes	See Magic 1. Over 11,000 Magic 1/2s ordered by 19 countries. All-sector dogfight and interception.
Matra BAe Dynamics 37 avenue Louis-Breguet, F-78146 Vélizy-Villacoublay Cedex Telephone: +33 1 34 88 30 00 Facsimile: +33 1 34 65 12 15	Super 530D	a) 149.4 (3.795) b) 24.4 (62.0)	a) 10.4 (26.3) b) 606 (275)	21+ (40+)	Mach 4.5+	Moving tail fins	Solid-propellant rocket	Semi-active radar homing	a) 66 (30) HE fragmentation b) Active radar proximity fuze	All-weather, all-sector, all-altitude to 85,000 ft (26,000 m). Mirage III, Mirage F1, Mirage 2000, Rafale. 530D/F used by 6 countries
Matra BAe Dynamics 37 avenue Louis-Breguet, F-78146 Vélizy-Villacoublay Cedex Telephone: +33 1 34 88 30 00 Facsimile: +33 1 34 65 12 15	Super 530F	a) 139.4 (3.54) b) 34.7 (88.0)	a) 10.4 (26.3) b) 540 (245)	19 (35)	Mach 4.5	Moving tail fins	Dual-thrust solid-propellant rocket	Semi-active radar homing	a) 66 (30) HE fragmentation b) Radar proximity fuze	Mirage III, Mirage F1, Mirage 2000, Rafale

Manufacturer	Designation	a) Length ins (m) b) Span ins (cm)	a) Diameter ins (cm) b) Weight lb (kg)	Range naut miles (km)	Speed	Control	Propulsion	Guidance	a) Warhead lb (kg) b) Fuzing	Comments and Platform(s)
Germany										
Daimler-Benz Aerospace/LFK PO Box 801109, D-81663 Munich Telephone: +49 89 6 07-0 Facsimile: +49 89 6 07 26481	A3M (see Comments for new EURAAM)	a) 144.1 (3.66)	a) 7 (18) b) 384 (174)	54 (100)		Moving tail fins	Boron-loaded, variable-flow, ducted rocket	IMU + active radar homing	a) HE fragmentation b) Radar proximity fuze	Proposed for Eurofighter. EURAAM is a rocket/ramjet AAM that could be test fired in the year 2000 (unguided tests initially). DASA Ulm Ka-band active radar seeker, with passive secondary X-band
Bodenseewerke-Gerätetechnik GmbH PO Box 101155, D-88641 Überlingen Telephone: +49 7551 89-6114 Facsimile: +49 7551 89-6274	IRIS-T	a) 118 (3.0) b) 13.8 (35.0)	a) 5.0 (12.7) b) 191.8 (87)	6.5 (12)		Thrust vectoring	Solid-propellant rocket	Passive IIR homing	a) 25 (11.4) HE b) Active laser	Short-range missile planned for Tornado, Eurofighter, etc. Saab Dynamics contributes at missile system level and the IIR seeker. Highly agile. IOC about 2002
India										
Defence R&D Lab	Astra							Inertial + active radar		LCA
Israel										
Rafael Armament Development Authority, Missile Division PO Box 2250/30, Haifa 31021 Telephone: +972 4 990 8503 Facsimile: +972 4 990 6257	Python 3	a) 118.1 (3.00) b) 33.9 (86.0)	a) 6.3 (16.0) b) 265 (120)	0.25 – 8 (0.5 – 15)	Mach 3.5	Moving canard fins	Solid-propellant rocket	Passive IR homing	a) 24.25 (11.0) HE fragmentation b) Active laser proximity fuze	Third generation, all-aspect, short/medium-range. Kfir, F-4, F-5, F-15, F-16, Mirage III, Mirage F1, Mirage 2000, Pantara, MiG-21-2000, J-7. Offered to Ecuador 1997
Rafael Armament Development Authority, Missile Division PO Box 2250/30, Haifa 31021 Telephone: +972 4 990 8503 Facsimile: +972 4 990 6257	Python 4 & Rafael/ Lockheed Martin Python 4I (see Comments)	a) 118 (3.0) b) 13.8 (35)	a) 6.3 (16.0) b) 234 (108)	8.1 (15)		Moving canards	Smokeless solid-propellant rocket	All aspect 2-colour passive IR homing	a) 24.25 (11.0) HE fragmentation b) Active laser	Fourth generation. Kfir, F-15I, F/A-18?, F-16. Lockheed Martin of the USA is jointly developing (under May 1998 agreement) Python 4I, the 'improved' missile having a new IR seeker and larger-range motor.
Rafael Armament Development Authority, Missile Division PO Box 2250/30, Haifa 31021 Telephone: +972 4 990 8503 Facsimile: +972 4 990 6257	Shafrir 2	a) 102.4 (2.60) b) 25.2 (64.0)	a) 6.3 (16.0) b) 205 (93)	2.7 (5)		Moving canard fins	Double-base solid rocket	All-aspect 2-colour passive IR homing	a) 24.25 (11.0) HE fragmentation b) Contact & proximity fuzes	F-4, F-15, F-16, Mirage III, Kfir, A-4
Rafael Armament Development Authority, Missile Division PO Box 2250/30, Haifa 31021 Telephone: +972 4 990 8503 Facsimile: +972 4 990 6257	5th Generation MRAAM			Medium			Rocket	Imaging IR & active radar homing		Development thought to have begun in mid-1990s, for trials from 1997-98. Possible seeker technology co-operation with US company
Italy										
Alenia Divisione Sistemi Missilistici Via Tiburtina Km 12.4, I-00 131 Roma Telephone: +39 06 41971 Facsimile: +39 06 4131133 or 4131436	Aspide Mk1	a) 145.7 (3.70) b) 39.4 (100.0)	a) 8.0 (20.3) b) 485 (220)	18.9 (35)	Mach 4	Moving wings	Single-stage solid-propellant rocket	Semi-active radar homing	a) 77 (35) fragmentation b) Active-radar proximity fuze	F-104S
Alenia Divisione Sistemi Missilistici Via Tiburtina Km 12.4, I-00 131 Roma Telephone: +39 06 41971 Facsimile: +39 06 4131133 or 4131436	Aspide Mk2	a) 143.7 (3.65) b) 24 (64)	a) 8.4 (21.2) b) 507 (230)	21.6 (40)	Mach 4	Moving wings	Single-stage solid-propellant rocket	Active radar homing	a) 77 (35) fragmentation b) Active-radar proximity fuze	Eurofighter
Japan										
Mitsubishi Electric 5-1, Marunouchi 2-chome, Chiyoda-ku, Tokyo 100 Telephone: +81 3 3212 3111 Facsimile: +81 3 3212 9865	AAM-3 (Type 90)	a) 118 (3.0) b) 25.2 (64)	a) 5 (12.7) b) 201 (91)	2.7 (5)		Moving canard fins?	Solid-propellant rocket	Passive IR homing	a) 33 (15) HE b) Contact & active laser proximity fuzes	F-4, F-15, F-2
Mitsubishi Electric (Address, etc, as above)	AAM-4 MRAAM	a) c.158 (c.4.0)	b) c.507 (c.230)	Medium				Active radar homing		Planned for F-15J from 1999 and later F-2
Mitsubishi Electric (Address, etc, as above)	XAAM-5			Short		Highly agile, with narrow & very long fins		IIR homing		Short-range AAM for IOC from early next century. Initial funding from JDA's 1998 budget. NEC IIR seeker. Over ±60° off-boresight angles for acquisition
Toshiba	Type 91							IR homing		OH-1 helicopter
Pakistan										
Pakistan Ordnance Factories Wah Cantt, nr Islamabad	designation unknown			Short				Passive IR homing		Trials from late 1980s
Romania										
Ploest plant	A-95-MH (data estimated)	a) 82.5 (2.09) b) 15.4 (39.0)	a) 4.7 (12.0)		Perhaps Mach 2.5?	Moving canard fins	Solid-propellant rocket	Passive IR homing	a) 7.7 (3.5) HE b) Active radar proximity fuze	Developed from Russian R-60, but with changes to seeker and motor. For at least SOCAT Puma

Manufacturer	Designation	a) Length ins (m) b) Span ins (cm)	a) Diameter ins (cm) b) Weight lb (kg)	Range naut miles (km)	Speed	Control	Propulsion	Guidance	a) Warhead lb (kg) b) Fuzing	Comments and Platform(s)
Russia										
GMKB Vympel 90 Volokolamskoye Shosse, Moscow, 123424 Telephone: +7 095 491 0239 Facsimile: +7 095 490 2222	K-30			c.16? (c.30?)		Vectored thrust		Passive IR homing	a) HE	New dogfight missile for Russian fighters
Novator Yekaterinburg	KS-172 (AAM-L)	a) 236 (6.0); 291 (7.4) with booster	a) 15.75 (40) b) 1,654 (750)	216 (400)		Cruciform tail surfaces	Solid-propellant rocket & solid-propellant tandem booster	Inertial + command up-dates, then active-radar terminal homing	a) Adaptive HE fragmenting b) Active-radar proximity fuze	Su-35, MiG 1-42, Su-32FN, Su-35/37, S-37
GMKB Vympel 90 Volokolamskoye Shosse, Moscow, 123424 Telephone: +7 095 491 0239 Facsimile: +7 095 490 2222	R-3S (AA-2 Atoll)	a) 111.7 (2.84) b) 20.8 (52.8)	a) 5.0 (12.7) b) 166 (75.3)	0.65 – 4.1 (1.2 – 7.6)	Mach 2.5?	Moving canard fins	Solid-propellant rocket	Passive IR homing	a) 24.9 (11.3) HE blast fragmentation b) Impact & optical proximity fuzes	MiG-21, MiG-23, MiG-27, Su-17, Su-20, Su-22
GMKB Vympel 90 Volokolamskoye Shosse, Moscow, 123424 Telephone: +7 095 491 0239 Facsimile: +7 095 490 2222	R-3R (AA-2C Atoll)	a) 134.7 (3.42) b) 20.8 (52.8)	a) 5.0 (12.7) b) 184.1 (83.5)	0.5 – 3.8 (1 – 7)	Mach 2.5?	Moving canard fins	Solid-propellant rocket	J-band semi-active radar homing	a) 24.9 (11.3) HE blast fragmentation b) Impact & optical proximity fuzes	Old missile, now used only with early versions of MiG-21
GMKB Vympel 90 Volokolamskoye Shosse, Moscow, 123424 Telephone: +7 095 491 0239 Facsimile: +7 095 490 2222	R-13M (AA-2D Atoll)	a) 113.2 (2.88) b) 23.2 (59.0)	a) 5.0 (12.7) b) 198.0 (89.8)	0.3 – 8.0 (0.6 – 15)	Mach 2.5?	Moving canard fins	Solid-propellant rocket	Passive IR homing	a) 24.9 (11.3) HE blast fragmentation b) Impact & RF proximity fuzes	MiG-21, MiG-23, MiG-27, Su-17, Su-20, Su-22, Su-25
GMKB Vympel 90 Volokolamskoye Shosse, Moscow, 123424 Telephone: +7 095 491 0239 Facsimile: +7 095 490 2222	R-23R (AA-7 Apex)	a) 175.6 (4.46) b) 39.4 (100.0)	a) 7.9 (20.0) b) 491.6 (223.0)	1 – 19 (1.8 – 35)	3,280 ft/sec (1,000 m/sec)	Moving tail fins	Solid-propellant rocket	Semi-active radar homing	a) 77.2 (35.0) HE fragmentation b) Proximity fuze	MiG-23
GMKB Vympel 90 Volokolamskoye Shosse, Moscow, 123424 Telephone: +7 095 491 0239 Facsimile: +7 095 490 2222	R-23T (AA-7 Apex)	a) 163.8 (4.16) b) 39.4 (100.0)	a) 7.9 (20.0) b) 478? (217?)	1 – c.14.6? (1.8 – c.27?)	3,280 ft/sec (1,000 m/sec)	Moving tail fins	Solid-propellant rocket	Passive IR homing	a) 77.2 (35.0) HE fragmentation b) Proximity fuze	MiG-23
GMKB Vympel 90 Volokolamskoye Shosse, Moscow, 123424 Telephone: +7 095 491 0239 Facsimile: +7 095 490 2222	R-24R (AA-7 Apex)	a) 177.2 (4.50) b) 38.3 (97.2)	a) 7.9 (20.0) b) 538 (244.0)	27 (50)	3,280 ft/sec (1,000 m/sec)	Moving tail fins	Solid-propellant rocket	Semi-active radar homing	a) 77.2 (35.0) HE fragmentation b) Proximity fuze	MiG-23
GMKB Vympel 90 Volokolamskoye Shosse, Moscow, 123424 Telephone: +7 095 491 0239 Facsimile: +7 095 490 2222	R-24T (AA-7 Apex)	a) 165.0 (4.19) b) 38.3 (97.2)	a) 7.9 (20.0) b) 522 (237)		3,280 ft/sec (1,000 m/sec)	Moving tail fins	Solid-propellant rocket	Passive IR homing	a) 77.2 (35.0) HE fragmentation b) Proximity fuze	MiG-23
GMKB Vympel 90 Volokolamskoye Shosse, Moscow, 123424 Telephone: +7 095 491 0239 Facsimile: +7 095 490 2222	R-27R (AA-10 Alamo A)	a) 160.6 (4.08) b) 38.3 (97.2)	a) 9.1 (23.0) b) 557.8 (253.0)	0.25 – 43 (0.5 – 80)		Moving canard fins	Solid-propellant rocket	Inertial + command updates, then semi-active radar homing	a) 86 (39) HE b) Active radar proximity fuze	MiG-21-93, MiG-29, Su-27, Su-33, Su-35, Su-39. AA-10 available to J-8II. R-27s have been produced by State Holding Company "Artem" of Kiev
GMKB Vympel 90 Volokolamskoye Shosse, Moscow, 123424 Telephone: +7 095 491 0239 Facsimile: +7 095 490 2222	R-27T (AA-10 Alamo B)	a) 149.5 (3.80) b) 38.3 (97.2)	a) 9.1 (23.0) b) 540.1 (245.0)	0.25 – 37.8 (0.5 – 70)		Moving canard fins	Solid-propellant rocket	Inertial + command updates, then passive IR homing	a) 86 (39) HE b) Active radar proximity fuze?	MiG-29, Su-27, Su-33, Su-35, Su-39
GMKB Vympel 90 Volokolamskoye Shosse, Moscow, 123424 Telephone: +7 095 491 0239 Facsimile: +7 095 490 2222	R-27EA	a) 188.2? (4.78?) b) 38.3 (97.2)	a) 10.2 (26.0) b) c.772 (c.350)	0.25 – 70 (0.5 – 130)		Moving canard fins	Solid-propellant rocket	Inertial + command updates, then active radar homing	a) 86 (39) HE b) Active radar proximity fuze	MiG-29, Su-27, Su-33, Su-35, Su-39
GMKB Vympel 90 Volokolamskoye Shosse, Moscow, 123424 Telephone: +7 095 491 0239 Facsimile: +7 095 490 2222	R-27EM	a) 188.2 (4.78) b) 38.3 (97.2)	a) 10.2 (26.0) b) 772 (350)	0.25 – 92 (0.5 – 170)		Moving canard fins	Solid-propellant rocket	Inertial + command updates, then passive IR homing	a) 86 (39) HE b) Active radar proximity fuze	MiG-29, Su-27, Su-33, Su-35, Su-39
GMKB Vympel 90 Volokolamskoye Shosse, Moscow, 123424 Telephone: +7 095 491 0239 Facsimile: +7 095 490 2222	R-27ER (AA-10 Alamo C)	a) 188.2 (4.78) b) 38.3 (97.2)	a) 10.2 (26.0) b) 772 (350)	0.25 – 70 (0.5 – 130)		Moving canard fins	Solid-propellant rocket	Inertial + command updates, then semi-active radar homing	a) 86 (39) HE b) Active radar proximity fuze	MiG-29, Su-27, Su-30, Su-33, Su-35, Su-39
GMKB Vympel 90 Volokolamskoye Shosse, Moscow, 123424 Telephone: +7 095 491 0239 Facsimile: +7 095 490 2222	R-27ET (AA-10 Alamo D)	a) 176.8 (4.49) b) 38.3 (97.2)	a) 10.2 (26.0) b) 765 (347)	0.25 – 64.75 (0.5 – 120)		Moving canard fins	Solid-propellant rocket	Inertial + command updates, then passive IR homing	a) 86 (39) HE b) Active radar proximity fuze	MiG-29, Su-27, Su-30, Su-33, Su-35, Su-39?

Manufacturer	Designation	a) Length ins (m) b) Span ins (cm)	a) Diameter ins (cm) b) Weight lb (kg)	Range naut miles (km)	Speed	Control	Propulsion	Guidance	a) Warhead lb (kg) b) Fuzing	Comments and Platform(s)
Russia (continued)										
GMKB Vympel 90 Volokolamskoye Shosse, Moscow, 123424 Telephone: +7 095 491 0239 Facsimile: +7 095 490 2222	R-27P/R-27EP	b) 38.3 (97.2)					Solid-propellant rocket	Passive radar homing		
GMKB Vympel 90 Volokolamskoye Shosse, Moscow, 123424 Telephone: +7 095 491 0239 Facsimile: +7 095 490 2222	R-33 (AA-9 Amos)	a) 163.4 (4.15) b) 46.5 (118.0)	a) 15.0 (38.0) b) 1,080 (490)	65 (120)			Solid-propellant rocket	Autopilot + semi-active radar homing	a) 103.6 (47) HE b) Impact & proximity fuzes?	MiG-31, option on Su-27
GMKB Vympel 90 Volokolamskoye Shosse, Moscow, 123424 Telephone: +7 095 491 0239 Facsimile: +7 095 490 2222	R-33A (AA-9 Amos)	a) c.164 (c.4.2) b) 46.5 (118.0)	a) 15.0 (38.0) b) c.1,102 (c.500)				Solid-propellant rocket	Autopilot + active/semi-active radar homing	b) Impact & proximity fuzes?	MiG-31, option on Su-27. Small cruciform forward fins added. Sometimes referred to as R-33S
GMKB Vympel 90 Volokolamskoye Shosse, Moscow, 123424 Telephone: +7 095 491 0239 Facsimile: +7 095 490 2222	R-37 (AA-13) & K-37M (see Comments)	a) 165 (4.2) b) 27.6 (70.0)	a) 15.0 (38.0) b) 1,102 (500)	189 (350)	2,158 kts (4,000 km/h)	Moving rear fins	Solid-propellant rocket	Inertial + semi-active radar homing	a) 132 (60) fragmentation b) Impact & proximity fuzes?	MiG-31M, 1-42, Su-32FN. K-37M for MiG-29SMT modernization and others (no data available at time of writing)
GMKB Vympel 90 Volokolamskoye Shosse, Moscow, 123424 Telephone: +7 095 491 0239 Facsimile: +7 095 490 2222	R-40RD (AA-6 Acrid)	a) 245.3 (6.23) b) 57.1 (145.0)	a) 12.2 (31.0) b) 1,016 (461)	1.08 – 43 (2 – 80)	Mach 4.5	Ailerons + moving canard fins?	Solid-propellant rocket	Semi-active radar homing	a) 83.7 (38.0) HE b) Impact & proximity fuzes?	MiG-25, MiG-31, Su-35
GMKB Vympel 90 Volokolamskoye Shosse, Moscow, 123424 Telephone: +7 095 491 0239 Facsimile: +7 095 490 2222	R-40TD (AA-6 Acrid)	a) 233.5 (5.93) b) 57.1 (145.0)	a) 12.2 (31.0) b) 992 (450)	16.2? (30?)	Mach 4.5	Ailerons + moving canard fins?	Solid-propellant rocket	Passive IR homing	a) 83.7 (38.0) HE b) Impact & proximity fuzes?	MiG-25, MiG-31, Su-35
GMKB Vympel 90 Volokolamskoye Shosse, Moscow, 123424 Telephone: +7 095 491 0239 Facsimile: +7 095 490 2222	R-60 (AA-8 Aphid)	a) 82.5 (2.09) b) 15.4 (39.0)	a) 4.7 (12.0) b) 95.9 (43.5)	0.16 – 4.0 (0.3 – 7.5)	Mach 2.5?	Moving canard fins	Solid-propellant rocket	Passive IR homing	a) 7.7 (3.5) HE b) Active radar proximity fuze	MiG-21, MiG-23, MiG-25, MiG-27, MiG-31, Mi-24, Su-17, Su-22, Su-24, Su-25, Su-27, Super Galeb, Iryda
GMKB Vympel 90 Volokolamskoye Shosse, Moscow, 123424 Telephone: +7 095 491 0239 Facsimile: +7 095 490 2222	R-60M & MK (AA-8 Aphid)	a) 84.2 (2.14) b) 15.4 (39.0)	a) 4.7 (12.0) b) 99.2 (45.0)	6.5 (12)	Mach 2.5?	Moving canard fins	Solid-propellant rocket	Passive IR homing	a) 7.7 (3.5) HE b) Laser proximity fuze?	MiG-21, MiG-23, MiG-25, MiG-27, MiG-29, MiG-31, Su-17, Su-22, Su-24, Su-25, Su-35, Su-39
GMKB Vympel 90 Volokolamskoye Shosse, Moscow, 123424 Telephone: +7 095 491 0239 Facsimile: +7 095 490 2222	R-73/R-73E/ R-73EL (AA-11 Archer)	a) 114.2 (2.90) b) 20.1 (51.0)	a) 6.7 (17.0) b) 232 (105)	0.16 – 16.2 (0.3 – 30)		Moving canard fins + thrust vectoring	Dual-thrust solid-propellant rocket?	Passive IR homing	a) 16.3 (7.4) b) Active radar or laser proximity fuze	MiG-21-93, MiG-21-2000, MiG-23B-98, MiG-27 upgrade, MiG-29, 1-42, S-80PT, Su-27, Su-30, Su-32/34, Su-33, Su-35, Su-37, Su-39, Ka-50, Ka-52
GMKB Vympel 90 Volokolamskoye Shosse, Moscow, 123424 Telephone: +7 095 491 0239 Facsimile: +7 095 490 2222	R-74ME	a) 114.2 (2.90) b) 20.1 (51.0)	a) 6.7 (17.0) b) 232 (105)	0.16 – 21.6 (0.3 – 40)		Moving canard fins & thrust vectoring	Dual-thrust solid-propellant rocket	Passive IR homing	a) 16.3 (7.4) b) Active radar or laser proximity fuze	MiG-29, Su-27, Su-33, Su-34, Su-35, Ka-50. Developed from the R-73 (Archer), with longer acquisition range due to new IR-sensitive element in head and wider off-boresight detection (±90° instead of ±60°)
GMKB Vympel 90 Volokolamskoye Shosse, Moscow, 123424 Telephone: +7 095 491 0239 Facsimile: +7 095 490 2222	R-77/R-77M (AA-12 Adder)	a) 141.7 (3.60) & longer for R-77M b) 27.56 (70)	a) 7.9 (20.0) b) 386 (175) or 408 (185) for R-77M	54 (100)	Mach 3	Moving rear lattice control surfaces	Solid-propellant rocket (probably dual-thrust for at least R-77M)	Inertial with datalink updates, then active or passive radar homing	a) 48.5 (22) HE b) Active radar proximity fuze	MiG-21-93, MiG-29, MiG-31, 1-42, Su-25, Su-30, Su-32, Su-34, Su-35, Su-37, Su-39, J-8II, Integral. AGAT seeker. R-77M has compact active radar seeker with digital processors and new antenna, plus folding fins and new warhead
GMKB Vympel 90 Volokolamskoye Shosse, Moscow, 123424 Telephone: +7 095 491 0239 Facsimile: +7 095 490 2222	RVV-AE-PD	a) 145.7 (3.7) b) 7.9 (20)	b) 496 (225)	86 (160)		See R-77	Combined rocket/ramjet	Inertial with datalink updates, then Doppler active or passive radar homing	a) 48.5 (22) HE b) Active radar proximity fuze	Similar to R-77
KB Mashinostroyeniya 140402 Kolomna, Moscow Region, Oksky Prospekt 42 Telephone: +7 096 61 33277 Facsimile: +7 096 61 33064	9M32M Strela-2M (SA-7b Grail) (see Comments for 9M36 Strela-3/SA-14)	a) 56.7 (1.44)	a) 2.8 (7.2) b) 21.8 (9.8)	0.43 – 2.3 (0.8 – 4.2)	Mach 1.7 (580 m/sec) maximum, Mach 1.49 (500 m/sec) average	2 moving canard fins	Improved solid-propellant booster & sustainer	Passive IR homing	a) 2.53 (1.15) fragmentation b) Contact & grazing	Mi-2, Mi-24, W-3, Gazelle. Strela-3 has length of 57.9 ins (1.47 m) and 24.2 lb (11 kg) weight but similar range
KB Mashinostroyeniya 140402 Kolomna, Moscow Region, Oksky Prospekt 42 Telephone: +7 096 61 33277 Facsimile: +7 096 61 33064	9M313 Igla-I (SA-16 Gimlet) & 9M39 Igla-V (SA-18 Grouse) (data for Gimlet)	a) 66.5 (1.69)	a) 2.8 (7.2) b) 23.6 (10.7)	2.7 – 3.67 (5 – 6.8) maximum		2 moving canard fins	Solid-propellant booster & sustainer	Passive IR homing	a) 2.80 (1.27) fragmentation? b) Contact & grazing	Ka-50, Ka-52, Mi-2, Mi-8AMT-Sh, Mi-17, Mi-24, Mi-28, Mi-35. SA-18 Grouse is generally similar

Manufacturer	Designation	a) Length ins (m) b) Span ins (cm)	a) Diameter ins (cm) b) Weight lb (kg)	Range naut miles (km)	Speed	Control	Propulsion	Guidance	a) Warhead lb (kg) b) Fuzing	Comments and Platform(s)
Russia (continued)										
Unknown	G3-X Vega		b) 75 (34)	2,625–39,370 ft (800–12,000 m)				Combined semi-active laser & IR		Mi-35
South Africa										
Denel, Kentron Division Jochemus Street, Erasmuskloof, PO Box 8322, Hennopsmeer 0046 Telephone: +27 12 428 0637 Facsimile: +27 12 428 0651	V-3C/Darter & A-Darter (Agile Darter)	a) 108.3 (2.75) b) 26.0 (66.0)	a) 6.2 (15.7) b) 196 (89)	0.15 – 5.4 (0.3 – 10)	Aircraft velocity + 1960 ft/sec (600 m/sec)	Moving canard fins. Tail surfaces + thrust vectoring for A-Darter	Solid-propellant rocket	Imaging IR homing	a) 35.3 (16.0) prefragmented HE b) Contact & laser proximity fuzes	Mirage III, Mirage F1, Cheetah, Puma, J-10? A-Darter service possibly 2005
Denel, Kentron Division Jochemus Street, Erasmuskloof, PO Box 8322, Hennopsmeer 0046 Telephone: +27 12 428 0637 Facsimile: +27 12 428 0651	R-Darter			c.27 (c.50)				Active radar homing		Medium-range AAM for IOC early next century. Under development?
Denel, Kentron Division Jochemus Street, Erasmuskloof, PO Box 8322, Hennopsmeer 0046 Telephone: +27 12 428 0637 Facsimile: +27 12 428 0651	U-Darter	a) 108.3 (2.75) b) 26.0 (66.0)	a) 6.2 (15.7) b) 211.6 (96.0)	0.22 – 5.4 (0.4 – 10.0)	Aircraft velocity + 2,130 ft/sec (650 m/sec)	Moving canard fins	Solid-propellant rocket	Passive 2-colour IR homing	a) 37.5 (17) prefragmented HE b) Contact & laser proximity	Cheetah?
Denel, Kentron Division Jochemus Street, Erasmuskloof, PO Box 8322, Hennopsmeer 0046 Telephone: +27 12 428 0637 Facsimile: +27 12 428 0651	LRAAM (Long-Range Anti-Aircraft Missile)	a) c.120 (c.3.0) b) c.16 (c.40)	a) 7.1 (18.0) b) c.287 (c.130)	54+ (100+)	Mach 2.3 - 3.0		Solid-propellant integral rocket/ramjets	Autopilot with datalink + passive IIR homing	a) 44 (20) HE	
Denel, Kentron Division Jochemus Street, Erasmuskloof, PO Box 8322, Hennopsmeer 0046 Telephone: +27 12 428 0637 Facsimile: +27 12 428 0651	V3/V3P/Kukri	a) 115.8 (2.94) b) 20.9 (53.0)	a) 5.0 (12.7) b) 161.8 (73.4)	0.16 – 1 (0.3 – 2) low-altitude; 0.16 – 2.2 (0.3 – 4) high-altitude	Aircraft velocity + 1640 ft/sec (500 m/sec)	Moving canard fins	Double-base solid-propellant rocket	Passive IR homing	a) Fragmentation, with Torpex 2A explosive b) Contact & proximity fuzes?	Mirage III, Mirage F1 & conversions. V3P carried by Rooivalk, with 2 colour seeker slaved to HMSD
Taiwan										
Chung Shang Institute of Science and Technology Tao Yuan Hsiang, Taipei Telephone: +886 3 471 2201	Tien Chien I (Sky Sword I)	a) 113.0 (2.87) b) 25.2 (64.0)	a) 5.0 (12.7) b) 198 (90)	2.7 (5.0)		Moving canard fins	Solid-propellant rocket	Passive IR homing	a) HE blast fragmentation b) Laser proximity fuze	Ching-Kuo, F-5, F-16, Mirage 2000
Chung Shang Institute of Science and Technology Tao Yuan Hsiang, Taipei Telephone: +886 3 471 2201	Tien Chien II (Sky Sword II)	a) 141.7 (3.60) b) 29.5 (75.0)	a) 8.0 (20.3) b) 419 (190)	21.6 (40)		Moving wings?	Solid-propellant rocket	Semi-active radar homing	a) Possibly 66 (30) HE fragmentation b) Radar proximity fuze	Ching-Kuo, F-16?, Mirage 2000?
United Kingdom										
Matra BAe Dynamics PO Box 19, Six Hills Way, Stevenage, Hertfordshire SG1 2DA Telephone: +44 1438 312422 Facsimile: +44 1438 753377	Active Sky Flash	a) 144.1 (3.66) b) 40.2 (102.0)	a) 8.0 (20.3) b) 459 (208)	21.6 (40)	Mach 4	Moving wings	Solid-propellant rocket	Active radar homing	a) 66 (30) fragmentation b) Puls~-Doppler proximity fuze	Was proposed for Tornado F.3
Raytheon Systems King's House, Kymberley Road, Harrow, Middlesex HA1 1YD Telephone: +44 181 861 2525 Facsimile: +44 181 863 0599	FMRAAM						Liquid-ramjet	2-way asynchronous datalink for mid-course guidance control & third party cueing and targeting		Evolved from AMRAAM. Industrial partners are Aerospatiale, Shorts, and Thomson-CSF. Eurofighter?
Shorts Missile Systems Alanbrooke Road, Castlereagh, Belfast BT6 9HB, Northern Ireland Telephone: +44 1232 458444 Facsimile: +44 1232 465172	Javelin	a) 54.7 (1.39) b) 10.8 (27.5)	a) 3.0 (7.6) b) 28.0 (12.7)	0.16 – 3.0 (0.3 – 5.5)	Mach 1+	Cruciform moving canard fins	Solid-propellant rocket	SACLOS	a) 6.0 (2.74) fragmentation b) Impact & proximity fuzes	A129
Matra BAe Dynamics PO Box 19, Six Hills Way, Stevenage, Hertfordshire SG1 2DA Telephone: +44 1438 312422 Facsimile: +44 1438 753377	Sky Flash	a) 144.1 (3.66) b) 40.2 (102.0)	a) 8.0 (20.3) b) 430 (195)	21.6 (40)	Mach 4	Moving wings	Solid-propellant rocket	CW semi-active J-band radar homing	a) 66 (30) continuous-rod b) Radar proximity fuze	Tornado F.3, JA37 Viggen, tested on F-16
Shorts Missile Systems Alanbrooke Road, Castlereagh, Belfast BT6 9HB, Northern Ireland Telephone: +44 1232 458444 Facsimile: +44 1232 465172	Starstreak	a) 55.1 (1.4) b) 9.85 (25)	a) 5.0 (12.7) b) 35.3 (16)	0.16 – 3.8 (0.3 – 7)	c. Mach 4 at sustainer burnout	Moving fins	Solid-propellant rocket booster, then unpowered	Laser beam-riding	a) 3 dense alloy darts containing HE (warhead is over 50% weight of dart) b) Delayed-action fuze	Shorts has received second contract from US Army for trials of Starstreak on Longbow Apache helicopter, in co-operation with Lockheed Martin and Boeing

Manufacturer	Designation	a) Length ins (m) b) Span ins (cm)	a) Diameter ins (cm) b) Weight lb (kg)	Range naut miles (km)	Speed	Control	Propulsion	Guidance	a) Warhead lb (kg) b) Fuzing	Comments and Platform(s)
United States of America										
Raytheon Systems Company 180 Hartwell Road, Bedford, MA 10730 Telephone: +1 617 274 5000 Facsimile: +1 781 860 2172 (Lexington)	AIM-7E (AAM-N-6B) Sparrow	a) 144.0 (3.66) b) 40.0 (101.6)	a) 8.0 (20.3) b) 452 (205)	23.8 (44)	Mach 3.7 at burnout	Moving wings	Solid-propellant rocket	Semi-active radar homing		F-4, F-14, F-15, F-16, F/A-18. Sparrow was formerly a Hughes product
Raytheon/former General Dynamics	AIM-7F Sparrow	a) 144.0 (3.66) b) 40.0 (101.6)	a) 8.0 (20.3) b) 504 (229)	21.6 (40)	Mach 3.7 at burnout	Moving wings	Solid-propellant rocket	Semi-active radar homing	a) 86 (39) continuous-rod b) Impact & RF proximity fuzes	F-2, F-4, F-14, F-15, F-16, F/A-18. Solid-state electronics, Doppler guidance and better ECM
Raytheon Systems Company 180 Hartwell Road, Bedford, MA 10730 Telephone: +1 617 274 5000 Facsimile: +1 781 860 2172 (Lexington)	AIM-7M Sparrow	a) 144.0 (3.66) b) 40.0 (101.6)	a) 8.0 (20.3) b) 508 (230)	0.3 – 24.3 (0.6 – 45)	Mach 2.5	Moving wings	Solid-propellant rocket	Monopulse semi-active radar homing	a) 86 (39) focussed blast fragmentation b) Impact & active-radar proximity fuzes	F-2, F-4, F-14, F-15, F-16, F/A-18. Monopulse version. Better in ECM and clutter environments
Raytheon Systems Company 180 Hartwell Road, Bedford, MA 10730 Telephone: +1 617 274 5000 Facsimile: +1 781 860 2172 (Lexington)	AIM-7P Sparrow	a) 144.0 (3.66) b) 40.0 (101.6)	a) 8.0 (20.3) b) 508 (230)	24.3 (45)		Moving wings	Solid-propellant rocket	Command via mid-course data uplink receiver, then semi-active radar homing	a) 86 (39) continuous-rod b) Impact & active-radar proximity fuzes	F-4, F-14, F-15, F-16, F/A-18. Better electronics and fuzes, for improved capability against anti-ship and cruise missiles
Raytheon Systems Company 180 Hartwell Road, Bedford, MA 10730 Telephone: +1 617 274 5000 Facsimile: +1 781 860 2172 (Lexington)	AIM-7R Sparrow	a) 144.0 (3.66) b) 40.0 (101.6)	a) 8.0 (20.3) b) 508 (230)			Moving wings	Solid-propellant rocket	Combined semi-active radar & passive IR seeker		F-4, F-14, F-15, F-16, F/A-18. More capable in sophisticated ECM environment
Ford Aerospace/Raytheon	AIM-9B Sidewinder	a) 111.4 (2.83) b) 20.9 (53.0)	a) 5.0 (12.7) b) 168 (76)	1.08 (2)		Moving canard fins	Solid-propellant rocket	Passive IR homing	a) 10.0 (4.5) blast-fragmentation b) IR proximity fuze	Has been widely used by NATO & others for close-range/dogfight
Ford Aerospace/Raytheon	AIM-9J Sidewinder	a) 120.9 (3.07) b) 22.0 (55.9)	a) 5.0 (12.7) b) 172.0 (78.0)	7.8 (14.5)	Mach 2.5	Moving canard fins	Solid-propellant rocket	Passive IR homing	b) Impact & proximity fuzes?	F-4
Ford Aerospace/Raytheon	AIM-9L Sidewinder	a) 113.0 (2.87) b) 25.2 (64.0)	a) 5.0 (12.7) b) 190.9 (86.6)	4.32 (8)	Mach 2.5	Moving canard fins	Solid-propellant rocket	Passive IR homing	a) 21.0 (9.5) annular blast-fragmentation b) DSU-21 laser proximity fuze	F-2, F-4EJ, C-101, F-14, F-15, F-16, F/A-18, Tornado, Tornado F.3, Sea Harrier, Harrier II, Gripen (as Rb 74), AMX/A-1, AH-1, P-3, A129, AH-64, Nimrod
Raytheon Systems Company 180 Hartwell Road, Bedford, MA 10730 Telephone: +1 617 274 5000 Facsimile: +1 781 860 2172 (Lexington)	AIM-9M Sidewinder (see Comments for AIM-9M-9)	a) 113.0 (2.87) b) 25.2 (64.0)	a) 5.0 (12.7) b) 190.9 (86.6)	8.7+ (16+)	Mach 2.5	Moving canard fins	Reduced-smoke solid-propellant rocket	Passive IR homing	a) 20.8 (9.4) blast-fragmentation b) Laser proximity fuze	F-14, F-15, F-16, F/A-18, F-117A, F-22, A-10A, Sea Harrier. All-aspect weapon. Better IRCCM, with further improvements for AIM-9M-9 version. Sidewinders no longer produced by Lockheed Martin/Loral
Raytheon Systems Company (Address, etc, as above)	AIM-9P-1 Sidewinder	a) 120.9 (3.07) b) 25.2 (64.0)	a) 5.0 (12.7) b) 180.8 (82.0)	4.32 (8)	Mach 2.5	Moving canard fins	Solid-propellant rocket	Passive IR homing	a) 26.5 (12.0) blast-fragmentation b) Laser proximity fuze	Used by export customers on various aircraft. Sidewinders no longer produced by Lockheed Martin/Loral
Raytheon Systems Company (Address, etc, as above)	AIM-9P-2 Sidewinder	a) 120.9 (3.07) b) 25.2 (64.0)	a) 5.0 (12.7) b) 180.8 (82.0)	4.32 (8)	Mach 2.5	Moving canard fins	Reduced smoke solid-propellant rocket	Passive IR homing	a) 26.5 (12.0) blast-fragmentation b) Laser proximity fuze	See above. Sidewinders no longer produced by Lockheed Martin/Loral
Raytheon Systems Company (Address, etc, as above)	AIM-9P-3 Sidewinder	a) 120.9 (3.07) b) 25.2 (64.0)	a) 5.0 (12.7) b) 180.8 (82.0)	4.32 (8)	Mach 2.5	Moving canard fins	Reduced-smoke solid-propellant rocket	Passive IR homing	a) 26.5 (12.0) blast-fragmentation b) Laser proximity fuze	See above. Sidewinders no longer produced by Lockheed Martin/Loral
Raytheon Systems Company (Address, etc, as above)	AIM-9P-4 Sidewinder	a) 120.9 (3.07) b) 25.2 (64.0)	a) 5.0 (12.7) b) 180.8 (82.0)	4.32 (8)	Mach 2.5	Moving canard fins	Solid-propellant rocket	Passive IR homing	a) 26.5 (12.0) blast-fragmentation b) Laser proximity fuze	See above. Sidewinders no longer produced by Lockheed Martin/Loral
Raytheon Systems Company (Address, etc, as above)	AIM-9R Sidewinder	a) 113.0 (2.87) b) 25.2 (64.0)	a) 5.0 (12.7) b) 191.8 (87.0)	4.32 (8)	Mach 2.5	Moving canard fins	Solid-propellant rocket	Optical-band homing	a) 21.0 (9.5) blast-fragmentation b) Laser proximity fuze	Sidewinders no longer produced by Lockheed Martin/Loral
Raytheon Systems Company (Address, etc, as above)	AIM-9S Sidewinder	a) 113.0 (2.87) b) 25.2 (64.0)	a) 5.0 (12.7) b) 190 (86.0)	4.32 (8)	Mach 2.5	Moving canard fins	Solid-propellant rocket	Passive IR homing	a) 22.5 (10.2) blast-fragmentation b) Laser proximity + impact fuzes	F-15, F-16. Sidewinders no longer produced by Lockheed Martin/Loral

Manufacturer	Designation	a) Length ins (m) b) Span ins (cm)	a) Diameter ins (cm) b) Weight lb (kg)	Range naut miles (km)	Speed	Control	Propulsion	Guidance	a) Warhead lb (kg) b) Fuzing	Comments and Platform(s)
United States of America (continued)										
Raytheon Systems Company 180 Hartwell Road, Bedford, MA 10730 Telephone: +1 617 274 5000 Facsimile: +1 781 860 2172 (Lexington)	AIM-9 Evolved Sidewinder (AIM-9X type)	a) c.120? (c.3?)	a) 5.0 (12.7) b) c.200? (c.90?)			Thrust vectoring	Solid-propellant rocket	Focal plane array sensor & Raytheon advanced tracker + passive IR homing	a and b) As for AIM-9M	Intended replacement in US forces and others for AIM-9M, via AIM-9X. Off-boresight type, possibly with pilot's helmet sight acquisition. Planned for USAF fighters, including F-22. Interest from Australia
Raytheon Systems Company 1151 East Hermans Road, PO Box 11337, Tucson, AZ 85734 Telephone: +1 520 794 3000 Facsimile: +1 520 794 1315	AIM-54C Phoenix	a) 169.3 (4.30) b) 36.0 (91.5)	a) 15.0 (38.0) b) 1,020.7 (463.0)	108+ (200+)	Mach 4+	Moving tail fins	Solid-propellant rocket	Inertial + semi-active & active radar homing	a) 132 (60) HE continuous rod b) Impact & radar proximity fuzes	F-14
Raytheon Systems Company 1151 East Hermans Road, PO Box 11337, Tucson, AZ 85734 Telephone: +1 520 794 3000 Facsimile: +1 520 794 1315	AIM-120A, B & C AMRAAM B & C in current production	a) 144.0 (3.65) b) 25.0 (63.5); 18 (46) for C	a) 7.0 (17.8) b) 345.0 (156.5)	30 (55)	Mach 4 at altitude	Moving tail fins driven by electric actuators (C has smaller fins)	Solid-propellant boost/sustain rocket. An enhanced rocket motor for retrofit & for new AMRAAM variants has been tested in Norway	Inertial with datalink updating + I-band active-radar homing	a) 48.5 (22.0) HE directed fragmentation b) Active radar proximity fuze	F-4F, F-14, F-15, F-16, F/A-18, F-22, JSF, Sea Harrier, Harrier II Plus, Gripen, Rafale, Viggen, Tornado, Eurofighter. Gencorp Aerojet 2-stage motor
Raytheon Systems Company 1151 East Hermans Road, PO Box 11337, Tucson, AZ 85734 Telephone: +1 520 794 3000 Facsimile: +1 520 794 1315	FIM-92A Stinger	a) 59.8 (1.52) b) 5.5 (14)	a) 2.7 (6.9) b) 35.2 (16)	0.1 – 1.62+ (0.2 – 3+)	Mach 2.2 (maximum)	Cruciform moving canard fins	Dual-thrust solid-propellant booster & sustainer	Passive IR homing	a) 6.6 (3.0) HE fragmentation b) Contact fuze	Tigre, A109K, A129, MG Defender, AH-60L, MH-60K, Kiowa Warrior, Comanche, AH-64, H-76 Eagle, KMH
Multi-national										
Matra BAe Dynamics/Raytheon	AIM-132 ASRAAM	a) 114.2 (2.90) b) 17.7 (45.0)	a) 6.5 (16.6) b) 192 (87)	<0.15 – 5.4 (<0.3 – 10)		Moving tail fins	Solid-propellant rocket (low signature)	Inertial + imaging IR homing	a) c.22 (c.10) HE blast fragmentation b) Active laser proximity fuze & impact	Advanced short-range air-to-air missile for Eurofighter, F-16, Rafale, F/A-18?, Harrier GR.7 and Tornado F.3
Matra BAe Dynamics/Saab/ Thomson-CSF	S225X & S225XR		a) c.7.9 (c.20)	54+ (100+)	Very high	Moving tail fins	Solid-propellant rocket (S225X) or ramjet (S225XR)	Inertial (probably with command link update) + active-radar homing	b) Active-radar or IR-based proximity fuze	Intended as a possible armament for export versions of Eurofighter and JAS 39 Gripen

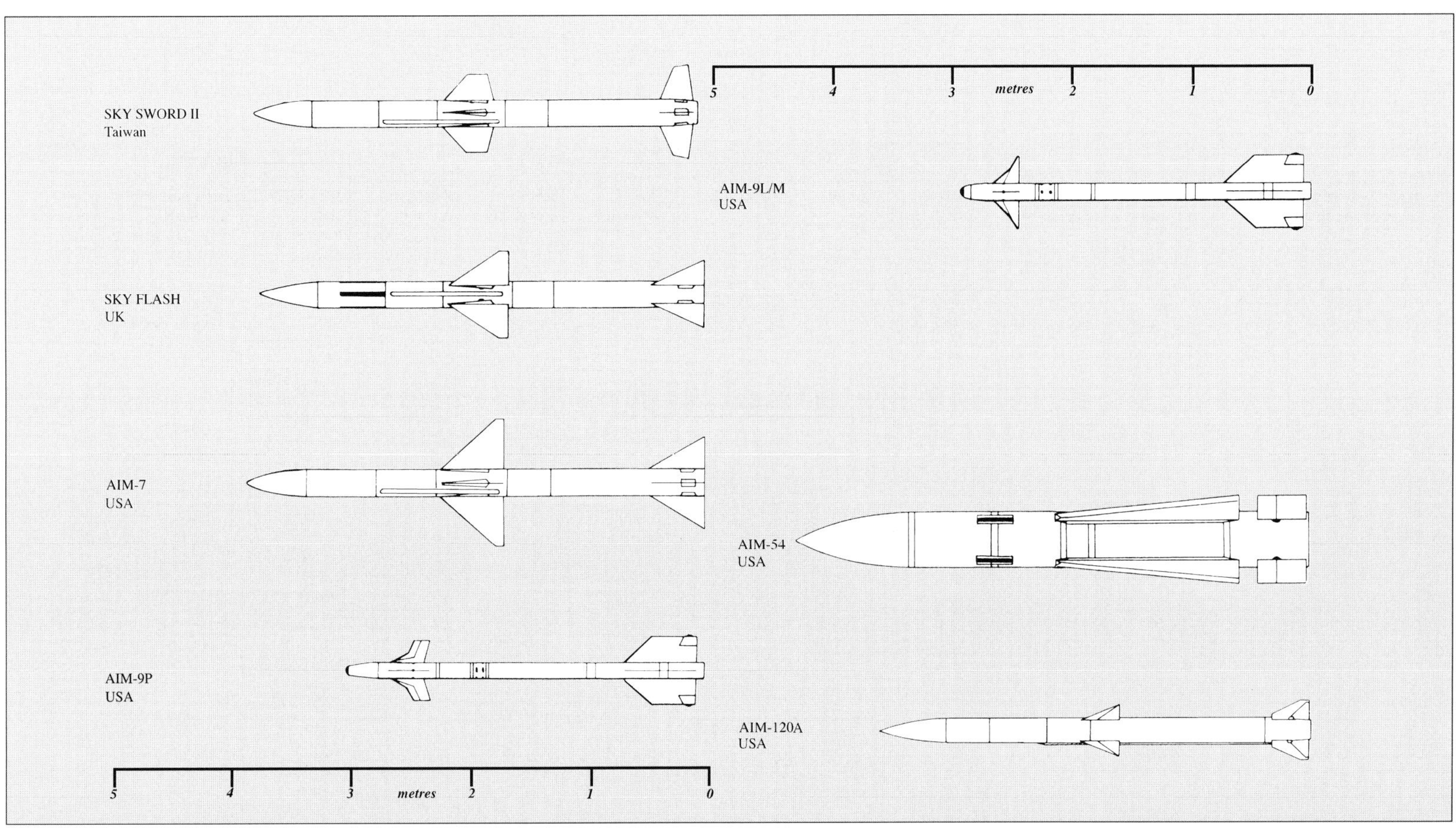

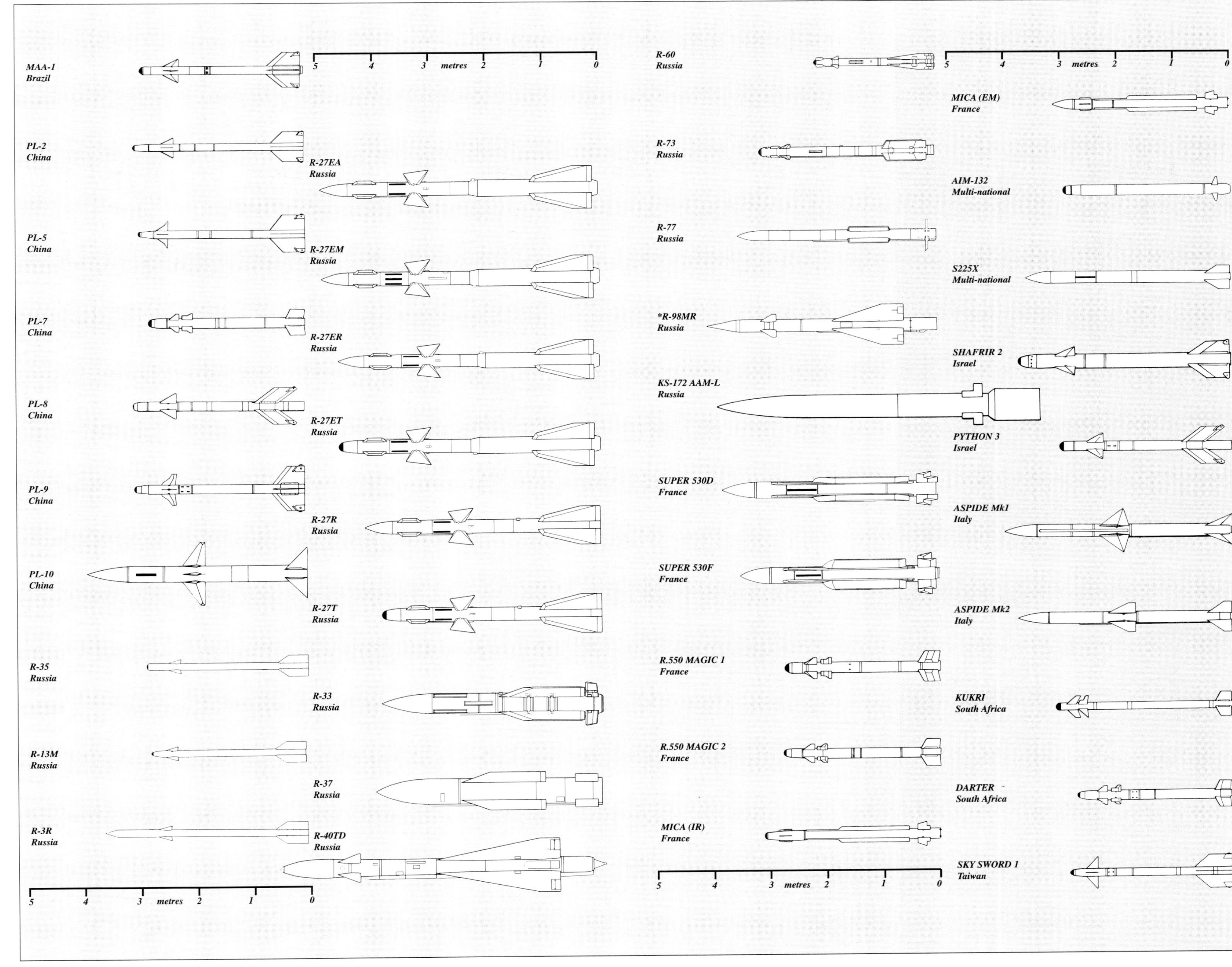
MAA-1
Brazil
PL-2
China
PL-5
China
PL-7
China
PL-8
China
PL-9
China
PL-10
China
R-35
Russia
R-13M
Russia
R-3R
Russia
5 4 3 metres 2 1 0
R-27EA
Russia
R-27EM
Russia
R-27ER
Russia
R-27ET
Russia
R-27R
Russia
R-27T
Russia
R-33
Russia
R-37
Russia
R-40TD
Russia
5 4 3 metres 2 1 0
R-60
Russia
R-73
Russia
R-77
Russia
*R-98MR
Russia
KS-172 AAM-L
Russia
SUPER 530D
France
SUPER 530F
France
R.550 MAGIC 1
France
R.550 MAGIC 2
France
MICA (IR)
France
5 4 3 metres 2 1 0
MICA (EM)
France
AIM-132
Multi-national
S225X
Multi-national
SHAFRIR 2
Israel
PYTHON 3
Israel
ASPIDE Mk1
Italy
ASPIDE Mk2
Italy
KUKRI
South Africa
DARTER
South Africa
SKY SWORD I
Taiwan
5 4 3 metres 2 1 0

Air-launched anti-ship

Manufacturer	Designation	a) Length ins (m) b) Span ins (cm)	a) Diameter ins (cm) b) Weight lb (kg)	Range naut miles (km)	Speed	Control	Propulsion	Guidance	a) Warhead lb (kg) b) Fuzing	Comments and Platform(s)
China										
China Precision Machinery Import Export Corporation (CPMIEC) 17 Wenchang Hutong, Xidan, PO Box 845, Beijing *or* International Trading Building, Shenzen 518014 Telephone: +86 755 225 1659 Facsimile: +86 755 222 1387	C-101 (CSS-X-5 Saples)	a) 228.35 (5.80), though also reported as 295 (7.5) b) 47.2 (120.0)	a) 29.9 (76.0) b) 4,210 (1,910)	45 (83)	Supersonic	Moving fins	Twin liquid-propellant ramjets & two solid-propellant rocket boosters	Inertial midcourse + active radar terminal homing	a) 660 (300) semi-armour-piercing (SAP)	H-5, H-6, SH-5
China Precision Machinery Import Export Corporation (CPMIEC) (Address, etc, as above)	Hai Ying 4/ C-201 (CSSC-7 Sadback)	a) 289.8 (7.36) b) 108.3 (275.0)	a) 30 (76) b) 3,836 (1,740)	81 (150)	Mach 0.8	Aerodynamic	Solid-propellant rocket booster & turbojet sustainer	Autopilot + active radar homing	a) 1,100 (500) HE	H-6?
China Precision Machinery Import Export Corporation (CPMIEC) (Address, etc, as above)	Ying Ji 1/ C-801 (CSSC-N-4 Sardine)	a) 183.1 (4.65), though also reported as 228.4 (5.80) b) 46.5 (118.0)	a) 14.2 (36.0) b) 1,444 (655)	4.4 – 21.6 (8 – 40)	Mach 0.9	Cruciform moving tail fins	Solid-propellant rocket booster & sustainer	Autopilot/ radar altimeter + active radar terminal homing	a) 363 (165) HE	H-6, JH-7
China Precision Machinery Import Export Corporation (CPMIEC) (Address, etc, as above)	Ying Ji 2K/ C-802K	a) 252 (6.39), though also reported as 208.7 (5.30) b) 65 (165)	a) 14.2 (36.0) b) 1,576 (715)	6 – 65 (15 – 120)	Mach 0.8 – 0.9	Cruciform moving tail fins	Turbojet & solid-propellant rocket booster	Autopilot/ radar altimeter + active radar terminal homing	a) 363? (165?) HE	H-6, Q/A-5, JH-7, helicopters
China Precision Machinery Import Export Corporation (CPMIEC) (Address, etc, as above)	Ying Ji 6/ C-601 (CAS-1 Kraken) (see Comments for C-611)	a) 290.6 (7.38) b) 94.5 (240.0)	a) 30 (76) b) 5,380 (2,440)	59.4 or 86 (110 or 160)	Mach 0.9	Aerodynamic	Liquid propellant rocket	Autopilot + active radar seeker	a) 1,131 (513) HE blast fragmentation	Q/A-5, H-6D, JH-7. Being replaced by new YJ-61 (C-611) with 108 naut mile (200 km) range
France										
Aerospatiale Missiles 2 rue Beranger, F-92322 Chatillon-sous-Bagneux Telephone: +33 1 47 46 21 21 Facsimile: +33 1 47 46 33 19	AM.39 Exocet	a) 185.0 (4.70) b) 43.3 (110.0)	a) 13.8 (35.0) b) 1,477 (670)	27 – 38 (50 – 70)	Mach 0.93	Cruciform moving tail fins	Solid-propellant booster & sustainer	Inertial/radar altimeter + active radar seeker	a) 363.7 (165) shaped charge/ fragmentation b) Delay + proximity fuze	AMX, Mirage 5, Mirage F1, Mirage 2000, Rafale, Jaguar, Atlantic/Atlantique, CN 235, Sea King, Super Frelon, Cougar, EH 101
Aerospatiale Missiles 2 rue Beranger, F-92322 Chatillon-sous-Bagneux Telephone: +33 1 47 46 21 21 Facsimile: +33 1 47 46 33 19	AS.15TT	a) 85.0 (2.16) b) 20.9 (53.0)	a) 7.3 (18.5) b) 212 (96)	8+ (15+)	920 ft/sec (280 m/sec)	Cruciform moving tail fins	Solid-propellant rocket	Command in azimuth + height control via radio altimeter	a) 65 (29.7) HE (derived from warhead in AS.12)	AS 565 Panther, C-212, Super Etendard and others
Aerospatiale Missiles 2 rue Beranger, F-92322 Chatillon-sous-Bagneux Telephone: +33 1 47 46 21 21 Facsimile: +33 1 47 46 33 19	ANS	a) 228 (5.8)	a) 14 (35.6) b) 1,984 (900)	81 – 97 (150 – 180)	*Mach 2.0+	*Moving tail fins	*Liquid-propellant ramjet	*Inertial and optional GPS active radar homing	a) *EH b) *Delayed	Designed to replace Exocet from about the year 2004. Extremely low approach to target and defence manoeuvring in terminal phase. Developed out of former Franco/German ANNG (anti-navire nouvelle géneration) programme. Data with asterisk denotes ANNG based information (provisional)
Germany										
Daimler-Benz Aerospace (former MBB)	AS34 Kormoran	a) 173.2 (4.40) b) 39.4 (100.0)	a) 13.5 (34.4) b) 1,323 (600)	16 (30)	Mach 0.9	Cruciform moving tail fins	Solid-propellant booster & sustainer	Cruise: inertial + radar altimeter; Attack: active radar seeker	a) P-charge 441 (200) HE	Tornado, F-104
Daimler-Benz Aerospace PO Box 801109, D-81663 Munich Telephone: +49 89 6 07-0 Facsimile: +49 89 6 07 26481	Kormoran 2	a) 173.2 (4.40) b) 39.4 (100.0)	a) 13.5 (34.4) b) 1,389 (630)	18.9 (35)	Mach 0.9	Cruciform moving tail fins	Solid-propellant booster & sustainer	Cruise: inertial + radar altimeter; Attack: active radar seeker or optical mode	a) 485 (220) semi-armour-piercing	Tornado. Industrial partner Aerospatiale. Can be used for stand-off attacks against ships from Tornado.
Israel										
Israel Aircraft Industries Elta Electronics Industries Division PO Box 330, Ashdod 77102 Telephone: +972 8 8572312 Facsimile: +972 8 8564568	Gabriel 3AS (see Comments for Gabriel Mk4LR)	a) 151.6 (3.85) b) 43.3 (110.0)	a) 13.4 (34.0) b) 1,323 (600)	32+ (60+)	Mach 0.73	Cruciform moving tail fins	Solid-propellant rocket	Cruise: inertial + radar altimeter; Attack: active radar homing	a) 330 (150) HE	F-4, A-4, Kfir, Sea Scan. Gabriel 4LR is a larger missile (length 185 ins, 4.7 m; diameter 17.3 ins, 44 cm; weight 2,116 lb, 960 kg) with a 108 naut mile (200 km) range

Manufacturer	Designation	a) Length ins (m) b) Span ins (cm)	a) Diameter ins (cm) b) Weight lb (kg)	Range naut miles (km)	Speed	Control	Propulsion	Guidance	a) Warhead lb (kg) b) Fuzing	Comments and Platform(s)
Italy										
Alenia (former OTO Melara and Sistel) Via Tiburtina Km 12.4, I-00 131 Roma Telephone: +39 06 41971 Facsimile: +39 06 4131133 or 4131436	Marte Mk 2	a) 190.6 (4.84) b) 38.6 (98.0)	a) 7.9 (20) fuselage, 12.4 (31.6) warhead b) 761 (345)	11+ (20+)	820 ft/sec (250 m/sec)	Cruciform centrebody wings?	Solid-propellant rocket booster & sustainer	Cruise: gyro control; Attack: active radar homing	a) 154 (70) SAP b) Contact & proximity fuzes	ASH-3D, MB-339, EH 101
Alenia (former OTO Melara and Sistel) Via Tiburtina Km 12.4, I-00 131 Roma Telephone: +39 06 41971 Facsimile: +39 06 4131133 or 4131436	Marte Mk 2a	a) 153.5 (3.9) b) 38.6 (98.0)	a) 7.9 (20) body, 12.4 (31.6) warhead b) 573 (260)	11+ (20+)	820 ft/sec (250 m/sec)	Cruciform centrebody wings?	Solid-propellant rocket	Cruise: gyro control; Attack: active radar homing	a) 154 (70) SAP b) Contact & proximity	MB-339
Alenia (former OTO Melara and Sistel) Via Tiburtina Km 12.4, I-00 131 Roma Telephone: +39 06 41971 Facsimile: +39 06 4131133 or 4131436	Marte Mk 2b	a) 153.5 (3.9) b) 38.6 (98.0)	a) 7.9 (20) body, 12.4 (31.6) warhead b) 573 (260)	32 (60)	820 ft/sec (250 m/sec)	Cruciform centrebody wings?	Solid-propellant rocket	Passive radar homing	a) HE fragmentation	Anti-radiation missile variant
Japan										
Mitsubishi Electric 5-1, Marunouchi 2-chome, Chiyoda-ku, Tokyo 100 Telephone: +81 3 3212 3111 Facsimile: +81 3 3212 9865	ASM-1 (see Comments for ASM-1C)	a) 155.5 (3.95) b) 47.2 (120.0)	a) 13.8 (35.0) b) 1,345 (610)	24+ (45+)	Mach 0.9	Moving tail fins	Solid-propellant rocket	Cruise: inertial + radar altimeter; Attack: active radar homing	a) 331 (150) SAP	F-1, F-2, F-4, P-3C. ASM-1 is Type 80. ASM-1C is Type 91 of 35 naut mile (65 km) range
Mitsubishi Electric 5-1, Marunouchi 2-chome, Chiyoda-ku, Tokyo 100 Telephone: +81 3 3212 3111 Facsimile: +81 3 3212 9865	ASM-2 (see Comments for ASM-3)			54, but perhaps 80+ (100, but perhaps 150+)	Subsonic?		Turbojet	Inertial midcourse + imaging IR terminal homing	a) HE	F-1, F-2, F-15J, F-16. NEC inertial navigation and IR seeker. The Japan Defence Agency is to launch the 'ASM-3' to eventually replace earlier missiles, with an integrated combined cycle rocket motor/ramjet and possibly combined active/passive radar and imaging IR guidance
Norway										
Kongsberg Defence & Aerospace PO Box 1003 N-3601 Kongsberg Telephone: +47 32 73 82 00 Facsimile: +47 32 73 85 86	AGM-119A Penguin Mk3	a) 125.2 (3.18) b) 39.4 (100.0)	a) 11.0 (28.0) b) 816 (370)	29.7 (55+)	Mach 0.8	Moving canard fins	Solid-propellant rocket	Inertial + IR homing	a) 309 (140) semi-armour-piercing HE b) Delayed-impact fuze	F-16, Rafale, Sea King
Kongsberg Defence & Aerospace PO Box 1003 N-3601 Kongsberg Telephone: +47 32 73 82 00 Facsimile: +47 32 73 85 86	AGM-119B Penguin Mk2 Mod 7	a) 118.5 (3.01) b) 55.9 (142.0)	a) 11.0 (28.0) b) 849 (385)	18.3 (34+)	Mach 0.9	Moving canard fins	Dual-thrust solid-propellant rocket	Inertial + IR homing	a) 264.5 (120) semi-armour-piercing HE b) Delayed-impact fuze	Surface ships & SH-60B
Russia										
Novator Yekaterinburg	AFM-L	a) c.315 (c.8)	b) c.4,409 (c.2,000)	135 (250)	722 – 787 ft/sec (220 – 240 m/sec) cruise; 2,297 ft/sec (700 m/sec) terminal phase		Turbojet + solid-propellant rocket	Inertial + active radar homing		
NPO Mashinostroyeniya	ASM-MS Alpha	a) c.256 & c.348 (c.6.5 & c.8.8)* b) c.62 & c.66.9 (c.1.6 & c.170)*	a) 24 (61) b) c.3,527 (c.1,600)	c.161.9 (c.300)	Mach 3		Turbojet with afterburner and rocket boost, though ramjet also reported	Inertial + GPS + multimode seeker for terminal phase	a) c.661 (c.300)	Su-32FN, Su-35/37 from about 2003. To cruise at 65,615 ft (20,000 m) and make final attack at 16 – 50 ft (5 – 15 m). A 4,000 kg ASM-MS5 derivative has also been reported. *both reported
MKB Raduga 2a Zhukovsky Street, Dubna, Moscow Region, 141980 Telephone: +7 096 21 24647 Facsimile: +7 096 21 23528	Kh-15S	a) 188.2 (4.78) b) 36.2 (92.0)	a) 17.9 (45.5) b) 2,646 (1,200)	Max 21.5 – 81 (40 – 150) depending on launch height & target radar cross-section	Mach 5 during the attack phase	Moving tail fins	Solid-propellant rocket	Inertial + active-radar terminal homing	a) 330 (150) semi-armour-piercing	Tu-22M, Tu-160
MKB Raduga 2a Zhukovsky Street, Dubna, Moscow Region, 141980 Telephone: +7 096 21 24647 Facsimile: +7 096 21 23528	Kh-22M/ Kh-22N (AS-4 Kitchen)	a) 458.7 (11.65) b) 118.1 (300.0)	a) 36.2 (92.0) b) 12,742 (5,780)	167.3 (310) for M, 188.9 (350) for N	1,943 kts (3,600 km/h)	Moving tail fins	Liquid-propellant rocket	Inertial + active radar seeker	a) 1,984 (900) HE	Tu-22M, Tu-95K-22
Zvezda Design Bureau, Zvezda-Strela, 7 Ilyicha Street, Kaliningrad, Moscow Region, 141070 Telephone: +7 095 519 5501 Facsimile: +7 095 519 4722	Kh 31A 2 (AS-17 Krypton) (see Comments for A-1)	a) 206 (5.23) b) 44.3 (112.5)	a) 14.2 (36.0) b) 1,323 (600)	37.8 (70)	3,281 ft/sec (1,000 m/sec)	Moving tail fins	Integrated rocket-ramjet	Inertial + active radar homing	a) 198 (90) semi armour piercing	MiG 21 93, MiG 29, Su 24, Su 25, Su-27, Su-30, upgraded *Fitter*, Su-33, Su-39. Leninets ARGS-35 seeker. Leninets has developed new 70 kg ARGS-K radar seeker suited to Kh-31A and Kh-35U, as coherent double RF-band multi-channel type with 32 naut mile (60 km) range. Kh-31A-1 version has 185 ins (4.7 m) length and 27 naut mile (50 km) range

Manufacturer	Designation	a) Length ins (m) b) Span ins (cm)	a) Diameter ins (cm) b) Weight lb (kg)	Range naut miles (km)	Speed	Control	Propulsion	Guidance	a) Warhead lb (kg) b) Fuzing	Comments and Platform(s)
Russia (continued)										
Zvezda Design Bureau, Zvezda-Strela, 7 Ilyicha Street, Kaliningrad, Moscow Region, 141070 Telephone: +7 095 519 5501 Facsimile: +7 095 519 4722	Kh-35 Uran (AS-20 Kayak)	a) 147.2 (3.74) b) 52.4 (133)	a) 16.5 (42.0) b) 1,168 (530), sometimes quoted as 1,058 (480)	2.7 – 70 (5 – 130)	985 ft/sec (300 m/sec)	Moving tail fins	Turbojet + tandem solid-propellant rocket booster	Inertial mid-course + active radar terminal homing	a) 320 (145) semi-armour-piercing/ incendiary	Tu-142M Bear F, Ka-27?, Ka-28, WIGE (eight on fuselage), Su-32FN, Su-39, MiG-21-93, MiG-29K. Leninets ARGS-35 seeker. Leninets has developed new 70 kg ARGS-K radar seeker suited to Kh-31A and Kh-35U, as coherent double RF-band multi-channel type with 32 naut mile (60 km) range
MKB Raduga 2a Zhukovsky Street, Dubna, Moscow Region, 141980 Telephone: +7 096 21 24647 Facsimile: +7 096 21 23528	Kh-41 (3M80) "Moskit"	a) 369.5 (9.39) b) 82.7 (210)	a) 30.0 (76.0) b) 9,921 (4,500)	81 – 135 (150 – 250), depending on altitude	1,510 kts (2,800 km/h)		Integral rocket-ramjet	Inertial mid-course + active or passive radar seeker	a) 661 (300) semi-armour piercing	Su-32FN, Su-33
MKB Raduga 2a Zhukovsky Street, Dubna, Moscow Region, 141980 Telephone: +7 096 21 24647 Facsimile: +7 096 21 23528	Kh-65SE (AS-15 Kent)	a) 237.8 (6.04) b) 122.0 (310.0)	a) 20.2 (51.4) b) 2,756 (1,250)	135 – 151 (250 – 280) (depending on launch altitude)	Mach 0.48 – 0.77	Moving tail fins	Turbofan mounted below rear fuselage	Inertial + terrain reference + active radar seeker	a) 904 (410) semi-armour-piercing	Tu-95 Bear H, Su-37. Conventionally armed, anti-ship version of the AS-15 cruise missile
Sweden										
Saab Dynamics SE-58188 Linköping Telephone: +46 13 18 60 00 Facsimile: +46 13 18 60 06	RBS15F and RBS15M (see Comments)	a) 171.3 (4.35) b) 55.1 (140.0)	a) 19.7 (50.0) b) 1,318 (598)	49+ (90+)	Mach 0.9	Moving tail fins	Turbojet	Inertial + frequency-agile active radar homing	a) 440 (200) HE semi-armour piercing	Viggen, Gripen. New-generation RBS 15M offers extended range (108 naut miles, 200 km), extremely low sea-skimming, sophisticated target discrimination and selection, high ECM resistance and stealth features
Taiwan										
Chung Shan Institute of Science & Technology Tao Yuan, Hsiang, Taipei Telephone: +886 3 471 2201	Hsiung Feng 2 (air-launched)	a) 153.5 (3.90) b) 35.4 (90.0)	a) 13.4 (34.0) b) 1,146 (520)	43 (80)	High subsonic	Cruciform moving tail fins	Turbofan	Inertial + active radar homing & IIR	a) 496 (225) semi-armour-piercing HE b) Contact	Ching-Kuo, AT-3A
United Kingdom										
Matra BAe Dynamics PO Box 19, Six Hills Way, Stevenage, Hertfordshire SG1 2DA Telephone: +44 1438 312422 Facsimile: +44 1438 753377	Sea Eagle	a) 163.0 (4.14) b) 47.2 (120.0)	a) 15.8 (40.0) b) 1,323 (600)	59.4 (110)	Mach 0.85	Cruciform moving tail fins	Turbojet (TRI-60.1 Microturbo)	Cruise: preset, inertial; Attack: active J-band radar homing	a) 507 (230) semi-armour piercing b) Delayed-impact fuze	Sea Harrier, Tornado, Jaguar, Shamsher, EH 101, Sea King. 3 user countries
Matra BAe Dynamics PO Box 19, Six Hills Way, Stevenage, Hertfordshire SG1 2DA Telephone: +44 1438 312422 Facsimile: +44 1438 753377	Sea Skua	a) 98.4 (2.50) b) 28.3 (72.0)	a) 9.8 (25) b) 324 (147)	8.1 (15)	Mach 0.85	Cruciform moving canard fins	Solid-propellant rocket	Semi-active I-band radar homing	a) 66 (30) blast fragmentation semi-armour-piercing b) Impact fuze with delay action	Light, all-weather. Lynx, AB-212, Sea King, SH-3D, H-76, C-212. Used by 5 navies.
United States of America										
Boeing Aircraft and Missile Systems PO Box 516, St Louis, MO 63166-0516 Telephone: +1 314 232 2800 Facsimile: +1 314 234 8296	AGM-84A Harpoon	a) 151.5 (3.852) b) 35.8 (91.0)	a) 13.5 (34.3) b) 1,145 (519.4)	67+ (124+)	Mach 0.85	Cruciform moving tail fins	Turbojet	Cruise: inertial + radar altimeter; Attack: active radar homing	a) Naval Weapons Centre 488.5 (221.6) HE penetration blast b) Contact (with time delay) + proximity fuzes	EH 101, F-16, F/A-18, B-52H, P-3, S-3, Nimrod, Fokker Enforcer Mk2, Rafale, Sea King. Trials on Harrier II, A-7 and CN 235
Boeing Aircraft and Missile Systems PO Box 516, St Louis, MO 63166-0516 Telephone: +1 314 232 2800 Facsimile: +1 314 234 8296	AGM-84 Harpoon Block 1G (Data based on Block 1D, which was abandoned. Boeing contracted to integrate reattack capability & improved guidance into new IG, delivered from 1997)	a) 174.8 (4.44) b) 32.6 (83.0)	a) 13.5 (34.3) b) 1,388 (629.5)	130 (240)	Mach 0.85	Cruciform moving tail fins	Turbojet	Cruise: inertial + radar altimeter; Attack: active radar homing	a) Naval Weapons Centre 488.5 (221.6) HE penetration blast b) Contact (with time delay) + proximity fuzes	Software and guidance system modifications (as retrofit kit), allowing reattack of target by using 'cloverleaf-shaped' search patterns.
Boeing Aircraft and Missile Systems PO Box 516, St Louis, MO 63166-0516 Telephone: +1 314 232 2800 Facsimile: +1 314 234 8296	AGM-84 Harpoon Block II (see Comments for AGM-84D)			a) 13.5 (34.3)	Mach 0.85	Cruciform moving tail fins. Vectored thrust control growth option	Turbojet	Incorporates GPS/INS from JDAM	As for AGM-84A plus optional submunition dispenser	Upgrade also to enable attack on land-based targets and improve lethality in congested environments. IOC by year 2000. AGM-84D is variant of Navy Harpoon for B-52Hs

C-801, China

ASM-1, Japan

AM.39 Exocet, France

AGM-119 Penguin, Norway

AS.15 TT, France

RBS15F, Sweden

AS34 Kormoran, Germany

Hsiung Fen 2, Taiwan

Gabriel 3AS, Israel

Kh-35U, Russia

Marte 2, Italy

Sea Skua, UK

Marte 2a, Italy

Sea Eagle, UK

Marte 2b, Italy

AGM-84 Harpoon USA

5 4 3 metres 2 1 0

5 4 3 metres 2 1 0

C-802K, China

C-101, China

C-201, China

C-601/CAS-1 Kraken China

Kh-65SE (AS-15) Kent, Russia

*KSR-5 Kingfish, Russia

Kh-41 Moskit, Russia

11 10 9 8 7 6 5 4 3 metres 2 1 0

Air-launched anti-tank

Manufacturer	Designation	a) Length ins (m) b) Span ins (cm)	a) Diameter ins (cm) b) Weight lb (kg)	Range naut miles (km)	Speed	Control	Propulsion	Guidance	a) Warhead lb (kg) b) Fuzing	Comments and Platform(s)
Argentina										
Instituto de Investigaciones Cientificas y Tecnicas de las Fuerzas Armadas (CITEFA) Zufriategui 4380, 1603 Villa Martelli, Buenos Aires Telephone: +54 1 331 2351 Facsimile: +54 1 331 6982	Mathogo	a) 39.4 (1.00) b) 17.7 (45.0)	a) 4.0 (10.2) b) 24.9 (11.3)	0.2 – 1.1 (0.35 – 2.1)	295 ft/sec (90 m/sec)	Wing-mounted spoilers	Solid-propellant booster & sustainer	CLOS via wire	a) 6.2 (2.8) HE	A109
Brazil										
Avibrás Industria Aerospacial Antiga Estrada de Paraibuna km 118, PO Box 229, 12201-970 São José dos Campos SP	FOG-MPM	a) c.59 (c.150)	a) 7.1 (18.0) b) 72.8 (33.0)	10.8 (20.0)			Solid-propellant rocket	Command via trailing optical fibre	a) HEAT	Helicopters. Former MAC-MP programme
China										
China North Industries Corporation (NORINCO) 7A Yuetan Nanjie, PO Box 2137, Beijing Telephone: +86 10 6354 2802 Facsimile: +86 10 6354 7569	Hongjian 8A (Red Arrow 8)	a) 33.86 (0.86) b) 12.6 (32.0)	a) 4.7 (12) b) 24.7 (11.2)	0.25 – 1.65 (0.5 – 3.1)	656 – 787 ft/sec (200–240 m/sec)	Deflector in sustainer efflux?	Solid-propellant booster & sustainer	SACLOS	a) 6.6 (3.0) HEAT	Harbin Z-9
China North Industries Corporation (NORINCO) 7A Yuetan Nanjie, PO Box 2137, Beijing Telephone: +86 10 6354 2802 Facsimile: +86 10 6354 7569	Hongian 8B (Red Arrow 8B)	a) 39.4 (1.0) b) 12.6 (32.0)	a) 4.7 (12) b) 27.5 (12.5)	2.1 (4.0)		Deflector in sustainer efflux	Solid-propellant booster & sustainer	SACLOS via wire	a) Tandem-charge HEAT b) Nose probe	Harbin Z-9?
France										
Aerospatiale Missiles 2 rue Beranger, F-92322, Chatillon-sous-Bagneux Telephone: +33 1 47 46 21 21 Facsimile: +33 1 47 46 33 19	AS.11	a) 47.6 (1.21) b) 19.7 (50)	a) 6.5 (16.4) b) 66.1 (30.0)	1.6 (3)		Deflector in sustainer efflux	Solid-propellant rocket	CLOS via wire	a) 9.9 (4.4) HEAT	Alouette, Gazelle
Aerospatiale Missiles 2 rue Beranger, F-92322, Chatillon-sous-Bagneux Telephone: +33 1 47 46 21 21 Facsimile: +33 1 47 46 33 19	AS.12	a) 73.6 (1.87) b) 25.6 (65)	a) 7.1 (18.0) b) 369.3 (167.5)	2.7 (5)		Deflector in sustainer efflux	Solid-propellant rocket	CLOS via wire	a) 66 (20) HEAT	Atlantic, Nimrod, Gazelle, Lynx, AB.212
India										
DRDO	NAG							Radio command link + imaging IR or millimetric-wave seeker	a) HEAT	Includes helicopters
Israel										
Rafael Armament Development Authority, Missile Division PO Box 2250/30, Haifa 31021 Telephone:+972 4 990 8503 Facsimile: +972 4 990 6257	NT-D (Spike?)			Short				Electro-optical guidance + fibre optic link	a) Tandem charge HEAT	Helicopters, including S-1W Huzar, A129 International. Possibly derived in some form from the US TOW system. Believed to be operational. Variant of Gill. Also the name Spike reported
Russia										
KB Mashinostroyeniya 140402 Kolomna, Moscow Region, Oksky Prospekt 42 Telephone: +7 096 61 33277 Facsimile: +7 096 61 33064	9M14 Malyutka (AT-3 Sagger)	a) 33.9 (0.86) b) 15.47 (39.3)	a) 4.9 (12.5) b) 24 (10.9)	0.25 – 1.6 (0.5 – 3.0)	377 ft/sec (115 m/sec)	Jetavator nozzles	Solid-propellant rocket	CLOS via wire. SACLOS via wire in Sagger-C	a) 5.7 (2.6) HEAT b) Impact	Mi-2URP, Mi-8, Mi-17, Mi-24, Gazelle
KB Mashinostroyeniya 140402 Kolomna, Moscow Region, Oksky Prospekt 42 Telephone: +7 096 61 33277 Facsimile: +7 096 61 33064	9M14M Malyutka-2 (AT-3 Sagger)	a) 38.8 (0.985) b) 15.47 (39.3)	a) 4.9 (12.5) b) 27.6 (12.5)	0.25 – 1.6 (0.5 – 3.0)	427 ft/sec (130 m/sec)	Jetavator nozzles	Solid-propellant rocket	SACLOS via wire	a) 7.7 (3.5) HEAT b) Impact	Mi-17MD
KB Tochmash Moscow	9M17M/P (AT-2 Swatter)	a) 45.7 (1.16) b) 26.8 (68.0)	a) 5.2 (13.2) b) 69.4 (31.5)	1.62 (3.0)	558 ft/sec (170 m/sec)	Elevons + moving canard fins	Single-stage solid-propellant rocket	CLOS via radio command link for M; SACLOS via radio command link for P	a) 15.4 (7) HEAT b) Impact	Mi-8, Mi-17, Mi-24
KB Mashinostroyeniya 140402 Kolomna, Moscow Region, Oksky Prospekt 42 Telephone: +7 096 61 33277 Facsimile: +7 096 61 33064	9M114 Shturm-V (AT-6 Spiral)	a) 72.0 (1.83) b) 11.8 (30.0)	a) 5.1 (13.0) b) 70.1 (31.8)	2.7 (5)	1,312 ft/sec (400 m/sec)	Moving canard fins	Solid-propellant rocket	SACLOS via radio command link	a) 16.3 (7.4) HEAT, with possibly optional fragmentation b) Impact	Mi-8AMT-Sh, Mi-24, Mi-28, Ka-29, W-3

Manufacturer	Designation	a) Length ins (m) b) Span ins (cm)	a) Diameter ins (cm) b) Weight lb (kg)	Range naut miles (km)	Speed	Control	Propulsion	Guidance	a) Warhead lb (kg) b) Fuzing	Comments and Platform(s)
Russia (continued)										
KB Mashinostroyeniya 140402 Kolomna, Moscow Region, Oksky Prospekt 42 Telephone: +7 096 61 33277 Facsimile: +7 096 61 33064	9M120 Ataka-V (AT-9 Spiral 2)	a) 72 (1.83) b) 12.8 (32.5)	a) 5.1 (13) b) 76 (34.5)	3.24 (6.0); 3.8 (7) for 9M120D	1,312 ft/sec (400 m/sec)	Moving canard fins	Solid-propellant rocket	SACLOS via radio command link	a) 16.3 (7.4) HEAT	Mi-8AMT-Sh, Mi-28, Mi-35. Improved variant of AT-6
KB Priborostroyeniya 300 001 Tula Telephone: +7 0872 440750 Facsimile: +7 0872 426139	9A4172 Vikhr (AT-16)	a) 97.2 (2.47) b) 14.5 (1.2)	a) 4.9 (12.5) b) 99.2 (45)	0.27 – 4.3/5.4 (0.5 – 8/10)	2,000 ft/sec (610 m/sec)		Solid-propellant rocket	Laser beam rider	a) 18 (8.0) shaped charge	Ka-50, Ka-52, Su-39, S-80PT
KB Priborostroyeniya 300 001 Tula Telephone: +7 0872 440750 Facsimile: +7 0872 426139	9M121 Vikhr M (AT-16)	a) 114 (2.9)	a) 4.9 (12.5) b) 99.2 (45)	5.4 (10)	Mach 1.8		Solid-propellant rocket	Laser beam rider	a) 18 (8.0) shaped charge	Ka-50, Ka-52, Su-39
South Africa										
Denel, Kentron Division Jochemus Street, Erasmuskloof, PO Box 8322, Hennopsmeer 0046 Telephone: +27 12 428 0637 Facsimile: +27 12 428 0651	ZT3 Swift	a) 53.2 (1.35) b) 15.8 (40.0)	a) 5.0 (12.7) b) 41.9 (19.0)	2.16 (4)		Cruciform rudders	Solid-propellant rocket	Automatic CLOS via laser command link	a) HEAT - tandem-charge warhead b) Impact	Puma/Oryx, Rooivalk
Denel, Kentron Division Jochemus Street, Erasmuskloof, PO Box 8322, Hennopsmeer 0046 Telephone: +27 12 428 0637 Facsimile: +27 12 428 0651	Mokopa ZT4/ZT6	a) 70.9 (1.8)	a) 7.0 (17.8) b) 114.6 (52)	0.27 – 4.3 (0.5 – 8.0)	1,740 ft/sec (530 m/sec)		Solid-propellant rocket boost/sustain motor	Digital autopilot + semi-active laser homing with articulated seeker head or millimetre-wave fire-and-forget homing	a) Tandem-shaped charge, HEAT, fragmentation/ penetrator options	Rooivalk
Denel, Kentron Division Jochemus Street, Erasmuskloof, PO Box 8322, Hennopsmeer 0046 Telephone: +27 12 428 0637 Facsimile: +27 12 428 0651	ZT35	a) 63 (1.60) b) 15.8 (40)	a) 5.0 (12.7) b) c.42 (c.19)	2.7 (5)		Rudders	Solid-propellant rocket	CLOS via laser command link?	a) Tandem shaped charge b) Impact	W-3WB Huzar
United Kingdom										
GEC-Marconi Defence Warren Lane, Stanmore, Middlesex HA7 4LY Telephone: +44 181 954 2311 Facsimile: +44 181 420 3900	Brimstone	a) 71 (1.805)	a) 7 (17.8) b) 107 (48.5)	4.3 (8)		As for Hellfire	Solid-propellant rocket	Digital autopilot & low-drift inertial measurement unit + advanced active millimetre wave radar seeker	a) HEAT, with tandem warhead or alternative Hellfire anti-ship blast fragmentation b) Crush fuze	Harrier GR7, Tornado, Eurofighter, L-159, helicopters. Ordered by RAF in 1996. Smart modular weapon, externally similar to Hellfire
United States of America										
Boeing Aircraft and Missile Systems/ Lockheed Martin. Joint venture name: Hellfire Systems Limited Liability Company	AGM-114A Hellfire	a) 64.0 (1.63) b) 13.0 (33.0)	a) 7.0 (17.8) b) 95 (43)	3.2 (6)	Subsonic	Aerodynamic surfaces on cruciform wings	Solid-propellant rocket	Semi-active laser homing	a) Firestone 18 (8) HEAT b) Contact	AH-1, AH-64, OH-58D, UH-60, HH-60H
Boeing Aircraft and Missile Systems/ Lockheed Martin. Joint venture name: Hellfire Systems Limited Liability Company	AGM-114B/C Hellfire (see Comments for AGM-114F)	a) 68.0 (1.73) b) 13.0 (33.0)	a) 7.0 (17.8) b) 100 (45.4)	4.4 (8)	Supersonic	Aerodynamic surfaces on cruciform wings	Solid-propellant rocket	Semi-active laser homing, IIR or radio frequency/IR	a) Firestone 18 (8) HEAT b) Contact	AH-1, AH-64, OH-58D, UH-60, HH-60H. AGM-114F has 71 ins (1.8 m) length and 108 lb (49 kg) weight
Boeing Aircraft and Missile Systems/ Lockheed Martin. Joint venture name: Hellfire Systems Limited Liability Company	AGM-114K Hellfire II	a) 64.0 (1.63) b) 13.0 (33.0)	a) 7.0 (17.8) b) 100 (45.4)	4.8 (9)	Supersonic	Aerodynamic surfaces on cruciform wings	Solid-propellant rocket	Semi-active laser homing	a) 18 (8) tandem shaped charge. Alternative anti-ship blast fragmentation b) Contact	Comanche, AH-1, AH-64, OH-58D, UH-60, HH-60H, A129
Lockheed Martin Electronics & Missiles/Northrop Grumman. Joint venture name: Longbow Limited Liability Company	AGM-114L Longbow Hellfire	a) 69 (1.75) b) 13.0 (33.0)	a) 7.0 (17.8) b) 107 (48.5)	4.4 (8)	Supersonic	Aerodynamic surfaces on cruciform wings	Solid-propellant rocket	Inertial + radar homing	a) Tandem shaped charge b) Contact	AH-64D, Comanche
Raytheon Systems Company 1151 East Hermans Road, PO Box 11337, Tucson, AZ 85734 Telephone: +1 520 794 3000 Facsimile: +1 520 794 1315	BGM-71A/B TOW	a) 46.5 (1.18) b) 17.7 (45.0)	a) 5.9 (14.9) b) 41.7 (18.9)	0.03 – 2.0 (0.065 – 3.75)	1,224 ft/sec (312 m/sec)	Cruciform rudders	Solid-propellant booster & sustainer	SACLOS	a) 7.7 (3.5) HEAT b) Contact	AH-1, MD500/530, A109, A129, Lynx, BO 105, Dauphin, Ecureuil
Raytheon Systems Company 1151 East Hermans Road, PO Box 11337, Tucson, AZ 85734 Telephone: +1 520 794 3000 Facsimile: +1 520 794 1315	BGM-71C Improved TOW	a) 57.1 (1.45) b) 17.7 (45.0)	a) 5.9 (14.9) b) 41.9 (19.0)	2 (3.75)	1,224 ft/sec (312 m/sec)	Cruciform rudders	Solid-propellant booster & sustainer	SACLOS	a) 8.8 (4.0) HEAT of increased diameter b) Contact	AH-1, MD500, A109, A129, Lynx, BO 105, Dauphin, Ecureuil, H-76 Eagle? Griffon?

Manufacturer	Designation	a) Length ins (m) b) Span ins (cm)	a) Diameter ins (cm) b) Weight lb (kg)	Range naut miles (km)	Speed	Control	Propulsion	Guidance	a) Warhead lb (kg) b) Fuzing	Comments and Platform(s)
United States of America (continued)										
Raytheon Systems Company 1151 East Hermans Road, PO Box 11337, Tucson, AZ 85734 Telephone: +1 520 794 3000 Facsimile: +1 520 794 1315	BGM-71D TOW 2	a) 61.0 (1.55) b) 17.7 (45.0)	a) 5.9 (14.9) b) 47.4 (21.5)	2 (3.75)	1,224 ft/sec (312 m/sec)	Cruciform rudders	Solid-propellant rocket booster & sustainer	SACLOS	a) 13.2 (6.0) HEAT b) Contact	AH-1, TOW Defender, A129, Super Lynx
Raytheon Systems Company 1151 East Hermans Road, PO Box 11337, Tucson, AZ 85734 Telephone: +1 520 794 3000 Facsimile: +1 520 794 1315	BGM-71D TOW 2A	a) 61.0 (1.55) b) 17.7 (45.0)	a) 5.9 (14.9) b) 47.4 (21.5)	2 (3.75)	1,224 ft/sec (312 m/sec)	Cruciform rudders	Solid-propellant rocket booster & sustainer	SACLOS	a) 13.2 (6.0) HEAT b) Contact	AH-1, A109CM, A129
Multi-national										
Euromissile Dynamics Group (EMDG) 12 rue de la Redoute, F-92260 Fontenay-aux-Roses, France Telephone: +33 1 41 13 27 80 Facsimile: +33 1 46 60 14 80	Trigat-LR	a) 59 (1.5) b) 7.9 (20)	a) 6 (15) b) 92.6 (42)	0.27 - 2.7 (0.5 - 5)	951 ft/sec (290 m/sec)	Cruciform fins	Solid propellant rocket	Passive IR homing	a) Tandem shaped charge	Fire-and-forget. Developed between Matra BAe Dynamics, Aerospatiale and Daimler-Benz Aerospace. Tigre, A129. Long-range version of Trigat-MR infantry missile
Euromissile 12 rue de la Redoute, F-92260 Fontenay-aux-Roses, France Telephone: +33 1 41 87 14 14 Facsimile: +33 1 46 61 64 67	HOT 1	a) 50.0 (1.27) b) 12.2 (31.0)	a) 5.4 (13.6) b) 50.7 (23.0)	0.04 – 2.1 (0.075 – 4.0)	787 ft/sec (240 m/sec)	Deflector in sustainer efflux	Solid-propellant booster & sustainer	SACLOS	a) 13.2 (6.0) HEAT	
Euromissile 12 rue de la Redoute, F-92260 Fontenay-aux-Roses, France Telephone: +33 1 41 87 14 14 Facsimile: +33 1 46 61 64 67	HOT 2/3	a) 51.2 (1.3) b) 12.2 (31.0)	a) 5.9 (15) b) 51.8 (23.5)	2.1 (4.0)		Deflector in sustainer efflux	Solid-propellant booster & sustainer	SACLOS	a) Heavier warhead of increased diameter, containing 9.0 lb (4.1 kg) of explosive	PAH-1, Tigre, A129, Lynx, Super Lynx

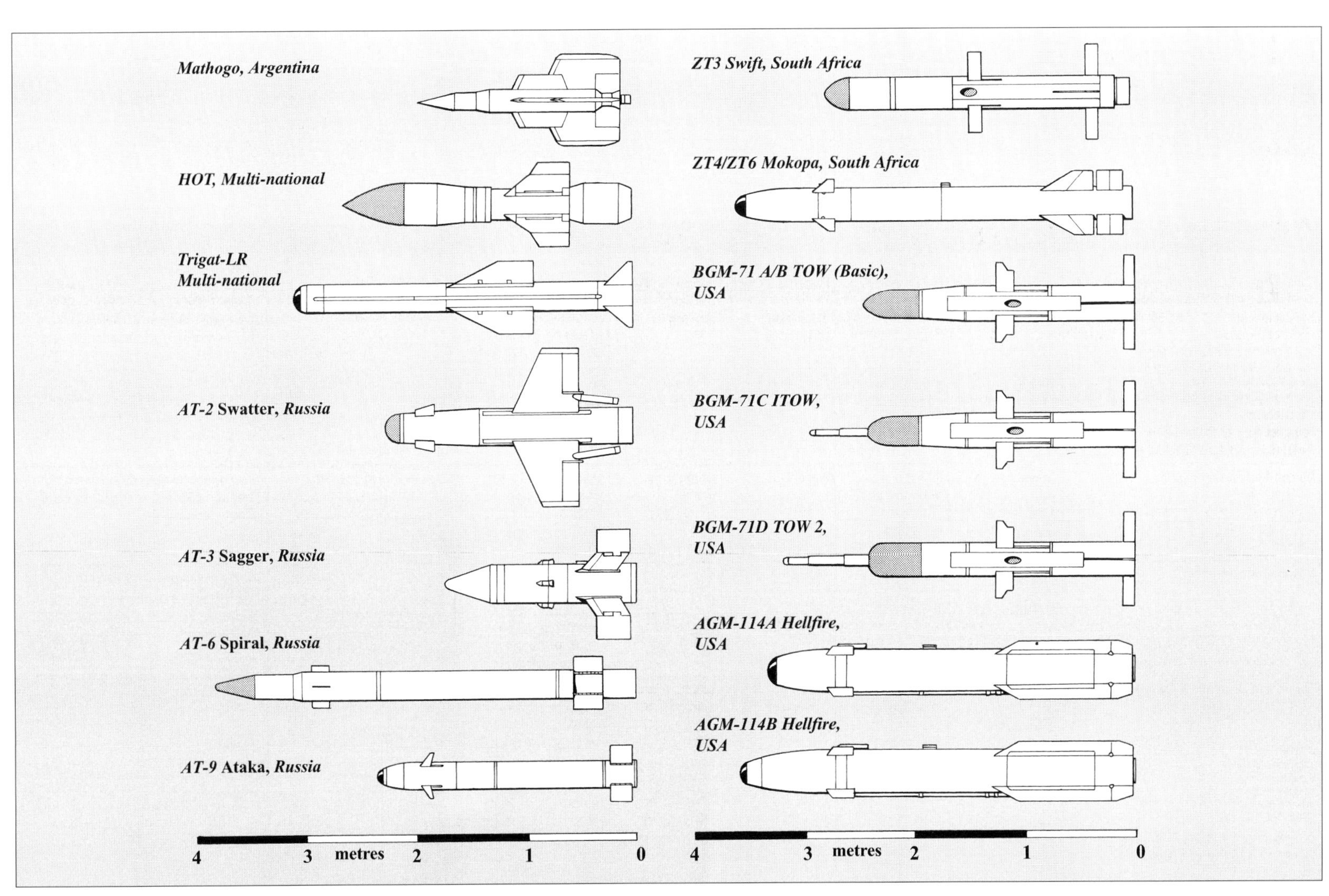

Airborne Radars

Radars are listed by nation, then alphabetically by designation.
Addresses, Telephone, Facsimile and E-mail numbers are given with the first entry for any particular company in each section.

Fighter, attack and bomber

Manufacturer	Radar designation a) Role	Type a) Operating frequency	Antenna type a) PRF (Hz) b) Pulse width (microsec)	Operating modes (air-to-air)	Operating modes (air-to-surface)	a) Tracking capacity b) Engagement capacity	a) Maximum range naut miles (km) b) Weight lb (kg)	Comments
China								
China Leihua Electronic Technology Research Institute (CLETRI). Wuxi. c/o Ministry of Electronic Industry, 46 Sanlihe, Fuwai Street, Beijing 100832. Telephone: +86 1068 20 81 14 Facsimile: +86 1068 21 85 62	JL-7 a) Air-to-air, air-to-ground (secondary)	Pulse (monopulse) a) X-band	Paraboloid	Search, track boresight	Air-to-ground ranging, attack	a) Single target b) Single target	a) Search 16 (30), track 8 (15) b) 254 (115)	Entered production in 1987. Later versions (JL-7A & JL-7AG) use TV raster displays and off boresight launch capability. Used in J-7 III.
China Leihua Electronic Technology Research Institute (CLETRI).	JL-10 a) Multirole	Pulse Doppler a) X-band	Planar a) Low, medium & high	Look-up, look-down & dogfight, range-while-search, TWS, boresight	Moving-target attack, real-beam mapping, air-to-ground ranging	a) Single target b) Single target	a) Look-up 43 (80), look-down 29 (54)	When seen at the 1993 Paris Air Show it was considered to be the first flat plate, slotted array radar to be developed in China. Anticipated for Chinese service version of FC-1.
China Leihua Electronic Technology Research Institute (CLETRI).	SR-4 a) Air-to-air?	Pulse a) I/J-band		Search, track, CW illumination	None?	a) Single target b) Single target	b) 88 (40)	Used in J-8 I.
Unknown.	T.266 a) Air-to-air?	Pulse?				a) Single target b) Single target		
China Leihua Electronic Technology Research Institute (CLETRI).	Type 317 a) Multirole	Pulse		Include ranging	Ground mapping, terrain avoidance, ranging	a) Single target b) Single target		
China Leihua Electronic Technology Research Institute (CLETRI).	Type 317a a) Multirole	Pulse (monopulse)			Ground mapping, terrain avoidance, ranging	a) Single target b) Single target	b) Lighter than Type 317	Thought to be used in J-8 II.
Unknown.	Unknown a) Missile guidance	Pulse?			Search, guidance for anti-ship missiles	a) Single target		
France								
Thomson-CSF Radars & Contre Mesures. 1 Blvd Jean Moulin, Elancourt, F-78852. Telephone: +33 1 34 59 60 00 Facsimile: +33 1 34 59 62 36	Agave a) Multirole	Pulse (monopulse) a) X-band	Inverse Cassegrain a) Variable b) Variable	Search, automatic tracking, ranging	Search, automatic tracking, target designation, mapping, air-to-ground ranging		a) Air 10-13.5 (18-25), sea 21.5-30 (40-55) b) 101 (46)	Agave was a joint development with EMD (now Dassault Electronique). Fitted in Super Etendard and Indian maritime strike Shamshers. Artificial beam sharpening improves quality of radar map in navigation mode.
Dassault Electronique. 55 quai Marcel Dassault, BP301, F-922214 Saint-Cloud. Telephone: +33 1 49 11 84 67 Facsimile: +33 1 46 02 57 58	Aida II a) Ranging	Magnetron a) X-band	Fixed lens	Air-to-air ranging	Air-to-surface ranging		b) 66 (30)	The fixed lens type antenna of just 5.9 ins (15 cm) made this radar highly suitable for aircraft with limited nose space.
Dassault Electronique.	Anemone a) Multirole	Pulse (monopulse) a) X-band	Planar	Linear scan search, continuous tracking	Search, track, track-while-scan, air-to-ground ranging, ground mapping		b) 132 (60)	Developed in co-operation with Thomson-CSF for the Super Etendard update programme.
Dassault Electronique.	Antilope 5/50 a) Attack	a) X-band	Planar		Terrain-following & ground mapping (interlaced if reqd), air-to-air & air-to-surface			Jointly developed with Thomson-CSF. Fitted in Mirage 2000 N and D.
Thomson CSF Radars & Contre Mesures.	Cyrano II a) Multirole	Pulse (monopulse) a) X-band	Inverse Cassegrain	Search, track, ranging	Ground mapping, terrain warning, ranging, navigation		b) 414 (188)	Used in Mirage III.

Manufacturer	Radar designation a) Role	Type a) Operating frequency	Antenna type a) PRF (Hz) b) Pulse width (microsec)	Operating modes (air-to-air)	Operating modes (air-to-surface)	a) Tracking capacity b) Engagement capacity	a) Maximum range naut miles (km) b) Weight lb (kg)	Comments
France (continued)								
Thomson-CSF Radars & Contre Mesures.	Cyrano IV & Cyrano IV-1 a) Multirole	Pulse (monopulse) a) X-band (8-10 GHz)	Inverse Cassegrain a) Variable b) Choice of 3	Search, track, dogfight, home-on-jam (IV-1 adds MTI look-down mode)			a) 52 (96) b) c.480 (c.217)	
Thomson-CSF Radars & Contre Mesures.	Cyrano IV-2 & Cyrano IV-3 a) Multirole	Pulse (monopulse) a) X-band (8-10 GHz)	Inverse Cassegrain a) Variable? b) Choice of 3?		Adds ground mapping, terrain avoidance & ranging		a) 52 (96) b) c.480 (c.217)	
Thomson-CSF Radars & Contre Mesures.	Cyrano IV-M & Cyrano IV-MR a) Multirole	Pulse (monopulse) a) X-band (8-10 GHz)	Inverse Cassegrain a) Variable? b) Choice of 3?	Search, track, interception, dogfight, home-on-jam	Optional contour mapping, terrain avoidance, blind let-down, air-to-ground ranging		a) 52 (96) b) 480 (217)	Retrofitted in a number of French Air Force F-1Cs. The MR version features ground and contour mapping for reconnaissance purposes.
GIE Radar. La Clef de St Pierre, 1 Blvd Jean Moulin, BP 6, Elancourt, F-78996. Telephone: +33 1 34 59 56 82 Facsimile: +33 1 34 59 70 37	RBE2 a) Multirole	Pulse Doppler a) Coherent X-band frequency generation; 4 independent channels (Σ, Az, El, G); analog to digital conversion	Phased array a) Low, medium & high	Look-up, look-down, with radar-to-missile datalinks interlaced with search & track-while-scan mode; dogfight	Terrain following, terrain avoidance, fixed & moving target search & track, high-resolution mapping, freeze & zoom, ranging, sea search, RCS assessment	a and b) Up to 40 targets tactical situation build-up; prioritization of 8 targets & simultaneous BVR firing at 4 targets		GIE is a legal entity associating Thomson-CSF and Dassault Electronique. The RBE2 for Rafale is the first European radar with a 2-plane electronic scanning antenna. The radar is passively scanned through a radant similar to the MiG-31 and B-1B radars. Cryo-cooling is said to give the radar a range that is the equivalent of transmitting with 30% greater power. Made up of 4 LRUs; antenna has high beam agility, very low side and scattered lobes, and ±60° azimuth/elevation.
Thomson-CSF Radars & Contre Mesures.	RC 400 a) Multimode	Pulse Doppler a) X-band	Planar a) Low, medium & high	All aspects, look-up, look-down, auto management of waveforms, multi-priority lock-on, simultaneous multi-target firing, combat modes, IFF	Air-to-ground: Ground mapping, DBS, range finding Air-to-sea: TWS 2 tracks, target calibration		a) 55 (102) b) 287 (130)	A compact, air-cooled radar for lightweight fighters and advanced trainers. Features azimuth beam compression for improved ground mapping. Flight testing was to begin during 1998. MAPO in Russia has opened discussions towards RC 400 for a MiG-29 upgrade.
Thomson-CSF Radars & Contre Mesures.	RDC (Radar Doppler Compact) a) Multirole	Pulse Doppler a) X-band (8-10 GHz)	Planar a) Medium & low	All-aspect search & tracking, range-while-search, TWS, single target track & various combat modes	Ground mapping, DBS, moving target detection, range finding, air-to-sea modes include BVR search & detection		b) c.220 (c.100)	The RDC radar was specially developed for retrofits on Mirage III, F1, F-5 and Russian aircraft.
Thomson-CSF Radars & Contre Mesures.	RDI (Radar Doppler à Impulsions) a) Air-to-air & air-to-ground	Pulse Doppler a) X-band	Planar a) High, medium, low	Search mode, IFF identification, tracking & combat. Intercept course & firing envelope missiles & guns	Ground mapping, contour mapping, air-to-ground ranging		a) 66 (122)	Developed in co-operation with ESD (now Dassault Electronique). Fitted in Mirage 2000B/Cs.
Thomson-CSF Radars & Contre Mesures.	RDM (Radar Doppler Multifunction) a) Multirole	Pulse Doppler a) X-band	Inverse Cassegrain a) 600-6,000 b) Pulse width according to selected mode	Search, track-while-scan, combat, intercept course, missile firing envelope & CW illuminator to fire Super 530D Doppler missile	Ground mapping, image freeze, terrain avoidance, air-to-ground ranging, GMTI Air-to-sea functions: long-range detection of naval targets & tracking with Doppler & non-Doppler modes		a) 60 (111) against fighter targets b) 441 (200)	Developed for the multirole version of the Mirage 2000 and widely used in export versions of the aircraft; Mirage 2000B, C (before upgrade), E. The transmitter offers random frequency agility or fixed frequency, according to the selected mode.
Thomson-CSF Radars & Contre Mesures.	RDY a) Multirole	Pulse Doppler a) X-band	Planar a) Low, medium & high	Look-up, look-down, velocity search, multi-target TWS with target priority, raid assessment, combat modes, single target track	Air-to-ground: terrain avoidance, ground mapping, DBS, air-to-ground ranging Air-to-sea: long-range detection & target tracking, target designation	a) 8 b) 4	a) 70 (130)	The RDY is one of the mainstays of the modernized Mirage 2000-5 combat system. Has auto waveform management for high, medium and low PRFs and features a Programmable Signal Processor (PSP). 37 Mirage 2000C airframes converted to Mirage 2000-5F standard (as 2000-50s) for the French Air Force and equipped with the RDY radar for service from 1999.

Manufacturer	Radar designation a) Role	Type a) Operating frequency	Antenna type a) PRF (Hz) b) Pulse width (microsec)	Operating modes (air-to-air)	Operating modes (air-to-surface)	a) Tracking capacity b) Engagement capacity	a) Maximum range naut miles (km) b) Weight lb (kg)	Comments
India								
Hindustan Aeronautics Ltd. PO Box 5150, 15/1 Cubbon Road, Bangalore 560 001. Telephone: +91 80 2866701 Facsimile: +91 80 2867140 E-mail: root@bnghal.kar.nic.in	Designation unknown a) Multirole (for LCA) Pulse Doppler			Look-up, look-down, track-while-scan	Ground mapping			Intended for the indigenous Light Combat Aircraft (LCA) .
Israel								
Israel Aircraft Industries, Elta Electronic Industries division. PO Box 330, Ashdod 77102. Telephone: +972 8 8572312 Facsimile: +972 8 8564568 E-mail: market@is.elta.co	EL/M-2001B a) Ranging	Pulse a) X-band		Air-to-air ranging	Air-to-ground ranging		b) under 22 (10)	Fitted in Israeli Air Force Kfirs. Target is detected visually and then acquired and tracked automatically by the radar. Also used to upgrade Romanian MiG-21 trainer and close air support versions.
Israel Aircraft Industries, Elta Electronic Industries division.	EL/M-2011 a) Multirole	Pulse Doppler a) X-band	Planar	Search, super-search, vertical scan, boresight	Ranging		a) 8 (15) b) 148 (67)	
Israel Aircraft Industries, Elta Electronic Industries division.	EL/M-2021B a) Multirole	Pulse Doppler a) X-band	Planar	Search, track-while-scan, single-target track	Ground mapping, terrain following & avoidance, ranging, DBS, air-to-sea search, beacon display in both air-to-air & air-to-ground modes	a) Several b) Single	b) 265 (120)	
Israel Aircraft Industries, Elta Electronic Industries division.	EL/M-2032 & -2032D a) Multirole	Pulse Doppler a) X-band	Planar	Look-up, look-down, track-while-scan, single-track, slewable ACM, HUD, boresight & vertical scan	Ranging, MTI, terrain avoidance, sea search, high resolution SAR mapping & mapping with real-beam DBS, expand & freeze	a) Several b) Single	a) Look-up 35-55 (65-102), look-down 30-45 (55-83) b) 171.9 -220 (78-100)*	* Weight depends upon antenna size, which can be adapted to aircraft's physical limitations. Used in update of Romanian MiG-21s and Chilean F-5s. Press reports suggest it has been proposed for update of Indian Harrier FRS.51s.
Israel Aircraft Industries, Elta Electronic Industries division.	EL/M-2035 a) Multirole	Pulse Doppler a) X-band	Planar	Look-up, look-down, track-while-scan, automatic lock-on, boresight		a) Several b) Single	a) 25 (46) b) 304 (138)	A version of the EL/M-2021B developed originally for the Lavi fighter. Used on Cheetah C.
Italy								
FIAR. via Montefeltro 8, 20156, Milan. Telephone: +39 02 357 90266 Facsimile: +39 02 357 90097	Grifo ASV P2801 a) Multirole	Pulse Doppler a) X-band	Planar	Search, range-while-search, track-while-scan, single-target track, combat	Track-while-scan, single-target track, sea search, ground mapping, freeze, terrain avoidance, air-to-ground ranging	a) Several	a) Air 19 (36), large warships 65 (120) b) 150 (68)	Developed for the maritime strike version of the AMX.
FIAR.	Grifo F, Grifo L & Grifo M3 a) Multirole	Pulse Doppler a) X-band	Planar a) Low, medium & high	Range-while-search, velocity search, track-while-scan, single-target scan, situation awareness, combat	Real beam & DBS ground mapping, air-to-ground ranging, sea mapping, surface MTI, surface moving-target track	a) Several for Grifo F & M3; 8 for Grifo L	b) 165 (75) for Grifo F, 176 (80) for Grifo M3*	*Antenna adds 33-44 (15-20) depending upon version. Recent contracts for aircraft updates in SE Asia include Mirage III, F-5 and F-7P. The -F version is intended for the F-5E/F retrofit market. L version used in L 159.
FIAR.	Grifo X a) Multirole	Pulse Doppler a) X-band	Planar a) Low, medium & high	Range-while-search, velocity search, track-while-scan, single-target scan, vertical-scan, HUD acquisition & boresight	Ground mapping, terrain avoidance, air-to-ground ranging, DBS	a) Several	b) 154 (70)	Used in Italian AMX.
FIAR.	Grifo 7 a) Air-to-air	Pulse Doppler a) X-band	Planar a) Low & medium	Look-up, look-down, super search, boresight	Air-to-ground ranging	a) Single-target?	b) 121 (55)	Used in Chinese F-7P. Offered for FC-1.
FIAR.	Pointer 2500 a) Ranging	a) X-band		Ranging	Ranging			Used in Chinese A-5M.
SMA/Tecnasa. SMA: Villa San Martino a Soffiano, I-50124 Florence. Telephone: +39 055 27501	SCP-01 Scipio a) Multirole	Pulse Doppler		Air-to-air, look-down, air combat	Air-to-ground & air-to-sea, ground ranging & mapping		b) 161 (73)	This radar was jointly developed by SMA and Tecnasa of Brazil, for AMX combat aircraft of the Brazilian Air Force.

Manufacturer	Radar designation a) Role	Type a) Operating frequency	Antenna type a) PRF (Hz) b) Pulse width (microsec)	Operating modes (air-to-air)	Operating modes (air-to-surface)	a) Tracking capacity b) Engagement capacity	a) Maximum range naut miles (km) b) Weight lb (kg)	Comments
Italy (continued)								
FIAR.	R21G/M1 Setter a) Multi-mode	Magnetron	Paraboloid	Includes look-down				An updated version of the R21G radar, it uses a new processor for improved capability.
Japan								
Mitsubishi Electric Corporation (MELCO). 2-3, Marunouchi 2-chome, Chiyoda-ku, Tokyo 100. Telephone: +81 3 3218 3306 Facsimile: +81 3 3218 3314	F-2 radar a) Multi-mode		Active phased array					Under development and testing for installation in the indigenous F-2 (former FS-X). Uses gallium-arsenide TX/RX modules. Due to enter service in 1999.
Mitsubishi Electric Corporation (MELCO).	J/AWG-11 & J/AWG-12 a) Multi-mode			Search & ranging for J/AWG-11	Ranging? For J/AWG-11			
Russia								
NPO Almaz. Moscow	Almaz-28 a) Attack				360° scanning		a) 5.4 (10)	Mast-mounted for Mi-28N. Twin antennae (millimetre and decametre wavelengths).
Phazotron. 1 Electrichesky Per, Moscow RF 123557. Telephone: +7 095 253 5613 Facsimile: +7 095 253 0495	FH-01 Arbalet a) Attack		Antenna width 47.2 ins (120 cm)	Control of missiles & guns	MTI ground & sea targets, mapping, terrain following & avoidance			Mast-mounted on Ka-52. Also used on Ka-50N and Ka-60.
Phazotron.	Zhuk 8II a) Multirole	Pulse Doppler	Planar	Fire control look-down, shoot-down		a) 10	a) 37.8 (70) in forward hemisphere, 21.6 (40) in aft hemisphere	Used in J-8 IIM.
Phazotron.	Komar (Gnat) a) Attack							Used for MiG-27 upgrade and podded for Su-22 upgrade in Komar-17 form.
Leninets. St Petersburg.	Kinzhal-5 a) Attack							Was to have been pod-mounted on Su-39. Used some Ukrainian parts. See page 78 for more details.
Phazotron.	Kopyo (Spear) a) Multirole	Pulse Doppler a) X-band	Planar	Track-while-scan, plus 3 automatic lock-on combat modes (vertical 2-bar scan, HUD & boresight)	Ground & sea search, plus real-beam & synthetic aperture mapping	a) 8 b) 2	a) Head-on 30 (57), tail-on 18.9 (35) b) 364 (165)	Used in MiG-21-93 upgrade and offered for MiG-23-98 upgrade. Uses technology from N-010 Zhuk developed for MiG-29M. MTBF 120 hours. Other users include Chinese FC-1.
Phazotron.	Kopyo 25 (N-027) a) Multirole	Pulse Doppler a) X-band	Planar (slotted flat of 20 ins, 50 cm diameter)	Air-interception, velocity search, range-while-search, single-target track, track-while-scan, HUD/vertical/ slewable search, boresight	Detection & target designation, air-to-surface & air-to-sea, mapping.		a) See Comments	Used in Su-39 in underfuselage pod. ±40° coverage in azimuth and +20°/-60° in elevation. Search range 108 naut miles (200 km) for large sea targets, 40.5 naut miles (75 km) for small sea targets, 13.5 naut miles (25 km) for tanks, and 31 naut miles (57 km) for aerial targets.
Phazotron.	Moskit (see Comments for Moskit-2) a) Multirole	Pulse Doppler	Planar	Look-up & look-down search/track, single-target track, air-combat	Real-beam & DBS ground mapping, fixed sea target indication, moving sea target tracking, sea target designation		a) 8 (15) against a fighter, 32 (60) against a ship b) 154 (70) for Moskit & 110 (50) for Moskit-2	Used in MiG-AC. Moskit-2 possible radar for Yak-131/133/135, MiG-21 upgrade (or alternative **Lev**) and MiG-23-98 upgrade.
NIIP.	N-001 S-27 Myech (Slot Back) as part of RLPK-27 radar attack system a) Air-to-air	Coherent pulse Doppler		Look-down/ shoot-down		a) 10 b) 1	a) About 54 (100) for fighter target	Used by Su-27, Su-30 and early Su-33.
Kunyavskiy.	N-003 Sapfir-23ML (High Lark 2) a) Air-to-air	Pulse Doppler? a) X-band		Version on MiG-23MLD has additional close-combat modes		b) Single target?	a) Search 46 (85), track 30 (55) b) Lighter than High Lark	
Kirpichev.	N-005 S-500 RP-25 Sapfir-25 a) Air-to-air	Pulse Doppler		Look-up, look-down		b) Single target	a) Search 62 (115), track 43 (80)	
NIIP.	N-006 RP-23P a) Air-to-air	Pulse Doppler a) X-band				b) Single target		

Manufacturer	Radar designation a) Role	Type a) Operating frequency	Antenna type a) PRF (Hz) b) Pulse width (microsec)	Operating modes (air-to-air)	Operating modes (air-to-surface)	a) Tracking capacity b) Engagement capacity	a) Maximum range naut miles (km) b) Weight lb (kg)	Comments
Russia (continued)								
NIIP.	N-007 S-800 SBI-16 Zaslon-A (Flash Dance) a) Air-to-air	Pulse Doppler a) X-band (9.0-9.5GHz)	Electronically scanned phased array (ESPA); antenna weight 661 lb (300 kg) & 43 ins (110 cm) diameter	Look-up, look-down. Search angles 70° each side in azimuth, +70°/-60° in elevation		a) 10 b) 4	a) See Comments b) More than 2,205 (1,000)	The first ESPA system to enter service; used in MiG-31. 151 naut mile (280 km) search range against AWACS type, 108 naut miles (200 km) against SR-71 type flying above 25,000 ft, 97 naut miles (180 km) against B-1, 64.7 naut miles (120 km) against F-16, and 35 naut miles (65 km) against cruise missile.
Unknown.	N-008 RP-23MLA a) Air-to-air	Pulse Doppler a) X-band				b) Single target		
Phazotron.	N-010 S-29M Zhuk (Beetle) a) Multirole	Pulse Doppler a) X-band	Planar	Look-down/ shoot-down	Automatic terrain following & terrain avoidance, real & synthetic aperture ground mapping with 50-65 ft (15-20 m) resolution & image freeze	a) 10 b) 4	a) 54+ (100+) maximum, 48 (90) against fighters in forward hemisphere & 21.6 (40) rear b) 551 (250)	Originally developed for MiG-29M. Now a derivative is fitted in Chinese J-8 IIM and has been associated with FC-1.
NIIP.	N-011/N-011M a) Multirole		Flat slotted. N-011M is phased array derivative	Track-while-scan. Look-down/ shoot-down	Ground mapping, terrain following & avoidance	a) 15 b) 4-6	a) 43-54 (80-100) fighter head-on, 16-21.5 (30-40) tail on; 108 (200) in air-to-surface mode	Coverage ±85° in azimuth, ±55° in elevation. Used by Su-35/–37.
Phazotron.	N-012						a) 2 (4)	Used as rearward facing radar in Su-35/-37 to supplement the main radar warning receiver. Also for 1-42?
NIIP.	N-014		Electronically-scanned phased array					Proposed for MiG MFI (1-42/1-44).
Phazotron.	N-019 S-29 Sapfir-29 (Slot Back) of the RLPK-29 radar attack system a) Air-to-air	Coherent pulse Doppler	Cassegrain	Look-down/ shoot-down		a) 10 b) Single target	a) Search 38 (70) in forward hemisphere & 19 (35) in rear for fighter targets, with 50% increase for large targets	Used in MiG-29. Search angles 67° each side in azimuth and +60°/-38° in elevation.
Phazotron.	N-019EA a) Air-to-air	Pulse Doppler	Cassegrain?				As NO-19 above	
Phazotron.	N-019ME & N-019M Topaz of the RLPK-29M radar attack system a) Air-to-air	Pulse Doppler	Cassegrain?			a) 10 b) 2	a) 54 (100) maximum, 38 (70) against surface targets	Used in MiG-29S/SD/SE/SM, plus upgrades and upgraded Malaysian aircraft. More jam resistant.
Unknown.	Obzor-MS (Clam Pipe) & Obzor-K a) Navigation/ attack							Used by Tu-95MS (Obzor-MS) and Tu-160 (Obzor-K).
Leninets.	Orion-A a) Attack	Pulse?		None			a) 81 (150)	Used on Su-24.
Leninets.	PN-AD (Down Beat) a) Nav/attack	a) X-band			No terrain avoidance (see Comments)		a) 175 (324)	Used in Tu-95K-22 & Tu-22M. Targets/AS-4 Kitchen missile. Tu-22M5 has new radar with terrain avoidance.
Leninets.	PSRS-2 Initsiativa-2B, -2K, -2M & -2ME a) Nav search/ attack	Pulse		None	Search & attack			Used by Mil Mi-14.
Nyenartouich.	RP-21, RP-21MA, R2L (Spin Scan) a) Air-to-air	Pulse a) X-band	a) 925-950 (search); 1,750-1,850 (track)			a) Single target b) Single target	a) Search 21 (40), track 16 (30)	
Unknown.	RP-21M (Spin Scan) a) Air-to-air	Pulse a) X-band	a) As above	Guidance for RS-2US missile		a) Single target b) Single target	a) As above	

Manufacturer	Radar designation a) Role	Type a) Operating frequency	Antenna type a) PRF (Hz) b) Pulse width (microsec)	Operating modes (air-to-air)	Operating modes (air-to-surface)	a) Tracking capacity b) Engagement capacity	a) Maximum range naut miles (km) b) Weight lb (kg)	Comments
Russia (continued)								
Volkov.	RP-22, 22M, 22SM or SMA Saphir-21 (Jay Bird) a) Air-to-air	Pulse a) Ku-band 12.9-13.2 GHz	a) 1,592-1,792; 2,042-2,048, 2,716-2,725 (for RP-22), -2,726 (for 22M) & -2,277 (for 22SM) b) 0.3-1.0			a) Single target b) Single target	a) Search 16 (30), track 8 (15) for RP-22; search 10.8 (20), track 5.4 (10) for RP-22M; search 10.8-13.5 (20-25), track 7.6-9.2 (14-17) for RP-22SM	Used in Su-20/22, MiG-21 & MiG-23. Search area 28° in azimuth and 17° 40' in elevation. Simplified version of Smerch A.
Volkov.	RP-25 Smerch A (Fox Fire) a) Air-to-air	Pulse a) X-band				b) Single target	a) Search 54 (100), track 38 (70) b) more than 1,100 (500)	
Phazotron.	RP-35 (former Zhuk PH) a) Multirole	Pulse Doppler a) X-band	Phased array	Target detection & velocity measurement, vertical & HUD search, wide-angle, boresight, raid-assessment	Real-beam ground mapping, DBS, synthetic aperture, enlargement, freeze, MTI, moving-target tracking, terrain avoidance	a) 24 b) 4 or 6-8	a) 89 (165) in velocity mode, 75 (140) in range mode, 35 (65) against receding targets b) 485 (220)	First seen at Farnborough '94, and was being tested in an Su-35. Used on MiG-35 and Su-35/-37? Formerly named Zhuk PH.
Phazotron.	RP-35 Improved (see Comments for Zhemchoug) a) Multirole	Pulse Doppler a) X-band	Phased array	As RP-35	As RP-35	a) 24 b) 6-8	a) 132 (245) in velocity mode, 99 (183) in range mode	Possibly used in Chengdu J-10 under name of Zhemchoug (Pearl) and MiG-29UB. Formerly named Zhuk PH Improved. Offered for MiG-23-98 upgrade in Zhemchoug form.
Kunyavskiy.	S-23 Sapfir-23D-Sh (High Lark) a) Air-to-air	Pulse Doppler a) X-band				b) Single target	b) Search 38 (70), track 30 (55)	Used in MiG-23B/G. Saphir-23 offered for MiG-23-98 upgrade.
Phazotron.	Zhuk 27 a) Multirole	Pulse Doppler a) X-band	Planar	Range-while-search, track-while-scan, vertical & HUD search, wide-angle, boresight	Real-beam ground mapping, DBS, synthetic-aperture enlargement, freeze, MTI, moving target tracking, ranging	a) 10-15 b) 4	a) Head-on 54 (100), tail-on 30 (55) b) 573 (260)	Used in new production Su-27, Su-27SMK/MKI, Su-30MK/MKI and Su-33, and possibly in Chinese J-10. Licence built in China.
Phazotron.	Sokol (Falcon)		Phased array			a) 24 b) 6 in air-to-air mode, 4 in air-to-surface mode	a) 43-97 (80-180) tail-on/head-on b) 606 (275)	Used in S-54/S-55.
A. Golenischev design team.	SRD-5 (Scan Fix) a) Ranging	Pulse a) S-band		Range only		a) Single target b) Single target	a) 1.6 (3)	Used in MiG-17/-19.
Unknown.	SRD-5M (High Fix) a) Ranging	Pulse a) X-band		Range only		a) Single target b) Single target	a) 5 (9.2)	Improved version of Scan Fix, used in Su-20C/D.
Phazotron.	Super Kopyo a) Multirole	Pulse Doppler a) X-band	Planar	Look-up, look-down, range-while-search, raid assessment, vertical & HUD search, wide-angle, boresight	Terrain avoid-ance, real-beam ground mapping, DBS, synthetic aperture, enlargement freeze, MTI, moving-target tracking, ranging	a) 8 air, 4 surface b) 2	b) 220 (100)	
Phazotron.	Super Kopyo PH a) Multirole	Pulse Doppler a) X-band	Active phased array	Look-up, look-down, with range-while-search, single-target track, air-combat	Real-beam ground mapping, DBS, 100:1 angular resolution synthetic aperture			
Unknown.	Uspekh-2A (Big Bulge) a) Nav/attack	a) X-band			Surface search & missile targeting, including mid-course guidance.		a) 230 (426)	Used in Tu-95RT & Ka-25T. Operates via a video link to missile launch platform.

Manufacturer	Radar designation a) Role	Type a) Operating frequency	Antenna type a) PRF (Hz) b) Pulse width (microsec)	Operating modes (air-to-air)	Operating modes (air-to-surface)	a) Tracking capacity b) Engagement capacity	a) Maximum range naut miles (km) b) Weight lb (kg)	Comments
Russia (continued)								
Istok Electronics. Fryasino.	Zaslon-M a) Air-to-air	Pulse Doppler a) X-band (9-9.5 GHz?)	Electronically scanned phased array	Look-up, look-down		a) 10 b) 6	a) Estimated 216 (400)	Used by MiG-31M.
Leninets.	Unknown (Sea Snake?) a) Multirole	Pulse Doppler	Phased array		Includes terrain-following & avoidance		a) 108-135 (200-250)	Used in Su-32FN; nose was extended to accommodate radar. High-resolution multi-function nav/attack radar.
Sweden								
Ericsson Microwave Systems AB. S-431 84 Mölndal. Telephone: +46 31 67 1000 Facsimile: +46 31 27 7891	PS-05/A a) Multirole	Pulse Doppler a) X-band	Planar a) Low, medium & high	Long-range search, multiple track-while-scan, short-range wide-angle scan, priority target tracking, raid assessment & missile mid-course update	Ground & sea priority target tracking, long-range search, ground mapping & ranging, DBS & SAR modes for high resolution		b) 344 (156)	This radar is in series production for the JAS 39 Gripen. 23.6 ins (60 cm) diameter lightweight, slotted waveguide, planar antenna, of 55 lb (25 kg) antenna plus platform weight.
Ericsson Microwave Systems AB.	PS-46/A a) Air-to-air	Pulse Doppler a) X-band	Cassegrain a) Low rate for look-up; medium rate for look-down	Look-down, search, track-while-scan, single-target track, auto & semi-auto HUD	Air-to-ground ranging, optional ground mapping		a) Look-down 27 (50) b) 661 (300)	An upgraded version was chosen for JA37 Viggen mid-life update.
Taiwan								
Unknown.	Golden Dragon 53 (GD-53) a) Multi-mode	Pulse Doppler a) X-band	Planar	Look-down/ shoot-down	40:1 Doppler beam sharpening. Sea search		a) Search 81 (150)	This radar is a locally modified version of the AN/APG-67(V). Uses a signal processing card, rather than a Programmable Signal Processor (PSP).
United Kingdom								
GEC-Marconi Avionics Limited. Crewe Toll, Ferry Road, Edinburgh EH5 2XS, Scotland. Telephone: +44 131 332 2411 Facsimile: +44 131 343 4011	AI-24 Foxhunter a) Multi-mode	FMICW* Pulse Doppler a) X-band	Cassegrain	Search, track, target illumination, track-while-scan			a) More than 100 (185)	Because of size of scanner, a hydraulic servo system was developed for beam positioning. (*Frequency Modulated Interrupted Continuous Wave.)
GEC-Marconi Avionics Limited.	Blue Fox a) Air-to-air	Pulse a) X-band	Planar	Search, track	Search, track			Uses frequency agility to offset clutter effects of rough sea states. MAPO has considered its use in a MiG-29 upgrade.
GEC-Marconi Avionics Limited.	Blue Hawk a) Multirole	Pulse Doppler a) X-band (9.6-9.9 GHz)	Planar a) Low, medium & high (800 Hz-120 kHz)	Look-up, look-down, velocity search, HUD field of view & single target track	Ground mapping with DBS, surface target tracking, freeze-frame & 2 sea search modes	a) 10 in TWS	a) Look-up 44 (81), look-down 27 (50), ground mapping 80 (148) b) 236 (107)	Offered for FC-1 (Super 7 platform cancelled in 1996). This radar is a low-cost, retrofit solution for a wide range of aircraft.
GEC-Marconi Avionics Limited.	Blue Vixen a) Multirole	Pulse Doppler a) X-band	Planar a) Low, medium & high	Look-up, look-down, TWS, single target track, air-combat, air-to-air ranging	Sea search, air-to-ground ranging		b) 312 (141.5)	Used in RN Sea Harrier F/A Mk 2. Successful trials with AMRAAM took place in USA during 1994. MAPO has considered its use in a MiG-29 upgrade.
GEC-Marconi Avionics Limited.	Skyranger a) Air-to-air	Pulse a) X-band	Paraboloid	Gun & missile			a) 8 (15) b) 88 (40)	Chinese F-7M.
GEC-Marconi Avionics Limited.	Super Skyranger a) Air-to-air	Pulse Doppler a) X-band	Planar array	Air-to-air search, combat	Air-to-ground ranging		a) 30 (55.5) b) 121 (55)	Chinese F-7MG.
United States of America								
Raytheon Systems Company. 2501 S Highway 121, Lewisville, TX 75067-8127. Telephone: +1 972 462 6500 Facsimile: +1 972 462 6508 (formerly Hughes)	AN/APG-63 & AN/APG-63(V)1 generally similar a) Air-to-air	Pulse Doppler a) X-band	Planar a) Low, medium & high	Look-down, super search, vertical scan, boresight			a) 100+ (185+) b) 494 (224)	In 1979 this radar was fitted with a programmable signal processor (PSP), which improved performance and is the key to incorporating synthetic aperture radar (SAR) in the APG-63. (V)1 refers to a reliability/maintainability upgrade. F-15.
Raytheon Systems Company. (formerly Hughes)	AN/APG-65 a) Multirole	Pulse Doppler a) X-band	Planar a) Low, medium & high	Long-range velocity search, range-while-search, single target track, TWS, raid assessment, HUD acquisition, vertical scan, boresight	Real-beam & DBS mapping, medium-range SAR, fixed & moving target tracking, sea surface search, terrain avoidance, INS update	a) 10 b) 8	a) 39 (72) b) 341 (154.7)	Used in AV-8B Harrier II Plus, which is in service with USMC, Italian & Spanish navies. Also F/A-18 Hornet.

Manufacturer	Radar designation a) Role	Type a) Operating frequency	Antenna type a) PRF (Hz) b) Pulse width (microsec)	Operating modes (air-to-air)	Operating modes (air-to-surface)	a) Tracking capacity b) Engagement capacity	a) Maximum range naut miles (km) b) Weight lb (kg)	Comments
United States of America (continued)								
Northrop Grumman Electronic Sensors & Systems Div. PO Box 17319, MS A255, Baltimore, MD 21203-7319. Telephone: +1 410 765 4441 Facsimile: +1 410 993 8771	AN/APG-66 a) Multirole	Pulse Doppler a) X-band	Planar Array a) Low for A/A look-up & maps; medium for A/A look-down b) 0.286-8	Look-up search, look-down search, spotlight search, situation awareness, single target track, air combat mode, ECCM	Real-beam map, expanded map, 8:1 DBS mapping, sea search, maritime target track, air-to-ground ranging, beacon, freeze	a) 1 b) 1	a) Look-up 25-40 (46-74), look-down 20-30 (37-56) b) 297 (134.7)	Last variant - Block 15S. IFF integration. CW integration for AIM-7. F-16A/B initial installation. Also used in F-4 & A-4. Maritime patrol applications in Aerostat, Citation, Falcon.
Northrop Grumman Electronic Sensors & Systems Div.	AN/APG-66H a) Multirole	Pulse Doppler a) X-band	Planar a) Low A/A for look-up & maps; medium for A/A look-down b) 0.286-8	Look-up search, look-down search, spotlight search, situation awareness, track-while-scan, single-target track, air combat mode, ECCM	Real-beam map, enhanced map, expanded map, 8:1 DBS mapping, sea search, maritime target track, fixed target track, ground MTI, air-to-ground ranging, beacon freeze, fix taking	a) 1 b) 8	a) Look-up 25-40 (46-74) look-down 20-30 (37-56) b) 250 (113)	Radar Control Panel LRU removed. Digital signal processor & radar computer LRUs combined into one Signal Data Processor LRU. Full symbology, IFF. Hawk 200 initial installation. Used in AT-3, F-5, P-3, Citation OT-47B tracker aircraft, HU-25C. APG-66 type on Reims Vigilant Frontier.
Northrop Grumman Electronic Sensors & Systems Div.	AN/APG-66(V)1 a) Multirole	Pulse Doppler a) X-band	Planar array a) Low for A/A look-up & maps; medium for A/A look-down b) 0.286-8	Look-up search, look-down search, spotlight search, situation awareness, single target track, air combat mode, ECM, AMRAAM	Real-beam map, expanded map, 8:1 DBS mapping, sea search, maritime target track, air-to-ground ranging, beacon, freeze	a) 1 b) 1	a) Look-up 25-40 (46-74), look-down 20-30 (37-56) b) 297 (134.7)	F-16A/B installation, AMRAAM integration, CW integration for AIM-7, IFF.
Northrop Grumman Electronic Sensors & Systems Div.	AN/APG-66(V)2 a) Multirole	Pulse Doppler a) X-band	Planar array a) Low for maps; medium for A/A b) 0.179-4.11	Range while search, spotlight search, situation awareness, dual target SAM, SAM multi track, SAM in GM, weather awareness, track-while-scan, single target track, air combat mode, ECCM, AMRAAM	Real beam map, enhanced map, expanded map, 64:1 DBS mapping, sea search, maritime target track, ground MTI, air-to-ground ranging, beacon, freeze, fix taking	a) 10 b) 10	a) 30-36 (56-67) b) 260 (118)	Second generation signal data processing. Full colour symbology. NATO F-16A/B upgrade. Used in A-4.
Northrop Grumman Electronic Sensors & Systems Div.	AN/APG-66(V)3 a) Multirole	Pulse Doppler a) X-band	Planar array a) Low for maps; medium for A/A b) 0.179-4.11	Range while search, spotlight search, situation awareness, dual target SAM, SAM multi track, SAM in GM, track-while-scan, single target track, air combat mode, ECCM, AMRAAM	Real beam map, enhanced map, expanded map, 64:1 DBS mapping, sea search, maritime target track, fix target track, ground MTI, air-to-ground ranging, beacon, freeze, fix taking	a) 10 b) 10	a) 30-36 (56-67) b) 260 (118)	2nd generation signal data processing. Full colour symbology, CW integration for AIM-7. F-16 Block 20.
Lockheed Martin Ocean, Radar & Sensor Systems. PO Box 4840, Syracuse, New York 13221-4840. Telephone: +1 315 456 3828 Facsimile: +1 315 456 3881	AN/APG-67 a) Multirole	Pulse Doppler a) X-band	Planar a) Low, medium & high b) Variable	Look-up/down search, velocity search, air combat auto search & track (super search, vertical acquisition, boresight slewable), TWS, single target search, situation awareness	Real-beam ground map & expand, Doppler beam sharpening, sea with freeze. Air-to-ground ranging. Surface moving target indication/track	Single target track, situation awareness to target track-while-scan	a) Up to 80 (148). Fighter size targets at greater than 50 (93) b) 175 (79.5)	SAR/ISAR available option. Integrated with BVR missiles. Selected for South Korean Samsung KTX-2 in 1998.
Northrop Grumman Electronic Sensors & Systems Div.	AN/APG-68(V)5 a) Multirole	Pulse Doppler a) X-band	Planar a) Low for A/A look-up & maps; medium for search & track; high for velocity search b) 0.0625-4	Range while search, look-up search, velocity search, spotlight search, situation awareness, dual target SAM, track-while-scan, single target track, air combat mode, raid cluster resolution, ECCM, AMRAAM	Real beam map, enhanced map, expanded map, 64:1 DBS mapping, sea search, maritime target track, fix target track, ground MTI, ground moving target track, air-to-ground ranging, synthetic beacon, freeze, fix taking	a) 10 b) 10	a) Classified b) 379 (172)	Signal processing & radar computing functions combined into one Programmable Signal Processor (PSP) and Advanced PSP LRUs. Block 25/30/40 – PSP, Block 50 – APSP. New dual mode transmitter. First multi-mode radar to demonstrate 150 hours+ MTBF, over 300 hours MTBF with APSP. Used in USAF F-16.

Manufacturer	Radar designation a) Role	Type a) Operating frequency	Antenna type a) PRF (Hz) b) Pulse width (microsec)	Operating modes (air-to-air)	Operating modes (air-to-surface)	a) Tracking capacity b) Engagement capacity	a) Maximum range naut miles (km) b) Weight lb (kg)	Comments
United States of America (continued)								
Northrop Grumman Electronic Sensors & Systems Div.	AN/APG-68(V)7 a) Multirole	Pulse Doppler a) X-band	Planar array a) Low for A/A look-up & maps; medium for search & track; high for velocity search b) 0.0625-4	Range while search, long range search, velocity search with ranging, spotlight search, situation awareness, dual target SAM, track-while-scan, single target track, air combat mode, ECCM	Real beam map, enhanced map, expanded map, 64:1 DBS mapping, sea search, maritime target track, fixed target track, ground MTI, ground moving target track, air-to-ground ranging, synthetic beacon, freeze, fix taking	a) 10 b) 10	a) Classified b) 379 (172)	Signal processing & radar computing functions combined into one Programmable Signal Processor (PSP) and Advanced PSP LRUs. Block 25/30/40 – PSP, Block 50 – APSP. New dual mode transmitter. Demonstrated 150 hours+ MTBF, over 300 hours MTBF with APSP. Used in FMS F-16.
Northrop Grumman Electronic Sensors & Systems Div.	AN/APG-68(V)8 a) Multirole	Pulse Doppler a) X-band	Planar array a) Low for A/A look-up & maps; medium for search & track; high for velocity search b) 0.0625-4	Range while search, long range search, velocity search with ranging, spotlight search, situation awareness, dual target SAM, track-while-scan, single target track, air combat mode, ECCM	Real beam map, enhanced map, expanded map, 64:1 DBS mapping, sea search, maritime target track, fixed target track, ground MTI, ground moving target track, air-to-ground ranging, synthetic beacon, freeze, fix taking	a) 10 b) 10	a) Classified b) 379 (172)	Signal processing & radar computing functions combined into one Programmable Signal Processor (PSP) & Advanced PSP LRUs. Block 25/30/40 – PSP, Block 50 – APSP. New dual mode transmitter. Demonstrated 150 hours+ MTBF, over 300 hours MTBF with APSP. Used in FMS F-16.
Northrop Grumman Electronic Sensors & Systems Div.	AN/APG-68(V)X (see Comments for AN/APG-68 Agile Beam Radar) a) Multirole	Pulse Doppler a) X-band			Adds synthetic aperture ground mapping			Upgrade for F-16. Exciter and receiver upgrades, plus commercial processor. Agile Beam Radar for UAE F-16 Block 60s.
Raytheon Systems Company. (formerly Hughes)	AN/APG-70 a) Multirole	Pulse Doppler a) X-band	Planar a) Medium & high	Range-while-scan, velocity search, single target track, TWS, raid assessment, auto acquisition	Real-beam & high resolution mapping, precision velocity update, air-to-ground ranging		a) 100+ (185+)	In 1984 this radar replaced the APG-63 in the F-15. It is faster, has higher resolution and larger memory.
Raytheon Systems Company. (formerly Hughes)	AN/APG-71 a) Multirole	Pulse Doppler a) X-band	Planar	As AWG-9 but adds BVR target identification & raid assessment modes	Real-beam & DBS mapping, medium-range SAR, fixed & moving target tracking, sea surface search, terrain avoidance, INS update	a) 10 b) 8	a) 115+ (213+)	Used in F-14D.
Raytheon Systems Company. (formerly Hughes)	AN/APG-73 a) Multirole	Pulse Doppler a) X-band	Planar	Velocity search, range-while-search, single target track, TWS, raid assessment, situation awareness, gun acquisition, vertical scan & target acquisition	Higher resolution in air-to-ground mode; adds terrain following & clearance			Upgrade of APG-65 used in F/A-18s, featuring upgraded signal & data processing. International users of this radar in F/A-18s include Finland, Switzerland and Malaysia.
Northrop Grumman Electronic Sensors & Systems Div/Raytheon Systems Company.	AN/APG-77 a) Multirole	Pulse Doppler a) X-band	Active electronically scanned array	Not known	Not known			Developed in a joint venture with Raytheon Systems Company for F-22. The first fighter radar using an active electronically scanned array.
Raytheon Systems Company. (formerly Hughes)	AN/APQ-110 a) Terrain-following	a) X-band			Terrain-following & avoidance, ground mapping			Used in F-111A.
GE Aerospace. (now part of Lockheed Martin Ocean, Radar & Sensor Systems).	AN/APQ-113 a) Attack	Pulse a) Ku-band (16.0-16.4 GHz)	Paraboloid a) 337, 674, 2022 b) 0.4, 1.2, 2.4	Range search, target-acquisition, track	Navigation, weapon-delivery, ranging			Designed for F-111A & F-111E. Also used in Australian F-111C.
Northrop Grumman Electronic Sensors & Systems Div.	AN/APQ-120 a) Multirole	Pulse a) X-band	Paraboloid a) 500 or 1000 b) 0.4 or 2.0				b) 619 (281)	

Manufacturer	Radar designation a) Role	Type a) Operating frequency	Antenna type a) PRF (Hz) b) Pulse width (microsec)	Operating modes (air-to-air)	Operating modes (air-to-surface)	a) Tracking capacity b) Engagement capacity	a) Maximum range naut miles (km) b) Weight lb (kg)	Comments
United States of America (continued)								
Raytheon Systems Company.	AN/APQ-126(V) a) Attack	Pulse a) X-band	Paraboloid	Ranging	Terrain avoidance & following, ground mapping, ranging			Used in A-7D/E Corsair II and in A-7 variants supplied to Greece & Portugal.
Raytheon Systems Company.	AN/APQ-140 a) Forward looking, multi-mode	a) X-band	Phased array					Tested during 1971 in a USAF KC-135.
SEI Systems & Electronics Inc. 201 Evans Lane, St Louis, MO 63121-1126. Telephone: +1 314 553 4678 Facsimile: +1 314 553 4950 E-mail: ssherman@SEISTL.com	AN/APQ-153 a) Air-to-air	Pulse a) X-band	Paraboloid	Search, auto acquisition & ranging. Boresight steering in missile mode, gunnery mode.			b) 110 (50)	Widely used in the F-5E.
Northrop Grumman Norden Systems. 10 Norden Place, PO Box 5300, Norwalk, CT 06856. Telephone: +1 203 852 7884 Facsimile: +1 203 852 7858	AN/APQ-156 a) Attack	Pulse a) X-band	Paraboloid + fixed		Terrain following, terrain-avoidance, ground mapping, search, tracking, beacon tracking		b) c.507 (c.230)	
SEI Systems & Electronics Inc.	AN/APQ-157 a) Air-to-air	Pulse	Paraboloid	Search, boresight, missiles, guns				
SEI Systems & Electronics Inc.	AN/APQ-159(V)-1/-2/-3/-4 a) Air-to-air	Pulse a) X-band	Paraboloid a) Medium for receding targets; high for approaching	Search, boresight, missiles, guns			b) 139 (63) for AN/APQ-159(V)1	This was the standard radar for the F-5F.
SEI Systems & Electronics Inc.	AN/APQ-159(V)-5 a) Air-to-air	Pulse a) X-band	Planar a) Medium for receding targets; high for approaching	Search, boresight, missiles, guns			a) Search 18 (34), track 12 (22)	Formerly used in Spanish Air Force upgrade programme for Mirage IIIEs.
SEI Systems & Electronics Inc.	AN/APQ-159(V)-7 a) Multirole	Pulse a) X-band	Planar a) Medium for receding targets; high for approaching	Search, boresight, missiles, guns	Adds air-ground			Used in former update programme for Spanish Air Force Mirage IIIEs. Also in F-5E/F.
Northrop Grumman Electronic Sensors & Systems Div.	AN/APQ-164 a) Attack & multi-mode radar	Pulse Doppler a) X-band	Phased array, 2-axes, electronically scanned		Ground MTI & track, terrain following, terrain avoidance, navigation, precise conventional weapon targeting & delivery. High-resolution SAR, monopulse ground moving map mode, A-A mode operation, weather mode			This radar is vital to the all weather targeting & navigation of the B-1B weapon system to conduct precise conventional all-weather strikes against time urgent targets that are fixed, moved & moving.
Lockheed Martin Electronics & Missiles. 5600 W Sand Lake Road, Orlando, FL 32819-8907. Telephone: +1 407 356 2211 Facsimile: +1 407 356 2080	AN/APQ-169(V1/V2) a) Attack	a) Ku-band	Paraboloid b) Down to 0.25				a) 200 (370)	Used in F-111 tactical fighter.
Raytheon Systems Company.	AN/APQ-171 a) Attack	Pulse	Twin units		Terrain following, terrain avoidance, ground mapping			Refers to updated version of APQ-146, to enhance reliability and facilitate maintenance on F-111s.
Raytheon Systems Company.	AN/APQ-172 a) Forward looking	Pulse (monopulse) a) X-band	Paraboloid		Ground mapping, terrain following			Improved version of APQ-99.
SEI Systems & Electronics Inc.	AN/APQ-175(V) a) Multimode	Pulse a) X-band	Paraboloid a) 925, 420, 250 b) 0.53, 2.35				a) 240 (445)	
Raytheon Systems Company. (formerly Hughes)	AN/APQ-180 a) Attack	Pulse Doppler						Variant of the APG-70 with added modes. Used on AC-130H.

Manufacturer	Radar designation a) Role	Type a) Operating frequency	Antenna type a) PRF (Hz) b) Pulse width (microsec)	Operating modes (air-to-air)	Operating modes (air-to-surface)	a) Tracking capacity b) Engagement capacity	a) Maximum range naut miles (km) b) Weight lb (kg)	Comments
United States of America (continued)								
Raytheon Systems Company. (formerly Hughes)	AN/APQ-181 a) Attack	Synthetic aperture a) Ku-band	2, wing mounted, electronically-scanned phased arrays		21 modes, including terrain following, terrain avoidance, ground mapping, motion sensing, target detection & tracking, weapon delivery		b) 2,101 (953)	This complex, liquid-cooled radar, used in the B-2, is integrated with the aircraft's defence management system.
Northrop Grumman Norden Systems.	AN/APS-130 a) Attack	Pulse a) X-band	Paraboloid + fixed		Terrain following, terrain avoidance, ground mapping, search, tracking, beacon tracking			
Raytheon Systems Company. (formerly Hughes)	AN/AWG-9 a) Air-to-air	Pulse Doppler a) X-band	Planar a) High	Velocity search, range-while-search, track-while-scan		a) 24 b) 6		Developed as part of the long-range Phoenix missile system in the F-14A.
Lockheed Martin Electronics & Missiles.	Longbow* a) Attack *(Developed in co-operation with Northrop Grumman ES&SD - former Westinghouse)	a) Millimetre-wave	Integrated RF interferometer		Target search, detection, location & classification & prioritization of fixed & mobile targets. Also missile fire-control			Longbow provides adverse weather fire and forget anti-armour targeting. Used in AH-64D Apache Longbow, Westland WAH-64 Apache and eventually for the RAH-66 Comanche.
Raytheon Systems Company.	Tornado Nose Radar (TNR) a) Multirole	Pulse a) Ku-band		Search, track, air-to-air ranging	Terrain mapping, manual & auto terrain following			Used in IDS & ECR versions of Tornado. Built since 1980 by a consortium of GEC-Marconi Avionics, FIAR and Daimler-Benz Aerospace (DASA). Gained design authority in 1984. DASA is now developing a radar improvement programme using DBS to offer SAR capability.
Lockheed Martin Electronics & Missiles.	Designation not yet assigned a) Multirole	a) X-band		Look-up, look-down, search, track, boresight, super search, vertical	Mapping, DBS, MTI, freeze, sea-search, air-to-ground ranging		a) Look-up 30 (56), look-down 19 (35) against fighter sized targets b) 229 (104)	
Multi-national								
GEC-Thomson-DASA-Airborne Radar (GTDAR)	Airborne Multi-role Solid state Active-array Radar (AMSAR) a) Multirole	Technology demonstrator Pulse Doppler a) X-band						Launched in 1993, this programme marks the advent of the next generation of radar. A first batch of trilateral active modules has already been produced.
Euroradar consortium headed by GEC-Marconi Avionics, with Telefunken Systemtechnik, FIAR & INISEL	ECR 90 a) Multirole	Pulse Doppler a) X-band	Planar (scans mechanically in azimuth, electronically in elevation) a) Low, medium & high	Look-up, look-down. Multi-target track-while-scan	Has air-to-surface modes			Features multiple missile guidance (AMRAAM, Aspide); non-co-operative target identification & adaptive waveforms. Based on Blue Vixen technology.
Thompson-CSF/Phazotron	Phathom a) Multirole	Pulse Doppler	Active phased array a) Medium & high	Long range search, look-up & look-down, boresight, vertical search, HUD acquisition, sector scan, raid assessment	Ground attack, ground mapping, MTI, terrain avoidance, sea search & attack	a) 8 b) 4	a) 37.8? (70?) b) c.265 (c.120)	Believed to combine elements of Kopyo-25 with processing from RDY. Used in Su-39.

Sea, land and air surveillance

Manufacturer	Radar designation a) Role	Type a) Operating frequency	Antenna type a) Scan rate (rpm) b) Peak output (kW)	a) PRF (Hz) b) Pulse width (microsec)	Operating modes	a) Maximum range naut miles (km) b) Weight lb (kg)	Comments
Australia							
Defence Science and Technology Organisation (DSTO).	Ingara a) Land surveillance	a) X-band			Surface search, spotlight, SAR, MTI	a) 60 (111)	An experimental system fitted in a C-47.
Canada							
Litton Systems Canada Limited. 25 City View Drive, Etobicoke, Ontario M9W 5A7. Telephone: +1 416 249 1231 Facsimile: +1 416 245 0324	AN/APS-503 a) Sea surveillance	Pulse a) X-band (9.2-9.4 GHz)	Paraboloid a) 30 b) 50	a) 400 b) 0.5	Surface search	b) 99 (45)	A lightweight radar for helicopter operations and used in the Sea King.
Litton Systems Canada Limited.	AN/APS-504(V)3 a) Sea surveillance	Pulse a) X-band (9.2-9.4 GHz)	Paraboloid b) 100	b) 0.5 or 2.4	Surface search		Developed from the APS-503 for the Tracker. Has proved popular as a surveillance radar for coastal monitoring. It has been refined to permit aircraft such as the EMB-111 to offer an ASW and ASV capability. Most recently fitted in Y8.
Litton Systems Canada Limited.	AN/APS-504(V)5 a) Sea surveillance	Pulse a) X-band (8.9-9.4 GHz)	Paraboloid b) 100		Surface search		Used in Do-228MP, CN-235; in service with US Navy, Egyptian Air Force and Taiwan. This latest variant uses pulse compression and frequency agility for optimal detection of small targets in high sea states. Used in MR version of Y8.
MacDonald, Dettwiler & Associates Ltd, Remote Sensing. 13800 Commerce Parkway, Richmond, BC V6V 2J3. Telephone: +1 604 278 3411 Facsimile: +1 604 278 1837 E-mail: srybak@mda.com	IRIS (Integrated Radar Imaging System) a) Surveillance	a) X-band			Wide swathe, high resolution	a) 54 (100) b) 882 (400)	
Litton Systems Canada Limited.	LASR-2 (Litton Airborne Search Radar-2) a) Sea surveillance	Pulse a) X-band (9.2-9.4 GHz)	Paraboloid a) Choice of 3 b) 100	a) Choice of 4 b) Choice of 2	Surface search	b) 170 (77)	A development of the APS-504, with increased peak power output. Offers a range of antenna sizes, with 3 different rates of rotation.
CAL Corporation, 1050 Morrison Drive, Ottawa, ON K2H 8K7 Telephone: +1 613 820 8280 Facsimile: +1 613 820 2994 E-mail: info@calcorp.com	Saffire (Synthetic Aperture Fixed Focus Imaging Radar Equipment) a) Ground surveillance	Sideways looking a) X-band (9.25 GHz)	Twin Microstrip b) 200	a) 550-1100 b) 230 nanosec	Surface mapping	b) Various	
CAL Corporation.	SLAR 100 a) Ground surveillance	Sideways looking a) X-band (9.25 GHz)	b) 200	a) 800 b) 0.23	Surface mapping	a) 54 (100) b) 588 (267)	This radar has been used in Dash 7 and L-188 for ice monitoring duties.
CAL Corporation.	SLAR 300 a) Ground surveillance	Sideways looking a) X-band	Twin Microstrip b) 250		Surface mapping	a) 45 (83)	SAR and MTI processing options available.
China							
China Leihua Electronic Technology Research Institute (CLETRI). Wuxi. c/o Ministry of Electronic Industry, 46 Sanlihe, Fuwai Street, Beijing 100832. Telephone: +86 1068 20 81 14 Facsimile: +86 1068 21 85 62	Type 698 a) Sea surveillance	Sideways looking a) X-band	Paraboloid		Surface search, MTI	a) 32 (60). Capable of detecting a periscope in sea State 4 at 9 (17) b) 507 (230)	Although not a new radar, it was being promoted at the 1993 Paris Air Show.
France							
Thomson-CSF Radars & Contre Mesures, 1 Blvd Jean Moulin, Elancourt, 78852. Telephone: +33 1 34 59 60 00 Facsimile: +33 1 34 59 62 36	Agrion (Appareil de Guet de Recherche et d'Identification d'Objectif Naval – Surveillance Equipment for Naval Target Search and Identification) a) Sea surveillance/missile tracking	Pulse a) X-band	Paraboloid		Surface search, missile guidance for AS 15TT		Uses pulse compression and frequency agility techniques with the addition of a monopulse tracking device and a matched antenna.

Manufacturer	Radar designation a) Role	Type a) Operating frequency	Antenna type a) Scan rate (rpm) b) Peak output (kW)	a) PRF (Hz) b) Pulse width (microsec)	Operating modes	a) Maximum range naut miles (km) b) Weight lb (kg)	Comments
France (continued)							
Dassault Electronique. 55 quai Marcel Dassault, BP 301, F-92214 Saint-Cloud. Telephone: +33 1 49 11 84 67 Facsimile: +33 1 46 02 57 58	DAV a) Air-to-air surveillance	a) S-band			Detects low & medium altitude threats, including hovering helicopters. Identifies, classifies & designates targets & air-to-air missile control	a) Multi target auto track up to 4.8 (9)	2 prototypes have been delivered to French MoD. First production equipment had been scheduled for 1998.
Thomson-CSF Radars & Contre Mesures.	DRAA 2 a) Sea surveillance/ ASW	Pulse a) X-band	Paraboloid		Surface search, tracking, coastal mapping, beacon		Used in Alize and Atlantic under designation -2A and -2B.
Eurocopter (Cougar & operator's consoles); Thompson-CSF (Target Radar); Dassault Electronique (Agatha secure data links & ground stations).	Horizon (Hélicoptère d'Observation Radar et d'investigation sur Zone) a) Land surveillance	Pulse Doppler a) X-band	a) 2° 24' or 8° per second		High resolution ground mapping, MTI	a) 108 (200)	First system delivered to French Army on 24 June 1996. Mounted on a Cougar AS 532 helicopter. A prototype version (Orchidée) performed well in the Gulf conflict. Studies have been made for installation of the system in Black Hawk, Mi-17 and CH-47 helicopters.
Thomson-CSF Radars & Contre Mesures.	Iguane (Instrument de Guet pour Navale Embarque – Surveillance Device for Shipborne Naval Aircraft) a) Sea surveillance	Pulse a) X-band	Paraboloid		Surface search	a) 150 (278)	Was chosen to update the Alize & Atlantique Nouvelle Generation (ANG) programme. Uses frequency agility.
OMERA-Segid (now part of Thomson-CSF)	ORB-31 a) Sea surveillance/ missile targeting	Pulse	Paraboloid		Surface search, navigation, weather, missile fire control	a) 43 (80) b) 165 (75)	This is a family of radars intended for helicopters & small fixed wing aircraft. Designator letters indicated role (for example, 'D' refers to Super Frelon).
OMERA-Segid (now part of Thomson-CSF)	ORB-32 a) Sea surveillance/ missile targeting	Pulse	Paraboloid b) 80		Surface search, navigation, weather, missile fire control	a) 49 (90) b) Various	Family of radars based upon the ORB-31. Typically the WTD version is a reconnaissance & target designation radar.
Thomson-CSF Radars & Contre Mesures.	Raphael/SLAR 2000 a) Reconnaissance	Sideways looking			High resolution mapping, mobile target detection & real-time &/or batch processing of data on the ground		French Air Force Mirage F1 CRs have used the system in Bosnia, in a pod mounting with datalink to the ground.
Thomson-CSF Radars & Contre Mesures.	Varan (Veille Aéroportée Radar Anti-Navire – Airborne Anti-ship Search Radar) a) Sea Surveillance	Pulse a) X-band	Paraboloid b) Low	b) Several	Surface search. Freeze frame & electronic magnification are provided	a) 130 (240)	This is basically an Iguane radar fitted with a smaller antenna and used in the Falcon 20 Gardian of the French Navy. It can be fitted or retrofitted with an Analyseur Coherent Numerique pour Doppler Aéroportée (ANACONDA) for the generation of high resolution images and SLAR capability.
Iraq							
Unknown.	Tiger G a) Air surveillance	Pulse Doppler a) S-band	Paraboloid? a) 12?			a) 65 (120) for ground level; the operational range was obviously much higher at altitude & reported as 189 (350)	This was a locally modified version of a French-made ground radar. It was mounted in an Il-76, the radome being fitted over the rear cargo ramp area. Known as Baghdad 1, it first appeared at the 1989 Baghdad arms fair. It is known that 10 of these radars were supplied c. 1987.
Israel							
Israel Aircraft Industries, Elta Electronic Industries division. PO Box 330, Ashdod 77102. Telephone: +972 8 8572312 Facsimile: +972 8 8564568 E-mail: market@is.elta.co	EL/M-2022 & EL/M-2022A a) Sea surveillance		Planar		Long-range, high-resolution surveillance, navigation, weather, airborne MTI, wide area DBS, classification, multi-target TWS, imaging		At Asian Aerospace '94, IAI announced a specialized avionic package to convert the An-72 Coaler into a Maritime reconnaissance aircraft (An-72P) using this radar.
Israel Aircraft Industries, Elta Electronic Industries division.	EL/M-2055 a) Land surveillance				Strip mode for wide range search & detection, high resolution spotting mode, MTI & wide area DBS surveillance	b) under 88 (40)	Designed as a compact, low-cost SAR payload, intended to fill a gap in UAVs used for tactical realtime battlefield surveillance. Said to be easy to upgrade for naval surveillance and imaging mode. Features extensive built-in test (BIT).

Manufacturer	Radar designation a) Role	Type a) Operating frequency	Antenna type a) Scan rate (rpm) b) Peak output (kW)	a) PRF (Hz) b) Pulse width (microsec)	Operating modes	a) Maximum range naut miles (km) b) Weight lb (kg)	Comments
Israel (continued)							
Israel Aircraft Industries, Elta Electronic Industries division.	EL/M-2075 Phalcon a) Air surveillance	a) L-band	Airframe mounted conformal phased arrays	a) Medium & low	Medium PRF search & track; low PRF helicopter detection, long-range search	a) Reportedly either 215 (400) or 200 (370)	At Paris Air Show '93, this system was first exhibited on a B707 intended for Chile. The configuration offered 280° coverage, but by adding 2 further arrays the full 360° coverage can be obtained. The system is being mounted on a Beriev A50 (modified Il-76) to suit a Chinese AEW requirement. C-130J, B767 and A310 AEW&C proposals.
Italy							
SMA. Villa San Martino a Soffiano, I-50124 Florence. Telephone: +39 055 27501 Facsimile: +39 055 714934	AM/APS-717 a) Land & sea surveillance	a) X-band	Planar		Search, ASV, navigation, ground mapping		Used in HH-3F.
FIAR. via Montefeltro 8, 1-20156, Milan. Telephone: +39 02 357 903 00 Facsimile: +39 02 334 009 81	Creso P2132 a) Land surveillance	Pulse Doppler	Planar		Land surveillance, MTI target detection & tracking		Designed for installation in AB 412 helicopters.
SMA.	MM/APS-705/705A a) Sea surveillance	Pulse a) X-band	Paraboloid a) 20 & 40 b) 25	a) 650, 1600 b) 0.05, 1.5	SAR, ASW, mapping	b) 176 (80)	Designed for helicopters, this radar is used in AB212, AB412 and SH-3D. A back-to-back antenna option was available. APS-705A is an upgrade with additional modes and improved processing.
SMA.	MM/APS-706 a) Sea surveillance/ missile targeting	Pulse a) X-band	Back-to-back paraboloids		Surface search, navigation, missile fire control		Used in SH-3D.
SMA.	MM/APS-707 a) Sea surveillance	Pulse a) X-band	Paraboloid		Surface search, surface mapping, target designation		This is a simpler, lighter version of the APS-705.
Eliradar.	MM/APS-784 (HEW-784) a) Sea surveillance	a) X-band			Sea search, ASW, weather		Was designed to suit the Italian Navy EH 101. Eliradar is a partnership of SMA and FIAR.
Japan							
NEC. 5-7-1 Shiba 5-chome, Minato-ku, Tokyo. Telephone: +81 3 3798 6681 Facsimile: +81 3 3798 6684	NEC-SAR a) Land & sea surveillance	Sideways looking a) X-band			Surface mapping		
Poland							
Unknown.	ARS-100 (ARS-400 – see Comments) a) Sea surveillance & navigation	a) Modified X-band	a) 7.5 & 15			a) 60 (111)	Replaced SRN-441XA in M-28RM, from which it is derived. Later versions to have ARS-400.
Russia							
Vega-M. 34 Kutuzovsky Prospekt, 121170 Moscow Telephone: +7 095 249 2933 Facsimile: +7 095 148 7996	Igla a) Sea surveillance?	Sideways looking	Phased array				Used in Il-20.
Leninets. St Petersburg.	Korshun-N a) Sea surveillance/ ASW	Pulse a) J-band			360° surface search & ASW/attack		Used in Tu-142M Bear-F.
Vega-M.	Kvant a) Air & land surveillance	Pulse Doppler a) S-band	a) 6		Can track up to 120 targets simultaneously	a) Search 108 (200) for fighter size target at altitudes up to 30,000 m; maximum 189-200 (350-370)	Used in An-71. 6 revolutions per minute. Target position within accuracy of 1.3 naut miles (2.5 km).
Unknown.	Osminog a) Search and navigation					97 (180) against large ship while flying at 2,100-2,400 m; 16 (30) against submerged submarine	Used in Ka-27, Ka-28, and Ka-32S and Ka-327.
Vega-M.	Nit (Thread) a) Sea surveillance?	Sideways looking a) Ku-band	Phased array			a) 43 (80) b) 882 (400)	Used in Il-20 & 24N.
NNIIRT. Nizhny Novgorod	E-801 Oko (Eye) a) Air & sea surveillance	Pulse Doppler a) Decametric	19 ft 8 ins × 3 ft 3 ins (6 × 1 m) a) 10		Air surveillance (tracks up to 10 targets, surface search)	a) 54-81 (100-150) against a fighter, 135 (250) against ships b) Antenna 441 (200)	Used in Ka-31. Folded horizontally for cruise and lowered into vertical position and rotated when in use (360° every 10 seconds).

Manufacturer	Radar designation a) Role	Type a) Operating frequency	Antenna type a) Scan rate (rpm) b) Peak output (kW)	a) PRF (Hz) b) Pulse width (microsec)	Operating modes	a) Maximum range naut miles (km) b) Weight lb (kg)	Comments
Russia (continued)							
Unknown.	Sabla & Shompol a) Land surveillance	Sideways looking					MiG-25RBS for Sabla; MiG-25RBSh for Shompol.
Vega-M.	Shtyk a) Reconnaissance	Sideways looking					Used in Su-24MR Fencer-E. Under consideration for S-80PT.
Unknown.	a) Land surveillance	Synthetic aperture sideways looking a) VHF (125 cm) & C-band (4 cm)			5-10 m resolution at 4 cm wavelength, or 20-40 m resolution at 1.25 m wavelength		Used in M-55B.
Unknown.	Type 12-M a) Sea surveillance/ ASW						Used in Mi-14PL.
Vega-M.	Shmel, Shmel-2 & Shmel-M a) Air surveillance	Pulse Doppler a) S-band	a) 6		Can track 50-60 targets simultaneously	a) 124 (230) for fighter size target at low altitude, 162-189 (300-350) at high altitude, and 216 (400) for large target b) 44,092 (20,000) total mission system	Shmel on A-50, Il-76 Adnan-9?; Shmel-2 on A-50M and Shmel-M on A-50U.
Leninets.	Strizh (Swift) a) Surveillance				Search zone ±135°	a) Search 10.8-119 (20-230) depending on size of target	Used by Il-114 and S-80PT. ±135° search area. Up to 20 targets can be tracked simultaneously.
KB Priborostroyeniya. 300001 Tula. Telephone: +7 0872 440750 Facsimile: +7 0872 426139	Liana (Flat Jack) a) Air surveillance	Pulse?					EW radar used on Tu-126 Moss SUWACS & Il-76TD.
Leninets. St Petersburg.	Berkut-95 (Wet Eye) a) Sea surveillance/ ASW	a) Ku-band			Surface search		Used on Il-38, Tu-142 Bear-F.
Sweden							
Ericsson Microwave Systems/ Swedish National Defence Research Establishment (FOA). Ericsson: S-431 84 Mölndal. Telephone: +46 31 67 1000 Facsimile: +46 31 27 7891	Carabas 1 (Coherent All Radio Band Sensing) a) Land surveillance, ground & foliage penetration	Ultra-wide-band synthetic aperture radar a) 20-90 MHz	2 inflatable booms, using ram air to maintain shape			a) 5.4 (10)	Tested on a Swedish Air Force Sabreliner in 1993 and has also been involved with tests in the US.
Ericsson Microwave Systems, Swedish National Defence Research Establishment (FOA).	Carabas II a) Land surveillance, ground & foliage penetration	Ultra-wide-band synthetic aperture radar a) 20-90 MHz	2 aramid fibre probe antennae			a) c.5.4+ (c.10+) b) c.330 (c.150) less antennae	Fitted with a more powerful transmitter to increase range. Reports indicate that the system is being studied for possible use in a UAV.
Philips Elektronikindustrier.	Hera a) Sea surveillance/ missile targeting	Pulse	b) 100				Developed for helicopters. Used a transceiver of French origin.
Ericsson Microwave Systems AB.	Erieye a) Air & sea surveillance	Pulse Doppler a) S-band	Active phased array	a) Low & medium		a) Fighter size target 189 (350), low flying cruise missile 81 (150). Instrumented range 243 (450) b) 2,910 (1,320)	Erieye is seen as an effective alternative to conventional rotodome AEW systems. Initially fitted on a Saab 340B for AEW&C. Other installations include the ERJ145. In Oct 1996 a development agreement was signed with Lockheed Martin for installation on a C-130.
United Kingdom							
GEC-Marconi Avionics Limited. Crewe Toll, Ferry Road, Edinburgh EH5 2XS, Scotland. Telephone: +44 131 332 2411 Facsimile: +44 131 343 4011	Argus 2000 a) Air surveillance	Pulse Doppler a) S-band	Twin paraboloids		Air & maritime surveillance		Being evaluated for the Chinese AEW programme; developed from radar in Nimrod AEW. Can provide 360° coverage.
MEL. (became part of Thorn-EMI, now Racal Radar Defence Systems)	ARI 5955 a) Sea surveillance/ ASW	Magnetron a) X-band	Paraboloid a) 60 b) 15	a) 800 b) 0.5	Air & sea search, ASW	a) 50 (93) b) 149 (67.6)	Developed for helicopter use. Used in UK Sea King & Wessex and by a number of overseas countries. World's first helicopter-borne 360° radar.
Racal Avionics. 88 Bushey Road, Raynes Park, London SW20 0JW. Telephone: +44 181 946 8011 Facsimile: +44 181 946 7530	ASR 360 a) Sea surveillance	Magnetron a) X-band	Slotted waveguide a) 23 b) 25	b) 0.05, 0.25, 1.0	Surface search	a) over 60 (111) b) 233.7 (106) for single display, 388 (176) for dual display	Based on marine radars originally developed by the Decca Navigator Company. Used in Jetstream 31, Cessna 337, Cessna Titan and Shorts Skyvan.
GEC-Marconi Avionics Limited.	Blue Kestrel 5000 a) Sea surveillance/ ASW	Pulse compression a) X-band	Planar array	a) Selectable		b) 225 (102)	A pulse compression radar developed for the EH 101 Merlin.

Manufacturer	Radar designation a) Role	Type a) Operating frequency	Antenna type a) Scan rate (rpm) b) Peak output (kW)	a) PRF (Hz) b) Pulse width (microsec)	Operating modes	a) Maximum range naut miles (km) b) Weight lb (kg)	Comments
United Kingdom (continued)							
GEC-Marconi Avionics Limited.	Blue Kestrel 6000 a) Sea surveillance/ ASW	Pulse Doppler a) X-band	Planar array	a) Selectable	Includes stand-off target classification & air target detection	b) 276 (125)	This radar combines the pulse compression techniques of the 5000 variant with pulse Doppler technology derived from Blue Vixen.
GEC-Marconi Avionics Limited.	Blue Kestrel 7000 a) Sea surveillance/ ASW	Pulse Doppler a) X-band	Planar array	a) Selectable	Includes stand-off target classification & air target detection	b) 190 (86)	New, multimode, lightweight version of Blue Kestrel family.
Thorn EMI (now Racal Radar Defence Systems). Racal Radar Defence Systems. Manor Royal, Crawley, West Sussex RH10 2PZ. Telephone: +44 1293 528787 Facsimile: +44 1293 542818	Marec II (Maritime Reconnaissance Radar) a) Sea surveillance	Magnetron a) X-band (9.345 GHz)	Paraboloid a) 60 b) 85	a) 200, 400 b) 0.4, 2.5	Surface search	a) over 100 (185) b) 187 (85)	Used in Do 228.
Thorn EMI. (now Racal Radar Defence Systems)	Searchwater (ARI 5980) a) Sea surveillance & AEW	Pulse	Paraboloid a) Multiple b) 65	a) Multiple b) Multiple	Surface search, navigation, target-classification, missile fire control & AEW	a) Classified b) c.2,000 (c.907)	Used in Nimrod & Sea King AEW, and was the first UK radar to be completely software controlled. One set was flight tested in a US Navy P-3. Further systems sold to Spanish Navy for SH-3D AEW. SH-5?
Thorn EMI. (now Racal Radar Defence Systems)	Searchwater 2 a) Sea surveillance	Pulse	Paraboloid a) Multiple b) 65	a) Multiple b) Multiple	Surface search, navigation, target classification	a) Classified b) c.1,322 (c.600)	Maritime patrol aircraft.
Racal Radar Defence Systems.	Searchwater 2000 MR a) Sea surveillance	Pulse Doppler a) X-band	Paraboloid a) Multiple b) 50	a) Multiple b) Multiple	Surface search, ASW, ISAR, SAR, target profiling, weather	a) Classified b) c.308 (c.140)	High degree of commonality with Searchwater 2000 AEW. Chosen for RAF Nimrod 2000 with a contract for 21 radars over an 8 year period.
Racal Radar Defence Systems.	Searchwater 2000 AEW a) AEW	Pulse Doppler a) X-band	Paraboloid a) Multiple b) Classified	a) Multiple b) Multiple	AEW	a) Classified b) c.1,543 (c.700)	Replacement for Royal Navy Sea King AEW system.
Racal Radar Defence Systems.	Searchwater 2000 (SW2000MS) a) Maritime & surveillance	Pulse Doppler a) X-band	Paraboloid or flat plate (slotted) a) 60 (variable) b) over 10	a) Multiple b) Multiple	Surface search, ASW, air-to-air, ISAR, SAR, radar profiling, ground mapping, MTI	a) over 200 (370), depending on target b) under 220 (100)	A new product intended for use in light to medium size fixed-wing aircraft and helicopters.
MEL. (became part of Thorn EMI, now Racal Radar Defence Systems)	Sea Searcher (ARI 5991) a) Sea surveillance/ ASW	Magnetron a) X-band	Paraboloid a) 30 b) 85	a) 400 b) 0.4, 2.5	Air & sea search, ASW	a) 125 (231)	Development of ARI 5955, with new, high-power transmitter.
GEC-Marconi Avionics Limited.	Seaspray Mk1/Mk3 a) Sea surveillance/ missile targeting	Pulse a) X-band	Paraboloid b) 90	a) Choice of 3 b) Choice of 2	Search, navigation, missile guidance for Sea Skua	b) 165 (75)	Lynx, Sea King, AB212, Super Lynx.
GEC-Marconi Avionics Limited.	Seaspray 2000 a) Sea surveillance	Pulse a) X-band	Paraboloid b) 90	a) Choice of 4 b) Choice of 2	Search, navigation, ground mapping	b) 176 (80)	A lightweight radar used in Reims Vigilant, Do 228, Defender 4000, and Super Puma. Performance optimized for paramilitary surveillance.
GEC-Marconi Avionics, Limited.	Seaspray 3000 a) Sea surveillance/ missile targeting	Pulse a) X-band	Paraboloid b) 90	a) Choice of 4 b) Choice of 2	Search, navigation, missile guidance for Sea Skua	b) 198 (90)	Used in Lynx, Sea King, AB212, F-27 & fast patrol boats.
GEC-Marconi Avionics Limited.	Seaspray 4000 a) Sea surveillance	Pulse a) X-band	Paraboloid	a) Selectable b) Selectable	Search, navigation	b) 176 (80)	Combines advanced pulse compression with digital signal processing.
Thorn EMI. (now Racal Radar Defence Systems)	Skymaster a) Air & sea surveillance	Pulse Doppler a) X-band	Paraboloid a) 60 b) 85	a) Multiple b) Multiple	Look-up, look-down, surface search	a) Classified b) c.904 (c.410)	Used in B-N Defender as a low-cost AEW. Has frequency agility, pulse compression & fully stabilized antenna.
Thorn EMI. (now Racal Radar Defence Systems)	Super Marec a) Sea surveillance	Magnetron a) X-band	Paraboloid a) 60 b) 85	a) 200, 400 b) 0.4, 2.5	Surface search	a) over 100 (185) b) c.165 (c.75)	Upgraded version of Marec II, with additional software and new display. Used by the Indian Coast Guard for the Do 228MP fleet.
MEL. (became part of Thorn EMI, now Racal Radar Defence Systems)	Super Searcher a) Sea surveillance	Pulse a) X-band	Planar array & paraboloid a) 60 b) 85 (Agile)	a) 300, 400, 2 kHz, 5 kHz b) 0.2, 0.5, 2.5	Surface search, ASW, ground mapping	a) over 125 (231) b) 165-198 (75-90)	Used by S-70, Sea King, EMB-111, Dominie, Do 228MP and Gulfstream GIV.

Manufacturer	Radar designation a) Role	Type a) Operating frequency	Antenna type a) Scan rate (rpm) b) Peak output (kW)	a) PRF (Hz) b) Pulse width (microsec)	Operating modes	a) Maximum range naut miles (km) b) Weight lb (kg)	Comments
United States of America							
Northrop Grumman Norden Systems. 10 Norden Place, PO Box 5300, Norwalk, CT 06856. Telephone: +1 203 852 7884 Facsimile: +1 203 852 7858	AN/APG-76 a) Multi-mode/ long-range stand-off surveillance & targeting	Pulse Doppler a) Ku-band			Wide area surveillance, targeting, simultaneous SAR & slow speed GMTI, air-to-air self defence, precision weapon delivery	b) 625 (283.5)	Only tactical operational radar system with simultaneous SAR/GMTI for real-time, all-weather detection of critical mobile targets. A pod version was installed & demonstrated on a USN S-3B (project Gray Wolf) and a USAF F-16.
Motorola Inc, Space & Systems Technology Group. PO Box 9040, 8220 E Rooswell Road, Mail Drop R7212, Scottsdale, AZ 85252-9040. Telephone: +1 602 441 8586 Facsimile: +1 602 441 6702	AN/APS-94F a) Reconnaissance	Sideways looking a) X-band	Back-to-back slotted waveguides		Ground mapping, MTI	a) 54 (100)	Used in OV-1B/D, P-3, UH-1. Could be used with a film-recorder and datalink under designation UPD-7.
General Electric. (now part of Lockheed Martin Ocean, Radar & Sensor Systems)	AN/APS-111 a) Air surveillance	Pulse a) UHF (c.400 MHz?)	Yagi array				Developed by modifying the AN/APS-96 (used in E-2A/B – not in production or supported) for land surveillance. Just 2 examples completed under XN-1 programme. No longer supported.
Raytheon Systems Company. 2501 S Highway 121, Lewisville, TX 75067-8127. Telephone: +1 972 462 6500 Facsimile: +1 972 462 6508	AN/APS-115 a) Sea surveillance/ ASW	a) X-band	2 paraboloids		Ocean surveillance		Used in P-3C, US-1A. There is a single antenna control unit; 1 antenna is mounted in nose of aircraft and the other in the tail to offer 360° coverage.
Raytheon Systems Company.	AN/APS-116 a) Sea surveillance/ ASW	a) X-band	Paraboloid		Periscope detection, surface search		Used in S-3A, CP-140 Aurora.
Raytheon Systems Company.	AN/APS-124 a) Sea surveillance/ ASW		Planar		Fast scan surveillance, long & medium range search, navigation	a) 160 (296) b) 210 (95)	Developed for the SH-60B ASW helicopter.
Raytheon Systems Company.	AN/APS-127 a) Sea surveillance		Planar				Used in HU-25A of USCG.
Telephonics Corp. 815 Broad Hollow Road, Farmingdale, NY 11735. Telephone: +1 516 755 7000 Facsimile: +1 516 755 7644	AN/APS-128 a) Sea surveillance	a) X-band (9.375 GHz)	Planar a) 15 or 60 b) 100	a) 267, 400, 1200, 1600 b) 0.5, 2.4, optional 0.1	Search, weather	a) 200 (370) as weather radar. Large tankers at 100 (185) b) 174 (79)	Widely used, typically in E-9A, Do 228MP, C-212MP and EMB-111.
Motorola Inc Space & Systems Technology Group.	AN/APS-131 a) Sea surveillance	Sideways looking	Back-to-back slotted waveguides		Sea surface mapping		Used in HU-25A of US Coast Guard.
Raytheon Systems Company.	AN/APS-134(V) a) Sea surveillance/ ASW	Pulse a) X-band (9.5-10 GHz)	Paraboloid a) 6, 40, 150 b) 500	a) Low, 500, 2000	Surveillance, search, navigation, periscope-detection, track-while-scan	a) 150 (278)	Used in P-3B/C/P, Maritime Enforcer, Maritime Mk 2, Sentinel Mk 2, Reims Vigilant Surmar.
Motorola Inc, Space & Systems Technology Group.	AN/APS-135 a) Sea surveillance	Sideways looking	Slotted waveguide		Sea surface mapping		Used in HC-130, Fokker Sentinel Mk 2. Similar to APS-131 except for antenna mounting.
Raytheon Systems Company.	AN/APS-137(V) & (V)2 a) Sea surveillance/ ASW	Pulse Doppler a) X-band (c.9.75 GHz)	Paraboloid or planar in helicopters		Includes long-range radar imaging, OTH targeting, ISAR, target classification		S-3B, P-3C, US Coast Guard C-130; AN/APS-137(H) in helicopters.
Raytheon Systems Company.	AN/APS-137B(V)5 a) Sea/land surveillance	Pulse Doppler a) X-band	Paraboloid		Selectable resolution for target detection & identification, providing real-time data to Battle Group Commander		Has Inverse Synthetic Aperture Radar (ISAR) and conventional SAR modes. Several systems currently being delivered for US Navy P-3Cs and international customers via Foreign Military Sales (FMS).
General Electric. (now part of Lockheed Martin Ocean, Radar & Sensor Systems)	AN/APS-138 a) Air surveillance	Pulse Doppler a) UHF	Yagi array a) 6		Air surveillance, limited ground surveillance		Used in E-2C, P-3AEW. Updated version of APS-125. Also in C-130AEW.
Lockheed Martin Ocean, Radar & Sensor Systems. PO Box 4840, Syracuse, New York 13221-4840. Telephone: +1 315 456 3828 Facsimile: +1 315 456 3881	AN/APS-139 a) Air surveillance	Pulse Doppler a) UHF	Yagi array a) 6		Air surveillance with improved ECCM, improved ground surveillance		Updated version of APS-138. Used in E-2C (Grp I).
Telephonics Corp.	AN/APS-143(V)/(V)2 a) Sea surveillance	a) X-band	Paraboloid or planar b) 10	a) 390, 750, 1510, 2500 b) 5.0 & 17.0	Surveillance, track-while-scan, missile guidance, SAR	a) over 200 (370) b) 180 (81.6)	Used in DHC-8, Beech 200T. Optional Inverse SAR. Chosen for SH-2G(A) ordered by Australian Navy. (V)2 version used in shipborne aerostats. Saab SAR-200.
Telephonics Corp.	AN/APS-143(V)3 a) Sea surveillance	a) X-band	Paraboloid or planar b) 8	a) 400, 800, 1510, 2500 b) 5.0 & 17.0	Surveillance, track-while-scan, missile guidance, SAR	a) over 200 (370) b) 180 (81.6)	Used in S-70 and Dauphin upgrade ASW helicopter.

Manufacturer	Radar designation a) Role	Type a) Operating frequency	Antenna type a) Scan rate (rpm) b) Peak output (kW)	a) PRF (Hz) b) Pulse width (microsec)	Operating modes	a) Maximum range naut miles (km) b) Weight lb (kg)	Comments
United States of America (continued)							
AIL Systems Inc. 415 Commack Road, Deer Park, NY 11729-4591. Telephone: +1 516 595 5000 Facsimile: +1 516 595 6639	AN/APS-144 a) Land surveillance	Pulse Doppler a) Ku-band	Paraboloid		Surveillance, MTI, SAR imaging of fixed targets, auto cueing of co-mounted E-O sensors	a) Long-range search 2.7-10.8 (5-20), near-range search 1.6-5.3 (3-10) b) MTI 54.9 (25) MTI/SAR 69.1 (31.3)	Developed for the US Army, this radar provides high resolution MTI & cueing capability for both manned aircraft & UAVs. Said to be the only airborne MTI radar capable of detecting small vehicles & personnel from platforms travelling at speeds of 80-120 kts.
Lockheed Martin Ocean, Radar & Sensor Systems.	AN/APS-145 & -145 Plus a) Air surveillance	Pulse Doppler a) UHF	Yagi array a) 5	b) Choice of 3?	Air and ground surveillance. Can track over 2,000 targets & control 40 interceptions simultaneously	a) 260+ (483+)	Updated version of APS-139. Used in E-2C (Grp II) Hawkeye, C-130/J AEW and P-3AEW.
Telephonics Corp.	AN/APS-147 a) Multimode				Aircraft track-while-scan, small target & periscope detection, missile targeting, coastal mapping, ISAR, SAR/MTI		Developed for update of US Navy SH-60 to 'R' standard.
Northrop Grumman Electronic Sensors & Systems Div. PO Box 17319, MS A255, Baltimore, MD 21203-7319. Telephone: +1 410 765 4441 Facsimile: +1 410 993 8771	AN/APY-1 a) Air & sea surveillance	Pulse Doppler a) S-band	Slotted planar array a) 6	a) High or low	Elevation scan, non-elevation scan, beyond the horizon, passive, maritime		This radar is the key to operational effectiveness of the E-3A AWACS. Digitized radar data is passed in near-real time to the aircraft's central processor and displays. Radar System Improvement Program (RSIP) upgrades include long PD modes.
Northrop Grumman Electronic Sensors & Systems Div.	AN/APY-2 a) Air & sea surveillance	Pulse Doppler a) S-band	Slotted planar array a) 6	a) High or low	Elevation scan, non-elevation scan, beyond the horizon, passive, maritime		Initially developed for the NATO AWACS aircraft, this radar was produced by the Westinghouse Command & Control Division and the former AEG-Telefunken in Germany. Radar System Improvement Program (RSIP) upgrades include long PD modes. RSIP upgrade being retrofitted on NATO & UK fleets. Used by E-3 and 767 AWACS.
Northrop Grumman Norden Systems.	AN/APY-3 JSTARS (Joint Surveillance & Target Attack Radar System) a) Land surveillance	Sideways looking phased array a) X-band	Slotted phased array		Wide area surveillance/ MTI, sector search, SAR, radar/fixed target indicator.	b) Radar antenna – 1,750 (794)	The heart of JSTARS is the surveillance & target acquisition radar currently installed & operational in the E-8C. Proven in Desert Storm & Bosnia.
Loral Defense Systems. (now part of Lockheed Martin)	AN/UPD-4 & AN/UPD-9 a) Reconnaissance	Sideways looking a) X-band	Slotted waveguide		Ground mapping, MTI	a) 30 (55) b) 622 (282)	Used in RF-4. UPD-4 refers to a system comprising a SAR officially designated AN/APD-10 Radar Mapping Set, a ground based ES-83A Correlator-Processor Set and AN/APM-321 test bench set. Originally developed by Goodyear Aerospace Corp.
Loral Defense Systems. (now part of Lockheed Martin)	AN/UPD-6 a) Reconnaissance	Sideways looking a) X-band	Slotted waveguide		Ground mapping, MTI	a) 30 (55) b) 622 (282)	Subject of a production contract in 1976, this was a special version for the German Air Force.
Loral Defense Systems. (now part of Lockheed Martin)	AN/UPD-8 a) Reconnaissance	Sideways looking a) X-band	Slotted waveguide		Ground mapping, MTI	a) 50 (93)	Used in RF-4. An updated version of UPD-4, offering greater range.
Raytheon Systems Company. (formerly Hughes)	ASARS-2 (Advanced Synthetic Aperture Radar System) a) Reconnaissance	Sideways looking a) X-band	'V'-shaped planar		Ground mapping, MTI		Originally developed for TR-1; -2 announced in 1977 and flown in U-2R. Also for Raytheon ASTOR programme.
Raytheon Systems Company. (formerly Hughes)	HISAR (Hughes Integrated Surveillance & Reconnaissance System) a) Reconnaissance	Sideways looking a) X-band			Air-to-air search, wide area search, strip map, spot, sea surveillance, wide-area MTI, combined SAR/MTI strip mode with 18 ft (5.5 m) resolution. SAR spot mode resolution 5.9 ft (1.8 m)	a) 54 (100) b) 496 (225) for radar version	System demonstrated at 1997 Paris Air Show in a King Air 200. The basic system is radar only; options include FLIR, long-range optical sensors, sigint sensors, radio, datalinks and ground stations. US Army RC-7B.
ERIM International. PO Box 134008, Ann Arbor, MI 48113-4008. Telephone: +1 313 994 1200 Facsimile: +1 313 994 5782 E-mail: ausherman@erim-int.com	IFSARE (Interferometric SAR for digital terrain Elevations)	Sideways looking a) X-band	Interferometer				This radar is mounted in a Learjet and is coupled to a ground-based processing facility. Processing software jointly developed by ERIM and JPL. System currently operated worldwide by Intermap Technologies, Inc. Is the first commercially viable interferometric SAR system and has been deployed to Bosnia.

Manufacturer	Radar designation a) Role	Type a) Operating frequency	Antenna type a) Scan rate (rpm) b) Peak output (kW)	a) PRF (Hz) b) Pulse width (microsec)	Operating modes	a) Maximum range naut miles (km) b) Weight lb (kg)	Comments
United States of America (continued)							
Northrop Grumman Electronic Sensors & Systems Div.	MESA (Multi-role Electronically Scanning Aircraft system) a) Air, sea & land surveillance	a) L-band	3 arrays in 'top hat' configuration for 737AEW&C		Air, sea and surface surveillance. See page 164 for further details	a) 190 (352)	Tested on BAC One-Eleven; offered for C-130, P-3, B737. 360° steerable beam arrays (with 288 modules).
Motorola Inc Space & Systems Technology Group.	SLAMMR (Side-Looking Airborne Modular Multi-mission Radar) a) Sea surveillance	Sideways looking a) X-band	Twin slotted waveguide		Sea surface mapping, optional MTI	a) 80 (148)	Used in maritime surveillance role in C-130 & B737. Now being considered for new ocean meteorology reconnaissance project.
Raytheon Systems Company.	SV 2022 a) Sea surveillance & small target detection				High resolution pulse-compression & scan-to-scan processing to reduce sea & rain clutter. 32 target track-while-scan capability	a) 12-122 (22-226)	Used in ATR 42MP.
Northrop Grumman Electronic Sensors & Systems Div.	TESAR (Tactical Endurance Synthetic Aperture Radar) a) Land surveillance	a) Ku-band	Planar (1 axis electronic mechanical gimbals) b) 1.050		MTI, SAR; in the latter mode continuous, fully-focused, high-resolution, near real-time strip map imagery is formed on either side of the aircraft	a) 5.4-15 (10-28) depending upon mode selected b) 165 (74.9)	Under contract to the US Army, TESAR is for use in the Predator UAV. Also currently flying in the Sherpa and Islander test beds & PC-XII Eagle. Uses a commercial off-the-shelf (COTS) processor. US Army awarded a $16.2 million contract in June 1997, with deliveries starting in 1998.
Multi-national							
AlliedSignal/ FIAR.	RDR-1500/-1500B a) Land & sea surveillance	a) X-band	Planar array b) 10	a) 200, 800, 1600 b) 0.1, 0.5, 2.35	Surface search, sea search, terrain mapping, weather avoidance, beacon detection	a) 160 (300) b) 93.47 (42.4)	This was a joint programme to develop a lightweight radar in 1981. It is based on the RDR-1300C. Used in A109, AB412, P.166, Do 228MP, AS 555SN Fennec, Reims Vigilant, Bell 230 Special Missions, Lynx, Sea King for SAR, Panther, Super Puma.
Thomson-CSF/ Daimler-Benz Aerospace. Wörthstrasse 85, D-89077 Ulm, Germany. Telephone: +49 731 393 5207 Facsimile: +49 731 392 4108 E-mail: Michael.Bischoff@VS.Dasa.De	Ocean Master a) Sea surveillance	Multi-mode a) X-band	Paraboloid a) 6-30 auto select with mode b) 6	a) 300 Hz-3.2 kHz	Long-range detection of all types of sea targets, multi-target tracking (track-while-scan), ship classification/ identification by use of high resolution	b) 159 (72)	In use by France, Pakistan, Indonesia and Japan, the latter for modernization of US-1A SAR aircraft. Other aircraft include Atlantic 1, Do 228MP, Falcon 20, Falcon 50, Fokker F-27, NC-212, CN 235, NBO 105 and Puma. Auto track of 32 targets; uses inverse SAR and SAR techniques. Several antenna reflector sizes are available.

Navigation and weather

Manufacturer	Radar designation a) Role	Antenna Type a) Operating frequency	Power output (kW) a) PRF (Hz) b) Pulse width (microsec)	Operating modes	Display	a) Maximum range naut miles (km) b) Weight lb (kg)	Comments
China							
China Leihua Electronic Technology Research Institute, (CLETRI). Wuxi. c/o Ministry of Electronic Industry. 46 Sanlihe, Fuwai Street, Beijing 100832. Telephone: +86 1068 20 81 14 Facslmile: +86 1068 21 85 62	WXR-350 a) Weather	Planar a) X-band	5 b) 1.0 & 5.5	Weather, ground mapping, navigation	Colour	a) 353 (654) b) 28.6 (13)	Produced under licence in China under an agreement signed with Collins Commercial Avionics in 1992. Used in Y7-100/-200.
France							
Thomson-CSF Radars & Contre Mesures. 1 Blvd Jean Moulin, Elancourt, F-78852. Telephone: +33 1 34 59 60 00 Facsimile: +33 1 34 59 62 36	ORB-37 a) Weather	Planar a) X-band	10 b) 2.5 & 0.4	Weather, ground mapping, beacon homing	Monochrome		Antenna rotates at low rate for weather and higher rate for mapping. Used in C-160.
Thomson-CSF Radars & Contre Mesures.	Arcana a) Navigation	Synthetic aperture		Advanced pulse Doppler air-to-ground modes			Used to update navigation in Mirage IV-P.

Manufacturer	Radar designation a) Role	Antenna Type a) Operating frequency	Power output (kW) a) PRF (Hz) b) Pulse width (microsec)	Operating modes	Display	a) Maximum range naut miles (km) b) Weight lb (kg)	Comments
Russia							
Unknown.	Buran D a) Weather	a) X-band	20 a) 250-1500 b) 0.5-6	Weather, ground-mapping, beacon interrogation	Colour	a) 300 (550)	
Leninets. St. Petersburg	Strizh a) Navigation/attack			Up to 20 targets tracked simultaneously		a) 10.8 (20) for small target, 108-119 (200-220) for large ship	S-80PT.
	Groza-42 (Thunderstorm) a) Weather						Used by Yak-42. Optional 7A813 Groza for Mi-26.
Phazotron. 1 Electrichesky Per, Moscow RF 123 557. Telephone: +7 095 253 5613 Facsimile: +7 095 253 0495	Gukol 1, Gukol 2, Gukol 3 & Gukol 4 a) Navigation & weather	a) X-band, except Gukol 4 which adds UHF-band	0.5 for Gukol 1, the others all 1.5	Real-beam ground mapping, DBS, synthetic aperture, enlarge, freeze, weather & turbulence detection, hazard warning, beacon interrogation	Colour	a) 189 (350) for Gukol 1, 242 (450) for Gukol 2 & 324 (600) for Gukol 3 & 4 b) 33 (15) for Gukol 1, 55 (25) for Gukol 2, 62 (28) for Gukol 3 & 132 (60) for Gukol 4	Used in a variety of light aircraft, transports (including Tu-330 and An-70) and tankers. Gukol considered for S-80PT, among others.
Unknown.	Kontur-10 a) Weather						Used in Be-32.
Leninets. St Petersburg	Kupol 2-76 & Kupol 3-76 a) Navigation						Used in Il-76. Kupol-2 is civil, Kupol-3 military.
Unknown.	PBR-4 Rubin 1 a) Mapping						Used in Tu-16.
Unknown.	RBP-4 (Short Horn) a) Navigation & bombing	a) Ku-band	a) 313-316, 496-504, 624-626 & 1249-1253 b) 1.0-1.9, 0.5-1.4, 0.4-1.3 and 0.01-0.9				Used in Tu-22, Tu-95, Yak-28, Ka-25PL. Features frequency agility with both circular and sector scans.
Unknown.	RPSN-3N Emblema a) Navigation & weather						Used in An-26.
United States of America							
Sperry Marine Inc. 1070 Seminole Trail, Charlottesville, VA 22901. Telephone: +1 804 974 2000 Facsimile: +1 804 974 2259	AN/APN-59 a) Multifunction	a) X-band	Various PRFs & pulse lengths depending upon mode selection	Weather, navigation, search, beacon homing		b) Typically 185 (84)	Used in C-130E/H, HC-130P/N, WC-130H, LC-130H, MC-130P, AC-130H, EC-130E/H, C-135, KC-135, RC-135. In 1993 the APN-59(X) was offered as a direct backfit on a box-by-box basis. Improvements include lower power requirements and more efficient antenna. Currently the subject of a replacement programme.
AlliedSignal Commercial Avionics Systems. 400 N Rogers Road, Olathe, KS 66062-1212. Telephone: +1 913 782 0400 Facsimile: +1 913 791 1302	AN/APN-215(V) a) Multifunction	Planar a) X-band	10 a) 200, 800 b) 0.5, 2.35	Weather, ground mapping, surface search	Colour	a) 240 (445)	Based on the commercial RDR-1300 radar. Used in HH-2, C-130, RU-38A, King Air.
AlliedSignal Commercial Avionics Systems.	AN/APN-234 a) Multifunction	Planar a) X-band	10 a) 200, 800 b) 0.5, 2.35	Weather, ground mapping, land & sea search	Colour	a) 240 (445)	Used in C-2A, P-3B. Similar to APN-215 but has sea search capability.
Raytheon Systems Company. 2501 S Highway 121, Lewisville, TX 75067-8127. Telephone: +1 972 462 6500 Facsimile: +1 972 462 6508	AN/APN-237A a) Navigation	a) Ku-band		Normal, weather, ECCM, Low Probability of Intercept (LPI) & Very Low Clearance (VLC)			This is terrain-following radar of the LANTIRN system used on F-15E, F-15I, F-15S & F-16C/D. Provides low-level day/night navigation, including adverse weather conditions blind letdown from altitude.
Northrop Grumman Electronic Sensors & Systems Div. PO Box 17319, MS A255, Baltimore, MD 21203-7319. Telephone: +1 410 765 4441 Facsimile: +1 410 993 8771	AN/APN-241 a) Multifunction	Planar a) X-band	0.116 peak	Weather, windshear, ground mapping, skin paint, beacon, station-keeping, flight plan, traffic collision avoidance	Colour	a) 320 (592) b) 205 (93)	Used in C-130J.
Raytheon Systems Company.	AN/APQ-122(V) & (V)5 a) Multifunction	a) X-band & Ku-band; X-band for (V)5		Ground mapping, weather, beacon interrogation		a) 200 (370)	Used in C-130E, E-4B. Developed for use with adverse weather aerial delivery system (AWADS) aircraft. Has been updated with addition of a scan converter. More than 300 APQ-122 radars of all variants were delivered during the 1970s and early 1980s.

Manufacturer	Radar designation a) Role	Antenna Type a) Operating frequency	Power output (kW) a) PRF (Hz) b) Pulse width (microsec)	Operating modes	Display	a) Maximum range naut miles (km) b) Weight lb (kg)	Comments
United States of America (continued)							
Raytheon Systems Company.	AN/APQ-122(V)8 a) Multifunction	a) X-band		Ground mapping, terrain following, weather, beacon interrogation		a) 200 (370)	Used in MC-130E Combat Talon I aircraft. In 1996 US Air Force awarded a US$8.9 million contract to upgrade the radar's receiver/transmitter on 42 sets. The work is expected to be completed by September 1999.
Raytheon Systems Company.	AN/APQ-168 a) Multifunction			Ground mapping, terrain following, terrain avoidance, ranging		b) 249 (113)	Used in the HH-60 Night Hawk, the radar is mounted in a pod on the forward fuselage.
SEI Systems & Electronics Inc. 201 Evans Lane, St Louis, MO 6312-1126. Telephone: +1 314 553 4678 Facsimile: +1 314 553 4950 E-mail: ssherman@SEISTL.com	AN/APQ-170 a) Multifunction	X-band circular antenna is mounted above 2 back-to-back Ku dishes. a) X-band & Ku-band		Ground mapping, terrain following, terrain avoidance, ranging, weather & beacon	4 CRTs		MC-130H Combat Talon II. This is virtually 2 radars in 1. X-band is optimized for terrain following/avoidance and beacon location. Ku-band is used for ground map generation, weather detection and radar beacon location. If necessary X-band can be used for these functions.
Raytheon Systems Company.	AN/APQ-174/174B a) Multifunction	Planar a) Ku-band		Ground mapping, terrain following, terrain avoidance, ranging, weather & beacon		b) 238 (108)	Used in CH-47, MH-47, HH-60, MH-60 and V-22. A derivative of LANTIRN terrain following radar. Intended for low altitude operation by day or night. The US Army has tested the -174B for use in special operations MH-60K and MH-47E helicopters.
SEI Systems & Electronics Inc.	AN/APQ-175 & AN/APQ-175X a) Multifunction	Paraboloid a) X-band & K-band. X-band for APQ-175X	90 a) 925, 420, 250 b) 0.53, 2.35	Ground mapping, weather & beacon		a) 240 (445)	C-130 all-weather airborne delivery system (AWADS) aircraft. Intended as a replacement for APQ-122(V).
AlliedSignal Commercial Avionics Systems.	AN/APS-133 (Types 1 & 2) & (V) a) Multifunction	Paraboloid a) X-band	65 a) 200 – Type 1 200, 800 – Type 2 b) 0.4 - 5	Weather, ground mapping, navigation + air-to-air search & track, beacon interrogation	Colour	a) 300 (555) b) 100 (45.5)	Developed from RDR-1F and used in C-5, C-141, KC-10, E-3, E-4, E-6, EC-24A, NKC-135A and CN 235M. C-17 uses AN/APS-133(V) version.
Rockwell Collins Inc. 400 Collins Rd NE, Cedar Rapids, IA 52498. Telephone: +1 319 295 1000 Facsimile: +1 319 295 5429	FMR-200X a) Weather	Phased array flatplate a) C-band (5.44 GHz)	0.120 a) 180 - 3000 b) 0.8 - 20	Weather, turbulence, ground mapping, predictive windshear, skin paint aircraft detection	Colour	a) 320 (593) b) 74.3 (33.7)	For flight-deck upgrade of USAF C-135 & KC-135. Collins supplied this radar which is a military version of the WXR-700. Features include skin paint capability to allow radar detection and separation between tankers during multiple tanker refuelling operations. Also used in Danish C-130 upgrade.
Narco Avionics Inc. 270 Commerce Drive, Fort Washington, PA 19034. Telephone: +1 215 643 2905 Facsimile: +1 215 643 0197 E-mail: narco@netreach.net	KWX-56 a) Multifunction	Planar	7.5 a) 1-10 b) 3.5	Weather, ground mapping, navigation	3 colour	a) 160 (296) b) 18.4 (8.35)	Narco took over production of this radar in 1985.
Narco Avionics Inc.	KWX-58 a) Multifunction	Planar	7.5 a) 1-10 b) 3.5	Weather, ground mapping, navigation	4 colour	a) 320 (593) b) 19.8 (8.98)	Narco took over production of this radar in 1985.
Northrop Grumman Electronic Sensors & Systems Division.	LPCR 130-1 a) Multifunction?		Low power		Colour		C-130.
Honeywell Business & Commuter Aviation Systems. 5353 W. Bell Road, Glendale, AZ 85308. Telephone: +1 602 436 8000 Facsimile: +1 602 436 7100	Primus 40 & 50 a) Search radar				Monochrome	a) 300 (556)	Used in IAR Puma.
Honeywell Business & Commuter Aviation Systems.	Primus 90 a) Weather	Planar a) X-band	a) 121		Colour	b) 44.9 (20.37)	Used in Y-7 and a wide range of light aircraft.
Honeywell Business & Commuter Aviation Systems.	Primus 100 ColoRadar a) Weather	Paraboloid a) X-band	b) 4.0 & 10	Weather, navigation	Colour	a) 200 (370)	This is a colour version of the earlier WeatherScout II.
Honeywell Business & Commuter Aviation Systems.	Primus 200 ColoRadar a) Weather	Planar a) X-band	b) 4.0 & 11	Weather, navigation	Colour	a) 200 (370)	This radar is the result of design update of Primus 100 with lighter units, more compact display and a planar antenna.
Honeywell Business & Commuter Aviation Systems.	Primus 300SL ColoRadar a) Weather	Planar a) X-band		Weather, navigation	Colour	a) 300 (556) b) 32.3-39.7 (14.7-18.0)	This radar was seen as a second generation colour set with options of 3 antenna sizes. Intended for turboprop/jet twin types.
Honeywell Business & Commuter Aviation Systems.	Primus 400 a) Weather	Planar a) X-band		Weather, navigation	Colour		Used in Falcon 50/50EX.

Manufacturer	Radar designation a) Role	Antenna Type a) Operating frequency	Power output (kW) a) PRF (Hz) b) Pulse width (microsec)	Operating modes	Display	a) Maximum range naut miles (km) b) Weight lb (kg)	Comments
United States of America (continued)							
Honeywell Business & Commuter Aviation Systems.	Primus 440 a) Weather	a) X-band	10			b) 14 (6.35)	Features Rain Echo Attenuation Compensation Technique (REACT). Selected for Loadmaster.
Honeywell Business & Commuter Aviation Systems.	Primus 450 a) Weather	Planar	1.3			a) 300 (556) b) 22.99 (10.43)	Features Rain Echo Attenuation Compensation Technique (REACT). Is EFIS and LSZ-850 (lightning sensor) compatible. Intended for business aircraft.
Honeywell Business & Commuter Aviation Systems.	Primus 500 a) Weather	Planar a) X-band (9.375 GHz)	10	Weather, navigation, beacon navigation	Colour	a) 200 (370) b) 29.2 (13.29)	This radar can interrogate, receive, process and display transponder beacons. A separate beacon receiver gain control lowers receiver gain for close-in operation with high power beacons.
Honeywell Business & Commuter Aviation Systems.	Primus 650 a) Weather	Planar a) X-band	1.3	Weather	Colour	a) 300 (556) b) 22.99 (10.43)	This radar has a flight plan facility for route overlay. Features REACT and is EFIS and LSZ-850 (lightning sensor) compatible. This is an integrated system whereby the transmitter, receiver & antenna are combined in a single unit for ease of installation. Intended for the business aircraft market. Used in 328, Citation Bravo and Ultra, and Learjet 45.
Honeywell Business & Commuter Aviation Systems.	Primus 660 a) Weather		10			b) 14 (6.35)	High power successor to Primus 650. Features REACT.
Honeywell Business & Commuter Aviation Systems.	Primus 700/701 a) Weather	Planar	10 a) Choice of 4 b) Choice of 6 (shortest is 100 nanosecs)	Weather, turbulence, navigation (plus beacon navigation on 701)	Colour	a) 300 (556) b) 35.93 (16.3)	Introduced in 1990 at the Dallas Heli-Expo, these radars were aimed at the helicopter market. The 701 features decoded beacon symbol, select course and clear zone during missed approach. Auto tilt keeps radar beam centred on surface beacon. Has REACT and is used in the Mi-17KF, S-76, Black Hawk and 412EP as option.
Honeywell Business & Commuter Aviation Systems.	Primus 708A (& 800 – see Comments) a) Weather	Planar	15 b) 2 for Primus 708A	Weather, ground mapping, navigation	Colour	a) 300 (556)	This turbulence detecting radar was designed for ARINC 708 digital interface. Has a variety of display options including TCAS. Typically used in A320, B747-400, MD-90 and MD-11. Large corporate jet and turboprop users include ATR 42 and Dash 8 for Primus 800.
Honeywell Business & Commuter Aviation Systems.	Primus 870 a) Weather	Planar a) X-band		Weather (including turbulence detection), ground mapping, navigation	Colour	a) 300 (556) b) 23.98 (10.88)	Used in Citation VII and Falcon 900B/900EX. Optional for Fairchild Dornier 328.
Honeywell Business & Commuter Aviation Systems.	Primus 880 a) Weather	Planar a) X-band	10			b) 14 (6.35)	High power successor to the Primus 870. Features REACT and Altitude Compensated Tilt (ACT) to reduce pilot workload. A target alert facility gives notice of potential hazardous weather directly ahead of the aircraft. Used by Citation Excel, Hawker 800XP.
AlliedSignal Commercial Avionics Systems.	RDR-1FB a) Weather	Paraboloid a) X-band	65 a) 200 b) 0.5 & 5.0	Weather, air-to-air mapping, ground mapping, navigation beacon tracking	Colour	a) 300 (556) b) 107.8 (48.9)	RDR-1F used in C-130H.
AlliedSignal Commercial Avionics Systems.	RDR-4A a) Weather	Planar a) X-band		Weather, navigation	Colour	a) 320 (593)	Used in B737, B747, B757, B767, A300, A310, Be-200 and Yak-142. Was chosen by Boeing as standard equipment on 757/767 aircraft and is fully compatible with EFIS systems.
AlliedSignal Commercial Avionics Systems.	RDR-4B a) Weather	Planar a) X-band		Weather, navigation, wind shear detection/avoidance	Colour	a) 320 (593)	First certificated in 1994, the RDR-4B gives 30-60 seconds warning of wind shear, which is automatic below 2,300 ft (700 m) above ground. Used in larger aircraft as it requires a 30 ins (76 cm) diameter antenna.
AlliedSignal Commercial Avionics Systems.	RDR-150 Colorvision/ Weathervision a) Weather	Paraboloid or Planar a) X-band	8 b) 3.5	Weather, ground mapping, navigation	Monochrome or colour	a) 160 (296) b) 18.5-23.2 (8.4-10.5)	A weather alert feature causes red storm cells to flash.
AlliedSignal Commercial Avionics Systems.	RDR-160 a) Weather	Paraboloid a) X-band	6	Weather, ground mapping	Monochrome or colour	a) 160 (296) b) 15 (6.8)	Used in Beech 1900. To save weight and ease installation, the antenna, transmitter and receiver are combined in a single unit.

Manufacturer	Radar designation a) Role	Antenna Type a) Operating frequency	Power output (kW) a) PRF (Hz) b) Pulse width (microsec)	Operating modes	Display	a) Maximum range naut miles (km) b) Weight lb (kg)	Comments
United States of America (continued)							
AlliedSignal Commercial Avionics Systems.	RDR-230HP a) Weather	Planar a) X-band	5	Weather, ground mapping	Monochrome or colour		
AlliedSignal Commercial Avionics Systems.	RDR-1100 a) Weather	Planar a) X-band	8	Weather, ground mapping	Monochrome or colour		
AlliedSignal Commercial Avionics Systems.	RDR-1200 a) Weather	Planar	10	Weather, ground mapping & navigation	Monochrome or colour		
AlliedSignal Commercial Avionics Systems.	RDR-1300 & -1300C a) Weather	Planar a) X-band	10			a) 320 (593) b) 34.98 (15.87)	Users include Sea King for forward looking. RDR-1300C in HH-60J.
AlliedSignal Commercial Avionics Systems.	RDR-1400C a) Weather	12 ins (30.5 cm) flat plate phased array (18 ins, 45.7 cm optional) a) X-band	10 b) 2	Weather, mapping, beacon identification, beacon track, OBS track, optional check list & moving map display	Colour	a) 240 (444.7) b) 25.70 (11.66)	System offers a beacon tracking mode as well as checklist storage and display capability. Do 228 Pollution surveillance aircraft, Y-12(II), AH-60L, Super Puma, Dauphin.
AlliedSignal Commercial Avionics Systems.	RDR-2000 a) Weather	Planar	4	Weather	Colour	b) 25.70 (11.66)	First of a new generation of Vertical Profile ® radars. System scans vertically at azimuth selected by pilot using track line. Offers independent dual indicator operation. Users include EC135 and Dauphin (as option).
AlliedSignal Commercial Avionics Systems.	RDR-2100 a) Weather	Planar	6	Weather	Colour	b) 25.70 (11.66)	Vertical Profile radar includes multifunction display, fault annunciation and TILT readout on CRT.
AlliedSignal General Aviation Avionics. 400 N Rogers Road, Olathe, KS 66062-1212. Telephone: +1 913 782 0400 Facsimile: +1 913 791 1302	RDS-81 a) Weather	12 ins (30.5 cm) flat plate phased array (10 ins, 25.4 cm available) a) X-band	1 a/b) Separate PRF and pulse width for each range	Weather, attenuation compensation	Colour	a) 240 (445) b) 19.4 (8.8)	Features a multifunction display, fault annunciation and TILT readout on CRT. Pulse width varies with distance. Used in C-90SE, Do 228, M28, L 410.
AlliedSignal Commercial Avionics Systems.	RDS-82 & RDS-83 a) Weather	Planar a) X-band	1 for RDS-82	Weather	Colour	a) 240 (445) b) 19.8 (9.0) for RDS-83	Based on ARINC 429 and used the colour Magenta to indicate areas of heavy rainfall.
AlliedSignal Commercial Avionics Systems.	RDS-84VP a) Weather	Planar a) X-band	1.3 a) 128, 1086 b) 0.8 - 15.3	Weather	Colour	b) 26.5 (12)	VP - Vertical Profile for thunderstorm assessment. This radar can compensate for signal attenuation.
AlliedSignal Commercial Avionics Systems.	RDS-86 a) Weather	Planar a) X-band	1.3	Weather, navigation	Colour	a) 320 (593) b) 22 (10)	Features include automatic tilt and range limiting, antenna stabilization and long-range navigation mode. Intended for Jetstream 61 and was part of the Falcon 20 avionics retrofit package.
Rockwell Collins Inc.	RNS-300 a) Weather	a) X-band	5 b) 1.0 & 5.6	Weather, ground mapping, navigation	Colour	a) 354 (656) b) 28.6 (13.0)	When introduced to the market, it was said to be the only radar capable of plotting intersecting course lines using data from dual nav aids or area navigation system. No longer in production.
Rockwell Collins Inc.	RNS-325 a) Weather	a) X-band	5	Weather, navigation	Colour	a) 300 (556)	The '300' family is basically the WXR-300 with additional processing to display aircraft position on weather map. No longer in production.
Rockwell Collins Inc.	RTA-854 a) Weather			Weather, navigation			Used by Challenger 604. RTA-800 for new Citation CJ1 and CJ2.
Rockwell Collins Inc.	TWR-850 a) Weather	Planar a) X-band	0.24	Weather, turbulence detection	Colour	a) 300 (556) b) 19.8 (9)	Solid-state Doppler turbulence detection. Separate function selection for each pilot (eg. mode, range, etc). Said to be the first weather radar for smaller aircraft which could detect and display turbulence using Doppler techniques. Used in Beech 1900D, Raytheon Premier I and N-250.
Honeywell Business & Commuter Avionics Systems.	WeatherScout II a) Weather	Paraboloid a) X-band	0.22 b) 4.0 & 10	Weather	Monochrome	a) 120 (222) b) 4.8 (2.18)	Popular with owners of single-engined and light twins. Often pod mounted on leading edge of wing.
Rockwell Collins Inc.	WXR-200A a) Weather	Paraboloid or planar a) X-band	5 b) 1.0 & 5.5	Weather	Monochrome	a) 180 (333) b) 22.7 (10.3)	No longer in production, this was the smallest radar in the Collins range. It featured a memory enhancement technique to enhance picture quality.
Rockwell Collins Inc.	WXR-250A a) Weather	Planar a) X-band	5 b) 1 & 5.5	Weather, navigation	Monochrome	a) 240 (445)	Users include L 610G.

Manufacturer	Radar designation a) Role	Antenna Type a) Operating frequency	Power output (kW) a) PRF (Hz) b) Pulse width (microsec)	Operating modes	Display	a) Maximum range naut miles (km) b) Weight lb (kg)	Comments
United States of America (continued)							
Rockwell Collins Inc.	WXR-270 a) Weather	Planar a) X-band	5 b) 1 & 5.5	Weather, navigation	Colour	a) 240 (445)	Users include EMB-120.
Rockwell Collins Inc.	WXR-300 a) Weather	Planar a) X-band	5 b) 1.0 & 5.5	Weather, ground mapping, navigation	Colour	a) 353 (654) b) 28.6 (13.0)	Black matrix CRT display with alphanumeric read-out of range and function. Also co-produced in China, at Wuxi, under licence agreement. No longer in production in USA.
Rockwell Collins Inc.	WXR-350 a) Weather	Planar a) X-band	5 b) 1.0 & 5.5	Weather, ground mapping, navigation	Colour	a) 300 (556)	Display on Collins EFIS and/or MFD. Users include Beech 1900D Airliner, CN 235.
Rockwell Collins Inc.	WXR-700C a) Weather	Phased array flat plate a) C-band (5.44 GHz)	0.23 a) 180-1440 b) 2.0-20	Weather, ground mapping, navigation & Doppler turbulence	Colour	a) 320 (593) b) 74.3 (33.7)	Standard ARINC 708 radar in C-band.
Rockwell Collins Inc.	WXR-700X a) Weather	Phased array flat plate a) X-band	0.12 a) 180-3000 b) 0.8-20	Weather, navigation, ground mapping, turbulence, predictive windshear detection	Colour	a) 320 (593) b) 74.3 (33.7)	In 1994 predictive windshear capability offered by modification kits. System warns pilots of microburst/windshear up to 10 naut miles (18.5 km) or 90 seconds ahead of aircraft. This capability is retrofittable to existing radars. Used by upgraded KC-135s.
Rockwell Collins Inc.	WXR-800 a) Weather				Colour		Optional for Bell (Agusta) BA 609. Avanti.
Rockwell Collins Inc.	WXR-840 a) Weather	Planar 12 ins (30 cm), 14 ins (36 cm), 18 ins (46 cm) a) X-band	0.24 a) Variable b) Variable	Weather, ground mapping	Colour	a) 300 (556)	Used in Learjet 60, Beechjet 400A, N-250. Optional for 1900D.
Rockwell Collins Inc.	WXR-850 a) Weather			Weather, ground mapping, etc.	Colour	a) 6-range radar: 10, 25, 50, 100, 200 & 300 (19, 46, 92, 185, 370 & 556)	Used in Astra SPX. ±15° antenna angle. 14 looks (scan) per minute of 120°. Pressurized wave guide for high altitude operations.

↑ First Boeing 757 transport was converted to perform as a flying laboratory in support of the Lockheed Martin F-22 Raptor fighter programme, to integrate and flight test the F-22's highly integrated avionics. The first modification to the structure was the fitting of an F-22 nose, to house the AN/APG-77 radar. The 'sensor wing' modification followed in August 1998, allowing the start of full-scale avionics testing in late 1998. Electronic warfare and communication, navigation and identification sensors are mounted directly on the sensor wing, which was designed to simulate the sensor positioning found on the F-22 wing. Full-scale avionics testing is now underway.

Airport Runway
Lengths, Designators (orientations) & Bearing Strengths

This section provides details of the designator (indicating also orientation), length and load-bearing strength of the longest runway at the world's major airports (some non-commercial aerodromes are also included for reference value). The criterion adopted in selecting the airports to be included is that they should have the longest runways in any particular country, normally of at least 9000 ft (2743 m), except where exclusion on this basis would result in a self-governing area, or a major or capital city not being represented. *Note that in this section commas are not used in runway length figures.*

Runway weight bearing capacity is shown by one of the following methods:

ACN/PCN system:
Aircraft Classification Number (ACN), calculated by accounting for the aircraft type, pavement type, and subgrade category.
Pavement Classification Number (PCN) expresses the bearing strength of a runway pavement for unrestricted operations, using the following codes. Type of Pavement: R - Rigid, F- Flexible. Pavement sub-grade category: A - High, B - Medium, C - Low, D - Ultra low. Maximum tyre pressure authorised: W - High, no limit, X - Medium, max 217 psi, Y - Low, max 145 psi, Z - Very low, max 73 psi. Pavement evaluation method: T - Technical evaluation, U - From actual past use by aircraft.

Load Classification Group (LCG) is related to **Load Classification Number (LCN)**, LCG I being the greatest strength.

LCG	LCN
I	101-120
II	76-100
III	51-75
IV	31-50
V	16-30
VI	11-15
VII	10 and under

Thousands of Kilogrammes (all-up weight of aircraft, dependant upon type of undercarriage assembly), where S = Single wheel, T = Twin wheel, B = Bogie, DB = Double Bogie. Thus 54S/220T/470B/830DB indicates 54000 kg AUW for single wheel, 220000 kg for twin wheel, 470000 kg for single bogie, 830000 kg for double bogie.
Thousands of Kilogrammes per principal undercarriage assembly, using S, T, B and DB as above (for Algeria, France, Ireland, Luxembourg, Morocco, Netherlands and Switzerland).

All-up weight (AUW) in kilogrammes

Isolated Single-Wheel (ISWL), maximum permissible weight in Kilogrammes.

Aircraft type, e.g. B747, indicating that the runway is suitable for aircraft having all-up weights no greater than the maximum all-up weight of that type.

THE FOLLOWING DETAILS ARE FOR GENERAL REFERENCE AND ARE NOT TO BE USED FOR FLIGHT PLANNING PURPOSES.

Based on material supplied by, and reproduced in part with the kind permission of, Racal AERAD.

Airport (Aerodrome) name	Designator (orientation) and length of longest runway		Runway LCN/PCN
AFGHANISTAN			
Kabul	11/29	11483 ft (3500 m)	ISWL 55000
Kandahar	05/23	10500 ft (3200 m)	ISWL 20400
ALASKA (see also USA)			
Anchorage International	06R/24L	10897 ft (3321 m)	PCN 52/F/A/X/T
Anchorage (Elmendorf)	05/23	10000 ft (3048 m)	PCN 52/F/A/X/T
Cold Bay	14/32	10415 ft (3174 m)	PCN 33/F/A/X/T
Fairbanks International	01L/19R	10300 ft (3139 m)	PCN 50/F/A/X/T
ALBANIA			
Tirana (Rinas)	18/36	9022 ft (2750 m)	—
ALGERIA			
Adrar (Touat)	04/22	9843 ft (3000 m)	PCN 87/F/A/W/T
Algiers (Houari Boumedienne)	05/23	11500 ft (3505 m)	43S/45T/74B
Annaba (El Mellah)	01/19	9843 ft (3000 m)	40S/40T/56B
Djanet (Tiska)	13/31	9843 ft (3000 m)	30S/38T/65B
El Golea	18/36	9843 ft (3000 m)	35S/65T/75B
Ghardaia	13/31	10171 ft (310 m)	ISWL 35000
Hassi Messaoud (Oued Irara)	01/19	9842 ft (3000 m)	27S/40T/65B
Illizi (Takhamalt)	09/27	9843 ft (3000 m)	86 tonnes
Oran (Es Senia)	07/25	10039 ft (3060 m)	ISWL 25000
Tamanrasset	03/21	11811 ft (3600 m)	ISWL 40000
Tebessa	11/29	9843 ft (3000 m)	PCN 59/F/D//W/T
Tiaret (Bou Chekif)	09/27	9843 ft (3000 m)	33S/38T/60B
Timimoun	06/24	9843 (3000 m)	PCN 52/F/A/W/T
Zarazaitine (In Amenas)	05/23	9843 ft (3000 m)	ISWL 35000
ANGOLA			
Luanda	05/23	12139 ft (3700 m)	LCN 105
Menonque	13/31	11483 ft (3500 m)	B707
Saurimo	14/32	11155 ft (3400 m)	DC-8
ARGENTINA			
Buenos Aires (Ezeiza)	11/29	10827 ft (3300 m)	172S/220T/386DB
Cataratas del Iguazu	12/30	10828 ft (3300 m)	58S/76T/121B/260DB

Airport (Aerodrome) name	Designator (orientation) and length of longest runway		Runway LCN/PCN
ARGENTINA			
Comodoro Rivadavia	07/25	9022 ft (2750 m)	56S/157B/365DB
Cordoba	18/36	10499 ft (3200 m)	43S/150B/350DB
Mendoza (El Plumerillo)	18/36	9885 ft (3013 m)	60S/160B/330DB
Moron	01/19	11811 ft (3600 m)	26S/34T/54B
Rio Gallegos	07/25	11647 ft (3550 m)	58S/87T/330DB
ARMENIA			
Yerevan (Zvartnots)	09/27	12631 ft (3850 m)	PCN 35/R/B/X/T
ASCENSION ISLAND			
Ascension Island (Wideawake)	14/32	10000 ft (3048 m)	70S/100T/250B/364DB
AUSTRALIA			
Adelaide	05/23	8294 ft (2528 m)	PCN 72/F/D/1400/U
Alice Springs	12/30	8000 ft (2438 m)	PCN 60/F/B/1750/U
Brisbane	01/19	11483 ft (3500 m)	PCN 97/F/D/1750/T
Cairns	15/33	10489 ft (3197 m)	PCN 90/F/D/1750/U
Canberra	17/35	8800 ft (2682 m)	PCN 45/F/B/1400/U
Darwin International	11/29	10906 ft (3324 m)	PCN 66/F/C/1400/U
Melbourne International	16/34	12000 ft (3658 m)	PCN 79/F/C/1750/U
Perth International	03/21	11300 ft (3444 m)	PCN 55/F/A/1400/T
Sydney (Kingsford Smith)	16R/34L	13000 ft (3962 m)	PCN 67/F/A/1750/U
AUSTRIA			
Graz	17/35	9055 ft (2760 m)	PCN 36/R/B/W/T
Innsbruck	08/26	6562 ft (2000 m)	PCN 45/R/B/W/T
Klagenfurt	10/28	8924 ft (2720 m)	PCN 37.5/R/B/W/T
Linz	09/27	9219 ft (2810 m)	PCN 55/F/C/W/T
Salzburg	16/34	9022 ft (2750 m)	PCN 55/R/B/W/T
Vienna (Schwechat)	16/34	11811 ft (3600 m)	PCN 70/F/C/W
AZERBAIJAN			
Baku (Bina)	18/36	10499 ft (3200 m)	PCN 150/F/W/A/T
AZORES			
Lajes	15/33	10865 ft (3312 m)	Unlimited

Airport (Aerodrome) name	Designator (orientation) and length of longest runway		Runway LCN/PCN
AZORES			
Santa Maria	18/36	10000 ft (3048 m)	LCN 200
BAHAMAS			
Freeport	06/24	11000 ft (3353 m)	PCN 73
Nassau International	14/32	11000 ft (3353 m)	PCN 73
BAHRAIN			
Bahrain International	12/30	13002 ft (3963 m)	LCN 100
BANGLADESH			
Chittagong	05/23	10000 ft (3048 m)	PCN 40/F/C/Y/T
Dhaka (Zia International)	14/32	10499 ft (3200 m)	PCN 50/R/B/X/U
BARBADOS			
Barbados (Grantley Adams International)	09/27	11000 ft (3353 m)	PCN 75/R/B/W/T
BELARUS			
Minsk	13/31	11942 ft (3640 m)	PCN 60/R/B/X/T
BELGIUM & LUXEMBOURG			
Antwerp (Deurne)	11/29	4954 ft (1510 m)	PCN 30/F/A/W/U
Beauvechain	04L/22R	10085 ft (3074 m)	LCN 50
Brussels (National)	07L/25R	11936 ft (3638 m)	PCN 64/F/A/W/U
Charleroi (Brussels South)	07/25	8366 ft (2550 m)	PCN 56/F/A/W/U
Florennes	08/26	11103 ft (3384 m)	LCN 45
Kleine Brogel	05/23	10158 ft (3096 m)	LCN 45
Liege	05R/23L	10784 ft (3287 m)	PCN 56/F/A/W/U
Luxembourg	06/24	13123 ft (4000 m)	PCN 65/F/A/W/U
Ostend	08/26	10499 ft (3200 m)	PCN 56/F/A/W/U
BELIZE			
Belize (Phillip S.W. Goldson Int'l)	07/25	7100 ft (2164 m)	PCN 61/F/C/W/U
BENIN			
Cotonou (Cadjehoun)	06/24	7874 ft (2400 m)	PCN 53/F/B/X/T
BERMUDA			
Bermuda	12/30	9713 ft (2960 m)	52S/120T/161B
BHUTAN			
Paro	15/33	6512 ft (1985 m)	LCN22
BOLIVIA			
Cochabamba (Jorge Wilsterman)	13/31	12467 ft (3800 m)	PCN 48/F/B/X/T
La Paz (J.F. Kennedy Int'l)	10/28	13123 ft (4000 m)	PCN 46/R/A/X/U
Santa Cruz (El Trompillo)	15/33	9144 ft (2787 m)	PCN 48/F/C/X/U
Santa Cruz (Viru Viru)	15/33	11482 ft (3500 m)	PCN 57/R/B/X/T
Tarija	13/31	10006 ft (3050 m)	PCN 48/F/C/X/T
BOSNIA-HERZEGOVINA			
Mostar	16/34	7874 ft (2400 m)	LCN 60
Sarajevo (Butmir)	12/30	8530 ft (2600 m)	LCN 80
BOTSWANA			
Francistown	11/29	7218 ft (2200 m)	LCN 40
Gaborone (Seretse Khama Int'l)	08/26	9843 ft (3000 m)	PCN 75/R/B/W/T
Kasane	08/26	6562 ft (2000 m)	PCN 15/F/A/W/T
Maun	08/26	6561 ft (2000 m)	PCN 18/F/B/X/T
BRAZIL			
Belo Horizonte (Tancredo Neves)	16/34	9843 ft (3000 m)	PCN 60/F/A/W/T
Brasilia International	11/29	10496 ft (3199 m)	PCN 76/F/B/X/T
Campinas (Viracopos)	15/33	10630 ft (3240 m)	PCN 56/F/B/X/T
Natal (Augusto Severo)	16L/34R	7447 ft (2270 m)	PCN 41/F/A/X/T
Recife (Guararapes)	18/36	9846 ft (3001 m)	PCN 63/F/B/X/T
Rio de Janeiro (Galeao Int'l)	10/28	13123 ft (4000 m)	PCN 78/R/A/W/T
Salvador (Dois de Julho)	10/28	9859 ft (3005 m)	PCN 74/F/B/X/T
Sao Jose dos Campos	16/34	8780 ft (2676 m)	PCN 71/F/A/X/T
Sao Paulo (Guarulhas)	09L/27R	12140 ft (3700 m)	PCN 85/F/B/W/T
BULGARIA			
Burgas	04/22	10499 ft (3200 m)	PCN 60/R/B/X/T
Plovdiv	13/31	8202 ft (2500 m)	PCN 38/R/A/X/T
Sofia	09/27	9186 ft (2800 m)	PCN 38/F/A/W/T
Varna	09/27	8202 ft (2500 m)	PCN 60/R/B/X/T
BURKINA FASO			
Bobo-Dioulasso	06/24	10827 ft (3300 m)	PCN 57/F/B/X/T
Dedougou	15/33	8202 ft (2500 m)	DC-3
Ouagadougou	04/22	9842 ft (3000 m)	PCN 59/F/B/X/T
BURUNDI			
Bujumbura	17/35	11811 ft (3600 m)	PCN 75/F/A/X/U
CAICOS ISLANDS			
Grand Turk	11/29	6335 ft (1931 m)	—
Providenciales International	10/28	7600 ft (2316 m)	PCN 52/F/A/X/T
CAMBODIA			
Phnom-Penh (Pochentong)	05/23	9842 ft (3000 m)	AUW 183000
CAMEROUN			
Douala	12/30	9350 ft (2850 m)	PCN 59/F/C/X/U
Garoua	09/27	11155 ft (3400 m)	PCN 71/F/C/X/T
Yaounde (Nsimalen)	01/19	11155 ft (3400 m)	PCN 71/F/C/W/U
CANADA			
Abbotsford	07/25	8000 ft (2438 m)	PCN 54/F/A/Y/T
Bagotville	11/29	10000 ft (3048 m)	46S/113T/148B
Calgary International	16/34	12675 ft (3863 m)	PCN 111/F/D/W/T
Edmonton International	02/20	11000 ft (3353 m)	PCN 93/R/C/W/T
Gander	04/22	10500 ft (3200 m)	PCN 54/F/A/W/T
Goose	08/26	11050 ft (3368 m)	PCN 67/F/A/W/T
Halifax International	06/24	8800 ft (2682 m)	PCN 61/F/B/W/T
Hamilton	12L/30R	8000 ft (2438 m)	PCN 87/F/D/X/T
Iqaluit	18/36	9000 ft (2743 m)	PCN 54/F/A/W/T
London	15/33	8800 ft (2682 m)	PCN 70/F/C/X/T
Moncton	11/29	8000 ft (2438 m)	PCN 70/F/C/W/T
Montreal (Dorval)	06L/24R	11000 ft (3353 m)	PCN 70/F/C/W/T
Montreal (Mirabel)	06/24	12000 ft (3658 m)	PCN 68/R/A/W/T
North Bay	08/26	10000 ft (3048 m)	PCN 61/F/B/W/T
Ottawa	14/32	9648 ft (2941 m)	PCN 67/F/A/W/T
Quebec	06/24	9000 ft (2743 m)	PCN 71/R/C/W/T
Stephenville	10/28	10000 ft (3048 m)	PCN 67/F/A/X/T
Toronto	15L/33R	11050 ft (3368 m)	PCN 79/R/B/W/T
Val D'or	18/36	10000 ft (3048 m)	PCN 70/F/C/Y/T
Vancouver	08R/26L	11000 ft (3353 m)	PCN 93/R/C/W/T
Winnipeg	18/36	11000 ft (3353 m)	PCN 79/R/B/W/T
CANARY ISLANDS			
Gran Canaria (Las Palmas)	03L/21R	10170 ft (3100 m)	PCN 65/F/A/W/V
Lanzarote	04/22	7874 ft (2400 m)	PCN 50/F/C/W/T
La Palma	01/19	7218 ft (2200 m)	PCN 34/F/A/W/T
Tenerife Norte	12/30	11155 ft (3400 m)	ISWL 26000
Tenerife Sur (Reina Sofia)	08/26	10499 ft (3200 m)	86B
CAPE VERDE REPUBLIC			
Sal (Amilcar Cabral)	02/20	10729 ft (3270 m)	PCN 58/F/A/W/T
CAROLINE ISLANDS			
Koror (Babelthaup)	09/27	7200 ft (2195 m)	25S/79T/143B
CAYMAN ISLANDS			
Cayman Brac (Gerrard-Smith)	08/26	6000 ft (1829 m)	PCN 50/F/B/X/U
Grand Cayman (Owen Roberts)	08/26	7000 ft (2134 m)	PCN 50/F/B/W/U
CENTRAL AFRICAN REPUBLIC			
Bangui (M'poko)	17/35	8530 ft (2600 m)	PCN 59/F/B/X/T
CHILE			
Calama (El Loa)	09/27	9478 ft (2889 m)	PCN 40/F/A/X/T
Iquique (Gen Diego Aracena)	18/36	10990 ft (3350 m)	PCN 40/F/A/X/T
Isla De Pascua (Mataveri)			
Easter Island	10/28	10827 ft (3300 m)	PCN 65/F/C/W/T
Punta Arenas (President Ibanez)	07/25	9154 ft (2790 m)	PCN 40/F/A/W/T
Santiago (A.M. Benitez)	17/35	10499 ft (3200 m)	PCN 63/F/B/W/T
CHINA (PEOPLE'S REPUBLIC)			
Beijing/Peking	18L/36R	12467 ft (3800 m)	PCN 108/F/C/W/T
Chengdu (Shuangliu)	02/20	9186 ft (2800 m)	PCN 50/R/B/W/T
Dalian (Zhoushnizi)	10/28	10827 ft (3300 m)	PCN 67/R/B/W/T
Guangzhou/Canton (Baiyun)	03/21	11089 ft (3380 m)	PCN 58/R/B/X/T
Hong Kong (Kai Tak)	13/31	11130 ft (3392 m)	PCN 65/F/A/W/T
Kunming (Wujiaba)	03/21	11155 ft (3400 m)	PCN 63/R/B/X/T
Lanzhou (Zhongchuan)	18/36	11155 ft (3400 m)	PCN 35/R/B/W/T
Sanya	08/26	11155 ft (3400 m)	PCN 78/R/B/W/T
Shanghai (Hongqiao)	18/36	11155 ft (3400 m)	PCN 58/R/C/X/T
Shenzhen (Huangtian)	15/33	11155 ft (3400 m)	PCN 72/R/B/W/T
Tianjin (Binhai)	16/34	10499 ft (3200 m)	PCN 50/R/B/X/T
Urumqi (Diwopu)	07/25	10499 ft (3200 m)	PCN 52/R/B/W/T
Xi'an (Xianyang)	05/23	9843 ft (3000 m)	PCN 60/R/B/W/T
Xichang (Qingshan)	18/36	11811 ft (3600 m)	PCN 56/R/B/W/T
COLOMBIA			
Barranquilla (Cortissoz)	04/22	9843 ft (3000 m)	273DB
Bogota (Eldorado)	13/31	12467 ft (3800 m)	363DB
Cali (Alfonso Bonilla Aragon)	01/19	9843 ft (3000 m)	293DB
Cartagena (R. Nunez)	18/36	8530 ft (2600 m)	77.3B/233DB
Rionegro (J.M. Cordova)	18/36	11483 ft (3500 m)	PCN 82/F/C/X/T
COMORES & MAYOTTE ISLANDS			
Dzaoudzi (Pamandzi)	16/34	6070 ft (1850 m)	PCN 26/F/C/W/T
Moroni (Prince Said Ibrahim)	02/20	9514 ft (2900 m)	B747
CONGO (Democratic Republic of – formerly Zaire)			
Gbadolite	08/26	10499 ft (3200 m)	—
Goma	18/36	9843 ft (3000 m)	15S/30T/60B
Kinshasa (Ndjili)	06/24	11811 ft (3600 m)	20S/40T/100B
Kisangani (Bangoka)	13/31	11483 ft (3500 m)	20S/40T/100B
Lubumbashi	07/25	10335 ft (3150 m)	18S/38T/80B
CONGO (People's Republic of)			
Brazzaville (Maya Maya)	06/24	10827 ft (3300 m)	PCN 69/F/C/X/U
Pointe Noire	17/35	6562 ft (2000 m)	PCN 20/F/B/X/T

Airport (Aerodrome) name	Designator (orientation) and length of longest runway		Runway LCN/PCN
COOK ISLANDS			
Rarotonga	08/26	7640 ft (2329 m)	LCN 100
COSTA RICA			
Alajuela (Juan Santa Maria)	07/25	9880 ft (3011 m)	B747
Liberia International			
(Daniel Oduber Quiros)	07/25	9022 ft (2750 m)	PCN 68/F/C/X/T
CÔTE d'IVOIRE (IVORY COAST)			
Abidjan			
(Felix Houphouet Boigny)	03/21	8858 ft (2700 m)	PCN 53/F/A/X/T
Bouake	03/21	10827 ft (3300 m)	B747
Yamoussoukro	05/23	9843 ft (3000 m)	DC-8
CROATIA			
Dubrovnik (Cilipi)	12/30	10827 ft (3300 m)	LCN 80
Pula	09/27	9678 ft (2950 m)	PCN 80/F/B/W/T
Rijeka (Krk)	14/32	8202 ft (2500 m)	LCN 65
Split	05/23	8366 ft (2550 m)	PCN 49/R/C/W/T
Udbina	13/31	9022 ft (2750 m)	—
Zadar	14/32	8202 ft (2500 m)	LCN 85
Zagreb (Plesa)	05/23	10669 ft (3252 m)	PCN 75/R/D/X/T
CUBA			
Camaguey			
(Ignacio Agramonte)	07/25	9843 ft (3000 m)	PCN 57/F/B/X/T
Cayo Largo Del Sur	12/30	9843 ft (3000 m)	—
Ciego de Avila	07/25	11680 ft (3560 m)	PCN 57/F/B/X/T
Havana			
(Jose Marti International)	05/23	13123 ft (4000 m)	PCN 57/F/B/X/T
Holguin	05/23	10253 ft (3125 m)	—
Santiago de Cuba			
(Antonio Maceo)	09/27	13123 ft (4000 m)	PCN 50/F/A/X/T
Varadero	06/24	11483 ft (3500 m)	PCN 52/F/A/X/T
CYPRUS			
Akrotiri	10/28	8999 ft (2743 m)	LCG II
Larnaca	04/22	8858 ft (2700 m)	PCN 80/F/D/W/U
Pafos International	11/29	8858 ft (2700 m)	PCN 80/F/C/W/T
CZECH REPUBLIC			
Brno (Turany)	10/28	8694 ft (2650 m)	PCN 48/R/A/X/T
Ostrava (Mosnov)	04/22	11483 ft (3500 m)	PCN 50/R/A/X/T
Prague (Ruzyne)	06/24	12188 ft (3715 m)	PCN 62/R/B/X/T
Vodochody	10/28	8005 ft (2440 m)	PCN 19/R/B/X/T
DENMARK			
Aalborg	08L/26R	8694 ft (2650 m)	PCN 42/R/D/X/U
Billund	09/27	10171 ft (3100 m)	PCN 110/F/A/X/T
Copenhagen (Kastrup)	04L/22R	11811 ft (3600 m)	PCN 80/F/C/X/U
Esbjerg	08/26	8530 ft (2600 m)	PCN 60/F/A/W/T
Karup	09R/27L	9623 ft (2933 m)	LCN 65
Tirstrup (Aarhus)	10R/28L	8885 ft (2708 m)	PCN 76/R/B/X/U
Vojens (Skrydstrup)	11L/29R	9940 ft (3030 m)	LCN 90
DJIBOUTI			
Djibouti (Ambouli)	09/27	10335 ft (3150 m)	24S/35T/85B
DOMINICAN REPUBLIC			
Puerto Plata	08/26	10105 ft (3080 m)	34/S
Santo Domingo			
(De las Americas)	17/35	11000 ft (3353 m)	34/S
ECUADOR			
Guayaquil (Simon Bolivar)	03/21	8005 ft (2440 m)	PCN 63/F/C/X/T
Latacunga (Cotopaxi)	18/36	12139 ft (3700 m)	PCN 72/F/C/X/U
Manta (Eloy Alfaro)	05/23	9186 ft (2800 m)	45S/57T
Quito (Mariscal Sucre)	17/35	10236 ft (3120 m)	PCN 42/F/B/X/T
EGYPT			
Abu Simbel	15R/33L	9842 ft (3000 m)	PCN 70/F/B/W/U
Alexandria	04/22	7218 ft (2200 m)	PCN 48/F/D/X/U
Aswan	17/35	11155 ft (3400 m)	PCN 60/F/B/W/U
Asyut	13/31	9843 ft (3000 m)	PCN 45/F/C/W/U
Cairo International	05L/23R	10827 ft (3300 m)	PCN 70/F/B/W/U
Hurghada	16/34	13123 ft (4000 m)	PCN 70/F/C/W/U
Luxor	02/20	9843 ft (3000 m)	PCN 70/F/C/W/U
Mersa Matruh	15/33	9843 ft (3000 m)	PCN 40/F/B/W/U
New Valley (El Kharga)	18/36	9843 ft (3000 m)	PCN 28/F/C/X/U
Port Said	10/28	7710 ft (2350 m)	PCN 35/F/C/X/U
Sharm-El-Sheikh			
International	04L/22R	10105 ft (3080 m)	PCN 65/F/B/W/U
Taba	04/22	9843 ft (3000 m)	PCN 70/F/B/W/U
EL SALVADOR			
San Salvador (El Salvador Int'l)	07/25	10499 ft (3200 m)	B747
EQUATORIAL GUINEA			
Malabo (Santo Isabel)	05/23	9646 ft (2940 m)	DC-10
ERITREA			
Asmara	07/25	9843 ft (3000 m)	PCN 40/F/B/X/T
Assab	12/30	11483 ft (3500 m)	LCN 20

Airport (Aerodrome) name	Designator (orientation) and length of longest runway		Runway LCN/PCN
ESTONIA			
Parnu	03L/21R	8202 ft (2500 m)	—
Tallinn (Ulemiste)	09/27	10072 ft (3070 m)	PCN 60/F/B/X/T
ETHIOPIA			
Addis Ababa (Bole International)	07/25	12139 ft (3700 m)	PCN 65/F/D/X/T
Bahar Dar	04/22	9843 ft (3000 m)	—
Dire Dawa			
(Aba Tenna Dejaznatch Yilma)	15/33	8858 ft (2700 m)	PCN 30/R/B/W/U
Makale (Alula Aba Nega)	11/29	9843 ft (3000 m)	—
FALKLAND ISLANDS			
Mount Pleasant	10/28	8497 ft (2590 m)	PCN 90/F/C/W/T
FAROE ISLANDS			
Vagar	13/31	4101 ft (1250 m)	PCN 28/F/A/X/U
FIJI			
Nadi International	02/20	10500 ft (3200 m)	PCN 59/F/C/X/U
FINLAND			
Halli	08/26	8530 ft (2600 m)	PCN 34/F/B/X/T
Helsinki (Vantaa)	04/22	11286 ft (3440 m)	PCN 102/F/B/W/T
Ivalo	04/22	8202 ft (2500 m)	PCN 100/F/A/X/T
Jyvaskyla	12/30	8530 ft (2600 m)	PCN 67/F/A/W/T
Kauhava	17/35	8858 ft (2700 m)	PCN 24/F/D/X/T
Kuopio	15/33	9186 ft (2800 m)	PCN 45/F/A/W/T
Oulu	12/30	8202 ft (2500 m)	PCN 45/F/A/W/T
Rovaniemi	03/21	9842 ft (3000 m)	PCN 46/F/B/W/T
Tampere (Pirkkala)	06/24	8858 ft (2700 m)	PCN 46/F/C/X/T
Turku	08/26	8202 ft (2500 m)	PCN 90/F/A/W/T
FRANCE			
Avord	06/24	11483 ft (3500 m)	16S/22T/39B
Basle (Mulhouse)	16/34	12795 ft (3900 m)	25S/33T/85B
Bordeaux (Merignac)	05/23	10170 ft (3100 m)	25S/33T/70B
Brest (Guipavas)	08R/26L	10171 ft (3100 m)	PCN 45/F/C/W/T
Chateauroux (Deols)	04/22	11483 ft (3500 m)	44R/C/W/T
Clermont Ferrand (Aulnat)	08/26	9892 ft (3015 m)	28S/33T/53B
Evreux (Fauville)	04/22	9826 ft (2995 m)	PCN 69/R/C/W/T
Grenoble (St. Geoirs)	09/27	10007 ft (3050 m)	35S/40T/65B
Istres (Le Tube)	15L/33R	12090 ft (3685 m)	16.8S/26T/60B
Lille (Lesquin)	08/26	9268 ft (2825 m)	PCN 62/F/C/W/U
Lyon (Satolas)	18R/36L	13123 ft (4000 m)	30S/43T/78B
Marseille (Provence)	14L/32R	11483 ft (3500 m)	35S/40T/80B
Mont de Marsan	09/27	10499 ft (3200 m)	37S/45T/82B
Nantes Atlantique	03/21	9514 ft (2900 m)	27S/33T/53B
Paris (Charles de Gaulle)	10/28	11860 ft (3615 m)	80R/C/W/T
Paris (Le Bourget)	07/25	9843 ft (3000 m)	35S/40T/70B
Paris (Orly)	07/25	11975 ft (3650 m)	80F/C/W/T
Tarbes (Ossun Lourdes)	02/20	9843 ft (3000 m)	28S/40T/72B
Toulouse (Blagnac)	15R/33L	11483 ft (3500 m)	PCN 58/R/B/W/U
FRENCH ANTILLES			
Fort de France (Le Lametin)	09/27	10827 ft (3300 m) (*first 1000 ft weight restricted)	45S/45T/75B*
Pointe a Pitre (Le Raizet)	11/29	11499 ft (3505 m)	40S/45T/75B
FRENCH GUIANA			
Cayenne (Rochambeau)	08/26	10500 ft (3200 m)	PCN 52/F/D/W/U
FRENCH OCEANIA			
Hao	12/30	11089 ft (3380 m)	DC-8
Noumea (La Tontouta)	11/29	10663 ft (3250 m)	46S/46S/70B
Tahiti (see TAHITI)			
GABON			
Franceville (Mvengue)	15/33	10105 ft (3080 m)	PCN 59/F/B/X/T
Libreville	16/34	9843 ft (3000 m)	PCN 59/F/C/X/T
GAMBIA			
Banjul	14/32	11810 ft (3600 m)	LCN 80/H/J
GEORGIA			
Sukhumi	12/30	11942 ft (3640 m)	PCN 45/R/B/W/T
Tbilisi (Novoalekseevka)	13/31	8202 ft (2500 m)	PCN 44/R/B/X/T
GERMANY			
Berlin (Schoenefeld)	07R/25L	9843 ft (3000 m)	PCN 140
Berlin (Tegel)	08L/26R	9918 ft (3023 m)	35S/50T/90B
Cologne-Bonn	14L/32R	12516 ft (3815 m)	PCN 75/F/B/W/T
Dusseldorf	05L/23R	8858 ft (2700 m)	PCN 100/R/B/W/T
Frankfurt (Main)	07L/25R	13123 ft (4000 m)	PCN 74/R/A/W/T
Hamburg	15/33	12028 ft (3666 m)	PCN 65/F/A/W/T
Hannover	09L/27R	12467 ft (3780 m)	PCN 68/R/B/W/T
Ingolstadt	07R/25L	9646 ft (2940 m)	LCN 92
Munich	08/26	13123 ft (4000 m)	PCN 90/R/A/W/T
Nurnberg	10/28	8858 ft (2700 m)	PCN 65/R/B/W/T
Schwerin (Parchim)	06/24	9843 ft (3000 m)	PCN 55/R/B/W/T
Stuttgart	07/25	10974 ft (3345 m)	PCN 80/R/C/X/T
GHANA			
Accra (Kotoka International)	03/21	9800 ft (2987 m)	PCN 70/F/B/W/T
GIBRALTAR			
Gibraltar	09/27	6000 ft (1829 m)	LCG III

Airport (Aerodrome) name	Designator (orientation) and length of longest runway		Runway LCN/PCN
GREECE			
Alexandroupolis (Dimokritos)	07/25	8530 ft (2600 m)	LCN 80
Andravida	16/34	10171 ft (3100 m)	LCN 80
Araxos	18/36	9810 ft (2990 m)	LCN 45
Athens (Central)	15L/33R	11483 ft (3500 m)	LCN 100
Heraklion (Nikos Kazantzakis)	09/27	8990 ft (2740 m)	LCN 60
Kasteli	02/20	9568 ft (2916 m)	LCN 30
Kavala (Megas Alexandros)	05R/23L	9843 ft (3000 m)	LCN 80
Khania (Souda)	11/29	11811 ft (3600 m)	LCN 80
Larisa	08/26	11941 ft (3640 m)	LCN 45
Limnos	04/22	9843 ft (3000 m)	LCN 80
Nea Anchialos	08/26	9810 ft (2990 m)	LCN 45
Rhodes (Diagoras)	07/25	10696 ft (3260 m)	LCN 100
Tanagra	10/28	9810 ft (2990 m)	LCN 45
GREENLAND			
Sondrestrom (Kangerlussuaq)	10/28	9236 ft (2815 m)	12S/71T/80ST/ 150TT/382DDT
Thule	15/33	10007 ft (3050 m)	155S/220T/440TT
GRENADA			
Point Salines	10/28	9000 ft (2743 m)	LCN 86
GUATEMALA			
Flores (Santa Elena Int'l)	10/28	10000 ft (3048 m)	B747
Guatemala Int'l (La Aurora)	01/19	9800 ft (2987 m)	ISWL 27272
GUINEA-BISSAU			
Bissau (Osvaldo Vieira)	03/21	10499 ft (3200 m)	LCN 75
GUINEA			
Conakry (Gbessia)	06/24	10827 ft (3300 m)	B747
GUYANA			
Georgetown (Cheddi Jagan Int'l)	06/24	7500 ft (2286 m)	PCN 40/R/A/W/T
HAITI			
Port au Prince (Mais Gate)	09/27	9974 ft (3040 m)	Takes C-135
HAWAII (see also USA)			
Honolulu International	08L/26R	12360 ft (3767 m)	45S/91T/181B
HONDURAS			
La Ceiba (Goloson)	06/24	9678 ft (2950 m)	LCN 74
San Pedro Sula (La Mesa)	04L/22R	9416 ft (2870 m)	—
HUNGARY			
Budapest (Ferihegy)	13L/31R	12162 ft (3707 m)	PCN 75/R/B/X/T
ICELAND			
Akureyri	01/19	6365 ft (1940 m)	LCN 40
Egilsstadir	04/22	6562 ft (2000 m)	LCN 58
Keflavik	02/20	10056 ft (3065 m)	LCN 90
Reykjavik	02/20	5987 ft (1825 m)	LCN 20
INDIA			
Arkonam	06L/24R	11040 ft (3365 m)	LCN 80
Bangalore	09/27	10850 ft (3307 m)	PCN 54/F/A/W/T
Calcutta (N.S. Chandra Bose Int'l)	01R/19L	11900 ft (3627 m)	PCN 63/F/C/W/T
Chennai (Madras)	07/25	12001 ft (3658 m)	PCN 56/F/C/W/T
Delhi International	10/28	12500 ft (3810 m)	PCN 55/F/B/W/T
Goa (Dabolim)	08/26	11253 ft (3430 m)	—
Mumbai (Jawaharlal Nehru Int'l)	09/27	11447 ft (3489 m)	PCN 65/F/C/W/T
Nagpur	14/32	10500 ft (3200 m)	PCN 41/R/B/W/T
Srinagar	13/31	11980 ft (3652 m)	LCG IV
INDIAN OCEAN			
Cocos Island	15/33	8000 ft (2438 m)	PCN 30/F/A/1400/U
Diego Garcia	13/31	12000 ft (3658 m)	C5A
INDONESIA			
Bali International	09/27	9843 ft (3000 m)	PCN 83/F/C/X/T
Batam (Hang Nadim)	04/22	13205 ft (4025 m)	PCN 79/F/C/X/T
Biak (Kaisiepo)	11/29	11713 ft (3570 m)	PCN 81/F/D/Y/T
Jakarta (Soekarno-Hatta Int'l)	07R/25L	12008 ft (3660 m)	PCN 120/R/D/W/T
Surabaya (Juanda)	10/28	9843 ft (3000 m)	PCN 73/F/C/X/U
IRAN			
Abadan	14R/32L	10170 ft (3100 m)	PCN 60/F/C/X/T
Ahwaz	12/30	11100 ft (3383 m)	LCN 40
Ardabil	14/32	10826 ft (3300 m)	PCN 50/F/D/Y/T
Bam	12/30	11155 ft (3400 m)	PCN 40/F/B/Y/T
Bandar Abbass	03/21	12020 ft (3664 m)	LCN 95
Bushehr	13L/31R	14058 ft (4285 m)	LCN 80
Charbahar (City)	09L/27R	12000 ft (3658 m)	LCN 100
Esfahan	08L/26R	14435 ft (4400 m)	LCN 100
Kerman	16/34	12623 ft (3847 m)	PCN 50/F/C/X/T
Mashhad (Shahid Hashemi Nejad)	13R/31L	12861 ft (3920 m)	PCN 60/F/B/X/T
Rasht	09/27	10007 ft (3050 m)	LCN 75
Shiraz International	11L/29R	14219 ft (4334 m)	PCN 85/F/C/W/T
Tabriz	12/30	12000 ft (3658 m)	LCN 70
Tehran (Mehrabad)	11L/29R	13123 ft (4000 m)	PCN 50/F/A/X/T
Yazd	13/31	13452 ft (4100 m)	PCN 60/F/B/X/T
Zahedan International	17R/35L	14000 ft (4267 m)	LCN 70

Airport (Aerodrome) name	Designator (orientation) and length of longest runway		Runway LCN/PCN
IRAQ			
Baghdad (Saddam International)	15L/33R	13123 ft (4000 m)	LCN 100
Basrah International	14/32	13123 ft (4000 m)	PCN 72/R/C/W/T
IRELAND			
Baldonnel (Casement)	11/29	6000 ft (1829 m)	23S/30T/60B
Connaught	09/27	7546 ft (2300 m)	PCN 52/F/A/W/T
Cork	17/35	7000 ft (2134 m)	PCN 55/R/C/W/U
Dublin	10/28	8652 ft (2637 m)	PCN 70/R/B/W/T
Kerry	08/26	6562 ft (2000 m)	PCN 44/F/C/W/T
Shannon	06/24	10500 ft (3200 m)	PCN 75/R/C/W/U
ISRAEL			
Eilat (J. Hozman)	03/21	6234 ft (1900 m)	PCN 36/F/B/X/T
Jerusalem (Atarot)	12/30	6447 ft (1965 m)	PCN 15 & 28/F/C/X/T
Ovda	02R/20L	9843 ft (3000 m)	PCN 44/F/B/Y/U
Tel Aviv (Ben Gurion Int'l)	08/26	11998 ft (3657 m)	PCN 84/F/B/Y/U
ITALY			
Alghero (Fertilia)	03/21	9843 ft (3000 m)	PCN 80/F/B/W/T
Amendola	11/29	9121 ft (2780 m)	—
Ancona (Falconara)	04/22	9816 ft (2992 m)	LCN 80
Bergamo (Orio al Serio)	11/29	9186 ft (2800 m)	LCN 90
Bologna	12/30	8038 ft (2450 m)	LCN 100
Brindisi (Casale)	14/32	8625 ft (2629 m)	LCN 90
Cagliari (Elmas)	14/32	9203 ft (2805 m)	PCN 79/F/B/W/T
Catania (Fontanarossa)	08/26	8366 ft (2550 m)	PCN 70/F/B/W/T
Decimomannu	17/35	9809 ft (2990 m)	ISWL 27000
Genoa (Sestri)	11/29	9925 ft (3025 m)	ISWL 35000
Grosseto	03/21	9868 ft (3008 m)	ISWL 44000
Milan (Linate)	18L/36R	8005 ft (2440 m)	ISWL 30000
Milan (Malpensa)	17L/35R	12844 ft (3915 m)	PCN 70
Naples	06/24	8661 ft (2640 m)	ISWL 28000
Palermo (Punta Raisi)	07/25	11220 ft (3420 m)	PCN 52/F/B/W/U
Pisa	04R/22L	9820 ft (2993 m)	LCN 90
Rimini	13/31	8337 ft (2541 m)	LCN 65
Rome (Ciampino)	15/33	7208 ft (2197 m)	ISWL 35000
Rome (Fiumicino)	16R/34L	12795 ft (3900 m)	LCN 100
Trieste (Ronchi dei Legionari)	09/27	9843 ft (3000 m)	PCN 90/F/A/W/T
Turin (Caselle)	18/36	10827 ft (3300 m)	PCN 115/F/B/X/T
Venice (Tessera)	04R/22L	10827 ft (3300 m)	LCN 120
Verona (Villafranca)	05/23	9797 ft (2986 m)	LCN 90
JAMAICA			
Kingston	12/30	8786 ft (2678 m)	70T/136B
Montego Bay (Sangster Int'l)	07/25	8705 ft (2653 m)	PCN 63/F/A/W/T
JAPAN			
Chitose Apt (New)	01/19	9840 ft (3000 m)	PCN 83/F/C/X/T
Chitose A/D (Old)	18L/36R	9840 ft (3000 m)	61S/87T/202B
Kadena	05L/23R	12100 ft (3688 m)	—
Kagoshima	16/34	9843 ft (3000 m)	PCN 58/F/A/X/T
Misawa	10/28	10000 ft (3048 m)	29S/77T/117B
Nagasaki	14/32	9840 ft (2999 m)	PCN 58/F/A/X/T
Nagoya	16/34	8990 ft (2740 m)	PCN 97/F/D/X/T
Naha	18/36	9840 ft (2999 m)	PCN 83/F/C/X/T
Osaka (Itami)	14R/32L	9840 ft (2999 m)	PCN 83/F/C/X/T
Osaka (Kansai International)	06/24	11483 ft (3500 m)	PCN 100/F/C/X/T
Shimojishima	17/35	9840 ft (2999 m)	PCN 63/F/B/X/T
Tokyo (Haneda)	16L/34R	9843 ft (3000 m)	PCN 140/F/B/X/T
Tokyo International (Narita)	16/34	13123 ft (4000 m)	PCN 140/F/C/X/T
Tokyo (Yokota)	18/36	11000 ft (3353 m)	68S/136T/217B
JOHNSTON ISLANDS			
Johnston Atoll	05/23	9000 ft (2743 m)	100S/175T/350B
JORDAN			
Amman (Queen Alia International)	08R/26L	12008 ft (3660 m)	—
Amman (Marka)	06/24	10781 ft (3286 m)	LCN 75
Aqaba	02/20	9843 ft (3000 m)	PCN 42/R/A/W/T
KAZAKHSTAN			
Aktyubinsk	13/31	10171 ft (3100 m)	PCN 19/R/A/X/T
Almaty	05/23	14436 ft (4400 m)	PCN 39/R/B/X/T
KENYA			
Kisumu	07/25	6693 ft (2040 m)	PCN 35/F/B/X/U
Mombasa (Moi)	03/21	10991 ft (3350 m)	PCN 67/F/C/W/T
Nairobi (Jomo Kenyatta)	06/24	13507 ft (4117 m)	PCN 80/F/A/W/U
KIRIBATI			
Tarawa (Bonriki)	09/27	6600 ft (2012 m)	LCN 30
KOREA (DEMOCRATIC PEOPLE'S REPUBLIC)			
Pyongyang (Sunan)	01/19	13123 ft (4000 m)	PCN 53/R/A/W/U
KOREA (REPUBLIC)			
Cheju International	06/24	9843 ft (3000 m)	PCN 83/F/C/W/T
Kwangju	04/22	9300 ft (2835 m)	PCN 60/R/B/W/T
Pusan (Kimhae International)	18/36	9000 ft (2743 m)	PCN 58/R/D/X/T
Seoul (Kimpo International)	14L/32R	11811 ft (3600 m)	PCN 100/F/C/W/T
KUWAIT			
Kuwait International	15L/33R	11483 ft (3500 m)	PCN 63/F/A/W/T

Airport (Aerodrome) name	Designator (orientation) and length of longest runway		Runway LCN/PCN
KYRGYSTAN			
Bishkek (Manas)	08/26	13780 ft (4200 m)	PCN 56/R/A/X/T
LAO PEOPLE'S DEMOCRATIC REPUBLIC			
Vientaine (Wattay)	13/31	9843 ft (3000 m)	PCN 43/R/B/W/T
LATVIA			
Riga International	18/36	8366 ft (2550 m)	PCN 110/F/A/W/T
LEBANON			
Beirut International	18/36	10663 ft (3250 m)	LCN 120
LEEWARD ISLANDS			
Antigua (V.C. Bird)	07/25	9000 ft (2743 m)	LCN 80
St. Kitts (Robert L. Bradshaw)	07/25	8002 ft (2439 m)	LCN 70
LESOTHO			
Maseru (Moshoeshoe 1)	04/22	10499 ft (3200 m)	PCN 52/F/B/W/T
LIBERIA			
Monrovia (Roberts International)	04/22	11000 ft (3353 m)	160B
LIBYA			
Benghazi (Benina)	15L/33R	11811 ft (3600 m)	LCN 90
Kufra	02/20	12008 ft (3660 m)	LCN 90
Labraq (El Beida)	10/28	11811 ft (3600 m)	LCN 100
Sebha International	13/31	11811 ft (3600 m)	LCN 85
Tripoli International	09/27	11811 ft (3600 m)	LCN 100
Tripoli (Mitiga)	11/29	11000 ft (3353 m)	LCN 100
LINE ISLANDS			
Christmas Island (Cassidy)	08/26	6895 ft (2101 m)	ISWL 14000
LITHUANIA			
Kaunas	08/26	9022 ft (2750 m)	PCN 50/F/B/X/T
Siauliai	14/32	11483 ft (3500 m)	PCN 70/R/B/W/U
Vilnius	02/20	8202 ft (2500 m)	PCN 49/F/D/X/T
LUXEMBOURG			
see Belgium & Luxembourg			
MACAU			
Macau	16/34	10827 ft (3300 m)	PCN 57/R/B/W/T
MACEDONIA			
Ohrid	02/20	8366 ft (2550 m)	LCN 31
Skopje	16/34	8038 ft (2450 m)	LCN 70
MADAGASCAR (incl Reunion Island)			
Antananarivo (Ivato)	11/29	10170 ft (3100 m)	PCN 59/F/B/X/T
Saint-Denis (Gillot)	12/30	10500 ft (3200 m)	53/F/B/W/U
MADEIRA			
Funchal	06/24	5906 ft (1800 m)	PCN 60/F/B/X/T
Porto Santo	01/19	9843 ft (3000 m)	ISWL 35000
MALAWI			
Blantyre (Chileka)	10/28	7628 ft (2325 m)	PCN 50/F/A/W/T
Lilongwe International	14/32	11614 ft (3540 m)	PCN 80/F/B/W/T
MALAYSIA & BRUNEI			
Brunei International (Bandar Seri Begawan)	03/21	12000 ft (3658 m)	PCN 70/F/C/W/T
Johor Bahru	16/34	11004 ft (3354 m)	PCN 59/F/B/X/U
Kota Kinabalu	02/20	9800 ft (2987 m)	PCN 59/F/B/X/U
Kuala Lumpur International	15/33	12400 ft (3779 m)	PCN 59/F/B/X/T
Penang International	04/22	10000 ft (3048 m)	LCN 70
MALDIVES			
Male International	18/36	11024 ft (3360 m)	PCN 66/F/A/W/U
MALI			
Bamako (Senou)	06/24	8858 ft (2700 m)	PCN 59/F/B/X/T
MALTA			
Malta (Luqa)	14/32	11627 ft (3544 m)	PCN 100
MARIANA ISLANDS			
Guam International	06L/24R	10015 ft (3052 m)	61S/107T/177B/355B
Guam (Anderson)	06R/24L	11182 ft (3408 m)	32S/105T/218B
MARSHALL ISLANDS			
Majuro (Marshall Islands Int'l)	07/25	7900 ft (2408 m)	55S/78T/132B
MAURITANIA			
Atar	04/22	9843 ft (3000 m)	DC-9
Nouakchott	05/23	9843 ft (3000 m)	PCN 53/F/A/X/T
MAURITIUS			
Mauritius (Sir Seewoosagar Ramgoolam Int'l)	14/32	8500 ft (2591 m)	PCN 80/F/D/X/T
MEXICO			
Acapulco International	10/28	10824 ft (3299 m)	PCN 48/R/B/X/T
Aguascalientas	17/35	9843 ft (3000 m)	PCN 46/F/C/X/T
Cancun	12/30	11484 ft (3500 m)	PCN 64/F/C/X/T
Cuernavaca	02/20	9094 ft (2772 m)	PCN 30/F/C/Z/T
Durango	03/21	9515 ft (2900 m)	45S/78T/171B
Guadalajara (Don Miguel Hidalgo)	10/28	13120 ft (3999 m)	PCN 56/R/B/X/T
Leon (De Guanajuato)	13/31	11483 ft (3500 m)	PCN 53/F/C/Y/T
Mexico City (B. Juarez Int'l)	05R/23L	12795 ft (3900 m)	PCN 97/F/B/X/U
Monterrey International	11/29	9843 ft (3000 m)	PCN 59/R/B/X/T
Morelia	05/23	11155 ft (3400 m)	—
Puebla	17/35	11812 ft (3600 m)	B727
Puerto Vallarta	04/22	10171 ft (3100 m)	PCN 48/F/B/X/T
San Luis Potosi	14/32	9843 ft (3000 m)	—
Tijuana	09/27	9711 ft (2960 m)	PCN 59/R/B/X/U
Toluca	15/33	13779 ft (4200 m)	PCN 33/F/A/X/T
Zacatecas	02/20	9843 ft (3000 m)	PCN 44/F/C/Y/T
MIDWAY ISLANDS			
Midway (Henderson)	06/24	7900 ft (2408 m)	195S/260T/390B
MOLDOVA			
Kishinau	08/26	11778 ft (3590 m)	PCN 26/R/B/Y/T
MONGOLIA			
Ulaanbaatar (Buyant-Ukhaa)	14/32	10170 ft (3100 m)	PCN 47/R/A/X/U
MOROCCO			
Agadir (Al Massira)	10/28	10499 ft (3200 m)	PCN 46/F/A/W/T
Agadir (Inezgane)	10/28	9547 ft (2910 m)	PCN 54/F/B/W/U
Casablanca (Mohamed V)	17/35	12205 ft (3720 m)	32S/58T/100B
Dakhla	03/21	9843 ft (3000 m)	B727
Errachidia (Moulay Ali Cherif)	13/31	9843 ft (3000 m)	PCN 45/F/A/W/T
Fess (Saiss)	10/28	10499 ft (3200 m)	PCN 45/F/A/W/T
Marrakech (Menara)	10/28	10171 ft (3100 m)	PCN 42/F/B/W/U
Quarzazate	12/30	9843 ft (3000 m)	PCN 46/F/A/W/T
Oujda (Angad)	06/24	9843 ft (3000 m)	PCN 40/F/B/W/U
Rabat (Sale)	04/22	11483 ft (3500 m)	PCN 41/F/B/W/U
Tangier (Boukhalf)	10/28	11483 ft (3500 m)	PCN 42/F/B/W/U
MOZAMBIQUE			
Beira	12/30	7874 ft (2400 m)	PCN 44/F/A/X/U
Chimoio	01/19	7874 ft (2400 m)	PCN 26/F/B/X/U
Maputo	05/23	12008 ft (3660 m)	PCN 40/F/A/X/U
MYANMAR			
Shante	01/19	8500 ft (2591 m)	AUW 154500
Yangon (Mingaladon)	03/21	8100 ft (2469 m)	PCN 50/R/B/W/T
NAMIBIA			
Grootfontein	08/26	11680 ft (3560 m)	LCN 74
Ondangwa	08/26	9750 ft (2972 m)	LCN 65
Windhoek International	08/26	14869 ft (4532 m)	LCN 84
NAURU			
Nauru	12/30	7050 ft (2149 m)	PCN 40/F/A/W/T
NEPAL			
Kathmandu (Tribhuvan)	02/20	10007 ft (3050 m)	PCN 54/F/A/W/T
NETHERLANDS			
Amsterdam (Schiphol)	06/24	11483 ft (3500 m)	PCN 82/R*/C/1.7/T *(non-standard construction)
Arnhem (Deelen)	02/20	9678 ft (2950 m)	LCN 30
Eindhoven	04/22	9843 ft (3000 m)	LCN 45
Maastricht Aachen	04/22	8202 ft (2500 m)	PCN 71/F/C/X/T
Rotterdam	06/24	7218 ft (2200 m)	PCN 70/R*/D/X/T *(composite construction)
NETHERLANDS ANTILLES			
Aruba (Reina Beatrix)	11/29	9000 ft (2743 m)	PCN 48/R/A/X/T
Curacao [Hato] (Willemstad)	11/29	11188 ft (3410 m)	LCN 100
NEW ZEALAND			
Auckland International	05/23	11926 ft (3635 m)	PCN 65/R/B/W/T
Christchurch International	02/20	10784 ft (3287 m)	PCN 60/F/B/X/U
Wellington International	16/34	6350 ft (1935 m)	PCN 57/F/B/X/U
NICARAGUA			
Managua (Augusto Cesar Sandino Int'l)	09/27	8000 ft (2438 m)	PCN 52/F/B/X/U
NIGER			
Niamey	09/27	9843 ft (3000 m)	PCN 59/F/B/X/T
NIGERIA			
Abuja International	04/22	11811 ft (3600 m)	LCN 100
Akure	03/21	9186 ft (2800 m)	LCN 100
Ilorin	05/23	10171 ft (3100 m)	LCN 90
Jos	10/28	9843 ft (3000 m)	LCN 50
Kaduna (New)	05/23	9843 ft (3000 m)	LCN 100
Kano (Mallam Aminu Int'l)	06/24	10827 ft (3300 m)	LCN 90
Lagos (Murtala Muhammed)	01L/19	12795 ft (3900 m)	LCN 110
Maiduguri	05/23	9843 ft (3000 m)	LCN 90
Minna	05/23	11155 ft (3400 m)	LCN 90
Odegi	06/24	9843 ft (3000 m)	—
Port Harcourt	03/21	9843 ft (3000 m)	LCN 100
Sokoto	08/26	9843 ft (3000 m)	LCN 85

Airport (Aerodrome) name	Designator (orientation) and length of longest runway		Runway LCN/PCN
NIUE ISLAND			
Niue International (Hanan)	10/28	7684 ft (2342 m)	LCN 50
NORWAY			
Banak	17/35	9134 ft (2784 m)	PCN 70/F/A/W/U
Bergen (Flesland)	17/35	9531 ft (2905 m)	PCN 70/F/A/X/T
Bodo	08/26	9813 ft (2991 m)	PCN 65/R/B/X/T
Hardstad/Narvik (Evenes)	18/36	8720 ft (2658 m)	PCN 65/F/A/W/T
Orland	16/34	8904 ft (2714 m)	PCN 50/F/B/X/U
Oslo (Fornebu)	06/24	7776 ft (2370 m)	PCN 70/F/B/X/T
Oslo (Gardermoen)	01/19	10449 ft (3185 m)	PCN 65/F/B/X/T
Stavanger (Sola)	18/36	8383 ft (2555 m)	PCN 65/F/A/W/U
Trondheim (Vaernes)	09/27	9062 ft (2762 m)	PCN 50/F/A/X/T
OMAN			
Muscat (Seeb)	08/26	11762 ft (3585 m)	PCN 60/F/A/X/J
Salalah	07/25	10958 ft (3340 m)	PCN 60/F/A/X/U
PAKISTAN			
Islamabad (Chaklala)	12/30	10997 ft (3352 m)	LCN 85
Karachi	07L/25R	10500 ft (3200 m)	LCN 83
Lahore	18/36	8999 ft (2743 m)	A300
Mianwali	06/24	10000 ft (3048 m)	—
Nawabshah	02/20	9000 ft (2743 m)	PCN 32/R/C/X/T
Quetta (Samungli)	13/31	12000 ft (3658 m)	LCN 70
PANAMA & CANAL ZONE			
Panama (Tocumen)	03R/21L	10007 ft (3050 m)	PCN 140/R/C/X/U
PAPAU NEW GUINEA			
Port Moresby (Jacksons)	14L/32R	9022 ft (2750 m)	PCN 70/F/C/X/U
PARAGUAY			
Asuncion (Silvia Pettirossi)	02/20	11000 ft (3353 m)	PCN 55/F/G/W/T
Guarani	05/23	11155 ft (3400 m)	PCN 66/F/C/X/T
PERU			
Anta (G.A. Grazziani)	16/34	10007 ft (3050 m)	PCN 19/F/B/Y/U
Arequipa (R. Ballon)	09/27	9777 ft (2980 m)	PCN 39/F/B/X/T
Cuzco	09/27	11155 ft (3400 m)	PCN 52/F/C/X/T
Jauja	12/30	9416 ft (2870 m)	PCN 35/F/C/X/U
Juliaca	11/29	13780 ft (4200 m)	PCN 30/F/C/X/T
Lima Callao International	15/33	11506 ft (3507 m)	PCN 42/R/A/W/T
Pisco	03/21	9908 ft (3020 m)	PCN 59/F/B/X/T
Puerto Maldonado	18/36	11483 ft (3500 m)	PCN 69/R/C/X/T
PHILIPPINES			
Clark International	02L/20R	10500 ft (3200 m)	PCN 60/R/B/X/U
Mactan (Lapu Lapu)	04/22	9091 ft (2771 m)	PCN 58/R/B/W/U
Manila International	06/24	12261 ft (3737 m)	PCN 114/F/D/W/U
PHOENIX ISLAND			
Canton Island	09/27	6000 ft (1829 m)	—
POLAND			
Gdansk	11/29	9186 ft (2800 m)	PCN 51/R/C/X/T
Krakow (JPS International)	08/26	8366 ft (2550 m)	PCN 52/R/B/W/T
Mielec	09/27	8196 ft (2498 m)	PCN 40/F/B/E/T
Poznan (Lawica)	11/29	8202 ft (2500 m)	PCN 49/F/A/X/T
Rzeszow (Jasionka)	09/27	8209 ft (2502 m)	PCN 41/R/B/X/T
Warsaw (Okecie)	15/33	12106 ft (3690 m)	PCN 70/F/C/X/T
PORTUGAL			
Alverca	04/22	9810 ft (2990 m)	LCN 14
Faro	10/28	8169 ft (2490 m)	PCN 80/F/A/W/T
Lisbon	03/21	12483 ft (3805 m)	PCN 80/F/B/W/T
Oporto (Francisco Sa Carneiro)	17/35	11417 ft (3480 m)	PCN 90/F/C/W/T
PUERTO RICO			
Aguadilla (Rafael Hernandez)	08/26	11700 ft (3566 m)	70S/106T/206B
Roosevelt Roads	06/24	11000 ft (3353 m)	55S/84T/153B
San Juan (Luis Munoz Marin Int'l)	08/26	10000 ft (3048 m)	PCN 61/F/B/X/T
QATAR			
Doha	16/34	15000 ft (4572 m)	LCN 100
ROMANIA			
Bucharest (Otopeni)	08/26	11483 ft (3500 m)	ISWL 45000
Constanta (Kogalniceanu)	18/36	11483 ft (3500 m)	ISWL 45000
Timisoara (Giarmata)	11/29	11483 ft (3500 m)	ISWL 45000
RUSSIA			
Abakan	02/20	10660 ft (3249 m)	PCN 74/F/B/W/T
Anadyr	01/19	11483 ft (3500 m)	PCN 32/R/A/W/T
Irkutsk	12/30	9072 ft (2765 m)	PCN 72/R/C/X/T
Kaliningrad (Khrabrovo)	06/24	10827 ft (3300 m)	PCN 29/R/C/X/T
Khabarovsk	05R/23L	13123 ft (4000 m)	PCN 55/R/B/X/T
Krasnoyarsk	11/29	12139 ft (3700 m)	PCN 80/R/B/Y/T
Magadan (Sokol)	10/28	11325 ft (3452 m)	PCN 42/R/A/X/T
Mineralnyye Vody	12/30	12795 ft (3900 m)	PCN 44/R/B/X/T
Moscow (Domodedovo)	14L/32R	12480 ft (3804 m)	PCN 78/R/C/X/T
Moscow (Sheremetievo)	07R/25L	12139 ft (3700 m)	PCN 70/R/B/X/T
Moscow (Vnukovo)	02/20	10039 ft (3060 m)	PCN 100/R/C/X/T
Novosibirsk (Tolmachevo)	07/25	11808 ft (3599 m)	PCN 82/R/C/X/T
Petropavlovsk-Kamchatsky	16/34	11155 ft (3400 m)	PCN 52/R/B/X/T
St. Petersburg (Pulkovo)	10R/28L	12408 ft (3782 m)	PCN 74/R/C/X/T
Sochi	06/24	9350 ft (2850 m)	PCN 44/R/C/X/T
Ufa	14R/32L	12336 ft (3760 m)	PCN 57/R/A/W/T
Vladivostok (Knevichi)	07L/25R	11483 ft (3500 m)	PCN 52/R/B/X/U
Yakutsk	05R/23L	11155 ft (3400 m)	PCN 63/R/C/X/T
RWANDA			
Kigali	10/28	11483 ft (3500 m)	LCN 50
SAMOA (WESTERN & AMERICAN)			
Samoa (Pago Pago)	05/23	9000 ft (2743 m)	148S/190T/380B/775DB
SAO TOME & PRINCIPE			
Principe (Jorge Gorgulho)	17/35	4298 ft (1310 m)	N2501
Sao Tome	11/29	7284 ft (2220 m)	ISWL 50000
SAUDI ARABIA			
Abha	13/31	10991 ft (3350 m)	PCN 56/F/A/W/T
Al Ahsa	16/34	10039 ft (3060 m)	PCN 58/R/B/X/T
Al Baha	07/25	10991 ft (3350 m)	PCN 60/F/B/X/T
Al Jouf	10/28	10827 ft (3300 m)	PCN 34/R/B/W/T
Arar (Badanah)	10/28	10007 ft (3050 m)	PCN 35/R/B/W/T
Bisha	18/36	10007 ft (3050 m)	PCN 27/F/A/X/T
Dhahran	16R/34L	12008 ft (3660 m)	B747
Gassim	15/33	9843 ft (3000 m)	PCN 56/F/A/W/T
Gizan	15/33	10007 ft (3050 m)	PCN 34/F/B/W/T
Guriat	10/28	10007 ft (3050 m)	PCN 34/F/B/W/T
Hail	18/36	10827 ft (3300 m)	PCN 42/R/C/W/T
Jeddah (King Abdul Aziz)	16R/34L	12467 ft (3800 m)	PCN 52/R/B/W/T
Jubail	17/35	13123 ft (4000 m)	B747
Khamis Mushait	06/24	12467 ft (3800 m)	B737
Madinah (Prince Mohamad Abdul Aziz)	17/35	12631 ft (3850 m)	PCN 64/F/A/X/T
Nejran	06/24	10007 ft (3050 m)	PCN 32/F/A/X/T
Ras Mishab	16/34	10610 ft (3234 m)	B737
Riyadh (King Khalid International)	15L/33R	13780 ft (4200 m)	PCN 70/F/B/W/T
Sharurah	08/26	11975 ft (3650 m)	PCN 52/F/A/X/T
Tabuk	06/24	10991 ft (3350 m)	PCN 42/R/B/W/T
Taif	07/25	12254 ft (3735 m)	PCN 53/F/A/W/T
Wadi Al-Dawasir	10/28	10007 ft (3050 m)	PCN 53/F/A/X/T
Wejh	15/33	10007 ft (3050 m)	PCN 32/R/B/W/T
Yenbo	10/28	10531 ft (3210 m)	PCN 34/F/B/X/T
SENEGAL			
Dakar (Leopold Sedar Senghor)	18/36	11450 ft (3490 m)	PCN 82/F/C/X/U
SEYCHELLES			
Seychelles International	13/31	9800 ft (2987 m)	LCN 100
SIERRA LEONE			
Freetown (Lungi)	12/30	10500 ft (3200 m)	LCN 80
SINGAPORE			
Singapore (Changi)	02L/20R	13123 ft (4000 m)	PCN 72/F/B/W/U
Singapore (Paya Lebar)	02/20	12400 ft (3779 m)	PCN 72/F/B/W/U
SLOVAK REPUBLIC			
Bratislava (M.R. Stefanik)	13/31	9678 ft (2950 m)	PCN 50/R/B/X/T
Kosice	01/19	10171 ft (3100 m)	PCN 55/F/C/W/T
Poprad (Tatry)	09/27	8530 ft (2600 m)	PCN 33/R/A/X/T
SLOVENIA			
Ljubljana	13/31	10827 ft (3300 m)	PCN 110/F/B/X/T
Maribor	15/33	8202 ft (2500 m)	LCN 72
SOLOMON ISLANDS			
Honiara (Henderson)	06/24	7218 ft (2200 m)	PCN 54/F/C/W/T
SOMALIA			
Berbera	05/23	13615 ft (4150 m)	B747
Kisimayu	05/23	12139 ft (3700 m)	LCN 70
SOUTH AFRICA			
Ausspannplatz	08/26	8402 ft (2561 m)	LCN 55
Bloemfontein	02/20	8396 ft (2559 m)	PCN 44/F/A/X/U
Cape Town International	01/19	10500 ft (3200 m)	PCN 57/F/A/X/U
Durban International	05/23	8015 ft (2443 m)	PCN 49/F/A/X/U
Johannesburg International	03L/21R	14495 ft (4418 m)	PCN 56/F/A/N/U
Kimberley	02/20	9843 ft (3000 m)	PCN 40/F/B/X/U
Lanseria	06L/24R	10000 ft (3048 m)	LCN 38
Mmabatho	04/22	14764 ft (4500 m)	LCN 100
Pretoria (Wonderboom)	11/29	6000 ft (1829 m)	LCN 40
Upington	17/35	16076 ft (4900 m)	PCN 50/F/A/X/U
Waterkloof	01/19	11000 ft (3353 m)	LCN 75
SPAIN			
Alicante	10/28	9843 ft (3000 m)	PCN 87/F/B/W/T
Almeria	08/26	10499 ft (3200 m)	LCN 80
Barcelona	07/25	10197 ft (3108 m)	PCN 86/F/A/W/T
Bilbao	12/30	8530 ft (2600 m)	PCN 60/F/B/Y/U
Granada	09/27	9514 ft (2900 m)	PCN 44/F/C/W/T
Ibiza	06/24	9186 ft (2800 m)	LCN 105
Madrid (Barajas)	15/33	13451 ft (4100 m)	PCN 91/F/B/W/T
Madrid (Torrejon de Ardoz)	05/23	13400 ft (4084 m)	SWL 120
Malaga	14/32	10500 ft (3200 m)	PCN 60/F/B/X/U

Airport (Aerodrome) name	Designator (orientation) and length of longest runway		Runway LCN/PCN
Minorca	01/19	7710 ft (2350 m)	PCN 45/F/A/X/T
Palma	06L/24R	10728 ft (3270 m)	LCN 120
Santiago	17/35	10499 ft (3200 m)	ISWL 35000
Seville	09/27	11024 ft (3360 m)	PCN 100/F/D/W/T
Seville (Moron)	03/21	11800 ft (3597 m)	45S/90T/180B
Valencia	12/30	8858 ft (2700 m)	PCN 54/F/C/W/T
Valladolid	05/23	9843 ft (3000 m)	PCN 58/F/A/W/T
Vitoria	04/22	11483 ft (3500 m)	LCN 89
Zaragoza	12R/30L	12198 ft (3718 m)	ISWL 41000
SRI LANKA			
Colombo (Katunayake)	04/22	10991 ft (3350 m)	PCN 85/F/B/X/T
SUDAN			
Dongola	17/35	9843 ft (3000 m)	LCN 60
Khartoum	18/36	9843 ft (3000 m)	LCG III
Nyala	04/22	9842 ft (3000 m)	LCN 40
Port Sudan	17/35	8202 ft (2500 m)	ISWL 2500
SURINAM			
Paramaribo (Johan A. Pengel)	11/29	11417 ft (3480 m)	PCN 52/F/A/W/T
SWAZILAND			
Matsapha (Manzini)	07/25	8530 ft (2600 m)	PCN 71/F/C/X/T
SWEDEN			
Gothenburg (Landvetter)	03/21	10823 ft (3299 m)	PCN 90/F/B/X/T
Malmo (Sturup)	17/35	9186 ft (2800 m)	PCN 80/F/B/X/T
Stockholm (Arlanda)	01/19	10830 ft (3301 m)	PCN 97/R/B/X/T
SWITZERLAND			
Berne (Belp)	14/32	4298 ft (1310 m)	PCN 40/F/B/X/T
Geneva (Cointrin)	05/23	12795 ft (3900 m)	PCN 60/R/B/W/T
Zurich	16/34	12140 ft (3700 m)	PCN 60/R/B/W/T
SYRIA			
Aleppo	09/27	9416 ft (2870 m)	PCN 55/F/C/X/U
Damascus International	05R/23L	11811 ft (3600 m)	PCN 80/R/C/W/T
Deir Zzor	10/28	9843 ft (3000 m)	PCN 18/R/C/W/T
Tabqa	09/27	9843 ft (3000 m)	B707
TAHITI			
Tahiti	04/22	11220 ft (3420 m)	PCN 53/F/A/W/U
TAIWAN			
Chia Yi	18/36	10007 ft (3050 m)	ESWL 18000
Kaohsiung International	09L/27R	10335 ft (3150 m)	PCN 69/R/C/X/T
Tainan	18L/36R	10007 ft (3050 m)	60S/130T/165B/250DB
Taipei International (Chiang Kai Shek)	05L/23R	12008 ft (3660 m)	100S/170T/266B/378DB
Taitung (Chih Hong)	04/22	10991 ft (3350 m)	ISWL 11400
TAJIKISTAN			
Dushanbe	09/27	10170 ft (3100 m)	PCN 26/R/B/X/T
TANZANIA			
Dar-es-Salaam	05/23	9843 ft (3000 m)	PCN 56/F/A/W/T
Kilimanjaro	09/27	11811 ft (3600 m)	LCN 100
Mwanza	12/30	10827 ft (3300 m)	PCN 65/F/C/X/U
Zanzibar (Kisauni)	18/36	8077 ft (2462 m)	PCN 42/F/A/W/T
TCHAD			
N'Djamena	05/23	9186 ft (2800 m)	PCN 63/F/C/X/U
THAILAND			
Bangkok	03L/21R	12139 ft (3700 m)	PCN 126/F/D/W/T
Chiang Mai	18/36	10171 ft (3100 m)	PCN 75/F/D/X/T
Phuket	09/27	9840 ft (3000 m)	PCN 69/F/C/X/T
Rayong	18/36	11499 ft (3505 m)	PCN 59/F/B/X/T
Songkhla (Hat Yai International)	08/26	10007 ft (3050 m)	PCN 60/F/C/X/T
Udon-Thani	12/30	10000 ft (3048 m)	PCN 33/R/C/X/T
U-Taphao	18/36	10499 ft (3200 m)	PCN 59/F/B/X/T
TOGO			
Lome (Tokoin)	05/23	9843 ft (3000 m)	PCN 59/F/B/X/T
TONGA			
Fua' Amotu	11/29	8763 ft (2671 m)	PCN 45/F/B/X/T
TRINIDAD & TOBAGO			
Port of Spain (Piarco)	10/28	10499 ft (3200 m)	B747
Scarborough (Crown Point)	11/29	9003 ft (2744 m)	PCN 60/F/A/W/T
TUNISIA			
Djerba (Zarzis)	09/27	10171 ft (3100 m)	PCN 52/F/B/Y/U
Monastir (Habib Bourguiba Int'l)	08/26	9679 ft (2950 m)	PCN 50/F/B/Y/U
Sfax (Thyna)	15/33	9842 ft (3000 m)	PCN 52/F/C/Y/U
Tozeur (Nefta)	09/27	10581 ft (3225 m)	PCN 48/F/B/Y/U
Tunis (Carthage)	01/19	10500 ft (3200 m)	PCN 56/R/B/W/U
TURKEY			
Adana (Incirlik)	05/23	10000 ft (3048 m)	LCN 80
Adana	05/23	9022 ft (2750 m)	PCN 100/F/A/X/T
Amasya (Merzifon)	05/23	10499 ft (3200 m)	LCN 50
Ankara (Akinci)	03/21	11024 ft (3360 m)	LCN 50
Ankara (Esenboga)	03R/21L	12310 ft (3752 m)	LCN 100

Airport (Aerodrome) name	Designator (orientation) and length of longest runway		Runway LCN/PCN
Antalya	18L/36R	11155 ft (3400 m)	PCN 80/F/B/Y/T
Batman	02/20	10000 ft (3048 m)	LCN 50
Dalaman (Mugla)	01/19	9843 ft (3000 m)	PCN 100/R/A/W/T
Diyarbakir	16/34	11644 ft (3549 m)	LCN 75
Erhac (Malatya)	03/21	10991 ft (3350 m)	LCN 50
Erzurum	08R/26L	12500 ft (3810 m)	LCN 65
Eskisehir (Anadolu)	09/27	10000 ft (3048 m)	LCN 50
Istanbul (Ataturk)	18/36	9843 ft (3000 m)	PCN 100/R/A/X/T
Izmir (Adnan Menderes)	16/34	10630 ft (3240 m)	PCN 120/F/C/W/T
Izmir (Kaklic)	17/35	10761 ft (3280 m)	PCN 45
Kars	06/24	11483 ft (3500 m)	PCN 68/R/A/X/T
Kayseri (Erkilet)	07R/25L	11152 ft (3400 m)	LCN 45
Konya	01/19	10991 ft (3350 m)	LCN 65
Merzifon	05/23	10500 ft (3200 m)	LCN 45
Mus	11L/29R	11647 ft (3550 m)	LCN 50
Sivas	01/19	12503 ft (3811 m)	LCN 45
TURKMENISTAN			
Ashkhabad	12/30	9842 ft (3000 m)	PCN 20/R/B/X/T
TUVALU			
Funafuti	03/21	5000 ft (1524 m)	LCN 15 at 80 psi
UGANDA			
Entebbe	17/35	12001 ft (3658 m)	LCN 100
Gulu	17/35	10200 ft (3109 m)	LCN 55
UKRAINE			
Kiev (Borispol)	18R/36L	11483 ft (3500 m)	PCN 62/R/C/X/T
Odessa	16/34	9186 ft (2800 m)	PCN 28/R/B/X/T
Simferopol	01L/19R	12159 ft (3706 m)	PCN 43/R/A/X/T
UNITED ARAB EMIRATES			
Abu Dhabi International	13/31	13451 ft (4100 m)	PCN 80/F/B/W/T
Abu Dhabi (Bateen)	13/31	10500 ft (3200 m)	LCN 80
Al Ain International	01/19	13123 ft (4000 m)	PCN 60/F/A/W/T
Dubai	12/30	13123 ft (4000 m)	PCN 70/F/B/W/T
Fujairah International	11/29	12303 ft (3750 m)	PCN 100/F/A/W/U
Ras Al Khaimah	16/34	12336 ft (3760 m)	LCN 80
Sharjah International	12/30	12336 ft (3760 m)	LCN 100
UNITED KINGDOM			
Aberdeen	16/34	6001 ft (1829 m)	PCN 40/R/B/X/T
Belfast (Aldergrove)	07/25	9110 ft (2777 m)	PCN 71/R/B/W/U
Belfast (City)	04/22	6000 ft (1829 m)	—
Birmingham	15/33	8547 ft (2605 m)	PCN 62/F/B/W/T
Boscombe Down	05/23	10537 ft (3212 m)	LCG III
Bournemouth	08/26	6030 ft (1838 m)	PCN 46/F/A/X/U
Brize Norton	08/26	10007 ft (3050 m)	PCN 81/F/B/W/T
Bristol	09/27	6598 ft (2011 m)	PCN 57/F/C/X/U
Cambridge	05/23	6447 ft (1965 m)	PCN 48/R/B/X/T
Campbelton	11/29	10003 ft (3049 m)	LCG III
Cardiff	12/30	7723 ft (2354 m)	PCN 50/F/A/W/T
Carlisle	07/25	6027 ft (1837 m)	PCN 29/F/C/X/T
Coningsby	08/26	9000 ft (2743 m)	LCG III
Coventry	05/23	5300 ft (1615 m)	PCN 29/F/A/W/T
East Midlands	09/27	7480 ft (2280 m)	PCN 63/R/C/W/T
Edinburgh	07/25	8400 ft (2560 m)	PCN 74/R/C/W/T
Exeter	08/26	6834 ft (2083 m)	PCN 53/F/B/X/U
Farnborough	07/25	7874 ft (2400 m)	LCG III
Glasgow	05/23	8720 ft (2658 m)	PCN 65/R/B/W/T
Guernsey	09/27	4800 ft (1463 m)	PCN 27/F/C/X/U
Humberside	03/21	7218 ft (2200 m)	PCN 55/F/R/B/X/T
Isle of Man	08/26	5751 ft (1753 m)	PCN 32/F/C/X/T
Inverness	06/24	6191 ft (1887 m)	PCN 40/F/C/X/T
Jersey	09/27	5597 ft (1706 m)	PCN 34/F/C/X/T
Leeds-Bradford	14/32	7382 ft (2250 m)	PCN 61/R/A/W/T
Liverpool	09/27	7500 ft (2286 m)	PCN 42/R/B/W/J
London (Gatwick)	08R/26L	10364 ft (3159 m)	PCN 78/R/B/W/T
London (Heathrow)	09L/27R	12802 ft (3902 m)	PCN 83/R/A/W/T
London (Stansted)	05/23	10000 ft (3048 m)	PCN 86/R/C/W/T
Luton	08/26	7087 ft (2160 m)	PCN 75/R/D/X/T
Manchester	06/24	10000 ft (3048 m)	PCN 94/F/C/W/T
Newcastle	07/25	7644 ft (2330 m)	PCN 65/F/B/W/T
Norwich	09/27	6043 ft (1842 m)	
Prestwick	13/31	9800 ft (2987 m)	PCN 85/R/C/W/T
Stornoway	18/36	7218 ft (2200 m)	PCN 47/F/A/W/T
Teesside	05/23	7516 ft (2291 m)	PCN 79/F/D/X/T
UNITED STATES OF AMERICA (see separate Alaska and Hawaii)			
Albuquerque	08/26	13375 ft (4077 m)	45S/95D/141DT
Atlanta (Wm. B. Hartsfield)	09L/27R	11889 ft (3624 m)	PCN 62/R/B/W/T
Atlantic City	13/31	10000 ft (3048 m)	39S/55D/159DT
Baltimore (Washington Int'l)	10/28	10500 ft (3200 m)	PCN 50/F/A/N/T
Bangor International	15/33	11438 ft (3486 m)	PCN 71/R/B/W/T
Birmingham International	05/23	8000 ft (2438 m)	80S/93D/159DT
Boston (Logan International)	15R/33L	10081 ft (3073 m)	PCN 61/F/B/W/U
Buffalo	05/23	8100 ft (2469 m)	34S/89D/204DT
Casper (Natrona County Int'l)	03/21	10600 ft (3231 m)	59S/77D/123DT
Charleston	15/33	9000 ft (2743 m)	174D/159DT/352DDT
Charlotte (Douglas)	18R/36L	10000 ft (3048 m)	PCN 61/R/B/W/T
Chicago (O'Hare)	14R/32L	13000 ft (3962 m)	PCN 72/R/C/X/T
Cincinnati (Northern Kentucky Int'l)	18R/36L	11000 ft (3353 m)	PCN 65/R/C/W/T

Airport (Aerodrome) name	Designator (orientation) and length of longest runway		Runway LCN/PCN
Cleveland	05R/23L	9000 ft (2743 m)	PCN 51/R/C/X/T
Colorado Springs (City of Colorado)	17L/35R	13500 ft (4115 m)	79D/154DT/340DDT
Columbus (Port Columbus)	10R/28L	10700 ft (3261 m)	46S/68D/136DT
Dallas-Fort Worth	17R/35L	13400 ft (4084 m)	PCN 60/R/B/X/U
Denver International	16/34	12000 ft (3658 m)	PCN 76/R/C/W/T
Des Moines	13L/31R	9000 ft (2743 m)	59S/82D/155DT
Detroit Metropolitan (Wayne)	03L/21R	12000 ft (3658 m)	PCN 70/R/C/X/T
Duluth International	09/27	10152 ft (3094 m)	34S/59D/104DT
Everett (Snohomish County)	16R/34L	9010 ft (2746 m)	PCN 71/F/B/X/T
Fargo (Hector Int'l)	17/35	9546 ft (2910 m)	46S/91D/182DT
Fort Lauderdale	09L/27R	9000 ft (2743 m)	PCN 71/F/B/X/T
Fresno	11L/29R	9222 ft (2811 m)	PCN 21/R/A/Y/T
Grand Junction (Walker Fld)	11/29	10501 ft (3201 m)	50S/82D/118DT
Great Falls	03/21	10500 ft (3200 m)	78D/127DT/190DDT
Houston International	14L/32R	12000 ft (3658 m)	PCN 71/R/B/X/U
Huntsville	18R/36L	10000 ft (3048 m)	34S/91D/385DDT
Indianapolis International	05L/23R	10005 ft (3049 m)	PCN 56/R/C/X/T
Jacksonville International	07/25	10000 ft (3048 m)	46S/95D/163DT
Kansas City International	01L/19R	10801 ft (3292 m)	PCN 62/F/B/W/T
Las Vegas	07L/25R	14505 ft (4421 m)	PCN 71/F/B/X/T
Long Beach	12/30	10000 ft (3048 m)	45S/77T/127B
Los Angeles International	07L/25R	12090 ft (3685 m)	36S/54T/95B/354DB
Louisville (Standiford Field)	01/19	10000 ft (3048 m)	34S/77D/164DT
Miami International	09R/27L	13000 ft (3962 m)	PCN 63/F/A/X/T
Milwaukee	01L/19R	9690 ft (2953 m)	PCN 70/R/C/W/T
Minneapolis	04/22L	11000 ft (3353 m)	29S/38D/68DT
Moses Lake (Grant County)	14L/32R	13501 ft (4115 m)	45S/91D/181DT
Nashville	13/31	11030 ft (3362 m)	34S/79D/113DT
Newark International	04R/22L	9300 ft (2835m)	PCN 62/F/A/W/T
Newburgh (Stewart)	09/27	11818 ft (3602 m)	79D/158DT/352DDT
New Orleans	10/28	10080 ft (3072 m)	PCN 94/F/D/X/U
New York (John F. Kennedy)	13R/31L	14572 ft (4441 m)	PCN 94/F/A/W/T
New York (La Guardia)	04/22	7000 ft (2134 m)	36S/77D/163DT
Niagara Falls	10L/28R	9125 ft (2781 m)	PCN 46/F/C/X/T
Norfolk International	05/23	9000 ft (2743 m)	91D/158DT/215DDT
Oakland International	11/29	10000 ft (3048 m)	41S/41T/88B
Ontario International	08L/26R	12200 ft (3719 m)	PCN 35/R/A/W/U
Orlando	18R/36L	12004 ft (3659 m)	75S/95D/182DT
Orlando (Sanford)	09L/27R	9600 ft (2926 m)	13S/77D/136DT
Palmdale	07/25	12002 ft (3658 m)	78D/205DT/353DDT
Philadelphia	09R/27L	10500 ft (3200 m)	91S/95D/159DT
Phoenix (Sky Harbor)	08L/26R	11001 ft (3353 m)	PCN 47/F/B/X/U
Pittsburgh	10R/28L	11500 ft (3505 m)	45S/102D/159DT
Portland International	10R/28L	11011 ft (3356 m)	PCN 63/F/A/X/T
Pueblo Memorial	08L/26R	10500 ft (3200 m)	PCN 26/F/C/X/T
Raleigh-Durham	05L/23R	10000 ft (3048 m)	86D/161DT/340DDT
Rapid City (Ellsworth)	13/31	13497 ft (4114 m)	59D/221DT/386DDT
Reno (Tahoe International)	16R/34L	11000 ft (3353 m)	34S/84D/159DT
Richmond International	16/34	9000 ft (2743 m)	57S/91D/154DT
Sacramento International	16R/34L	8600 ft (2621 m)	94D/185DT/385DDT
St Louis International	12R/30L	11019 ft (3359 m)	PCN 61/R/B/W/T
Salt Lake City	16L/34R	12000 ft (3658 m)	27S/91D/386DDT
San Antonio International	12R/30L	8500 ft (2591 m)	PCN 57/R/C/X/U
San Diego	09/27	9400 ft (2865 m)	PCN 61/R/A/W/T
San Francisco	10L/28R	11870 ft (3618 m)	12S/39T/72B
Savannah	09/27	9351 ft (2850 m)	34S/79D/127DT
Seattle Boeing Field (King County International)	13R/31L	10000 ft (3048 m)	PCN 34/R/A/X/T
Seattle (Tacoma)	16L/34R	11900 ft (3627 m)	PCN 62/F/B/X/T
Sioux Falls	03/21	9000 ft (2743 m)	91S/91D/201DDT
Spokane International	03/21	9000 ft (2743 m)	PCN 60/R/B/X/T

Airport (Aerodrome) name	Designator (orientation) and length of longest runway		Runway LCN/PCN
Syracuse (Hancock Int'l)	10/28	9005 ft (2745 m)	PCN 43/F/B/X/T
Tampa International	18R/36L	11002 ft (3353 m)	PCN 58/R/A/W/T
Tucson	11L/29R	10994 ft (3351 m)	91D/159DT/265DDT
Washington (Dulles)	01R/19L	11500 ft (3505 m)	PCN 81/R/C/W/U
Windsor Locks	06/24	9501 ft (2896 m)	PCN 54/F/A/W/T
URUGUAY			
Montevideo (Carrasco)	06/24	8858 ft (2700 m)	PCN 60/F/C/W/U
UZBEKISTAN			
Samarkand	09/27	10171 ft (3100 m)	PCN 29/R/C/X/T
Tashkent (Yuzhnyy)	08L/26R	13123 ft (4000 m)	PCN 84/F/B/X/T
VANUATU			
Port Vila (Bauerfield)	11/29	8535 ft (2601 m)	35S/45T/90B
VENEZUELA			
Caracas (Simon Bolivar)	09/27	11483 ft (3500 m)	B747
El Vigia	09/27	10630 ft (3240 m)	PCN 65/F/A/W/U
Maracaibo (La Chinita)	02R/20L	8169 ft (2490 m)	PCN 53/F/B/W/U
Maracay (El Libertador)	09/27	10400 ft (3170 m)	Takes C124
Margarita (Del Caribe)	09/27	10433 ft (3180 m)	AUW 360 tonnes
San Domingo	11/29	9990 ft (3045 m)	AUW 252 tonnes
Valencia	10L/28R	9843 ft (3000 m)	PCN 46/F/D/W/T
VIETNAM			
Danang	17L/35R	10000 ft (3048 m)	PCN 46/F/A/W/T
Hanoi (Noibai)	11/29	10499 ft (3200 m)	PCN 54/R/B/W/U
Hochiminh (Tansonnhat)	07L/25R	10000 ft (3048 m)	PCN 50/R/B/X/U
VIRGIN ISLANDS			
St. Croix (The Henry E. Rohlsen)	09/27	7612 ft (2320 m)	PCN 52/F/B/X/T
St. Thomas (Cyril E. King)	10/28	7000 ft (2134 m)	PCN 36/F/B/X/T
WAKE ISLAND			
Wake Island	10/28	9859 ft (3005 m)	100S/200T/350B
WINDWARD ISLANDS			
St. Lucia (Hewanorra International)	10/28	9000 ft (2743 m)	LCN 100+
YEMEN			
Abbs	09/27	9843 ft (3000 m)	—
Aden International	08/26	10168 ft (3099 m)	PCN 74/F/B/W/U
Hodeidah	03/21	9843 ft (3000 m)	LCN 75
Riyan (Mukalla)	06/24	9843 ft (3000 m)	PCN 60/F/B/W/U
Sadah	18/36	9843 ft (3000 m)	DC-6
Sanaa International	18/36	10669 ft (3252 m)	LCN 60
Taiz (Ganed)	01/19	9843 ft (3000 m)	LCN 60
YUGOSLAVIA (Federal Republic of)			
Banja Luka	17/35	8202 ft (2500 m)	LCN 61
Belgrade	12/30	11155 ft (3400 m)	PCN 65/F/C/X/T
Podgorica	18/36	8202 ft (2500 m)	LCN 80
Pristina	17/35	8202 ft (2500 m)	LCN 70
Tivat	14/32	8202 ft (2500 m)	LCN 85
ZAMBIA			
Lusaka International	10/28	13000 ft (3962 m)	LCN 135
ZIMBABWE			
Bulawayo	13/31	8491 ft (2588 m)	PCN 40/F/A/X/U
Harare International	05/23	15509 ft (4727 m)	PCN 50/F/A/W/T
Hwange (National Park)	08/26	14764 ft (4500 m)	PCN 25/F/B/Y/U
Victoria Falls	12/30	7500 ft (2286 m)	PCN 28/F/B/X/U

Index

How to use the Index:

a) All aircraft (with the exception of gliders/motorgliders and buoyant aircraft/airships) can be found in the first main Aircraft index. Separate indices (indexes) follow for the various other sections of the book.

b) Entries are strictly alphabetical. For cross references (for example, where *Panavia Tornado* under 'P' has been cross referenced as *Tornado, Panavia* under 'T'), alphabetical order applies to the part of the entry preceding the comma. For example:
Dracula, IAR AH-1RO: 311
Dragonfly, Moyes: 530
Dragonfly, Viking: 589
Dragonfly-6, Shijiazhuang: 405
Dragon Fly mod 333: 302-303
Dragon Fly srl: **302**
Dragon Lady, Lockheed Martin U-2S and ST: 169

c) Where numbers form the start of entries, these come before letters. Roman numerals are treated as the numbers they represent.

d) Page numbers in bold refer to company details with addresses.

Part 1 Aircraft

(see separate index for Gliders/Motorgliders & Buoyant Aircraft)

Part 2 Gliders & Motorgliders

Part 3 Spaceflight

Part 4 Buoyant Aircraft (airships)

Part 5 Engines

Part 6 Missiles

Part 7 Airborne Radars

AIRFORCE

AFGHANISTAN

ALBANIA

ALGERIA

ANGOLA

ARGENTINA

AUSTRALIA

AUSTRIA

BAHRAIN

BANGLADESH

BURKINA (UPPER VOLTA)

(BURMA) MYANMA

BURUNDI

CAMBODIA

CAMEROON

CANADA

CENTRAL AFRICAN REPUBLIC

CHAD

CHILE

DJIBOUTI

DOMINICAN REPUBLIC

ECUADOR

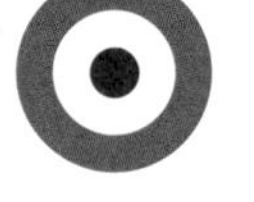
EGYPT

EIRE

EL SALVADOR

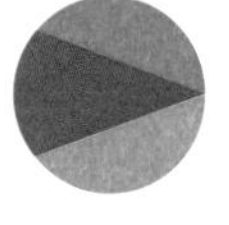
ERITREA

ETHIOPIA

FRANCE

HAITI

HONDURAS

HUNGARY

INDIA

INDONESIA

IRAN

IRAQ

ISRAEL

ITALY

LATVIA

LEBANON

LYBIA

LITHUANIA

MADAGASCAR

MALAWI

MALAYSIA

MALI

MALTA

NIGER

NIGERIA

NORWAY

OMAN

PAKISTAN

PANAMA

PAPUA NEW GUINEA

PARAGUAY

PERU

SINGAPORE

SLOVAKIA

SLOVENIA

SOMALIA

SOUTH AFRICA

SPAIN

SRI LANKA

SUDAN

SURINAM

TURKEY

UGANDA

UNITED KINGDOM

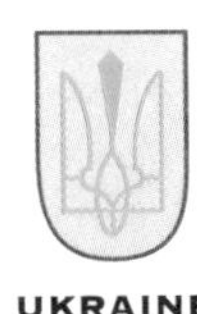
UKRAINE

UNITED ARAB EMIRATES

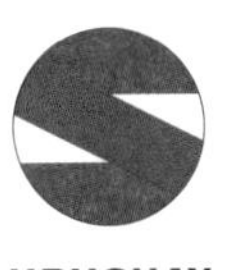
URUGUAY

USA

VENEZUELA

VIETNAM